Good Beer Guide 2007

Edited by

Roger Protz

Glenfiddich Drink Writer of the Year, 1997 and 2004

Deputy Editor

Jill Adam

Assistant Editor

Ione Brown

Campaign for Real Ale
230 Hatfield Road, St Albans,
Hertfordshire AL1 4LW

Contents

CAMRA Books Head of Publications: Joanna Copestick; Emma Lloyd, Publications Project Editor; Debbie Williams, Editorial Assistant

Thanks to the following at CAMRA head office: Chief Executive Mike Benner. The Campaigns, Marketing and Website team of Louise Ashworth, Iain Loe, Tony Jerome, Georgina Rudman, Jonathan Mail, Kate Foster and Owen Morris. Photo research: Samantha Jones. The Administration team: Cressida Feiler, John Cottrell, Malcolm Harding, Jean Jones, Gary Fowler, Michael Green, Carwyn Davies, Caroline Clerembeaux, Gillian Dale and Magdalena Madariova. Thanks to Peter Feiler for help with the Breweries section.

Beer Index compiled by Jeff Evans.

Thanks to 83,000 CAMRA members who carried out research for the pubs; Steve Westby for advising on new breweries; Julian Hough and the campaign's Regional Directors, who co-ordinated the pub entries; Paul Moorhouse for assembling the beer tasting notes; Dave Gamston and Paul Ainsworth for assembling and checking the National Inventory of pubs with historic interiors; and CAMRA's National Executive for their support and enthusiasm.

The Good Beer Guide production team: cover and colour section: Howells Design, London W13; county and brewery sections origination: Redbus, London W4; maps by David and Morag Perrott, PerroCarto, Machnylleth, Wales. Printed by William Clowes, Beccles, Suffolk.

Front cover photographs: Photolibrary.com (left); Alamy (right). Back cover photographs: Alamy

Published by the Campaign for Real Ale Ltd, 230 Hatfield Road, St Albans, Herts, AL1 4LW. Tel 01727 867201. Fax 01727 867670.

Email camra@camra.org.uk **Website** www.camra.org.uk

ISBN 10 1 85249 224 4

ISBN 13 978 1 85249 224 3

35 years young and fighting fit

As CAMRA marks another bibulous milestone, new challenges demand even greater vigilance to ensure a fair deal for all beer drinkers

THIRTY-FIVE YEARS IN THE LIFE of an organisation may not merit a silver or gold award, as is the case with 25 and 50 years respectively, but it nevertheless marks a significant milestone in the history of the Campaign for Real Ale. The world of beer and pubs has changed out of all recognition since the early 1970s, when the major battle was against the national brewers and their new keg beers.

But many of the key issues remain unchanged. CAMRA was born in a pub and the pub remains central to the campaign's activities. As Ted Bruning shows in this section, giant national companies now own vast swathes of Britain's pubs and these 'pubcos' too often restrict available beer to the heavily discounted products of the bigger breweries. To improve diversity for drinkers, we call for a 'guest beer' policy that would enable pub tenants to buy in cask beers of their choice from smaller breweries.

The success of CAMRA today destroys the media myth that there is no demand for real ale. The campaign's membership stands at an all-time high of 83,000 and the clamour by beer lovers for cask beer from independent producers forced CAMRA in 2006 to move its flagship Great British Beer Festival in London

Still rolling out the barrels: the 2006 Great British Beer Festival at Earls Court started with a procession of brewers' drays to stress the importance of the independent brewing sector

Photograph: Hazel Dunlop

Photograph: Hazel Dunlop

Colin Bocking of Crouch Vale Brewery celebrates winning the Champion Beer of Britain competition at Earls Court with Nigel Evans MP (left) and Roger Protz (right)

to the bigger facilities offered by Earls Court.

The Good Beer Guide has referred for several years now to a 'real ale revolution' in Britain. The impact of more than 500 micro-breweries means there is greater choice for drinkers today than at any time in CAMRA's history. The astonishing rise of the micro-brewery sector chimes with the demand by modern consumers for local products that avoid road miles and air miles that damage the environment. The world of small brewers is a green world.

It is a world that encourages women as well as men to drink good beer, as can be seen from the campaign's own members and from the people who flock to beer festivals throughout the country. CAMRA has been at the forefront of the initiative to match beer and food, which reaches out to a new audience and is attracting many of the country's leading chefs, as Susan Nowak shows in this section.

The new licensing laws in England and Wales were the result in part of a concerted effort by CAMRA to convince the government of the need for change. That change came despite a media rant against what was erroneously dubbed 'twenty-four drinking'. It is clear already that the change has led to a modern and sensible pub culture.

But the word complacency does not exist in CAMRA's lexicon. Thirty-five years on, the campaign faces up to the new challenges of the 21st century. In this issue of the guide we discuss not only measures to bring greater choice to pubs but also the equally pressing need to save breweries threatened by closure. Above all, we continue where we started in 1971: to promote real ale with passion and verve, and the pubs where it is sold.

Keep it in the community

The cull of regional breweries has to stop. **Roger Protz** outlines plans for management buy-outs and local co-operatives as the way to save drinkers' beers

THE LOSS OF REGIONAL BREWERIES is reaching the proportions of a Shakespearean tragedy, with as many dead bodies strewn around as in the finals acts of Hamlet and Macbeth. In recent years such highly regarded brewers as King & Barnes, Mansfield, Morland, Morrells, Ruddles and Vaux have disappeared. In 2005 Greene King bought and closed Ridley's in Essex and then moved north to siphon up Belhaven.

Not to be outdone, Wolverhampton & Dudley Breweries, which vies with Greene King as the biggest national brewer in Britain, bought the Cumbrian brewer Jennings. In June 2006, Greene King was on the march again, snatching Hardys & Hansons in Nottingham from under the nose of W&DB. Meanwhile Fuller's in London – rapidly becoming a national player thanks to the strength of its premium cask beer, London Pride – bought and closed Gale's of Horndean in Hampshire. The driving force for takeovers, mergers and closures

Going with the grain: Gale's traditional family-owned brewery in Hampshire, bought by Fuller's, is the size of company that is ideal for an employees' buy-out

is two-pronged: developing national brands such as Greene King IPA, Marston's Pedigree and London Pride, and building ever-bigger estates of pubs to counter the domination of the global brewers in the free trade sector. At one level, appreciative drinkers much prefer the cask beers of national and regional brewers to the globals' lagers and nitro-keg products. But the success of these brands should not be at the expense of the local beers from the breweries they buy, which only diminishes choice.

Greene King's promise to maintain some of the Ridley's brands, albeit brewed at Bury St Edmunds, was quickly broken. Only a couple remain, as seasonal rather than regular beers. Fuller's has already slimmed down the Gale's range, which is now brewed in London, and one wonders for how long Gale's Butser can share bar space with Fuller's London Pride. The same question arises with the bottle-fermented Gale's Prize Old Ale, as Fuller's has its own successful range of bottled real ales.

W&DB has invested substantially in Jennings, while Belhaven and its 275 pubs and massive free trade in Scotland offer a new market in a separate country for Greene King. These two breweries seem safe in the medium term. The future of Hardys & Hansons is unknown at present. Greene King made no comment about the future of the brewery at the time of the takeover and its track record is one of concentrating production at its much-expanded Suffolk plant. As H&H has little market penetration outside its own trading area, a gloomy view is that Nottingham drinkers will soon see the green umbrellas that already announce Greene King IPA in many parts of the country.

Beer factories

Speculation is idle. The main consideration is for breweries to remain in local hands. That is the only real safeguard for genuine beers brewed at source and not in a large beer factory several hundred miles away. While the success of the micro-brewery sector is mightily encouraging – around 60 new breweries are listed in this edition – the threat to independent family-owned breweries and their pub estates and cask beers is a challenge that cannot be ignored.

The mantra is familiar: takeovers and mergers cannot be stopped, especially when families that own breweries have gone cap-in-hand to find a buyer. In fact, the opposite is the case. If employees had had the opportunity, Gale's and Ridley's are perfect examples of small regionals that could have been saved. Both the Bowyer family that owned Gale's and the Ridley family followed the

Drink up and stub out

New licensing laws for England and Wales came into effect in November 2005. This enables pub owners to choose longer or flexible opening hours if approved by the licensing authorities. The Good Beer Guide has treble-checked the opening hours for listed pubs but they are still liable to change: the experience of the first 10 months of the new law is that many pubs have retained their old hours and some that chose to remain open longer have returned to 11pm closing during the week. It is advisable to check a pub's opening hours before making a long journey to visit it.

A ban on smoking in public places – including pubs and bars – in England and Wales is due to come into effect in the summer of 2007. A similar change was enacted in Scotland in March 2006. Many pub owners are developing heated outside patios for smokers. This edition of the guide continues to list internal smoke-free areas in pubs in England and Wales, as smoking in pubs will continue for most of the edition's life.

Photograph: Roger Protz

It's history now: England's oldest pub, the Trip to Jerusalem, below Nottingham Castle, was part of the bounty seized by Greene King when it bought Hardys & Hansons brewery in June 2006

advice of Dr Samuel Johnson, who, when involved in selling Thrale's London brewery in 1781, said: 'We are not here to sell a parcel of boilers and vats, but the potentiality of growing rich, beyond the dreams of avarice'. The pity is that the two families sold to bigger breweries and not to their own management, workforce and local communities.

Management buy-outs can succeed. Bass, when it was preparing its exit strategy from brewing, sold the Highgate Brewery in Wallsall to its management in 1995. In order to raise additional money for investment in new plant, Highgate eventually became part of the Aston Manor drinks group but it remains a successful independent brewery, with highly regarded brands, contract brewing for Coors and Smiles, and a growing pub estate.

The Old Crown pub in Hesket Newmarket in Cumbria and the adjoining brewery are both owned by co-operatives, made up of local people and others from Britain and abroad who love the pub and the beers. Dave Hollings of Co-operative and Mutual Solutions, who advised both co-ops, says the strength of the arrangement is that members can only each own the same number of shares and they must

Young's: a Pilgrim's Progress

In June 2006 Young & Co, the iconic brewer of cask beer in Wandsworth, south London, announced it would leave the site in October and would create, with Charles Wells of Bedford, a new company called the Wells & Young's Brewing Co. Wells and Young's will remain as separate pub companies but their beers will all be brewed in Bedford, the birthplace of John Bunyan. Young's was forced to look for a new site when Wandsworth Council announced it planned to redevelop the town centre. The brewery was unable to find suitable alternative premises in London and the move to Bedford gives the company the opportunity to use a plant with an annual capacity of 500,000 barrels. Young's needed additional brewing capacity.

be sold back to the co-ops if any members leave. But the Hesket Newmarket Brewery is tiny, with a weekly capacity of around 20 barrels. Can such arrangements work for breweries producing 20,000 barrels a year?

Dave Hollings believes they can and says there are advantages to family companies if they sell to their employees and allow them to pay over a period of, say, five years. Such an arrangement would mean the family could avoid paying Capital Gains Tax. If the family demands the full amount up front then the employees would have to raise the cash from loans or grants. But they wouldn't have to repay them immediately and could fund them from revenue. They could seek support from trade unions and local authorities: there are restrictions on local councils making loans and grants to commercial enterprises but they do have some scope.

The biggest business in the country that is owned and run by its employees is the John Lewis Partnership, which includes Waitrose, Peter Jones and Selfridges. Since the 1920s, when the son of the founder handed the company to its workforce, they have owned the shares and receive an annual distribution of the profits. Today

there are 64,000 partners in the business, which is effectively a giant workers' co-operative.

Hollings advice is for employees of independent breweries with shares available on the Stock Exchange to buy 5 per cent stakes in the companies and start to build up a bigger stake over time until they have a sufficient holding to enable them to influence company policies. When all the shares are owned by a family, the employees should approach the family for talks to ascertain whether they plan to continue to run the brewery or, as in the case of Gale's and Ridley's, they are looking for an exit strategy. If the latter is the case then the employees can discuss with the family the price they are looking for, and whether they would want all the money in advance or would accept payment over an agreed period.

Genuine roots

The strength and importance of small regional breweries is that they have genuine roots in local communities. Beer drinkers as well as employees have an interest in such breweries staying open and independent. The workforce need not stand alone in attempting to save breweries and jobs. They can join forces with consumers who may well offer influence and experience in such key areas as raising funds, legal structures and public relations. The experience of professional football shows just how effective supporters can be in rescuing failed clubs or helping struggling managements to stay in business.

Supporters Direct is a national organisation made up of 120 democratically-run supporters' groups that have taken an active interest in running their football clubs. There are to date 13 trusts in England and Wales that have stakes in their clubs. Scotland has no fewer than 28 trusts. Supporters in England have stakes in 30 per cent of Premiership clubs, 75 per cent of clubs in the Championship, 63 per cent of League One clubs and 79 per cent in League Two.

Brentford, Chesterfield, Rushden & Diamonds and Stockport County are clubs now owned and run by their supporters. Chesterfield had debts of £2 million but is now breaking even. The supporters are seeking a partnership with the local authority to widen community control and participation. A supporters' trust is now the part-owner of Lincoln City. The club was in administration in 2001 and was saved by a community buy-out, in which the local supporters' trust became a part-owner. The club has seen a rise in attendances at matches and in the last full season recorded a profit of £700,000.

It would be naïve to suggest that running a professional football club is analogous to owning and controlling a brewery. But the differences should not be exaggerated. Both have loyal fan bases and trusts involving both brewery employees, pub tenants and drinkers could play a crucial role in saving local breweries for their communities and protecting them from takeovers and closure.

At its annual members' meeting in 2006, CAMRA adopted a call to set up a special task group to investigate initiatives, such as co-ops and trusts, to save independent breweries. It is an idea whose time has come.

■ Further information from Co-operative & Mutual Solutions: 01254 706939; www.cms.coop; www.supporters-direct.org.

Saving the Lamb from the slaughter

Celebrity chefs are accepting the challenge of cooking in pubs and developing menus that match beer and real ale. **Susan Nowak** reports

IT'S AMAZING HOW MANY CELEBRITY CHEFS have been called to the bar. If they've got a TV listing or a Michelin star, chances are they'll pop up in the kitchen of the Pint & Platter. So what makes high-profile chefs such as Heston Blumenthal and Antony Worrall Thompson suddenly want to dish up pub grub? Could it be the growing reputation of pub food? Or the realisation that gastro-pubs are luring diners away from restaurants? Or a laddish desire to be street savvy? Or simply that the ambience of a British pub frees them from the tyranny of formal restaurant cuisine? They want food to be fun again...

That's certainly the case with Jean-Christophe Novelli, who sizzled in TV's Hell's Kitchen before fleeing swanky Auberge du Lac in Hertfordshire for the White Horse eight miles away in Harpenden.

'I think you are guaranteed to be more relaxed in a pub. I'm doing a lot of things I would not have permitted myself before, but cooking should not be to a formula,' he says. The Michelin starred chef has turned full circle; his first serious job in Britain was at Keith Floyd's former pub in Devon, where he learned to value local produce – and pull a pint. Even at the Auberge, signature dishes such as stuffed pigs' trotters and oxtail braised with liquorice were the sort of peasant cooking that goes so well with beer, now happily translated to his pub menu.

Novelli designed the beer menus for two CAMRA awards lunches and believes real ale is 'an important part of an English pub'. Two handpumps grace the bar of the White Horse, and he is committed to serving real ale in new gastro-pubs he plans around the M25.

Village centres destroyed

With countless TV credits and top culinary awards, Antony Worrall Thompson is one of the best-known chefs to go the pub route. But he has a different motive.

'It's actually to keep the pubs going because so many are being sold off as private houses and the centres of villages have been ripped out,' he told me shortly after acquiring the Lamb at Satwell, Oxfordshire. So did he save the Lamb from the slaughter?

'Undoubtedly. Some weeks it was doing less than a grand and it's very small. Already we've multiplied that figure by around 12,' he says.

Joint proprietor since 2004 of the Angel in Heytesbury, Wiltshire, a Greene King tenancy, in 2005 he took over the Greyhound in Rotherfield Peppard – 'a pub I've always had a soft spot for' – followed in 2006 by the Lamb, both free houses.

'I have Fuller's London Pride as house beer but I also like to support micro-breweries from this area such as Loddon and Butler's – and, of course, Brakspear,' says Worrall Thompson, who is also committed to sourcing local produce for his pubs.

He loathes the term gastro-pub. Perhaps the Angel comes closest, but he thinks he's persuaded its chefs to be 'less poncy – more bistro'. The Greyhound echoes the beefy menu of his fashionable London restaurants Notting Grill and Kew Grill, while the Lamb features old-fashioned country fare.

More than simple pie men: Jean-Christophe Novelli (previous page) and Antony Worrall Thompson have brought their culinary skills to pubs with rustic food and cask beers. Worrall Thompson's mission is to save rural pubs from closing

Photograph: Fran Nowak

'We call it "world in a stew" and nothing's over a tenner. We do dishes like braised oxtail, leg of mutton with caper sauce, steak and kidney pie, sausage and lentil casserole,' he says. Sometimes his chefs use beer, in a carbonnade or pork with stout and prunes, and many diners do drink beer, especially at the Lamb.

'I think the range of beers we serve is just right with traditional country dishes,' Worrall Thompson, a devotee of English ale, adds.

Ready, Steady, Cook! regular Phil Vickery grew up on Shepherd Neame beers in Kent. 'It worries me that the void between restaurant food in so-called gastro-pubs and the basic rubbish on offer in many pubs is so vast. What we miss is the simply cooked, tasty, good value for money food that was once the backbone of a great pub,' he says.

Vickery is making his own contribution by holding master classes for pub chefs, and originating beer dishes for Shepherd Neame pubs, such as lamb and mint cobbler with Spitfire. He supports beer with food and has found a novel way to promote it by serving shot glasses with a dish. So with marshmallow chocolate brownies you sip raspberry beer.

Real ale essential

Australia-born Roxy Beaujolais arrived in London by tramp steamer in 1973, and the following year became front-of-house at Ronnie Scott's in Soho. A self-taught cook, she's been chef to the Royal Shakespeare Company, made TV appearances, including Full on Food, and penned the recipe book Home from the Inn Contented. Her pub career began 20 years ago with the Nicholson's pub group at the Unicorn in St James's followed by the Three Greyhounds in Greek Street.

'I'm not a celebrity chef and I'm not a restaurateur; I'm a publican who just happens to like cooking,' says Roxy, who is landlady of two London pubs, the Seven Stars in Carey Street and Bountiful Cow in Eagle Street. She believes real ale is essential in a pub and is proud that the Seven Stars gained Cask Marque status in 2005

'I like what beer on handpump signifies. It is real, it is a live product, I have to be responsible for the quality, and the sort of people who are appreciative of the

Best shots: Phil Vickery offers tasters of beer and food at his master classes for chefs in Shepherd Neame pubs (left). Roxy Beaujolais (above) says cask beer is a live product and is the perfect companion for pub food

beer are appreciative of the sort of pub I run – no TV or machines, just chat,' she says. She likes to stock Fuller's and Young's – 'beers accessible to Londoners' – Adnams for its quality ales; and guests beers, especially her new discovery, Dark Star from Sussex.

'Someone from CAMRA said Hophead was the best beer in the world, so I thought "that's good enough for me". It's a light, flowery beer but bitter, too, and my customers can't get enough of it. I've also served their Espresso Stout, which my women drinkers really loved, and their IPA at 6.2 per cent just flew out.'

True to its name, main courses at the Bountiful Cow focus on beef from well-hung steaks to freshly ground burgers. Roxy cooks at the Seven Stars, which has gained several food awards, and reckons good pub food 'requires simplicity, good taste and a broad sense of rightness.'

Her blackboard menu might include lamb steak with barley, Napoli sausages with belly pork, potted shrimps with sourdough bread and occasionally home-pickled ox tongue. Beer is used in beef stews and game casseroles in winter – 'straight from the handpump it's cheaper than a bottle of wine'.

Not content with owning 'the best restaurant in the world', as the Fat Duck in Bray has been dubbed, three-Michelin star chef Heston Blumenthal, known for his scientific approach to cooking, took over the Hind's Head close by. He wanted neither gastro-pub nor 'some smart restaurant on a pub theme', but traditional pub food listed on a blackboard.

Typical dishes include pea and ham soup (£5.50), Lancashire hotpot (£14.75), roast cod with champ and parsley sauce (£13.50), and his take on a BLT sandwich, bacon with oven roast tomato and rocket (£4.50). You can quaff three real ales – always Greene King IPA, a Rebellion beer and a guest – maybe even 'buttered ale' because he plans occasional historic flavours in keeping with the Tudor building. But, definitely, no snail porridge.

■ Susan Nowak is co-editor, with Jill Adam, of Good Pub Food.

Pub giants are a threat to choice

Once brewers owned the pubs we drink in. But, argues **Ted Bruning**, it is non-brewing pubcos that rule the roost and restrict diversity of beer

WHO OWNS YOUR LOCAL? Bet you think it's a brewery. And 20 years ago, you'd probably have been right.

For in the late 1980s, the Big Six national brewers – Allied, Bass, Courage, GrandMet, Scottish & Newcastle and Whitbread – were at their height. They owned more than half the pubs in Britain, and most of the rest belonged to the 50 or so regional independent breweries that existed then.

But, following an investigation by the Monopolies Commission, the government decided to break the power of the Big Six. The 1990 Beer Orders set a ceiling of 2,000 pubs and told all brewers who owned more than that number to sell half of the surplus, or lease them free of tie, and to allow all their tenants to stock a guest cask beer of their choice.

Watery grave: Brakspear of Henley on Thames brewed magnificent beer but the management saw richer pickings from closing the brewery and just running pubs

The legislation didn't so much break the power of the Big Six as wipe them out, for within a few years all of them except S&N had ceased to exist. First they sold their pubs in batches to new non-brewing pub chains (hereinafter referred to as 'pubcos'), then they sold their breweries, too, becoming the Big Four instead. Along with S&N (which owns the Courage and John Smith's brands), the new powers are Carlsberg (Danish owner of Tetley), Coors (American owner of Worthington), and InBev (Brazilian and Belgian owner of almost everything else).

While the national brewers went through their various phases of meltdown, times were just as exciting for the pubcos they had spawned. For within a few years, two super-lean, super-mean predators, Enterprise Inns and Punch Taverns, had emerged from the pack to gobble up their competitors like a couple of grizzlies laying down fat for winter. They now own more than 9,000 pubs each.

Changing times

In the late 1980s the Big Six owned more than 30,000 pubs and the regionals owned 11,500 – a situation a Tory government thought merited investigation and radical regulation. Today, the pubcos own more than 30,000 pubs while the regionals own just 9,000 – a situation a Labour government isn't bothered about. How times change!

But does it matter? Yes. For since 1990 – bizarrely, you may think, given the intention of the Beer Orders – the nationals have actually increased their share of the British beer market and achieved global status; and unless independent brewers can get fair access to the pubcos' outlets, their future is at stake.

Cartoon: John Simpson

There are many reasons why the globals have continued to grow despite the Beer Orders. First, they've concentrated on lager, which few independents brew these days. Lager now outsells ale, and almost every lager font in every pub in the land belongs to a global brewer.

Second, they dominate the take-home trade, which in effect means the supermarkets. Pubs are losing sales to supermarkets, and apart from a few facings of 'premium bottled ales' from regional brewers, the vast bulk of supermarket beer is BOGOFF Carling.

Third, the globals have been the big beneficiaries from the closure of so many regionals in the last 10-15 years. They haven't actually bought any outright, and many of the victims – Morland, King & Barnes, Gale's, Ridley's – have fallen prey to other regionals. But the way things have worked out the production volume of some of the biggest of the disappeared ones – Greenalls and Vaux in particular – has gone to the globals.

The one sector of the market where

regional and smaller brewers can slug it out with the globals on anything like equal terms is the pub trade, where demand for real ale is still encouragingly strong and where under-promoted, lacklustre national brands just don't cut it. And some of the pubcos have opened their doors a crack to regional brewers' real ales. All right, they were mostly founded by ex-big brewery middle management who used big brewery loans to buy ex-big brewery pubs selling, of course, big brewery beers. But things have moved on since then and in almost any pubco house today you can find real ales from the likes of Adnams, Fullers, and Young's.

Begging bowl

But that leaves the most exciting and dynamic sector of the brewing industry – the country's 500 micro-brewers – standing at the kitchen door with a begging bowl and a hopeful expression. Some of the cannier among them have created brands of national significance such as Hop Back Summer Lightning, which are widely distributed. Others have managed to get their beers on pubco guest ale lists, or are supplied to pubco pubs through third-party distributors such as WaverleyTBS and Carlsberg UK. But for micros as a whole, the pickings in the pubco estates have been pretty thin.

After seeking access to this crucial market by various means, the Society of Independent Brewers (SIBA) discovered that the pubcos weren't hostile to the idea of listing its members' beers: if customers would buy them, pubcos were happy to sell them. But micros that wanted to deal with pubcos had to do so on the pubcos' terms, and what the pubcos wanted was a simplified logistical system that all suppliers had to conform to.

For the micro-brewer, this often meant delivering to a central depot hundreds of miles away, even if the beer was destined for a pub near the brewery; and then having to go back to the depot to retrieve empty casks that could have been collected from the pub. Clearly the game was hardly worth the candle, especially as pubcos aren't noted for the generous prices they pay.

So in 2003 SIBA came up with the Direct Delivery Scheme, under which a central office takes the publican's order and transmits it to the brewery concerned, which can deliver its beer direct to the pub and collect its own empties. All the billing and other paperwork are also carried out centrally, which suits the pubcos' purchasing and accounting systems. Both the big pubcos and several of the smaller ones are members of the scheme, as are the 150 SIBA brewers taking advantage of it to sell, at time of writing, 1,200 barrels a month to pubco tenants.

It's a good scheme: it allows micro-brewers' salesmen to target pubco pubs and plays to current concerns over 'food miles'. But it has drawbacks: for instance, if a tenant wants to join the scheme he has to get permission from his area manager, who might not be all that receptive to the idea. The result is that while the

CAMRA says: Bring back guest beer

The Campaign for Real Ale is calling for the restoration of the Guest Beer policy that was introduced as part of the Beer Orders in the 1990s by the then Conservative government. This gave tenants of national brewers the right to stock a cask beer of their choice. The policy was scrapped by the present government on the ludicrous grounds that it believes 'full and fair competition exists in the brewing industry'. CAMRA wants the policy restored but widened so that not only tenants but also managers – who are employees of breweries or pubcos – can choose guest beers independent of their landlords or employers. The policy should involve all companies that own more than 30 pubs.

The sky's the limit: Adnams in Suffolk has invested in a new brewhouse and warehouse to increase production of its beers whose quality has forced them on to the bars of the major pubcos

pubcos that have signed up to DDS own more than 20,000 pubs, only 1,000 get their beer via the scheme.

CAMRA is worried that even with DDS, the balance of power lies too much with the pubcos. There is nothing to stop them turning their backs on SIBA and the regionals and reverting to cheap national brands instead. It's conceivable they might do so. If that happened the entire independent brewing sector, not just the micros, would be in deep trouble.

So the campaign wants to go back to the 1990s, when the Beer Orders were in force and every national brewery tenant had the right to stock a guest cask ale of his choosing. Only we want it radically extended: first, to embrace all operators with more than 30 pubs, whether brewers or not; and secondly, to cover pub managers as well as tenants, so that operators can't get round it by converting tenancies into managed houses.

For one thing we've discovered, painfully, over the years is that there's very little we can do to stop breweries from closing – though as this edition of the guide shows, there is new thinking in this area. Where we have succeeded is in encouraging new ones to open – hundreds of them, in fact. In terms of the sheer number and variety of real ales on the market, this is a golden age for British brewers and beer drinkers. CAMRA's main aim is making sure brewers can get their beers into pubs so that drinkers can drink them.

■ Ted Bruning edits CAMRA's monthly newspaper, *What's Brewing*.

Beer Festival Calendar 2007

THE CAMPAIGN FOR REAL ALE'S BEER FESTIVALS are magnificent shop windows for cask ale and they give drinkers the opportunity to sample beers from independent brewers rare to particular localities. Beer festivals are enormous fun: many offer good food and live entertainment, and – where possible – facilities for families. Some seasonal festivals specialise in spring, autumn and winter ales. Festivals range in size from small local events to large regional ones. CAMRA holds two national festivals, for winter beers in January, and the Great British in August; the latter features around 500 beers. The festivals listed are those planned for 2007. For up-to-date information, contact the CAMRA website: **www.camra.org.uk** and click on 'CAMRA Near You'. By joining CAMRA – there's a form at the back of the guide – you will receive 12 editions of the campaign's newspaper What's Brewing, which lists every festival on a month-by-month basis. Dates listed are liable to change: check with the website or What's Brewing.

JANUARY

National Winter Ales Festival (Manchester)
Bent & Bongs Beer Bash (Atherton)
Burton Winter Festival
Cambridge Winter Festival
Derby Winter Festival
Exeter Winter Festival
Hitchin Winter Festival
Redditch Winter Festival

FEBRUARY

Battersea
Bishop Auckland
Bradford
Chelmsford Winter Festival
Chesterfield
Dorchester
Dover Winter Festival
Fleetwood
Gosport Winter Ales Festival
Hucknall
Liverpool
Pendle
Rotherham
Salisbury
Tewkesbury

MARCH

Bristol
Coventry
Darlington
Ely
Hitchin
Leeds
Leicester
Loughborough
London Drinker (Camden)
Oldham
St Neots
Sussex (Brighton & Hove)
Walsall
Wigan
York

APRIL

Banbury
Bexley
Bury St Edmunds
Chippenham
Dunstable
Maldon
Mansfield
Newcastle upon Tyne
Paisley
Reading
Stourbridge
Thanet

MAY

Alloa
Cambridge
Chester
Colchester
Doncaster
Beer on Broadway (Ealing)
Farnham
Fife
Lincoln
Macclesfield
Newark
Northampton
Stockport
Yapton

JUNE

Ashfield (Notts)
Catford
Colchester
Doncaster
Kingston (Surrey)
Plymouth
Salisbury
Scottish Traditional Beer Festival (Edinburgh)
Stalybridge
Southampton
South Downs (Lewes)
St Ives, Cornwall
Thurrock (Grays)
Wolverhampton
Woodchurch, near Ashford
Kent: Rare Breeds

JULY

Ardingly
Boston
Boxmoor (Hemel Hempstead)
Bromsgrove
Canterbury
Chelmsford
Cotswold
Derby
Devizes

Not a beard or beer belly in sight: women drinkers are happy drinkers at a CAMRA festival

Eden Valley (Kent)
Fenland
Hereford
Louth
Much Wenlock
Plymouth
Woodcote Steam Rally

AUGUST

Great British Beer Festival (London)
Barnstaple
Clacton
Harbury
Moorgreen
Peterborough
Mumbles
Worcester

SEPTEMBER

Abergavenny at Food Festival
Ayrshire
Birmingham
Bridgenorth/SVR
Burton upon Trent
Chappel (Essex)
Darlington
Erewash
Ipswich
Jersey
Keighley
Letchworth
Maidstone
Melton Mowbray
Nantwich
North Notts (Worksop/Retford)
Northwich
St Albans
St Ives, Cambs
Scunthorpe
Sheffield
Shrewsbury
Somerset
Southport
South Devon (Newton Abbot)
Tamworth
Ulverston
Quorn

OCTOBER

Alloa
Barnsley
Bath
Bedford
Wirral (Birkenhead)
Carmarthen
Croydon & Sutton (Wallington)
Dunfermline
Eastbourne
Falmouth
Gravesend
Hampshire Downs (Overton)
Harlow
Huddersfield
Hull
Middlesbrough
Norwich
Nottingham
Oxford
Poole
Quorn (Leicestershire)
Redhill
Solihull
Stoke-on-Trent
Swindon
Troon
Twickenham
Wakefield
Westmorland (Kendall)
Wirral
Worthing

NOVEMBER

Aberdeen
Accrington
Belfast
Bury
Dudley Winter Festival
Loughborough
Medway
Rochford
Watford
Woking
Wolverton, near Milton Keynes

DECEMBER

Cockermouth
Great Welsh Beer & Cider Festival (Cardiff)
Harwich & Dovercourt
Ipswich Winter Festival
Pigs Ear (Hackney)

Preserving our pub heritage

CAMRA's National Inventory lists pub interiors that have outstanding historic interest worth saving

THE NATIONAL INVENTORY is CAMRA's pioneering effort to identify and protect the most important historic pub interiors in the country. It has been part of the campaign's mission for the past 35 years to not only save real ale but also Britain's rich heritage of pubs. The main aim of the National Inventory has been to list those pub interiors that have remained much as they had been before the Second World War. They need to be protected and cherished in order that future generations can enjoy them – along with good beer.

National Inventory Part 1

Part 1 emphasises intactness. It lists pubs whose interiors have remained largely unaltered since World War Two and also certain exceptional examples from the post-War era (up to 1976)

ENGLAND

BUCKINGHAMSHIRE
West Wycombe: Swan

CAMBRIDGESHIRE
Peterborough: Hand & Heart

CHESHIRE
Alpraham: Travellers Rest
Barthomley: White Lion
Bollington: Holly Bush
Gawsworth: Harrington Arms
Macclesfield: Castle

CORNWALL
Falmouth: Seven Stars

CUMBRIA
Broughton Mills: Blacksmiths Arms
Carlisle: Cumberland Inn

DERBYSHIRE
Derby: Old Dolphin
Elton: Duke of York
Kirk Ireton: Barley Mow
Wardlow Mires: Three Stags' Heads

Black Horse, Preston, with its superb opulently curved bar

Samuel Smith's Cittie of York in London has a spectacular beamed roof and old wine butts

DEVON
Drewsteignton: Drewe Arms
Luppitt: Luppitt Inn
Topsham: Bridge Inn

DORSET
Pamphill: Vine
Worth Matravers: Square & Compass

DURHAM
Billy Row: Dun Cow
Durham City: Shakespeare; Victoria

ESSEX
Mill Green (Ingatestone): Viper

GLOUCESTERSHIRE & BRISTOL
Ampney St Peter: Red Lion Inn
Bristol: (centre) King's Head
Purton: Berkeley Arms
Willsbridge: Queen's Head

HAMPSHIRE
Steep: Harrow

HEREFORDSHIRE
Leintwardine: Sun Inn
Leysters: Duke of York

KENT
Ightham Common: Old House
Snargate: Red Lion

LANCASHIRE
Great Harwood: Victoria
Preston: Black Horse
Stacksteads: Commercial

LEICESTERSHIRE
Whitwick: Three Horseshoes

GREATER LONDON
Central London: (Hatton Garden, EC1) Old Mitre; (Smithfield, EC1) Hand & Shears; (Bloomsbury, WC1) Duke of York; (Holborn, WC1) Cittie of York
East London: (Dagenham) Eastbrook; (Ilford) Doctor Johnson
North London: (Harringay, N4) Salisbury; (Crouch End, N8) Queen's Hotel; (Tottenham, N17) Beehive
North West London: (Eastcote) Case is Altered; (Harrow) Castle; (South Kenton) Windermere
South East London: (Kennington, SE11) Old Red Lion
South West London: (West Brompton, SW10) Fox & Pheasant
West London: (Soho, W1) Argyll Arms: (Hammersmith, W8) Hope & Anchor; (Kensington, W8) Windsor Castle; (West Ealing, W13) Forester

GREATER MANCHESTER
Altrincham: Railway
Ashton-under-Lyne: March Hare

The King's Head, Suffolk – known as the Low House – has settles, open fires and beers on gravity

Chorlton on Medlock: Mawson
Eccles: Grapes; Lamb; Royal Oak; Stanley Arms
Farnworth: Shakespeare
Gorton: Plough
Heaton Norris: Nursery Inn
Manchester: (centre) Briton's Protection, Circus Tavern, Hare & Hounds, Peveril of the Peak
Rochdale: Cemetery Hotel
Salford: Coach & Horses
Stockport: Alexandra; Arden Arms; Swan with Two Necks
Westhoughton: White Lion

MERSEYSIDE
Birkenhead: Stork Hotel
Liverpool: (centre) Nook, Peter Kavanagh's, Philharmonic, Vines; (Walton) Prince Arthur
Lydiate: Scotch Piper
Waterloo: Volunteer Canteen

NORFOLK
Warham: Three Horseshoes

NORTHUMBERLAND
Berwick upon Tweed: Free Trade
Netherton: Star Inn

NOTTINGHAMSHIRE
Nottingham: (centre) Olde Trip to Jerusalem; (Sherwood) Five Ways

OXFORDSHIRE
Steventon: North Star
Stoke Lyne: Peyton Arms

SHROPSHIRE
Edgerley: Royal Hill
Selattyn: Cross Keys
Shrewsbury: Loggerheads

SOMERSET
Bath: Old Green Tree; Star
Faulkland: Tucker's Grave Inn
Midsomer Norton: White Hart
Witham Friary: Seymour Arms

STAFFORDSHIRE
Rugeley: Red Lion
Tunstall: Vine

SUFFOLK
Brent Eleigh: Cock
Bury St Edmunds: Nutshell
Ipswich: Margaret Catchpole
Laxfield: King's Head ('Low House')

SUSSEX (EAST)
Hadlow Down: New Inn

SUSSEX (WEST)
Haywards Heath: Golden Eagle
The Haven: Blue Ship

TYNE & WEAR
Newcastle upon Tyne: (centre) Crown Posada; (Byker) Cumberland Arms

WARWICKSHIRE
Five Ways: Case is Altered

WEST MIDLANDS
Birmingham: (Digbeth) Anchor, Market Tavern, White Swan, Woodman; (Handsworth) Red Lion; (Nechells) Villa Tavern; (Small Heath) Samson & Lion; (Sparkbrook) Marlborough; (Stirchley) British Oak
Bloxwich: Romping Cat; Turf Tavern
Dudley: Shakespeare
Oldbury: Waggon & Horses
Rushall: Manor Arms
Sedgley: Beacon Hotel
Wednesfield: Vine

WILTSHIRE
Easton Royal: Bruce Arms
Salisbury: Haunch of Venison

WORCESTERSHIRE
Bretforton: Fleece
Clent: Bell & Cross
Defford: Cider House ('Monkey House')
Worcester: Paul Pry Inn

Bennet's Bar in Edinburgh is a shrine to gleaming and immaculate Victorian design

YORKSHIRE (EAST)
Hull: (centre) Olde Black Boy, Olde White Harte

YORKSHIRE (NORTH)
Beck Hole: Birch Hall Inn
Harrogate: Gardeners Arms
York: Blue Bell; Golden Ball; Swan

YORKSHIRE (SOUTH)
Barnburgh: Coach & Horses
Doncaster: Plough
Sheffield: (centre) Bath Hotel

YORKSHIRE (WEST)
Bradford: (centre) Cock & Bottle, New Beehive
Halifax: Three Pigeons
Leeds: (centre) Adelphi, Whitelock's; (Burley) Cardigan Arms, Rising Sun; (Hunslet) Garden Gate; (Lower Wortley) Beech

WALES

MID WALES
Llanfihangel-yng-Ngwynfa: Goat
Llanidloes: Crown & Anchor
Welshpool: Grapes

NORTH EAST WALES
Ysceifiog: Fox

NORTH WEST WALES
Bethesda: Douglas Arms
Conwy: Albion Hotel

WEST WALES
Llandovery: Red Lion Inn
Pontfaen: Dyffryn Arms

SCOTLAND

BORDERS
Selkirk: Town Arms

DUMFRIES & GALLOWAY
Stranraer: Grapes

FIFE
Kincardine: Railway Tavern
Leslie: Auld Hoose

GRAMPIAN
Aberdeen: (centre) Grill

THE LOTHIANS
Edinburgh: (centre) Abbotsford, Bennet's Bar, H P Mather's Bar, Oxford Bar, Rutherford's; (Newington) Leslie's Bar

STRATHCLYDE
Glasgow: (centre) Horseshoe Bar, Steps Bar; (Shettleston) Portland Arms
Larkhall: Village Tavern
Lochgilphead: Commercial ('The Comm')
Paisley: Bull
Renton: Central Bar

TAYSIDE
Dundee: Clep; Speedwell Bar; Tay Bridge Bar

NORTHERN IRELAND

COUNTY ANTRIM
Ballycastle: Boyd's; House of McDonnell
Ballyeaston: Carmichael's
Bushmills: Bush House
Camlough: Carragher's

COUNTY ARMAGH
Portadown: Maguire's; Mandeville Arms (McConville's)

BELFAST
Belfast: (centre) Crown; (west) Fort Bar (Gilmartin's)

COUNTY FERMANAGH
Irvinestown: Central Bar

COUNTY LONDONDERRY
Limavady: Owen's Bar

National Inventory Part 2

Part 2 lists pub interiors which, although altered, have exceptional rooms or features of national historic importance. We also include (in italics)a number of outstanding pub-type rooms in other kinds of establishment, such as hotel bars.

ENGLAND

BEDFORDSHIRE
Broom: Cock
Luton: Painters Arms

BERKSHIRE
Aldworth: Bell

CUMBRIA
Carlisle: Redfern

DEVON
South Zeal: Oxenham Arms

DURHAM
Barningham: Millbank Arms

GLOUCESTERSHIRE & BRISTOL
Bristol: (centre) Palace Hotel
Duntisbourne Abbots: Five Mile House

HERTFORDSHIRE
Bishop's Stortford: Nag's Head

KENT
Cowden Pound: Queen's Arms

GREATER LONDON
Central London: (Blackfriars, EC4) Black Friar; (Holborn, EC4) Olde Cheshire Cheese; (Holborn, WC1) Princess Louise; (Covent Garden, WC2) Salisbury
East London: (Newham, E6) Boleyn
South East London: (Southwark, SE1) George Inn; (Herne Hill, SE24) Half Moon
South West London: (St James's, SW1) Red Lion; (Battersea, SW11) Falcon; (Tooting, SW17) King's Head
West London: (Fitzrovia, W1) Tottenham; (Marylebone, W1) Barley Mow; (Soho, W1) Dog & Duck; (Maida Vale, W9) Prince Alfred, Warrington Hotel; (Notting Hill, W11) Elgin Arms

GREATER MANCHESTER
Manchester: (centre) Marble Arch, Mr Thomas's
Stalybridge: *Railway Station Buffet*
Stockport: Queen's Head

MERSEYSIDE
Liverpool: (centre) Crown, Lion

NORTHUMBERLAND
Blyth: King's Head

NOTTINGHAMSHIRE
Arnold: Vale Hotel
West Bridgford: Test Match Hotel

SOMERSET
Huish Episcopi: Rose & Crown ('Eli's')

The Lion in Liverpool is a fine example of Merseyside pub architecture

The Old Swan is better known as Ma Pardoe's from the matriarch who ruled it for decades

SUSSEX (EAST)
Brighton: King & Queen
Hastings: Havelock

TYNE & WEAR
Gateshead: Central Hotel
Sunderland: Dun Cow; Mountain Daisy

WEST MIDLANDS
Birmingham: (Aston) Bartons Arms; (Hockley) Rose Villa Tavern; (Northfield) Black Horse
Coventry: Biggin Hall Hotel
Netherton: Old Swan ('Ma Pardoe's')
Smethwick: Waterloo Hotel
Upper Gornal: Britannia

WORCESTERSHIRE
Hanley Castle: Three Kings

YORKSHIRE (EAST)
Beverley: White Horse Inn ('Nellie's')
Bridlington: *Railway Station Buffet*
Hull: (centre) White Hart

YORKSHIRE (NORTH)
Middlesbrough: (centre) Zetland Hotel

YORKSHIRE (SOUTH)
Sheffield: (Carbrook) Stumble Inn

YORKSHIRE (WEST)
Heath: King's Arms

WALES

GLAMORGAN
Cardiff: (centre) Golden Cross

MID-WALES
Rhayader: *Lion Royal Hotel*

NORTH-WEST WALES
Bangor: *Snowdon Buffet Bar (Bangor Station)*

SCOTLAND

BORDERS
Oxton: *Tower Hotel*
Tweedsmuir: Crook Inn

THE LOTHIANS
Edinburgh: (centre) Cafe Royal, Kenilworth
Leith: Central Bar
Prestonpans: Prestoungrange Gothenburg

NORTHERN IRELAND

COUNTY FERMANAGH
Enniskillen: Blake's Bar

■ Pub Heritage Group maintains a further list of pubs that are closed or undergoing refurbishment and will require reappraisal. Details are published from time to time in CAMRA's newspaper What's Brewing.

The National Inventory is compiled by CAMRA's Pub Heritage Group
All photographs of National Inventory pubs by Michael Slaughter

Getting to nose you...

A brewers' scheme aims to widen the appreciation of complex cask ale. **Roger Protz** helps you to distinguish a Fuggle from a Golding

IF YOU FIND A FUGGLE a bit of a Challenger and a Golding makes you Bramling Cross, then you need friendly advice when it comes to appreciating the joys of real ale. In recent years, many brewers have started to list the hops they use on labels and beer mats while CAMRA contributes to a greater understanding of cask beer with the tasting notes published in the Good Beer Guide and other publications.

Now a major regional brewer, Everards of Leicester, has launched its Cyclops scheme, aimed as an easy introduction to real ale. The scheme was the brainchild of David Bremner, the company's head of marketing, who feels that over-fancy beer descriptions can deter people from making the switch from keg beer or lager to the greater complexities of cask ale.

David's scheme has a dual approach. The one-eyed Cyclops logo on beer mats and point-of-sale material in pubs gives a brief description of the colour of Everard's beers while hop and sugar lump symbols indicate the bitterness and sweetness of each brew. Simple tasting notes suggest what to expect from the aroma and flavour.

For example, Tiger Best Bitter is described as having an auburn or chestnut-brown colour, a spicy hop, malt and toffee aroma, while the taste has a good

Take a deep breath: the aroma of a beer will tell you a lot about the malt and hop character. Below, one of Everard's beer mats with tasting notes

bitter/sweet balance. The beer receives three hops and three sugar lumps to indicate bitterness and sweetness. The brewery's Sunchaser, on the other hand, is described as having a gold or straw colour, a delicate citrus fruit aroma and a subtle zesty, sweet taste. Bitterness is low, just one and a half hops, with three lumps for sweetness.

The scheme is aimed primarily at first-time younger beer drinkers who are new to cask ale and would like to try it but need to know where to start. This is a group whom independent brewers are keen to win over to cask beer rather than left to a few heavily advertised global brands. Women in particular, whose taste buds are more receptive to bitterness than are men's, are often deterred from drinking cask beer as they perceive the style to be too impenetrable. The Everard's scheme helps to show the diversity of flavours available and that some beers are relatively low in bitterness.

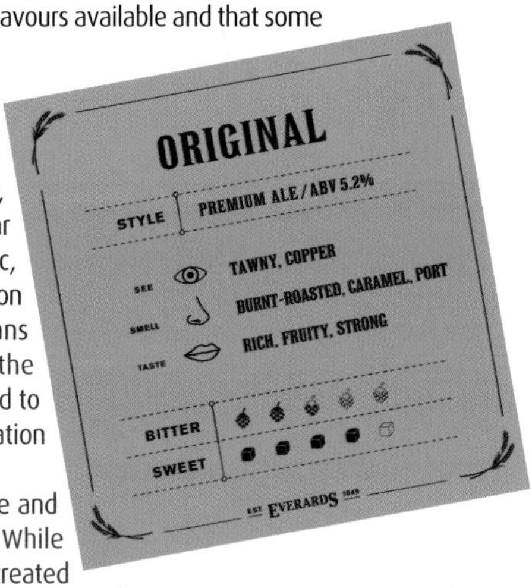

The scheme has been so well received that a large number of other brewers have adopted it. They include Badger, Caledonian, Camerons, Elgoods, Fuller's, Hook Norton, Refresh (Brakspear and Wychwood), Robinsons, Titanic, Wadworth, Charles Wells, Wolverhampton & Dudley and Woodforde's. This means that hundreds of pubs throughout the country will display information geared to increasing the knowledge and appreciation of our national drink.

CAMRA has welcomed the scheme and given it the campaign's full support. While cask beer, like any other drink, can be treated as a simple refresher, some idea of the ingredients that go into its manufacture can only heighten its perception and prove it is worthy of support in the age of global brands that are largely devoid of taste and character.

Malt

Barley malt is the basis of all beer. Even 'wheat beers' are a blend of barley malt as well as wheat. While brewers may use other grains, such as rye and oats to achieve different colours and textures, it is barley malt that provides the rich sugar or maltose that is fermented into alcohol.

Pale malt is the core grain: even midnight black porters and stouts are made primarily from pale malt, with darker grains blended in. On its own, pale malt will give a delightful juicy, biscuity, Ovaltine or cracker bread aroma and flavour to beer. Darker malts make their own contribution to aroma and taste as well as affecting the colour of beer. Crystal, amber, brown, black and chocolate malts give characteristics that range from nuts through raisins and sultanas to coffee and chocolate. Roasted barley, often used in stout, adds a pungent burnt and bitter grain element.

Hops

The hop plant does more than add bitterness to beer. The plant comes in scores of varieties: some add bitterness, others are used principally for their fine aroma. For example, many British craft brewers blend the traditional Fuggles and Goldings

Sip it and see: women drinkers detect bitterness more acutely than men. Tasting notes can help avoid disappointment

varieties, the first for its bitterness, the second for aroma. Hops balance the essential sweet nature of malt and add such characteristics as pine, resin, citrus fruit, fresh-mown grass, herbs, spices and pepper.

Other English hop varieties include Boadicea, Bramling Cross, Challenger, First Gold and Target. Many craft brewers import hops from North America, Australasia and western and central Europe to give their beers the aroma and flavour they seek. While English hops characteristically add bitterness, America hops are famous for their rich citrus notes – grapefruit in particular.

Water

Even the strongest beer is made up of 90 per cent water. The quality and character of water is essential to making good beer. Brewers don't just turn on the tap. Throughout the world, craft brewers who wish to make such British styles as India Pale Ale (IPA) and Bitter will add sulphates to their water. It was the sulphates in the spring waters of the Trent Valley that enabled brewers in Burton-on-Trent in the 19th century to perfect pale ale as a revolutionary new beer style long before the first golden lagers were produced. Today brewers will 'Burtonise' their water with such sulphates as gypsum and magnesium.

Yeast

Without yeast there can be no alcohol: it is this natural fungus that attacks the malt sugars produced during the brewing process and turns them into alcohol. As well as creating alcohol, yeast picks up and retains the flavours of the beer it makes. Fermentation also creates natural aromas and flavours similar to fruit. Many people look askance at the notion that beer made from grain can be 'fruity', but characteristics such as pineapple and blackcurrant are the result of yeast turning sugar into alcohol.

Knowing more about the brewing process and the skills and the ingredients involved help broaden the appeal of cask beer. That is the aim of the Everard's Cyclops scheme and CAMRA's tasting panels.

And if you think we are both saying that real ale is as complex and diverse as wine, the answer is simple: You bet!

Britain's classic beer styles

You can deepen your appreciation of cask ale and get to grips with all the beers listed in the Breweries section with this run-down on the main styles available

Mild

Mild was once the most popular style of beer but was overtaken by Bitter from the 1950s. It was developed in the 18th and 19th centuries as a less aggressively bitter style of beer than porter and stout. Early Milds were much stronger that modern interpretations, which tend to fall in the 3% to 3.5% category, though there are stronger versions, such as Gale's Festival Mild and Sarah Hughes' Dark Ruby. Mild ale is usually dark brown in colour, due to the use of well-roasted malts or roasted barley, but there are paler versions, such as Banks's Original, Timothy Taylor's Golden Best and McMullen's AK. Look for rich malty aromas and flavours with hints of dark fruit, chocolate, coffee and caramel and a gentle underpinning of hop bitterness.

Old Ale

Old Ale recalls the type of beer brewed before the Industrial Revolution, stored for months or even years in unlined wooden vessels known as tuns. The beer would pick up some lactic sourness as a result of wild yeasts, lactobacilli and tannins in the wood. The result was a beer dubbed 'stale' by drinkers: it was one of the components of the early, blended Porters. The style has re-emerged in recent years, due primarily to the fame of Theakston's Old Peculier, Gale's Prize Old Ale and Thomas Hardy's Ale, the last saved from oblivion by O'Hanlon's Brewery in Devon. Old Ales, contrary to expectation, do not have to be especially strong: they can be no more than 4% alcohol, though the Gale's and O'Hanlon's versions are considerably stronger. Neither do they have to be dark: Old Ale can be pale and burst with lush sappy malt, tart fruit and spicy hop notes. Darker versions will have a more profound malt character with powerful hints of roasted grain, dark fruit, polished leather and fresh tobacco. The hallmark of the style remains a lengthy period of maturation, often in bottle rather than bulk vessels.

Bitter

Towards the end of the 19th century, brewers built large estates of tied pubs. They moved away from vatted beers stored for many months and developed 'running beers' that could be served after a few days' storage in pub cellars. Draught Mild was a 'running beer' along with a new type that was dubbed Bitter by drinkers. Bitter grew out of Pale Ale but was generally deep bronze to copper in colour due to the use of slightly darker malts such as crystal that give the beer fullness of palate. Best is a stronger version of Bitter but there is considerable crossover. Bitter falls into the 3.4% to 3.9% band, with Best Bitter 4% upwards but a number of brewers label their ordinary Bitters 'Best'. A further development of Bitter comes in the shape of Extra or Special Strong Bitters of 5% or more: familiar examples of this style include Fuller's ESB and Greene King Abbot. With ordinary Bitter, look for a spicy, peppery and grassy hop character, a powerful bitterness, tangy fruit and juicy and nutty malt. With Best and Strong Bitters, malt and fruit character will tend to dominate but hop aroma and bitterness are still crucial to the style, often achieved by 'late hopping' in the brewery or adding hops to casks as they leave for pubs.

Golden Ales

This new style of pale, well-hopped and quenching beer developed in the 1980s as independent brewers attempted to win younger drinkers from heavily-promoted lager brands. The first in the field were Exmoor Gold and Hop Back Summer Lightning, though many micros and regionals now make their versions of the style. Strengths will range from 3.5% to 5%. The hallmark will be the biscuity and juicy malt character derived from pale malts, underscored by tart citrus fruit and peppery hops, often with the addition of hints of vanilla and sweetcorn. Above all, such beers are quenching and served cool.

IPA and Pale Ale

India Pale Ale changed the face of brewing early in the 19th century. The new technologies of the Industrial Revolution enabled brewers to use pale malts to fashion beers that were genuinely golden or pale bronze in colour. First brewed in London and Burton-on-Trent for the colonial market, IPAs were strong in alcohol and high in hops: the preservative character of the hops helped keep the beers in good condition during long sea journeys. Beers with less alcohol and hops were developed for the domestic market and were known as Pale Ale. Today Pale Ale is usually a bottled version of Bitter, though historically the styles are different. Marston's Pedigree is an example of Burton Pale Ale, not Bitter, while the same brewery's Old Empire is a fascinating interpretation of a Victorian IPA. So-called IPAs with strengths of around 3.5% are not true to style. Look for juicy malt, citrus fruit and a big spicy, peppery, bitter hop character, with strengths of 4% upwards.

Porter and Stout

Porter was a London style that turned the brewing industry upside down early in the 18th century. It was a dark brown beer – 19th-century versions became jet black – that was originally a blend of brown ale, pale ale and 'stale' or well-matured ale. It acquired the name Porter as a result of its popularity among London's street-market workers. The strongest versions of Porter were known as Stout Porter, reduced over the years to simply Stout. Such vast quantities of Porter and Stout flooded into Ireland from London and Bristol that a Dublin brewer named Arthur Guinness decided to fashion his own interpretation of the style. Guinness in Dublin blended some unmalted roasted barley and in so doing produced a style known as Dry Irish Stout. Restrictions on making roasted malts in Britain during World War One led to the demise of Porter and Stout and left the market to the Irish. In recent years, smaller craft brewers in Britain have rekindled an interest in the style, though in keeping with modern drinking habits, strengths have been reduced. Look for profound dark and roasted malt character with raisin and sultana fruit, espresso or cappuccino coffee, liquorice and molasses.

Barley Wine

Barley Wine is a style that dates from the 18th and 19th centuries when England was often at war with France and it was the duty of patriots, usually from the upper classes, to drink ale rather than Claret. Barley Wine had to be strong – often between 10% and 12% – and was stored for prodigious periods of as long at 18 months or two years. When country houses had their own small breweries, it was often the task of the butler to brew ale that was drunk from cut-glass goblets at the dining table. The biggest-selling Barley Wine for years was Whitbread's 10.9% Gold Label, now available only in cans. Bass's No 1 Barley Wine (10.5%) is occasionally brewed in Burton-on-Trent, stored in cask for 12 months and made available to CAMRA beer festivals. Fuller's Vintage Ale (8.5%) is a bottle-conditioned version of its Golden Pride and is brewed with different varieties of malts and hops every year. Many micro-brewers now produce their interpretations of the style. Expect massive sweet malt and ripe fruit of the pear drop, orange and lemon type, with darker fruits, chocolate and coffee if darker malts are used. Hop rates are generous and produce bitterness and peppery, grassy and floral notes.

Scottish Beers

Historically, Scottish beers tend to be darker, sweeter and less heavily hopped than English and Welsh ales: a cold climate demands warming beers. But many of the new craft breweries produce beers lighter in colour and with generous hop rates. The traditional, classic styles are Light, low in strength and so-called even when dark in colour, also known as 60/-, Heavy or 70/-, Export or 80/- and a strong Wee Heavy, similar to a barley wine, and also labelled 90/-. In the 19th century, beers were invoiced according to strength, using the now defunct currency of the shilling.

Choosing the pubs

Beer quality sets the pace...

THE GOOD BEER GUIDE IS UNIQUE. There are several pub guides available and in the main they concentrate on picture-postcard country pubs and food. This guide, on the other hand, starts with beer quality: hence its title. It is more than just a pub guide. The driving force of the Campaign for Real Ale is quality cask-conditioned draught beer and it has been the guide's belief for 34 years that if a landlord keeps his beer well and pours perfect pints, then everything else in his pub – welcome, food, accommodation and family facilities – are likely to be of an equally high standard. It's the beer that counts, not thatched roofs, carved wooden settles, inglenooks and, in one case, Thai vegetable schnitzels: German cuisine goes Oriental.

The heart of the guide is its pub section, offering more than 4,500 pubs throughout the country. They are all full entries. One pub guide says it offers 5,000 pubs but the editorial team only inspects 1,000 of them: the remainder are unchecked.

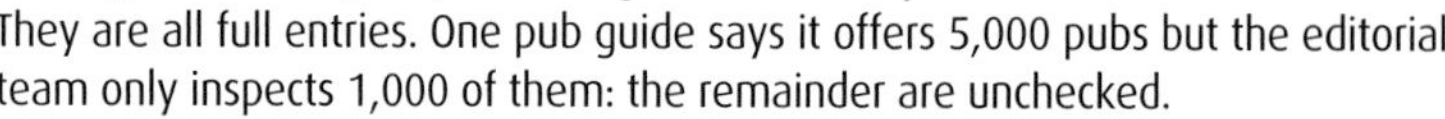

Every pub in the Good Beer Guide has been inspected many times by CAMRA members during the course of a year. They visit them to check that beer quality has not declined. The guide does not charge for entry, neither does it make do with questionnaires sent to publicans. Even as the guide goes to press, we will delete an entry if we receive a report about poor beer quality.

The guide is unique in several ways. It has an army of 83,000 unpaid CAMRA volunteers. They choose the entries, with detailed descriptions of beer, food, history, architecture, facilities and public transport available. There is a considerable turnover of pubs from edition to edition as CAMRA members delete those that have fallen below an acceptable standard or rotate pubs in an area with a substantial number of good outlets.

And it is not a guide to country pubs alone. CAMRA has campaigned to sustain rural pubs and they feature prominently in these pages. But drinkers visit urban pubs, too, and all the major towns and cities feature in the guide with an abundance of choice. We do not, for example, insult Leeds by listing just one pub, which is the case with one so-called pub guide.

As this is a guide to beer as well as pubs, we also offer our unique contribution to beer appreciation: the Breweries section. It is an annual snapshot of the industry, listing all the beers produced with strengths and tasting notes. It indicates breweries that have closed and new entrants to the industry. The section complements the pub listings, helping you to find the beers available, and stressing the enormous choice and diversity available.

■ You can keep your copy of the guide up to date by visiting the CAMRA website: www.camra.org.uk . Click on Good Beer Guide then Updates to the GBG 2007. You will find information on brewery changes to pubs and breweries.

England

BEDFORDSHIRE

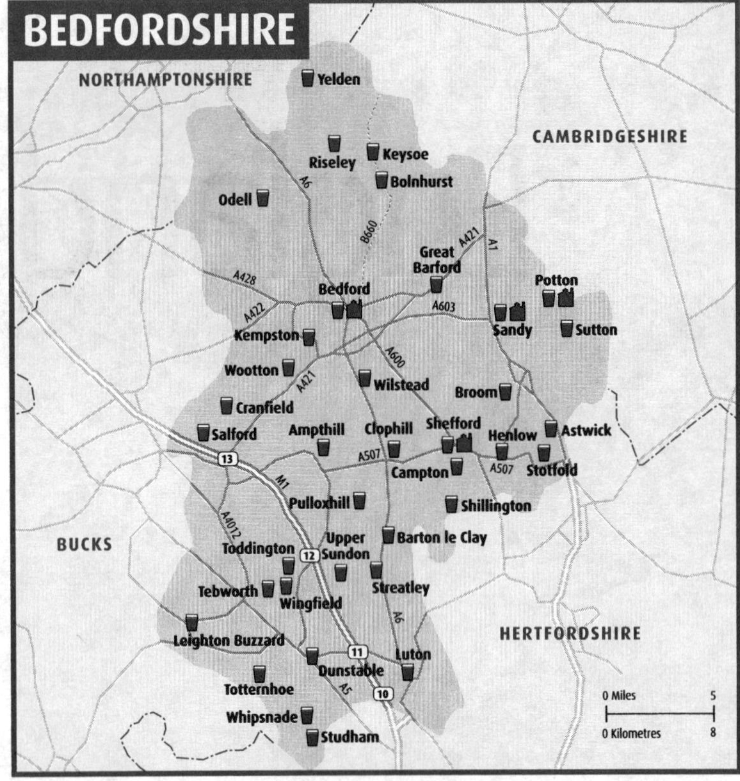

Ampthill

Queens's Head

20 Woburn Street, MK45 2HP

11-11; 12-10.30 Sun

(01525) 405016

Wells Eagle, Bombardier; guest beer [H]

Cosy 18th-century tavern in a historic area of Ampthill, close to the park and the Green Sands Ridge walk. Inside is a low-beamed bar frequented by locals, a lounge and a restaurant which is available for private functions. Home-cooked meals are available all day. Quarterly beer festivals are hosted. The pub's name refers to Catherine of Aragon who was imprisoned in Ampthill Castle while Henry VIII dissolved the monasteries and broke from the church in Rome.

Astwick

Tudor Oaks

1 Taylors Road, SG5 4AZ

11-11; 12-3.30, 7-10.30 Sun

(01462) 834133 tudoroaks.co.uk

Beer range varies [H]

Situated alongside the northbound A1 between Stotfold and Langford, a pleasant atmosphere awaits you at this large, one-room, multi-beamed bar and restaurant. Seven handpumps serve beers from regional and micro-breweries. Good food is available in the restaurant, with seafood and steak particularly recommended, and accommodation is available.

P

Barton le Clay

Bull Hotel

77 Bedford Road, MK45 4LL

12-2.30, 6-1am (2am Fri & Sat); 12-2.30, 6-midnight Sun

(01582) 705070

Adnams Bitter; Greene King IPA; McMullen AK, Shepherd Neame Spitfire [H]

Old, oak beamed pub in the centre of the village. Popular with a varied clientele, it has dominoes and darts teams. A pool table and dartboard are situated in the front bar. The main dining area is no-smoking and offers a children's menu (no food Thu eve). Outside the pub at the front is a small seating area. A large function room is available to hire.

P

Bedford

Cricketers Arms

35 Goldington Road, MK40 3LH

(on A428 E of town centre)

5-11; 12-11 Sat; 6.30-10.30 Sun

(01234) 303958 cricketersarms.co.uk

Hook Norton Hooky Bitter; guest beers [H]

Small, one-bar pub opposite the Bedford

INDEPENDENT BREWERIES

B&T Shefford
Old Stables Sandy
Potton Potton
Wells & Young's Bedford

Blues rugby ground. Popular with fans of the game and very busy on match days. Live rugby matches are shown on the two plasma screens at each end of the wood-panelled bar. The three rotating guest beers are usually from regional breweries, chosen from Punch Taverns' finest cask selection. No meals served Sunday evenings. ❀◗⊟⊬

Phoenix

45 St John's Street, MK42 0AB
(on A6 S of town centre)
✪ 11-11; 12-10.30 Sun
☎ (01234) 352862
Wells Eagle, Bombardier Ⓗ
Friendly local overflowing with Irish charm, facing a large traffic island south of the river. Built in 1900 and extended in the 1960s, the pub has a fine collection of old local photographs displayed in the lounge bar. Home-cooked lunches and evening meals are served Monday to Saturday. Car park access is from Kingsway (A6 northbound).
◖◗⇌(St Johns)⊟♣P

Wellington Arms

40-42 Wellington Street, MK40 2JX (just off gyratory system N of town centre)
✪ 12-11; 12-10.30 Sun
☎ (01234) 308033 ⊕ wellingtonarms.co.uk
Adnams Bitter; B&T Two Brewers, Shefford Bitter; guest beers Ⓗ
Sociable B&T tied house offering a wide range of regional and micro-brewery beers, plus real cider and perry, from 16 handpumps. A range of Belgian and other imported beers is available on draught and bottled. Breweriana appears to fill every nook and cranny. Food is limited to filled rolls. There is a courtyard for outdoor drinking. ❀⊟●⊡

Bolnhurst

Plough

Kimbolton Road, MK44 2EX
(on B660, S end of village)
✪ 12-3, 7-11 (closed Mon); 12-3 Sun
☎ (01234) 376274 ⊕ bolnhurst.com
Bateman XB; Potton Village Bike; guest beer Ⓗ
Recently refurbished pub and restaurant offering high quality food. The bar has a modern fireplace and plenty of seating. Through the bar the kitchen is visible. Outside is a large drinking area next to the car park. The pub is no-smoking throughout.
⚠Q❀◖◗♿⊟P⊬

Broom

White Horse

SG18 9NN (opp. village green)
✪ 12-3, 5.30-midnight; 12-4, 6-1am Sat; 12-10.30 Sun
☎ (01767) 313425 ⊕ whitehorsebroom.co.uk
Greene King IPA, Abbot; guest beers Ⓗ
A Grade II listed building, this friendly locals' pub has a welcoming feel. The third handpump dispenses a changing range of guest beers, usually from the Greene King stable. Excellent Sunday lunches are served. The pub runs several events throughout the year to raise money for local charities. ⚠❀◖◗⊞♿⛺P

Campton

White Hart

Mill Lane SG17 5NX
✪ 7-11; 5-11 Fri; 3-11 (1am summer) Sat; 12-4, 7-10.30 Sun
☎ (01462) 812567
Theakston Best Bitter; Courage Directors; John Smith's Bitter; guest beers Ⓗ
A Guide entry since 1976, the pub has been run by the same family for over 35 years. This 300-year-old Grade II listed free house has three bar areas. Exposed brickwork, wooden beams, quarry-tiled floors, inglenooks and bygone artefacts feature throughout. The pub hosts a monthly quiz and several teams including darts, crib, petanque and dominoes, and runs a golf society. The large garden has a well-equipped play area. ⚠❀♣P

Clophill

Stone Jug

10 Back Street, MK45 4BY (off A6, N end of village)
✪ 12-3, 6-11; 12-11 Fri; 11-11 Sat; 12-10.30 Sun
☎ (01525) 860526
B&T Shefford Bitter; John Smith's Bitter; Wadworth 6X; guest beers Ⓗ
Popular local at the northern edge of Clophill. Converted from 17th-century stone cottages, the single bar serves two drinking areas and a function/children's room. There is a patio at the rear and picnic benches at the front. Excellent home-made food is served Monday to Saturday. Parking can be difficult at busy times. Awarded CAMRA North Beds Pub of the Year 2005. Q⛀❀◖♣●P

Cranfield

Carpenters Arms

93 High Street, MK43 0DP
✪ 12-3 (not Mon-Thu), 6-11; 12-3, 7-10.30 Sun
☎ (01234) 750232
Wadworth 6X; Wells Eagle Ⓗ
Situated in the heart of Cranfield village, the 'Carps' is a light and airy modernised pub with wooden floors and cladding. Home-cooked meals are served in the popular, no-smoking lounge/restaurant. Traditional pub games are played in the bar. The large car park leads to a secure patio garden. Q❀◖◗⊞⊟♣P⊬

Dunstable

Globe

43 Winfield Street, LU6 1LS
✪ 12-11 (10.30 Sun)
☎ (01582) 512300 ⊕ globe-pub.co.uk
B&T Two Brewers, Shefford Bitter, Shefford Dark Mild, Dragonslayer; Everards Tiger; guest beers Ⓗ
This former keg-only local with a notoriously chequered past has miraculously reopened as B&T's third tied pub. Decorated with breweriana, the clean, bright bar offers no frills, just good beer. Twelve handpumps offer an ever-changing range of guest beers, as well as Belgian bottled beers and Weston's Old Rosie cider. Welcoming and dog friendly, the pub has quickly built a loyal following. Unusually, the dark mild is the second most requested beer.
Q♣●

Victoria
69 West Street, LU6 1ST
11-12.30am (1am Fri & Sat); 11-12.30am Sun
(01582) 662682
Beer range varies H
A frequent CAMRA local Pub of the Year, this thriving pub usually offers four ales including the house beer, Victoria Bitter, brewed by Tring brewery. The guests come from a range of micro-breweries. The main bar houses a dartboard and TV, mostly tuned to Sky Sports. Quarterly beer festivals are hosted. A patio area with heaters is at the rear and the small function room doubles as a family area. There is no admittance after 11pm. ❀◐♣

Great Barford

Anchor Inn
High Street, MK44 3LF
12-3, 6 (5.30 Fri)-11; 12-11 Sat; 12-4, 6.30-10.30 Sun
(01234) 870364
Wells Eagle; guest beers H
Busy village pub next to the church and overlooking the River Ouse. At least two guest beers are usually available from an extensive range. Good, home-cooked food is served in the bar and restaurant as well as an extensive wine list. The pub is popular with river users in summer. ♔Q◐◑P⚟

Henlow

Engineers Arms
68 High Street, SG16 6AA
12-midnight (1am Fri & Sat); 12-midnight Sun
(01462) 812284 engineersarms.co.uk
Everards Tiger; guest beers H
A real gem, this busy village meeting place now has 10 handpumps dispensing over 20 different beers a week, plus three real ciders and a perry. It hosts the village beer festival in October and mini festivals over the bank holiday weekends. Bedfordshire CAMRA Pub of the Year four years in a row; it was the East Anglia winner in 2003. ♔Q❀⊟♿♣●

Kempston

Half Moon
108 High Street, MK42 7BN
12-3, 6 (5 Fri)-11; 12-3.30, 7-11 Sat; 12-3.30, 7-10.30 Sun
(01234) 852464
Wells Eagle, Bombardier H
Welcoming local with a comfortable lounge and a spacious public bar. The attractive outdoor area has two boules pitches and a large grassed garden with play area. A quiz or bingo is held on Sunday evening. The pub is situated in the old part of town near the Great Ouse and convenient for riverside walks. Twice runner up in Charles Wells' community pub competition. ❀⊟🚌♣P

Keysoe

White Horse
Kimbolton Road, MK44 2JA (on B660 at Keysoe Row crossroads)
12-3, 5.30 (7 Mon)-11; 12-11 Sat; 12-10.30 Sun
(01234) 376363
Wells Eagle; guest beers H
Single-bar country pub with a thatched roof and low beams. It is one of the oldest pubs in the Charles Wells estate. Backing on to the bar area is a conservatory with a pool table and dartboard. Outside is a large garden with children's play area. There are normally two guest beers from the Charles Wells list available. No food is served on Monday or Sunday evening. ♔❀◐◑🚌♣P

Leighton Buzzard

Hare
10 Southcott Village, Linslade, LU7 2PR
12-midnight daily
(01525) 373941
Courage Best Bitter; Fuller's London Pride; Young's Bitter; guest beers H
Popular local pub overlooking the village green which attracts a good mix of drinkers. Over the years the village has expanded and it is now part of the town. A collection of historic photographs features in the pub. An annual St George's Day beer festival is held in a marquee in the large rear garden. Two regularly changing guest beers are usually on offer. ♔❀⇌♣P

Stag
1 Heath Road, LU7 8AB
12-1am; 12-10.30 Sun
(01525) 372710
Fuller's Discovery, London Pride, ESB, seasonal beers H
This tied house serves the full range of Fuller's beers except Chiswick which seems to have made way for Discovery. The tongue and groove walls dominate the interior of this deceptively large wedge-shaped inn. Late night opening is dependent on the level of trade earlier in the evening. ❀◐

Wheatsheaf
57 North Street, LU7 7EQ
11-11 (1am Fri & Sat); 12-11 Sun
(01525) 374611
Tring Jack O'Legs; guest beer H
Small pub with an island bar serving two rooms. An eclectic mix of regulars drinks here, ranging from the dominoes team to the rock music enthusiasts. Live music is played on Friday and Saturday night, with rock the favourite genre. The back room is larger than the cosy front bar and houses the stage, a pool table and dartboard. The Jack O'Legs changes occasionally; an additional guest beer is usually available at the weekend. ♣

Luton

Bricklayers Arms
16-18 Hightown Road, LU2 0DD
12-3, 5-11; 12-midnight Fri & Sat; 12-10.30 Sun
(01582) 611017
Everards Beacon, Tiger; guest beer H
Run by the same landlady for over 20 years, this somewhat quirky pub is popular with locals, especially on match days, when it can get busy. Two TVs show Sky Sports, and on Monday there is a quiz night. The three guest beers, on average eight a week, are usually sourced from micro-breweries. Belgian beers,

bottled and draught, are also stocked. Weekday lunchtime snacks are available. ❀≠♣P

English Rose

46 Old Bedford Road, LU2 7PA

⏲ 12-11 daily

☎ (01582) 723889 🌐 englishroseluton.co.uk

Beer range varies 🄷

Voted CAMRA local Pub of the Year 2006, this friendly corner pub has the atmosphere of a village local in town. The three frequently-changing beers are chosen from a range of breweries. Food is served at lunchtime during the week and until 6pm on Saturday, with a takeaway service available. The convivial bar staff have a basic knowledge of British sign language. The quiz on Tuesday evening is a highlight and there is a pool table. The large garden is popular in summer. Conveniently located for the station. ❀◐◑≠

Odell

Bell

Horsefair Lane, MK43 7AU

⏲ 11.30-3, 6-11; 12-4.30, 6-11 Sat; 12-4.30, 7-10.30 Sun

☎ (01234) 720254

Greene King IPA, Ruddles County, Abbot 🄷

Handsome, thatched village inn with a large garden near the river Great Ouse. With the Harrold-Odell country park just down the lane, this is a popular stop-off for walkers. Sympathetic refurbishment and a series of linked but distinct seating areas help retain a traditional pub atmosphere. Small menu portions are available at lunchtime.

♨Q❀◐◑🚌(124)P⚟

Potton

Bricklayers Arms

1 Newtown, SG19 2GH

⏲ 12-11 (12.30am Fri & Sat); 12-11 Sun

☎ (01767) 262332 🌐 thebricklayerspotton.co.uk

Adnams Broadside; Greene King IPA, Abbot 🄷

Recently refurbished locals' pub with a large bar and garden with a welcoming atmosphere. Three real ales are served with pride by the landlord. Pub games include darts and a petanque team has recently been formed with an area of the garden developed to accommodate the game. ❀♿♣P

Old Coach House

12 Market Square, SG19 2NP

⏲ 12-2.30, 5-11; 12-11 Sun

☎ (01767) 260221 🌐 pottoncoachhouse.co.uk

Adnams Bitter; Potton Shambles, Shannon; guest beers 🄷

Large Georgian coaching inn facing the market square. The tap for local brewery Potton, the pub is known to regulars as the Shambles – also the name of one of Potton's ales. Recently redecorated, it has a large front bar, a smaller bar and dining area at the rear, and a restaurant. ☕❀🛏◐◑P⚟

Pulloxhill

Cross Keys

13 High Street, MK45 5HB

⏲ 12-3, 6-11; 12-3, 7-10.30 Sun

☎ (01525) 712442

Adnams Broadside; Wells Eagle, Bombardier 🄷

Old, oak-beamed inn near the top of the hill in a pretty village – a popular venue for dining due to home-made specials and an extensive wine list. A small area to the side of the main bar is no-smoking. The large function room is used by local groups and clubs. The extensive grounds include a children's play area next to the car park. ❀◐◑⛺P⚟

Riseley

Fox & Hounds

High Street, MK44 1DT

⏲ 11-2.30, 6-11; 12-3, 7-10.30 Sun

☎ (01234) 708240

Wells Eagle, Bombardier; guest beers 🄷

Old village inn, originally two 16th-century cottages complete with priest's hiding hole. With a reputation for good food, charcoal-grilled steak, sold by weight and served with salad, is a speciality (not Sat lunch). The dining room can be reserved for parties but booking is unnecessary for bar meals – relax and enjoy your pint while your food is cooked. The large, lawned garden has a covered patio with heaters for inclement weather. Q❀◐◑🚌P

Salford

Red Lion Country Hotel

Wavendon Road, MK17 8AZ (2 miles N of M1 jct 13)

⏲ 11-2.30, 6-11; 12-2.30, 7-10.30 Sun

☎ (01908) 583117 🌐 redlioncountryinn.com

Wells Eagle, Bombardier 🄷

Traditional country hotel serving a fine selection of home-cooked food in the bar and no-smoking dining room. The bar, warmed by an open fire in winter, offers a selection of board games. The large garden includes a covered area and a safe children's playground. The hotel offers well-furnished rooms, some with four-poster beds. Charles Wells' top wine pub for the last two years. ♨Q❀🛏◐◑⊟♿🚌♣P

Sandy

Sir William Peel

39 High Street, SG19 1AG

⏲ 11-11; 12-10.30 Sun

☎ (01767) 680607

Everards Beacon; guest beers 🄷

Traditional pub with a single U-shaped bar, which can be smoky at times. Two guest beers, from micro-breweries, change often. No food is available but a chip shop and Indian restaurant are on either side of the pub.

❀♿⛺≠P

Shefford

Brewery Tap

14 North Bridge Street, SG17 5DH

⏲ 11.30-11; 12-10.30 Sun

☎ (01462) 628448

B&T Shefford Bitter, Shefford Dark Mild, Dragonslayer; Everards Tiger; guest beer 🄷

A short walk from the B&T Brewery, this tap was resurrected and renamed by B&T in 1996.

The single bar serves two areas and a family room. Access to the patio garden and car park is through an archway next to the pub. The bar has an interesting collection of breweriana and old bottled beers. Occasional live music and entertainment is hosted on Friday evening. ☎❀♣P

Shillington

Musgrave Arms

16 Apsley End Road, SG5 3LX

12-3, 4.30-11; 12-11 Sat; 12-10.30 Sun

☎ (01462) 711286 themusgravearms.co.uk

Greene King IPA, Abbot H

Splendid country pub with original Tudor beams. Dominoes and petanque are popular here. The no-smoking restaurant serves good home-cooked meals (not Sun eve or Mon), with steak night on Tuesday and Thursday. Children and dogs are permitted in the bar. The monthly quiz is on a Monday and live music is also once a month on a Friday. Q❀♣P

Stotfold

Stag

35 Brook Street, SG5 4LA

4 (1 Fri; 12 Sat)-11; 12-10.30 Sun

☎ (01462) 730261

Adnams Bitter; guest beers H

Friendly village free house with an L-shaped bar and games area. A drinker's paradise, Adnams Bitter is always on tap, along with two frequently changing guests, often from local micro-breweries. Food is served on occasional themed curry or chilli nights. Live music and games nights are held regularly. A haunt for steam enthusiasts. ❀P

Streatley

Chequers

171 Sharpenhoe Road, LU3 9PS

12-11.30 (12.30am Fri & Sat); 12-11 Sun

☎ (01582) 882072

Greene King IPA, Morland Original, Abbot, Old Speckled Hen; guest beers H

In the centre of the village next to the church, the Chequers is Georgian in origin but has been sympathetically extended. Unusually for the area, oversized glasses are used. A single L-shaped bar offers food all day. The pub is popular with walkers from the Chiltern Way nearby. The garden has a play area and hosts monthly Sunday afternoon jazz sessions. Accommodation is available in five guest rooms. ❀♣P

Studham

Red Lion

Church Road, LU6 2QA

12-3, 5-11; 11-11 Fri & Sat; 12-10.30 Sun

☎ (01582) 872530

Adnams Bitter; Fuller's London Pride; Greene King IPA; Tring Colley's Dog; guest beer H

Overlooking the village common, this welcoming local pub has a lounge bar, snug and a no-smoking dining room serving a good range of home-cooked food (no food Sun or Mon eve). There is usually at least one beer from a local brewer and real cider has recently been added to the list. Dogs are welcome in the bar. The village of Studham is popular with walkers and visitors to Whipsnade Zoo. Ramps are provided to aid access to the pub.
Q☎❀P

Sutton

John O'Gaunt

30 High Street, SG19 2NG

12-3, 7-11; 12-3, 7-10.30 Sun

☎ (01767) 260377

Greene King IPA, Abbot; guest beers H

An excellent village pub with lots of character serving good food, with occasional folk music evenings. Welcoming and traditional, with two bars and a large garden, the pub has a timeless feel to it. In winter the bar is warmed by an open fire. The pub is active in community life and the lounge is decorated by the Sutton village quilt. No food is served on Sunday evening. Q❀♣P

Tebworth

Queen's Head

The Lane, LU7 9QB

12-3 (not Tue & Wed), 6-11; 12-3, 6-11 Sun

☎ (01525) 874101

Adnams Broadside; G **Wells Eagle;** H **guest beers** G

Traditional two-bar village local with a public bar, popular for darts and dominoes, and a lounge, which offers a quiz on Thursday and live music on Friday evening. A large garden is at the rear. No food is served but customers are welcome to bring their own. The pub has featured in the Guide for over 20 years under the present landlord, who also has a career as an actor with innumerable appearances on stage, radio and TV. ❀♣P

Toddington

Oddfellows Arms

2 Conger Lane, LU5 6BP

5-11 (midnight Fri); 12-midnight Sat; 12-11 Sun

☎ (01525) 872021

Adnams Broadside; Fuller's London Pride; guest beers H

Attractive 15th-century pub facing the village green with a heavily beamed and brassed L-shaped bar. The no-smoking restaurant becomes a bar when food service has finished. There are over 20 bottled Belgian beers to choose from, all served in their correct glasses. The varied menu offers good food (Tue-Sat eves and Sun lunch). Beer festivals are usually held in the spring and autumn. Tables on the small patio area are an added attraction. ❀

Sow & Pigs

14 Church Square, LU5 6AA

11 (12 Sun)-midnight

☎ (01525) 873089 sowandpigs.co.uk

Greene King IPA, Abbot; guest beers H

This 19th-century commercial inn has featured in every edition of the Guide. It has one long, narrow bar heated by open fires, decorated with pigs, golf memorabilia and paintings of the pub by local artists. Excellent home-made food is offered daily (12-4pm) and tapas-styles snacks are served in the evening. Banquets can be booked for larger parties, served in the heavily-oaked banquet room upstairs. A well-planted patio garden is to the rear. Comfortable and reasonably-priced accommodation is available.
⛰Q✿🛏◐♣P

Totternhoe

Cross Keys
201 Castle Hill Road, LU6 2DA
⏲ 11.30-3, 5.30-11; 11.30-11 Sat; 11-11 Sun
☎ (01525) 220434
Adnams Broadside; Greene King IPA, Abbot; guest beer (summer) Ⓗ
Voted by local CAMRA as Most Improved Pub 2005, this attractive, Grade II listed, thatched building dating from 1433 has undergone a massive refurbishment programme following a fire. The quaint restaurant area, which is no-smoking during food service times, offers lunchtime and evening meals daily (not Sun eve). Barbecues are a regular event during the summer, held in the large garden which enjoys extensive views of Aylesbury Vale and Ivinghoe Beacon. ✿◐◑♣P

Upper Sundon

White Hart
56 Streatley Road, LU3 3PQ
⏲ 11-11; 12-10.30 Sun
☎ (01525) 872493
Wells Eagle; guest beers Ⓗ
Friendly, mock Tudor, two-bar village local, tucked away in a side-street in this semi-rural scattered village. Close to Sundon Hills country park, it is a popular stop off for visitors. The pub has low beams and leaded windows, and gardens at the front and rear. A large selection of malt whiskies is stocked.
✿⊟♣P

Whipsnade

Old Hunter's Lodge
The Cross Roads, LU6 2LN
⏲ 11-3, 5-11; 12-3, 7-10.30 Sun
☎ (01582) 872228 🌐 old-hunters.com
Greene King IPA, Abbot; guest beer Ⓗ
The Lodge is a 15th-century thatched inn with a comfortable lounge. Two guest beers are usually sourced from micro-breweries. A large dining area provides food throughout the week. The Lodge has six guest rooms including a bridal suite with four-poster bed. Handy for nearby Whipsnade Zoo, one of Europe's most important centres for breeding and conserving rare animals.
⛰✿🛏◐◑⊟P

Wilstead

Woolpack
2 Bedford Road, MK45 3HW
⏲ 5-11 Mon; 12-11.30 (1am Fri & Sat); 12-11.30 Sun
☎ (01234) 742318
Greene King IPA, Old Speckled Hen; guest beers Ⓗ
Friendly village local where visitors are very welcome. Guest ales change regularly and a beer festival is held in August. The open fire adds to a cosy atmosphere – note the old well in the corner. The car park leads to a pretty patio garden. Good, home-cooked food is served at lunchtime and in the evening you are welcome to bring in your own supper from nearby takeaways. Live music is played most weekends. ⛰✿◐🚌♣P

Wingfield

Plough
Tebworth Road, LU7 9QH
⏲ 12-midnight daily
☎ (01525) 873077
Fuller's London Pride, ESB, seasonal beers; guest beer Ⓗ
Attractive thatched village inn dating from the 17th century. Beware the low doorway and beams. The bar is decorated with paintings of rural scenes, many featuring ploughs. The conservatory is no-smoking and used by drinkers and diners; good food is available daily except Sunday evening. There are tables outside the front of the pub and the prize-winning enclosed rear garden is illuminated at night.
⛰✿◐◑P⚟

Wootton

Chequers
Hall End, MK43 9HP
⏲ 11.30-2.30, 5.30-11; 12-10.30 Sun
☎ (01234) 768394
Wells Eagle Ⓗ
Originally a farmhouse, the pub has heavy wooden beams and a low ceiling creating an intimate atmosphere. The large, lawned garden with outdoor tables and chairs is popular in summer. A wide range of interesting food is served Wednesday to Sunday lunchtime and Tuesday to Saturday evening. ⛰✿◐◑⊟♿⛺♣P

Yelden

Chequers
High Street, MK44 1AW
⏲ 12-2 (not Mon & Tue), 5-11; 12-midnight Fri & Sat; 12-10.30 Sun
☎ (01933) 356383
Fuller's London Pride; Ⓗ **Greene King Abbot;** Ⓖ **Taylor Landlord; guest beers** Ⓗ
Traditional village pub offering five real ales and two ciders. Families are welcome in the skittles area. Good, home-cooked pub meals are served in the no-smoking lounge, with occasional ticket-only guest chef days. The extensive rear garden hosts an annual spring bank holiday beer and cider festival. The village of Yelden is on the Three Shires Way footpath and boasts the impressive earthworks of an abandoned Norman castle.
⛰🐄✿◐◑⛺🚌♣🍎P⚟

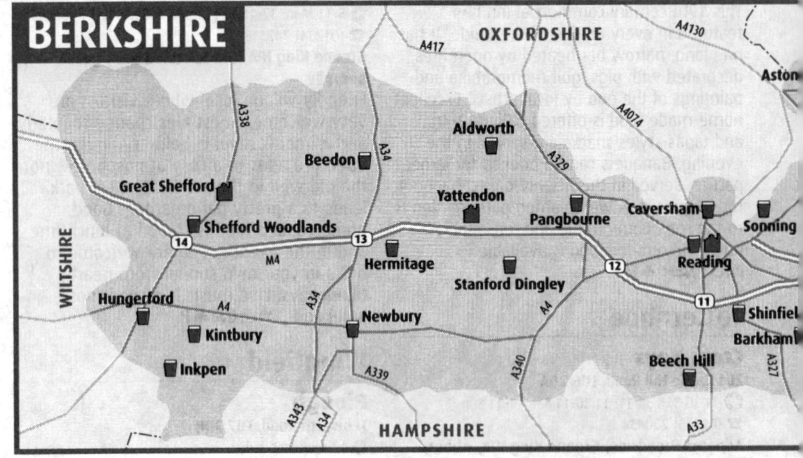

Aldworth

Bell ☆

Bell Lane, RG8 9SE (off B4009) OS555796
✪ 11-3, 6-11; closed Mon; 12-3, 7-10.30 Sun
☎ (01635) 578272
Arkell's 3B, Kingsdown; West Berkshire, Maggs Mild, seasonal beers Ⓗ

Genuine, unspoilt village ale house run by the same family for 200 years. Close to the Ridgeway, it is popular with walkers and cyclists. The garden is delightful and provides access to the village cricket ground. West Berkshire Brewery's monthly ales are available as well as local Uptons farmhouse cider. The locals' tipple of a 50/50 mix of Kingsdown and 3B is known here as 'two-stroke'. Delicious home-made filled rolls and soup are recommended. Winner of CAMRA regional Pub of the Year 2005.
⛼Q♉❀♣♣P

Aston

Flower Pot

Ferry Lane, RG9 3DG
✪ 11-3, 6-11 (11-11 Sat & summer); 12-11 Sun
☎ (01491) 574721
Brakspear Bitter, Special, seasonal beers Ⓗ

Red brick building in a rural location near the Thames Path; an ideal starting point for a walk to Henley on Thames or Hambledon Lock. The pub has a fishing theme reflecting its location and the walls are decorated with various stuffed animals. The large garden is surrounded by fields where you might see a variety of interesting fowl. Traditional pub fare is served in generous portions at reasonable prices. ⛼Q❀⛟☾◗⊟P

Barkham

Bull

Barkham Road, RG41 4TL (on B3349)
✪ 11-3, 5.30-11; 12-3, 7-10 Sun
☎ (0118) 976 0324 🌐 thebullatbarkham.com
Adnams Bitter, Broadside; Courage Best Bitter; Theakston XB, Old Peculier Ⓗ

Comfortable and friendly country pub away from the centre of the village. The large single bar has an adjoining dining area in a former outbuilding with an exposed beamed roof. The bar has etched windows and a distinctive fireplace with a tiled hearth. Excellent home-cooked food is served including Barkham Blue, a distinctive locally-produced cheese. ⛼❀☾◗P⚟

Beech Hill

Elm Tree

Beech Hill Road, RG7 2AZ
✪ 12-11 daily
☎ (0118) 988 3505 🌐 the-elmtree.com
Adnams Bitter; Fuller's London Pride; Greene King IPA Ⓗ

Independent establishment just west of the A33 near Stratfield Saye House and Wellington Country Park. The century-old building is fronted by a tropical patio garden overlooking beautiful countryside. The restaurant has an excellent reputation. The Clock Room has a wood fire and dozens of weird and wonderful clocks. Ladies, the unconventional decor in the toilets should not be missed! ⛼Q❀P

Beedon

Langley Hall Inn

Oxford Road, World's End, RG20 8SA
✪ 11-3, 5.30-11; 11-11 Fri & Sat; 11.30-6.30 Sun
☎ (01635) 248332 🌐 langley-hall-inn.co.uk
West Berkshire Good Old Boy; guest beer Ⓗ

Single-bar pub with areas for drinking and dining. The inn has a good reputation for food made with high-quality local produce – specialising in fresh fish including shellfish. Tapas are available 5-7pm. The decor is minimal – note the petanque ladder and trophy, the court in the garden is built to international specifications. There are three bedrooms for overnight accommodation.
⛼❀⛟☾◗⊟(6, 9)♣P

INDEPENDENT BREWERIES

Butts Great Shefford
West Berkshire Yattendon
Zerodegrees Reading

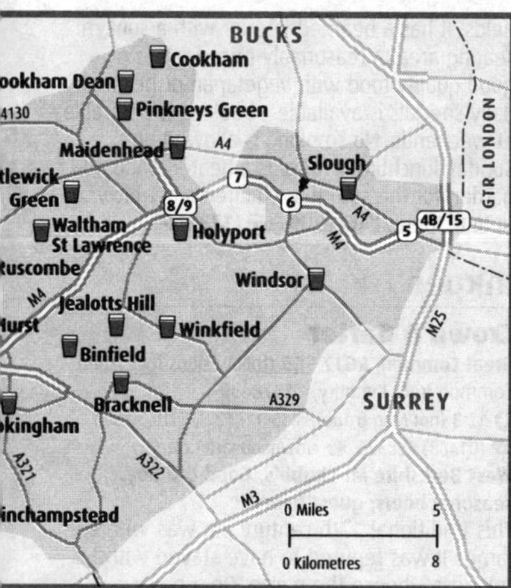

Binfield

Victoria Arms

Terrace Road North, RG42 5JA

11.30-11 (midnight Fri & Sat); 12-11 Sun

☎ (01344) 483856

Fuller's Discovery, London Pride, ESB, seasonal beers; guest beers H

Local village pub with a real fire, TV and an enormous bottled beer collection lining the rafters of the main bar. There is a small no-smoking area and a dining area offering a wide range of freshly-made food. In summer the garden is a pleasant place to spend a summer evening. The landlord is a Master Cellarman.

Bracknell

Old Manor

Grenville Place, High Street, RG12 1BP

9am-midnight (1am Fri & Sat); 9am-midnight Sun

☎ (01344) 304490

Greene King Abbot; Marston's Pedigree; guest beer H

A former manor house dating back to Tudor times, this Wetherspoon's is a genuinely historic building. It has two bars, the main one serving four changing guest beers as well as the regular choices. Children are welcome until 8.30pm if dining. Smoking is not allowed in the pub though it is permitted on the outside covered and heated patio.

Caversham

Griffin

10-12 Church Road, RG4 7AD

11-11.30; 12-10.30 Sun

☎ (0118) 947 5018

Courage Best Bitter, Directors; Theakston XB; guest beers H

Just out of Caversham's bustling centre, the Griffin is a large, comfortable, homely pub. It takes its name from the griffins on the coat of arms of Lord Craven, reputed to be the first owner. A Chef & Brewer pub, it serves a wide selection of meals and snacks ranging from ham, egg and chips to chef's specials, with roasts on Sunday. The pub can be busy in the evening.

Cookham

Bounty

Riverside, SL8 5RG (footpath from station car park, across bridge, along towpath) OS893868

12-10.30 (winter closed Mon-Fri; 12-dusk Sat); 12-10.30 (12-dusk winter) Sun

☎ (01628) 520056

Rebellion IPA, Mutiny, guest beers H

Fronting the River Thames, there is no road access to this inn – even the beer arrives by boat. The front room has a boat-shaped bar and is decorated with flags and other nautical memorabilia. The pub is no-smoking throughout. A large patio and a garden with children's play area make the pub ideal for families. Food is served until the early evening. Limited free mooring and camping are available – ask at the bar. (Bourne End)

Cookham Dean

Jolly Farmer

Church Road, SL9 9PD

11.30-11 (11.45 Fri); 12-10.30 Sun

☎ (01628) 482905 jollyfarmercookhamdean.co.uk

Brakspear Bitter; Courage Best Bitter; Young's Bitter; guest beer H

Brick and flint 18th-century pub opposite the village green and church, owned by the village since 1987. The public bar has a cosy open fire while the larger Dean bar is used by diners and drinkers. A more formal small dining room is also used to host the annual St George's Day and Hallowe'en beer festivals. No evening meals are served Sunday or Monday. The large garden has a play area for children. Q P

Finchampstead

Queen's Oak

Church Lane, RG40 4LS (follow signs to Finchampstead church) OS793639

11-11; 12-10.30 Sun

☎ (0118) 973 4855

Brakspear Bitter, Special, seasonal beers H

This pub, mentioned in the Domesday Book, has a warm, rural feel to it. It is very popular with walkers who come here to drink or dine after exploring the local footpaths. There is one small no-smoking bar and a larger bar with restaurant area. In the summer there is a barbecue in the large garden. Aunt Sally is played here and there is play equipment for children. Q P

Hermitage

Fox Inn

High Street, RG18 9RB

12-2.30 (3 Sat), 5-11 (midnight Fri & Sat); 12-11 Thu; 11-4, 6.30-10.30 Sun

☎ (01635) 201545

Fuller's London Pride; Shepherd Neame Master Brew, Spitfire; guest beers H

This much improved village pub is divided into three areas, with the central bar separated from the restaurant area by a partition. The constantly changing guest beer is often sourced from small breweries, including local micros. Real cider is usually available in the summer. Various themed food nights are held including pasta and pizza on Monday and curry on Wednesday. ⛼❀⇆◑◗⊟♣●P⚟

Holyport

Belgian Arms

Holyport Street, SL6 2JR

⊙ 11-3, 5.30-11; 11-11 Fri & Sat; 12-10.30 Sun

☎ (01628) 634468

Brakspear Bitter, Special Ⓗ

Holyport village green has been the centre of many activities over the years, including international cricket. Where better to watch them from than this excellent village pub? Originally called the Eagle, the name was changed during WWI after German POWs saluted the pub sign as they were marched by. ⛼Q❀◑◗P

Hungerford

Downgate

13 Down View, Park Street, RG17 0ED

⊙ 11-11; 12-11 Sun

☎ (01488) 682708 ⊕ the-downgate.co.uk

Arkell's 2B, 3B, seasonal beers Ⓗ

Cosy, relaxing pub divided into three areas, one with a real fire. On the edge of this small market town, the pub overlooks Port Down on Hungerford Common and tables in the garden enjoy pleasant views. Award-winning hanging baskets adorn the pub in summer. Displays of former brewers' 'barrel bushes', past currencies and photographs of old Hungerford decorate the interior. A collection of old blow lamps and model aircraft are suspended from the ceiling. Good value, traditional pub food includes Sunday roasts. ⛼❀◑◗⥈⊟(13)♣

Hungerford Club

3 The Croft, RG17 0HY

⊙ 7-11; 12-3, 7-11 Sat & Sun

☎ (01488) 682357

Fuller's Chiswick, London Pride; guest beers Ⓗ

Popular social club, behind the main street, converted from cottages at the start of the 20th century. The emphasis here is on sports and games with bowls and tennis outside and traditional pub games inside. Table bowls is played in winter on the snooker tables. Photographs of club members who were killed during the World Wars decorate the snooker room. There are always two guest beers. Show a copy of this Guide or a CAMRA membership card for entry. ❀⥈⊟(13)♣P

Hurst

Green Man

Hinton Road, RG10 0BP (off A321)

⊙ 11-3, 5.30-11; 12-3.30, 6-10.30 Sun

☎ (0118) 934 2599 ⊕ thegreenman.uk.com

Brakspear Bitter, Special, seasonal beers Ⓗ

A licensed hostelry since 1602, this charming country pub is in a rural setting overlooking fields. It has a beamed interior with a sunken seating area. A reasonably-priced range of good quality food with vegetarian dishes and daily specials is available – booking is advisable at weekends. No smoking is allowed on Sunday lunchtime. There is a heated patio and garden for the summer. Children are welcome until 8.30pm. ⛼Q❀◑◗♿⊟(128)P⚟

Inkpen

Crown & Garter

Great Common, RG17 9QR (follow signs for Inkpen Common from Kintbury) OS378639

⊙ 12-3 (not Mon & Tue), 5.30-11; 12-3, 7-10.30 Sun

☎ (01488) 668325 ⊕ crownandgarter.com

West Berkshire Mr Chubb's, Good Old Boy, seasonal beers; guest beers Ⓗ

This traditional 17th century inn was where James II was reputed to have stayed with his mistress – hence the name. On a more macabre note, the corpses of murderers hanged at nearby Coombe gibbet were laid out in the inn's barn. Set in stunning countryside, the pub offers freshly cooked, traditional English food in the no-smoking restaurant, eight bedrooms and an interesting selection of local and guest ales in the atmospheric bar area, dominated by a huge inglenook fireplace. ⛼❀⇆◑◗♿⊟(13)♣●P

Swan

Craven Road, RG17 RDX (follow signs for Inkpen from Hungerford Common) OS359643

⊙ 11-2.30 (3 Sat), 7 (6 Wed-Sat)-11; 12-3, 6-10.30 Sun

☎ (01488) 668326 ⊕ theswaninn-organics.co.uk

Butts Jester, Traditional, seasonal beers; West Berkshire Maggs Mild; guest beers Ⓗ

An organic shop, large no-smoking area, flagstoned games room, oak beamed restaurant and ten rooms for accommodation have all been added to this 17th-century pub over the last 10 years, along with a large suntrap patio. However, the public bar area is still the main focus for locals who come here for lively conversation and good beer. The excellent bar meals are mostly organic and the beef comes from the owners' nearby farm. Well-thought out ramping inside and out makes the site wheelchair friendly. ⛼❀⇆◑◗♿⊟(13)♣P⚟

Jealotts Hill

New Leathern Bottle

Maidenhead Road, RG42 6ET (on A3095 N of Bracknell)

⊙ 12-2.30, 5-11; 12-11 Sat; 12-7 Sun

☎ (01344) 421282

Fuller's London Pride, seasonal beers; guest beer Ⓗ

Pass through the enclosed gardens with children's play equipment to reach the pub's small front bar, which opens into a larger room. The food here is recommended – monthly Sunday roasts, curry night buffet, sausages and mash, specials and a children's menu, with a 10% discount for seniors. No evening meals are served Sunday or Monday. Quiz night is Wednesday. You are guaranteed a warm welcome from Brett and Angie. ⛼❀◑◗P⚟

Kintbury

Dundas Arms

53 Station Road, RG17 9UT (opp. station) OS386671
⏲ 11-2.30, 6-11; 12-2.30 (closed eve) Sun
☎ (01488) 658263 🌐 dundasarms.co.uk
Ramsbury Gold; Sharp's Eden; West Berkshire Mr Chubb's, Good Old Boy; guest beers Ⓗ
Run by the Dalzell-Piper family for almost 40 years, this 18th-century inn is in an attractive location between the canal and the river. It offers good value, high quality English rustic cooking, en-suite riverside accommodation and an excellent range of cask ales served by friendly and knowledgeable staff. There are pleasing views from the restaurant and the canal and riverside seating. The pub is no-smoking throughout. No food is served on Sunday or Monday evening. Q❀🛏◑⇌🚌(13)P⚟

Littlewick Green

Cricketers

Coronation Road, SL6 3RA
⏲ 11-3, 5-11; 11-11 Thu-Sat; 12-10.30 Sun
☎ (01628) 822888
Badger K&B Sussex, Best, Tanglefoot, seasonal beers Ⓗ
Three-bar pub overlooking the village green, with a cricketing theme, naturally. Check out the splendid old clock. Children are welcome in the bar. Home-cooked food is available at lunchtime and every evening except Sunday. Badger beers are unusual for the area.
🔥⚇❀🛏◑♣P⚟

Maidenhead

Maidenhead Conservative Club

32 York Road, SL6 1SF
⏲ 10.30-2.30, 5.30-11; 10.30-11 Fri & Sat; 12-3, 7-11 Sun
☎ (01628) 620579
Fuller's Discovery, London Pride, seasonal beers; Greene King IPA; guest beers Ⓗ
Friendly real ale outlet close to the station. The club steward is a CAMRA member and this is reflected in the beer quality. Two guest ales are always available, as well as bottle-conditioned beers. Monday is crib night, Tuesday and Wednesday darts, and a quiz is held on Sunday evening. Food is available at lunchtime. Show this Guide or a CAMRA membership card to get in. ◐⇌🚌

Greyhound

92-96 Queen Street, SL6 1HT
⏲ 9am-midnight (1am Fri & Sat); 9am-midnight Sun
☎ (01628) 779410
Greene King Abbot; Marston's Burton Bitter, Pedigree; Shepherd Neame Spitfire; guest beers Ⓗ
The original Greyhound inn – now a bank – was where Charles I met his children before his execution in 1649. This large Wetherspoon's near the station offers up to six guest beers including Loddon and Rebellion plus Westons Old Rosie on handpump. Converted to a Lloyd's No.1 in 2005, it now has an additional quiet room with low-level music in the evening. A quiz is held on Sunday evening. ◑♿⇌🚌●⚟

Portland Arms

16 West Street, SL6 1RL
⏲ 12-3, 5-11; 12-11 Fri & Sat; 12-10.30 Sun
☎ (01628) 634649
Brakspear Bitter; Fuller's Chiswick, ESB Ⓗ
One of the few traditional town pubs left in the area, situated in a back road just off the high street. Basic pub food is available at lunchtime and early evening. Visitors can play pool on the newly installed table. A degree of flexibility in opening hours occurs, dependent on how busy the pub is. Accommodation is now available in the new rear extension. Street parking is difficult but there is a pay and display car park nearby. 🛏◑⇌🚌♣

Newbury

Gun

142 Andover Road, Wash Common, RG14 2NE (on A343)
⏲ 12-11 daily
☎ (01635) 47292
Adnams Broadside; Courage Best Bitter; Greene King Old Speckled Hen; Shepherd Neame Spitfire; Wadworth 6X; guest beer Ⓗ
Old fashioned, down to earth local a mile from the town centre. The public bar has pool, a juke box, pinball and TV; the quieter lounge has a small no-smoking area. There has been a pub on this site since the time of the Civil War – the first Battle of Newbury raged nearby. There are rumours of a resident ghost. The guest beer usually comes from a regional brewery. No meals are served Sunday evening. ❀◑🚌(1, 12)P⚟

Pangbourne

Cross Keys

Church Road, RG8 7AR
⏲ 12-11; 12-10.30 Sun
☎ (0118) 984 3268
Greene King IPA; Ruddles Best Bitter; guest beer Ⓗ
A friendly welcome, fine ales, good food and a comfortable bed await you at this ancient coaching inn. Originally two buildings dating from the 16th and 18th centuries, it retains the wooden and flagstone floors and timber beams. Vintage trombones hang from the beams. The bare brick and panelled walls are festooned with old prints. Evening meals are served Tuesday – Sunday.
🔥❀🛏◑⇌🚌(132, 142)

Pinkneys Green

Stag & Hounds

1 Lee Lane, SL6 6NU (W of A308 on Pinkneys Drive)
⏲ 12-3, 6-11; 12-11 Sat summer; 12-4, 7-10.30 (12-10.30 summer) Sun
☎ (01628) 630268
Beer range varies Ⓗ
This country free house was a regular entry in the Guide until 2001. After a period of change the pub has been in steady hands again for a couple of years and is now back on form. It offers five real ales including a Rebellion beer and usually a mild. The public bar is cosy, the lounge has a real fire and tables for dining. The large garden is popular in summer. A skittles alley in the self-

contained function room can be hired.
♔Q❀◐◑⊟♣P

Reading

Allied Arms
57 St Mary's Butts, RG1 2LG
⏲ 12-11; 12-10.30 Sun
☎ (0118) 959 0865 ⊕ allied-arms.com
Fuller's London Pride; Loddon Hullabaloo; guest beer Ⓗ
The Butts, near St Mary's Church, was where medieval folk practised archery. A traditional two-roomed pub dating from 1828, it has a delightful suntrap garden. The publicans have worked wonders over the last few years to ensure a quality pint and a welcoming atmosphere. Occasional beer festivals are held. Opposite the Broad Street mall, it can be busy, particularly on London Irish rugby match days with a noisy but good-natured crowd. ❀⊟⇌⊞⚟

Butler
89-91 Chatham Street, RG1 7DS
⏲ 11.30-11 (11.30 Fri & Sat); 12-10 Sun
☎ (0118) 959 5500
Fuller's London Pride, ESB, seasonal beers Ⓗ
Until the 1970s this pub was Butler & Sons High Class Wine Merchant, with an otherwise unnamed public house. Butler's marketed the Reading Abbey range of wines and spirits and even bottled Guinness for the local area. The pub has a well-hidden garden including remnants of the wine cellar and railway tracks. The area may be redeveloped but the Butler will stay. ♔◐⇌⊞(17, 37, 38)P

Corn Stores
10 Forbury Road, RG1 1SE
⏲ 11.30-11; closed Sun
☎ (0118) 951 2340
Fuller's Discovery, London Pride, ESB, seasonal beers Ⓗ
An intriguing conversion of a former grain warehouse, this bar looks both modern and historic at the same time. Two minutes' walk from the station, it is popular with after-work drinkers. At other times you can settle into one of the comfy sofas and relax with an excellent pint. You may even get table service if the barman is not too busy. The bar offers the same menu as the Italian restaurant upstairs. ◐◑♿⇌⊞

Eldon Arms
19 Eldon Terrace, RG1 4DX
⏲ 11-3, 5.30 (7 Sat)-11.30 (midnight Fri & Sat); 12-3, 7-11.30 Sun
☎ (0118) 957 3857
Wadworth IPA, 6X, seasonal beers Ⓗ
Interesting Wadworth's back street local close to the Royal Berkshire Hospital, run by the longest serving publicans in the area. The public bar has darts, cribbage and music at the weekend; entering the quiet lounge feels like going back in time. A small, pleasant patio garden provides outdoor drinking in fine weather. This is one of the few Reading pubs to stock mild on a regular basis. Meals are served Monday-Saturday. Q❀◐⊟♣

Hobgoblin
2 Broad Street, RG1 2BH
⏲ 11-11; 12-10.30 Sun
☎ (0118) 950 8119
Beer range varies Ⓗ
Not to be missed by the real ale enthusiast, this pub offers three West Berkshire Brewery beers and five ever-changing guests to a happy band of regulars and visitors. The walls and ceiling of the bar are covered with pump clips from the thousands of beers sold over the years. Wood-panelled snugs in the back room add an intimate touch. ❀⇌⊞●

Retreat
8 St John's Street, RG1 4EH
⏲ 4.30-11; 12-11.30 Fri & Sat; 12-11 Sun
☎ (0118) 957 1593 ⊕ retreatpub.co.uk
Loddon Hoppit; Ringwood Best Bitter; guest beers Ⓗ
Multiple award-winning pub tucked away in the middle of a terrace, close to the Royal Berks hospital. A wide range of real ales is complemented by a selection of Belgian bottled beers and one or two draught ciders or perries. A traditional two-roomed house, the front room is for conversation and the back bar has a pool table. Q⊟⊞♣●

Three Guineas
Station Approach, RG1 1LY
⏲ 10.30-11 daily
☎ (0118) 957 2743
Tetley Bitter; Young's Bitter; guest beers Ⓗ
Converted from part of the railway station offices and booking hall, the name reflects the prize for a competition held in 1904 to choose the name of the express train from London to Plymouth. The bar is dominated by a large screen TV showing sporting events. The pub can be noisy on Friday and Saturday evenings and when the London Irish rugby team is playing at 'home' in Reading. There are screens showing train departure times in the bar. ❀◐⇌⊞

Ruscombe

Royal Oak
Ruscombe Lane, RG10 9JN
⏲ 12-3, 5-11; closed Sun and Mon eve winter; 12-4, 6-10.30 Sun
☎ (0118) 934 5190 ⊕ burattas.co.uk
Brakspear Bitter; Fuller's London Pride Ⓗ
This pub has a modern interior yet retains many original features. It has a variety of comfortable seating. A good range of bistro-style food is available as well as two or three course set menus. The large garden has extensive seating and there is a fenced off area with ducks and chickens roaming free. ❀◐◑⊞(127)P⚟

Shefford Woodlands

Pheasant
Ermin Street, RG17 7AA
⏲ 11-11; 12-10.30 Sun
☎ (01488) 648284
Butts Jester; Loddon Hoppit; Wadworth 6X Ⓗ
High on the Downs with expansive views over the Kennet Valley, this isolated pub

caters for the local racing stables as well as visitors. Wooden imitation horse stalls line the red painted walls. Although half the pub is dedicated to dining, a friendly and vocal bunch of regulars ensures that an old-fashioned country pub atmosphere is maintained. There is no intrusive piped music but the TV is turned on for horse racing. ⌂◐♣P

Shinfield

Magpie & Parrot

Arborfield Road, RG2 9EA (on A327 E of village)
⏲ 12-7; 12-3 Sun
☎ (0118) 988 4130
Fuller's London Pride; guest beer Ⓗ
Hard to find due to minimal signposting, this pub is worth the effort to seek out for its warm welcome and friendly atmosphere. The intimate bar area is an extension of the sitting room and features an amusing collection of curios. Winner of local CAMRA Pub of the Year 2006, occasional beer festivals are held here. ⌂Q❀🚌(144)♣P

Slough

Rose & Crown

312 High Street, SL1 1NB
⏲ 11-11; 12-10.30 Sun
☎ (01753) 521114
Beer range varies Ⓗ
The oldest pub on Slough High Street, dating back to the late 16th century. Two bars serve a constantly changing range of beers from three handpumps. Real cider is sometimes available. In July the pub holds a beer festival. Entertainment includes darts, karaoke on a Friday night, and occasional live music. There is a large-screen TV in one bar for important sporting events.
❀⇌🚌♣●

Wheatsheaf

15 Albert Street, SL1 2BE
⏲ 12-11 daily
☎ (01753) 522019
Fuller's Discovery, London Pride, ESB, seasonal beers Ⓗ
Once a bakery but licensed since 1897, this traditional local is in the Upton area. It has a comfortable single bar and pleasant patio garden. Thursday is quiz night and poker night is Sunday. There are occasional art exhibitions. Over 25s only are allowed in the bar. There is limited pay & display parking nearby. ⌂❀◐♣

Sonning

Bull Hotel

High Street, RG4 6UP (next to St Andrew's Church)
⏲ 11-3, 5.30-11 (11.30 Fri); 11-11.30 Sat; 12-10.30 Sun; open all day in summer
☎ (0118) 969 3901
Fuller's Gale's Butser, London Pride, HSB, seasonal beers; guest beer Ⓗ
This rambling 16th-century hotel is full of character, with various drinking areas, lots of exposed beams and attractive gardens. Located in a tranquil Thames-side village, the Bull is mentioned in JK Jerome's Three Men in a Boat. Very popular on a fine day, food is served in the bars or the quality restaurant. Beer is served through a sparkler which can be removed on request.
⌂Q❀🛏◐🚌(127)P⚟

Stanford Dingley

Bull

RG7 6LS (on Yattendon/Burnt Hill road)
⏲ 12-3, 6-11; 12-3, 7-10.30 Sun
☎ (0118) 974 4409 🌐 thebullatstanforddingley.co.uk
Brakspear Bitter; West Berkshire Good Old Boy; guest beers Ⓗ
This 15th-century country pub is situated in a picturesque village in the Pang Valley. It has a saloon bar and dining room, both no smoking, and a tap room with exposed wattle and daub wall. A large garden allows families to relax with their children in a safe environment. No evening meals Sunday.
⌂Q❀🛏◐🍴♿▲♣P⚟

Waltham St Lawrence

Bell

The Street, RG10 0JJ (next to church)
⏲ 12-3, 5-11; 12-11 Sat; 12-10.30 Sun
☎ (0118) 934 1788 🌐 thebellinn.biz
Beer range varies Ⓗ
Delightful village pub that attracts drinkers and diners. The building dates from circa 1400 and was bequeathed for the benefit of the parish in 1608. The two cosy main bars have log fires while the no-smoking family room offers more space – and a view down the old well. The pub's house beer, No 1, is brewed by West Berkshire. Popular with walkers in summer, morris dancers may also put in an appearance.
⌂Q🍼❀◐🚌(53a)♣P⚟

Star

Broadmoor Road, RG10 0HY (on B3024 Twyford-Windsor road) OS834767
⏲ 11.30-2.30, 6 (6.30 Sat)-11; 12-3 Sun
☎ (0118) 934 3486 🌐 thestar-inn.co.uk
Wadworth IPA, 6X Ⓗ
Comfortable, friendly countryside pub on a back road between Reading and Windsor. It has a spacious dining area plus smoking and no-smoking drinking areas. The interior features wood panelling and brick fireplaces, one with a log fire in winter. Fishing rods adorn the beams. ⌂❀◐🚌(53a)P⚟

Windsor

Black Horse

290 Dedworth Road, SL4 4JR
⏲ 11-2.30, 5-11; 11-midnight Fri & Sat; 12-10.30 Sun
☎ (01753) 861953
Fuller's London Pride; Young's Bitter; guest beer Ⓗ
This community local in Windsor's western suburb supports football, cribbage and darts teams. Darts night is Thursday and occasional quizzes and live music are hosted. A skittles alley, available to hire, can be set up in the garden in summer. Major sporting events are shown on TV. Children are welcome during

the day. Buses to and from Windsor town centre stop outside. No food is served on Sunday. ♛❀◐🚌P

Carpenters Arms

4 Market Street, SL4 1PB

✪ 11-11 (midnight Fri); 10-midnight Sat; 10-11 Sun

☎ (01753) 755961

Beer range varies 🄷

Close to the castle, the pub is situated in a cobbled street behind the Guildhall, a popular civil wedding venue. Although in a tourist area, it maintains a regular local clientele as well as visitors. Built around 1518, this historic building used to be linked to the castle by a tunnel, now bricked up. Five handpumps serve an ever-changing selection of real ale from breweries countrywide. ❀◐◑⇌(Windsor & Eton Central)🚌⁄

Swan

9 Mill Lane, Clewer Village, SL4 5JG

✪ 5.30-11; 12-11 Sat; 12-10.30 Sun

☎ (01753) 862069

Courage Best Bitter; Fuller's Gale's HSB; guest beer 🄷

Traditional, friendly, 18th-century back-street pub, cosy in winter with a wood-burning fire. It is mainly frequented by locals but its close proximity to Windsor and the racecourse makes it a good watering hole for visitors. Children and dogs are welcome in the bar. There is a dartboard in one corner and the pub also holds regular quizzes. ♛Q⇄♣●P

Trooper

97 St Leonards Road, SL4 3BZ

✪ 11-11; 12-10.30 Sun

☎ (01753) 670123

Fuller's Gale's HSB, seasonal beers 🄷

Full of character, this 19th-century coaching inn is situated just beyond the end of Windsor's main shopping street and within walking distance of the castle. The main bar is always busy, with office workers at lunchtime, and locals in the evening, particularly when live sport is on TV. A covered garden room serves as a dining room. A rare outlet for Gale's in this area. No food is served on Sunday evening. ❀⇄◐◑⇌(Windsor & Eton Central)

Winkfield

Old Hatchet

Hatchet Lane, SL4 2EE

✪ 12-11; 12-10.30 Sun

☎ (01344) 899911

Fuller's Discovery, London Pride, ESB, seasonal beers 🄷

Attractive and welcoming country pub. Originally built as a small row of woodmans' cottages, it has many authentic features including flagstone and quarry tiles, beams and large fireplaces. The rear of the pub has been turned into a formal restaurant with an interesting and varied menu. New soft furnishings give a cosy feel although this is still a real beer drinkers' pub. Live music is hosted occasionally. ♛❀◐◑♿P⁄

Wokingham

Broad Street Tavern

29 Broad Street, RG40 1AU

✪ 12-11; 12-3, 7-10.30 Sun

☎ (0118) 977 3706

Wadworth IPA, 6X, JCB, Bishop's Tipple; guest beers 🄷

Splendid, welcoming town-centre pub that attracts a varied clientele. A central corridor divides two comfortable front rooms and leads to the lively bar area. The comfortable lounge hosts live music on Thursday evening. Major rugby and cricket matches are shown on a large screen TV. The bar stays open until midnight Thursday-Saturday (no entry after 11pm). Beer festivals are held four times a year. Outside is a patio garden where summer barbecues are held. It was local CAMRA Pub of the Year for 2003-5. Q❀◐⇌🚌⁄

Rifle Volunteer

141 Reading Road, RG41 1HD (on A329)

✪ 11-11; 12-5.30, 7-10.30 Sun

☎ (0118) 978 4484

Courage Best Bitter; Fuller's London Pride; guest beer 🄷

Dating from the 1850s, this pub has a large single bar and a small no-smoking family room. Live sport on TV, darts, a Sunday night quiz and a pub football team make this pub a firm favourite with locals and beer enthusiasts alike. The guest beers often come from local micros including Hogs Back and West Berkshire. Food is served at lunchtime during the week. ♉❀◐♣P⁄

Ship Inn

104 Peach Street, RG40 1XH

✪ 12-11 (midnight Thu-Sat); 12-11 Sun

☎ (0118) 978 0389

Fuller's Discovery, London Pride, ESB, seasonal beers 🄷

Local CAMRA Pub of the Year 2006, this 400-year-old building was an 18th-century stagecoach stop. A rustic brick and wood beamed decor is enhanced by a real log fire. Ship lights, barrels and milk churns adorn the mock gallery in the main dining area – note the risqué ship's figurehead. Good air conditioning and a high timber roof make this a virtually smoke-free pub. The friendly burble of locals is undisturbed by the TV which has the sound off and quiet piped music. ♛◐◑P

Victoria Arms

1 Easthampstead Road RG40 2EH

✪ 12-11 (midnight Fri & Sat); 12-11 Sun

☎ (0118) 978 3023

Taylor Landlord; guest beers 🄷

A first appearance in the Guide for this small local. It was presented with a Most Improved Pub award by the local CAMRA branch in 2006. The single room interior is divided by a large central fireplace. A strategically placed TV means that Sky Sports can be viewed throughout the pub. The new landlord intends to add beers from local micros to his guest list. ♛◐◑♣

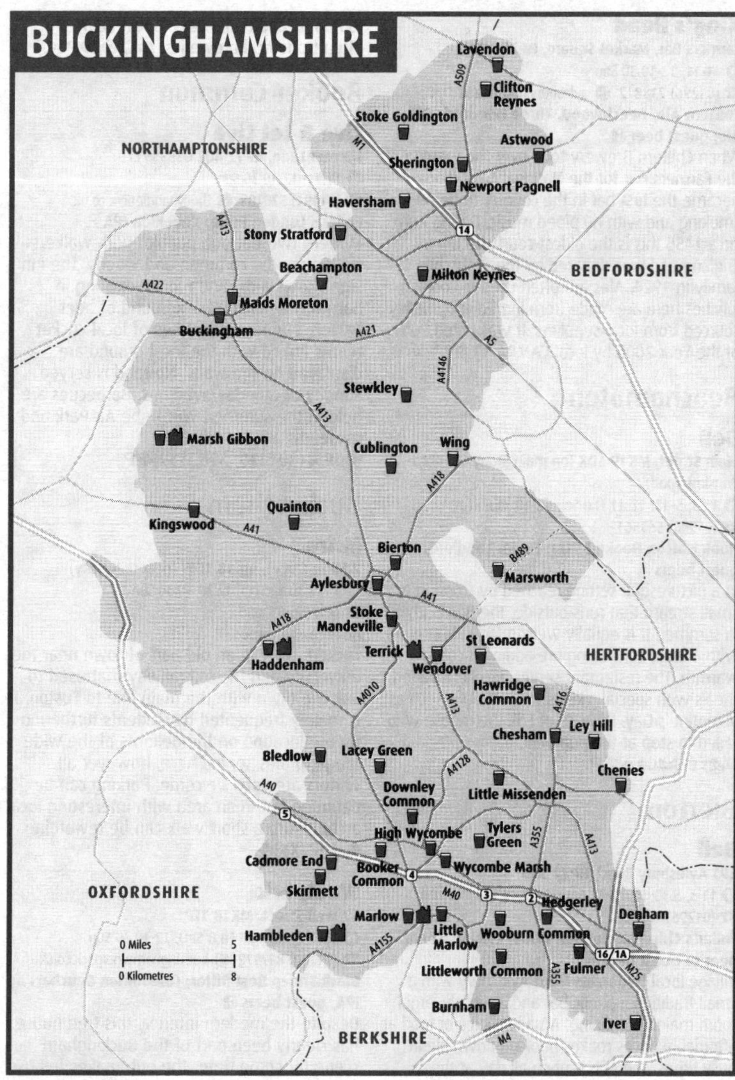

Astwood

Old Swan

8 Main Road, MK16 9JS (off A421)

11-3, 6-11; closed Mon; 12-3.30 Sun

☎ (01234) 391351

Everards Beacon, Tiger; guest beer Ⓗ

Low beamed 17th-century free house located half way between Bedford and Milton Keynes, just inside the county boundary. A large assortment of blue and white china and an impressive water jug collection adorn the interior. The restaurant regularly has game and fish dishes on the specials board, sourced from local suppliers (booking recommended).

Aylesbury

Hop Pole

83 Bicester Road, HP19 9AZ

12-11 (midnight Fri & Sat); 12-11 Sun

☎ (01296) 482129

Vale Best Bitter; guest beers Ⓗ

A sign outside boasts 'Aylesbury's Permanent Beer Festival' and with handpumps offering up to nine guest ales including mild and porter, the pub lives up to its claim. With myriad micro-brewery beers on offer, this is Vale Brewery's sole outlet in the town. A total refurbishment has transformed a run-down old boozer into a venue that attracts discerning drinkers from far and wide. The food, freshly prepared in house, is becoming more and more popular.

INDEPENDENT BREWERIES

Chiltern Terrick
Old Luxters Hambleden
Oxfordshire Ales Marsh Gibbon
Rebellion Marlow
Vale Haddenham

King's Head

Farmers Bar, Market Square, HP20 2RW
11-11; 12-10.30 Sun
☎ (01296) 718812 aylesburykingshead.co.uk
Chiltern Ale, Beechwood, Three Hundreds Old Ale; guest beer Ⓗ
When Chiltern Brewery took over the running of the Farmers Bar for the National Trust it became the first bar in the country to be no-smoking and with no piped music. Dating from circa 1455 this is the oldest courtyard inn in England and was donated by the Rothschild family in 1924. Ales are often used in cooking; lunches here are made from ingredients freshly sourced from local suppliers. It was voted Pub of the Year 2006 by local CAMRA. Q❀ⓒ♿⇌

Beachampton

Bell

Main Street, MK19 6DX (on main Stony Stratford-Winslow road)
12-3, 5-11; 12-11 Thu-Sat; 12-10.30 Sun
☎ (01908) 563861
Hook Norton Hooky Bitter; Taylor Landlord; guest beers Ⓗ
In a picturesque setting reached by crossing a small stream that runs outside, the Bell is idyllic in summer. It is equally welcoming in winter with a large central log fire adding a cosy warmth. The restaurant serves excellent varied meals with special menus for occasions such as Valentine's Day. Beware of Erik the moose who failed to stop at the pub wall.
⛰❀ⓒ◑♿ΔP

Bierton

Bell

191 Aylesbury Road, HP22 5DS
11-3, 5.30-11; 11-11 Sat; 12-10.30 Sun
☎ (01296) 436055
Fuller's Chiswick, London Pride, ESB, seasonal beer or guest beer Ⓗ
Village local two miles from Aylesbury with a small traditional public bar and a slightly larger room mainly for dining. A wide choice of food at affordable prices makes booking advisable at busy times. The pub is open all day at the weekend and is a popular venue for watching sporting events on the wide-screen TV. Occasional live music is played on Sunday evening featuring local blues bands. ◑🚌♣P

Bledlow

Lions of Bledlow

Church End, HP27 9PE (off B4009 between Chinnor and Princes Risborough) OS776020
11.30-3, 6-11; 12-10.30 (12-4, 7-10.30 winter) Sun
☎ (01844) 343345
Wadworth 6X; guest beers Ⓗ
Rambling, unspoilt, Grade II listed 16th-century free house, complete with beams, inglenooks and a large log fire. Originally three shepherds' cottages, notes and pictures illustrating the pub's earlier days are displayed. There is a restaurant and large bar with wide-ranging blackboard menus. The extensive garden is busy in summer with walkers and families; tables at the front enjoy a picturesque setting at the junction of footpaths and bridleways. Guest beers are often from local breweries. ⛰Q❀◑P⚡

Booker Common

Live & Let Live

Limmer Lane, HP12 4QZ OS835917
11-11; 12-10.30 Sun
☎ (01494) 520105 theliveandletlive.co.uk
Fuller's London Pride; Rebellion IPA Ⓗ
Modern two-bar pub popular with walkers on the nearby common and woods. The inn sign shows a cat and mouse existing in harmony against a background of beer barrels. Numerous pictures of local cricket teams linked with the local ground are displayed on the walls. No food is served Sunday or Monday evenings. Barbecues are held in the summer. Wycombe Air Park and museums are close by.
❀◑🚌(30, 315, 326, 339)♣P

Buckingham

Mitre

2 Mitre Street, MK18 1DW (near university)
7 (12.30 Sat)-11; 12.30-10.30 Sun
☎ (01280) 813080
Beer range varies Ⓗ
Tucked away in an old part of town near the university and the old railway that used to link the town with the main line to Euston. It is mainly frequented by students furthering their education on the delights of the wide range of ales served here, however all visitors are very welcome. Parking can be daunting but in an area with interesting local architecture a short walk can be rewarding.
⛰❀🚌(X5)♣

Woolpack

57 Well Street, MK18 1EP
10-11 (midnight Fri & Sat); 12-10.30 Sun
☎ (01280) 817972 buckinghamwoolpack.co.uk
Black Sheep Best Bitter; Caledonian Deuchars IPA; guest beers Ⓗ
Despite the modern interior, this free house has clearly been part of the Buckingham scene for some time. The pub makes full use of the new relaxed opening hours – opening at 10am in typical old market town style. A good, varied food menu is offered. Children are welcome in the no-smoking back room where there are toys to keep them occupied. Regular live music adds to a pub for all.
⛰❀◑🚌(X5)P⚡

Burnham

George

20 High Street, SL1 7JH
12-11; 12-10.30 Sun
☎ (01628) 605047
Courage Best Bitter, Directors; guest beers Ⓗ
Recently refurbished and refreshed with a new landlord taking over from the previous 37-year incumbent. This Grade II listed 16th-century coaching inn, once the old magistrate's court, is believed to be the oldest pub in Burnham High Street. Currently around 10 guest ales a month are offered, although there are sometimes more if

requested. Over-21s only, however well-behaved dogs are welcome. ⌂❀▭♣P

Cadmore End

Old Ship

Marlow Road, HP14 3PN (on B482 between Lane End and Stokenchurch)

12-2.30 (not Mon), 5.30-10 (11 summer); 12-3, 7-10 Sun

☎ (01494) 883496

Brakspear Bitter; Young's Bitter; guest beers Ⓖ

This small country pub is one of the classic gems of the Chilterns. Despite handpumps on the bar, all ales are gravity-dispensed and carried up from the cellar. A free house, it serves a constantly changing range of guest beers, including ales from local breweries. Meals are available at all times except Sunday evening and Monday lunchtime. The large garden has a covered seating area situated below road level. A pub not to be missed. ⌂Q❀◐▭♣P⊬

Chenies

Red Lion

WD3 6ED (off A404 between Chorleywood and Little Chalfont)

11-2.30, 5.30-11; 12-3, 6.30-10.30 Sun

☎ (01923) 282722

Vale Best Bitter; Wadworth 6X; guest beers Ⓗ

This outstanding traditional village pub with a long-serving landlord features in this Guide year after year. With the emphasis on drinking, it claims to be 'a pub that serves food', however the food is high quality, served in the main bar or small dining room. The tiny one-table, two-chair snug at the back adds to the cosy feel. The house beer, Lion Pride, is brewed by Rebellion. Ben's comes from the Vale Brewery. Close to Chenies Manor and good walking country, it is well worth a visit. Q❀◐♿▭P

Chesham

Rose & Crown

264 Waterside, HP5 1PY

12-11 (midnight Fri & Sat); 12-11 Sun

☎ (01494) 786465

Fuller's Discovery, London Pride, seasonal beers; guest beer Ⓗ

Traditonal local community pub with two bars. A large-screen TV shows sporting events. A full range of Fuller's bottled beers is available as well as Belgian bottled beers. The landlord's dog is a South African ridgeback; customers' dogs are welcome. Live music is held on the third Saturday of the month with local groups playing. The pub organises golfing trips. ⌂❀◐⊖▭▭♣P

Clifton Reynes

Robin Hood

MK46 5DR (off A509, S of Olney); OS903512

12-3, 6.30-11; closed Mon; 12-3, 7-10.30 Sun

☎ (01908) 711574 ⊕ therobinhoodpub.co.uk

Greene King IPA, Abbot; guest beer Ⓗ

An all-year-round gem. The food is of the highest quality and prepared to order. The conservatory is a no-smoking haven for diners and drinkers. Look out for numerous pictures of the legendary Nottingham outlaw as well as the list of landlords going back hundreds of years. No meals are served on Sunday evening. ⌂Q❀◐▭▲♣⊬

Cublington

Unicorn

High Street, LU7 0LQ

12-3, 5-11; 12-11 Sat; 12-10.30 Sun

☎ (01296) 681261

Greene King IPA; Shepherd Neame Spitfire; Young's Bitter; guest beer Ⓗ

This is now a thriving free house, rescued from closure in 2004 by three village families. The long, low-ceilinged bar has open fires at each end. Guest beers are from independent or local micro-breweries. Food is available at all sessions either in the bar or a small dining area. The large garden has been much improved over the past couple of years. Pub games include darts and bridge. ⌂Q❀◐♣P

Denham

Falcon

Village Road, UB9 5BE

12-3, 5-11; 11-11 Sat (summer); 12-10.30 Sun

☎ (01895) 832125 ⊕ falconinn.biz

Taylor Landlord; Wells Bombardier; Young's Bitter; guest beer Ⓗ

Dating back more than 500 years, this inn overlooks the village green in the fascinating Denham preservation area. This friendly bar retains some olde worlde charm with timber beams and two open hearths. Steps lead down to a back room, and up to the toilets. Attractive en-suite guest rooms are available. The brasserie features a varied menu and a selection of tapas. Q❀⇌◐⇌▭●⊬

Downley Common

Le de Spencer Arms

The Common, HP13 5YQ (across common from village) OS849959

12-3, 6-11; 12-11 Fri & Sat; 12-10.30 Sun

☎ (01494) 535317

Fuller's Chiswick London Pride, ESB, seasonal beers; guest beers Ⓗ

Family-oriented brick and flint building remotely situated off Downley Common. It has numerous secluded areas and a small room off the bar. In summer there are barbecues and two mini beer festivals under canvas. Pub games include mole in the hole. A much-frequented pub for ramblers in the area, food is served every lunchtime and Friday and Saturday evenings. Sunday roasts are popular. ⌂Q❀◐▭(31)♣P

Fulmer

Black Horse

Windmill Road, SL1 6DH

11-3, 5.30-11; 11-11; 12-10.30 Sun

☎ (01753) 663183

Greene King IPA, Abbot; guest beers Ⓗ

This 17th-century three-bar pub is central to village life, hosting charity events and supporting local sporting activities. The original bars are now complemented by the addition of an old cellar room which can be used for dining or drinking, and the restaurant which overlooks the extensive garden. The central bar's frontage is constructed from timber salvaged from a WWII APR hut. ⚠Q❀◑▶P

Haddenham

Green Dragon

8 Churchway, HP17 8AA

12-2.30, 6.30-11; 12-3 Sun

☎ (01844) 291403 eatatthedragon.co.uk

Caledonian Deuchars IPA; Vale Wychert Ale; Wadworth 6X Ⓗ

Award-winning pub over 350 years old. Although famed for its food, its warm and friendly atmosphere means it is still a great place to visit if you just want a beer. Good value food offers on Tuesday and Thursday mean that it can get busy, so it is always wise to ring ahead if you are in a large party. Q❀◑▶P⚟

Hambleden

Stag & Huntsman

RG9 6RP (opposite churchyard) OS785866

11-2.30 (3 Sat), 6-11; 12-3, 7-10.30 Sun

☎ (01491) 571227 stagandhuntsman.co.uk

Rebellion IPA; Wadworth 6X; guest beer Ⓗ

Arcadian, unspoilt gem situated in a brick and flint National Trust village. It has three contrasting bars: a snug public bar, a larger rear lounge and a cosy front bar accessed through a curtain. Food is served in the dining room as well as throughout the pub. The ever-changing guest beers come from local and west country breweries. A weekend beer festival is held in early September. Thatchers dry cider is stocked at this past local CAMRA Pub of the Year.

⚠❀⇌◑▶⊟♣●P

Haversham

Greyhound

2 High Street, MK19 7DT

12-2.30 (3 Sat), 5.30-11; 12-3, 7-10.30 Sun

☎ (01908) 313487

Greene King IPA, Abbot Ⓗ

The only pub in the village, the proprietors have strived to make it a true community pub. Good, wholesome food is available and Sunday lunches are popular. A motorcycle club is based here along with various other local sports teams. Opening hours may extend to midnight occasionally and children are welcome until 9pm. CAMRA local Pub of the Year in 2005. ⚠❀◑▶⊟♣P

Hawridge Common

Full Moon

HP5 2UH (between Chesham and Tring)

12-11; 12-10.30 Sun

☎ (01494) 758959

Adnams Bitter; Draught Bass; Brakspear Special; Fuller's London Pride; guest beers Ⓗ

In a village known for its DH Lawrence connection, this 17th-century pub has a Wethereds brewery lantern still hanging over the front door and a windmill close by. Inside it has one large beamed bar and two eating areas with food served throughout. A pergola-covered patio and garden is delightful in summer and children and dogs are welcome. A popular pub with walkers on the common opposite. Q❀◑▶♿♣P

Hedgerley

White Horse

Village Lane, SL2 3UY

11-2.30, 5-11; 11-11 Sat; 12-10.30 Sun

☎ (01753) 643225

Greene King IPA; Rebellion IPA; guest beers Ⓖ

A real village pub, this family-owned free house usually serves seven ales on gravity dispense, five of which change frequently and come from small breweries all over the country. Belgian beers and two real ciders are also available. Voted local CAMRA Pub of the Year and a finalist Cider Pub of the Year in 2005, it hosts an annual beer festival over the Whitsun bank holiday offering over 100 beers. ⚠Q❀◑⊟♣●P

High Wycombe

Belle Vue

45 Gordon Road, HP13 6EQ (100 yds from station, platform 3 exit)

12-3, 5-11; 12-11 Sat; 12-10.30 Sun

☎ (01494) 524728

Beer range varies Ⓗ

Friendly, 150-year old purpose-built community pub with a range of three varying beers from the Punch Taverns selection. Frequented mainly by locals, there is live music on Saturday evening, a quiz on Thursday and darts matches on Tuesday. Across the valley from the pub are wooded hills. ⚠❀⇌⊟(33, 307)♣

Iver

Swan

2 High Street, SL0 9NG

10-midnight (2am Fri & Sat); 12-11 Sun

☎ (01753) 655776 theswaniver.co.uk

Fuller's London Pride; Greene King IPA; guest beers Ⓗ

Opposite the lovely old church at the village centre crossroads, this outwardly traditional 16th-century coaching inn has recently been totally refurbished, although many of the original features remain. While it is still a drinkers' pub, it now offers fine dining too. It is a rare outlet for the Grand Union Brewery located a few miles away. No food is served on Monday. ❀◑▶⊟P⚟

Kingswood

Plough & Anchor

Bicester Road, HP18 0RB

12-3, 6-11; 12-5.30 Sun

☎ (01296) 770251

Fuller's London Pride; guest beer Ⓖ

Comfortable 16th-century roadside pub,

catering mainly for diners but drinkers are welcome. The beers are served on gravity by a custom-built dispense and cooling system. The guest beer is sourced from regional or micro-breweries and is usually under 4% ABV. The open fire is fuelled by some of the largest logs you will ever see, and burns continuously from October to April. A patio area is available for outdoor drinking.
⩩❀◑◗⊟(16)P

Lacey Green

Whip

Pink Road, HP27 0PG
⏲ 11-11; 12-10.30 Sun
☎ (01844) 344060 ⊕ whipinn.co.uk
Draught Bass; Greene King IPA, Old Speckled Hen; guest beers Ⓗ
Delightful 150-year-old free house with outstanding views close to many walks including the Ridgeway Path. Real cider or perry is sometimes dispensed from a polypin on the bar. A beer festival is held during May as well as the annual alternative Oktoberfest in a marquee with live jazz. Nearby is the oldest working smock windmill in the country – a Chiltern Society restoration. No food is served on Sunday evening. ⩩Q❀◑◗⊟(323, 324)♣●

Lavendon

Horseshoe

26 High Street, MK46 4HA (on A428)
⏲ 12-3 (not Mon), 5.30-11; 12-6 Sun
☎ (01234) 712641
Wells Eagle; guest beers Ⓗ
Roadside pub in the centre of the village with two bars: one is a typical locals' public bar, the other a comfortable lounge with an area for dining. There is one guest ale on handpump in each bar, both from the Wells list, so ask what is available. The food menu is varied with an emphasis on fresh fish.
⩩❀◑◗⊟♣P⚟

Ley Hill

Swan

Ley Hill Common, HP5 1UT
⏲ 12-11 (12-3.30, 5.30-11 winter); 12-4, 6-10.30 Sun
☎ (01494) 783075 ⊕ swanleyhill.com
Adnams Bitter; Brakspear Bitter; Fuller's London Pride; Taylor Landlord; guest beer Ⓗ
Originally three timber-framed cottages, this old-style country pub faces the local cricket pitch and is close to Ley Hill golf club. Themed food evenings are a highlight, with Spanish tapas, Italian and Portuguese, and fish is a speciality. Jazz evenings are held all year round. The small front garden leads to a larger rear garden. ⩩Q❀◑◗⊟●P

Little Marlow

King's Head

Church Road, SL7 3RZ (on A4155 between Marlow and Bourne End)
⏲ 11-11; 12-10.30 Sun
☎ (01628) 484407
Fuller's London Pride; Taylor Landlord; guest beers Ⓗ
Charming 14th-century inn in a picturesque village with a 12th-century church. The heavily beamed interior includes a log fire that creates a warm atmosphere in winter. Good home-cooked dishes from an extensive menu are very popular. The spacious garden is pleasant in summer and families are welcome. A regular in this Guide, four handpumped ales are always available. ⩩❀◑◗♿P

Little Missenden

Crown

HP7 0RD (off A413, Amersham end of village)
⏲ 11-2.30, 6-11; 12-3, 7-10.30 Sun
☎ (01494) 862571
Adnams Bitter; Young's Bitter; Ⓗ **guest beers** Ⓖ/Ⓗ
Timeless village pub run by the same family for over 90 years, with 25 consecutive years in this Guide. The single-room interior is served by a small bar edged with built-in wall seats. There are four handpumps with an occasional guest on gravity. Weston's Old Rosie cider is always available. The absence of music and games machines accentuates the traditional atmosphere. Shove ha'penny and shut the box are played. Pub food is served at lunchtime except Sunday.
⩩Q❀◑♿♣●P

Littleworth Common

Jolly Woodman

Littleworth Road, SL1 8PF OS936835
⏲ 11-11; 12-10.30 Sun
☎ (01753) 644350
Brakspear Bitter; Caledonian Deuchars IPA; Fuller's London Pride; guest beer Ⓗ
Country pub close to Burnham Beeches, popular for its range of beers, good food and live Monday-night jazz sessions. The bar area features a collection of old beer bottles, and agricultural implements and a rowing scull are suspended from the rafters. Real fires in winter and the garden in summer add to the appeal. ⩩❀◑◗P

Maids Moreton

Wheatsheaf

Main Street, MK18 1QR (off A413, Buckingham-Towcester road) OS705355
⏲ 12-3, 6-11; 12-3, 6-10.30 Sun
☎ (01280) 815433 ⊕ thewheatsheaf.uk.com
Brains Rev James; Hook Norton Hooky Bitter; Tring Side Pocket for a Toad Ⓗ
Ancient village pub, as you can tell from the nooks and crannies and the sloping floor. Sympathetically extended, it now has an attractive conservatory for dining where children are welcome. The location is handy for National Trust's Stowe Park and Silverstone race circuit. No food is served on Sunday evening and booking is advisable at other times. The staff will remove the sparklers if requested. ⩩☕❀◑◗P⚟

Marlow

Prince of Wales

1 Mill Road, SL7 1PX (250 yds from station)

⏲ 11-11 (midnight Fri); 12-10.30 Sun
☎ (01628) 482970
Adnams Bitter; Brakspear Bitter; Fuller's London Pride; guest beer Ⓗ
Friendly side-street local with two connecting bars: a comfortable public bar that leads to a no-smoking room where excellent Thai cuisine is served. A recent extension to the main bar has added a cosy seating area. The guest beer is often the monthly special from Rebellion Brewery. A stone's throw from Marlow High Street and handy for the station, the pub is also a short diversion from the Thames Path for walkers. ❀🛏◑◗♿⇌P⚟

Three Horseshoes
Burroughs Grove Hill, SL7 3RA OS876890
⏲ 11.30-3, 5-11; 11.30-11 Fri & Sat; 12-5, 7-10.30 Sun
☎ (01628) 483109
Rebellion Mild, IPA, Smuggler, Mutiny, seasonal beers Ⓗ
Acclaimed tap for the local Rebellion Brewery, the pub was closed for several years before Rebellion transformed what was a dilapidated building to the success story that it is today. A former local CAMRA Pub of the Year, it serves six brewery ales including the monthly special. An extensive value-for-money food menu is always popular. A secluded garden is attractive in summer. ♨Q❀◑◗🚌P⚟

Marsh Gibbon

Plough
Church Street, OX27 0HQ
⏲ 12-11; 12-10.30 Sun
☎ (01869) 278759
Greene King IPA; Oxfordshire Ales Triple B, Marshmellow Ⓗ
Situated in a quiet Domesday village, this 16th-century pub has two bars and a restaurant. One bar is no-smoking and the other has pool, darts and live sport on TV. Bar food is served throughout the day with Sunday lunches a speciality and curry and steak evenings. Aunt Sally is played in season. The Oxfordshire Ales Brewery is half a mile away. ❀◑◗🍺🚌(16)P⚟

Marsworth

Angler's Retreat
Startops End, HP23 4LJ (on B489, opp. Startops reservoir car park) OS918141
⏲ 11-11; 12-10.30 Sun
☎ (01442) 822250
Fuller's London Pride; Tring Side Pocket for a Toad; guest beers Ⓗ
Country pub near two reservoirs famous for wild birds and close to the Grand Union Canal. The interior has a fishing theme. The guest list varies, with dark beers including mild, stout and porter predominating. Two mini beer festivals are held in April and October. Home-cooked food is served daily. The no-smoking conservatory, garden and small aviary make the pub popular with families. Dogs are welcome. ♨❀◑◗🚌♣P⚟

Red Lion
90 Vicarage Road, HP23 4LU (off B489, by canal bridge 130)
⏲ 11-3, 5 (6 Sat)-11; 12-3, 7-10.30 Sun
☎ (01296) 668366
Fuller's London Pride; Vale Best Bitter; guest beers Ⓗ
A Guide regular, this fine 17th-century village pub is close to the Grand Union Canal. The quiet lounge has comfortable sofas and a small restaurant, the popular public bar has an open fire and games area. Darts, bar billiards, shove ha'penny and skittles (by prior arrangement) are all played. Children are permitted in the games area only and dogs are welcome. The rear door provides wheelchair access.
♨Q☕❀◑◗🍺🚌♣●P

Milton Keynes

Victoria
Vicarage Road, Bradwell Village, MK13 9AQ
⏲ 11-midnight (1am Fri & Sat)
☎ (01908) 316355
Fuller's London Pride; guest beers Ⓗ
An old village local though not far from the central part of the new city. The decor is more modern than the exterior. Due to the successful introduction of a guest ale, a second is now a regular feature, both often from micro-breweries. The range increases even more during the annual August bank holiday beer festival. Regular quiz nights and darts and pool matches make this a true community pub. ❀◑🚌♣●P

Newport Pagnell

Cannon
50 High Street, MK16 8AQ
⏲ 11-11 (midnight Fri & Sat); 12-11 Sun
☎ (01908) 211495
Banks's Bitter; Marston's Pedigree; guest beers Ⓗ
With 10 consecutive years in the Guide, local CAMRA's Pub of the Year 2006 is situated right in the centre of town and its beer prices are excellent for the area. Once the home of Cannon Brewery, it has retained a number of the old outbuildings at the rear of the pub. Note the military memorabilia, particularly the old uniform preserved in a glass case. The car park can be reached via Creed Street. ♨♣🚌P

Quainton

George & Dragon
The Green, HP22 4AR
⏲ 12-11 (midnight Fri & Sat); 12-10.30 Sun
☎ (01296) 655436
Fuller's London Pride; Hook Norton Hooky Bitter; Young's Bitter; guest beer Ⓗ
Two-bar local on a sloping village green overlooked by a tall windmill. The lower bar offers reasonably priced meals with vegetarian and children's options. Cheap lunches are on offer for older people on Tuesday and bargain-priced steaks on Tuesday evening (no food Sun eve or Mon lunch). Voted Pub of the Year 2006 by the local council, it is no-smoking throughout. The Buckinghamshire Railway Centre, just outside the village, is popular with steam

and railway history enthusiasts.
ᗰQ◑⊟♣P⊬

St Leonards

White Lion

Jenkins Lane, HP23 6NN (4 miles from Chesham on Wendover road) OS918069
⊙ 11.30-midnight; 12-11.30 Sun
☎ (01494) 758387
Greene King IPA; guest beers Ⓗ
Down-to-earth, friendly hostelry serving excellent simple food. The highest pub in the Chilterns, its nautical theme is slightly quirky, but adds to the experience. The main bar has an open fire and there are two smaller side rooms. Its proximity to the Ridgeway and Chiltern paths makes it popular with walkers, and dogs are welcome. A mild festival is held in late spring. A favourite pub with local CAMRA members.
ᗰQ♉❀◑♿♣P⊬

Sherington

White Hart

1 Gun Lane, MK16 9PE (off A509, follow signs to village) OS892468
⊙ 12-3, 5-11; 12-4, 7-10.30 Sun
☎ (01908) 611953 ⊕ whitehartsherington.com
Fuller's London Pride; Young's Bitter; guest beers Ⓗ
A previous local CAMRA Pub of the Year, the White Hart manages to achieve the right balance between offering five quality real ales and serving superb gourmet food. The annual beer and sausage festival held over the May bank holiday is a highlight. Cottage beers are often on the guest list though ales can come from anywhere in the UK. Good accommodation is available across the car park from the pub. Booking for food is essential. ᗰQ❀⇌◑♣●P

Skirmett

Frog

RG9 6TG (off M40 jct 5, through Ibstone to Skirmett) OS775903
⊙ 11.30-3, 6-11; 12-4 (10.30 summer) Sun
☎ (01491) 638996 ⊕ thefrog.tablesir.com
Adnams Bitter; Rebellion IPA; guest beers Ⓗ
With fine views across the countryside, this 300-year-old free house lies in the beautiful Hambleden Valley. The Frog is a family owned pub exuding warmth and tranquillity. It offers a fine restaurant and high-quality accommodation. Guest beers often come from local breweries. Snacks are available in the bar where an inviting log fire burns in winter. Food is cooked to order; specials are available daily. Theme nights are a regular feature. ᗰQ❀⇌◑♣P⊬

Stewkley

Swan

Chapel Square, High Street, LU7 0HA
⊙ 12-1am (2am Fri & Sat); 12-10.30 Sun
☎ (01525) 240285
Courage Best Bitter; guest beers Ⓗ
Close to the village centre, the Swan is a lively local appealing to all. Originally three cottages, the pub dates from the 16th century and retains many oak beams and an attractive inglenook. A ghost named Valerie is said to make her presence felt occasionally. Guest ales are often local, from Tring Brewery or other independents. Freshly prepared food is available daily. Live music is played on most Saturdays and a popular folk jam session is hosted on some Wednesdays. ❀◑♣P

Stoke Goldington

Lamb

16-20 High Street, MK16 8NR (on B526)
⊙ 12-3, 5-11; 12-11 Sat; 12-10.30 Sun
☎ (01908) 551233
⊕ thelambstokegoldington.moonfruit.com
Nethergate IPA; guest beers Ⓗ
A Guide regular for a number of years, the owners strive to make this pub an asset to the community. Guest ales come from all over the UK. The daft dog now has a companion again (the previous one sadly passed away). The increasingly rare Northamptonshire skittles can be played here. Sunday lunches are enormous and great value. Belgian beer lovers will enjoy the bottled Duvel, cider fans the Westons Old Rosie. Ring ahead to check Sunday opening hours in winter. ᗰQ❀◑♣●P⊬

Stoke Mandeville

Bull

5 Risborough Road, HP22 5UP
⊙ 12-3, 5.30-11; 12-11 Fri & Sat; 12-10.30 Sun
☎ (01296) 613632
Fuller's London Pride; Tetley Bitter; Wells Bombardier Ⓗ
Small pub situated on a main road, well served by public transport. The front bar is popular with locals, especially sports fans who gather to watch football and horse racing on TV. The comfortable lounge bar at the back tends to be quieter and leads out to a large, secure garden. Popular with families in summer, the garden has plenty to keep children amused. Q❀⊟≹⊟♣P

Stony Stratford

Fox & Hounds

87 High Street, MK11 1AT (on old A5)
⊙ 11-11; 12-10.30 Sun
☎ (01908) 563307
⊕ stonystratford.co.uk/foxhound.html
Beer range varies Ⓗ
Situated just north of the town centre, this pub has been transformed and now has a more modern feel to it. A small side room has become a dining area. 'The' real ale pub in town, it offers an ever-changing list of four guest ales. At the heart of the local music scene, a small stage has now been added. The pub gets very busy on music nights (usually Thursday). ❀◑⊟⊟♣P⊬

Tylers Green

Horse & Jockey

Church Road, HP10 8EG

⌚ 11.30-3, 5-11; 11.30-11.30 Fri & Sat; 12-11 Sun
☎ (01494) 815963 🌐 horseandjockeytylersgreen.co.uk
Adnams Bitter, Broadside; Brakspear Bitter; Fuller's London Pride; Greene King Abbot Ⓗ
A traditional local near Tylers Green church; the building was converted into a pub in 1821. The single room is U-shaped with a food counter to the left and the dartboard to the right. Food is available all week, lunchtimes and evenings. The main car parking area is on the opposite side of the road.
⩩❀◐◑♣P

Wendover

Pack Horse

29 Tring Road, HP22 6NR
⌚ 12-11 (midnight Fri & Sat); 12-10.30 Sun
☎ (01296) 622075
Fuller's Chiswick, London Pride, seasonal beers; guest beers Ⓗ
Small, friendly village pub situated at the end of a terrace of thatched cottages known as the Anne Boleyn cottages. The pub, a free house, dates from 1769 and has been owned by the same family for 43 years. It is on the Ridgeway Path and the wall above the bar is decorated with RAF squadron badges denoting connections with nearby RAF Halton. The pub runs men and women's darts teams, dominoes and crib.
⇌♣

Wing

Queen's Head

9 High Street, LU7 0NS
⌚ 11.30-11; 12-10.30 Sun
☎ (01296) 688268
Fuller's London Pride; Greene King IPA; Hook Norton Old Hooky Ⓗ
Welcoming locals' pub in the centre of the village with an increasing number of real ales. The 16th-century building features real log fires in the main bar and restaurant, where good home-made specials are served all week. The excellent no-smoking adult-only snug is comfortably equipped with leather sofas, with board games available at every table. Outside is a lovely patio and large garden.
⩩❀◐◑♣P⍻

Wooburn Common

Royal Standard

Wooburn Common Road, HP10 0JS (follow signs to Odds Farm) OS923876
⌚ 12-11; 12-10.30 Sun
☎ (01628) 521121
Caledonian Deuchars IPA; Ⓗ **Hop Back Summer Lightning;** Ⓖ **guest beers** Ⓖ/Ⓗ
Popular semi-rural roadside pub, a short detour from the A40, and well worth it. Ten ales, five on handpump, five on gravity, greet the discerning drinker. A dark beer, stout, porter or mild is usually among the gravity dispensed beers. The local real ale fraternity enjoys lively banter here, adding to a congenial atmosphere created by drinkers and diners. A large real fire warms the pub in winter. Disabled car parking is available. ⩩Q❀◐◑♿P

Wycombe Marsh

General Havelock

114 Kingsmead Road, HP11 1HZ
⌚ 12-2.30, 5.30-11; 11-11 Fri & Sat; 12-10.30 Sun
☎ (01494) 520391
Fuller's Chiswick, Discovery, London Pride, ESB, seasonal beers Ⓗ
An imposing building on a road that runs paralled to, and south of, the M40. It boasts 15 consecutive appearances in this Guide and has been run by the same licensee since Fuller's bought it. The garden is pleasant in warmer weather. Lunchtime food is served daily except Saturday. Evening meals are only available on Friday. ⩩❀◑P

Red Lion

551 London Road, HP11 1ET (on main A40 between M40 jct 2 and Wycombe centre)
⌚ 12-11 (closed Mon); 12-10.30 Sun
☎ (01494) 440083 🌐 redlionrocks.co.uk
Fuller's London Pride; Rebellion Mild; guest beers Ⓗ
Rejuvenated 1930s pub in a prominent position on the A40 opposite the shopping centre. Inside is a series of different areas with a large screen at one end, a pool table at the other, and a stage in the middle. Live music is played every day with blues on Tuesday and an acoustic jam on Sunday afternoon. An annual beer festival is held in June. ⩩❀🚌P

Smoking ban

A ban on smoking in public places – including pubs – in England and Wales is due to come into effect during the summer of 2007. A similar ban is already in operation in Scotland. Many pubs are preparing for the ban in England and Wales by planning heated outside patios and other areas for smokers. This edition of the guide continues to list areas set aside for non-smokers as such arrangements will continue for most of the life of this edition.

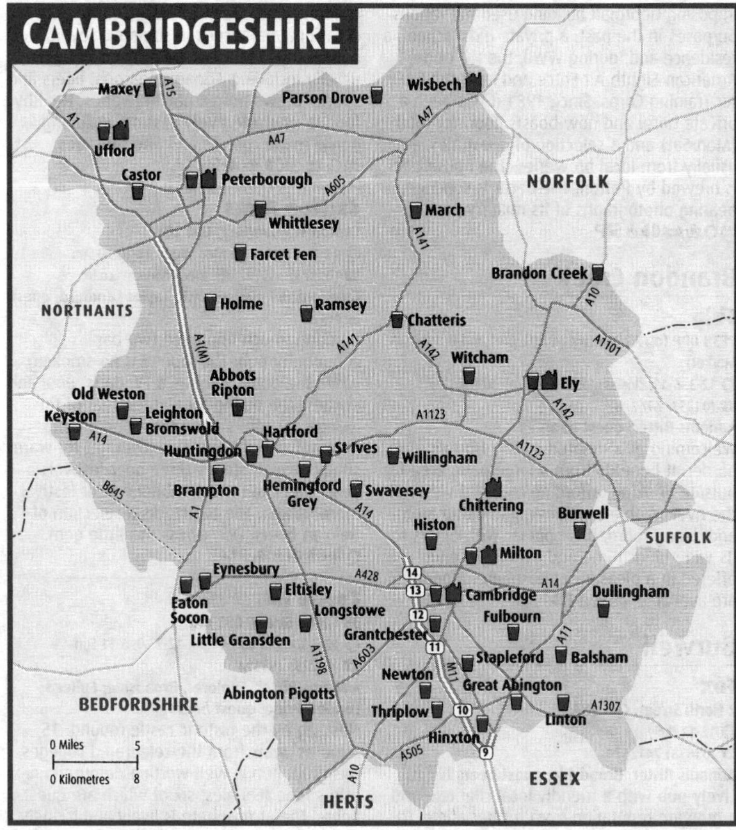

Abbots Ripton

Three Horseshoes

Moat Lane, PE28 2PA (on B1090)

11.30-3, 6-11; closed Mon; 12-5 Sun

(01487) 773440

thethreehorseshoes.com

Adnams Bitter, Broadside; Oakham JHB; guest beers

Part of the De Ramsey estate, this is a picturesque pub in a village of thatched cottages. A small, listed thatched pub that has been carefully refurbished and extended, the quarry-tiled, original oak-beamed pub area has been sensitively retained as a family room. The extensions include a comfortable, large lounge bar, a restaurant and accommodation. The menu offers varied modern cuisine.

Abington Pigotts

Pig & Abbot

High Street, SG8 0SD (off A505 through Litlington) OS306444

12-3, 6-11; 12-11 Sat; 12-10.30 Sun

(01763) 853515 pigandabbot.co.uk

Adnams Bitter; Fuller's London Pride; guest beers

Deceptively large Queen Anne period pub in a picturesque and surprisingly remote part of the south Cambridgeshire countryside. Run by a mother and daughter team, it has a comfortable restaurant and lounge bar where a large inglenook holds a wood-burning stove, creating a cosy atmosphere. An imaginative menu makes this pub a popular choice for food. Various guest beers are offered, often from Woodforde's or Timothy Taylor.

Balsham

Black Bull

27 High Street, CB1 6DJ

11.30-2.30 (3 Sat), 6-11; 12-3, 7.30-10.30 Sun

(01223) 893844 blackbull-balsham.co.uk

Greene King IPA; guest beers

Large, Grade II listed thatched pub dating from 1700 that has been much altered but retains plenty of its original character. Authentic beamed bars are set around a central island. Two restaurant areas offer a wide selection of food including fresh fish, locally sourced meat and vegetarian dishes, at all sessions except Sunday evening and Monday lunchtime. The licensee stocks a changing selection of beers from micro-breweries.

Brampton

Grange

115 High Street, PE28 4RA

11-11; 12-10.30 Sun

(01480) 459516 grangehotelbrampton.co.uk

Greene King IPA; guest beers

Imposing Georgian building used for various purposes in the past: a private girls' school, a residence and, during WWII, the HQ of the American Eighth Air Force and later the RAF Air Training Corps. Since 1981 it has been a private hotel and now boasts gourmet food (Mon-Sat) and a selection of guest ales, usually from local breweries. The house beer is brewed by Potton. The decor is subdued, bearing photographs of its military past.

Brandon Creek

Ship

PE38 0PP (on A10 between Littleport and Downham Market)

12-3, 6-11; closed Mon; 12-4, 6-10.30 Sun

(01353) 676228

Adnams Bitter; guest beers H

Welcoming pub situated on the Norfolk border. It benefits from a large patio area for outside drinking, affording pleasant views of the river. With a spacious no-smoking area and dining room, it is popular with diners for its varied lunchtime and evening menus offered in a pleasant atmosphere. Moorings are available.

Burwell

Fox

2 North Street, CB5 0BA

12-11 daily

(01638) 741267

Adnams Bitter, Broadside; guest beers H

Lively pub with a friendly local clientele and a growing reputation from further afield. It takes pride in offering a genuine alternative to the other dining and drinking establishments in the village, with guest ales rarely found in the region and authentic Mexican cuisine in the evenings (no food Sun or Mon lunchtime). The dining room offers a calm, modern contrast to the traditional public bar. There is a patio and a large garden for the summer. A cider is sometimes stocked.

Cambridge

Cambridge Blue

85-87 Gwydir Street, CB1 2LG

12-2.30 (3 Sat), 5.30-11; 12-2.30, 6-10.30 Sun

(01223) 361382

City of Cambridge Hobson's Choice; Elgood's Black Dog; Oakham JHB; Woodforde's Wherry; guest beers H

A pub for conversation, operating a no-mobile phone policy. No-smoking throughout, it welcomes well-behaved children (and dogs). The large garden hosts occasional barbecues in summer. Seven handpumps feature a wide range of beers, usually including Adnams seasonal beers and special brews from small breweries. Healthy food is available every session, including home-made choices and fine sausages.

Carlton Arms

Carlton Way, Arbury, CB4 2BY

11-11 (11-3, 5-11 Mon-Wed); 12-10.30 Sun

(01223) 355717 thecarltonarms.co.uk

Caledonian Deuchars IPA; Taylor Landlord; guest beers G

Cracking, much improved two-bar community pub. The lounge is no-smoking, while the public bar has a TV, darts, pool and skittles. The dining area at the rear of the lounge bar offers good food, and a patio area in front of the pub is just right for warm sunny days. It stages three beer festivals a year; check out the Cambridge beer festival memorabilia. The bar stocks a selection of Belgian beers. Don't miss this little gem.

Castle Inn

38 Castle Street, CB3 0AJ

12-2.30, 5 (6 Sat)-11.30; 12-2.30, 6-11 Sun

(01223) 353194

Adnams Bitter, Explorer, Broadside; Fuller's London Pride; guest beers H

Nestling by the historic castle mound, 15 minutes' walk from the celebrated colleges, this great pub is well worth a detour. It offers nine real ales, six of which are guest beers. The atmosphere is lively and friendly. An open fire welcomes you in winter months, while a suntrap patio makes it a pub for all seasons. Food is available at every session.

Champion of the Thames

68 King Street, CB1 1LN

11-11; 12-11 Sun

(01223) 352043

Greene King IPA, Abbot; guest beer H

Traditional, two-room, city-centre pub, popular with locals and students alike. The two wood-panelled bars feature low ceilings, sturdy tables and many interesting nooks and crannies. The eponymous sportsman appears in the superb etched glazing and various sketches and prints. It stands in the middle of the infamous 'King Street run' pub crawl.

Flying Pig

106 Hills Road, CB2 1LQ

12 (7 Sat)-11; 7-11 Sun

Adnams Bitter, Broadside; Fuller's London Pride; Greene King Abbot; Shepherd Neame Spitfire H

City pub, close to the station, with an L-shaped interior and separate games room. Pigs are much in evidence in the decor, along with a variety of posters, both old and new. A lot of the light comes from candles on the tables. The pub was recently threatened by a proposed redevelopment, but after local outcry it was saved. Bar billiards can be played here.

INDEPENDENT BREWERIES

Cambridge Moonshine Cambridge
City of Cambridge Chittering
Elgood's Wisbech
Fenland Ely
Hereward Ely
Milton Milton
Oakham Peterborough
Ufford Ufford

Free Press
Prospect Row, CB1 1DU (behind police station)
✪ 12-2.30 (3 Sat), 6-11; 12-2.30, 7-10.30 Sun
☎ (01223) 368337
Greene King XX Mild, IPA, Abbot; guest beers Ⓗ
Saved from demolition in the 1970s, this thriving little traditional pub has been no-smoking since 1992 (and mobile phones are banned too). Features include a snug and a walled garden. Food is available every session (except Sun eve); a healthy selection includes home-made soups and pastas. As a Greene King tenancy, the guest beers are from the company's portfolio. ⌂Q✿◑♣⊁☐

Green Dragon
5 Water Street, CB4 1NZ (off Chesterton High St)
✪ 11-11; 11-4, 7-11 Sun
☎ (01223) 505035
Greene King XX Mild, IPA, Abbot; guest beers Ⓗ
Built in the 1500s as a coaching inn and located near the river, it makes a good stop, or starting point, for a walk along the Fen Rivers Way. A fire in a large inglenook greets you in the winter and there is a garden by the river for the summer. It serves excellent food and is popular for watching sport on TV amid friendly company. ⌂✿◑

Kingston Arms
33 Kingston Street, CB1 2NU
✪ 12-2.30, 5-11; 12-midnight Fri & Sat; 12-11 Sun
☎ (01223) 319414 ⊕ kingston-arms.co.uk
Crouch Vale Brewers Gold; Elgood's Black Dog; Hop Back Entire Stout; Oakham JHB; Taylor Landlord; guest beers Ⓗ
Ten handpumps dispensing regular and guest beers, an excellent wine list and award-winning food combine to make this a busy pub. If you wish to dine, booking is advisable. No keg beer or cider is stocked. The sheltered garden has canopies and heaters for cool evenings in summer. Free wireless Internet access is an added bonus. ⌂Q✿◑⇌♣

Live & Let Live
40 Mawson Road, CB1 2EA
✪ 11.30-2.30, 5.30 (6 Sat)-11; 12-3, 7-10.30 Sun
☎ (01223) 460261
Adnams Bitter; Everards Tiger; Nethergate Umbel Ale; guest beers Ⓗ
Traditional, 19th-century back-street local where wood panelling and timber floors enhance the genuinely friendly atmosphere. Seven real ales are on offer, including a wide variety of guests, the cider is from Cassels, and it also stocks a selection of bottled Belgian beers. Food, of a high standard is served at every session. Live acoustic music is performed on Saturday evening. Q◑♿⇌♣●⊁

Castor

Prince of Wales Feathers
38 Peterborough Road, PE5 7AL
✪ 12-3 (not Tue or Thu), 5-11.30 (midnight Fri); 12-midnight Sat; 12-11.30 Sun
☎ (01733) 380222
Adnams Bitter; Greene King Ruddles County; John Smith's Bitter; guest beer Ⓗ
Refurbished village local: only one bar but divided into different areas to serve a varied clientele. It retains the original stained glass windows. Monthly live music is performed and a quiz is held on Sunday evening. A small patio to the side of the pub is an attraction in summer. Lined glasses are available on request. Lunches are served Friday and Saturday. ⌂Q✿◐♿⊟⊁☐

Chatteris

Walk the Dog
34 Bridge Street, PE16 6RN
✪ 12-2.30, 6.30-11; 12-3.30, 7-10.30 Sun
☎ (01354) 693695
Adnams Bitter; Fuller's London Pride; guest beers Ⓗ
Real ale drinkers are especially welcome at this family-owned, single-room community pub. This free house always serves a selection of frequently-changing guest ales and bottle-conditioned beers. Games are played including Scrabble, chess, dominoes, darts, crib and petanque. A sailing group and a golf society are also based here. Regular themed evenings include a cheese night on Friday, and a Sunday quiz. Four large benches at the front of the pub provide a popular summer suntrap. Food is served weekdays. ⌂Q✿◐⊟♣P

Dullingham

Boot
18 Brinkley Road, CB8 9UW
✪ 11-2.30, 5-11; 11-11 Sat; 12-2.30 (closed eve) Sun
☎ (01638) 507327
Adnams Bitter, Broadside; guest beers Ⓗ/Ⓖ
Splendid village pub, truly at the hub of its community. The single, L-shaped bar, open-plan with a low ceiling, is decorated in brown and cream. A locals' pub but welcoming to visitors, children are permitted until 8pm. Food is served at lunchtime except Sundays at Cambridge CAMRA's Pub of the Year 2005. ⌂✿◐⇌♣P

Eaton Socon

Rivermill Tavern
School Lane, PE19 8GW
✪ 11-11 (midnight Fri); 10.30-11 Sun
☎ (01480) 219612
Adnams Broadside; Greene King IPA, Abbot; guest beers Ⓗ
Popular pub, converted from a flour mill at Eaton Socon lock on the River Great Ouse. It has a galleried area above the main bar and children are well catered for in a family room. Extensive bar snacks feature a Mexican selection. Live music is popular, with two sessions a week (Wed and Fri eves). A quiz is held on Sunday evening. Moorings are available. Up to two guest beers from independent breweries are stocked. ⛭✿◑P

Eltisley

Leeds Arms
2 The Green, PE19 6TG (off A428)
✪ 11.30-2.30, 6.30-11; 12-4, 6.30-11 Sun
☎ (01480) 880283
Wells Eagle; guest beers Ⓗ
Georgian pub, named after the Leeds family

of Croxton, whose estate was extended to include Eltisley in the 18th century. Different areas are divided by oak beams and screens, while two large fireplaces feature at opposite ends of the main bar. Traditional pub food is served daily. The extensive restaurant is available for functions and meetings. Accommodation includes three twins and six single rooms, all en-suite. ⛫Q❀⛼◐◑⛟P⚟

Ely

Prince Albert

62 Silver Street, CB7 4JF

(100 yds from Barton Rd car park)

⏲ 11-3.30 (not Tue), 6.30 (6 Fri)-11.30; 12-3.30, 7-10.30 Sun

☎ (01353) 663494

Greene King XX Mild, IPA, Abbot; guest beers Ⓗ

Traditional, friendly local next to the old Cambridgeshire Militia staff quarters. A regular CAMRA local and regional award winner, the present landlord and wife team have run this six-handpump gem for 16 years. Excellent, home-made lunches are available, except Tuesday and Sunday. The suntrap beer garden is a regular Greene King in Bloom area winner. The pub is free from background music and games machines. Q❀◐♿⇌♣

Town House

60-64 Market Street, CB7 4LS

⏲ 11-11 (1am Fri-Sat); 12-10.30 Sun

☎ (01353) 664338

Oakham JHB; guest beers Ⓗ

City-centre pub within sight of the cathedral, serving guest beers that change weekly. On Sunday evening it stages a well-attended quiz. On Friday and Saturday nights the pub stays open until 1am with a DJ running a disco, and can be busy. An annual beer festival is held in the summer with a wide selection of beers served in the garden. ❀◐⚟

West End House

16 West End, CB6 3AY

⏲ 12-3, 6-11; 12-11 Fri & Sat; 12-4, 7-10.30 Sun

☎ (01353) 662907

Adnams Bitter; Greene King IPA; guest beers Ⓗ

Traditional pub replete with old beams, small windows and low ceilings. Just outside the city centre, it is well worth seeking out. The pub is divided into four drinking areas, including a small snug room. A small, enclosed garden often has a marquee put up in summer for special events and private parties. Guest beers frequently come from the local Fenland Brewery. ⛫❀◐♣

Eynesbury

Chequers

St Mary's Street, PE19 2TA

⏲ 12-2, 7-11; 12-2 (closed eve) Sun

☎ (01480) 472116 🌐 thechequers.co.uk

Beer range varies Ⓗ

Warm, welcoming old pub with a wealth of exposed beams. Areas are set aside for customers to enjoy the excellent bar meals. Built in the 16th century, and one of the oldest houses in Eynesbury, it housed manor courts in the 18th century. It has seen many additions and much restoration over the years. Two cask beers are on sale, often from East Anglian micro-breweries. ⛫Q❀◐◑⛟P

Farcet Fen

Plough

Milk & Water Drove, Ramsey Road, PE7 3DR

(on B1095, S of A605)

⏲ 12-11; 12-10.30 Sun

☎ (01733) 844307 🌐 theploughfarcet.co.uk

Elgood's Black Dog; Oakham JHB; guest beers Ⓗ

Isolated Fenland pub with a reputation for good food and ale. Refurbished for structural reasons, the pub has lost the real fire but gained a dining area. The bar, with a farming theme, has a beamed ceiling and leather settees. A large tropical fish tank divides the room. Children are welcome and there is an outdoor play area. Smoking is permitted in the public bar, which contains a bar billiards table. Live music is featured on Friday. No evening meals are served in winter. ❀◐◑⊟♿⛺♣P⚟

Fulbourn

Six Bells

9 High Street, CB1 5DH

⏲ 11.30-3, 6-11.30; 12-11.30 Fri & Sat; 12-11 Sun

☎ (01223) 880244

Adnams Bitter; Greene King IPA; Tetley Burton Ale; guest beers Ⓗ

An open log fire, the landlord's cheery welcome and fine, home-cooked food are three of the ingredients that make this former coaching inn an archetypal village pub. It also happens to sell excellent ale – three regular beers, plus a surprisingly diverse choice of guests mean the customer always has something to look forward to. Food is served in the restaurant and bar (eve meals Tue-Sat). Live jazz twice monthly and a large garden are added attractions. ⛫Q☕❀◐◑⊟♿♣●P

Grantchester

Blue Ball Inn

57 Broadway, CB3 9NQ

⏲ 11-3, 6-11; 12-10.30 Sun

☎ (01223) 840679

Adnams Bitter; guest beer Ⓗ

Small, yet cosy pub, full of friendly locals, and no draught lagers! Established in 1767, it holds the oldest licence in Grantchester, and displays a full list of landlords since then. Games such as shut the box, ring the bull and shove-ha'penny are played, while live blues music is performed on Thursday evening. An authentic, traditional and relaxing experience centred on conversation and the community; children are not admitted here. ⛫Q❀⛼♣●

Great Abington

Three Tuns

75 High Street, CB1 6AB

⏲ 12-2.30, 6-11; 12-11 Sat; 12-10.30 Sun

☎ (01223) 891467

Greene King IPA; Nethergate seasonal beers; guest beers Ⓗ

Revitalised, two-bar free house, opposite the

village cricket green, that draws a wide range of customers. The small dining room is no-smoking and there is a slightly larger main bar. An excellent, authentic Thai menu is available Monday-Saturday, plus a proper roast on Sunday (booking is advisable; no eve meals Sun). A changing beer range includes two guests from the likes of Adnams, City of Cambridge, Taylor or Woodforde's. Folk musicians visit some Sunday evenings. ♨❀◑◗▲P⚟

Hartford

King of the Belgians

27 Main Street, PE29 1XU

⊙ 11-3.30, 5.30-11; 11-11 Fri & Sat; 12-10.30 Sun

☎ (01480) 452030 ⊕ kingofthebelgians.co.uk

Beer range varies Ⓗ

Dating from the 16th century, this was originally the local pub for the small, picturesque village of Hartford, before it was absorbed into the town of Huntingdon. It is believed that Oliver Cromwell, who had a farm nearby, used to frequent the establishment. Comprising a public bar and a restaurant, the ceiling in the bar displays a collection of aviation-related memorabilia of British and international units from the Cold War era, as well as other flying-related mementos. The pub was once called the King of the Prussians, but the name was changed during WWI. A constantly changing range of up to three real ales is on offer, and good value pub food is also available. Q❀◑◗⊟P

Hemingford Grey

Cock

47 High Street, PE28 9BJ (off A14, SE of Huntingdon)

⊙ 11.30-3, 6-11; 12-4, 6.30-10.30 Sun

☎ (01480) 463609 ⊕ cambscuisine.com

Earl Soham Victoria Bitter; Woodforde's Wherry; guest beers Ⓗ

Stylish bar in a village pub, offering outstanding real ales from East Anglian brewers and excellent cuisine in the restaurant. The convivial bar has modest furnishings, a real fire and a sociable food-free environment. There is a covered patio for smokers. The cask beers are well chosen and the restaurant is widely acclaimed with a daily fresh fish board, meat and game dishes and a range of superb sausages; booking is usually necessary. ♨Q❀◑◗⊟P⚟

Hinxton

Red Lion

32 High Street, CB10 1QY

⊙ 11-3.30, 6-11.30; 12-4.30, 7-11 Sun

☎ (01799) 530601 ⊕ redlionhinxton.co.uk

Adnams Bitter; Greene King IPA; Woodforde's Wherry; guest beer Ⓗ

Friendly, community pub, frequented by a wide cross-section of villagers. It began life as a coaching inn in the 16th century. An extension housing the restaurant does not detract at all from the older part of the building, which is cosy and comfortable with sofas in a variety of seating areas. The large garden features secluded spots and (occupied) dovecotes near the back. ♨Q❀◑◗♣●P

Histon

Red Lion

27 High Street, CB4 4JD

⊙ 10.30-3, 5 (4 Fri)-11; 10.30-11 Sat; 12-6, 7-10.30 Sun

☎ (01223) 564437

Elgood's Black Dog; Everards Tiger, Sunchaser; Oakham Bishops Farewell; guest beers Ⓗ

Two-bar free house with a quiet(ish) lounge where food is served and a more boisterous public bar, displaying a fine collection of bottled beers. Breweriana featured throughout includes old pub signs and water jugs. Two beer festivals are held annually: an Easter 'apertif' and the main event in September with a marquee in the garden and live entertainment. An extensive range of Belgian beers includes three on draught. Popular monthly curry nights and other special events are staged. The garden has a petanque piste. ♨❀◑⊟♣●P

Holme

Admiral Wells

41 Station Road, PE7 3PH

⊙ 12-2.30, 5-11; 12-11 Sat; 12-10.30 Sun

☎ (01487) 831214

Everards Tiger; Woodforde's Wherry; guest beers Ⓗ

Recently refurbished Victorian inn, said to be the lowest pub in England. Situated next to the East Coast mainline railway, it is named after one of the pallbearers at Nelson's funeral. Up to six real ales plus a traditional cider are available in the two drinking areas, the no-smoking lounge and dining room. Booking is recommended for the popular restaurant, particularly at weekends. There is a large, shady garden to one side. ♨❀◑◗♣●P

Huntingdon

Old Bridge Hotel

1 High Street, PE29 3TQ (on ring road, by river)

⊙ 11-11; 12-10.30 Sun

☎ (01480) 424300

Adnams bitter; guest beers Ⓗ

Sumptuous splendour is provided in this handsome hotel bar with a relaxing, welcoming environment for local beer drinkers and residents. The 18th-century building, once a private bank, sits alongside the River Great Ouse in the birthplace of Oliver Cromwell. Imaginative high quality food and wine are served in a relaxed atmosphere on the stylish mural-adorned 'terrace' or in the intimate, more formal dining room. ♨Q❀⇌◑◗⇌⊟P⚟

Keyston

Pheasant

Village Loop, PE28 0RE (on B663, 1 mile S of A14)

⊙ 12-3, 6-11; 12-3, 7-10.30 Sun

☎ (01832) 710241 ⊕ huntsbridge.com

Adnams Bitter; guest beers Ⓗ

Part of the small Huntsbridge group of pubs, which offer high quality food, fine wines and

well-kept cask ales, the Pheasant has been created from a row of thatched cottages in an idyllic setting. The village is named after Ketil's Stone, probably an Anglo-Saxon boundary marker. It boasts a splendid lounge bar and three dining areas, including the Red Room restaurant in a rear extension. Local micro-breweries' products usually feature.
⛫Q❀◑◗P⚟

Leighton Bromswold

Green Man
37 The Avenue, PE28 5AW (1 mile N of A14)
✪ 12-3 (not Tue-Thu), 7-11; closed Mon; 12-3, 7-10.30 Sun
☎ (01480) 890238 🌐 greenmanpub.org
Nethergate IPA; guest beers 🄷
Delightful local in a charming village on a high ridge (the Bromswold) not far from the Northamptonshire border. The Green Man provides a congenial focus for a small village community and attracts visitors from a wide area for good food and an interesting, frequently-changed beer range, with typically three guest ales and Belgian and British bottled real ales. Hood skittles is a popular game here. A real fire adds atmosphere in winter. No food is served on Sunday evening. ⛫♉❀◑◗♣P⚟

Linton

Crown Inn
11 High Street, CB1 6HS
✪ 12-2.30 (3 Fri), 5.30 (5 Fri)-11; 12-11 Sat; 12-8 Sun
☎ (01223) 891759
Beer range varies 🄷
Situated at the north end of one of the most varied and picturesque streets in the area, the Crown is a long, thin pub divided into drinking areas and a no-smoking restaurant. The space is imaginatively used in the narrow but cosy main bar, enhanced by attractive window seats. Note the Watneys Red Barrel lantern hanging in one of the bay windows. Excellent home-cooked food is available in the bar and restaurant at all sessions except Sunday evening. ⛫❀🛏◑◗P

Little Gransden

Chequers
71 Main Road, SG19 3DW (on B1046)
✪ 12-2, 7-11; 11-11 Fri & Sat; 12-6, 7-10.30 Sun
☎ (01767) 677348
Oakham JHB; guest beers 🄷/🄶
The hub of this small village: a local in the true sense of the word, run by the same family for the last 56 years. A well researched and documented history around the walls makes interesting reading. The excellent, unspoilt public bar with bench seating and roaring fire has been complemented by the addition of a comfortable lounge. There is always an interesting guest beer to try here. Check out the collection of beer festival glasses. ⛫♉❀⊟♿⊡♣P

Longstowe

Red House
134 Old North Road, CB3 7UT
✪ 12-3, 5.30-11 (midnight Fri); 12-midnight Sat; 12-10.30 Sun
☎ (01954) 718480 🌐 theredhousepub.co.uk
Greene King IPA; guest beers 🄷
Former coaching inn, meticulously recreated as the epitome of a country pub; in fact you almost feel as if you are entering the parlour of the local squire, with stuffed animals and hunting scenes on the walls, and candles on the tables creating a genteel atmosphere. The restaurant section, recently extended into the adjoining barn, includes an old organ among other curios. Meals are served all day at the weekend. Guest beers are often unusual brews for the area. ⛫❀◑◗P

March

King William IV
107 High Street, PE15 9LH
✪ 12-3, 5.30-midnight; 12-3, 7-midnight Sun
☎ (01354) 653378
Greene King IPA, Morland Original; Taylor Landlord; guest beers 🄷
Red-brick 1930s style pub unspoilt by ugly modern tat. The bar is split into two sections and has a brick surround fireplace. Popular with local residents for early evening meals, a dining room is located to the rear, but meals can be eaten in the bar (no eve meals Sun). Accommodation is available in three en-suite double rooms. Not far from the boat moorings on the river, a small patio is open in summer. Winter opening hours may vary.
Q❀🛏◑◗♿⇌⊡P

Maxey

Blue Bell
37-39 High Street, PE6 9EE
✪ 5.30 (12 Sat)-midnight; 12-4.30, 7.30-11 Sun
☎ (01778) 348182
Abbeydale Absolution; Fuller's London Pride; Oakham JHB; guest beers 🄷
Superb village pub dating from 1645, built of local limestone, winner of local CAMRA Pub of the Year 2006. It has been sympathetically modernised retaining low beams and flagstones. Six beers are normally available and a free buffet is served on Sunday lunchtime. Friday is Hawaiian shirt night! ⛫Q⊟♣

Milton

Waggon & Horses
39 High Street, CB4 6DF
✪ 12-2.30 (3 Sat), 5-11 (midnight Fri; 6-11.30 Sat); 12-3, 7-10.30 Sun
☎ (01223) 860313
Elgood's Black Dog, Cambridge, Golden Newt, seasonal beers; guest beers 🄷
This imposing, mock-Tudor, one-room pub, featuring an impressive collection of hats, is Elgood's most southerly house. The large garden is safe for children and has a slide, swings and a petanque terrain. A challenging quiz is held on Wednesday. Baltis are the speciality on Thursday's menu but all meals are good value and recommended. Bar billiards is still popular here and shove-ha'penny is also played. The real cider

comes from local producer, Cassels. ⛫❀◑♣●P⊬Ō

Newton

Queen's Head

Fowlmere Road, CB2 5PG

⌚ 11.30-2.30, 6-11; 12-2.30, 7-10.30 Sun

☎ (01223) 870436

Adnams Bitter, Broadside, seasonal beers Ⓖ

Classic, two-roomed village local with a great deal of history; a (short) list of all the licensees going back to 1729 is on display. This is one of the few pubs to have appeared in every edition of this Guide to date. Before the outbreak of WWI George V and the Kaiser drank together here. The head on the pub's sign is that of Anne of Cleves. Good, simple pub food is available. Cider from Crones or Cassels is stocked. ⛫Q◑⊟♿⛺♣●P⊬

Old Weston

Swan

Main Street, PE28 5LL (on B660, N of A14)

⌚ 12-2.30 (not Mon-Fri), 6.30 (7 Sat)-11; 12-3.30, 7-10.30 Sun

☎ (01832) 293400

Adnams Bitter, Broadside; Greene King Abbot; guest beers Ⓗ

Dating from the 16th century, this oak-beamed village pub started life as two private houses that were later merged, and has evolved and grown over the years. At the end of the 19th century the pub had its own brewery. There is a central bar with a large inglenook, a dining area and a games section offering hood skittles, darts and pool. On Saturday and Sunday a varied menu of traditional pub food is available, including home-made puddings. ⛫Q♉❀◑♣P

Parson Drove

Swan

Station Road, PE13 4HA

⌚ 5.30 (5 Fri)-11; 12-3.30, 7.30-11 Sat; 12-10.30 Sun

☎ (01945) 700291

Elgood's Black Dog, Cambridge, Pageant Ale; guest beer Ⓗ

Situated in a large spread-out Fenland village, the pub is well used by the locals. The beamed, single-roomed bar is L-shaped, with a bar billiards table at one end. Meals are served in the dining room. Live music is sometimes performed on Saturday evenings. ⛫❀◑⛺🚌P

Peterborough

Bogarts

17 North Street, PE1 2RA

⌚ 11-11 (2am Fri & Sat); 12-10.30 Sun

☎ (01733) 890839 🌐 bogarts.co.uk

Everards Tiger, Sunchaser, Original; guest beers Ⓗ

Former home-brew shop, this small, city-centre bar is tucked down a side street off Westgate. Alterations mean that the former kitchen has gone and all meals are now served from Melillos Restaurant at the rear. Bare brick walls and subdued lighting make for a relaxing atmosphere. The large patio hosts regular beer festivals. Live music is featured fortnightly; there are also quiz nights and DJ battle nights. An animation club meets every other Monday. No entry after 11pm; no lunches are served Monday. ❀◑♿⇌🚌

Brewery Tap

80 Westgate, PE1 2AA

⌚ 12-11 (1.30am Fri & Sat); 12-11 Sun

☎ (01733) 358500

Oakham JHB, White Dwarf, Bishops Farewell; guest beers Ⓗ

Former labour exchange, converted into an airy, spacious public house. Home to Oakham Ales, it is now under threat of demolition as the North Westgate area of Peterborough is redeveloped. The whole of the upper area is no-smoking. It often stages live music at the weekends when there may be a door charge. Excellent Thai food is cooked by Thai chefs. The 12 real ales always include a mild, and Belgian bottled beers are stocked. Dress code is smart casual. ◑⇌⊬

Charters

Town Bridge, PE1 1DB

⌚ 12-11 (2am Fri & Sat); 12-11 Sun

☎ (01733) 315700 🌐 bluesontheboat.co.uk

Oakham JHB, White Dwarf, Bishops Farewell; guest beers Ⓗ

Large Dutch barge moored near Town Bridge, owned by the same group as Oakham Ales. Normally 12 real ales are available, with extra ones in the cellar. Beers are all usually also available by gravity on request. With over 500 guest beers a year, a mild is always stocked as well as a stout or porter during the winter months. The large garden houses a marquee where regular beer festivals are held. The upper deck of the barge houses East, a fine restaurant serving oriental food. Live bands means a door charge on Friday and Saturday evenings. ♉◑⇌🚌♣⊬

Coalheavers Arms

5 Park Street, Woodston, PE2 9BH

⌚ 12-2 (not Mon-Wed), 5-11; 12-11 Fri & Sat; 12-10.30 Sun

☎ (01733) 565664

Beer range varies Ⓗ

Small, single-roomed, back-street pub that is very much a local. Refurbished by a group of businessmen including Milton Brewery, the real ales are a mix of Milton and guests, always including a mild. A real cider and Belgian bottled beers are also stocked. The large popular garden is used to stage two annual beer festivals on May bank holiday weekend and three weeks after Peterborough beer festival. The opening hours are extended in summer. Q❀⇌🚌●Ō

Drapers Arms

29-31 Cowgate, PE1 1LZ (next to bus and rail stations)

⌚ 9am-midnight (1am Fri-Sat); 9am-midnight Sun

☎ (01733) 847570

Courage Directors; Greene King Abbot; Marston's Pedigree; guest beers Ⓗ

One of Wetherspoon's first no-smoking pubs, refurbished in 2005. Wood panelled walls display pictures of the city in bygone days. Popular with a varied clientele, food theme nights are held, while quiz nights, jazz sessions and soothing Sunday lunchtime music recitals are some of the main attractions. Intimate enclosed tables and seating form part of the large drinking and dining area. Handy for bus and railway stations. Q❀◐◑♿⇌🚌⅟

Goodbarns Yard

64 St Johns Street, PE1 5DD

✪ 11-midnight (1.30am Fri & Sat); 12-11 Sun

☎ (01733) 551830

Adnams Broadside; Caledonian Deuchars IPA; guest beers 🄶

Situated at the edge of the city centre, the pub looks modern and uninviting from the outside but is, in fact, a warm and welcoming local. All beers are served by gravity from the cellar. Snacks are available all day and children are welcome. Sunday lunches are also provided. The front conservatory is no-smoking. The bar houses a large-screen TV as football is popular here.

Hand & Heart ☆

12 Highbury Street, Millfield, PE1 3BE

✪ 11-11 daily

☎ (01733) 564653

Caledonian Deuchars IPA; John Smith's Bitter; Wychwood Hobgoblin; guest beers 🄷

Splendid, unspoilt, 1930s community local where a warm welcome is assured. Its two rooms are accessed via an impressive black and white tiled corridor. The public bar features a war memorial. The rear smoke room has no bar, just a serving hatch. A more ornate servery provides drinks in the corridor. Darts, dominoes and crib are played and a cheese club meets monthly (last Thu). A renovated garden adds to the charm; children are welcome early on in the back room. ♨Q❀🚌♣⅟

Palmerston Arms

82 Oundle Road, Woodston, PE2 9PA

✪ 12 (4 Mon)-11 (midnight Fri & Sat); 12-11.30 Sun

☎ (01733) 565865

Beer range varies 🄶

Stone pub that dates back to the 17th century. A Bateman house, it normally offers three Bateman's ales plus up to 11 others, all served directly from casks in the cellar. The pub has no handpumps and sells no keg beers. Three traditional ciders and/or perries, Belgian and German bottled beers and a large choice of single malts add variety. Mirrors and other breweriana adorn the walls and an extensive collection of ale jugs hang from the beams in the bar. A small, sheltered outdoor area is popular in summer. No entry after 10.30pm.

Q🚌♣

Wortley Arms

The Wortley Almshouses, Westgate, PE1 1QA

(next to bus station)

✪ 11.30-11; 12-10.30 Sun

☎ (01733) 348839

Samuel Smith OBB 🄷

This gem underwent a sympathetic refurbishment a few years ago to provide six drinking areas, and was rewarded by a well-deserved accolade from CAMRA. The original floor and fireplace were discovered 20 feet under the pub floor, which is now covered in hand-made tiles. Pictures of the Wortley Montague family adorn the walls of this former workhouse, one of whom, Edward, was MP for the city in the 18th century. Charles Dickens is said to have been inspired by this pub to write his classic Oliver Twist.

♨Q◐⇌🚌⅟

Ramsey

Jolly Sailor

43 Great Whyte, PE26 1HH

✪ 11-2, 5.30-11; 11-3, 6-11 Sat; 12-3, 7-10.30 Sun

☎ (01487) 813388

Adnams Broadside; Bateman XB; Jennings Cumberland Ale; Wells Bombardier; guest beers 🄷

This Grade II listed building has been a pub for over 400 years; the interior has three linked rooms. Welcoming and friendly, it attracts an older clientele who enjoy the fine beer and good conversation free from intrusive music. No food is served. Guest beers are available at weekends and a pub quiz is held on the last Sunday of the month.

♨Q❀🚌♣P

St Ives

Floods Tavern

27 The Broadway, PE27 5BX

✪ 11.30 (12 winter)-11 (midnight Thu; 1am Fri & Sat); 12-10.30 Sun

☎ (01480) 467773

Elgood's Cambridge, Greyhound Strong, seasonal beer 🄷

Lively town bar named after a banker formerly employed by the bank that occupied these premises in the 19th century. Dramatic enlarged photographs on the interior walls illustrate the other type of flood that the area is renowned for. The idyllic outdoor drinking area overlooks the River Great Ouse and its water meadow. It hosts karaoke on Thursday and live music most Friday and Saturday evenings, while the Tavern Club, a showcase for new young bands, takes place monthly (fourth Sun).

♨❀◐♣

Oliver Cromwell

13 Wellington Street, PE27 5AZ

✪ 11-11 (12.30am Fri & Sat); 12-11 Sun

☎ (01480) 465601

Adnams Bitter, Broadside or seasonal beer; Oakham JHB; Woodforde's Wherry; guest beers 🄷

Warm, congenial and sociable, wood-panelled bar close to the old town river quay. Built as a cottage in the 18th century, it was a beer house from the 1840s, with its own brewery until 1920. A glass floor provides a view down an old well, possibly once used for the brewing. Entertainment includes a monthly quiz, live music on occasional Sunday afternoons, and acoustic music on the first and last Thursday evenings of the month. ❀◐🚌⅟

Stapleford

Longbow

2 Church Street, CB2 5DS
✪ 11-3, 6-11.15 (midnight Sat); 11-midnight Fri; 12-3, 7-11 Sun
☎ (01223) 566855
Adnams Bitter; guest beers 🄷
A plaque above the bar lists former landlords of this friendly pub going back to the 1800s. It remains a traditional centre for village entertainment: the games room, annexed to the main bar, provides games, including bar billiards, pool and darts, while petanque is popular during warmer months. Five real ales are on offer, with guests often from Archers and Woodforde's; Cassells local cider is stocked. Live music is performed most weekends. ❀◑≋(Shelford)♣●P

Swavesey

White Horse Inn

1 Market Street, CB4 5QG
✪ 12-2.30, 6-11; 11.30-11 Sat; 12-10.30 Sun
☎ (01954) 232470
Beer range varies 🄷
Hub of the village with exposed beams and pictures giving an idea of its past 480 years. Usually Caledonian Deuchars IPA is supplemented by one or more guest beers in summer and a small beer festival in May. Open fires and good food make travellers feel at home. The large public bar allows games, with an added games/family room to the rear. The no-smoking lounge bar is comfortable and spacious with a restaurant area. ⛰❀◑⊟⊟♣⚟

Thriplow

Green Man

2 Lower Street, SG8 7RJ
✪ 12-3, 6-11; closed Mon; 12-3 (closed eve) Sun
☎ (01763) 208855 ⊕ greenmanthriplow.co.uk
Beer range varies 🄷
Comfortable, quiet, friendly pub near the Duxford Imperial War Museum. The menu offers GM-free dishes of high quality. Pictures of the village and pub adorn the walls while pump clips on the ceiling show what you might have missed – guest beers are the norm here, not the exception. Tables on the green outside allow for outdoor drinking. ⛰Q❀◑♿P

Ufford

White Hart

Main Street, PE9 3BH
✪ 12-11 (midnight Fri & Sat summer); 12-5 (11 summer) Sun
☎ (01780) 740250
Adnams Bitter; Oakham JHB; Ufford Idle Hour; guest beer 🄷
Restored old stone farmhouse with two bars. The public bar displays some interesting artefacts, while in the lounge high quality food is served all day. Ufford Ales Brewery is across the car park; visits are available. The back of the pub looks out onto a patio and large gardens. ⛰Q❀⛟◑⊟♿♣P

Whittlesey

Boat

2 Ramsey Road, PE7 1DR
✪ 12-11 daily
☎ (01733) 202488
Elgood's Black Dog, Cambridge, Golden Newt, Pageant Ale, seasonal beers; guest beers 🄶
Traditional local where strangers are welcome, stocking a good selection of single malt whiskies. During Saturday night's live music sessions any musicians are welcome to join in. Popular with anglers, a large screen shows Premiership football matches. It is a main calling point during the Whittlesey Straw Bear Festival. Note the boat-shaped bar-front in the lounge. Mentioned in the Domesday Book, it offers good value accommodation.
Q❀⛟⊟♿≋⊟♣P⚟

Bricklayers Arms

9 Station Road, PE7 1UA
✪ 11-5, 7-11; 11-11 Fri & Sat; 11-5, 7-11 Sun
☎ (01733) 262593
John Smith's Bitter; guest beers 🄷
Excellent local with a long, plainly furnished public bar and a cosy no-smoking lounge, it attracts a mixed bunch of regulars of all ages. The large garden is popular in summer. Close to the railway station, buses and boat moorings, the pub is HQ for the Whittlesey Straw Bear Festival. A good range of guest beers always includes a mild on offer at a discounted price. ❀⊟♿≋⊟♣P⚟▯

Willingham

Three Tuns

43 Church Street, CB4 5HS
✪ 12-3, 5 (6 Sat)-11; 12-3, 7-10.30 Sun
☎ (01954) 203243
Greene King XX Mild, IPA, Old Speckled Hen; guest beers 🄷
Classic, village local with a smart, comfy lounge but the lively public bar is the place to be. Visitors are always welcome to join in the constant banter at the bar or just sit and listen in. It is a rare outlet for Greene King's delicious dark mild. Booking is advisable for the legendary Sunday lunches, featuring freshly-cooked, locally-sourced ingredients (lunches Fri-Sun; eve meals Thu-Sat). The delightful back garden is huge. ❀◑⊟♣P

Witcham

White Horse

7 Silver Street, CB6 2LF (off A142)
✪ 12.30-3 (not Mon, Tue, Thu or Fri), 6.30-midnight (1am Fri & Sat); 12-3, 7-midnight Sun
☎ (01353) 778298
Adnams Bitter; guest beers 🄷
A warm welcome awaits at this quiet village pub, that offers two changing guest beers and excellent home-cooked food. The public bar area boasts a large mural of Southwold. There is a no-smoking dining area, with a small lounge to relax in. During WWII it was frequented by New Zealanders from the local airfield and veterans return to revisit still. Q❀◑⊟P

CHESHIRE

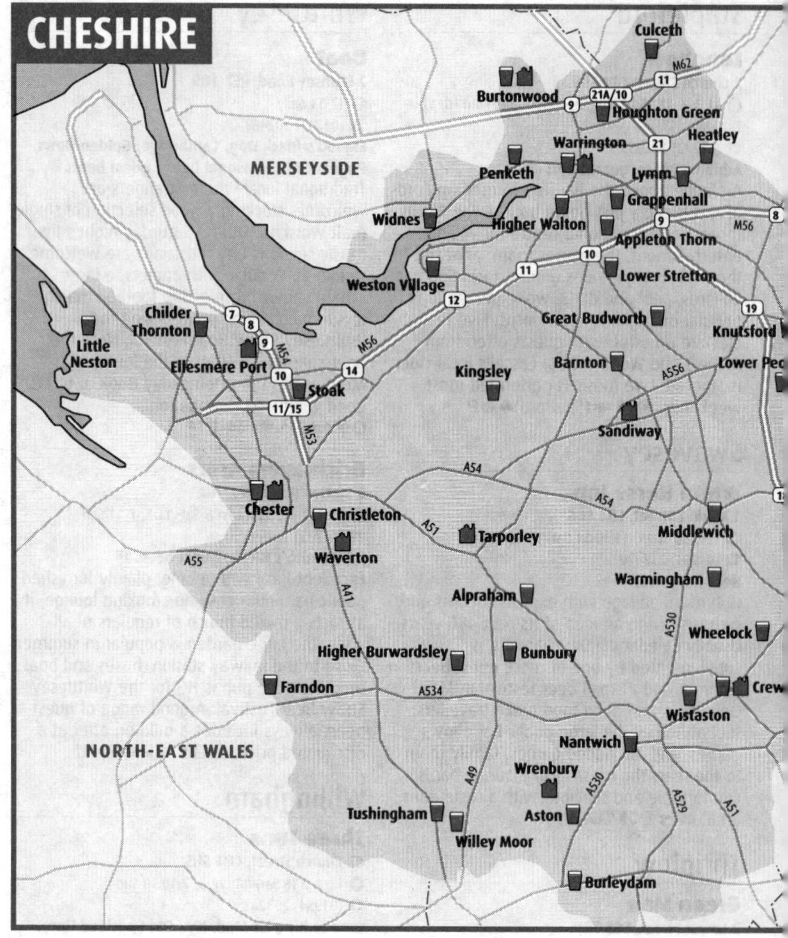

Alpraham

Travellers Rest ☆

Chester Road CW6 9JA (on A51, north of village)
✪ 6.30-11; 12-4.30, 6-11 Sat; 12-3, 7-10.30 Sun
☎ (01829) 260523
Caledonian Deuchars IPA; Tetley Bitter 🄷
Family-run genuine free house where both locals and visitors are guaranteed a friendly welcome. This roadside pub is Victorian in origin, with a modest extension built in 1937, and its four-roomed interior has a wonderful and relaxing 1950s feel to it – no electronic distractions here. This is a rare example of an unspoilt rural pub that has been run with care and dedication by the same family for more than 100 years.
Q⊞🚌♣P

Appleton Thorn

Appleton Thorn Village Hall

Stretton Road, WA4 4RT (on B5356)
✪ 7.30-midnight Thu-Sat; closed Mon-Wed; 1-4, 7.30-10.30 Sun
☎ (01925) 261187 🌐 atvh.org
Beer range varies 🄷
This ex-school, a former national CAMRA Club of the Year, is now a thriving village hall offering an ever-changing range of six beers from regional and micro-breweries. The attractive sandstone building houses a small, comfortable, lounge and large hall, which acts as a bar area. There is a small pool room attached. To the rear is a garden area and bowling green. The club holds regular events in the hall including live music.
Q❀♿🚌P⚡

Aston

Bhurtpore

Wrenbury Road, CW5 8DQ
(1/4 mile W of A530, 5 miles S of Nantwich)
✪ 12-2.30 (3 Sat), 6.30-11.30 (midnight Fri & Sat); 12-11.30 Sun
☎ (01270) 780917
Beer range varies 🄷
This large free house has been run by the same family for many years. A wide and ever changing range of real ales is always on handpump, including milds and porters. Additionally, real ciders and continental beers are served, along with an extensive range of Belgian bottled beers. The excellent food menu includes vegetarian,

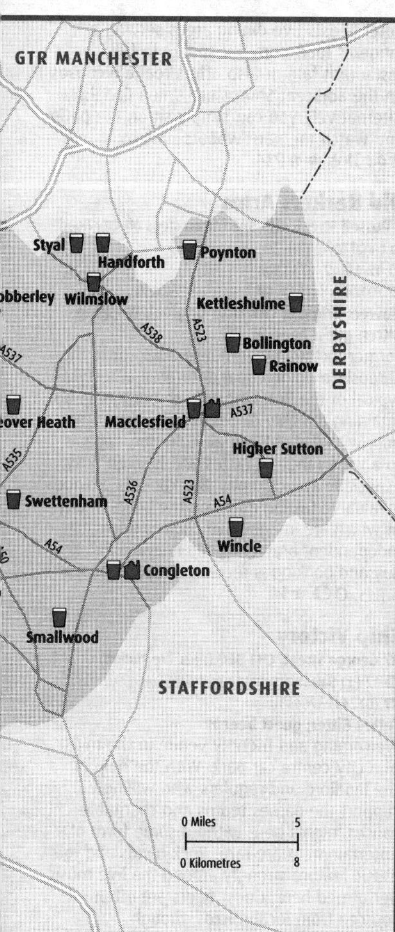

fish and curry options. A beer festival is held in summer at this CAMRA Regional Pub of the Year 2005.
⚐Q❀◐◑⊟⇌(Wrenbury)♣●P⊬

Barnton

Barnton Cricket Club

Broomsedge, Townfield Lane, CW8 4QL (200yds from A533 via Stonehayes Lane)
⊙ 6.30-midnight (12.30am Thu & Fri); 5-12.30am Sat; 12-11.30 Sun
☎ (01606) 77702 ⊕ barntoncc.co.uk
Archers Village; Boddingtons Bitter; Hydes Mild, 1863; guest beers Ⓗ
Show a CAMRA membership card for entry to this popular multi-sports club that features squash and bowls as well as cricket. A strong commitment to real ale and an annual beer festival in November ensure that this is a premier drinking venue in mid-Cheshire. There is a spacious function room with large TV showing major sporting events, and a pool table, plus a smaller, quieter no-smoking lounge to the side. A national finalist in CAMRA's Club of the Year 2004.
❀◐◑♿♣P⊬

Bollington

Poachers Inn

95 Ingersley Road, SK10 5RE
⊙ 12-2 (not Mon), 5.30-11; 12-2, 7-midnight Sat; 12-10.30 Sun
☎ (01625) 572086 ⊕ thepoachers.org
Copper Dragon Scotts 1816; Taylor Landlord; guest beers Ⓗ
Genuine free house offering three regularly changing guest beers, often from local brewery Storm. The a la carte restaurant serves good quality, reasonably-priced home-made fare (not Mon). Food is also available in the bar. Converted from five terraced stone cottages, the real log fire in winter and delightful suntrap garden in summer attract ramblers from the nearby Gritstone Trail and Peak District National Park. The pub runs quiz nights and golf days.
⚐❀◐◑P

Bunbury

Dysart Arms

Bowes Gate Road, CW6 9PH
⊙ 11.30-11; 12-10.30 Sun
☎ (01829) 260183 ⊕ dysartarms-bunbury.co.uk
Thwaites Original; guest beers Ⓗ
Dating back to the mid-1700s and an inn since the late 1800s, the Dysart (which formerly housed an abattoir) is a classic English village pub, with lovely open fires, bookcases scattered all around, lots of old oak and a really pleasant garden. A central bar serves an open-plan layout. A Brunning & Price pub, it is committed to cask beer, often from independent micros, and the local Weetwood beers are usually on sale. Good quality food is recommended.
⚐Q❀◐◑P⊬

Burleydam

Combermere Arms

Whitchurch Road, SY13 4AT (on A525 E of A530 jct)
⊙ 12-11; 12-10.30 Sun
☎ (01948) 871223
⊕ combermerearms-burleydam.co.uk
Caledonian Deuchars IPA; Flowers IPA; guest beers Ⓗ
Few pubs have a more rural setting than this one, and the recent refurbishment by Brunning & Price only helps to enhance the feeling of tranquillity, even though the pub now appears twice the size. Beer from local

INDEPENDENT BREWERIES

Beartown Congleton
Borough Arms Crewe
Burtonwood Burtonwood
Coach House Warrington
Northern Sandiway
Paradise Wrenbury
Spitting Feathers Waverton
Station House Ellesmere Port
Storm Macclesfield
WC Chester
Weetwood Tarporley
Woodlands Wrenbury

micros and locally-sourced good quality food with an imaginative menu (served all day) complete the transformation of this ever-popular inn. Westons Old Rosie is available. Public transport is scarce.
⛰Q❀◑♿●P🚭

Burtonwood

Fiddle i'th Bag

Alder Lane, WA5 4BJ OS584930
🕘 12-11; 12-10.30 Sun
☎ (01925) 225442
Beer range varies Ⓗ
It is well worth going out of your way to find this highly individual pub packed with an ever-increasing collection of unusual items ranging from a stuffed cockerel to remnants of WWII aircraft. The open plan bar area is complemented by a quiet room to the right of the entrance. Four changing cask ales are available as well as good food. Easily accessible from Sankey Valley Park, the pub overlooks fields to the distant M62.
⛰Q❀◑♿P

Chester

Bear & Billet

94 Lower Bridge Street, CH1 1RU
🕘 12-11 (11.30 Wed & Thu; midnight Fri & Sat); 12-10.30 Sun
☎ (01244) 311886
Okells Bitter; guest beers Ⓗ
Fine historic 17th-century building with much original woodwork on display both inside and out. A large wooden-floored bar at street level is divided into three areas; there is an open fire and a large plasma TV. A distinctive and spacious sitting/dining room is on the first floor and a function room on the second floor. Outside is a small yard with tables. A good selection of real ales and continental beers is always available.
⛰❀◑

Carlton Tavern

1 Hartington Street, Handbridge, CH4 7BN
🕘 5.30-11.30; 12-11.30 Sat; 12-10.30 Sun
☎ (01244) 676688 🌐 thecarlton.co.uk
Hydes Bitter, seasonal beers Ⓗ
This enterprising suburban pub just across the river from the city centre dates back to the 1920s and was built on the site of an existing pub. A large central bar serves three rooms; an extensive collection of old prints of Chester adorns the walls. Tuesday is quiz night and monthly folk music sessions are hosted. Public Internet access is available.
⛰🚌♣

Mill Hotel

Milton Street, CH1 3NF (by canal)
🕘 11-midnight; 12-11.30 Sun
☎ (01244) 345635 🌐 millhotel.com
Weetwood Best Bitter; guest beers Ⓗ
City centre hotel housed in a former corn mill dating from the 1930s. It is a beer festival every day here with up to 16 real ales on handpump including three house beers, a guest mild and a guest real cider. Three plasma screens show sports. The hotel boasts five dining areas serving a range of food from bar snacks to full restaurant fare. It also offers real ale cruises on the adjacent Shropshire Union Canal. Alternatively you can simply sit on the patio and watch the narrowboats pass by.
❀🛏◑♿⇌●P🚭

Old Harkers Arms

1 Russell Street, CH3 5AL (down steps off City Road to canal towpath)
🕘 12-11; 12-10.30 Sun
☎ (01244) 344525 🌐 harkersarms-chester.co.uk
Flowers Original; Thwaites Original; Wapping Bitter; guest beers Ⓗ
Former Victorian warehouse adjacent to the Shropshire Union Canal decorated in a style typical of the Brunning & Price pub group but retaining a highly distinctive character. The pub, with its light and airy interior, appeals to a wide range of tastes and is often busy, especially at weekends. Blackboards provide invaluable tasting notes on the beers, many of which are imaginative choices from independent brewers. Food is available all day and booking is recommended at busy times. Q◑⇌🚭

Ship Victory

47 George Street, CH1 3EQ (near fire station)
🕘 12 (11 Sat)-midnight; 12-midnight Sun
☎ (01244) 376453
Tetley Bitter; guest beer Ⓗ
Welcoming and friendly venue in the midst of a city-centre car park. With the help of the landlord and regulars who willingly support the games teams and charitable causes, nights here without some form of entertainment are rare. Rock bands and folk music feature strongly among the live music performed here. Guest beers are often sourced from local micros, though Abbeydale beers are always well received. Despite planned local development work it is hard to imagine this pub not surviving.
⇌♣

Telford's Warehouse

Tower Wharf, CH1 4EZ
🕘 12-11 (1am Wed; 12.30am Thu; 2am Fri & Sat); 12-1am Sun
☎ (01244) 390090 🌐 telfordswarehouse.com
Taylor Landlord; Weetwood Eastgate Ale; guest beers Ⓗ
Popular, converted former warehouse in a stunning location on Chester's canal basin. Artefacts from the industrial age scattered around the pub include a crane that forms the centrepiece of the ground floor. A large glass frontage allows views of passing barges below. The lower bar, which opens in the evening, accommodates the pub's thriving live music scene. Upstairs is an array of comfy leather sofas and an extensive dining area. The menu is supplemented by blackboard specials. Note: there may be an admission charge on some evenings. ❀◑♣P🚭

Union Vaults

44 Egerton Street, CH1 3ND
🕘 11-midnight; 12-10.30 Sun

☎ (01244) 400556
Caledonian Deuchars IPA; Phoenix Arizona; guest beer Ⓗ
Small, friendly, hard drinking street corner local nestling in a large scale property development halfway between the railway station and city centre. A split level pub, the lower area houses a popular bagatelle table and wall-mounted TV. Upstairs is a quieter lounge area where on week nights you may join in one of the impromptu folk evenings. Parking is difficult. ⇌♣

Childer Thornton

White Lion
New Road, CH66 5PU (off A41)
⊙ 11.30-11.30 (midnight Fri & Sat); 12-11.30 Sun
☎ (0151) 339 3402
Thwaites Mild, Original, Lancaster Bomber Ⓗ
Small, friendly country pub on the outskirts of Ellesmere Port. Some original features such as the brick fireplace have been retained while a new small room has been created from part of the kitchen. The snug is popular with families at lunchtimes. A former CAMRA regional Pub of the Year, it offers excellent value meals (not Sun) – try the home-made chicken tikka. ♨Q❀◑P

Christleton

Plough Inn
Plough Lane, CH3 7PT
⊙ 12-midnight; 12-11 Sun
☎ (01244) 336096
Theakston Mild, Best Bitter; guest beers Ⓗ
This 18th-century red-brick former farmhouse pub has been extended several times over recent years into a large country-style pub-restaurant. Although open-plan, there are three distinct areas – public bar, no-smoking lounge and restaurant – which are all served from the large central bar. Up to nine real ales are available including most of the range from the nearby Spitting Feathers brewery. The busy, award-winning restaurant has a policy of using local produce including home-grown vegetables and home-reared livestock (booking is recommended).
Q❀◑▶⊟♿♣P⊬

Congleton

Beartown Tap
18 Willow Street, CW12 1RL (on A54 Buxton road)
⊙ 12-2, 4-11; 12-11 Fri & Sat; 12-10.30 Sun
☎ (01260) 270990 ⊕ beartownbrewery.co.uk
Beartown Kodiak Gold, Bearskinful, Polar Eclipse, Black Bear; guest beer Ⓗ
Welcoming local just yards from the Beartown Brewery. Opened in 1999, this was the brewery's first pub and such is the beer quality that it won regional CAMRA Pub Of The Year in 2003 and 2004. Guest beers are usually sourced from other micros and there is generally another Beartown beer available. Real cider is also stocked and a good selection of Belgian bottled beers. Street parking can be found immediately outside the pub. ♨Q⇌♣●⊬

Castle Inn
Castle Inn Road, Dane-in-Shaw, CW12 3LP (on A527)
⊙ 12-11; 12-10.30 Sun
☎ (01260) 277505
Taylor Landlord; guest beers Ⓗ
Converted from 18th-century cottage buildings around 1820, the pub is just yards from the Staffordshire border and is popular with walkers on the Biddulph Valley Way nearby. A choice of up to three guest ales includes a mix of well-known offerings from larger brewers and interesting ales from smaller micros. The varied home-cooked menu includes vegetarian options. Children are welcome in the restaurant area. Quiz night is Tuesday. Q❀◑▶⊟♿♣P⊬

Congleton Leisure Centre
Worral Street, CW12 1DT
⊙ 10-1 (not Mon), 7-11 (9.30 Sat); 8-10.30 Sun
☎ (01260) 271552
Beer range varies Ⓗ
Unusually, a municipal leisure centre that sells an ever-changing choice of three real ales from micro-breweries. Efforts have been made to create a pub environment in the bar: the walls are adorned with brewery posters and pump clips from the beers sold. The bar has a snug feel and is no smoking. It is open to everyone – there is no entrance fee and no need to use the sporting facilities. Q⛱♿⇌P⊬

Queen's Head
Park Lane, CW12 3DE (opp. station, at bridge 75 of Macclesfield Canal)
⊙ 11-midnight (2am Fri & Sat); 12-midnight Sun
☎ (01260) 272546
Draught Bass; Courage Directors; Greene King Abbot; Tetley Bitter; guest beers Ⓗ
Canalside pub with its own moorings, popular with locals and canal users. The huge garden has a children's play area and stages occasional events in summer. Originally built for the railway trade, the pub has enjoyed a revival in recent years under the current landlord. Guest beers change frequently, often coming from local breweries. The accommodation has been recently refurbished. It was local CAMRA Pub of the Season winter 2005.
❀⛟◑▶⇌♣P⊬

Crewe

Angel
Victoria Street, CW1 2PU (below street level in Victoria Centre)
⊙ 10-7; 10-9 Fri & Sat; closed Sun
☎ (01270) 212003
Oakwell Barnsley Bitter Ⓗ
Welcoming pub in the Victoria Centre. Open plan but divided into a number of discrete areas, some are for dining and others for drinking. Prices for ale are even cheaper than the nearby Wetherspoon's and lunches are also good value. Occasional charity horse race nights are held on Saturday. ◑⛟

Borough Arms
33 Earle St, CW1 2BG
⊙ 7 (3 Fri)-11; 12-4, 7-11 Sat; 12-3, 7-10.30 Sun

☎ (01270) 254999

Beer range varies Ⓗ

Friendly free house, deservedly popular with locals and visitors alike. A cornucopia of real ales awaits the serious and dedicated imbiber. Though open plan in layout it has three distinct drinking areas, free from music, pool and fruit machines. Nine constantly changing real ales are available, mainly from micros, as well as two beers from the Borough Arms Brewery located in the basement. There is also an excellent range of Belgian beers.

British Lion

58 Nantwich Road, CW2 6AL

12-4 (Mon & Sat), 7-11; 12-11 Fri; 12-10.30 Sun

☎ (01270) 214379

Tetley Dark Mild, Bitter; guest beers Ⓗ

Busy town pub handy for Gresty Road, home of Crewe Alex FC. It can get crowded on match days and closes at 3pm for home fixtures. Known locally as the Pig, its nickname recalls the rumoured escape of a pig from the nearby livestock market many years ago. Home to darts, dominoes and quiz teams, this is one of a few local outlets for draught mild. Two guest beers from local micros are usually available.

Culcheth

New Inn

474 Warrington Road, WA3 5QX (on A574)

12-midnight; 12-10.30 Sun

☎ (01925) 763391

Caledonian Deuchars IPA; Greene King Old Speckled Hen; guest beers Ⓗ

Situated on the Warrington to Leigh road, this pub has a lounge and bar area as well as a no-smoking restaurant. Dominoes, darts and pool are played in the bar with Sky TV showing football and rugby. A large decked area outside is popular for alfresco drinking and dining. Blackboard specials complement the daily main menu. Draught cider is available in summer.

P

Farndon

Farndon Arms

High Street, CH3 6PU

11.30-3, 5 (7 Sun)-midnight

☎ (01829) 270570 farndonarms.com

Adnams Bitter; John Smith's Bitter; guest beers Ⓗ

Formerly known as the Raven, with ground-floor etched windows still showing the original name, this black and white half-timbered pub is situated centrally in this picturesque village, just 200 metres from the river bordering Wales. Although now one-roomed, there are three distinct areas including a dining area and an upstairs restaurant serving a good range of dishes as well as traditional pub food. Occasional live music is hosted. Q P

Grappenhall

Grappenhall Ex-Servicemen's Club

Chester Road, WA4 2QG (on A56)

6.30 (4 Thu & Fri)-midnight; 12-midnight Sat & Sun

☎ (01925) 261702

Beer range varies Ⓗ

Well established, thriving and comfortable private club in close proximity to the picturesque village of Grappenhall, situated 400 yards from the Bridgewater Canal. The club officers and steward are fully committed to a high standard of cask ales, dispensed from three pumps at very reasonable prices. There are two large refurbished lounges, a function room, games rooms and floodlit bowling green with a seating area. Large-screen TVs show sport and there is snooker, pool and darts. Your CAMRA membership card gains admission.

Q P

Great Budworth

George & Dragon

High Street, CW9 6HF (off A559)

11.30-3, 5-11; 11.30-11 Fri & Sat; 11.30-10.30 Sun

☎ (01606) 891317

Beer range varies Ⓗ

Situated at the heart of this delightful village opposite the 14th-century church and the stocks, the George & Dragon is a classic rural Cheshire pub. Built in 1722, it has an unusual pub sign extending from one corner. There is a welcoming lounge to the front and a bar with pool to the rear. Upstairs is a restaurant, though food is served throughout the pub. A blackboard above the bar describes the guest beers. Newspapers are provided. Q P

Handforth

Railway

Station Road, SK9 3AB (opp. railway station)

12-11; 12-3, 7-11 Sat; 12-3, 7-10.30 Sun

☎ (01625) 523472

Robinson's Hatters, Unicorn, Old Tom Ⓗ

This is a busy and welcoming pub with a good local following. The main bar was recently refitted and displays an interesting collection of pictures and brassware. Smaller rooms off the bar include a no-smoking dining area for lunchtime meals, Tuesday to Friday, and a locals' bar. The pub is renowned for its impressive floral displays in summer. P

Heatley

Railway

42 Mill Lane, WA13 9SQ

12-11 daily

☎ (01925) 752742

Boddingtons Bitter; Taylor Landlord; guest beer Ⓗ

They don't make pubs like this any more. Many different-sized rooms provide diverse facilities to accommodate varying local needs. Folk is the most regular of the many different types of live music hosted here. A large, open, grassed play area is ideal for children. Local CAMRA's Pub of the Year 2006 is ideally located for walkers on the Trans-Pennine trail or by the River Bollin.

P

Higher Burwardsley

Pheasant Inn

CH3 9PF
11-11; 11-10.30 Sun
(01829) 770434 thepheasantinn.co.uk
Weetwood Best Bitter, Eastgate Ale, Old Dog; guest beer H
Nestling among the Peckforton Hills, this charming rural pub is in an ideal location for hikers walking the Sandstone Trail or for visitors to the nearby Candle Workshops. The emphasis here is on quality ales and food in a relaxed atmosphere, with Sunday lunchtimes especially popular. During winter months take advantage of the cosy open fires, while in warmer weather the seating area outside offers breathtaking views over the Cheshire plain.

Higher Sutton

Hanging Gate

Meg Lane, SK11 0NG (follow Ridge Hill Rd from village centre for 1½ miles)
12-3, 7 (5.30 Fri)-11; 12-11 Sat; 12-10.30 Sun
(01260) 252238
Hydes Bitter, Jekyll's Gold, seasonal beers H
Unusual building, dating from 1621, built on the edge of the hill, with an extensive view across the Cheshire Plain to the Welsh mountains. It has small, cosy rooms and a large dining area. Warm and welcoming, the family-run pub is popular with walkers and diners, and has a well-deserved reputation for its home cooked food (booking recommended). The pub can become very busy on summer weekends and weekend evenings.

Higher Walton

Warrington Sports Club

Walton Lea Road, WA4 6SJ (off A56)
6-11 (11.30 Thu & Fri); 11.30-11.30 Sat; 11.30-10.30 Sun
(01925) 263210 warringtonsportsclub.co.uk
Taylor Golden Best; guest beers H
Large club on the south side of town yet in the heart of Cheshire countryside near Walton Gardens. It has large playing areas for cricket, rugby and hockey plus squash courts inside. The spacious lounge has a large screen TV and the function room has a stage for live entertainment. Up to six real ales are on offer on handpump. A beer festival is held around Easter. CAMRA members are welcome as guests but must be signed in (show card). Note that closing hours may vary depending on the season – ring to check.

Houghton Green

Plough

Mill Lane, WA2 0SU
11.30-11 (11.30 Thu & Sat); 11-midnight Fri; 12-11 Sun
(01925) 815409
Fuller's London Pride; Wells Bombardier; guest beers H
This pub dating from 1774 is in the northern part of Warrington, formerly rural but now swallowed up by housing estates. It was extended in the late 1980s and now has a strong emphasis on food. However it still retains a village pub feel with its bowls team and green, despite its proximity to the M62. Quiz night is Thursday and live music is played on Friday.

Kettleshulme

Swan Inn

SK23 7QU (on B5470)
12-3 (not Mon), 5.30-midnight (12.30am Thu & Fri); 12-12.30am Sat; 12-11 Sun
(01663) 732943 the-swan-inn-kettleshulme.co.uk
Marston's Burton Bitter; guest beers H
Village pub saved from closure in 2005 when it was bought by a group of locals and reopened. The 15th-century stone building has a small, quaint interior with two cosy rooms featuring timber beams, stone fireplaces and an open fire in winter. Two frequently changing guest beers, usually from micros, supplement the regular Marston's Bitter. Families and walkers are welcome at this excellent inn in a picturesque Peak District national park village surrounded by good walking country and close to Windgather Rocks.

Kingsley

Red Bull

The Brow, WA6 8AN
12-3, 5.30 (6 Sat)-midnight (1am Fri & Sat); 12-3, 7-midnight Sun
(01928) 788097
Beer range varies H
This typical village pub is well worth seeking out (turn off the main road through the village at the post office). The single bar, with a small no-smoking area to the left, has six handpumps featuring a constantly changing range of beers mainly from local micros. The home-prepared food is recommended. There is a quiz night on Tuesday and live music every six weeks on a Saturday featuring a range of styles including blues and swing.

Knutsford

Cross Keys

52 King Street, WA16 6DT
11.30-2.30, 5.30-11 (11.30 Thu & Fri); 11.30-11.30 Sat; 12-3, 7-10.30 Sun
(01565) 750404 knutsfordcrosskeys.co.uk
Caledonian Deuchars IPA; Taylor Landlord; Tetley Bitter; guest beers H
Set on an attractive shopping street, this former 18th-century coaching inn was largely rebuilt in 1909. A glass and timber screen separates the lounge from the vault with its pool table and TV. Bar meals are served at lunchtimes, or you can dine in the restaurant, reached by a barrel-vaulted tunnel that doubles as a no-smoking area. The fine choice of cask ales sets the Cross Keys apart: a gleaming bank of polished brass handpumps dispenses three constantly changing guest beers. Real cider is often available.

Little Neston

Harp

19 Quayside, CH64 0TB

⌚ 11-11.30 (midnight Fri & Sat); 12-11.30 Sun

☎ (0151) 336 6980

Holt Bitter; Taylor Landlord; Titanic Iceberg; guest beers 🄷

A former coalminers' inn, this pub can be difficult to find but is well worth the effort. Converted from two cottages, it has a public bar and lounge/family room. Set in a glorious location overlooking the Dee estuary (a popular location for twitchers), it can be cut off at high tide. The outside drinking area is a superb spot for watching the breathtaking sunsets over north Wales. No glasses are allowed outside so if you want to avoid plastic, bring your own pewter tankard. No food is served Monday. ⩩Q⊱❀◖⊟P

Lower Peover

Crown

Crown Lane, WA16 9QB

⌚ 11.30-3, 5.30-11; 12-10.30 Sun

☎ (01565) 722074

Boddingtons Bitter; Caledonian Deuchars IPA; Flowers IPA; Greene King Old Speckled Hen; Taylor Landlord; Tetley Dark Mild 🄷

This traditional country inn was a local CAMRA Pub of the Season in 2005. It has an L-shaped bar which divides into a locals' area where darts and dominoes are played and a comfortable lounge. Good, home-cooked food made with locally sourced ingredients where possible is served in the no-smoking dining area (not Sun eve or Mon lunch). The regular beers are usually supplemented by a guest, often from a local micro. There is a cobbled patio for outdoor drinking. ⩩❀◖◗♣P

Lower Stretton

Ring o' Bells

Northwich Road, WA4 4NZ (on A559 off M56 jct 10)

⌚ 12-2.30 (3 Thu-Sat), 5.30 (7 Sat)-11; 12-4, 7-10.30 Sun

☎ (01925) 730556

Fuller's London Pride; Tetley Bitter; guest beer 🄷

Situated on the edge of the Cheshire countryside to the south of Warrington, this popular roadside local is a genuine country pub. With no juke box or games machine, lively conversation among the locals dominates the main bar. There are two quieter side rooms, one no-smoking. A folk night is held on the first Tuesday of the month. Boules is played in summer. ⩩Q❀♣P⍁

Lymm

Barn Owl

Warrington Lane, Agden Wharf, WA13 0SW (off A56)

⌚ 11-11 (midnight Fri; 1am Sat); 12-11 Sun

☎ (01925) 752020 🌐 thebarnowlinn.co.uk

Marston's Burton Bitter, Pedigree; guest beers 🄷

This former boatyard building affords views over the Bridgewater Canal and countryside beyond. Walkers on the opposite towpath can summon the pub's ferry by ringing a bell. It entices hungry diners to savour the home-cooked food and drinkers to sample the two guest beers that change often. Despite its rural location the pub enjoys a thriving trade and hosts regular live music sessions. ❀◖◗♿♣P

Spread Eagle

47 Eagle Brow, WA13 0AG

⌚ 11-11 (midnight Fri & Sat); 12-10.30 Sun

☎ (01925) 757467

Lees GB Mild, Bitter, seasonal beers 🄷

Situated by the lower dam and a short stroll from the Bridgewater Canal, this large, traditional pub is an integral part of the old village centre. A small public bar and a cosy snug, complete with real fire, complement the lounge and large restaurant area, serving a variety of meals all day every day. The pub is popular with the local community and passing trade from the canal. A function room occupies part of the first floor. ⩩Q❀◖◗⊟♿

Macclesfield

British Flag

42 Coare Street, SK10 1DW

⌚ 5.30 (5 Sat)-11; 12-3, 7-10.30 Sun

Robinson's Hatters, Unicorn, 🄷 **Old Tom (winter),** 🄶 **seasonal beers** 🄷

This is an old-fashioned and friendly town local where four rooms surround a central bar. Pub games are popular, including table skittles, and one room is dedicated to pool. The tap room, apart from darts and dominoes, is home to the landlord's trophy cabinet of Macclesfield Town FC memorabilia. There is also a large-screen TV for sport. In the 1860s the pub was a ginger beer brewery; it now serves as the local for the staff and old boys of the neighbouring King's School. ≹♣

Dolphin

76 Windmill Street, SK11 4HS

⌚ 12-2.30, 5.30-11; 12-11 Sat; 12-10.30 Sun

☎ (01625) 616179

Robinson's Hatters, Unicorn, 🄷 **Old Tom (winter);** 🄶 **guest beers** 🄷

This friendly pub is very much a community local but also welcoming to visitors. A central bar separates the two drinking areas; a further room provides an ideal venue for meetings. The original glass door is a distinctive feature. Robinson's award-winning Old Tom is always available during the winter; home cooked food is served Monday-Saturday. A past CAMRA Pub of the Season award winner. ⩩⊱◖⊟≹♣

Plough

32 Prestbury Road, SK10 1AU

⌚ 11-midnight (1am Fri & Sat); 12-midnight Sun

☎ (01625) 422097

Caledonian Deuchars IPA; Tetley Bitter; Young's Bitter; guest beers 🄷

Busy, comfortable, traditional end of terrace pub on the edge of the town centre with a good mix of customers. Multi-roomed with a central bar, it has an ocean liner theme. It runs many pub teams including Nine Card Don and crown green bowls in nearby West Park. The yard is festooned with flower baskets in summer. There are usually three guest beers, often from smaller independent breweries. ❀◐⊟⇌♣

Prince of Wales

33 Roe Street, SK11 6UT
⏲ 11.30-11 (midnight Fri & Sat); 12-10.30 Sun
☎ (01625) 424796 🌐 portersprinceofwales.co.uk
Caledonian Deuchars IPA; Theakston Bitter; guest beers Ⓗ
Comfortable and friendly town-centre pub attracting a varied clientele. Look out for the mosaics made by the landlady at the front entrance and in the small backyard, and also for the fish tank separating the gents' toilets from the bar area. One roomed but with quieter corners, it has a real fire in winter. The pub supports teams in local sports leagues. Three constantly-changing guest beers usually come from independent breweries. ♔❀⇌♣

Waters Green Tavern

98 Waters Green, SK11 6LH
⏲ 11.30-3, 5.30-11; 11-3, 7-11 Sat; 12-3, 7-10.30 Sun
☎ (01625) 422653
Greene King IPA; guest beers Ⓗ
Handy for both the train and bus stations, this popular town pub has won numerous awards from the local branch of CAMRA. Seven ales are normally available, frequently including a dark beer, regularly from Roosters, Oakham and Phoenix and other small breweries. There are three distinct drinking areas offering plenty of corners for a quiet pint, as well as darts, crib and dominoes, and a pool room to the rear. Traditional home cooked food is served at lunchtime except Sunday. ♔◐⇌⛟♣●

Middlewich

Big Lock Inn

Webbs Lane, CW10 9DN
⏲ 11-11; 11-10.30 Sun
☎ (01606) 833489
Black Sheep Best Bitter; Phoenix Wobbly Bob; Tetley Bitter; guest beers Ⓗ
Named after lock number 75 on the Trent & Mersey Canal, the inn's balcony and patio overlooking the canal are very popular. In warmer weather there are tables outside. The interior is divided into several areas; the front bar shows Sky Sports on large and small screens, there is a snug and a restaurant where a good range of quality food is served. Dogs are welcome in the bar. ❀◐◑♣P

Royal British Legion

100 Lewin Street, CW10 9AS
⏲ 12-3, 7-11; 12-11.30 Sat; 12-3, 7-10.30 Sun
☎ (01606) 833286
Hydes Dark Mild, Original Bitter; guest beers Ⓗ
A firm supporter of real ale, this large club has won several awards including local CAMRA Club of the Year in 2005. There is a spacious lounge where an annual beer festival is held in October, a games room with snooker tables, a comfortable no-smoking room and a rear bar with TV. Show a copy of this guide or a valid CAMRA membership card for entry. ❀⊟⛟♣P⊬⊡

Mobberley

Roebuck

Mill Lane, WA16 7HX (signed from B5085)
⏲ 12-3, 5-11; 12-11 Sat; 12-10.30 Sun
☎ (01565) 873322
Greene King Old Speckled Hen; Taylor Landlord; Tetley Bitter; guest beer Ⓗ
Originally a traditional pub, this fashionable restaurant has a wine bar atmosphere. The three open rooms have timber and tiled floors and scrubbed wood tables. A log fire warms in winter. The adventurous menu offers excellent home-cooked food with prices not unreasonable for the location. Although the emphasis is on dining here, the gleaming handpumps dispense a good range of quality beer including a regularly changing guest ale. ♔❀◐◑P⊬

Nantwich

Black Lion

29 Welsh Row, CW5 5ED (just outside town centre over river bridge)
⏲ 4-11; 1-11 Sat; 1-10.30 Sun
☎ (01270) 628711
Titanic White Star; Weetwood Best Bitter, Old Dog, Oasthouse Gold Ⓗ
Close to the River Weaver and Shropshire Union Canal, the date 1664 appears above the door of this black and white half-timbered free house. Three drinking areas and a heated conservatory all have candle-lit tables. Local micro-brewed ales are served. Wednesday is quiz night and chess is played by the locals. A bluegrass band performs on Thursday, and there is more live music on Friday and Saturday evenings. Dogs are welcome. ♔❀⇌♣

Penketh

Ferry Tavern

Station Road, WA5 2UJ
⏲ 12-3, 5.30-11; 12-11 Sat; 12-10.30 Sun
☎ (01925) 791117 🌐 theferrytavern.com
Boddingtons Bitter; Courage Directors; Greene King Old Speckled Hen; guest beers Ⓗ
Situated between the Sankey Canal and River Mersey on the Trans Pennine Trail, the pub is popular with walkers, cyclists and locals. A large outdoor drinking area is well used in summer. Three guest ales, traditional ciders and a large range of Scotch and Irish whiskies are stocked. Look out for special promotions for drinkers with a current CAMRA membership card. The pub is dog friendly.
♔Q☋❀⊟⛟●P

Peover Heath

Dog Inn

Wellbank Lane, WA16 8UP (off A50 at Whipping Stocks Inn and continue for 2 miles) OS792735
⏲ 11.30-3, 4.30-11; 11.30-11 Sat; 12-10.30 Sun
☎ (01625) 861421 🌐 doginn-overpeover.co.uk
Copper Dragon Scotts 1816; Moorhouses Black Cat; Weetwood Best Bitter Ⓗ
Historic rural pub on a quiet lane south of

Knutsford. The comfortable bar area has a real fire and pool, darts and dominoes are played. Two dining rooms, one no-smoking, offer a full and varied menu (booking is advisable at weekends). Food is served all day on Sunday. Cask mild is always available. A front patio and beer garden are available for outdoor drinking. Beer festivals are held in summer. Popular quizzes are held on Thursday and Sunday; live entertainment is hosted usually once a month on Friday. ⛬Q❀⛺◐◑⊟♿♣P

Poynton

Royal British Legion

Georges Road West, SK12 1JY

✪ 12-11; 12-10.30 Sun

☎ (01625) 873120

Beer range varies Ⓗ

Extensive, comfortable and welcoming club that brings a much needed variety of real ale to Poynton. The changing guest beers are invariably from micro-breweries. A beer festival is held twice a year in spring and autumn and the club hosts regular social evenings and live entertainment. Non members can be signed in. ⊟♣P

Rainow

Highwayman

Macclesfield Road, SK10 5UU (on B5470)

✪ 12-3, 5-1am; 12-1am Sat; 12-midnight Sun

☎ (01625) 573245

Thwaites Original, Lancaster Bomber, seasonal beers Ⓗ

Dating from the late 15th century, the name recalls a local highwayman who could spot unwary travellers a mile off from a nearby vantage point. A welcome haven in a remote area, the pub enjoys idyllic views over Cheshire to Winter Hill. A maze of connecting rooms, with three log fires, it serves daily specials and traditional home-cooked food. Live music is played on Wednesday and quizzes are held every other Friday. Families are welcome. ⛬Q♉❀◐◑♣P⚟

Smallwood

Blue Bell Inn

Spen Green, CW11 2XA

✪ 12-3, 5-11; 12-11 Fri & Sat; 12-10.30 Sun

☎ (01477) 500262

Black Sheep Best Bitter; Caledonian Deuchars IPA; Greene King Ruddles County; guest beer Ⓗ

Originally a farm pub, the Blue Bell lies nestled alongside the old farm buildings. This countryside local has three rooms – there is no music and conversation is the main form of entertainment. The garden is ideal for families – large, well maintained and safely enclosed. ⛬Q❀◐♣P⚟

Stoak

Bunbury Arms

Little Stanney Lane, CH2 4HW (signposted off A5117)

✪ 12-midnight; 12-10.30 Sun

☎ (01244) 301665

Weetwood Best Bitter; guest beers Ⓗ

Built in the 16th century, this attractive red-brick pub is situated in a tiny hamlet, bordering a small wood, with moorings on the Shropshire Union Canal close by. Comprising a small public bar and smart open plan lounge, there are four handpumps regularly serving a range of guest ales from local breweries. This traditional yet busy gastropub is a hidden gem and a popular retreat for walkers and cyclists alike, filling the usually tranquil garden during the summer months. ⛬Q❀◐◑⊟♿⛺♣●P

Styal

Ship

Altrincham Road, SK9 4JE (off B5166)

✪ 11.30-11 (midnight Fri & Sat); 12-10.30 Sun

☎ (01625) 523818

Taylor Landlord; Theakston Best Bitter; Wells Bombardier; guest beers Ⓗ

Located close to Styal Country Park, Quarry Bank Mill and Manchester Airport, this multi-roomed pub started serving beer when it was a farm outhouse or shippon, shortened to ship. The oak-panelled snug, named the Pilot's Room, contains a model ship and a grandfather clock, and is furnished with settles. It hosts a chess club on Tuesday. There are normally up to four guest ales. Meals are served until 9pm followed by a light 'munchies' menu until closing time. There is live music on Saturday evening. The pub hosts an annual beer festival.
❀⛺◐◑⚌♣P⚟

Swettenham

Swettenham Arms

CW12 2LF (off A535) OS800672

✪ 11.30-3, 6-11; 12-10.30 Sun

☎ (01477) 571284 🌐 swettenhamarms.co.uk

Beartown Kodiak Gold; Hydes Original Bitter; Moorhouses Pride of Pendle; guest beers Ⓗ

This picturesque, award-winning free house is situated down a narrow country lane. The comfortable bar has an open fire in winter and hosts live music on Wednesday. For fine days there is ample outdoor seating alongside an arboretum and the pub's own lavender field. High quality food is served at lunchtime and in the evening, all day on Sunday. The guest beers usually include an ale from Storm and other local micros.
⛬❀◐◑P⚟

Tushingham

Blue Bell Inn

SY13 4QS (signed Bell o' t'Hill from A41)

✪ 12-3, 6-11; 12-3, 7-11 Sun

☎ (01948) 662172

Salopian Shropshire Gold; guest beers Ⓗ

Dating from the 14th century in parts, this timber-framed, atmospheric pub is just off the A41 main road. A cobbled front leads to an ancient, heavy front door. The main bar, popular with regulars, is a place for conversation; visitors are made welcome. A further bar is used for dining. Guest beers usually come from micros. The pub is dog-friendly. ⛬Q♉❀◐◑⛺♣P⚟

Warmingham

Bear's Paw

School Lane, CW11 3QN

✪ 5 (12 Sat)-11; 12-10.30 Sun

☎ (01270) 526317 🌐 thebearspaw.co.uk

Tetley Bitter; guest beers Ⓗ

The imposing red-brick frontage of this 19th-century hotel hides a more modern interior with wood panelling in a 1920s style. Open plan, with raised seating opposite a long bar, there is also a stylish restaurant and pleasant garden. Bar snacks are available, with meals served all day at weekends, and there are 12 en-suite bedrooms. Although the emphasis here is on food, the licensees are keen supporters of real ale and the guest beers often come from local small breweries. ❀🛏◑♿P⊬

Warrington

Lower Angel

27 Buttermarket Street, WA1 2LY

✪ 10-midnight; 11-1am Fri & Sat; 12-4 Sun

☎ (01925) 633299

Tetley Mild, Bitter, Burton Ale; guest beer Ⓗ

Traditional, unspoilt, two-roomed, town-centre pub, comprising a public bar and a more comfortable lounge. Note the music selection on the juke box. A winner of many CAMRA local and regional awards over the years. ⊟⇌(Central)

Ring o' Bells

131 Church Street, WA1 2TL

✪ 12-11; 12-10.30 Sun

☎ (01925) 634035

Greene King Old Speckled Hen; guest beers Ⓗ

Situated next to St Elphins parish church, a short walk from the town centre, the pub has a traditional feel with wood panelling and comfortable furniture. A single bar serves several drinking and eating areas including a family dining area at the rear. An upstairs function room is available. Two changing guests complement the regular beer. ♨❀◑⇌ (Central)

Tavern

25 Church Street, WA1 2SS

✪ 2-11; 12-11 Fri & Sat; 12-10.30 Sun

☎ (01925) 577990

Beer range varies Ⓗ

The town centre's only true free house, it offers a range of up to six beers sourced from micro-breweries. This one-roomed pub has light wood floors and furniture, with a covered courtyard to the rear. It gets very busy when rugby league matches are showing on TV, especially if Wolves are at home. Bottled cider, Belgian beers and imported lagers are offered together with a range of Scotch and Irish whiskies. ❀⇌(Central)

Weston Village

Prospect Inn

Weston Road, WA7 4LD

✪ 12-11; 12-10.30 Sun

☎ (01928) 651280

Adnams Bitter; Cains Bitter; Tetley Dark Mild; guest beers Ⓗ

This out of the way pub is well worth a visit for the best selection of real ale in Halton. The public bar hosts a pool table and dartboard. The main lounge is a comfortable room where food is served at lunchtime and in the evening. Sunday lunch is very popular and booking is essential. Regular folk nights are held on Monday and a quiz on Tuesday. A free buffet is available every Friday and Saturday evening. Q❀◑⊟♿P

Royal Oak

187 Heath Road South, WA7 4RP

✪ 12-11.30; 12-11 Sun

☎ (01928) 580908

Wells Bombardier; guest beers Ⓗ

Situated in the centre of Weston Village, this recently refurbished pub caters for the local community, offering darts, dominoes and dice in a comfortable open plan bar. Traditional pub fare is served daily and the reasonably-priced Sunday lunch menu is popular (no food Sun eve). Saturday nights are occasionally spiced with live entertainment. Outside is a large enclosed garden for the summer months. Q❀◑♿♣⊬

Wheelock

Commercial

2 Game Street, CW11 3RR

(off Crewe Rd, near canal bridge)

✪ 12-11 (12.30am Fri & Sat); 12-10.30 Sun

☎ (01270) 760122

John Smith's Bitter; Thwaites Original; Weetwood Best Bitter; guest beers Ⓗ

Family run free house close to bridge 154 on the Trent & Mersey Canal. The pub dates back to the opening of the canal in 1777. Once known as the New Inn, it originally provided stabling for horses working on the canal. There are three rooms, two with snooker tables, a cosy snug and a public bar. The interior is classic Birkenhead Brewery with a BB mat and signage in the gents' toilet. Westons Old Rosie is sold. Children are welcome until 9pm. The pub is dog friendly. ♨Q❀⊟🚌♣●P⊬

Widnes

Church View

Lunts Heath Road, WA8 9RY

✪ 12-11 (11.30 Fri & Sat); 12-10.30 Sun

☎ (0151) 424 3296

Tetley Bitter; Theakston Mild; guest beers Ⓗ

Friendly pub on the edge of town with a large, single-room, split-level interior, divided into smaller areas for dining. The decor features dark wood and stained glass, and there are two interesting ceiling lights inside the main entrance. There is a TV in the bar area. Food is served from noon until 8pm. Q❀◑♿P⊬

Four Topped Oak

2 Hough Green, WA8 4PE

✪ 12-11; 12-midnight Sun

☎ (0151) 257 8030

Cains Bitter; Fuller's London Pride; guest beer Ⓗ

Comfortable, quiet pub with a relaxing atmosphere. Decorated in a modern style, it has many separate areas. There is a large patio for summer drinking and cosy fires during the winter, making this a pleasant pub for all seasons. No children under 14 are allowed on the premises, including the outside areas. Q❀◐◗♿P

Willey Moor

Willey Moor Lock Tavern

Tarporley Road, SY13 4HF (300 yds off A49) OS534452

✪ 12-2.30 (3 summer), 6-11; 12-2.30 (3 summer), 7-10.30 Sun

☎ (01948) 663274

Beer range varies Ⓗ

Accessed by a footbridge over the Llangollen Canal, the Willey Moor was a former lock keeper's cottage. This genuine free house always has an esoteric range of guest beers, including one from Thwaites. It is popular with canal boaters and walkers on the nearby Sandstone Trail. The interior is comfortably furnished with padded wall seats, local watercolour paintings and a collection of teapots. There are cosy real fires in the winter months and an outside terrace with an enclosed beer garden for the summer. ♨❀◐◗P

Wilmslow

Rifleman's Arms

113 Moor Lane, SK9 6BY (off A34)

✪ 12-11; 12-10.30 Sun

☎ (01625) 537235

Boddingtons Bitter; Cains Bitter; Greene King Abbot; Theakston Mild; guest beers Ⓗ

Some distance from the town centre, this is a popular locals' pub. The spacious interior has a central bar serving the lounge area and adjoining pool room. There is a vault or public bar where darts and crib are played, and dogs are welcome. Regular events include quiz and jazz nights. The highlight of the menu is the sausage emporium offering eight types of sausage, available weekdays at lunchtime and early evening. The garden is fully enclosed, making it safe for children. ❀◐◗⊟♿⊟♣P

Wincle

Ship

SK11 0QE (off A64 near Danebridge) OS652962

✪ 12-3, 7 (5.30 Fri)-11; closed Mon; 12-11 Sat; 12-10.30 Sun

☎ (01260) 227217

Fuller's London Pride; Lancaster Duchy; guest beers Ⓗ

One of the rare regular Fuller's outlets in the area, this attractive 16th-century sandstone village inn is popular with locals, walkers and diners and can become very busy on summer weekends. On the edge of the Dane Valley, the pub is divided into two bars plus a cosy snug, a small dining area and a further raised area for families. The drinks menu features a range of bottle-conditioned beers with tasting notes. The pub has a good reputation for its imaginative food menu. Local CAMRA Pub of the Year 2006, it holds a beer festival on August bank holiday. ♨Q❀◐◗●P

Wistaston

Rising Sun

Middlewich Road, CW2 8SB (on A530 between Marshfield Green and Nantwich)

✪ 11-11 (midnight Fri & Sat); 11-10.30 Sun

☎ (01270) 213782

Beer range varies Ⓗ

This pub offers a constantly changing range of beers from across the nation on nine regular handpumps. Fourteen more pumps are added for regular beer festivals. The interior has a homely atmosphere with plenty of exposed wooden beams. There is a diverse menu of excellent home-cooked food. The garden is well equipped for alfresco dining or drinking. Westons Old Rosie and other ciders are sold. ♨❀◐◗♿●P⚟

Fishing for beer

Ah! My beloved brother of the rod, do you know the taste of beer – of bitter beer – cooled in the flowing river? Take your bottle of beer, sink it deep, deep in the shady water, where the cooling springs and fishes are. Then, the day being very hot and bright, and the sun blazing on your devoted head, consider it a matter of duty to have to fish that long, wide stream. An hour or so of good hammering will bring you to the end of it, and then – let me ask you avec impressement – how about that beer? Is it cool? Is it refreshing? Does it gurgle, gurgle, and 'go down glug' as they say in Devonshire? Is it heavenly? Is it Paradise and all the Peris to boot? Ah! If you have never tasted beer under these or similar circumstance, you have, believe me, never tasted it all all.

Francis Francis, By Lake and River, 16th century

Pubs Transport – 2007

BUSES

Bus Traveline

Most bus timetable enquiries are now dealt with through the National Traveline which is operated under a standard call number by local authorities across the UK for countrywide information:-
Telephone: 0870 608 2608
Textphone: 0870 241 2216

Information & Journey Planner Websites – some may cover other transport modes.

TBC public transport information:
www.xephos.com

National transport enquiries:
www.traveline.org.uk www.pti.org.uk

Timetable directory & most websites:
www.barrydoe.co.uk

BUSES, TRAMS & TRAINS
Other sources of information can be found through your local County, District or Unitary Council or Passenger Transport Executive (see Websites below) to ascertain correct contact details. Details of train operating company telephone numbers together with Network Rail, Rail Regulator and Association of Train Operating Companies appear in full in the National Rail Timetable (from some main stations and W H Smith shops). Some tram operators are shown in this, too. Other operators appear in the **www.ukbus.co.uk** website.

www.ukbus.co.uk Station Master Bus & Train Information & Journey Planners with telephone numbers

www.arriva.co.uk Arriva Buses, Trams & Trains

www.arrivabus.co.uk Arriva Buses

www.firstgroup.com First Group Buses, Trams & Trains

www.stagecoachplc.com Stagecoach Buses, Trams & Trains

www.go-ahead.com Go Ahead Group

www.tfl.gov.uk for all types of transport in London

www.lothianbuses.co.uk for Edinburgh & Lothian area **www.translink.co.uk** Northern Ireland, Belfast, Ulsterbus & Rail

www.transdevplc.co.uk London, Bournemouth, North Yorkshire & East Lancashire

Other large Bus Groups include East Yorkshire Motor Services (Hull, Manchester & Scarborough), Preston Bus, Wellglade Trent (Derby & Nottingham), often with websites for their local operating companies. Council owned bus companies include Blackburn, Blackpool, Bournemouth, Cardiff, Eastbourne, Halton, Ipswich, Isle of Man, Islwyn, Lothian Buses (Edinburgh), Newport, Northern Ireland, Nottingham, Plymouth, Reading, Rossendale, Thamesdown (Swindon), and Warrington.

OTHER INFORMATION WEBSITES
Other important local authority public transport websites often give information – the main ones in urban areas are as follows:-

PTEs & UAs in Urban Areas:-

www.gmpte.gov.uk Greater Manchester

www.merseytravel.gov.uk Merseyside

www.nexus.org.uk Tyne & Wear

www.centro.org.uk West Midlands

www.southyorks.org.uk South Yorkshire

www.wymetro.com West Yorkshire

www.spt.co.uk Glasgow & Strathclyde

www.edinburgh.gov.uk Edinburgh & Lothian

www.cardiff.gov.uk Cardiff area

www.tfl.gov.uk London

Many of the other Shire Counties & UAs have a website, often **www.** ending in **.gov.uk**

COACHES

National Express . Scottish City Link

For longer distance coach service timetables & planners contact National Express – their line numbers are:-
08705 808080 www.nationalexpress.co.uk

Scottish Citylink
08705 505050 Website: www.citylink.co.uk

TRAINS

National Train Information Line

The national hotline for all train information is:-
08457 484950 Minicom: 0845 60 50 600

Other Rail Timetable & Fare Information + Journey Planning Websites

Enquiries:
www.nationaltrainenquiries.co.uk
www.networkrail.co.uk

Planning:
www.travelinfosystems.com

Current state of rail services:
www.nationalrail.co.uk

Booking services:
www.thetrainline.com

London:
www.tfl.gov.uk (Covers Buses, Trams, Underground, River, Docklands Rail and Victoria Coach Station)

Europe & Foreign:
www.raileurope.co.uk www.railchoice.co.uk

Many of the above websites often refer to a further local site for additional detailed information, and most of the train operating companies also have websites.

The lists shown are not exhaustive due to space limitations but many smaller operators have websites too.

For other information about transport websites, Ale Trails, CAMRA transport related activities and other contacts, but **NOT** timetable or service enquiries, please contact the CAMRA Public Transport.

Advisory Group on e-mail:
dave@cunningham57.freeserve.co.uk or by post or email via CAMRA Headquarters.

ALE TRAILS: Many local authorities and some operators have a programme of local public transport based Ale Trails with publicity leaflets listing timetables and pubs to visit. These help both transport and local pubs. Contact your local council for details.

Important Note: Don't rely on information from websites being 100% accurate and up-to-date – contact the appropriate telephone enquiry service to check before travelling.

CORNWALL

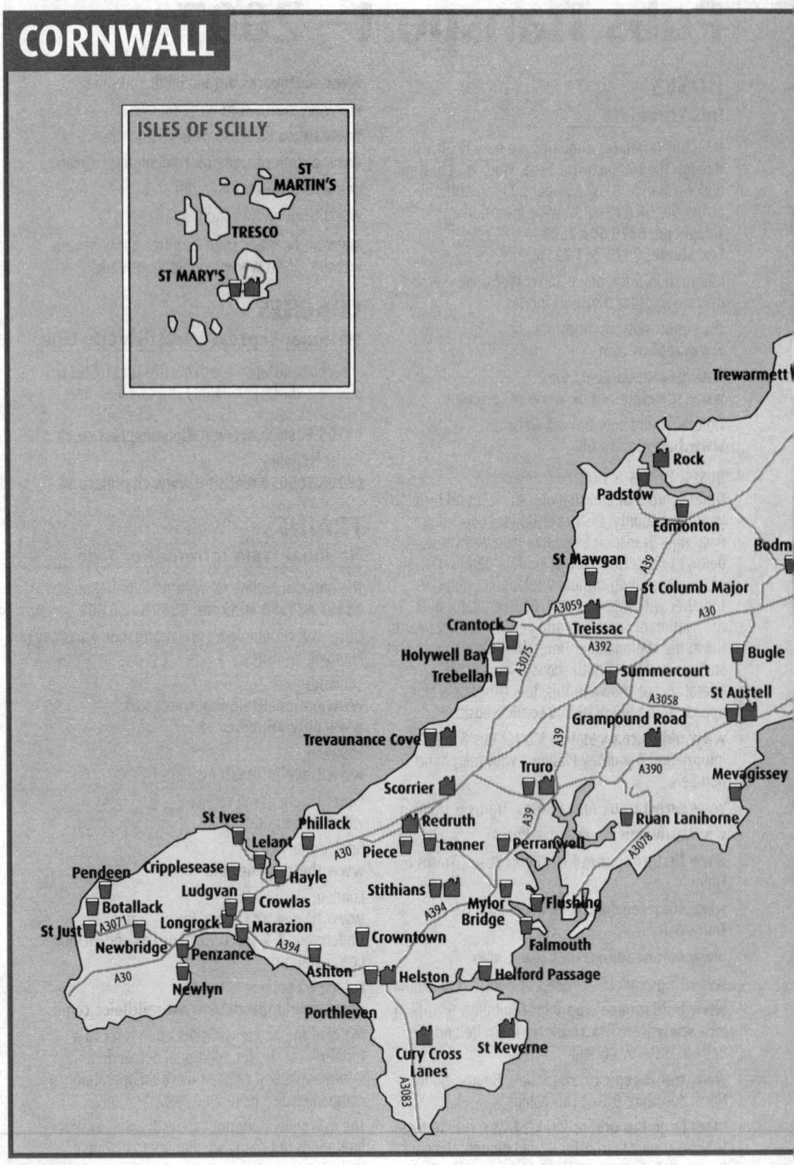

Ashton

Lion & Lamb

Fore Street, TR13 9RW (on A394 3 miles W of Helston)

12-11 daily

☎ (01736) 763227

Sharp's Doom Bar; Shepherd Neame Spitfire; guest beers Ⓗ

Welcoming family-run hostelry with an award-winning summer floral display enhancing the outdoor seating at the front of the pub. A quieter grass area is by the car park at the back, with camping for five tents. Four real ales are available in winter and six in summer. Bar snacks are available throughout opening hours and the service is always cheerful. Live entertainment is hosted on Friday evening and some Saturdays – the local choir is always popular.

❀◑ ⛺ 🚌 P

Blisland

Blisland Inn

The Green, PL30 4JF

11.30-11; 12-10.30 Sun

☎ (01208) 850739

Beer range varies Ⓗ /Ⓖ

Overlooking the green in this quaint moorland village, this CAMRA favourite is well worth the short drive off the A30 to visit. Up to seven beers and ciders are always available, many from micro-breweries both local and further afield. House beers and special promotional prices offer good value. A former CAMRA National

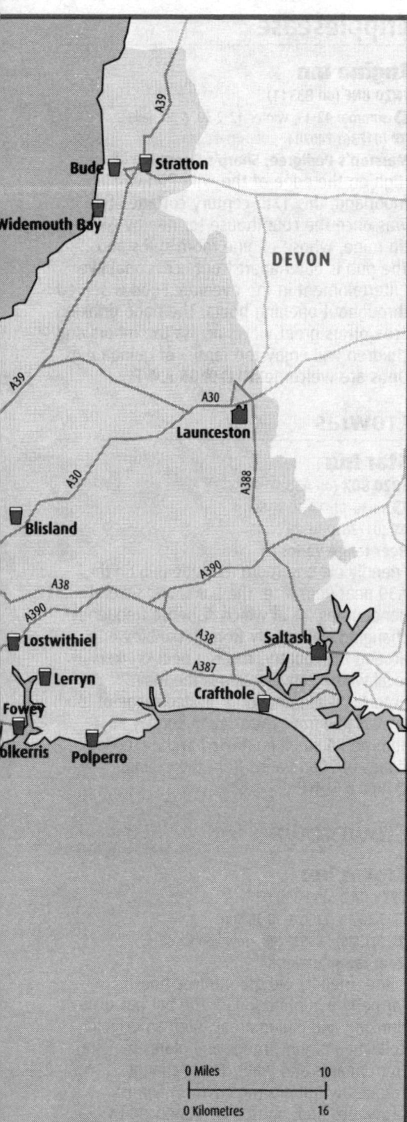

Pub of the Year and four times local winner, the pub has a strong community focus. Good value meals are popular with visitors and walkers. A no-smoking area and children's room are available. Dogs are welcome.
♨Q☺❀◑◐♣●P⊁

Bodmin

Bodmin Jail

Berrycoombe Road, PL31 2NR
(off Bodmin ring road)
✪ 10-11 daily
☎ (01208) 76292
Brains Rev James; Greene King IPA; guest beer Ⓗ
On the site of the once infamous Bodmin Jail, the pub has recently been refurbished to create a comfortable bar and lounge/dining area. A tour of the prison museum is a must. The guest ale varies regularly but is always from a Cornish brewery. The restaurant offers freshly-cooked, locally-sourced food, and fine wines are also available. Children are welcome.
Q☺❀◑◐⊟▲⊡P

George & Dragon

3 St Nicholas Street, PL31 1AB
✪ 11-11; 12-10.30 Sun
☎ (01208) 72514
St Austell Tinners, Tribute Ⓗ
Small, single bar locals' pub with a welcoming atmosphere on the edge of the town centre. Lively conversation is the main entertainment here. The pub fields teams in the local euchre, darts and pool leagues, and can be crowded on match nights. Good lunchtime bar snacks are reasonably priced. The preserved Bodmin & Wenford steam railway, which connects to the main line in summer, is a few minutes' walk away. B&B offers good value accommodation.
Q☺❀⇌⊡♣

Botallack

Queen's Arms

TR19 7QG (off B3306)
✪ 12-3 (not winter), 4-11; 12-11 Sat and summer; 12-10.30 Sun
☎ (01736) 788318
Beer range varies Ⓗ
Traditional village local, beamed and built of granite, not far from the coastal path. Up to three ever-changing Cornish ales, plus Tallack Tipple, the house beer brewed by Skinner's, are on handpump. A single bar serves several drinking areas including the family room, and there is a spacious garden. Mining pictures on the walls reflect the once-dominant local industry. Renowned for its imaginative and high-quality food, the pub also holds a beer festival in September.
♨Q☺❀◑◐▲⊡P

Bude

Bencoolen Inn

Bencoolen Road, EX23 8PJ
✪ 11 (12 winter)-11; 12-10.30 summer
☎ (01288) 354694

INDEPENDENT BREWERIES

Ales of Scilly St Mary's
Atlantic Treisaac
Bathtub Stithians
Blackawton Saltash
Blue Anchor Helston
Doghouse Scorrier
Driftwood Trevaunance Cove
Keltek Redruth
Lizard St Keverne
Organic Cury Cross Lanes
Ring O'Bells Launceston
St Austell St Austell
Sharp's Rock
Skinner's Truro
Wooden Hand Grampound Road

Ring O'Bells Dreckly; Sharp's Doom Bar, Own; guest beer (summer) [H]
Spacious, friendly and welcoming pub, popular with all ages. A guest beer is added in summer and several more during Bude Jazz Festival at the end of August. The pub is named after a locally wrecked ship which foundered in 1862 on its way from Liverpool to Bombay – some of the ship's timbers were used in the pub's construction. You can read the account of the wreck, which occupies one of the walls. Accommodation is available summer only. P

Bugle

Bugle Inn

57 Fore Street, PL26 8PB (on A391)
10-midnight daily
(01726) 850307 bugleinn.co.uk
St Austell IPA, Tinners, Dartmoor Best, Tribute [H]
Friendly local in the centre of the village, named after the sound of the horn as the stagecoach passed through. Located in the centre of Corwall, it is an ideal base for touring the county – the Eden Project is three miles away. Meals are served all day with breakfast from 8am. Entertainment includes darts, pool, a juke box and live music on most Sunday evenings. Accommodation is available in five en-suite rooms. P

Crafthole

Finnygook Inn

PL11 3BQ (on B3247)
summer 12-11; 12-10.30 Sun; winter 12-3, 6-11; 12-11 Fri & Sat; 12-3, 6-10.30 Sun
(01503) 230338 finnygook.co.uk
Sharp's Doom Bar; guest beers [H]
Silas Finny, leader of a local gang of smugglers, died in a skirmish with revenue men nearby. Locals claim that his gook (ghost) still sometimes make its presence felt. This free house offers an interesting variety of ales in traditional surroundings with low beamed ceilings and a wealth of brass and copper ornaments. Bar and restaurant menus are available with cream teas in summer. Live music is played at weekends and a 10-day music and real ale festival is held in August. P

Crantock

Old Albion

Langurroc Road, TR8 5RB
12 (2 winter Mon-Thu)-midnight; 12-11 Sun
(01637) 830243
Courage Best Bitter; Skinner's Betty Stogs; guest beers [H]
Picture-postcard, partly-thatched village pub tucked away on a lane leading to the church. The pub has a history of involvement in smuggling and inside are secret tunnels leading to the church and the beach. Particularly busy in summer, visitors are attracted by the good value meals, pleasant outdoor drinking area, the safe, sandy beach nearby and numerous camping and caravan facilities. P

Cripplesease

Engine Inn

TR20 8NF (on B3311)
summer 12-11; winter 12-2.30, 6-11 daily
(01736) 740204
Marston's Pedigree; Sharp's Doom Bar [H]
High on the edge of the wild Penwith moorland, this 17th-century cottage-style inn was once the counthouse for nearby Giew tin mine, whose engine room still stands. The pub is quiet apart from occasional live entertainment in the evening. Food is served throughout opening hours. The patio drinking area offers great views across the moors and children will enjoy the family of guinea pigs. Dogs are welcome. Q P

Crowlas

Star Inn

TR20 8DX (on A30)
11.30-11; 12-10.30 Sun
(01736) 740375
Beer range varies [H]
Friendly old one-room roadside pub on the A30 near Penzance. The bar sports several handpumps, all of which dispense frequently-changing ales mostly from micro-breweries around the country. This is a beer drinkers' local where conversation is the main entertainment, though a limited range of food is available from Thursday to Sunday in summer. A small boat used in the Crowlas floods of 2003 hangs from the ceiling.
Q P

Crowntown

Crown Inn

TR13 0AD (on B3303)
5.30-11; 12-3, 7-10.30 Sun
(01326) 565538 crownlodges.co.uk
Beer range varies [G]
Large, friendly old granite free house, formerly a hunting lodge. The bar has distinct drinking and dining areas, with an eclectic collection of jugs, mugs and plates hanging from beams and walls. Beers change frequently but are mostly from Cornish breweries and, unusually, dispensed by gravity straight from the cellar, despite the handpumps. Sunday lunch is served. There is a pool room and accommodation is in lodges at the rear of the pub. Q P

Edmonton

Quarryman Inn

PL27 7JA (off A39)
12-10.30; 12-11 Fri & Sat & summer; 12-10.30 Sun
(01208) 816444
Beer range varies [H]
Popular free house where 'dogs are welcome and children tolerated', says the landlord. Full of character, the decor is eclectic in this cosy, convivial pub which divides into a public and lounge bar with a dining area. The excellent food is made using local produce. A first-class beer menu generally includes a Skinner's brew and guests are from the brewer's range.

Warning: this is a mobile-free zone so switch off or fall foul of the landlord!
⛫Q❀◐◑⛺🚌P

Falmouth

Mason's Arms

31 Killigrew Street, TR11 3PW
⏲ 11-11 (1am Fri & Sat); 12-11 Sun
☎ (01326) 311061
St Austell Tribute 🄷
Traditional town centre pub favoured by locals with a cosy, tiny single bar. The interior has a seafaring theme, with a collection of nautical flags decorating the ceiling. No food is served but you are welcome to bring your own if you wish. ⛫⇌🚌

Oddfellows Arms

Quay Hill, TR11 3HG
⏲ 12-11; 12-10.30 Sun
☎ (01326) 318530 🌐 theoddfellowsarms.co.uk
Sharp's Eden Ale, Special; 🄷 **guest beers** 🄶
Small but perfectly formed – the pub consists of a tiny main bar and a pool room. Breathtakingly good Sharp's Eden and Special, along with a top class and constantly changing choice of guests straight from the barrel, provide excellent fuel for the lively and highly entertaining exploits of the regulars, many of whom can be found arguing over recipes way in advance of the pub's annual 'cakefest' – a jolly affair held in June each year. A true gem of a back street local. ⇌🚌♣

Seven Stars ☆

1 The Moor, TR11 3QA
⏲ 11-3, 6-11; 12-3, 7-10.30 Sun
☎ (01326) 312111
Draught Bass; Sharp's Special; Skinner's Cornish Knocker; guest beers 🄶
A timeless classic, Cornwall's only entry in CAMRA's National Inventory of pubs with interiors of outstanding historic interest. Tear your gaze away from the dizzying collection of key fobs and you will spot the bespoke stillage which supports 18 gallon casks of Bass below, and firkins of guest ales a-top. The pub, with regulars providing a hubbub of lively bar banter, has been carefully watched over for more than 50 years by landlord and parish priest Rev Barrington Bennetts.
Q❀⇌🚌●

Flushing

Seven Stars

3 Trefusis Road, TR11 5TY (off A393 at Penryn)
⏲ 11-11; 12-10.30 Sun
☎ (01326) 374373
Skinner's Betty Stogs, Cornish Knocker, seasonal beers 🄷
Central village pub with tables outside overlooking the Penryn River. Inside is a large, well-furnished L-shaped bar and a restaurant serving good, reasonably-priced food – fish is a speciality and the Cornish pasties are home-made. The pub is popular with locals and visitors; access is possible via the passenger ferry from Falmouth.
⛫Q❀◐◑

Fowey

Lugger Inn

5 Fore Street, PL23 1AQ
⏲ 11-11.30; 11-11 Sun
☎ (01726) 833435
St Austell Tinners, Tribute, HSD 🄷
Small, friendly, one-bar town centre pub with large no-smoking area, popular with locals and visitors. The building is dated 1633 but the front is more modern, with small leaded windows. The interior sports ship memorabilia and a large mural depicting Cornish luggers on the river. In the summer, outdoor tables on the main street are always in demand. An extensive menu of excellent home-cooked food including fresh local seafood is available daily. Q❀⇔◐◑🚌⅟

Hayle

Cornish Arms

86 Commercial Road, TR27 4DJ (B3301 between Copperhouse and Hayle)
⏲ 11.30-2.30, 5.30-11; 11-11 Sat; 12-10.30 Sun
☎ (01736) 753237
St Austell IPA, Tinners, Tribute, Dartmoor Best, HSD 🄷
Convivial, roomy two-bar local, popular with a broad mix of the community. The public bar has a pool table and the spacious lounge a dartboard. A recent extension at the back serves as a restaurant area and there is a garden beyond. One of the few pubs to feature the full range of St Austell's real ales, as the array of handpumps testifies, pub games including euchre are played here.
⛫Q❀◐◑⊟⛺⇌🚌♣P

Helford Passage

Ferry Boat Inn

TR11 5LB (N of Helford river, near Mawnan Smith)
⏲ 10 (11.30 Sun)-midnight
☎ (01326) 250625
St Austell Tinners, Tribute, HSD 🄷
In an idyllic creekside position overlooking its own beach and the Helford river, this large open-plan pub has a spacious single bar room with a small, more intimate annexe. The bar is set into three stone arches. The walls and beamed ceilings are festooned with an eclectic mix of nautical bric-a-brac including a whole ship's mast, while the wooden furniture is supplemented with comfortable sofas. Families are welcome. ⛫❀⇔◐◑P

Helston

Blue Anchor

50 Coinagehall Street, TR13 8EU
⏲ 10.30-midnight (11 Sun)
☎ (01326) 562821
Blue Anchor Spingo, Jubilee, Middle, Special, seasonal beer 🄷
Rambling, unspoilt 15th-century building with a thatched roof and its own brewery at the rear. Conversation is the main entertainment in the two small bars with no games machines or juke box to intrude. An indoor skittle alley has its own bar, popular for group functions. The occasional seasonal

beer may be a winter warmer or commemorative brew. A 'bragget' or honey and herb-based beer appears in summer.
♔Q♉❀🛏◑⊟🚌♣

Holywell Bay

St Piran's Inn

TR8 5PP
⏲ summer 11 (12 Sun)-midnight; winter 5 (11 Fri & Sat)-midnight; 12-3.30 Sun
☎ (01637) 830205
St Austell Tribute; Shepherd Neame Spitfire; guest beers Ⓗ
Close by a scenic bay, this beachside free house was originally two coastguards' cottages. The beamed interior is spacious but homely, with wood furnishings, bric-a-brac and an open fire in winter. The range of beer stocked varies with the season and a good value, high quality food menu is offered. A quiet, family-friendly pub, it also has a large outdoor drinking area and children's play area. Due to its proximity to the beach there may be a refundable car parking charge in summer. ♔Q♉❀◑♿⛺🚌P

Lanner

Lanner Inn

The Square, TR16 6EH (on A393 Redruth-Falmouth road)
⏲ 12-2 (not Mon), 4.30-11; 12-2, 7-10.30 Sun
☎ (01209) 215611
Sharp's Own; guest beer Ⓗ
Small and busy community pub where the landlord varies the guest beers regularly on the recommendation of his regulars. The emphasis here is on real ale and conversation – no food is served. Pub games including darts, euchre, pool, dominoes and quizzes are popular. A delightful orchard doubles as the garden and children's play area in summer. Good value B&B accommodation is available.
♔Q❀🛏⊟🚌♣P

Lelant

Watermill Inn

Lelant Downs, TR27 6LQ
⏲ 11-11; 12-10.30 Sun
☎ (01736) 757912
Ring O' Bells Dreckly; Sharp's Doom Bar; guest beer Ⓗ
Set in beautiful surroundings, this two-storey 18th-century free house was formerly a mill. Downstairs, the traditional single-room pub features the original working waterwheel complete with millstones. The bar is divided into drinking and dining areas and an extensive bar menu is available. Upstairs, the former mill loft is an evening-only restaurant where local seafood is a speciality. Over the mill stream is an extensive garden.
♔Q❀◑⛺⇌(Lelant Saltings)🚌P⊬

Lerryn

Ship Inn

Fore Street, PL22 0PT
⏲ 11-midnight (winter 11-3, 6-midnight); 12-midnight Sun
☎ (01208) 872374 🌐 theshipinnlerryn.co.uk
Beer range varies Ⓗ
Charming, traditional gem of a village pub near the river Fowey, in good walking territory. The slate-floored public bar offers up to five real ales; Bass is always available as well as a selection from Skinner's and Sharp's ranges. Haye Farm draught cider, made nearby, is also served. The pub offers excellent value bar meals, a more formal restaurant area and a garden.
♔❀🛏◑⊟●

Longrock

Mexico Inn

Gladstone Terrace, TR20 8JB (off A30)
⏲ 11-2.30, 5-11 (midnight Fri & Sat); 12-11 Sun
☎ (01736) 710625
Sharp's Doom Bar, Eden Ale; Skinner's Betty Stogs Ⓗ
Once part of a mine, this local free house has a single L-shaped beamed bar and bare granite walls, with a no-smoking extension at the rear. Popular in summer, it is a short walk from the beach. A wide range of good quality food is available in the bar and restaurant. Beers from Skinner's and Sharp's may vary. Tables on the pavement outside and a small terrace at the rear provide alfresco drinking. Families and dogs are welcome. Parking is limited. ♔Q♉❀◑♿🚌P⊬

Lostwithiel

Globe Inn

3 North Street, PL22 0EG
⏲ 12-2.30, 6-11; 12-2.30, 7-10.30 Sun
☎ (01208) 872501 🌐 globeinn.com
Sharp's Doom Bar; Skinner's Betty Stogs; guest beers Ⓗ
Cosy and friendly 13th-century pub in the narrow streets of this old town, close to the station and medieval stone bridge over the river. The rambling one-bar inn has several drinking and eating areas and a restaurant to the rear. Although the pub is mainly oriented towards food, drinkers are more than welcome. It gets its name from the ship on which a member of the family of the one-time owners was killed in a sea battle in 1813. Q❀🛏◑⛺⇌♣

Ludgvan

White Hart

TR20 8EY (on B3309)
⏲ 12-3, 5.30-11 (10.30 Sun)
☎ (01736) 740574
Draught Bass; Flowers IPA; Greene King Abbot; Sharp's Doom Bar Ⓖ
This 14th-century granite inn stands next to the village church. The quaint single-room interior reflects its age with wood furnishings, panels and partitions creating an authentic atmosphere. Warmed by two large wood-burning stoves, this is a bar for quiet conversation. All beer is served direct from the cask. Good-quality food, made with local produce, is served in generous portions. Limited parking is shared with the church.
♔Q❀◑🚌P

Marazion

King's Arms

The Square, TR17 0AP

11-2.30, 6-11; 11-11 Fri & Sat; 12-10.30 Sun

(01736) 710291

St Austell Tribute, HSD H

Old market corner pub opposite the ferry quay to St Michael's Mount, busy with tourists in 'the season'. There is one small but comfortable family-friendly bar, with several tables outside on the pavement. Tuesday is quiz night and on the first Thursday of the month there is a live jam session with visitors welcome to join in. An extra ale from the St Austell range may appear in summer.

Mevagissey

Harbour Tavern

Jetty Street, PL26 6UH (on harbourside)

10.30-midnight daily

(01726) 842220

Skinner's Betty Stogs, Figgy's Brew; guest beer H

Overlooking the harbour in this bustling fishing village and originally a fish store, the pub is now a well-established house popular with locals and tourists of all ages. The large, square bar room has a raised area in the corner with plenty of tables for diners. Home-cooked food is served with local fish dishes a favourite choice. Accommodation with sea views is available. Parking can be difficult in summer.

Ship Inn

Fore Street, PL26 6UQ

10 (12 Sun)-midnight daily

(01726) 843324

St Austell HSD, Tinners, Tribute H

Full of character, this old pub in the centre of town has wood-clad walls and a slate-flagged floor. The bar is one long room with many nooks and crannies giving a more cosy feel. It is rumoured that Ship regulars in bygone times were involved with smuggling and wrecking. Food is served all day in summer. En-suite accommodation includes two family rooms.

Mylor Bridge

Lemon Arms

Lemon Hill, TR11 5NA (off A393 at Penryn)

11-3, 6-11; 12-3, 7-10.30 Sun

(01326) 373666

St Austell Tinners, Tribute, HSD H

One-bar friendly village centre pub popular with local sports teams. Families with children are made most welcome here and there is a patio/garden for the summer. Good home-cooked food is available. The present licensees have recently celebrated 10 years in residence. The ales from St Austell may vary from time to time.

Newbridge

Fountain Inn

TR20 8QH (on A3071)

11.30-11 (midnight summer; 11.30-2, 4-11 Jan-Feb); 12-10.30 Sun

(01736) 364075

St Austell IPA, Tinners, Black Prince, Tribute, HSD H

Welcoming old Grade II listed inn and former Cornwall CAMRA Pub of the Year. The one-bar building has solid stone walls and a flagstone floor, and a carpeted dining area with a real fire in an enormous granite fireplace. Some bar tables are made from old wooden casks with redundant dartboards as tops. Renowned locally for its good food and quality ales, the pub welcomes families and dogs.

Newlyn

Tolcarne Inn

Tolcarne Place, TR18 5PR

10.30-3, 6.30-midnight; 12-midnight Sun

(01736) 363074

Courage Best Bitter; Sharp's Special; guest beer H

Round the corner from the fish market, close by the sea wall, this 300-year-old inn attracts a loyal following throughout the year. Inside is a long bar and dining area, outside a patio. Highly-rated home-cooked food is prepared with locally-sourced ingredients, including freshly-caught fish. The guest beer changes regularly. Parking is limited – you need a permit from the bar staff at busy times. Jazz features on Sunday lunchtime; you will often find the landlord making up a duo. The pub lies on the Cornish cycle route. Q

Padstow

Golden Lion Inn

Lanadwell Street, PL28 8AN

11 (12 Sun)-11

(01841) 532797

Draught Bass; Sharp's Cornish Coaster, Doom Bar; H **guest beer** G

Old, unspoilt free house situated away from the busy harbour area, offering a friendly welcome to locals and visitors alike. The public bar with its low ceiling is partitioned to create a family and dining area; there is also a lounge and patio with seating outside. A good selection of bar food is available. On the first of May – 'obby 'oss day – the pub becomes the 'stable' for the red 'oss, from which it energetically emerges!

Pendeen

North Inn

TR19 7DN (on B3306)

11-midnight (1am Fri & Sat); 12-11 Sun

(01736) 788417

St Austell IPA, Tinners, Black Prince (winter), Tribute, HSD (summer) H

Welcoming locals' pub in an old mining village; a former Cornwall CAMRA Pub of the Year. The single large room is decorated with pictures and artefacts from nearby Geevor, the last working mine to be closed in the Pendeen area and now a mining museum. The inn is in a popular location for walkers, with nearby cliffs and the coastal path. Accommodation is available as well as camping round the back. A small upstairs restaurant affords outstanding views over the sea. ⛰Q❀⇌◐◗⛺⊟P

Penzance

Alexandra Inn

Alexandra Road,Wherrytown, TR18 4LY

⊕ 11.30-2.30, 5-11; 11.30-11 Sat; 12-10.30 (winter 12-3, 6-10.30) Sun

☎ (01736) 365165

Sharp's Own; Skinner's Heligan Honey; guest beer Ⓗ

Situated between the sea front and Mount's Bay rugby club, this popular local community pub offers friendly and efficient service all round. The landlord keeps up to six real ales, mainly Cornish, and a real cider. No food is served at lunchtime in winter. The sheltered garden is pleasant in summer. Pub games includes Scalextric on a track that folds to become a dartboard. Cornwall CAMRA's Pub of the Year 2006 offers accommodation, advance booking only. Q❀⇌◐◗♿♣●

Pirate Inn

Alverton Road, TR18 4PS

⊕ 10.30-11.30; 12-11.30 Sun

☎ (01736) 366094 ⊕ pirateinn.co.uk

Beer range varies Ⓗ

Typical two-bar Cornish country pub in an old granite building dating back to 1624 but converted from a farmhouse in the 1950s. Up to six ales are on offer, a mix of national brands and local brews, usually from Skinner's, Sharp's and Ales of Scilly. The capacious garden includes a play area and chickens; well-behaved children and dogs are welcome. No food is served on Sunday evening. Folk night is Tuesday. ⛰Q❀⇌◐◗⊟⊟♣●P

Tremenheere

4-8 Market Place, TR18 2JA

⊕ 9am-midnight (1am Fri & Sat); 9am-midnight Sun

☎ (01736) 335350

Greene King Abbot; Marston's Burton Bitter, Pedigree; Skinner's Cornish Knocker; guest beers Ⓗ

Named after Lord Tremenheere of Penzance, this Wetherspoon town centre conversion has a large open-plan interior on two levels. Up to nine real ales and a cider, usually Sheppy's, are on handpump; polypins of Weston's Old Rosie and vintage ciders are in the cooling cabinet. Food is served all day. A small, fully-enclosed yard has patio heaters and sun shades. ❀◐◗⇌⊟●⚡

Perranwell

Royal Oak

TR3 7PX

⊕ 11-3, 6-11; 12-3, 7-10.30 Sun (hours vary in summer)

☎ (01872) 863175

Draught Bass; Flowers IPA; Sharp's Special Ⓗ

Small, friendly cottage pub dating from the 18th century, now a free house with a deserved reputation for good beer and food. Tapas are available at the bar which has a cosy drinking area. Good public transport links connect not only to Truro but also to both coasts. The pub is on the Truro-Falmouth rail ale trail; the station is a 10-minute walk. Q❀◐◗⇌⊟P

Phillack

Bucket of Blood

14 Churchtown Road, TR27 5AE

⊕ 12-2.30 (not Mon), 6-11; 11.30-3, 6-11 Sat; 12-4, 7-10.30 Sun

☎ (01736) 752378

St Austell Dartmoor Best, HSD Ⓗ

Near the dunes of Hayle Towans, this friendly old local gets its name from a gory legend involving the pub's well. Recently refurbished to render the pub structure safe, the single bar room houses a pool table at one end and a cosy drinking and dining area at the other with settles and a recently-exposed old fireplace. Beware of the very low beams overhead! An extra ale from the St Austell range appears in summer. ⛰☋❀◐◗⛺♣P

Piece

Countryman Inn

TR16 6SG (on Four Lanes-Pool road)

⊕ 11-11; 12-10.30 Sun

☎ (01209) 215960

Courage Best Bitter; Greene King Old Speckled Hen; Sharp's Doom Bar; Skinner's Cornish Blonde, Heligan Honey; Theakston Old Peculier Ⓗ

Lively country pub, formerly a grocery shop for miners, set high among the old copper mines near Carn Brea. There are two bars, the larger hosting some form of live entertainment every night, and on Sunday lunchtime there is a raffle in support of local charities. A range of 10 ales is available including the house beer from Sharp's called No-Name, because it was never given one! Food is available all day. ⛰☋❀◐◗⊟⛺P

Polkerris

Rashleigh Inn

PL24 2TL

⊕ 11-midnight (12.30 Fri & Sat); 11-midnight Sun

☎ (01726) 813991

Sharp's Doom Bar; Taylor Landlord; guest beers Ⓗ

Drive down a steep, narrow lane or divert off the coastal path to reach the inn, overlooking a small harbour with a sandy beach. This is a perfectly secluded spot to enjoy excellent real ales including the house beer, Rashleigh Bitter, brewed by Sharp's. Inside, comfortable furnishings, beamed ceilings and open fires create a cosy ambience. Good food is available including an a la carte menu. ⛰Q❀◐◗⛺●P

Polperro

Blue Peter

Quay Road, PL13 2QZ (end of fish quay)

⊕ 11-11; 12-10.30 Sun

☎ (01503) 272743

Sharp's Doom Bar; guest beers Ⓗ

Named after the naval flag that signals 'crew on board, ready to sail', this family-run free house with sea views is near the outer harbour, on the south west coast path. A changing range of ales from west country independents complements the excellent home-cooked food (lunchtime only). Low ceilings, old beams, traditional decor and a friendly welcome make this pub popular with fishermen, locals and visitors; children are welcome upstairs. Live music is held at weekends. Dog friendly – please ask for a biscuit. ⛫◖🚌🍎

Porthleven

Atlantic Inn

Peverell Terrace, TR13 9DZ (above harbour)
🕐 11-11; 12-10.30 Sun
☎ (01326) 562439 🌐 santi.me.uk
Skinner's Betty Stogs, Figgy's Brew; guest beer 🄷
From its lofty vantage point above the town, the recently refurbished Atlantic enjoys fine views over the harbour and bay through its picture windows and from the outside terrace. The bar is constructed like a ship's hull, and furnished with a mix of settles, benches and chairs. To the rear is a quiet lounge and restaurant decorated with murals. Children, and dogs on leads, are welcome. Guest beers often include a third brew from Skinner's. ⛫❀◖◗♿P

Ruan Lanihorne

King's Head Inn

TR2 5NX
🕐 12-2.30 (closed Mon winter), 6-11; 12-2.30, 6.45-11 Sun
☎ (01872) 501263
Beer range varies 🄷
On the Fal estuary, within the Roseland Peninsula, nestles this delightful family-run free house, renowned for its superb food and drink. The homely interior has a single bar and two dining areas. Quiet and traditional in style, log fires add winter warmth and charm. Full of character, the decor reflects village history. A sun terrace and quaint sunken garden provide space for outdoor drinking and dining. The house beer, King's Ruan, is brewed by Skinner's. No food is served on Sunday evening. ⛫Q❀◖◗P

St Austell

Western Inn

West Hill, PL25 5EY
🕐 12-midnight daily
☎ (01726) 72797
St Austell Tinners, Tribute, seasonal beer 🄷
One of six pubs bought by the St Austell Brewery from the Treluswell Brewing Company of Penryn in 1943. Until the late 1960s the interior was split into many back rooms and a snug but it is now a single bar with a dining area at one end and a raised area at the other for playing pool and darts. A convivial pub popular with all ages, it offers reasonably priced home-cooked food. Quiz night is Sunday. ⛫❀◖◗♿⛺⇌🚌♣P

St Columb Major

Ring O' Bells

3 Bank Street, TR9 6AT
🕐 12-2 (not Mon, Wed & winter), 5-11; 12-3, 7-10.30 Sun
☎ (01637) 880259
Sharp's Doom Bar, Eden Ale; guest beer (summer) 🄷
Atmospheric 15th-century free house opened to celebrate the parish church tower, hence the name. A former brew-pub, it is the oldest hostelry in town. The narrow frontage belies the extensive beamed, slate-floored, three-bar interior. Each bar has its own character and custom: the young frequent the front bar, older drinkers relax in the middle and the back. The rustic decor, wood furnishings and wood-burning stoves give a traditional feel. The former brewery is now a cosy restaurant offering a cosmopolitan menu. ⛫Q❀◖◗🚌♣

St Ives

Golden Lion

High Street, TR26 1RS
🕐 11-11; 12-10.30 Sun
☎ (01736) 793679
Courage Best Bitter; Sharp's Eden Ale; Skinner's Cornish Knocker; guest beer 🄷
A former coaching inn, now a thriving, welcoming town centre pub, where the locals drink. Recently refurbished, it has two bar rooms and an eye-catching mural of staff and customers adorning the corridor that links the two. The convivial front bar draws drinkers who like to chat while the rear games bar, with access to the courtyard garden, suits families and younger drinkers. High-quality food made using local produce is always popular – specialities are the fish and home-made pies. The Skinner's beer may vary. Q❀◖◗🄿♿⛺⇌🚌♣

St Just

King's Arms

5 Market Square, TR19 7HF
🕐 11-11; 12-10.30 Sun
☎ (01736) 788545
St Austell Tinners, Tribute; guest beer 🄷
Situated in the town square, this granite building was originally three 14th-century cottages. The rambling interior reflects the inn's history. A single L-shaped bar serves the many diverse areas within. The flagstone entrance, low exposed beam ceilings, open fire and wooden furnishings add character. Outside seating at the front facing the square is popular in summer. Food is home cooked using local produce. The pub is home to the Cape Singers; be prepared for impromptu singsongs. ⛫Q❀🛏◖◗♿⛺🚌♣

Star Inn

1 Fore Street, TR19 7LL
🕐 11 (12 Sun)-11
☎ (01736) 788767
St Austell Tinners, Dartmoor Best, Tribute, HSD 🄷
Popular 18th-century granite inn, reputedly the oldest in St Just. The atmospheric single bar interior reflects a long association with tin mining. Flags of the Celtic nations adorn the beamed ceiling. This is primarily a drinkers' pub where locals spin a yarn or two, though quality pub grub is served in the adjoining refurbished 'snuggery' in summer.

The beer range varies with the season. A sample of each ale stands in front of its handpump. ♨Q☺❀⌂◗♿⛟♣

St Mary's, Isles of Scilly

Atlantic Inn

The Bank, Hugh Town, TR21 0HY
⏲ 11-11; 12-10.30 Sun
☎ (01720) 422323
St Austell Tinners, Tribute, HSD ⊞
Arguably the best pub in town for beer and conversation, this spacious, busy, open-plan pub with beamed ceilings and a small outside patio overlooks St Mary's harbour. Three real ales are supplemented by one or two more from the St Austell range in summer; prices are much the same as on the mainland. A good range of food is served in the dining room. Children are welcome. Q❀◗▲⚟

St Mawgan

Falcon Inn

TR8 4EP
⏲ 11-3, 6-11; 12-3, 7-11 Sun
☎ (01637) 860225 🌐 thefalconinn-newquay.co.uk
St Austell Tinners, Tribute, HSD ⊞
In an idyllic setting in the unspoilt valley of Lanherne, this 16th-century country pub offers a friendly welcome. Very quiet, without juke box or games machine, the single bar is warmed by an open fire in winter. Excellent food is served in the dining room, where local art is on display. Family friendly, the large award-winning gardens include a play area and there is a games room. Q❀◗▲P

Stithians

Seven Stars Inn

Church Road, TR3 7DH
⏲ 12-2.30 (2 Tue), 7 (5 Fri)-11; 12-11 Sat; 12-10.30 Sun
☎ (01209) 860003
Beer range varies ⊞
Lively village local, home to the tiny Bathtub Brewery, originally built as a farmhouse extension to serve the drinking needs of local tin miners. The landlord changes the four beers regularly, favouring ales from Sharp's, Skinner's, Bathtub and other local breweries. The original rooms have been opened out to form one drinking area; a modern extension houses the pool table. Good quality and value pub meals are available (no food on Mon eve or Tue). ♨❀◗⛟♣●⚟

Stratton

King's Arms

Howells Road, EX23 9BX (on main road from A39 to Launceston)
⏲ 12-2.30, 6.30-11; 12-11 Fri & Sat; 12-10.30 Sun
☎ (01288) 352396
Exmoor Ale; Ring O' Bells Dreckly; Sharp's Doom Bar; guest beer ⊞
A popular local in the heart of this ancient market town. Originally a 17th-century coaching inn, the name reflects the town's political loyalties after the Civil War – the battle of Stamford Hill took place near here in 1643. The two simply-furnished bars retain many original features including the well-worn Delabole slate flagstone and wooden floors, and a small bread oven exposed in the lounge during refurbishment. A second guest ale may appear in summer. ♨Q❀⌂◗⊟♿▲⛟♣●P

Summercourt

London Inn

1 School Road, TR8 5EA (off A30 at village crossroads)
⏲ 12-2.30 (not winter Mon-Thu), 6 (5 Fri)-midnight; 12-2.30, 7-10.30 Sun
☎ (01872) 510281
Beer range varies ⊞
Former 17th-century coaching inn on the old London Road, now a lively, family-friendly free house where a warm welcome is assured. The spacious interior is divided by wooden screens to create drinking and dining areas. The eclectic decor features Laurel and Hardy figurines set among wooden furnishings and coach lamp lighting. Beers are rotated from the Skinner's, Sharp's and St Austell ranges, with an occasional guest in summer. The pub is central to the annual village fair celebrations in September. ♨Q❀◗▲⛟P

Trebellan

Smugglers' Den Inn

TR8 5PY (off Cubert Road from A3075)
⏲ summer 11-midnight; 12-10.30 Sun; winter 11.30-2.30 (not Mon-Wed), 6-11; 12-3, 6-10.30 Sun
☎ (01637) 830209 🌐 thesmugglersden.co.uk
Beer range varies ⊞
Former 16th-century farmhouse tucked away down a narrow lane. Once a haunt for smugglers, the original oak-beamed ceilings, paved courtyards to the front and rear, cosy corners filled with curios and a roaring log fire add to the olde-worlde charm. Reputedly haunted by several ghosts too. Occasional jazz or folk evenings are held and beer festivals feature throughout the year. The range of real ales favours Cornish breweries and Addlestones cider is served in summer. ♨Q☺❀◗♿▲♣●P⚟

Trevaunance Cove

Driftwood Spars Hotel

TR5 0RT
⏲ 11(12 Sun)-midnight
☎ (01872) 552428 🌐 driftwoodspars.com
Driftwood Cuckoo Ale; St Austell HSD; Sharp's Doom Bar, Own; Tetley Bitter; guest beer ⊞
By the coast, this vibrant family-run hotel with micro-brewery attracts surfers and cliff walkers. A former mine warehouse and sail loft, it is built from granite, slate and enormous ships' spars. The three-bar nautical-themed interior includes a fine collection of ships' clocks as well as beamed ceilings, leaded light windows and granite fireplaces. There is lift access to the upper bar, an excellent fish and game restaurant

with adjoining sun terrace. Live music and theatre are both frequently staged.

Trewarmett

Trewarmett Inn

PL34 0ET

11-3, 6.30-midnight; 12-3, 7-11 Sun

(01840) 770460

Beer range varies H

Traditional village local, once a kiddleywink – an inn that sold beer but a wink would get you a drop of the hard stuff – for workers at the nearby quarry. It has low beams, slate floors, stone walls and an open fireplace in its two drinking rooms and dining area. The raised garden offers distant sea views. The ales – up to five in summer – are normally all Cornish. Folk music features here, with instruments hanging from the walls and a 'folk and cask' festival in September.

Truro

City Inn

Pydar Street, TR1 3SP

12-11.30; 11-12.30am Fri & Sat; 12-11.30 Sun

(01872) 272623

Courage Best Bitter; Sharp's Doom Bar; Skinner's Betty Stogs; guest beer H

Busy two-bar community pub away from the shopping centre, about 10 minutes from the bus station. The comfortable lounge bar has several drinking corners and sports an impressive collection of water jugs, while the bar is more spartan and sports-oriented. The pub offers up to five ales from a variety of micro and regional breweries. The garden is a sun trap in summer and there is a covered drinking area to the side.

Rising Sun Inn

TR1 1ED

11-midnight (12.30am Fri & Sat); 12-11.30 Sun

(01872) 273454

Greene King Abbot; Sharp's Doom Bar; guest beer H

Frequented mainly by locals, and a short, steep uphill walk from the city centre, this feels like a village pub in a city environment. It has two bars and a large extension that houses the pool table. An imaginative menu is available every day, plus a Sunday carvery (booking advised). Guest ales from the Punch Taverns' monthly list vary regularly. A 10-minute walk from the bus station, car parking is limited.

Widemouth Bay

Bay View Inn

Marine Drive, EX23 0AW (minor road next to coast path from Bude to Widemouth Bay)

11-11; 12-10.30 Sun

(01288) 361273 www.bayviewinn.co.uk

Sharp's Doom Bar, Own H

Small, welcoming hotel in a lovely location near the coastal path with unrivalled views over a popular surfing beach and the bay. Inside is a bar, dining room, family room and conservatory, and outside a children's play area in the garden. The decor includes a display of old photographs of the local area. The house beer, Bay View Sunset, is brewed by Skinner's. Up to two guest ales are available during the summer.

The beauty of hops

When Sean Franklin, who runs Roosters Brewery in Yorkshire, described hops as the 'grapes of brewing' he opened a debate that has led to a much greater appreciation of the role of the small green plant in brewing. There are many varieties of hops: global brewers use 'high alpha' varieties (high in alpha acids) purely for bitterness. Craft brewers prefer to use varieties that deliver aroma and flavour as well as bitterness. The two most widely used English hops are Fuggles and Goldings, often blended together in the same beer, the Fuggle primarily for bitterness but with earthy and smoky notes, the Golding for its superb resiny, spicy and peppery character. Bramling Cross delivers rich fruity (blackurrant) notes, Challenger has a citrus/lime edge while the workhorse of the hop fraternity, Target, offers citrus and pepper. First Gold is the most successful of the new 'hedgerow' varieties that grow to only half the height of conventional hops and are therefore easier to pick. It offers piny and apricot notes. American varieties used in Britain include Willamette (an offshoot of the Fuggle) and Cascade, both of which give rich citrus/grapefruit aromas and flavours. The Styrian Golding (actually a type of Fuggle) from Slovenia is widely used as an aroma hop in Britain for its luscious floral and citrus character.

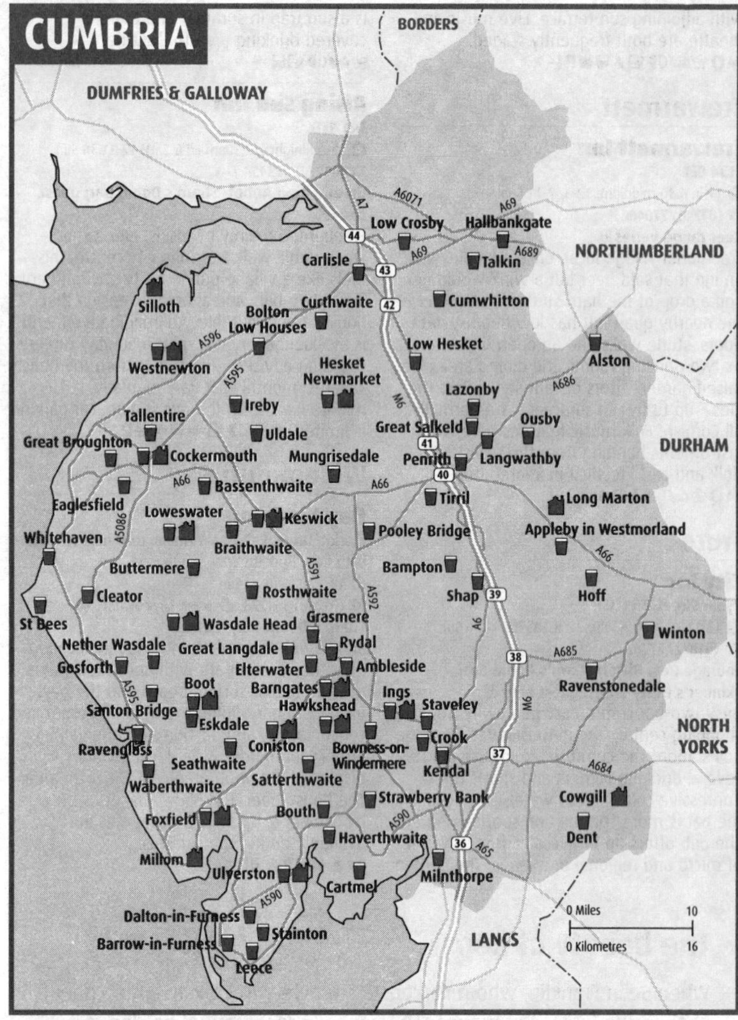

Alston

Cumberland Hotel

Townfoot, CA9 3HX

11-11; 12-10.30 Sun

☎ (01434) 381875 cumberlandalston.co.uk

Jennings Cumberland Ale; guest beers Ⓗ

Three handpumps offer guests from Cumbrian and Scots breweries as well as micros. The pub is situated at the bottom of the town, near the river, surrounded by good walking country. Alston is a pleasant town with many local attractions including a narrow gauge steam railway. The standard of the cuisine is high; Sunday roasts are a speciality. Q❀⇌◑◐♿▲♣P

Ambleside

Golden Rule

Smithy Brow, LA22 9AS

(200 yds off A591 towards Kirkstone)

11-midnight; 12-midnight Sun

☎ (015394) 32257

Robinson's Hatters, Old Stockport, Hartleys XB, Cumbria Way, Unicorn, Double Hop Ⓗ

Long-standing Guide entry, popular with locals and visitors of all ages. Eschewing meals, piped music and pool, one room houses a dartboard and games machine, while the no-smoking room at the rear has a TV tuned to terrestrial stations. A sheltered suntrap patio to the rear has bench seating. One of the regular beers is usually replaced by a seasonal brew. The pub has a disabled WC. ⛫Q❀♿♣⚡

Appleby in Westmorland

Golden Ball

High Weind, CA16 6RD (off Boroughgate)

12 (4 Mon & winter Thu)-midnight; 12-midnight Sun

☎ (017683) 51493

Jennings Bitter; Marston's Bitter; guest beers Ⓗ

Little changed over several decades, this traditional, side-street pub retains a strong local following, supplemented by railway buffs visiting the nearby Settle-Carlisle line. The simply furnished lounge and the bar, with TV and games, are both served from a central bar counter. Q❀⇌◑ ⊟≠♣

Bampton

Mardale Inn

CA10 2RQ

✪ 12-3 (summer only), 6-11; 6-10.30 Sun; closed Jan

☎ (01931) 713244 ⊕ mardaleinn.co.uk

Beer range varies Ⓗ

Village pub, formerly the St Patrick's Well Inn, set in picturesque countryside. Usually a Tirril beer is accompanied by a local guest on the handpumps. Above average quality meals are served in the dining room. No-smoking throughout, no juke box, TV or pool disturb the peace, but lots of puzzles and newspapers are provided. Benches in the lane outside allow drinkers to take the air. Nearby is Haweswater Reservoir – home to a golden eagle – Shap Abbey and the Coast-to-Coast route. ♨Q❀⇌◑⊭

Barngates

Drunken Duck

LA22 0NG (off B5286) OS351031

✪ 11.30-11; 12-10.30 Sun

☎ (015394) 36347 ⊕ drunkenduckinn.co.uk

Barngates Cracker Ale, Tag Lag Ⓗ

Home of the Barngates Brewery, two more of its draught beers are usually on sale, as well as bottled Belgian beers. Brewery tours can be arranged. The pub has been extensively renovated to give a pleasing mix of Lakeland and modern styles. In summer you can sit outside and enjoy the magnificent Lakeland views. Accommodation and meals are both high quality; food is served in the restaurant and the bar during the afternoon and evening; the building is no-smoking throughout. ♨❀⇌◑ ⋏P⊭

Barrow-in-Furness

Furness Cricket Club

Oxford Street, LA14 5PR

✪ 8 (2 Sat & Sun matchdays)-11 daily

☎ (01229) 825339 ⊕ furness.play-cricket.com

Beer range varies Ⓗ

Established in 1892, the club is a recent convert to the Barrow real ale scene. The adoption of cask beer has been enthusiastically welcomed by the regulars. The single draught ale is usually increased to two on matchdays when the club has extended opening hours. Although a private cricket club, CAMRA members are admitted. Take bus No. 1A to get here. Q❀♿⊟♣

Bassenthwaite Lake

Pheasant Inn

CA13 9YE (S off A66, W end of lake)

✪ 11.30-2.30, 5.30-10.30 (11 Fri & Sat); 12-2.30, 6-10.30 Sun

☎ (017687) 76234 ⊕ the-pheasant.co.uk

Draught Bass; Jennings Cumberland Ale; Theakston Best Bitter Ⓗ

This 500-year-old coaching inn enjoys a well deserved reputation as a traditional country hotel. The bar's special character is due to the rich red-brown patina of the walls and the antique furniture. The Pheasant offers a selection of fine wines and whiskies and there is a choice of bar meals or the excellent restaurant. Local CAMRA's Pub of the Season, winter 2005 stands in extensive gardens, near the 'Bass' lake and the northern fells. ♨Q❀⇌◑ ⊟♿⋏P

Bolton Low Houses

Oddfellows Arms

New Street, CA7 8PA (off A595, 12 miles W of Carlisle)

✪ 12-3 (not Mon-Thu), 7 (6 Fri & Sat)-11; 12-10.30 Sun

☎ (016973) 44452

Thwaites Original, Lancaster Bomber Ⓗ

This tiny village is on a tranquil bypass off the main road between Carlisle and Cockermouth. On the edge of the Lake District National Park, this welcoming pub benefits from stunning views of the fells at the back of Skiddaw. Two drinking areas are served from a single bar. The food is all freshly cooked to order, using the best of local ingredients. ❀◑⋏P

Boot

Brook House Inn

CA19 1TG OS176008

✪ 9am-midnight; 12-10.30 Sun

☎ (019467) 23288 ⊕ brookhouseinn.co.uk

Theakston Best Bitter; guest beers Ⓗ

Haven of quality food and uncommon beers, right by the last station on the narrow gauge Ravenglass and Eskdale steam railway. It is owned and run by a dedicated group of family members spanning several generations. Set in a delightful valley, popular with walkers, campers, railway enthusiasts and real ale drinkers, this is as close to heaven as it gets. It always offers a Yates beer and up to seven guests. All Boot's pubs collaborate on popular, twice yearly week-long beer festivals. ♨❀⇌◑⋏≠(Dalegarth R&ER)●P⊭

Woolpack Inn

CA19 1TH (1 mile E of Boot) OS190010

✪ 11-11 (phone to check in winter); 12-10.30 Sun

INDEPENDENT BREWERIES

Barngates Barngates
Beckstones Millom
Bitter End Cockermouth
Coniston Coniston
Cumbrian Hawkshead
Dent Cowgill
Derwent Silloth
Foxfield Foxfield
Great Gable Wasdale Head
Hardknott Boot
Hawkshead Hawkshead
Hesket Newmarket Hesket Newmarket
Jennings Cockermouth
Keswick Keswick
Loweswater Loweswater
Abraham Thompson Barrow-in-Furness
Tirril Long Marton
Ulverston Ulverston
Watermill Ings
Yates Westnewton

☎ (019467) 23230 🌐 woolpack.co.uk
Beer range varies Ⓗ
Surrounded by magnificent scenery, this pretty, rambling inn sits at the foot of dramatic, twisting Hardknott Pass. This friendly, highly individual inn is run by owners who are passionate about good local cask ales and quality food prepared from fresh ingredients. Brewing their own Hardknott beer ties in with these ideals; they also serve five guests from Cumbrian micros and guest ciders. On some evenings live music is performed. It is a lovely 20-minute walk to the Ravenglass and Eskdale Railway terminus. ♨Q❀⇔◐⊟▲♣●P⚟

Bouth

White Hart

LA12 8JB (off A590, 6 miles NE of Ulverston)
⏲ 12-2, 6-11; 12-11 Sat & Sun
☎ (01229) 861229 🌐 bed-and-breakfast-cumbria.co.uk
Black Sheep Best Bitter; Jennings Cumberland Ale; Tetley Bitter; guest beers Ⓗ
Country pub that has been opened out over recent years and is now deceptively large. Low, beamed ceilings, two real fires and hearty food add to its traditional rural Lakeland ambience. It became the first entirely no-smoking pub in 2004. Animal lovers should be aware that a fair number of stuffed beasts adorn the bar area. The large patio at the back of the pub is heated to extend outside drinking time. ♨❀⇔◐▲♣P⚟▯

Bowness-on-Windermere

Royal Oak

Brantfell Road, LA23 3EG
⏲ 11-11 (midnight Fri & Sat); 11-11 Sun
☎ (015394) 43970 🌐 royaloak-windermere.co.uk
Coniston Bluebird; Greene King Old Speckled Hen; guest beers Ⓗ
Friendly local which, despite being just off the village centre, is sought out by visitors. It comprises a no-smoking family/dining room to the left of the bar area, raised seating to the right and an upper level with pool table and juke box. The meals here are good value. A framed certificate proclaims the pub as the official start/finish of the Lake to Lake walk, which stretches 163 miles from Windermere to Kielder in Northumberland. ♨❀⇔◐♣P⚟

Braithwaite

Coledale Inn

CA12 5TN (off Whinlatter Rd, left at Coledale sign)
⏲ 12-11 daily
☎ (017687) 78272 🌐 coledale-inn.co.uk
Jennings Bitter; Yates Bitter; guest beer Ⓗ
This country inn looks out over the village of Braithwaite towards the Skiddaw range, and is ideally situated for walkers. Two bars serve real ale; dogs are welcome in the Georgian Bar that features traditional Lakeland oak carving. The guest beer may be from Theakston or one of the Cumbrian breweries. The building dates from 1824, when it was a woollen mill. It then became a pencil factory, using locally mined graphite, before being extended in Victorian times. ♨❀⇔◐▲♣P

Buttermere

Fish Hotel

CA13 9XA (off B5289 from Keswick)
⏲ 10.30-3, 6-11; 10.30-11 Sat & Sun
☎ (017687) 70253 🌐 fish-hotel.co.uk
Jennings Bitter, Sneck Lifter; guest beers Ⓗ
Family-owned, stone built hotel in a lovely setting between Buttermere and Crummock Water. With a spacious, comfortable bar area, much used by hikers, climbers and visitors to the area. Seven handpumps dispense largely Cumbrian beers. Good value meals offer a wide choice including vegetarian food. Winter beer options are reduced due to the quieter trade, the owners preferring to concentrate on quality. Q❀⇔◐♿▲P

Carlisle

Carlisle Rugby Club

Warwick Road, CA1 1CW
(off A69, by Carlisle United FC)
⏲ 7 (5.30 Fri & Sat)-11 (12.30-11 Sat in rugby season); 12-3, 7-10.30 Sun
☎ (01228) 521300
Theakston Best Bitter; Yates Bitter; guest beer Ⓗ
Recently extended and renovated following the substantial damage sustained during Carlisle's worst flood in 100 years, this club is a winner in Cumbria CAMRA's annual awards. A guest ale is always put on at weekends during the rugby season; it can get crowded when Carlisle United play at home. Show this Guide or a CAMRA membership card to be signed in. Q❀P⚟

Howard Arms

107 Lowther Street, CA3 8ED
⏲ 11-11; 12-10.30 Sun
☎ (01228) 532926
Theakston Best Bitter; guest beer Ⓗ
Reckoned to serve the best pint of Theakston's in the city, it now offers a regular guest, too. Popular throughout the day, the pub attracts a constantly changing clientele. The exterior boasts a superb green tiled façade, while inside a number of linked drinking areas are served by a compact bar. The rear area houses a large-screen TV for major sporting events. The rooms are decorated with memorabilia from the State Management days and the theatre that once stood opposite. ❀◖⇌

Jovial Sailor

40 Caldcotes, CA2 7AA
(follow hospital signs, W from centre)
⏲ 12 (11 Sat)-11; 12-10.30 Sun
☎ (01228) 532761
Theakston Best Bitter; guest beer Ⓗ
The unusual name for a pub in a landlocked city is explained by its proximity to a long-gone canal basin. The narrow bar displays some interesting old adverts. The lounge is divided into three areas for pool, darts and general seating. There are seats, too, in the rear yard where you can relax with a pint assailed by the aroma of baking biscuits from the factory next door. ♨❀P

King's Head

Fisher Street, CA3 8RF (behind old town hall)
10-11; 12-10.30 Sun
(01228) 533797
Yates Bitter; guest beer Ⓗ
The King's Head is one of the older pubs in the city centre, where many pictures of Carlisle through the ages are on display. It has a dartboard at the back of the room. A plaque outside explains why Carlisle is not in the Domesday Book. The pub is close to the tourist area of Carlisle, with the castle, cathedral and the Lanes shopping centre.

Near Boot

Whiteclosegate, CA3 0JA (take A689 N from centre)
12-2.30 (not winter Mon), 5.30 (4 Fri)-11; 12-10.30 Sun
(01228) 540100 nearboot.com
John Smith's Bitter; Theakston Mild; guest beers Ⓗ
The unusual name of this 18th-century inn alludes to the nearside boot when riding from Carlisle! Redesigned by the State Management scheme's architect, Harry Redfern, alas the rear aspect, which was typical of his work, was largely altered by a recent extension. The former bowling green, now a garden, affords excellent views over the city to the Caldbeck Fells. Traditionally furnished, the Boot has two small, cosy 'rooms' at the front and an open-plan area to the side and rear.
(179)P

Cartmel

King's Arms

The Square, LA11 6QB
11-11; 11-10.30 Sun
(015395) 36220
Black Sheep Best Bitter; Hawkshead Bitter; Jennings Cumberland Ale; Taylor Landlord; guest beers Ⓗ
Surprisingly spacious village pub that has a good mix of rooms and open-plan areas. Exposed beams combine with brass and copperware to create a warm, relaxed ambience. The restaurant overlooks the ducks on the little River Eea as it passes through the village, which is always busy with tourists in summer – however, the four pubs cope admirably with the influx. A drinking house has existed on this site for over 900 years.

Royal Oak

The Square, LA11 6QB
11-11; 12-10.30 Sun
(015395) 36259 theroyaloakinn.co.uk
Black Sheep Best Bitter, Riggwelter; Camerons Castle Eden Ale; guest beer Ⓗ
This pub, which is ideally located on Cartmel's village square, is best described as traditional. A firm favourite of locals and tourists alike, the bar meals, decor and atmosphere are all excellent. A welcoming open log fire and oak-beamed ceilings give a rustic appeal. An extensive enclosed garden is an added attraction for families.
Q

Cleator

Brook

Trumpet Terrace, CA23 3DX
11-midnight (1am Fri & Sat); 11-midnight Sun
(01946) 811635
Taylor Landlord; Yates Fever Pitch; guest beers Ⓗ
Situated on the main Cleator to Egremont road, this newly refurbished, lively village pub offers a cosy, candlelit interior. The Sunday lunches are proving very popular and music features strongly here, with local bands on Friday evening and the occasional jam session on a Sunday. Quiz night is Thursday. The licensee is committed to real ale and varies the range as much as he can.

Cockermouth

Bitter End

15 Kirkgate, CA13 9PJ (off Market Place)
12-2.30 (11.30-3 Fri & Sat); 6-midnight (11 Mon; 11.30 Tue & Wed); 12-3, 6-11 Sun
(01900) 828993 bitterend.co.uk
Bitter End Cockermouth Pride, Cuddy Lugs; Jennings Bitter, Cumberland Ale, Sneck Lifter; guest beers Ⓗ
The Bitter End Brewery, which can be seen through a glass screen behind the back bar area, boasts equipment, installed in 2004, that started out producing ales in New Jersey. The pub comprises three areas; the front bar has a welcoming open fire. Note the collection of Cockermouth photographs and memorabilia. Popular for dining, particularly weekends and evenings, a well attended free quiz takes place on Tuesday at local CAMRA Pub of the Year 1999-2002.

Swan Inn

56 Kirkgate, CA13 9PH (off Market Place)
11-2 (not Mon or Tue), 6-11.30 (midnight Fri); 11.30-midnight Sat; 12-4.30, 6.30-11 Sun
(01900) 822425
Jennings Dark Mild, Bitter Ⓗ
This welcoming local is one of the oldest in Cockermouth, and retains much of its earlier character. Cosy, with its flagged floor and low beams, it is warmed by an open fire in the front bar in winter. The pub fields two quiz teams and is the watering-hole for the Cockermouth Mechanics Band. Q

Coniston

Sun

LA21 8HQ (up hill from the Black Bull)
12-11; 12-10.30 Sun
(015394) 41248
Coniston Bluebird; Hawkshead Bitter; guest beers Ⓗ
Pub and hotel, dating back to the 16th century, situated up the hill from the main part of Coniston village. A typically Lakeland bar area, with its slate floor, boasts a stunning solid fuel range which is heavenly to sit and drink by in winter. It always serves two beers from local breweries – one from the village. In summer there is no better venue for enjoying your beer while taking in the magnificent views of Coniston Old Man.
QP

Crook

Sun Inn

LA8 8LA (on B5284)
⊙ 12-2.30, 6-11; 12-11 Sat; 12-10.30 Sun
☎ (015398) 21351
Coniston Bluebird; Theakston Best Bitter; guest beers Ⓗ
Country inn, retaining many original features. The bar area is separated from the no-smoking dining room by a part wall containing a two-way fireplace. Noted for its high quality meals (served all day Sat and Sun), booking is essential in the evenings. The pub enjoys fine views across extensive farmland to Scout Scar, and there are plenty of low-level and woodland walks in the vicinity. ♨Q❀◑◗⛺P⍉

Cumwhitton

Pheasant Inn

CA8 9EX (4½ miles SE of Warwick Bridge)
⊙ 6-11 (closed Mon); 12-3, 7-10.30 Sun
☎ (01228) 560102 🌐 thepheasantatcumwhitton.com
Beer range varies Ⓗ
Originally a farm cottage, to which a pub was added around 1810, the building, once known as the Red Lion, has had various extensions and internal alterations to arrive at the popular hostelry it is today. The bar and games room feature stone-flagged floors and a roaring fire in winter, while the carpeted dining room offers a comfortable environment in which to enjoy the excellent food on offer, including Sunday lunch. Upstairs is a function room. ♨❀🛏◗⛺♣P

Curthwaite

Royal Oak

CA7 8BG (off A595, 2 miles S of Thursby)
⊙ 12-2, 5-11; 10-11 Fri & Sat; 12-10.30 Sun
☎ (01228) 710219
Jennings Cumberland Ale, Cocker Hoop; guest beers Ⓗ
At the centre of a small village community that fully supports its pub. The large 30-seater restaurant is popular with regulars as well as visitors, offering a variety of meals made with local ingredients. Although off the beaten track it is one of the nearest pubs to Carlisle selling Jennings beers. ❀◑◗⛺♣P

Dalton-in-Furness

Brown Cow

10 Goose Green, LA15 8LP (below St Mary's Church, on road to Barrow)
⊙ 12-11; 12-10.30 Sun
☎ (01229) 462553
Beer range varies Ⓗ
Possibly 900 years old, this family-run pub, with a big, no-smoking restaurant upstairs, provides a cosy place for sampling good food and drink. One central bar serves three distinct areas, one of which is warmed by a coal fire. Nestling below the tower of the parish church, on the extreme western edge of town, it has a paved, raised patio and garden, which can be covered and heated when required. Fuller's London Pride is normally available. ♨❀🛏◑◗⇌🚌(6)♣P

Dent

Sun Inn

Main Street, LA10 5QL
⊙ 11-11; 12-10.30 Sun
☎ (015396) 25208
Dent Aviator, Kamikaze, seasonal beers Ⓗ
Standing on an ancient cobbled street, at the centre of this popular Dales village, the Sun has an L-shaped bar, with an open hearth and dartboard. A no-smoking side area can be curtained off. A games room offers pool and other amusements. It is traditionally seen as the tap to Dent Brewery, which is two miles along the dale towards Dent Station (another two miles further on). ♨Q❀🛏◑◗♿♣●P⍉

Eaglesfield

Black Cock

CA13 0SD (off A5086 S of Cockermouth)
⊙ 8-11 (midnight Fri & Sat); 12-11 Sun
☎ (01900) 822989
Jennings Bitter Ⓗ
At the heart of the village, the Black Cock is a treat to be savoured. A pub since the 17th century, not much has changed here since the 1960s. Low beams and oak panelling set off the gleaming brassware, while a real fire adds to the atmosphere in winter. A daytime bus service runs through the village between Cockermouth and Cleator Moor. ♨Q🚌

Elterwater

Britannia Inn

LA22 9HP
⊙ 10-11; 12-10.30 Sun
☎ (015394) 37210 🌐 britinn.co.uk
Coniston Bluebird; Jennings Bitter; Taylor Landlord; guest beers Ⓗ
This 400-year-old pub overlooks the village green, which often acts as an overflow to the terraced patio (as pictured on the cover of the 2006 edition of this Guide). The entrance lobby, with seating, leads to the main bar and dining room (all no-smoking), and finally, the back room. Free from piped music, pool, games machines and TV, it offers home-made meals based on local produce; snacks are available during the afternoon. Sunday is quiz night. ♨Q❀🛏◑◗⛺🚌(516)P⍉

Foxfield

Prince of Wales

LA20 6BX (opp. station)
⊙ 2.45 (12 Fri & Sat)-11; closed Mon & Tue; 12-10.30 Sun
☎ (01229) 716238 🌐 princeofwalesfoxfield.co.uk
Beer range varies Ⓗ
Winner of numerous awards and current holder of Cumbria CAMRA Pub of the Year, this pub provides beers from all over England as well as from its two house breweries, Foxfield and Tigertops, always including a mild. The pub's location, next to a rural station and a bus stop, has helped make its regular themed mini beer festivals a great success. ♨Q❀🛏🛏⇌🚌(X7)♣P🍺

Gosforth

Gosforth Hall Hotel

CA20 1AZ

☼ 12-2.30, 4-midnight (varies winter, phone to check); 5-11 Sun

☎ (019467) 25322 ⊕ gosforthhallhotel.co.uk

Hawkshead Bitter; Theakston Best Bitter; Yates Fever Pitch Ⓗ

Full of history and character, this former pele tower and fortified farmhouse boasts the largest sandstone arch fireplace surviving in England and a 1673 crest in the bar. This comfortable, atmospheric hostelry offers an extensive menu and is completely no-smoking. The large, landscaped garden houses a boules pitch that hosts tournaments and runs a boules ladder from Easter until October. Do not be surprised to come across people in medieval costume – it means a banquet is in progress. ⌂Q❀⇌◑⊟⅄♣P⊬

Grasmere

Dale Lodge Hotel (Tweedies Bar)

Langdale Road, LA22 9SW

☼ 11-11 (midnight summer); 12-10.30 Sun

☎ (015394) 35300 ⊕ dalelodgehotel.co.uk

Beer range varies Ⓗ

At the centre of a popular tourist village, Tweedies derives its name from its former role as a woollen mill shop. The bar and no-smoking dining room have stone-flagged floors, wood furniture and a fine, wood-burning stove; meals are served in both rooms. At the rear is a games room. It usually offers a beer from Scotland and one from Taylors, but the range changes frequently. In summer the open top No. 599 runs between Grasmere and Bowness. ⌂❀⇌◑⊟●P⊬

Great Broughton

Punchbowl Inn

19 Main Street, CA13 0YJ (off A66)

☼ 7 (12 Fri & Sat)-11; 12-10.30 Sun

☎ (01900) 824708

Jennings Bitter; guest beers Ⓗ

Welcoming, traditional village pub, run by the same landlord for 30 years – it has featured in this Guide for most of them. The building dates back to the 17th-century. Pictures of local rugby league players cover the walls and a collection of water jugs hangs from the low ceiling behind the bar. The licensees are active fundraisers for a number of charities. ⌂♣

Great Langdale

Old Dungeon Ghyll Hotel

LA22 9JY

☼ 11-11; 12-10.30 Sun

☎ (015394) 37272 ⊕ odg.co.uk

Black Sheep Special; Jennings Cumberland Ale; Theakston XB, Old Peculier; Yates Bitter; guest beers Ⓗ

The Hikers bar adjoining the hotel is geared up for outdoor types, with its solid floor, bench seating and a kitchen range that is handy for drying wet clothing. The patio commands stunning views of the surrounding Langdale fells. Good, sturdy pub food is available, while the hotel has a more sedate bar and dining room (where booked meals are served at 7.30pm). The National Trust campsite opposite is open in summer. ⌂Q❀⇌◑⅄⊟(516)●P

Great Salkeld

Highland Drove Inn

CA11 9NA (off B6412, between A686 and Lazonby)

☼ 12-3 (not Mon), 6-midnight; 12-midnight Sat & Sun

☎ (01768) 898349 ⊕ highland-drove.co.uk

John Smith's Bitter; Theakston Black Bull Bitter; guest beer Ⓗ

Saved from closure in 1998, this popular 18th-century inn, on the old Scottish drovers route south, has been carefully extended and upgraded, while maintaining a traditional atmosphere. The owners have used local sandstone, reclaimed timber and exposed brickwork to lend an air of authenticity. Local CAMRA Pub of the Year 2005 and 2006 also boasts an award-winning restaurant. ⌂❀⇌◑⊟⅄♣P

Hallbankgate

Belted Will

CA8 2NJ (on A689 Alston road, 4 miles E of Brampton)

☼ 5 (12 Sat & Sun)-midnight

☎ (016977) 46236 ⊕ beltedwill.co.uk

Marston's Pedigree; guest beer Ⓗ

The unusual pub name comes from Lord William Howard of nearby Naworth Castle who was nicknamed Belted Will by Sir Walter Scott on account of the broad belt he wore. At the northern tip of the Pennines, the pub is ideally situated for all types of outdoor activities, including hiking, cycling, pony trekking, golf, fishing and birdwatching at the UK's largest inland RSPB reserve. Locals and tourists, drinkers and diners all receive a wam welcome here. ⌂❀⇌◑♣

Haverthwaite

Anglers Arms

LA12 8AJ (off A590, opp. steam railway)

☼ 11.30-midnight (1am Fri & Sat); 11.30-midnight Sun

☎ (015395) 31216

Copper Dragon Golden Pippin; Moorhouses Pride of Pendle, Pendle Witches Brew; Tetley Bitter; guest beers Ⓗ

Just off the main road, this pub caters for locals and tourists. The thriving back bar is a regulars' haunt while meals are served in the main lounge. With a good beer range – six more than listed here, including local brews and a dark mild – and regular beer festivals it is surely a contender for the prime real ale house in Furness. The decor features witches in the back bar, Furness railway memorabilia in the lounge and an electric train. ❀◑⊟⊟(X35)●

Hawkshead

King's Arms Hotel

Market Square, LA22 0NZ

☼ 11-11; 12-10.30 Sun

☎ (015394) 36372 ⊕ kingsarmshawkshead.co.uk

Coniston Bluebird; Hawkshead Bitter, seasonal

beers; guest beer Ⓗ
Cosy, often busy pub, dating back to Elizabethan times, in the same family for over 25 years. An unusual roof support comes in the form of a sculpture by local artist John Whitworth. A spacious dining room ensures that diners are unlikely to struggle to find a table, while additional outside seating overlooks the square. Beers are typically local and carry-outs are available. It stocks a fine selection of malts, cider in summer and serves 'draught' mulled wine in winter. ⛫❀⇌◑◐♿⛺●

Hesket Newmarket

Old Crown

CA7 8JG
⚙ 12-3 (not Mon & Tue), 5.30-11; 12-3, 7-10.30 Sun
☎ (016974) 78288 🌐 theoldcrownpub.co.uk
Hesket Newmarket Great Cockup Porter, Blencathra Bitter, Skiddaw Special, Doris's 90th Birthday Ale, Old Carrock Strong Ale Ⓗ
The pub always stocks the full range of Hesket Newmarket beers from the brewery situated in the barn at the rear. The pub belongs to a co-operative that was set up to ensure that it remained as the brewery tap. Voted eighth best pub in the country by the trade paper, Morning Advertiser, it was also local CAMRA's Pub of the Season, winter 2005. At the centre of the village the Old Crown has received several royal visitors. ⛫Q❀◑◐⛾⛺♣

Hoff

New Inn

CA16 6TA (on B6260)
⚙ 12 (7.30 Mon)-midnight; 12-midnight Sun
☎ (017683) 51317
Tirril Bewsher's Best Bitter; guest beers Ⓗ
A pub since 1823, although briefly converted to residential use, it made a welcome return as a village local in 2001. The bar area features a stone-flagged floor and oak furniture, with a raised fireplace at one end and a dining area at the other. The pump clips affixed to the black ceiling beams are a testament to the enthusiasm with which guest beers are sourced. Home-cooked meals are served Wednesday-Sunday. It hosts regular live music evenings – mostly folk and blues. ⛫Q❀⇌◑◐♿⛺♣P

Ings

Watermill Inn

LA8 9PY (off A591, turn by the church)
⚙ 12-11; 12-10.30 Sun
☎ (01539) 821309 🌐 watermillinn.co.uk
Black Sheep Best Bitter; Moorhouses Black Cat; Theakston Old Peculier; guest beers Ⓗ
Multi-award winning, family run mecca for real ale, sporting 16 handpumps: eight in the family-friendly bar and eight in the dog-friendly bar that has viewing windows into the cellar and new on-site brewery. Watermill's own beers and other local micros' products are regularly available, as well as an above average choice of draught and bottled continental beers. Bar meals are served most of the day, undisturbed by piped music, machines or TV. It hosts a monthly story telling evening (first Tue). ⛫Q⛱❀⇌◑◐♿🚌(555)♣●P⚟

Ireby

Lion

CA7 1EA (E of A595)
⚙ 12-3 (not Mon-Fri), 6-midnight; 12-3, 7-11 Sun
☎ (016973) 71460 🌐 irebythelion.co.uk
Beer range varies Ⓗ
A house ale, Iree-by, brewed by the award-winning Hesket Market Brewery is occasionally sold, complementing three other ales, with at least one from a Cumbrian brewer. The pub sits at the centre of a quiet rural town, which is really just a village with a market cross. It features wood panelling from local churches, but the bar came from a pub in Leeds. The Lion supplies beer for the annual folk festival in May. No meals are served Monday evening. ⛫Q❀◑◐♣

Kendal

Burgundy's Wine Bar

19 Lowther Street, LA9 4DH
⚙ 11.30-3.30 (not Mon-Wed), 6.30-11 (not Mon); 7-10.30 Sun
☎ (015397) 33803 🌐 burgundyswinebar.com
Yates Fever Pitch; guest beers Ⓗ
Town-centre bar on three levels, with games machines in the lower, seating in the upper and bar service in the middle. A wide range of draught and bottled continental lagers supplements the changing guest beers. The bar hosts the Cumbria Micros Beer Challenge and St George's Day celebrations each spring and stages weekly live jazz (Thu eve). Bus and train connections are nearby. ⇌●

Castle Inn

Castle Street, LA9 7AA
⚙ 11.30-11 (midnight Fri & Sat); 12-11 Sun
☎ (015397) 29983
Tetley Bitter; guest beers Ⓗ
Lying within walking distance of all the town-centre amenities, the Castle is a popular pub offering good value meals at lunchtime and lively evenings among the local commuity; it has a raised games area. The bar always offers a Dent and a Jennings beer as well as a guest. Notable features are the fish tank in the lounge wall and an original Duttons window in the bar. Nearby, the ruined castle was the birthplace of Catherine Parr. ❀◑⇌♣

Rifleman's Arms

4-6 Greenside, LA9 4LD
⚙ 6 (12 Fri-Sun)-midnight
☎ (015397) 23224
Caledonian Deuchars IPA; Tetley Bitter; guest beers Ⓗ
It is well worth the steep climb from the town centre to this 'village' local that stands opposite an impressive, tree scattered green. Very much at the heart of its edge of town community, the building occupies part of a 17th-century barn, which incorporates the original 'Postman Pat' post office with its

distinctive commemorative plaque. It hosts folk evenings (Thu) and a quiz on alternate Sundays. Families and their dogs are welcome. Pavement seats allow for some outside drinking. ✿♣

Keswick

Dog & Gun

2 Lake Road, CA12 5BT

✪ 11 (12 winter)-11 (11.30 Thu; midnight Fri & Sat); 12-11 Sun

☎ (017687) 73463

Theakston Best Bitter, Old Peculier; Yates Bitter; guest beers 🄷

Lively, yet cosy central pub, replete with flagstone floors and low beams. A chip-free zone, it is renowned for its Hungarian goulash and serves a good wine selection to accompany the varied menu. It supports the Keswick mountain rescue team, raising funds through its Thursday quiz; see the gallery of mountain climbing pictures around the walls. Well-behaved dogs are welcome. It is handy for the Theatre by the Lake and the Moot Hall. ♕◐▶⛺

Langwathby

Shepherds Inn

Village Green, CA10 1LW

(on A686, 5 miles NE of Penrith)

✪ 12-3, 6.30-11 (6-midnight summer); 12-midnight Sat; 12-3, 6.30-11 (12-midnight summer) Sun

☎ (01768) 881335 🌐 shepherds-inn.co.uk

Black Sheep Best Bitter; guest beer 🄷

On the green of a large village on the River Eden, this inn is frequented by regulars and tourists on the scenic Penrith-Alston road. Local attractions include an ostrich farm and Long Meg stone circle. The split-level interior comprises a bar down some stairs and an upper level that opens out onto an enclosed garden. The guest beer is often from a Scottish micro-brewery, while local produce is used extensively in the kitchen. Langwathby Station is on the Settle-Carlisle line. ♕✿🛏◐▶⇌♣P

Lazonby

Joiners Arms

Townfoot, CA10 1BL

(on B6413, 5 miles NE of Penrith)

✪ 11-12.30am (1.30am Fri & Sat); 11-12.30am Sun

☎ (01768) 898728

Hesket Newmarket Doris's 90th Birthday Ale; guest beer 🄷

A cottage built in the 18th century later became an ale house, then in 2004 the premises were refurbished by a local couple. The bar leads to a dining area where meals are mostly based on local produce, then down some steps to a games room or to the garden at the back. The village is well situated, overlooking the River Eden and is on the scenic Carlisle-Settle railway line. No lunches are served on Tuesday. ♕Q✿🛏◐▶⛺⇌♣

Leece

Copper Dog

LA12 0QP (3 miles E of Barrow in Furness, off A5087)

✪ 11.30-3, 5-11; 11.30-midnight Fri & Sat; 12-11 Sun

☎ (01229) 877088

Tetley Bitter; guest beers 🄷

Spacious village pub serving fresh food in the large dining area. It concentrates largely on its food trade, but does offer good ales, with two guests that change frequently, a varied wine list and a wide range of bottled beers. Diners can look out onto expansive country views. ♕QP◐▶🚌(10)P

Loweswater

Kirkstile Inn

CA13 0RU

(off B5289, 5 miles from Cockermouth via Lorton)

✪ 11-11; 11-10.30 Sun

☎ (01900) 85219 🌐 kirkstile.com

Coniston Bluebird; Loweswater Melbreak Bitter, Rannerdale; guest beers 🄷

Home of Loweswater Brewery, this Lakeland inn sits below Melbreak in a stunning setting 'twixt Loweswater and Crummock Water. Low ceilings and stone walls add character. Outdoor seating affords views across the Buttermere Valley. Totally no-smoking, it comprises a single bar with three seated areas, plus a restaurant serving good food. Local CAMRA's Pub of the Year 2003 to 2005 offers two Loweswater guest beers and another from Yates. ♕Q✿🛏◐▶♿P⊁⊍

Low Crosby

Stag Inn

Main Street, CA6 4QN (off A689)

✪ 12-3, 6-midnight (11-midnight Sat & Easter-Sept); 11-11 Sun

☎ (01228) 573210

Jennings Mild (summer), Bitter, Cumberland Ale, Sneck Lifter 🄷

Renowned locally for its good food and range of Jennings beers, the Stag stands on the Hadrian's Wall footpath at the centre of a peaceful village. Four rooms radiating off the bar all feature low, beamed ceilings and stone-flagged floors. The upstairs restaurant offers an extensive menu. Like much of the village, the Stag was badly affected by the devastating floods of January 2005, but that has not prevented it from becoming local CAMRA's runner-up Pub of the Year 2006. ♕✿◐▶🚌♿♣P⊁

Low Hesket

Rose & Crown

CA4 0HG (on A6 between Carlisle and Penrith)

✪ 12-3 (not Mon-Thu), 6-11.30 (midnight Fri & Sat); 12-3, 6.30-11 Sun

☎ (016974) 73346

Jennings Mild, Bitter, Cumberland Ale 🄷

Long-standing roadside inn, one of the few to have survived the M6 taking the traffic (and potential custom) away. It can get busy at mealtimes (Fri-Sun lunchtimes and Tue-Sun eves), but a good welcome is always assured. The walls are adorned with old-fashioned pictures on the theme of travel and transport, and some seating is provided by old coach seats. Although close to Carlisle, this is a quiet rural village, easy to find on the A6. ♕Q◐▶P

Milnthorpe

Cross Keys Hotel

1 Park Road, LA7 7AD

12-1am daily

☎ (015395) 62115 thecrosskeyshotel.co.uk

Robinson's Hartleys XB, Unicorn, Double Hop Ⓗ

Imposing, roadside hotel with an L-shaped bar, no-smoking dining room and an upstairs function suite. It is convenient for visiting Levens Hall, noted for its topiary garden, and the nearby Morecambe Bay coast, renowned for its shifting sands and views of the Lake District fells. A number code may be needed to exit the car park. ♔⇌ⒹⒹ♿⊟(555)P

Mungrisdale

Mill Inn

CA11 0XR (1½ miles N of A66)

11-11; 12-10.30 Sun

☎ (01768) 779632 the-millinn.co.uk

Jennings Bitter, Cumberland Ale; guest beer (summer) Ⓗ

Do not confuse this 17th-century coaching inn with the hotel next door. Ideally located for low and high level walks in the beautiful Lake District, it benefits from stunning views down the valley. Home-made food is all freshly prepared from local produce; award-winning pies are a speciality. In 2004 it was named Cumbrian Business of the Year – a fitting tribute to the hard work put in by the licensees to provide drink, food and accommodation of the highest standard. ♔❀⇌ⒹⒹ♣P⚡

Nether Wasdale

Screes Inn

CA20 1ET (E off A595, 5 miles NE of Ravenglass)

11-11; 12-10.30 Sun

☎ (019467) 26262 thescreesinnwasdale.com

Black Sheep Best Bitter; Coniston Bluebird; Yates Bitter; guest beer Ⓗ

Multi-level, multi-roomed country pub with a dining room. It hosts occasional live music – folk or jazz. Popular with walkers, it is a first-class source of real ale in this tiny hamlet, hidden deep in the heart of the national park, close to Wastwater, Great Gable and Scafell Pike. With the Strands (opposite) it jointly hosts the annual Wasdale Real Ale Festival. Home-cooked fare is based on local produce, with vegetarian choices and Sunday lunches served. ♔Q❀⇌ⒹⒹ⊟♿▲♣P⚡

Ousby

Fox Inn

CA10 1QA (2 miles S of A686 near Melmerby)

6-11; 12-3, 7-10.30 Sun

☎ (01768) 881374

Tirril Old Faithful; guest beer Ⓗ

After a period in the doldrums, opening just on Friday and Saturday evenings, new owners have transformed the Fox since taking over in 2004, twice extending the restaurant and refurbishing the bar and spacious lounge. Situated near the foot of Cross Fell on the northern Pennines, it is popular with those seeking the great outdoors. It has had its own static caravan site for many years, augmented in 2006 by a touring site for 20 vans. Sunday lunch is served. ♔⇌❀Ⓓ▲♣P

Penrith

Gloucester Arms

Great Dockray, CA11 7DE

11-11 (midnight Fri & Sat); 12-10.30 Sun

☎ (01768) 863745 gloucesterarms.co.uk

Greene King Old Speckled Hen; Taylor Landlord; guest beer Ⓗ

The oldest pub in Penrith, this welcoming, beamed inn with a warm, cosy atmosphere, claims historical links to Richard III. Traditional bar meals are served throughout the pub, which has a no-smoking drinking area and restaurant serving excellent home-cooked food. Large parties are welcome to book meals and Sunday lunch is served here. ♔❀ⒹⒹ⊟⇌P⚡

Lowther Arms

3 Queen Street, CA11 7XD

11-11 (midnight Fri & Sat); 11.30-3, 6-10.30 Sun

☎ (01768) 862792

Theakston Best Bitter, seasonal beers; guest beers Ⓗ

Coaching inn off the old A6 route, it has recently been extended, but without compromising the building; this gives a slight step between the levels. A past winner of various awards from CAMRA and In Bloom competitions, it can be busy at mealtimes, but is always welcoming. Drinkers are spoilt for choice, with a range of up to eight real ales usually available. ♔QⒹⒹ⇌

Pooley Bridge

Sun Inn

CA10 2NN

12-11; 12-10.30 Sun

☎ (017684) 86205

Jennings Bitter, Cumberland Ale, Sneck Lifter, seasonal beers Ⓗ

The pub enjoys a brisk dining trade in its no-smoking, wood-panelled top bar and an equally steady liquid one in the more basic lower bar. It also has a no-smoking dining room and a large, safe garden that is well used in summer by families, often with their dogs. A short walk away the steamer pier on Ullswater offers popular summer trips to Patterdale at the other end of the lake. ♔Q❀⇌ⒹⒹ⊟▲⊟(108)♣P⚡

Ravenglass

Ratty Arms

CA18 1SN (through mainline station)

11-midnight; 12-midnight Sun

☎ (01229) 717676

Greene King Ruddles Best; Jennings Bitter; Theakston Best Bitter; guest beers Ⓗ

Railway-themed pub on Ravenglass Station platform, in a former station building at the junction of two railways: mainline passengers can cross the line and transfer to the La'al Ratty for narrow gauge steam trains running deep into pretty Eskdale. Added attractions are a railway museum, visitor shop and play area, with Muncaster Castle, a Roman bathhouse and a pretty tidal inlet, rich in wildlife, all nearby. Excellent, good value food is served all day and two guest beers are usually stocked. ♨Q♉❀◑♿▲⇌P⚟

Ravenstonedale

King's Head Inn

CA17 4NH (village signed off A685)

⏲ 11 (6 winter Mon & Tue)-midnight; 11-midnight Sun

☎ (015396) 23284 🌐 kings-head.net

Black Sheep Best Bitter; guest beers Ⓗ

The enthusiasm for real ale here can be detected in the array of pump clips and guest beer lists in the cosy bar area. Down some steps is a games room; to the left is a lounge and large dining room, both no-smoking. Note the huge collection of water jugs. Upstairs a former courtroom is now used for meetings. The beckside garden is a haven for red squirrels. The Settle-Carlisle railway line passes through Kirkby Stephen West Station nearby. ♨Q❀⛟◑▲♣●P⚟

Rosthwaite

Scafell Hotel

CA12 5XB

⏲ 11-11; 11-10.30 Sun

☎ (017687) 77208 🌐 scafell.co.uk

Black Sheep Best Bitter; Theakston Best Bitter, XB, Old Peculier; guest beers H

Traditional country hotel in the heart of the Lake District. Real ales are served in the large Riverside Bar, which has a pool table at one end. Popular with walkers, dogs are welcome. Guest ales – two at busy times – are usually from local breweries and there is a choice of more than 60 malt whiskies. Meals are served in the bar or the formal dining room in the main building. ♨❀⛟◑▲P⚟

Rydal

Glen Rothay Hotel (Badger Bar)

LA22 9LR

⏲ 11-11; 11-10.30 Sun

☎ (015394) 34500

Beer range varies Ⓗ

Roadside inn dating from 1624, full of rustic charm, with beams, oak panels and elaborate fireplaces. The bar area has bench seating and copper-topped tables, while a cosy side room has alcove seating and armchairs. The beers are usually from local breweries. Meals are served in the bar and impressive dining room, from where you may see badgers in the grounds in the evening – the animals feature in the decor. Ideally placed for gentle walks and visiting Rydal Mount – Wordsworth's last home. ♨❀⛟◑🚌(555)P

St Bees

Manor House Hotel

11-12 Main Street, CA27 0DE

⏲ 12-2 (not winter Mon), 4-11; 12-11 Fri-Sun

☎ (01946) 822425 🌐 stbees.org.uk

Greene King Old Speckled Hen; guest beers Ⓗ

Converted, 18th-century manor house in a pleasant coastal village where local attractions include an imposing early 12th-century priory, sandy beaches, cliffs with nesting seabirds and the starting point of the Coast-to-Coast walk. The bar (named after Wainwright's walk) is popular with villagers and visitors alike and the landlord regularly changes the two guest beers. Good food is served in both bars and the restaurant (no meals Mon). ♨Q❀⛟◑⊟▲⇌♣P

Santon Bridge

Bridge Inn

CA19 1UX (off A595) OS11106

⏲ 11-11; 12-10.30 Sun

☎ (019467) 26221 🌐 santonbridgeinn.com

Jennings Bitter, Cumberland Ale, Cocker Hoop, Sneck Lifter, seasonal beers Ⓗ

Home of the immensely popular World's Biggest Liar competition, this pub has a wealth of charm and history, with creaking floors, low beams and warming fires. In summer, you can relax outside by the river, taking in the lovely mountain and woodland views in a still, peaceful atmosphere. Tasty, home-cooked food and a comprehensive range of Jennings beers makes this historic but homely pub well worth a visit. ♨Q❀⛟◑▲P⚟

Satterthwaite

Eagle's Head

LA12 8LN (4 miles S of Hawkshead)

⏲ 12-3.30 (not Mon), 7-11; 12-2.30, 6.30-11 Fri & Sat; 12-2.30, 7-10.30 Sun

☎ (01229) 860237

Barngates Cat Nap; Hawkshead Bitter; Theakston Best Bitter Ⓗ

The road from Hawkshead to Satterthwaite winds through the Grizedale Forest. This building, which dates from the late 15th century, has been a watering-hole since the 16th century. A warm, welcoming and comfortable country inn, it attracts locals, walkers and holidaymakers for good food and ale. The house beer, Eagleshead, is brewed by Moorhouses. The pub is often closed early in the week in winter – phone to check. ♨Q❀⛟◑▲P

Seathwaite

Newfield Inn

LA20 6ED (7 miles N of Broughton in Furness) OS227950

⏲ 11-11; 12-10.30 Sun

☎ (01229) 716208 🌐 newfieldinn.co.uk

Caledonian Deuchars IPA; Jennings Cumberland Ale; Theakston Old Peculier; guest beer Ⓗ

A fell walkers' oasis, this free house in the tiny hamlet of Seathwaite in the Duddon Valley prides itself on serving both good food and quality ales. Meals are served 12-9pm daily. Situated in Wordsworth's favourite valley, this unspoilt pub has welcomed travellers since the 17th century and boasts a noteworthy slate floor in the main bar and a riotous history. ♨Q♉❀◑⊟▲♣P⚟

Shap

Greyhound Hotel

Main Street, CA10 3PW (on A6)
⌚ 11-11; 12-10.30 Sun
☎ (019317) 16474 🌐 greyhoundhotel.co.uk
Jennings Bitter, Cumberland Ale; Tetley Bitter; guest beers Ⓗ
Imposing roadhouse, entered through a revolving door to a spacious bar offering a variety of drinking and seating areas. Of particular note is the wall-mounted, large-scale copy of Wainwright's famous map of Westmorland. There is a no-smoking dining room and a games room. Bunkhouse accommodation is popular with walkers on the Coast-to-Coast route. Easily accessible from junction 39 of the M6.
⛫Q❀⇌◐◑♿⛺🚌(106/7)♣P

Stainton

Stagger Inn

Long Lane, LA13 0NN
⌚ 12-2.30, 5.30-11; 12-11 Fri & Sat, 12-10.30 Sun
☎ (01229) 462504
Coniston Bluebird; Hawkshead Bitter, seasonal beers; Jennings Cumberland Ale Ⓗ
Stunning, country village pub dating from the 18th-century that underwent extensive refurbishment in November 2004, resulting in a blend of old features and modern luxury. Beer here is reasonably priced and the food is excellent, with lunchtime and early evening offers. The smartly attired staff are attentive and friendly. The delightful landscaped garden is a bonus.
⛫❀◐◑♿🚌(11)⚡

Staveley

Eagle & Child Hotel

Kendal Road, LA8 9LP
⌚ 11-11; 12-10.30 Sun
☎ (015398) 21320 🌐 eaglechildinn.co.uk
Beer range varies Ⓗ
The three-sided bar area displays an abundance of memorabilia, and offers a variety of seating arrangements. Up to five ales are normally supplied by northern micro-breweries, while good value food includes special offers during the week. The function room is in the style of a medieval banqueting hall. It has a garden at the rear and another across the road, with river frontage where bank holiday beer festivals are staged. The Kentmere Valley nearby is popular with walkers. ⛫❀⇌◐◑⛺🚌(555)♣🍎P

Strawberry Bank

Masons Arms

LA11 6NW OS413895
⌚ 11.30-11; 12-10.30 Sun
☎ (015395) 68486 🌐 strawberrybank.com
Black Sheep Best Bitter; Hawkshead Bitter; Taylor Landlord; guest beer Ⓗ
Picturesque pub set in the Lyth Valley. Famous for a large bottled beer range, one of its draught ales is always from the local Hawkshead Brewery. No-smoking throughout, two solid fuel ranges and three seating areas make this a great pub for winter drinking, while a large patio with heaters allows an extended outdoor summer season. The meals here are above average in quality. ⛫Q❀⇌◐◑P⚡

Talkin

Blacksmith's Arms

CA8 1LE (3 miles S of Brampton, left off B6413)
⌚ 12-3, 6-11 daily
☎ (016977) 3452 🌐 blacksmithsarmstalkin.co.uk
Jennings Cumberland Ale; Yates Bitter; guest beer Ⓗ
One of the most popular pubs in the area, the Blackies has for many years enjoyed a reputation for good food and beer in convivial, relaxed surroundings, be it in the bar, lounge, garden room or Old Forge restaurant. Local amenities include Brampton golf course, Talkin Tarn country park and, a few miles further on, Hadrian's Wall. Many other country pursuits are possible locally as the pub lies on the fringe of an area of outstanding natural beauty. ⛫Q❀⇌◐◑⛺P⚡

Tallentire

Bush Inn

CA13 0PT
⌚ 12-3 (not Mon-Thu), 6-midnight (not Mon); 12-11 Sun
☎ (01900) 823707
Jennings Bitter; guest beers Ⓗ
Reopened in 2005 under the stewardship of experienced and welcoming licensees from an award-winning Fylde pub, the Bush is a thriving hub, hosting inter-village darts matches and a Sunday quiz. The Grade II listed building with stone-flagged bar area has been refurbished but retains its traditional appearance and standards. A former coaching inn and ex-State Management outlet, it always offers two guest beers from a wide area, invariably micro-brewery products. The restaurant is a recent addition. Q❀♣P

Tirril

Queen's Head Inn

CA10 2JF
⌚ 12-3, 6-midnight; 12-midnight Fri & Sat; 12-10.30 Sun
☎ (017688) 63219 🌐 queensheadinn.co.uk
Tirril Bewsher's Best, Brougham Ale, Old Faithful, Academy Ale Ⓗ
This venerable building has been much adapted over the years, but retains the best of its original features. The part-flagged, part timber-floored front bar boasts massive beams and an award-winning inglenook; the back bar houses a pool table and juke box. The multi-level dining room was converted from separate dwellings. In August it hosts a Cumbrian beer and sausage festival, offering a score each of bangers and ales. A beer from another brewery is added in summer.
⛫❀⇌◐◑⊟♣P

Uldale

Snooty Fox

CA7 1HA
⌚ 6.30 (6 Fri)-11; 12-2, 6.30-10.30 Sun

☎ (016973) 71479
Beer range varies 🄷
When it first opened, the pub was called the George and Dragon; the name change occurred in the 1980s. The house beer Uld Ale is brewed by the famous Hesket Newmarket Brewery and three guests can be sampled in both bars. An ideal base for exploring the area known as 'Back o' Skiddaw' and the Caldbeck Fells, it is also close to the Solway coast. Meals are freshly prepared from local produce at Solway CAMRA's Pub of the Season spring 2005. ♨❀🛏◐◑⊟♿♣P

Ulverston

Farmers Arms
Market Place, LA12 7BA
⏲ 10-11; 10-10.30 Sun
☎ (01229) 584469 🌐 farmersrestaurant-thelakes.co.uk
Yates Sun Goddess; guest beers 🄷
Busy, pub, serving good quality meals and snacks, both in the upper level restaurant and the bar area. A good choice of wines and coffee complements the six cask ales. The front terrace, complete with heaters and a canopy, overlooks the activity of the town centre, ideal for watching the world go by. The pub stages a weekly quiz on Thursday. ❀◐◑⛺⇌🚌(6)

King's Head
14 Queen Street, LA12 7AF
⏲ 11.30-11 (midnight Fri & Sat); 12-10.30 Sun
☎ (01229) 588064
Jennings Bitter, Cumberland Ale, Cocker Hoop, Sneck Lifter; guest beers 🄷
Quiet, town-centre former coaching inn, dating from the 17th century, where the garden with its own bowling green at the rear is a true oasis on a hot summer's day. Recent renovations revealed an original well in the dining area, now illuminated beneath a glass floor. Good value meals and good conversation are assured. ❀🛏◐◑⛺⇌🚌(6)♣

Waberthwaite

Brown Cow Inn
LA19 5YJ (2 miles SE of Ravenglass on A595)
⏲ 11.30-11.30 (12.30am Fri & Sat); 12-11.30 Sun
☎ (01229) 717243 🌐 browncowinn.com
Beckstones Iron Town; Jennings Cumberland Ale; Theakston Best Bitter; guest beer 🄷
Once a farm and barn on the old packhorse route between Bootle and Ulpha, visitors are welcome at this community-focused pub where they will find a friendly atmosphere. An open-plan arrangement allows ample space for traditional games, and there is a no-smoking snug next to the dining room, where home-cooked food incorporates local produce, with Chinese and Indian dishes a speciality. The four ales vary, but local breweries Jennings and Beckstones are normally represented. ♨Q❀🛏◐◑⊟♣P🚭⊔

Wasdale Head

Wasdale Head Inn
CA20 1EX (E off A595 at Gosforth) OS187087
⏲ 11-11; 12-10.30 Sun
☎ (019467) 26229 🌐 wasdale.com
Great Gable Liar, Great Gable, Burnmoor Pale, Wasd'ale, Illgill IPA, Yewbarrow 🄷
Majestically situated at the foot of England's highest mountains and well off the main roads, deep in Wasdale, past Wastwater, this famous pub is a wonderful centre for walking and climbing. It was once the abode of Will Ritson, raconteur and the World's Biggest Liar. Now the home of Great Gable Brewery, a comprehensive range of its beers is served in the walkers' bar, while home-cooked food in the bar and restaurant is based on local produce. ♨Q♉❀🛏◐◑⊟⛺♣P🚭⊔

Westnewton

Swan Inn
CA7 3PQ (from Aspatria take B5301 N)
⏲ 6-11 (not Wed; opens 12-2 Fri & Sat summer); 12-2, 6-11 Sun
☎ (016973) 20627 🌐 theswaninnwestnewton.co.uk
Yates Fever Pitch, Sun Goddess 🄷
The beer at the Swan does not have far to travel, as it is brewed in the village. A Yates guest may supplement the regular ales on occasion. The pub comprises a bar with a pool table and a restaurant where meals prepared from locally sourced ingredients are served; no meals are available on Tuesday. The Swan also has two guest rooms. ♨🛏◑♣

Whitehaven

Bransty Arch
Bransty Row, CA28 7XE (opp. Tesco)
⏲ 9am-midnight (1am Fri & Sat); 12-10.30 Sun
☎ (01946) 517640
Greene King Abbot; Marston's Burton Bitter, Pedigree; guest beers 🄷
Spacious, split-level pub, this popular Wetherspoon's outlet offers a staggering 15 real ales at all times, including a good selection of Jennings beers and guests from around the country. Beer festivals are held several times a year. The licensee and staff are evidently committed to real ale. Lying close to the attractive harbour and convenient for the station, this pub can get busy at weekends and in the evening. ◐◑♿⇌🍎

Winton

Bay Horse Inn
CA17 4HS (village is signed off A685)
⏲ 12-3 (not Mon), 6-midnight; 12-3, 6-11.30 Sun
☎ (017683) 71451
Beer range varies 🄷
Overlooking the green, this is a fine example of a traditional, privately owned, village local. Farmhouse-style doors lead into the stone-flagged bar area, where dogs are welcome, and on to a raised games room at the rear. An adjoining room, with a small bar counter, is set out for dining, while a further room, featuring an unusual fireplace, provides additional space. The beer is usually from Hawkshead, Titanic or Fuller's, plus one or two changing guests. ♨Q❀🛏◐◑🍎P

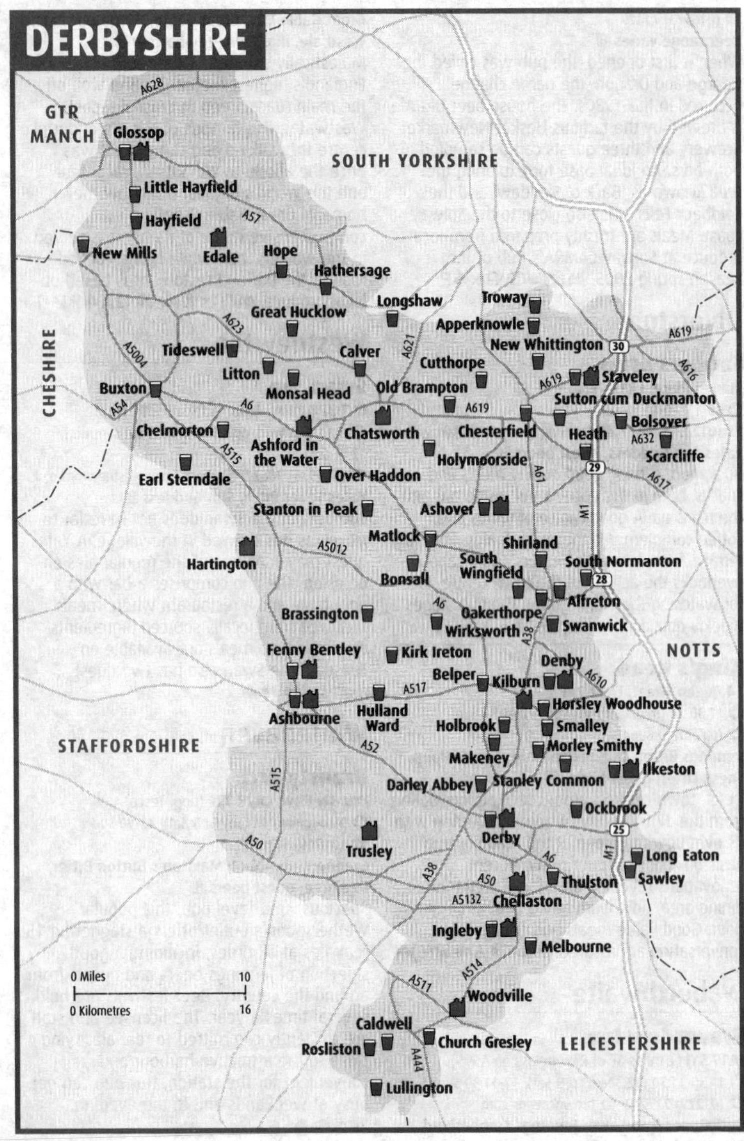

Alfreton

Victoria Inn

80 Nottingham Road, DE55 7EL (on B600)
1 (12 Sat)-11; 12-10.30 Sun
☎ (01773) 520156
Taylor Landlord; guest beers Ⓗ
Extensively refurbished, busy but friendly two-roomed local served by a central bar. The lounge features an illuminated aquarium, while pump clips of previously featured beers are displayed on beams in the public bar, which has a pool table and Sky TV. Guest beers change regularly and showcase local micro-breweries; a summer beer festival is held. The outdoor terrace houses long alley skittles. Alfreton Town football ground is nearby. Catch the No. 91 or 92 Derby-Mansfield bus or Red Arrow.

Apperknowle

Barrack Hotel

Barrack Road, S18 4AU (off main road to Unstone)
6-midnight (1am Fri); 12-3, 7-1am Sat; 12-4, 8 (7 summer)-midnight Sun
☎ (01246) 416555
Tetley Bitter; guest beers Ⓗ
Situated high above the Drone Valley and enjoying spectacular panoramic views, this mid 19th-century stone building has been carefully refurbished, retaining part of the original bar facade. Guest beers are usually from local micro-breweries. All cooked food is home prepared: lunchtime meals are restricted to the weekend; evening meals are available until 8pm, Tuesday-Saturday (book for Sat). The name is a reference to the ancient practice of bear baiting – 'the

Barracking Bear', rather than a nearby military installation. ❀♣◑🚌♣P

Ashbourne

Green Man & Black's Head Royal Hotel

St Johns Street, DE6 1GH

⌚ 11-11; 12-11 Sun

☎ (01335) 345783

Draught Bass; Leatherbritches Ashbourne Ale, seasonal beers; Marston's Pedigree; guest beers Ⓗ

Warmly praised by Boswell in his famous biography of Samuel Johnson, the Green Man has retained its old gallows sign across Ashbourne's main street. A rambling 300-year-old coaching inn with stone steps from a cobbled yard, it is warmed by open fires in winter. Nearby the ball is 'turned up' for the start of the Royal Shrovetide football game and mementos feature throughout. Local breweries are showcased and an August bank holiday beer festival is held.

♨Q❀🛏◑🍽♿🚌(ONE, 109)⚡

Ashover

Old Poets' Corner

1 Butts Road, S45 0EW

⌚ 12-2.30, 5-11; 12-11 Fri & Sat; 12-10.30 Sun

☎ (01246) 590888 🌐 oldpoets.co.uk

Greene King Abbot; Ⓗ/Ⓖ **Taylor Landlord; guest beers** Ⓗ

Beautiful, mock-Tudor building with open fires, hop-strewn oak beams, church pews and candlelit tables, creating a relaxed atmosphere. Eight handpumps serve three house beers (one from Tower) plus a range from regional and micro-breweries (usually including one strong dark ale), ciders, Belgian beers and fruit wines. Local CAMRA Pub of the Year 2006, this enterprising establishment hosts regular live music, poetry readings, folk evenings, a weekly quiz and three seasonal beer festivals a year.

♨Q❀🛏◑♿⛺♣🍎P

Belper

Cross Keys

Market Place, DE56 1FZ

⌚ 12-11; 12-10.30 Sun

☎ (01773) 599191

Bateman Mild, XB, XXXB, seasonal beers; Draught Bass; guest beer Ⓗ

This early 19th-century pub was formerly used as accommodation for visiting theatre troupes, and as a meeting place for Druids and Oddfellows. It has also witnessed at least one murder! Two-roomed, with a central bar, the pub has enjoyed a renaissance since being bought by Bateman, all of whose beers have proved popular locally; regular beer festivals are held. Bar billiards and shove-ha'penny are played. ♨Q❀🍽♿⇌🚌♣

Queen's Head

29 Chesterfield Road, DE56 1FF

⌚ 4 (12 Fri & Sat)-11; 12-10.30 Sun

☎ (01773) 825525 🌐 thequeenshead.freeuk.com

Caledonian Deuchars IPA; Tetley Bitter, Burton Ale; guest beers Ⓗ

Built during the Victorian era, this popular roadside inn comprises three rooms with a central bar, an upstairs function room and a pleasant patio area, providing panoramic views over the town and countryside. The public bar has a real fire and old photographs of Belper. Reputedly haunted, the pub hosts regular themed beer festivals, quizzes and entertainment, usually blues or folk, at the weekends. It is a short walk from the market place. ♨Q❀🍽🚌♣🍎

Bolsover

Blue Bell

57 High Street, S44 6HF

⌚ 12-3, 6.30-11; 12-3, 7-10.30 Sun

☎ (01246) 823508 🌐 bolsover.uk.com

Camerons Strongarm; guest beers Ⓗ

This family-run, former coaching inn retains the low, oak beamed ceiling in its two main drinking areas. The garden sits atop a crumbling cliff face, affording panoramic views across to the Peak District. Look out for the 'Neglected Shed' beer festivals held in the ancient stables, and the knights in armour who can provide unusual entertainment after a hard day dashing around the neighbouring castle grounds. An excellent range of quality guest beers makes every visit worthwhile. Q🚂🚌♣P

Bonsall

Barley Mow

The Dale, DE4 2AY

⌚ 6-11; closed Mon; 12-midnight Sat; 12-11 Sun

☎ (01629) 825685 🌐 barleymowbonsall.co.uk

Greene King Abbot; Whim Hartington Bitter; guest beers (occasional) Ⓗ

With its cellar hewn out of the solid rock behind, this 17th-century pub is always full of surprises. Live music on Saturday evening and events such as world hen races, UFO spotting, marrow dressing and the landlord's guided walks make this one of the most fascinating

INDEPENDENT BREWERIES

Bottle Brook Kilburn
Brunswick Derby
Danelaw Chellaston
Derby Derby
Derventio Trusley
Edale Edale
Falstaff Derby
Funfair Ilkeston
Haywood Bad Ram Ashbourne
Howard Town Glossop
Leadmill Denby
Leatherbritches Fenny Bentley
Old Poets Ashover
Peak Ales Chatsworth
Spire Staveley
John Thompson Ingleby
Thornbridge Ashford in the Water
Tollgate Woodville
Townes Staveley
Whim Hartington

pubs in the area. The excellent food is always interesting and varied. ♨Q✿◑◐▲

King's Head

62 Yeoman Street, DE4 2AA

⏲ 12-2.30 (not Mon), 6.30-midnight; 12-2.30, 7-midnight Sun

☎ (01629) 822703

Bateman Valiant, XB, seasonal beers; guest beers Ⓗ

The King's Head is generally accepted as being the oldest inn in Bonsall and said to date back to 1649 (Charles I lost his head). The current premises were built in 1677 and are steeped in history. The first innkeeper, John Abell, engraved his name on a wooden beam that can be seen just inside the entrance to the pub, when his first son was born. This is one of a handful of Bateman's houses in Derbyshire. ♨Q✿◑◐P⊬

Brassington

Olde Gate Inne

Well Street, DE4 4HJ (off A5023)

⏲ 12-2.30, 6-11; 12-3, 7-10.30 Sun

☎ (01629) 540448

Marston's Pedigree, seasonal beers; guest beer Ⓗ

Family-run, ivy-clad gem, built in 1616, now Grade II listed and reputedly haunted. Oak beams feature throughout, with gleaming copper utensils hanging around three open fireplaces. The main bar boasts pewter jugs and a black-leaded range, while a pipe rack in the snug dates from the 17th century. An extensive menu includes home-cooked dishes and game in season (no food Mon eve). Boules is played here. The tourist attraction of Carsington Water is nearby. No children under 10 are admitted.
♨Q✿◑◐♿▲♣P⊬

Buxton

Baker's Arms

26 West Road, SK17 6HF

⏲ 11-3, 6 (4 Fri)-midnight; 12-midnight Sat & Sun

☎ (01298) 24404 🌐 uk-sites.com/bakersarmsbuxton

Marston's Burton Bitter, Pedigree; guest beers Ⓗ

Small, friendly, two-room town-centre pub entered via a welcoming porch. The simple bench seating and small tables surround a central L-shaped bar. If you are confident in playing in confined spaces, you can try a game of darts, just one of many sports supported by the pub. The success of the pub teams can be judged from the impressive contents of the trophy cabinet. Regular guest beers come from the Marston's range. ✿▲⇌▣♣

Buckingham Hotel (Ramsey's Bar)

1 Burlington Road, SK17 9AS

⏲ 12-2, 6-midnight; 12-3, 6-midnight Sun

☎ (01298) 70481 🌐 buckinghamhotel.co.uk

Thornbridge Jaipur IPA; Wells Bombardier; guest beers Ⓗ

An extensive, friendly hotel with an outstanding public bar that feels like a well-appointed gentlemen's club. A range of interesting beers, usually from independent and micro-breweries, makes the bar popular with real ale drinkers. The name stems from the fact that number one Burlington Road used to be the studio and home of noted local artist George Ramsey. The food here is recommended. ✿🛏◑◐♿▲⇌▣P

George Hotel

The Square, SK17 6AZ

⏲ 11-12.30am daily

☎ (01298) 24711

Kelham Island Pale Rider; guest beers Ⓗ

Centrally located and spacious inside, the George continues to make friends and expand its trade. Always bustling, especially in the evenings when live music is a regular feature, there is a constantly-changing range of guest beers. Outdoor drinking is possible in summer on the pleasant patio. The good, home-cooked lunches are highly recommended. Regular beer festivals are a recent introduction. ♨✿◑▲⇌▣♣

Caldwell

Royal Oak

Main Street, DE12 6RR

⏲ 11-midnight (1am Fri & Sat); 11-midnight Sun

☎ (01283) 761486

Marston's Pedigree; guest beers Ⓗ

This friendly, 18th-century free house is a genuine community pub. There is a small, narrow bar with a low, beamed ceiling at the front, and stairs leading to a smart split-level lounge with an open fire and beamed ceiling. The latter was recently renovated by customers to recreate its mid 20th-century look. Cyclists and ramblers are welcome, as are families in the lower part of lounge. Occasional themed food evenings are held. Locally-made preserves and honey can be bought. Limited parking. ♨✿⊟▲♣P

Calver

Bridge Inn

Calver Bridge, S32 3XA (on A623)

⏲ 11.30-3 (3.30 Sat), 5.30-11; 12-3.30, 7-10.30 Sun

☎ (01433) 630415

Hardys & Hansons Bitter, Olde Trip, seasonal beers Ⓗ

Sturdy, stone pub with a room on either side of the central bar area. Both rooms are comfortably furnished and feature collections of local guide books, some antique fire-fighting equipment and an array of hats. The long-standing landlord has won awards from the brewery. The pub boasts a pleasant garden overlooking the River Derwent and Arkwright's Calver Mill, now converted into apartments. No evening meals are served on Monday or winter Sunday. ♨Q✿◑◐♿▲▣P⊬🍷

Chelmorton

Church Inn

Main Street, SK17 9SL

⏲ 12-3.30, 6.30-11 (11-11 summer Sat); 12-3, 7-10.30 (12-10.30 summer) Sun

☎ (01298) 85319 🌐 thechurchinn.co.uk

Marston's Burton Bitter, Pedigree; guest beers Ⓗ

Set in beautiful surroundings opposite the church, this village pub caters for both walkers and locals alike. Even though the main room is laid out with dining tables, and good, home-cooked, food is on offer, a cosy pub atmosphere is maintained. The low ceiling and welcoming fire make this an excellent pub serving great beer. There is a pleasant outdoor area for summer drinking. Guest accommodation is now available

Chesterfield

Derby Tup

387 Sheffield Road, Whittington Moor, S41 8LS

11.30-3, 5-11; 11.30-11 Fri & Sat; 12-10.30 Sun

☎ (01246) 454316

Bateman XXXB; Burton Bridge Top Dog Stout; Copper Dragon Golden Pippin; Everards Original; Taylor Landlord; guest beers H

No frills Tynemill pub offering a good selection of beers, real cider and continental bottles. Split into three rooms, all of which bear frosted windows harking back to the days when the pub was called the Brunswick Hotel, the larger public bar features a collection of framed pump clips. The back room and small snug are no-smoking. It offers a good value lunchtime menu and hosts a Sunday quiz. Q

Market Hotel

New Square, S40 1AH

11-11; 7.30-10.30 Sun

☎ (01246) 541691

Greene King Abbot; Marston's Pedigree; Taylor Landlord; Tetley Bitter; guest beers H

Located in the town centre, with views of New Square market place, this is a busy, but friendly local. Traditionally furnished with historic photographs of the area, flagstone floors and wooden fittings, the pub comprises a single L-shaped room with a central bar. For the moment, smoking is permitted in all areas. Reasonably-priced lunches are served. Popular with all ages, it can get crowded on market days and weekend evenings

Peacock

412 Chatsworth Road, Brampton, S40 3BQ (on A619)

12-4, 5.30-11; 12-11 Fri & Sat; 12-10.30 Sun

☎ (01246) 275115

Adnams Broadside; Black Sheep Best Bitter; Caledonian Deuchars IPA; Tetley Bitter; guest beer H

Popular, friendly two-room pub with an open fire in the lounge. The central bar offers a good selection of real ales, including a guest beer. To the rear is a large garden ideal for families in summer, with an additional seating area at the front. Entertainment includes darts, dominoes, a Monday evening quiz and a folk night most Thursdays. It has the distinction of winning both local and Derbyshire CAMRA Pub of the Year 2005. Q

Portland Hotel

West Bars, S40 1AY

9am-midnight (1am Fri & Sat); 9am-midnight Sun

☎ (01246) 245410

Greene King Abbot; Marston's Burton Bitter, Pedigree; Theakston Best Bitter; guest beers H

The larger of two Wetherspoon establishments in town, just off the smaller market square, it is understandably busy on market days. Formerly a railway hotel, it is now a Wetherspoon lodge with accommodation. It offers a wide range of beers, often showcasing Wentworth Brewery, and food with themed evening menus on Tuesday (steaks), Wednesday (Chinese) and Thursday (curry). Q P

Red Lion

570 Sheffield Road, Whittington Moor, S41 8LX

12-11; 12-10.30 Sun

☎ (01246) 450770

Old Mill Mild, Bitter, Bullion, seasonal beers H

Traditional two-roomed pub served by a central bar. This southernmost outlet for Old Mill beers is also one of Chesterfield's few regular stockists of a cask mild. The interior has some attractive stained glass and the walls are decorated with interesting local pictures including photographs of the old trams that used to pass by. There is a wide-screen TV in the public bar and occasional live music is hosted. P

Royal Oak

1 The Shambles, S40 1PX (accessed by walkway from Market Place)

11-11 (7 Mon & Tue); closed Sun

☎ (01246) 237700

Caledonian Deuchars IPA; Greene King Abbot; Stones Bitter; guest beers H

Located in the Shambles area, this is said to be the town's oldest pub, first licensed in 1772. Made up of two distinct buildings, the older is reputed to date back to the 16th century. The two bars are accessible by separate entrances but both are served by a central bar on two levels. The top bar is no-smoking and has an impressive high ceiling and exposed roof timbers. A range of up to six cask ales is available.

Church Gresley

Rising Sun

77 Church Street, DE11 9NR

12-midnight; 12-11 Sun

☎ (01283) 217274

Draught Bass; Marston's Pedigree H

Built by Bass in 1889 and one of the last inns to incorporate stables, this lively free house stands near Gresley Rovers football ground. It consists of an L-shaped drinking area, with an arch linking a busy public bar to a marginally quieter lounge and another small lounge beyond. Features include an unusual porch, bar tops inlaid with around 6,500 old pennies, and an old red telephone box. A function room upstairs boasts impressive carved oak beams.

Cutthorpe

Gate Inn

Overgreen, S42 7BA

11.30-11; 12-10.30 (Sun)

☎ (01246) 276923

Black Sheep Best Bitter; Caledonian Deuchars

IPA; Fuller's London Pride; guest beer 🄷
Large, isolated rural pub commanding spectacular views over the surrounding countryside. Situated atop the picturesque Cordwell Valley and ideally suited for walkers, the pub, built from the local gritstone, features an L-shaped bar serving four well-kept ales (endorsed by Mr Fuller himself!), a welcoming open fire and two well-appointed dining rooms. Bar snacks are available at lunchtimes while the excellent evening meals feature home-prepared ingredients from local suppliers. Diners with specific dietary requirements (e.g. coeliacs) are catered for.
⛬❀◑◗♿⛺P

Darley Abbey

Abbey Inn

Darley Street, DE22 1DX
⏲ 11.30-2.30, 6-11; 12-11 Sat; 12-10.30 Sun
☎ (01332) 558297
Samuel Smith OBB 🄷
This erstwhile, 15th-century guesthouse is all that remains of the Augustinian Abbey of St Mary De Pratis, the most powerful abbey in Middle England before the Dissolution. Rescued from long neglect in 1978, it won a national award for the conversion to its present use. The upper level bar is reached by an impressive stone spiral staircase and boasts original church pews for seats. This complements a lower-level bar, with stone-flagged floor and roaring fire. Darley Park is nearby. ⛬Q❀◑◗▢♣P

Derby

Leadmill Old Stables Bar

Park Hall, Park Hall Road, DE5 8PX (off B6179)
⏲ 5 (12 Sat)-11; closed Mon-Thu; 12-10.30 Sun
☎ (01332) 883577 🌐 leadmillbrewery.co.uk
Bottle Brook range; Leadmill range; guest beers 🄷
Set in the grounds of the imposing Park Hall, this converted stable building now acts as the tap for the Leadmill Brewery, directly opposite. With a proper stable door, sawdust-covered floor, wooden furniture, low lighting and much brewery memorabilia, the place has real atmosphere. An impressive range of 12 handpumps adds to the overall drinking experience, which resulted in the local CAMRA Pub of the Year award in 2005. Catch the No. 91/92 Derby-Mansfield bus. Denby Pottery is nearby.
Q❀▣♣●P▯

Derby

Alexandra Hotel

203 Siddals Road, DE1 2QE
⏲ 11-11; 12-3, 7-10.30 Sun
☎ (01332) 293993
Castle Rock Elsie Mo, Harvest Pale; Marston's Pedigree; guest beers 🄷
Named after the Danish princess who married the Prince of Wales (later Edward VII) in 1863, the Alex was originally the Midland Coffee House. The end wall once advertised Zacharia Smith's Shardlow Ales, but both sign and brewer have slipped into history. Long a Shipstone's house, it subsequently went to Bateman's and latterly to Tynemill, since when it has been a strong champion of small breweries. Two roomed, with a central bar; the pub was the birthplace of Derby CAMRA in 1974.
Q❀⇔◑◗▢♿⇌▣♣●P⅟

Babington Arms

11-13 Babington Lane, DE1 1TA (off St Peter's St)
⏲ 9am-midnight (1am Fri & Sat); 9am-midnight Sun
☎ (01332) 383647
Wyre Piddle seasonal beers; Falstaff seasonal beers; guest beers 🄷
Probably the best Wetherspoon's house, in the country, winning the company's pretisgious Cask Ale Pub of the Year and also local CAMRA City Pub of the Year in 2005. Showcasing an amazing range of beers from its 17 handpumps, it stages regular themed brewery weekends. Originally a furniture store, now fronted with a verandah for fair-weather drinking, the pub stands in the former grounds of Babington House. The first performance of Bram Stoker's Dracula was given in the neighbouring Grand Theatre in 1924. Q❀◑◗♿▣●⅟

Brunswick Inn

1 Railway Terrace, DE1 2RU
⏲ 11-11; 12-10.30 Sun
☎ (01332) 290677
Brunswick Father Mike's, Railway Porter, Second Brew, Triple Hop; 🄷 guest beers 🄶 /🄷
Originally built as the centrepiece of a railway village, it was closed in 1974 and fell into disrepair. Eventually rescued and restored, it opened as Derby's first multiple real ale house some 14 years later. A purpose-built brewery was added and it rapidly became one of the best-known free houses in the country before being sold to Everards in 2002. Things remain unchanged however and the pub was crowned Local CAMRA City Pub of the Year 2004.
Q☋❀◑♿⇌▣●⅟

Crompton Tavern

45 Crompton Street, DE1 1NX
⏲ 11-11; 12-10.30 Sun
☎ (01332) 733629
Marston's Pedigree; Taylor Landlord; guest beers 🄷
Tucked away down a cul-de-sac off Green Lane and lit up with fairy lights, the former Queen's Hotel was originally a guesthouse for visiting thespians at the nearby Grand Theatre. Two doors open on to different sides of the same U-shaped room, with wings on each side of a central bar. The walls frequently double as a gallery for local artists. A pleasant rear garden is a welcome fair-weather haven. ⛬❀▣♣

Falstaff

74 Silverhill Road, Normanton, DE23 6UJ (1 mile from centre)
⏲ 12-11; 12-10.30 Sun
☎ (01332) 342902 🌐 falstaffbrewery.co.uk
Falstaff Phoenix, Smiling Assassin, seasonal beers; guest beers 🄷

Known locally as 'the Folly' and reputedly haunted, this former Allied pub was originally a latter-day coaching inn before the surrounding area was built up, closing it in. Now free of tie, its on-site brewery has made it the best real ale house in Normanton. The curved bar is flanked on one side by a small lounge, with Offilers Brewery memorabilia and an open fire in winter, and on the other by a games room with occasional entertainment. Not posh, but a real local. ♨Q❀⊟♣●⅟

Flowerpot

23-25 King Street, DE1 3DZ

⊙ 11-11 (midnight Fri & Sat); 12-11 Sun

☎ (01332) 204955

Marston's Pedigree; Oakham Bishops Farewell; Whim Hartington IPA; guest beers Ⓖ/Ⓗ

Just up from the cathedral and round Clockhouse Corner, this is one of the pubs that spearheaded Derby's free trade expansion in the 1990s to become a virtual showcase for small breweries. Much extended from its original premises, it reaches far back from the small, roadside frontage and divides into several interlinking rooms. The furthest provides the stage for a lively, ongoing gig scene and another houses a glass cellar wall, revealing row upon row of stillaged firkins. Q❀◖◗⊟♿⊟●

Furnace Inn ☆

9 Duke Street, DE1 3BX (upriver from market place)

⊙ 11-11; 12-3, 6.30-10.30 Sun

☎ (01332) 331563

Hardys & Hansons Bitter, Mild, Olde Trip, seasonal beers Ⓗ

Just off St Mary's Bridge with its 15th-century chapel, the pub stands on the west bank of the Derwent at the edge of Darley Park. The name preserves its close connection with Handyside's Britannia foundry of which it was once part. Although opened out, it retains distinct drinking areas around a central bar. Scenes of bygone Derby adorn the walls and bar top. A bustling community local, it provides a handy watering-hole for riverside cyclists and walkers. ❀♿⊟♣P

Olde Dolphin Inne ☆

5A Queen Street, DE1 3DL

⊙ 10.30-midnight; 12-11 Sun

☎ (01332) 267711

Adnams Bitter; Black Sheep Best Bitter; Caledonian Deuchars IPA; Draught Bass; Greene King Abbot; guest beers Ⓗ

Standing below the great gothic tower of the cathedral, the timber-framed Dolphin is Derby's most picturesque and oldest surviving pub, although much restored latterly. The beamed interior divides into bar, upper and lower lounges, snug and an upstairs steak bar, each with its own character. Reputedly haunted, regular themed evenings are supplemented by beer festivals in February and July, which spreads out on to a splendid, raised rear patio. It is a real gem and not to be missed. ♨Q❀◖◗⊟♿⊟P⅟

Rowditch Inn

246 Uttoxeter New Road, DE22 3LL (1 mile from centre)

⊙ 12-2 (not Mon-Fri), 7-11; 12-2, 7-10.30 Sun

☎ (01332) 343123

Marston's Pedigree; guest beers Ⓗ

The pub stands on the borough's ancient boundary, once marked by a defensive dyke or rough ditch (hence Rowditch). A plain-fronted but warmly welcoming roadside pub, its unexpectedly deep interior divides into two drinking areas and a small snug. A downstairs cellar bar opens occasionally, and the long rear garden is a positive haven in warmer weather. An extensive collection of pump clips adorns the bar area. Winner of local CAMRA City Pub of the Year. ♨❀♣⅟

Smithfield

Meadow Road, DE1 2BH (downriver from market place)

⊙ 11-11; 12-10.30 Sun

☎ (01332) 370429 ⊕ thesmithfield.co.uk

Burton Bridge Top Dog Stout; Kelham Island Pale Rider; Oakham Bishops Farewell, JHB; Whim Hartington IPA; guest beers Ⓗ

Bow-fronted riverside pub built to serve the cattle market, which has since moved to a new site, leaving the Smithy in a bit of a backwater. A long, basic bar is flanked on one side by a games/TV room that admits children until 9pm, and on the other by a cosy lounge with stone fireplace and old settles, overlooking a pleasant riverside patio. Exceptional beer helped earn the pub local CAMRA's Pub of the Year award in the past. ♨☺❀◖⊟⊟♣P

Station Inn

12 Midland Road, DE1 2SN

⊙ 11.30-2.30, 5 (7 Sat)-11; 11.30-11 Fri; 12-3, 7-10.30 Sun

☎ (01332) 608014

Draught Bass; Ⓖ **Black Sheep Best Bitter; Caledonian Deuchars IPA; guest beers** Ⓗ

This modest pub, but for its elaborate frontage and stained glass, was named after the Midland Railway's classical station nearby, which was needlessly swept away in 1983 to be replaced by the present uninspiring edifice. A traditional bar, with panelled counter, cast iron footrail and quarry-tiled floor, is flanked by a games area to the right and a large lounge to the rear that acts as a dining area and function room. Many cellar awards attest to the skills of the licensee. ◖⊟♿⇌⊟♣▯

Wardwick Tavern

15 The Wardwick, DE1 1HA (near library)

⊙ 11-11; 12-10.30 Sun

☎ (01332) 332677

Tetley Bitter; guest beers Ⓗ

This handsome, three-storey, Grade II listed, red-brick building replaces a much older stone building, the stately fireplace of which can still be seen inside. An iron plaque beside the door marks the height of the Great Flood in 1842. Alton's Wardwick Brewery, which used the union system, extended far to the rear, being taken over first by Strettons, then by Allsopps, later Ind

Coope, who converted their front offices into this attractive pub with bare floorboards and wooden settles. ❀♣◑⊟⚟

Earl Sterndale

Quiet Woman

SK17 9SL (off B5053)

☼ 12-3.30, 7-11; 12-3.30, 7-10.30 Sun

☎ (01298) 83211

Jennings Dark Mild; Marston's Burton Bitter, Pedigree; guest beers Ⓗ

The epitome of the rural village inn, this totally unspoilt and charming pub appears to be caught in a time warp. Hard to find in the idyllic setting of the Peak District National Park, efforts to track it down will be amply rewarded with a great pint and settles around the fire. It is popular with walkers, who stock up on the local eggs, cheese and pork pies on sale over the bar. A folk club is hosted on Sunday. Why the Quiet Woman? The answer is on the pub sign outside. ♨Q♉❀⛺⊟♣P

Fenny Bentley

Bentley Brook Inn

DE6 1LF (on A515)

☼ 11-11; 12-10.30 Sun

☎ (01335) 350278 ⊕ bentleybrookinn.co.uk

Leatherbritches Ashbourne Ale, Bespoke, Goldings, Hairy Helmet; Marston's Pedigree; guest beers Ⓗ

Just inside the National Park and set back off the main road, this attractive inn is home to Leatherbritches Brewery, an award-winning restaurant, a smokehouse, a Victorian kitchen garden, a bakery and a shop selling local produce, plants and bottled real ales. The annual spring bank holiday Peak Booze and Blues festival, featuring over 150 beers, is held in a large marquee in its extensive grounds, with camping facilities. Affording fine views and superb facilities, the pub is the ideal base for Derbyshire's major tourist attractions. ♨♉❀⛟◑♿⛺♣●P⚟

Glossop

Crown Inn

142 Victoria Street, SK13 8HY

☼ 5-11; 11.30-11 Fri & Sat; 12-10.30 Sun

☎ (01457) 862824

Samuel Smith OBB Ⓗ

A fine example of a pub serving the community, this corner, terraced local is on the Hayfield Road out of the town, but a comfortable walk from the centre. Built in 1846, it has been a Smith's house since 1977 – the only one in the entire High Peak area. An attractive curved bar serves two side snugs (one no-smoking) and a pool/games room. Old pictures of Glossop and country prints add to a traditional atmosphere. Its beer prices are the cheapest in the area. ♨Q❀♿⇌♣⚟

Friendship

3 Arundel Street, SK13 7AB

☼ 4-midnight;12-3, 7-11 Sun

☎ (01457) 855277 ⊕ thefriendship.co.uk

Robinson's Hatters, Unicorn, seasonal beers Ⓗ

Street-corner local with an open-plan lounge and a rear tap room, which retains its 1950s look through ongoing sympathetic refurbishment. It is popular with spectators at Glossop's cricket and football clubs, which are both nearby. A secluded and well-stocked garden is open to children until 8pm. A choice of 30-plus malt whiskies complements the well-kept ales. Over the front door is one of the diminishing number of the brewery's impressive lamps dating from around 1900. ♨❀⇌⊟♣⚟

Globe

144 High Street West, SK13 8HJ

☼ 5-2am; closed Tue; 1-1am Sun

☎ (01457) 852417 ⊕ globemusic.org

Beer range varies Ⓗ

Seven hand-pulled beers from various micro-breweries such as Abbeydale, Kelham Island, Shaws, Storm, Ossett and the local Howard Town breweries, as well as cider and perry jugged from the cellar, and a British bottled beer selection attract customers young and old. Live music features strongly with an upstairs room hosting concerts on Friday and Saturday evenings. Downstairs, Monday is folk night, Wednesday the popular quiz and a local resident band plays on Thursday. A vegetarian only menu is popular. No admittance after 10.45pm. Q❀◗♿⇌⊟●

Old Gloveworks

Unit 1 Riverside Mill, George Street, SK13 8AY

☼ 12-midnight (1 am Fri-Sat); closed Mon-Wed; 12-10.30 Sun

☎ (01457) 858432 ⊕ thegloveworksglossop.com

Beer range varies Ⓗ

This converted glove mill is completely free of tie, selling six changing beers from local and regional breweries. A roof terrace and front patio give views over Glossop Brook and Harehills Park. Thursday from 5pm is curry night, always with a vegetarian choice, followed by a quiz. Friday and Saturday are disco nights and on Sunday from 4pm a live group or artist performs. An age restriction of 25 ensures a trouble-free atmosphere, although children are admitted during the day at the landlord's discretion. ❀◐⇌⊟P

Star Inn Ale House

2-4 Howard Street, SK13 7DD

☼ 2 (12 Sat)-11 (midnight Fri & Sat); 12-10.30 Sun

☎ (01457) 853072

Beer range varies Ⓗ

Highly regarded by locals and the first and last stop off for visitors by public transport – bus and train termini are within yards of the door. Run by long-standing CAMRA members, the beers are mainly from micro-breweries, both local and from further afield. At least one cider is available on draught, usually Westons Old Rosie, supplemented by several good bottled ciders. Pictures of bygone Glossop, wood floors and a tap room served by a hatch add to the atmosphere. ⛟⇌⊟♣●P

Great Hucklow

Queen Anne Inn

Main Road, SK17 8RF

⏲ 12-2.30 (not Tue), 6.30 (6 Fri)-11; 12-3, 6-11 Sat; 12-3, 7-10.30 Sun
☎ (01298) 871246 🌐 thequeenanne.net
Adnams Bitter; guest beers Ⓗ
The Queen Anne was first granted a licence in 1704, although it was functioning as an ale house as early as 1577. The village thrived on lead mining in the 18th century and a Unitarian chapel remains from this period. The pub has low ceilings, beams and brasses, and a high-backed settle. Pets and walkers are welcome. The guest beers often come from the Storm Brewery from where a band also comes to perform occasionally. The pub is closed all day Monday between New Year and Easter. ⌂☕❀⇌◑♿⛺♣P⊬⊔

Hathersage

Little John Hotel
Station Road, S32 1DD
⏲ 12-11; 12-10.30 Sun
☎ (01433) 650225
Beer range varies Ⓗ
Customers here have a choice of several beers from one brewery in any given week, the selected company being rotated on a weekly basis, with the most popular being Archers, Kelham Island and Storm. They can also choose from four seating areas: a lounge, a bar, a family room and a function area, all smartly furnished. Food is home cooked and portions are generous, with meals available all day at the weekend. Folk singers perform monthly (second Sat).
⌂☕❀⇌◑⊟♿⛺⇌▭♣P⊬

Millstone Inn
Sheffield Road, S32 1DA
⏲ 11.30-3, 7-11; 11.30-11 Fri-Sun and summer weekdays
☎ (01433) 650258 🌐 millstoneinn.co.uk
Black Sheep Best Bitter; guest beers Ⓗ
The pub originally served the nearby millstone quarry and is now popular with climbers and walkers. Inside there is one bar area furnished with country tables and upholstered chairs. Guest beers are supplied by Abbeydale, Kelham Island and Wentworth. A beer festival is held over August Bank Holiday weekend. Customers have the use of a free wireless Internet facility. In addition to bar meals, a high quality terrace restaurant specialises in fish dishes. ⌂❀⇌◑▭♣P⊬⊔

Hayfield

Royal Hotel
Market Street, SK22 2EP
⏲ 12-11 (1am Fri & Sat); 12-11 Sun
☎ (01663) 742721 🌐 theroyalhayfield.co.uk
Boddingtons Bitter; Hydes Bitter; guest beers Ⓗ
A former vicarage, this imposing stone pub stands near the church and cricket ground in an attractive Peak District village. The traditional interior boasts original oak panels and pews that create a relaxing atmosphere, further enhanced by real fires in winter. A restaurant and function room complete the facilities. Meals are served all day on Saturday and Sunday. An annual beer festival is staged in early October.
⌂Q❀⇌◑♿⛺▭P⊬

Heath

Elm Tree
Mansfield Road, S44 5SE (1 mile from M1 jct 29)
⏲ 11-3, 5-11; 11.30-11 Sat; 12-10.30 Sun
☎ (01246) 850490 🌐 elmtree.members.beeb.net/
Beer range varies Ⓗ
The only pub in the village, this popular hostelry boasts fine home-cooked food as well as two regularly-changing guest ales. The interior divides into two bar areas and a dining area. The large, well maintained gardens to the side and rear afford great views, yet the pub is just a mile from the motorway. ❀◑⊟⛺♣P

Holbrook

Dead Poets Inn
38 Chapel Street, DE56 0TQ
⏲ 12-2.30, 5-11; 12-11 Fri & Sat; 12-10.30 Sun
☎ (01332) 780301
Greene King Abbot; Marston's Pedigree; guest beers Ⓖ/Ⓗ
Built in 1800 and formerly known as the Cross Keys, the pub has undergone a remarkable transformation in recent times to create an inn with a real medieval feel. Its two rooms contain high-backed pews, stone-flagged floors, low lighting, a real fire and inglenook. Once free, now an Everards house, it was so named because its former owner believed that many of our famous poets gained inspiration from atmospheric taverns such as this; poetry readings are held monthly (first Tue). ⌂Q❀◑▭♣♠P

Holymoorside

Lamb Inn
16 Loads Road, S42 7EU
⏲ 5 (4 Fri)-11; 12-3, 7-11 Sat; 12-3, 7-10.30 Sun
☎ (01246) 566167
Adnams Bitter; Fuller's London Pride; John Smith's Bitter; Taylor Landlord; guest beers Ⓗ
Cosy and cheerful local where everyone is made welcome, including dogs and walkers (after removing their muddy boots). Winner of many Chesterfield CAMRA awards, a roaring fire provides a focal point in winter. In summer the outdoor drinking area hosts occasional jazz concerts. The Stagecoach service 25 from Chesterfield stops nearby.
⌂Q❀⊟▭♣P

Hope

Cheshire Cheese
Edale Road, S33 6ZF
⏲ 12-3, 6-11; 12-11 Sat; 12-4, 6-10.30 Sun
☎ (01433) 620381 🌐 cheshirecheesehope.co.uk
Black Sheep Best Bitter; Tetley Bitter; Whim Hartington Bitter; guest beers Ⓗ
Guest beers are supplied by micro-breweries in Cheshire, Derbyshire and South Yorkshire. There are three seating areas in this 16th-century free house, furnished with upholstered chairs and benches; the lower section becomes a restaurant at mealtimes.

Food is served all day until 8.30pm on Sunday. Children are welcome, except in the immediate vicinity of the bar. Take care outside: the car park is small and the road narrow. ⌂Q❀⇔◐▲P⁄

Horsley Woodhouse

Old Oak Inn

176 Main Street, DE7 6AW (on A609)

⊙ 5 (4 Fri)-11; 12-11 Sat; 12-10.30 Sun

☎ (01332) 881299

Bottle Brook range; Leadmill range; guest beers Ⓗ

Once a farmhouse, the Old Oak was under threat of demolition when it was acquired and renovated by the Denby-based Leadmill Brewery in 2003. Four interconnected rooms and a courtyard provide a variety of drinking spaces with real fires and hanging hops giving the pub a genuine homely atmosphere. Eight handpumps, occasional beer festivals and live music help to make it another example of a recent, successful village pub revival. ⌂Q❀⊟(125)♣●P⁄◻

Hulland Ward

Black Horse Inn

DE6 3EE (on A517)

⊙ 12-2.30, 6-11; 12-3, 7-10.30 Sun

☎ (01335) 370206

Beer range varies Ⓗ

This traditional, 300-year-old country inn stands in an elevated village, in some of the most picturesque country outside the Peak, close to Carsington Water. Its split-level, multi-roomed drinking area, with low, beamed ceilings and quarry-tiled floors, is served by a central bar, offering rotating guest ales. An extensive bar menu is complemented by a popular Sunday carvery in the restaurant. Some guest rooms boast four-poster beds. ❀⇔◐⊟(109)♣P⁄

Ilkeston

Dewdrop

24 Station Street, DE7 5TE (50 yds from A6096)

⊙ 12-2.30 (4 Sat), 7-11; 12-4, 7-10.30 Sun

☎ (0115) 932 9684

Castle Rock Harvest Pale; Oakham Bishops Farewell; Taylor Best Bitter; guest beers Ⓗ

Victorian, street-corner local boasting a multi-roomed interior, with the lounge and a no-smoking snug both warmed by open fires, while the bar has a free juke box and a pool table. The original lobby bears a plaque commemorating the stay of the inventor of the 'bouncing bomb' Barnes Wallis during WWII. This winner of local CAMRA Pub of the Year 2004 and 2005 adds guests from micro-breweries such as Glentworth and Oakham at the weekend to satisfy demand. ⌂Q❀⊟⁄

Ilford Club

93 Station Road, DE7 5LJ (on A6096)

⊙ 2-5.30 (not Mon-Fri), 7.30 (7 Sat)-midnight; 12-midnight Sun

☎ (0115) 930 5789

Beer range varies Ⓗ

Situated by the Erewash Canal with boat moorings nearby, this former local CAMRA Club of the Year is now a free house. Beers are sourced mainly from micros, with Whim and Crouch Vale usually prominent. Traditional pub games including snooker are popular in this single-room establishment. Children are admitted on Saturday and Sunday lunchtimes. With advance notice the friendly landlord will open outside usual hours for groups. ❀⊟(27)♣◻

Needlemakers' Arms

Kensington Street, DE7 5NY (10 mins walk from town centre)

⊙ 6.30-11; 12-11.30 Fri & Sat; 11-11 Sun

☎ (07986) 634427

Caledonian Deuchars IPA; guest beers Ⓗ/Ⓖ

Created by knocking two former workers' cottages into one, this popular pub takes its name from the former needlemaking factory nearby. The beer range usually consists of frequently-changing guests, both on handpump and jugged from the cellar. There is a pool and family/function room to the rear, with a quiet lounge area to the left of the bar where a quiz is staged on Thursday evening. Traditional pub games are also popular in local CAMRA's Pub of the Year 2006. Q☋❀⊟♣P

Ingleby

John Thompson Inn

Ingleby Lane, DE73 1HW (off A514)

⊙ 10.30-2.30, 5-11; 12-2, 7-10.30 Sun

☎ (01332) 862469

John Thompson JTS XXX, Porter, seasonal beers; Tetley Burton Ale Ⓗ

John Thompson is the former fruit grower who revived Derbyshire's brewing industry in 1977, having made his family home into a highly individual pub eight years earlier. Comprising a large, comfortable lounge with smaller rooms opening off, the pub is rich in local interest, displaying many prints and watercolours. Close to the banks of the River Trent, in open country just outside the village, it has a spacious patio and large garden with the brewery housed in outbuildings. ☋❀◐♿♣P⁄

Kirk Ireton

Barley Mow ☆

Main Street, DE6 3JP (off B5023)

⊙ 12-2, 7-11; 12-2, 7-10.30 Sun

☎ (01335) 370306

Hook Norton Old Hooky; Marston's Pedigree; Whim Hartington IPA; guest beers Ⓖ

Set in an olde-worlde village overlooking the Ecclesbourne Valley, this exceptionally characterful, gabled Jacobean building was originally a farmhouse. Several interconnecting rooms of different sizes and character have low, beamed ceilings, mullioned windows, slate-topped tables, well-worn woodwork and open fires set in stone fireplaces. A small serving hatch reveals a stillage with up to six beers dispensed straight from the cask. There are

few pubs remaining like this rural gem.
♔Q❀⇆⅄♣●P⚟

Little Hayfield

Lantern Pike

45 Glossop Road, SK22 2NG
⏲ 12-11 (1am Fri & Sat); 12-11 Sun
☎ (01663) 747590 ⊕ lanternpikeinn.co.uk
Black Sheep Best Bitter; Caledonian Deuchars IPA; Taylor Landlord; Tetley Bitter Ⓗ
This unaltered country pub, built as a farmhouse in 1783, was licensed in 1844. Nestling under the hill that gives the pub its name, it is handy for walking Kinder Scout and the accommodation here is popular with ramblers. Food is offered all day until 10pm. Claims to fame are that scriptwriter Tony Warren penned the first eight Coronation Street episodes at the pub and in 1927, the landlady was found murdered, with a carving knife stuck in her head.
♔♉❀⇆◑⅄⊟P⚟

Litton

Red Lion

Main Street, SK17 8QU
⏲ 12-3, 6-11; 12-11 Fri & Sat; 12-10.30 Sun
☎ (01298) 871458
Black Sheep Best Bitter; Oakwell Barnsley Bitter; Shepherd Neame Spitfire; guest beer Ⓗ
This small, cosy, three-roomed pub is graced by an enormous fireplace. It overlooks the pleasant village green, complete with stocks, and spring daffodils. It keeps a collection of local guide books and displays many interesting photographs. Customers are a mix of locals and visitors to the Peak District. A quiz is staged on Monday evening, monthly in winter and more frequently at other times. No meals are served on Sunday evening. Guest beers come from local breweries such as Peak Ales and Thornbridge Hall. ♔Q❀⇆◑⅄♣

Long Eaton

Hole in the Wall

6 Regent Street, NG10 1JX
⏲ 10-midnight (1am Fri & Sat); 12-midnight Sun
☎ (0115) 973 4920
Draught Bass; Nottingham Rock Ale Bitter, EPA; Taylor Landlord; guest beers Ⓗ
Over 100 years old, this free house has been run by the same licensee for the past 20 years and featured in this Guide for the last 14. Close to the town centre and the Erewash Canal, it offers two drinking areas: a lively bar and quiet lounge. Breweriana and CAMRA awards adorn both rooms where you can sample an excellent, changing range of beers, mostly supplied by micro-breweries. In the garden there is an enclosed skittle alley and barbecue. ❀⊟⊟♣●

Royal Oak

349 Tamworth Road, NG10 3LU (1 mile from town centre)
⏲ 11-11; 12-11 Sun
☎ (0115) 983 5801
Beer range varies Ⓗ
This large, friendly pub has taken advantage of the deal between SIBA and Enterprise Inns to supply guest beers to supplement the regulars such as Fuller's London Pride and Wadworth 6X. It benefits from a large car park, and separate children's play area, while moorings on the Erewash Canal at the rear attract boaters. The bar has a pool table, darts and Sky TV and a quiz is held on Wednesday evening. Home-made food includes a vegetarian option and children's menu. ❀◑⊟♿⅄⇌⊟♣P⚟

Twitchell Inn

Howitt Street, NG10 1ED (off High St)
⏲ 9am-midnight (1am Fri & Sat); 9am-midnight Sun
☎ (0115) 972 2197
Greene King Abbot; Marston's Pedigree; guest beers Ⓗ
Formerly a wine bar, this is a smaller than average Wetherspoon's pub but all the better for it, hidden on a side street off the main shopping centre. Apart from the regular Wetherspoon ales, it stocks beers from the local Nottingham brewery. Two no-smoking family areas are well decorated and display old photographs of Long Eaton. Food is served all day, every day. The pub is a short walk from the Market Place and five minutes from main bus routes.
♉◑♿⊟●P⚟

Longshaw

Grouse Inn

S11 7TZ (on A625)
⏲ 12-3, 6-11; 12-11 Sat; 12-10.30 Sun
☎ (01433) 630423
Banks's Bitter; Caledonian Deuchars IPA; Marston's Pedigree; guest beers Ⓗ
The Grouse stands in isolation on a bleak moorland but main road access to Sheffield makes it deservedly popular. It is ideally placed for walkers on the local gritstone edges, of which the pub displays some fine photographs. The family have run the pub since 1965 and have accumulated other collections, such as bank notes and cigarette cards. There is a lounge at the front and a smaller bar and conservatory at the rear. No evening meals are served Monday evening.
♔Q♉❀◑♣P⊓

Lullington

Colvile Arms

Main Street, DE12 8EG
⏲ 12-2 (not Mon-Fri), 6-11; 12-3, 7-10.30 Sun
☎ (01827) 373212
Draught Bass; Marston's Pedigree; guest beer Ⓗ
Popular, 18th-century free house, leased from the Lullington Estate, at the heart of an attractive hamlet at the southern tip of the county. The public bar comprises an adjoining hallway and snug, each featuring high-backed settles with wood panelling. The bar and a comfortable lounge are situated on opposite sides of a central serving area. A second lounge/function room overlooks the garden and bowling green. Two quiz teams and the local cricket and football teams meet here. ❀⊟♣P

Makeney

Holly Bush Inn

Holly Bush Lane, DE56 0RX OS352447
⏲ 12-3, 5-11; 12-11 Fri & Sat; 12-10.30 Sun
☎ (01332) 841729
Archers Golden; Greene King Ruddles County; [H] **Marston's Pedigree;** [G] **Taylor Landord;** [H] **guest beers** [H]/[G]
Grade II listed, and once a farmhouse with a brewery on the Strutt Estate, this late 17th-century, former Offilers' house positively oozes character. It stood on the Derby turnpike before the Strutts opened the valley route in 1818; Dick Turpin is known to have drunk here. The wooden snug is sandwiched between two bars with open fires. Regular beer festivals are staged.
⌂Q♘❀⊟⊞P

Matlock

Boathouse

110 Dale Road, DE4 3PP
⏲ 11.30-2.30, 5-11; 11.30-11 Wed-Sat; 12-11 Sun
☎ (01629) 581519
Hardys & Hansons Bitter, Olde Trip, seasonal beers [H]
This pub, now part of the Hardys and Hansons tenanted estate, was built before 1750. It has also operated as a mortuary for a smallpox outbreak and on two separate occasions, a brothel. The pub takes its name from the ferry that it formerly operated on the nearby River Derwent. Popular with diners from nearby education offices, tourists and walkers; fish dishes are a speciality on the menu. There are five en-suite guest rooms.
⌂Q♘♣⊭◐⇌⊞♣P

Melbourne

Blue Bell

53 Church Street, DE73 1EJ
⏲ 11-11; 12-10.30 Sun
☎ (01332) 865764
Shardlow Golden Hop, Reverend Eaton's Ale, Special Bitter, seasonal beers; guest beers (occasional) [H]
In a prime spot close to the hall and Norman church, in a well-pubbed locality, the Blue Bell stands out as the Shardlow Brewery tap, although it is several miles from the brewery itself. The bar of this old country pub bears a sporting emphasis, while the lounge opens on to a patio with barbecue. Run on traditional lines with seasonal beers and a house mild, occasional guests are available too. ❀⊭◐⊟⛺⊞(68, 68A, 68B)♣

Monsal Head

Monsal Head Hotel

DE45 1NL (on B6465)
⏲ 11.30-11; 12-10.30 Sun
☎ (01629) 640250 🌐 monsalhead.com
Taylor Landlord; Theakston Best Bitter, Old Peculier; Whim Hartington Bitter; guest beers [H]
Real ale is served mainly in the Stables Bar, behind the main hotel. This bar is what remains from an earlier inn and retains its original floor and vestiges of individual stalls for horses. The hotel stands in a beauty spot overlooking the limestone Monsal Dale and can get crowded, so visit on a quiet evening or when the weather is fine enough to allow drinkers to spill out on to the ample forecourt. Guest beers are often local, from the likes of Peak Ales or Thornbridge Hall.
⌂Q❀⊭◐⛺♣P

Morley Smithy

Three Horseshoes

Main Road, DE7 6DF (on A608)
⏲ 11.30-11; 12-10.30 Sun
☎ (01332) 834395
Marston's Pedigree, seasonal beers; guest beers [H]
An attractive, white painted, rural pub on the main Derby-Heanor road and H1 bus route. Modestly modernised inside, its long, narrow, single room is centrally divided by an archway separating a smart, food-oriented lounge from the plainer, quarry-tiled bar with open fire and fake beams. An old photo shows the original thatched inn that also served as a smithy, which was pulled down around 1910. Farm-laid eggs can be bought at the bar. ⌂Q❀◐♿⊞♣P

New Mills

Pack Horse Inn

Mellor Road, SK22 4QQ
⏲ 12-3, 5-11; 12-11 Sat; 12-10.30 Sun
☎ (01663) 742365 🌐 packhorseinn.co.uk
Tetley Bitter; guest beers [H]
The owners of this enterprising public house have now completed a sympathetic stone extension at this well established bed and breakfast stop for tourists and businessmen. There is a spacious, beautifully-lit dining room, too. Walk uphill from New Mills or cadge a lift because the effort is worth it – the owners choose their guest beers with a lot of imagination. ⌂Q❀⊭◐⊞P

New Whittington

Wellington

162 High Street, S43 2AN
⏲ 11-11 (12.30am Fri & Sat); 12-11 Sun
☎ (01246) 450879
Camerons Strongarm; guest beers [H]
Within easy reach of Chesterfield and the surrounding area by bus (Nos. 25, 50 and 99 stop outside), this is a simple but comfortable, two-roomed local. Twice-weekly quizzes, monthly live music and great themed menu evenings reinforce community links. Add to this a pool table that is free at all times, good food and five cask ales and you are on to a winner.
❀◐⊟♿⊞♣P⊓

Oakerthorpe

Anchor Inn

DE55 7LP (on B6013)
⏲ 12-3, 6.30-11; 12-11 Sat; 12-10.30 Sun
☎ (01773) 833575
Cropton Honey Gold, Monkmans Slaughter, Two Pints, seasonal beers [H]

This mid 18th-century bay fronted building can be picked out at the roadside by a huge 18ft dredger's anchor. Little of the original features remain however, apart from a stone wall surrounding the fireplace and a few beams believed to originate from ship's timbers. Long and rambling inside with four distinct areas separated by stone archways, an unusual reverse swan-neck handpull system dispenses Cropton beers – rare in these parts.
Q⛅❀◑⊟♿P⚡

Ockbrook

Royal Oak

55 Green Lane, DE72 3SE
(off A5, follow Ilkeston signs)
✪ 11.30-2.30 (3 Sat), 6-11; 12-3, 7-10.30 Sun
☎ (01332) 662378
Draught Bass; guest beers Ⓗ
Set back from the road across a cobbled courtyard, this fine pub is a former CAMRA regional Pub of the Year winner. In the same family since coronation year and little changed since then, each of the five rooms has its own distinctive character and clientele. Three ever-changing guest beers are supplemented by an annual beer festival in October. Excellent home-cooked food is served. Separate gardens cater for adults and families. Catch the No.9 bus from Derby, daytime only. Q❀◑♿🚌♣P⚡

Old Brampton

George & Dragon

Main Road, S42 7JG OS336718
✪ 12-4, 7-11 Mon; 12-11 Tue-Sat; 12-10.30 Sun
☎ (01246) 567821
Adnams Bitter; Marston's Pedigree; guest beers Ⓗ
Typical country pub and village local, situated opposite the medieval church with its 63-minute clock face. This 200-year-old pub has intriguing ghost stories to tell. A haven for walkers and their dogs, it is within easy reach of the Peak District, Chesterfield, woodland and local reservoirs. Warmed by an open log fire, the pub serves a good selection of hand-pulled guest ales and plays host to occasional beer festivals, folk sessions and a Tuesday quiz. 🔥❀⛺🚌♣●P

Over Haddon

Lathkil Hotel

DE45 1JE (off B5055, Bakewell-Monyash road) OS206665
✪ 11.30-3, 7-11; 11.30-11 Sat; 12-10.30 Sun
☎ (01629) 812501 🌐 lathkil.co.uk
Whim Hartington Bitter; guest beers Ⓗ
Standing above Lathkill Dale, this popular free house enjoys one of the most outstanding views of the Peak District from its front window, which could explain why an inn has existed on this spot since the Georgian period. The traditional styled bar has an open fire and serves a wide selection of ales. Accommodation and good quality, home-cooked food are also available at this regular local CAMRA award winner.
🔥Q⛅❀🛏◑♣▯

Rosliston

Bull's Head

Burton Road, DE12 8JU
✪ 12-3, 7-11 daily
☎ (01283) 761705
Draught Bass; Marston's Pedigree; guest beer Ⓗ
Late 19th-century, brick-built free house with a comfortable public bar and smart, cosy lounge, both featuring open fires and beamed ceilings, plus a large function room in a converted stable block. A collection of china bulls is displayed behind the bar, and interesting encased models of a Burton Union brewing system can be found in the public bar and the function room. Guest beers appear at the weekend. The National Forest Forestry Centre is located about half a mile away. 🔥◑⊟⛺🚌♣P⚡

Sawley

Harrington Arms

392 Tamworth Road, NG10 3AU (on B6540 near River Trent & marina)
✪ 11-11.30 (11 Mon; 12.30am Fri & Sat); 11-11.30 Sun
☎ (0115) 973 2614
Hardys & Hansons Best Bitter, Olde Trip, seasonal beers Ⓗ
A regular entry in this Guide, this former coaching inn stands near the Trent and Mersey Canal. After a recent refurbishment it now offers a no-smoking restaurant (open all day), better disabled facilities and a fourth handpump. A large outdoor drinking area plays host to a successful August bank holiday beer festival. A wide range of bar meals complements the excellent choice of freshly-cooked international cuisine served in the restaurant.
🔥Q❀◑♿⇌(Long Eaton)🚌P⚡

Scarcliffe

Horse & Groom

Rotherham Road, S44 6SU (on B6417)
✪ 12-11; 12-3, 7-10.30 Sun
☎ (01246) 823152
Draught Bass; Greene King Abbot; Tetley Bitter; guest beers Ⓗ
This excellent rural free house, a past Derbyshire CAMRA Pub of the Year, has neither loud music nor slot machines. It consists of a tap room where the art of conversation reigns supreme and a lounge with a copper-topped bar. Up to six real ales are available as well as an impressive range of malt whiskies. Children are welcome in the covered verandah behind the pub. Accommodation is in three self-catering cottages. Q⛅❀🛏⊟♿⛺🚌♣P

Shirland

Hay Inn

135 Main Road, DE55 6BA
✪ 4.30 (6 Mon)-11.30; 12-midnight Sat; 12-10.30 Sun
☎ (01773) 835383
Hardys & Hansons Mild; Theakston Best Bitter; guest beers Ⓗ
Ex-Brampton Brewery pub, dating from around 1980, this free house is a flagship

real ale outlet run by long-standing, award-winning CAMRA members. Served via a central bar, this comfortable local offers an interesting range of three changing guest beers, a real cider and a selection of Belgian bottled beers and country wines. Impressive attention to detail – from the decor to summer hanging baskets – a weekly quiz and twice-yearly beer festivals make it well worth seeking out. ⛺🚌♣🍎P

Smalley

Bell Inn

35 Main Road, DE7 6EF (on A608)
11.30-3, 5-11; 11-11 Sat; 12-10.30 Sun
☎ (01332) 880635
Adnams Broadside; Mallard Duckling; Oakham JHB; Whim Hartington Bitter, IPA; guest beers Ⓗ
This mid 19th-century inn has three rooms and a large, attractive child-friendly garden. Brewing and other memorabilia adorn the walls. Top quality beer and food have helped make the Bell local CAMRA Pub of the Year 2006. Situated near Shipley Country Park, it can be reached via the Derby-Heanor H1 bus service, which stops right outside. Accommodation is offered in three flats in a converted stable adjoining the pub. ⛫Q❀🛏◑🗔♿🚌P

South Normanton

Clock Inn

107 Market Street, DE55 2AA
4-11.30; 11-11.30 Sat; 12-11 Sun
☎ (01773) 811396 🌐 theclockinn.co.uk
Everards Tiger; Marston's Bitter; guest beer Ⓗ
Traditional free house consisting of a no-smoking lounge, bar and a garden to the rear. The number of CAMRA awards and Cask Marque certificates displayed in the lounge attest to the beer quality. The guest beer goes on at the weekend and a selection of malt whiskies is stocked. The No. 92 bus stops outside. Q🚸❀🗔♿🚌P⚡

Royal Oak

78 Water Lane, DE55 2EE (off M1 jct 28)
12-11.30; 12-11 Sun
☎ (01773) 861337
Morland Old Speckled Hen; guest beers Ⓗ
This multi-roomed free house boasts gardens at both front and rear. A collection of ornamental brass around the bar and exposed beams in the main area add to the traditional atmosphere. Three guest beers are usually available with local micro-breweries well supported. Quiz night is Thursday and pub games are available. The No. 92 bus stops outside. ⛫❀🗔🚌♣P

South Wingfield

Old Yew Tree

51 Manor Road, DE55 7NH (on B5035)
5-11; 12-3, 6.30-11 Sat; 12-4, 7-10.30 Sun
☎ (01773) 833763
Cottage seasonal beers; Marston's Pedigree; guest beers Ⓗ
A regular Guide entry, this busy, family-run free house is situated near the magnificent remains of the 15th-century Wingfield Manor, destroyed by Cromwell during the Civil War. Guest beers regularly showcase local micro-breweries. Good home-cooked food, including excellent Sunday lunches (no food Sun eve), draws people from near and far. The pub has won the Amber Valley Clean Air award in the past. There is limited parking space. ⛫❀◑♿⛺P⚡

Stanley Common

White Post Inn

237 Belper Road, DE7 6FT (on A609)
11-11; 12-10.30 Sun
☎ (0115) 930 0194
Beer range varies Ⓗ/Ⓖ
This large, white-painted, roadside inn on the main thoroughfare is surrounded by some fine country, away from the built-up sprawl. Three interlinking rooms are served by a central bar, with one used as a dining area where good home-cooked food is served. An interesting range of up to five changing guest beers is supplemented by occasional beer festivals, which in summertime spill out on to the pleasant rear garden. ⛫Q🚸❀◑🗔♿🚌♣P⚡

Stanton in Peak

Flying Childers

Main Road, DE4 2LW (off B5056, Bakewell-Ashbourne road)
12-2 (not Mon & Tue or winter Wed & Thu), 7-11; 12-3, 7-11 Sat & Sun
☎ (01629) 636333
Black Sheep Best Bitter; Wells Bombardier; guest beer Ⓗ
Created from four cottages in the 18th century, this unspoilt, characterful free house offers changing guest beers, often sourced from Archers and local micros. A real fire, settles and beams enhance the cosy, timeless bar, while the lounge has a gas fire and leather seating. Home-made soups and cobs are available at lunchtime. It hosts a monthly quiz night (fourth Thu) and occasional entertainment. Walkers and dogs are welcome – it is a handy watering-hole for the magical Stanton moor. ⛫Q❀🗔⛺⇌♣P

Staveley

Speedwell Inn

Lowgates, S43 3TT
6-11; 6-10.30 Sun
☎ (01246) 474665
Townes IPA, Lowgate Light, Speedwell Bitter, Staveley Cross, Staveleyan; guest beer (occasional) Ⓗ
Home of the Townes Brewery since 1998, this unassuming pub has twice won the local CAMRA Pub of the Year award. Simple and comfortable surroundings provide real ale lovers with a desirable venue. Townes produces regular special brews and holds an annual beer festival early in December. Occasional guest beers are also offered, as well as a small range of Belgian bottled beers. Q🚌♣⚡

Sutton Cum Duckmanton

Arkwright Arms

Chesterfield Road, S44 5JG
(on A632 between Chesterfield and Bolsover)
11-11; 12-10.30 Sun
(01246) 232053
Greene King Abbot or Morland Old Speckled Hen; Marston's Pedigree; guest beers H

There is always a warm welcome at this mock-Tudor fronted free house. The public bar is separated from the lounge by a horseshoe-shaped bar; the dining room is to the rear. All three are made cosy by open fires. It stocks an excellent range of ales with changing guests, normally from five micro-breweries. Beer festivals are held on the Easter and August bank holidays, supplement by regular mini events throughout the year. Evening meals are served weekdays. Bolsover Castle is nearby. P

Swanwick

Steam Packet Inn

Derby Road, DE55 1AB (on B6179)
12 (11 Sat)-11.30 (midnight Fri & Sat); 12-11.30 Sun
(01773) 602172
Adnams Bitter; Black Sheep Best Bitter; Caledonian Deuchars IPA; Everards Tiger; Young's Bitter; guest beers H

Land-locked Swanwick does not see many steam packets come or go. A rumour that the name arose from the use of the pub as a pay office by the steam railway sounds improbable. Centrally situated next to the church, this traditional 19th-century inn has not been drastically altered inside and retains lounge and bar areas. Beer festivals are staged in April and October. Lunches are served Thursday-Sunday, evening meals Friday.
Q (91, 92) P

Thulston

Harrington Arms

4 Grove Close, DE72 3EY (off B5010)
11.30-3 (not Mon), 6-11; 11.30-11 Sat; 12-10.30 Sun
(01332) 571798
Draught Bass; guest beers H

Formerly two cottages refronted to stand out, and brightly lit after dark, the pub has been smartly modernised without losing its cottagey feel, with low, beamed ceilings, wood-clad walls and open fires. The restaurant serves good food. The house beer, Earl of Harrington, is from Wicked Hathern. Elvaston Castle Country Park, former estate of the Earls of Harrington, is nearby. The magnificent iron gates at the entrance were spoils of the Napoleonic Wars from Spain.

Tideswell

Star

High Street, SK17 8LD
3-11.30; 12-midnight Sat; 12-11 Sun
(01298) 872397
Jennings Bitter; Marston's Burton Bitter; guest beer H

Lively local in the village centre, although not as the address implies on the main road, but up a side street. It consists of three small rooms around a central bar – one houses a TV, another a pool table. The third, no-smoking, room is popular for meals, which are served daily until 8pm. The pub is smartly furnished and decorated throughout. The beer range is now from the Wolverhampton and Dudley group, with usually three ales on.

Troway

Gate Inn

Main Road, S21 5RU (from B6056 turn off at minor road by Black-a-Moor pub)
12-3, 7-11; 12-3, 7-10.30 Sun
(01246) 413280
Jennings Sneck Lifter; Marston's Burton Bitter; guest beer H

A hidden gem to be found up a narrow country lane in North Derbyshire. Relax and soak up the charm of this small, friendly pub in good walking country on the south side of the Moss Valley. Now in its 12th year under the current tenants, it has featured in this Guide for the past 11. The real ales may be enjoyed beside a log fire in winter or in the award-winning garden in the summer.
Q P

Wirksworth

Royal Oak

North End, DE4 4FG (off B5035)
8-11; 12-3, 7.30-10.30 Sun
(01629) 823000
Draught Bass; Taylor Landlord; Whim Hartington IPA; guest beers H

Excellent little traditional local in a stone terrace near the market place, illuminated at night by fairy lights. The bar features some good breweriana and old local pictures. The Oak combines a long-standing reputation for Bass with a choice of guests. Wirksworth (or Wuzzer, as it is affectionately known) is well pubbed and others are worthy of a visit, too.
Q (R61)

Good health

A glass of bitter beer or pale ale, taken with the principal meal of the day, does more good and less harm than any medicine the physician can prescribe.

Dr Carpenter, 1750

DEVON

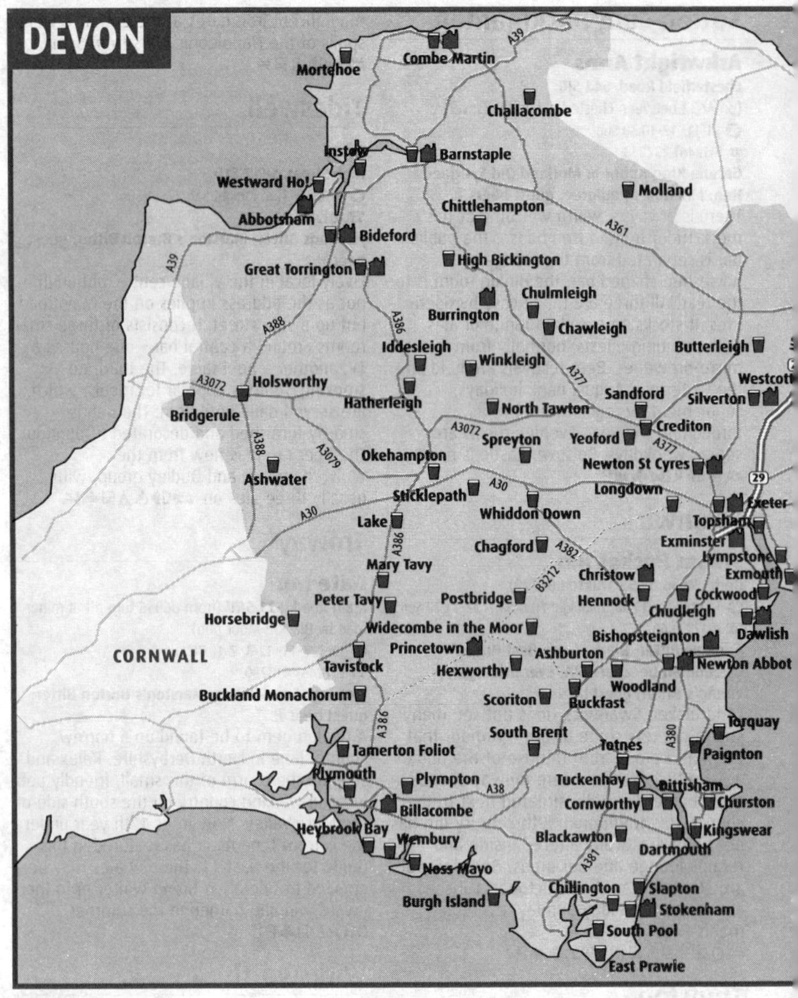

Ashburton

Exeter Inn

26 West Street, TQ13 7DU

11-2.30, 5-11 (midnight Fri & Sat); 12-3, 7-10.30 Sun

☎ (01364) 652013

Badger First Gold; Greene King IPA Ⓗ

This friendly local, the oldest public house in Ashburton, was constructed in 1131 (with additions in the 17th century) to house the workers that built the nearby church. The inn was used by Sir Francis Drake on his journeys to London. The main bar is L-shaped, rustic and wood-panelled, with a canopy. There are two main drinking areas either side of the entrance hallway and a further bar at the rear is served by a small hatch. Q ♣

Ashwater

Village Inn

EX21 5EY (off A388, midway between Launceston and Holsworthy)

12-2.30 (3 Sat), 6-11; 12-3, 6-10.30 Sun

☎ (01409) 211200 villageinnpub.co.uk

Exmoor Ale; Sharp's Doom Bar; guest beers Ⓗ

Busy pub set on the village green where a well-maintained, Mediterranean-style patio and a conservatory add to its appeal. There is a large car park to the rear. A games room is just one of several drinking areas. On the green is a children's play area. Facilities for disabled patrons are good. Although off the main road, it is easy to find and well worth the effort. ♣P

Axminster

Lamb Inn

Lyme Road, EX13 5BE

11.30-3, 5-midnight; 11.30-2am Fri & Sat; 11.30-midnight Sun

☎ (01297) 33922

Branscombe Vale Branoc; St Austell Tinners; guest beer Ⓗ

Situated half a mile from the town centre on the Lyme road, this pleasant free house is popular with locals of all ages, and is home to one of the local football teams. An attractive garden at the rear contains two boules pistes. Major sporting events are shown on a large-screen TV. Check out the

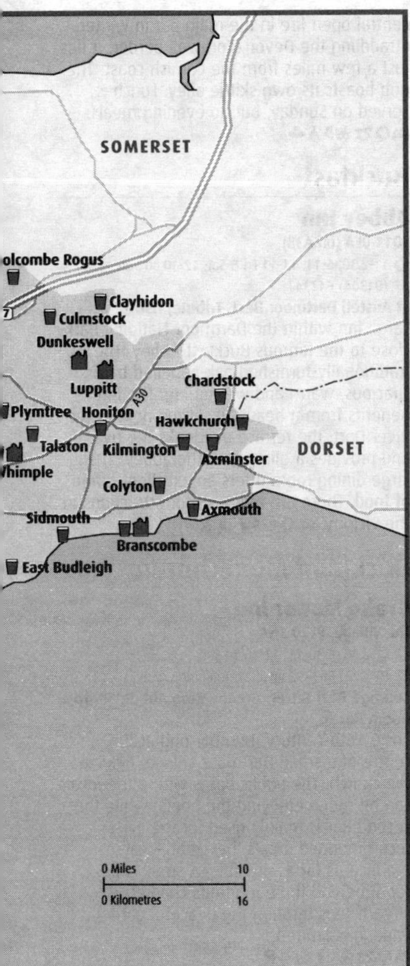

landlady's collection of Toby jugs. This is a traditional pub with modern touches. ✿♣P

Red Lion

Lyme Street, EX13 5AY

⏲ 11-midnight (1.30am Fri & Sat); 12-midnight Sun

☎ (01297) 32016

Beer range varies Ⓗ

A busy town-centre pub, 50 yards from a public car park, with a large bar and a room for dining. It offers a comprehensive and varied menu, reasonably priced, with specials and theme nights as added attractions. Three wide-screen TVs provide good sports coverage and music. The beer range from four handpumps constantly varies – usually featuring two local beers and two others, mostly from Wales and the South. ◐⇌♣

Axmouth

Harbour Inn

EX12 4AF

⏲ 11-3, 6-11 (11-11 Easter-Sept); 12-3, 7-10.30 Sun

☎ (01297) 20371

Badger First Gold, Tanglefoot; Otter Bitter, seasonal beers Ⓗ

The tidal part of the River Axe, just around the corner from this old pub, is a well known spot for birdwatchers, and the pub is also near the end of the famous Undercliffe walk from Lyme Regis. Acquired by Hall & Woodhouse in 2005, little has changed at the Harbour. The main bar features an enormous fireplace, always in use in winter, and there is more dining space beyond the bar. Children are welcome in the skittle alley in summer. ⌂Q✿◐♿▲P⚟

Barnstaple

Panniers

33/34 Boutport Street, EX31 1RX

⏲ 9am-midnight (1am Fri & Sat); 9am-midnight Sun

☎ (01271) 329720

Exmoor Stag; Greene King Abbot; Shepherd Neame Spitfire; guest beers Ⓗ

Pleasant and efficient Wetherspoon's outlet that was converted from an arcade of shops. Conveniently situated in the centre of town directly opposite the Queen's Theatre, it is close to the Pannier Market, from which it takes its name. The split-level interior offers several distinct seating areas and displays prints of local scenes and history. The garden is a suntrap and offers cover and heating for the less clement weather. Cider is supplied by Sheppy's and Westons. ✿◐♿⇌●⚟

Reform Inn

Reform Street, Pilton, EX31 1PD

⏲ 11.30-11; 12-10.30 Sun

☎ (01271) 329994

Barum Original, Breakfast, Firing Squad Ⓗ

Well-established local at the heart of its community. The skittle alley is the place to be for the annual green man beer festival in July. Pool and music are played in the large bar, while the smaller, lounge bar is quieter and designated as a no-smoking area. The pub hosts live music twice monthly on a Friday. The beers are supplied by Barum Brewery, located behind the pub. ✿⊟⇌♣⚟

INDEPENDENT BREWERIES

Barum Barnstaple
Beer Engine Newton St Cyres
Blackdown Dunkeswell
Branscombe Vale Branscombe
Burrington Burrington
Clearwater Great Torrington
Combe Martin Combe Martin
Country Life Abbotsham
Exe Valley Silverton
Gargoyles Dawlish
Jollyboat Bideford
O'Hanlon's Whimple
Otter Luppitt
Princetown Princetown
Red Rock Bishopsteignton
Scattor Rock Christow
South Hams Stokenham
Summerskills Billacombe
Tarka Barnstaple
Teignworthy Newton Abbot
Topsham & Exminster Exminster
Warrior Exeter

Bideford

King's Arms

7 The Quay, EX39 2HW
11-11 daily
(01237) 475196
Adnams Broadside; Butcombe Bitter; Greene King Abbot; Jollyboat Grenville's Renown H
River quayside inn that boasts a great seafaring history and much character. The pub has a single, long bar with a tiny snug at one end. Old photos of the quay adorn the walls at the front of the pub, which is below sea level at high tide. There is also a higher room at the rear near the cellar. Parking is possible opposite the pub on the quay.

Blackawton

George Inn

Main Street, TQ9 7BG (signed off A3122 Dartmouth-Halwell road) 05805509
12-3 (may vary), 6-11; 12-11.30 Sat; 12-10.30 Sun
(01803) 712342
Palmer Copper Ale; Princetown Jail Ale; Teignworthy Spring Tide; guest beers H
Friendly, unspoilt village local, with two bars warmed by a double-sided wood-burning stove, and another room. It sources real ales from small breweries and specialises in Belgian beers and rare malt whiskies. Hogwash cider from Cornworthy is available in summer. An impressive selection of home-made food is served (not Mon lunchtime) using local South Hams suppliers. Child and dog friendly, it has a new children's play area at the rear. The south-facing patio and garden afford pleasant rural views. Q P

Branscombe

Fountain Head

Street, EX12 3BG (western end of village)
11-3, 6-11; 12-3, 6-10.30 Sun
(01297) 680359
Branscombe Vale Branoc; guest beer H
This traditional pub, popular with walkers, is over 500 years old and was once a forge and cider house. It retains wood-panelled walls and flagstone floors, while a sympathetic refurbishment in 2005 exposed the inglenook. A beer festival is held in June. The house beer, Jolly Jeff, is brewed by Branscombe Vale, and the guest ale is usually supplied by the same brewery. The cider is from Green Valley. Good food is served at reasonable prices. Q P

Bridgerule

Bridge Inn

EX22 7EJ
(W of bridge over River Tamar)
12-2.30 (not Mon-Fri), 6.30-11; 12-3.30, 6.30-10.30 Sun
(01288) 381316
Fuller's London Pride; guest beers H
The sign outside reads 'the only pub west of the Tamar, but still in Devon'. This low-beamed local offers a warm, friendly welcome to all visitors, enhanced by a central open fire in the main bar in winter. Straddling the Devon/Cornwall border, it lies just a few miles from the Cornish coast. The pub boasts its own skittle alley. Lunch is served on Sunday, but no evening meals. Q

Buckfast

Abbey Inn

TQ11 0EA (off A38)
11-2.30, 6-11; 11-11 Fri & Sat; 12-10.30 Sun
(01364) 642343
St Austell Dartmoor Best, Tribute, HSD H
Large inn within the Dartmoor National Park, close to the famous Buckfast Abbey. The traditionally-furnished oak-panelled bar is spacious, warm and welcoming. The inn benefits from a beautiful setting next to the River Dart; the terrace overlooks the river, and provides a glimpse of the abbey. The large dining room offers an excellent range of food. There are many visitor attractions in the vicinity. Q P

Buckland Monachorum

Drake Manor Inn

The Village, PL20 7NA
11-2.30, 6.30-11; 12-10.30 Sun
(01822) 853892 drakemanorinn.co.uk
Courage Best Bitter; Greene King Abbot; Sharp's Doom Bar H
Cosy, 16th-century, two-bar pub at the centre of a small Dartmoor village, next to the church. The public bar is where the locals can be found enjoying the beers, while the second bar is mainly used for the recommended meals, based on local produce as far as possible. A small cellar room behind the bar admits children. A stream runs through the peaceful garden. Parking is limited.
Q P

Burgh Island (Bigbury)

Pilchard Inn

TQ7 4BG (walk from Bigbury car park, or take half-hourly sea tractor, check tides and times with pub)
11-11 daily
(01548) 810514
Beer range varies H
The tidal Burgh Island, with its Art Deco hotel and clifftop scenery, is a truly stunning setting for this ancient stone pub. The atmospheric, completely no-smoking hostelry is popular with walkers and families, even out of season, and the food, although not cheap, enjoys a good reputation. Three ales are usually stocked, with the emphasis on West Country beers, particularly Teignworthy and Sharp's. Heron Valley cider is sold. Q

Butterleigh

Butterleigh Inn

EX15 1PN
12-2.30, 6-11; 12-3, 7-10.30 Sun
(01884) 855407
Cotleigh Tawny; Otter Ale; guest beer H

Great country pub in a charming location, this splendid 400-year-old Devon cob building is full of character. There is a main bar and lounge with a modern but sympathetically-styled dining room. The open fire in the bar and the wood-burner in the lounge make this a warm, welcoming place in winter. In summer, you can sit in the attractive, secluded garden and enjoy the views of the surrounding rolling hills. The guest beer is usually from a local micro-brewery.
⛫Q❀⇌◐◑♣P

Chagford

Ring O' Bells

44 The Square, TQ13 8AH

⏲ 9.30am (10 Sat)-3, 5 (6 Sat)-midnight; 12-3, 6-midnight Sun

☎ (01647) 432466 🌐 ringobellschagford.co.uk

Butcombe Bitter; St Austell IPA; Teignworthy Reel Ale Ⓗ

This 400-year-old country inn, a former courthouse, is full of character, with a huge fireplace, exposed beams and comfortable furnishings. An extensive and reasonably-priced wine list accompanies a daily changing menu of local produce. A good selection of bottled beers is stocked; the cider varies. The main bar and lounge are supplemented by a dining area and lawned rear garden. Accommodation is available – breakfasts are served from 8.30am.
⛫Q♉❀⇌◐◑♿⛺♣●⚟

Sandy Park Inn

Sandy Park, TQ13 8JW (on A382, Moretonhampstead-Whiddon Down road)

⏲ 12-11 daily

☎ (01647) 433267 🌐 sandyparkinn.co.uk

Otter Bitter; St Austell Tribute; Ⓗ **guest beers** Ⓗ/Ⓖ

Thatched free house, circa 17th century, near Castle Drogo (NT). The characterful main bar boasts exposed beams and pews around the tables, while the spacious, no-smoking snug off the bar is dominated by a huge table. The no-smoking restaurant offers an intimate atmosphere and a menu of mainly local produce, with a specials board that changes regularly. It keeps an extensive wine list, but a limited bottled beer range. There is parking for just five cars at the front.
⛫Q♉❀⇌◐◑⛺♣●P⚟

Challacombe

Black Venus

EX31 4TT (on B3358 between A399 and Simonsbath) OS693411

⏲ 12-2, 6-11; 12-2.30, 6.30-10.30 Sun

☎ (01548) 763251

Beer range varies Ⓗ

This 18th-century village inn has low beams, a hop-strewn ceiling and plenty of character in its bar, supplemented by a dining area and games room. There are normally three ales, including a St Austell's beer, although this may be reduced in winter. With a campsite nearby this is a good base for walks over the western side of Exmoor. The name Black Venus appears to refer to a flock of sheep, which used to be kept in the field opposite. Q❀◐◑⛺♣P

Chardstock

George Inn

Chard Street, EX13 7BX

⏲ 12-2.30 (3 Sat), 6-11; 12-3, 7-10.30 Sun

☎ (01460) 220241 🌐 george-inn.co.uk

Branscombe Vale Branoc, seasonal beers; guest beer Ⓗ

Grade II listed, attractive, 15th-century thatched church house at the heart of a rural village; it is popular with locals and visitors alike. The spacious interior has three bar areas, a dining room, games room and a skittle alley. The ales and the produce for the extensive menu are sourced locally. Among its notable features are a superb linenfold screen and graffiti from 1600s. ⛫Q❀⇌◐◑♣P

Chawleigh

Earl of Portsmouth

The Square, EX18 7HJ

⏲ 11-3, 5.30-11; 11-11 Sat; 12-10.30 Sun

☎ (01769) 580204 🌐 earlofportsmouth-pub.co.uk

Barum Firing Squad; Beer Engine Rail Ale; guest beers Ⓗ

Rebuilt by the Earl of Portsmouth 1869, this excellent village local serves three beers from Devon micro-brewers all year round, plus Scrumpy cider from Winkleigh. The single bar is warmed by a log fire in winter and is home to Eric, the African Grey parrot. Locally-produced food is served in the bar or restaurant, for which Sue the chef continues to win plaudits – her beef fillet medallions and chicken breast fillets are particularly popular. ⛫❀◐◑♣●P

Chillington

Open Arms

TQ7 2LD (on A379, E of Kingsbridge)

⏲ 11-2.30, 6-11; 12-3, 7-11 Sun

☎ (01548) 581171

Draught Bass; Exmoor Ale; Princetown Jail Ale; guest beer Ⓗ

Unpretentious free house, this village local lies on the narrow main road between Kingsbridge and Dartmouth. An excellent range of ales includes a well-chosen guest, or try a glass of real Devon cider. Home-cooked food is served all day. Daily specials are chalked up – depending on the fish catch. Family friendly, the pub hosts occasional live music. ⛫Q♉❀◐◑⛺♣🚌●⚟

Chittlehampton

Bell Inn

The Square, EX37 9QL (off B3227, S Molton-Torrington road)

⏲ 11-3, 6-midnight; 11-midnight Sat; 12-11 Sun

☎ (01769) 540368 🌐 thebellatchittlehampton.co.uk

Beer range varies Ⓗ/Ⓖ

Busy, late 18th-century, village-centre pub with a child-safe garden and a conservatory dining area. It has a single bar, plus a games

room. The landlord is as enthusiastic as the locals when it comes to ale, football and cricket. The pub normally stocks a large range of ales, some handpumped, some on gravity, which are listed on a board. The cider is Thatchers. Much of the food served, including game, is locally sourced.
❀◑♿⛺♣●⚟

Chudleigh

Bishop Lacy

52-53 Fore Street, TQ13 0HY

✪ 12-midnight (1am Fri & Sat); 12-midnight Sun

☎ (01626) 854585

Fuller's London Pride; Princetown Jail Ale; Ⓖ guest beers Ⓗ

Grade II listed, this 14th-century church house is now a bustling local. It has built up a reputation for serving a good selection of real ales. The pub has two bars, both warmed by real fires, and one is no-smoking. Home-cooked food is served in a no-smoking restaurant area. Beer festivals are a regular event at this local CAMRA Pub of the Year 2000 (and regional winner in 1998). Children and dogs are welcome.
♛Q◑⊟⛺🚌♣⚟

Chulmleigh

Old Court House

South Molton Street, EX18 7BW

(200 yards from town centre)

✪ 11.30-midnight daily

☎ (01769) 580045 🌐 oldcourthouseinn.co.uk

Cotleigh Tawny; Sharp's Doom Bar; guest beers Ⓗ

Thatched country inn in a Grade II listed building. On the upper level you can see the authentic Royal House of Stuart coat of arms in a room that was used as a court house when Charles I stayed here. The cosy bar serves all areas, while good food is available in the bar or dining room. The cider is Thatchers Dry. Quizzes are staged on Thursday evening in support of various local good causes. ♛❀🛏◑♣●

Red Lion

East Street, EX18 7DD (off B3096)

✪ 11-11; 12-11 Sun

☎ (01769) 580384 🌐 redlionchulmleigh.co.uk

Barum Original; St. Austell Dartmoor Ⓗ

Grade II listed, 17th-century (15th-century in part) coaching inn, centrally located in this small town. The single, partitioned bar serves all areas, with three handpumps supplying two local real ales and Thatchers Cheddar Valley cider. Excellent food is served, with an emphasis on local produce – look for the quality statement in the restaurant listing local food providers. Apparently there is a friendly ghost who removes kitchen items, returning them a few days later. ♉❀🛏◑♣●P

Churston

Weary Ploughman

Dartmouth Road, TQ5 0LL

✪ 11-11; 12-11 Sun

☎ (01803) 844702

Sharp's Doom Bar; John Smith's Bitter; guest beers Ⓗ

Next to the steam railway station, this previous local CAMRA Pub of the Year enjoys a good reputation for its variety of real ales, sourced mainly from local breweries. The restaurant serves top of the range pub food at reasonable prices. It usually offers three guest ales and a draught Belgian beer. The large, open-plan bar includes a child-friendly area. The pub hosts barbecues in summer and an August beer festival.
Q❀🛏◑♿⛺⇌(Steam Rlwy)🚌P⚟

Clayhidon

Half Moon Inn

EX15 3TJ

✪ 12-3 (not Mon), 6-11; 12-3, 7-10.30 Sun

☎ (01823) 680291

Cotleigh Tawny; St Austell Tribute; guest beer Ⓗ

Traditional country inn, set in the Blackdown Hills, near the Somerset border. It is thought to have been constructed by and for the stonemasons building the church in the 18th century. There is a little used public right of way through the pub to the church (used on Rogation Sunday). The pub affords outstanding views of the Culm Valley. Bollhayes cider is sold.
♛♉❀◑⛺♣●P⚟

Cockwood

Anchor

EX6 8RA (on A379 between Starcross and Dawlish)

✪ 11-11; 12-10.30 Sun

☎ (01626) 890203

Fuller's London Pride; Greene King Abbot, Old Speckled Hen; Otter Ale; Taylor Landlord; Wadworth 6X Ⓗ

Eye-catching pub, in a stunning setting on an old harbour, populated by small boats and swans. It boasts genuine old timbers, low beams and high-backed settles. Offering as good a fresh fish and shellfish menu as anywhere in the UK, plus plenty of sensibly-priced snacks, it fully warrants its long list of prestigious awards. Six ales, including local brews, make this a busy pub all year round, run by an experienced landlord and efficient staff. ♛Q❀◑⛺🚌P

Colyton

Gerrard Arms

Rosemary Lane, EX24 6LN

✪ 11-3, 5.30 (6 Sat)-midnight (1am Fri & Sat); 12-3, 7-1am Sun

☎ (01297) 552588

Draught Bass; Ⓗ Branscombe Vale Branoc; Ⓖ guest beer Ⓗ

Busy, one-bar pub next to the church in this delightful little town with lots of lovely old cottages, tangled narrow streets and alleyways. The home-made food is good value, with a traditional roast available on Sundays. In summer the lunchtime session may run on. Colyton Station on the Seaton tramway is a level walk of under a mile, or take the connecting horse-drawn wagon service to the pub's door. ❀◑⛺⊖

Combe Martin

Castle Inn

High Street, EX34 0HS
⏲ 12 (4 Mon)-2.30am; 12-10.30 Sun
☎ (01271) 883706 🌐 castleinn.info
Beer range varies Ⓗ/Ⓖ
Situated about halfway along a claimant to the title of Britain's longest street, this is a proper pub. It features reclaimed floorboards, an elm-topped bar and four changing ales from small brewers all year round, supplemented by Winkleigh cider. It also serves good food. Amenities include darts, pool, skittles, table football and big screens for sport. It hosts regular live music and an August beer festival. Well-behaved children (and dogs) are welcome.
♨ᘐ❀◑◗♿⛺♣●P

Cornworthy

Hunter's Lodge Inn

TQ9 7ES (off A381, between Totnes and Kingsbridge)
⏲ 11.30-3, 6.30-11; 12-3, 6.30-11 Sun
☎ (01803) 732204 🌐 hunterslodgeinn.co.uk
Teignworthy Reel Ale; guest beers Ⓗ
Lively village pub, mentioned in the Domesday Book, that has maintained its variety and quality of beers. This comfortable, low beamed bar with a log fire has a welcoming atmosphere, despite being home, apparently, to a resident ghost. Three real ales are normally available and it has earned an excellent reputation for home-cooked food using the best of local ingredients. It hosts live music and quiz nights and sponsors the village football team (average age, 40). ♨Q❀◑◗⛺P

Crediton

Crediton Inn

28a Mill Street, EX17 1EZ (opp. Somerfield)
⏲ 11-11; 12-2, 7-10.30 Sun
☎ (01363) 772882 🌐 crediton-inn.co.uk
Fuller's London Pride; Sharp's Doom Bar; guest beers Ⓗ
Just off the town centre, this well-established, friendly, free house is a regular entry in this Guide. Four ales are always available, with guests typically coming from independent breweries. The skittle alley doubles as a function room and the pub runs its own angling club and cricket team. It hosts occasional quiz and theme nights. The menu is modest, but the food is good at local CAMRA's Pub of the Year 2005.
◑◗🚌♣P

Culmstock

Culm Valley Inn

EX15 3JJ
⏲ 12-4, 6-11; 11-11 Sat; 12-10.30 Sun
☎ (01884) 840354
Beer range varies Ⓖ
You will find this 300-year-old village inn by the River Culm, close to where it emerges from the Blackdown Hills. The car park was formerly the railway sidings of the Tiverton light railway and the pub was previously called the Railway Inn. It offers some 10 guest beers that change frequently, from small breweries. For the menu, local produce is used – often free range and organic.
♨Q❀⇄◑◗♣●P⁄

Dartmouth

Cherub Inn

13 Higher Street, TQ6 9RB
⏲ 11-11; 12-10.30 Sun
☎ (01803) 832571
Sharp's Doom Bar; guest beers Ⓗ
This Grade II listed pub that dates back to the 12th century is the oldest building in Dartmouth. Behind its quaint Tudor façade a small, cosy, beamed bar offers meals every lunchtime and evening. A tight, steep staircase leads to the restaurant that has a good reputation for local fish and seafood. Three beers (two in winter) supplement the house beer from Summerskills. Q◑◗⛺●

Ship in Dock

1 Ridge Hill, TQ6 9PE (at foot of hill from naval college)
⏲ 11-11.30; 12-11 Sun
☎ (01803) 835916 🌐 theshipindock.co.uk
Banks's Bitter; Wychwood Hobgoblin; guest beer Ⓗ
In a 16th-century listed building, the pub overlooks the River Dart estuary. The cosy bar bears a nautical theme and features a blazing fire in winter. A second room is up a couple of steps, with service through a hatchway down to the bar itself. Food is limited to snacks, such as sandwiches and pasties. With moorings a mere 20 or so yards away, the pub is convenient for visiting sailors, and welcomes dogs as well as seadogs. ♨Q❀⇄♣

Dawlish

Smugglers' Inn

27 Teignmouth Road, EX7 0LA (on A379 coast road to Teignmouth)
⏲ 11-11; 12-10.30 Sun
☎ (01626) 862301
Draught Bass; Teignworthy Reel Ale; guest beers Ⓗ
Unusually for a large roadhouse, this is free of tie and run by the owners. It benefits from a big car park and lovely coastal views. Comfortably furnished, it has a large, popular restaurant and caters happily for families without a noisy playground. The four handpumps serve a national brew and three local Devon ales, including one from Scattor Rock. It stages regular entertainment, occasional live music and beer festivals that are well supported. The facilities for disabled customers are commendable.
♨Qᘐ❀◑◗♿⛺⇌🚌♣P

Dittisham

Ferry Boat Inn

Manor Street, TQ6 0EX
⏲ 11-midnight; 11-11 Sun
☎ (01803) 722368
Draught Bass; Brakspear Bitter; Wychwood Hobgoblin; Young's Bitter Ⓗ

With scenic views of the River Dart, this Punch Taverns pub is accessible by boat, car or foot. A listed building, it has dark wooden beams, old local photos on the walls and flags on the ceiling. From a small kitchen upstairs a variety of food can be ordered, including a range of specials. With a good choice of beers, too, this is a really pleasant pub. Mobile phone use is penalised by a donation to charity. ♨◑◗

East Budleigh

Sir Walter Raleigh

22 High Street, EX9 7ED (off A376)

⏲ 11.45-2.30, 6-11; 12-2.30, 7-10.30 Sun

☎ (01395) 442510

Adnams Broadside; Otter Bitter; Wells Bombardier Ⓗ

Pleasant, 16th-century village pub, close to Sir Walter Raleigh's birthplace of Hayes Barton. Consisting of a bar and adjoining restaurant, this friendly pub is well patronised by locals. Diners are offered a wide range of pub favourites as well as more adventurous choices. Children are not encouraged in this pub that is free from piped music and gaming machines. Q◑◗▲

East Prawle

Pig's Nose Inn

TQ7 2BY

⏲ 12-2.30, 7-11 (closed winter Mon); 12-2.30, 7-11 (not winter eve) Sun

☎ (01548) 511209 🌐 pigsnoseinn.co.uk

Fuller's London Pride; South Hams Devon Pride, Ⓖ **Eddystone** Ⓗ

Old, three-roomed smugglers' inn, set on the village green. Children and dogs are welcome in its cluttered interior with a maritime ambience. Occasional live music, performed at weekends in a hall adjoining the pub, draws a crowd. The beer, largely on gravity, is stored in a specially-made rack behind the bar in an old alcove. It is a haven for birdwatchers and coastal walkers alike. Home-made, wholesome food is provided using local ingredients at local CAMRA's Pub of the Year 2005.

♨♉❀◑◗▲♣●

Exeter

Brook Green Tavern

31 Well Street, EX4 6QL

⏲ 4 (12 Sat & summer Fri)-11; 12-10.30 Sun

☎ (01392) 495699

Caledonian Deuchars IPA; Fuller's London Pride; Taylor Landlord; guest beers Ⓗ

Traditional pub serving the local community where the friendly landlady always offers six beers. Close to St James Park football ground, it is also student-friendly. It fields two football teams and hosts meetings of the Victorian cricket team. It stages occasional live entertainment and is renowned for its Sunday lunches and Thursday evening's 'curry and a pint'. Close to St James's Station, it is a five-minute walk from the city centre.

♉❀⇄◑◗♿⇌(St James's)🚌P

City Gate

City Gate Hotel, Iron Bridge, North Street, EX4 3RB

⏲ 11-midnight; 12-11.30 Sun

☎ (01392) 495811 🌐 citygatehotel.co.uk

Young's Bitter, Special, Waggledance; guest beer Ⓗ

A short walk from the High Street, this previously closed hotel has been carefully refurbished by Young's. The original entrance leads into an open bar area and hotel reception for the 15 guest rooms. Reasonably-priced food is served throughout, but restricted to snacks outside usual mealtimes. The large patio garden is framed by part of Exeter's old city wall. There is a small function room. Young's bottled beers are available to take away at favourable prices.

♨Q❀⇄◑◗♿⇌(Central/St David's)⚡

Double Locks Hotel

Canal Bank, EX2 6LT (road access from Marsh Barton trading estate)

⏲ 11-midnight; 12-10.30 Sun

☎ (01392) 256947

O'Hanlons Royal Oak; Otter Ale; Young's Bitter, Special, Waggledance; Ⓗ **guest beers** Ⓖ

An excellent mix of families, students, cyclists, walkers and their dogs makes this a busy pub all year round. Lovely log fires in winter and the canalside settting in good weather are particular attractions. All day food and an excellent range of ales (up to nine in summer, mainly on gravity), make this a worthwhile visit. Camping is available (phone ahead). ♨Q❀◑◗▲●P

Great Western Hotel

St David's Station Approach, EX4 4NU

⏲ 11-11; 12-10.30 Sun

☎ (01392) 274039 🌐 greatwesternhotel.co.uk

Adnams Broadside; Branscombe Vale Branoc; Fuller's London Pride; O'Hanlon's Yellowhammer; Taylor Landlord; guest beers Ⓗ

Built at the time of Brunel's opening of the railway in the mid-1880s, the Loco Bar displays many photographs and memorabilia of the bygone age of steam. The split-level bar keeps seven regular ales and always at least five, mostly local, guests that turn over rapidly. Ample portions are served on the extensive bar menu, and full meals can be enjoyed in the Brunel Restaurant. A few pavement benches allow for outdoor drinking.

❀⇄◑◗⇌(St David's)🚌⚡

Old Firehouse

50 New North Road, EX4 4EP (near Debenhams)

⏲ 12-2.30 (not Sat); 5 (6 Sat)-1am; 6-midnight Sun

☎ (01392) 277279

Topsham & Exminster Ferryman; Warrior Tomahawk; Wychwood Hobgoblin; guest beer Ⓗ

Popular, city-centre pub; its intimate, friendly atmosphere is only disturbed by the hum of conversation. Four beers include an organic guest whenever possible. Scrubbed wooden tables and benches add character, with candles lighting cosier corners. Upstairs, the dining and drinking area is much airier. Good value food is freshly prepared on the premises. The pub is five minutes' walk from Exeter bus station and Central railway

station. Work is in hand on alterations on the first floor and disabled toilet facilities.
Q❀◐⇌(Central)⊟

Well House Tavern
16-17 Cathedral Yard, EX1 1HO
⊙ 11-11; 12-10.30 Sun
☎ (01392) 223611
Beer range varies Ⓗ
This pub benefits from a large front window overlooking the lovely cathedral green at the historic heart of the city. It forms part of the Royal Clarence Hotel, which includes chef Michael Caine's restaurant. The house beer (Well House Ale) brewed by Otter, is complemented by five guest beers that change regularly and Grays cider. This pub is a must for any visitor to the city.
Q◐⇌(Central)⊟●

Exmouth

Grove
The Esplanade, EX8 1AS
⊙ 11-midnight daily
☎ (01395) 272101
Young's Bitter, Special, Waggledance, seasonal beers Ⓗ
Large Young's house, at the western end of the Esplanade, 10-15 minutes' walk from the town centre, with good bus and train services (buses also run along the Esplanade in the holiday season). Good food is served 12-10pm daily in the bar or upstairs no-smoking restaurant that benefits from panoramic views across the sea and Exe estuary. Families are welcome and the large garden is popular in summer when the pub gets busy. It hosts a quiz on Thursday evening.
⚔❀◐♿⇌⊟⚡

Powder Monkey
2-2a The Parade, EX8 1RJ
⊙ 9am-midnight (1am Fri & Sat); 9am-midnight Sun
☎ (01395) 280090
Blackawton Headstrong; Exmoor Stag; Greene King Abbot; Marston's Pedigree; guest beers Ⓗ
Attractive period building, once the offices of the local Herald and Journal newspaper, now a Wetherspoon's house. With a pleasant front patio, it is situated conveniently 300 yards or so from the station, and buses pass the door; Exmouth's main shopping area is two minutes' walk. A relaxed atmosphere pertains in the central seating area and the interconnected rooms. It hosts a quiz on Sunday evening.
⚔Q☕❀◐♿⇌⊟♣●⚡

Great Torrington

Torrington Arms
New Street, EX38 8BX
⊙ 11-midnight (1am Thu-Sat); 11-midnight Sun
☎ (01805) 622280
Clearwater Cavalier; Green King Abbot; guest beer Ⓗ
Situated on the main road through town, this former Railway Inn was renamed the Torrington Arms after the railway's demise. The open-plan bar and dining area is decorated with photographs depicting the escapades of the local charity fundraising group, the 'Cavaliers', over the last 35 years. At the rear is a patio and a function room converted from a barn. ⚔❀⇌◐♣

Hatherleigh

Tally Ho!
14 Market Street, EX20 3JN
⊙ 12 (11 Tue & Sat)-11 (1am Sat); 12-11 Sun
☎ (01837) 810306 🌐 hatherleigh.org.uk/tallyho
Clearwater Cavalier; guest beers Ⓗ
Towards the top of the main street of this small market town, stands this pleasant 15th-century inn with low beams and woodblock flooring. The central bar serves a number of drinking areas and the restaurant. Winkleigh cider is sold. A self-contained brewery at the rear has supplied the pub in the past, but currently is unfortunately inactive. ⚔Q❀⇌◐●

Hawkchurch

Old Inn
The Street, EX13 5XD (1 mile off B3165, opp. church)
OS343004
⊙ 12-3.30, 6.30-11 daily (closed Mon Oct-Easter)
☎ (01297) 678309 🌐 hawkchurch.com
Cotleigh Tawny; guest beers Ⓗ
Traditional one-roomed inn, situated in a quiet village off the beaten track. The first inn on the site was built in the 1540s, but then deliberately burnt down with adjoining properties in 1806 and rebuilt. Although food-oriented, the bar area is well set-up. Popular with walkers, guest accommodation includes a family room and smaller self-contained units converted from the skittle alley. The bar and restaurant are closed to non-residents on Mondays from October until Easter. Q❀⇌◐▲♣P

Hennock

Palk Arms
Church Road, TQ13 9QB
⊙ 12-2, 7-11 (midnight Fri & Sat); 12-2, 7-11 Sun
☎ (01626) 836584
Princetown Jail Ale; guest beer Ⓗ
Set high above the Teign Valley, this quintessential rustic pub in an out of the way location rewards the journey. Reputedly 16th century, it has recently had a new lease of life thanks to the quality of its ever-changing guest beer. It incorporates a small shop and post office. You are assured of a warm welcome from locals – and the cavernous log fire. Live music is performed every Saturday evening. Bar billiards, bar skittles and shove-ha'penny are played. ⚔❀◐♣

Hexworthy

Forest Inn
PL20 6SD (off B3357, Two Bridges-Dartmeet road)
⊙ 11.30-2.30, 6-11 daily
☎ (01364) 631211 🌐 theforestinn.co.uk
Teignworthy Reel Ale, Beachcomber; guest beers Ⓗ
Country inn situated in the Dartmoor forest,

well worth seeking out for a quick drink, a meal or a longer stay. Walkers, riders, anglers, canoeists, children and dogs are all welcome. Devon beers and cider are offered as well as a wide range of food and accommodation, including en-suite guest rooms and a bunkhouse. The bars are furnished with comfortable chesterfields, and there are separate areas for diners. Horses can be stabled by prior arrangement. ⛫Q♨❀⛟◐◑●P

Heybrook Bay

Eddystone Inn

Heybrook Drive, PL9 0BN (follow tourist signs, Langdon Crt to Heybrook)

✪ 12-3, 6-11; 12-11 Sat and summer; 12-10.30 Sun

☎ (01752) 862356

Sharp's Doom Bar, Wills Resolve; guest beers 🄷

Spacious bar and restaurant where an outdoor terrace affords splendid panoramic views over the bay to the Eddystone Lighthouse. It is ideal for walkers as it lies close to the coastal path, is dog-friendly and is open all day, every day in summer. Good value, freshly-cooked meals are prepared from local produce as far as possible, with a selection of six vegetarian dishes and a Sunday carvery. A Tuesday quiz night is staged fortnightly. Darts and pool are played. ❀◐◑▲♣P

High Bickington

Golden Lion Inn

North Road, EX37 9BB (on B3212 between A377 and A3124)

✪ 12-3 (not winter), 4.30-11; 12-11 Sat; 12-10.30 Sun

☎ (01769) 560213

Cotleigh Tawny, Barn Owl 🄷

This 17th-century inn lies on the main road through the village. The single bar is partitioned down the middle. Plentiful pictures and a number of books on display portray local village life and history. The small but comfortable dining room doubles as a children's room. Lunches are served daily in summer, just Saturday and Sunday the rest of the year. The bar is dog-friendly. It is close to a golf course and convenient for fishing on the Taw. Q♨◐◑♣P

Holcombe Rogus

Prince of Wales

TA21 0PN

✪ 12-3, 6-11; 11-11 Sat; 12-10 Sun

☎ (01823) 672070

Courage Best Bitter; guest beers 🄷

Not far from the Somerset border and the Grand Western Canal, which is popular with cyclists and walkers, this 17th-century country pub boasts unusual cash register handpumps. The recently extended dining area includes smart new toilets. Home-cooked food caters for vegetarians. A large log-burning stove warms the bar area. Pool and darts facilities are well used by local teams. The attractive walled garden is a bonus. Up to five real ales change regularly. ⛫Q❀⛟◐◑♣●P

Holsworthy

Rydon Inn

Rydon Road, EX22 7HU (½ mile W of Holsworthy on A3072, Bude road)

✪ 11.30-3, 5.30-11 (closed winter Mon); 12-3, 6-10.30 (not winter eve) Sun

☎ (01409) 259444 🌐 rydon-inn.com

Sharp's Doom Bar 🄷

A spacious, modern extension to an original Devon longhouse, this free house and restaurant is ideally situated for the market town of Holsworthy and just a few miles from the north Cornish coast. The central thatched bar serves all sections, including a conservatory and a large no-smoking/children's area offering award-winning food. The house bitter, Triple H, is a blend of Dreckly and Bodmin Boar ales from Ring o' Bells Brewery. The cider is Thatchers Dry. Families with well-behaved children are welcome. ⛫Q♨❀◐◑♿●P⅟

Honiton

Holt

178 High Street, EX14 1LA

✪ 10.30-3, 5.30-11 (midnight Fri & Sat); 11-4 Sun

☎ (01404) 47707 🌐 theholt-honiton.com

Otter Bitter, Bright, Ale Head 🄷

Otter Brewery has a done a fine job in converting what was a wine bar to its first pub. It comprises a good, cosy bar at street level, and a dining area upstairs; both are smart, incorporating much exposed wood in the decor. The kitchen is in full view, and as well as the restaurant menu, tapas-style snacks are usually available (no evening meals are served Sun). ◐◑♿⇌

Horsebridge

Royal Inn

PL19 8PJ (off A388, Tavistock-Launceston road)

✪ 11.30-3, 6.30-11; 12-3, 7-10.30 Sun

☎ (01822) 870214 🌐 royalinn.co.uk

Draught Bass; Sharp's Doom Bar; 🄷 **guest beers** 🄶

Originally built by monks as a nunnery, the pub overlooks an old bridge over the River Tamar, connecting Devon and Cornwall. It features half-panelling and stone floors in the bar and lounge, both are traditional in style. A further room off the lounge is no-smoking. The terraced gardens are suitable for children, who are welcome until 9pm. Guest beers are usually served from the barrel. The food is recommended. Bar billiards is played here. ⛫Q❀◐◑♣P⅟

Iddesleigh

Duke of York

EX19 8BG (off B3217, next to church) OS570083

✪ 11-11; 12-10.30 Sun

☎ (01837) 810253

Adnams Broadside; Cotleigh Tawny; guest beers 🄶

The 'Duke' is a 15th-century inn and free house situated in a quiet village. A friendly, relaxing atmosphere is enhanced by the exposed beams and inglenooks. The cider is Sam's Dry from nearby Winkleigh. Some food is supplied from the landlord's farm and served in the bar and dining rooms; a set menu is available in the evening until 9.30pm. Although remote, this 15th-century pub can get busy with locals and walkers on the Tarka Trail. ♕Q❀⇌◐♣●

Instow

Wayfarer Inn

Lane End, EX39 4LB (off N end of esplanade)
✪ 11-11; 12-10.30 Sun
☎ (01271) 860342 ⊕ thewayfarerinstow.co.uk
Country Life Old Appledore; Otter Bitter; Sharp's Doom Bar; guest beers Ⓖ
Traditional, family-run inn situated in a pretty coastal village. The pub boasts a suntrap garden, an enclosed outdoor eating area and a skittle alley. Locally-sourced, fresh food is served throughout the day, including fish caught from the pub's own boat (on which fishing can be arranged for residents). The pub is convenient for the South-West Coast Path and the restored Instow signal box. Instow esplanade is served by frequent bus services. ❀⇌◐●⊬

Kilmington

New Inn

The Hill, EX13 7SF (off A35)
✪ 11-2.30, 6-11; 12-3, 7-10.30 Sun
☎ (01297) 33376
Palmer Copper Ale, IPA Ⓗ
Cosy, thatched Devon longhouse that was rebuilt after a major fire in 2004, but retains a warm atmosphere. One benefit to have resulted from the fire was the provision of excellent toilet facilities. Secluded gardens and the landlord's aviaries are attractive outdoor features, while a well-used skittle alley is home to nine local teams. Regular quizzes and other events maintain this pub's position at the heart of village life. Q❀◐♿⚠⊟P⊬

Old Inn

EX13 7RB
✪ 12-2.30 (3 Sat), 6-11; 12-3, 7-10.30 (not winter) Sun
☎ (01297) 32096
Branscombe Vale Branoc; Otter Bitter, Ale; guest beer Ⓗ
Thatched roadside pub on the main A35, with a big car park. There is a major emphasis on quality food, with plenty of fish on the specials menu, mainly sourced from the local fishing village of Beer. Outside there is a pleasant patio and a raised lawn with tables, and inside, a restaurant, no-smoking lounge and bar with cricketing memorabilia. The beers are usually from the south west (except for the Czech Budvar lager) and lovingly tended by the landlord. ♕Q❀◐⊟P⊬

Kingswear

Ship Inn

Higher Street, TQ6 0AG
✪ 12-midnight (12-3, 6-midnight winter Mon-Thu); 12-11.30 Sun
☎ (01803) 752348 ⊕ theshipinnkingswear.co.uk
Adnams Bitter; Otter Ale; guest beers Ⓗ
Situated at the end of the steam railway line, this bustling, 15th-century, family-run village pub stands next to the church. Local CAMRA's Pub of the Year 2006 enjoys outstanding views of the River Dart from the dining room and terrace. The comfortable bar on the left has darts and other games, while the cosy lounge bar bears a ship theme; both are warmed by log fires. The restaurant has a well-deserved reputation for local fish dishes. ♕Q❀◐⚠⇌(Steam Rlwy)

Lake

Bearslake Inn

EX20 4HQ (on A386)
✪ 11-3, 6-11; 12-4 Sun
☎ (01837) 861334 ⊕ bearslakeinn.com
Beer range varies Ⓗ/Ⓖ
Bearslake Inn is a 13th-century Devon longhouse. Inside this family-run hostelry you will find a bar offering a range of quality real ales from the local area. The interior features exposed beams and timbers, flagstone floors and low ceilings. On the edge of Dartmoor by the Granite Way, it affords views of rugged landscape and granite tors and is ideally situated for walking, horse riding, fishing and cycling. With a fine restaurant and splendid accommodation, it nonetheless remains a real pub. ♕Q♉❀⇌◐♿⚠♣●P⊬

Longdown

Lamb Inn

EX6 7SR (on B3212, Exeter-Moretonhampstead bus route)
✪ 12-3, 6-11; closed Mon; 12-10.30 Sun
☎ (01392) 811711
Teignworthy Reel Ale; guest beers Ⓗ
Open-plan village pub, consisting of a restaurant and bar with open fires. Well decorated, it is furnished with sofas, armchairs, tables and traditional bar stools. Four handpumps offer beers from micro-breweries; four-pint jugs come at a reduced price. A wide range of draught and bottled Belgian beers – some uncommon – is displayed on a chalkboard with tasting notes. The cider is Grays. A good choice of home-cooked meals often includes a main course cooked with Belgian beer on the specials list. ♕Q♉❀⇌◐⊟♣●P⊬

Lympstone

Redwing Inn

Church Road, EX8 5JT (off A376 before Exmouth)
✪ 11.30-3, 6-11; 11.30-11 Sat; 12-10.30 Sun
☎ (01395) 222156
O'Hanlon's Royal Oak; Otter Bitter; Palmer IPA; guest beer Ⓗ
This active village pub is a genuine free house. The public bar and lounge are separate, but linked by a common bar. The dining room, off the lounge, serves a good choice of meals. Regular entertainment includes a Monday evening quiz and live music (Tue and Fri, plus occasionally summer Sun). Bottle-conditioned O'Hanlon's Port Stout and Thatchers draught cider are

stocked. The pub has a garden and patio. An hourly daytime bus service stops within a mile of the pub. Q❀◑⊟≠●P

Mary Tavy

Elephant's Nest

Horndon, PL19 9NQ

✪ 12-3, 6.30-11; 12-3, 6.30-10.30 Sun

☎ (01822) 810273

Palmer Copper Ale, IPA; guest beers Ⓗ

Intriguingly renamed, from the New Inn, by a previous landlord, this 16th-century pub affords magnificent views over Dartmoor from its large garden. The bar remains traditional, despite featuring many elephantine items, including a mural, figurines and curios; note the word 'elephant' spelt in many different languages on the beams. Two further rooms off the bar are suitable for children. It supports local cricket, rugby and pony clubs. ♔Q☕❀◑♣●P⊬

Molland

London Inn

EX36 3NG (3 miles off B3227) OS807285

✪ 11.30-2.30, 6-11; 11-2.30, 7-11 Sun

☎ (01769) 550269

Cotleigh Tawny; Exmoor Ale Ⓖ

Delightful, 15th-century, former coaching inn next to the church, nestling in the hills beneath Exmoor. The pub comprises several small rooms and a restaurant, all boasting stone walls and beamed ceilings; its walls are laden with displays connected with shooting, hunting and fishing. It can be busy during the shooting season, and attracts both locals and visitors. The pub has a skittle alley situated across the road. ♔Q❀⊟◑

Mortehoe

Chichester Arms

EX34 7DU

✪ 12-3, 6.30-11; 12-11 Sat and summer; 12-10.30 Sun

☎ (01271) 870411

Barum Original; Cottage Somerset & Dorset Ale; Greene King Ruddles Best Bitter; guest beers Ⓗ

This friendly village free house is particularly popular in summer, but busy all year. It still has gas lighting. Food, made on the premises, is served in the restaurant, bar, or outside. The games room houses a skittle alley and other games are available. In a picturesque location, there are fine coastal walks on NT land; the long distance footpath leads to expansive beaches at nearby Woolacombe. Children are welcome in summer when food is served daily (meals Wed-Sun other periods). ☕❀◑▲P⊬

Newton Abbot

Locomotive Inn

35-37 East Street, TQ12 2JP (100 yds from hospital)

✪ 11-11; 12-10.30 Sun

☎ (01626) 365249

Adnams Broadside; Draught Bass; guest beers Ⓗ

Cosy, three-roomed, 17th-century inn at the town centre. The main, L-shaped bar has a large open fire, a TV with a sofa for viewers and a dartboard. Another small bar and seating area is available next to what was the old sherry bar. At the rear is a pool room, with a small serving hatch through to the main bar. Up to four real ales are stocked, as well as Westons Old Rosie cider. ♔⊟♿≠⊟♣●

Newton St Cyres

Beer Engine

EX5 5AX (off A377, by station)

✪ 11-11; 12-11 Sun

☎ (01392) 851282

Beer Engine Rail Ale, Piston Bitter, Sleeper Heavy, seasonal beers Ⓗ

Detached, late 19th-century former railway hotel with a most pleasant public bar, polished floors, a roaring log fire and ceiling beams adorned with hops. There is always a warm welcome here and in the restaurant. The secluded patio and barbecue area afford views over open countryside. You can make an appointment to visit Devon's oldest working brewery (opened in 1983) in the basement. ♔Q☕❀◑♿≠♣P⊬☐

North Tawton

Railway Inn

Whiddon Down Road, EX20 2BE (1 mile S of village) OS666001

✪ 12-3 (not Mon-Thu), 6-11; 12-3, 7-11 Sun

☎ (01837) 82789

Teignworthy Reel Ale; guest beers Ⓗ

Set in a rural location, the Railway is a friendly, single-bar pub that is part of a working farm. It stands next to the former North Tawton Station (closed 1971), which it predates; the bar decor includes railway memorabilia and old station photos. The beer range is generally from the West Country, as is the cider (usually Grays) stocked in summer. The dining room is popular in the evening (no food Thu eve); light meals are served at lunchtime. ♔◑♣●P

Noss Mayo

Ship Inn

PL8 1EW

✪ 11.30-11; 12-10.30 Sun

☎ (01752) 872387 🌐 nossmayo.com

Butcombe Blonde; Princetown Jail Ale; St Austell Tribute; Summerskills Tamar; guest beer Ⓗ

This former Plymouth CAMRA Pub of the Year is situated on the River Yealm, with its own moorings (check with pub for details). Comfortable seating inside and out allows guests to enjoy the smoke-free atmosphere, and gaze at the river. With a second pub, the Turtley Corn Mill, the owners are able to maintain their policy of sourcing local products for their kitchen and bar.
♔Q❀◑♿♣P⊬

Okehampton

Plymouth Inn

26 West Street, EX20 1HH

✪ 11-midnight daily

☎ (01837) 53633

Beer range varies Ⓖ
Situated near the bridge over the West Okement River at the western end of town, the Plymouth is a friendly pub that brings the welcome and atmosphere of a village pub to an old market town. Walking and cycling groups are informally organised in summer and two beer festivals are held each year (normally May and Nov). The changing beer range places the accent on West Country breweries. ❀◑♣

Paignton

Isaac Merritt

54-58 Torquay Road, TQ3 3AA
⏲ 10 (9am Sat)-midnight; 9am-midnight Sun
☎ (01803) 556066
Courage Directors; Greene King Abbot; Marston's Burton Bitter, Pedigree; guest beers Ⓗ
This busy, town-centre pub was local CAMRA Pub of the Year in 2001 and a Wetherspoon's award-winner in 2004. It is easily accessible to wheelchair users, and has a designated ground-floor toilet. The changing range of superb quality real ales is augmented by mini-beer festivals every Sunday and Monday, with the chosen beers sold at reduced prices. Good value meals are served all day. Q◑♿⇌🚌●⊬

Peter Tavy

Peter Tavy Inn

PL19 9NN
⏲ 12-2.30 (3 Fri), 6-11; 12-2.30, 6-10.30 Sun
☎ (01822) 810348
Blackawton Original Bitter; Princetown Jail Ale; Sharp's Doom Bar; guest beers Ⓗ
In a quiet village on the edge of Dartmoor, a good range of local beers can be found in the pub's small central bar. There are also two larger rooms, one of which is a no-smoking/ family room. A patio and hidden garden are added attractions. The pub is renowned for its food, however drinkers are made welcome. The inn is situated on the No.27 cycle route, near a caravan and camping site. ⛫Q♨❀⇄◑⛺P⊬

Plymouth

Artillery Arms

6 Pounds Street, Stonehouse, PL1 3RH
(behind Stonehouse Barracks and Millbay Docks)
⏲ 11-11; 12-10.30 Sun
☎ (01752) 262515
Draught Bass; guest beers Ⓗ
Opening at 9am for breakfast (no alcohol), this corner pub at the rear of the Brittany Ferries terminal has a single bar, plus a no-smoking dining area where good value, home-made food is served (no meals Sun). This is very much a community pub, sponsoring charity fundraising events, including monkey races; a 'beach party' is held in February. Although not the easiest pub to locate in the back streets of Stonehouse, it is well worth the effort. ⛫◑

Blue Peter

68 Pomphlett Road, Plymstock, PL9 7BN
⏲ 11 (12 winter)-11 (midnight Fri & Sat); 11-10.30 Sun
☎ (01752) 402255
Beer range varies Ⓗ
Local CAMRA Pub of the Year two years running, this two-bar pub is in a part of Plymouth where real ale is scarce. The lounge area, with alcove seating, is where most meals are taken, while the public bar contains a large sports screen and games area, and can be used for live entertainment. Beer festivals are held – check with the pub for details. The pub is on a frequent bus route, No. 7/7A from the city centre to Turnchapel.
⛫❀◑⊟⛺🚌♣●P⊬

Boringdon Arms

Boringdon Terrace, Turnchapel, PL9 7TQ
⏲ 11-11; 12-11 Sun
☎ (01752) 402053 🌐 bori.co.uk
Draught Bass; Butcombe Bitter; Otter Ale; RCH Pitchfork; Summerskills Best Bitter; guest beer Ⓗ
Recent renovations have made this former regional CAMRA Pub of the Year even more popular. Situated in a waterside village on the coastal footpath, Turnchapel is well served by road and water taxis from the Barbican. Beer festivals are held on the last weekend of odd numbered months. The 'Bori' has a reputation for its hot meals, which can be taken out in the enclosed garden that was created from part of a redundant quarry. ⛫Q♨❀⇄◑⊟♣

Britannia

1 Wolseley Road, Milehouse, PL2 3AE (near football ground)
⏲ 9am-midnight (1am Fri & Sat); 9am-midnight Sun
☎ (01752) 607596
Greene King Abbot; Marston's Burton Bitter, Pedigree; Shepherd Neame Spitfire; guest beers Ⓗ
Typical Wetherspoon's conversion from a run-down Edwardian pub into a fine, busy local that serves its community well. The Britannia mostly attracts regulars, however as it is the closest pub to Home Park, home of Plymouth Argyle FC, supporters also visit on match days when the atmosphere becomes more lively but remains friendly. The pub stands at one of the city's busiest road junctions, opposite the bus station and roughly half a mile from the railway station.
⛫Q❀◑♿⇌🚌⊬

Clifton

35 Clifton Street, Greenbank, PL4 8JB
⏲ 3.45-11; 12-midnight Fri-Sun
☎ (01752) 266563
Draught Bass; Worthington's Bitter; guest beers Ⓗ
Clifton Classic is a house beer brewed by local brewer Summerskills for this spacious, back-street pub not far from the city centre. Warm and friendly, the pub fields many competitive teams. The Clifton was once considered the luckiest pub in Britain as it numbered no fewer than three National Lottery millionaires among its regulars. Addlestones and Thatchers ciders are stocked. ⇌(North Rd)♣●

Dolphin Hotel
14 The Barbican, PL1 2LS
10 (9am summer)-midnight; 11.30-10.30 Sun
☎ (01752) 660876
Draught Bass G
The most famous pub on the Barbican, it is unspoilt and remains unmodernised. The original windows still bear the logo of the Octagon Brewery. Numerous paintings of the landlord by famous artists are an unusual feature here. It stands near the Mayflower Steps from where the Pilgrim Fathers left for a new life in the New World, and was the first place the Tolpuddle Martyrs stayed on their return to England. Q

Fawn Private Members Club
39 Prospect Street, PL4 8NY
12-11; 12-10.30 Sun
☎ (01752) 660540 thefawnclub.co.uk
Courage Best Bitter; guest beers H
Named after the now-scrapped HMS Fawn, and previously a Whitbread pub, CAMRA members are welcome here with a valid, current membership card. Regular visitors will be required to join. Many members are keen followers of rugby and other televised sports, and support the club's darts, pool and euchre teams, while others just come to enjoy the ambience and reasonable prices. The house beer, Fawn Ale, is supplied by Sharp's and two guest ales are also available as well a cider.

Fisherman's Arms
31 Lambhay Street, PL1 2NN (on Barbican near Citadel army base)
12 (5 Mon)-11; 12-10.30 Sun
☎ (01752) 661457
St Austell Tinners, Tribute, HSD H
Reputedly the second oldest pub in Plymouth, hidden away behind the famous Barbican, it has a warm and friendly atmosphere and serves home-cooked food. Its location makes it popular both with locals, who head for the lively public bar, and tourists who generally settle in the lounge, which has a raised area at the rear especially suitable for dining. Although limited to St. Austell beers, the quality has improved under the current licensees and the community feel has returned.

Fortescue
37 Mutley Plain, Mutley, PL4 6JQ
11-11 (midnight Thu-Sat); 12-10.30 Sun
☎ (01752) 660673
Draught Bass; Blue Anchor Spingo Special; Greene King Abbot; guest beers H
This lively local is frequented by a broad section of the community and conversation flourishes. On Thursday the popular cellar bar hosts an acoustic evening and at weekends various alternative DJs play anything but chart music. A perfect Sunday can be spent here: a home-cooked roast, washed down with Spingo and rounded off by the quiz. The patio garden draws a crowd in summer. The pub displays some interesting cricketing memorabilia.

Maritime
19 Southside Street, Barbican, PL1 2LD
11-11; 12-10.30 Sun
☎ (01752) 664898
Beer range varies H
Situated at the heart of the historic Barbican, opposite the old customs house, the pub has entrances on Southside Street and Quay Road. The former leads into a comfortable, carpeted lounge section with tables for dining and easy chairs. The Quay entrance leads into a bar with a slate floor, dominated by a large TV and sound system. Although there are no partitions between the two areas, they are quite distinct. Take your pick.

Prince Maurice
3 Church Hill, Eggbuckland, PL4 6RJ
11-3, 7-11; 11-11 Fri & Sat; 12-10.30 Sun
☎ (01752) 771515
Adnams Broadside; Courage Best Bitter; Greene King Old Speckled Hen; RCH East Street Cream; Summerskills Best Bitter; guest beers H
A village pub atmosphere pervades this cosy, friendly pub, next to the green and church in Eggbuckland, which is now a suburb of the city. Four times local CAMRA Pub of the Year, it continues to sell eight beers, plus Thatchers Cheddar Valley cider. The pub is named after the Royalist general whose headquarters were nearby during the siege of Plymouth. P

Providence
20 Providence Street, PL4 8JQ
5-midnight; 4-1am Fri; 1-1am Sat; 1-midnight Sun
☎ (01752) 228178
South Hams XSB, Eddystone; Summerskills Best Bitter; guest beers H
Intimate, one-bar, street-corner local in a terrace near the city centre. The Providence is a meeting place for local members of the Sealed Knot Society. It is handy for the railway station, the city centre and Mutley Plain. The draught cider, which is Thatchers Cheddar Valley, must be asked for as it is kept out of the bar to maintain its optimum temperature.

Pym Arms
16 Pym Street, Devonport, PL1 4RG
11-1.30 (not Mon-Wed), 4-11; 12-10.30 Sun
☎ (01752) 561823
Princetown Jail Ale; guest beers G
A long, single-roomed pub at the end of a terrace, with bare beams and floorboards. Close to the Torpoint Ferry, it is also near the historic Devonport Dockyards, from where many of its customers come. Two or three ales are served straight from the cask and a real cider (mostly Thatchers Cheddar Valley) is usually available. Q ≠ (Devonport)

Sippers
18 Millbay Road, PL1 3LH
11-10.30 (11 Fri & Sat); 12-10.30 Sun
☎ (01752) 670668 sipperspub.co.uk
Fuller's London Pride; Greene King Old Speckled Hen; guest beers H
This pub is located just off the city centre, between the Pavilions Leisure Centre and the ferry port. It is spread over four levels, two of

which are designated as no-smoking. The pub has stone floors and the walls are covered with naval and other memorabilia. The unusual name refers to an old naval rum ration. Up to five real ales are kept. ❀◑◐⚟

Thistle Park Brewhouse
32 Commercial Road, Coxside, PL4 0LE
(between National Aquarium and Vue cinema)
⏲ 11-2.30am; 12-4am Fri & Sat; 12-1.30am Sun
☎ (01752) 204890
South Hams Devon Pride, XSB, Sutton Comfort, Eddystone, seasonal beers 🄷
Friendly pub, undergoing a makeover at the time of writing, which will provide it with a new restaurant area, dance floor and improved disabled access. All the beers are from the South Hams Brewery (formerly Sutton Brewery that was actually located in the pub – the brewery's relocation has made the pub's refurbishment possible). Note the extended opening hours. Live music is staged every weekend. If you feel brave (and have a strong jaw) try the biltong – a delicacy from South Africa. ◑◐♿●⚟

Plympton

Lyneham Inn
PL7 5AT (on old A38 towards Exeter)
⏲ 12-3, 5-11; 12-11 Fri & Sat; 11.30-10.30 Sun
☎ (01752) 336955 🌐 oldmanorinns.com
Draught Bass; Palmer IPA; guest beers 🄷
Large inn, just outside Plympton, where a long bar serves two separate seated areas (one of which is no-smoking) and a spacious conservatory providing further seating. It is one of three houses owned by Old Manor Inns, the others are in Torbay. Two regular and two guest ales are offered on handpump, the guests sourced from regional breweries. The pub is popular for meals and families are welcome; an outdoor play area is provided. ♛❀◑◐♿▲P⚟

Plymtree

Blacksmith's Arms
EX15 2JU
⏲ 12-2.30 (not Mon or Tue), 6-11 (not Mon); 12-4, 7-10.30 Sun (not winter)
☎ (01884) 277474
O'Hanlon's Firefly, Yellowhammer; guest beer 🄷
Delightful, 18th-century village free house, with open fires, oak beams and blacksmith's tools. A blackboard lists events for the month ahead, including occasional quizzes and live music. Skittles, boules and darts are played here. Reasonable prices are charged for the good food that is sourced locally and has built up a good reputation. Opening hours on Monday and Tuesday may vary, so phone to check if travelling far.
♛Q❀◑◐♣●P

Postbridge

Warren House Inn
PL20 6TA (on B3212, Two Bridges-Moretonhampstead road)
⏲ 11-11 (11-5 winter Mon-Wed); 12-10.30 Sun
☎ (01822) 880208
Badger Tanglefoot; Otter Ale; Ringwood Old Thumper; guest beer 🄷
The interior of this isolated Dartmoor inn, the third highest pub in England, features exposed beams and wood-panelled walls, complemented by rustic benches and tables. The open fire in the bar has apparently not gone out since 1845; it smoulders away gently in the background all year round. Lunch and evening menus offer home-cooked dishes based on locally-sourced ingredients and include vegetarian options. There is a spacious family room. Tables outside afford breathtaking views of the moors. ♛Q♉❀◑◐▲●P⚟

Sandford

Lamb Inn
The Square, EX17 4LW
⏲ 9am (11 Sat)-11 (midnight Fri & Sat); 11-10:30 Sun
☎ (01363) 773676
Beer Engine Rail Ale, Piston Bitter; 🄷 **guest beer** 🄶
This 16th-century former coaching inn is located at the heart of the village. Now a free house, it features two Beer Engine beers and one guest; the cider is from Sandford Orchards. The food is based on local ingredients, mostly seasonal organic produce. All meals are cooked to order and you can enjoy a coffee or light snack from 9am during the week in the garden. The skittle alley functions as an occasional cinema and hosts open-mike evenings for local bands. ♛❀◑◐🚌♣●

Scoriton

Tradesman's Arms
TQ11 0JB
⏲ 12-2.30, 6-11; 12-4 Sun
☎ (01364) 631206
Badger First Gold; Princetown Dartmoor IPA; guest beers 🄷
Traditional, country village pub, originally an ale house built for the tin miners in the 17th century. It comprises a single, open-plan L-shaped bar, with a small additional seating area for diners. Good food, prepared as far as possible from local produce, is served (not Sun eve) and special dietary needs are catered for, especially diabetic and gluten-free. There are gated areas outside for summer dining and an inside room that can be used by families or for meetings.
♛Q♉❀◑◐●P⚟

Sidmouth

Swan Inn
37 York Street, EX10 8BY (400 yds from seafront lifeboat station)
⏲ 11-2.30 (3 Sat), 5.30-11; 12-3, 7-10.30 Sun
☎ (01395) 512849
Young's Bitter, Special, Winter Warmer 🄷
Situated in the winding back streets of this quaint seaside town, originally cottages and a shop, it became an inn in 1890. Just a short walk from the seafront and main shopping area but in a quiet location, there is evening parking opposite and all day

public parking just two minutes' walk away. Beams and open fireplaces help create a cosy, traditional atmosphere. The nearest bus stop is a four-minute walk.
♨Q❀◐◑♿🚌♣⚟

Silverton

Lamb Inn

Fore Street, EX5 4HZ
⏲ 11.30-2.30, 6-11 (1am Thu; 2am Fri); 11.30-2am Sat; 12-11 Sun
☎ (01392) 860272
Draught Bass; Exe Valley Dob's Best Bitter; guest beers [H]/[G]
Family-run village pub characterised by stone floors, stripped timber and old pine tables and chairs. Most ales served are by gravity from a temperature controlled stillage behind the bar; the two guests are changed monthly. A multi-purpose function room/skittle alley and bar is well used by local teams. Good value, home-cooked food includes a specials board with vegetarian options. ♨◐◑♣

Slapton

Queen's Arms

TQ7 2PN (800 yds from beach, off A379)
⏲ 11-3, 6-11; 12-3, 7-10.30 Sun
☎ (01548) 580800
Sharp's Doom Bar; Teignworthy Reel Ale; guest beers [H]
South Devon free house with a single bar where the traditional mood is enhanced by a large open fire. Two or three real ales are stocked, depending on the time of year, plus a good range of bottled beers. A full menu includes a take-away service; Sunday lunchtime roasts in winter are worth booking. Many old photos depict wartime evacuation. The walled garden allows for alfresco drinking. Children (and dogs) are welcome. ♨❀◐◑⛺🚌♣P

South Brent

Royal Oak

Station Road, TQ10 9BE
⏲ 12-11 (11.45 Fri & Sat); 12-11 Sun
☎ (01364) 72133 🌐 royaloak.net
Draught Bass; Teignworthy Reel Ale; guest beers [H]
Busy pub at the centre of the village on the edge of Dartmoor. The main L-shaped bar is surrounded by a large open-plan area with comfortable leather sofas to relax in. Alternatively visitors can sit at the wood-panelled bar and enjoy the excellent range of real ales. At the back is the restaurant/function room converted from the old skittle alley, where good quality food is served. Beer festivals are held occasionally. Q◐◑⛺

South Pool

Millbrook Inn

TQ7 2RW (off A379 at Chillington, E of Kingsbridge) OS776402
⏲ 12-3, 6-11; 12-3, 6-10.30 Sun
☎ (01548) 531581
Draught Bass; [G] **Palmer IPA; guest beers** [H]
This pub is situated at the head of the Salcombe estuary, accessible by boat. The main section dates back to the 17th century, with the top bar, where children are welcome, added later. The pub is busy in summer with most of its trade coming from boaters and walkers. It is famed for its crab sandwiches. Dogs are also welcome. At the back you can watch ducks swimming in the stream. Heron Valley cider is stocked in summer.
♨Q❀◐◑⊟♣●⚟

Spreyton

Tom Cobley Tavern

EX17 5AL (leave A30 at Whiddon Down, onto A124, then right)
⏲ 12-3, 6-midnight (6.30-10.30 Mon; 6-1am Fri & Sat); 12-3, 7-11 Sun
☎ (01647) 231314
Clearwater Cavalier; [G] **Cotleigh Tawny;** [H] **Country Life Old Appledore;** [G] **Sharp's Doom Bar; St Austell Tribute;** [H] **guest beers** [H]/[G]
Local CAMRA's Pub of the Year 2006, the Tom Cobley offers an exceptional beer range with eight regular ales; altogether, there are usually four on handpump and up to 10 on gravity. A thriving village pub, with a modest bar and a spacious dining room at the rear, it is popular for food as well as beer with locals and others in the know. Booking is recommended for all meals, but especially Sunday lunch. It has four guest rooms.
♨Q⛷❀🛏◐◑⊟♿♣P

Sticklepath

Devonshire Inn

EX20 2NW (on old A30)
⏲ 11-3, 5.30-11; 11-11 Fri & Sat; 12-3, 7-10.30 Sun
☎ (01837) 840626
St Austell Tinners, HSD [G]
At the end of what was originally a terrace of Elizabethan cottages in a North Dartmoor village, the Devonshire is an unspoilt thatched local with low beams and a large open fire. A leat running past the back wall helps cool the stillage for the gravity dispensed beers, as well as powering the waterwheels of the NT's Finch Foundry Museum nearby. The Exeter-Okehampton bus (X9) stops outside and a number of footpaths access the Dartmoor countryside nearby. ♨Q❀◐🚌♣P

Taw River Inn

EX20 2NW (5 miles E of Okehampton)
⏲ 12-midnight; 12-11 Sun
☎ (01837) 840377
Draught Bass; Greene King Abbot; St Austell Tribute; Sharp's Doom Bar [H]
North Devon CAMRA Pub of the Year 2005 and 06, the Taw River is an active village local on the old A30. The large single bar is usually lively as numerous sports and pub games are pursued by the regulars. The area is popular for walking in summer, while the Finch Foundry Museum (NT) is just across the road. The Exeter-Okehampton (X9) bus stops nearby. ♨❀◐◑🚌♣P

ENGLAND

Stokenham

Tradesman's Arms

TQ7 2SZ (250 yds from A379)
11.30-3, 6-11; 12-3, 7-10.30 Sun
☎ (01548) 580313 thetradesmansarms.com
Brakspear Bitter; Draught Bass; South Hams Devon Pride, Eddystone; guest beer H

Pleasant free house in the South Hams, frequented by local drinkers. Reputed to be 500 years old, with beamed ceilings and a real fire, interconnecting rooms off the bar provide ample seating and tables. The quiet pub permits an excellent atmosphere in which to savour the Brakspear ale on offer or those from the local South Hams Brewery, and the extensive menu. The landlord's previous pub was in the Chilterns, hence the Brakspear connection. ⛫Q❀◖◗⛺🚌●⚟

Talaton

Talaton Inn

EX5 2RQ (from A30 follow ESCOT Park signs for 2 miles)
12-3, 7-10.30 daily
☎ (01404) 822214
Fuller's London Pride; O'Hanlon's Yellowhammer; Otter Bitter; guest beers H

Excellent example of a country pub. The 16th-century building in a small village has a large bar that draws in the locals. The restaurant, with a no-smoking bar area, serves a good value menu, including lunchtime specials and offers for older people. The large skittle alley is well used. Generally, it sells four real ales, two from local breweries. ⛫Q◖◗♿♣P⚟

Tamerton Foliot

Seven Stars Inn

Seven Stars Lane, PL5 4NN
12-11 (midnight Fri & Sat); 12-11 Sun
☎ (01752) 772901
Courage Best Bitter; Sharp's Doom Bar; guest beers H

Reputedly Plymouth's oldest pub, with parts dating back to the 13th century, its history is linked to that of the local church. Close to Tamerton Creek (SSSI), Warleigh Point Nature Reserve, and enjoying good access to Dartmoor, the pub welcomes families. It organises occasional brewery visits and regular beer festivals, featuring up to eight extra ales and ciders. An outside area is provided for summer drinking, dining and barbecues. It hosts a Sunday evening quiz and monthly jazz (first Mon). ⛫Q❀◖◗P⚟

Tavistock

Trout & Tipple

Parkwood Road, PL19 0JS
(on A386 to Okehampton, past Kelly College)
12-2.30 (not Tue), 6-11; 12-2.30, 6 (7 winter)-10.30 Sun
☎ (01822) 618886 troutandtipple.co.uk
Princetown Jail Ale; guest beers H

Just a mile north of Tavistock, this hostelry features a traditional, hop-strewn bar with a large no-smoking conservatory and dining area. A small games room and patio complete the picture. Nearby is a trout fishery. Children are welcome until 9pm. This friendly pub, where dogs are accepted, stocks a changing cider and seasonal beers from Teignworthy; the ceiling bears a plethora of pump clips from past ales. It stages beer festivals in February and October. ⛫Q❀◖◗⛺●P⚟

Topsham

Bridge Inn ☆

EX3 0QQ (by River Clyst on Exmouth road)
12-2, 6-10.30 (11 Fri & Sat); 12-2, 7-10.30 Sun
☎ (01392) 873862 cheffers.co.uk
Beer range varies G

This Grade II listed building has been owned and run by the same family since 1897, and was visited by the Queen in 1998. The snug, small room and old malt house, which occasionally hosts music, are all no smoking. Numerous picnic tables overlook the river. A minimum of six beers is always stocked, dispensed from the cellar; 'thirds' glasses are provided for some of the stronger seasonal ales and tasting sessions. Snacks prepared from local produce are available at lunchtime. ⛫Q❀⇌🚌P⚟

Globe Hotel

Fore Street, EX3 0HR
11-11 (midnight Fri & Sat); 12-11 Sun
☎ (01392) 873471 globehotel.com
Draught Bass; Butcombe Bitter; Fuller's London Pride; St Austell Dartmoor Best; Sharp's Doom Bar; guest beer H

Set in a beautiful, historic estuary town, this 17th-century former coaching inn is popular with tourists and business people as well as locals. Food served (not Sun) in the restaurant or the bar places an emphasis on good local produce. There is a skittle alley in the Malt House; occasional live music is performed and Topsham Folk Club meets on Sunday. In winter you can warm up by an open fire. Children are welcome in the back room. ⛫Q❀🛏◖◗♿⇌🚌♣P

Torquay

Buccaneer Inn

43 Babbacombe Downs Road, TQ1 3LN (on the downs)
12 (11 Sat)-11 (midnight Fri & Sat summer); 12-10.30 Sun
☎ (01803) 312661
St Austell Tribute, HSD H

Family-run St Austell house overlooking the clifftop gardens, with superb views across Lyme Bay. The single, spacious, wood-panelled bar has a designated area for pool and darts. Children are admitted until 7pm. Home-cooked food is available Easter-October, and Sunday lunch all year. An extra St Austell beer is stocked in summer. The front forecourt provides extra space for drinkers. It is a short walk from the model village and cliff railway, and the steep descent to Babbacombe Beach is nearby. ❀◖◗♿♣

Crown & Sceptre

2 Petitor Road, St Marychurch, TQ1 4QA

☉ 12-4, 5.30-11; 12-midnight Fri; 12-4, 6.30-midnight Sat; 12-4, 7-11.30 Sun

☎ (01803) 328290

Courage Best Bitter; Fuller's London Pride; Greene King Abbot, Old Speckled Hen; Young's Special; guest beers Ⓗ

This 200-year-old coaching house boasts over 30 years of unbroken entries in this Guide, under the stewardship of the same landlord. The collections of chamber pots and pennants and the open fire impart character inside, while outdoors there are two small, enclosed gardens. This well supported, community pub, selling five regular and three guest ales at all times, encourages live music (jazz Tue and Sun eves; folk most Fris). Food is served Monday-Saturday. Dogs are made very welcome here. ⌂Q❀◑◗⊟♣P

Hole in the Wall

6 Park Lane, TQ1 2AU (off end of Torwood St)

☉ 11-midnight daily

☎ (01803) 200755

Greene King IPA; Sharp's Doom Bar; Shepherd Neame Spitfire; Theakston Mild; Wells Bombardier; guest beers Ⓗ

Tucked away behind the harbour, Torquay's oldest inn (circa 1540), with its beamed ceilings and cobbled floors worn smooth over the centuries, is a real ale oasis in the town centre. Its hospitality is enjoyed by seafarers, business people, locals and holidaymakers. Dogs on leads are welcome. The narrow passageway outside, boasting award-winning floral displays, acts as a pleasant alfresco drinking area. ❀◑◗⊡⚡

Totnes

Rumours

30 High Street, TQ9 5RY

☉ 11-11 (11.30 Fri & Sat); 6-10.30 Sun

☎ (01803) 864682

Beer range varies Ⓗ

In the style of a wine bar/bistro, Rumours offers a changing range of real ales and a good selection of bottled continental beers and lagers. Imaginative food, expertly cooked, is based on locally-sourced ingredients, and so the menu changes often. No meals are served Sunday lunchtime. This is a popular venue providing a relaxed and convivial ambience. ◑◗

Tuckenhay

Maltster's Arms

Bow Creek, TQ9 7EQ

(signed from A381, Totnes-Kingsbridge road)

☉ 11-11 daily

☎ (01803) 732350 🌐 tuckenhay.com

Princetown Dartmoor IPA; guest beers Ⓗ

Superb old pub, overlooking the peaceful Bow Creek, with boat moorings available on the tidal River Dart and ample waterside seating. It hosts excellent barbecues and occasional live music outdoors. The two cosy rooms are linked by a long, narrow bar. Live music is sometimes staged on Friday evenings. The pub fields a cricket team. The restaurant serves good food and boasts fine views of the wooded valley. A discount applies to accommodation for card-carrying CAMRA members. Heron Valley cider is sold in summer. ⌂Q☺❀⛟◑◗♿♣●P

Wembury

Odd Wheel

Knighton Road, PL9 0JD

☉ 12-3, 6.30-11; 12-11 Sat; 12-4, 7-10.30 Sun

☎ (01752) 862287

Courage Best Bitter; Princetown Jail Ale; Shepherd Neame Spitfire; Skinner's Spriggan Ale; South Hams XSB Ⓖ

Friendly village pub where the comfortable lounge bar offers an extensive menu, with fish a speciality. The dog-friendly public bar houses a pool table and dartboard. Live jazz sessions take place on Thursday evenings. The bus stop outside is on a regular route to Plymouth. Ducks and chickens roam freely on the small patio, while the orchard is home to ponies, goats and pot-bellied pigs – a favourite with children. ⌂Q❀◑◗⊟♿▲⊡♣P

Wembury Club

Southland Park Road, PL9 0HH (off Church Rd)

☉ 7.30 (8 Fri; 4 Sat)-11; 12-11 Sun

☎ (01752) 862159

Theakston Best Bitter; guest beers Ⓗ

Although this is a private club, CAMRA members and their families are made most welcome in this excellent drinking establishment. It offers changing guest beers that are generally rarely available elsewhere, sold at sensible and uniform prices, regardless of strength. The landlord relishes the opportunity to obtain more uncommon beers on request; he also stocks over 30 bottled beers and an excellent cider choice. The club is near a picturesque marine conservation area, which is popular with walkers.

⌂Q☺❀◑⊟♿▲♣●P

Westcott

Merry Harriers

EX15 1SA (on B3181 between Exeter and Cullompton)

☉ 11-11 (midnight Fri & Sat); 11-11 Sun

☎ (01392) 881254

Cotleigh Tawny, seasonal beers; O'Hanlon's Firefly, Yellowhammer, Royal Oak Ⓗ

This traditional pub, formerly thought to be a blacksmith's, has a friendly atmosphere. The lounge bar is welcoming and cosy with a log fire and beamed ceilings. The child-friendly dining area is just through the bar, with an impressive menu and specials board featuring local produce. There is seating outside and a spacious car park plus accommodation behind the pub. Addlestones cider is sold.

⌂Q❀⛟◑⊟●P

Westward Ho!

Pig on the Hill

Pusehill, EX39 5AH OS426282
✪ 12-3, 6.30-11; 12-3, 7-10.30 Sun
☎ (01237) 425889
Country Life Old Appledore, Pot Wallop, Golden Pig, Country Bum; guest beers Ⓗ
Converted and extended farmhouse with a bar and two dining areas, bearing a porcine theme. The pub is family- and dog-friendly. Outside is a sheltered patio and a large garden, overlooking pig and goat pens; the pub hosts a petanque club in the grounds. Formerly the home of the Country Life Brewery, the bar still stocks its beers. The coastal footpath is within easy reach and the pub has holiday cottages to rent. The cider sold here is Addlestones.
❀◐▲♣●P

Whiddon Down

Post Inn

EX20 2QT (close to A30, Whiddon Down roundabout)
✪ 11-11; closed Tue; 12-10.30 Sun
☎ (01647) 231242
Beer range varies Ⓗ
Built in the 16th century as a post office on the old coaching road, the Post is a pleasant country pub. Handy for the A30, it caters well for modern travellers (meals served 11-11); food is home cooked, using local produce and seasonal game. The central bar serves three rooms, with the two side rooms generally laid out for diners. The ales follow a West Country theme and the cider (Grays) is local. This pub is now no-smoking throughout.
♔Q❀◐♣●P⚡

Whimple

New Fountain Inn

Church Road, EX5 2TA (leave A30 E of Exeter at Daisymount, follow signs)
✪ 12-3, 6.30-11; 12-3, 7-10.30 Sun
☎ (01404) 822350
O'Hanlon's Firefly; Teignworthy Reel Ale; guest beers (occasional) Ⓖ
Friendly local in a lovely village, serving good value, home-cooked food. Do not be fooled by the handpumps – they are for advertisement only – the beers are served direct from the cellar. In January wassailing takes place near the original home of Whiteways Cider; the village heritage centre stands at the rear of the pub's car park. This inn is well worth searching out.
♔Q❀◐⇌♣P

Widecombe-in-the-Moor

Rugglestone Inn

TQ13 7TF (¼ mile from village centre) OS721766
✪ 11.30-3, 6.30-12.30am; 12-3, 6.30-11.30 Sun
☎ (01364) 621327
Butcombe Bitter; St Austell Dartmoor Best; guest beer Ⓖ
Unspoilt, cosy pub in a splendid Dartmoor setting. The small bar area has seating and a stone floor; beer is also served through a hatch in the passageway. The lounge, with an open fire, welcomes children. The pub is named after a local 'logan' stone. Across the stream, a large grassed seating area has a shelter for use in bad weather. A wide selection of home-cooked food is served. The pub's large car park is just down the road.
♔Q♉❀◐⊟♿▲●P⚡

Winkleigh

King's Arms

Fore Street, EX19 8HX
✪ 11-11; 12-10.30 Sun
☎ (01837) 83384 🌐 hatherleigh.org.uk/kingsarms
Butcombe Bitter; Sharp's Cornish Coaster, Doom Bar Ⓗ
At the heart of this picturesque village, this thatched inn has a warm, cosy feel, enhanced by the low ceiling and a log fire in the split-level bar. The cider is Winkleigh's Sam's Dry, from down the road. Excellent, locally-produced food is served in the bar or the multi-roomed restaurant that displays army memorabilia and boasts a covered well. Visitors might be interested to ask about the antics of the two ghosts, George and Cecilia.
♔Q❀◐♣●▽

Woodland

Rising Sun

TQ13 7JT (signed from Plymouth-bound A38) OS790697
✪ 12-3, 6-11; 12-3, 7-11 Sun
☎ (01364) 652544 🌐 risingsunwoodland.co.uk
Princetown Jail Ale; guest beer Ⓗ
Well-ordered, rural pub, with a strong emphasis on food for which it has been awarded many accolades - it is renowned for its pies. It comprises a spacious, open-plan area used mainly by diners, with a long, single bar where small screens offer some privacy. The children's area is off the main bar. The extensive grounds are pleasant, with a children's play area. Accommodation is available and the pub is suitable for parties and functions.
♔Q♉❀⛟◐▲P

Yeoford

Mare & Foal

The Village, EX17 5JD
(turn right out of station, then 2 mins' walk)
✪ 12-3, 6-11; closed Mon; 11-11 Sat & Sun
☎ (01363) 84348 🌐 mareandfoal.co.uk
Beer range varies Ⓗ
Set in beautiful countryside, easily accessible from the real ale trail along the Exeter-Barnstaple Tarka Line, this 17th-century pub has been run by new owners since July 2005. It offers three changing West Country ales and an extensive menu based, as far as possible, on locally sourced, organic produce. Meals are cooked to order and the menu changes weekly, if not daily. You will always find a warm atmosphere here, with well-behaved children welcome, and dogs on leads accepted. ♔♉❀◐⊟♿⇌♣P

CAMRA's Beers of the Year

The beers listed below are CAMRA's Beers of the Year. They were short-listed for the Champion Beer of Britain competition in August 2006, and the Champion Winter Beer of Britain competition in January 2006. The August competition judged Dark and Light Milds; Bitters; Best Bitters; Strong Bitters; Golden Ales; Speciality Beers; and Real Ale in a Bottle, while the winter competition judged Old Ales and Strong Milds; Porters and Stouts; and Barley Wines. Each beer was found by panels of trained CAMRA judges to be consistently outstanding in its category, and they all receive a 'full tankard' [■] symbol in the Breweries section.

DARK AND LIGHT MILDS
Bazens' Black Pig
Brains Dark
Elgoods Black Dog
Grainstore Rutland Panther
Hook Norton Hooky Dark
Mighty Oak Oscar Wilde
Naylor's Sparky's Mild

BITTERS
Acorn Barnsley Bitter
Castle Rock Harvest Pale
Durham Magus
E&S Bargee
Elgoods Cambridge Bitter
Farmers A Drop of Nelson's Blood
Holden's Black Country Bitter
Hydes Traditional Bitter
Nottingham Rock Ale Bitter
Sharp's Doom Bar
Triple fff Alton Pride
Woodforde's Wherry
George Wright Longboat
Young's Bitter

BEST BITTERS
Batham's Best Bitter
Copper Dragon Scotts 1816
Fuller's London Pride
Harvey's Sussex Best Bitter
High House Nel's Best
Kelburn Red Smiddy
Mallard Duckling
Potton Village Bike
St Austell Tribute
Surrey Hills Shere Drop
Triple fff Moondance
Woodforde's Nelson's Revenge
Woodlands IPA
Wye Valley Butty Bach

STRONG BITTERS
Blue Moon Hingham High
Bullmastiff Son of a Bitch
Fuller's ESB
Oakham Bishop's Farewell
Thornbridge Jaipur IPA
Weetwood Oasthouse Gold
York Centurion's Ghost Ale

GOLDEN ALES
Copper Dragon Golden Pippin
Crouch Vale Brewers Gold
Dark Star Hophead
Everards Sunchaser
Holden's Golden Glow
Hop Back Summer Lightning
Tomos Watkin Cwrw Haf

OLD ALES AND STRONG MILDS
Buffy's Mild
Gales Festival Mild
Goffs Black Knight
Kelburn Ca-Canny
Orkney Dark Island
Sarah Hughes Dark Ruby
Young's Winter Warmer

PORTERS AND STOUTS
Bath Fertility
Battersea Power Station Porter
Bazens' Knoll Street Porter
Beowulf Dragon Smoke Stout
E&S 1872 Porter
Fuller's London Porter
Hop Back Entire Stout

BARLEY WINES
Abbeydale Last Rites
Adnams Tally Ho
Exmoor Beast
Hogs Back A Over T
Isle of Skye Cuillen Beast
Orkney Skullsplitter
Robinson's Old Tom
Woodforde's Norfolk Nip

SPECIALITY BEERS
Cairngorm Trade Winds
Enville Ginger
Green Jack Orange Wheat
Oakham White Dwarf
Williams Fraoch
Wolf Straw Dog
Wylam Bohemia

REAL ALE IN A BOTTLE
Durham Temptation
Fuller's 1845
Greene King Hen's Tooth
Harvey's Extra Double Stout
Hogs Back BSA
Hop Back Summer Lightning
Titanic Stout
Woodforde's Nelson's Revenge
Worthington's White Shield
Wye Valley Dorothy Goodbody's Wholesome Stout
Young's Special London Ale

CHAMPION WINTER BEER OF BRITAIN
Hogs Back A Over T

CHAMPION BEER OF BRITAIN 2006
Crouch Vale Brewers Gold

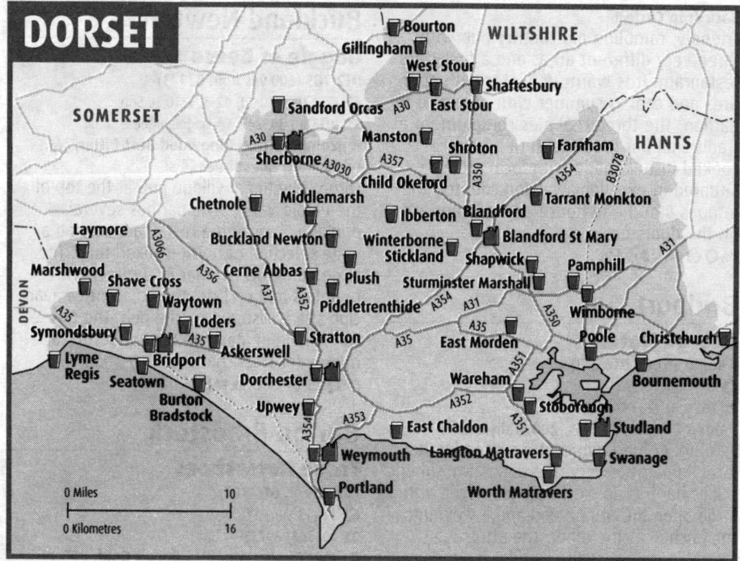

Askerswell

Spyway Inn

DT2 9EP (signed off A35, 4 miles E of Bridport)
OS529933
☼ 12-3, 6-11 daily
☎ (01308) 485250 🌐 spyway-inn.co.uk
Otter Bitter, Ale; guest beers Ⓖ

Smugglers' inn dating from the 16th century perched above the village on the approach to the ancient Eggardon Hill earthwork fort. Popular with walkers and diners, this is an idyllic country pub, busy in summer, with an exceptional garden including children's play area. The small but charming lounge has a welcoming fire, settles and a low-beamed ceiling. Two further rooms are mainly used for dining – the high quality food made with locally sourced ingredients is very popular. The beer is from local brewers and served direct from the barrel. ⌂Q❀⇌◑ΛP⊬

Blandford

Railway

Oakfield Street, DT11 7EX
☼ 11.30-1am daily
☎ (01258) 456374
Badger First Gold; Ringwood Best Bitter; guest beers Ⓗ

Popular back-street Victorian pub that dates back to when there was a railway line and station opposite. However it has embraced the 21st century with large multi-screen TVs, even at the bar. It also makes the most of extended drinking hours, remaining open until the early morning. ❀◑♣

Bournemouth

Goat & Tricycle

27-29 West Hill Road, BH2 5PP
☼ 12-3, 5-11; 12-11.30 Fri & Sat; 12-3, 7-11.30 Sun
☎ (01202) 314220
Wadworth IPA, 6X, JCB, seasonal beers; guest beers Ⓗ

The Goat, as it is known by the regulars, is popular with locals and tourists. Originally two neighbouring pubs, they were joined together by owners Wadworth's, retaining original features, split levels and a delightful courtyard garden. The bar features 10 handpumps with regularly changing guest beers. Good value, hearty food is served at this CAMRA award winner. ⌂❀◑♿

Porterhouse

113 Poole Road, Westbourne, BH4 8BY
☼ 10.30-11 (midnight Fri & Sat); 12-11 Sun
☎ (01202) 768586
Ringwood Best Bitter, Fortyniner, Old Thumper, seasonal beers; guest beer Ⓗ

Cosy, Ringwood-owned pub with a bustling atmosphere, where conversation dominates. Full of character, it has a wooden floor, oak panelling and hops adorning the bar. It sells the full range of Ringwood beers and an excellent choice of changing guests as well as Cheddar Valley cider. East Dorset CAMRA Pub of the Year six times. A simple menu is served weekdays. Q◐⇌(Branksome)●

Bourton

White Lion

High Street, SP8 5AT (1 mile off A303 between Zeals and Wincanton)
☼ 12-3, 6-11; 12-4, 7-10.30 Sun
☎ (01747) 840866
Fuller's London Pride; Greene King IPA; Hop

INDEPENDENT BREWERIES

Badger Blandford St Mary
Dorset Weymouth
Goldfinch Dorchester
Isle of Purbeck Studland
Palmer Bridport
Sherborne Sherborne

Back Crop Circle Ⓗ
Friendly, rambling old country pub with three very different areas and a first-class restaurant. It is warm in winter with open fires and cool in summer with access to the garden. The three real ales complement a traditional bar menu featuring home-cooked dishes made with local produce. Situated in excellent walking country, the famous Stourhead house and gardens are on the doorstep.
Q P

Bridport

George Hotel
4 South Street, DT6 3NQ
10-11; 10-4 Sun
☎ (01308) 423187
Palmer Copper Ale, IPA, 200, Tally Ho! Ⓗ
Ex-hotel in the town centre owned by the local Palmer Brewery. The dark, atmospheric public bar has an old-fashioned decor, with a large open fire at one end and a view into the kitchen at the other. The attractive family room across the corridor is simply furnished with a wooden floor. Popular with a mixed clientele, the pub can be crowded at times. Prices are above average for Palmer's beer. Food is available at lunchtime only Monday-Saturday – the well-filled sandwiches and fishcakes are delicious. Dogs are welcome.

Greyhound
East Street, DT6 3LF (next to town hall)
9am-midnight (1am Fri & Sat); 9am-midnight Sun
☎ (01308) 421905
Courage Best Bitter, Directors; Greene King Abbot; Marston's Burton Bitter, Pedigree; guest beers Ⓗ
Prominently placed in the town centre, this large Grade II listed ex-hotel has been extensively refurbished by JD Wetherspoon and decorated in Georgian style inside and out. Inside is a large main bar with numerous adjoining rooms, making this a spacious and popular all-day venue for a mixed clientele; weekend evenings are busy with young revellers. Five regular and two changing guest beers are served and sometimes a real cider, all at bargain prices. Occasional beer festivals are hosted.

Tiger Inn
14-16 Barrack Street, DT6 3LY
12 (5 winter)-11; 12-midnight Sat & Sun
☎ (01308) 427543
Branscombe Vale Draymans; Fuller's London Pride; guest beer Ⓗ
Early 19th-century community pub in a side street five minutes' walk from the town centre. The single bar has ample seating, a gas fire and a TV showing sporting events. To the rear is a dining area offering a good, varied menu, prepared on the premises. At the back is a skittles alley and outdoor patio area. Families and dogs are welcome.

Buckland Newton

Gaggle of Geese
DT2 7BS (600 yds from B3143)
12-2.30, 6.30-11; 12-3, 7-10.30 Sun
☎ (01300) 345249 gaggleofgeese.co.uk
Butcombe Bitter; Ringwood Best Bitter, Fortyniner; guest beer Ⓗ
Large, traditional village pub at the top of the Piddle Valley. The bar has several drinking areas and a restaurant serving a wide selection of home-cooked food. The large garden is popular in summer with ramblers and cyclists. The adjacent caravan club site is also run by the pub. The Goose Fair is held in May and September to raise money for local charities.
Q P

Burton Bradstock

Three Horseshoes
Mill Street, DT6 4QZ
11 (12 Sun)-11
☎ (01308) 897259
Palmer Copper Ale, IPA, Dorset Gold, 200 Ⓗ
Attractive, thatched pub in a pretty village close to Chesil Beach. The restaurant and bar menus specialise in locally produced organic meat and local fish – there is little choice for vegetarians. Cosy in winter with low beams and a log fire, in summer the outdoor seating area at the front is a suntrap. This is one of the few pubs that serve Tally Ho! when it is available.
(X53)P

Cerne Abbas

Red Lion
Long Street, DT2 7JF (in main square)
6.30-11.30; 12.30-11.30 Sat; 12.30-10.30 Sun
☎ (01300) 341441
Beer range varies Ⓗ
Friendly, traditional local pub, popular with village residents. This historic building has a restored wood-panelled interior with attractive stained glass windows. Beers change regularly with guests often coming from local and south-westerly breweries. A fine place to enjoy a good pint by the fire with friends.

Chetnole

Chetnole Inn
DT9 6NU
11-2.30, 6.30-11; 12-3, 7-10.30 Sun
☎ (01935) 872337
Branscombe Vale Branoc; Butcombe Bitter; Palmer IPA; guest beer Ⓗ
This classic country pub, opposite the church, is a 20-minute stroll along country lanes from Chetnole Halt on the Weymouth to Bristol line, and makes an excellent day out. The public bar is warmed by a blazing fire, and there is a skittle alley behind. Excellent food is served in the lounge, restaurant or garden on sunny days. Guest beers come from west country brewers, and there is a beer festival at Easter.
Q P

Child Okeford

Saxon Inn

Gold Hill, DT11 8HD

12-2.30 (4 Sat), 7-11; 12-11 Sun

(01258) 860310

Butcombe Bitter; Ringwood Best Bitter; guest beers H

Hidden away at the north end of the village, this pub was converted from 300-year-old cottages in the early 1950s. Look for the pub sign by the road – the pub itself is up a short driveway. A corner bar serves both the main room with its open fire and comfortable lounge with wood-burning stove. Guest ales often come from the Hidden Brewery. Food is cooked to order with daily specials chalked up (no food Sun eve). Q P

Christchurch

Olde George Inn

2A Castle Street, BH23 1DT

11-11 (11.30 Thu; midnight Fri & Sat); 11-11 Sun

(01202) 479383

Ringwood Fortyniner; guest beers H

Former 15th-century coaching inn situated at the bottom of Christchurch High Street. It is linked to the nearby Priory and castle by now closed off tunnels. It has two rooms, one of which is no-smoking. Outside is a courtyard with patio heaters and extra seating. On Sunday the barn bar is open for a carvery. A wide range of tasty dishes is on the menu. There is a skittles alley and function room to hire. Q

Thomas Tripp

10 Wick Lane, BH23 1HX

10-11; 12-11 Sun

(01202) 490498 thomas-tripp.co.uk

Ringwood Fortyniner H

Named after a legendary local smuggler, the pub is at the Priory end of town near the Red House Museum. Frequent live bands and DJs play in the evening from Wednesday to Sunday and the pub can be quite boisterous, though always friendly. There is a quieter bar area and seating outside in the partially-covered garden. Good lunchtime food is prepared by the new 'celebrity' chef.

Dorchester

Blue Raddle

9 Church Street, DT1 1JN

11.30-3 (not Mon), 6.30-11; 12-3 Sun

(01305) 267762

Otter Bitter; Sharp's Doom Bar; guest beers H

A warm welcome awaits at Dorchester's only genuinely independent free house. Situated just two minutes' walk from the town centre, it attracts a mixed clientele of all ages. A choice of cask ales usually centres on West Country breweries and the excellent real food is home cooked. The town car park is close by. Q

East Chaldon

Sailor's Return

DT2 8DN (1 mile S of A352) OS791834

11-11; 12-10.30 Sun

(01305) 853847 sailorsreturn.com

Hampshire Strong's Best Bitter; Ringwood Best Bitter; guest beers H

This thatched inn on the fringe of a small hamlet provides a welcome stop for ramblers on the nearby Dorset Coastal Path. It can be very busy on summer weekends. Excellent food is served throughout the numerous flagstone-floored rooms although the main area retains the feel of a local public bar. Up to seven beers are served in high season, as well as Westons traditional cider. A tented beer festival is held in late spring. P

East Morden

Cock & Bottle

BH20 7DL (on B3075, off A35 near Wareham)

11-3, 6-11; 12-3, 7-10.30 Sun

(01929) 459238

Badger K&B Sussex, First Gold, Tanglefoot H

Lovely, unspoilt village pub. An open fire is the main feature in the 'happy chatter' (public bar). Well-used by locals, the pub attracts a lot of custom for its award-winning food, served in the cosy dining area (booking is recommended for weekend meals). Reasonably-priced bar snacks are also served. The garden is well situated to enjoy a summer pint. Disabled facilities are good with easy wheelchair access.
Q P

East Stour

King's Arms

East Stour Common, SP8 5NB (on A30 W of Shaftesbury)

12-3, 5.30-11; 12-midnight Sat; 12-10.30 Sun

(01747) 838325 thekingsarmsdorset.co.uk

Fuller's London Pride; Palmer Copper Ale; guest beer H

Imposing, multi-roomed, single-bar country pub alongside the A30. After recent renovation it now has a garden room leading to an enclosed garden and patio. Two of the three beers often come from Palmer. Food here is excellent – the a la carte menu has a Scottish theme although made with locally sourced ingredients. Live, acoustic music is played on the first and third Sunday of the month – bring your own instrument. Q P

Farnham

Museum Inn

DT11 8DE

12-3, 6-11; 12-3, 7-10.30 Sun

(01725) 516261 museuminn.co.uk

Taylor Landlord; guest beer H

Originally built for visitors to the local museum, this part-thatched country inn retains its flagstone floors and large inglenook despite a recent extensive refurbishment. It is always worth a visit for the changing guest beer and varied food menu. Situated in excellent walking country, Larmer Tree Gardens and Cranborne Chase are nearby. Q P

Gillingham

Buffalo

Lydfords Lane, Wyke, SP8 4NS (100 yds from B3081, Wincanton road)
⏲ 12-3, 5.30 (6 Sat)-11 (midnight Fri & Sat); 12-3, 7-11 Sun
☎ (01747) 823759
Badger K&B Sussex, First Gold, seasonal beers ⊞
This pub gets its name from the logo of the former Matthews Brewery nearby. It has the feel of a country pub despite its location on the edge of town. A community pub, it is home to various social clubs. The interior has been refurbished but retains much of its original character. Outside is a decked area and large garden. The pub is renowned for good food and holds regular themed food nights (no meals Sun eve). ♛Q❀◐◑♿♣P

Phoenix Inn

The Square, SP8 4AY
⏲ 10-2.30 (3 Sat), 7-11; 12-3, 7-10.30 Sun
☎ (01747) 823277
Badger K&B Sussex, First Gold, seasonal beers ⊞
Friendly town-centre pub built in the 15th century, originally a coaching inn complete with its own brewery. A cosy, one-bar pub, it has no games machines, just background piped music. There is a separate dining area with an extensive menu and an outside drinking area in the square. ♛❀◐◑⛺⇌

Smouldering Boulder

Queen Street, SP8 4DZ
⏲ 12-11; closed Mon; 12-4 Sun
☎ (01747) 823988
Beer range varies ⊞
This single bar, two-roomed pub was until recently an obscure wine bar. It is now a thriving real ale outlet offering up to three beers, often including a house beer from Branscombe Vale. There is a patio for outdoor drinking. Backgammon is played here. ❀⇌♣

Ibberton

Crown Inn

Church Lane, DT11 0EN
⏲ 12-3, 7-11; closed Mon; 12-3, 7-10.30 Sun
☎ (01258) 817448
Butcombe Bitter; Palmer IPA; guest beer ⊞
Delightful, unspoilt pub in a peaceful lane near the village church. A small brook runs alongside the idyllic lawned garden. The main bar retains its original flagstone floor. A small area off the bar has been recently redecorated and furnished with leather sofas and comfortable chairs – the perfect place to enjoy a pint in front of the fire on a cold winter evening. ♛Q♉❀◐◑♣P

Langton Matravers

King's Arms Hotel

27 High Street, BH19 3HA
⏲ 12-3, 6-11; 12-3, 7-10.30 Sun
☎ (01929) 422979
Ringwood Best Bitter; Fortyniner; guest beers ⊞
Dating back to 1743, this lovely four-room pub features the original flagstone floors. Adorning the walls are paintings and photographs of the local area. In the early days the front room was formally the village morgue and the rest of the building was the inn. Outside is a large garden with a shed housing a pool table. The pub is ideally situated for exploring the Purbecks.
♛Q♉❀◐◑⊟♣

Laymore

Squirrel Inn

TA20 4NT (just off B3162 towards Winsham) OS387048
⏲ 11-2.30, 6.30-late; 12-late Sun
☎ (01460) 30298 🌐 squirrelinn.co.uk
Branscombe Vale BVB; Otter Bitter; Sharps's Special ⊞
Red brick, family friendly pub with a large garden and children's play equipment. The food menu changes constantly – all dishes are cooked to order using local produce, with steaks featuring on Wednesday. A beer festival is held in the garden in summer and the local Ashen Faggot Festival is hosted annually on the 6th of January. The large bar is partitioned into different areas. The pub holds a 24-hour licence.
♛❀⛟◐◑♿⛺♣●P⊭

Loders

Loders Arms

DT6 3SA
⏲ 11.30-3, 6-11 (extended hours in summer); 12-3, 6-10.30 Sun
☎ (01308) 422431 🌐 lodersarms.co.uk
Palmer Copper Ale, IPA, 200 ⊞
Charming inn standing in a pretty village in the River Asker Valley. The garden overlooks medieval field terraces carved into the surrounding hills. Good food is served in the bar and restaurant made with local ingredients. The pub is popular with local farmers and villagers and is home to several skittles teams. Camping is available in a field beyond the car park. ♛Q❀⛟◐◑⛺♣●P

Lyme Regis

Nag's Head

32 Silver Street, DT7 3HS
⏲ 11-2, 5-11; 11-11 Fri & Sat; 12-10.30 Sun
☎ (01297) 442312
Otter Ale; guest beers ⊞
Old brick and flint coaching inn a short walk from the town centre with magnificent views along the Jurassic Coast from the garden. It has two linked bar areas and a games room. Live music features every Saturday night plus Wednesdays in summer. There are three or four real ales, including Sark Lark house beer from the Dorset Brewing Company and guest ales from independent breweries nationwide. B&B accommodation is available. ♛❀⛟⛺♣

Volunteer

31 Broad Street, DT7 3QE
⏲ 11-11; 12-10.30 Sun
☎ (01297) 442214
Fuller's London Pride; guest beers ⊞
Double-fronted pub in the heart of the town

with a low-beamed bar and pleasant family/dining room. This historic pub was named after the regiment founded in 1794 to fend off the French. The bar has a cosy olde-worlde atmosphere and is popular with locals. The house beer, Donegal, is brewed by Branscombe Vale. Excellent, wholesome pub food is served in the bar and dining room. ◑ ⅄

Manston

Plough

Shaftesbury Road, DT10 1HB (on B3091, 2 ½ miles NE of Sturminster Newton)

11.30-2.30, 6.30-11; 12-10.30 Sun

☎ (01258) 472484

Palmer Copper Ale, IPA; Ⓗ **guest beers** Ⓗ/Ⓖ

Traditional stone-built country inn believed to be more than 400 years old. The single large bar is welcoming and the pub is no-smoking throughout. Outside, the large garden has a petanque rink. A beer festival is held in July. Guest ales are usually served straight from the cask.

Q ◑ ♿ ⅄ ♣ P ⚟

Marshwood

Bottle Inn

DT6 5QJ (on B3165)

12-3, 6.30-11 (closed winter Mon); 12-3, 7-10.30 Sun

☎ (01297) 678254 thebottleinn.co.uk

O'Hanlon's Royal Oak; Otter Bitter Ⓗ

This thatched inn is billed as 'the first and last' pub in Dorset. The front, no-smoking bar leads through to a large back bar where games are played and live music is performed. The large garden plays host to the world famous nettle-eating contest in June, as well as an annual beer festival. Vegetarian dishes and organic produce feature on the menu. On the Liberty Trail, the pub stands in excellent walking country.

◑ ⅄ ♣ P ⚟

Middlemarsh

Hunter's Moon

DT9 5QN (on A352)

11-3, 6-11 daily

☎ (01963) 210966 huntersmoon.co.uk

Beer range varies Ⓗ

The charming owner has transformed the 400-year-old derelict former White Horse into a quality real ale country pub with a homely and welcoming atmosphere. Brewery memorabilia line the walls, with jugs, cups and tankards hanging from the ceiling. Small alcoves and corners line the interesting L-shaped room. The menu is innovative, specialising in local game. The beers come from Palmer, St Austell and Sharp's. Q ◑ ♿ P ⚟

Pamphill

Vine Inn ☆

BH21 4EE (off B3082)

11-3, 7-10.30 (11 Thu-Sat); 12-3, 7-10.30 Sun

☎ (01202) 882259

Fuller's London Pride; Ⓗ **guest beers** Ⓖ

Delightful pub, built as a bakehouse over 200 years ago, close to the National Trust's Kingston Lacey House and Badbury Rings. No-smoking throughout, its interior is of historic interest with two small bars and a games room. The guest beer is usually from a small regional or micro-brewery. Bulmers cider is served on gravity. Popular with walkers and cyclists, dogs are permitted. The attractive garden has ample seating. Sandwiches and ploughman's are served at lunchtime.

Q ◑ ♣ P ⚟

Piddletrenthide

Poachers Inn

DT2 7QX

11-11 daily

☎ (01300) 348358 thepoachersinn.co.uk

Butcombe Bitter; Palmer Tally Ho!; Ringwood Fortyniner Ⓗ

Quality village inn with sloping lawns leading down to the twinkling River Piddle which runs through the bottom of the garden. Improvements have mushroomed since the current owners took over in 2004, with a beer range including at least three real ales that vary according to requests from customers. Here you will find farmers in boots mingling happily with diners who have come for the fine cuisine and residents staying in the attractive en-suite accommodation. The newly refurbished restaurant features local artwork.

Q ◑ ♿ P

Plush

Brace of Pheasants

DT2 7RQ (off B3143)

12-3, 6.30-11.30 (10.30 Sun)

☎ (01300) 348357 braceofpheasants.co.uk

Beer range varies Ⓖ

Very much a gastro pub, here you will find excellent ales, super company, congenial surroundings and fantastic food. Guest ales change constantly, as does the local cider, served straight from the cask.

Q P

Poole

Angel

28 Market Street, BH15 1HD

11-11; 12-10.30 Sun

☎ (01202) 666800

Ringwood Best Bitter, Fortyniner, Old Thumper, seasonal beers; guest beer Ⓗ

A welcome return to the Guide for the Angel, Ringwood Brewery's tied house in Poole. Sitting in the shadow of the historic Guildhall, there has been an inn on this site since 1789; the present building dates from 1890. A central bar serves a single large room subtly divided into different areas. Note the glass viewing point that reveals the immaculately clean cask cellar. Evening meals are served 5-8pm Thursday to Saturday. Live music is on Thursday.

◑ ♿ ≠ ♣

Bermuda Triangle
10 Parr Street, Lower Parkstone, BH14 0JY
11-2.30, 5-11 (midnight Fri); 11-midnight Sat; 12-11 Sun
☎ (01202) 748087
Beer range varies Ⓗ
This pub is a mecca for real ale drinkers, with 198 different ales dispensed from four handpumps in the last year. Speciality German lagers are also served. A cosy pub, the wood-panelled walls are adorned with a variety of nautical miscellany relating to the mystery of the Bermuda Triangle. Taped music in the evening adds to the atmosphere. A former CAMRA East Dorset Pub of the Year. ❀⇌(Parkstone)

Blue Boar
29 Market Close, BH15 1NE
11-3, 5-11; 12-11 Sat; 12-10.30 Sun
☎ (01202) 682247
Fuller's Discovery, London Pride, ESB, seasonal beers; guest beer Ⓗ
Just off the high street, this former free house was recently acquired by Fuller's – its only tied outlet in the area. Originally a merchant's house dating from 1750, it has steps leading up to the nautically themed lounge bar. Good value Sunday lunches are served. The atmospheric cellar bar features live music on Wednesday (folk night) and Friday. The second floor boasts a rather plush function room with bar. Q❀◐⇌

Brewhouse
68 High Street, BH15 1DA
11-11; 12-10.30 Sun
☎ (01202) 685288
Milk Street Mermaid, Beer, seasonal beers Ⓗ
Popular town-centre pub owned by Frome's Milk Street Brewery. This split-level room is served by a single bar. The front area overlooks the High Street; at the rear are pool tables. East Dorset CAMRA Pub of the Year in 2005, it sells excellent beers at competitive prices. ⇌♣

Queen Mary
68 West Street, BH15 1LD
12-3, 6-11; 12-10.30 Sun
☎ (01202) 661701
Palmer Copper Ale, 200; Sharp's Doom Bar; guest beers Ⓗ
A short stroll from the High Street, this cosy old Poole pub has its own set of traffic lights. It is a regular outlet for Palmer's beers. The single room is divided into two areas: one hosts darts while the other is for dining. The food is good value, particularly the Sunday roast served 12-8.30pm. Making a welcome return to the Guide under new tenants, the pub was local CAMRA Pub of the Season in autumn 2005. ⚠❀◐◑⇌♣P

Royal Oak & Gas Tavern
25 Skinner Street, BH15 1RQ
11-11; 12-11 Sun
☎ (01202) 672022
Ringwood Best Bitter, Fortyniner; guest beer (occasional) Ⓗ
Traditional local back-street pub, dating from 1798. Many original features remain – note the windows and wood-panelled walls. At the rear is a large family room that doubles as a function room. An enclosed garden hosts barbecues and a small beer festival. This pub is a haven of peace during the busy summer season. Sunday lunch is served. Q❀◑♿⇌♣⚟

Portland

Clifton
Grove, DT5 1DA (signed from A354)
11-11; 12-10.30 Sun
☎ (01305) 820473
Beer range varies Ⓗ
Friendly local close to the imposing Victorian prison and ideally situated for exploring Portland's rugged coastline. The large single bar has a family dining area and there is also a restaurant. Four constantly changing beers from regional and micro-brewers are available plus Westons or Cheddar Valley cider. The food menu is varied and reasonably priced with an extensive wine list. A popular beer festival is held in May. ❀◐◑♣P

Sandford Orcas

Mitre Inn
DT9 4RU (village signed from B3148) OS626205
11.30-2.30 (not Mon), 7-11; 12-2.30, 7-10.30 Sun
☎ (01963) 220271
Greene King Abbot; guest beers Ⓗ
Mind your head when you enter the Mitre! The welcome is warm, home-cooked food is excellent, there is plenty of comfortable seating including armchairs in the bar, and there is fine real ale to enjoy. Flagged floors extend from the bar area to the dining room. Well-behaved children are welcome. Outside is an elevated garden. No food is served on Monday. Beers are selected from the Punch Tavern guest list. ⚠Q❀◐◑♿♣P

Seatown

Anchor Inn
DT6 6JU (½ mile S of Chideock)
11-3, 6-11 (11-11 summer); 12-10.30 Sun
☎ (01297) 489215
Palmer Copper Ale, IPA, 200 Ⓗ
Dramatically situated on the edge of the beach, nestling under the 600ft Golden Cap on the coastal path, this comfortable pub is predictably busy in summer. Out of season it is quieter and a good time to take a look at the photographs on the walls and occasional fossil on display. Opening hours vary according to the season and the weather conditions. Public parking is available opposite the pub. ⚠Q❀◐◑▲♣P⚟

Shaftesbury

Crown
40 High Street, SP7 8JG
10.30 (10 Sat)-11; 12-10.30 Sun
☎ (01747) 852902
Badger K&B Sussex, First Gold, seasonal beers Ⓗ
Originally a 19th-century coaching inn, this is a friendly single-room, single-bar town

hostelry in the heart of historic Shaftesbury. It is close to the famous Gold Hill and abbey ruins. An interesting brick and wood fireplace is reputedly from the abbey. Seating is mainly a long settle down one wall. Access is via the old coach archway and courtyard. ⛰❀♣

Mitre

23 High Street, SP7 8JE
✪ 10.30-midnight; 12-11 Sun
☎ (01747) 853002
Young's Bitter, Special, seasonal beers Ⓗ
Historic pub at the top of Gold Hill overlooking the beautiful Blackmore Vale. Popular with all ages, there is something for everyone here from real ale and cream teas to good pub food. The pub runs crib and darts teams and hosts charity quiz nights. A cosy fire warms in winter while the decking outside provides stunning views in summer. A real gem. ⛰♉❀◑♿♣⚟

Shapwick

Anchor

West Street, DT11 9LB (off B3082)
✪ 11-3, 6-11 daily
☎ (01258) 857269 🌐 anchoratshapwick.com
Ringwood Best Bitter; guest beers Ⓗ
In the heart of the delightful Stour Valley lies the village of Shapwick. Opposite the village cross is this splendid 19th-century family-run pub. The main bar is open-plan with a central serving area and a small games room. Home-cooked meals are prepared to order with vegetarians catered for and local Dorset dishes a speciality. A popular stop for walkers and cyclists on the Stour Valley Way in summer. ❀◑♣●P

Shave Cross

Shave Cross Inn

DT6 6HW (2½ miles W of B3162 Bridport-Broadwindsor road) OS415980
✪ 11-3, 6-11 (11-11 summer); 12-3, 7-10.30 (12-10.30 summer) Sun
☎ (01308) 868358
Branscombe Vale Branoc; guest beer Ⓗ
A classic rural pub – stone built and thatched with an idyllic garden and steeped in history. The local owners have saved this remote pub from closure and are sympathetically restoring it. A small flagstoned bar with a large, welcoming fireplace leads to the restaurant. There is a second bar in the skittle alley/function room. Accommodation is available in adjoining buildings. The house beer is from the Dorset Brewing Company in Weymouth and Thatchers cider is available in summer. ⛰Q♉❀◑♿⛺♣●P

Sherborne

Digby Tap

Cooks Lane, DT9 3NS
✪ 11-2.30, 5.30-11; 11-3.30, 6-11 Sat; 12-3, 7-10.30 Sun
☎ (01935) 813148
Beer range varies Ⓗ
The town's only remaining true free house is situated close to the abbey, railway station and town centre. It has four drinking areas, all with flagged floors and cosy corners. A popular locals' pub but visitors are made welcome. However, mobile phones are discouraged and an inadvertent ring will incur a 'fine'. Three or four ever-changing beers are served, mostly from independent brewers in the south west. Good pub food is served on weekday lunchtimes. ♉❀🛏◑♿≋♣●

Shroton (Iwerne Courtney)

Cricketers

Main Street, DT11 8QD (off A350)
✪ 11 (12 Sun)-3, 7-11
☎ (01258) 860421
Badger First Gold; Greene King IPA; guest beers Ⓗ
As the name suggests, this traditional village pub has a cricketing theme. Memorabilia adorn the walls and the handpumps are in the style of cricket bats. Situated below Hambledon Hill, the pub is popular with walkers and tourists as well as locals. There is a large public bar with games area and a dining area where excellent food is served. Award-winning accommodation is available. Q♉❀🛏◑♿⛺♣P⚟

Stoborough

King's Arms

3 Corfe Road, BH20 5AB (adjacent to B3075)
✪ 11-3, 5-11.30; 11-11.30 Fri & Sat; 11-10.30 Sun
☎ (01929) 552705
Ringwood Best Bitter; guest beers Ⓗ
This 400-year-old listed building played host to Cromwell's troops in1642 at the time of the siege of Corfe Castle. A long, slim pub renowned for its food, it has a large no-smoking restaurant and a split level bar. The riverside dining area is very popular with families in summer. At least two real ales are served and a cider from Cheddar Valley. ⛰Q♉❀◑●P⚟

Stratton

Saxon Arms

The Square, DT2 9WG (on A37 3 miles W of Dorchester)
✪ 11-2.30, 5.30-11; 11-11 Sat; 12-10.30 Sun
☎ (01305) 260020
Ringwood Best Bitter; guest beers Ⓗ
This new pub has already established itself as a community inn at the heart of village life. Stone built and thatched with flagstone floors and an open fire, it has a suntrap terrace at the front. The extensive menu attracts diners from near and far. A good range of beers changes regularly. ⛰Q❀◑♿P

Studland

Bankes Arms Hotel

Watery Lane, BH19 3AU
✪ 10-11 daily
☎ (01929) 450225
Isle of Purbeck Fossil Fuel, Solar Power, Studland Bay Wrecked; guest beers Ⓗ

Home of the Isle of Purbeck Brewery and situated in a picturesque village in the heart of the Purbeck heritage area, this pub is a gem. The cosy Purbeck stone built pub offers a range of nine ales and an excellent menu. The huge cliff top garden hosts an annual beer festival in August and offers views over Poole Bay and Old Harry Rocks.

Sturminster Marshall

Black Horse

Blandford Road, BH21 4AQ (on A350 1 mile N of A31)

12-2.30, 6-10.30; 1-11 Fri & Sat; 12-10.30 Sun

(01258) 857217

Badger First Gold; guest beer H

Cosy, traditional pub on the outskirts of the village. Locals and visitors flock here to enjoy the excellent food or a pint in front of the fire on a cold winter's evening. The L-shaped room is full of character with wooden furnishings. A popular quiz is held on Sunday. P

Swanage

Red Lion

63 High Street, BH19 2LY

10.30-11; 11-10.30 Sun

(01929) 423533 redlionswanage.co.uk

Caledonian Deuchars IPA; Ringwood Best Bitter; Taylor Landlord; guest beer H

Popular two-roomed pub in the town centre, dating back to the 17th century and retaining many traditional features. Five real ales are available and six ciders. Good value meals are served from an extensive menu. Live music occasionally features and a range of pub games is played. The garden is busy in summer. Accommodation is now offered – the pub's location makes it a good base for exploring the Purbecks.

Q P

Symondsbury

Ilchester Arms

DT6 6HD

11.30-3, 6-late; 12-3, 6-late Sun

(01308) 422600

Palmer Copper Ale, IPA, Dorset Gold, Tally Ho! H

Delightful stone built and thatched village pub with a large inglenook fire which burns throughout the winter months. The single bar has seven tables where home-cooked food is served to complement the three real ales and draught cider. There is also a restaurant but it is advisable to book ahead at the weekend. Children are not allowed in the bar. A small stream with mature willow trees runs alongside the garden. P

Tarrant Monkton

Langton Arms

DT11 8RX

11-midnight; 12-11.30 Sun

(01258) 830225 thelangtonarms.co.uk

Ringwood Best Bitter; guest beers H

Set in a peaceful village in the north Dorset countryside, this pub offers excellent food, real ales including a house beer from Hop Back and accommodation. It has a no-smoking restaurant, tap room with pool table and large dining room/function room with skittle alley. Since the old, thatched part of the pub was burned down in a major fire in 2004 it has had a major rebuild and new phoenix logo, and is once again a highly successful enterprise. Wedding catering is a speciality.

P

Upwey

Royal Standard

700 Dorchester Road, DT3 5LA

11-3, 7-midnight; 12-midnight Sat & Sun

(01305) 812558

Butcombe Bitter; Palmer Copper Ale; Ringwood Fortyniner H

Comfortable two-roomed local on the outskirts of Weymouth. The wood-panelled public bar is generally busier than the comfortable lounge with its distinctly homely feel. The interior reflects the publican's interest in model railways and classic motorbikes. You will also find rats and ferrets in cages, cats prowling the bars and an eagle owl in an aviary outside. Although customers are welcome to use the Internet facilities here, mobile phones are frowned upon and you risk a fine if yours rings. The choice of draught ales is complemented by bottled Belgian beers. Q P

Wareham

Duke of Wellington

East Street, BH20 4NN

11-11 daily

(01929) 553015

Camerons Castle Eden Ale; Isle of Purbeck Fossil Fuel; Ringwood Best Bitter; guest beers H

Busy pub in the middle of the town, popular with real ale drinkers from near and far. In the past year more than 150 guest beers have been served. The snug lounge has wood panelling and open fires and there is a no-smoking restaurant offering an extensive menu. The pleasant courtyard garden is a delightful place for a drink in the summer.

Q

Waytown

Hare & Hounds

DT6 5LQ (off A3066 near Netherbury)

11-3 (not Mon), 6.30-11; 12-3, 7-10.30 Sun (11-11 Sat & Sun summer)

(01308) 488203

Palmer Copper Ale, IPA, 200 or Tally Ho! G

Tucked away in a small hamlet, this unspoilt pub offers Palmer's ales on gravity dispense. A single counter serves two drinking areas. The garden has superb views. Situated in one of the prettiest parts of west Dorset and surrounded by many walks, this is an ideal place to stop off. No food is served on Sunday evening or Monday in winter. Taunton traditional cider is stocked.

Q P

West Stour

Ship Inn

SP8 5RP (on A30)

⏲ 12-3, 6-11; 12-3, 7-10.30 Sun

☎ (01747) 838640 ⊕ shipinn-dorset.com

Palmer Dorset Gold; Ringwood Best Bitter; guest beer [H]

Imposing traditional stone coaching inn built around 1750. Although recently refurbished throughout, the pub retains much of its original character. The pub has fine views across Blackmore Vale and the pleasant gardens include a tranquil water feature. This family-friendly pub is renowned for excellent fresh home-cooked food (no meals Sun eve). Dogs are welcome.

♛Q❀⇆◑♣P

Weymouth

Boot Inn

High Street, DT4 8QT

⏲ 11-11; 12-10.30 Sun

☎ (01305) 770327

Ringwood Best Bitter, Fortyniner, Old Thumper, seasonal beers; guest beers [H]

Weymouth's oldest pub is hidden behind the fire station. The wood-floored bar area leads to small rooms at each end with comfortable seating and warming fires. The full Ringwood beer range is supplemented with guest beers and Cheddar Valley cider. The pub's popularity can lead to a spillage of customers onto the pavement in fine weather. An old-fashioned pub where conversation dominates, it was voted regional CAMRA Pub of the Year in 2005.

♛Q❀≠♣●

Queen's Hotel

7 King Street, DT4 7BJ

⏲ 12-11 (12-2, 4.30-11 winter); 12-11 Sun

☎ (01305) 786326

Dorset Weymouth JD 1742, Steam Beer; guest beers [H]

Situated opposite the railway station, this large pub has a lounge, public bar and pool room. A keen supporter of local breweries, particularly Dorset Brewing Company, the licensee has rejuvenated this establishment. Good value, wholesome food is served.

♛Q☋⇆◑⊟≠⚟

Weatherbury Hotel

7 Carlton Road North, DT4 7PX

⏲ 12-11; 12-10.30 Sun

☎ (01305) 786040

Fuller's London Pride; guest beers [H]

Single bar pub in a residential area, divided into different areas with a TV screen in each one. Well-behaved children are welcome. Alongside the London Pride there is a frequently changing range of guest beers. For outside drinking there is a patio by the front door. ☋❀⇆P

Wimborne

Crown & Anchor

6 Wimborne Road, Walford, BH21 1NN

⏲ 11-2.30 (3 Sat), 6-11; 12-4, 6.30-10.30 Sun

☎ (01202) 841405

Badger First Gold, seasonal beers [H]

Built in 1823, this pub is beside the River Allen and overlooks Walford Craft Mill. The single-room L-shaped bar is cosy and quietly welcoming. The pub is popular for its home-cooked food (booking advisable at weekends). There is a small garden by the river. The centre of Wimborne with its 12th century minster is a short walk from here.

♛Q❀◑P

Winterborne Stickland

Crown

North Street, DT11 0NJ (2½ miles N of A354)

⏲ 12-2.30, 6.30-11; 12-3, 7-10.30 Sun

☎ (01258) 880838

Ringwood Best Bitter, Fortyniner, seasonal beers; guest beer [H]

This 18th-century Grade II listed inn sits in the middle of a peaceful Dorset village. A two-room pub, the inglenook dominates the front bar with a low-beamed dining room at the back. There is an unusual thatched games room in the courtyard.

♛Q☋❀◑♿▲♣P⚟

Worth Matravers

Square & Compass ☆

BH19 3LF (off B3069) OS974777

⏲ 12-3, 6-11; 12-11 Sat; 12-3.30, 7-10.30 Sun

☎ (01929) 439229

Ringwood Best Bitter; guest beers [G]

Stunning pub perched atop the Jurassic coastline. Run by generations of the Newman family for 100 years, it has featured in every edition of the Guide. More than 200 years old, with original flagstone floors, it oozes character from every nook and cranny. Beer is dispensed at a serving hatch in the corridor. It hosts a Pumpkin and Beer festival on the first Saturday in October and a cider festival in November. It is also renowned for its live music. A museum alongside displays fossils found in the area.

♛Q❀♣●

Steak and Bass

'Lets have filleted steak and a bottle of Bass for dinner tonight. It will be simply exquisite. I shall love it.' 'But my dear Nella,' he exclaimed, 'steak and beer at Felix's! It's impossible! Moreover, young women still under twenty-three cannot be permitted to drink Bass.'

Arnold Bennett, The Grand Babylon Hotel, 1902

DURHAM

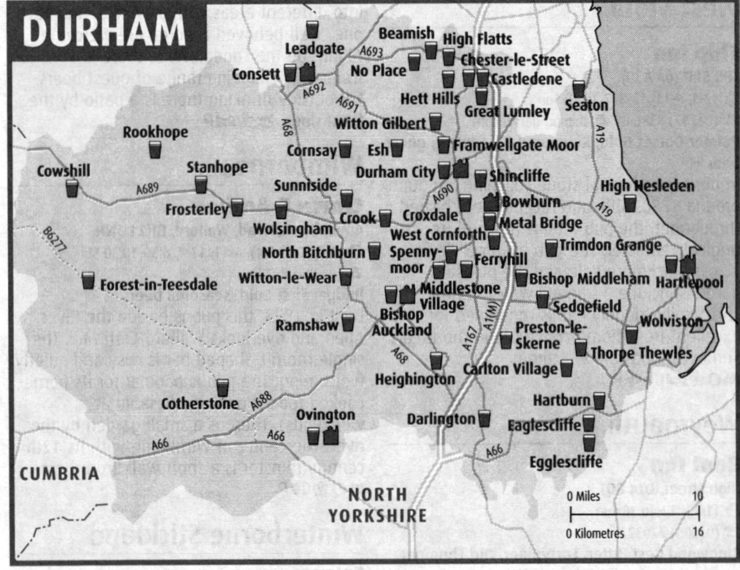

Co Durham incorporates part of the former county of Cleveland

Beamish

Sun

Beamish Open Air Museum, DH9 0RG (follow signs for Beamish, then catch tram)
11 (12 Sun)-3.30 (4.30 summer)
(0191) 370 2908
Theakston Old Peculier; guest beers
Traditional pub, formerly situated in Bishop Auckland. Step back in time in an authentic replica of a 1913 pub with sawdust on the floor and an antique till on the bar. Mounted animals on display represent the taxidermist's art. Sample Temperance drinks here, including sarsaparilla. Serial killer Mary Ann Cotton stayed here during her incarceration at Durham. ♣P

Bishop Auckland

Grand Hotel

Holdforth Crest, DL14 6DU (near Asda car park)
6 (12 Fri & Sat)-11; 12-10.30 Sun
(01388) 601956 the-grand-hotel.co.uk
Beer range varies
This large free house goes from strength to strength. As well as opening the Wear Valley Brewery in outbuildings in summer 2005, it was voted local CAMRA Pub of the Year in 2005. The brewery is gaining a good reputation and two or three of its beers are usually available in the pub, as well as up to five guest beers and a cider. A beer festival is held in August. Quiz night is Thursday and live music is hosted on Saturday and sometimes Friday (see website for details). It is a five-minute walk from the railway station. ♣P

Pollards

104 Etherley Lane, DL14 6TU
11-11; 12-10.30 Sun
(01388) 603539
Camerons Bitter, Strongarm; guest beers
Now under new management, the pub offers three guest ales. The newly refurbished kitchen provides meals on weekday lunchtimes (not Mon) and every evening. Two roaring open fires are very welcoming on cold evenings. Darts and dominoes are played. ♣P

Tut 'n' Shive

68 Newgate Street, DL14 7EQ
11-midnight (1am Fri & Sat); 11-midnight Sun
(01388) 603252
Beer range varies
This popular town centre pub has recently been refurbished throughout. It offers two regularly changing guest ales and Westons Old Rosie cider. Bar meals are available during the day and live bands (usually rock) are a regular and welcome feature. Close to the bus and railway stations.

Bishop Middleham

Cross Keys

9 High Street, DL17 9AR (1 mile from A177)
12 (5 Mon)-11; 12-10.30 Sun
(01740) 651231
Marston's Pedigree; Wells Bombardier; guest beer
Fine example of a comfortable family-run village local with a highly-recommended restaurant. A spacious open-plan lounge/bar with exposed beams is complemented by a large restaurant/function room serving a full a la carte menu (booking advised). A three-

INDEPENDENT BREWERIES

Camerons Hartlepool
Consett Ale Works Consett
Durham Bowburn
Four Alls Ovington
Hill Island Durham City
Wear Valley Bishop Auckland

mile circular village walk starts opposite (leaflets available in the pub). Quiz night is Tuesday. Teeside Tornados Bike Club meets on Wednesday and the pub fields its own football team. ⛰❀◐◑

Carlton Village

Smith's Arms

TS21 1EA

✪ 12-midnight; closed Mon; 12-10.30 Sun

☎ (01740) 630471

Caledonian Deuchars IPA; guest beer Ⓗ

This Victorian red-brick end-of-terrace pub is in the centre of this quiet village and at the heart of the community. The bustling public bar is crowded on big-match days. The comfortable lounge with its cosy settees tempts you to stay for just one more pint. The newly refurbished restaurant in the old stables offers a wide range of upmarket food including English specialities. Q❀◐◑⊟♣P

Castledene

Smiths Arms

Brecon Hill, DH3 4HE

✪ 4 (12 Sat)-11; 12-10.30 Sun

☎ (0191) 385 6915

Black Sheep Best Bitter; Courage Directors; Taylor Landlord; guest beers Ⓗ

Despite being well tucked away, this country pub is very popular with drinkers and diners, particularly at weekends. Regulars gather in the snug public bar with its real fire in winter, where two guest ales are available. There is a comfortable lounge with a floor that slopes somewhat disconcertingly – it's not the drink, honest. The games room houses a pool table. The high quality restaurant is upstairs. ⛰Q◑⊟♣P

Chester-le-Street

Butchers Arms

Middle Chare, DH3 3QD (off Front St)

✪ 11-11 (midnight Thu-Sat)

☎ (0191) 388 3605 🌐 4durhamcounty.co.uk

Camerons Strongarm; Marston's Pedigree; guest beers Ⓗ

Ideal for the discerning drinker and diner, this pub enjoys a good reputation for beer and home-cooked food. Pies and freshly delivered fish are specialities. Bedrooms are available for travellers from afar. Tea and coffee are served here. Small meetings can be accommodated. Note the fine array of porcelain artefacts. ⛟◐⇌⚡

Grange Club

Pelaw Grange Stadium, Drum Road, DH3 2AF (signed from Barley Mow roundabout on A167)

✪ 6.30 (7 Tue & Fri)-11; closed Wed; 12-4, 7-10.30 Sun

☎ (0191) 410 2141 🌐 pelawgrange.co.uk

Black Sheep Best Bitter; guest beer Ⓗ

The Grange Club at the greyhound stadium includes a large open bar where children are welcome, a panoramic restaurant and a concert room, all overlooking the track. The club serves two cask ales. Reasonably-priced bar meals are available on race nights. With a loyal clientele the club has a lively atmosphere, especially on race nights (Mon, Thu, Sat). Managed by a CAMRA member, this is the only greyhound stadium in Britain with real ales, an annual beer festival and trips to local micros. ❀◑♿P

Consett

Grey Horse

115 Sherburn Terrace, DH8 6NE (off A692 between Consett and Leadgate)

✪ 12-11.30 (midnight Wed-Sat); 12-11.30 Sun

☎ (01207) 502585

Hadrian & Border Gladiator Ⓗ

A welcome return to the Guide for this charming, friendly pub with great beer and a warm atmosphere. Two open fires blaze in winter. Pump clips on display reveal the diverse guest ales policy. Regular beer festivals are popular with locals and visitors to the area. The Coast-to-Coast cycle route is nearby. ⛰Q♨❀⊟⊟ (765) ♣●

Cornsay

Blackhorse Inn

Old Cornsay, DH7 9EL (2 miles W of B6301 Cornsay Colliery road)

✪ 7-11; 12-2.30, 8-10.30 Sun

☎ (0191) 373 4211 🌐 blackhorsebar.co.uk

Black Sheep Best Bitter; guest beers Ⓗ

Remote west Durham village pub overlooking the picturesque Gladdow Valley. The comfortable, contemporary bar has an adjoining restaurant which is also used for local functions and events. Evening meals are served Tuesday to Saturday. An annual beer festival takes place over the Easter weekend. Q❀◑⛺♣P

Cotherstone

Red Lion

DL12 9QE (on B6277 Barnard Castle to Middleton in Teesdale road)

✪ 12-3 (Sat only), 7-11; 12-4, 7-10.30 Sun

☎ (01833) 650236

Jennings Cumberland Ale; Wells Bombardier; guest beer Ⓗ

Typical Teesdale stone-built village inn. The main bar has a beamed ceiling, half-panelled walls and an open fire, and a large adjoining room serves bar meals. A la carte evening meals are served in the small dining room. Food is only available at the weekend, with dishes made from local Cotherstone cheese a speciality. Up to three real ales are stocked including a guest from a local micro-brewery. Dogs and children are welcome. ⛰Q❀◐◑⊟⛺♣P

Cowshill

Cowshill Hotel

DL13 1JQ

✪ 12-2.30 (may vary), 7-11; 12-2.30, 7-10.30 Sun

☎ (01388) 537236

Tetley Bitter Ⓗ

The nearest pub to the Kilhope lead mining centre, this free house has been in the same family for more than 45 years. Excellent food is served at the weekend – booking is

recommended. The surrounding hills provide good terrain for walkers and cyclists but at this high altitude the weather can be extreme at times. If visiting by bus check return times before travelling.
⛰Q◐◑⛺🚌(101)♣P

Crook

Colliery

High Jobs Hill, DL15 0UL

⏲ 12-3 (may vary Mon), 6-11; 12-10.30 Sun

☎ (01388) 762511

Camerons Strongarm; Courage Directors Ⓗ

High above Crook on the Durham road, this pleasant hostelry enjoys a good reputation for its fine food. Far enough out of town to be off the 'circuit' and still without a juke box, this is a place to relax and converse.
Q◐◑🚌(46)P⚡

White Swan

66 Hope Street, DL15 9HT

⏲ 11-11.30; 12-10.30 Sun

☎ (01388) 764478

Beer range varies Ⓗ

Small, friendly pub offering two guest ales from independent breweries. Since the return of cask ales the pub has gone from strength to strength and is very busy at weekends with locals. Live music features on Saturday night. The present licensees previously ran the Surtees and uphold the same high standards here. ❀🚌♣

Croxdale

Daleside Arms

Front Street, DH6 5HY (on B6288, 3 miles S of Durham, off A167)

⏲ 3 (7 Tue; 12 Sat)-midnight (11 Mon-Wed); 11-8 Sun

☎ (01388) 814165

Beer range varies Ⓗ

This family-run local is an example of how a rural pub can be successful by doing the simple things well, offering an interesting range of guest ales and good-value home-cooked food (available Sun lunch and Wed-Fri eve, booking advisable). Try the chilli if you dare. Sporting relics decorate the bar. Check out the stunning floral displays which have won prestigious awards. Q❀◐◑🛏♿P

Darlington

Binns Department Store

1-7 High Row, DL3 7HH

⏲ 9-5.30 (6 Fri & Sat); 11-5 Sun

☎ (0870) 160 7273

House of Fraser department store in the heart of the pedestrianised town centre with a well-stocked bottled beer section in the basement wine shop. Over 200 quality beers are available, including scores of Belgian and British bottle-conditioned ales. It sells a good choice of badged glasses too. ♿⇌

Britannia

Archer Street, DL3 6LR (next to ring road, W side of town centre)

⏲ 11.30-3, 5.30-11; 11.30-11 Fri & Sat; 12-10.30 Sun

☎ (01325) 463787

Camerons Strongarm; John Smith's Bitter; guest beers Ⓗ

Warm, friendly, much-loved local CAMRA award-winning pub, a bastion of cask beer for 140 years, situated across the ring road from the town centre but away from the frenetic 'circuit'. It retains much of the appearance and layout of the private house it originally was: a modestly enlarged bar and domestic-proportioned parlour (used for meetings) sit either side of a central corridor. Listed for historic associations, it was the birthplace of teetotal, 19th-century publisher, JM Dent. Up to four guest beers are available. ⛰Q♿⇌♣P🍺

Darlington Cricket Club

South Terrace, DL1 5JD (off Feethams South)

⏲ 7.30 (7 Fri; 12 Sat)-midnight; 12-11.30 Sun

☎ (01325) 250044

Camerons Strongarm; guest beer Ⓗ

Traditional-style pavilion at the historic Feethams ground where Durham County CC plays occasional fixtures. The comfortable lounge is decorated with local cricketing memorabilia. There is a TV for sport and a snooker room. The function room overlooks the cricket field. The bar opens earlier when there is a match. Members select the guest beer each month. Show this Guide or CAMRA membership card for entry. ❀⇌♣P

Darlington Snooker Club

1 Corporation Road, DL1 6AE (1/4 mile N of centre)

⏲ 11-11 (2am Fri & Sat); 12-10.30 Sun

☎ (01325) 241388

Beer range varies Ⓗ

This first-floor, family-run and family-oriented private snooker club offers a warm, friendly welcome. Up to three guest beers are available in the single bar, while a small, comfortable TV lounge is provided for those not playing on one of the 10 top quality snooker tables. Twice yearly, the club plays host to a professional celebrity. CAMRA's regional Club of the Year 2004 and 2005 welcomes CAMRA members on production of a current membership card or this Guide.
Q👶⇌(North Rd)♣🍺

Number Twenty-2

22 Coniscliffe Road, DL3 7RG

⏲ 12-11; closed Sun

☎ (01325) 354590 🌐 villagebrewer.co.uk

Village White Boar, Bull, Old Raby; guest beers Ⓗ

Town-centre ale house with a passion for cask beer; it has won numerous CAMRA awards since opening in 1995. Huge curved windows and a high ceiling give it an airy spaciousness even when busy. Thirteen handpumps serve 11 beers including up to six guests, mainly from small micro-breweries countywide. This is the home pub of Village Brewer beers, commissioned from Hambleton by the licensee. Hambleton Nightmare is sold here as Yorkshire Stout and Burton Bridge Festival as Classic Burton Ale. 🛏♿⇌🍺

Old Yard Tapas Bar

98 Bondgate, DL3 7JY

⏲ 11-11; 12-10.30 Sun

☎ (01325) 467385 🌐 tapasbar.co.uk

John Smith's Magnet; Theakston Old Peculier; guest beers 🄷
Interesting mixture of town centre bar and Mediterranean-style taverna, where a range of six real ales is sold alongside sangria, ouzo, tapas and mezes. Four guest beers are stocked and, although it is a thriving restaurant, it is perfectly acceptable to simply pop in for a pint. Licensed for pavement drinking, tables are set out in summer. The TV shows sport only. ❀◑◗

Quakerhouse
1-3 Mechanics Yard, DL3 7QF (off High Row, through alley next to Binns)
⏲ 11 (12 Sun)-midnight
☎ (07845) 666643 🌐 quakerhouse.net
Jarrow Rivet Catcher; guest beers 🄷
Hidden jewel, based in one of Darlington's oldest buildings in the historic yards area of the town. Local CAMRA's Pub of the Year 2006 stocks up to nine guest beers from micro-breweries countrywide, plus a cider. There is live music on Wednesday evening (door charge after 7.30pm). An upstairs function room is available for hire. Food is served on Saturday lunchtime. ♿≉●

Durham City

Colpitts
Colpitts Terrace, DH1 4EG (on A690)
⏲ 2 (12 Thu-Sat)-11; 12-10.30 Sun
☎ (0191) 386 9913
Samuel Smith OBB 🄷
This gem of a pub remains little changed, sitting in a time warp in the heart of the city. Situated on a corner, this local still has an off-sales hatch. Coal fires warm in winter. In line with Sam Smith's policy it has no music; entertainment is provided by conversation. If you love unpretentious and interesting pubs then this is a must.
⛼Q♉❀⊟♿≉♣⚟

Dun Cow
37 Old Elvet, DH1 3HN
⏲ 11 (10 Sat)-11; 12-10.30 Sun
☎ (0191) 386 9219
Caledonian Deuchars IPA; Camerons Castle Eden Ale; guest beer 🄷
Dating from the 16th or 17th century – opinion varies – this friendly, atmospheric pub is a must for visitors to Durham City. The front bar is a cosy snug, while the larger lounge is accessed down an alley. See the plaques on the alley wall for the link with the St Cuthbert's legend. This pub boasts the highest sales of Castle Eden in the country.
Q❀◑⊟≉♣⚟

Half Moon
New Elvet, DH1 3AQ (by Elvet Bridge)
⏲ 11-11 (midnight Fri & Sat); 12-11 Sun
☎ (0191) 383 6981
Draught Bass; Taylor Landlord; guest beers 🄷
This deservedly popular pub, run by the same landlord for 25 years, continues to flourish. Its listed interior is split into two crescents – hence the name – on two levels. The upper half is a drinking area favoured by locals and the lower half is a lounge area with seating. A large screen shows Sky Sports. The pub is busy at the weekend, particularly Saturday evening. It hosts regular mini-beer festivals, with Durham Brewery ales featuring as guests. Wheelchair access is good. Q❀⊟♿≉

Victoria Inn ☆
86 Hallgarth Street, DH1 3AS
⏲ 11.45-3, 6-11; 12-2, 7-10.30 Sun
☎ (0191) 386 5269
Big Lamp Bitter; guest beers 🄷
This authentic Victorian pub has listed status outside and in, featuring in CAMRA's National Inventory of heritage pubs. Its tiny snug and coal fires create an olde-worlde atmosphere. Superb real ales are sold alongside a wide range of malt and Irish whiskies. This friendliest of establishments, run by the same licensee for 30 years, is simply a must for visitors to the city. Awarded Durham CAMRA Pub of the Year in 2003 and 2005. ⛼Q⇆◑⊟≉♣

Water House
65 North Road, DH1 4TM
⏲ 9am-midnight (1am Fri & Sat); 9am-midnight Sun
☎ (0191) 370 6540
Courage Directors; Greene King Abbot; Marston's Pedigree; Shepherd Neame Spitfire; guest beers 🄷
Wetherspoon's made several attempts to open a pub in Durham City, but this busy hostelry in the former waterboard offices is now well established. A long, narrow split-level building opens out into three areas. Although one of the smaller pubs in the group, it serves a good range of guest ales. Beers from local breweries feature with Wylam, Mordue and Darwin making regular appearances. Q♉◑◗♿≉⚟

Woodman Inn
23 Gilesgate, DH1 1QW
⏲ 12-midnight; 12-11.30 Sun
☎ (0191) 386 7500
Beer range varies 🄷
The first pub in Durham City to introduce a no-smoking drinking area, the Woodman serves as the tap for Durham Brewery, offering its ales as part of a range of six cask beers usually available. Regular beer festivals are held, including themed German events. The licensee's love of border terriers is evident by the pictures on the wall. ❀≉🚌(63, 64)⚟

Eaglescliffe

Cleveland Bay
718 Yarm Road, TS16 0JE
⏲ 11-12.30am daily
☎ (01642) 780275
Beer range varies 🄷
This 180-year-old whitewashed double-fronted pub dominates the junction of the A67 and A135. A long-term devotee of real ale, the licensee has recently adopted a most successful policy of stocking rotating guest ales, with cask ale sales more than trebling. The pub dates back to the days of the Stockton and Darlington Railway, whose coal drops can still be seen from the car park. Q❀⊟♿≉(Allens West)♣P⊡

Egglescliffe

Pot & Glass

Church Road, TS16 9DQ

12-2, 6-11 (5.30-midnight Fri; 6-midnight Sat); 12-10.30 Sun

(01642) 651009

Draught Bass; Caledonian Deuchars IPA; Jennings Cumberland Ale; guest beers

The sort of pub we would all like to have as our local – the Pot & Glass is at the centre of village life and runs darts and cricket teams. It is situated opposite the church, whose graveyard is the last resting place of former licensee Charlie Abbey. Charlie, who was also a cabinet maker, gave the pub much of its character, crafting the ornate bar fronts from old country house furniture. The two rapidly rotating guest beers are from micro-breweries or regionals. No meals are served on Sunday. Q P

Esh

Cross Keys

Front Street, DH7 9QR (3 miles off A691, between Durham and Consett) OSNZ2044

12-3, 5.30 (6.30)-11; 12-10.30 Sun

(0191) 373 1279

Black Sheep Best Bitter; Tetley Bitter

Pleasant, 18th-century pub in a picturesque village where a varied menu offers vegetarian and children's choices. A comfortable locals' bar complements the lounge overlooking the River Browney Valley. Delft racks display porcelain artefacts, some of which portray the old village. (725)P

Ferryhill

Surtees Arms

Chilton Lane, DL17 0DH

4 (12 Sat)-11; 12-10.30 Sun

(01740) 655724

Bateman XXXB; Shepherd Neame Spitfire; guest beers

A genuine free house, the pub offers the only real ale in Ferryhill. Up to five beers are available at very reasonable prices. A large, multi-roomed pub, it has a restaurant and upstairs function room. Popular karaoke nights are held monthly. Ask the landlord about his range of waistcoats. Lunchtime meals are served at weekends.
Q (2, 112)

Forest-in-Teesdale

Langdon Beck Hotel

DL12 0XP (on B6277 6 miles W of Middleton-in-Teesdale) OS853313

11-11; 12-10.30 Sun

(01833) 622267 langdonbeckhotel.com

Black Sheep Best Bitter, Emmerdale; Jarrow Rivet Catcher; guest beers

Situated high in the Pennines in some of the finest countryside in England, this country inn has long been a destination for walkers, fishermen and those seeking tranquillity. Now this rejuvenated gem offers a range of beers including up to two guests from local micro-breweries, plus excellent food and accommodation. It has a 24 hour licence. The spectacular High Force and Cauldron Snout waterfalls are a short walk away, and the Pennine Way passes close by in Upper Teesdale. Q P

Framwellgate Moor

Tap & Spile

Front Street, DH1 5EE

12-3 (not Mon), 6 (5 Fri)-11; 12-3, 7-10.30 Sun

(0191) 386 5451

Beer range varies

This ever popular pub continues to set a high standard, providing great atmosphere and excellent conversation. With its wooden floors and three rooms, it is a typical ale house. It now stocks a rotating range of mainly local ales in tip top condition. Check out the displays of holiday 'tat', 'kindly' donated by customers. Q

Frosterley

Black Bull

Bridge End, DL13 2SL (W end of village)

11-11 (4 Mon); 12-10.30 Sun

(01388) 527784

Copper Dragon Golden Pippin; Durham Magus; guest beers

Since new owners have taken over this true free house, the keg lager and nitro-beer have been replaced by four handpumped ales plus traditional cider and perry. A high standard of catering ensures that the food is always in demand and booking is essential (eve meals Tue-Sat). Tuesday nights feature popular live music sessions from many traditional performers. Situated opposite the steam Weardale Railway Station, guests can drift back in time while enjoying a fine pint.
Q (101) P

Great Lumley

Old England

Front Street, DH3 4JB (near Co-op)

11-11 (lounge: 6.15-11 & 11-3 Fri & Sat); 12-10.30 (lounge: 12-3, 6.30-10.30) Sun

(0191) 388 5257

Beer range varies

This friendly, family-run pub usually has three guest beers on tap, including ales from Northumberland and Durham. The spacious, comfortable, split-level lounge is divided into distinct areas by stylish panels. The atmosphere is peaceful, attracting a regular clientele, including diners (no-smoking tables available). The public bar is more lively, with a pool table, dartboard, satellite and projection TV. Other entertainment includes a quiz held twice a week. P

Hartburn

Masham Hotel

87 Hartburn Village, TS18 5DR

11-11 (11.30 Fri & Sat); 12-4, 7-10.30 Sun

(01642) 580414 themasham.co.uk

Draught Bass; Black Sheep Special; guest beer

Old, mid-terrace local run by a long-established cask beer family. With a recent

refurbishment there is a growing emphasis on good, home-cooked food here, though the pub's origins as a house serving the public have not been lost, and the pub is very popular for its real ales. Good garden and patio facilities provide an outdoor warm weather alternative.
Q❀◖◗⊟♣P⅍

Parkwood Hotel
64-66 Darlington Road, TS18 5ER
✪ 12-3, 5-11.30; 12-midnight Sat; 12-11 Sun
☎ (01642) 587933
Camerons Strongarm; Greene King Abbot; guest beer Ⓗ
Originally a large Victorian house and unchanged in outward appearance, the Parkwood is set in a leafy, suburban area. Once the home of the Ropner family, local ship owners and civic benefactors, the hotel offers a friendly welcome to all. The licensee is determined to keep the bar as a pub and not allow diners to take it over (no meals Sun eve). Demand for real ale continues to grow. Quality accommodation is available.
❀⇌◖◗🚌(98, 99)P

Hartlepool

Brewery Tap
Stockton Street TS24 7QS
✪ 11-4; closed Mon; 11-4 Sun
☎ (01429) 868686 🌐 cameronsbrewery.com
Camerons Strongarm; guest beers Ⓗ
Imaginative conversion of what was once the Stranton Inn into a multi-purpose building: brewery tap, shop, bistro and starting point for brewery tours. A friendly and welcoming atmosphere prevails. The range of Camerons cask ales, including some from the Lion's Den micro-plant, reflects the manager's long interest in serving real ale – his pubs have featured in the Guide many times. A two-for-one menu is served in the bistro on weekdays. ◖⇌P⅍

Causeway
Vicarage Gardens, Stranton, TS24 7QT (beside Stranton Church)
✪ 11-11 (midnight Fri & Sat); 12-10.30 Sun
☎ (01429) 273954
Banks's Original, Bitter; Camerons Strongarm; Marston's Old Empire Ⓗ
One of several gems in a town with a burgeoning reputation for real ale. This fine red-brick Victorian watering-hole has recently been extended into the once derelict shop next door to provide better facilities for the ever-popular live music hosted on most evenings. The two small side rooms, one no-smoking, remain, served by a hatch in the corridor. Boasting a massive annual turnover of real ale and a large, loyal clientele, the Causway is a lively and vibrant meeting place. No food is served on Sunday.
Q❀◖⊟⇌♣⅍▯

Jackson's Arms
Tower Street, TS24 7HH
✪ 12-midnight (2am Fri & Sat); 11-midnight Sun
☎ (01429) 862413
Beer range varies Ⓗ
Typical street-corner local with an interesting history – it was once offered as a prize in a raffle. The two bars, with leather seating along the walls, are bustling and busy; one caters for pool and darts players. Four handpulls dispense an ever-changing choice of guest ales, often from small or micro-breweries. The pub has a strong sense of local identity, but provides a warm and friendly welcome to regulars and visitors alike. Q⊟⇌♣

Ward Jackson (Lloyds No 1)
Church Square, TS24 7EY
✪ 9am-midnight (1am Fri & Sat); 9am-midnight Sun
☎ (01429) 850140
Beer range varies Ⓗ
Formerly the main Hartlepool branch of Barclay's Bank and now part of Wetherspoon's Lloyds No 1 chain, this pub looks most unpromising from the outside – all 1960s glass and chrome. It is also very much a pub that attracts younger drinkers. However, the enthusiastic management majors heavily on cask ales, with the local Camerons Brewery featuring frequently. Unusually, cask cider is always available too. Three guest beers are stocked. ◖◗♿⇌●

White House
Wooler Road, TS26 0DR (at Grange Rd roundabout)
✪ 11-11; 12-10.30 Sun
☎ (01429) 224392
Draught Bass; Camerons Strongarm; guest beers Ⓗ
Once a Roman Catholic boys' grammar school, its former pupils would surely approve of the conversion (no, not that sort of conversion!) into a warm and welcoming pub. Relax and enjoy one of four or five real ales while reading the newspapers in comfortable leather armchairs. There are numerous areas and alcoves, some with open fires. Occasional beer festivals are held. ♨Q❀◖◗P⅍

Heighington

Bay Horse
28 West Green, DL5 6PE
✪ 11-midnight; 12-11.30 Sun
☎ (01325) 312312
Black Sheep Best Bitter; Jennings Cumberland Ale; John Smith's Magnet; guest beers Ⓗ
Picturesque, historic, 300-year-old pub overlooking the village's largest green. Its exposed beams and stone walls offer traditional surroundings, partitioned into distinct drinking and dining areas, with a large restaurant extending from the lounge. Food plays a prominent role, with excellent home-cooked meals available as well as bar snacks. The bar area gives drinkers the chance to enjoy the beer range in the evening, which includes up to three guest ales; the cider is Westons Old Rosie.
❀◖◗⊟♿♣●P▯

George & Dragon
4 East Green, DL5 6PP (behind church)
✪ 12-3 (not Mon), 5-11; 12-11 Fri & Sat; 12-10.30 Sun
☎ (01325) 313152
Black Sheep Best Bitter; Caledonian Deuchars

IPA; Wells Bombardier; guest beers [H]
Friendly village pub where locals warmly welcome visitors. An old coaching inn complete with stables, it has been refurbished in a modern style with a bar and spacious lounge. Meals are served in the lounge, while a conservatory-style restaurant area offers excellent home-cooked food. Regular live music is hosted on alternate Sundays. Two guest ales help ensure this is a pub for lovers of good beer. ❀◑⊟♣P⍰

Locomotion No. One

Heighington Station, DL5 6QG
⌚ 11-midnight; 12-10.30 Sun
☎ (01325) 320132 🌐 locomotionone.co.uk
John Smith's Bitter; guest beers [H]
This family-run pub occupies the former stationmaster's house at Heighington Station, next to the level crossing where the first ever locomotive to haul a passenger train was hoisted on to the track in 1825. An excellent range of real ales including up to three guests is enjoyed by locals and visitors alike. A terrace occupies the original platform with an additional courtyard for outdoor drinking. An extensive menu is served in the pub or upstairs restaurant (no food Sun eve). Beware, the last train leaves early. ♨❀◑♿≋♣P

Hett Hills

Moorings

DH2 3JU (from Chester-le-Street, follow B6313 under viaduct) OSNZ2451
⌚ 12-11.30 (10.30 Sun)
☎ (0191) 370 1597 🌐 themooringsdurham.co.uk
Black Sheep Special; Rudgate Battleaxe; Theakston Cool Cask [H]
Impressive pub on two levels bearing a nautical theme. The bar and bistro serve food all day, with a wide choice of traditional home-cooked English fare. The upstairs restaurant, overlooking the west Durham hills, offers classic French cuisine, including lobster and other seafood. ♞❀◑P⊬

High Flatts

Plough

DH2 1BL (between Chester le Street and Stanley)
⌚ 2 (1 Sat)-11; 12-10.30 Sun
☎ (0191) 388 2068
Wadworth 6X; guest beers [H]
Traditional country pub close to Chester-le-Street town centre with a regular bus service passing the door. The present landlord introduced cask ales to the pub with great success. Quizzes are held three times a week attracting contestants from a wide area. Brass and copper implements adorn the walls together with photographs of a bygone age. The panoramic views take in the Angel of the North and Penshaw Monument. Quoits is played in the bar. There is an airstrip outside. ❀♿▲🚌♣P⊬

High Hesleden

Ship Inn

TS27 4QD ($^3/_4$ mile S of B1281)
⌚ 11 (12 Sat)-3, 6-11; 12-8 Sun
☎ (01429) 836453
Beer range varies [H]
Spacious two-room village inn which became no-smoking throughout in March 2006. The bar and lounge/restaurant both have a nautical theme with model ships and photographs of old warships. The rooms are well furnished and decorated in traditional style including a large gilt-edged mirror. An extensive menu ranges from bar snacks to a la carte and a changing chef's menu. ♨Q❀⇌◑⊟♣P⊬

Leadgate

Jolly Drovers

DH8 6RR (at A692/Ebchester Rd jct)
⌚ 11-11 daily
☎ (01207) 503994
Beer range varies [H]
Traditional cosy British pub with an equal emphasis on serving food and drink. A wide range of beer and cider is offered as well as bottled beers from foreign brewers. A small selection of good, tasty food, value for money prices and excellent, efficient service make the pub very popular and busy, particularly for Sunday lunches. There is a TV in the bar and piped music. ◑P

Metal Bridge

Old Mill

Thinford Road, DH6 5NX (signed off A177) OS303352
⌚ 12-11 (10.30 Sun)
☎ (01740) 652928 🌐 theoldmill.uk.com
Beer range varies [H]
This spacious rural inn, situated a mile south of junction 61 on the A1(M), was formerly a flour and wood mill. It offers a choice of three real ales, often featuring the Durham Brewery. Renowned for the quality of its food, all freshly prepared in house, it offers an extensive menu complemented by a good range of specials. Accommodation includes en-suite facilities. ❀⇌◑♿P⊬

Middlestone Village

Ship Inn

Low Road, DL14 8AB
⌚ 4 (12 Fri & Sat)-11; 12-10.30 Sun
☎ (01388) 810904
Beer range varies [H]
Closed down by Vaux as unviable, the pub was reopened after a vigorous campaign by a local CAMRA member. Now a thriving village inn, it goes from strength to strength – the brewery is no more but the Ship sails on, regularly winning local and regional CAMRA awards. Six ales from local and regional breweries are on offer, and more than 1,000 beers have now been sampled. Twice-yearly beer festivals in May and December offer additional beers. A true community hostelry, its regular clientele comes from far and wide. On clear days enjoy magnificent views from the rooftop patio.
♨❀♿🚌(7, 7A)♣P⍰

No Place

Beamish Mary Inn

DH9 0QH (off A693, Chester-le-Street to Stanley road)
⌚ 12-11 (10.30 Sun)
☎ (0191) 370 0237
Beer range varies Ⓗ
Family-run pub in a former pit village, with open fires and a collection of memorabilia from the 1920s and 1930s. Live music is performed thrice weekly and a folk club meets on Wednesday in the stables. Up to 10 ales are stocked, including a Big Lamp house beer. A beer festival is staged in January. The pub whose theme is 'all dressed up and no place to go', has received many CAMRA awards. ♨🛏◐ ⊡♿♣●P

North Bitchburn

Red Lion

North Bitchburn Terrace, DL15 8AL
⌚ 12-3, 7-11; 12-3, 7-10.30 Sun
☎ (01388) 763561
Beer range varies Ⓗ
Popular village free house that usually has three ales from independent breweries on offer. The house ale – Jenny Ale – comes from Camerons; a contribution to the local hospice is made for every pint sold. The dining room affords superb views over rural Wear Valley. ♨❀◐🚌(1B)♣P

Ovington

Four Alls

The Green, DL11 7BP (2 miles S of Winston and A67)
⌚ 7 (6 Fri)-11; 12-11 Sat; 12-10.30 Sun
☎ (01833) 627302
Tetley Bitter; guest beer Ⓗ
Friendly 18th-century inn opposite the green in what is known as the 'Maypole village'. Note the unusual Victorian sign denoting The Four Alls: 'I govern all (Queen), I fight for all (Soldier), I pray for all (Parson), I pay for all (Farmer)'. The pub consists of a bar, games room and restaurant serving excellent value food. The pub is the home of the Four Alls Brewery, whose beers alternate with guests from micros countrywide; phone first if wanting to try the popular Four Alls beers as they tend not to last. ♨Q☺❀🛏◐♣P

Preston-le-Skerne

Blacksmiths Arms

Preston Lane, DL5 6JH
(1/2 mile from A167 at Gretna Green)
⌚ 11.30-2, 6-11; closed Mon; 12-10.30 Sun
☎ (01325) 314873
Beer range varies Ⓗ
Welcoming, extended free house in a rural location, known locally as the Hammers. A long corridor separates the bar, lounge and restaurant. The beamed lounge is furnished in a farmhouse style complete with Welsh dresser. It has an excellent reputation for home-cooked food, while up to three guest beers come from micro-breweries countrywide. A previous local CAMRA Rural Pub of the Year winner, it even has a helicopter landing pad. Q☺❀◐ ⊡♿♣P

Ramshaw

Bridge

1 Gordon Lane, DL14 0NS
⌚ 11-midnight; 12-11.30 Sun
☎ (01388) 832509
Beer range varies Ⓗ
Community pub by the river and caravan park in a pleasant location, ideal for exploring rural Teesdale and Weardale. Reasonably priced accommodation is available. It offers two ales mainly from independents in the north east. The pub can be busy at the weekend and during the holiday season and is a favourite haunt for residents of the camp site who make use of the fish and chip shop, tuck shop and bingo. ♨❀🛏◐ ⛺🚌(82)P

Rookhope

Rookhope Inn

DL13 2BP
⌚ 11-11; 12-10.30 Sun
☎ (01388) 517215
Beer range varies Ⓗ
Once closed down as unviable, the pub is now run as a village amenity by the Saint Aiden's Trust. A brewery is to open nearby. Situated at a convenient location close to the Coast-to-Coast cycle route, meals and accommodation are provided.
♨Q🛏◐ ⛺🚌(102)♣P

Seaton

Seaton Lane Inn

Seaton Lane, SR7 0LP (on B1404, just off A19)
⌚ 11.30-midnight (1am Fri); 12-midnight Sun
☎ (0191) 581 2038
Taylor Landlord; Theakston Best Bitter; Young's Special; guest beer Ⓗ
The front of the building which houses the bar was originally a 17th-century blacksmith's cottage. Adjacent to the bar is a cosy lounge and split-level restaurant. Live bands perform on the decking in the ample garden in summer and on bank holidays, weather permitting.
♨Q❀◐ ⊡P

Sedgefield

Ceddesfeld Hall

Sedgefield Community Association, Rectory Row, TS21 2AE (behind church)
⌚ 7.30-10.30; 8-11 Fri; 9-11 Sat; 7.30-10.30 Sun
☎ (01740) 620341
Beer range varies Ⓗ
This is a private club where CAMRA members and guests are most welcome. Originally built as the parsonage in 1791, it comes complete with a resident ghost, the Pickled Parson. The club has a small bar, a comfortable, spacious lounge and meeting rooms. Set in its own spacious grounds, it is ideal for a summer evening. Run by volunteers from the Sedgefield Community Association, it hosts a variety of local groups. An annual beer festival is held on the first weekend in July.
Q❀♿P⊓

Nag's Head

8 West End, TS21 2BS

12-2.30, 5-11 (midnight Wed-Fri); 12-midnight Sat; 12-11 Sun

(01740) 620234

Taylor Landlord; Theakston Cool Cask; guest beers H

Situated just off the centre of the village, close to Sedgefield racecourse, this free house is run as a traditional local to attract all age groups; families with well-behaved children are most welcome. There is a comfortable bar and a smaller no-smoking lounge, while the restaurant serves dishes prepared with fresh local produce including locally-caught seafood. Meals are also served in the bar (eve meals Tue-Sat).

Shincliffe

Avenue Inn

Avenue Street, DH1 2PT (off A177)

12-11 daily

(0191) 386 5954 theavenue.biz

Caledonian Deuchars IPA; Camerons Strongarm H

This friendly out of town pub is thriving once again. The menu offers traditional home-cooked fare including specials and traditional Sunday lunch (no food Sun eve). A dominoes competition on Thursday evening and the Monday night quiz are popular with locals and guests alike. Historic Durham City is a mile away. A wealth of public footpaths nearby makes the pub a handy base for walkers and cyclists exploring the surrounding countryside. P

Spennymoor

Frog & Ferret

Coulson Street, DL16 7RS (on A688/B6288 roundabout)

12-midnight (11 Sun)

(01388) 818312

Beer range varies H

A welcome addition to Spennymoor and this Guide, this comfortable pub is a genuine free house with four real ales including some from local micro-breweries. Newly refurbished, the pub has a central bar with comfortable seating on three sides. The cosy interior – a mix of stone, brick and wood – plus a solid fuel stove, encourages you to settle in for the night. A quiz is held on Sunday and a pop music quiz once a month. Q

Stanhope

Grey Bull

17 West Terrace, DL13 2PB

2 (12 Sat)-11; 12-10.30 Sun

(01388) 528177

Beer range varies H

Friendly local at the west end of the village, near the ford and open air swimming pool. Now owned by W&D, this Jennings pub offers two ales from its list. This is a popular watering hole for walkers and cyclists exploring the dale, with roads leading north and south across some spectacular moorland terrain. (101)

Sunniside

Moss Inn

78 Front Street, DL13 4LX

11-11; 12-10.30 Sun

(01388) 730447

Black Sheep Best Bitter; guest beer H

Village free house with a reputation for fine food and ales – well worth seeking out in an area that is a cask ale desert. A spacious restaurant and function room are busy at weekends. The bar offers a fine selection of malt whiskies to complement the food. (1B)

Thorpe Thewles

Hamilton Russell Arms

Bank Terrace, TS21 3JW

12-11.30 daily

(01740) 630757 hamiltonrussell.co.uk

Wells Bombardier; Marston's Pedigree; guest beers H

Named in celebration of the marriage of Gustavson Hamilton and Emma Maria Russell in 1928, this impressive pub was formerly part of the Marchioness of Londonderry's estate. There are several distinct drinking areas, a snug and a games room, and a spacious no-smoking dining area. The extensive sunny garden has fine views. A varied menu includes many fish and vegetarian options. P

Trimdon Grange

Dovecote Inn

Salters Lane, TS29 6EP (on B1278)

7 (12 Fri-Sun)-11

(01429) 880391

Beer range varies H

This free house dates back to at least 1820, growing an extra storey in 1927, resulting in a distinctive tall but narrow appearance. Situated on the outskirts of a former mining village, it is very much a locals' pub. There used to be a dovecote built into one corner – hence the name. Its single large room houses a popular pool table and dartboard; quiz night is Tuesday.

West Cornforth

Hare & Hounds Inn

Garmondsway, DL17 9DT (1 mile S of Coxhoe on A177)

12-3, 6-11; closed Mon; 12-11 Sat; 12-10.30 Sun

(01740) 654661

Jennings Cumberland Ale; guest beer H

Originally called the Fox Inn, the pub dates back to 1771, when it was part of a farm and coaching inn. Now owned by Enterprise Inns and run by tenants who appreciate real ale, it comprises a large L-shaped bar and a restaurant that doubles as a lounge; exposed beams feature throughout. It specialises in meals based on locally sourced produce, particularly beef. P

Square & Compass

7 The Green, DL17 9JQ (off Coxhoe-W Cornforth road)

12-2.30 (Mon only), 7-midnight; 11.30-midnight Fri &

Sat; 12-midnight Sun
☎ (01740) 653050
Beer range varies Ⓗ
Thriving local situated at the top of the green, in the oldest part of the village and quite different from the rest of 'Doggy' (the locals' name for the place). The pub comprises a large, L-shaped, open-plan bar/lounge and a smaller games room. This free house is popular with all ages, hosting a quiz on Thursday and entertainment on Saturday. ❀♿♣

Witton Gilbert

Glendenning Arms

Front Street, DH7 6SY (off A691, 3 miles from Durham)
⌚ 4 (3 Fri; 12 Sat)-midnight; 12-11.30 Sun
☎ (0191) 371 0316
Black Sheep Best Bitter; Greene King Abbot; Wells Bombardier Ⓗ
Popular village local with a welcoming bar and a cosy, no-smoking lounge. Refurbished two years ago, it has retained the character that makes it a regular in the Guide. The bar has original 1970s Vaux handpulls in red and white. Small functions can be catered for in the lounge. The pub is a meeting place for local clubs and football teams.
⌂Q❀⊞P⚟

Travellers Rest

Front Street, DH7 6TQ (off A691, 3 miles from Durham)
⌚ 11-11; 12-10.30 Sun
☎ (0191) 371 0458
Theakston Best Bitter; guest beers Ⓗ
Country-style pub offering an extensive food menu. The open plan interior is divided into three sections with the bar at the centre: a restaurant, drinking area and conservatory. Most of the pub is no-smoking including the conservatory where families are welcome. There is a large car park and garden area. Steak night is Monday, a quiz and hot buffet are offered on Tuesday and a music quiz is on Sunday evening. ⌂Q♨❀◑P⚟

Witton le Wear

Dun Cow

19 High Street, Crook, DL14 0AY (just off A68)
⌚ 6 (12.30 Sat)-11; 12-10.30 Sun
☎ (01388) 488294
John Smith's Bitter; Wells Bombardier Ⓗ
This village free house date from 1799. A community pub, no pool, games machines or music feature here, although the TV is switched on for special occasions including Sunderland matches. It is close to Low Barns nature reserve, Hamsterley Forest and Harperley POW Camp. The bus service is limited. ⌂Q❀⛺🚌(85, 88)P

Wolsingham

Black Bull

27 Market Place, DL13 3AB
⌚ 11-11; 12-11.30 Sun
☎ (01388) 527332
Ansells Best Bitter; Caledonian Deuchars IPA Ⓗ
Large hostelry in the market place, providing first-rate food and lodgings. It can be busy with a younger crowd at weekends and during men's and women's darts nights – also on the evenings when Weight Watchers meet in the town hall opposite! The hotel is an ideal place to take a break for those exploring the historic streets of Wolsingham or stopping off on the steam operated Weardale Railway a mile away.
⌂Q❀🛏◑⊞⛺🚌(101 X21)♣

Wolviston

Ship

50 High Street, TS22 5JX
⌚ 12-3, 5-11.30; 12-3, 7-10.30 Sun
☎ (01740) 644420
Black Sheep Best Bitter; guest beer Ⓗ
The old stables behind the Ship are all that remains of the original coaching stop – the present building is around 150 years old. The pub is renowned for its home-cooked food, with no hint of portion control or microwave, drawing diners from a wide area (no food Sun eve). The licensee follows a vigorous real ale policy – guest beers change every couple of days. ❀◑♣P⚟

Wellington

31-33 High Street, TS22 5JY
⌚ 12-11 (midnight Thu-Sat)
☎ (01740) 646901
Draught Bass; Taylor Landlord; guest beer Ⓗ
This fine old whitewashed pub with pantiled roof sits alongside the old road north, proudly proclaiming Bass Burton Ales in raised plasterwork. The Wellington has sold draught Bass for many years. The interior is open plan, but with a comfortable lounge area. Live music often features in the large upstairs function room. The pub offers a warm and friendly welcome to all. No food is served on Sunday evening. ❀◑♣P

Your shout

We would like to hear from you. If you think a pub not listed in the guide is worthy of consideration, please let us know. Send us the name, full address and phone number (if known). If a pub in the guide has given poor service, we would also like to know. Write to Good Beer Guide, CAMRA, 230 Hatfield Road, St Albans, Herts, AL1 4LW or email **camra@camra.org.uk**

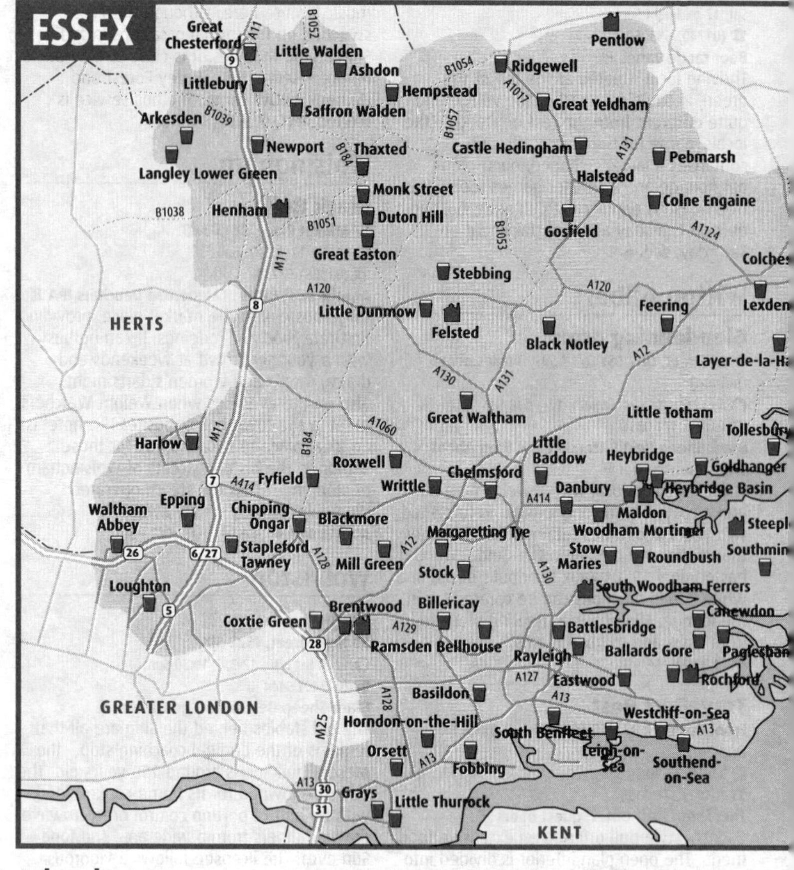

Arkesden

Axe & Compasses

Wicken Road, CB11 4EX (2 miles N of B1038)
OS483344
⏲ 11.30-2.30, 6-11; 12-3, 7-10.30 Sun
☎ (01799) 550272 ⊕ axeandcompasses.co.uk
Greene King IPA, Abbot, Old Speckled Hen Ⓗ

Partly thatched, 17th-century village inn, with a public bar and an award-winning restaurant. This friendly, community pub is the centre of village life where the locals in the public bar tend to be interested in, and talk to, strangers. It is frequented by walkers on the extensive footpath network in this pleasant area where three counties meet; the Harcamlow Way long distance path passes nearby.
♨Q✿◐◑⊟♣P

Ashdon

Rose & Crown

Crown Hill, CB10 2HB (5 miles NE of Saffron Walden)
OS587422
⏲ 12-2, 6-11; 12-4, 7-10.30 Sun
☎ (01799) 584337
Adnams Bitter; Greene King IPA, Abbot; guest beers Ⓗ

This 16th-century, three-roomed pub reveals much character of historical interest. Reputedly haunted, the Cromwell Room still bears its original decoration. Access at the front is via steps. Evening meals are served Monday-Saturday; the weekly fish and chips night is a speciality. The main bar is no-smoking. ♨Q✿◐◑P⊬

Ballards Gore (Stambridge)

Shepherd & Dog

Gore Road, SS4 2DA (between Rochford and Paglesham)
⏲ 12-3, 6-11; 6.30-10.30 Sun
☎ (01702) 258279 ⊕ shepndog.com
Beer range varies Ⓗ

Fine, rural pub in comfortable cottage style. Local CAMRA's Pub of the Year 2004 has been voted Rural Pub of the Year for the second year running. Up to four excellent real ales generally come from micro-breweries and are often unusual for the area. The no-smoking restaurant serves good meals, and snacks are available in the bar. Cider is stocked in summer. Children are allowed in the restaurant or the spacious garden. There is a daytime bus service (not Sun). Q✿◐◑⊟♠P

Basildon

Moon on the Square

1-15 Market Pavement, SS14 1DF
⏲ 9am-midnight (1am Sat); 9am-midnight Sun

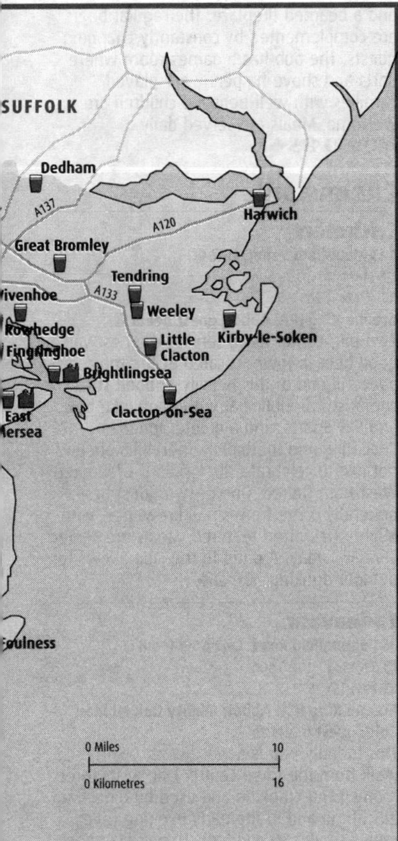

☎ (01268) 520360
Courage Directors; Greene King Abbot; Marston's Burton Bitter, Pedigree; guest beers Ⓗ
Good, busy, Wetherspoon's outlet serving a wide selection of guest ales. Easy to find, near the railway and bus stations, it stands on the corner of Basildon market. Curry, Chinese and quiz evenings are weekly events and it hosts at least two beer festivals a year. Meals are served all day from 9am. Q◐◑≠🚌⊬

Battlesbridge

Barge
Hawk Hill, SS11 7RE
(off A130/A132, follow signs to antiques centre)
⏲ 11-11; 12-10.30 Sun
☎ (01268) 732622
Adnams Bitter, Broadside; Greene King IPA, Abbot; guest beers Ⓗ
Traditional Essex weatherboarded building dating from the 17th century although remodelled in the last decade. It is situated close to the tidal River Crouch and draws plenty of customers from the adjacent antiques centre. Both the pub and centre get busy at the weekend. Beers are normally rotated on five handpumps, and guests are often chosen by drinkers. An annual beer festival is held around St George's Day.
❀◐◑♿≠♣⊬

Billericay

Coach & Horses
36 Chapel Street, CM12 9LU (near B1007)
⏲ 11-11; 12-10.30 Sun
☎ (01277) 622873
Adnams Bitter; Greene King IPA, Abbot; guest beers Ⓗ
Welcoming beer drinkers' pub close to the High Street. This regular Guide entry caters for all ages. It stands on the site of the tap room of the Crown, a one-time coaching inn. The bright, comfortable bar is adorned with prints and photographs, plus impressive collections of jugs and elephants. Good quality food is served, specialising in home-made pies.
⛰❀◐◑≠🚌P

Black Notley

Vine Inn
105 Witham Road, CM77 8LQ (SO767208)
⏲ 12-2.30, 6.30-11; 12-4, 7-11 Sun
☎ (01376) 324269
Adnams Bitter, Broadside; guest beer Ⓗ
The Vine is a 16th-century free house, comprising an open-plan bar/restaurant with log-burning stoves at each end. An unusual feature in the bar is the compact mezzanine galleried area with seating for six people, accessible via a steep, straight, wooden staircase. The restaurant side is a designated no-smoking area where hearty, home-cooked food is served. There is a frequent bus service from Braintree.
⛰❀◐◑🚌P

Blackmore

Leather Bottle
Horsefayre Green, CM4 0RL OS603009
⏲ 11-11; 12-10.30 Sun
☎ (01277) 821891 🌐 theleatherbottle.net
Adnams Bitter, Broadside; guest beers Ⓗ
Large village pub, mainly occupied by a good quality restaurant. The bar to the left is nonetheless popular with locals. The two or three guest beers usually include one brew of around 5% ABV; the cider is Westons Old Rosie. An annexe to the bar has various games, but the fruit machine is silent. Sunday meals are served 12-4pm.
⛰❀◐◑⊞♣●P

INDEPENDENT BREWERIES

Blanchfields Rochford
Brentwood Brentwood
Crouch Vale South Woodham Ferrers
Famous Railway Tavern Brightlingsea
Farmer's Ales Maldon
Felstar Felsted
George & Dragon Foulness
Mersea Island East Mersea
Mighty Oak Maldon
Nethergate Pentlow
Saffron Henham
Star Steeple

Brentwood

Rising Sun

144 Ongar Road, CM15 9DJ (on A128)
❂ 3 (12 Sat)-11; 12-10.30 Sun
☎ (01277) 213749
Brakspear Bitter; Taylor Landlord; guest beers Ⓗ
This much improved local just outside the town centre brings a good choice of real ales to an area where the choice for beer drinkers is limited. A rare regular outlet for Brakspear, there are also two guest beers. This is a community-focused pub where the local clubs meet, regular quizzes are held on a Monday evening and darts is popular.
❀⊟♣P

Brightlingsea

Railway Tavern

58 Station Road, CO7 0DT (on B1029)
❂ 5 (3 Fri; 12 Sat)-11; 12-3, 7-10.30 Sun
☎ (01206) 302581 🌐 geocities.com/famousrailway
Crouch Vale Crouch Best; Railway Tavern Crab & Winkle Mild, seasonal beers; guest beers Ⓗ
The landlord started brewing mild here some years ago – Crab & Winkle went on to become CAMRA's Champion Mild of East Anglia. Two fermenters now allow a range of seasonal beers to be brewed exclusively for the pub, supplemented by guests from micros. Very much a local, where visitors are welcomed, the rear bar has become chic, but retains the original railway memorabilia. After the annual cider festival in May a week in autumn is devoted to Essex beers.
⛫Q☋❀⊟⛺♣●

Canewdon

Chequers Inn

High Street, SS4 3QA
❂ 12-4.30 (11-6.30 Sat), 7-11; 12-10.30 Sun
☎ (01702) 258251
Fuller's London Pride; Greene King IPA, Abbot; Mighty Oak Maldon Gold; guest beer Ⓗ
Spacious, 17th-century inn at the centre of a pretty village, this quiet pub comprises several comfortable rooms and an outdoor paved drinking area. It supports local community groups, including cricket and crib teams. Canewdon's famous church and stocks are nearby; local legend suggests that while the church tower stands Canewdon will have six witches! Excellent, well-priced food, including vegetarian options, is served daily at lunchtime and Thursday-Saturday evenings. Mighty Oak usually supplies the guest beer. Daytime buses run Monday-Saturday. Q☋❀◑◗🚌●P⚡

Castle Hedingham

Wheatsheaf

2 Queen Street, CO9 3EX
(on B1058, 1 mile from A1017)
❂ 12-midnight (1am Fri & Sat); 12-midnight Sun
☎ (01787) 460555
Greene King IPA, Old Speckled Hen; guest beer Ⓗ
Run by a friendly landlord, in an ancient village, this Grade I listed, 15th-century building boasts carved beams, a tiled floor and a beamed fireplace. The regular beers are complemented by constantly-changing guests. The pub has a games room where darts and shove-ha'penny are played. Families with well-behaved children are welcome. Meals are served daily.
⛫Q❀◑◗⊟♿♣P

Chelmsford

Cricketers

143 Moulsham Street, CM2 0JT
❂ 11-11; 12-10.30 Sun
☎ (01245) 261157
Greene King IPA, Abbot; guest beers Ⓗ
Two-bar, corner local, serving the best value good beer in town. Located at the more peaceful end of this heavily-pubbed street, it comprises a public bar with pool, juke box and Sky Sports, and a quieter lounge. Cricketing and football memorabilia abound – not just to celebrate the landlord's favoured West Ham United. One or two guest beers generally come from small breweries, with Mighty Oak often featured. Meals are served Sunday-Friday. A patio to the side allows for outdoor drinking. ❀◑⊟♣

Endeavour

351 Springfield Road, CM2 6AW (on B1137)
❂ 11-11; 12-10.30 Sun
☎ (01245) 257717
Greene King IPA, Abbot; Mighty Oak Maldon Gold; guest beers Ⓗ
This friendly pub is a worthwhile 15-minute walk from the town centre. One of its three rooms is no-smoking and used by diners at lunchtime and in the early evening (eve meals served Fri and Sat). Two guest beers are kept – one is always a mild between September and May (Hardys and Hansons for the past two winters). Westons cider is sold. Regular fundraising events for charity include a Sunday meat raffle and a bank holiday quiz. ⛫◑◗●⚡

Original Plough

28 Duke Street, CM1 1HY (next to station)
❂ 11-11 (midnight Thu-Sat); 11-11 Sun
☎ (01245) 250145
Greene King IPA; Taylor Landlord; guest beers Ⓗ
Spacious, open-plan, town-centre pub, attracting a varied clientele. The landlord is a keen rugby fan, but he will show other sports if the occasion demands it. Mild and other dark beers are often available. There is no smoking at the bar and another no-smoking area is provided at lunchtime. Evening meals, served Monday-Thursday, finish at 8pm. The pub hosts occasional live music (rock and soul). ❀◑◗⥮♣P⚡

Queen's Head

30 Lower Anchor Street, CM2 0AS (near cricket ground and B1007)
❂ 12-11; 11-11.30 Fri & Sat; 12-11 Sun
☎ (01245) 265181 🌐 queensheadchelmsford.co.uk
Crouch Vale Crouch Best, Brewers Gold; guest beers Ⓗ
Welcoming, back-street local, where the six guest ales always include a mild and a second dark beer. Good value lunches are

served Monday-Saturday (and Sunday if there's a cricket match in Chelmsford). Quiz night is Tuesday and live jazz is performed monthly on the afternoon of the last Sunday. It hosts a well-attended annual beer festival in September. It was chosen by local CAMRA as Pub of the Year for the fifth time in 2006. ♨Q❀◐♿♣●P

White Horse

25 Townfield Street, CM1 1QJ (behind station by entrance to Selex Communications)

⏲ 11.30-11; 12-10.30 Sun

☎ (01245) 269556

Adnams Broadside; Caledonian Deuchars IPA; Greene King IPA; Theakston Mild; Young's Bitter; guest beers Ⓗ

Tucked away on a corner of a back street, the White Horse has seen a succession of landlords recently, but now appears to be settled. The single, long, narrow bar has bar billiards at one end, darts at the other and Sky Sports everywhere! Guest beers tend to be sourced from the larger regional and family breweries. It is home to an active golf society and various other games teams. Lunches are served weekdays. ◐⇌♣

Woolpack

23 Mildmay Road, CM2 0DN (near A138)

⏲ 11-11 (midnight Fri & Sat); 12-11 Sun

☎ (01245) 259295

Greene King IPA, Ruddles Best, Abbot; guest beers Ⓗ

Winner of local CAMRA's Most Improved Pub award for 2005, this ex-Ridleys' house makes the most of the guest beers allowed by Greene King, with five ales normally on handpump. Darts and pool can be played in the public bar, while the larger lounge leads to a third room down a step. The menu includes speciality sausages that are produced locally – the variety changes every week; evening meals are served Monday-Friday. ❀◐◑⊕P

Chipping Ongar

Cock Tavern

218 High Street, CM5 9AB (on A128)

⏲ 11-11 (midnight Fri & Sat); 12-10.30 Sun

☎ (01277) 362615 🌐 thecocktavernongar.co.uk

Greene King IPA; guest beers Ⓗ

Typical Gray's house over 400 years old, frequented by all ages and loyal locals. Darts and crib teams meet here. The meals are home made, not home cooked. A public (pay) car park is next to the pub; good daytime bus services run to Epping and Brentwood, but are limited evenings. A function room with handpumps can be hired and live music is staged most weekends. Three guest beers are usually sourced from micro-breweries and cider is sold in summer. ♨◐◑🚌♣●

Clacton-on-Sea

Old Lifeboat House

39 Marine Parade East, CO15 6AD (near A133, almost on seafront)

⏲ 11-11 (closed winter Mon); 12-10.30 Sun

☎ (01255) 688004

Shepherd Neame Best Bitter, Spitfire, seasonal beers Ⓗ

As the name suggests, this pleasantly refurbished pub was once home to Clacton's lifeboat. Naturally, the interior bears an RNLI theme, with photographs, paintings and memorabilia, including a ship's clock and bell. Although a free house, the regular beers both come from Shepherd Neame, but guests are added in peak periods. ❀◐⇌🚌P

Colchester

Bricklayers

27 Bergholt Road, CO4 5AA (on A134/B1508, near North Station)

⏲ 11-3, 5.30-11; 11-midnight Fri; 11-11 Sat; 12-3, 7-11 Sun

☎ (01206) 852008

Adnams Bitter, Explorer, Broadside, seasonal beers; Fuller's London Pride; guest beers Ⓗ

Friendly, busy local, handy for the North Station and on many bus routes. It comprises a public bar, with pool and darts, a lounge bar on three levels and a no-smoking conservatory. It is run by a CAMRA award-winning landlord and his family, who offer good quality home-cooked lunches (not Sat) – arrive early for the popular Sunday roast. The full range of Adnams ales is complemented by guests; the cider is Crones.

❀◐⇌(North)♣🚌●P⚡

British Grenadier

67 Military Road, CO1 2AP (opp. military church)

⏲ 12 (11 Tue)-2.30, 5-11.40 (12.10am Fri); 11-12.10am Sat; 12-3, 7-11.40 Sun

☎ (01206) 500933

Adnams Bitter, Broadside, seasonal beers; guest beers Ⓗ

A deserved second time winner of local CAMRA's Town Pub of the Year, this cosy, two-bar hostelry is well worth the short walk from the Town station. The publicans have built up a reputation for their friendly welcome and fine beer quality, with regular guest beers adding variety. Darts and pool teams are well supported and the Sunday evening quizzes generally prove to be both popular and entertaining. Oversized beer festival glasses are available on request.

❀⇌(Town)🚌♣🍺

Dragoon

82 Butt Road, CO3 3DA (on B1026, near police station)

⏲ 11-midnight (1am Fri & Sat); 11-midnight Sun

☎ (01206) 573464

Adnams Bitter, Explorer, Broadside, seasonal beers; guest beers Ⓗ

Ten minutes from the High Street, this perennial favourite has a spacious lounge, a public bar area, with dartboard and pool table and a small garden. En route to the town's football ground, it can get busy on match days when both home and away supporters congregate to sample Dragoon's famous chilli, washed down by Adnams' finest or a guest beer. Lunches are served daily except Saturday (unless there is a match), a traditional roast is offered on Sunday. ❀◖≠(Town)⊟♣

Fox & Fiddler

1 St John's Street, CO2 7AA
⌚ 11-11 (midnight Fri & Sat); 12-10.30 Sun
☎ (01206) 560520
Mighty Oak English Oak; guest beers Ⓗ
Friendly, town-centre free house, dating back to 1420. Allegedly haunted, it is a stop-off point on the town's Thursday evening ghost walk. A small front bar leads to two larger drinking areas, where good home-cooked food is served at lunchtime (not Mon) and Wednesday evening (try the steak and ale pie). A changing range of ales regularly highlights local breweries, especially Mighty Oak. Live music is performed most Saturday evenings. The enclosed patio is a summer suntrap. ❀◖≠(Town)⊟

Hospital Arms

123-125 Crouch Street, CO3 3HA (on A1124, opp. Essex County Hospital)
⌚ 12-midnight (1am Fri & Sat); 12-midnight Sun
☎ (01206) 573572 🌐 hospitalarms.co.uk
Adnams Bitter, Explorer, Broadside, seasonal beers; Fuller's London Pride; guest beer Ⓗ
With a comfortable, raised lounge and front bar (both no-smoking) and three further drinking areas, 'Ward 9' attracts an eclectic clientele, for whom conversation and drinking quality beer are of prime importance – no loud music, darts or pool here. Patio heaters allow the chat to continue outside after the sun has set. Occasional barbecues supplement the varied lunchtime menu (try the Sunday roast) and themed food evenings. It is well worth the 10-minute walk from the High Street. Q❀◖⊟⚟

Odd One Out

28 Mersea Road, CO2 7ET (on B1025)
⌚ 4.30 (12 Fri; 11 Sat)-11; 12-10.30 Sun
☎ (01206) 513958
Archers Best Bitter; guest beers Ⓗ
Colchester's best value real ale pub, the multi award-winning Oddie, is 15 minutes' walk from the High Street. Up to six guest ales from brewers countrywide include at least one dark beer, and are supplemented by two or three real ciders, over 50 Scottish malts and 10 Irish whiskeys. The front bar is no-smoking and a small function room can be hired. Scrabble and chess are played and the pub fields a cricket team. Cheese rolls keep hunger pangs at bay. ♨Q❀≠(Town)⊟♣●⚟

Rose & Crown Hotel

51 East Street, CO1 2TZ (200 yds from A133/A1232 jct, near Rollerworld)
⌚ 11-2.30, 6-11; 11-11 Sat; 12-10.30 Sun
☎ (01206) 866677 🌐 rose-and-crown.com
Adnams Broadside; Tetley Bitter Ⓗ
Dating from the 14th century, this is the oldest coaching inn in the oldest recorded town in England. Heavily beamed and pleasantly lit, the inn has comfortable seating areas in the bar and friendly staff. Best known as a first-rate hotel and restaurant, non-residents are always welcome in the bar. Rose and Crown Bitter is Adnams Bitter rebadged, but the staff do not mislead when asked. An extensive bar menu complements the full a la carte selection offered in the restaurant. Parking is limited. ♨⇌◖◗⊟P

Colne Engaine

Five Bells

Mill Lane, CO6 2HY (off A1124 at Earls Colne, down Station Rd)
⌚ 12-3, 7-midnight; 12-midnight Fri-Sun
☎ (01787) 224166 🌐 fivebells.net
Greene King IPA; guest beers Ⓗ
Sympathetically refurbished pub, retaining many original features such as exposed beams. Set in a peaceful village, views from the pub terrace take in the undulating surrounding countryside and the Colne Valley. Local micro-breweries are well supported by a varying range of guest beers, while the dining room also offers local produce on its modern English menu. Jazz bands perform on Friday evenings and alternate Sundays. ♨❀◖◗⊟♿♣P⚟

Coxtie Green

White Horse

173 Coxtie Green Road, CM14 5PX
(1 mile W of A128) OS564959
⌚ 11.30-11 (midnight Fri & Sat); 12-11 Sun
☎ (01277) 372410
Adnams Bitter; Fuller's London Pride; guest beers Ⓗ
Great little country local of two bars: a cosy, comfortable saloon and a public bar with a dartboard. The atmosphere is relaxed and friendly, with a good mix of customers. Since the demise of Ridleys, the bar now offers four guest beers from all over the UK. Regular golf and angling competitions are organised and a beer festival is held in July in the large garden that has a children's play area. Cider is usually available; no food is served Sunday. ❀◖♿♣●P

Danbury

Griffin

64 Main Road, CM3 4DH (on A414)
⌚ 12-11; 12-10.30 Sun
☎ (01245) 222905
Adnams Broadside; guest beers Ⓗ
Food-oriented Chef and Brewer benefiting from a beer-loving landlord who exploits his guest beer options to the full. The Mighty Oak seasonal range from nearby Maldon often features among the choices on the bar. The building is over 400 years old and numbers Sir Walter Scott among its famous visitors. Food is served all day and the menu always includes various fresh fish dishes. The Griffin is no-smoking throughout. ♨❀◖◗P⚟

Dedham

Sun Inn

High Street, CO7 6DF (on B1029, opp. church)
⌚ 12-11; 12-6 Sun

☎ (01206) 323351 🌐 thesuninndedham.com

Adnams Broadside; guest beers Ⓗ

This 15th-century inn has a large, no-smoking bar and a wood-panelled smoking room, offering three guest ales from local micro-breweries. It is renowned for the high quality meals served in its spacious restaurant and an excellent wine list. The large garden is an additional attraction. Children are welcome and may take advantage of the large range of board games provided. Four en-suite guest rooms include one with a four-poster bed.

⛫Q❀⇄◐◑♣P⊬

Duton Hill

Three Horseshoes

CM6 2DX (½ mile W of B184, Dunmow-Thaxted road) OS606268

✪ 12-2.30 (not Mon-Wed; 12-3 Sat), 6-11; 12-3, 7-10.30 Sun

☎ (01371) 870681

Bateman XB; guest beers Ⓗ

Cosy village local, where the large garden overlooks the Chelmer Valley and farmland. It hosts an open-air theatre in July (the landlord is a former pantomime dame). The wildlife pond is home to frogs and newts. A millennium beacon, breweriana and a remarkable collection of Butlins' memorabilia are features of this unpretentious pub. A beer festival is held over the late spring bank holiday. The repainted pub sign depicts a famous painting, 'The Blacksmith', by local resident Sir George Clausen. ⛫❀♣P

East Mersea

Courtyard Café

Mersea Island Vineyard, Rewsalls Lane, CO5 8SX (off B1025 from Colchester, then follow vineyard signs) OSTM039123

✪ 11-4 daily (closed Tue and winter Mon-Wed)

☎ (01206) 385900 🌐 merseawine.com

Mersea Island Mud Mild, Yo Boy, Skippers Bitter Ⓗ

Hot and cold snacks, tea and cakes – and the brewery tap – all in one place. Worth seeking out as a rare outlet for this growing brewery, the modern, single-room Courtyard Café has a large outdoor seating area that benefits from views over the Colne Estuary. Its own wines are also available and tours of the brewery and vineyard can be booked. B&B and self-catering accommodation are available (see website or phone for details).

Q❀◐♿⛺P⊬

Eastwood

Oakwood

564 Rayleigh Road, SS9 5HX (on A1015)

✪ 11-11 (midnight Fri & Sat); 11-11 Sun

☎ (01702) 429000 🌐 theoakwood.co.uk

Beer range varies Ⓗ

Popular, two-room pub with a garden. One area houses pool tables and a dartboard and shows live sport on TV; the smaller bar is quieter, with comfortable seating and a piano. Note the original stained glass windows that are preserved in the ceiling between the stage and the bar. It hosts live entertainment on Saturday evening. No evening meals are served on Sunday. The pub is on a good bus route between Southend and Rayleigh. ❀◐◑🚌♣P

Epping

Forest Gate

Bell Common, CM16 4DZ (off B1393, opp. Bell Hotel) OS45011

✪ 10-2.30, 5-11; 12-3 (3.30 summer), 7-10.30 Sun

☎ (01992) 572312

Adnams Bitter, Broadside; Nethergate IPA; Ⓗ **guest beers** Ⓗ/Ⓖ

Timeless, 17th-century, genuine country free house, owned and run by the same family for many years, specialising in real ale. Situated on the edge of Epping Forest, it is popular with walkers. Free from juke box, music and fruit machines, you use a mobile phone here at your peril. Snacks are usually available, including the renowned turkey broth. A large, lawned area at the front of the pub is used for summer drinking; dogs are welcome. ⛫Q🍺❀🍎P

Feering

Sun Inn

3 Feering Hill, CO5 9NH (on B1024, off A12)

✪ 12-3, 6-11; 12-3, 6-10.30 Sun

☎ (01376) 570442 🌐 suninnfeering.com

Beer range varies Ⓗ

It is well worth taking the train to nearby Kelvedon station to visit this superb pub. Full height exposed beams separate three cosy drinking areas, warmed by log fires in winter. Up to six changing guest beers are offered, usually including a dark ale; micro-breweries are well represented and a cider is stocked. Home-cooked food ranges from snacks to exotic main courses and the menu changes daily. To the rear of the pub is a large garden and barbecue area.

⛫❀◐◑⇚(Kelvedon)🚌♣🍎P

Fingringhoe

Whalebone

Chapel Road, CO5 7BG (take B1025 towards Mersea, turn off at Abberton)

✪ 11-3, 5.30-11; 11-11 Sat; 11-10.30 Sun

☎ (01206) 729307

Greene King IPA; guest beers Ⓗ

Grade II listed, early 18th-century pub at the centre of this pretty village that also boasts a 12th-century church. The large, open bar and dining area is no-smoking throughout but ashtrays are provided in the garden. Up to three guest beers are generally sourced from micro-breweries. Good quality, home-cooked food is offered on a varying menu. Popular with walkers, dogs are also welcome. The extensive garden affords fine views over the river valley. ⛫❀◐◑🚌P⊬

Fobbing

White Lion

Lion Hill, SS17 9JR (near B1420) OS716839

✪ 12-3, 5.30-11; 12-midnight Fri & Sat; 12-11 (12-3.30, 7-11 winter) Sun

☎ (01375) 673281
Archers Village; Greene King Old Speckled Hen; guest beer Ⓗ
Circa 17th-century, friendly village pub with 18th-century extensions, incorporating beams from Thames sailing barges. Barge owners stored their sails in the pub's loft. Note the growing display of local photos and memorabilia. The village is associated with the Peasants Revolt against the poll tax in 1381. Home-cooked lunches are served (not Sun); there is a designated no-smoking area. Children are welcome until 9pm. The guest beer is a national brand; the cider is Addlestones. ఠ❀🛏◐●P⊬⊟

Fyfield

Queen's Head

Queen Street, CM5 0RY (off B184)
⊕ 11-3.30 (4 Sat), 6-11; 12-3.30, 7-10.30 Sun
☎ (01277) 899231
Adnams Bitter, Broadside; guest beers Ⓗ
Busy, 15th-century country pub in the middle of the village. It retains a cosy feel, with a long bar, some partitions, a beamed ceiling and a real fire in winter. The popular food can at times dominate the pub, leading to crowding. The garden backs on to the River Roding where you can feed the ducks. It usually stocks four guest beers from micro-breweries. ♨❀◐◑●P

Goldhanger

Chequers

The Square, CM9 8AS (400 yds from B1026)
⊕ 11-11; 12-10.30 Sun
☎ (01621) 788203 🌐 thechequersgoldhanger.co.uk
Caledonian Deuchars IPA; Flowers IPA; guest beers Ⓗ
Busy 15th-century pub, local CAMRA Pub of the Year 2006. With low ceilings and exposed beams throughout, the large, central bar is surrounded by small, characterful rooms: dining area, tap, no-smoking snug, and a games room with bar billiards. The cosy public bar displays local memorabilia, including agricultural and fishing equipment. An extensive, reasonably-priced menu is served (no food Sun eve except monthly curry eve – booking essential). A beer festival is held in March and a vintage car rally in October.
♨Qఠ❀🛏◐◑⊟⛺♣P⊬

Gosfield

King's Head

The Street, CO9 1TP
⊕ 12-3, 6-11 (midnight Fri & Sat); 12-10.30 Sun; Sat & Sun summer
☎ (01787) 474016
Greene King IPA; guest beers Ⓗ
Situated in a pretty village this charming 16th-century pub has been faithfully restored. Timbered throughout and with inglenooks, the lounge bar has comfy leather sofas while the public bar has a pool table. Fresh, home made food is served from an imaginative bar menu or a varied a la carte menu offered in the conservatory dining room (no meals Sun eve). Guest ales come from well-known brewers. Do not miss the Gosfield summer scarecrow festival.
♨Q❀◐◑⊟P

Grays

Theobald Arms

141 Argent Street, RM17 6HR
(5 mins' walk from Grays Station, down King's Walk)
⊕ 11-3, 5-11; 11-11 Fri & Sat; 12-4, 7-11 Sun
☎ (01375) 372253
Courage Best Bitter; guest beers Ⓗ
Real, traditional pub with a public bar and an unusual hexagonal pool table. The changing selection of three guest beers showcases local independent breweries. In addition to real ales it stocks a range of unusual bottled beers. It is universally popular and the meals, served weekdays, are much appreciated. There is some outside seating for summer drinking. ❀◐⊟♿⇌♣⊬

White Hart

168 High Street, RM17 6HR
⊕ 12-3, 5-11; 12-11 Fri & Sat; 12-11 Sun
☎ (01375) 373319
Crouch Vale Brewers Gold, guest beers Ⓗ
Much improved and rejuvenated traditional local just outside the town centre, with views of the River Thames. Guest ales usually include a mild or other dark beer. Pool is played here and there is meeting/function room available. The landlord was until recently running the local CAMRA Club of the Year nearby. ❀⊟⇌P

Great Bromley

Cross Inn

Ardleigh Road, CO7 7TL (on B1029)
⊕ 12-2 (not Mon or Tue), 6.30-11; 12-3, 7-10.30 Sun
☎ (01206) 230282
Greene King IPA; Woodforde's Wherry; guest beer Ⓖ
Quiet, warm and friendly free house where the single bar feels like someone's front room, with an open hearth, comfortable seating and fresh flowers. The landlord is a previous Guide-listed pub owner and the landlady is a dog-lover, with two friendly huskies (remember to close the gate!). Booking is advised for the meals, served Wednesday-Saturday, as sometimes community events are held, when food may not be available. It hosts an annual beer and folk music festival (usually in May).
♨Q❀◐◑♣P⊬

Snooty Fox

Frating Road, CO7 7JW (off A133 at Frating crossroads)
⊕ 11-2am; 11-11 Sun
☎ (01206) 251065
Greene King IPA; guest beers Ⓗ
Truly traditional English inn, replete with beamed ceilings, flagstone floors and horse brasses – there is even a meadow at the rear. Having acquired a reputation recently for its food, the pub has been purchased by a CAMRA award-winning landlord who is now expanding the beer range to include

ales from micro-breweries, and stocking real ciders (Westons Old Rosie and others). The food ranges from wholesome baguettes to a full restaurant menu prepared by international chefs. ⛫Q❀◑◗♿⊟♣●P

Great Chesterford

Crown & Thistle

High Street, CB10 1PL (near B1383, close to M11/A11 jct)

✪ 12-3, 6-11 (midnight Thu; 11.30 Fri & Sat); 12-5 (7-11 summer) Sun

☎ (01799) 530278

Greene King IPA; guest beers Ⓗ

Popular pub, frequented by locals, including the cricket team. Great Chesterford is an interesting village and the pub, built in 1546 as the Chequers, was expanded to serve as a coaching inn in 1603 and renamed at the same time. According to legend, James I stopped here on his way to London for the coronation. The bar boasts a magnificent inglenook. A patio has seating for outdoor drinking. No evening meals are served on Sunday. ⛫❀⇚◑◗Å⇌P

Plough

High Street, CB10 1PL (100 yds off B184)

✪ 11.30-3, 5.30-11.30; 12-midnight Sat; 12-11 Sun

☎ (01799) 530283 🌐 ploughatchesterford.co.uk

Greene King IPA; guest beers Ⓗ

Although at the edge of the village, this pub is at the heart of its community – indeed it was awarded Greene King Community Pub of the Year in 2004. The landlord is testing the whole reach of the brewery's guest beer list, offering three guests at all times. Good pub food (not Mon eve) is served inside and out, although the bar is kept free for drinkers; booking is advised for Sunday lunch. A large fenced area houses an adventure playground. ⛫Q⊂❀◑◗♿⇌♣P

Great Easton

Swan

The Endway, CM6 2HG (3 miles N of Dunmow off B184) OS606255

✪ 12-3, 6-11; 12-3, 7-10.30 Sun

☎ (01371) 870359 🌐 swangreateaston.co.uk

Adnams Bitter; guest beers Ⓗ

A warm welcome is assured in this 15th-century free house in an attractive village. A log-burning stove, exposed beams and comfortable sofas feature in the lounge; pool and darts are played in the public bar. All meals are prepared to order, the majority home made from local produce; no frozen ingredients are used (no meals Sun eve). The chef looks after the beer that complements the food. The lounge bar and restaurant are no-smoking.
⛫Q❀◑◗⊟♣P⊬

Great Waltham

Rose & Crown

Minnow End, Chelmsford Road, CM3 1AG (850 yds W of B1008) OS701131

✪ 11.30-3, 5.30-1am; 11.30-1am Sat; 12-1am Sun

☎ (01245) 360359

🌐 roseandcrowngreatwaltham.co.uk

Fuller's London Pride; Shepherd Neame Spitfire; guest beers Ⓗ

Rural pub where a log fire burns in the inglenook. Old flintlock and percussion guns on the walls reflect the rural heritage of this part of Essex. It offers good ales and a country menu of local produce cooked in traditional dishes and served in the restaurant or bar. It organises monthly racing trips with breakfast in the pub, a coach to the racecourse and dinner at the pub on return. A front patio provides outdoor seating for summer drinking.
⛫Q❀◑◗P⊬

Great Yeldham

Waggon & Horses

High Street, CO9 4EX (on A1017)

✪ 11-11; 12-10.30 Sun

☎ (01787) 237936 🌐 waggonandhorses.net

Greene King IPA, Abbot; guest beers Ⓗ

Guest beers are only sourced from local brewers, such as Mauldons or Wolf, and Storm cider, also produced locally, is always available. This 16th-century inn is a busy village hostelry, and everyone is made welcome. Food, served every day, is especially popular at weekends. Sixteen rooms in an annexe overlooking the garden provide overnight accommodation. The friendly landlord is a long-term supporter of real ale.
⛫⇚◑◗♣●P

Halstead

Dog Inn

37 Hedingham Road, CO9 2DB (on A1124)

✪ 4 (11.30 Sat)-11; 12-11 Sun

☎ (01787) 477774

Adnams Bitter, Broadside; Elgood's Black Dog; guest beers Ⓗ

A quiet pub, within easy walking distance of the town centre, which is well served by buses. Bar snacks and more substantial meals complement the range of guest ales. It makes an ideal stop after a country walk, especially in summer when you can sit in the garden and watch a game of petanque while enjoying a barbecue. En-suite accommodation is available. The pub hosts occasional beer festivals (phone for details).
⛫⊂❀⇚◑⊟⊟♣P⊬

White Hart Inn

15 High Street, CO9 2AA (at A131/A1124 crossroads)

✪ 10-11 (1am Fri & Sat); 12-10.30 Sun

☎ (01787) 475657

Adnams Bitter; Mauldons Bitter; guest beers Ⓗ

Former coaching inn dating from the 15th century in a friendly market town. With two traditional bars and an open fire, this popular pub is an ideal refreshment stop after a hard day's shopping. It always stocks a guest ale, while the varying menu includes light options, vegetarian choices and children's portions. The B&B accommodation is recommended. ⛫❀⇚⊟P

Harlow

William Aylmer

Aylmer House, Kitson Way, CM20 1DG

10-midnight (1am Fri & Sat); 10-midnight Sun

(01279) 620630

Greene King Abbot, Shepherd Neame Spitfire; Theakston Best Bitter; guest beers H

Spacious, busy Wetherspoon's house, with a large, no-smoking lounge. Framed details of local medical pioneer William Aylmer are displayed. Regular customers are augmented by families dining and some younger drinkers going on to nightclubs at the end of the week. Food is served until an hour before closing.

Harwich

New Bell Inn

Outpart Eastward, CO12 3EN

(200 yds from eastern end of A120)

11-3, 7-midnight (1am Fri & Sat); 12-4, 7-midnight Sun

(01255) 503545

Greene King IPA; Nethergate Priory Mild; guest beers H

Harwich, once a bustling seaport, retains a strong sense of community and history and nowhere reflects this better than this excellent pub that buzzes with conversation and is an untiring supporter of local events. The front bar is the hub, but it leads to a quieter rear bar, a seating area and a modest garden. The food is classic but imaginative pub fare, while the beer range includes guests from local breweries and an ever-present mild. (Town)P

Hempstead

Bluebell Inn

High Street, CB10 2PD (on B1054, between Saffron Walden and Haverhill)

11.30-3.30, 6-11; 11.30-11 Fri & Sat; 12-10.30 Sun

(01799) 599199

Adnams Bitter, Broadside; Woodforde's Wherry; guest beers H

Late 16th-century village pub with 18th-century additions, reputed to be the birthplace of Dick Turpin; the bar displays posters about his life. The restaurant serves excellent meals from an extensive menu. The large bar has a log fire. Ample seating is provided outside, with a children's play area at the rear. Six real ales often include a guest from a Fenland brewery; Aspall cider comes from Suffolk. Local CAMRA's Pub of the Year 2005 hosts a folk evening on Tuesday. Q P

Heybridge

Maltsters Arms

Hall Road, CM9 4NJ (near B1022)

12-11.30; 12-11 Sun

(01621) 853880

Greene King IPA, Abbot; guest beers G

This well-supported Grays' house is a single-bar local where a warm welcome is extended to drinkers and their dogs. Step in straight off the pavement to enjoy the pleasant atmosphere that is enhanced by collections of bottles and copper bric-a-brac. It can be busy at lunchtime with locals and ramblers; no meals are served but they do offer a selection of rolls. The patio overlooks the old course of the tidal river. Q

Heybridge Basin

Old Ship

CM9 4RX (follow sign from Goldhanger road)

10am-1am; 12-midnight Sun

(01621) 854150

Adnams Broadside; Greene King IPA; Mighty Oak Maldon Gold; Shepherd Neame Spitfire; guest beer H

Benefiting from a pleasant view over the waters of Heybridge Basin, this pub is popular with sailors and is handy for walkers on the canal towpath. The food is good, hence the pub can get quite busy on sunny days. It was built some 200 years ago at the same time as the canal, which is one of the oldest in the world. Paintings by local artists and sailing memorabilia adorn the walls. A function room upstairs seats 50. P

Horndon-on-the-Hill

Bell Inn

High Road, SS17 8LD (near B1007)

11-2.30 (3 Sat), 5.30 (6 Sat)-11; 12-4, 7-10.30 Sun

(01375) 642463 bell-inn.co.uk

Draught Bass; G **Greene King IPA; guest beers** H

Busy, 15th-century coaching inn, where the beamed bars feature wood panelling and carvings. Note the unusual hot cross bun collection – a bun is added every Good Friday. The hilltop village, now relieved by a bypass, has a restored woolmarket. The award-winning restaurant is no-smoking. The pub boasts five honeymoon suites. Up to five guest ales are stocked, including beers from Essex breweries. Q P

Kirby-le-Soken

Red Lion

32 The Street, CO13 0EF (on B1034)

11.30-11.30; 12-11 Sun

(01255) 674832

Greene King IPA; guest beers H

This family-run pub has developed an excellent reputation for its variety of real ales and also offers an extensive bar and restaurant menu. The delightful garden, with solid decking, includes a children's play area; at the height of summer the Red Lion is surrounded by colourful flowers in hanging baskets and containers. It was voted local CAMRA's Pub of the Year in 2005.

P

Langley Lower Green

Bull

CB11 4SB (turn off B1038 at Clavering) OS436345

12-2 (3 Sat), 6-11; 12-3, 7-10.30 Sun

(01279) 777307

Greene King IPA, Abbot, seasonal beers H

Classic, Victorian village local, with its original cast iron lattice windows and fireplaces. It sits in a tiny, isolated hamlet,

less than a mile from the Hertfordshire border, and a little further from Cambridgeshire. The pub is supported by a devoted band of regulars, including football and cricket teams. This friendly pub in beautiful rolling countryside is worth the effort to find; a long distance footpath, the Harcamlow Way, passes within a mile. Meals can be arranged with advance notice.
Q❀⊟♣P⁄

Layer-de-la-Haye

Donkey & Buskins

CO2 0HU (on B1026, S of Colchester) OS974209
❂ 11-3, 6-11; 11-11 Sat; 12-11 Sun
☎ (01206) 734774
Greene King IPA; Tindall Best Bitter; guest beers Ⓗ
Unspoilt free house, comprising a public bar, three no-smoking areas and a large, secluded rear garden. A rare Essex outlet for Tindall Brewery, it serves up to four ales, often including beers from the yet more rarely encountered Mersea Island Brewery. It also stocks a range of fine wines. An extensive menu includes good value Sunday roasts. A regular quiz is staged on Sunday evening. The guest accommodation here is recommended. ♨Q❀⊟♿P⁄

Leigh-on-Sea

Broker

213-217 Leigh Road, SS9 1JA
❂ 11-11 (midnight Fri & Sat); 12-11 Sun
☎ (01702) 471932 🌐 brokerfreehouse.co.uk
Everards Tiger; Fuller's London Pride; St Austell Tribute; Shepherd Neame Spitfire; Young's Bitter; guest beers Ⓗ
Family-run free house that has featured in every edition of this Guide since 1996. It has a garden at the rear and a small pavement seating area. This sporty, community pub organises local charity fundraising events, including quizzes or live music on Sunday evening. Bar and restaurant meals are served lunchtime (12-6 Sun) and Tuesday-Saturday evenings. Children are welcome until 7.30pm in a sectioned-off, no-smoking area of the bar. Two guest beers are stocked.
❀⟨Chalkwell⟩♣

Elms

1060 London Road, SS9 3ND (on A13)
❂ 9am-midnight (1am Fri & Sat); 9am-midnight Sun
☎ (01702) 474687
Courage Best Bitter, Directors; Greene King Abbot; Marston's Pedigree; Shepherd Neame Spitfire; guest beers Ⓗ
Busy roadhouse on the A13. The name originates from the farmhouse that previously occupied the site. Wetherspoon's refurbishment has created a spacious, comfortable pub with many alcoves providing seating. The large front garden has a deep hedge to reduce the noise from the main road. Many photographs and pictures recall past inhabitants, the history of Leigh-on-Sea and the old town. Food is available all day until 11pm. Westons Vintage Organic and Old Rosie are stocked. Q❀♿●P⁄

Lexden

Crown Inn

235 Lexden Road, CO3 4DA (at A133/A1124 jct)
❂ 11.30-2.30, 5-midnight; 11.30-midnight Sat; 12-11 Sun
☎ (01206) 572071
Beer range varies Ⓗ
On the western outskirts of Colchester and well served by bus routes, the recently refurbished Crown is split into three rooms. The large public bar houses the dartboard, the lounge bar is no-smoking and the dining area can be hired for functions. The pub benefits from a large car park and enclosed garden. It offers up to eight changing beers, including one each from Mighty Oak and Cottage. Good quality home-cooked food is served daily, with an additional menu Wednesday-Sunday. ❀⊟♣P⁄

Little Baddow

Rodney

North Hill, CM3 4TQ OS778080
❂ 11-11; 11-10.30 Sun
☎ (01245) 222385
Greene King IPA, Old Speckled Hen; guest beer Ⓗ
A pub since the early 1800s, when it sold beer from the old Chelmsford Brewery, the Rodney was built as a farmhouse around 1650 and has served as a grocer's and bakery. This comfortable, two-roomed, beamed building comprises a public bar with a pool table, a small snug and a compact drinking/dining area, displaying brasses, posters, pump clips and seafaring prints. The food is all home made and includes good value daily specials. Q❀⊟♣P

Little Clacton

Apple Tree

The Street, CO16 9LF (on B1441)
❂ 11-11; 12-10.30 Sun
☎ (01255) 861026
Fuller's London Pride; Mighty Oak Oscar Wilde; guest beers Ⓖ
The new landlord, no stranger to Guide entries, has taken over this popular pub and continues to serve quality real ales direct from the cask. Changes to the interior have made the pub more spacious and comfortable, while the exterior has been relieved of its fluorescent yellow paint – much to everyone's delight. ❀♣P

Little Dunmow

Flitch of Bacon

The Street, CM6 3HT (850 yds S of B1256) OS656216
❂ 12-3 (not Mon), 5.30-11; 12-5, 7-10.30 Sun
☎ (01371) 820323
Fuller's London Pride; Greene King IPA; guest beers Ⓗ
The pub sign shows a side or flitch of bacon – the prize awarded to a married couple who have not argued for a year; this ancient ceremony still takes place. Of note, too, are the old signs advertising Bass and Worthington in bottles. Step down into a beamed bar area that has a large fireplace and leads to the no-smoking restaurant at

the rear. A good range of food is served to complement the well-kept beer at this traditional, friendly rural pub. ⌂Q✿⇌◐◑

Little Thurrock

Traitor's Gate

40-42 Broadway, RM17 6EW
(on A126, 1 mile E of Grays town centre)
⏲ 12-11; 12-10.30 Sun
☎ (01375) 372628
Beer range varies Ⓗ
Friendly pub that appeals to a varied, local clientele – an excellent example of how a good pub can attract a busy trade; it displays an amazing collection of pump clips showing the 1,500 or so beers sold over the last few years. The pub hosts music nights (Fri and Sat) and has an impressive selection of recorded music. Sport is shown on TV. The garden won the Thurrock in Bloom award in 2004 and 2005. Home-made bar snacks are available. ✿♣

Little Totham

Swan

School Road, CM9 8JL (2 miles SE of B1022, between Tiptree and Maldon) OS889117
⏲ 11-11; 12-10.30 Sun
☎ (01621) 892689 ⊕ theswanpublichouse.co.uk
Adnams Bitter; Crouch Vale Brewers Gold; Mighty Oak Oscar Wilde, Maldon Gold; guest beers Ⓖ
Archetypal, 17th-century, heavily beamed village pub: the unspoilt public bar has a dartboard, while the comfortable saloon has open fires and an air filtration system. A national CAMRA Pub of the Year winner, it has a large garden; muddy boots and dogs are welcome. Walkers may eat their own food by arrangement. It stocks country fruit wines, Belgian beers, cider and perry in season; the house beer Totham Parva is brewed by Mighty Oak. The June beer festival is a must.
⌂Q✿◐⊟♿⛺♣●P⊓

Little Walden

Crown

High Street, CB10 1XA (on B1052, 2 miles NE of Saffron Walden)
⏲ 11.30-2.30 (3 Sat), 6-11; 12-10.30 Sun
☎ (01799) 522475
Adnams Broadside; City of Cambridge Boathouse Bitter; Greene King IPA; guest beers Ⓖ
Charming, beamed country pub, boasting a large walk-through fireplace. The pub offers an extensive menu, with evening meals available Tuesday–Saturday. Racked cask stillage is used for dispensing an excellent range of beers. This recently extended, 18th-century pub, in a quiet country hamlet, attracts locals and business customers from Saffron Walden. It is used for club meetings and hosts trad jazz on Wednesday evening. New overnight accommodation should be open in 2007.
⌂Q♉✿◐◑♿♣P⅟

Littlebury

Queen's Head

High Street, CB11 4TD
(on B1383, old A11, 1 mile NW of Saffron Walden)
⏲ 12-3, 5.30-11; 12-3, 7-10.30 Sun
☎ (01799) 522251 ⊕ queensheadinnlittlebury.co.uk
Greene King IPA, Morland Original; guest beers Ⓗ
Once a strategic roadhouse on the old A11, it is now a homely, 15th-century village pub supporting local football and cricket teams, and a golf society. The spacious single bar has many period features – an inglenook, exposed beams and a large settle, dominated by an imposing circular bar counter. The landlord promotes the guest beers supplied by Greene King. The dining room offers home-cooked meals (Tue-Sun), based on local produce. Six new en-suite guest rooms are now available.
⌂Q✿⇌◐◑♿♣P⅟

Loughton

Victoria Tavern

165 Smarts Lane, IG10 4BP (near A121)
⏲ 11-3, 5-11; 12-10.30 Sun
☎ (0208) 508 1779
Adnams Bitter; Greene King IPA; Harveys Sussex Best Bitter; Taylor Landlord Ⓗ
Old-fashioned, dark wood-panelled pub with a bar to match. Photographs of Loughton vie for wall space with a display of blue and white plates. The dining area is no smoking. It has two fireplaces, but only one real fire. Backgammon is played here. ⌂Q✿◐◑⊖♣P

Maldon

Blue Boar Hotel

Silver Street, CM9 4QE
⏲ 11-11; 12-11 Sun
☎ (01621) 855888 ⊕ blueboarmaldon.co.uk
Adnams Bitter; Farmer's Nelson's Blood, Blue Boar Bitter, Pucks Folly, seasonal beers Ⓖ
Independently run, ancient coaching inn at the heart of this historic town. Both bars retain plenty of olde-worlde charm and there is a no-smoking area to the rear. Farmer's Ales (ex-Maldon) are supplied by the brewery in the stable block across the yard. The pub hosts regular jazz sessions and folk music. In warm weather beers can be enjoyed in the patio or in the yard between the bars and the hotel. Q✿⇌◐◑P⅟⊓

Queen's Head

The Hythe, CM9 5HN
⏲ 10.30-11; 12-10.30 Sun
☎ (01621) 854112
Greene King IPA, Abbot; Mighty Oak Maldon Gold, Burntwood; guest beer (occasional) Ⓗ
Quayside pub, some 600 years old, on the River Blackwater. Old sailing barges are moored nearby. There is a spacious outdoor seating area with sun umbrellas and an outside bar for summer use. The front bar, warmed by a log fire, is a local meeting place. Food can be consumed in the restaurant or elsewhere; the extensive menu is supplemented by daily specials. Children are allowed in the restaurant. Good disabled

access and WC facilities are provided.
⩩Q❀◐◑⊟♿

Swan Hotel

73 High Street, CM9 5EP
⊙ 11-11; 12-10.30 Sun
☎ (01621) 853170
Greene King IPA, Abbot; Mighty Oak Maldon Gold; guest beer Ⓗ
Late 14th-century, town-centre hostelry that retains many period features. Always busy, with customers of all ages, it is popular with visitors to the area. It stages regular quiz nights and pool and dominoes are also played. The large function hall (the Bewick suite) is used for live events and a monthly farmers market. A pleasant area is set aside for dining; the food and accommodation are recommended. The guest ale changes weekly; sparklers will be removed on request.
⇌◐◑P⊡

Warwick Arms

185 High Street, CM9 5BU
⊙ 12 (11 Sat)-11; 12-10.30 Sun
☎ (01621) 850122
Greene King IPA; Mighty Oak Maldon Gold; guest beers Ⓗ
This High Street drinkers' pub boasts two open fires. Pool and darts are played and it stages live music most weekends. Friendly staff and locals contribute to its relaxed atmosphere. Guest beers are often from local breweries, Farmer's Ales and Mighty Oak. No under-18s are admitted on Friday or Saturday evenings. The pub has a meeting room on the first floor. Tables behind the pub allow for some outdoor drinking.
⩩❀P⊡

Margaretting Tye

White Hart Inn

Swan Lane, CM4 9JX (off Galleywood Rd) OS684011
⊙ 11.30-3, 6-11 (midnight Fri & Sat); 12-10.30 Sun
☎ (01277) 840478 🌐 thewhitehart.uk.com
Adnams Bitter, Broadside; Mighty Oak IPA; Ⓗ **guest beers** Ⓖ
Large pub, comprising an L-shaped bar and a conservatory, hidden away in farmland between Chelmsford and Ingatestone. Six guest beers are always available on gravity, all served from the temperature-controlled cellar. Home-made daily specials supplement the regular menu; food is served all day Sunday. The expansive grounds include a children's play area and a pets' corner. Beer festivals are held in June and at the end of October.
⩩Q⊳❀◐◑♿▲♣P⚟

Mill Green

Viper ☆

Mill Green Road, CM4 0PT OS641018
⊙ 12-3, 6-11; 12-11 Sat; 12-10.30 Sun
☎ (01277) 352010
Mighty Oak Oscar Wilde; guest beers Ⓗ
This isolated, unspoilt country pub is now run by the long-standing cellarman and the owner's daughter, but continues much as before. Viper ales are commissioned from the Mighty Oak Brewery. The three guest ales also tend to favour Mighty Oak or Nethergate, but could come from anywhere in the country. The cider is Wilkins or Westons. The pub comprises three rooms: a lounge, a wood-panelled snug and a public bar. A beer festival is held in September.
⩩Q❀◐⊟♣●P

Monk Street

Farmhouse Inn

CM6 2NR (off B184 between Dunmow and Thaxted)
⊙ 11-midnight daily
☎ (01371) 830864 🌐 farmhouseinn.org
Greene King IPA; Mighty Oak Maldon Gold Ⓗ
Built in the 16th-century, this former Dunmow Brewery pub was enlarged to incorporate a restaurant (in the old cart shed) and accommodation; the bar is in the original part of the building. The quiet hamlet of Monk Street overlooks the Chelmer Valley, two miles from historic Thaxted, and is convenient for Stansted Airport and the M11. A well in the pub garden is no longer used, but did supply the hamlet with water during WWII. Cider is sold in summer. ❀⇌◐◑●P⚟

Newport

Coach & Horses

Cambridge Road, CB11 3TR (on B1383, old A11)
⊙ 11-3, 6-11.30; 11-5 Sun
☎ (01799) 540292
Adnams Bitter, Broadside; Young's Bitter; guest beers Ⓗ
An attractive, friendly pub, a former coaching inn on the old turnpike to Newmarket, where an interest in horseracing is still apparent in the decor. Most of the building dates from 1520. A large open fire warms customers on cold winter days. Separate family and dining areas, together with a fine and varied range of food, have made this a popular place to dine (no meals Sun eve). The landlord's Great Dane (sadly just the one now) is large but also friendly.
⩩⊳❀◐◑♿P⚟

Orsett

Foxhound

18 High Road, RM16 3ER (on B188)
⊙ 11-3.30, 6-11.30; 11-11.30 Sat; 12-4.30, 7-11 Sun
☎ (01375) 891295
Courage Best Bitter; Greene King IPA; guest beer Ⓗ
Two-bar village local that is at the centre of social life in Orsett. It has a comfortable saloon and a basic, but characterful public bar. The guest beers are usually from the Crouch Vale portfolio or other independent breweries. The Fox's Den restaurant provides excellent meals at lunchtime and Wednesday-Saturday evenings (booking necessary); it is also available for functions and business meetings. Quiz nights are held regularly.
⩩❀◐◑⊟♿♣P

Paglesham

Punch Bowl

Church End, SS4 2DP
(from A127, head E on B1013)
11.30-3, 6.30-11; 12-3, 7-11 Sun
(01702) 258376
Adnams Bitter; guest beers H
Dating from the 16th century, this former sailmaker's house in white Essex board is in a quiet, one-street village. The single, beamed bar is decorated with vintage artefacts and pictures. The small, no-smoking restaurant to the side offers an extensive, reasonably priced menu, served by friendly, helpful staff. The bar always stocks an Archers beer, plus two guests, often from Nethergate. There are south-facing tables in front of the pub and more in the children's play area at the rear. P

Pebmarsh

King's Head

The Street, CO9 2NH (4 miles NE of Halstead) OS852335
12-3, 6-11; closed Mon; 12-10.30 Sun
(01787) 269306
Greene King IPA; Woodforde's Wherry; guest beers H
As befits a village local over 500 years old, the King's Head boasts an array of oak beams. Guest beers are sourced from micro-breweries, while good quality, home-cooked food is served in the restaurant area. Family friendly, the pub is popular with walkers, although difficult to reach by public transport. There are benches at the front and rear for summer drinking, and two bouncy castles are provided for children (one exclusively for toddlers). P

Ramsden Bellhouse

Fox & Hounds

Church Road, CM11 1PW (50 yds from railway bridge)
11.30-11; 12-10.30 Sun
(01268) 710286
Greene King IPA; Mighty Oak Maldon Gold; guest beers H
Recently refurbished, this classy mock-Tudor pub is both a friendly local and ideal for people passing through the village. It usually offers a good choice of ales; guests include Archers. Westons cider is sold. The pub is situated in a rural location with plenty to keep children amused. The restaurant offers a good menu all day, specialising in pies of the day, plus vegetarian options. Every summer the pub hosts a well-attended beer festival in the spacious garden. P

Rayleigh

Roebuck

138 High Street, SS6 7BU (on A129)
9am-midnight (1am Fri & Sat); 9am-midnight Sun
(01268) 748430
Greene King Abbot; Marston's Pedigree; Shepherd Neame Spitfire; guest beers H
Friendly Wetherspoon's house in the High Street on the site of the Rev James Pillington's Baptist School – photographs in the pub recall its former schooldays. It stocks an excellent choice of guest ales and the beer festivals are well attended here, as are curry evenings (Thu). Meals are served all day until 11pm. Children are welcome in a sectioned off no-smoking area. Outside drinking is possible on the pavement. The cider is Westons.
Q

Ridgewell

White Horse Inn

Mill Road, CO9 4SG (on A1017, midway between Halstead and Haverhill) OS737410
11-3 (not Mon), 6-11; 12-10.30 Sun
(01440) 785532 ridgewellwh.com
Beer range varies G
Essex CAMRA's Pub of the Year 2006 is a real ale haven, offering at least three or four (often more) beers from a wide variety of breweries both local and nationwide, from casks behind the bar. Biddenden and Westons ciders are served straight from the cellar. A delightful restaurant offers home-cooked food at reasonable prices with occasional themed menus. For those wanting to explore the beautiful countryside of north Essex, accommodation is available in the luxurious motel.
P

Rochford

Blanchfields Bar

1 Southend Road, SS4 1HA
11-11; 12-10.30 Sun
(01702) 544015 blanchfields.co.uk
Beer range varies H
The changing range of up to eight real ales from micro-breweries was no doubt a strong reason for local CAMRA members voting the Blanchfields brewery tap their Pub of the Year in 2006. It also stocks three guest ciders. Recently refurbished with comfortable sofas, the pub has a no-smoking policy until 6pm. The excellent food is good value. It hosts live music and themed evenings as well as regular beer festivals.
P

Golden Lion

35 North Street, SS4 1AB
11.30-11 (2am Fri-Sun)
(01702) 545487
Adnams Bitter; Crouch Vale Brewers Gold; Greene King Abbot; guest beers H
Classic, 16th-century Essex weatherboarded pub with stained glass windows and hops above the bar. A regular local CAMRA award winner, it often sells interesting guest beers – check out the pump clips on the ceiling. The juke box, which caters for most tastes, can be loud at times - Friday evenings for example - but quiet corners can be found. An unobtrusive TV shows major sports events and others on request. Meals are served Tuesday-Friday. Children are not admitted.

Roundbush (Purleigh)

Roundbush Inn

Roundbush Road, CM9 6NN (on B1010)
⏲ 11-2.30 (4 Sat), 6 (5 Fri)-11; 12-10.30 Sun
☎ (01621) 828354
Greene King IPA; guest beers Ⓖ
Traditional, friendly local, frequented by inhabitants of many of the surrounding villages. The beers are served direct from the cask and can be enjoyed in two comfortable bars that have recently been refurbished. Chalkboards attest to the landlord's love of cooking; the cosy dining room is the ideal place to try out his food. The pub fields darts teams and customers play cribbage. Varied music is performed twice monthly (Thu). The pub owns the adjoining café that opens for breakfast.
⌂Q❀◐◑♣P

Rowhedge

Albion

High Street, CO5 7ES (approx. 3 miles S of Colchester)
⏲ 12-3 (not Mon), 5-11; 12-11 Thu-Sat; 12-10.30 Sun
☎ (01206) 728972
Beer range varies Ⓗ/Ⓖ
This village free house is considerably more friendly than in the days when a Customs and Excise man was hanged here – but the noose remains as a reminder. Benefiting from views over the River Crouch towards Wivenhoe, a foot ferry operates in summer. The changing beer range includes many from micro-breweries, both local and from further afield. Three beer festivals are staged, two to coincide with St George's Day and Regatta Day in June. Boules and other games are played. ❀⛟♣

Roxwell

Chequers

The Street, CM1 4PD (next to church)
⏲ 5-11; 12-2.30, 6-11 Sat; 12-3.30, 7-10.30 Sun
☎ (01245) 248240
Greene King IPA, Abbot; guest beer Ⓗ
This 17th-century village inn has retained much of its original structure. The hum of conversation dominates in the single bar; background music is subdued – if present at all – and even the pool table is confined to a separate room. The landlord will open weekday lunchtimes by prior arrangement for parties. ⌂❀♣P⚟▯

Saffron Walden

Old English Gentleman

11 Gold Street, CB10 1EJ (50 yds E of B184/B1052 jct)
⏲ 11-midnight (11 Mon); 11-12.30am Fri & Sat; 11-11 Sun
☎ (01799) 523595
Adnams Bitter; Greene King IPA; guest beers Ⓗ
This 18th-century, town-centre pub, has log fires and a welcoming atmosphere. It serves a selection of guest beers and an extensive tapas-style lunchtime menu that changes regularly. Filled baguettes and sandwiches are also available in the bar or the no-smoking dining area where various works of art are on display. Saffron Walden is busy on Tuesday and Saturday – market days. The pub has a pleasant patio at the rear.
⌂❀◐

Railway

Station Road, CB10 3HQ
⏲ 12-3, 6-11 (midnight Thu-Sat); 12-3, 6-11 Sun
☎ (01799) 522208
Adnams Bitter; Draught Bass; guest beers Ⓗ
Typical, 19th-century, town-centre railway tavern, recently refurbished to a high standard, where railway memorabilia includes model trains over the bar and in the garden. The single large bar has a mix of furniture and fittings that helps to convey a relaxed atmosphere. An extensive menu of good food ranges from traditional pub fare to tapas (no meals Sun eve). ❀◐◑P

Temeraire

55 High Steet, CB10 1AA (on B184)
⏲ 9am-midnight (12.30am Fri & Sat); 9am-midnight Sun
☎ (01799) 516975
Greene King IPA, Abbot; Marston's Pedigree; guest beers Ⓗ
Spacious Wetherspoon's house in a former workingmen's club on the main thoroughfare of this attractive market town. Named after a battleship featured in a famous painting by Turner, its tenuous local connection is explained in displays around the pub. Beer festivals are staged three times a year. The well-trained staff assiduously apply a 'try before you buy' policy. A pleasant, secluded outside drinking area at the rear is a bonus. It draws a young crowd evenings and weekends.
Q⏰❀◐◑♿P⚟

South Benfleet

Hoy & Helmet

24-32 High Street, SS7 1NA (on B1014, near Benfleet Station)
⏲ 11-11 (midnight Fri & Sat); 12-11 Sun
☎ (01268) 792307
Adnams Broadside; Courage Directors; Greene King IPA; guest beers Ⓗ
Situated in a conservation area, this Grade II listed pub has many rooms on different levels. The pool room has fruit machines and televised sport, another has a large open fire and low beams, while the restaurant is completely no-smoking. This busy pub, attracting locals and commuters, always offers a guest ale and serves a fine selection of food until 9.30pm. A seafood stall nearby is open most evenings. It benefits from a large garden and car park.
⌂❀◐◑⇌(Benfleet)⛟♣P⚟

Southend-on-Sea

Cork & Cheese

10 Talza Way, Victoria Plaza, SS2 5BG (near A13/A127)
⏲ 11-11; closed Sun
☎ (01702) 616914 🌐 corkandcheese.co.uk
Draught Bass; Nethergate IPA; guest beers Ⓗ
Large, friendly pub located on the lowest

level of the Victoria Plaza shopping centre within easy reach of two local railway stations. The walls and ceiling are covered in breweriana collected by the current owner. Five times local CAMRA Pub of the Year, it offers a changing range of guest beers – over 3,000 since early 1992; the cider is Cheddar Valley. Good quality, home-cooked lunches are served weekdays in the upstairs restaurant.
❀◐⇌(Victoria/Central)🚌♣●

Southminster

Station Arms

39 Station Road, CM0 7EW (near B1021)
✪ 12-2.30, 6 (5.30 Thu & Fri)-11; 2-11 Sat; 12-4, 7-11 Sun
☎ (01621) 772225 ⊕ thestationarms.co.uk
Adnams Bitter; Crouch Vale Brewers Gold; Dark Star Hophead; guest beers 🄷
This rare example of a traditional weatherboarded local thrives by providing an excellent range of real ales, catering for the connoisseur. At least 10 guests are sold every week, with two on at any time, as well as Westons cider. Beer festivals are held in January, late May and August bank holidays in the pub's restored barn. Local CAMRA's Pub of the Year stages regular live music. The enclosed patio garden is a plus.
⾕Q❀⇌♣●

Stapleford Tawney

Moletrap

Tawney Common, CM16 7PU (3 miles E of Epping, 1½ miles SW of Toot Hill) OS500013
✪ 11-2.30, 6.30 (6 summer)-11; 12-4, 7-10.30 Sun
☎ (01992) 522394
Fuller's London Pride; guest beers 🄷
Great old country pub, enjoying superb views. The guest beers mostly come from small or micro-breweries, with usually one from Crouch Vale. It serves good, home-cooked food that can be enjoyed in summer in a brilliant outside drinking and dining area. It is a popular pub and due to its small size it can get busy. Although hard to find, it is well worth the effort.
⾕Q❀◐◑P⚟

Stebbing

White Hart

High Street, CM6 3SQ (2 miles N of B1256, old A120)
✪ 11-3, 5-11; 11-11 Sat; 12-10.30 Sun
☎ (01371) 856383
Adnams Bitter; Greene King IPA; guest beers 🄷
Timbered, 15th-century inn in a picturesque village. This friendly, comfortable pub features exposed beams, eclectic collections – from chamber pots to cigarette cards – an old red post box in an interior bar wall and a section of exposed lathe and plaster wall behind a sheet of glass. A community pub, it is used by several local teams, including badminton, indoor bowls and cricket. Good value food is served daily. Live music is performed on Sunday afternoon and occasionally on Saturday evening. ⾕Q❀◐◑♣P

Stock

Hoop

21 High Street, CM4 9BD (on B1007)
✪ 11-11 (12.30am Fri; midnight Sat); 12-10.30 Sun
☎ (01277) 841137 ⊕ thehoop.co.uk
Adnams Bitter; Crouch Vale Brewers Gold; guest beers 🄷/🄶
This 14th-century weatherboarded pub underwent extensive work at the end of 2005, but retains a rustic theme. A larger bar area, inside toilets and upstairs restaurant specialising in fish and game dishes have been added. Bar meals are also served. At least four changing guest beers (usually dispensed on gravity) are available. The large garden is the setting for a long-established beer festival over the spring bank holiday. No. 100 bus runs through the village, between Billericay and Chelmsford.
Q☺❀◑♿🚌●⚟

Stow Maries

Prince of Wales

Woodham Road, CM3 6SA (near B1012) OS830993
✪ 11-11; 12-10.30 Sun
☎ (01621) 828971
Beer range varies 🄷
Attractive, 17th-century pub in a tiny village. Three open-plan drinking areas are warmed by real fires; in summer meals may be served in the converted barn or the raised garden. The beers may include something from Dark Star or Farmer's Ales, complemented by a range of draught Belgian ales and Westons Old Rosie cider. Themed menu evenings add variety to the good value food that is all prepared in house. The annual firework display is awesome. Accommodation is planned for 2007. ⾕Q☺❀◐◑●P⚟

Tendring

Cherry Tree Inn

Crow Lane, CO16 9AP (on B1035)
✪ 11-3, 6-11; closed Mon; 12-4 Sun
☎ (01255) 830340
Adnams Bitter; Greene King IPA; guest beers 🄷
The pub's interior is divided into three discrete sections. The main bar is where regulars meet to chat while the other two areas provide secluded dining in a pub renowned for the quality of its food. The stars of this rural house, the landlord and his wife, always welcome you with a smile and the latest village news.
⾕❀◐◑🚌P

Thaxted

Star

Mill End, CM6 2LT (on B184)
✪ 12-midnight (1am Sat); 12-10.30 Sun
☎ (01371) 830368
Adnams Bitter, Broadside, seasonal beer; guest beer 🄷
Frequented by locals and visitors alike, the Star has been opened up, but exposed beams and a large hearth have been retained. Thaxted itself is an architectural

gem, with its steep High Street, guildhall, almshouses and its parish church of cathedral proportions. The church holds a month-long annual music festival and the town also hosts a gathering of morris dancers when teams from all over the country dance in the streets, pubs and surrounding villages. ⌂❀◐♣P

Tollesbury

King's Head

1 High Street, CM9 8RG (on B1023, 5 miles SE of Tiptree)

⏲ 12-11 (midnight Fri & Sat); 12-10.30 Sun

☎ (01621) 869203

Adnams Bitter; Greene King IPA; guest beers Ⓗ

Situated on the main square, this 17th-century free house is an essential watering-hole for any visitor to this charming village on the Blackwater Estuary. It receives regular visits from motorcycling clubs, and hosts monthly folk and 'open mike' nights (not karaoke). The public bar houses a dartboard and pool table, while a large screen shows Sky Sports in the adjoining bar. The beers are reasonably priced, it stocks up to three guests, with one usually a dark ale. ⌂❀⊟🚌♣P

Waltham Abbey

White Lion

11 Sun Street, EN9 1ER

⏲ 11-1am (2am Fri & Sat); 11-1am Sun

☎ (01922) 718673

McMullen AK Ⓗ

Small, one-bar, one-beer pub in the pedestrianised shopping area, a short walk from the abbey and the abbey gardens. The pub fields a number of darts teams in the local leagues and stages live music at weekends. Note: if business is slack in the week, it may close earlier than the stated times, so check before travelling. Children are welcome in summer. ♣

Weeley

White Hart

Clacton Road, Weeley Heath, CO16 9ED (on B1441)

⏲ 12-2.30, 4.30-11 (10 Mon); 12-11 Fri; 11-11 Sat; 12-10.30 Sun

☎ (01255) 830384

Beer range varies Ⓗ

Weeley, although nicknamed 'Blasted Heath', can nevertheless be welcoming on a winter's night, particularly this family-run pub where the real ale acts as a magnet for drinkers from near and far. The single, L-shaped bar is large enough to house a dartboard, pool table and Sky TV while still allowing for conversation. The beer range varies constantly and micro-breweries are supported. The food is recommended. ❀⛺🚌♣P🍺

Westcliff-on-Sea

Cricketers

228 London Road, SS0 7JG (on A13)

⏲ 11-1am (2am Fri & Sat); 11-1am Sun

☎ (01702) 343168

Fuller's London Pride; Greene King IPA, Abbot; guest beers Ⓗ

Large, street-corner pub, officially Southend's oldest licensed premises, this Gray's house has always sold real ale. Frequent theme nights have made it a bustling part of the community, while the hall at the rear continues to attract many great musical acts (see the website: rigamusicbar.co.uk). It stocks up to three real ciders and beer festivals are now a regular feature. Under-18s are welcome before 8pm. Tables in the car park are provided for outside drinking. ❀◐♿⇌(Southend Victoria)🚌●P

Wivenhoe

Horse & Groom

55 The Cross, CO7 9QL

(on B1028, approx. 1 mile from station)

⏲ 10.30-3, 5.30 (6 Sat)-11 (midnight Fri); 12-4.30, 7-10.30 Sun

☎ (01206) 824928

Adnams Bitter, Broadside, seasonal beers; guest beer Ⓗ

Friendly local at the edge of a pleasant village. The pub comprises a cosy saloon bar and a large, busy, public bar. In addition to the Adnams beers, a guest is always available from its generous portfolio. Good value, home-cooked food is served lunchtimes, except Sunday. It is accessible by bus from Colchester, or via the Wivenhoe trail, a popular walking and cycling path along the River Colne. ❀◐⊟🚌♣P

Woodham Mortimer

Hurdlemakers Arms

Post Office Road, CM9 6SU (near A414)

⏲ 12-3, 6.30-11.30; 12-midnight Sat; 12-11 Sun

☎ (01245) 225169

Greene King IPA, Abbot; guest beers Ⓗ

Country pub with a community focus and excellent large garden – it was the recipient of local CAMRA's Most Improved Pub award in 2005. The energetic tenants host many special events throughout the year, while darts, crib and dominoes can be enjoyed at any time in the unspoilt public bar. The cosy lounge incorporates the no-smoking dining area. Three guest beers change frequently and often include a dark beer and one from local brewer, Mighty Oak. ⌂Q❀◐◑⊟♣P

Writtle

Wheatsheaf

70 The Green, CM1 3DU (off A1060)

⏲ 11-3, 5-11; 11-midnight Fri & Sat; 12-11 Sun

☎ (01245) 420695 🌐 wheatsheafph-writtle.co.uk

Greene King IPA, Abbot; Mighty Oak Oscar Wilde, Maldon Gold, Burntwood Ⓗ

Small, traditional pub near the village green. Free from piped music, the TV is switched on only occasionally. The pub appeals to a cross-section of the community and visitors will always find a conversation to join in. Monthly folk nights are held on the third Friday. The last entry is 30 minutes before closing. There is a patio for outside drinking in fine weather. Q❀⊟♣P

GLOUCESTERSHIRE & BRISTOL

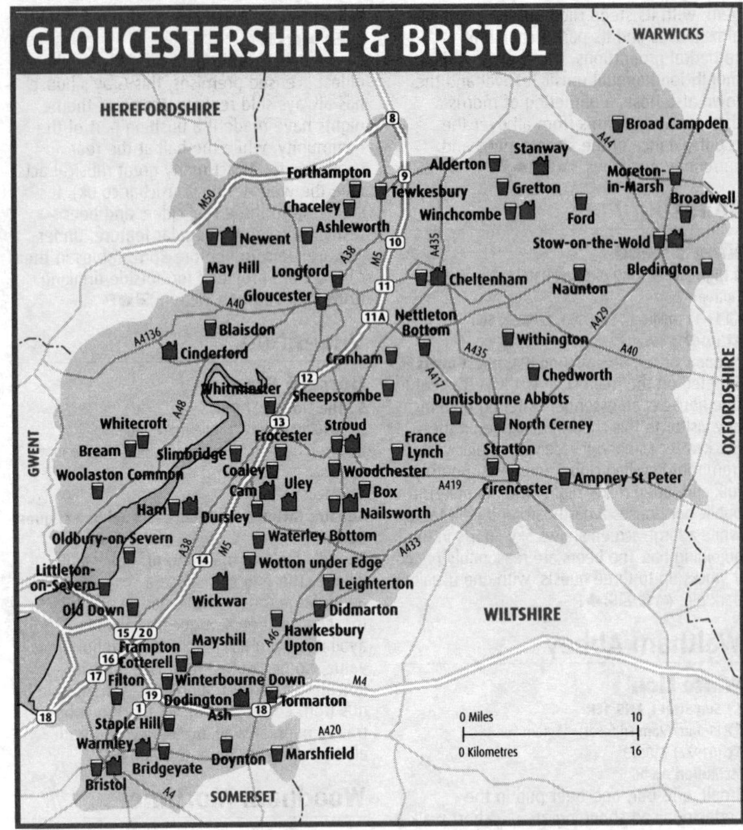

Alderton

Gardeners Arms

Beckford Road, GL20 8NL
(follow brown signs from B4077)
☉ 12-2.30, 6-11; 12-2.30, 6.30-10.30 Sun
☎ (01242) 620257
Beer range varies Ⓗ
Listed, 16th-century, oak beamed free house at the heart of a quiet village. Four handpumps serve a changing range of beers from a weekly menu. The lounge features an original well, local photographs and a piano. The pub hosts Whitsun and Christmas mini-beer festivals (focusing on local brewers), charity events and monthly fun quizzes. An extensive, home-cooked range includes bar meals, fresh fish specials, theme nights and takeaways. Live music is performed on Friday evening.
⩩❀◐♿♣P⅟

Ampney St Peter

Red Lion ☆

GL7 5SL (on A417)
☉ 12-2 (not Mon-Fri), 6-10.30 (9.30 Mon-Wed); 12-2, 7-10.30 Sun
☎ (01285) 851596
Hook Norton Hooky Bitter; Taylor Golden Best or Landlord Ⓗ
Superb, 400-year old pub caught in a time warp: the two tiny flagstoned rooms with open fires are well preserved and little appears to have changed since the veteran landlord was a babe in arms. Without a bar counter, service is from the corner of one room. One beer is available winter weekdays, two at other times. Two pub signs grace the frontage, one is in the distinctive oval frame of the old Stroud Brewery. Opening times may vary.
⩩Q❀⊟P

Ashleworth

Boat Inn

The Quay, GL19 4HZ OS819251
☉ 11.30-2.30 (3 Sat; not Wed), 7-11; closed Mon; 12-3, 7-10.30 Sun
☎ (01452) 700272 🌐 boat-inn.co.uk
Beer range varies Ⓖ
An absolute gem – an unspoilt, tranquil haven on the bank of the River Severn, owned by the same family for 400 years. It serves beer direct from the cask, the range coming from smaller local breweries. Several rooms are furnished with antiques. The courtyard has some tables under cover. A rare no-smoking pub, it is a frequent local CAMRA award-winner. Rolls and ploughman's are available at lunchtime.
⩩Q❀●P⅟

Blaisdon

Red Hart

GL17 0AH (off A4136, E of Longhope) OS703169
⏲ 11.30-3, 6-11; 12-3.30, 6.30-10.30 Sun
☎ (01452) 830477
Hook Norton Hooky Bitter; Tetley Bitter; guest beers Ⓗ
Lovely pub in the small village of Blaisdon on the outskirts of the Royal Forest of Dean, where five real ales can be sampled at any time. A log fire, low ceilings and flagstone floors make this a special place for special occasions. The large garden and patio area are popular in summer for barbecues and have plenty of space for children to play safely. The food is excellent.
♔Q❀◑◐♣P

Bledington

King's Head

The Green, OX7 6XQ
⏲ 11-3, 6-11; 12-10.30 Sun
☎ (01608) 658365 🌐 kingsheadinn.net
Hook Norton Hooky Bitter; guest beers Ⓗ
Delightful, 16th-century, honey coloured stone inn overlooking the village green with its brook and ducks. The original old beams, inglenook with kettle and military brasses, flagstone floors and high-backed settles and pews help creat a convivial atmosphere. Top quality food is served in the restaurant (booking advised). Twelve rooms offer charming accommodation.
♔Q♉❀⇌◑◐⊟⅄⇌(Kingham)♣P

Box

Halfway House

GL6 9AE (southern edge of Minchinhampton Common) OS856003
⏲ 12-midnight; 12-10.30 Sun
☎ (01453) 832631
Moles Molecatcher; Otter Ale; Taylor Landlord; Wickwar BOB; guest beers Ⓗ
Recently refurbished, this 300-year-old pub is set on the edge of Minchinhampton Common, near the village of Box. The food is all home made and apart from the fish and seafood, which is delivered daily from St Mawes in Cornwall, it is based on fresh local produce. Separate from the stylish restaurant, the public bar area retains its village pub appeal and hosts a quiz on Monday evening with free bar food (no meals are served Mon).
◑◐♠P⚡

Bream

Rising Sun

High Street, GL15 6JF (opp. Cenotaph)
⏲ 12-2.30, 6.30-11; 12-11 Sat (and summer Fri); 12-2.30, 7-10.30 (12-11 summer) Sun
☎ (01594) 564555
Freeminer Speculation; guest beers Ⓗ
Welcoming, 200-year-old stone pub, affording spectacular views over the forest. A large building, it houses a friendly main bar with overspill into adjoining rooms, two restaurants and a large function room with its own bar. An enclosed garden with seating provides a pleasant summer venue. With new accommodation in five guest rooms and a central location within the forest, this is a popular base for visitors.
♔♉❀⇌◑◐♿⅄♣P

Bridgeyate

White Harte

111 London Road, BS30 5NA (on A420, 2 miles E of Kingswood)
⏲ 11-3, 5 (6 Sat)-11; 12-3, 7-10.30 Sun
☎ (0117) 967 3830
Bath Gem; Butcombe Bitter; Courage Best Bitter; Marston's Pedigree Ⓗ
Unspoilt country pub, dating from 1860, situated at a busy crossroads on the A420. The bar divides into two areas, one for diners, with beamed ceilings. A large green at the front is popular in summer. The pub runs a golf society and hosts a weekly quiz on Monday evening; cribbage is also played here. There is a limited bus service. ❀◑⊟♣P

Bristol: Central

Bag o' Nails

141 St Georges Road, Hotwells, BS1 5UW (5 minutes' walk from the cathedral)
⏲ 12-2 (not Mon), 5.30-11; 12-11 Fri & Sat; 12-10.30 Sun
☎ (0117) 940 6776 🌐 bagonails.org.uk
Beer range varies Ⓗ
Small, friendly, unspoilt, gaslit terraced pub with wood panelling and bare floorboards. The Bag is a real ale drinker's delight. The beer mainly comes from small independents and micro-breweries with often 12 different ales to sample in a week, and usually six or eight beers sold at one time. It also stocks a good range of bottled beers and stages two beer festivals a year. Lunchtime opening hours may vary. **Q♣**

Bell

Hillgrove Street, Stokes Croft, BS2 8JT (off Jamaica St)
⏲ 12-2, 5-midnight; 4-1am Sat; 12-midnight Sun
☎ (0117) 909 6612
Butcombe Bitter, Blond, Gold; seasonal or guest beer Ⓗ
Lively, two-roomed pub, 10 minutes' walk from the Broadmead shopping centre. It

INDEPENDENT BREWERIES

Bath Ales Warmley
Battledown Cheltenham
Bristol Beer Factory Bristol
Cotswold Spring Dodington Ash
Donnington Stow-on-the-Wold
Eagles Bush Ham
Freeminer Cinderford
Goff's Winchcombe
Nailsworth Nailsworth
Severn Vale Cam
Stanway Stanway
Stroud Stroud
Uley Uley
Whittington's Newent
Wickwar Wickwar
Zerodegrees Bristol

enjoys a busy lunchtime food trade and is popular with office workers and staff from nearby hospitals, while on Friday evening it attracts drinkers on their way to the clubs. Well frequented by music fans, DJs spin discs nightly in one of the rooms from 10pm. Beer can be taken away in five litre containers. Sunday roast lunches are served. Buses stop on nearby Cheltenham Road. ❀◐◑🚌

Bridge Inn

16 Passage Street, BS2 0JF (over river bridge from Temple fire station)
⏲ 11.30-11; 7-10.30 Sun
☎ (0117) 949 9967
Bath SPA, Gem; guest beer Ⓗ
Small and friendly, this one room pub enjoys a thriving trade on weekday lunchtimes from the surrounding offices whose workers make short work of the jacket potatoes and chilli dishes. The walls are adorned with film stills and posters. Continuous but not deafening background pop music is played. The pub has close ties with Bath Ales, who often supply the guest beer. GWR radio station stands opposite. Tables are put out on the pavement in summer. ◐≠ (Temple Meads)🚌

Bunch of Grapes

8 Denmark Street, BS1 5DQ
(near Hippodrome Theatre)
⏲ 11-midnight; 12-midnight Sun
☎ (0117) 987 0500 🌐 thebunchofgrapes.co.uk
Beer range varies Ⓗ
Lively, single bar pub, set just off the city centre, selling four changing real ales, mostly from local micro-breweries. The rear of the L-shaped interior hosts live music of all styles most evenings, including rock, blues and acoustic sessions, but Monday is quiz night. The excellent juke box compensates for when no-one is performing. Located opposite the stage door of the Hippodrome, the pub is decorated with posters from theatre productions. Meals are served 12-7pm (6pm Sun). ◐

Cornubia

142 Temple Street, BS1 6EW
(opp. fire station by former Courage Brewery)
⏲ 12 (6 Sat)-11; closed Sun
☎ (0117) 925 4415
Otter Bitter; guest beers Ⓗ
A choice of seven real ales from micro-breweries plus a traditional cider are served at this popular, mid 19th-century Grade II listed pub. Originally a pair of Georgian houses built some 100 years earlier, the name Cornubia is of Cornish origin. The L-shaped pub gets crowded, especially early in the evening, and it is currently undergoing an overdue, but gentle internal refurbishment. Note the limited weekend opening hours. Several buses stop in nearby Victoria Street. ❀◐≠ (Temple Meads) 🚌●P

Cotham Porter Stores

15 Cotham Road, South Cotham, BS6 5TZ (follow Cotham Brow from Cheltenham Rd for 400 yards)
⏲ 12-11 daily 🌐 cothamporterstores.co.uk
Shepherd Neame Spitfire; guest beers Ⓗ
Classic, traditional cider house, now gaining similar recognition for beer, selling at least two real ales alongside Thatchers, Cheddar Valley and one or two guest ciders. The long, narrow bar tapers into a snug seating area. Note the mural, which is rumoured to have been painted by John Lennon in 1963. The pub fields a cricket team in summer, while sport is often shown on TV. The atmosphere can get smoky when busy. It frequently opens later than the stated time. 🚌♣●

Hare on the Hill

41 Thomas Street North, Kingsdown, BS2 8LX
(up steep hill from lower Cheltenham Rd area)
⏲ 12-2.30, 5-11; 12-11.30 Fri & Sat; 12-11 Sun
☎ (0117) 908 1982
Bath SPA, Gem, Barnstormer, seasonal beers Ⓗ
The pub is situated in the residential Kingsdown suburb above the city, not far from Cheltenham Road. Bath Ales' first pub, it stocks its full range of regular and seasonal beers plus the odd guest ale and over 25 malt whiskies. It also hosts occasional beer festivals. There is a large-screen TV for sport and a dartboard at the back of the bar. Live acoustic music is performed most Sunday evenings. Pictures by local artists are displayed for sale. ◐◑🚌♣

Highbury Vaults

164 St Michael's Hill, Kingsdown, BS2 8DE
⏲ 12-midnight; 12-11 Sun
☎ (0117) 973 3203
Bath Gem; Brains SA; St Austell Tribute; Young's Bitter, Special; guest beer Ⓗ
This dark, wood-panelled pub with bare floorboards is frequented by locals and students. There is a small front bar and a larger back room, which is split into smaller areas. The rear garden is partially covered and heated to allow for year round use. Good value, home-cooked food is served at lunchtime and weekday evenings. Although open until midnight, there is no admission after 11pm. The pub is on the No. 9 bus route and others stop nearby. Q❀◐◑🚌

Hillgrove Porter Stores

53 Hillgrove Street North, Kingsdown, BS2 8LT
(off Dove St)
⏲ 4-midnight; 12-midnight Sun
☎ (0117) 944 4780
Butcombe Bitter; Mathews Brassknocker; St Austell Tribute; guest beers Ⓗ
Now completely free of tie, this fine community pub offers a warm welcome and four changing guest beers to augment the regular offerings. An ale board gives details of what's on and brief tasting notes. On Monday all ales are reduced in price and on other evenings the 'ale of the day' is reduced until 8pm. Sunday is quiz night and the pub may open at lunchtime for televised rugby international games. ⊬

Hope & Anchor

38 Jacobs Well Road, Hotwells, BS8 1DR
⏲ 12-11; 12-10.30 Sun
☎ (0117) 929 2987
Beer range varies Ⓗ
Here we have a genuine free house offering a good range of up to six real ales. The beers change frequently, with West Country brews

featuring prominently and many favourites returning on a regular basis. The pub is deservedly popular, not only for its beers, but also for its good quality food, served all day until an hour before closing. The terraced garden at the back up a few steep steps is a pleasant spot for a drink in warm weather. Several buses stop in nearby Park Street and Anchor Road.
❀◐◑🚌

Horts

49 Broad Street, BS1 2EP
⏲ 11-midnight (1am Fri & Sat); 12-midnight Sun
☎ (0117) 925 2520
Young's Bitter, Special, seasonal beers Ⓗ
Large but cosy, town-centre pub with a long, single bar and several distinct drinking areas. Up to six real ales and two traditional ciders – Thatchers Dry and Cheddar Valley – are stocked at most times. A projection screen TV is available for major sporting events, while two pool tables and a function room are available for hire. Live jazz is performed on Sunday afternoon. No meals are served Sunday evening. There is a pleasant outdoor seating area for summer. The pub has a wheelchair WC. ❀◐◑♿⇌ (Temple Meads)●

King's Head ☆

60 Victoria Street, BS1 6DE (300 yds from Temple Meads)
⏲ 11 (6.30 Sat)-11; 12-3, 7-11 Sun
☎ (0117) 927 7860
Bath Gem; Courage Best Bitter; Hook Norton Old Hooky; Sharp's Doom Bar Ⓗ
The pub dates back to the 1600s but boasts an outstanding late Victorian interior. The single narrow bar leads to a cosy 'tramcar' snug. Photographs and drawings of old Bristol adorn the walls, while a collection of well polished glass is displayed behind the bar. Used by office workers at lunchtime and locals of all ages in the evening, four pavement tables are available in summer. Good food is served weekday lunchtimes. It lies on several bus routes. ❀◐⇌ (Temple Meads) 🚌

Old Fishmarket

59-63 Baldwin Street, BS1 1QZ
⏲ 12-11 (midnight Fri & Sat); 12-11 Sun
☎ (0117) 921 1515
Butcombe Bitter; Fuller's Discovery, London Pride, ESB, seasonal beers Ⓗ
Converted from a former fishmarket, this was Fuller's first Bristol pub. The main drinking area is dominated by a long, carved wooden bar topped with black marble. To the right sofas are provided for relaxed drinking and viewing the big screen (sporting events draw a crowd), while behind the bar is a more intimate snug area. An enclosed courtyard offers a quiet drinking space (and wheelchair access). Sunday is quiz night. Thai food is served all day until 9pm. ◐◑♿⇌(Temple Meads) 🚌⚡

Orchard Inn

12 Hanover Place, BS1 6XT (off Cumberland Rd)
⏲ 12-3, 5-11; 12-3, 7-10.30 Sun
☎ (0117) 926 2678
Bath Gem; guest beers Ⓗ
Homely, street-corner free house, close to the historic SS Great Britain and Matthew (when in dock). It is often busy, being frequented by locals, business people and passing trade. It is known for the quality of its ciders – Thatchers Dry, Cheddar Valley and Moles Black Rat – as well as the real ales. The guest beers change frequently, and are normally sourced from West Country brewers such as Butcombe, Wickwar and Sharp's. Excellent lunches are served weekdays.
❀◐♣●

Reckless Engineer

Temple Gate, BS1 6PO (opp. station approach road)
⏲ 11-11 (1am Fri & Sat); 12-11 Sun
☎ (0117) 922 0487
Butcombe Bitter; Otter Ale; guest beers Ⓗ
At time of survey in 2006, this spacious one bar pub was undergoing refurbishment, but should now feature a raised wooden floor and a stage. The pub hosts live music – usually rock bands – on most Friday and Saturday evenings, with free admission for card-carrying CAMRA members; it also boasts a good rock juke box. One or two guest beers are always on sale in the fully air-conditioned bar. Sunday meals are served 12-4pm. The pub is well served by public transport.
◐◑⇌ (Temple Meads)🚌♣

Zerodegrees

53 Colston Street, BS1 5BA (near Bristol Royal Infirmary)
⏲ 12-midnight daily
☎ (0117) 925 2706 🌐 zerodegrees.co.uk
Zerodegrees Wheat Ale, Pale Ale, Pilsner, Black Lager, seasonal beers Ⓟ
Winner in the New Build category of the 2005 CAMRA Pub Design awards, it was built on the site of an old tramshed, in contemporary industrial style. The high-tech brewery is on full view. A 250-seat restaurant is spread over two floors, featuring an open kitchen. There is a spacious drinking area around the bar with flat screen TVs that are silent except for major sporting events. Music is piped throughout the building. All beers are served at cool temperatures.
❀◐◑🚌 (20,21)

Bristol: North

Inn on the Green

2 Filton Road, Horfield, BS7 0PA (on A38, opp. sports centre, near Memorial Stadium)
⏲ 11-3, 6-11; 11-11 Sat; 12-11.30 Sun
☎ (0117) 952 1391
Butcombe Bitter, Gold; Fuller's London Pride; guest beers Ⓗ
Offering at least 10 guest beers and three ciders, this open-plan pub is divided into three distinct sections to cater for the community it serves. At the centre is the bar, with a mix of seating and tables; to the left is a quiet, comfy lounge. To the right, the old skittle alley offers seating, tables, pool, fruit machines, juke box and big TV screens. Independent chefs supply a wide variety of meals, oriented towards the beer drinker. Children are welcome at lunchtime.
Q❀◐◑🚌 (75, 76, 77, 585)●P⚡

Miners Arms

136 Mina Road, St Werburghs, BS2 9YQ
(300 yds from M32)
✪ 4 (12 Fri & Sat)-11 (midnight Thu-Sat); 12-11 Sun
☎ (0117) 955 6718
Butcombe Bitter; Caledonian Deuchars IPA; Fuller's London Pride; Wadworth 6X; guest beers Ⓗ
Located near St Werburgh's City Farm and Bristol Climbing Centre (in a converted church), this excellent, two-roomed, street-corner local is worth a visit. The split-level interior houses a hop-adorned bar where you can try the ale of the day at a discount until 9pm. Well behaved dogs are welcome. Parking is not easy but the No. 5 or 25 bus stops in St James St, a short walk from the pub. The gents toilets are reminiscent of football ground facilities of the 1970s. ⛫🚌♣

Robin Hood's Retreat

197 Gloucester Road, BS7 8BG (on A38)
✪ 12-3, 5-11 (midnight Thu-Sat); 12-11 Sun
☎ (0117) 924 8639
Beer range varies Ⓗ
Transformed from a down-at-heel Victorian, red-brick boozer into a quality pub, the refurbishment has provided charm and character through the lighting, furnishings, flooring and decor. The bar at the front of this relatively compact, L-shaped pub stocks up to eight beers from independent breweries. Top of the range, classic British pub food is served (no meals Sun eve or Mon), while a select range of wines includes organic varieties. Children are welcome at lunchtime. Q◐◑♿🚌●

Wellington

Gloucester Road, Horfield, BS7 8UR
(on A38 by Horfield Common)
✪ 12-11 (midnight Fri & Sat); 12-11 Sun
☎ (0117) 951 3022
Bath SPA, Gem, Barnstormer, seasonal beers; guest beer (occasional) Ⓗ
Large, red-brick pub close to Bristol Memorial Stadium, it was local CAMRA's Pub of the Year 2004 and joint 2005 winner. This traditional pub has a spacious L-shaped bar with a good-sized no-smoking area. It stocks a fine range of bottled beers. Free live blues music is performed on Sunday and Monday. It serves a good selection of food that is well worth trying. ❀◐◑P⊬

Bristol: South

Coronation

18 Dean Lane, Southville, BS3 1DD (near river footbridge off Coronation Rd)
✪ 4 (12 Sat)-11; 12-10.30 Sun
☎ (0117) 940 9044
Hop Back GFB, Best Bitter, Crop Circle, Summer Lightning, seasonal beers; guest beer Ⓗ
This brightly lit, bustling corner local is Hop Back's only Bristol pub. The single bar has an elevated, no-smoking snug area. It usually stocks five Hop Back draught ales, however limited cellar space means some can run out. It also sells Hop Back's bottle-conditioned beers, and Westcroft's award-winning cider. There are no pub games, juke box or other loud distractions, but live music and quizzes do take place. Food is limited to pizzas, served 6-9pm daily. Q🚌(24)●⊬

Shakespeare

1 Henry Street, Totterdown, BS3 4UD
✪ 4.30 (12 Sat)-11 (midnight Fri & Sat); 12-10.30 Sun
☎ (0117) 907 8818 🌐 theshakey.co.uk
Bath Gem; Sharp's Cornish Coaster; guest beers Ⓗ
Known locally as the Shakey, this street corner pub, in a hilltop suburb lies within easy reach of the station. It offers up to three guest beers, mainly from local and regional brewers, and, occasionally, Thatchers Cheddar Valley cider. A pool table stands at the far end of the U-shaped bar. An outside drinking area at the rear is heated, while a small front patio provides extra seating. Food is limited to snacks during the week, but a full Sunday lunch is served (booking advised).
⛫❀≠(Temple Meads)🚌(54, 356)●

Bristol: West

Adam & Eve

7 Hope Chapel Hill, Hotwells, BS8 4ND
✪ 4 (12 Fri & Sat)-11 (midnight Thu-Sat); 12-10.30 Sun
☎ (0117) 929 1508
Sharp's Eden Ale; guest beers Ⓗ
Traditional pub, full of nooks and crannies, attracting a mixed clientele who come both for the excellent beer range and the good quality food. It stocks up to five real ales from small, independent breweries, often local. One of the beers may occasionally make way for a second cider to supplement the regular Addlestones, particularly in summer. A selection of board games is available and a book exchange. Meals are served daily from opening time until 9pm. Buses to Weston and North Somerset stop nearby.
◐◑🚌●

Port of Call

3 York Street, Clifton, BS8 2YF
(off top of Blackboy Hill)
✪ 12-2.30, 5.30-11; 12-11 Sat; 12-5 Sun
☎ (0117) 973 3600
Draught Bass; Butcombe Blond; Caledonian Deuchars IPA; Sharp's Cornish Coaster; Theakston Old Peculier; guest beers Ⓗ
Local CAMRA's Pub of the Year 2005 serves up to 12 beers, including many guests, in a warm, cosy and friendly atmosphere. The quality of the beer is well matched by good home-made food; the Sunday lunch is particularly popular and booking is advised. Pictures of old local pubs vie with maritime and fishing memorabilia. Children are welcome in the pleasant garden, but not dogs. Large unfamiliar groups are discouraged and disabled access is tricky. Q❀◐≠(Clifton Down)🚌

Post Office Tavern

17 Westbury Hill, Westbury on Trym, BS9 3AG
✪ 11-11; 12-10.30
☎ (0117) 940 1233
Draught Bass; Ⓖ **Bath SPA; Butcombe Bitter; Courage Best Bitter; Otter Bitter; guest beer** Ⓗ
This elegant Victorian building at the top of Westbury Hill was once the village post office and still bears evidence of its past function, including an old red telephone box. A lively

community pub, it hosts a quiz on Tuesday and Thursday evenings and regulars like to watch sporting events, especially rugby. Lunches are served Monday to Saturday and pizzas are available in the evening. The pub operates a tidy dress code. One area is no-smoking. Q❀◐🚌(1, 20)⚟

Prince of Wales

84 Stoke Lane, Westbury on Trym, BS9 3SP

⌚ 11-11; 12-10.30 Sun

☎ (0117) 962 3715

Draught Bass; Bath SPA; Butcombe Bitter, Gold; Courage Best Bitter; Fuller's London Pride Ⓗ

Busy, Butcombe house, popular with lunchtime diners when a choice of good food is available (no meals served Sun). There are various seating areas, with one designated as no-smoking at mealtimes. Unusual prints and sporting memorabilia adorn the walls. The lower level informal seating area leads to an attractive garden. Sporting events, particularly rugby, are shown on a foldaway TV screen. Butcombe's popular Brunel IPA is available as a winter beer. Q❀◐

Royal Oak

50 The Mall, Clifton, BS8 4JG (just off the Downs)

⌚ 12-11; 12-4 Sun

☎ (0117) 973 8846

Draught Bass; Courage Best Bitter; Sharp's Cornish Coaster, Doom Bar Ⓗ

Set at the heart of Clifton village, this popular pub has been under the same ownership for nearly 10 years. The roomy single bar is split level, with exposed floorboards throughout and stone walls in the lower level. Inspect the photographs of former Bristol rugby teams and see if you can spot the landlord. A traditional roast is served on Sunday.
◐🚌(8, 9)

Victoria

20 Chock Lane, Westbury on Trym, BS9 3EX
(in small lane behind churchyard)

⌚ 12-2.30, 5.30-11; 12-3, 5.30-11 Sun

☎ (0117) 950 0441 🌐 thevictoriapub.co.uk

Draught Bass; Butcombe Bitter; Wadworth IPA, 6X; guest beer Ⓗ

Down a lane behind the parish church, the Victoria's hillside garden is a delight in summer. The bar has a no-smoking area and displays pictures of Westbury when it was a village in its own right. The pub enjoys a busy food trade with home-cooked meals served at lunchtime and early evening (until 8pm), pizzas are available until 10pm. Social events include quiz nights, live music and themed menus.
❀◐◑⚟

White Horse

24 High Street, Westbury on Trym, BS9 3DZ

⌚ 11-11; 12-10.30 Sun

☎ (0117) 950 7622

Draught Bass; Bath Gem; Butcombe Bitter; Sharp's Cornish Coaster Ⓖ

This charming pub is known locally as the Hole in the Wall, as one bar serves the Georgian extension via a window of the original building. All the beers are served directly from the barrel, kept in a 14th-century vault. Seating in the various bars ranges from ancient carved wooden settles to modern furniture. Children are allowed in any room without a bar until 7pm. It can be smoky and busy at weekends. Bus Nos. 1, 20 and others serve the pub.
Q❀🚌♣●

Broad Campden

Bakers Arms

GL55 6UR (signed from B4081)

⌚ 11.30-2.30, 4.45-11; 11.30-11 Fri, Sat & summer; 12-10.30 Sun

☎ (01386) 840515

Donnington BB; Stanway Stanney Bitter; Taylor Landlord; Wells Bombardier; guest beer Ⓗ

Dating from 1724, this fine old country pub was Gloucestershire CAMRA Pub of the Year 2005 and local winner for three of the last four years. A local outlet for the superb Stanney Bitter, this truly genuine free house is characterised by Cotswold stone walls, exposed beams and an inglenook. Excellent value, home-cooked food can be enjoyed in the no-smoking dining room, but debit or credit cards are not accepted.
♨Q❀◐◑♣●P

Broadwell

Fox Inn

The Green, GL56 0UF (off A429)

⌚ 11-2.30, 6-11; 12-2.30, 7-10.30 Sun

☎ (01451) 870909

Donnington BB, SBA Ⓗ

Attractive, one-bar, stone pub overlooking the village green. Original flagstone flooring remains in the main bar area, where jugs hang from the beams. Addlestones cider is sold here. Good, traditional pub food is served (not Sun eve) in the no-smoking dining room. Tables are set out in the rear garden, where Aunt Sally is played; there is a caravan site in the field behind. This friendly pub is a convenient refreshment stop for visitors to the NT's Chastleton House.
♨Q❀◐◑⛺♣●P

Chaceley

Old Ferry Inn

Stock Lane, GL19 4EQ OS865298

⌚ 11.30-3, 7-11 (11.30-11 summer Sat); closed Tue; 12-3, 7-11 Sun

☎ (01452) 780333 🌐 oldferry.co.uk

Wickwar Coopers WPA; Wye Valley Butty Bach; guest beers Ⓗ

Set on the western bank of the River Severn, the pub's name derives from the ferry crossing that existed here for hundreds of years, taking people to the 11th-century Odda's Chapel in Deerhurst. Altered and extended over the past 200 years, it is now a friendly pub with a large public bar, comfortable lounge and a restaurant serving good value food. Busy all year, a blazing fire helps draw the customers in winter, and the locals make visitors feel welcome.
♨Q❀◐◑🛏♿⛺♣●P⚟

Chedworth

Seven Tuns

Queen Street, GL54 4AE (near church) OS053121
12-3.30, 6-11; 11-11 Sat & summer; 12-10.30 Sun
(01285) 720242
Young's Bitter, Special, seasonal beers H
This rare outlet for Young's beers in Gloucestershire is unspoilt, spacious and attractively located in one of England's longest villages. Good food on an extensive menu is accompanied by a comprehensive wine list and served in separate dining areas. With two bars, the whole premises are well furnished, displaying local artefacts and photographs. The recently refurbished function room and skittle alley can be hired.

Cheltenham

Adam & Eve

8 Townsend Street, GL51 9HD (near Tesco superstore)
10-2, 4-11; 10-11 Sat; 12-2, 4-10.30 Sun
(01242) 690030
Arkell's 2B, Moonlight, seasonal beers H
Run by the same landlady for 27 years, this friendly, unpretentious terraced local is 15 minutes' walk from the town centre. While parking is limited, it is readily accessible by bus, with Stagecoach services C, H and 41 passing nearby. The public bar, with its adjoining skittle alley and separate lounge form a strong community focus. The pub is home to skittle and quiz teams. Books are sold on a table at the bar to raise funds for charity.

Bath Tavern

68 Bath Road, GL53 7JT
11-11; 12-10.30 Sun
(01242) 256122
Bath SPA, Gem H
This single bar free house was kept for over 100 years by the Cheshire family. Now run by young management, keen to keep pub traditions, it draws a mixed clientele, but the younger element is being encouraged. Local produce is freshly cooked on the premises – Sunday lunch is popular. Music is maintained at a background level, but the volume may rise on weekend evenings. Often busy, the atmosphere is always warm. Etched and stained glass windows help retain a traditional feel.

Cheltenham Motor Club

Upper Park Street, GL52 6SA
(access from London Rd, A40 is via Crown Passage)
12-3 (not Mon-Fri), 7-midnight; 12-2, 7-midnight Sun
(01242) 522590 cheltmc.com
Beer range varies H
Card-carrying CAMRA members are welcome at this friendly club, just outside the town centre in the former Crown pub. Three regularly changing ales, Thatchers cider, bottled porters, various foreign beers and a perry are normally stocked. Gloucestershire CAMRA's 2006 Club of the Year has a no-smoking bar with a games room leading off. Parking is limited, but Stagecoach service B stops nearby.

Jolly Brewmaster

39 Painswick Road, GL50 2EZ
12-11; 12-10.30 Sun
(01242) 772261
Caledonian Deuchars IPA; Greene King IPA; Hook Norton Old Hooky; guest beers H
Featured in CAMRA's Good Cider Guide, this busy pub retains the feel of an old-fashioned local. Built as a coaching inn in 1854, it has retained the distinctive etched windows and two original open fires. The unusual, horseshoe-shaped bar boasts six handpumps, three of which offer changing guest beers. Thatchers medium cider and Westons perry are also sold on draught. Sunday lunch is served and the courtyard barbecue is free to hire – bring your own food. Both smokers and dog owners are welcome here.

Kemble Brewery Inn

27 Fairview Street, GL52 2JF
11.30-2.30 (3 Fri), 5.30-11 (midnight Fri); 11.30-11.30 Sat; 12-4, 7-10.30 Sun
(01242) 243446
Taylor Landlord; Wye Valley Hereford Pale Ale; guest beers H
A small, but deservedly popular back-street local, this former Cheltenham CAMRA Pub of the Year is hard to find but well worth the effort. Six real ales are usually available, often including a local beer. Good value, home-made lunches are served. The first owner came from Kemble and made cider pressed from apples grown in the back garden, now an attractive walled drinking area. Tuesday is quiz night. The pub can become smoky on race days or if near neighbours, Cheltenham Town, are at home.

Royal Oak

43 The Burgage, Prestbury, GL52 3DL
11.30-2.30, 5.30-11 (11.30-11 summer); 12-10.30 Sun
(01242) 522344 royal-oak-prestbury.co.uk
Archers Best Bitter; Taylor Landlord; guest beers H
Handy for the races, this small, popular local in Prestbury already operates a smoking ban in all enclosed spaces. Smokers have to head for the large garden that leads to a skittle alley-cum-function room. The public bar, where snacks are available, features exposed beams, while the lounge serves as a dining room until 9pm. All food is home made and regularly features fresh fish and Cotswold game. Two beer festivals are held annually. Parking is limited, but Stagecoach service A stops nearby.

Sudeley Arms

25 Prestbury Road, GL52 2PN (near Pittville Gates)
11-11; 12-10.30 Sun
(01242) 510697
Goff's Jouster; Taylor Landlord; guest beers H
Built in 1826, this friendly pub is close to Cheltenham Town football ground. Loosely divided into public bar, lounge and snug, it is listed in CAMRA's Good Cider Guide and the Football and Real Ale Guide. Five handpumps are in regular use and Westons cider is always available. Stagecoach service A passes the pub, which is a five minute walk from the town centre. Visiting football fans and racegoers are always well looked after here.

Swan
37 High Street, GL50 1DX
🕘 12-11 (midnight Fri & Sat); 12-10.30 Sun
☎ (01242) 584929
Beer range varies Ⓗ
A cosmopolitan crowd gathers at Cheltenham CAMRA's Pub of the Year 2005 and 2006, where three real ales from micro-breweries are normally stocked, with local brewers featuring regularly. The varied menu offers excellent food at lunchtime and Monday-Thursday evenings. Moles Black Rat cider is usually sold. The large public car park at the rear leads to the courtyard drinking area and no-smoking conservatory. The Swan hosts a Monday quiz, live music and theme nights and exhibits work by local artists. ❀◑●⊬

Cirencester

Corinium Hotel
12 Gloucester Street, GL7 2DG
(off A435 at traffic lights)
🕘 11-11; 12-10.30 Sun
☎ (01285) 659711 🌐 coriniumhotel.co.uk
Fuller's London Pride; Uley Pig's Ear or Laurie Lee's Bitter; guest beer Ⓗ
An understated frontage conceals an agreeable two-star hotel that was originally an Elizabethan wool merchant's house. The charming courtyard entrance leads to a comfortable lounge, opening from a small flagstoned bar. An attractive, comfortable restaurant and pleasant walled garden complete the picture. ❀🛏◑♿P

Twelve Bells
Lewis Lane, GL7 1EA (off A435 roundabout)
🕘 11-3, 5-11; 12-3.30, 6.30-10.30 Sun
☎ (01285) 644549
Beer range varies Ⓗ
Beer drinkers' haven, an old, panelled pub warmed by open fires in all three rooms. The landlord, who has a wry sense of humour, holds court in the lively front bar, but the rear rooms are quieter. Choose from five changing guest beers and an excellent, wide-ranging menu of freshly prepared meals using ingredients from local suppliers. Portions are substantial – abandon all diets ye who enter here! Winner of local CAMRA Pub of the Year 2006. ♨☕❀◑♿▲

Coaley

Fox & Hounds
The Street, GL11 5EG
🕘 12-3 (not Mon or Tue), 7-11; 12-11 Sat; 12-3, 7-10.30 Sun
☎ (01453) 890366
Uley Bitter; guest beers Ⓗ
Situated in an attractive country village, this 300-year-old Cotswold stone free house has one cosy bar with a low, beamed ceiling and a wood-burning stove. The function room houses a skittle alley and dining area, which serves an extensive home-cooked menu at reasonable prices. At the front is a roadside seating area. The pub is famous for its jazz, Irish and Cajun music performed on Saturday and occasionally on Friday. A house beer is brewed by Severn Vale. ♨Q❀◑♣●P

Cranham

Black Horse
GL4 8HP (off A46 or B4070) OS896129
🕘 12-3, 6.30-11; closed Mon;12-3, 8-10.30 Sun
☎ (01452) 812217
Archers Special; Hancock's HB; Whittington's Cats Whiskers; Wickwar BOB; guest beer Ⓗ
A rural gem, approached up a side road in the lower part of Cranham village. Be sure to duck as you enter this genuine free house and beware the landlord's corny humour, honed over 20 years in situ. A log fire is a welcoming sight in the main bar; there is a small lounge and two more rooms upstairs for meals. A blackboard lists country-style, home-cooked dishes and the sandwiches, too, are good value; no food is served on Sunday evening. ♨Q❀◑⊟♣P

Didmarton

King's Arms
The Street, GL9 1DT (on A433) OS818875
🕘 11-3, 6-11; 11-11 Fri-Sun
☎ (01454) 238245
Uley Bitter; guest beers Ⓗ
The low-key frontage belies the warm, welcoming interior of this sympathetically refurbished 17th-century coaching inn. The style and comfort of the pub gradually increase as you progress around the central counter from the hop-strewn games/public bar to the excellent restaurant. The food is imaginative; half portions are available for children. The well-maintained walled garden is an added attraction. ♨❀🛏◑⊟♣P⊬

Doynton

Cross House Inn
High Street, BS30 5TF
(1 mile N of A420, on outskirts of Wick)
🕘 11.30-3, 6-11; 12-4, 6-10.30 Sun
☎ (0117) 937 2261
Bath Gem; Courage Best Bitter; Fuller's London Pride; Greene King Old Speckled Hen; guest beer Ⓗ
This stone inn has played a major part in village life for over 200 years. The large, single room bar has an open fire at one end to keep the chills away and a dartboard at the other. Excellent food is offered in both the main bar and the restaurant, set at a lower level. Beers from the local Cotswold Spring Brewery are sometimes sold here. ♨❀◑♣P

Duntisbourne Abbots

Five Mile House ☆
Old Gloucester Road, GL7 7JR (off A417 at services sign, S of Texaco garage)
🕘 12-3, 6-11; 12-3, 7-11 Sun
☎ (01285) 821432
Beer range varies Ⓗ
Refurbishments of unspoilt pubs with Grade II listed interiors are rarely as successful as this. The tiny bar, virtually unchanged and free of food, leads to a smart dining room that offers a wide choice of excellent food and wines. To the left of the entrance is a small tap room created by two venerable curved settles

around a wood-burning stove; steps lead down to a snug and the converted cellar. The pub usually has three real ales on offer.
⚘Q❀◐◑♣P

Dursley

Old Spot Inn

Hill Road, GL11 4JQ (next to bus station)
☉ 11-11; 12-10.30 Sun
☎ (01453) 542870 ⊕ oldspotinn.co.uk
Uley Old Ric; guest beers Ⓗ
Genuine free house named after the Gloucester Old Spot pig. Sympathetically restored by the owner, Ric, this 100-year-old pub's intimate atmosphere is enhanced by log fires and brewery memorabilia. Three of the five drinking areas are no-smoking. It offers five guest beers, mainly from micro-breweries, and a wholesome menu, served 12-8pm (12-5pm at weekends). A convivial local on the Cotswold Way, the secluded garden has a boules piste. Gloucestershire CAMRA's Pub of the Year 2006 stands opposite a free car park. ⚘Q❀◐◑♣⚟

Filton

Ratepayers Arms

Filton Sports & Leisure Centre, Elm Park, BS34 7PS
(signed from mini-roundabout on A38 by police station)
☉ 6 (12 Sat)-11.30 (11 Mon-Wed); 12-2.30, 7-11 Sun
☎ (01454) 866697
Butcombe Bitter; guest beers Ⓗ
Up to four changing guest beers are available at this pub that is unusual in being part of a sports centre. It is an excellent place to relax with a pint, whether or not you take part in active sport, as you can also watch sport on the big-screen TV. It hosts karaoke on Monday evenings and a monthly charity quiz is usually held on the fourth Sunday. No-smoking throughout, it offers a limited range of bar snacks. ◐◑♿⇌(Abbey Wood)🚌(75, 309)P⚟

Ford

Plough Inn

GL54 5RU (on B4077, 5 miles W of Stow-on-the-Wold)
☉ 11-midnight daily
☎ (01386) 584215 ⊕ theploughinnatford.co.uk
Donnington BB, SBA Ⓗ
This former 16th-century courthouse offers superb Donnington Ales, including the rarely seen XXX Mild during May and June. Horseracing chat is commonplace in the bar areas, with their low, beamed ceilings, flagstone floors and inglenooks. This is hardly surprising as the gallops of trainer Jonjo O'Neill are just across the road. Local CAMRA's Pub of the Year 2004 enjoys a fine reputation for food and has a large beer garden with a play area for children. ⚘❀🛏◐◑♿⛺♣●P

Forthampton

Lower Lode Inn

GL19 4RE OS878317
☉ 12-3 (not winter Mon or Tue), 6-midnight; 12-midnight Sat & Sun
☎ (01684) 293224 ⊕ lowerlodeinn.co.uk
Donnington BB; Goff's Tournament; Hook Norton Old Hooky; Sharp's Doom Bar; guest beers Ⓗ
Standing in three acres of lawned river frontage, looking across the River Severn to Tewkesbury Abbey, this brick-built pub has been licensed since 1590. A popular stop-over for boaters using the public mooring facilities, it has a private slipway on to the river. There is a Camping and Caravan Club hideaway site and day fishing is available. A ferry operates across from Tewkesbury to Lower Lode's picnic area (April-Oct); the approach roads are liable to winter flooding.
⚘Q☙❀🛏◐◑♿⛺♣P⚟

Frampton Cotterell

Rising Sun

43 Ryecroft Road, BS36 2HN
☉ 11.30-3.30, 5.30-11.30; 11.30-11.30 Fri & Sat; 12-11 Sun
☎ (01454) 772330
Draught Bass; Butcombe Bitter; Sharp's Doom Bar; Wadworth 6X; Wickwar Coopers WPA; guest beers Ⓗ
Three-roomed free house that usually stocks five or six real ales, with the accent on local breweries. The main bar has flagstoned floors and displays prints of the locality. The conservatory doubles as a no-smoking restaurant, while at present the upper rear level is a dining area for smokers. Children are welcome until 8.30pm. Cribbage and skittles are played here. The pub occasionally stays open until 1am. There is a limited bus service. ☙❀◐◑🚌♣P⚟

France Lynch

King's Head

GL6 8LT
☉ 12-3, 6-11; 12-11 Sun
☎ (01453) 882225
Taylor Landlord; Young's Bitter; guest beers Ⓗ
Friendly, single-bar pub, hidden away at the heart of a village of winding lanes, but well worth finding. The village name implies Huguenot connections; French and Flemish weavers came to this wool-rich part of the Cotswolds in search of work. The pleasant garden has a safe play area for children and a crèche is provided on Friday evening (7-9pm). Live music is performed on Monday evening – jazz, blues and folk. No food is served Sunday evening.
⚘Q☙❀◐◑♣P

Frocester

George Inn

Peter Street, GL10 3TQ
☉ 11.30-2.30, 5-11; 11-11 Fri & Sat; 12-10.30 Sun
☎ (01453) 822302 ⊕ georgeinn.co.uk
Black Sheep Best Bitter; Caledonian Deuchars IPA Ⓗ
Warm and friendly village pub where the home-cooked food is based on local produce. The George, at the foot of Frocester Hill, has been dispensing hospitality since the early 18th century, when it was a coaching inn serving the route between Gloucester and Bath. Once called the Royal Gloucestershire Hussars, it was renamed in 1998. It serves at

least two guest beers that change often and Westons Old Rosie cider. It hosts the occasional mini beer festival.
♨Q❀⇆◑⊟♣●P⚟

Gloucester

Dick Whittington

100 Westgate Street, GL1 2PE
⏲ 10-midnight; 12-midnight Sun
☎ (01452) 502039
Mighty Oak Oscar Wilde; St Austell Tribute; Sharp's Doom Bar; Wells Bombardier; guest beers 🄷
Behind an imposing Georgian frontage is a 14th-century building that was the Whittington family's town house from 1311 to 1546. It was converted to an ale house in the 1980s, but the current owner has created a more contemporary ambience. Home-cooked food is served 10am-10pm Tuesday-Saturday and Sunday lunches get heavily booked. Four guest beers mainly come from local brewers, including Bath Ales. It won local CAMRA's Pub of the Year award in 2005 and 2006. Q❀◑⇌

Fountain Inn

53 Westgate Street, GL1 2NW
⏲ 10.30-11 (midnight Fri & Sat); 12-11 Sun
☎ (01452) 522562 🌐 fountainglos.co.uk
Caledonian Deuchars IPA; Fuller's London Pride; Greene King Abbot; Wickwar BOB; guest beer 🄷
Records suggest that ale has been served on this site since 1216, although the present pub dates from the 17th century. The single, L-shaped bar, with its carved stone fireplace is warm and welcoming, while the overflow Orange Room is smart and modern. The large courtyard, with its colourful display of flowers, is usually packed in summer. An eclectic mix of dishes cooked to order is available throughout the day (except winter Sun eve). The cider is Westons Traditional Scrumpy. Q❀◑♿⇌♣●⚟

Linden Tree

73-75 Bristol Road, GL1 5SN (on A430, S of docks)
⏲ 11.30-2.30, 6-11; 11.30-11 Sat; 12-10.30 Sun
☎ (01452) 527869
Wadworth IPA, 6X, JCB, seasonal beers; 🄷 **guest beers** 🄶
The stark external appearance gives no indication of the smart yet homely bar within this popular community pub. Heavy stools line the bar, with a mix of tables and chairs at either end, while a small lounge area is almost hidden behind the open log fire. The skittles extension opens up for extra space when needed. Eight real ales are the norm, with guests coming mainly from family brewers. Substantial home-cooked meals (not served Sat or Sun eves) and bargain accommodation complete the picture. ♨Q❀⇆◑⊟♣

New Inn

16 Northgate Street, GL1 1SF
⏲ 11-11 (1am Thu; 2.30am Fri & Sat); 12-10.30 Sun
☎ (01452) 522177 🌐 newinnglos.com
Beer range varies 🄷
Shakespeare probably acted in the courtyard of this Grade I listed, galleried inn that dates from 1455 – occasionally visiting players still perform here. It comprises a coffee shop, restaurant, Regency function room and a rear bar, providing night club style entertainment at weekends. The main bar offers up to eight real ales from local craft brewers as well as Palmer, RCH and Sarah Hughes; the cider is Westons Old Rosie. The guest accommodation has been refurbished and special weekend rates apply to CAMRA members.
❀⇆◑⇌♣●

Gretton

Royal Oak

GL54 5EP (1½ miles from Winchcombe)
⏲ 12-3, 6-11; 12-4, 7-10.30 Sun
☎ (01242) 604999
Goff's Jouster; Hop Back Summer Lightning; guest beers 🄷
Deservedly popular Cotswold pub, where the family owners pride themselves on knowing their customers individually and what they like to drink. Supporters of Gloucestershire breweries, they often showcase guest ales from Donnington, Goff's or Wickwar. Home-cooked food can be enjoyed in the conservatory that affords outstanding views across the vale. A beer and music festival is held in July. Steam trains on the Gloucestershire Warwickshire Railway pass the end of the garden. ♨Q❀◑♣P

Ham

Salutation

Ham Green, GL13 9QH (from Berkeley take road signed to Jenner Museum) OS681984
⏲ 12-2.30 (not Mon) 5-11; 11-11 Sat; 12-10.30 Sun
☎ (01453) 810284
Eagles Bush Kestrel, Golden Eagle; guest beers 🄷
Country pub in the Severn Valley, within walking distance of Berkeley Castle and the Jenner Museum. This brew-pub is frequented by friendly locals. Three guest beers are sourced from micro-breweries, two ciders come from Gwatkin and it also stocks the occasional perry. The three bar areas include a no-smoking dining room that serves traditional home-cooked food. The pub is popular with walkers and its garden is safe for children. Q❀◐⊟♣●P⚟

Hawkesbury Upton

Beaufort Arms

High Street, GL9 1AU (on A46, 6 miles N of M4 jct 18)
⏲ 12-11; 12-10.30 Sun
☎ (01454) 238217 🌐 beaufortarms.com
Wickwar BOB; guest beers 🄷
Cotswold stone, two-bar pub, frequented by locals and passing customers. The main bar boasts two ancient dentist's chairs and a collection of brewery and local memorabilia. The no-smoking dining area serves good value food and displays paintings by local artists for sale. Added attractions include a skittle alley/function room and an attractive garden, featuring a six-foot wood carving of a silver yale (mythical beast). A frequent local CAMRA Pub of the Year, it won the Gloucestershire award in 2004.
♨Q☕❀◑⊟♿♣●P⚟

Leighterton

Royal Oak

The Street, GL8 8UN (off A46)

✪ 11-3, 6-midnight; 12-3.30, 7-midnight Sun

☎ (01666) 390250

Sharp's Doom Bar; Wickwar BOB; guest beers 🄷

This 300-year-old village hostelry serves the portion of the population that is resistant to gastropubs. Although now opened up into a single bar, massive columns break up the space into more intimate areas. Meals are served in a separate dining area. The four real ales and the standard pub fare all represent good value, making the Royal Oak well worth finding.

ᗑ❀◑◐♿♣P

Littleton-on-Severn

White Hart

High Street, BS35 1NR (signed from B4461)

✪ 12-2.30, 6-11; 12-11 Sat & Sun

☎ (01454) 412275

Young's Bitter, Special, seasonal beers; guest beers 🄷

Originally a farmhouse dating back to the late 17th century, this country inn is characterised by low ceilings, oak beams, flagstone floors and inglenooks. The interior boasts many nooks and crannies – try a crawl through the various drinking areas off the main bar. A sunny patio and large front garden add to its appeal. Child friendly, it is surrounded by countryside and benefits from views over the Severn estuary. En-suite accommodation is in a converted barn.

ᗑQ♘❀🛏◑◐🀫♣P⊬

Longford

Queen's Head

84 Tewkesbury Road, GL2 9EJ (on A38 N of A40 jct)

✪ 11-3 (2.30 Mon & Tue), 5.30 (6 Sat)-11; 12-3, 7-10.30 Sun

☎ (01452) 301882

Ringwood Best Bitter; Sharp's Doom Bar; Stonehenge Pigswill; Taylor Landlord; Wye Valley Butty Bach 🄷

Bedecked with flower baskets all summer, this 18th-century free house attracts business people and local residents. The public bar features a stone-flagged floor and a smart array of sporting pictures. The lounge is smoke-free and has two distinct dining areas set back from the bar. The award-winning food is extremely popular and evening booking is strongly recommended. No children are admitted. CAMRA's Gloucester area Country Pub of the Year 2006 sells Moles Black Rat cider.

◑◐🀫🚌🍎P⊬

Marshfield

Catherine Wheel

High Street, SN14 8LR

✪ 12-3, 5.30-11; 12-11 Sat; 12-10.30 Sun

☎ (01225) 892220

Abbey Bellringer; guest beers 🄷

Beautifully restored Georgian pub on the village High Street with a pretty dining room. The extensive main bar leads down from the original wood-panelled area, via stone-walled rooms to the cosy patio garden at the rear. In winter there is a superb open fire to warm your feet at. The pub usually has three guest beers to choose from. Food, served in the bar or garden, is imaginative and well presented (no lunches Mon or eve meals Sun).

ᗑQ❀🛏◑◐P

May Hill

Glasshouse

GL17 0NN (off A40 W of Huntley) OS710213

✪ 11.30-3, 6.30-11; 12-3, 7-10.30 Sun

☎ (01452) 830529

Draught Bass; Butcombe Bitter; guest beers 🄷

Delightful old pub, sympathetically extended using reclaimed timbers and stone to blend in with the original building. Divided into three bars, exuding charm and character, one houses an old, black-leaded range, and another a roaring log fire. Low, beamed ceilings, flagstone floors and nooks and crannies all add to the cosy atmosphere. A historic yew hedge with a seat makes a lovely focal point in the garden. The food here is recommended.

ᗑQ❀◑◐🍎P

Mayshill

New Inn

Badminton Road, BS36 2NT

(on A432, between Coalpit Heath and Nibley)

✪ 11.45-2.30, 5.30-11; 12-11 Sat; 12-10.30 Sun

☎ (01454) 773161

Draught Bass; guest beers 🄷

Superb 17th-century roadside inn, where the original parts date back to 1550. Three guest beers that change regularly are sourced from breweries near and far. Carpeted and cosy throughout, the front bar is warmed by a real fire in winter, while the main bar area features settles and window seats. Booking is recommended for the good food, which is served all day at the weekend; children are welcome until 8.45pm. Bus Nos. X42, 342 and 581 stop right outside.

ᗑ❀◑◐🚌P

Moreton-in-Marsh

Inn on the Marsh

Stow Road, GL56 0DW (on A429, S end of town)

✪ 12-2.30, 7-11; 11-3, 6-11 Fri, Sat & summer; 12-3, 7-10.30 Sun

☎ (01608) 650709

Banks's Original; Marston's Burton Bitter, Pedigree; guest beer 🄷

This charming pub is a rare house in the area for the Wolverhampton & Dudley Brewery. A former bakery, baskets hanging from the rafters are a reminder of Moreton's basket weaving history. The main area features comfortable armchairs, old photographs and hanging hops. Food, served in the conservatory, has a Dutch East Indies influence; you can also try the Dutch game of Schoolen. The landlord, now in his 10th year here, always offers an interesting guest.

Q❀◑◐♿⛺🚆♣P⊬

Nailsworth

George Inn

Newmarket, GL6 0RF

11-3, 6.30-11; 12-3, 7-11 Sun

☎ (01453) 833228

Moles Tap Bitter; Taylor Landlord; Uley Bitter, Old Spot 🄷

Village local, looking south over the valley above Nailsworth. The George is a 15-minute walk from the Forest Green Rovers ground. Three chimneys confirm that the inn was originally three cottages, becoming a pub in 1820 and renamed in 1910 to honour the incoming King George V. The food is renowned and can be eaten in the small restaurant or in the bar (booking is advisable).

Q❀◑▶P

Naunton

Black Horse

GL54 3AD (off B4068) OS119234

11-3, 6-11; 11-11 Sat; 12-10.30 Sun

☎ (01451) 850565

Donnington BB, SBA 🄷

Traditional Cotswold stone village inn replete with black beams, stripped stonework, flagstone flooring, wooden settles and cast iron framed tables. The pub sign shows a black horse with unusually positioned legs! Home-cooked food is served in the old snug (no eve meals Sun or Mon in winter). Unspoilt Naunton boasts a magnificent 16th-century dovecote and an old mill that can be discovered on the Black Horse walk – pick up a leaflet in the pub. Dogs are welcome here.

Q❀⇌◑▶♿▲♣P

Nettleton Bottom

Golden Heart

GL4 8LA (on A417)

11-3, 5.30-11; 11-11 Fri & Sat; 12-10.30 Sun

☎ (01242) 870261

Marston's Pedigree; Taylor Golden Best; guest beers 🄷

The 300-year-old free house may stand almost alone beside a very busy (and dangerous) section of single carriageway road, but inside bucolic peace reigns supreme. The small bar is hidden beyond a huge open fireplace and overlooks a patio and garden that lead to cow pastures. Only highest quality meats are used for the pub's national prize winning meals (served all day Sun). Guest beers come from local craft brewers and an adventurous beer festival is held over August bank holiday weekend.

⛫Q❀⇌◑▶P⊭

Newent

George

Church Street, GL18 1PU (off B4215 and B4216)

11-11; 12-10.30 Sun

☎ (01531) 820203 georgehotel.uk.com

Hancock's HB; Whittington's Cats Whiskers; guest beers 🄷

Lively, town-centre hotel bar with a central serving area and seating. It is quiet at the front while a dartboard, fruit machines and TV screens are provided at the rear. The restaurant is reached by a corridor behind the bar (no food Sun eve). A games room above the restaurant has snooker and table football. There is a large patio in the courtyard of this former coaching inn. A beer festival takes place during Newent Onion Fair in September.

⛫❀⇌◑▶♣P

North Cerney

Bathurst Arms

GL7 7BZ OS019079

12-3, 6-11; 12-3, 7-10.30 Sun

☎ (01285) 831281

Hook Norton Hooky Bitter; Wickwar Cotswold Way; guest beer 🄷

Enterprising, 17th-century village pub with flagstone floors and a stove in an inglenook. It offers everything you would expect from a Cotswold pub – even the tiny River Churn runs through the garden. Excellent food is served in both the bar and the smart restaurant. The kitchen also cooks the lunches for the village primary school (Jamie Oliver would be impressed). The accommodation is recommended.

⛫❀⇌◑▶P

Old Down

Fox

The Inner Down, BS32 4PR (1½ miles from A38)

12-3, 6-11 daily

☎ (01454) 412507

Draught Bass; Flowers IPA; Moles Best Bitter; Sharp's Doom Bar; guest beers 🄷

This welcoming, 18th-century pub is well respected for its beers, with one or two guests including a local brew usually on sale. Moles Black Rat cider is also stocked. Smartly furnished, it has low ceilings and exposed beams. The family room at the back of the pub is no-smoking. Food is popular and bookings are taken for weekend meals (no eve meals Sun). Live music is performed sometimes on Saturday evenings and the pub may stay open longer at the weekend.

⛫ᗢ❀◑▶♣●P⊭

Oldbury on Severn

Anchor Inn

Church Road, BS35 1QA

11.30-2.30, 6.30-11; 11.30-11 Sat; 12-10.30 Sun

☎ (01454) 413331

Draught Bass; Butcombe Bitter; Otter Bitter; Theakston Old Peculier; guest beer 🄷

Converted riverside mill, the main bar is L-shaped with a beamed ceiling, open fire and settles. The public bar is smaller, displaying local photographs. The guest ale changes every Thursday, but the accent here is on food, with a varied menu to choose from; children are welcome in the dining room at the rear of the building. The large rear garden is safely fenced and has a boules piste at the end. A footpath leads to the River Severn.

⛫Q❀◑▶⊟♿♣P

Sheepscombe

Butcher's Arms

GL6 7RH (signed from A46/B4070) OS892104
⊙ 11.30-3, 6.30 (6 Fri & Sat)-11.30; 12-11 Sun
☎ (01452) 812113 ⊕ cotswoldinns.co.uk
Moles Tap Bitter; Otter Ale; Wye Valley Bitter, seasonal beers Ⓗ
Cosy, 17th-century village pub and restaurant cooking fresh produce. It is part of Blenheim Inns, a privately-owned company that breathes life into tired pubs. Quoits is played here. The pub sign of a butcher supping ale with a pig tied to his leg is probably the most photographed in the country. It is thought that butchering went on here when Henry VIII hunted deer in Sheepscombe Valley. On Sunday meals are served all day.
♨Q❀◐◑♣P⊬⊓

Slimbridge

Tudor Arms

Shepherd's Patch, GL2 7BP
(from A38 1 mile beyond Slimbridge village)
⊙ 11-11; 12-10.30 Sun
☎ (01453) 890306
Uley Pig's Ear; Wadworth 6X; guest beers Ⓗ
Family-operated free house that draws much of its custom from canal users and visitors to the famous Wildfowl and Wetlands Trust site. Recent improvements to the premises include a new kitchen and dining room. The modern lodge alongside offers accommodation, while a separately owned caravan and camping site is immediately to the rear. Home-cooked food is served all day in summer. Three guest beers come mainly from local craft brewers, while the cider is Moles Black Rat.
❀⇔◐◑♿⛺♣●P⊬

Staple Hill

Humpers Off-Licence

26 Soundwell Road, BS16 4QW (on A4017)
⊙ 12-2, 5-10.30 daily (12-10.30 summer Sat & Sun)
☎ (0117) 956 5525
Butcombe Bitter, Gold; RCH Pitchfork; guest beers Ⓗ
Independent offie selling up to three guest beers where prices are extremely reasonable. Cider drinkers are also well catered for, with up to three to choose from. It also stocks an expansive range of bottled beers, many bottle-conditioned. Bring your own container or buy one here. A wide selection of polypins is stocked in December. This is very much a local institution. ●

Stow-on-the-Wold

Queen's Head

The Square, GL54 1AB
⊙ 11-11; 12-10.30 Sun
☎ (01451) 830563
Donnington BB, SBA Ⓗ
Centrally located in the main square, this Donnington house is a near-perfect example of a Cotswold town pub, virtually unchanged since the 17th century. It attracts locals and tourists alike – and welcomes dogs. The two bars are adorned with interesting pictures and artefacts, while flowers on the tables throughout are a nice touch. Although the pub has no car park of its own there is plenty of space in the square where there is also a bus stop. Q❀◐◑🚌⊬

Stratton

Drillman's Arms

34 Gloucester Road, GL7 2JY (on old A417, N of A435 jct)
⊙ 11-2.30, 5.30-11; 11-11 Sat; 12-4, 7-11 Sun
☎ (01285) 653892
Archers Best Bitter; Sharp's Doom Bar; guest beers Ⓗ
Do not be put off by the obtrusive fruit machines in the lounge. The low, beamed ceilings, open fires, horse brasses, brewery pictures and four real ales more than compensate and give this popular old local a welcoming atmosphere. Reasonably priced standard pub fare is served but evening meals must be booked in advance. A small beer festival is staged on August bank holiday. Tables at the front of the pub allow for outside drinking in summer. Parking is limited. ♨❀◐◑♣P

Stroud

Golden Fleece

Nelson Street, GL5 2HN
⊙ 12-3, 5-11; 12-midnight Fri & Sat; 12-11 Sun
☎ (01453) 764850
Badger Tanglefoot; Caledonian Deuchars IPA; Fuller's London Pride; Hook Norton Old Hooky; guest beers Ⓗ
The single bar has two alcoves decorated with musical instruments and jazz memorabilia; live music is performed on Thursday. Open fires and a south-facing walled garden are added attractions at this homely pub. Meals are served only on Sunday lunchtime. The nearest public car park is only 50 yards away and charges do not apply after 6pm.
♨❀⇌♣

Queen Victoria

5 Gloucester Street, GL5 1DG
⊙ 11-11 (later Fri & Sat); 12-10.30 Sun
☎ (01453) 762396
Beer range varies Ⓗ
This imposing building formerly housed the Gloucester Street forge and records show that it was owned by the Nailsworth Brewery in 1891. The large, single bar offers a constantly-changing range of at least four real ales. This community pub fields quiz, darts and pool teams in local leagues. The spacious function room hosts beer festivals at least once a year and live music on Thursday, Friday and Saturday evenings. ♨❀⇌♣

Tewkesbury

Berkeley Arms

8 Church Street, GL20 5PA
⊙ 11.30-3, 5-11; 11-11 Fri & Sat; 12-4, 7-10.30 Sun
☎ (01684) 293034
Wadworth IPA, 6X, JCB; guest beers Ⓗ

Superb, 15th-century, half-timbered Grade II listed building. The public bar entrance is on the street, while the lounge is accessed via one of Tewkesbury's many alleyways at the rear. A barn, believed to be the oldest non-ecclesiastical building in this historic town, is used for dining in summer. Good value food includes specials (no meals Mon). Live music is performed on Saturday evening at Tewkesbury CAMRA's Pub of the Year 2006.
Q◑◗⊟⛺🚌(41, 71)♣

White Bear

Bredon Road, GL20 5BU (N of High St)
⏲ 10-midnight daily
☎ (01684) 296614
Beer range varies Ⓗ
On the edge of the town centre, this good value, family-run lively pub attracts a varied clientele and can be noisy on busy evenings. The single L-shaped bar houses a dartboard and pool table. The three guest beers change often and include many from smaller and local breweries. Near Tewkesbury Marina, the pub is popular with river users. Crib, darts, skittles and pool teams compete in local leagues. Live music is often performed on Sunday.
❀⛺🚌(41, 71)♣🍎P⊍

Tormarton

Portcullis

High Street, GL9 1HZ (close to M4 jct 18)
⏲ 12-3, 6-11; 12-3, 7-10.30 Sun
☎ (01454) 218263
Butcombe Gold; Otter Bitter; Uley Pig's Ear; guest beers Ⓗ
The focal point of the village, built in the 1700s, the modest virginia creeper-covered frontage belies its spacious, unassuming main bar, frequented by locals. The friendly landlord extends a warm welcome to all, and takes pride in his fine selection of beers from micro-breweries. The oak-panelled restaurant provides freshly cooked meals at reasonable prices; evening meals are served Monday-Friday.
♛Q❀🛏◑◗♣P

Waterley Bottom

New Inn

GL11 6EF (signed from North Nibley; OS map recommended) OS758964
⏲ 12-2.30 (not Mon), 6-11; 12-11 Sat; 12-10.30 Sun
☎ (01453) 543659
Cotleigh Tawny; Wye Valley Hereford Pale Ale, Butty Bach; guest beers Ⓗ
Free house, nestling in a tiny hamlet in a scenic valley surrounded by steep hills. During the 19th century it was a cider house frequented by mill workers taking the footpath to Dursley. It has a cosy lounge/dining area with a pair of ancient beer engines on display and a small public bar. The child-friendly garden has a terraced, decked area with a pool table. It offers an imaginative menu (not Mon) and en-suite accommodation. Thatchers and Westons cider are sold.
♛Q❀🛏◑◗⊟♣🍎P

Whitecroft

Miners Arms

The Bay, GL15 4PE
(on B4234, near railway crossing) OS619062
⏲ 12-11; 12-10.30 Sun
☎ (01594) 562483 🌐 minersarms.org
Holden's Bitter; guest beers Ⓗ
This traditional free house is the hub of its community and has been restored to a good standard. The skittle alley doubles as a blues venue once a month; quoits is played in the bar and boules in one of the gardens. The back garden is safe for children. Steam trains on the Dean Forest Railway line stop at the station behind the pub. Offering four real ales, four draught ciders and a occasional guest perry, the Miners Arms was voted CAMRA Cider and Perry Pub of the Year in 2005.
♛❀⊟♿⛺⇌(Dean Forest Rlwy)♣🍎P

Whitminster

Old Forge Inn

GL2 7NP (on A38, near M5 jct 13)
⏲ 12-11 (may be midnight Thu-Sat); 12-10.30 Sun
☎ (01452) 741306
Black Sheep Best Bitter; Butcombe Bitter; Greene King IPA; guest beer Ⓗ
Largely timber framed, 16th-century building, bearing an odd mix of windows. It was a pub even before it became a forge – see the swan sign at the door. A short bar serves two rooms – one is favoured for food, which is served all day at the weekend. The menu includes a children's section and daily specials. A homely atmosphere is enhanced by the lively landlady, her aquarium and her decor. In summer outdoor games, including chess, are played on the patio. Q❀◑◗⛺♣P

Winchcombe

Corner Cupboard Inn

83 Gloucester Street, GL54 5LX (on B4632, S end of town)
⏲ 11-11; 12-10.30 Sun
☎ (01242) 602303 🌐 cornercupboard.co.uk
Greene King IPA; Stanway Stanney Bitter; guest beer Ⓗ
This former 16th-century farmhouse, built using stones from Winchcombe Abbey ruins, is now a traditional Cotswold pub with a small smoke room and a back lounge, replete with heavy beams, stripped stone and an inglenook. Note the two old corner cupboards that gave the pub its name. Local Stanney Bitter is a favourite with locals and visitors alike. A sign on the floor records that 'Gwen Marshall slipped here 1962'! Buses from Cheltenham stop outside, but only at lunchtime. ♛Q❀◑◗⊟♿🚌♣P🚭

Winterbourne Down

Cross Hands Inn

85 Down Road, BS36 1BZ (on road from Winterbourne to Badminton Road)
⏲ 12 (11 Sat)-11 daily
☎ (01454) 850077
Courage Best Bitter; guest beers Ⓗ
Friendly, stone-built village free house,

dating back to the 17th century. The main bar is spacious and airy, with a snug and an alcove dedicated to traditional games. Note the interesting array of old sewing machines. The pub welcomes dogs and there is a large garden at the rear. It now offers four guest beers that change often; the cider is from Taunton. Unfortunately, there is no local bus service and parking is limited.
♔🚂❀♣●

Withington

King's Head

King's Head Lane, GL54 4BD (off Yanworth Road, SE of village) OS036153

⏲ 11-2.30, 6-11; 12-3, 7-10.30 Sun

☎ (01242) 890216

Hook Norton Hooky Bitter; Wickwar Cotswold Way, seasonal beers ⊞

It is well worth the effort to find this unspoilt village local. The pub has been run by the same family for nearly 100 years and is a true free house, full of interesting photographs. Food is not normally available. This stone-built pub is popular with walkers, cyclists and visitors to the nearby NT property of Chedworth Villa. Children are allowed in the lounge anteroom. Nine men's morris and quoits are played here. Westons cider is stocked. ♔Q❀⊟♣●P

Woodchester

Ram Inn

Station Road, GL5 5EQ (signed from A46)

⏲ 11-11; 12-10.30 Sun

☎ (01453) 873329

Archers Village; Otter Ale; Uley Old Spot; Whittington's Nine Lives; guest beers ⊞

The Ram is more than 400 years old and stands in superb walking country near Woodchester Mansion. A recently completed extension has provided new toilet facilities and wheelchair access. This is a dog-friendly village pub that stocks an excellent range of beers, mostly from local producers. The food is highly recommended, too.
♔Q❀◑♿♣P🚭

Woolaston Common

Rising Sun

GL15 6NU (1 mile off A48 at Woolaston) OS590009

⏲ 12-2.30 (not Wed), 6.30-11; 12-3, 7-10.30 Sun

☎ (01594) 529282

Fuller's London Pride; Wye Valley Bitter; guest beer ⊞

Lovely 350-year-old country pub affording spectacular views over the Forest of Dean. The landlord, who has been here for 28 years, has made sympathetic improvements during that time. The pub now comprises a large main bar and a cosy snug. It features in the circular pub walks of the Forest of Dean and is popular with ramblers. All visitors are assured of a friendly welcome and a varied menu of good, home-cooked food (no meals Wed). Q❀◑P

Wotton Under Edge

Falcon

Church Street, GL12 7HB (foot of one-way high st)

⏲ 11-11; 12-10.30 Sun

☎ (01453) 521005 🌐 easywell.co.uk/falcon/

Bath SPA; Sharp's Cornish Coaster; Theakston Old Peculier; guest beers ⊞

This 17th-century listed inn on the Cotswold Way was sympathetically restored in 2002 and enjoys a good reputation for the quality of its real ales and cider. The public and lounge bars have wood-burning stoves for a cosy atmosphere. Food can be enjoyed in no-smoking areas at lunchtime and in the evenings. Live music is performed occasionally. A minimum of four real ales including two guests is stocked at all times.
♔Q◑⊟♿♣●🚭

Beers suitable for vegetarians and vegans

Isinglass

A number of cask and bottle-fermented beers in the Good Beer Guide are listed as 'suitable for vegetarians and vegans'. The main ingredients used in cask beer production are malted grain, hops, yeast and water, and these present no problems for drinkers who wish to avoid animal products. But most brewers of cask beer use isinglass as a clearing agent: isinglass is derived from the bladders of certain fish, including the sturgeon. Isinglass is added to a cask when it leaves the brewery and attracts yeast cells and protein, which fall to the bottom of the container. Other clearing agents – notably Irish moss, derived from seaweed – can be used in place of isinglass and the guide feels that brewers should take a serious look at replacing isinglass with plant-derived finings, especially as the sturgeon is an endangered species. Vegans avoid dairy products: lactose, a bi-product of cheese making, is used in milk stout, of which Mackeson is the best-known example.

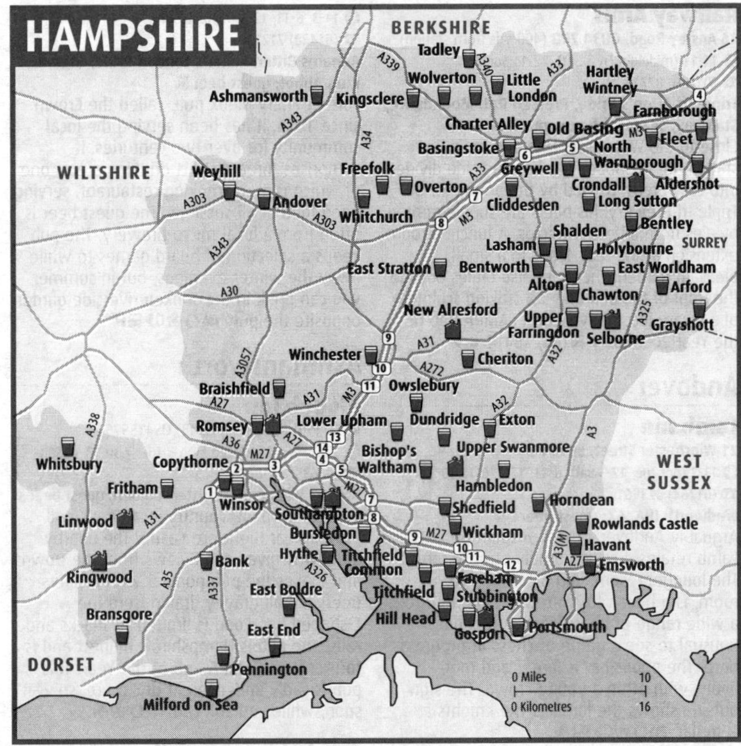

Gale's Brewery has been bought and closed by Fuller's. The beers are now brewed in London.

Aldershot

Garden Gate

4 Church Lane East, GU11 3BT (S edge of town)
12-3 (not Mon), 5.30 (5 Mon)-11; 12-11 Fri & Sat; 12-10.30 Sun
☎ (01252) 321051
Greene King IPA, Abbot, seasonal beers H
Originally built to serve German soldiers during the reign of Queen Victoria, this former two-bar pub has been carefully converted. Bench seating, wood-panelled walls and half-frosted bay windows number among its attractive features. Thursday is quiz night and the pub hosts live bluegrass music monthly (third Mon).

Royal Staff

37A Mount Pleasant Road, GU12 4NN
12-3, 5-midnight (1am Fri); 12-1am Sat; 12-11 Sun
☎ (01252) 408012
Fuller's London Pride, seasonal beers H
At the top of a steep hill, overlooking Aldershot's football ground, this pub mostly caters for local drinkers. The L-shaped bar boasts etched windows and ornate glass lampshades. The TV is often tuned to football. The pub hosts a popular meat draw and a quiz on Sunday. Fuller's beer festivals are enthusiastically supported and other Fuller's regular beers can sometimes be found on the bar.

Alton

Eight Bells

33 Church Street, GU34 2DA
11-11; 12-10.30 Sun
☎ (01420) 82417
Ballard's Midhurst Mild, Best Bitter; guest beers H
Excellent free house, just outside the town centre on the old Alton to Odiham turnpike. The building dates from 1640 and is steeped in history. Opposite stands the ancient St Lawrence Church, around which the Civil War battle of Alton was fought. The pub has one small, oak-beamed bar with a further drinking area at the rear and a bijou garden, housing a well. Hearty, filled rolls will help keep hunger pangs at bay. Q ♣

King's Head

Market Street, GU34 1HA
10 (11 Wed & Thu)-11; 12-10.30 Sun
☎ (01420) 82313
Courage Best Bitter; guest beer H
Popular, market town free house, retaining its two-bar layout, that has been run by the same family for 20 years. The regular Courage Best – a reminder of Alton's brewing history – is complemented by a changing guest. The pub has a policy of supporting local breweries and welcomes recommendations from customers, so you can always be sure of a good pint here. The pub regularly participates in local charity and sporting events. No food is served Sunday.
Q ♣

Railway Arms

26 Anstey Road, GU34 2RB (400 yds from station)
⏲ 11-11 (midnight Fri & Sat); 12-11 Sun
☎ (01420) 82218
Triple fff Alton's Pride, Pressed Rat, Moondance, Stairway, seasonal beers; guest beers [H]
Close to the Watercress Line and main line station, the U-shaped bar has one side divided into cosy areas. Owned by the proprietor of Triple fff Brewery, his beers are supplemented by ales from a host of micros. A function room extension at the rear, leads to a small, pleasant garden. There are also tables outside the front of the pub under a striking sculpture of a steam locomotive. Local CAMRA Pub of the Year 2006. ❀ ≉ 🚌 (64, X64) ♣ ● ⚟

Andover

Lamb Inn

21 Winchester Street, SP10 2EA
⏲ 11-3 (not Tue; 12-3 Sat), 6-11; 12-3, 6-10.30 Sun
☎ (01264) 323961
Wadworth IPA, 6X; guest beers [H]
Arguably Andover's most unspoilt pub, the Lamb retains a cosy, homely atmosphere. The lounge, resembling a cottage sitting room, is a haven for conversation and offers a wide range of board games; it is not unusual to see a game of chess in progress here. The public bar is larger and more lively, with often a young crowd. The sign outside shows the lamb of the Knights Templar. ♨ Q ❀ ◑ ⊟ ♣

Wyke Down Country Pub & Restaurant

Picket Piece, SP11 6LK (follow signs for Wyke from A303)
⏲ 11-2.30, 6-11; 11-2.30, 6-10.30 Sun
☎ (01264) 352048 🌐 wykedown.co.uk
Exmoor Ale; guest beers [H]
This spacious country pub is based around an extended, beamed barn in which many old agricultural implements are displayed. The large restaurant draws customers from a wide area and is also used for functions. A comfortable conservatory and adjacent games rooms complete the facilities in the main building. Outside there is a campsite, children's play area, golf driving range and a swimming pool. Several annual events take place in the grounds. ☋ ❀ ◑ Å ♣ P ⚟

Arford

Crown

Arford Road, GU35 8BT (200 yds N of B3002) OS826365
⏲ 11-3, 6-11; 12-3, 7-10.30 Sun
☎ (01428) 712150
Adnams Bitter; Fuller's London Pride; Greene King Abbot; guest beer [H]
Former Friary Meux pub, called the Crown since 1876, it has been serving the local community for over two centuries. It comprises three distinct drinking areas, one of which is a no-smoking restaurant, serving good food at all sessions. The guest beer is often from a local micro-brewery. The pub keeps a selection of board games to while away the winter evenings, but in summer you can drink in the sunken riverside garden opposite the pub. ♨ Q ❀ ◑ 🚌 P

INDEPENDENT BREWERIES

Crondall Crondall
Hampshire Romsey
Itchen Valley New Alresford
Oakleaf Gosport
Red Shoot Linwood
Ringwood Ringwood
Stumpy's Upper Swanmore
Triple fff Selborne
White Star Southampton
Winchester Southampton

Ashmansworth

Plough Inn

RG20 9PU (1 mile off A343) OS415575
⏲ 12-2.30, 6-11; closed Mon & Tue; 7.30-10.30 Sun
☎ (01635) 253047
Archers Village, Best Bitter, Golden; guest beer [G]
Superb, unspoilt, country local in a small village near Highclere Castle. The nearby Ridgeway gives good views from the Downs and makes the pub popular with walkers. Beers are all gravity drawn from the L-shaped bar. Food is limited to snacks and rolls. The pub is Hampshire's highest and is a former local CAMRA Pub of the Year. This pub is sadly under threat of closure, so visit soon, while you still can. ♨ Q ❀ ♣

Bank (near Lyndhurst)

Oak Inn

Pinkney Lane, SO43 7FE
(off A35, 1¼ miles W of Lyndhurst) OS287072
⏲ 11-3, 6-11; 11-11 Sat & summer; 12-10.30 Sun
☎ (023) 8028 2350 🌐 oakinn.co.uk
Hop Back Summer Lightning; Ringwood Best Bitter; guest beers [P]
This completely no-smoking, 18th-century pub in a New Forest hamlet is a world apart from the busy A35 nearby. One of the treasures of the rustic, L-shaped bar is the fireplace decorated with Minton tiles showing Shakespearean scenes that came from the home of Alice Liddle (Alice in Wonderland). Small breweries are well represented, particularly during the two annual beer festivals in early July and December. Excellent food is served (all day Sun) with seafood from Poole and Selsey a speciality. ♨ ❀ ◑ 🚌 P ⚟

Basingstoke

Basingstoke & North Hants Cricket Club

Fairfields Road, RG21 3DR
⏲ 12-3, 5-11; 12-11 Fri & Sat; 12-10.30 Sun
☎ (01256) 331646 🌐 basingstoke-sports-club.co.uk
Adnams Bitter; Fuller's Discovery, London Pride; Greene King IPA; Ringwood Best Bitter; guest beers [H]
The club was founded by Colonel John May, owner of May's Brewery, which ceased brewing in the late 1940s. Although a members – only club CAMRA members are welcome on production of a valid

membership card. The club offers snooker and pool, and has squash courts. Outside there is seating facing the main cricket pitch. ❀♣P🍺

Queen's Arms

Bunnian Place, RG21 7JE (100 yds from station)

11-11; 11-10.30 Sun

☎ (01256) 465488

Courage Best Bitter; Fuller's London Pride; Wadworth 6X; guest beers H

Convenient for the station, this pub provides an oasis of stability in a town that is undergoing constant change. One of the few Basingstoke pubs that does not set out to appeal to the 'alcopops' generation, its clientele ranges from students to pensioners, enjoying the cosy interior that is conducive to conversation. Although an Enterprise house, the licensees make every effort to bring a wide range of real ales to their customers as possible, from the SIBA list. ❀◐⊟≋♣

Soldier's Return

80 Upper Sherborne Road, Oakridge, RG21 5RB (opp. playing field)

11-2.30, 5.30-11; 11-11 Fri & Sat; 12-10.30 Sun

☎ (01256) 322449

Courage Best Bitter; guest beers H

Some 150 years old, the pub is on the north side of town near the A339 ring road. A focus for the local community, it is often frequented by football teams wanting a beer after their game and it also serves as a meeting place for the local motorcycle action group. The public bar can be lively at times. Outside seating overlooks the playing fields. Lunches are served Monday-Saturday. Q❀◐⊟♣P

Bentley

Bull Inn

GU10 5JH (on dual carriageway between Alton and Farnham)

11-11; 12-10.30 Sun

☎ (01420) 22156

Courage Best Bitter; Fuller's London Pride; Hogs Back TEA; Young's Bitter H

This fine brick building stands a mile east of Bentley and is convenient for walkers enjoying the Alice Holt Forest; dogs are welcome. It comprises two, low-ceilinged bars, one of which leads to a restaurant. Old pictures of towns in the vicinity adorn the walls. The local bus stops outside and it is a gentle 30-minute stroll to the station. ❀◐🚌

Bentworth

Star

Church Street, GU34 5RB (off A339) OS665402

12-3, 5-11; 12-11 Fri & Sat; 12-10.30 Sun

☎ (01420) 561224 🌐 star-inn.com

Fuller's London Pride; Ringwood Best Bitter; guest beers H

Dating back to 1841, this friendly free house has a bar warmed by open fires and an adjacent, quiet, no-smoking restaurant offering freshly-cooked meals. A social hub for the village community, its enthusiastic staff put on an active social calendar, including Tuesday curry evening and live music Friday and Sunday evenings. Background music is kept to a low volume at other times. Visitors are always made welcome. ⛫❀◐🚌♣P

Bishop's Waltham

Bunch of Grapes

St Peter's Street, SO32 1AD (follow signs to church)

11-2, 6-11; 12-2, 7-10.30 Sun

☎ (01489) 892935

Courage Best Bitter; Greene King IPA G

This listed building houses a welcoming pub that is now no-smoking throughout. Although it has been immaculately redecorated, it has not changed essentially in the last decade. The golf club is as active as ever, and still has a waiting list. Work is continuing to make the top garden as attractive as the rest of the facilities. Q❀♣⚞

Braishfield

Newport Inn

Newport Lane, SO51 0PL (lane opp. phone box) OS373249

12-2.30, 6-11; 12-2.30, 7-10.30 Sun

☎ (01794) 368225

Fuller's Gale's Butser, London Pride, Gale's HSB H

The Newport does not embrace ephemeral tastes: seekers of this year's trend will be disappointed. However, the many loyal customers of this completely unspoilt, two-bar pub – for decades run by the same family – revel in the unchanging delights offered here. Good beer, simple, but justly praised snacks based around bread, ham and cheese, Saturday evening singalongs accompanied by the landlady on the piano, conversation and occasional Thursday evening folk music are the perennial attractions here. ⛫❀⊟🚌♣P

Wheatsheaf

Braishfield Road, SO51 0QE

11-midnight daily

☎ (01794) 368372 🌐 wheatsheafbraishfield.co.uk

Caledonian Deuchars IPA; Hook Norton Old Hooky; Ringwood Best Bitter; Taylor Landlord; guest beers H

Village pub that benefits from a strong local following. The bar has been refurbished and displays an eclectic mix of artefacts ranging from old tools to the top of an old petrol pump. The careful use of low lighting and candles on the tables, blended with soft jazz in the background, creates a warm, friendly atmosphere in which to enjoy the well presented and highly regarded food. Two guest beers change regularly. Dogs are welcome here. ⛫Q❀◐♿⛺🚌P⚞

Bransgore

Three Tuns

Ringwood Road, BH23 8JH (N from A35 at Hinton)

11.30-11; 12-10.30 Sun

☎ (01425) 672232

Caledonian Deuchars IPA; Ringwood Best Bitter, Fortyniner; Taylor Landlord Ⓗ
Picture postcard village inn, dating from the 17th century, where the interior does not disappoint, with its pleasant mix of old beams and lighter wood. The spacious main bar has some tables for diners but also plenty of room for drinkers. There is also a more formal restaurant and a snug bar (where smoking is permitted), either side of the main area. An extensive, high quality menu is served every day (12-9.15pm Sun); fresh soups and local produce feature.
⛫Q❀◑◗♿⊟P⁄

Bursledon

Jolly Sailor
Land's End Road, Old Burlesdon, SO31 8DN (park at Bursledon Station, follow signed footpath)
☺ 11-11 (midnight Fri & Sat); 11-11 Sun
☎ (023) 8040 5557
Badger K&B Sussex, First Gold, Tanglefoot, seasonal beers Ⓗ
Famous riverside pub on the Hamble that has recently been enlarged, but maintains much of its character in its floorboards, flagstones and fireplaces. The single bar serves several interconnected rooms and dining areas. In addition to the garden a covered jetty provides sheltered outdoor seating and access for those arriving by boat. However, road access and parking are not so easy, so the short steep walk from the station car park may be a better option.
⛫❀◑◗⇌

Vine Inn
High Street, Old Bursledon, SO31 8DJ
(¾ mile from Lowford) OS485092
☺ 12-2.30 (not Mon-Thu), 5.30-11; 12-4, 7-10.30 Sun
☎ (023) 8040 3836
Greene King IPA, Abbot Ⓖ
Unpretentious, single-bar pub with a welcoming atmosphere, situated in a deceptively rural area in the midst of the Solent conurbation – the surrounding maze of roads is effectively a cul-de-sac, so the pub relies on local trade. The comfortable bar, replete with exposed beams, a collection of copper teapots, books and bric-a-brac, eschews modernity and the handpumps on the bar have now been rendered redundant by the casks behind the bar. ⛫⇔⇌♣

Charter Alley

White Hart
White Hart Lane, RG26 5QA (1 mile W of A340) OS593577
☺ 12-2.30 (3 Sat), 7-11; 12-10.30 Sun
☎ (01256) 850048 ⊕ whitehartcharteralley.com
Loddon Ferrymans Gold; Otter Ale; Stonehenge Spire Ale; West Berkshire Maggs Mild; guest beers Ⓗ
The oldest building in the village, put up next to the forge in 1819, it was the place where folk stopped to natter, hence 'chatter alley' which later became Charter Alley. A delightful rural ambience is enhanced by oak beams and log fires. The landlord has designed a beautiful terraced garden, which is a real suntrap, but offers shady areas and water features for a lovely, peaceful drink. The pub has nine new en-suite guest rooms. A cider is stocked occasionally.
⛫Q❀⇔◑◗⊞♣●P⁄◘

Chawton

Greyfriar
Winchester Road, GU34 1SB (opp. Jane Austen's house)
☺ 12-11; 12-10.30 Sun
☎ (01420) 83841 ⊕ thegreyfriar.co.uk
Fuller's Discovery, London Pride, ESB, seasonal beers Ⓗ
Welcoming hostelry, attracting locals and visitors alike for the full range of Fuller's beers. Originally three cottages, the pub includes a no-smoking restaurant and designated areas for non-smokers in the bar. The menu changes daily and has gained an excellent reputation. A function room is available. Fuller's Best Country Village Pub 2005 boasts a pleasant garden. Stagecoach bus No. 205 stops nearby. ❀◑◗⊟P⁄

Cheriton

Flower Pots
SO24 0QQ (½ mile N of A272 between Winchester and Petersfield)
☺ 12-2.30, 6-11; 12-3, 7-10.30 Sun
☎ (01962) 771318
Beers range varies Ⓖ
This two bar, red-brick Victorian pub was the home of the Cheriton Brewhouse, which is expected to reopen before the next edition of this Guide appears. The cider is Westons. Near the source of the River Itchen and a mile from the Civil War battlefield (1644), it is popular with walkers. Good food is served daily (not Sun eve); the Wednesday curry evening is run by an Indian chef. An adjacent barn has been converted to provide high class guest accommodation.
⛫Q❀⇔◑◗⊞▲●P

Cliddesden

Jolly Farmer
Farleigh Road, RG25 2JL (on B3046)
☺ 12-11 (midnight Thu-Sat); 12-10.30 Sun
☎ (01256) 473073
Beer range varies Ⓗ
Busy, listed village pub, close to Basingstoke, offering an interesting selection of four beers from the Punch Taverns list, plus a couple of ciders. The second, quiet, bar may be used by children and non-smokers when it is not reserved for functions. A large garden at the rear provides a secluded area for a peaceful drink, with a covered, heated patio for cooler evenings. ↭❀◑◗♣●P

Copythorne

Empress of Blandings
Romsey Road, SO40 2PE (on A31 between Cadnam and Ower)
☺ 11-11; 12-10.30 Sun
☎ (023) 8081 2321

Badger K&B Sussex, First Gold, Tanglefoot, seasonal beers Ⓗ
First listing in this Guide for a new pub, handsomely converted from a restaurant in 2004. The spacious building in colonial style features much light oak panelling and floors, lofty ceilings and two open fires. The single bar offers many large alcoves, including a smoking area. Food, from a wide-ranging menu, is available daily until 9pm. The pub benefits from two small gardens. Conveniently located on the eastern approach to the New Forest, the No. 31 bus (Cadnam-Southampton) stops nearby.
♔❀◐◑♿🚌P⊬

Dundridge

Hampshire Bowman

Dundridge Lane, Bishop's Waltham, SO32 1GD (1½ miles E of B3035) OS578184
⏲ 12-3, 6-11; 12-11 Fri & Sat; 12-10.30 Sun
☎ (01489) 892940 🌐 hampshirebowman.com
Ringwood Fortyniner; guest beers Ⓖ
Sympathetic alterations, due for completion in June 2006, will provide additional seating and improved access to the garden, via a new patio. Billed as a 'beer house that serves food' the pub offers an increasingly rare opportunity to sample gravity-dispensed beers including three or four guests with a local bias. It also hosts an annual beer festival. Meals are served all Saturday (until 9pm) and Sunday (until 7pm). Children are welcome until 9pm.
♔Q❀◐◑♿⛺♣P⊬

East Boldre

Turfcutters' Arms

Main Road, SO42 7WL (1½ miles SW of Beaulieu, off B3054) OS374004
⏲ 11-3, 6-11; 11-11 Fri & Sat; 12-10.30 Sun
☎ (01590) 612331
Ringwood Best Bitter, Fortyniner, seasonal beers; Wadworth 6X Ⓗ
In a tiny, timeless New Forest village, the pub is close to the Motor Museum, Abbey and Palace at Beaulieu and the 18th-century ship-building village of Buckler's Hard. Three rooms (two no-smoking) offer an unselfconsciously rustic setting in which to enjoy good ale, home-made food (including local game) and a choice of some 40 malt whiskies. The bookshelves and camera collection offer plenty of interest to browsers. Accommodation is in an adjoining converted barn. No evening meals are served Sunday.
♔❀🛏◐◑🚌P⊬

East End

East End Arms

Lymington Road, SO41 5SY (2¼ miles E of IOW ferry terminal) OS361968
⏲ 12-3, 6-11; 12-10 Sun
☎ (01590) 626223
Ringwood Best Bitter, Ⓗ **Fortyniner; guest beer** Ⓖ
Small, unpretentious pub, tucked away in a remote corner of the New Forest. The cosy public bar, full of local artefacts, is preferred by the regulars and dogs are welcome here, too. The larger, comfortable lounge, where children are admitted, is used by customers wanting a quiet drink and diners. Booking is recommended for meals (eve meals served Tue-Sat). The garden provides useful extra capacity for summer visitors.
♔Q❀◐◑🚌♿♣P

East Stratton

Northbrook Arms

SO21 3DU (off A33, 8 miles N of Winchester)
⏲ 11-11; 12-10.30 Sun
☎ (01962) 774150 🌐 northbrookarms.co.uk
Fuller's Gale's HSB; Otter Bitter; Ringwood Best Bitter; guest beers Ⓗ
At the end of a row of unusual thatched cottages, this dog-friendly pub overlooks the green where there are plenty of tables, and petanque is played. Inside is a bar with tiled floor, plus two further areas, one no-smoking, used mainly for dining (no food winter Mon). At the rear is a skittle alley with bar billiards, darts and a snooker table. It stocks two guest beers that change frequently and cider, such as Westons Old Rosie, is often available.
♔Q❀🛏◐◑♣●P⊬

East Worldham

Three Horseshoes

Caker Lane, GU34 3AE
⏲ 12-3, 6-11 daily
☎ (01420) 83211
Fuller's Gale's Butser, London Pride, Gale's HSB, seasonal beers Ⓗ
First licensed in 1834, but in part 300 years old, it was purchased by Gale's (now Fuller's) in 1930. Reputedly haunted (the upstairs bar is spook-free), the single ground-floor bar is laid out in informal areas. The attractive, no-smoking restaurant serves a range of daily home-made specials (no food Sun eve). A useful stop for walkers on the ancient Hangers Way from Alton to Selborne and beyond, the pub once provided refreshment for workers in the long-gone, hop-growing district.
♔Q❀🛏◐◑🚌P

Emsworth

Coal Exchange

21 South Street, PO10 7EG
⏲ 10.30-3.30, 5.30-11; 10.30-midnight Fri & Sat; 12-11 Sun
☎ (01243) 375866
Fuller's Gale's Butser, London Pride, Gale's HSB Ⓗ
When this green-tiled pub was built in the 17th century it doubled as a pork butchery and ale house. The people of Emsworth also used it as a place to trade their produce with coal delivered to the nearby harbour, hence the name. Commercial traffic has been replaced by pleasure boating and the harbour is now full of yachts. Award-winning food is served at lunchtime, while early arrival is recommended for the poplar curry (Tue) and international (Thu) evenings.
♔❀◐⇌

Lord Raglan

35 Queen Street, PO10 7BJ

⏲ 11-3, 6-11; 11-11 Sat & Sun

☎ (01243) 372587 🌐 thelordraglan.com

Fuller's Gale's Butser, London Pride, Gale's HSB 🄷

Traditional flint building alongside Slipper Mill pond and the county boundary with West Sussex. One bar has been converted into a cosy restaurant, while the other, surprisingly large bar hosts live music on Sunday evening. Excellent, home-cooked food, served daily, represents good value. The garden at the rear affords views of the mouth of the River Ems and the harbour. The pub is a rare outlet in these parts for traditional cider (Bulmers). ⛰Q❀◐◑⇌●

Exton

Shoe

Shoe Lane, SO32 3NT

⏲ 10-3, 6-11; 10-3, 6-10.30 Sun

☎ (01489) 877526

Wadworth IPA, 6X; guest beers 🄷

As you might expect from a pub bearing this name, it has a large number of shoes on display – note the display case in one room and the impossibly large shoe above the fire in another. The pub has an unusual bar, with access at the back to the rooms behind. By the time this Guide is published work will have been completed to give wheelchair access. ⛰❀◐◑⊟♿P⚟

Fareham

Lord Arthur Lee

100-108 West Street, PO16 0PE

⏲ 9am-midnight (1am Fri & Sat); 9am-midnight Sun

☎ (01329) 280447

Courage Directors; Greene King Abbot, Old Speckled Hen; Ringwood Fortyniner or Old Thumper; guest beers 🄷

In common with most Wetherspoon's pubs, this one now has a flat-screen TV, but fortunately the volume is usually turned right down and all that it shows is the news headlines. The pub is named after the Viscount Lee who had a hand in the Prime Minister's country residence, Chequers. The pub offers up to six guest ales and stages regular beer festivals. It gets busy after the shops close with weary shoppers fortifying themselves for the journey home.
Q◐◑♿⇌⚟

Farnborough

Prince of Wales

184 Rectory Road, GU14 8AL (near North Station)

⏲ 11.30-2.30, 5.30-11; 11.30-11 Fri & Sat; 12-10.30 Sun

☎ (01252) 545578

Badger Tanglefoot; Fuller's London Pride; Hogs Back TEA; Ringwood Fortyniner; Young's Bitter; guest beers 🄷

Renowned free house where the long-standing licensee has set a benchmark for pub atmosphere, beer choice and quality. Three traditionally-styled drinking areas make the interior roomy yet snug for the affable locals to enjoy. Five guest pumps typically offer ten beers a week, plus a keenly priced session beer that changes monthly. The month of May sees a great selection of mild ales and a beer festival is held in mid-October. No food is served on Sunday. Q❀◐⇌(North)P

Fleet

Prince Arthur

238 Fleet Road, GU51 4BX

⏲ 9am-midnight (12.30am Fri & Sat); 9-midnight Sun

☎ (01252) 545578

Courage Best Bitter; Greene King Abbot; Hogs Back TEA; Ringwood Old Thumper; Shepherd Neame Spitfire; guest beers 🄷

Situated towards the southern end of Fleet's high street, the Prince Arthur is a Wethespoon's on a fairly human scale. Real ale is clearly a priority here, with up to three guest beers that often showcase local breweries, such as Hog's Back, Itchen Valley and Triple fff. Westons Old Rosie or Vintage cider is sometimes available. Q❀◐◑♿🚌⚟

Freefolk

Watership Down

RG28 7NJ (off B3400)

⏲ 12-3, 6-11 (11.30 Fri & Sat); 12-3, 7-10.30 Sun

☎ (01256) 892254

Young's Bitter; guest beers 🄷

Welcoming free house with one bar but several drinking areas, including a conservatory, used mostly by diners, a heated patio and large gardens with an area for children. Named after Richard Adams's book, the pub boasts an impressive collection of penny arcade machines and a table football machine. Five handpumps serve a changing range of ales, always including a real mild. Popular with walkers and cyclists, buses stop close to local CAMRA's Pub of the Year 2006 winner.
❀◐◑♣P⚟

Fritham

Royal Oak

SO43 7HJ (1 mile S of B3078) OS232141

⏲ 11.30-2.30 (11-3 summer), 6-11; 11-11 Sat; 12-10.30 Sun

☎ (023) 8081 2606

Hop Back Summer Lightning; Ringwood Best Bitter, Fortyniner; guest beers 🄶

Small, thatched gem at the end of a New Forest track. The main bar leads into several interconnecting rooms served through a hatchway. Beers are mostly from small, local breweries. Black beams, low doorways, boarded floors and colour-washed walls are all as you would expect. Lunchtime food is simple but good. A vast, tabled garden hosts barbecues, hog roasts and a mid-September beer festival. The log fires are delightful. Perfect for walkers, cyclists and equestrians (facilities provided); dogs abound. ⛰Q❀◐

Gosport

Clarence Tavern

1 Clarence Road, PO12 1BB

⏲ 11-11;12-10.30 Sun

☎ (023) 9252 9726
Oakleaf Bitter, Hole Hearted, Blake's Gosport Bitter [H]
The roof covering the largest room in the Clarence came from the Isle of Wight; at one end the old equipment from the former Chapel Brewery can still be seen. The brewery has been moved across the road and renamed Oakleaf, but the Clarence is still regarded as the brewery tap. It hosts beer festivals over the Easter and August bank holiday weekends. Three double rooms have recently been opened for B&B guests. ⌂❀⇄◐▶P

Queen's Hotel
143 Queen's Road, PO12 1LG
⊙ 11.30-2.30 (not Mon-Thu), 5-11; 11.30-11 Sat; 12-3, 7-10.30 Sun
☎ (023) 9258 2645
Ringwood Fortyniner; Rooster's Yankee; Young's Bitter; guest beers [H]
Back-street local, with many CAMRA awards to its credit. Weekend closing times are flexible, with an extra half hour available, depending on customer demand. The bar normally stocks one or two guest beers, plus a beer of the month. The focal point of the bar is an old open fireplace with a carved wood surround. Bar snacks are served on Friday lunchtime. The beer festival is an established event in October. Real cider is served in summer. ⌂♣●

Grayshott

Fox & Pelican
Headley Road, GU26 6LG
⊙ 11-11; 12-10.30 Sun
☎ (01428) 604757
Fuller's Gale's Butser, London Pride, Gale's HSB [H]
Large pub of several interlinked areas that cater well for family groups, ramblers and real ale fans alike. The large garden, equipped with barbecue and children's playthings, is well used when weather permits, while in winter a big log fire literally provides a warm welcome. Pool is played and a large screen meets the needs of TV sports fans. Evening meals are served Tuesday-Saturday. There is a bus stop outside the pub.
⌂❀◐▶⊟P⚡

Greywell

Fox & Goose
The Street, RG29 1BY (off A287, just S of M3 jct 5)
⊙ 11-11; 12-11 Sun
☎ (01256) 702062
Courage Best Bitter; Wychwood Hobgoblin; Young's Bitter; guest beer [H]
Popular, 16th-century pub set in an attractive village, with a large field behind used for camping and village events. In a good walking area, with Basingstoke Canal close by, the pub is child-friendly and customers may take well-behaved dogs inside or stay in the garden with them. Games are provided along with local newspapers.
⌂❀◐▶⊟⛺♣P

Hambledon

Bat & Ball
Hyden Farm Lane, PO8 0UB (2½ miles from village on Clanfield road)) OS677167
⊙ 11.30-3 (12-3.30 Sat), 6-11; 12-4, 7-10.30 Sun
☎ (023) 9263 2692
Fuller's Gale's Butser, London Pride, Gale's HSB [H]
This pub surely needs no introduction as it is nationally renowned as the cradle of cricket. The single bar is full of memorabilia of the great game, and it is as much a museum as a pub. How better to enjoy a match than with a beer? Set high on Broadhalfpenny Down, the boundary line between Hambledon and Clanfield is still marked on the floor, it used to bisect the bar – a significant fact when the parishes operated different licensing hours. ⌂❀◐▶♿♣P

Vine
West Street, PO7 4RW
⊙ 11.30-3, 6-11; 12-4, 7-10.30 Sun
☎ (023) 9263 2419
Ringwood Best Bitter; guest beers [H]
A large, deep well is a prominent feature of this pub. As the chalk below is porous, the water level changes rapidly during a storm, resulting in locals zooming in to take a peek to decide if a flood is likely. A pub with masses of character, the Vine dates from the 16th century; it has been opened out somewhat since it was built, but it remains unspoilt. No evening meals are served Sunday. The cider is Addlestones.
⌂Q❀◐▶●

Hartley Wintney

Waggon & Horses
High Street, RG27 8NY
⊙ 11-11 (midnight Fri & Sat); 12-11 Sun
☎ (01252) 842119
Courage Best Bitter; [H] **Fuller's Gale's HSB;** [G] **guest beers** [H]
True village pub where the lively public bar contrasts with a quieter lounge. Although packed on weekend evenings, it is still a great place to drink, and the guest beer changes frequently. A winner of many local CAMRA awards, it is as welcoming to first-timers as it is to all the regulars. At the rear of the pub is a pleasant courtyard garden. No food is served Sunday. ⌂Q❀◐⊟

Havant

Old House at Home
2 South Street, PO9 1DA
⊙ 11-11; 12-10.30 Sun
☎ (023) 9248 3464
Fuller's Gale's Butser, London Pride, Gale's HSB [H]
Despite the date of 1339 being carved in the outside wall, this pub began life in the 16th century as five cottages. Nonetheless, it is one of the oldest buildings in town, having survived the fire of 1760. Other claims to fame are that its beams came from the Spanish Armada and the last dancing bear in England performed here. Once a bakery, the remains of the oven can still be seen in the surprisingly large lounge bar. ⌂❀◐⊟⇌

Hill Head

Crofton

48 Crofton Lane, PO14 3QF
11-11; 12-10.30 Sun
☎ (01329) 314222
Caledonian Deuchars IPA; Greene King Old Speckled Hen; ⒽH guest beers Ⓖ/Ⓗ
Modern estate pub in a housing area once occupied by strawberry fields. The guest beers are from Punch Taverns (Innspired) and Oakleaf Hole Hearted appears quite often. The pub has four handpumps, with up to two extra casks on stillage in the cellar, but plans were in hand to install more handpumps on the bar during 2006. The function room houses a skittle alley that gets booked up well in advance. Home-cooked food is served all day at weekends at local CAMRA's Pub of the Year 2006.
Q❀◐ ♣P

Holybourne

Queen's Head

20 London Road, GU34 4EG (opp. Grange Hotel)
12-midnight (1am Fri & Sat); 12-11 Sun
☎ (01420) 86331
Greene King IPA, Ruddles Best Bitter, seasonal beers; guest beer Ⓗ
Reputedly of 18th-century origin, but much extended, this traditional pub comprises two rooms, one of which is a large, no-smoking lounge for drinkers and diners. Food is based on local produce and comes in hearty portions (no eve meals winter Sun-Tue). Regular music performances take place through the year. Cribbage is played here. The extensive garden features a children's play area; dogs are welcome. Stagecoach 64/X64 service (Winchester-Guildford) stops nearby. ❀◐ ⇌(Alton) ♣P

Horndean

Brewers Arms

1 Five Heads Road, PO8 9NW
12-2 (2.30 Fri; not Mon); 5-11 (midnight Fri); 12-4, 6-midnight Sat; 12-3, 7-11 Sun
☎ (023) 9259 1325
Courage Directors; Fuller's London Pride; Ringwood Best Bitter; guest beers Ⓗ
Pre-war pub, set back off the main Portsmouth road. It is referred to by regulars as 'a proper pub' – a genuine local where people come to drink and chat. Up to three guest ales are available at the weekend, including beers from local SIBA breweries. Pump clips adorn the walls around the bar – most of the beers shown have been sold here. Occasional live music is staged on a Saturday evening. Dog owners are welcome to bring their four-legged friends. Q❀ P

Hythe

Lord Nelson

5 High Street, SO45 6AG (in central shopping precinct)
11-11 (midnight Fri & Sat); 11-11 Sun
☎ (023) 8084 2169
Ringwood Best Bitter; Taylor Landlord; Wadworth 6X Ⓗ
Old-fashioned, maritime pub, circa 1740, in the town centre, alongside the last working pier train in the country. Popular with locals, it comprises two small bars at the front, a no-smoking snug in the middle and a large bar at the back, affording views over Southampton Water. The food, mostly home made, is simple but reasonably priced fare. The pub hosts live music on Friday evening and a quiz on Wednesday. There is ramped access and a wheelchair WC.
Q◐ ♿♣

Kingsclere

Swan Hotel

Swan Street, RG20 5PP
11-3, 5.30-11.30; 12-4, 7-11 Sun
☎ (01635) 298314 🌐 swankingsclere.co.uk
Young's Bitter; guest beers Ⓗ
Traditional inn, frequented by an eclectic mix of customers, serving four regularly changing handpumped beers from local micro-breweries and regionals. One of the country's oldest coaching inns dating from 1449, retaining many original oak beams and fireplaces, it is a Grade II listed building. Associated with the Bishop of Winchester for 300 years, it has been a pub since 1600. As befits a true inn, good food is served in the bar or dining room, and there are nine en-suite bedrooms. Q❀◐♿♣P

Lasham

Royal Oak

GU34 5SJ (off A339 between Alton and Basingstoke)
12-11; 12-10.30 Sun
☎ (01256) 381213 🌐 royaloak.uk.com
Fuller's Gale's HSB; Hogs Back TEA; Ringwood Best Bitter; Triple fff Moondance; guest beers Ⓗ
Over 200 years old the Royal Oak has two bars, including a no-smoking lounge. It is situated in the centre of a quiet village next to Lasham Airfield, well known for its gliding club. Excellent fresh food is served daily lunchtime and evening, and all day on Sunday. A large car park, beautiful garden and picturesque surroundings make this pub popular with ramblers and cyclists; children are welcome. It stands on the Stagecoach 28 bus route. Q❀◐ ♣P

Little London

Plough Inn

Silchester Road, RG26 5EP (1 mile off A340, S of Tadley)
12-2.30 (3 Sat), 5.30-11;12-3, 7-10.30 Sun
☎ (01256) 850628
Ringwood Best Bitter, seasonal beers; Ⓗ guest beers Ⓖ
Wonderful, popular village pub, with an informal atmosphere. This is a sympathetically restored cottage where in winter you can enjoy a glass of porter in front of a cheery log fire. A good range of baguettes is usually available (not Sun eve). Musicians perform popular songs monthly (second Tue). A lovely secluded garden at the side of the pub is an added attraction.

The location is ideal for ramblers visiting the Roman ruins at nearby Silchester or Pamber Wood. ⛫Q❀♣P

Long Sutton

Four Horseshoes

The Street, RG29 1TA (1 mile E of village) OS748471
⏲ 12-3 (not Mon), 6.30-11; 12-3, 6.30-10.30 Sun
☎ (01256) 862488 🌐 fourhorseshoes.com
Fuller's London Pride; guest beers 🄷
Traditional country pub on the outskirts of the village, next to Lord Wandsworth College. Three dining areas radiate from a spacious central bar that houses a large collection of horse brasses and novelty keyrings. Next to the car park is a garden with a large play area for children and a boules pitch. Two or three guest beers are stocked, invariably including a mild, which is the landlord's favourite tipple. Daytime buses run every two hours (return journeys must be booked). ⛫Q☕❀🛏◖◗🚌♣P

Lower Upham

Woodman

Winchester Road, SO32 1HA (on B2177 by B3037 jct)
⏲ 12-2.30 (6 Sat), 7.15-11 (midnight Fri & Sat); 12-6, 7.15-11 Sun
☎ (01489) 860270
Greene King IPA; guest beers 🄷
Dating partly from the 17th century, the Woodman offers two contrasting bars: a cosy lounge, bedecked with Toby jugs, and a public bar suited to a more gregarious clientele. The bar offers one or two guest beers from Greene King, while whisky lovers can choose from nearly 200 malts! In summer, fine floral displays bring a blaze of colour to the pub's frontage. A meat draw takes place weekly on Friday, while 'Sausage Saturday' is an annual, albeit movable, feast. ⛫❀🚂🚌♣P🃏

Milford on Sea

Red Lion

32 High Street, SO41 0QD
⏲ 11.30-2.30, 6-11; 12-3, 7-10 (not winter eve) Sun
☎ (01590) 642236
Fuller's London Pride; Ringwood Best Bitter; guest beers 🄷
Friendly, comfortable, 18th-century village pub with a relaxed atmosphere, notable for its feature fireplace and photographs of submarines on the walls. The no-smoking dining area can be used by drinkers after the diners finish their meals. A central ramp enables wheelchair access. Pool and darts are played and occasional bands perform. The large, lawned garden is away from traffic. Real cider is sold in summer. Accommodation is in two double and one twin en-suite rooms. ⛫❀🛏◖◗♿♣🍎P🚭

North Warnborough

Lord Derby

Bartley Heath, RG29 1HD (off A287)
⏲ 11.30-3, 5.30-11; 11.30-11 Wed-Sat; 11.30-10.30 Sun
☎ (01256) 702283
Fuller's London Pride; Moorhouses Pendle Witches Brew; guest beer 🄷
This is primarily a restaurant, but has a separate drinking area with a stone-flagged floor. Exposed beams and posts are strewn with hop garlands. The former main road outside has been cut off by the motorway and provides useful extra parking, except on the first Wednesday of the month (bikers' day) when it is full of expensive motorbikes. No food is served on that day or on any Sunday evening. ❀◖◗♿P

Old Basing

Crown

The Street, RG24 7BW (next to Old Basing House ruins)
⏲ 11-3, 5.30-11; 11-11.30 Fri & Sat; 12-10.30 Sun
☎ (01256) 321424
Fuller's London Pride; Theakston Old Peculier; guest beers 🄷
The Crown sits alongside the remains of Old Basing House, which Cromwell's troops are said to have attacked from the pub. Members of the Sealed Knot, who recreate historic battles that took place nearby, gather annually for a beer festival arranged by the pub, when strong ales feature. One bar is no-smoking, the other a cosy snug. Guest beers are chosen to celebrate themes, such as patron saints, poets and sporting events. The No. 8 bus from Basingstoke centre stops outside. ❀◖◗🚌P

Overton

Greyhound

46 Winchester Street, RG25 3HS
⏲ 11-1.30, 4.30-11; 11-2, 6-11 Sat; 12-2, 7-10.30 Sun
☎ (01256) 770241
Caledonian Deuchars IPA; Greene King IPA, Abbot; Wadworth 6X 🄷
Being a short walk from the village centre helps the Greyhound to retain a cosy local atmosphere. The single bar combines a comfortable lounge area with a games section where pool and darts are played. As befits its local clientele, the pub supports team in most games. The loos are outside, so a warm up by the log fire is advised before venturing forth in winter. There is a small patio for summer use. ⛫❀♣

Owslebury

Ship Inn

SO21 1LT (off B2177, 1½ miles N of Marwell Zoo)
⏲ 11-3, 6-11; 11-11 Fri-Sun
☎ (01962) 777358
Greene King IPA, Morland Original, Abbot 🄷
Picture postcard country pub, where one bar is established as a restaurant, serving an excellent menu, while the other retains a cosy, traditional atmosphere. Meals are served all day Friday-Sunday, 11am-11pm and special menus are laid on for events such as Valentine's Day and Christmas. The garden features a covered area and a well-protected pond. Children are always welcome. Teams play in darts, cribbage and petanque leagues. Wheelchair access is via the car park entrance. ⛫❀◖◗♿♣P

Pennington (Lymington)

Musketeer

26 North Street, SO41 8FZ (off A337, at White Hart roundabout)

⏲ 11.30-2.30, 5.30-11; 11.30-11.30 Fri & Sat; 12-11 Sun

☎ (01590) 676527

Courage Best Bitter; Ringwood Best Bitter, Fortyniner; guest beers Ⓗ

Imposing pub, built in 1906 after a fire destroyed the previous inn. Pub sign aficionados will delight in the unusual bronze sign outside. Inside this community local is a rectangular single bar, warmed by two log fires, with tables and comfortable seating. The small patio is ideal for summer drinking. The pub fields two darts teams and hosts a weekly quiz (Tue). An annual beer festival is held over August bank holiday. ⩕❀◖⊟♣P

Portsmouth

Bridge Tavern

54 East Street, Old Portsmouth, PO1 2JJ

⏲ 11-11; 12-10.30 Sun

☎ (023) 9275 2992

Fuller's Gale's Butser, London Pride, Gale's HSB Ⓗ

Originally a small, one-storey harbourside pub, drawing a mixed clientele of fisherman and locals, it was refurbished and has grown beyond recognition into an imposing edifice on two floors. Different levels, nooks and crannies add interest. The Bridge is worth finding for the excellent ale served in pleasant surroundings by an attentive and helpful staff. No meals are served Sunday evening. ◖◗⍁

Cellars at Eastney

56 Cromwell Road, Southsea, PO4 9PN

⏲ 12-11.15 (11.30 Fri & Sat); 12-11 Sun

☎ (023) 9282 6249 🌐 thecellars.co.uk

Hop Back Summer Lightning; Ringwood Best Bitter, Fortyniner Ⓗ

Street-corner, community local situated opposite the old Royal Marine barracks and a short walk from the RM Museum. The single bar houses a small stage that hosts live music several evenings a week (details on website). At the rear is a small conservatory. The Cellars is a rare outlet for Ringwood beers in the area and stocks a good range of wines. Displayed in the bar is the plate for the licensee from 1839-1969, of interest to former servicemen. ●

Fifth Hants Volunteer Arms

74 Albert Road, Southsea, PO5 2SL

⏲ 12-midnight (1am Fri & Sat); 12-midnight Sun

☎ (023) 9282 7161

Fuller's London Pride, Gale's HSB, Festival Mild Ⓗ

Birthplace of the local CAMRA branch, this street-corner pub is one of the few in the vicinity to retain its two bars. The lively public bar features a collection of hard hats, an overcooked pizza and a chiming clock. The quieter lounge displays the certificates to show the pub's many appearances in this Guide. All in all, this is an excellent, traditional watering-hole in an area of modernised pubs. It hosts a quiz on Sunday evening. ⊟♣

Florence Arms

18-20 Florence Road, Southsea, PO5 2NE

⏲ 12-11 (maybe later weekends); 12-10.30 Sun

☎ (023) 9287 5700

Adnams Broadside; Young's Bitter, Special; guest beers Ⓗ

Back-street pub, well worth seeking out, as its regularly changing guest beers are often unusual. The cider is Addlestones. Two bars each offer their own particular charm, while the third bar is used mainly as a restaurant for the tasty weekday meals. In the evening, food is served 6.30-8.30pm. The pub is convenient for Southsea's shops and seafront. Q◖◗♿●⍁

Hole in the Wall

36 Great Southsea Street, PO5 3BY

⏲ 4-11; 12-2, 4-midnight Fri; 12-midnight Sat; 12-11 Sun

☎ (023) 9229 8085

Oakleaf Nuptu'ale, Hole Hearted; guest beers Ⓗ

Small, welcoming pub, with a cosy rear snug. The absence of loud music, Belgian beers, Thatchers cider and a choice of up to 30 wines makes this an ideal venue for all who value good food, drink and conversation. O'Hagan's sausages and mash and savoury puddings are served; Monday and Tuesday are chilli nights. The pub is usually packed for the Thursday evening quiz. Four-pint jugs are sold at reduced prices before 9pm. No admittance after 11pm, Friday and Saturday. Q◖◗♣●⍁▯

Old Customs House

Gun Wharf Quay, PO1 3TY

⏲ 10-midnight (1am Fri & Sat); 10-11 Sun

☎ (023) 9283 2833 🌐 theoldcustomshouse.com

Fuller's Gale's Butser, London Pride, Gale's HSB Ⓗ

High quality conversion to a pub of a former naval office building, once a pay office. No expense has been spared to produce an environment that is conducive to a lively and pleasant evening. Comprising several rooms, it is much more than the sum of its parts and well worth a visit for residents or visitors to Portsmouth. ❀◖◗♿⇹(Harbour)⍁

Old House at Home

104 Locksway Road, Milton, PO4 8JR

⏲ 10-midnight (1am Fri & Sat); 12-midnight Sun

☎ (023) 9273 2606

Caldenian Deuchars IPA; Fuller's London Pride, Gale's HSB; Young's Special; guest beers Ⓗ

A community pub in all senses, it was recently voted by the trade paper Morning Advertiser as Meridian Community Pub of the Year 2006 – an award that was richly deserved. The pub usually stocks four real ales, from Scotland to Hampshire, with seasonal guests added in summer. Good food is served at lunchtime and early evening, with the lounge bar doubling as a dining area at the weekend. ⩕❀◖◗⊟♿♣P

Pembroke

20 Pembroke Road, Old Portsmouth, PO1 2NR

⏲ 10-midnight (11 Mon); 12-4, 7-11 Sun

☎ (023) 9282 3961

Draught Bass; Fuller's London Pride; Greene King Abbot Ⓗ

Built in 1711, this single-bar, horseshoe-shaped pub on a corner site was originally named the Little Blue Line and is mentioned in the novels of Captain Marryat. The name was changed in 1900. All kinds of naval memorabilia are displayed in the bar that has an L-shaped servery run by friendly staff. This rare haven for discerning drinkers attracts a varied clientele. The ales are extremely good and it offers probably the best pint of Pride in Portsmouth. ♨◐♿

Royal Marine Artillery Tavern

58 Cromwell Road, Southsea PO4 9PN

✪ 3 (12 Sat)-11 (midnight Fri & Sat); 12-11 Sun

☎ (023) 9282 0896

Fuller's Gale's Butser, London Pride, Gale's HSB; guest beers Ⓗ

Typical, back-street pub frequented by local drinkers, that stands right outside the main gate to the old Royal Marine barracks from which it takes its name. It stages live entertainment most weekends and it houses the last surviving skittle alley in Portsmouth. A real fire provides a warm glow in winter. Within walking distance of the Eastney seafront, it is also convenient for the Royal Marines Museum. ♨❀⛺♣

Sir Loin of Beef

152 Highland Road, Southsea, PO4 9NH

✪ 11-11.30 (midnight Fri & Sat); 12-11 Sun

☎ (023) 9282 0115

Hop Back Summer Lightning; guest beers Ⓗ

True free house where the beers are mostly sourced from southern independent breweries. It also stocks a wide range of bottle-conditioned ales. The pub has a contemporary feel, bearing a nautical theme, with submarine paraphernalia in abundance and a klaxon is used to call time. A quiz is held on Sunday evening. ⛺

Still & West Country House

2 Bath Square, Old Portsmouth, PO1 2JL

✪ 10-11; 11-10.30 Sun

☎ (023) 9282 1567

Fuller's Gale's Butser, London Pride, Gale's HSB; guest beers Ⓗ

One of the oldest pubs in Old Portsmouth, this large establishment affords stunning vistas of the harbour and the best view of the newly opened Spinnaker Tower. The downstairs bar bears interesting ceilings and a diverse collection of maritime memorabilia. Excellent food is served, with fish a speciality. Well worth finding, the pub can get crowded on sunny days in high summer, when the patio comes into its own. ❀◐◑♿≢(Harbour)

Thatchers

95 London Road, Northend, PO2 0BN

✪ 10-11 (midnight Fri & Sat); 12-10.30 Sun

☎ (023) 9266 2146

Greene King Abbot; guest beer Ⓗ

Attractive pub in a shopping centre, which was extensively remodelled and refurbished five years ago: the two bars have gone to make way for a more modern, split-level layout with an L-shaped servery to one side. The interior has been finished to a high standard – the best in the vicinity – it is a true racehorse among carthorses. Thatchers is now a pleasant refreshment stop for Northend shoppers, offering a frequently changed guest beer. Children are welcome until 5pm. ❀◐♿⊬

Winchester Arms

99 Winchester Road, Buckland, PO2 7PS

✪ 12 (4 Mon)-11 daily

☎ (023) 9266 2443

Oakleaf Hole Hearted, Blake's Gosport Bitter; Shepherd Neame Spitfire; guest beers Ⓗ

Friendly, two-bar local, hidden among the terraced back streets. The former home of the now defunct Buckland Brewery, the brewer now plies his trade at Oakleaf. Children and dogs are welcome here. It stages live music on Sunday and an acoustic session on Wednesday evening, while Monday is quiz night. The pub fields darts and football teams and hosts the local science fiction group's monthly meetings (second Tue). It may stay open until midnight at the weekend if busy. ♨Q❀⊟♣⊬

Romsey

Abbey Hotel

11 Church Street, SO51 8BT

✪ 11-3, 6-11; 12-3, 7-10.30 Sun

☎ (01794) 513360 🌐 abbeyhotelromsey.co.uk

Courage Best Bitter, Directors; Young's Bitter Ⓗ

The Abbey was built in the 1860s to replace a victim of road widening. It passed from Fuller's to Strong's, then to Courage, whose tenure is evident in the lintel above the entrance. Its handsome black and white gables face the east end of Romsey Abbey, while the interior is divided in two, with one area designated no-smoking during food service (no meals Sun eve). The whole pub is quiet enough for easy conversation. Splendid, award-winning floral displays gladden the heart. ♨Q❀⇄◐◑≢⊟P

Old House at Home

62 Love Lane, SO51 8DE (next to Waitrose car park)

✪ 11-3, 5-11 (midnight Fri & Sat); 12-4, 7-10.30 Sun

☎ (01794) 513175

Fuller's Gale's Butser, London Pride, Gale's HSB Ⓗ

Romsey's only thatched pub is a welcoming, efficiently run establishment, popular with all ages. The three discrete areas, two of which are reserved for non-smokers, offer comfortable settings in which to enjoy good quality English food that makes much use of local ingredients. Deeply satisfying cooked breakfasts are served 9.30-11.30am; lunch is the only meal served on Sunday, which is quiz night. There is no entry at the weekend after 11pm. ❀◐◑≢⊟P⊬

Star Inn

13 Horsefair, SO51 8EZ (200 yds N of market place)

✪ 12-2.30, 5-11 (midnight Fri); 12-midnight Sat; 12-3, 7-11 Sun

☎ (01794) 516353 🌐 thestarinnromsey.co.uk

Wadworth IPA, 6X, JCB, seasonal beers Ⓗ

Standing outside the old Strong's Brewery gates, the pub was once the brewery tap, although it started life in the 17th century as a weaver's house. A broad single bar has a dartboard on the left and an inglenook with easy chairs to the right. Evening entertainment includes varied live music (Sat), folk sessions (Wed) and a Sunday quiz. Food is available Wednesday-Sunday lunchtimes, and Wednesday-Friday early evening. ⌂❀🛏◐◑≋🚌♣

Rowlands Castle

Castle

1 Finchdean Road, PO9 6DA

⏲ 11-11 (midnight Fri & Sat); 11-11 Sun

☎ (023) 9241 2494

Fuller's Gale's Butser, London Pride, Gale's HSB; guest beer Ⓗ

Typical village pub behind the railway bridge, by the entrance to Stanstead House. Both bars have open hearths, wall panelling and bare boards or flagstones. Walkers and dogs are welcome in the public bar, while the no-smoking lounge doubles as a restaurant; meals are served all day (until 3.30pm Sun). The pub is well known locally for its home-made pies, while fish and chips wrapped in newspaper are sold on Friday evenings. A themed menu is featured on Monday evening. ⌂Q❀◐◑⊞♿≋♣P⚟

Selborne

Selborne Arms

High Street, GU34 3JR

⏲ 11-3, 6 (5.30 Fri)-11 (11-11 summer Sat); 12-11 Sun

☎ (01420) 511247

Courage Best Bitter; Ringwood Fortyniner; guest beers Ⓗ

Traditional village pub retaining log fires and other original features in a building that dates back to the 1600s. It is located at the bottom of Selborne Hanger and the famous zigzag path carved by naturalist Gilbert White. The guest beers in this free house showcase local micro-breweries' products, while the award-winning menus also feature local produce. The extensive, grassed garden is popular in summer; it boasts a children's play area and a fantastic barbecue. ⌂Q❀◐◑⊞🚌(72, X72)●P⚟

Shalden

Golden Pot

Odiham Road, GU34 4DJ (on B3349, 1 mile N of village)

⏲ 11-midnight (1am Fri & Sat); 12-midnight Sun

☎ (01420) 80655

Greene King IPA, Ruddles County, Abbot, Old Speckled Hen; guest beers Ⓗ

This pub continues to demonstrate how Greene King beer should taste, while maintaining an excellent reputation, too, for its menus that are based on local produce and fresh fish. Meals may be enjoyed in the light, airy, no-smoking dining area. Ghosts reputedly haunt the premises, including two Polish airmen whose aircraft crashed in the garden during WWII. The pub name is derived from the local area. It hosts monthly folk evenings (second Tue) and has a skittle alley. ⌂Q❀◐◑♣P⚟

Shedfield

Wheatsheaf Inn

Botley Road, SO32 2JG (on A334)

⏲ 12-11; 12-10.30 Sun

☎ (01329) 833024

Ringwood Fortyniner (summer), XXXX Porter (winter); guest beers Ⓖ

Friendly pub with a lively public bar and a small lounge. Between six and eight beers are served straight from casks mounted on a two-tier stillage behind the bar. At least one Oakleaf beer is usually stocked; the cider is Thatchers Cheddar Valley. A beer festival is held annually over the late spring bank holiday. Dogs on leads are admitted. The car park is across a busy main road. Blues, jazz or Irish music is staged on Saturday evening. Q❀◐♣●P

Southampton

Bitter Virtue (off-licence)

70 Cambridge Road, SO14 6US (take Alma Rd from The Avenue, by church, 250 yds)

⏲ 10.30-8.30 (not Mon); 10.30-2 Sun

☎ (023) 8055 4881 🌐 bittervirtue.co.uk

Beer range varies Ⓖ

Splendid beer shop that truly deserves its Highly Recommended designation from the 2006 drinks retailing industry awards. Just beers and ciders are sold here: the bottled beer range includes products from the UK, Belgium, Germany, Holland, the Czech Republic and the USA. Draught beer is also available from both local breweries and others further afield. It stocks a good selection of Belgian glasses, plus books and T-shirts. 🚌

Crown

9 Highcrown Street, SO17 1QE (off Highfield Lane)

⏲ 11-11; 12-11 Sun

☎ (023) 8031 5033

Draught Bass; Flowers Original; Fuller's London Pride; Hampshire Strong's Best Bitter; Ringwood Best Bitter Ⓗ

Comfortable, busy pub that attracts a healthy mix of customers of all ages from the nearby university, many of whom come to enjoy the good value food that dominates one side of the single bar (reservations necessary at weekends). Lively conversation is aided by the absence of fruit machines. Children are welcome on the covered, heated patio. The car park is in Hawthorn Road. ❀◐◑P

Dolphin Hotel

30 Osborne Road South, St Denys, SO17 2EZ (by footbridge from St. Denys Station)

⏲ 12-11; 12-10.30 Sun

☎ (023) 8039 9369

Adnams Broadside; Fuller's London Pride, Gale's HSB; Ringwood Fortyniner; Taylor Landlord; guest beers Ⓗ

Shown on Southampton's 1878 'drink map', this single-bar pub was once owned by the Coopers Brewery. The interior retains cosy corners; the cellar doors in the middle of the floor show how the bar has been remodelled. Eight handpumps serve regular and guest ales, while an imaginative menu of home-cooked food is served daily, except Monday. Live music is performed twice a week when the pub may stay open until midnight. There is a pleasant garden for outdoor drinking. ⛰❀◐◑⇌(St Denys)P⊬

Duke of Wellington

36 Bugle Street, SO14 2AH (off A33, Town Quay road)
⏲ 11-11; 12-10.30 Sun
☎ (023) 8033 9222
Ringwood Best Bitter; Wadworth IPA, 6X; guest beers 🄷
This Grade II listed building has been an inn since 1490 when it was called the Brewe House, but the cellar dates from 1210. It acquired its current name in 1815. A short walk from the Town Quay, it offers three guest ales and an extensive menu of home-cooked food (no meals Sun eve). It has a no-smoking room, another room for private functions and a small terrace by the pavement for outdoor drinking. Wheelchair access is at the rear. ⛰Q❀◐◑♿●⊬

Guide Dog

38 Earl's Road, Bevois Valley, SO14 6SF (100 yds W of Bevois Valley road)
⏲ 3 (12 Sat)-11; 12-10.30 Sun
☎ (023) 8022 5642
Beer range varies 🄷
Single-roomed, back-street town pub, formerly Wadworth's, but now a genuine free house where six handpumps dispense a changing range of beers from micro-breweries, both local and from far afield. Hundreds of neatly displayed pump clips show beers previously sold here. An interesting selection of bottled beers, mainly Belgian, is also stocked. Two annual beer festivals are staged at this local CAMRA Pub of the Year winner in 2005. It is an ideal pre- or post-match venue for Southampton FC games. 🚌♣

Humble Plumb

Commercial Street, Bitterne, SO18 6LY
⏲ 11.30-2.30, 5-11; 11.30-11 Sat; 12-10.30 Sun
☎ (023) 8043 7577
Wadworth IPA, 🄷 **6X,** 🄶 **seasonal beers; guest beers** 🄷
Friendly, family local with a spacious L-shaped bar and plenty of seating in the tranquil garden that has a covered area. The bar boasts nine working handpumps of which six offer guest beers that change weekly, showcasing smaller breweries whenever possible. The guests are listed on a blackboard and customers are invited to 'try before you buy'. It hosts a regular Monday quiz and a meat draw on Sunday afternoon. Good food is served (no meals Mon). Dogs are welcome. ❀◐◑♿🚌P⊬

Park Inn

37 Carlisle Road, Shirley, SO16 4FN (off Romsey Rd)
⏲ 11.30-midnight daily
☎ (023) 8078 7835
Wadworth IPA, 6X, JCB; guest beers 🄷
Although now a single bar, the Park retains a two-bar feel. Dating from the 1800s this Wadworth's house was owned by Barlow's until 1929 before passing to Brickwood's then Whitbread. Note the collection of mirrors around the walls. Outside drinkers can sit at tables in the walled forecourt. Sandwiches are served at lunchtime. ❀♣

Platform Tavern

Town Quay, SO14 2NY
⏲ 12-11 (11.30 Thu; midnight Fri & Sat); 12-11 Sun
☎ (023) 8033 7232 🌐 platformtavern.com
Fuller's London Pride; Itchen Valley Godfathers; guest beers 🄷
This stone-floored single bar, built in 1872 incorporates parts of the old city walls. Live music (jazz, blues and soul), good food, an African themed décor and candlelight, all contribute to a relaxing café-style ambience. Two changing guest beers supplement the regulars. Food is available every day - all day at weekends. There is a pavement area dedicated to outside drinkers. Just occasionally an admission charge is levied for special music events. ❀◐◑🚌

Richmond Inn

108 Portswood Road, Portswood, SO17 2FW
⏲ 11-midnight or 1am daily
☎ (023) 8055 4523
Greene King IPA, Abbot; guest beers 🄷
Two bar pub, dating from the 1870s: a busy, lively public bar housing a dartboard, juke box and TV, and a quieter, more comfortable lounge – both can sometimes be smoky. The two bars share a lovely antique brass till. Pictures of the great liners associated with Southampton are displayed. A pleasant, well-maintained garden houses a function room. Staff are happy to remove sparklers on request. The Richmond may stay open until 1am on Friday and Saturday if trade demands. ❀⊟⇌(St Denys)🚌♣

South Western Arms

38-40 Adelaide Road, St Denys, SO17 2HW (next to St Denys Station)
⏲ 3-11.30; 12-1am Fri & Sat; 12-11.30 Sun
☎ (023) 8032 4542
Caledonian Deuchars IPA; Fuller's London Pride; Hop Back Summer Lightning; Ringwood Best Bitter; guest beers 🄷
Another pub that featured on the 1878 'drink map' of Southampton, this thriving ale house is on two levels. The upper level offers table football, pool and a wide-screen TV. Draught and bottled beer festivals supplement the already generous supply of regular beers and six guests; various ciders are also stocked. A recent CAMRA regional Pub of the Year, it was a national finalist in 2004. A pleasant courtyard is used for drinking and barbecues in summer.
❀⇌(St Denys)♣●P

Waterloo Arms

101 Waterloo Road, Freemantle, SO15 3BS
⏲ 12-11 daily
☎ (023) 8022 0022
Hop Back GFB, Crop Circle, Entire Stout, Summer Lightning, seasonal beers; guest beers 🄷
Cosy, one-bar local in a quiet residential area, benefiting from a secluded garden at the rear and a new, no-smoking, conservatory for families to use. Beer

festivals are held twice a year (May and Sept) and the pub operates a 'try before you buy' policy on its ales. It stocks a selection of country wines and serves good food. Dogs are welcome at this pub, just a short walk from Millbrook Station. Polypins and minipins are available to take away.
(Millbrook)

Wellington Arms

56 Park Road, Freemantle, SO15 3DE (Mansion Rd jct)
12-midnight daily
(023) 8022 0356
Adnams Bitter; Fuller's London Pride; Greene King Abbot; Hook Norton Old Hooky; Ringwood Best Bitter; guest beers
Dating from the 1860s, this corner local was called the Swan until 1975. A Punch Taverns house, it is a treasure trove of Iron Duke memorabilia; also note the many old coins set into the bar counter. There are two bars, with a designated no-smoking area and a garden/patio. It stages live jazz most Sunday evenings, a quiz on Thursday and a bridge club meets on Monday evening.
(Central/Millbrook)

Stubbington

Golden Bowler

122 Stubbington Lane, PO14 2NQ
11-11; 12-10.30 Sun
(01329) 662845 thegoldenbowler.co.uk
Theakston XB; guest beers
Family-run, 1960s free house, originally a Victorian country property attached to a nursery. Opening hours are frequently extended to 11.30pm or midnight at the weekend, according to customer demand. Three guest beers are normally kept, with local breweries usually represented and real cider is now a regular feature. The restaurant serves the same menu as the main bar area (no food Mon eve). A multi-purpose TV/function room has conference facilities. Live music is occasionally performed on Saturday evening. P

Tadley

Bishopswood Golf Club

Bishopswood Lane, RG26 4AT (6 miles N of Basingstoke, off A340) OS591617
11-11 (9.30 Mon; winter hours vary); 12-7 Sun
(0118) 981 2200
Beer range varies
A golf club is not generally a place to find any, not to mention good quality, real ale, but this is an exception. A warm, friendly atmosphere pertains in the comfortable lounge (dress code applies) that boasts an unusual central fireplace. Snooker is played. Outside, a pleasant raised terrace overlooks the course. Visitors are welcome to local CAMRA's Club of the Year, three years running. One beer is usually from Brains or and West Berkshire, accompanied by another guest.
P

Titchfield

Queen's Head

High Street, PO14 4AQ
11-3 (not Mon), 6-11; 12-3, 7-10.30 Sun
(01329) 842154
Fuller's London Pride; guest beers
The pub is named after Catherine of Braganza who married Charles II and was first commemorated by an inn sign in the late 18th century. The left-hand bar is now a restaurant (eve meals are served Tue-Sat), while the other bar, crammed with old local photographs, has a raised seating area. The old entrance to the off-licence can still be seen across the black and white chequerboard stone floor in the foyer.
P

Wheatsheaf

East Street, PO14 4AD
12-3, 5 (6 Sat)-11;12-3, 7-10.30 Sun
(01329) 842965
Fuller's London Pride; guest beers
Near the centre of this ancient and picturesque village, the Wheatsheaf, which offers three guest beers, is regularly listed in this Guide. The largest room is its busiest, usually full of jocular locals. A tiny snug, a dining room and an extensive outside seating area complete the facilities. Of particular note are the unusual carvings on the ceiling beams. The pub has limited parking space – arrive early if you need to park. No lunches are served on Wednesday.
P

Titchfield Common

Sir Joseph Paxton

272 Hunts Pond Road, PO14 4PF
12-11 (11.30 Wed & Thu; midnight Fri & Sat); 12-11 Sun
(01489) 572125
Caledonian Deuchars IPA; Wells Bombardier; guest beer
The pub name derives not from the man who was responsible for building the Crystal Palace, but from a variety of strawberry that he developed, in an area famous for growing the fruit. The pub's dimly lit interior offers many cosy corners, while at the rear an area is dedicated to snooker. The large garden was only slightly reduced in size by the construction a few years ago of an extension. The pub benefits from an extensive car park. P

Upper Farringdon

Rose & Crown Inn

Crows Lane, GU34 3ED (off A32)
12-3, 6-11; 12-11 Sat; 12-10.30 Sun
(01420) 588231
Adnams Bitter; Courage Best Bitter; Greene King IPA; Triple fff Moondance, Stairway
In a village just off the beaten track, this friendly pub, with an L-shaped bar, progresses from a seating area near a log fire through formal tables to a modern restaurant (no food Mon eve). Families may find that the large garden and boxed games in the bar help to keep children occupied.

Imaginative food is supplemented by lunchtime bar snacks. Dogs and walkers are always welcome. The inn stages regular Monday jazz evenings. ♨Q❀◐⊟♣P

Weyhill

Weyhill Fair

SP11 0PP (near Andover)

⏲ 11.15-3, 6 (5 Fri)-11; 12-3, 7-10.30 Sun

☎ (01264) 773631 🌐 weyhillfair.co.uk

Fuller's Chiswick, London Pride, ESB; guest beers Ⓗ

This single-bar pub on the main road from Andover was recently acquired by Fuller's, however, local breweries are also represented on its six handpumps. Nearby is the Weyhill Fairground, site of the famous sheep fairs, and now a popular crafts centre. Buses stop outside the pub, which stands on a good cycle route to Andover. ❀◐♿⊟P⊬

Whitchurch

Prince Regent

104 London Road, RG28 7LT (on Basingstoke road)

⏲ 11-11; 12-11 Sun

☎ (01256) 892179

Hop Back Summer Lightning; Otter Bitter; Stonehenge Pigswill Ⓗ

Unspoilt free house – a true local - that has very welcoming owners; be prepared to be drawn into some interesting conversations. The single-bar pub overlooks the Test Valley and is well worth the walk up from the town. It fields crib, quiz and pool teams, and the local ferret club meets here in the cellar. Buses stop outside for the nearby towns of Winchester, Andover and Basingstoke. ❀♣P

Whitchurch Sports & Social Club

Longmeadow Sports Centre, Winchester Road, RG28 7RB (S edge of town)

⏲ 11-2.30 (winter Wed-Sat only), 7-11; 12-10.30 Sun

☎ (01256) 892493

Fuller's London Pride; Hampshire King Alfred's Ⓗ

The excellent facilities at this club tend to be underrated by the townsfolk, but two large, contrasting bars provide a welcoming atmosphere. It is home to Whitchurch FC and an indoor bowling club whose green can be viewed from the lounge bar. It also houses a squash club. It stages regular events, ranging from astronomy sessions to disco parties. The club stands opposite the tranquil Millennium Meadow. CAMRA members can be signed in on production of a valid membership card. ❀⊟♿●P

White Hart Hotel,

The Square, RG28 7DN

⏲ 11 (7am for breakfast)-11; 12-10.30 Sun

☎ (01256) 892900 🌐 whitehartotelwhitchurch.co.uk

Arkell's 3B, Kingsdown Ⓗ

Impressive coaching inn, dating from 1461, where the emphasis is on good service. Divided into several areas, the pub displays the work of local artists and live music is a regular attraction. It opens for breakfast and coffee at 7am and sells cream teas in the summer. It stands opposite the birthplace of the late Lord Denning, Master of the Rolls and the people's right to demonstrate was won in the square outside the pub just over 100 years ago. ♨Q⇄◐⊟♿⇌P

Whitsbury

Cartwheel

SP6 3PZ (2½ miles W of A338 at Breamore) OS129188

⏲ 11.30-2.30 (3 Sat), 5.30-11; 12-10.30 Sun

☎ (01725) 518362 🌐 cartwheelinn.co.uk

Ringwood Best Bitter; Fortyniner, Old Thumper, seasonal beers; guest beer (occasional) Ⓗ

Easily missed, as it resembles a pair of red-brick cottages, the Cartwheel comprises a pleasant bar with low ceiling and a log fire, plus a dining room where good food is served every day. Pictures show the local racing stables – indeed the pub was re-opened by Desert Orchid in 2004. This remote and immaculately preserved part of Hampshire is ideal walking country, but the only public transport is the bookable C61 bus service from Fordingbridge.

♨Q❀◐♿⊟♣P

Wickham

Greens

The Square, PO17 5JQ

⏲ 11-3, 6-11; closed Mon; 12-3, 7-10.30 (not winter eve) Sun

☎ (01329) 833197

🌐 btinternet.com/~a.kingshott/greens/greens.htm

Fuller's London Pride; guest beers Ⓗ

Advertised as a restaurant and pub, the building is about 100 years old. The modern, entirely no-smoking interior is divided into several areas including a function room. The gourmet menu has received exceptional reviews in the local newspaper. The emphasis on food has resulted in real ale being served in oversized glasses, which is unusual for the area. One or two guest beers are stocked, mostly well-known brands. The garden overlooks Wickham water meadows and hosts special events in summer. ❀◐♿⊬▯

Wickham Wine Bar

The Square, PO17 5JN

⏲ 11.30-2.30, 5.30-midnight; closed Sun

☎ (01329) 832732 🌐 wickhamwinebar.com

Oakleaf Hole Hearted Ⓗ

This Grade II listed, 15th-century timber-framed building is a no-smoking wine bar and restaurant that also sells real ale (no keg). The ground-floor bar has retained the original vaulted oak beams and an open log fire. The two-storey upstairs restaurant boasts a 16th-century wall painting. The bar stays open until 1am for diners, but may close earlier, depending on customer demand. The menu changes frequently, and generally offers fresh fish and local game. Live jazz is performed on Wednesday evening. ♨Q◐⊬

Winchester

Bell

83 St Cross Road, St Cross, SO23 9RE (on B3335 at edge of the city)

⏲ 11-3, 5-11; 11-11 Fri, Sat & summer; 12-4, 7-10.30 Sun
☎ (01962) 865284
Greene King IPA, Old Speckled Hen, seasonal beer or guest beer Ⓗ
Proper, two-bar pub, allowing a choice of comfortable drinking areas: a quiet, carpeted, conversational lounge (no-smoking at lunchtime) or a busy, cosmopolitan, flagstoned public bar that leads to a large, safe garden with play equipment. The Bell adjoins the Hospital of St Cross, England's oldest (1132) almshouse; it is a tranquil mile-long stroll from the city through the water meadows that inspired Keats's ode To Autumn. A varied menu of good food includes Sunday roasts (no meals Wed eve).
⌂Q❀◐◑⊟⊟P⚡

Black Boy
1 Wharf Hill, SO23 9NQ (off B3330, Chesil St)
⏲ 11-3, 5-11; 12-3, 7-10.30 Sun
☎ (01962) 861754
Hop Back Summer Lightning; Ringwood Best Bitter; guest beers Ⓗ
Centuries old, rambling building of interconnected rooms surrounding a central bar. Guest beers come from small local breweries. A converted barn serves as a restaurant Tuesday–Saturday; another room, with a working Aga is a farmhouse kitchen. The pub resembles an eccentric folk museum: a lathe on a mantelpiece, a wall of buckets, watches on the ceiling, a Victorian butcher's display and a stuffed donkey number among its 'exhibits'. No food is served Sunday evening or Monday and Tuesday lunchtimes.
⌂Q❀◐◑♣

Fulflood Arms
28 Cheriton Road, SO22 5EF (take Western Rd off Stockbridge Rd)
⏲ 12-2 (not Tue), 5-11; 12-11 Fri; 11-11 Sat; 12-11 Sun
☎ (01962) 622006
Greene King IPA, Abbot; guest beer Ⓗ
Glazed brickwork and etched windows are evidence of this 19th-century pub's association with the former Winchester Brewery. Once a multi-roomed pub, it now has a single bar bearing all the clutter and intimacy of a real local, with bar billiards, darts and TV for entertainment. It has a no-smoking area and small patios at the front and rear. It will stay open until midnight on Friday and Saturday if trade demands.
❀≷♣⚡

Hyde Tavern
57 Hyde Street, SO23 7DY (on B3047)
⏲ 12-2 (3 Sat), 5 (6 Sat)-11 (midnight Fri & Sat); 12-11.30 Sun
☎ (01962) 862592
Greene King IPA, guest beer Ⓗ
This small, medieval, timber-framed pub is not only an architectural gem, but it is run by a proper landlady who has the gift of making every guest feel valued. The front bar, below street level, features low beams and sagging floors and ceilings. The cosy rear bar displays a plethora of sporting paraphernalia. Some say the pub is haunted and King Alfred's grave is close by. The secluded garden is delightful.
Q❀⊟≷♣

Wykeham Arms
75 Kingsgate Street, SO23 9PE (by the entrances to Cathedral Close and college)
⏲ 11-11; 12-10.30 Sun
☎ (01962) 853834
Fuller's Gale's Butser, London Pride, Gale's HSB Ⓗ
Rambling, Georgian inn with many rooms, adjoining the city's ancient Kingsgate. Bric-a-brac covers every available space – old school desks make convenient tables – Nelsonia abounds and a variety of artefacts, including (allegedly) 2,000 pewter mugs, fills every inch. Often busy but always civilised, it is a conversational haven away from 21st-century pressures. Booking is recommended for the award-winning food (no meals Sun eve) and the accommodation is of an equally high standard. ⌂Q❀⛟◐◑

Winsor

Compass Inn
Winsor Road, SO40 2HE
⏲ 11-11; 12-11 Sun
☎ (023) 8081 2237
Fuller's London Pride, Gale's HSB; Greene King Abbot; Ringwood Best Bitter; guest beer (summer) Ⓗ
Spick and span pub in a one-street hamlet, east of the New Forest. Its modest, white-painted brick exterior belies the spacious interior: a comfortable lounge with polished wood furniture, fresh flowers and a log-burning stove; a homely dining room and a smart public bar with a pool table. Good value food is available daily, with smoking restricted during dining hours. Beer festivals are held over May and August bank holidays. The No. 31 bus (Cadnam-Southampton) passes the door.
⌂Q❀◐◑▲⊟●P

Wolverton

George & Dragon
Wolverton Townsend, RG26 5ST (1 mile E of A339, 3½ miles SW of Tadley)
⏲ 12-3, 5.30-11; 12-3, 7-10.30 Sun
☎ (01635) 298292
Brakspear Special; Fuller's London Pride; Wadworth IPA; West Berkshire Mr Chubb's; guest beers Ⓗ
Oak beams festooned with dried hops, and a huge open hearth burning logs in winter characterise this 300-year-old inn, run by the same landlord for 21 years. It provides a superb setting in which to relish the good selection of beers, while diners sit at candlelit tables to enjoy good home-cooked cuisine in a romantic atmosphere. The large garden is set in an orchard where children can play. The function room, with bar and skittle alley, caters for parties.
⌂Q❀⛟◐◑●♣P

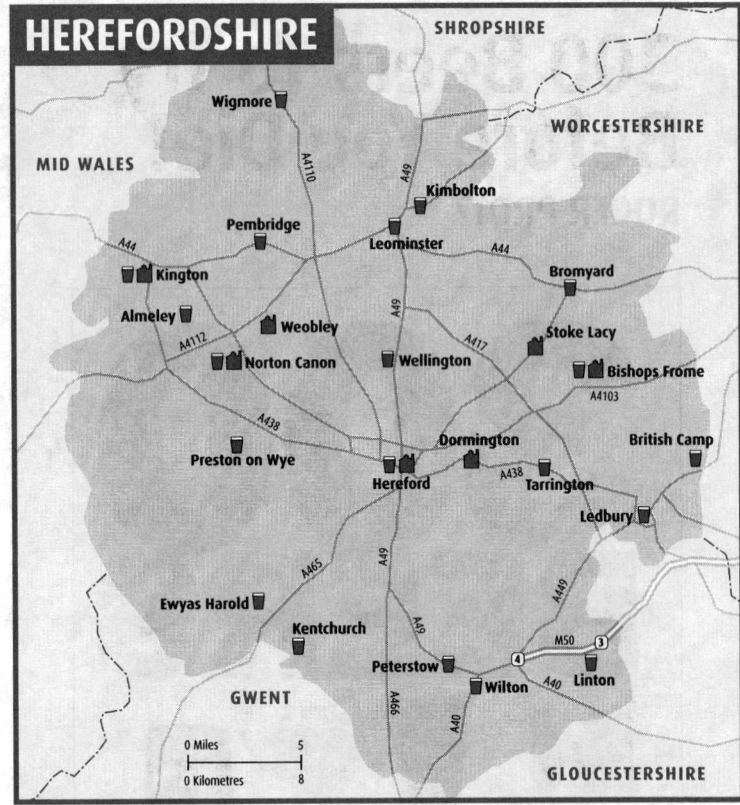

Almeley

Bells Inn

HR3 6LF OS334515

12-3 (not Tue or Thu), 7-11; 12-11 Sat & Sun

(01544) 327216

Wye Valley Bitter; guest beer H

From the car park, where horses may sometimes be seen at the hitching rail, this unpretentious stone-built village pub is entered through the former jug and bottle. It has a large low-ceilinged bar and a second, no-smoking, room which doubles as family room and dining area. Outside is a double petanque piste. Traditional, home prepared meals are served in the evening (Thu-Sat) and Sunday lunchtime. The guest beer is generally from local brewers. There is live music on some Saturday evenings.

P

Bishops Frome

Green Dragon

WR6 5BP (just off B4214)

12-2 (summer Tue-Thu), 5-11; 12-11 Fri & Sat; 12-4, 7-11 Sun

(01885) 490607

Taylor Golden Best; Theakston Best Bitter; Wye Valley Butty Bach; guest beer H

A welcome return for this iconic pub, a mecca for real ale in the 1970s and 80s, and now as popular as ever. A splendid 17th-century, multi-roomed, low-beamed inn, it has a warren of flagstone bars and an inglenook forming the centrepiece of the main bar, as well as a real fire in every room. The TV and function room doubles as a restaurant. Conversation is allowed to flourish here. Food is served (not Sun) with steaks a speciality. Draught local cider is available in summer.

P

British Camp

Malvern Hills Hotel

Jubilee Drive, WR13 6DW (on A449)

10-11 daily

(01684) 540690 malvernhillshotel.co.uk

Malvern Hills Black Pear; Wye Valley Bitter, Hereford Pale Ale; guest beers H

Large landmark hotel located high on the Malvern Hills, near the British Camp Hill Fort. It is popular with locals and particularly with

INDEPENDENT BREWERIES

Arrow Kington
Bridge Street Brewing suspended
Dunn Plowman Kington
Marches Dormington
Mayfields Bishops Frome
Shoes Norton Canon
Spinning Dog Hereford
Wild's Weobley
Wye Valley Stoke Lacy

walkers (dogs and well-behaved children are welcome – the latter until 5.30pm). There is a genuine commitment to quality cask beers: five pumps adorn the main bar, with guest beers from local breweries. An airy restaurant offers affordable quality dining, along with bar meals in the main bar. A new conservatory, as well as outside seating, makes this an ideal venue for a fine day. ♛❀⇆◐◑♿♣P⚡

Bromyard

Rose & Lion

5 New Road, HR7 4AJ

☺ 11-3, 5-11; 11-midnight Fri & Sat; 12-midnight Sun

☎ (01885) 482381

Wye Valley Bitter, Hereford Pale Ale, Butty Bach; guest beer Ⓗ

Situated just off the High Street, this traditional and unspoiled three-roomed pub has all the necessary ingredients: a friendly public bar, a cosy lounge, a good buzz and a pleasant garden in which to drink good ale. It enjoys a loyal following among locals, while always welcoming visitors. A folk jam session is held on Sunday evening. Rent for the garden is paid annually to owners Wye Valley in home grown parsnips. Q❀⊟♣P

Ewyas Harold

Dog Inn

HR2 0EX (just off B4347)

☺ 10-midnight (1am Fri & Sat); 10-11 Sun

☎ (01981) 240598 ⊕ thedoginn.net

Brains Rev James; guest beer Ⓗ

Dating from 1509, this friendly, stone-built village inn has been the Bell, Dog, Castle and now the Dog again. Consisting of a main bar plus games room and restaurant, its beers are drawn from local and regional breweries and draught Gwatkins cider is occasionally available. Home-prepared and locally-sourced meals are served in the restaurant and, at lunchtimes, also in the bar. Live music features from time to time, and a beer festival is held annually in the summer. ♛Q❀⇆◐◑♣●⚡

Hereford

Barrels

69 St Owen Street, HR1 2JQ

☺ 11-11.30 (midnight Fri & Sat); 11-11.30 Sun

☎ (01432) 274968

Wye Valley Bitter, Hereford Pale Ale, Butty Bach, Dorothy Goodbody's Wholesome Stout , seasonal beers Ⓗ

Once home to Wye Valley Brewery, and still the brewery's flagship outlet, the pub stocks most of the beer range, plus Thatchers Traditional Cider. Voted Herefordshire CAMRA Pub of the Year 2003, its four rooms cater for all age groups. A pool table occupies one bar, and another has a large-screen TV for major sporting events – otherwise conversation rules. Freed from brewery activities, the rear courtyard now provides a great outdoor drinking area, and is the venue for the August bank holiday charity music and beer festival. ❀⊟⇌♣●

Kings Fee

49-53 Commercial Road, HR1 2BJ

☺ 9am-midnight daily

☎ (01432) 373240

Greene King Abbot; Marston's Pedigree; guest beers Ⓗ

Wetherspoon conversion of an old supermarket, highly commended in the 2004 CAMRA National Pub Design Awards. The large, open-plan main bar leads to an elevated family area (where children are welcome until 5pm) and a courtyard. Decor is contemporary in style, and features local history panels and woodcut prints by a local artist. It has brought to Hereford a welcome choice of guest ales, plus Westons cider and perry, at reasonable prices. Good value food is served all day. The pub is no-smoking throughout. Q☋❀◐◑♿⇌●⚡

Victory

88 St Owen Street, HR1 2QD

☺ 3 (11 summer)-11 (midnight Fri & Sat); 12-10.30 Sun

☎ (01432) 274998

Spinning Dog Organic Bitter, Herefordshire Owd Bull, Herefordshire Light Ale, Top Dog, Organic Oatmeal Stout; guest beers Ⓗ

Home of Hereford's Spinning Dog Brewery, you will find most of its beers here, plus the city's best range of real ciders and perry including Westons and Bridge Farm. The main bar is made of timber with bare wooden floors, and the bar servery is in the shape of a galleon. The unusual nautical theme continues through to a large narrow bar and skittle alley to the rear. A key venue for local bands on Saturday and Sunday evenings, it holds mini-beer festivals twice a year. Meals are served on Saturday and Sunday only. ♛☋❀◐⊟⇌♣●

Kentchurch

Bridge Inn

HR2 0BY (on B4347)

☺ 12-3 (not Mon or Tue), 5-11; 12-3, 7-10.30 Sun

☎ (01981) 240408

Beer range varies Ⓗ

Situated in a beautiful location close to the Welsh border on the banks of the River Monnow, the building probably dates from the 14th century. It comprises a welcoming single front bar plus a restaurant with excellent views and boasts riverside gardens and a petanque piste for those summer days. The freshly-prepared food ranges from bar snacks to full à la carte (not served Sun eve). Guest beers are from regional and local breweries, usually including one from Wye Valley. Beer festivals are held on spring and August bank holidays.
♛Q❀⇆◐◑▲♣P

Kimbolton

Stockton Cross

HR6 0HD (on A4112, W of village)

☺ 12-3, 7-11 (not Mon eve); 12-3 Sun

☎ (01568) 612509

Teme Valley This; Wye Valley Butty Bach Ⓗ

Single bar black and white pub dating from the 16th century and retaining some

interesting original features. Long and narrow, it has a drinking area at one end of the bar while the dining area at the other end includes two cosy alcoves set either side of a large fireplace. The food, including a good vegetarian choice, is sourced locally and freshly prepared to order so there may be a short wait – allowing time to enjoy a good pint and quiet conversation.
♛❀◐◗P⊬

Kington

Olde Tavern

22 Victoria Road, HR5 3BX

⚙ 7 (6.30 Tue-Fri)-midnight (1am Fri); 12-3, 6-1am Sat; 12-3, 7-11.30 Sun

☎ (01544) 230122

Dunn Plowman Brewhouse Bitter, Sting, Shirehorse Ale, Railway Porter 🄷

A pub for the connoisseur and a two-room time warp, voted Herefordshire & Worcestershire CAMRA Pub of the Year in 2005. The tap for the nearby Dunn Plowman Brewery, there is always a warm welcome from staff and locals alike. Regulars take an active part in pub games and the Kington festivals. The recently opened Jake's Bistro to the rear offers a varied menu using home-produced and locally-sourced food (weekends only).Q❀◗⊟♣

Ledbury

Prince of Wales

Church Lane, HR8 1DL

⚙ 11-11 daily

☎ (01531) 632250

Banks's Bitter; Brains Rev James; Sharp's Doom Bar; guest beer 🄷

Tucked away down a beautiful, narrow, cobbled street towards the church, this superb 16th-century timbered pub has a front and back bar. Always bustling with locals and visitors alike, it holds a popular folk jam session on Wednesday evening and is home to a number of pub games teams. Run with a real verve, good value, simple bar meals and Sunday roasts feature, along with Westons cider and perry. Parking is available in the town car parks.
♨❀◐⊟⇌♣●

Talbot Hotel

14 New Street, HR8 2DX

⚙ 11-3, 5-11 (midnight Fri); 11-midnight Sat; 11-4, 7-11 Sun

☎ (01531) 632963 ⊕ visitledbury.co.uk/talbot

Wadworth IPA, 6X; Wye Valley Butty Bach; guest beer 🄷

Excellent black-and-white half-timbered hotel dating back to 1596. The heavily beamed bar surrounds an island servery, dividing into a range of relaxing and comfortable drinking areas. The beautiful oak-panelled dining room, with its fine carved overmantle, was once the scene of fighting between Cavaliers and Roundheads. Traditional bar snacks are available and English and continental dishes are served in the restaurant, all made with local ingredients. Live music is hosted occasionally. An ideal place to spend a relaxing short break, on-street parking is available nearby.
♛⊭◐◗⇌♣

Leominster

Bell Inn

39 Etnam Street, HR6 8AE

⚙ 12-11; 12-10.30 Sun

☎ (01568) 612818

Hobsons Town Crier; Wye Valley Bitter; guest beer 🄷

Joint winner of Herefordshire CAMRA Pub of the Year 2005, this friendly, modernised pub with its single island U-shaped bar has a light and airy feel, with a pleasant garden to the rear. Live music features here – folk on Tuesday evening and band on Thursday. On-street parking outside is free and there is a large car park nearby. Reasonably priced, home-made pub food is served at lunchtime. Regular beers are complemented by often adventurous guest beers from micros – both local and from afar. ♛❀◐⇌♣

Black Horse

74 South Street, HR6 8JF

⚙ 11-2.30, 6-11; 11-11 Sat; 12-3, 7-10.30 Sun

☎ (01568) 611946

Dunn Plowman Brewhouse Bitter; Hobsons Town Crier; guest beers 🄷

Enthusiastically-run, if somewhat unassuming ex-coach house. Once home to the fledgling Dunn Plowman Brewery, it is still noted for its excellent range of beers. It has a traditional public bar, a narrow lounge area – resplendent in 1980s red decor – and a separate dining area to the rear. Bar snacks and meals are served (not Sun eve), with Sunday lunches a speciality. Games include petanque, table skittles and quoits. Car park access is via the narrow courtyard entrance. Addlestones cider is served.
Q♨❀◐◗⊟⇌♣●P

Grape Vaults

2-4 Broad Street, HR6 8BS

⚙ 11-11; 12-10.30 Sun

☎ (01568) 611404

Banks's Original, Bitter; Marston's Pedigree; guest beers 🄷

Herefordshire CAMRA Pub of the Year runner-up for 2004 and once a 'hard-core' cider house, this is an unadulterated treat. The original wood-panelled single main bar is resplendent with snug, roaring fire and bench seating. Good conversation is guaranteed in this cosy haven – the TV is only turned on for major rugby games. The gents toilet is probably the smallest in England. Conventional English pub food is served (not Sun) at affordable prices, made with local ingredients. There is always a guest beer from Wood.
♛Q◐◗⇌

Radnorshire Arms

85 Bargates, HR6 8HB

⚙ 5-11; 12-11 Sat & Sun

☎ (01568) 613872

Adnams Bitter; guest beer Ⓗ
Workaday locals' two-bar pub, run with real love by the landlady, a short walk from the town centre. It has a small lounge and a well-appointed public bar with TV, plus a separate elevated area with gaming machines. Laurel & Hardy keep watch over the lounge. The guest beer is sourced from a local micro-brewery, often Spinning Dog. ♔Q⊟♣

Linton

Alma Inn

HR9 7RY (off B4221, W of M50 jct 3) OS659255
✪ 12-3 (not Mon-Fri), 6.30 (6 Fri & Sat)-11; 12-3, 7-10.30 Sun
☎ (01989) 720355 ⊕ almainnlinton.co.uk
Butcombe Bitter; RCH Pitchfork; guest beers Ⓗ
Frequent Herefordshire CAMRA Pub of the Year, the Alma was joint winner again in 2005. The Alma is that enigma – a very successful village pub that does not serve food. A large but cosy lounge with roaring fire contrasts with a basic pool room and a quieter, no-smoking 'other room'. Run with real passion, the Alma champions small and local breweries. The extensive hillside gardens are the venue for an ambitious Blues & Ale festival held in June or July each year.
♔Q❀⅄♣P⚟

Norton Canon

Three Horseshoes

HR4 7BH (on A480)
✪ 12-3 (Wed, Sat only), 6-11; 12-3, 7-10.30 Sun
☎ (01544) 318375
Shoes Norton Ale, Canon Bitter, Peploe's Tipple, Farriers Ale Ⓗ
Recovering from a major fire in March 2006 that fortunately left the bars largely unscathed, the pub is home to Shoes Brewery. A public bar leads through to a larger pool room, or there is the small, cosy lounge furnished with an ad hoc collection of comfortable old sofas, chairs and a piano. Farriers Ale, at 15% ABV, is now available on draught as well as in bottles. The bus stop is half a mile from the pub (services 461/462 from Hereford), alight at the 'Weobley Turn'.
♔Q☋❀⊟⊞♣P

Pembridge

New Inn

Market Square, HR6 9DZ (on A44)
✪ 11-3, 6-11; 12-3, 7-10.30 Sun
☎ (01544) 388427
Black Sheep Best Bitter; Dunn Plowman Brewhouse Bitter; Fuller's London Pride Ⓗ
Imposing old building facing the market square with outdoor seating. The public bar is resplendent with flagstone floor, large settle and fireplace; there is also a lounge, dining/drinking/family area and a downstairs restaurant. The heavily-beamed interior is decorated with hop bines and traditional furniture creates a homely feel. Draught Westons Old Rosie and bottled Dunkertons Black Fox cider are available.
♔Q☋❀⇌◐⊟♣●P

Peterstow

Red Lion

Winters Cross, HR9 6LH (on A49, just NW of village)
✪ 12-2.30, 6-11.30 (12.30am Fri); 12-12.30am Sat; 12-11 Sun
☎ (01989) 730202
Otter Bitter; Taylor Landlord; guest beers Ⓗ
The Red Lion was delicensed in the 1970s but, unusually, reverted to a pub a few years later after a sympathetic renovation. A single bar serves drinking and dining areas including a conservatory. The home-prepared food ranges from bar snacks to full meals, many of which are offered as 'light bite' options: booking is advisable at most times. Guest beers come from local micros or regional breweries. Facilities include an outdoor adventure playground for children. The regular Hereford-Ross No. 38 bus service stops outside. ♔☋❀◐♿⅄⊞♣P

Preston On Wye

Yew Tree

HR2 9JT
✪ 7-midnight (1am Fri & Sat); 12-3, 7-11 Sun
☎ (01981) 500359
Beer range varies Ⓖ
Pleasantly eccentric and unspoilt single bar drinkers' establishment located in a quiet hamlet near the River Wye. Comfortable and welcoming, it is home to boules, pool and quiz teams, while in the summer it is popular with fishermen and canoeists. The beer, which tends to alternate between local or regional breweries, is served direct from a cask behind the small bar. Draught Thatchers Heritage Cider is also available. Often also open on Saturday lunchtimes in summer; it hosts monthly live music on Saturdays.
♔Q❀⅄♣●P

Tarrington

Tarrington Arms

HR1 4HX (on A438)
✪ 12-3, 7-11; 12-3, 7-10.30 Sun
☎ (01432) 890796 ⊕ tarringtonarms.co.uk
Wood Shropshire Lad; guest beer Ⓗ
Late-Georgian red brick ex-hotel with colonnade entrance, it has two bars and a restaurant with a distinct refectory atmosphere. The smaller lounge bar features old photos of the hop-picking industry and contrasts with an archetypal public bar. The guest beer is from a small regional or micro-brewery. The food strikes a rare balance – high quality but at an affordable price – with a fish night each third Wednesday of the month. No food is served on Sunday evening. The Hereford-Ledbury No. 476 bus stops outside. ♔❀⇌◐⊟⊞♣P⚟

Wellington

Wellington Inn

HR4 8AT (½ mile W of A49)
✪ 12-3 (not Mon), 6-11; 12-3, 7-10.30 Sun
☎ (01432) 830367
Hobsons Best Bitter; Wye Valley Butty Bach; guest beers Ⓗ

Thriving, traditional village hostelry with a welcoming public bar, where wooden benches contrast with opulent leather sofas. A separate barn-style restaurant is popular with diners. Winner of the Tastes of Herefordshire 2005, food is a real speciality, with bar snacks, an elaborate lunchtime and evening menu, and carvery on Sunday. The bar has interesting local photographs, board games and newspapers. Guest beers are mainly from micro-breweries, and Westons First Quality cider is served. Hereford-Leominster bus No. 492 stops outside.
⛰❀◐◑🚌♣P

Wigmore

Olde Oak

HR6 9UJ (on A4110)
⏲ 12-3, 6-11; 12-11 Sat; 12-3, 7-10.30 (12-10.30 summer) Sun
☎ (01568) 770247
Wye Valley Butty Bach; Three Tuns Three 8; guest beers Ⓗ
Timber-framed two-bar village pub with a comfortable public bar featuring bare stone walls and beams. The lounge at the back leads to a restaurant in the conservatory. Home-made bar and restaurant meals are served every day except Sunday evening. Children and dogs are welcome. The interesting regular beers are complemented by guest beers from local micros or regional brewers, with an accent on Welsh products.
⛰Q⛲❀◐◑🚌♣P

Wilton

White Lion

Wilton Lane, HR9 6AQ (just off B4260)
⏲ 12-11; 12-10.30 Sun
☎ (01989) 562785 🌐 whitelionross.co.uk
Fuller's London Pride; Hook Norton Old Hooky; Wye Valley Hereford Pale Ale; guest beer (summer) Ⓗ
Attractive pub in a riverside setting affording views of the rivers Wye and Ross. The bar is open plan with exposed beams and stonework and a large stone fireplace. The restaurant is in a room called the gaol, which was originally part of a prison house adjoining the pub. English cuisine, freshly prepared from local ingredients, is served here and in the bar. The attractive garden leads down to the river.
⛰❀🛏◐◑⛺🚌♣P

The language of beer

Nose: the aroma. Gently swirl the beer to release the aroma. You will detect malt: grainy and biscuity, often likened to crackers or Ovaltine. When darker malts are used, the nose will have powerful hints of chocolate, coffee, nuts, vanilla, liquorice, molasses and such dried fruits as raisins and sultanas. Hops add superb aromas of resins, herbs, spices, fresh-mown grass and tart citrus fruit – lemon and orange are typical, with intense grapefruit notes from some American varieties. Sulphur may also be present when waters are 'Burtonised': ie gypsum and magnesium salts have been added to replicate the famous spring waters of Burton-on-Trent.

Palate: the appeal in the mouth. The tongue can detect sweetness, bitterness and saltiness as the beer passes over it. The rich flavours of malt will come to the fore but hop bitterness will also make a substantial impact. The tongue will also pick out the natural saltiness from the brewing water and fruit from darker malts, yeast and hops. Citrus notes often have a major impact on the palate.

Finish: the aftertaste, as the beer goes over the tongue and down the throat. The finish is often radically different to the nose. The aroma may be dominated by malt whereas hop flavours and bitterness can govern the finish. Darker malts will make their presence felt with roast, chocolate or coffee notes; fruit character may linger. Strong beers may end on a sweet or biscuity note but in mainstream bitters, bitterness and dryness come to the fore.

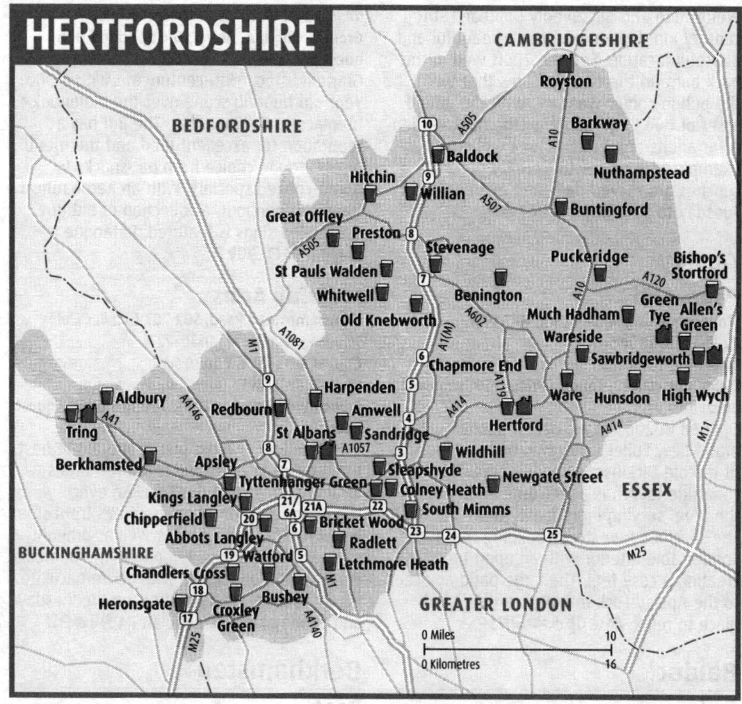

Abbots Langley

Compasses

95 Tibbs Hill Road, WD5 0LJ

⏲ 11-11 (11.30 Fri & Sat); 12-3.30, 7-11 Sun

☎ (01923) 262870

Courage Best Bitter; Fuller's London Pride; Greene King Abbot; Shepherd Neame Spitfire Ⓗ

Welcoming 18th-century inn with all the attributes of a good local, sympathetically modernised with a new patio area. Good pub food is served in the two bars and a dining area. Four real ales are usually available as well as 90 whiskies. Note the Victorian photographs of life in Yorkshire – ask the landlord for an explanation. The garden has a children's playhouse – children are not permitted in the bar.

❀⇄◑♿🚌(W6)P

Aldbury

Valiant Trooper

Trooper Road, HP23 5ER

⏲ 11.30-11; 12-10.30 Sun

☎ (01442) 851203

Fuller's London Pride; Oakham JHB; Tring Jack O'Legs; guest beers Ⓗ

The central bar has original low beams and is decorated in contemporary style but with tiled and wooden floors, scrubbed pine tables and open fires giving a traditional twist. A converted stable adjoining the pub has seating for 40 diners. Good ale and food makes this a popular destination for cyclists and walkers. No meals are served on Sunday or Monday evenings. Children are not allowed in the bar area.

♨Q❀◑🚌P⊬

Allen's Green

Queen's Head

CM21 0LS OS455168

⏲ 12-2.30 (not Mon & Tue), 5-11; 11-11 Fri & Sat; 12-10.30 Sun

☎ (01279) 723393 🌐 shirevillageinns.co.uk

Fuller's London Pride; Ⓗ **Buntingford Pargetters;** Ⓖ **guest beers** Ⓗ/Ⓖ

Small, traditional village inn with an enormous garden, popular with cyclists, walkers and locals. In the middle of nowhere, it is well worth the effort to find. With one dark mild, two ciders and a perry always available, the third weekend of the month is Beer Lovers Weekend with around 10 beers from small local and rare breweries on sale. Beer festivals are also held on bank holiday weekends. There is no TV, juke box or gaming machines at CAMRA local Pub of the Year 2006. ♨❀♿●P

Amwell

Elephant & Castle

Amwell Lane, AL4 8EA OS167132

⏲ 12-2.30, 5.30-11; 12-11 Sat; 12-10.30 Sun

☎ (01582) 832175

Greene King IPA, Morland Original, Abbot Ⓗ

INDEPENDENT BREWERIES

Alehouse St Albans
Buntingford Royston
Green Tye Green Tye
McMullen Hertford
Red Squirrel Hertford
Sawbridgeworth Sawbridgeworth
Tring Tring

Welcoming and deservedly popular 18th-century inn, hidden away in a beautiful and peaceful location. See the 200ft well in the back bar and the two real fires that warm the pub in colder weather. With the added asset of two large gardens (the back garden is for adults only), this is an excellent example of a successful country pub. Lunches are served daily and evening meals Tuesday to Saturday. ⛼❀◐◑♣P

Apsley

Paper Mill

Stationers Place, Apsley Lock, HP3 9RH

☺ 11-11; 12-10.30 Sun

☎ (01442) 288800

Fuller's Discovery, London Pride, ESB, seasonal beers Ⓗ

Opened in 2005 in a blaze of publicity, this brand new Fuller's pub was built on the site of the old Dickinsons paper works. This canalside tavern is a welcome addition to the area, serving high quality food and drink. The spacious two-storey building has a comfortable interior with an open fire creating a cosy feel. The large patio adjacent to the Apsley Lock marina is a delightful place to relax. ⛼❀◐◑♿⇌⊟P⚡

Baldock

Cock

43 High Street, SG7 6BG

☺ 12-1.30 (Wed only), 5-11 (11.30 Fri); 12-2.30, 5-11.30 Sat; 12-3.30, 7-11 Sun

☎ (01462) 892366

Greene King IPA, Abbot, Old Speckled Hen; guest beers Ⓗ

Dating from the 17th century, the inn has a beamed interior with split-level drinking areas. The pub is no smoking throughout. Greene King's XX Mild is regularly available with the occasional use of a cask breather. Baldock is an ancient market town on the old Great North Road coaching route. Market day is Wednesday when the pub is open at lunchtime. ⛼❀♿⇌⊟⚡

Barkway

Tally Ho

London Road, SG8 8EX (S end of village)

☺ 11.30-3, 5.30-11; 12-3, 6-11 Sat; 12-3 Sun

☎ (01763) 848389

Nethergate Suffolk County; guest beers Ⓟ

This friendly rural free house provides a regular outlet for the Buntingford Brewery, with at least one beer from its range always available, as well as ales from other local independents. Dark beers, milds and porters can usually be found here. With a convivial atmosphere and stimulating conversation, visitors are made welcome. Bar snacks are served as well as fresh home-cooked meals in the restaurant. A whisky menu offers 52 varieties. ⛼Q❀◐◑P

Benington

Bell Inn

Town Lane, SG2 7LA

☺ 12-3, 6.30-11 (7-10.30 Sun)

☎ (01438) 869270 ⊕ bellbenington.co.uk

Greene King IPA, Abbot, Old Speckled Hen; guest beers Ⓗ

Grade II listed, 15th-century inn with a 300-year-old hunting scene over the inglenook fireplace in the main bar. The inn has a reputation for excellent food and the menu offers a good choice from bar snacks to home-cooked specials. With an aeronautical theme throughout, a collection of antique enamelled signs is featured. Petanque is played. ⛼Q❀◐◑P

Lordship Arms

42 Whempstead Road, SG2 7BX (3 miles E of Stevenage via B1037) OS308227

☺ 12-3, 6-11; 12-3, 7-10.30 Sun

☎ (01438) 869665

Crouch Vale Brewers Gold; Young's Bitter; guest beers Ⓗ

This excellent one-bar pub is one of the best free houses in Herts and is a three-times local CAMRA Pub of the Year. An ever-changing selection of beers comes from small breweries far and wide, as well as draught cider and fruit wines. Telephone memorabilia decorate the pub inside with an immaculate garden outside. Curry night is on Wednesday and Sunday lunch is popular. ⛼❀◐●P▯

Berkhamsted

Boat

Gravel Path, Ravens Lane, HP4 2EF

☺ 11-11 (midnight Fri & Sat); 12-11 Sun

☎ (01442) 877152

Fuller's Discovery, London Pride, ESB; guest beer Ⓗ

New build pub opened in 1989, with one large main bar containing different areas and seating. One wall features a collection of photographs of the author Graham Greene who was born in the town. The patio facing the Grand Union Canal is popular. The guest beer comes from Fuller's. ❀◐◑⇌⊟P⚡

Crystal Palace

Station Road, HP4 2EZ

☺ 11-11 (midnight Fri & Sat); 12-10.30 Sun

☎ (01442) 862988

Greene King IPA, Old Speckled Hen; guest beer Ⓗ

Built in 1854, this friendly locals' pub has two contrasting bars. The public has a TV showing sporting events and hosts pub games while the quieter saloon offers views of the Grand Union Canal. Outdoor seating overlooking the canal is popular. The castle remains nearby are where William the Conqueror accepted the nation's defeat after the Battle of Hastings in 1066.
❀◐◑⊞♿⇌⊟♣P

Lamb

227 High Street, HP4 1AJ

☺ 11-11, 12-11 Sun

☎ (01442) 862615

Adnams Bitter; Fuller's London Pride; Greene King IPA; Tring Ridgeway Ⓗ

A recent refurbishment has changed the seating to make better use of space in this traditional pub, and a no-smoking area has also been created. However, the original character of the building remains unchanged with low beams and wooden furnishings helping to retain an old-fashioned feel. Essentially a drinkers' pub but food is served at weekday lunchtimes. ❀◖≠🚌♣⊬

Bishop's Stortford

Half Moon

31 North Street, CM23 2LD

⊙ 11-11.30 (12.30am Wed-Sat); 12-11.30 Sun

☎ (01279) 834500

Caledonian Deuchars IPA; Fuller's London Pride; Wychwood Hobgoblin; guest beers Ⓗ

Friendly, lively town centre pub. Three guest beers are usually on offer. The rambling 16th-century building includes a no-smoking bar and a large function room with a stage, home to regular live blues, acoustic, folk, jazz and comedy nights as well as quiz evenings. In summer you can enjoy a barbecue in the garden. ♨Q❀◖⊟≠♣●⊬

Jolly Brewers

170 South Street, CM23 3BQ

⊙ 12-3, 5.30-1.30am; 12-2am Fri & Sat; 12-1.30am Sun

☎ (01279) 836055

Greene King IPA; Taylor Landlord; guest beers Ⓗ

Town centre pub taking full advantage of the new licensing laws. Opened in 1882, it was originally named the Teetotallers, which was soon changed for obvious reasons. Two bars and a pool and games room dominate the more relaxed saloon. No food is served in the evening Friday to Sunday. Last entry is at midnight. ❀⊟◖◗♿≠P

Bricket Wood

Black Boy

79 Old Watford Road, AL2 3RU (off A405)

⊙ 10.30-11; 12-10.30 Sun

☎ (01923) 672444

Fuller's London Pride; guest beers Ⓗ

Dating from 1751, this Grade II listed building was extended in the 1930s. The bar area has original oak beams and a flagstone floor with two seating areas at either end. It is a serious games pub with two darts teams, four football teams and a flourishing golf society. Outdoor drinking can be enjoyed in the sloping garden which is set on three levels. Food is served weekdays. ❀◖P

Buntingford

Crown

17 High Street, SG9 9AB

⊙ 12-3, 6-11; 12-3 Sun

☎ (01763) 271422

Everards Tiger; guest beers Ⓗ

Now in its 17th year, the Crown holds the local CAMRA record for consecutive years in the Guide. The town centre pub has a large front bar, no-smoking back bar and a function room. Outside is a covered patio and secluded garden. Though the emphasis here is on drinking rather than dining, there are regular themed speciality food nights as well as fish and chips on Thursday and Friday. Crossword fans find the reference books useful. ♨Q❀◖◗🚌(700, 331)⊬

Brambles

117 High Street, SG9 9AF

⊙ 12-11; 12-10.30 Sun

☎ (01763) 273158

Fuller's London Pride, ESB; guest beers Ⓗ

Originally the Chequers, the pub has opened under a new name after many years of closure, with two bars both warmed by real fires. Six handpumps dispense real ale with more planned and cask beer now outsells keg and lager. Buntingford Brewery beers are usually available. ♨❀⊟🚌(700, 331)P⊡

Bushey

Swan

25 Park Road, WD23 3EE (off High Street)

⊙ 11-11; 12-10.30 Sun

☎ (020) 8950 2256

Greene King Old Speckled Hen; Jennings Cumberland Ale; Young's Bitter, Special Ⓗ

Small, one-bar back street locals' pub. The walls are adorned with CAMRA awards, old photographs and other items of interest. The Ladies' lavatory is outside, accessed via the garden. Snacks including rolls and pies are available all day. ♨❀🚌♣

Chandlers Cross

Clarendon Arms

Redhall Lane, WD3 4LU OS066983

⊙ 11 (12 Sun)-midnight (may close earlier)

☎ (01923) 270929

Courage Best Bitter; Greene King Old Speckled Hen; Wells Bombardier; guest beers Ⓗ

The single L-shaped bar room has three drinking and dining areas. Food highlights include a tapas menu, Sunday lunchtime carvery and a Saturday barbecue in summer. Popular with walkers, the pub is set in a area of commons and undulating woodland, though just a couple of miles from Watford. Access by public transport is limited to an infrequent bus service. ♨❀◖◗🚌(352)P⊬

Chapmore End

Woodman

30 Chapmore End, SG12 0HF OS328164

⊙ 12-2.30 (not Mon), 5.30-11 (midnight Fri); 12-11 Sat & Sun

☎ (01920) 463143 🌐 woodmanpub.com

Greene King IPA, Abbot, seasonal beers; guest beers Ⓖ

In a quiet hamlet off the B158, this totally unspoilt gem has been sensitively updated. The two-bar pub has gravity-dispensed real ale from cooled casks in the cellar behind the public bar. A local favourite is 'Mix': half IPA, half Abbot. Speciality themed meal evenings are held on alternate Thursdays. The large garden at the rear has a safe children's play area. The pub holds numerous special events. ♨Q❀◖⊟♣P⊬

Chipperfield

Royal Oak

1 The Street, WD4 9BH

⊙ 12-3, 6-11; 12-3, 7-10.30 Sun

☎ (01923) 266537

Adnams Broadside; Fuller's London Pride; Young's Bitter; guest beer Ⓗ
Long-standing Guide entry situated on the lower edge of the village. The public bar has many upholstered beer casks, and walls adorned with historic car photographs, local drawings and a large matchbook collection. The saloon is more open, furnished with horse brasses and brewery mirrors. Children are admitted if eating in the saloon. No lunches are served on Sunday. Book for evening meals. ᗰQ❀◐◑♿P

Colney Heath

Crooked Billet

88 High Street, AL4 0NP
✪ 11-2.30, 5.30-11; 11-11 Sat; 12-10.30 Sun
☎ (01727) 822128
Young's Special; guest beers Ⓗ
Popular and friendly cottage-style village pub dating back over 200 years with a lively public bar. Greene King IPA is usually available plus at least two guests often from local micro-breweries. Good value food is served at lunchtime and on Friday and Saturday evening. An ideal starting or finishing point for local footpath walks, this family-friendly pub has a large garden with children's play equipment. ᗰQ❀◐◑♣P

Croxley Green

Sportsman

2 Scots Hill, WD3 3AD (on A412)
✪ 12-11; 12-10.30 Sun
☎ (01923) 443360 ⊕ croxleygreen.com/sportsman
Tring Side Pocket for a Toad; guest beers Ⓗ
Unusual sporting equipment adorns the walls and ceiling while darts and pool dominate the front part of the bar. Live music takes over on many evenings – usually blues, jazz or folk. A separate 'shed' is used for occasional beer festivals. Quiz night is Wednesday. ❀◐♣P

Great Offley

Red Lion

Kings Walden Road, SG5 3DZ (off A505)
✪ 12-midnight; 12-10.30 Sun
☎ (01462) 768281 ⊕ redlionoffley.com
Thwaites Lancaster Bomber; Young's Bitter; guest beers Ⓗ
Traditional country pub set in idyllic countryside with a good reputation for food. Fresh fish on Wednesday with exceptional chips made from locally grown potatoes and the speciality Red Lion pancake are highlights of the varied menu, served in the bar or no-smoking conservatory restaurant. There is a large fire in the cosy main bar. An annual beer festival is held on the spring bank holiday. ᗰ☕❀⇄◐◑♣P⁄

Harpenden

Cross Keys

39 High Street, AL5 2SD
✪ 11-12 (1am Fri & Sat); 12-11 Sun
☎ (01582) 763989
Fuller's London Pride; Taylor Landord; Rebellion IPA Ⓗ
Charming two-bar pub with a fine pewter bar top, flagstone floors and original oak-beamed ceiling from which hangs a collection of pewter tankards belonging to customers past and present. The main bar has two refectory tables. It boasts a secluded, attractive garden. Officially the Rebellion is a guest ale but due to its popularity it is always available. Lunches are served daily except Sunday. Q❀◐⊟≠

Malta

110 Lower Luton Road, Batford, AL5 5AH
✪ 12-11.30 (12.30am Fri & Sat); 12-11.30 Sun
☎ (01582) 765654
Greene King IPA; Shepherd Neame Spitfire; guest beer Ⓗ
Since the introduction of top quality beer several years ago it has gone from strength to strength. The landlord has recently introduced a further handpump due to the increasing popularity of his beers. This one-bar pub serves mainly locals and a little passing trade. Originally dating from 1756 and located further along the River Lea, it was moved to its current site in 1800. ᗰQ❀◐♣

Heronsgate

Land of Liberty, Peace & Plenty

52 Long Lane, WD3 5BS (800 yds from M25, jct 17) OS023949
✪ 11-11 (midnight Fri); 12-midnight Sat; 12-11 Sun
☎ (01923) 282226 ⊕ landoflibertypub.com
Fuller's London Pride; Young's Bitter; guest beers Ⓗ
Welcoming country pub serving a changing range of three or more micro guest beers. Real cider and perry are available plus authentic continental lagers. Bottled real ale and more than 10 bottled Belgian beers are also sold. The single bar is comfortably fitted out in traditional style, decorated with historical breweriana. A large garden with a petanque pitch is popular in summer. Special events include beer tastings. Herts CAMRA Pub of the Year 2006. ᗰ❀◐♣●P▽

Hertford

Black Horse

29-31 West Street, SG13 8EZ
✪ 12-2 (not Tue; 2.30 Fri), 5-11; 12-11 Sat & Sun
☎ (01992) 583630 ⊕ blackhorseherts.co.uk
Greene King IPA, Abbot, seasonal beers; guest beers Ⓗ
Early 19th-century timbered pub which has a country feel to it. Situated in one of Hertford's most attractive streets, it is near the start of the Cole Green Way. Handy on match days for Hertford Town football club supporters, the Horse is renowned for its own RFU-affiliated rugby team. Good value home-made food is served lunchtime and evening (not Sun) and children are allowed until 8pm. ᗰ❀◐◑≠(North/East)♣

Old Cross Tavern

8 St Andrew Street, SG14 1JA
✪ 12-11; 12-10.30 Sun
☎ (01992) 583133
Crouch Vale Brewers Gold; Fuller's London Pride;

Mighty Oak IPA; Taylor Landlord; guest beers Ⓗ
Superb town free house offering a friendly welcome. Eight real ales – usually including a dark beer of some distinction – come from brewers large and small. Beer festivals are held over the spring bank holiday and in October. Excellent home-made lunches are served at CAMRA local runner up Pub of the Year 2005. ⚜Q❀◖⇌(North/East)♣●

White Horse
33 Castle Street, SG14 1HH
⊙ 12-2.30, 5.30-11; 12-11 Fri & Sat; 12-10.30 Sun
☎ (01992) 501950 🌐 castlestreetparty.org.uk
Adnams Bitter; Fuller's Chiswick, London Pride, ESB, seasonal beers; guest beers Ⓗ
Charming old timber-framed building with two downstairs bars and no-smoking rooms upstairs (children welcome until 9pm). Guests of character come from craft brewers. Country wines are also stocked. Beer festivals are held over the early May and August bank holiday weekends. Home-made lunches are served every day. Monday night features the Gastronomic Tour, a set menu of dishes from around the world.
⚜Q❀◖⇌(North/East)♣⚟

High Wych

Rising Sun
CM21 0HZ (1 mile W of Sawbridgeworth) OS464141
⊙ 12-2.30, 5.30-11; 12-11 Sat; 12-10.30 Sun
☎ (01279) 724099
Courage Best Bitter; guest beers Ⓖ
Known locally as Sid's after its former long-term landlord, currently divided into a bar, saloon with serving hatch and a games room. It has never had a handpump installed and hopefully never will – hence all beers are dispensed on gravity. Traditional home-cooked food is available in a mobile phone free zone. ⚜Q❀◖

Hitchin

Half Moon
57 Queen Street, SG4 9TZ
⊙ 12-2.30, 5-midnight; 12-1am Fri & Sat; 12-11 Sun
☎ (01462) 452448
Adnams Bitter; Young's Special; guest beers Ⓗ
This split-level one-bar pub dates back to 1748 and was once owned by Hitchin brewer W&S Lucas. It sells two guests, often from local breweries, cider and perry and a good choice of wines. Twice-yearly beer festivals are hosted. An interesting selection of home-prepared food is available (not Tue eve). Monthly quiz nights and curry nights are popular in this friendly community pub with a loyal clientele.
⚜❀◖◗♣●P⚟

King's Arms
16 Bucklersbury, SG5 1BB
⊙ closed Mon; 12-2.30, 7.30-11 (6-1am Fri, 7.30-1am Sat); 7.30-11 Sun
☎ (01462) 459544
Adnams Bitter, Broadside; Caledonian Deuchars IPA; guest beer Ⓗ
Run by the same landlord for more than 30 years. First opened in 1806 in a much older Grade II listed building, it retains the feel of a multi-roomed old-style pub despite 1960s refurbishment. To the rear is a conservatory and patio heated in winter. The pub gets popular with younger drinkers at the weekends. ⚜❀◖◗P

Nightingale
Nightingale Road, SG5 1RL (on A505)
⊙ 12-midnight (11 Tue & Thu); 11-midnight Sat; 12-10.30 Sun
☎ (01462) 457448
Nethergate Umbel Magna, seasonal beers; Wychwood Hobgoblin Ⓗ
This friendly free house is around 150 years old and reputed to have three ghosts. It was formerly owned by Fordhams of Ashwell, whose name is set into the exterior stonework. The interior is open plan but retains the layout of the original rooms, with distinct seating areas. Two guest beers, often from Nethergate, are served. Traditional entertainment includes darts, pool, card and board games.
❀⇌♣●P

Sunrunner
24 Bancroft, SG5 1JW
⊙ 12-3, 5-11; 12-midnight Fri & Sat; 12-11 Sun
☎ (01462) 440717
Draught Bass; Potton Shannon IPA; guest beers Ⓗ
The Sunrunner, housed in an 18th-century building, is a mini beer festival in its own right. With six changing guest beers, mainly from small or new micros, including stouts, porters and milds, there is always something different to try. Paulainer and Leffe are on draught. Cider drinkers have Weston's Old Rosie and another guest, and fruit wines are sold. Home-cooked lunches are served. The pub has a loyal clientele but visitors are always welcome. ◖●

Hunsdon

Fox & Hounds
2 High Street, SG12 8NH (on B180, S end of village)
⊙ 12-4, 6-11 (not Mon & Tue eve); 12-6 Sun
☎ (01279) 843999
Adnams Bitter, Broadside; guest beers Ⓗ
Genuine free house, a 300-year-old restored yeoman's house with tall ceilings, oak beams and bare wood tables. The emphasis at this gastro pub is on food; the menu changes daily with fresh and seasonal food served in the large dining room or in the bar. A large selection of bottled Belgian beers is available. The garden is large.
⚜Q❀◖◗🚌(351)P⚟

Kings Langley

Saracen's Head
47 High Street, WD4 9HU
⊙ 11-2.30 (3 Sat), 5 (6 Sat)-11; 12-3, 7-10.30 Sun
☎ (01923) 400144
Fuller's London Pride, ESB; Tring Ridgeway; guest beer Ⓗ
Enter through the low doorway of this single-bar pub, dating from 1619, and step down into the cosy atmosphere of this free house. It features low ceilings, beams, a

wood-burning open fire and collections of beer bottles, water jugs and antique telephones. Outside are award-winning hanging basket displays. There is an active golf society, now in its sixth year. Lunches are served Monday to Saturday. ♨◖🚌P

Letchmore Heath

Three Horseshoes

The Green, WD25 8ER
⏲ 11.30-11 daily
☎ (01923) 856084
Greene King IPA; Shepherd Neame Spitfire; guest beers Ⓗ
A beer house since the 18th century, the earliest part of the building is the 16th-century timber hall with its 17th-century frontage. Substantial reconstruction took place in 1803. The pub has featured in films and numerous TV programmes since the 1920s. Facing the common, it has two bars: a flagstoned public and oak-beamed lounge. ♨Q❀◖◗⊟♿P⚡

Much Hadham

Bull Inn

High Street, SG10 6BU
⏲ 12-3, 6-11; 12-3, 7-10.30 Sun
☎ (01279) 842668
Caledonian Deuchars IPA; Greene King IPA; guest beer Ⓗ
Pub with a quiet atmosphere at the north end of this long, delightful village. Food can dominate at busy times, but drinkers are always welcome in the bar. The food is a mix of traditional English and continental styles. The guest beer changes frequently. ♨Q❀◖◗♿🚌(351)P

Newgate Street

Coach & Horses

61 Newgate Street Village, SG13 8RA
⏲ 11-11; 12-10.30 Sun
☎ (01707) 872326
Adnams Bitter; Black Sheep Best Bitter; Greene King IPA Ⓗ
Old, ivy-covered pub situated next to an attractive church on an ancient road which runs through the village. Popular with horse riding clubs, classic car societies and vintage motorcycle clubs, this Punch Taverns pub offers a friendly welcome to all. ♨❀◖P

Nuthampstead

Woodman Inn

Stocking Lane, SG8 8NB (signed off A10)
⏲ 11-11; 12-4, 7-10.30 Sun
☎ (01763) 848328 🌐 thewoodman-inn.co.uk
Adnams Bitter; Nethergate IPA; guest beers Ⓗ
A welcome return to the Guide for this 17th-century free house with an L-shaped bar and wonderful open fires. The recently extended restaurant offers house specials and snacks (no food Sun eve). Ideally located for visiting local attractions such as Duxford Imperial War Museum. During WWII the USAF 398th Bomber Group was based nearby and much memorabilia is displayed. ♨Q❀⛺◖◗P⊡

Old Knebworth

Lytton Arms

Park Lane, SG3 6QB OS229202
⏲ 11-11; 12-10.30 Sun
☎ (01438) 812312
Adnams Bitter, Broadside; Fuller's London Pride; guest beers Ⓗ
Nineteenth-century Lutyens house situated on the edge of Knebworth Park with two bars and a no-smoking conservatory. Ten ales are usually available here from a mix of regional and micro-brewers. An interesting range of continental beers supplements the real ales and ciders. Outside is an attractive decked patio and garden. Beer festivals are held at least twice a year. ♨❀◖◗♣●P⚡

Preston

Red Lion

The Green, SG4 7UD (2 miles S of Hitchin)
⏲ 12-3, 5.30-11; 12-3, 7-10.30 Sun
☎ (01462) 459585
Young's Bitter; guest beers Ⓗ
Attractive Georgian-style free house on the village green. It was the first community-owned pub in Great Britain. The guest beers, many from micro-breweries, are constantly changing. Fresh home-cooked food (no meals Tue eve) is served, with many of the ingredients sourced locally. The pub runs several cricket teams and fundraises for charity. A regular CAMRA award winner. ♨Q❀◖◗⊟♿♣●P

Puckeridge

Crown & Falcon

33 High Street, SG11 1RN
⏲ 11.30-2.30, 5.30 (6.30 Sat)-11; 12-4.30, 7-10.30 Sun
☎ (01920) 821561 🌐 crown-falcon.demon.co.uk
Adnams Bitter; McMullen AK; Shepherd Neame Spitfire; guest beers Ⓗ
A public house since around 1530, with the 'Crown' half of the name taken much later from a defunct pub in the village. Changes to the interior layout can be traced on plans displayed in the bar. It is now one large open plan room with a separate no-smoking restaurant. The guest beer changes weekly. Darts and bar billiards are popular. The Falcon is mentioned in Samuel Pepys' diary of 1662 – he bought the landlord's boots for four shillings. ♨❀◖◗🚌(700, 381)P

Radlett

Red Lion

78-80 Watling Street, WD7 7NP
⏲ 11-midnight; 12-11.30 Sun
☎ (01923) 855341
Young's Bitter, Special, seasonal beers Ⓗ
This Victorian hotel opposite the railway station was originally a temperance house. It now has a large, split level bar plus a 60-seater restaurant. There are 14 guest rooms and a function room. Meals are served in both the bar and restaurant. A flower-bedecked patio is at the front of the building. ♨❀⛺◖◗♿≠P⚡

Redbourn

Cricketers

East Common, AL3 7ND

12-11 (11.30 Thu, midnight Fri & Sat; 10.30 Sun)

(01582) 792410

Fuller's London Pride; guest beers H

Two-bar pub on the prestigious common, now the village's only free house following a change of ownership in 2004. A selection of Fuller's beers is dispensed alongside two guest ales – Rebellion IPA is a regular. Freshly made home-cooked food is prepared on the premises. The 250-year-old Redbourn Cricket Club is on the common. Q

St Albans

Boot

4 Market Place, AL3 5DG

12-11; 11-midnight Sat; 12-11 Sun

(01727) 857533

Beer range varies H

Charming 16th-century, low-ceilinged pub at the heart of the city's market place opposite the clock tower. It is a pleasant refuge from the city centre youth circuit pubs. Five beers from the Punch Taverns Finest Cask selection may be on handpump. Addlestones cider and a large selection of wines and malt whiskies are also available. Freshly-made food featuring locally-produced meat and fish is served. Tuesday is open mike night.

Farriers Arms

35 Lower Dagnall Street, AL2 4MJ (off A5183)

12-2.30 (not Mon), 5.30-11; 12-11 Sat; 12-10.30 Sun

(01727) 851025

McMullen AK, Country, seasonal beer; guest beers H

Classic back-street local, it is the only pub in St Albans never to have forsaken real ale. A plaque on the wall outside marks the first meeting of the Hertfordshire branch of CAMRA. The split-level interior has a small area fronting the bar for stand-up drinking, darts and cards. The back room has more comfortable seating. Both bars are free of gaming machines but there is a TV for sports. Parking can be difficult.

Garibaldi

61 Albert Street, AL1 1RT

12-11 (11.30 Fri & Sat); 12-11 Sun

(01727) 855046

Fuller's Chiswick, Discovery, London Pride, ESB, seasonal beers; guest beers H

Traditional, welcoming, back-street local within walking distance of the cathedral. The bar is centrally located with seating and room to stand all around. The pub is named after the Italian patriot who unified Italy in the 19th century. Barbecues are held in summer and a beer festival in August. Lunches are not served on Sunday and Monday. ≠(Abbey)

Goat Inn

37 Sopwell Lane, AL1 1RN

12-3, 5-11; 12-11.30 Fri & Sat; 12-11 Sun

(01727) 833934

Adnams Broadside; Caledonian Deuchars IPA; Shepherd Neame Spitfire; guest beer H

Built at the end of the 15th century, a short walk from the cathedral and situated on the old coaching route from London, it retains the old carriage arch. Food is served in a dining area at the rear. Westons Old Rosie cider and a wide selection of wines and whiskies are available. Dominoes, shove ha-penny and board games are popular, and bar billiards is played. ≠(Abbey)

Lower Red Lion

34-36 Fishpool Street, AL3 4RX

12-2.30, 5.30-11; 12-11 Sat; 12-10.30 Sun

(01727) 855669 lowerredlion.com

Oakham JHB; guest beers H

Two-bar, 17th-century coaching inn near the cathedral and Roman Verulamium. This genuine free house serves seven guest beers from micro-breweries. It now features beers brewed by one of the licensees at the Verulam Brewery, under the name Alehouse. Dutch, Czech and Belgian bottled beers and malt whiskies are available as well as real cider in summer. A beer festival is held every few weeks. Chess night is Monday. Sunday roasts are recommended.

Q P

Portland Arms

63 Portland Street, AL3 4RA

12-3, 5.30-11 (midnight Fri); 12-midnight Sat; 12-11 Sun

(01727) 844574

Fuller's Chiswick, Discovery, London Pride, ESB, seasonal beers H

Back-street community pub tucked away in a residential area, handy for St Michaels and the Roman Museum. The tenants are members of the Campaign for Real Food and the pub serves a wide range of meals (eve meals Tue-Sat) with meat supplied by a local farm. Takeaway fish and chips is also available. Music night is Sunday.

Q P

White Lion

91 Sopwell Lane, AL1 1RN

12 (5.30 Mon)-11; 12-11 Sun

(01727) 850540 thewhitelionph.co.uk

Black Sheep Best Bitter; Young's Special; guest beers H

Traditional 16th-century two-bar pub a short walk from the cathedral. Six handpumps dispense two regulars plus four guests from the Punch Taverns range. The large garden has a barbecue, children's play areas and a petanque pitch. Quality home-cooked food is served (not Mon or Sun eve). Live music is played on Tuesday night. A music and beer festival is held on the August bank holiday weekend. ≠(Abbey)

St Pauls Walden

Strathmore Arms

London Road, SG4 8BT

12-2.30 (not Mon), 5 (6 Mon)-11;12-11 Fri & Sat; 10-10.30 Sun

(01438) 871654

Fuller's London Pride; Woodforde's Wherry; guest beers H

Refurbished pub on the Bowes-Lyon estate divided into drinking, dining and games areas. The pub is close to the church and is popular with local bellringers. The landlord keeps a collection of bottled beers behind the bar. Evening meals are served Thursday to Saturday. Local CAMRA Pub of the Year for 2004, it hosts several beer festivals.
Q❀◐◑⛺♣●P

Sandridge

Green Man

High Street, AL4 9DD
11-3, 5.30-11.30; 11-11.30 Fri & Sat; 12-11 Sun
☎ (01727) 854845 thegreenman-sandridge.co.uk
Adnams Broadside; Caledonian Deuchars IPA; G Greene King IPA, H Abbot; G guest beer H
This 1880s Victorian one-bar red-brick pub is in the centre of the village. It is the only pub in the area to serve three of its ales straight from the cask – located in a ground-floor cellar nearby. A locals' pub, run by the same landlord for the last 19 years, it extends a warm welcome to all discerning ale drinkers.
Q❀◐◑♣P

Sawbridgeworth

Gate Inn

81 London Road, CM21 9JJ
11.30-2.30, 5.30-11; 11.30-11 Fri & Sat; 12-10.30 Sun
☎ (01279) 722313 the-gate-pub.co.uk
Rebellion IPA; guest beers H
Local community three-roomed pub and home to the Sawbridgeworth Brewery. The front saloon/snug is used by locals and is quiet while the back bar is preferred by younger drinkers and is sports oriented. The snug is often used as a stillage for the many mini beer festivals. The pub is renowned for stocking a large selection of rare and unusual beers and a Sawbridgeworth beer is often a guest. A large beer festival is held in the car park several times a year.
❀◐♿⇌♣●P⚟

Sleapshyde

Plough

Sleapshyde Lane, AL4 0SD (off A414)
11.30-2.30, 5.30-11; 12-3, 7-10.30 Sun
☎ (01727) 823720
Fuller's London Pride; Greene King IPA, Abbot H
Old village pub with a wealth of exposed beams and an inglenook fireplace. An imaginative menu offers good value food. The pub is a popular meeting place for local groups and regular games night are hosted.
Q❀◐◑♣P

South Mimms

White Hart

St Albans Road, EN6 3PJ
11-11; 12-10.30 Sun
☎ (01707) 642122
McMullen AK, Country H
Originally a coaching inn on the Great North Road, this 400-year-old building still has the stables at the rear. A traditional pub with a post-war interior, the public bar is lively with darts and crib teams. The lounge has been opened out to extend the dining facilities (no food is served Sun eve). The raised sunny garden overlooks farmland.
❀◐◑♿♣P

Stevenage

Our Mutual Friend

Broadwater Crescent, SG2 8EH
(off A602 Broadhall Way)
12-11 (11.30 Fri & Sat); 12-3, 7-10.30 Sun
☎ (01438) 312282
Caledonian Deuchars IPA; guest beers H
Thriving community pub brought back from the cask ale graveyard four years ago. Since then it has gone from strength to strength, now sporting six real ales, real cider and perry plus a small range of Belgian bottled beers. A regular beer festival brightens up January. Locals drink alongside visitors who come for the good beer and regular pool and darts matches. Winner of many local CAMRA awards including Most Improved Pub and Pub of the Year 2006. Q❀♣●P

Squirrel Tavern

Chells Way, SG2 0NH (off Six Hills Way)
11.30-11; 12-10.30 Sun
☎ (01438) 312037
Greene King IPA; Potton Gold H
This medium-sized town pub is a local CAMRA Community Pub winner. The large open bar area offers plenty of seating and a split-level area for quiet drinking. The pub runs active darts, pool and dominoes teams and regular charity fundraising events are held. Outside at the front is a small garden. Meals are served 1-7pm (not Wed).
❀◐◑♣P

Tring

King's Arms

King Street, HP23 6BE
12 (11.30 Sat)-2.30 (3 Fri), 7-11; 12-4, 7-10.30 Sun
☎ (01442) 823318
Wadworth 6X; guest beers H
Hidden in the back streets of Tring, this 1830s pink pub is a frequent local CAMRA Pub of the Year and a long-time entry in this Guide. It serves an ever-changing array of five ales and the occasional cider. Excellent freshly-cooked food is made with local ingredients. There are two real fires with unusual windowed chimneys. The canopied patio is heated during the cooler months. Children are welcome at lunchtime.
Q❀◐◑●⚟

Tyttenhanger Green

Plough

AL4 0RW (off A414 via Highfield Lane)
11.30-3 (11-3.30 Sat), 6-11; 12-3.30, 7-10.30 Sun
☎ (01727) 857777
Fuller's London Pride, ESB; guest beers H
Deservedly busy country free house with an ever-changing range of up to six guest beers. Excellent value food makes it a popular lunchtime destination. The large garden has children's play equipment and

there is an indoor conservatory area for families. Worth visiting for the large collection of bottled beers and the idiosyncratic beermats. 🜂Q☋❀◖♿♣P

Ware

Crooked Billet

140 Musley Hill, SG12 7NL (via New Rd from High St)

⊙ 12-2.30 (Tue only), 5.30-11 (midnight Fri); 12-midnight Sat; 12-11.30 Sun

☎ (01920) 462516

Greene King XX Mild, Abbot; guest beer Ⓗ

This justifiably popular local is well worth tracking down. There are two main bar areas, one relaxed and cosy, the other more lively with a pool table and Sky Sports on TV. Carlisle United fans will be given the red carpet treatment! The beers usually include the hard-to-find Greene King Mild, though it may not be on in the summer. 🜂❀♿♣

Rose & Crown

65 Watton Road, SG12 0AE

⊙ 12-2.30, 5-11; 12.30-2.30, 5-midnight Thu; 12-1am Fri & Sat; 12-11 Sun

☎ (01920) 462371

McMullen AK, Country; guest beer Ⓗ

Wonderful pub with a landlord who takes great pride in his cellar, winning numerous cellarmanship awards over the years. As well as quality ale, superb home-cooked food is also served (no eve meals Sun-Tue). The pub was built with famous local hitch bricks and at the back is a colourful garden that is easy to miss from the road. There is a covered and heated conservatory, children's play area, an aviary and a petanque piste. ❀◖◗♿⇌♣P

Wareside

Chequers

SG12 7QY (on B1004) OS395155

⊙ 12-3, 6-11; 12-10.30 (12-3, 6-10.30 winter) Sun

☎ (01920) 467010

Greene King IPA; guest beers Ⓖ

Warm, friendly 16th-century pub situated in beautiful Hertfordshire countryside, excellent for walking and cycling. All draught ales are gravity dispensed, normally including a dark mild, stout or porter. Guests are usually from small independent brewers. Good, well-priced food includes vegetarian options and a children's menu. Children are welcome before 9pm. 🜂Q❀🛏◖◗⊟🚌(M3, M4)P

Watford

Southern Cross

41 Langley Road, WD17 4PP

⊙ 11-11 (11.30 Thu-Sat); 12-10.30 Sun

☎ (01923) 256033

Caledonian Deuchars IPA; Theakston Mild; Wells Bombardier; guest beers Ⓗ

Thriving, large, open-plan bar with a central serving area, currently half no-smoking. Three guest beers from the Beer Seller list are usually served and the introduction of mild has been a great success. A regular general knowledge quiz is held on Thursday and Sunday. Board games are available. ❀🛏◖◗⇌(Junction)🚌P⍁

Whitwell

Maiden's Head

67 High Street, SG4 8AH

⊙ 12-3, 5-11; 12-4, 6-11 Sat; 12-4, 7-11 Sun

☎ (01438) 871392

McMullen AK, Country; guest beers Ⓗ

One of the flagship McMullen pubs, the Maiden's Head has been a regular Guide entry for the last 22 years. The walls are adorned with photographs, paintings and awards and there is a collection of Dinky toys. Popular with ramblers, the pub has won the 'Ted and Josie' award for best community pub and also the CAMRA East Anglian Pub of the Year. Evening meals are served Tuesday-Saturday. 🜂❀◖◗⊟♣P

Wildhill

Woodman

Wildhill Road, AL9 6EA (between A1000 and B158) OS265068

⊙ 11.30-2.30, 5.30-11; 12-2.30, 7-10.30 Sun

☎ (01707) 642618

Greene King IPA, Abbot; McMullen AK; guest beers Ⓗ

This small, friendly village pub offers up to three guest beers from regional and micro breweries near and far, with prices some of the cheapest in the area. Popular with office workers for lunch, it is also busy on Sunday, although no food is served on that day. The large garden is lovely in summer. It is a favourite watering hole for sports fans and the pub runs its own fantasy Formula 1 competition. The pub has won numerous awards including local CAMRA Pub of the Year a record seven times. Q❀◖♣P

Willian

Fox

SG6 2AE (800 yds from A1(M) jct 9 via Baldock Lane)

⊙ 12-11; 12-10.30 Sun

☎ (01462) 480233 🌐 foxatwillian.co.uk

Adnams Bitter; Fuller's London Pride; Woodforde's Wherry; guest beer Ⓗ

Recently refurbished, bright and airy pub with a large bar and restaurant area in a village setting on the fringes of Letchworth. In the evening the restaurant serves a high quality, somewhat pricey menu with the emphasis on seafood. At lunchtime a cheaper bar food menu is available (not Sun). The guest ale changes regularly and a good selection of wines is on offer. ❀◖◗♿P⍁

Beer: a high and mighty liquor – **Julius Caesar**

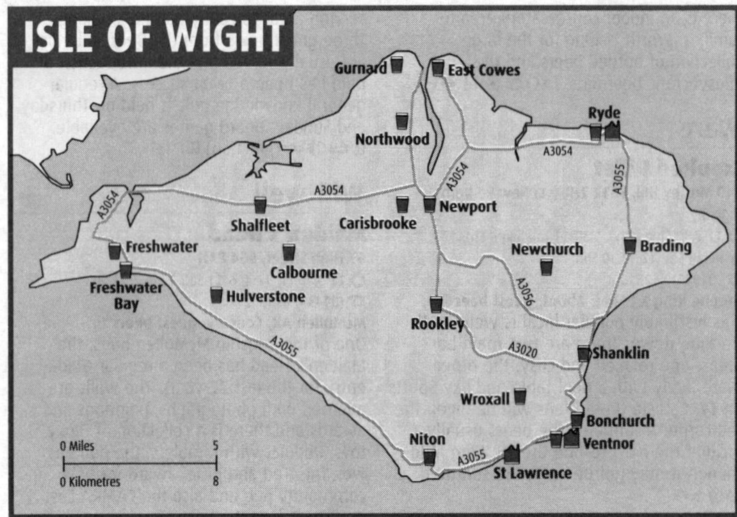

Bonchurch

Bonchurch Inn

The Chute, PO38 1NU (off Shanklin to Ventnor road)
✪ 11-3, 6.30-11; 12-3, 7-10.30 Sun
☎ (01983) 852611 🌐 bonchurch-inn.co.uk
Courage Best Bitter, Directors; Greene King Ruddles Best, Ruddles County Ⓖ
Superbly preserved stone pub, tucked away in a Dickensian courtyard, formerly the stables of the adjacent Manor House. Little has changed since it first gained its licence in the 1840s, making this one of the most unspoilt pubs on the island. As well as featuring in an episode of TV's The Detectives, there are mementos and keepsakes from many of the stars who have visited. There is a pergola outside and an Italian restaurant across the courtyard.
Q ❀ ◑ ♣ P ⊬

Brading

Yarbridge Inn

Yarbridge, PO36 0AA (left at traffic lights between Brading and Sandown)
✪ 11-11 (11-3, 5-11 winter); 12-10.30 Sun
☎ (01983) 404212 🌐 yarbridgeinn.co.uk
Moorhouses Pendle Witches Brew; Oakleaf Hole Hearted; RCH East Street Cream; Taylor Landlord; Ventnor Golden; guest beer Ⓗ
Previously known as the Anglers, this is a very pleasant single-bar pub with an interesting selection of changing ales. It has a dining area where the menu includes a specials board and choice of roast on Sunday. Outside is a safe area for children with an adventure playground and a paved area with parasols. There is plenty of railway memorabilia, a model train and the Brading to Sandown line at the bottom of the garden. ❀ ◑ ▲ ≢ ♣ P ⊬

Calbourne

Blacksmiths Arms

Park Cross, Calbourne Road, PO30 5SS (on B3401 Carisbrooke to Calbourne road)
✪ 11 (12 Sun)-11
☎ (01983) 529263
Fuller's London Pride; Itchen Valley Fagin's; Shepherd Neame Spitfire; Taylor Landlord; Ventnor Golden; Young's Special; guest beer Ⓗ
Historic country pub near the start of the Tennyson Trail with superb panoramic views of the Solent and the mainland. The pub is known locally as the 'Betty Haunt' – Betty Haunt Lane is where a local lass was rumoured to have lost her life for telling tales to the excise men. In fact it means 'between hunts', although the pub is said to be haunted. The cosy public bar leads to a pool room and outside is a children's play area. The pub may stay open later except on Sunday, if customers wish.
Q ❀ ◑ ▲ P ⊬

Carisbrooke

Waverley

2 Clatterford Road, PO30 1PA
✪ 11-11 (midnight Fri & Sat); 12-10.30 Sun
☎ (01983) 522338
Archers Best Bitter; Hampshire King Alfred's, Ironside; Ventnor Golden, Old Ruby; Yates' Undercliff Experience; guest beer Ⓗ
Large local at the village crossroads that has retained its individual rooms. The present incumbent, with a record of successful pubs in the area, has quickly built a reputation for good quality food and an ever-changing range of interesting beers. Local memorabilia is displayed around the walls and a large-screen TV is switched on for big occasions. There is plenty of room for well-behaved children and a large, safe play area outside.
❀ ◑ ♣ P ⊬

INDEPENDENT BREWERIES

Goddards Ryde
Ventnor Ventnor
Yates' St Lawrence

East Cowes

Ship & Castle

21 Castle Street, PO32 6RB

11 (12 Sun)-11

(01983) 290522

Greene King Abbot; Shepherd Neame Spitfire; guest beers

This gem is just how you imagine a street corner pub should be – a cosy retreat for when the wind is whistling across the Red Funnel car park and the rain lashing down from the floating bridge. Despite the small bar there are always at least four beers on offer and a guest that changes weekly to keep the locals in suspense. Bustling on match nights, four darts teams and Sky TV keep sports fans happy.

Freshwater

Prince of Wales

Princes Road, PO40 9ED

11-11; 12-10.30 Sun

(01983) 753535

Archers Dark Mild, Best Bitter; Boddingtons Bitter; Greene King Abbot; Ringwood Fortyniner; Wadworth 6X; guest beer

This fine, unspoilt town pub is run by possibly the longest-serving landlord on the island. A strong games section adds to the lively atmosphere. Just off the main Freshwater shopping centre, it has a large garden for hot summer days and a pleasant snug bar to sample the ales in winter. No need to phone for a taxi home – the landlord has one. Q P

Freshwater Bay

Fat Cat

Sandpipers, Coastguard Lane, PO40 9QX

11-midnight daily

(01983) 758500 sandpipershotel.com

Black Sheep Best Bitter; Mordue Workie Ticket; Ringwood Best Bitter, Old Thumper; Young's Special; guest beer

A real gem, tucked away within the Sandpipers Hotel and situated between Freshwater Bay and the Afton Nature Reserve. It stocks an ever-changing range of ales. This pub is well worth a visit, especially at the end of March for the biggest real ale festival on the island with 60 ales on offer. For children there is an adventure playground and a cosy playroom with games and amusements. The hotel offers fine dining. Q P

Gurnard

Portland Inn

2 Worsley Road, PO31 8JN

11-11 (midnight Fri & Sat); 12-10.30 Sun

(01983) 292948

Bateman Valiant; Jennings Cocker Hoop; Young's Special; Ventnor Golden; guest beers

This building has been a bakery, a hardware store and a grocer's and now serves as a community local. A recent conversion into the depths of the premises has created an attractively refurbished, multi-purpose area that boasts a huge TV screen where children can bring their own videos and see them as never before. The Gurnard Firework Charity was formed here to raise funds and support local charities.

Woodvale Hotel

1 Princess Esplanade, PO31 8LE (on the seafront)

11-11; 12-10.30 Sun

(01983) 292037 the-woodvale.co.uk

Badger Tanglefoot; Fuller's London Pride; Greene King Abbot, Old Speckled Hen; Taylor Landlord; guest beers

Just a short walk along the esplanade from Cowes stands the splendid former Mew Langton Hotel. Within yards of the water's edge it offers a grandstand view of the racing yachts and shipping movements, not to mention the odd power boat race. Recently renovated to a high standard, it now has a function room upstairs and five spectacular letting rooms. Enjoy summer days or balmy evenings in the large garden. An excellent selection of food is available all day. P

Hulverstone

Sun Inn

Main Road, PO30 4EH

11-11; 12-10.30 Sun

(01983) 741124 sun-hulverstone.com

Draught Bass; Shepherd Neame Spitfire; Taylor Landlord; Wadworth 6X; Wychwood Hobgoblin; guest beer

This 600-year-old building at the heart of rural west Wight has a charming garden and uninterrupted views to sea. It has built up a strong following for food, which is served all day, with a weekly curry night and music evening. It now has a large restaurant and caters for wedding parties in the new extension. Well-behaved children are welcome. P

Newchurch

Pointers Inn

High Street, PO36 0NN

11-3, 6-11; 12-11 Sun

(01983) 865202

Fuller's London Pride, Gale's HSB; guest beers

Ancient village local with a warm, cosy atmosphere where families are welcome. The no-smoking lounge/restaurant has been integrated with the old public bar. The restaurant has a fine reputation for its home-cooked food. The large garden has a petanque terrain. The village church next door has an unusual wooden steeple.

Newport

Prince of Wales

36 South Street, PO30 1JE (opp. bus station)

10.30-11; 12-10.30 Sun

(01983) 525026

Archers Best Bitter; Greene King IPA; Hop Back Crop Circle; Jennings Sneck Lifter; guest beers

Formerly the tap to the now demolished Green Dragon, this excellent mock-Tudor,

single-bar, street-corner local has established a fine reputation for its ales. Although in the centre of town, this is very much a local, which has resisted the temptation to be 'tarted up', and still retains the atmosphere of a public bar.
⛫Q◑♣●

Niton

Buddle Inn

St Catherine's Road, PO38 2NE
(follow signs to St Catherine's lighthouse)
⌚ 11-11 (midnight Fri & Sat); 12-10.30 Sun
☎ (01983) 730243
Adnams Bitter; Goddards Fuggle-Dee-Dum; Taylor Landlord; Ventnor Golden; Yates' Undercliff Experience; guest beers Ⓗ
Originally a farmhouse dating from the 16th century, this was reputedly a haunt for smugglers during the 18th century. Though extensively refurbished in recent years, it retains the original flagstones, beams and inglenook. The adjoining public bar was a cattle shed until 1934 when it became a dance hall. A popular pub in the summer, there is large outdoor area to enjoy the pub's south-facing vista. The good quality food is highly recommended and there is always a choice of at least six ales.
⛫Q❀◑◗⊟⛺

White Lion

High Street, PO38 2AT
⌚ 11-11 (midnight Sat); 11-11 Sun
☎ (01983) 730293
Archers Golden; Badger Tanglefoot; Draught Bass; Crouch Vale Brewers Gold; Greene King Abbot; Yates' Undercliff Experience Ⓗ
Picturesque pub in the centre of the village. The new landlord has made a big impression since his arrival, completely overhauling the premises and adding a new kitchen. The pub has a fine reputation for its food and the Sunday roast is a sell out. From the cellar comes a succession of frequently changing ales, with at least one from an island brewery. ⛫Q♉❀◑◗⊟♿⛺P

Northwood

Travellers Joy

85 Pallance Road, PO31 8LS (on A3020, Yarmouth road out of Cowes)
⌚ 11-2.30, 5-midnight; 11-midnight Fri & Sat; 12-3, 7-11 Sun
☎ (01983) 298024
Archers Golden; Caledonian Deuchars IPA; Goddards Special Bitter; Oakleaf Nuptu'ale; Ventnor Old Ruby Ale; guest beers Ⓗ
Offering one of the best choices of cask ales on the island, this well renovated and extended old country inn was the island's first beer exhibition house. Local drinkers owe much to the Travellers Joy, and CAMRA members have voted it local Pub of the Year on no fewer than five occasions. It always has at least eight beers on offer from national, local and micro-breweries. A good range of home-cooked food is also served.
⛫♉❀◑◗⛺♣●P⚟

Rookley

Chequers Inn

Niton Road, PO38 3NZ (on A3020, Rookley to Niton road)
⌚ 11-11; 12-10.30 Sun
☎ (01983) 840314 ⊕ chequersinn-iow.co.uk
Courage Best Bitter, Directors; Fuller's Gale's HSB; Ventnor Golden; Wadworth 6X; guest beers Ⓗ
This country pub at the heart of the island benefits from beautiful views. Considering its present popularity after an extensive rebuild, it is astonishing that Whitbread closed the pub and sold it. Dating back to the mid-1880s, it was once a customs and excise house. These days it is heavily food- and family-oriented but still retains a flagstone-floored public bar and a fine pint of beer. Good children's facilities include a large outdoor play area and baby changing room.
⛫Q♉❀◑◗⊟♿⛺♣●P

Ryde

Solent Inn

7 Monkton Street, PO33 1JW
⌚ 11-11; 12-10.30 Sun
☎ (01983) 563546
Banks's Bitter; Oakleaf Hole Hearted, Blake's Gosport Bitter; Ventnor Old Ruby Ale; Wells Bombardier; guest beers Ⓗ
Excellent street-corner local with a warm, welcoming atmosphere. The pub has an impressive record for excellence and was the 2004 and 2005 Isle of Wight CAMRA Pub of the Year, offering an ever-changing range of six ales. Live music is performed at least three times a week and a friendly quiz is staged on one night. Q❀⊟⇌(Esplanade)♣

Shalfleet

New Inn

Mill Road, PO30 4NS
⌚ 12-3, 6-11 (10.30 Sun)
☎ (01983) 531314
Draught Bass; Fuller's London Pride; Goddards Special Bitter; Greene King IPA; Ventnor Golden Ⓗ
The New Inn has stood at the entrance to Mill Road for 300 years. An ancient and largely unspoilt country local, it has a flagstone floor and huge log fire. The seafood, for which the pub is noted, continues to entice locals from inland and yachtsmen from Shalfleet Creek. The roaring log fire is a delight in the winter and, for the summer, there is a sheltered garden to the rear. The pub is no-smoking throughout and well-behaved children are welcome. ⛫❀◑◗P

Shanklin

Chine Inn

Chine Hill, PO37 6BW
⌚ 11.30-midnight (12-4, 7-11; 11.30-11 Sat winter); 12-10.30 Sun
☎ (01983) 865880
Archers Village; Greene King Abbot; Hampshire Ironside; Oakleaf Hole Hearted; Taylor Landlord; guest beer Ⓗ
This pub is a gem. The building, which has stood since 1621, must have some claim to

being one of the oldest buildings with a licence on the island. Completely refurbished with a new kitchen, it has retained plenty of the original charm for which it was well known. On a summer's day when the sky is blue and the sun's rays are dancing on Sandown Bay, there is no finer view in England than from here.

King Harry's Bar

6 Church Road, Old Village, PO37 6NU

11-11 (later Fri & Sat); 12-10.30 Sun

☎ (01983) 863119

Fuller's ESB; Hampshire Pride of Romsey; Young's Bitter, Special; guest beers H

Charming 19th-century thatched property with two established Tudor bars and Henry VIII Kitchen that specialises in steaks and grills. The large garden, floodlit at night, has a stream, natural wild flowers and ferns. Adjacent, Shanklin Chine leading to the beach was once the route of PLUTO (the wartime Allied pipeline). A totally refurbished bar area has seen an increase in the number of handpumps. Well-behaved children are welcome. P

Ventnor

Volunteer

30 Victoria Street, PO38 1ES (near bus terminus)

11-11 (midnight Fri & Sat); 12-10.30 Sun

☎ (01983) 852537 volunteer-inn.co.uk

Butcombe Bitter; Courage Best Bitter, Directors; Greene King Abbot, Old Speckled Hen; Ventnor Golden; guest beers H

Built in 1866, the Volunteer is probably the smallest pub on the Isle of Wight. It operated as a beer house between 1869 and 1871 and retains many original features of the traditional drinkers' pub. Always highly rated in the annual local CAMRA Pub of the Year awards, it achieved first place in 2003. No chips, no children, no fruit machines, no video games, just a pure adult drinking house; this is one of the few places where you can still play rings.

Q♣

Wroxall

Four Seasons

2 Clarence Road, PO38 3BY

10.30-midnight; 11-11.30 Sun

☎ (01983) 854701

Fuller's Gale's HSB; Greene King Abbot; Ringwood Best Bitter; guest beers H

Formerly known as the Star, this pub was brought back to life after a disastrous fire. It is now a successful village pub with an island-wide reputation for excellent food. The beer range may vary but will usually include an island brew.

Q♣P

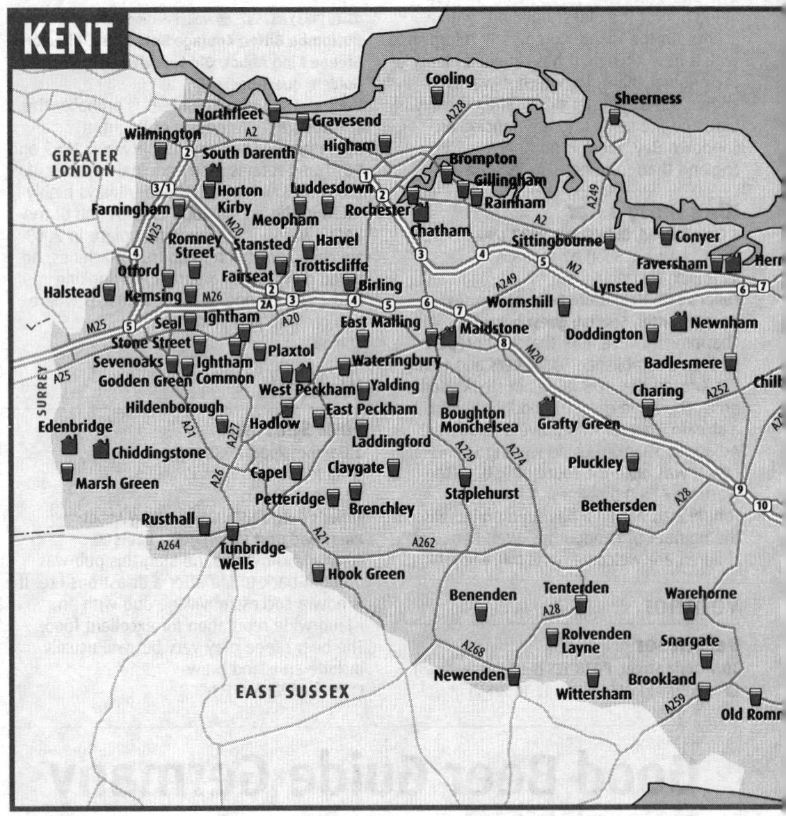

Badlesmere

Red Lion

Ashford Road, ME13 0NX

(on A251)

✪ 12-3 (not Mon), 6 (5 Fri)-11; 12-midnight Sat; 12-10.30 Sun

☎ (01233) 740320

Fuller's London Pride; Greene King Abbot; Shepherd Neame Master Brew Bitter; guest beer Ⓗ

Welcoming roadside free house of exposed beams and low ceilings dating from 1546. Where there are now casks of beer, there were once coffins as the cellars have served as a morgue. The guest beer range often includes some rarities. Beer festivals are held over the Easter and August bank holiday weekends. Cider is sold in summer. Ingredients for the home-cooked food are sourced from local farmers and growers (no meals Sun eve or Mon). Bands perform on Friday evening.

ጰ❀◑▲⊟♣●P

Barfrestone

Yew Tree Inn

Barfreston Road, CT15 7JH

✪ 12-11; 12-10.30 Sun

☎ (01304) 831619 ⊕ barfreston.com

Hopdaemon Incubus; guest beers Ⓗ

Next to the Norman church in a picturesque village, this friendly, traditional pub has several bars (two no-smoking) and a family room. The pub showcases beers from local Kent micro-breweries; a mild beer and a real local cider are always available. Good, genuinely home-cooked, local seasonal fresh food is served – 50% of the menu is vegetarian. The Yew Tree offers excellent value for both beer and meals. Local folk musicians perform (Thu eve) and pub games are played.

ᗢ❀◑⊟

Benenden

Bull

The Street, TN17 4DE

✪ 12-midnight daily

☎ (01580) 240054

Harveys Sussex Best Bitter: Larkins Traditional; Rother Valley Level Best; guest beers Ⓗ

Sizeable, 17th-century pub in a central position, next to the green where the village cricket team plays. The Bull's comfortable interior features wood floors, oak beams and a large inglenook. Meals can be taken in the bar or restaurant, which serves a popular Sunday lunchtime carvery. Later on Sunday afternoon performances of live music are staged in the public bar. Accommodation is of a high standard at local CAMRA's Pub of the Year 2006.

ጰ❀⇔◑▲⊟(297)♣●P

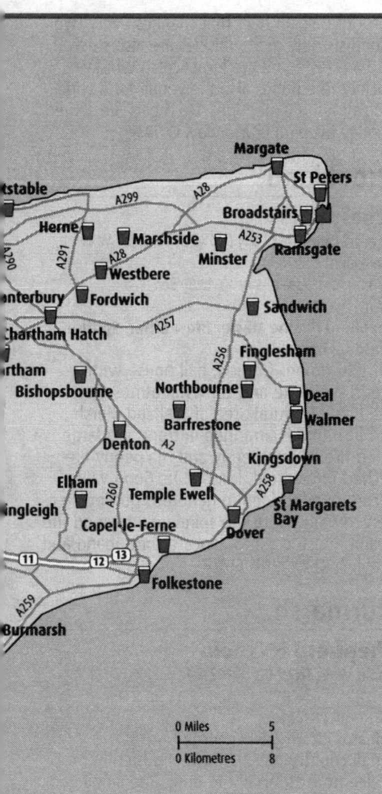

Bethersden

George

The Street, TN26 3AG (off A28)

⏲ 12-11; 12-10.30 Sun

☎ (01233) 820235

Brakspear Bitter; Greene King Old Speckled Hen; Ⓖ Harveys Sussex Best Bitter; guest beer Ⓗ

Traditional village pub with a public bar and a saloon bar incorporating a dining area. Dating from the early 18th century, recent work has exposed the original interior brick walls and fireplaces. Three guest beers and Biddendens cider are normally stocked. Beer festivals are held to celebrate St George's Day and over the last week in July. The garden has a large children's play area. Proper pub food, all home made, is served Tuesday-Saturday and Sunday lunchtime. ♨❀◐◑⊟●P

Birling

Nevill Bull

1 Ryarsh Road, ME19 5JW

⏲ 11-3, 6.30-11; closed Mon; 12-3, 7-10.30 Sun

☎ (01732) 843193

Adnams Bitter; Shepherd Neame Master Brew Bitter; guest beer Ⓗ

Spacious, well-appointed pub at the centre of a dormitory village. The name change to Nevill Bull dates from 1953, in memory of a local noble, Michael Nevill, killed in WWII. The main, mock-beamed bar area has comfortable, red upholstered bench seating; the restaurant is no-smoking. The same good value, varied menu is available in both sections (children permitted throughout the pub if dining); no food is served Sunday evening. There is no TV and games machines are turned down low. ♨Q❀◐◑🚌(58)P

Bishopsbourne

Mermaid

The Street, CT4 5HX

⏲ 12-3.30, 6-11; 12-11 Sat; 12-3.30, 7-11 Sun

☎ (01227) 830581

Shepherd Neame Master Brew Bitter, seasonal beers Ⓗ

Well worth the short detour from the A2, this attractive community pub is just off the North Downs Way. Dogs are welcome with well-behaved owners. The front bar has been sensitively refurbished, while the other bar retains its split-level floor and welcoming hearth. No food is served on Sunday. ♨Q❀⇄◐♿♣⚟

Boughton Monchelsea

Cock Inn

Heath Road, ME17 4JD (on B2163)

⏲ 11-11; 12-10.30 Sun

☎ (01622) 743166

Young's Bitter, Special, seasonal beers Ⓗ

This 400-year-old coaching inn has been in the Young's tied estate since 1999 after some years as a Beefeater. Built to provide lodgings for Canterbury pilgrims, the Cock is now a superb country pub, serving excellent food and beers in spacious, welcoming surroundings. Meals are served (not Sun eve) in the bar and restaurant. Seafood is a speciality and theme nights feature the cuisine of different countries. Seasonal beers are usually available. ♨❀◐◑🚌(59)♣P

Brenchley

Halfway House

Horsmonden Road, TN12 7AX (½ mile SE of village)

⏲ 12-11 daily

☎ (01892) 722526 🌐 halfway-house-brenchley.co.uk

Adnams Broadside; Elgood's Black Dog; Harveys Sussex Best Bitter; Larkins Chiddingstone; Westerham Special Bitter Ale 1965; Ⓖ guest beer Ⓗ

With the layout of the pub rearranged to accommodate casks at the back of the bar, and two beer festivals a year, the preference of the owner is clear. This quaint, 18th-century coaching house comprises six oak-

INDEPENDENT BREWERIES

Goacher's Maidstone
Hopdaemon Newnham
Larkins Chiddingstone
Millis South Darenth
Nelson Chatham
Ramsgate Broadstairs
Shepherd Neame Faversham
Swan on the Green West Peckham
Westerham Edenbridge
Whitstable Grafty Green

beamed, timber floored rooms, some displaying old Kentish farm implements. Mild ale and Chiddingstone cider make regular appearances. Good, sensibly-priced food is served. Three en-suite guest rooms and a large children's play area complete the picture. ⌂Q☺❀⇌◑◗♣♠P

Broadstairs

Brown Jug

204 Ramsgate Road, CT10 2EW
12-3, 6-11; 12-11 Sat; 12-10.30 Sun
☎ (01843) 862788
Beer range varies H
Charming, olde-worlde pub, featuring leaded windows, a knapped flint façade and outside toilets. Formerly tied to Cobbs of Margate, the pub was linked to a nearby farm by a series of tunnels and was almost certainly involved in smuggling during the early 19th century. Look for the water clock that plays Little Brown Jug, and the framed print depicting soldiers from the Napoleonic Wars outside the pub. ⌂Q❀⊟⇌(Dumpton Pk)⊟♣P

Lord Nelson

11 Nelson Place, CT10 1HQ
11-midnight; 12-11 Sun
☎ (01843) 861210
Greene King IPA, Abbot, seasonal beers H
Friendly local, pleasantly situated in a conservation area near the sea. Originally a draper and tailors' premises, it was converted to a pub in 1815 and named after the great Admiral Nelson, whose body had famously been preserved in a barrel of spirits on HMS Victory, which moored in Broadstairs Harbour after the battle of Trafalgar. The one-roomed bar is decorated with naval memorabilia and the ceiling is covered with maritime charts. Impromptu live music performances take place during folk week. ⌂☺❀⇌

Neptune's Hall

1-3 Harbour Street, CT10 1ET
11-11; 12-10.30 Sun
☎ (01843) 861400
Shepherd Neame Master Brew Bitter, Kent's Best, Spitfire H
Early 19th-century gem, noted for its particularly fine bar fitments, a short walk from the seafront. Folk music is popular here and it is one of the main venues for live music during the town's August folk week. The pleasant back garden hosts barbecues in fine weather. The well-kept Shep's beers ensure the pub stays busy with both locals and visitors. ❀◑⊟⇌♣

Brompton

King George V

1 Prospect Row, ME7 5AL
11.45-11; 9am-2am Fri; 9am-3am Sat; 12-10.30 Sun
☎ (01634) 842418
Adnams Bitter; Goacher's Mild; Harveys Sussex XX Mild; guest beer H
This pub, close to Chatham's Historic Dockyard, displays much naval and military memorabilia. It serves four ales including a mild, and a draught Belgian beer that changes every two months. Thirty malt whiskies are also stocked, and are tasted by the local Scotch Whisky Society. The pub is also the venue for a wine club's monthly meetings. No meals are served Sunday evening or Monday. Q◑◗⊬

Brookland

Woolpack

Beacon Lane, TN29 9TJ (off A259, 1 mile SW of Brookland) OS978245
11-3, 6-11; 11-11 Sat; 12-10.30 Sun
☎ (01797) 344321
Shepherd Neame Master Brew Bitter, Spitfire, seasonal beers H
Ancient timber-framed, hall house with a warm welcome and convivial atmosphere in the beautiful rural area of Walland Marsh. Old furniture is arranged in front of a large open fire. Shove-penny and -ha'penny are etched into an old, long table. Good value, recommended food in generous portions is served daily. Note the spinning wheel on the ceiling, once used to allocate contraband and wool. ⌂Q☺❀◑◗⊟♣P

Burmarsh

Shepherd & Crook

Shear Way, TN29 0JJ OS102321
11-3 (maybe 4), 7-11; 12-5, 7-11 Sat & Sun
☎ (01303) 872336
Adnams Bitter; guest beer H
Small country pub that offers a friendly welcome – especially to dogs. The single room contains the bar and dining area. Formerly a Mackeson's pub, it is now a thriving, family-run free house. One guest beer is always available, sourced from breweries near and far. Traditional English food is popular, all home cooked from local ingredients wherever possible. No meals are served on Sunday or Tuesday. The pub is on the Romney Marsh cycle route. ⌂Q❀◑◗♣

Canterbury

King's Head

24 Wincheap, CT1 3RY (on A28 towards Ashford)
12-2.30, 4.45-midnight; 12-midnight Sat; 12-11.30 Sun
☎ (01227) 462885
Beer range varies H
Traditional, friendly and unspoilt local, well worth the 15-minute walk from the city centre. Dating from the 15th century, the building is Grade II listed. Exposed beams, hanging hops and bric-a-brac all add to its character. Bar billiards and darts are played indoors, while bat & trap matches are held in summer in the attractive garden. The dining room serves good value food. Guest beers are usually sourced from micro-breweries. Q⇌◑◗⇌(East)♣P

Phoenix

67 Old Dover Road, CT1 3DB
11-11; 12-4, 7-10.30 Sun
☎ (01227) 464220 thephoenix-canterbury.co.uk
Greene King Abbot; Theakston Mild; Wells Bombardier; Young's Bitter; guest beers H

Cosy, corner pub where cricket memorabilia abounds – the Phoenix is handy for the county ground. A changing range of two guest beers comes from all over the UK and this is the only Canterbury pub to feature a permanent mild. A well-attended beer festival is staged in December, showcasing a wide range of seasonal beers. Fun quizzes are held weekly (Wed eve). Food is good value and comes in generous portions (no meals Thu eve). Q✿🛏◐◑♿⇌(East)♣P

Unicorn Inn

61 St Dunstans' Street, CT2 8BS (by level crossing)
✪ 11-11 (midnight Fri & Sat); 11-11 Sun
☎ (01227) 463187 🌐 unicorninn.com
Caledonian Deuchars IPA; Shepherd Neame Master Brew Bitter; guest beers 🄷
This comfortable, 1604 pub stands near the ancient Westgate and boasts an attractive suntrap garden. Bar billiards can be played, and a quiz, set by regulars, is held weekly on Sunday evening. The two guest beers often include a brew from Hopdaemon. Imaginative food is prepared from high quality local ingredients (no meals Sun eve); the excellent value menu ranges from pub favourites to exotic specials. ♨✿◐◑⇌(West)♣⚟

Capel

Dovecote Inn

Alders Road, TN12 6FU (½ mile W of A228, between Colts Hill and Tudeley) OS643441
✪ 12-3, 5.30-11.30 (midnight Fri & Sat); 12-5, 7-11 Sun
☎ (01892) 835966
Adnams Broadside; Badger K&B Sussex Bitter; Harveys Sussex Best Bitter; Larkins Chiddingstone; 🄶 **guest beer** 🄷
Welcoming, traditional pub in an idyllic rural location. The back wall of the bar is lined with mock barrels, through which four or more ales and Chiddingstone cider are dispensed from casks kept in a cool room behind. Food is available at all sessions, including tasty Swiss rösti dishes. Parts of the bar and restaurant are no-smoking areas. Themed events include a quiz on alternate Wednesdays. The pleasant garden has a children's climbing frame and a patio dining area. ♨Q✿◐◑♿●P⚟

Capel-le-Ferne

Royal Oak

New Dover Road, CT18 7HY (on B2011)
✪ 11.30-11 (11.30 Fri & Sat); 12-10.30 Sun
☎ (01303) 244787
Hancock's HB; Shepherd Neame Master Brew Bitter; guest beers 🄷
At the Dover end of the clifftop straggle known as Capel-le-Ferne, the Royal Oak enjoys a prime location with views over the channel seascape. Originally a long barn, it has a games area/public bar in an extension. This no-nonsense but friendly house offers quality and value for money. It maintains a strong local focus but takes visitors easily in its stride, especially from nearby caravan sites in summer. Buses pass the door, even after dark. ✿⛺🚌♣P

Charing

Bowl

Egg Hill Road, TN27 0HG (at Five Lanes jct) OS950154
✪ 5-11; 12-midnight Fri & Sat; 12-11 Sun
☎ (01233) 712256 🌐 bowlinn.co.uk
Fuller's London Pride; guest beers 🄷
Historic free house in a remote location on top of the North Downs. It is signed from both the A20 and A251. The Bowl always offers three guest beers. A regular CAMRA award-winner, it stages a beer festival in mid-July. In summer the garden can be used for camping (booking essential), while in winter the pub is warmed by a magnificent open fire. Snacks are available until 9.45pm. Note the unusual hexagonal pool table. ♨Q✿⛺♣P

Chartham

Artichoke Inn

Rattington Street, CT4 7JG
✪ 11-2.30 (4 Sat), 7-11 (midnight Fri & Sat); 12-5, 7-11 Sun
☎ (01227) 738316
Shepherd Neame Master Brew Bitter, Spitfire, seasonal beers 🄷
The quaint, half-timbered exterior hints at the age of this pub, built in the 14th century as a hall house. One half is given over to dining, the other half is a cosy, beamed bar with a large fireplace. Quiz and race nights, darts and bat & trap feature among the regular activities, with occasional performances of live music. Evening meals are served on Friday and Saturday. ♨✿◐◑⇌♣P⚟

Chartham Hatch

Chapter Arms

The Street, CT4 7LT
✪ 10-11; 12-10.30 Sun
☎ (01227) 738340
Shepherd Neame Master Brew Bitter, Spitfire, seasonal beers; guest beer 🄷
Set among orchards on the outskirts of the village, this 19th-century pub is festooned with flowers and boasts splendid, large gardens. An array of musical instruments hangs from the ceiling of the main bar and live jazz is performed regularly. The pub lays on candlelit dinners twice a month on a Tuesday, Sunday lunches, and in summer cream teas and barbecues (Sunday afternoon). A popular destination for walkers and diners, it is just over a mile from Chartham Station. ♨✿◐◑🄿♣P⚟

Chilham

White Horse

The Square, CT4 8BY (1 mile from station)
✪ 10-midnight (1am Fri & Sat); 12-11.30 Sun
☎ (01227) 730355
Beer range varies 🄷
Facing the castle, this 15th-century pub is one of the beautiful houses in Chilham's square that featured on TV in a Miss Marple story. Next to the church, it was the home of a 17th-century vicar whose ghost reputedly haunts the superb inglenook; his

story is recorded nearby. The pub serves breakfast from 9am; evening meals Tuesday-Saturday. Barbecues, fancy dress nights and live music are staged here. Four real ales change frequently. ⌂Q❀◐◑♣

Claygate

White Hart

TN12 9PL (on B2162)
✪ 11-11 daily
☎ (01892) 730313
Goacher's Light; Shepherd Neame Master Brew Bitter, Spitfire; guest beer Ⓗ
Popular Victorian free house, set among orchards and hop gardens. The two bars, both with open fires, offer a warm, welcoming atmosphere. The adjoining dining area, seating up to 60, serves excellent home-cooked food and can cater for diabetic and gluten-free diets. A special flambé menu on Monday and monthly theatre supper nights add variety. The acre of garden provides a pleasant retreat, with frequent barbecues and pig roasts. Children are welcome. ⌂Q❀◐◑⊟♿▲⊞(26)♣P

Conyer

Ship

The Street, ME9 9HR
✪ 11.30-3 (not Mon), 6-11; 11.30-11 Sat; 12-10.30 Sun
☎ (01795) 520778
Adnams Bitter; Caledonian Deuchars IPA; Shepherd Neame Master Brew Bitter, Spitfire Ⓗ
This pub is situated in an isolated settlement next to a creek off the Swale estuary. It is popular with boat owners who can moor nearby and there are many resident houseboats. Furthermore, it is an excellent place to end a long walk through the surprisingly pretty countryside. The bar has bare floorboards and a large brick fireplace for the winter months. In summer you can sit outside for a view of the creek. There is a separate restaurant. ⌂❀◐◑

Cooling

Horseshoe & Castle

The Street, ME3 8OJ
✪ 11.30 (5.30 Mon)-11 (12.30am Fri & Sat); 12-11.30 Sun
☎ (01634) 221691 🌐 horseshoeandcastle.co.uk
Adnams Bitter; Larkins Chiddingstone; guest beers Ⓗ
This pub nestles in the quiet village of Cooling, near a ruined castle that was once owned by Sir John Oldcastle, on whom Shakespeare's Falstaff was modelled. The local graveyard was used in the film of Great Expectations, when young Pip was surprised by the convict, Magwitch. Pool, darts, petanque and bat & trap can be played here. Seafood is a speciality (no meals Mon). The cider is Addlestones. ⌂Q❀⇌◐◑♣●

Deal

Bohemian

47 Beach Street, CT14 6HY (on seafront, by pier)
✪ 11-11 (midnight Thu-Sat); 9am-11.30 Sun
☎ (01304) 374843
Adnams Broadside; Caledonian Deuchars IPA; Woodforde's Wherry; guest beer Ⓗ
In a prime position on the seafront, opposite the pier, the pub's interior bears an appropriately bohemian decor, with comfy couches – a fine example of a congenial modern pub. It stocks an imaginative range of real ales, plus a wide selection of bottled beers from Belgium and further afield – even Cooper's Australia is regularly featured. Westons organic cider is also often sold. A keen Norwich City fan, the landlord considers this hostelry the honorary HQ of Kent Canaries. ❀◐◑⇌●

Deal Hoy

16 Duke Street, CT14 6DU
✪ 12-11; 12-8 Sun
☎ (01304) 363972 🌐 dealhoy.co.uk
Shepherd Neame Master Brew Bitter, Spitfire, seasonal beers Ⓗ
In this Guide for the third year, but fortunately still a best-kept secret. Tucked away in a Victorian terrace off the High Street in the north end of town, the pub has a modern, relaxed interior. Shepherd Neame beer at its best can be enjoyed out in the enlarged garden in summer. Purely a drinkers' pub, although it does host occasional barbecues in good weather. ❀⇌

Prince Albert

187-189 Middle Street, CT14 6LW
✪ 6-11; 12-11 Sun
☎ (01304) 375425
Beer range varies Ⓗ
A short stroll from the town centre in the conservation area, this Grade II listed building is noted for its unusual corner entrance with curved double doors. It also boasts etched Fremlins windows. The cosy bar is welcoming and offers a frequently changed choice of three beers; pump clips on the wall testify to the turnover. The atmospheric, candlelit restaurant features exposed floorboards and an open hearth. Steps lead down to an attractive courtyard garden. ⌂❀⇌◑⇌

Ship

141 Middle Street, CT14 6JZ
✪ 11-11; 12-11 Sun
☎ (01304) 372222
Caledonian Deuchars IPA; Hop Back Summer Lightning; Shepherd Neame Master Brew Bitter Ⓗ
Traditional, two-bar pub in Deal's 18th-century old town, within 100 yards of the sea. The cosy rear bar, with padded benches against the walls, has steps leading out to the small garden. The larger front bar houses a piano and bar servery. Nautical prints and memorabilia are displayed. Live music (folk-style) is played on Thursday evening. ❀⇌

Denton

Jackdaw

The Street, CT4 6QZ (on A260)
✪ 11-11; 12-10.30 Sun
☎ (01303) 844663
Beer range varies Ⓗ

This historic pub featured in the film Battle of Britain and displays RAF memorabilia. It was named after the Jackdaw of Rheims from the Ingoldsby Legends. Up to four guest ales, mainly from regional breweries, are selected from the Enterprise Inns list, but local Shepherd Neame Spitfire is served as a house beer. Meals are served all day in the dining area. Lydden racing circuit is nearby and buses stop outside. ❀ⒹP

Doddington

Chequers Inn

The Street, ME9 0BG

11-3, 7 (6 summer Fri)-11; 11.45-11 Sat; 11.45-3, 7-10.30 Sun

Shepherd Neame Master Brew Bitter, Spitfire Ⓗ

Ancient hostelry at the centre of a downland village. It has two distinctly different bars and many noteworthy features, not least the fireplace in the saloon that gives a timeless feel to the place in winter. Ingredients for the kitchen are sourced from local producers – the sausages are made in the village and the cheesemaker frequents the saloon bar. No evening meals are served Monday. This multi-award winning pub has a well-used outside drinking area. ❀ⒹP

Dover

Blakes

52 Castle Street, CT16 1PJ (off market sq)

11.30-11; 12-10.30 Sun

☎ (01304) 202194 blakesofdover.com

Beer range varies Ⓗ

Fine cellar bar, with restaurant above, below one of Dover's main thoroughfares. The stillage comprises six self-tilting mounts; six casks, plus handpumps and 56 malt whiskies make this a haven for the serious drinker. There is always a stout on handpump but keg beers and lagers are remarkable for their absence. A great atmosphere and fine hosts make this a refuge from the bustling street above and persuaded local CAMRA members to vote it Pub of the Year 2006. ❀Ⓓ⇌(Priory)

Red Lion

Charlton Green, CT16 2PS (off one-way system)

11-midnight daily

☎ (01304) 202899

Fuller's London Pride; Wells Bombardier Ⓗ

Warm, friendly pub with a great social calendar, the Red Lion fields teams for darts, skittles and football. It has its own golf society and a skittle alley in the secluded back garden. The pub offers a big-screen TV for important matches and runs a Friday night meat raffle. A popular destination for locals and workers in nearby industry, it draws a great crowd of older people at lunchtime. ❀ⒹP

White Horse

St James Street, CT16 1QF (next to sports centre)

4-11; 1-10.30 Sun

☎ (01304) 242974

Ringwood Fortyniner; Taylor Landlord; Young's Special; guest beer Ⓗ

The oldest of Dover's pubs, its roots go back to the 14th century; this characterful pub has bags of character, approachable hosts and a great atmosphere. To find Ringwood Fortyniner is most unusual in this part of the country. The pub offers plenty of space on several levels and a raised garden. Old sewing machine treadles are used for some tables. Check out the walls for signatures of cross-channel swimmers and details of their times.
❀⇌(Priory)

East Malling

King & Queen

1 New Road, ME19 6DD

10-2.30, 6-11; 10-11 Fri; 11-11 Sat; 11-3.30 Sun

☎ (01732) 842752

Black Sheep Special; guest beers Ⓗ

This 16th-century inn is at the heart of a village mentioned in the Domesday Book. Now justifiably known for its good food, an a la carte menu is served daily except Sunday when it is replaced by a traditional roast lunch. Guest beers are often from local breweries – a board on the wall provides tasting notes for customers who may be unfamiliar with the range on offer. The pub opens earlier for tea and coffee Monday-Saturday.
❀Ⓓ⇌P

Rising Sun

125 Mill Street, ME19 6BX

12-11; 12-10.30 Sun

☎ (01732) 843284

Goacher's Light; Shepherd Neame Master Brew Bitter; guest beer Ⓗ

This family-run, beamed village local is deservedly popular with discerning drinkers for its sensible pricing policy and adventurous choice of guest ales. A base for sporting clubs and societies, the large-screen TV makes it a convivial venue for major sports events. The dartboard is Kent-style (no trebles). A U-shaped bar separates the comfortable seating area from the main darts section. No under-14s are admitted, but they are welcome in the spacious garden. ❀Ⓓ⇌(58)

East Peckham

Bush, Blackbird & Thrush

194 Bush Road, Peckham Bush, TN12 5LW

(1 mile NE of Peckham via Pound Rd) OS664500

11-3 (not Mon), 6-11; 12-3, 6-10.30 Sun

☎ (01622) 871349

Shepherd Neame Master Brew Bitter, Spitfire, seasonal beers Ⓖ

Fine, 15th-century tile-hung Kentish building, on the fringe of East Peckham village, with a long pub tradition. This Shepherd Neame house serves ales straight from the casks, which are set into the main wall behind the bar. The pub is divided into two rooms, separated by a large brick fireplace burning logs in winter, with the bar on the left and the dining area on the right. They serve traditional pub food (eve meals Tue-Sat). Bat & trap can be played.
Q❀ⒹP

Elham

Rose & Crown

High Street, CT4 6TD

12-midnight (1am Fri & Sat); 12-midnight Sun

☎ (01303) 840226 ⊕ roseandcrownelham.co.uk

Shepherd Neame Master Brew Bitter, Kent's Best, Spitfire; seasonal beers Ⓗ

Charming, 16th-century country inn that joined the Shepherd Neame estate in 2005. The bar has two fires with cosy sofas, and separates neatly into dining and drinking areas. There is also a no-smoking restaurant. All food is home produced, using local suppliers; fish is a speciality. The garden overlooks the pretty Elham Valley. There are six en-suite rooms in the converted stable block. ♨Q❀⇄◑◗🚌P

Fairseat

Vigo

Gravesend Road, TN15 7JL (on A227)

12-4 (not Mon-Fri), 6-11; 7-10.30 Sun

☎ (01732) 822547

Harveys Sussex Best Bitter; Westerham Black Eagle; Young's Bitter; guest beers Ⓗ

Traditional ale drinkers' haven, a former drovers' inn at the top of a steep hill on the North Downs. It has recently undergone refurbishment, but retains its traditional bar of quiet character, with a large open fireplace at one end. Daddlums, a rare form of Kentish table skittles, is still played here. Seasonal beers from Harveys and Westerham are usually available. Totally no-smoking throughout. ♨Q⊟⛺🚌(308)♣P⊁

Farningham

Chequers

87 High Street, DA4 0DT

12-11; 12-10.30 Sun

☎ (01322) 865222

Fuller's London Pride, ESB; Taylor Landlord; guest beers Ⓗ

Thriving, one-bar, small corner local in an attracive riverside village. Under new ownership since 2005, the pub now features decorative murals depicting local scenes. It is close to the Darent Valley footpath and accessible by major roads, although parking is difficult. Up to eight beers, including a rotating range of guests, usually favour Kent micro-breweries. Nearby cottages display notable flower arrangements in spring and summer. No food is served on Sunday. ◑♣

Faversham

Bear Inn

3 Market Place, ME13 7AG

10.30-3, 5.30-11.30; 10.30-midnight Fri & Sat; 11.30-10.30 Sun

☎ (01795) 532668

Shepherd Neame Master Brew Bitter, Kent's Best, Spitfire, seasonal beers Ⓗ

Only a handful of pubs left in the country retain a layout similar to that of the Bear: three distinct bars off a side corridor. The characterful front, snug and rear bars all boast wood panelling. The building dates from 1504. The nearby historic Guildhall can in warmer months be admired from chairs and tables outside the pub. Fine, home-cooked English dishes are served. The pub is popular with folk musicians. ❀◑⊟⇌

Chimney Boy

59 Preston Street, ME13 8PG

11-11 (midnight Fri & Sat); 12-11 Sun

☎ (01795) 532007

Shepherd Neame Master Brew Bitter, Kent's Best, seasonal beers Ⓗ

This two-storey, 18th-century building started life as a private house. Rumour has it that it was a convent at one time, however by 1885 it had become the Limes Hotel. In 1931 Shepherd Neame purchased the hotel and in 1970, during refurbishment, some steps up the chimney were discovered and the pub was renamed the Chimney Boy. The upstairs function room hosts many clubs and societies, including the perennially popular Faversham folk club. ♨❀◑◗⇌♣P

Crown & Anchor

41 The Mall, ME13 8JN

10.30-3, 5.30-11; 10.30-4, 6-11 Sat; 12-3.30, 7-10.30 Sun

☎ (01795) 532812

Shepherd Neame Master Brew Bitter Ⓗ

This large, red-brick pub stands on the Mall, just a short stroll from the town centre and close to the station. Owned by the town's brewery since 1847, it is run by one of the longest-serving licensees in the area and you can be assured of a friendly welcome. The lost art of conversation can be rediscovered in this true community pub as there is no TV or background music. The goulash is as authentic as the landlord is Hungarian. Q◑⇌♣

Mechanics Arms

44 West Street, ME13 7JG

11-11; 12-10.30 Sun

☎ (01795) 532693

Shepherd Neame Master Brew Bitter Ⓗ

Small, unassuming, traditional local that enjoys a loyal following. It was built in the early 17th century but many features were hidden by a new front, added in the 19th century. The licensee holds Shepherd Neame's Master of Beer award. Food is only served on special occasions, otherwise a home-made pickled egg may quell a few hunger pangs. In summer the almost-secret garden comes into its own. Most sporting events are shown on TV. ❀⇌♣

Phoenix

98-99 Abbey Street, ME13 7BH

11-3, 6-11 (1am Fri); 11-1am Sat; 12-4 Sun

☎ (01795) 532757

Beer range varies Ⓗ

Historic Abbey Street contains many fine, old buildings, not least the Phoenix. A lovely inglenook divides the main bar, while wood panelling and low beams feature throughout. The pub, which includes a restaurant area, was once part of a medieval hall dating from around 1330. Two or three beers are offered, often including brews from Rother Valley in East Sussex. The large garden is lovely in summer. Thai food is served (no meals Sun eve). ⌂Q❀◐◑⇌P⁄

Shipwright's Arms

Ham Road, Hollowshore, ME13 7TU OS017636

11-3, 6-11 (closed winter Mon); 12-3, 6-10.30 Sun

☎ (01795) 590088

Beer range varies Ⓖ

Romantic, historic house at the confluence of Faversham and Oare creeks, surrounded by marshes. Dating from the mid-19th century, it is full of interesting nooks and crannies. The beers are sourced solely from Kentish breweries, served from the cask; Shipwrecked is a house ale from Goacher's. This multi-award winner was Kent CAMRA Pub of the Year 2005. The large garden, well-used in summer, is popular with walkers. Primarily a drinkers' pub, home-cooked food is served (not Sun eve or Mon lunchtime). ⌂Q❀◐◑♣P⁄

Sun Inn

10 West Street, ME13 7JE

11-11 (11.30 Fri & Sat); 12-11 Sun

☎ (01795) 535098 🌐 sunfaversham.co.uk

Shepherd Neame Master Brew Bitter, Spitfire, seasonal beers Ⓗ

Ancient pub, originally a 15th-century hall, but much altered every century since; it has been sympathetically extended to provide a restaurant (no eve meals Sun) and guest rooms. The main room features well-preserved oak panelling, some 16th-century, and a beautiful old fireplace. In summer the rear garden fills up, and there are tables in the pedestrianised street at the front. This is one of West Street's venerable buildings, near the historic market place.
⌂❀⇆◐◑♿⇌⁄

Windmill Inn

Canterbury Road, Preston, ME13 8LT

12-midnight (1am Fri & Sat); 12-4, 7-11 Sun

☎ (01795) 536505

Shepherd Neame Master Brew Bitter, seasonal beers Ⓗ

The two-bar pub lies on Watling Street, the old Roman road from Chester to Dover, Its name is derived from the Preston Mill that stood close by until it was demolished in the early 1940s. The pub retains many original features, including a windmill etched into the glass of the door to the front bar, which has a no-smoking section at one end. The inn keeps a few guest rooms.
⌂⇆◐◑⊟⇌♣P⁄

Finglesham

Crown

The Street, CT14 0NA (on A258)

11-3, 6-11 (midnight Fri); 11-midnight Sat; 11-11 Sun

☎ (01304) 612555 🌐 thecrownatfinglesham.co.uk

Shepherd Neame Master Brew Bitter; guest beers Ⓗ

In a quiet rural village, the Crown offers up to five real ales, with at least one brewed in the region. A varied social calendar through the year offers a monthly beer club, themed food nights and quizzes. Bat & trap is played during the summer, replaced by cribbage on winter evenings. The Crown beer festival is held in August. Well-behaved dogs are welcome, but not at meal times. Buses pass only on Sunday. ❀◐◑⛺♣P

Folkestone

British Lion

10 The Bayle, CT20 1SQ (just off town centre)

12-4, 7-11; 11-11 Sat; 12-4, 7-10.30 Sun

☎ (01303) 251478

Greene King IPA, Abbot; guest beers Ⓗ

An ale house has stood on this site since 1460. A comfortable, relaxed atmosphere prevails in this pub that is close to all the facilities of the town centre. The pub fields a quiz team, and cribbage and chess are played regularly. The interior is decorated with some fine old prints from the pub's former Whitbread days, including a scene featuring the closed Chiswell Street brewery. Two guest beers are normally stocked. No meals Tuesday evening. ⌂❀◐◑♣

Chambers

Radnor Chambers, Cheriton Place, CT20 2BB

12-11 (midnight Fri & Sat); 7-10.30 Sun

☎ (01303) 223333

Adnams Bitter; Ringwood Old Thumper; guest beers Ⓗ

Surprisingly spacious cellar bar with a café upstairs under the same ownership. Three guest beers normally include Kentish ales, as well as those from further afield, and are supplemented by Biddenden and Cheddar Valley ciders. Beer festivals are held over Easter and August bank holiday weekends. The food, which includes Mexican and European choices plus daily specials, is served every lunchtime and Sunday-Thursday evenings. ◐◑⇌(Central)♣●

East Cliff Tavern

13-15 East Cliff, CT19 6BU

4 (12 Fri; 11 Sat)-midnight; 12-midnight Sun

☎ (01303) 251132

Beer range varies Ⓗ

This back-street, two-bar, split-level pub is hidden along a terraced street across the harbour railway line. Its walls are decorated with old photos of Folkestone. It normally sells two beers, often from Kentish micros such as Hopdaemon or Ramsgate. Biddenden dry cider is also stocked. The glass cabinet on the bar keeps a range of chocolate and Anadin! This popular pub is well worth searching out above the harbour. Q♣●

Guildhall

42 The Bayle, CT20 1SQ (top of the old High St)

12-11 (midnight Fri & Sat); 12-10.30 Sun

☎ (01303) 251393

Draught Bass; Greene King IPA; guest beers Ⓗ

Welcoming and traditional pub, close to the town centre, with a single bar that offers two guest beers. Large windows give the pub a light, airy feel. The Bayle is an attractive old area of town, where Charles Dickens once lived and started working on Little Dorritt. It is handy for the shops and cinema. ❀◐♣P

Fordwich

Fordwich Arms

King Street, CT2 0DB (500 yds from A28 at Sturry)
⏲ 11-midnight (1am Fri & Sat); 12-midnight Sun
☎ (01227) 710444
Flowers Original; Shepherd Neame Master Brew Bitter; Wadworth 6X; guest beers Ⓗ
Classic 1930s building, now listed in Kent CAMRA's Regional Inventory. This attractive local has a large bar with a superb fireplace and a woodblock floor and a dining room; excellent meals are served in both areas (no food Sun eve). The garden and terrace overlook the River Stour. The pub hosts regular folk music sessions and themed evenings. Fordwich claims to be England's smallest town – its fine old town hall is next to the pub. ⛫Q❀◐◗⇌(Sturry)P

Gillingham

Barge

63 Layfield Road, ME7 2QY
⏲ 7 (4 Fri; 12 Sat)-11; 12-11 Sun
☎ (01634) 850485 🌐 folkatthebarge.co.uk
Beer range varies Ⓗ
This single-bar town house boasts five handpumps, four of which change constantly. A well-known music venue, the first Wednesday in the month is 'Bards at the Barge' night when anyone can pick from an array of musical instruments – from a harp to guitar – and play. It is much more like being in Ireland than Medway. The pub also hosts various charity events in the summer. The garden affords superb views of the River Medway. ❀⇌♣

Frog & Toad

Burnt Oak Terrace, ME7 1DR
⏲ 11-11; 12-10.30 Sun
☎ (01634) 852231 🌐 thefrogandtoad.com
Fuller's London Pride; Harveys Sussex XX Mild; guest beers Ⓗ
Busy pub, serving the local community. Note the carpet design linked to the pub's name. More than 500 pump clips represent beers that have been sold at the bar or during one of the beer festivals, which are staged regularly, including each bank holiday. The pub also serves more than 30 Belgian beers, each in its own branded glass; one is kept on draught. It holds summer barbecues and meat raffles. Meals are served Monday-Thursday. Q❀◐◗⇌

Roseneath

79 Arden Street, ME7 1HS
⏲ 12-midnight; 12-11 Sun
☎ (01634) 852553
Fuller's London Pride; guest beers Ⓗ
A welcome return to the Guide for this single-bar town house. The present owner has now been at the pub for 18 years. The walls have been knocked back to reveal the original brickwork, which adds to the character of the place. The large garden hosts music and barbecue events monthly throughout the summer. The pub sponsors three football teams and for the less active, a football table is provided. Six handpumps offer some surprising choices. ❀⇌♣

Upper Gillingham Conservative Club

541 Canterbury Street, ME7 5LF
⏲ 11-2.30 (3 Sat), 7-11; 12-2.30, 7-10.30 Sun
☎ (01634) 851403
Shepherd Neame Master Brew Bitter; guest beers Ⓗ
To gain entry to the club you will need a current CAMRA membership card or the latest edition of this Guide. Three handpumps serve ales up to the mid-4% ABV range. There are rooms for snooker and TV, while the lounge has a wheelchair ramp at the entrance. Welcoming and cosy, this has been local CAMRA Club of the Year for the last seven years and a previous national runner-up.
♿⇌♣

Will Adams

73 Saxton Street, ME7 5EG
⏲ 12-3 (not Mon-Fri), 7-11; 12-4, 8-11 Sun
☎ (01634) 575902
Beer range varies Ⓗ
Voted Medway CAMRA Pub of the Year 2006, this back-street pub, that always has a friendly welcome, is named after a local adventurer and seaman. Two guest beers of varying strengths, Budweiser Budvar, a draught cider and a large selection of malt whiskies provide drinkers with plenty of choice. A magnet for Gillingham football supporters, it also welcomes away fans and gets busy on match days. ❀⇌●

Godden Green

Buck's Head

Park Lane, TN15 0JJ 05553551
⏲ 12-3, 5.30-11; 12-3.30, 5.30-11 Sun
☎ (01732) 761330
Shepherd Neame Master Brew Bitter, Spitfire Ⓗ
Happy to admit children and dogs, this friendly pub is in a hamlet behind Knole Park, due east of Sevenoaks. This area is popular with hikers and the pub is a good place to seek refreshment when walking in the park or the many footpaths. The interior features exposed beams, wood panelling, framed pictures, horse brasses, and copper and brass items. Food is served in the restaurant or bar, which often stocks seasonal beers. ⛫❀◐◗🚌♣P🍺

Gravesend

Crown & Thistle

44 The Terrace, DA12 2BJ (off inner ring road)
⏲ 11-11; 12-10.30 Sun
☎ (01474) 326049 🌐 crownandthistle.org.uk
Daleside Shrimpers; guest beers Ⓗ
Small Georgian terraced pub between the Thames and town centre. A convivial atmosphere prevails, free from games machines and intrusive music. With three changing guests, over 1,000 different beers have featured since the pub reopened in 2001; Westons cider is stocked. Chinese, Indian and Thai meals can be ordered at the bar from local outlets to eat on or off the premises. Summer barbecues are held in the small garden. It was CAMRA National Pub of the Year in 2003. ❀◐◗⇌●⚟

Ship & Lobster

Mark Lane, Riverside, Denton, DA12 2QB

11-11; 12-4 Sun

☎ (01474) 324571

Daleside Shrimpers; guest beers [H]

On the Thames at the eastern end of Gravesend, the pub can be reached from Gravesend by following Ordnance Road, past the canal basin, through the industrial estate to the end of Mark Lane. The original 18th-century Ship features in Charles Dickens' Great Expectations. It bears a nautical theme and is home to local fishermen for whom takeaway meals are offered. On Sunday it provides an excellent home-cooked roast (booking essential). Two rotating guest beers and Westons cider are sold. ⌂❀◐♣●

Hadlow

Two Brewers

Maidstone Road, TN11 1DN

12-11; 12-10.30 Sun

☎ (01732) 850267

Harveys Hadlow Bitter, Sussex Best Bitter, Armada Ale, seasonal beers [H]

Friendly, two-bar village pub, much improved by Harveys. The walls show pictures of the village and the closed Kenward and Courts Brewery. Two Harveys beers are served from the barrels in the public bar and its seasonal brews are normally available. The Hadlow Bitter is brewed using hops from the local hop farm. Food is served and well-behaved children are welcome. A regular bus service from Tonbridge Station stops nearby and runs until late in the evening. ❀◐◑♿🚌P⚟

Halstead

Rose & Crown

Otford Lane, TN14 1 7EA OS489611

12-11 daily

☎ (01959) 533120

Larkins Traditional; Whitstable East India Pale Ale; guest beers [H]

Two-bar, flint-faced free house, dating from 1860 then named the Crown. It was part of Fox and Sons' estate and later owned by Style and Winch. The bars show pictures of the pub and village in earlier times. In this Guide for 12 consecutive years, it has a policy of offering four regularly-changing guest ales. A mainly home-made menu is served daily; Sunday lunch is recommended and well-behaved children are welcome. ⌂Q⚙❀◐◑♿♣P

Harvel

Amazon & Tiger

Harvel Street, DA13 0DE

12-3, 6-11; 12-11 Fri-Sun

☎ (01474) 814705

Beer range varies [H]

This bustling village local at the heart of its community is associated with Harvel cricket club whose ground is behind the pub. This rather austere, 1914 brick building was reputedly deliberately styled as a private house to avoid offending the sensibilities of the congregation of the local chapel. The two distinctive bars are pleasantly furnished and offer three guest beers from independent brewers. A quiz is staged on Monday evening. Evening meals are served Thursday-Saturday. ⌂❀◐◑⛺♣P

Hastingleigh

Bowl

The Street, TN25 5HU

12-midnight (1 am Fri & Sat); 12-11 Sun

☎ (01233) 750354

Adnams Bitter; Fuller's London Pride; Harveys Sussex Best Bitter; guest beer [H]

Lovingly restored village pub. This listed building retains many period features including a tap room - now used for playing pool, but the pub is thankfully free from games machines. Photographs of historical interest are on display. The welcoming landlord serves well-kept beers, including seasonal brews, and ciders – usually Biddenden. No hot food is available. ⌂❀●

Herne

Smuggler's Inn

1 School Lane, CT6 7AN

11-11 (1am Fri & Sat); 11-11 Sun

☎ (01227) 741395

Shepherd Neame Master Brew Bitter, seasonal beers [H]

Friendly local in an attractive village with a smuggling history, situated just inland from Herne Bay. Parts of the pub are 400 years old; the saloon bar is characterised by a low ceiling, hanging hops, wood panelling and a ship's binnacle. The public bar is more modern, with pool and darts. Bat & trap is played in the garden. The tiny Butcher's Arms across the road is also worth a visit. Q❀◑♿🚌♣

Hernhill

Three Horseshoes

46 Staple Street, ME13 9UA OS080601

12-2, 6-11; 12-11 Fri & Sat; 12-4, 7-10.30 Sun

☎ (01227) 750842 🌐 3shoes.co.uk

Shepherd Neame Master Brew Bitter, [G] **Spitfire, seasonal beers** [H]

Beautiful pub in an archetypal Kentish location, affording views over the orchards of Mount Ephraim House to the church at Hernhill in the distance. A haphazard array of furniture greets the visitor in two separate drinking (and dining) areas. Good pub food is served, but not on Sunday evening or Monday. The 'Shoes is noted for its annual wheelie bin grand prix in July! A bus runs two-hourly (not Sun). ⌂Q❀◐◑⛺🚌♣P

Higham

Stonehorse

Dillywood Lane, ME3 8EN (off B2000 Cliffe road)

11-3, 6-11; 11-11 Fri & Sat; 12-3, 7-10.30 Sun

☎ (01634) 722046

Beer range varies [H]

Country pub with large garden on the edge of Strood, surrounded by fields and handy for walks. The rare, unspoilt public bar boasts a wood-burning range, darts and a bar billiards table. A quiz is held on Sunday evening. Good value food is served Monday-Saturday. The beer range includes a real mild. ♨Q❀◐◑⊟♣P

Hildenborough

Cock Horse

London Road, TN11 8NM OS553499

✪ 11-3 (12-2 Mon), 5.30 -11 (8 Mon); 12-3, 6-1 am Sat; 12-3 Sun

☎ (01732) 835232

Shepherd Neame Master Brew Bitter, Spitfire Ⓗ

A friendly atmosphere pertains at this 15th-century pub with low beams. The huge open hearth is very appealing on cold winter nights. Originally a Courage house, known as the Old Cock, outside is an unusual two-tier decked area with heating, leading to a garden area and stream. Popular with walkers, the pub also has good access for disabled people. Home-cooked food is chalked up daily on a blackboard; Sunday lunch recommended (no meals Sun eve); booking is advised. ♨Q❀◐◑♿⇌P⊬

Hook Green

Elephant's Head

Furnace Lane, TN3 8LJ (on B2169)

✪ 12-3, 4.30-11; 12-11 Sat; 12-10.30 (9 winter) Sun

☎ (01892) 890279

Harveys Hadlow Bitter, Sussex Best Bitter, Armada Ale, seasonal beers Ⓗ

Built in 1489 and formerly part of the famous Culpepper family estate, it has been a pub since 1768 – read the interesting history inside. The well-preserved interior includes an inglenook with a log fire in the winter, oak beams hung with hops and a conservatory. Outside facilities include a garden and children's play area. Now a Harveys house, it serves a varied menu (not Sun or Mon eve), including traditional English dishes, fish and children's meals. A darts team plays here regularly. ♨Q⛄❀◐◑♣P

Horton Kirby

Bull

3 Lombard Street, DA4 9DF

✪ 12 (4 Mon)-11 (midnight Fri & Sat); 12-10.30 Sun

☎ (01322) 862274 ⊕ thebullpub.co.uk

Beer range varies Ⓗ

Refurbished village pub where the large landscaped garden affords a wide view across Darent Valley. The new, top-notch, kitchen offers good food. Three changing beers are selected by the landlord from enterprising micro-breweries, including the local Millis Brewing Company. A central bar divides a no-smoking area to the right from the remainder of the pub. Quiz nights are held on Monday and a successful cribbage league on Tuesday. ❀◐◑♿♣⊟(414)●⊬

Ightham

Chequers

The Street, TN15 9HH

✪ 11-3, 6-11; 12-3, 7-10.30 Sun

☎ (01732) 882396

Greene King IPA, Abbot, seasonal beer; guest beer Ⓗ

Pleasant, convivial, former coaching inn dating from the 17th century at the village centre. It enjoys a good local reputation for its food (booking essential). Diners are accommodated throughout, with a no-smoking area at one side; the other side is dominated by a large stone fireplace. The Chequers supports charities including Kent Air Ambulance. ♨Q❀◐◑⊟(308, 222)P

Ightham Common

Old House ☆

Redwell Lane, TN15 9EE (½ mile SW of Ightham Village, between A25 and A227) OS590559

✪ 7-11 (9 Tue); 12-3, 7-11 Sat; 12-3, 7-10.30 Sun

☎ (01722) 822383

Daleside Shrimpers; Ⓖ **Flowers IPA;** Ⓗ **Oakham JHB;** Ⓖ **guest beers** Ⓖ

Tucked away down a steep, narrow, country lane, this brick and tile-hung cottage pub is a classic. The pub sign has disappeared and it feels like a private house offering drinks to loyal friends. The building dates from the 17th century: the larger room features a Victorian wood-panelled bar counter and a huge inglenook; the smaller one has the atmosphere of a quiet parlour. Beers are served from a stillage by gravity in this remarkable survivor from a bygone era. ♨Q⊟♣P

Kemsing

Rising Sun

Cotmans Ash Lane, TN15 6XD (phone for directions) OS563599

✪ 11-3, 6-11; 12-3, 7-10.30 Sun

☎ (01959) 522683

Beer range varies Ⓗ

Isolated hilltop hostelry in scenic downland near several local footpaths, therefore popular with walkers and cyclists. The pub sign is fading and not easy to spot from the road. Partly 16th century, this former hunting lodge has a flint exterior and an oak beamed interior, displaying an abundance of old agricultural implements. An ancient African Grey parrot resides by the large open fireplace. Up to five beers from local and regional micro-breweries are stocked. ♨Q⛺♣P▯

Kingsdown

King's Head

Upper Street, CT14 8BJ

✪ 12-2.30 (not Mon-Thu), 5-11; 12-3, 6-11 Sat; 12-10.30 Sun

☎ (01304) 373915

Fuller's London Pride; Goacher's Light; guest beer Ⓗ

Split-level pub, dating back to the turn of the 18th/19th century, although the original structure is probably a lot older. It is situated halfway along the main village street as it runs down to the sea. The lower bar has a display of old firearms and a fine, frosted glass door bearing the name of a defunct local brewery, Thompson of Walmer. A secluded garden at the rear houses a skittle alley. Home-cooked food includes fresh fish and curries. The pub stocks a good selection of malt whiskies. ⛫♉❀◑♣⁄

Laddingford

Chequers Inn

Lees Road, ME18 6BP

✪ 12-3, 5-11; 12-11 Sat & Sun

☎ (01622) 871266

Adnams Bitter; Fuller's London Pride; guest beers Ⓗ

Attractive, 15th-century village pub, with a good community spirit. The frontage is a picture in summer, with colourful window boxes and hanging baskets. The entrance opens onto the main bar; to the left is a split-level dining area, to the right a small, cosier room, all simply furnished. A beer festival is held in late April, showcasing some 30 beers. The food is excellent; daily specials and theme nights provide variety. ⛫Q❀⛟◐◑⛍(26)♣P

Luddesdown

Cock Inn

Henley Street, DA13 0XB OS664672

✪ 12-11; 12-10.30 Sun

☎ (01474) 814208

Adnams Bitter, Broadside; Goacher's Mild; Harveys Sussex Best Bitter; Shepherd Neame Master Brew Bitter; guest beers Ⓗ

Local CAMRA Pub of the Year and Kent runner-up in 2005, this enterprising, independently-owned free house offers at least seven real ales. The landlord devises and hosts a well-attended quiz on Tuesday evening. Excellent, home-cooked food is served in the bar, including pie made with locally-shot game in season (no meals Sun eve). Rooms are available for meetings and petanque is played in the garden. Deservedly popular, this pub is well worth finding. ⛫Q❀◐◑⊟⅄♣P

Lynsted

Black Lion

ME9 0RJ

✪ 11-3, 7-11; 11-11 Sat; 12-3, 7-10.30 Sun

☎ (01795) 521229

Goacher's Mild, Light, seasonal beers Ⓗ

At the centre of a picturesque village, this is a shrine to Goacher's Brewery, some distance from its Maidstone base. A friendly pub sought out by drinkers from all around, the main room has open fires at both ends, providing genuine warmth in winter. A second, smaller room has a pool table and dartboard. Timber floors throughout add character. In summer the focus shifts to the large garden alongside the pub. There is a two-hourly bus service (not eve or Sun). ⛫Q❀◐◑⛍P

Maidstone

Druid's Arms

24 Earl Street, ME14 1PP (opp. Hazlitt Theatre)

✪ 11-11 (midnight Thu-Sat); 12-11 Sun

☎ (01622) 758516

Greene King Morland Original, Ruddles County, Abbot, Old Speckled Hen; guest beers Ⓗ

This town-centre pub was the original Hogshead. It stands next to the new Fremlins Walk shopping centre that replaced the old Fremlins Brewery. A mixed clientele enjoys live music on Thursday and Saturday in the heated, covered courtyard. Lively piped music is played in the split-level bar that hosts a quiz on Monday. It offers changing guest ales and regular beer festivals. Meals are served 12-6.30pm daily. ⛫❀◐♿⇌(East)

Fox

85 Hartnup Street, ME16 8LT

✪ 11-11 (midnight Thu-Sat); 12-11 Sun

☎ (01622) 729530

Flowers IPA; Fuller's London Pride; Goacher's Dark; Young's Bitter Ⓗ

Open-plan, corner pub in an established residential area in the west of town. The friendly landlord, who has a passion for music, always offers a warm welcome. Live music is performed most Saturday evenings during autumn and winter. Excellent value lunches are served Monday-Saturday; tapas are served in summer. At the weekend, the Fox may stay open until 1am if trade demands. Dogs are welcome at this pub, which is a rare outlet for Goacher's Dark Ale. Parking is limited. ◐P

Pilot

23-25 Upper Stone Street, ME15 6EU

✪ 12-3, 6-11; 12-4, 7-midnight Sat, 12-5, 7-midnight Sun

☎ (01622) 691162

Harveys Sussex Best Bitter, Armada Ale, seasonal beers; guest beer Ⓗ

This 17th-century, town-centre pub is the only Harveys' house in Maidstone; the four handpumps offer mild as well as other seasonal beers. There is a welcoming log fire in the bar and another in the family room. To the rear of the pub is a secluded patio with a petanque pitch. Good value pub food is available weekday lunchtimes and live music is performed every Sunday. ⛫Q♉❀◐♣

Rifle Volunteer

28 Wyatt Street, ME14 1EU

✪ 11-3, 6 (7 Sat)-11; 12-3, 7-10.30 Sun

☎ (01622) 758891

Goacher's Mild, Light, Crown Imperial Stout Ⓗ

Local CAMRA Pub of the Year 2005, the single bar is free from fruit machines and music. The pub fields two quiz teams in the local league. The lunches represent excellent value. If you want a good, old-fashioned pub where you can enjoy conversation with a variety of customers, this is the place for you. Q◐⇌(East)♣

Margate

Northern Belle

4 Mansion Street, CT9 1HE

✪ 11-11; 12-10.30 Sun

☎ (07748) 691270

Shepherd Neame Master Brew Bitter, seasonal beers Ⓗ

This small, down-to-earth seafarers' tavern, up a tiny lane opposite the harbour, is the oldest standing pub in town. It resulted from combining two fisherman's cottages built around 1680 that stood right at the water's edge, and was first known as the Waterman's Arms, then the Aurora Borealis. Its present name derives from an American merchant ship that ran aground in 1857. It had a subtle refit in 2004, and always has two real ales on handpump.
⊟≉♣

Orb Inn

Chapel Hill, Ramsgate Road, CT9 4EU
✪ 11-midnight; 12-11 Sun
☎ (01843) 220663
Shepherd Neame Master Brew Bitter, Spitfire; seasonal beers Ⓗ
This former Guide regular is making a welcome return following a couple of changes of licensee. In Victorian times, horsedrawn traffic would stop on the road between Margate and Ramsgate and traces still remain of the forge at this pub. There are also two sealed tunnels, reputedly used in Elizabethan times by Catholics escaping persecution. It is now a Shepherd Neame house, but was previously tied to Rigdens, Thomson & Wotton, and Whitbread.
⩕❀ⅭP♣P

Marsh Green

Wheatsheaf Inn

TN8 5QL (on B2028 through village centre)
✪ 11-11; 12-11 Sun
☎ (01732) 864091 🌐 thewheatsheaf.net
Harveys Sussex Best Bitter; guest beers Ⓗ
Spacious pub, comprising several drinking areas, including a no-smoking conservatory, displaying old photographs. The bar stocks up to eight real ales that change frequently, with usually a mild and local brews in the range. Biddenden cider is sold. An annual beer festival is held in early summer, to coincide with the village fête, offering over 30 ales on gravity and a hog roast. Home-cooked food, with vegetarian options, is served daily. ⩕Q♉❀ⅭⅮ⊟♿♣●P⅟

Marshside

Gate Inn

Boyden Gate, CT3 4EB (off A28)
✪ 11-2.30 (4 Sat), 6-11; 12-4, 7-10.30 Sun
☎ (01227) 860498
Shepherd Neame Master Brew Bitter, Spitfire, seasonal beers Ⓖ
Splendid village pub, in this Guide for 31 years under the same landlord. His commitment to the local community includes organising fundraising events and hosting traditional entertainment such as mummers' plays, hoodeners and morris dancing. The bars have tiled floors and log fires. The excellent, good value food (no eve meals Mon or winter Tue) is based on fresh local ingredients. Close to the Saxon Shore Way and the Wantsum Walk, the pub is popular with hikers and cyclists.
⩕Q♉❀ⅭⅮ⛺♣P⅟

Meopham

George

Wrotham Road, DA13 0AH (on A227)
✪ 11-11; 12-10.30 Sun
☎ (01474) 814198
Shepherd Neame Master Brew Bitter, Spitfire, Bishops Finger, seasonal beers Ⓗ
Attractive former coaching inn located in the historic centre of a long village, near the parish church. Believed to date from the 15th century, it reopened in the late 1990s, when it was rescued from semi-dereliction. Inside the Kentish weatherboarded exterior are two bars in contrasting styles, and a restaurant serving excellent quality food until 9pm. There is a paved, heated courtyard, a large garden and a floodlit petanque pitch. ⩕❀ⅭⅮ🚌(308)♣P

Minster (Thanet)

New Inn

2 Tothill Street, CT12 4AG
✪ 11.30-3, 6 (5 Tue)-11; 11.30-11 Wed-Thu; 11.30-midnight Fri & Sat; 12-10.30 Sun
☎ (01843) 821294
Beer range varies Ⓗ
Welcoming village local that offers good ale, home-cooked food and live music to villagers and visitors alike. A regularly changing guest ale is sourced from local independent or micro-breweries. The extensive garden is popular in summer. This former Cobbs' house retains the brewery's stained glass windows at the front. No food is served on Sunday evening or Monday. ❀ⅭⅮ≉♣P

Newenden

White Hart

Rye Road, TN18 5PN
✪ 11-11; 12-10.30 Sun
☎ (01797) 252166
Fuller's London Pride; Harveys Sussex Best Bitter; Rother Valley Level Best; guest beer Ⓗ
Reputedly haunted, this 500-year-old free house stands right on the Sussex border. Its main feature is perhaps the magnificent inglenook with seats. The no-smoking restaurant serves excellent food and the pub has six guest bedrooms. It is convenient for Northiam Station on the Kent and East Sussex Light Railway, which runs to Tenterden and Bodiam Castle (NT). The pub has a boules pitch.
⩕Q❀🛏ⅭⅮ⛺≉(Northiam K&ES Rlwy)♣P

Northbourne

Hare & Hounds

The Street, CT14 0LG (signed from A258 and A256)
✪ 11-3, 6-11; 12-3, 7-10.30 Sun
☎ (01304) 365429
Fuller's ESB; Harveys Sussex Best Bitter; Shepherd Neame Spitfire; Taylor Landlord; guest beer Ⓗ
The area's flagship no-smoking pub, this friendly country inn offers a fine selection of real ales, wines and soft drinks. The fifth handpump usually dispenses an interesting guest ale. The menu specialises in free range and local produce, with an extensive list of

innovative vegetarian dishes. Hops decorate the split-level bar that is divided into three comfortable sections, warmed by open fires. The pub supports the local cricket team and other worthy causes. ⛫Q❀◐◑P⚟

Northfleet

Campbell Arms

1 Campbell Road, DA11 0JZ

✪ 12-11; 12-10.30 Sun

☎ (01474) 320488

Courage Best Bitter; Daleside Shrimpers; guest beers 🄷

Edwardian, back-street corner local in a residential area, bordering Gravesend. A welcoming, popular community pub, it fields darts, pool and football teams. Note the Mann, Crossman and Paulin Brewery mirror behind the bar. The two guest beers are competitively priced and always include at least one draught mild. It is within walking distance of Gravesend town centre, but far enough away from the madding crowd. ❀⇌(Gravesend)♣

Earl Grey

177 Vale Road, DA11 8BP (off Perry St)

✪ 12-11; 12-10.30 Sun

☎ (01474) 365240

Shepherd Neame Master Brew Bitter, Spitfire, seasonal beers 🄷

Late 18th-century cottage-style building, with a Kentish brick and flint exterior, rarely seen in this area. This friendly community pub consists of an L-shaped bar with a raised seating area at one end. Located at the Perry Street end of Vale Road, it is handy for buses into Gravesend, including the No. 499 that runs late into the evening. ❀🚌♣P

Old Romney

Rose & Crown

Swamp Road, TN29 9SQ (off A259)

✪ 11.30-11 (later for functions); 12-10.30 Sun

☎ (01797) 367500 🌐 roseandcrown-oldromney.co.uk

Greene King IPA, Abbot; Taylor Landlord; guest beer 🄷

Situated just off the A259, this welcoming free house overlooks the open countryside of Romney Marsh. Built originally as two cottages, in 1689 it became a pub and still retains two bars, together with a no-smoking conservatory. Reasonably-priced meals and filled baguettes are available (no food Sun eve). The pub welcomes dogs and supports a range of games including shove-ha'penny, petanque, cribbage, pool, darts and quizzes. The guest beers are usually from local micro-breweries; Biddenden cider is sold in summer.
⛫Q❀⛟◐◑⊟♿⛺♣●P⚟

Otford

Bull

High Street, TN14 5PG

✪ 11-11; 12-10.30 Sun

☎ (01959) 523198

Greene King IPA; guest beers 🄷

A Victorian exterior fronts a timber-framed Tudor building. Of note are the chiming of the old grandfather clock, the 17th-century wood panelling and two large stone fireplaces, which were brought here from the ruined Otford Palace. Good food is available all day throughout this no-smoking pub; chalkboards display the varied menus and fresh fish is a house speciality. Three guest beers come from independents; one handpump normally offers Dudley's Choice – the current recommendation of the cellarman. ⛫Q◐◑⇌P

Petteridge

Hopbine

Petteridge Lane, TN12 7HE OS667413

✪ 12 (11 Sat)-2.30, 6-11; 12-3, 7-10.30 Sun

☎ (01892) 722561

Badger K&B Sussex Bitter, First Gold, seasonal beers 🄷

In this Guide for 17 years, this Hall & Woodhouse pub serves three Badger beers, including seasonal brews, plus Westons Old Rosie cider. A favourite with locals from the hamlet of Petteridge and surrounding villages, it serves good, traditional pub food daily, except Wednesday. Well-behaved children are welcome in the pub and the safe garden, and dogs are admitted. The pub fields a darts team and is the base for a walking group called the Hopbine Amblers.
⛫Q❀◐◑♣●P⚟

Plaxtol

Golding Hop

Sheet Hill, TN15 0PT

✪ 11-3, 6 (5.30 Fri)-11; 11-11 Sat; 12-3 (4 summer), 7-10.30 Sun

☎ (01732) 882150

Adnams Bitter; Young's Special, seasonal beers; guest beers 🄶

Old whitewashed, cottagey pub, nestling in a valley, surrounded by orchards. It is noted for its range of ciders, one made on the premises. The interior has four rooms spread over three levels, featuring white walls, oak beams and a log-burning stove. Petanque and bar billiards are played. Outside is a flower-filled terraced garden by a stream. Eggs are often for sale from the resident ducks, geese and chickens. Meals are served Wednesday-Sunday. ⛫❀◐◑♣●P

Pluckley

Dering Arms

Station Road, TN27 0RR

✪ 11.30-3, 6-11; closed Mon; 12-3 Sun

☎ (01233) 840371

Goacher's Gold Star 🄷

This attractive pub is easy to find, opposite Pluckley Station. Built in the 1840s as a hunting lodge for the Dering estate, it was designed as a replica of the main manor house, on a smaller scale. It features distinctive windows and stone-flagged floors. The regular house beer, Dering Ale, is brewed by Goacher's. The pub is renowned for its good food, especially fish, and hosts regular gourmet evenings. ⛫Q❀⛟◐◑⇌P

Rainham

Angel

Station Road, ME8 7UH
12-11 (midnight Fri & Sat); 12-9 Sun
(01634) 360219
Beer range varies H
Corner pub in a semi-rural position, this popular local was Medway CAMRA's Pub of the Year in 2004 and 2005. Of the three handpumps one offers Whitstable's pale ale, the others change constantly and sometimes showcase rare beers. The Angel is well worth the walk. ⌂❀≋♣P

Mackland Arms

213 Station Road, ME8 7PS (400 yds N of station)
10-11; 12-10.30 Sun
(01634) 232178
Shepherd Neame Master Brew Bitter, seasonal beers H
Small, mid-terrace local, with an L-shaped bar area. It attracts a wide range of customers, from builders to bankers. The main reason to visit is to chat and drink, but major sports fixtures are shown on TV. ❀≋♣

Ramsgate

Churchill Tavern

19-22 The Paragon, CT11 9JX
11-11 (midnight Fri & Sat); 12-10.30 Sun
(01843) 587862 churchilltavern.co.uk
Beer range varies H
The Churchill combines a modern, brasserie-style restaurant with a traditional English pub. Affording superb views across the English Channel and busy harbour, it is popular with locals, visitors and students from the nearby language school. The current owners rebuilt the interior in 1986 as an English country pub, using authentic reclaimed materials, including stained glass; the bar was built from 19th-century oak church pews. It was voted Thanet CAMRA Pub of the Year 2004. ⌂◐♣

Foy Boat

8 Sion Hill, CT11 9HZ
11-11; 12-10.30 Sun
(01843) 591198
Greene King IPA, Abbot; Ramsgate Gadds No. 3; Young's Bitter H
Warm, welcoming pub, occupying a commanding position overlooking the Royal Harbour. The building is a sympathetic late 1940s replacement for the original pub that was bombed in 1941. The only Foy Boat in the country, this former Thomson & Wotton house was reputedly the model for the Channel Packet in Ian Fleming's Goldfinger. It gets busy at lunchtime with diners, particularly on Sunday when meals are served until 6pm; there is a restaurant on the first floor. ⇄◐♣

Montefiore Arms

1 Trinity Place, CT11 7HJ
12-2.30 (not Wed), 7-11; 12-3, 7-10.30 Sun
(01843) 593265
Beer range varies H
Traditional, Victorian pub serving well-presented, varied ales to appreciative locals – it was chosen by Thanet CAMRA to be their Pub of the Year 2005. The pub name commemorates the local Jewish philanthropist, Sir Moses Montefiore – see the impressive marquetry depicting his coat of arms. Quiz and darts teams are well supported here and the Sunday meat raffle is a favourite event. The pub is hidden up a cul-de-sac, off Hereson Road, but near the Thanet loop bus stop. ≋(Dumpton Pk)♣

St Lawrence Tavern

High Street, St Lawrence, CT11 0QN
11-11; 12-11 Sun
(01843) 592337
Beer range varies H
The real ale flagship of the Thorley Taverns chain, the St Lawrence was built in 1969 as a Whitbread-Cobb house, called the White Horse. A popular, friendly local, it serves imaginative bar snacks and has a busy restaurant. The beer range often features locally-brewed ales, with a least one from an independent brewery. CAMRA events such as Mild Day and Pubs Week are always keenly supported. ❀◐♣P

Rochester

Britannia Bar Café

376 High Street, ME1 1DJ
10-11 (2am Fri & Sat); 12-11 Sun
(01634) 815204 britannia-bar-cafe.co.uk
Beer range varies H
Busy at lunchtimes, attracting a mainly business clientele, the pub serves an extensive and popular daily menu, plus traditional Sunday lunches (eve meals Mon-Thu); breakfasts are also served (10-noon). A friendly, cosy atmosphere extends into the evening. A stylish bar leads out into a small walled garden that is a suntrap in summer. Occasional live music is performed and a monthly quiz is staged.
Q❀◐≋(Rochester/Chatham)

Cooper's Arms

10 St Margaret's Street, ME1 1TL (behind cathedral)
11-2.30, 5.30-11; 11-11 Fri & Sat; 12-10.30 Sun
(01634) 404298
Courage Best Bitter, Directors; guest beers H
Just off the High Street, in the shadow of the cathedral and castle, this ancient inn features in the Domesday Book and is a contender for the oldest pub in Kent. The two bars contain items of historical interest, including the original fireplace uncovered a few years ago during renovation work. Good quality lunches are served. If you happen to see a monk, it could be the resident ghost.
⌂Q❀◐≋(Rochester/Strood)P

Good Intent

83 St John Street, ME1 1YL
12-midnight daily
(01634) 843118
Beer range varies H
The only original building left in a completely redeveloped area, this two-bar local in Rochester's Troy Town area sources its three changing beers from small breweries. It is a short walk from the castle, cathedral and High Street. The public bar

houses a pool table, while bar billiards can be played in the saloon. The safe, enclosed south-facing garden gives access to the quiet saloon bar. Occasional live music and barbecues are staged. Q P

Man of Kent

6-8 St John Street, ME1 1YN (200 yds off A2)
12-11 (midnight Fri & Sat); 12-11 Sun
(01634) 818771
Beer range varies H
Small, back-street pub with a single L-shaped bar. The rare tiled exterior advertises Style & Winch, the Maidstone brewery that closed long ago. Seven handpumps showcase beers from Kent micro-breweries. Two Kentish ciders are also stocked – one on handpump, one top pressure. Also on draught are three German and two Belgian fruit beers, as well as a wheat beer. Some 30 bottled continental beers and local ciders add yet more variety.

Rolvenden Layne

Ewe & Lamb

26 Maytham Road, TN17 4LN (1 mile from Rolvenden towards Wittersham)
11-11; 12-5 Sun
(01580) 241837
Adnams Bitter; Greene King Old Speckled Hen; Harveys Sussex Best Bitter H
Near Great Maytham Hall on the High Weald landscape trail from Tenterden stands this pleasantly restored country pub. Warmed by log fires, it provides a great environment in which to relax, enjoy good beer and fine wine, accompanied by excellent food. Served by the No. 294 bus from Rolvenden (not every day), it is within easy walking distance of the Wittersham Road station on the Kent & East Sussex steam railway. Dogs are welcome in the bar, but not the no-smoking restaurant. Q P

Romney Street

Fox & Hounds

TN15 6XR (2 miles up hill from Eynsford war memorial) OS550614
12-midnight daily
(01959) 525428
Harveys Sussex Best Bitter; guest beers H
Remote country pub in a hamlet east of Otford village. A friendly watering-hole for ramblers and loyal regulars, it welcomes children and has a large, secluded garden. Old-fashioned games such as shove-ha'penny and shut the box can be played here. Three changing guest beers are sourced from regional and local brewers. Not the easiest pub to find – ring for directions if you get lost. Evening meals are served Wednesday-Saturday; no meals are available on Monday. A wheelchair ramp can be provided. Q

Rusthall

Beacon

Tea Garden Lane, TN3 9JH (400 yds off A264, opp. cricket pitch)
11-11; 12-10.30 Sun
(01892) 524252 the-beacon.co.uk
Harveys Sussex Best Bitter; Larkins Traditional; Taylor Landlord H
Perched on an outcrop of sandstone, this bar and restaurant affords beautiful views over its 17 acres of grounds and beyond. The bar boasts a magnificent ornate plastered ceiling, two large sofas in front of an open hearth and a collection of old wirelesses on the shelves above. Food is served in four rooms; the menu is based on local ingredients with seafood a speciality. The function room downstairs has a bar and is licensed for weddings. Fishing and camping are possible in the grounds. P

St Margaret's Bay

Coastguard

CT15 6DY (2 miles E of A258)
11-11; 12-10.30 Sun
(01304) 853176 thecoastguard.co.uk
Beer range varies H
Set below the famous white cliffs, the pub looks out over the Straits of Dover towards France. Formerly the Green Man, it suffered shelling in the war and was subsequently rebuilt and altered, and now comprises two bars, plus a spacious outside terrace for drinkers. Excellent fresh food includes an award-winning cheeseboard. The varying beer range usually offers three ales that concentrate on micro-breweries, frequently local. It also stocks a good range of continental bottled beers. P

St Peters

White Swan

17 Reading Street, CT10 3AZ
11-2.30, 6 (5 Thu & Fri)-11; 11-11 Sat; 12-3, 7-10.30 Sun
(01843) 863051
Beer range varies H
Built in 1913 on the foundations of an 18th-century smuggling inn, the White Swan boasts an ever-changing roster of real ales, notable for their scarcity in this part of Kent. A large Thomson and Wotton sign outside and a Fremlins' elephant in the saloon bar indicate the pub's previous brewery ties. A warm welcome awaits any visitor to this backwater on the Isle of Thanet and local CAMRA's Pub of the Year 2006. Q

Sandwich

Fleur de Lis

6-8 Delf Street, CT13 9BZ
10-11; 11-10.30 Sun
(01304) 611131 thefleur-sandwich.co.uk
Greene King IPA; Wadworth 6X; guest beer H
Friendly inn near the Guildhall at the centre of this ancient Cinque Port. The Fleur dates back to 1642 when it was the meeting place for Royalist volunteers fighting for Charles I. On offer is a changing range of guest beers from a variety of independent breweries, including Kent micros. The rambling interior is divided into a number of drinking and dining areas, serving exciting food and a selection of wines by the glass. Live music is performed on Friday.

Seal

Crown Inn

16 High Street, TN15 0AJ

11-11; 12-10.30 Sun

(01732) 761023

Greene King IPA; Harveys Sussex Best Bitter; Young's Bitter H

This Grade II listed public house offers a warm welcome and boasts a 16th-century inglenook. Light bar food is available lunchtimes from Tuesday to Friday, and a traditional roast is offered on Sunday. This community-focused pub, with pool, darts, and bat & trap, fields teams that play at local league level. The large garden is floodlit. Look out for planned mini-beer festivals. P

Sevenoaks

Anchor

32 London Road, TN13 1AS

11-3 (4 Fri), 6 (7.30 Sat)-midnight (12.30am Fri & Sat); 12-5, 7-11 Sun

(01732) 454898

Harveys Sussex Best Bitter; guest beer H

Friendly, town-centre pub, popular with all ages and local CAMRA Pub of the Year 2005. Good value food is served (not Sun) – Christmas lunches are recommended. An unusual feature is the curved entrance doors – the inner and outer doors form an almost completely circular lobby. Live blues music is performed monthly (first Wed). The landlord is the longest serving in the Sevenoaks area enjoying a good reputation for maintaining consistent high quality. Bus services are limited evenings and weekend.

Halfway House

London Road, TN13 2JD (5 mins' walk from station)

12-3, 5-11; 12-11 Sat & Sun

(01732) 457108

Greene King IPA; guest beer H

Two-bar community pub, run as a traditional local, with no pool table or juke box. Beer is mainly from the Greene King range with an occasional guest beer and seasonal offerings. The food is mostly home made and is acquiring a growing reputation; evening meals are served daily except Sunday. The pub is home to a variety of darts, quiz and soccer teams. An open quiz is held most Saturday evenings. P

Oak Tree

135 High Street, TN13 1XA

10-11.30 daily

(01732) 742615

Courage Best Bitter; Westerham British Bulldog, Sevenoaks Bitter H

Originally a farmhouse for the Farm on the Vine, once the largest hop grower in the area, the front elevation of the building has not changed much since the early part of the last century. The interior is partly wood panelled, the rest is in a more modern style of later construction. The pub is the only stockist of Westerham beers in the town centre. Used by all ages, it draws a predominantly young crowd at the weekends and evenings.

Sheerness

Red Lion

61 High Street, Blue Town, ME12 1RW

11-11; 12-10.30 Sun

(01795) 664354

Beer range varies H

Set in the historic Blue Town area of Sheerness, where the High Street still has cobblestones. Inside you will find maritime memorabilia, including old photographs of naval ships associated with the dockyard opposite. Three changing beers are sourced from regional and micro-breweries. No meals are served but a free buffet is provided all day Sunday. Unusually the cellar entrance is outside the pub. Even more unusual is the concrete gnome factory located behind the pub.

Sittingbourne

Long Hop

80 Key Street, ME10 1YU (on A2)

11.30-11; 12-10.30 Sun

(01795) 425957

Shepherd Neame Master Brew Bitter; guest beer H

Situated on the busy A2, west of the town centre, in the parish of Borden. Although traffic may speed past, once inside all is peaceful and you are barely aware of the main road a few feet away. Part of this rustic-looking local dates back 200 years. Originally the British Queen, the name changed after refurbishment some 20 years ago. The current name reflects its situation opposite a cricket ground. Half-hourly buses pass the pub (two-hourly Sun).

P

Snargate

Red Lion ☆

TN29 9UQ (on B2080, 1 mile W of Brenzett)

12-3, 7-11; 12-3, 7-10.30 Sun

(01797) 344648

Goacher's Mild, Light; guest beers H

Beautiful, unspoilt, award-winning pub on the remote Walland Marsh. It hosts several beer festivals annually – the main one takes place in June. The walls are decorated with WWII and Women's Land Army posters. This pub is a haven for good conversation in an environment redolent of a bygone age. Do not miss the chance of a game of toad in the hole. Dogs are welcome.

Q P

Stansted

Black Horse

Tumblefield Road, TN15 7PR (1 mile N of A20, jct 2)

OS606621

11-11; 12-10.30 Sun

(01732) 822355

Larkins Traditional; guest beers H

Large, Victorian building in a downland village, accessible from three motorways. The focus of local community life and an ideal stop for walkers and cyclists, the

emphasis here is on home-cooked food, real ales and ciders. The pub hosts a Kent week in July, when all produce is from the county. Recommended for families and accommodation, a family-run Thai restaurant is open Tuesday-Saturday evenings, while Sunday lunches represent especially good value.
⛫Q♨❀⇌◑◗♿⚠●P⚟🥃

Staplehurst

Lord Raglan

Chart Hill Road, TN12 0DE OS786472
⊙ 12-3, 6.30-11.30; closed Sun
☎ (01622) 843747
Goacher's Light; Harveys Sussex Best Bitter; guest beer 🄷
Hops decorate the bar of this Guide regular that is deservedly popular with locals and visitors alike. No music or other distractions interrupt the flow of conversation. Excellent snacks and full meals are always available and may be eaten in the bar or restaurant. Two log fires keep customers warm in winter, while in summer the garden catches the evening sun. Well-behaved children and dogs are welcome. The guest beer changes often and Double Vision cider is sold.
⛫Q❀◑◗●P

Stone Street

Padwell Arms

TN15 0LY (1½ miles S of A25 via Church Rd, then turn right)
⊙ 12-3, 6-11.30; 12-4, 7-11 Sun
☎ (01732) 761532
Badger First Gold; Harveys Sussex Best Bitter; Larkins Traditional; guest beer 🄷
Traditional village free house, offering a range of eight real ales. A blackboard is updated daily to display which beers are on handpump. An extensive selection of fine wines and good quality, home-cooked food is also available. Set in magnificent orchards and rolling countryside, this is a real haven for walkers and families alike. The patio garden is an ideal spot to sit and enjoy a pint, while admiring the view.
⛫Q❀◑◗♿♣P⚟

Temple Ewell

Fox

14 High Street, CT16 3DU
⊙ 11-3.30, 6-11; 12-4, 7-11 Sun
☎ (01304) 823598
Caledonian Deuchars IPA; guest beers 🄷
Just outside Dover, in scenic countryside close to Kearsney Abbey, the congenial atmosphere of this pub suits all tastes, and the dining area is unobtrusive (no meals Sun eve). Although water in the garden stream flows intermittently these days (if at all), a steady supply of quality beers always flows freely. Of the four beers usually stocked, three will be rotating guests from small breweries. Traditional games are played and the garden houses a skittle alley.
⛫❀◑◗♿⇌(Kearsney)♣P

Tenterden

White Lion Hotel

The High Street, TN30 6BD
⊙ 10-11 (midnight Fri & Sat); 10-10.30 Sun
☎ (01580) 765077
Adnams Broadside; Greene King IPA; guest beer 🄷
This former coaching inn dating from the 15th century is popular with all ages and boasts many original features. The drinking area in front of the hotel gets busy in summer. Country fare and international cuisine is served in both the bar and restaurant. The guest beer may be from the Westerham Brewery set up only in 2004. The hotel has 15 en-suite bedrooms, some with four-poster beds; it makes an ideal base for exploring the best of traditional Kent. ❀⇌◑◗⇌P

Trottiscliffe

Plough

Taylors Lane, ME19 5DR
⊙ 11.30-3, 6 (6.30 Sat)- 11; 12-3 (closed eve) Sun
☎ (01732) 822233
Adnams Bitter, Broadside; Harveys Sussex Best Bitter 🄷
Welcoming pub nestling in the foothills of the North Downs in the quaint village of Trottiscliffe, pronounced locally as Trosley. Weatherboarding and timbered ceilings are indications of the 1483 origins of this pub. It is home to a friendly ghost affectionately known as Alice. A narrow bar divides the pub: on one side a no-smoking restaurant serves home-cooked food, including renowned local sausages and mash (no food Mon eve); the comfortable saloon is deceptively spacious. Families and dogs are welcome. ⛫Q❀◑◗⚠♣

Tunbridge Wells

Crystal Palace

69 Camden Road, TN1 2QL
⊙ 11-11.30 (1am Fri & Sat); 11-11.30 Sun
☎ (01892) 548412
Harveys Sussex XX Mild, Best Bitter, seasonal beers 🄷
If you want to watch Sky Sports with a good pint of Harveys in your hand – maybe a seasonal brew – this is the place. Not far from the top shopping area, this well-run pub is popular with the locals. It benefits from a pretty garden with a play area for children. Live music is performed monthly (last Sat). An added attraction is the bar billiards table. ❀♣

Grove Tavern

19 Berkley Road, TN1 1YR
⊙ 12-11 daily
☎ (01892) 526549
Harveys Sussex Best Bitter; guest beers 🄷
This small pub is possibly the oldest building in Tunbridge Wells, just off Grove Park in the old village area. It enjoys a good reputation for serving a fine pint and offers a friendly atmosphere where people can chat or have a game of pool. It is a favourite watering-hole for some local CAMRA members. ⛫⇌♣

Rose & Crown

47 Grosvenor Road, TN1 2AY

10.30-11.30; 12-3.30, 7-10.30 Sun

(01892) 522427

Greene King IPA; Wadworth 6X; Young's Bitter; guest beers H

Friendly little Victorian pub frequented by locals and situated near the town centre. It offers a good choice of real ales from six handpumps. Food served at lunchtime is good home-made fare that is reasonably priced and consequently very popular. This is an old-fashioned pub in which to relax or if you wish, watch major televised sporting events.

Sankey's

39 Mount Ephraim, TN4 8AA

11-11 (midnight Fri & Sat); 12-11 Sun

(01892) 511423 sankeys.co.uk

Harveys Sussex Best Bitter; Larkins Traditional H

Recently refurbished, but still quirky pub, cluttered with memorabilia. Bare floorboards and an open hearth give it a homely air. Continental draught beers are sold from handpumps and there are plans to dispense the real ales from the barrel; the winter ales change frequently. Chiddingstone cider is stocked. The bar is at street level, while the basement houses a restaurant, serving good food with fish a speciality. Live music is performed on some Sundays.

Walmer

Berry

23 Canada Road, CT14 7EQ

11-2.30 (not Tue or Thu), 5.30-11 (midnight Fri); 11-midnight Sat, 11.30-11 Sun

(01304) 362411

Harveys Sussex Best Bitter; Woodforde's Wherry; guest beers H

The Berry is well worth the short detour inland from Walmer Green and the seafront. Formerly known as the Green Beret and traditionally a watering-hole for marines, prospects must have seemed bleak when the barracks across the road closed a decade ago. However, doom was averted and the pub survives as a thriving concern, providing a welcoming focus for the local community. An interesting beer range is sourced from regional breweries. (Deal)P

Warehorne

Woolpack

Church Road, TN26 2LL

11.30-3 (not Mon), 6-11; 12-4, 7-10.30 Sun

(01233) 733888

Harveys Sussex Best Bitter; guest beer H

Rural, 16th-century free house, opposite the village church. The bar features beams, hops and a large inglenook. There is also a lounge, warmed by a log-burning stove, and a no-smoking restaurant where home-cooked food includes weekly specials and a popular Wednesday carvery. The guest beer is often supplied by a Kent or Sussex brewer, while the house beer is produced by Goacher's. Outdoor tables are provided for summer drinking. P

Wateringbury

North Pole

434 Red Hill, ME18 5BJ (3/4 mile N of village) OS549696

11-11; 12-10.30 Sun

(01622) 812392

Badger K&B Sussex; Fuller's London Pride; Greene King Abbot; Wells Bombardier; guest beer H

Built in 1826 as a private venture, together with adjacent cottages and stabling, it was soon acquired by Jude Hanbury, then by Whitbread as can be seen from the etched bay windows. French doors lead from the bar via a staircase down to the large, enclosed garden. The no-smoking restaurant has subdued lighting and displays pictures for sale from a local artist. Earlybirds may get a special offer on meals when two dine together. Cider is sold in summer. QP

Westbere

Olde Yew Tree Inn

32 Westbere Lane, CT2 0HH

11.30-3, 6-11; 11.30-11 Fri; 11.30-midnight Sat; 12-4, 7-10.30 (12-10.30 summer) Sun

(01227) 710501 yeoldeyewtreeinn.co.uk

Beer range varies H

Beautiful, 14th-century, black & white half-timbered hall house that has been a pub since 1824. Many original features, including beams and an inglenook, have been retained, while the bar is in a modern extension that blends in well. The garden overlooks Westbere lakes, and the Stour Valley walk is close by. The guest beers are usually sourced from Kentish brewers. Good food is served; booking is recommended at the weekend (no eve meals winter Sun). QP

West Peckham

Swan on the Green

The Green, ME18 5JW

(1 mile W of B2016, Seven Mile Lane) OS644525

11-3 (4 Sat), 6-11; 12-5 (8 summer) Sun

(01622) 812271 swan-on-the-green.co.uk

Swan Whooper Pale, Trumpeter, seasonal beers H

At the end of a no-through road, the Swan enjoys an enviable position by the church and village green where cricket is played. Although licensed since 1658, the interior is modern with a timber floor and light, airy atmosphere. A mecca for diners and drinkers alike, it offers up to six beers (sometimes seasonal brews) produced behind the pub and good food (eve meals Tue-Sat). Walkers often stop here and can sit on the green in summer, undisturbed by traffic. QP

Whitstable

Four Horseshoes

62 Borstal Hill, CT5 4NA (on Canterbury road)

12 (11 Sat)-11; 12-10.30 Sun

(01227) 273876

Shepherd Neame Master Brew Bitter, Spitfire H

Friendly, traditional pub on the bus route

between Whitstable and Canterbury. The typically Kentish building, with its long, low weatherboarded front, dates from 1638 and was originally a blacksmith's forge. It comprises three small, interconnecting rooms that have a welcoming, old-fashioned feel. Bat & trap is played in the garden that offers 'bring your own' barbecue facilities. ⌂Q❀♣P

New Inn

30 Woodlawn Street, CT5 1HG
11-11; 12-4, 7.30-11 Sun
☎ (01227) 264746
Shepherd Neame Master Brew Bitter Ⓗ
Back-street corner pub, part of Whitstable's heritage. The long narrow bar was originally divided into tiny drinking areas, discernible from the etched glass windows. A small snug room can be used by families. Note the original matchboarded ceilings. Licensees of 10 years' standing maintain a strong community spirit; visitors can join in with pool or darts in the games area or participate in the robust debates that occur at the bar. The Chinese takeaway opposite will deliver to the pub. ⇌♣

Prince Albert

Sea Street, CT5 1AN (opp. Horsebridge Gallery)
11.30-11; 12-10.30 Sun
☎ (01227) 273400
Fuller's London Pride; Greene King IPA; guest beer Ⓗ
Just a few yards from the beach and popular restaurants, this small, friendly, one-bar pub stands opposite the new Horsebridge development. Note the original Thomson and Wotton windows and the line showing the level reached by the 1953 flood. The small, secluded garden is a real suntrap and a pleasant summer lunch venue. The excellent home-cooked food includes fisherman's and steak and oyster pies. ❀⇌

Ship Centurion

111 High Street, CT5 1AY
11-11; 12-7 Sun
☎ (01227) 264740
Beer range varies Ⓗ
The only pub in town always to serve mild, this busy, central free house is festooned with colourful hanging baskets in summer. Fascinating photographs of old Whitstable hang in the bar. It hosts live entertainment on Thursday evening. Home-cooked bar snacks often feature authentic German produce (the only food on Saturday is schnitzel). A public car park is in Middle Wall nearby. ⇌

Wilmington

Cressy Arms

1 Hawley Road, DA1 1NP (on A225, Dartford boundary)
12-11; 12-10.30 Sun
☎ (01322) 287772
Courage Best Bitter; guest beers Ⓗ
Small, unpretentious corner pub on the A225 just outside Dartford, but within reasonable walking distance of the town centre. It is served by several buses, including the No. 477 late in the evening. The landlord is a motor enthusiast and one side of the truncated V-shaped bar is bedecked with pictures of Ford vehicles, while three glass cabinets display model Ford cars of various vintages. Two rotating guest beers supplement the regular ale. ❀♣

Wittersham

Swan Inn

1 Swan Street, TN30 7PH (on B2028 between Rye and Tenterden)
11-midnight (2am Fri & Sat); 12-2am Sun
☎ (01797) 270913 swan-wittersham.co.uk
Goacher's Light; Harveys Sussex Best Bitter; Rother Valley Smild; guest beers Ⓗ
This dog-friendly, 17th-century drovers' inn has recently been sympathetically refurbished without destroying its two-bar character. The pub offers seven beers, including a mild – several on gravity dispense – and two draught ciders, usually Biddenden and Double Vision. Special events staged here include summer and winter beer festivals, live music and a conker championship. Good food is available, and a warm welcome is assured at all times at local CAMRA Pub of the Year 2006.
⌂Q❀(312)P

Wormshill

Blacksmiths Arms

The Street, ME9 0TU
7-11 (not Mon); 12-3 Sun
☎ (01622) 884386
Beer range varies Ⓗ
Situated on the long Street, this is a small, 17th-century pub in a village close to the Kentish North Downs. A brick-floored bar and an open log fire are pleasing features. A candlelit restaurant serves Sunday lunch and evening meals; the excellent home-cooked menu specialises in fish dishes. Frequently-changing beers from across the country are on offer. The cosy bar is popular with locals, and its rural location means that many walkers and cyclists drop in for a pint.
⌂❀P

Yalding

Walnut Tree

Yalding Hill, ME18 6JB
11.45-3, 6-11; 11.45-11 Fri & Sat; 12-10.30 Sun
☎ (01622) 814266
Adnams Bitter; Fuller's London Pride; Harveys Sussex Best Bitter; guest beer Ⓗ
Originally an oak beamed, Kentish Yeoman's house, circa 1492, red brick walls were added later, as was the extension that is now the restaurant. An inglenook dominates the small upper area. Step down to the lower bar in the extension that stands outside the original ground-floor end wall that was removed. Hops, brassware, cricketing pictures and memorabilia decorate the walls. The pub is noted for its good food made from fresh local produce wherever possible.
⌂❀(23, 26)P

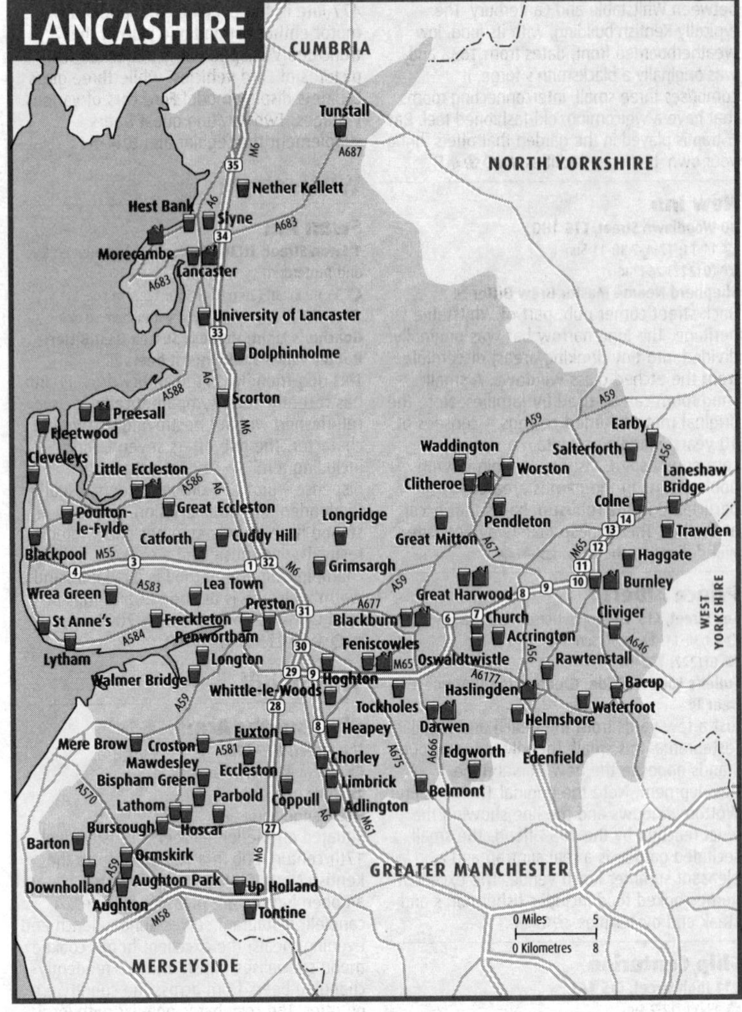

Accrington

Alma Inn

388 Manchester Road, BB5 2QG

✪ 2 (12 Sat)-11 (midnight Fri & Sat); 12-11 Sun

☎ (01254) 390424

Beer range varies Ⓗ

Small local selling two constantly-changing beers. The pub is open plan with a central bar flanked by seating areas on both sides. There is also a games room with a pool table. The pub is popular with the locals and can get busy. ❀♣

Peel Park Hotel

Turkey Street, BB5 6EW (200 yds from A679 next to the old football ground)

✪ 12-11.30 daily

☎ (01254) 235830

Tetley Bitter; guest beers Ⓗ

This pub goes from strength to strength. The restaurant/function room has now become the no-smoking room, as the place just gets busier. Strong community links mean that it fields a number of teams in the local leagues. A regular quiz takes place on Thursday evening and the pub football team plays on the old Accrington Stanley ground across the road. Lunches are served Wednesday-Sunday. ⌂❀◐♣P⊬

Adlington

Spinners Arms

23 Church Street, PR7 4EX (on A6)

✪ 12-11; 12-2, 5-11 Tue; 12-10.30 Sun

☎ (01257) 483331

Coniston Bluebird; Taylor Landlord; guest beers Ⓗ

Situated on the main road through Lower Adlington, the Spinners is a cosy local dating from 1838. It has a sizeable bar area with alcoves, plus a no-smoking dining section. At the front of the pub is an attractive outdoor drinking space. The bar's six handpumps offer a selection of micros' beers usually of Scottish or northern origin, including a dark mild. There is another Spinners in the top part of the village so be sure to get the right one! ⌂❀◐⇌⊟♠P⊬

Aughton

Derby Arms

Prescot Road, L39 6TA
(midway between Kirkby and Maghull)
❂ 11.30-11 (midnight Fri & Sat); 11.30-10.30 Sun
☎ (01695) 422237
Tetley Mild, Bitter; guest beers Ⓗ
The Derby Arms is not an easy pub to find but it is worth the effort – the beers on offer are often drawn from the smaller brewers and the atmosphere is always friendly and comfortable. In summer there is pleasant outside seating at the front, and in the winter a real fire warms the no-smoking room. A good staging post for walkers, the Derby Arms also serves good value, wholesome food. ♨❀◐▭♣P⊬

Bacup

Crown

19 Greave Road, OL13 9HQ (off Todmorden Road)
❂ 5-midnight; 12-1am Sat; 12-midnight Sun
☎ (01706) 873982
Pictish IPA; guest beer Ⓗ
Fascinating, traditional stone pub built in the style of the mid-Pennines. The welcoming, cosy atmosphere is just right for a quiet social evening – no children or dogs are admitted. You can play bar skittles and enjoy superb sandwiches. The bar offers up to two guest beers and soon you may be able to sample ales from the new Barearts Brewery, set up by a former landlord. ♨Q❀▭♿♣P⊬

Barton

Blue Bell

Southport Road, L39 7JU (on A5147)
❂ 11-midnight daily
☎ (01704) 841406 🌐 thebluebellhotel.co.uk
Beer range varies Ⓗ
In the heart of the countryside, the Blue Bell is a friendly pub, working hard to meet the needs of both locals and passing visitors. An ideal place to break a walk, it offers high quality, good value food as well as traditional pub games and live music some evenings. Its most distinctive feature, though, is the superb animal farm for children, with sheep, hens, rabbits and goats – even a Shetland pony! ♨♉❀◐▭▭♣P⊬

Belmont

Black Dog

4 Church Street, BL7 8AB (on A675 S of Blackburn)
❂ 12-11; 12-10.30 Sun
☎ (01204) 811218
Holt Mild, Bitter Ⓗ
Owned by Holt since 1952, but originally a farmhouse. It became a pub in 1825; part of the bar area has been used for the village court in the past. Holt's seasonal brews are sometimes to be found here. The bar menu is good value; no meals are served on Tuesday evening, but food can be enjoyed all day Saturday and Sunday. Mobile phones are banned – those caught using one pay a charity 'fine'. Outside drinking is possible in a small, cobbled area. ❀▭◐P⊬

Bispham Green

Eagle & Child

Malt Kiln Lane, L40 3SG (off B5246)
❂ 12-3, 5.30-11; 12-10.30 Sun
☎ (01257) 462297
Thwaites Original; guest beers Ⓗ
Outstanding, 16th-century local, boasting antique furniture and stone-flagged floors. Renowned for its food, a popular feature is the monthly themed menu evening (first Mon), when booking is advisable. An annual beer festival is held over the first May bank holiday in a marquee behind the pub. Tables around the bowling green offer wonderful views of the surrounding countryside, while the front of the pub overlooks the village green. ♨Q❀◐♿●P⊬

Blackburn

Station

391 Preston Old Road, Cherry Tree, BB2 5LW
(next to Cherry Tree Station)
❂ 3-12.30am; 12-1am Fri & Sat; 12-11.30 Sun
☎ (01254) 201643
Thwaites Mild, Original, seasonal beers Ⓗ
Much improved pub on the old road out to Preston. Named after the adjacent Cherry Tree Station, served by trains from Preston to Colne, it is also handy for travellers along the Leeds-Liverpool Canal. The pub lies in the heart of Cherry Tree 'village', once a small community but now swallowed up by Blackburn's suburban sprawl, from which it draws most of its custom. Its open-plan design features much light wood around a central bar area. A small side patio allows for outside drinking. ❀⇌(Cherry Tree)♣P

Blackpool

Churchills

83-85 Topping Street, FY1 3AF (100 yds from Church St, near Winter Gardens)
❂ 10-midnight (1am Fri & Sat); 11-midnight Sun
☎ (01253) 622036
Bateman XXXB; Greene King Ruddles County, Old Speckled Hen; Wells Bombardier Ⓗ
Conversation flows freely in this bustling, town-centre pub, where Guinness memorabilia and wartime posters add to the warm, relaxed lunchtime atmosphere. However, things liven up greatly in the evening with regular 'psychic' nights, quizzes, 'boozy' bingo, karaoke and guest artists all through the weekend. If you

INDEPENDENT BREWERIES

Bowland Clitheroe
Bryson's Morecombe
Fuzzy Duck Preesall
Hart Little Eccleston
Hopstar Darwen
Lancaster Lancaster
Moonstone Burnley
Moorhouses Burnley
Porter Haslingden
Red Rose Great Harwood
Three B's Feniscowles
Thwaites Blackburn

enjoy a sing-song, this is the place to come. Darts and dominoes teams play here, too. An extensive, good value menu is served 11-6pm. ◐≠(North)♣

Dunes

561 Lytham Road, FY4 1RD (500 yds from airport)
✪ 11-11 (midnight Thu-Sat); 12-11 Sun
☎ (01253) 403854
Boddingtons Bitter; Greene King IPA; Theakston Best Bitter; Wells Bombardier; guest beers Ⓗ
True local community pub with a public bar, the Dunes offers up to four guest ales, usually sourced from micro-breweries, and often a beer from the local Hart Brewery. It holds a quiz on Thursday and Sunday evenings. Meals finish at 7.30pm. A heated, flower-decked patio allows for outside drinking in front of the pub. It stands on the No. 11 and No. 68 bus routes. Cribbage is played here. The pub is well worth a visit. ❀◐ ♿≠(Squires Gate)♣P

Highlands

206 Queens Promenade, Bispham, FY2 9JS
(near Bispham tram stop, Red Bank Rd)
✪ 12 (4 Thu)-midnight; 12-midnight Sun
☎ (01253) 354877
Thwaites Original, Lancaster Bomber Ⓗ
Originally two houses, this popular seafront pub appeals to locals and visitors alike. The main bar area has modern decor; families are welcome in the dining area. The pub offers 'two for one' on the excellent choice of main courses and was awarded the Thwaites' Snack Pub of the Year title in 2005. The games room houses a pool table and it fields various games teams. Perfectly placed for trams to Blackpool and Fleetwood, tables in front of the pub afford sea views. ❀◐♿⊖♣P⚡

New Road Inn

244 Talbot Road, FY1 3HL (near North Station)
✪ 10.30-11 (midnight Fri & Sat); 11-10.30 Sun
☎ (01253) 628872
Jennings Dark Mild, Cumberland Ale, Sneck Lifter; guest beers Ⓗ
Talbot Road was the new road in to town from the Layton Hall estate in the early 1840s, with the first railway to Blackpool following nearby in 1846. This pub is a classic 1930s local with impressive, original Art Deco features as well as consistently good beer. The single central bar serves the main lounge, a games room and a comfortable no-smoking room at this local CAMRA award winner. The forecourt has facilities for outdoor drinkers. ❀≠(North)♣⚡

Pump & Truncheon

Bonny Street, FY1 5AR (opp. police station)
✪ 11 (9am Sat)-11 (midnight Fri & Sat); 9am-midnight Sun
☎ (01253) 751176 🌐 pump&truncheon.co.uk
Boddingtons Bitter; guest beers Ⓗ
Convivial, town-centre pub offering a changing range of often seasonal, nationally and locally sourced beers on eight handpumps. It hosts its own beer festivals. Awards include the local CAMRA Pub of the Season winter 2006 and Blackpool Tourism Pub of the Year 2005. There is entertainment at weekends with a late licence, and various pub games. Good home-cooked food is available. In the oldest part of Blackpool, the original pub dates back to the 1870s. ◐⊖(Central Pier)♣

Saddle Inn

286 Whitegate Drive, FY3 9PH (at A583 jct)
✪ 12-11 (midnight Thu-Sat); 12-11 Sun
☎ (01253) 607921
Draught Bass; Thwaites Original; guest beers Ⓗ
Blackpool's oldest pub, established in 1770, it comprises a main bar and two side rooms. The first is a cosy, wood-panelled room, displaying pictures of sporting heroes. The second is used as a no-smoking dining area and features pictures of the brewing art. The pub generally offers a choice of four guest beers. The menu includes daily specials (served Mon-Fri, 12-2pm and 5-7pm; Sat and Sun 12-3pm). A large patio provides ample space for outside drinking. Bus Nos. 2, 4 and 61 serve the pub. Q❀◐♿P⚡

Shovels

260 Commonedge Road, FY4 5DH
(on B5261, ½ mile from A5230 jct)
✪ 11.30-11 (midnight Thu-Sat); 12-11 Sun
☎ (01253) 762702
Beer range varies Ⓗ
This large, award-winning pub has twice been local CAMRA's Pub of the Year. It offers six changing beers, usually from micros and brew-pubs. The pub holds a week-long beer festival every year in October. It is home to a number of sports teams and Thursday is quiz night. An extensive menu (served 12-9.30pm) offers fresh daily specials. ❀◐♿(14)♣P⚡

Burnley

Bridge Bier Huis

2 Bank Parade, BB11 1UH (behind shopping centre)
✪ 12-midnight (2am Fri & Sat); closed Mon & Tue; 12-midnight Sun
☎ (01282) 411304 🌐 thebridgebierhuis.co.uk
Hydes Original Bitter; guest beers Ⓗ
This smart bar caters for beer connoisseurs: the five guest handpumps mainly offer micro-breweries' products. It also stocks five draught foreign beers, plus 40 bottled beers from around the world. No juke box or slot machines disturb the conversation, although live music is sometimes performed, with an 'open mike' session monthly (last Sun). Occasional beer festivals are held. Bands play throughout Easter as part of the Burnley Blues Festival. The pub opens Tuesday if Burnley FC are at home. Q◐≠(Central)♣

Coal Clough

41 Coal Clough Lane, BB11 4PG
✪ 12-midnight daily
☎ (01282) 423226 🌐 coalcloughpub.co.uk
Cains Bitter; Worthington's Bitter; guest beers Ⓗ
True end-of-terrace, community local that is always busy. Don, dominoes and darts are played in the games room, while the main room stages entertainment on Tuesday and Thursday evenings, plus Sunday teatime. The Masseys' Bitter is brewed to an old recipe from the sadly defunct Burnley Brewery, while the two guest beers are from micro-breweries more often than not. Beer

festivals are occasionally held.
≠(Barracks)♣

Ministry of Ale
9 Trafalgar Street, BB11 1TQ
✪ 5 (12.30 Wed & Thu; 12 Fri & Sat)-midnight; 12-midnight Sun
☎ (01282) 830909 🌐 ministryofale.co.uk
Moonstone Black Star; guest beers Ⓗ
A warm, friendly welcome is guaranteed at this small brew-pub, five minutes' walk from the station. Good beer (the brewery can be seen in the front room) and conversation are the order of the day here. Another Moonstone beer and two guests supplement the Black Star. Two foreign draught beers have been added to the range, plus a selection of bottled foreign beers. Regular art exhibitions are an unusual feature here. Q≠(Manchester Rd)♣

Burscough

Slipway
48 Crabtree Lane, L40 0RN (off A59)
✪ 12-11.30; 12-10.30 Sun
☎ (01704) 897767
Thwaites Original, Lancaster Bomber Ⓗ
The Slipway is an attractive, canalside pub that actually has a slipway for trailer boats. In the summer it is possible to sit beside the canal in an extensive garden with children's play facilities and watch the boats passing through the swing bridge. Inside, the bar's decorations continue the boating theme.
Q❀◐▶♿≠(New Lane)♣P

Catforth

Running Pump
Catforth Road, PR4 0HH (½ mile from B5269 jct)
✪ 11-midnight; 12-midnight Sun
☎ (01772) 690265 🌐 therunningpump.co.uk
Robinson's Unicorn Ⓗ
This three-roomed village pub is named after the spring-fed water pump built into the front wall. Chatty, friendly locals make visitors feel immediately welcome. A small front tap room, favoured by local drinkers, and a comfortable rear lounge with blazing log fires in winter, are served from a central bar area. Diners can enjoy expertly-cooked, hearty English bar meals in the lounge, or dine in the à la carte restaurant (no food Mon; Sun meals 12-9pm). ♨◐▶P

Chorley

Malt 'n' Hops
50-52 Friday Street, PR6 0AH (behind station)
✪ 12-11; 12-10.30 Sun
☎ (01257) 260967
Beartown Kodiak Gold; guest beers Ⓗ
The pub was converted from a corner shop in 1988. The Victorian-style decor gives the single room a period atmosphere, emphasising its purpose as a place for people who like to drink in convivial surroundings. Quiz night is Wednesday. The eight handpumps usually serve four Beartown beers and four guests. Bar snacks are served all day. At Chorley station, take the platform two exit. Ample car parking is available in front of the pub. ❀≠🚌

Potter's Arms
42 Brooke Street, PR7 3BY (next to Morrisons)
✪ 11-11.30 (midnight Fri & Sat); 12-11 Sun
☎ (01257) 267954
Moorhouses Premier; Tetley Bitter; Three B's Doff Cocker Ⓗ
Small, friendly free house named after the owners, Mr and Mrs Potter, situated at the bottom of Brooke Street, alongside the railway bridge. The central bar serves two games areas, while the two comfortable lounges are popular with locals and visitors alike. The pub displays a fine selection of photographs from the world of music, as well as local scenes. Regular darts and dominoes nights are well attended. ≠🚌♣P

Prince of Wales
9-11 Cowling Brow, PR6 0QE (off B6228)
✪ 11-11; 12-10.30 Sun
☎ (01257) 413239
Jennings Bitter, Cumberland Ale, seasonal beers; guest beers Ⓗ
This stone terraced pub stands in the south-eastern part of town, not far from the Leeds–Liverpool Canal. Its unspoilt interior incorporates a traditional tap room, a games area, a large lounge and a comfortable snug, complete with real fire. There is photographic evidence of the licensee's love of jazz, plus collections of brewery artefacts and saucy seaside postcards. It stocks a fine selection of malt whiskies and serves sandwiches on request. ♨❀⊟🚌♣⚟▯

Church

Stag Inn
1 Bank Street, BB5 4HH
✪ 12-11 (midnight Fri & Sat); 12-10.30 Sun
☎ (01254) 399906
Holt Bitter; guest beers Ⓗ
Typical, street-corner local, comprising a comfortable lounge and a busy tap room. The regulars enjoy games such as dominoes and darts, which are played competitively against other local pub teams. The area has a number of homes for the elderly and the pub organises many events especially for them. This is a perfect example of a successful community pub. ⊟≠♣

Cleveleys

Victoria Hotel
183 Victoria Road West, FY5 3PZ
✪ 11-11; 12-10.30 Sun
☎ (01253) 853306
Samuel Smith OBB Ⓗ
Locals' pub housed in an impressive corner building, comprising a large main bar and smaller back room. The main bar is open plan with Tudor-styled decor of panelling, tapestries and beautiful stained glass windows. There is plenty of space for diners away from the main bar area and the food is reasonably priced. Cleveleys town centre is five minutes' walk away, where the tram and bus stops are located; the no. 11 bus stops nearby. ♨Q❀◐▶⊟♿🚌P⚟▯

Clitheroe

New Inn

Parson Lane, BB7 2JT (from interchange, head S towards castle)
⏲ 11-11; 11-10.30 Sun
☎ (01200) 443653
Coach House Gunpowder Mild; Copper Dragon Golden Pippin; Moorhouses Premier; Taylor Landlord; guest beers 🄷
Nestling below the castle ruins, this busy ale house retains many original features. A central bar connects four rooms, two of which are warmed by real fires. Six guest bedrooms of a high specification have recently been opened in the adjacent stone building, thus leaving the pub's character unchanged. The market and car parking are nearby. Folk music is performed at weekends, especially on a Friday evening. A meeting place for many local societies, this pub is dog-friendly. ⩕Q❀⛟≹♣

Cliviger

Queen Hotel

412 Burnley Road, BB10 4SU (on A646, 4 miles from Burnley)
⏲ 1-11 daily
☎ (01282) 436712
John Smith's Bitter; guest beers 🄷
Small, friendly, roadside local with two rooms, both warmed by coal fires in winter. Good conversation and beer are the norm here, free from music and machines. Situated amid the spectacular scenery of the Cliviger Gorge, the pub displays a good collection of old photographs of its people and the countryside. Walkers are welcome to bring food to eat here. Three guest beers are usually sourced from micro-breweries. ⩕Q⊟♿♣P

Colne

Admiral Lord Rodney

Mill Green, Waterside Road, BB8 0TA
⏲ 12-midnight; 12-10.30 Sun
☎ (01282) 866565
Archers Best Bitter, IPA; Goose Eye Barm Pot; guest beers 🄷
An oasis for real ale lovers in Colne, this popular, friendly local has been on this site since the 1790s; see the display of the history of the local area. Robert Neil featured the pub in his novel Song of Sunrise. It has recently been purchased by Archers of Swindon as its first house. Home-made meals, with fish dishes a speciality, are served until 8.30pm Tuesday-Sunday. The car park is across the road. ⩕❀◐≹♣

Coppull

Red Herring

Mill Lane, PR7 5AN (off B5251)
⏲ 12-11 (11.30 Fri & Sat); 12-11 Sun
☎ (01257) 470130
Beer range varies 🄷
In a village dominated by keg outlets, this real ale oasis, formerly the offices of the imposing mill next door, was converted to a pub some years ago. The bar serves a large single room and extension. TV sports fans are well catered for, as are anglers, who use the millpond opposite. It hosts regular music nights and free barbecues. Handy for trainspotters, it stands by the West Coast main line. Food serving times may vary. Beers are usually from micro-breweries. ❀◐♿⊟♣P

Croston

Grapes

67 Town Road, PR26 9RA
⏲ 12-11 (midnight Fri & Sat); 12-11 Sun
☎ (01772) 600225
Greene King IPA; guest beers 🄷
Old whitewashed pub, situated close to the cross from which the village takes its name. The Grapes has been an inn since at least 1799; the building has also been used as a custom house and a magistrates' court in the past. A small bar serves a compact lounge, but there are two rooms at the front, plus a restaurant at the back. Five guest beers are usually stocked. ⩕♨❀◐◑♿≹⊟P⚟

Cuddy Hill

Plough at Eaves

Eaves Lane, PR4 0BJ (1 mile off B5269)
⏲ 12-3, 5.30-11; 12-midnight Sat; closed Mon (except Apr-Sep 7-11); 12-10.30 Sun
☎ (01772) 690233 🌐 ploughateaves.com
Thwaites Original, Lancaster Bomber 🄷
Not the easiest of pubs to find but a real gem with a history going back to 1645, located on an old drovers' road. Cromwell fought a major battle nearby. Inside this low, white-painted building with a two-storey neighbour, is a collection of ornamental plates and horse brasses, along with a roaring fire in winter. The low black beams have now been raised slightly after the main beams started to give about two years ago. The menu offers a variety of reasonably-priced food. ⩕Q♨❀◐◑⊟♿♣P⚟

Darwen

Black Horse

72 Redearth Road, BB3 2AF (near Sainsbury's)
⏲ 12-midnight daily
☎ (01254) 873040
Hopstar Dizz Danny, Spinning Jenny's Smokey Joes; Three B's Stoker's Slake; guest beers 🄷
Lively community local that stocks quality ales and cider. Its annual rare beer festivals showcase over 30 ales. Held in January, late May bank holiday and November, they draw visitors from far and wide. Monthly mini festivals also take place. Darwen's own brewery, Hopstar, provides the beers that take pride of place on the bar. Meal deals are offered during the afternoon. Picnic tables cover the large, enclosed, flagged yard. ❀◐♿≹♣●

Pub

210 Duckworth Street, BB3 1PX (100 yds N of town centre on A666)
⏲ 12-11; 12-10.30 Sun
☎ (01254) 708404
Beer range varies 🄷
Succinctly-named, friendly, corner local near

the town centre. Open plan, retaining the Matthew Brown Brewery's original red lion tiles in the main entrance, the corner door leads to a narrow tap room area down one side, with a large-screen TV in one corner. A juke box, games machines, pool and football tables will keep you entertained. The central circular bar is adorned with pump clips of previous guest beers. A summer drinking area is provided behind the pub. ❀≑(Darwen)♣

Dolphinholme

Fleece

Bay Horse, LA2 9AQ (½ mile W of village)

⚙ 12-11; 12-10.30 Sun

☎ (01524) 791233

Beer range varies Ⓗ

At first sight, this former farmhouse is in the middle of nowhere, but as the nearby village and the country beyond have no pubs, it is the local for quite a large community. The old-fashioned hall features an oak settle; the main bar, oak-beamed and with pews and (usually) a roaring fire is to the right, the dining room to the left. The beer range grows from two guests in winter to six in summer; Moorhouses and Bryson's often feature. ❀◐P

Downholland

Scarisbrick Arms

2 Black-a-Moor Lane, L39 7HX (at A5147 jct)

⚙ 12-2.30, 5-11; 12-11 Sat & Sun

☎ (0151) 526 1120

Beer range varies Ⓗ

The Scarisbrick Arms is, given its isolated position, surprisingly adventurous in its beer selections, which usually include a product from the local Southport Brewery range. Positioned alongside a canal, it is an excellent place to stop on a walk, with a large garden and children's play area. The pub itself is spacious and offers good food at reasonable prices. There is folk music on Wednesday evenings. Q❀◐P⁄

Earby

Red Lion

70 Red Lion Street, BB18 6RD

(follow signs to youth hostel from A56)

⚙ 12-3, 5-11; 12-11 Sat & Sun

☎ (01282) 843395

Copper Dragon Black Gold, Best Bitter; Tetley Bitter; Theakston Best Bitter; guest beers Ⓗ

Friendly, two-roomed village local next to the youth hostel and popular with walkers. It offers an extensive menu, with food served in the lounge bar every day; the home-made pies are a speciality. It was voted Pub of the Year by local CAMRA in 2004. Seats in front of the pub allow for summer drinking in the fresh air. Q❀◐♣P⁄

Eccleston

Original Farmers Arms

Towngate, PR7 5QS (on B5250)

⚙ 11.30-midnight (12.30am Fri & Sat); 11.30-11.30 Sun

☎ (01257) 451594

Boddingtons Bitter; Phoenix Arizona; Taylor Landlord; Tetley Bitter; guest beers Ⓗ

This white-painted village pub has expanded over the years into some cottages next door, allowing for a substantial dining area. However, the original part of the pub is still used mainly for drinking. The two or three guest ales are changed frequently. Meals are served throughout the day, seven days a week, and there are four guest rooms. Bus Nos. 113 (Preston-Wigan), 347 (Chorley-Southport) and C7 from Chorley serve the pub. ❀◐P

Edenfield

Coach Horses

163 Market Street, BL0 0HJ

(off A56 on B6527 towards Rawtenstall)

⚙ 12-11 (midnight Fri & Sat); 12-11 Sun

☎ (01706) 822252

Moorhouses Black Cat, Pride of Pendle, Blond Witch; Phoenix Pale Moonlight; George Wright Kings Shillin' Ⓗ

Pleasant family pub, where a spacious dining area offers a traditional English menu, including local black pudding. The comfortable bar stocks four real ales on handpull, as well as a selection of continental lagers and a range of coffees and wines. ◐♿P⁄

Edgworth

Black Bull

167 Bolton Road, BL7 0AF

⚙ 11.30-midnight; 12-midnight Sun

☎ (01254) 852811

Lees Bitter; Tetley Bitter; guest beers Ⓗ

Traditional country pub, two cottages joined together. Until 1995 only the front rooms were licensed (but not for spirits) and no women were admitted – they had to use the back 'nanny pen' kitchen, now the lounge. In these more enlightened times the bar unites both areas, with handpumps at each end. The guest beers change regularly. The award-winning bistro restaurant provides excellent food. Ornate decorations at the front complete the picture. ❀◐♣P

Euxton

Euxton Mills

Wigan Road, PR7 6JD (at A581 jct)

⚙ 12-3.30, 5-11.30; 11.30-11.30 Fri & Sat; 12-11 Sun

☎ (01257) 264002

Burtonwood Bitter; guest beers Ⓗ

Village pub, the recipient of several Best Kept Pub awards; it is particularly attractive in the summer months, with numerous hanging baskets full of flowers outside. Low ceilings and doors help create a cosy atmosphere inside. Two or three guest beers are always available, and three times a year the pub holds a beer festival. It has long enjoyed a widespread reputation for good food. ❀◐≑(Balshaw Lane)P

Talbot

10 Balshaw Lane, PR7 6HX

⚙ 12-11 (midnight Fri & Sat); 12-11 Sun

☎ (01257) 411531

Theakston Mild, Best Bitter; guest beers Ⓗ
Large, modern pub that is comfortably furnished throughout. The lounge is on two levels, with a raised section providing a refuge from the busier area near the bar. The public bar is accessed through an archway. Making its first ever appearance in this Guide, the pub has steadily built up a good reputation, and usually offers two guest beers. No food is served on Tuesday, or Monday and Saturday evenings.
◑ ⊞ ≠ (Balshaw Lane) ▣ ♣ P ⊬

Feniscowles

Feildens Arms

673 Preston Old Road, BB2 5ER (at A674/A6062 jct)
✪ 12-12.30am (1.30am Fri & Sat); 12-12.30am Sun
☎ (01254) 200988
Black Sheep Best Bitter; Flowers IPA; Three B's Tackler's Tipple; guest beers Ⓗ
Welcoming stone pub at a busy road junction, easily reached from the M65. Run by former regulars, the landlord always has a guest mild on handpump and favours bitters from the likes of Moorhouses, Phoenix and Marston Moor. It hosts occasional live entertainment and live football is shown regularly.
⩩ ❀ ≠ (Pleasington) ▣ (123, 124, 152) ♣ P

Fleetwood

Steamer

1-2 Queens Terrace, FY7 6BT (next to market)
✪ 10-midnight (1am Fri & Sat); 10-midnight Sun
☎ (01253) 771756 🌐 sugarvine.com
Wells Bombardier; guest beers Ⓗ
The Steamer was built opposite the ferry terminal in 1842 and named after the London-Scotland ferry that docked here. The spacious, open-plan single bar features wood panelling. There are photos of early 20th-century Fleetwood life, while ships enhance the nautical theme. It was voted local CAMRA Winter Pub of the Season 2005. Good value meals are available (eve meals Thu-Sat); children are welcome in the no-smoking room until 7pm. Snooker and pool can be played here. ♉ ◑ ♿ ♣ ⊬

Thomas Drummond

London Street, FY7 6JY (between Lord St and Dock St)
✪ 9am-midnight (1am Fri & Sat); 9am-midnight Sun
☎ (01253) 775020
Marston's Burton Bitter; Shepherd Neame Spitfire; Theakston Best Bitter; guest beers Ⓗ
This pub's open-plan design includes both family and child-free no-smoking areas. An interesting pictorial history of Fleetwood lines the walls. Food is served 9am-11pm daily (children's last orders at 5pm). The steak club is on Tuesday, China club Wednesday and curry night Thursday. Bottled foreign beers and cider are stocked. Other facilities include a cash machine, an outdoor area and a range of coffees. In 2005 this pub received local CAMRA's Silver award.
♉ ❀ ◑ ♿ ⊖ (Preston St) ⊬

Wyre Lounge Bar

Marine Hall, The Esplanade, FY7 6HF
(250 yds from pier)
✪ 12-3.30 (4 Fri, Sat & summer), 7-11; 12-4, 7-10.30 Sun
☎ (01253) 771141 🌐 marinehall.co.uk
Courage Directors; Moorhouses Pendle Witches Brew; Phoenix Navvy; guest beers Ⓗ
Located within the Marine Hall complex on the lower Promenade, this has twice won local CAMRA's Pub of the Year award. The outside drinking area affords great views over Morecambe Bay and the Lakeland fells, and is popular in summer due to its proximity to the beach. The beers are sourced from breweries both local and further afield. In the nearby gardens crown green bowls, crazy golf and pitch and putt can be played. ❀ ♿ ⊖ (Ferry Terminal) P

Freckleton

Coach & Horses

6 Preston Old Road, PR4 1PD
(behind war memorial, off A584)
✪ 11-midnight (1am Fri & Sat); 11-midnight Sun
☎ (01772) 632284
Boddingtons Bitter; guest beers Ⓗ
At the centre of a large village, the pub's main lounge boasts a welcoming fire in winter, and a corner glass cabinet showing off sporting and local brass band trophies. A side room has a TV but no juke box or pool table. The pub hosts a golfing society. Lunches are served weekdays, sandwiches are available Saturday. Bus nos. 61 and 70 from Preston, Blackpool and Kirkham stop nearby. ⩩ Q ❀ ◐ ♿ ▣ P

Great Eccleston

White Bull

The Square, PR3 0ZB (opp. bus stop in village centre)
✪ 11 (4.30 Tue)-11; 12-10.30 Sun
☎ (01995) 670203
Black Sheep Best Bitter; Caledonian Deuchars IPA; Tetley Bitter; guest beers Ⓗ
Comfortable, 18th-century former coaching inn, with cream walls and dark wood. The family that took over in August 2005 brought many years of experience in the catering and licensed trade with them; indeed it was voted runner-up in the local CAMRA Pub of the Year awards in 2005. Wholesome, freshly-cooked dishes, based on local produce, are served daily (except Tue) with traditional roasts added to the menu on Sunday. Daily newspapers are provided. ⩩ Q ♉ ❀ ◑ ♿ Ⓐ P

Great Harwood

Royal Hotel

Station Road, BB6 7BE (Accrington road)
✪ 12-11 (midnight Fri & Sat); 12-10.30 Sun
☎ (01254) 883541 🌐 rockandroyal.co.uk
Beer range varies Ⓗ
The tap for the nearby Red Rose Brewery, it offers eight beers, including a number of guests from near and far, and always at least two dark beers, plus a good range of bottled beers. A beer festival is held over May day bank holiday. Music lovers enjoy regular free entertainment in the concert room (see website). Well served by public transport from Blackburn, Accrington and

Manchester, the Royal is a handy stop for visitors to Ribble Valley and Pendle Witch country. ❀⇄Ⓐ♣▯

Victoria ☆

St John's Street, BB6 7EP (behind St John's Church)

4.30 (3 Fri; 12 Sat)-11; 12-10.30 Sun

☎ (01254) 885210

Beer range varies Ⓗ

Built in 1905 by Alfred Nuttall, the Victoria or 'Butcher Brig' boasts a wealth of original features. There is floor to ceiling glazed tiling in the lobby and dark wood throughout the five rooms, including the no-smoking snug. On the horseshoe bar the regular Bowland Gold is accompanied by seven other beers, sourced mainly from small breweries across the north of England and Scotland; Copper Dragon, Phoenix and Durham often feature. The pub sits on a cycleway. Q❀Ⓐ♣⚟

Great Mitton

Aspinall Arms

Mitton Road, BB7 9PQ

(on B6246, between Clitheroe and Whalley)

12-3, 6-11.30; 12-11 Sat; 12-10.30 Sun

☎ (01254) 826223 aspinallarms.co.uk

Beer range varies Ⓗ

Parts of the building date back to the 17th century, and it was originally called the Boat, after the ferry across the nearby River Ribble. Beers on the four handpumps change regularly; breweries featuring recently have included Copper Dragon, Moorhouses, Phoenix, Salamander and Wychwood. Food is excellent value – check the specials board first. Tables are provided in the large garden, overlooking the Ribble. Occasional music evenings are staged, and quizzes on alternate Tuesday evenings. ⩩❀⇄ⒹP

Grimsargh

Plough

187 Preston Road, PR2 5JR (on B5269)

11-11; 12-10.30 Sun

☎ (01772) 652235 theplough-grimsargh.co.uk

Moorhouses Pride of Pendle; Taylor Landlord; guest beers Ⓗ

Dating from 1785, this award-winning country pub, a focal point of village life, retains many original features, including oak beams, open fires and antique furniture. Free of tie, usually the five cask beers on offer are from regional and micro-breweries. Excellent home-cooked food is served, using local ingredients whenever possible. Smoking is only permitted in the vault. A bowling green, outdoor drinking area, regular quizzes, theme nights and social events are added attractions. ⩩❀ⒹⒹ♿♣P⚟

Haggate

Sun Inn

1 Burnley Road, BB10 2JJ (2 miles from Burnley centre, past hospital)

1-midnight; 12-1am Fri & Sat; 12-midnight Sun

☎ (01282) 428785

Moorhouses Premier Ⓗ

Friendly village pub on the north-eastern edge of Burnley, next to moorland and farmland. Two local football teams use this pub, which also fields a pool team. It hosts a regular quiz, plus live entertainment on alternate Saturdays. This old building, with oak beams and a relaxing atmosphere, is a tenanted pub owned by Punch Taverns, serving local beer; besides the Premier, two other Moorhouses' brews alternate. A seated area behind the pub allows for outdoor drinking. ⩩❀♿Ⓐ♣P⚟

Heapey

Top Lock

Copthurst Lane, PR6 8LS

(alongside canal at Johnson's Hillock)

11-11; 12-10.30 Sun

☎ (01257) 263376

Black Sheep Best Bitter; Coniston Bluebird; Taylor Best Bitter; guest beers Ⓗ

In October an annual beer festival is held at the picturesque Top Lock, which sits beside the Leeds-Liverpool canal at the series of locks called Johnson's Hillock. This fine country pub combines a single bar downstairs with an upstairs dining room. A regular meeting place for walkers, narrowboat owners and diners, the eight handpumps dispense at least five guest beers, including a dark mild and a cask stout, mostly sourced from micro-breweries. The cider varies. Thursday is music night. ❀Ⓓ♿♣P

Helmshore

Robin Hood

288 Holcombe Road, BB4 4NP

(600 yds from A6177/B6214 jct)

4 (2 Sat)-11 (midnight Fri & Sat); 2-10.30 Sun

☎ (01706) 213180 robinhoodinn-helmshore.co.uk

Tetley Bitter; guest beers Ⓗ

Featured in past Guides, the pub is now run by the ex-barmaid. An extra guest is now served, often from Moorhouses. This locals' pub is small: even the bar is sideways on with the beer engines mounted against a wall. Although it has been opened out, distinct areas have been retained, as well as two open fires. Nearby are the Helmshore Textile Museum and Musbury Fabrics factory outlet. The Helmshore circular bus runs past the front door linking the pub with both Haslingden and Rawtenstall. ⩩❀♣

Hest Bank

Hest Bank

2 Hest Bank Lane, LA2 6DN

11.30-11; 11.30-10.30 Sun

☎ (01524) 824339

Black Sheep Best Bitter; Caledonian Deuchars IPA; Taylor Landlord; guest beer Ⓗ

Read inside the history of this pub, as the last stop for travellers beginning the perilous crossing of the sands. Transport developments and suburban sprawl have cut it off from the sea, but left it with a pleasant canalside garden. To the left, the locals' bar is in the older part of the pub with the oldest room behind; to the right, linked rooms on different levels are used mainly by diners. It is served by bus No. 5. ⩩Q❀ⒹⒶ♣P⚟

Hoghton

Royal Oak

Blackburn Old Road, Riley Green, PR5 0SL
(at A675/A674 jct)
✪ 11.30-3, 5.30-11; 11.30-11 Sat; 12-10.30 Sun
☎ (01254) 201445
Thwaites Mild, Original, Lancaster Bomber, seasonal beers Ⓗ
Stone pub on the old road between Preston and Blackburn, near the Riley Green Basin on the Leeds–Liverpool Canal. The Royal Oak is popular with diners and drinkers alike. Rooms (including a dining room) and alcoves radiate from the central bar. Low, beamed ceilings and horse brasses give the pub a rustic feel. This Thwaites' tied house is a regular outlet for its seasonal beers. Nearby Hoghton Tower, which is steeped in history, can be visited. ♨Q✿◐◑🚌P⚡

Sirloin

Station Road, PR5 0DD (off A675, near level crossing) OS360426
✪ 12 (4 Mon)-midnight (1.30am Sat); 12-midnight Sun
☎ (01254) 852293 🌐 thyme-restaurant.co.uk
Beer range varies Ⓗ
The atmosphere in this small, 250-year-old, family-run country coaching inn is friendly; even the ghosts are benign. It is near Hoghton Towers, where King James I knighted a loin of beef. His coat of arms hangs over a fireplace and sirloin steak is a speciality in the pub and adjoining restaurant (meals served 12-midnight Tue-Fri; 12-6pm Sat and Sun). Three handpumps dispense beers that are often from Lancashire micro-breweries; a dark beer, either mild or porter, is usually available. ♨✿◐◑♿🚌♣P⚡

Hoscar

Railway Tavern

Hoscar Moss Road, L40 4BQ (1 mile from A5209)
✪ 12-11; 12-10.30 Sun
☎ (01704) 892369
Jennings Bitter; Tetley Mild, Bitter; guest beers Ⓗ
The Railway Tavern, as its name implies, is immediately adjacent to a small station on the Southport-Manchester line, and dates back to the opening of the railway in the 19th century. There are few reasons for alighting here, other than to enjoy the beers and food the Tavern offers (be warned: there are no trains Sun). The pub is a natural place to break a walk or cycle ride, and there is a pleasant garden at the back. Cider is sold in summer. ♨✿◐◑⊞♿⇌●P

Lancaster

Bobbin

8 Chapel Street, LA1 1HH (by bus station)
✪ 11.30-midnight (11 Thu-Sat); 11.30-midnight Sun
☎ (01524) 32606
Everards Beacon, Tiger; Thwaites Lancaster Bomber; guest beers Ⓗ
Substantial, late 19th-century corner pub. The single large bar, renovated in 1997 with a varnished floor and conspicuous curtains, bears a Lancashire cotton industry theme, consisting mainly of unlikely objects fastened to the walls. This is Lancaster's Goth pub so the music on the juke box is loud and fast. Bomber is sold as Bobbin Beer. It stages a quiz Tuesday, live music Thursday. ✿◐♿⇌♣●

Collegian Club

Gage Street, LA1 1UH (near town hall)
✪ 11 (11.30 Mon; 12 Tue)-3 (not Wed), 7-11; 11-11 Sat; 12-3, 6-10.30 Sun
☎ (01524) 65329
🌐 http://hometown.aol.co.uk/collegianclub/
Jennings Cumberland Ale; guest beers Ⓗ
Just an ordinary working men's club – except for the beer range! It was founded in 1933, but the decor and fittings appear to be of 1960s vintage. The bar is dominated by a snooker table; upstairs is a function room, with no real ale. It usually offers Cumberland Ale or something else from Jennings and often a second cask beer. CIU affiliated – people carrying this Guide are welcomed. ⇌♣

John O' Gaunt

53 Market Street, LA1 1JG (off A6)
✪ 11-11 daily
☎ (01524) 65356 🌐 yeoldejohnogaunt.co.uk
Black Sheep Best Bitter; Caledonian Deuchars IPA; Greene King Abbot; Jennings Bitter, Cumberland Ale; guest beer Ⓗ
A pub with the status of treasured local institution. A handsome bow-windowed frontage hides this narrow pub where the walls are crammed with a variety of objects collected by the previous licensee – beermats, jazz posters, photos of musicians and award certificates. At lunchtime most of the customers come from nearby banks and offices, in the evening it draws many regulars. Live music in a variety of styles is performed most week nights. Pies are usually available outside meal times. ✿◐⇌

Penny Bank

51 Penny Street, LA1 1XF
✪ 11-11 (1am Fri & Sat); 11-11 Sun
☎ (01524) 847666
Boddingtons Bitter; Caledonian Deuchars IPA; Tirril Old Faithful; guest beers Ⓗ
Formerly a Hogshead, this is a new addition to the plethora of excellent drinking establishments in the city centre. Retaining the open-plan layout, but updating with comfier seating, lighter decoration and more sunlight has made this a very popular lunchtime venue for shoppers and a favourite for evening drinkers. No food is served Sunday. ◐♿⇌

Sun Hotel & Bar

63 Church Street, LA1 1ET (off A6)
✪ 11-midnight (12.30am Fri & Sat); 12-11.30 Sun
☎ (01524) 66006 🌐 thesunhotelandbar.co.uk
Lancaster Duchy, Blonde, JSB; Thwaites Lancaster Bomber; guest beers Ⓗ
Dramatic alterations have been carried out at this inn, while retaining much exposed stonework and bare floors. Various original features have been left on view, including five fireplaces and an old door. A rather small bar with open space for drinkers to stand is supplemented by a larger extension where works by local artists are exhibited.

Breakfast is served from 7.30am; cheeseboard is available until 9pm. ❀⇌◐⇌

Three Mariners

Bridge Lane, LA1 1EE (near Parksafe car park)
12-midnight daily
☎ (01524) 388957
Beer range varies Ⓗ

Commonly claimed to be Lancaster's oldest pub. It certainly looks old and many of the beams and stones are ancient, but it has suffered some rebuilding and underwent a comprehensive and quite successful revamp in 2005. Built into the side of a hill, the cellar is at first-floor level. The narrow strip of cobbles at the front, with tables, is all that remains of Bridge Lane. Six handpumps showcase Black Sheep, Jennings, Thwaites, Copper Dragon and Moorhouses. Weekend meals finish at 5pm. ⌂❀◐⇌

Water Witch

Tow Path, Aldcliffe Road, LA1 1SU (on canal towpath near Penny St bridge)
11-midnight daily
☎ (01524) 63828 thewaterwitch.co.uk
Lancaster Duchy, JCB; Thwaites Lancaster Bomber; guest beers Ⓗ

Former canal company stable block that assumed its present name and use in 1978 – the first true canalside pub on this canal. Wedged between the towpath (with seating) and a retaining wall, it is long and narrow. The spartan decor features much bare stonework and flagstone floors. A mezzanine floor and the space underneath, both used mainly by diners, are no-smoking. Numerous buses stop here (Infirmary). ❀◐⇌

White Cross

White Cross Industrial Estate, South Road, LA1 4XT (behind Town Hall)
12-11 (12.30am Fri & Sat); 12-11 Sun
☎ (01524) 33999
Caledonian Deuchars IPA; Greene King Old Speckled Hen; guest beers Ⓗ

On the corner of an extensive complex of Victorian textile mills, now converted to other uses, this old chemical store became a pub in 1988. Features of the old structure are visible to the sharp-eyed. The wide open spaces and general style give the appearance of a circuit pub, but many of the customers are locals, nipping in from work or college. French windows open onto the canal towpath where there are tables and a waterbus stop. Sunday meals finish at 5pm. ❀◐⇌♣P

Yorkshire House

2 Parliament Street, LA1 1PB
(S end of Greyhound Bridge)
7 (2 Sat)-11 (1am Fri & Sat); 2-11.30 Sun
☎ (01524) 64679 yorkshirehouse.enta.net
Everards Beacon, Tiger; guest beers Ⓗ

Unusual in this area, the pub hosts a vibrant live music scene in the upstairs venue with performers from all over the country. The single-room bar is one of the only pubs in the city to serve a guest cider on handpump. A welcoming atmosphere ensures that this is always a busy, thriving haven for the night-time drinker. ⌂❀●

Laneshaw Bridge

Emmott Arms

Keighley Road, BB8 7HX
12-midnight; 12-11 Sun
☎ (01282) 868660
John Smith's Bitter; Taylor Golden Best, Landlord; Tetley Bitter; guest beer Ⓗ

Friendly roadside pub on the main Colne-Keighley Road. Named after a local family, the Emmotts has operated as a free house under the same landlord for many years. Popular with diners throughout the day, it offers a carvery every lunchtime. The interior has two main rooms: one has an open fire, the other, Internet access. There is a small garden to the rear. Domino players are welcome here. ⌂❀◐♿♣P

Lathom

Ship

4 Wheat Lane, L40 4BX (off A5209, by Leeds-Liverpool Canal)
11.30-11 (midnight Sat); 12-10.30 Sun
☎ (01704) 893117
Moorhouses Black Cat, Pride of Pendle, Pendle Witches Brew; Theakston Bitter; Wells Bombardier; guest beers Ⓗ

Situated at the junction of two canals, the Ship, locally known as the Blood Tub for reasons obscurely connected to the making of black puddings, is a picturesque 200-year-old pub with a wide range of beers on offer (usually including at least one Phoenix beer), an occasional cider and reasonably-priced food. It is supposedly haunted, the ghost presumably knowing a good pub when it found one. Q❀◐♿♣●P⊬

Lea Town

Smith's Arms

Lea Lane, PR4 0RP
12-11.30 (12.30am Fri & Sat); 12-11.30 Sun
☎ (01772) 760555
Thwaites Mild, Original, Thoroughbred, Lancaster Bomber, seasonal beers Ⓗ

Roughly seven miles from central Preston, served by daytime buses, this recently renovated country pub has retained its traditional feel but gained improved facilities, including full disabled access and a covered patio with an interesting water feature. There is a large no-smoking area. The pub sells the full range of Thwaites beers including the seasonal brews. Good, traditional food is on offer, using local ingredients when possible (served all day Sun, 12-8pm). ⌂❀◐♿⛺♣P⊬

Limbrick

Black Horse

Long Lane, PR6 9EE (1 mile SE of Chorley)
12-11 (midnight Fri & Sat); 12-10.30 Sun
☎ (01257) 264030
Caledonian Deuchars IPA; Theakston Best Bitter; guest beer Ⓗ

Situated by the River Yarrow, the Black Horse claims to be one of England's oldest pubs, dating back to 997AD and holding a continuous licence since 1577. The remains of the original pub can be seen in the cellar. A single bar serves two lounges, both with real fires, and two games rooms; beware the sloping floor at the bar. In summer it is popular with walkers from nearby reservoirs and local cricketers, playing on the neighbouring field. ♨❀◐◑♣P⊬

Little Eccleston

Cartford Hotel

Cartford Lane, PR3 0YP (½ mile from A586)

⊛ 12-3, 6.30-11; 12-10.30 Sun

☎ (01995) 670166 ⊕ cartfordinn.co.uk

Boddingtons Bitter; Fuller's London Pride; guest beers ⊞

Numerous CAMRA awards, including local Pub of the Year 2006, adorn the walls of the bar in this former farmhouse. The pub stands by the toll bridge across the River Wyre. The Hart Brewery, which usually supplies one or two of up to six changing guest beers, is located next door. The food is popular. Hotel guests can make use of the pub's fishing rights. One not to miss. ♨❀⇄◐◑Ⓐ♣P⊬

Longridge

Corporation Arms

Lower Road, PR3 2YJ (near B6243/B6245 jct)

⊛ 11-11 (midnight Fri & Sat); 12-10.30 Sun

☎ (01772) 782610 ⊕ corporationarms.co.uk

Beer range varies ⊞

Constructed in 1750 on the site of an older building, this family-run country inn was renamed in the 1930s when Preston Corporation built the nearby reservoirs. This comfortable and relaxing pub is largely no-smoking. Beers are often from the area's independent breweries. Excellent food is served all day, often incorporating local ingredients. The old horse trough outside was reputedly used by Oliver Cromwell to water his horse on his way to the Battle of Preston. ♨♉❀⇄◐◑⊟♣P⊬

Forrest Arms

1 Derby Road, PR3 3JR

⊛ 4-midnight; 12-1am Fri-Sun

☎ (01772) 786612

Beer range varies ⊞

From the stoney exterior of this pub you pass into a bright, modern interior decorated in light colours, displaying modern art and football memorabilia. Three handpumps sit on a central island bar, an unusual feature for Lancashire. The house beer, Thyme, is Bank Top's GSM, rebadged by the brewery. The pub holds regular music nights and a twice-yearly beer festival. Good value food is served, often using locally-sourced ingredients (Tue-Thu 6-8pm; Fri-Sun 12-6pm). ❀◐◑⊟♣⊬

Longton

Dolphin

Marsh Lane, PR4 5JY

(down Marsh Lane 1 mile, take right fork)

⊛ 12-2.30am daily

☎ (01772) 612032

Beer range varies ⊞

Isolated country pub, on the edge of the marshes by the Ribble Way, comprising two bars, where smoking is permitted, and a no-smoking conservatory used by diners. A function room hosts the annual August beer festival. Food is served 12-11pm daily. An outside play area is provided for children. The range of four or five beers includes a mild; cider is sold in summer. A free mini-bus service from local villages can be arranged by this local CAMRA award winner. ♨♉❀◐◑⊟♣●P

Lytham

Hastings

26 Hastings Place, FY8 2LZ (off Church Rd)

⊛ 12-11.30 (midnight Fri & Sat); 12-11.30 Sun

☎ (01253) 732839

Caledonian Deuchars IPA; Moorhouses Pride of Pendle, Pendle Witch's Brew; Wadworth 6X; guest beers ⊞

This former Conservative Club enjoys a quiet and civilised location, as reflected in the smart decor. Home-cooked food complements up to 12 cask ales on offer, while the upstairs bar (Orangery) keeps a fine selection of world beers, with Leifmanns Kriek and Küppers Kölsch on draught. CAMRA's National Club of the Year 2005 admits CAMRA members free of charge on production of a membership card. ❀◐◑⊟♿⇌♣⊬

Taps

Henry Street, FY8 5LE (off west beach, A584)

⊛ 11-11 (midnight Fri & Sat); 11-11 Sun

☎ (01253) 736226 ⊕ thetaps.com

Greene King IPA; guest beers ⊞

Winner of many awards, this enduringly popular, side-street local attracts a wide variety of customers. Bare brick walls and floorboards reveal the influence of the Hogshead chain, but give way to turf (honestly!) when the open golf plays locally. Children are admitted until 7pm; free bar snacks are served on Sunday lunchtime. The Taps can be busy in the evening, but service is always attentive and friendly. Six guest ales change frequently; Taps Bitter is brewed for the pub by Titanic. ♨Q❀◐♿⇌♣●

Mawdesley

Black Bull

Hall Lane, L40 2QY (off B5246)

⊛ 12-midnight; 12-11 Sun

☎ (01704) 822202

Black Sheep Best Bitter; Caledonian Deuchars IPA; Jennings Cumberland Ale; Lees Bitter; guest beer ⊞

A pub since 1610, the low-ceilinged, stone building boasts some magnificent oak beams. Older village residents know the pub as 'Ell 'Ob' – a reference to a coal fired cooking range. There is a games room upstairs and a boules pitch outside. Certificates in the bar record the pub's success in Lancashire's Best-Kept Village competition and there are awards for its hanging baskets. Bus No. 347 passes three times a day (Chorley-Southport; not Sun). No evening meals are served Monday. ♨❀◐◑♿⊟♣P⊬

Robin Hood

Bluestone Lane, L40 2QY (off B5250) OS506163
11.30-11; 12-10.30 Sun
(01704) 822275 robinhoodinn.co.uk
Caledonian Deuchars IPA; Jennings Cumberland Ale; Taylor Landlord; guest beers H
Charming, white-painted inn at the crossroads between the three old villages of Mawdesley, Croston and Eccleston. The 15th-century building was substantially altered in the 19th century. In the same family for over 30 years, it enjoys a reputation for good food, but still finds room for drinkers, offering three guest ales. Bar food is served all day at the weekend; Wilson's Restaurant, upstairs, is open Tuesday–Sunday evenings. The no. 347 bus runs weekdays from Chorley and Southport. ❀◐◑P⊬

Mere Brow

Legh Arms

82 The Gravel, PR4 6JX (near A565/B5246 jct)
12-11; 12-10.30 Sun
(01772) 812359
Caledonian Deuchars IPA; Taylor Landlord; Tetley Bitter; Wells Bombardier H
Situated a short distance from the entrance to the Tarleton Leisure Lakes, the Legh Arms is a quiet, unspoilt pub where walkers and visitors to the lakes can relax. The pub has two bars and its own house beer, Fetlers, brewed by Tetley. A perfect local with a popular public bar, it would be worth moving to Mere Brow to sup here.
Q❀◐◑&P⊬

Nether Kellet

Limeburner's Arms

32 Main Road, LA6 1EP
7.30-midnight; 12-2am Sun
(01524) 732916
Beer range varies H
Once, within living memory, most country pubs were like this: no food, no juke box, plain and simple furnishings. The landlord is a DIY enthusiast and improvements are slowly happening, but not so as to change the character of the place; at present the side room is a work in progress. Unsurprisingly, most customers are locals; the landlord is also a farmer. Old photos in the bar reward study. A single cask beer comes from the region. Take buses Nos. 84 or 85 to get here. QP⊬

Ormskirk

Hayfield

22 County Road, L39 1NN (on A59)
12-11 (midnight Fri & Sat); 12-11 Sun
(01695) 571157
Beer range varies H
Spacious and comfortable open-plan pub, with an L-shaped bar, slightly away from the centre of Ormskirk. It usually offers an adventurous beer range drawn from the smaller brewers. A winner of many CAMRA awards over the years, it is popular with local students and is particularly lively at the weekends. Q❀◐◑&P

Yew Tree

Grimshaw Lane, L39 1PD (off A59)
11.30-3; 6-11; 12-11 Sat; 12-4, 7-10.30 Sun
(01695) 572261
Cains Dark Mild, Bitter; Robinson's Unicorn; Theakston Best Bitter; guest beers H
The Yew Tree is a perfectly kept reminder of the way pubs on housing estates used to be in the 1950s, when the pub was still the hub of the community. When you visit, check out, for example, the traditional tap room and the walled garden. The beer range always includes beers from local breweries such as Cain's and Robinson's. Reasonably-priced food is available, including Sunday lunches. Q❀◐◑&P

Oswaldtwistle

Coach & Horses

Haslingden Old Road, BB5 3SN (on B6236)
12-3, 5.30-11 (not Mon or winter Tue); 12-11 Fri & Sat; 12-10.30 Sun
(01706) 213825 coachandhorsesinn.com
Beer range varies H
The beer is excellent, the food is exceptional. Two real ales usually come from local breweries; cider is sold in summer. A specials board lists mouth-watering delights, while the menu forms the basis of good cuisine (served all day Sun). Public transport is non-existent on this road, but at weekends many hikers from the adjoining moors make use of the pub's amenities. Both diners and drinkers can sit anywhere in the pub including the two no-smoking areas.
◐◑P⊬

Parbold

Wayfarer

1-3 Alder Lane, WN8 7NL (on A5209)
12-3, 5.30-11 (midnight Fri & Sat); 12-10.30 Sun
(01257) 464600
Beer range varies H
A conversion of a row of 18th-century cottages, initially to a restaurant and now a pleasant rural pub, with low, beamed ceilings and cosy little nooks and crannies. Three handpumps provide a varying beer range, usually from Skipton, Copper Dragon or Tetley. Reasonably-priced bar meals make it a popular stop, especially in summer and weekends, being close to the Leeds-Liverpool Canal and Parbold Hill, with its panoramic views stretching from the Welsh hills to Blackpool Tower and beyond.
❀◐◑&P⊬

Pendleton

Swan with Two Necks

Main Street, BB7 1PT (off A59)
12-3 (not Mon; 12-2.30 Sat), 7 (6 Fri & Sat)-11; closed Tue; 12-10.30 Sun
(01200) 423112
Beer range varies H
The ideal village pub, beer is given top priority here, with four handpumps. One of the guests is likely to come from Phoenix, while others may be from Salamander, Lancaster, Skinner's, Hop Back or Copper Dragon. Tasting notes are

usually provided on a chalkboard behind the bar. The pub may seem small at first, but two rooms are tucked behind the bar. Pendle Hill is nearby, so walkers drink here nearly all year round. Look for the amazing collection of teapots. ♨Q❀◑P

Penwortham

Black Bull

83 Pope Lane, PR1 9BA

✪ 11-11; 12-10.30 Sun

☎ (01772) 752953

Greenalls Bitter; Theakston Mild, Best Bitter; guest beer ⊞

Attractive, cottage-style pub that has managed to retain a village atmosphere, despite its location in a well-populated area. On entering, a narrow passageway leads through to a central bar serving a number of drinking areas. A pub that has continued to serve a real mild, it is also a rare outlet for the fast disappearing Greenalls Bitter. In the last year a new landlord has further improved the beer choice with the addition of one or two guests. ◖⊟⛟♣P

Fleece

39 Liverpool Road, PR1 9XD (on A59)

✪ 11-11 (midnight Thu-Sat); 12-11.30 Sun

☎ (01772) 745561

Boddingtons Bitter; guest beers ⊞

Old coaching inn, situated close to Penwortham's most prominent feature, the former water tower. Facing onto the main road, a cosy village inn appearance is maintained, but inside the pub has seen several refurbishments over the years. At the back, a former bowling green now serves as an outdoor drinking area and children's playground. Three or four guest beers are usually stocked. ❀◑⛟♣P⚟

Poulton-le-Fylde

Old Town Hall

5 Church Street, FY6 7AP

(in pedestrianised town centre)

✪ 11-11 (11.30 Thu-Sat; later in summer); 11-11.30 Sun

☎ (01253) 892257

Black Sheep Best Bitter; Greene King Old Speckled Hen; Theakston Best Bitter; guest beer ⊞

Lively, large, single-roomed pub with high ceilings and an airy feel. TV screens in different parts of the pub cater for football and racing fans. Children are welcome if dining. The lunchtime menu includes many excellent value options; locally baked pies are a particular favourite. Upstairs is a recently refurbished lounge bar and function room that hosts folk music and karaoke evenings on a regular basis. ◖♿⇌

Preesall

Black Bull

Park Lane, FY6 0NW (on B5377)

✪ 12-3, 5-11; 12-midnight Sat & Sun

☎ (01253) 810294

Black Sheep Best Bitter; Caledonian Deuchars IPA; Taylor Landlord ⊞

Cosy, multi-roomed, friendly village local, dating back to the 14th century, replete with low beams, alcoves and a small dining room. Once three separate dwellings, the upper floors were added later. Excellent value meals are based on locally-sourced produce; try Jim's mixed grill. An upstairs function room is available for special occasions. Children are welcome. The No. 2C bus runs from Blackpool to Knott End, stopping outside the pub. Q❀◑♿⛟♣P⚟

Preston

Ashton Institute

10-12 Wellington Road, PR2 1BU

(by Slingers Motorcycles)

✪ 7 (4 Fri & Sat)-11 (may open earlier for TV sports events); 4-11 Sun

☎ (01772) 726582

Beer range varies ⊞

Private club, formerly two terraced houses. The oldest club still in its original premises in Preston (opened 04/04/44), one room is available for hire, the other has pool and snooker. An annual beer festival is held over the last weekend in October at this former local CAMRA Club of the Year. Show a CAMRA membership card or this Guide to be signed in. Thwaites normally supplies one beer, supplemented by at least one more independent brew. Take Preston bus No. 24 or 25 to St Michaels church. ⛟♣

Black Horse ☆

166 Friargate, PR1 2EJ

✪ 10.30-11; 12-4 (closed eve) Sun

☎ (01772) 204855

Robinson's Hatter's, Cumbria Way, Unicorn, Double Hop, seasonal beers ⊞

Classic, Grade II listed building in the main shopping area, close to the historic open market. With its exquisite tiled bar and walls and superb mosaic floor, it is an English Heritage/CAMRA award winner. The two front rooms bear photos of old Preston. The famous hall of mirrors seating area is to the rear. See the memorabilia of a previous landlord set in a glass partition. The modern upstairs bar (no real ale) usually opens at weekends. ⇌⛟

Finney's Sports Bar

1 East View, Deepdale Road, PR1 5AS

✪ 2 (12 Fri & Sat)-midnight; 12-10.30 Sun

☎ (01772) 250490

Tetley Bitter; guest beers ⊞

Multi-screened, multi-channel sports venue at the town end of Deepdale Road. It has a large bar and raised games areas to the right and left, plus a small dance floor. Handy for Preston North End, various football shirts adorn the walls. It hosts karaoke on Friday and Saturday evenings, when tracksuits may not be worn. Two guest beers from small breweries and micros are usually kept. Outside tables are provided in front of the pub. ❀⛟♣

Fox & Grapes

15 Fox Street, PR1 2AB

✪ 12-11 (midnight Fri & Sat); 12-11 Sun

☎ (01772) 561149

Beer range varies ⊞

Small, friendly, back-street oasis, close to the

bustling shopping centre. Six handpumps dispense a changing range of real ales. An impressive collection of beer mats adorns the walls, while motorcycle memorabilia, table football, and the 60-year-old framed press articles on old Preston pubs (many long gone) all add interest. It hosts occasional live music, and a chess club for those who enjoy quieter pursuits. ⇌⊟♣

Market Tavern

33-35 Market Street, PR1 2ES

10.30-9 (11 Thu; midnight Fri & Sat); 12-9 Sun

☎ (01772) 254425

Beer range varies Ⓗ

Popular, town-centre local, overlooking the Victorian outdoor covered market. Over 400 different guest beers from far and wide were sold in 2005, and it offers a fantastic selection of imported bottled beers, plus German and French wheat beers on draught. Outside seating is available in summer. No juke box or TV interferes with conversation at this former local CAMRA Pub of the Year. No food is sold, but you are more than welcome to bring your own. ❀⇌⊟

New Britannia

6 Heatley Street, PR1 2XB (off Friargate)

11-midnight; 11-11 Sun

☎ (01772) 253424

Boddingtons Bitter; Camerons Castle Eden Ale; Goose Eye Brontë Bitter; Marston's Pedigree; guest beers Ⓗ

This single bar, town-centre pub attracts real ale enthusiasts from a fair distance. It enjoys an excellent reputation for the high quality and choice of its beers – a recent change in management has seen no reduction in quality. Four guest beers usually include one from the Timothy Taylor range. The tasty, home-made food, served weekdays, represents good value. A small patio to the rear allows for some outdoor drinking. It stages three beer festivals a year. ❀◖⇌⊟●

Old Black Bull

35 Friargate, PR1 2AT

10.30-11 (midnight Fri & Sat); 12-10.30 Sun

☎ (01772) 823397

Boddingtons Bitter; Cains Bitter; guest beers Ⓗ

Mock-Tudor fronted, city-centre pub. A small front vault, a main bar with distinctive black and white floor tiles, two comfortable lounge areas and a pool table combine to make it a popular venue. The patio is a bonus in summer. Live music is performed Saturday evening and Sky Sports is available. Up to seven guest beers are usually sourced from micros or small independents. Twice winner of local CAMRA's Pub of the Year, it serves a good range of food at competitive prices. ❀◖⊟♿⇌⊟♣

Old Vic

78 Fishergate, PR1 2UH (opp. station)

11.30-midnight (1am Fri & Sat); 12-1am Sun

☎ (01772) 254690

Black Sheep Best Bitter; Marston's Pedigree; Theakston Best Bitter; guest beers Ⓗ

Friendly, comfortable, family-run pub across the road from Preston Station, handy for rail travellers. It can therefore get busy during Preston North End home games. Look for the old Preston photographs and the china collection. Five cask beers are usually on offer. The lunches (served all afternoon) are home made, using fresh ingredients where possible. There are regular theme nights and other events, and the pub runs darts, football and pool teams and a golf society. ❀◖⇌⊟♣⅟

Olde Dog & Partridge

44 Friargate, PR1 2AT

11-2, 6-1.30am (may close early); 11-1.30am Sat; 12-11.30 Sun

☎ (01772) 252217

Fuller's London Pride; Highgate Dark; Taylor Landlord; guest beers Ⓗ

Long-established classic rock music venue, although the nearby university influences the clientele. The decor has a strong military theme. Good value basic lunches are available (not Sun) and it is handy for evening takeaways. A long-serving DJ performs on Sunday and Thursday. Guest beers are often from White Shield (formerly Bass Museum) Brewery. A former Bass pub, performing superbly under Punch, it is a rare outlet for real cider and mild in the city centre. ◖⇌⊟♣●

Stanley Arms

24 Lancaster Road, PR1 1DD (next to Guild Hall)

11-11; 12-10.30 Sun

☎ (01772) 254004

Theakston Best Bitter; guest beers Ⓗ

This pub is close to but not part of the 'circuit', and handy for the bus station. Five guest beers at all times come from all over the country. The single lounge bar tends to be busy. It has a no-smoking restaurant/function room upstairs. An impressive, ornate, listed building, the pub's name refers to the Earls of Derby, once landowners in the area. Pavement tables allow for summer drinking. ❀◖◗●⇌⊟

Waterfront

Navigation Way, Ashton, PR2 2YP (on Preston Marina)

9am-11 (12.30am Thu; 1am Fri & Sat); 10-11 Sun

☎ (01772) 721108

Boddingtons Bitter; Taylor Landlord; guest beers Ⓗ

1980s pub on Preston Marina near the recently opened steam railway. Split into two, a bar area and restaurant, real ale is available in both sections. Quiz night (Thu) sees a late bar as do the weekend live acts and entertainment. It is busy during the Marina festival, while the garden is popular all summer. Guest beers are taken from Fuller's, Hydes and other regionals. Take Preston bus No. 27/127 (alight after Morrisons) or Stagecoach service 75. ❀◖◗♿⊟P⅟

Rawtenstall

Craven Heifer

264 Burnley Road, BB4 8LA (½ mile N of town centre on A682)

6 (11 Sat)-11; 12-11 Sun

☎ (01706) 214757

Moorhouses Black Cat, Premier, Pride of Pendle, Blond Witch, Pendle Witches Brew; guest beer Ⓗ

A recent Moorhouses' acquisition and an excellent place to sample all of its beer range. There is a large lounge that has been extended over the river (view the ducks) and a smaller bar room. Sport can be watched on a large screen. Thursday is quiz night, and entertainment is staged on Saturday evening. A guest beer is usually available. ⊟

St Anne's

Trawlboat

Wood Street, FY8 1QR (just off square)
✪ 9am-midnight (1am Fri & Sat); 9am-midnight Sun
☎ (01253) 783080
Greene King Abbot; Marston's Burton Bitter, Pedigree; Theakston Old Peculier; guest beers Ⓗ
This sympathetic, yet contemporary Wetherspoon conversion of former solicitors' offices has a café-bar ambience during the day, becoming more lively on weekend evenings. A patio, with windbreaks and large parasols (heated in winter) accommodates smokers; the pub itself is no-smoking throughout, one of the first in the Wetherspoon estate. Children are welcome until 9pm. Up to three guest ales and Westons Old Rosie cider are stocked.
♨Q❀◑◐♿⚌●⚟

Salterforth

Anchor

Salterforth Lane, BB18 5TT (200 yds from B6383)
✪ 12-midnight daily
☎ (01282) 812186
Caledonian Deuchars IPA; Courage Directors; John Smith's Bitter; Theakston Best Bitter; guest beer Ⓗ
Popular with boaters and locals, this historical, canalside village pub sits on the summit level of the Leeds and Liverpool Canal. Seats and moorings for boats are provided next to the inn. Food is served (all day Sun) in a no-smoking dining area. The cellar features an unusual collection of stalactites and stalagmites formed by water seeping through the limestone – viewing by arrangement with the licensee (during quiet periods). ♨❀◑◐⅄P

Scorton

Priory

The Square, PR3 1AU (½ mile off A6 at Little Chef)
✪ 11-11.30 (midnight Thu & Fri); 9am-midnight Sat & Sun
☎ (01524) 791255 ⊕ theprioryscorton.co.uk
Thwaites Lancaster Bomber; guest beers Ⓗ
Scorton offers no tourist attractions in the usual sense, nevertheless, trippers, coach parties and cycle club runs regularly converge on the place, many ending up in the Priory. This is first and foremost a restaurant, but the former blacksmith's shop at one end of the range of buildings houses a fully-licensed bar. The furniture here, too, is mostly dining-room style. In the evening a fair number of locals gather. ♨❀⛟◑◐P

Slyne

Slyne Lodge

92 Main Road, LA2 6AZ (on A6)
✪ 11-11; 12-10.30 Sun
☎ (01524) 825035 ⊕ slynelodge.co.uk
Jennings Dark Mild, Bitter, Cumberland Ale; guest beer Ⓗ
Elegant, Georgian house with a terraced garden. It was a country club until 1981 when it gained a full licence. It has a large central servery, dark wood panelling and a log fire. There is a modern conservatory on one side and a rustic, galleried restaurant on the other. The latter extends into the old stables where the house's original owner kept horses he raced at Ascot. ❀◑◐⛍ (55, 555) ♣P

Tockholes

Royal Arms

Tockholes Road, BB3 0PA
✪ 12-11; 12-10.30 Sun
☎ (01254) 705373
Three B's Bobbin's Bitter; guest beers Ⓗ
This village pub is the closest to Darwen Tower and Roddlesworth walks. Two houses knocked into one, with back-to-back fireplaces, this is a four-roomed, cosy little retreat. Hops hang from beams, walls reveal original stonework and the wood or stone floors happily cater for walkers with dogs. The beers come from local micros. It has won awards for its service and cuisine (booking advisable); meals are served until 9pm (not Tue) and regular special theme nights are a feature. ♨❀◑◐P

Tontine

Delph Tavern

Sefton Road, WN5 8UJ (off B5206)
✪ 11.30-midnight (1am Fri & Sat); 12-11.30 Sun
☎ (01695) 622239
Hydes Bitter; Moorhouses Pride of Pendle; guest beers Ⓗ
Large, multi-roomed pub that has been opened out but retains a separate vault. It caters for all ages, which creates a friendly atmosphere aided by a warm welcome. Good value meals are served in the dining area, to complement the reasonably-priced beer. Children are welcome, except in the vault. Darts and dominoes are played in the local league.
♉❀◑◐⊟♿⚌(Orrell)♣P

Trawden

Sun Inn

Back Colne Road, BB8 8PG (alight bus at St Mary's Church, follow signs) OS910385
✪ 7 (5 Wed-Fri)-11.30; 12-midnight Sat; 12-11.30 Sun
☎ (01282) 867985
Copper Dragon Black Gold, Best Bitter, Golden Pippin, Scotts 1816 Ⓗ
Tucked away at the village centre, the Sun Inn has been acquired by Copper Dragon Brewery as its third tied house. All Copper Dragon beers are available on the bar. Home-cooked food is served evenings (Wed-Sun), plus weekend lunchtimes. The main lounge and dining area is supplemented by a snug/public bar and two large private function rooms. A local jazz band performs on Tuesday evening. Outside is a small seated area and a large car park.
Q❀◑◐⊟♣P

Tunstall

Lunesdale

LA6 2QN (on A683)
⏲ 11-3, 6-11; closed Mon; 12-3, 6-10.30 Sun
☎ (01524) 274203
Black Sheep Best Bitter; guest beer Ⓗ
Clean, modern decor characterises this pub: white walls, scrubbed tables and varnished floorboards. There is a small servery, surrounded by several rooms, one has pool and table football, while at the other end there is a restaurant; the main room is also mostly used for eating. Bus Nos. 81 and 81A serve the pub.
◑🚌P

University of Lancaster

Furness College Bar

Bailrigg, LA1 4YG (first college on south spine)
⏲ 12 (6 Sat)-11; 7-10.30 Sun (liable to close in vacations)
☎ (01524) 592954
Beer range varies Ⓗ
Student bar of early 1970s vintage: pink bricks and matchboarding, teal paint and chiaroscuro, with plenty of standing room. The eight handpumps are not all in use all the time, but offer a mix of local(ish) brews, remote rarities and old favourites. Various ciders and a perry are stocked. Furness is near the middle of campus, well-signposted; the bar is directly off the main campus. It is well served by buses.
❀🚌(2, 2A, X2, 3, 4)♣🍎P

Graduate College Bar

Alexandra Park, LA2 0PF (SW of main campus, signed Alexandra Park)
⏲ 7 (6 Fri)-11; 8-11 Sun
☎ (01524) 592824 🌐 gradbar.co.uk
Beer range varies Ⓗ
Modern student bar, more like a pub than most and (as the name suggests) the age range is slightly higher than most of the campus bars. Between two and eight beers are stocked: Hawkshead, Copper Dragon, Acorn and Barngates feature regularly. A major beer festival at the end of June is worth the detour. Bus Nos. X2, 3 and 4 call nearby. Make sure you find the correct stop for the return trip.
❀🚌♣🍎P

Up Holland

Old Dog

6 Alma Hill, WN8 0NW (off A577, near parish church)
⏲ 5-midnight (1am Fri & Sat); 5-11.30 Sun
☎ (01695) 623487
Banks's Bitter; guest beers Ⓗ
Halfway up the steep Alma Hill, this small stone pub is worth the climb. Recently refurbished, it retains much of its character, including an original Greenall Whitley etched window, and one showing the pub name. Its four small, heavily beamed rooms are all on different levels and are served from a central bar. The rear rooms benefit from wonderful views across Wigan to the West Pennines. The pub is home to a wine tasting group and quiz team.
Q❀♣

White Lion

10 Church Street, NN8 0ND
(off A577, opp. parish church)
⏲ 5-midnight (1am Fri & Sat); 12-midnight Sun
☎ (01695) 622727
Thwaites Bitter, Lancaster Bomber Ⓗ
This multi-level pub is built into the hillside opposite the parish church. Inside are four rooms: two lounges, a games room to the rear and a small snug at the front. Photographs of old Up Holland adorn the walls of the front lounge, which also houses a large screen, popular for watching sport. The pub is reputedly haunted, possibly by local highwayman George Lyon, who is buried in the churchyard opposite. Q♣P

Waddington

Lower Buck

Edisford Road, BB7 3HU (behind church)
⏲ 12-midnight; 12-11.30 Sun
☎ (01200) 423342
Black Sheep Best Bitter; Moorhouses Black Cat, Premier, Blond Witch; Taylor Landlord; guest beers Ⓗ
With real fires in most rooms, the Lower Buck provides a warm welcome throughout the year. The landlord specialises in guest beers from local micro-breweries such as Three B's and Bowland. Bottle-conditioned beers are stocked and seasonal brews from Moorhouses are sometimes available. Popular with locals and visitors, including walkers in the nearby Forest of Bowland, bar meals are served and there is a restaurant upstairs. 🔥Q❀◑⍻

Walmer Bridge

Walmer Bridge Inn

65 Liverpool Old Road, PR4 5QE
⏲ 4 (12 Sat)-midnight; 12-10.30 Sun
☎ (01772) 612296
Robinson's Unicorn; guest beers Ⓗ
Village local comprising a comfortable lounge and a lower level vault. Pictures of bygone Walmer Bridge and Longton include some of Longton's old Pyes/Wilkins Breweries, (now long gone). Guest beers are from the pub group list. A play area for children is provided in the garden. Bus services stop outside. This was local CAMRA's Pub of the Season winter 2005/06. Cider is sometimes stocked in summer. ❀⊟🚌♣🍎P

Waterfoot

Jolly Sailor

Booth Road, BB4 9BD
(200 yds off B6238 Burnley road)
⏲ 12-midnight (1am Sat); 12-midnight Sun
☎ (01706) 226340
Caledonian Deuchars IPA; Jennings Cumberland Ale; Taylor Landlord Ⓗ
Spacious, traditional pub offering four regular real ales and one guest. Popular with students, it stages live music, including jam sessions every two weeks. A friendly local, where good conversation is the norm, it is two miles from the local steam railway, and the M66 motorway to Manchester. 🔥❀◑⊟♿♣P⍻

Whittle-le-Woods

Royal Oak

216 Chorley Old Road, PR6 7NA (off A6)

3-11; 2.30-midnight Fri; 12-midnight Sat; 1-10.30 Sun

(01257) 276485

Black Sheep Best Bitter; Taylor Landlord; guest beer H

This small, terraced, village local was built in 1820 to serve the adjacent branch of the Leeds-Liverpool Canal extension (now filled in). A regular local CAMRA award winner, it has been in this Guide for over 30 consecutive years. Long and narrow, it has a small bar/lounge and a games room. Very much a community pub, it is frequented by mature motorcycle enthusiasts. Note the etched windows from the long-gone Nuttalls Brewery.

Worston

Calf's Head

BB7 1QA (100 yds from A59 Clitheroe bypass)

11-11 daily

(01200) 441218 calfshead.co.uk

Jennings Bitter, Cumberland Ale; guest beers H

Two guest beers are always available in this large inn, just off the Clitheroe bypass. Friendly service is guaranteed in the comfortable bar area. Menu boards abound to allow you to choose your food at leisure. No smoking is permitted in any of the three restaurant areas. The large garden boasts a stream with free range ducks. Eleven en-suite bedrooms complete the facilities, set in the beautiful Pendle countryside.

Wrea Green

Villa

Moss Side Lane, PR4 2PE (¼ mile outside village on B5259)

12-11 daily

(01772) 684347 villahotel-wreagreen.co.uk

Copper Dragon Scotts 1816; Jennings Cumberland Ale H

The bar and restaurant were originally part of a 19th-century gentleman's residence. Enjoy sitting in the luxurious deep leather chairs and settees in the oak-panelled area by the fireplace. Bar meals here outshine food served in many restaurants. The Villa has won awards, including Best Small Hotel, Best Restaurant, and multiple CAMRA Pub of the Season. Jazz evenings are held on the first Friday of the month. The pub has a wheelchair WC.

LEICESTERSHIRE & RUTLAND

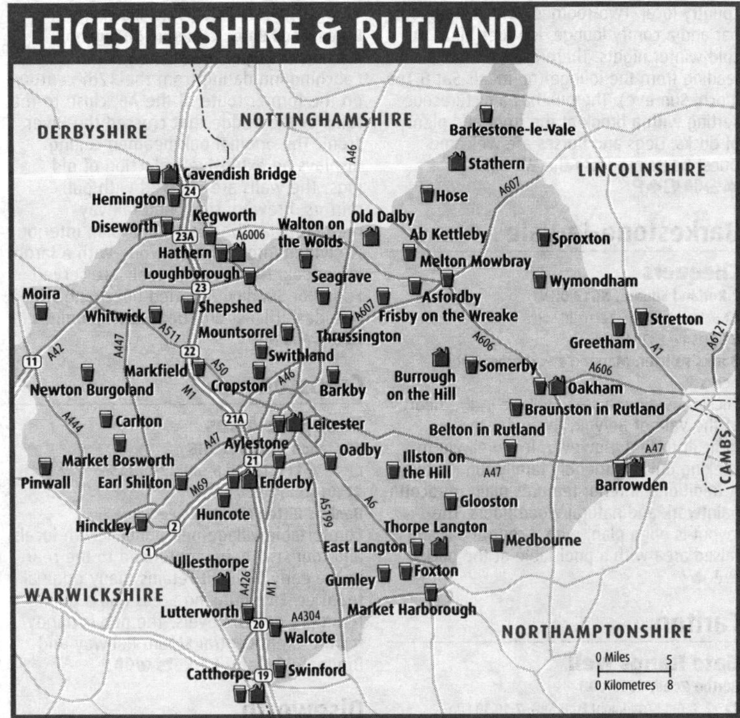

LEICESTERSHIRE

Ab Kettleby

Sugar Loaf

Nottingham Road, LE14 3JB

11-11; 12-10.30 Sun

☎ (01664) 822473

Draught Bass; Fuller's London Pride; Marston's Burton Bitter; guest beers H

Atmospheric 17th-century coaching inn with a Georgian facade on the main road to Nottingham. Inside is a bar, lounge/dining area and conservatory. Three guest beers are offered, often including brews from the nearby Belvoir Brewery. Home-cooked food is served all day. Q P

Asfordby

Horseshoes

Main Street, LE14 3SA

12 (11 Tue & Sat)-3, 7-11; 12-3, 7-10.30 Sun

☎ (01664) 813392

Bateman Mild, XB; Tetley Bitter H

This friendly locals' pub is in the centre of the village. Unusually for the area it is a Bateman's house. Three regular real ales are offered including a mild. The pub has a garden and function room. The bus stop is right outside the door.

INDEPENDENT BREWERIES

Barrowden Barrowden
Bells Ullesthorpe
Belvoir Old Dalby
Brewster's Stathern
Dow Bridge Catthorpe
Everards Enderby
Grainstore Oakham
Hoskins Leicester
Langton Thorpe Langton
Parish Burrough on the Hill
Shardlow Cavendish Bridge
Wicked Hathern Hathern

Aylestone

Black Horse

65 Narrow Lane, LE2 8NA

5-11; 12-midnight Fri & Sat; 12-11 Sun

☎ (0116) 283 2811

Everards Beacon, Tiger, seasonal beers; guest beers H

Cracking three-bar community local dating from late Victorian times. It offers a comfortable lounge and smoke-free snug. All bars have open log fires in winter. There is a function room upstairs and a large garden with a children's play area. A long alley skittles room is available for hire. A short distance from the Grand Union Canal and Great Central Way, the pub is popular with boaters and walkers. Q

Barkby

Brookside

35 Brookside, LE7 3QO (off Barkby Holt Lane)

12-2.30 (not Tue), 5.30-11 (midnight Fri & Sat); 12-4, 7-10.30 Sun

☎ (0116) 260 0092

Banks's Bitter; Camerons Strongarm; Marston's Pedigree; guest beers H

Cheery and welcoming pub with the air of a

country local. Two-roomed, with a traditional bar and a comfy lounge, log fires blaze on cold winter nights. There is a restaurant leading from the lounge (no meals Sat & Tue lunch, Sun eve). The pub has a picturesque setting with a brook at the front and plenty of ducks. Dogs and horses are welcome. Guest beers are from the W&D list.
⛰❀◐◑⊟♣P

Barkestone-le-Vale

Chequers
2 Rutland Square, NG13 0HN
⏲ 6-11; 12-11 Sat; 12-10.30 Sun
☎ (01949) 842947
Banks's Bitter; Marston's Pedigree; guest beers Ⓗ
Tucked away in a small village in the heart of the Vale of Belvoir, this pub can be difficult to find. However, it is well worth seeking out this friendly family-run hostelry. A traditional interior features plain terracotta paintwork and natural wood floors. The layout is open plan, with a central bar and a raised area with a pool table at the back.
❀♿♣

Carlton

Gate Hangs Well
Barton Road, CV13 0DB
⏲ 12-3, 6-11 (midnight Fri & Sat); 7-10.30 Sun
☎ (01455) 291845
Draught Bass; Greene King Abbot; Marston's Burton Bitter, Pedigree Ⓗ
Traditional, welcoming village inn near Market Bosworth, convenient for Bosworth Battlefield and the preserved railway line. A central bar serves the recently refurbished seating areas. Sandwiches and rolls are made to order. Singers provide entertainment on Wednesday and Saturday evenings. Popular with walkers and cyclists, there is a pleasant garden for the summer and a conservatory where families with children are welcome until mid evening. A consistently good free house. ⛰Q❀♣P

Catthorpe

Cherry Tree
Main Street, LE17 6DB
⏲ 12-2.30, 5-11; 12-11 Sat; 12-10.30 Sun
☎ (01788) 860430
Marston's Pedigree; guest beers Ⓗ
With a committed team and ongoing refurbishment, the future looks bright for this two-roomed village free house. The new kitchen provides an excellent range of food including the popular Sunday roast (no food Sun eve). Frequently changing guest beers often include ales from the local Dow Bridge Brewery. There is a garden to enjoy in summer. Pub games include table skittles. Close to the M1/M6 and A5. ⛰Q❀◐◑⛺♣P

Cavendish Bridge

Old Crown
DE72 2HL
⏲ 11-midnight (1am Fri & Sat); 12-midnight Sun
☎ (01332) 792392 🌐 oldcrown.batcave.net
Burtonwood Bitter; Camerons Strongarm; Marston's Pedigree; guest beers Ⓗ
Coaching inn dating from the 17th-century on the former route of the A6, close to the ruins of the bridge that crossed the River Trent. The original oak-beamed ceiling displays an extensive collection of old jugs. The walls are covered with pub mirrors, brewery signs and railway memorabilia. The cosy, open-plan interior is divided into two areas, one with a large inglenook. No evening meals are served Friday or Sunday. A varied beer range includes at least one beer from Jennings.
⛰❀🛏◐◑🚌P

Cropston

Bradgate Arms
15 Station Road, LE7 7HG
⏲ 11.30-11 (11.30 Fri & Sat); 12-10.30 Sun
☎ (0116) 234 0336
Banks's Bitter; Marston's Pedigree Ⓗ
Comfortable village pub popular with locals and tourists. Though extended to the rear in the early 1990s it retains many original features. Five drinking areas and a dining room are on two levels. The pub is handy for the Great Central Steam Railway and Bradgate Country Park. ❀◐◑P

Diseworth

Plough Inn
33 Hall Gate, DE74 2QJ
⏲ 11.30-3, 5-11; 11.30-11 Fri & Sat; 12-10.30 Sun
☎ (01332) 810333 🌐 theploughdiseworth.co.uk
Draught Bass; Caledonian Deuchars IPA; Marston's Pedigree; guest beers Ⓗ
Cosy multi-roomed pub with parts dating back to the 13th century. Low beamed ceilings and exposed brickwork are just some of the original features discovered during renovation work in the 1990s. The walls display an interesting range of old photographs of the local area. The Duck lounge (watch the low ceiling) is no-smoking and there is a restaurant serving good food.
⛰❀◐◑🚌P⚟

Earl Shilton

Dog & Gun
72 Keats Lane, LE9 7DR
⏲ 12-2.30 (not Mon-Thu), 5.30-11; 11.30-3.30, 5.30-11 Sat; 12-3, 7-10.30 Sun
☎ (01455) 842338
Banks's Original; Marston's Burton Bitter, Pedigree Ⓗ
Built behind the original pub, which was demolished in 1932, the pub is set back from the rest of the buildings on the street. It has three rooms including a bar with a tiled floor and a large log fire, and a snug. Meals are served at lunchtimes and evenings. With a number of walking routes in the area, the pub runs its own rambling club, as well as participating in many charity events. The attractive garden is a regular award winner.
⛰❀◐◑⊟♣P

East Langton

Bell Inn

Main Street, LE16 7TW

⏲ 12-2.30, 7 (6.30 Fri & Sat)-11; closed Mon; 12-5 Sun

☎ (01858) 545278

Greene King IPA, Abbot; Langton Caudle Bitter [H]

This 17th-century listed building is in the heart of Leicestershire's hunting country. Low beams and an open log fire add to the pub's appeal. Food is freshly prepared from local ingredients (no food Sun eve). The Langton Brewery, which used to brew in buildings behind the pub, has now moved to Thorpe Langton.

⌂Q❀⇆◐◑♿🚌(44)♣P

Enderby

New Inn

51 High Street, LE19 4AG

⏲ 12-2.30 (3 Sat; not Mon), 7 (5.30 Fri)-11; 12-3, 7-10.30 Sun

☎ (0116) 286 3126

Everards Beacon, Tiger, Original; guest beers [H]

Friendly, low-beamed village local, dating from 1549. This pub has two main rooms with a central bar, plus lounge. Acquired by founder William Everard in 1887, it was the first for the family brewery, although it had already gained its current name owing to a transfer of licence from a previous location nearby. Long alley skittles, darts and a full-size snooker table are part of the games culture here. Guest beers are from Everards Old English Ale Club.

⌂Q❀◐🚌♣P

Foxton

Foxton Locks Inn

Bottom Lock, Gumley Road, LE16 7RA

⏲ 11-11 daily

☎ (0116) 279 1515

Caledonian Deuchars IPA; Greene King Old Speckled Hen; Theakston Best Bitter, Old Peculier; guest beers [H]

This recently refurbished canalside inn sits at the foot of Foxton Locks, a major attraction on the Grand Union Canal. The canal director's office, once upstairs, has been recreated at the rear of the pub, complete with a collection or original share certificates on display. Outdoor seating runs down to the canal bank where boats may be moored. Families are welcome inside the pub which is no-smoking throughout. Blankets are available for outdoor drinkers.

❀◐◑♿▲P⚟

Frisby-on-the-Wreake

Bell Inn

2 Main Street, LE14 2NJ

⏲ 12-2.30, 6 (7 Sat)-11; 12-3, 7-10.30 Sun

☎ (01664) 434237

Greene King IPA, Abbot; guest beers [H]

This welcoming village local, dating back to 1759, is situated in a small village to the south of the river Wreake. The comfortable lounge/bar features oak beams, flagstone floors and an open fire. There is a family room and restaurant (no food Wed lunch or Sun eve). Two regular beers are complemented by three guests, often from breweries far afield.

⌂Q☕❀◐◑🚌P

Glooston

Old Barn Inn

Andrews Lane, LE16 7ST

⏲ 12-3, 6.30-11; closed Mon; 12-3, 6.30-11 Sun

☎ (01858) 545215

Bateman XB; Greene King IPA; guest beers [H]

This 16th-century rural inn is situated in a village that is a little off the beaten track, but well worth the detour. Low ceilings, oak beams and an open fire help to create a warm, welcoming atmosphere. Good food is served at lunchtime and in the evening. The house beer, Old Barn Bitter, is brewed by Langton Brewery. Westons cider is available in summer.

⌂☕❀◐◑♣●P

Gumley

Bell Inn

2 Main Street, LE16 7RU

⏲ 11-3, 6-11; 12-3 (closed eve) Sun

☎ (0116) 279 2476

Draught Bass; Bateman XB; Greene King IPA; guest beers [H]

This early 19th-century free house is popular with locals as well as a commuting urban clientele. Cricketing memorabilia adorns the entrance hall and fox hunting scenes hang on the walls of the bar and dining room. The beamed interior has an L-shaped bar and a no-smoking dining room serving an extensive menu. The pub has a large patio garden but children and dogs are not permitted here. ⌂Q❀◐◑♣P

Hathern

Dew Drop Inn

49 Loughborough Road, LE12 5HY

⏲ 12-2.30, 6-11; 12-3, 7-11 Sat; 12-3, 7-10.30 Sun

☎ (01509) 842438

Hardys & Hansons Mild, Bitter, Olde Trip, seasonal beers [H]

Traditional two-roomed local run by a long-established landlord who makes all visitors feel like regulars. A visit to the toilets is a must with their tiled walls and original features. A good range of malt whiskies is stocked, and cobs are available to order at lunchtime. ⌂Q❀🚆🚌♣P

Hemington

Jolly Sailor

21 Main Street, DE74 2RB

⏲ 11.30-2.30, 4.30-11; 11-11 Sat; 12-10.30 Sun

☎ (01332) 810448

Draught Bass; Greene King Abbot; Kelham Island Gold; M&B Mild; guest beers [H]

This 17th-century building is thought to have once been a weaver's cottage. A pub since the 19th century, it retains many original features including old timbers, open fires

and a beamed ceiling – a convenient place to hang the collection of blow lamps and beer mugs. The restaurant is available for functions and meetings. Draught cider is served. No food is available on Sunday. Local CAMRA Pub of the Year 2006.
♨Q❀◑♿🚌●P

Hinckley

New Plough Inn

24 Leicester Road, LE10 1LS (on B4668 opp. fire station)
✪ 5-11; 12-2.30, 6-11 Sat; 12-2.30, 6-10.30 Sun
☎ (01455) 615037
Marston's Burton Bitter, Pedigree Ⓗ
Built in 1900, this traditional roadside pub has a comfortable lounge with original wooden settles. The walls are adorned with local rugby memorabilia. The exterior features shields of local rugby clubs. Table skittles is played and the pub runs its own team. There is an outdoor area for drinking in summer. Dogs are welcome. ❀♣P

Hose

Black Horse

21 Bolton Lane, LE14 4JE
✪ 12-2 (not Mon-Thu), 7-midnight; 12-4, 7-10.30 Sun
☎ (01949) 860336
Adnams Bitter; Castle Rock Harvest Pale; Fuller's London Pride; guest beers Ⓗ
Traditional pub with a lounge featuring wooden beams and a brass-ornamented brick fireplace. Pictures and blackboard menus for food and drink surround a wooden corner bar (no food Sun eve). The unspoilt public bar, decorated with pictures and mirrors, has a tiled floor, wooden furniture and a brick fireplace. The rustic, wood-panelled restaurant serves good food using local produce.
♨Q❀◑⊟♿♣P⅍

Huncote

Red Lion

Main Street, LE9 3AU
✪ 12-2.30 (not Mon), 5-11; 12-11 Sat; 12-10.30 Sun
☎ (0116) 286 2233 🌐 red-lion.biz
Everards Beacon, Tiger; guest beers Ⓗ
Built in 1892, the Red Lion is a friendly local with a warm welcome. With beamed ceilings throughout, it has a cosy lounge with a wooden fireplace and log fire. The bar has an adjoining dining area and a separate pool room. The sizeable garden has picnic tables and a children's play area. The pub serves good value home-cooked lunches. Long alley skittles can be played by prior arrangement.
♨Q❀◐🚌♣P⅍

Illston on the Hill

Fox & Goose

Main Street, LE7 9EG (off B6047 near Three Gates)
✪ 12-2 (not Mon), 5.30 (7 Mon)-11; 12-2.30, 7-10.30 Sun
☎ (0116) 259 6340
Everards Beacon, Tiger, Original; guest beers Ⓗ
Cosy, unspoilt pub with a timeless feel, tucked away in the village and well worth seeking out. A fascinating collection of local mementos and hunting memorabilia is on display. In 1997, when structural work was needed, all the items on the walls were photographed and later returned to exactly the same place. That's how unchanged it is! Popular annual events include a conker championship, onion-growing competition and a fundraising auction for local charities.
♨Q❀⊟♣

Kegworth

Red Lion

24 High Street, DE74 2DA
✪ 11.30-11; 12-10.30 Sun
☎ (01509) 672466
Adnams Bitter; Archers Golden; Banks's Original; Courage Directors; Greene King Abbot; guest beers Ⓗ
Georgian building standing on the 19th-century route of the A6 London to Glasgow road. It has three small bars with bench seating and original features, and a no-smoking family/function room. Various flavoured Polish and Ukrainian vodkas, a good selection of malt whiskies, and up to four guest beers are stocked. There is a skittle alley and petanque courts. Outside is a large garden with children's play area. No food is served on Sunday.
♨Q🛏❀⇌◑⊟♣●P⅍

Leicester

Ale Wagon

27 Rutland Street, LE1 1RE
✪ 11-11; 12-3, 7-10.30 Sun
☎ (0116) 262 3330 🌐 alewagon.co.uk
Hoskins Hob Best Mild, Brigadier, Bitter, White Dolphin, Tom Kellys Stout, Ⓟ EXS; guest beers Ⓗ
A friendly local atmosphere pervades the 1930s interior of this pub, run by the Hoskins family. It boasts an original oak staircase and has two rooms with tiled and parquet floors and a central bar. There is always a varied selection of Hoskins Brothers ales and guests available. The pub is popular with rugby fans and real ale drinkers visiting the town. Voted Leicester CAMRA Pub of the Year in 2004.
♨⊟⇌🚌♣⅍

Black Horse

1 Foxon Street, LE3 5LT (on A47 Braunstone Gate)
✪ 3 (12 Sat)-midnight (11 Mon); 7-midnight Sun
☎ (0116) 254 0030
Everards Beacon, Tiger, Best Bitter, seasonal beers; guest beers Ⓗ
Small, cosy street-corner pub – the only traditional pub left on Braunstone Gate, now surrounded by wine bars. With all the character of a lively local, it has two rooms and a central bar. There is a general knowledge quiz on Wednesday and Sunday – the longest running in Leicester. Live music is hosted on Monday, Tuesday and Thursday with an acoustic session on Saturday evening. Up to five guest beers are from Everards Old English Ale Club, and Westons Old Rosie cider is sold.
⊟🚌●

Criterion
44 Millstone Lane LE1 5JN
✪ 12-11; 12-10.30 Sun
☎ (0116) 262 5418
Oakham JHB, Bishops Farewell; guest beers Ⓗ
Two-roomed city centre pub built in the 1960s. Formerly an M&B house, a collection of international brewery memorabilia adorns the walls. A large selection of imported bottled beers is stocked as well as up to 10 guest beers from micro and regional breweries. Popular live music sessions are held on Saturday afternoon and Thursday evening. Home-baked Italian-style pizzas are the house speciality (Tue-Sat). Regular beer festivals are held. The pub is busy on match days with football and rugby supporters. Winner of Leicester CAMRA City Pub of the Year in 2006.
❀◐◑🚌♣

Globe
43 Silver Street, LE1 5EU
✪ 11-11 (1am Fri & Sat); 12-10.30 Sun
☎ (0116) 262 9819
Everards Beacon, Sunchaser, Tiger, Original, seasonal beers; guest beers Ⓗ
Almost 30 years ago, this city-centre pub was hailed as Everards' first pub to return to a full real ale range after seven years as keg only. Major renovations in 2000 moved the bar to the centre of the pub and created four drinking areas. The yard became part of the pub interior. There is a snug, and gas lighting throughout (electric too). An upstairs room is regularly used for Leicester CAMRA meetings; its first meeting was held here in 1974, as well as its 25-year bash. A friendly welcome awaits all.
◐⊟🚌♿

Leicester Gateway
52 Gateway Street, LE2 7DP
✪ 11 (12 Sat)-11; 12-10.30 Sun
☎ (0116) 255 7319
Castle Rock Harvest Pale; Everards Tiger; guest beers Ⓗ
A warm welcome greets all visitors to this friendly free house in a converted hosiery factory. Six real ales are usually available with up to nine at busy times. Imported bottled beers are also stocked. Home-made food is served all day and the Sunday lunchtime carvery is always popular. Quiz night is Sunday. Close to both Leicester City football and Tigers rugby grounds, the pub is busy on match days. ◐◑🚌♣●⚡

Out of the Vaults
24 King Street, LE1 6RL
✪ 12-11; 12-10.30 Sun
☎ (07976) 222378
Beer range varies Ⓗ
City centre free house serving up to 12 real ales, specialising in small independent and micro-brewery beers. Real ale enthusiasts visit regularly for the frequent beer festivals. Close to the rugby and football grounds, the pub is busy with supporters on match days. The bar room is accessible from New Walk as well as King Street. Leicester CAMRA City Pub of the Year in 2005. ⇌🚌●▯

Shakespeare's Head
Southgates, LE1 5SH
✪ 12-midnight (1am Fri & Sat); 12-11 Sun
☎ (0116) 262 4378
Oakwell Old Tom Mild; Barnsley Bitter Ⓗ
This two-roomed local was built alongside the underpass in the 1960s and has changed little since then – it retains all the charm of a typical town pub of its era. It has two large glass doors leading to an off-sales area with a bar to the left and lounge to the right. Formerly a Shipstones pub, it now sells Oakwell beers at reasonable prices.
◐⊟♿🚌♣

Swan & Rushes
19 Infirmary Square, LE1 5WR
✪ 12-11; 12-10.30 Sun
☎ (0116) 233 9167
Oakham JHB, Bishops Farewell; guest beers Ⓗ
Triangular, two-roomed 1930s pub in the city centre with the atmosphere of a country pub. Up to five real ales are usually available and a good selection of imported bottled beers. Two German beer festivals and cheese and cider festivals are held as well as real ale events. A popular pub close to Leicester Royal Infirmary and the football and rugby grounds, it is often busy.
❀◐⊟🚌●♣⚡

Talbot
4 Thurcaston Road, LE4 5PF
✪ 11.30-3 (4 Fri), 6-11; 11.30-4, 6.30-midnight Sat; 12-4, 7-10.30 Sun
☎ (0116) 266 2280
Ansells Mild, Best Bitter; Marston's Pedigree Ⓗ
There has been a pub on this site since the 15th century and the cellars date back to the 12th century, owned by the church until the 19th century. This friendly local in the heart of old Belgrave consists of two lounge areas. Handy for the historic Belgrave Hall (reputed to be haunted), Abbey pumping station and the National Space Centre, it is a 10-minute walk from the Great Central Railway (steam) Leicester North station which connects with Rothley, Quorn and Loughborough.
♨❀◐🚌♣P

Tudor
100 Tudor Road, LE3 5HT
✪ 12-2.30, 5-11; 11-11 Thu & Fri; 11-11.30 Sat; 12-10.30 Sun
☎ (0116) 262 0087
Everards Beacon, Tiger Ⓗ
A corner pub in a terraced area with a Victorian exterior. Inside are two rooms – a bar and a lounge. There is a function room upstairs with table skittles. Darts and pool are also played. ⊟♣

Loughborough

Albion
Canal Bank LE11 1QA
✪ 11-3 (4 Sat), 6-11; 12-3, 7-10.30 Sun
☎ (01509) 213952
Archers Best Bitter; Brains Dark; guest beers Ⓗ
This canalside pub was built in the late 18th century at the same time as the Loughborough Canal. It has a bar, darts room

and quiet lounge (no-smoking until 8pm). Outside is a patio with an aviary. The house beer, Albion Special, is brewed for the pub by the local Wicked Hathern Brewery. Take care if driving to the pub along the narrow towpath. ⌂Q❀◐◗≠⊟♣P⊬

Plough Inn

28 Thorpe Acre Road, LE11 4LF

✪ 12-3, 7-11; 12-11 Sat; 12-10.30 Sun

☎ (01509) 214101

Draught Bass; M&B Mild; guest beers ⊞

Dating from around the early 19th century the building was part of the original Thorpe Acre village and is now surrounded by modern houses. The pub's unusual appearance is due to a change in road layout that has resulted in the back of the pub adjoining the road. To the 'front' of the pub are gardens and a children's play area. The split-level interior has the bar and front entrance lower than the lounge, which is accessed via steps leading from the road. Live entertainment is hosted most weekends. Q❀⊟⊟♣P

Swan in the Rushes

21 The Rushes, LE11 5BE

✪ 11-11 (midnight Fri & Sat); 12-10.30 Sun

☎ (01509) 217014

Adnams Bitter; Archers Golden; Castle Rock Rushes Gold, Harvest Pale ⊞

Three-room Tynemill pub with separate no-smoking rooms, comprising a comfortable lounge, family room and the Vaults with a juke box and wooden bench seating. Up to six guest beers are available including a mild, as well as real cider and perry. There is also a limited range of continental bottled and draught beers, and a selection of malt whiskies and country wines. Upstairs the skittle alley/function room hosts live music and twice-yearly beer festivals. Well-behaved dogs are welcome. ⌂Q☎❀⇄◐◗⊟♿≠⊟●P⊬

Tap & Mallet

36 Nottingham Road, LE11 1EU

✪ 5-11; 11.30-11 Sat; 12-10.30 Sun

☎ (01509) 210028

Churchend Gravediggers; Courage Best Bitter; guest beers ⊞

Genuine free house situated on a direct route from the railway station to the town centre. The five guests are from micro-breweries, often from the east or north-east midlands, and usually beers that are rarely seen in the Loughborough area. Draught cider or perry is also stocked. The pub has a single room split into two, and there is a pool table. The lounge can be partitioned off for private functions. Outside, the secluded walled garden has children's play equipment and a pets' corner. Cobs are available all day. ⌂❀≠⊟♣●

Lutterworth

Fox Inn

34 Rugby Road, LE17 4BN (off M1 jct 20 on A426)

✪ 12-3, 5-11; 12-11 Fri & Sat; 12-3, 7-10.30 Sun

☎ (01455) 552677

Adnams Bitter; Greene King Old Speckled Hen; Taylor Landlord; guest beer ⊞

Warm and welcoming pub with an L-shaped open plan interior featuring real log fires. The room is richly decorated with many items of motor racing and rallying memorabilia, plus rugby football shirts and footballs. RAF and other aircraft photographs are also on the walls. A good menu including a specials board is available daily. ⌂❀◐P

Unicorn Inn

29 Church Street, LE17 4AE (on one-way system near church)

✪ 10.30-11 (midnight Fri & Sat); 12-11.30 Sun

☎ (01455) 552486

Draught Bass; Greene King IPA; M&B Brew XI; Robinson's Unicorn ⊞

Busy and friendly traditional town centre corner pub run by the same landlord for 25 years. The large public bar is well supported by local teams playing darts and skittles. Football and rugby matches are shown on large-screen TVs. The quieter lounge has its own bar decorated with many photographs of old Lutterworth. Inexpensive lunchtime snacks and meals are served throughout the week. ⌂❀⇄◐⊟♣P

Market Bosworth

Olde Red Lion Hotel

1 Park Street, CV13 0LL

✪ 11 (10 Wed)-2.30, 5.30-11; 10-11.30 Fri & Sat; 11-10.30 Sun

☎ (01455) 291713

🌐 yeolderedlionmarketbosworth.com

Banks's Original, Bitter; Camerons Bitter; Greene King Abbot; Marston's Pedigree; Theakston Old Peculier; guest beers ⊞

Popular with all ages, the hotel is situated near the old market square. It has a large beamed bar and dining area with an open fire in winter. The range of beers, including two guests, is extensive. A varied menu offers good food at sensible prices, served daily at lunchtime and in the evening (Tue-Sat). Accommodation includes bedrooms with four-poster beds. ⌂❀⇄◐◗P⊬

Market Harborough

Cherry Tree

Church Walk, Kettering Road, Little Bowden, LE16 8AE

✪ 12-2.30, 5-11 (12.30am Fri & Sat); 12-11 Sun

☎ (01858) 463525

Everards Beacon, Tiger, Original ⊞

This spacious pub has low beams and a thatched roof. Drinkers and diners can choose from many alcoves and seating areas. Although the pub is situated in Little Bowden it is very much part of the Market Harborough community. A beer festival is held over the August bank holiday. Guest beers are from Everards Old English Ale Club. ❀◐◗≠♣⊬

Markfield

Bull's Head

23 Forest Road, LE67 9UN (½ mile from M1 jct 22)

✪ 3 (2 Fri)-11.30; 11-midnight Sat; 12-11.30 Sun

☎ (01530) 242541

Banks's Original; Marston's Burton Bitter, Pedigree Ⓗ
Long-established two-roomed local tucked away in the corner of the village with a friendly welcome for all. A typical village inn, it is full of traditional character.
Q⊟♣

Medbourne

Nevill Arms
12 Waterfall Way, LE16 8EE
12-2.30, 6-11; 12-3, 7-11 Sun
☎ (01858) 565 288
Adnams Bitter; Fuller's London Pride; Greene King Abbot; guest beers Ⓗ
The initials MGN over the door are those of Captain Nevill, who was heir to the nearby Holt estate when this former coaching inn was rebuilt in 1863 after the original building was destroyed by fire in 1856. Folklore suggests that a spark caused the fire after the village blacksmith wagered that he could support an anvil on his chest while a horseshoe was forged on it. A warm welcome awaits inside the heavily-beamed bar with its large inglenook.
⌂❀⇌0▶♣P

Melton Mowbray

Crown Inn
10 Burton Street, LE13 1AE
11-3, 7-11; 11-11 Sat; 12-4, 7-10.30 Sun
☎ (01664) 564682
Everards Beacon, Tiger, Original; guest beers Ⓗ
Sociable, two-bar pub run by a long-serving landlord. In the centre of town, the pub is popular with workers and shoppers at lunchtime. Smoking is not permitted in the lounge when lunches are being served. Owned by Everards, the pub offers at least one guest ale in addition to the Everards range. Access is easy by bus and the train station is nearby. No food is served on Sunday and Monday, or Friday and Saturday evenings. ⌂Q0▶⊟⇌⊟

Harboro Hotel
49 Burton Street, LE13 1AF
11-11; 12-10.30 Sun
☎ (01664) 560121 harborohotel.com
Beer range varies Ⓗ
An 18th-century coaching inn close to the station and town centre. The comfortable bar serves four guest beers and a range of draught and bottled German and Belgian beers. There are two lounges, one with comfortable sofas. Meals and bar snacks are served daily except Sunday evening. There are good bus links and the railway station is nearby. See the website for details of beer festivals. ⇌0▶♿⇌P

Moira

Woodman
1 Shortheath Road, DE12 6AL
12-11; 12-10.30 Sun
☎ (01283) 218316
Greene King Abbot; Marston's Pedigree; Wells Bombardier; guest beer Ⓗ
Formerly called the Rawdon Arms after the local mine which closed in the 1980s. The walls are covered with commemorative plates depicting local coal mines, the last of which closed in 1990. There is a separate pool room that can be converted to a dining area or meeting room. This popular pub was local CAMRA Most Improved Pub in 2004.
❀⊟♣P

Mountsorrel

Swan Inn
10 Loughborough Road, LE12 7AT
12-2.30, 5.30-11; 12-11 Sat; 12-3, 7-10.30 Sun
☎ (0116) 230 2340 jvf.co.uk/swan
Greene King Ruddles County; Theakston Best Bitter, XB, Old Peculier; guest beers Ⓗ
Traditional 17th-century coaching inn, formerly called the Nag's Head, under the present ownership since 1990. The split-level bar has stone floors, bench seating and low ceilings. There is a small dining area with a polished wood floor that leads off a further room which can be used for dining or drinking. Westons bottled cider is stocked. Good quality, interesting food is cooked to order and the menu changes fortnightly. Outside is a secluded riverside garden with moorings available locally.
⌂❀⇌0▶⊟P

Newton Burgoland

Belper Arms
Main Street, LE67 2SE
12-midnight (1am Fri & Sat); 12-midnight Sun
☎ (01530) 270530
Marston's Pedigree; guest beers Ⓗ
Genuine village free house dating from 1290, with a warm, friendly atmosphere. Reputed to be the oldest pub in Leicestershire, it has many historical artefacts, even a ghost, '5 to 4 Fred'. The pub has one large low-beamed bar with several alcoves. Four frequently-changing guest beers are usually available. Food, from snacks to a la carte and specials, is served every lunchtime and evening, either in the bar or dining area. The location is ideal for exploring the surrounding countryside. ⌂Q❀0▶ÅP

Oadby

Cow & Plough
Stoughton Farm Park, Gartree Road, LE2 2FB
12-3, 5-11 daily (12-11 summer Tue-Sun)
☎ (0116) 272 0852
Fuller's London Pride; Steamin' Billy Bitter, Skydiver; guest beers Ⓗ
Situated in a converted farm building with a no-smoking conservatory, the pub is decked out with breweriana. It is home to Steamin' Billy beers, named after the owner's Jack Russell featured on its logo, and brewed under licence by Grainstore of Oakham. A guest mild and Westons cider are always available. Twice CAMRA's East Midlands Pub of the Year, it was also Leicester Pub of the Year in 2005 and 2006.
Q❀0▶⊟♿⊟♣●P⚟

Pinwall

Red Lion

Main Road, CV9 3NB (at B4116/B5000 jct 1 mile from A5)
❂ 12-11; 12-10.30 Sun
☎ (01827) 712223
Draught Bass; Greene King IPA, Abbot; Marston's Pedigree; Taylor Landlord; guest beer 🄷
This rural, cosy, unspoilt locals' pub is one of only five or six buildings that make up Pinwall – a village so tiny that it does not even appear on most maps. The Red Lion includes a restaurant and six-room accommodation; room prices may be negotiated at weekends. Evening meals are not served on Sunday. ♨Q✿🛏◐◑♣P

Seagrave

White Horse

6 Church Street, LE12 7LT
❂ 12-12.30, 5.30-11; 12-11 Sat; 12-10.30 Sun
☎ (01509) 814715
Greene King IPA, Abbot; Wadworth 6X 🄷
Cosy two-roomed pub with open fires and a piano in the lounge where local groups and enthusiasts meet for a folk night on Thursday. The bar is popular with the local darts and dominoes teams. Prints of horse racing adorn the walls along with plates depicting hunting scenes. The bus service is limited. ♨✿◐◑⊟🚌♣P

Shepshed

Black Swan

21 Loughborough Road, LE12 9DL
❂ 7-midnight; 12-3, 5 (6 Sat)-1am Fri & Sat; 12-midnight Sun
☎ (01509) 502659
Adnams Broadside; Draught Bass; Greene King Abbot; Taylor Landlord; guest beer 🄷
Situated in a prominent position close to the town centre, this multi-roomed pub has been modernised and rejuvenated by the present licensees. The main room has two drinking areas, both with comfortable seating. A further small room can be used by families. The upstairs restaurant serves good quality food (Thu eve, Fri and Sat lunch and eve and 12-5pm Sun). Shepshed Dynamo football ground is nearby. Q♘✿🛏◐◑🚌P

Somerby

Stilton Cheese

High Street, LE14 2QB
❂ 12-3, 6-11; 12-3, 7-10.30 Sun
☎ (01664) 454394
Grainstore Ten Fifty; Marston's Pedigree; Tetley Bitter; guest beers 🄷
Late 16th-century pub built in the local ironstone, as are most of the buildings in the village. Tall customers in particular will notice the wide range of pump clips on the low beams (mind your head). There are two rooms, one no-smoking, and a function room. A varying real cider is always available. A popular pub for dining – booking is advisable. ♨Q♘✿◐◑♣P⊬

Three Crowns Inn

39 High Street, LE14 2QB
❂ 12-2.30, 6.30 (5.30 Fri)-11; 12-10.30 Sun
☎ (01664) 454777
Draught Bass; Greene King IPA; Parish Special; guest beer 🄷
Traditional village pub on the main street. This 15th-century hostelry was given by Sir Richard Sutton to Brasenose College, Oxford, in 1508. The interior is cosy and full of character with a large open fireplace. Ales from the local Parish Brewery are available. There is live music on the first Saturday of the month. ♨Q✿◐◑♿▲♣P

Sproxton

Crown Inn

Coston Road, LE14 4QB
❂ 5 (12 Sat)-11; 12-10.30 Sun
☎ (01476) 860035
Greene King XX Mild, IPA, Abbot 🄷
Unspoilt, creeper-covered, stone building on the edge of the Vale of Belvoir, popular with locals and visitors. The bar has several comfy chairs, an open fire and a small TV in the corner. Four handpumps serve beers from the Greene King stable, including the cask mild. A full food menu is offered and there is a room set aside for dining (no food weekday lunchtime or Sun eve). ♨✿◐◑⊟♿♣P

Swinford

Chequers

High Street, LE17 6BL
❂ 12-2.30 (3 Sat; not Mon), 6-midnight; 12-3, 7-11 Sun
☎ (01788) 860318 🌐 chequersswinford.co.uk
Adnams Bitter; guest beers 🄷
This popular, friendly village pub has been run by the same family for 18 years. A traditional inn, it caters for all ages. Bar meals are served including vegetarian options and daily specials (not Sun eve). Three cask beers are usually available, with two regularly changing guests. Table skittles is played in the bar area. The large garden with benches and children's play area is popular in summer. An annual beer festival is held in July. ✿◐◑▲♣P

Swithland

Griffin Inn

174 Main Street, LE12 8TJ
❂ 11-11; 12-10.30 Sun
☎ (01509) 890535 🌐 griffininnswithland.com
Everards Beacon, Tiger, Original; guest beers 🄷
Friendly and welcoming local with three comfortable rooms, a restaurant, function room and long alley skittles. Set in the heart of Charnwood Forest, there are many cycling and walking routes nearby. Swithland Reservoir, Bradgate Park and the preserved Great Central Railway are also close. Meals are served all day on Saturday and Sunday and light snacks every afternoon including Dickinson and Morris pork pies. The guest beer is from the Everards Old English Ale Club. ♨Q✿◐◑♿♣P⊬

Thrussington

Blue Lion

5 Rearsby Road, LE7 4UD
✪ 12-2.30 (not Wed), 5.30-11; 12-3, 6-11 Sat; 12-3, 7-10.30 Sun
☎ (01664) 424266
Marston's Burton Bitter, Pedigree; guest beer Ⓗ
Late 18th-century rural pub that was once two cottages. Recently refurbished, it has a comfortable lounge where you can enjoy good value pub food including meat provided by the local butcher. The bar is the heart of the pub, where locals meet to challenge each other to high pressure darts and dominoes matches, refereed by licensees Mandy and Bob. Note the extensive collection of teapots – 160 at the last count. There is a secluded garden and petanque pitch at the rear of the pub.
⛫❀◐◑⊟⛺🚌♣P

Walcote

Black Horse

25 Lutterworth Road, LE17 4JU (on A4304 1 mile E of M1 jct 20)
✪ 12-2, 5-midnight; closed Mon & Tue; 12-midnight Fri & Sat; 12-10.30 Sun
☎ (01455) 552684
Oakham JHB; Taylor Landlord; guest beers Ⓗ
It is well worth taking a short detour from the M1 to visit this roadside free house at the heart of the community. Locals mix with visitors attracted by the renowned home-cooked Thai food, for which the pub has built up an excellent reputation over the last 20 years. There are usually four guest beers sourced from independent breweries.
⛫❀◐◑🚌(58)P⚡

Walton-on-the-Wolds

Anchor Inn

2 Loughborough Road, LE12 8HT
✪ 12-3 (not Mon), 6.30-11; 12-3, 7-10.30 Sun
☎ (01509) 880018
Adnams Bitter; Marston's Pedigree; Taylor Landlord; guest beer Ⓗ
Situated in an elevated position in the centre of the village, the pub has an open plan, comfortable L-shaped lounge with an open fire. Prints and photographs of classic cars and village scenes adorn the walls. One corner is dedicated to sporting memorabilia and trophies. Good quality food is served Tuesday to Saturday, and a roast on Sunday lunchtime. A mild, often from Theakston, is usually available. Local morris dancers perform in the car park in summer. A paddock is available by arrangement.
⛫Q❀◐◑🚌P

Whitwick

Three Horseshoes ☆

11 Leicester Road, LE67 5GN
✪ 11-3, 6.30-11; 12-2, 7-10.30 Sun
☎ (01530) 837311
Draught Bass; M&B Mild; Marston's Pedigree Ⓗ
Grade II listed building that features in CAMRA's National Inventory of pubs with interiors of outstanding historic interest. Its nickname, 'Polly's', is thought to refer to a former landlady, Polly Burton. Originally two separate buildings, they were joined possibly in 1882. The long bar has a quarry-tiled floor and open fires, wooden bench seating and pre-war fittings. The small snug is similarly full of character. The original outside toilets are still in use.
⛫Q⊟🚌♣

Wymondham

Berkeley Arms

Main Street, LE14 2AG
✪ 12-3 (not Mon), 6-11; 12-3, 7-10.30 Sun
☎ (01572) 787587
Greene King IPA; Marston's Pedigree; guest beer Ⓗ
Large stone-built pub in the centre of the village. The interior has been modernised while retaining the character of the building. The pub is popular with diners as well as drinkers and can become quite busy. One guest ale is always available alongside the regulars, as well as Addlestones real cider.
⛫Q❀◐◑♿●P

RUTLAND

Barrowden

Exeter Arms

28 Main Street, LE15 8EQ (next to duck pond)
✪ 12-2.30 (not Mon), 6-11; 12- 3, 7-10:30 Sun
☎ (01572) 747247
Barrowden Beach Boys, Bevin Boys, Danny Boys; Greene King IPA; guest beers Ⓗ
Collyweston stone-built pub overlooking the village green and duck pond. Inside, there is one long room with a dining area at one end (no food served Sun eve or Mon). Smoking and use of mobile phones are not permitted. A barn at the end of the garden houses the Barrowden Brewery (once the Blencowe Brewery), now under new ownership. The garden has excellent views across the Welland Valley on sunny days. Petanque is played. Three letting rooms are available.
⛫Q❀🛏◐◑♿♣P⚡

Belton in Rutland

Sun Inn

24 Main Street, LE15 9LB (½ mile from A47)
✪ 12-1.30, 6-11; 12-10.30 Sun
☎ (01572) 717227
Banks's Bitter; guest beer Ⓗ
This cosy pub is tucked away in a small, quiet village and is well worth a detour from the nearby A47. It was originally a Phipps pub until it was swallowed up by Watneys in the early 1970s. On three floor levels, including a games room, little has changed since the 1960s. It has an unusual washer on nail system for recording drinks left in by locals. This typical country local is unspoilt by the passage of time.
⛫Q❀🚌♣

Braunston in Rutland

Old Plough Inn

2 Church Street, LE15 8QY

☼ 11-11 (midnight Sat); 12-10.30 Sun

☎ (01572) 722714

Grainstore Cooking, Ten Fifty; guest beers Ⓗ

One of just a few pubs owned by the Grainstore Brewery, this popular inn has a bar and comfortable low-beamed lounge, conservatory/restaurant and patio garden. Not all the pub's spirits come in bottles: footsteps and slamming doors have been heard long after closing time. Two guest beers are usually on handpump.

Greetham

Plough

23 Main Street, LE15 7NJ

☼ 11-3, 5-11; 11-11 Thu-Sat; 12-10.30 Sun

☎ (01572) 813613

Beer range varies Ⓗ

Stone-built pub with a comfortable carpeted bar and open fire. There is a smaller no-smoking room. A mild is always available, as well as Westons Old Rosie cider. The kitchen specialises in fresh food made with local ingredients and baguettes sold by the foot. The pub has a quiz team, petanque and darts teams, hosts the Greetham reading circle and provides community Internet facilities. Pub games include devil among the tailors, quoits, Jenga, solitaire, dominoes and cribbage. In other words, this is a genuine village local.

Oakham

Grainstore

Station Approach, LE15 6RE

☼ 11-11 (midnight Fri & Sat); 11-11 Sun

☎ (01572) 770065 ⊕ grainstorebrewery.com

Grainstore Rutland Panther, Cooking, Triple B, Ten Fifty; guest beers Ⓗ

The pub and brewery derive their name from the former Victorian grainstore they occupy, situated next to the railway station. The large bar has wooden flooring and steel pillars that support the upper floor where the brewery is located. Part of the brewery can be seen through a glass panel in the bar. A good selection of Belgian bottled beers is also stocked. Wooden chairs and tables on the hardstanding area in front of the pub are popular for outdoor drinking in summer.

Stretton

Jackson Stops

Rookery Lane, LE15 7RA

☼ 12-2.30, 6.30-11; closed Mon; 12-3 Sun

☎ (01780) 410237

Oakham JHB; guest beer Ⓗ

This 17th-century inn with whitewashed stone walls is situated in the heart of the village. It has four dining rooms offering good value food and excellent service. The public bar has a real fire and stocks a small but interesting range of bottled beers. Traditional games include nurdling, which is played in only one other pub in England. Ask how the pub got its name!

What is real ale?

Real ale is also known as cask-conditioned beer or simply cask beer. In the brewery, the beer is neither filtered nor pasteurised. It still contains sufficient yeast and sugar for it to continue to ferment and mature in the cask. Once it has reached the pub cellar, it has to be laid down for maturation to continue, and for yeast and protein to settle at the bottom of the cask. Some real ale also has extra hops added as the cask is filled, a process known as 'late hopping' for increased flavour and aroma. Cask beer is best served at a cellar temperature of 11-12 degrees C, although some stronger ales can benefit from being served a little warmer. Each cask has two holes, in one of which a tap is inserted and is connected to tubes or 'lines' that enable the beer to be drawn to the bar. The other hole, on top of the cask, enables some carbon dioxide produced during secondary fermentation to escape. It is vital that some gas, which gives the beer its natural sparkle or condition, is kept within the cask: the escape of gas is controlled by inserting porous wooden pegs called spiles into the spile hole. Real ale is a living product and must be consumed within three or four days of a cask being tapped as oxidation develops.

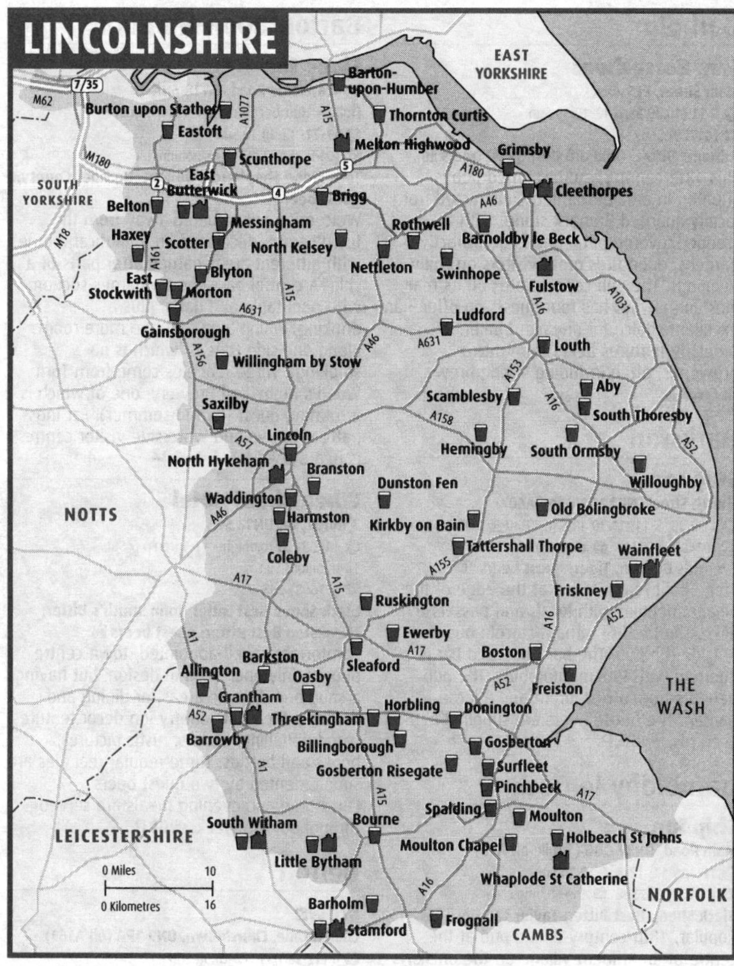

Aby

Railway Tavern

Main Road, LN13 0DR (off A16 via S Thoresby)

12-12.30 daily (closed winter Tue)

☎ (01507) 480676

Bateman XB; Everards Tiger; guest beer Ⓗ

Cosy village pub off the beaten track close to Claythorpe Watermill, offering good food and a guest beer that changes often. With open fires and beams aplenty, it also displays railway memorabilia, including the original Aby platform sign. It holds a quiz night on Wednesday and is known for its excellent theme nights and games in support of local charities. Dogs are welcome at this pub, which has good local walks and fishing nearby. ₼Q❀◑♿♣P

Allington

Welby Arms

The Green, NG32 2EA (1 mile from A1 Gonerby Moor roundabout)

12-2.30, 6-11; 12-4, 6-10.30 Sun

☎ (01400) 281361

Draught Bass; John Smith's Bitter; Taylor Landlord; guest beers Ⓗ

Picture postcard village inn, ideally placed for visits to Belvoir Castle, Isaac Newton's birthplace and the historic town of Stamford. It provides comfortable accommodation, as well as good food in the no-smoking dining area. There are usually six beers on offer, with three weekly changing guests. A monthly quiz (third Mon) attracts teams from a wide area. The pub is a regular in this Guide. ₼Q❀⇆◑♿P

INDEPENDENT BREWERIES

Bateman Wainfleet
Blue Bell Whaplode St Catherine
Blue Cow South Witham
DarkTribe East Butterwick
Fugelstou Fulstow
Highwood/Tom Wood Melton Highwood
Melbourn Stamford
Newby Wyke Little Bytham
Oldershaw Grantham
Poachers North Hykeham
Riverside Wainfleet
Willy's Cleethorpes

Barholm

Five Horseshoes

Main Street, PE9 4RA
⏲ 5-11 (10.30 Sat); 12-10.30 Sun
☎ (01778) 560238
Adnams Bitter; Oakham JHB; guest beers Ⓗ
This 18th-century, multi-roomed pub is situated in a quiet hamlet. Constructed from locally quarried Barnack stone, with a creeper-covered patio and large attractive gardens, open fires greet visitors on chilly evenings. The pub concentrates on its real ales and always has four guests on offer – an excellent choice for any ale drinker. It regularly features beers from micro-breweries, often including strong brews.
♔Q⇄▲

Barkston

Stag Inn

Church Street, NG32 2NB (off A607)
⏲ 11-2.30, 5-11; 11.30-11 Sat; 12.30-3, 6-10.30 Sun
☎ (01400) 250363 🌐 the-stag.com
Everards Beacon, Tiger; guest beers Ⓗ
Stone built roadside inn at the edge of the village, popular with locals and passers-by alike. The local Grantham-Lincoln bus stops outside the pub. The bare-boarded bar is adorned with RAF memorabilia. The pub benefits from a restaurant and a large garden. The house beers are supplied by Everards. ✿♿🚌P

Barnoldby le Beck

Ship Inn

Main Road, DN37 0BG (1 mile off A18)
⏲ 12-3, 6-11; 12-3, 6-10.30 Sun
☎ (01472) 822308 🌐 the-shipinn.com
Black Sheep Best Bitter; Taylor Landlord Ⓗ
Popular, 18th-century dining pub at the centre of an affluent village on the outskirts of Grimsby. A fine example of a traditional country inn, with a friendly atmosphere and an open fire, the pleasant interior is largely wood panelled displaying memorabilia on the walls and ceiling. The restaurant at the rear serves excellent fare, specialising in seafood often caught by the landlord's own fishing boats. The patio has benches for summer drinking.
♔Q✿P⊁

Barrowby

White Swan

High Road, NG32 1HN (off A1 and A52)
⏲ 11.30-midnight (1am Fri & Sat); 11.30-midnight Sun
☎ (01476) 562375
Adnams Bitter, Broadside; Greene King IPA; guest beer Ⓗ
Village pub, comprising two bars: a quiet, comfortable lounge and a larger public bar with music, a pool table and dartboard where sporting memorabilia line the walls. The garden, off the car park, is some way from the pub, but has shady trees and swings for children. Good, simple food is served at lunchtime.
Q✿◑⊟♣P

Barton-upon-Humber

Sloop Inn

81 Waterside Road, DN18 5BA
(follow Humber Bridge viewing signs)
⏲ 11-11; 12-10.30 Sun
☎ (01652) 637287 🌐 sloopinn.net
Tom Wood Shepherd's Delight, Bomber County; guest beer Ⓗ
Welcoming pub situated away from the town centre, decorated on a nautical theme, with different areas named after parts of a ship. A central bar serves a games section with pool table and darts, plus a drinking/dining area and two more rooms along one side (one of which is no-smoking). Three real ales come from Tom Wood's Highwood Brewery, one of which is a rotating guest (two in summer). Far Ings nature reserve and Waterside visitor centre is nearby. ✿◑◗♿▲≠♣⊁

Wheatsheaf Hotel

3 Holydyke, DN18 5PS
⏲ 11-3.30, 5-midnight; 11-1am Fri & Sat; 12-midnight Sun
☎ (01652) 633175
Black Sheep Best Bitter; John Smith's Bitter; Theakston Best Bitter; guest beers Ⓗ
Comfortable, well-appointed, town-centre pub, mainly open-plan in design, but having a snug and discrete areas for dining and drinking. Pleasant country inn decor features wood panelling, beams, rustic pictures, books and bottles. Three regular real ales are supplemented by two guest beers. Lunchtime and evening meals are served throughout the week. ✿◑◗P

Belton

Crown

Church Lane, Churchtown, DN9 1PA (off A161)
⏲ 4 (12 Sat)-11; 12-10.30 Sun
☎ (01427) 872834
Marston's Pedigree; Theakston Best Bitter; Tom Wood Best Bitter; guest beers Ⓗ
Difficult to find but well worth the effort, this friendly local is a haven for the discerning beer drinker. No smooth beers are kept and no food is served. The Highwood (Tom Wood) Bitter has recently become a fixture, while beers from the nearby Glentworth Brewery are served on a rotating basis. A games room is situated at the back of the pub. ♔✿♣P

Wheatsheaf

152 Westgate Road, DN9 1QB (from A161 follow Westgate Rd towards Sandtoft)
⏲ 5-midnight (1am Fri & Sat); 5-midnight Sun
☎ (01427) 872504
Caledonian Deuchars IPA; Everards Tiger; guest beers Ⓗ
Family-run village pub with a friendly atmosphere. All ages are catered for here with weekend entertainment ranging from live rock bands to a piano, which is played on Sundays. The owners are committed to real ale, offering a variety of guest beers, but no food. The garden is a recent addition, while the decor is a somewhat curious mix

of Hollywood legends and photos of Old Belton. ♨❀♣P

Billingborough

Fortescue Arms

27 High Street, NG34 0QB
⏲ 12-3, 5.30-11; 12-11 Sun
☎ (01529) 240228
Fuller's London Pride; Greene King IPA; Tetley Burton Ale Ⓗ

Grade II listed, fine country inn set in a village with spring wells. The oak-beamed bar and lounge have that country feel and tubs of plants, shrubs and vines brighten three sides of the pub. Home-made food is popular. Nearby is the site of Sempringham Abbey with a monument to Gwenllian, daughter of the Prince of Wales, who was confined to the priory in the 12th century. Stone from the Abbey was used to build parts of the inn. ♨Q❀◐▮▣♿▲P

Blyton

Black Horse

93 High Street, DN21 3JX
⏲ 5-midnight (1am Fri & Sat); closed Mon; 7-11 Sun
☎ (01427) 628277
Greene King IPA; Tom Wood Dark Mild, Best Bitter Ⓗ

Now under new ownership, this village local has been revitalised after some quiet years. A good selection of fine real ales has been introduced. The pub has become a focal point for the community, providing a meeting place for village groups. An extension, doubling the size, is due for completion in summer 2006 and will increase facilities, while retaining the values of a traditional village local. Phone for details of B&B and food availability. ♨❀♿♣P

Boston

Ball House

Wainfleet Road, PE21 9RL (on A52, 2 miles from town centre)
⏲ 11.30-3, 6.30-11; 12-3, 7-10.30 Sun
☎ (01205) 364478 🌐 the ballhouse.co.uk
Bateman XB, XXXB Ⓗ

A cheery welcome greets customers old and new to this early 13th-century, mock-Tudor pub that stands on the site of an old Cannonball store. Award-winning floral displays can be enjoyed during the summer. There is a play area and plenty of seating in the pleasant gardens. A varied menu offers excellent home-cooked meals and snacks, using local grown produce; small adult portions are available. Monthly theme nights are hosted from January-July. ♨Q♨❀◐▮♿P⚟

Carpenters Arms

20 Witham Street, PE21 6PU (2 mins' walk from market place)
⏲ 12-11 daily
☎ (01205) 362840
Bateman XB, Valiant, XXXB; guest beers Ⓗ

This is a multi-roomed, low-ceilinged, traditional local situated in the maze of side streets off the medieval Wormgate, and overlooked by the magnificent Boston Stump. Bateman's is the house beer but a guest is usually available. There is a patio area outside for sunny days. Lunch is served on a Sunday but be sure to book. ♨❀▣♿🚌

Coach & Horses

86 Main Ridge, PE21 6SY (near football ground)
⏲ 5 (6 Fri)-11; 11-3, 7-11 Sat; 12-3, 7-10.30 Sun
☎ (01205) 362301
Bateman XB, XXXB Ⓗ

Just off the town's ring road, John Adams Way, and situated near Boston United's football ground, this one-roomed pub fields thriving pool, dominoes and darts teams. You need to get in early on match days. It is well worth the walk from the town centre to try the XXXB. No food is served, but the popular Eagles fish and chip outsales and café is nearby. ♨❀🚌♣▯

Cowbridge

Horncastle Road, PE22 7AX (on B1183, N of town)
⏲ 11-3, 6-11; 12-4, 7-10.30 Sun
☎ (01205) 362597
Greene King Old Speckled Hen; Theakston Mild, Best Bitter; guest beers Ⓗ

Just out of town, this pub is popular with drinkers and diners. It separates into three main areas: the public bar is a no-nonsense drinking and darts environment, with a large array of football scarves; the smaller lounge is cosy with an open fire and it opens out into a restaurant that serves excellent, freshly-cooked food. The pub is frequented by members of Boston Golf Club, which is just up the road. ♨Q♨❀◐▮▣♿♣P

Eagle

144 West Street, PE21 8RE (300 yds from station)
⏲ 11-11 (11.30 Wed & Thu, midnight Fri & Sat); 11-11 Sun
☎ (01205) 361116
Banks's Bitter; Castle Rock Harvest Pale; Taylor Landlord; guest beers Ⓗ

This Tynemill pub remains the best choice for real ale in Boston. The L-shaped bar houses a pool table and large screen for live sports. There is a small, cosy lounge with open fire. It usually stocks four guest beers, plus cider from Stowford Press and Biddenden. The function room is home to Boston Folk Club. Wednesday is midweek supper night and Thursday is quiz night. Twice monthly (Sun) when musicians play live, the bar closes at midnight. ♨Q❀▣♿⇌🚌♣●

Moon Under Water

6 High Street, PE21 8SH
⏲ 9am-midnight (1am Fri & Sat); 9am-midnight Sun
☎ (01205) 311911
Bateman XXXB; Greene King Abbot; Marston's Burton Bitter, Pedigree; Wells Bombardier; guest beers Ⓗ

Large, lively, town-centre pub near the tidal section of the River Witham. Formerly a government building, an imposing central staircase leads from the lounge up to the toilets. A spacious conservatory-style dining area is supplemented by a second no-

smoking, child-friendly dining room adjacent to the lounge. It offers four guest ales and a good range of continental beers. Local history around the walls highlights the characters associated with Boston.
❀◐◗♿⇌⊬

Ship Tavern

Custom House Lane, PE21 6HH (off South Sq)
⏲ 11-11; 12-10.30 Sun
☎ (01205) 358156
Bateman Mild, XB; Greene King IPA; guest beer Ⓗ
Town-centre pub opposite the quayside behind the old custom house and near the Guildhall and theatre. A traditional pub with one large L-shaped room, plenty of brewery memorabilia is displayed including some good photos of now demolished local pubs. Popular with students, it gets busy on match days with football supporters. In the summer a small patio is used for outside drinking.
❀⇌🚌♣🥛

Bourne

Smith's

25 North Street, PE10 9AE
⏲ 11-11 (midnight Fri & Sat); 12-11 Sun
☎ (01778) 426819
🌐 smithsofbourne.co.uk
Fuller's London Pride; Oakham JHB; guest beers Ⓗ
Winner of the national CAMRA/English Heritage conversion to pub use award, this former grocer's, in a three-storey listed Georgian building, is now a superb pub. Bars are situated to the front and rear of the ground floor and on the upper floor, with several attractively designed drinking areas throughout the building. There is a large, well-equipped patio and garden. The pub regularly has guest beers. If you miss lunch, a cheeseboard is available until 7pm.
🔥🍼❀◐🍴♿♣

Branston

Waggon & Horses

1 Rectory Lane, LN4 1NA
⏲ 12-2, 5-midnight (4-1am Fri); 12-1am Sat; 12-midnight Sun
☎ (01522) 791356
Draught Bass; John Smith's Bitter; guest beers Ⓗ
Unpretentious, brick-built roadhouse-style pub at the centre of a commuter village. The Waggon was built in the 1950s, to replace a Warwicks house on the same site, as can be seen from the photographs in the comfortable lounge bar. The lively public bar features pool, a dartboard and TV. The varied guest beers appear each Thursday for the weekend. Saturday is live music night and Monday evening is quiz time. A bus service runs from Lincoln (not Sun). ❀🍴🚌♣P

Brigg

Black Bull

3 Wrawby Street, DN20 8JH
⏲ 11-3 (4 Thu), 7-11.30 (11 Wed); 11-midnight Fri & Sat; 12-3, 7-11 Sun
☎ (01652) 652153
John Smith's Bitter; Tom Wood Harvest Bitter; guest beer Ⓗ
Popular, friendly, town-centre pub that gets busy on market days (Thu and Sat). There is a no-smoking dining room where children are welcome. It offers a changing guest beer. The car park to the rear is adjacent to the patio area. Brigg can be reached by bus from Scunthorpe and Barton (and by train on a Saturday on the Sheffield-Cleethorpes line). ❀◐⇌🚌♣P⊬

Yarborough Hunt

49 Bridge Street, DN20 8NF (across bridge from market place)
⏲ 10-11 (midnight Thu-Sat); 10-11 Sun
☎ (01652) 658333
Greene King IPA; Tom Wood Best Bitter; guest beers Ⓗ
Recipient of the CAMRA/English Heritage Joe Goodwin award in 2006, this former Sargeants Brewery tap has been carefully restored. Built in the early 1700s, the pub retains original features and its four rooms are simply furnished. Four rotating guest beers and Westons Old Rosie cider are supplemented by Belgian beers and over 50 malt whiskies. Wood-burning stoves and a heated patio keep you warm. No food is served but you are welcome to bring sandwiches. Trains only run on Saturday.
🔥Q❀♿⇌♣🍎⊬

Burton-upon-Stather

Ferry House

Stather Road, DN15 9DJ (follow campsite signs through village)
⏲ 7 (12 Sat)-11; 12-11 Sun
☎ (01724) 721504
Beer range varies Ⓗ
Friendly village local in a picturesque location next to the River Trent. It has a large open-plan bar-cum-lounge, plus another, no-smoking, suntrap lounge overlooking the river. A single rotating guest beer is drawn from national, regional and micro-breweries. It stages two beer festivals a year, Easter and summer. The pub welcomes families and provides an outdoor play area with bouncy castle. A cask beer club (Mon-Wed) offers discounted beer. Live music is performed outdoors on summer weekends. ❀♿⛺P⊬

Cleethorpes

No. 2 Refreshment Room

Station Approach, DN35 8AX
⏲ 9am-1am; 10-midnight Sun
☎ (07905) 375587
M&B Mild; Hancock's HB; Hardys & Hansons Olde Trip; guest beers Ⓗ
A warm and friendly welcome awaits at this single-roomed free house located on the railway station, adjacent to the promenade and beach. In addition to five real ales, this local CAMRA Pub of the Year 2004 and 2005 offers an increasing range of single malt whiskies. A quiz night is held on Thursday and a free buffet is provided on Sunday evening. The pub is also close to the bus terminus. ❀⇌🚌

Willy's

17 Highcliff Road, DN35 8RQ

11-11 (2am Fri & Sat); 11-11 Sun

☎ (01472) 602145

Bateman XB; Willy's Original; guest beers Ⓗ

Modern bar but in traditional style, from where the adjacent brewhouse can be viewed. The beer range includes ales from micro-breweries and Willy's occasional specials. Good value, home-cooked food is served at lunchtime (plus Mon, Tue and Thu eves). The pub affords excellent views of the promenade, beach, river and the Yorkshire coastline, and gets busy in summer when visitors flock to the resort to enjoy the water sports and annual kite festival. Frequent buses run from the town centre.

Coleby

Bell Inn

3 Far Lane, LN5 0AH

11-3, 5.30-11; 12-10.30 Sun

☎ (01522) 810240 thebellinncoleby.co.uk

Beer range varies Ⓗ

The Bell is tucked away behind the church in a typical Lincoln cliff village. The pub, although undoubtedly food led serving excellent meals, actively welcomes drinkers. Three beers are selected from the more interesting breweries on the Carlsberg-Tetley finest cask list. The decked area behind the pub is ideal for alfresco summer drinking, while the bar's real fire warms customers on winter evenings. Overnight accommodation is available - high demand means early booking is advisable. Q P

Donington

Black Bull

Market Place, PE11 4ST

11-11; 12-10.30 Sun

☎ (01775) 822228

John Smith's Bitter; Wells Bombardier; guest beers Ⓗ

Busy village local, just off the A52, whose success shows in the steady growth of its real ale range. Two handpumps feature a constantly-changing selection of guest beers from small brewers as well as larger regionals. There is a traditional feel to the bar, with its low, beamed ceilings and old wooden settles. The adjacent restaurant offers a good choice of evening meals. Tables in the car park permit outdoor drinking. Buses run from Boston and Spalding (not Sun). P

Dunston Fen

White Horse

LN4 3AP (follow brown signs from B1188, 6 miles) OS138663

12-3, 7-11; 12-midnight Sat; 12-11 Sun

☎ (01526) 398341 whitehorseinn.biz

Beer range varies Ⓗ

Remote free house on the bank of the River Witham. Normally a Poacher's beer is accompanied by one or two ales from other micros depending on the time of year. A popular tented beer festival is held over the August bank holiday weekend. The menu changes often and includes seasonal local produce. A large children's play area is provided, plus free overnight moorings for boating customers. The pub has changed hands but in most respects remains unchanged. P

East Butterwick

Dog & Gun

High Street, DN17 3AJ (off A18, at Keadby Bridge)

6 (5 Thu & Fri)-11 (midnight Fri); 12-midnight Sat; 12-11 Sun

☎ (01724) 782324

John Smith's Bitter; guest beers Ⓗ

Small, but busy, village-centre pub consistently supplying quality ales. Locals and visitors can enjoy a welcoming real fire in its traditional, cheerful atmosphere in winter and a pleasant drink on the bank of the River Trent in summer. The pub now houses the DarkTribe Brewery, which produces a wide range of beers to suit all palates. The pub showcases these in rotation giving its eager customers a variety of tastes to savour, including seasonal offerings. Q P

East Stockwith

Ferry House

27 Front Street, DN21 3DJ

11.30-3, 6.30-11; closed Mon; 12-10.30 Sun

☎ (01427) 615276

John Smith's Bitter; Webster's Bitter; guest beers Ⓗ

Village free house beside the River Trent that caters for locals and enjoys a thriving food trade (booking sometimes required). Prices are reasonable for food of high quality that is all cooked on the premises. The large bar has facilities for pool, darts and dominoes, there is a dining room and a function room. Three guest bedrooms with Trent views provide keenly-priced B&B. Two guest beers from independent brewers are offered. A quiz is held on alternate Wednesday evenings. P

Eastoft

River Don Tavern

Sampson Street, DN17 4PQ

(on A161 Goole-Gainsborough road)

5 (12 Sat)-midnight; 7.30-11 Mon & Tue; 12-midnight Sun

☎ (01724) 798040

John Smith's Bitter; guest beers Ⓗ

Welcoming village local in the Isle of Axholme. The open plan design offers discrete areas for dining and drinking. In summer you can take your drink into the orchard at the rear. Dark beams and agricultural implements on the walls give a distinct rural ambience. It offers three guest beers (two in winter). Good value food includes hot skillet meals and a weekend carvery, served Wednesday-Friday 5-9pm (12-9 Sat and Sun). An annual beer festival is staged in summer. P

Ewerby

Finch Hatton Arms

43 Main Street, NG34 9PH
✪ 12-3, 6-11 daily
☎ (01529) 460363 🌐 finchhattonarms.co.uk
Everards Tiger; Riverside Dixon's Major; guest beers Ⓗ
Substantial country inn built in the early 1870s. It was purchased by Lord Winchelsea in 1875 and given his family name until the mid-1960s. The pub sign on the well includes the Finch Hatton family motto, 'with a clear conscience'. Now a free house and fully-equipped small hotel it retains the charm of its past, enhanced by local artefacts inside and out. The extensive menu caters for all tastes and pockets. Cribbage can be played here. ♨Q❀⊨◐◑⊟♣P⍁

Freiston

King's Head

Church Road, PE22 0NT
✪ 11-2.30, 6.30-11; 11-11.30 Sat; 12-10.30 Sun
☎ (01205) 760368
Bateman Mild, XB Ⓗ
This welcoming village local is a regular finalist in Bateman's floral display competition – it looks a treat in summer months. Good, home-cooked food represents excellent value and is ideal for those with a hearty appetite. Pub games are played and it fields local league teams in darts and dominoes. Amenities include the Wash Banks for angling and bird watching. ♨Q❀◐◑⛺♣P⊓

Friskney

Barley Mow

Sea Lane, PE22 8SD
(on A52, between Boston and Skegness)
✪ 12-3, 6.30-11; closed Mon & Tue; 12-11 Sat; 12-10.30 Sun
☎ (01754) 820883
Bateman Mild, XB; guest beers Ⓗ
Situated on the busy Boston-Skegness road, this 300-year-old hostelry is known locally as the Barley Mow (pronounced Cow). Frequented by locals and visitors alike, it is especially popular in the summer months. A wide selection of home-cooked meals features on an imaginative menu. A conservatory adds to the atmosphere at this gem of a pub. ♨♉❀◐◑♿⊟P

Frognall

Goat

155 Spalding Road, PE6 8SA
✪ 11.30-2.30, 6-11; 11.30-2.30, 6-10.30 Sun
☎ (01778) 347629
Beer range varies Ⓗ
Friendly, cosy pub with comfortable surroundings, consisting of a bar and two dining areas and real fires to welcome you on chilly evenings. A changing selection of guest beers, often from small and brand new micro-breweries, is supplemented by a growing range of Belgian beers and 50-plus malt whiskies. In July the pub hosts its annual beer festival with over 25 real ales to choose from. The pub offers hot and cold home-cooked food. ♨Q❀⊨◐◑♿●P

Gainsborough

Eight Jolly Brewers

Ship Court, Silver Street, DN21 2DW
(next to council offices)
✪ 11-midnight daily
Bateman XXXB; guest beers Ⓗ
Pleasant, town-centre pub near the River Trent, a former carpenter's workshop. The bar is on the ground floor with the upper floor providing two additional areas, sometimes used for meetings. The landlord has established a thriving weekly music night (Thu); entry is free. This multiple CAMRA award winner always stocks eight draught beers including ales from Glentworth and the landlord's Maypole Brewery in Newark. Biddenden cider, Belgian Leffe on draught, bottled beers and fruit wines add variety. Q⇌(Lea Rd)⊟♣●⍁

Elm Cottage

139 Church Street, DN21 2JU
(100 yds W of football ground)
✪ 11 (9 Tue)-3, 6-11 (1am Thu); 11-1am Fri & Sat; 12-11 Sun
☎ (01427) 615474
Jennings Cumberland Ale; John Smith's Bitter Ⓗ
One-roomed pub served by a central bar. It first appeared on the town map in 1853, and was once owned by Hewitts of Grimsby. Headquarters for football, cricket and darts teams in local leagues, it hosts a quiz on Tuesday evening, occasionally replaced by live music. Two bay windows to the front have seating. Pictures of local interest are displayed around the pub. Breakfast is served on Tuesday, while the regular lunchtime menu is replaced by a carvery on Sunday. ❀◐◑♣P

Gosberton

Bell

High Street, PE11 4NJ
✪ 11.45-11; 12-10.30 Sun
☎ (01775) 840186
Beer range varies Ⓗ
A change of hands in 2004 transformed the fortunes of this small, friendly local, which now offers a regularly changing selection of four handpumped ales from both large and small brewers. The comfortable bar features old photographs of the village and the pub over the years. Bar meals are available all day and there is live music most weekends. Tables in the car park allow for some outdoor drinking. Buses run from Boston and Spalding (not Sun). ♨❀◐◑♿⊟P

Gosberton Risegate

Duke of York

105 Risegate Road, PE11 4EY
✪ 12 (6.30 Mon)-11; 12-3.30, 7-10.30 Sun
☎ (01775) 840193
Bateman XB; Black Sheep Best Bitter; guest beers Ⓗ
Excellent pub with a long record for providing

good value beer and food. The comprehensive, changing beer range always offers something of interest. Playing an active role in its local community, the pub supports charities, sports teams and other social activities. There is a large garden and children's play area, while goats and other animals are an added attraction. The arch above the public bar indicates the pub's former Bateman's ownership. ⚲❀◐◑▲♣P▯

Grantham

Blue Bell

64 Westgate, NG31 6LA
11-midnight; 12-11 Sun
☎ (01476) 570929
Newby Wyke Bear Island, seasonal beers; guest beers Ⓗ

Three-roomed local, popular with all ages, situated at the west end of the market place, five minutes' walk from the rail and bus stations. A busy bar contrasts with a quiet lounge that is available for private functions; the games room has pool and darts. There is a decked outside drinking area at the rear. The beer is supplied by the local Newby Wyke Brewery. It hosts occasional live music at the weekends. ❀⊟≉⊟P

Lord Harrowby

65 Dudley Road, NG31 9AB (½ mile E of town centre, near A52)
4 (12 Sat)-11; 12-10.30 Sun
☎ (01476) 563515
Draught Bass; Tom Wood Best Bitter; guest beer Ⓗ

This friendly pub with two bars offers a variety of activities, but no food. Darts, crib and dominoes are played on Tuesday evenings and darts again on Friday. Every other Friday there is a karaoke session while on the third Friday of the month you can listen to jazz in front of a real fire. Test your general knowledge every Sunday evening at the quiz. ⚲⊟♣

Nobody Inn

9 North Street, NG31 6NU (on corner opp. Asda car park)
12-11 (midnight Sat); 12-10.30 Sun
☎ (01476) 5665288 nobodyinn.com
Draught Bass; Bateman XB; Oakham JHB; guest beers Ⓗ

Small, friendly, independently owned free house, popular with all ages and a mecca for sports fans – all major sports events are shown. The house beer, Grantham Gold, is brewed for the pub by Newby Wyke. Look out for the hidden entrance to the toilets through the bookcase. Café-style tables and chairs are set out on the pavement during the summer months. ❀≉

Tollemache Inn

St Peter's Hill, NG31 6QF (at St Catherine's Rd jct)
9am-midnight (1am Fri-Sat); 9am-midnight Sun
☎ (01476) 594696
Greene King Abbot; Marston's Pedigree; guest beers Ⓗ

Sympathetic Wetherspoon conversion of an old Co-op. The pub is named after Frederick Tollemache, a former Liberal MP, whose statue stands outside the front door. The ever-changing beer range includes the pub's own Tolle Tipple from local brewer Oldershaw, who also produced a special brew for the pub's tenth anniversary in 2005. The pub benefits from a large no-smoking section and an outdoor drinking area with patio heaters. Q❀◐◑♿≉⊬

Grimsby

Hope & Anchor

148 Victoria Street, DN31 1NX
12-midnight (2am Fri & Sat); 12-midnight Sun
☎ (01472) 500706
Tetley Bitter; guest beers Ⓗ

Town-centre pub with a modern, open, spacious layout. A favourite with office staff at lunchtime and early evening, it manages to retain its local pub atmosphere. It serves up to four guest beers, mostly from regional brewers. Convenient for the bus terminus and Freshney Place shopping centre, lunches are served Monday-Saturday. There is a patio for summer drinking. ❀◐≉⊟♣

Rose & Crown

Louth Road, DN33 2HR
11-11 (midnight Fri & Sat); 12-11 Sun
☎ (01472) 279931
Draught Bass; Bateman XXXB; Taylor Landlord; Tetley Bitter; guest beer Ⓗ

First entry in this Guide since 1986 and a welcome return for this friendly local serving the Scartho area of Grimsby and others wishing to eat and drink in a comfortable, relaxed place. It is much changed internally since the early days, following stylish refurbishment and re-opening as one of Mitchells & Butlers' Ember Inns. It is now smoke-free throughout, but has a heated patio area for smokers. Beer festivals twice a year showcase small breweries. ⚲❀◐◑♿⊟P⊬

Swigs

21 Osborne Street, DN31 1EY (between station and town hall)
9am-11; 12-10.30 Sun
☎ (01472) 354773
Tom Wood Shepherd's Delight; Willy's Original; guest beers Ⓗ

One-roomed, town-centre pub close to bus and rail stations, it is the sister pub to Willy's in Cleethorpes and is popular with all ages. Substantial, good value, home-cooked food includes vegetarian options and breakfast. The environment is continental in style, but the bar back is from an old church. It stages occasional quiz and acoustic evenings. It offers two changing guest beers and has regular 'happy hours'. Tuesday is student night. There is an option to remain open until 2am. ◐≉⊟♣

Tap & Spile

Haven Mill, Garth Lane, DN31 3AF (behind Freshney Place shopping precinct)
12-11; 12-10.30 Sun
☎ (01472) 357493
Caledonian Deuchars IPA; Theakston XB; Wychwood Hobgoblin; guest beers Ⓗ

Spacious, one-roomed pub, a former flour mill where old stone, brick and woodwork have been retained. Good quality, wholesome food is served Tuesday-Saturday. It stages quiz nights on Monday and Thursday and music most weekends, including acoustic blues. A welcome retreat away from the brash town centre disco bars, the pub's balcony overlooks the river. ❀◐◑≹⊟♣

Wheatsheaf

47 Bargate, DN34 5AD

⏲ 12-11 (midnight Thu-Sat); 12-11 Sun

☎ (01472) 246821

Bateman XB; Taylor Landlord; Tetley Bitter; guest beer Ⓗ

Well refurbished, grand public house, now one of Mitchells & Butlers' Ember Inns. The emphasis is on good food and ales, friendly service and a relaxing atmosphere. The split-level layout encompasses various seating areas and is no-smoking throughout; smokers may use the patio. Two beer festivals a year feature products from small breweries. The pub benefits from a regular bus service. ❀◐◑♿≹⊟P⊬

Yarborough Hotel

29 Bethlehem Street, DN31 1JN (next to station)

⏲ 9am-midnight (1am Fri & Sat); 9-midnight Sun

☎ (01472) 268283

Bateman Mild; Greene King Abbot; Marston's Pedigree; Shepherd Neame Spitfire; guest beers Ⓗ

Impressive, spacious Victorian building, formerly a hotel, but now a Wetherspoon's pub. Centrally located next to the station, on numerous bus routes, it offers the largest selection of cask ales in Grimsby, plus a guest cider. The pub serves a house beer called Yarborough Gold, brewed locally by Tom Wood. The interior is largely wood panelled with a no-smoking area at the rear, served by its own bar. Good value meals are served all day. Q❀◐◑♿≹●⊬

Harmston

Thorold Arms

High Street, LN5 9SN (off A607)

⏲ 12-3 (not Mon or Tue), 6-11 (hours may vary); 12-11 Sun

☎ (01522) 720358 🌐 thoroldarms.co.uk

Beer range varies Ⓗ

This stone-built, 17th-century building has a cosy bar area warmed by an open fire, and relaxing sofas. Situated just off the busy A607, the No. 1 bus runs close to the village, which has the Viking Way running through it. No regular beers are kept, but 135 different ales have been sold during the last year. A beer festival is held over August bank holiday. The restaurant doubles as a meeting room. Board games are available at this pub which is now entirely no-smoking. ♨Q❀◐◑⊞♿⊟♣P⊬

Haxey

Loco

31-33 Church Street, DN9 2HY (from A161, follow B1396 into village)

⏲ 12-midnight; 3-1am Fri & Sat; 3-mdidnight Sun

☎ (01427) 752879

John Smith's Bitter; guest beers Ⓗ

Unusual pub, converted from the village Co-op during the 1980s. Decorated with railway memorabilia, it is a must for railway buffs. Further interest is provided by Kashmir Sidings, the pub's Indian restaurant and takeaway (open Tue-Sun eves). At least one guest beer is always available. Extensive refurbishment is planned for 2006-07 to include disabled access. The pub participates in the annual Haxey Hood game on January 6th. ◑♣

Hemingby

Coach & Horses

Church Lane, LN9 5QF (1 mile from A158)

⏲ 12-2 (not Mon or Tue), 7 (6 Wed-Fri)-11; 12-3, 7-10.30 Sun

☎ (01507) 578280

🌐 coachandhorses.mysite.wanadoo-members.co.uk

Bateman Mild; Riverside Dixon's Major; guest beers Ⓗ

Welcoming free house in a village on the edge of the picturesque Lincolnshire Wolds, a little way off the busy Skegness Road. Next to the church, this low, white-painted building looks, and is, delightful. A central open hearth separates the pool area from the main bar. The pub is noted for its reasonably-priced, home-cooked meals, available Wednesday-Sunday (not Sun eve). ♨Q❀◐◑⛺♣P

Holbeach St Johns

Plough

1 Jekils Bank, PE12 8RF (4 miles S of Holbeach on B1168)

⏲ 12-11; 12-10.30 Sun

☎ (01406) 540654

Adnams Bitter; Oakham Bishops Farewell; guest beers Ⓗ

Popular with all ages, and with pub games playing a prominent part, this local makes an important contribution to village life. Sky Sports TV is here for those who want to watch, but there is also plenty of local chat. A skittle alley is available by prior arrangement, as some furniture rearranging is needed. Guest beers are often seasonal offerings from Jennings or Oakham Brewery – much favoured by the landlord. No food is served Tuesday; Sunday meals are available 12-5pm. ❀◐◑♿⛺♣P

Horbling

Plough Inn

Spring Lane, NG34 0PF

⏲ 12-3, 5-11; 12-11 Fri-Sun

☎ (01529) 240263

Beer range varies Ⓗ

Unusual pub owned by the parish council in a quiet village, built in 1832. In addition to the bar/lounge, the snug is surely one of the smallest and most intimate of its kind. Low beams and doorways add to its character. Beers are usually from Lincolnshire breweries and others close by. Home-made

food is served and it stages theme nights: Wednesday is a regular steak night.
Q❀◐◑♣P

Kirkby on Bain

Ebrington Arms

Main Street, LN10 6YT
✪ 12-3, 6-midnight; 12-11 Sun
☎ (01526) 354560
Bateman XB; Greene King Abbot; Woodforde's Wherry; guest beers H
Attractive country pub close to the River Bain, comprising a low, beamed bar/lounge. Dating back to 1610, it was used by airmen during WWII; coins still slotted into the ceiling beams were for beer when they returned from missions. Ebrington Bitter is a house beer brewed by Tom Wood. Booking is advised for the popular restaurant. The garden has an awning to protect outside drinkers if the weather turns cool. There is a Caravan Club site within a mile of the pub.
⩩Q❀◐◑♿⅄♣P

Lincoln

Golden Eagle

21 High Street, LN5 8BD (1 mile S of city centre)
✪ 11-11; 12-11 Sun
☎ (01522) 521058
Bateman XXXB; Castle Rock Harvest Pale; Everards Beacon; guest beers H
Once a Georgian coaching inn, this traditional two-roomed pub has a function room upstairs. Beyond the rear car park is a large garden and a petanque pitch. Children are welcome in the cosy front lounge, with its pub games and the lively, modern, rear bar. Friday is quiz night and it hosts an autumn beer festival. Castle Rock's Wildlife Trust beers, up to six guest ales, two real ciders and continental bottled beers add to its appeal and represent good value.
Q❀⊟♣●P

Jolly Brewer

27 Broadgate, LN2 5AQ
✪ 12-11 (1am Fri & Sat); 12-10.30 Sun
☎ (01522) 528583 🌐 thejollybrewer.co.uk
Taylor Landlord; Young's Bitter; guest beers H
Bare boards, a real fire, imitation Art Deco and a cosmopolitan clientele characterise this city-centre pub. Food is served weekdays (12-2pm and 5-7pm) and Sunday lunchtime. Music features large here – live bands on Saturday evening, open mike sessions (Wed eve), and an interesting selection on the juke box. A patio area behind the pub acts as a concrete garden and, in good weather, as an occasional live music space. The guest cider is often Westons. ⩩❀◐◑⇌●P

Morning Star

11 Greetwell Gate, LN2 4AW (200 yds E of cathedral)
✪ 11-11; 12-11 Sun
☎ (01522) 527079
Draught Bass; Greene King Ruddles Best Bitter, Abbot; Tetley Bitter; Wells Bombardier; guest beer H
It can be a squeeze getting into this popular little pub, where conversation is the usual entertainment. Reputed to have first been an inn in the 18th century, and a couple of minutes' walk from the cathedral, it offers good value food at lunchtime (meals are served Mon-Sat 12-2pm). The pub is a regular sponsor of the nearby Lincoln RFC.
Q⛾❀◐🚌♣P⚟

Peacock Hotel

23 Wragby Road, LN2 5SH
✪ 11.30-11; 12-11 Sun
☎ (01522) 524703
Hardys & Hansons Mild, Bitter, Olde Trip, seasonal beers H
Busy pub at a main road junction near the cathedral. The main drinking section leads to the dining area where good quality food is served 12-9pm daily, including a Sunday roast. The bar area has two TVs for sports events and also hosts regular darts and dominoes games. This former Whitbread house sells the full range of Hardys & Hansons' beers, including its seasonal ales.
◐◑⊟♣P

Queen in the West

12-14 Moor Street, LN1 1PR (off A57 Carholme Rd)
✪ 12-3, 5.30-11; 11-11.30 Fri & Sat; 12-10.30 Sun
☎ (01522) 880123
Greene King Old Speckled Hen; Shepherd Neame Spitfire; Taylor Landlord; Wells Bombardier; guest beers H
One of the area's few remaining truly independent free houses, with continuity of ownership since 1989. A limestone farm building, converted to a public house in the 1860s, it is rumoured that a monarch once stayed here, and that her eerie effigy can be seen some days peering from the wall of the houses opposite. A central bar serves two rooms, which feature oak beams and stonework. Customers come for a quiet drink and conversation. Occasionally live music is performed in summer. ⊟♣

Sippers

26 Melville Street, LN5 7HW
✪ 11-midnight; 12-midnight Sun
☎ (01522) 527612
Caledonian Deuchars IPA; John Smith's Bitter; guest beers H
Sippers has been a Guide entry for many years. Its regular beers are supplemented by up to five guests from small independent brewers. Once the Crown and Cushion, this comfortable pub is conveniently placed, close to bus and rail stations. It can be busy on weekday lunchtimes, but there is ample seating tucked away. Musicians perform regularly on Sunday. Lunches are served Monday-Saturday. ◐⇌🚌♣

Strugglers Inn

83 Westgate, LN1 3BG (under NW corner of castle)
✪ 11-11 (midnight Thu-Sat); 12-10.30 Sun
☎ (01522) 535023
Draught Bass; Bateman Mild; Black Sheep Best Bitter; Fuller's London Pride; Taylor Landlord; guest beer H
Friendly pub, in the historic uphill quarter of

Lincoln, under the shadow of the castle wall. The bustling bar contrasts with the cosy snug, with its open fire and pictures of old Lincoln. The pretty patio flower garden is used in winter with a sturdy, heated marquee for shelter. A fortnight-long beer festival is held each October, boosted by themed nights throughout the year. Exceptional home-cooked fresh meals come with real chips (served Tue-Sat). ⅏Q❀◖⊟

Tap & Spile

21 Hungate, LN1 1ES (100 yds E of police station)
✪ 12-midnight daily
☎ (01522) 534015 ⊕ tapandspilelincoln.co.uk
Caledonian Deuchars IPA; Wells Bombardier; guest beers Ⓗ
The former White Horse is a real pub, away from the nearby trendy, city-centre bars. Old advertising slogans and pictures of blues legends adorn the rugged decor. Three intimate walk-through drinking sections have replaced the original rooms, served from a central bar. Six guest beers and a range of Lindisfarne Wines are stocked. Sunday evening is 'open mike' followed by a general knowledge quiz, Thursday hosts circular chess and Friday live music. No food is served Sunday. ◖⇌♣●⅔

Treaty of Commerce

173 High Street, LN5 7AF
✪ 11-11; 12-10.30 Sun
☎ (01522) 541943
Bateman XB, XXXB, seasonal beers; guest beers Ⓗ
Bearing a unique name, this pub was built in 1788. Located just south of Lincoln's notorious level crossing, a short walk from bus and rail stations, it is near the retail heart of the city. A Bateman's house, it always has three of its beers, as well as up to three guests. An unusual feature is the wooden barrel-vaulted ceiling at the far end of the single long bar. The good value lunches are filling. ❀◖⇌⊟

Victoria

6 Union Road, LN1 3BJ
✪ 11-11 (11.30 Fri & Sat); 12-11 Sun
☎ (01522) 536048
Bateman XB; Taylor Landlord; guest beers Ⓗ
Well-known pub in the shadow of the castle and within easy reach of the cathedral. Part of the thriving Tynemill chain, it hosts two beer festivals (summer and Christmas) each year, and stocks six guest beers at any time, including a mild. The cider is Biddendens. Children are allowed in the 'Link' and the outside drinking area in summer.
Q❀◖⊟♣●⅔

Little Bytham

Willoughby Arms

Station Road, NG33 4RA
✪ 12-3, 5-11; 12-11 Sat & Sun
☎ (01780) 410276 ⊕ willoughbyarms.co.uk
Beer range varies Ⓗ
Lincolnshire CAMRA Pub of the Year 2004 enjoys a country setting. The award-winning Newby Wyke Brewery behind the pub usually supplies three beers to the bar. Wednesday is curry night; food can be ordered in the bar or no-smoking restaurant (not Mon). Westons Old Rosie is always available, alongside occasional guest ciders. The pub stages a monthly quiz night and occasional beer festivals. Well appointed accommodation is available. ⅏❀⇎◖◗●P⊟

Louth

Boar's Head

12 Newmarket, LN11 9HH
✪ 12-3 (not Mon or Tue; 9.30am-3 Thu), 5-11; 11-11 Sat; 12-11 Sun
☎ (01507) 603561
Bateman Mild, XXB, seasonal beers; guest beers Ⓗ
Situated next to the cattle market, a short distance from the town centre, the Boar's Head has real fires in winter and always a warm welcome. Pub games include darts, pool, shove-ha'penny and dominoes. There are two main rooms – one no-smoking – plus the old snug, which now houses the pool table. A council car park is next to the pub.
⅏Q⇎◖⊟♣⅔

Masons Arms Hotel

Cornmarket, LN11 9PY
✪ 10-11 (midnight Fri & Sat); 12-11 Sun
☎ (01507) 609525 ⊕ themasons.co.uk
Bateman XB, XXXB; Marston's Pedigree; Taylor Landlord; guest beers Ⓗ
Licensed as the Bricklayer's Arms in 1782, the present name was adopted in 1801. The mid 19th-century façade of this early 18th-century Grade II listed building, with its balcony and canted bays to the ground floor, is a commanding presence on the town's bustling market place. Once one of Louth's principal posting inns, and home to the Masonic Lodge, today the Masons is a thriving family-run hotel. ⇎◖◗⊟

Newmarket Inn

133 Newmarket, LN11 9EG
✪ 7 (6 Wed & Fri)-11; 12-3, 7-11 Sun
☎ (01507) 605146
Adnams Bitter; Young's Bitter; guest beer (occasional) Ⓗ
Friendly, relaxed local, open evenings only except Sunday. Opened out into a single bar in the 1970s, the L-shaped room is a pleasantly decorated retreat in which to sample the landlord's well-kept ales. Meals are served in both the bar and the bistro (Wed-Sat eves and Sun lunchtime); booking is advisable. Tables and benches in front of the pub allow you to drink outside. ❀◗♿P

Wheatsheaf Inn

62 Westgate, LN11 9YD
✪ 11-3, 5-11; 11-11 Sat; 12-4, 7-10.30 Sun
☎ (01507) 606262
Black Sheep Best Bitter; Flowers Original; guest beers Ⓗ
Attractive, traditional inn dating back to 1625, in a Georgian terrace, close to St James Church, which boasts the tallest spire of any parish church in England. The three rooms are all warmed by coal fires in winter. Well-behaved dogs are welcome in the outside drinking area. A beer and bangers

festival is held annually at the end of May. Daily specials are offered on the home-cooked menu. It stocks a house beer (Tipsy Toad) and three or four guests. ⩕Q❀◑P

Woolpack Inn

Riverhead Road, LN11 0DA (1 mile E of town centre)
⊙ 11-3 (not Mon), 5-11; 11-11 Sat; 11-10.30 Sun
☎ (01507) 606568
Bateman Mild, XB, XXXB, seasonal beers; Greene King IPA, Abbot; guest beers Ⓗ
Old, friendly pub, out of the town centre. Dating back to 1770, as the name suggests the pub was once used to store wool as well as serve beer. The pub comprises two L-shaped bars, with lovely fires, and serves wonderful home-cooked food (not Mon). A good-sized back garden is ideal for families in the summer. Buses run in daytime. ⩕Q❀◑◗⊟♿⊟♣P⊁

Ludford

White Hart Inn

Magna Mile, LN8 6AD
⊙ 12-2 (not Mon-Wed, 5.30-11; 12-3, 6-11 Sat; 12-4, 7-11 Sun
☎ (01507) 313489
Hardys & Hansons Bitter; guest beers Ⓗ
Thought to have first been used as a public house in 1742, this two-roomed rural village pub, close to the Viking Way, is very popular with hikers and ramblers. It always offers four changing guest beers; the licensees pride themselves on serving real ale from micro-breweries. All food served is home made with ingredients from local suppliers. The guest accommodation is separate from the pub. Well-behaved dogs are welcome. ⩕Q❀⊨◑◗♣P

Messingham

Bird in the Barley

Northfield Road, DN17 3SQ (on A159, Gainsborough road)
⊙ 11.30-3 (not Mon), 5.30 (6.30 Mon)-11; 12-3, 6-10.30 Sun
☎ (01724) 764744
Marston's Pedigree; guest beers Ⓗ
Comfortable roadside inn decorated in rustic style with beams, bare bricks and rural artefacts. Quiet and welcoming, with an emphasis on food, real ale is also promoted with tasting notes and a try-before-you buy policy. One or two rotating guest beers are supplemented by draught Hoegaarden. Quizzes are held on Sunday and Monday evenings, when food is not served. The bar displays an impressive array of pump clips from featured beers. ⩕❀◑◗♿P

Horn Inn

61 High Street, DN17 3NU
⊙ 11-11; 12-10.30 Sun
☎ (01724) 762426
John Smith's Bitter; guest beers Ⓗ
Friendly, family-run local offering a warm welcome to regulars and passing trade. Two rotating guest ales sourced through SIBA are served in comfortable TV-free surroundings. The open-plan layout features coal fires, rural artefacts and settles built by a previous landlord. It serves excellent, home-cooked lunches (booking recommended Sun). Entertainment includes live music (Wed), and a quiz (Mon). On the main road through the village, buses pass the door. ⩕Q❀◑♿⊟(351, 353)♣P

Morton

Crooked Billet

1 Crooked Billet Street, DN21 3AG
⊙ 12-midnight (1am Fri & Sat); 12-midnight Sun
☎ (01427) 612584
Beer range varies Ⓗ
Large, Victorian pub where a central bar serves three rooms. The games room houses a pool table, juke box and Sky TV and hosts occasional live music. The smoke room boasts a display of local pre-war photos, while the middle room is used for bingo and quizzes. The pub is the headquarters for local sports teams, including fishing. The beers come from a variety of breweries. ⩕Q⊟⊡

Moulton

Swan

13 High Street, PE12 6QB
⊙ 11-11; 12-10.30 Sun
☎ (01406) 370349
Adnams Broadside; Tetley Bitter; Wells Bombardier; guest beer Ⓗ
Family-run pub that enjoys a good reputation for its ale and food. Ideally situated at the village centre, it narrowly escaped the 'Moulton tornado', which badly damaged the church opposite. The tallest windmill in the country also survived unscathed and proudly stands nearby. A TV caters for sports fans in the public bar, while the pleasant garden is popular with families. Cider is sold in summer. ⩕❀◑◗⊟♣●P

Moulton Chapel

Wheatsheaf

4 Fengate, PE12 0XL
⊙ 12-2 (not Mon), 5.30-11; 12-3, 7-11 Sat; 12-3, 7-10.30 Sun
☎ (01406) 380525
Beer range varies Ⓗ
The heart of this village pub is the small, quarry-tiled bar, with its splendid range, complete with oven and boiler and glowing fire. A stack of logs by its side completes the timeless picture, with no muzak, games or TV to distract from eavesdropping on the local gossip. A realistic stocking policy of one ale at a time, often from a micro, ensures a quality pint. Excellent food is served in two smart dining rooms. ⩕Q❀◑◗Å♣P

Nettleton

Salutation

Church Street, LN7 6NP (on A46)
⊙ 12-3, 6-11.30; 7-10.30 Sun
☎ (01472) 851228
Flowers IPA; Taylor Landlord; Wadworth 6X; guest beer Ⓗ
This friendly, relaxing pub on the Grimsby-

Lincoln bus route is not only popular with locals but also with walkers – the Viking Way and Lincolnshire's highest point (near Normanby-le-Wold radar station) are nearby. It has a dining area next to the bar and a family room. The pub hosts a monthly themed food night, live music (last Fri of month) with a resident band and open mike sessions. A large garden houses farm animals, rabbits and guinea pigs.
♨☺❀◐◑♿⛺🚌♣P⚡

North Kelsey

Butcher's Arms

Middle Street, LN7 6EH

⊙ 4 (12 Sat)-midnight (1.30am Fri & Sat); 12-midnight Sun

☎ (01652) 678002

Tom Wood Best Bitter, Harvest Bitter; guest beer Ⓗ

Traditional village pub of open-plan design, decorated in rural fashion with hop bines, rustic furnishings and beer memorabilia. The cosy feel is enhanced by small, discrete areas. An attractive outdoor drinking space is framed by mature trees. Owned by the local Highwood Brewery, it serves a rotating guest beer; at busy times a third Tom Wood beer may be added. Table skittles can be played here. A disabled toilet is provided.
♨❀♿♣P

Oasby

Houblon Arms

Village Street, NG32 3NB (between A52 and B6403)

⊙ 12-2, 7-11; closed Mon; 12-2.30, 6-11 Sat; 12-3, 7-11 Sun

☎ (01529) 455215

Everards Tiger; Greene King Abbot; guest beers Ⓗ

Local CAMRA's Country Pub of the Year 2006 nestles at the village centre, where time slips by so easily. The traditional flagstone floor and a large inglenook are notable features. The dining room serves good home-cooked food, expertly presented, that tastes as good as it looks (no food Sun eve). B&B accommodation is provided in four cottages. Named after the first Governor of the Bank of England (John Houblon), this pub should not be missed if passing this way.
♨Q❀🛏◐◑♿P⚡

Old Bolingbroke

Black Horse Inn

Moat Lane, PE23 4HH

⊙ 2.30-midnight; 2.30-5.30, 8-midnight Thu; 5-1.30am Fri; 12.30-1am Sat; 12-midnight Sun

☎ (01790) 763388

Bateman Mild; Fuller's ESB; Harviestoun Schiehallion; Theakston Old Peculier; Young's Bitter; guest beers Ⓗ

A warm welcome is assured in this old country inn. The castle remains and the roses of Henry IV and the Duke of Lancaster from 1366 are features of this lovely village. The inn stages regular beer festivals. The food is prepared from local organic produce; Friday is Grimsby fish night, and Saturday speciality night (booking advisable). Ploughmans lunches are available at the weekend. Ring to check opening times and food availability.
♨Q❀◑⊟♿♣P

Pinchbeck

Bull Inn

1 Knight Street, PE11 3RA

⊙ 12-2.30, 5.30-11; 12.30-2.30, 5-midnight Fri; 12-midnight Sat; 12-11 Sun

☎ (01775) 723022

Greene King Old Speckled Hen; John Smith's Bitter; guest beers Ⓗ

Situated on the old main road in the village centre, the Bull was the birthplace of the Fenland branch of CAMRA, when it was a Barnsley Brewery house in the 1970s. It now offers an excellent real ale choice, and regularly features beers from small breweries nationwide. The distinctive bar features a carved bull's head on the front, with the bar rail representing its horns. Tables in the car park allow for some outside drinking. Buses run from Spalding and Boston (not Sun). ♨Q☺❀◐◑♿🚌P

Rothwell

Blacksmith's Arms

Hill Rise, LN7 6AZ

⊙ 12-3, 5-11.30; 12-11.30 Sat; 12-11 Sun

☎ (01472) 371300

Black Sheep Best Bitter; Greene King Abbot; Tom Wood Shepherd's Delight; guest beer Ⓗ

Tucked away on the edge of the Lincolnshire Wolds and close to the Viking Way, the Blackies is popular with locals and visitors alike. The pub has recently been redecorated, which has given the main bar a more contemporary feel, with a pool table added in the small side bar. Anvil Ale is the house beer from Tom Wood's Highwood Brewery. The food is well worth a try.
♨❀◐◑♿♣P

Ruskington

Potters

3 Chestnut Street, NG34 9DL

⊙ 12 (11 Fri & Sat)-3 (not Mon), 5-11; 12-3, 7-10.30 Sun

☎ (01529) 832777

Bateman XB; Black Sheep Special; guest beers Ⓗ

Former garage and car showroom converted into a snooker club (hence its name), it has now been given a new lease of life as a comfortable, smart pub. Its convivial atmosphere makes it popular with all ages, and its reputation for beer and food is growing. A full-sized snooker table is available to members. ◐◑⇌P

Saxilby

Anglers

65 High Street, LN1 2HA

⊙ 11-2.30, 6-11 (midnight Fri); 11-12.30am Sat; 12-midnight Sun

☎ (01522) 702200

Greene King IPA; Theakston Best Bitter; guest beers Ⓗ

Uncomplicated, comfortable village pub,

home to darts, pool, crib, dominoes and golf teams. The local history society, drama group and others often meet here. There are also shove-ha'penny and skittles boards available. The pub, one of four in the village, was originally the Railway. Great pictures of old Saxilby feature in the lounge. The Fossdyke Canal runs through the village; its moorings are well used. ❀⊟⇌⊟♣P

Scamblesby

Green Man

Old Main Road, LN11 9XG
(off A153, Horncastle-Louth road)
✪ 12-midnight daily
☎ (01507) 343282
Black Sheep Best Bitter; Young's Bitter; guest beer 🄷
This 200-year-old pub is run by motorcycle and ale loving licensees, and is frequently visited by walkers and visitors to the nearby Cadwell Park race circuit. The bar features a games area, an open fire and Harry the pub dog, while the quiet lounge offers a couple of rocking chairs and fine views. Good value food is served daily. Motorcycle prints and photos adorn the walls – some are for sale. ♛Q☋❀⇋◐◑⊟⛺♣P

Scotter

White Swan

9 The Green, DN21 3UD
✪ 11.30-3.30, 6.30-midnight; 11.30-1am Fri & Sat; 11.30-midnight Sun
☎ (01724) 762342
John Smith's Bitter; Webster's Yorkshire Bitter; Tom Wood Bomber County; guest beers 🄷
Traditional village local with an attached hotel. Open-plan, with distinct drinking areas and a spacious dining facility, low ceilings and coal-effect gas fires provide a cosy, friendly environment. It attracts locals and those who travel to dine here. The garden overlooks the river with its resident ducks. Two rotating guest beers come from independent breweries. Q☋❀⇋◐◑♿P

Scunthorpe

Blue Bell

1-7 Oswald Road, DN15 7PU
✪ 9am-midnight (1am Fri & Sat); 9am-midnight Sun
☎ (01724) 863921
Greene King Abbot; Marston's Burton Bitter, Pedigree; guest beers 🄷
Town-centre Wetherspoon's of open-plan design, but with a raised, no-smoking area for diners and families. The large, L-shaped bar to one side serves up to three guest beers, plus two real ciders. Popular for meals during the day and early evening, it can get busy at weekends due to the influx of circuit drinkers. The pub hosts two beer festivals annually, during spring and autumn. Q❀◐◑♿⇌⊟●

Honest Lawyer

70 Oswald Road, DN15 7PG
✪ 11-11 (midnight Fri & Sat); 12-11 Sun
☎ (01724) 849906
Daleside Bitter; Taylor Landlord; guest beers 🄷
Friendly, single-roomed pub near the station and town centre. Wood decor throughout bears strong evidence of the pub's legal theme. The bar is long and narrow, with a snug area at the end housing a large TV (popular with football fans); daily newspapers are provided. Six real ales are offered – four are rotating guests – and Addlestones cider. Upstairs is the Gallows Restaurant (open Wed-Sat eves). The pub can get busy weekend evenings. ❀◑♿⇌⊟●

Malt Shovel

219 Ashby High Street, DN16 2JP
✪ 11-11 (midnight Fri & Sat); 12-10.30 Sun
☎ (01724) 843318
Bateman XXXB; Courage Directors; John Smith's Bitter; Theakston Old Peculier; guest beers 🄷
Private snooker facilities (membership available) and a lounge bar are combined under the same roof. The three rotating guest beers show a recent pleasing commitment to cask mild (mixed being a traditional steelworker's thirst slaker). The pub can get busy at lunchtime and early evening for good value food, otherwise a quiet drink can be enjoyed in the comfortably furnished, spacious room. Oak beams, leaded windows and a brick fireplace enhance the country inn feel, despite its shopping area location. Q❀◐◑

Sleaford

Barge & Bottle

Carre Street, NG34 7TR
✪ 9-11 (midnight Thu-Sat); 12-10.30 Sun
☎ (01529) 303303 🌐 thebargeandbottle.co.uk
Greene King IPA, Abbot; Tetley Bitter; Theakston Old Peculier; guest beers 🄷
Modern, open-plan pub modelled on a pub group design, but independently owned. A selection of nine real ales often includes seasonal favourites. An outside seating area overlooks the River Slea, and a footbridge leads to the new Hub crafts centre and the historic Navigation House. The pub is well known for its restaurant that serves a wide range of meals at reasonable prices. ❀◐◑♿⇌⍁

South Ormsby

Massingberd Arms

Brinkhill Road, LN11 8QS (1½ miles from A16 turn at Swaby)
✪ 11.30 (6 Mon)-11; 11-11 Fri-Sun
☎ (01507) 480492
Beer range varies 🄷
Set in an area of outstanding natural beauty, this welcoming pub is an ideal stopping place for walkers, cyclists and passing motorists. Dating back to the 19th-century it is named after the local lord of the manor. Fine, home-made food is based on local butcher's produce and served with fresh vegetables grown locally; bar snacks are available until 7pm. ♛Q❀◐◑♣P⍁

South Thoresby

Vine Inn

LN13 0AS (off A16)
✪ 12-3 (not Tue), 7-11; 12-3, 7-10.30 Sun
☎ (01507) 480273 ⊕ alford.info/vineinn
Bateman XB; guest beers Ⓗ
Delightful, 15th-century inn featuring open fires, exposed beams, local pictures and a display of old lemonade bottles. The garden to the side is popular with families in summer. Good, home-cooked food is available in the bars or restaurant. An ideal base for exploring the Lincolnshire Wolds, the pub offers en-suite accommodation (dogs are welcome). A quiz held every Saturday sends all proceeds to Lincolnshire Air Ambulance.
⛫Q❀⇌◑◐⊟♿♣P

Spalding

Olde White Horse

Churchgate, PE11 2RA (opp. town bridge)
✪ 11.30-11; 12-10.30 Sun
☎ (01775) 766740
Samuel Smith OBB Ⓗ
This 450-year-old, thatched coaching inn overlooks the River Welland. A popular meeting place for customers of all ages, it has a cosy lounge and adjoining dining room. The larger stone-floored, public bar is usually frequented by young people. This Sam Smith's pub offers excellent value beer and cheerful, efficient service from the hosts and staff. A wide range of pub meals includes Sunday roasts, served 12-6pm. A short stroll leads to historic Ayscoughfee Hall and Gardens. Q❀◑◐⊟⇶P

Red Lion Hotel

Market Place, PE11 1SU
✪ 11-11; 12-10.30 Sun
☎ (01775) 722869 ⊕ redlionhotel-spalding.co.uk
Draught Bass; Fuller's London Pride; Greene King Abbot; Marston's Pedigree Ⓗ
Busy hotel bar in the market place. A haven from the bustle of everyday life, its warm, friendly atmosphere, and rich mix of local people, welcomes visitors to the Fens. The Spalding Blues Club presents fortnightly bands in the Blues Café to the rear of the main bar. It is only two minutes from the Welland with its pleasant riverside walks. A monthly farmer's market is held nearby (first Sat). ⛫Q❀⇌◑◐⇶⊟

Stamford

Green Man

29 Scotgate, PE9 2PA
✪ 11-midnight; 12-midnight Sun
☎ (01780) 753598
Caledonian Deuchars IPA; John Smith's Bitter; guest beers Ⓗ
Stone-built, former coaching inn dating from 1796, with a split-level, L-shaped bar. Beer festivals are held each Easter and September on the secluded patio. A good range of European bottled beers and seven real ciders is stocked. No food is served on Sunday.
⛫❀⇌◑⇶⊟♣●▯

Otter's Pocket

20 All Saints Street, PE9 2PA
✪ 11-midnight; 12-11 Sun
☎ (01780) 762169 ⊕ theotterspocket.co.uk
Fuller's London Pride; Hop Back Summer Lightning; Oakham Bishops Farewell; Taylor Landlord; Wells Bombardier Ⓗ
Formerly the Albion, the bar covers one long room leading to a raised drinking area. Over-21s only are admitted to this sports-oriented pub. A selection of three draught Belgian beers are always on offer, together with bottled Belgian beers. Live jazz is performed on summer Sundays.
⛫◑⇶⊟

Periwig

7 All Saints Place, PE9 2AG
✪ 11-11 (midnight Wed & Thu; 1am Fri & Sat); 12-10.30 Sun
☎ (01780) 762169
Fuller's London Pride; Oakham JHB; Ufford Idle Hour; guest beers Ⓗ
Formerly the Marsh Harrier, this pub has been completely updated. Covering two floors and popular with all ages, it has plasma screens throughout the bars showing live sports coverage. Guest beers are regularly sourced from micro-breweries. A no-smoking area is available at lunchtime and a cheeseboard is served 12-7pm.
◑♿⇶⊟⚟

Surfleet

Ship Inn

154 Reservoir Road, PE11 4DH (off A16 S of A152 jct, follow brown signs)
✪ 11-3, 6-midnight; 12-11 Sun
☎ (01775) 680547 ⊕ shipinnsurfleet.com
Adnams Broadside; guest beers Ⓗ
The original Ship was demolished in 2004 and only some flagstones in the entrance and a model on the bar recall the old pub. The larger, new inn boasts four guest bedrooms. On the banks of the River Glen, where it becomes tidal and joins the Welland, the area is popular with dinghy sailors. The McMillan Way footpath passes the pub. Bar meals are served daily and the upstairs restaurant affords views over the river.
⛫Q⇌◑◐♿P

Swinhope

Click'em Inn

LN8 6BS (on B1203, 2 miles N of Binbrook)
✪ 12-3 (not Mon), 7-11 (11.30 Fri); 11.30-11.30 Sat; 12-3, 7-10.30 Sun
☎ (01472) 398253
Greene King Abbot; Shepherd Neame Spitfire; guest beers Ⓗ
Country pub set in the picturesque Lincolnshire Wolds. The unusual name originates from the counting of sheep through a nearby clicking gate. It is popular with both locals and diners due to the good, home-cooked food served in the bar and conservatory. The pub serves a house beer called Click'em Bitter, as well as changing guest beers

and a real cider (varies). It was voted local CAMRA's Country Pub of the Year for the last four years.
Q❀◑♣●P

Tattershall Thorpe

Bluebell Inn

Thorpe Road, Woodhall Spa, LN4 4PE
✪ 12-3, 7-11; 12-3, 7-10.30 Sun
☎ (01526) 342206
Greene King IPA; Taylor Landlord; Tom Wood Bomber County; guest beer Ⓗ
You step back in time when you enter this lovely 13th-century inn, one of Lincolnshire's oldest. There is a large open fire and the beamed ceilings are very low. The walls are covered with signed photos from WWII RAF squadrons who used the pub, including the famous 617 Dambusters. A no-smoking lounge is provided for diners or drinkers.
⛬Q❀◑⊟♿♣P⚟

Thornton Curtis

Thornton Hunt Inn

DN39 6XW (on A1077, between Wooton and Barton)
✪ 12-3, 6.30-11; 12-3, 7-10.30 Sun
☎ (01469) 531252 🌐 thornton-inn.co.uk
Taylor Landlord; Tetley Bitter; Tom Wood Shepherd's Delight Ⓗ
Well-appointed village local situated opposite a picturesque church. It places a strong emphasis on food, with involvement in the 'Tastes of Lincolnshire' project, but this is backed up by a good selection of real ales. The dining room is open seven nights a week. The decor is rustic, with exposed beams, brasses and rural pictures. Accommodation is available in six en-suite rooms. It stands one mile from the ruins of Thornton Abbey.
Q❀⛿◑♿P

Threekingham

Three Kings Inn

Saltersway, NG34 0AU
✪ 12-3 (not Tue), 7-11; closed Mon; 12-3, 7-11 Sun
☎ (01529) 240249
Draught Bass; Fuller's London Pride; Taylor Landlord; guest beer Ⓗ
Attractive rural coaching inn, built around 1700. The name comes from three Danish kings slaughtered here in 870 at the Battle of Stow; look for the stone effigies above the front door. The old original coat of arms hangs outside. The stone courtyard, now indoors, gives a genuine coaching inn feel, while the lounge and dining areas have attractive wood panelling. Apparently Dick Turpin's father-in-law once held the licence here.
⛬Q❀◑♿♣P⚟

Waddington

Three Horseshoes

Old High Street, LN5 9RF (off A607)
✪ 12-4, 7-11; 12-12.30am Fri; 11-12.30am Sat; 12-11 Sun
☎ (01522) 720448
John Smith's Bitter; guest beers Ⓗ
This traditional village local is situated at the heart of the village, within easy access of Lincoln; the half-hourly No. 1 bus service runs through the village. Featured brewery nights are organised occasionally, and there is always a good selection of guest beers, often from micro-breweries. Darts, dominoes and shove-ha'penny are all played, while the pub fields teams for football, darts and even fishing.
⛬❀◐⊟🚌♣P

Wainfleet

Bateman's Visitor Centre

Salem Bridge Brewery, PE24 4JE
✪ 11.30-3.30 (not winter Mon or Tue); eves by appointment
☎ (01754) 880317 🌐 bateman.co.uk
Bateman Mild, XB, Salem Porter, XXXB, seasonal beers Ⓗ
A chance to sample a comprehensive range of those 'good honest ales' at source. The brewery's core brands are always available, as well as seasonal beers. The Mill Bar is on the ground floor of the famous mill, next to the Brewery Experience exhibition, with its many interesting artefacts. An unusual place to drink, it offers indoor and outdoor games and a good selection of Lincolnshire food specialities.
Q❀◐⊟♿⛺⇌🚌♣P⊓

Willingham by Stow

Half Moon

23 High Street, DN21 5JZ
✪ 12-2 (not Mon-Wed), 5-11; 12-11 Sat & Sun
☎ (01427) 788340
Caledonian Deuchars IPA; guest beers Ⓗ
Popular and cosy village pub, just off the main road. It always serves two or three real ales that change frequently. The home-cooked food is a must – the fish and chip suppers are excellent (lunches served Thu & Fri; eve meals Thu-Sat). Various traditional games are played and the pub is headquarters of the local football teams. A beer festival usually takes place in the summer.
⛬Q❀◑⊟♣⊓

Willoughby

Willoughby Arms

Church Lane, LN13 9SU (on Alford-Skegness road)
✪ 12-2 (not Mon; 12-3 Sat), 7-11; 12-3, 7-10.30 Sun
☎ (01507) 462387
Bateman XB; guest beers Ⓗ
Willoughby was the home of Captain John Smith of Pocahontas fame, and the pub commemorates this; see the plaque affixed outside. The pub is friendly and welcoming with a great coal fire. It stocks an array of changing guest beers. The pub hosts many quizzes and auctions for charity and puts on celebration nights, such as St Patrick's Day. Children are welcome, as are well-behaved dogs.
⛬❀◑♣P

GREATER LONDON

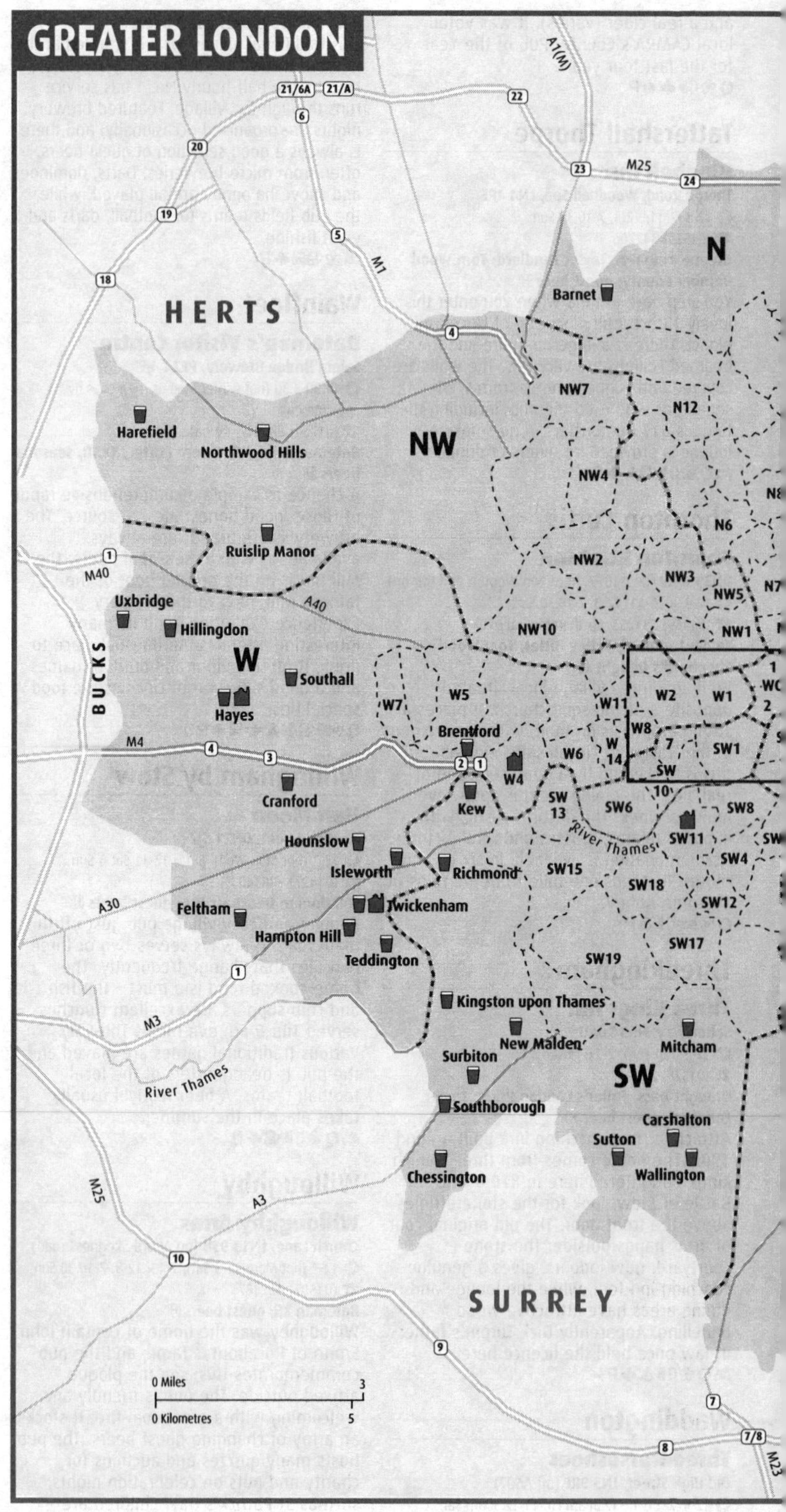

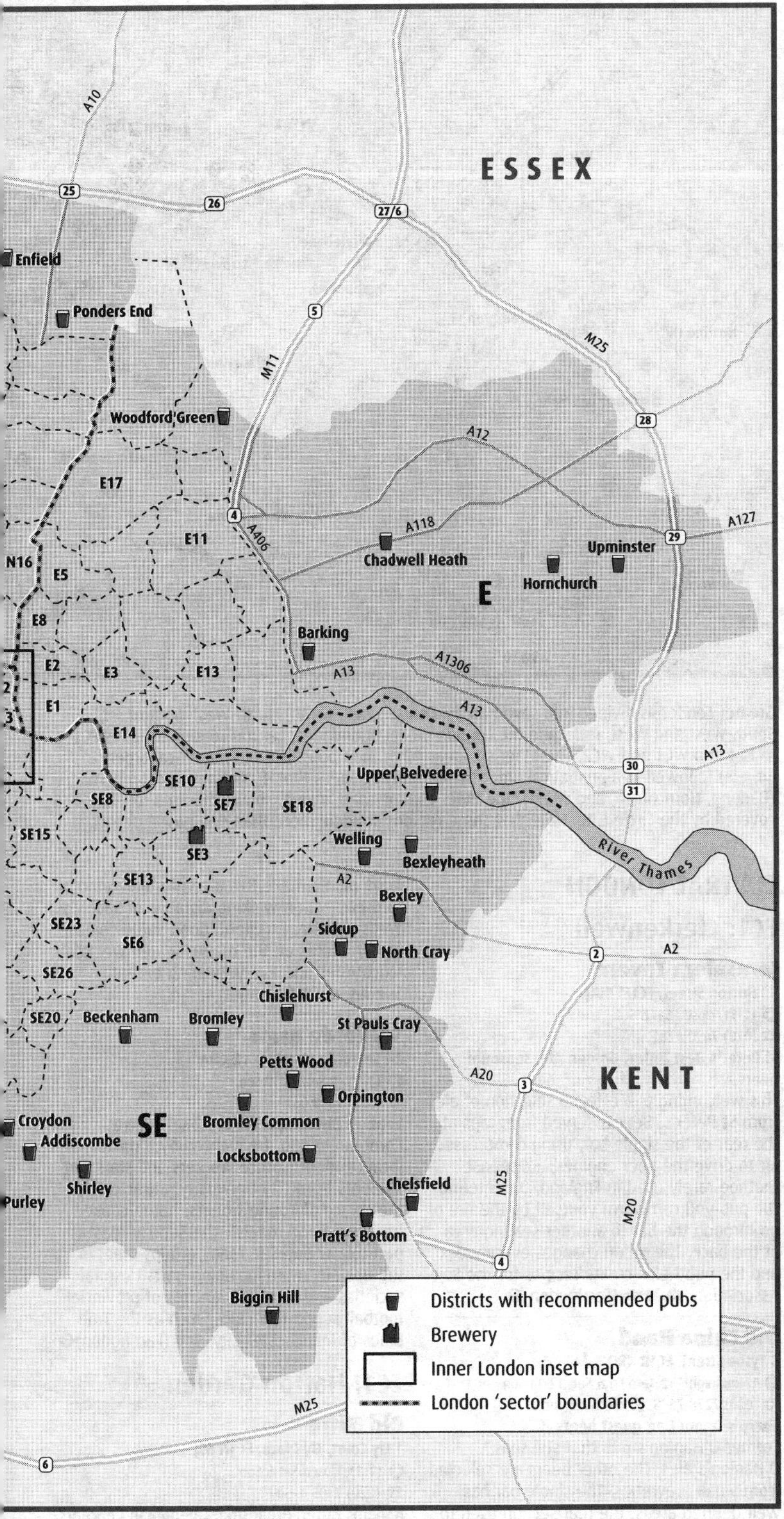
ESSEX
KENT
E
SE
Enfield
Ponders End
Woodford Green
E17
E11
N16
E5
E8
E2
E3
E13
E1
E14
SE10
SE7
SE8
SE18
SE15
SE3
SE13
SE23
SE6
SE26
SE20
Chadwell Heath
Upminster
Hornchurch
Barking
Upper Belvedere
Welling
Bexleyheath
Bexley
Sidcup
North Cray
Chislehurst
Beckenham
Bromley
St Pauls Cray
Petts Wood
Orpington
Bromley Common
Croydon
Addiscombe
Locksbottom
Shirley
Purley
Chelsfield
Pratt's Bottom
Biggin Hill
River Thames
A10
A12
A118
A127
A406
A13
A1306
A2
A20
M11
M25
M20
25
26
27/6
5
28
4
29
30
31
2
3
6
Districts with recommended pubs
Brewery
Inner London inset map
London 'sector' boundaries

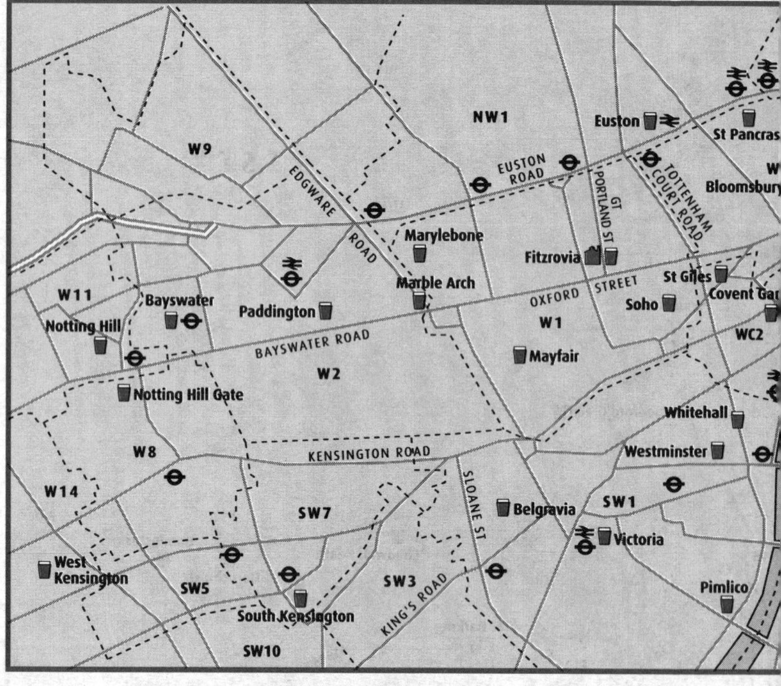

Greater London is divided into seven areas: Central, East, North, North-West, South-East, South-West and West, reflecting the London postal boundaries. Central London includes EC1 to EC4 and WC1 and WC2. The other six areas have their pubs listed in numerical order (E1, E4, etc) followed in alphabetical order by the outlying areas that do not have postal numbers (Barking, Hornchurch, and so on). The Inner London map, above, shows the area roughly covered by the Circle Line. Note that some regions straddle more than one postal district.

CENTRAL LONDON

EC1: Clerkenwell

Jerusalem Tavern

55 Britton Street, EC1M 5UQ

11-11; closed Sat & Sun

☎ (020) 7490 4281

St Peter's Best Bitter, Golden Ale, seasonal beers Ⓐ

This welcoming pub offers a selection of ales from St Peter's. Beer is served from taps at the rear of the single bar, using compressed air to drive the beer engines, a dispense method rarely used in England. On entering the pub you can warm yourself by the fire or go through the bar to another seating area at the back. The menu changes every week and the pub helps create recipes for the Soil Association. ⇌(Farringdon)⊖

Old China Hand

8 Tysoe Street, EC1R 4RQ

12-midnight; 12-1am Fri & Sat; 12-11 Sun

☎ (020) 7278 7678 oldchinahand.co.uk

Sharp's Doom Bar; guest beers Ⓗ

Former O'Hanlon's pub that still sells O'Hanlon's ales. The other beers are selected from small breweries. The single bar has well-defined areas, the rear section used to be the garden. Minimalist bare walls, subdued lighting, solid wooden furniture and large plants make this a comfortable place to drink, within walking distance of Sadler's Wells Theatre. Excellent, good value Chinese food features on the menu, served weekday lunchtimes and every evening except Sunday. ⊖(Angel)

Sekforde Arms

34 Sekforde Street, EC1R 0HA

11-11 (9 Sat); 11-9 Sun

☎ (020) 7608 0615

Young's Bitter, Special, seasonal beers Ⓗ

Community pub, frequented by a mix of local residents, office workers and staff and students from City University, attracted by the choice of Young's beers, home-cooked bar snacks and meals – the Sunday roast is particularly popular. Many groups meet in the upstairs room including Barts Hospital societies and London branches of provincial football supporters clubs, such as the True Blues of Manchester City. ⇌(Farringdon)⊖

EC1: Hatton Garden

Old Mitre ☆

1 Ely Court, Ely Place, EC1N 6SJ

11-11; closed Sat & Sun

☎ (020) 7405 4751

Adnams Bitter, Broadside; Caledonian Deuchars IPA; guest beers Ⓗ

Hidden away down an alley between Hatton

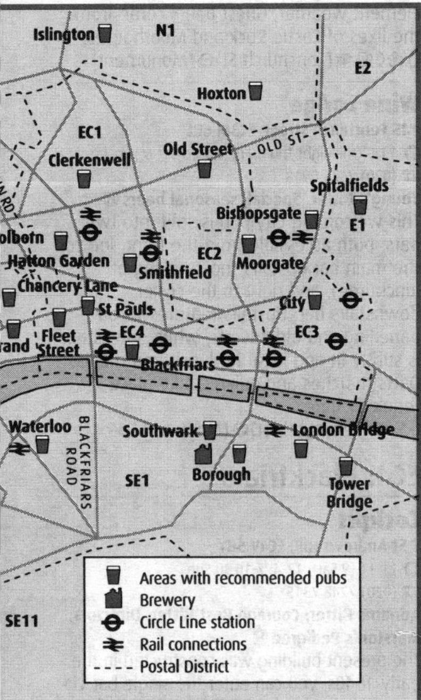

Garden and Ely Place, this gem is well worth seeking out. Originally the servants' quarters of the Bishop of Ely's Palace (and thus nominally in Cambridgeshire), the Mitre is a true haven from the city bustle. Superbly kept regular beers are joined by monthly guests from the larger micro-breweries. Toasties, sausages, pork pies and scotch eggs help keep hunger pangs at bay.
Q❀⊟≠(Farringdon/City Thameslink) ⊖(Chancery Lane)

EC1: Old Street

Masque Haunt

168-172 Old Street, EC1V 9PB
9am-11.30; 9am-11 Sun
☎ (020) 7241 4195
Courage Best Bitter, Directors; Fuller's London Pride; Greene King Abbot; Marston's Pedigree; Shepherd Neame Spitfire; guest beers Ⓗ
A light and airy Wetherspoon's shop conversion on the edge of the city, frequented by a loyal band of regulars, both locals and commuters. Pleasant and efficient staff make this one of the chain's best pubs. Guest beers from west London brewery Grand Union are to be found on most visits as they are a particular favourite of the manager. Such is their popularity that the brewery delivers directly on a weekly basis.
◖◗≠⊖🍎

Old Fountain

3 Baldwin Street, EC1V 9NU
11-11; closed Sat & Sun
☎ (020) 7253 2970
Adnams Broadside; Fuller's Discovery, London Pride; guest beer Ⓗ
A single bar pub on two levels with, unusually, entrances opening onto different streets. This comfortable pub, offering keenly priced food, draws its custom from local businesses and the adjacent Moorfields Eye Hospital. The full time cellarman keeps the beers in tip-top condition at this friendly free house, with the London Pride being the best for some distance. A large aquarium in one corner gives a peaceful alternative to the TV opposite. ❀◖≠⊖

EC1: Smithfield

Butchers Hook & Cleaver

61-63 West Smithfield, EC1A 9DY
11-11; closed Sat & Sun
☎ (020) 7600 9181
Fuller's Chiswick, Discovery, London Pride, ESB, seasonal beers Ⓗ
Situated near Smithfield Market, St Barts Hospital and the Museum of London, the pub displays photographs of the local area. To the right of a large, semi-circular bar is a no-smoking area, while the left-hand side is dominated by a large TV screen. A wrought iron spiral staircase leads to a balcony where waitress service is provided at lunchtime.
◖◗♿≠(Farringdon)⊖(Barbican)⚟

EC2: Bishopsgate

Dirty Dick's

202 Bishopsgate, EC2M 4NR
11-midnight; 11.30-11 Sat; closed Sun
☎ (020) 7283 5888
Young's Bitter, Special, seasonal beers Ⓗ
Renowned city hostelry evoking Hogarth's London. The name commemorates Nathaniel Bentley, a London dandy who was so devastated by the death of his fiancée that afterwards he dressed shabbily and refused to wash. Wooden fixtures in Georgian style impart a welcoming feel to all areas of the pub: main bar, upstairs restaurant and downstairs vaults. The pub serves a good range of snacks and meals.
◖◗≠(Liverpool St)⊖⚟

EC2: Moorgate

Red Lion

1 Eldon Street, EC2M 7LS
11-11; closed Sat & Sun
☎ (020) 7247 5381
Caledonian Deuchars IPA; Fuller's London Pride; Greene King IPA, Abbot; Young's Bitter; guest beers Ⓗ
Small, two-bar corner pub, serving regular guest beers from the larger micros and

INDEPENDENT BREWERIES

Battersea SW11
Brew Wharf SE1
Bünker WC2
Fuller's W4
Grand Union Hayes
Mash W1
Meantime SE7
Twickenham Twickenham
Young's (moved to Bedford October 06)
Zerodegrees SE3

national brewers. The handpumps in the upstairs bar are not used, however the friendly staff are happy to send beer up. The downstairs bar features snob screens (not original) and Victorian brass water fountains. Food is served until 9pm, with speciality pies and sausages changing daily.
Q◖◗⇌(Liverpool St)⊖♣

EC3: City

Counting House

50 Cornhill, EC3V 3PD
✪ 11-11; closed Sat & Sun
☎ (020) 7283 7123
Fuller's Chiswick, Discovery, London Pride, ESB, seasonal beers; guest beers Ⓗ
Previously a bank, this pub consists of a single, large oval bar with an upstairs seating area. The former manager's offices to the rear are used as function rooms. A war memorial, thought to be the only one actually in a public house, commemorates the bank staff who died in the Great War. The building dates back to 1893 and part of it is built on a Roman basilica that was incorporated into the walls of the strong room.
Q◖◗⇌(Liverpool St)⊖(Monument/Bank)

Elephant

119 Fenchurch Street, EC3M 5BA
✪ 11-9 (midnight Thu & Fri); closed Sat & Sun
☎ (020) 7623 8970
Young's Bitter, Special, seasonal beers Ⓗ
The upstairs bar boasts much woodwork, and is just right for a perfect pint of Young's. Downstairs the atmosphere is better suited to a sit down drink while watching sport on the large TV screen or for a conversation with friends. The upstairs bar closes at 8pm; the downstairs is then accessible by the side entrance in Hogarth Passage.
◖⊟⇌(Fenchurch St)⊖(Monument)

Lamb Tavern

10-12 Leadenhall Market, EC3V 1LR
✪ 11-9 (11 Wed; midnight Thu & Fri); closed Sat & Sun
☎ (020) 7626 2454
Young's Bitter, Special; seasonal beers Ⓗ
Magnificent Grade II listed pub in an unusual setting: Leadenhall Market is full of small retailers of quality produce and the Lamb fits in perfectly. The main bar and mezzanine floor are frequently packed, and drinkers overflow into the market area, which is covered. A notable feature is the beautifully tiled basement.
Q❀◖◗⇌(Liverpool St)⊖(Monument/Bank)

Swan

Ship Tavern Passage, 78 Gracechurch Street, EC3V 1LY
✪ 11-11; closed Sat & Sun
☎ (020) 7283 7712
Fuller's Chiswick, London Pride, seasonal beers; guest beers Ⓗ
Small two-bar pub that was granted the first 24-hour licence for use on special occasions. Despite this, early closing is the norm here, so go early or ring before visiting late in the evening. A narrow ground floor bar is supplemented by a covered passageway outside that is popular with drinkers in clement weather. Guest beers come from the likes of Castle Rock and Moorhouses.
Q❀◖⊟⇌(Fenchurch St)⊖(Monument)

Wine Lodge

145 Fenchurch Street, EC3M 6BL
✪ 11-9 (midnight Thu & Fri); closed Sat & Sun
☎ (020) 7626 0918
Young's Bitter, Special, seasonal beers Ⓗ
This welcoming City pub is split into two bars, both accessible from the front: left for the main bar upstairs (no-smoking at lunchtime), and right to the cosier downstairs bar. Upstairs features wood panelling and old adverts, while downstairs is subtly lit and ideal for lunchtime meals. Darts matches and quizzes take place regularly here.
◖♿⇌(Fenchurch St)⊖(Monument)⚞

EC4: Blackfriars

Cockpit

7 St Andrews Hill, EC4V 5BY
✪ 11-11 (9 Sat); 12-4, 7-10.30 Sun
☎ (020) 7248 7315
Adnams Bitter; Courage Best Bitter, Directors; Marston's Pedigree Ⓗ
The present building was constructed in the early 1840s; you can enter the single bar via an unusual curved door. Originally called the Cockpit, the name was changed to the Three Castles to disassociate the pub from the 'sport' of cockfighting, but it was renamed again to commemorate it being the last venue to stage a legal cockfight. With a welcoming atmosphere, it is one of the few pubs in the area to open at the weekend. ◖⇌⊖♣

EC4: Fleet Street

Old Bank of England

194 Fleet Street, EC4 2LT
✪ 11-11; closed Sat & Sun
☎ (020) 7430 2255
Fuller's Chiswick, Discovery, London Pride, ESB, seasonal beers Ⓗ
A pub since 1995, it was built in 1888 as the law courts' branch of the Bank of England, and is Grade I listed. This highly atmospheric pub relates its history by means of prints and newspaper articles. Three brass chandeliers hang from an ornate plastered ceiling above the central oval bar. Legend has it that tunnels under the pub were used by Sweeney Todd to go to Mrs Lovett's pie shop. Meals are served all day until 9pm (8pm Fri).
◖◗⇌(Blackfriars)⊖(Temple/Chancery Lane)

EC4: St Pauls

Paternoster

2-4 Queens Head Passage, Paternoster Square, EC4M 7DZ
✪ 10-11; 12-4 Sat & Sun
☎ (020) 7248 4035
Young's Bitter, Special; seasonal beers Ⓗ
Newly-built Young's house in the Paternoster Square development to the north of St Paul's Cathedral. A dark wood bar and floor with leather 'clubman' sofas and chairs provide a comfortable environment for drinkers and

diners alike. There is a raised no-smoking section in the centre of the bar. Good disabled access is an asset in this more than adequate replacement for the Master Gunner (also Young's) formerly on this site.
◖◗♿≠(Farringdon)⊖⚡

WC1: Bloomsbury

Calthorpe Arms

252 Grays Inn Road, WC1X 8JR

⏲ 11-11.30 (midnight Fri & Sat); 12-10.30 Sun

☎ (020) 7278 4732

Young's Bitter, Special, seasonal beers 🄷

Single-bar pub with a restaurant/meeting room upstairs. It was once used as a temporary magistrates' court after the first recorded murder of an on-duty policeman in 1830. The long-standing tenant ensures a cheerful, friendly atmosphere. A busy lunchtime and early evening trade is assured from the surrounding offices and hospitals, with regulars tending to visit later and at weekends. Meals include daily specials (eve meals served weekdays). Pavement benches are provided at this twice CAMRA North London Pub of the Year winner.
❀◖◗≠(King's Cross)⊖(Russell Sq)

Lamb

94 Lamb's Conduit Street, WC1N 3LZ

⏲ 11-midnight; 12-4, 7-10.30 Sun

☎ (020) 7405 0713

Young's Bitter, Special, seasonal beers 🄷

Nestling in the shadow of Great Ormond Street Hospital is this splendid, Grade II listed Georgian pub, noted for its exquisite green tiling and mosaic frontage. The interior does not disappoint either, with its island bar, snob screens and green leather banquettes. A forerunner of the juke box, a polyphon, can be played in aid of charity. Children are not permitted here. Food is served 12-2.30pm all week and 6-9pm Monday-Thursday and Saturday.
Q❀◖◗≠(Kings Cross)⊖(Russell Sq)

Rugby Tavern

19 Great James Street, WC1N 3ES

⏲ 11-11; closed Sat & Sun

☎ (020) 7405 1384

Shepherd Neame Master Brew Bitter, Spitfire, seasonal beers 🄷

The pub name probably owes more to the fact that it was built on land donated by the founder of Rugby School than any innate connection to the game, although prints celebrating the sport abound. Its location in a quiet backwater, with seating in a pedestrianised zone, makes it an attractive proposition for a summer pint. Serving the local residential and office community, it gets busy late afternoon and early evening. The upstairs function room doubles as a restaurant. ❀◖◗⊖(Russell Sq)♣

WC1: Holborn

Cittie of Yorke ☆

22 High Holborn, WC1V 6BS

⏲ 11.30-11; closed Sun

☎ (020) 7242 7670

Samuel Smith OBB 🄷

Close to the Holborn Bars, the historic entrance to London, a pub has stood on this site since 1430. Rebuilt in 1695 as the Gray's Inn Coffee House, it is now a three-bar pub, the cellar bar being part of the 17th-century structure. Now Grade II listed, it boasts a hugely impressive interior. A rare triangular stove is still in use, with an underfloor chimney. Despite the exceptional surroundings the beer prices here are competitive and the food is good.
♨Q◖◗♿≠(Farringdon)⊖(Chancery Lane)♣⚡

Penderel's Oak

283-288 High Holborn, WC1V 7HJ

⏲ 9am-1am; 9am-midnight Sun

☎ (020) 7242 5669

Fuller's London Pride; Greene King Abbot; Marston's Burton Bitter, Pedigree; guest beers 🄷

Typical Wetherspoon's conversion of former office premises, displaying shelves of dusty books. The ground floor is mainly used by tourists and diners; the basement bar, with TV screens tuned to sport, can be noisy. The pub boasts award-winning toilet facilities. Meals are served from opening through to 11pm. This large Wetherspoon's serves four changing guest beers. Benches allow for some outdoor drinking.
Q❀◖◗♿⊖🍎⚡

Princess Louise ☆

208 High Holborn, WC1V 7EP

⏲ 11 (12 Sat)-11; 12-10.30 Sun

☎ (020) 7405 8816

Samuel Smith OBB 🄷

Grade II listed Victorian masterpiece. Built in 1854, with an interior by WB Simpson dating back to the end of the 19th century, this pub is an essential part of any visit to central London. The visitor will find an interior of stained and gold embossed glass, polychrome tilework, a patterned ceiling and the original mahogany bar; downstairs are the contemporary gents' WCs. Named after Queen Victoria's fourth daughter, it sells proper Samuel Smith's products without adjuncts at a keen price. Q◖◗⊖

WC1: St Pancras

Mabel's Tavern

9 Mabledon Place, WC1H 9AZ

⏲ 11-11; 12-10.30 Sun

☎ (020) 7387 7739

Shepherd Neame Master Brew Bitter, Kent's Best, Spitfire, Bishops Finger, seasonal beers 🄷

Bright and comfortable pub, halfway between Euston and King's Cross/St Pancras stations. The long, single bar serves the main drinking area between the no-smoking alcove on the left and a raised area with coal-effect gas fire to the right. The pub attracts office staff at lunchtime, tourists and locals in the evenings and at weekends. The Shepherd Neame Best Cellar award 2005 testifies to the beer quality (only three beers offered at weekends). A few seats are available outside. Winner of CAMRA North London Pub of the Year 2006.
❀◖◗≠(Kings Cross/Euston)⊖⚡

Skinners Arms
114 Judd Street, WC1H 9NT
☉ 11-11; closed Sat & Sun
☎ (020) 7837 6521
Greene King IPA, Abbot; Taylor Landlord; guest beer Ⓗ
Former Greene King corner pub; the mock-Victorian interior extends to the curtains, bar counter, mirrored pillars, stained glass and flocked wallpaper. A raised seating area to the left and a rear no-smoking section complete what must surely become the waiting room of choice for the discerning Eurostar traveller of the future.
⛼Q◐ ⇌(Kings Cross)⊖⊬

WC2: Chancery Lane

Knights Templar
95 Chancery Lane, WC2A 1DT
☉ 9am-11.30; 11-7 Sat; closed Sun
☎ (020) 7831 2660
Fuller's London Pride; Greene King IPA; Marston's Pedigree; Shepherd Neame Spitfire; guest beers Ⓗ
Imposing Wetherspoon's conversion of a listed former bank. Its scroll remains above the entrance, which leads into a grand high-ceilinged bar with many decorative features retained and enhanced. A metal sculpture of a knight as its centrepiece commemorates the Knights Templar, a military order who rendered service to the Crown as bankers until dissolved by the Pope in 1312. Upstairs, three interconnected no-smoking, mezzanine level rooms for discreet liaisons can also be hired for functions. Q⛾♿⊖⊬

Seven Stars
53-54 Carey Street, WC2A 2JB
☉ 11 (12 Sat)-11; 12-10.30 Sun
☎ (020) 7242 8521
Adnams Bitter, Broadside; Harveys Sussex Best Bitter; guest beer Ⓗ
A delightful, old-fashioned, narrow Grade II listed pub dating from 1602, opposite the Royal Courts of Justice. The walls of this little pub are decorated with film posters with a legal theme and pictures of famous judges. Food is available every day until 9pm. Upstairs toilets are reached via a narrow staircase behind the bar. Q◐⊖

WC2: Covent Garden

Freemasons Arms
81-82 Long Acre, WC2E 9NG
☉ 12-11; 12-9 (may close earlier) Sun
☎ (020) 7836 3115
Shepherd Neame Master Brew Bitter, Spitfire; seasonal beers Ⓗ
Smartly furnished lounge bar with a polished floor, mirrors and raised seating area. Since its Charringtons days in the 1980s, it has passed to Sam Smith, Greene King and now Shepherd Neame who awarded it their Pub of the Year in 2006. The first floor has two function rooms. Home-cooked food is served 12-3, 5-9 weekdays, 12-9 Saturday and 12-4.30 Sunday. The pub's Masonic connections are indicated by the symbols on the frontage. ◐♿⊖

Harp
47 Chandos Place, WC2N 4HS
☉ 11-11; closed Sun
☎ (020) 7836 4291
Black Sheep Best Bitter; Harveys Sussex Best Bitter; Taylor Landlord; guest beers Ⓗ
Narrow, bustling, mirror-lined drinkers' pub, with a thespian character, popular with musicians and stage hands from the adjacent London Coliseum. Owned by the Punch Group, it offers a good selection of guest beers, mostly from regional breweries. There is a no-smoking room upstairs. Dating from the 18th century, it dropped 'Welsh' from its name in 1995. The TV is tuned to football but without any sound. Q⇌(Charing Cross)⊖⊬

WC2: St Giles

Angel
61-62 St Giles High Street, WC2H 8LE
☉ 11.30 (12 Sun)-11; 1-10.30 Sun
☎ (020) 7240 2876
Samuel Smith OBB Ⓗ
Classic local with three distinct drinking areas. The public bar has chess tables, darts, theatre posters and TV for sports. The main bar has tall, curtained windows, chandeliers, a fireplace and leather chairs. A tiled passageway, used for outdoor drinking on summer afternoons, leads to the small, cosy saloon bar. Meals are served until 9pm (6pm Sun). A tavern has stood here since the 16th-century, it is one of the handful of Sam Smith's London pubs retaining handpumps.
⛼Q❀◐⊟⊖(Tottenham Crt Rd)♣

WC2: Strand

Devereux
20 Devereux Court, WC2R 3JJ
☉ 11-11 (11.30 Thu-Fri); closed Sat & Sun
☎ (020) 7583 4562
Greene King Old Speckled Hen; Wells Bombardier; guest beers Ⓗ
Smart, comfortable lounge bar run by Punch group in an alleyway off the Strand. Dating from 1844 and Grade II listed, it offers a changing range of guest beers, mainly from regionals, chalked up on a board. There is optional table service for drinks and food, which is served all day. The clientele includes office workers and members of the legal profession. An upstairs restaurant opens at lunchtime. ◐⊖(Temple)⊬

Edgar Wallace
40-41 Essex Street, WC2R 3JE
☉ 11-11 (11.30 Fri); closed Sat & Sun
☎ (020) 7353 3120
Adnams Bitter; guest beers Ⓗ
Popular, single-bar corner pub run by Enterprise Inns with an adventurous range of guest beers from micros supplied by SIBA brewers. The house beer, EPA, is from Nethergate. Food, served 12-8pm, includes British tapas-style snacks, such as fishfinger sandwiches. Upstairs is a lunchtime restaurant/function room. Originally the Essex Head and frequented by Samuel Johnson, it was rebuilt in 1891 and renamed in 1995. It hosts up to three beer festivals a year. ◐⊖(Temple)

EAST LONDON

E1: Spitalfields

Pride of Spitalfields

3 Heneage Street, E1 5LJ
⏲ 11-11; 12-10.30 Sun
☎ (020) 7247 8933
Crouch Vale Brewers Gold; Fuller's London Pride, ESB; guest beers Ⓗ
Located close to Brick Lane, the curry centre of East London, this friendly, back-street local has an open fire in winter, and gets very busy. Old pictures of the area add interest to the small, single bar, which offers varying guest beers. It hosts quiz and race nights and evening meals can be booked. Some seats are available at the front for summer drinking. It may close early Sunday evening. ⛫❀◑⊖(Aldgate East/Shoreditch)♣

E1: Whitechapel

Black Bull

199 Whitechapel Road, E1 1DE
⏲ 11-11 (midnight Sat); 12-11 Sun
☎ (020) 7247 6707
Nethergate Suffolk County, Augustinian Ale, seasonal beers Ⓗ
The pub's mock-Tudor frontage serves as a landmark at the corner of Vallance Road. A true free house, it offers a range of the excellent Nethergate beers. The spacious, open-plan area is served by a single bar at the rear. Frequented by market traders and staff from the Royal London Hospital, it shows major sports events on a large screen. Cards and dominoes are played here. The pub closes early on Sunday if quiet. ⊖(Whitechapel)♣

E2: Bethnal Green

Camel

277 Globe Road, E2 0JD
⏲ 11-11; 12-10.30 Sun
☎ (020) 8983 9888
Adnams Bitter, Broadside Ⓗ
This camel has risen from the sands of abandonment and neglect. Shut and threatened with demolition, it reopened after much petitioning by locals. They have been well rewarded by its renaissance. It serves Adnams ales and gourmet pie and mash (food is served 12.30-9pm). The pub has traditional character, a brown tiled exterior, a single long bar and 1940s design wallpaper. Close to York Hall, a once famous boxing venue, it displays a photograph of notable 1940s and 50s British pugilists. ◐◑≠⊖⊁

E3: Bow

Coborn Arms

8 Coborn Road, E3 2DA
⏲ 11-11.30 (midnight Thu-Sat); 12-11 Sun
☎ (020) 8980 3793
Young's Bitter, Special, seasonal beers Ⓗ
Friendly local purchased by Young's in 1984 and extended into number six next door. Now open plan with a central bar, it retains distinct drinking areas. Although not classed as a sports pub, it does have a large screen tuned to sports channels and a dartboard is housed in its own room. The sign is a work of fiction – it was discovered that the Coborn family (local benefactors) was not entitled to bear arms. Meals are served all day (1-9pm) at the weekend. ❀◐◑♿⊖(Mile End)♣

E5: Clapton

Anchor & Hope

15 High Hill Ferry, E5 9HS (800 yds N of Lea Bridge Rd along River Lea)
⏲ 11 (12 Sat)-11; 12-10.30 Sun
☎ (020) 8806 1730
Fuller's London Pride, ESB, seasonal beers; guest beers Ⓗ
Though there is no saloon, food or car park, the pub does however provide good beer and a great community spirit. It also fields a darts team. Built alongside the River Lea, it is popular with walkers and cyclists who drink on the river path. The new landlord has introduced brewery specials and guest beers. ⛫≠♣

Princess of Wales

146 Lea Bridge Road, E5 9BQ
⏲ 11.30-11; 12-10.30 Sun
☎ (020) 8533 3463
Young's Bitter, Special; seasonal beers Ⓗ
Renowned venue on the bank of the River Lea, where a core of local regulars is supplemented by many walkers, cyclists and boaters, especially at weekends and in summer. The original Victorian lounge and public bars have been sensitively modernised. It serves a selection of bar meals and a popular Sunday roast. Ample parking is a bonus. Take a 15-minute walk down the river for a view of the 2012 Olympics site. ⛫❀◐◑⊟≠♣P

E8: Hackney

Pembury Tavern

90 Amhurst Road, E8 1JH
⏲ 12-11 daily
☎ (020) 8986 8597
Beer range varies Ⓗ
Closed due to a fire and reopened after extensive rebuilding, the Tavern boasts an impressive 16 handpumps serving a good selection of beers from Milton Brewery in Cambridge, plus varying guests from micros. No smoking, no Guinness and no big brand keg lager here, but it does sell draught Budvar, a good selection of bottled beers, mostly from Belgium, and a choice of single malts. Real cider or perry is usually available, too. It has pool and bar billiard tables. Q◐◑♿≠(Hackney Downs/Central)♣●⊁🍷

E11: Leytonstone

Birkbeck Tavern

45 Langthorne Road, E11 4HL
⏲ 11-11 (midnight Fri & Sat); 12-11 Sun
☎ (020) 8539 2584
Beer range varies Ⓗ
This excellent pub, tucked away behind

Leyton tube station, is a revolving festival of micro-brewery beers – it serves some 350 in a year and is a must for connoisseurs of good real ale. A real pub, it fields two darts teams. No food is served, but rolls are available at lunchtime. The pub has an extensive garden. ❀⊖(Leyton)♣

E11: Wanstead

Duke of Edinburgh

79 Nightingale Lane, E11 2EY

11-11 (11.30 Thu; midnight Fri & Sat); 12-11 Sun

☎ (020) 8989 0014

Adnams Broadside; Greene King IPA; Young's Bitter H

A proper back-street pub that has survived 100 years. Originally two bars, it has been opened out, with a recent extension that is no-smoking. It features a dark wood interior, housing a large screen and two plasma TVs for sport. Meals are served 11-8pm daily. It hosts live music and karaoke (both once a month). You can play darts here or try your hand at shove-ha'penny – a fast disappearing pub game. Say hello to the pub dog. ❀◑◗⊖(Snaresbrook)♣P⍀

George

159 High Street, E11 2RL

9am-midnight (12.30am Fri & Sat); 9am-midnight Sun

☎ (020) 8989 2921

Courage Directors; Greene King Abbot; Marston's Pedigree; guest beers H

A Wetherspoon outlet that was actually a pub in its former life. Spacious, and now open-plan, it is split into several drinking areas, including an upstairs bar and a family section. Previously the George Hotel, one of Grand Met's keg pubs, it retains the etched windows. A strange feature is an enormous chair in the shape of a mythical creature. The terrestrial TV is tuned to sport; the manager is a rarity – a Leyton Orient supporter. Sheppy's cider is sold. ❀◑◗♿⊖●⍀

Nightingale

51 Nightingale Lane, E11 2EY

11-11 (midnight Thu-Sat); 12-11 Sun

☎ (020) 8530 4540

Courage Best Bitter; guest beers H

Traditional, friendly pub in an area known as Mob's Hole, where highwaymen used to meet. Originally several bars and a jug and bottle off-licence, it has been opened up to give a central bar, but has retained two rooms – one for non-smokers. Six beers are always stocked here and six of them change frequently. It also stocks a large range of whiskies. ◑♿⊖(Snaresbrook)⍀

E13: Plaistow

Black Lion

59-61 High Street, E13 0AD

11-3, 5-11; 11-11 Wed-Sat; 12-10.30 Sun

☎ (020) 8472 2351

Courage Best Bitter; guest beers H

Although rebuilt in the early 18th century, a coaching inn has stood on this site for over 600 years. The long public bar shows TV sport. The quieter lounge bar is accessed by the door to the side of the pub. At the rear, the old stables have been converted to a function room with its own bar. A cobbled yard leads to the garden of this historic pub. ❀◑◗⊖

E14: Limehouse

Grapes

76 Narrow Street, E14 8BP

12-3, 5.30-11; 12-11 Sat; 12-10.30 Sun

☎ (020) 7987 4396

Adnams Bitter; Marston's Pedigree; Taylor Landlord H

Riverside pub that has hardly changed over the years. Built in 1720 after the original pub burned down, it is a Grade II listed building with a wealth of dark wood and old prints. A deck overlooks the Thames. This was one of five pubs used by Dickens to create 'six jolly fellowship porters' in his novel Our Mutual Friend. A renowned fish restaurant upstairs is an added attraction. The pub is dog-friendly but mobile phones are banned.

Q❀◑◗⊖(Limehouse/West Ferry DLR)♣⍀

E17: Walthamstow

Nag's Head

9 Orford Road, E17 9LP (10 mins walk from Walthamstow Central)

4-11; 4-10.30 Sun

☎ (020) 8520 9709

Adnams Broadside; Fuller's London Pride; Mighty Oak Oscar Wilde; guest beers H

Community pub in the heart of historic Walthamstow. The 12th-century parish church and local history museum are nearby. Built in 1857 as a coaching inn, the pub itself looks modern. Facilities here include a community notice board, bicycle park, a seating area with benches at the entrance and a large stone-paved garden with tables, chairs and heaters at the back. There is always a mild on handpump and a range of Belgian bottled beers to choose from.

❀⇌⊖(Walthamstow Central)

Village

31 Orford Road, E17 9NL

12-11; 12-10.30 Sun

☎ (020) 8521 4398

Adnams Broadside; Courage Directors; Greene King IPA; guest beers H

Set in the heart of a conservation area, it is a surprise to discover that this comfortable local in a quiet side street has only been a pub for about 16 years. It has a long, single bar that leads to a cosy snug. The paved garden behind the pub appeals to many on sunny days. ❀◑◗⇌⊖ (Walthamstow Central)

Barking

Britannia

1 Church Road, IG11 8PR (near A123)

11-3, 5-11; 12-11 Sat & Sun

☎ (020) 8594 1305

Young's Bitter, Special, seasonal beers H

The architecture of the Britannia is a tribute to Barking's nautical past, once boasting

England's largest fishing fleet. The saloon bar is a comfortable home-from-home for most locals and is normally quiet, in contrast to the noisier public bar with its bare boards, juke box, TV, darts and pool. Bar meals are excellent value, available Sunday-Friday. Entertainment is also occasionally staged in this friendly local. The surrounding area has changed dramatically with new apartments replacing the old flats.
Q❀◖⊟⇌⊖♣P

Chadwell Heath

Eva Hart

1128 High Road, RM6 4AH (at A118/Station Rd jct)
⏲ 9am-midnight daily
☎ (020) 8597 1069
Greene King IPA, Abbot; Marston's Burton Bitter, Pedigree; Shepherd Neame Spitfire; guest beers Ⓗ
Pleasant and comfortable Wetherspoon's converted from a former police station; a haven in a locality where real ale is sparse. It usually offers two or three guest beers, plus Westons Old Rosie cider. It has extensive no-smoking areas on both the ground floor and balcony, where children are welcome until 7pm. Eva Hart, a local music teacher, was one of the oldest Titanic survivors. Good value meals are served 12-10pm (and breakfasts 9-11am) daily. ❀◖◗♿⇌P●⊬

Hornchurch

Chequers

North Street, RM11 1ST (near A124 at Billet Lane jct)
⏲ 11-11; 12-10.30 Sun
☎ (01708) 442094
Ansells Best Bitter; Draught Bass; Tetley Bitter; Young's Bitter Ⓗ
Genuine local that has managed to retain much of its character. Situated on a large traffic island, it sells excellent value beers and is definitely a drinkers' pub. This busy local enjoys a keen darts following, fielding several teams. A TV in an area at the end of the bar shows sporting events. It is a regular local CAMRA Pub of the Year contender.
⇌(Emerson Pk)♣P

Upminster

Crumpled Horn

33-37 Corbets Tey Road, RM14 2AJ (on B1421)
⏲ 11-11 (midnight Fri & Sat); 12-11 Sun
☎ (01708) 226698
Adnams Broadside; Banks's Bitter; Marston's Pedigree; guest beer Ⓗ
Opened in September 2000, this W&D Pathfinder Inn (formerly Wizard) is an attractive conversion of former shops, near the centre of Upminster. The guest ale changes regularly, providing a welcome boost to the limited local real ale scene, augmented by occasional beer festivals. A prize quiz is held on Tuesday evening. Meals are served 12-9pm (8pm weekends). The pub's name, chosen in a competition, refers to a nearby, long-defunct dairy that was sadly demolished at the end of 2003.
◖◗♿⇌⊖⊬

Woodford Green

Cricketers

299-301 High Road, IG8 9HG (on A1099)
⏲ 11 (11.30 Sat)-11; 12-10.30 Sun
☎ (020) 8504 2734
McMullen AK, Country; guest beer Ⓗ
Winner of local CAMRA Pub of the Year 2006. Pleasant local with a comfortable saloon bar and a more basic public, with a dartboard. The saloon displays insignia plaques for all 18 first class cricket counties, together with a number of photos of Sir Winston Churchill, for many years the local MP – his statue stands on the green almost opposite. The guest beer changes monthly and the meals, including special deals for older people, are hearty and good value (no food Sun). The garden boasts a petanque pitch.
❀◖⊟♿♣P

Traveller's Friend

496-498 High Road, IG8 0PN (on A104)
⏲ 12-11 (midnight Fri); 12-5, 7-11 Sun
☎ (020) 8504 2435
Adnams Broadside; Archers Best Bitter; Courage Best Bitter; Greene King Abbot; guest beer Ⓗ
Excellent, genuine local on a slip road off the busy main road. This comfortable, friendly pub features oak-panelled walls and rare original snob screens. Run by a couple who hail from South Wales, they have been making everyone welcome and serving great beers for quite a few years now. They offer a guest ale at all times and host a beer festival in April. Parking is limited, but several buses stop nearby. No food is served Sunday. Q❀◖♿⊟P

NORTH LONDON

N1: De Beauvoir Town

Talbot

109 Mortimer Road, N1 4JY
⏲ 4.30 (12 Sat)-11 (midnight Fri & Sat); 12-10.30 Sun
☎ (020) 7254 0754
Adnams Broadside; Harveys Sussex Best Bitter Ⓗ
Revived and much improved corner pub in De Beauvoir Town that gets busy with after work drinkers and diners. It now features an appetising evening menu accompanied by an extensive wine range. A weekend brunch is available until 4.30pm. Bare floorboards and plenty of uncovered brickwork, with mainly wooden tables and chairs and a few sofas, help create a relaxed and comfortable ambience. It has a garden and an upstairs room for hire with a rooftop balcony.
❀◗⇌(Dalston Jct)

N1: Hoxton

Eagle

2 Shepherdess Walk, N1 7LB
⏲ 12-midnight (1am Fri & Sat); 12-midnight Sun
☎ (020) 7533 7681
Caledonian Deuchars IPA; Fuller's London Pride; Taylor Landlord; guest beers Ⓗ
Once the site of the Eagle Tavern, where Marie Lloyd first publicly performed, the pub

was made famous in the song Pop goes the Weasel. Leather workers would pawn or 'pop' their tools (weasels) for a drink. The present, open-plan pub is modern with large picture windows and a pleasant, secluded garden. The beer range can change. Meals are served until 10pm (8.30pm Sun).
❀◖◗≠(Old St)⊖

Prince Arthur

49 Brunswick Place, N1 6EB

⊛ 11-midnight; 12-6.30 (may vary) Sun

☎ (020) 7253 3187

Shepherd Neame Master Brew Bitter, Kent's Best, Spitfire Ⓗ

Friendly, back-street local, run by the same landlord now for 27 years. An oasis from the rush of nearby City Road, it has some outside seating. Inside the front section has seating at tables, while the rear houses a regularly used dartboard. The decor bears a sporting motif, including photographs of the landlord's boxing days, and the TV shows sports events. Unobtrusive background music plays. Light snacks are always available. Sunday hours may be extended if trade warrants it. ❀≠(Old St)⊖♣

Wenlock Arms

26 Wenlock Road, N1 7TA

⊛ 12-midnight (1am Fri & Sat); 12-midnight Sun

☎ (020) 7608 3406 ⊕ wenlock-arms.co.uk

Adnams Bitter; guest beers Ⓗ

Early 19th-century back-street pub, near the site of the long-demolished Wenlock Brewery. A classic real ale establishment, famous with beer tourists from afar, it nonetheless has a strong community focus. Eleven consecutive years in this Guide and local CAMRA Pub of the Year four times, it offers up to eight real ales, always including a mild, plus a real cider and perry and a good range of draught and bottled continental beer. It hosts live jazz several times a week. Substantial snacks are served.
♨⊖(Old St)♣●

N1: Islington

Compton Arms

4 Compton Avenue, N1 2XD

⊛ 12-11; 12-10.30 Sun

☎ (020) 7359 6883

Greene King IPA, Abbot; guest beer Ⓗ

Handy for concerts at the nearby Union Chapel, this is a small, cottage-style building whose compact dimensions and beams heighten the country pub atmosphere. The main area is bare-boarded, with bottle-glass panelled windows. To the rear of the bar is a smaller room, while a lower lounge leads to a pleasant patio courtyard. The guest beer, not from the Greene King portfolio, adds variety. It can get crowded when Arsenal play at home.
❀◖◗≠(Highbury & Islington)⊖

Crown

116 Cloudesley Road, N1 0EB

⊛ 12-11; 12-10.30 Sun

☎ (020) 7837 7107

Fuller's Discovery, London Pride, seasonal beers; guest beers Ⓗ

This 1820s pub is now a Grade II listed building on CAMRA's Regional Inventory. Originally at least four bars, it has been opened up around an island bar, featuring much etched glass and some original Victorian, ornate snob screens, divorced from their original setting. It offers an extensive, modern British menu, which is served all day at the weekend. The pleasant outdoor terrace is a bonus in London.
♨Q❀◖◗⊖(Angel)

Island Queen

87 Noel Road, N1 8HD

⊛ 12-11.30; 12-midnight Fri & Sat; 12-11.30 Sun

☎ (020) 7704 7631

Draught Bass; Fuller's London Pride; guest beer Ⓗ

Listed on CAMRA's Regional Inventory for its interior, this 1851 pub retains many features, including a full height timber and glass screen in the back room. A corridor leads to a no-smoking upstairs lounge that boasts a mosaic. Also of note are the impressive cut and etched glasswork and tall mirrors. A varied menu is designed to suit all tastes, and includes a Sunday roast. It stocks Belgian bottled and draught beers. This dog-friendly pub has outside tables for fine weather. ♨Q❀◖◗⊖(Angel)♣⊬

Narrow Boat

119 St Peters Street, N1 8PZ

⊛ 11-midnight; 12-10.30 Sun

☎ (020) 7288 0572

Adnams Bitter, Broadside; Fuller's London Pride; Harveys Sussex Best Bitter Ⓗ

A long pub on two levels running alongside Regent's Canal. Outside it displays some of its Victorian origins while inside the decor is distinctly light and modern, following an impressive refurbishment. Large picture windows open in summer while TV screens satisfy the footie aficionados. On Friday, Saturday and Sunday food is served throughout the day until 9.30pm. ◖◗⊬

N4: Harringay

Oakdale Arms

283 Hermitage Road, N4 1NP

⊛ 12-11; 12-10.30 Sun

☎ (020) 8800 2013 ⊕ individualpubs.co.uk/oakdale

Milton Pegasus, seasonal beers; guest beers Ⓗ

Rare example of a cosmopolitan community local that does everything well. Cask mild and stout often feature on the eight handpumps, strong draught ales are stocked in winter and a changing cider is always available. Good value food is freshly made (no food Sun eve) and it offers an astonishing choice of 27 curries on Friday. It is home to an enthusiastic cricket team. Three beer festivals are held annually and more unusually, the local church conducts services here on Sunday morning.
❀◖◗⊖(Seven Sisters)♣●P⊓

Salisbury ☆

1 Grand Parade, Green Lanes, N4 1JX

⊛ 5-midnight (1am Thu); 3-2am Fri; 12-2am Sat; 12-11 Sun

☎ (020) 8800 9617
Fuller's Discovery, London Pride, ESB, seasonal beers Ⓗ
The Salisbury is worth visiting for the magnificent Victorian architecture alone as this Grade II listed building has a glorious interior. It also serves good food, although this is no gastropub, but very much a pub for drinkers. As well as the two bars, there is a further room at the back that includes the kitchen. Occasionally DJs and musicians perform here and a quiz is staged on Monday evening.
◑ ⊖(Turnpike Lane)⊬

N6: Highgate

Flask
77 Highgate West Hill, N6 6BU
⏲ 12-11; 12-10.30 Sun
☎ (020) 8348 7346
Adnams Broadside; Taylor Landlord; guest beers Ⓗ
Built in the 17th century, with the original bar still evident, the Flask features a mix of timber floorboards, brick fireplaces, old prints and a quirky collection of chairs and tables. The regular and guest ales are backed up by foreign draught and bottled beers, while an extensive menu caters for all appetites; meals are served all day at the weekend. The heated and partly covered outdoor drinking area, complete with bar and barbecues, compensates for any lack of interior space.
Q ◑ ♣ ⊬

Red Lion & Sun
25 North Road, N6 4BE
⏲ 12-midnight (1am Fri-Sun)
☎ (020) 8340 1780
Greene King IPA, Abbot Ⓗ
Pub built in 1920s mock-Elizabethan style, with seating areas on three sides of the bar, panelled walls, a cast iron stove and a carved bar-back facing the street. Old prints, drawings, photographs and a collection of china dogs and toby jugs complete the decor. Jazz is sometimes performed on a Tuesday evening, while multiple TV sets show sporting events. Food is served daily (all day Sat & Sun until 7pm). Occasionally a guest beer from Greene King is sold.
◑ ⊖P

Wrestlers
98 North Road, N6 4AA
⏲ 4.30-12 (1am Fri); 12-1am Sat; 12-11 Sun
☎ (020) 8340 4297
Fuller's London Pride; Greene King IPA, Abbot; Young's Bitter Ⓗ
The pub originally dates from 1547, with a fireplace possibly of that age, but it was rebuilt in mock Tudor style in 1921. It is an occasional venue for the Swearing of Horns ceremony, welcoming strangers to Highgate. Much of the 1920s feel remains, although partitions have been removed, and the current tenant has installed subdued wall lighting. This is a locals' pub, with board games available; the TV is only used for special events. Sunday lunch is popular (12-4.30pm). ◑⊖

N7: Holloway

Coronet
338-346 Holloway Road, N7 6NJ
⏲ 9am-11.30pm daily
☎ (020) 7609 5014
Courage Directors; Greene King Abbot; Marston's Burton Bitter, Pedigree; Theakston Best Bitter; guest beers Ⓗ
An exceptional and sympathetic Wetherspoon's conversion of a former cinema. This striking building is an oasis in Holloway, stocking at least five guest ales. The former grandeur of the 1940s cinema is still discernible, and includes a decommissioned cinema projector. Known locally for exceptional beer quality and range, combined with great value prices, it serves a standard Wetherspoon's menu.
Q ◑ ≠ (Upper Holloway) ⊖ (Holloway Road) ⊬

N8: Crouch End

Harringay Arms
153 Crouch Hill, N8 9HX
⏲ 12-11.30 (midnight Fri & Sat); 12-11.30 Sun
☎ (020) 8340 4243
Adnams Broadside; Caledonian Deuchars IPA; Courage Best Bitter; Wells Bombardier Ⓗ
Small, cosy pub with a friendly atmosphere. Although a small TV shows sport at low volume at one end of the bar, this is a quiet pub where conversation rules. The wood-panelled interior displays pictures that show the history of the pub and the locality. At the rear is a small courtyard. Three of the four beers listed are stocked at any one time. Filled rolls are available lunchtime and early evening. Quiz night is Tuesday. Q ♣

N8: Hornsey

Three Compasses
62 High Street, N8 7NX
⏲ 11-11 (midnight Fri & Sat); 12-11 Sun
☎ (020) 8340 2729
Caledonian Deuchars IPA; Fuller's London Pride; Taylor Landlord; guest beers Ⓗ
Friendly, welcoming pub that appeals to all ages, with background music playing. Very much a pub for drinking, but good food is also served daily. The main bar is light and airy, especially when the doors are opened out in warm weather. The back bar has a different feel, with a pool table and skylight. Major sporting events are shown in the back bar, which hosts occasional live music. Quiz night is Monday.
◑ ≠⊖(Turnpike Lane)♣⊬

N12: North Finchley

Elephant Inn
283 Ballards Lane, N12 8NR
⏲ 11-11 (midnight Fri & Sat); 12-10.30 Sun
☎ (020) 8343 6110
Fuller's Discovery, London Pride, ESB; seasonal beers Ⓗ
The Elephant Inn (formerly Moss Hall Tavern) is a long established Fuller's house. Described by patrons as a cracking Fuller's

local, it is one of the best pubs in North Finchley. The beers are particularly well cared for and served by dedicated staff. Always welcoming, the pub hosts a popular Monday quiz night, plus various themed evenings. A real log fire and extensive wood panelling add character to the two large bars; an outside heated drinking area is a bonus. ⛼Q❀◖◗♿♣

N16: Stoke Newington

Daniel Defoe

102 Stoke Newington Church Street, N16 0LA
⏲ 1-11 (midnight Fri & Sat); 12-11 Sun
☎ (020) 7254 2906
Wells Eagle, Bombardier; St Austell Tribute; guest beer Ⓗ
Popular corner house now focused on informal dining rather than sports as before. It was renamed in honour of the local author of Robinson Crusoe fame. Meals are served all day until 9.30pm (7pm Fri-Sun). The Wells beers bring a little bit of no-nonsense Bedfordshire into trendy Stokey. ❀◖◗≢

Rose & Crown

199 Stoke Newington Church Street, N16 9ES
⏲ 11.30-11; 12-10.30 Sun
☎ (020) 7254 7497
Adnams Bitter; Marston's Pedigree; guest beer Ⓗ
Close to historic Clissold House and Park, this is the 'gateway' to central Stoke Newington's nightlife. This inter-war Truman's house retains many period features, including the distinctive wood-panelling. The pub is ideal for lazy Sunday afternoons. The en-suite accommodation is recommended. ⛟◖≢

N21: Winchmore Hill

Dog & Duck

74 Hoppers Road, N21 3LH
⏲ 12-11 (midnight Fri & Sat); 12-10.30 Sun
☎ (020) 8886 1987
Greene King IPA, Abbot; Taylor Landlord; Wadworth 6X Ⓗ
The landlord here has created a popular haven for locals wishing to gather for a chat. The interior of this small pub is open plan, with the bar running part of the way along the left wall, leaving the right wall free to display photos of the area in bygone times. TV screens may show football and rugby. The small rear garden provides a secluded retreat in summer. ❀≢

Orange Tree

18 Highfield Road, N21 3HA
⏲ 12-midnight (1am Fri & Sat); 12-midnight Sun
☎ (020) 8360 4853
Greene King IPA, Ruddles County; guest beer Ⓗ
Tucked away down a side street, just off Green Lanes, this popular pub is well worth finding. It attracts a sporty crowd, with a big-screen TV, pool table and darts team. The garden has a play area and hosts summer barbecues; ice lollies are sold for children. The pub has been voted local CAMRA Pub of the Year several times. There is no admittance after 11pm. Parking is limited. ❀≢♣P

Winchmore Hill Cricket Club

The Paulin Ground, Ford's Grove, N21 3ER
⏲ 7 (12 Sat)-11; 12 (may vary)-10.30 (6 winter) Sun
☎ (020) 8360 1271 🌐 winchmorehill.org
Greene King IPA; guest beers Ⓗ
Long established and popular sports club, just off Green Lanes. It stocks at least three guest beers from various breweries across the UK. Families are catered for and there is a TV, pool table and dartboard. A beer festival is held to coincide with cricket week in August. Meals are usually available at lunchtime during the summer. Local CAMRA's Club of the Year for the last three years, it admits visitors on production of this Guide or a CAMRA membership card.
❀◖🚌(329, 125)♣P⚟

Barnet

Olde Monken Holt

193 High Street, EN5 5SU
⏲ 12-11 (midnight Thu-Sat); 12-10.30 Sun
☎ (020) 8449 4280 🌐 yeoldemonkenholt.com
Adnams Broadside; Courage Best Bitter; Greene King IPA; guest beers Ⓗ
This thoughtfully refurbished town pub is named after General Monk who camped in Barnet en route to restore Charles II to the throne. Four different areas include the cosy 'snob's corner', a dining section, a sports/music room and a light, restful conservatory. It hosts a quiz Tuesday evening, crib on Monday, acoustic music Sunday from 7pm (all musicians welcome) and occasional bands on Saturday evening. Enjoy the Mediterranean style courtyard in the summer. Weekend meals (Fri-Sun) are served 12-5pm. ❀◖◗♿♣

Sebright Arms

9 Alston Road, EN5 4ET
⏲ 12-3 (not Mon), 5-11 (midnight Wed); 12-1am Fri & Sat; 12-10.30 Sun
☎ (020) 8449 6869
McMullen AK, Country; guest beer Ⓗ
Two-bar, back-street local built by McMullen in 1872, both bars have open fireplaces. The public bar houses a dartboard and a piano that is played by whoever volunteers. The larger saloon bar has armchairs in an alcove beside an open log fire. This bar can be hired for functions. The garden has a children's play area. Evening meals are available on Friday. No admittance after 10.30pm on Friday or Saturday.
⛼❀◖⊟♣P

Enfield

King & Tinker

Whitewebbs Lane, EN2 9HJ (between Bullsmoor Lane and Crews Hill)
⏲ 12-11; 12-10.30 Sun
☎ (020) 8363 4111
Adnams Bitter; Greene King IPA, Old Speckled Hen; Tetley Bitter Ⓗ
Accessible from M25 junctions 24 and 25, this historic country pub with a single bar

and a restaurant retains many original features and all its charm. Situated in ancient royal hunting grounds, it is named after an encounter between James I and a tinker. Convenient for the vast Crews Hill nurseries, Capel Manor gardens, parkland, open countryside and a public golf course, it attracts families, walkers, horse riders and visitors to nearby Whitewebbs Museum of Transport.
♛☕❀◐▲P

Wonder
1 Batley Road, EN2 0JG
⏲ 11-11; 12-10.30 Sun
☎ (020) 8363 0202
McMullen AK, Country; guest beer Ⓗ
Victorian two-bar pub just outside Enfield Town. This gem of a local is cosy and unspoilt and has a loyal local clientele. This McMullen house usually offers a guest ale. The saloon is decorated with various prints and the public bar houses a piano that is played regularly at weekends; jazz is also performed on Sunday. Monday is crib night. A basic range of food is available. A patio at the front allows for some outdoor drinking.
♛❀◐⊟♿⇌(Gordon Hill)♣P

Ponders End

Picture Palace
Howards Hall, Lincoln Road, EN3 4AQ (Hertford Rd jct)
⏲ 9am-midnight (1am Fri & Sat); 9am-midnight Sun
☎ (020) 8344 9690
Courage Directors; Fuller's London Pride; Greene King Abbot; Marston's Pedigree; guest beers Ⓗ
Standing at a busy crossroads and served by buses from all directions, the pub normally keeps five guest beers in an area that is dire for real ale. Built as a cinema in the 1920s, Wetherspoon's has restored the interior to its former glory. A large mural of Laurel and Hardy and other silent movies stars is a reminder of its former use. Two alcoves off the main hall are designated as no-smoking areas.
Q❀◐♿⇌(Southbury/Ponders End)🚌P⚡

NORTH-WEST LONDON

NW1: Camden Town

Quinns
65 Kentish Town Road, NW1 8NY
⏲ 11-12 (2am Thu-Sat); 12-midnight Sun
☎ (020) 7267 8240
Greene King IPA, Abbot; guest beers Ⓗ
Unlike the average Camden watering-hole this pub has no security guards, a relaxed environment and a convivial atmosphere! Although attracting a mainly young crowd, it is probably the closest thing to a true community pub in this part of NW1. A free house, it boasts a 100-foot bar counter, discrete TV screens and a spacious seating area. Noteworthy for selling over 60 continental beers, listed behind the bar, it also offers two or three draught British beers. Good food is reasonably priced for the area. ◐⇌(Kentish Town)⊖

NW1: Euston

Doric Arch
1 Eversholt Street, NW1 1DN
⏲ 11 (10 Sat)-11; 11-6 (may extend) Sun
☎ (020) 7383 3359
Fuller's Discovery, London Pride, ESB; Hop Back Summer Lightning; guest beers Ⓗ
Formerly the Head of Steam, located at the east side of the bus station right in front of the railway station, with a single bar on the first floor reached by two entranceways. The pub's impressive collection of railway artefacts remains and Fuller's continues to encourage a range of guest beers from the likes of Archers, Cottage, Castle Rock and Dark Star, with a mild often available, as well as two Westons ciders and seasonal perries. ◐⇌⊖♣⚡

NW1: Primrose Hill

Princess of Wales
22 Chalcot Road, NW1 8LL
⏲ 11-midnight; 11-11 Sun
☎ (020) 7722 0354
Adnams Bitter; Fuller's London Pride; guest beer Ⓗ
Corner pub in a quiet enclave of inner London suburbia. A large bar has plenty of seating with french windows that are fully opened in summer when plastic tables and chairs are put out on the pavement. A reasonably priced menu of various (not 'gastro') dishes is an added attraction. There is no admission after 11pm. Live jazz is performed Thursday evening and Sunday afternoon. ◐⊖(Chalk Farm)

NW2: Cricklewood

Beaten Docket
50-56 Cricklewood Broadway, NW2 3DT
⏲ 9am-11 (12.30am Fri & Sat); 9am-11 Sun
☎ (020) 8450 2972
Courage Best Bitter, Directors; Greene King Abbot, Old Speckled Hen; guest beer Ⓗ
Due to a long period under the same management, this typical Wetherspoon's conversion of a retail premises has become a beacon for real ale. A series of well-defined drinking areas disguises the vastness of the place. The pub's name refers to a losing betting slip: plenty of prints and paraphernalia reinforce the theme. Benches are outside all year. A local CAMRA Pub of the Season winner, it offers a no-smoking children's family food area and menu – last orders 5pm. Q❀◐♿⇌⚡

NW3: Hampstead

Duke of Hamilton
23 New End, NW3 1JD
⏲ 12-11; 12-10.30 Sun
☎ (020) 7794 0258
Fuller's London Pride, ESB; guest beers Ⓗ
Five minutes from Hampstead tube, this back-street classic is in a quiet street. Twice local CAMRA Pub of the Year and 15 years in this Guide under the present owner/landlord, the Duke's formula is

simple: excellent beer, reasonable prices and a warm welcome. The 200-year-old single-bar pub, named after a Civil War Royalist, has a strong community focus, drawing a cosmopolitan Hampstead crowd, and fields its own cricket and rugby teams. The large terrace is always busy in summer. ❀◐⊖♣

Holly Bush

22 Holly Mount, NW3 1HE

11-11; 12-10.30 Sun

☎ (020) 7435 2892 🌐 thehollybushpub.com

Adnams Bitter, Broadside; Fuller's London Pride; Harveys Sussex Best Bitter; guest beers Ⓗ

One of Hampstead's best hidden pubs, situated in a quiet residential area just off the High Street. Grade II listed and steeped in history, this pub is in CAMRA's Regional Inventory. Very much a community pub, it has an interesting layout of several small rooms, plus a large one for non-smokers at the rear. Good food, with some dishes incorporating ale, is freshly prepared on the premises. This pub is well worth a visit; cider is sold in summer. ♛Q◐◑⊖♣♣⚡

Spaniards Inn

Spaniards Road, NW3 7JJ

11-11; 10-11 Sat & Sun

☎ (020) 8731 6571

Adnams Bitter; Fuller's London Pride; Marston's Old Empire; guest beers Ⓗ

Multi-roomed pub dating back to 1585, with wooden floors, beams and settles. Two guest beers, sometimes seasonal brews, are usually offered. Four themed beer festivals are held during the year. Food is served all day, including weekend breakfasts; the main menu lists a suggested beer to match each item. The extensive outdoor drinking space has its own bar. The area has strong Keats associations and a poetry group meets here weekly. Close to Hampstead Heath and Kenwood House, children are welcome.
♛Q❀◐◑♣P⚡

NW4: Hendon

Greyhound

52 Church End, NW4 4JT

12-11; 12-10.30 Sun

☎ (020) 8457 9730

Young's Bitter, Special, seasonal beers Ⓗ

With a strong community focus, the Greyhound lies in the village area of Hendon, next to the local history museum, Church Farmhouse and an 18th-century church with a churchyard worth exploring. Three main drinking areas around a single bar cater for all. RAF memorabilia commemorate the former RAF Hendon base. The pub is a football-free zone, cosy and relaxed. Monday is quiz night. Low volume background music is usually blues. It serves traditional pub lunches with evening meals available on Saturday. ❀◐♣

NW5: Dartmouth Park

Dartmouth Arms

35 York Rise, NW5 1SP

11 (10.30 Sat)-11; 10.30-10.30 Sun

☎ (020) 7485 3267 🌐 dartmoutharms.co.uk

Adnams Bitter; guest beers Ⓗ

Relaxed, welcoming, two-bar pub that is central to its community. There is much that is distinctive about this place: artworks for sale in the back room, books for sale in the front bar, a cigar-vending machine and regular wine tastings. Above average food is served (all day at weekends), ranging from fry-ups to more adventurous dishes. The landlord promotes bottled ciders and perries to supplement the varying draught cider. It is a thoroughly civilised place without being stuffy.
♛❀◐◑⇌(Gospel Oak) ⊖(Tufnell Pk)♣

NW5: Kentish Town

Junction Tavern

101 Fortess Road, NW5 1AG

12-11; 12-10.30 Sun

☎ (020) 7485 9400 🌐 junctiontavern.co.uk

Caledonian Deuchars IPA; guest beers Ⓗ

Corner pub on the main road, with a side door leading into a wood-panelled and mirrored bar. Overlooking the main road, the restaurant serves gastro-style food. Behind the main bar is a beautiful conservatory overlooking a flourishing garden with seating. The three guest beers turn over rapidly and the pub stages regular beer festivals when 20 firkins are stillaged on the bar. Dogs are welcome.
❀◐◑♿⇌⊖(Tufnell Pk)

NW7: Mill Hill

Rising Sun

137 Marsh Lane, Highwood Hill, NW7 4EY

12-11; 12-10.30 Sun

☎ (020) 8959 1357

Adnams Bitter; Greene King Abbot; Young's Bitter Ⓗ

Dating back to the 17th century, this pub in the rural outskirts of north London retains a genuine country pub feel, with its small bar, low ceilings, benches and two small rooms (one no-smoking). It still has outside toilets and is reputedly haunted. Once owned by Sir Stamford Raffles, now by Punch, it has a renowned restaurant in a converted barn, warmed by an open fire. In winter a quiz is held on Monday evening. Children are welcome until 7pm.
Q♨❀◐◑🚌(251)♣P⚡

NW10: Harlesden

Grand Junction Arms

Acton Lane, NW10 7AD

11-midnight; 12-10.30 Sun

☎ (020) 8965 5670

Young's Bitter, Special Ⓗ

Imposing pub alongside the Grand Union Canal (moorings available), offering three contrasting bars together with extensive gardens, a patio and children's amusments. The front bar has pool tables and a TV for sport. The middle bar is more intimate and regularly features sport on a smaller TV. The beamed back bar opens on to the canal and welcomes children until 7pm at weekends.

Music or karaoke may feature on a Friday evening. Meals are served 12-9pm.
❀◐◑⊟♿⇌⊖P

Harefield

King's Arms
6 Park Lane, UB9 6BJ
⏲ 11-11 (midnight Fri & Sat); 12-11 Sun
☎ (01895) 825485
Adnams Broadside; Fuller's London Pride; Greene King IPA; guest beers 🄷
Although very much a locals' pub, a warm welcome and a relaxed atmosphere awaits everyone. There are three distinct drinking areas, one of them doubling as a restaurant. Traditional pub food is available at lunchtime, while excellent, good value Thai food, cooked and served by Thais, is offered in the evening (no food Sun). ❀◐◑♣P

Northwood Hills

William Jolle
53 The Broadway, Joel Street, HA6 1NZ
⏲ 9am-midnight (1am Fri & Sat); 9am-midnight Sun
☎ (01923) 842240
Courage Best Bitter, Directors; Greene King Abbot; Marston's Pedigree; guest beers 🄷
This converted showroom is now a Wetherspoon's pub with a large open interior. There is a no-smoking family area with a heated patio that is open during part of the winter. This friendly pub offers good value beers and food. It hosts several beer festivals throughout the year and special food nights such as curries, steaks, roasts and Wetherspoon's famous two for the price of one menu. ◐◑♿⊖●⚟

Ruislip Manor

JJ Moons
12 Victoria Road, HA4 0AA
⏲ 9am-midnight (1am Fri & Sat); 9am-midnight Sun
☎ (01895) 622373
Courage Best Bitter, Directors; Fuller's London Pride; Greene King Abbot; Marston's Pedigree; guest beers 🄷
Busy Wetherspoon's pub overseen by one of the group's longest serving managers. The pub has an area at the back of the main bar set aside for diners and non-smokers. This converted shop stands opposite the tube station. A typical pub from this company, it is always reliable and represents good value.
❀◐◑♿⊖●⚟

SOUTH-EAST LONDON

SE1: Borough

Market Porter
9 Stoney Street, SE1 9AA
⏲ 6-8.30am, 11-11; 11-midnight Sat; 12-10.30 Sun
☎ (020) 7407 2495
Harveys Sussex Best Bitter; guest beers 🄷
Popular pub, recently refurbished and extended to provide much needed extra space, especially on Friday and Saturday when the farmers market opposite is in full swing. The increased bar area now allows up to 10 guest beers to be stocked. The upstairs function room has been converted into a restaurant. It was voted local CAMRA Pub of the Year in 2005.
◐◑♿⇌(London Bridge)⊖●

Royal Oak
44 Tabard Street, SE1 4JU
⏲ 11 (6 Sat)-11; 12-6 Sun
☎ (020) 7357 7173
Harveys XX Mild, Pale Ale, Sussex Best Bitter, seasonal beers 🄷
Harveys' only tied pub in London, this traditional local is sought out by beer enthusiasts from far-flung corners of the country. It consists of two rooms and an entrance lobby (the old off-sales counter) with a central bar and an attractive function room upstairs for hire. The original Tabard Inn was destroyed by fire in 1676, rebuilt as the Talbot and eventually demolished in 1873. Today CAMRA's regional Pub of the Year 2003 would make the previous landlords proud. Q◐◑⇌(London Bridge)⊖

Wheatsheaf
6 Stoney Street, SE1 9AA (at edge of Borough Market)
⏲ 11-11; closed Sun
☎ (020) 7407 7242
Young's Bitter, Special, seasonal beers 🄷
Market pub that has changed little over the years. A former Courage house, listed in CAMRA's Regional Inventory for historic pub interiors, and reprieved from demolition for the Thames Link 2000 project, it won Young's Cellarmanship Award 2004/5. A menu of hot dishes changes daily, all freshly made using ingredients from Borough Market. Charity events, held in conjunction with the market workers, can range from live music to film shows. A TV shows major sporting events but not Saturday football.
♨Q❀◐◑⊟♿⇌⊖(London Bridge)♣

SE1: Southwark

Charles Dickens
160 Union Street, SE1 0LH
⏲ 11.30-11; 12-8 Sun
☎ (020) 7401 3744 🌐 thecharlesdickens.co.uk
Adnams Bitter, Regatta; guest beers 🄷
This great little free house is a must to visit. The rustic, cosy atmosphere of the warm and welcoming interior invites you to indulge in the delicious menu served for lunch and dinner. Originally the JP Prince, it was renamed around 1911 when Lant Street School also changed its name to Charles Dickens School. The author lived in neighbouring Lant Street as a boy, when in 1824 his father was in Marshalsea Prison for debt.
◐◑♿⊖ (Southwark/Borough)

Lord Clyde
27 Clennam Street, SE1 1ER (off Southwark Bridge Rd)
⏲ 11 (12 Sat)-11; 12-6 Sun
☎ (020) 7407 3397
Adnams Broadside; Fuller's London Pride; Greene King IPA; Shepherd Neame Spitfire; Wells Bombardier; Young's Bitter 🄷

This back-street local was rebuilt in 1913. One of the two bars is dominated by a TV for football fans. The exterior boasts a ceramic fascia in Truman's livery. It has been altered but retains traditional charm, with tongue and groove wall panelling, a serving hatch and a most effective open fire. The clientele are local regulars. Tucked away off the trunk road, the Clyde is easily missed. Despite City beer prices it is recommended for the relaxing environment.
⚠ (London Bridge)⊖(Borough)

Shipwrights Arms
88 Tooley Street, SE1 2TF
11-midnight (1am Fri & Sat); 11.30-11 Sun
☎ (020) 7378 1486
Adnams Bitter; Shepherd Neame Spitfire; guest beer 🄷
Spacious, single-room pub with an island bar where the traditional decor features a large tile picture of the Pool of London. It always offers three real ales on handpump. It is convenient for tourist attractions such as the London Dungeon and the South Bank complex. A large function room is available for hire. (London Bridge)⊖

SE1: Tower Bridge

Bridge House
218 Tower Bridge Road, SE1 2UP
11-11; 12-10.30 Sun
☎ (020) 7407 5818
Adnams Bitter, Broadside, seasonal beers 🄷
The only pub in London owned by Suffolk brewers Adnams, it enjoys a splendid location, well worth the walk across the Tower Bridge approach. Notable for its modern, stylish decor, it has a no-smoking dining room downstairs and an upstairs function room for hire. Four Adnams beers are usually stocked, as well as a decent wine list. A contemporary menu is served all day until 10.30pm and even the nibbles are good quality. ⊖(Tower Hill)

Pommelers Rest
196-198 Tower Bridge Road, SE1 2UN
10-midnight (1am Fri & Sat); 10-midnight Sun
☎ (020) 7378 1399
Courage Best Bitter; guest beers 🄷
Expansive premises divided into three sections, music-free and no-smoking throughout with effective air-conditioning and low lighting. Comfortable furnishings are not crowded together. The beer range includes changing guests and a house beer, Tower Bridge, brewed by Itchen Valley. Wireless Internet connection is a useful amenity. Wetherspoon's usual food offers and themed meal days apply here.
Q ⊖(London Bridge)

SE1: Waterloo

King's Arms
25 Roupell Street, SE1 8TB
11-11; 12-10.30 Sun
☎ (020) 7207 0784
Adnams Bitter; Fuller's London Pride; Greene King IPA; Shepherd Neame Spitfire 🄷
Traditional back-street local, near Waterloo, nestling in an unspoilt residential area of SE1. The main area consists of two wood-panelled bars displaying London memorabilia, while the third room to the rear – The Court Yard – is packed full of exhibits. The pub was used 18 years ago to film the great Dalek battle in TV's Dr Who.
Q (Southwark)⊖

Mulberry Bush
89 Upper Ground, SE1 9PP
11-11; 12-7.30 Sat; closed Sun
☎ (020) 7928 7940
Young's Bitter, Special; seasonal beers 🄷
Charming pub just a walk up from the Southbank Centre, home of the Royal Festival Hall, National Theatre and Film Theatre. It is popular with concertgoers, locals and business people alike. The main bar includes a raised seating area and leads to a bright conservatory to the rear, which provides a refreshing contrast to the pub's traditional decor. (Waterloo/Blackfriars)
⊖ (Temple/Southwark)

SE6: Catford

Catford Ram
9 Winslade Way, SE6 4JU
11-11; 12-10.30 Sun
☎ (020) 8690 6206
Young's Bitter, Special, seasonal beers 🄷
At the Broadway entrance to the Catford Mews shopping centre, this pub is popular with shoppers and market traders. It has a large, raised seating area and is comfortably air-conditioned. Sporting events are shown on the big-screen TV but kept to a reasonable volume. Just behind the Broadway Theatre, it is handy for interval drinks and also for the Catford beer festival held in June. ♿

Rutland Arms
55 Perry Hill, SE6 4LF
12-11; 12-10.30 Sun
☎ (020) 8291 9426
Adnams Bitter, Broadside; Fuller's London Pride, ESB; Young's Bitter, Special 🄷
Traditional, unpretentious, family-run local with a friendly atmosphere, half a mile from Catford railway station. An impressive choice of six real ales is permanently available. Snacks are provided during the week and at lunchtime on Sunday; sandwiches are sometimes available. The biggest attraction for music lovers is the live R&B on Thursday evening and jazz on Tuesday and Saturday.
♿ (Catford Bridge)♣

SE8: Deptford

Dog & Bell
116 Prince Street, SE8 3JD
12-11; 12-10.30 Sun
☎ (020) 8692 5664 thedogandbell.com
Fuller's London Pride, ESB; guest beers 🄷
Voted 2004 CAMRA London Regional Pub of the Year, this tucked away little gem is popular with local residents and fans of great beer from all over the capital. The

main bar area leads to another room with ample seating for diners and drinkers and an 80-year-old bar billiard table. The menu has been extended in recent months and occasional curry nights feature. The changing beer range is supported by a good choice of Belgian beers and whiskies.
♛Q❀◖◗⇌♣

SE10: Greenwich

Ashburnham Arms

25 Ashburnham Grove, SE10 8UH
✪ 11-11; 12-10.30 Sun
☎ (020) 8692 2007
Shepherd Neame Master Brew Bitter, Best Bitter, Spitfire, Bishops Finger, seasonal beers 🄷
Excellent, back-street local that has been owned by Shepherd Neame since the mid-1970s and certainly does the brewery proud. The warm, friendly pub is light and airy. It benefits from a back garden for summer drinking and a cosy conservatory for when the temperature drops. You can play bar billiards here or choose from a stack of newspapers and magazines if you just want a quiet pint on your own. No food is served Monday. ❀◖◗⇌⊖(DLR)♣

Plume of Feathers

19 Park Vista, SE10 9LZ
✪ 11-11; 10-midnight Wed, Fri & Sat; 12-11 Sun
☎ (020) 8858 1661
Adnams Bitter; Fuller's London Pride; guest beers 🄷
This regular Guide entry is a pleasant back-street local. The central, three-sided bar is surrounded by seating. A comfortable hostelry, it attracts discerning drinkers from the throngs of tourists to Greenwich. You can choose from an extensive bar menu or dine in the restaurant; Lebanese dishes are a speciality here (eve meals Tue-Sat). In summer drinkers take advantage of the walled garden, which has a safe play area for children.
Q❀◖◗⇌(Maze Hill)⊖(DLR Cutty Sark)

Richard I (Tolly's)

52-54 Royal Hill, SE10 8RT
✪ 11-11 (midnight Fri & Sat); 12-10.30 Sun
☎ (020) 8692 2996
Young's Bitter, Special, Winter Warmer, seasonal beers 🄷
Traditional two-bar pub, formerly a cottage dating back to the 18th century and once owned by Tolly Cobbold Brewery, which accounts for its alternative name. Now owned by Young's, it earns a regular place in this Guide. It boasts a great garden at the back, ideal for those perfect summer nights of long pints.
❀◖♿⇌⊖(DLR)

SE13: Lewisham

Dacre Arms

11 Kingswood Place, SE13 5BU
✪ 12-11; 12-10.30 Sun
☎ (020) 8852 6779
Courage Best Bitter; Greene King IPA; guest beers 🄷
Welcoming, cosy, back-street local in a quiet residential area off Dacre Park, between Lee High Road and Lee Terrace. The single, wood-panelled bar room bears extensive collections of plates, mugs and old photos of the pub. TV is available for major sporting events but is mostly switched off to allow for friendly conversation between customers and staff. The well-kept garden is popular in the summer months. The pub offers up to three guest ales.
Q❀⇌(Blackheath)

Watch House

198-204 Lewisham High Street, SE13 6JP
✪ 9am-11; 12-10.30 Sun
☎ (020) 8318 3136
Courage Best Bitter, Directors; Greene King Abbot; Marston's Pedigree; guest beers 🄷
Bustling, town-centre pub, catering for a varied clientele. It has kept the early Wetherspoon's layout, with areas broken up by wooden partitions, thus avoiding the company's more recent penchant for completely open-plan designs. The usual range of good value food associated with this pub chain is complemented by a wide variety of guest beers. The Watch House is named after the original village green, now a pedestrianised shopping centre.
❀◖◗♿⇌⊬

SE15: Peckham

Gowlett

62 Gowlett Road, SE15 4HY
✪ 12-midnight (1am Sat); 12-10.30 Sun
☎ (020) 7635 7048 🌐 thegowlett.com
Beer range varies 🄷
Now firmly established as a neighbourhood pub and winner of LBC's Living London Award 2005, the Gowlett goes from strength to strength, and now offers organic bottled cider and wines. Stone-baked pizzas are cooked to order lunchtime and evenings, except Monday. It hosts live jazz and board game evenings, and DJs hit the decks from late afternoon on Sunday. Children are welcome until 9pm. A changing display of modern art adds interest to South East London CAMRA's Pub of the Year 2004.
❀◗♿⇌(Peckham Rye)♣

SE18: Plumstead Common

Old Mill

1 Old Mill Road, SE18 1QG
✪ 11.30-11.30 (12.30am Fri); 12-10.30 Sun
☎ (020) 8244 8592
Beer range varies 🄷
Originally an 18th-century cornmill, beer has been served here since 1848; the original windmill (minus sails) is just visible above the roof. Inside you will find an L-shaped bar, with friendly staff. This free house has been transformed since the present landlord took over in 2003. The large back garden boasts an aviary and hosts a beer festival in July. Lunches are served Monday-Saturday, free snacks on Sunday. The landlord occasionally signals last orders on his drum kit. ❀◖

SE18: Woolwich

Prince Albert (Rose's)

49 Hare Street, SE18 6NE

11-11; 12-3 (closed eve) Sun

(020) 8854 1538

Beer range varies H

Near Woolwich Ferry, Rose's is a fantastic free house; quiet, with a friendly atmosphere, it also offers good value accommodation. It serves three changing real ales in proper oversized lined glasses – no short measures here! It also stocks a selection of Belgian beers. Excellent rolls have generous fillings (it can be hard to find the bread). The pub sports an interesting collection of old brewery memorabilia.
Q ≠ (Woolwich Arsenal) ♣

SE19: Crystal Palace

Railway Bell

14 Cawnpore Street, SE19 1PF

12 (4 Mon-Wed)-11 (1am Fri & Sat); 12-11 Sun

(020) 8670 2844

Young's Bitter, Special, seasonal beers H

Friendly, back-street Young's house, off Gypsy Hill, which has adapted its opening hours to suit local demand. A short walk from the railway station, the bar features railway pictures and models. The U-shaped, split-level single bar has a dartboard. The pub has won awards in the past for its garden. ≠ (Gipsy Hill) ♣

SE19: Upper Norwood

Postal Order

32-33 Westow Street, SE19 3RW (between A214 Westow Hill and A212 Church Rd)

9am-midnight daily

(020) 8771 3003

Courage Directors; Greene King Abbot; Marston's Bitter, Pedigree; guest beers H

Smaller than average Wetherspoon's pub converted from a former post office and sorting office in 2004. Prints of local historic interest adorn the walls. There are plenty of tables and comfortable sofas. Guest ales are displayed on a blackboard with interchangeable hook-on plaques. The no-smoking area at the back of the pub admits children until 9pm when accompanying adult diners. Food is served all day until 10pm.
Q ≠ (Crystal Palace)

SE20: Penge

Moon & Stars

164-166 High Street, SE20 7QS

9am-11; 12-10.30 Sun

(020) 8776 5680

Courage Directors; Greene King Abbot; Hop Back Summer Lightning; Marston's Pedigree; Shepherd Neame Spitfire; guest beers H

Spacious Wetherspoon's, built in 1994, incorporating interesting architectural features such as wood and stone panelling inside. One wall consists of tables in individual booths for a quiet, cosy atmosphere. It usually offers at least six guest ales, ranging from old favourites to new beers from independent breweries. Extremely popular with a wide cross-section of the local community, you need to arrive early when the regular beer festivals are held. Q ≠ (Penge E/Clock House) ⊖ (Beckenham Rd Tramlink) P

SE23: Forest Hill

Blythe Hill Tavern

319 Stanstead Road, SE23 1JB

11-11 (midnight Thu-Sat); 12-11 Sun

(020) 8690 5176

Courage Best Bitter; Fuller's London Pride; guest beer H

Traditional corner pub on the South Circular, halfway between Catford and Forest Hill. Three unspoilt, cosy, wood-panelled rooms, each with its own bar, retain many original features and are individually themed: one with breweriana, one dedicated to jockey Lester Piggott, and one featuring golf. All have a large-screen TV for sport. The pub stocks a good selection of malt whiskies. Outside is a small paved drinking area and a fenced garden with slides for children.
Q ≠ (Catford/Catford Bridge)

Capitol

11-21 London Road, SE23 3TW

9am-midnight (1am Fri & Sat); 9am-midnight Sun

(020) 8291 8921

Courage Best Bitter; Greene King Abbot, Old Speckled Hen; Marston's Pedigree; Shepherd Neame Spitfire; guest beers H

Large Wetherspoon cinema conversion, combining modern decor with many original features. A no-smoking family area at the back gives a sense of being on stage, as you look back up at the old cinema circle. No music is played, however major sporting events are shown on screen. In common with other outlets in the chain, the Capitol now stocks an increased range of bottled foreign beers and ciders. Breakfast is served from 9am. ≠

SE26: Sydenham

Dulwich Wood House

39 Sydenham Hill, SE26 6RS

12-11 (midnight Thu-Sat); 12-10.30 Sun

(020) 8693 5666

Young's Bitter, Special, seasonal beers H

A constant Guide entry for the past 20 years, and originally a private residence for Sir Joseph Paxton, architect of the nearby Crystal Palace, fittingly photos and newspaper articles relating to that edifice are displayed. The front bar retains much of its original charm, while at the rear, the no-smoking area is in a sympathetic extension. Children are welcome in the covered, heated terrace and extensive garden, but not in the pub. Wheelchair access is via the garden.
Q ≠ (Sydenham Hill) P

Addiscombe

Claret Free House

5a Bingham Corner, Lower Addiscombe Road, CR0 7AA

11.30-11 (midnight Fri & Sat); 12.30-11 Sun
(020) 8656 7452 claretfreehouse.co.uk
Palmer IPA; guest beers H
Small, friendly local at the centre of Addiscombe. A true free house, it has twice been Croydon CAMRA's Pub of the Year. The only outlet in London to serve Palmer IPA, it also offers a changing selection of guest beers, many from small breweries; see the list on the blackboard. Light snacks are available at lunchtime. The pub has ample seating and a TV for sport, but no loud music. It is a real oasis for ale and cider lovers. ⊖(Tramlink)♣

Cricketers
47 Shirley Road, CR0 7ER (on A215 opp. Bingham Rd)
12-11.30 (12.30am Fri & Sat); 12-11 Sun
(020) 8655 3507
Harveys Sussex Best Bitter; Taylor Landlord; guest beers H
Popular 'Brewers' Tudor' pub. Stripped woodwork and stressed effect panelling give a light and airy feel. Quite games oriented with pool, darts and touch-screen games machines and sports TV, it gets busy in the evenings especially on quiz night (Thu). Quieter at lunchtimes with diners, meals are served until 7pm (5pm Sun). The only permanent outlet for Landlord in the area, it also offers two rotating guest beers from the Enterprise list.
⊖(Blackhorse Lane)♣P

Oval Tavern
131 Oval Road, CR0 6BR (off A222)
12-3, 4.30-11; closed Fri; 12-midnight Sat; 12-10.30 Sun
(020) 8686 6023 theoval.co.uk
Beer range varies H
Old-fashioned, traditional, back-street local where you can hear live blues every Wednesday and Sunday; it is very much part of the local music scene. Sunday roasts are good value, while sociable barbecues are held in the large garden in summer. It forms part of an excellent pub crawl with a Fuller's pub around the corner and the Claret 10 minutes' walk away. Occasional beer festivals are staged. ≥(E Croydon)⊖(Lebanon Rd Tramlink)♣

Beckenham

Jolly Woodman
9 Chancery Lane, BR3 6NR
12-11; 12-10.30 Sun
(020) 8663 1031
Adnams Best Bitter; Caledonian Deuchars IPA; Fuller's London Pride; Harveys Sussex Best Bitter; guest beers H
This is a friendly, back-street, basic, quiet local that benefits from a strong regular trade and discerning drinkers from further afield. Originally an ale house, it has one bar and two rooms. The front one serves food and is no-smoking; home-made lunches are available weekdays. It has a gas fire and a patio garden. There is disabled access through a side gate.
Q

Bexley

Black Horse
63 Albert Road, DA5 1NJ
10-11.30 (12.30 Fri & Sat); 11-11.30 Sun
(01322) 523371
Courage Best Bitter; guest beers H
Friendly, back-street local, offering good value lunches in comfortable, uncrowded surroundings. The open-plan bar is split in two: the front and left providing an open space with a dartboard, while to the right is a smaller, more intimate area and bar, leading to the garden. The pub supports a golf society. The publican aims to put on a different beer every time one of his two guest pumps runs out. ≥♣

King's Head
65 Bexley High Street, DA5 1AA
11-11 (midnight Fri & Sat); 11-11 Sun
(01322) 526112
Greene King IPA, Morland Original, Abbot H
Popular pub, busy at lunchtime and early evening with commuters from Bexley railway station nearby. Dating from the 16th-century, this is one of the oldest buildings in historic Bexley village; it has been a pub for around 300 years. Its weatherboarded exterior makes it a local landmark, the interior has many original oak beams (and a few replacements following Victorian alterations). Sunday lunch is served in the function room. ≥P

Old Wick
9 Vicarage Road, DA5 2AL
12-11 (11.30 Fri & Sat); 12-11 Sun
(01322) 524185
Shepherd Neame Kent's Best, Spitfire, seasonal beers H
Excellent pub on the road from Bexley Village to Dartford. It changed its name from the Rising Sun in 1996. The welcoming, cosy interior is enhanced by subdued lighting and friendly staff. It benefits from a regular, local clientele, but has a no dogs rule. It is a rare outlet for Shepherd Neame Porter in season.
≥P

Bexleyheath

Prince Albert
2 Broadway, DA6 7LE (Erith Rd/Watling St jct)
11-2.30, 4.30-11; 11-midnight Fri & Sat; 12-11 Sun
(020) 8303 6309
Shepherd Neame Kent's Best, Spitfire, Bishops Finger, seasonal beers H
Cosy corner local that has been knocked through but retains a two-bar atmosphere. Upstairs is a highly rated restaurant. At least three beers are available at any one time from Shepherd Neame. The bars are bedecked with a profusion of quaint brass lamps surrounded by a huge collection of hanging brass ephemera. The seating is comfortable, but the pub can be noisy. P

Robin Hood & Little John
78 Lion Road, DA6 8PF
11-3, 5.30 (7 Sat)-11; 12-4, 7-10.30 Sun
(020) 8303 1128

Adnams Bitter; Brains Rev James; Brakspear Bitter; Fuller's London Pride; Harveys Sussex Best Bitter; guest beers Ⓗ
Excellent little back-street pub, dating from the 1830s. It offers a wide range of well-kept real ales, mostly from independents, including Westerham Brewery. Family run since 1980, home-cooked lunches (not served Sun) always feature an Italian pasta dish. Eat at tables converted from old Singer sewing machines at this regular CAMRA London Pub of the Year winner. Over 21s only are admitted. ❀ↄ

Rose

179 Broadway, DA6 7ES (opp. Christ Church)
11-11 (midnight Fri & Sat); 12-11.30 Sun
☎ (020) 8303 3846
Adnams Broadside; Greene King IPA; Harveys Sussex Best Bitter; Young's Bitter Ⓗ
Attractive, double bay-windowed pub, handy for the central shopping area in Bexleyheath. A horseshoe-shaped bar helps create a cosy atmosphere. The single room has comfortable seating and music kept at a reasonable level. A small drinking area outside at the front and patio garden at the rear add to its appeal. Lunches are served Monday-Saturday. ❀ↄ

Royal Oak (Polly Clean Stairs)

Mount Road, DA6 8JS
11-3, 6-11; 11-11 Sat; 12-3, 7-10.30 Sun
☎ (020) 8303 4454
Courage Best Bitter; Fuller's London Pride; guest beer Ⓗ
Converted from the village store to become a pub in the 1850s, this attractive brick and weatherboarded building with its country style now seems out of place in a residential suburb. Thankfully the rural charm has been maintained inside. The nickname derives from a house-proud landlady who used to wash the front steps every day. Lunchtime snacks (not served Sun) are prepared to order. Children are allowed in the garden. The pub is on the B13 bus route. Q❀P

Biggin Hill

Old Jail

Jail Lane, TN16 3AX (1 mile from A233)
11.30-3, 6-11; 12-11 Sat; 12-10.30 Sun
☎ (01959) 572979
Greene King IPA; Harveys Sussex Best Bitter; guest beer Ⓗ
This 200-year-old pub is located at the eastern extremity of Biggin Hill towards Cudham. It displays memorabilia of the former fighter station, now a civil airport, including numerous wall plates picturing WWII aircraft. Although quite large, the pub has a cosy feel with supporting beams at one end, giving the impression of separate rooms. Children are allowed throughout. The R2 bus stops outside. ❀ↄ◗P

Bromley

Bitter End Off-Licence

139 Masons Hill, BR2 9HW
12-3 (not Mon), 5-10 (9 Mon); 11-10 Sat; 12-2, 7-9 Sun
☎ (020) 8466 6083 🌐 thebitterend.biz
Beer range varies Ⓖ
If you have not visited this rare real ale off-licence, then you should take the opportunity. It sells real ale and cider by the pint in takeaway containers, or by the polypin. It also stocks a large range of bottled beers, foreign imports and ciders. All this in one place and pleasant staff, too. Go on, spoil yourself! ⇌(South)

Bromley Labour Club

HG Wells Centre, St Marks Road, BR2 9HG
11-11 (midnight Fri & Sat); 12-11 Sun
☎ (020) 8460 7409
Shepherd Neame Master Brew Bitter; guest beer Ⓗ
Comfortable, friendly club with a spacious bar and a paved seating area to the side and rear of the building. Card-carrying CAMRA members are welcome. A former CAMRA South-East London Club of the Year, it is a good place for escaping from the crowds and shops in Bromley High Street. ❀⇌(South)♣

Partridge

194 High Street, BR1 1HE
11-11; 12-10.30 Sun
☎ (020) 8464 7656
Fuller's Chiswick, London Pride, ESB, seasonal beers Ⓗ
This pub used to be a branch of the NatWest Bank and still has something of the atmosphere of an old-fashioned market town bank. An impressive, well-built, stone-faced building, the old manager's office is now a cosy snug, and much dark woodwork features. The bar has been carefully built to replace the counters. The Partridge appeals to the more mature customer.
Q❀ↄ◗♿⇌(North/South)

Red Lion

10 North Road, BR1 3LG
11-11; 12-11 Sun
☎ (020) 8460 2691
Greene King IPA, Abbot; Harveys Sussex Best Bitter; guest beers Ⓗ
With its sagging shelves of old books lining the walls, the Red Lion resembles a cosy study, inviting customers to bring out their newspapers or books to read over a pint of one of the five ales on offer. Beyond the bar is an original tiled floor and a dartboard. The outdoor drinking area at the front has pleasing flower displays all year. Although near the station, this pub has the feel of a village local. Meals are served until 7pm.
Q❀ↄ◗⇌(North)♣

Tom Foolery

204-206 High Street, BR1 1PW
11-11 (11.30 Fri & Sat); 12-10.30 Sun
☎ (020) 8290 2039
Fuller's Discovery, London Pride, seasonal beers Ⓗ
This pleasant pub was Fuller's Pub of the Year in 2004. A spacious, open-plan bar close to the town centre, it imparts a relaxed atmosphere with programmed background music. It hosts an Elvis night every couple of months and operates a strict over 21 policy. It has a no-smoking area and a small patio garden at the rear. Good facilities are

provided for disabled drinkers. ❀◑♿⇌(North/South)⚡

Bromley Common

Two Doves

37 Oakley Road, BR2 8HD

⏲ 12-3, 5-11 (11.30 Fri); 12-11.30 Sat; 12-11 Sun

☎ (020) 8462 1627

Young's Bitter, Special, Waggledance, seasonal beers Ⓗ

The traditional façade, with its original leaded windows, draws you into the attractively decorated interior of this small one-bar pub with comfortable seating. At the rear is a light and airy conservatory that overlooks an immaculate garden. The No. 320 bus from Bromley High Street stops outside. Q❀◑🚌♣⚡

Chelsfield

Five Bells

Church Road, BR6 7RE

⏲ 11-11 (midnight Fri & Sat); 12-10.30 Sun

☎ (01689) 821044

Courage Best Bitter; Greene King IPA, Old Speckled Hen; Harveys Sussex Best Bitter; Shepherd Neame Spitfire Ⓗ

Welcoming, two-bar village pub dating back to the 17th century. After many decades in the same family, the pub now has a new landlord who has further developed the food operation while maintaining the excellent beer quality. Lunches are served all week with the evening restaurant open from Thursday to Saturday; it has already achieved a reputation for traditional Sunday roasts. Darts has recently returned to the pub to complement the existing games. The R3 bus from Orpington stops nearby. ❀◑🍴🚌♣P⚡

Chislehurst

Bull's Head

Royal Parade, BR7 6NR

⏲ 11-11 (midnight Fri & Sat); 12-11 Sun

☎ (020) 8467 1727

Young's Bitter, Special, seasonal beers Ⓗ

Early 19th-century, red-brick, creeper-clad hotel, comfortably furnished; wood panelling enhances the cosy atmosphere. The new restaurant serves lunches, plus a Sunday carvery from noon until 5pm. It also offers barbecues in summer. Children are welcome in the no-smoking lounge until 6.30pm. The function room caters for weddings, salsa groups and singles nights. It can be very busy on a Friday evening. 🛏❀🛏◑🍴P⚡

Queen's Head

2 High Street, BR7 5AN

⏲ 12-midnight daily

☎ (020) 8295 2873

Young's Bitter, Special; guest beer Ⓗ

The oldest pub in Chislehurst, it has recently undergone a complete refurbishment with modern decor, but provides cosy areas surrounding the bar. It offers a good selection of light and main meals. A garden at the back next to the pond hosts summer barbecues and seats are also provided in front of the pub looking onto the High Street. Tuesday and Sunday are quiz nights. No children are allowed in the pub. P

Croydon

Beer Circus

282 High Street, CR0 1NG

⏲ 5 (12 Fri & Sat)-midnight; 6-midnight Sun

☎ (07910) 095945 🌐 thebeercircus.co.uk

Dark Star Hophead; guest beers Ⓗ

This gem of a corner bar is dominated by grey office blocks. Three real ales from southern micro-breweries usually include Dark Star's Hophead, accompanied by four regular foreign beers, two guests on draught and real cider. Occasional beer festivals are held at Croydon CAMRA's Pub of the Year 2005. Printed copies of the 300-strong bottled beer list can be found in folders on the bar. Q🍎

Dog & Bull

24 Surrey Street, CR0 1RG (behind Grants Centre multiplex)

⏲ 11-11 (midnight Thu & Fri; 12.30am Sat); 12-10.30 Sun

☎ (020) 8667 9718

Young's Bitter, Special, Winter Warmer, seasonal beers Ⓗ

Grade II listed, 18th-century building, possibly the oldest in Surrey Street, home of Croydon's market. The ground-floor island bar is flanked by two adjoining, bare-boarded drinking areas. The rear area has a big-screen TV for major sporting events, while the side area is no-smoking during meals service (eve meals finish at 8pm). Outside, via the bar, is a large, well-equipped garden – no dogs (or bulls) admitted. Q❀◑⇌(East/West)⊖(George St/Church St Tramlink)⚡

Princess Royal

22 Longley Road, CR0 3LH (off A213/A235)

⏲ 12-3, 5.30-11; 12-11 Fri; 12-5, 7-11 Sat; 12-2.30, 8-10.30 Sun

☎ (020) 8689 7862

Banks's Original; Fuller's London Pride; Greene King IPA, Abbot Ⓗ

A real local, also known as the Glue Pot, with a friendly atmosphere. Tucked away from the bustle of Croydon, it offers a range of excellent, home cooked meals, plus daily specials and popular Sunday roasts. One of the few pubs in Croydon with a secluded garden, it hosts summer barbecues. It supports active darts teams (men's and women's) and hosts a monthly charity quiz. ❀◑⇌(West)⚡

Royal Standard

1 Sheldon Street, CR0 1SS

⏲ 12-midnight (1am Fri & Sat); 12-11 Sun

☎ (020) 8688 9749

Fuller's Chiswick, London Pride, ESB, seasonal beers Ⓗ

Excellent back-street local, virtually under the flyover and behind Wandle Road car park. It can get crowded early evenings, with the 'suited' brigade, but attracts a more cosmopolitan clientele later in the evening

and at weekends. The garden (across the road) has waitress service in summer. Children can be catered for (but their own menu is not always available). Regulars are keen on rugby union, with most games shown. A cricket bat signed by the 2002 Surrey team is displayed.
Q❀◐⊖(George St/Church St Tramlink)

Ship of Fools
9-11 London Road, CR0 2RE
9am-midnight (1am Fri & Sat); 9am-midnight Sun
☎ (020) 8681 2835
Courage Best Bitter, Directors; Greene King Abbot; Marston's Pedigree; Shepherd Neame Spitfire; guest beers Ⓗ
Busy Wetherspoon's in Croydon's main shopping area. The name relates to Sebastian Brant's medieval religious treatise and the pub displays items on this subject as well as prints of local historical interest. It usually stocks three or four guest ales and at least one real cider, and hosts beer festivals in spring and autumn. Children are welcome in the no-smoking dining area until 9pm if accompanying adult diners.
◐◑♿⇌(West)⊖(Tramlink)●⚡

Skylark
34-36 South End, CR0 1DP
9am-midnight daily
☎ (020) 8649 9909
Courage Best Bitter, Directors; Greene King Abbot; Marston's Pedigree; guest beers Ⓗ
Mid-1990s conversion of a former gym and health club, now easily the best of the quartet of Wetherspoon's pubs in Croydon. Up to seven guest beers are sold at any one time. The downstairs bar is less noisy than upstairs where plasma TV screens and music feature. Meals are served up to one hour before closing. Children are welcome until 8pm. There are several good Indian restaurants nearby. Q❀◐◑♿⇌(South)●⚡

Locksbottom

Olde Whyte Lion
Farnborough Common, BR6 8NE (on A21)
11-11; 12-10.30 Sun
☎ (01689) 852631
Shepherd Neame Master Brew Bitter, Spitfire, seasonal beers Ⓗ
Once a halfway coaching house between London and Dover, this black and white fronted building dates back to the 17th century. Inside, however, it is modern and comfortable with a spacious dining area, where dishes include home-made pies. It boasts an outstanding walled garden at the rear, with heated decking and fairy lights in the trees. On the main road, parking is possible to the side of the pub. A local walking group makes this its starting point once a month. ⛰❀◐◑♿P

North Cray

White Cross
146 North Cray Road, DA14 5EL
11-11; 12-10.30 Sun
☎ (020) 8300 2590
Courage Best Bitter, Directors; guest beer Ⓗ
Although situated on a dual carriageway, this pleasant pub's setting otherwise remains rural. The front part of the bar is a locals' haunt, while the rest of the pub is comfortable for both drinking and dining. Popular for food, meals are served all day, every day. The changing guest beer is often sourced from a micro-brewery. The late Sir Edward Heath was an occasional visitor here.
Q❀◐◑P

Orpington

Cricketers
93 Chislehurst Road, BR6 0DQ
12-3, 5-11; 12-11 Sat & Sun
☎ (01689) 812648
Adnams Bitter, Broadside; guest beer Ⓗ
Just five minutes' walk from the town centre, this family-run free house is a world away from High Street chains. The friendly bar staff make everyone welcome, while the landlord was awarded Barman of the Year 2005 by the local paper. The main bar area has recently been refurbished and there is a no-smoking family room to the rear, with table football and electronic games. This is a dog-friendly pub. ☺❀♿⚡

Harvest Moon
141-143 High Street, BR6 0LQ
9am-11; 9am-10.30 Sun
☎ (01689) 876931
Courage Best Bitter; Greene King Abbot; Marston's Pedigree; Shepherd Neame Spitfire; guest beers Ⓗ
The larger, often boisterous front bar of this High Street Wetherspoon's shop conversion now includes TV screens for sporting events. The pub tapers to a quiet, more cramped seating area to the rear. The decor features wood panelling throughout and many historical prints relating to the area. There is usually a good choice of guest beers to supplement the standard range. ◐◑♿⇌⚡

Petts Wood

Sovereign of the Seas
109-111 Queensway, BR5 1DG
10-11 (11.30 Fri & Sat); 10-11 Sun
☎ (01689) 891606
Courage Best Bitter; Greene King Abbot; Marston's Pedigree; Shepherd Neame Spitfire; guest beers Ⓗ
Converted shop in an uninspiring suburban centre. The front part is normally lively, with two TV screens mercifully silent most of the time. The rear part of the pub is no-smoking, popular with diners and families – children are welcome until 8pm. There is pavement seating at the front and a small garden to the rear. It normally stocks up to six guest ales from micro-breweries from all over the UK and offers the usual Wetherspoon's value for money. ❀◐◑♿⇌⚡

Pratt's Bottom

Bull's Head
Rushmore Hill, BR6 7NQ

⏲ 11-11; 12-10.30 Sun
☎ (01689) 852553
Courage Best Bitter; Shepherd Neame Spitfire; guest beer Ⓗ
Thriving village pub situated on the Green Street Green circular country walk. A popular watering-hole for thirsty ramblers and cyclists, children (and dogs) are welcome. The pub produces a quarterly guide listing the various theme nights, golf society events and quiz evenings. Good value food is usually served all day until 8pm (but check if planning an evening meal). The R5 bus stops outside. ⛰❀◖◗🚌♣P

Purley

Foxley Hatch

8-9 Russell Hill Parade, Russell Hill Road, CR8 2LE
(on island site on A23 one-way system)
⏲ 9am-midnight (12.30am Fri & Sat); 9am-midnight Sun
☎ (020) 8763 9307
Courage Best Bitter; Greene King Abbot; Marston's Pedigree; guest beers Ⓗ
Wetherspoon's formula is applied here to a former shop premises – though smaller than the group's current ambitions. An L-shaped drinking area leads to a no-smoking/dining section at the rear where children are welcome until 9pm. It usually offers at least four interesting guest ales and two real ciders from Westons. It runs all the usual Wetherspoon's promotions and beer festivals. Last food orders are taken at 11pm. ◖◗♿≷●⊁

St Pauls Cray

Bull Inn

Main Road, BR5 3HS
⏲ 11-11; 12-10.30 Sun
☎ (01689) 821642
Flowers Original; Greene King Old Speckled Hen; Shepherd Neame Master Brew Bitter Ⓗ
Partly-weatherboarded 18th-century, two-bar pub, with a real fire, near the Cray River. It is popular with locals as well as customers from the neighbouring offices. The cosy saloon bar has a no-smoking area for drinkers and diners; disabled access is via Sandy Lane into the bar. Food is served until 2.45pm. Tuesday is quiz night. ⛰❀◖⊟♿⊁

Shirley

Orchard

116 Orchard Way, CR0 7NN
(between A232 and A214 at Radnor Walk)
⏲ 12-midnight; 12-10.30 Sun
☎ (020) 8777 9011
Fuller's London Pride; Harveys Sussex Best Bitter; guest beer (occasional) Ⓗ
Modern, well designed pub, hidden behind a large cedar tree in the Monk's Orchard district of Shirley. It comprises two bars, one with tables in alcoves. Sports TV competes with more traditional pub games such as darts and cribbage; the pub fields two darts teams and a football side. This privately-owned free house sometimes offers a guest beer at the weekend. No food is served Sunday. The No. 367 bus stops in the Glade, a 10-minute stroll away. ◖♿🚌♣P

Sidcup

Alma

10 Alma Road, DA14 4EA
⏲ 11-3, 5.30-11; 11-midnight Fri; 11-4, 6-midnight Sat; 12-3, 7-11 Sun
☎ (020) 8300 3208
Courage Best Bitter; Fuller's London Pride; guest beer (occasional) Ⓗ
Back-street local, near Sidcup Station, popular with commuters. The pub dates from 1868 when it was called the Railway Tavern. It has a fair-sized garden that is popular in summer. A mainly older clientele enjoys the well-kept beers here in a traditional pub atmosphere. It always stocks a range of bottled beers from various brewers, but not always bottle-conditioned. Lunches are served on weekdays. Parking is limited. Q❀◖≷♣P

Charcoal Burner

Main Road, DA14 6QL
⏲ 11-11 (midnight Fri & Sat); 11-10.30 Sun
☎ (020) 8300 0313
Courage Best Bitter; Fuller's London Pride; Greene King IPA Ⓗ
From the outside the pub looks like a typical brick-built 1960s or '70s estate establishment. But on entering, the character of the pub changes to give a cosy feel with small cubbyholes for quiet drinkers. It has a dining room area and the staff offers a friendly welcome to all. While it has a limited variety of real ales they are reasonably priced. Q❀◖◗⊟

Portrait

7 Elm Parade, Main Road, DA14 6NF (near police station)
⏲ 11-11; 12-10.30 Sun
☎ (020) 8302 8757
Greene King Old Speckled Hen; guest beers Ⓗ
This Barracuda Group house, voted its Pub of the Year in 2005, was converted from retail premises. Drinking areas on two levels provide a choice of small and large booths and open-plan seating. It has become popular with diners, and offers special drink deals. The evening customers are mainy young, and the atmosphere is friendly. It now keeps three guest beers that change often, always including one from Archers and Westerham. Food is served all day (last orders 9pm). ◖◗♿

Upper Belvedere

Victoria

2 Victoria Street, DA17 5LN
⏲ 11-11 (midnight Thu-Sat); 12-10.30 Sun
☎ (01322) 433773
Adnams Bitter; Shepherd Neame Spitfire Ⓗ
Pleasant, back-street local run in a traditional manner. A cosy horseshoe-shaped bar displays sporting memorabilia on one side and old local photographs on the other. An attractive outside drinking area is ideal for summer evenings. Lunches are served

weekdays. You can play shove-ha'penny, backgammon, cribbage and other games here. ❀◐♣

Welling

New Cross Turnpike

55 Bellegrove Road, DA16 3PB

9am-11.30

☎ (020) 8304 1660

Courage Best Bitter; Greene King Abbot; Marston's Pedigree; Shepherd Neame Spitfire; guest beers H

Split level Wetherspoon's pub with a light and airy atmosphere. Seating is on four levels including a gallery and two patios. The pub benefits from good public transport links. Food is served all day from 9am. Disabled facilities include a wheelchair lift. Guest beers change regularly. It attracts younger drinkers in the evening.

Q❀◐♿⇌

SOUTH-WEST LONDON

SW1: Belgravia

Duke of Wellington

63 Eaton Terrace, SW1W 8TR

11-11; 12-10.30 Sun

☎ (020) 7730 1782

Shepherd Neame Master Brew Bitter, Spitfire, Bishops Finger H

For many years a Whitbread house until it was acquired by Shepherd Neame, this small, late Georgian tavern was built in 1862 and named in honour of the 'Iron Duke', Arthur Wellesley, to celebrate the Battle of Waterloo. This is a dog-friendly establishment that shows Sky Sports.

❀◐⊖(Sloane Sq)

Horse & Groom

7 Groom Place, SW1X 7BA

11-11 (midnight Thu & Fri); closed Sat & Sun

☎ (020) 7235 6980

Shepherd Neame Master Brew Bitter, Kent's Best, Spitfire H

Marvellous pub, first licensed in 1846 as a beer house, with wood-panelling and a cosy atmosphere. An upstairs room houses a dartboard and can be used by families or hired for functions; the whole pub can be booked at the weekend. Snacks such as sandwiches can be ordered in advance for meetings and other events. Tables and chairs are put outside in good weather.

❀◐⇌(Hyde Pk Corner)⊖

Nag's Head

53 Kinnerton Street, SW1X 8ED

11-11; 12-10.30 Sun

☎ (020) 7235 1135

Adnams Bitter, Broadside H

Run by the same landlord for a long time, this smashing place serves well-kept Adnams. The two unspoilt bars are on two levels – the front one boasts the lowest counter in London, if not the country. First licensed as a beer house in 1840, it was acquired by Benskins in the late 19th century. Meals are served all day at the weekend (an evening surcharge of £1.50 on all meals starts at 2.30pm). Seats at the front allow for some outside drinking.

Q❀◐⊖(Hyde Pk Corner)

Star Tavern

6 Belgrave Mews West, SW1X 8HT

11-11; 12-10.30 Sun

☎ (020) 7235 3019

Fuller's Chiswick, Discovery, London Pride, ESB, seasonal beers H

The tiny front room of this attractive mews tavern opens up into a comfortable and spacious seating area. One of only two London pubs to have appeared in every edition of this Guide since 1974, it was West London CAMRA Pub of the Year in 2006. The Star is well known for its excellent food served at reasonable prices. A dubious claim to fame is that the Great Train Robbery was planned here. ◐⊖(Knightsbridge)

SW1: Pimlico

Morpeth Arms

58 Millbank, SW1P 4RW

11-11; 12-10.30 Sun

☎ (020) 7834 6442

Young's Bitter, Special, seasonal beers H

On the site of the old Millbank prison, near Tate Britain, this 2004 West London CAMRA Pub of the Year stands opposite the MI6 building across the Thames. A welcoming local, it is also popular with tourists. Its Victorian-style interior features an L-shaped bar with a mirrored bar back and a smaller public bar area to the rear. The upstairs, no-smoking dining room can be hired for functions. Snacks are available in the evening. Q❀◐⇌(Vauxhall)⊖

SW1: Victoria

Cask & Glass

39-41 Palace Street, SW1E 5HN

11-11; 12-8 Sat; closed Sun

☎ (020) 7834 7630

Shepherd Neame Master Brew Bitter, Kent's Best, Spitfire H

Comfortable, back-street local, first licensed in 1862 as a beer house called the Duke of Cambridge; the pub continued to serve beer only in half-pints for a long time. The name changed in 1962 and it traded under Watney colours for some years. Wood-panelled with low ceilings, the pub displays an impressive collection of model aeroplanes. Q❀⇌⊖

Jugged Hare

172 Vauxhall Bridge Road, SW1V 1DX

12-11.30; 12-11 Sun

☎ (020) 7828 1543

Fuller's Chiswick, Discovery, London Pride, seasonal beers H

Situated in a residential and business area near the ailing Tachbrook Street market, this pub is a conversion of a NatWest bank into a Fuller's themed Ale and Pie house, with mock Victorian decor. It is popular with business people, locals and visitors to the nearby Royal Horticultural Halls. The no-

smoking area was the bank manager's office. The upstairs balcony can be booked for functions. A TV allows customers to catch up with sport. Food is served all day.
◑ ≉ ⊖ ⊬

SW1: Westminster

Adam & Eve

81 Petty France, SW1H 9EX
✪ 11-11; closed Sat & Sun
☎ (020) 7222 4575
Courage Best Bitter; Fuller's London Pride; guest beers 🄷
This 1880 pub, like many former Watney's houses, was designed by the famous architect JJ Newton. It has retained its Victorian character, including mirrors, wood panelling and the turn of the (previous!) century high-relief wallpaper. The beer range always includes a Young's brew and the landlady, who looks after the cellar herself, delights in serving Young's and Fuller's beers side by side. She also offers three guests. Terrestrial TV is used for sporting events. Meals are served weekdays 12-9.30pm.
◑ ⊖ (St James's Pk) ⊬

Buckingham Arms

62 Petty France, SW1H 9EU
✪ 11-11 (5.30 Sat); 12-5.30 Sun
☎ (020) 7222 3386
Young's Bitter, Special, seasonal beers 🄷
No-nonsense pub – just for talking and drinking. Built in 1780, this former hat shop became a pub in 1820, but was not mentioned in this Guide until 1974! One of just two London pubs to have appeared in every edition, it displays the certificate and plaque to prove it. The single spacious bar has blue velvet seating. Look out for the charming charity box that tells your fortune for a small donation. Games are available on request. ◑ (St James's Pk) ♣ ⊬

Royal Oak

2 Regency Street, SW1P 4BZ
✪ 11-11; closed Sat; 12-4 Sun
☎ (020) 7834 7046
Young's Bitter, Special, seasonal beers 🄷
Saved from demolition by a campaign run by the locals and CAMRA, this was a Watney's house for some years until acquired by Young's. It dates back to 1831 (rebuilt in 1872) and is handy for the Royal Horticultural Halls. In the main its customers are local workers but it attracts a lot of passing trade, too. Tables and chairs allow for some outside drinking. Nearby is a Grade II listed gents'.
Q ❀ ◐ ≉ (Victoria) ⊖ (St James's Pk)

Sanctuary House Hotel

33 Tothill Street, SW1H 9LA
✪ 11-11; 12-10.30 Sun
☎ (020) 7799 4044
Fuller's Chiswick, Discovery, London Pride, ESB, seasonal beers 🄷
A modern mural on the rear wall encapsulates the history of this former sanctuary for monks in several scenes but some of them are a tad depressing, showing brothers sick or in pain. However, framed prints throughout show monks in happier times supping pints of ale. This comfortable pub serves the full range of Fuller's ales and has 34 guest rooms above. Meals are served all day until 9pm.
⇌ ◑ ♿ ≉ (Victoria) ⊖ (St James's Pk) ⊬

Speaker

46 Great Peter Street, SW1P 1HA
✪ 12-11; closed Sat; 12-4 Sun
☎ (020) 7222 1749
Shepherd Neame Spitfire; Young's Bitter; guest beers 🄷
Formerly the Elephant and Castle, this small, quiet, back-street pub is situated near New Scotland Yard and the Home Office. Its homely feel attracts civil servants and politicians taking a lunch break: note the apt cartoons. As with most pubs in the area a division bell is used to call MPs back to the House. At other times locals from the small neighbouring estates come in for a drink.
Q ◐ ⊖ (St James's Pk)

SW1: Whitehall

Lord Moon of the Mall

16-18 Whitehall, SW1A 2DY
✪ 9am-11.30 (midnight Fri & Sat); 9am-11 Sun
☎ (020) 7839 7701
Courage Best Bitter; Fuller's London Pride; Greene King Abbot; Marston's Pedigree; Shepherd Neame Spitfire; guest beers 🄷
Former grand banking hall: high ceilings and windows, historic photos and Georgian paintings fit the bill here. Its spacious, open bar with comfortable seating is warm, welcoming and friendly and offers shelves of books to read – not borrow! It affords views from the rear to Admiralty Arch and St James's Park. The pub stocks a good range of bottled beers and cider.
Q ☕ ◑ ⊖ ≉ (Trafalgar Square/Charing Cross) 🍏 ⊬

SW4: Clapham

Manor Arms

128 Clapham Manor Street, SW4 6ED
✪ 1 (4 Oct-Mar)-11.30; 12-1am Fri & Sat; 12-11 Sun
☎ (020) 7622 2894
Black Sheep Best Bitter; Everards Tiger; Taylor Landlord; guest beers 🄷
Minutes away from the bustle of Clapham High Street, here is an oasis of peace. The narrow bar area has sufficient space to escape from the TV which shows sporting events. There is a marquee at the rear (no children admitted), which is ideal for a quieter pint, but children are welcome on the front patio. Two guest beers include one from Adnams. Clapham Manor Baths stand opposite. ❀ ≉ (High St) ⊖ (North)

SW6: Parsons Green

White Horse

1-3 Parsons Green, SW6 4UL
✪ 11-midnight (1am Fri & Sat); 11-midnight Sun
☎ (020) 7736 2115
Adnams Broadside; Fuller's ESB; Harveys Sussex

Best Bitter; Oakham JHB; Rooster's Yankee; guest beers Ⓗ
Internationally renowned, the pub runs monthly beer festivals, stocks a wide range of foreign beers and hosts 'Beer Academy' courses. The large bar, with benches and leather settles, is warmed by an open fire. It is also famous for its food, served in the bar, the no-smoking restaurant at the rear or the upstairs restaurant that doubles as a function room. Barbecues are held at the front of the pub Thursday-Sunday in summer and in winter when Chelsea play at home.
♛Q❀◑♿⊖

SW7: South Kensington

Anglesea Arms

15 Selwood Terrace, SW7 3QG
⏲ 11-11; 12-10.30 Sun
☎ (020) 7373 7960
Adnams Bitter, Broadside; Brakspear Bitter; Fuller's London Pride; guest beers Ⓗ
This thriving pub has sold good real ale since CAMRA first started. Built in 1827 and licensed two years later, it is convenient for the museums, the Royal Albert Hall and Hyde Park, so attracts tourists as well as locals and business people. It is almost a village pub in a fashionable area. As befits a pub close to Christie's showrooms it features rare and fascinating paintings on its wood-panelled walls. Q❀◑⊖⍁

SW8: South Lambeth

Priory Arms

83 Lansdowne Way, SW8 2PB
⏲ 11-11; 12-10.30 Sun
☎ (020) 7622 1884
Adnams Bitter, Broadside; Harveys Sussex Best Bitter; guest beers Ⓗ
Award-winning, family-run free house where recent innovations have not altered the atmosphere. Two rotating guest beers are still changed regularly – over 4,000 have been offered. It hosts a regular quiz and is home to backgammon and chess clubs. Sunday roasts (served until 5pm) are recommended and vegetarians are well catered for. This community pub stocks Thatchers Dry Cider, 25 malt whiskies, a choice of wines and a range of German bottled and draught beers. An upstairs family room is open on Sunday.
❀◑⇌(Vauxhall)⊖(Stockwell)♣●

Surprise

16 Southville, SW8 2PP
⏲ 11-11; 12-10.30 Sun
☎ (020) 7622 4623
Young's Bitter, Special, seasonal beers Ⓗ
Long-time favourite making a welcome return to this Guide. A beer house until the 1950s, it is still very beer oriented. The Surprise has its own boules pitch nearby. It now stands on its own in a quiet cul-de-sac, but nearby development could change this. Regulars have always raised large amounts for local charities with sponsored events. It stages occasional live music events.
♛Q❀◐⇌(Vauxhall)⊖(Stockwell)♣

SW9: Brixton

Beehive

407-409 Brixton Road, SW9 7DG
⏲ 9am-midnight daily
☎ (020) 7738 3643
Courage Best Bitter, Directors; Greene King Abbot; Marston's Pedigree; guest beers Ⓗ
Thriving, single-bar pub that attracts a wide-ranging clientele. Good beer quality is guaranteed by the high turnover of cask ales, with always at least four guests. At the rear is a quiet no-smoking area. Panelled walls display pictures of the locality around the 1930s. Tables in booths allow people to meet and linger. Food is served all day, including breakfast from 9am. Westons Old Rosie draught cider is stocked. ◑⇌⊖●⍁

Trinity Arms

45 Trinity Gardens, SW9 8DR
⏲ 11-11 (midnight Fri & Sat); 12-10.30 Sun
☎ (020) 7274 4544
Young's Bitter, Special, seasonal beers Ⓗ
Single-bar pub, with a garden, that draws its custom from the town centre, including town hall staff, and tends to get busy in the evening. It was built in 1850 and named after Trinity Asylum, which was founded in 1824 in nearby Acre Lane by Thomas Bailey. Rock fans enjoy a drink here before a concert at the Brixton Academy. The Trinity Arms was voted SW London CAMRA Pub of the Year for 2004. Weekday lunches are served. ❀◐⇌⊖

SW9: Clapham

Landor

70 Landor Road, SW9 9PH
⏲ 12-11.30 (midnight Fri & Sat); 12-10.30 Sun
☎ (020) 7274 4386 🌐 landortheatre.co.uk
Fuller's London Pride; Greene King IPA; guest beers Ⓗ
Spacious, single-bar Victorian pub, divided into several distinct areas, displaying a variety of pictures and artefacts. It stocks two guest beers, one from a family brewer, another from a small producer such as Battersea, Rebellion or Hogs Back. An intimate theatre upstairs (Tue-Sat) stages a variety of performances from plays to cabaret. Part of the pub can be booked for functions. Meals are served all day Saturday, 1-5pm Sunday (no food Mon). You can play pool and watch Sky Sports here.
❀◑⇌(High St)⊖(North)

SW10: Chelsea

Chelsea Ram

32 Burnaby Street, SW10 0PL
⏲ 11-11; 12-10.30 Sun
☎ (020) 7351 4008
Young's Bitter, Special, seasonal beers Ⓗ
Back-street local, near Chelsea Harbour and the Lots Road auction rooms. Drinkers always receive a warm welcome in this friendly pub. The interior has been modernised in keeping with the sophisticated nature of the area; an assortment of wooden furniture and bare

floorboards gives it a distinctive and spacious feel. It offers good quality meals on a varied menu, including daily specials. Q❀◐◑🚭

SW11: Battersea

Beehive

197 St John's Hill, SW11 1TH

⏲ 11-midnight (1am Fri & Sat); 11-midnight Sun

☎ (020) 7564 1897

Fuller's London Pride, ESB 🄷

Excellent little single-bar local in an area that has become trendy in recent years with the development of several drinking and dance venues. A Fuller's tied house, rare for this part of town, it is furnished with light wooden tables and chairs. Excellent home-cooked food is served lunchtime (except Sat). Sporting events on terrestrial TV are shown at this former CAMRA SW London Pub of the Year. ❀◐♣

Castle

115 Battersea High Street, SW11 3HS

⏲ 12-11; 12-10.30 Sun

☎ (020) 7228 8181

Young's Bitter, Special, seasonal beers 🄷

Always reliable for its beer quality, this popular Battersea pub goes from strength to strength. A heated marquee area (the 'jumbrellas') is the latest addition to this Guide regular, which is justifiably sought out for its excellent food, including freshly prepared stews, fish dishes and Sunday roasts. The specials on the menu are good value. The pub serves a diverse range of customers, including dog-owners – no doubt to the chagrin of the two resident cats.
❀◐◑⇌(Clapham Jct)P

Eagle Ale House

104 Chatham Road, SW11 6HG

⏲ 12-11; 12-10.30 Sun

☎ (020) 7228 2328

Battersea Bitter; Black Sheep Best Bitter; Fuller's London Pride; Taylor Landlord; guest beers 🄷

A haven for real ale drinkers away from the bustle of trendy Northcote Road. Its unspoilt, somewhat chaotic interior features old carpets, big leather sofas and dusty book and bottle collections. Four semi-regular ales are complemented by three changing guests from micro-breweries. Only major sporting events are shown on a retractable big screen. The garden is covered by a heated marquee for winter use. A real gem.
♨❀◐◑♿⇌(Clapham Jct)♣🍎

Prince Albert

85 Albert Bridge Road, SW11 4PF

⏲ 12-11; 12-10.30 Sun

☎ (020) 7228 0613

Battersea Bitter; Greene King IPA; Young's Bitter; guest beer 🄷

Comfortable, spacious, Victorian pub, overlooking Battersea Park, just south of Battersea Bridge. A 15-minute walk across the park takes you to Battersea Park and Queenstown Road railway stations. Sympathetically refurbished in 2003, it is open plan around a central bar but has two distinct drinking areas: one is a comfortable lounge and the other more akin to a public bar. It is a rare outlet for local Battersea Bitter. Outside seating is provided in summer. An adventurous menu is served.
❀◐◑♿

SW12: Balham

Nightingale

97 Nightingale Lane, SW12 8NY

⏲ 11-midnight; 12-midnight Sun

☎ (020) 8673 1637

Young's Bitter, Special, seasonal beers 🄷

Still by far the best bet in Balham for atmosphere and beer. In marked contrast to some pubs, a recent refurbishment here has maintained the country local ambience that attracts regulars and visitors in large numbers. A small conservatory acts as a children's room, while the garden is a real suntrap in summer. A full menu is served daily, 12-10pm. It stages a monthly quiz. Dogs are made welcome with a free biscuit and water bowl.
♨ꝏ❀◐◑♿⇌(Wandsworth Common)
⊖(Clapham Sth)♣🚭

SW13: Barnes

Coach & Horses

27 Barnes High Street, SW13 9LW

⏲ 11-midnight; 12-midnight Sun

☎ (020) 8876 2695

Young's Bitter, Special, seasonal beers 🄷

One of only 28 Young's pubs known to have sold beers from the Ram Brewery since before 1831 when the Young family took control. A regular in this Guide, it remains a cosy, welcoming local. The small single bar retains fine etched windows and dark wood panelling. The large garden, which hosts barbecues in summer, has a well-equipped children's play area. Excellent meals are served all day. The large function room is an asset to the community.
❀◐◑⇌(Barnes Bridge)

Red Lion

2 Castelnau, SW13 9RU

⏲ 11-11; 12-10.30 Sun

☎ (020) 8748 2984

Fuller's Discovery, London Pride, ESB, seasonal beers 🄷

Large roadside pub by the entrance to the Wetlands Centre. Extended over the years and sympathetically refurbished, it has been opened out to provide one spacious drinking and dining area with comfortable seating. Close to Barnes Common and pond, it has a village atmosphere and is dog- and family-friendly. Excellent food is available from a varied, upmarket menu; arrive early for Sunday lunch (no bookings). Barbecues are held in summer. ♨❀◐◑♿P

SW15: Putney

Bricklayers Arms

32 Waterman Street, SW15 1DD

⏲ 12-11 (may close some weekday afternoons); 12-10.30 Sun

☎ (020) 8780 1155 🌐 bricklayers-arms.com
Taylor Golden Best, Best Bitter, Landlord, Ram Tam (winter); guest beer Ⓗ
The oldest pub in Putney in its original building (1826), this is a homely, family-owned, community pub with a country atmosphere. Tucked away in a cul-de-sac behind Putney High Street, it benefits from a suntrap garden. Children are welcome until 9pm. Peaceful background music plays and a wood fire burns in winter. A remarkable rescue of a pub that had been closed with redevelopment in view, although original fittings were sadly lost.
⚘❀◐◑⇌⊖(Putney Bridge)♣

Olde Spotted Horse
122 Putney High Street, SW15 1RG
⏲ 11-midnight (1am Fri & Sat); 12-11.30 Sun
☎ (020) 8788 0246
Young's Bitter, Special, seasonal beers Ⓗ
Behind a mock-Tudor façade, complete with a carved wooden horse, replaced in 2002, lies a modern, but at heart traditional, pub that welcomes a cross section of the local community. Although a busy pub, its size affords a generous amount of seating and a refuge from the bustling High Street. Pub food, including pizzas, burgers and roasts on Sundays, is served all day.
◐◑⇌⊖(East/Putney Bridge)⚟

SW15: Roehampton

Angel
11 Roehampton High Street, SW15 4HL
⏲ 11-midnight; 12-10.30 Sun
☎ (020) 8788 1997
Young's Bitter, Special, seasonal beers Ⓗ
A Young's house since 1872, the pub dates back to 1617 in a part of historic Roehampton that is well worth exploring. A new management team has kept up the same high standards of beer, but the food business is run separately. The public bar remains the hub, while the saloon continues to attract locals and visitors. Buses run from Hammersmith and Clapham Junction. ◐◑⊟♣

SW17: Summerstown

Prince of Wales
646 Garratt Lane, SW17 0NT
⏲ 11-11; 12-10.30 (may close 4-7) Sun
☎ (020) 8947 3190
Young's Bitter, Special Ⓗ
Three-roomed pub on the corner of busy Garratt Lane, drawing a mainly local clientele. It boasts some fine external tiling, while the interior, which features pillars and an embossed ceiling, has earned it a place in CAMRA's London Regional Inventory. Weekday lunches are served. There is a seafood stall outside, while Wimbledon Greyhound Stadium and the Sunday market are both close by.
⚘♘❀◐⇌(Earlsfield)♣P

SW18: Southfields

Gardeners Arms
268 Merton Road, SW18 5JL
⏲ 11-11.30 (midnight Fri & Sat); 12-11.30 Sun
☎ (020) 8874 7624
Young's Bitter, Special, seasonal beers Ⓗ
This 1930s corner house bears distinctive green tiling. A horseshoe bar divides the pub into two sections, one of which was extended into a former shop in 1989 to create a large seating area. First leased by Young's in 1875, it bought the property in 1915. Daily newspapers are provided, Sky Sports shown and a quiz is staged on Tuesday. Lunches are served weekdays. It is roughly 10 minutes' walk from Southfields tube or central Wandsworth.
❀◐⊖♣

SW18: Wandsworth

Freemasons
1 North Side, Wandsworth Common, SW18 2SS
⏲ 12-11; 12-10.30 Sun
☎ (020) 7326 8580 🌐 freemasonspub.com
Everards Tiger; Taylor Landlord Ⓗ
The Freemasons has had many guises over the years, most recently as a fish restaurant, but its transformation into a lively gastropub serving excellent food and real ales has ensured its entry into this Guide for the second year. The pub retains some original features and boasts unusual canister-style handpumps. It attracts a mainly young crowd, particularly at the weekend, but a calmer atmosphere prevails during the week. Well worth the short trek up the hill from Clapham Junction.
❀◐◑♿⇌(Clapham Jct)

Grapes
39 Fairfield Street, SW18 1DX
⏲ 11-midnight; 12-midnight Sun
☎ (020) 8874 3414
Young's Bitter, Special, Winter Warmer, seasonal beers Ⓗ
Unspoilt and beautifully maintained corner pub from the early-19th century, with a single U-shaped bar. The piano is used for occasional recitals, at other times quiet background music is played and some sport is shown on the TV. There is a garden, patio and conservatory at this SW London CAMRA Pub of the Year 2005. This friendly local is not one to pass by.
❀◐⇌(Town)

Spread Eagle
71 Wandsworth High Street, SW18 2PT
⏲ 11-midnight; 11-11 Sun
☎ (020) 8877 9809
Young's Bitter, Special, seasonal beers Ⓗ
Spacious, opulent late Victorian pub situated at the heart of Wandsworth. The unspoilt interior fully justifies its inclusion in CAMRA's Regional Inventory for London. The pub has three distinct areas: the comfortable main bar with imposing etched mirror, serving as a backdrop to a long bar; the public bar with a pool table and giant TV screen; and the quiet dining room. Meals are served Monday-Saturday 12-3pm and weekday evenings. A fine combination of ornate elegance and good beer.
⚘Q◐◑⊟⇌(Town)

SW19: South Wimbledon

Princess of Wales

98 Morden Road, SW19 3BP (on A2)
⏲ 11-midnight; 12-11 Sun
☎ (020) 8542 0573
Young's Bitter, Special, seasonal beers Ⓗ
A Young's pub for 130 years, brightened by hanging baskets, the central bar divides the establishment into two drinking areas, one with a dartboard. The Stane Street by Hilaire Belloc mentions the pub; the ancient road passed nearby. Twinned with the Horse Brass pub in Portland, Oregon, patrons make occasional exchange visits. A pub for conversation, free from music or TV, the games machines are quiet. Weekend barbecues are held throughout summer. Deen City Farm nearby benefits from charity collections. Q❀◖◗⊖(Morden Rd)♣P

Sultan

78 Norman Road, SW19 1BT
⏲ 12-11 (midnight Fri & Sat); 12-11 Sun
☎ (020) 8542 4532
Hop Back GFB, Entire Stout, Summer Lightning, seasonal beer or guest beer Ⓗ
Hop Back's only tied house in London, this 1950s back-street local has won many CAMRA awards and recognition from other publications for its food and drink. The smaller of the two bars, which houses a dartboard, opens in the evening. Wednesday is beer club night (6-9pm), offering discounted cask beers. A weekend beer festival is held in September. Quiz night is Tuesday. ❀⊟♿⊖(Colliers Wood)

Trafalgar

23 High Path, SW19 2JY (Pincott Rd/High Path jct)
⏲ 12 (11 Wed-Fri)-11; 12-11 Sun
☎ (020) 8542 5342 🌐 thetraf.com
Fuller's Gale's HSB; Taylor Golden Best; guest beers Ⓗ
Small, friendly, one-bar corner house, dating from the 1860s and extended in 1906, with two distinct areas and much Nelson memorabilia. The beer range can vary, with two or three constantly changing guests often coming from small breweries such as Downton, Grand Union and Sharp's. A wide selection of milds is added during May. Monday is quiz night and there is Sky Sports on TV. Weekday lunches are available. ♨❀◖⊖(S Wimbledon/Morden Rd)♣

SW19: Wimbledon

Hand in Hand

6 Crooked Billet, SW19 4RQ
⏲ 11-11; 12-10.30 Sun
☎ (020) 8946 5720
Young's Bitter, Special, seasonal beers Ⓗ
A Wimbledon institution: this former bakehouse was once owned by members of the Watney family (before they set up the infamous brewery). A beer house since the 1870s, the pub has distinct drinking areas, including a no-smoking family room and a small games room. In summer, drinkers spill out on to the green across the narrow access road. This pub has won awards, including SW London CAMRA's Pub of the Year.
♨👪❀◖◗♣⚟

Carshalton

Greyhound Hotel

2 High Street, SM5 3PE (on A232)
⏲ 11-midnight; 12-midnight Sun
☎ (020) 8647 1511 🌐 greyhoundhotel.net
Young's Bitter, Special, seasonal beers Ⓗ
Despite some opening out, the pub retains enough nooks and corners to allow it to cater happily for its varied clientele. First recorded in 1706 as the Dog, it is actually two buildings in contrasting yet sympathetic styles. A 2000 refurbishment of local CAMRA's Pub of the Year 2005 brought the atmospheric old cellar into use. An elegant Greyhound mosaic marks the entrance to the Swan Bar, which is warmed by an open fire and affords views over the pretty pond.
♨Q❀🛏◖◗♿⇌P⚟

Railway Tavern

47 North Street, SM5 2HG (on B277)
⏲ 12-2.30, 5-11; 12-11 Sat; 12-10.30 Sun
☎ (020) 8669 8016
Fuller's London Pride, ESB, seasonal beers Ⓗ
You are certain of a superb pint of ale at the home of Fuller's Master Cellarman award winner from 2002-05. This small hostelry, near the station entrance, is a haven for railway enthusiasts for its pictures and artefacts from the steam era. Very much a local, you can try your hand here at shut the box or other traditional games. Bar lunches are served weekdays, just filled rolls on Saturday. The attractive patio garden is an added attraction. ❀⇌♣

Chessington

North Star

271 Hook Road, Hook, KT19 1EQ (on A243)
⏲ 11 (12 Fri & Sat)-midnight; 12-11 Sun
☎ (020) 8391 9811
Adnams Bitter; Draught Bass; Caledonian Deuchars IPA; Wells Bombardier; guest beers Ⓗ
Community pub, dating back 150 years, that draws a mixed clientele. One area of this large pub is no-smoking. Good food is served all day until 8pm, with snacks available until last orders. Unobtrusive background music only affects some areas of the pub, which is home to a golf society and Sunday football club. The cellarman has clocked up 35 years behind the bar here. An annual beer festival is held in the autumn. ♨❀◖◗♿🚌P⚟

Kew

Coach & Horses Hotel

8 Kew Green, TW9 3BH
⏲ 11-midnight daily
☎ (020) 8940 1208 🌐 coachhotelkew.co.uk
Young's Bitter, Special, seasonal beers Ⓗ
This wonderful 17th-century coaching inn, opposite the Royal Botanic Gardens, underwent sensitive renovation in 2001 to provide 31 guest rooms. Its function room for 50 people adjoins an atrium licensed to hold civil weddings. Good quality home-

cooked food includes a fresh fish menu with daily specials, served in the bar or the wood-panelled, no-smoking dining area.
(Bridge/Gardens)
(Gardens)P

Inn at Kew Gardens

292 Sandycombe Road, TW9 3NG
11-11 (midnight Thu-Sat); 11-10.30 Sun
(020) 8940 2220 innatkewgardens.com
Fuller's London Pride; Greene King IPA; Hogs Back TEA; guest beers H
Once a hotel bar, the recently renovated inn now occupies the hotel's ground floor and is run as a separate operation. Stripped window frames, bare boards and flower vases create a modern, spacious and welcoming air. Six ales are on offer, while the lunch and evening meal menus are extensive. Between the station and gardens, it is ideal for refreshment after a long walk.
(Kew Gardens)

Kingston upon Thames

Canbury Arms

49 Canbury Park Road, KT2 6LQ
9am-11 Mon-Sat; 9am-10.30 Sun
(020) 8255 9129 thecanburyarms.com
Fuller's Gale's HSB; Harveys Sussex Best Bitter; Hogs Back TEA; Hook Norton Old Hooky; guest beer H
Large, 19th-century, opened-out pub. Recently refurbished, it is no-smoking throughout. A changing range of guest beers and a varied food menu including light bites and breakfasts cater for all tastes. The decor of the former Canbury Hotel is imaginative and modern with timber floors and monochrome pictures. Children are welcome until 7pm; a play area is provide in a heated tent outside. Q P

Park Tavern

19 New Road, KT2 6AP (off B351)
11-11; 12-10.30 Sun
Fuller's London Pride; Taylor Landlord; Young's Bitter; guest beers H
Originally two cottages, but a pub now for over 150 years, its customers are mostly locals from the Richmond Park area. The central bar serves the whole pub and the patio. Guest beers often come from small breweries. Sporting events are shown on TV. Take time to look at the varied collection of memorabilia.

Spring Grove

13 Bloomfield Road, KT1 2SF
11-11 (midnight Fri & Sat); 12-10.30 Sun
(020) 8549 9507
Young's Bitter, Special, seasonal beers H
Traditional public house in a quiet back-street location. This large pub is divided into several areas, each with its own working fireplace. The pub fields pool and darts teams. Children are not allowed inside but can use the garden, which often hosts summer barbecues. Occasional live entertainment is staged on Sunday evenings. The comprehensive food menu includes daily specials and Sunday roasts. Q

Willoughby Arms

47 Willoughby Road, KT2 6LN
10.30-midnight; 12-midnight Sun
(020) 8546 4236 thewilloughbyarms.com
Caledonian Deuchars IPA; Fuller's London Pride; Wells Bombardier; guest beers H
Renowned for the quality of its real ale and its charismatic landlord, this Victorian pub in the back streets of north Kingston is a regular meeting place for the Society for the Preservation of Beer from the Wood. The landlord runs beer festivals for St George's Day and Hallowe'en, which also showcase real cider. The pub houses a sports bar and a quieter saloon, while upstairs the function room hosts live bands. The garden is used for summer barbecues.

Wych Elm

93 Elm Road, KT2 6HT
11-midnight; 12-11 Sun
(020) 8546 3271
Fuller's Chiswick, Discovery, London Pride, ESB, seasonal beers H
Award-winning pub, not only for its beer but also its floral displays. This traditional, homely pub has been under the stewardship of the same landlord for over 20 years. Unusually for the area, it boasts a public bar as well as an attractive garden. It often sells one-off draught versions of Fuller's bottled beers. Good quality, home-made lunches are served Monday-Saturday.

Mitcham

Queen's Head

70 Cricket Green, CR4 4LA
11-midnight (1am Fri & Sat); 12-11 Sun
(020) 8648 3382 queens-mitcham.com
Shepherd Neame Master Brew Bitter, Spitfire, seasonal beers H
This 1930s building stands opposite the historic cricket green. The main room, with a juke box, hosts occasional live acoustic music, while sports TV and games machines are in the smaller room. All hot food is prepared by the licensees, who came from the restaurant business, including Sunday roasts and summer barbecues. Fish and chips to eat in or take away are available on Friday evening. Customers support five darts teams and charity events during the year, including the Easter tug-of-war.
(Tramlink)P

New Malden

Woodies

Thetford Road, KT3 5DX
11-11; 12-10.30 Sun
(020) 8949 5824
Adnams Broadside; Fuller's London Pride, ESB; Young's Bitter; guest beers H
Originally a cricket pavilion, then a clubhouse and now a free house, the pub is still extensively decorated with sporting memorabilia. It can be a little hard to find. The three guest beers change constantly and are sourced from breweries far and wide. It has one drinking area, partly segregated for

diners and families. The patio area is a favoured spot for summer drinking. ♔❀◖🚌P

Richmond

Red Cow

59 Sheen Road, TW9 1YJ
⏲ 11-11.30; 12-10.30 Sun
☎ (020) 8940 2511 🌐 redcowpub.activehotels.com
Young's Bitter, Special, seasonal beers Ⓗ
Sympathetically restored, this popular local is a few minutes' walk from Richmond's shops and station. There are three distinct drinking areas where rugs on bare floorboards and period furniture create a traditional atmosphere. The first floor has four en-suite bedrooms. Good lunches are served daily, and evening meals Monday-Thursday until 8.30pm. Tuesday is quiz night and live music is performed on Thursday evening.
♔❀🛏◖◗⇌⊖

Roebuck

130 Richmond Hill, TW10 6RN
⏲ 11-11 (midnight Fri & Sat); 12-10.30 Sun
☎ (020) 8948 2329
Beer range varies Ⓗ
Overlooking the World Heritage view of Petersham Meadows and the Thames, this 200-year-old, reputedly haunted pub is close to Richmond Park Gate. Patrons are welcome on the terrace opposite to enjoy the view cherished by their forbears and highwaymen for 500 years. Three beers change regularly, and award-winning pies and sausages form the basis of an extensive menu (served all day Sat and Sun). Bar billiards is played.
♔❀◖◗♣

Waterman's Arms

12 Water Lane, TW9 1TJ
⏲ 11-11 (midnight Fri & Sat); 12-10.30 Sun
☎ (020) 8940 2893
Young's Bitter, Special, seasonal beers Ⓗ
Historic pub, one of the oldest in Richmond (rebuilt 1895), retaining its Victorian two-bar layout. In a lane leading to the White Cross and the river, generations of watermen have drunk here and some, along with others in riparian occupations, still do. In the 1950s it was a lunchtime stop for the Swan Uppers en-route from Blackfriars to Henley. Good Thai food is served all day until 10pm. The upstairs room hosts a Monday folk club.
♔Q❀◖◗⇌⊖

White Cross

Riverside, Water Lane, TW9 1TJ
⏲ 10-midnight daily (may vary according to demand)
☎ (020) 8940 6844
Young's Bitter, Special, seasonal beers Ⓗ
A prominent feature on Richmond's waterfront, the pub dates from 1835, but a stained glass panel is a reminder that it stands on the site of a former convent of the Observant Friars, whose insignia was a white cross. It is reached by steps for good reason – the river often floods here. An island bar serves two side rooms (one a mezzanine); an unusual feature is a working fireplace beneath a window. A ground-level patio bar opens at busy times. ♔Q❀◖⇌⊖

Southborough

Cap in Hand

174 Hook Rise North, KT6 5DE (at A3/A243 jct)
⏲ 10-midnight daily
☎ (020) 8397 3790
Courage Best Bitter; Greene King Old Speckled Hen; Marston's Pedigree; Theakston Old Peculier; guest beers Ⓗ
Popular, spacious Wetherspoon's, now no-smoking throughout, although smokers can retire to the heated, covered patio. The building dates back to 1934 and photos show celebrities born locally and other famous people. The open-plan layout is divided into different areas with tables and chairs or booths. The large conservatory at the front is the designated family area until 9pm. The house beer is brewed by Itchen Valley. It runs themed food nights: steak Tuesday, Chinese Wednesday, Thursday curry and fish on Friday. Q🐎❀◖◗♿🚌●P⚡

Surbiton

New Prince

117 Ewell Road, KT6 6AL (on A240)
⏲ 12-11 (midnight Fri & Sat); 12-11 Sun
☎ (020) 8296 0265
Fuller's London Pride, Gale's Butser, HSB, seasonal beers Ⓗ
A short distance from the town centre, this 19th-century pub bears traditional decor in its large front bar and smaller back bar that doubles as a function room. Children are welcome until 7pm. A wheelchair ramp is provided at the rear entrance. Ales can be sampled to help you decide on your pint.
🐎❀◖♿⇌🚌⚡

Waggon & Horses

1 Surbiton Hill Road, KT6 4TW (on A240)
⏲ 11-11.30 (midnight Fri & Sat); 12-11 Sun
☎ (020) 8390 0211
Young's Bitter, Special, seasonal beer Ⓗ
Victorian pub on a former coaching route; it comprises several drinking areas and a function room. Parking may be difficult but the pub is conveniently situated just off the Kingston-Surbiton bus route. Tuesday is quiz night. The pub often sells Young's occasional brews. Meals are served 12-9pm daily.
Q🐎❀◖◗♿⇌🚌♣P⚡

Sutton

Little Windsor

13 Greyhound Road, SM1 4BY (off A232, E of centre)
⏲ 12-11.30 (midnight Fri & Sat); 12-11 Sun
☎ (020) 8643 2574
Fuller's Discovery, London Pride, ESB; guest beer Ⓗ
Once the Windsor Castle, this pub formally adopted its nickname which, despite subsequent extension, is still appropriate. The drinking area is wrapped around the L-shaped bar with additional space in the extension to the rear. At the back is a garden, and a couple of tables at the front of the pub also permit outdoor drinking. A discount on ales applies on weekday

afternoons. Lunches are served Monday-Saturday. ❀◖⇌

Lord Nelson

32 Lower Road, SM1 4QP
⏲ 12-11; 12-4, 7-10.30 Sun
☎ (020) 8642 4120
Young's Bitter, Special Ⓗ
Excellent local situated in the New Town area. A Young's hostelry since 1888, the exterior boasts green and brown tiling and etched windows. The recently refurbished interior comprises two distinct drinking areas, separated by the length of the attractive bar. Darts and crib are played. Home-cooked lunches are served weekdays. The pleasant garden is a bonus. The pub stands on the 154 bus route. ❀◖🚌♣

Old Bank

2 High Street, SM1 1HN
⏲ 11-11; 12-10.30 Sun
☎ (020) 8661 7525
Adnams Bitter; Fuller's London Pride; Greene King Old Speckled Hen; guest beers Ⓗ
This former bank and subsequent brew-pub is now part of the Barracuda Group. Situated next to Sutton Station it attracts a varied clientele throughout the day. The deep single bar has a raised section at the far end. Five handpumps dispense ales from the larger independents. A similar number of TV screens, normally mute, display news and sport. Food is served 12-9pm daily. Cribbage can be played. There is a patio at the rear. ❀◖◗♿⇌♣

Robin Hood

52 West Street, SM1 1SH
⏲ 11-11; 12-11 Sun
☎ (020) 8643 7584
Young's Bitter, Special, seasonal beers Ⓗ
Convenient for Sutton's main thoroughfare, this cosy, single-bar pub is very much a venue for the local community. The landlord won Young's Best Kept Cellar management award in 2005 after two years as runner-up. It hosts the annual national home-brewing championships in November. Games include shove-ha'penny, chess and dominoes. Bar snacks are always available. There is a small patio at the rear and a function room with a bar can be hired. Winner of local CAMRA Pub of the Year 2006. ❀◖◗⇌♣

Wallington

Duke's Head Hotel

The Green, 6 Manor Road, SM6 0AA (A237/A232 jct)
⏲ 11-midnight; 12-11.30 Sun
☎ (020) 8401 7410 🌐 dukesheadsurrey.co.uk
Young's Bitter, Special, seasonal beers Ⓗ
Historic pub overlooking the village green of the original manor of Wallington. The Duke's Head has been owned by Young's Brewery since 1832, but there was a pub here long before then. It consists of a basic public bar housing a dartboard and a comfortable saloon bar with wood panelling and a fine clock. A hotel and restaurant have been added to the pub. It has its own garden and the green is often used for outdoor drinking in summer. ♛Q❀🛏◖◗🚌♣P

Whispering Moon

25 Ross Parade, Woodcote Road, SM6 9QT (by station)
⏲ 9am-midnight (1am Fri & Sat); 9am-midnight Sun
☎ (020) 8647 7020
Greene King Abbot, Old Speckled Hen; Marston's Burton Bitter, Pedigree; guest beers Ⓗ
Across the road from the station, Wetherspoon's formula has been applied to a former small cinema premises. A single bar serves an open-plan L-shaped lounge that incorporates an elevated drinking area. The regular beer range is augmented by changing guests, usually from micro-breweries. Just up the road is Wallington Hall – home of Croydon & Sutton CAMRA's annual October beer and cider festival. ◖◗♿⇌🍎⚡

WEST LONDON

W1: Fitzrovia

King & Queen

1-2 Foley Street, W1W 6DL
⏲ 11-11; 11-10.30 Sun
☎ (020) 7636 5619
Adnams Bitter; St Austell Tribute; Wells Bombardier Ⓗ
Behind the attractive Grade II listed, red-brick Edwardian façade, the spacious main bar on the ground floor of this corner pub doubles as a portrait gallery of British royalty and sports teams. Upstairs, the function room houses an impressive collection of brewery-themed mirrors. The landlord knows what his locals like so the beer range is stable. Behind the bar you will find a vast and intriguing collection of whiskies. ❀◖◗⊖(Goodge St)

One Tun

58-60 Goodge Street, W1T 4ND
⏲ 11-11; 11-10.30 Sun
☎ (020) 7209 4105
Young's Bitter, Special, seasonal beers Ⓗ
The recent closure of the Middlesex Hospital has not lessened the crowds in this popular pub. Dominated by a dark wood island bar, it boasts a fine collection of prints and an intricately carved mirror frame - maybe former regular Jimi Hendrix checked his reflection here. The musical spirit lives on as rock tunes are played over a quality sound system. Sports on a large-screen TV and the Tuesday quiz help keep the devoted locals entertained. No lunches are served on Sunday. ❀◖◗⇌(Euston)⊖(Goodge St)♣

W1: Marylebone

Carpenters Arms

12 Seymour Place, W1H 7NE
⏲ 11-11; 12-10.30 Sun
☎ (020) 7723 1050
Fuller's London Pride; Harveys Sussex Best Bitter; Young's Bitter; guest beers Ⓗ
A comfortable, friendly, neighbourhood

atmosphere belies the pub's close proximity to Oxford Street and Marble Arch. Tables near the windows are slightly elevated in this popular meeting place. One of the three regular beers listed above will be on handpump, supported by three changing guests. Drinkers of all ages mingle happily here, watching sport on TV; there is a dartboard at the rear and another in the function room upstairs. ❀⊖(Marble Arch)♣

Duke of Wellington

94A Crawford Street, W1H 2HQ
✪ 11-11; 12-10.30 Sun
☎ (020) 7724 9435
Adnams Bitter; Wells Bombardier 🄷
Popular pub, just a few minutes' walk from Edgware Road Station. Carpeted throughout, an eye-catching display stand contains bottled Belgian and British beers and pewter tankards. Another display is devoted to the Duke of Wellington – among the memorabilia you can find a cheque written by the Duke in 1828. A third collection – Toby jugs – hangs above the bar.
Q◐⊖(Edgware Rd)

W1: Mayfair

Coach & Horses

5 Hill Street, W1J 5LD
✪ 11.30-11; closed Sat & Sun
☎ (020) 7355 1055
Shepherd Neame Kent's Best, Spitfire, seasonal beers 🄷
Always a friendly welcome awaits at this pub with an imposing bar. The back bar is a Georgian Grade II listed corner building. A tasty menu lists fish and chips, home-cooked ham and free range eggs, baked potatoes, sarnies, salads and puds – try the apple crumble, as well as home-baked organic baguettes. The oldest surviving pub in Mayfair (see the plaque outside), dating from 1744, it boasts leaded windows and interesting art on the walls. ◐⊖(Green Park)

W1: Soho

Coach & Horses

29 Greek Street, W1D 5DH
✪ 11-11; 12-10.30 Sun
☎ (020) 7437 5920
Draught Bass; Fuller's London Pride; Tetley Bitter; Wells Bombardier 🄷
Famous Soho local of the late Jeffrey Bernard and the staff of Private Eye magazine, displaying many relevant cartoons on the walls. The pub was recreated for the set of the play Jeffrey Bernard Is Unwell – the oft-stated reason for the absence of his newspaper column. This well-lit, traditional corner pub with wood-panelling and well-worn upholstered benches and chairs offers a wide choice of quality ales. A diverse mix of regulars, local workers, tourists and theatregoers keeps the staff busy.
⊖(Leicester Sq)

Dog & Duck ☆

18 Bateman Street, W1D 3AJ
✪ 11-11; 12-10.30 Sun
☎ (020) 7494 0697
Fuller's London Pride; Taylor Landlord; guest beers 🄷
The dog and duck motif is evident all around the pub in tiles and mosaics dating from 1897. Not the largest pub in London, but bay windows give the illusion of space upstairs in the George Orwell bar where the author used to drink. This Grade II listed building has comfortable green leather seating and a large AG Symonds mirror with its trademark red hopleaf. Meals are served every day 12-9pm. ◐⇌(Charing Cross)⊖(Piccadilly/Leicester Sq)

Pillars of Hercules

7 Greek Street, W1D 4DF
✪ 12-11; 12-10.30 Sun (closed Sun Jan & Feb)
☎ (020) 7437 1179
Young's Bitter; guest beers 🄷
This site has harboured a pub called the Pillars of Hercules since the 17th century, although the original was demolished. It was mentioned in Dickens' Tale of Two Cities. A varied clientele of office workers, media types and concertgoers quaff their way through a changing range of 25-30 guest beers each month. A quirky DJ performs on Wednesday evening, playing a mixture of reggae, rockabilly, ska and C&W (all vinyl) from a converted supermarket trolley. Meals are served 12-8pm daily.
❀◐⊖(Tottenham Crt Rd)

Ship

116 Wardour Street, W1F 0TT
✪ 12-11; closed Sun
☎ (020) 7437 8446
Fuller's Discovery, London Pride, ESB 🄷
Fuller's pub that has been beautifully refurbished, with etched glass windows and mirrors, a long, classic wooden bar with brass footrail and mirrors behind. An eclectic choice of music, covering Brit rock, punk, metal and indie attracts a mixed crowd of young locals, tourists, musicians and clubbers. John Lennon, Hendrix, the Who and the Clash are all reputed to have drunk here in the past. A limited menu is served at lunchtime. ◐⊖(Tottenham Ct Rd)

W2: Bayswater

King's Head

33 Moscow Road, W2 4AH
✪ 11-11; 12-10.30 Sun
☎ (020) 7229 4233
Adnams Broadside; Fuller's London Pride; Greene King IPA; Young's Bitter; guest beers 🄷
A single, large room incorporating a small no-smoking area, popular with young people and tourists from the busy Queensway shopping precinct. It can get noisy and smoky later in the evening. Five handpumps offer regular beers and a changing guest; it also stocks a good range of foreign beers. Photographs of the Bernard brewery are displayed. Sporting events are shown on TV.
◐⊖(Bayswater/Queensway)

Prince Edward

73 Princes Square, W2 4NY

🕐 11-11; 12-10.30 Sun
☎ (020) 7727 2221
Badger K&B Sussex, First Gold, Tanglefoot; guest beers Ⓗ
Listed building built in 1858 as the Princes Hotel on the corner of a leafy Victorian square. Inside is a smartly furnished lounge bar with a central island bar. Note the fine black and white photographs, etched glass mirrors and coloured, leaded glass panels. Lunches are served 12-3pm, evening meals 5.30-10pm (9pm Sun). ❀ⓛⓓ⊖⚟

W2: Marble Arch

Tyburn
18-20 Edgware Road, W2 2EN
🕐 10-11; 12-10.30 Sun
☎ (020) 7723 4731
Courage Best Bitter; Fuller's London Pride; Greene King Abbot; Marston's Pedigree; guest beers Ⓗ
Opened in 2000 in former shop units under an office block, the Tyburn is ultra-modern in style with large curved, floor-to-ceiling windows, black tiled and polished wood floors and metal tables and chairs. Red and blue lights highlight the pub's name and ownership. The pub takes its name from the Tyburn tree that stood nearby and was used for public executions until 1783.
ⓛⓓ♿⊖⚟

W2: Paddington

Mad Bishop & Bear
Upper Level, The Lawn, Paddington Station, W2 1HB (accessible via escalator from station concourse)
🕐 9am (7.30am Sat)-11; 10-10.30 Sun
☎ (020) 7402 2441
Fuller's Chiswick, Discovery, London Pride, ESB, seasonal beers; guest beers Ⓗ
This Fuller's pub is situated above Paddington Station with access via an escalator. Furnished and fitted to a high standard, attractive mirrors and lighting, including a prominent chandelier, create a sophisticated impression; many prints depict clerical and aristocratic subjects. It is a relaxing refuge from the hustle and bustle of the station below, despite the piped music. Breakfast is served from opening until midday; the pub may close early if quiet.
ⓛⓓ⇌⊖

Victoria
10A Strathearn Place, W2 2NH
🕐 11-11; 12-10.30 Sun
☎ (020) 7724 1191
Fuller's Chiswick, London Pride, ESB, seasonal beers Ⓗ
Imposing pub with a wood-panelled interior and a narrow central section. Upstairs are two function rooms with plush furnishings and fittings from the old Gaiety Theatre in the Strand. The pub, with its white-painted stucco exterior, dates from 1839 and is Grade II listed. It was reputedly visited by Queen Victoria after the opening of the rebuilt Paddington Station in 1854. It was for many years a Charringtons house. Tuesday is quiz night.
⛼Q❀ⓛⓓ⇌⊖(Lancaster Gate)

W4: Chiswick

Bell & Crown
72 Strand-on-the-Green, W4 3PH
🕐 11-11 daily
☎ (020) 8994 4164
Fuller's Chiswick, London Pride, ESB, seasonal beers Ⓗ
Busy riverside pub, where the conservatory at the rear and the patio overlook the Thames. The wood-panelled interior is warmed by an open fire in winter. Opened in 1787 as the Bell, it was rebuilt in 1907 on condition that the licence of a neighbouring pub (the Crown) be surrendered. Good meals are freshly prepared. Children are welcome in the conservatory. It is handy for Kew Bridge station. ⛼Q❀ⓛⓓ♿⇌(Kew Bridge)

George & Devonshire
8 Burlington Lane, W4 2QE
🕐 11-11; 12-10.30 Sun
☎ (020) 8994 1859
Fuller's Chiswick, London Pride, ESB, seasonal beers Ⓗ
One of Fuller's oldest tied houses, it was purchased in 1701, together with two cottages for £70. It is said that Dick Turpin drank here before his ride to York. Just yards from the brewery, it was the George until 1823, when the name was changed to avoid confusion with the nearby George IV. Rare in the area for retaining separate saloon and public bars, with individual entrances, this attractive red-brick pub has some outdoor seating. No food is served Sunday.
❀ⓛ⊟♣P⚟

Old Pack Horse
434 Chiswick High Road, W4 5TF
🕐 11-11; 12-10.30 Sun
☎ (020) 8995 2872
Fuller's Chiswick, London Pride, ESB, seasonal beers Ⓗ
Well-preserved corner pub that consists of five distinct drinking areas and a large Thai restaurant (open daily 12-10pm) at the back. Known as the Lower Packhorse until 1812, this became one of Fuller's showpiece houses when it was rebuilt with a fine Edwardian frontage in 1910.
Q❀ⓛⓓ⊖(Chiswick Pk)

W5: Ealing

Castle
36 St Mary's Road, W5 5EU
🕐 10-midnight (1am Fri & Sat); 10-midnight Sun
☎ (020) 8567 3285
Fuller's Chiswick, Discovery, London Pride, ESB, seasonal beers; guest beer (occasional) Ⓗ
Old-style local that attracts a mixed bunch of regulars, from students attending Thames Valley University opposite to sporting enthusiasts who enjoy the extensive coverage of football and rugby matches, when the pub can get busy. Among the several drinking areas there is a tiny snug, a

raised no-smoking area and a secluded patio. It serves Thai cuisine and more traditional pub fare. ❀ ◐ ♿ ⊖ (South) ⊬

Ealing Park Tavern

222 South Ealing Road, W5 4RL

11-11; 12-10.30 Sun

☎ (020) 8758 1879

Beer range varies Ⓗ

Large, open 18th-century inn with understated bistro-style decor. Five handpumps serve an ever-changing variety of guest beers, often including unusual, local or seasonal brews. Free from electronic games machines, the low background music permits conversation. The top-rated restaurant serves a daily changing menu (no food Mon lunchtime). The only cider served here is French – imported Breton cider in bottles. ♨ ❀ ◐ ⊖ (South)

Questors Grapevine Club

12 Mattock Lane, W5 5BQ

7-11; 12-2.30, 7-10.30 Sun

☎ (020) 8567 0011 🌐 questors.org.uk/grapevine

Fuller's London Pride, seasonal beers; guest beers Ⓗ

Last year, this friendly theatre bar, which has been local CAMRA Club of the Year several times, reached the last four in the national awards. The staff are all volunteers and real ale fans, which shows in the quality of the beers. Usually four beers are stocked, many from small breweries. Although primarily for members of the Questors Theatre, guests are welcome in the bar – just sign the visitors' book on arrival.

Q ♿ ⇌ (Broadway) ⊖ ♣ P

Red Lion

13 St Mary's Road, W5 5RA

11-11(1am Fri & Sat); 12-10.30 Sun

☎ (020) 8567 2541

Fuller's Chiswick, Discovery, London Pride, ESB, seasonal beers; guest beers (occasional) Ⓗ

This single-bar pub was greatly enlarged in a major 2002 refurbishment. While this has allowed a greater emphasis to be placed on food, the essential character of the original front section remains virtually unchanged. It is also known as Stage 6 because of its location opposite Ealing Studios – a link reinforced by old photographs lining the walls. It was local CAMRA Pub of the Year 2002-04.

Q ❀ ◐ ⇌ (Broadway) ⊖ (South)

Wheatsheaf

41 Haven Lane, W5 2HZ

12 (11 Sat)-11; 12-10.30 Sun

☎ (020) 8997 5240

Fuller's Chiswick, Discovery, London Pride, ESB, seasonal beers Ⓗ

Friendly local, tucked away up a side street, just north of Ealing town centre. Inside, it is deceptively large, with wood much in evidence. A small, semi-partitioned area at the front leads to a comfortable saloon that itself leads on to a more open space at the rear. Several TVs show sport, but it is possible to escape them. ◐ ⇌ (Broadway) ⊖

W6: Hammersmith

Andover Arms

57 Aldensley Road, W6 0DL

12-11 (11.30 Fri & Sat); 12-3.30, 7-10.30 Sun

☎ (020) 8741 9794

Fuller's Chiswick, London Pride, ESB, seasonal beers Ⓗ

Marvellous pub, dating from 1853 and acquired by Fuller's in 1991. A back-street local well hidden in the centre of Brackenbury Village, Aldensley Road also sports an increasingly rare independent butcher's shop. A small restaurant area and kitchen have been built into the pub, serving Thai food of a high quality. Snob screens at the bar have been retained here. It hosts a regular quiz on Sunday evening.

Q ◐ ⊖ (Ravenscourt Pk)

Brook Green Hotel

170 Shepherd's Bush Road, W6 7PB

11-midnight daily

☎ (020) 7603 2516 🌐 brookgreenhotel.co.uk

Young's Bitter, Special, seasonal beers Ⓗ

Dating from 1886, this Victorian pub conveys an impression of grandeur with large windows, high ceilings and chandeliers. Sympathetically refurbished, many imposing features remain, including much woodwork, ornate mirrors and an impressive fireplace. Comfortable lounge-style seating and a real fire are provided in the main bar. Sky TV is available for major sporting events and darts can be played. The basement bar is a function room and entertainment venue, staging comedy, jazz and blues. The overnight accommodation is competitively priced. ♨ 🛏 ◐ ⊖ ♣ ⊬

Dove

19 Upper Mall, W6 9TA

11-11; 12-10.30 Sun

☎ (020) 8748 9474

Fuller's Discovery, London Pride, ESB, seasonal beers Ⓗ

Popular, historic, Grade II listed riverside pub dating from the 18th-century. James Thompson composed Rule Britannia here in an upstairs room. The main wood-panelled bar is slightly elevated, while the tiny public bar at the front lays claim to being the smallest in Britain. The rear terrace, boasting a fruit-bearing vine, leads to another terrace overlooking the Thames. If you arrive late during the boat race you will never get in.

Q ❀ ◐ ⊟ ⊖ (Ravenscourt Pk)

Plough & Harrow

120-124 King Street, W6 0QU

9am-11.30; 9am-10.30 Sun

☎ (020) 8735 6020

Courage Best Bitter, Directors; Fuller's London Pride; Greene King Abbot; Marston's Pedigree; guest beers Ⓗ

Opened in 2002 in the former car showroom that had occupied the site since the 1959 demise of the original Plough & Harrow, the spacious interior is in modern style with an Art Deco influence, with largely tiled flooring and a rear carpeted area reserved for families, diners and non-smokers. There is a smaller enclosed lounge at the back while the upper floors are occupied by a Holiday Inn. A tavern has existed on this site since 1419. Q♉◑⊖(Ravenscourt Pk)⚡

Salutation
154 King Street, W6 0QU
☼ 11-11; 12-10.30 Sun
☎ (020) 8748 3668
Fuller's Chiswick, Discovery, London Pride, ESB, seasonal beers Ⓗ
First licensed in 1727, the present pub, with its unusual tiled exterior dates from 1910. The large lounge bar has some raised seating areas and a fine fireplace. It was visited by the late Queen Mother in 1989 in her role as patron of the London Garden Society to inspect the floral display. ❀◐⊖(Ravenscourt Pk)

W7: Hanwell

Fox
Green Lane, W7 2PJ
☼ 11-midnight (1am Fri & Sat); 11-12 Sun
☎ (020) 8567 3912
Caledonian Deuchars IPA; Fuller's London Pride; Taylor Landlord; guest beers Ⓗ
A pub has stood on this site for 200 years; the present encumbent can be dated to the early 20th century. Although popular with locals, it also attracts boaters and walkers from the nearby Grand Union Canal. An active community involvement includes participating in the Hanwell carnival and other events. The Easter beer festival is now a firm fixture, showcasing many of the guest ales on offer over the year. ♨Q❀◐♣P

W8: Notting Hill Gate

Churchill Arms
119 Kensington Church Street, W8 7LN
☼ 11-11 (midnight Thu-Sat); 12-10.30 Sun
☎ (020) 7727 4242
Fuller's Chiswick, Discovery, London Pride, ESB, seasonal beers Ⓗ
Superb pub, run by the same licensee now for many years. It dates from 1824 and for the first 18 months was named the Bedford Arms. There are a number of references here to WS Churchill (but the pub was not named after Sir Winston). Also on display is a framed collection of 1,500 butterflies. A no-smoking Thai restaurant serves meals all day from noon until 10pm (10.30pm Sun). ◑⊖⚡

Uxbridge Arms
13 Uxbridge Street, W8 7TQ
☼ 12-11; 12-10.30 Sun
☎ (020) 7727 7326
Brakspear Bitter; Fuller's London Pride; Greene King IPA Ⓗ
Popular, back-street local, a short walk from Notting Hill Gate tube. The pub displays an interesting collection of bric-a-brac above the bar and many prints along the wood-panelled walls. The TV is switched on for special sporting events. Benches outside on the pavement allow for some outside drinking in fine weather. Q❀⊖

W11: Notting Hill

Cock & Bottle
17 Needham Road, W11 2RP
☼ 12-11; 12-10.30 Sun
☎ (020) 7229 1550
Fuller's London Pride; Hogs Back TEA Ⓗ
Hard to find off the busy Westbourne Grove, this haven has preserved many features that existed before its name changed from the White Swan, including the leaded coloured glass panels, a snob screen and a large fireplace. Locals like to watch TV in the saloon bar, other visitors can talk by the fire in the lounge. Beware of the anti-clockwise clock that makes you lose track of time. Tuesday is quiz night. Weekday lunches are served. ❀◐⊖(Notting Hill Gate/Westbourne Pk)

W14: West Kensington

Crown & Sceptre
34 Holland Road, W14 8BA
☼ 11-11 (midnight Fri & Sat); 12-10.30 Sun
☎ (020) 7602 1866
Beer range varies Ⓗ
Dating from 1856, its makeover a few years back transformed it from a rundown local to a pub with a reputation for both quality and good value. It retains its traditional bar, with an inscription of the pub above it, and a glass frontage. The layout is split level, with a no-smoking area at the rear. It serves up to three beers supplied by Theakston and micro-breweries. Meals include authentic Mexican dishes and steaks on Wednesday. Quiz night is Tuesday. ❀◑♿⇌(Olympia)⊖♣⚡

Radnor Arms
247 Warwick Road, W14 8PX
☼ 12-11; 12-10.30 Sun
☎ (020) 7602 7708
Everards Tiger; guest beers Ⓗ
The building stands out on the busy Earls Court one-way system, because of redevelopment all around. It was threatened with demolition, but a recent petition helped secure its reprieve. This single-bar pub has a traditional feel, with wooden floors and a collection of beer bottles, glasses and jugs. The only regular stockist of Everards Tiger in west London, it attracts workers from nearby council and inland revenue offices, as well as locals who play chess and Connect Four regularly. ⇌(Olympia) ⊖♣

Brentford

Brewery Tap
47 Catherine Wheel Road, TW8 8BD
☼ 12-midnight daily
☎ (020) 8560 5200
Fuller's Chiswick, London Pride, ESB, seasonal beers; guest beers Ⓗ
Originally the tap of the William Gomm Brewery (acquired by Fuller's in 1980), the pub is of Victorian origin, and it is reached by steps as the river used to flood here. Renowned for its regular jazz (Tue and Thu eves), it stages other music every evening except Monday (quiz night) and Wednesday which is quiet. Lunches are popular (book

Sun); on weekdays meals are served until 7.30pm. There are patios to the front and rear, where well-behaved dogs are welcome. ❀◑◗⇌♣

Express Tavern

56 Kew Bridge Road, TW8 0EW

⏲ 11.30-11 (midnight Thu & Fri); 6.30-midnight Sat; 12-10.30 Sun

☎ (020) 8560 8484

Draught Bass; Young's Bitter; guest beers Ⓗ

Over 200 years old, this friendly local at the northern end of Kew Bridge has too much history to detail, but if you are interested in the origins of Brentford FC, the former Brentford market, Brentford's pubs, the 'Buffalos' and indeed CAMRA, you have to come here. Noted locally for its Bass and Young's Bitter (still known here as pale ale), its two bars, quiet mock-manorial lounge and garden provide a haven from the busy road. ♨Q❀◑⊟⇌(Kew Bridge)

Magpie & Crown

128 High Street, TW8 8EW

⏲ 11-midnight (1am Thu-Sat); 12-midnight Sun

☎ (020) 8560 5658

Beer range varies Ⓗ

Mock-Tudor pub, set back from the High Street, with outside tables at the front and a rear patio (equipped with a cycle rack). Four changing ales (nearly 1,600 in 10 years) have made it a magnet for beer lovers. Up to three varying ciders (occasionally perry) are offered, plus draught Budvar, Fruli, Hoegaarden and Paulaner, and a range of continental bottled beers. CAMRA's local Pub of the Year 1999 and 2000 offers Thai food (eve meals Tue-Sat), bar billiards and other games. ❀◑◗⇌♣●

Cranford

Jolly Gardeners

144 High Street, TW5 9WB

⏲ 11-midnight (2am Fri & Sat); 12-11 Sun

☎ (020) 8897 6996

Beer range varies Ⓗ

Small locals' pub where the distinct bars are connected via an archway. The single beer is constantly rotated and often comes from a small brewer. A friendly atmosphere pertains in this former Benskins house, with occasional live music performed on a Saturday evening in the large public bar. The lunches are prepared on the premises. ❀◑♣P

Queen's Head

123 High Street, TW5 9PB

⏲ 11-midnight; 12-11 Sun

☎ (020) 8897 0722

Fuller's Chiswick, Discovery, London Pride, ESB, seasonal beers Ⓗ

There are several interesting aspects to this large roadhouse, built in the 1930s. It stands on the site of the first pub in the country to be granted a full licence and is situated on a shopless High Street. It was the venue for the formation of the local CAMRA branch in 1974 – at the time it was one of just six pubs in the area to sell real ale. Q❀◑◗P

Feltham

Moon on the Square

30 The Centre, High Street, TW13 4AU

⏲ 9am-midnight (1am Fri & Sat); 9am-midnight Sun

☎ (020) 8893 1293

Courage Best Bitter, Directors; Greene King Abbot; Shepherd Neame Spitfire; guest beers Ⓗ

This real ale oasis continues to flourish in a changing Feltham. The interior betrays it as an early Wetherspoon's outlet: wood panels and glass-partitioned booths with pictures and history panels depicting how Feltham has altered over the years. The welcome is warm and genuine and it always offers eight ales, often including a Scottish beer (reflecting the manager's origins) and Westons cider. Families with children are welcome in the no-smoking area.
◑◗♿⇌●⚟

Hampton Hill

Roebuck

72 Hampton Road, TW12 1JN

⏲ 11-11 (11.30 Fri & Sat); 12-4, 7-11 Sun

☎ (020) 8255 8133

Badger First Gold, Tanglefoot; Young's Bitter; guest beers Ⓗ

Entering this welcoming haven you are struck by the eclectic bric-a-brac: fishing rods on the ceiling; framed banknotes from around the world; a life-sized carving of an Indian chief and a host of transport memorabilia of all kinds. Working traffic lights change for last orders and closing time. The pub boasts a compact, award-winning garden and a summerhouse for cooler evenings. Two guest beers change monthly; lunches are served weekdays.
♨❀⊟◑⇌(Fulwell)

Hayes

Botwell Inn

25-29 Coldharbour Lane, UB3 3EB

⏲ 9am-midnight (1am Fri & Sat); 9am-midnight Sun

☎ (020) 8848 3112

Courage Best Bitter, Directors; Greene King Abbot; Marston's Burton Bitter, Pedigree; Shepherd Neame Spitfire; guest beers Ⓗ

A large Wetherspoon shop conversion, this pub regularly features guest beers from the local Grand Union Brewery, a popular choice with regulars and casual visitors alike. The many seating areas, including both outdoor amenities front and rear, allow non-smokers and families to enjoy a pleasant atmosphere. The area is associated with George Orwell, who taught at a nearby school. ❀◑◗♿⇌⚟

Hillingdon

Star

Blenheim Parade, Uxbridge Road, UB10 0LY (Near Pole Hill Rd jct)

⏲ 11-11 (1am Fri & Sat); 12-10.30 Sun

☎ (020) 8577 1096

Fuller's London Pride Ⓗ

This is a proper locals' pub. The landlady, Lily, is 'mum' to many of her regulars. It is not uncommon to see three generations

from one family supping together. Although not that old, the pub has a fair amount of dark wood and a very homely feel. The only food that is served is the Sunday roast.
Q❀♣⊬

Hounslow

Moon under Water

84-86 Staines Road, TW3 3LF

⌚ 10-11; 12-10.30 Sun

☎ (020) 8572 7506

Greene King Abbot; Hop Back Summer Lightning; Marston's Burton Bitter; guest beers Ⓗ

Early Wetherspoon's shop conversion, since enlarged, in typical style displaying local history panels and photos in the smoking area and booths. Very popular, it has a broad customer base from local regulars to others who travel from further afield; all receive a friendly welcome. It usually has three guest ales – far more at festival times. Unusually, the Monday club beer discounts apply only to the real ales. The large, no-smoking area accommodates families.
Q❀◖◗♿⇌⊖(Central)♣●⊬

Isleworth

Red Lion

92-94 Linkfield Road, TW7 6QJ

⌚ 11-11 (midnight Fri & Sat); 12-11 Sun

☎ (020) 8560 1457 🌐 red-lion.info

Young's Bitter; guest beers Ⓗ

Spacious, two-bar free house with a strong community focus. There is often something going on: a production on stage or in the garden by its own theatre group; live music (weekend eves); a quiz (Thu); or one of its four annual beer festivals. It offers eight beers, usually with tasting notes provided, and a draught cider. Lunches are served weekdays at local CAMRA's Pub of the Year 2003 and 2004. ❀◖⊟⇌♣●

Royal Oak

128 Worton Road, TW7 6EP

⌚ 12-11; 12-10.30 Sun

☎ (020) 8560 2906

Fuller's Chiswick, London Pride, ESB; seasonal beers or guest beer Ⓗ

Dating from 1843, the Royal Oak is a gem in an entirely residential area by the Duke of Northumberland's River. It is very traditional with dark wood partitions, etched glass and bric-a-brac, including a miniature bottle collection. Old photos of local interest adorn the walls and ceiling alongside the long-serving landlord's many awards. It has a riverside patio, TV at the back for sports, and food is served all day.
❀◖◗

Southall

Conservative & Unionist Club

Fairlawn, High Street, UB1 3HB

⌚ 11.30-2.30 (3 Fri & Sat), 7 (6 Fri & Sat)-11; 12-3, 7-10.30 Sun

☎ (020) 8574 0261

Rebellion IPA, seasonal beers; guest beers Ⓗ

Hidden down an alley beside the fire station, this gem welcomes card-carrying CAMRA members or anyone with this Guide, regardless of political persuasion. Weekday lunches are reasonably priced; there are four snooker tables and live music is performed monthly (last Sat). ❀◖⇌♣P

Teddington

Lion

27 Wick Road, TW11 9DN

⌚ 12-11 (11.30 Wed & Thu; midnight Fri & Sat); 12-11 Sun

☎ (020) 8977 3199 🌐 thelionpub.co.uk

Adnams Broadside; Caledonian Deuchars IPA; Fuller's London Pride; Sharp's Doom Bar; guest beer Ⓗ

Victorian single-bar, corner pub, sympathetically modernised and recently extended to give additional space for dining as well as wheelchair access. Food (not served Sun eve) ranges from traditional to modern English cuisine. Live music in the bar on Saturday evening is mostly blues; Wednesday is quiz night. Pool is played here. Twice-yearly beer festivals are held; barbecues are hosted in the garden. It is a short walk from Hampton Wick Station.
⛰❀◖◗♿⇌(Hampton Wick)♣⊬

Queen Dowager

49 North Lane, TW11 0NT

⌚ 11-11; 12-10.30 Sun

☎ (020) 8943 3474

Young's Bitter, Special, seasonal beers Ⓗ

Just off the main street but easily missed, this comfortable local is close to Teddington's main car park (behind Tesco). There has been a pub on the site since 1747 but the present building dates from 1906; it commemorates William IV's consort, Queen Adelaide, who returned to Teddington as Ranger of Bushy Park on his death. This recently modernised and extended pub serves cooked lunches every day. Bar billiards can be played here.
❀◖⇌♣⊬

Twickenham

Cabbage Patch

67 London Road, TW1 3SZ

⌚ 11-midnight; 12-11.30 Sun

☎ (020) 8892 3874

Adnams Broadside; Caledonian Deuchars IPA; Fuller's London Pride; Wells Bombardier; guest beers Ⓗ

Named after the site of the nearby rugby stadium, this pub is a favourite watering-hole for fans on match days. The landlord and his family, of over 25 years standing, provide a warm welcome. Six seating areas cater for all tastes. The freshly prepared food represents good value and the Sunday lunches are renowned. It has an upstairs disco and occasionally hosts live R&B music.
❀◖◗⊟♿⇌⊬

Fox

39 Church Street, TW1 3NR

⌚ 11-11 (12.30am Thu-Sat); 11-11 Sun

☎ (020) 8892 1535

Caledonian Deuchars IPA; Fuller's London Pride;

Hogs Back TEA; Twickenham Original; guest beers H
Twickenham's oldest pub (known originally as the Bell) dates from around 1670 and changed its name to the Fox in the early 1700s. Its function room was built as the Assembly Rooms around 1900. Step down from the street into the small bar where a good selection of real ales is always available, and try the home cooking. The Fox is favoured by the locals in this attractive area. ⌂Q❀◐⇌

Old Anchor

71 Richmond Road, TW1 3AW
☉ 12-11 (midnight Fri-Sat); 12-10.30 Sun
☎ (020) 8892 2181
Youngs Bitter, Special, seasonal beers H
Rebuilt in the early 20th century (originally the 1830s Anchor), the pub features much light wood - in the bar, panelling, furniture and floor - enhancing the welcome and attracting both regular and passing custom. Sunday lunches, using only locally-sourced organic ingredients, are popular as are the 'serious' sandwiches available at all times. In summer the ample paved garden is attractive. Quiz night is Thursday.
Q❀◐◑⇌

Prince Albert

30 Hampton Road, TW2 5QB
☉ 11-11 (midnight Fri & Sat); 11-11 Sun
☎ (020) 8894 3963
Fuller's Chiswick, Discovery, London Pride, ESB, seasonal beers H
Originally opened as the Star Brewery in 1840, the pub later became unofficially known as 'Whiffen's'– it was run by three generations of the same family whose name is still displayed behind the bar. Nowadays the Albert is popular for excellent beer, its convivial atmosphere and Thai food. It is divided into three areas, with a sports screen in one for fans. In summer the attractive garden and patio are popular. Live music is staged Saturday evenings.
❀◐◑♿⇌(Strawberry Hill)

Prince Blucher

124 The Green, TW2 5AG
☉ 11-11 (midnight Fri & Sat); 12-11 Sun
☎ (020) 8894 1824
Fuller's Chiswick, Discovery, London Pride, ESB, seasonal beers; H **guest beer** G
Historic 1815 pub, probably the only one remaining in the UK still to pay homage to Wellington's left flanker at Waterloo. Four distinct bar areas suit most tastes, with a large screen at the rear drawing crowds for major rugby and football events. The landlord offers home-made food all day, while summer hog roasts and barbecues in the child-friendly garden are an added attraction. Food and ale festivals are the pub's latest venture.
⌂Q❀◐◑⇌(Strawberry Hill)P⅍

Turk's Head

28 Winchester Road, TW1 1LF
☉ 12-11 (11.30 Thu; midnight Fri & Sat); 12-10.30 Sun
☎ (020) 8892 1972
Fuller's Discovery, London Pride, ESB, seasonal beers H
Beatles fans (some even from Japan) come here to see the pub location for a scene from A Hard Day's Night. The Bearcat Comedy Club has been bringing top comedians every Saturday night to the function room for over 20 years. Rugby fans form human pyramids on match days and try to stick stamps on the high ceiling. Built in 1902, it remains a genuine local corner pub offering fine beers and food.
⌂❀◐◑♿⇌(St. Margaret's)⅍

Uxbridge

Load of Hay

33 Villier Street, UB8 2PU
☉ 11-11.30; 12-11.30 Sun
☎ (01895) 234676
Fuller's London Pride; guest beers H
Genuine free house that sells a changing range of beers. There are usually three guest ales, mostly sourced from small, independent breweries. The building was originally the officers' mess of the Elthorne Light Militia, becoming a pub in the 1870s. The main part of the pub was once the stable block. The small, quiet front bar is the venue for frequent darts matches. A quiz is held each Tuesday and there is live music on Saturday. Parking is limited. ❀◐◑♣P⅍

Gone for a Burton

Burton-on-Trent is almost wholly given up to the manufacture of beer. The place is nothing more than a huge brewery or nest of breweries. Then there is Bass – his extensive beer-mills covering a hundred acres of land, and using two or three hundred quarters of malt every day, requiring the barley grown on sixty thousand acres of good English land, besides the hops grown on two thousand acres – yearly rolls into the groggeries of London and other great towns in England something like a million barrels of beer.

John B Gough, 1880

GREATER MANCHESTER

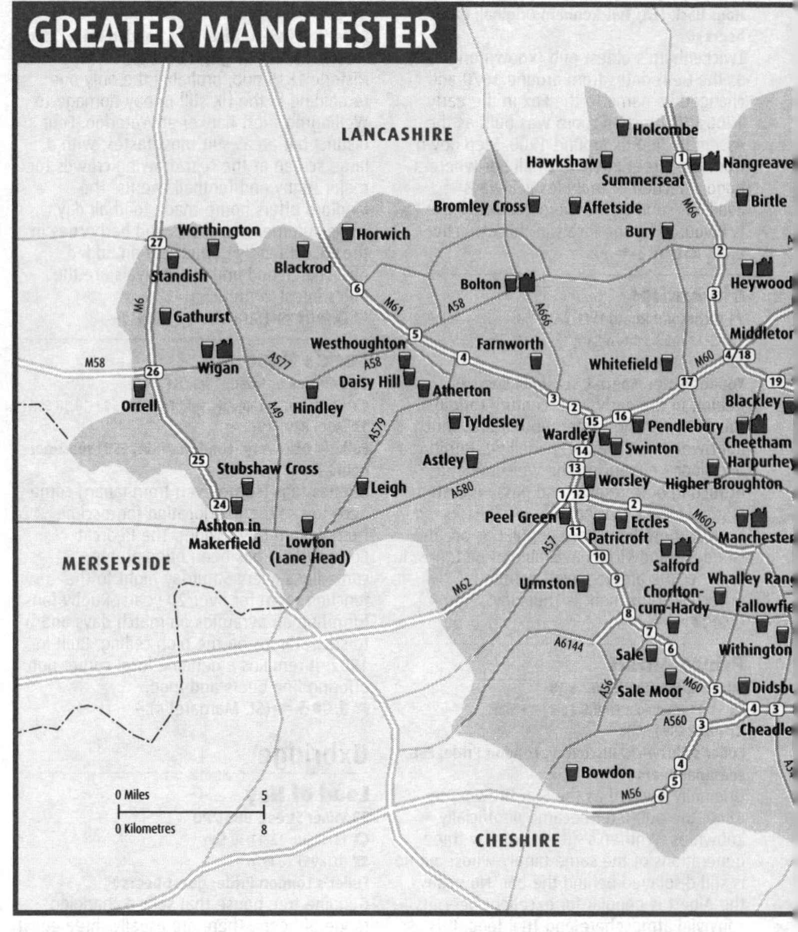

Affetside

Pack Horse

52 Watling Street, BL8 3QW
(approx 2 miles NW of Walshaw) OS755136
✪ 12-3, 5-11; 12-midnight Sat & Sun
☎ (01204) 883802
Hydes 1863, Original Bitter, seasonal beers Ⓗ
This country pub benefits from panoramic views, thanks to its situation high up on a Roman road. The bar area and cosy lounge (with real fire) are the original parts of the pub, dating from the 15th century. It has a function and pool room, while the Hightop Bar is used as a family room. Many stories are told relating to the ghost of the local man whose skull is on view behind the bar.
⌂Q≋❀◑▲P

Ashton-in-Makerfield

Ashton Jubilee Club

167-169 Wigan Road, WN4 9ST
✪ 8 (7.30 Fri & Sat)-midnight; 8-midnight Sun
☎ (01942) 202703
Beer range varies Ⓗ
Warm, friendly, social club with a welcoming atmosphere. At least one changing cask ale of consistently good quality and competitively priced is sold. It offers the usual social club entertainment (quiz, karaoke, bingo, themed nights) and occasional live entertainment in the main function room. There is a small lobby bar area, and two meeting rooms without bar service. Non-members are admitted, subject to constraints on frequency of visits and payment of a nominal admission charge (half price to CAMRA members).
⇌(Bryn)♣P♖

Ashton-under-Lyne

Dog & Pheasant

528 Oldham Road, Waterloo, OL7 6PQ
✪ 12-11 (11.30 Fri & Sat); 12-11 Sun
☎ (0161) 330 4849
Banks's Original; Marston's Burton Bitter, Pedigree; guest beers Ⓗ
Nicknamed the Top Dog, this popular, friendly local stands near the Medlock Valley Country Park. A large bar serves three areas, plus another room at the front. An extensive menu of good value food (not served Sun eve) includes vegetarian options. On Tuesday and Thursday evenings it stages a quiz. The pub is home to a local hiking group known as the Bog Trotters. Marston's Old Empire is

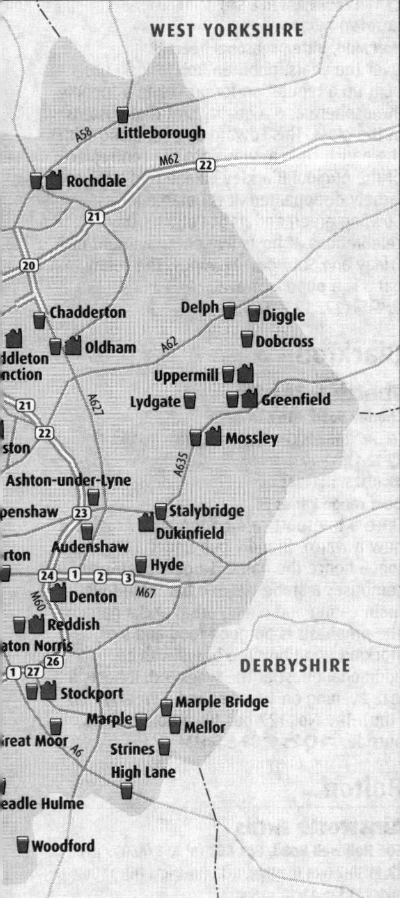

a regular guest beer. The No. 409 bus stops outside. ⛺❀◑◗▭P

Junction Inn

Mossley Road, Hazlehurst, OL6 9BX

⌚ 12-3, 5-midnight; 12-midnight Sat & Sun

☎ (0161) 343 1611

Robinson's Hatters, Unicorn, seasonal beers Ⓗ

Small pub of great character that remains little changed, close to open countryside and Ashton golf course. Built of local stone in the 19th century, it is the first building out of town that is not of brick construction. The small, cosy rooms make it welcoming and the unpretentious tap room is traditional in every respect. The home-made rag puddings are well worth a try; early evening meals are served Tuesday-Friday. A pavement patio allows for outdoor drinking. Q❀◑◗ ▭♣P

Oddfellows Arms

1-7 Alderley Street, Hurst, OL6 9LJ

⌚ 11-1am daily

☎ (0161) 330 6356

Robinson's Hatters, Unicorn, seasonal beers Ⓗ

The 'Oddies', on a corner terrace, has been in the same family since 1914. A small hatch and screen leads to the fine polished bar with its stained glass and nooks and crannies; a small tap room and vestry are to the left. Adjoining the lounge is the no-smoking Tom's Room, named after the late landlord. There is a walled patio to the side, used for free barbecues in summer, which houses a Koi carp pool. Q❀▭≈▭(38, 39)⚡

Astley

Cart & Horses

221 Manchester Road, M29 7SD

⌚ 12-11 (1am Fri & Sat); 12-10.30 Sun

☎ (01942) 870751

Holt Mild, Bitter Ⓗ

Popular roadside local, noted for its excellent Holt's frontage, complete with roof sign, etched windows and cobbled front space. Inside, the large, open-plan lounge manages to contain distinct sections, and there is a raised no-smoking area that leads to the patio and garden. The single bar serves both the lounge and tap room. ❀◑◗ ▭♣P⚡

Atherton

Atherton Arms

6 Tyldesley Road, M46 9DD

⌚ 11.30-midnight (1am Fri & Sat); 12-10.30 Sun

☎ (01942) 882885

Holt Mild, Bitter Ⓗ

This spacious, town-centre pub bears reminders of the club it once was. Beyond the double doors lies a comfortable hallway, complete with a serving hatch. Off the hall is a large lounge, the setting for weekend karaoke. For sports fans, the tap room houses pool and snooker tables and has ample seating for watching TV sport. To the rear is a concert room that occasionally hosts entertainment of various kinds and is available for hire. ▭♣P

Pendle Witch

2-4 Warburton Place, M46 0EQ

⌚ 4-midnight; 12-10.30 Sun

☎ (01942) 884537

Moorhouses Black Cat, Premier, Pendle Witches

INDEPENDENT BREWERIES

3 Rivers Reddish
All Gates Wigan
Bank Top Bolton
Bazens' Salford
Boggart Hole Clough Moston
Greenfield Greenfield
Holt Cheetham
Hydes Manchester
Lees Middleton Junction
Leyden Nangreaves
Lowes Arms Denton
McGuinness Rochdale
Marble Manchester
Mayflower Wigan
Millstone Mossley
Owl Oldham
Phoenix Heywood
Pictish Rochdale
Robinson's Stockport
Saddleworth Uppermill
Shaws Dunkinfield

Brew, seasonal beers; guest beers [H]
Access to the popular Pendle is from an alley off Market Street. This small, one-roomed pub has a raised seating area, cosy benches and standing room in front of the bar, which is home to the landlady's collection of Pendle witches. The pub hosts regular rock nights and frequent beer festivals. The garden is a summer suntrap.

Old Issacs
48 Market Street, M46 0EQ
⏲ 11-midnight; 12-11 Sun
☎ (01942) 895229
Beer range varies [H]
Refurbishment and renaming of the former Wheatsheaf has made an improvement to the pub and the town centre. Two front lounges have been brought into use – one for non-smokers, the other for diners and drinkers. The main room boasts a large fireplace, surrounded by comfortable chairs, with a raised seating area to one side. From the bar you can watch the busy chef through a viewing window, working to provide an excellent menu at reasonable prices. Two Phoenix beers are stocked. Q◑⊁

Audenshaw (Guide Bridge)

Boundary
2 Audenshaw Road, M34 5HD
(opp. station)
⏲ 11-midnight; 12-11 Sun
☎ (0161) 330 1679
Beer range varies [H]
A conservatory and dining room have been added to the already extensive frontage of this pub, allowing even greater capacity in the spacious interior that is split evenly between a lounge (serving the cask ale) and a tap. Micro-breweries are showcased on the array of five handpumps. Good value meals are served all day until 9pm. The large car park is the scene of an annual beer festival in June, which attracts boaters from the adjacent Ashton Canal.
❀◑⊟⇌(Guide Bridge)♣P

Birtle

Pack Horse Inn
Elbut Lane, BL9 7TU (off B6222) OS836125
⏲ 12-11; 12-10.30 Sun
☎ (0161) 764 3620
Lees Bitter, seasonal beers [H]
Traditional, country inn with a large car park, close to several footpaths and bridleways, so it attracts walkers and riders as well as locals. There is a small snug with a TV and coal fire, a restaurant area and a conservatory as well as the main bar area. Food is served throughout, with table service in the restaurant. Most of the premises is no-smoking. The south-facing patio and garden, affording fine views, are a bonus in warm weather. ⩩❀◑⊟♿P⊁

Blackley

Golden Lion
47 Old Market Street, M19 8DX (off Rochdale Rd)
⏲ 11-11 (midnight Fri & Sat); 11-11 Sun
☎ (0161) 740 1944
Holt Mild, Bitter, seasonal beers [H]
Over the years, publican Bob Jasinski has built up a reputation for providing a friendly atmosphere and a quality pint that glistens in the glass. This Edwardian pub, along with the parish church, was once the centrepiece of the original Blackley village that has now largely disappeared. It is notable for its bowling green and its St Patrick's Day celebrations. It hosts live entertainment on Friday and Saturday evenings. The sunny patio is a popular draw.
❀⊟🚌(17, 123, 163)♣

Blackrod

Thatch & Thistle
Chorley Road, BL6 5LA
(on A6 towards Chorley, 1 mile from M61 jct 6)
⏲ 12-11; 12-10.30 Sun
☎ (01257) 474044
Beer range varies [H]
Once a transport café on the busy A6, this is now a warm, friendly pub under a thatched roof – hence the name. Largely open-plan, it comprises a stone-flagged bar, with four main eating and dining areas and a garden. The emphasis is on good food and ales, stocking two Bank Top beers with an additional guest at the weekend. It hosts a jazz evening on Tuesday and a weekly quiz (Thu). The No. 127 bus from Bolton stops outside. ⩩Q🛏❀◑♿🚌P⊁

Bolton

Ainsworth Arms
606 Halliwell Road, BL1 8BY (at A58/A6099 jct)
⏲ 11.30-2 (not Tue-Thu), 5-11 (midnight Fri); 11.30-midnight Sat; 12-10.30 Sun
☎ (01204) 840671
Taylor Landlord; Tetley Mild, Bitter; guest beers [H]
Near Smithills Hall, a Grade I listed building, this is a dog-friendly local. The bar serves several areas: one is raised with alcoves, another is a basic tap room complete with bell pushes in use until 1981. It has a long association with football, and is the meeting place for many local sports teams; the juke box is only switched on by request. Lunches are served Friday–Sunday and breakfasts are strongly recommended. Guest beers come from small, independent breweries. Q❀◐♣

Barrister's Bar
7 Bradshawgate, BL1 1HJ
(on A575, near market cross)
⏲ 12-1am (2am Fri & Sat); 12-1am Sun
☎ (01204) 365174
Bank Top Flat Cap, Port O Call; Moorhouses Pride of Pendle, Blond Witch, Pendle Witches Brew [H]
Barrister's, for over 25s only, is part of the Swan Hotel, a listed building dating from 1845. Formerly the Malt and Hops bar, it was closed for many years until a change of ownership in 2004. The wood-panelled interior remains the same, but some comfortable chairs have been added. The regular beer range is supplemented by guest ales, primarily from Moorhouses and Bank

Top (who also provide the house beer, Judges Chambers). It also stocks a few Belgian bottled beers. ❀◖≠

Bob's Smithy

1448 Chorley Old Road, BL2 3BQ
(uphill from A58 ring road)
☉ 4.30 (12 Sat)-11 (midnight Fri & Sat); 12-11 Sun
☎ (01204) 842622
Bank Top Flat Cap; Taylor Landlord; Tetley Mild, Bitter; guest beers Ⓗ
The pub is named after a blacksmith who allegedly spent more time here than he did at work. This stone-built inn has been in existence for around 200 years. On the edge of the moors, it is handy for walkers as well as visitors to the Reebok Stadium. A genuine free house, it usually offers beers from small, independent breweries. Buses Nos. 125 and 126 from Bolton stop outside. ⌂❀🚌P

Brooklyn

Green Lane, Great Lever, BL3 2EF (1½ miles from town centre, off B6536)
☉ 12-11 (11.30 Thu; midnight Fri & Sat); 12-11 Sun
Holt Mild, Bitter Ⓗ
This imposing, brick Victorian house, boasting a notable mansard roof and ornamental chimneys, was built in 1859 and licensed in 1926. The central bar serves a comfortable tap room and several more large rooms, with elaborately moulded plasterwork on the ceilings and walls. The extensive grounds include a bowling green, outside drinking area, woodland and a car park. On Sunday meals are served 12-6pm; Wednesday curry evenings are popular. ❀◖◗⊟♣P

Lodge Bank Tavern

260 Bridgeman Street, BL3 6SA
☉ 2-midnight; 12-2am Fri & Sat; 12-midnight Sun
☎ (01204) 531946
Lees Bitter Ⓗ
Welcoming local, near Bobby Heywood's Park (with free use of floodlit pitches). The main room is conveniently divided into three small areas, and there is a pool room at the back of the bar. Karaoke, on Friday and Saturday evenings, is always well-attended – and loud! The only Lees pub in Bolton, it was the last to change its ale house status to a full licence. Well-behaved dogs are welcome. ❀≠♣P

Pepper Alley

7-13 Bank Street, BL1 1TS
(on A575 near market cross)
☉ 11-11; 12-10.30 Sun
☎ (01204) 391533
Holt Mild, Bitter Ⓗ
This large Holt's house opened in 2001, incorporating the former Millstone on Crown Street, and extending into a former restaurant on Bank Street. It has two distinct drinking areas: the former Millstone frontage has been refurbished and this part of the building retains a traditional pub feel with small alcoves, while the Bank Street extension is a modern, open-plan bar. Several TVs show sporting events and comedy evenings are staged monthly (last Thu). ❀◖≠

Sweet Green Tavern

127 Crook Street, BL3 6DD (opp. Sainsbury's, off A579)
☉ 11-11; 12-10.30 Sun
☎ (01204) 392258
Tetley Bitter; guest beers Ⓗ
This friendly local is situated on the edge of the town centre close to the bus/rail interchange. It comprises four small rooms served by a long bar, including an unspoilt vault. Its name reflects the original character of the area, 'a place of fragrant gardens', prior to 19th-century industrial development, which has in turn been replaced by a supermarket. Five guest beers are regularly served, usually featuring a mild. ⌂❀⊟≠♣P

Bromley Cross

Flag Inn

50 Hardmans Lane, BL7 9HX (off B6472)
☉ 12-11 (midnight Fri & Sat); 12-11 Sun
☎ (01204) 598267
Greene King IPA; guest beers Ⓗ
Enterprising management and seven guest beers, sourced from small independent breweries, make this beer drinker's mecca well worth seeking out. Bank Top seasonal brews are usually stocked. The building dates back over 300 years – the old brick-arched cellars were originally stables. A spacious, open-plan interior has TV screens for sports enthusiasts, but they do not dominate or impede conversation. It gets busy at weekends. Bar snacks are available at lunchtime (and early eve Mon-Thu). ⌂❀◖◗≠

Bowdon

Stamford Arms

The Firs, WA14 2TF (opp. church, up hill from B5160)
☉ 11.30-11 (11.30 Thu; midnight Fri-Sat); 12-11 Sun
☎ (0161) 928 1536
Boddingtons Bitter; Greene King IPA, Abbot; Marston's Pedigree; Wells Bombardier; guest beers Ⓗ
This large, low, attractive building near the church has served the people of Bowdon since Victorian times and retains a high proportion of local customers. The long bar faces a spacious seating area, with low ceilings. It has a no-smoking section and an elevated lounge suitable for functions. This former Boddingtons' house now offers a good choice of five regular beers plus guests. A raised, grassy area in front of the pub is used for outside drinking. ❀◖◗🚌P⊬

Bury

Dusty Miller

87 Crostons Road, BL8 1AL (at B6213/B6214 jct)
☉ 12-11; 12-10.30 Sun
☎ (0161) 764 1124
Moorhouses Black Cat, Premier, Blond Witch, Pendle Witches Brew Ⓗ
Proudly traditional local catering for a mixed clientele. Its position at a busy road junction makes parking difficult, but it is well worth making the effort to visit. Divided into two

rooms, served by a central bar, it also has a covered courtyard and outdoor seating for summer drinking. Bar snacks are usually available, but it is advisable to ring first. The Dusty Miller is one of just a small number of Moorhouses' tied pubs. ❀⊟

Trackside

East Lancs Railway, Bolton Street Station, BL9 0EY
12-midnight; 12-11 Sun
☎ (0161) 764 6461
Beer range varies Ⓗ
Free house with nine handpumps that also sells various ciders and perry direct from the cellar and a range of foreign beers. Simple wooden tables and chairs impart a traditional railway buffet mood. The vast array of pump clips on poles attached to the ceiling bear testimony to the beers that have been sold here. Quiet during the day, it can be busy at weekends when the ELR holds special events. Chairs and tables on the platform allow for summer drinking.
Q❀◐♿⇌(Bolton St)⊖⊟●

Chadderton

Horton Arms

19 Streetbridge Road, OL1 2SZ
(beneath motorway bridge)
12 (11.30 Fri & Sat)-midnight Mon-Thu; 12-10.30 Sun
☎ (0161) 624 7793
Lees GB Mild, Bitter Ⓗ
Pleasant, well-run pub where a large, open-plan space is neatly divided into distinct drinking areas, decorated with brasses. A side room houses a TV for major sporting events. Popular with locals and passing trade, thanks to its location on the B6195, despite its semi-urban location, the pub bears a country feel. Excellent home-cooked meals are served daily at lunchtime and early Friday evening (4.30-7pm). There are benches in front of the pub for fair weather drinking. ❀◐◑P

Cheadle

Cheshire Line Tavern

Manchester Road, SK8 2NZ (on B5095)
12-11; 12-10.30 Sun
☎ (0161) 428 3352 cheshireline.co.uk
Banks's Original; Marston's Pedigree Ⓗ
Hidden gem, only visible from the M60. At first glance this converted station appears to be a large, single-roomed restaurant. But closer inspection reveals it is a pub at heart, with an island bar carrying handpumps and a drivers' bar serving soft drinks, tea and coffee. The food is recommended. The pub hosts a quiz on Tuesday and weekly meetings of a Mini car owners club (Wed). This is a wonderful place for eating, drinking and relaxation, either inside or on the spacious patio. ⚲❀◐◑♿⇌(E Didsbury)P⊬

Cheadle Hulme

Church

90 Ravenoak Road, SK8 7EG (on A5149)
11-11; 12-10.30 Sun
☎ (0161) 485 1897
Robinson's Hatters, Old Stockport, Unicorn, seasonal beers Ⓗ
A Robinson's house since 1880, this attractive pub has been run by the same family for over 30 years. Two comfortable lounges are warmed by open fires; the rear lounge doubles as Edwardo's Restaurant. There is also a small vault behind the bar. Service is always efficient, even during busy periods, and the pub remains as popular as ever, enjoying a strong local following. Seasonal beers replace Old Stockport as available. ⚲Q❀◐◑⊟♣P

Cheetham

Queen's Arms

6 Honey Street, M8 8RG
(250 yds from A665 at top of Red Bank)
12-11; 12-10.30 Sun
☎ (0161) 834 4239 queensarmsmanchester.co.uk
Phoenix Bantam; Taylor Landlord; guest beers Ⓗ
Just outside Manchester's northern quarter, the uphill walk is rewarded by the sight of this two-roomed pub's impressive tiled Empress Brewery façade. A large garden to the rear, overlooking the industrialised Irk Valley and the city's evolving panorama, contains a play area for supervised children. Up to six guest beers are sourced from micro-breweries and a range of bottled and draught continental beers is stocked. A quiz is held on Tuesday evening.
⚲❀◐⇌(Manchester Victoria)⊖●

Chorlton-cum-Hardy

Bar

533 Wilbraham Road, M21 0UE
12-11 (midnight Thu; 1am Fri & Sat); 12-12.30am Sun
☎ (0161) 861 7576
Marble Manchester Bitter, Ginger Marble; guest beers Ⓗ
This popular, suburban bar welcomes customers of all ages, making it a true community local. The spacious no-smoking area is the ideal place in which to enjoy the excellent food, based on locally-sourced ingredients. The beers are from Marble and other micro-breweries in the vicinity, and the bar offers plenty of foreign bottled beers to try. The quiet juke box means conversation is not hampered. The patio has picnic tables. ❀◐◑⊬

Beech

72 Beech Road, M21 9EZ
11-11 (midnight Fri & Sat); 11-11 Sun
☎ (0161) 881 1180
Caledonian Deuchars IPA; Marston's Pedigree; Taylor Best Bitter, Landlord; guest beers Ⓗ
Busy, three-roomed local, close to the village green, it is lively most evenings and weekends, attracting customers of all ages. Irish musicians play on Monday evenings and a quiz is held every Thursday. All major sporting events are shown on TV. A paved seating area in front of the pub and a garden to the rear are both well used on warm evenings. The Beech has earned 10 consecutive entries in this Guide. ❀⊟♣

Marble Beer House

57 Manchester Road, M21 9PW

12-11 (midnight Tue-Sat); 12-midnight Sun

☎ (0161) 881 9206

Marble GSB, Manchester Bitter, Ginger Marble, Lagonda IPA, seasonal beers; guest beers Ⓗ

Café-bar, converted in 1998 from a beer shop, stocking the full range of Marble beers, plus two guests from micro-breweries and a guest cask cider. It can get crowded in the evening, and the outdoor seating is occupied all year round in mild weather. Children are welcome until 5pm. Chess, dominoes and backgammon are played. No meals are served but snacks from the award-winning Unicorn Wholefood Co-operative opposite are available; its produce, like the Marble beers, is vegan and organic. Q❀⊟♣●

Daisy Hill

Rose Hill Tavern

321 Leigh Road, Westhoughton BL5 2JQ (on B5235)

12-11 (11.30 Fri & Sat); 12-11 Sun

☎ (01942) 811529

Holt Mild, Bitter Ⓗ

Large, busy pub, now opened out, but retaining the outline of its old layout, with two rooms taken up by games of all sorts. It is often referred to by locals as the 'Bug' since an orphanage (the Bug House) was demolished to make way for the pub in 1899, a year after the railway came to the village. Originally owned by the Oldfield Brewery of Poolstock, Wigan, its crest can still be seen over the front door. ❀⇌♣P

Delph

Royal Oak (Th'heights)

Broad Lane, Heights, OL3 5TX

(1 mile above Denshaw Rd) OS982090

7-11; 12-5, 7-10.30 Sun

☎ (01457) 874460

Black Sheep Best Bitter; guest beers Ⓗ

Isolated, 250-year-old stone pub on a packhorse route overlooking the Tame Valley. In a popular walking area, it benefits from outstanding views. It comprises a cosy bar and three rooms, each with an open fire. The refurbished side room boasts a hand-carved stone fireplace, while the comfortable snug bears exposed beams. Good home-cooked food (eve meals Fri-Sun) often features game and home-bred pork. The house beer is brewed by Moorhouses. Guests include brews from Phoenix and Millstone. ⛼Q❀◗P⚟

Didsbury

Didsbury

852 Wilsmlow Road, M20 2SQ

(on A5145 by Fletcher Moss Gdns)

12-11 (midnight Fri & Sat); 12-11 Sun

☎ (0161) 445 5389

Courage Directors; Theakston Best Bitter; Wells Bombardier; guest beers Ⓗ

Look beyond the Chef & Brewer corporate family dining pub-restaurant with its faux-rustic interior and you will encounter a hugely popular eating house that dispenses excellent ales from eight handpulls. Unlikely as this may seem, it is a testament to the skill and commitment of the cellar and management team. Do not be afraid to reserve a table solely for drinking. The Didsbury even hosts a beer festival twice a year. ❀◖◗⇌(E Didsbury)⊟P

Fletcher Moss

1 William Street, M20 6RQ (off Wilmslow Rd, A5145)

12-11 (midnight Fri & Sat); 12-11 Sun

☎ (0161) 438 0073

Hydes Mild, Bitter, Jekyll's Gold, seasonal beers Ⓗ

This ivy-covered, back-street pub has two traditional snugs (one no-smoking) and a large conservatory. The central bar serves top quality Hydes' beers – even its Welsh mild. This Hyde's tied house is adorned with many old pictures of the brewery. There is no food or football here, just conversation in a friendly, relaxed atmosphere. Q♿⊟P⚟

Diggle

Diggle Hotel

Station Houses, OL3 5JZ (½ mile off A670) OS011081

12-3, 5-midnight; 12-midnight Sat & Sun

☎ (01457) 872741

Black Sheep Best Bitter; Jennings Cumberland Ale; Taylor Golden Best, Landlord; guest beer Ⓗ

Stone pub in a pleasant hamlet near the Standedge canal tunnel under the Pennines. Built as a merchant's house in 1789, it became an ale house and general store on the construction of the railway tunnel in 1834. Affording fine views of the Saddleworth countryside, this makes a convenient base in a popular walking area. With a bar area and two rooms, the accent is on home-cooked food (served all day Sat and Sun). Brass bands play on alternate summer Sundays. Q❀⛺◖◗♣P⚟

Dobcross

Navigation Inn

21-23 Wool Road, OL3 5NS

(on A670, next to Huddersfield Narrow Canal)

12-2.30, 5-11 (midnight Fri); 12-11 Sat; 12-10.30 Sun

☎ (01457) 872418

Moorhouses Pride of Pendle; Taylor Golden Best; Wells Bombardier; guest beers Ⓗ

This stone canalside pub was built in 1806 to serve the navvies cutting the Standedge tunnel. The open-plan bar and L-shaped interior feature a collection of old brass band photos; live concerts are staged on alternate Sunday afternoons in summer. It is the venue for annual events such as the beer walk (spring) and the Rushcart Festival (Aug). Three guest beers normally include a local micro-brewery's brew. Home-cooked meals with weekday special offer lunches are popular (no food Sun eve). Q❀◖◗P⚟

Swan Inn (Top House)

The Square, OL3 5AA

12-3, 5-11 (midnight Thu-Sat); 12-4, 7-11 Sun

☎ (01457) 873451
Jennings Dark Mild, Bitter, Cumberland Ale, Cocker Hoop, Sneck Lifter; guest beers ⊞
Built in 1765, for the Wrigley family of chewing gum fame, part of the building was later used as a police court and cells. Overlooking the attractive village square, the pub has been well renovated, with flagged floors and three rooms, plus a fine function room that caters for 80 people. It gets busy during the Whit Friday brass band contest and the August Rushcart Festival. Imaginative, home-cooked food features dishes from around the world (no food Sun eve); booking advisable. ♨Q❀◖◗⚟

Eccles

Albert Edward

142 Church Street, M30 0LS (opp. library)
⏲ 12-11; 12-10.30 Sun
☎ (0161) 707 1045
Samuel Smith OBB ⊞
Small, friendly, town-centre pub, recently renovated by the brewery. It has a small, wood-panelled bar, with a standing area to the left of the entrance, and a stone-floored snug to the right. There is also a comfortable, no-smoking room and a larger room at the back, leading to a small yard with seating for warm weather. An Eccles town heritage plaque on the side of the pub acts as a reminder of the town's weaving tradition. ♨Q❀♿⇌⊖♣⚟

Lamb Hotel ☆

33 Regent Street, M30 0BP (on A57, opp. tram terminus)
⏲ 11.30-11 (11.20 Fri & Sat); 12-10.30 Sun
☎ (0161) 787 7297
Holt Mild, Bitter ⊞
Totally rebuilt in 1906, this Holt's house retains most of its Edwardian features. Its four rooms include a vault and a billiards room that is richly adorned with French polished mahogany, etched glass, an ornate fire surround and tiling. At its heart is a splendid central bar, graced with more curved etched glass and polished wood. The exterior is equally highly decorated with red brick mouldings, a balustered parapet, lofty chimneys and a circular corner tower topped by a copper cupola.
Q⊟⇌⊖(Terminus)⊡♣P

Fallowfield

Friendship

353 Wilmslow Road, M14 6XS (on B5093)
⏲ 12-11 (midnight Fri & Sat); 12-11 Sun
☎ (0161) 224 5758
Hydes 1863, Original Bitter, Jekyll's Gold, seasonal beers; guest beers ⊞
Prominently positioned in a student area, this busy pub draws a mix of locals as well as students. The semi-circular bar dominates the spacious drinking area. An extension to the rear, opened in 2004, has provided more space for watching sport on the big screens. The guest ale is usually from another independent brewery. Good value food is served daily 12-5pm (4pm weekends). The raised patio affords a view of what is reputed to be Europe's busiest bus route.
❀◖⊡♣P⚟

Farnworth

Britannia

34 King Street, BL4 7AF (opp. bus station, off A6053)
⏲ 11-11; 12-10.30 Sun
☎ (01204) 571629
Moorhouses Premier ⊞
Busy local next to the market, with a basic, but spacious vault and a smaller lounge, both served by a central bar. The pub offers well-priced Moorhouses Premier and sometimes another beer from the brewery as well as inexpensive, home-cooked lunches every day. Mini-outdoor beer festivals on May and August bank holidays are well attended. Behind the pub is a free car park. Children are welcome until 4.30pm.
❀◖⊟⇌♣

Gathurst

Bird I'th Hand

386 Gathurst Road, WN5 0LH
(on B5206, 400 yds from Gathurst Station)
⏲ 12-11.30 (3am Fri & Sat); 12-11.30 Sun
☎ (01942) 212006
Beer range varies ⊞
Two-roomed pub, where one room is dedicated to all day dining, from light bites to full a la carte, including a vegetarian menu and a Sunday carvery. An unusual feature of the main bar is an eagle lectern, while the impressive array of pump clips displayed above the bar is evidence of the variety of beer dispensed by the three handpumps. The bar houses three TV screens and even the restaurant has a discreet TV. Children are welcome until 9pm.
❀◖◗♿⇌(Gathurst)P

Gorton

Vale Cottage

Kirk Street, M18 8UE (on foot from A57, take path by side of Gorton Butterfly Garden)
⏲ 12-3, 5 (7 Sat)-11; 12-4, 7-10.30 Sun
☎ (0161) 223 2477
Taylor Landlord; Wells Bombardier ⊞
Tucked away in Gore Brook conservation area, this feels like a country pub. On a warm day, a home-cooked lunch (served Sun-Fri) in the garden is a joy. Low, beamed ceilings indicate that parts of the building date back to the 17th century. Despite a rumoured resident ghost, it has a relaxed, friendly atmosphere with quiet background music. Quiz nights – general knowledge Tuesday, music Thursday – are popular and musicians perform monthly (last Wed) at local CAMRA's Pub of the Year 2006.
Q❀◖⊡P

Great Moor

Crown

416 Buxton Road, SK2 7TQ (on A6)
⏲ 11-11 (midnight Fri & Sat); 12-11 Sun

☎ (0161) 483 4913 🌐 crow-bar.co.uk
Robinson's Hatters, Unicorn, Double Hop, seasonal beers Ⓗ
This impressive, three-gabled house was built by former Stockport brewer, Bell & Co. Decorated with a collection of coloured drawings of old Stockport, the wooden screen with wrought iron arches above is an unusual feature. Note, too, the decorated tiles by the front and rear entrances. Sporting events are shown on the large, wall-mounted screens. With its attractive outdoor drinking area overlooking its bowling green, this is a great summer pub. ❀⇌(Woodsmoor)🚌♣P

Greenfield

King William IV
134 Chew Valley Road, OL3 7DD (on A669)
🕐 12-midnight daily
☎ (01457) 873933
Caledonian Deuchars IPA; Lees Bitter; Tetley Bitter; guest beers Ⓗ
Detached stone pub at the village centre, comprising a central bar area and two rooms. A cobbled forecourt with benches allows for outdoor drinking. It offers two changing guest beers and food is served most days until 7pm. Handy for walks over the Moors, the Nos. 180 and 183 buses from Manchester and Oldham pass by. The pub is the centre of village life, participating in the annual beer walk and Ruschart Festival (Aug) and hosting the Whit Friday brass band contest. ❀◑⇌♣P

Railway
11 Shaw Hall Bank Road, OL3 7JZ (opp. station)
🕐 12-midnight (1am Thu-Sat); 12-midnight Sun
☎ (01457) 872307
Caledonian Deuchars IPA; John Smith's Bitter; Taylor Landlord; Wells Bombardier; guest beer Ⓗ
Unspoilt pub where the central bar and games area draw a good mix of old and young. The tap room boasts a log fire and old Saddleworth photos. In a picturesque area, it provides a good base for various outdoor pursuits and affords beautiful views across Chew Valley. The venue for live Cajun, R&B, jazz and pop music on Thursday, Friday (unplugged) and Sunday, it also hosts top class entertainment every month. Westons cider is served by gravity dispense. ♨❀⇆🀫⛺⇌♣🍎P

Harpurhey

Junction Inn
1-5 Hendham Vale, Queen's Road, M9 5SF (on A6010, near A664 jct)
🕐 11-11; 12-10.30 Sun
☎ (07910) 472403
Holt Bitter, seasonal beers Ⓗ
A free house close to Queen's Park, this crescent-shaped pub, with its imposing brick exterior, is popular with the locals. A well-used juke box and regular Saturday night discos set the tone for entertainment. It comprises a vault and two further rooms, with an open fire, a no-smoking section and many original features. ♨🀫⊖(Woodlands Rd)🚌♣P⁄

Hawkshaw

Red Lion
81 Ramsbottom Road, BL8 4JS (on A676)
🕐 12-3, 6-11; 12-11 Sat; 12-10.30 Sun
☎ (01204) 856600
Jennings Bitter, Cumberland Ale; guest beers Ⓗ
Attractive stone pub, nestling in a picturesque village. Inside you will find a single, large room that is usually full of friendly locals. The excellent menu of freshly-prepared dishes means that the pub is also popular with diners who can choose to eat either in the pub or the adjacent restaurant. Meals are served all day Saturday and Sunday. Guest beers often come from Bank Top or Phoenix. ⇆◑🚌P

Heaton Norris

Navigation
11 Manchester Road, SK4 1TY (on A626)
🕐 12-11; 12-10.30 Sun
☎ (0161) 480 6626
Beartown Bearskinful, Polar Eclipse, Black Bear, Bruins Ruin, Wheat Bear; guest beers Ⓗ
Well worth the quarter mile walk up Lancashire Hill from Stockport town centre, the Navigation is Beartown's only pub in the area. This former local CAMRA Pub of the Year keeps almost the full range of Beartown beers, a regular guest, various ciders and a perry. Recently refurbished, the lounge and vault are smart but comfortable. Entertainment includes a monthly folk night, occasional quizzes and televised sport in the vault. This pub is thriving in an area where others have suffered. ❀🀫🚌🍎P

Nursery ☆
258 Green Lane, SK4 2NA
(off A6 by Dunham Jaguar garage)
🕐 11.30-3, 5.30-11; 11.30-midnight Fri & Sat; 12-11.30 Sun
☎ (0161) 432 2044
Hydes Mild, Original Bitter, Jekyll's Gold, seasonal beers Ⓗ
CAMRA's national Pub of the Year 2001, and a Guide regular, the Nursery is a classic, unspoilt 1930s pub, hidden away in a pleasant suburb. The multi-roomed interior includes a traditional vault with its own entrance and a spacious wood-panelled lounge, used by diners at lunchtime. The home-made food draws customers from miles around (set lunches only on Sun); children are welcome if dining. The pub's immaculate bowling green – an increasingly rare feature – is well used by local league teams. ❀◐🀫♣🚌P

Heywood

Wishing Well
89 York Street, OL10 4NS
(on A58 towards Rochdale)
🕐 12-11 (midnight Thu-Sat); 12-11 Sun
☎ (01706) 620923
Black Sheep Best Bitter; Moorhouses Pride of Pendle; Phoenix Bantam, White Monk; Taylor Landlord; guest beers Ⓗ
Popular free house, on the Rochdale side of

the town centre, worth visiting for the wide range of beers and clientele. Each of several comfortable drinking areas is equipped with a smoke filter unit. The efforts of the long-standing landlord are reflected in the quality of the beer and various awards received over the years; guest ales are sourced from 12 local micro-breweries. The beers can be served in the adjoining award-winning restaurant. Popular jam sessions are held on Thursday. ♣(471)P

High Lane

Royal Oak

Buxton Road, SK6 8AY

12-3, 5.30-11 (12-11 school summer hols); 12-3, 6-10.30 Sun

☎ (01663) 762380

Burtonwood Bitter; guest beer Ⓗ

Well-appointed pub, with a pleasing exterior, on a busy main road. Although open-plan, there are three distinct drinking areas – one is used for games. Live entertainment is staged most Fridays. An innovative menu is served at all sessions. The pub frequently offers two guest beers. The garden and play area are added attractions. Q P

Higher Broughton

Star

2 Back Hope Street, M7 2FR (near A56/B6187 jct)

1.30-11; 1.30-10.30 Sun

☎ (0161) 792 4184

Robinson's Hatters, Unicorn Ⓗ

Tucked away along a cobbled street in a conservation area, this low-fronted pub can be hard to find. The small vault, housing a narrow bar and TV, is the haunt of locals, and leads to a larger games room with a pool table and music, where well-attended quizzes are staged on Sunday evening. A visit to the Ladies entails a trip across the courtyard. ♣

Hindley

Edington Arms

186 Ladies Lane, WN2 2QJ (off A58, next to station)

12-11.30 (12.30am Fri & Sat); 12-11.30 Sun

☎ (01942) 256769

Holt Mild, Bitter Ⓗ

Also known as the Top Ale House, the Edington is a cosy, welcoming pub. The single bar is centrally situated in the front lounge. Behind this is the games room that leads out to the garden. Standing next to the Liverpool-Manchester line station, it is easily accessible and an ideal stop on a 'rail and ale' crawl. Music is featured most weekends. ♣P

Hare & Hounds

31 Ladies Lane, WN2 2QA

4 (5 Tue; 12 Sat)-11; 12-11 Sun

☎ (01942) 511948

Moorhouses Black Cat, Premier; guest beers Ⓗ

Small, somewhat basic pub, between the station and the town centre. Once upon a time, all urban pubs were like this, with a cosy lounge with a roaring fire on one side and a bar/vault on the other. The lounge displays pictures of bygone Hindley and the long-defunct Wigan casino. The bar has plenty of standing room and is decorated with photos and posters from the golden age of boxing. The pub boasts the best selection of beers for several miles. ♣

Holcombe

Shoulder of Mutton

BL8 4LZ

12-3, 5-11; 12-11 Sat & Sun

☎ (01706) 822001

Greene King IPA; Taylor Landlord; guest beers Ⓗ

At the heart of a picturesque village, this pub was originally known as the Lower House. Built in 1751, its frontage and a side elevation are constructed from finely cut stone, typical of the period. Famed as a cockfighting venue in the 19th century, today you are more likely to find diners enjoying the excellent, home-cooked meals (served all day at the weekend). The large main room is complemented by a no-smoking family dining area. P

Horwich

Crown

1 Chorley New Road, BL6 7QJ (at A673/B6226 jct)

11-11 (midnight Fri & Sat); 12-11.30 Sun

☎ (01204) 690926

Holt Mild, Bitter Ⓗ

Spacious pub on the edge of town, handy for the Reebok Stadium, Rivington Pike and the West Pennine moors. Mainly open plan, it comprises a well-furnished drinking area, a vault and a games room at the rear. This friendly pub serves good value food. Sunday evenings are busy, when locals take part in free and easy singalongs; Wednesday is quiz night. The pub is a well known and imposing local landmark. (Blackrod)♣P

Original Bay Horse

206 Lee Lane, BL6 7JF (on B6226, 200 yds from A673)

1-midnight; 12-12.30am Fri & Sat; 12-midnight Sun

☎ (01204) 696231

Lees Bitter; Taylor Landlord; guest beers Ⓗ

Dating back to 1777, this stone pub with small windows has been run by the same family for many years. The little bar is always busy with local drinkers; a Bank Top beer is always available as is Westons Old Rosie cider. The low ceilings add to the ambience. Live sports coverage on TV is popular. Q♣P

Hyde

Cheshire Ring

72 Manchester Road, SK14 2BJ

2 (1 Thu-Sat)-11; 1-10.30 Sun

☎ (0161) 366 1840

Beartown Kodiak Gold, Bearskinful; guest beers Ⓗ

One of the oldest pubs in Hyde. After a period in the doldrums, the place has been comprehensively overhauled by Beartown Brewery – a shining example of how such a task should be tackled. Seven handpulls offer guests from Beartown and other breweries.

Continental lagers, including Budvar and Budvar Dark, three ciders or perries (only one displayed) and a range of bottled beers provide plenty of variety. A warm welcome is assured in this friendly pub, with low volume background music.
(Central/Flowery Field) P

Queen's Hotel
23 Clarendon Place, SK14 2ND
11-11 daily
(0161) 368 2230
Holt Mild, Bitter, seasonal beers H
Imposing building at the heart of this bustling market town, Queen's is a true community pub, attracting drinkers of all ages and from all walks of life. The keenly-priced ales are sometimes supplemented by a Holt seasonal offering. Well laid out in a simple style, comprising four distinct areas/rooms, visitors are assured of finding a cosy niche. The pub may stay open later for events. The bus station – two minutes' walk – is served by regular buses from all directions (Central/Newton)

Sportsman
57 Mottram Road, SK14 2NN
11-2am; 12-2am Sun
(0161) 368 5000
Moorhouses Black Cat; Phoenix Bantam; Pictish Brewers Gold; Plassey Bitter; Taylor Landlord; Whim Hartington Bitter H
True free house, offering six regular beers and two guests, as well as a range of continental lagers. Its loyal following keeps this pub at the heart of the community, but passing visitors slot in seamlessly and are soon involved in bar chat if they wish. The pub fields a pool team, and a chess club is based here. The upper room houses a full-sized snooker table. This previous local CAMRA Pub of the Year should not be missed. (Newton) P

Leigh

Bowling Green
110 Manchester Road, WN7 2LD
11-12.30am (1am Wed & Thu); 11-2am Fri & Sat; 12-12.30am Sun
(01942) 673964
Holt Bitter; John Smith's Bitter H
Close to Butts Bridge Marina on the Bridgewater Canal (Leigh branch), this large roadside pub caters equally for the local community and visitors. The large, open-plan lounge sports numerous alcoves, affording plenty of room for the golf society and share club, as well as the weekly quizzes (Sun and Thu). The tap room can be restful, unless darts, dominoes or pool teams are practising their skills. The dining room is also used by drinkers. Children are welcome until 9pm.
Q P

Musketeer
15 Lord Street, WN7 1AB
12-midnight (1am Fri & Sat); 12-11 Sun
(01942) 701143
Boddingtons Bitter; Jennings Cumberland Ale; guest beers H

CAMRA's former regional Pub of the Year is a popular, two-roomed, town-centre local. The lounge bar is split into separate drinking areas, including a snug, with standing room in front of the bar; regular entertainment is staged here. The tap room, adorned with pictures of local and national Rugby League players, is frequented by rugby supporters on match days. Parking at the pub is limited but there are public car parks nearby. P

Waggon & Horses
68 Wigan Road, WN7 5AY (1 mile from town centre)
7 (4 Fri)-midnight; 12-1am Sat; 12-11 Sun
(01942) 673069
Hydes Light, Dark, Bitter H
Good, local community pub that attracts customers of all ages. Separating the bar from the L-shaped lounge is a large hearth. The lounge has comfortable bench seats that provide good views of the big-screen TV, used for sporting events. For a quiet pint, the bar serves a snug. The games room, which houses a pool table, is home to the darts and dominoes teams. Children are welcome until 8pm.

Littleborough

Moorcock
Halifax Road, OL15 0LD (on A58)
11.30-midnight; 11.30-11.30 Sun
(01706) 378156 themoorcockinn.com
Taylor Landlord; guest beers H
Built as a farmhouse in 1641 and first licensed in 1840, this gem, nestling in the Pennine foothills, is worth a visit for the view alone. Although boasting a fine 80-seat restaurant, the pub section is kept apart by clever use of floor space. Three guest beers, usually from local brewers, are served in agreeable surroundings. The pub is close to the Pennine Way so ramblers and equestrians stop by; tethers are provided for horses. Six rooms are available for overnight guests. P

White House
Blackstone Edge, Halifax Road, OL15 0LG
(on A58, top of hill)
12-3, 6.30-midnight; 12.30-10.30 Sun
(01706) 378456 whitehousepub.co.uk
Beer range varies H
The Pennine Way passes this 17th-century coaching house, situated 1,300 feet above sea level, a landmark that benefits from panoramic views of the surrounding moors, all the way to Cheshire and Wales. This family-run hostelry gives a warm friendly welcome in its two bars, with log fires in each. Guest beers, Westons cider, continental bottled beers and a range of wines complement the excellent menu and daily specials board. Meals are served in two spacious dining areas (all day Sun).
Q P

Lowton (Lane Head)

Travellers' Rest
443 Newton Road, WA3 1NX (on A572 between Lowton and Newton)

12-11 (midnight Fri & Sat); 12-11 Sun
(01925) 224391
Marston's Pedigree; guest beers H
This cosy, roadside inn has been serving travellers on the stretch of road between Leigh and Newton-le-Willows for many years. The pub has a restaurant, but meals are served throughout, with the restaurant specialising in Greek cuisine. The bar area is ideal for a pint and a chat, and has discrete areas for those seeking peace and quiet.
P

Lydgate

White Hart

51 Stockport Road, OL4 4JJ (at A669/A6050 jct)
12-midnight; 12-11 Sun
(01457) 872566 thewhitehart.co.uk
Lees Bitter; Taylor Golden Best, Landlord; Tetley Bitter; guest beers H
Detached, stone, free house dating from 1788, commanding impressive views over the hills above Oldham. Adjoining the village church and school, the pub has four rooms, two used for dining. The small snug has its own servery and the main bar boasts eight handpumps. A new extension, with bar, is used for gourmet meals and weddings. It makes an excellent base for visiting Saddleworth's moors and villages, with 18 en-suite rooms and food from an award-winning chef. Buses from Manchester and Oldham to Greenfield pass nearby.
Q P

Manchester City Centre

Bar Fringe

8 Swan Street, M4 5JN (50 yds from A665/A62 jct)
12-11; 12-10.30 Sun
(0161) 835 3815
Beer range varies H
Belgian-style 'brown bar', well known for its robust welcome. The long, single room has recently been refurbished. It offers up to five real ales from breweries such as Dent, Slater's and Boggart Hole Clough. Several continental beers, both on draught and bottled, are also stocked and Thatchers Cheddar Red cider, kept chilled in the fridge is a popular choice. Meals are served until 6pm (4pm Sat and Sun). The nearest bus station is at Shudehill.
(Victoria)(Shudehill)

Beer House

6 Angel Street, M4 4BR
12-11; 12-10.30 Sun
(07868) 897075
Moorhouses Black Cat, Pendle Witches Brew; Phoenix Bantam, Wobbly Bob; guest beers H
Famous free house now returning to its former glory. The single room is dominated by the bar that dispenses up to eight guest beers at the weekend from all over the UK and clearly listed on the large beer board. The house beer, Premium Blonde is brewed by Phoenix. Real cider and perry often come from Herefordshire. The upstairs pool room occasionally hosts live music; opening hours may be extended. This is an essential stop on the northern quarter drinking circuit.
(Victoria)(Shudehill)P

Britons Protection ☆

50 Great Bridgewater Street, M1 5LE
(opp. Bridgewater Hall)
11-11; 12-10.30 Sun
(0161) 236 5895
Jennings Cumberland Ale; Robinson's Unicorn; Tetley Bitter; guest beers H
Historic pub, dating from 1811 and Grade II listed, reputed to have been a recruiting post for men who died at the Battle of Waterloo. Now it is famous for its splendid multi-roomed interior, all dim lights and low ceilings, offering the privacy that modern pubs lack. It usually sells five cask ales, with guests often from Coach House, and keeps a range of malt whiskies. Lunches are served weekdays. It may close early when there is a big football match on.
(Oxford Rd)(G-Mex)

Castle Hotel

66 Oldham Street, M4 1OE (off Piccadilly Gdns)
1 (12 Sat)-11; 12-11 Sun
(0161) 236 6515 castlepub.org.uk
Robinson's Hatters, Old Stockport, Cumbria Way, Unicorn, Old Tom, seasonal beers H
Every Robinson's real ale (subject to availability) can be sampled in the Stockport regional brewer's sole pub in the city centre. It attracts a cosmopolitan crowd, with some young faces, drawing customers from near and far. It maintains links with Norway and the Czech Republic, since football's Euro '96. This characterful house, comprising a bar, lobby, parlour and back room, is a Grade II listed building on the Piccadilly bus route.
(Victoria)(Market St)

City Arms

46-48 Kennedy Street, M2 4BQ (near town hall)
11-11; 12-11 Sat; 12-8 Sun
(0161) 236 4610
Tetley Dark Mild, Bitter; guest beers H
Busy little two-roomed pub, sandwiched between the Vine Inn and the Waterhouse. In 2006 it received a local CAMRA award for 12 consecutive years in this Guide. It can be hectic at lunchtime with office workers, due to its policy of serving food within five minutes. The early evening can be again busy, giving way to a quieter period later when the 'local' mood is regained. The six changing guest beers include a 'guess the mystery ale' on Friday.
(Oxford Rd)(St Peters Sq)

Dutton Hotel

37 Park Street, Strangeways, M3 1EU (200 yds from A665/A6042 jct)
11.30-11; 12-10.30 Sun
(0161) 236 0944
Hydes Original Bitter, Jekyll's Gold or seasonal beer H
Back-street, corner pub, near the site of the former Boddingtons Brewery. Three rooms radiate from a central bar, each containing various ornaments and collectors' items, including a trademark Hydes' anvil that marks the original entrance to the pub. A

friendly clientele generates a local ambience in an establishment that is not actually in a residential area. It is, however, convenient for visitors to the nearby MEN Arena.
❀≷⊖(Victoria)🚌♣

Font Bar

7-9 New Wakefield Street, M1 5ND
⏲ 12-1am; closed Sun
☎ (0161) 236 0944 🌐 fontbar.com
Beer range varies Ⓗ
The Font is a distinctively modern drinking place built into a railway arch alongside Oxford Road Station, handy for the BBC's new Broadcasting House. Home-cooked food at bargain prices is available all day until 8pm. It stages regular live music, shows local art and holds a beer festival. The two guest beers are usually from local or Yorkshire breweries. It has excellent access, with a lift connecting the two floors.
◑♿≷(Oxford Rd)⊖(St Peters Sq)

Hare & Hounds ☆

46 Shudehill, M4 4AA (opp. transport interchange)
⏲ 11-11; 12-10.30 Sun
☎ (0161) 832 4737
Holt Bitter; Tetley Bitter Ⓗ
Classic, Grade II listed building where ornate tiling, mahogany woodwork and leaded glass feature in a three room linear layout. It boasts a community spirit, and singalongs around the piano are more redolent of a local pub than a city-centre hostelry. Situated opposite the transport interchange, it is an ideal place to start or finish a tour of the northern quarter. Wheelchair access is via the back door on Salmon Street. It occasionally stays open late.
♿≷(Victoria)⊖(Shudehill)🚌♣

Jolly Angler

47 Ducie Street, M1 2JW (behind Piccadilly Station)
⏲ 12-3, 5.30-11; 12-4, 8-10.30 Sun
☎ (0161) 236 5307
Hydes Original Bitter, seasonal beers Ⓗ
Small, basic and friendly street-corner local. The bar serves two rooms on either side of the entrance; the smaller one is warmed by a real fire. Regular evening music sessions take place and the Villeann Pipers often perform. Seasonal ales are sometimes available. The pub can get busy if Manchester City are playing at home as the new stadium is not far away.
♨≷(Piccadilly)⊖🚌♣

Knott

374 Deansgate, M3 4LY
⏲ 12-11.30 (midnight Thu; 12.30am Fri & Sat); 12-11.30 Sun
☎ (0161) 839 9229
Marble Manchester Bitter, Ginger Marble, Lagonda IPA; guest beers Ⓗ
Built into a railway arch in historic Castlefield, the Knott has established itself as a pub for good beer lovers from all walks of life. Its unusual layout, furniture and outside balcony (best tried in summer) all add to the atmosphere. As well as guests from local micros, draught and bottled beers from Belgium and Germany and a couple of ciders are stocked. It serves up a menu as varied as the selection on the juke box.
❀◑≷(Deansgate)⊖(G-Mex)●⚡

Lass O' Gowrie

36 Charles Street, M1 7DB (off Oxford Rd, A34)
⏲ 11-11 (midnight Thu-Sat); 12-10.30 Sun
☎ (0161) 273 6932 🌐 thelass.co.uk
Black Sheep Best Bitter; Greene King IPA, Abbot, Old Speckled Hen; guest beers Ⓗ
Boasting 10 handpumps to serve its clientele of BBC workers and academics from the nearby university, the Lass O' Gowrie is a great place for thirsty thinkers. At weekends, livelier crowds appear in search of a good pint or match on the large screen. 'Beer tickers' will be impressed by the range and quality of guest beers from Titanic, Bank Top and Beartown. Traditional pub food is popular, supplemented with daily specials.
◑🚌⚡

Marble Arch ☆

73 Rochdale Road, M4 4HY
(300 yds from A664/A665 jct)
⏲ 11.30-11 (midnight Thu-Sat); 12-10.30 Sun
☎ (0161) 832 5914 🌐 marblebeers.co.uk
Beer range varies Ⓗ
Free house incorporating the vegan Marble micro-brewery. The shap granite entrance opens into a narrow lounge, featuring an infamous sloping mosaic floor that leads down to the bar. This room has green tiled walls, a brown tiled barrel-vaulted ceiling with a decorative drinks frieze, and a McKenna's Brewery mirror. To the rear of the bar is a no-smoking room with a view into the brewery. An extensive menu complements five Marble beers and five micro-brewery guests (eve meals finish at 7.30pm; 5.30pm Sun).
♨❀◑≷(Victoria)⊖(Shudehill)🚌♣●⚡

Rain Bar

80 Great Bridgewater Street, M1 5JG
⏲ 11-11.30 (12.30am Fri & Sat); 12-10.30 Sun
☎ (0161) 235 6500
Lees GB Mild, Bitter, Moonraker, seasonal beers Ⓗ
Lees flagship pub, converted from an umbrella factory in 1999, two minutes' walk from Bridgewater Concert Hall. The patio overlooks the Rochdale Canal and is surrounded by trendy flats. Set over three floors, the ground floor is traditional, with much wood and a stone floor; on the first floor a no-smoking restaurant is open during the day, while the top floor has a private room for hire. Meals are served 12-9pm (8pm Sun). Thursday is quiz night. Children are not admitted. ❀◑♿≷(Oxford Rd/ Deansgate)⊖(St Peters Sq/G-Mex)🚌

Sandbar

120 Grosvenor Street, All Saints, M1 7HL
(off Oxford Rd, A34/B5117 jct)
⏲ 12-11 (midnight Thu-Sat); 6-10.30 Sun
☎ (0161) 273 3141 🌐 sandbaronline.net
Phoenix Navvy; guest beers Ⓗ
Converted from two Georgian terraced houses, Sandbar revels in its eclectic appearance and bohemian atmosphere.

Close to the university, it is popular with students, but attracts a good mix of customers. Of the two guest ales, typically one is a light and one a dark beer. It always stocks a real cider or perry that usually changes monthly, plus an impressive range of draught and bottled continental beers. Meals, served weekdays, include hearty Polish dishes.

Sinclairs Oyster Bar

2 Cathedral Gates, M3 1SW (behind cathedral)

11-11; 12-10.30 Sun

(0161) 834 0430

Samuel Smith OBB

The bar moved for the second time in its history when in 1999 it was taken down brick by brick and rebuilt 100 yards away to the exact same layout, even down to the low beams and wood panelling. The narrow bar area can get congested, but there are two small rooms behind. Upstairs is another bar with a lounge and other small rooms. Meals are served until 8pm. In 2005 Sinclairs became Manchester's first all no-smoking pub. Q (Victoria) (Shudehill)

Smithfield Hotel & Bar

37 Swan Street, M4 5JZ (100 yds SE of A664/A665 jct)

12-11; 12-10.30 Sun

(0161) 839 4424

Robinson's Hatters; guest beers

The long, narrow, single room has a central bar with a pool table dominating the entrance and an area resembling a parlour at the rear where the TV is usually on in the background. The main attraction here, though, is the eight handpumps dispensing rare finds from micro-breweries and a house beer from Phoenix. The occasional beer festivals offer more choice with cellar jugs. Note the extensive range of pump clips on the ceiling. The affordable accommodation is recommended.

(Victoria) (Shudehill)

White Lion

Liverpool Road, M3 4NQ

10.30-11; 11-10.30 Sun

(0161) 832 7373

Taylor Landlord; guest beers

Situated on a corner, this was once an old-fashioned, multi-roomed local, but is now a single bar with a central serving area. There is plenty of seating throughout and picnic benches on a paved area to the side allow for outdoor drinking. The White Lion offers a good range of beers, with up to four guests at any time. (G-Mex)

Marple

Hatters Arms

81 Church Lane, SK6 7AW

12-11; 12-10.30 Sun

(0161) 427 1529 hattersmarple.co.uk

Robinson's Hatters, Unicorn, Old Tom, seasonal beers

At the end of a row of hatters' cottages, this small stone pub is everyone's idea of a local, replete with small rooms and wooden panelling. Service bells are still nominally in use and the pub pursues an active social life. This is one of only 20 pubs that qualify to serve Robinson's Old Tom on draught.

Railway

223 Stockport Road, SK6 3EN

11.45-11; 12-10.30 Sun

(0161) 427 2146

Robinson's Hatters, Unicorn

This impressive pub opened in 1878, alongside Rose Hill Station, whose Manchester commuters still number among its customers. The pub is little changed externally and is handy for walkers and cyclists on the nearby Middlewood Way. There are two airy, open-plan, relaxing rooms and an outside drinking area. It is deservedly popular. (Rose Hill)P

Marple Bridge

Lane Ends

Glossop Road, SK6 5DD

12-2.30 (not Mon), 4-11; 12-11 Fri & Sat; 12-10.30 Sun

(0161) 427 5226

Caledonian Deuchars IPA; guest beer

It is a long uphill pull here from Marple Bridge, but the Glossop–Hazel Grove bus passes the door. This stone pub borders on some lovely countryside and benefits from delightful views from the front. It is now open plan, but its window spaces, a hint of two levels with some secluded seating, give it a fairly intimate feel. Take time to look at the old local photos. Home-cooked food is served. The garden has a children's play area. P

Mellor

Oddfellows Arms

73 Moor End Road, SK6 5PT

12-3, 5.30-11; closed Mon; 12-6 Sun

(0161) 449 7826

Adnams Bitter; Marston's Burton Bitter; Phoenix Arizona; guest beer

Extremely popular for its food, this elegant, stone pub enjoys an attractive village setting. The traditional interior has been modernised somewhat of late, but its flagged floors and open fires make it particularly seductive in winter. In summer you can sit out at tables on a sunny patio.

QP

Royal Oak

134 Longhurst Lane, SK6 5PJ

(1 mile from Marple Bridge)

5.30-midnight; 12-midnight Sat & Sun

(0161) 427 1655

Robinson's Hatters, Unicorn, Double Hop

Convivial village pub serving a choice of Robinson's beers. The excellent rear garden boasts impressive views. An integral Thai restaurant serves authentic cuisine in the evening (all day Sun). It is one of a sadly diminishing band of unchanging locals that has been doing an excellent job for many years – long may it continue.

Q

Middleton

Tandle Hill Tavern

14 Thornham Lane, Slattocks, M24 2HB (1 mile along unmetalled road off A664 or A627) OS898091
5.30-midnight; 12-midnight Sat & Sun
(01706) 345297
Lees GB Mild, Bitter H

Reached by a pleasant mile walk along a pot-holed lane, this comfortable, two-roomed, hidden gem is a haunt of the local farming community, as well as walkers from the country park in which it is situated. A roaring log fire is a great draw in winter, and dogs are always welcome. Soup and sandwiches are available on Saturday, with a full lunch served only on Sunday. The rear courtyard is a suntrap in summer.

Mossley

Britannia Inn

217 Manchester Road, OL5 9AJ
11-11; 12-11 Sun
(01457) 832799
Marston's Burton Bitter, Pedigree or Old Empire; guest beers H

The Britannia faces the Manchester to Huddersfield railway line and is only a few yards from Mossley station. This impressive grit-stone building is semi-open plan, with a bar, lounge and games areas, plus a small patio drinking area at the front. A quiet dining area was added in 2005; meals are served until 7pm (5pm Sun). The pub's range of guest beers has increased steadily over the years. Q

Church Inn

82 Stockport Road, OL5 0RF
12-midnight; 12-11 Sun
(01457) 832021
Thwaites Mild, Original, Lancaster Bomber; guest beers H

This traditional, northern, end of terrace, town pub was recently taken over by Thwaites, having previously been a free house and once part of Oldham Brewery's tied estate. A subsequent refurbishment has not altered its character significantly, and it has retained a tap room. Popular with all ages, it is home to the Mossley morris men. Note the attractive tilework in the vestibule.
P

Rising Sun

235 Stockport Road, OL5 0RQ
5-midnight; 2-midnight Sun
(01457) 834436
Archers Village; Black Sheep Best Bitter; Shaws Golden Globe; guest beers H

Mossley's only surviving truly free house is aptly named as it affords fine views over the Tame Valley to Saddleworth Moor. At the north end of town, it is just under a mile from the station. The interior is semi-open plan, with a games room (used by the local Blue Grass Boys on Tue eve). A pavement patio allows for some outdoor drinking. Local micro-breweries' beers are often stocked, as well as an interesting range of vodkas and single malts.

Tollemache Arms

415 Manchester Road, OL5 9BG
12-midnight (1am Fri & Sat); 12-midnight Sun
(01457) 834555
Robinson's Hatters, Old Stockport, Unicorn, H **Old Tom (winter)** G

The Tollmache Arms is a popular, traditional local. It lies about a mile north of the station, on the valley floor, squeezed between Manchester Road and the Huddersfield Narrow Canal. Much of the original timber and glasswork in the interior has been retained. The patio, between the road and the canal, has direct access from the towpath.
P

Nangreaves

Lord Raglan

Mount Pleasant, BL9 6SP OS810154
12-2.30, 7 (5 Fri)-11; 12-11 Sat; 12-10.30 Sun
(0161) 764 6680
Leyden Nanny Flyer, Light Brigade, Raglan Sleeve; seasonal beers H

This inn is the home of the Leyden Brewery and several of its beers always feature on the bar. The Leyden family has run this charming country local for half a century. It is decorated throughout with many items of interest, including antique glassware and pottery, old photographs and pictures. The pub is renowned for its good food; the chef is also the head brewer. P

Oldham

Ashton Arms

28-30 Clegg Street, OL1 1PL
11.30-11 (11.30 Fri & Sat); 11.30-10.30 Sun
(0161) 630 9709
Beer range varies H

A friendly welcome awaits in this mid-terrace, split-level, traditional pub. Situated in the town-centre conservation area, opposite the old town hall, this free house provides up to six real ales plus a permanent cider and various continental beers. A seat by the 200-year-old stone fireplace makes a change from the trendy outlets nearby. Local micro-breweries are showcased in the array of guest beers. Meals are served weekdays until 6pm (3pm Fri). (Mumps)

Gardener's Arms

Dunham Street (Millbottom), Lees, OL4 3NH (near Huddersfield Rd)
12-midnight; 12-11 Sun
(0161) 624 0242
Robinson's Hatters, Unicorn H

About two miles east of Oldham centre, near the Waterhead bus terminus, the pub stands on an old route to Yorkshire, by the River Medlock. Overshadowed by one of the many old mills in this area, a pub has stood on this site since around 1800; this one was rebuilt after 1926 when Robinson's acquired it. Many features remain from that time in the largely original room layout; the fireplaces, wood and tilework are typical of the period.

Royal Oak
172 Manchester Road, Werneth, OL9 7BN
(on A62 opp. Werneth Park)
✪ 2-midnight; 12-11 Sun
☎ (0161) 624 5795
Robinson's Hatters, Unicorn Ⓗ
Traditional pub, retaining separate rooms around a central bar. This popular, community local boasts wood panelling, old-fashioned cast iron radiators and an old Gledhill cash register, which is still in use. Regular bus services stop nearby, and Werneth Station is about 15 minutes' walk. Although the pub is in a restricted parking zone, a small car park is nearby. Q♿🚌♣

Openshaw

Legh Arms
741 Ashton Old Road, M11 2HD (on A635)
✪ 11-11; 12-11 Sun
☎ (0161) 223 4317
Moorhouses Black Cat, Pendle Witches Brew; guest beers Ⓗ
Local CAMRA's Pub of the Year 2005 is a true drinkers' pub, run by a licensee who is as passionate about his beer as he is about nearby Manchester City FC. The once multi-roomed layout has been opened up, yet it retains quiet drinking areas away from the pool and darts – played on an unusual log end board. Outside, an enclosed area has raised decking for casual drinking and may accommodate barbecues or a bouncy castle for children in summer. ❀⇌(Ashburys)♣●

Orrell

Robin Hood
117 Sandy Lane, WN5 7AZ
✪ 2-midnight; 12-1am Fri & Sat; 12-11 Sun
☎ (01695) 627429
Beer range varies Ⓗ
This small, sandstone pub could easily go unnoticed, tucked away as it is in a residential estate. However, its reputation for serving excellent home-cooked food (Thu-Sun, booking advisable), accompanied by three rotating guest beers (often including Old Speckled Hen or Caledonian Deuchars IPA), ensures that this is not the case. One of the two bar areas is pretty much given over to diners during meal times. Not surprisingly, the decor bears a Robin Hood theme. Q◐⇌♣P

Patricroft

Stanley Arms
295 Liverpool Road, M30 0QN
✪ 12-midnight; 12-11.30 Sun
☎ (0161) 788 8801
Holt Mild, Bitter Ⓗ
Neat, tidy and tiny (compared with other Holt's Edwardian palaces in the area), sums up this rare tenancy (one of just three now), acquired by Holt in 1909. It was built in the 1850s as the Red Lamp. The side entrance on Liza Ann Street opens into the lobby with a single table. Across the bar is the popular vault. The 'best room' is accessed from the lobby, while at the end of a corridor lined with photographs is a third room. ⊟⇌♣

Peel Green

Grapes Hotel
439 Liverpool Road, M30 7HD
(on A57, near M60 jct 11)
✪ 11-11 (midnight Fri & Sat); 12-11 Sun
☎ (0161) 789 6971
Holt Mild, Bitter Ⓗ
A red-brick building from 1903, the Grapes retains many original features: etched glass, polished mahogany, wall tiles, ornate fireplaces and mosaic floors. It still has its billiards room, but this is only used for pool now. In all there are five rooms, including a busy vault and a no-smoking parlour. Its size and attractive appearance have led to it being frequently used as setting for film and TV dramas. ⛫♘⊟🚌♣P⊬

Pendlebury

Lord Nelson
653 Bolton Road, M27 4EJ
(on A666 Bolton-Manchester road)
✪ 11-11; 12-10.30 Sun
☎ (0161) 794 3648
Holt Mild, Bitter Ⓗ
The Nelson is essentially a two-roomed 1960s pub where back-to-back bars serve a roomy vault and a massive square lounge with a stage. However, a small corner near the lounge door resembles a snug, although the bustle in the main room can still impinge. A projector TV in the vault frequently shows sporting events. Most pubs around here have lost their real ale in the last 10 years, leaving only this pub and next door (Newmarket) selling cask Holt's, and the Windmill opposite stocking Sam Smith's. ⊟⇌(Swinton)🚌♣P

Reddish

Thatched Tavern
54 Stanhope Street, SK5 7AQ (behind Houldsworth Sq off B6167)
✪ 11.30-11; 12-10.30 Sun
☎ (0161) 285 0900
Boddingtons Bitter; Tetley Dark Mild, Bitter; guest beer Ⓗ
In an area almost devoid of good pubs, it is well worth seeking out this gem of a street-corner local, hidden away behind Houldsworth Square. Once you track it down you will find a warm welcome in the comfortable lounge and traditional vault, both about to be refurbished as the Guide went to press. Look for the photo of the builders standing outside their handiwork in 1882, when Reddish was far more rural than it is today. ❀⊟🚌♣

Rochdale

Albion
600 Whitworth Road, OL12 0SW
✪ 12-2.30, 5-11 (midnight Fri); 12-midnight Sat; 12-10.30 Sun
☎ (01706) 648540

Lees Bitter; Taylor Best Bitter, Landlord; guest beers Ⓗ
A true free house with a bistro attached. The pub's growing reputation for good food makes it popular with locals and visitors alike. There is always a good range of real ales with three or more guest beers on handpump. The pub offers good value bar food as well as bistro meals, many having an African flavour; a varied selection of wine is also stocked. The walls are hung with paintings by a local artist, which are for sale.

Baum

33-37 Toad Lane, OL12 0NU
(follow signs for Co-op Museum)
11.30-11 (midnight Fri & Sat); 11.30-11 Sun
☎ (01706) 352186
Boddingtons Bitter; Taylor Golden Best; guest beers Ⓗ
Delightful pub in the conservation area, right next door to the world's first Co-op, and facing the splendid St Mary's Church. The Baum stocks two guest ales and a variety of continental bottled beers. It is a split-level house, with a no-smoking area at the rear and an upstairs function room. Outside is a huge space, boasting two boules pistes. Excellent meals, including vegetarian options, are served daily.

Flying Horse Hotel

37 Packer Street, Town Hall Square, OL16 1NJ
(by town hall)
11-11; 11-midnight Fri-Sun
☎ (01706) 646412 theflyinghorsehotel.co.uk
Lees Bitter; Taylor Best Bitter, Landlord; guest beers Ⓗ
Impressive stone building by the side of an equally impressive town hall. Built as a hotel in the early 20th century, its warm, friendly atmosphere attracts a varied clientele. Two guest beers – usually from Phoenix – are served alongside the regulars in the large, pleasantly decorated, open-plan lounge. Evening meals are available Monday-Thursday. Centrally located, close to all the town's amenities, it is convenient for bus and train travellers. P

Healey Hotel

172 Shawclough Road, OL12 6LW
(on B6377, opp. nature reserve)
3 (12 Sat)-midnight; 12-11.30 Sun
☎ (01706) 645453
Robinson's Unicorn, seasonal beers Ⓗ
End of terrace stone pub, close to Healey Dell nature reserve, frequented by the reserve's visitors as well as locals. It retains many original architectural features including the bar, tiled walls and oak doors. The multi-room layout includes a no-smoking room, which displays pictures of the locality and houses the TV. The main bar and lounge area are decorated with film star portraits. The extensive space outdoors is a bonus.
Q

Merry Monk

234 College Road, OL12 6AF (at A6060/B6222 jct)
12-11; 12-5, 7.30-10.30 Sun
☎ (01706) 646919
Hydes Mild, Original Bitter, Jekyll's Gold; guest beers Ⓗ
Small, friendly local – a proper pub – welcoming to all. This Victorian detached property, licensed since the 1850s and a free house since 1984, comprises a small bar area, a lounge adorned with photos of old Rochdale and a games room. The pub supports strong darts and quiz teams and boasts a petanque piste. The guest beer varies, but is usually from a micro-brewery, making this a haven for anyone who enjoys well-kept beer and good company.

Regal Moon

The Butts, OL16 1HB (next to central bus station)
9am-midnight (1am Fri & Sat); 9am-midnight Sun
☎ (01706) 657434
Greene King Abbot; Marston's Burton Bittter, Pedigree; Shepherd Neame Spitfire; guest beers Ⓗ
Imposing Wetherspoon's cinema conversion at the centre of Rochdale, handy for the main shopping areas. It has a raised no-smoking and family area, while the rest of the pub, which has retained the cinema's woodwork, is well laid out around the original pillars. A striking, tail-coated mannequin sits at an organ over the single, long bar that serves an excellent choice of up to 10 cask ales. Food, from breakfast through to evening meals, is available daily.
Q

Sale

Railway

35 Chapel Road, M33 7FD (200 yds behind town hall)
12-11 (midnight Thu; 12.30am Fri; 11.30 Sat); 12-midnight Sun
Robinson's Hatters, Unicorn, Double Hop, seasonal beers Ⓗ
This small Robinson's house lies just off the town centre. Its unusual white cladding can easily be spotted from the nearby canal bridge. The interior has benefited from a refit, making it more attractive to its local clientele and those visiting the new Sale Waterside Theatre complex. Wheelchair access is via the back door. The car park is small. P

Sale Moor

Legh Arms

178 Northenden Road, M33 2SR
(at A6144/B5166 jct)
11.30-11 (11.30 Thu; midnight Fri & Sat); 12-11.30 Sun
☎ (0161) 973 7491
Holt Mild, Bitter Ⓗ
Spacious, multi-roomed pub at the centre of Sale Moor village, under 15 minutes' walk from Brooklands and Sale metrolink stations. A true community pub, it stages quizzes (Mon and Wed), karaoke (Thu and Sun) and live entertainment on Saturday. It also hosts competitions in summer on the bowling green. Two large TV screens show sport, but there is a room for those who want a quiet drink. It stocks the full range of Holt's bottled

beers. Lunches are served Wednesday-Sunday. Q✿◐⊟♣P⅄

Salford

Crescent

18-21 Crescent, M5 4PF (on A6, near university)
⌚ 11-11; 12-10.30 Sun
☎ (0161) 736 5600
Bazens' Black Pig Mild; Hydes Bitter; Phoenix Thirsty Moon; Rooster's Special; guest beers Ⓗ
Popular, long-standing Guide entry, known to pre-date the 1830 Beerhouse Act. An island bar serves a mix of university staff, students and beer enthusiasts in three rambling, bare-boarded rooms. The vault hosts regular beer festivals, while the bar normally sells up to six guests from micro-breweries, together with a good choice of draught and bottled foreign beers. The food is good quality and value, particularly on Wednesday's curry night. The enclosed back garden is an added attraction.
♨✿◐◗≈(Crescent)⊟♣●P▢

King's Arms

11 Bloom Street, M3 2AN
⌚ 12-1am; 12-6 Sun
☎ (0161) 832 3605
Bazens' Pacific Bitter, Flatbac; Caledonian Deuchars IPA; guest beers Ⓗ
An impressive structure, outside and in, notable for its buttresses and gothic arches; the main bar is lofty, with a curved outer wall. Across the corridor is a smaller room. Beers change regularly, but usually include Bazens and other micro-breweries' products. The extensive lunch menu (not served Sat) represents good value. A large, domed room upstairs stages plays and live music. Phone to check if open if travelling far as it may close early or be hosting a private party.
Q✿◐≈(Central)⊟P

Stalybridge

British Protection

Hough Hill Road, SK15 2HB
⌚ 4.30-midnight; 3-2am Fri;12-2am Sat; 12-midnight Sun
☎ (0161) 338 5432
Banks's Bitter; guest beer Ⓗ
This community local lies to the south of the new canalside development and Tesco superstore, making it a convenient stop for boaters on the Huddersfield Narrow Canal. Originating as a beer house in the 1840s, it passed through Swales Brewery ownership in 1899 and, much later, Boddingtons in 1970. The bar serves several welcoming rooms, including a tap, which are frequented by all ages. The guest beers are from the W&D portfolio. ♨Q⊟≈⊟♣

Stalybridge Station Buffet Bar ☆

Platform 1, Stalybridge Station, Rassbottom Street, SK15 1RF
⌚ 11 (10am for food)-11; 12-10.30 Sun
☎ (0161) 303 0007 🌐 buffetbar.freewebspace.com
Boddingtons Bitter; Flowers IPA; guest beers Ⓗ
An international institution among beer aficionados, the Buffet Bar continues to follow a successful path, bringing an astonishing variety of beers to an appreciative public. With eight handpumps, an impressive total of over 6,000 different beers has been notched up since 1997. Four rooms, individually furnished, and a blazing fire create a haven for the enjoyment of ale, conversation and simple home cooking (10am-8pm) – do not miss the black peas. All drinkers should visit at least once in their lifetime. ♨Q◐◗≈⊟●P

Standish

Dog & Partridge

33 School Lane, WN6 0TG (off A49, towards M6)
⌚ 12-11.30 (midnight Fri & Sat); 12-11 Sun
☎ (01257) 401218
Tetley Mild, Bitter; guest beers Ⓗ
A central bar stocks four guest beers, mostly from micro-breweries and occasionally the local Mayflower Brewery, plus a real cider. One side of the pub is popular for watching TV sport, while the other side is quieter and now designated as no-smoking. Fresh flowers enhance the decor. Outside a heated patio has an awning for sunny weather. ✿●P⅄

Stockport

Arden Arms ☆

23 Millgate, SK1 2LX (behind Asda)
⌚ 12-midnight; 12-11.30 Sun
☎ (0161) 480 2185 🌐 ardenarms.com
Robinson's Hatters, Unicorn, Double Hop, Ⓗ **Old Tom (winter),** Ⓖ **seasonal beers** Ⓗ
Now a permanent Guide entry, this National Inventory and Grade II listed, multi-roomed pub was CAMRA's runner-up for national Pub of the Year 2004. Along with the chequerboard floor tiling, of particular note is the snug, accessible through the glassed-in bar. High quality lunches complement Robinson's fine ales, including Old Tom from a cask on the bar in winter. Real fires make this pub extra special. Parking is limited.
♨Q✿◐⊟P⅄

Armoury

31 Shaw Heath, SK3 8BD (on B5465, near station)
⌚ 10.30-midnight; 11-midnight Sun
☎ (0161) 477 3711
Robinson's Hatter, Unicorn, Ⓗ **Old Tom (winter)** Ⓖ
Prominent corner pub, opposite the King's and Cheshire Regiment's TA centre. This former Bells Brewery house comprises three rooms: a lounge, vault and rear lounge – the latter two being popular for darts and quiet conversation. Darts enjoys enthusiastic support here, with teams playing four evenings a week. A defunct fireplace, now covered with an impressive beaten copper screen, provides a focus in the lounge, while photos of old Edgeley add interest. The Bells glass in each door is remarkable.
Q✿⊟≈⊟♣

Blossoms

2 Buxton Road, Heaviley, SK2 6NU (at A6/A5102 jct)
⌚ 12-3, 5-11; 11.30-11 Sat; 12-10.30 Sun
☎ (0161) 477 2397

Robinson's Hatters, Unicorn, [H] Old Tom (winter) [G]
Situated at a busy road junction, this multi-roomed Victorian gem, built as a coaching house, retains its original layout of a lobby bar and three rooms. The rear 'smoke' room boasts an elegant carved fire surround and unusual stained glass window panels. Two lodges of the Antediluvian Order of Buffaloes meet here. The emphasis is on quality beers, epitomised by the cask of Old Tom on the bar in winter. The lunch menu includes excellent pies made on the premises.
Q◖⊟♿⇌(Davenport)🚌♣P

Olde Vic

1 Chatham Street, Edgeley, SK3 9ED (behind station)
⏲ 5-11; 7-11 Sat & Sun
☎ (0161) 480 2410
Beer range varies [H]
Jolly, welcoming one-roomed free house run in irrepressible style. Particularly busy when Sale Sharks play at home, no-one is a stranger for long in this well-run pub (strictly no swearing). Five handpumps dispense a changing range of guest beers, usually from micros; pick out the pump clips on the ceiling, among the bric-a-brac. Pub dog Molly can hear a crisp packet rustle from half a mile away. Note that the pub is closed at lunchtime. Westons vintage cider is sold.
♨✿⇌🚌●

Railway

1 Avenue Street, Portwood, SK1 2BZ
(opp. Peel Centre)
⏲ 12-11; 12-10.30 Sun
☎ (0161) 429 6062
Porter Floral Dance, Bitter, Porter, Sunshine, seasonal beers; guest beers [H]
This Porter Brewery flagship is a pub for the discerning drinker, with something for everyone. No less than 11 handpumps dispense the full Porter range, including seasonal and one-off brews, plus three guest beers at the weekend. Beers from new breweries installed by Dave Porter are often showcased. The guest cider varies. Bar billiards is played here. Proper, home-made lunches are served Monday-Saturday. This must-visit pub is threatened once again by a redevelopment scheme, so get there while you can. ✿◖🚌♣●

Thatched House

74 Churchgate, SK1 1YJ (off market place)
⏲ 8-11; closed Mon; 7-1am Fri; 3-2am Sat; 3-midnight Sun
☎ (0161) 355 1910 🌐 thatched-live.co.uk
Black Sheep Best Bitter; Boddingtons Bitter; guest beers [H]
The Thatched House is Stockport's premier live music venue – staging mostly hard rock, metal and punk – this is not a quiet pub. Notable architectural details are the etched windows and a mosaic in the porch. The main bar doubles as the stage; to the left is a pool room and beyond this the garden with tables, benches and a barbecue. It stocks two guest ales, two real ciders and a wide range of good quality bottled beers.
✿🚌●

Three Shires

32 Great Underbank, SK1 1NB
⏲ 11-11 (9 Mon & Tue); 12-9 Sun
☎ (0161) 477 4579
Beer range varies [H]
This Tudor building, circa 1580, was a former town house of Leghs of Adlington. Now offering three cask ales, quality food and wines in immaculate but cosy surroundings, it blends old-fashioned and modern styles, welcoming both family diners and business people. The owner is justifiably proud of the freshly-prepared food. Two handpumps normally supply Copper Dragon ales, with the third promoting a micro-brewery beer.
◖◗🚌

Tiviot

8 Tiviot Dale, SK1 1TA
⏲ 11-11; 12-4 (closed eve) Sun
☎ (0161) 480 4109
Robinson's Hatters, Unicorn, [P] Old Tom [G]
A real, old fashioned, town-centre pub where the four rooms, including a vault and dining room, are decorated with photographs of old Stockport and Tiviot Dale in particular. The good value lunches (served Tue-Sat) attract shoppers, so it is busy during the day. In the evening the pub tends to be quieter, supported by a loyal band of regulars. ◖⊟🚌P

Strines

Sportsman's Arms

105 Strines Road, SK6 7GE
⏲ 12-3, 5-11; 12-11 Sat; 12-10.30 Sun
☎ (0161) 427 2888
Boddingtons Bitter; Cains Bitter; guest beers [H]
On a direct bus route (358) from Stockport, this pub keeps an enterprising choice of guest beers in an area where variety is at a premium. Striking views down the Goyt Valley can be enjoyed through a picture window. In winter, you can gaze instead into the welcoming log fires. The food trade is an important element here, but the beer drinker is never forgotten.
♨Q✿◖◗⊟♿🚌♣P

Stubshaw Cross

Cross Keys

76 Golborne Road, WN4 8XA (on B5207, off A58)
⏲ 4 (6 Mon; 12 Fri & Sat)-midnight; 12-11.30 Sun
☎ (01942) 727965
Beer range varies [H]
Built in 1893, this is the only pub in Stubshaw Cross. An old-fashioned local, it offers a friendly welcome. It has rooms for the pool, dominoes and darts teams, while the main room around the bar is open plan. In 2003 it won Wigan CAMRA's New Cask Outlet award. Sky TV allows fans to watch football, rugby league, cricket and other sports. Most Saturdays the pub hosts karaoke. Families with children are welcome until 8pm. Snacks are available on request.
✿♿♣

Summerseat

Footballers Inn

28 Higher Summerseat, BL0 9UG OS788145
⏲ 2 (12 Sat)-11.30 (midnight Fri & Sat); 12-11 Sun
☎ (0120) 488 3363 🌐 footballersinn.co.uk
Caledonian Deuchars IPA; Hydes Original Bitter; Taylor Landlord; guest beers 🄷

In the quiet village of Summerseat, this friendly, family-run pub caters for all. One large room is divided into several drinking areas. The bar boasts six cask ales, often including one from a micro-brewery. The pub runs numerous social events, including a popular quiz evening. Enjoy the excellent views from the rear garden where you can play petanque, or even practise your golf swing on the covered driving range. Dog-friendly, this pub is a wi-fi hot spot.
❀⇌(E Lancs Steam Rlwy)♣P

Swinton

Farmers Arms

160 Manchester Road, M27 5TP (on A6, opp. Victoria Park)
⏲ 11-11; 12-10.30 Sun
☎ (0161) 281 5599
Black Sheep Best Bitter; Boddingtons Bitter; Theakston Mild, Best Bitter 🄷

Opened in the 1830s as a beer house attached to a smithy, the exterior has hardly been altered since then. Although the interior was gutted in the early 1990s, the work was done sympathetically, with low ceilings and exposed beams giving an impression of age. Known locally as the Red House, a nickname acquired in the late 19th century, the pub opens at 9.30am but beer is only sold to customers having breakfast.
❀◐◑⊟⊡♣P

White Lion

242 Manchester Road, M27 4TS (at A6/A572 jct)
⏲ 3 (12 Sat)-11; 12-10.30 Sun
☎ (0161) 288 0434
Robinson's Hatters, Unicorn, seasonal beers 🄷

This late 18th-century pub has been extended and altered internally, most recently to take in the site of a derelict adjoining cottage. It comprises a large main lounge with angled seating and some partitioning, a roomy vault and a small, new snug between the two. At the rear a spacious annexe displays memorabilia of Swinton Lions RLFC whose ground stood opposite the pub. This room is used for meetings and hosts a Monday folk club.
Q♉❀⊟⊡♣P

White Swan

186 Worsley Road, M27 5SN
(on A572, 100 yds N of A580)
⏲ 12-11; 12-10.30 Sun
☎ (0161) 794 1504
Holt Mild, Bitter 🄷

Smart, well cared for pub where a central bar serves a small vault, a larger space converted from two rooms and a comfortable, wood-panelled lounge that features stained glass windows and a collection of swans. A large function room at the back caters for families, darts matches and sports fans watching televised events. Regulars in the vault play an unusual, sometimes noisy, dice game on the bar in the evenings. ♉⊟⊡♣P

Tyldesley

Half Moon

115-117 Elliot Street, M29 8FL
⏲ 11-4, 7-midnight; 12-midnight Sat; 12-11 Sun
☎ (01942) 873206
Holt Bitter 🄷

Well-kept local, popular with all ages due to its atmosphere, friendly local landlord serving good beer and its central location in the town. The main lounge has various seating areas around the walls, only interrupted by doors and the bar, and there are some nooks in which to stand and chat over a pint. There is a further lounge and a patio for summer use that affords a panoramic view of Winter Hill. ❀♣

Mort Arms

235-237 Elliot Street, M29 8FL
⏲ 12-midnight (1am Sat); 12-11 Sun
☎ (01942) 883481
Holt Mild, Bitter 🄷

Splendid 1930s pub that has undergone just a few alterations since it was built. The main entrance provides access to the tap room and the lounge, both served by a central bar. The lounge is split in two (one of the alterations) but retains much wood panelling and etched glass; it hosts a friendly quiz on Thursday. The vibrant tap room is ideal for chatting or dominoes. ⊟⊖♣

Uppermill

Cross Keys

OL3 6LW (off Running Hill Gate)
⏲ 11-11 (midnight Fri & Sat); 12-11 Sun
☎ (01457) 874626
Lees GB Mild, Bitter, Moonraker, seasonal beers 🄷

Overlooking Saddleworth Church, this attractive, 18th-century stone building has exposed beams throughout. The bar boasts a stone-flagged floor and a Yorkshire range. The centre for many activities, including mountain rescue, a clay pigeon club and the Saddleworth Runners, it is busy during annual events, such as the folk festival (July), the road and fell race, and Rushcart Festival (both Aug). It hosts folk nights (Wed and Sun) in the barn. Good value food is served until 6.45pm. Children are welcome.
♨Q♉❀◐◑⊟♣P

Waggon Inn

34 High Street, OL3 6HR
⏲ 11.30-11 (midnight Fri & Sat); 12-10.30 Sun
☎ (01457) 872376 🌐 thewaggoninn.co.uk
Robinson's Unicorn, seasonal beers 🄷

This mid 19th-century stone pub in a picturesque village stands opposite Saddleworth Museum and the Huddersfield Narrow Canal. With a central bar, three rooms and a restaurant, it now offers high quality, en-suite B&B. It is the venue for many annual events, including the Whit

Friday brass band contest, the July folk festival, and in August the 'Yanks' weekend and Rushcart Festival. Good quality home-cooked food includes seniors and early bird specials and themed events (no eve meals Thu). Q❀⇌◐◑⊟⅄⇌(Greenfield)♣P

Urmston

Lord Nelson

49 Stretford Road, M41 9LG

✪ 11-11 (11.30 Fri & Sat); 11-11 Sun

Holt Mild, Bitter 🄷

Originally built as a courthouse in 1805, shortly after Nelson's death at Trafalgar, it was rebuilt in 1877 and licensed as a public house. Formerly an ale house, known as a rum pub for its lively and eccentric characters, it has mellowed with the passing of time. The no-smoking room is a front snug that survived an early 1990s refurbishment. Quiz night is Tuesday, while discos are hosted on Saturday. Sky Sports TV is available; children are not admitted.
❀⊟⇌♣P⚟

Wardley

Morning Star

520 Manchester Road, M27 9QW (on A6 near motorway flyover)

✪ 12-11 (midnight Fri & Sat); 12-10.30 Sun

☎ (0161) 794 4927

Holt Mild, Bitter 🄷

Popular community pub situated between Swinton and Walkden. The Edwardian building has a much altered interior, with a large back lounge, a smaller front lounge and a traditional vault that caters for the avid darts and dominoes players. Entertainment is provided on Saturday evening and quizzes are held on Wednesday. Excellent value and highly recommended lunches are served weekdays from the award-winning kitchen. A small paved area at the side allows for some outside drinking.
❀◐⊟⇌(Moorside)⊟♣P

Westhoughton

Brinsop Country Inn

584-592 Chorley Road, BL5 3NJ (on A6, 500 yds from A6027 roundabout)

✪ 12-3, 5.30-11; 12-11 Fri & Sat; 12-10.30 Sun

☎ (01942) 811113

Thwaites Bitter; guest beers 🄷

Genuine free house on the busy A6, midway between Westhoughton and Horwich. The five guest beers change frequently. The main drinking area is comfortably furnished and there is a no-smoking room to the left of the bar. The restaurant serves home-cooked food and bar meals are available at all times. Just 20 minutes' walk from the Reebok Stadium, it can be busy on match days; visiting away fans are welcome.
Q❀◐◑⊟⇌(Horwich Parkway)P⚟

Whalley Range

Hillary Step

199 Upper Chorlton Road, M16 0BH

✪ 4 (12 Sat)-11.30 (12.30am Fri & Sat); 12-11 Sun

☎ (0161) 881 1978

Thwaites Thoroughbred; guest beers 🄷

Recently converted from a newsagent's shop, this lively, modern bar is completely no-smoking. The central bar divides the pub into two distinct areas. Low volume music is sometimes played, otherwise it is a mainly conversational pub. Three guest beers are usually from local micro-breweries, such as Phoenix. Olives and other nibbles keep hunger pangs at bay. It sells a good choice of wines by the glass and some interesting bottled ciders, for example, Thatchers' single varietals, and coffee is available. ❀⚟

Whitefield

Eagle & Child

Higher Lane, M45 7EY

✪ 12-11 (11.30 Fri & Sat); 12-10.30 Sun

☎ (0161) 766 3024

Holt Mild, Bitter 🄷

Large, black and white pub set back from the road. It has an L-shaped main bar and a cosy back room. The well-kept bowling green at the rear is popular in summer. The building dates from 1936, replacing the original hostelry built in 1802, which was the first pub to open on Higher Lane – the other five are long gone. Once a Whitefield Brewery pub, it has been a Holt's house since 1907. ❀◐⊟⊖(Besses o' th' Barn)P

Wigan

Anvil

Dorning Street, WN1 1ND (by bus station)

✪ 11-11; 12-10.30 Sun

☎ (01942) 239444

Hydes Bitter; Phoenix Arizona; guest beers 🄷

A great atmosphere is enhanced by the provision of several draught Belgian beers at local CAMRA's Pub of the Year 2005. It attracts a mixed clientele and gets busy on football and rugby match days – the large room on the right caters for sports enthusiasts. Plans are in hand for its own brewery (next to the parish church). You are assured of a warm reception here.
❀◐⊟⇌(North Western/Wallgate)

Berkley

27 Wallgate, WN1 1LD

✪ 12-11 (midnight Fri & Sat); 12-10.30 Sun

☎ (01942) 242041

Theakston Mild, Old Peculier; guest beers 🄷

Open-plan bar, once a coaching house, it won an award from local CAMRA as best new cask outlet in 2006. Clever design means that the comfortable, split seating areas give the impression of distinct sections and the wide-screen TVs can be avoided by drinkers who prefer not to watch sport; one area is no-smoking. Children are welcome from noon until 3pm, and food is served daily until 8pm. A first-floor function room is available for hire.
◐◑⇌(Wallgate/North Western)⚟

Bowling Green Hotel

106 Wigan Lane, WN1 2LF

⏲ 3 (12 Fri & Sat)-11 (1am Sat); 12-11 Sun
☎ (01942) 519871
Caledonian Deuchars IPA, 80/-; Greene King Old Speckled Hen; Tetley Dark Mild, Bitter; guest beers Ⓗ
The guest ales change frequently at this popular pub, comprising a lively vault and two well-appointed lounges, one no-smoking. The large garden at the rear of the pub gets busy in summer, especially for barbecues. Daily newspapers are provided. Dominoes, darts and pool are played here. It hosts live music at the weekend, with an open mike session on Sunday evening.
⛬❀◐◑⊟♿⇌♣⊬

Brocket Arms

Mesnes Road, Swinley, WN1 2DD
⏲ 9am-midnight; 8am-1am Fri & Sat; 9am-midnight Sun
☎ (01942) 403500
Greene King Abbot; Marston's Pedigree Ⓗ
This former small hotel has been restored to its original use and now offers function rooms and overnight accommodation. The 1950s exterior opens into a light, airy, open-plan room that has been skilfully divided to provide distinct sections. Customers have a choice of intimate booths with fixed benches or more flexible seating to accommodate groups of all sizes. A large, no-smoking area and a patio for use in good weather are added attractions.
❀⛾◐◑♿P⊬

Moon under Water

5-7A Market Place, WN1 1PE
⏲ 9am-midnight (1am Fri & Sat); 9am-midnight Sun
☎ (01942) 323437
Courage Directors; Greene King Abbot; Marston's Pedigree; guest beers Ⓗ
The former Halifax Building Society office was converted into Wigan's first (and largest) Wetherspoon's pub. The no-smoking area on the first floor is also accessible from the Weind (Wigan's historic shopping street). It gets extremely busy at lunchtime and weekends. Food is available all day until 11pm. Selected sports programmes are shown on a large screen.
Q◐◑♿⇌(North Western/Wallgate)⊬

Old Pear Tree

44 Frog Lane, WN1 1HG (400 yds from town centre and bus station)
⏲ 12-midnight daily
☎ (01942) 243677
Burtonwood Bitter; Marston's Pedigree; guest beers Ⓗ
Welcoming hostelry, reputed to be the oldest purpose-built pub in Wigan. A two-minute walk from the town centre, its low ceilings and heavy beams create an impression of a local country inn. An authentic vault houses a dartboard and dominoes tables, while sports events are shown on large screens. Warmed by coal fires, the pub has some quiet alcoves and displays old football and rugby photographs. Up to four guest beers are supplied by W&D. Sunday meals finish at 5pm.
⛬Q❀◐◑⊟⇌(Wallgate/North Western)⊞♣

Orwell

Wallgate, WN3 4EU
⏲ 12-11 (9 Mon-Wed if quiet); 12-9 Sun
☎ (01942) 323034 🌐 wiganpier.co.uk
Beer range varies Ⓗ
Spacious, comfortable pub based in a converted wharfside building at the heart of the Wigan Pier tourist attraction. It has four handpumps for real ale, but only one or two are in use during the week. The two floors above are used for weddings and other events. The Sunday afternoon carvery offers good value. The Orwell is the closest pub in this Guide to the JJB Stadium, while the home of Wigan Athletic FC is a 10-minute walk up the canal bank.
❀◐♿⇌(North Western/Wallgate)

Royal Oak

111-115 Standishgate, WN1 1XL
(on A49, N of centre)
⏲ 4-midnight; 12-1am Fri & Sat; 12-midnight Sun
☎ (01942) 323137 🌐 royaloakwigan.co.uk
Mayflower Myles Best Bitter; Tetley Bitter; guest beers Ⓗ
Multi-roomed pub, served by a long bar stocking foreign draught and bottled beers and draught cider. The Royal Oak is the tap for the on-site Mayflower Brewery and stocks the full range of its beers. It hosts live music, beer and food festivals. The attractive, well-kept garden is available for summer barbecues.
❀♿⇌(North Western/Wallgate)♣●⊬▯

Withington

Victoria

438 Wilmslow Road, M20 3BW (on B5093)
⏲ 11.30-11; 12-10.30 Sun
☎ (0161) 434 2600
Hydes Mild, Original Bitter, Jekyll's Gold, seasonal beers Ⓗ
Traditional pub that keeps traditional opening hours, the Victoria is popular with students and locals, welcoming anyone over 18. In 2005 it celebrated 100 years as a Hydes' house, then went on to win the brewery's Cellar of the Year award out of 85 pubs. This spacious, open-plan building includes a snug that houses a billiard table. It can get lively when football matches are enjoyed on the big screen. The patio allows for outdoor drinking in summer. ❀⊞♣

Woodford

Davenport Arms (Thief's Neck)

550 Chester Road, SK7 1PS (on A5102)
⏲ 11-3.30, 5.15-11; 11-11 Sat; 12-3, 7-10.30 Sun
☎ (0161) 439 2435
Robinson's Hatters, Unicorn, Old Tom (winter), seasonal beers Ⓗ
A real pub, surrounded by 'identikit' dining venues, it has been run by the same family for over 70 years. Resembling an old red-brick farmhouse, it features impressive floral displays in spring and summer. The cosy rooms are warmed by real fires, with smokers confined to the tap room, in line with CAMRA's policy on this issue. The

excellent food is mostly home made, with some adventurous specials. The large, attractive garden is set well away from the road. ⛰Q⛵❀◐⊟♣P⚡

Worsley

Barton Arms

2 Stablefold, M28 2ED
(on B5211, ¼ mile from M60 jct 13)
⏲ 12-11; 12-10.30 Sun
☎ (0161) 727 9321
Black Sheep Best Bitter; Caledonian Deuchars IPA; Fuller's London Pride Ⓗ
This half-timbered, multi-gabled structure belies its age – it was built in the 1990s. It comprises seven quite distinct sections, with pillars, partitions and half walls breaking up the interior. Placing an emphasis on food from the Ember Inns menu, it gets busy at lunchtime, even midweek. The cask ales are chosen by customers voting from a list of 14 from national or regional breweries – all 'safe' beers. Accompanied children over 14 are admitted for meals (served all day until 8pm). Q❀◐◑♿P⚡

Bridgewater

23 Barton Road, M28 2PD (on B5211)
⏲ 11-11; 12-10.30 Sun
☎ (0161) 794 0589
Bank Top Flat Cap; Greene King IPA; Phoenix Arizona; guest beers Ⓗ
Standing opposite one of Britain's oldest canals and the Duke of Bridgewater's boat house, this former Boddingtons' house is enjoying a new lease of life after years in the doldrums. Now staging beer festivals twice yearly, it always has eight or more beers on handpump. Several distinct drinking areas surround the main central bar, with its tiled floor. The large garden is popular at weekends. Food is served all day until 9pm. Quizzes and weekend discos are regular events. ❀◐◑♿⊟♣●P⚡

Worthington

Crown Hotel

Platt Lane, WN1 2XF (between A49 and A5106)
⏲ 12-11; 12-10.30 Sun
☎ (0800) 686678 🌐 thecrownatworthington.co.uk
Beer range varies Ⓗ
Enjoying a new lease of life, the Crown Hotel now offers five cask beers. The landlord sources guest ales from micro-breweries around the country, and it is a rare outlet for Mayflower beers. High quality, home-made food is served in the bar and no-smoking conservatory restaurant. A large, decked sun terrace at the rear has patio heaters. The upstairs function room hosted the Crown's first beer festival in 2006. This local CAMRA Pub of the Year winner 2006 has 10 en-suite bedrooms. ⛵❀🛏◐◑P⚡

White Crow

Chorley Road, WN1 2XL (on A5106 between Standish and Coppull)
⏲ 12-3, 5.30-11; 12-11 Fri-Sun
☎ (01257) 474344
Boddingtons Bitter; guest beers Ⓗ
Commodious pub, refurbished in olde-worlde style, with a games area and large TV screen tucked away at one end and a no-smoking dining area and children's room at the other. It serves an extensive menu and has earned a deserved reputation for its good food. Close to Worthington Lakes, the pub benefits from a large car park and children's play area, next to the stables at the rear. It usually stocks three guest beers. There is a wheelchair WC. ⛰⛵❀◐◑♿♣P⚡

Spores for thought

Yeast is a fungus, a single cell plant that can convert a sugary liquid into equal proportions of alcohol and carbon dioxide. There are two basic types of yeast used in brewing, one for ale and one for lager. (The yeasts used to make the Belgian beers known as gueuze and lambic are wild spores in the atmosphere.) It is often said that ale is produced by 'top fermentation' and lager by 'bottom fermentation'. While it is true that during ale fermentation a thick blanket of yeast head and protein is created on top of the liquid while only a thin slick appears on top of fermenting lager, the descriptions are seriously misleading. Yeast works at all levels of the sugar-rich liquid in order to turn malt sugars into alcohol. If yeast worked only at the top or bottom of the liquid, a substantial proportion of sugar would not be fermented. Ale is fermented at a high temperature, lager at a much lower one. The furious speed of ale fermentation creates the yeast head and with it the rich, fruity aromas and flavours that are typical of the style. It is more accurate to describe the ale method as 'warm fermentation' and the lager one as 'cold fermentation'.

MERSEYSIDE

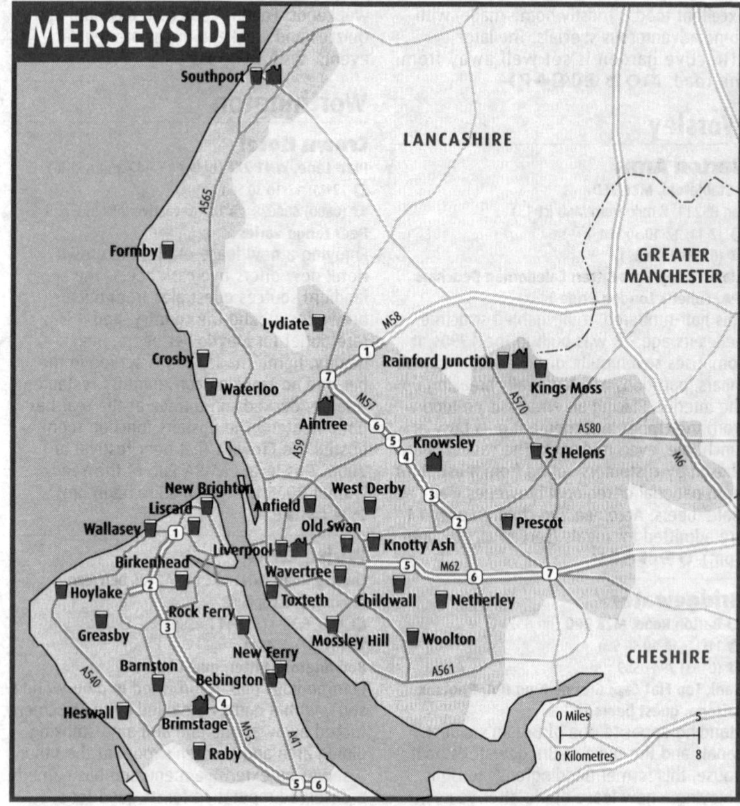

Barnston

Fox & Hounds

107 Barnston Road, CH61 1BW

⏲ 11-11; 12-10.30 Sun

☎ (0151) 645 7685

Marston's Pedigree; Theakston Best Bitter, Old Peculier; Webster's Yorkshire Bitter; guest beers 🄷

Large roadside pub in picturesque Barnston Dale. A lounge, converted from tea rooms, complements the original snug and traditional tiled bar. Local photographs adorn the walls and each room has a real fire in winter. The sheltered stone courtyard is a welcoming stop-off on the local CAMRA summer pubs walk. ⛰Q🚸❀◐⊟♿♣P

Bebington

Rose & Crown

57 The Village, CH63 7PL

⏲ 12-11; 12-10.30 Sun

☎ (0151) 643 1312

Thwaites Original, Lancaster Bomber 🄷

Former coaching inn built in 1732, now a thriving suburban pub with a bar and games room. Satellite TV is prominent. Nearby is Port Sunlight Village, founded by William Hesketh Lever in 1888 to house his soap factory workers. In the Village is the Lady Lever Art Gallery, home to one of the most beautiful collections of art in the country. ⊟⇌(Port Sunlight)♣P

Traveller's Rest

169 Mount Road, CH63 8PJ

⏲ 12-11 (11.30 Wed & Thu; midnight Fri & Sat); 12-11 Sun

☎ (0151) 608 2988

Caledonian Deuchars IPA; Flowers IPA; Greene King Abbot; Taylor Landlord; Wells Bombardier; guest beers 🄷

Former coaching inn, reputed to be over 300 years old. This popular hostelry has a country pub feel, decorated throughout with brasses and bric-a-brac. Beers are available from a central bar serving two other rooms (one no-smoking), and regularly include brews from local micros. A regular winner of local CAMRA awards, the pub is a big fundraiser for local charities. It is busy with fans visiting nearby Tranmere Rovers' ground, Prenton Park. Award-winning food is served at lunchtime (not Sun).
Q◐♿⚟

INDEPENDENT BREWERIES

Brimstage Brimstage
Cains Liverpool
Cambrinus Knowsley
Canavans Aintree
Higson's Liverpool
Southport Southport
Wapping Liverpool
George Wright Rainford

Birkenhead

Brass Balance

39-47 Argyle Street, CH41 6AB
9am-midnight (1am Fri & Sat); 9am-midnight Sun
(0151) 650 8950
Cains Bitter, 2008; Marston's Bitter, Pedigree; guest beers Ⓗ
Busy town centre pub handy for Birkenhead bus station, three railway stations and the Mersey ferry to Liverpool. Excellent food at reasonable prices is served all day until 9pm. Family friendly and no smoking, it is a popular meeting place for shoppers, office workers and locals. Micro-brewery beers feature regularly, and there is at least one beer festival a year. Q❀◑◗♿⇌(Hamilton Sq/Conway Pk/Central)🚌♣⚟

Stork Hotel ☆

41-43 Price Street, CH41 6JN
11.30-11; 12-10.30 Sun
(0151) 647 7506
Beer range varies Ⓗ
Built in 1840, this highly ornate pub has a wonderful mosaic floor, etched glass and carved wood. It retains its original wall fittings plus an ornate circular bar with leaded stained glass. The main bar serves two further rooms including the no-smoking 'news room', still with its original bell pushes. Winner of many local CAMRA awards, the pub is listed in CAMRA's National Inventory of historic interiors and is Grade II listed. ❀◑⇌(Hamilton Sq/Conway Pk)

Crosby

Crosby

75 Liverpool Road, L23 5SE
12-11; 12-10.30 Sun
(0151) 924 2574
Beer range varies Ⓗ
Large pub on the main road close to Crosby village. Recently comfortably refurbished, it has an open plan main bar with window alcoves and a pool table area. There is a small, attractive garden. The pub can be very busy at times, especially when sports events are shown on several large screens. At other times it is reasonably quiet although there are occasional live bands and discos. ❀

Crow's Nest

63 Victoria Road, L23 7XY
11.30-11; 12-10.30 Sun
(0151) 924 6953
Cains Bitter; guest beers Ⓗ
This popular community local, housed in a Grade II listed building, has a cosy bar with a tiny snug and comfortable lounge. The interior features a tiled floor and original etched windows. Friendly staff ensure a warm welcome; see the blackboard for forthcoming ales. Outside tables are available for summer drinking at this suburban gem. Q❀⊟⇌(Blundellsands/Crosby)P

Stamps Wine Bar

4 Crown Buildings, L23 5SR
10.30-11; 12-10.30 Sun
(0151) 286 2662 stampsbistro.co.uk
Beer range varies Ⓗ
This bistro/bar was once the local post office. The upper floor is a pleasant, peaceful place to spend time chatting and reading. The lower floor with bare bricks and floorboards provides a comfortable and inviting ambience. Food is served until 9pm. The pub is well known for its live music sessions and attracts a varied clientele. ◑◗♿⇌(Blundellsands/Crosby)

Formby

Freshfield Hotel

1a Massams Lane, Freshfield, L37 7BD
12-11 (midnight Fri & Sat); 12-11 Sun
(01704) 874871
Caledonian Deuchars IPA; Greene King IPA, Ruddles County, Abbot; guest beers Ⓗ
Flagship pub in the area south of Southport with an impressive array of beers always on offer, many from smaller brewers. Unpretentious in design, the pub is a perfect place for a drink after a visit to the nearby Red Squirrel reserve where the National Trust supports the endangered animal almost as effectively as the Freshfield supports endangered ales. ♨❀◑⇌(Freshfield)🚌♣P

Greasby

Irby Mill

Mill Lane, CH49 3NT
12-11 (midnight Fri & Sat); 12-11 Sun
(0151) 604 0194
Cains Bitter; Caledonian Deuchars IPA; Greene King Ruddles Best Bitter; Jennings Cumberland Ale; Taylor Landlord; guest beers Ⓗ
Traditional rural pub built in 1980 on an ancient mill site. Two rooms are linked by a narrow bar. An ale drinkers' haven with 13 handpumps, it has won many CAMRA awards. A favourite haunt of locals and country walkers from nearby Royden Park and Wirral Country Park, it is also close to West Kirby and Hoylake beaches. Always friendly and busy, it serves excellent, good value food until 8pm every day, specialising in rump steaks. ♨Q❀♿P⚟

Heswall

Dee View

Dee View Road, CH60 0DH
12-11 (midnight Fri & Sat); 12-11 Sun
(0151) 342 2320
Cains Bitter; Caledonian Deuchars IPA; Taylor Landlord; Tetley Bitter; guest beer Ⓗ
Homely local with a single bar, offering a warm welcome and six handpulled beers, many from micro-brewers. It sits on a hairpin bend opposite the war memorial and famous mirror. Monday is curry night and Tuesday offers a popular and entertaining pub quiz. Evening meals are available Sunday-Thursday. ❀◑◗♣P

Johnny Pye

Pye Road, CH60 0DB (next to bus station)
11-11 (11.30 Thu; midnight Fri & Sat); 12-11 Sun
(0151) 342 8215
Banks's Bitter; Marston's Burton Bitter Ⓗ
Situated on the site of the old bus depot,

this lively, modern pub is named after a local entrepreneur. Johnny Pye is also associated with other buildings nearby, and he was responsible for starting the local bus service. An autographed cartoon of footballer Gordon Banks adorns the bar; the pub has a wide-screen TV, a strong football following and a darts team. Well-priced food is on offer with authentic curries on Thursday night (no meals Sun eve). ❀◐◑♿🚌♣P⅟

Hoylake

Ship Inn

Market Street, CH47 3BB

11.30-11; 12-11 Sun

☎ (0151) 632 4319

Caledonian Deuchars IPA; Fuller's London Pride; Flowers IPA; Jennings Bitter; Wadworth 6X; Wells Bombardier; guest beers Ⓗ

Popular town centre pub, first licensed in 1754 (recent testing has dated the building to 1730). Although modernised in recent years into one L-shaped bar area, old beams have been retained in the back lounge. Twelve real ales are on offer, with good value bar meals served every lunchtime and in the evening (not Sun). The large, secluded garden at the rear has a pond. On Monday night a jazz band plays. ❀◐◑⇌(Manor Rd)P

Kings Moss

Collier's Arms

57 Pimbo Road, WA11 8RD (off B5205 to Rainford, follow Houghwood Golf Club signs)

12-11; 12-10.30 Sun

☎ (01744) 892894

Beer range varies Ⓗ

Nestling in a hamlet between Billinge and Rainford, this cosy pub is part of a row of traditional miners' cottages. The interior has stone floors and mining memorabilia. An extensive food menu is offered and the pub can get busy with diners. Families are welcome and high chairs are available (no eve meal Sun). ♨Q❀◐◑⊟●⅟

Liscard

Clairville

48 Wallasey Road, CH45 8PB

9am-midnight (1am Fri & Sat); 9am-midnight Sun

☎ (0151) 346 8960

Cains Bitter; Marston's Pedigree; guest beers Ⓗ

This Wetherspoon pub was originally a supermarket. A large, airy, modern establishment, it has a no smoking/family area. Meals are served all day. Popular with shoppers and workers during the day, it is a short walk from the main shopping area and town centre bus stops. In the evening it attracts a clientele of all ages. Regular beers come from local micro-breweries including Garton and George Wright and there is an interesting range of guests. Westons real cider is available. ◐◑♿⇌🚌●⅟

Liverpool: Anfield

Strawberry Tavern

Breckfield Road South, L6 5DR

11.30-11; 12-10.30 Sun

☎ (0151) 260 6158

Oakwell Old Tom Mild, Barnsley Bitter Ⓗ

An Oakwell house, the Strawberry continues to serve both its beers. The interior is divided to give a separate games area with pool table and dartboard. Lying between Breck Road and West Derby Road, the pub is a welcome oasis for thirsty fans visiting Liverpool Football Club. If you visit during the afternoon, you may notice that many customers are laden with Asda carrier bags – the pub is evidently an essential stop off after a visit to the supermarket! ❀⊟♿♣P

Liverpool: Childwall

Childwall Abbey

Childwall Abbey Road, L16 5EY

11-11 (11.30 Mon; midnight Fri & Sat); 11.30-11 Sun

☎ (0151) 722 5293

Beer range varies Ⓗ

Fine 17th-century listed building with panoramic views of the valley and village church. Despite its name it was never an abbey and resembles a castle. Now one of Wolverhampton & Dudley's Pathfinder pubs, it offers up to three changing real ales. The three drinking areas have been refurbished and part of the lounge is no smoking. The back bar has a plasma screen showing Sky Sports. Outside is a grassed children's play area and bowling green. Food, including daily specials, is served until 8.15pm (7.45pm Sun). Q❀⇄◐◑♿P⅟

Liverpool: City Centre

Augustus John

Peach Street, L3 5TX (on University campus)

11-11; 2-11 Sat; 4-7 Sun

☎ (0151) 794 5507

Beer range varies Ⓗ

Named after the painter, the pub was officially opened in 1969 by his son Caspar. Formerly a Tetley's pub, it is now owned by Liverpool University and usually offers two house bitters (Tetley's and Hydes) and three rotating guest beers from regional and micros around the country, plus a guest scrumpy. Beer festivals are held annually, coinciding with the Liverpool beer festival. Popular with university students and staff, there is a pool table, piped music via an IT games box and big screen TV for live sports events. ❀♿⇌(Lime St)⊖(Central)

Baltic Fleet

33 Wapping, L1 8DQ

12 (11 Sat)-11; 12-10.30 Sun

☎ (0151) 709 3116

Wapping Bitter, Summer Ale, Stout; guest beers Ⓗ

Located near the Albert Dock, the building is Grade II listed and based on the 'flat iron' principle. The interior has a nautical theme and mysterious tunnels in the cellar have led to much speculation among the customers of a dark period in history involving smuggling and press gangs. The beer range comes from the pub's own Wapping Brewery, supplemented by two guest ales. Food is served downstairs, with Sunday roasts making a comeback. ♨Q◐⊖(James St)●⅟

Blackburne Arms
24 Catharine Street, L8 7NL
10-midnight (1am Fri & Sat); 11-midnight Sun
(0151) 707 1249
Black Sheep Best Bitter; Caledonian Deuchars IPA; Taylor Landlord; guest beers H
Although at the end of a Georgian terrace this building is deceptive as the exterior only dates from the 1930s. The interior, which was gutted in the 1960s or 70s, was sensitively restored in early 2006 to give it a more traditional feel and turn some of the rooms into accommodation. Located at the edge of the city centre near the University and Philharmonic Hall, this is very much a local pub. (Central)

Carnarvon Castle
5 Tarleton Street, L1 1DZ
10-11 (8 Mon-Wed); 12-6 Sun
(0151) 709 3153
Cains Bitter; Courage Directors; Marston's Pedigree; Theakston Mild, Best Bitter H
Dating from the latter part of the 19th century, Carnarvon's ceramic frontage dominates a row of uninteresting modern shop fronts. The traditional interior includes a wood-panelled back room. The pub is decorated with memorabilia and photographs. The homely atmosphere is popular with shoppers and locals alike. Toasted sandwiches are available to order. A full English breakfast is served from 10am and Sunday roasts from noon. (Lime St)(Central)

Cracke
13 Rice Street, L1 9BB (near Philharmonic Hall)
12-11 (midnight Fri & Sat); 12-10.30 Sun
(0151) 709 4171
Cains Bitter; Phoenix Old Oak Ale, Wobbly Bob; guest beers H
A mid Victorian back street boozer that has not been so much altered as extended. It gets its name because it was originally so small, consisting of what is now the tiny public bar. What used to be the back room is called The War Office because it was the place where people who wanted to bore about the Boer War were despatched. However the pub has been extended all around it so this is now in the middle. (Lime St)(Central)

Crown Hotel ☆
43 Lime Street, L1 1JQ
11-11; 12-10.30 Sun
(0151) 707 6027
Fuller's London Pride; guest beers H
This architectural gem is just a few seconds' walk from Lime Street Station. The Grade II listed building boasts an Art Nouveau-style interior; the two downstairs rooms retain the original decoration. A function room is available upstairs. A small range of beers is served from a large bar. Reasonably-priced food is served until the early evening. The friendly staff welcome a wide variety of patrons. (Lime St)(Central)

Dispensary
87 Renshaw Street, L1 2SP
12.30-11; 12-midnight Fri & Sat; 12.30-10.30 Sun
(0151) 709 2160
Cains Mild, IPA, Bitter, FA; guest beers H
Former Tetley's pub originally called the Grapes (the old name is displayed above the bar). It was bought by Cains and converted into a replica of a one-room Victorian street-corner local. The brewery was rewarded with the CAMRA/English Heritage Refurbishment award. It sells two constantly-changing guest beers. The pub is popular with both regulars and shoppers. (Lime St)(Central)

Doctor Duncan's
St John's House, St John's Lane, L1 1HF (on Queen's Square)
11.30-11; 12-10.30 Sun
(0151) 709 5100
Cains Mild, IPA, Bitter, FA, seasonal beers; guest beers H
Cains' flagship managed house, usually serving the full range of its beers plus four guests on handpump. A small bar leads to back lounges and the Grade II-listed tiled room, which was the original entrance to the Pearl Assurance building, designed by Alfred Waterhouse in 1896-8. Dr Duncan implemented a public health policy to combat cholera epidemics in Liverpool around 1850. This friendly pub can get busy, particularly on Friday and Saturday evenings with people enjoying a night out. (Lime St)

Everyman Bistro
5-9 Hope Street, L1 9BH (beneath the Everyman Theatre)
12 (11 Sat)-midnight (2am Thu-Sat); closed Sun
(0151) 708 9545 everyman.co.uk
Beer range varies H
A pub, restaurant and theatre bar in one. Although under separate management from the theatre, they enjoy a close relationship. Do any other pubs ring a bell at the end of the interval? It comprises three rooms: the first has a bar, the second serves food and the third is used as an overflow or as a function room. No attempt is made to separate diners and drinkers but you may bump into Macbeth at the bar late on a Friday night. Q(Lime St)(Central)

Fly in the Loaf
13 Hardman Street, L1 9AS
12-11 (midnight Fri & Sat); 12-10.30 Sun
(0151) 708 0817
Okells Bitter, Maclir, Dr Okells IPA, seasonal beers; guest beers H
The second Manx Cat Inn to be opened on the mainland by the IOM brewer Okells. The previous Kirklands bakery, whose slogan was 'no flies in the loaf', has been tastefully refurbished to a Steve Holt design with ecclesiastic fittings. There are usually up to seven guest beers from micro-breweries and a good selection of foreign bottled beers. The Fly attracts a wide cross section of customers from students to theatregoers. The home-cooked meals are excellent, especially the Sunday roasts. (Lime St)(Central)

Globe
17 Cases Street, L1 1HW (opp. Central Station)

⊙ 11-11; 12-10.30 Sun
☎ (0151) 707 0067
Cains Mild, Bitter; guest beers Ⓗ
Small, two-roomed Victorian pub in the city centre, close to Central Station and Clayton Square shopping area. Offering a good selection of real ales, this friendly little pub is popular with regulars and thirsty shoppers, and can get very busy. However, it is well worth a visit; watch out for the sloped floor between the two rooms. A plaque commemorating the inaugural meeting of the Merseyside branch of CAMRA hangs in the small, quiet back room.
⇌(Lime St)⊖(Central)

Lion Tavern ☆
67 Moorfields, L2 2BP
⊙ 11-11; 12-10.30 Sun
☎ (0151) 236 1734
Caledonian Deuchars IPA; Highgate Dark; Lees Bitter; Young's Bitter; guest beers Ⓗ
The Lion Tavern is named after the locomotive that originally worked the Liverpool to Manchester railway. A Grade II listed building, the interior of the pub has undergone numerous changes. The original building was very much smaller. In 1915 the adjoining licensed premises was acquired, the two buildings amalgamated and the existing corridor layout established. The Lion attracts a mixed clientele throughout the day including local office staff and journalists. Bar food is available, with speciality cheeses and hand-made pork pies recommended.
⇌(Lime St)⊖(Moorfields)

Peter Kavanagh's ☆
2-6 Egerton Street, L8 7FY (off Catherine St)
⊙ 12-midnight (1am Fri & Sat); 12-midnight Sun
☎ (0151) 709 3443
Cains Bitter; Greene King Abbot; guest beers Ⓗ
The original terraced structure of this wonderful back street pub, with stained glass windows and wooden shutters, is more than 150 years old. Over the years the pub has expanded into two adjoining houses, resulting in lots of small, interestingly shaped rooms. Two snugs boast period wall paintings by Eric Robertson, and wooden benches with carved arms, said to be caricatures of Peter Kavanagh. The staff are happy to tell visitors about the pub's history, and point out its many features. Q

Poste House
23 Cumberland Street, L1 6BU
⊙ 11-11; 12-10.30 Sun
☎ (0151) 236 4130
Cains Mild, Bitter; guest beer Ⓗ
Compact, busy pub dating back to 1820, tucked away just off Dale Street. It has two cosy rooms and a warm, welcoming environment. It was saved from demolition by a campaign led by regular customers, local newspapers and CAMRA members. This hospitable little pub will now be integrated into the development scheme that was meant to replace it. Charles Dickens is one of a number of famous people who are said to have visited this characterful pub over the years. ⇌(Lime St)⊖(Moorfields)

Roscoe Head
24 Roscoe Street, L1 2SX
⊙ 11.30 (12 Sat)-midnight; 12-11 Sun
☎ (0151) 709 4365
Jennings Bitter; guest beers Ⓗ
Quiet pub, run by the same family for over 20 years, which has appeared in every edition of the Guide. The pub has recently been refurbished but has retained the original layout with four small rooms. Weekday meals are served. Sky Sports is now shown. Q⇌(Lime St)⊖(Central)

Ship & Mitre
133 Dale Street, L2 2HJ (by Birkenhead tunnel entrance)
⊙ 12-11; 12-10.30 Sun
☎ (0151) 236 0859 shipandmitre.com
Beer range varies Ⓗ
This pub was probably once full of Art Deco splendour but, like so many pubs, the interior was ripped out to turn it into a ship (hence the present name). While the architecture may not be what it was the beer range is impressive with up to 12 beers plus two ciders or perries as well as around 100 different imported bottles. The pub also holds quarterly beer festivals when up to 70 beers are available.
⇌(Lime St)⊖(Moorfields)♣

Swan Inn
86 Wood Street, L1 4DQ
⊙ 12-11 (2am Thu-Sat); 12-10.30 Sun
☎ (0151) 709 5281
Hydes Bitter; Phoenix Best Bitter, Wobbly Bob; Theakston Old Peculier; guest beers Ⓗ
Next door to the FACT Arts Centre just off Bold Street, there are plans for refurbishment for this pub. Currently it is a smoky den with dark spaces and a popular loud rock juke box. The smoke will go but the character of the place is likely to change little. Set on three floors, only the ground floor has real ale. Four guest beers are normally available. Traditionally a bikers' pub, it now attracts a wider range of customers. ♿⇌(Lime St)⊖(Central)

Thomas Frost
177-187 Walton Road, Kirkdale, L4 4AJ (opp. Aldi on A59)
⊙ 9am-11.30 daily
☎ (0151) 207 8210
Beer range varies Ⓗ
This branch of Wetherspoon's occupies the ground floor of a former drapery store. Thomas Frost had a single shop on the site in 1885 and later expanded to occupy the whole block. The layout is open plan, broken only by a few supporting pillars, providing a light and airy feel to this pleasant venue. It usually offers a wider range of real ales than most Wetherspoon outlets. ♿

Thomas Rigby's
23-25 Dale Street, L2 2EZ
⊙ 11.30-11; 11.30-10.30 Sun
☎ (0151) 236 3269

Okells Bitter, seasonal beers; guest beers Ⓗ
Thomas Rigby (1815-1856) was a wholesale wine and spirit dealer. The Grade II listed buildings that bear his name once comprised offices and a pub called the George. Today, you will find an extensive world beer selection and up to four changing guest beers from a range of breweries here. Award-winning hot and cold food, including daily specials, is served until 7pm. There is one no-smoking room with a friendly and efficient table service.
❀◖◗ ⊟ ≈(Lime St)⊖(Moorfields)⚟

Welkin

7 Whitechapel, L1 6DS
10-midnight (1am Fri & Sat); 12-midnight Sun
☎ (0151) 243 1080
Beer range varies Ⓗ
A Wetherspoon house, the Welkin is situated in the busy city centre shopping area, close to the Cavern Quarter. It offers a changing choice of beers, including seasonal options, and holds a series of beer festivals throughout the year. Good value food is available all day; look out for the ever-popular curry nights, steak nights and Sunday roasts. The pub opens early for breakfast, with tea or coffee.
◖◗ ♿ ≈(Lime St)⊖(Central)⚟

White Star

2-4 Rainford Gardens, L2 6PT
11.30-11; 12-10.30 Sun
☎ (0151) 231 6861 🌐 thewhitestar.co.uk
Beer range varies Ⓗ
Rare traditional pub located among the more glitzy establishments of the Mathew Street area. The White Star abounds with local memorabilia and pictures of White Star liners. Twinned with bars in the Czech Republic and Norway, it has a strong sporting theme, and regularly broadcasts football matches on a big screen. House beers are from Lancashire's Bowland range.
◖⊟≈(Lime St)⊖(Central/Moorfields)

Liverpool: Knotty Ash

Wheatsheaf

186 East Prescot Road, L14 5NG
11-midnight (1am Fri & Sat); 11-midnight Sun
☎ (0151) 228 5080
Cains Bitter Ⓗ
Multi-roomed pub that has retained the etched windows of the nearby Joseph Jones Brewery some 80 years after its demise. It is probably the only pub in Liverpool still offering a table service in the lounge and snug. The bar shows televised sports.
Q⊟🚌(8, 9, 10, 61)P

Liverpool: Mossley Hill

Storrsdale

43-47 Storrsdale Road, L18 7JY
3-11; 2-11.30 Fri; 12-11.30 Sat; 12-11 Sun
☎ (0151) 724 3464
Taylor Landlord Ⓗ
Sizeable two-roomed local with a comfortable wood-panelled lounge and stone-floored bar with a dartboard and juke box. No music is played in the lounge. Leaded windows and attractive exterior tiling reflect the 1930s construction. Popular with a mix of locals, students and thirsty sporty types from the nearby playing fields, all are drawn by the friendly, relaxed atmosphere. Sky football is shown. A small yard to the side has tables and benches for outdoor drinking in summer. Q❀⊟≈♣

Liverpool: Netherley

Falcon

Caldway Drive, L27 0YB
12-midnight (1am Fri & Sat); 12-11 Sun
☎ (0151) 498 9994
Oakwell Barnsley Bitter Ⓗ
Spacious pub on the edge of the Netherley estate. This Oakwell tied house is a rare suburban outlet for real ale. It hosts karaoke on Saturday evening and bingo on Tuesday and Friday afternoons. A patio allows for outdoor drinking. ❀⊟♿🚌(165, 169, 883)♣P

Liverpool: Old Swan

Albany

40-42 Albany Road, L13 3BJ
12-midnight; 12-10.30 Sun
☎ (0151) 220 3871
Cains Bitter; Theakston Mild; guest beer Ⓗ
This pub has been converted from two houses. There are two bar areas and a no-smoking snug. Increasing demand for real ale has led to the addition of a weekly guest beer. All major sporting events are shown on TVs. 🚌(60)♣⚟

Liverpool: Toxteth

Brewery Tap

35 Grafton Street, L8 5XJ (adjoins Cains Brewery)
11-11; 12-10.30 Sun
☎ (0151) 709 2129
Cains Mild, IPA, Bitter, FA, seasonal beers Ⓗ
Cains' tap, set within the walls of the brewery, usually has the full range of its beers on handpump. Formerly the Grapes (the name is still in the terracotta façade), it hosts brewery tours. An interesting collection of breweriana, especially beer labels from former Merseyside breweries, is on display. ❀◖🚌(4)●P

Liverpool: Wavertree

Willowbank

329 Smithdown Road, L15 3JA
12-11 (11.30 Wed & Thu; midnight Fri & Sat); 12-11 Sun
☎ (0151) 733 5782
Greene King IPA; Marston's Pedigree; Shepherd Neame Spitfire; guest beers Ⓗ
Now part of the Spirit Group, this Victorian pub is a classic ale house. Several guest beers are available, often from smaller breweries. The pub is popular with locals as well as numerous students who live locally. All football matches and other sports are shown on the TVs situated around the pub, including one outside on the patio. Weekend meals are served 12-6pm. Beer festivals are held in March, June, October and December. Quiz night is Wednesday. Children are welcome until 6pm. ❀◖◗⊟♿●P

Liverpool: West Derby

Halton Castle

96 Mill Lane, L12 7JD

12-11 (midnight Thu-Sat); 12-11 Sun

☎ (0151) 270 2013

Cains Bitter; Marston's Pedigree Ⓗ

Traditional Victorian pub divided into several rooms including a public bar. An outside area provides a pleasant place for drinking in good weather. A rare outlet for real ale in the suburbs, the pub is supplied with bitter from the local Cains Brewery. ❀⊞ (12, 13)P

Royal Standard

1 Deysbrook Lane, L12 9EY

12-11 daily

☎ (0151) 220 9675

Cains Bitter Ⓗ

A pleasant suburban pub. The single L-shaped bar is made up of alcoves with old photographs of the local area on the walls. Part of the bar serves as a small restaurant while food is being served (12-8.30pm Mon-Sat). Children are welcome until 9pm. ❀ (61)

Liverpool: Woolton

Gardeners Arms

101 Vale Road, L26 7RW

4 (2 Fri)-11; 12-midnight Sat; 12-11 Sun

☎ (0151) 428 1443

Cains Bitter; Caledonian Deuchars IPA; Tetley Mild; John Smith's Bitter; guest beer Ⓗ

Small, back-street local hidden behind flats but easily accessible from the city centre by bus (alight at Allerton Golf course, walk through the flats). A warm and friendly community pub, the atmosphere is relaxed and visitors are made welcome. It caters for local sports and is home to a number of teams including golf and women's netball. Note the Titanic History of Events displayed on the back wall. Sky TV is available and a quiz is held on Tuesday evening. Almost half the pub is no-smoking. Q (176, 177)⊬

White Horse

2 Acrefield Road, L25 5JL

12-11 (midnight Sat & Sun)

☎ (0151) 428 1862

Cains Bitter; guest beers Ⓗ

This cosy local dates from the time when Woolton was a separate village, and has been run for many years by the same landlord. The smoke-free environment is appreciated by customers. Three drinking areas and a central bar with wood panelling and brasswork create a warm, relaxing atmosphere. Good value food is available including a daily special. Is this the only pub in the country to offer a home delivery service for Sunday lunches? Customers can watch Sky TV. Two guest beers are available, usually from regional brewers. ❀◑⊬

Lydiate

Scotch Piper ☆

Southport Road, L31 4HD

12-3, 5.30-11 (1am Fri); 12-1am Sat; 12-midnight Sun

☎ (0151) 526 0503

fortunecity.com/millenium/ellerburn/53/

Banks's Bitter; guest beer Ⓗ

Picturesque Grade II listed pub on the Southport road (A5147) just outside Lydiate. Each of the three rooms has its own real fire, but most regulars try to squeeze into the tiny front bar! With a warm welcome for all, the Piper is popular with locals and visitors alike; bikers congregate on Wednesday. The pub features in CAMRA's National Inventory of pubs with historic interiors.
⌂Q❀ (300)♣P

New Brighton

Clarence Hotel

89 Albion Street, CH45 9JQ (behind Hotel Victoria)

11.30-11; 12-10.30 Sun

☎ (0151) 639 3860

Cains Bitter; Caledonian Deuchars IPA; guest beers Ⓗ

Friendly suburban pub with a bar, lounge and dining/function room. Handpumps situated in the lounge, not the bar, dispense a varied range of up to three guest beers. No meals are served on Monday, Tuesday or Thursday evening. Winner of many local CAMRA awards including Wirral Pub of the Year 2005, it holds an excellent annual beer festival every July. It is a five minute walk from New Brighton Station. ❀◑♿⊖

Magazine Hotel

7 Magazine Brow, CH45 1HP

11-11 (11.30 Fri); 11.30-11.30 Sat; 12-10.30 Sun

Draught Bass; Black Sheep Best Bitter; Fuller's London Pride; guest beers Ⓗ

Dating from 1759, this pub is full of character with a central bar area and three adjoining rooms. Situated above the riverfront promenade, it affords extensive views over the River Mersey. Two rooms are no-smoking. The guest beer is usually from a regional or national brewery. Good value home-cooked bar food is served every lunchtime and early evening on Thursday and Friday only. The garden is superb.
⌂Q❀◑♣P⊬

New Ferry

Freddie's Club

36 Stanley Road, CH62 5AS

5 (12 Sat)-11; 12-11 Sun

☎ (0151) 645 3023

Beer range varies Ⓗ

Small, cosy club in the back streets of New Ferry, Freddie's is a welcome oasis in an area considered to be a beer desert. Entry is either by showing a CAMRA membership card or current Good Beer Guide. A comfortable lounge bar serves two changing guest beers. It was voted Wirral CAMRA Club of the Year 2004 for its consistently good beer quality. An attached snooker room houses two full-sized tables. Q♿P

Prescot

Clock Face

54 Derby Street, L34 3LL (off jct 2 M57)

✪ 11-11; 12-10.30 Sun
☎ (0151) 292 4121
Thwaites Original, Lancaster Bomber 🄷
Located on the hillside approach to Prescot, this elegant former mansion house on the Lord Derby estate was converted in the 1980s, yet retains much of its former splendour, with sympathetic decor and furnishings. The central bar serves several areas. The pub is reputedly home to three ghosts. ❀⇌◖P

Raby

Wheatsheaf Inn

Raby Mere Road, CH63 4JH (from M53 jct 4 take B5151)
✪ 11.30-11; 12-10.30 Sun
☎ (0151) 336 3416
Greene King Old Speckled Hen; Tetley Bitter; Theakston Best Bitter, Old Peculier; Thwaites Original; Wells Bombardier; guest beer 🄷
Thatched pub of great character rebuilt after a fire in 1611. Wirral's oldest pub, known locally as the Thatch, it originally dates from the 13th century. It is reputed to be home to a ghost called Charlotte, who died at the pub. The main bar with nine handpumps serves two further rooms and a no-smoking dining room (eve meals Tue-Sat). The walls are decorated with photos of old Raby. The pub's antiquity is betrayed by the low beamed ceiling and doorways – mind your head!
♛Q♉❀◖◗♿P

Rainford Junction

Junction

News Lane, WA11 7JU (from A570 follow Rainford Jct Station signs)
✪ 12-11; 12-10.30 Sun
☎ (01744) 882876 🌐 thejunctionrainford.co.uk
Weetwood Old Dog Bitter; guest beers 🄷
Friendly community local opposite Rainford Junction Station. Guest beers come from Weetwood and local brewers including George Wright. A central bar serves the lounge and games room, with darts, dominoes and pool. Home to several local clubs and a popular live music venue, it hosts a bluegrass night on Wednesday and folk nights Thursday and Sunday. Quiz night is Monday. Outside is a children's play area.
❀⇌◖◗⊟⇌♣P

Rock Ferry

Lord Napier

28 St Paul's Road, CH42 3UZ
✪ 12-11.30 (midnight Fri & Sat); 12-10.30 Sun
☎ (0151) 643 9341
Beer range varies 🄷
Traditional street corner local with two rooms – a basic bar and comfortable lounge. A Guide regular in the 1980s, the return of the licensee from that period has sparked a return to form. The pub is a brisk 20 minutes' walk from Tranmere Rovers football ground. The beer range varies though it often features ales from Archers or Copper Dragon. ⊟⇌♣

St Helens

Abbey Hotel

1 Hard Lane, Denton's Green, WA10 6TL (off A570, 1 mile N of town centre)
✪ 12-11; 12-10.30 Sun
☎ (01744) 25649
Holt Mild, Bitter, seasonal beers 🄷
A former coaching inn, just off the A570 to the north of the town heading towards Rainford, this Holt's pub has been tastefully refurbished retaining many original features. The central bar area serves five rooms (one no-smoking), each with its own character. Traditional pub games, including dominoes and pool, are played in the games room. There is a large screen showing most popular sporting broadcasts. Quiz night is Thursday. Private parties can be catered for.
Q❀◖◗♣P⚟

Beecham's Bar

Water Street, WA10 1PZ (under Beecham's clock tower)
✪ 12-11; closed Sun
☎ (01744) 623420
Beer range varies 🄷
This comfortable and modern bar, situated in a listed building next to the College, is a haven for real ale lovers. It features at least four guest beers and offers CAMRA members a 10% discount on production of a valid card on pints only. Students also receive 10% discount. There is a refurbished and extended no-smoking area with sofas and low tables. Sports events are screened.
◖♿⇌(Central)⚟🍸

Glass House

5 Market Street, WA10 1NE
✪ 9am-midnight (1am Fri-Sat); 9am-midnight Sun
☎ (01744) 762310
Greene King Abbot; Marston's Pedigree; guest beers 🄷
This former discount store just off the main shopping street is a Wetherspoon conversion. The town has a historical association with glass making, hence the name. There is disabled access from the Chalon Way entrance, with a chair lift from the patio area to the main bar. Children are welcome in the lower area if dining. A large screen TV shows big sporting events. The pub can be busy at weekends and opens early for breakfast. ❀◖◗♿⇌(Central)⚟

Griffin Inn

Church Lane, Eccleston, WA10 5AD (from A570 St Helens take B5201 to Prescot)
✪ 12-11; 12-10.30 Sun
☎ (01744) 27907 🌐 griffininn.co.uk
Cains Bitter; Marston's Pedigree; guest beers 🄷
Situated on the outskirts of St Helens at Eccleston, the current building dates back to 1812, with an impressive sandstone frontage. A rotating guest beer complements the regular ales. The central bar serves all areas, including a lounge with a large-screen TV. Bar meals are available, and the restaurant serves a full menu. A decked patio area to the rear overlooks the children's play area. Quiz night is

Wednesday. There is a late bar when Saints play at the nearby rugby ground.
❀⇄◐P⊁

Sutton Oak
73 Bold Road, WA9 4JG (on B5204)
✪ 4-11; 12-midnight Fri & Sat; 12-11 Sun
☎ (01744) 813442 ⊕ suttonoak.co.uk
Beer range varies 🄷
Newly refurbished family-friendly pub close to the station, serving at least three guest beers, usually from independent breweries, plus a real cider. A large-screen TV shows sports events in the bar. Patio doors lead to an extensive garden with children's play area where barbecues are hosted in summer and a marquee is erected for a beer festival over the August bank holiday. Other seasonal beer festivals are held plus an Easter cider festival. The pub runs an angling club.
❀⊟♿⇌(Junction)♣●P▯

Turks Head
49-51 Morley Street, WA10 2DQ
✪ 2 (12 Sat)-11; 12-11 Sun
☎ (01744) 751289
Beer range varies 🄷
A distinctively designed building with its own turret, this imposing pub divides into three areas. Well-stocked bookcases and a huge collection of spirit miniatures (empty) and medicine bottles adorn the walls. The Turk's Head motif is visible throughout, on the etched glass and bar front of the central split-level serving area, which is home to 12 handpulls, offering a changing range of up to 10 real ales. There are five fonts for continental beer and a large collection of bottled beers is available. A large screen shows popular sporting events and there is a pool table and dartboard. There are regular in-pub beer festivals, music evenings, quiz nights and a curry night on Thursday. ♨◐●

Southport

Ainsdale Conservative Club
630 Liverpool Road, Ainsdale, PR8 3BH
✪ 5 (12 Sat)-midnight; 12-11 Sun
☎ (01704) 578091
Beer range varies 🄷
Due to a dedicated bar manager, this local community pub offers at least one interesting guest beer from anywhere in the UK, as can be seen by the display of pump clips. Settle into one of the comfortable seats in the large, L-shaped room or just chat with the locals at the bar. Two TV screens show sports and other major events and live entertainment is occasionally staged. Show this Guide or your current CAMRA membership card for entry.Q❀⇌♣⊁

Barons Bar (Scarisbrick Hotel)
239 Lord Street, PR8 1NZ
✪ 11-11 (11.30 Fri-Sat); 12-11 Sun
☎ (01704) 543000
⊕ scarisbrickhotel.com/baronsbarbeerfestival.co.uk
Moorhouses Pride of Pendle; Tetley Bitter; guest beers 🄷
The Baron's Bar is a comfortable lounge bar in one of Southport's leading hotels. The decor is baronial but the atmosphere is neither figuratively nor literally stuffy. The Bar has established itself as a flagship for real ales in the area and has hosted several Independent Brewer competitions. It runs an annual beer festival with its own website which starts at 6am on May 1st. The beer range is adventurous and a real cider is often available too. Q♉❀♿⇌⊟●

Berkeley Arms
19 Queens Road, PR9 9HN
✪ 4 (12 Fri & Sat)-11; 12-10.30 Sun
☎ (01704) 500811 ⊕ berkeley-arms.com
Adnams Bitter; Banks's Bitter; Hawkshead Bitter; Marston's Pedigree; Moorhouses Black Cat; Taylor Landlord 🄷
This pub is a regular in the Guide despite several changes of name. It is the only pub for miles around to serve Hawkshead Bitter but all its beers are in excellent condition and reasonably priced. Although it is a small hotel it functions fully as a pub and is much larger than it appears from the road. The pizzas are a speciality.
Q♉❀⇄◗⇌⊟♣P⊁

Bold Arms
59-61 Botanic Road, Churchtown, PR9 7NE
(2 miles N of town, near Botanic Gardens)
✪ 11.30-11; 12-10.30 Sun
☎ (01704) 228192
Tetley Dark Mild, Bitter; guest beers 🄷
The oldest inn in town, formerly a coaching house dating from the 17th century, this attractive pub is in the centre of Churchtown – the oldest and quaintest part of Southport. It always has interesting guest ales on offer, usually coming from smaller brewers. In winter there are real fires in several rooms and in summer the garden is delightful.
♨♉❀◐⊟♿⊟(49, 49A)♣P⊁

Cheshire Lines
81 King Street, PR8 1LQ
✪ 11.30-midnight (1am Thu-Sat); 12-midnight Sun
☎ (01704) 532178
Tetley Dark Mild, Bitter 🄷
One of Southport's oldest pubs, the Cheshire Lines is named after the old railway line that used to serve Southport to the south, though it predates the line by a century. Situated in a road dominated by small hotels and bed and breakfast establishments, it is very much a local, offering comfortable drinking space (the snug has newspapers for the solitary drinker), good wholesome food at reasonable prices and two well-kept beers. There are tables outside at the front.
♨❀◐⊟♣

Guest House
16 Union Street, PR9 0QE (side street off Lord St)
✪ 11-11; 12-10.30 Sun
☎ (01704) 537660
Beer range varies 🄷
One of the most attractive pubs in Southport, with flower baskets overhanging the entrance, the Guest House has interesting

interior decorative features – glass tiling over the bar, a tiled entrance hall and much wood panelling. A good range of beers usually includes something from the local Cains Brewery as well as ales from small breweries further afield. At the back there is a delightful small garden for the summer. A regular winner of local CAMRA awards. Q❀⇌🚌

London
14 Windsor Road, PR9 0SR
12-midnight (1am Fri & Sat); 12-11 Sun
☎ (01704) 542885
Oakwell Old Tom Mild, Barnsley Bitter Ⓗ
Traditional community pub a mile inland from the centre of Southport with a full range of pub games on offer – darts, dominoes, pool and even a bowling green. Trophies line the walls, showing that the pub's clientele is rather good at these games. No doubt the excellent Barnsley Bitter and Old Tom Mild help – this is the only pub in the area to offer these beers. Despite all the activity here, the pub is spacious enough to ensure that it never gets too crowded. ❀⇌🚌(43, 44, 300)♣P

Masons Arms
44 Anchor Street, PR9 0UT (off London St)
11-1am daily
☎ (01704) 534123
Robinson's Unicorn, seasonal beers Ⓗ
In an area dominated by ale-free bars, the Masons Arms is a welcome oasis. A small, traditional back-street pub one minute from Southport Station, the Masons is the only place in town regularly offering the local Robinson's beers. In winter a real fire greets you in the small snug on your left as you enter where you will find newspapers left out for the solitary drinker. ❀⇌🚌

Sir Henry Segrave
93-97 Lord Street, PR8 1RH
9am-midnight daily
☎ (01704) 530217
Greene King Abbot; Marston's Burton Bitter, Pedigree; guest beers Ⓗ
A Wetherspoon's pub, the Sir Henry Segrave has all the chain's customary virtues – a wide range of cask ales at reasonable prices, good food at equally good prices and plenty of space to eat and drink in. The building itself was once a Victorian department store and is of some interest architecturally on the outside. This was one of the first pubs in England to adopt a no-smoking policy throughout. Q❀ ♿🚌

Windmill
12-16 Seabank Road, PR9 0EL
11.30-11 (midnight Thu-Sat); 12-10.30 Sun
☎ (01704) 547319
Moorhouses Black Cat; Theakston Best Bitter; guest beer Ⓗ
Traditional pub with many small corners, old prints on the wall and old-fashioned furnishings. Run by the same licensees for 15 years, it remains unspoilt and comfortable, but also offers live music, quizzes and karaoke. The food is excellent value and the beer is consistently well kept. There is a particularly pleasant garden at the front for summer drinking. ❀ 🚌♣

Wallasey

Cheshire Cheese
2 Wallasey Village, CH44 2DH
12-11 (midnight Fri & Sat); 12-11 Sun
☎ (0151) 630 3641
Tetley Bitter; Theakston Mild; guest beers Ⓗ
Wallasey's oldest licensed premises, William of Orange stayed here back in 1690. He would no doubt approve of the quality of ales and service today. The present landlord has transformed this previously run down local in a short space of time and been rewarded with local CAMRA's Publican of Year award 2005. Quiz nights, regular themed evenings and beer festivals show the pub's commitment. The public bar features a growing collection of sporting memorabilia and there is a lounge and snug. Q❀ ⇌♣

Farmers Arms
225 Wallasey Village, CH45 3LG
11.30-11; 12-10.30 Sun
☎ (0151) 638 2110
Cains Bitter; Tetley Bitter; Theakston Mild, Best Bitter Ⓗ
This friendly, popular pub has enjoyed 15 consecutive entries in the Guide under the same licensee, who has been here for more than 20 years. Multi-roomed, it has a front bar, side snug and rear lounge. The pub runs its own golf society, popular with all ages. Quiz night is Tuesday. Good quality bar meals are served on weekday lunchtimes. Wirral CAMRA Pub of the Year, 2004, it is a short walk from Wallasey Village and Grove Road stations. Q❀ ⇌(Grove Rd)

Waterloo

Volunteer Canteen ☆
45 East Street, L22 8QR
12-11; 12-10.30 Sun
☎ (0151) 928 4676
Cains Bitter; guest beer Ⓗ
This cosy, traditional local has a central bar serving both the public bar and the lounge where photographs of old Liverpool, Crosby and Waterloo decorate the walls. The 'Volly' provides table service, these days a rarity, and runs its own golf society and darts team. It has a relaxed atmosphere without the intrusion of a juke box – just friendly banter and the daily newspapers. Q⇌

Well coude he know a draught of London ale – **Geoffrey Chaucer**

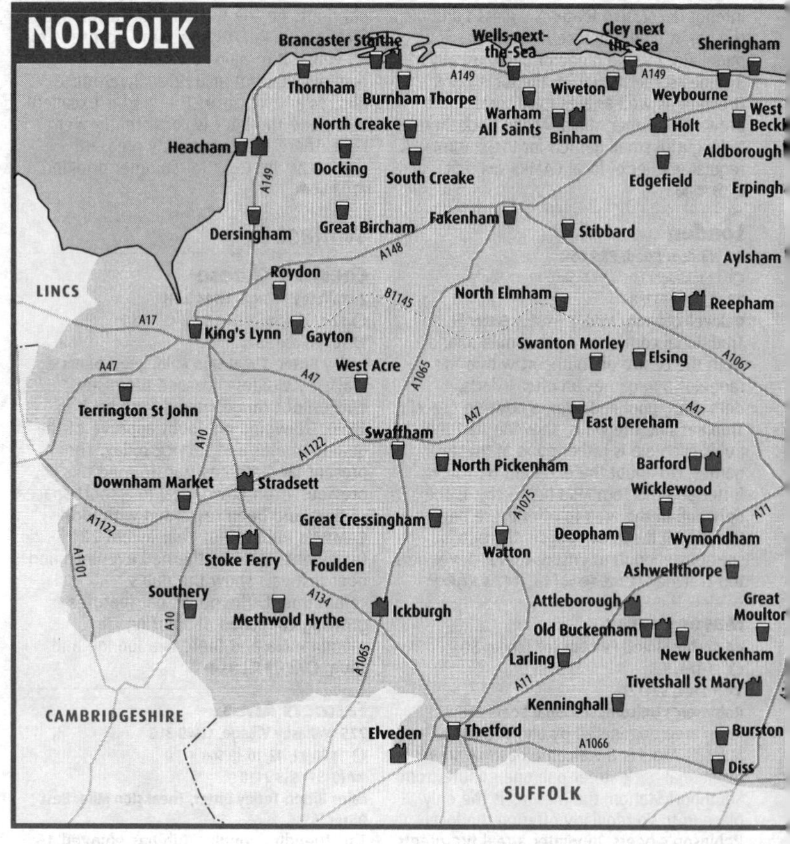

Aldborough

Old Red Lion

The Green, NR11 7AA
⌚ 12-11; 12-10.30 Sun5
☎ (01263) 761451
Adnams Bitter; Winter's Golden; Ⓗ guest beers Ⓖ
This classic, old north Norfolk local is situated on the edge of one of the county's largest village greens, and offers great views of the cricket matches that take place in summer. The pub consists of one main bar with exposed beams and an adjoining room used mostly by diners. The beers often come from Winter's Brewery; meals and cider are available in summer. Aldborough is close to the coast. ⛼❀⊭◐◑♣🍏P⊁

Ashwellthorpe

White Horse

51-55 The Street, NR16 1AA
⌚ 12-3.30 (not Mon-Fri), 5.30-11.30 (midnight Thu-Sat); 12-3.30 Sun
☎ (01508) 489721
Fuller's London Pride; guest beers Ⓗ
Pleasant, village-centre pub that has retained its original beams and an inglenook that houses a wood-burning stove. It has a large garden at the rear and hosts regular charity events. The pub is reputedly haunted by a ghost called Maude who enters through a bricked-up doorway. Guest beers come from regionals and micros. The White Horse no longer serves food. ⛼Q❀⊟♿♣P

Aylsham

Feathers

54 Cawston Road, NR11 6EB (on B1145, W of market place)
⌚ 12-11; 12-10.30 Sun
☎ (01263) 732314
Wells Bombardier; Young's Bitter; guest beers Ⓗ
The Feathers is a brick and flint Victorian building on the outskirts of the historic market town of Aylsham. This friendly local has a very cosy feel in its two bars. The pub is festooned with a wide variety of memorabilia including old boxing photos, china jugs, beer mats, old farm implements and brewery posters. Q❀♣

Barford

Cock Inn

Watton Road , NR9 4AS
⌚ 12-3, 6-11; 12-3, 7-11 Sun
☎ (01603) 757646
Blue Moon Easy Life, Sea of Tranquillity, seasonal beers Ⓗ
The Blue Moon Brewery stands at the rear of this 18th-century, former coaching inn. Games are played in one bar, which has timber flooring and a woodburner. A second, smaller bar leads to the excellent restaurant

where diners can enjoy good quality food in a cosy environment. The garden has a croquet lawn. Q P

Binham

Chequers Inn

45 Front Street, NR21 0AL OS007438

11.30-2.30, 6-11; 12-2.30, 7-11 Sun

(01328) 830297 binhamchequers.co.uk

Front Street Binham Cheer, Callums Ale, Unity Strong; guest beer H

At the heart of a charming north Norfolk village, near the medieval priory (English Heritage), the pub consists of one long bar with a real fire at each end; one end is no-smoking. Now home to its own brewery, Front Street, it sells three regular ales and some occasional brews, as well as guests from other local breweries. Liefmans Kriek on draught plus a range of continental bottled beers add variety. An extensive menu of home-cooked food is served. P

Brancaster Staithe

Jolly Sailors

Main Road, PE31 8BJ

11-11; 12-10.30 Sun

(01485) 210314 jollysailors.co.uk

Brancaster IPA, Old Les; guest beers H

Busy throughout the year with locals, sailors and birdwatchers, the pub's three small rooms around the bar are cosy and intimate in winter and cool in the summer. A restaurant, conservatory and large garden complete the choice of drinking areas. The on-site brewery produces the house beers, which are supplemented by a changing guest. Freshly cooked food from locally sourced ingredients is available 12-9pm. Q P

White Horse

Main Road, PE31 8BY

11-11; 12-10.30 Sun

(01485) 210262 whitehorsebrancaster.co.uk

Adnams Bitter; Fuller's London Pride; Woodforde's Wherry; guest beer H

The bar area of this award-winning hotel and restaurant maintains a genuine, warm pub feel. Bare floors and scrubbed pine furniture set off the walls covered in local photographs and artists' exhibits. The feel is bright but cosy. The outside terrace affords unrivalled views over Scolt Head Island and the extensive saltmarshes. Bar billiards is played here. The accommodation is in 15 en-suite rooms. P

Burnham Thorpe

Lord Nelson

Walsingham Road, PE31 8HL (off B1355)

11-3, 6-11; closed winter Mon; 12-3, 6.30-10.30 Sun

(01328) 738241 nelsonslocal.co.uk

Fox Nelson's Blood; Greene King IPA, Abbot; Woodforde's Wherry, Nelson's Revenge G

Situated in Nelson's birthplace, this pub has changed little over the past 370 years. Drinks are served direct from the tap room; there is no bar. You can sit on the same high-backed settle that Nelson once occupied. He entertained the whole village to a final meal here in 1793. A shrine to the

INDEPENDENT BREWERIES

Blackfriars Great Yarmouth
Blue Moon Barford
Brancaster Brancaster Staithe
Buffy's Tivetshall St Mary
Bull Box Stradsett
Chalk Hill Norwich
Elveden Elveden
Fat Cat Norwich
Fox Heacham
Front Street Binham
Humpty Dumpty Reedham
Iceni Ickburgh
Norfolk Cottage Norwich
Reepham Reepham
Spectrum Barford
Tindall Seething
Tipples Norwich
Uncle Stuarts Lingwood
Wagtail Old Buckenham
Waveney Earsham
Why Not Thorpe St Andrew
Winter's Norwich
Wissey Valley Stoke Ferry
Wolf Attleborough
Woodforde's Woodbastwick
Yetman's Holt

local hero, memorabilia can be found throughout. Usually five beers are stocked and you can sample the rum-based drink sold as Nelson's Blood. Children are welcome. ♨Q❀◑♿▲♣P

Burston

Crown

Crown Green, IP22 5TW
✪ 12-2 (not Mon or Tue), 5-11; 12-11 Fri & Sat; 12-9 Sun
☎ (01379) 741257 🌐 burstoncrown.co.uk
Adnams Bitter; Elgood's Pageant Ale; Woodforde's Nelson's Revenge, Admiral's Reserve; guest beers Ⓖ
Dating from 1580 and standing at the centre of a south Norfolk village, this red-brick pub has an extensive car park and a garden. The interior layout consists of a bar area with pool table and juke box, a no-smoking lounge with a welcoming log fire in the large inglenook and some comfortable armchairs. A wide range of meals and snacks are served in the restaurant, Wednesday-Saturday. Kingfisher cider is sold. ♨❀◑♣●P⊬

Buxton

Old Crown

Crown Street, NR10 5EN (on B1354)
✪ 12-2, 5-11; 11-11 Sat; 12-10.30 Sun
☎ (01603) 279958
Adnams Bitter, Broadside; Woodforde's Wherry; guest beers Ⓗ
In the village centre, this gabled pub has recently undergone extensive refurbishment both internally and externally. The interior is now very modern with new furnishings and carpets, but has retained some of the original exposed beams to show that it is in fact an old inn. The three main rooms comprise a lounge, games room with pool and darts and a no-smoking restaurant serving home-cooked food. Children (and dogs) are welcome. The private Bure Valley narrow gauge line is nearby. ❀◑▣♣P

Caister-on-Sea

Ship Inn

2 Victoria Street, NR30 5HA
✪ 10-midnight (2am Fri & Sat); 12-11 Sun
☎ (01493) 728008
Greene King IPA, Old Speckled Hen; guest beer Ⓗ
Charming village local, near the centre of this pleasant little resort on the east coast. Conveniently situated for the beach a few hundred yards away, it is also close to Britain's only completely independent lifeboat station. It has a cosy, L-shaped bar warmed by a real fire and a dining room where meals are served at lunchtime and in the evening. The patio is brightened by many floral baskets. ♨♉❀◑⊕▣♣P

Chedgrave

White Horse

5 Norwich Road, NR14 6ND
✪ 12-3, 6-11.30 daily
☎ (01508) 520250
Adnams Bitter, Broadside; Flowers IPA; Taylor Landlord; Ⓖ **guest beers** Ⓗ
Characterful pub, dating back to the 1700s. It has an L-shaped bar serving two drinking areas. One has a Victorian glazed tiled fireplace, bare floorboards, a pool table and comfortable seating. Step down to the carpeted lounge area (no-smoking) and the small dining area that serves a variety of meals. A new restaurant should be open when this Guide is published, offering an extensive menu based on local produce. Outside is a patio and a bowling green. ♨Q❀◑♿▲▣♣P⊬

Cley next the Sea

Three Swallows

Newgate Green, NR25 7TT (½ mile S of A149)
✪ 11-11;12-10.30 Sun
% (01263) 740526
Adnams Bitter; Greene King IPA, Abbot Ⓗ
Alongside the village green, this family-friendly pub affords superb views across the Glaven Valley. The three rooms feature traditional half panelling and timber flooring throughout, with an interesting array of ancient photographs. An extensive menu ranges from snacks to three-course meals and the pub offers a good wine list. A great base for birdwatching, walking and exploring the coastline, it offers good accommodation. The green provides a wonderful setting for a pint of good East Anglian beer in the fresh air. ♨Q♉❀⇌◑♿▲P⊬

Coltishall

Railway Tavern

Station Road, NR12 7JL (on B1150, N of village)
b 12-3, 5-11; 12-11 Fri-Sun 🌐 railwaycoltishall.co.uk
☎ (01603) 738316
Beer range varies Ⓗ
This fine brick and flint, 17th-century pub is a good example of a friendly, rural local. Its three rooms comprise a main bar, games room with darts and pool and a TV lounge. A Wolf beer is normally stocked. The food is home cooked. Sunday is quiz night and occasional live music is performed. Above the bar, a blackboard lists popular local Norfolk phrases with translations for those not familiar with the dialect. The large rear garden houses some disused 19th-century limekilns. ♨❀◑⊕♣P

Deopham

Victoria Inn

Church Road, NR18 9DT (½ mile N of church)
OS051008
✪ 12 (5 Mon)-11; 12-4, 7-10.30 Sun
☎ (01953) 850783
Spectrum 42; Wolf Golden Jackal; Woodforde's Wherry; guest beer Ⓗ
Slightly tucked away, this free house is a friendly and welcoming village local, with comfy chairs set around the fire. It supports active pool and darts teams and caters for families. The food includes vegetarian options and midweek specials; evening meals are served Tuesday-Saturday. It hosts

monthly live music or karaoke. The guest bedrooms have en-suite facilities. ♨❀⇔◐◑♣P

Dersingham

Feathers Hotel

Manor Road, PE31 6LN

⏲ 10.30-11 (midnight Fri); 10.30-10.30 Sun

☎ (01485) 540207 🌐 thefeathershotel.co.uk

Adnams Bitter; Draught Bass; guest beers 🄷

This fine carrstone hotel is a former coaching house. Royal connections and its position, roughly half a mile from Sandringham, make it deservedly popular with tourists. The Sandringham bar features a roaring log fire in winter, while the Saddle bar is no-smoking. Across from the main hotel entrance, the Stable bar attracts a young crowd with regular live music. Food is available in all the bars, or in the restaurant. The large garden has playthings for children. ♨Q❀⇔◐◑🚌P⊬

Diss

Cock Inn

63 Lower Denmark Street, IP22 4BE

⏲ 12-11; 12-10.30 Sun

☎ (01379) 643633

Adnams Bitter; Greene King Old Speckled Hen; guest beer 🄷

This 16th-century beamed pub faces a large green, which acts as an outdoor drinking area, on the south side of the market town. It has one bar, serving three real ales to three comfortable drinking areas, with wood furniture and leather sofas. A drinkers' pub (no food), it gets busy at weekends when music is performed. ♨Q❀♿🚌♣

Docking

Railway Inn

Station Road, PE31 8LY (on B1153 Brancaster road) OS766374

⏲ 12-3, 6-11.30; 12-11 Sat; 12-10.30 Sun

☎ (01485) 518620

Buffy's Bitter; Woodforde's Nelson's Revenge, Admiral's Reserve; guest beer 🄷

Superb village local in the same ownership for more than 20 years. The warmth and friendliness of the staff and regulars make visitors feel at home. There are facilities for hearing impaired customers, with some staff fluent in sign language. A log fire in winter and outside seating in summer make this inn a must. An excellent menu includes a £5 board; Tuesday is curry night. A bowling green and remains of a former railway line add interest. ♨☖❀⇔◐◑♣P

Downham Market

Crown Hotel

12 Bridge Street, PE38 9DH

⏲ 10-11; 12-10.30 Sun

☎ (01366) 382322

Adnams Bitter; Greene King IPA, Abbot; guest beers 🄷

Fine, 17th-century coaching inn at the heart of the traditional town centre. It is popular with both locals and visiting ale lovers. In the single bar, with its beamed ceiling, a good choice of beers from independent breweries is regularly featured. Mouth-watering food is an added attraction, perhaps to compensate for the 'bread riots' that occurred here in 1816 when hungry agricultural workers kept the justices of the peace 'prisoners' at the Crown until the militia arrived. ♨❀⇔◐◑♿⇌🚌P

Earsham

Queen's Head

Station Road, NR35 2TS (off A143 near Bungay)

⏲ 12-3, 5-11; 12-3, 7-10.30 Sun

☎ (01986) 892623

Beer range varies 🄷

Home of the Waveney Brewery, this 17th-century inn on the Suffolk border is a real gem. It is divided internally into a main bar with a red tiled floor and wooden furniture, an adjacent games room split by a large fireplace with welcoming fire, and a dining room that also has two fireplaces. The Waveney beers are supplemented by two guests. Part of the car park has been landscaped recently to create an attractive garden. ♨❀◐▲🚌♣P□

East Dereham

George Hotel

Swaffham Road, NR19 2AZ (near war memorial)

⏲ 10-11 (midnight Fri & Sat); 10-11 Sun

☎ (01362) 696801

Adnams Bitter, Broadside; Fuller's London Pride; Greene King Old Speckled Hen; Woodforde's Wherry; guest beer 🄷

Welcoming bar in a market town hotel, open to non-residents. It serves an excellent range of traditional bar meals and has an a la carte restaurant. The new conservatory provides a pleasant, no-smoking drinking area, while the comfortable bar area features wood panelling and pictures of local historical interest. The guest beer, which changes regularly, comes from an East Anglian brewer. ♨❀⇔◐◑🚌P⊬

Edgefield

Three Pigs

Norwich Road, NR24 2RL (on B1149)

⏲ 11-3, 6.30-11; 12-3, 6.30-10.30 Sun

☎ (01263) 587634

Adnams Bitter, Broadside; Greene King IPA; Woodforde's Wherry; guest beers 🄷

Large free house, convenient for all the attractions of north Norfolk. The two-roomed bar area is spacious and comfortable while the adjacent restaurant serves excellent home-cooked meals. You may find as many as six guest beers here at a time. Jazz sessions are held once a month. A touring caravan park stands next to the pub's large car park. ♨Q❀◐◑▲🚌♣P⊬

Elsing

Mermaid

Church Street, NR20 3EA

⏲ 12-2.30, 7 (6 Fri & Sat)-11; 12-3.30, 6.30-11 Sun
☎ (01362) 637640
Adnams Broadside; Wolf Golden Jackal; Woodforde's Wherry; guest beers (occasional) Ⓖ
Lovely inn next to the parish church in a small, picturesque village in the upper Wensum Valley. The single long bar has a log fire and dartboard at one end and pool table at the other. All the real ales are served by gravity, guest beers are added in summer and during the winter shooting season. Good quality, home-cooked meals are served. Popular with walkers, the pub boasts two gardens and there is a fishing lake nearby. ♨✿◐◑▲♣P

Erpingham

Spread Eagle

Eagle Lane, NR11 7QA OS191318
⏲ 11-3, 6.30-11 (midnight in high season); 11-midnight Sat; 12-4, 7-11 Sun
☎ (01263) 761591 🌐 thespreadeagleinn.com
Adnams Bitter, Broadside; Woodforde's Wherry; guest beers Ⓗ
The original building dates back to the 17th century and it was the Woodforde's tap until the brewery moved to Woodbastwick in 1989. The interior consists of a long, open-plan room with the bar in the centre. At one end is a games room with comfy sofas and at the other a no-smoking restaurant and family area. Home-cooked meals are also served in the bar. A monthly quiz is staged. The pub welcomes dogs.
♨♉✿◐◑▲P⚟

Fakenham

Bull

41 Bridge Street, NR21 9AG
⏲ 10-midnight (12.30am Fri & Sat); 12-10.30 Sun
☎ (01328) 853410
Elgood's Black Dog; Woodforde's Wherry; guest beers Ⓗ
Pleasant pub, popular with all ages. The light, modern and spacious room boasts an impressive solid ash bar and oak plank flooring; leather sofas and artworks enhance the decor. The open-plan interior is divided into three sections: the bar, a no-smoking zone and an area where children are made welcome. Disabled facilities are good. Four new guest rooms offer en-suite accommodation. Food includes occasional speciality evenings. ♨♉✿🛏◐♿▲⚟

Foulden

White Hart

White Hart Street, IP26 5AW
⏲ 11-3, 7-midnight; 11-midnight Thu-Sat; 11-12.30 Sun
☎ (01366) 328638
Adnams Bitter, Broadside; Greene King IPA, Abbot; guest beers Ⓗ
Very much a traditional village pub at the centre of its community, this family-run establishment runs regular charity quizzes and other events. The guest beer changes often, so is never boring. The home-cooked food is a well known feature here. The small garden is home to some pet animals that children may visit. ♨✿🛏◐◑▲♣P

Gayton

Crown

Lynn Road, PE32 1PA (on B1145)
⏲ 12-3, 6-11; 11-midnight Fri & Sat; 12-11.30 Sun
☎ (01553) 636252
Greene King XX Mild, IPA, Abbot; Old Speckled Hen; guest beer Ⓗ
A true gem, this pub was voted local CAMRA Pub of the Year in 2004. A rare outlet for the superb XX Mild, it serves excellent food in both the pub and the large dining room. There is also a games room. At the centre of village life, the pub is well supported by locals, especially for music evenings and special events. With gardens front and back and a huge log fire in the main bar in winter, this is a pub for all seasons.
♨Q♉✿◐◑⊟♿🚌P⚟

Geldeston

Locks

Locks Lane, NR34 0HW
⏲ 12-12.30am (1 am Fri & Sat); winter hours may vary; 12-12.30am Sun
☎ (01508) 518414 🌐 geldestonlocks.co.uk
Green Jack Canary, Orange Wheat, Grasshopper, Gone Fishing; guest beers Ⓗ
Quintessential Broads pub, owned by the Green Jack Brewery. The building dates back to the 1600s, although it has been extended. The bar is lit by candles, enhancing the exposed beams and bare brickwork. The superb fireplace houses a wood-burning stove. Gardens lead down to the river which with Sunday afternoon entertainment is the perfect spot to while away an hour or so. Live music is performed on Thursday and Saturday, Friday is curry night.
♨Q♉✿◐◑●P

Wherry

7 The Street, NR34 0LB
⏲ 12-midnight (1am Fri & Sat); 12-midnight Sun
☎ (01508) 518371
Adnams Bitter, Broadside Ⓗ
The original part of this building dates back to the 1670s – it is a cosy room with a quarry-tiled floor; look for the framed history of the pub and its site. The modern extension was added during the 1970s. The pub is one of the few in the area where the card game phat is played regularly.
♨Q✿◐◑▲♣P⊡

Gorleston-on-Sea

Albion

87 Lowestoft Road, NR31 6SH
⏲ 11-11; 12-11 Sun
☎ (01493) 661035
Black Sheep Best Bitter; Buffy's Polly's Folly; Greene King IPA; Wells Bombardier; guest beer Ⓗ
Comfortable, urban, street-corner local on the southern side of Gorleston. This former Steward and Patteson house suffered considerable damage during WWII. It serves a wide range of real ales, including guests. The pub has a separate pool room and extensive car park. It is owned by the same company as the New Entertainer. 🚌♣P

Lord Nelson

33 Trafalgar Road West, NR31 8BS

11-11 (midnight Fri & Sat); 12-10.30 Sun

(01493) 301084

Adnams Bitter, Broadside; Bateman XB, XXXB; guest beers H

This two-bar pub has recently changed hands and come under Bateman's ownership. The beer quality remains very good. One bar displays a collection of cigarette lighters and much Nelson memorabilia. It also has a conservatory and function room. Although tucked away, this pub is well worth seeking out.

New Entertainer

80 Pier Plain, NR31 6PG

12-11; 12-10.30 Sun

(01493) 441643

Greene King IPA; guest beers H

Formerly the Suffolk Hotel, the building dates back to the 1800s. Its most notable feature is the original Lacon's window. The bar is divided into a carpeted lounge with comfortable seating and a bare-boarded area with a pool table. The pub is completely surrounded by roads, so care is needed when leaving. It stocks a good range of Belgian beers, in case the six guest ales do not provide you with enough choice! Q

Great Bircham

King's Head

Lynn Road, PE31 7RJ

11-11; 12-10.30 Sun

(01485) 578265 kings-head-bircham.co.uk

Adnams Bitter; Fuller's London Pride; Woodforde's Wherry; guest beer H

This is not a typical village local. The old pub has been completely refurbished in a modern style, with stainless steel and pale wood complementing the abstract art. The highly-rated restaurant is more Notting Hill than Norfolk, but features fresh, local produce. Do not be put off if all you want is a drink – the welcome is friendly and the beer excellent, and it runs quiz nights like a proper pub.

Great Cressingham

Windmill Inn

Water End, IP25 6NN

11-3, 5-11; 11-11 Sat; 12-10.30 Sun

(01760) 756232

windmillinn-greatcressingham.com

Adnams Bitter, Broadside; Greene King IPA; guest beers H

This pub has been in the same family for 45 years and is hugely popular, especially in holiday periods. Its many rooms cater for all tastes, from snug drinking areas to airy conservatories overlooking the ample gardens. It offers six real ales and an enormous range of meals. Q P

Great Moulton

Fox & Hounds

Frith Way, NR15 2HE

7-11; closed Mon; 12-2.30, 7-10.30 Sun

(01379) 677506

Adnams Bitter; Greene King IPA H

Parts of the original building of this inn are 500 years old; in the 1600s it underwent 'modernisation'. Today it retains many ancient features such as a very low ceiling with many exposed beams – anyone over 5ft 8in tall has to take care! A large red-brick fireplace holds a roaring log fire in winter, and is surrounded by comfortable sofas. The restaurant offers an extensive menu.

Q P

Great Yarmouth

Gallon Pot

1 Market Place, NR30 1NB

10-11; 12-10.30 Sun

(01493) 842230

Adnams Bitter; Fuller's London Pride; Greene King Old Speckled Hen; Woodforde's Wherry H

This 1960s building replaced the previous pub that was destroyed by bombs during WWII. Occupying a prime site on the west side of Great Yarmouth's historic market place, it has a spacious, open-plan interior, with a raised area at one end and a no-smoking cellar bar where families are welcome. In addition to a good range of four real ales, it is popular for its home-cooked food, which is served all day.

Mariners Tavern

69 Howard Street South, NR30 1LN

11-midnight (2am Fri & Sat); 12-11 Sun

(01493) 332299

Beer range varies H

Situated close to the town centre, this delightful red-brick and flint building sells a rotating range of between six and eight real ales, many of which come from local breweries. The main bar is complemented by a smaller no-smoking room where families with children are welcome. Live music is staged on Saturday evening – usually folk, blues or jazz, definitely no karaoke. In summer part of the car park is set with tables and chairs for outside drinking.

Q P

Red Herring

24-25 Havelock Road, NR30 3HQ

11.30-3.30 (5 Fri & Sat), 6.30-midnight (1am Fri & Sat); 11.30-midnight Sun

(01493) 853384

Greene King IPA, Abbot; M&B Mild; guest beers H

Tucked away in a residential area, just back from the seafront, this friendly corner local bucks the trend for many Yarmouth pubs. Opposite the award-winning Time and Tide Museum, this pub is a must to visit. Well used by both locals and holidaymakers, the open-plan bar has a pool area that can be partitioned off. Pictures of old Yarmouth line the panelling above the bar. The cider is Westons Old Rosie.

St John's Head

58 North Quay, NR30 1JB

12 (11 summer)-midnight; 12-midnight Sun

(01493) 843443

Elgood's Cambridge; guest beers Ⓗ
This red-brick pub dates back to the 18th century. Situated near the quayside, it is also convenient for Yarmouth (Vauxhall) Station. Fairly small, the single bar still manages to fit in a pool table and wide-screen TV at one end. Four real ales are sold at competitive prices and Addlestones cider is always stocked. ❀≠(Vauxhall)⊟♣●P

Happisburgh

Hill House

NR12 0PN
✪ 12-3, 7-11.30; 12-11.30 Thu-Sun
☎ (01692) 650004
Beer range varies Ⓗ
Outstanding coastal hideaway, once the haunt of Sir Arthur Conan Doyle, who wrote a Sherlock Holmes novel here. The range of six real ales blossoms to over 40 during the pub's midsummer beer festival week. This is an atmospheric, 500-year-old pub that has some good modern touches, such as disabled access. ♨Q♉❀⇄◐◑♿♣P⊬

Heacham

Fox & Hounds

22 Station Road, PE31 7EX
✪ 12-11; 12-10.30 Sun
☎ (01485) 570345 ⊕ foxbrewery.co.uk
Adnams Broadside; guest beers Ⓗ
Busy, one-roomed local that is popular with both regulars and visitors. The home of Fox Brewery, three of the six beers served are from the brewery itself, while other micro-breweries' products are also featured. It stocks a range of foreign bottled beer and draught cider from the Norfolk Cider Company. Entertainment includes live music on Tuesday evening and a quiz on Thursday. Two beer festivals are held here each year, in March and mid-July. ❀◐◑⊟●P⊓

Hedenham

Mermaid

Norwich Road, NR35 2LB (on B1332, Norwich-Bungay road)
✪ 12-2.30 (not Tue-Thu), 7-11; 12-4, 7-10.30 Sun
☎ (01508) 482480
Greene King IPA; Tindall Best Bitter; guest beers Ⓗ
Dating from the 17th century, this terracotta-coloured coaching inn, with a large rear garden (where customers may camp), is on the main Bungay to Norwich road. The semi-open plan interior features exposed beams and a mix of wooden and upholstered chairs. One area houses a pool table and the pub is dominated by a large fire. One or two guest beers are added in the summer season. Home-cooked food is served in the dining area. ♨Q❀◐⛺⊟♣P

Horsey

Nelson Head

Beach Road, NR27 3LT (300 yds off B1159)
✪ 11-3, 6-11; 12-3, 6-10.30 Sun
☎ (01493) 393378
Woodforde's Wherry, Nelson's Revenge, Norfolk Nog Ⓗ
Situated just off the coast road, this old pub affords panoramic views across the fields of this part of Norfolk, and is popular with naturalists, artists and walkers, as well as locals. Many paintings in the bar feature Nelson, of course, but the small dining room also displays the work of local artists for sale. The pub serves three local ales and good food. A log fire is a focal point in winter. ♨Q♉❀◐◑⊡P

Ingham

Swan

Sea Palling Road, NR12 9AB (1 mile NE of Stalham on B1151) OS390260
✪ 12-3, 6-11; closed Mon winter; 12-10.30 (12-3 winter) Sun
☎ (01692) 581099
Woodforde's Wherry, Great Eastern, Nelson's Revenge, Admiral's Reserve; guest beer Ⓗ
Delightful, thatched, flint pub, part of a 14th-century terrace. The split-level, smoke-free interior boasts a wealth of warm brick, flint and beams. A wide choice of excellent home-prepared meals is served in the dining room, and in summer a special alfresco menu is available in the secluded courtyard. High quality en-suite accommodation in a separate building is available all year. In a pleasant rural setting near the church, the Swan is handy for the coast and the Broads. Q❀⇄◐◑♣P⊬

Kenninghall

Red Lion

East Church Street, NR16 2EP (opp. church)
✪ 12-3, 6.30-11; 12-11 Fri & Sat; 12-10.30 Sun
☎ (01953) 887849
Fuller's London Pride; Greene King IPA, Abbot; Woodforde's Wherry; guest beer Ⓗ
Licensed since 1722 and believed to be 400 years old, this lovely pub has wood and pamment floors throughout and has retained the original fireplaces in all areas. Exposed beams, pictures and various artefacts around the walls lend a rustic feel; there is a wonderful snug area with a high-backed settle. To the rear is a patio drinking area and a well-used bowls green. Live music is staged occasionally. ♨Q❀⇄◐◑P

King's Lynn

Live & Let Live

18 Windsor Road, PE30 5PL
✪ 11.30 (1 Mon)-11 (midnight Fri & Sat); 11.30-11 Sun
☎ (01553) 764990
Beer range varies Ⓗ
Lively, back-street, community pub just off London Road, with two bars. The larger public bar has a pool table and a screen for watching sport, while the lounge is smaller and more cosy. Four real ales are kept, generally including a bitter, a strong beer and – rare in this district – a mild. It is also one of the few outlets in the area to sell Westons cider (ask at the bar). ⊡≠♣●⊬⊓

Stuart House Hotel
35 Goodwins Road, PE30 5QX
✪ 6-11; 7-10.30 Sun
☎ (01553) 772169 ⊕ stuart-house-hotel.co.uk
Beer range varies Ⓗ
Cosy hotel bar and restaurant that always has three real ales on the bar. Quietly situated near the centre of King's Lynn, it is close to the park and within walking distance of the bus and rail stations. A beer festival is held in the grounds during the last week of July. Regular Friday night entertainment often features blues bands. Open evenings only (except by arrangement), it is recommended for bar and restaurant meals and its accommodation. ♨❀⇔◗P

White Horse
9 Wootton Road, PE30 4EZ
✪ 11-11; 12-10.30 Sun
☎ (01553) 763258
Bateman XB; Greene King IPA; guest beer Ⓗ
Thriving, traditional local with a public and lounge bar, near the Gaywood Clock. It features in CAMRA's East Anglian Regional Inventory for pub interiors. Three beers are available, one of which is a changing guest, occasionally from a micro-brewery. Regulars gather here to watch football in the public bar that has a large screen as well as a TV, and to play pub games such as dominoes. ⊟⊟♣P⊽

Larling

Angel Inn
NR16 2QU (off A11, between Thetford and Norwich)
✪ 10-11 daily
☎ (01953) 717963
Adnams Bitter; guest beers Ⓗ
Be sure to detour from the A11 to visit the superb Angel Inn, where you will find five top-notch ales from micro-breweries all over the UK; one will be a mild, a rarity in such a rural area. And do sample the delicious, home-cooked food (booking advisable for the restaurant). A watering-hole for the local farming community; football fans en route for Norwich are also welcome (the landlord is a keen Norwich City fan). A beer festival is held in summer. ♨❀⇔◖◗⊟⅄≷(Harling Rd, limited service)♣P⊽

Lessingham

Star Inn
School Road, NR12 0DN (300 yds from Happisburgh coast road) OS284389
✪ 12-3, 7-midnight daily
☎ (01692) 580510 ⊕ thestarlessingham.co.uk
Buffy's Bitter; Greene King IPA; guest beers Ⓗ
Pleasant country pub, consisting of a long public bar with a woodburner at one end and a tame jackdaw at the other! Situated at a minor crossroads, just west of the village and coast road, the pub has a large garden. The small, no-smoking restaurant is recommended; vegetarian options always feature on the menu. The Star usually offers three guest beers from micro-breweries. The pub may open an hour earlier in the summer. ♨Q❀⇔◖◗♿♣●P

Methwold Hythe

Green Man
IP26 4QP
✪ 12-4 (not Tue-Fri); 7-1am; closed Mon;12-4, 7-11 Sun
☎ (01366) 728537
Elgood's Black Dog; Greene King IPA Ⓗ
The core of this pub was built in 1632 on a crossroads at the centre of what was then a small port (hythe) on the edge of the fens. In the last two years the landlord has succeeded in creating the impression that his customers are guests in his home. He keeps a superb pint of mild, while his wife turns out excellent food. The atmosphere is jovial and this pub is well worth a detour. ♨❀◖◗⅄♣P

New Buckenham

King's Head
Market Place, NR16 2AN
✪ 12-2.30, 7-11.30; 12-3, 7-11.30 Sun
☎ (01953) 860487
Adnams Bitter; guest beer Ⓗ
Set beside the village green, this friendly, conversational, two-bar pub, which dates from the early 16th century, served as a coaching inn between London and Norwich. The front (no-smoking) bar is more of a lounge, in contrast to the larger pamment-floored back bar, which is warmed by a woodburner in the inglenook. Good value, home-cooked food comes in generous portions (no meals Mon). ♨❀◖◗♣⊁

North Creake

Jolly Farmers
1 Burnham Road, NR21 9JW
✪ 12-2.30, 7-11; closed Mon & Tue winter; 12-2.30, 7-10.30 Sun
☎ (01328) 738185 ⊕ jollyfarmers-northcreake.co.uk
Adnams Bitter; Woodforde's Wherry; guest beer Ⓖ
Just eight miles from the north Norfolk coast and three from the upmarket haunts of Burnham Market, this pub manages to retain a down-to-earth ambience. It has two bars: one with a pool table mainly for drinkers, and another with stripped pine tables and chairs that is geared up for diners. The Red Room is suitable for families and used for private functions. Food is freshly cooked from local produce and the pub keeps a good selection of wine and whiskies. ♨❀◖◗⊟P⊁

North Elmham

Railway
40 Station Road, NR20 5HH (on B1145)
✪ 11-midnight daily
☎ (01362) 668300
Beer range varies Ⓗ
Typical village community local, this brick and flint building lies to the east of the village centre, next to the old Dereham-Fakenham railway line. The pub dates from the mid-19th century, just after the line opened. It comprises a main lounge, where old, comfy chairs surround an open fire, a section for diners to enjoy the home-cooked

food and a bar area that houses a pool table. A variety of real ales mostly comes from East Anglian brewers. ♨❀◐◑▲P⊬

North Pickenham

Blue Lion

Houghton Lane, PE37 8LF
⏲ 12-11 (midnight Fri & Sat); 12-11 Sun
☎ (01760) 440289
Greene King IPA; guest beers [H]
A late 17th-century 'dog leg'-shaped building in the village centre, the Blue Lion concentrates on beer drinkers and does not allow children to remain after 8pm. Being one of the few country pubs in Norfolk to stay open all day ensures its local popularity, as do its successful fundraisers and quiz held on alternate Sundays. ♨❀▲♣P

Norwich

Alexandra Tavern

16 Stafford Street, NR2 3HH (off Dereham Rd)
⏲ 10.30-11 (midnight Fri & Sat); 12-11 Sun
☎ (01603) 627722
Chalk Hill Tap, CHB; guest beers [H]
Victorian, street-corner local: this is effectively a two-bar pub, even though at the northern end there is no door. An interesting mix of memorabilia adorns the walls. The real ales come from the local Chalk Hill Brewery, with guests from micro-breweries. Evening meals finish at 7pm. The landlord made his name in the pub trade for contesting, and winning, a battle against Inntrepreneur's leasing terms. He has also rowed across the Atlantic in aid of charity! ♨❀◐◑⊟🚌♣

Beehive

30 Leopold Road, NR4 7PJ (between Newmarket and Unthank Road)
⏲ 12-2.30, 5.30-11 (midnight Fri); 12-midnight Sat; 12-3, 7-11.30 Sun
☎ (01603) 451628 🌐 beehivepubnorwich.co.uk
Fuller's London Pride; Greene King IPA; Hop Back Summer Lightning; Wolf Golden Jackal, Wolf in Sheep's Clothing; guest beers [H]
Genuine suburban local, this two-roomed, ex-Courage pub stocks a good range of ales, including a mild and porter. Home to a Lodge of the Royal and Ancient Order of Buffalos, it maintains sporting links with rugby, golf, football and darts. Very much a community pub, it attracts customers of all ages. The comfortable lounge boasts several chesterfield sofas to relax on with a pint. It holds regular quiz nights and wine tastings in the upstairs function room, and summer barbecues. ❀◐🚌♣P

Cider Shed

98-100 Lawson Road, NR3 4LF
(10 mins from Anglia Sq)
⏲ 12-11.30 (12.30am Fri & Sat if busy); 12-11 Sun
☎ (01603) 413153 🌐 theshednorwich.co.uk
Adnams Bitter; Fat Cat Bitter, Top Cat; Taylor Landlord; [H] **guest beers** [H]/[G]
Consult the website for the regular music events staged here, including Sunday jazz. Under the same ownership as the Fat Cat, and brewing its beers next door under the direction of former Woodforde's maestro, Ray Ashworth, this recently opened free house is a 10-minute walk from Anglia Square. The pub's name is apt for its layout and pride of place goes to the giant redwood bar top. Home of Dr Zog's secondhand book emporium, this pub is a must. ❀🚌(21, 22)♿♣●P

Champion

101 Chapelfield Road, NR2 1SE (opp. shopping mall)
⏲ 10-11 (midnight Fri & Sat); 12-10.30 Sun
☎ (01603) 765611
Belhaven 80/-Ale; Blackfriars Sygnus Bittergold; Greene King IPA, Abbot; Woodforde's Wherry [H]
Traditional, Victorian pub in the city centre, convenient for the New Chapelfield shopping centre. It maintains a friendly atmosphere among its varied clientele who are attracted by the fine local ales. The pub boasts notable collections of water and Toby jugs and boxing memorabilia. A small function room is used by various pub teams. Lunches are served, but between 11am and 9pm you can order Indian and Chinese takeways to eat in the back lounge (cutlery and plates provided). ♨◐⊟🚌♣

Coach & Horses

82 Thorpe Road, NR1 1BA (400 yds from station)
⏲ 11-midnight (1am Fri & Sat); 11-midnight Sun
☎ (01603) 477077
Chalk Hill Tap, CHB, Dreadnought, Flinknapper's Mild, Old Tackle; guest beer [H]
You can spot the pub by its façade, which is reminiscent of the old French quarter of New Orleans, and two giant parasols covering a heated seating area. The large, L-shaped bar serves the entire range of Chalk Hill beers - the brewery next door is visible through a glass partition. Good food is served all day in generous portions. This popular pub attracts sports fans as most televised games are shown on several screens throughout the bar. Burnards cider is sold. ♨❀◐◑≹●P

Duke of Wellington

91-93 Waterloo Road, NR3 1EG
⏲ 12-11; 12-10.30 Sun
☎ (01603) 441182
Elgood's Black Dog; Fuller's London Pride; [H] **Hop Back Summer Lightning; Oakham Bishops Farewell;** [G] **Wolf Golden Jackal;** [H] **guest beers** [G]
Superb community local. A former Norwich CAMRA Pub of the Year, it serves a cornucopia of beers, with an astonishing 10-14 in the tap room behind the bar. A mecca for drinkers in the north of the city, it hosts a beer festival over the late August bank holiday weekend, which is renowned for its beer choice. Held under canvas at the rear of the pub, this is a pleasant spot throughout the summer. Folk music is performed on Tuesday evenings. ♨❀🚌♣

Fat Cat

49 West End Street, NR2 4NA (off Dereham Rd)
⏲ 12 (11 Sat)-1am (midnight Fri & Sat); 12-10.30 Sun
☎ (01603) 624364 🌐 fatcatpub.co.uk
Adnams Bitter; Elgood's Black Dog; Fat Cat

Bitter, Top Cat; Taylor Landlord; Woodforde's Wherry; guest beers 🄷
A magnet for beer drinkers, with a superb range of over 20 real ales on handpump and gravity. The pub now sells beers from its own Fat Cat Brewery, which are brewed across town at the Cider Shed pub. It also offers a wide range of Belgian beers. Twice winner of CAMRA's prestigious National Pub of the Year award, it offers a warm welcome to all in a pub adorned with a wealth of brewery memorabilia all around the walls and alcoves. ❀🚌(19, 20, 21, 22)🍎

King's Arms

22 Hall Road, NR1 3HQ
⏲ 11-11.30; 11-midnight Fri & Sat; 12-11 Sun
☎ (01603) 766361
Adnams Bitter, Broadside; Bateman Mild, XB, XXXB; Wolf Coyote; guest beers 🄷
The pub stages an impressive four beer festivals a year (seasonal) and a monthly quiz. Now a Bateman's house, the range and quality of the ales remain superb, with always a dark beer stocked. Food is available at lunchtime and if nothing on the menu appeals you can bring in your own from local takeaways. The pub gets busy on match days, as it is only a short walk from the football ground. The pub has a wheelchair ramp and WC. ❀◐♿🚌♣🚭▯

King's Head

42 Magdalen Street, NR3 1SE (5 mins' walk from Anglia Sq)
⏲ 12-midnight; 12-11 Sun
☎ (01603) 620468 🌐 kingshead.gb.com
Beer range varies 🄷/🄶
This pub has been drastically improved and refurbished after two enthusiastic CAMRA members acquired it. They took a year to sympathetically renovate and restore the listed building and reopened in May 2005 with a strict policy of not serving any keg beer, just cask-conditioned ales from Norfolk breweries. They now source from further afield (ie Suffolk) and offer a wide range of continental bottled beers and guests from around the world. Popular with the local TV studio staff, it offers a warm welcome to all. Q🚌🍎🚭▯

Nelson

122 Nelson Street, NR2 4DR (off Dereham Rd)
⏲ 12-11; 12-10.30 Sun
☎ (01603) 626362 🌐 nelsonpub.co.uk
Caledonian Deuchars IPA; Woodforde's Wherry; Wychwood Hobgoblin; guest beers 🄷
Community oriented pub, split into two distinct areas with a large garden at the rear that hosts barbecues in summer. Occasional beer festivals are held in spring and autumn and various musical events take place during the week. It stocks a good range of rums and gins (the Nelson influence) and you can purchase memorabilia of the admiral here. The owners strive to offer a truly caring, community atmosphere. Buses 19, 20, 21 and 22 serve the pub. ❀🚌♣P

Reindeer

10 Dereham Road, NR2 4AY (on A1074 100 yds from A147 jct)
⏲ 11-11; 10-midnight Fri & Sat; 10-11 Sun
☎ (01603) 762223
Elgood's Black Dog, Cambridge, Golden Newt, Greyhound Strong; guest beers 🄷
Just off the inner ring road, to the west of the city centre, this pub was acquired by Elgood's in 2003 and reopened as a tied house after extensive refurbishment in 2004, selling its full range of beers alongside an impressive guest list. One long, cavernous main bar has a raised section to one side and a no-smoking area to the rear. Well-supervised children are welcome. Note the old red telephone box in the corner.
❀◐◗🚌♣P🚭

Rosary Tavern

95 Rosary Road, NR1 4BX (2 mins' walk up pathway from station)
⏲ 11.30-11 daily
☎ (01603) 666287
Black Sheep Best Bitter; Caledonian Deuchars IPA; 🄷 **guest beers** 🄷/🄶
Just up the hill from the station, this pub plays host to many clubs and sports teams, including the Norfolk Pipe Smoking club who meet in the rear conservatory. Its new landlord aims to continue the tradition of serving quality ales in a friendly atmosphere. The single bar pub houses a rare bar billiards table for this part of the country. The garden is popular in summer, and the pub gets busy with football supporters on match days.
❀◐⇌(Norwich Thorpe)🚌♣🍎

Trafford Arms

61 Grove Road, NR1 3RL (behind Sainsbury's)
⏲ 11-11 (midnight Fri & Sat); 12-11.30 Sun
☎ (01603) 628466 🌐 traffordarms.co.uk
Adnams Bitter; Tetley Bitter; Woodforde's Wherry; guest beers 🄷
Norwich CAMRA Pub of the Year 2005, and deservedly so. Very much a community pub, the landlord is a fanatical Norwich City supporter. The games are naturally shown on TV here, but so are other major sporting events. The pub is now divided into two areas – the left-hand side is strictly no-smoking and includes the main dining area (no eve meals Sun), while on the right there is a pool table and TV. A beer festival is staged around Valentine's Day.
❀◐◗🚌♣🍎P🚭

Wig & Pen

6 St Martins at Palace Plain, NR3 1RN (near Law Courts)
⏲ 11-midnight (1am Fri & Sat); 12-5 Sun
☎ (01603) 625891 🌐 thewigandpen.com
Adnams Bitter; Buffy's Hopleaf; guest beers 🄷
Near the cathedral and law courts, this pub is cosy and inviting, and serves excellent food. Offering a wide range of changing guest ales, it is popular with locals as well as drinkers who travel in from further afield. It hosts a Scottish themed beer festival at the beginning of the year, mostly featuring micro-breweries. The small back dining area doubles as a meeting room. The spacious patio is well used in summer.
🏰❀◐◗⇌🚌♣

Old Buckenham

Gamekeeper
The Green, NR17 1RE
11.45-11; 12-10.30 Sun
☎ (01953) 860397 🌐 thegamekeeperfreehouse.com
Adnams Bitter, Broadside Ⓗ
Situated on the village green, this 17th-century pub has a pamment-floored bar area, with a truly rustic feel enhanced by exposed beams and a brick inglenook. One area of the pub is dedicated to drinking and darts, while another is used for dining, with food served at all sessions. The larger of the two function rooms houses a skittle alley. The house beer is brewed by Wolf.
⩩❀⇆◐◑♣P⚟

Poringland

Royal Oak
44 The Street, NR14 7JT (on B1332 between Norwich and Bungay)
12-3, 5-11; 12-midnight Fri & Sat; 12-11.30 Sun
☎ (01508) 493734
Adnams Bitter; Caledonian Deuchars IPA; Woodforde's Wherry; Ⓗ **guest beers** Ⓖ/Ⓗ
This 19th-century pub has a spacious, semi open-plan interior with a number of distinct drinking areas: a large bar, several small lounges and a space for games with pool and darts. The pub participates in darts and crib leagues and stages a quiz on Sunday evening. Occasional live music can be heard. It sells anything up to ten guest beers at a time. No food is served but customers may bring in fish and chips from the shop next door. Q❀⊟♣●P⊓

Reedham

Reedham Ferry Inn
Ferry Road, NR13 3HA
10.30-3, 6.30-11 (11-11 summer); 11-10.30 Sun
☎ (01493) 700429 🌐 archerstouringpark.co.uk
Adnams Bitter, Broadside; Woodforde's Wherry; guest beers (summer) Ⓗ
Widely regarded as Broadland's premier riverside pub, this superb 17th-century inn boasts beamed ceilings, stone floors and a collection of rural tools. The historic ferry across the River Yare is the last on the Broads. High quality ales are matched by a choice of fine home-prepared meals, with locally-caught fish, game and seafood a speciality. Themed evenings offer dishes and wine from around the world. It hosts a folk festival in September. A caravan site and extensive moorings are available.
⩩Q⛫❀◐◑⊟♿⅄⇌⊟P

Reepham

King's Arms
Market Place, NR10 4JT
11.30-3, 5.30-11; 12-3, 7-10.30 Sun
☎ (01603) 870345
Adnams Bitter; Greene King Abbot; Taylor Landlord; Woodforde's Wherry; guest beer Ⓗ
Centrally situated in the market place, this pub has been carefully modernised to an open-plan design, but has retained plenty of exposed beams and old fireplaces that give a cosy feel. At the rear is a conservatory and a small garden. A range of six real ales is usual here, as well as lunchtime and evening meals. Sunday lunchtime jazz sessions are staged in the courtyard in summer. There is ample parking space on the market place.
⩩Q❀◐◑⊟♣

Roydon

Three Horseshoes
146 Lynn Road, PE32 1AQ
12-11 (midnight Thu-Sat); 12-11.30 Sun
☎ (01485) 600362
Adnams Broadside; Greene King IPA; guest beers Ⓗ
Lying at the heart of its community, this lovely pub, built from local carrstone, has a snug bar and restaurant serving good food. It supports the local cricket team and many other activities, including live music some weekends. It also stages occasional beer festivals. Two guest beers change often. Families with children are welcome here. The outdoor drinking area at the front is brightened by flower containers.
⩩❀◐◑⊟♣P

Union Jack
30 Station Road, PE32 1AW
4 (12 Mon, Fri & Sat)-midnight; 12-midnight Sun
☎ (01485) 601347
Beer range varies Ⓗ
This is a rare village drinkers' pub that relies solely on wet trade – food is only available on special occasions. It offers two or three guest beers that change frequently, mostly around 4% ABV, which are chosen in consultation with the regulars. It stages two beer festivals a year, in May and September. The pub supports many activities, including darts, dominoes, football and cribbage, and trophies abound. Live music is performed some weekends. ⩩❀⊟♣P

Salhouse

Bell
3 Lower Street, NR13 6RW (on B1140)
12-3, 5.30-11; 12-11 Fri & Sat; 12-11 Sun
☎ (01603) 721141
Buffy's Bitter; Wolf Golden Jackal; guest beers Ⓗ
Typical rural community local with a friendly atmosphere, comprising a lounge and public bar and a small dining area that serves an excellent range of home-cooked food. Vegetarian dishes are popular here and a blackboard shows a list of specials that change often. Cider is sold in summer. The pub has a large car park at the front and a garden to the rear. ❀◐◑⊟⊟♣●P⚟

Sheringham

Lobster
13 High Street, NR26 8JP
10-11 (midnight Fri & Sat); 10-11 Sun
☎ (01263) 822716 🌐 the-lobster.com
Adnams Bitter; Greene King Abbot; guest beers Ⓗ
On the main street, near the seafront, this large pub has two bars. The lounge is

divided into several areas with dark wood and a homely atmosphere throughout. The Stables bar is no-smoking. Food is served all day, with breakfast starting at opening time; afternoon tea is available 3-6pm. Offering 10 ales, a selection of foreign bottled beers and 39 single malts, it is not difficult to find something to your taste to drink here. ⛫Q☕❀◐ ⊟♿⇌⊟⚡

Windham Arms

15-17 Wyndham Street, NR26 8BA
⏲ 11-midnight daily
☎ (01263) 822609
Adnams Bitter, Broadside; Marston's Pedigree; Woodforde's Wherry; guest beers Ⓗ
On a side street, close to the seafront and its beautiful beach, this cosy pub consists of two bars. In the lounge you can spend time reading all the old sayings and proverbs on the walls; one end is suitable for diners as it has larger tables. The pub attracts a mixed clientele, from locals to holidaymakers. It has a good outside drinking area and a family room. ⛫Q☕❀◐ ⊟⇌⊟

Shotesham

Globe

The Common, NR15 1YG (on unclassified road 1 mile S of Stoke Holy Cross)
⏲ 12-11 (midnight Fri & Sat); 12-10.30 Sun
☎ (01508) 550475
Adnams Bitter; Greene King IPA Ⓖ
In an area popular with walkers, the pub stands in a small village a few miles south of Norwich, overlooking a picturesque valley. A warm welcome always awaits in this friendly rural hostelry that has a small main bar and a dining area. Beers dispensed by gravity and hot or cold food are available all day. Children are welcome to amuse themselves in the large garden. ❀◐ ⊟⊟♣P

Skeyton

Goat Inn

Long Road, NR10 5DH OS250244
⏲ 11-3, 6-11; 12-3, 6.30-11 Sun
☎ (01692) 538600 🌐 goatinnskeyton.co.uk
Adnams Bitter; Woodforde's Wherry; guest beers Ⓗ
Greatly extended, 16th-century thatched country pub set in over seven acres of grounds, serving a wide rural community. Many events are held in the grounds, including a classic car show in May. Old farming tools and local photographs are displayed. A varied menu, supplemented by daily specials, is served in both the bar and restaurant. A house beer is produced by Woodforde's for summer. ❀◐ ▲P⚡

Smallburgh

Crown

NR12 9AD (on A149)
⏲ 12-3 (not Mon), 5.30 (7 Sat)-11; 12-3 (closed eve) Sun
☎ (01692) 536314
Adnams Bitter; Greene King IPA, Abbot; guest beers Ⓗ
Very much a traditional inn, dating back to the 15th century, the Crown is close to the Broads and coast, but far enough away to maintain a relaxed character. Bar snacks are served or full meals in the dining room. Unusually, the pub keeps a small range of premium rums. The garden at the rear is a peaceful refuge for those wishing to escape from the summer bustle of the Broads; no children under 14 are admitted. ⛫Q❀⇄◐ ♣P

South Creake

Ostrich

Fakenham Road, NR21 9PB (on B1355, Burnham Market road) OS864355
⏲ 12-3, 6-11 (12-11 summer); 12-3, 5-10.30 (12-10.30 summer) Sun
☎ (01328) 823320 🌐 ostrichinn.co.uk
Greene King IPA, Abbot; Woodforde's Wherry; guest beer Ⓗ
Well modernised village inn, dating from the 17th century. Excellent, freshly prepared meals are served here and in the summer the garden is a perfect spot for relaxed dining. In the winter the partly divided bar area is warm and cosy. A restored large barn is used for functions and the pub offers overnight accommodation. ⛫❀⇄◐ ♿P⚡

Southery

Old White Bell

20 Upgate Street, PE38 0NA
⏲ 11 (3 Wed)-11; 12-10.30 Sun
☎ (01366) 377057 🌐 oldwhitebell.co.uk
City of Cambridge Rutherford IPA; guest beers Ⓗ
True local free house serving a village community, situated just off the busy A10, between Ely and King's Lynn. An open-plan pub with a small restaurant, you will inevitably find football shown on the TV and indeed, the pub runs its own soccer team – White Bell Wanderers (see the website). An outlet for City of Cambridge ales, it also offers a fine selection of guests. This basic but brilliant pub was local CAMRA's Pub of the Year 2006. ◐ ⊟♣P

Stibbard

Ordnance Arms

Guist Bottom, NR20 5PF (on A1067)
⏲ 12-2.30 (not Mon-Fri), 5.30-midnight; 12-10.30 Sun
☎ (01328) 829471 🌐 ordnancearms.co.uk
Adnams Bitter; Draught Bass; Greene King Abbot Ⓗ
Old country inn on the main road between Norwich and Fakenham. The main bar, warmed by a log fire, leads through to another small room used for pool and darts. A third drinking area has a tiled floor and old pine furnishings. The pub is well known for its Thai restaurant (open evenings), which has gained a good reputation for oriental cuisine over the past few years. ⛫Q❀◗⊟P

Stoke Ferry

Bluebell

Lynn Road, PE33 9SW (off A134)
⏲ 12-3, 5-11; 11-11 Fri & Sat; 12-10.30 Sun

☎ (01366) 502056
Adnams Bitter; Greene King IPA 🄷
Small village pub that is rebuilding a community spirit in this industrial village. The former home of Wissey Valley Brewery and Tony Hook beers, their ales can still be found on the bar. It is a great place to eat and well worth the diversion off the A134 for a meal or just an enjoyable pint of ale. ♨❀◑P

Strumpshaw

Shoulder of Mutton

Norwich Road, NR13 4NT
⏲ 11-11; 12-10.30 Sun
☎ (01603) 712274
Adnams Bitter, Broadside; Greene King IPA; guest beer 🄷
Traditional village pub, deservedly popular with locals and visitors alike. Noted for its fine quality ales and an extensive choice of home-prepared meals served in the restaurant (booking advisable), it hosts occasional themed evenings. No food is served Sunday evening, but kippers can be purchased to take home. The spacious public bar has pool, darts and crib, while in summer, petanque is played in the large garden. It is close to an RSPB reserve with a nature walk and the boating centre of Brundall. ❀◑⊟♣P

Swaffham

Lydney House Hotel

Norwich Road, PE37 7QS
⏲ 10.30-2.30, 7-10.30; closed Sun
☎ (01760) 723355
🌐 lydney-house.demon.co.uk
Woodforde's Wherry, Nelson's Revenge; guest beers 🄶
This small hotel continues its tradition of serving excellent ales straight from the barrel. The guest beers are usually local. The bar offers many traditional pub games that can be quite entertaining. A full menu is served as well as bar meals (no food Sun). The hotel is situated on the eastern side of Swaffham's beautiful medieval church. Look out, too, for the town's two giant wind turbines. ♨Q❀🛏◑♿🚌♣P

Swanton Morley

Darby's

142 Elsing Road, NR20 4NY
(off B1146, E end of village)
⏲ 11.30-3, 6-11; 11.30-11 Sat; 12-10.30 Sun
☎ (01362) 637647
Adnams Bitter, Broadside; Badger Tanglefoot; Theakston Mild; Woodforde's Wherry; guest beers 🄷
Darby's is a traditional rural pub replete with timber flooring, exposed beams, plain brick walls and rustic tables. The main bar boasts a large inglenook, while a side room has a well with a glass viewing window. Pictures of local historical interest, breweriana and old agricultural tools cover the walls. It offers one of the largest ranges of real ales of any Norfolk country pub, and good food is produced from local ingredients. The large garden has a children's play area. ♨❀◑▲P⚟

Terrington St John

Woolpack

Main Road, PE14 7RR
⏲ 11.30-2.30, 6.30-11; 12-3, 7-10.30 Sun
☎ (01945) 881097
Greene King IPA; Wells Eagle; guest beers 🄷
The Woolpack is dominated by the larger than life personality of the Aussie landlady, Lucille. A fan of modern art and an artist in her own right, her Art Deco style restaurant features specially commissioned tapestries. The good food served here naturally has an antipodean flavour – try the 'bird cake'. It is best to book for meals, particularly at weekends. Celebrating a birthday or other special event can be an unforgettable experience here. ♨❀◑🚌P

Thetford

Albion

93-95 Castle Street, IP24 2DN
⏲ 11-2.30 (3 Fri & Sat), 5 (6 Fri)-11; 12-3, 7-10.30 Sun
☎ (01842) 752796
Greene King IPA, Abbot 🄷
In a quiet area of town, the Albion forms part of a row of cottages, overlooking Castle Park, towards the ramparts of Castle Hill. This excellent, two-roomed pub has a cosy, relaxing ambience. The upper room is good for conversation, while the lower room has a pool table, darts and TV. There is an intimate patio for summer drinking. Parking can be difficult. ♨Q❀P

Thornham

Lifeboat

Ship Lane, PE36 6LT (signed off A149 coast road)
⏲ 11-11; 12-10.30 Sun
☎ (01485) 512236 🌐 lifeboatinn.co.uk
Adnams Bitter; Greene King IPA, Abbot; Woodforde's Wherry; guest beer 🄷
This 16th-century former smugglers' haunt is beautifully situated on the edge of the saltmarshes. The heavily beamed bar has been well preserved, and unchanged over many decades; dark and cosy, it is lit by hanging oil lanterns. Walkers, children and dogs are all made very welcome. The historic bar is complemented by an extensive restaurant, spacious conservatory and enclosed outdoor drinking area. Local seafood, including Brancaster mussels in season, is a speciality. The cider is Westons Old Rosie. ♨Q❀🛏◑🚌♣●P⚟

Trunch

Crown

Front Street, NR28 0AH (next to church)
⏲ 12-3 (3.30 Sat), 5.30-11; 12-3.30, 7-10.30 Sun
☎ (01263) 722341 🌐 trunchcrown.co.uk
Bateman Dark Mild, XB, XXXB; Greene King IPA; guest beers 🄷
Unusually, this is a Bateman's house – a rarity in Norfolk. It stocks the full range of the Lincolnshire brewers' ales, including the

mild, which is kept on gravity dispense at quiet times, as well as seasonal and guest beers. Check the website for details of the annual beer festival and other events. A small dining room, serving food from Wednesday-Sunday, caters in style for hungry visitors. ♔❀◐◑ ⛺P

Walcott

Lighthouse

Coast Road , NR12 0PE

⌚ 11-11 daily

☎ (01692) 650371 🌐 thelighthouseinn.co.uk

Greene King IPA; guest beers Ⓗ

Large, friendly, community-centred pub, on the Norfolk coast, where the regular clientele is augmented by visitors, particularly in summer. Meals are available all day until 10.30pm daily. Families are well catered for, with good facilities, but a quieter dining room is also provided. Other areas can be partitioned off and a large marquee, erected in summer, gives further accommodation. It hosts an annual firework spectacular in November, but the beer range may be restricted during the winter months. ♔♉❀◐◑⛺♣P

Warham All Saints

Three Horseshoes ☆

Bridge Street, NR23 1NL

⌚ 11.30-3, 6-11; 12-3, 6-10.30 Sun

☎ (01328) 710547

Greene King IPA; Ⓗ **Woodforde's Wherry;** Ⓖ **guest beer** Ⓗ

This early 18th-century flint pub, listed in CAMRA's National Inventory, is a rural gem. The three stone-floored rooms all contain old cast iron fireplaces and are adorned with old paintings, photos and other memorabilia. Particularly notable features are the game of Norfolk Twister, which dates back to 1830 and is an old form of roulette with a wheel set in the ceiling, a 1930s one-armed bandit and a grandfather clock. The pub serves delicious, home-cooked food and offers overnight accommodation. ♔Q❀⛟◐◑♿♣●P⍻

Watton

Breckland Wines

80 High Street, IP25 6AH

⌚ 9-9 daily

☎ (01953) 881592

Beer range varies Ⓖ

Brilliant, beer-friendly off-licence that offers local Iceni ales, alongside bottle-conditioned beers from numerous East Anglian micros, as well as breweries from all over the UK, Europe and even further afield. The owner has a knowledgeable staff who will guide you to some great beers – and children will love the choice of sweets. 🚌

Wells-next-the-Sea

Edinburgh

Station Road, NR23 1AE

⌚ 11-2.30, 7-11; 11-11 Sat (and summer Fri); 12-3, 7-10.30 Sun

☎ (01328) 710120

Draught Bass; Hancock's HB; guest beer Ⓗ

Spacious, Victorian pub on the main shopping street – but do not expect big High Street names, as this is a lovely old town that maintains its individuality. The pub is a rare outlet for Draught Bass, a tradition that remains from the days when Midlanders came to north Norfolk by train for their holidays. Just one bar, but the lounge has an area called Jack's Bar, and a restaurant at one end. Children are welcome away from the bar. ♔Q❀⛟◐◑⊟⛺🚌🍷

West Acre

Stag

Low Road, PE32 1TR

⌚ 12-2.30, 7(5 Fri, 6.30 Sat summer)-11; closed Mon; 12-2.30, 7-10.30 Sun

☎ (01760) 755395

Beer range varies Ⓗ

West Acre is famous for the summer theatre in the Priory ruins and the old chapel. However, close behind comes the village local, transformed over the last few years. There always seems to be something going on – maybe a hog roast, quiz night or a beer festival. Even on an ordinary day there will be at least three interesting beers to choose from, with increasingly adventurous selections. The food is good, too, at local CAMRA's Pub of the Year 2005. ♔❀◐◑♿♣P🍷

West Beckham

Wheatsheaf

Church Road, NR25 6NX (1 mile S of A148)

⌚ 11.30-3, 6.30-11; 12-3, 7-10.30 Sun

☎ (01263) 822110 🌐 wheatsheaf.org.uk

Greene King IPA; Woodforde's Wherry, Nelson's Revenge; guest beers Ⓗ

Situated on the top of the Holt-Cromer ridge behind Sheringham Woods, this building was a farmhouse until it was converted into a public house in the 1980s. Beers on sale here come mainly from local brewers, particularly Woodforde's. The main bar is supplemented by a games room down the corridor. Three self-catering cottages are available throughout the year within the grounds of the pub, which benefits from an extensive car park. ♔Q❀⛟◐◑⛺♣P

Weybourne

Ship

The Street, NR25 7SZ

⌚ 12-3, 6-11; closed Mon; 12-11 Sat; 12-4 Sun

☎ (01263) 588721 🌐 shipinnweybourne.co.uk

Beer range varies Ⓗ

Victorian brick and flint building that boasts Steward & Patteson Brewery windows and an impressive verandah. It stands opposite the church and priory ruins at the village centre. With its two bars, retaining timber floors and original features, plus a welcoming open fire, the pub is popular with walkers on the coastal path and visitors to the nearby military museum and steam railway. It hosts an Easter beer festival. The

food, from locally sourced produce, comes in generous portions (no food Sun).
⛫❀◐◗⊟♿▲⊟♣●P⚡

Wicklewood

Cherry Tree

116 High Street, NR18 9QA

⏲ 12-3, 6-11; 12-11 Wed & Sun; 12-midnight Fri & Sat

☎ (01953) 606962 ⊕ thecherrytreewicklewood.co.uk

Buffy's Bitter, Hopleaf, Norwegian Blue; guest beer Ⓗ

Single bar, village pub, with an unusual bar top. The drinking area contains some really comfy chairs and sofas and is divided by a central fireplace; the larger bare-boarded area is no-smoking. In the dining area, the evening menu (served Tue-Sat) includes a varied list of pies, including vegetarian and vegan options; real Norfolk ice cream is also on offer. The pub hosts monthly themed evenings. The guest beers are from Buffy's range. ❀◐◗P⚡

Winterton-on-Sea

Fisherman's Return

The Lane, NR29 4BN (off B1159)

⏲ 11.30-2.30, 6-11; 11.30-11 Sat; 12-10.30 Sun

☎ (01493) 393305 ⊕ fishermans-return.com

Adnams Bitter, Broadside; Greene King IPA; Woodforde's Wherry, Norfolk Nog; guest beers Ⓗ

This 17th-century brick and flint-faced pub at the heart of a charming Norfolk coastal village is just five minutes' walk from the beach. It serves a wide range of beers, mostly from local breweries, and home-cooked food is available at lunchtime and evening. It has a separate family/function room. Close to the Broads and the resort town of Great Yarmouth, the pub has three en-suite guest rooms.
⛫☕❀⊟◐◗⊟♣●P

Wiveton

Bell

Blakeney Road, NR25 7TL

(4 miles NW of Holt on B1156, opp. church)

⏲ 12-2.30, 6.30-11; closed winter Mon; 12-2.30 (closed eve) Sun

☎ (01263) 740101 ⊕ wivetonbell.co.uk

Woodforde's Wherry, Nelson's Revenge; guest beer (summer) Ⓗ

Archetypal country hostelry where brasses and beams abound. Overlooking the village church, with a large garden to the rear and benches at the front, this is an ideal spot for a meal and a pint – or a glass of wine as the list is as extensive as the menu. Pews, settles and olde-worlde tables and chairs lend an authentic rustic air. Originally the Bluebell, the building, now several hundred years old, has been sympathetically cared for over the years.
⛫❀◐◗♣P⚡

Woodbastwick

Fur & Feathers

Slad Lane, NR13 6HQ

⏲ 11.30-3, 6-11 (10.30 Mon); 12-10.30 Sun

☎ (01603) 720003

Woodforde's Mardlers, Wherry, Great Eastern, Nelson's Revenge, Norfolk Nog, Admiral's Reserve Ⓗ

Converted from three old cottages in the early 1990s and situated next to the brewery, this pub is effectively Woodforde's tap. It sells the entire range of its beers, plus a house ale that Woodforde's brews just for the pub. Fairly food-oriented, providing an extensive menu of home-cooked food, a new dining room has recently been added. Large, landscaped gardens and an ample car park add to the appeal. Q◐◗P

Wymondham

Feathers

13 Town Green, NR18 0PN

⏲ 11-2.30, 7-11; 11-midnight Fri & Sat; 12-midnight Sun

☎ (01953) 605675

Adnams Bitter; Greene King Abbot; Marston's Pedigree; guest beers Ⓗ

Interesting pub that bears unusual decor and offers various seating areas. This free house keeps the widest range of ales in town, plus a draught cider. It attracts a mixed clientele and the meals service does not dominate the pub. Monthly folk nights are held in the upstairs clubroom (last Sun). Elgood's supplies the house beer.
❀◐◗⊟♣●

Railway

Station Road, NR18 0JY (by station exit)

⏲ 11-11; 12-8 Sun (later in summer)

☎ (01953) 605262 ⊕ the railwaypub.com

Adnams Bitter; guest beers Ⓗ

As its name suggests, this imposing building stands next to the award-winning Wymondham Station, which is 15 minutes from Norwich on the Cambridge line and a short stroll from the historic market cross. Recently refurbished and revitalised, the pub consists of a spacious, comfortable bar with a dining area adjacent, leading to a lower bar. An extensive menu is supplemented by blackboard specials (booking advised at weekends). Meals are served all day Saturday from 12-9.30pm and until 6pm on Sunday.
⛫❀◐◗⇶⊟●P

Why America was founded

For we could not now take time for further search (to land our ship) our victuals being much spent especially our beer.

Log of the Mayflower

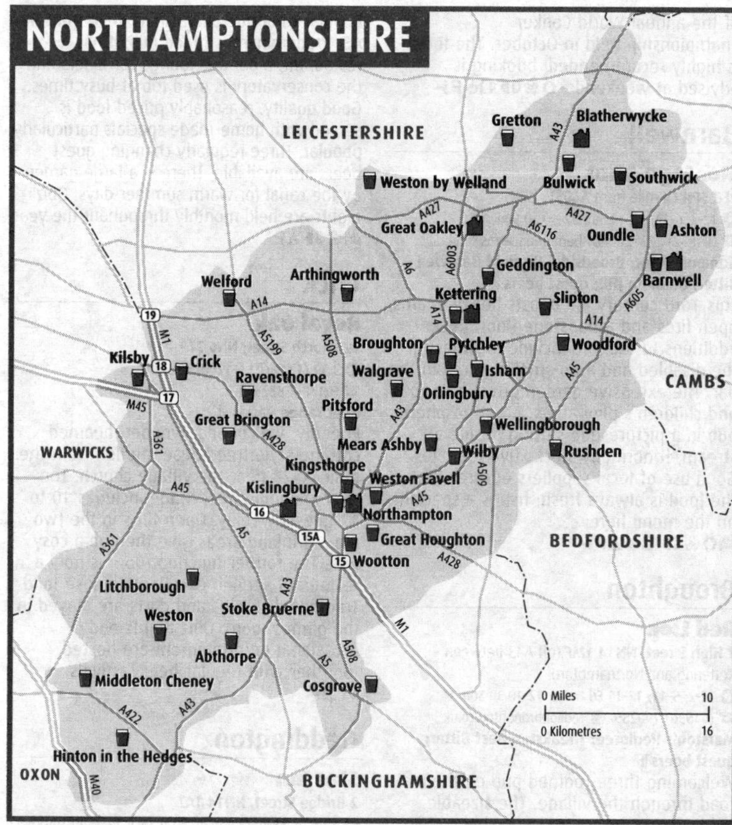

Abthorpe

New Inn

Silver Street, NN12 8QR (off A5/A43)
🕐 12-3, 5-11; 12-11 Fri & Sat; 12-3, 7-11 Sun
☎ (01327) 857306
Hook Norton Hooky Bitter, Old Hooky, seasonal beers H
Quiet, country pub, hidden in a cul-de-sac off a corner of the village green, providing the locals with a popular amenity. Built from mellow sandstone, the New Inn was once a thatched farmhouse, although it is now tiled. The comfortable interior has an inglenook in the bar area and a restaurant on a lower level in the Elton John snug. Hard to find but well worth the effort.
⛺Q❀◑♣P⚟

Arthingworth

Bull's Head

Kelmarsh Road, LE16 8JZ (off A508)
🕐 12-3, 6-11; 12-10.30 Sun
☎ (01858) 525637
Everards Tiger, Original; Wells Eagle; guest beers H
Large 19th-century village pub, converted from a former farmhouse. Threatened with closure, the Bull was taken over by enterprising owners who have turned it around. Recently refurbished, the L-shaped bar has log fires and secluded drinking areas. The dining room is separate from the main bar. With four excellent guest beers and the popular August bank holiday beer festival, it was a recent local CAMRA Pub of the Season award winner. There are eight en-suite rooms for overnight stops.
⛺Q❀⇌◑♿♣P⚟

Ashton

Chequered Skipper

The Green, PE8 5LD
🕐 11.30-3, 6-11; 11.30-11 Sat; 11.30-10.30 Sun
☎ (01832) 273494
Oakham JHB; guest beers H
Attractive, thatched pub in the heart of the Rothschild's model village of Ashton. A fire nine years ago meant that the whole of the interior had to be refurbished, and the pub now has a modern, clean appearance. Usually four real ales and Aspalls Suffolk cider are available all year round. The outside drinking area is the village green, scene

INDEPENDENT BREWERIES

Digfield Barnwell
Frog Island Northampton
Great Oakley Great Oakley
Hoggleys Kislingbury
Nobby's Kettering
Potbelly Kettering
Rockingham Blatherwycke

of the annual World Conker Championship held in October. The food is highly recommended; booking is advised at weekends. Q❀◐◑⊞♿P⊁

Barnwell

Montagu Arms

PE8 5PH (¼ mile from A605)

✪ 12-3, 6-11; 12-11 Sat; 12-10.30 Sun

☎ (01832) 273726 ⊕ themontaguarms.co.uk

Adnams Bitter, Broadside; Digfield Barnwell Bitter; Oakham JHB; guest beers Ⓗ

This 16th-century inn boasts heavy beams, open fires and a flagstone floor. Recent additions to the pub include facilities for the disabled and a no-smoking area in the bar. The extensive garden offers petanque and children's play areas. An atmospheric pub in a picturesque setting beside a stream, it normally stocks five real ales. Good use of local suppliers ensures that the food is always fresh; fish is a speciality on the menu here.
⛫Q❀◐◑⊞♿⅄P⊁

Broughton

Red Lion

7 High Street, NN14 1MF (off A43 between Kettering and Northampton)

✪ 12-2, 5-11; 12-11 Fri & Sat; 12-10.30 Sun

☎ (01536) 790239 ⊕ redlionbroughton.co.uk

Marston's Pedigree; Theakston Best Bitter; guest beers Ⓗ

Welcoming three-roomed pub on the main road through the village. The sizeable public bar serves up to six real ales, two from local brewers. Northants skittles is played in the games room. For good food, try the restaurant on the other side of the pub. With friendly staff and locals, this is well worth a visit.
Q❀◐◑⊞♿♣P⊓

Bulwick

Queen's Head

Main Street, NN17 3DY (½ mile off A43)

✪ 12-3, 6-11 (closed Mon); 12-4.30, 7-10.30 Sun

☎ (01780) 450272

Shepherd Neame Spitfire; guest beers Ⓗ

Situated in the centre of the village opposite the church, the pub has a public bar and three restaurant areas. The bar has stone walls, low painted beams and a flagstone floor, complemented by a wood-burning stove. The five handpumps always provide beers from micro-breweries such as Newby Wyke and Church End. A high quality, traditional English menu is available, with game often appearing on the specials board (no eve meals Sun).
⛫Q❀◐◑⊞♿♣

Cosgrove

Navigation Inn

Thrupp Wharf, MK19 7BE (off A508 Castlethorpe road)

✪ 12-3, 5.30-11; 12-11 Sat; 12-11.30 Sun

☎ (01908) 543156

Greene King IPA; guest beers Ⓗ

Popular canalside pub a short drive from the A5. Predominantly a food pub, it has a restaurant, a bar and lounge for diners and the conservatory is used too at busy times. Good quality, reasonably priced food is served with home-made specials particularly popular. Three regularly changing guest beers are available. There is a large garden by the canal for warm summer days. Quiz nights are held monthly throughout the year.
⛫❀◐◑⅄P

Crick

Royal Oak

22 Church Street, NN6 7TP

✪ 3.30 (12 Sat)-11; 12-10.30 Sun

☎ (01788) 822340

Beer range varies Ⓗ

Friendly, welcoming, wooden-beamed cottage-style free house, hidden from the main A428 near the village church. The ever-changing beer range includes 10 to 12 guests weekly. Open fires in the two main drinking areas give the pub a cosy feel. The former function room is now a restaurant serving excellent Chinese food. Traditional skittles and darts are played in the games room. Quiz nights and occasional entertainment are hosted, together with regular beer festivals.
⛫❀♣

Geddington

Star Inn

2 Bridge Street, NN14 1AZ

✪ 12-3, 6-11.30 (12.30am Fri & Sat); 12-7 (11 summer) Sun

☎ (01536) 742386 ⊕ star-inn-geddington.com

Greene King IPA; guest beers Ⓗ

Stone-built pub opposite what is considered to be the finest of the surviving Eleanor Crosses, built by Edward I in 1295 to mark the nightly resting place of Queen Eleanor's coffin on her last journey from Nottingham to London. The Star has a three-sided bar with a wood-panelled snug with comfy settees, lounge and dining room. Upstairs is a pool room. The pub is popular for its good food and guest ales which always include a local brew. ⛫❀◐◑⊞♿♣P⊁

Great Brington

Althorp Coaching Inn (Fox & Hounds)

Main Street, NN7 4EW (2 miles W of A428)

✪ 11-11 (11.45 Fri & Sat); 12-10.30 Sun

☎ (01604) 770651

Fuller's Discovery, London Pride; Greene King IPA, Abbot; Potbelly Redwing; guest beers Ⓗ

Olde-worlde pub particularly popular in the summer due to its proximity to Althorp House, the former home of Princess Diana. The listed stone building with a thatched roof and oak beams has flagstone floors and a huge inglenook. Outside is an enclosed courtyard and floral garden which are delightful in summer. The adventurous menu is served lunchtime and evening in both

the bar and cellar restaurant. Up to five guest beers are available.
⛫Q✿◐◑P⚟

Great Houghton

White Hart

39 High Street, NN4 7AF (off A428)
✪ 12-3, 5 (6 Sat)-11; 12-4, 7-10.30 Sun
☎ (01604) 762940
Everards Tiger, Original; Greene King IPA; guest beers [H]
Attractive stone-built thatched village pub on the outskirts of Northampton. Its exposed walls, beams and low ceilings create a cosy, intimate atmosphere. Good, reasonably priced food is served daily in three dining and drinking areas. To the rear is an attractive garden for warmer days. Several local clubs meet here. Q✿◐◑⊟P⚟

Gretton

Hatton Arms

Arnhill Road, NN17 3DN (off A6003)
✪ 12-2, 5 (6 Sat)-11; 12-10.30 Sun
☎ (01536) 770268 ⊕ thehattonarms.co.uk
Marston's Pedigree; Greene King IPA; guest beers [H]
Traditional thatched country pub and restaurant, parts of which date back to the 14th century, hidden away in the village overlooking the Welland Valley. The no-smoking lounge always serves a guest ale from a local micro. Good food is available in the restaurant with regular themed nights throughout the year. The pub participates in the annual Welland Valley beer festival in June. ⛫Q✿◐◑⊟♿P⚟

Hinton in the Hedges

Crewe Arms

Sparrow Corner, NN13 5NF (off A43/A422)
✪ 6-11; 12-10.30 Sun
☎ (01280) 705801 ⊕ thecrewearms.com
Hook Norton Hooky Bitter, Old Hooky; guest beers [H]
Stone-built genuine free house tucked away down a lane in a village that can be hard to find. It has been recently refurbished after a two year closure and uncertain future. Fortunately two locals bought the pub to maintain a central village amenity. With several rooms and many nooks and crannies, it is often described as a Tardis. Dining is popular here but the pub maintains a cosy bar area. Guest beers are from micro-breweries and change weekly. ⛫✿◑♿P

Isham

Lilacs

39 Church Street, NN14 1HD (off A509)
✪ 12-3, 5.30-1am (1.30am Fri & Sat); 12-4, 8-12.30am Sun
☎ (01536) 723948
Greene King IPA, Ruddles Best Bitter, Abbot; guest beers [H]
Three-roomed 17th-century local inn, right at the heart of the community. The pub's name refers to a breed of rabbit, pictured on the sign outside. It has a busy bay-fronted lounge, cosy snug and a large games room. Popular with all ages, it is home to various car clubs and other events are held here throughout the year. Guest beers are from the Greene King list. ⛫♉✿◐⊟♣P

Kettering

Alexandra Arms

39 Victoria Street, NN16 0BU
✪ 2-11; 12-midnight Fri & Sat; 12-11 Sun
☎ (01536) 522730
Marston's Burton Bitter; guest beers [H]
Back street pub that goes from strength to strength, now with Nobby's Brewery in the cellar and a Nobby's beer always available. With a constantly changing beer range, over 2,000 different ales have been served through the 10 handpumps in just three years. There is a smoke-free bar and lounge at the front and a larger back bar with Sky TV, darts and Northants skittles. The bar is full of brewery memorabilia and pump clips decorate the ceiling. Winner of local CAMRA Pub of the Year 2005, this is a pub not to be missed. ✿⇄⊟⇌♣⚟

Piper

Windmill Avenue, NN15 6PS (opp. Wicksteed Park)
✪ 11-3, 6-11; 12-10.30 Sun
☎ (01536) 513870
Hook Norton Old Hooky; Oakham White Dwarf; Theakston Best Bitter; guest beers [H]
Excellent 1950s two-roomed pub serving a good range of beers from the Enterprise Inns list, with six changing guests described in detail on the chalkboard. These are complemented with a real cider and a good choice of fruit wines. The quiet lounge has a no-smoking policy. The bar/games room is more lively with pool and Sky TV. Two beer festivals are held a year. On Sunday evening there is a quiz. Q✿◐◑⊟♿♣●P⚟

Sawyers

44 Montague Street, NN16 8RU
✪ 1 (12 Fri & Sat)-11; 1-11 Sun
☎ (01536) 484800 ⊕ sawyersvenue.co.uk
Oakham JHB; Shepherd Neame Spitfire; [H] **guest beers** [H]/[G]
Town centre pub that has recently become a major music venue. It hosts regular alternative music nights from Tuesday to Sunday featuring jam sessions, jazz, blues, acoustic, rock and metal bands. The pub acts as the tap for the local award-winning Potbelly Brewery, with two ales always available plus additional pins on gravity on band nights. A Newby Wyke brew is also stocked. ✿♿⇌P

Kilsby

George

Watling Street, CV23 8YE (at A361/A5 jct)
✪ 11.30-3 (not Mon), 5.30 (6 Sat)-11; 12-5, 7.30-11 Sun
☎ (01788) 822229
Fuller's London Pride; Greene King IPA, Abbot; guest beers [H]
The George, now with new signage reflecting the village's connection with George Stephenson and the railway, is a fine country local. A wood panelled lounge and

refurbished dining room are joined by a rear bar which can be used for private functions. Close to the A5 and junction 18 of the M1, it is an excellent place to stop off for great beer and food. No food is served on Sunday evening. Q❀⇌◑◗⊟♣P

Kingsthorpe

Queen Adelaide

50 Manor Road, NN2 6QJ

11.30-3, 5.30-11; 11.30-11 Fri & Sat; 12-10.30 Sun

☎ (01604) 714524 🌐 queenadelaide.com

Adnams Bitter, Broadside; Greene King IPA; guest beers [H]

Kingsthorpe is a traditional English village mentioned in the Domesday Book but now part of Northampton. Situated up a small hill just beyond the village green, this pretty, white-painted, listed pub has an ironstone frontage. Inside, the split-level front bar has Northants skittles in the lower room, while the upper room has a homely wooden snug area. The rear lounge/dining area leads to a pleasant back garden. The landlord has increased the number and variety of guest beers and introduced Old Rosie cider. Runner up local CAMRA Pub of the Year 2005.

❀◑⊟♿♣●

Litchborough

Old Red Lion

4 Banbury Road, NN12 8JF

11.30-2.30 (3 Sat & Sun), 6.30-11

☎ (01327) 830250

Banks's Bitter; Marston's Pedigree; guest beer [H]

Cosy, compact stone village pub with possibly the longest serving landlord in the county. Totally unspoilt, it has flagstone floors, wooden beams and a huge inglenook. A small passage leads to a pool room on one side and Northants skittles on the other. The pub fields a number of games teams. The raised garden is popular with families in summer. The only amenity in the village, the pub is busy with locals, walkers and cyclists. The guest beer is from Banks's monthly list.

⌂Q☎❀♿♣P⊓

Mears Ashby

Griffins Head

28 Wilby Road, NN6 0DX

11.30-midnight (1am Fri-Sun)

☎ (01604) 812945

Adnams Bitter; Greene King IPA; Young's Bitter; guest beers [H]

Stone-built village pub in the heart of the community. Warm and welcoming, it has a comfortable lounge with a log fire, a back bar and a small dining area serving good quality food. The central U-shaped bar offers three changing guest ales. ⌂Q◑◗⊟♿P

Middleton Cheney

New Inn

45 Main Road, OX17 2ND

12-3, 7-midnight; 12-midnight Sat; 12-11 Sun

☎ (01295) 710399 🌐 newinn.tablesir.co.uk

Adnams Broadside; Fuller's London Pride; Hook Norton Hooky Bitter; Wadworth 6X; guest beers [H]

Built in the 17th century, this traditional stone pub is on the main road through the village. Inside there is a long open bar and a dining room to the side. The local Oxfordshire game of Aunt Sally is played in the extensive garden. The pub holds an annual beer festival at the end of July.

⌂Q❀◑◗♣P⊬

Northampton

Lamplighter

66 Overstone Road, NN1 3JS

5-11; 12-midnight Sat; 12-6 Sun

☎ (01604) 631125

Beer range varies [H]

This Victorian corner-terraced pub is gaining a good reputation by word of mouth for its real ale, pub grub and welcoming atmosphere. Inside, the walls have been knocked through but the remaining arches create different comfortable seating areas. Four handpumps dispense a changing range of beers from micros and regionals. Popular quiz nights are held on Wednesday and Friday. Lunches are served Saturday and Sunday, evening meals Monday to Friday.

⌂❀◑◗♣

Malt Shovel Tavern

121 Bridge Street, NN1 1QF (opp. Carlsberg factory)

11.30-3, 5-11; 12-3, 7-10.30 Sun

☎ (01604) 234212 🌐 maltshoveltavern.com

Frog Island Natterjack; Fuller's London Pride; Tetley Bitter; guest beers [H]

Award-winning free house full of brewery memorabilia reflecting Northampton's brewing heritage. The Shovel is the tap for the Great Oakley Brewery, with up to four of its beers available. With up to 11 cask beers regularly stocked, as well as a selection of English country wines and malt whiskies, this is a discerning drinkers' paradise. Blues bands perform on Wednesday evening and there is a popular quiz once a month. CAMRA Regional Pub of the Year in 2004.

Q❀◑♿⇌🚌●

Racehorse

15 Abington Square, NN1 4AE

12-midnight daily

☎ (01604) 631997

Beer range varies [H]

Lively town centre pub with a varied beer range and eclectic clientele – a great place to escape from shopping. Seven rotating guest beers often include ales from Hampshire breweries. The pub is divided into two and has a large back room for live bands and other functions. Regular barbecues are held in the large rear garden in summer. Children are not allowed in the pub but are welcome in the garden. ❀🚌♣●P

Romany

Trinity Avenue, NN2 6JN (½ mile E of Kingsthorpe Village)

11.30-11.30; 12-11 Sun

☎ (01604) 714647

Fuller's London Pride; Newby Wyke Bear Island; Oakham JHB; Theakston Best Bitter; guest beers [H]

This 1930s roadhouse-style pub offers up to 12 beers, real cider and perry, as well as a selection of bottled beers. The two-room pub hosts live bands and sporting events, fielding local teams. The landlord offers a discount to CAMRA members on Tuesday and Wednesday evening. Off the beaten track but well worth a visit. ✿◖⊟⊞♣●P

Victoria Inn

2 Poole Street, NN1 3EX

⊙ 4 (12 Sat)-11; 12-10.30 Sun

☎ (01604) 633660

Beer range varies Ⓗ

Comfortable corner-terraced, back-street local close to the racecourse and handy for the Balloon Festival in August. With four handpumps, one usually serves a Vale Brewery ale and the others changing guest beers. Northants skittles and pool are played here. The pub is busy on most evenings with a music quiz on Tuesday, general knowledge quiz on Wednesday evening and live music on Friday. ♣

White Elephant

Kingsley Park Terrace, NN2 7HG (N side of racecourse)

⊙ 11-11; 12-10.30 Sun

☎ (01604) 711202

Beer range varies Ⓗ

Recently modernised, the pub is named the White Elephant because of the nearby racecourse which closed down 100 years ago. A mixed clientele includes students from the local university. A quiz night is held on Tuesday and live music played every other Thursday. The games area has pool tables. Five guest beers are rotated. ✿◖◗♿

Orlingbury

Queen's Arms

11 Isham Road, NN14 1JD (off A43, S of Kettering)

⊙ 11-2.30, 5.30 (5 Sat)-11; 12-3, 6-10.30 Sun

☎ (01933) 678258

Adnams Bitter; Caledonian Deuchars IPA; Fuller's London Pride; Taylor Landlord; Tetley Bitter Ⓗ

Fine inn just around the corner from the village green. The pub dates back to about 1750 and was originally called the King's Arms but changed its name in 1840 for the coronation of Queen Victoria. The central lounge has three distinct areas plus a no-smoking snug and dining room. The large garden has children's play equipment. Up to three guest beers are available. No food is served on Sunday evening. ✿◖◗P⊬

Oundle

Ship Inn

18 West Street, PE8 4EF

⊙ 11-midnight; 12-11 Sun

☎ (01832) 273918 ⊕ theshipinn-oundle.co.uk

Oakham JHB; Theakston XB; guest beers Ⓗ

Grade II listed building in the main street, 100 yards from the town centre. The pub is reputedly haunted by a previous landlord who threw himself from an upstairs window. The Ship is divided into several drinking areas, creating a homely and cosy atmosphere. It is often busy with live jazz on the last Sunday of the month, quiz night on Tuesday, jam sessions on most Wednesdays and discos on Friday and Saturday. ⛫Q✿⛺◖◗⊟♿⊞♣●P

Pitsford

Griffin Inn

25 High Street, NN6 9AD (off A508)

⊙ 12-2.30 (not Mon), 5.30 (6 Sat)-11; 12-2.30, 7-11 Sun

☎ (01604) 880346

Fuller's London Pride; Greene King IPA, Abbot; Young's Bitter Ⓗ

Ironstone village pub dating from the 18th century close to the Pitsford Reservoir country park. It has two traditional bar areas, one no-smoking. The lounge leads to a restaurant at the rear where excellent home-cooked food is served from a varied menu (booking advisable). The Sunday evening quiz is very popular. Q✿◖◗⊟P⊬

Pytchley

Overstone Arms

Stringers Hill, NN14 1EU (off A43/A14)

⊙ 11-2.30, 6.30-11; 12-2.30, 6.30-10.30 Sun

☎ (01536) 790215

Adnams Bitter; Marston's Pedigree; guest beers Ⓗ

Large stone village pub with a small bar and no-smoking restaurant. The bar has a real fire and pictures of hunting scenes on the walls. The popular restaurant serves excellent food and booking is advisable. The extensive gardens are a welcome attraction in summer. Two guest beers are stocked, one changes weekly and the other monthly. ⛫Q✿◖◗P

Ravensthorpe

Chequers

Chequers Lane, NN6 8ER (off A428)

⊙ 12-3, 6-11; 12-11 Sat; 12-3, 7-10.30 Sun

☎ (01604) 770379

Fuller's London Pride; Greene King IPA; Jennings Bitter; guest beers Ⓗ

The Chequers started life as a farmhouse in a rural village among rolling countryside and close to three reservoirs. This Grade II listed building features an L-shaped bar and a dining room to the rear where good value food is served (eve meals Tue-Sat). Quiz nights are held and crib and darts are played. Across the yard is a games room housing Northants skittles and a pool table. Two guest beers are always available. ⛵✿◖◗♣P

Rushden

Rushden Historical Transport Society

Station Approach, NN10 0AW (off inner ring road)

⊙ 12-3 (not Mon-Fri), 7.30-11; 12-3, 7-10.30 Sun

☎ (01933) 318988 ⊕ rhts.co.uk

Fuller's London Pride; guest beers Ⓗ

Rushden Station was a victim of branch line cutbacks before it had a chance to succumb to 20th-century progress. Consequently the local transport society acquired a well-preserved relic of the old LMS railway, complete with gas lighting. What was the ladies' waiting room is now the club bar and the station platform is an outdoor drinking area. Recent improvements include converting one end of a coach into a Northants skittles room and the other to a no-smoking lounge. The friendly welcome and good range of well-kept beers from micros have earned regular CAMRA awards. Day membership is £1. ⌂Q❀♣⊬▯

Slipton

Samuel Pepys

Slipton Lane, NN14 3AR (off A6116)
⊙ 12-3, 6-11; 12-11 Sat; 12-10.30 Sun
☎ (01832) 731739 ⊕ thesamuelpepys.net
Greene King IPA; Oakham JHB; Potbelly Aisling; guest beers Ⓗ
Excellent country pub and restaurant on the outskirts of the tiny village of Slipton. Formerly the Red Cow, this stone building dates back to the 1600s. There are two drinking areas, one a traditional public bar, the other a popular lounge for drinkers and diners. The conservatory restaurant serves fine cuisine and booking is advisable. There is a large garden for drinking and dining in summer. Three guest ales are dispensed on gravity all year round. ⌂❀◐◑⊟P

Southwick

Shuckburgh Arms

Main Street, PE8 5BL
⊙ 12-2 (not Mon & Tue), 6-11; 12-10.30 Sun
☎ (01832) 274007
Fuller's London Pride; Oakham JHB; guest beer Ⓗ
Located at the centre of the village next to the village hall, this pub has two rooms, one with a large real fire. The spacious, enclosed garden at the rear is adjacent to the village cricket pitch. Traditional home-cooked food is popular and well priced. Up to three beers are available throughout the year.
⌂Q❀◐◑♿⊟⛺P

Stoke Bruerne

Boat Inn

Shutlanger Road, NN12 7SB (opp. Canal Museum)
⊙ 11-3, 6-11; 11-11 Fri, Sat & summer; 12-10.30 Sun
☎ (01604) 862428 ⊕ boatinn.co.uk
Marston's Burton Bitter, Pedigree, Old Empire; guest beers (summer) Ⓗ
Popular thatched canalside pub with many drinking and dining areas. The Rose & Castle morris dancers are a regular sight on the dockside in good weather. Northants skittles is played here. In summer the pub runs its own canal trips. Children are welcome in the bistro and lounge. ⌂Q⊟♣P

Walgrave

Royal Oak

Zion Hill, NN6 9PN (2 miles off A43)
⊙ 12-3, 5.30-11; 12-10.30 Sun
☎ (01604) 781248
Adnams Bitter; Greene King Abbot; guest beers Ⓗ
This big old ironstone building has been a pub since 1840. The front bar has three distinct areas and the small, comfortable lounge has a dining area to the rear. There are usually three guest ales, plus an extensive menu with reasonable prices. Across the yard is a games room where Northants skittles is played. The garden has a children's play area. ⌂Q❀◐◑♣P

Welford

Wharf Inn

NN6 6JQ (on A5199 N of village)
⊙ 12-midnight daily
☎ (01858) 575075 ⊕ wharfinn.co.uk
Banks's Bitter; Marston's Pedigree; guest beers Ⓗ
Formerly the George Inn, this new entry to the Guide was built to provide accommodation for travellers following the opening of the Welford arm of the Grand Junction Canal. Today this popular brick inn has a main bar and an extensive dining area. Its landscaped, enclosed garden provides the ideal starting point for five historic walks – a guide to these is available in the pub. Three rotating guest beers often include one from a local micro-brewery. ⌂Q❀🛏◐◑⊟♿P⊬

Wellingborough

Locomotive

111 Finedon Road, NN8 4AL (on A510 next to industrial estate)
⊙ 11-11; 12-3, 7-10.30 Sun
☎ (01933) 276600
Theakston Black Bull Bitter; guest beers Ⓗ
Within three years the hard-working management have turned what was once a run down local into a thriving community free house catering for real ale drinkers and traditional pub games players. The pub has three rooms – a lounge with railway art and a real fire, a games room with Northants skittles and pool and a cosy public bar (note the working train set above the bar). Three or four changing guest beers come from micros and regionals. Quiz night is the last Friday of the month. Lunches are served Monday to Friday. ⌂Q❀◐⊟♣P

Old Grammarians Association

46 Oxford Street, NN8 4JH (off one-way system)
⊙ 11-3, 7-11; 12-11 Fri & Sat; 12-10.30 Sun
☎ (01933) 226188
Greene King IPA; Hook Norton Hooky Bitter, Old Hooky; guest beers Ⓗ
Close to the town centre, this sports and social club is friendly and welcoming. The spacious main bar is next to a smaller lounge plus a function/games room. Access is from the large rear car park with a stairlift for wheelchair users. Four changing micro-brewery beers are usually available. The club hosts an annual beer festival in association with the local chamber of commerce.
☋◐◑♿♣P

Weston

Crown

2 Helmdon Road, NN12 8PX
⊙ 12-3 (not Mon & Tue), 6-11; 12-3, 6-11 Sun
☎ (01295) 760310
Black Sheep Best Bitter; Greene King IPA; Hook Norton Hooky Bitter; guest beer Ⓗ

Large 16th-century locals' pub at the heart of this rural village. Formerly a farmhouse, it has stone-flagged floors, oak beams and open fires. Inside are three bars and a family restaurant serving good food. A function room is available for local clubs and special events. Dogs are welcome here. ⌂❀◗⊟♣

Weston by Welland

Wheel & Compass

Valley Road, LE16 8HZ (off B664)

✪ 12-3, 6-11; 12-10.30 Sun

☎ (01858) 565864

Banks's Bitter; Greene King Abbot; Marston's Burton Bitter, Pedigree; guest beer Ⓗ

Multi-roomed pub in a rural location, popular with locals and visitors. A separate restaurant area has been built recently to increase space in the bar. Good value food from an extensive menu is served all day. The large rear garden attracts families in summer with benches and seats plus swings and slides for children. The pub participates in the Welland Valley Beer Festival held in June. ⌂Q❀◖◗P

Weston Favell

Bold Dragoon

48 High Street, NN3 3JW (off A4500)

✪ 11-3, 5.30-11; 11-11 Fri & Sat; 12-10.30 Sun

☎ (01604) 401221

Fuller's London Pride; Greene King IPA, Abbot; guest beers Ⓗ

Thirties pub hidden away down the High Street of a village that has been swallowed up by Northampton. Owned by Churchill Taverns, it has maintained its reputation as a real ale pub, with four regular and four changing guest beers. The house beer is Churchill's Pride, brewed by Highgate. It is also popular as a food pub with the conservatory doubling as a restaurant. The central serving area divides the public bar and pool table at the front from the split-level lounge, conservatory and garden at the rear. Q❀◖◗⊟♿♣P

Wilby

George Inn

117 Main Road, NN8 2UB (on A4500)

✪ 12-11; 12-10.30 Sun

☎ (01933) 222902

Bateman XB; Courage Best Bitter; guest beers Ⓗ

Stone-built pub in a village situated close to the former A45 that is now almost a part of Wellingborough. Inside is a cosy lounge with an open fire. To the rear is a dining area, as well as the garden and children's play area with views of the Nene Valley. A popular music venue, live music is played on Thursday, Friday and Sunday evenings. Up to three guest beers are available, mainly from micros. Food is served on Tuesday, Wednesday and Saturday evenings. ⌂❀◖◗♣P

Woodford

Duke's Arms

83 High Street, NN14 4HE (off A14)

✪ 12-11 (10.30 Sun)

☎ (01832) 732224 🌐 dukesarms.co.uk

Greene King IPA, Abbot; guest beers Ⓗ/Ⓖ

Now with new owners, the pub makes a welcome return to the Guide. The bar has been carefully refurbished and plasterwork removed to reveal the original stone wall interior. Two rooms have been opened out to enlarge the bar and the former lounge is now the dining room. Overlooking the green, the pub was once called the Lords Arms then renamed in honour of the Duke of Wellington who was a regular visitor to the village. To the rear is a games room with Northants skittles, pool and darts. Guest beers are often from Church End and Oakham. No food is served on Sunday evening. ⌂♉❀◖◗⊟♿♣●P

Wootton

Wootton Working Men's Club

High Street, NN4 6LW (near M1 jct 15, off A508 towards Northampton)

✪ 12-2 (3 Sat; not Thu), 7 (4.30 Fri)-11 (11.30 Fri); 12-10.30 Sun

☎ (01604) 761863

Great Oakley Wot's Occurring; guest beers Ⓗ

The ironstone exterior is evidence that this club was once a pub, the Red Lion, which was rescued from closure to become what is now a premium outlet for real ale. The club has a bar, a quiet lounge, concert room and a games room featuring Northants skittles. A previous local CAMRA Club of the Year, it has featured in the Guide for many years. Up to five changing guest beers are stocked. Show this Guide or CAMRA membership card for admittance. Q♉♣P⚟

Sorry, Dobbin

When I conducted a beer-rating session last year, I wrote that most American beers taste as if they were brewed through a horse. This offended many people in the American beer industry, as well as patriots who thought I was being subversive in praising foreign beers. Now I must apologise. I have just read a little-known study of American beers. So I must apologise to the horse.

Mike Royko

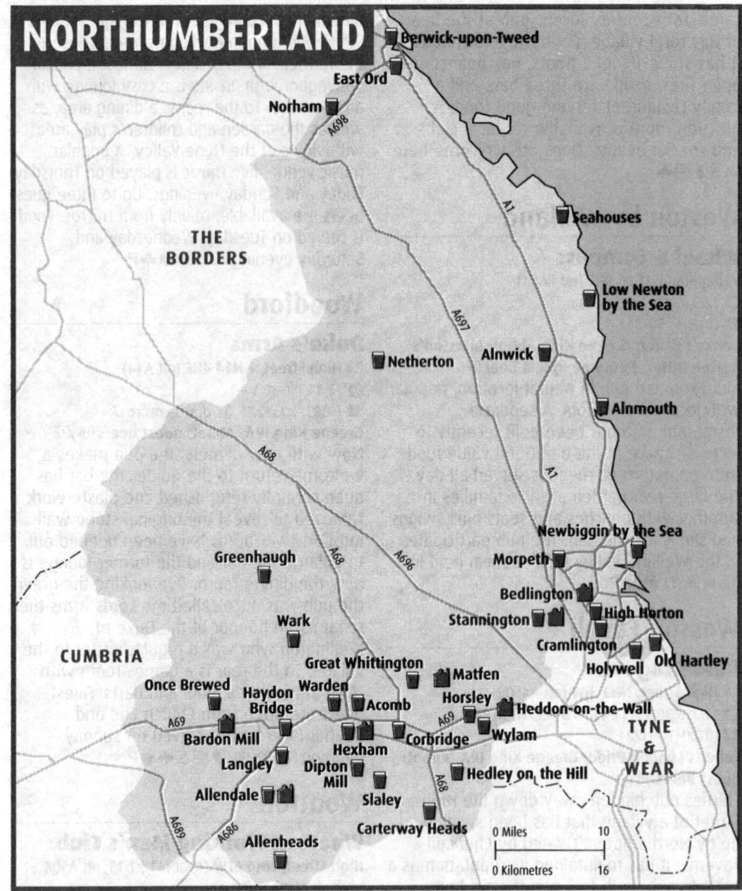

Acomb

Miners Arms

Main Street, NE46 4PW

12-2.30, 5-midnight; 12-midnight Fri-Sun

(01434) 603909 theminersacomb.com

Black Sheep Best Bitter; Yates Bitter; guest beers H

The pub's name is a reminder of the once prominent mining industry in this area. An unusual central staircase divides the pub into two drinking areas: a small cosy bar and a comfortable lounge with a real fire. Four real ales are always on handpump. The dining room is to the rear.

(880, 882)

Allendale

Golden Lion

Market Place, NE47 9BD

12-1am (2am Fri-Sun)

(01434) 683225

Draught Bass; Black Sheep Best Bitter; Wylam Gold Tankard; guest beer H

Large, 18th-century pub in the main square catering for a mix of locals, cyclists, ramblers and tourists attracted to this area of outstanding natural beauty. The bar hosts live Irish music on the last Thursday of the month and the local choir practises here on a Tuesday night. On the walls are pictures of the local tar barrel procession – the tar barrel committee meets at the pub.

(688)

Allenheads

Allenheads Inn

NE47 9HJ

12-4, 7-11; 12-11 Fri & Sat; 12-10.30 Sun

(01434) 685200 theallenheadsinn.co.uk

Black Sheep Best Bitter; Greene King Abbot; guest beers H

Built in the 18th century as the family home of Sir Thomas Wentworth, the inn is now the social heart of a village claiming to be the highest in England. It features an extensive, eclectic assembly of memorabilia, antiques and equipment throughout its many rooms – public bar, games, lounge and dining. The

INDEPENDENT BREWERIES

Allendale Allendale
Barefoot Stannington
Hexhamshire Hexham
High House Matfen
Northumberland Bedlington
Redburn Bardon Mill
Wylam Heddon on the Wall

bar attracts hikers, walkers and cyclists on the Coast-to-Coast cycle route that passes nearby. ⛫❀◐🚌(688)♣P

Alnmouth

Red Lion Inn

22 Northumberland Street, NE66 2RT

⏲ 12-3, 6-11 (closed winter Mon); 12-11 Sat; 12-10.30 Sun

☎ (01665) 830584

Black Sheep Best Bitter; guest beers Ⓗ

Former 18th-century coaching inn with a cosy, wood-panelled lounge bar. The dining room has two red lions in the windows. Note the unusual murals in the gents' featuring Northumbrian castles. Raised decking in the garden provides marvellous views across the River Aln estuary. The pub is handy for the town golf course and some of the best sandy beaches in the county. No-smoking throughout, dogs are welcome. ⛫❀🛏◐🚌(518)♣P

Alnwick

John Bull Inn

12 Howick Street, NE66 1UY

⏲ 7-11; 12-3, 7-11 Sat; 12-3, 7-10.30 Sun

☎ (01665) 602055 🌐 john-bull-inn.co.uk

Beer range varies Ⓗ

Self-styled as a 'back street boozer', the inn was purpose-built in 1832, possibly as the Alnwick Brewery tap. As well as offering a wide range of quality real ales, often from local micro-breweries, it also stocks over 100 malt whiskies and a large selection of Belgian bottled beers. There are no gaming machines, electronic music or juke box, but it does have a board games corner for 'big kids' including Triominoes (three-sided dominoes). The pub holds a leek show and annual beer festival to coincide with the Alnwick Fair. Q❀♣

Tanners Arms

Hotspur Place, NE66 1QF

⏲ 12-3 (not winter), 5-midnight (12.30am Fri); 12-12.30am Sat; 12-midnight Sun

☎ (01665) 602553

Beer range varies Ⓖ/Ⓗ

Stone built, ivy clad pub in a residential area just off Bondgate Without. Its bare walled single room interior has flagstone floors, bench seating and a popular juke box. Five handpumps dispense a range of beers, showcasing regional micro-breweries; three more ales on gravity appear in summer. The pub hosts the annual Alnwick Strongman competition and occasional beer festivals. It is handy for visiting Hotspur Tower and not far from the entrance to Alnwick Gardens. 🚌

Berwick-upon-Tweed

Foxtons

26 Hide Hill, TD15 1AB

⏲ 10-11 (closed Sun)

☎ (01289) 303939

Caledonian Deuchars IPA, 80/- Ⓗ

An unusual regular in the Guide, Foxtons is more like a busy coffee shop than a pub in appearance and style. However, among the wine and food, this enterprising establishment, particularly noted for its scones and shortbread, also serves real ale. Non-diners are more than welcome. Handily situated for the Maltings Art Centre to the rear, it is a short stroll from the extensive Elizabethan town walls and the River Tweed with its famous swans. ❀◐⇌🚌

Pilot

31 Low Greens, TD15 1LX

⏲ 12-midnight (10.30 Sun)

☎ (01289) 304214

Beer range varies Ⓗ

Stone-built terraced local dating back to the 19th century – note the 1916 photograph inside. A central drinking passageway with an attractive mosaic floor and service hatch leads to three further rooms. The wood-panelled public bar features various brass nautical artefacts, old wooden beams and an open coal fire. It sells two beers, often from north-eastern micros. The pub regularly hosts a wide variety of musical evenings and runs darts and quoits teams. ⛫🛏◐🀫⇌🚌

Carterway Heads

Manor House Inn

DH8 9LX (on A68 S of Corbridge)

⏲ 12-3, 6-11; 12-3, 6-10.30 Sun

☎ (01207) 255268

Courage Directors; Greene King Old Speckled Hen; Theakston Best Bitter; Wells Bombardier; guest beer Ⓗ

Welcoming country inn near Derwent Reservoir, enjoying splendid views over the Derwent Valley. Guest ales usually come from local micro-breweries, and Westons Old Rosie cider is stocked. Excellent home-cooked food is served in the bar and restaurant. Accommodation is also available here. ⛫❀🛏◐●P

Corbridge

Angel Inn

Main Street, NE45 5LA

⏲ 10 (10.30 Sun)-11

☎ (01434) 632119

High House Auld Hemp, Nel's Best; Taylor Landlord; guest beers Ⓗ

Large, three-roomed coaching inn dating from 1726 in the centre of town. The bar has recently been refurbished and offers 30 single malt whiskies. The wood-panelled lounge has comfortable sofas and armchairs. Food is popular, with local ingredients used whenever possible.
⛫Q❀🛏◐♿⇌🚌(604, 685)P⚟

Dyvels

Station Road, NE45 5AY

⏲ 11.30-11; 12-10.30 Sun

☎ (01434) 633633

Caledonian Deuchars IPA; guest beers Ⓗ

Traditional inn with a warm, cosy atmosphere. This stone-built, three-roomed pub is situated near the railway station. No smoking throughout, it has a garden for summer drinking. Handy for the nearby Tynedale rugby club. ⛫♉❀🛏◐♿⇌P⚟

Cramlington

Plough

Middle Farm Buildings, NE23 9DN
11-3, 6-11; 11-11 Thu-Sat; 12-10.30 Sun
☎ (01670) 737633
Theakston XB; guest beers Ⓗ
In the centre of a former mining village, this fine pub faces the parish church. Once a farm, the old buildings were sympathetically converted to the present establishment some years ago. The bar is small and busy with a door to the outside seating area. The lounge, containing the handpumps, is large and comfortable with a round 'gin gan' acting as an extra sitting room. Ever-changing guest beers are often from local micro-brewers. ❀◑◐ ♿ ⇌ P

Dipton Mill

Dipton Mill Inn

Dipton Mill Road, NE46 1YA (2 miles from Hexham on Whitley Chapel road)
12-2.30, 6-11; 12-4, 7-10.30 Sun
☎ (01434) 606577
Hexhamshire Devil's Elbow, Shire Bitter, Devil's Water, Whapweasel, Old Humbug; guest beers Ⓗ
The tap for Hexhamshire Brewery, this is a small low-ceilinged pub with a cosy atmosphere and warm welcome. The landlord brews excellent beers which are sold in the pub. Guest beers are occasionally offered. Great home-cooked meals complement the ales – try the ploughmans! The large garden has a stream running through it and there is plenty of countryside to explore. ⩕Q❀◑◐ ●

East Ord

Salmon Inn

TD15 2NS
11-3, 5-11; 11-11 Fri & Sat; 12-10.30 Sun
☎ (01289) 305227
Caledonian Deuchars IPA, 80/-; guest beers Ⓗ
On the main street, this is very much a locals' pub attracting a wide range of customers of all ages. Many are tempted by the home-cooked food prepared with locally sourced ingredients – game is a speciality. The bar has a real fire together with a pool table and TV. A large marquee in the garden caters for the frequent overspill. Handy for the Tweed Cycle Way and fishing on the River Tweed; dogs are welcome.
⩕❀◑◐ ▲ (23)P

Great Whittington

Queen's Head Inn

NE19 2HP
12-2.30, 6-11; closed Mon; 12-3, 7-10.30 Sun
☎ (01434) 672267
Hambleton Bitter Ⓗ
Dating from the 15th century, the Queen's Head is reputedly the oldest inn in the county. It is the only regular outlet in Northumberland for the Hambleton Brewery, providers of the house beer, Queen's Head Bitter. Set in the heart of Hadrian's Wall country, the pub is popular with tourists. The extensive food menu is recommended – all made with local produce where possible. The small, friendly bar is warmed by a roaring fire. ⩕Q◑◐P

Greenhaugh

Hollybush Inn

NE48 1PW
5.30-11; closed Mon winter; 12-11 Sat; 12-3, 7-10.30 Sun
☎ (01434) 240391
High House Nel's Best; guest beer Ⓗ
Formerly a drovers' inn, the pub is in a row of cottages and dates back to the 17th century. It is the only public house in England's largest and least populated parish. Cosy and welcoming, do not be surprised if you are invited to share a table with friendly locals. The emphasis is on conversation here: there is no television, piped music or gaming machines. Note the Victorian range: its oven is still in regular use. The garden offers marvellous views of the local scenery. Only one beer is served during winter.
⩕Q❀ ◑◐

Haydon Bridge

General Havelock

9 Ratcliff Road, NE47 7HU
12-2.30, 7-11; closed Mon; 12-2.30, 7-10.30 Sun
☎ (01434) 684376
Beer range varies Ⓗ
A pub with a well-deserved reputation for fine food, with the emphasis on local produce. There are usually one or two of northern England's finest micro-brewed ales on offer here. The rear garden extends down to the River Tyne. Hadrian's Wall is just a few miles to the north. Haydon Bridge lies halfway between Hexham and Haltwhistle.
⩕Q❀◑◐ ⇌ (685)♣

Hedley on the Hill

Feathers

NE43 7SW
12-3 (not Mon-Fri), 6-11; 12-3, 7-10.30 Sun
☎ (01661) 843607
Beer range varies Ⓗ
Outstanding pub set in a hamlet high above the Tyne Valley with views of the three counties that surround it. There are two bars, both with exposed stone walls and wood beams. High quality home-made food complements the four real ales on offer. The pub holds a mini beer festival at Easter culminating on Monday with the famous uphill barrel race – the winners are rewarded with a prize of real ale. ⩕Q❀◑◐ ♣P

Hexham

Tap & Spile

1 Eastgate, NE46 1BH
11-11 (midnight Fri & Sat); 12-3, 7-10.30 Sun
☎ (01434) 602039
Black Sheep Best Bitter; Caledonian Deuchars IPA; guest beers Ⓗ
Classic, town centre, street corner pub split into two areas, one no-smoking, both served

from a central bar. Guest beers reflect the owning pub company's limited choice, but there should always be something to take your fancy. No food is served on Sunday. Regular live music nights are held. Situated in the centre of Hexham, the Abbey is nearby. Q◐⊟⇌♣

High Horton

Three Horseshoes

Hatherley Lane, NE24 4HF (off A189 N of Cramlington, follow A192) OS276794

✪ 11-11; 12-10.30 Sun

☎ (01670) 822410

Greene King Abbot; Tetley Bitter, Burton Ale; guest beers Ⓗ

Much extended former coaching inn at the highest point in the Blyth Valley, affording excellent views of the Northumberland coast. The pub is open plan with bar and dining areas plus a conservatory. Known locally as 'the Shoes', it is dedicated to real ale with seven handpumps serving three regular beers and a constantly changing list of guests including brews from local micros. Regular beer festivals are held.

Q❀◐◑⊟(X25, X26)P⁄

Holywell

Fat Ox

NE25 0LJ

✪ 12-11; 12-10.30 Sun

☎ (0191) 237 0964

Mordue Workie Ticket; guest beers Ⓗ

Situated close to the county boundary near Seaton Delaval, this traditional pub is in the heart of the village. The cosy half-timbered bar offers a warm welcome to all. It serves quality cask ales with guests including beers from the Scottish Courage list and local micro Mordue. ❀

Horsley

Lion & Lamb

NE15 0NS

✪ 12-3, 6-11; 12-11 Fri & Sat; 12-10.30 Sun

☎ (01661) 852952

Caledonian Deuchars IPA; High House Nel's Best; Marston's Pedigree; guest beers Ⓗ

Well-appointed multi-room roadside pub in the centre of the village. Parts of the building date from 1718 with resulting low-beamed ceilings – the inscription 'Mind ya heed' is not just there for decorative purposes. Despite an emphasis on food (no meals Sun eve), drinkers are well catered for by the six handpumps in the bar. A garden to the rear offers stunning views of the Tyne Valley. Bus No 685 Newcastle-Carlisle stops outside. ♨Q❀◐◑⊟⊟(685)P⁄

Langley

Carts Bog Inn

NE47 5NW (3 miles off A69 on A686 to Alston)

✪ 12-3, 5-11; 12-11 Sat; 12-3, 7-10.30 Sun

☎ (01434) 684338

Beer range varies Ⓗ

Traditional, unspoilt country pub serving a discerning local community as well as visitors to the area. Dating from 1730, it is built on the site of an ancient brewery (circa 1521). A large, unusual fire divides the two rooms. The name is derived from a steeply-banked corner on the old road where, on wet days, the horse-drawn carts were invariably bogged down. Popular for Sunday lunch, you are assured a warm welcome at any time. The house beer, Bog Bitter, is from Mordue. ♨Q❀◐◑P

Low Newton by the Sea

Ship Inn

Newton Square, NE66 3EL (off B1340)

✪ 11-3, 8 (6 Fri)-11; 11-11 Sat and summer; 12-10.30 Sun

☎ (01665) 576262

Black Sheep Best Bitter; guest beers Ⓗ

Despite its location in a very quiet village, the Ship can be busy most of the time, even in winter. Set among a row of old whitewashed stone fishermen's cottages around the village green, it is almost on the beach. Ideal for coastal walkers, car drivers must use the village car park and walk down the hill to the pub. An excellent choice of guest ales from local micro-breweries is available. This is an ideal place to take a break when exploring the Northumberland coastline. Evening meals are not always available in winter.

♨Q❀◐◑Å♣⁄

Morpeth

Joiners Arms

3 Wansbeck Street, NE61 1XZ

✪ 12-11; 11-11 Fri & Sat; 12-10.30 Sun

☎ (01670) 513540

Draught Bass; Caledonian Deuchars IPA; Fuller's London Pride; Tetley Bitter; guest beers Ⓗ

This Fitzgerald's owned pub is a friendly place to enjoy a good pint of real ale. Just a short stroll from the town centre, it is popular with locals and visitors. The lounge has a pleasant view over the River Wansbeck. Its guest list often features beers from local micro-breweries. Tuesday is the night for quiz fans. Q⊟

Tap & Spile

23 Manchester Street, NE61 1BH

✪ 12-2.30, 4.30-11; 12-11 Fri & Sat; 12-10.30 Sun

☎ (01670) 513894

Beer range varies Ⓗ

If you like Tap & Spile pubs then this one will certainly appeal. Popular with locals and visitors alike, the pub boasts eight handpumps serving a variety of real ales and Westons Old Rosie cider. There is a bar and comfortable, quiet lounge where children are welcome. Northumbrian pipers play on Sunday lunchtime. Snacks are served Thursday to Sunday lunchtime, at other times you are welcome to bring your own food. Q⊟⊟●

Netherton

Star Inn ☆

NE65 7HD (off B634 from Rothbury)

🕐 7.30-10 Tue, Wed & Sun; 7.30-11 Fri; 7.30-10.30 Sat
☎ (01669) 630238
Camerons Castle Eden Ale [G]
Entering this gem, privately owned and unchanged for the last 80 years, feels like going into the living room of a private house rather than a pub. The beer is served on gravity straight from the cellar at a hatch in the panelled entrance hall. The bar area is basic with benches around the wall. It is the only pub in Northumberland to appear in every edition of this Guide. Children are not allowed in the bar. Please ring to check opening hours.
QP

Newbiggin by the Sea

Queen's Head
7 High Street, NE64 6AT
🕐 10-midnight; 12-10.30 Sun
☎ (01670) 817293
John Smith's Bitter; guest beers [H]
Multi-roomed, traditional pub with lots of character and some unusual oval tables. The landlord introduced guest ales, often from local micro-breweries, when he took over the pub three years ago and has now sold over 700 different brews. The large collection of pump clips behind the bar makes an interesting topic of conversation – how many of the ales have you tried?
🀫🀫

Norham

Masons Arms
16 West Street, TD15 2LB
🕐 12-3, 7-11; 12-3, 7-10.30 Sun
☎ (01289) 382326
Belhaven 80/-; Caledonian Deuchars IPA; guest beer [H]
Cosy, wood-panelled bar with a welcoming real fire at its heart and an eclectic assembly of tools, water jugs and fishing equipment hanging from the ceiling. The pub hosts regular ceilidh music evenings reflecting both northern Northumbrian and southern Scottish musical traditions. It also runs a leek club. The pub is well-situated for attractions including the 12th-century castle at the end of the village, the Tweed Cycle Way, and local golf courses. No food is served Sunday evenings.
⛰❀⇌◐◑🀫🚌(23)

Old Hartley

Delaval Arms
Old Hartley, NE26 4RL (at jct of A193/B1325)
🕐 12-3, 6-11; 12-11 Sat; 12-10.30 Sun
☎ (0191) 237 0489
Beer range varies [H]
Multi-roomed Grade II listed building dating from 1748 with a listed water storage tower in the garden and great views up and down the Northumberland coast. To the left as you enter the pub there is a room served through a hatch from the bar and to the right a room where children are welcome. In the public bar the landlord has introduced guest ales. Quality, affordable meals (not Sun eve) complement the beer.
Q☺❀◐◑🀫P

Once Brewed

Twice Brewed Inn
Military Road, Bardon Mill, NE47 7AN (on B6318)
🕐 11-11; 12-10.30 Sun
☎ (01434) 344534 🌐 twicebrewedinn.co.uk
Beer range varies [H]
Originally a coaching inn, the pub dates back to the 17th century. It now provides excellent modern facilities including an IT suite with Internet connection. Hard to find, it is situated on the Military Road midway between Newcastle upon Tyne and Carlisle. Set among breathtaking scenery, it stands in the shadows of Steel Rigg, one of the most dramatic parts of Hadrian's Wall. Very busy during the tourist season, it is a rural transport interchange. The staff are trained in sign language.
Q☺⇌◐◑♿🚌♣P⚡

Seahouses

Olde Ship Hotel
7-9 Main Street, NE68 7RD
🕐 11-11 daily
☎ (01665) 720200 🌐 seahouses.co.uk
Draught Bass; Black Sheep Best Bitter; Courage Directors; Greene King Ruddles County; Hadrian & Border Farne Island; guest beers [H]
Originally a farmhouse built in the 18th century, this recently modernised hotel has been owned by the same family for almost a century. A Guide regular for many years, it features a large collection of maritime brass instruments including a nameplate from the wrecked SS Forfarshire of Victorian heroine Grace Darling fame. Situated by the harbour, the hotel is in an ideal location for boat trips to the Farne Islands.
⛰Q❀⇌◐◑🀫♿🚌♣P⚡

Slaley

Travellers Rest
NE46 1TT (on B6306, 1 mile N of village)
🕐 12-11; 12-10.30 Sun
☎ (01434) 673231
Black Sheep Best Bitter; Marston's Pedigree; guest beers [H]
Licensed for over 100 years, this welcoming inn started life in the 16th century as a farmhouse. Living up to its name, it offers visitors an excellent choice of guest beers, wonderful food and accommodation. The bar has several distinct cosy areas and a large open fire, stone walls, flag floors and comfortable furniture. Food is served (not Sun eve) in the bar as well as the restaurant – the menu is extensive and features local produce. Children are welcome and there is a safe play area beside the pub.
⛰Q❀⇌◐◑P

Stannington

Ridley Arms
NE61 6EL

⏲ 11.30-11; 12-10.30 Sun
☎ (01670) 789216
Black Sheep Best Bitter; Taylor Landlord; guest beers Ⓗ
An excellent Fitzgerald House with several rooms, some no-smoking. Ramps and wide doors allow easy access for disabled visitors. Eight handpumps with guests from local micros and good food cater for all tastes. Efficient air conditioning ensures a pleasant atmosphere for drinkers and diners who do not wish to be disturbed by smoking or food smells. A quiz night is held on Tuesday. Q❀◑♿P⚟

Warden

Boatside Inn

NE46 4SQ (off A69)
⏲ 11-11 (10.30 Sun)
☎ (01434) 602233 🌐 boatsideinn.co.uk
Beer range varies Ⓗ
Recently refurbished after flooding, the Boatside is an attractive country pub, set in good walking and cycling country, between the River South Tyne and the wooded Warden Hill, near the rural Tyne Valley railway line. The World Heritage site of Hadrian's Wall is within easy reach. Good, home-cooked food is served from a menu that changes often. Boatside cottages offer B&B or self-catering accommodation for a longer stay. Activities at the pub include darts and quoits. Children are welcome. ♨❀⛟◐◑♿P⚟

Wark

Battlesteads Hotel

NE48 3LS
⏲ 11-11; 12-10.30 Sun
☎ (01434) 230209 🌐 battlesteads-hotel.co.uk
Wylam Gold Tankard; guest beers Ⓗ
Traditional 17th-century farmhouse inn close to Hadrian's Wall and the National Park. The cosy bar room has an interesting bar front converted from a 200-year-old dresser, and a big inglenook. Live folk music is played on most evenings and there is a large garden. The excellent accommodation includes ground floor rooms providing disabled access. ♨Q❀⛟◐◑⊟♿P

Wylam

Boathouse

Station Road, NE41 8HR
⏲ 11-11; 12-10.30 Sun
☎ (01661) 853431
Wylam Gold Tankard; guest beers Ⓗ
Outstanding two-room pub located next to the level crossing at Wylam railway station. The bar groans under the constant use of its nine handpumps. The Boathouse is the tap for Wylam Brewery and offers all of its beers as available. George Stephenson of Rocket fame was born nearby; his cottage can be visited just across the River Tyne. Meals are served at the weekend. Winner of CAMRA Northumberland Pub of the Year 2006. ♨Q❀◐⊟⇌♣●P

NOTTINGHAMSHIRE

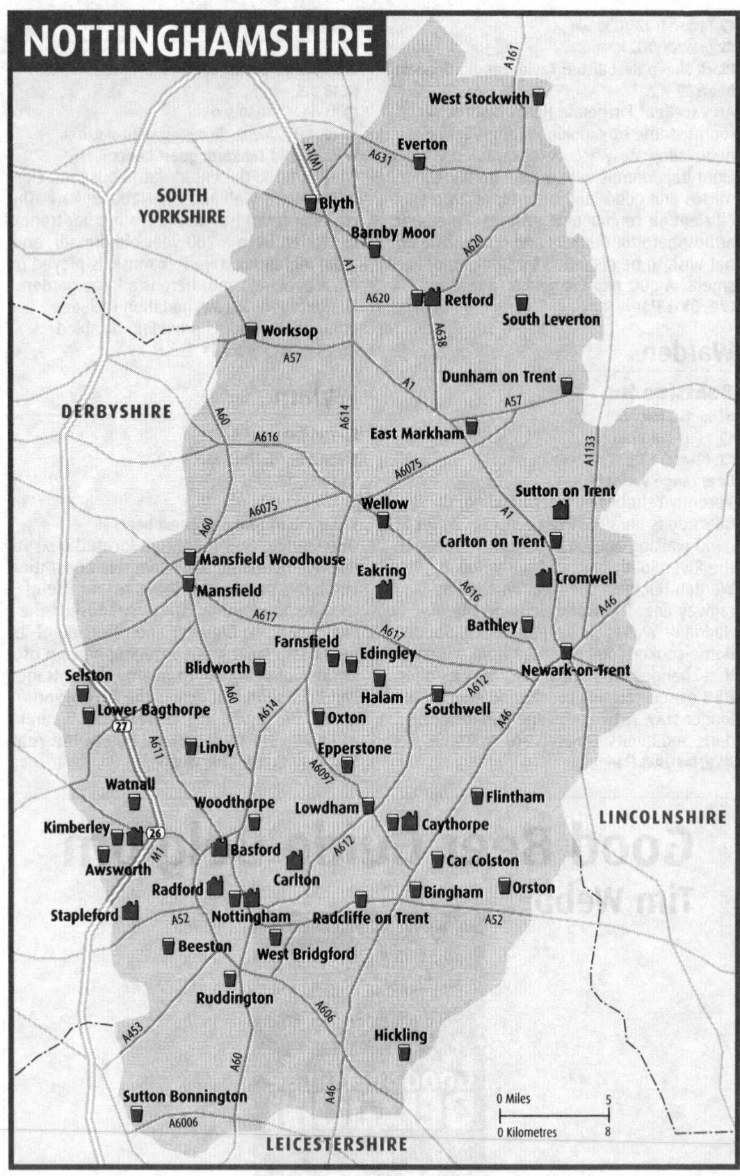

Awsworth

Gate

Main Street, NG16 2RN (just off A610)

12-1am (2am Fri & Sat); 12-1am Sun

☎ (0115) 932 9821

Hardys & Hansons Mild, Best Bitter, seasonal beers Ⓗ

Traditional three-roomed inn with a public bar, lounge and pool room. Popular with all age groups, this cosy and friendly pub is a timeless example of a fine local pub. The collection of old photographs in the bar depicts the railway connection in the local area. Outdoor skittles and an upstairs function room are also available.

Q ♣P

Barnby Moor

White Horse

Great North Road, DN22 8QS (on A638)

11 (12 Sun)-11

☎ (01777) 707721

Beer range varies Ⓗ

A new entry in the Guide, this attractive village pub has a large lounge bar with a dining area and a smaller public bar area. Four to six changing cask ales are available, most originating from local micro-breweries. The walls in the lounge bar are covered with paintings, some connected to the local Grove & Rufford Hunt which has its kennels across the road.

QP

Bathley

Crown

Main Street, NG23 6DA
✪ 11-3, 7-2am; 11-2am Fri-Sun
☎ (01636) 702305
Banks's Riding Bitter, Bitter; guest beer ⊞
Popular, unspoilt village local – the hub of its community. Well-kept beers provide a backdrop for a successful food operation. The Doll Museum at Cromwell, Southwell and Laxton are all nearby. ♨❀◐◑♣P

Beeston

Malt Shovel

1 Union Street, NG9 2LU
✪ 11-11 (midnight Fri & Sat); 12-11 Sun
☎ (0115) 922 2320
Nottingham Rock Mild, Rock Bitter; guest beers ⊞
Hidden away down a side street, this friendly establishment has been transformed by a bold refurbishment. Although it has only one room, thoughtful use of furnishings and decor creates a sense of separate drinking areas. Wooden floors, bright colours and cosy leather sofas provide a comfortable yet light and airy feel. There is a good value lunchtime menu (no meals Sun eve), curry night (Wed) and regular live music. ♨❀◐◑♿●P

Victoria Hotel

85 Dovecote Lane, NG9 1JG (off A6005 by station)
✪ 11-11; 12-11 Sun
☎ (0115) 925 4049 ⊕ victoriabeeston.co.uk
Castle Rock Harvest Pale, Hemlock; Everards Tiger; guest beers ⊞
This former Nottingham CAMRA Pub of the Year is popular with drinkers and diners alike. The multi-roomed layout allows for a dining area, no-smoking area and a separate bar. Twelve beers are served, including a stout and a mild, all from regional and micro-brewers. Two real ciders are also available. Freshly cooked food, including a wide vegetarian choice, is available all day. Music festivals are held. ♨Q❀◐◑⊟♿♣●P⊬

Bingham

Horse & Plough

25 Long Acre, NG13 8AF
✪ 11-11 (11.30 Fri & Sat); 12-11 Sun
☎ (01949) 839313
Caledonian Deuchars IPA; Wells Bombardier; guest beers ⊞
Warm, friendly one-room free house with an olde-worlde cottage style interior and flagstone floor. Six cask ales are always available including four frequently changing guests. The pub, which has a 'try before you buy' policy, is housed in a former Methodist chapel and was once a bookies and a butchers. The first floor restaurant serves a varied menu and is popular with diners from near and far. Bar food is served weekday lunchtimes (no eve meals Mon). ◐◑♿⇌

Blidworth

Black Bull

Main Street, NG21 0QH
✪ 5-midnight; closed Mon; 12-2.30, 7-11.30 Sun
☎ (01623) 792291
Black Sheep Best Bitter; Tetley Bitter; guest beers ⊞
Three-roomed, beamed local at least 400 years old in parts. The public bar with log-burning stove, lounge and snug are all served from a central bar. Live music is played on most weekends, folk music on Sunday evening. The pub is popular with walkers. Recent guest beers have been Spitfire, Brains SA, Taylor Landlord and Wells Bombardier. ♨Q≿❀⊟⊞♣P⊬

Blyth

Red Hart

Bawtry Road, S81 8HG
✪ 12-midnight (11.30 Sun)
☎ (01909) 591221
Beer range varies ⊞
An attractive village pub situated in the centre of Blyth – a previous winner of best-kept village. The interior includes a lounge and bar areas with a reasonably-sized dining room. Regularly changing guest ales come from micro-breweries including the local Broadstone Brewery. Restaurant quality food at pub prices is served daily. ♨Q❀◐◑⛺⊞P

Car Colston

Royal Oak

The Green, NG13 8JE (½ mile from A46)
✪ 11.30-3 (not Mon), 6-midnight; 11.30-midnight Sat & Sun
☎ (01949) 20247
Banks's Mansfield Cask; Marston's Bitter; guest beer ⊞
This impressive country pub situated on England's largest village green has two main rooms – a lounge and restaurant on one side and a bar with comfortable seating on the other. Note the bar's interesting brickwork ceiling – a legacy from the pub's previous life as a hosiery factory. The pub boasts a good food menu (not Sun eve) – the mouth-watering range of puddings is particularly popular. A skittle alley is at the rear.
♨Q❀◐◑⛺♣P⊬

Carlton on Trent

Great Northern

Ossington Road, NG23 6NT (400 yds from A1)

INDEPENDENT BREWERIES

Alcazar Basford
Broadstone Retford
Castle Rock Nottingham
Caythorpe Caythorpe
Full Mash Stapleford
Hardys & Hansons Kimberley (bought by Greene King June 06)
Holland Kimberley
Magpie Nottingham
Mallard Carlton
Maypole Eakring
Milestone Cromwell
Nottingham Radford
Springhead Sutton on Trent

⏲ 12-midnight (1am Fri & Sat); 12-midnight Sun
☎ (01636) 821348
Hardys & Hansons Mild, Best Bitter, Olde Trip, seasonal beers 🄷
Large single-roomed pub with a beamed ceiling accommodating a games area, dining area and central bar. Traditional pub games sit alongside a pool table and fruit machine. Situated outside the village adjacent to the railway line, this pub has excellent disabled access and a garden next to the large car park. The stained glass panels in oak surrounds adjoining the bar are a reminder of the steam age. ♨☕❀◐◑♿♣P

Caythorpe

Black Horse Inn
29 Main Street, NG14 7ED
⏲ 12-2.30, 5 (6 Sat)-11; closed Mon; 12-4, 7 (8 winter)-10.30 Sun
☎ (0115) 966 3520
Caythorpe Dover Beck; guest beers 🄷
This 18th-century free house has been in the same family for 37 years. It features a comfortable lounge, a gem of a snug bar with hatch servery, inglenook, bench seats, beams and wood panelling. Bar food, mostly cooked to order using fresh ingredients, is very popular – booking is essential. The Caythorpe Brewery operates from outbuildings at the back. Guest beers often come from local micro-breweries. ♨Q❀◐◑⊟♣P

Dunham on Trent

White Swan
Main Street, NG22 0TY (on A57)
⏲ 10-11 (10.30 Sun)
☎ (01777) 228307
Beer range varies 🄷
Attractive village pub with separate lounge and bar areas and a reasonably-sized dining room. Regularly changing guest ales including beers from the local Broadstone Brewery are usually available. Good, reasonably-priced home cooked food is served daily. The pub is well situated for anyone wishing to have a day fishing on the Trent. ♨Q❀◐◑P

East Markham

Queen's Hotel
High Street, NG22 0RE (1/2 mile from A1)
⏲ 12-11; 12-10.30 Sun
☎ (01777) 870288
Beer range varies 🄷
One of two pubs in East Markham selling real ales, this cosy house has a friendly atmosphere enhanced by an open fire in winter. A single bar serves the lounge, pool room and dining area. Food is available Tuesday-Sunday. There is a large garden area at the rear of the premises where you can enjoy a drink on a warm summer day. ♨Q❀◐◑♣P

Edingley

Old Reindeer
Main Street, NG22 8BE (off A614)
⏲ 12-11 (10.30 Sun)
☎ (01623) 882253
Banks's Mansfield Cask; Marston's Pedigree; guest beers 🄷
Although recently renovated to provide a sumptuous new restaurant, great care has been taken to maintain the ambience of this fine old 18th-century village pub, with six real ales on handpump from W&D's range of 30 ales, always in very good condition. With an attractive garden plus good parking this is an excellent pub for all seasons, serving top quality food. Pub games and activities are organised. Accommodation is available in en-suite rooms. Q❀⇌◐◑♿♣P

Epperstone

Cross Keys
Main Street, NG14 6AD
⏲ 12-3 (not Mon), 6-midnight; 12-midnight Sun
☎ (0115) 966 3033
🌐 piczo.com/crosskeyspubepperstone
Hardys & Hansons Best Bitter, Olde Trip, seasonal beers 🄷
Delightful, quiet, rural pub, popular with walkers in the summer months, with eight different walks all starting from the pub. It has two rooms, a lounge/dining room and a bar. Outside there is a large garden and play area for children. A minimum of three beers is always available. The home-cooked food menu includes daily specials and a vegetarian selection. Fresh fish dishes are available Wednesday to Saturday.
Q❀◐◑⊟♿🚌(61)⚟

Everton

Blacksmith's Arms
Church Street, DN10 5BQ
⏲ 10-midnight daily
☎ (01777) 817281 🌐 blacksmiths-everton.co.uk
John Smith's Bitter; Theakston Old Peculier; guest beers 🄷
Regular winner of local CAMRA Pub of the Season awards, this 18th-century free house stands at the heart of the village. Drinking areas include the locals' bar with its original tiled floor and the games room (formerly the old smithy). The comfortable lounge area leads to a large restaurant where the emphasis is on fresh, home-cooked food (booking is advisable). Outside is a Mediterranean-style garden; en-suite accommodation is available in the converted stables. ♨Q☕❀⇌◐◑⊟♿P

Farnsfield

Plough Inn
Main Street, NG22 8EA (off A614)
⏲ 11-3, 5.30-11;11-11 Sat; 12-10.30 Sun
☎ (01623) 882265
Marston's Pedigree; guest beers 🄷
This recently refurbished inn has been tastefully decorated. A comfortable pub for a quiet drink, the interior includes a snug with cosy armchairs, bar and open-plan lounge. It is very popular with locals and visitors. A wide range of traditional pub games is available. ♨Q❀◐◑⊟♿♣P⚟▯

Red Lion

Main Street, NG22 8EY
🕘 11-3, 6-midnight; 11-3, 6-10.30 Sun
☎ (01623) 882304
Banks's Riding Bitter; Marston's Pedigree; guest beers 🄷
Friendly, family-run local on the main street of this rural village close to Sherwood Forest. Popular with locals and visitors, it serves good home-cooked food in its no-smoking restaurant area. Dominoes is popular, played by the landlord and locals. An ever-changing range of guest beers is always in tip top condition. ♨Q✿◑◗♿♣P

Flintham

Boot & Shoe

Main Street, NG23 5LA
🕘 12-3, 6-11; 12-11 Sat; 12-10.30 Sun
☎ (01636) 525246 🌐 bootandshoe.net
Beer range varies 🄷
The pleasant village pub atmosphere is not spoiled by a TV hidden to one side of the bar, enabling the art of conversation to be upheld. Food is served from an extensive menu made up of home-made fare. ♨✿🛏◑◗P

Halam

Wagon & Horses

The Turnpike, NG22 8AE (off B6386, 1 mile W of Southwell)
🕘 11.30-3, 5.30-11; 11-11; 12-10.30 Sun
☎ (01636) 813109
Thwaites Original, Thoroughbred, Lancaster Bomber; guest beers 🄷
Situated in an unspoilt village, the pub has a rustic charm with its low-beamed ceiling and exposed brickwork. It is close to Southwell with its historic minster and restored workhouse, and near Sherwood Forest. Good quality, home-cooked food is served at reasonable prices. Q✿◑◗♣P

Hickling

Plough

Main Street, LE14 3AH
🕘 12-3, 5.30-11; 12-11 Fri & Sat; 12-10.30 Sun
☎ (01664) 822225
Adnams Broadside; Caledonian Deuchars IPA; Greene King Ruddles Best Bitter; Taylor Landlord 🄷
Situated opposite the Hickling Basin, part of the Grantham Canal, this attractive pub is popular with walkers and cyclists using the towpath. The main bar is upstairs while downstairs is a second bar, a small function room and a pool room. An annual beer festival is held over the August bank holiday. No meals are served Sunday evening. ♨☕✿◑◗⊟♿♣P⚟

Kimberley

Nelson & Railway

12 Station Road, NG16 2NR
🕘 11-11.30; 12-11 Sun
☎ (0115) 938 2177
Hardys & Hansons Best Bitter, Olde Trip, seasonal beers 🄷
Traditional local, within sight of Hardys & Hansons Brewery, set back from the main road behind a large front garden which is popular in summer. The friendly bar offers a warm welcome to all and there is a cosy beamed lounge with an adjoining dining area and a rear garden. The pub is renowned for its good value food and accommodation. ✿🛏◑◗⊟♿🚌(R1)♣P⚟

Stag Inn

67 Nottingham Road, NG16 2NB (on A610)
🕘 5 (1.30 Sat)-11; 12-10.30 Sun
☎ (0115) 938 3151
Adnams Bitter; Caledonian Deuchars IPA; Highgate Dark; Marston's Pedigree; Taylor Landlord; guest beer 🄷
Full of character, this quiet and welcoming two-room village pub dates from 1537. The interior features low beams and settles, old-fashioned slot machines in full working order and old photographs of Shipstones – the former brewery that once owned the pub. The spacious rear garden and children's play area are popular in summer and during the end-of-May annual bank holiday weekend beer festival.
Q✿♿🚌(R1)♣P

Linby

Horse & Groom

Main Street, NG15 8AE
🕘 12-11; 12-10.30 Sun
☎ (0115) 963 2219
Beer range varies 🄷
Charming and unspoilt village pub dating back to 1800. This multi-roomed establishment is Grade II listed and boasts an inglenook in the public bar, a snug and roaring open fires. The Green Room welcomes families and is no-smoking. There is a conservatory and garden with a children's play area. Fine food is available at lunchtime (eve meals Fri and Sat).
♨Q☕✿◑◗⊟🚌(141)P⚟

Lowdham

Old Ship Inn

Main Street, NG14 7BE (400yds N of A612)
🕘 12-11; 12-10.30 Sun
☎ (0115) 966 3049
Courage Directors; John Smith's Bitter; Wells Bombardier; guest beers 🄷
Traditional village inn close to the Nottingham-Southwell road. The split-level public bar has a juke box, dart board and pool table. The beamed lounge has two distinct areas, one of which leads through to the restaurant, which can be booked for large groups or buffets. The home-cooked food is made with fresh local produce and the guest beers are usually from local micros. ✿🛏◑◗⊟≹🚌(90)♣P⚟

Lower Bagthorpe

Dixies Arms

School Road, NG16 5HF (1½ miles from M1 jct 27)
🕘 12-11; 12-10.30 Sun
☎ (01773) 810505

Greene King Abbot; Theakston Best Bitter; guest beer 🄷
Built in the late 1700s, Dixies offers a friendly welcome to all. Locals and visitors alike can be found warming themselves around the real fires in the public rooms, playing darts or dominoes, or gossiping in the snug. The pub's unspoilt character and amiable atmosphere attract a big following, with full houses at weekends for the live music on Saturday and quiz on Sunday. On weekdays it is quieter and a haven for real ale drinkers. ♨❀⊟▲♣P

Shepherds Rest

Wansley Lane, NG16 5HF (2 miles from M1 jct 27)
🕒 12-11; 12-10.30 Sun
☎ (01773) 811337
Caledonian Deuchars IPA; Greene King Abbot; Wells Bombardier; guest beer 🄷
Family-run pub, dating back to the 1700s and reputedly haunted. An extensive garden includes a children's play area and benches in an idyllic countryside setting. The freshly prepared and home-cooked food can be enjoyed in the garden, weather permitting. Exposed beams, flagstone floors and open fires in the bar and restaurant add to the ambience. Evening meals are served Tuesday to Saturday. ♨❀◐◑⊟♣P⊬

Mansfield

Bold Forester

Botany Avenue, NG18 5NF (on A38 1/2 mile from station)
🕒 11-11.30 (12.30am Fri & Sat); 12-midnight Sun
☎ (01623) 623970
Greene King IPA, Ruddles County, Abbot, Old Speckled Hen; guest beers 🄷
An open-plan pub with split levels, a dining area, a small snug, partitions and support pillars, creating an impression of privacy. Background music is not intrusive and the TV can be avoided. The pool table in a separate area is much used. It offers a wide selection of well-kept real ales from all over the UK and hosts a yearly beer festival to celebrate St George's Day. With excellent meals served all day, this has proved to be one of Mansfield's flagship real ale pubs. ❀◐◑♿≢●P⊬

Court House

Market Place, NG18 1HX
🕒 9am-midnight (1am Fri & Sat); 9am-midnight Sun
☎ (01623) 412720
Greene King Abbot; Marston's Pedigree; Milestone Black Pearl; Nottingham Bullion; Springhead Roaring Meg 🄷
Excellent Wetherspoon's conversion where a good range of well-kept beers at some of the best prices in the area is complemented by reasonable wines and spirits. The pub was formerly the town court house and has been tastefully converted in typical Wetherspoon's style with an extra large dining area and a central bar. A deceptively large pub inside a seemingly small building. Q⛺◐◑≢

Railway Inn

9 Station Street, NG18 1EF
🕒 10.30-11.30 (8 Tue); 12-5 Sun
☎ (01623) 623086
Bateman XB, seasonal beers; Greene King IPA 🄷
The Railway has survived due to the local support from both CAMRA and the community who use this pub. Excellent lunchtime meals, served throughout the afternoon, offer first class value for money. Three real ales are always available at some of the best prices in the local area. A good selection of canned and bottled beer and ciders is offered at discounted prices. The three course Sunday lunch is a must, available until 4pm at £5.95. Q⛺❀◐◑≢♣

Widow Frost

Leeming Street, NG18 1NB
🕒 9am-midnight (1am Fri & Sat); 9am-midnight Sun
☎ (01623) 666790
Greene King Abbot; Marston's Pedigree; Shepherd Neame Spitfire; guest beers 🄷
An exceptionally spacious single-roomed pub with a larger than usual no-smoking area for both diners and drinkers. As in all Wetherspoon's, alcohol is available from 9am with your good value breakfast. A basic Wetherspoon's menu is supplemented with daily specials on the bar. Local history displayed around the walls makes interesting reading. The usual Sunday lunch is excellent value. Q⛺◐◑♿≢●

Mansfield Woodhouse

Greyhound

82 High Street, NG19 8BD
🕒 12-11 (midnight Fri & Sat); 12-10.30 Sun
☎ (01623) 464403
Greene King Abbot; Theakston Mild; Webster's Yorkshire Bitter; guest beers 🄷
This stone-built pub, reputedly dating from the 17th century, has featured in the Guide for more than 14 years. Located near the old market square, this popular, friendly pub has two rooms – a lively tap room with pool table and traditional pub games plus a quiet, comfortable lounge. Up to six real ales are on offer. Quiz nights are held twice a week. Q❀⊟♿≢♣P▽

Star Inn

Warsop Road, NG19 9LE (on A6075 at crossroads)
🕒 12-3, 5-11 (10.30 Sun)
☎ (01623) 403110
Tetley Bitter; guest beers 🄷
This friendly pub is popular with locals. The cosy bar has a pool room leading off it and both can be busy. The comfortable lounge is ideal for conversation and a quiet drink. Up to five real ales are available and the ever-changing range makes this a pub always worth a visit. Food may be eaten in the lounge or bar. Q❀◐◑⊟♿≢♣P

Newark-on-Trent

Castle

5 Castlegate, NG24 1AZ
🕒 11-11 (midnight Sat); 12-10.30 Sun
☎ (01636) 640733
Beer range varies 🄷
The 'country pub in the town' wording adorning the interior perfectly describes this

delightful pub. Half-timbered panelled walls, settles, mirrors, hops and old pictures add character. Regularly-changing guest beers often from local micros feature among the six handpumps. Quiz night is Monday and jazz is played on Friday. Bar snacks are available but if you want something more substantial try the Mayse next door (owned, like the Castle, by the Yardglass Pub Co). ⌕≠(Castle)⊟♣

Castle & Falcon

10 London Road, NG24 1TW (50 yds from Beamond Cross)

12 (11 Fri)-3 (not Tue-Thu), 7-11; 12-3, 7-10.30 Sun

☎ (01636) 703513

John Smith's Bitter; guest beers Ⓗ

Within walking distance of the town centre in the shadow of the old James Hole Brewery, this friendly pub has all the atmosphere of a local. A 19th-century inn, it served the London to York run. A public bar with pool table, separate lounge and conservatory provide plenty of space to enjoy quality ale. It offers a wide and varying selection of guest beers and testers are always available. There is a small outdoor seating area for summer use. ❀≠(Castle)⊟♣

Mail Coach

13 London Road, NG24 1TN
(25 yds from Beamond Cross)

4.30-midnight; 12-midnight Fri-Sun

☎ (01636) 605164

Flowers IPA, Original; guest beers Ⓗ

Beer Guide stalwart, appearing for its 17th consecutive year. The regular beers are supplemented by an imaginative selection of regularly changing guests, mostly sourced locally. The pub itself is roomy, divided into three distinct areas. There is a real fire at both ends of the pub. Good value meals are served at lunchtime and live bands play occasionally, usually on Thursday evening. Although licensed until midnight the pub closes when the last customer goes home. ⌂Q❀⇆◑≠(Castle)⊟P

Nottingham: Central

Bell Inn

18 Angel Row, Old Market Square, NG1 6HL

10.30-12.30am; 10-midnight Sun

☎ (0115) 947 5241 thebell-inn.com

Hardys & Hansons Mild, Best Bitter, Olde Trip, seasonal beers; guest beers Ⓗ

The 2006 Nottingham Pub of the Year, this three-roomed traditional pub in the Market Square offers a wide selection of guest ales, many from micros. A labyrinth of Norman caves exists beneath the pub – cellar tours take place on Tuesday evening. Food is served in the Belfry restaurant and some of the bars. A cafe-style pavement drinking area operates during the summer months. The back bar hosts live music and occasional beer festivals. Q❀◑◐⊟⊖(Old Market Sq)

Cock & Hoop

25-27 High Pavement, Lace Market, NG1 1HF

12-11 (midnight Thu; 1am Fri & Sat); 12-10 Sun

☎ (0115) 852 3231

Fuller's London Pride; Nottingham Rock Bitter; guest beers Ⓗ

A varied clientele is attracted to this no-smoking, air-conditioned, split-level pub opposite the Galleries of Justice in the popular Lace Market area. Downstairs is a comfortable lounge formed out of the former cellar while the upstairs area features a solid pewter bar top dispensing five beers, the guests often from local breweries. Freshly-cooked food is served daily until the early evening. Q◑◐♿≠⊖(Lace Market)⊟⚟

Gatehouse

Toll House Hill, NG1 5FS

11-midnight; 12-11 Sun

☎ (0115) 947 3952

Nottingham Rock Bitter; guest beers Ⓗ

Fully refurbished in 2005; the interior is bright and furnished with a variety of chairs, benches and comfortable settees. In the summer the front of the pub is opened out with sliding doors and additional seating provided on the enclosed pavement area overlooking the busy Maid Marian Way roundabout. The beer range is dispensed from four handpumps and local micro-breweries are often showcased. Handy for both the Playhouse and Theatre Royal; evening meals are served weekdays. Q❀◑◐♿⊖(Royal Centre)⊟

Kean's Head

46 St Mary's Gate, NG1 1QA

10-11 (midnight Fri & Sat); 12-10.30 Sun

☎ (0115) 947 4052

Bateman XXXB; Castle Rock Harvest Pale, Elsie Mo; guest beers Ⓗ

Named after a pub that once stood nearby, the Kean's Head was purchased by the Tynemill pub group in 2004. It was the first no-smoking real ale outlet in Nottingham. The former hostelry was named in honour of the 19th-century actor Edmund Kean, who once performed at the original Theatre Royal that stood on St Mary's Gate in the historic Lace Market district. This one-room pub offers freshly-prepared food from an ever-changing menu. Occasional live music is played. ◑◐♿≠⊖(Lace Market)⊟⚟

Lincolnshire Poacher

161 Mansfield Road, NG1 3FR (on A60 500 yds N of city centre)

11-11 (midnight Thu-Sat); 12-11 Sun

☎ (0115) 941 1584

Bateman XXXB; Castle Rock Poacher's Gold, Harvest Pale; Everards Tiger; guest beers Ⓗ

Two-roomed, traditional pub, with a no-smoking room and conservatory to the rear, plus an enclosed patio. The pub is popular with diners and the real ale fraternity doing the Mansfield Road crawl. It was probably the first pub in Nottingham to sell an ever-changing range of up to 11 real ales from micro-breweries on a regular basis, always including a mild or porter. It also stages regional brewery themed nights. An extensive food menu, half vegetarian, is available. ❀◑◐♣●⚟⊟

Newshouse

123 Canal Street, NG1 7HB
11-11, 12-10.30 Sun
(0115) 950 2419
Castle Rock Daily Gold; Everards Tiger; guest beers H
Straightforward, friendly, two-roomed local. At one time the national news used to be read out to customers – hence the name. Memorabilia from BBC Radio Nottingham and the local Evening Post adorn the walls. Look for the brewery names etched into ceramic wall tiles in the public bar. Sport is shown on TV, and played in a more gentle fashion on the resident bar billiards table and dartboard. Beer choice is excellent, catering for all tastes, light and dark.
(Station St)P

Old Moot Hall Inn

27 Carlton Road, NG3 2DG (near ice stadium)
11-11; 10.30-midnight Sat (doors close 11); 12-10.30 Sun
(0115) 954 0170
Oakham JHB; guest beers H
Originally a chapel, and retaining some of its original features, this two-storey building has been beautifully converted to a warm and friendly local. Eight guest handpumps offer up to 30 ales from many different micro-breweries each week. A Highwood house, this real ale mecca is worth seeking out.

Olde Trip to Jerusalem ☆

1 Brewhouse Yard, NG1 6AD (below castle)
10.30-11 (midnight Thu-Sat); 11-11 Sun
(0115) 947 3171 triptojerusalem.com
Hardys & Hansons Mild, Best Bitter, Olde Trip, seasonal beers; guest beers H
The world famous Olde Trip to Jerusalem is reputed to date from 1189. It has a number of rooms downstairs, some cut out of the castle rock. Upstairs, the Rock Lounge is home to The Cursed Galleon (hence the house beer). A newly-opened museum room houses a tapestry depicting Nottingham's history. Meals are served until 6pm. The top bar can be reserved for private functions. Winner of the English Heritage/CAMRA award 2004. Q(Station St)

Sir Charles Napier

209 North Sherwood Street, NG1 4EQ
11.30-11; 12-11 Sun
(0115) 941 0420
Beer range varies H
Adjacent to the Arboretum gates, this lively, two-roomed, back street local dates back over 200 years and used to be owned by the original Nottingham Brewery. A patio area at the rear of the pub gives the impression of a Tuscan garden. Screen sports are regularly shown on TV and there is a pool table and bar billiards. Artwork is exhibited on the walls from students of the nearby University. Three guest beers change frequently.

Vat & Fiddle

12-14 Queen's Bridge Road, NG2 1NB
11-11 (midnight Fri & Sat); 12-11 Sun
(0115) 985 0611
Castle Rock Nottingham Gold, Harvest Pale, Hemlock, Elsie Mo; guest beers H
This deservedly popular and friendly pub is close to the railway station and tram terminus. The Castle Rock Brewery tap, it dispenses four of its beers plus an ever-changing selection of guests from its ten handpumps. A guest mild is always available, together with a traditional cider and around 70 whiskies. An extension was completed in 2006 to add additional rooms including a viewing panel into the brewery.
Q(Station St)

Nottingham: North

Fox & Crown

33 Church Street, Basford, NG6 0GA
12-11; 12-10.30 Sun
(0115) 942 2002
Alcazar Ale, New Dawn, Vixen's Vice, seasonal beers; guest beers H
Situated a couple of miles from the city centre, the Alcazar Brewery tap attracts beer lovers from near and far. A centre bar and modern wooden furnishings give the pub a spacious feel. The numerous handpumps serve at least six Alcazar beers and one or more guests. The sunken patio to the rear is a pleasant spot for a summer drink. The pub is renowned for its excellent Thai food.
Q(David Lane/Basford)(69)P

Gladstone

45 Loscoe Road, Carrington, NG5 2AW (off A60 Mansfield road)
5-11 (11.30 Fri & Sat); 12-11.30 Sun
(0115) 912 9994
Caledonian Deuchars IPA; Fuller's London Pride; Greene King Abbot; Nottingham EPA; Taylor Landlord; guest beers H
Small, friendly, two-room back-street hostelry dating from around 1880, serving the local community. The public bar displays sporting memorabilia and sporting events are shown on TV. The lounge is home to a library of books for customers to read. Thursday is quiz night and the Carrington Folk Club meets in the upstairs function room on Wednesday night. Nottingham Brewery beers can usually be found here.

Horse & Groom

462 Radford Road, Basford, NG7 7EA
11-11 (11.30 Fri & Sat); 12-11 Sun
(0115) 970 3777 horseandgroombasford.co.uk
Caledonian Deuchars IPA; Wells Bombardier; guest beers H
The former Shipstone's Brewery stands just a few yards to the south of this popular pub. Access is via several steps up to the front door, although disabled access is available on request. The small bar area accommodates eight handpumps, serving mainly micro-brewery beers. The pub is split into several distinct areas and has a function room. (Shipstone St)(60, 62)

Lion Inn

44 Mosley Street, New Basford, NG7 7FQ
12-midnight; 12-11 Sun
(0115) 970 3506

Draught Bass; Bateman XB, XXXB; guest beers Ⓗ
Situated adjacent to Shipstone Street tram stop, the Lion overlooks the now defunct Shipstone's Brewery buildings. A renowned music venue, live bands play on weekend evenings, plus other one-off nights. There is a central bar that serves up to ten beers from both regional and local breweries. A real cider is also available on gravity. Good value meals are served. The pub may shut early if not busy.
(Shipstone St) (60, 62) P

Nottingham: West

Plough

17 St Peters Street, Radford, NG7 3EN
12-3, 5-11; 12-11 Fri & Sat; 12-10.30 Sun
☎ (0115) 970 2615
Nottingham Rock Mild, Rock Bitter, Legend, EPA, Bullion; guest beers Ⓗ
This 1840s local acts as the tap for the Nottingham Brewery, which is situated to the rear of the pub. Up to nine cask ales are served in this former Nottingham CAMRA Pub of the Year. The traditional layout allows for Sky TV in one room and quiet drinking in the other. Curry and a Pint is served on Tuesday evening and a quiz with free chilli takes place on Thursday. Sunday lunches are served.
Q (28, 30) P

Orston

Durham Ox

Church Street, NG13 9NS
12-3, 6-11; 11.30-11 Sat; 12-3, 6-10.30 Sun
☎ (01949) 850059
Fuller's London Pride; Greene King IPA; Marston's Burton Bitter, Pedigree; guest beers Ⓗ
Delightful village pub popular with locals and visitors alike. It has a garden and pavement café tables in summer and a roaring fire in winter. There is ample parking and hitching rails for horses (and ferrets). The bar room has an interesting whisky collection in one half and aviation pictures and memorabilia in the other. Filled rolls can be made to order. Pub games are played.
Q P

Oxton

Olde Bridge Inn

Nottingham Road, NG25 0SE (off A6097 at roundabout)
11-11; 12-10.30 Sun
☎ (0115) 965 2013
Everards Beacon, Sunchaser, Tiger; Wells Bombardier; guest beers Ⓗ
Elegant rural pub close to the village centre. The interior comprises a bar, lounge, snug, garden room and restaurant. There are usually six beers available plus a varied wine and spirit range. Two rooms are no-smoking. The creative menu features excellent local produce, including vegetarian options. There is a carvery on Sunday. The pub is popular with cyclists and ramblers exploring the area. The large garden has three patios.
P (61)

Radcliffe on Trent

Black Lion

Main Road, NG12 2FD
11.30 (11 Sat)-11; 12-10.30 Sun
☎ (0115) 933 2138
Courage Directors; Greene King IPA; Taylor Landlord; guest beers Ⓗ
Comfortable, spacious pub at the centre of the village, serving three regular beers and three changing guests. Children can dine in the smart lounge, half of which is no-smoking. The public bar has a large screen TV for sport. An upstairs function room hosts regular live music. Food is served from 12-8.30pm, with the emphasis on home-cooked dishes and an extensive specials board. The enclosed garden with children's play area is popular with families and houses an annual beer festival. P

Retford

Rum Runner

Wharf Road, DN22 6EN (50 yds from fire station)
10am-1am daily
☎ (01777) 860788
Bateman XB, XXXB; guest beers Ⓗ
This popular town centre pub, now owned by Bateman Brewery, was a past local CAMRA Pub of the Year and is a regular Pub of the Season. The local Broadstone Brewery is situated in outbuildings at the rear and the brewer can be seen at work from the lounge area or garden. Three guest ales are always available, often including a Broadstone beer; as well as a good selection of foreign bottled beers. The lounge area has a couple of soft sofas, and can get busy at the weekends.

Ruddington

Three Crowns

23 Easthorpe Street, NG11 6LB
12-3, 5-11; 12-11 Sat; 12-10.30 Sun
☎ (0115) 921 3226
Adnams Bitter; Nottingham Rock Ale Mild, EPA; Taylor Landlord; guest beers Ⓗ
Smart and popular single bar village local also known as the Top House. The name refers to the pub's chimney pots. The pub is also home to the well respected Luk Pra Tor Thai restaurant, open Tuesday to Saturday evenings (booking advisable). Thai bottled beers are sold. Look for the Tuk-Tuk.

White Horse

60 Church Street, NG11 6HG
12-11 (10.30 Sun)
☎ (0115) 9844550 whitehorse-inn.co.uk
Black Sheep Best Bitter; Jennings Cumberland Ale; Wells Bombardier; guest beers Ⓗ
Excellent two-roomed local built in the 1930s by Home Brewery, now essentially a free house. The no-smoking lounge is carpeted, with comfortable upholstered settles, stools and chairs. The public bar has bare floorboards, a dartboard, pool table and TV. Both rooms have interesting old local photographs on the walls. The garden drinking area is superb in summer with patio

heaters for cooler evenings. There is a building at the rear where frequent beer festivals are held. Q☕❀◐◑⊟⊟♣P⊬

Selston

Horse & Jockey

Church Lane, NG16 6FB OS464539
⊙ 12-3, 5-11; 12-3, 7-10.30 Sun
☎ (01773) 781012
Draught Bass; [H] Greene King Abbot; Taylor Landlord; [G] guest beers [H]/[G]
This friendly village local, dating back to 1664, is reputedly haunted. The interior has a main bar, snug and lounge with cast iron range. Low-beamed ceilings, flagstone floors and open fires give a warm and cosy feel. You are welcome to play pool or a selection of pub games in the games room. Up to nine real ales are available at any one time. Winner of several local CAMRA awards and Nottinghamshire CAMRA Pub of the Year 2004. ♨Q❀♿♣P

South Leverton

Plough Inn

Town Street, DN22 0BT
⊙ 10-1am (midnight Sun)
☎ (01427) 880323
Greene King Ruddles County; guest beers [H]
A recent winner of the local CAMRA Pub of the Season Award, this small, friendly village pub also houses the local Post Office. Situated opposite the village hall, you could drive through the village and not see it, but then you would miss out on a little gem. Some of the seating appears to be old church pews. The locals will make you feel welcome. Q❀⛺♣P

Southwell

Old Coach House

69 Easthorpe, NG25 0HY (on A612 heading to Upton)
⊙ 4 (12 Sat & Sun)-midnight
☎ (01636) 813289
Beer range varies [H]
This street corner pub has yet again been voted Newark CAMRA pub of the year and was one of four finalists in the CAMRA Pub of the Year 2005. There is an ever-changing range of beers, always including one mild. A traditional pub with a central bar serving several drinking areas, it has real fires in winter. A novel patio lends itself to outdoor drinking during the summer. A short walk from the centre of the town, there is always a friendly welcome here. ♨Q❀⊟♣●

Sutton Bonnington

King's Head

75 Main Street, LE12 5PE
⊙ 12-2, 6-midnight; 12-midnight Sat; 12-10.30 Sun
☎ (01509) 672331
Banks's Mansfield Cask; Marston's Pedigree; guest beer [H]
Warm and friendly community-focused local that attracts a diverse clientele. The bar area displays various artefacts from the local village, creating a mini museum as a reminder of the history of the south Notts neighbourhood. The lounge has an open fire burning during colder months. ♨Q❀⊟♣P

Watnall

Royal Oak

25 Main Road, NG1 1HS (on B600)
⊙ 12-midnight daily
☎ (0115) 938 3110
Hardys & Hansons Best Bitter, Olde Trip, seasonal beers [H]
This popular roadside pub has a homely feel to it. A cosy upstairs lounge is open at weekends. The log cabin to the rear is used for occasional bands and the pub's renowned beer festivals. Pool is played in the back room and sport is shown on an unobtrusive TV. In fine weather you can sit outside at the rear or the front. The car park is across the road. Q❀♿⊟(331, 125)♣P

Wellow

Olde Red Lion

Eakring Road, NG22 0EG
⊙ 11.30-3.30, 6-11; 11-11 Sat; 12-10.30 Sun
☎ (01623) 861000
Caledonian Deuchars IPA; Fuller's London Pride; Wells Bombardier [H]
Regular winner of local CAMRA Pub of the Season awards, this 400-year-old pub with exposed beams stands opposite the village green and maypole. The walls of the bar are covered in old photographs and maps that depict the history of both the pub and the village. There is a small lounge bar and restaurant where good home-cooked food is served daily. Clumber and Rufford country parks and Center Parcs Holiday Village are nearby. May Day is very busy when children from the village dance round the maypole. Q❀◐◑⛺♣P⊬

West Bridgford

Southbank Bar

1 Bridgford House, Trent Bridge, NG2 5GJ
⊙ 11 (10 Sat)-midnight (11 Tue & Wed; 1am Fri & Sat); 10-midnight Sun
☎ (0115) 945 5541 ⊕ southbankbar.co.uk
Caledonian Deuchars IPA; Fuller's London Pride; Mallard Duck 'n' Dive; Taylor Landlord [H]
Large, lively bar on Trent Bridge, handy for the cricket and both football grounds. It has comfortable seating and a patio overlooking the Trent. An independently owned free house, it always offers beer from Mallard. The Globe, its sister pub, is just over the bridge. A varied and interesting selection of food is available, including breakfast at the weekend from 10am. Live music is played most evenings. Several TVs show sport. ❀◐◑♿

Stratford Haven

2 Stratford Road, NG2 6BA
⊙ 10.30-11 (midnight Thu-Sat); 12-11 Sun
☎ (0115) 982 5981
Adnams Broadside; Bateman XB; Caledonian Deuchars IPA; Castle Rock Nottingham Gold, Harvest Pale; guest beers [H]
Busy, gimmick-free Tynemill pub, tucked

away next to the Co-op between the town centre and Trent Bridge cricket ground. Named as the result of a competition in the local press, the winning entry is on display. The beer range includes at least one mild and Castle Rock house beers. Monthly brewery nights are usually accompanied by live music. A good menu is available, including vegetarian options, but no chips. Q❀◐◑♿🍎⊬

Test Match ☆

Gordon Square, NG2 5LP

10.30-11.30 (midnight Fri & Sat); 12-11.30 Sun

☎ (0115) 981 1481

Hardys & Hansons Best Bitter, Olde Trip, seasonal beer H

Art Deco masterpiece lovingly restored to highlight the original features. The main entrance is via a revolving door opening directly into the spacious lounge. This has a fine stairway leading to the upstairs cocktail bar. A separate public bar with pool table can be reached via the main entrance or through a side door. The cricket theme is reflected in the front lounge area in large, impressive murals. The pub is a recent winner of an English Heritage award. ❀◐◑⊟♿🚌(6)♣P⊬

West Stockwith

White Hart

Main Street, DN10 4ET

11-1am daily

☎ (01427) 890176

Taylor Landlord; guest beers H

Small country pub with a little garden overlooking the River Trent, Chesterfield Canal and West Stockwith Marina. One bar serves the through bar, lounge and dining area. Daleside beers are often available to accompany the freshly-cooked food. The area is especially busy during the summer, due to the volume of river traffic. West Stockwith is where the Chesterfield Canal joins the River Trent. Q❀◐◑♿⛺♣P

Woodthorpe

Vale ☆

Mansfield Road, NG5 3GG

12-11 (midnight Fri & Sat); 12-11 Sun

☎ (0115) 926 8864

Adnams Broadside; Castle Rock Elsie Mo; McEwans 80/-; Taylor Landlord; guest beers H

This late 1930s pub sits on a prominent corner position near the site of the original owners, Home Brewery. The main entrance leads to a timber and glass porch. Inside there is much original wood panelling. There is a separate bar and a family dining/no-smoking area to the rear of the lounge. Six beers are stocked and good value food is available all day. A popular quiz is held every Sunday. ❀◐◑⊟♿🚌(25)P⊬

Worksop

Kilton Inn

Kilton Road, DN22 6EN

11-12.30am (1.30am Fri & Sat); 11-12.30am Sun

☎ (01909) 473828 🌐 kiltoninn.co.uk

Greene King Abbot; John Smith's Bitter; Stones Bitter H

A new entry in the Guide, this is a popular pub with very active darts, dominoes and pool teams, situated on the edge of Worksop town centre. A single bar serves a large open plan space divided into three areas. To one side of the bar is a quiet area with seating; the dartboard and pool table are at the other end of the room. The pub has received industry awards for its beer quality. ⇌🚌♣P

Mallard

Station Approach, S81 7AG

5 (2 Fri; 12 Sat)-11; 12-4 Sun

☎ (01909) 530757

Beer range varies H

Local CAMRA Pub of the Year 2004 and regular winner of Pub of the Season, this welcoming pub was formerly the Worksop station buffet. Two real ales are always on handpump together with a large selection of foreign bottled beers and country fruit wines. A further room is available downstairs for special occasions such as the three beer festivals the pub holds each year. Q⛺⇌🚌P

Regency Hotel

Carlton Road, S81 7AG (opp. railway station)

11-2, 7-11; 12-2, 7-10.30 Sun

☎ (01909) 474108

John Smith's Magnet; guest beers H

Large hotel situated opposite Worksop railway station on the edge of the town centre. Following its inclusion in the 2005 Guide the Regency has now added a third handpull, allowing it to dispense two guest ales as well as John Smith's Magnet. It has one bar and a dining area. The pub is popular at lunchtime due to a good selection of reasonably priced food. Q❀◐◑⛺⇌🚌P

Shireoaks Inn

Westgate, S80 1LT (200 yds from market)

11.30-4, 6-11; 11.30-11 Sat; 12-4.30, 7-10.30 Sun

☎ (01909) 472118

Beer range varies H

Warm, friendly pub, converted from cottages. The public bar houses a pool table and large screen TV. There is a comfortable lounge bar and dining area where tasty home-cooked food represents good value for money. The two handpulls dispense varying guest ales. A small outside area with tables is available in summer. Q❀◐⊟⛺⇌🚌♣⊬

Keep your Good Beer Guide up to date by visiting www.camra.org.uk, click on *Good Beer Guide* then *Updates to the GBG 2007* where you will find information about changes to breweries.

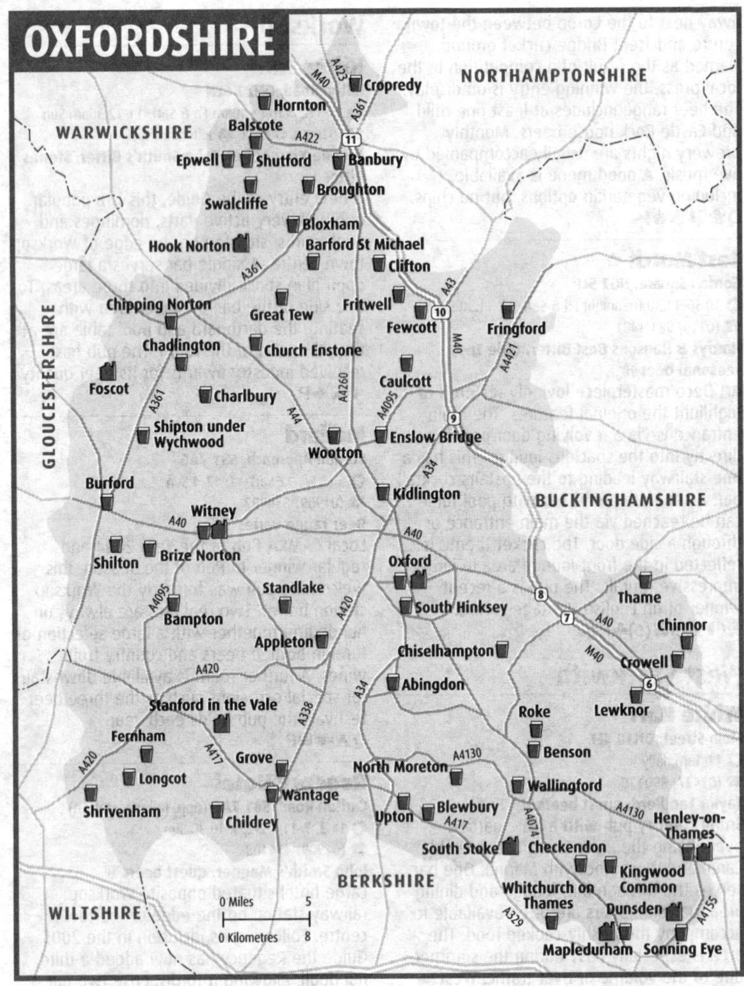

Abingdon

Brewery Tap

40-42 Ock Street, OX14 5BZ

11-midnight (1am Fri & Sat); 12-4, 7-11 Sun

(01235) 521655 brewerytap.net

Greene King Morland Original, Old Speckled Hen; guest beer Ⓗ

Set in the former Morland Brewery grounds, this Grade II listed, award-winning conversion of the sales office has been owned by the same family since 1993. The attractive interior features panelled walls, stone floors and an open fire. This pub is a popular lunchtime venue offering an innovative menu. The historic town centre, old abbey buildings and the River Thames are nearby.

White Horse

189 Ock Street, OX14 5DW

11-11 (midnight Fri & Sat); 12-11 Sun

(01235) 524490

Greene King IPA, Abbot, Morland Original; guest beer Ⓗ

This Grade II listed former coaching inn, close to the town, has recently been extended but retains its original character and pleasant atmosphere. A busy pub with an award-winning garden, locals, visitors, children and pets are all made welcome. Host to football, darts and Aunt Sally teams playing in local leagues, it also holds quiz nights and seasonal events. Quality food is reasonably priced.

INDEPENDENT BREWERIES

Appleford Brightwell-cum-Sotwell
Brakspear Witney
Butler's Mapledurham
Cotswold Foscot
Hook Norton Hook Norton
Loddon Dunsden
Lovibonds Henley-on-Thames
Old Bog Oxford
Ridgeway South Stoke
White Horse Stanford in the Vale
Windrush Witney
Wychwood Witney

Appleton

Plough

Eaton Road, OX13 5JR

⊙ 12-2.30 (not Wed), 6-11; 12-3, 7-10.30 Sun

☎ (01865) 862441

Greene King XX Mild, IPA, Morland Original; guest beer 🄷

Classic local in the centre of the village. Visitors are assured of a warm welcome as soon as they set foot inside the door. There are three interconnected rooms served from a single bar. The lounge – almost a snug – and public bar both have a coal fire in winter. Earnest debate and lively conversation are the main sources of entertainment here, with the landlord joining in. ♛Q❀🛏⊟⛺♣P

Balscote

Butcher's Arms

OX15 6SQ (½ mile S of A422 Banbury-Stratford road)

⊙ 12-2 (not Mon or Tue; 3 Sat), 6.30-midnight; 12-3, 7-midnight Sun

☎ (01295) 730750

Hook Norton Hooky Bitter, seasonal beers; guest beers 🄷

Village pub built from the local honeyed Hornton stone. A single large room provides a comfortable drinking area and games room. There is a small library, TV and pool table. Hearty, good value meals are served on Friday, Saturday and Sunday lunchtime. Popular folk music sessions are held every second Wednesday. It is a good starting or finishing point for a country walk.
♛Q◖◗🚌♣P

Bampton

Morris Clown

High Street, OX18 2JW

⊙ 5-11 (midnight Fri); 12-midnight Sat; 12-11 Sun

☎ (01993) 850217

Brakspear Bitter; Courage Best Bitter; guest beer 🄷

The single bar is decorated with Toulouse Lautrec-style murals and has a bar billiards table. The pub's name reflects its morris dancing connections – the village has upheld the tradition for 600 years and a major morris dancing festival is held every Whit Monday. The guest beer is usually from a local micro. Franziskaner wheat beer is available in bottles.
♛❀♣🍎P

Banbury

Bell Inn

Middleton Road, Grimsbury, OX16 4QJ

⊙ 1-4, 7-midnight; 12-midnight Sat; 12-4.30, 8-11 Sun

☎ (01295) 253169

Hancock's HB; Highgate Dark; guest beers 🄷

A favourite watering hole for the local community and a regular entry in the Guide, it has a comfortable lounge with a blazing fire and a traditional bar with a pool table where crib and other games are played. Two or three guest beers are usually available.
♛❀⊟⇄🚌♣P

Olde Reindeer

47 Parsons Street, OX16 5NA

⊙ 11-11; 12-3 (closed eve) Sun

☎ (01295) 264031

Hook Norton Hooky Dark, Hooky Bitter, Old Hooky, seasonal beer; guest beer 🄷

This historic 16th-century inn is not to be missed if you are in the area. It is reported to be the location where Oliver Cromwell stayed during the Civil War. Ask to see the Globe Room with its old wood panelling. The main bar has beamed ceilings, more wood panelling, a wooden floor and an open fire in winter. The pub is a recent winner of a Best Kept Cellar award.
♛Q♉❀◖♿⇄🚌♣P

Woolpack at Banbury Cross

28 Horsefair, OX16 0AE

⊙ 11-2.30, 5-11; 12-4.30 Sun

☎ (01295) 265646 ⊕ banbury-cross.co.uk/woolpack

Adnams Bitter; guest beers 🄷

A welcome addition to the local real ale scene, this pub has recently had a sympathetic refurbishment. The building has been a public house for more than 150 years and is believed to have taken its name from the former sheep market. It has two bars, one no-smoking. Food is served in both bars or the restaurant at the back. At least two guest beers are usually available. Q◖◗⇄🚌🚭

Barford St Michael

George Inn

Lower Street, OX15 0RH

(1½ miles off B4031 6 miles SW of Banbury)

⊙ 12-3 (Sat), 7-11; 12-4, 7-10.30 summer Sun

☎ (01869) 838226

Greene King IPA; guest beers 🄷

Charming thatched village inn dating from 1672. There is a pool table in the back bar and regular quiz evenings are held. Live folk or pop bands play occasionally. Themed food evenings are also popular. The large rear garden has splendid countryside views – you are welcome to bring a picnic. With its own labrador, this is a dog-friendly pub.
♛❀♿⛺♣P

Benson

Three Horseshoes

2 Oxford Road, OX10 6LX

⊙ 11-3, 5.30-midnight; 11-midnight Sat; 12-11 Sun

☎ (01491) 838242 ⊕ thethreehorseshoesbenson.co.uk

Brakspear Bitter; guest beer 🄷

Small, cosy, multi-roomed 17th-century local with a lively clientele. A free house, it has been under the same ownership since 1986. It has a dining room, no-smoking area, covered patio and large enclosed garden with playground. The guest beer usually comes from Loddon Brewery or another local micro. An extensive food menu is available and a wide choice of wines. ♛Q♉❀◖◗P🚭

Blewbury

Barley Mow

London Road, OX11 9NU

⊙ 11-11; 12-10.30 Sun

☎ (01235) 850296
Archers Best Bitter; Greene King Morland Original ⊞
1930s roadhouse situated on the main road. Until 1986 it was owned by Bass Charrington and the sign outside retains the trademark Charrington lettering of that era. Inside is a small saloon bar, public bar with pool table and a large, bright conservatory where reasonably-priced meals are served.
⇌◖◗⊟♣P⊬

Bloxham

Elephant & Castle

Humber Street, OX15 4LZ (off A361 4 miles W of Banbury)
⊙ 11-3, 5-11; 11-11 Sat; 12-10.30 Sun
☎ (01295) 720383
Hook Norton Hooky Bitter, seasonal beers; guest beers ⊞
Welcoming 16th-century coaching inn with a wide carriage entrance to the garden, car park and front doors. The original bread oven remains in the restaurant area. Home-cooked meals and snacks are available at lunchtime Monday-Saturday. Open fires blaze in winter. Chas, the friendly landlord, has run this pub for 34 years. Accommodation is available in two new double rooms with views to the church.
ᗑQ❀⇌◖⊟♿⊟♣P

Brize Norton

Masons Arms

Burford Road, OX18 3NN
⊙ 12-3, 6.30-11; 12-4, 6.30-10.30 Sun
☎ (01993) 842567
Wells Bombardier; guest beers ⊞
There is an amiable welcome from the landlord at this unadorned and homely free house, a Cotswold stone building with log fires near Burford. The bar divides the interior into the comfy, music-free lounge and the public bar, with quiet background music (but the volume rises when Plymouth are on TV!). Outside are small colourful gardens with seating, one lawned for Aunt Sally. It can be noisy with the RAF airbase across the field.
ᗑQ♉❀♿⊟♣P

Broughton

Saye & Sele Arms

Main Road, OX15 5ED (3 miles W of Banbury on B4035)
⊙ 11.30-2.30 (11-3 Sat), 7-11; 12-3, 7-10.30 Sun
☎ (01295) 263348
Adnams Bitter; Wadworth 6X; guest beers ⊞
Built with local Hornton stone, this imposing village pub lies on the edge of the Broughton Castle grounds. There are always two guest ales to try in the beamed and flagstoned bar. Good food with friendly service and a regularly changing menu help make the restaurant popular (booking is advised) – note the huge collection of water jugs. The shady garden and patio are perfect for a summer drink after a walk around the castle grounds. Q❀◖◗♿⊟♣P

Burford

Royal Oak

26 Witney Street, OX18 4SN (off A361)
⊙ 11-2.30 (not Tue), 6.30-11; 11-11 Sat; 11-3, 7-10.30 Sun
☎ (01993) 823278
Wadworth IPA, 6X; guest beer ⊞
Tucked away in a side street, this is a genuine local with a traditional pub atmosphere. The flagstoned front bar leads to a long, carpeted side bar with a bar billiards table. The walls are decorated with photographs and memorabilia. An ancient clock chimes melodiously. Around 1,000 tankards hang from the ceilings. Excellent home-made food using local produce is served. Walkers are welcome.
ᗑQ❀⇌◖◗⛺⊟♣●P

Caulcott

Horse & Groom

Lower Heyford Road, OX25 4ND (on B4030 between Middleton Stoney and Lower Heyford)
⊙ 11-3, 6-11; 12-3, 7-10.30 Sun
☎ (01869) 343257
Hook Norton Hooky Bitter; guest beers ⊞
A small country pub with a big welcome and cosy atmosphere. An excellent choice of three frequently-changing guest beers is available, with the emphasis on brews from local small and micro-breweries. Good a la carte meals and speciality sausages are served in the bar or restaurant. Twice local CAMRA Pub of the Year, the pub is set in gentle, scenic walking country. ᗑQ❀◖◗

Chadlington

Tite Inn

Mill End, OX7 3NY (off A361 2 miles S of Chipping Norton)
⊙ 12-2.30, 6.30-11; closed Mon; 12-3, 7-10.30 Sun
☎ (01608) 676475 🌐 titeinn.com
Ramsbury Bitter; Sharp's Doom Bar; guest beers ⊞
Family-run Cotswold stone free house run by the same owners for 20 years. The attractive garden offers fine views, and colourful shrubs line the path from the car park. Two comfortably-furnished connecting bars and a restaurant are supplemented by the garden room in summer. Excellent freshly prepared food and six real ales are served. The pub is a focus for village activities including an annual pantomime, cricket team and Easter egg rolling. Winner of local CAMRA Pub of the Year 2005, the pub is no-smoking throughout. ᗑQ♉❀◖◗♿⛺⊟♣●P⊬

Charlbury

Olde Three Horseshoes

Sheep Street, OX7 3RR
⊙ 7-11; 5-midnight Fri; 12- midnight Sat; 12-11.30 Sun
☎ (01608) 810780
Wizard Apprentice, seasonal beers; guest beers ⊞
This pub is a favourite venue for quizzes, darts matches and, in the summer, Aunt Sally. An antique kitchen stove warms the

cosy, quiet front bar. There is also a back bar, family room with TV and function room. Authentic Thai food is served in a spacious back room (Tue-Sat). A selection of beers from the Wizard Brewery is always available. ⛫Q⛰❀◗⊟⛺⇌⊟♣P

Rose & Crown

Market Street, OX7 3PL

⏲ 12-11 (midnight Wed & Thu; 1am Fri); 11-1am Sat; 12-11 Sun

☎ (01608) 810103 🌐 theroseandcrownpub.com

Young's Bitter; guest beers Ⓗ

Popular, traditional, town-centre free house, more than 20 years in the Guide. Simply furnished, it has a split level bar with no-smoking lounge, plus a patio courtyard. On the Oxfordshire Way long distance path, walkers are welcome to bring their own picnics. A pub for the discerning drinker, six real ales are offered – the best selection in the area. A strong supporter of micro-breweries, the Rose & Crown has been North Oxon CAMRA Pub of the Year three times. Regular music nights feature local and touring musicians. ❀⛺⇌⊟♣⚟

Checkendon

Black Horse

Burncote Lane, RG8 0TE (off A4074)

⏲ 12-2, 7-11; 12-2, 7-10.30 Sun

☎ (01491) 680418

Butler's Oxfordshire Bitter; West Berkshire Old Father Thames, Good Old Boy Ⓖ

This 300-year-old pub has been run by generations of the same family for over a century. Full of olde-worlde charm, it is hidden away up a lane that at first glance appears to lead to nowhere. However it is well worth seeking out and is popular with locals and visitors, walkers and horse riders. This is not a food pub, but baguettes are usually available at lunchtime. ⛫Q❀⛺P

Childrey

Hatchet

Main Street, OX12 9UF (on B4001)

⏲ 12-2.30 (3 Sat), 7-11; 12-3.30, 7-10.30 Sun

☎ (01235) 751213

Greene King Morland Original; guest beers Ⓗ

Situated not far from the duck pond in this picture postcard village, the Hatchet offers a warm welcome and a fine array of ales to suit all tastes. The interior of the pub is open plan with a quieter drinking and dining area off to one side. As well as the usual pub games, there is shove ha'penny and an Aunt Sally pitch. It was a well-deserved winner of local CAMRA Pub of the Year in 2004. ❀◖◗⊟♣P

Chinnor

Red Lion

3 High Street, OX39 4DL (on B4009)

⏲ 12-3, 5-11; 12-11 Fri & Sat; 12-10.30 Sun

☎ (01844) 353468

Greene King IPA; Loddon Ferryman's Gold; Young's Special; guest beers Ⓗ

This 300-year-old friendly village local was originally three cottages. It is situated near the village centre but within easy access of the fine Chiltern countryside and a local steam railway. The outside drinking area has been refurbished and wooden decking added. Quiz nights are held monthly. Guest ales usually change three times a week. No evening meals are served Sunday. ⛫Q❀◖◗♣P

Chipping Norton

Chequers

Goddards Lane, OX7 5NP

⏲ 11-11; 12-10.30 Sun

☎ (01608) 644717 🌐 chequers-pub.co.uk

Fuller's Chiswick, London Pride, ESB, seasonal beers Ⓗ

Town centre pub with a warm, welcoming atmosphere and friendly service from the long-serving licensees and their efficient team. Divided into four seating areas, subdued lighting and simple furnishings create a pleasant ambience. There is a separate meeting room and courtyard restaurant serving traditional food (not Sun eve). It is a convenient meeting point for the adjacent theatre. ⛫Q◖◗⊟

Chiselhampton

Coach & Horses

Watlington Road, OX44 7UX (B480/B4015 jct)

⏲ 11.30-11; 11-3.30 Sun

☎ (01865) 890255 🌐 coachhorsesinn.co.uk

Hook Norton Hooky Bitter, Hooky Dark Ⓗ

Dating back to the 16th century, this pub has a bar and four dining areas where you can enjoy good quality food. Plenty of beams, exposed brickwork and open log fires create a traditional feel. For summer there is a patio and lawn. To the rear nine chalet-style bedrooms offer attractive accommodation. ⛫❀⛿◖◗♿P

Church Enstone

Crown

Mill Lane, OX7 4NN (off A44)

⏲ 12-3 (not Mon), 6-11; 12-3 (closed eve) Sun

☎ (01608) 677262 🌐 crowninnenstone.co.uk

Hook Norton Hooky Bitter; Wychwood Hobgoblin; guest beers Ⓗ

Dating from the 17th century, this Cotswold stone pub is a gem. An inglenook and local photographs add to the character. The no-smoking restaurant features fresh fish, seafood and game (in season), made with local produce (no food Mon). The pub is popular with locals and visitors who enjoy pleasant conversation without intrusive music or games machines. It is an ideal place to visit after a walk in the surrounding countryside. The front patio and rear garden are delightful in summer. ⛫Q❀◖◗⊟P

Clifton

Duke of Cumberland's Head

Main Street, OX15 0PE (on B4031)

⏲ 12-2.30 (not Mon), 6.30-11; 12-3 Sun

☎ (01869) 338534

Caledonian Deuchars IPA; Hook Norton Hooky Bitter; guest beers Ⓗ
Built in 1645, this attractive, peaceful pub, situated close to the canal, is popular, especially at weekends. Named after Prince Rupert, who led the King's troops in the battle of Edgehill in 1642, the low-beamed lounge has a large fireplace with a cosy log fire. The no-smoking dining room has exposed stone walls. Three excellent real ales, together with over 30 whiskies, await you at this warm, welcoming pub.
⛼Q☺❀⇆◐◑♿⊟P⊬

Cropredy

Red Lion

8 Red Lion Street, OX17 1PB
⏲ 12-2.30 (3.30 Sat), 6 (5.30 Tue & Fri)-11; 12-3.30, 6.30-10.30 Sun
☎ (01295) 750224 🌐 redlioncropredy.co.uk
Hook Norton Hooky Bitter; guest beers Ⓗ
A warm welcome awaits at this traditional Oxfordshire pub situated just a few yards from the Oxford Canal. In the heart of Cropredy – winner of best kept Oxfordshire village in 2005 – the garden is a delight in summer. An extensive food menu is offered. Two of the four rooms have real fires and there are usually three guest beers available.
⛼Q☺❀◐◑♿♣P⊬

Crowell

Shepherd's Crook

The Green, OX39 4RR (off B4009 between Chinnor and M40 jct 6) OS744997
⏲ 11.30-3, 5-11; 11-11 Sat; 12-10.30 Sun
☎ (01844) 351431
Batham Best Bitter; Otter Bitter; Young's Bitter; guest beers Ⓗ
In the foothills of the Chilterns, this comfortable inn is renowned for its wide selection of beers – the landlord is a real ale fanatic. He is also a former fish merchant and his fresh fish comes direct from the West Country, while excellent steak and kidney pies and steaks come from the local butcher. The pub is a rare outlet for Batham; local beers also feature. A beer festival is held on the August bank holiday weekend. Dogs are welcome here.
⛼Q❀◐◑♣●P

Enslow Bridge

Rock of Gibraltar

OX5 3AY (off A4260, signed to Bletchingdon)
⏲ 11-1am; 12-1am Sun
☎ (01869) 331373
Beer range varies Ⓗ
Historic, traditional free house built in 1787, by the side of the Oxfordshire Canal between Thrupp and Lower Heyford. This two-storey pub has a large, open bar and offers a choice of up to three constantly changing ales. Food is served in the bar or downstairs restaurant. Well behaved dogs are welcome in the bar area or large canalside garden.
⛼☺❀◐◑P

Epwell

Chandler's Arms

OX15 6LH (off B4039 Banbury to Shipston road) OS353403
⏲ 11-11 (1am Fri & Sat); 12-10.30 Sun
☎ (01295) 780344
Hook Norton Hooky Bitter, Old Hooky, seasonal beers; guest beers Ⓗ
Traditional, cosy, two-roomed village pub in an area popular with walkers near the Warwickshire border. The pub has evolved over the years but retains its original character and remains a rural idyll. The lounge area screens rugby internationals on TV. Pub games are played, including Aunt Sally in season. Food is served all day every day.
Q❀◐◑⊟⊟♣●P

Fernham

Woodman Inn

SN7 7NX (on B4508)
⏲ 11-3, 5-11; 11-11 Fri & Sat; 12-10.30 Sun
☎ (01367) 820643
Beer range varies Ⓖ
This charming 17th-century inn has been a public house since 1652. Reopened in 2004 after a three-year closure, it remains unchanged except for new lavatories. Four real ales are available, all dispensed by gravity. The excellent food menu is renowned locally and the pub can be busy with drinkers and diners, but there is plenty of room and ample seating for all.
⛼Q❀♿⊟♣●P

Fewcott

White Lion

Fritwell Road, OX27 7NZ (near jct 10, M40, 300 yds off B4130) OS539279
⏲ 7 (5.30 Fri; 12 Sat)-midnight; 12-6.30 Sun
☎ (01869) 346639
Beer range varies Ⓗ
A true free house, the White Lion is popular with CAMRA members who come for the four constantly changing ales. This village local has a cosy yet spacious bar with a games room for darts and pool. Families are welcome and there is a large, quiet garden at the rear. ⛼❀♿⊟♣P

Fringford

Butchers Arms

Stratton Audley Road, OX27 8EB (off A4421) OS604285
⏲ 12-1.30am; 12-11.30 Sun
☎ (01869) 277363
Adnams Broadside; Marston's Pedigree; guest beers Ⓗ
Cosy stone-built pub with comfortable seating and an open fire overlooking the village cricket pitch. High quality, traditional pub food served in the bar or restaurant complements the good ale. A pub for the community, it holds regular quiz nights and pub games. Dogs on leads are welcome in the bar. Food is available throughout the day. ❀◐◑♿⛺⊟♣P⊟

Fritwell

King's Head

92 East Street, OX27 7QF (2 miles W of jct 10, M40)
✪ 12-midnight; 12-10 Sun
☎ (01869) 346738 ⊕ thekingsheadfritwell.co.uk
Hook Norton Hooky Bitter; guest beers Ⓗ/Ⓖ
Ever popular, this village local has a welcoming open fire and small garden. Three or four ales are offered on handpump or gravity. A bottled beer festival is held in the spring along with other events – check the website for details. Traditional pub food is served daily, except Monday.
♨❀◑🚌♣P

Great Tew

Falkland Arms

19-21 The Green, OX7 4DB (off A361 and B4022)
✪ 11.30-2.30 (3 Sat), 6-11 (11.30-11 summer Sat); 12-3, 7-10.30 (12-10.30 summer) Sun
☎ (01608) 683653 ⊕ falklandarms.org.uk
Wadworth IPA, 6X, seasonal beers; guest beers Ⓗ
Set in a picturesque thatched village, this award-winning pub is a haven for visitors with an unspoilt, relaxed atmosphere where mobile phones are banned. Simple wooden furniture and flagstone and bare board floors, and an inglenook fireplace to warm you in winter, add to the olde-worlde character. Drinking vessels and old artefacts hang from the oak beams. Up to four guest ales are offered and a range of whiskies. High-quality food is served (not Sun eve).
♨Q❀⇌◑●

Grove

Volunteer

Station Road, OX12 0DH (on A338, 2 miles N of Wantage)
✪ 11-midnight (1am Thu-Sat); 12-midnight Sun
☎ (01235) 769557 ⊕ the-volunteer-inn.co.uk
Hook Norton Hooky Dark, Hooky Bitter, 303AD, Old Hooky, seasonal beers; guest beers Ⓗ
Popular open-plan pub, one of Hook Norton's more remote outposts. The Volunteer was originally built to serve the former Wantage Road station and the terminus of the old Wantage tramway. Outside in the courtyard there is a pitch for Aunt Sally, the traditional pub game found mostly in Oxfordshire. Westons Old Rosie cider is available in summer. Meals are served at lunchtime except Monday. ❀◑🚌♣●P

Henley-on-Thames

Bird in Hand

61 Greys Road, RG9 1SB (200 yds SW of A4155)
✪ 11.30-2.30, 5-11; 11.30-11 Sat; 12-10.30 Sun
☎ (01491) 575775
Brakspear Bitter; Fuller's London Pride; Hook Norton Hooky Dark; guest beers Ⓗ
Henley's only genuine free house, this friendly, one-bar, town centre local was local CAMRA's Pub of the Year 2006. The large, secure garden has an aviary, pond and pets, and is reached through the family room. Two guest beers often come from micro-breweries. The landlord is a rugby fan and big matches are shown on a plasma screen. Reasonably priced lunches are served weekdays. ᗢ❀◑Δ≠♣

Rose & Crown

56 New Street, RG9 2BT
✪ 11-3, 6-11; 11-11 Sat; 11-6 Sun
☎ (01491) 578376 ⊕ roseandcrownhenley.co.uk
Brakspear Bitter Ⓗ
Small, town-centre pub near the Thames, that can get busy with patrons of the nearby Kenton Theatre. You can sink into one of the large leather armchairs in the lounge or drink outside in the enclosed patio garden. Spot the well in the floor of the main bar. A full menu is served, but Friday is fish and chips day and a range of roasts is offered on Sunday until 5pm. ❀⇌◑◗Δ≠

Hornton

Dun Cow

West End, OX15 6DA
✪ 6-1am; 12-11 Sat; 12-10.30 Sun
☎ (01295) 670524 ⊕ drunkenmonk.co.uk
Hook Norton Hooky Bitter; Wells Bombardier; guest beers Ⓗ
Classic, hidden-away, thatched, low beamed and flagstone-floored pub in a remote village close to the Warwickshire border. It was a butcher's slaughterhouse until 1840 and retains much of its character. With a wide choice of guest ales, bottled beers and rural wines, you may well find something you have not tried before. You can play pool at the bottom of the garden near the ducks. There are beer festivals in February and July.
♨Qᗢ❀◗⊟♿🚌♣●P⚟

Kidlington

King's Arms

4 The Moors, OX5 2AJ
✪ 11-3, 5.30-11.30; 11-midnight Fri & Sat; 12-11.30 Sun
☎ (01865) 373004
Greene King IPA; Wells Bombardier; guest beer Ⓗ
Popular two-bar local in the old part of Kidlington. Good food is available at lunchtime for under a fiver. The heated, covered patio is used for traditional games throughout the year. Local CAMRA Country Pub of the Year 2003, it serves an interesting range of guest beers. Frequent beer festivals are held supporting local breweries. ᗢ❀◑⊟♣P

Kingwood Common

Unicorn

Colmore Lane, RG9 5LX (off B481 towards Stoke Row)
✪ 12-3, 6-11; 12-3, 6-10.30 Sun
☎ (01491) 628452
Brakspear Bitter, seasonal beers; Hook Norton Hooky Dark Ⓗ
Welcoming and pleasant pub for drinking and dining, popular with locals as well as visitors. The Unicorn goes from strength to strength and has recently added a new one-room suite for hire with a gym, private garden and broadband connection.
♨Q❀⇌◑♣P

Lewknor

Leather Bottle

1 High Street, OX49 5TH
11-2.30, 6-11; 12-3, 7-10.30 Sun
(01844) 351482
Brakspear Bitter, Special, seasonal beers H
Wonderful old public house with an immaculate interior. Spacious drinking and dining areas are spread over three rooms. An open fire and central servery divide the two bars and there is a no-smoking area and family room. With consistently good ale and an extensive menu featuring home-made specials, this is a pub well worth seeking out. It has only missed one edition of this Guide.

Longcot

King & Queen

Shrivenham Road, SN7 7TL (off B4508)
12-3, 6-11; closed Mon; 12-3, 7-10.30 Sun
(01793) 783611 kingandqueenlongcot.co.uk
Caledonian Deuchars IPA; Courage Best Bitter; guest beers H
It is thought that this pub was constructed around 200 years ago to cater for navvies working on the nearby Wilts & Berks Canal. It boasts a view of the famous 3000-year-old Uffington White Horse. Inside is an extensive open plan drinking area and a restaurant serving organic meat and local produce. Bar billiards, table skittles and boules are played here.

Mapledurham

Pack Saddle

Chazey Heath, RG4 7UD (on A4074)
11-3, 6-11; 11-11 Fri & Sat; 12-10.30 Sun
(0118) 946 3000 thepacksaddleinn.co.uk
Wadworth IPA, 6X, JCB, seasonal beers H
Located on the Mapledurham Estate, a few miles from the famous house, this genuine old pub is popular with locals and visitors. The front bar is mainly for drinking with a huge fireplace, substantial beams and agricultural and equine paraphernalia. The back bar is no-smoking and used for dining. The food, freshly made with the emphasis on traditional English fare, is recommended for its good value and quality (booking is advisable). The large garden has a children's play area and there is a paddock for beer festivals.

North Moreton

Bear at Home

High Street, OX11 9AT
12-3, 6-11 (midnight Thu; 1am Fri & Sat); 12-3, 6-11 Sun
(01235) 811311 bear-at-home.co.uk
Taylor Landlord; guest beers H
Dating from the 16th century, the Bear has recently been revitalised by a local family who also run an antiques business – many items on display at the pub are for sale. The pub backs on to the village cricket green and Aunt Sally is played in summer. The bar has a relaxed feel with comfortable sofas and an open fire. Three real ales are usually available, at least one from a micro-brewery.

Oxford

Angel & Greyhound

30 St Clements Street, OX4 1AB
11 (12 winter)-midnight; 12-midnight Sun
(01865) 242660
Young's Bitter, Special, seasonal beers H
Popular pub over the Magdalen Bridge in the St Clements area of Oxford, named after the local Angel meadow. It has a spacious open-plan single bar. A full range of Young's beers is available, both draught and bottled. Good pub food is served at lunchtimes and evenings. Patios front and rear are busy in fine weather; the rear patio has a covered, heated area. There is a wide range of board games available plus bar billiards and darts.

Eagle & Child

49 St Giles, OX1 3LU
11.30-11.30 (12.30am Fri & Sat); 12-11 Sun
(01865) 302925
Adnams Broadside; Caledonian Deuchars IPA; Fuller's London Pride; guest beer H
This sprawling, long and narrow pub overlooking the Lamb and Flag and St Giles has recently been awarded a Pubs in Time plaque for its involvement in shaping history – famous writers including CS Lewis and JR Tolkein met here regularly. The pub's name comes from the Earl of Derby's crest – his family were once local landowners. The two front bars are rare classics. The pub is popular with students and tourists who come for the wide range of good beers.

Harcourt Arms

Cranham Terrace, Jericho, OX2 6DG
12-2, 5.30-11 (midnight Fri & Sat); 12-2, 7-11 Sun
(01865) 310630
Fuller's Chiswick, Discovery, London Pride, ESB, seasonal beers H
Street corner Jericho pub, once an Ind Coope house but for many years now a fine Fuller's outlet. Background jazz, board games, newspapers and two relaxing log fires create a relaxed atmosphere. Recently refurbished but retaining its original character, the pub has gained an extra handpump for Fuller's seasonal beer. Note the collection of banknotes from around the world. Toasted sandwiches are served until late on week nights.

Hobgoblin

172 Cowley Road, OX4 1UE (opp. Tesco)
12-11; 12-10.30 Sun
(01865) 439496
Beer range varies H
Busy pub with a single open-plan bar; the clientele is a mix of locals and students. It has a large garden and patio that fill up quickly in the summer months – in colder weather the patio is covered by a marquee. Large screens show sporting events. A 20% discount on real ale is offered to card carrying CAMRA members.

King's Arms

40 Holywell Street, OX1 3SP

✪ 10.30-midnight daily

☎ (01865) 242369

Young's Bitter, Special, seasonal beers; Wadworth 6X; guest beers Ⓗ

A historic Oxford institution dating from 1607, the interior is a warren of different rooms. For a quiet pint head for the back rooms – the large front bar is the student haunt. Unusually for a Young's house, guest beers from regional or larger micro-breweries are often available alongside Young's seasonal ales. Q❀◑⊟⅄

Lamb & Flag

12 St Giles, OX1 3JS

✪ 11-11 (midnight Sun); 12-10.30 Sun

☎ (01865) 515787

Fuller's London Pride; Palmer IPA; Shepherd Neame Spitfire; Skinner's Betty Stogs; Theakston Old Peculier; guest beer Ⓗ

Originally a 15th-century coaching inn, the pub is now owned by St John's College who once attempted to close it and convert it to student accommodation. Now a flagship for Oxford CAMRA, this rambling multi-roomed pub serves town and gown alike. The Palmer's and Skinner's beers are rare for the area. Lamb and Flag Gold is brewed by Palmer – look out for Tally Ho! at Christmas. Q◐⇌

Masons Arms

2 Quarry School Place, Headington Quarry, OX3 8LH

✪ 5 (11 Sat)-11; 12-4, 7-10.30 Sun

☎ (01865) 764579 ⊕ masonsquarry.co.uk

Black Sheep Best Bitter; Caledonian Deuchars IPA; St Austell Tribute; guest beers Ⓗ

This family-run community pub is full of character and charm. It is home to local darts and Aunt Sally teams. Guest ales change weekly and it hosts an annual beer festival. The Old Bog Brewery situated on the premises produces a range of beers available in the pub – see the website for details. The covered, heated, decking area is popular all year round and the function room can be booked for private events. ❀⊟♿⊟♣●P

Rose & Crown

14 North Parade Avenue, OX2 6LX

✪ 10-midnight (no entry after 11pm)

☎ (01865) 510551 ⊕ rose-n-crown.co.uk

Adnams Bitter, Broadside; Hook Norton Old Hooky Ⓗ

Popular three-room single bar pub located in a smart, narrow street of shops, galleries and restaurants just to the north of the city centre. A good mix of students, locals and academics enjoy the hospitality and lively conversation in unspoilt surroundings with no intrusive music, gaming machines or mobile phones. There is a small no-smoking cottage room that can be booked for private events and a covered, heated garden. Prices reflect the affluence of the surrounding area. Q❀◑⊟⅄

Turf Tavern

7 Bath Place, OX1 3SU

✪ 11-11; 12-10.30 Sun

☎ (01865) 243235 ⊕ theturftavern.co.uk

Beer range varies Ⓗ

Though recently taken over by Greene King, this pub retains its traditional character and excellent beer range – up to 11 real ales are offered as well as Westons Old Rosie cider. Three flagstoned patios, heated by coal braziers in winter, ease the pressure in the two bars during busy term times. Check the pub's website for popular 'meet the brewer' evenings. An annual beer festival is held in October. Q❀◑●⅄

Roke

Home Sweet Home

OX10 6JD (off B4009) OS628934

✪ 11.30-2.30; 6.30 (6 Fri & Sat & summer)-11; 12-4 Sun

☎ (01491) 838249

Beer range varies Ⓗ

Large, rambling listed building with oak beams and open fires. Drinkers and diners receive a friendly welcome in the long bar opposite the entrance. Excellent home-cooked food, often including spit-roasted meat, is served in the restaurant or in the bar, with an interesting specials list. Two Loddon beers are supplemented by a guest ale. The pub runs a beer festival offering a wide choice of micro-brewery ales over the spring bank holiday.

♨Q☋❀◑♿P

Shilton

Rose & Crown

OX18 4AB (off B4020)

✪ 11.30-3, 6-11.30; 11.30-11.30 Fri & Sat; 11.30-11 Sun

☎ (01993) 842280

Young's Bitter; guest beers Ⓗ

Situated in a picturesque village with a duck pond, this cosy 300-year-old free house has a single bar with bare stone walls and tiled floors. Simply furnished with wooden settles, it has an inglenook and interesting pictures on the walls. The restaurant offers a short menu featuring local produce. The bar stocks Hook Norton's seasonal beers. The garden is attractive in summer and there is a field at the rear used for special events. Popular with walkers, dogs are welcome.

♨Q❀◑♿▲⊟♣P

Shipton under Wychwood

Shaven Crown

High Street, OX7 6BA (on A361 between Burford and Chipping Norton)

✪ 12-2.30, 5-11; 12-11 Sat; 12-10.30 Sun

☎ (01993) 830330 ⊕ theshavencrown.co.uk

Hook Norton Hooky Bitter; guest beers Ⓗ

Situated in the heart of the village, this 700-year-old free house with a warm and friendly atmosphere welcomes drinkers and diners. Many original features remain including the 14th-century gateway. The Monks Bar is traditionally furnished with booth seating and a heavily beamed ceiling. It has a large open fire and leaded windows look out onto the delightful courtyard. Three real ales are always available. Well-behaved children are welcome. ♨Q❀⇔◑⊟⇌⊟P

Shrivenham

Prince of Wales

High Street, SN6 8AF

12-3, 6-11; 12-3 Sun

(01793) 782268 powshrivenham.co.uk

Wadworth IPA, 6X, G JCB, seasonal beers; guest beers H

Grade II listed, family-friendly pub with a good menu of home-cooked food including specials and Sunday roasts. Tuesday is quiz night; board games and newspapers are always available. A beer festival is held in late May and barbecues on bank holiday Mondays. The pub organises regular visits to breweries and beer festivals.

Shutford

George & Dragon

Church Lane, OX15 6PG (3 miles off A422)

12-2.30, 6-11; closed Mon; 12-10.30 Sun

(01295) 780320 georgeanddragon.co.uk

Hook Norton Hooky Bitter; guest beers H

This thriving free house is set in the heart of the village in the shadow of the nearby church. A sympathetic restoration has created a lively bar area with inglenook fireplace, quarry tiled floor and traditional furnishings. The restaurant is renowned locally for its wholesome food. Beers change regularly, often coming from smaller breweries. There is a small area for outdoor drinking.

Sonning Eye

Flowing Spring

Henley Road, RG4 9RB (on A4155 near Playhatch)

11.30-11; 12-10.30 Sun

(0118) 969 3207

Fuller's Chiswick, Discovery, London Pride, ESB H

Popular country local with a large riverside garden with swings and a slide. The traditional wood panelled interior has a coal fire, dartboard and no-smoking area. A balcony – heated on cool summer evenings – overlooks the large garden. Traditional pub food is served every lunchtime and Wednesday-Saturday evenings. Walkers and cyclists come from the surrounding countryside and cycle paths. The pub dogs like to snuggle up to drinkers sitting near the fire.

South Hinksey

General Elliot

Manor Road, OX1 5AS

11-midnight daily

(01865) 739369 generalelliot.co.uk

Vale Best Bitter; guest beers H

This pleasant village local has gone from strength to strength since being taken over and renovated by Vale Brewery. Although the excellent food is very popular, it is the cask ale that is the main draw here. Three changing guest beers are offered, usually from micros, often including a second Vale beer. A quarterly beer festival is held. The large garden is popular in good weather. Many visitors take the footpath across the fields from Oxford to get here.

Standlake

Black Horse

81 High Street, OX29 7RH

11-3, 6-11 (midnight Fri); 11-midnight Sat; 12-10.30 Sun

(01865) 300307 theblackhorse.demon.co.uk

Hook Norton Hooky Bitter; guest beers H

Black and white building at one end of the long, wide High Street in this old village. This friendly pub has been an inn since 1679 but the building is older and once belonged to Henry VIII. It has two smart but comfortable bars and a restaurant. Good quality food is served throughout the pub. There are two guest beers and Old Hooky is often added in summer.

Swalcliffe

Stag's Head

The Green, OX15 5EJ (6 miles W of Banbury on B4035)

12-2.30 (not Mon), 6-11; 11.30-3, 6-11 Sat; 12-4 Sun

(01295) 780232

Hook Norton Hooky Bitter; guest beers H

Charming thatched 15th-century inn set in the heart of this pretty village, with a historic tithe barn close by. The cosy, atmospheric pub, with oak beams and an inglenook fireplace, has wooden pews and tables. Popular home-made food uses locally sourced ingredients. The guest beers change frequently although often with a northern theme. There is a delightful garden for relaxing in summer.

Thame

Birdcage

9 Cornmarket, OX9 3DX

12-midnight (11 Mon; 1am Fri & Sat); 12-11 Sun

(01844) 260381 birdcagepub.co.uk

Beer range varies H

Originally the market house, this 13th/14th century building is one the oldest in the 800-year-old market town of Thame. The exterior, with its oversailing corner, is much photographed. Recent sympathetic refurbishment inside has retained many ancient features while creating a number of drinking areas and a dining area. The two real ales change regularly although Wells Bombardier is a favourite and sometimes beers from Rebellion are sold.

Upton

George & Dragon

Reading Road, OX11 9JJ

12-2.30 (not Mon), 5.30-11; 12-1am Fri & Sat; 12-11 Sun

(01235) 850723 georgeanddragon.info

Beer range varies H

This pub is ideally located for walkers on the Ridgeway Path. An authentic old three-room pub, with wood beams, brasses and a large fireplace, it has a welcoming atmosphere. Customers are encouraged to borrow from or add to the shelf of books in the main bar. Good quality, reasonably priced pub food is served. The garden has a children's play area. ♔❀◐▲♣P⊬

Wallingford

Cross Keys

48 High Street, OX10 0DB

✪ 12-3, 5-11; 12-11 Fri & Sat; 12-10.30 Sun

☎ (01491) 826377

Brakspear Bitter, Special, seasonal beers; Hook Norton Hooky Dark Ⓗ

Unspoilt 17th-century pub in a Grade II listed building retaining original features including exposed beams, fireplaces and an internal cellar. The carpeted public bar has a juke box, games machine and steps up to a games room. The wood-floored lounge leads to a function room. This friendly cask ale-oriented pub serves as a hub to the local community. The large, fenced garden, with children's play area, stands on what are believed to be Saxon town ramparts. Winner of local CAMRA Pub of the Year in 2005. ♔❀◐⊟▲♣●P

Wantage

Royal Oak Inn

Newbury Street, OX12 8DF (300 yds S of Market Place along A338)

✪ 5.30-11; 12-2.30, 7-11 Sat; 12-2, 7-10.30 Sun

☎ (01235) 763129 🌐 royaloakwantage.tripod.com

Wadworth 6X; Ⓗ/Ⓖ **West Berkshire Maggs Mild,** Ⓖ **Dr Hexter's Wedding Ale, Dr Hexter's Healer; guest beers** Ⓗ/Ⓖ

Thriving corner pub with a beer-loving landlord of many years' standing, whose name features on two West Berkshire ales served here. Photographs of ships bearing the Royal Oak name adorn the walls, as do many CAMRA awards. The smaller public bar with table football is frequented by a younger crowd. The larger lounge has a bar front of oak leaves and acorns formed from wrought iron, although it is mostly hidden by more than 200 real ale pump clips. ⛟⊟♣●

Shoulder of Mutton

38 Wallingford Street, OX12 8AX (200 yds E of Market Square on A417)

✪ 12-11 daily

☎ (07836) 380543 🌐 shoulderofmuttonwantage.com

Butts Traditional; guest beers Ⓗ

Voted local CAMRA Pub of the Year in 2006, this popular and welcoming town pub has remained largely unchanged since its inception in 1820. There is a cosy snug plus public and lounge bars with traditional decor and furnishings. The lounge has a computer with Internet access. In summer enjoy the small paved area at the back festooned with hanging baskets. ♔❀⊟⊟♣

Whitchurch on Thames

Greyhound

High Street, RG8 7EL

✪ 12-3, 6-11; 12-3, 7-10.30 Sun

☎ (0118) 984 2160

Flowers Original; Greene King IPA; Shepherd Neame Spitfire; Wells Bombardier Ⓗ

Whitchurch on Thames is a picturesque south Oxfordshire village, with a population of around 700, lying within the Chilterns area of Outstanding Natural Beauty. Most of the village, reached by a 100-year-old lattice girder toll bridge, is designated a conservation area. The pub's single L-shaped bar has a very low ceiling and plenty of beams, wood panelling and bric-a-brac. There is a small garden and limited parking. Q❀◐⇌(Pangbourne)P

Witney

House of Windsor

11 West End, OX28 1NQ

✪ 12-2.30, 6-11; 12-3, 6-midnight Fri & Sat; 12-midnight Sun

☎ (01993) 704277

Caledonian Deuchars IPA; St Austell Tinners; Taylor Landlord; guest beers Ⓗ

Popular free house once threatened with closure. An interesting range of guest beers is complemented by good value meals served at lunchtime. Watch your step when entering. Treasure the Tinners Ale – it is rare for the area. Support this pub or lose it. ♔Q❀◐

New Inn

111 Corn Street, OX28 6SU

✪ 5 (4 Fri)-11; 12-11 Sat; 12-10.30 Sun

☎ (01993) 703807

Brakspear Bitter; Black Sheep Best Bitter; St Austell Dartmoor Best; Wychwood Hobgoblin; guest beers Ⓗ

The landlord, an honorary Maasai elder, is an aficionado of ale and intellectual conversation. The pub can be quiet until the nearby Wychwood Brewery workers arrive. The cosy lounge has encyclopaedias and reference books; the public bar is for the young at heart with bay window seats, open log fire, large TV and music – live at weekends. A Cotswold stone barn beyond the fishpond is the venue for beer festivities and pub games. ♔Q❀♿⊟♣P⊡

Wootton

Killingworth Castle

Glympton Road, OX20 1EJ (on B4027)

✪ 12-3, 7-11 (midnight Wed, Fri & Sat); 12-3, 7-10.30 Sun

☎ (01993) 811401 🌐 killingworthcastle.co.uk

Greene King IPA, Abbot, Morland Original Ⓗ

Dating from 1637, this charming coaching inn has a long beamed bar with a log-burning stove and a smaller rear bar with games including bar billiards. Simple pine furniture and timber and flagstone floors are complemented by bookcases and old rural artefacts. Popular with locals, tourists and walkers, this is a long-established music venue with live music every Friday. The garden is spacious and there is comfortable accommodation in a modern barn conversion. Excellent pub food is available. ♔Q♉❀⛟◐♣P

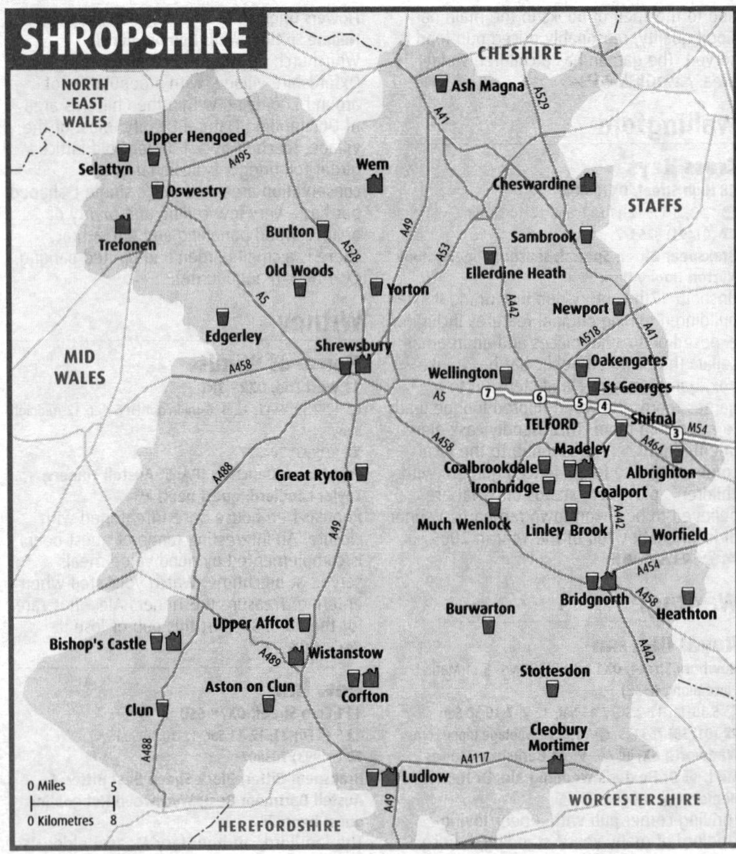

Albrighton

Harp Hotel

40 High Street, WV7 3JF
12-11; 12-10:30 Sun
☎ (01902) 374381
Holden's seasonal beers; guest beers Ⓗ

Basic two roomed local pub which gets busy on music nights. An internationally-known jazz venue, pictures of some of the artists who have played at the Harp are displayed in the lounge. Terry, the landlord, has been proprietor for 23 years and holds two mini beer festivals each year, with beer coming from local breweries and further afield. Bulmers Traditional cider is stocked. Summer drinking is pleasant by the green to the front of the pub. ❀⊟♿⛺⇌♣●P

Ash Magna

White Lion

SY13 4DR (off A525 2 miles from Whitchurch)
12-3 (Sat only), 6-11; 12-4, 7-11 Sun
☎ (01948) 663153
Draught Bass; Taylor Landlord; Worthington's Bitter; guest beers Ⓗ

Situated in the heart of the village, this pub is the focal point of the community. The landlord and his wife have run award-winning pubs in other parts of the county and their experience shows. The lounge bar is warm and welcoming with golf memorabilia and the busy public bar displays real ale artefacts. The landlady is from Germany and dishes from her native country feature on the food menu. A former CAMRA local Pub of the Year. ♨Q❀◗⊟♣P⊡

Aston on Clun

Kangaroo

Clun Road, SY7 8EW (on B4368)
12-3 (not Mon & Tue), 6-11; 2-11 Fri; 12-11 Sat & Sun
☎ (01588) 660263 kangarooinn.co.uk
Titanic Mild; Wells Bombardier; guest beers Ⓗ

INDEPENDENT BREWERIES

All Nations Madeley
Bridgnorth Bridgnorth
Corvedale Corfton
Dolphin Shrewsbury
Hanby Wem
Hobsons Cleobury Mortimer
John Roberts Three Tuns Bishop's Castle
Lion's Tail Cheswardine
Ludlow Ludlow
Offa's Dyke Trefonen
Salopian Shrewsbury
Six Bells Bishop's Castle
Wood Wistanstow
Worfield Madeley

Cosy village local with a small lounge, public bar, games room and dining area. Good home-cooked food is served (not Sun-Tue eves); the themed evenings are recommended. The pub supports the nearby annual Arbour tree redressing ceremony at the end of May, hosts summer barbecues and an annual beer festival on August bank holiday, and is part of the Clun Valley Beer Festival at the beginning of October. The Bike-roos meet here on Sunday afternoon. It is also a Broadplace (in conjunction with Switch on Shropshire) with the provision of broadband access, printing facilities, web cam links and more. There are also on-site recycling facilities. Outside is a large garden and patio. ♛Q✿◐◑▲⇌♣P⊬

Bishop's Castle

Castle Hotel

Market Square, SY9 5BH

✪ 10.30-2.30, 6-11; 12-2.30, 7-10.30 Sun

☎ (01588) 638403

Hobsons Mild, Best Bitter; Six Bells Big Nev's; guest beers Ⓗ

Fine 17th-century hotel with superb views across Bishop's Castle and over to Wales. The impressive interior retains original woodwork and furnishings. Excellent home-cooked food (not Mon lunch or Sun eve) is served by attentive staff throughout the hotel. The Castle is an active supporter of the annual Bishop's Castle Real Ale Festival, held in July. Outside is a magnificently landscaped terrace. ♛Q✿⛟◐◑⊟⊡(553)♣P

Six Bells

Church Street, SY9 5AA

✪ 12-2.30 (not Mon), 6-11 (midnight Thu-Sat); 12-11 (winter 12-3, 7-11) Sun

☎ (01588) 638930

Six Bells Big Nev's, Goldings, seasonal beers Ⓗ

Popular with visitors and locals alike, the Six Bells brewery tap is undergoing continuing improvements and alterations. An inglenook and log fire warm the traditional wooden beamed bar. Excellent freshly-prepared food (not Sun eve) is served in the lounge/dining area which is furnished to reflect its 17th-century origins. The pub is an active supporter of the town's Real Ale Festival, usually sporting 20 guest ales and hosting live music in the rear courtyard. ♛Q✿◐◑⊟♿⊡♣

Bridgnorth

Bell & Talbot

2 Salop Street, High Town, WV16 4QU (400 yds W from town centre)

✪ 5-midnight; 12-2.30, 5.30-11 Sun

☎ (01746) 763233 🌐 odleyinns.co.uk

Batham Best Bitter; Hobsons Town Crier; Holden's Bitter; guest beers Ⓗ

In 1831 this old coaching inn was also a wet-fish shop and retains some quaint features. The small bar displaying sporting equipment is home to the local quiz team. The larger music bar, with its ceiling display of records and instruments, hosts live music every Friday and Sunday. The pub holds two beer festivals, spring and autumn, and all guest beers are selected from breweries within a radius of 35 miles. Bar meals are served Thursday-Sunday evenings. There is a large conservatory at the rear. ♛⛟◑⇌(SVR)♣

Black Boy

58 Cartway, WV16 4BG

✪ 10-1am (2am Fri & Sat); 10-1:30am Sun

☎ (01746) 764691

Banks's Bitter; Caledonian Deuchars IPA; Hook Norton Hooky Bitter; Hopback Summer Lightning; Wells Bombardier; guest beers Ⓗ

Compact and cosy pub with a friendly atmosphere run by the youngest landlord in Bridgnorth and possibly Shropshire. This 17th-century inn has an 18th-century fireplace with a Minton tile surround found in a skip in Shrewsbury 26 years ago. Pub games include darts, dominoes and Trivial Pursuit played against other Shropshire pubs. A top-name jazz concert is held once a month. The main bar is no-smoking. The patio affords views over the River Severn and Bridgnorth landscape. The Cliff Railway and Severn Valley Railway are nearby. ♛✿⇌(SVR)♣⊬

Black Horse

4 Bridge Street, Low Town, WV15 6AF

✪ 5-12; 12-midnight Sat & Sun

☎ (01746) 762415

Banks's Original, Bitter; Batham Best Bitter; Enville Ale; Hobsons Town Crier; guest beers Ⓗ

Classic, mid-1700s ale house comprising two rooms: a small front bar with an antique bar fitting and dartboard, and a larger room with a wood-panelled main bar typical of the period. Both rooms have large screen TVs, mainly for sports events. The courtyard is pleasant for outdoor drinking and boasts marvellous floral displays in summer. The restaurant and accommodation were refurbished a couple of years ago and are recommended. This is a popular venue for anglers after a hard day on the nearby River Severn. Guest beers include seasonal ales. ✿⛟◐◑⊟♿⇌(SVR)P⊽

Friars Inn

3 St Mary's Street, High Town, WV16 4DW (entrance in Central Court off High St or St Mary's St)

✪ 12-2, 5-11; 12-11 Sat & summer; 12-10.30 Sun

☎ (01746) 762396 🌐 virtual-shropshire.co.uk/friarsinn

Enville Ale; Holden's Golden Glow; guest beers Ⓗ

Tucked away in a quiet courtyard off the High Street, this is one of the oldest surviving inns in Bridgnorth. First licensed in 1828 as a posting house, it has been a brewery, cider house and blacksmiths. Inside old pictures and ornaments adorn the pleasant bar and no-smoking dining area. Guest beers are usually selected from local Shropshire or West Midlands breweries. In summer planters and hanging baskets decorate the courtyard seating area. Q✿⛟◐◑⇌(SVR)⊬

Railwayman's Arms

Severn Valley Railway Station, Hollybush Road, WV16 5DT

✪ 11.30-4, 6-11; 11-11 Sat; 12-10:30 Sun

☎ (01746) 764361 🌐 svr.co.uk

Batham Best Bitter; Hobsons Best Bitter; guest beers Ⓗ
Owned by SVR, this licensed refreshment room dating from 1900 attracts beer drinkers and steam railway enthusiasts from around the country. The platform drinking area is perfect for soaking up the atmosphere of the steam era. An abundance of fine railway memorabilia adorns the walls. Three guest beers tend to be from smaller, often local, brewers. 'Ma Pardoe's' Bumble Hole is a frequent guest and some bottled beers are available. An exceptionally busy drinking spot, it is a free house and hosts a CAMRA beer festival in the car park every September. Many themed weekends are held on the station and trains. ⋒Q❀⇌(SVR)●P⊡

Burlton

Burlton Inn

Burlton, SY4 5TB (on A528 between Shrewsbury and Ellesmere)
✪ 11-3, 6-11; 12-3, 7-10:30 Sun
☎ (01939) 270284 ⊕ burltoninn.co.uk
Banks's Bitter; guest beers Ⓗ
Attractive rural free house situated near the North Shropshire lakes. Recently refurbished, it offers three changing guest ales along with award-winning home-cooked food made with local produce. Although the emphasis is on food, drinkers are welcomed in a quiet drinking area and comfy lounge. Tucked away behind the inn is cottage style accommodation with six en-suite bedrooms. ⋒Q❀⇔⊂⊃♿P

Burwarton

Boyne Arms

WV16 6QH (on B4364 Bridgnorth-Ludlow road)
✪ 10-3, 6-midnight; 11-midnight Sat & Sun
☎ (01746) 787214
Draught Bass; Hobsons Town Crier; Taylor Landlord; Wood Shropshire Lad; guest beers Ⓗ
Fine example of an 18th-century coaching inn with two bars and a restaurant area. Seven handpulls supply four regular and three guest beers. Draught cider is also available. Food is served daily from midday (not Sun eve) and many new fish dishes have been added to the extensive menu. The rear garden is fully enclosed and the children's area is RoSPA certified. Easy to find because of the large green frog on a bike outside. ⋒Q❀⇔⊂⊃⊟Å♣●P⚟

Clun

White Horse Inn

The Square, SY7 8JA
✪ 11-midnight (1am Fri & Sat); 12-midnight Sun
☎ (01588) 640305 ⊕ whi-clun.co.uk
Hobsons Mild, Best Bitter; Salopian Shropshire Gold; Three Tuns XXX; Wye Valley Butty Bach; guest beers Ⓗ
Comfortable, 18th-century coaching inn and post house standing in the old market square at the centre of a wonderfully timeless town, described by A E Housman as 'one of the quietest places under the sun'. This friendly local, two minutes from the castle, has an L-shaped bar with low beams and new adjoining no-smoking dining room. A range of board games can be borrowed and the excellent, reasonably-priced food is home made. Weston's First Quality cider and a range of foreign bottled beers are stocked. Relax over a quiet pint in the secluded garden at the rear. The attractive guest rooms are recommended. ⋒Q❀⇔⊂⊃Å♣●⊡

Corfton

Sun Inn

SY7 9DF (on B4368 Bridgnorth-Craven Arms road)
✪ 12-2.30, 6-midnight; 12-3, 7-midnight Sun
☎ (01584) 861239 ⊕ thesuninn.netfirms.com
Corvedale Katie's Pride, Norman's Pride, Secret Hop, Dark and Delicious; guest beers Ⓗ
Dating from the 17th-century, this family-run pub is set in scenic Corvedale between Wenlock Edge and Clee Hills. The pub acts as a tourist information point for the many visitors, walkers and cyclists who drop in. The cask and bottle-conditioned ales available in the pub are produced in the micro-brewery in the garden. A wide range of good value home-cooked meals is offered, made with local produce. ❀⊂⊃⊟♿Å♣●P⚟

Edgerley

Royal Hill ☆

SY10 8ES (midway between Pentre and Melverley) OSSJ3517
✪ 12-2, 5-midnight; 12-midnight Sat & Sun
☎ (01743) 741242
Salopian Shropshire Gold; guest beer Ⓗ
Set on a quiet road with its garden bordering the River Severn, this delightful pub dating from the 18th-century looks out toward the Breidden Hills and is well worth seeking out. The recently extended but well-preserved building comprises a number of cosy rooms and a tiny bar where visitors are warmly welcomed. Camping and caravans are permitted at the back of the pub's grounds. Food is served on various evenings during the week but not to a set menu so it is best to telephone ahead. ⋒Q☋❀⊟♣

Ellerdine Heath

Royal Oak

TF6 6RL (midway between A53 and A442) OS603226
✪ 12 (11 Sat)-11; 12-10.30 Sun
☎ (01939) 250300
Hobsons Best Bitter; Salopian Shropshire Gold; Wye Valley Hereford Pale Ale; guest beers Ⓗ
Locally known as the Tiddly, this friendly country pub is always awash with conversation. The new extension with disabled access has made the pub more spacious but without changing the rural character of this popular meeting place. Keen prices for drinks and food ensure it is always lively (no food Tue). The central bar has a roaring fire and there is a games room and outside play area for children. The annual cider festival (late July) attracts a huge following, with Cheddar Valley stocked all year. ⋒Q❀⊂⊃♿Å♣●P

Great Ryton

Fox Inn

SY5 7LS (5½ miles S of Shrewsbury, 1 mile E of A49 Dorrington) OSSJ4903

✪ 12-2.30 (not Mon), 7-11 (midnight Sat); 12-3.30, 7-1am Sun

☎ (01743) 718499

Hobsons Best Bitter; Jennings Cumberland Ale; Three Tuns XXX; Salopian Shropshire Gold; guest beers Ⓗ

Country pub nestling under the Stretton Hills. At the heart of the local community, the Fox is popular with locals and visitors from neighbouring villages. Local beers are always stocked and it hosts an annual beer festival. The lunchtime bar menu is good and there is an extensive quality food menu in the evenings. ♨Q✿◑⊟●P⊬⊓

Heathton

Old Gate Inn

WV5 7EB (between B4176 and A458 near Halfpenny Green) OS814923

✪ 12-2.30 (Not Mon), 6.30-11; 12-3, 7-10.30 Sun

☎ (01746) 710431 ⊕ oldgateinn.co.uk

Salopian Golden Thread; Taylor Landlord; guest beers Ⓗ

A long-standing entry in this Guide and deservedly so. This 16th-century two bar free house in a rural location offers top quality beer and food. The traditional and homely rooms with open fires provide a warm and relaxed atmosphere. Real flowers abound too. The landlord displays a personal letter from Timothy Taylor's brewer testifying to the excellent nature of product that he sampled here. There is also an extensive menu incorporating a fresh fish 'specials' board. Luxury en-suite accommodation is new. ♨✿⇐◑♿P⊬

Linley Brook

Pheasant Inn

Briton's Lane, WV16 4TA (400 yds from B4373) OS680979

✪ 12-2, 7 (6.30 summer)-11; 12-3, 7 (6.30 summer)-10.30 Sun

☎ (01746) 762260 ⊕ the-pheasant-inn.co.uk

Beer range varies Ⓗ

A fine example of an unspoilt, traditional pub, set in a beautiful remote area in perfect walking country. There are two rooms, both with real fires, one with bar billiards. The ale is sourced from local breweries, and a good value menu is offered with food from a local butcher and greengrocer. The Pheasant has been in the Guide for 23 consecutive years and is highly recommended. ♨Q✿◑⊟P

Ludlow

Church Inn

The Buttercross, SY8 1AW

✪ 12-11 (11.30 Fri & Sat); 12-11 Sun

☎ (01584) 872174 ⊕ thechurchinn.com

Hobsons Mild, Town Crier; Hook Norton Hooky Bitter, Old Hooky; Three Tuns Cleric's Cure; guest beers Ⓗ

Situated in the centre of Ludlow, close to the castle and market square, the Church is the only free house within the town walls and local CAMRA Pub of the Year 2005. The landlord, a former mayor of Ludlow and also owner of the reopened Charlton Arms at Ludford Bridge, is a great advocate of real ale. Guests always supplement the inn's regular beers. The upstairs bar affords a wonderful view of the South Shropshire Hills and Ludlow Church. Four of the inn's nine guest and family rooms feature spa baths. ♨Q⇐◑⇌⊬⊓

Nelson Inn

Rocks Green, SY8 2DS (on A4117 Kidderminster Road from Ludlow bypass)

✪ 12-2.30, 5 (7 Tue)-midnight; 12-midnight Fri-Sun

☎ (01584) 872908

Nottingham Extra Pale Ale; St Austell Tribute; guest beers Ⓗ

A traditional beer house on the outskirts of Ludlow, the Nelson Inn dates back some 300 years. The bar has a pool table, darts, quoits and a juke box featuring 1970s and '80s music. The lounge is decked out with musical instruments on the walls. Occasionally, spontaneous music events occur. It holds its own beer festivals at Easter and early September in conjunction with Ludlow's Food and Drink Fair. The tasty real chips on the menu are highly recommended. Real cider and, from time to time, perry are sold. ✿◑⊟♿⊟♣●P

Much Wenlock

George & Dragon

2 High Street, TF13 6AA

✪ 12-11 (1am Fri; midnight Sat); 12-10.30 Sun

☎ (01952) 727312

Greene King IPA, Abbot; Hobsons Town Crier; Taylor Landlord; guest beers Ⓗ

An intimate bar and snug restaurant is hidden behind an attractive but unassuming frontage. Dating from 1714, this award-winning market town local is a focal point for the area, welcoming regulars and visitors. Four regular ales and one guest, which changes weekly, are all on handpull. The cosy restaurant bases its excellent menu on local produce (no eve meals Wed or Sun) and booking is advisable for Friday and Saturday evenings. The locally produced 'faggots & paes' are to die for. The restaurant and bar area are no-smoking. Every effort is made to accommodate wheelchairs within the limits of the aged building. ♨Q◑♿⊬

Newport

Fox

Pave Lane, Chetwynd Aston, TF10 9LQ (off A41)

✪ 12-11; 12-10.30 Sun

☎ (01952) 815940 ⊕ fox-newport.co.uk

Taylor Landlord; Thwaites Original; Wood Shropshire Lad; guest beers Ⓗ

Recently refurbished Edwardian-style ex-Joules pub with intact original Joules fireplace. The sunny, spacious rooms are warmed by coal- and log-burning fires. Six handpulls serve three regular and three guest ales. There are no-smoking rooms and dogs are allowed in the front bar. An extensive menu with locally sourced ingredients caters for all tastes and pockets. Outside there is a large south-facing terrace. Children under 14 are not allowed after 7pm. ♨Q❀◑◗♣P⊬

Old Woods

Romping Cat

SY4 3AX

✪ 12-2.30 (not Mon, Wed or Fri), 6-11; 12-3.30, 7-11 Sat; 12-2.30, 7-10.30 Sun

☎ (01939) 290273

Draught Bass; Caledonian Deuchars IPA; Hobsons Best Bitter; guest beers 🄷

This roadside country pub is popular with locals and townsfolk alike due in no small part to its guest beer policy as well as the regular ales. There are usually three guests from the lesser-known breweries. A drinkers' pub, no food is served in the cosy bar with its open coal fire. This year the Cat celebrates its 10th consecutive year in the Good Beer Guide and has raised many thousands of pounds for charity. A pleasant patio area is open in summer, enhanced by an attractive floral display. ♨Q❀♣P⊡

Oswestry

Fox Inn

Church Street, SY11 2SU

✪ 11.30 (7 Mon)-11.30; 12-10.30 Sun (winter hours vary)

☎ (01691) 679669

Banks's Riding Bitter; guest beers 🄷

Town centre pub with timber-beamed rooms. A small, cosy front bar leads to a larger room with a big log fire, and two further no-smoking rooms. At the rear of the pub is a courtyard where barbecues are held in summer. A small art gallery features local artwork for sale. Live music is held once a month. The pub has a strict no swearing policy. Five cask ales are available and there are two cask ciders from Westons. No food is served Sunday or Monday evenings. ♨Q❀◑◗♣●⊬

Sambrook

Three Horse Shoes

TF10 8AP (½ mile E of A41)

✪ 12-2 (not Mon), 5 (4 summer Tue-Fri); 11-10.30 Sun (11-11 summer Sat & Sun)

☎ (01952) 551133

Salopian Shropshire Gold; St Austell Tribute; guest beers 🄷

Situated about five miles north of Newport, this pub is well worth a visit. A drinkers' paradise, there are regular and changing guest ales and an occasional mild. The quarry-tiled bar has a real fire and there is a no-smoking lounge and dining room. Visitors come from near and far to talk, drink and play traditional pub games in a music-free ambience. The garden is very attractive in summer. ♨Q❀◑◗⊟♿♣●P⊬

Selattyn

Cross Keys ☆

Glyn Road, SY10 7DH (on B4579 Oswestry-Glyn Ceiriog road)

✪ 7 (6 Fri)-1am; 12-4, 7-1am Sun

☎ (01691) 650247

Salopian Shropshire Gold; guest beers 🄷

A Guide regular, situated next to the church in a small village close to the Welsh border and Offa's Dyke. The building, dating from the 17th-century, has been a pub since 1840 and is CAMRA National Inventory listed. No-smoking throughout, the cosy, small bar has a quarry-tiled floor and real fire, and there are two further rooms and a larger function room. Irish music is played on Thursday evening. It opens at lunchtime for parties by prior arrangement. Accommodation is available in a self-catering cottage attached to the pub. ♨Q⊱❀⇋⊟▲♣P⊬

Shifnal

White Hart

4 High Street, TF11 8BH

✪ 12-3, 5-11; 12-11 Fri -Sun

☎ (01952) 461161

Adnams Broadside; Enville Ale; Holden's Mild, Bitter; guest beers 🄷

Five times winner of local CAMRA Pub of the Year, including 2006. This half-timbered inn with oak-beamed interior is a beacon for drinkers for miles around who come to relish the seven ales, fine wines, good company and great atmosphere. Excellent food is available at lunchtimes (not Sun). In summer enjoy the garden and new patio. Q❀◑⇌♣P

Shrewsbury

Abbey Hotel

83 Monkmoor Road, SY2 5AZ (15 min from Shrewsbury Railway Station via Castle footbridge)

✪ 11.30-11 (midnight Fri & Sat); 12-11 Sun

☎ (01743) 264991

Fuller's London Pride; M&B Mild, Brew XI; guest beers 🄷

Currently enjoying a new lease of life, the Abbey offers a choice of nine cask beers including six guests, generally sourced from smaller breweries. Tasting notes are thoughtfully provided at the bar. The spacious lounge bar has open and secluded seating areas. The venue, popular with groups and societies, hosts bi-weekly quiz nights in aid of charity. Beer festivals are a regular feature. Occasional cask lager is available. Children under 14 years are not permitted. ♨Q❀◑◗♿P⊬

Admiral Benbow

24 Swan Hill, SY1 1NF

✪ 12-2.30 (Fri only), 5-11; 12-11 Sat; 7-10.30 Sun

☎ (01743) 244423

Greene King IPA; guest beers 🄷

Conveniently situated just off Shrewsbury's main square, this spacious free house specialises in its variety of Shropshire ales; up to five are normally available together with a smaller choice of local cider, and sometimes perry, during the summer. Early records date this pub to 1835; the present name was adopted in 1861 in tribute to the local sailor. A small room off the bar is

available for functions. Children are not permitted and under 30s are served at the management's discretion. Outside seating is available during the summer months.
♔Q✿⊟≠♣●

Armoury

Victoria Quay, Victoria Avenue, SY1 1HH (near Welsh Bridge on the town centre side of Shrewsbury)
⏲ 12-11 (10.30 Sun)
☎ (01743) 340525 🌐 armoury-shrewsbury.co.uk
Outlaw IPA; Salopian Shropshire Gold; guest beers Ⓗ
Once an armoury, the building was renovated in 1995 and renamed. A quiet pub during the day, it becomes much livelier in the evening. Two regular and six changing guests aim to please a wide range of tastes. Tasting notes are provided on chalkboards. Some 70 or more malt whiskies are also available. Excellent food is served and children are welcome until 9pm. Board games are available on request. ♔Q◐◑≠

Coach & Horses

Swan Hill SY1 1NP (near Music Hall)
⏲ 11.30-midnight (12.30am Fri & Sat); 12-11.30 Sun
☎ (01743) 365661
🌐 vixentrading.com/odley/coach&horses.htm
Phoenix Arizona; Salopian Shropshire Gold; guest beers Ⓗ
Set in a quiet street off the main shopping area, the Coach & Horses provides a peaceful haven. In summer it has magnificent floral displays. Victorian in style, the pub has a wood-panelled bar, a small side snug area and a large lounge where meals are served. Bar snacks are available until 2.30pm. Addlestones Cloudy cider is also sold. Live music, electro-acoustic in the main, is hosted most Sunday evenings.
Q◐◑♿≠●

Loggerheads ☆

1 Church Street SY1 1UG (off St Mary's St)
⏲ 11-11 (midnight Thu-Sat); 12-3, 8-11 Sun
☎ (01743) 355457
Banks's Original, Bitter, Mansfield Cask; Draught Bass; Marston's Pedigree; guest beer Ⓗ
Situated in the town centre, this 18th-century Grade II listed establishment is a classic among urban pubs and features in CAMRA's National Inventory of Pub Interiors. The small bar provides a servery to three rooms, one of which was, until 1975, reserved for 'Gents Only'. The pub hosts spontaneous folk music and regular poetry readings. Food is available at lunchtime (not Sun) and during summer evenings.
Q◐◑⊟≠♣

Prince of Wales

30 Bynner Street, Belle Vue, SY3 7NZ (via Belle Vue Rd and Trinity St)
⏲ 12-2, 5-11; 12-midnight Fri-Sun
☎ (01743) 343301 🌐 princeofwaleshotel.co.uk
Greene King IPA; St Austell Tribute; Salopian Golden Thread; guest beers Ⓗ
Welcoming two-roomed traditional community local with a relaxed atmosphere. The large decked suntrap to the rear overlooks the pub's bowling green and an 18th-century maltings. Popular themed evenings are always well attended and usually raise money for a charitable cause. Darts, bowls, dominoes and quiz teams are in abundance. Home-made lunches are served daily made with locally-sourced produce. An annual beer festival is held in May/June. Awarded local CAMRA Pub of the Year 2006, a good range of beers and a real cider are always available here.
♔Q✿◐⊟♿♣●P⊡

Three Fishes

Fish Street, SY1 1UR
⏲ 11.30-3, 5-11; 11.30-11.30 Fri & Sat; 12-4, 7-10.30 Sun
☎ (01743) 344793
Caledonian Deuchars IPA; Taylor Landlord; guest beers Ⓗ
A CAMRA award-winning pub, this 15th-century building stands in the shadow of two churches, St Alkmond's and St Julian's, within the maze of streets and passageways in the medieval quarter of the town. Freshly-prepared food is available at lunchtime and early evening (not Sun eve). The pub offers a range of up to six local and national beers, with some dark beers featuring regularly. One of the first pubs to introduce a no-smoking throughout policy.
Q◐◑≠⚟

Wheatsheaf

50 High Street, SY1 1ST
⏲ 11-midnight; 12-11 Sun
☎ (01743) 272702
Banks's Bitter; Marston's Old Empire; guest beers Ⓗ
Comfortable town-centre, street-corner pub with a view to St Julian's church, popular with regulars, visitors and shoppers. Three distinct bar areas are adorned with many pictures of Old Shrewsbury. Food is served at lunchtime (not Sun) made from locally sourced produce. Beer festivals are held in March and October. In fine weather street seating is provided. ✿◐≠♣

Woodman Inn

32 Coton Hill, SY1 2DZ (½ mile from station on the Ellesmere road, A528)
⏲ 4 (2 summer)-11; 12-10.30 Sun
☎ (01743) 351007
Beer range varies Ⓗ
Half brick and timbered black and white corner pub originally built in the 1800s but destroyed by fire in 1923 and rebuilt in 1925. It has a wonderful oak-panelled lounge with two real log fires and traditional settles. The bar has the original stone-tiled flooring, wooden seating, log fire and listed leaded windows. The courtyard seating area is decorated with award-winning floral displays in summer. The pub is reputedly haunted by an ex-landlady who died when the pub burnt down.
♔Q✿◐⊟≠♣

Stottesdon

Fighting Cocks

1 High Street, DY14 8TZ
⏲ 6-midnight; 5-1am Fri; 12-midnight Sat; 12-11.30 Sun

☎ (01746) 718270
Hobsons Best Bitter, Town Crier; guest beers 🄷
An ale house since 1830, this pub and its shop are the hub of activity for the village and local community. There is live music most Saturday nights and a beer festival every autumn. Inside there are beamed ceilings, a cosy bar area with log fire, and two dining areas. On the walls old photos and newspaper cuttings depict the pub's long history. Excellent award-winning food is served (eve meals Tue-Sat) made only with fresh locally-sourced produce.
⚲Q❀◐◑♿⛺♣P

Telford: Coalbrookdale

Coalbrookdale Inn
12 Wellington Road, TF8 7DX
✪ 12-3, 5-11; 12-midnight Fri & Sat; 12-10.30 Sun
☎ (01952) 433953 ⊕ coalbrookdaleinn.co.uk
Hobsons Town Crier; Three Tuns XXX; Wye Valley Hereford Pale Ale; guest beers 🄷
This well-supported pub offers a good range of seven ales, together with excellent freshly-prepared food. While the character of the pub has changed a little since it was awarded CAMRA National Pub of the Year, it still offers a very warm welcome to all visitors both old and new. There is always a good ebb and flow of conversation in the pub with no games machines or music to interrupt it. The Museum of Iron, opposite, is worth a visit. Real cider is available in summer. ⚲Q❀◐◑●P⊁

Telford: Coalport

Shakespeare Inn
High Street, TF8 7HT (near Tar Tunnel and China Museum)
✪ 5-11; 12-11 Sat & Sun
☎ (01952) 580675 ⊕ shakespeare-inn.co.uk
Enville Ale; Everards Tiger; guest beers 🄷
A warm, welcoming family run pub, with wonderful views of the Severn Gorge, ideally situated for the Coalport China and Tar Tunnel museums. Also nearby is the Silkin Way which leads to the Blists Hill Museum. A good selection of guest ales changes frequently. The tempting menu of excellent home-cooked dishes (eve meals Tue-Sat) is always popular so booking in advance is strongly advised. A youth hostel is next door.
Q❀🛏◐◑♿P⊁

Telford: Ironbridge

Golden Ball
Newbridge Road, TF8 7BA (near jct Madeley Rd/Wesley Rd)
✪ 12-11; 12-10:30 Sun
☎ (01952) 432179 ⊕ goldenballinn.com
Everards Tiger; guest beers 🄷
An inn since 1728, set in the heart of Shropshire in historic Ironbridge Gorge near the museums. If you only have time to visit one pub in the area, this is the one not to be missed. Once a brew house, it retains many period features including the original fireplace, water pump, wooden beams and floors. Friendly, efficient staff and a wide choice of guest beers make for a real ale haven. Fresh, high quality home-cooked food is served daily. Outside is a quiet garden and picturesque courtyard.
⚲Q❀🛏◐◑♿♣●P⊁🗍

Robin Hood Inn
33 Waterloo Street, TF8 7HQ
✪ 10-midnight (10.30 Sun)
☎ (01952) 433100 ⊕ yeolderobinhoodinn.co.uk
Holden's Bitter, Golden Glow, Special; guest beers 🄷
Overlooking the river Severn and the space age Jackfield Bridge, this historic hostelry has a warm, friendly atmosphere. Three regular and three guest beers are served plus draught cider. Food is traditional, sourced locally where possible, and good value. Every first Wednesday in the month there is live Irish music, and on the second Tuesday live folk music. En-suite accommodation is available. Q❀🛏◐◑♿♣●P⊁

Telford: Madeley

All Nations
20 Coalport Road, TF7 5DP (off Legges Way)
✪ 12-3, 5-midnight; 12-midnight Fri-Sun
☎ (01952) 585747
Worfield Coalport Dodger Mild, Dabley Ale; guest beers 🄷
A hostelry since 1831, this one-room establishment is always lively. One of just four existing home-brew pubs on CAMRA's inception, it now accommodates the Worfield Brewery in the original brew house. A mix of locals, tourists and 'beer hounds' frequents this pub. The landlord is an ex-rugby player and televised rugby fixtures always feature. During matches the television is perched on top of two 36-gallon barrels! Food comprises hearty rolls, pork pies and pickled eggs. ⚲Q❀🗔♣●P🗍

Telford: Oakengates

Crown Inn
Market Street, TF2 6EA
✪ 12-3, 5-11; 12-11 Wed-Sun
☎ (01952) 610888 ⊕ crown.oakengates.com
Hobsons Best Bitter; guest beers 🄷
Popular three-room community pub adorned with beer and transport memorabilia. The 14 cooled handpulls have dispensed over 5,000 different beers in 11 years. A mild, stout or porter is always served and one pump is reserved for cider or perry. Continental draught and bottled beers along with country wines and a large selection of malt whiskies, oversized eggs, strong cheese and potatoes are also available. Twice a year (first weekend of May and Oct), 20 handpulls are added for beer festivals. Regular events include live bands, folk music, acoustic evenings, quiz nights, themed beer sessions and baking competitions. ❀◐🗔⇌♣●P⊁

Station Hotel
42 Market Street, TF2 6DU
✪ 10-11; 10.30-4, 7-11 Sun

☎ (01952) 612949 🌐 station-hotel.net
Holden's Golden Glow; Salopian Shropshire Gold; guest beers Ⓗ
Genuine free house in the main street of this busy town with two distinctive drinking areas. The front room has a quarry-tiled floor and the walls are adorned with pictures, posters and bric-a-brac, while the lounge at the rear has a comfortable seating area. There is an ever-changing menu of guest beers dispensed via six handpumps. Festivals for beer, cider and perry, and continental brews feature throughout the year. There is no hot food but the 'monster' baps are legendary.
♔❀⊟⇶♣●⅟

Telford: St Georges

St Georges Sports & Social Club
Church Road, TF2 9LU
⏲ 7-midnight; 5-12.30am Fri; 12-12:30am Sat; 12-midnight Sun
☎ (01952) 612911
Banks's Original, Bitter; Wye Valley Hereford Pale Ale; guest beers Ⓗ
This club is a regular winner of CAMRA awards for enthusiastic support and promotion of real ale. Beers are mainly showcased from Shropshire and Black Country breweries, but not exclusively so. CAMRA members are particularly welcome. The outside drinking area overlooks grounds used by Shropshire Cricket Club and the club is also a base for many other local sports teams.
♘❀♣P⅟

Telford: Wellington

Cock Hotel
148 Hollyhead Road, TF1 2DL
⏲ 4 (12 Thu)-11.30; 12-midnight Fri & Sat; 12-4, 7-11 Sun
☎ (01952) 244954 🌐 cockhotel.co.uk
Archers Dark Mild; Hobsons Best Bitter; Wye Valley Hereford Pale Ale; guest beers Ⓗ
This popular 18th-century coaching inn is a regular winner of local CAMRA awards. The hop-festooned main bar serves all drinking areas, including two no-smoking rooms and an old stable courtyard outside. The cosmopolitan clientele is able to enjoy lively conversation with no games machines or music to intrude. The eight ever-changing handpulls always include a mild, a stout or porter along with a cider, normally Thatchers Cheddar Valley. A well-stocked foreign bottle section and pork pies are also popular.
Q❀⇄⊟⇶♣●P⅟

Upper Affcot

Travellers Rest Inn
SY6 6RL (on A49 between Church Stretton and Craven Arms)
⏲ 11-11; 12-10.30 Sun
☎ (01694) 781275 🌐 travellersrestinn.co.uk
Draught Bass; Hobsons Mild, Best Bitter; Wood Shropshire Lad; guest beers Ⓗ
There is a warm welcome for travellers and locals alike at this large roadside inn on the busy A49. Accompanying the excellent beers is a wide-ranging menu of good food served all day. There is a spacious no-smoking conservatory for diners and a games area with pool table and darts. Children are welcome. Overnight accommodation includes two rooms adapted for wheelchairs.
Q❀⇄◐◑♿▲♣●P⅟

Upper Hengoed

Last Inn
SY10 7EU (off B4579 at Weston Rhyn sign, 3 miles N of Oswestry)
⏲ 10-1.30am; 12-11.30 Sun
☎ (01691) 659747
Wood Parish Bitter; guest beers Ⓗ
Large pub at a rural crossroads with an inn sign exhibiting a lengthy Latin tag. This former cobbler's workshop has six cask ales on offer from micro and regional breweries. Beyond the bar is a large games room and an extensive function room that hosts folk evenings and other entertainment. An impressive display of brewery trays and various items of brewery memorabilia are on show. Home to the Last Inn Runners club.
♔Q♘◑♣P

Worfield

Dog Inn (Davenport Arms)
Main Street, WV15 5LF (off A454 3 miles E of Bridgnorth)
⏲ 12-2.30, 7-11; 12-3, 7-10:30 Sun
☎ (01746) 716020
Courage Best Bitter; Theakston Mild; Wells Bombardier Ⓗ
Traditional pub in a sleepy village with two rooms, one predominantly for dining. An extensive menu of home-made food is available until 9.15pm. Fresh fish is a speciality. The pub has a friendly atmosphere and families are welcome. Nearby and worth a visit is Lower Hall, a superb example of a Tudor building set in magnificent gardens.
♔Q❀◐◑⊟♿♣P⅟

Yorton

Railway Inn
SY4 3EP (200 yds from station)
⏲ 12.30 (12 Sun)-4, 7-11
☎ (01939) 220240
Salopian Heaven Sent; Wadworth 6X; Wood Shropshire Lad; guest beers Ⓗ
Stepping inside the Railway Inn is like going back in time. Little has changed since 1936 when the owners first moved in. Then a Southam's pub, it became a free house in 1972 when the family purchased it from Whitbread. Until 1980 an adjacent smallholding provided milk to local dairies. The small bar is extremely popular with locals and railway travellers with its settles and quarry-tiled floors. Local beers are predominant plus three guests and two ciders from Thatchers and Westons. Snacks such as sandwiches may be available on request. ♔Q❀⊟⇶♣●P⅟

SOMERSET

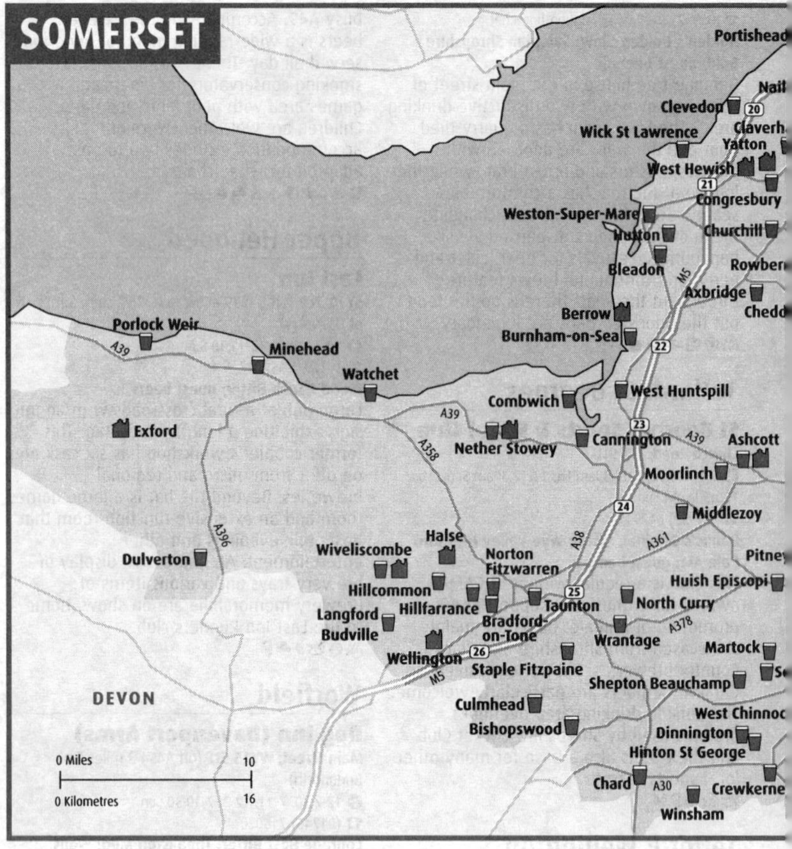

Ash

Bell

3 Main Street, TA12 6NS

12-2 (closed winter Mon & Tue), 6-11; 12-3, 7-10.30 Sun

(01935) 822727 thebellatash.co.uk

Butcombe Bitter; Sharp's Doom Bar; guest beers

Pleasant pub in the village centre. Its one-bar appears to be split into different areas because of the furniture layout. The piano is well used and the pub often stages live blues music in the function room that doubles as a skittle alley. Quiet recorded jazz plays in the background in the bar where good food is served (not Sun or Mon eves); Sunday lunch is popular. Quiz nights are held. P

Ashcott

Ring O'Bells

High Street, TA7 0PZ (off A39)

12-2.30, 7-11; 12-2.30, 7-10.30 Sun

(01458) 210232 ringobells.com

Beer range varies

Central village pub near the church and village hall, with a large garden to the rear. The pub has been run by the same family for nearly 20 years. The function room is busy and there is a no-smoking dining room that serves award-winning food. The ales are often from local breweries and the cider also comes from a local producer, Wilkins. It was voted Somerset CAMRA Pub of the Year in 1998. P

Axbridge

Crown Inn

St Mary's Street, BS26 2BN

12-3, 5-11; 12-11 Sat & Sun

(01934) 732518 axbridgecrown.co.uk

Sharp's Doom Bar; guest beers

Free house, just off the main square of the historic village of Axbridge The cosy front bar boasts a big open fireplace. Local teams gather regularly for competitive games of table skittles. The back bar has a more modern feel, with a pool table and games machine. The skittle alley doubles as a family room. Bar food is served all day at reasonable prices. Most beers come from Sharp's. (126)

Babcary

Red Lion

TA11 7ED

12-3, 6-11; 12-3 Sun

(01458) 223230

Beer range varies

Dating from the 14th century, the pub is in the village centre. The lounge bar and

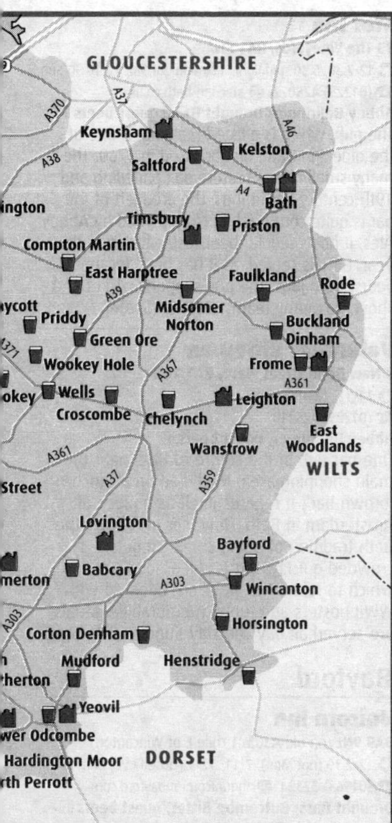

excellent restaurant have recently been refurbished, retaining flagged floors and beams. The back bar features ancient furniture and plenty of traditional bar games. Beers from Teignworthy Brewery are usually sold and guests are also often from south-western producers. When they are not too busy, the bar staff are happy to go to the cellar and pour the beer straight from the barrels. ⚘❀◑⊟♿⛺♣P

Bath

Bell

103 Walcot Street, BA1 5BW

⌚ 11.30-11; 12-10.30 Sun

☎ (01225) 460426 🌐 walcotstreet.com

Abbey Bellringer; Bath Gem; Hop Back Summer Lightning; Otter Bitter; RCH Pitchfork; guest beers Ⓗ

The Bell has live bands performing on Monday and Wednesday evenings and Sunday lunchtime. There is a long main bar and a number of seating areas. At the back is a large, terraced garden with plenty of seating. Posters for local gigs and forthcoming events in the Walcot area are displayed. A mini-launderette and WiFi facilities have been added. ❀◑⇌(Spa)♣

Hop Pole

Albion Buildings, Upper Bristol Road, BA1 3AR

⌚ 12-11 (midnight Fri & Sat); 12-11 Sun

☎ (01225) 446327

Bath SPA, Gem, Barnstormer; guest beers Ⓗ

Bath Ales' first pub in Bath, the Hop Pole is a friendly place, situated between Victoria Park and the River Avon. Normally six real ales are available – four from Bath; a range of bottled foreign beers and cider is also stocked. High quality food is available most lunchtimes and evenings. An alleyway connects to the river towpath, part of the Bath-Bristol cycle path. ❀◑♣⚡

King William

36 St Thomas Street, BA1 5NN

⌚ 12-3, 5-midnight (11.30 Sun)

☎ (01225) 428096

Palmers Copper Ale; guest beers Ⓗ

The pub underwent refurbishment in 2004, transforming a rather dubious venue to a more civilised place with an emphasis on good beer and food. The main bar is split into two areas; both are quite small and can get crowded. The pub always features beers from Palmer and Milk Street. ⚘◑

King William IV

54 Combe Road, Combe Down, BA2 5HY

⌚ 10-11; 12-7 Sun

☎ (01225) 833137 🌐 kingwilliampub.com

Butcombe Bitter; guest beers Ⓗ

Built in 1825, it was named in honour of William IV for commissioning the local Bath stone for Buckingham Palace. The recently refurbished L-shaped bar is decorated with local prints. In addition to the skittle alley, there is an enclosed courtyard used in summer, along with a south-facing terrace. The guest beers change often. ❀◑♣P

Old Green Tree ☆

12 Green Street, BA1 2JZ

⌚ 11-11; 12-10.30 Sun

☎ (01225) 448259

RCH Pitchfork; Wickwar BOB; guest beers Ⓗ

This is a classic, traditional, unspoilt pub. Situated in a 300-year-old building, an atmosphere of dim cosiness pervades all

INDEPENDENT BREWERIES

Abbey Ales Bath
Berrow Berrow
Blindmans Leighton
Butcombe Wrington
Cotleigh Wiveliscombe
Cottage Lovington
Dunkery Exford
Exmoor Wiveliscombe
Glastonbury Somerton
Juwards Wellington
Keynsham Keynsham
Matthews Timsbury
Milk Street Frome
Moor Ashcott
Newmans Yatton
Odcombe Lower Odcombe
RCH West Hewish
Stowey Nether Stowey
Taunton Vale Halse
Yeovil Yeovil

three of the small, oak-panelled rooms. The panelling dates from the 1920s. The comfortable lounge bar at the front is decorated with pictures of WWII aircraft. During Bath's annual Fringe Festival, these are replaced by the works of selected local artists. The pub can get crowded but the back bar is no-smoking. ♨Q◐⇌(Spa)♣⊬

Pig & Fiddle

2 Saracen Street, BA1 5PL

✪ 11-11 (midnight Fri & Sat); 12-10.30 Sun

☎ (01225) 460868

Abbey Bellringer; guest beers Ⓗ

Large, busy but friendly town-centre pub close to the rugby ground that draws a mixed clientele. One end is an old shop front, the other an outside courtyard with drinking benches. The decor is an esoteric mix of rugby memorabilia, such as signed shirts, a pair of signed Olympic skis and an oar from the coxed eight Olympic gold medalists. Guest beers usually come from local breweries. ❀◐◑⇌(Spa)♣●

Raven

6-7 Queen Street, BA1 1HE

✪ 11-11 (midnight Fri-Sat) 12-10.30 Sun

☎ (01225) 310324

Beer range varies Ⓗ

Situated in a small, cobbled street near Queen Square, just off Milsom Street, the pub has reverted to its original name after many years as Hatchetts. It has been extensively refurbished for a more upmarket feel and has a no-smoking bar and dining area upstairs. Acoustic music is performed on alternate Tuesdays. The house beer is brewed by Blindmans. ◐⇌(Spa)⊬

Royal Oak

Lower Bristol Road, Twerton, BA2 3BW

✪ 12-midnight (11.30 Sun)

☎ (01225) 481409

Beer range varies Ⓗ

This new free house is an oasis in a beer desert. If visiting the city do make the effort to come – you will not be disappointed. The pub is a three-minute walk down Brook Road from Oldfield Park Station and the regular No 5 bus passes the door. Up to ten beers of all styles come from micro-breweries around the country but local brews feature strongly too. It hosts Irish music on Wednesday and offers a traditional Sunday roast. ♨Q❀◐⇌(Oldfield Pk)🚌♣●P⊬

Salamander

3 John Street, BA1 2JL

✪ 11.30-11; 12-10.30 Sun

☎ (01225) 428889

Bath SPA, Gem, Barnstormer; guest beers Ⓗ

This former 18th-century coffee house has undergone many changes over the years and now features the familiar Bath Ales style, with bare floorboards, wood panelling and hanging hops. It can quickly get crowded. Subtly divided downstairs, it has a restaurant upstairs where food includes beer-themed meals. The pub stocks a selection of bottled Belgian beers; Bath Ales merchandise and beers to take home can also be purchased. ◐◑⇌(Spa)⊬

Star Inn ☆

23 The Vineyards, BA1 5NA

✪ 12-2.30, 5.30-midnight; 12-midnight Sat; 12-10.30 Sun

☎ (01225) 425072 🌐 star-inn-bath.co.uk

Abbey Bellringer; Draught Bass; guest beers Ⓗ

The pub, which is a listed building, is one of the oldest in Bath, first licensed in 1760. The many small rooms feature oak panelling and 19th-century bar fittings; the area left of the bar is quite comfortable. Now owned by Abbey Ales, it hosts regular beer festivals during the year. Bass is served, as it has been for many years, from jugs. The pub supports cricket and shove-ha'penny teams. ♨Q⇌(Spa)♣

Volunteer Rifleman

3 New Bond Street Place, BA1 1BH

✪ 11-11; 12-10.30 Sun

☎ (01225) 425210

Abbey Bellringer, guest beers Ⓗ

One-bar pub in the centre of Bath near the main shopping area. Modelled on a Dutch 'brown bar', it regards itself as a piece of Amsterdam in Bath. However, it follows the Bath tradition of being small, so gets crowded quickly, but is still a good place in which to relax. The walls are adorned with WWII posters and rugby memorabilia. Meals are served all day Tuesday-Sunday. ◐⇌(Spa)

Bayford

Unicorn Inn

BA9 9NL (on old A303, 1 mile E of Wincanton)

✪ 12-2.30 (not Mon), 7-11; 12-3 (closed eve) Sun

☎ (01963) 32324 🌐 theunicorninnbayford.com

Draught Bass; Butcombe Bitter; guest beers Ⓗ

Access to this 270-year-old pub is via an impressive coach arch into the courtyard. The single bar comprises three distinctive areas in one room. There are usually two keenly priced guest beers available, often from local micros. Fish is a speciality on a good menu that is served at all sessions. There is en-suite accommodation in four guest rooms. The pub gets busy on Wincanton race days. ♨Q❀🛏◐◑P⊬

Bishopswood

Candlelight Inn

TA20 3RS (½ mile N of A303)

✪ 12-2.30, 7 (6.30 Fri & Sat)-11; 12-2.30, 7-10.30 Sun

☎ (01460) 234476

Butcombe Bitter, Gold; guest beer Ⓖ

Free house, dating back to the 17th century, replete with low beams and exposed stone. One large room is divided into different areas by partitions, and there is a skittle alley that doubles as a function room. The handpumps are not used except to show what ales are on offer. It serves good food, with some dishes available to take away. The River Yarty flows through the garden. ♨Q❀◐◑⛺♣P

Bleadon

Queen's Arms

Celtic Way, BS24 0NF (¼ mile from A370)

✪ 11.30-3, 5-11; 11-11 Fri & Sat; 12-10-30 Sun

☎ (01934) 812080

Bath Gem; Butcombe Bitter, Blond; guest beers Ⓖ
The oldest of Bleadon's three pubs, it stands in the village centre. Three rooms converge onto the bar that has a no-smoking area and garden sales hatch. At first sight, this might appear to be a pub that puts the emphasis on food, but the beer is top-notch with a good variety of guests. Just off the main road, you could think you are deep into the country here, but Weston-Super-Mare is just a mile to the north. ⌂Q❀◐▶⅄⊟(83)●P⊁

Bradford-on-Tone

White Horse Inn

Regent Street, TA4 1HF (off A38)
⊙ 11.30-3, 5.30-11; 12-3, 7-10-30 Sun
☎ (01823) 461239
Cotleigh Tawny; guest beers Ⓗ
Very much a community pub at the village centre, the post office and shop are in outbuildings. One or two guest beers are sourced from local and national breweries. The beautiful large garden hosts barbecues in summer, while in winter open fires warm both bars. The skittle alley (with its own bar) doubles as a function room; bar billiards can be played in the main bar. Excellent home-cooked food is served (booking advised), and international evenings are a feature.
⌂❀◐▶⊟♣P⊁

Buckland Dinham

Bell

High Street, BA11 2QT (on A362)
⊙ 12-3, 6-11; 12-2.30, 7-10.30 Sun
☎ (01373) 462956 ⊕ bellatbuckland.co.uk
Butcombe Bitter; Fuller's London Pride; guest beers Ⓗ
This 16th-century inn is the centre for most village activities. The bar, which is divided into several drinking areas, offers four real ales. An ancient barn has been converted to accommodate live music and beer festivals – a regular fest is planned for August. ⌂❀◐▶⅄P

Burnham-on-Sea

Dunstan House

8 Love Lane, TA8 1EU (next to hospital)
⊙ 11-11; 12-10.30 Sun
☎ (01278) 784343
Young's Bitter, Special, seasonal beers Ⓗ
Spacious roadside pub owned by Young's, with a long bar with split-level dining areas. It has a garden room at the side and there is outside seating and a play area for children. The pub caters for all ages and attracts a good mix of customers. The food, ales and accommodation are all recommended here.
⌂ಠ❀⇔◐▶♿⅄⊟P⊁

Cannington

Rose & Crown

30 High Street, TA5 2HF (off A39)
⊙ 12-11; 12-10.30 Sun
☎ (01278) 653190
Caledonian Deuchars IPA; Greene King IPA, Abbot, Old Speckled Hen; guest beer Ⓗ
Atmospheric, friendly pub, dating back to the 17th century. The single bar, with a tiled floor and roaring fire in winter, enjoys a loyal local following and lively conservation is the norm. The bar houses a pool table, table skittles and, more unusually, a range of games hand-made by locals. The exposed beams are covered with interesting objects donated by regulars – a real curiosity pub - it also houses a collection of clocks. The garden has won several Pubs in Bloom awards. ⌂❀⇔⊟♣P

Chard

Bell & Crown

Coombe Street, Crimchard, TA20 1JP
(follow Combe St Nicholas signs from High St)
⊙ 12-2.30 (not Mon; 12-5 Sat), 7-11 (midnight Fri & Sat); 12-5, 7-11 Sun
☎ (01460) 62470
Branscombe Vale Draymans; Otter Bitter; guest beers Ⓗ
Converted from cottages to give a typical village-style pub, quite near the town centre. Five or six ales are mostly West Country brews, and always include a Sharp's product; Westons Farmhouse Scrumpy is also stocked. Beer festivals are held regularly, spilling out into the new garden and patio if weather permits. The skittle alley doubles as a function room. Food is served at lunchtime, with the evenings dedicated to beer. Qಠ❀◐⅄⊟♣●P

Cheddar

White Hart

The Bays, Cheddar Gorge, BS27 3QW
(behind Fortes Ice Cream Parlour)
⊙ 12-2.30, 5.30-11; 12 (11 summer)-11 Sat; 12-11 Sun
☎ (01934) 741261 ⊕ thewhitehartcheddar.co.uk
Butcombe Bitter; Greene King Old Speckled Hen; Wadworth 6X Ⓗ
Delightfully welcoming local near Cheddar Gorge. A no-smoking, family dining room is to the right of the entrance; the large main bar has a cosy, relaxed atmosphere, dominated by the fireplace. Engaging photos of regulars' day trips add interest. At the rear is a large garden and a car park. An excellent range of food is served all day, Sunday lunches are available once a month (first Sun). It also hosts regular music and quiz nights. The cider is Thatchers. ⌂ಠ❀◐▶♣●P⊁

Chelynch

Poachers Pocket

BA4 4PY
⊙ 12-3, 6-midnight (1am Fri & Sat); 12-3, 7-midnight Sun
☎ (01749) 880220 ⊕ poachers-pocket.co.uk
Butcombe Bitter; Cotleigh Tawny; Wadworth 6X; guest beers Ⓗ
A part 14th-century village pub with an emphasis on food. The bar area and adjacent function room/skittle alley are popular with locals. The pub offers a good choice of three regular real ales, plus a guest beer and draught cider. In recent years it has hosted annual beer and cider festivals and also supports local arts and folk music events. A folk club meets here on the second Sunday of the month. ⌂❀◐▶♣●P

Churchill

Crown Inn

The Batch, Skinners Lane, BS25 5PP
(off A38, ¼ mile S of A368 jct)
✪ 11-11; 12-10.30 Sun
☎ (01934) 852995
Draught Bass; Bath SPA; Palmer IPA; RCH Hewish IPA, PG Steam; guest beers Ⓖ
Step back in time and visit a real pub. Several small rooms with stone-flagged floors, warmed by two log fires, offer an assortment of seating to encourage the enjoyment of a wide range of ales and ciders. Excellent food is served and in fine weather, inspiring views from the patio gardens are a bonus. Easy access by bus No. 121 from Bristol or Weston-super-Mare (not eves) means a good time can be had by all. ⛫Q✿◑⊟⛺⊡♣P

Claverham

Claverham Village Hall

Bishop's Road, BS49 4NP (off A370 at Cleeve)
✪ 12-2 (not Mon-Thu), 7-11; 12-10.30 Sun
☎ (01934) 830020 ⊕ claverhamvillagehall.co.uk
Butcombe Bitter; guest beer Ⓗ
The bar forms part of the village hall, which was built in 1999. Run by volunteers, it is well supported by the local community. The people in charge of the bar are enthusiastic supporters of real ale and organise a successful annual beer festival at the beginning of July as well as various themed events throughout the year. This venue proves that a modern building can provide a pleasant drinking environment. Bus No. 353 stops almost outside. ✿♿⛺⊡♣P

Clevedon

Old Inn

9 Walton Road, BS21 6AE (on Portishead road)
✪ 10-11.30 (midnight Fri & Sat); 11-11 Sun
☎ (01275) 340440 ⊕ theoldinnclevedon.co.uk
Courage Best Bitter; Greene King Old Speckled Hen; guest beers Ⓗ
Delightful old inn, one large beamed room that once served the carriage trade from Weston to Portishead. The current landlady's great grandmother also ran the pub. A wonderful community feel is sometimes enhanced by piano playing or other jollity. The two guest beers are often adventurous or unusual. Tasty pub food offers good value. The garden is an added attraction. Buses 364, X7, X24 and X25 pass close but beware, they move in mysterious ways! Ask a local. ⛫Q✿⛟◑⊡♣P

Salthouse

Salthouse Road, BS21 7TY (on seafront)
✪ 10-11 (midnight Fri & Sat); 12-11.30 Sun
☎ (01275) 343303
Butcombe Gold; Sharp's Doom Bar; Shepherd Neame Spitfire Ⓗ
Large pub with views of the sea and the historic pier. Since a major 2004 refit, the pub is split in two: half for drinkers and half for diners (no meals Sun eve). The drinking section has a lovely wooden round bar with several divided areas to give a relaxed ambience. Outside, a large patio overlooks the salthouse field with its miniature railway. Coastal path walks number among the local amenities. ⛾✿◑⊟♿⊡P⊬

Combwich

Anchor Inn

Riverside, TA5 2RA
✪ 7 (12 Fri & Sat)-midnight; 12-10.30 Sun
☎ (01278) 653612
Beer range varies Ⓗ
Situated by the River Parrett, this friendly 17th-century pub serves a constantly-changing range of West Country beers and benefits from a large car park, garden and function room. Popular with both locals and visitors, it is the first pub on the Parrett Trail that runs the length of the river – enjoy a walk along it to build up a thirst. ⛫Q⛾✿◑⊟♿⛺⊡♣P

Compton Martin

Ring O' Bells

Main Street, BS40 6JE (on A368)
✪ 11.30-3, 6-11; 12-3, 6.30-11 Sun
☎ (01761) 221284
Butcombe Bitter, Blond, Gold; guest beer Ⓗ
Large, traditional village inn of multiple rooms, including a dedicated family room, baby changing facilities and a child-friendly garden. The restaurant, family room and lounge are all no-smoking. The main bar has a real fire in winter. It is popular for well-priced meals, but there is always room if you just want a drink. The guest beer comes from the likes of Wadworth, Fuller's or Timothy Taylor. ⛫Q⛾✿◑⊟⊡(672)♣P⊬

Congresbury

Old Inn

Pauls Causeway, BS49 5DH (off A370 at Ship & Castle)
✪ 12-11.30 (12.30am Fri & Sat); 12-11 Sun
☎ (01934) 832270
Young's Bitter, Special, seasonal beers; guest beer Ⓗ
Popular, 16th-century village local owned by Young's, offering three of its beers, one of them seasonal, and a regular guest ale. This cosy pub boasts a wonderful inglenook burning chunky logs during the winter. Low ceilings throughout give the two main rooms character. Note that the bar area has leather straps hanging from the ceiling to steady yourself after one too many! No food is served. ⛫Q✿⊡(X1, 353)♣P

Corton Denham

Queen's Arms

DT9 4LR (3 miles from A303) OS636225
✪ 11-3, 6-11; 11-11 Sat; 12-10.30 Sun
☎ (01963) 220317 ⊕ thequeensarms.com
Butcombe Bitter; Taylor Landlord; guest beers Ⓗ
Friendly, village pub, featuring wood and flagstone flooring, old pews, tables and chairs. Real ale holds a prominent place alongside the Cheddar Valley cider, bottled beers and a good wine list. It serves mulled wine (and occasionally mulled cider) in winter. In the village centre, the pub is in good walking and

horse-riding country; dogs and muddy boots are welcome (no dogs in the bedrooms). The dining room is no-smoking, and good quality food is served throughout. ⌂Q❀⇌◑●P

Crewkerne

Old Stagecoach Inn

Station Road, TA18 8AL

⏲ 11-2, 6-11; 12-2, 6-11 Sun

☎ (01460) 72972

Beer range varies H

The ideal pub to have next to a station: accommodation, large garden, good parking and, to top it all, interesting beers and food. The hours are flexible if notice is given, and the licensees aim to fulfil customers' needs. The real ales are from West Country breweries and the range of Belgian beers is probably the best in Somerset. The annual Belgian beer evening is popular. Food includes dishes cooked with beer, and some with a Cajun influence, alongside more traditional fare. ⌂Q❀⇌◑⇌⊟♣P

Croscombe

Bull Terrier

Long Street, BA5 3QJ

⏲ 12-2.30, 7-11 daily (closed winter Mon)

☎ (01749) 343658 ⊕ bullterrierpub.co.uk

Butcombe Bitter; guest beers H

Originally the Rose and Crown in 1612, it was renamed in 1976. The fine beams and inglenook in the main bar are part of the original construction. Two main rooms at the front of the pub are mainly used by diners. Locals congregate in the common bar at the back. The landlord offers a good choice of four real ales plus draught cider. Traditional games are played and the pub holds a prominent place in the local pub quiz league. Q❀⇌◑⊟♣●P⊁

George Inn

Long Street, BA5 3QH

⏲ 12 (11.45 Sat)-3, 7 (6 Fri)-11; 12-3, 7-11 Sun

☎ (01749) 342306

Butcombe Bitter; guest beers H

An early landlord, Mr James George, introduced his own coinage in 1666, depicting George and the Dragon. This 17th-century former coaching inn has been sympathetically refurbished since 2000 by the present landlord whose use of personal photographs and mementos gives the feel of being welcomed into a family home. It comprises a large main bar with a smaller, adjacent no-smoking area and a dining room. A skittle alley is in an outbuilding in the back garden. ⌂❀⇌◑♿♣●P⊁

Culmhead

Holman Clavel

TA3 7EA (¼ mile off B3170)

⏲ 11-11; 12-3, 7-10.30 Sun

☎ (01823) 421432

Butcombe Bitter, Gold; guest beers H

The only pub in England to bear this unusual name, the eponymous Clavel is a lintel above the fireplace made of Holm Oak. The menu features local fish and game in season and has dishes to suit all tastes and budgets. Guest ales come from both micro and regional independent brewers. The pub is allegedly haunted by the ghost of a defrocked monk, but a warm, friendly welcome is assured. ⌂Q❀◑▲♣P

Dinnington

Dinnington Docks

Lower Street, TA17 8SX

⏲ 11.30-3.30, 6-11; 12-3, 7-10.30 Sun

☎ (01460) 52397

Butcombe Bitter; guest beers H

Fabulous village pub that always seems to be full of locals enjoying the ales, cider and hearty meals from the traditional, home-cooked menu. You can get your hair cut in the pub on the fourth Tuesday of each month. Dogs and walkers are welcome in the L-shaped bar that is decorated with railway photographs and curiosities for those of an enquiring nature to examine. Beers from Cottage Brewery and west country guests supplement the Butcombe Bitter. ⌂❀◑♿♣●P

Draycott

Red Lion

Wells Road, BS27 3SN (on A371)

⏲ 12 (4 Mon)-midnight; 12-midnight Sun

☎ (01934) 743786

Beer range varies H

Genuine free house, built in 1640 as a cider house; nowadays the landlord likes to support west country micro-breweries. The pub is handy for walkers on the nearby West Mendip Way. Good value home-cooked meals are served (not Mon), with special deals for older people on Wednesday and Thursday. Pub games include shove-ha'penny and a skittle alley, there is a wide-screen TV and occasional live music. Thatchers and Rich's ciders are stocked. ⌂❀◑▲⊟(126)♣●P⊁

Dulverton

Rock House Inn

1 Jury Road, TA22 9DU

⏲ 11-11 (midnight Fri & Sat); 12-11 Sun

☎ (01398) 323131 ⊕ rockhouseinn.co.uk

Cotleigh Tawny; guest beers H

Lively free house at the top of this bustling Exmoor town. Built on the side of a rock face, it was first licensed in 1837, although part of the property is said to be much older. The single bar is where locals congregate and it can get smoky, but there is an adjoining lounge area and a no-smoking family room. No food is served during the week, just a roast lunch on Sunday. Rich's farmhouse cider is sold. ⌂▲⊟●

Woods

4 Bank Square, TA22 9BU (near church)

⏲ 11-3, 6-midnight; 12-3, 7-11 Sun

☎ (01398) 324007

Exmoor Ale; Otter Head; guest beer G

Formerly a bakery, this popular and unpretentious bar serves both beer-loving locals and visitors wanting to eat in the open-plan restaurant where excellent locally produced food is served. The interior is rustic with a wood-burning stove in winter, wooden floors and bar, country paraphernalia and three beers served straight from the cool room behind the bar. It is a rare regular outlet for Otter Head. Friendly staff and sturdy bar food add to its attraction. ⌂Q❀◐♿⛺🚌●

East Harptree

Castle of Comfort

BA40 6DD (on B3134 at jct with minor roads)
✪ 12-3, 6-11 daily
☎ (01761) 221321 ⊕ castle-of-comfort.co.uk
Butcombe Bitter; guest beers Ⓗ
Splendid, sprawling inn, on an isolated crossroads in the Mendip Hills, not really in East Harptree at all. The name is said to derive from the time when it housed condemned criminals for their last night before execution. The pub is popular for food and it is not always easy to find a seat for a drink at busy times. Guest beers come from all over the UK. The child-friendly garden is pleasant in summer. ⌂Q❀◐♣●P

East Woodlands

Horse & Groom

BA11 5LY (1 mile S of A361/B3092 jct) OS792446
✪ 11.30-2.30 (not Mon), 6.30-11; 12-3, 7-10.30 Sun
☎ (01373) 462802
Blindmans Buff; Taylor Landlord; Wadworth 6X; guest beers Ⓖ
A warm welcome awaits at this pub on the edge of Longleat estate and safari park at the end of a road that seems endless. The pub boasts an open fire and flagstone floors with an intimate public bar, free from piped music. The conservatory has been turned into a restaurant and snacks are available in the bar. The large garden provides good views of the country. ⌂Q❀◐⊟⛺●P

Faulkland

Tucker's Grave ☆

BA3 5XF (on A366, 1 mile E of village) OS752552
✪ 11.30-3, 6-11; 12-3, 7-10.30 Sun
☎ (01373) 834230
Draught Bass; Butcombe Bitter Ⓖ
This is a real treasure of a local that has not changed much since it was built in the mid-17th century. All beers and ciders are served direct from the cask in an alcove rather than a bar. A good clientele is drawn from all walks of life and many visitors come from miles around. Tucker hanged himself in 1747 and is buried at the crossroads, as immortalised in a song by the Stranglers. ⌂Q❀♣●P

Frome

Griffin Inn

Milk Street, BA11 3DB
✪ 5-11 (1am Fri & Sat); 12-10.30 Sun
☎ (01373) 467766 ⊕ milkstreet.5u.com
Milk Street Nick's, Beer; guest beers Ⓗ
Situated in the older part of Frome, the Griffin is owned by the Milk Street Brewery. A small brewhouse out the back, in a former adult cinema, produces a wide range of ales, which are on sale alongside guest beers. The single bar has retained many original features – open fires, etched glass windows and wood floors – in this basic but popular pub. Live music is performed some evenings. The small garden is open in the evening. ⌂❀⇌♣P⊡

Green Ore

Ploughboy Inn

BA5 3ET (at A39/B3135 jct)
✪ 11-2.30, 6.30-11; closed Mon; 12-3, 7-11 Sat & Sun
☎ (01761) 241375
Butcombe Bitter; Otter Ale; Palmer Best Bitter Ⓗ
Roadside free house with a neat and tidy appearance. The L-shaped room features a real fire and subdued lighting; outside is a pleasant courtyard, extensive patio area and lawn. Ample parking is a plus. The three real ales are subject to occasional change. Easily spotted if approaching from Bristol in particular (look for the plough affixed to the whitewashed walls). ⌂❀◐🚌(375/376)P

Hardington Moor

Royal Oak

Moor Lane, BA22 9WW (off A30 at Yeovil Court Hotel)
✪ 12-3 (not Mon), 7-midnight (11 Mon); 12-4, 7-11 Sun
☎ (01935) 862354
Branscombe Vale Branoc; guest beers Ⓗ
You will find the Royal Oak set back from the road in the lower part of the village. On Thursday evening, it hosts the long-standing 'bike and chips' night. This well-supported pub fields skittle teams and stages an annual beer festival. The cider is made from apples collected from the orchards next to the pub. Traditional bar food is supplemented by special dishes. ⌂❀◐♿♣●P

Henstridge

Bird in Hand

2 Ash Walk, BA8 0RA (100 yds S of A30/A357)
✪ 11-2.30, 5.30-11; 11-11 Sat; 12-3, 7.30-10.30 Sun
☎ (01963) 362255
Beer range variess Ⓗ
Friendly stone-built village pub with low ceilings, exposed beams and open fires. A games room with skittle alley and TV is accessed from the main bar. The landlord's policy is to present an ever-changing selection of real ales, including seasonal beers. The home-cooked bar snacks are not to be missed. ⌂Q❀◐♿♣●P

Hillcommon

Royal Oak

TA4 1DS (on B3227)
✪ 11.30-3, 6 (6.30 winter)-11; 12-3, 6 (6.30 winter)-11 Sun
☎ (01823) 400295
Cotleigh Tawny; RCH Pitchfork; Sharp's Doom Bar; guest beer Ⓗ
Village pub on the main road, frequented by local drinkers as well as diners. The single, large, open-plan bar is set for diners, but there is always seating for drinkers. A selection of bottled beers supplements the

four handpumps. There is a beautiful, large garden at the rear. Food is locally sourced and booking is advised for the carvery served on Thursday and Sunday; discounts are offered to older people on Tuesday and Thursday. ❀◑⊟♣P⊬

Hillfarrance

Anchor

TA4 1AW (1 mile off A38 or A358 near Oake) OS166246
⌚ 11-11; 12-10.30 Sun
☎ (01823) 461334
Branscombe Vale Branoc; O'Hanlon's seasonal beers; Ⓗ guest beers Ⓗ/Ⓖ
Catering for both beer drinkers and diners, this large village pub has four handpumps, two of which offer guest beers. Several rooms include a cosy bar, a family/games room and a large function room where the Sunday carvery is served. Food is locally sourced and home made. Accommodation consists of four double rooms. Outside is a car park, garden and licensed camping facilities. A beer festival is held on August bank holiday. ♛☎❀⇌◑♿▲P⊬

Hinton St George

Lord Poulett Arms

High Street, TA17 8SE
⌚ 12-3, 6.30-11 daily
☎ (01460) 73149 ⊕ lordpoulettarms.co.uk
Beer range varies Ⓖ
Stone-flagged floors and a bar-mounted gravity stillage provide the first impressions on entering this charming village pub. Antique furniture is a feature of the restaurant, contrasting with the exciting modern menu on offer. The bar has a well-stocked magazine rack and library, encouraging customers to linger by the fire. Outside, a charming Mediterranean garden, complete with petanque court, leads to a further, secluded garden with a pelota wall that dates from Napoleonic times.
♛Q❀⇌◑⊟♿♣●P

Horsington

Half Moon

BA8 0EF (200 yds off A357)
⌚ 12-2.30 (3 Sat), 6-11; 12-3, 7-10.30 Sun
☎ (01963) 370140 ⊕ horsington.co.uk
Wadworth 6X; guest beers Ⓗ
Just off the A357, this spacious village pub is a delight for the real ale aficionado, with its friendly service and choice of ales. The landlord endeavours to strike a balance between local and national breweries, stocking up to six ales, with local micros such as Blindmans, Hobdens and Milk Street often featuring. A beer festival is held annually in May, providing an opportunity to try a further 20 or so beers. Accommodation is in a separate cottage-style building.
♛Q☎❀⇌◑♣●P

Huish Episcopi

Rose & Crown (Eli's) ☆

Wincanton Road, TA10 9QT (on A372)
⌚ 11.30-2.30, 5.30-11; 11.30-11 Fri & Sat; 12-10.30 Sun
☎ (01458) 250494
Teignworthy Reel Ale; guest beers Ⓗ
This traditional thatched inn, known locally as Eli's, has been in the same family for generations. The character and unusual features have remained unchanged, offering an experience redolent of a bygone era. The pub is divided into several cosy rooms, with drinks served in the flagstoned tap room. Good, wholesome pub food is served at lunchtime and early evening. Rich's cider is sold. Q☎❀◑⊟♿♣●P

Hutton

Old Inn

Main Road, BS24 9QQ
⌚ 11.30-11 (midnight Fri & Sat); 12-11 Sun
☎ (01934) 812336
Greene King IPA, Ruddles Best Bitter, Old Speckled Hen, guest beers Ⓗ
Spacious, single room pub with an area for dining. The extensive menu is designed to suit most tastes and budgets. The landlord makes good use of the brewery's guest beer policy, with two guests always available, from all parts of Britain, often ales rarely seen in the area. The village is a regular winner of the Britain in Bloom competition.
❀◑⊟(4, 5A)P

Kelston

Old Crown

Bath Road, BA1 9AQ (3 miles from Bath, on A431)
⌚ 11-11; 12-10.30 Sun
☎ (01225) 423032
Draught Bass; Bath Gem; Butcombe Bitter, Blond, Gold; Wadworth 6X Ⓗ
Attractive, multi-roomed, 18th-century former coaching inn owned by Butcombe Brewery. The old beer engine in the bar, flagstone floors, open fires and settles all help to create a friendly atmosphere. A selection of good quality, imaginative meals, including fresh fish dishes, is served in the restaurant and bar areas. In summer barbecues are sometimes held in the large, pleasant garden, while in winter head for the bar, where Butcombe's seasonal Brunel IPA is served. ♛Q❀⇌◑⊟(319, 332)P⊬

Langford Budville

Martlet Inn

TA21 0QZ
⌚ 12-3, 7-11; closed Mon; 12-4 (closed eve) Sun
☎ (01823) 400262
Cotleigh Tawny; Exmoor Ale; Sharp's Doom Bar; guest beer Ⓗ
Comfortable old village inn that has seen some improvements over the years, yet remains unspoilt. The main bar has flagstone floors, low exposed beams, a large woodburner and a fireplace that divides off the no-smoking dining room. Steps lead to the no-smoking lounge bar and the child-free front patio garden – there is a large rear family garden with play equipment. Excellent home-cooked food and a large skittle alley/function room complete the

facilities. Cider is stocked in summer.
♛Q❀⇌◑◐⊟♣●P⁄

Lower Odcombe

Masons Arms

BA22 8TX

✪ 12-2.30, 6-midnight daily

☎ (01935) 862591 ⊕ the-masons-arms.co.uk

Odcombe No1; guest beers Ⓗ

Friendly thatched village local, recently revitalised by experienced licensees. The Odcombe Brewery is in the small brewhouse at the rear of the pub. Good food is served, using local produce, and children are catered for. Theme nights are staged every Thursday and a quiz night on the first Sunday of the month. Guest beers are sometimes selected by the customers. ❀⇌◑◐▲⊟♣●P

Martock

White Hart Hotel

East Street, TA12 6JQ (next to the Pinnacle)

✪ 12-2 (not Mon; 12-3 Sat), 5.30-midnight (2am Fri & Sat); 12-3 (closed eve) Sun

☎ (01935) 822005 ⊕ whitehart hotelmartock.co.uk

Otter Bitter; guest beers Ⓗ

This family-run free house offers two guest beers, typically from Sharp's, Cottage, Dorset, Sherborne or Church End. Bar food and an extensive restaurant menu, including special dishes, is prepared by a resident chef at all sessions except Monday evening. The hotel has several bedrooms, some en-suite. The bar features chesterfield sofas around the fireplace and a piano that is sometimes played early evening. It attracts a good mix of visitors and locals. The skittle alley sees regular action. ⇌◑◐▲⊟♣P

Middlezoy

George Inn

42 Main Road , TA7 0NN (off A372)

✪ 12-3 (not Mon), 7-midnight; 12-3, 7-11.30 Sun

☎ (01823) 698215

Butcombe Bitter; guest beers Ⓗ

This 17th-century pub has retained many of its original features, such as exposed beams, fireplaces, and the stone-flagged floor. Home-cooked food is served in the no-smoking dining room (lunches Tue-Sat, eve meals Wed-Sat). An excellent selection of changing real ales is supplemented by regular beer festivals. The George was voted Somerset CAMRA Pub of the Year 2000.
♛Q❀◑◐P⁄

Midsomer Norton

White Hart ☆

The Island, BA3 2HQ

✪ 11-11; 12-10.30 Sun

☎ (01761) 418270

Draught Bass; Butcombe Bitter Ⓖ

This pub is a gem of Victorian design. Its multi-room layout has not changed in years and it is worth a visit for this alone. In addition to the Victoriana, memorabilia from the past mining heritage of the area are displayed alongside old pub pictures. The beers are served direct from the cask and there is usually a choice of two ciders. This popular local in the centre of town provides good bar snacks. ♛❀⇌◑⊟♣●

Minehead

Queen's Head

Holloway Street, TA24 5NR (off The Parade)

✪ 12-3, 5.30-11; 12-11 Sat; 12-3, 6.30-11 Sun

☎ (01643) 706000

Exmoor Gold, Hart; St Austell Tribute; guest beers Ⓗ

Situated in a side street, just off The Parade, this popular town pub sells up to eight ales. The spacious single bar has a raised seating area for dining and families. There is a games room at the rear. Good value food is served daily, 12-2pm and 7-9pm – try the home-made pies. Twice yearly beer festivals are held. ◑◐▲⇌(W Somerset Rlwy)⊟♣

Moorlinch

Ring O'Bells

Pit Hill Lane, TA7 9BT (signed from A39)

✪ 12-3 (not Mon), 5-11; 12-11 Sat; 12-10.30 Sun

☎ (01458) 210358

Beer range varies Ⓗ

Spacious, welcoming village pub with a large, carpeted public bar housing a pool table, dartboard and juke box. The restaurant is located in the lower lounge bar where good value home-cooked meals are served. The opening hours are flexible, depending on trade. The pub usually offers a varied selection of three real ales. Moorlinch Vineyard is not far away. ♛Q☎◑◐⊟♿⊟P⁄

Mudford

Half Moon

Main Street, BA21 5TF (on A359)

✪ 12-11; 12-10.30 Sun

☎ (01935) 850289

⊕ visitwestcountry.com/thehalfmoon

RCH beer range Ⓖ

Large, 17th-century inn, which although restored, has retained its character. A rare outlet in south Somerset for RCH beers, two are normally kept on stillage behind the bar. Westons cider is sold. Excellent food is served all day. The Half Moon has 13 en-suite bedrooms. An excellent car park at the side of the building makes disabled access easy. ♛Q❀⇌◑◐♿⊟●P⁄

Nailsea

Blue Flame

West End, BS48 4DE (turn off A370 at Chelvey)

✪ 12-3, 6-11; 12-10.30 Sun

☎ (01275) 856910

Fuller's London Pride; RCH East Street Cream; guest beer Ⓗ

Lovely, rustic, 19th-century pub, unaltered for many years, comprising two rooms, one with a bar, and a snug. Coal fires help create a cosy atmosphere in winter. Live music is performed twice a month (first and third Tue). The large rear garden is ideal for families in summer. Camping is possible, but telephone first. Food is limited to filled rolls. ♔Q❀⚐♣●P

Nether Stowey

Rose & Crown

St Mary's Street, TA5 1LJ (off A39, Bridgwater-Minehead road)

⏲ 12-midnight daily

☎ (01278) 732265

Beer range varies Ⓗ

This 16th-century pub sits at the centre of a pretty village at the foot of the Quantocks. A busy, traditional hostelry, it sells mostly West Country beers. The restaurant attached serves home-grown vegetables to accompany the locally sourced meat and fish on its a la carte menu. Bar meals are also available and cream teas in summer. The walled Victorian garden is an added attraction. Conveniently situated for Coleridge Cottage and hill walking, the pub offers accommodation. ♔Q☕❀⛟◐⊟▣♣●

North Curry

Bird in Hand

Queen's Square, TA3 6LT

⏲ 12-3, 6 (5.30 Fri)-11; 12-4, 7-11 Sat; 12-3, 7-10.30 Sun

☎ (01823) 490248

Otter Bitter; guest beers Ⓗ

Village local with low, beamed ceilings and a central fireplace in the front bar. The restaurant at the rear of the pub serves a varied menu including dishes made with local produce at reasonable prices. Outside drinking areas are provided at the front and rear of the pub. The guest beers change often and Rich's cider is sold. ♔Q❀◐⚐▣♣●P

North Perrott

Manor Arms

Middle Street, TA18 7SG

⏲ 11-11; 12-10.30 Sun

☎ (01460) 72901 ⊕ manorarmshotel.co.uk

Butcombe Bitter; Fuller's London Pride; O'Hanlon's Royal Oak; guest beers Ⓗ

Friendly, attentive service is the norm at this 16th-century village inn that was converted from cottages. This well arranged pub has gone from strength to strength, serving good food alongside up to 10 ales that may come from any part of the UK. The pub has a dining area at each end. A radio plays gently at one end of the bar, but the rest of the pub is quiet. Not to be missed. ♔Q❀⛟◐▣P

Norton Fitzwarren

Cross Keys

TA2 6NR (at A358/B3227 jct W of Taunton)

⏲ 11-11; 12-10.30 Sun

☎ (01823) 333062

Beer range varies Ⓗ

Large Chef and Brewer house, divided into cosy areas, with exposed beams and nick-nacks. A wide-ranging menu is augmented by daily chef's specials. Two monthly guest beers from the likes of Fuller's and RCH supplement two others that change more frequently from regional and micro-breweries. There is also a small selection of bottled Belgian and German beers. Beer festivals are held twice a year and it hosts a monthly jazz evening. The large garden has a stream running nearby. ♔☕❀◐▣P⚟

Pitney

Halfway House

Pitney Hill, TA10 9AB (on B3153) OS451278

⏲ 11.30-3, 5.30-11 (midnight Fri & Sat); 12-3.30, 7-11 Sun

☎ (01458) 252513 ⊕ thehalfwayhouse.co.uk

Branscombe Vale Bitter; Butcombe Bitter; Hop Back Crop Circle, Summer Lightning; Teignworthy Reel Ale; guest beers Ⓖ

Traditional village pub serving a wide variety of local ales, alongside a range of international bottled beers. Excellent, home-cooked food (not served Sun) is based on local produce. There is no juke box or fruit machine to disturb the buzz of conversation at CAMRA's national Pub of the Year 1996 (and frequent Somerset winner). A real gem of a pub. ♔Q❀◐⚐▣(54)♣●P

Porlock Weir

Ship Inn

TA24 8PB (take B3225 from Porlock)

⏲ 11-11; 12-10.30 Sun

☎ (01643) 862753 ⊕ theanchorhotelandshipinn.co.uk

Cotleigh Barn Owl; Exmoor Ale, Gold; guest beer Ⓗ

Possibly the best view from any pub in Somerset, overlooking the small harbour and Bristol Channel towards the South Wales coast. Located in the Exmoor National Park, it is over 400 years old and the adjacent Anchor Hotel dates from the early 1800s. Good bar and restaurant food is served by friendly staff. Ideal for walkers, the Ship is close to Porlock village and the famous hill. The large local pay and display car park can be busy during holiday periods. ♔☕❀⛟◐♿▣P⚟▯

Portishead

Windmill Inn

58 Nore Road, BS20 6JZ

⏲ 11-11; 12-10.30 Sun

☎ (01275) 843677

Draught Bass; Butcombe Gold; Courage Best Bitter; RCH Pitchfork; guest beers Ⓗ

Spacious, split-level free house with a large tiered patio to the rear, at the edge of town, affording panoramic views over the Severn estuary. A beamed ceiling, pictures and various artefacts give the pub a warm atmosphere. A varied menu is served all day. The guest ales often come from local breweries, and the cider is Thatchers. The No. 359 bus serves the pub. ☕❀◐♿▣●P

Priddy

Hunter's Lodge

BA5 3AR (at minor crossroads 1 mile from Priddy) OS549501

⏲ 11.30-2.30, 6.30-11; 12-2, 7-10.30 Sun

☎ (01749) 672275

Blindmans Mine Beer; Butcombe Bitter; guest beers Ⓖ

Timeless, classic roadside inn, at an isolated crossroads near Priddy, the highest village in Somerset. Often frequented by cavers and walkers, three rooms for drinkers include one with a flagged floor and barrels behind the bar. The landlord has been here nearly 40 years. Home-cooked food is simple, but tasty and good value. Folk musicians drop in for a session on Tuesday evening. The pub has a pleasant, secluded garden. ♨Q✿◑⊟♣●P

Queen Victoria Inn

Pelting Drove, BA5 3BA
(on minor road to Wookey Hole)
✪ 12-3 (not Mon, or winter Tue-Fri) 7-11; 12-11 Sat & Sun
☎ (01749) 676385
Butcombe Bitter, Blond (summer), Gold; Sharp's Doom Bar; Wadworth 6X Ⓖ/Ⓗ
Tradtional free house, a pub since 1851. Two rooms boast low ceilings, flagged floors and log fires. It has barely changed in decades and is a lovely haven from the cold in winter months. Popular during Priddy Folk Festival in July and the annual fair in August, children (and dogs) are admitted. Reasonably priced, home-cooked food is a speciality, but you cannot book in advance. ♨Q✿◑⛺♣●P

Priston

Ring of Bells

BA2 9EE
✪ 7-11; 12-3, 6.30-11 Fri & Sat; 12-3, 7-10.30 Sun
☎ (01761) 471467
Draught Bass; Greene King IPA, Ruddles Best, Old Speckled Hen Ⓗ
Traditional old English pub, providing a real fire, real ale and real atmosphere. A cheerful landlord and friendly customers combine to make this a welcome stop. Substantial bar meals are served in convivial surroundings. A pub set in the heart of a pretty village, it is well worth visiting for several good rural walks. ♨✿◑⛺♣P

Rode

Cross Keys

20 High Street, BA11 6NZ (off A361, midway between Frome and Trowbridge) OS803537
✪ 11.30-2.30 (not Mon), 6-11; 12-3; 7-10.30 Sun
☎ (01373) 830900
Butcombe Bitter; guest beers Ⓗ
Reopened in 2004 following ten years of closure. It was originally the tap of the long closed Fussell's Brewery and more latterly a Bass depot. Sympathetically restored, it has succeeded in bringing back a strong village trade. A passageway – a feature in itself with its deep well – links the two bars. There is also a large restaurant area (once the Bass depot canteen). The guests regularly feature Wadworth 6X, beers from the nearby Blindman's brewery, and other local micros. ♨Q✿⛟◑⊟⛺♣P

Rowberrow

Swan Inn

Rowberrow Lane, BS25 1QL (just S of A38/A368 jct)
✪ 12-3, 6-11; 12-3, 7-10.30 Sun
☎ (01934) 852371
Draught Bass; Butcombe Bitter, Gold; guest beer Ⓗ
Believed to date from the late 17th or early 18th century, this Butcombe tied house enjoys a pleasant setting, nestling beneath the nearby Dolebury iron age hillfort. A convenient stop for walkers on the Mendip Hills, the emphasis here is on home-cooked food, but not to the detriment of customers just wanting a drink. The walls bear an interesting collection of artefacts. Thatchers cider is sold. ♨Q✿◑●P

Saltford

Bird in Hand

58 High Street, BS31 3EJ (approx. 400yds from A4)
✪ 11-3 (3.30 Sat), 6-11; 12-3.30, 6-10.30 Sun
☎ (01225) 873335 🌐 birdinhandsaltford.co.uk
Abbey Bellringer; Butcombe Bitter; Courage Best Bitter; guest beer Ⓗ
Dating back to 1869, this is a smart, carpeted, single bar in the old High Street. Around the walls a fine collection of plates (mostly depicting birds), photographs and pictures give it a homely feel. Decidedly food-oriented, the dining room is in a fairly recent conservatory extension that offers good views of the garden and hills beyond. There is also a small family area. The Avon Valley Cycleway runs behind the pub. ✿◑♿🚌●P⚡

Shepton Beauchamp

Duke of York

North Street, TA19 0LW
✪ 12-3 (not Mon), 6.30-11 (6-midnight Fri); 12-midnight Sat; 12-3, 6.30-11 Sun
☎ (01460) 240314
Fuller's London Pride; Sharp's Doom Bar; Teignworthy Reel Ale; guest beers Ⓗ
Friendly village pub, popular with locals and home to numerous darts and skittles teams. On a hot summer's day, sit outside on the raised pavement and watch village life go by. The restaurant serves good value meals (not winter Sun or Mon eve). The pub has a pool room and a garden at the rear. ♨✿◑🚌♣P

Somerton

Half Moon

West Street, TA11 6QQ
✪ 11-3, 6.30 (5 Fri)-midnight (1am Fri & Sat); 11-3, 6.30-midnight Sun
☎ (01458) 272401 🌐 halfmoon-somerton.co.uk
Wadworth 6X; guest beers Ⓗ
Large public house, built in 1903, set in a small shopping district of Somerton. The public bar is sports oriented, with two dartboards and a pool table, which are well supported by local teams. The extensive menu offers steak nights and special meals for older people every lunchtime except Sunday. Booking is advised for the popular Sunday lunches in the no-smoking dining room. The pub usually keeps four real ales, Burrow Hill cider and a selection of bottled beers. ⏰✿⛟◑⊟⛺🚌♣●P⚡

South Petherton

Brewer's Arms

18 St James Street, TA13 5BW (1/2 mile off A303)

11.30-2.30, 6-11 (midnight Fri & Sat); 12-10.30 Sun

(01460) 241887

Otter Bitter; guest beers (H)

Busy, friendly old pub at the village centre. The pub's guest beer book shows over 1,200 entries. A blackboard gives tasting notes for the current three and forthcoming guest beers. It stages two annual beer festivals: one in late May, the other, showcasing Somerset beer and cider, on August bank holiday. The next door restaurant is now part of the pub. A true community pub for all, it was Somerset CAMRA runner-up in the Pub of the Year 2006 awards.

Staple Fitzpaine

Greyhound Inn

TA3 5SP

12-3, 6-11; 12-10.30 Sun

(01823) 480227

Hancock's HB; Otter Ale; guest beer (H)

In a beautiful part of Somerset between Taunton and the Blackdown Hills, this Grade II listed 16th-century, former hunting lodge has a flagstoned bar area and several connecting rooms, revealing old timbers and natural stone walls. It offers an extensive menu and the food is freshly prepared to order. The guest beers come from anywhere in the country. P

Street

Two Brewers

38 Leigh Road, BA16 0HB

11-2.30, 6-11 (11.30 Fri & Sat); 11.30-2.30, 6-11 Sun

(01458) 442421 thetwobrewers.co.uk

Courage Directors; Greene King Ruddles County; guest beers (H)

Large town pub that has a long single bar, carpeted throughout, with a good sized area for diners. The extensive menu includes vegetarian and children's meals. The pub has its own newsletter, which shows the beer and food available at the time of issue as well as a list of frequent and occasional guest beers. The pub benefits from an attractive garden at the rear. Q P

Taunton

Coal Orchard

30 Bridge Street, TA1 1TX

9am-midnight (1am Fri & Sat); 9am-midnight Sun

(01823) 477330

Courage Directors; Greene King Abbot; Marston's Pedigree; guest beers (H)

Large Wetherspoon's shop conversion decorated in an Art Deco style, in keeping with the building. Tall stools next to the long front windows allow you to watch the world go by. There is a large no-smoking area and a quiet paved garden. Guest beers regularly showcase breweries from Somerset and the surrounding counties while mini festivals offer up to six beers from one of the local breweries.

Eagle

46 South Street, TA1 3AF

6-11.30 (midnight Fri); 12-3, 7-midnight Sat; 12-3, 7-11.30 Sun

(01823) 275713

Otter Bitter; guest beer (H)

Games-oriented town pub with two dartboards, two pool tables and two skittle alleys, one of which doubles as a function room. The building dates from the Victorian era and boasts an outdoor terrace for enjoying the summer evenings. Guest beers change regularly and can come from all parts of the country but are often from west country breweries.

P

Wyvern Club

Mountfields Road, TA1 3BJ

7-11; 4 (5.30 summer)-11.30 Sat; 12-3, 7-10.30 Sun

(01823) 284591 wyvernclub.co.uk

Exmoor Ale; guest beers (H)

This large, busy sports and social club offers a variety of West Country beers, which change frequently. Normally three different breweries' ales are on offer at club prices. Meals are available until 9pm, plus Sunday lunchtime. The club premises are available for daytime meetings. Show this Guide or your CAMRA membership card to be signed in as a guest. A real ale festival is held in October.

P

Wanstrow

Pub

Station Road, BA4 4SZ

12-2.30 (not Mon; 12-3 Fri & Sat), 6-11; 12-3, 7-10.30 Sun

(01749) 850455

Draught Bass; Blindmans Mine Beer, seasonal beers; Greene King IPA; guest beers (H)

This is a gem, a friendly village local where the lounge bar with open fire and flagstone floors leads to a small restaurant. The pub is a regular outlet for the nearby Blindmans' Brewery and in addition serves up to six guest beers on handpump or gravity. Blindmans' seasonal beers are also offered, plus two ciders. Games include skittles, bar billiards and ring the bull. A limited but imaginative menu is served; all food is home made. Q P

Watchet

Star Inn

Mill Lane, TA23 0BZ

12-3, 6.30-midnight; 12-4, 6.30-1am Fri & Sat; 12-4, 7-midnight Sun

(01984) 631367

Beer range varies (H)

Three 15th-century cottages knocked into a single building make up this popular pub near the marina on the road to Blue Anchor. The beer range concentrates on brews from West Country micros and always includes Archers, Cottage and Cotleigh ales, while guests come from the likes of Bath Ales, Otter and Newmans. The pub consists of three, low-ceilinged rooms with the bar in the main one. Home-cooked food is served at Somerset CAMRA's Pub of the Year 2006. ⛫☕❀◐▲⇌(W Somerset Rlwy)⊟♣P⊬

Wells

City Arms

69 High Street, BA5 2AG

⊙ 9am-11 (11.30 Fri & Sat); 12-10 Sun

☎ (01749) 673916 ⊕ thecityarmsatwells.co.uk

Butcombe Bitter; guest beers ⊞

The City Arms became a public house in 1810, having been the city jail for the preceding 200 years. The main bar retains the atmospheric small barred windows and low, vaulted ceilings from its former existence. The former Keeper's Bar has recently been refurbished as a patisserie and bistro, with a modern, coffee bar ambience. One of the few free houses in Wells, the landlord prides himself on maintaining a choice of six real ales at all times. ☕❀◐♣●

West Chinnock

Muddled Man

Lower Street, TA18 7PT

⊙ 11-2.30, 7-midnight; 12-midnight Fri-Sun

☎ (01935) 881235

Beer range varies ⊞

A warm welcome always awaits at this traditional free house, set among the hamstone cottages of Lower Street. The pub is as keen on selling a good pint as it is on providing traditional meals. The skittle alley has been built to act as a function room and is well heated. The local cider is from Burrow Hill. ⛫❀◐♣●

West Huntspill

Crossways Inn

TA9 3RA (on A38)

⊙ 12-3, 5.30-11; 12-10.30 Sun

☎ (01278) 783756 ⊕ crossways-inn.com

Flowers IPA; Fuller's London Pride; guest beers ⊞

This 17th-century inn has been in the same hands for over 25 years. The guest ales change frequently. The food menu is chalked on a large blackboard by the bar and it hosts occasional themed events such as Burns Night or Beaujolais Nouveau day. There is a bistro and no-smoking area for diners. The pub is divided into different areas, making it cosy and comfortable. There is a skittle alley and jazz sessions are held in the summer. Rich's cider is sold. ⛫Q❀⇔◐⊟♣●P

Weston-super-Mare

Off the Rails

Station Approach, BS23 1XY (on railway station)

⊙ 7am-1am; 9am-1am Sun

☎ (01934) 415109

RCH Hewish IPA; guest beers ⊞

Genuine free house, conveniently situated for travellers, that doubles as the station buffet, selling snacks, sandwiches and magazines. Two guest beers come from West Country breweries with an occasional ale from further afield – the landlord is happy to receive suggestions from regulars. Two-pint carry-out containers are useful for train travellers. Thatchers traditional cider is stocked. There is a free juke box and a Tuesday night quiz for entertainment. ⇌●

Raglan Arms

42-44 Upper Church Road, BS23 2DX

⊙ 12-midnight (1am Fri & Sat); 12-11 Sun

☎ (01934) 418470

Beer range varies ⊞

Since its takeover by the present licensee in 2004, this has become a CAMRA favourite. The lounge bar houses a piano, a real fire and all the handpumps. It always stocks between two and six ales from south-western micros, such as RCH, Butcombe, Newmans and Bath Ales. Live acoustic music is performed on Friday evening and occasionally at the weekend. Take bus Nos. 1, 100 and 101 to get here. ⛫Q⊡⊟

Wick St Lawrence

Ebdon Arms

Lilac Way, BS22 9WE (600 yds from Worle Cemetery)

⊙ 11-11; 12-10.30 Sun

☎ (01934) 513005

Draught Bass; Butcombe Bitter; Fuller's London Pride; RCH Hewish IPA, East Street Cream; guest beer ⊞

Recently-built pub in a modern residential area, the main bar is spacious and comfortable and incorporates a dining area. A function room/sports bar houses a skittle alley, pool, darts and a large-screen TV. At the rear is an enclosed garden and seating area. The broad menu includes daily specials and Sunday roasts. Ample car parking is available. Owned by Celtic Inns, Thatchers cider is available. ❀◐▲⊟(5A)♣●P

Wincanton

Uncle Tom's Cabin

51 High Street, BA9 9JU

⊙ 11-11 (midnight Fri & Sat); 12-11 Sun

☎ (01963) 32790

Butcombe Bitter; guest beers ⊞

The only thatched building left in Wincanton, which in part dates back to the 15th century, it was originally a shop but opened as a pub in 1861. Just inside is the original hatch where cider was served, now sadly blocked in. Outside, at the back, is a pleasant courtyard garden. Beware where you sit though as the long bench in the side bar is jokingly called death-row. It hosts occasional live music evenings. Thatchers cider is sold. ⛫❀♿♣●

Winsham

Bell Inn

11 Church Street, TA20 4HU

⊙ 12-2.30 (not Mon; 12-3 Sat), 7-11; 12-3, 7-10.30 Sun

☎ (01460) 30677

Branscombe Vale Branoc; guest beers ⊞

Popular pub at the village centre, comprising a large, open-plan bar and a function room where darts and skittles are played. Two or three reasonably priced ales are usually stocked. The patio hosts many village

activities. This pub offers good value food; the home-made pies are a speciality. Children are welcome.
⛬Q❀◑♣P

Wiveliscombe

Bear Inn

10 North Street, TA4 2JY (200 yds N of B3227)
☼ 11-11 (midnight Thu-Sat); 12-11 Sun
☎ (01984) 623537
Cotleigh Tawny, Golden Eagle; Sharp's Doom Bar; guest beers Ⓗ
Former coaching inn and lively community pub just away from the town centre. It has a comfortable bar with a pool area. Children are welcome; there is a large garden and play space at the back. The old brewing centre of Wiveliscombe is ideal as a base for exploring Exmoor and the Brendon Hills. Guest beers include seasonals from nearby Cotleigh Brewery. Home-made pizzas can be eaten in or taken away.
⛬❀◑♿♣P

Wookey

Burcott Inn

Wookey Road, BA5 1NJ (on B3139, 2 miles W of Wells)
☼ 11.30-2.30 (12-3 Sat), 6-11; 12-3, 7-10.30 Sun
☎ (01749) 673874
Beer range varies Ⓗ
Popular country pub that boasts a copper-topped, L-shaped bar, always serving two or three ales, and a real log fire. The stone roadside inn is characterised by low beams, pine tables and flagstone flooring. Darts and shove-ha'penny are played in the games room. The garden houses the remains of an old cider press and benefits from good views of the Mendip Hills. The chef's freshly prepared food, including daily specials, is served throughout the pub, Tuesday-Saturday. ⛬Q❀◑♣P⚟

Wookey Hole

Wookey Hole Inn

BA5 1BP (opp. caves)
☼ 12-3, 6-11 (1am Fri & Sat); 12-4.30 Sun
☎ (01749) 676677 🌐 wookeyholeinn.com
Beer range varies Ⓗ
Unusual conversion of an old village pub, where the emphasis is on high quality 'fusion' food. The main room comprises a split-level dining room and two smaller drinking areas. A smaller family room doubles as an overspill dining area. The style is more continental café-bar than country pub, but it works. The beer range includes three guests, a house beer - Wook Ale - and several draught Belgian beers; Wilkins cider is sold, too. It hosts live jazz Sunday lunchtime.
⛬❀◑⛺P⚟

Wrantage

Canal Inn

TA3 6DF (on A378, 4 miles SE of Taunton)
☼ 12-2 (not Mon), 5-11; 12-3, 7-10.30 Sun
☎ (01823) 480210 🌐 canalinn.com
Beer range varies Ⓖ/Ⓗ
Roadside pub, reopened after a long campaign, which has since won several awards, including Somerset CAMRA's Pub of the Year in 2005. Four ales are usually sourced from local breweries and Blackdown brews the house beer, Canal Ditchwater. Belgian beers and Burrow Hill cider are also sold. A summer beer festival is held annually and a farmers market monthly. An extensive menu features theme nights and monthly fresh fish evenings. A large garden is an asset; dogs and boots are welcome.
⛬❀◑⛺♣P

Yeovil

Great Western

47 Camborne Grove, BA21 5DG
☼ 12-2, 5-midnight; 12-midnight Fri-Sun
☎ (01935) 431051 🌐 greatwestern-pub.co.uk
Buttercombe Bitter; Wadworth 6X, seasonal beers; guest beers Ⓗ
Comfortable, friendly local with wood and flagstone floors and railway memorabilia. A corner of the room houses the dartboard and bar billiards table, and there is a TV for important sporting events. The skittle alley hosts league matches and can be hired for functions. Tuesday is quiz night. Good value food (not Mon) includes Sunday lunches, served 2-6pm. Conveniently situated for Pen Mill station on the Bristol-Weymouth line.
❀◑♣⚟

Pall Tavern

15 Silver Street, BA20 1HW
☼ 11-1am (3am Fri & Sat); 12-10.30 Sun
☎ (01935) 476521
Greene King Ruddles Best, Old Speckled Hen; guest beer Ⓗ
Pronounce the name of this excellent local 'pal' and you get a good idea of its character. It really is a village inn in the town centre, a comfortable, single bar that plays subdued music from the 1950s and '60s. Good value food (not served Mon) is served in the bar and no-smoking dining area. Despite opening hours that match those of the nearby nightclubs, the atmosphere and clientele here are totally different. Well-behaved dogs are welcome.
❀◑♣

Quicksilver Mail

168 Hendford Hill, BA20 2RG (at A30/A37 jct)
☼ 11-midnight (1am Fri & Sat); 12-10.30 Sun
☎ (01935) 424721
Adnams Broadside; Butcombe Bitter; guest beer Ⓗ
Friendly pub on the western outskirts of town, named after an express mail coach. Note the pub sign, a modern reproduction of an earlier version, displayed in the comfortable bar, which also has some interesting old photos. Good value food is served and Sunday lunch is available. Well-behaved children (and dogs) are welcome. Addlestones Cloudy cider is sold. The skittle alley doubles as a function room.
❀◑♣P

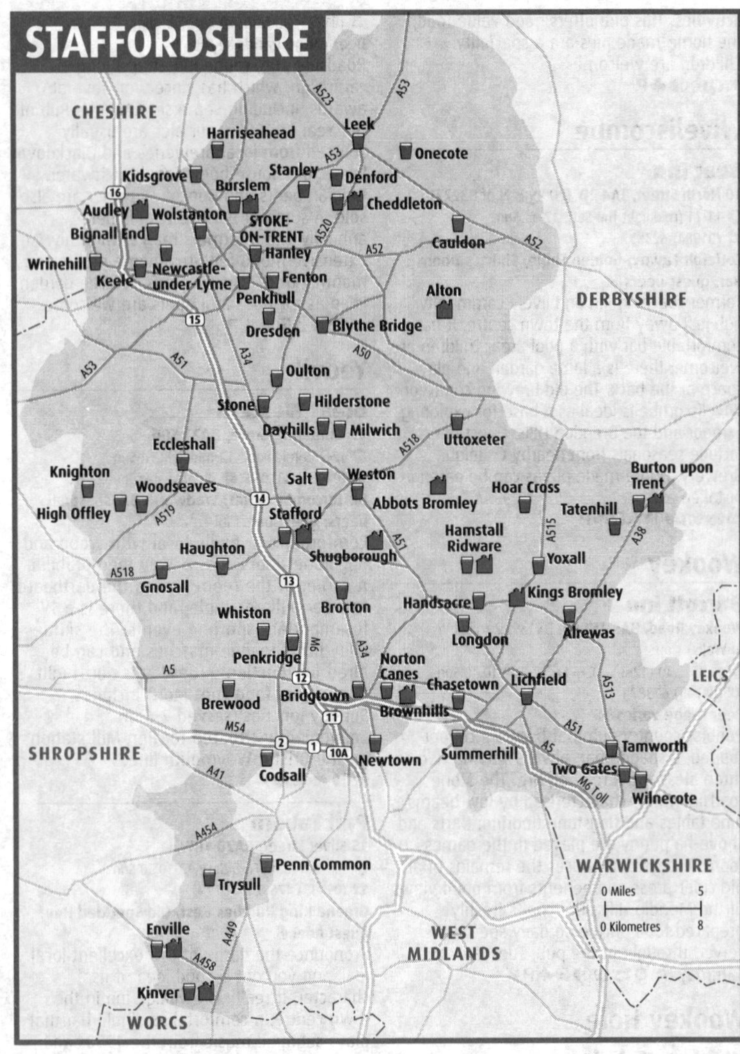

Alrewas

Crown Inn

7 Post Office Road, DE13 7BS (off Main Street)
🕘 12-2.30, 5-11; 12-11 Sat; 12-10.30 Sun
☎ (01283) 790328
Draught Bass; Marston's Pedigree; Wells Bombardier; guest beer Ⓗ
This 500-year-old former coaching inn once housed the village post office. Near the Trent & Mersey Canal, families, boaters and walkers are welcome. Good value home-cooked food includes Thursday fish night and a carvery on Sunday (no eve meals winter Sun or Mon). Live music – jazz, r&b, or folk – is performed most Monday evenings. ⌂Q❀◑◐▣▲⊟♣P⚞

Bignall End

Bignall End Cricket Club

Boon Hill, ST7 8LA (off B5500)
🕘 7-11; 12-11 Sat; 12-3, 7-10.30 Sun
☎ (01782) 720514
Fuller's London Pride; Wells Bombardier; guest beers Ⓗ
Traditional village cricket club, in a semi-rural location, established over 100 years. The large club house comprises a comfortable lounge bar and a billiard room with full-sized snooker table downstairs, plus a spacious function room upstairs. Enjoy panoramic views across Cheshire from the cricket field. The club hosts a popular annual beer festival and a 'biker' rally. CAMRA members are admitted as guests. ❀♿⊟P

Plough

2 Ravens Lane, ST7 8PS
(on B5500, ½ mile E of Audley)
🕘 12-3, 7-11; 12-midnight Fri & Sat; 12-10.30 Sun
☎ (01782) 720469
Beer range varies Ⓗ
Ever-popular, family-owned village pub, thrice CAMRA Potteries Pub of the Year, including 2005. The local Town House Brewery beers are regularly on sale along with Banks's Bitter and a changing range of guest ales, mainly from

micros. It also stocks a selection of bottled beers. It comprises a busy, traditional bar and a split-level lounge with dining area where good value meals are served (not Sun eve).
❀◑◐⛼♿🚌♣P

Blythe Bridge

Black Cock

393 Uttoxeter Road, ST11 9NT
⏲ 12-3, 5-11; 12-2.30, 7-11 Sun
☎ (01782) 392388
Beer range varies 🄷
Unspoilt village pub renowned for its good beer and food. The bar boasts seven handpulls offering a frequently-changing choice of ales, making this the hardest decision of your visit. Stand-up drinkers congregate by the bar of this two-room, totally smoke-free pub while comfortable seating is provided for those who prefer to relax. The pub hosts two quizzes each week. Q❀◑◐⇌🚌P⚡

Brewood

Bridge Inn

22 High Green, ST19 9BD (5 mins' walk from village centre)
⏲ 12-3, 5-11; 12-11 Fri & Sat; 12-11 Sun
☎ (01902) 851999
Banks's Original, Bitter; Marston's Burton Bitter; guest beers 🄷
Comfortable, traditional village pub, situated on the Staffordshire Way and the Shropshire Union Canal, the pub is naturally popular with walkers and boaters. Dogs are also welcome, with drinks available for them in the bar. Home-cooked food, including specials chalked up on a board, is served in the lounge and restaurant to the rear of the building. The Bridge hosts occasional live music evenings. ♨Q❀◑◐⛼♿🚌P

Swan Hotel

15 Market Place, ST19 9BS
⏲ 11.45-2.30 (4 Sat), 7-11; 12-10.30 Sun
☎ (01902) 850330
Courage Directors; Theakston XB; guest beers 🄷
A former regional CAMRA Pub of the Year, this old coaching inn has a low, beamed bar area with a snug at either side displaying pictures of old Brewood. Seasonal log fires add to the cosy atmosphere, but note the unusual collection of witches' figures suspended from the beams. An upstairs skittle alley hosts folk nights (see www.brewoodfolk.org.uk). ♨Q🚌♣P

Bridgtown

Stumble Inn

264 Walsall Road, WS11 3JL
(just off A34/A5/M6 toll jct)
⏲ 12-2 (not Sat), 6-11 (5-midnight Fri & Sat); 12-11 Sun
☎ (01543) 502077
Banks's Original; Taylor Landlord; guest beers 🄷
Comfortable, one-room pub where the split-level interior includes an area for pool and darts, plus a small function room. Popular with the local community, the pub stages regular charity events. An emphasis on music sees a lively disco every Friday, live music every Saturday and jam or showcase nights for new local talent on alternate Tuesdays. Weekday lunches represent excellent value.
❀◑♿⇌🚌♣P

Brocton

Chetwynd Arms

Cannock Road, ST17 0ST (on A34)
⏲ 11-midnight; 12-10.30 Sun
☎ (01785) 661089
Banks's Original, Bitter; Marston's Pedigree; guest beer 🄷
Local CAMRA Pub of the Year 2004, its bustling public bar, offering pub games, is a haven for drinkers, while the comfortable lounge caters for both drinkers and diners; meals are served all day until 9.30pm (8.30pm Sun). The garden includes an excellent children's play area. The location is ideal for visitors to Shugborough Hall and Cannock Chase, an area of outstanding natural beauty.
Q❀◑◐⛼♿🚌♣P⚡

Burton upon Trent

Burton Bridge Inn

24 Bridge Street, DE14 1SY (on A511)
⏲ 11.30-2.15, 5-11; 12-2, 7-10.30 Sun
☎ (01283) 536596
Burton Bridge Golden Delicious, Bitter, Porter, Festival, seasonal beers; guest beer 🄷
This 17th-century pub is the flagship of the Burton Bridge Brewery estate and fronts the brewery itself. Sensitively renovated and extended in 2000, it has two rooms served from a central bar. The smaller front room, with wooden pews, displays many awards and brewery memorabilia. The oak beamed and panelled back room is no-smoking. The beer range is supplemented by a fine selection of malt whiskies and fruit wines. No meals are served Sunday. A function room and skittle alley are upstairs. ♨Q❀◑🚌♣⚡

Coopers Tavern

43 Cross Street, DE14 1EG (off Station St)
⏲ 12-2.30, 5-11; 12-2.30, 7-10.30 Sun
☎ (01283) 532551

INDEPENDENT BREWERIES

Beowulf Brownhills
Black Hole Burton upon Trent
Blythe Hamstall Ridware
Brothers Abbots Bromley
Burton Bridge Burton upon Trent
Enville Enville
Kinver Kinver
Leek Cheddleton
Marston's Burton upon Trent
Old Cottage Burton upon Trent
Peakstones Rock Alton
Quartz Kings Bromley
Shugborough Shugborough
Slater's Stafford
Titanic Burslem
Tower Burton upon Trent
Town House Audley

Draught Bass; Tower Thomas Salt's Bitter; guest beers Ⓗ/Ⓖ
Originally the Bass Brewery bottle store, this classic, unspoilt 19th-century ale house, once the Bass Brewery tap, is now a privately owned free house. The intimate inner tap room, renowned for lively conversation, has barrel tables and bench seats. The beer is served from a small counter, next to the cask stillage, using a mixture of gravity and handpumps; Hop Back Summer Lightning is added at the weekend, and fruit wines are served. The more comfortable lounge often hosts folk music.

Derby Inn

17 Derby Road, DE14 1RU (on A5121)
11.30-3, 5.30-11; 11.30-11 Thu & Sat; 11.30-midnight Fri; 12-11 Sun
☎ (01283) 543674
Marston's Pedigree, Ⓗ **Owd Rodger (winter)** Ⓖ
This friendly, brick-built local, situated towards the northern edge of the town, has changed little since the 1950s. The basic bar features railway pictures and related memorabilia, plus some interesting old, yellowing newspaper cuttings above the bar counter. In the smarter, wood-panelled lounge the theme is one of horse racing. Very much a community pub, where locally produced fruit, vegetables and preserves are sold in the bar, it offers a step back in time to a more relaxed pace of life.
Q P

Devonshire Arms

86 Station Street, DE14 1BT
11.30-2.30, 5.30-11; 11.30-11.30 Fri & Sat; 12-3, 7-10.30 Sun
☎ (01283) 562392
Burton Bridge Golden Delicious, Bitter, Porter, Stairway to Heaven; guest beer Ⓗ
Popular old pub, dating from the 19th century and Grade II listed: one of four Burton Bridge Brewery hostelries in the town. It comprises a small public bar and a larger, comfortable lounge to the rear, with a no-smoking area off to one side. Note the 1853 map of Burton, old photographs, and unusual arched wooden ceilings. The patio has a fountain. Continental bottled beers and English fruit wines are stocked. Food is served all day Friday and Saturday; no meals Sunday. P

Elms Inn

36 Stapenhill Road, Stapenhill, DE15 9AE (on A444)
12-11 daily
☎ (01283) 535505
Draught Bass; guest beer Ⓗ
Busy free house, overlooking the River Trent. Built as a private house in the late 19th-century, this is one of Burton's original 'parlour pubs'. Recently renovated in a Victorian style, with the small public bar and snug at the front, and the larger, no-smoking lounge to the rear, an intimate, friendly atmosphere has been retained. Social activities include a walking club, race trips, a Tuesday quiz and summer barbecues. A Tower beer is always stocked.
Q P

Plough

7 Ford Street, Stapenhill, DE15 9LE (off Rosliston Rd)
12-3.30, 7-midnight daily
☎ (01283) 548160 theploughstapenhill.co.uk
Marston's Pedigree; guest beers Ⓗ/Ⓖ
Local CAMRA Pub of the Year 2004, this suburban free house dates back to the 19th century. The single, large room is partitioned into distinct areas, served from a central counter where the guest beers (up to seven, including a Blythe brew and at least one mild) are listed on a board. It hosts live entertainment most weekends and four beer festivals during the year.
P

Wetmore Whistle

93 Wetmore Road, DE14 1SH
(600yds N from western end of Trent Bridge, A511)
12-3, 4.30-11; 12-midnight Fri & Sat; 12-3, 6.30-11 Sun
☎ (01283) 515762
Draught Bass; Ⓖ **Bateman XXXB; Castle Rock Harvest Pale;** Ⓗ **Marston's Pedigree;** Ⓖ **guest beers** Ⓗ
A run-down local a little off the beaten track has been refurbished and revitalised by Tynemill and its new landlady. Two rooms, linked by a brick arch, have wooden floors and part wood-panelled, part tiled walls. The music room hosts live music on Saturday evening and Sunday lunchtime. The dining room opens at 8am (not Sun) for breakfast; evening meals can be arranged. A new 'classic'. P

Cauldon

Yew Tree

ST10 3EJ (off A52 and A523)
11-2.30, 6-11; 12-2.30, 7-10.30 Sun
☎ (01538) 308348
Draught Bass; Burton Bridge Bitter Ⓗ
Renowned, award-winning country pub that has been in the same family for 45 years. Near the Manifold Valley, the Yew Tree is packed with antiques and curios and offers a warm welcome. Pub games are popular. A monthly folk music evening is held (first Tue). Good value snacks include pork pies and pickled eggs – not to be missed. Coach House brews the house beer, Grays Dark Mild. Q P

Chasetown

Uxbridge Arms

2 Church Street, WS7 8QL (opp. Spot Garage)
12-3, 5.30-11; 12-1am Fri & Sat; 12-midnight Sun
☎ (01543) 674853
Draught Bass; guest beers Ⓗ
Busy, corner local, a short distance from Chasewater Country Park. The large public bar features an unusual round pool table. Meals are served in the bar, the extended lounge and the Haycroft restaurant upstairs. Four guest beers are available and the pub offers a wide choice of fruit and country wines, plus 50 malt whiskies. P

Cheddleton

Boat Inn

Basford Bridge Lane, ST13 7EQ

⌚ 12-3, 6-11; 12-midnight Fri & Sat; 12 – 11 Sun
☎ (01538) 360683 🌐 the-boatinn.co.uk
Marston's Pedigree; guest beers Ⓗ
Set in the Churnet Valley close to the steam railway, this beautiful canalside pub has everything you would want from a rural hostelry. It benefits from a large outside eating and drinking area, which is covered and heated during winter. The pub itself has all the trappings of a country inn: brassware and copper ornaments adorn the shelves and mantelpieces. A sympathetic extension has been added to the rear for diners.
❀◑P

Codsall

Codsall Station
Chapel Lane, WV8 2EJ
⌚ 11.30-2.30, 5-11; 11.30-11 Fri & Sat; 12-10.30 Sun
☎ (01902) 847061
Holden's Mild, Bitter, Golden Glow, Special, seasonal beers; guest beer Ⓗ
Created from the waiting room and offices of a Grade II listed former station building, the pub has won local CAMRA awards every year since 2001. The interior, divided into a bar, lounge, snug and conservatory, displays worldwide railway memorabilia. Steam locomotives can occasionally be spotted from the terrace, while the floodlit boules piste is the site of an annual beer festival in early September. Evening meals are served Tuesday-Saturday. Q❀◑♿⇌🚌♣P

Dayhills

Red Lion
Uttoxeter Road, ST15 8RU
(3½ miles E of Stone on B5027)
⌚ 6-11; 4-midnight Fri, 12-10.30 Sun
☎ (01889) 505474
Draught Bass; Ⓗ/Ⓖ Worthington's Bitter; guest beer Ⓗ
This welcoming country pub is known locally as the Romping Cat. Unspoilt and full of character, along with the adjoining farm it has been in the same family since 1920. The main room has a timeless feel, with its quarry tiled floor, meat hooks in the ceiling and inglenook. The atmosphere is undisturbed by music, gaming machines or TV. Draught Bass may be served straight from the cask in winter. ⛰Q♣P

Denford

Holly Bush
Canal Side, ST13 7JJ (½ mile S of New Inn on A53)
⌚ 11-11; 12-11 Sun
☎ (01538) 371819
Courage Directors; Fuller's London Pride; Marston's Pedigree; guest beers Ⓗ
Beautifully situated, next to the Cauldon Canal and close to the Deep Hayes Country Park, this pub boasts original features, including a quarry tiled floor, open fires and a traditional bar. Food is available in the bar area or in the restaurant extension. Live music is performed on Thursday. Dogs on leads are permitted in the large rear garden.
⛰Q❀◑⊟P⚟

Eccleshall

George
Castle Street, ST21 6DF
⌚ 11-11; 12-10.30 Sun
☎ (01785) 850300 🌐 thegeorgeinn.freeserve.co.uk
Slater's Bitter, Original, Top Totty, Premium, Supreme, seasonal beer Ⓗ
The brewery has outgrown the extended outbuilding behind the pub, but the six handpulls serving nearly the full range of Slater's award-winning ales are still the main attraction at the George. Originally a 17th-century coaching inn but sadly neglected for much of the last century, it has thrived under the Slater family's ownership and now boasts attractive bar and lounge areas and 10 luxurious guest rooms. Excellent meals are served all day. ⛰🛏◑🚌P

Enville

Cat
Bridgnorth Road, DY7 5HA (on A458)
⌚ 12-2:30 (3 Sat), 6.30 (7 Mon & Tue)-11; 12-5:30 Sun
☎ (01384) 872209 🌐 theenvillecat.co.uk
Enville Ale; guest beers Ⓗ
The lounge of this country pub dates back to the 16th century and is warmed by a powerful log burner. The snug and smoke room interconnect and both have real fires; there is also a no-smoking family/function room. For summer there is a garden and courtyard, adorned with hanging baskets. Bar snacks are augmented by home-made seasonal dishes and daily specials, using local produce wherever possible. No meals are served Monday. Up to five guest beers usually include others from Enville.
⛰Q⛴❀◑♣P⚟

Gnosall

Royal Oak
Newport Road, ST20 0BL (on A518)
⌚ 12-midnight daily
☎ (01785) 822362
Greene King IPA, Abbot; Highgate Dark Mild; guest beers Ⓗ
This well-run pub comprises a traditional, dog-friendly bar and a separate lounge. The guest beers are sourced from micro-breweries whenever possible. A wide range of home-cooked food, including a good vegetarian selection, is served in the lounge. The pub has an upstairs function room with a skittle alley for hire. There is a large garden with a climbing frame and swings.
⛰❀◑⊟🚌♣P⚟

Hamstall Ridware

Shoulder of Mutton
Yoxall Road, WS15 3RZ
⌚ 12-3 (not Mon-Thu); 7-11; 12-3, 7-11 Sun
☎ (01889) 504488
Draught Bass; guest beer Ⓗ
Busy village free house with a good reputation for food (advance booking advisable; eve meals Tue-Sat). The smart public bar at the front has a cosy nook to one side with brick fireplace, and a board

with some local historical snippets (there is a link between the village and Jane Austen) and photographs. The comfortable no-smoking lounge has an open area around the bar counter, with two adjacent small rooms for dining. The pub always stocks a beer from nearby Blythe Brewery.
♛Q❀◑◗⊟⅄♣P⁄

Handsacre

Old Peculiar

The Green, WS15 4DP

⏲ 12-2 (not Mon or Tue), 5.30–11; 12-3, 7-10.30 Sun

☎ (01543) 491891

Theakston Mild, Best Bitter, Old Peculier; Marston's Pedigree; guest beers Ⓗ

A warm welcome is assured in this cosy free house in the village centre; a one-roomed pub split into three areas. Good value food, served both lunchtime and evening is popular with locals and visitors alike. Regular guest beers are usually supplied by local micro-breweries. Good quality accommodation is available, and the pub is only two minutes' walk from the Trent & Mersey Canal. ❀⛟◑◗⊞♣P

Harriseahead

Royal Oak

42 High Street, ST7 4JT

⏲ 12-3 (not Mon-Fri), 7-11; 12-3, 7-10.30 Sun

☎ (01782) 513362

Copper Dragon Black Gold; Courage Directors; Fuller's London Pride; John Smith's Bitter; guest beers Ⓗ

Two-roomed, 19th-century free house, deservedly popular with locals. Two changing guest beers come from small micro-breweries. An upstairs function room provides extra space during beer festivals. A selection of 15 Belgian bottled beers is supplemented by a Belgian draught. Monthly quizzes are held in aid of local charities. Outside the designated no-smoking area, air-conditioning filters the smoke. ♛⊟⊞♣●P⁄

Haughton

Bell

Newport Road, ST18 9EX (on A518)

⏲ 12-3, 6-11; 12-10.30 Sun

☎ (01785) 780301

Banks's Original; Marston's Burton Bitter, Pedigree; guest beers Ⓗ

This friendly local free house has one large L-shaped room; the lounge area is no-smoking and serves excellent food (no meals Sun eve). The bar has Sky TV for football and horse racing fans. The building is over 200 years old and was originally a farm; photos and memorabilia are on display. Two guest beers change regularly. ❀◑◗⊞P⁄

High Offley

Anchor

Peggs Lane, Old Lea, ST20 0NG (by bridge 42 of Shropshire Union Canal) OS775256

⏲ 12-3 (not winter Mon-Fri), 8-11 (not winter Mon-Thu); 12-3, 7-11 (not winter eve) Sun

☎ (01785) 284569

Wadworth 6X Ⓖ

On the Shropshire Union Canal, this Victorian inn is a rare example of an unspoilt, country pub. It has two small bars where the cask ale and cider are served from jugs. This free house has been run by the same family since 1870, when it was called the Sebastopol. It boasts a large, award-winning garden with a canalware gift shop at the rear. Not easily found by road, but well worth seeking out. ♛Q❀⊟⅄♣●P

Hilderstone

Roebuck

Sandon Road, ST15 8SF (on B5066)

⏲ 3-11; 12-midnight Fri; 12-1am Sat; 12-10.30 Sun

☎ (01889) 505255

Marston's Burton Bitter; guest beers Ⓗ

Revitalised village pub with a cosy lounge/bar and a games room. Two guest beers are stocked. Home-cooked food is served Tuesday to Saturday evenings and Friday to Sunday lunchtimes. Tuesday is curry night, while on Friday it might be Chinese, Mexican, fresh fish or pasta. Entertainment includes a buskers' night on Wednesday; on most Saturday evenings there is a live act, disco or karaoke. ♛❀◑◗♣P

Hoar Cross

Meynell Ingram Arms

Abbots Bromley Road, DE13 8RB

⏲ 12-11 (midnight Fri & Sat); 12-10.30 Sun

☎ (01283) 575202 🌐 themeynell.co.uk

Marston's Pedigree; Taylor Landlord; guest beer Ⓗ

Unspoilt village pub in a pleasant rural setting. Once a farmhouse, dating from the early 16th century when it formed part of the Earl of Shrewsbury's estate, it has retained original beams and quarry tiled floors. The pub was named after the Meynell family who owned nearby Hoar Cross Hall. There are smoking and no-smoking bar areas, a snug served through a hatch, a restaurant and an attractive paved courtyard. It enjoys a good reputation for food (no meals Sun eve, when live music may be staged). Q❀◑◗⊟P⁄

Keele

Keele Postgraduate Association (KPA)

Horwood Hall, University of Keele, ST5 5BJ

⏲ 11 (5 Sat)-midnight (not Mon); 11-1am Fri; 7-midnight Sun

☎ (01782) 584228

Beer range varies Ⓗ

Founded in 1967 as Keele Research Association, it changed its name and moved to the present venue behind the Students Union in 1994. It always offers at least two cask beers from small independents and micros, plus quality fresh food served in its bistro and on its suntrap patio. Quiz night is Tuesday and Thursday is folk evening, but music is also performed on other evenings. Local CAMRA's first Club of the Year in 2001, this private members club admits CAMRA members as guests. ❀◑◗♿⊞♣●⁄

Kidsgrove

Blue Bell

25 Hardingswood, ST7 1EG (off A50, near Tesco)
⌚ 7.30-11 (not Mon); 1-4, 7-11 Sat; 12-10.30 Sun
☎ (01782) 774052 🌐 bluebellkidsgrove.co.uk
Beer range varies Ⓗ
This canalside free house was Staffordshire CAMRA Pub of the Year 2000–02 and is a frequent Potteries winner. Six ever-changing cask beers come from a wide range of breweries. Real cider and/or perry plus German and Czech beers provide real choice. No juke box, TV or games machines distract from a classic pub. On Sunday evening folk musicians perform at this dog-friendly, no-smoking pub. Q❀⇌⊟●P⊬

Kinver

Constitutional Social Club

119 High Street, DY7 6HL
⌚ 5-11 (midnight Fri); 11.30-midnight Sat; 12-10.30 Sun
☎ (01384) 872044
Banks's Original, Bitter; Wye Valley Hereford Pale Ale; guest beers Ⓗ
Rambling club situated on the High Street. There are three main areas: a smart restaurant serving excellent food, a large snooker room and a bar dispensing up to six guest beers from myriad breweries at reasonable prices. The club enjoys an enviable sporting reputation and hosts regular quiz and music nights. Meals are served Sunday lunchtime and Wednesday to Saturday evenings; booking advised. Card-carrying CAMRA members are welcome but must be signed in.
❀◖◗♿⊟♣P⊓

Cross

Church Hill, DY7 6HZ
⌚ 12-11 daily
☎ (01384) 872435
Enville Ale; Greene King Abbot; guest beers Ⓗ
Situated a few hundred metres from the Staffs and Worcester Canal, this pub brewed its own beers in the 19th century and has scarcely changed since that time, although sadly the brewery is long gone. It has maintained a strong community feel in its small, cosy lounge and the larger, more basic public bar. The adjacent Tudor house is of particular architectural note as it has been faithfully restored and become an award-winner. ♨❀⊟⊟●P

Plough & Harrow

82 High Street, DY7 6HD
⌚ 4 (2 Fri)-11; 12-10.30 Sun
☎ (01384) 872659
Batham Mild, Best Bitter, XXX (winter) Ⓗ
Community pub, affectionately nicknamed the Steps, deservedly popular with locals, cyclists and walkers alike. The front bar sees locals and visitors intermixing and engaging in lively conversation, while the plusher lounge is more comfortable. Note the Batham's breweriana and old advertising posters. Good food is served all day at weekends at reasonable prices. Cider is stocked in summer. ❀◖◗⊟♣●P

Knighton

Haberdasher's Arms

ST20 0QH (between Adbaston and Knighton)
OS753275
⌚ 12.30 (5 Wed)-midnight; 12.30-1am Fri & Sat; 12-midnight Sun
☎ (01785) 280650
Banks's Original, Bitter; guest beer Ⓗ
Traditional community pub, built about 1840, offering a warm, friendly welcome. This former local CAMRA Pub of the Year has four compact rooms all served from a small bar. The large garden is used for events such as the annual potato club show. It is well worth the drive through leafy country lanes to get here. ♨Q❀⊟⛺♣P

Leek

Den Engel

11-13 Stanley Street, ST13 5HG
⌚ 5-11; 11-11.30 Wed & Thu; 11-midnight Fri & Sat; 12-10.30 Sun
☎ (01538) 373751
Beer range varies Ⓗ
This building has been refurbished in contemporary Belgian bar style. The bar stocks 11 draught Belgian beers and 150 different bottled Belgian beers (plus matching glasses), in addition to cask ales from independent brewers. The bar has two rooms: the no-smoking front room overlooks the street, while the back room overlooks the courtyard. Note: no admittance after 11pm at weekends.
❀⊬

Wilkes' Head

16 St Edward Street, ST13 5DS
⌚ 12 (3 Mon)-11; 12-10.30 Sun
☎ (01538) 383616
Whim Arbor Light, Hartington Bitter, IPA, seasonal beers; guest beers Ⓗ
The second oldest pub in Leek boasts records of it operating as a pub back in the 1740s. The licensee is an enthusiastic musician and holds weekly live sessions on Monday evening, as well as organising three annual music festivals, and providing one of the area's best juke boxes. The landlord does, however, operate a strict dress code – if you are wearing a tie, you won't be served! ❀P

Lichfield

Acorn

12-18 Tamworth Street, WS13 6JJ
⌚ 11-midnight (1am Fri & Sat); 11-midnight Sun
☎ (01543) 263400
Greene King Abbot; Marston's Pedigree Ⓗ
Well-run Wetherspoon's pub in which customers request a choice of beers; these comprise a mix of light, dark and heavy. The children's area welcomes families from 9am to 7.30pm, serving children's food. A plasma screen shows sports channels, while themed food nights and beer festivals keep the regulars coming. A range of bottled beer complements the handpumped offerings.
◖◗⇌(City)⊟●⊬

Duke of Wellington

Birmingham Road, WS14 9BJ

⏲ 12-11; 12-10.30 Sun

☎ (01543) 263261

Fuller's London Pride; Marston's Pedigree; guest beers Ⓗ

Sympathetically converted, this open-plan local has been divided into three distinct drinking areas. Look out for the midweek themed food evenings, when booking is advised. For those who like to drink outside during summer there is a large, enclosed lawned garden with patio area to the rear. The licensee's hard work and high standards have transformed the 'Welly' into a favourite haunt for local real ale enthusiasts. ❀◐⇌(City)🚌♣P

George & Dragon

28 Beacon Street, WS13 7AJ

⏲ 11-11 (midnight Thu-Sat); 12-11 Sun

☎ (01543) 253667

Banks's Original, Bitter; Marston's Pedigree; guest beer Ⓗ

Compact, two-roomed pub to the north of the cathedral and close to Beacon Park. The public bar is complemented by a cosy lounge where you can discover the story of the second siege of Lichfield in 1643 when Royalists led by Prince Rupert bombarded the cathedral from a mound above the pub garden. The pub is just five minutes' walk from the city centre. ❀⊟⇌(City)🚌♣P

King's Head

21 Bird Street, WS13 6PW

⏲ 10-11 (midnight Thu-Sun)

☎ (01543) 256822

Marston's Burton Bitter, Pedigree; guest beers Ⓗ

Since a change of ownership, the King's Head has received much care and attention and become an excellent venue in which to enjoy a decent pint. Trad jazz is played on Thursday evening, all-comers' jam sessions are on Friday and different live bands perform on Saturday (free admission). A plaque claims that the former coaching inn is the birthplace of the Staffordshire Regiment and military paraphernalia adorns the walls. Good value food is served weekday lunchtimes and Thursday evening. ❀◐⇌(City)🚌⚟

Queen's Head

4 Queen Street, WS13 6QD

⏲ 12-11 (11.30 Fri & Sat); 12-3, 7-11 Sun

☎ (01543) 410932

Adnams Bitter; Marston's Pedigree; Taylor Landlord; guest beers Ⓗ

Lichfield's mecca for lovers of real ale, this elongated single-roomed pub is well worth the short walk from the city centre. Two guest beers, often from micros, supplement the three regular beers. Good value, home-cooked lunches are served (not Sun) with bread, cheese and pate available at all sessions from a specialist counter. Q◐⇌(City)🚌

Longdon

Swan with Two Necks

40 Brook End, WS15 4PN (off A51)

⏲ 12-3, 7-11; 12-10.30 Sun

☎ (01543) 490251

Adnams Bitter; Caledonian Deuchars IPA; Taylor Landlord; guest beer Ⓗ

A Guide entry for over 25 years, this excellent, friendly village local plays a central role in the community, providing the beer choices of the regulars. The landlord and his staff offer a warm welcome at a pub with real fires. A varied and appetising menu is served every day in the restaurant (all day Sun until 8.30pm). ♨Q❀◐◑P

Milwich

Green Man

ST18 0EG (on B5027)

⏲ 12-2.30 (not Mon-Wed), 5-11; 12-11 Sat; 12-10.30 Sun

☎ (01889) 505310 🌐 greenmanmilwich.com

Adnams Bitter; Draught Bass; Marston's Pedigree; guest beers Ⓗ

A pub since 1775, this free house offers guest beers from regional and micro-breweries nationwide - see the website for forthcoming guest beers. Westons or Thatchers cider is stocked. The current licensee is in his 16th year at the pub and a list of his predecessors, dating back to 1792, is displayed. Popular with walkers and cyclists, the bar houses a 16-seat restaurant (lunch Thu-Sun; eve meals Tue-Sat). Local CAMRA pub of the Year 2006.
♨❀◐◑🚌♣●P⚟

Newcastle-under-Lyme

Arnold Machin

37 Ironmarket, ST5 1PB

⏲ 8am-11pm (12.30am Fri & Sat); 8am-11pm Sun

☎ (01782) 557840

Draught Bass; Greene King Abbot; guest beers Ⓗ

Wetherspoon's conversion situated in the town's former post office that was built in 1914. The pub name is a tribute to the locally-born sculptor responsible for designing the Queen's portrait on postage stamps. With regular guests, the pub offers one of the more adventurous beer ranges in town. It is handy for Newcastle bus station.
Q♨❀◐◑♿🚌●⚟

Museum

29 George Street, ST5 1JU (on A52)

⏲ 12-11; 12-10.30 Sun

☎ (01782) 623866

Draught Bass; Worthington's Bitter; guest beers Ⓗ

If you imagine a traditional British boozer, you would probably think of a pub like the Museum: warm, friendly and comfortable. The bar houses a TV and pub games are often played. The lounge is altogether quieter, ideal for a chat or just a peaceful pint. Two guest beers are usually available, along with a real cider. Well worth a visit. Q◐⊟🚌♣●

Old Brown Jug

41 Bridge Street, ST5 2RY

⏲ 6-midnight (11 Mon; 1am Wed); 12-1am Fri & Sat; 12-12.30am Sun

☎ (01782) 711393 🌐 theoldbrownjug.co.uk

Marston's Pedigree; guest beers Ⓗ

This pub has a traditional feel with wooden

floors and large tables. It is a popular drinking spot in the town, especially on music nights: Wednesday is jazz night and various styles are performed on Sunday. The new licensing laws have enabled it to be a late night venue all week. The large rear garden attracts summer drinkers. Real cider is always stocked (often Westons). The bus station is nearby. ❀▣♣●

Newtown

Ivy House

62 Stafford Road, WS6 6AZ (on A34)

✪ 12-2.30, 5-11; 11-11 Sat; 12-3, 7-11 Sun

☎ (01922) 476607

Banks's Original, Bitter; Marston's Pedigree; guest beers Ⓗ

Walsall CAMRA (Staffs) Pub of the Year 2005 was first listed as an ale house in 1824. This 200-year-old building is a traditional pub with a country feel, as its garden backs onto farmland. It comprises three rooms on two levels, one of which doubles as the restaurant, serving excellent value meals (no food Mon eve). A visit is highly recommended and a warm welcome assured. ⩕Q❀◖◗▣P⚟

Norton Canes

Railway Tavern

63 Norton Green Lane, WS11 9PR (off Walsall Rd)

✪ 12-2, 5-midnight; 12-midnight Fri & Sat; 12-11.30 Sun

☎ (01543) 279579

Banks's Original, Bitter; Greene King IPA; Highgate Dark; guest beers Ⓗ

Recently extended and altered internally, the pub has a single room with a spacious no-smoking area. The fully enclosed garden contains a patio drinking area, children's play equipment and a large grassed area suitable for ball games. Twice local CAMRA Pub of the Year, real cider is stocked in summer.❀◖◗♿♣●P⚟

Onecote

Jervis Arms

ST13 7RU (on B5053, off Leek-Ashbourne road)

✪ 12-3, 7-11; 12-10.30 Sun

☎ (01538) 304206

Worthington's Bitter; guest beers Ⓗ

This family-friendly pub must come close to perfection. Lying within the Peak District national park, not far from Alton Towers, you enter the garden over a small river – just lovely on a hot summer's day. The landlord is a real ale fanatic and sources beers from micro-breweries throughout the UK. Beer festivals are staged during the year, when camping is available. Food ranges from bar snacks to a full menu. ⛱❀◖◗⛺♣P⚟

Oulton

Brushmaker's Arms

8 Kibblestone Road, ST15 8UW (500 yds W of A520)

✪ 12-3, 6-11; 12-3, 7-11 Sun

☎ (01785) 812062

Marston's Pedigree; Worthington's Bitter; guest beer Ⓗ

Built in 1865 and thought to be named after a local cottage industry, this pub is an example of a local that has retained its traditional public bar and lounge. The unspoilt bar has photos of the area in the past and a TV; the lounge is intimate and comfortable. There are no gaming machines or juke box. Guest ales include favourites from Archers and Black Sheep. The patio garden is busy in summer. ⩕Q❀⊟▣♣P

Penkridge

Horse & Jockey

Market Street, ST19 5DH

✪ 12 (11.30 Sat)-midnight (2am Fri & Sat); 12-midnight Sun

☎ (01785) 716299

Worthington's Bitter; guest beers Ⓗ

Three real ales are always available here; the beer changes when a barrel empties so regulars can experience up to 25-30 different ales a month! The pub has a bar, lounge and garden, with play area. Live music evenings are staged weekly and the pub hosts occasional quizzes, race nights and summer barbecues as well as a magnificent firework display on November 5th. Lunches are served Monday-Saturday. ❀◖⊟⇌▣♣⚟

Railway

Clay Street, ST19 5AF (on A449)

✪ 12-3, 5-11; 12-midnight Fri & Sat; 12-10.30 Sun

☎ (01785) 712685

Banks's Original, Bitter; Ⓟ **Black Sheep Best Bitter; Greene King Abbot, Old Speckled Hen** Ⓗ

This 16th-century, Grade II listed building became a pub in 1834 to serve the workers building the Birmingham to Liverpool railway (who were banned from nearby hostelries). The pub, which has also been a mortuary and an auctioneers, is today owned by Punch Taverns. A large, grassed area is used as a children's play area and for outside drinking. On Sunday meals are served 12-5. ⩕Q⛱❀◖◗⊟♿⇌▣♣P⚟▯

Penn Common

Barley Mow

Pennwood Lane, WV4 5JN (follow signs for Penn Golf Club from A449) OS949902

✪ 12-2.30, 6-11; 12-11 Sat; 12-10.30 Sun

☎ (01902) 333510

Banks's Original; Flowers Original; Greene King Abbot; guest beers Ⓗ

Small pub with low, beamed ceilings, dating from the 1600s, on the West Midlands border. A small extension was added in the 1990s. The 'Mow' enjoys a well deserved reputation for food, with meat supplied from the landlord's own award-winning butcher's shop. Next to the local golf course, the pub is a short walk over the Seven Cornfields from Wolverhampton. Q❀◖◗P

Salt

Holly Bush

ST18 0BX

✪ 12-11 (midnight Fri & Sat); 12-11 Sun

☎ (01889) 508234 ⊕ hollybushinn.co.uk

Adnams Bitter; Marston's Pedigree; guest beer Ⓗ

The Holly Bush is believed to be the second English inn to be granted a licence, and the oldest part of the building is still thatched. With extensions and alterations having taken place over the centuries, there are now three distinct areas: a bar towards the middle of the pub, a no-smoking dining room and a snug, mainly occupied by diners. Many awards have been won for the superb yet reasonably priced meals. Q❀◖◗⊟P

Stafford

Bird in Hand

Victoria Square, ST16 2AQ

✪ 12-11 (midnight Fri & Sat); 12-10.30 Sun

☎ (01785) 252198

Courage Best Bitter; Fuller's London Pride; Wells Bombardier; guest beer Ⓗ

Described as one of Stafford's most customer friendly pubs, the 'Bird' benefits greatly from having retained four separate and very different rooms: a traditional yet comfortable public bar, a quiet, cosy snug, a large lounge with TVs and a big games room for pool enthusiasts. Meals are served Monday to Saturday. It stands midway between the station and the town centre; opposite is the crown court, while the famous Ancient High House is also nearby. ❀◖⊞≢⊟♣

Greyhound

12 County Road, ST16 2PU (opp. jail)

✪ 4.30 (2 Fri; 12 Sat)-11; 12-11 Sun

☎ (01785) 222432

Beer range varies Ⓗ

The Greyhound has experienced a remarkable transformation; closed and threatened with conversion to another use after failing under pub company ownership, it is now thriving as one of the few genuine free houses around Stafford. A few minutes' walk from the town centre, the Greyhound, a pub since the 1830s, retained its separate bar and lounge during a sensitive 2002 refurbishment. Six to eight handpulled ales from micro and regional brewers are usually available. ♨❀⊞⊟♣P

Lamb

Broad Eye, ST16 2QB

✪ 11-11; 12-10.30 Sun

☎ (07946) 403433

Banks's Original; Everards Tiger; Marston's Pedigree; guest beer Ⓗ

Although next to the busy Chell Road and surrounded by car parks and supermarkets, the Lamb retains something of the atmosphere of a street-corner local. Bought by Punch 10 years ago, the pub has since been carefully refurbished. The Lamb's regular customers are joined during the evening by drivers stationed at the nearby lorry park and during the day by shoppers taking advantage of the exceptionally good value meals served lunchtimes (not Sun) and weekday evenings. ◖◗≢⊟♣

Luck Penny

62 Crab Lane, ST16 1SQ (on Trinity Fields estate)

✪ 11-11 (midnight Fri & Sat); 12-11 Sun

☎ (01785) 603503

John Smith's Bitter; Marston's Pedigree; guest beer Ⓗ

Deservedly popular estate pub that has been run by the same licensee for a quarter of a century, making him currently the longest-serving pub landlord in the Stafford area. Built in the late 1960s at the same time as the surrounding houses, this community-based pub supports several sports and games teams. Visitors can expect good service and great value food (no meals Sun eve). ❀◖◗⊞♿⊟♣P

Spittal Brook

106 Lichfield Road, ST17 4LP (1 mile SE of centre)

✪ 12-3, 5-11; 12-11 Sat; 12-4, 7-10.30 Sun

☎ (01785) 245268

Black Sheep Best Bitter; Everards Tiger; Jennings Cumberland Ale; Marston's Pedigree; guest beer Ⓗ

Formerly the Crown, the pub reverted to the original name of its locality in 1998. This thriving, two-roomed ale house, adjacent to the West Coast mainline, fields darts, cribbage, water polo and netball teams and a golfing society. The premises are licensed for civil weddings. Entertainment includes a folk night (Tue) and a quiz (Wed). Addlestones Cloudy cask cider is sold. No food is served Sunday evening. ♨❀⇌◖◗⊞♿⊟♣●P

Tap & Spile

59 Peel Terrace, ST16 3HE (off B5066)

✪ 4.30 (2 Fri; 12 Sat)-11.30; 12-10.30 Sun

☎ (01785) 223563

Wells Bombardier; guest beers Ⓗ

Thriving beer house, selling an incredible volume and variety of cask ales – usually eight to choose from – sourced from a wide range of regional and micro-breweries. Built early last century, the name change from the Cottage by the Brook, 13 years ago, coincided with a sensitive refurbishment, four distinct drinking areas being retained. The first pub locally with a no-smoking area, it also has a free bar billiards table and fields several sports teams. ♨❀⊟♣⚟

Stanley

Travellers Rest

Tompkin Lane, ST9 9LX (approx. 1 mile from A53/B5051 jct) OS933523

✪ 12-3, 6-11; 12-3, 7-10.30 Sun

☎ (01782) 502580

Marston's Burton Bitter, Pedigree; guest beers Ⓗ

Popular village local with a traditional feel inside. Described by the landlord as a restaurant with a bar, this is nonetheless a genuine free house, offering three rotating guest beers from independent and micro-breweries. The food menu is extensive and popular, lunchtime and evening. There is seating outside by the road, at this Ideal stop for walkers in the Staffordshire Moorlands or visitors to the Potteries. ♨Q❀◖◗⊟P⚟

Stoke on Trent: Burslem

Bull's Head

14 St John's Square, ST6 3AJ

✪ 3 (12 Fri & Sat)-11; 12-10.30 Sun

☎ (01782) 834153

Titanic Best Bitter, Iceberg, Anchor, White Star, seasonal beers; guest beers Ⓗ

The jewel in Burslem's crown, this two-roomed, town-centre pub is only 10 minutes' walk from Vale Park. The bar houses a juke box and bar billiards table, while the quieter wood-panelled lounge is warmed by a real fire. Serving by far the best selection of real ale in the town, this pub is busy at weekends and on match days. Although owned by Titanic Brewery, two guest ales are usually available; it also hosts occasional themed mini-beer festivals. ⚜Q❀⊟⊞♣●

Stoke on Trent: Dresden

Princess Royal

34 Carlisle Street, ST3 4HA

⏲ 12-midnight; 12-11 Sun

☎ (01782) 335488

Draught Bass; Greene King IPA, Ruddles County, Abbot; guest beer Ⓗ

This traditional multi-roomed pub is a little gem in the back streets of Dresden. On entry to the right is the public bar with an open Victorian fireplace. At the centre of the pub is the TV room with a large screen for sports. Towards the rear is a games area with pool, darts and table football. In summer the landlord hosts barbecues in the garden, weather permitting of course. ⚜❀⊟⊞♣

Stoke on Trent: Fenton

Malt 'n' Hops

259 King Street, ST4 3EJ

⏲ 12-4, 7-11; 12-3, 7-10.30 Sun

☎ (01782) 313406

Beer range varies Ⓗ

One of the few free houses in the city, this long-established hostelry has been in the same ownership for almost two decades. Comprising a single room greatly extended over the years, the split levels give the impression of a separate traditional bar and comfortable lounge. Ever-changing beers from small breweries and micros make this very much a beer oriented pub. The house beers are brewed by Tower. Belgian beers are also stocked. ≠(Longton)⊞

Potter

432 King Street, ST4 3DB

⏲ 12 (11 Sat)-11; 12-10.30 Sun

☎ (01782) 311968

Coach House Dick Turpin; Greene King Abbot; guest beers Ⓗ

Established, genuine, traditional free house that appeals to customers of all ages. Three excellent guest beers are backed up by the regular ales. This three-roomed pub comprises a main bar, another room set aside for games, and a back snug that doubles as a meeting room. A minor refurbishment has not changed the original feel of this 100-year-old house. It gets busy for televised sport, but a warm welcome awaits all visitors. ⚜≠(Longton)⊞♣

Stoke on Trent: Hanley

Coachmaker's Arms

65 Lichfield Street, ST1 3EA (off A5008, Potteries Way ring road)

⏲ 12-11.30 (midnight Fri & Sat); 7-10.30 Sun

☎ (01782) 262158

Draught Bass; guest beers Ⓗ

Rare survivor of a Potteries town pub, retaining its separate room layout. Radiating off the tiled drinking passage, each of the four rooms has its own character. The 'Coach' offers its own culture, despite its position just outside the official 'cultural quarter'. It hosts occasional acoustic music and jazz. A mild and stout feature on the expanding array of handpumps. Children are welcome until 7pm. ⚜Q⛴⊟⊞♣

Stoke on Trent: Penkhull

Beehive Inn

103 Honeywall, ST4 7HU (off A52, Hartshill road)

⏲ 4-1am; 2-2am Fri & Sat; 12-11.30 Sun

☎ (01782) 846947 🌐 beehiveinn.com

Marston's Pedigree; guest beers Ⓗ

Deservedly popular local on the hill above Stoke. Something of a shrine to Stoke City fans, due to the collection of club memorabilia, it gets busy on home match days when it opens early (call to check). It hosts a Tuesday quiz, plus occasional social events. Meals are served 4-8pm weekdays and at the weekend. The beer range was recently increased to four guests that change weekly. ⚜❀◗⊞♣P

Greyhound Inn

5-6 Manor Court Street, ST4 5DW

⏲ 11-3, 5-11 (midnight Thu); 11-midnight Fri & Sat; 12-11 Sun

☎ (01782) 848978 🌐 thegreyhoundinn.co.uk

Greene King Old Speckled Hen; Marston's Pedigree; Wadworth 6X; guest beers Ⓗ

In the centre of a village now enveloped by the city, parts of the Greyhound date back to the 17th century, while another section used to act as the manor courtroom until the 1840s. The pub comprises three rooms: the public bar with darts and pool, a comfortable lounge and a snug leading off. No evening meals are served Sunday or Monday; Tuesday is curry night. ⚜Q❀◖◗⊟⊞♣

Stone

Swan

18 Stafford Street, ST15 8QW (on A520, by Trent & Mersey Canal)

⏲ 11-11 (midnight Tue & Wed; 1am Thu-Sat); 12-11 Sun

☎ (01785) 815570

Coach House Gunpowder Mild, John Joule Old Knotty, Old Priory, Victory; guest beers Ⓗ

This Grade II listed building was carefully renovated in 1999. To date beers from over 300 breweries have been served, with up to six guests at any one time. Tuesday is quiz night and live music is performed up to three nights a week. A free buffet is served every Sunday at 12.30pm and lunchtime snacks are offered Tuesday-Saturday. An annual beer festival is held in the garden during the second week of July. No under-18s are admitted. ⚜❀◖♿≠⊞●

Summerhill

Boat

Walsall Road, WS14 0BU (on A461)
✪ 12-3, 6-11; 12-11 Sun
☎ (01543) 361692
Beer range varies Ⓗ
A new car park and a large, secure, stylish patio set the standard for the Boat. The extended building has several dining and bar areas in which to enjoy the delectable food and varying guest beers. Always offering one beer from a local micro, this free house enjoys the ability to select beers nationwide. Having built up a reputation for incredible food, the owners now seek to increase beer consumption, with the emphasis on a varied range. Q❀◐◑♿🚌P

Tamworth

Albert

32 Albert Road, B79 7JS (near station)
✪ 12-11 (12.30am Thu-Sat); 12-10.30 Sun
☎ (01827) 64694
Banks's Original, Bitter; Marston's Pedigree; guest beer Ⓗ
A former local CAMRA Pub of the Year, this town-centre, friendly hotel is handy for the station. Good quality food is served and guest beers tend to come from the Wolverhampton & Dudley Marston's range. Thursday is quiz night. A secluded patio to the rear complements the front drinking area on the roadside; both spaces are well used in summer. ⛰❀🛏◐◑⊟♿≹🚌♣P

Market Vaults

7 Market Street, B79 7LU
✪ 12-3, 6-11; 12-3, 7-11 Sun
☎ (01827) 69653
Banks's Bitter; guest beers Ⓗ
Cosy, two-roomed, traditional pub, centrally situated in one of the older parts of the town, close to Tamworth's historic castle. The statue of Sir Robert Peel, founder of the modern police force, stands in the same street. Old photographs of the town adorn the walls of the bar, which offers a regularly changing guest beer. Good value lunches are served daily. Q❀◐⊟≹🚌

Sir Robert Peel

13-15 Lower Gungate, B79 7BA (in pedestrian area next to new registry office)
✪ 12-11 (midnight Thu-Sat); 12-11.30 Sun
☎ (01827) 300910
Beer range varies Ⓗ
This busy, town-centre pub is a regular haunt for CAMRA members. It is a friendly, family-run business that takes pride in the 'real' aspects of life, by offering regular live music and keeping a real ale corner of the bar that offers two regularly changing guest beers as well as draught Leffe and Hoegaarden. This pub is a must for real ale, real music and real people. ≹🚌♣

Tatenhill

Horseshoe

Main Street, DE13 9SD
✪ 11-11 (11.30 Thu-Sat); 12-11 Sun
☎ (01283) 564913
Marston's Pedigree Ⓗ
This old village coaching inn, dating back to the late 17th-century, has retained much of its charm despite extensive renovation over the years. The wood-panelled public bar has a homely feel (note the list of tenants going back to 1860), and several linked rooms feature low, beamed ceilings, breweriana and domestic and agricultural artefacts. It is locally renowned for its meals, which are available all day. The garden includes an enclosed play area. ⛰❀◐◑⊟♿P

Trysull

Bell

Bell Lane, WV5 7JB
✪ 11.30-3, 5-11; 11.30-11 Sat; 12-10.30 Sun
☎ (01902) 892871
Batham Best Bitter; Holden's Bitter, Golden Glow, Special, seasonal beers; guest beer Ⓗ
This 18th-century building stands on the site of a much older pub next to the medieval church in the centre of the village. There are three distinct rooms: a lounge with an inglenook; a more basic bar that is popular with locals and ramblers (dogs welcome); and a restaurant. The meals, largely home made, are cooked to order (eve meals served Wed-Sat). The Staffs & Worcs Canal is nearby. The guest beer usually comes from a micro-brewery. ❀◐◑⊟♿🚌P⌷

Two Gates

Bull's Head

446 Watling Street, B77 1HW (at A51/B5404 jct)
✪ 12-2.30, 6.30-11; 12-3, 7-11 Sat; 12-2.30, 7-11 Sun
☎ (01827) 287820
Marston's Pedigree; guest beer Ⓗ
Community local, which although situated in a housing area, bears the appearance of a Victorian farmhouse. This two-roomed pub has a split-level lounge leading out to the patio, and a small, friendly bar. It enjoys a keen sporting following, including a long-standing golf society, and hosts quiz nights. Q❀⊟≹(Wilnecote)🚌(115, 116, 117)♣P

Railway Inn

409 Watling Street, B77 5AD
✪ 12-11 daily
☎ (01827) 262937
Draught Bass Ⓗ
Basic, three-roomed traditional drinker's pub, right next door to Wilnecote Station, its three handpumps all dispense high quality Draught Bass. All the usual pub games are played in this welcoming local which has a separate pool room. The main drinking area is the public bar, where the walls are adorned with railway memorabilia. For a more peaceful pint try the lounge, which is called the clubroom. ⛰Q♉⊟≹(Wilnecote)🚌♣P

Uttoxeter

Bank House

Church Street, ST14 8AG (opp. St Mary's Church)
✪ 11-11; 12-11 Sun
☎ (01889) 566922 🌐 bankhousehotel.info

Greene King Abbot; Marston's Pedigree; Taylor Landlord; guest beer 🄷
Built in 1776 and situated just a short distance from the town centre, this fine looking building was once the first bank in Uttoxeter. The original bank vault can still be seen in what is now the restaurant, but instead of holding cash it now contains condiments. The hotel has conference facilities and boasts an impressive, unsupported, oak staircase. The racecourse is nearby. ⛫❀⇄◖◗♿⛺≋🚌P

Weston

Woolpack

The Green, ST18 0JH
✪ 11-11 (midnight Fri & Sat); 11.30-11 Sun
☎ (01889) 270238
Banks's Original, Bitter; Marston's Pedigree; guest beer 🄷
Known locally as the Inn on the Green, the Woolpack is a welcoming village local with an extensive dining area. Four bays inside reflect the pub's origins as a row of cottages, and it is recorded as having been owned by the Bagot family in the 1730s. Over the years the low-ceilinged pub has been thoughtfully extended, while retaining the original bar area. ⛫❀◖◗⊟⛺🚌♣P

Whiston

Swan

ST19 5QH (in Penkridge, take turn at George & Fox pub) OSSJ8914
✪ 12-3 (not Mon), 5-11; 12-11 Sun
☎ (01785) 716200
Holden's Mild, Bitter; guest beer 🄷
Although in a remote situation, high quality ales and superb food combine to make this a thriving pub. Built in 1593, it burnt down and was rebuilt in 1711; the oldest part today is the small bar housing an inglenook. The lounge features an intriguing central double-sided log fire. On Sunday meals are served all day until 8.30pm; Aberdeen Angus steaks and game pie are specialities here and vegetarians are catered for.
⛫Q❀◖◗⊟♿🚌♣P⊬

Wilnecote

Red Lion Inn

Quarry Hill, B77 5BS
✪ 12-3, 5 (7 Sat)-11; 12-11 Thu & Fri; 12-3, 7.30-11 Sun
☎ (01827) 280818
Draught Bass; guest beer 🄷
Two-roomed community pub situated on the old Roman road (Watling Street). It comprises a large lounge with a smaller bar-cum-games room. The welcoming landlord takes pride in serving quality ale. The pub is happy to admit dogs on leads. In summer you can enjoy a quiet pint in the outdoor drinking area. ❀⊟♣P

Wolstanton

New Smithy

21 Church Lane, ST5 0EH
✪ 12 (11 Sat)-11; 12-10.30 Sun
☎ (01782) 740467
Everards Beacon, Tiger; Lancaster Duchy; Marston's Pedigree; guest beers 🄷
This village pub is frequented by all ages. Strangers to the area find it hard to believe that it was once threatened with demolition, until a band of locals successfully fought to save the pub. It is now leased to a local beer wholesaler who also owns the Lancaster Brewery, hence the continued presence of its beers. A changing beer choice and good management will stand this pub in good stead for the future. If you want a seat you need to arrive early – especially at the weekend. Westons cider is always stocked. ❀🚌♣●⊬

Woodseaves

Cock

Newport Road, ST20 0NP (just N of A519/B5405 jct) OS799254
✪ 12-3, 5-midnight; 12-1am Fri & Sat; 12-midnight Sun
☎ (01785) 284270
Banks's Original, Bitter; Wells Bombardier 🄷
The Cock was originally a farmhouse with a brewhouse added in the 19th century, and has remained virtually unchanged for over 100 years. The present hosts have been at the Cock for 11 years and make visitors welcome. Good value food is served as a set meal between 12 and 3pm weekdays. On Saturday sandwiches are available until 7pm. The Shropshire Union Canal is within walking distance. ⛫Q❀◖⊟🚌♣P

Wrinehill

Crown

Den Lane, CW3 9BT (off A531, between Newcastle and Crewe)
✪ 12-3 (not Mon), 6-11; 12-4, 6-10.30 Sun
☎ (01270) 820472
Adnams Bitter; Banks's Original; Marston's Bitter, Pedigree; guest beer 🄷
Busy, family-owned village free house with a commitment to real ale. It won the 'Britain in Bloom' regional gold award in 2003 and 2004. No pool, TV or games machines spoil the peace. The excellent varied menu includes steaks, fresh fish, vegetarian and vegan options. There are two no-smoking areas in the comfortable lounge bar, complete with open fires. ⛫❀◖◗♿P⊬

Yoxall

Golden Cup

Main Street, DE13 8NQ (on A515)
✪ 12-3, 5-midnight (1am Fri & Sat); 12-11.30 Sun
☎ (01543) 472295 🌐 thegoldencup.com
Marston's Pedigree; guest beer 🄷
Impressive, family run, 300-year-old inn at the centre of the village, opposite St Peter's church, bedecked with attractive floral displays for much of the year. The smart L-shaped lounge caters for diners with an extensive menu on offer. The award-winning pub gardens stretch down to the River Swarbourn and include a camping area for caravans and motor homes only. Regular beer festivals are held.
⛫Q❀⇄◖◗⊟♿⛺♣P

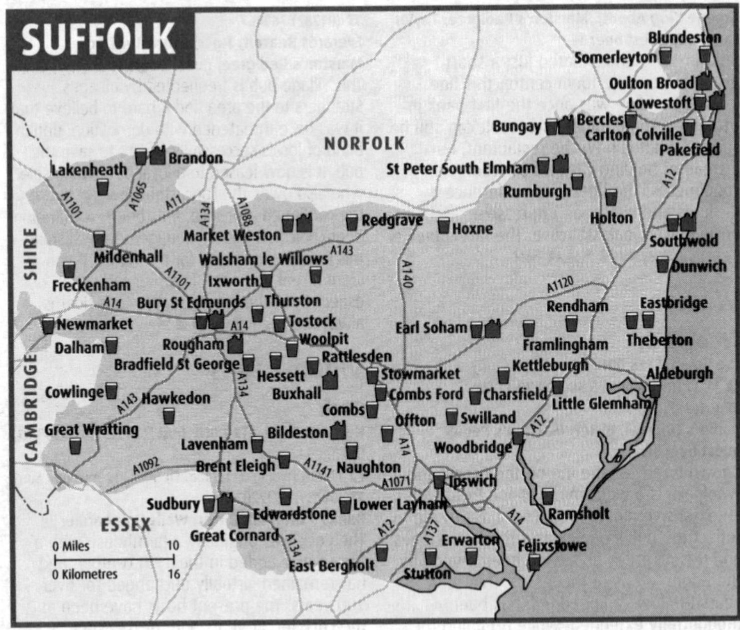

Aldeburgh

Mill Inn

Market Cross Place, IP15 5BJ (opp. Moot Hall)
11-11; 12-10.30 Sun
☎ (01728) 452563 millinnaldeburgh.co.uk
Adnams Bitter, Broadside; seasonal beers H
Street corner inn opposite the ancient Moot Hall with a small no-smoking restaurant where fresh locally-caught fish is a speciality. During the winter there are themed food evenings. It is popular not just with tourists but also locals including some of the lifeboat crew. After a bracing walk across the shingle beach to see the scallops it is the ideal place to stop for refreshments. No food is served Sunday evening (or Winter Mon eve). Q❀⇌◐🚌♣⅄

White Hart

222 High Street, IP15 5AJ
11-11; 12-10.30 Sun
☎ (01728) 453205
Adnams Bitter, Explorer, Broadside; seasonal beers H
Single-room pub which was formerly the public reading room. Popular with locals and holidaymakers, it is conveniently situated next door to Aldeburgh's renowned fish and chip shop. An interesting selection of nautical memorabilia adorns the wood-panelled walls and the small open fire warms the room in winter. The pub is dog friendly. ⌂❀♿▲🚌♣

Beccles

Bear & Bells

Old Market, NR34 9AP (adjacent to bus station)
11.30-3, 5.30-11; 12-3, 7-10.30 Sun
☎ (01502) 712291
Adnams Bitter; Greene King IPA; guest beers H
Large, Victorian town centre pub by the bus station and close to the River Waveney. In the open-plan interior is a spacious bar area with restaurant to one side (booking advisable). The ceiling is adorned with porcelain jugs. The large function room doubles as an overflow dining area. The pub is renowned for wholesome food. Mobile phones must be switched off. ❀◐⇌🚌P

Blundeston

Plough

Market Lane, NR32 5AN
12-3, 7 (6.30 Fri & Sat)-11.30; 12-3, 7-10.30 Sun
☎ (01502) 730261
Adnams Bitter; guest beers H
Mock-Tudor style inn with exposed beams in a large village dominated by the church with the tallest round tower in East Anglia. It has a restaurant, main bar serving up to five real ales, and a pool room. The large, attractive garden is popular in the summer. Charles Dickens mentions the inn as the birthplace of

INDEPENDENT BREWERIES

Adnams Southwold
Bartrams Rougham
Brandon Brandon
Cox & Holbrook Buxhall
Earl Soham Earl Soham
Green Dragon Bungay
Green Jack Lowestoft
Greene King Bury St Edmunds
Kings Head Bildeston
Mauldons Sudbury
Old Cannon Bury St Edmunds
Old Chimneys Market Weston
Oulton Oulton Broad
St Peter's St Peter South Elmham

David Copperfield – hence the Dickensian memorabilia. ⌂❀◐◑♣P

Bradfield St George

Fox & Hounds

Felsham Road, IP30 0AB

⊙ 12-2.30, 6-11 (closed Mon); 12-2.30, 7-10.30 Sun

☎ (01284) 386379

Adnams Bitter; guest beers Ⓗ

On the village outskirts, close to the historic coppiced woodland of the Suffolk Wildlife Trust. Free of tie, the pub has been restored in Victorian style. The comfortable, attractive interior is fronted by a glazed dining area. The public bar has a wood-block floor, wood-burning stove and pine seating. En-suite accommodation is available. Q❀⇌◐◑

Brandon

Bell

48 High Street, IP27 0AQ

⊙ 11-11 (1am Fri & Sat); 12-11 Sun

☎ (01842) 810465

Beer range varies Ⓗ

High street local with its coaching inn origins still visible. Fine blocked-in 'tax windows', of which Brandon has many, are proudly displayed. The spacious interior has a single handpump hidden behind a bar pillar, often dispensing beers from Brandon Brewery just 200 yards down the street. The pub's car park is hard to access. ❀⇌♣P

Brent Eleigh

Cock ☆

Lavenham Road, CO10 9PB

⊙ 12-3, 6-11; 12-3, 7-10.30 Sun

☎ (01787) 247371

Adnams Bitter; Greene King IPA, Abbot Ⓗ

An absolute gem! This pub manages to transport you back in time. In winter both tiny bars are snug and warm; in summer with the doors open the bar is at one with its surroundings. Good conversation is guaranteed – sit and listen and you will soon become involved. Close to Lavenham and the beautiful Brett Valley, the comfortable accommodation is recommended. The pub is 'CAMROT' (Campaign for Real Outside Toilets) approved. Do not miss it. Q❀⇌⊟♣●P

Bungay

Green Dragon

29 Broad Street, NR35 1EE

⊙ 11-3, 5-11; 11-midnight Fri; 12-midnight Sat; 12-3, 7-11 Sun

☎ (01986) 892681

Green Dragon Chaucer Ale, Gold, Bridge Street, Ⓗ **seasonal beers** Ⓖ/Ⓗ

Bungay's only brew-pub close to the town centre. The brewery is situated in outbuildings adjacent to the car park (tours by arrangement). This lively pub has a public bar and lounge, plus a room for families which leads to the secluded garden surrounded by a hop hedge. Up to four draught beers are on handpump and sometimes bottle-conditioned beers are also available. Curry night is Wednesday, food is not served at other times. ⌂☺❀⊟▲P

Bury St Edmunds

Elephant & Castle

2 Hospital Road, IP33 3JT

⊙ 12-2.30, 5-11; 12-11 Sat & Sun

☎ (01284) 755570

Greene King IPA, Abbot; guest beer Ⓗ

'The Trunk' is a Victorian street corner pub fronting onto Hospital Road. Access to the car park is from the main Parkway Road. Despite overlooking a busy junction the two bars of this community pub have a village local feel to them. The front bar is no-smoking during lunchtime. The rear bar is the hub for many games teams including football, darts, cribbage and dominoes. Outside is a large garden with children's play area. ❀◐◑⊟♣P

Old Cannon Brewery

86 Cannon Street, IP33 1JR

⊙ 12-3 (not Mon), 5-11; 12-3, 7-10.30 Sun

☎ (01284) 768769 🌐 oldcannonbrewery.co.uk

Adnams Bitter; Old Cannon Best Bitter, Gunner's Daughter, seasonal beers; guest beers Ⓗ

Formerly the St Edmund's Head, this excellent brew-pub is on the site of the original Cannon Brewery. Now in private hands, it is a true free house. The Cannon serves good quality food (not Sun or Mon) and comfortable accommodation is available. ⌂Q❀⇌◐◑♿⇌P▯

Rose & Crown

48 Whiting Street, IP33 1NP

⊙ 11.30-11; 11.30-3, 7-11 Sat; 12-2.30, 7-10.30 Sun

☎ (01284) 755934

Greene King XX Mild, IPA, Abbot; guest beer Ⓗ

Suffolk CAMRA Pub of the Year 2005, the pub occupies a prominent street corner location within sight of Greene King's Westgate Brewery. The 19th-century red brickwork and tile facade front a timber structure from the 17th century or earlier. A welcoming, no frills local, good value lunches are served Monday to Saturday. Q❀◐⊟♣

Carlton Colville

Bell

The Street, NR33 8JR

⊙ 11-11.30; 12-10.30 Sun

☎ (01502) 582873

Oulton Bitter, Nautilus, Gone Fishing, seasonal beers; guest beer Ⓖ

An Oulton Ales inn with car parking at the front and a large garden at the back. The open-plan bar with flagstone flooring throughout has an original central fireplace dividing the drinking area from the restaurant. The no-smoking section doubles as a family room. Just a mile away, the East Anglian Transport Museum is well worth a visit. ⌂☺❀◐◑P

Charsfield

Three Horseshoes

The Street, IP13 7PY

⊙ 11.30-2.30, 7-11; 12-3, 7-10.30 Sun

☎ (01473) 737330
Adnams Bitter; guest beers Ⓗ
Small village local with two bars, one simply furnished with a tiled floor and cosy fire, the other more modern with an attractive restaurant annexe. Outside is the car park and a well-kept garden. The village was featured in the local history film Akenfield and a new publication, Return to Akenfield, focuses on the area again. ⾕☺❀◑◐⊟⋀⊟(72)♣P⁄

Combs

Gardeners Arms
Moats Tye, IP14 2EY
⊙ 12-2.30 (not Mon), 6-11; 12-2.30 Sun
☎ (01449) 673963
Greene King IPA; guest beers Ⓗ
Two-bar pub: one mainly for dining, the other for drinking. The dining area is no-smoking with an open fire in winter and the drinking area is more eclectic with a mix of furniture including a piano and pool table. An interesting menu is offered with food made from locally sourced ingredients. The pub is dog friendly. Accommodation is planned. ⾕❀◑◐♿♣P⁄

Combs Ford

Gladstone Arms
2 Combs Ford, IP14 2AP (on Stowmarket to Ipswich road)
⊙ 11-3, 5 (7 Sat)-11; 12-4, 7-10.30 Sun
☎ (01449) 612339
Adnams Bitter, Broadside; guest beer Ⓗ
A regular appearance in the Guide is testimony to the consistently excellent beer quality here. Situated in a suburb of Stowmarket, this attractive old pub is warm and welcoming with a roaring fire in winter. Excellent value home-cooked food includes vegetarian options. The pub is an ideal place to stop off before or after the football at Ipswich. No food is served on Sunday or Monday evenings. ⾕❀◑◐♿⊟P

Cowlinge

Three Tuns
Queens Street, CA8 9QD (6 miles N of Haverhill on A143, turn left)
⊙ 12-2 (not Mon & Tue), 5.30 (6 Mon; 5 Fri)-11; 12-11 Sat; 12-10.30 Sun
☎ (01440) 821847
Adnams Bitter, Broadside; guest beers Ⓗ
A local gem, this heavily beamed bar festooned with hop bines and furnished with comfortable sofas is a delightful place to relax and enjoy good ale in traditional surroundings. Good beer, food and conversation prevail in this village inn, with a roaring fire in winter and attractive garden for summer. Bar snacks are available. The restaurant offers a good, imaginative menu. ⾕Q❀◑◐P

Dalham

Affleck Arms
Brookside, CB8 8TG
⊙ 5-11, 12-3; 6.30-11 Sat; 12-10.30 Sun
☎ (01638) 500306
Adnams Bitter; Greene King IPA; guest beers Ⓗ
Attractive thatched pub in the north west corner of rural Suffolk welcoming walkers, visitors and locals alike. Two regular, frequently changing guest ales, usually from smaller breweries, complement the two local beers. An interesting menu offers excellent food (lunches Sat and Sun; eve meals Tue to Sat). In summer, sit on the bank of the stream that passes the front door or try the sheltered rear patio for outdoor dining and drinking.
⾕❀⊭◑◐♿P

Dunwich

Ship
St James Street, IP17 3DT
⊙ 11-11; 12-10.30 Sun
☎ (01728) 648219 ⊕ shipinndunwich.co.uk
Adnams Bitter, Broadside; Mauldons seasonal beers Ⓗ
Situated in the main street of what is now a small village, although once one of the largest East Anglian ports until it was lost to the sea. This former smugglers' haunt is popular with locals and visitors to the area. The main bar has a flagstone floor and wood-burning stove. There is a conservatory and dining room where children are welcome. Outside is a patio and large garden with a fine and ancient fig tree. Dogs on leads are welcome in the bar.
⾕Q❀⊭◑◐⋀P

Earl Soham

Victoria
The Street, IP13 7RL (on A1120)
⊙ 11.30-3, 6-11; 12-3, 7-10.30 Sun
☎ (01728) 685758
Earl Soham Victoria Bitter, Sir Roger's Porter, Albert Ale, seasonal beers Ⓗ
Timeless and unchanging, this village pub attracts visitors from far and wide. The traditional interior has simple furnishings, bare floorboards and an open fireplace. The superb beer is brewed a few yards away. An interesting menu offers good value home-cooked meals at lunchtime and evenings. The pub can be busy at times but is always worth a visit.
⾕Q☺❀◑◐⊟♣P

East Bergholt

Hare & Hounds
Heath Road, CO7 6RL
⊙ 12-11; 12-10.30 Sun
☎ (01206) 298438
Adnams Bitter; guest beers Ⓗ
Excellent, friendly, traditional local situated in the birthplace of the world famous landscape painter John Constable. Built in the 15th century it retains a pargetted (deep plaster relief) ceiling, circa 1590, in the lounge. This fine pub offers something for everyone, including a family room, pleasant garden and separate public bar. Food is served at lunchtime. The village church has a unique wooden bell cage in the churchyard.
⾕Q❀◑⊟⋀⊟♣P

Eastbridge

Eel's Foot
Leiston Road, IP16 4SN
⌚ 12-3, 6-11; 11-11 Sat; 12-10.30 Sun
☎ (01728) 830154 🌐 theeelsfootinn.co.uk
Adnams Bitter, Broadside; seasonal beers Ⓗ
Close to the RSPB bird reserve at Minsmere, this cosy inn is popular with locals and visitors. It offers a varied and interesting menu of excellent home-cooked food. A new building at the rear provides accommodation and there is a large garden with plenty of outside seating. Local musicians play on Thursday evening and all are welcome to come and join in. A traditional folk night is hosted on the last Sunday of the month. Dogs are permitted. ♨Q❀⛟◐◑▲♣P

Edwardstone

White Horse
Mill Green, CO10 5PX OS951429
⌚ 5-11; 12-3, 5-11 Sat & Sun
☎ (01787) 211211
Adnams Bitter; Greene King IPA; guest beers Ⓗ
Hard to find, the pub is hidden down the winding lanes and undulating countryside leading to the River Box. The public bar is quarry tiled and half wood panelled. An annual dark beer festival in May adds to the interesting range of beers, always including a mild – a rarity in these parts. A meeting place for local clubs, there are two holiday cottages to let and camping and caravanning on site. Evening meals are served Tuesday to Sunday. Q❀⛟◑⊟▲♣●P

Erwarton

Queen's Head
IP9 1LN OS215346
⌚ 11-3, 6.30-11; 12-3, 7-10.30 Sun
☎ (01473) 787550
Adnams Bitter; Greene King IPA; guest beers Ⓗ
Attractive, heavily-timbered 18th-century pub in lovely countryside with splendid views across the river Stour. An extensive food menu includes good vegetarian options. A range of pub games includes bar billiards and shove ha'penny. The walls are adorned with seafaring and local photographs, with nautical charts in the Gents'. The pub is an ideal place to stop off for walkers and cyclists on the Shotley Peninsula. ♨❀◐◑⊟♣P

Felixstowe (Walton)

Half Moon
303 Walton High Street, IP11 9QL
⌚ 12-2.30 (not Mon), 5-11; 12-11 Sat; 12-3, 7-10.30 Sun
☎ (01394) 216009 🌐 halfmoonfelixstowe.com
Adnams Bitter, Broadside; guest beers Ⓗ
Friendly two-bar community local just outside the town which retains the feel of a pub of yesteryear. Traditional pub games and good conversation can be enjoyed without the distraction of games machines or muzak. Part of one bar is a screened no-smoking area. Books (and spectacles!) are available to customers and regular quiz nights are held. Look for the humorous messages on the pavement blackboard and the 'current word'. ♨Q❀⊟▲⊟♣P⚞

Framlingham

Station
Station Road, IP13 9EE (on B1116)
⌚ 12-2.30, 5-11; 12-2.30, 5-10.30 Sun
☎ (01728) 723455
🌐 earlsohambrewery.co.uk/the station/
Earl Soham Gannet Mild, Victoria Bitter, Albert Ale, seasonal beers Ⓗ
Popular town bar set in a former station premises. Unfortunately the branch line closed in 1952. The main bar is a cosy mixture of public bar and scrubbed tables while the back bar is smaller and quieter. Prominent in the main bar is a five-handpull font of German silver. An excellent, varied menu is available every day except Sunday evening. The brewer himself may often be found close to the bar during evening sessions. ♨Q☋❀◐◑⊟P

Freckenham

Golden Boar Inn
The Street, IP28 8HZ
⌚ 12-11; 12-4.30 Sun
☎ (01638) 723000
Adnams Bitter; Fuller's London Pride; guest beers Ⓗ
Superbly remodelled old coaching inn retaining many interesting original features. Ask the landlord about the history of the imposing fireplace to the left when entering. A good-sized bar for drinkers, popular with locals, has been retained despite the emphasis on dining. Excellent meals are prepared using fresh ingredients with a range of blackboard specials. ❀⛟◐◑♿P

Great Cornard

King's Head
115 Bures Road, CO10 0JE (on B1508)
⌚ 4 (12 Fri & Sat)-11; 12-10.30 Sun
☎ (01787) 319253
Greene King IPA, Abbot, Old Speckled Hen; guest beers Ⓗ
This traditional community pub serves what, with a population of nearly 10,000, must be one of the largest villages in the country. The building dates from the early 1500s. It has been a coaching inn and in the late 1800s had its own brewery. Greene King bought the pub in the 1930s and guest beers are from the Greene King list. The pub fields teams in darts, crib and pool. ♨❀◐▲♣P

Great Wratting

Red Lion
School Road, CB9 7HA (on B1061 2 miles N of Haverhill)
⌚ 11-2.30, 5-11; 11-1am Fri & Sat; 12-3, 7-10.30 Sun
☎ (01440) 783237
Adnams Bitter, Broadside, seasonal beers; guest beers Ⓗ
An amazing collection of brass and copper greets you as you enter this fine village local. The friendly landlord offers a warm

welcome along with good beer and food, served in both the bar and restaurant. Try the Adnams seasonal ales and guest beers from a range of breweries. The huge back garden has views over the surrounding countryside. Check out the jaw bones of a whale around the front door as you enter.
⌂❀◐◑P

Hawkedon

Queen's Head

Rede Road, IP29 4NN

✪ 5 (12 Sat)-11; 12-10.30 Sun

☎ (01284) 789218

Adnams Bitter; Greene King IPA; guest beers Ⓗ

Heavily beamed, 15th-century flagstone floored pub with a roaring fire in winter, situated in a picturesque village. Up to six cask-conditioned ales are available along with excellent, imaginative food (eve meals Fri and Sat). Occasional events such as live music, theatre, suppers and games evenings are held. Outside are a patio and large garden for summer drinking. The highly successful beer festival held in July has become an annual event. ⌂Q❀◐◑▲♣●P

Hessett

Five Bells

The Street, IP30 9AX

✪ 12-3 (not Mon), 5 (6 Sat)-11; 12-4, 7-10.30 Sun

☎ (01359) 270350

Greene King IPA, Abbot; guest beer Ⓗ

Close to the A14 (Beyton junction) but off the beaten track, in the centre of this pretty village and opposite the Norman church, the heavily-timbered Bells is a cosy pub. Two bars either side of the entrance lobby have log fires in large fireplaces. The massive Tudor brick post holding the sign above the entrance is said to be all that remains of the entry to a long-demolished stately home. A record of landlords back to 1753 is framed in the bar. ⌂Q❀◐◑♣P

Holton

Lord Nelson

Mill Road, IP9 8PP

✪ 11.30-3, 6.30-midnight; 12-3, 7-11 Sun

☎ (01986) 873275

Adnams Bitter; Taylor Landlord; guest beer Ⓗ

Now part of Admiral Inns, this traditional village pub is divided into two bars, one with a pool table and the other for dining and drinking. The walls and ceilings are adorned with seafaring artefacts and Nelson memorabilia. Good value food is prepared with local produce (booking advisable for Sunday lunch). The landlord is an Ind Coope Master Cellarman. There is a car park at the side and large garden at the rear.
❀◐◑⊟▲♣P

Hoxne

Swan

Low Street, IP21 5AS

✪ 11-3, 6-11; 12-10.30 Sun

☎ (01379) 668275 ⊕ hoxneswan.co.uk

Adnams Bitter, Broadside; Ⓖ **guest beers** Ⓗ

Large, high-ceilinged, multi-roomed, 15th-century timber-framed pub in an attractive, historic village. There are bare boards and scrubbed tables in the two main rooms with carpeted dining areas. Excellent home-cooked food features dishes in keeping with the character of the building, such as venison and wild boar, on a frequently changing menu. The large garden is a pleasant place for a drink in summer. An annual beer festival is held on spring bank holiday. ⌂Q❀◐◑⊟♣P

Ipswich

Dales

216 Dales Road, IP1 4JY

✪ 11-2.30, 4.30-11; 11.30-2.30, 6.30-11 Sat; 12-2.30, 7-10.30 Sun

☎ (01473) 250024

Adnams Bitter; Greene King IPA; guest beers Ⓗ

Well-run 1960s free house in a suburban area offering a good choice of beer and food. The comfortable lounge and the bar are separated by French doors which are opened up for quiz nights and special themed dining events. Access to the patio and garden is through the lounge. The pub has wheelchair access to all bars from the pavement, with disabled parking close by. Good value lunches are served Monday to Friday, steak nights are Tuesday, Thursday and Saturday. Sunday roasts and barbecues are popular and the pub boasts the best loos in town. ❀◐◑⊟♿P

Dove Street Inn

76 St Helens Street, IP4 2LA

✪ 12-midnight; 12-11 Sun

☎ (01473) 211270 ⊕ dovestreetinn.co.uk

Beer range varies Ⓗ/Ⓖ

After two years of hard work by the landlord and landlady of this street corner inn, the pub now offers a wide selection of local and not so local beers and ciders. With up to 10 beers on handpump and 10 on gravity, there is always something different to try. Seasonal beer festivals held in a marquee may offer more than 60 beers. The pub has three rooms: a main bar, quiet lounge and delightful no-smoking snug.
⌂Q❀◐◑⊟♿⊟(66, 2, 5)♣●P⊬▯

Emperor

293-295 Norwich Road, IP1 4BP

✪ 12-midnight (11 Sun)

☎ (01473) 743600

Ansells Mild; Young's Bitter; guest beers Ⓗ

A haven for local real ale drinkers in an area not noted for quality real ale. The pub caters for all with regular beer festivals, friendly conversation, pool, darts, TV sports, occasional music and an open fire. The patio overlooks the only Suffolk steel quoits beds currently in use in the town.
⌂❀◐♿⊟♣P⊬

Fat Cat

288 Spring Road, IP4 5NL

✪ 12-11 (1am Fri & Sat); 12-11 Sun

☎ (01473) 726524 ⊕ fatcatipswich.co.uk

Adnams Bitter; Ⓗ Crouch Vale Brewers Gold; Fuller's London Pride; Ⓖ Woodforde's Wherry; Ⓗ guest beers Ⓖ
Always a joy to visit, this ten-year-old pub is a superb reconstruction of a basic bareboards local, decorated with original tin advertising signs and posters. A wide range of keenly priced guest ales is always on offer. The surprisingly large garden and patio are popular in summer. The spacious conservatory provides additional room away from the servery during busy periods. No children under 14 or dogs. Q❀⇌(Derby Rd)🚌(2, 75)●

Greyhound

9 Henley Road, IP1 3SE
⏲ 11-2.30, 5-11 (midnight Fri); 11-11 Sat; 12-10.30 Sun
☎ (01473) 252862
Adnams Bitter, Explorer, Broadside, seasonal beers; guest beer Ⓗ
Comfortable Adnams pub a short walk from the town centre and near the museum and Christchurch Park. Since the present landlord took over this pub it has been in every issue of the Guide and he is justifiably proud of the pub's reputation. High quality freshly prepared food is available. There is an outdoor drinking area for the summer. Do not miss it if you are in town. ❀◐◑🚌P⊬

Lattice Barn

973 Woodbridge Road, IP4 4NX
⏲ 12-11 (midnight Fri & Sat); 12-10.30 Sun
☎ (01473) 727737
Greene King IPA; guest beer Ⓗ
A welcome new entry to the Guide, this pub has undergone a lot of work in the past year by the enthusiastic landlord and is definitely worth a visit. Situated on the outskirts of the town, handy for the hospital, it is easily accessible by bus. An interesting, comfortable pub, it has Sky TV for sports fans. 🔥❀🚌(66)♣P

Lord Nelson

81 Fore Street, IP4 1JZ
⏲ 11-2.30 (not Sat unless Ipswich Town are at home), 5-11; 12-4, 7-10.30 Sun
☎ (01473) 254072 🌐 ipswichlordnelson.com
Adnams Bitter, Broadside, seasonal beers Ⓗ
Grade II listed building, originally two timber-framed cottages. Adorned with Nelson and nautical memorabilia, the pub's interior is largely open plan. There has been a pub on this site since at least 1672; between 1790 and 1805 it was known as Noah's Ark. A handy location for the rapidly developing wet dock area. No food is served on Sunday evening. ❀◐◑♿⇌♣⊬

Mannings

8 Cornhill, IP1 1DD
⏲ 11-11; 12-5.30 Sun
☎ (01473) 254170
Adnams Bitter, Broadside; Fuller's London Pride; guest beer Ⓗ
A gem of a pub by the town hall in the town centre. Outdoor tables and chairs in summer provide the ideal place to sit and watch the world go by. A perfect location to watch Ipswich Town football club show off their trophies on the town hall balcony. The ales are excellent quality although perhaps a tad expensive. ❀◐♿⇌🚌

Ixworth

Greyhound

49 High Street, IP31 2HJ
⏲ 11-2.30, 6-11; 12-3, 7-10.30 Sun
☎ (01359) 230887
Greene King XX Mild, IPA, Abbot, seasonal beers Ⓗ
Situated in Ixworth's pretty High Street, which is now free from traffic since the bypass, this traditional pub has three bars including a lovely central snug. The whole community is made welcome here. The heart of the building dates back to Tudor times. At the rear of the car park the stable block bears witness to its historic past. It is one of the few remaining outlets for XX Mild in west Suffolk. Good value lunches and early evening meals are served in the no-smoking restaurant. Q❀◐◑◑♣P⊬

Kettleburgh

Chequers

The Street, IP13 7JT
⏲ 12-2.30, 6-11; 12-3, 6-10.30 Sun
☎ (01728) 723760 🌐 thechequers.net
Elgood's Black Dog; Greene King IPA; guest beers Ⓗ
Friendly rural pub with a large single bar, comfortably furnished with an unusual array of woodland cuttings on the ceiling. The choice of food ranges from simple bar snacks to an a la carte menu. The garden is over an acre and is popular in summer with its pretty riverside views. Part of the outdoor area was once the Deben Brewery which was demolished in Victorian times after a previous landlord failed to pay his malt duty. B&B accommodation is superb.
🔥❀◐◑Ʌ🚌(118)♣P⊬

Lakenheath

Brewer's Tap

54 High Street, IP27 0AU
⏲ 12-11 daily
☎ (01842) 862328
Beer range varies Ⓗ
Village-centre pub of character; a good find for real ale fans being truly 'free' in an area dominated by one brewer (Greene King). Local beers are usually available and some from 'abroad' (Suffolk dialect for anything not local) are allowed. Do not be put off by the small frontage – an extension and patio at the rear make the pub more spacious than it appears. A public car park is nearby. ❀◐♣

Lavenham

Angel

Market Place, CO10 9QZ
⏲ 11-11; 12-10.30 Sun
☎ (01787) 247388 🌐 lavenham.co.uk/angel
Adnams Bitter, Broadside; Greene King IPA; Nethergate Suffolk County Ⓗ
First licensed in 1420, this family-run inn is at the heart of England's finest medieval village. It sits opposite the Guildhall and

overlooks the market cross. No-smoking throughout, it is a busy place for food and drinking space can be at a premium at peak times. The menu changes daily with all meals prepared from fresh ingredients on the premises. There are eight comfortable, well-equipped guest rooms with good value mid-week breaks available. ⋔Q❀⇌◐⍉

Little Glemham

Lion Inn

Main Road, IP13 0BA (on A12)
⌚ 12-2.30, 6-11; closed Mon; 12-3, 7-10.30 Sun
☎ (01728) 746505
Adnams Bitter, Broadside; guest beer 🄷
Deceptively large, open-plan pub beside the A12, one of just a few pubs now to be found on this road. It has enjoyed a considerable revival in fortune since the current owners took over and visitors are assured a warm welcome. A monthly quiz night on Tuesday and regular themed food nights are popular. The menu features locally sourced ingredients prepared on the premises. No smoking is allowed throughout the pub. ⋔♨❀◑◐⊟(64)P⍉

Lower Layham

Queen's Head

The Street, IP7 5LZ
⌚ 12-3 (not Mon-Thu), 7-11; 12-3, 7-10.30 Sun
☎ (01473) 827789
Beer range varies 🄷
This ancient pub dates back over 700 years, with a wealth of beams and, allegedly, a resident ghost. The walls are festooned with historic photographs and artefacts. The present landlord rescued the pub from virtual closure and transformed it into one of the finest in Suffolk. Four ales usually include one from Cox & Holbrook. Excellent evening meals including vegetarian options are served from Wednesday to Sunday. ⋔Q❀◑◐⊡⅄P

Lowestoft

Oak Tavern

Crown Street West, NR32 1SQ
⌚ 10.30-11; 12-10.30 Sun
☎ (01502) 537246
Adnams Bitter; Greene King Abbot; guest beers 🄷
On the north side of town, this lively drinkers' pub is festooned with Belgian memorabilia. The open-plan bar divides into two areas with a pool table and Sky TV (for sporting events only) at one end and at the other a four-handpump display selling all real ales at the same price. A large range of continental beers, mainly from Belgium, is also available. ❀⇶P

Triangle Tavern

29 St Peter's Street, NR32 1QA
⌚ 11-11 (midnight Thu; 1am Fri & Sat); 12-10.30 Sun
☎ (01502) 582711
Green Jack Canary, Orange Wheat, Grasshopper, Gone Fishing, seasonal beers; 🄷 **guest beers** 🄷/🄶
Two-roomed pub with a comfortable front bar with wooden floor and a cartwheel hanging from the ceiling festooned with hops. A corridor leads to the open-plan bar and pool table. With a beer festival every three months, the pub is referred to locally as Lowestoft's permanent real ale festival. Live music is staged on Thursday and Friday evenings. The flagship for the Green Jack Brewery attached to the pub, it serves a full range of its excellent ales. ⋔⊡⇶●

Market Weston

Mill Inn

Bury Road, IP22 2PD
⌚ 12-3 (not Mon), 5-11; 12-3, 7-11 Sun
☎ (01359) 221018
Adnams Bitter; Greene King IPA; Old Chimneys Military Mild; guest beer 🄷
Run by the same landlady for more than 10 years, this imposing white brick and flint inn is situated on the B1111 crossroads on the outskirts of the village. The large single bar layout has a welcoming atmosphere with a good log fire in winter. Free of tie, this is the closest outlet for Old Chimneys Brewery on the other side of the village. An interesting range of beers complements the varied menu of home-made meals (no food Mon eve). ⋔Q◑◐♣P

Mildenhall

Queen's Arms

42 Queensway, IP28 7JY
⌚ 12-2.30, 5-11.30; 12-11.30 Fri-Sun
☎ (01638) 713657 🌐 queensarmsmildenhall.co.uk
Greene King IPA, Abbot; guest beers 🄷
Comfortable and homely pub used as a community centre by the locals. A small Greene King based beer festival is held in the large garden on August bank holiday when the cycle rally comes to town. Guest beers are from the Greene King list and some Belgian beers are stocked. The car park is small. ❀⇌⅄♣P

Naughton

Wheelhouse

Whatfield Road, IP7 7BS (450yds from B1078)
⌚ 5 (12 Fri & Sat)-11; 12-10.30 Sun
☎ (01449) 740496
Beer range varies 🄷
Dating back over 500 years, this part-thatched pub is full of character. The superb quality and variety of the interesting beer range – usually three to five different ales – attracts visitors from miles around to this rural gem. Expect to see several bicycles propped up outside as it is a popular destination for country bike rides. Food is restricted to sandwiches and baguettes. An open fire in winter adds to the warm, welcoming atmosphere. ⋔Q❀♿⊟♣P⍉

Newmarket

Five Bells

15 St Mary's Square, CB8 0HZ (behind Rookery shopping centre)
⌚ 11 (12 Sun)-11
☎ (01638) 602868

Beer range varies Ⓗ
Sold by Greene King last year, this popular local now has a vastly improved range of beer available. Situated away from the busy high street, it has a lively atmosphere, especially when darts and petanque teams are visiting. The large garden to the rear houses the petanque terrain and regular weekend barbecues are held in summer. Parking in front of the pub is limited, a public car park is 300 yards away. ⊞❀♣

Offton

Limeburners
Willisham Road, IP8 4SF
⏲ 4.30 (12 Fri & Sat)-11; 12-10.30 Sun
☎ (01473) 658318 🌐 limeburners.co.uk
Adnams Bitter; Greene King IPA; guest beers Ⓗ
Although known as the Offton Limeburners, the pub is just inside the parish of Willisham. This roadside local gets its name from the disused lime kiln in the old quarry opposite. The relatively new, award-winning, traditional fish and chip shop attached to the pub serves takeaways or you can eat in the pub (no eve meals Wed). Lively busking sessions are held on Sunday evening as well as monthly music events and a quiz night on the second Thursday of the month.
❀◐◑♿🚌P

Pakefield

Ship Inn
95 Stradbroke Road, NR33 7HW
⏲ 11-11; 12-10.30 Sun
☎ (01502) 562592 🌐 theshipinnlowestoft.com
Oulton Bitter, Nautilus, Gone Fishing, seasonal beers Ⓗ
The entrance to this Oulton Ales pub has a pair of doors with the Bullard's logo engraved on glass, leading to two main bars. A large central bar serves both rooms. This spacious pub has a modern appearance with wood panelling and flooring throughout, and nautical memorabilia adorning the walls. A selection of continental bottled beers as well as the Oulton range is available. At the rear is a candlelit restaurant.
◐◑🚂P

Ramsholt

Ramsholt Arms
Dock Road, IP12 3AB (signed off B1083) OS307415
⏲ 11-11 (11-3, 6-11 winter) daily
☎ (01394) 411229
Adnams Bitter, Broadside, seasonal beer Ⓗ
Cosy and isolated pub set on the foreshore of the River Debden, with outstanding views of the river and local countryside. The pub has long had a tradition for good food and ale and is popular with local sailors and walkers. The menu features mainly fish dishes with some meat and children's options. There are several dining areas and a comfy snug. Children and dogs are welcome.
⊞Q🐴❀◐◑P⚡

Rattlesden

Five Bells
High Street, IP30 0RA
⏲ 12-midnight (11.30 Sun)
☎ (01449) 737373
Beer range varies Ⓗ
Set beside the church on the high road through the village, this is a good old traditional Suffolk drinking house – few of its kind survive. Three well chosen ales on the bar are usually sourced direct from the breweries. The cosy single room has a games room on a lower level. ⊞Q❀●

Redgrave

Cross Keys
The Street, IP22 1RW
⏲ 12-2.30, 6-11; 12-2.30, 7-10.30 Sun
☎ (01379) 898510
🌐 crosskeysredgrave.co.uk
Greene King IPA; guest beers Ⓗ
Fairly modern in style with exposed brickwork, wood panelling and carpet throughout, the pub has two good-sized bars. One serves as the public bar and games room with pool and darts, the other is no-smoking and used as restaurant and lounge. Regular live music is hosted on Saturday night and food is available with a good range of curries alongside other dishes. No food is served on Sunday evening or Monday. ⊞🐴❀◐◑♣P⚡

Rendham

White Horse
Bruisyard Road, IP17 2AF
⏲ 12-2.30, 6-11; 12-3, 7-10.30 Sun
☎ (01728) 663497
Earl Soham Victoria Bitter; Mauldons Suffolk Pride; Taylor Landlord; guest beers Ⓖ
Opposite the 14th-century church, this genuine free house is popular with locals and visitors, particularly walkers. An excellent and varied menu featuring locally-sourced produce includes curry night on Thursday and takeaway fish and chips on Friday. Occasional live music is played and a charity quiz night held on the first Monday of the month. An annual beer festival is hosted on the August bank holiday weekend.
⊞Q❀◐◑⛺🚌♣P⚡🥛

Rumburgh

Rumburgh Buck
Mill Road, IP19 0NT
⏲ 11.45-3, 6.30-11; 12-3, 7-10.30 Sun
☎ (01986) 785257
Adnams Bitter, seasonal beers; guest beers Ⓗ
Full of character, this splendid pub was originally the guest house for the medieval priory. It has a long, narrow front bar with a games room extension. The back rooms are now dining areas where you can enjoy good food made with local ingredients (booking recommended). The original bar area is timber framed with a flagstone floor. There is an aviary in the garden. A popular

local at the heart of village life, it holds folk music evenings, quiz nights and sporting events. ❀◖◗⊟⛺♣P⊬

St Peter South Elmham

St Peter's Hall

NR35 1NQ (follow sign from A144 or B1062)
OS336854
✪ 11-3, 6-11; 11-11 Sat; 12-10.30 Sun
☎ (01986) 782322 ⊕ stpetersbrewery.co.uk
St Peter's beer range Ⓗ
Situated in unspoilt rural surroundings, this impressive moated churchlike hall has its own resident black swans. The back bar dates from 1280 and the medieval hall was extended in 1539 using 14th-century architectural salvage from a nearby derelict monastery. The furnishings are mainly 17th and 18th century. Good food is served made with local organic produce where possible (booking is recommended). St Peter's Brewery is across the courtyard in former agricultural buildings.
♨Q❀◖◗♿P

Somerleyton

Duke's Head

Slugs Lane, NR32 5QX
✪ 11-3, 6.30-11; 11-11 Sat & summer; 12-10.30 Sun
☎ (01502) 730281 ⊕ somerleyton.co.uk
Adnams Bitter; Greene King IPA; Green Jack Orange Wheat; guest beer Ⓗ
Situated in a picturesque village close to the railway station, overlooking the marshes near the River Waveney, this Broads pub is owned by Somerleyton Estates. The interior includes a public bar, lounge and restaurant. The large garden is busy with families in the summer. A converted barn in the grounds is used for musical events and occasional beer festivals. The food menu features local produce and changes seasonally (booking is advised).
♨❀◖◗⊟⛺⇌P

Southwold

Nelson

42 East Street, IP18 6EJ
✪ 10.30-11; 12-10.30 Sun
☎ (01502) 722079
Adnams Bitter, Broadside, seasonal beers Ⓗ
Busy town pub next to the Sailor's Reading Room museum and a stone's throw from the sea. It has three drinking areas, children are allowed in the side bar and outside on the shady patio. Decorated with naval artefacts, the main bar has a flagstone floor and welcoming open fire in winter. The pub is renowned for its good value food and full range of Adnams beers.
♨ᘏ❀◖◗⛺

Stowmarket

Royal William

53 Union Street East, IP14 1HP
✪ 11-3, 6 (5 Fri; 7 Sat)-11; 12-3, 7-10.30 Sun
☎ (01449) 674553
Greene King IPA; St Austell Tribute, guest beers Ⓖ
Unpretentious, small back-street local which has scarcely changed since it was granted a full licence 40 years ago; previously it held an ale licence only. Darts, crib, dominoes and conversation are as popular as ever. The well-kept beers are served on gravity, the casks kept on a stillage in a small room behind the bar. Conveniently situated just around the corner from the fine Victorian railway station.
❀⇌⊟♣

Stutton

Gardeners Arms

Manningtree Road, IP9 2TG
✪ 12-3, 6-11 (not Mon eve); 12-3, 6-10.30 Sun
☎ (01473) 328868
Adnams Bitter; Greene King IPA; guest beers Ⓗ
Friendly local ideally located for walkers and visitors to the area. Excellent food is served at lunchtime and early evening in the bar or dining area. Outside is a patio, two gardens, a fishpond and a bandstand where live music is played on summer Sundays. Note the enormous blacksmith's bellows suspended from the ceiling in the bar.
♨Q❀◖◗⊟♣P

Sudbury

Waggon & Horses

Acton Square, CO10 1HJ
✪ 11-3.30, 7 (5 Wed-Fri)-11; 11-4, 7-11 Sat; 12-4, 7-10.30 Sun
☎ (01787) 312147
Greene King IPA; guest beers Ⓗ
Local in the town's back streets, behind Market Hill. As well as several drinking areas, there is a games section with pool and darts and a small dining area. Guest beers are from the Greene King list. Food is home cooked with frequent special menus (booking is advisable). The new Phoenix Court flats nearby are built on the site of the defunct Phoenix Brewery, so named because it rose from the ashes of a fire in 1890. ♨Qᘏ❀⇔◖◗⇌♣

Swilland

Moon & Mushroom

High Road, IP6 9LR
✪ 11.30-2.30 (not Mon), 6-11; 12-2.30, 6-10.30 Sun
☎ (01473) 785320
Buffy's Norwich Terrier, Hopleaf; Crouch Vale Brewers Gold; Wolf Bitter; Woodforde's Wherry, Norfolk Nog; guest beers Ⓖ
Full of character, this cosy village pub has oak beams, low ceilings and an open fire. The decor is simple with tiled floors, scrubbed tables and photographs of the local area on the walls. The fine range of beers from local independents makes the pub always worth a visit, though it can be busy, especially at weekends. Good food made with locally sourced ingredients is served in the small smoke-free dining area (eve meals Tue-Sat). The toilets are outside. An unspoilt gem in a changing world.
♨Q❀◖◗⊟P

Theberton

Lion

The Street, IP16 4RU
12-2.30, 6-11; 12-3, 7-10.30 Sun
☎ (01728) 830185 🌐 thelioninn.co.uk
Adnams Bitter; Woodforde's Wherry; guest beers [H]
Detached red brick pub opposite the thatched, round-towered church which is well worth a look. A single bar serves the main drinking and dining area. Outside is a patio and garden. Guest beers are often from local East Anglian breweries and complement the home-made food. Quiz night is Wednesday and live jazz is played on the first Sunday of the month. Well-behaved dogs are welcome. Camping is allowed at the rear of the pub.
♨❀◑ ▲P

Thurston

Fox & Hounds

Barton Road, IP31 3QT
12-2.30, 5-11; 12-midnight Fri & Sat; 12-10.30 Sun
☎ (01359) 232228 🌐 thurstonfoxandhounds.co.uk
Adnams Bitter; Greene King IPA; guest beers [H]
This pub was saved from closure a few years ago, thanks mainly to CAMRA activists, and since then has gone from strength to strength. Now a regular entry in the Guide, four cask ales are always on offer, with an extra two at the weekend. Good, home-cooked food is served. The public bar has a pool table and there is a no-smoking area in the quieter, more comfortable lounge.
❀🛏◑ ⊟♿▲⇌♣P⚟

Tostock

Gardeners Arms

Church Road, IP30 9PA
11.30-3, 6.30-11; 12-3.30, 7-10.30 Sun
☎ (01359) 270460
Greene King IPA, Abbot; guest beers [H]
Situated in a charming village just two miles off the A14, this fine 14th-century building retains the original low beams and stone floor in the public bar. Darts, pool and crib are played here. The large lounge has a big open fireplace. Home-cooked food is served in the 'potting shed' (not Sun eve) and tasty snacks throughout the pub. The large, enclosed garden and patio are wonderful for families in summer.
♨❀◑ ⊟▲♣P

Walsham le Willows

Blue Boar

The Street, IP31 3AA
12-2.30, 5-midnight (1am Fri); 12-1am Sat; 12-midnight Sun
☎ (01359) 258533
Adnams Bitter; [H] **Woodforde's Wherry;** [G] **Caledonian Deuchars IPA;** [H] **guest beers** [H]/[G]
An ale house most of the time since 1420, this excellent village pub is well worth a visit. The friendly landlord particularly welcomes CAMRA members. Regular themed food nights and live music nights are hosted. A 20-tub beer festival is held annually on May bank holiday in a large marquee in the garden. ♨❀◑ ♣P

Woodbridge

Bell & Steelyard

103 New Street, IP12 1DZ
12-3, 6-midnight (12.30am Fri); 12-12.30am Sat; 12-10.30 Sun
☎ (01394) 382933 🌐 yeoldbell.co.uk
Greene King IPA, Abbot, guest beers [H]
Large and impressive timber-framed building incorporating the historic 'steelyard' on the front wall overhanging the street. The two bars are simply furnished with bare wood floors and high ceilings. An airy conservatory and garden are to the rear. Good food is served (not Sun eve). Traditional games played here include bar billiards and darts. This friendly, cosy pub where children are welcome is always worth a visit.
♨Q⛁❀◑ ♿⇌⊟♣⚟

Cherry Tree

73 Cumberland Street, IP12 4AG
7.30am-11; 9am-11 Sun
☎ (01394) 384627 🌐 thecherrytreepub.co.uk
Adnams Bitter, Explorer, Broadside, seasonal beers; guest beers [H]
Busy single bar close to the town centre. The large island-style servery helps to divide the space in this Grade II listed building. To the rear is an old timber barn which has been converted to provide accommodation. The garden has a children's play area and seating for summer days. A wide range of food is served daily from breakfast onwards.
♨Q⛁❀🛏◑ ⊟♣P⚟

Woolpit

Bull

The Street, IP30 9SA
11 (11.30 Sat)-3, 6-11; 12-2.30, 7-10.30 Sun
☎ (01359) 240393 🌐 bullinnwoolpit.co.uk
Adnams Bitter; guest beers [H]
Large inn, on the main Ipswich to Cambridge road through the centre of this historic village. A garden with a children's play area leads off the car park beside the pub. Inside, choose between the community-minded front bar, hosting varied charity events throughout the year, a games room, a comfortable conservatory and spacious restaurant at the rear. Wholesome home-cooked food is served (not Sun eve).
⛁❀🛏◑ ⊟♣P

> Where village statesmen talked with looks profound
> And news much older than the ale went round.
> **Alfred, Lord Tennyson**

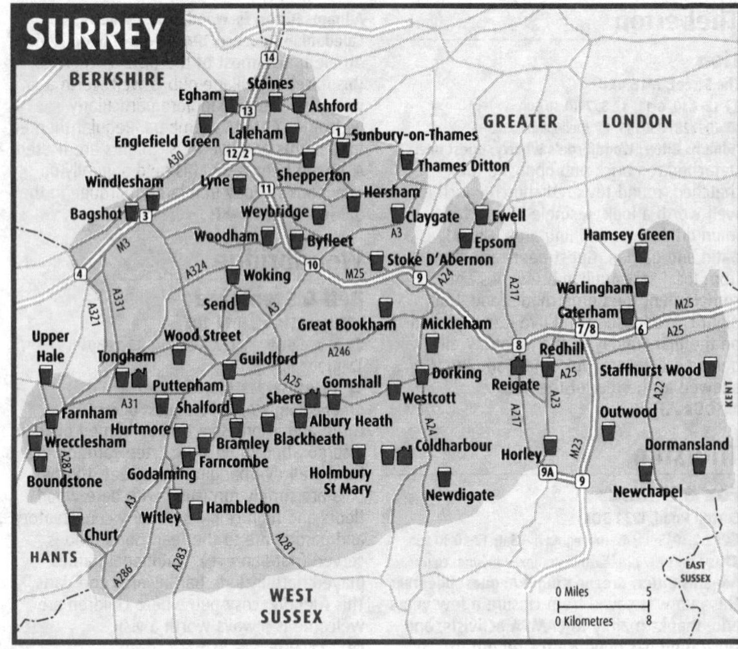

Albury Heath

William IV

Little London, GU5 9DG OS066467

11-3, 5.30-11; 12-3, 7-10.30 Sun

☎ (01483) 202685

Flowers IPA; Hogs Back TEA; Surrey Hills Ranmore Ale, Shere Drop, seasonal beers Ⓗ

Beers from local micro-brewers are featured at this secluded pub, dating from the 16th century. A wood-burning fire warms the flagstoned, wood-beamed bar in winter, while in summer there are picnic tables on the front lawn. There is a dining room up a few steps and a function room upstairs. Good value English home-made meals are served (not on Sun eve). Shove ha'penny is played here. ♨Q❀◑♣P

Ashford

Ash Tree

Convent Road, TW15 2HW (on B378)

11-11 (midnight Fri & Sat); 12-10.30 Sun

☎ (01784) 252362

Fuller's Chiswick, London Pride, ESB, seasonal beers Ⓗ

Recently refurbished Fullers-managed pub built in the early 1960s in a residential area outside the town centre. It is now a single bar with a large TV showing sport, a pool table, live music and a quiz night. Thai food is a speciality, available in the old public bar or to take away. Sunday roasts are also popular. At the back is outdoor patio seating. Situated on several bus routes, it is a 20-minute walk from the rail station.
❀◑🚌P

INDEPENDENT BREWERIES

Hogs Back Tongham
Leith Hill Coldharbour
Pilgrim Reigate
Surrey Hills Shere

Bagshot

Foresters Arms

173 London Road, GU19 5DH (on A30)

12-2.30, 5.30-11; 12-3, 7-11 Sun

☎ (01276) 472038

Courage Best Bitter; Fuller's London Pride; Hogs Back TEA; Taylor Dark Mild; guest beers Ⓗ

Traditional rural pub renowned for its range of seven well-kept cask ales, including three guests, and good food ranging from sandwiches to roasts. The adjoining skittle alley with its own bar is popular with skittles groups and for private functions. The pub runs a keen golf society, so much so that a two-bay practice golf net has been installed behind the pub. ❀◑🚌(34, 500)♣P

Blackheath

Villagers

Blackheath Lane, GU4 8RB OS035462

12-3, 6-11; 12-11 Fri & Sat; 12-11 Sun

☎ (01483) 893152 🌐 thevillagersinn.co.uk

Hogs Back TEA; Surrey Hills Shere Drop, seasonal beers; Taylor Landlord Ⓗ

The 'pub on the hill' is in fine walking country, a 30-minute stroll from Chilworth Station. Food is important here (not Sun eve), with a fine fish menu. Drinkers are well catered for too, in the stone-flagged public bar where dogs are welcome. Children are allowed in the daytime and there is a roof terrace, heated in winter. Live music is played on Tuesday evening.
♨❀🛏◑🚂P

Boundstone

Bat & Ball

Bat & Ball Lane, GU10 4SA (via Upper Bourne Lane off Sandrock Hill Rd)
⏲ 11-3, 5.30-11; 11-11 Fri & Sat; 12-10.30 Sun
☎ (01252) 792108 🌐 thebatandball.co.uk
Hogs Back TEA; Young's Bitter; guest beers Ⓗ
At the hub of several footpaths, the pub is easier to find on foot than by car. With wood-panelled walls and oak beams, it is decked out with cricket memorabilia. The bar area has terracotta floor tiles, wooden furniture and an open log fire. Doors lead to an ample pergola used as a family room with a TV at one end. The sunny garden has children's play equipment. The house beer, Bat & Ball Bitter, is Hampshire Ironside rebadged, and there are three further guests. ♨☡❀⛟◐♿🚌P⚡

Bramley

Jolly Farmer

High Street, GU5 0HB (on A281)
⏲ 11-11; 12-10.30 Sun
☎ (01483) 893355 🌐 jollyfarmer.co.uk
Beer range varies Ⓗ
The frontage of this pub is a delight, with hanging baskets full to overflowing in season. There are six real ales on offer from a diverse range of breweries. The bar area has subdued lighting and contains much local-interest memorabilia as well as a number of stuffed animals. There is also a feature fish tank. The dining area offers varied menus and specials. Opening hours may vary – phone in advance to be sure. ♨❀◐🚌P

Byfleet

Plough

104 High Road, KT14 7QT (off A245)
⏲ 11-3, 5-11; 12-3, 7-10.30 Sun
☎ (01932) 353257
Courage Best Bitter; Fuller's London Pride; guest beers Ⓗ
One of the best pubs for miles around with seven ever-changing guest beers. With two magnificent fires and 18th-century timbers, this is a real pub in every sense, where conversation dominates. Three drinking areas include one with large tables for groups to gather. Children are permitted in the no-smoking conservatory (enter via the car park). The hidden garden is an easily-missed asset, a haven of tranquillity in summer. Lunches are served Monday to Friday.
♨Q☡❀◐🚌♣P⚡

Caterham

Clifton Arms

110 Chaldon Road, CR3 5PH (on B2031)
⏲ 11.30-2.30, 4-11 (midnight Fri); 12-midnight Sat; 12-11 Sun
☎ (01883) 343525
Fuller's London Pride; Young's Bitter; guest beers Ⓗ
Former Charrington house which displays a vast collection of artefacts relating to local history and militaria – it could almost claim to be an extension of the local East Surrey Museum! It is a comfortable and cosy place to while away your time and enjoy a drink, whether it is a beer or one of the ciders, sometimes perry too. The back room doubles as a restaurant (eve meals Tue-Sat) and, on Saturday night, a rock 'n' roll disco is held.
❀◐🚌●P

King & Queen

34 High Street, CR3 5UA (on B2030)
⏲ 11-11; 12-10.30 Sun
☎ (01883) 345438
Fuller's Chiswick, London Pride, ESB, seasonal beers Ⓗ
Welcoming 400-year-old red brick and flint pub which has evolved since the 1840s from three former cottages, one of which was a bakery. The pub was one of Caterham's early ale houses and still retains three distinct areas – a front bar facing the high street, a high-ceilinged wooden beamed middle room with inglenook, and a small lower level rear area leading to a patio. Its name refers to Britain's only joint monarchy, William and Mary. No meals are served on Sunday.
♨Q❀◐⊟🚌♣P

Churt

Crossways

Churt Road, GU10 2JE (on A287)
⏲ 11-3.30, 5-11; 11-11 Fri & Sat, 12-4, 7-10.30 Sun
☎ (01428) 714323
Courage Best Bitter; Ringwood Fortyniner; Ⓗ **guest beers** Ⓖ
Situated on a busy road in good walking country, the Crossways attracts a good mix of locals, travellers and ramblers. The guest beers, usually around five at a time, are drawn straight from the cask in the cellar and four real ciders are on stillage behind the bar. Good, traditional home-cooked lunches are served Monday to Saturday. A popular beer festival is held every year offering up to 45 beers. Awarded local CAMRA Pub of the Year for 2005 and 2006.
Q❀◐⊟⛺🚌(1A)♣●P

Claygate

Foley Arms

Hare Lane, KT10 0LZ
⏲ 11-midnight daily
☎ (01372) 462021
Young's Bitter, Special, seasonal beers Ⓗ
Run by a landlord with 20 years' experience and passionate about real ale, this traditional two-bar Victorian village pub was named after a family of local landowners. It incorporates an old stables now used as a gym for Foley Boxing Club and there is also a spacious hall for hire. The large garden has a patio and children's play area. Blues music nights are hosted.
♨Q❀◐⊟♿⇌🚌(K3)🚌♣P

Griffin

58 Common Road, KT10 0HW OS161635
⏲ 11 (12 Sun)-midnight
☎ (01372) 463799
Fuller's London Pride; Oakham JHB; Young's

Bitter; guest beers (occasional) 🄷
Small, back street free-house in a residential area run by a landlord of 15 years' standing. It has two bars – the public is lively with a TV and darts, the saloon quieter – separated by a glass leaded light partition with a small door. Both bars have fireplaces made from local brick. The front windows are original, advertising Mann, Crossman & Paulin. There is a small rear garden and larger fenced front patio with heaters. Evening meals are served Friday and Saturday.
⛰Q❀◑◐⊟♿⇌▭(K3)♣P⚟

Coldharbour

Plough Inn

Coldharbour Lane, RH5 6HD OS152441
✪ 11.30-11; 12-10.30 Sun
☎ (01306) 711793 ⊕ ploughinn.com
Leith Hill Hoppily Ever After, Crooked Furrow, Tallywhacker; Ringwood Fortyniner; Shepherd Neame Spitfire 🄷
Situated close to Leith Hill (the highest point in south-east-England) and in superb walking country. Originally on a coaching route from London to the south coast, parts of the pub date from the 17th century. It is worth a visit for its own ales, brewed in an outbuilding at the back, and excellent food. The large garden comes into its own in summer.
⛰❀⇐◑◐♣P

Dorking

Cricketers

81 South Street, RH4 2JU (on A25 one-way system, westbound)
✪ 12-11; 12-10.30 Sun
☎ (01306) 889938
Fuller's Chiswick, London Pride, ESB, seasonal beers 🄷
Small, traditional town-centre pub with bare brick walls covered in Fuller's beer advertisements and old photographs. Perhaps the best feature of the pub is the lovely Georgian walled garden which is a summer suntrap. One of three Fuller's pubs in a row, the Cricketers is a good place to enjoy a pint in friendly surroundings. A TV is switched on for major sporting occasions.
❀▭♣

King's Arms

45 West Street, RH4 1BU (on A25 one-way system eastbound)
✪ 11-11 (11.30 Wed; midnight Fri & Sat); 12-3, 7-11 Sun
☎ (01306) 883361
Fuller's London Pride; Greene King IPA; guest beers 🄷
Attractive 16th-century inn situated in a street renowned for its antique shops. The split-level bar has low beams and leaded windows. At the rear is a cosy restaurant for evening meals only (not Sun or Mon). Food is served at lunchtime in the bar. On Wednesday and Sunday evenings a variety of live music is played. Guest beers, usually two, are mostly sourced from micro-breweries and change frequently.
❀◑◐⇌(West)▭P

Old House at Home

24 West Street, RH4 1BY (on A25 one-way system eastbound)
✪ 11-11 (1am Fri, 2am Sat); 12-11 Sun
☎ (01306) 889664
Young's Bitter, Special, seasonal beers 🄷
This well-renovated 15th-century inn is a successful blend of the old and the new. Divided into four areas, the single bar has wooden floors and good solid tables and there is a function room. Flat-screen TVs show sporting events. Outside is an attractive garden. Customers must be in the pub by 11pm to make use of the extended hours. ❀◑⇌(West)▭⚟

Dormansland

Old House At Home

63 West Street, RH7 6QP (signed from village, off Dormans Road) OS402422
✪ 11.30-3.30, 6-midnight; 12-4, 7-midnight Sun
☎ (01342) 832117
Shepherd Neame Master Brew Bitter, 🄷 **Kent's Best** 🄶 **Spitfire, seasonal beers** 🄷
Traditional old pub hidden on the western side of the village, with the main bar dating back to the 16th century. The bar at the side was added later and the restaurant at the back serves good quality home-made food (no food Sun eve). There is a patio for outdoor drinking. Hours may vary and last entry is around 11.30pm. An extra Shepherd Neame beer is added occasionally.
⛰❀◑◐⇌▭(236, 409)♣P

Egham

Crown

38 High Street, TW20 9DP (on B388)
✪ 11.30-11 (midnight Fri & Sat); 12-10.30 Sun
Adnams Bitter, Broadside; Fuller's London Pride; Greene King Abbot; guest beers 🄷
Large, cosy, traditional pub split into different drinking areas including a no-smoking conservatory at the back. Unobtrusive TV screens show sporting events. A local CAMRA Pub of the Year, guest ales served here include offerings from Archers and Hogs Back. Beer festivals feature during the year.
❀◑◐⇌▭♣⚟

Englefield Green

Barley Mow

TW20 0NX (off A328)
✪ 11.30-11; 11.30-10.30 Sun
☎ (01784) 431857
Adnams Broadside; Caledonian Deuchars IPA; Fuller's London Pride; Greene King Old Speckled Hen; Wadworth 6X 🄷
Opposite the village green, the pub is sited where the victim of the last public duel in England died in 1852. His ghost is reputed to haunt this old weather-boarded pub. The interior has recently been revamped and at the back is a large south-facing garden with children's play area. The landlord is an accomplished bongo player and sometimes gives an impromptu performance.
❀◑◐▭

Happy Man

12 Harvest Road, TW20 0QS (off A30) OS997708
11-11.30 (midnight Fri & Sat); 12-10.30 Sun
(01784) 433265
Hop Back Summer Lightning; guest beers H
Originally two Victorian cottages, around 125 years ago they were converted to become a beer house to serve the labourers constructing nearby Royal Holloway College, one of the most impressive Victorian structures close to London. The internal layout has barely changed and it still feels as though you are drinking in the landlord's front room. More than 120 pump clips are testament to the ever-changing beer range at this back-street pub.

Epsom

Barley Mow

12 Pikes Hill, KT17 4EA (off A2022, Upper High St)
12-11 (midnight Fri & Sat); 12-10.30 Sun
(01372) 721044
Fuller's Chiswick, Discovery, London Pride, ESB, seasonal beers H
Originally three cottages built for gravel workers, they were converted into a pub some years ago and extended more recently. A popular, well-run hostelry in a side street just out of the town centre, it has one long central bar with seating areas surrounding it. The decor is traditional with a mixture of wooden boards, tiles and carpeting. A conservatory leads to the garden. Upper High Street car park is nearby.

Jolly Coopers

84 Wheelers Lane, KT18 7SD (off B280 via Stamford Green Road)
12-11 (midnight Thu-Sat); 12-10.30 Sun
(01372) 723222
Harveys Sussex Best Bitter; guest beer H
A locals' pub set back from the road in a residential area. To the left is the lounge where you will find the handpumps. Cosy, quiet and carpeted with a small brick fireplace, it has bench seating around the walls and a piano. To the right is the more popular public bar with a bare herringbone wood floor and heavily beamed ceiling. Between the two bars is a small seating area. P

Symonds Well

30 South Street, KT18 7PF (on A24)
12-3, 5-11; 12-1am Fri & Sat; 12-10.30 Sun
(01372) 723158
Greene King Abbot; Young's Bitter; guest beers H
Previously called the Magpie, it was renamed after an Epsom yeoman called John Symonds, who discovered a well nearby in 1667, claimed to have medicinal properties. Situated on the one-way system at the west end of town, the pub has a central bar with seating areas around it, and a further room at the back. The front bar area has etched windows looking out on to the busy road, a wood floor, panelling, benches and an open gas fire with brick surround. Past scenes of Epsom races decorate the walls.

Ewell

Wheatsheaf

34 Kingston Road, KT17 2AA (off A240/B2200)
11-11; 12-10.30 Sun
(020) 8393 2879
Wells Bombardier; Young's Bitter; guest beers H
Friendly local built in 1858, though an ale house has been on this site since 1456. Situated opposite the old mill and Hogsmill River Park, the comfortable two-roomed pub is served by one bar. The bar back is made from leaded windows from the long-gone Isleworth Brewery. Both rooms have open fires, the walls are decorated with bygone local scenes and unusual pictures of local drinkers. The well-kept large rear garden holds occasional barbecues and the pub's frontage has impressive floral displays in summer. Live music is played on Saturday night. (West) (406, K10)

Farncombe

Cricketers

37 Nightingale Road, GU7 2HU
12-11; 12-midnight Fri & Sat; 12-11 Sun
(01483) 420273
Fuller's Chiswick, Discovery, London Pride, ESB H
Friendly back-street local attracting a good mix of all ages. Founded by a former Surrey and England cricketer Julius Caesar (really) it retains its cricketing theme. One central bar serves three drinking areas and a dining area. There is a front terrace and an elevated rear garden for outdoor drinking. Note the Good Beer Guide awards on proud display.

Farnham

Hop Blossom

Long Garden Walk, GU9 7HX (off A287)
12-3, 5-11; 12 (11 Sat)-midnight Fri & Sat; 12-11 Sun
(01252) 710770
Fuller's Chiswick, London Pride, ESB, seasonal beers; guest beer H
Popular traditional pub tucked away in a small lane in the centre of town. The modest L-shaped bar area has a real fire at one end – crumpets and chestnuts are sometimes provided in winter – and an adjoining conservatory. A large no-smoking room for diners, drinkers and families is at the rear. Live acoustic and jazz music are held on Tuesday and Thursday. Good food includes a curry night on Wednesday and roast on Sunday. Dogs are welcome.
Q

Lamb

43 Abbey Street, GU9 7RJ (off A287)
11-2.30, 5-11; 11-midnight Fri & Sat; 12-10.30 Sun
(01252) 714133
Shepherd Neame Kent's Best, H **Spitfire,** G **seasonal beers** H/G
A community pub in the best tradition. The quieter end of the bar is for conversation and home to a successful quiz team, the other end has a pool table and two TVs screening important footie matches. Good live bands play on most Friday nights and

the pub can become crowded. Outside is an attractive terrace at rooftop level. Although the pub is beer oriented, the food is excellent and great value (no food Tue eve or all day Sun). ♨❀◐◑⇌⊟♣

William Cobbett

Bridge Square, GU9 7QR

☼ 11-11 (midnight Fri & Sat); 12-10.30 Sun

☎ (01252) 726281

Courage Best Bitter; Fuller's London Pride; guest beers Ⓗ

Birthplace of the 18th-century social reformer William Cobbett, the inn's flagstone floors and low beams testify to its 16th-century origins. The interior has several interlinked small areas downstairs (one with a football table) and a pool room upstairs with four tables. Popular with all ages, the atmosphere is friendly and lively, and the pub is particularly busy when live music features in a marquee behind the pub. ❀◐⇌⊟♣P

Godalming

Red Lion

1 Mill Lane, GU7 1HF

☼ 11-11 (11.30 Thu); 1am Fri & Sat; 12-11 Sun

☎ (01483) 415207

Harveys Sussex Best Bitter; guest beers Ⓗ

Wonderful free house of enduring popularity with five ever changing and imaginative guests complemented by an extensive Belgian beer selection. The saloon is small and intimate with hop vines, numerous pump clips adorning the ceiling and prints of old Godalming. The public bar is larger with historical connections – in 1696 it was the Oddfellows Hall and later the grammar school attended by Jack Phillips, the ill-fated Titanic radio operator. Regular themed beer festivals are held at Easter and Halloween. No food is served on Sunday evening or all day Monday. Q❀◐◑⊟⇌⊟

Gomshall

Compasses

50 Station Road, GU5 9LA (on A25)

☼ 11-11; 12-10.30 Sun

☎ (01483) 202506

Hogs Back TEA; Surrey Hills Ranmore Ale, Shere Drop; guest beers (summer) Ⓗ

Originally called God Encompasses, the name has contracted over time. Dating from 1830, this former Surrey Trust Company pub stands on the banks of the Tillingbourne – a small bridge spans the river to reach the garden. The ghost of a girl who was drowned in the stream is reputed to haunt the pub. The pub's restaurant serves good home-cooked food (no meals Sun eve). There is live music on Friday night. ❀⇆◐◑⇌⊟(21,25,32)P

Great Bookham

Anchor

KT23 4AH (off A246 via Eastwick Road)

☼ 11-3, 5.30-11; 12-3, 7-10.30 Sun

☎ (01372) 452429

Courage Best Bitter, Directors; guest beer Ⓗ

Grade II-listed 16th century inn with beamed ceilings, exposed brick walls and wooden floors throughout, and an inglenook with a welcoming real fire in winter. The bar is adorned with hop vines. The landlord of this traditional local has been in residence for more than 15 years. A popular pub, it can get busy in the evening. Quality meals are served at lunchtime Monday to Saturday. Children are not allowed in the bar.
♨Q❀◐⊟(479)♣P

Guildford

Keystone

3 Portsmouth Road, GU2 4BL (on A3100)

☼ 12-11 (midnight Fri & Sat); 12-7 Sun

☎ (01483) 575089 ⊕ thekeystone.co.uk

Black Sheep Best Bitter; Wadworth 6X; guest beers Ⓗ

Over 21s town-centre pub with a stylish interior. Access is from the main road or via the heated patio at the rear. Excellent home-made food is cooked to order (no food Fri-Sun eve). Live music sessions are held, often acoustic on Saturday, with jazz on the first Wednesday of the month – see the website for event details. Chess, backgammon and Jenga are played and there are books to read while you enjoy your pint. ❀◐◑⇌⊟

Varsity Bar

University of Surrey, Egerton Road, GU2 7XU (off A3 at university exit, near hospital)

☼ 12-11; 12-8.30 Sat; 12-10.30 Sun

☎ (01483) 689974

⊕ www.unisport.co.uk/varsity_bar.htm

Beer range varies Ⓗ

University sports bar open to all; access is via the downstairs shop. Three varying beers are always available, often from local independent brewers. A British cask and European bottled beer festival is held annually in November, as well as mini festivals throughout the year. The bar can be busy on match days (Wed and Sat) but quieter at other times. Quiz night is the first Monday of the month. Sports matches are shown on the large-screen TV. The food is good and burgers highly recommended (not Sun lunch or Fri-Sun eve). ◐◑⊟P

Hambledon

Merry Harriers

Rock Hill, Hambledon Road, GU8 4DR OS968392

☼ 11-3 (4 Sat), 6-11; 12-4, 7-10.30 Sun

☎ (01428) 682883

Greene King IPA; Hogs Back TEA; Hop Back Crop Circle; guest beer Ⓗ

Small and unpretentious country pub well off the beaten track run by the same family for nearly 40 years. The single bar has a strong local community focus but warmly welcomes visitors including walkers. A collection of old chamber pots and stamped pint-measure ceramic mugs hangs from the ceiling and the more traditional wooden Surrey slats cover the walls. Food is good value (eve meals Fri and Sat only) and the sign outside proclaiming 'warm beer and lousy food' is to be ignored. Camping and caravan facilities are opposite. ♨♘❀◐◑▲♣●P

Hamsey Green

Good Companions

Limpsfield Road, CR6 9RH (on B269)

12-11.30 (midnight Fri & Sat); 12-11 Sun

☎ (020) 8657 6655 thegoodcompanions.com

Westerham Black Eagle SPA, British Bulldog, Sevenoaks Bitter 7X, seasonal beers Ⓗ

Dating from the 1930s, this large family-run establishment is split into a main bar, restaurant and no-smoking lounge. The Westerham beers are a popular choice and food is available all day in the bar except Sunday evening. A large-screen TV shows major sporting events and there is a pool table in the bar. Thursday is 'open mike' night and there is a disco on the last Saturday of the month. See the website for forthcoming events.

(403)P

Hersham

Royal George

130 Hersham Road, KT12 5QJ (off A244)

11-11 (midnight Fri & Sat); 12-11 Sun

☎ (01932) 220910

Young's Bitter, Special Ⓗ

Built in 1964, this local has two spacious bars. A friendly atmosphere and a blazing fire in each bar make it a popular hostelry for all ages. The pub is named after a ship from the Napoleonic wars, which accounts for some of the pictures on the walls. A wide range of home-cooked food is available (not Sun eve). The pub raises a lot of money for charity and a quiz is held on Tuesday evening.

(218)P

Holmbury St Mary

King's Head

Pitland Street, RH5 6NP (off B2126)

12-11 (10.30 Sun)

☎ (01306) 730282

Greene King IPA; King Horsham Best Bitter; Surrey Hills Shere Drop; guest beers Ⓗ

Tucked away in a side road, this pub concentrates on beers from micro-breweries. The ales are served from a vintage integral six pump beer engine. An adventurous home-made menu includes pheasant and wild boar (no eve meals Sun and Mon). The bar has several rooms and an open fireplace, with a sloping beer garden outside. Set in the midst of the Surrey Hills, this is a popular stop-off for walkers.

(21)P

Horley

Coppingham Arms

263 Balcombe Road, RH6 9EF (on B2036)

11.30 (12 Sun)-11

☎ (01293) 782283

Greene King Old Speckled Hen; Harveys Sussex Best Bitter Ⓗ

Traditional 300-year-old pub built from two cottages on the edge of Horley. Inside is one main room divided into three areas. The older part splits into public and saloon bars, while a more modern extension is used for dining too (no eve meals winter Sun). The public bar holds a pool table. Live music is held on the last Friday of the month. Closing time may be extended when the pub is busy.

P

Hurtmore

Squirrel Inn

Hurtmore Road, GU7 2RN (off A3)

11-11; 12-10.30 Sun

☎ (01483) 860223

Fuller's London Pride; guest beers Ⓗ

Comfortably furnished lounge bar divided into smoking and no-smoking areas. There is a good choice of food ranging from bar snacks to full main meals, including vegetarian dishes, served in the bar or dining room. Outside is the garden and heated patio. Hot air balloon flights are available here during the summer months.

(46)P

Laleham

Feathers

The Broadway, TW18 1RZ (on B377)

12-11 (midnight Fri & Sat); 12-10.30 Sun

☎ (01784) 453561

Fuller's London Pride; guest beers Ⓗ

Traditional village free house a short walk from the River Thames. The central bar serves two drinking areas. Three guest beers from micros change rapidly. Good food made with local ingredients is served from noon to 9pm. A beer festival is hosted during the first week of July, with occasional mini events throughout the year. The patio garden at the back provides shady outdoor drinking and there are benches outside at the front.

(218,438)

Lyne

Royal Marine

Lyne Lane, KT16 0AN (off B386) OS012663

12-2.30, 5.30-11; 11-2.30, 6.30-11 Sat; 12-3 Sun

☎ (01932) 873900

Courage Best Bitter; Hogs Back TEA; guest beers Ⓗ

North Surrey's best kept secret is well worth seeking out. Converted 160 years ago from two cottages, its name commemorates the occasion when Queen Victoria reviewed her Crimean troops on nearby Chobham Common. The interior features much Marine memorabilia and a guest book for Marines past and present. Two of the four handpumps dispense constantly changing guest beers, often including a mild.

Q(P3)P

Mickleham

King William IV

4 Byttom Hill, RH5 6EL (off A24, southbound) OS174538

11-3, 6-11; 12-10.30 Sun

☎ (01372) 372590

Adnams Bitter; Badger First Gold; Hogs Back TEA; guest beer (summer) Ⓗ

Splendid pub nestling on the side of a hill on the scenic North Downs with great views over Norbury Park and the Mole Valley. Full of character, it has just two small bars but the secluded garden provides more room for drinkers in summer. As well as the range of beers, food is a major attraction (no eve meals Sun). Parking is available at the bottom of the hill.
♨Q❀◖◗▭(465)♣P

Newchapel

Blacksmith's Head

Newchapel Road, RH7 6LE (on B2028, off A22)
✪ 11-3, 5.30-11; 12-3, 6-11 Sat; 12-7 Sun
☎ (01342) 833697 ⊕ theblacksmithshead.co.uk
Fuller's London Pride; Harveys Sussex Best Bitter; guest beers Ⓗ
Built in the 1920s on the site of a former forge, this one-bar country free house has a restaurant area to the side and provides quality accommodation. Food is freshly prepared with restaurant, bar and tapas menus to choose from – Portuguese influences reflect the nationality of the licensees. Occasional quizzes are held and two regularly changing guest beers come from small independents or micros.
♨❀⇌◖◗▲♣P

Newdigate

Surrey Oaks

Parkgate Road, RH5 5DZ (between Newdigate and Leigh) OS205436
✪ 11.30-2.30, 5.30-11; 11.30-3, 6-11 Sat; 12-10.30 Sun
☎ (01306) 631200 ⊕ surreyoaks.co.uk
Harveys Sussex Best Bitter; Surrey Hills Ranmore Ale; Taylor Landlord; guest beers Ⓗ
A frequent CAMRA local Pub of the Year winner, the 'Soaks' serves myriad guest beers, mostly from micro-breweries, with two always available often including a dark ale. The central part of the bar, dating from the 16th century, has a low-beamed ceiling and flagstone floors. The dining room serves excellent home-cooked food (no eve meals Sun and Mon). Outside is a large garden and a boules pitch. A beer festival is held over the late spring and August bank holidays when the pub is open all day. The pub is no-smoking throughout.
♨Q❀◖◗♣●P⚟

Outwood

Castle Inn

Millers Lane, RH1 5QB OS317453
✪ 12-3, 5.30-11; 12-11 Sat; 12-8 Sun
☎ (01342) 842754
Adnams Broadside; Fuller's London Pride; Harveys Sussex Best Bitter; guest beer Ⓗ
A food-oriented pub where the tables may all be booked by diners at busy times. The main area is L-shaped with a small no-smoking area, warmed by an open fire, and a dining area. Outside is covered decking with heaters, a patio and children's play space. Guest beers change frequently.
♨Q❀◖◗♿P⚟

Puttenham

Good Intent

62 The Street, GU3 1AR (off B3000)
✪ 11-3, 6-11; 11-11 Sat; 11-10.30 Sun
☎ (01483) 810387
Ringwood Best Bitter; Theakston Old Peculier; Young's Bitter; guest beers Ⓗ
A haven of tranquillity in an unspoilt village, yet easily accessible from the nearby A31 (Hogs Back). The L-shaped room, with low beams and hops over the bar, has dining areas at either end separated by a magnificent fireplace. Special food nights include fish and chips on Wednesday (no eve meals Sun and Mon). Welcoming to all, including dogs, this atmospheric pub is well worth heading out into the countryside for.
♨Q❀◖◗P

Redhill

Garland

5 Brighton Road, RH1 6PP (on A23, S of town centre)
✪ 11-midnight (1am Fri & Sat); 12-3, 7-midnight Sun
☎ (01737) 760377
Harveys Sussex XX Mild, Hadlow Bitter, Sussex Best Bitter, Armada, seasonal beers Ⓗ
A Victorian street corner local, this is the place to come for the best Harveys you will find anywhere. The entire range is sold along with any seasonal beers the landlord can get hold of – the record is 12 different beers on sale at one time. The pub is an oasis of tradition in a town full of chain pubs. See if you can spot the large collection of clowns, most of which are above the bar. Darts is popular here. Customers must be in the pub by 11pm for late opening hours. Food is served Monday to Friday. ❀◖≢▭♣P

Home Cottage

3 Redstone Hill, RH1 4AW (just off A25 behind station)
✪ 11-11.30; 12-10.30 Sun
☎ (01737) 762771
Young's Bitter, Special, seasonal beers Ⓗ
Large, mid-19th century community pub with three distinct drinking areas. The front bar has a relaxing atmosphere warmed by a real fire and offers an interesting bank of five handpumps. The back bar is the public bar. The no-smoking conservatory is a family room where children are welcome. There is also a large room available for hire. The pub hosts monthly music and comedy nights.
♨♉❀◖◗≢▭P⚟

Send

New Inn

Send Road, GU23 7EN (on A247)
✪ 11-11; 12-10.30 Sun
☎ (01483) 762736
Adnams Bitter; Fuller's London Pride; Greene King Abbot; Ringwood Best Bitter; guest beers Ⓗ
Situated on the Wey Navigation, one of Britain's oldest commercial waterways dating from the 1660s. Nowadays this single bar with three drinking areas plays host to recreational boaters, walkers and drivers escaping the Woking concrete jungle. The

garden, with its barbecue, is very popular in summer. The present pub replaces an old inn on the other side of the road and was originally a mortuary – it is claimed that the phrase 'a stiff drink' originated here.
Q✿◑🚌(436,463)P

Shalford

Queen Victoria

Station Row, GU4 8BY (on A281)
⏲ 11-11; 12-10.30 Sun
☎ (01483) 561733
Fuller's London Pride; Greene King IPA; guest beer Ⓗ
Traditional pub about two miles from Guildford. A busy establishment, it is well supported by local residents. Many original features remain including the bay windows. A small children's area at the back leads to a paved garden. Special food evenings are a highlight throughout the year. The guest beer is from a local brewery. 🔥✿◑⇌🚌

Shepperton

Barley Mow

67 Watersplash Road, TW17 0EE (off B376)
⏲ 12-11; 12-10.30 Sun
☎ (01932) 225326
Courage Best Bitter; Hogs Back TEA, seasonal beers; guest beers Ⓗ
A gem of a traditional local with five handpumps offering three constantly changing guests and cider from Mr Whiteheads available straight from the cask. At least one beer festival is held a year. The single-room horseshoe-shaped bar is decorated with bottled beers and pump clips. The friendly crowd of regulars enjoys quiz night on Thursday, live jazz on Wednesday and rock 'n' roll or blues on Saturday. An eclectic menu includes goat curry. Local CAMRA Pub of the Year in 2004.
✿◑♿🚌(218,400,438)♣P

Staffhurst Wood

Royal Oak

Caterfield Lane, RH8 0RR OS407485
⏲ 11-11 (closed 3-5 winter Mon & Tue); 12-10.30 Sun
☎ (01883) 722207
Adnams Bitter; Harveys Sussex Best Bitter; Larkins Traditional; Ⓗ **guest beers** Ⓗ/Ⓖ
Friendly rural free house well worth seeking out. Inside you are likely to find at least one barrel of beer perched on the bar and a good selection of bottled Belgian beers close at hand. Good-quality meals made from locally-sourced ingredients are served in the bar and restaurant (not Sun eve). One of the guest beers is from the Westerham Brewery – look out for the pies made with its ale. Views from the garden are superb. A popular stop-off for ramblers, dogs are welcome.
🔥✿◑🚃♣🍎P⊁

Staines

George

2-8 High Street, TW18 4EE (on A308)
⏲ 9am-midnight (1am Fri & Sat); 9am-midnight Sun
☎ (01784) 462181
Courage Best Bitter; Greene King Abbot; Marston's Pedigree; Shepherd Neame Spitfire; guest beers Ⓗ
Popular new-build Wetherspoon pub opposite the old town hall and war memorial. The large downstairs bar has several booths and a spiral staircase leading to the quieter no-smoking upstairs bar. On Friday and Saturday evenings the pub tends to become a waiting room for the local nightclubs but beer quality is always assured. Guest ales usually include an offering from Loddon. The cider is Weston's Old Rosie. Q◑♿⇌🚌🍎⊁

Wheatsheaf & Pigeon

Penton Road, TW18 2LL (off B376)
⏲ 11-11; 12-10.30 Sun
☎ (01784) 452922
Courage Best Bitter; Fuller's London Pride; Hogs Back TEA; guest beers Ⓗ
Splendid community pub offering a warm welcome to all, from locals to Thames Path walkers (if they can find it!). Up to three guest beers are served. The pub hosts an August bank holiday weekend beer festival and street party with tug of war and barbecue. A wide range of food from bar snacks to curries and steaks is served (no food Mon eve). Quiz night is Tuesday. Conversation dominates but an unobtrusive TV shows sport.
✿◑🚌P⊁

Stoke D'Abernon

Old Plough

2 Station Road, KT11 3BN (off A245)
⏲ 11.30-11; 12-10.30 Sun
☎ (01932) 862244 🌐 dabernons-restaurant.co.uk
Courage Best Bitter; guest beers Ⓗ
Dating from the late 16th century, this roadside pub features in a Sherlock Holmes novel. A full food menu is available in the conservatory but a lighter menu is served in the bar. Children are welcome until 7pm. Guest beers are selected from all over the country but local micros are sometimes represented. The garden is popular in summer and includes a children's play area.
🔥✿◑⇌🚌(408)P⊁

Sunbury-on-Thames

Hare & Hounds

132 Vicarage Road, TW16 7QX (off Sunbury Cross)
⏲ 11-11 (midnight Fri & Sat); 11-10.30 Sun
☎ (01932) 761478
Fuller's Chiswick, London Pride, ESB, seasonal beers Ⓗ
After several years in the doldrums this large, comfortable roadside inn has undergone a renaissance thanks to the current landlord. Its previous, somewhat dubious, reputation has been swept aside and visitors are now assured of a warm welcome and ales in excellent condition. There is a large garden and patio area and beer festivals are planned twice a year.
✿◑♿⇌🚌(235)P⊁

Thames Ditton

George & Dragon

High Street, KT7 0RY (on B364)
11-11; 12-10.30 Sun
☎ (020) 8398 2206
Shepherd Neame Master Brew Bitter, Kent's Best, Spitfire, seasonal beers Ⓗ
Popular village local set back from the road. The open plan interior is divided into several areas, one no-smoking at lunchtime, with two bars. Pictures of the local area adorn the wood-panelled walls. Live music is played on Tuesday evening. Evening meals are served Wednesday to Saturday. Local CAMRA Pub of the Year 2005. Q (514,515)P

Tongham

Hogs Back Brewery Shop

Manor Farm, GU10 1DE (off A31)
9am-8.30; 9am-6 Sat; 10-4.30 Sun
☎ (01252) 783495 hogsback.co.uk
Beer range varies Ⓖ
Off-licence attached to the award-winning brewery selling Hogs Back beers on draught to take away, plus the brewery's full range of bottle conditioned ales. Thousands of other bottled beers from around the world are available including a wide selection from the UK. The brewery can be viewed from a gallery in the shop. A 5% discount on draught beers is available to card-carrying CAMRA members. P

Upper Hale

Ball & Wicket

104 Upper Hale Road, GU9 0PB (on A3016)
4 (12 Sat)-11; 12-10.30 Sun
☎ (01252) 735278
Hogs Back TEA; Itchen Valley Hampshire Rose, Winchester Ale; guest beers Ⓗ
Situated opposite the local village cricket green, the pub has a single bar with a wooden floor and low beams. With a strong local following the emphasis is on conversation and background music is unobtrusive. There is a large-screen TV used for major sporting events. A quiz is held on Sunday night and a meat raffle on Friday.
P

Warlingham

Hare & Hounds

633 Limpsfield Road, CR6 9DZ (on B269)
12-11; 12-10.30 Sun
☎ (01883) 623952
Fuller's London Pride; Tetley Bitter; guest beers Ⓗ
On the edge of the green belt, this modestly-sized one-bar community pub has an intriguing extension and a beer garden to the rear. Smartly refurbished during 2005, the walls are decorated with many period photographs of the local area. It serves guest beers from local micro-breweries including Westerham and King. Pub food is served from noon until 7pm (3pm Sun). Live music is played on Saturday evening.
(403, 409, 411)P

Westcott

Prince of Wales

Guildford Road, RH4 3QE (on A25)
11-11; 12-10.30 Sun
☎ (01306) 889699
Fuller's Chiswick Bitter, London Pride, ESB Ⓗ
A small entrance hall leads to a light and airy L-shaped room with an area set aside for diners. Good food is served at lunchtime and in the evening, with takeaway meals also available. There is a room where pool and darts are played. Set below road level is a pleasant garden.
(21,22,32)P

Weybridge

Jolly Farmer

41 Princes Road, KT13 9BN (off A317)
11-3, 5.30-11; 12-3, 7-11 Sun
☎ (01932) 856873
Hop Back Odyssey, Summer Lightning; Young's Bitter; guest beers Ⓗ
Comfortable, friendly, back-street, mid-Victorian pub with a low-beamed ceiling. The L-shaped bar is surrounded by upholstered bench seats. There are large mirrors and pictures of old Weybridge decorating the walls and a collection of Toby jugs on the high shelving. The large garden is popular in summer. Q

Old Crown

83 Thames Street, KT13 8LP (off A317)
10-11; 12-10.30 Sun
☎ (01932) 842844
Courage Best Bitter, Directors; Young's Bitter; guest beer Ⓗ
Attractive, Grade II-listed, 17th-century weatherboarded pub sited at the confluence of the rivers Thames and Wey. There is access to the pub for small boats. The interior is divided into four wood-panelled areas, each with a different feel. The conservatory at the rear of the lounge is no-smoking. The garden overlooks the river. An interesting range of food is served at this welcoming family-run pub (no eve meals Sun-Tue).
Q P

Windlesham

Bee

School Road, GU20 6PD (on B386)
12-11; 12-10.30 Sun
☎ (01276) 479244
Courage Best Bitter; Hogs Back TEA; Hop Back Summer Lightning; Young's Bitter; guest beer Ⓗ
The present landlord bought this pub several years ago and since then it has featured every year in the Good Beer Guide. A simple country pub on the outskirts of the village, it offers four regular cask ales and a guest. A range of hot and cold traditional pub food is served (not Sun eve or Mon). In the summer much use is made of the garden, equipped with a barbecue and children's play area. It hosts occasional live music, including outdoor jazz in the summer.
(500)P

Half Moon

Church Road, GU20 6BN (off B386)
11-3, 5.30-11.30; 12-4, 7-11 Sun
(01276) 473329
Hogs Back TEA; Hop Back Summer Lightning; Sharp's Doom Bar; Taylor Landlord; Theakston Old Peculier; guest beer H
A true free house, owned by the Sturt family since 1909. Set in rural Surrey, the pub has a large garden including a Wendy house for children and a slide. Complete refurbishment of the cellar in 2005 has ensured the quality of the five regular ales and one guest. The pub also has a reputation for good traditional English food including game shot locally (no food Sun eve). Wheelchair access is excellent. Q (500)P

Witley

White Hart

Petworth Road, GU8 5PH (on A283)
11-3.30, 5.30-11; 12-3.30, 7-10.30 Sun
(01428) 683695
Shepherd Neame Master Brew Bitter, Spitfire, seasonal beers H
First licensed in 1700, the inn was originally used as a hunting lodge by Richard III. Warm and welcoming to all including dogs, there is a comfortable lounge and a cosy side bar with TV and fire. The dining room serves good quality home-made food (not Sun eve). There are rumoured to be three ghosts haunting the building – note the drawing of two of them by a psychic investigator in the public bar. The garden has a climbing frame and roundabout. (71)

Woking

Wetherspoons

51-57 Chertsey Road, GU21 5AJ
9am-11.30 (12.30am Fri & Sat); 9am-11.30 Sun
(01483) 722818
Courage Directors; Hogs Back TEA; Marston's Burton Bitter, Pedigree; Shepherd Neame Spitfire; guest beers H
One of the best in the Wetherspoon's chain, with friendly and efficient staff dispensing four rapidly changing guests. With an ideal town-centre location handy for the railway station and bus bays, the pub is unofficially known as the 'waiting room'. The theme is HG Wells – note the invisible man and the time machine clock that goes backwards on the ceiling operated by a push button. Though lively and bustling, particularly at weekends, a retreat can always be found in the no-smoking area. Q

Woodham

Victoria

427 Woodham Lane, KT15 3QE (on B385)
11-11; 12-10.30 Sun
(01932) 345365
Greene King IPA; Harveys Sussex Best Bitter; guest beers H
Large pub split into drinking and dining areas. Up to four cask ales are usually available, sometimes fewer in quiet times to maintain quality. A welcome local outlet for Harveys, the guests are often unusual for the area. Good food includes a carvery on Saturday evening and Sunday lunchtime. Quiz night is Sunday. The inn's sign features the Penny Black stamp.
(West Byfleet) (P1,472)P

Wood Street

Royal Oak

89 Oak Hill, GU3 3DA
11-3 (3.30 Sat), 5-11; 12-3.30, 7-10.30 Sun
(01483) 235137
Courage Best Bitter; Hogs Back TEA; guest beers H
Welcoming free house with a local reputation for being the best around. An ever-changing selection of beers is dispensed via the four guest pumps, in a range of strengths, with a mild always available. Pump clips above the bar indicate forthcoming beers to look forward to. Thatchers cider is available straight from the tub. Popular lunchtime food (Mon-Sat) is highly recommended. A large back garden has swings for children and is a pleasant spot to relax in warmer weather.
(16,17) P

Wrecclesham

Sandrock

Sandrock Hill, Boundstone, GU10 4NS (off B3384)
OS830444
12-11; 12-10.30 Sun
(01252) 715865 thesandrock.com
Batham Best Bitter; guest beers H
Small, two-roomed pub in the south of Farnham. Eight regularly changing real ales are excuse enough to visit this Good Beer Guide stalwart, but now there is the added benefit of award-winning home-cooked food (no food Sun eve). However, good beer remains the focal point of the pub. There is an excellent bar billiards table in one of the rooms and live music is sometimes hosted.
Q P

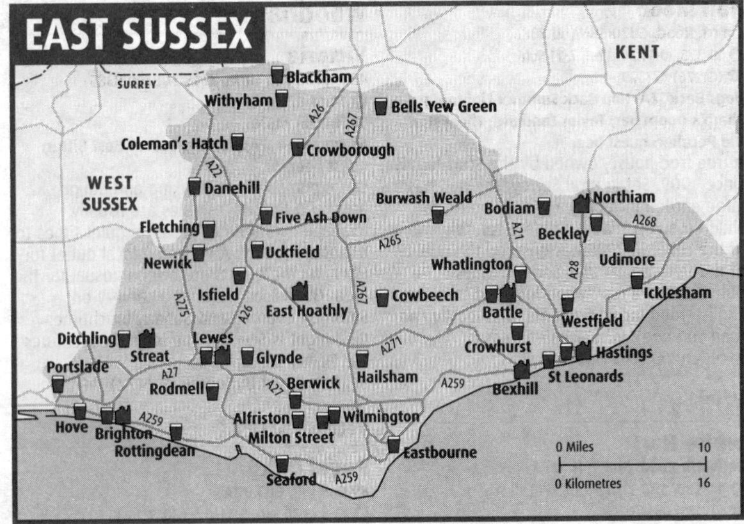

SUSSEX (EAST)

Alfriston

Smugglers Inn

Waterloo Square, BN26 5UE (by market cross)
☼ 11-2.30 (3 Sat), 6.30-11; 12-3, 7-10.30 Sun
☎ (01323) 870241
Courage Directors; Harveys Sussex Best Bitter, XXX Old Ale; White seasonal beers ⊞
This comfortable old-fashioned village inn dating from the mid-14th century has a relaxed atmosphere, free from electronic noise. The main bar area has been recently restored to its full glory after a car crashed into the front entrance. An impressive inglenook, hops and horse race day tickets stuck on the beams, give the pub a country feel. Good value, tasty bar food is available. It draws walkers on the South Downs Way and other visitors to this popular village.
Q❀◑▶🚌⁄

Battle

Chequers Inn

Lower Lake, TN33 0AT (on A2100/Marley Lane jct)
☼ 11-11 (midnight Fri & Sat); 11-10.30 Sun
☎ (01424) 772088
Fuller's London Pride; Harveys Sussex Best Bitter; guest beers ⊞
This 15th-century inn south of the High Street features exposed beams and open fires. The no-smoking dining room boasts a large inglenook. The terrace, to the rear of the pub, is pleasant and in summer hosts occasional concerts by local brass bands. The back garden overlooks the Hastings battlefield.
♨❀◑▶⇌🚌♣P

Beckley

Rose & Crown

Northiam Road, TN31 6SE (opp. B2188/B2165 jct)
☼ 11-12.30am; 12-11.30 Sun
☎ (01797) 252161
Fuller's ESB; Harveys Sussex Best Bitter; Taylor Landlord; guest beers ⊞
Well established free house situated at the western end of this long village. Loyally supported by locals, it attracts a good mix of drinkers and diners. A choice of four or five beers makes this rural gem a must for visitors and villagers alike, dogs are most welcome. ♨Q❀◑▶♣P

Bells Yew Green

Brecknock Arms

TN3 9BJ
☼ 12-3, 5.30-11; 12-3, 7-10.30 (not winter eve) Sun
☎ (01892) 750237
Harveys Hadlow Bitter, Sussex Best Bitter ⊞
Good, traditional ale house dating from the 1850s, serving excellent beer and good quality food. The public and saloon bars are both small and comfortable with open fires. Recently refurbished with Harveys Brewery pictures adorning the walls of the no-smoking saloon bar, home-made pies are a speciality on a varied food menu. Very much the hub of the community, it supports the local cricket team. ♨Q❀◑▶⇌P⁄

Berwick

Cricketers' Arms

BN26 6SP (S of A27, W of Drusilla's roundabout)
☼ 11-3, 6-11; 11-11 Sat & Mon-Fri summer; 12-10.30 Sun
☎ (01323) 870469 🌐 cricketersberwick.co.uk
Harveys Sussex Best Bitter, Armada Ale, seasonal beers Ⓖ
Once two cottages, and a pub since the 18th century, it was extended in 1981 in keeping with its original character. Harveys beers are served straight from the cask. There is plenty of room to sit in the pleasant gardens in summer or by the real fires in the bars in the winter. A popular stop for walkers on the nearby South Downs, toad in the hole can be played here. Meals are served all day at the weekend (12-9pm).
♨Q❀◑▶♣P⁄

Blackham

Sussex Oak

TN3 9UA (on A264)
✪ 11-3, 6-11; 12-3, 6.30-10.30 Sun
☎ (01892) 740273
Shepherd Neame Master Brew Bitter, Kent's Best, Spitfire Ⓗ
Excellent country pub, the Sussex Oak was a deserved winner of the local CAMRA Pub of the Year award in 2003. It is run by a friendly couple who offer a good range of meals, often with an Asian or Irish accent to reflect their origins. It hosts occasional food themed nights, however, the pub is worth seeking out at any time for a quiet pint.
Q ❀ ◐ ⇌ (Ashurst)P

Bodiam

Castle

TN32 5UB (opp. castle entrance)
✪ 11-3, 6-11; (11-11 summer Sat); 12-10.30 Sun
☎ (01580) 830330
Shepherd Neame Master Brew Bitter, Spitfire, seasonal beers Ⓗ
Rural Shepherd Neame pub in the scenic Rother Valley on the Kent border. Bodiam Castle, the impressive NT property, is opposite. An extensive menu, featuring local produce, is displayed in the main bar above the imposing fireplace. This pleasant pub is ideal for a peaceful pint.
Q ❀ ◐ ⇌ (Kent & E Sussex Rlwy) P

Brighton

Basketmakers Arms

12 Gloucester Road, BN1 4AD
✪ 11-11.30 (12.30am Thu-Sat); 12-11.30 Sun
☎ (01273) 689006
Fuller's London Pride, Gale's Butser, HSB, seasonal beers Ⓗ
Corner local by the North Laine area of the city. Prior to takeover by Fuller's, this was a Gale's tied house, and still usually stocks most of the Gale's range, together with seasonal beers and Fuller's guest beers. It also keeps an extensive selection of malt whiskies. This establishment is convenient for theatres and is popular for its good quality and value food. ◐ ⇌

Battle of Trafalgar

34 Guildford Road, BN1 3LW
✪ 12-11 (midnight Fri & Sat); 12-11 Sun
☎ (01273) 327997
Fuller's London Pride; Harveys Sussex Best Bitter; guest beers Ⓗ
Popular pub, a short walk up a steep hill from the station. Four handpumps serve regular and guest ales. The small frontage is deceptive for the size and shape of this pub. The decor features pictures of old sea battles and other nautical memorabilia. Live music is sometimes staged (Sun eve); background music (jazz or blues) is kept at a sensible level. Weekend meals are served 12-5pm. ❀ ◐ ⇌

Bugle

24 St Martin's Street, BN2 3HJ
✪ 4 (3 Fri; 12 Sat)-11 (midnight Fri & Sat); 12-11 Sun
☎ (01273) 607753
Fuller's London Pride; Harveys Sussex Best Bitter, Armada Ale Ⓗ
Two-bar local with a strong Irish influence, displaying pictures of Irish authors. The courtyard is a suntrap. Live music is performed (Wed eve and Sun afternoon). Situated west of the busy Lewes Road, parking is extremely difficult here. A good Brighton mix of students and other local residents frequent this pub. Children are welcome until 8.30pm.

Cobblers Thumb

10 New England Road, BN1 4GG
✪ 12-midnight daily
☎ (01273) 605636
Harveys Sussex Best Bitter; Wells Bombardier; Young's Waggledance; guest beers Ⓗ
Although based on an Australian theme, the pub retains the appearance of a traditional, street-corner local. Note the old name of the New England Inn on the outside. The interior still bears the original fittings, and old-fashioned adverts adorn the walls. A quiet games room lies off the main bar area to the rear and live music is performed weekly. Coopers Sparkling Ales feature in the range of bottled beers on sale. ❀ ♣

Dover Castle

43 Southover Street, BN2 9UE
✪ 12-11.30 (midnight Fri & Sat); 12-11.30 Sun
☎ (01273) 688276 dovercastle.co.uk
Shepherd Neame Kent's Best, Bishops Finger, seasonal beers Ⓗ
Corner pub that has been modernised, but not ruined, at the heart of the Hanover area. It is popular with all ages. Various items of local art and sculpture can be purchased here. A DJ or live music can be enjoyed on Friday and Saturday evenings. The menu features both traditional and Eurasian dishes. At the rear is a walled garden with a covered heated area where supervised children are permitted. ❀ ◐ ♿ (37) ♣ ⅟

Evening Star

55-56 Surrey Street, BN1 3PB (400 yds S of station)
✪ 12 (11.30 Sat)-11 (midnight Fri & Sat); 12-11 Sun
☎ (01273) 328931 eveningstarbrighton.co.uk
Dark Star Hophead, Original, seasonal beers; guest beers Ⓗ
Deserved winner of Regional CAMRA Pub of the Year 2005, free from pool tables, fruit machines or TV, this is a must for any beer-loving tourist to Brighton. Alongside Dark Star's own beers, real ciders and guest ales can be sampled, together with foreign beers on draught and in bottles. Live music is performed most Sundays and occasional

INDEPENDENT BREWERIES

1648 East Hoathly
Fallen Angel Battle
Filo Hastings
Harveys Lewes
Kemptown Brighton
Rectory Streat
Rother Valley Northiam
White Bexhill

beer festivals are held. Filled rolls are available at lunchtime. ❀◖⇌⊟●

Lord Nelson

36 Trafalgar Street, BN1 4ED (near station)
✪ 11-midnight (1am Fri & Sat); 12-11 Sun
☎ (01273) 695872 🌐 thelordnelsoninn.co.uk
Harveys Sussex XX Mild, Hadlow Bitter, Best Bitter, Armada Ale, seasonal beers Ⓗ
Friendly pub in the North Laine area: two small bars, the right-hand one leads through to a back room then a conservatory drinking area that doubles as a gallery for local artists – note the tree growing in the middle! The left-hand bar has a pull-down screen for sports. The pub features regularly on the local CAMRA ale trail. Children are welcome until 8pm. ♨♉◖⇌⊟♣●

Prestonville Arms

64 Hamilton Road, BN1 5DN
✪ 5-11; 12-midnight Fri & Sat; 12-11 Sun
☎ (01273) 701007
Fuller's London Pride, Gale's Butser, HSB, seasonal beers Ⓗ
Street-corner local on a triangular site in a residential area – its bar is on two levels, reflecting its hilly location. There is a no-smoking area on the upper level, which leads to a pleasant garden patio. It hosts a music quiz on Tuesday and a general knowledge one on Sunday. It offers a good choice of well-presented, home-cooked food. ❀◖◗⇌⚟

Sir Charles Napier

50 Southover Street, BN2 9UE
✪ 4-11; 3-12.30am Fri; 12-12.30am Sat; 12-11 Sun
☎ (01273) 601413
Fuller's London Pride, Gale's Best, HSB, seasonal beers; guest beers Ⓗ
Traditional, friendly street-corner local in the Hanover area of the city. It displays items relating to Admiral Sir Charles Napier. One of the most popular pub quizzes in the city is held every Sunday evening. It also stages various theme nights, such as St George's, St Patrick's and Beaujolais Nouveau night. The good value Sunday lunches are popular. The rear, walled garden gets a lot of usage in summer. Q❀♿⊟♣

Burwash Weald

Wheel Inn

Heathfield Road, TN19 7LA (on A265)
✪ 12-11; 12-10.30 Sun
☎ (01435) 882758
Harveys Sussex Best Bitter; guest beers Ⓗ
Large, popular village pub with a car park and garden. The pub comprises a games room, a spacious bar and a restaurant. The beers change every week. The pub hosts weekly events, such as live music and quizzes, and a monthly curry night. Pool and bar billiards can be played here. ♨❀◖◗♿⛺♣P

Colemans Hatch

Hatch Inn

TN7 4EJ (400 yds S of B2110) OS452335
✪ 11.30-2.30, 5.30-11 (11-11 summer Sat); 12-10.30 Sun
☎ (01342) 822363 🌐 hatchinn.co.uk
Harveys Sussex Best Bitter; Larkins Traditional; guest beers Ⓗ
Originally three cottages dating from the 15th century, it has been a pub for the past 200 years. Inside the attractive, weatherboarded exterior is a cosy bar, with scrubbed tables and low beams. Convenient for Ashdown Forest (Winnie the Pooh country), the pub is much appreciated by walkers, diners and drinkers. A recent addition is a pair of Concorde seats. Local breweries are well supported. No food is served Monday evening. ♨Q❀◖◗P⚟

Cowbeech

Merrie Harriers

BN27 4JQ (off A271, NE of Hailsham)
✪ 11.30-3 (4 Sat), 6-11; 12-4, 6-10.30 Sun
☎ (01323) 833108 🌐 merrieharriers.co.uk
Harveys Sussex Best Bitter; guest beers Ⓗ
Dating from the 1620s and Grade II listed, this traditional village pub serves excellent food, sourced locally where possible, and freshly prepared. The public bar features an inglenook, the lounge bar is set for diners; both have beamed ceilings. The no-smoking restaurant overlooks the garden, which slopes down into the Weald. The guest beer is often from WJ King. ♨Q❀◖◗♿P

Crowborough

Coopers Arms

Coopers Lane, TN6 1SN (follow St. John's Rd from Crowborough Cross for ½ mile)
✪ 12-2.30 (not Mon or Tue; 12-3 Sat), 6 (5.30 Fri)-11; 12-3, 6-11 Sun
☎ (01892) 654796
Greene King IPA; guest beers Ⓗ
Hidden gem, serving first class real ale, including many old favourites as well as new brews sourced from all over the country. The decor is simple, and being improved all the time – a dining room is the latest addition and meals are excellent. Regular themed beer festivals with live music are held; milds are featured throughout May and it offers a continental bottled beer menu. ❀◖♿⛺♣P

Wheatsheaf

Mount Pleasant, Jarvis Brook, TN6 2NF
✪ 12-11 (12-3, 5-11 Mon); 12-10.30 Sun
☎ (01892) 663756
Harveys Sussex XX Mild, Hadlow Bitter, Best Bitter, Armada Ale, seasonal beers Ⓗ
The recently updated central square bar now serves all Harveys regular ales. There are three distinct drinking areas, one of which is no-smoking at lunchtime, when good quality meals are served. A popular late May bank holiday beer festival is held in a marquee in the landscaped garden, and the pub also hosts monthly live music.
♨Q❀◖◗♿⇌⊟♣P

Crowhurst

Plough Inn

TN33 9AW (1 mile from station)
✪ 11-2.30, 6-11; 11.30-midnight Sat; 12-4, 6-11 Sun
☎ (01424) 830310

Harveys Sussex Best Bitter, Armada Ale, seasonal beers; guest beer (occasional) Ⓗ
Excellent village local; a free house that chooses to sell Harveys ales, with an occasional guest beer from local micros. It has a small restaurant and a no-smoking area. This pub supports local sports teams and the rest of the community well. Toad in the hold and boules are played here. Live music is sometimes performed in the bar.
♛Q✿◐♣P⊁

Danehill

Coach & Horses

School Lane, RH17 7JF (off A275)
✪ 12-3, 6-11; 12-4, 7-10.30 Sun
☎ (01825) 740369
Harveys Sussex Best Bitter; guest beers Ⓗ
This rural, two-bar free house boasts an award-winning restaurant. The large front garden has a children's play area, but the rear patio is just for adults. The guest beers change regularly and can include some unusual beers. The pub is convenient for Ashdown Forest, Sheffield Park Gardens and the Bluebell Railway. No food is served Sunday evening. ♛Q✿◐⊟▲▣(270)P

Ditchling

White Horse

16 West Street, BN6 8TS
✪ 11-11; 12-10.30 Sun
☎ (01273) 842006
Harveys Sussex Best Bitter; guest beers Ⓗ
This Guide regular is a family-run free house dating from the 16th century. It is situated opposite the village church, close to the Anne of Cleve's house. A dining room is available, but meals may be taken in the bar. A dedicated games area can be found at the back of the pub. Occasional live music is played here. ✿◐▣♣

Eastbourne

Buccaneer

10 Compton Street, BN21 4BW
✪ 11-11; 12-10.30 Sun
☎ (01323) 732829
Draught Bass; Greene King Abbot; Tetley Bitter; guest beers Ⓗ
Large, open pub situated at the heart of Eastbourne's theatreland. Always welcoming, it offers a choice of five or six real ales, including three changing guests. The pub is popular at all times of the day, attracting a good mix of locals and visitors. The front bar is decorated with old theatre posters of past productions. The raised, no-smoking seated area at the back overlooks Devonshire Park.
◐⇌▣⊁

Hurst Arms

76 Willingdon Road, BN21 1TW (on A2270)
✪ 11-11; 12-10.30 Sun
☎ (01323) 721762
Harveys Sussex Best Bitter, Armada Ale, seasonal beers Ⓗ
Friendly, Victorian local with two bars: a lively public with pool, darts, a wide-screen TV and a juke box; and a homely lounge that feels like someone's front room. Harveys beers are served to an unfailing high standard, confirmed by the brewery's Cellar of the Year award. A quiet rear garden is supplemented by a front patio by the road.
Q✿⊟♿

Lamb

36 High Street, B21 1HH (old town, A259)
✪ 10.30-11 (midnight Fri & Sat); 10.30-11 Sun
☎ (01323) 720545
Harveys Hadlow Bitter, Sussex Best Bitter, Armada Ale, seasonal beers Ⓗ
Dating from 1180, this unspoilt landmark in the old town has three bars, one of which is partly arranged as a restaurant. The other two – public and lounge – both have oak beamed ceilings, with bare boards and carpeting respectively. The menu offers a good range of freshly-prepared food, with frequently-changing specials.
♛Q◐⊟♿⇌▣

Five Ash Down

Fireman's Arms

TN22 3AN (200 yds from A26)
✪ 11.30-3, 5-11; 11-11 Sat; 12-10.30 Sun
☎ (01825) 732191
Courage Directors; Harveys Sussex Best Bitter Ⓗ
Recently refurbished and redecorated two-bar village local. An extensive menu, representing good value and quality, is served in the bar area or the no-smoking restaurant. There is a monthly quiz (first Tue) and open mike music sessions (last Tue). The bar is decorated with paddle steamer and railway memorabilia. Biddenden cider is sold. ♛✿◐⊟♿▣●P

Fletching

Griffin Inn

TN22 3SS
✪ 12-11 (midnight Fri & Sat); 12-11 Sun
☎ (01825) 722890
⊕ thegriffininn.co.uk
Badger Tanglefoot; Harveys Sussex Best Bitter; King Horsham Best Bitter Ⓗ
A bit of a legend in Fletching, attracting visitors from far and wide for its restaurant food and four-poster beds. The cosy, low-ceiling bar areas, joined by an interesting back corridor, offer a mix of comfortable and practical furniture. The large back garden faces Sheffield Park. Live jazz Friday evening and Sunday lunchtime helps pack the place.
♛Q✿⇔◐⊟▲P

Glynde

Trevor Arms

The Street, BN8 6SS (over bridge from station)
✪ 11-11; 12-10.30 Sun
☎ (01273) 858208
Harveys Sussex Best Bitter, seasonal beers Ⓗ
Village pub of four rooms (including two no-smoking areas), this Harveys tied house serves good quality and value food at all sessions. Vintage car owners regularly gather at the pub and the locality is popular with

walkers. Glyndebourne is close by, and impromptu music performed by musicians from the opera house may be heard in the garden on summer Sundays.
Q❀◑◗⇌🚌♣P⚟

Hailsham

Grenadier

67 High Street, BN27 1AS (on A295)
✪ 11-11 (11.30 Fri & Sat); 12-10.30 Sun
☎ (01323) 842152 ⊕ thegrenny.com
Harveys Sussex XX Mild, Sussex Best Bitter, seasonal beers Ⓗ
This 200-year-old pub was used by the Grenadier Guards as a drinking house. Since Harveys refurbished the exterior in 2003 the splendid sign of a Grenadier makes a fine feature. Traditional games – toad in the hole, shove-ha'penny, table skittles and darts – are played in the public bar while the saloon has a quieter, more relaxed atmosphere. A large play area for children is provided in the garden. ❀◑⊟♿🚌♣P

Hastings

First In Last Out

14 High Street, Old Town, TN34 3ET
✪ 11-11; 12-10.30 Sun
☎ (01424) 425079 ⊕ thefilo.co.uk
FILO Crofters, Ginger Tom, Cardinal (winter), Gold (summer) Ⓗ
Home of the FILO Brewery since 1985, four beers are usually available. The large bar is heated by an attractive open log fire in the centre, and has plenty of alcove-style seating. Organic, freshly-cooked food is available Tuesday-Saturday. The pub hosts a beer festival most bank holidays.
⌂Q◑Å🚌♣

White Rock Hotel

1-10 White Rock, TN34 1JU (on A259)
✪ 10-11; 12-10.30 Sun
☎ (01424) 422240 ⊕ thewhiterockhotel.co.uk
Harvey's Sussex Best Bitter; Rother Valley Boadicea Ⓗ
This is a completely no-smoking bar, next to the theatre and opposite the pier. The bar, part of the hotel, offers ample seating areas and a spacious terrace. It serves beers from Sussex independent breweries, including 1648, Dark Star and White. A range of freshly-prepared food is available, starting with a popular full breakfast.
Q❀🛏◑♿⇌🚌⚟

Hove

Downsman

189 Hangleton Way, BN3 8ES (by Dyke Railway Trail)
✪ 11-4, 6-11; 12-4, 7-11 Sun
☎ (01273) 711301
Harveys Sussex Best Bitter; Itchen Valley Fagin's; guest beers Ⓗ
This 1950s building is like a country pub in a suburban environment. Extensively refurbished over the last six years, this friendly, family-run pub comprises two large bars and a dining area (no eve meals Sun). Archaeological excavations during construction found the remains of two medieval cottages from the lost village of Hangleton. These were reconstructed as one cottage at the Weald and Downland Museum. ⌂❀◑◗⊟♿🚌♣P

Neptune

10 Victoria Terrace, Kingsway, BN3 2WB
✪ 12-1am (2am Fri & Sat); 12-midnight Sun
☎ (01273) 324870 ⊕ theneptunelivemusicbar.co.uk
Dark Star Hophead; Greene King Abbot; Harveys Sussex Best Bitter; guest beer Ⓗ
This popular pub stages live music on Friday and Sunday evenings. It has one long, narrow bar, having been knocked through from three small bars in the 1960s. Originally a ship's chandlers, and at about 150 years old, it is one of Hove's oldest pubs. Music photos and posters cover the walls. The rest of the decor is quite basic, with bare boards, rugs and dark, wood-panelled walls. ♿🚌♣

Sussex Cricketer

Eaton Road, BN3 3AF (at entrance to cricket ground)
✪ 12-11 (midnight Thu-Sat); 11-11 Sun
☎ (01273) 771645
Greene King Old Speckled Hen; Harveys Sussex Best Bitter; guest beers Ⓗ
Although located within the Sussex County ground there is no cricketing memorabilia in this open-plan single bar pub, which is part of the Ember Inns chain. Instead there are local prints on the walls, flame-effect fires and comfy seating. At least three real ales are offered plus a wide (but pricey) range of wines and a typical pub chain food menu. Parking is available if there is no cricket match. ❀◑◗♿🚌⚟

Icklesham

Queen's Head

Parsonage Lane, TN36 4BL (off A259, opp. village hall)
✪ 11-11; 12-10.30 Sun
☎ (01424) 814552 ⊕ queenshead.com
Beer range varies Ⓗ
Welcoming country inn, slightly off the beaten track, but still busy. It stocks five or six varied ales of increasing strength, which combined with excellent, affordable meals, make this a must to visit. Built in 1632, this cosy, timber-framed building with three log fires, benefits from superb views over Brede Valley. Live music is performed at local CAMRA's Pub of the Year 2005.
⌂❀◑◗🚌♣●P⚟♢

Isfield

Laughing Fish

Station Road, TN22 5XB (2 miles S of Uckfield)
✪ 11.30-11 daily
☎ (01825) 750349 ⊕ laughingfishonline.co.uk
Greene King IPA, Morland Original; guest beers Ⓗ
Comfortable, Victorian pub next to the Lavender Line railway station; both are well worth a visit. There are drinking and dining areas available for non-smokers. The well-kept garden includes a children's play space. A popular pub on local CAMRA's ale trail,

good food is served, (no eve meals Sun). Look for the laughing fish etched into the porch window. ⋒Q❀◐◑⛺♣P⊬

Lewes

Brewers Arms
91 High Street, BN7 1XN
⏲ 10-11; 12-10.30 Sun
☎ (01273) 479475
Harveys Sussex Best Bitter; guest beers Ⓗ
Two bar pub; in the rear bar, which houses a juke box, you are allowed to smoke. It features a sports mural on the wall alongside pictures of old Lewes and a display of shotgun cartridges. Traditional pub games, including toad in the hole and shut the box, are played here. Biddenden cider is served. Evening meals finish at 6.45pm.
◐◑⇌🚌♣●⊬

Elephant & Castle
White Hill, BN7 2DJ (off Fisher St)
⏲ 11.30-11.30; 12-11 Sun
☎ (01273) 473797
Harveys Sussex Best Bitter; guest beers Ⓗ
The only building on White Hill, it stocks an unusual range of guest beers, such as Black Sheep. The pub tends to draw a young clientele. Local organic produce is incorporated in the menu where possible, including their burgers and specials. Around the building are various stuffed and mounted animal heads. Obliging staff make this pub well worth finding. ⋒◐⇌🚌♣●

Gardener's Arms
46 Cliffe High Street, BN7 2AN
⏲ 11-11; 12-10.30 Sun
☎ (01273) 474808 🌐 gardenersarmslewes.com
Harveys Sussex Best Bitter; guest beers Ⓗ
This is a genuine free house, situated in Cliffe, close to the River Ouse and Harveys Brewery. It is run by a football-loving landlord whose strong allegiances are evident in the pub. Normally six real ales and Black Rat cider are available in this pub that was runner-up in local CAMRA's Pub of the Year 2005. It is five minutes' walk from Lewes bus station. 🚌♣●

Lewes Arms
1 Mount Place, BN7 1YH
⏲ 11-11 (midnight Fri & Sat); 11-11 Sun
☎ (01273) 473152
Greene King IPA, Abbot; Harveys Sussex Best Bitter Ⓗ
Historic, unspoilt, curved-fronted pub built into the castle ramparts. A small front public bar complements a rear saloon bar. There is a games room where children are allowed until 8pm and darts and toad in the hole can be played. The function room is home to the local folk club. Mobile phones are banned but dogs are welcome. Biddendens cider is stocked. ⋒Q❀◐⊟⇌🚌♣●

Milton Street

Sussex Ox
BN26 5RL (signed off A27) OS534041
⏲ 11-3, 6-11; 12-3, 6-10.30 (12-5 winter) Sun
☎ (01323) 870840 🌐 thesussexox.co.uk
Dark Star Hophead; Harveys Sussex Best Bitter; guest beer Ⓗ
Superb country pub, deep into the South Downs near the Long Man of Wilmington. A traditional wooden interior offers a small continental-style bar with plenty of seating to the side plus a dining room. The real ale is always in tip-top condition, with golden ales to the fore. The bar and restaurant food is high quality. This pub provides the perfect escape from the rigours of modern life, with a laid-back atmosphere.
⋒❀◐◑P⊬

Newick

Royal Oak
1 Church Road, BN8 4JU
⏲ 11-11; 12-10.30 Sun
☎ (01825) 722506
Fuller's London Pride; Harveys Sussex Best Bitter, seasonal beers Ⓗ
Warm, friendly, 16th-century local in the beautiful village of Newick. This oak-beamed pub features an exposed wattle and daub panel between the bars. A roomy public bar connects to a cosy saloon area, featuring a large inglenook and a further dining area. A good range of home-made traditional pub food is served (not Sun eve). The local cricket club is based here. Dogs are welcome. Stowford Press cider is sold.
⋒Q❀◐◑⊟🚌(31, 121)♣●P

Portslade

Stanley Arms
47 Wolsley Road, BN41 1SS
⏲ 2 (12 Sat)-11; 12-10.30 Sun
☎ (01273) 430234 🌐 thestanley.com
Beer range varies Ⓗ
Genuine, family-run free house offering a varied range of beers, mainly from small and micro-breweries on four handpumps. Ten bottled Belgian beers (£2 on Mon) plus Westons perry and bottled organic cider are on sale. Three beer festivals are held in February, June and September. A small garden hosts barbecues. A large plasma TV shows many sporting events. Although mainly a quiet pub, it does stage regular live music. Children are welcome until 8pm.
⋒Q☺❀⊟⇌(Fishersgate)🚌(2, 46)♣▯

Rodmell

Abergavenny Arms
Newhaven Road, BN7 3EZ
⏲ 11-3, 5.30-11; 11-11 Sat; 12-11 Sun
☎ (01273) 472416 🌐 abergavennyarms.com
Harveys Sussex Best Bitter; guest beers Ⓗ
Once a Domesday-listed Sussex barn, the oak timbers are from wrecks of the Spanish Armada. The spacious no-smoking bar area features a large fireplace and an array of china mugs and memorabilia. There is a larger, split-level dining area, and a public bar where smoking is permitted. It hosts occasional Sunday quizzes. Popular with walkers, dogs are welcome.
⋒Q❀◐◑⊟⛺🚌(123)♣P⊬

Rottingdean

Black Horse

65 High Street, BN2 7HE (off A259)
⌚ 10.30-11; 12-10.30 Sun
☎ (01273) 302581 🌐 theblackhorse.co.uk
Greene King IPA, Abbot, seasonal beers ⊞
Friendly, 16th-century local in an attractive seaside village, three miles east of Brighton. The large public bar is connected to a spacious, split-level saloon via a small, no-smoking snug. No food is served but sandwiches purchased form the nearby bakery may be consumed. Both bars have TV for major sporting events. ⊟⊡♣⊬

St Leonards

Bull

530 Bexhill Road, TN38 8AY (on A259)
⌚ 12-11; 12-10.30 Sun
☎ (01424) 424984 🌐 the-bull-inn.com
Shepherd Neame Master Brew Bitter, Kent's Best, Spitfire, seasonal beers ⊞
Welcoming roadside pub, noted for its range of Shepherd Neame beers. This local also offers an excellent menu (book at weekends; no food Sun eve). There is a dining room and a car park at the rear, which offers much more space than appears at first. The large rear garden has barbecue facilities. The pub is convenient for the Glynde Gap shops. ⌂Q◐◑♿⊡♣P

Dripping Spring

34 Tower Road, TN37 6JE (off A2100)
⌚ 11-11 daily
☎ (01424) 434055 🌐 thedrippingspring.com
Adnams Broadside; Harveys Sussex Best Bitter; Young's Bitter; guest beers ⊞
This treasured pub, tucked away in the bohemian part of St Leonards, is a must for real ale fans. Serving seven different real ales at any one time, it caters for all tastes. Beer festivals are planned throughout the year with beers served from the cellar and old bakery in an enclosed patio at cellar level. The cider is from Biddenden.
Q❀⇌(Warrior Sq)⊡♣●

Horse & Groom

4 Mercatoria, TN38 0EB
⌚ 11-11; 12-10.30 Sun
☎ (01424) 420612 🌐 sussex200.com
Adnams Broadside; Greene King IPA; Harveys Sussex Best Bitter; Rother Valley Boadicea ⊞
This is St Leonards' first pub, built in 1829. A first-class free house it is welcoming and comfortable, with olde-worlde charm and manners. A horseshoe-shaped bar serves two separate bars, with a further quieter room to the rear. A good selection of lunchtime food is served Monday-Saturday. The little patio is useful in summer.
Q❀◐⇌(Warrior Sq)⊡

Seaford

Wellington

33 Steyne Road, BN25 1HT (200 yds from seafront)
⌚ 11-11 (midnight Fri & Sat); 11-11 Sun
☎ (01323) 890032
Greene King IPA, Abbot, Old Speckled Hen; Harveys Sussex Best Bitter; guest beers ⊞
Situated in the old part of the town, facing what was once the harbour of this ancient Cinque Port, the Wellington has a spacious, comfortably furnished saloon bar, a small public bar with a TV showing sporting events, and a well-appointed, no-smoking room where children are allowed. It is one of a few Greene King pubs still offering Harveys as a guest, and is well worth seeking out. Evening meals are served Monday-Thursday. Some pavement seating is provided. ⌂Q☋❀◐◑⊟⇌⊡♣⊬

Uckfield

Alma

Framfield Road, TN22 5AJ (on B2102)
⌚ 11-3, 5-11; 11-11 Fri & Sat; 12-10.30 Sun
☎ (01825) 762232
Harveys Sussex XX Mild, Sussex Best Bitter, XXXX Old Ale, seasonal beers ⊞
Now under new management, this pleasant pub continues to serve a good selection of Harveys beers. There is a public bar where games are played, including shove-ha'penny, and a darts team flourishes. The saloon is comfortable and has a small no-smoking area. There is a little garden next to the car park. The pub is roughly five minutes' walk from the town centre, station and bus routes. Food is now served on Sunday with popular roast lunches (no food on Tue lunchtime or Sat eve).
❀◐◑⊟♿⇌⊡♣P⊬

Udimore

King's Head

Rye Road, TN31 6BG (on B2089, W of village)
⌚ 11-4 (not winter Mon), 5.30-11; 12-4, 7-10.30 (not winter) Sun
☎ (01424) 882349
Harveys Sussex Best Bitter; guest beers ⊞
Built in 1535, and extended in the 17th century, this traditional village ale house boasts exposed beams, two open fires and a very long bar, that was installed in the 1930s and has to be seen (and leant on) to be believed. The pub serves excellent, home-cooked food and has a no-smoking dining room (lunches Tue-Sun; eve meals Mon-Sat). Situated in an area of outstanding natural beauty, there are many scenic walks nearby. ⌂Q☋❀◐◑♿♣P

Westfield

Old Courthouse

Main Road, TN35 4QE
⌚ 12-11; 12-10.30 Sun
☎ (01424) 751603 🌐 oldcourthousepub.co.uk
Harveys Sussex Best Bitter; guest beers ⊞
The pub is central to the village and community-focused. The main bar, with open fire and low ceilings, has traditional games, together with the unusual ten pin billiards. There is a smaller, no-smoking bar. Hot food is served all day (except Wed, and winter Sun eve). A roast of the day is served Sunday lunchtime, and the first Friday of

each month is curry night. A mini-beer festival is held over August bank holiday weekend.

Whatlington

Royal Oak

Woodmans Green, TN33 0NJ (on A21)
11-11 (10.30 Mon); 12-10.30 Sun
(01424) 870492 whatlington.com
Harveys Sussex Best Bitter; guest beers
Excellent, weatherboarded roadside inn, five miles from Hastings. Mind your head on the low ceilings – there are many beams in its split-level interior. The restaurant area is no-smoking; a deep indoor well is an unusual feature and a splendid large inglenook holds a roaring log fire in winter. It hosts occasional music sessions, the highlight being the wassail in January that involves toasting the health of the apple tree. Good food is served from an extensive menu.

Wilmington

Giant's Rest

The Street, BN26 5SQ (off A27)
11-3, 6-11; 11-11 Sat; 12-10.30 Sun
(01323) 870207 giantsrest.co.uk
Harveys Sussex Best Bitter, Old Ale; Hop Back Summer Lightning (summer); Taylor Landlord; guest beers
This popular Victorian hostelry is the perfect resting place for many – not just long men. An extensive range of excellent food, much of which is sourced locally, complements traditional real ales. Unusual games and puzzles abound, with at least one to each of the numerous tables. The interior is mainly wood, with an airy spacious feel; saucy Beryl Cook prints on the walls help lighten the mood. Entertainment is often provided by local morris men dancing in the street.

Withyham

Dorset

Castlefields, TN17 4BD (on B2110)
11.30-3 (not Mon), 6-11; 12-3, 7-10.30 Sun
(01892) 770278
Harveys Hadlow Bitter, Sussex Best Bitter; seasonal beers
Popular with walkers and visitors to nearby Ashdown Forest, this attractive village pub is set back from the road behind a small green with picnic tables. The pub dates back to the 15th century – a cosy bar with oak floors is complemented by a small no-smoking saloon bar that leads to the restaurant. Roast lunches are served on Sunday (no eve meals); booking for meals is advisable summer weekends.

SUSSEX (WEST)

Amberley

Sportsman

Crossgates, BN18 9NR
(½ mile E of village) OS039134
11-11; 12-10.30 Sun
(01798) 831787 amberleysportsman.co.uk
Fuller's London Pride; Greene King XX Mild; Harveys Sussex Best Bitter
This convivial 17th-century rural free house is frequented by walkers, diners and locals. There are three bars, each having its own character, a conservatory restaurant and a patio, both of which afford views of Amberley Wild Brooks. This pub is home of the Miserable Old Buggers Club, whose members raise money for children's charities.

Ardingly

Oak Inn

Street Lane, RH17 6UA
12-3, 5-11; 11-11 Fri, Sat & summer; 12-10.30 Sun
(01444) 892244
Harveys Sussex Best Bitter; Taylor Landlord; guest beer
Dating from the 16th century, and originally a row of labourers' cottages, the pub's characterful interior features an inglenook and many low beams, plus the 'grey lady' who haunts the establishment. The restaurant serves a wide range of food (not Sun eve). Walkers are welcome. It is close to the South of England Showground and the Bluebell Railway.

Arundel

King's Arms

36 Tarrant Street, BN18 9DN
11-3, 5.30-11; 11-11 Sat; 12-10.30 Sun
(01903) 882312
Fuller's London Pride; Hop Back Summer Lightning; Young's Special; guest beer
Warm, welcoming free house, popular with locals and visitors alike, this has been a pub for about 500 years, and retains its community focus. Built on a split level, the main bar is a lounge, where the handpumps are situated. A smaller snug, off to the right, leads to the patio. The lower bar has a juke box with 1970s rock music. Fines imposed on customers using mobile phones are donated to the RNLI.

Swan Hotel

27-29 High Street, BN18 9AG
11-11; 12-10.30 Sun
(01903) 882314
Fuller's London Pride, Gale's HSB; guest beer
You are assured of a friendly welcome at this pub/hotel that has been restored to a high standard, with wooden fittings and a large collection of old local photographs. The bar displays the original pub sign, dated 1850. Most areas are no-smoking and a good selection of food is available (all day in season). It stages monthly live music nights. NB: the beer range may change following the closure of Gale's Brewery.

Ashurst

Fountain

Horsham Road, BN44 3AP (on B2135)
11.30-11; 12-10.30 Sun
(01403) 710219

Fuller's London Pride; Harveys Sussex Best Bitter; Wychwood Hobgoblin; Young's Bitter; guest beer Ⓗ
Fine, 16th-century pub and restaurant with oak beams and flagstone floors. The guest beer on stillage behind the bar is chosen from Sussex breweries. Several cosy rooms preserve the large log fire front bar for imbibers and locals. The back bar accommodates both drinkers and diners, while the recommended restaurant is a discrete entity in the pub. A refurbished barn is available for skittles and functions. Outside a cottage garden overlooks the village duckpond.
♔Q❀◑◐♿●P

Barns Green

Queen's Head

Chapel Road, RH13 0PS
⏲ 11-2.30, 6-11; 12-10.30 Sun
☎ (01403) 730436
Badger K&B Sussex Bitter; Fuller's London Pride; King Horsham Best Bitter Ⓗ
Traditional village pub, dating back to 1643. It boasts a wealth of exposed beams and a large inglenook that burns logs; horse brasses abound. The pub is proud of its home cooking, with a popular Sunday lunch carvery (no meals Sun eve). ♔❀◑◐P⊁

Bepton

Country Inn

Severals Road, GU29 0LR (1 mile SW of Midhurst) OS870206
⏲ 11.30-3, 5-midnight; 11.30-12.30am Fri & Sat; 12-midnight Sun
☎ (01730) 813466
Ballard's Midhurst Mild; Fuller's London Pride; Young's Bitter; guest beers Ⓗ
Popular local in a quiet spot, serving changing guest beers from independent brewers. An easy walk down the lane from Midhurst, a single bar serves two distinct drinking areas; on one side with a log fire, the dining area enjoys a busy trade (no food Sun eve). Outside at the front there are tables, while the extensive rear garden is equipped with children's play equipment. Closing may be extended on busy nights.
♔Q❀◑◐🚌(60)♣P

Bosham

White Swan

Station Road, PO18 8NG (on A259 roundabout)
⏲ 12-2.30, 5-11; 12-11 Fri-Sat; 12-10.30 Sun
☎ (01243) 576086
Hop Back Crop Circle, Summer Lightning; Ringwood Old Thumper; guest beers Ⓗ
An inn for 300 years, this roadside local is spacious yet cosy, with beams, bare brick walls and open fires. It lies on the No. 700 Brighton-Southsea bus route, 100 yards from the railway station. No food is served at any time – the former dining area now houses a pool table. The skittle alley has gone, but the pleasant patio area remains. Addlestones cider is sold.
♔❀⇌(Bosham)🚌♣●P

Burgess Hill

Watermill Inn

1 Leylands Road, RH15 0QF
⏲ 11-11; 12-10.30 Sun
☎ (01444) 235517
Fuller's London Pride; Greene King Old Speckled Hen; Young's Bitter; guest beers Ⓗ
Large pub, made very cosy by the welcoming landlord and staff. Apart from the excellent beer, it boasts an impressive art gallery started by a previous landlord. Noted runner, Cecil Bowles, who held many trophies and ran against the world record holder in the 1920s, was a local resident. There are many beautiful walks in the vicinity; dog owners and ramblers are frequent visitors. Lunches are served Friday-Sunday. Westons Old Rosie cider is sold in summer. ♔Q❀◑⇌(Wivelsfield)♣●P▯

Byworth

Black Horse

RH15 0QF (off A283, 1 mile SE of Petworth)
⏲ 11.30-11; 12-10.30 Sun
☎ (01798) 342424
O'Hanlon's Yellowhammer; Skinner's Betty Stogs; guest beers Ⓗ
Friendly, unspoilt, 16th-century village pub, originally the local tannery. The traditional atmosphere is most apparent in the front bar area with its large fireplace, old flagstones and exposed beams. There are distinctive areas for diners and an old spiral staircase leads to the function room. One of the finest pub gardens in Sussex is steeply terraced and affords good Downs views.
♔Q♉❀◑◐⊟P

Camelsdale

Mill Tavern

Liphook Road, GU27 3QE (on B2131)
⏲ 12-3, 5.30-11; 12-11 Sat; 12-10.30 Sun
☎ (01428) 643183
Fuller's London Pride; Hogs Back TEA; Ringwood Best Bitter, Fortyniner; Taylor Landlord; guest beers Ⓗ
This 15th-century mill now makes a wonderful country pub, full of character. The main bar, with heavy beams, a log fire, bare wooden floor and charming decor, is supplemented by two dining rooms, offering an extensive menu; all food is prepared on the premises and largely home made. A must for serious beer drinkers, it also caters well for families with babies and young children who enjoy the spacious family room and large garden. ♔♉❀◑◐⊟♿P

Charlton

Fox Goes Free

East Dean Lane, PO18 0HU (½ mile E of A286 at Singleton) OS889130
⏲ 11-11; 12-11 Sun
☎ (01243) 811461 🌐 foxgoesfree.com
Arundel Sussex Mild; Ballard's Best Bitter; guest beers Ⓗ
Popular Sussex flint pub in a downland valley close to Goodwood and its various

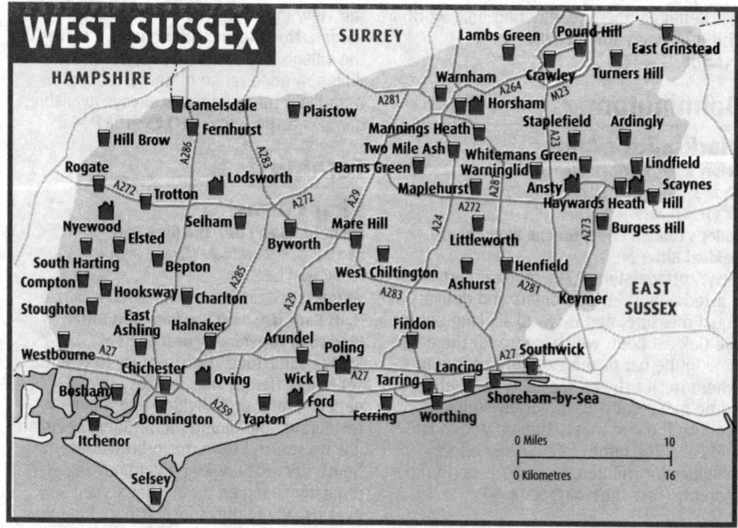

attractions. With red-brick floors, inglenooks and many original features retained during its 400 year history, it oozes character. Concentrating on quality beers and food, coupled with friendly service it benefits from five en-suite bedrooms with excellent views. The large garden is popular in summer. A house ale is provided by Arundel Brewery.

Chichester

Bell Inn

3 Broyle Road, PO19 6AT (opp. Festival Theatre)
11.30-3, 5-11.30; 12-3, 7-11.30 Sun
☎ (01243) 783388
Beer range varies H

Attractive city local opposite the Festival Theatre. Half-timber panelling and rustic brickwork contribute to the homely atmosphere. Popular with locals and theatregoers alike, a good selection of typical pub fare is available at all sessions except Sunday evening. A sheltered suntrap garden to the rear is a bonus. Three handpumps deliver two guest beers from the Enterprise range plus one from an independent or micro-brewery. Q P

Four Chesnuts

243 Oving Road, PO19 4EQ
12-11 (midnight Fri & Sat); 12-10.30 Sun
☎ (01243) 779974
Oakleaf Hole Hearted; Tetley Dark Mild; guest beers H

Outside the city centre, this pub is well worth the walk. Converted to a single bar some time ago, it retains its distinctive drinking areas. The skittle alley doubles as a dining room at busy times, and as the venue for beer festivals. Up to three guest beers are sourced from small regional breweries. Traditional pub food includes home-made pasties (no food Sun eve or Mon). Some evenings feature music (Tue, and folk Sat) as well as darts, pool and quizzes.
P

Compton

Coach & Horses

The Square, PO18 9HA (on B2146)
11.30-2.30, 6-11; 12-3, 7-10.30 Sun
☎ (02392) 631228
Fuller's ESB; guest beers H

This 16th-century pub lies in a remote but charming village that is sometimes cut off by downland streams. The front bar features two open fires and a bar billiards table. The back bar, now the restaurant (closed Sun eve and Mon), is the oldest part of the pub, boasting plenty of exposed beams. Up to five guest beers from independent breweries are usually available. There are seats outside in the village square.
Q

Crawley

George

High Street, RH10 1BS
11-11; 12-11 Sun
☎ (01293) 524215
Fuller's London Pride; Harveys Sussex Best Bitter H

Nice, old town-centre hotel with a bar. Split into two rooms: one has a TV, while the other, larger room features oak panels around the bar. Following a takeover by a new company, it has only recently started selling ale after much campaigning by locals.

INDEPENDENT BREWERIES

Arundel Ford
Ballard's Nyewood
Custom Haywards Heath
Dark Star Ansty
Gribble Inn Oving
Hammerpot Poling
Hepworth Horsham
King Horsham
Langham Lodsworth
Pitfield Haywards Heath
Welton's Horsham

It is definitely the one watering-hole worth a visit in Crawley town centre. P

Donnington

Blacksmith's Arms

Selsey Road, PO20 7PR (on B2201)
11-3, 5.30-11; 11-11 Sat; 12-10.30 Sun
(01243) 783999
Fuller's London Pride; Greene King Abbot; Oakleaf Bitter [H]
Cosy, cottage-style, 17th-century, part Grade II listed pub. It attracts diners and drinkers in equal measure, and is worth seeking out for the Oakleaf beer, which is rare for the area. Dine in the bar or the excellent restaurant where fresh fish is a speciality. Everything is home made daily, using locally-sourced produce (no eve meals Sun, or Mon in Jan and Feb). The large, safe garden offers activities for children. Live jazz is performed monthly (first Thu). Q P

East Ashling

Horse & Groom

PO18 9AX (on B2178, 2½ miles NW of Chichester)
12-3, 6-11; 12-6 (closed eve) Sun
(01243) 575339 horseandgroomchichester.com
Dark Star Hophead; Harveys Hadlow Bitter; Hop Back Summer Lightning; Young's Bitter [H]
Local CAMRA's Pub of the Year 2005, this 17th-century inn has been skilfully extended, using knapped Sussex flints. The large fireplace (once a forge) houses a fine old range, while the flagstone floor, old settles and half-panelled walls in the bar underpin its character. Diners enjoy a diverse, high quality menu of home-made dishes in the comfortable restaurant (no food Sun eve). Accommodation is in oak-beamed, en-suite rooms in a converted 17th-century flint barn. Q P

East Grinstead

Ship

Ship Street, RH19 4EG (on B2110)
11-11; 12-11 Sun
(01342) 312089
Young's Bitter, Special, seasonal beers [H]
Relaxing pub on the outside edge of town just away from the centre. Seating areas in both bars are small, offering large armchairs, plus stools at the bar. One bar is quiet, the other has a TV and games. It has a pleasant garden to the rear, but the car park is small. This is a good option for a drink when visiting East Grinstead. P

Elsted

Three Horseshoes

GU29 0JY (E end of village)
11-2.30, 6-11; 12-3, 7-10.30 Sun
(01730) 825746
Ballard's Best Bitter; Fuller's London Pride; Taylor Landlord; guest beers [G]
Former drovers' inn, ideal for cosy winter evenings with its small, low, beamed rooms and open fires, or equally so in summer for the view of the Downs from the large garden. No-smoking throughout, it serves as the village local, with one room set aside for dining. A good range of home-cooked traditional country food is always available; game is a speciality. Q P

Fernhurst

King's Arms

Midhurst Road, GU27 3HA (on A286)
11.30-3, 5.30-midnight (1am Fri & Sat); 12-3.30 (closed eve) Sun
(01428) 652005 kingsarmsfernhurst.com
Hogs Back TEA; King Horsham Best Bitter; Ringwood Fortyniner; guest beers [H]
Sussex sandstone, 17th-century free house set below Henley Hill. The cosy, wood-panelled interior is divided into a bar, restaurant, and dining room. Guest beers are always sourced from micro-breweries; the house beer is brewed by Ventnor. The regularly changing menu (not served Sun eve) usually features local fish and game. Outside is an enclosed garden and a camping field (24 hours notice is required to move the cows!) and a Sussex barn for functions. Q (70) P

Red Lion

8 The Green, GU27 3HY
11.30-3, 5-11; 11.30-11 Thu-Sat; 12-10.30 Sun
(01428) 643112
Fuller's Chiswick, London Pride, ESB, seasonal beers; guest beers (occasional) [H]
Idyllically set beside the village green, the Red Lion has been a pub since 1592. Inside is a single bar with a low, timbered ceiling and two side rooms, while outside customers can drink at the front overlooking the green or in the large rear garden. The pub is popular with both locals and diners, but no food is served on Sunday or Monday evenings. (70)P

Ferring

Henty Arms

2 Ferring Lane, BN12 6QY (N of level crossing)
11-3, 5.30-midnight; 11-midnight Thu-Sat; 12-4, 6.30-midnight Sun
(01903) 241254
Caledonian Deuchars IPA; Fuller's London Pride; Greene King Ruddles County; Young's Bitter; guest beers [H]
Friendly village pub: the public bar (with a no-smoking area) houses a TV, juke box, darts, pool and other games; the lounge bar is quieter with a no-smoking restaurant attached. Good food is served at reasonable prices. It hosts a Sunday night quiz and is used by the village cricket club. Well-behaved children are welcome until 9pm. A garden beer festival is staged in July. It is a 15-minute walk from Goring Station along a footpath. Q (700) P

Findon

Findon Manor Hotel

High Street, BN14 0TA
11-2.30, 6-11; 12-10.30 Sun

☎ (01903) 872733 🌐 findonmanor.com
Black Sheep Best Bitter; Greene King Abbot; Harveys Sussex Best Bitter; guest beer H
Built in the 16th century, Findon Manor was originally a rectory belonging to Magdalen College, Oxford and remained so until the 1930s. Real ale is served in the Snooty Fox bar. Warmed by a log fire in winter, it offers a cosy, convivial atmosphere and attracts a varied clientele. Children are welcome. Top quality food is available (smoking is banned during food serving times). ⛫Q❀⛟◑P

Halnaker

Anglesey Arms
Stane Street, PO18 0NQ (on A285)
⏲ 11-3, 5.30-11.30; 11-11 Sat; 11-11.30 Sun
☎ (01243) 773474 🌐 angleseyarms.co.uk
Adnams Bitter; Caledonian Deuchars IPA; Hop Back Summer Lightning; Young's Bitter H
Family-run, listed Georgian pub consisting of a wood and flagstone-floored public bar with a log fire, and a comfortable restaurant, renowned for good food using local seasonal produce; steaks and fresh fish are specialities (Sun lunch booking essential). Cribbage, darts and cricket are played by pub teams. It has a two-acre back garden and numerous flowering baskets in the front in summer. Westons Old Rosie cider is sold in summer.
⛫Q❀◑⊟♿⛺🚌(99, 55)♣●P

Haywards Heath

Duck
27 Wivelsfield Road, RH16 4EF
⏲ 11-11 daily
☎ (01444) 410663 🌐 the-duck.co.uk
Fuller's Gale's HSB; Harveys Sussex Best Bitter H
Friendly town pub that stages regular quiz nights. This traditional local, with cosy corners, places an emphasis on quality beer. Sandwiches and bar snacks, including pickled eggs, are available at lunchtime. Traditional pub games include darts, shove-ha'penny, and fives and threes; the public bar houses a pool table. ⛫❀⊟🚌♣P

Henfield

Plough
High Street, BN5 9HP
⏲ 11-11.30 (midnight Fri & Sat); 12-10.30 Sun
☎ (01273) 492280
Fuller's London Pride; Harveys Sussex Best Bitter; King Horsham Best Bitter H
At the centre of Henfield High Street, this former coaching house has a modern look to the exterior and a cosy single bar inside. Guns, horse brasses and mellow brick give a traditional feel. A restaurant area runs down the left-hand side, offering a Tapas menu as well as English food. ⛫❀◑⛺🚌(17, 100)♣

Hill Brow

Jolly Drover
GU33 7QL (on B2070, opp. B3006 jct)
⏲ 11-2.30, 6-11; 12-3 (closed eve) Sun
☎ (01730) 893137
Fuller's London Pride; Greene King Abbot; Ringwood Best Bitter; Taylor Landlord; guest beer H
Built in 1820 by a drover, this watering-hole lies on the old A3, just outside Liss. A family-run, country local, the atmosphere is enhanced by original beams, a huge log fire and two chesterfield sofas; note the bar price list from the 1950s. The well-proportioned bar and dining area offer over 20 home-made daily specials. Swamp Donkey cider is pressed on the premises and available bottled at the bar.
⛫Q❀◑P

Hooksway

Royal Oak
PO18 9JZ (¼ mile NE of B2141) OS815162
⏲ 11.30-2.30, 6 (7 winter)-11; closed Mon; 12-3, 7-10.30 (not winter eve) Sun
☎ (01243) 535257
Beer range varies H
Tucked away in a valley close to the South Downs Way, this 15th-century rural gem became a lunch stop for the 'guns' on West Dean estate shoots. King Edward VII was a frequent patron, but now walkers and cyclists enjoy its peaceful setting. Reasonably-priced, home-cooked food complements the four ales which include Hooksway Bitter from Hampshire Brewery, and usually a strong dark beer. Opening times/days can vary – phone if travelling far; it is closed Tuesdays following bank holidays.
⛫Q☕❀◑⛺♣P⊁

Horsham

Black Jug
31 North Street, RH12 1RJ
⏲ 12-11; 12-10.30 Sun
☎ (01403) 253526 🌐 blackjug-horsham.co.uk
Adnams Broadside; Greene King Old Speckled Hen; Welton's Horsham Bitter; guest beers H
Lively, bustling, town-centre pub, with a friendly atmosphere – now totally no-smoking. A large conservatory leads to an outside seating area, and there is plenty of seating in both bars. A local meeting place and easy to get to, it offers good quality meals, served all day until 9.30pm, at affordable prices – try the Sunday roasts. The house beer, Black Jug, is brewed in Horsham by Welton's.
❀◑⇌

Malt Shovel
15 Springfield Road, RH12 2PG
⏲ 11-11; 12-11 Sun
☎ (01403) 254543 🌐 maltshovel.com
Fuller's Gale's Best Bitter; Taylor Best Bitter; Tetley Mild; guest beers H
Large, one-bar pub just outside the town centre on the ring road. The old-style interior has all wooden chairs and an old-fashioned bar front. The real fire is lovely when the weather is cold. The walls are lined with old pictures. This pub has long supported CAMRA, running a Mild Day event each year and their own beer festivals.
⛫❀◑⇌●P

Itchenor

Ship Inn

The Street, PO20 7AH (100 yds from harbour)
11.30-11; 12-10.30 Sun
☎ (01243) 512284
Ballard's Best Bitter; Itchen Valley Godfathers; guest beers Ⓗ
The pub sits a short distance from the waterfront in the main village street. Although built in the 1930s it has character due to the wood panelling and yachting memorabilia. Two of the rooms are dedicated to dining – a wide range of traditional meals is served, with locally-caught fish a speciality. Up to four beers are available, all from small or local micro-breweries. ⌂Q❀⇌◑⊟♣P

Keymer

Greyhound Inn

Keymer Road, BN6 8QT
11-3, 6-11; 11-11 Fri & Sat; 12-10.30 Sun
☎ (01273) 842645
Adnams Bitter; Courage Best Bitter; Harveys Sussex Best Bitter; guest beers Ⓗ
Comfortably furnished old pub with wood-panelled decor throughout, situated opposite the church of St Cosmas and St Damian. Bar billiards can be played in the small public bar. A large collection of ceramic beer and beverage mugs hangs from the low beams in the saloon and dining areas; the latter is tucked away behind the inglenook. No food is served Monday evening.
⌂Q❀◑⊟⊟♣P

Lambs Green

Lamb Inn

RH12 4RG (off A264)
11.30-3, 5.30-11; 12-3, 7-10.30 Sun
☎ (01293) 871336 thelambinn.info
King Horsham Best Bitter, Red River, seasonal beers Ⓗ
This delightful country pub is (so far) WJ King's only tied house. The drinking area extends into a large no-smoking conservatory, while drinkers are surrounded by dark oak beams and cosy nooks in the bar. An unusual feature is the double-sided open fireplace. Traditional, home-cooked food is available. The friendly, welcoming bar staff can serve you bottle-conditioned ales, Biddendens cider, or one of the wide range of wines. ⌂❀◑●P

Lancing

Crabtree

140 Crabtree Lane, BN15 9NQ (N of station)
12-11 daily
☎ (01903) 755514
Fuller's London Pride; guest beers Ⓗ
The Crabtree is a 1930s-style pub, with a large, sporty public bar, and a smaller lounge/dining area adorned with aviation memorabilia, topped by an attractive cupola. Three rotating guest beers are offered, mainly sourced from small local breweries. Primarily a community pub, it is beginning to attract customers from further afield. The pleasant garden has a safe play area for children. No food is served Monday; a Thai menu features Wednesday-Saturday evenings. Q❀◑⊟⇌P

Lindfield

Stand Up Inn

47 High Street, RH16 2HN
11.30-11; 12-10.30 Sun
☎ (01444) 482995
Dark Star Hophead, Original, seasonal beers; guest beers Ⓗ
This popular hostelry in the village centre has recently been taken over by the owners of the Evening Star in Brighton and reopened following alterations and redecoration. The pub reverted to its original name after many years as the Linden Tree. The extensive beer range is mainly from Dark Star, plus guests. Bar snacks are available at lunchtime. Two real ciders are usually sold, at least one on handpump. ⌂❀⊟(30, 82)♣●⚟

Witch Inn

1 Sunte Avenue, RH16 2AB
12-2.30, 5-11; 12-11 Fri & Sat; 12-10.30 Sun
☎ (01444) 414504 thewitchinn.co.uk
Greene King Old Speckled Hen; Harveys Sussex Best Bitter Ⓗ
Dating back to at least 1746, this family-oriented pub has been run by former Brighton and Republic of Ireland footballer Gerry Ryan for the past 20 years. His collection of framed football shirts makes an interesting focal point in this friendly, split-level free house. It enjoys a good reputation for its organic, locally-sourced, home-cooked food. A plasma screen shows major sporting events. Well-behaved children (and dogs) are welcome. ❀◑⊟

Littleworth

Windmill

Littleworth Lane, RH13 8EJ (from A24 or A272, head for Partridge Green) OS193205
11.30-3, 5.30 (6 Sat)-11; 12-3, 7-10.30 Sun
☎ (01403) 710308
Badger K&B Sussex Bitter, First Gold, Tanglefoot Ⓗ
Still proudly displaying the old King & Barnes livery, this unspoilt rural gem offers two contrasting bars: a comfortable saloon caters for diners, while a real old-fashioned public bar, festooned with agricultural implements, has bar billiards and darts. The pleasant garden is blessed with an idyllic setting. The menu is based on home-cooked dishes: fish and chips on Friday and a selection of Thai and Indian curries. ⌂Q❀◑⊟♿♣●P

Mannings Heath

Dun Horse Inn

Brighton Road, RH13 6HZ
11-11; 12-10.30 Sun
☎ (01403) 265783 dunhorseinn.co.uk
Fuller's London Pride; Taylor Landlord Ⓗ
Two-bar pub on a village road junction. Note the stained glass windows promoting Rock Ales that date back to 1926 when the pub

was rebuilt. The recently extended snug bar offers Sussex pub games and bar billiards. The saloon bar to the right houses the main bar and is no-smoking. Although a roadhouse, on the Horsham-Brighton bus route, the pub is very much a village local. Evening meals are served Tuesday-Saturday. ⩕❀⇆◑♣P⊬

Maplehurst

White Horse

Park Lane, RH13 6LL OS190246

✪ 12-2.30, 6-11.30; 11.30-2.30, 6-12.30am Fri & Sat; 12-3, 7-11.30 Sun

☎ (01403) 891208

Harveys Sussex Best Bitter; Welton's Pride 'n' Joy; guest beers ⊞

Delightful country pub, family run for 24 years. It is forbidden to take yourself seriously in the bars (unless talking beer). The landlord champions small breweries. It has been a Guide entry for over 20 years and local CAMRA Pub of the Year three times. Children are welcome in the no-smoking conservatory, with views over the spacious garden and countryside. Real local cider is sold. No fruit machines or piped music, conversation rules here. No food is served Monday. ⩕Q❀◑♣●P⊬

Mare Hill (near Pulborough)

White Horse Inn

RH20 2DY (1 mile E of Pulborough on A283)

✪ 11-3, 5-11; 11-11 Sat; 12-10.30 Sun

☎ (01798) 872189

Fuller's Chiswick, London Pride, ESB, seasonal beers; guest beer (occasional) ⊞

Pleasant pub with a popular restaurant. The front bar overlooks the Downs and Pulborough Brooks; walkers (and dogs) are welcome. The snug bar, with garden view and the front bar have log fires in winter. A no-smoking bar is on a lower level. Bar food features a varied range of home-made burgers. ⩕Q❀◑P⊬

Plaistow

Sun Inn

The Street, RH14 0PX

✪ 12-3 (not Mon), 7-11; 12-3 (closed eve) Sun

☎ (01403) 871313

Fuller's Gale's Best Bitter ⊞

Quiet, friendly, village local comprising two small bars - a sunken, corner bar to the left and a bar to the right that is dominated by an inglenook. A small room off this bar is mainly used for dining. Brick floors and exposed beams feature throughout. Evening meals are served Thursday-Saturday, lunches Tuesday-Saturday. Whatever beer they decide to sell following closure of Gale's is bound to be served in tip-top condition. ⩕Q❀◑⊟P

Pound Hill

Tavern on the Green

Grattons Drive, RH10 3BA

✪ 10-11; 12-10.30 Sun

☎ (01293) 882468

Harveys Sussex Best Bitter; guest beers ⊞

Opened in 1975 and still run by members of the same family, for a while it had the distinction of being the only Crawley New Town neighbourhood pub to be a free house. It has an attractive open-plan, modern interior and is situated in one of the leafier suburbs of Crawley. Guest ales are often from local craft brewers, such as WJ King. ❀◑♿⇌(Three Bridges)♣P

Rogate

White Horse Inn

East Street, GU31 5EA (on A272)

✪ 11-3, 6-11.30 (midnight Fri); 11-midnight Sat; 12-10.30 Sun

☎ (01730) 821333

Harveys Sussex Best Bitter, Hadlow Bitter, Armada Ale, seasonal beers ⊞

This 16th-century coaching inn boasts oak beams, flagstone floors and a huge log fire. A Harveys tied house, you can expect up to five beers to be available, including all their seasonal brews. One half of the pub is used for dining; the large range of meals includes steaks and vegetarian choices. The pub fields its own cricket, football and darts teams. No food is served Sunday evening. ⩕Q❀◑♣P

Scaynes Hill

Sloop Inn

Sloop Lane, RH17 7NP OS385244

✪ 12-3, 6-11 (5.30-11.30 Fri);11.30-11.30 Sat; 11.30-11 Sun

☎ (01444) 831219

Greene King IPA, Ruddles County, Abbot, seasonal beers; guest beers ⊞

Deep in the beautiful Sussex countryside, next to the River Ouse and near the Bluebell preserved railway line, low-ceilinged cottages were converted to a pub in 1815. The public bar area (where smoking is allowed) is decorated with railway memorabilia. An independent guest beer is sometimes stocked. Good food is served throughout the pub and garden. It hosts a music festival in July. ⩕Q❀◑⊟♿♣P⊬

Selham

Three Moles

GU28 0PN (off A272) OS935206

✪ 12-2, 5-11; 11.30-11 Sat; 12-10.30 Sun

☎ (01798) 861303 🌐 thethreemoles.co.uk

Skinner's Betty Stogs; guest beers ⊞

Moles abound at this characterful, bijou country pub, hidden in the Rother Valley, built in 1872 to serve Selham Station; the railway is defunct but this welcoming free house thrives, stocking a mild plus three guest beers from small breweries. The name refers to the coat of arms of the owners, the Mitford Family. This frequent local CAMRA Pub of the Year hosts a garden beer festival in June. The Worthing-Midhurst bus No. 1 stops at Halfway Bridge, a pleasant mile's walk. ⩕Q❀⛺♣P

Selsey

Lifeboat

Albion Road, PO20 0DJ

⏲ 11-3, 6-11 (11-11 summer weekends); 12-4, 7-10.30 Sun

☎ (01243) 603501

Arundel ASB; Fuller's London Pride; guest beer [H]

Situated close to the beach and lifeboat slipway, this pleasant, friendly pub comprises two bars and an adjoining restaurant that serves home-cooked meals including locally-caught fish and Selsey crab salads. The garden and patio area are popular in summer with both locals and holidaymakers. Nautical photographs abound at this favourite watering-hole of lifeboat crew and local fishermen. Car parking is limited. Q❀◐◑⊟♿♣P

Shoreham-by-Sea

Buckingham Arms

35-39 Brunswick Road, BN43 5WA

⏲ 11-11; 11-10.30 Sun

☎ (01273) 453660

Greene King XX Mild; Harveys Sussex Best Bitter; Hop Back Summer Lightning; Ringwood Best Bitter; Taylor Landlord; guest beers [H]

A warm welcome is guaranteed at this friendly town pub opposite the station. It offers eleven beers on handpump – five are changing guests – plus a cider. There is something for everyone at this busy pub that draws a good mix of customers. It hosts regular live music, a plasma screen shows major sporting events, and beer and cider festivals are staged in February and August. ❀◐⇌⊟♣●P

Red Lion

Old Shoreham Road, BN43 5TE

⏲ 11.30-11; 12-10.30 Sun

☎ (01273) 453171

Beer range varies [H]

A regular Guide entry in a town full of good pubs. Situated 10 minutes north of the centre and station (follow the river) in 'old' Shoreham, the Red Lion stands opposite the airport, which makes it popular on air show days. An Adur beer festival is held each Easter with a marquee covering the back garden. This ancient ale house is not designed for tall people, but the top bar, with river views, has more headroom. Beers are from small breweries. ♨Q❀◐◑⊟(12)P⍁

South Harting

Ship

North Lane, GU31 5PZ (on B2146)

⏲ 11-11; 12-10.30 Sun

☎ (01730) 825302

Ballard's Wassail; Cheriton Pots Ale; Palmer IPA; guest beer [H]

Friendly, 17th-century free house built using old ship's timbers. There is a small public bar and a larger lounge/restaurant where good value meals are served (not Tue or Sun eves, Feb-Sep); booking is recommended at weekends. An enclosed garden flanks the B2146. The guest beer is always from an independent or micro-brewery. ♨Q❀◐◑⊟♣P

Southwick

Romans

Manor Hall Road, BN42 4NG

⏲ 12-11; 11-11 Sat; 12-10.30 Sun

☎ (01273) 592147

Beer range varies [H]

Once a basic pub the Romans has been transformed into a true community hostelry, fielding its own football, hockey, darts, pool and bar billiards teams. Live music is staged every Sunday and a quiz on Monday. Two regular beer festivals add to its appeal. Built in the 1930s, the pub retains many original features. The large, child-friendly garden boasts an aviary. The name comes from a Roman building nearby, now beneath the church. No evening meals are served Sunday. ♨❀◐◑⊟♿⇌⊟♣●P⊡

Staplefield

Jolly Tanners

Handcross Road, RH17 6EF (on B2114)

⏲ 11-3, 5.30-11; 11-11 Sat; 12-10.30 Sun

☎ (01444) 400335 🌐 jollytanners.com

Elgood's Black Dog; Fuller's Chiswick, London Pride; Harveys Sussex Best Bitter; guest beers [H]

This ever-popular village local continues to serve four regular cask ales, including a mild, and a changing guest beer. It boasts a large, well-maintained garden much used by families. The well-prepared meals are popular with locals and customers from further afield; early arrival is recommended for dining. Several clubs meet here including the Goon Preservation Society. Occasional beer festivals are staged at this family-run pub. ♨Q❀◐◑♣P⍁

Stoughton

Hare & Hounds

PO19 9JQ (off B2146) OS802115

⏲ 11-3, 6-11; 11-11 Fri, Sat & summer; 12-10.30 Sun

☎ (02392) 631433

Fuller's Gale's HSB; Itchen Valley Hampshire Rose; Taylor Landlord; Young's Bitter; guest beers [H]

Traditional country pub, in a beautiful downland valley – an ideal base for walking. A large dining room serves fresh local produce. The public bar, warmed by an open fire, is the locals' choice. Altogether there are three open fires, which along with stone flagged floors, beams and simple furniture give it a wonderful atmosphere. Outside is a paved drinking area at the front and a garden at the back. ♨Q❀◐◑⊟♣P⍁

Tarring

George & Dragon

1 High Street, BN14 7NN (opp. post office)

⏲ 11-11 (midnight Fri & Sat); 12-10.30 Sun

☎ (01903) 202497

Courage Directors; Harveys Sussex Best Bitter; Hop Back Summer Lightning; Young's Bitter; guest beers [H]

Originally the White Horse (a tavern has been on this site since 1610) the George and Dragon offers a cosy ambience, friendly staff and a competitive pricing policy, that all contribute to its popularity among Tarring folk. In a timber-framed building, a large bar leads to a games room and a secluded snug. The garden has been revamped and holds the annual beer festival on August bank holiday. Note the original Watneys sign behind the bar. Dogs are welcome. ⛰Q🍺❀◖⊟⇌(W Worthing)P⊬

Vine

27-29 High Street, BN14 7NN

🕐 12-11 (midnight Fri & Sat); 12-10.30 Sun

☎ (01903) 202891

Badger K&B Sussex Bitter, First Gold, Tanglefoot; Gribble K&B Mild Ale; Hop Back Summer Lightning; guest beers Ⓗ

Situated on Tarring's historic High Street, this welcoming pub keeps up to nine real ales, including seasonal brews. The remains of an old brewery still exist, and during the recent careful refurbishment, wooden panels were revealed from the building's first use as a school. The garden has a children's play area and the patio is heated with a 'jumbrella'. The pub hosts live music. Evening meals are served Monday-Thursday. Q❀◖◗⇌(W Worthing)P

Trotton

Keeper's Arms

GU31 5ER (on A272) OS838222

🕐 12-3; 6.30-11; closed Mon; 12-3 (closed eve) Sun

☎ (01730) 813724 🌐 keepersarms.co.uk

Ballard's Best Bitter Ⓗ

Delightful country pub, situated close to the River Rother. An oak floor, wood-panelled walls, beams and homely soft furnishings around a log fire allow for total relaxation. Note the collection of intriguing ornaments and artefacts from the landlady's travels. Reservations are recommended for the excellent restaurant. The raised front patio affords views over the valley and is a popular spot in summer for watching the world go by. ⛰Q❀◖◗♣P

Turners Hill

Crown at Turners Hill

East Street, RH10 4PT (at main crossroads)

🕐 10-midnight (1am Fri & Sat); 12-10.30 Sun

☎ (01342) 715218 🌐 thecrownatturnershill.co.uk

Adnams Broadside; Greene King Old Speckled Hen; Harveys Hadlow Bitter, Sussex Best Bitter; guest beers (summer) Ⓗ

This truly old English pub prides itself on good ale, hospitality and service. The 16th-century, oak-beamed interior provides ample space for drinkers and diners alike, while the garden and patio provide additional seating in summer. The pub is popular with locals and visitors and runs a beer festival every autumn. Good, fresh food is served from local suppliers. Regular buses stop outside. ⛰❀◖◗⊟P⊬

Red Lion

Lion Lane, RH10 4NU (off North St, B2028) OS342357

🕐 11-3, 5.30-11; 11-11 Sat; 12-10.30 Sun

☎ (01342) 715416

Harveys Sussex Best Bitter, seasonal beers Ⓗ

The local CAMRA branch was formed in this interesting, tile-hung pub, back in 1974. Split-level, replete with beams and an inglenook, it is home to a marbles team and a folk club meets monthly. During the summer it stages occasional outdoor music events and barbecues. A dark beer is available all year round and the excellent home-cooked lunches (not Sun) come highly recommended (no chips). ⛰❀◖♣P

Two Mile Ash

Bax Castle

Two Mile Ash Road, RH13 0LA (off B2237)

🕐 11.30-3, 6-11 daily

☎ (01403) 730369

Banks's Bitter; Harveys Sussex Best Bitter; Marston's Bitter, Pedigree Ⓗ

This traditional English pub is popular with locals and visitors alike. Parts of the building are 600 years old and the pub consists of a number of adjoining rooms clustered around the friendly bar. Food can be eaten in the bar area or the large restaurant. In the summer months you can enjoy a drink in the front garden, while in the winter you can get cosy by a roaring fire. ⛰Q❀◖◗♣P

Warnham

Sussex Oak

2 Church Street, RH12 3QW

🕐 11-11; 12-10.30 Sun

☎ (01403) 265028 🌐 thesussexoak.co.uk

Adnams Bitter; Fuller's London Pride; Taylor Landlord; Young's Bitter; guest beers Ⓗ

Still serving the best pint north of Horsham, the pub is gaining a reputation for the extensive beer festivals it stages regularly on bank holidays. It stocks an interesting variety of guest beers. An attractive, 16th-century pub, standing opposite the church, a cosy inglenook holds a roaring log fire in winter. A variety of home-cooked food is served in the no-smoking restaurant. Popular with families, it boasts a large garden. There is a bus service to Horsham. ⛰Q❀◖◗♿♣P⊬

Warninglid

Half Moon

The Street, RH17 5TR (on B2115, 1 mile W of A23)

🕐 11.30-2.30, 5.30-11; 12-10.30 Sun

☎ (01444) 461227

Black Sheep Best Bitter; Harveys Sussex Best Bitter; guest beers Ⓗ

This attractive village local has been under threat of closure in recent years. Now with a new owner, careful redecoration of the two bars on split levels has retained much of its original character. A good range of food is served, and most customers prefer to eat in the larger, lower bar which is no-smoking. ⛰Q❀◖◗P⊬

Westbourne

Cricketers

Commonside, PO10 8TA (northern edge of village)

🕐 5 -11.30; 12-midnight Fri; 11-midnight Sat; 12-11 Sun

☎ (01243) 372647

Beer range varies Ⓗ

Hard to find on the northern edge of the

village, this 300-year-old pub is worth seeking out. Now a thriving free house, its five handpumps deliver guest beers usually from Sussex and Hampshire micro-breweries. The comfortable L-shaped bar is part wood panelled and hops are draped from the ceiling. Darts and bar billiards are played here. 🜲❀♣P

Stag's Head

The Square, PO10 8UE

🕐 12-3, 5-11; 12-midnight Fri & Sat; 12-10.30 Sun

☎ (01243) 372393

Hogs Back TEA; Oakleaf Hole Hearted; Ringwood Best Bitter Ⓗ

This popular pub features beers from local small breweries. Actively dog-friendly, it enjoys a thriving local trade. A compact restaurant serves an interesting menu of good value English and continental cuisine, sourced locally by the French chef (no meals Sun eve or Mon lunch). With exposed brickwork and wood panelling, the log fire in winter and carpeting throughout enhance the cosy atmosphere. Summer sees the small suntrap patio garden a riot of colour from hanging baskets and planters. 🜲Q❀◐◑♣

West Chiltington

Five Bells

Smock Alley, RH20 2QX OS091172

🕐 12-3, 6-11; 12-4.30, 7-10.30 Sun

☎ (01798) 812143

🌐 westchiltington.com/five_bells

Palmer Copper Ale; guest beers Ⓗ

This idyllic country free house is somewhat off the beaten track. The clued-up licensees maintain an inspired choice of five beers, including a mild. In the winter there is usually a wooden barrel on the bar serving one of the guest beers. Biddenden cider also comes straight from the barrel. The food is excellent and the pub now has five double rooms for B&B. 🜲Q❀🛏◐◑♿🍎P

Whitemans Green

Ship Inn

RH15 5BY (N of Cuckfield at B2115/B2036 jct)

🕐 12-2.30, 5-11; 12-11 Sat; 12-3, 7-10.30 Sun

☎ (01444) 413219

Beer range varies Ⓖ

Friendly, single-bar, village local with a games room and no-smoking dining area. Handpumps are for decoration only, since the beer is served by gravity dispense from a cool room behind the bar. This free house is family run and has a comfortable interior with sofas around an unusual double-sided fireplace. Good food is served, with a changing range of specials supplementing the regular menu. 🜲❀🛏◐◑🂠🚌(40)P

Wick

Dewdrop Inn

96 Wick Street, BN17 7JS

🕐 10.30-3, 5.30-11; 10.30-11 Sat; 10.30-10.30 Sun

☎ (01903) 716459

Fuller's Gale's Butser Bitter; Ringwood XXXX Porter Ⓗ

Part of a Victorian terrace of houses, this anachronistic former Gale's pub – now a free house – has a cosy lounge bar adorned with mirrors, copper maps and a series of Ringwood Porter posters. In contrast, the public bar is spacious and minimalist. You are assured a warm welcome. If Ringwood Porter is not available it is normally replaced by a seasonal guest beer.

Q🂠♣

Worthing

Selden Arms

41 Lyndhurst Road, BN11 2DB (near hospital)

🕐 11 (12 Sat)-11; 12-10.30 Sun

Beer range varies Ⓗ

Genuine free house and community pub that has been local CAMRA's Pub of the Year since 2000. It offers conviviality and a choice of six ever-changing ales, often including a dark beer, plus Belgian bottled beers. It hosts an annual beer festival in January and occasional live music. Photographs of old Worthing hostelries adorn the walls. A small no-smoking area is provided. Food (Mon-Sat) comes in liberal amounts and is good value.

🜲◐⇌(Central)♣⚟

Swan

79 High Street, BN11 1DN (opp. Lidl store)

🕐 11-2.30, 6-11 (midnight Fri); 11-midnight Sat; 12-11 Sun

☎ (01903) 232923

Greene King Abbot; Harveys Sussex Best Bitter; Shepherd Neame Spitfire Ⓗ

Five minutes' walk east from the town centre, this 19th-century oasis has all the rustic charm one might associate with a village local, as it is adorned with beams, brasses and various agricultural implements. Take time out from 21st-century shopping to enjoy what is undoubtedly Worthing's best pint of Harveys Best Bitter. The Swan is relaxed by day, and more lively in the evening, with music nights, darts and bar billiards.

🜲❀◐⇌(Central) ♣

Yapton

Maypole Inn

Maypole Lane, BN18 0DP (off B2132, pedestrian access from Lake Lane) OS978041

🕐 11.30-midnight; 1am Fri & Sat (no entry after 11pm); 12-midnight Sun

☎ (01243) 551417

Arundel Sussex Mild; Ringwood Best Bitter; Skinner's Betty Stogs; guest beers Ⓗ

Regional CAMRA Pub of the Year 2004 and local winner in 2006, this small, flint-built pub is tucked away from the village centre. Maypole Lane was cut off by the railway in 1846 and the pub has enjoyed quiet isolation ever since. The cosy lounge boasts a log fire and an imposing row of seven handpumps, dispensing beers from local and regional independents. The public bar houses a juke box, darts and pool; a skittle alley can be booked.

🜲Q🍼❀◐♿⛺♣🍎P

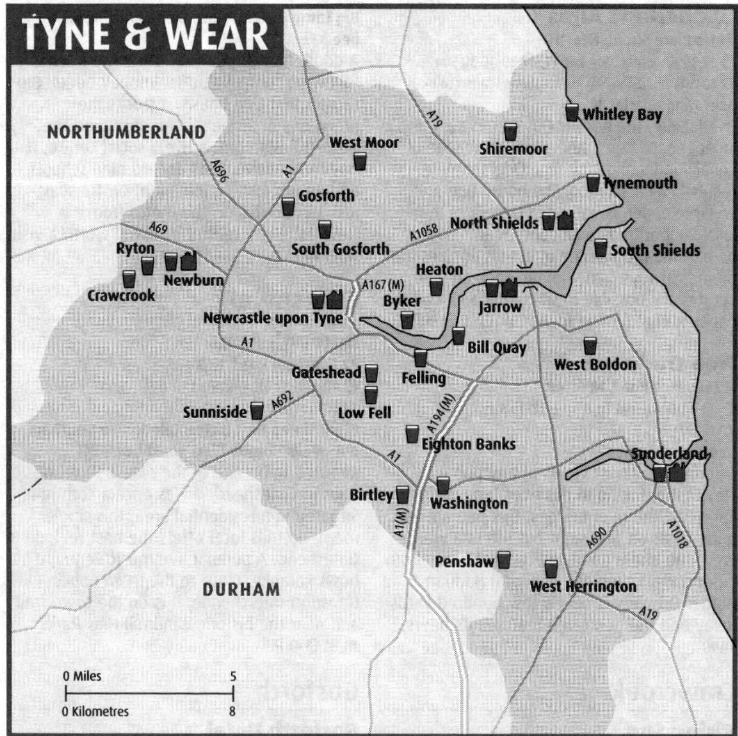

Bill Quay

Albion

Reay Street, NE10 0TY

4-11 (midnight Fri); 12-midnight Sat; 12-11 Sun

☎ (0191) 469 2418

Jarrow Bitter, Swinging Gibbet, Rivet Catcher, seasonal beers; guest beers Ⓗ

One of only three pubs owned by the local Jarrow Brewery, it stocks not just its own multiple CAMRA award-winning real ales but those from other micros in the north east too. Overlooking the widest part of the River Tyne, the comfortable lounge bar with large-screen TV has fascinating views across heavily-industrialised Tyneside. There is a pool table in the conservatory. Regular live music and weekly quizzes are hosted. The Coast-to-Coast cycle route and Keelman's Way Walk are nearby.

⊖(Pelaw)♣●P

Birtley

Moulders Arms

Peareth Terrace, Birtley Lane, DH3 2LW

11-3, 5.30-11; 12-3, 7-10.30 Sun

☎ (0191) 410 2949

Boddingtons Bitter; Jennings Cumberland Ale; guest beer Ⓗ

Just off the main road, this community pub is at the centre of the local social scene. Managed by a tenant with many years' experience of running Good Beer Guide favourites, it has a large, comfortable split-level lounge and a smaller, livelier public bar with wooden beams. A strong supporter of local charities, it runs its own long-standing golf society and darts teams and hosts a weekly quiz. The pub is reputed to be home to a ghost whose main activity seems to be moving things about!

❀◐ ⊞P

Byker

Cluny

36 Lime Street, NE1 2PQ

11.30-11 (midnight Thu; 1am Fri & Sat); 12-10.30 Sun

☎ (0191) 230 4475 theheadofsteam.com

Beer range varies Ⓗ

You will find a good range of draught and bottled British and foreign beers on offer here, as well as excellent home-made food. A popular live music venue, the pub also has a gallery holding regular displays of art. Situated in a building converted from an 1840s industrial mill, the large number of artists working in the surrounding studios ensures a wide variety of customers. Located in a part of Newcastle undergoing sympathetic redevelopment, the pub is close to Ouseburn Farm and next to the National Centre for Children's Books.

Q◐♿⊖●⚟

INDEPENDENT BREWERIES

Big Lamp Newburn
Bull Lane Sunderland
Darwin Sunderland
Hadrian & Border Newcastle upon Tyne
Jarrow Jarrow
Mordue North Shields

Cumberland Arms ☆
James Place Street, NE6 1LD
12.30 (4 winter Mon-Fri)-11; 12.30-10.30 Sun
☎ (0191) 265 6151 ⊕ thecumberlandarms.co.uk
Beer range varies Ⓗ
Overlooking the historic Ouseburn valley, this independent free house supplies a range of equally independent beers. Ciders are regularly available too. The house beer, Wylam Rapper, is named in honour of the local Rapper traditional dance teams based here. A full programme of events ensures that there is always something happening here, yet it is still possible to sit quietly and read the paper or chat among friends. ♨Q❀⊖●P

Free Trade Inn
St Lawrence Road, NE6 1AP
11-11 (midnight Fri & Sat); 12-11 Sun
☎ (0191) 265 5764
Beer range varies Ⓗ
Offering the finest views of any pub in Newcastle, taking in the river Tyne, Baltic, Sage and the river bridges, this pub appears quite basic on first sight but offers a warm welcome and a good selection of beers from independent brewers. The local Hadrian & Border Brewery is only a few hundred yards away and the pub often features its beers. ♨❀

Crawcrook

Rising Sun
Bank Top, NE40 4EE
11-11; 12-10.30 Sun
☎ (0191) 413 3316
Black Sheep Best Bitter; Mordue Workie Ticket; Wells Bombardier; guest beers Ⓗ
A warm welcome awaits at this lively local offering the best range of ales for miles. An extensive food menu is available and the conservatory provides a comfortable place for dining. Drinkers have a choice of areas to enjoy their pint. The hub of the local community, the pub is run by long-serving licensees. It is situated half a mile south of the main village crossroads. ❀◑▣(10)P

Eighton Banks

Lambton Arms
Rockliffe Way, NE9 7XR
11-11 daily
☎ (0191) 487 8137 ⊕ lambtonarms.co.uk
Greene King IPA, Abbot, Old Speckled Hen; guest beers Ⓗ
The first no-smoking pub in the area, the Lambton Arms is now a well-established inn and restaurant. Although largely a food establishment, it proudly claims to be a cask ale specialist too, with four handpumps offering a good range of ales varying in strength. The quiz nights on Tuesday and Thursday are always popular. ❀◑⊞♿●P

Felling

Wheatsheaf
26 Carlisle Street, NE10 0HQ
5 (12 Fri & Sat)-11; 12-10.30 Sun
☎ (0191) 420 0659
Big Lamp Bitter, Prince Bishop Ale, seasonal beers Ⓗ
A good, honest pub that attracts a keen following for its value-for-money beers. Big Lamp's first tied house, it stocks the brewery's occasional beers including the powerful Blackout. A lively social centre, it has competitive darts and domino schools, and an impromptu folk night on Tuesday. Just 10 minutes on the metro from Newcastle city centre, it is well worth a visit. ♨⊖♣

Gateshead

Borough Arms
82 Bensham Road, NE8 1PS
12-3, 6-11; 12-midnight Fri & Sat; 12-11 Sun
☎ (0191) 478 1323
Black Sheep Best Bitter; Caledonian Deuchars IPA; Wells Bombardier; guest beers Ⓗ
Reputed to be one of the oldest surviving pubs in Gateshead, it was once a corn mill. Situated in a residential area, this single room, no frills local offers the best real ale in Gateshead. A popular live music venue, it hosts karaoke. Close to the main public transport interchange, it is on the town trail and near the historic Windmill Hills Park. ♨❀⊖♣P

Gosforth

Gosforth Hotel
Salters Road, NE3 1HQ
10-11; 11-12.30am Fri & Sat; 11-10.30 Sun
☎ (0191) 285 6617
Black Sheep Best Bitter; Fuller's London Pride; Marston's Pedigree; Taylor Landlord; Tetley Bitter; guest beers Ⓗ
On the corner of a busy road junction, this lively pub has a mixed clientele of students, locals and business people. As well as areas for drinking with large tables there are a number of comfortable sofas to relax in. The small, comfortable snug, decorated with old photographs, opens in the evening. ◑⊞⊖(Regent Centre)

Heaton

Chillingham Arms
Chillingham Road, NE6 5XN (opp. metro station)
11-11; 12-10.30 Sun
☎ (0191) 265 5915
Black Sheep Best Bitter; Mordue Workie Ticket; Theakston Best Bitter; guest beers Ⓗ
Run by Newcastle's best and most real ale friendly pub chain, Sir John Fitzgerald, this large, two-roomed pub is in an area popular with students east of Newcastle city centre. Seven beers and one cider are available. The public bar has a pool table, juke box and Sky TV; the lounge is quieter. An upstairs function room is available. ◐⊞♿⊖●P

Jarrow

Robin Hood
Primrose Hill, NE32 5UB
11-11 (11.30 Fri & Sat); 12-11 Sun
☎ (0191) 428 5454

Jarrow Bitter, Rivet Catcher, Joblings Swinging Gibbet, seasonal beers; guest beers Ⓗ
CAMRA regional Pub of the Year 2005 goes from strength to strength and has built a loyal following since it opened in 2002. There is a variety of rooms including a restaurant and, beyond the heavy church doors, an impressive bar. Its walls are adorned with photographs of the famous Jarrow crusade alongside CAMRA beer awards which have deservedly come thick and fast. The Jarrow Brewery adjoins the pub. Two guest beers are stocked and regular beer festivals hosted.
⛫❀◖◗⊟♿⊖(Fellgate)●P

Low Fell

Aletaster
706 Durham Road, NE9 6JA
✪ 12-11 (midnight Fri); 11-midnight Sat; 12-11 Sun
☎ (0191) 487 0770
Bateman XXXB; Jennings Cumberland Ale; Marston's Pedigree; Mordue Workie Ticket; Theakston Best Bitter; Wychwood Hobgoblin; guest beers Ⓗ
Styled as an ale house, this suburban pub has bare boards in the public bar but carpet in the cosy snug. It is still recognisable as a member of the Scottish & Newcastle T&J Bernard chain that it once was. With 10 cask conditioned beers available at all times it offers the widest selection of real ales in the area. Westons Old Rosie cider is served too – a rarity on Tyneside. Occasional beer festivals are held as well as a weekly quiz and, from time to time, live music.
❀⊟♣●P

Newburn

Keelman
Grange Road, NE15 8NL
✪ 11-11; 12-10.30 Sun
☎ (0191) 267 1689
Big Lamp Bitter, Summerhill Stout, Prince Bishop Ale, seasonal beers Ⓗ
The tap for Big Lamp, both the pub and brewery are housed in this converted Grade II listed water pumping station. A conservatory has extended the dining and drinking areas to accommodate the growing band of Big Lamp converts sampling the full range of its products. Situated near to the Coast-to-Coast cycle way, Hadrian's Wall Path and Tyne Riverside Country Park. ❀◖◗⊟P⊬

Newcastle upon Tyne

Bacchus
High Bridge, NE1 6BX
✪ 11.30-11; 7-10.30 Sun
☎ (0191) 261 1008
Harviestoun Bitter & Twisted; Taylor Landlord; guest beers Ⓗ
Popular pub with a comfortable seating area looking out onto the narrow street outside. There is plenty of standing room with high tables and a raised seating area at the back. Themed to look like the first class lounge of an ocean liner, the no-smoking snug has photographs of civil and military ships and north east shipbuilding yards. The pub only opens on Sunday lunchtime if Newcastle United is at home. A range of foreign bottled beers is stocked. ◖≠⊖(Monument)⊬

Bodega
125 Westgate Road, NE1 4AG
✪ 11-11 (midnight Fri & Sat); 12-10.30 Sun
☎ (0191) 221 1552
Big Lamp Prince Bishop Ale; Durham Magus; Mordue Workie Ticket; guest beers Ⓗ
A multiple winner of local CAMRA Pub of the Year awards. Its proximity to China Town, the Newcastle United football ground and the theatre ensures a mixed clientele. Match days – live or televised – are particularly busy. Note the striking original stained glass ceiling domes in the two main areas.
◖≠⊖(Central)●

Bridge Hotel
Castle Garth, NE1 1RQ
✪ 11.30-11; 12-10.30 Sun
☎ (0191) 232 6400
Caledonian Deuchars IPA; guest beers Ⓗ
Next to the high level bridge built by Stephenson and opposite the 'new' castle which gives the city its name, the pub and garden offer fine views of the River Tyne and the Gateshead Quayside. Inside is a spacious bar divided into a number of seating and standing areas. Railway and brewery memorabilia adorn the walls. The upstairs function room is home to reputedly the oldest folk club in the country. Music events are hosted most nights.
❀◖≠⊖(Central)⊬

Crown Posada ☆
33 Side, NE1 3JE
✪ 11 (12 Sat)-11; 12-10.30 Sun
☎ (0191) 232 1269
Draught Bass; Mordue Five Bridge Bitter; Taylor Landlord; guest beers Ⓗ
An architectural gem with an unusual high ceiling and stained glass windows, this small pub is a welcome oasis just off Newcastle's throbbing Quayside. A tiny snug – three-deep is packed – and larger lounge area combine to provide an excellent place to enjoy a well-kept ale or two. On the walls are photographs of the city and river in days past. There is no juke box, TV or background music other than an electric record player on the end of the bar here. **Q**≠⊖(Monument)

Duke
High Bridge, NE1 1EN
✪ 11-11; 12-10.30 Sun
☎ (0191) 261 8852
Caledonian Deuchars IPA; Mordue Geordie Pride, IPA; Tetley Bitter; Wells Bombardier; guest beers Ⓗ
Busy city centre pub close to the infamous Bigg Market with a friendly atmosphere. Recently refurbished, the pub is bright and cheerful with comfortable seating and plenty of standing room. Formerly the Duke of Wellington, pictures of the famous military man line the walls. Note, also, a picture of a previous owner called Stokoe whose main claim to fame was his size. The pub can be

busy when live sport is televised on match days. ◑≠⊖(Monument)

Fitzgeralds
60 Grey Street, NE1 6AF
✪ 11-11; 7-10.30 Sun
☎ (0191) 230 1350
Black Sheep Best Bitter; Mordue Workie Ticket; guest beers Ⓗ
On the finest street in the city designed by John Dobson, the narrow frontage leads to a large pub well fitted and furnished. The interior is on several levels with seating around the walls. Steps lead down to the spacious bar area with plenty of standing room and high tables. The pub can be busy especially at weekends.
◑≠⊖(Monument)

Head of Steam
1 Neville Street, NE1 1EU
✪ 12-1am (midnight Sun)
☎ (0191) 232 4379
Beer range varies Ⓗ
The pub has an unusual layout with nothing on the ground floor except the ladies and gents. The bar is upstairs and a music venue downstairs. Its location opposite the railway station ensures a steady flow of customers enjoying a pint before or after their journey, and in the evening travellers are joined by drinkers on the growing 'Central Station' circuit. One of a chain of Head of Steam houses, the pub holds special events and themed festivals. ≠⊖

Hotspur
103 Percy Street, NE1 7RY
✪ 11-11; 12-10.30 Sun
☎ (0191) 232 4352
Courage Directors; McEwan's 80/-; Theakston Old Peculier; guest beers Ⓗ
Large single roomed pub in the university area, popular with students and staff from the nearby Royal Victoria infirmary. Independent Scottish beers are a particular favourite of the manager and there is usually at least one available. The popularity of the pub ensures a rapid turnover of beers and the quality is always good. Wide windows and large wall mirrors create a light and airy feel although the pub can be full on match days. ◑⊖(Haymarket)

New Bridge
2 Argyle Street, NE1 6PE
✪ 11-11; 12-10.30 Sun
☎ (0191) 240 2617
Beer range varies Ⓗ
This cosy bar is on the outskirts of the city centre. The single room interior is divided by partitions. Customers include regulars, real ale visitors and lunch trade. A large-screen TV shows sport; Thursday is quiz night. A Fitzgerald's house, the New Bridge offers the cheapest beers of six in the city.
◑⊖(Manors)♣

Newcastle Arms
57 St Andrews Street, NE1 5SE
✪ 11-11; 12-10.30 Sun
☎ (0191) 260 2490
Caledonian Deuchars IPA; guest beers Ⓗ
An impressive selection of ales greets the visitor here, and occasional guest cider too. Beers are sourced from breweries up and down the country, guaranteeing a treat every time. The exterior of the pub features an interesting curved glass window and decorative tiling. Within earshot of Newcastle United's football ground, the pub is always busy on match days. ⊖(St James)

Tilley's
Westgate Road, NE1 4AG
✪ 12-11 (midnight Thu; 1am Fri & Sat); 12-midnight Sun
☎ (0191) 232 0692
Caledonian Deuchars IPA; Hopback Summer Lightning; guest beers Ⓗ
Part of the Head of Steam chain, the beer range is complemented by a selection of draught and bottled continental beers. The two-roomed interior includes a no-smoking room reached by a flight of stairs and a larger L-shaped area with bar stools and comfortable seating. The room has a light and airy feel with advertisements and prints on the walls. Food is served until 5pm.
◑≠⊖(Central)♠⚟

North Shields

Magnesia Bank
Camden Street, NE30 1NH
✪ 11-11 (midnight Thu-Sat); 12-10.30 Sun
☎ (0191) 257 4831 ⊕ magnesiabank.co.uk
Durham Magus; Mordue Workie Ticket; guest beers Ⓗ
Opened in 1989 in a converted Georgian bank, this excellent town centre pub is a past local CAMRA Pub of the Year. It is the brewery tap for Mordue and stocks up to six guest ales at any one time. Excellent meals are served in the Garden restaurant and themed international food nights are a speciality. It is also a venue for live music and comedy nights. ♨Q◑⊖⚟

Oddfellows
7 Albion Street, NE30 2RJ
✪ 11-11; 12-10.30 Sun
☎ (0191) 257 4288 ⊕ oddfellowspub.co.uk
Greene King Abbot; Hadrian & Border Gladiator; Jarrow Bitter Ⓗ
The walls of this friendly, small, single-room lounge bar are covered with historic maps, photographs of pre-war North Shields and newspaper cuttings of former local boxing heroes. The pub has strong sporting connections and football matches are shown on the large-screen TV. The landlord fundraises for charities and the darts team has most of the top 16 professional players signed up to play when in the area.
✿♿⊖♣

Porthole
11 New Quay, NE29 6LQ
✪ 11-11 (midnight Wed-Sat); 12-10.30 Sun
☎ (0191) 257 6645
Courage Directors; guest beers Ⓗ
Dating from 1834 and rebuilt around 1900, the Porthole is situated close to the North

Shields ferry landing. It has two bars separated by a food serving area. Local breweries are chosen to provide the guest ales. A lunchtime jazz club is held on Wednesday and there is also live entertainment on Friday and Sunday evenings. ❀◐⊖♣⚡

Prince of Wales

2 Liddell Street, NE30 1HE

12 (7 Tue)-11; 12-11.30 Sun

☎ (0191) 296 2816

Samuel Smith OBB H

There are records of this pub dating back to 1627, but the current building, faced with green glazed brick, dates from 1927. The premises lay empty for some years before being restored in traditional style by Sam Smith's and reopened in 1992. A rare outlet for Sam Smith's this far north, it is well worth a visit. Crab sandwiches and fish and chips are served at lunchtime and are highly recommended. ♨Q♉❀◐⊟⊖♣⚡

Teac Fiddlers

112 Church Way, NE29 6PB

11-11; 12-10.30 Sun

☎ (07790) 679725

Draught Bass; Caledonian Deuchars IPA; Jennings Cumberland Ale; guest beer H

Opened in January 2005, this pub has shown a commitment to supplying real ale to a high standard. It is the only pub in the area that is no smoking throughout. As the name suggests, it has an Irish theme and its music nights may feature traditional Irish tunes. ◐⊖⚡

Penshaw

Monument

Village Lane, DH4 7ER (off A183, signed to Old Penshaw)

12-11 (10.30 Sun)

☎ (0191) 584 1027

Jennings Cumberland Ale H

Delightful one-room bar overlooking the green with Penshaw monument a short walk away. The bar has a stone fireplace with a real fire. The walls are adorned with photographs of old Penshaw and the monument itself. There is a pool room at the rear and a garden for summer drinking. A popular locals' pub, visitors are also warmly welcomed. Toasties are available at lunchtime. ♨❀♿P

Ryton

Olde Cross

Barmoor Lane, NE40 3QP

4-11 (midnight Fri); 12-midnight Sat; 12-10.30 Sun

☎ (0191) 413 4689

Black Sheep Best Bitter; Caledonian Deuchars IPA; Taylor Landlord; Wells Bombardier H

Thriving local in a picturesque setting by the old village green and the cross that gives the pub its name. The beer range may rotate between the four regular ales. There is an outdoor area for drinking and a function room upstairs available to hire. Ryton Willows, a country park with pleasant riverside walks, is just down the hill. ❀⚡

Shiremoor

Shiremoor House Farm

Middle Engine Lane, NE29 8DZ

11-11; 12-10.30 Sun

☎ (0191) 257 6302

Mordue Workie Ticket; Taylor Landlord; guest beers H

Award-winning Fitzgerald conversion of a derelict stone-built farm retaining many original features including the conical, raftered 'gin-gan'. The pub's well-deserved reputation for its beer quality and good food means it can be very busy at times. There is no juke box, pool table or games machines. Well worth a visit. Q♉❀◐◑P⚡

South Gosforth

Victory

Killingworth Road, NE3 1SY

12-11 (midnight Fri & Sat); 12-11 Sun

☎ (0191) 285 1254

Caledonian Deuchars IPA; Courage Directors; Theakston Best Bitter; Wells Bombardier; guest beers H

Established on this site in 1861, the pub is named after Nelson's flagship. Small and open plan, the interior is divided into drinking areas with a low-beamed ceiling, traditional wooden decor and two fireplaces. A piano provides the entertainment. Six handpumps on the bar serve the regular ales and two guests, usually from local micros. There is also a good malt whisky selection. Quiz night is Tuesday. Quiet in the afternoons, the pub can be busy at the weekend with tables outside in summer. ♨Q❀◐♿⊖P

South Shields

Alum Ale House

River Drive, NE33 1JR

11-11; 12-10.30 Sun

☎ (0191) 427 7245

Banks's Bitter; Marston's Pedigree; guest beers H

Old-fashioned, two-roomed pub close to the market place and ferry landing – an ideal waiting room for the North Shields ferry. Relaxed and friendly, the Alum is a firm favourite on the town centre circuit. Two regular beers are complemented by four frequently changing guests. A small range of bottled beer is also available. ❀⊖

Bamburgh

Bamburgh Avenue, NE34 6SS (on coast road)

11-11; 12-10.30 Sun

☎ (0191) 454 1899

Greene King IPA, Abbot; guest beer H

Spacious, open plan pub at the finishing line of the Great North Run. The interior has a games area with two pool tables and a large-screen TV at one end and a lounge with raised seating areas for dining at the other. The regulars help to choose the guest beers. In summer there is seating outside affording excellent views over the Leas to the North Sea. ♉❀◐◑ÅP

Dolly Peel
137 Commercial Road, NE33 1SH
✪ 11-11 (midnight Thu-Sat); 12-11 Sun
☎ (0191) 427 1441
Black Sheep Best Bitter; Caledonian Deuchars IPA; Courage Directors; Taylor Landlord; guest beers 🄷
This small, quiet, two-roomed pub has been a regular in the Guide for more than 20 years. Situated close to the banks of the Tyne, it is part of the Mill Dam circuit and can be busy at weekends. A former CAMRA local Pub of the Year, the landlord has maintained the high standards of his predecessors. Attracting a mostly mature clientele, there is no music or TV. The pub gets its name from an 18th-century local fishwife. ◖▲⊖(Chichester)P◻

Maltings
2 Claypath Lane NE33 4PG (opp. town hall)
✪ 12-11 (11.30 Fri & Sat); 12-11 Sun
☎ (0191) 427 7147
Jarrow Bitter, Rivet Catcher, Joblings Swinging Gibbet, Westoe IPA, seasonal beers; guest beers 🄷
Part of the award-winning Jarrow Brewery estate, this new, traditional-style pub with an L-shaped lounge and small bar room is built in a former restaurant. The U-shaped bar has 13 handpumps, 10 reserved for Jarrow beers, the others for guests and cider. A baby grand piano is played at weekends. Two beer festivals are held in March and October. Q◖◗⊖●P

Riverside
3 Mill Dam, NE33 1QH
✪ 11.30-11 (midnight Fri & Sat); 12-10.30 Sun
☎ (0191) 455 2328
Black Sheep Special; Courage Directors; John Smith's Bitter; Taylor Landlord; guest beers 🄷
Popular corner-site pub in the Mill Dam area a short distance from the market place. Two guest beers supplement the regular range. The pub attracts a varied clientele and is handy for the Custom House concert and theatre venue which stands close by. The Tuesday night quiz generates keen competition. ❀⊖●

Stag's Head
45 Fowler Street, NE33 1NS
✪ 11-11 (midnight Fri & Sat); 12-11.30 Sun
☎ (0191) 427 2911
Draught Bass 🄷
Small but busy pub with an unspoilt interior including a ground floor bar and upstairs lounge. A real ale oasis in an area dominated by circuit drinking establishments, you will find probably the finest Bass in the town here. Visitors and regulars alike are guaranteed a warm welcome. It can be very busy on disco and karaoke nights. ♔⊖

Steamboat
51 Coronation Street, Mill Dam, NE33 1EQ
✪ 12-midnight; 12-11.30 Sun
☎ (0191) 454 0134
Black Sheep Best Bitter; Caledonian Deuchars IPA; Greene King Old Speckled Hen; Wells Bombardier; guest beers 🄷
This traditional riverside tavern is one of the oldest in town. The bar is decorated with nautical memorabilia. A popular inn, it gets especially busy at weekends. Close to the ferry landing and the Custom House theatre, it is handy for pre- or post-performance drinks. The long-standing landlord and staff offer a warm welcome. ◖◗⊖♣

Trimmers Arms
Commercial Road, NE33 1RW
✪ 11.30-11 (1am Thu-Sat); 12-10.30 Sun
☎ (0191) 454 5550 🌐 trimmers-arms.co.uk
Draught Bass; Bateman XXXB; Courage Directors; Jarrow Rivet Catcher; John Smith's Bitter; Stones Bitter; guest beers 🄷
Built in 2004 on the site of a pub with the same name that never opened because of WWII. This three-roomed pub comprises a quality seafood restaurant, small private function room called Nelson's Boardroom and a bar on two levels. Large-screen TVs show football on match days.
◖◗♿⊖(Chichester)●P

Sunderland

Clarendon
143 High Street East, SR1 2BL (follow signs to docks on B1293)
✪ 11 (12 Sun)-11
☎ (0191) 510 3200
Bull Lane Nowtsa Matter, Ryhope Tug, seasonal beers; guest beer 🄷
After refurbishment in 2005 this traditional dockside pub reopened as the home of Bull Lane Brewery – Sunderland's first brew-pub. The single-room building has views across the River Wear of the redeveloped north shore. It offers a friendly welcome to visitors and regulars with three ales on offer and the first chance to try new beers from the brewery. A new entry to the Guide, it is well worth a visit. Q♿🚌(14A)♣●

Cliff
Mere Knolls Road, SR6 9LG
✪ 12-11 (midnight Fri & Sat); 12-midnight Sun
☎ (0191) 548 6200
Courage Directors; Marston's Pedigree; guest beer 🄷
In a quiet residential area, this single-room, open-plan pub has a raised games area and TV, but the volume is kept at a low level. Monitors on the beer fonts allow you to continue viewing while ordering your beer. Guest ales are often from micro-breweries. Quizzes are held on Tuesday and Wednesday. ♿⊖(Stadium of Light)

Fitzgeralds
10-12 Green Terrace, SR1 3PZ
✪ 11-11 (midnight Fri & Sat); 12-10.30 Sun
☎ (0191) 567 0852
Beer range varies 🄷
A magnificent range of beers awaits you at this large Art Deco-style pub in the heart of the city's café-bar and nightclub circuit. Ten handpumps offer nine real ales mostly from micro-breweries and one changing cider. Popular with local workers, shoppers and students during the day, it is even livelier in

the evening. The small Chart room is quieter than the main bar and hosts the Monday night quiz. A past local CAMRA Pub of the Year and regional winner.
❀◑⇌⊖(University)●

Ivy House

7 Worcester Street, SR2 7AW
⊙ 11-11; 12-10.30 Sun
☎ (0191) 567 3399
Darwin Evolution, Ghost Ale; Taylor Landlord; guest beers Ⓗ
Tucked away in a side street near Park Lane interchange, the Ivy is a large open-plan bar popular with a wide mix of customers including students from the nearby university. Local bands perform in the bar on Thursday. Six handpumps dispense three regular beers complemented by up to three guests. The same landlord has managed this pub for many years. No food is served Sunday. ◑⇌⊖(Park Lane)

King's Arms

Beech Street, SR4 6BU (behind B&Q warehouse)
⊙ 11-11 (midnight Fri & Sat); 12-10.30 Sun
☎ (0191) 567 9804
Taylor Landlord; guest beers Ⓗ
Situated off the beaten track, this unspoilt, traditional pub is over 150 years old. It has two rooms, each with a real fire, and friendly staff offer a warm welcome. With nine handpumps on the bar, there is something to suit all tastes. The garden has a large marquee which hosts live music. Awarded CAMRA local Pub of the Year 2005.
⩩❀⊖(University/Millfield)●

Rosedene

Queen Alexandra Road, Tunstall, SR2 9BT
⊙ 11-11 (11.30 Sat); 12-11 Sun
☎ (0191) 528 4313
Greene King IPA, Abbot, Old Speckled Hen; guest beers Ⓗ
Large, multi-room former Georgian house in substantial grounds with a large conservatory. Catering for a wide clientele, the beer range is supplemented by three guest ales. The restaurant offers high quality meals. Quizzes are held on Monday and Wednesday and live music is hosted occasionally. ⩩Q❀◑♿P

Saltgrass

Hanover Place, Deptford, SR4 6BY
⊙ 11-11 (midnight Fri & Sat); 12-10.30 Sun
☎ (0191) 565 7229
Draught Bass; Black Sheep Best Bitter; Caledonian Deuchars IPA; guest beers Ⓗ
Traditional two-roomed pub with a low ceiling, it gets its name from the tough saltgrass that was here before the shipyards. The public bar has a nautical theme. A welcoming real fire and friendly staff await you on cold winter days and there is a patio for outdoor drinking in the summer. The no-smoking lounge becomes a busy restaurant from Wednesday to Sunday. The walls feature pictures of old Deptford. Curry night is Monday and quiz night Tuesday.
⩩❀◑⊖(Millfield)●P

Sunniside

Potter's Wheel

Sun Street, NE16 5EE
⊙ 11.30-11; 12-10.30 Sun
☎ (0191) 488 3628
Caledonian Deuchars IPA; guest beers Ⓗ
Part of the Fitzgerald's chain, this spacious village pub has several seating areas served by one main bar. It offers continually rotating guest ales from all parts of the country, with local breweries featuring regularly among the handpumps. In previous times the building was a nightclub with a star attraction – Mandy Rice-Davies! ❀◑♿P⊬

Tynemouth

Cumberland Arms

17 Front Street, NE30 4DX
⊙ 12-11; 12-10.30 Sun
☎ (0191) 257 1820 🌐 cumberlandarms.co.uk
Courage Directors; McEwan's 80/-; Theakston Best Bitter; guest beers Ⓗ
Split-level pub with two bars each dispensing six real ales. The dining area is at the rear of the building, serving good value meals. One of the guest ales is often a mild. The pub can become busy at weekends when live football matches are shown on the large-screen TV – the manager is a big football fan. ◑♿⊖

Tynemouth Lodge Hotel

Tynemouth Road, NE30 4AA
⊙ 11-11; 12-10.30 Sun
☎ (0191) 257 7565 🌐 tynemouthlodgehotel.co.uk
Draught Bass; Belhaven 80/-; Caledonian Deuchars IPA; guest beer Ⓗ
This attractive, externally-tiled free house, built in 1799, has been in every issue of the Guide since 1984 when it was taken over by the present owner. The comfortable, single-room lounge bar is noted in the area for always having Scottish real ales on tap, and for selling reputedly the highest volume of Draught Bass on Tyneside. It is next to Northumberland Park and near the Coast-to-Coast cycle route. Q❀⊖P

Washington

Courtyard

Arts Centre, Biddick Lane, Fatfield, NE38 8AB
⊙ 11-11 (midnight Fri & Sat); 12-11 Sun
☎ (0191) 417 0445
Taylor Landlord; guest beers Ⓗ
Café-bar within the Arts Centre owned by Sunderland council, with seven handpumps offering the largest range of beers in Washington plus real cider and perry. Beers are sourced from independent breweries from the north east and nationally. Events include live music on Monday and curry and quiz night on Thursday. Beer festivals are held in March and August. ❀◑♿●P⊬

Sandpiper

Easby Road, Biddick, NE38 7NN (400 yds from Biddick Lane)
⊙ 11-11; 12-10.30 Sun
☎ (0191) 416 0038

Greene King IPA, Abbot, Old Speckled Hen; guest beers Ⓗ

In a residential area, the two-roomed pub has six handpumps including three guests. A good selection of wines is also available. Substantial meals are served at reasonable prices. Sky TV is shown here. A quiz is held on Tuesday and Saturday is music night. Children are welcome while food is available until 8pm (3pm Sun). ❀◑♿♣P

Steps

Spout Lane, NE38 7HP

✪ 11-11; 12-10.30 Sun

☎ (0191) 415 7001

Beer range varies Ⓗ

Small, comfortable lounge bar in an old village close to Washington Old Hall. A locals' pub, it is quiet during the day and lively at weekend evenings when it attracts a younger clientele. There are quizzes on Wednesday and Sunday and dominoes is popular. A regular Guide entry since 1999, this gem is well worth a visit. ◑♣

West Boldon

Black Horse

Rectory Bank, NE36 0QQ

✪ 11-11; 12-10.30 Sun

☎ (0191) 536 1814

Darwin Evolution; guest beers Ⓗ

Next to a fine church, this old pub has a cosy L-shaped bar and a renowned local restaurant. Live music is played on Sunday. A supporter of the local Darwin Brewery, Evolution is always on one of the two handpumps. Q❀◑P

West Herrington

Stables

DH4 4ND (off B1286 signed W Herrington)

✪ 3.30-11 (midnight Fri); 12-midnight Sat; 12-11 Sun

☎ (0191) 584 9226

Black Sheep Best Bitter; guest beer Ⓗ

Welcoming, atmospheric pub with an eclectic collection of horse-related photographs and memorabilia. A barn conversion, the interior retains the original beams with wooden furnishings. Happy hour is 3.30-7pm Monday to Friday and the pub is busy during these times. A small room off the bar is quieter and there is an area for games in the main bar. ♔Q♨❀♿P

West Moor

George Stephenson

Great Lime Road, NE12 7NJ

✪ 12-11 daily

☎ (0191) 268 1073

Caledonian Deuchars IPA; McEwan's 80/-; guest beers Ⓗ

Much altered over the last century, the pub retains two largely separate drinking areas which, when required, can become a single room by opening the dividing doors. A patio offers outdoor drinking in the shadow of the east coast main line. A well-established music venue, live bands play on several evenings and the occasional Sunday afternoon – phone for details. Two guest beers change frequently, often from smaller or local breweries.
❀P

Whitley Bay

Briar Dene

71 The Links, NE26 1UE

✪ 11-11; 12-10.30 Sun

☎ (0191) 252 0926

Beer range varies Ⓗ

Every day is a beer festival at this Fitzgerald's pub, with eight handpumps dispensing constantly-changing beers from all over the country, including many that are not usually available in this area. Once a toll house, it enjoys a well-earned reputation for good quality beer and food. The attractively-lit lounge has coloured, leaded glass above the bar and overlooks the links, St Mary's lighthouse and the sea. The smaller rear bar has a TV, pool and darts. Former local CAMRA Pub of the Year. ❀◑⊟♿⅄P⊬

Fitzgeralds

2-4 South Parade, NE26 2DT

✪ 11-11 (1am Fri & Sat); 12-midnight Sun

☎ (0191) 251 1255

Beer range varies Ⓗ

Large, friendly town centre pub near the metro and bus services. It can be very busy at the weekend, with a wider range of real ales usually available during the week. Like most of the Fitzgerald's pubs, the food is good value and popular. The present licensee's last pub was a regular in the Guide and he is now turning this one around to match his high standards.
◑♿⊖⊬

Rockliffe Arms

Algernon Place, NE26 2DT

✪ 11-11; 12-10.30 Sun

☎ (0191) 253 1299

Beer range varies Ⓗ

A compact Sir John Fitzgerald one-room community pub offering old-style drinking in pleasant surroundings. Enter by the snug or the lounge doors that are attractively decorated with stained glass. The single bar is divided to serve two distinct drinking areas. Regular darts and dominoes nights are held. Tuesday is quiz night.
❀⊖♣

> Is there anywhere in this damned place where we can get a decent bottle of Bass?
>
> **Alfred, Lord Tennyson,** during a public performance of one of his poems, **1862**

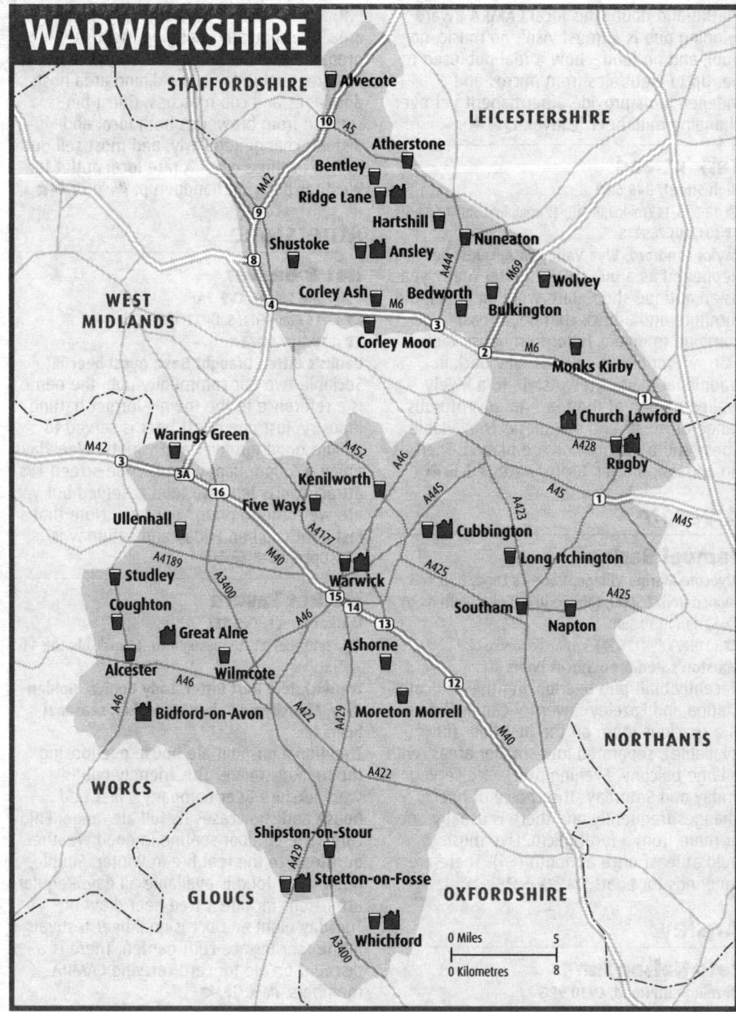

Alcester

Holly Bush

Henley Street, B49 5QX

12-11 (1am Fri & Sat); 12-11.30 Sun

☎ (01789) 762482

Black Sheep Best Bitter; Cannon Royall Fruiterer's Mild; Purity Pure Gold; Uley Bitter; guest beers H

Traditional local in an historic market town. Recent restoration work has brought the garden and function room back into use, as well as three more rooms, making a total of five including the public bar. A beer festival is held during the Alcester & Arden Folk Festival at midsummer, plus an Oktoberfest. Regular folk sessions are usually twice a month (Tue & Fri) and spontaneous music may be expected at any time. Several times winner of CAMRA local branch Pub of the Month, August 2001, in What's Brewing, the CAMRA newspaper.

Three Tuns

34 High Street, B49 5AB

12-11; 12-10.30 Sun

☎ (01789) 762626

Goff's Jouster; Hobsons Best Bitter; guest beers H

Do not be fooled by the double-front and bulls-eye windows making the Tuns look like an antique shop. Inside there are low beams, a stone floor and an exposed area of

INDEPENDENT BREWERIES

Atomic Rugby
Church End Ridge Lane
Frankton Bagby Church Lawford
North Cotswold Stretton-on-Fosse
Purity Great Alne
Rugby Rugby
Shakespeare's Bidford-on-Avon
Slaughterhouse Warwick
Tunnel Ansley
Warwickshire Cubbington
Wizard Whichford

wattle-and-daub. This local CAMRA award-winning pub is a 'must visit': no music, no pool, and no food – how a real pub used to be. Up to eight ales from micros and independents provide a permanent yet ever-changing mini beer festival. Q🚌♣

Turk's Head

High Street, B49 5AD

12-3, 5-11 (midnight Fri); 12-midnight Sat; 12-11 Sun

☎ (01789) 765948

Taylor Landlord; Wye Valley HPA; guest beer Ⓗ

Reopened as a pub in 1999 after many years as an antique shop. Bare wooden floors, old furniture and a brick chimney breast combine to give a Tudor farmhouse feel. Narrow fronted, it extends way back in traditional market town style to a lovely walled garden at the rear. An adventurous range of meals and bar snacks is available. Chess and backgammon are played. There is no admission after 11pm. ⛰❀◐◑♿🚌♣

Alvecote

Samuel Barlow

Alvecote Marina Village, Robey's Lane, B78 1AS

(signed from B5000, Tamworth to Polesworth road)

12-11 (10.30 Sun)

☎ (01827) 898175 🌐 samuelbarlow.co.uk

Marston's Pedigree; guest beers Ⓗ

Recently built pub overlooking the Alvecote Marina and Fazeley-Coventry Canal. The bar is a spacious room on the first floor (lift available), separated into smaller areas, with a large balcony. Evening meals are served Friday and Saturday. The choice of beer changes frequently and there is usually one or more from a local micro. Live music is held at least once a month (Fri). There are moorings for boats. ⛰❀◑♿P

Ansley

Lord Nelson Inn

Birmingham Road, CV10 9PG

12-2.30, 5.30-11; 12-11 Sat; 12-10.30 Sun

☎ (024) 7639 2305

Draught Bass; Tunnel Late Ott, Trade Winds, seasonal beers; guest beer Ⓗ

Renowned for its food as well as its beer, the pub features regularly in the Guide. Run by the same family for over 30 years, it has two restaurants and a bar, all with a nautical theme. Trafalgar Day is celebrated with a gala meal, ceremony and beer festival. The Tunnel Brewery (a separate venture) can be viewed from the garden and carry-outs are available. Beer appreciation courses are held in the Victory restaurant. ❀◐◑🖵🚌P

Ashorne

Cottage Tavern

CV35 9DR (1½ miles from B4100 at Fosse Way Island) OS303577

12-3 (not Mon), 5-11; 12-11 Sat; 12-10.30 Sun

☎ (01926) 651410

John Smith's Bitter; guest beers Ⓗ

Friendly village pub with a welcoming atmosphere. A cosy log fire warms the traditional drinking area at one end of the bar; at the other is a no-smoking dining area. The regularly changing menu is prepared by a local chef. When not in use for the great value food, the dining area hosts dominoes and crib matches. Guest beers, sourced from breweries both local and distant, change regularly, and most sell out in two or three days. A rare local outlet for Westons perry on handpump. ⛰❀◐◑♣●

Atherstone

Hat & Beaver

130 Long Street, CV9 1AF

12-11 (2am Fri & Sat); 12-10.30 Sun

☎ (01827) 720082

Banks's Bitter; Draught Bass; guest beer Ⓗ

Sociable two-bar community pub; the name is a reference to the town's former hatting industry. Just one guest beer is served to ensure good turnover and variety. Weekdays enjoy a 6-8pm happy hour. Wide-screen TVs attract sports fans. No food is served but you are welcome to bring your own. Note that last admission on Friday and Saturday is 11.30pm. ❀⇌🚌♣P

Market Tavern

Market Street, CV9 1ET

12(10 Tue)-11; 10-midnight Fri; 11-midnight Sat; 11-11 Sun

Warwickshire Best Bitter, Lady Godiva, Golden Bear, Churchyard Bob, King Maker, seasonal beers Ⓗ

Traditional unspoilt ale house overlooking the market square. This friendly pub is Warwickshire Beer Company's first tied house and showcases its full ale range. Enjoy café-style outdoor seating in good weather or retreat to the real fire in winter. Simple, good value food is available all day. Regular attractions include a free beer draw on Tuesday night and occasional beer festivals in the rear terrace-cum-garden. There is a discount on ale for card-carrying CAMRA members. ⛰❀◐◑⇌

Bedworth

Bear & Ragged Staff

50 King Street, CV12 8JA

11-midnight (1am Fri & Sat); 12-midnight Sun

☎ (024) 7649 4340

Greene King Abbot; Marston's Pedigree; guest beers Ⓗ

Long, narrow Wetherspoon's pub converted from a toyshop. There are photographs and articles about the history of Bedworth spread around the pub. The rear section is used as a family area with a TV. Outside there is a patio with hanging baskets and pot plants. It stocks up to six guest beers, many from local micro-breweries. ❀◐◑♿⇌🚌●⚡

Bentley

Horse & Jockey

Coleshill Road, CV9 2HL

(on B4116, 2½ miles SW of Atherstone)

12-3, 5.30-11; 12-11 Fri-Sun

☎ (01827) 715236

Draught Bass; Brewster's Hophead; Fuller's

London Pride; Shepherd Neame Spitfire; guest beers Ⓗ
Old whitewashed country pub with a strong local trade. The multi-room layout includes a time-warp bar with scrubbed wooden tables, open fire and quarry tiles. The lounge has been carefully extended into the stable without destroying the character of the building. Two changing guest beers complement the regular ales; Brewster's is unusual for the area. No food is available on winter Sunday evenings. The attractive garden has a children's play area.
⛫❀◑◐⊟♣P

Bulkington

Olde Chequers Inn

Chequers Street, CV12 9NH
⏲ 12-3, 6-11; 12-11 Thu-Sat; 12-10.30 Sun
☎ (024) 7631 2182 🌐 oldechequersinn.com
Draught Bass; M&B Brew XI; guest beers Ⓗ
Situated in the centre of the village, games are popular here, with darts, dominoes, crib and football teams. The bar has an array of pump clips showing guest beers from local as well as regional breweries. Leading from the main bar is a passageway to two games rooms, the larger of which can be hired.
⛫♨❀♿🚌(56, 750 and 775)♣P

Weavers Arms

12 Long Street, Ryton, CV12 9JZ
⏲ 12-3, 5-11; 12-11 Fri & Sat; 12-5, 7-10.30 Sun
☎ (024) 7631 4415
Draught Bass; guest beers Ⓗ
Over a 100 years ago the hamlet of Ryton was known for its weaving, hence the pub's name. The attractive family-run free house has a split-level stone-floored bar and a small wood-panelled games room. The lounge has been refurbished and is now no-smoking. Guest beers are from small regional and local brewers. Lunches are served Tuesday-Saturday. ⛫❀◑⊟🚌♣⚟

Corley Ash

Saracen's Head

Tamworth Road, CV7 8BP (on B4098)
⏲ 12-2.30, 5.30-11; 12-11 Fri & Sat; 12-4, 6-10.30 Sun
☎ (01676) 540853
Flowers Original; Ringwood Best Bitter; Wadworth 6X; guest beer Ⓗ
Imposing three-storey detached pub with a garden and children's play area. Inside are two rooms, a dining room and larger split-level stone and wood floored bar decorated with horse brasses and brass plates. The dartboard has its devotees but is not intrusive. Meals are popular. The knowledgeable landlord is dedicated to real ale. ❀◑◐🚌♣●

Corley Moor

Bull & Butcher

Common Lane, CV7 8AQ (1½ miles from B4098)
⏲ 10-midnight (breakfast from 9am) daily
☎ (01676) 540241
Draught Bass; M&B Brew XI; guest beer Ⓗ
Busy village local with separate rooms and a newly extended dining area, serving good value meals featuring local produce. The real pies (not the usual casserole with a lid on) are recommended. One of the rooms is completely unspoiled with an authentic range and high-backed settle – wonderful on a cold winter's night! The extensive outdoor area is ideal for children. Flowers are abundant and there are fine views over the moor. ⛫Q❀◑◐⊟♿⛺♣P⚟

Coughton

Throckmorton Arms

Coughton Hill, B49 5HX (on A435 between Studley and Alcester)
⏲ 12-11; 12-10.30 Sun
☎ (01789) 766366 🌐 thethrockmortonarms.co.uk
Hook Norton Hooky Bitter; St Austell Tribute; Wye Valley Butty Bach; guest beers Ⓗ
Large roadside hotel with a welcoming atmosphere due to the friendly staff and real fire. It is situated close to Coughton Court of 'Gunpowder Plot' fame. The lounge and snug are served from a single bar. The hotel is popular with business people for overnight stays and with visitors on weekend breaks. A pleasant no-smoking restaurant is next to a large patio overlooking fields. Food ranges from snacks to full home-cooked meals.
⛫❀🛏◑◐♿P⚟

Cubbington

Queen's Head

20 Queen Street, CV32 7NA
⏲ 12-11; 12-10.30 Sun
☎ (01926) 429949
Ansells Mild, Best Bitter; Draught Bass; guest beer Ⓗ
Traditional 19th-century village pub providing a welcoming cosy haven for drinkers to sample their 'usual' or to experiment with one of the ever-changing guest beers. Pump clips from featured beers adorn the bar ceiling. The interior is divided into an attractively furnished lounge, a refurbished bar and a pool room. Note the old photographs of the village. The meeting point for many village clubs and societies, sporting enthusiasts are well catered for on 'big match' days. Q❀⊟♿🚌♣P

Five Ways

Case is Altered ☆

Case Lane, CV35 7JD (off Five Ways Road near A4141/A4177 jct) OS225701
⏲ 12-2.30, 6-11; 12-2, 7-10.30 Sun
☎ (01926) 484206
Greene King IPA; Hook Norton Old Hooky; Ⓖ **guest beer** Ⓗ
Traditional 350-year-old rural pub. Gravity beers are dispensed by antique cask pumps from a stillage behind the bar. Mobile phones, dogs, children and computers are barred. There is a bar billiards table in the entrance corridor that takes old sixpence coins – available from the bar. Memorabilia from old Leamington breweries decorate the bar. Roaring log fires in the colder months add to the charm. One guest beer is usually from a local brewery. ⛫Q❀♿♣P

Hartshill

Stag & Pheasant

The Green, CV10 0SW

3 (12 Thu)-midnight; 12-12.30am Fri & Sat; 12-11.30 Sun

(024) 7639 3173

Draught Bass; Flowers Original; Marston's Pedigree; guest beer Ⓗ

Two-roomed pub overlooking the village green, ideally situated for walkers using the nearby Hartshill Hayes country park and canal users. The guest beer is usually from local breweries Church End or Tunnel. Traditional pub lunches are served; Chinese food features every night except Monday which is curry and chilli night. A summer beer festival is held every June.

Kenilworth

Old Bakery

12 High Street, CV8 1LZ (near A429/A452 jct)

5.30 (5 Fri & Sat)-11; 12-2, 7-10.30 Sun

(01926) 864111 oldbakeryhotel.co.uk

Hook Norton Hooky Bitter; Taylor Landlord; guest beers Ⓗ

This attractively restored former bakery is situated in the heart of Kenilworth Old Town; the perfect place for a pint after a stroll around the neighbouring Abbey fields and the castle ruins. Recently awarded the National Clean Air gold award, it was the first pub in Warwickshire to become no-smoking throughout. As well as two inside drinking areas, there is an attractive outside patio around an old well. Disabled access is from the rear car park. Q P

Royal Oak

36 New Street, CV8 2EZ

4(12 Sat)-11; 12-10.30 Sun

(01926) 853201

Ansells Best Bitter; Marston's Pedigree; Taylor Landlord; Wells Bombardier Ⓗ

A lively local with a friendly atmosphere, situated near old Kenilworth. The main bar with adjoining lounge features a juke-box and dartboard, there is also a games room with pool table. Sport is popular here, with golf and West Bromwich Albion memorabilia adorning the walls and active darts and pool teams. The big screen is rolled out for sporting events. The attractive rear garden is popular in summer and quizzes are held on Sundays.

Virgins & Castle

7 High Street, CV8 1LY (A429/A452 jct)

11-11.30; 11-11 Sun

(01926) 853737

Everards Tiger, Original; Fuller's London Pride; Wells Bombardier; guest beer Ⓗ

A merger between the Two Virgins and the Castle Tavern, the pub dates from 1777, though its origins may go back to the 1500s. There is a main bar serving the lounge and three snugs, with wood panelling and exposed beams. The heated terrace is popular throughout the warmer months. There is an adventurous menu of Japanese and Filipino cuisine alongside more traditional favourites. Limited parking is available in the high street. Q

Long Itchington

Harvester Inn

6 Church Road, CV47 9PG

12-2.30, 6-11; 12-3, 6-10.30 Sun

(01926) 812698 theharvesterinn.co.uk

Hook Norton Hooky Bitter, Old Hooky; guest beer Ⓗ

The 21st consecutive year in the Guide for this village local – the owners took over in 1984. A genuine free house, it has an outside drinking area and is an easy walk from the Grand Union Canal. The unchanging interior features several historic photographs of the village, but it is also keeping up with the times as a WiFi hotspot. The current guest beer is listed on its website.

P

Monks Kirby

Denbigh Arms

Monks Kirby, CV23 0QX

12-3 (not Mon), 6.30-11; 12-11 summer Sat; 12-3, 6.30-10.30 Sun

(01788) 832303

Caledonian Deuchars IPA; Greene King Abbot; Taylor Landlord; Theakston XB; guest beer Ⓗ

Beautiful, unspoilt, traditional village inn dating back to the 17th century, opposite the second largest church in Warwickshire. The central bar serves all the linked rooms and there is a no-smoking snug. An extensive menu is available. Outside there is seating on the front and rear lawns and a children's play area. Q P

Moreton Morrell

Black Horse

CV35 9AR (near Fosse Way and M40 jct 12)

11.30-3, 6.30-11; 12-3, 7-10.30 Sun

(01926) 651231

Hook Norton Hooky Bitter; guest beer Ⓗ

An unchanging village pub that appears to be set in a time warp from the 1960s; artefacts that once belonged to the landlord's mother have never been moved. The juke-box features mostly Beatles-era music, while a pool table in the back room is popular with younger folk. The peaceful rear garden overlooking the Warwickshire countryside is popular. The guest beer is usually from a small independent brewery. Q

Napton

Bridge at Napton

Southam Road, CV47 8NQ (on A425 by Oxford Canal bridge 111)

12-3, 6-11 (closed winter Mon); 12-11 summer Sat; 12-10.30 (3 winter) Sun

(01926) 812466 thebridgeatnapton.co.uk

Beer range varies Ⓗ

A place in this year's Guide follows a number of recent awards. Two or three changing ales are on offer. There are three drinking areas, an upmarket restaurant and a large garden. Spend some time in the loos to study the cartoons on the walls. The excellent website has details of forthcoming live bands and how to book a meal deal including a boat trip aboard 'Bumble'. A canal mooring and winding hole are adjacent. A charity beer and bands festival is held in July. ⛼Q❀◗⊟⊟P

Nuneaton

Lloyds Bar

10 Bond Street, CV11 4BX

⏲ 7-11; 7-10.30 Sun

☎ (024) 7637 3343

Beer range varies Ⓗ

Well placed for the town centre, situated between the railway and bus stations. Up to 14 real ales from breweries far and wide, often rare and hard to find, are available, with pump clips from past beers displayed around the split-level bar. Regular quiz nights and other events are held. ◖◗⇌⊟

Ridge Lane

Church End Brewery Tap

109 Ridge Lane, CV10 0RD (two miles SW of Atherstone) OS295947

⏲ 6 (12 Fri & Sat)-11; closed Mon-Wed; 12-10.30 Sun

☎ (01827) 713080 ⊕ churchendbrewery.co.uk

Beer range varies Ⓗ

A deserving Warwickshire CAMRA Pub of the Year, 2004 and 2005, with eight hand pumps dispensing ales fresh from the brewery visible from the bar as well as real ciders and Belgian bottles. Cheeky poster decor adds a humorous touch. A recent extension – the Vestry – opens during busy periods. Food arrangements vary – check beforehand. Hidden behind houses, look for the sandwich board opposite the unmarked drive. The meadow-style garden is attractive in summer. Q❀◖⛺⊟♣P⚟◻

Rugby

Alexandra Arms

72 James Street, CV21 2SL

(next to multi-storey car park)

⏲ 11.30-3, 5-11; 11.30-11 Fri & Sat; 12-10.30 Sun

☎ (01788) 578660 ⊕ alexandraarms.co.uk

Fuller's London Pride; Greene King IPA, Abbot; guest beers Ⓗ

Awarded Rugby CAMRA Pub of The Year in 2005 for the seventh time, the pub is now home to a micro-brewery at the back. Guest beers include milds, stouts and porters from a wide range of breweries. Addlestones cider is also available on draught. The comfortable L-shaped lounge is where lively debate flourishes among the locals. The games room is a favourite with rock fans attracted by the well-stocked juke-box. Skittles and bar billiards are also played. The garden serves as a venue for summer beer festivals with open and covered seating.

Q❀◖⊟♿⇌⊟♣

Fighting Cocks

39 Cymbeline Way, Bilton, CV22 6JZ

⏲ 12 (4 Mon)-11; 12-midnight Fri & Sat; 12-10.30 Sun

☎ (01788) 810628

Greene King IPA; Wells Bombardier; guest beers Ⓗ

A warm, friendly, convivial atmosphere awaits in this community pub where families are welcome. Filled rolls are always available along with five real ales with rotating guest beers. Beer festivals are held in the spring and autumn. Quiz night is every other Sunday and live music is played on Saturday. Sky Sports is shown on a large screen. Darts, skittles and pool are played.

♣⊟P

Half Moon

32 Lawford Road, CV21 2DY

⏲ 3.30 (12 Fri)-11; 12-midnight Sat; 12-11 Sun

☎ (01788) 550216

Courage Directors; Greene King IPA, Abbot; guest beers Ⓗ

This small mid-terraced pub is a five minute' walk from town. Friendly locals always make you feel welcome. Originally two terraced houses that have been knocked into one, it has plenty of wooden seating and tables. The walls are adorned with pictures of old Rugby.

⛼⊟♣

Merchants Inn

5-6 Little Church Street, CV21 3AW

⏲ 12-midnight (1am Sat); 12-midnight Sun

☎ (01788) 571119 ⊕ merchantsinn.co.uk

B&T Shefford Bitter; Everards Tiger; guest beers Ⓗ

Well-established ale house with a warm, cosy atmosphere, wooden seating, comfortable sofas, flagstone floors and an abundance of brewery memorabilia. The pubs stocks seven guest ales and a superb selection of Belgian beers, ciders, wines and malt whiskies. Home-cooked food is served. On Tuesday evening the pub becomes a popular live music venue. A beer festival is hosted in spring and autumn; the pub is actively involved in the brewery historical society. Warwickshire CAMRA Pub of the Year 2003.

◖♿⊟♣⚈⚟

Raglan Arms

50 Dunchurch Road, CV22 6AD (next to Rugby School playing fields)

⏲ 7 (5 Fri)-11; 11.30-4, 7-11 Sat; 11.30-4, 7-10.30 Sun

☎ (01788) 544441

Ansells Mild, Best Bitter; Fuller's London Pride; Marston's Pedigree; guest beers Ⓗ

Traditional pub with a friendly welcome, run by an ex-England international Rugby player. It stands opposite the famous close at Rugby school where the game was invented. The pub plays host to darts, dominoes, crib, soccer and hockey teams in local leagues. It is one of the few remaining town pubs to permanently stock milds among its well-kept ales. A small outside drinking area and car park are at the rear of the pub.

⛼Q❀⊟⊟♣

Squirrel Inn

33 Church Street, CV21 3PU

⏲ 11-11; 12-10.30 Sun

☎ (01788) 544154

Greene King Abbot; Marston's Pedigree; guest beers Ⓗ

Probably the smallest pub in the area and

consequently everyone is made to feel welcome. Dating from the early 19th century, it is also one of the oldest buildings in Rugby. Now a single room, many years ago it was three tiny rooms, and the boundaries are still clearly evident. Despite its size live music is played every other Saturday. Games and newspapers are available. Q♣

Victoria Inn

1 Lower Hillmorton Road, CV21 3ST

12-2.30, 6-11 (5.30-midnight Fri); 1-midnight Sat; 12-4, 7-11.30 Sun

☎ (01788) 544374

Greene King IPA; guest beers

Street-corner, two-room local. The bar doubles as a games room where darts and pool are played. The lounge is a lovely Victorian design retaining many of its original features; a comfortable place to sit and enjoy one of the fives ales that are available. Quiz night (Wed) is popular. ♣

Shipston-on-Stour

Black Horse

Station Road, CV36 4BT

11-11; 12-11 Sun

☎ (01608) 661617

Everards Tiger; Greene King IPA, Abbot; guest beer

Ancient stone-built pub for the discerning drinker – the only thatched building in Shipston. The licence dates back to 1540, and it was brewing illegally before that. The cosy and welcoming lounge has a large inglenook and real log fires. Aunt Sally is played here, as are crib, darts and dominoes. An informal folk musicians' session happens monthly. ♣P

Shustoke

Griffin Inn

Church Road, B46 2LB (on B4116 on sharp bend)

12-2.30, 7-11; 12-3, 7-10.30 Sun

☎ (01675) 481205

Everards Tiger; Hook Norton Old Hooky; Marston's Pedigree; RCH Pitchfork; Theakston Old Peculier; guest beers

With six regular beers and four that change constantly, you are assured of something new to try on every visit. Real fires, an isolated rural setting and charismatic landlord draw customers from far and wide. Enjoy the superbly kept beer in this unspoilt English country inn. Food is served at lunchtime, Monday to Saturday. A spacious conservatory overlooks the garden with its fine rural vista. QP

Southam

Stoneythorpe Hotel

10 Warwick Road, CV47 0HN

10.30-11; 12-10.30 Sun

☎ (01926) 812365 thestoneythorpehotel.co.uk

Fuller's London Pride; guest beers

The building was founded in 1774 as an eye hospital by Dr. Henry Lilley-Smith and the architecture reflects its history. Note the unusual pointed arched windows. In 1823 the world's first dispensary was established here, celebrated by a nearby monument and in the naming of the hotel's bar. Relax in the comfortable, airy lounge while enjoying ales from near and far. A beer festival is held in June. QP

Stretton-on-Fosse

Plough

GL56 9QX

11.30-3 (not winter Mon), 6-11; 12-3, 7-11 Sun

☎ (01608) 661053

Ansell Mild; Hook Norton Hooky Bitter; guest beers

Stone-built village pub dating from the 17th century with a traditional salt box built into the walls. The bar enjoys a thriving local trade and is a rare outlet for mild in south Warwickshire. Food is served in the no-smoking dining room (not Sun eve). An excellent public children's playground is just the other side of the street. The first Sunday of the month is quiz night and there is a folk session 'second Sun'. ♣P

Studley

Little Lark

108 Alcester Road, B80 7NP (Tom's Town Lane jct)

12-3, 6-11; 12-11 Sat; 12-3, 6.30-10.30 Sun

☎ (01527) 853105

Adnams Bitter, Broadside; Ansells Mild; guest beers

Popular village local with three drinking areas served by a central bar. The interior has a newspaper theme, with framed front pages adorning the walls. Good quality reasonably priced meals, cooked by the licensee, are served seven days a week. Traditional country wines and a selection of single malt whiskies are available. The pub hosts two cheese festivals every year.
Q♣

Ullenhall

Winged Spur

Main Street, B95 5PA

12-11; 12-10.30 Sun

☎ (01564) 792005 thewingedspur.com

Flowers IPA; guest beers

An unassuming open-plan village pub, with nooks and crannies creating different drinking areas. The name derives from the Knight family crest – the spur was the medieval symbol of knighthood. Up to three guest beers as well as two ciders are available. Good food, including vegetarian, is served daily with changing specials. Sunday is quiz night. Awarded local CAMRA Most Improved Pub in 2004. QP

Warings Green

Blue Bell Cider House

Warings Green Road, B94 6BP (S of Cheswick Green – off Ilshaw Heath Road) OS129742

11-11; 12-10.30 Sun

☎ (01564) 702328

Beer range varies

Popular free house with a patio and garden

overlooking the canal. Two or three real ales and four draught ciders are usually available, often from local micro-breweries as well as national brands. There is a real community spirit among the locals with regular quiz nights and occasional live music. The good beer and reasonably priced food, including vegetarian and children's options, attract boaters, walkers, cyclists and fishing parties in summer. Evening meals are available Easter to December.

Warwick

Cape of Good Hope

66 Lower Cape, CV34 5DP (end of road)

12-11; 12-10.30 Sun

(01926) 498138 capeofgoodhope.co.uk

Greene King IPA, Abbot; Tetley Bitter; Ⓗ Weatheroak Keystone Hops Ⓖ; guest beers Ⓖ/Ⓗ

Friendly canalside pub, easier to find by boat. Inside are two rooms; live music is hosted on a Friday night in the bar overlooking the canal. The quieter lounge at the back is ideal for enjoying good value meals – Sunday roasts are served until 9pm. Look out for the impressive collection of bank notes from around the world.

Q P

Millwright Arms

67 Coten End, CV34 4NU

winter 12-2.30, 5.30-11 (midnight Fri & Sat); 12-2.30, 5.30-11 Sun; Summer 12-11 (midnight Fri & Sat) daily

(01926) 496955 millwrightarms.co.uk

Adnams Broadside; Black Sheep Bitter; Caledonian Deuchars IPA; Greene King IPA; guest beer Ⓗ

Half-timbered 16th-century Tudor coaching inn. The multi-room interior features exposed beams and fine old settles and benches. The small bar room at one end is set at right angles to the main bar, with a snug and dining room to the side. There are no smoking areas in all rooms. Home-cooked food is excellent; English breakfasts are a speciality (not Sun; booking recommended). Well-behaved children and dogs are welcome. The large garden has an outside bar open in summer.

Q P

Old Fourpenny Shop

27-29 Crompton Street, CV34 6HJ (near racecourse, between A429 and A4189)

12-2.30 (3 Sat), 5.30-11; 12-11 Fri; 12-3, 6-10.30 Sun

(01926) 491360 fourpennyshophotel.co.uk

RCH Pitchfork; guest beers Ⓗ

Located near the racecourse, this was once a racing inn and stables. Later it became famous with the canal navvies for cheap coffee and rum – the origin of the name. Now famous for the diversity and quality of the guest beers, this is the 'Shop's' 16th consecutive entry in the Guide. A blackboard behind the bar lists the beers, locals order by number. The front lounge is decorated in contemporary earthy colours, the restaurant at the rear in cooler tones.

Q P

Simple Simon

105 Emscote Road, CV34 5QY

11.30-11.30 daily

(01926) 400333

Greene King IPA; guest beers Ⓗ

A return to the Guide for this main-road town pub situated close to the Grand Union Canal. Inside are two bars and a further seating area to the rear with real fires. The public bar has a pool table and a large TV screen for sports. The lounge hosts live music sessions three or four times a week. A now demolished pie factory nearby may explain the current name. One guest beer is from Slaughterhouse Brewery, located behind the shops opposite.

Whichford

Norman Knight

CV36 5PE (facing village green)

12-2 (not Mon & Tue), 7-11 (not winter Mon); 12-3, 7-11 Sat; 7-midnight Sun

(01608) 684621 thenormanknight.co.uk

Wizard Apprentice, One For The Toad, seasonal beers Ⓗ

Pub with stone-flagged floors and exposed timbers facing the village green, named after John de Mohun (d.1376), one of the original Garter Knights, who is buried in the nearby church. Popular with locals, it offers a warm welcome to visitors. The Wizard brewery started here in 2003 and three of its beers are always available, more in summer. An enthusiastic outpost of Aunt Sally as well as dominoes and shove ha' penny. Evening meals are available Friday and Saturday. P

Wilmcote

Masons Arms

Aston Cantlow Road, CV37 9XX

11.30-2.30, 5.30-11; 12-10.30 Sun

(01789) 297416

Beer range varies Ⓗ

Traditional 19th-century pub with real fires and a pleasant conservatory dining room, handy for Mary Arden's House and the station and canal. The name comes from the former quarry behind the pub. Games includes bar skittles, nine men's morris, Jenga and shove ha' penny.

Wolvey

Blue Pig

Hall Road, LE10 3LG (set back from village square)

12-2.30, 5.30 (5 Fri)-11; 12-11 Sat; 12-10.30 Sun

(01455) 220256

Greene King IPA, Ruddles County, Abbot, Old Speckled Hen; guest beer Ⓗ

Lovely old pub in a quiet setting near the heart of the village. There is a small outside seating area at the front and a garden at the rear. The long split-level L-shaped bar has low ceilings and old settles. It is decorated with traditional farm implements, pitchforks and tankards. The food is always in great demand, particularly good lunchtime specials. Regular quiz nights are held.

P

WEST MIDLANDS

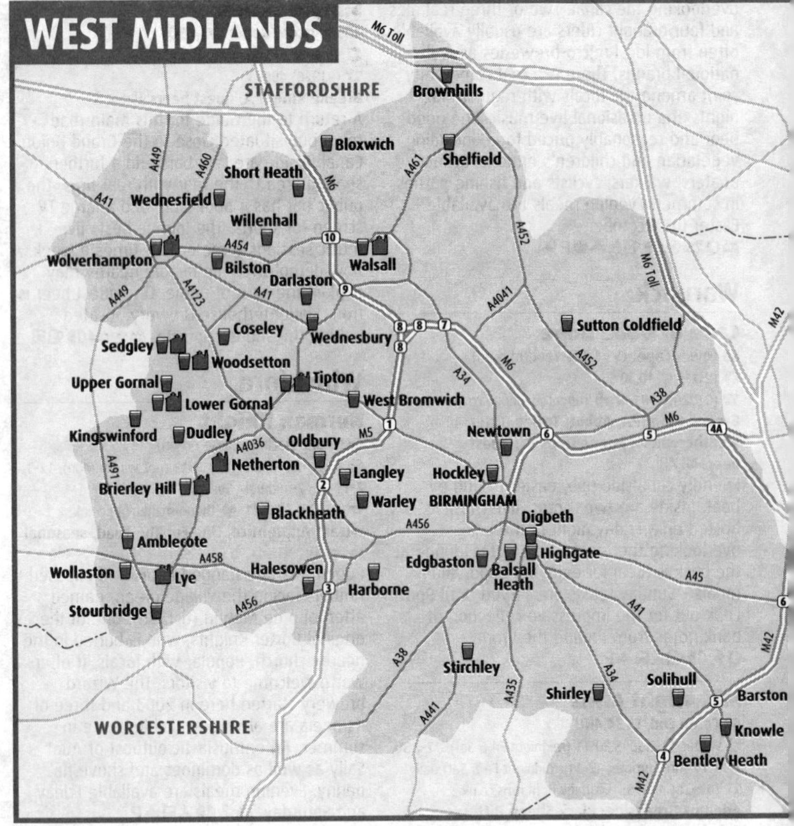

Amblecote

Robin Hood

119 Collis Sreet, DE8 4EQ (on A4102 off Brettell Lane, A461)

12-3, 6-11; 12-midnight Sat; 12-11 Sun

(01384) 821120

Batham Best Bitter; Enville Ale; Salopian Shropshire Gold; guest beers H

Situated on a one-way street forming the main route between Brierley Hill and Stourbridge, the pub regularly offers four guest beers. It is also noted for its excellent varied menu. A lively quiz takes place on the first Tuesday evening of the month. En-suite accommodation is available, including a family room.

P

Swan

10 Brettel Lane, DY8 4BN

12-2.30 (not Tue -Thu), 7-11; 12-11 Sat & Sun

(01384) 76932

Beer range varies H

Free house consisting of a comfortable lounge and a public bar with a TV for watching sporting events. This is a friendly, neighbourhood pub where the regulars support many local charities, such as the air ambulance service. It always has three real ales that change frequently to give variety. The garden is a delightful suntrap.

Balsall Common

Railway

547 Station Road, CV7 7EF (by Berkswell Station)

12-11 daily

(01676) 533284

Adnams Broadside; Draught Bass; Hook Norton Best Bitter; Taylor Landlord H

Small, 19th-century one-bar pub, handy for Berkswell Station, from where trains run between Coventry and Birmingham every 30 minutes. It can get busy early evening as commuters call in on their way home. It is also convenient for the nearby National Exhibition Centre. Children are not admitted to the pub, but are welcome in the garden. Wheelchair access is at the rear.

(Berkswell)P

Barston

Bull's Head

Barston Lane, B92 0JU

11-2.30, 5-11; 11-11 Sat; 12-10.30 Sun

(01675) 442830

Adnams Bitter; Black Sheep Best Bitter; guest beers H

Genuine village local, with a history as a coaching inn going back to 1490. It has three beamed rooms: the restaurant is in the oldest part of the building, while the two bars both have real fires and horse racing memorabilia. Thrice winner of the local

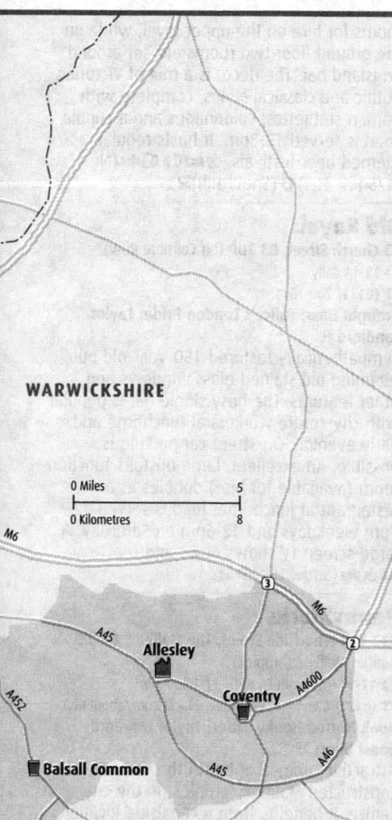

CAMRA Pub of the Year, it supports independent breweries and has appeared in this Guide for 14 consecutive years. The excellent food is based on seasonal produce (no meals Sun eve). Well worth a visit.
⛫Q❀◑▀☗♣P

Bentley Heath

Drum & Monkey

177 Four Ashes Road, B93 8ND
⌚ 11-11; 12-10.30 Sun
☎ (01564) 772242
Hobsons Best Bitter; guest beers Ⓗ
One of the Chef & Brewer chain, serving upmarket pub food using fresh produce. Lots of exposed beams and brickwork give an olde-worlde feeling without being tacky. The name may come from the blasting powder carriers working on construction of the nearby railway - the powder monkeys. And the drum would be the receptacle the powder was stored in. ⛫❀◑♿P

Bilston

Olde White Rose

20 Lichfield Street, WV14 0AG
⌚ 12-11 (11.30 Fri & Sat); 12-11 Sun
☎ (01902) 498339
Beer range varies Ⓗ
The Olde White Rose offers 12 changing real ales, plus cider, perry and a good choice of bottled foreign beers. Add to this the excellent food, including a carvery, and it becomes a must to visit. Entertainment includes quizzes (Tue and Wed) and folk music on Thursday. The garden is popular in summer and its bierkeller can be hired for private functions. Close to both metro and bus stations, the No. 79 Woverhampton-Birmingham bus stops nearby.
❀◑♿⊖(Bilston Central)☗●

Sir Henry Newbolt

45-47 High Street, WV14 0EP
⌚ 11-midnight (1am Fri & Sat); 11-midnight Sun
☎ (01902) 404636
Enville White; Greene King Abbot; guest beers Ⓗ
Typical Wetherspoon's conversion of an old cinema building that opened in 2000. Its frontage, designed to blend in with nearby buildings, means you can easily walk past the pub without realising. The name commemorates a famous Bilston poet. Food is served all day every day until 11pm.
Q❀◑♿☗⊖(Bilston Central)●⚟

Trumpet

58 High Street, WV14 0EP
⌚ 11-3, 7.30-11; 12-3, 7.30-11 Sun
☎ (01902) 493723 🌐 trumpetjazz.org
Holden's Mild, Bitter, Golden Glow, seasonal beers Ⓗ
Busy, compact but characterful, one-room local, serving Holden's national award-winning ales at reasonable prices. Music memorabilia and cartoons of locals adorn the walls, while the ceiling is festooned with musical instruments. Live jazz is performed here seven nights a week all year round. No meals, but cobs are available. Smoking is tolerated in this well-ventilated bar.
❀⊖(Bilston Central)☗

Birmingham: Balsall Heath

Old Moseley Arms

53 Tindal Street, B12 9QU
⌚ 12-11.30; 12-11 Sun
☎ (0121) 440 1954
Black Sheep Best Bitter; Enville Ale, Ginger; Greene King Abbot Ⓗ
Back-street pub, set on the end of a terrace surrounded by the local play area. Live music is staged every Sunday upstairs in the pool room. Tuesday and Thursday are curry nights. The pub fields one cricket team and is regularly visited by a second. The juke box caters for all, including the oldies! A truly multicultural establishment, it numbers

INDEPENDENT BREWERIES

Banks's Wolverhampton
Batham Brierley Hill
Black Country Lower Gornal
Highgate Walsall
Holden's Woodsetton
Sarah Hughes Sedgley
Olde Swan Netherton
Rainbow Allesley
Toll End Tipton
Windsor Castle Lye

among its customers the local Harley Davidson garage owner and friends. It is 10 minutes from Edgbaston cricket ground.
❀⊟🚌

Birmingham: City Centre

Bull

1 Price Street, B4 6JU (off St Chads Queensway)
✪ 12-11; closed Sun
☎ (0121) 333 6757
Adnams Broadside; Ansells Mild; Marston's Pedigree; guest beer Ⓗ
One of Birmingham's oldest pubs, this friendly, back-street local is near Aston University and the hospital. Two main rooms share the bar in the middle, with a small, quiet room at the rear. One cannot miss the extensive collections of plates, cups and water jugs alongside old photographs of Brum. The guest beer changes frequently and a varied menu is served. This Punch Taverns award winner boasts etched Ansells Ales windows.
Q❀⇄◑♿≠(Snow Hill)⊖🚌♣⊓

Corner House

29a Newhall Street, B3 3PU
✪ 12-11 (midnight Thu-Sat); closed Sun
☎ (0121) 200 2423
Enville White; Greene King IPA; guest beers Ⓗ
Formerly part of the Hogshead chain, the pub is located in the business area of the city, frequented by office workers at lunchtime/early evening and by students later on. Music is played most days, but is not obtrusive. The pool table sees plenty of action, especially on Thursday when there is no charge. ◑♿≠(Snow Hill/New St)⊖(Snow Hill)🚌⚡

Old Fox

54 Hurst Street, B5 4TD
✪ 11.30-midnight (2am Thu-Sat); 12-midnight Sun
☎ (0121) 622 5080
Everards Tiger; Greene King Old Speckled Hen; Marston's Pedigree; Tetley Bitter; guest beers Ⓗ
Situated opposite the Hippodrome Theatre and Birmingham's restored Victorian back-to-back houses, near the Arcadian, Chinese Quarter and the Bullring. Popular in the evening with theatregoers, the central bar serves both the bare-boarded smaller public area and the carpeted main lounge, which are connected by an open doorway. On display are posters and photographs of the stars, including Charlie Chaplin, who reputedly drank here. Good value snacks and meals include a matinee menu. Guest ales come from independents and micros.
❀◑♿≠(New St)🚌

Old Joint Stock

4 Temple Row West, B2 5NY (opp. St. Philip's Cathedral)
✪ 11-11; closed Sun
☎ (0121) 200 1892
Fuller's Chiswick, Discovery, London Pride, ESB, seasonal beers; guest beer Ⓗ
Grade II listed building, formerly the Joint Stock Bank, bearing an impressive illuminated façade. The pub has function rooms for hire on the upper level, while on the ground floor two rooms are set around an island bar. The decor is a mix of Victorian gothic and classical styles, complete with Roman statuettes, colonnades and a cupola. Food is served 12-8pm. It hosts regular themed beer festivals. ❀⇄◑⊟≠(New St/Snow Hill)⊖(Snow Hill)🚌

Old Royal

53 Church Street, B3 2DP (off Colmore Row)
✪ 12-11 daily
☎ (0121) 200 3841
Draught Bass; Fuller's London Pride; Taylor Landlord Ⓗ
Sympathetically restored 150-year-old pub, retaining old stained glass windows and other features. The busy single bar is popular with city-centre workers at lunchtime and early evening. On-street car parking is possible. An excellent, large upstairs function room (available for hire) doubles as a restaurant at lunchtime; food is served 12-8pm weekdays and 12-6pm on Saturday. A large-screen TV shows news and sport.
◑♿≠(Snow Hill)⊖🚌

Pennyblacks

132-134 Wharfside Street, The Mailbox, B1 1XL (within Mailbox complex)
✪ 11-11 (midnight Fri-Sat); 11-10.30 Sun
☎ (0121) 632 1460 🌐 penny-blacks.com/about.php
Hook Norton Hooky Bitter; Taylor Landlord; guest beers Ⓗ
Attractive, upmarket bar in the recently-constructed Mailbox complex, in the city centre. It benefits from a canalside location, with outside tables in front. Note the unusual stillaging arrangement, with barrels racked behind the bar area. Up to four guests are sourced from small producers, with occasional mini-festivals showcasing individual breweries such as Church End. It serves good English food all day; look out for the dishes with ale in the recipe. It attracts drinkers wanting a relaxed pint and diners.
❀◑♿≠(New St/Snow Hill)⊖(Snow Hill)🚌⚡

Prince of Wales

84 Cambridge Street, B1 2NP (behind National Indoor Arena and Rep Theatre)
✪ 12-11; 12-10.30 Sun
☎ (0121) 643 9460
Adnams Broadside; Ansells Mild; Everards Tiger; Taylor Landlord; Wells Bombardier; guest beer Ⓗ
Rare community local in the centre of Birmingham, under new management. Frequented by local residents and real ale enthusiasts alike, the pub has a lively core of loyal customers – one has his own reserved seat with an engraved plaque to prove it! It can become busy after shows at the nearby National Indoor Arena. It hosts live music on Sunday afternoon. ◐≠(Snow Hill)⊖🚌

Sack Of Potatoes

10 Gosta Green, B4 7ER
✪ 11.30-11 (midnight Thu & Fri; 1am Sat); 12-midnight Sun
☎ (0121) 503 5811
Black Sheep Best Bitter; guest beers Ⓗ

Popular with students, office workers and firefighters, this corner pub has retained some original fixtures and fittings. The U-shaped bar and distinct seating areas, with a mix of bare boards and carpeted floors, display old Birmingham photos on the walls. Outside seating is available on warmer days when the pub can be busy. The food is good value and the beer prices low for the area; guests are from the M&B portfolio. A small, quiet room at the back shows major events on Sky Sports.
❀◐ ⊟≢(Snow Hill)⊖⊟⅟

Shakespeare
31 Summer Row, B3 1JJ
⏲ 11.30 (12 Sat)-11 (midnight Fri & Sat); 12-6 Sun
☎ (0121) 214 5081
M&B Brew XI; guest beers Ⓗ
Extensively but well restored city-centre pub, near Broad Street, and at the heart of Summerrow nightclub complex. The traditional bar has a small hatch to serve the rear snug. It is popular with early evening office workers and students. Changing guest ales and an annual mini-beer festival in April add to its appeal. Food is served until late. Look out for the superb engraved Mitchells & Butlers mirror. Summer barbecues are held in the pleasant garden.
Q❀◐♿≢(New Street/Snow Hill)⊖(Snow Hill)⊟

Stage
Paradise Place, B3 3HJ
⏲ 12-11 (1am Thu-Sat); 12-10.30 Sun
☎ (0121) 212 2524
Taylor Landlord; guest beer Ⓗ
Ideally positioned for the NIA and Birmingham Rep, and for the many events that take place in nearby Centenary Square, the pub is owned by the landlord of the Prince of Wales nearby (see above). Live music is performed at the weekend, and quizzes occasionally staged in the week. The pub meals are excellent. ❀◐♿≢(New St/Snow Hill)⊖(Snow Hill)⊟

Tap & Spile
Regency Wharf, Gas Street, B1 2JT (off Broad St)
⏲ 11-11 (2am Fri & Sat); 11-11 Sun
☎ (0121) 632 5602
Adnams Bitter; Fuller's London Pride; Greene King IPA; Marston's Pedigree; Wells Bombardier; Young's Bitter Ⓗ
Rather expensive, two-storey pub off Birmingham's busy Broad Street. Both bars are fairly narrow and can get quite crowded. The downstairs bar opens out onto the canal where drinkers can watch passing pleasure boats and the canalside skyline. Both bars are adorned with plaques recording the history of the local area. This previous Guide entry has shown an improvement in beer quality. ≢(New St)⊟

Wellington
37 Bennetts Hill, B2 5SN
⏲ 10-midnight daily
☎ (0121) 200 3115 🌐 thewellingtonrealale.co.uk
Black Country Bradley's Finest Golden, Pig on the Wall, Fireside; guest beers Ⓗ
At the current Birmingham CAMRA Pub of the Year you will find a warm, friendly atmosphere in which to sample a superb range of beers: 2,610 different ales were sold during 2005 to a mixed clientele. The commitment to ale was matched by a changing range of real ciders and foreign bottled beers and it hosts quarterly beer festivals. No food is served, but you can bring your own (cutlery provided). It is five minutes' walk from the stations.
Q♿≢(New St/Snow Hill)⊖(Snow Hill)⊟●⅟

Woodman
106 Albert Street, B5 5LG (opp. Millennium Point)
⏲ 11-midnight (2am Fri & Sat); 11-midnight Sun
☎ (0121) 643 1959
Everard's Original, Tiger; guest beer Ⓗ
Situated opposite Millennium Point and adjacent to the historic Curzon Street Railway Station, the pub has recently reopened after a period of closure for interior renovation. It now features a long L-shaped bar and a lounge with pool table, served through a hatch. Bar snacks and sandwiches are the only food available until the refurbishment of the kitchen has been completed.
⊟≢(New St/Moor St)⊟

Birmingham: Digbeth

Anchor ☆
308 Bradford Street, B5 6ET
⏲ 11-midnight; 12-11 Sun
☎ (0121) 622 4516k
Ansells Mild; Tetley Bitter; guest beers Ⓗ
Local CAMRA Pub of the Year three times over, the Anchor is a Grade II listed building. The bar is split by an unusual three-quarter height partition; there is a lounge at the rear and a 'quiet man's room' for non-smokers. It always offers a wide selection of cask ales, bottled foreign beers and at least one cider. It is popular with travellers passing through Digbeth coach station.
Q❀◐⊟♿≢(New St/Moor St)⊟●⅟

White Swan ☆
276 Bradford Street, B12 0QY
⏲ 12-3, 4.15-11; 11-11 Fri & Sat; 12-4, 7-10.30 Sun
☎ (0121) 622 2586
Banks's Original, Bitter; Marston's Burton Bitter, Pedigree Ⓗ
This classic, unspoilt pub is situated just off the city's Irish quarter, a 10-minute walk from the city centre. The bar is unaltered, except for the addition of a large-screen TV. The small lounge is free from music or TV for those wanting a quiet drink.
≢(New St/Moor St)⊟

Birmingham: Edgbaston

MAC (Midlands Arts Centre)
Cannon Hill Park, B12 9QH (opp. Edgbaston cricket ground)
⏲ 12-11; 12-10.30 Sun
☎ (0121) 440 3838 🌐 macarts.org.uk
Beer range varies Ⓗ
Bar with a commitment to real ale within a mixed-use arts centre - theatre, cinema,

galleries and children's activities - located in Cannon Hill Park, the city's largest green space. Particularly suitable for families, the pub is fully accessible throughout for disabled customers. The courtyard drinking area stages live music and barbecues in fine weather. The pizzas are good value (served eves) and the Mac café is open for lunch. Two beers are always available from a range of eight. Visit the website for events.
❀O♿🚌P⚟

Birmingham: Harborne

Bell Inn

11 Old Church Road, B17 0BB (10 mins' walk from A4040)
✪ 12-11 (midnight Thu-Sat); 12-11 Sun
☎ (0121) 427 0934
Caledonian Deuchars IPA; guest beers Ⓗ
In an upmarket suburb, this pub retains a rural feel, situated next to St Paul's churchyard. The main beamed room is decorated in warm colours with modern prints. At the rear a large patio overlooks an L-shaped bowling green, the scene of regular club matches in summer. The servery hatch in the corridor has two handpumps and usually stocks a guest session bitter. The food is good value, especially the Sunday lunches (eve meals weekdays). Sunday is quiz night.
❀O◗🚌P

New Inn

74 Vivian Road, B17 0DJ
(5 mins from A4040/High St)
✪ 12-11 (11.30 Thu); 12-midnight Fri &Sat; 12-11 Sun
☎ (0121) 427 5062
Banks's Original, Bitter; Marston's Pedigree Ⓗ
Multi-roomed pub, previously a coaching inn. The public bar at the front is the haunt of the regulars; the bar back is 100 years old and a well-preserved example. There is a cosy snug off the corridor and a large lounge area to the side, boasting several interesting features: plasterwork ceiling panels, tiled floors, and a metal-plated bar front. The conservatory leads to improved patio seating, overlooking a bowling green and club pavilion. The lunches are reasonably priced. Tuesday is quiz night.
❀O⊞♿P

White Horse

2 York Street, B17 0HG (off High St)
✪ 11-11.30 (11 Mon; midnight Fri & Sat); 12-11 Sun
☎ (0121) 427 6023
🌐 whitehorseharborne.homestead.com/home.html
Greene King IPA, Abbot; Marston's Pedigree; Shepherd Neame Spitfire; guest beers Ⓗ
Suburban pub, a 10-minute bus ride from the city centre and handy for Harborne High Street. It features a central island bar with a recently refurbished snug at the front. It can get busy for televised sport, screened in both the front and back rooms. It offers a good range of guest beers and a decent menu, served until 6pm (3pm Sun). A rare outlet for real cider, which comes from the cellar in excellent condition.
❀O◗♿🚌●

Birmingham: Highgate

Lamp

257 Barford Street, B5 6AH
✪ 12-5am daily
☎ (0121) 622 2599
Church End Gravediggers; Everards Tiger; Stanway Stanney Bitter; guest beers Ⓗ
This friendly, one-bar pub, tucked away at the rear end of the market, draws a loyal clientele from all walks of life. It is the city's only outlet for Stanway beers. The well-equipped function room hosts live music at the weekend and is a popular venue for various railway society meetings during the week. Q♿⇌(New St)🚌

Birmingham: Hockley

Black Eagle

16 Factory Road, B18 5JU (in Jewellery Quarter)
✪ 11.30-3, 5.30-11; 11.30-11 Fri & Sat; 12-3 (closed eve) Sun
☎ (0121) 523 4008
Ansells Mild, Best Bitter; Marston's Pedigree; guest beers Ⓗ
Rebuilt in 1895, the pub has two bars, a comfortable lounge and restaurant and has retained most of its original features, including Minton tiles. An annual beer festival is held in the pleasant garden each July. One of the three guest beers is usually from Beowulf Brewery.
❀O◗⊖(Soho Benson Rd)🚌

Birmingham: Newtown

Bartons Arms ☆

144 High Street, B6 4UP (at A34/B4144 jct)
✪ 12-11; 11-10.30 Sun
☎ (0121) 333 5988 🌐 bartons-arms.co.uk
Oakham JHB, White Dwarf, Bishops Farewell; guest beers Ⓗ
This magnificent, large pub is Grade II listed and on the CAMRA National Inventory of pub interiors. Tiled throughout, the semi-circular public bar features the original etched snob screens. A spacious dining area at the back is a peaceful contrast to the main bar area. The pub is always busy. Good value, authentic Thai food is served daily. The cider is Westons. Several buses pass this way, including the 33, 51, 113, 168 and 951.
O◗🚌●P⚟

Birmingham: Stirchley

British Oak ☆

1364 Pershore Road, B30 2XS
✪ 11-11.30 (1am Sat); 12-10.30 Sun
☎ (0121) 458 1758
Beer range varies Ⓗ
Extensive, former M&B pub, now owned by Punch Taverns. It offers a constantly-changing range of up to four guest ales, often from micro-breweries. Good value hearty meals are served, with curry specials during quiz night on Monday. Families with children are welcome in the attractive 1930s-style dining room, which looks out onto the patio and large garden. The public bar is at the front of the building, with an

adjacent snug and other smaller rooms. ❀◐◑ ⊟ ⇌ (Bournville) ⊟ P

Highbury Inn

Dads Lane, B13 8PQ (10 mins' walk from A441)

12-11; 12-10.30 Sun

☎ (0121) 414 1529

Banks's Original; Jennings Cumberland Ale; M&B Brew XI Ⓗ

Large, community local with a public bar at the front, a games area, lounge bar and a function room that doubles as a family area, leading to an extensive garden at the rear with children's play facilities. Bar snacks are available weekday lunchtimes. It is close to the Rea Valley cycle path and Cannon Hill Park. It now regularly has Westons cider on draught. A big screen in the public bar shows sports events and music videos.

❀ ⊟ ♿ ⊟ ● P

Blackheath

Bell & Bear

71 Gorsty Hill Road, Rowley Regis, B65 0HA (on A4099, Halesowen Road)

11.30-11; 12-11 Sun

☎ (0121) 561 2196

Taylor Landlord; guest beers Ⓗ

Fine, 400-year old building, set back from the busy main road. The area is enjoying an industrial renaissance, with the growth of the nearby Business Park. The pub benefits from an extensive patio and garden to the rear, which afford superb views over the Black Country and beyond. Seven real ales are normally available and food is served every day, 12-9pm. Quizzes are held twice a week. ❀◐◑ P ⊬

Bloxwich

Sir Robert Peel

104 Bell Lane, WS3 2JS (on A4124)

12-11 (midnight Fri & Sat); 12-11 Sun

☎ (01922) 470921

Caledonian Deuchars IPA; Highgate Dark; Wells Bombardier; guest beers Ⓗ

Situated a short walk from the town centre, this welcoming pub is well worth a visit. The friendly atmosphere extends from the bar, where traditional pub games are played, through to the more relaxed lounge. Diners are catered for in the smoke-free restaurant or in the lounge if you prefer (booking is recommended). The function room is well used by local clubs and organisations. The pub usually keeps four real ales.

Q❀◐◑ ⊟ ♿ ⇌ ⊟ ♣ P

Turf Tavern ☆

13 Wolverhampton Road, WS3 2EZ (opp. Bloxwich Park)

12-3, 7-11 daily

☎ (01922) 407745

Titanic Mild; guest beers Ⓗ

Grade II listed building, known locally as Tinky's, that has been in the same family ownership for over 130 years. The three rooms are dominated by the bar with its splendid tiled floor. Tinky's is a haven for quiet conversation, which only adds to its character. Outside, the courtyard serves as a pleasant summer drinking area. The pub is no-smoking throughout. Q❀ ⊟ ♿ ⇌ ⊟ ⊬

Brierley Hill

Rose & Crown

161 Bank Street, DY5 3DD (on B4179)

12-2 (3.30 Fri & Sat), 6-11; 12-3.30, 7-10.30 Sun

☎ (01384) 77825

Holden's Mild, Bitter, Special, seasonal beers; guest beer Ⓗ

This traditional, side-street pub was originally two terraced properties. The lounge has a cosy, relaxed atmosphere with friendly clientele. One end of the small bar is dominated by the dartboard; a recent conservatory extension adds welcome extra space. Good value pub food is served Monday-Saturday. The changing guest beer comes from a variety of small breweries. It is five minutes' walk from the High Street, which is served by several bus routes.

❀◐◑ ⊟ ⊟ ♣ P

Vine (Bull & Bladder)

10 Delph Road, DY5 2TN

12-11; 12-10.30 Sun

☎ (01384) 78293

Batham Mild, Best Bitter, XXX (winter) Ⓗ

Classic, unspoilt brewery tap with an ornately decorated façade proclaiming the Shakespearian quotation: 'Blessings of your heart, you brew good ale'. Nothing could be more apt for this elongated pub with a labyrinthine layout. The rooms have contrasting characters: the front bar is small and staunchly traditional, while the larger rear bar, which houses the dartboard, is decorated in tartan. The lounge and rear room are homely. Good value lunches are served weekdays. Q❀◐ ⊟ ⊟ ♣ P

Brownhills

Prince of Wales

98 Watling Street, WS8 7NP (on A5)

7 (5 Mon; 4.30 Fri)-midnight; 12-1am Sat; 11.30-midnight Sun

☎ (01543) 372551

Banks's Original; Beowulf Heroes Bitter Ⓗ

Cheerful, friendly corner local on the A5, near Chasewater Park and the light railway. The recently extended single room houses a large-screen TV for sporting events. It can be busy on Wednesday evening (when a free buffet is served) and Friday and Saturday evenings. Simple, filled rolls are generally available. Parking can be difficult. ❀♣

Royal Oak

68 Chester Road, WS8 6DU (on A452)

12-3.30, 6-11 (midnight Fri & Sat); 12-3.30, 7-11 Sun

☎ (01543) 452089 theroyaloakpub.co.uk

Banks's Original; Caledonian Deuchars IPA; Greene King Abbot; Taylor Landlord; Tetley Bitter; guest beer Ⓗ

Known locally as the Middle Oak, this pub has gone back to its roots, once again decorated in 1930s Art Deco style. Games are played in the traditional bar, while the comfortable lounge has a relaxed

atmosphere. There is a no-smoking dining room and a new, large garden off the patio drinking area to the rear.
Q❀◐◑⊟♿🚌♣P⊬

Coseley

New Inn

35 Ward Street, WV14 9LQ (backs onto A4123)
⏲ 4-11; 12-11.30 Sat; 12-10.30 Sun
☎ (01902) 676777
Holden's Mild, Bitter, seasonal beers 🄷
Cosy, one-room local, best approached from the car park off Birmingham New Road. From the corridor you enter the lounge housed in a late 20th-century extension. At the far end is the old bar area in the 19th-century part of the building. They are separated by the bright, modern bar counter that is the hub of the pub. Evening meals (Tue-Sat) and Sunday lunches are served. The bus (from Brum or Wolverhampton) stops at Roseville; the station is a 10-minute walk. ⛫❀◑♿⇌🚌(126)♣●P⊬

Coventry

Beer Engine

35 Far Gosford Street, CV1 5DW
⏲ 12-11 daily
☎ (024) 7626 7239 🌐 thebeerengine.net
Black Sheep Best Bitter; guest beers 🄷
Town pub, a single room near Coventry University, boasting its own art gallery that showcases works by local artists. A popular venue for live bands every Saturday, impromptu sessions often happen on other evenings (see website). Meals are only served on Sunday lunchtime, however customers are welcome to bring in their own, as the surrounding area is full of cosmopolitan food outlets. No children are admitted. ⛫❀♣

City Arms

1 Earlsdon Street, Earlsdon, CV5 6EP
⏲ 9am-midnight (1am Fri & Sat); 9am-midnight Sun
☎ (024) 7671 8170
Greene King Abbot; Marston's Pedigree; guest beers 🄷
Spacious, open-plan pub in typical Wetherspoon style. A Grade II listed building, the back room is geared up for families and dining. Locally known as Ma Cooper's, it runs the Tuesday steak club and Thursday curry club, typical of the chain. It offers up to six guest beers, often including one from Church End. Westons Old Rosie and Organic ciders are stocked. This family-oriented pub is a mile from city centre at the heart of Earlsdon. Q⛾❀◐◑♿🚌●P⊬

Craven Arms

58 Craven Street, Chapelfields, CV5 8DW (1 mile W of city centre, off Allesley Old Road)
⏲ 11-midnight (1am Fri & Sat); 11-midnight Sun
☎ (024) 7671 5308
Flowers Original; Greene King Abbot; Sarah Hughes Dark Ruby; guest beer 🄷
Thriving, traditional, corner pub where the new landlord was previously the cellarman for over a decade and clearly knows how to keep a good pint. The Dark Ruby was chosen as a regular beer following a pub ballot. An integral part of the famous 'Craven Street crawl', the pub comprises a lounge and an area for pool and darts. Barbecues are held in summer, and live music features heavily on Sunday evening. ⛫❀🚌♣

Farmhouse

215 Beechwood Avenue, Earlsdon, CV5 6HB (300 yds from Canley Station)
⏲ 11-11; 12-10.30 Sun
☎ (024) 7671 4332
Hardys & Hansons Bitter, Olde Trip, seasonal beers 🄷
Next to Hearsall Common, this is Coventry's only Hardys & Hansons' pub. It provides a no-smoking restaurant area on one side and a comfortable (partly no-smoking) drinking area with pool table, games machine and TV on the other. A monthly changing beer from the brewery is usually available. It gets busy when there is a fair or circus on the common. Family fun days are planned, and the pub benefits from a large garden with seating and a children's play area.
❀◐◑♿⇌(Canley)🚌P⊬

Gatehouse Tavern

46 Hill Street, CV1 4AN (near jct 9 of inner ring road)
⏲ 11-3, 5-11; 11-midnight Thu-Sat; 12-10.30 Sun
☎ (024) 7663 0140
Draught Bass; guest beers 🄷
Small pub, converted by the landlord from the gatehouse of the now demolished Leigh textile mill. It boasts probably the largest pub garden in the city centre. The stained glass windows depict the six nations as befits its sporting theme. The pub usually offers two guest beers from Church End Brewery. No meals are served Saturday evening or Sunday. ❀◐◑⇌🚌

Greyhound Inn

Sutton Stop, Hawkesbury Junction, CV6 6DF (1 mile along Blackhorse Rd from B4113 jct)
⏲ 11-11; 12-10.30 Sun
☎ (024) 7636 3046 🌐 thegreyhoundinn.com
Highgate Dark; Marston's Pedigree; guest beers 🄷
Winner of the 2005 Godiva Award for Best Pub in Coventry and Warwickshire, this traditional canalside inn dates back to around 1830 and has retained many original features. The no-smoking restaurant serves an extensive menu created by an award-winning chef. It hosts regular beer festivals in April and September. A canalside terrace, rear garden and another quiet garden at the side, where meals can be served, all add to its appeal. ⛫Q❀◐◑🚌♣●P

Hare & Hounds

Watery Lane, Keresley End, CV7 8JA (off Bennetts Rd)
⏲ 11-11; 12-11 Sun
☎ (024) 7633 2716 🌐 hareandhounds.co.uk
Adnams Broadside; Draught Bass; M&B Brew XI; Greene King Abbot, Old Speckled Hen; guest beer 🄷
Near the former site of one of Coventry's pits, the pub dates back 150 years, when it was a coaching inn. It has been renovated,

but the tiny original bar, behind the main pub still stands (now a listed building). It has a pavilion, where various activities and music events are held, while the public bar houses table skittle tables and a dartboard. The restaurant area serves traditional pub food, vegetarian options and more adventurous chef's specials. ♛Q❀◐◑⊟🚌(36)♣●P⚟

Nursery Tavern

38-39 Lord Street, Chapelfields, CV5 8DA (1 mile W of city centre, off Allesley Old Rd)

✪ 12-11.30; 11-midnight Fri & Sat; 12-11 Sun

☎ (024) 7667 4530

Courage Best Bitter; John Smith's Bitter; Theakston Mild; Wells Bombardier; guest beers 🄷

Popular community pub in a Victorian terrace, which stocks seven beers, including three guests. Customers include Rugby Union and Formula 1 supporters, as is evident from the paraphernalia. Musical events have now been introduced in the rear room of this three-roomed pub, which also hosts quizzes and traditional games. The pub has been staging beer festivals in June and December for over 10 years. Thatchers dry cider is stocked. Q♉❀◑🚌♣●

Old Windmill

22-23 Spon Street, CV1 3BA

✪ 10.30-11 (midnight Fri & Sat); 12-midnight Sun

☎ (024) 7625 2183

Caledonian Deuchars IPA; Greene King Ruddles County, Old Speckled Hen; Theakston Old Peculier; Wychwood Hobgoblin; guest beers 🄷

Popular old pub, one of the oldest in Coventry. Traces of the old brewhouse remain in one of the many small rooms, while low beams and flagstone floors are much in evidence throughout. Situated in the entertainment quarter, there is a constant ebb and flow of customers. The pub is known as Ma Brown's after a former licensee. Normally two guest beers are available, and Westons Old Rosie cider is stocked. ♛◑⇌🚌●

Rose & Woodbine

40 North Street, Stoke Heath, CV2 3FW

✪ 12-4, 7-11; 12-11.30 Fri & Sat; 12-5, 7-11 Sun

☎ (024) 7645 1480

Banks's Original; Draught Bass; guest beer 🄷

Built for the Northampton Brewing Company, the pub no longer serves Brew XI, but offers an expanding range of regional beers and sometimes a local micro-brewery's product. Games played include darts, dominoes and pool, and it is the meeting place for two homing pigeon societies. It runs discos on Saturday and Sunday, but most of the time is a quiet pub, popular with locals of all ages. Children are welcome until 7pm. A ramp now gives some disabled access. ❀◑⊟🚌♣

Town Wall Tavern

Bond Street, CV1 4AH (behind Belgrade Theatre)

✪ 11-11.30; 11-10.30 Sun

☎ (024) 7622 0963

Adnams Bitter, Broadside; Draught Bass; M&B Brew XI; guest beer 🄷

Actors and journos' pub, close to the theatre and newspaper offices. One of the few traditional, two-bar pubs left in the city, the donkey box is an unusual feature; yes, you can get a donkey in there - ask for the story. The landlord has his own bakery, so check out the rolls and sandwiches. Westons Old Rosie cider is sold. No meals are served Sunday. A no-smoking area is provided 11-3pm, Monday-Saturday. ♛◑⊟⇌🚌●⚟

Whitefriars Olde Ale House

114-115 Gosford Street, CV1 5DL

✪ 11-midnight; 12-1am Fri & Sat; 12-11 Sun

☎ (024) 7625 1655

Everards Tiger; guest beers 🄷

A recent pub, but the original structure dates back to the early 14th century. Many changes over the years include the addition of chimneys in a 16th-century modernisation. In 1850 the building was combined with its 17th-century neighbour to form a butcher's shop. The latest renovations used bricks reclaimed from the old Daimler factory. Many old features are still discernible today - it is worth a look upstairs. The pub normally offers a splendid choice of five well chosen ales. ♛Q❀◑♿🚌♣

Darlaston

Prince of Wales

74 Walsall Road, WS10 9JT

✪ 2 (12 Fri & Sat)-11; 12-10.30 Sun

☎ (0121) 526 6244

Holden's Bitter, Golden Glow; guest beer 🄷

Black Country local comprising two rooms. The long, narrow bar is decorated with advertising mirrors; darts is played at one end. The small, comfortable lounge is family friendly and displays a number of photos of the local swimming and football clubs. At the rear is a garden with a play area and bench seating. It hosts occasional music and quiz nights. ❀◑⊟♣

Dudley

Lamp Tavern

116 High Street, DY1 1QT

✪ 12-2.30, 5-11; 12-11 Fri & Sat; 12-10.30 Sun

☎ (01384) 254129

Batham Mild, Best Bitter, XXX (winter) 🄷

Lively Batham's local, with a spacious, welcoming front bar, and a dining area where good value weekday lunches are served. At the rear of the pub, the old Queen's Cross Brewery has been converted into a venue, staging regular music and comedy nights. Bed and breakfast accommodation is in the adjacent Lamp Cottage (discount for CAMRA members). ❀🛏⊟♿🚌P

Halesowen

Coombs Wood Sports & Social Club

Lodgefield Road, B62 8AA (off A4099 to Blackheath)

✪ 7.30 (7 Fri)-11; 12.30-11 Sat; 12-10.30 Sun

☎ (0121) 561 1932

Beer range varies 🄷

Housed in a cricket pavilion, originally built

for employees of the local steel works, this family-friendly club continues to prosper long after the factories have been demolished. It runs various sports teams and has a pool table and big-screen TV to provide entertainment for the less energetic. Five real ales, including a mild, are normally available. Hot and cold snacks are served Friday-Sunday evenings. Show a CAMRA membership card or copy of this Guide to gain admission. ❀♣

Hawne Tavern

78 Attwood Street, B63 3UG (off A458 ½ mile W of town centre)

✪ 4.30 (12 Sat)-11; 12-10.30 Sun

☎ (0121) 602 2601

Bank Top Dark Mild; Banks's Bitter; Batham Best Bitter; guest beers Ⓗ

This side-street free house has earned its place in this Guide since 1999. Of late, it offers four regular and six changing guest beers, mostly from micro-breweries. The bar has partitioned seating areas and more seating beyond, plus a pool table and dartboard. On the other side is a small, comfortable lounge. At the back the enclosed garden is popular in warm weather. No food is served on Sunday, but lunches are available on Saturday.

⛼Q❀⊖♣⊡

Somers Sports & Social Club

The Grange, Grange Hill, B62 0JH (at A456/B4551 jct)

✪ 12-2.30, 6-11; 12-2, 7-10.30 Sun

☎ (0121) 550 1645

Banks's Bitter; Batham Mild, Best Bitter; Enville Ale; Olde Swan Original; Taylor Landlord; guest beers Ⓗ

On the green belt side of the bypass, the club occupies a large, 250-year-old house set in its own extensive grounds. It usually offers five regular and five guest ales, all listed on a board behind the long bar. The main bar and adjacent lounge provide ample seating, or you can sit out on the patio, overlooking the bowling green. Show a CAMRA membership card or this Guide to gain admission. Groups of five or more should phone in advance. ❀P

Waggon & Horses

21 Stourbridge Road, B63 3TU (on A458, ½ mile from bus station)

✪ 12-11.30 (12.30am Fri & Sat); 12-11.30 Sun

☎ (0121) 550 4989

Bank Top Dark Mild; Batham Best Bitter; Enville Ale; Nottingham Extra Pale Ale; Oakham White Dwarf; guest beers Ⓗ

Its regular beers, supplemented by guests - many from micros and small local brewers - make this pub a must for the enlightened drinker. The long bar is complemented by quieter seating at each end. The pub has a national reputation and is also popular with locals, creating a great atmosphere. Real cider, draught Belgian beers and fruit wines are sold, and tasty home-made sandwiches are available 12-6.30pm, Monday-Saturday. A charity quiz is held alternate Wednesdays at this dog-friendly establishment. Q●⅟

Kingswinford

Bridge

110 Moss Grove, DY6 9HH (on A491)

✪ 12-3, 5-11:30; 12-11:45 Fri & Sat; 12-11:30 Sun

☎ (01384) 352356

Banks's Original, Bitter; guest beers Ⓗ

This welcoming pub is housed in a mid 19th-century building. The comfortable bar is popular for traditional games and local gossip; at the rear is a cosy lounge. It hosts occasional live entertainment at weekends, while in summer the well-equipped garden stages barbecues and a bouncy castle is installed for children. One or two guest beers come from the Wolverhampton and Dudley list. Sandwiches are made to order. It is 10 minutes' walk from the centre of Kingswinford. ⛼❀⊖♣P⊡

Park Tavern

182 Cot Lane, DY6 9QG (off A4101 and A491)

✪ 12-11; 12-3, 7-11 Sun

☎ (01384) 287178

Batham Best Bitter; guest beers Ⓗ

Two-roomed local, dating from the 19th century. The comfortable lounge has a quiet, cosy atmosphere, conducive to the art of conversation; its layout allows for a number of seating areas. The livelier bar is sport and games-oriented, and shows Sky Sports on TV. Up to three guest beers are selected from the Punch Taverns' list. Broadfield House Glass Museum is nearby and it is a 10-minute walk to the centre of Kingswinford. ❀⊖♣P

Knowle

Vaults

St John's Close, B93 0JU (off High St, A4141)

✪ 12-2.30, 5-11; 12-11.30 Fri & Sat; 12-11 Sun

☎ (01564) 773656

Ansells Mild; Greene King IPA; Tetley Bitter, Burton Ale; guest beers Ⓗ

Over 10 years in this Guide, and voted Solihull CAMRA Pub of the Year three years running, this is a haven for discerning drinkers. Two guest beers, often from micro-breweries, supplement the regular ales and Westons Old Rosie cider. Check out the fishing memorabilia and specimen catches on display; ask the landlord about the one that got away. It hosts occasional beer festivals, pickled onion and sloe gin competitions. Lunches are served Monday-Saturday. There is a public car park nearby. ●

Langley

Crosswells

Whyley Walk, B69 4SB

✪ 12-11 (midnight Fri & Sat); 12-11 Sun

☎ (0121) 552 2629

Marston's Pedigree; Olde Swan Entire; guest beer (occasional) Ⓗ

Well-appointed, busy local hostelry, with a large carvery restaurant and function room that plays host to local bands. The traditional bar and cosy lounge offer an occasional guest ale from the central bar. Food is served all day, every day throughout the pub. At the end of the High Street, it stands on a bus route, a short walk from the railway station. ◐⊞♿⇌(Langley Green)⊟♣P⊬

Model

Mitford Road, B69 4PZ (1 min walk from High St)
✪ 11.30-11.30 (midnight Fri & Sat); 12-11 Sun
☎ (0121) 532 0090
Greene King Abbot; Taylor Landlord; guest beer (occasional) ⒽH
True community pub at the heart of Langley, well served by buses and a short walk from Langley Green Station. The U-shaped bar is divided into two distinct areas. A pleasant conservatory, which is used as a no-smoking dining room, serves excellent value meals all week, supplemented by the chef's specials on Friday and Saturday evenings (no food Sun). Throughout the summer months the local pigeon fanciers club meets here before its races. ♨❀◐♿⇌(Langley Green)⊟♣P

Lower Gornal

Black Bear

86 Deepdale Lane, DY3 2AE
✪ 5 (4 Fri)-11; 12-11 Sat; 12-10.30 Sun
☎ (01384) 253333
Beer range varies Ⓗ
Charming, traditional pub, originally an 18th-century farmhouse. It is built on a hillside, supported by massive buttresses, and affords views over the southern Black Country. The split-level, L-shaped room has discrete and comfortable seating areas. Between four and seven beers, sourced mainly from small breweries, change frequently. It is 10 minutes' walk from Gornal Wood bus station. ♨❀⊟♣⊬

Five Ways

Himley Road, DY3 2PZ (at B4175/4176 jct)
✪ 12-11.30 (1am Fri & Sat); 12-10.30 Sun
☎ (01384) 252968
Batham Best Bitter; guest beer (occasional) Ⓗ
This already vibrant roadside pub is set to become even busier as it takes advantage of the extended opening hours. Its J-shaped single lounge, housing a large TV screen, sweeps round to a quieter bar area. Weekday lunches are served. A raised decked area at the rear is used for outside drinking. ❀◑♿⊟♣P

Fountain

8 Temple Street, DY3 2PE (on B4157, near Gornal Wood bus station)
✪ 12-11; 12-10.30 Sun
☎ (01384) 242777
Enville Ale; Everards Tiger; Greene King Abbot; Hook Norton Old Hooky; RCH Pitchfork; guest beers Ⓗ
Excellent free house serving nine real ales, traditional cider, draught and bottled Belgian beers and 20 fruit wines. The rear garden is a suntrap in summer. Popular with locals and visitors, the lively bar is complemented by an elevated dining area serving food 12-9pm, except Sunday evening. Twice winner of Dudley CAMRA's Pub of the Year award, it hosts beer festivals at Easter and in October. ❀◐♿⊟♣●P⊬

Old Bull's Head

1 Redhall Road, DY3 2NU (at Temple St, B4175 jct)
✪ 4 (2 Fri)-11; 12-11 Sat & Sun
☎ (01384) 231616 🌐 oldbullshead.co.uk
Black Country Bradley's Finest Golden, Pig on the Wall, Fireside, seasonal beers; guest beers Ⓗ
Impressive, late Victorian pub of two rooms. The larger lounge bar is popular for crib and dominoes. A raised area at one end serves as a stage several evenings a week for live entertainment. There is also a sports lounge with pool table, dartboard and a large-screen TV for sport. Black Country Ales Brewery is at the rear of the pub; two guest beers are normally stocked, sourced from various breweries. Gornal Wood bus station is a five minute walk. ♨❀⊞⊟♣●P

Oldbury

Wagon & Horses ☆

17a Church Street, B69 3AD (opp. Sandwell Council House)
✪ 12-11 (midnight Fri & Sat); 12-10.30 Sun
☎ (0121) 552 5467
Enville White; Oakham JHB; guest beers Ⓗ
National Inventory listed pub, noted for its splendidly ornate tiled walls, panelled ceiling and Holt Brewery etched windows. Frequented by office workers, locals and visitors alike, it offers a peaceful haven from the town centre. It comprises a bar, lounge and a passageway that is used as an extra drinking space. Food is served mainly weekday lunchtimes and Wednesday-Friday evenings, 5.30-7.30pm. It hosts a monthly quiz. ♨Q◐⊞♿⇌(Sandwell/Dudley)⊟P⊬

Sedgley

Beacon Hotel ☆

129 Bilston Street, DY3 1JE (on A463)
✪ 12-2.30 (3 Sat), 5.30 (6 Sat)-11; 12-3, 7-10.30 Sun
☎ (01902) 883380
Sarah Hughes Pale Amber, Surprise Bitter, Dark Ruby, seasonal beers; guest beers Ⓗ
Authentic Victorian tap, with a tower brewery to match, centred around a short corridor and a tiny island bar with snob screens. It has four contrasting rooms: a small, Spartan tap room, a cosy snug, an imposing main lounge and a family room in the rear extension overlooking an outdoor play area. Go through the lounge to admire the conservatory's exotic plants. One or two guest beers are sold in addition to the home-brewed delights. Cheese cobs are available. Q♉❀⊟♣P

Bull's Head

27 Bilston Street, DY3 1JA
✪ 10-midnight; 11-midnight Sun
☎ (01902) 661676
Holden's Mild (occasional), Bitter, Golden Glow, Special, seasonal beers Ⓗ
Open-plan, L-shaped, community pub with a pleasant ambience that attracts locals and visitors alike. Wherever you come from, you are assured of a warm welcome. The boisterous bar contrasts with the more sedate lounge extension. It can get crowded

at the weekend. There is a 20p per pint discount on draught beers 10-4pm weekdays. ❀⊟♿⊟●⊟

Mount Pleasant (Stump)

144 High Street, DY3 1RH (on A459)

⏲ 6 -11; 12-3, 7-10.30 Sun

Beer range varies Ⓗ

Lovingly restored and reopened after a long period of closure, this 'Gornal stone', brick and timber faced pub, has rapidly established a fine reputation in this area of real ale excellence. Behind the front bar is a convivial lounge with alcove seating and a warming coal-fired stove. Further back and slightly lower is another cosy area, also with its own stove. No smoking is permitted except in the enclosed passageway at the side of the lounge areas. Up to eight real ales are offered, including beers from RCH and other small micros. ⌂❀⊟⊟♣P⊬

Shelfield

Four Crosses

11 Green Lane, WS4 1RN (off A461)

⏲ 12-11; 12-3, 7-10.30 Sun

☎ (01922) 682518

Banks's Original, Bitter; guest beers Ⓗ

Traditional, good old-fashioned pub, with an open fire in the saloon and a welcoming lounge. Over 200 years old, it has retained notable features such as the mosaic flooring and stained glass in the entrance. Pub games are played here. Children, accompanied by adults, may use the passageway. ⌂Q❀⊟⊟♣P⊬

Shirley

Bernie's Real Ale Off-Licence

266 Cranmore Boulevard, B90 4PX (200 yds off Stratford Rd)

⏲ 12-2 (not Mon; 11.30-1.30 Wed), 6-10 (5.30-9 Fri); 11-3, 5-9 Sat; 12-2, 7-9 Sun

☎ (0121) 744 2827

Beer range varies Ⓗ

The business of Bernie's is to sell real ale of quality and diversity. It stocks the most interesting range of beers from micro-breweries that you will find anywhere in the Solihull area. Its owners have built a reputation for always serving a perfect pint. If you are unsure which beer to buy, a sampling service is offered together with advice and a warm welcome. ⊟

Short Heath

Duke of Cambridge

82 Coltham Road, WV12 5QD

⏲ 12-3.30 (not Mon or Tue), 7-11; 12-3.30, 7-10.30 Sun

☎ (01922) 408895

Greene King Old Speckled Hen; Highgate Dark; Taylor Landlord; Worthington's Bitter; guest beers Ⓗ

Convivial, family-run free house converted from 17th-century farm cottages but licensed for nearly 200 years. The main rooms benefit from electronic air cleaners. The public bar has a solid fuel stove. The lounge is split into two halves by a wall containing an aquarium; the front half showing the original exposed beams. Both rooms feature display cases of model commercial vehicles. The large family room houses pool and bar football tables. ⌂Q⊟⊟⊟♣P

Solihull

Field House

10 Knightcote Drive, Monkspath, B91 3JU (off Monkspath Hall Rd)

⏲ 12-11 (midnight Thu-Sun)

☎ (0121) 711 8011

Caledonian Deuchars IPA; Fuller's London Pride; M&B Brew XI; guest beers Ⓗ

Part of the Ember Inns chain, this modern pub is attractively decorated and comfortably furnished, featuring four large, coal-effect fires and pleasant patio areas. It normally stocks four or five well-known ales, changing often and featuring more unusual brews during festival periods and promotions. Often busy, it attracts a wide age range, but only welcomes children if they are over 14 and dining. Food is served every day until 8pm, after which some light snacks are available. ❀◑♿⇌(Widney Manor)⊟P⊬

Golden Acres

Rowood Drive, Damsonwood, B92 9NG (off Damson Lane)

⏲ 12-11 (midnight Fri & Sat); 12-11 Sun

☎ (0121) 704 9002

Beer range varies Ⓗ

On a housing estate, the pub has done much to alleviate its severe 1960s façade by installing abundant floral displays in summer. Inside there is a public bar and a comfortable lounge. Since being taken over by enthusiastic licensees this pub, which seemed in terminal decline, has sprung back to life. As for the beer, sometimes the usual regionals are stocked but frequently it offers two guests from micros. The food (not served Tue) is also available to take away. ⌂❀◑⊟⊟●P

Stourbridge

Garibaldi

19 Cross Street, DY8 3XE (take Greenfield Ave exit from New Road, third left)

⏲ 12-11; 12-4.30, 7-10.30 Sun

☎ (01384) 373390 🌐 garibaldiinn.co.uk

Banks's Original, Bitter; Marston's Pedigree; guest beers Ⓗ

Stourbridge's best kept secret, not far from the town ring road, but it can be hard to find, so follow the directions carefully. The welcome you will receive makes the effort worth while. Traditional games can be played in the bar or you can play pool in the family room. The lounge is quiet during the day but hosts live music (folk, Irish, and so on) most evenings. ⊟◑⊟♣P

Royal Exchange

75 Enville Street, DY8 1XW (on A458)

⏲ 1 (12 Sat & summer)-11; 12-10.30 Sun

☎ (01384) 396726

Batham Mild, Best Bitter, seasonal beers Ⓗ

The lively bar, small, quiet lounge and large

patio are all accessed from a narrow passageway. The upstairs room is not normally open, but is available for private hire or meetings. There is a public car park opposite. Drinkers are always made very welcome, and snacks are usually available. Q❀⊟♣

Shrubbery Cottage

28 Heath Lane, DY8 1RQ (near Oldswinford traffic lights)
⊙ 11.30-11; 12-10.30 Sun
☎ (01384) 377598
Holden's Bitter, Golden Glow, Special, seasonal beers Ⓗ
Cosy, welcoming pub, with a spacious, open bar area. The pub has a barbecue in the garden and its own miniature putting green. At one end of the bar, the large-screen TV often shows golf or football. The pub has been recently refurbished and now provides full disabled access from the car park.
❀◑♿⇌(Junction)🚌P

Sutton Coldfield

Bishop Vesey

63 Boldmere Road, B73 5UY (in Boldmere central shopping area)
⊙ 11-11 daily
☎ (0121) 355 5077
Courage Directors; Marston's Burton Bitter, Pedigree; guest beers Ⓗ
Refurbished in 2005, this Wetherspoon's is named after the Sutton Coldfield benefactor. The pub is now no-smoking throughout, but provision has been made for smokers with a canopied patio area at the rear. It has the usual open-plan layout but has upstairs seating; children are allowed in designated areas. It stages themed food evenings, a weekly quiz and regular mini-beer festivals, run by a friendly and efficient staff. A main bus route is within 200 yards.
❀◑♿⇌(Wylde Green)🚌●⊬

Crown

Walsall Road, Four Oaks, B74 4RA (on A454, opp. Crown Lane)
⊙ 12-11 (2am Thu-Sat); 12-11 Sun
☎ (0121) 309 7994
M&B Brew XI; guest beers Ⓗ
Magnificent, large, post-war brick building, recently refurbished to Ember Inn's high standard. It has plenty of individual seating areas and a large, curved bar to accommodate all customers comfortably. Good quality food is offered on a varied, reasonably priced menu, 12-8pm daily; bistro-style snacks are available later. A good range of cask ales is provided by a landlord who is keen to offer unusual brews. With two no-smoking areas and a heated patio, there is a niche here for all.
❀◑♿⇌(Butler's Lane)🚌P⊬

Laurel Wines

63 Westwood Road, Banners Gate, B73 6UP (200 yds off A452, near Sutton Park)
⊙ 5-10; 3-10.30 Fri; 12-10.30 Sat; 12-2, 6-9 Sun
☎ (0121) 353 0399
Batham Best Bitter; Enville Ale; Taylor Landlord; guest beers Ⓖ
This real ale off-licence is well known across the Midlands for its constantly-changing range of guest beers sourced nationwide. Requested ales can be sampled before purchase; you can bring your own container or buy one here. It also stocks British and foreign bottled beers and the usual off-licence goods. For functions, beer can be supplied and set up in your home.

Station

Station Street, B73 6AT (near southbound platform)
⊙ 12-11 (midnight Fri & Sat); 12-10.30 Sun
☎ (0121) 362 4960
Taylor Landlord; guest beer Ⓗ
Spacious, town-centre pub, catering for enthusiasts of real ale and real food of all ages. Well used by rail passengers owing to its proximity to the platform, it is a popular meeting place at all times of day. An interesting menu is served. The upstairs function room hosts a sell-out Thursday night comedy club and impromptu music sessions often occur. The garden has been recently refurbished and it also boasts a heated bandstand. ⛼❀◑⊟♿⇌🚌♣

Wylde Green

Birmingham Road, B72 1DH (on A5127 between A452 and A453)
⊙ 11-11 (midnight Fri & Sat); 12-11 Sun
☎ (0121) 373 1340
Hardys & Hansons Bitter, Olde Trip; guest beer Ⓗ
The pub is on the site of a former coaching inn adjacent to a crown bowling green with its own club; a pleasurable sight for visitors during the bowling season. Excellent food is provided from a la carte menus, while a less expensive choice is also available for older patrons. The beer is unusual for the area.
❀◑🚌

Tipton

Rising Sun

116 Horseley Road, DY4 7NH (off B4517)
⊙ 12-2.30, 5-11; 12-11 Sat; 12-10.30 Sun
☎ (0121) 530 2308
Banks's Original; Oakham JHB; guest beers Ⓗ
Imposing Victorian hostelry, comprising two distinct rooms. The bright bar is adorned with pictures of local sporting heroes. The comfortable lounge is divided in two by a screen, and each section is warmed by an open fire. In summer, the back yard opens for drinking and occasional functions. Up to six guest beers supplement the two regular brews. Great Bridge bus station nearby has frequent services to Dudley, West Bromwich and Birmingham.
⛼❀⊟🚌♣●

Waggon & Horses

131 Toll End Road, Ocker Hill, DY4 0ET (on A461)
⊙ 5 (12 Fri & Sat)-11; 12-3.30, 7-10.30 Sun
☎ (0121) 502 6453
Banks's Original; Olde Swan Entire; Toll End Black Bridge; guest beers Ⓗ
Thriving, community brew-pub of mock-Tudor design. The spacious public bar houses a well-used dartboard and an open fire. The

plusher, more comfortable lounge has a relaxed atmosphere. Toll End Brewery at the rear is set in a landscaped garden with an attached conservatory drinking area. Two or three of its beers are often amongst the guests.
⛫♨❀⊟♿⊖(Wednesbury Parkway)⊟♣●

Upper Gornal

Britannia (Sally's) ☆

109 Kent Street, DY3 1UX (on A459)

⊙ 12-3, 7-11; 12-11 Fri & Sat; 12-10.30 Sun

☎ (01902) 883253

Batham Mild, Best Bitter, XXX (winter) ⊞

The real gem of this National Inventory listed pub is the wood-panelled tap room, called Sally's Bar after a former landlady; beer is still occasionally dispensed in this room from the handpulls attached to the wall. The pub also has a friendly main bar and a comfortable back parlour. Originally a brew-pub, built around 1780, brewing ceased in 1959, although the brewhouse is still intact and adjoins the delightful backyard drinking area. ⛫♨❀⊟♿⊟♣⚟

Walsall

Arbor Lights

127-128 Lichfield Street, WS1 1SY (off A4148 ring road at Arboretum island)

⊙ 10-11; 12-11 Sun

☎ (01922) 613361 🌐 arborlights.co.uk

Beer range varies ⊞

Opened in 2003, this modern, open-plan, town-centre pub is popular with drinkers and diners alike. There is a large dining area where good, locally sourced food is served from midday (booking recommended especially at weekends). The pub's name is derived from the nearby Arboretum Illuminations, which are known locally as 'the lights'and held annually in September. Three rotating guest beers are always available; Westons Old Rosie cider is stocked in summer. ◐♿≠⊟●⚟

Fountain

49 Lower Forster Street, WS1 1XB

⊙ 12-midnight daily

☎ (01922) 629741

Caledonian Deuchars IPA; Fuller's London Pride; guest beer ⊞

Small, two-roomed Victorian local in a conservation area. Sympathetically modernised, with restrained, comfortable decor, it displays a collection of photographs of old Walsall. Good pub food includes home-made pies and Sunday roasts (eve meals served Tue-Sat). Convenient for local history and leather museums, this friendly community pub on the edge of the town centre makes a welcome break from the circuit. Q◐⊟≠⊟♣⚟

Lyndon House Hotel

9-10 Upper Rushall Street, WS1 2HA

⊙ 11-11.30; 12-11 Sun

☎ (01922) 612511

Courage Directors; Greene King Abbot; Highgate Dark; Theakston Best Bitter; guest beer ⊞

Formerly the Royal Exchange, now a one-roomed pub with an island bar. The woodwork and beams may be imported but the result is a warm, cheerful and comfortable venue. The pub is part of a tardis-like complex that contains a hotel, Italian restaurant and a balcony drinking area for the summer. At the top of Walsall market, it is popular with the business community. A real slice of Walsall life, it provides a pleasant aperitif for the many nearby restaurants. ⛫Q❀⊟⊟

Rose & Crown

55 Old Birchills, WS2 8QH (off A34)

⊙ 12-midnight (1am Fri & Sat); 11-midnight Sun

☎ (01922) 720533

Black Country Pig on the Wall; guest beers ⊞

Grade II listed, this three-roomed corner pub dates from 1901. You enter into a central corridor that also serves as a drinking area. The long bar, with its superb back bar, has real character and a good atmosphere. It hosts live entertainment on Saturday evening, karaoke (Fri eve and Sun afternoon) and a quiz on Sunday evening. A pool table, function room and Sky Sports are also available. Guest beers are from independent breweries. ⛫♨⊟⊟♣

Tap & Spile

5 John Street, WS2 8AF

⊙ 12-3, 6-11; 12-3, 7-11 Sun

☎ (01922) 627660

Oakham JHB; Theakston Best Bitter; guest beers ⊞

Small, friendly, back-street local. It comprises a comfortable bar, warmed by a coal fire in winter, a cosy lounge and a corridor drinking area. Known as The Pretty Bricks, due to glazed tiling on its frontage, this pub has a place in CAMRA history: it is one of the pubs from where CAMRA was launched nationally in 1972 and where Walsall CAMRA was founded in that same year. Good pub food (served Tue-Sat) includes warm spicy chicken salad and baltis. It is convenient for the Leather Museum.
⛫Q❀◐⊟⊟♣

Walsall Cricket Club

Gorway Road, WS1 3BE (off A34, by university campus)

⊙ 8 (7 Fri; 12 Sat)-11; 12-11 Sun

☎ (01922) 622094 🌐 walsallcricketclub.com

Marston's Burton Bitter; guest beers ⊞

Established in 1830, the club has occupied this site since 1907. The comfortable, single-room clubhouse lounge displays cricket memorabilia as you would expect. The bar is staffed by members. On match days the cricket can be viewed through panoramic windows; in good weather the lounge is opened onto the patio area. Beer festivals are staged. Entry to the club for non-members is by showing this Guide or a CAMRA card. Q❀P⊔

White Lion

150 Sandwell Street, WS1 3EQ

⊙ 12-11 (midnight Fri & Sat); 12-11 Sun

☎ (01922) 628542

Adnams Bitter; Fuller's London Pride; Greene King IPA, Old Speckled Hen; Highgate Dark; guest beers Ⓗ
Imposing, late Victorian, back-street local. The classic, sloping bar, with its deep end and shallow end, is one of the best in town. A plush, comfortable lounge caters for the drinker who wants to languish, while the pool room has two tables. This pub is a great community melting-pot: caught at the right moment, an instant party. The cider is Westons Old Rosie.
❀⊟⊟♣●

Warley

Plough

George Road, B68 9LN
✪ 2 (12 Sat)-11 (midnight Fri & Sat); 12-11 Sun
☎ (0121) 552 3822
Adnams Bitter; Banks's Original; Draught Bass; Marston's Pedigree; guest beer Ⓗ
This whitewashed, former farmhouse is a genuine local, tucked away in a residential area. Enter through the lounge and a series of four small areas leads gently upwards through to a sports bar with a pool table. The decor takes you back to the 1950s, resulting in a comfortable, homely ambience where locals are happy to chat to visitors. The outdoor seating area and garden are pleasant on a warm day.
❀⊟⊟♣P

Wednesbury

Old Blue Ball

19 Hall End, WS10 9ED
✪ 12-3, 5-11; 12-11 Fri; 12-4.30, 7-11 Sat; 12-3.30, 7-10.30 Sun
☎ (0121) 556 0197
Everards Original; Highgate Dark; Taylor Landlord; guest beers Ⓗ
Grade II listed building: the small bar is decorated with cigarette and drinks mirrors, while a drinking passage displays a potted history of Everards Brewery and a collection of pump clips. The snug is quiet. The large family room is popular with darts players. The garden at the rear has plenty of bench seating and a children's play area. Table football is played on an open veranda.
Q❀⊟⊟♣

Olde Leathern Bottel

40 Vicarage Road, WS10 9DW
✪ 12-2.30 (not Mon), 6-11; 12-2, 6-11.30 Fri; 12-11.30 Sat; 12-4, 7-11 Sun
☎ (0121) 505 0230
Worthington's Bitter; guest beers Ⓗ
Set in cottages dating from 1510, the bar and no-smoking snug have bench seating, while the split-level lounge features soft furnishings. Drinkers can also stand in the passage, and additional seating is available out in the rear yard. The pub is decorated throughout with old photos and prints. Good value home made meals include a vegetarian selection and children are welcome to dine here. It hosts the local history society and stages a Sunday evening quiz. ⛰❀◐⊟⊟P⚟

Wednesfield

Pyle Cock

Rookery Street, WV11 1UN
(on old Wolverhampton road)
✪ 10.30-11 (11.30 Fri & Sat); 11-11 Sun
☎ (01902) 732125
Banks's Original, Bitter; Ⓟ **guest beers** Ⓗ
Splendid, traditional pub, dating back to the 1860s, offering its customers a choice of three rooms. It now has three guest handpumps to give plenty of alternatives to the regular beers. The landlord was awarded the Mild Merit award by local CAMRA for his commitment to serving excellent mild. A friendly welcome is assured here and visitors find they are soon drawn into conversation. It lies on showcase bus route No. 559 from Wolverhampton, with frequent services day and evening. ❀⊟⊟P

Royal Tiger

41 High Street, WV11 1ST
✪ 11-12 (1am Fri & Sat); 11-12 Sun
☎ (01902) 307816
Banks's Original, Bitter; Greene King Abbot; Marston's Burton Bitter; guest beers Ⓗ
Modern, purpose-built pub, opened in 2000. It offers a range of real ales, Westons Old Rosie cider and a typical Wetherspoon's menu. The patio at the rear, near the canal, is used in the summer. The pub lacks a car park, but it is well served by showcase route No. 559 with its regular service.
❀◐⊟●⚟

West Bromwich

Old Crown

56 Sandwell Road, B70 8TJ (200 yds off High St)
✪ 12-4, 5-11; 12-11 Fri & Sat; 12-3.30, 7-10.30 Sun
☎ (0121) 525 4600
Beer range varies Ⓗ
Vibrant, back-street free house within 10 minutes' walk of the town centre. Four ever changing guest ales are always on sale here, with many supplied by local micro-breweries. It can get busy at lunchtime and early evening due to its competitively priced curries and baltis (no meals Sat or Sun, or Mon eve).
◐⊖(Dartmouth St)⊟♣

Vine

152 Roebuck Street, B70 6RD
✪ 11.30-2.30, 5-11; 11.30-11 Fri; 12-11 Sat; 12-10.30 Sun
☎ (0121) 553 2866
Beer range varies Ⓗ
At first sight, this is a regular, traditional, corner pub, but once past the building's original tiny snug, smoke room and back room, it opens out into a vast glass-roofed extension, with a barbecue room beyond that. The yard has been tented over to create overspill space for diners. Famous for its food, served all day at the weekend, including traditional pub dishes, curries, baltis and vegetarian choices, the good value barbecues are particularly popular. One guest beer is served.
◐⇌(Smethwick Galton Bridge)⊟⊡

Wheatsheaf

379 High Street, B70 9QW

11-11.30 (midnight Fri & Sat); 11-11.30 Sun

☎ (0121) 553 4221

Holden's Mild, Ⓟ Bitter; Ⓟ/Ⓗ Golden Glow, Special, seasonal beers Ⓗ

Every high street should have at least one pub like this classic town house, with its lively, basic front bar and plush, more genteel lounge tucked away from the hustle and bustle at the rear. Beloved of office workers during the week, footie fans at weekends and horse racing enthusiasts all week long, it serves good value lunches (extended on Sat when Baggies are at home). The cider is Thatchers Cheddar Valley.

(Guns Village/Dartmouth St)

Willenhall

Falcon

Gomer Street West, WV13 2NR

12-11; 12-10.30 Sun

☎ (01902) 633378

Greene King Abbot; Oakham JHB; Olde Swan Mild; RCH Pitchfork; guest beers Ⓗ

Genuine free house, offering up to eight cask ales, mainly from small breweries. A short walk from the town centre and two minutes from the No. 529 Walsall-Wolverhampton bus route, this friendly pub has two rooms: a busy bar and a quieter rear lounge. This local CAMRA Pub of the Year winner 2005 fields darts, crib and cricket teams. Willenhall Lock Museum is nearby.

Wollaston

Foresters

Bridgnorth Road, DY8 3PL (on A458 towards Bridgnorth)

12-2.30, 6-11; 12-3, 7-10.30 Sun

☎ (01384) 394476

Enville Ale; Marston's Pedigree; guest beers Ⓗ

This friendly local is well known for high quality and good value food (eve meals served Tue-Sat). The T-shaped room conveniently provides an area for diners and is home to the Foresters Golf Society. Regular quizzes are held, usually on the first and third Sundays of the month. An event not to be missed is the annual fun run with the proceeds going to charity.

P

Unicorn

145 Bridgnorth Road, DY8 3NX (on A458 towards Bridgnorth)

12-11; 12-4, 7-10.30 Sun

☎ (01384) 394823

Batham Mild, Best Bitter, seasonal beers Ⓗ

Former brewhouse, purchased by Batham in the early 1990s, which has earned the reputation of being one of the busiest pubs serving one of the best pints in the estate. The remains of the old brewhouse are visible at the side of the pub, but would be costly to renovate. The pub itself is a basic two-roomed house, mainly for drinkers as food is limited to lunchtime sandwiches. 'Unspoilt by progress' is an apt description of this pub.

Q P

Wolverhampton

Chindit

113 Merridale Road, WV3 9SE

2 (12 Sat)-midnight; 12-midnight Sun

☎ (01902) 425582

Caledonian Deuchars IPA; guest beers Ⓗ

Street-corner local opened after WWII as a tribute to local men who served with the South Staffordshire Regiment, taking part in the 1944 Chindit campaign in Burma. The pub comprises two rooms: a comfortable lounge and a bar with pool table. Up to three guest beers are offered, usually from local micro-breweries. Live music is staged on Friday evening and an outdoor beer festival held over May Day weekend.

P

Combermere Arms

90 Chapel Ash, WV3 0TY (On A41 Tettenhall road)

11-3, 5.30-11; 12-11 Fri & Sat; 12-10.30 Sun

☎ (01902) 421880

Banks's Original, Bitter; guest beers Ⓗ

Multi-roomed local with a no-smoking bar, snug and lounge off the central corridor, leading to a covered courtyard and outside seating in the garden area. It is worth a trip to the gents, off the courtyard, to admire the tree growing in the middle. A quiz is held on Tuesday evening. Bar lunches are available weekdays.

P

Great Western

Sun Street, WV10 0DJ

11-11; 12-10.30 Sun

☎ (01902) 351090

Batham Best Bitter; Holden's Mild, Bitter, Golden Glow, Special; guest beers Ⓗ

Historic, listed pub opposite the closed former low-level Great Western Railway Station. A Holden's house, it is the only city-centre outlet for Batham and Holden's beers. Good value food is served at record speed at lunchtime. The railway and Wolverhampton Wanderers memorabilia are well worth perusing. P

Hog's Head

186 Stafford Street, WV1 1NA

12-11 (midnight Fri & Sat); 12-11 Sun

☎ (01902) 717955

Caledonian Deuchars IPA; Greene King Old Speckled Hen; Hook Norton Old Hooky; Taylor Landlord; guest beers Ⓗ

Built in 1889 as the Vine, the name is still evident in the brickwork. For about 100 years it sold Butler's ales. It closed in 1984 and reopened as the Hog's Head in 1998. The pub is locally listed for its superb terracotta exterior. It attracts a varied clientele except Friday and Saturday when 18-25 year olds dominate and the noise level can soar.

(St George's)

Moon under Water

53-55 Lichfield Street, WV1 1EQ (opp. Grand Theatre)
11-midnight (1am Fri & Sat); 9am-midnight Sun
☎ (01902) 422447
Marston's Burton Bitter, Pedigree; guest beers Ⓗ
Open-plan Wetherspoon's pub converted from the former Co-op store in 1995. The decor features photographs illustrating the history of Wolverhampton. Popular with theatregoers, as the Grand Theatre is directly opposite, it can get busy on weekend evenings with drinkers going on to the clubs. The usual Wetherspoon menu is served until 11pm. Ever-changing guest beers include Enville and Highgate products. It is convenient for both the railway and bus stations.
◑ ⇌ ⊖ (St George's) ⊟ ⁄

Newhampton

19 Riches Street, WV6 0DW
11-11 (midnight Fri & Sat); 12-11 Sun
☎ (01902) 745773
Caledonian Deuchars IPA; Courage Best Bitter, Directors; Greene King Abbot; Theakston Old Peculier; guest beers Ⓗ
Multi-roomed local boasting an unexpectedly large garden where games facilities include a bowling green and boules piste. The Newhampton serves its local community and customers from further afield, as its function room is a thriving venue for folk and other music. It also has a smoke room, pool room and bowls pavilion bar. The home-made food, including good vegetarian options, is recommended.
❀ ◑ ♣

Posada

48 Lichfield Street, WV1 1DG (opp. art gallery)
12-11.30 (1am Fri & Sat); 12-11.30 Sun
☎ (01902) 429011
Adnams Broadside; Caledonian Deuchars IPA; Wells Bombardier; guest beers Ⓗ
Grade II listed, city-centre hostelry behind an imposing tiled frontage. The interior of this small, narrow pub features more original tiling, a magnificent bar back and a tiny, intimate alcove. The pub has been revitalised by new management and regularly stocks five guest beers, of which one is usually a mild.
❀ ◑ ⇌ ⊖ (St George's) ⊟

Shoulder of Mutton

62 Wood Road, Tettenhall Wood, WV6 8NF (up Holloway from Compton island, A454)
11.30-2.30, 5-11 (midnight Fri); 11.30-midnight Sat; 12-11 Sun
☎ (01902) 756672
Banks's Original, Bitter; guest beer Ⓗ
One-roomed pub with low ceilings and oak beams, in the Tettenhall Wood area of the city. A warm welcome is assured here, as is good value, traditional home-cooked food at lunchtime. The games room is served from a hatch and can be used by families or booked for meetings. It has a patio area with space for barbecues. Occasional live entertainment is staged on weekday evenings.
Q ❀ ◑ ♿ ⊟ ♣ P ⁄

Stile

3 Harrow Street, Whitmore Reans, WV1 4PB (off Newhampton Rd E)
12-11; 12-10.30 Sun
☎ (01902) 425336
Banks's Original, Bitter; Ⓟ **guest beer** Ⓗ
Late Victorian pub that has been given local listing status. With its small smoke room, club room and public bar, it is a truly community-focused place. An old stable block dating back to the 1860s (which is the only reminder of the previous pub on the site) overlooks the unusual L-shaped bowling green. It gets crowded on Wolves match days as it is close to the football ground. Regular buses stop on Newhampton Road East, a five-minute walk away.
❀ ◑ ♿ ⊟ ♣

Swan (at Compton)

Bridgnorth Road, Compton, WV6 8AE
(at Compton island, A454)
11-11 (11.30 Thu; midnight Fri & Sat); 12-11 Sun
☎ (01902) 754736
Banks's Original, Bitter; Marston's Pedigree Ⓗ
Grade II listed inn in the Compton area of the city. A basic unspoilt gem with a convivial atmosphere, the traditional bar features wooden settles, exposed beams and a faded painting of a swan dating from 1777. The bar and L-shaped snug are both supplied from a central servery. The lounge has Sky TV for sports, and doubles as a games room, with a dartboard.
Q ❀ ⊟ ♣ P

Tap & Spile

35 Princess Street, WV1 1HD
11-11; 11-10.30 Sun
☎ (01902) 713319
Banks's Bitter; guest beers Ⓗ
City-centre pub consisting of a narrow bar, two snugs and a small paved area for outside drinking. A large-screen TV and three others showing major sporting events and music make it popular with both clubbers and Wolves fans on match days. Beers from local micro-breweries, obtained through the SIBA direct delivery scheme, often feature as guests. The cider is Westons Old Rosie. It is handy for the bus station.
❀ ♿ ⇌ ⊖ (St George's) ⊟ ♣

Woodsetton

Park Inn

George Street, DY1 4LW (on A457, 200 yds from A4123)
12-11; 12-10.30 Sun
☎ (01902) 661279
Holden's Mild, Bitter, Golden Glow, Special, seasonal beers Ⓗ
Bright and breezy suburban brewery tap, just off the main Wolverhampton-Dudley and Tipton-Sedgley thoroughfares. Its U-shaped main bar has a raised area for dining and is dominated by a large TV screen. A more tranquil spot can be found in the adjacent conservatory; there is also a games room. Reasonably-priced food is available (no meals Mon eve). Coseley railway station is about 20 minutes' walk from the pub. ❀ ◑ ⊟ ♣ P

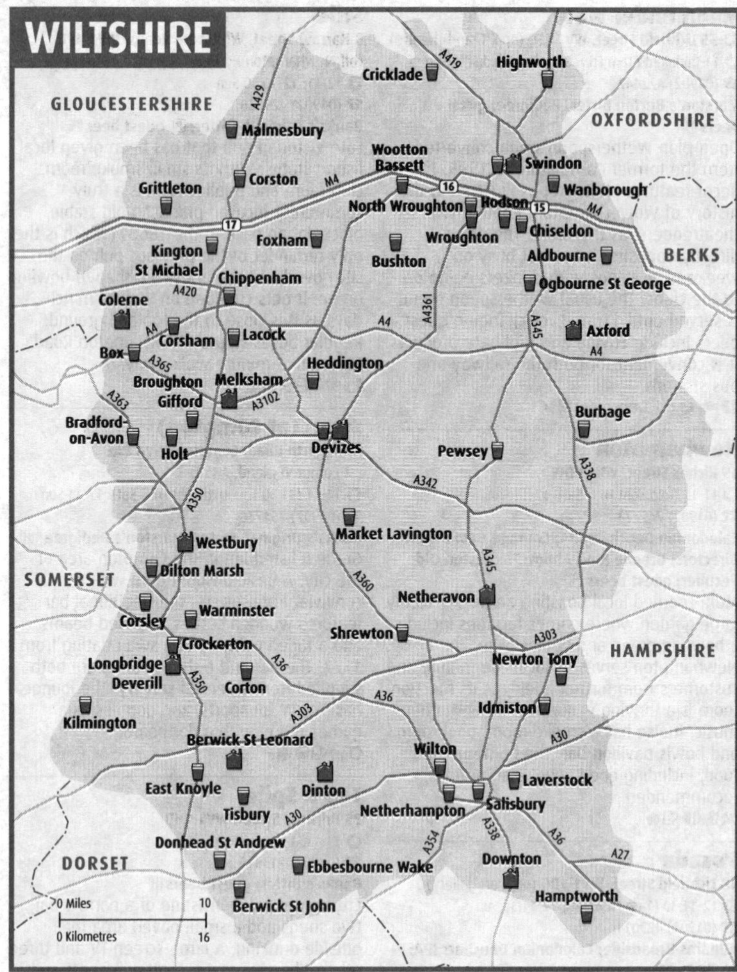

Aldbourne

Masons Arms

11 West Street, SN8 2BS

⏲ 6-11; 12-3, 7-10.30 Sun

☎ (01672) 540124

Fuller's London Pride; Wadworth IPA; guest beers Ⓗ

Friendly local with two small, intimate bars full of character and chit chat – note the 3D pub sign. The pub runs dominoes, crib and darts teams. Beer festivals are held twice a year in May and September during the Aldbourne carnival. A mild beer is usually available. Q❀⊟♣

Berwick St John

Talbot

The Cross, SP7 0HA (S of A30, 5 miles E of Shaftesbury)

⏲ 12-2.30, 6-11; 12-4 Sun

☎ (01747) 828222

Draught Bass; Ringwood Best Bitter; Wadworth 6X; guest beer Ⓗ

Situated in rolling downland countryside, tucked away in a pretty village, this old stone building has a single bar with a huge inglenook fireplace. The pub is popular with regulars as well as walkers and tourists exploring the Downs and Ebbe Valley, or the nearby regimental badges carved into the hillside. Four beers are usually available complementing the good value pub food.

⛫Q❀◑◐♿♣●P

INDEPENDENT BREWERIES

Archers Swindon
Arkell's Swindon
Box Steam Colerne
Downton Downton
Hidden Dinton
Hop Back Downton
Keystone Berwick St Leonard
Moles Melksham
Ramsbury Axford
Stonehenge Netheravon
Wadworth Devizes
Wessex Longbridge Deverill
Westbury Westbury

Box

Bear
High Street, SN13 8NJ (on A4)
⏲ 11-3, 5-11; 11-11 Fri & Sat; 12-10.30 Sun
☎ (01225) 743622 🌐 bearatbox.co.uk
Box Rev Awdry, Tunnel Vision, Blind House; Wadworth 6X; guest beer Ⓗ
A genuine local, this smart, comfortable pub on the main road also welcomes drinkers from far and wide who come for the beers brewed in the pub's own brewery, Box Steam. Although the brewery is not on the premises, there are usually a couple of its beers on handpump, as well as guests. The food has a very good reputation. Paintings by local artists are displayed on the walls. ♔Q❀⇌ᗡ◗♿P

Bradford-on-Avon

Bunch of Grapes
14 Silver Street, BA15 1JY
⏲ 11-11 (midnight Fri & Sat); 12-10.30 Sun
☎ (01225) 863877
Young's Bitter, Special, seasonal beers; guest beers Ⓗ
Town-centre pub, easily recognisable by the grapevine growing over the side. This welcoming pub has been a well-deserved regular in the Guide for years. The narrow bar is divided into three drinking areas and there is a restaurant upstairs (booking advisable) serving good value food. There is a carvery every Sunday and theme nights once a month. The small pub can get busy at times, making it feel crowded. A rare Young's pub in the area. ❀ᗡ◗≹

Rising Sun
231 Winsley Road, BA15 1QS
⏲ 12-11; 12-10.30 Sun
☎ (01225) 862354
Beer range varies Ⓗ
Popular local on the outskirts of Bradford at the top of a hill. It has two bars: the lounge, which is small and quiet with pictures of various cricket pavilions adorning the walls, and the larger and livelier saloon, with a big TV screen. The friendly locals and the pub's ancient spaniel offer visitors a warm welcome. Live music is played at weekends. ♔❀♣●▯

Broughton Gifford

Bell on the Common
SN12 8LX (2 miles W of Melksham, off B3107)
⏲ 11-11; 12-10.30 Sun
☎ (01225) 782309
Wadworth IPA, 6X, seasonal beers Ⓗ
Handsome old pub standing on the edge of the extensive village green. Inside are two contrasting bars: the smart bar, with a copper top, attached to the restaurant, and the public bar which is very much a locals' hangout, complete with wooden settles and old tables. Its wonderful 'old' wooden floor is in fact a recent addition. A games room is next to the public bar. The garden is large and safe for families, and in summer holds barbecues. The food in the restaurant is highly rated. ♔♉❀ᗡ◗⊟♣P

Burbage

Three Horseshoes
1 Stibb Green, SN8 3AE (off A346 bypass, through village)
⏲ 12-2 (not Mon), 6-11; 12-2, 7-10.30 Sun
☎ (01672) 810324
Wadworth IPA, 6X; guest beer Ⓗ
Traditional thatched pub by the village green, near to Savernake Forest and the Kennet & Avon canal. The home-cooked food is highly recommended; a variety of pies and other traditional dishes is served (no food Mon). Guest beers come from Wadworth's list. The pub is adorned with railway pictures and other artefacts. ♔Q❀ᗡ◗⊟P⚟

Bushton

Trotting Horse
SN4 7PX (S of Wootton Bassett between A4361 and A3102) OS063778
⏲ 5-11; 12-2.30, 6.30-11 Sat; 12-2.30, 7-10.30 Sun
☎ (01793) 731338
Archers Village; Wadworth 6X; guest beers Ⓗ
Traditional roadside pub with two bars, one with an old bar billiards table. A no-smoking dining area is to the rear. The menu offers a good selection of dishes, served at weekend lunchtimes and evenings Tuesday to Saturday. The landlord features beers from small local breweries among his guest ales. ♔Q❀ᗡ◗♿♣P⚟

Chippenham

Four Seasons
6 Market Place, SN15 3HD
⏲ 11-11 (1am Thu; 2am Fri & Sat); 11-midnight Sun
☎ (01249) 444668
Fuller's Discovery; London Pride, ESB Ⓗ
Lively town centre pub in the market place next to the Buttercross, serving fine Fuller's ales. Reasonably-priced lunchtime meals are excellent. Live local bands feature as part of a regular programme of evening entertainment. A big screen shows sports fixtures. An ideal spot to take time out from the busy town centre. ᗡ≹⊟

Chiseldon

Patriots Arms
6 New Road, SN4 0LU
⏲ 12-2, 5.30-11; closed Mon; 12-11 Sat; 12-10.30 Sun
☎ (01793) 740331 🌐 patriotsarms.co.uk
Courage Best Bitter; Wadworth 6X; West Berkshire Mr Chubb's; guest beer Ⓗ
There is something for everyone at this multi-roomed pub which welcomes families and diners alongside casual drinkers. A large family room opens on to the secure garden where a huge wooden playship, HMS Patriot, is berthed. As well as the public bar there is a lounge and no-smoking restaurant. On the menu is a mixture of traditional and modern dishes; fresh meat is supplied by the local butcher (no food available Sun eve or Mon). The award-winning landlord ensures that the beer is no after-thought, either.
Q♉❀⇌ᗡ◗⊟⛺⊟♣P⚟

Corsham

Hare & Hounds

48 Pickwick, SN13 0HY

⏲ 12-3, 6-11; 12-11 Fri & Sat; 12-10.30 Sun

☎ (01249) 701106

Bath Gem; Caledonian Deuchars IPA; guest beers Ⓗ

This busy community pub on the old London to Bath coaching road is in easy reach of many tourist attractions including Bath itself, the medieval village of Lacock and Castle Combe. Divided into three drinking areas, there is a large lounge and two public bars. It hosts at least one beer festival every year and guest beers are always available. A variety of good food is always on the menu.

🔥Q❀◖◗⊟♿🚌(231/232)P⚟

Two Pigs

38 Pickwick, SN13 9BU

⏲ 7-11; 12-2.30, 7-10.30 Sun

☎ (01249) 712515 🌐 twopigs.freeserve.co.uk

Hop Back Summer Lightning; Stonehenge Pigswill, Danish Dynamite; guest beers Ⓗ

A real gem, this lively free house has a rustic bar, flagstone floor and wood panelled walls. The outside covered seating area is called 'the Sty' and the swine theme features throughout. With a strong commitment to real ale and an ever-changing range of guest beers, the pub has featured in the Guide for the last 18 years. It has been local CAMRA Pub of the Year several times. Live blues is staged on Monday evening. Over-21s only are admitted. 🔥❀

Corsley

Cross Keys

Lyes Green, BA12 7PB (off A362 Corsley Heath roundabout, Frome-Warminster road) OS821462

⏲ 12-3, 6.30-11; 12-4, 7-10.30 Sun

☎ (01373) 832406 🌐 crosskeyscorsley.co.uk

Wadworth IPA, 6X, JCB; guest beer Ⓗ

There is a warm, friendly ambience at this 18th-century pub with a large open fire in the bar. Excellent bar food and restaurant meals are served. The landlord and staff are happy to help and a good portfolio of guest beers makes the pub always worth a visit. There is an attractive, award-winning garden for outdoor drinking. A new function suite, the Oak Apple Room, has recently opened. Situated close to Longleat House and safari park.

🔥Q❀◖◗♣P

Corston

Radnor Arms

SN16 0HD (on A429 between M4 jct 17 and Malmesbury)

⏲ 11-midnight (1am Fri & Sat); 12-10.30 Sun

☎ (01666) 823389 🌐 radnor-arms.co.uk

Hook Norton Hooky Bitter; Young's Bitter; guest beers Ⓗ

Welcoming, 19th century stone-built pub on the main road through the village with a friendly landlord and bar staff. Good value food is served including speciality sausages. The pub has a new skittles alley and hosts skittles and darts leagues. There are occasional beer festivals, hog roasts and live music.

🔥Q❀◖◗♿♣●P

Corton

Dove

BA12 0SZ (on Wylye Valley road, S of Sutton Veny) OS934405

⏲ 12-2.30, 6-11; 12-3, 6-11 Fri & Sat; 12-3, 7-10.30 Sun

☎ (01985) 850109 🌐 thedove.co.uk

Hop Back GFB; Shepherd Neame Spitfire; guest beers Ⓗ

Village pub in the picturesque Wylye valley. Guest beers (one in winter, two in summer) may include Butcombe Bitter, Sharp's Doom Bar, Taylor Landlord and a Milk Street beer. Food is excellent with a varied range of lunchtime meals and a more sophisticated evening menu using local ingredients including game and fish. Children are permitted in the candlelit conservatory and the restaurant. There is a large garden. Corton is situated on the Wiltshire cycleway.

🔥Q❀🛏◖◗♿⛺♣●P⚟

Cricklade

Red Lion

74 High Street, SN6 6DD

⏲ 12-11 (midnight Fri & Sat); 12-10.30 Sun

☎ (01793) 750776

Moles Best Bitter; Ramsbury Gold; Sharp's Doom Bar; Wadworth 6X; guest beers Ⓗ

Friendly, 16th-century ale house serving a variety of up to nine real ales from small local breweries. Food is served in what used to be the back bar and is now the restaurant (no food Mon). A past winner of CAMRA South West Regional Pub of the Year.

🔥❀🛏◖◗♿

Crockerton

Bath Arms

Clay Street, BA12 8AJ (off A350 N of Longbridge Deverill) OS863422

⏲ 11-3, 6-11; 12-3, 6-10.30 Sun

☎ (01985) 212262

Courage Best Bitter; Wessex Naughty Ferret, Crockerton Classic; guest beers Ⓗ

Fairly large yet cosy and inviting pub on the edge of Crockerton. It has a single, long bar with two drinking areas and a restaurant at the end serving good quality food. Popular with locals as well as visitors from further afield, the pub has a picturesque garden where barbecues and village events are often held. A fine outlet for beers from the nearby Wessex brewery as well as one or two guests. It is near the Longleat estate and picturesque Shearwater boating lake.

🔥Q❀◖◗⛺P

Devizes

British Lion

9 Estcourt Street, SN10 1LQ

⏲ 12-11 (midnight Thu-Sat); 12-11 Sun

☎ (01380) 720665
Beer range varies Ⓗ
Genuine free house with a varied clientele – from bikers, bankers, builders, mayors and mechanics to servants civil and uncivil, teachers and the unteachable, they are all here. The landlord supports as many small, independent breweries as he can and offers the best range of beer in town. A little gem. ♨❀♣●P

Hare & Hounds

Hare & Hounds Street, SN10 1LZ
⏲ 12-11 (midnight Fri & Sat); 12-11 Sun
☎ (01380) 723231
Wadworth IPA, 6X, JCB, seasonal beers Ⓗ
Community-focussed back-street local with the feel of a village pub. The pub dates back several centuries and each landlord or landlady has applied their own stamp without ever completely obliterating what was there before. This Guide regular provides a benchmark for what Wadworth beers should taste like. ♨❀◑♿♣P

Southgate

SN10 5BY
⏲ 12-11 (1am Thu; 4am Fri & Sat); 12-11 Sun
☎ (01380) 722872
Beer range varies Ⓗ
Popular roadside pub with a varied clientele run by a friendly Italian landlord. The U-shaped bar has three drinking areas where you can enjoy a range of guest ales and foreign beers complemented by a good selection of spirits. Outside is a small patio and a function room that hosts occasional live music and an annual beer festival at Easter. The pub can be busy at the weekend. ♨❀♿♣●P

Dilton Marsh

Prince of Wales

94 High Street, BA13 4DZ
⏲ 12-2.30 (3 Sat; not Mon or Tue), 7 (5.30 Fri)-11 (midnight Fri & Sat); 12-3, 7-11 Sun
☎ (01373) 865487
Wadworth 6X; Young's Bitter; guest beers Ⓗ
Friendly village local with a single bar serving two drinking areas plus a small pool table annexe and a skittle alley. It offers a wide variety of guests, mostly session beers, often including ales from Cornish brewers Sharp's. The pub participates in local skittles, crib and pool leagues. There is a weekly Sunday evening quiz. Moles (not necessarily the beer) are something of a feature at the pub. The pub sign is factually incorrect – can you spot the error? ❀◑▶⇌♣P

Donhead St Andrew

Forester Inn

Lower Street, SP7 9EE (1 mile N of A30 at Ludwell)
⏲ 11-3, 6(5 Fri)-11; 12-3.30, 7-10.30 Sun
☎ (01747) 828038
🌐 foresterinndonheadstandrew.co.uk
Ringwood Best Bitter; guest beers Ⓗ
Traditional 16th-century stone-built multi-roomed inn featuring original beamed ceilings and an inglenook fireplace. The house bitter is supplied by Sharp's and its beers often feature among the guests. The pub is renowned for the quality of its food and offers gourmet dining and wine tasting. It is home to bridge players and golf societies. It has a friendly, relaxed atmosphere and a pleasant garden. ♨☕❀🛏◑▶P

East Knoyle

Seymour Arms

The Street, SP3 6AJ
⏲ 12-3, 7-11; closed Mon; 12-3, 7-10.30 Sun
☎ (01747) 830374
Wadworth IPA, 6X, JCB Ⓗ
Large ivy-covered red brick pub in the heart of the village where Sir Christopher Wren was born, named after the family of Jane Seymour, third wife of Henry VIII. The inn is very much at the centre of the local community. The building was originally a farmhouse and the single bar has a number of discrete areas. The pleasant garden has a children's play area. The pub enjoys a good reputation for high quality food (no meal Sun eve). ♨Q❀🛏◑▶♿P

Ebbesbourne Wake

Horseshoe Inn

SP5 5JF OS993239
⏲ 12-3, 6.30-11.30; 12-4 Sun
☎ (01722) 780474
Otter Bitter; Ringwood Best Bitter; guest beers Ⓖ
Unspoilt 18th-century inn in a remote rural setting at the foot of an old ox drove. This friendly pub has two small bars, a restaurant and a conservatory. You are welcome to pop in for a pint and a chat or enjoy good food made with local ingredients. The bars house an impressive collection of old farm implements, tools and lamps. The four beers are served direct from casks that are stillaged behind the bar. Service is either via the bar or the original serving hatch just inside the front door. Thatcher's cider is offered. There is a pleasant garden and B&B accommodation. ♨Q❀🛏◑▶🚌●P

Foxham

Foxham Inn

SN15 4NQ (follow signs to Foxham off B4069 Chippenham to Lyneham road) OS976772
⏲ 12-2.30 (3 Sat; not Mon), 7-11; 12-3, 7-10.30 Sun
☎ (01249) 740665 🌐 thefoxhaminn.co.uk
Bath Gem; Wadworth 6X; guest beer Ⓗ
Typical brick-built English pub in the centre of a small village. A free house with a friendly atmosphere, it concentrates mainly on local beers. Food dominates with an extensive menu of home-cooked food featuring produce from local high-quality suppliers – fish is a speciality in summer. The pub has a single bar with dining areas, or you can eat outside under the new pergola. Slightly off the beaten track, it is well worth a detour for an excellent pint and good food. ♨Q❀◑▶♿P

Grittleton

Neeld Arms

The Street, SN14 6AP
12-3, 5.30-11.30; 12-3.30, 7-11 Sun
(01249) 782470 neeldarms.co.uk
Wadworth IPA, 6X; guest beers H
Cosy, comfortable 17th-century inn, set in a beautiful and unspoilt south Cotswold village. The ever-changing range of guest beers means that there is always something of interest to try. A log fire is welcoming in winter. A good selection of home-made food is offered. Popular with locals and visitors, the pub is heavily involved with the community. It is close to tourist attractions including Castle Combe, Malmesbury and Bath. MQ⚘⇌(D♣P⁄

Hamptworth

Cuckoo Inn

Hamptworth Road, SP5 2DU OS244197
11.30-2.30, 5.30-11; 11.30-11 Sat; 12-10.30 Sun
(01794) 390302
Hop Back GFB, Summer Lightning; Ringwood Best Bitter; guest beers G
Beautiful, thatched pub within the New Forest national park. Inside are four small rooms, three served from the same bar. Ales are dispensed direct from the cask, racked in the ground floor cellar. At least three guest ales, more in summer, are available alongside Frams Scrumpy cider. The large garden has a quiet, adults-only space as well as an area with swings for children. An annual beer festival is held in late summer. MQ⚘(D♣P

Heddington

Ivy

Stockley Road, SN11 0PL (2 miles off A4 from Calne)
12-3 (4 Sat), 6.30-11; 12-4, 7-10.30 Sun
(01380) 850276
Wadworth IPA, 6X, seasonal beers G
This thatched village inn was originally three 15th-century cottages. It has evolved from a pub serving just drinks and snacks 25 years ago to a popular hostelry with a well-deserved reputation for good food (booking for the restaurant is advisable, eve meals Thu-Sat). It remains the focal point for a dispersed and ever changing village. Calne Wigglybus can be booked up to a week in advance for travel between the surrounding area and Heddington. MQ⚘(D♣P

Highworth

Rose & Crown

19 The Green, SN6 7DB (off A361) OS200922
12-midnight (1am Thu-Sat); 12-11.30 Sun
Courage Best Bitter; Wadworth 6X; Wells Bombardier; guest beers H
This pub dates from at least 1768 when it was sold for £25. It has passed through the hands of many now departed breweries since 1821 including Dixons, Bowlys, Simonds, Courage and Ushers. Today it is a friendly local that stages regular live music and outdoor events. It has the largest pub garden in Highworth and boules is played here. A wide range of malt whiskies is available. ⚘(D♣

Hodson

Calley Arms

SN4 0QG (off B4005)
12-2.30, 5.30-11; 11.30-2.30, 6.30-11 Sat; 12-10.30 Sun
(01793) 740350
Wadworth IPA, 6X, seasonal or guest beer H
Cosy country pub on the edge of the village. The open plan bar has a raised dining area at one end. Outside is a large board with directions for a two and a half mile walk to Coate Water Country Park. Cyclists will find a cycle path to the same destination starts half a mile down the road to Chiseldon. A varied menu, including plenty of specials, is available every day except Sunday evening. MQ⚘(DP

Holt

Tollgate Inn

Ham Green, BA14 6PX (on B3105 between Bradford on Avon and Melksham)
12-2.30, 6-11; closed Mon; 11.30-2.30 Sun
(01225) 782326 tollgateholt.co.uk
Beer range varies H
A gem of an old village pub with an upmarket atmosphere with sofas in the bar. The range of four to five ales, which changes every week, is imaginative with a good selection of local beers and many from smaller brewers from further away. The food in both the upstairs restaurant and the bar is excellent. The garden at the rear overlooks a pretty valley. M⚘⇌(DÅP⁄

Idmiston

Earl of Normanton

Tidworth Road, SP4 0AG (on A338)
11-3, 6-11; 12-3, 7-10.30 Sun
(01980) 610251 earlofnormanton.co.uk
Hop Back Summer Lightning; guest beers H
This popular roadside pub boasts an enviable selection of real ales. The five handpumps feature local breweries, often including a beer from Triple fff. Appetising and good value food is served and there is a small but pleasant garden, albeit a little steep. Accommodation is available separately from the pub. This was Salisbury CAMRA Pub of the Year in 2002. M⚘⇌(DP

Kilmington

Red Lion Inn

BA12 6RP (on B3092 to Frome 3 miles N of A303 Mere)
11.30-2.30, 6.30-11; 12-3, 7-10.30 Sun
(01985) 844263
Butcombe Bitter; Butts Jester; guest beers H
Originally a farmworker's cottage, this National Trust owned pub is more than 400 years old. It is close to Stourhead house and gardens, next to an old coach road and the South Wiltshire Downs. The single bar is mainly stone-flagged with a real fire at each

end and a smaller no-smoking room to one side. Excellent, value for money food is served at lunchtime. Walkers and dogs are welcome. ♨Q❀◑♣●P

Kington St Michael

Jolly Huntsman

The Street, SN14 6JB

⊙ 11.30-2.30, 6-11 (midnight Fri & Sat); 12-3, 7-10.30 Sun

☎ (01249) 750305

Greene King IPA; Wadworth 6X; guest beers Ⓗ

Stone-built pub in the main street of a village with a Cotswolds feel. The village church's bells are hung anti-clockwise – most unusual. The pub has an extensive food trade but also provides much of interest for those just wanting a drink. Guest beers usually include one from Wychwood and two more from local or more distant micros. Various entertainment is held in the pub including live music and games. ♨⇌◑♣P⊬

Lacock

Bell Inn

The Wharf, Bowden Hill, SN15 2PJ

⊙ 11.30-2.30, 6-11; 11.30-11 Sat; 12-10.30 Sun

☎ (01249) 730308

Bath Gem; Wadworth 6X; guest beers Ⓗ

This freehold house is on the line of the Wilts & Berks Canal. Though the canal is disused, the Chippenham to Melksham cycle path runs past the pub. On the edge of the National Trust village of Lacock, the Bell is renowned for its food, served all day at the weekend. The pub is smoke free with a garden room for smokers. It holds a beer festival in summer and winter. Local CAMRA Pub of the Year for 2003 and 2005. ❀◑♿Δ♣●P⊬

Rising Sun

32 Bowden Hill, SN15 2PP (1 mile E of Lacock)

⊙ 12-3 (not Mon), 6-11.30; 12-11.30 Sat & Sun

☎ (01249) 730363

Moles Tap Bitter, Best Bitter, Molecatcher, seasonal beers Ⓗ

Lovely stone-built, flagstone floored pub with extensive views of the Avon Valley from the conservatory and large garden. Inside are displays of birds in glass cases and an array of jugs and tankards hanging from the beams. An idyllic setting to sample the full range of Moles beers as well as good food – special dietary requirements can be catered for – telephone in advance for requests or booking. ♨Q❀◑●P

Laverstock

Duck Inn

Duck Lane, SP1 1PU

⊙ 12-11 daily

☎ (01722) 327678

Hop Back GFB, Odyssey, Crop Circle, Summer Lightning Ⓗ

Recently refurbished, this single-room pub is mainly no-smoking, although smoking is permitted in the pool and darts area. Occasionally a seasonal or guest beer replaces one of the regular beers. Westons Old Rosie is served. The patio and garden are pleasant in summer. Food is served all week except Sunday evening and winter Monday lunchtime. Live music is hosted once a month. Dogs are welcome. ♨Q❀◑♿♣●P⊬

Malmesbury

Whole Hog

8 Market Cross, SN16 9AS

⊙ 11-11; 12-10.30 Sun

☎ (01666) 825845

Archers Best Bitter; Wadworth 6X; Young's Bitter; guest beers Ⓗ

Located between the 15th-century market cross and Abbey church, the building has at various times served as a cottage hospital, gas showroom and café/restaurant, before becoming licensed premises. With a warm, friendly atmosphere, the pub is popular with locals and visitors alike. Meals can be eaten in the bar or dining area (no food Sun eve). Cider is sold in summer. Q◑●

Market Lavington

Green Dragon

26 High Street, SN10 4AG

⊙ 12-3.30, 5.30-midnight; 12-midnight Thu-Sun

☎ (01380) 813235

Wadworth IPA, 6X, JCB, seasonal beers; guest beer Ⓗ

This pub led the revival of real ale in the village, now joined by the Drummer Boy just down the road. The landlord of this comfortable and welcoming pub used to run the Cavalier in Devizes, which also featured in the Guide. It has an enclosed garden area with a pets' corner, petanque pitch and barbecue area. Like most successful village pubs, there is something for everyone here. ♨❀⇌◑♿Δ♣●P⊬

Netherhampton

Victoria & Albert

SP2 8PU (opp. church)

⊙ 11-3, 5.30 (5 Fri & Sat)-11; 12-3, 7-10.30 Sun

☎ (01722) 743174

Beer range varies Ⓗ

Classic country pub built in 1540 with a thatched roof and a lovely, large garden. A log fire and low beams add to the cosy atmosphere. The four constantly changing real ales are from small, independent brewers – over 1,200 different beers have been drunk in the last three years. All food is prepared in the pub and the menu ranges from snacks to restaurant meals. Dogs are welcome at Salisbury CAMRA Pub of the Year 2005. ♨Q☋❀◑♣P

Newton Tony

Malet Arms

SP4 0HF (1 mile off A338) OS215403

⊙ 11-3, 6-11; 12-3, 7-10.30 Sun

☎ (01980) 629279

Palmer Best Bitter; guest beers Ⓗ

Classic country pub named after a local family who are well represented in the village churchyard. There are two comfortable bars and a restaurant – the larger bar features a huge fireplace and a window reputed to come from an old galleon. Of the four beers, there is usually one from Stonehenge Ales and Butts Barbus Barbus makes a frequent appearance; the cider is Westons Old Rosie. A blackboard menu based on fresh, local ingredients changes daily. ⛫Q❀◑◗♠P

North Wroughton

Check Inn

79 Woodland View, SN4 9AA

11.30-3.30, 6-midnight; 11.30-1am Fri & Sat; 12-midnight Sun

☎ (01793) 845584 🌐 checkinn.co.uk

Beer range varies [H]

Genuine free house serving eight real ales plus imported lager and bottled beers. Guest beers change frequently and are usually from local and independent breweries. The roadside pub has been cut off by the M4 and isolated in a cul-de-sac. It has a terraced drinking area at the front and boules can be played in the back garden. Good home-cooked food is available at reasonable prices. It was national CAMRA Pub of the Year runner up in 2005.
⛫Q❀⇆◑◗♿♣♠P⍁

Ogbourne St George

Inn with the Well

Marlborough Road, SN8 1SQ (off A346)

12-2.30 (not Mon), 6-11; 12-2.30 (closed eve) Sun

☎ (01672) 841445 🌐 theinnwiththewell.co.uk

Wadworth 6X; guest beer [G]

The pub gets its name from the 90ft well in the dining room (the glass cover is supposed to be bullet proof). Originally a coaching inn dating from 1647, the pub is well placed for walking the Ridgeway or the Og Valley. The handpumps are just for show – the beer is served by gravity straight from the cellar. Good food is recommended (not available Mon). Q❀⇆◑◗⛺♣P

Pewsey

Coopers Arms

37-39 Ball Road, SN9 5BL (off B3087) OS168600

6 (12 Sat)-11; 5-midnight Fri, 12-10.30 Sun

☎ (01672) 562495

Fuller's London Pride; Wadworth 6X; guest beers [H]

This thatched pub takes some finding, but is well worth the effort to seek out. In the main bar there is an open fire in winter, and there are rooms for pool and television. Live music is performed regularly. The pub is ideally situated for walkers on the White Horse Trail. ⛫❀⛺P

Salisbury

Deacons

118 Fisherton Street, SP2 7QT

5 (4 Fri; 12 Sat)-11; 12-10.30 Sun

☎ (01722) 504723

Hop Back GFB, Summer Lightning; Sharp's Doom Bar; guest beers [H]

This traditional, friendly drinkers' pub, popular with a mixture of locals and visitors, is convenient for the city centre and railway station. The front bar has an open gas fire in a traditional hearth and woodblock flooring. The back bar has table football. ⇆⇌♣⍁

King's Arms

99 Fisherton Street, SP2 7SP

12-11; 12-6 Sun

☎ (01722) 337811

Hop Back GFB; Ringwood Best Bitter; guest beer [H]

Family-run pub with two long rooms – one with comfortable seating, ideal for a quiet pint; the other more lively with pool and darts. The large garden is a real suntrap and barbecues are held in summer. Pub teams play in local crib, darts and pool leagues, and live music is occasionally hosted. The guest beer is often from Moles, or Ringwood Fortyniner.
❀⇆◑⊟⇌♣

Rai d'Or

69 Brown Street, SP1 2AS

12.30-2 (not Mon-Thu), 5-11; closed Sun

☎ (01722) 327137 🌐 raidor.co.uk

Beer range varies [H]

This historic free house dating from 1292 retains its original atmosphere with wooden floors and panelled benches. The name originated over 700 years ago when it was a brothel and tavern in the old red light district of Salisbury. The landlord provides a warm welcome and excellent Thai food is served at all times. The beer comes from small local breweries, frequently including Stonehenge or Downton. ◑◗♣⍁

Village Freehouse

33 Wilton Road, SP2 7EF (on A36 near St Paul's roundabout)

12-midnight daily

☎ (01722) 329707

Downton Quadhop; Taylor Landlord; [H] **guest beers** [H]/[G]

This friendly city local serves at least three ever-changing guest beers chosen by customers. It specialises in beers unusual in the area, normally including a mild or stout, making it the only regular outlet for such ales in the city. A local, traditional cider is sometimes available. Close to the station, it is popular with visitors by rail, and railway memorabilia adorn the walls. Cricket, rugby and football are shown on a small TV. Local CAMRA Pub of the Year in 2001 and 2004. ⇌♣

Winchester Gate

113-117 Rampart Road, SP1 1JA

12-11 daily

☎ (01722) 322834

Hop Back seasonal beers; Taylor Landlord; guest beers [H]

Welcoming 17th-century former coaching inn on the site of the city's east tollgate. Now a two-bar free house, it offers an interesting range of beers including two guests. Cider or perry is often available on draught. Live music is played on Friday and Saturday evening with a popular open mike session once a month. The large garden has a petanque terrain that is well used in summer. Fresh filled rolls are available at all times. ⛰❀⊟♣●P

Wyndham Arms

27 Estcourt Road, SP1 3AS

4.30-11.30; 3-1am Fri; 12-midnight Sat; 12-11.30 Sun

☎ (01722) 331026

Hop Back GFB, Odyssey, Crop Circle, Summer Lightning, seasonal beers; guest beers Ⓗ

The original home of the Hop Back brewery, although brewing has long since moved to nearby Downton. A carved head of Bacchus greets you as you enter the pub. A genuine local, it caters for all. Inside is a small bar and two further rooms, one no-smoking. Local CAMRA Pub of the Year 2006 is all about beer, with six real ales and a fine selection of bottled beers. ♣⅍

Shrewton

George Inn

London Road, SP3 4DH OS069445

12-3 (not Tue), 6-11; 12-4, 7-11 Sun

☎ (01980) 620341

Courage Best Bitter; guest beers Ⓗ

Friendly two-roomed pub with the lounge mainly used for food. Originally a brewery, the building has been a pub since 1841. A beer festival is held on August bank holiday weekend in the garden and covered patio. The skittle alley is available for hire. Three guest beers often include one from Archers and another from a local brewery. Food is not available on Tuesday evening. ⛰❀◐♣⅍

Swindon

Gluepot

5 Emlyn Square, SN1 5BP

11-11; 12-10.30 Sun

☎ (01793) 523935

Hop Back GFB, Odyssey; Crop Circle; Entire Stout, Summer Lightning; seasonal beers; guest beers Ⓗ

Friendly and welcoming, this one-bar pub serves primarily Hop Back beers with occasional guests. Five traditional ciders are available. Built in the mid-19th century in the heart of Brunel's railway village, the pub is a short walk from the steam museum and Swindon station. The lunch menu (served Tue-Sat) is good value and highly recommended. There is a regular meat raffle and buffet on Sunday and occasional live music. Dogs are welcome. Q❀◐⇌●

Steam Railway

14 Newport Street, SN1 3DX

12-11 daily

☎ (01793) 538048

Fuller's London Pride; Wadworth 6X; Wells Bombardier; guest beers Ⓗ

Large pub that was expanded years ago and can be quite noisy at weekends. The traditional real ale bar has a low ceiling and wood panelling; it has nine handpumps offering a regularly changing selection of guest beers. The bar gets busy when major sporting events are shown on TV but at other times you can enjoy a quiet drink here. Meals are served daily including a roast on Sunday. The pub is home to RATS (real ale tasting society) and the RATS beer festival is held in May. ⛰❀◐♿♣

Wheatsheaf

32 Newport Street, SN1 3DP

12-11 daily

☎ (01793) 523188

Wadworth IPA, 6X, JCB, seasonal beers; guest beers Ⓗ

Popular two-bar town pub dating from the 1820s. The small public bar retains its original features and the large, welcoming back bar has a rustic decor. Ales are still served from the original cellar. Meals are available daily including a popular roast on Sunday. Q⇄◐⊟♣

Tisbury

Boot Inn

High Street, SP3 6PS

11-2.30, 7-11; 12-4 Sun

☎ (01747) 870363

Beer range varies Ⓖ

This fine village pub, built of Chilmark stone, has been licensed since 1768. The landlord has been here since 1976 and maintains a relaxed, friendly atmosphere appealing to locals and visitors alike. Three beers are served direct from the casks stillaged behind the bar. Good food is available and there is a spacious garden. ⛰❀◐⅄⇌♣P

Wanborough

Harrow Inn

High Street, SN4 0AE

12-2.30, 6-midnight; 12-3, 7-midnight Sun

☎ (01793) 790622 theharrowinnwanborough.com

Adnams Bitter; Wadworth 6X; guest beers Ⓗ

This thatched pub is the oldest in Wanborough, retaining many interesting features. It has a Grade II listed dog grate and many concealed cupboards in the eaves which were used by smugglers to hide their illegal goods. Today's more law abiding citizens can enjoy guest beers and good food (not Sun eve). Live music is played on Sunday evening. ⛰Q❀◐P

Plough

High Street, SN4 0AE

12-3, 5-11; 12-11 Fri; 12-3, 7-10.30 Sun

☎ (01793) 790523

Draught Bass; Caledonian Deuchars IPA; Fuller's London Pride; Moles Tap Bitter; Wadworth 6X Ⓗ

Recently re-thatched, this Grade II listed building has a cosy interior with beams, low doorways and large open fireplaces. The wide beer range is complemented by a good choice of food with excellent specials (no food Sat lunchtime or all day Sun). As well as traditional pub games the pub hosts a boules competition each May on its own piste. ⛰Q❀◐♿⊟♣P

Warminster

Fox & Hounds
6 Deverill Road, BA12 9QP
✪ 11-11 daily
☎ (01985) 216711
Ringwood Best Bitter; Wessex Warminster Warrior; guest beer Ⓗ
Friendly, two-bar local just off the town centre. One bar is a cosy snug, the other includes an area for pool and an unobtrusive TV. The two real ciders from Rich's and Thatchers are a mainstay of the pub. A regular outlet for the nearby Wessex micro-brewery, the guest beer is also usually sourced from a local micro.
♔Q❀⊟♿≠♣●

Rose & Crown
57 East Street, BA12 9BZ
✪ 4-11; 12-midnight Sat; 12-10.30 Sun
☎ (01985) 214964
Beer range varies Ⓗ
Refurbished by new landlords in 2005, this is a bright and cosy single-bar real ale emporium just off the town centre. A number of original features have been revealed for the first time in years. Popular with a clientele of all ages, television and background music are unobtrusive. The six guest beers vary although they are usually sourced from local micros.
♔❀≠♣●⚡

Wilton

Bear Inn
12 West Street, SP2 0DF
✪ 11-3, 4.30-midnight; 12-3, 6-midnight Sun
☎ (01722) 742398
Badger First Gold, Tanglefoot Ⓗ
Traditional public house dating from 1750 with a beamed front bar and games area with a pool table. Outside is a large, quiet walled garden. Pub games are popular with teams featuring in the local leagues. The art of conversation is alive and well at this friendly pub where visitors are warmly welcomed by staff and locals. Parking is available in the nearby market square.
♔❀◐◑♣

Wootton Bassett

Five Bells
Wood Street, SN4 7BD
✪ 12-3, 5-midnight; 12-midnight Fri-Sun
☎ (01793) 849422
Fuller's London Pride; guest beers Ⓗ
Cosy, thatched local with a low, beamed ceiling. It first opened before 1841 and absorbed a neighbouring cottage in 1921. The bar sports five handpumps for one regular and four guest beers. There is another pump for real cider. A large blackboard displays a good selection of lunchtime meals. Themed food evenings are held on Wednesday. A beer festival offering more than 20 beers is held in August. Winner of the Bassett in Bloom competition several times.
♔❀◐♣●

Wroughton

Carters Rest
High Street, SN4 9JU
✪ 12-3, 5-11 (1am Fri); 12-1am Sat; 12-10.30 Sun
☎ (01793) 812288
Archers Best Bitter; Fuller's London Pride; Hop Back Crop Circle; guest beers Ⓗ
Built some time after 1866, this large, two-room pub with a friendly atmosphere was extensively refurbished in the early 1990s when it was owned by Archers. Decorated with plenty of beer-related memorabilia, it keeps up to eight real ales. It hosts a quiz night every Thursday – get there early to find a seat. ♔Q❀⊟♣P

News from beer's front line

CAMRA members receive a free monthly newspaper, with its special Beer supplement. It's packed with information about beer, brewing and pubs, and will keep you informed about all the latest developments in the world of beer. The paper also lists CAMRA beer festivals and branch activities.

What's Brewing is worth the price of CAMRA membership alone. Sign up for membership, using the forms at the back of the guide.

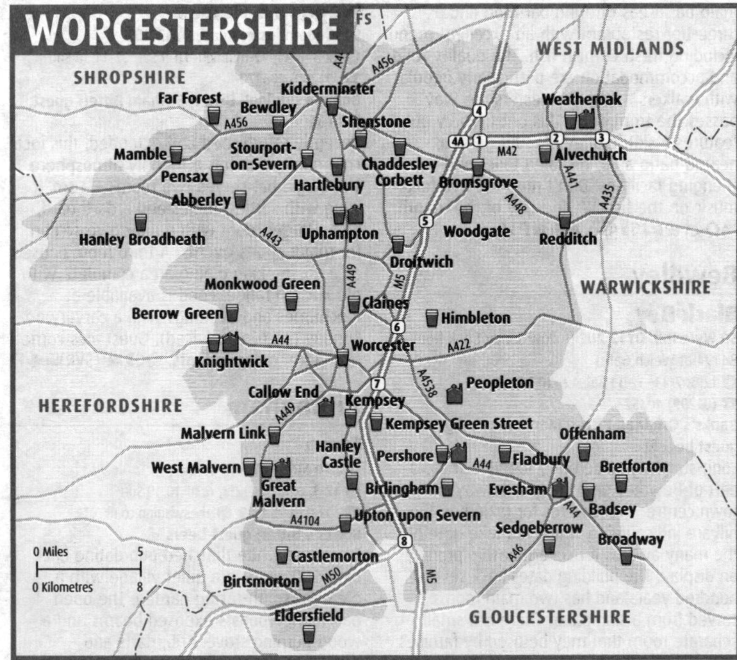

Abberley

Manor Arms

Netherton Lane, WR6 6BN (signposted off B4202)

12-3 (not Mon), 6-midnight; 12-midnight Sun

(01299) 896507 themanorarms.co.uk

Flowers IPA; Hook Norton Old Hooky; Taylor Landlord; Wye Valley Hereford Pale Ale; guest beer

Situated in a quiet village, this 300-year-old building with beamed ceilings is more than just a pleasant and welcoming 'local' pub and hotel; it is also an enjoyable family and pet-friendly destination for lunch on a day out. The Worcestershire Way and its many linking pathways are close by. A varied menu is served in the lounge, bar, and quiet, no-smoking restaurant. A beer festival is held in summer. P

Alvechurch

Weighbridge

Scarfield House, Scarfield Hill, B48 7SQ

12-3 (4.30 in summer), 7-11; 12-3 (4.30 in summer), 7-10.30 Sun

(0121) 445 5111 the-weighbridge.co.uk

Beer range varies

It is hard to believe that only five years ago this small, attractive hostelry (2005 CAMRA local Pub of the Year) was a house and private social club. Situated adjacent to the Marina, it has established itself as a popular retreat for boaters, weekend walkers and commuters making their way home from the station next door. The pub offers two separate lounges and a public bar, serving good value, home-cooked food every day except Tuesday and Wednesday. An autumn beer festival is an established event. The regular ale, Tillerman's Tipple, is brewed for the pub by Weatheroak Ales who have a real ale off-licence nearby. Q P

Badsey

Round of Gras

47 Bretforton Road, WR11 7XQ

11-11 daily

(01386) 830206 roundofgras.co.uk

Flowers IPA; Uley Pigs Ear; guest beers

Open-plan roadside inn on the eastern edge of the village with an attractive garden. It is named in honour of the asparagus that is the speciality of this part of the Vale of Evesham: 'gras' features prominently on the menu from April to June, and other locally-sourced ingredients are used in cooking all year round. Two guest beers are often from micros or independents. P

Berrow Green

Admiral Rodney

WR6 6PL (on B4917)

11-3 (not Mon), 5-11; 11-11 Sat; 12-10.30 Sun

(01886) 821375 admiral-rodney.co.uk

Wye Valley Bitter; guest beers

Light, airy country pub serving three guest ales, often from local micro-breweries, as well as real cider and perry. There are three

INDEPENDENT BREWERIES

Brandy Cask Pershore
Cannon Royall Uphampton
Evesham Evesham
Malvern Hills Great Malvern
St George's Callow End
Teme Valley Knightwick
Weatheroak Weatheroak
Wyre Piddle Peopleton

main bar areas offering bar food and a three-tier restaurant with an excellent menu including fresh Cornish fish. The quality food and accommodation are particularly popular with walkers as the Worcestershire Way passes the front door. This pet-friendly pub features a skittle alley, floodlit garden, heated patio area, disabled toilet and baby changing facilities. Don't miss the live folk music on the first Wednesday of the month. ⛫Q❀⇌◐⊞♿⛺♣●P⚟

Bewdley

Black Boy

50 Wyre Hill, DY12 2UE (follow Sandy Bank from B4194 at Welch Gate)

⏲ 12-3, 7-11; 12-11 Sat; 12 -10.30 Sun

☎ (01299) 403523

Banks's Original, Bitter; Marston's Pedigree; guest beer Ⓗ

Long-standing guide entry found in the old part of Bewdley up a steep hill away from the town centre. The rewards for taking on the hill are indisputable when you take note of the many awards for cellarmanship proudly on display. The building dates back several hundred years and has two main rooms served from a single bar. There is a small separate room that may be used by families at the landlord's discretion. Guest beers come from Banks's guest list. ⛫Q❀⊞⊟♣

Hop Pole

Hop Pole Lane, DY12 2QH (¾ mile out of Bewdley on B4190)

⏲ 12-3 (not Mon & Tue), 4-11; 12-11 Fri & Sat; 12-10.30 Sun

☎ (01299) 409244

Banks's Original, Bitter; Marston's Pedigree; guest beer Ⓗ

Popular community pub that caters for all. Sympathetically refurbished, it now consists of one long U-shaped room featuring an old kitchen range at one end and a dining area and pool room at the other. Between these is a long, wooden bar and drinking area with plenty of natural wood fittings. Guest beers come from Banks's guest list. Good, traditional, home-cooked food is served in the bar and restaurant. Well-behaved children are welcome; there is a children's menu. ❀◐⛺⊟♣P⚟

Mug House

5 Severnside North, DY12 2EE

⏲ 12-11.15-(midnight Fri & Sat); 12-11.30 Sun

☎ (01299) 402543 🌐 mughousebewdley.co.uk

Taylor Landlord; Wye Valley Hereford Pale Ale; guest beers Ⓗ

Situated right by the River Severn, the pub's name originates from the time when deals were struck between trow haulers and carriers over a mug of ale. A welcoming fire greets thirsty drinkers, and fine food is served in the restaurant, with live lobster a speciality. Guest beers come from breweries such as RCH, Titanic and Beowulf and the house beer, Mug's Gayme, is brewed by Wye Valley. The May Day weekend beer festival is a regular fixture and local English wine is often available. ⛫Q❀⇌◐⇐(SVR)⊟●

Waggon & Horses

91 Kidderminster Road, DY12 1DG

⏲ 12-3, 6-11; 12-midnight Fri & Sat; 12-11.30 Sun

☎ (01299) 403170

Banks's Original, Bitter; Batham Bitter; guest beer Ⓗ

Recently refurbished and extended, this local community pub has a friendly atmosphere. The single bar serves two rooms – a small snug with settles, tables and a dartboard, and a larger room with a roll-down screen for major sports events. A third room is used as a no-smoking dining area complete with old kitchen range. Food is available at lunchtimes and evenings with a carvery on Sunday (booking advised). Guest ales come from local independents. ❀◐⇐(SVR)⊟♣P

Birlingham

Swan

Church Street, WR10 3AQ

⏲ 12-3, 6.30-11; 12-3, 6.30-10.30 Sun

☎ (01386) 750485 🌐 theswaninn.co.uk

Banks's Bitter; guest beers Ⓗ

Black and white thatched pub dating back over 500 years in a quiet village with a pleasant south-facing garden. The open bar/lounge boasts exposed beams and a wood-burning stove. Crib, darts and dominoes are played in the bar and traditional home-cooked food is served in the conservatory at the rear. Over 400 different guest beers have been served in the last year and beer festivals are held in May and September. Laminated maps of local walks are provided and dogs are welcome. The landlord and landlady speak Japanese. ⛫❀◐♣●P⚟

Birtsmorton

Farmers Arms

Birts Street, WR13 6AP (off B4208)

⏲ 11-4, 6-11; 12-4, 7-11 Sun

☎ (01684) 833308

Hook Norton Hooky Bitter, Old Hooky; guest beer Ⓗ

Classic black and white village pub, tucked away down a quiet country lane. A large stone-flagged bar area with a splendid inglenook is complemented by a cosy lounge area with low beams. Good value, home-made food is served every day. The guest beer usually comes from a small independent brewer, often local. The spacious, safe garden with swings provides fine views of the Malvern Hills. ⛫Q❀◐⊞P

Bretforton

Fleece Inn ☆

The Cross, WR11 7JE (near church)

⏲ summer 11-11 (1am Fri & Sat); 11-11 Sun; winter 11-3, 6-11 (5-midnight Fri); 11-1am Sat; 12-11 Sun

☎ (01386) 831173 🌐 thefleeceinn.co.uk

Hook Norton Hooky Bitter; Purity Pure Ubu; Uley Pig's Ear; guest beers Ⓗ

Famous old National Trust owned village pub recently reopened following a fire that all but gutted much of the interior. Fortunately the public area escaped almost unscathed, including the world-famous collection of 17th-century pewter-ware. The restoration has been excellent and the pub remains one of the stars of CAMRA's National Inventory of Historic Pub Interiors. Visitors may drink inside or in the orchard, which is delightful for families in fine weather and the site of the famous asparagus auction in the (very short) season. ♔Q❀⇔◐♿🚌♣🍎⁄

Broadway

Crown & Trumpet
Church Street, WR12 7AE

⌚ 11-3, 5-11; 11-11 Sat & summer; 11-10.30 Sun
☎ (01386) 853202 🌐 cotswoldholidays.co.uk

Greene King Old Speckled Hen; Hook Norton Hooky Bitter, Old Hooky; Stanway seasonal beers; Taylor Landlord Ⓗ

Fine 17th-century Cotswold stone inn on the road to Snowshill, complete with oak beams and log fires along with plenty of Flowers brewery memorabilia. The pub is popular with locals, tourists and walkers alike, who all enjoy a good menu offering specials made with locally grown fruit and vegetables. An unusual range of pub games is played here including ring the bull, and there is often live music on Saturday evening. The Stanway seasonal beers rotate; some are brewed exclusively for the pub. ♔❀⇔◐♿▲🚌♣P

Bromsgrove

Hop Pole
78 Birmingham Road, B61 0DF
(200 yds from town centre)

⌚ 12 (4 Mon-Wed)-11 (11.30 Fri & Sat); 12-11 Sun
☎ (01527) 870100 🌐 hop-pole.com

Worfield OBJ; guest beers Ⓗ

This revitalized one-room pub was Redditch & Bromsgrove CAMRA Pub of the Autumn Season in 2004. The daytime atmosphere is light and bright with a varied lunchtime menu served Thursday to Saturday. The inviting enclosed garden is sunny in the afternoons. The pub hosts local live bands of many musical styles in the evenings from Friday to Sunday. On a quieter note, Monday is quiz night. ❀◐🚌

Ladybird
2 Finstall Road, Aston Fields, B60 2DZ (on A448)

⌚ 11-11; 12-10.30 Sun
☎ (01527) 878014 🌐 ladybirdinns.co.uk

Batham Best Bitter; Hobsons Best Bitter; guest beers Ⓗ

Formerly the Dragoon, it was renamed by its new owner Chris Bird in memory of his late wife whose picture hangs over the fireplace in the lounge. Over recent years it has grown and now boasts a front bar for drinkers, light and airy no-smoking lounge with polished wooden floors, function room, restaurant, garden and 45-room hotel. Its location by the railway station makes it popular with tourists. ❀⇔◐◑♿⇌🚌P⁄

Red Lion
73 High Street, B61 8AQ (by bus station)

⌚ 10.30-midnight; 11-3, 7-11 Sun
☎ (01527) 835387

Banks's Hanson's Mild, Original, Bitter; guest beers Ⓗ

Busy one-room pub in the main shopping street, famous for its slogan 'Smooth pour is never sold here'. Seven real ales, including interesting guests, are complemented by two draught Belgian beers and fruit wines. The simple bar meals served at lunchtime (hot food available Thu-Sat) are exceptional value and Monday night is curry night. Live music is hosted on most Thursdays. The pub has won many CAMRA awards and beer festivals are held regularly. There is a covered patio. ❀◐🚌♣P

Castlemorton

Plume of Feathers
Gloucester Road, WR13 6JB (on B4208) OS788388

⌚ 12-11; 12-10.30 Sun
☎ (01684) 833554

Batham Best Bitter; Greene King Old Speckled Hen; Hobsons Bitter; guest beers Ⓗ

Classic country pub on the edge of Castlemorton Common with splendid views of the Malvern Hills from its front garden – the ideal starting point for walks across the common and onto the hills. The main bar has a wealth of beams and a real fire while a small side room offers TV and darts and a no-smoking room caters for diners. Occasional live music is played and a beer festival is held in mid summer. The local bus runs on Saturdays, otherwise it is a pleasant walk over the common from nearby Welland. ♔Q☕❀◐▲🚌P

Chaddesley Corbett

Fox Inn
Bromsgrove Road, DY10 4QN

⌚ 11.30-2.30, 5-11; 11.30-11 Sat; 12-10.30 Sun
☎ (01562) 777247 🌐 foxinn-chaddesleycorbett.co.uk

Enville Ale; Theakston Best Bitter; guest beer Ⓗ

Roadside pub to the south of this attractive village with a comfortable interior. The L-shaped lounge has a pool room to the side and there is an air-conditioned, no-smoking restaurant area. The popular, good value carvery is available at lunchtime Tuesday to Sunday and Wednesday and Friday evening. A comprehensive range of main meals and snacks is also served throughout the pub every day. The guest beer is usually from an independent micro-brewer.
♔❀◐◑♿🚌♣🍎P

Swan
DY10 4SD

⌚ 11-3, 6-11; 11-11 Sat; 12-3, 7-11 Sun
☎ (01562) 777302

Batham Mild, Best Bitter, XXX (winter) Ⓗ

Dating from 1606, this popular oak-beamed pub includes a traditional bar, large lounge featuring trad jazz Thursday, small snug and restaurant serving evening meals from Thursday to Saturday. Lunch is available daily (no hot food Mon). An ever-changing snapshot of village life and gossip, the bar welcomes locals and visitors. A convenient watering-hole for walkers, well-behaved dogs are welcome. The extensive gardens are ideal for families during the summer months. Westons Old Rosie cider is available.

Talbot

DY10 4SA

11-3, 5.30-11; (11-11 summer Sat); 12-3, 6-10.30 Sun

(01562) 777388 talbotinn.net

Banks's Original, Bitter; guest beers

There has been an inn standing on this site in the heart of the village since 1600. This historic, picturesque half-timbered black and white inn has a bar with pool table, two wood-panelled lounges (one no-smoking) and a restaurant upstairs. The varied and interesting menu is prepared on the premises using fresh and local produce. The large patio area is shaded by a grape vine, ideal for eating and drinking out in the summer.

Claines

Mug House

Claines Lane, WR3 7RN

11-3, 6-11; 11-11 Sat & Sun

(01905) 456649

Banks's Hanson's Mild, Bitter; guest beers

Picturesque village pub on the edge of Worcester and next door to Claines church. The classic multi-room interior includes a central bar serving two rooms and a third room used as a snug. The decor reflects the historic building and the bar is warmed by a real fire in winter. Banks's beers are served by electric dispense with two constantly changing guest beers on handpump. The garden has seating and superb views.

Droitwich

Hop Pole Inn

40 Friar Street, WR9 8ED

12-11; 12-10.30 Sun

(01905) 770155 thehoppoleatdroitwich.co.uk

Wye Valley Hereford Pale Ale, Butty Bach; guest beer

Traditional 300-year-old inn with a Grade II listed Queen Anne style frontage. The interesting interior with exposed beams includes a central serving area, dining areas and pool room. Ideal for a relaxing lunchtime drink and excellent value meal; in the evening the pub is livelier with younger pub-goers. Various events are held throughout the week – check the website or ring for details. The large garden includes a gazebo.

Eldersfield

Greyhound

GL19 4NX (N of B4211/B4213 jct) OS814305

11.30-2.30 (3 Sat), 7 (6 Fri & Sat)-11; 12-3, 7-10.30 Sun

(01452) 840381 greyhoundinn.co.uk

Butcombe Bitter; guest beers

Worth the effort needed to find it, the Greyhound offers a traditional country pub experience with wood burning stoves, pub games including quoits, and beer dispensed straight from the cask (up to three guests). The public bar and lounge areas are no-smoking throughout, though smoking is permitted in the skittle alley and garden. The annual beer festival is held in June.

Far Forest

Plough

Cleobury Road, DY14 9TE (½ mile from A456/B4117 jct) OS730744

12-3, 6-11.30; 11-11 Sat; 12-10.30 Sun

(01299) 266237 nostalgiainns.co.uk

Beer range varies

Busy, popular country pub and restaurant with a number of drinking and eating areas served from the main bar. The front room is for drinkers only and there is a large dining area that extends into the conservatory. The beer range varies, with ales from Wood, Wye Valley and Enville featuring regularly. For diners, there is a renowned carvery and extensive menu choice. Food is served all day Sunday (booking essential). Children are allowed in the dining areas.

Fladbury

Chequers Inn

Chequers Lane, WR10 2PZ (signed from village)

11.30-3, 5.30-11; 12-3 Sun

(01386) 860276 chequersinnfladbury.co.uk

Black Sheep Best Bitter; Fuller's London Pride; Hook Norton Hooky Bitter; guest beer

Large, welcoming inn dating from 1372, set back from the village green. The spacious open bar, once three separate rooms, boasts exposed beams and a range fire at one end. The restaurant, at the rear of the pub, serves a wide range of food, making best use of locally-produced ingredients. The recently refurbished walled garden has views to Bredon Hill. Seven bedrooms are available for overnight guests.

Great Malvern

Great Malvern Hotel

Graham Road, WR14 2HN (by Church Street crossroads)

10-11; 11-10.30 Sun

(01684) 563411 great-malvern-hotel.co.uk

Wood Shropshire Lad; guest beers

Busy public bar in a hotel located a short walk from the Malvern Theatre complex; an ideal venue for pre- or post-performance refreshment. The guest beer often comes from a local brewery including the nearby Malvern Hills Brewery. Meals are served in the bar and the adjoining no-smoking brasserie area (no food on Sun), or you can relax in the comfortable lounge with sofas and daily newspapers. The station is a short walk away and buses stop nearby.

Hanley Broadheath

Fox Inn

WR15 8QS (on B4204)

5-11.30 (midnight Thu); 12-1am Fri & Sat; 12-11 Sun

(01886) 853189

Batham Best Bitter; Hobsons Best Bitter; guest beers Ⓗ
This busy 400-year-old timbered rural village pub is a gem well worth seeking out. It has become a community focal point to the extent that a local resident delivers the Batham's! Two different guest beers are always available. Many varied community events are held including the Foxstock beer and music festival (first weekend Aug) and lawnmower Grand Prix in an adjacent field. The Thai landlady serves authentic Thai food Thursday to Saturday evenings. ⌂◗⊟♣●P

Hanley Castle

Three Kings ☆

Church End, WR8 0BL (signed off B4211) OS838420
✪ 12-3, 7-11; 12-3, 7-10.30 Sun
☎ (01684) 592686
Butcombe Bitter; Hobsons Best Bitter; guest beers Ⓗ
Unspoilt 15th-century country pub on the village green near the church run by the same family for 95 years. A former CAMRA national Pub of the Year, it also features in CAMRA's National Inventory of Historic Interiors. The three-room interior comprises a small snug with large inglenook, serving hatch and settle wall, family room (without bar) and 'Nell's Lounge' with another inglenook and original beams. Three interesting guest ales often come from local breweries. Regular live music sessions are hosted. A popular beer festival is held every November.
⌂Q☺❀◖◗⊟●

Hartlebury

Hartlebury British Legion

Millridge Way, Waresley, DY11 7LD (off A449, down a track on Waresley Ct Rd)
✪ 12-2 Tue only, 8 (7 Sat)-11; 12-4.30, 8-11 Sun
☎ (01299) 250252
Cannon Royall Fruiterer's Mild; guest beers Ⓗ
Welcoming club on the edge of Hartlebury with a large open-plan lounge bar and pool table and a smaller room to the side. The four guest beers are usually from micro-breweries and sold at reasonable prices. Food is available in the evening on Monday and Tuesday (plus lunch), Friday and Saturday. Bring a copy of this Guide or a CAMRA membership card to get signed in. Voted CAMRA West Midlands Region Club of the Year for 2005.
☺❀◗♿⇌♣●P

Himbleton

Galton Arms

Harrow Lane, WR9 7LQ
✪ 12-2 (not Mon), 4.30-11; 12-11 Sun
☎ (01905) 391672
Banks's Original, Bitter; Wye Valley Hereford Pale Ale; guest beer Ⓗ
Popular village local with a warm, welcoming atmosphere. Formerly known as the Harrow Inn, the building has been a pub since the 1800s and displays a list of landlords dating back to 1881. The main bar area retains the original beams. Food is served in the bar or dining room (no food Mon eve). Guest beers come mainly from local micro-breweries. Real cider is usually available. ⌂Q☺❀◖◗♿♣●P

Kempsey

Walter de Cantelupe

34 Main Road, WR5 3NA
✪ 12-2.30, 6-11; closed Mon; 12-2.30, 7-10.30 Sun
☎ (01905) 820572 ⊕ walterdecantelupeinn.com
Cannon Royall Kings Shilling; Hobsons Best Bitter; Taylor Landlord; guest beer Ⓗ
Fascinating free house named after the 13th-century Bishop of Worcester. The bar area features a large inglenook, and there is a high quality food menu. Ploughmans and sandwiches made with local bread and cheeses are a speciality, complementing the wide selection of beers and wines. Dogs are welcome in the attractive walled garden. Regular events include an all-day outdoor paella party in June.
⌂Q❀⊭◖◗P⊓

Kempsey Green Street

Huntsman Inn

Green Street, WR5 3QB (take Post Office Lane from Kempsey on A38)
✪ 12-3.30 (Sat only), 5-midnight; 12-3.30, 5-midnight Sun
☎ (01905) 820336
Batham Best Bitter; Everards Beacon, Tiger Ⓗ
Originally a farmhouse, this exposed beamed 300-year-old pub welcomes visitors with its friendly atmosphere. The cosy free house boasts real fires and brims with character throughout the bar, lounge and restaurant. Reasonably priced home-cooked food is popular with locals and visitors. An attractive garden is situated to the side and the impressive skittle alley has its own bar.
⌂Q☺❀◖◗⊟♣●P

Kidderminster

Boar's Head Tap House

39 Worcester Street, DY10 1EW
✪ 11.30-11 (12.30am Thu-Sat); 7-11.30 Sun
☎ (01562) 68776 ⊕ thetaphouse.co.uk
Banks's Bitter; guest beers Ⓗ
Popular town centre Victorian pub. The cosy lounge has wood panelling and a wood-burning stove. The main bar leads into a large covered and heated courtyard where live music is staged on Thursday and Sunday evenings. There is also a tented garden area for the summer. Note also the Pop Art style paintings. A range of guest beers from the Banks's list is on offer and there is a free mineral water dispenser for drivers.
⌂Q❀◖♿⇌⊟●

King & Castle

SVR Station, Comberton Hill, DY10 1QX
✪ 11-3, 5-11; 11-11 Sat; 12-10.30 Sun
☎ (01562) 747505
Batham Best Bitter; guest beers Ⓗ
Popular with locals and visitors to the Severn Valley Railway, the K&C is a replica of a GWR refreshment room. As you would expect there

is plenty of seating and even a carpet with the GWR logo. There is a varied selection of guest beers, many from local independents, with Enville Mild often found on busy weekends. Royal Piddle is brewed especially for the pub by Wyre Piddle. Food is served 12-2pm daily and 7-9pm Friday to Sunday when trains are running. A WC with wheelchair access is available on the platform.

Knightwick

Talbot

Knightwick, WR6 5PH (on B4197, 400 yds from A44 jct) OS572560
11-11; 12-10.30 Sun
(01886) 821235 temevalley.co.uk
Hobsons Best Bitter; Teme Valley This, That, seasonal beer H
It is not hard to see why the Talbot was voted Worcester CAMRA Pub of the Year for 2005. Nestling in a beautiful riverside location, away from the hustle and bustle of everyday life, it is all that a classic 14th-century coaching inn should be. The restaurant serves great quality food made with local ingredients. The Teme Valley Brewery is located behind the hotel. A highlight in the calendar is the Green Hop Festival held in early October.

Malvern Link

Nag's Head

21 Bank Street, WR14 2JG (uphill from Malvern Link station, left at traffic lights)
11-11.15 (11.30 Fri & Sat); 12-11 Sun
(01684) 574373
Banks's Bitter; Greene King IPA; Marston's Pedigree; guest beers H
This award-winning pub is located at the top of Malvern Link common and enjoys stunning views across the hills. Formerly a row of cottages, it has several rooms in which to enjoy a wide range of ever-changing beers. A rack of newspapers is provided for those wanting a quiet read. At weekends and in the evenings the pub has a lively atmosphere and can be busy. In winter heated marquees are erected in the gardens to allow more drinking space. The Nag's Tail restaurant serves food until 9pm when the room reverts to a bar.

Mamble

Sun & Slipper

Mamble, DY14 9JL (signed from A456)
12-3, 6.30-midnight (1 am Fri & Sat); closed Mon; 12-4, 7-midnight Sun
(01299) 832018
Banks's Original, Bitter; Hobsons Best Bitter; guest beer H
Very much at the centre of village life on the old village green, this solid, country pub has a small, cosy bar with pool table and a separate dining room with a log-burning stove. There are old photos of the village in the hallway while the bar has new seating, a bar of light oak and fresh flower displays. The food is very good; menus change monthly.

Monkwood Green

Fox

Monkwood Green, WR2 6NX (follow signs to Wichenford off A443) OS803601
12-2.30 (not Mon-Thu), 5-11; 12-5, 7-10.30 Sun
(01886) 889123
Cannon Royall Arrowhead, Muzzle Loader; guest beer H
Friendly, rural, single-bar village local dating from Georgian times with good views of the Malvern Hills to the south. The guest beer usually comes from a local micro and the pub is a rare outlet for Barkers farmhouse cider and award-winning perry. The centre for many local events, various pub games are played here and there is a skittle alley and indoor air rifle shooting. A music night is held on the last Friday of the month. Opening hours and food availability are flexible.

Offenham

Bridge Inn

Boat Lane, WR11 8QZ (follow signs to Riverside Pub)
11-midnight; 12-11 Sun
(01386) 446565 bridge-inn.co.uk
Caledonian Deuchars IPA; Donnington BB; guest beers H
Traditional country free house dating back to the 1700s with its own moorings and a garden leading down to the Avon – the perfect place for whiling away those lazy summer afternoons by the riverside. Known locally as the Boat, it has a good reputation for meals produced with locally grown fruit and vegetables, which are served in the restaurant area.

Pensax

Bell

Pensax, WR6 6AE (on B4202, Clows Top-Great Witley)
12-2.30 (not Mon), 5-11; 12-10.30 Sun
(01299) 896677
Hobsons Best Bitter; guest beers H
You will find a warm welcome and friendly atmosphere at this award-winning pub. The bar serves at least four guest beers, two normally under 4% ABV, with local independents such as Cannon Royall, Malvern Hills and Windsor Castle often stocked. Westons Herefordshire perry and Old Rosie cider also feature. Children are welcome in the snug and no-smoking dining room where the menu offers good food prepared with local produce. The annual beer festival is on the last weekend of June.

Pershore

Brandy Cask

25 Bridge Street, WR10 1AJ
11.30-11.30 (midnight Fri & Sat); 11-11 Sun
(01386) 552602
Brandy Cask Whistling Joe, Brandy Snapper, John Baker's Original; guest beers H
Popular and lively town pub with its own brewery. Three of the home-brewed ales are constantly on handpump, with seasonal

brews including Ale Mary appearing regularly. Two imaginative guest beers and a real cider are also normally available. Good value home-cooked food is served in both the bar and restaurant (not winter Tue). The garden which fronts the river Avon is a joy in summer months. A regular beer festival is held in August. ⩕Q❀◐◑●

Redditch

Steps

163 Evesham Road, Headless Cross, B97 5EN (400 yds from A441/A448 roundabout, opposite church)
✪ 12-3, 5-11; 12-midnight Fri & Sat; 12-11 Sun
☎ (01527) 550448 🌐 stepsbarandbistro.co.uk
Hobsons Town Crier; guest beer Ⓗ

Trendy chrome bar that becomes a busy nightspot at weekends, with disco on Friday and local bands performing on Saturday. The no-smoking bar offers guest beers from local independents. Opening early for food only, a breakfast buffet is available until 11am (12 Sat and Sun). Lunch is served Monday-Friday 12-2pm. There is a relaxing sofa area and pleasant patio garden. Steps sponsors a local football team. Quiz night is Thursday. ❀◐♿🚌⚡

Sedgeberrow

Queen's Head

1 Main Street, WR11 7UE (on B4078)
✪ 12-3, 5.30-11; 12-4, 6.30-10.30 Sun
☎ (01386) 881447
Greene King IPA; guest beers Ⓗ

Village pub on the southern edge of the Vale of Evesham. Run by friendly owners, visitors receive a warm welcome. The regular beer is complemented by up to two guest beers, usually from local micros, and a traditional cider from Thatchers. A good menu is available (not Mon) and children are allowed in the no-smoking lounge area. ◐◑⊟♣●⚡

Shenstone

Plough

Shenstone Village, DY10 4DL (off A450/A448)
✪ 12-3, 6-11; 12-3, 7-10.30 Sun
☎ (01562) 777340
Batham Mild Ale, Best Bitter, XXX (winter) Ⓗ

Traditional country pub serving Batham's beers at reasonable prices. A single bar serves a cheery public bar and lounge, both with real fires. Many pictures of the Falklands war decorate the walls. Children are allowed in the large covered courtyard. There is no cooked food here but bar snacks are available. ⩕Q⛴❀⊏⊐⛺P

Stourport-on-Severn

Bird in Hand

Holly Road, DY13 9BA (off B4193 by canal)
✪ 11-11; 12-10.30 Sun
☎ (01299) 822385
Enville Ale; Flowers IPA; Taylor Landlord; Wadworth 6X Ⓗ

This canalside pub is a 10-minute walk along the towpath from the town. A small, cosy snug is to the left of the entrance; the comfortable main room is divided into three with plenty of seating and a warm atmosphere. The pub serves good value food with special themed food nights. In summer, enjoy a pint sitting outside by the canal. Saturday is quiz night. ⩕❀◐⊟P⚡

Old Crown

8 Bridge Street, DY13 8XB
✪ 9.30 (alcohol from 11)-12.30am; 12-10.30 Sun
☎ (01299) 825693
Banks's Original; Greene King Abbot; Marston's Burton Bitter Ⓗ

The drinking area outside this Wetherspoon's pub overlooks Brindley's historic river basins and the river bridge. Inside is one large room with plenty of seating and a long single bar down one side. Old photos of canal basins of note decorate the walls. The family area is at the back; children are welcome until 9pm. Q⛴❀◐♿⛺🚌P⚡

Uphampton

Fruiterer's Arms

Uphampton Lane, WR9 0JW (off A449 at Reindeer pub) OS839649
✪ 12.30 (12 Sat)-3, 7-11; 12-3, 7-10.30 Sun
☎ (01905) 620305
Cannon Royall Fruiterer's Mild, Arrowhead, Muzzle Loader, seasonal beers; John Smith's Best Bitter Ⓗ

This cosy pub, tucked away down a country lane, is the brewery tap for Cannon Royall. Sporting guns, old local prints and many CAMRA awards adorn the walls of the wood-panelled lounge. The public bar is more basic. Good, home-cooked food is served. A little gem well worth seeking out for its reasonable prices. ⩕Q❀◐⊟♣P

Upton upon Severn

White Lion Hotel

High Street, WR8 0HJ
✪ 11-11; 12-10.30 Sun
☎ (01684) 592551 🌐 whitelionhotel.biz
Greene King Abbot; guest beers Ⓗ

Featuring in Henry Fielding's novel Tom Jones, this traditional inn dates from the 16th century. The welcome is unstuffy, warm and relaxed. Bar meals are available (not Sat eve or Sun lunch) or you can spoil yourself in the high quality restaurant. Three guest ales usually include one from a local brewery. The Lion & Pepperpot Beer Festival is held during the last bank holiday in May; other beer events complement Upton's music festivals. Q❀⊏⊐◐◑♿🚌P

Weatheroak

Coach & Horses

Weatheroak Hill, B48 7EA (Alvechurch to Wythall road)
✪ 11.30-11; 12-10.30 Sun
☎ (01564) 823386
Hobsons Mild; Weatheroak Light Oak, Ale, Keystone Hops; Wood Shropshire Lad; guest beers Ⓗ

Attractive rural pub, home of the Weatheroak Brewery, with a quarry-tiled public bar with real fire and functional seating, a comfortable split level lounge/bar and a modern no-smoking restaurant with disabled access and toilets. Meals are available in the restaurant and bar daily except Sunday evening. The large, family friendly garden and patio are popular in summer. A recipient of numerous local CAMRA awards, beer festivals are an added attraction. ⛼Q❀◑◐⊟♣●P

West Malvern

Lamb Inn

87 West Malvern Road, WR14 4NG (on B4232)

4.30 (12 Sat)-11; 12-10.30 Sun

☎ (01684) 577847

Adnams Broadside; Caledonian Deuchars IPA; guest beers Ⓗ

Thriving village local regularly packed for music nights (Sat, sometimes Fri) and open mike sessions (Thu). The main room containing the bar is festooned with flags and inflatable toys. A quieter second room has a skittle alley and further seating. Sunday lunch featuring ten vegetables is very popular – no other food is served. The road up to the car park is very steep. ❀♣●P

Woodgate

Gate Hangs Well

Woodgate Road, B60 4HG (off Hanbury road close to Stoke Prior) OS39662664

11-11.30 (midnight Fri & Sat); 11-11.30 Sun

☎ (01527) 821957

Banks's Bitter; guest beers Ⓗ

The inviting bar is a welcome sight when you enter this recently refurbished pub and restaurant. Log fires, snug areas, a pool table and a garden all add to the traditional country look and feel of this smart pub. Five guest ales usually include beers from local breweries. The owners take their food as seriously as their beer and offer the very best of fresh ingredients, cooked to order, served in a relaxed and comfortable atmosphere. ⛼❀◑◐♿▲⊟♣P⚟

Worcester

Bell

35 St Johns, WR2 5AG (W side of the Severn off A44)

10.30-2, 5-11 (11.30 Fri); 10.30-4, 7-11.30 Sat; 12-3, 7-11 Sun

☎ (01905) 424570

M&B Brew XI; guest beers Ⓗ

This pub is a popular local comprising a busy main bar with two side rooms, one of which doubles as a family room. Pub games feature, with a busy skittle alley at the rear. One of the guests is usually Fuller's London Pride, with two others frequently from local breweries. A modest selection of single malt whiskies is stocked. ❀⊟♣

Berkeley Arms

School Road, St Johns, WR2 4HF

12-3.30, 5-midnight; 12-12.30am Fri & Sat; 12-3.30, 7-11 Sun

☎ (01905) 421427

Banks's Hanson's Mild, Bitter, Original Ⓟ**; guest beer** Ⓗ

This compact local pub has two front rooms: one a basic public bar with a small TV used for sporting events, the other a more comfortably furnished lounge. A third room at the rear with a dartboard can be used for meetings or as a family room, and outside is a patio area for warmer weather. The guest beer is supplied by Wolverhampton & Dudley and is usually either a special from one of its own breweries or from one of the larger independents. ❀⊟⊟♣P

Cap 'n' Gown

45 Upper Tything, WR1 1JZ

11-midnight; 12-10.30 Sun

☎ (01905) 24208

Hook Norton Hooky Dark, Hooky Bitter, Old Hooky, seasonal beers Ⓗ

Busy single-room house with welcoming staff in an area of town popular for pubs and restaurants. A good range of Hook Norton beers is normally available, including mild and seasonals. There is a big screen TV that shows sports events but does not intrude at other times. ⇌(Foregate St)⊟♣

Dragon Inn

51 The Tything, WR1 1JT (on A449, 200 yds N of Foregate St)

12-3, 4.30-11 (11.30 Fri); 12-11 Sat; 12-3, 7-10.30 Sun

☎ (01905) 25845 🌐 thedragoninn.com

Beer range varies Ⓗ

This multi-award winning real ale paradise houses possibly the widest range of beers in Worcester. You will regularly see beers (including a stout or porter) from breweries as far apart as Lancashire and Cornwall. The traditional cider is usually from Thatchers or Rich's. A partially-covered patio garden allows for alfresco drinking in the summer. Good value lunchtime meals are available (not Sunday). Q❀◑⇌(Foregate St)⊟♣●

Green Man

40 The Tything, WR1 1JL

11-midnight; 12-11 Sun

☎ (01905) 330460

Beer range varies Ⓗ

Recently refurbished with flagstone floors and a bright, airy decor, this is very much a high-class food oriented pub, serving breakfast (not Sun), lunch and dinner. Five changing guest beers are always available. There is a small courtyard area outside as well as tables in the street. The upstairs area is no-smoking.
Q❀◑◐⇌(Foregate St)⊟⚟

Swan with Two Nicks

28 New Street, WR1 2DP

11-11 (1am Fri & Sat); 7-10.30 Sun

☎ (01905) 28190 🌐 theswanwithtwonicks.co.uk

Beer range varies Ⓗ

Historic real ale pub with four ever-changing beers, usually from local micros or small, mainly south-west, breweries and a choice of more than 60 malt whiskies. Hearty home-prepared lunchtime meals are served (not Sun) and children are welcome. Upstairs is the Luna retro 1970s cocktail bar and, at the rear, Drummonds venue bar with regular live music. Traditional cider or perry is available occasionally. ❀◑♿⇌●

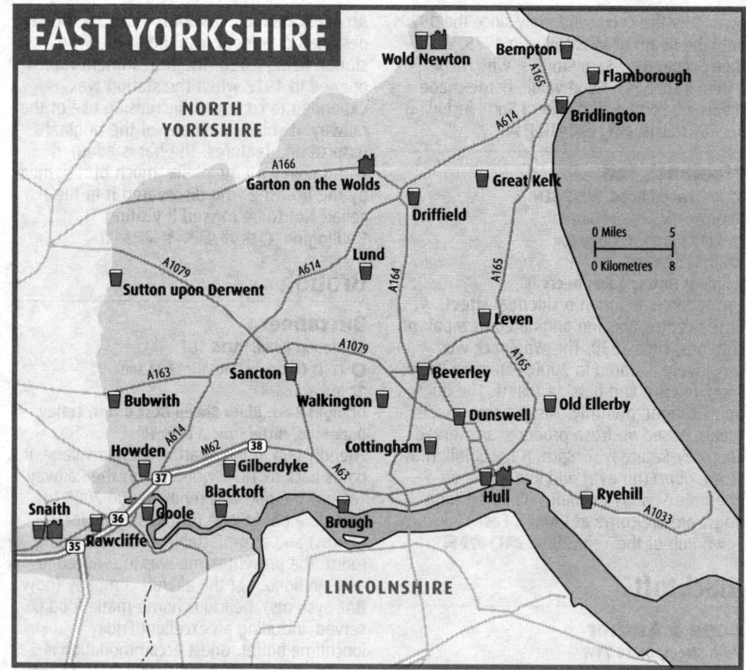

YORKSHIRE (EAST)

Bempton

White Horse Inn

30 High Street, YO15 1HB

⏲ 11.30-3 (4 Fri & Sat), 7-11 (11.30 Fri & Sat); 12-4.30, 7-11 Sun

☎ (01262) 850266

John Smith's Bitter; guest beers 🄷

Built in 1938, this former Moors and Robson's ale house still bears its distinctive blue-tiled roof. This community local has a comfortable, open-plan lounge with period wood panelling and a solid bar. The former tap room houses a pool table and dartboard. Two guest beers are stocked. Home-cooked food, served 12-2pm, includes locally-caught fish. The nearby RSPB sanctuary and cliffs attract walkers and birdwatchers. The EYMS 504 bus from Bridlington serves the village (not Sun). ♨❀◐⇌🚌♣P

Beverley

Durham Ox

48 Norwood, HU17 9HJ (300 yds E of bus station)

⏲ 10.30-11; 12-11 Sun

☎ (01482) 679444

John Smith's Bitter; Tetley Bitter; Wychwood Hobgoblin; guest beers 🄷

Two-roomed Victorian local near the new Tesco store that was built on the site of the former cattle market. The pub was refurbished about six years ago after consultation with CAMRA's local pub preservation officer. The lounge was extended to include a games area, but retains its original etched windows, public bar with wooden floor and off-sales hatch in the entrance lobby. The pub fields five darts and two dominoes teams. Off-street parking is possible directly opposite. Meals are served weekdays. ◑⊟🚌♣

Green Dragon

51 Saturday Market, HU17 8AA

⏲ 11-midnight; 12-10.30 Sun

☎ (01482) 889801

Beer range varies 🄷

This historic inn was renamed the Green Dragon in 1765. Enter the Tudor fronted building via a side passage and marvel at the length of the bar (42 feet). It dispenses ales mainly from Yorkshire micro-breweries such as Anglo Dutch, Cropton, Rudgate and Wold Top. Refurbished and substantially extended 10 years ago, sadly most internal fittings of note were lost, but some wood panelling remains. Meals are served daily until 7pm; quiz nights are Tuesday and Wednesday. Weekends are busy. ❀◑♿⇌🚌⚟

White Horse Inn (Nellie's) ☆

22 Hengate, HU17 8BL (behind bus station)

⏲ 11-11; 12-10.30 Sun

☎ (01482) 861973 🌐 nellies.co.uk

Samuel Smith OBB 🄷

One of Beverley's landmarks, this historic inn retains a multi-roomed interior with gas lighting and stone-flagged floors; all six rooms, including the large, no-smoking room upstairs, often have coal fires blazing. The building,

INDEPENDENT BREWERIES

Garton Garton on the Wolds
Old Mill Snaith
Whalebone Hull
Wold Top Wold Newton

owned by the Collinson family since the 1920s until the death of Miss Nellie in 1975, was then acquired by Sam Smith's, who made minimal changes. Good value, home-made meals are served all day until 5pm, including Sunday roasts. ⛰Q❀◑⊟⊟P⚟

Woolpack Inn

37 Westwood Road, HU17 8EN

(near Westwood, S of hospital)

✪ 6 (12 Sat)-11; 12-10.30 Sun

☎ (01482) 867095

Jennings Bitter; guest beers ⊞

Located in a Victorian residential street, west of the centre, this inn originated as a pair of cottages, circa 1830. The Woolpack was sensitively restored in 2000, retaining its cosy snug, log fire and outside toilets. The guest beers change monthly. Tasty, home-made meals, based on fresh produce, are served Thursday-Saturday, 6-8pm. It hosts folk music (Tue), quiz (Thu eve) and live music on alternate Sunday evenings. Children (and dogs) are welcome at CAMRA East Yorkshire Town Pub of the Year 2004. ⛰Q❀◗⊟

Blacktoft

Hope & Anchor

Main Street, DN14 7YW

(3½ miles S of Gilberdyke Station)

✪ 4-11; 12-10.30 Sun

☎ (01430) 440441

John Smith's Bitter; Theakston Mild; guest beer ⊞

Village local with a recently added conservatory that, like the outdoor tables, looks out across the River Ouse to Blacktoft Sands bird sanctuary. To the side is a children's play area. On the Trans Pennine Trail link, the pub is popular with walkers and cyclists, and with seamen who tie up at the nearby jetty. Note the collection of Laurel and Hardy figures. Old Mill Mild sometimes replaces the Theakston's. The village is served by South Cave-Goole, EYMS No. 160 bus (Wed and Sat only). ❀◐◗▲⊟P

Bridlington

Old Ship Inn

90 St John's Street, YO16 7JS (1 mile NW of centre)

✪ 11.30-11 (midnight Fri & Sat); 12-11 Sun

☎ (01262) 670466

John Smith's Bitter; Worthington's Bitter; guest beers ⊞

Thriving, former Vaux local, originally two dwellings. Alterations in the 1980s resulted in the present layout of a front lounge and snug and a large rear bar. The lounge walls are adorned with prints of famous sailing ships, while the snug resembles a small Victorian parlour displaying photographs of Yorkshire coastal scenes. The meals (not served Mon) are recommended. The rail station is less than a mile away and EYMS bus Nos. 1 and 2 go to the bus station. ☋❀◐◗⊟♣⚟

Station Buffet ☆

Station Approach, YO15 3EP

✪ 10-7 daily

☎ (01262) 673709 ⊕ stationbuffet.co.uk

Wold Top Mars Magic; guest beers ⊞

An application by CAMRA to have the buffet designated Grade II resulted in the whole station being listed. The refreshment rooms opened in 1912 when the station was expanded to cope with increasing use of the railway. It still bears many of the original fixtures and features. The bar is adorned with railway memorabilia, much of it owned by the licensee who discovered it in the cellar. Not to be missed if visiting Bridlington. Q❀◐◗⊟♿⇌⊟P⚟⊡

Brough

Buccaneer

47 Station Road, HU15 1DZ

✪ 12-11 (midnight Thu-Sat); 12-11 Sun

☎ (01482) 667435

Draught Bass; Black Sheep Best Bitter; Tetley Dark Mild, Bitter; guest beer ⊞

Friendly pub at the heart of the old village, it dates back to 1870 when it was the Railway Tavern. The pub was renovated in 2000 to provide a bar-lounge (displaying old local photos) and a comfortable 45-seater dining room. The present name was introduced in 1968 in honour of the aircraft company (now BAE Systems). Delicious home-made food is served, including an excellent Friday lunchtime buffet. Guest accommodation is due to open in 2007. ❀◐◗⇌⊟(155, X62)♣P

Bubwith

Jug & Bottle

50 Main Street, YO8 6LX (on A163)

✪ 5 (11 Fri & Sat)-9; closed Mon & Tue; 1-7 Sun

☎ (01757) 289707 ⊕ jugandbottle.co.uk

Taylor Landlord; guest beers ⊞

In the summer of 2006 this enterprising off-licence settled in to its new home further along the road in a recently restored former village school building. Guest beers are sourced from throughout the UK and customers' suggestions are always welcome. In addition to a good range of bottled beer and cider, it stocks an extensive selection of cheeses and unusual snacks, olives, crackers and much more. This shop is very much part of the village. Q⊟●⚟

Cottingham

King William IV

152 Hallgate, HU16 4BD

✪ 11-11 (11.30 Fri & Sat); 12-11 Sun

☎ (01482) 847340

Banks's & Hanson's Riding Bitter; Marston's Pedigree; guest beers ⊞

Two village-centre houses were converted to form a traditional bar and lounge, served by a central bar. At the rear an old brewery has been transformed into a function room where sport is shown on a plasma screen TV. The central fireplace in the lounge provides a welcoming focal point in winter, while in summer the terrace garden is a pleasant enclosed area for drinking. Q❀◐◗⊟♿⇌⊟♣⚟

Driffield

Bell

46 Market Place, YO25 6AN

⊙ 10-11; 12-3,, 7-10.30 Sun
☎ (01377) 256661 🌐 thebellindriffield.co.uk
Beer range varies Ⓗ
Local CAMRA's Town Pub of the Year 2005, this inn features a long, wood-panelled bar with red leather seating, substantial fireplaces, antiques and paintings that lend a quality feel. Two or three beers are kept, usually from Wold Top, Hambleton or Highwood breweries, but other micros are also represented. Over 300 malt whiskies are stocked. A covered courtyard has bistro seating. A splendid lunchtime carvery buffet is served Mon-Sat; the restaurant opens 7-9.30pm; Sunday lunch must be booked. Children are welcome until 7.30pm. Q☕🛏◐♿⇌🚌P⚡

Foundry

7 Market Walk, YO25 6BW (down passageway off market place)
⊙ 10-3 (not Wed; 10-4 Fri), 7-11; 10-11 Tue & Sat; 12-3 (closed eve) Sun
☎ (01377) 253874
Beer range varies Ⓗ
Local CAMRA Town Pub of the Year runner-up, the café and bar are housed in the only building that remains of the old Victoria Foundry complex. The ground floor is divided in two: a front area with a tiled floor, comfortable bench seating, tables and chairs and a raised rear area with sofas and low tables. The walls throughout are bare brick with heavy beams. Daily papers are provided. Up to five beers are available at weekends in this completely no-smoking hostelry. Q☕◐⇌🚌♣⚡▯

Mariner's Arms

47 Eastgate South, YO25 6LR
⊙ 3 (12 Sat)-midnight; 12-11 Sun
☎ (01377) 253708
Banks's Bitter; Camerons Bitter; guest beers Ⓗ
This street-corner local is well worth seeking out as an alternative to the John Smith's outlets that dominate the 'capital of the Wolds'. Formerly part of the Hull Brewery estate, its four small rooms have now become two: a basic bar and more comfortable lounge. Live sport is shown and the pub fields various sports teams. The long-standing licensees enjoy a loyal following among locals and offer a friendly welcome to all visitors. ❀⊟⇌🚌♣P

Rose & Crown

North Street, YO25 6AS (400 yds N of centre)
⊙ 12-midnight (11 Wed; 1am Thu & Fri); 11-1am Sat; 12-11 Sun
☎ (01377) 253041
John Smith's Bitter; guest beers Ⓗ
Family-run pub, opposite the town's Green Flag awarded park. It comprises a main bar/lounge and a pool room. Televised live sport is shown, Thursday is quiz night and regular entertainment is staged on Saturday evening. Numerous sports teams represent the pub. The two guest beers, mostly from independents, change every few days. Table service is available Thursday-Saturday evenings. Benches are provided outside for summer drinking. The EYMS No. 121 Hull-Scarborough bus and other services run regularly. ❀🚌♣P

Dunswell

Ship Inn

Beverley Road, HU6 0AJ (on main Hull-Beverley road)
⊙ 11-11 (11.30 Fri & Sat); 12-11 Sun
☎ (01482) 859160
Black Sheep Best Bitter; John Smith's Bitter; Taylor Landlord; guest beer Ⓗ
This white-painted inn fronting the old Hull-Beverley road once served traffic on the nearby River Hull, as reflected in the nautical memorabilia and decor. Two log fires warm the convivial interior that is partly divided to form a dining area with church pew seating. A newly-converted, detached extension provides overnight accommodation, aptly named the Ship's Quarters. Barbecues are held in the adjoining paddock. Meals are served all day until 7pm. 🔥❀🛏◐🚌♣P

Flamborough

Seabirds

Tower Street, YO15 1PD
⊙ 12-3, 6-midnight; closed winter Mon; 12-3, 6-11 (not winter eves) Sun
☎ (01262) 850242
John Smith's Bitter; guest beer Ⓗ
Once two rooms, this pub changed hands in 2003 and has been refurbished, resulting in a clean, contemporary look. The guest beer often comes from a local brewery. A range of home-cooked food, with vegetarian options, is based on local produce whenever possible. Camping is possible nearby; the pub is popular with walkers and bird enthusiasts – spectacular cliffs and Bempton RSPB Sanctuary are close by. EYMS buses 510 and 502 from Bridlington provide an occasional service. 🔥❀◐♿⛺🚌P

Ship Inn

Post Office Street, YO15 1JS
⊙ 11-11; 12-10.30 Sun
☎ (01262) 850454
John Smith's Bitter; Taylor Landlord; guest beer Ⓗ
Grade II listed, former 17th-century coaching inn at the village centre, that extends a warm welcome to locals and visitors alike. Dark wood abounds throughout and the original stained glass windows are intact, with external lettering identifying each room. Varied bar food includes vegetarian options and daily specials; the restaurant area is no smoking. The accommodation is reasonably priced. Walkers are welcome, as are dogs. Buses from Bridlington serve the village. 🔥🛏◐⊟⛺🚌(510)♣P

Gilberdyke

Cross Keys

Main Road, HU15 2SP (on B1230, W edge of village)
⊙ 12-2, 4-midnight; 12-1am Fri & Sat; 12-11 Sun
☎ (01430) 440310
Black Sheep Best Bitter; John Smith's Bitter; Tetley Bitter; guest beers Ⓗ
This pub on the old A63 (now bypassed by the M62) enjoys strong local support and attracts visitors from near and far. A listed building dated 1750, it was originally known as Mooks Inn after its Dutch owners,

changing to its current name, derived from the nearby crossroads, around 1800. It comprises a pool/bar room and bar/lounge with a split-level snug displaying traditional photographs. Guest beers vary.
⛫❀◑⊟♿⇌🚌♣●P⊬

Goole

Mackintosh Arms

13 Aire Street, DN14 5QE

⏲ 10-1am (midnight Mon; 2am Fri & Sat); 12-midnight Sun

☎ (01405) 763850

Tetley Dark Mild, Bitter, Imperial; guest beer Ⓗ

This friendly, characterful, town-centre pub is situated in a terrace near the docks. One of the three rooms set around the central bar is used for pool. Members of a motorcycle club, the Wobbly Goolies, meet here once a month to organise their charity events. The guest beer changes frequently. The pub hosts karaoke on Sunday and live music is performed monthly on the last Friday. ❀⇌♣P

Great Kelk

Chestnut Horse

Main Street, YO25 8HN (follow signs for Kelk)

⏲ 6 (5.30 Fri & Sat)-11; 12-10.30 Sun

☎ (01262) 488263

Black Sheep Best Bitter; guest beers Ⓗ

Built in 1793, this delightful Grade II listed, rural community pub is situated between the Wolds and Holderness. Darts, dominoes and chess are played here. It has a cosy bar with real fire and a comfortable games room that doubles as a daytime family room. The restaurant serves fine, home-cooked meals until 8.45pm daily (7.30pm Sun). Up to three guest beers are sold alongside draught Hoegaarden and Leffe; Belgian bottled beers are served in authentic glasses. ⛫Q❀◑♣●P⊬

Howden

Barnes Wallis

Station Road, North Howden, DN14 7LF (on B1228, near station)

⏲ 12-2 (3 Sat), 5 (6 Sat)-11; 12-10.30 Sun

☎ (01430) 430639 🌐 barneswallisinn.co.uk

John Smith's Bitter; guest beers Ⓗ

Friendly, one-roomed pub, close to Howden Station, a mile north of Howden. It features aviation memorabilia and artefacts relating to Barnes Wallis who worked in nearby Brough when designing airships and the Wellington Bomber. Changing guests usually include at least one dark beer. The large, secluded garden is ideal for children. Local charities are well supported here. Regular quizzes are held – the music one on Sunday afternoon is renowned for its difficulty. ⛫❀◑♿⇌♣P

Hull

Admiral of the Humber

1 Anlaby Road, HU1 2NT

⏲ 9am-midnight (1am Fri & Sat); 9am-midnight Sun

☎ (01482) 381850

Greene King Abbot; Marston's Burton Bitter, Pedigree; guest beers Ⓗ

Wetherspoon's second outlet in the city was converted from a former paint shop in 2000. One roomed, it has a raised no-smoking area for diners, a second no-smoking section and several booths on either side that each seat four. Westons Old Rosie and vintage organic ciders are available on draught, alongside up to seven guest beers. Meals are served until an hour before closing every day. It is a short walk from the station. ◑♿⇌⊬

Falcon

60 Falkland Road, Greatfield, HU9 5HA

⏲ 11-11 (midnight Fri & Sat); 11-11 Sun

☎ (01482) 713721

Lees Bitter; guest beers Ⓗ

On an outlying estate four miles from the centre in the eastern part of the city in an area where real ale choice is limited, this community local has been rejuvenated by the current licensee. Under his care the pub has gone from strength to strength and his customers will always find a mild here among the three guest beers. Craven Park, home of Hull Kingston Rovers Rugby League Club, is less than 15 minutes' walk away. ❀⊟🚌(42, 66)♣P

Gardeners Arms

35 Cottingham Road, HU5 2PP (near university)

⏲ 11 (12 Mon)-midnight; 12-midnight Sun

☎ (01482) 342396

Tetley Bitter; guest beers Ⓗ

Former local CAMRA Pub of the Year and a regular finalist, the Gardeners is situated on a main bus route. The original front bar has seen many alterations, but retains the matchwood ceiling that blends with the current ale house style. The large rear extension is comfortably furnished, housing several pool tables. Good value food is served 12-9pm every day. The six guest beers in the front bar usually include one each from Bateman and Black Sheep. It hosts three weekly quizzes. ❀◑♿🚌♣●P⊬

Hole in the Wall

115 Spring Bank, HU3 1BH

⏲ 1 (12 Fri & Sat)-11; 12-10.30 Sun

☎ (01482) 580354

Old Mill Mild; Rooster's Yankee; guest beers Ⓗ

Once an amusement arcade, converted in 2001, it offers up to four guest beers, mainly sourced from independents, including local breweries. All real ales are reduced in price Monday-Thursday. Featuring wood floors throughout, the spacious front bar has plenty of standing room and comfortable leather upholstered bench seating. Sports enthusiasts prefer the rear bar for its large-screen TV and pool table. It is handy for the KC Stadium and railway station – both 15 minutes' walk away. ❀⇆♿⇌🚌♣

Minerva Hotel

Nelson Street, HU1 1XE (near marina and Victoria Pier)

⏲ 11-11; 12-10.30 Sun

☎ (01482) 326909

Tetley Bitter; guest beers Ⓗ

Overlooking the Humber estuary and Victoria Pier, this famous pub, built in 1835, is a great place for watching the ships go by. Superb photos and memorabilia are a reminder of the area's maritime past. The central bar serves various rooms, including a tiny, three-seater snug. Noted for its excellent home-made food, evening meals are served until 8.30pm. The pub is connected to the Deep visitor attraction by a footbridge at the mouth of the River Hull.

Olde Black Boy ☆

150 High Street, HU1 1PS

12-11 (midnight Fri & Sat); 12-11 Sun

(01482) 326516 yeoldeblackboy.co.uk

Caledonian Deuchars IPA; Copper Dragon Golden Pippin; Rooster's Yankee; Springhead Roaring Meg; guest beers

Licensed in 1729, this town pub on the medieval cobbled High Street is a five-minute walk from the Deep. Note the leaded display front window and the carved head above the fireplace in the front snug. The upstairs rooms (used only occasionally) both feature stained glass windows and open fireplaces. It stocks two guest ales and Holy Island fruit wines. Folk music sessions take place monthly (first Mon). The pub was Grade II listed following a successful local CAMRA campaign. Q

Olde White Harte ☆

25 Silver Street, HU1 1JG

11-midnight (1am Fri & Sat); 12-midnight Sun

(01482) 326363

Caledonian Deuchars IPA; Greene King Old Speckled Hen; McEwan's 80/-; Theakston Old Peculier

Historic, 16th-century courtyard pub, reputedly the residence of the Governor of Hull when he resolved to deny Charles I entry to the city. An impressive staircase leads to the 'plotting room' and restaurant. The ground floor comprises two distinct areas, each with a bar. Award-winning floral displays, superb dark woodwork, stained glass windows and inglenooks feature. At the heart of the old town's commercial centre, it has a covered, heated outdoor drinking area. An extensive range of single malts is stocked. Q

Pave

16-20 Princes Avenue, HU5 3QA

11 (12 Mon)-11 (11.30 Fri & Sat); 12-11 Sun

(01482) 333181 pavebar.co.uk

Caledonian Deuchars IPA; Theakston Best Bitter, XB; guest beer

Cosmopolitan café bar; the result of a conversion in 2002. Single roomed, it incorporates a raised stage area with an open fire. Comfy sofas and leather seating attract diverse drinkers; it is especially popular at weekends. Live jazz is played on Sunday. A secluded garden and front patio are pleasurable in warmer months. A varied range of European draught and bottled beers is stocked. Food is served from opening until 7pm daily. (15, 115)

Three John Scotts

Lowgate, HU1 1XW

9am-midnight (1am Fri & Sat); 9am-midnight Sun

(01482) 381910

Greene King Abbot; Hop Back Summer Lightning; Marston's Pedigree; Tetley Bitter; Theakston Old Peculier; guest beers

Converted Edwardian post office opposite St Mary's church in the old town, this open-plan Wetherspoon's features modern decor and original art. Named after three past incumbents of the church, it now welcomes the bellringers on Tuesday evenings and twice on Sunday. The clientele is mixed at lunchtime, with circuit drinkers appearing at weekends. The rear courtyard has plentiful seating. It offers up to five guest beers, always incuding a Rooster's brew, plus Westons cider and perries. Food is served until 11pm daily.

Wellington Inn

55 Russell Street, HU2 9AB (on edge of city centre, 50 yds N of A165)

12-11 (midnight Fri; 1am Sat); 12-11 Sun

(01482) 329486 wellingtoninn.co.uk

Tetley Bitter; guest beers

Established in 2004, this free house was Hull and East Yorks CAMRA joint Pub of the Year 2005. Refurbished to a high standard, it boasts a walk-in cooler stocking over 100 European bottled beers. Up to seven guest beers are mainly sourced from Yorkshire and Lincolnshire independent breweries. Ciders, perries and European fruit beers add variety. No food is available but you are welcome to bring your own sandwiches. Outdoor drinking is next to the car park. P

Whalebone

165 Wincolmlee, HU2 0PA (500 yds N of North Bridge on W bank of river)

11-midnight daily

(01482) 226648

Highwood Best Bitter; Taylor Landlord; Whalebone Diana Mild, Neckoil, seasonal beers; guest beer (occasional)

Built in 1796 on the site of the old Lockwood's Brewery, the pub is situated on the former harbour in an old industrial area – look for the illuminated M&R Ales sign. The comfortable saloon bar is adorned with photos of bygone Hull pubs and the city's sporting heritage; CAMRA awards are also displayed. The Whalebone Brewery, housed in the adjacent building, started brewing in 2003. Two real ciders, bottle Belgian beers and Gale's country wines are sold, plus hot snacks.

Leven

Hare & Hounds

1 North Street, HU17 5NF

12 (4 Mon & winter Tue & Wed)-11 (1am Fri & Sat); 12-11.30 Sun

(01964) 542523

Tetley Bitter; guest beers

Standing at the village crossroads, this former coaching inn is an imposing building dating back to the early 1700s and once housed the local smithy. Comprising two rooms, the cosy front bar caters for the older generation, while younger drinkers gather in the back bar. Home to darts, dominoes and pool teams, the Sunday night quiz is also popular. Guest beers change on a fortnightly basis. Take the EYMS bus No. 240 from Hull or Hornsea. Q❀⊟▲⊟♣P⊁

Lund

Wellington Inn

19 The Green, YO25 9TE

✪ 12-3 (not Mon), 6.30-11; 12-3, 6.30-11 Sun

☎ (01377) 217294

Black Sheep Best Bitter; John Smith's Bitter; Taylor Landlord; guest beer Ⓗ

The Wellington enjoys a prime location on the green in this award-winning Wolds village. Most of its trade comes from the local farming community. It was totally renovated by the present licensee, and features stone-flagged floors, beamed ceilings and three real fires. This multi-roomed pub includes a no-smoking room, a games room and a candlelit restaurant serving evening meals, Tuesday-Saturday. Good quality food can be enjoyed at lunchtime from the bar menu and specials board. ⛼◑⊟♿♣P⊁

Old Ellerby

Blue Bell Inn

Crabtree Lane, HU11 5AJ

✪ 12-4 (not Mon-Fri), 7-11.30 (midnight Fri & Sat); 12-5, 7-11.30 Sun

☎ (01964) 562364

Black Sheep Best Bitter; Tetley Bitter; guest beers Ⓗ

The single room in this 16th-century inn has a rear games area and a snug to the right of the L-shaped bar. Tiled floors, beamed ceilings and horse brasses are features of this community-based pub that holds many fundraising events. The large garden houses a bowling green and a children's play area. EYMS Hull-Hornsea bus 230/240 runs twice daily (not Sun). It was CAMRA's East Yorkshire Pub of the Year in 1998, 2000 and 2003. ⛼Q❀▲⊟♣P

Rawcliffe

Jemmy Hirst at the Rose & Crown

26 Riverside, DN14 8RN

✪ 6 (5 Fri)-11 (midnight Sat); 12-10.30 Sun

☎ (01405) 831038 🌐 goolelink.co.uk/Pubs_and_Clubs

Taylor Landlord; guest beers Ⓗ

This pub is a gem, run by welcoming owners, their dog and loyal customers. Real ales in abundance are served here, many from local breweries. A real fire and book-lined walls invite you to stay longer. A walk along the river bank is recommended in summer to build up a thirst and there is a patio for warm evenings. After a few visits to the pub, you may find yourself considering the possibilities of moving here! ⛼❀♣P

Ryehill

Crooked Billet

Pitt Lane, HU12 9NN (400 yds off A1033, E of Thorngumbald)

✪ 11-1am (2am Fri & Sat); 12-midnight Sun

☎ (01964) 622303

Camerons Bitter; Jennings Bitter; guest beers Ⓗ

Unspoilt, 17th-century coaching inn featuring a stone-flagged floor, comfortable upholstered seating areas, horse brasses and old pictures of the pub. This two-roomed inn is a peaceful retreat. Guest beers are from Wolverhampton & Dudley's monthly list. Good quality, home-cooked food is served from Tuesday evening through to Sunday. At the heart of the local community, it supports cricket and darts teams and a Scrabble club. Regular buses run on the Hull-Withernsea route, EYMS Nos. 71, 75, 76 and 77. ⛼Q◑⊟♣P

Sancton

Star

King Street, YO43 4QP (on A1074)

✪ 12-2.30, 6.30-midnight; closed Mon; 12-2.30, 6.30-midnight Sun

☎ (01430) 827269 🌐 thestaratsancton.co.uk

Black Sheep Best Bitter; Fuller's London Pride Ⓗ

Lying south of Market Weighton, the Star was first licensed in 1710. Following a major refurbishment, it reopened in 2003 as a roadside pub and quality restaurant. Bar meals are served at lunchtime but evening meals are only available in the restaurant and booking is advised. Meals are created from high quality produce sourced locally. Further major alterations and extensions were planned for Autumn 2006 to provide wheelchair access and a guest beer and the pub plans to open every day. ❀◑⊟P⊁

Snaith

Brewers Arms

10 Pontefract Road, DN14 9JS

✪ 11-midnight; 12-11.30 Sun

☎ (01405) 862404

Old Mill Bitter, Old Curiosity, Bullion, seasonal beers Ⓗ

Just outside the centre of a small country town, this pub/hotel belongs to Old Mill Brewery and serves a full range of its beers, including seasonal offerings. The well-appointed interior is split into separate sections, including a no-smoking area. Visitors should not miss the floodlit well with its skeleton. Meals are served daily, with a Sunday carvery available 12-6pm. Snaith has a limited train service. ❀⊟◑⇌P⊁

Sutton upon Derwent

St Vincent Arms

Main Street, YO41 4BN (follow B1228 beyond Elvington)

✪ 11.30-3, 6-11; 12-3, 7-10.30 Sun

☎ (01904) 608349

Fuller's Chiswick; Old Mill Bitter; Taylor Landlord; Wells Bombardier; York Yorkshire Terrier; guest beers Ⓗ

York CAMRA's Pub of the Year 2006 is a typical whitewashed country inn, renowned for its range of Fuller's beers, including ESB direct from the barrel. Owned and run by the same family for many years, it is often busy with groups of regulars in its cosy bar. It also has a smaller bar/dining room, two further dining areas and a pleasant outside terrace. Note the large Fuller, Smith & Turner mirror. Q❀◑▲P

Walkington

Barrel Inn

35 East End, HU17 8RX
⏲ 4(12 Sat)-11; 12-10.30 Sun
☎ (01482) 868494
Thwaites Mild, Original, Thoroughbred, Lancaster Bomber, seasonal beers Ⓗ
Understated local, near the village pond, which started life as a blacksmith's and is rumoured to be haunted. The front bar features a log fire, beamed ceiling and comfortable seating. Fresh flowers and daily newspapers add to the atmosphere. One step up from the bar is the lounge, with a darts area off. Sky TV is available for all major sporting events. Children are welcome until 8pm. An hourly bus service (EYMS 180/182) runs between Beverley and Hessle. ⛫❀🚌♣▯

Wold Newton

Anvil Arms

YO25 3YL (2 miles from B1249)
⏲ 12-midnight daily
☎ (01262) 470279
John Smith's Bitter; Theakston Best Bitter; guest beer Ⓗ
Reputedly haunted, this Grade II listed building stands opposite the pond in a picturesque village on the edge of the Wolds. Sympathetically restored, it comprises a welcoming bar, games room with pool table and a restaurant that opens Friday and Saturday evenings and for Sunday lunch (booking essential). Bar snacks are also available at times. It fields darts and dominoes teams. The guest beer is likely to come from Hambleton, Daleside or Rudgate, however, local beers may also appear. ⛫Q☋❀◑▣♿♣●P⚟

YORKSHIRE (NORTH)

Appletreewick

Craven Arms

BD23 6DA (W end of village)
⏲ 11-3, 6.30-11; 11.30-11 Sat; 12-10.30 Sun
☎ (01756) 720270
Taylor Golden Best; Tetley Bitter; Wharfedale Folly Ale, Executioner, Folly Gold Ⓗ
Built in 1548 as a farm, the Craven Arms retains the original stone-flagged floor and fireplace. Recently returned to charming historical authenticity by an enthusiast, there are future plans to extend by building the first cruck barn for 500 years. The pub has close links with Wharfedale Brewery and most of its range is always on sale. The No. 74 Ilkley-Grassington bus serves the pub except Sunday. ⛫Q❀◑⛺🚌P⚟

New Inn

BD23 6DA (W end of village)
⏲ 12-3 (not Mon; 12-3.45 Sat), 7-11; 12-3, 7-10.30 Sun
☎ (01756) 720252
Daleside Bitter; John Smith's Bitter; Theakston Old Peculier Ⓗ
Small, friendly, unspoilt village local, which has featured in this Guide since 1988. It stocks a large range of bottled beers from around the world. Benefitting from fine views of the surrounding fells, walkers and cyclists are welcome; the Dales Way long distance footpath and the Dales cycle way pass close by and cyclists can make use of the pub's cycle livery for any maintenance. The No. 74 Ilkley-Grassington bus passes (not Sun). ⛫☋❀🛏◑⛺🚌P

Beck Hole

Birch Hall Inn ☆

YO22 5LE (1 mile NW of Goathland) OS823022
⏲ 11-3, 7.30-11 (not Mon eve); 11-11 May-Aug; 11-11 Sun
☎ (01947) 896245 🌐 beckholeweb.plus.com
Black Sheep Best Bitter; guest beers Ⓗ
Tiny gem of a pub, once the provisions store for the local ironstone industry, the Birch Hall was granted a licence in 1860 and has had just three licensees in the past 80 years. The store lives on as a sweet shop, sandwiched between the two bars, which serve one or two guest beers, often from local breweries, in additon to the regular Black Sheep. The website is worth visiting and includes a virtual pub tour with extensive historical notes. ⛫Q❀🛏▣⛺

Beckwithshaw

Smith's Arms

Church Row, HG3 1QW (on B6161)
⏲ 11-11; 12-10.30 Sun
☎ (01423) 504871
Courage Directors; Theakston Best Bitter; guest beer Ⓗ
Spacious and welcoming stone-built inn dating from the 19th century. Part of the pub used to be the village smithy. At the centre of its local community, the pub is also popular with visitors to this attractive area close to Harrogate. It enjoys a good reputation for the quality of its food. The guest beer is often from the local Daleside Brewery. ⛫Q❀◑♿P

Bedale

Three Coopers

2 Emgate, DL8 1AH (off High St)
⏲ 12-midnight (1am Fri & Sat); 12-midnight Sun
☎ (01677) 422153
Jennings Bitter, Cumberland Ale; Marston's Burton Bitter; guest beers Ⓗ
Easily accessible from the Wensleydale Railway station, this deceptively large market town pub is split into three main drinking areas on several levels. Famed for its Wednesday steak nights (booking essential), this lively pub serves a good range of Wolverhampton & Dudley beers. The decor is simple, with wooden floors and bare brickwork. ⛫❀◑⇌(Wensleydale Rlwy)🚌♣

Bellerby

Cross Keys

DL8 5QS (1 mile from Leyburn on A6108 Richmond road)
⏲ 11-3, 6-11; 11-11 Fri & Sat; 12-10.30 Sun
☎ (01969) 622256
John Smith's Bitter; Theakston Best Bitter; guest beers Ⓗ

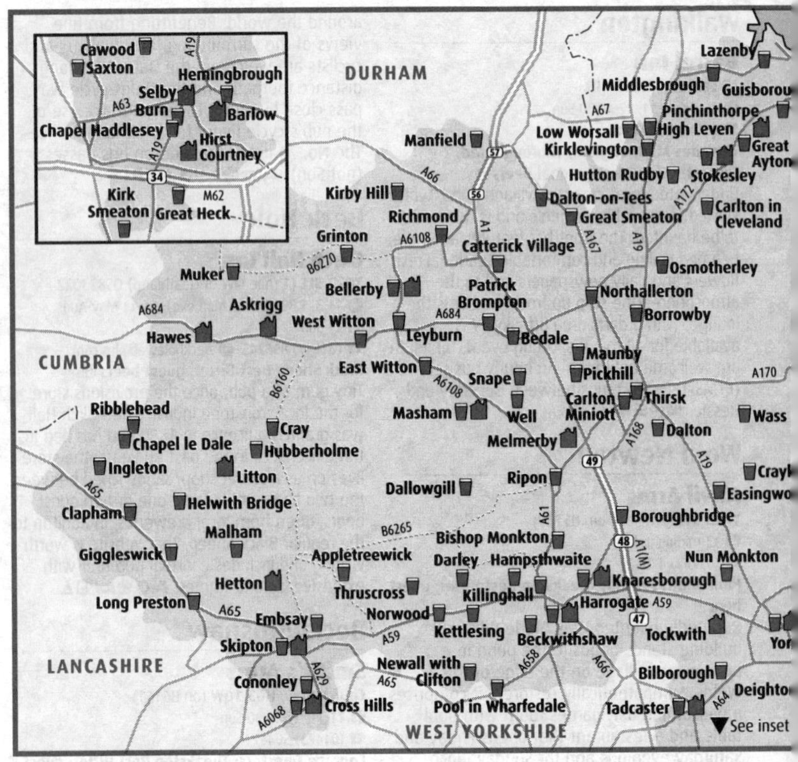

Lively village pub, well supported by locals and enjoying a good passing trade. The L-shaped bar is warmed by an open fire. Guest ales change frequently and now usually include a Wensleydale beer since the brewery relocated into the village. The pub hosts regular quizzes and games evenings. Families are welcome. ⌂☺❀◐♿♣P

This cosy, country pub is the centre of activity for the village. It supports many local clubs and societies and is an active fundraiser for the cricket team. Its two rooms are filled with unusual brasses. The May bank holiday hog roast takes place by the nearby stream that is also the scene of the August bank holiday plastic duck race. ⌂Q☺⇌◐▲⊟♣P

Bilbrough

Three Hares

Main Street, YO23 3PH (off A64, York-Leeds road)

⊕ 11-midnight; 11-11 Sun

☎ (01937) 832128 ⊕ thethreehares.co.uk

Black Sheep Best Bitter; John Smith's Bitter; Taylor Landlord; guest beers Ⓗ

Four miles west of York in a quiet village just off the main road, this attractive, white-painted pub was once the village forge. The smart interior is divided into several sections, one of which is a restaurant. Although the emphasis is on high quality meals, the management is keen to cater to drinkers, maintaining a distinct bar area that acts as the village local. Access from the car park in a lane behind the pub is via a heated outdoor terrace. Q❀◐⊟♣P

Bishop Monkton

Lamb & Flag

Boroughbridge Road, HG4 3QN (off A61)

⊕ 12-2 (not Mon), 5.30-11; 12-3, 7-10.30 Sun

☎ (01765) 677332

Daleside Bitter; Tetley Bitter; guest beer (summer) Ⓗ

Boroughbridge

Black Bull Inn

6 St James Square, YO51 9AR

⊕ 11-11 (midnight Fri & Sat); 12-10.30 Sun

☎ (01423) 322413

John Smith's Bitter; Theakston Black Bull Bitter; guest beer Ⓗ

Situated in the main square, this 13th-century, Grade II listed inn is extremely popular. One of the three drinking areas is designated no smoking; the beers are good value. The restaurant has been restored to its former glory, thanks to a complete refurbishment after suffering serious fire damage. Even the resident ghost is reported to have moved back in. An international menu is supplemented by a good choice of bar meals. This little gem is well worth a visit; limited parking. ⌂Q⇌◐▲♣P⚡

Borrowby

Wheatsheaf

YO7 4QP (1 mile off A19, trunk route)

⊕ 12-2.30 (not Mon-Fri), 5.30 (6 Sat)-11; closed Tue; 12-11 summer Sat; 12-4, 7-10.30 Sun

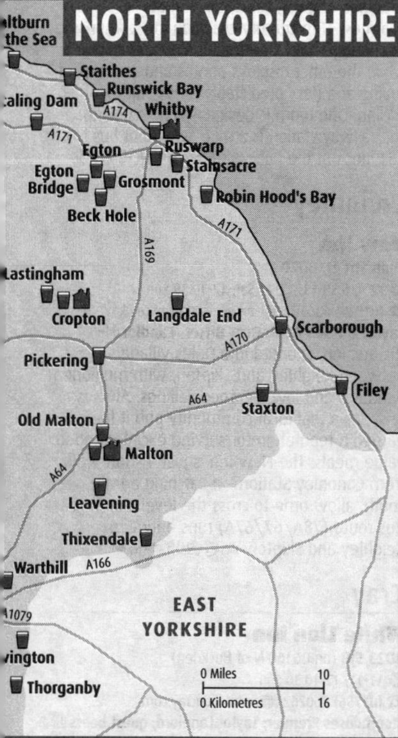

☎ (01845) 537274 🌐 borrowbypub.co.uk

Daleside Bitter; Tetley Bitter; guest beers Ⓗ

Small, and attractive 17th-century village inn, handy for the A19. The public bar features an imposing stone fireplace, low beams and a flagged floor. The addition of a new drinking area to the rear of the bar does not detract from the traditional feel. One or two guest ales are always available. Evening meals are served Wednesday-Saturday in the no-smoking dining room.

Burn

Wheatsheaf

Main Road, YO8 8LJ (on A19, 3 miles S of Selby)

12-11 daily

☎ (01757) 270614 🌐 selbynet.co.uk/wheatsheaf.html

John Smith's Bitter; Taylor Landlord; guest beers Ⓗ

Change of ownership in 2005 has not detracted from the popularity of this roadside inn. It stocks at least three reasonably priced guest beers, often from the nearby Brown Cow Brewery. Wholesome, home-cooked food is served, too (eve meals Thu-Sat). The narrow bar entrance, boasting a collection of bottled beers on a plate rack, opens into a lounge dominated by an enormous fireplace and decorated with agricultural and aeronautical memorabilia (Burn was a bomber aerodrome in WWII).

Carlton-in-Cleveland

Blackwell Ox

Main Street, TS9 7NU

11.30-11; 12-10.30 Sun

☎ (01642) 712287 🌐 theblackwellox.co.uk

Black Sheep Best Bitter; Worthington's Bitter; guest beers Ⓗ

Impressive village pub with a public bar and smaller rooms off. A wide range of food is served 12-2pm and 5.30-9pm, with Thai cuisine featuring strongly. The changing range of guest beer often includes micro-breweries' products. To the rear, the garden houses a camping and caravan site. The pub is cool in summer and warmed by open fires in winter.

Carlton Miniott

Dog & Gun

YO7 4NJ (on A61 to Ripon, 1 mile W of Thirsk Station)

12-3, 5.30-11.30; 12-11.30 Sat; 12-10.30 Sun

☎ (01845) 522150

Caledonian Deuchars IPA; John Smith's Bitter; Theakston Best Bitter; guest beers Ⓗ

Traditional pub with a large, comfortable main bar, a huge conservatory and a small bar housing a pool table. Restaurant and bar meals are served throughout. An attractive garden to the rear adjoins the pub's large car park and leads to a space for camping and visiting caravans. In the main bar, see the display of 'vintage' photos of locals – to qualify to appear in this gallery, the contender must be a native of and resident in the village.

Catterick Village

Bay Horse

38 Low Green, DL10 7LP (off main street)

12-midnight; 12-11.30 Sun

☎ (01748) 811383

Jennings Bitter, Cumberland Ale, Cocker Hoop; guest beers Ⓗ

Established village local facing the picturesque green and beck, just off the main through road and convenient for the A1 trunk route

INDEPENDENT BREWERIES

Abbey Bells Hirst Courtney
Black Dog Whitby
Black Sheep Masham
Brown Cow Barlow
Captain Cook Stokesley
Copper Dragon Skipton
Cropton Cropton
Daleside Harrogate
Hambleton Melmerby
Litton Litton
Malton Malton (brewing suspended)
Marston Moor Tockwith
Moorcock Hawes
Naylor's Cross Hills
North Yorkshire Pinchinthorpe
Rooster's Knaresborough
Rudgate Tockwith
Selby Selby
Samuel Smith Tadcaster
Theakston Masham
Wensleydale Bellerby
Wharfedale Hetton
York York
Yorkshire Dales Askrigg

and racecourse. With a largely open-plan, comfortable interior, this busy, friendly pub demonstrates a strong commitment to beer quality. Guest ales come from the Wolverhampton & Dudley range. Daytime buses serve the village. Q☎❀◐◑⊟♣P⊬⊓

Cawood

Ferry Inn

2 King Street, YO8 3TL (S side of river, near swing bridge)
⏲ 12-midnight (11 Mon-Wed); 12-11 Sun
☎ (01757) 268515
Caledonian Deuchars IPA; Taylor Landlord; Theakston Best Bitter; guest beers Ⓗ
Low ceilings, an inglenook, open fires and a terraced garden overlooking the river all combine to make this a popular overnight stop for visitors to York. The main bar has record of Cawood's connections with Cardinal Wolsey as Archbishop of York, as well as the great feast of 1464. This privately-owned village inn now serves good value food every day and opens early in the morning at the weekend. ⩩Q❀⇔◐◑Å⊟P⊬

Chapel Haddlesey

Jug Inn

Main Street, YO8 8QQ
(on A19, 5 miles N of M62 jct 34)
⏲ 5.30 (12 summer Sat)-11; closed Mon; 12-10.30 Sun
☎ (01757) 270307 🌐 thejuginn.co.uk
Beer range varies Ⓗ
This 300-year-old village pub is popular for its variety of beers and fresh, home-made food, based on local produce. A small central bar serves both the low-ceilinged lounge, where a collection of jugs hangs from the beams, and the public bar; both are warmed by open fires. A snug with easy chairs and a large garden backing up to the River Aire are added attractions. Privately owned, the Jug is well worth seeking out. ⩩Q❀◐◑⊞♿⊟♣P⊬

Chapel-le-Dale

Hill Inn

LA6 3AR (on B6255)
⏲ 12-3, 6-11; 12-11 Sat; closed Mon; 12-10.30 Sun
☎ (01524) 241256
Black Sheep Best Bitter; Dent Bitter, Aviator Ⓗ
Beloved of generations of hikers and potholers: well-worn paths run from here to both Whernside (Yorkshire's highest peak) and Ingleborough (its best known). It is also a destination for diners (booking advisable); puddings are a speciality here. Lots of exposed wood features in the bar, and some stonework. It hosts a monthly folk evening (last Fri). The nearest public transport is at Ribblehead Station (two miles). Note: the pub may be closed if there are no customers or bookings. ⩩Q❀◐◑ÅP

Clapham

New Inn

LA2 0HH
⏲ 11-11 daily
☎ (01524) 251203 🌐 newinn-clapham.co.uk
Copper Dragon Golden Pippin, Scotts 1816; Thwaites Original, Lancaster Bomber Ⓗ
Spacious, 18th-century coaching inn, comprising two lounge bars. One features oak panelling, while the other displays photos and cartoons of caving and (less predictably for the area) cycling. One room is designated no smoking. The railway station is a mile away, but bus No. 581 stops at the pub. ⩩❀⇔◐◑⊞Å⊟♣P⊬

Cononley

New Inn

Main Street, BD20 8NR
⏲ 12-3, 5.30-11; 12-11 Sat; 12-10.30 Sun
☎ (01535) 636302 🌐 newinncononley.co.uk
Taylor Golden Best, Best Bitter, Landlord Ⓗ
Historic inn, situated in a Dales village between Keighley and Skipton, with mullioned windows and low, beamed ceilings. Always busy, as a real local community pub it has earned a reputation for serving excellent good value meals. The New Inn is just a short walk from Cononley Station – if catching a train south, allow time to cross the level crossing. Bus route (78A/67/67A) runs between Keighley and Skipton. ⩩Q❀◐◑⇌⊟♣

Cray

White Lion Inn

BD23 5JB (on B6160 N of Buckden)
⏲ 11-11; 12-10.30 Sun
☎ (01756) 760262 🌐 whitelioncray.com
Moorhouses Premier; Taylor Landlord; guest beers Ⓗ
This traditional Dales inn boasts stone-flagged floors, an open fire and welcoming atmosphere. Popular with walkers, cyclists and anyone exploring the countryside, the accommodation provides an excellent base for those who enjoy the outdoors. The bar is situated in the main drinking area with raised seating at the back; there is a no-smoking room to the left. Copper Dragon beers feature regularly here. ⩩Q❀⇔◐◑Å⊟♣P⊬

Crayke

Durham Ox

West Way, YO61 4TE OS562474
⏲ 11-3, 6-11; 11-10.30 Sun
☎ (01347) 821506 🌐 thedurhamox.com
Beer range varies Ⓗ
This enterprising free house adopted its guest ale policy after a successful village beer festival. The comfortable interior includes a large dining area with stone-flagged floor, a huge open fire and panelling copied from 14th-century pew ends. The bar features stripped floorboards, another fireplace and a picture of the original Durham ox – an animal renowned for its exceptional size. High quality meals make use of local produce; a private dining room is available for parties. ⩩Q❀⇔Q◐◑⊞♿P

Cropton

New Inn

Woolcroft, YO18 8HH (5 miles off A170, Pickering-Kirkby Moorside road)
⏲ 11-11; 12-10.30 Sun
☎ (01751) 417330 🌐 croptonbrewery.co.uk

Cropton Endeavour, Two Pints, Yorkshire Moors, Monkmans Slaughter, seasonal beers; guest beers H
Charming old country inn on the edge of the North Yorkshire Moors national park. It enjoys strong local support and is welcoming to visitors, old and new. A good base for walkers, cyclists and horse riders, with good value accommodation, it is convenient for access to the North Yorkshire Moors Railway and the many attractions of Whitby, York and an abundance of other locations. Cropton Brewery, in the grounds, supplies most of the pub's ales; guided tours are available. Q P

Cross Hills

Old White Bear

6 Keighley Road, BD20 7RN (on A6068, near A629 jct)
11.30-11; 12-10.30 Sun
(01535) 632115
http://sleekweb.co.uk/Naylors/OWB.html
Naylors Sparkey's Mild, Mother's Best, seasonal beers H
Constructed in 1735, the building has served various purposes over the years as a hotel, brothel, council meeting room and dance hall, before becoming the pub it is today. It is partly no smoking. Children (and dogs) are welcome provided they are well behaved. A recent local CAMRA Pub of the Season award winner, as home to Naylor's Brewery it provides a showcase for its beers. Listed in CAMRA's Good Cider Guide, it is a good bet for handpulled cider and perry. Q P

Dallowgill

Drovers Inn

HG4 3RH (2 miles W of Laverton on road to Pateley Bridge) OS210720
12-3 (summer only), 7-11; closed Mon; 12-3, 6.30-11 Sat; 12-3, 6-10.30 Sun
(01765) 658510
Black Sheep Best Bitter; Hambleton Bitter; Old Mill Mild or Bitter H
This small, one-roomed pub out on the moors above Laverton has a tiny bar that manages always to offer three well-kept beers. Although most of the customers come from the surrounding area, walkers and visitors are made most welcome, and good food is served until 8.30pm. The opening times may often be extended as the pub has been granted a 24-hour licence. Tables are provided in the car park for outdoor drinking. Q P

Dalton

Moor & Pheasant

Dalton Moor, YO7 3JD
12-11 (midnight Mon; 2am Fri & Sat); 10-midnight Sun
(01845) 577268
John Smith's Bitter; guest beer H
This pub lies on the southern outskirts of the village, five miles south of Thirsk. A front bar with a pool table, darts area and french windows to the garden shares a servery with the lounge, which doubles as a dining area. Both rooms have an open fire. Good value meals are available (not Sun eve); discounts are offered to older people. Outside is a large play area for children and a private static caravan site. P

Dalton-on-Tees

Chequers Inn

DL2 2NT
12-3, 5.30-11; 12-10.30 Sun
(01325) 721213 chequers-dalton.co.uk
Banks's Bitter; guest beers H
Traditional inn dating back to the 1840s, consisting of a bar, lounge and restaurant, where a warm welcome is always guaranteed. Formerly known as the Crown and Anchor, this was once part of the now-defunct Fryer's Brewery estate. The landlord is passionate about real ale and at least two guest beers are sourced from micros countrywide. Regular gourmet evenings take place and a quiz is held every Wednesday. Q P

Danby

Duke of Wellington

2 West Lane, YO21 2LY OS708687
12-3 (not Mon), 7-11; 12-11 Fri & Sat; 12-3, 7-10.30 Sun
01287) 660351 danby-dukeofwellington.co.uk
Tetley Imperial, Daleside Bitter; guest beer H
Dating back to 1765, this inn at the heart of the North Yorkshire Moors has expanded over the centuries to encompass what was originally a row of cottages overlooking the village green. The timber-beamed bars and open fire create a warm and friendly atmosphere in which to eat, drink and relax. Used as a recruiting post during the Napoleonic War, there is a cast iron plaque of the Duke, unearthed during restoration, above the fireplace. Q

Darley

Wellington

HG3 2QQ (on B6451 near Harrogate)
11.30-11; 12-10.30 Sun
(01423) 780363
Black Sheep Best Bitter; Taylor Landlord; Tetley Bitter; guest beer H
Spacious, stone roadside inn, some 200 years old, nestling in a picturesque valley on the edge of the Yorkshire Dales. An ancient kitchen range, revealed during some alterations, has been restored to its former glory. Note, too, the Buffalo Bill memorabilia on the walls. On a bus route, the pub makes a good starting point for walking or cycling in the Dales, and has a good restaurant. Q P

Deighton

White Swan

YO19 6HA (on A19, 5 miles S of York)
11.30-2.30, 6.30-11; 11-11 Sat; 12-10.30 Sun
(01904) 728287
Banks's Bitter, Mansfield Cask; Marston's Pedigree; guest beer H
Now a focal point for residents of the nearby village, but once a drovers' inn on the road from Selby to York, the field opposite the pub is still known as the pinfold. No-smoking throughout, meals are served in the dining

areas of the front bar as well as the lounge/dining room. A comprehensive, good value menu is supplemented by a daily board and children's dishes. The tenant prepares the meals himself from fresh, local produce. Q❀◑⊟♣P⊁

Easingwold

George at Easingwold

Market Place, YO61 3AD

⊙ 11-2.30, 5-11; 12-2.30, 5-10.30 Sun

☎ (01347) 821698 ⊕ the-george-hotel.co.uk

Black Sheep Best Bitter; Moorhouses Pride of Pendle; Tetley Bitter; guest beers ⊞

The George occupies a prime position on Easingwold's cobbled market square, close to the market cross. Its origins date from the 18th century and the coaching trade. Today it is a comfortable country inn offering a full range of meals and well-equipped accommodation. The central bar serves various cosy rooms and drinking areas, popular as meeting places for visitors and locals alike. A rejuvenated beer range reflects the landlord's interest in matters Lancastrian. ᗑQ❀⇔◑♿⊟P⊁

East Witton

Cover Bridge Inn

DL8 4SQ (½ mile N of village on A6108, near Leyburn)

⊙ 11-midnight; 12-11.30 Sun

☎ (01969) 623250 ⊕ thecoverbridgeinn.co.uk

Black Sheep Best Bitter; John Smith's Bitter; Taylor Landlord; Theakston Best Bitter, Old Peculier; guest beers ⊞

Outstanding country inn at the point where the Rivers Ure and Cover meet. A CAMRA multi-award winner, it resembles a mini beer exhibition, with nine cask ales usually stocked. Fathom out the door latch (and mind your head) to enter the ancient public bar, with its splendid hearth and flagged floor. A tiny lounge leads out to a pleasant riverside garden with a play area. An enviable reputation for food makes it popular with diners. The bus service is infrequent. ᗑQᗢ❀⇔◑⊟Ă⊟♣P⊡

Egton

Horseshoe

YO21 1TZ

⊙ 11-3, 6-midnight daily (may close early in winter)

☎ (01947) 895274 ⊕ yehorseshoe.co.uk

John Smith's Bitter; Taylor Landlord; Tetley Bitter; Theakston Black Bull Bitter ⊞

Village-centre free house; the single L-shaped bar has a coal fire at each end, while traditional brasses and matchboxes decorate the beams. Old treadle sewing machines serve as tables. Originally known as the Horse Shoe Inn and Farm, it was sold by auction in 1864 (the lot included a roan cow in calf); some of the old farm buildings still remain. En-suite accommodation is provided and residents have use of a private lounge. The sheltered garden is a bonus. ᗑ❀⇔◑Ă⇌♣P

Wheatsheaf Inn

YO21 2TZ

⊙ 11-3 (not Mon), 5.30-11; 11.30-11 Sat; 12-10.30 Sun

☎ (01947) 895271

Black Sheep Best Bitter; Caledonian Deuchars IPA; guest beer ⊞

Grade I listed pub at the village centre. Church pew-style seats occupy the bar area, while the lounge bar bears a fishing theme, with numerous fly rods attached to the beams. The main bar and no-smoking dining room are warmed by coal fires, while a large grassed area to the front is ideal in warmer weather. Seasonal, local produce is the basis for the recommended menu. Popular with anglers, walkers and for special meals, the pub has four en-suite guest rooms. ᗑ❀⇔◑⊟Ă⇌P⊁

Egton Bridge

Horseshoe Hotel

YO21 1XE (down hill from Egton Station, over bridge)

⊙ 11.30-3, 6.30-11; 12-3, 7-10.30 Sun

☎ (01947) 895245

John Smith's Bitter; Theakston Black Bull Bitter; guest beers ⊞

Hidden away, this gem is popular with locals and visitors alike. The single bar, that gives access to a second room for non-smokers and children, is furnished with old settles. A large, raised grass area at the front is used for outdoor dining in summer, but there is also a restaurant. Easily reached from the station via the road or stepping stones across the Esk, it is a good start or finish point for walks on the moors or in the Esk Valley. ᗑQᗢ❀⇔◑Ă⇌P⊁

Elvington

Grey Horse

Main Street, YO41 4AG

(on B1228 6 miles SE of York)

⊙ 12-2.30 (not Mon or Tue), 5-11; 12-midnight Fri-Sat; 12-11 Sun

☎ (01904) 608335 ⊕ elvington.net/pub

Black Sheep Best Bitter; John Smith's Bitter; Taylor Landlord; guest beers ⊞

Situated opposite the village green, the pub's two rooms are served from a central bar. In summer outdoor seating is provided at the front and in the yard. The lounge displays photographs of the WWII bombers that used to fly from the nearby airfield, now the Yorkshire Air Museum. Guest beers change regularly and an excellent menu is served (no eve meals Mon or Tue). The pub fields darts and golf teams and Thursday is quiz night. ᗑQ❀⇔◑⊟♿Ă⊟♣P⊁

Embsay

Elm Tree Inn

5 Elm Tree Square, BD23 6RB

⊙ 11.30-3, 5.30-11; 12-3, 7-10.30 Sun

☎ (01756) 790717

Black Sheep Best Bitter; Goose Eye No-Eye Deer; Wells Bombardier; guest beers ⊞

Former coaching inn situated in the village square. Inside it has an open feel with oak beams and horse brasses. The large main bar is supplemented by a smaller no-smoking side room mainly used by diners. It always stocks at least one dark beer – usually a mild. Look for the worn mounting steps outside. Well situated for walking on the edge of the Yorkshire Dales National Park; Embsay and Bolton Abbey steam railway line is nearby. ❀⇄◑♿⇌🚌P⚡

Filey

Bonhommes Bar

Royal Crescent Court, The Crescent, YO14 9JH

⊙ 11-11; 12-10.30 Sun

☎ (01723) 512034

Caledonian Deuchars IPA; John Smith's Bitter; guest beers 🄷

The bar lies just off the fine Victorian Royal Crescent Hotel complex. From the 1950s it was known as the American Bar. The present name celebrates John Paul Jones, father of the American navy. His ship, the Bonhomme Richard, was involved in a battle off nearby Flamborough Head during the War of Independence. Live music is provided most Friday evenings, quizzes on Tuesday and Sunday evenings and an afternoon fun quiz on Saturday. ⇌♣

Giggleswick

Hart's Head Hotel

Belle Hill, BD24 0BA (from Settle take B6480 for 1/2 mile N towards Kirkby Lonsdale)

⊙ 12-2.30 (not Thu), 5.30-11; 11-11 Sat; 12-10.30 Sun

☎ (01729) 822086 🌐 hartsheadhotel.co.uk

Copper Dragon Scotts 1816; Tetley Bitter; guest beers 🄷

Welcoming, 18th-century coaching inn, now established as a regular entry in this Guide. The open-plan bar retains a multi-room feel with some comfortable sofas. As well as the excellent range of up to six cask beers on offer, mostly from local breweries, food features highly at this hostelry, as can be seen from the enormous blackboard menu at the entrance to the dining area. The refurbished cellar houses a full-sized snooker table. ⛫Q❀⇄◑🛏🚌♣P⚡

Great Ayton

Whinstone View

TS9 6QG (on B1292 1/2 mile from Great Ayton)

⊙ 12-9 (9.30 Sat); closed Mon; 12-4 Sun

☎ (01642) 723285 🌐 whinstoneview.com

Beer range varies 🄷

This bistro and pub is set in its own grounds on the edge of the North York moors. Beautiful and peaceful, the spacious, open-plan interior features much wood and other natural materials. A large veranda at the front overlooks the grounds and an adjacent caravan park. The Whinstone View enjoys a good reputation for meals and the seating is geared up for this. There are conference facilities upstairs. ⛫Q❀◑♿P⚡

Great Heck

Bay Horse

Main Street, DN14 0BQ (follow signs from A19)

⊙ 12-2, 5-11 (midnight Fri); 12-midnight Sat; 12-10.30 Sun

☎ (01977) 661125

Old Mill Bitter 🄷

An outlet for the local Old Mill Brewery, with a second beer usually available, the pub was converted from cottages. It is surprisingly light and bright but retains some old features, such as exposed beams and rails that are adorned with pottery and brassware. Although open-plan, it has retained three distinct areas; the raised restaurant offers an extensive menu (served all day until 8 or 9pm Sat and Sun). A patio at the rear is ideal for warm weather. ⛫❀◑P⚡

Great Smeaton

Bay Horse

Church View, DL6 2EH (on A167)

⊙ 12-3 (not Mon or Tue, 5 (5.30 Mon & Tue)-midnight; 12-midnight Sat; 12-10.30 Sun

☎ (01609) 881466

Black Sheep Best Bitter; John Smith's Bitter; Theakston XB; guest beers 🄷

Small, 18th-century free house, set in the middle of a row of roadside cottages in an atttractive village. Comprising a beamed lounge with a central fireplace, a bustling bar and a games room to the rear, it enjoys an excellent reputation for home-cooked food (no eve meals Mon). Up to two guest beers are sourced from micro-breweries countrywide. This former local CAMRA Rural Pub of the Year benefits from an enclosed garden with a small play area. ⛫Q❀◑♣⚡🗑

Grinton

Bridge Inn

DL11 6HH (on B6270 1 mile E of Reeth)

⊙ 12-midnight (1am Fri & Sat); 12-11 Sun

☎ (01748) 884224 🌐 bridgeinngrinton.co.uk

Jennings Cumberland Ale, Cocker Hoop; guest beers 🄷

Surrounded by magnificent Swaledale scenery and nestling beneath Fremington Edge, this country inn is understandably popular with ramblers and other visitors. Inside there is something for everyone: a comfortable hotel lounge and dining room, a central lounge and, on a lower level, a public bar and games room. Food is one of its strengths and the Bridge offers three guest beers from the Wolverhampton & Dudley range. There is a youth hostel a short walk away. ⛫Q☕❀⇄◑🛏⛺♣P

Grosmont

Crossing Club

Front Street, YO22 5QE (next to Co-op, 200 yds from station)

⊙ 8-11 daily

☎ (01947) 895040

Archers Village; guest beers (summer) 🄷

Interesting conversion completed by volunteers of the old Co-op delivery bay to a bar full of railway memorabilia, including an old crossing gate. Access is gained through a glass door (ring the bell). Well-behaved children and pets are welcome. Members demonstrate pride in their club through the hospitality they offer. In summer it stocks a further three guest beers and opens for special steam events outside the posted opening times. Q❀⛺⇌♣

Guisborough

Cross Keys Inn

Middlesbrough Road, TS14 6RW (on A171 Nunthorpe road)

⏲ 11-11; 12-10.30 Sun

☎ (01287) 610035

North Yorkshire Prior's Ale, Ruby Ale; guest beers Ⓗ

Originally a farmhouse selling refreshments to passing coachmen, it was converted to an inn during the 1820s, with the construction of the Middlesbrough and Guisborough railway. It became a Chef & Brewer establishment in 2002. The inn is divided into family and adult areas, using wood panelling and lintels, creating semi-secluded spaces for dining and drinking; salvaged pine furniture enhances the effect. Up to eight ales are stocked in summer – try a free tasting. Game and fish are specialities. ♨❀⇔◐◑♿P⚟

Globe

81 Northgate, TS14 6JP (opp. general hospital)

⏲ 4 (2 Thu & Fri; 12 Sat)-midnight; 12-11.30 Sun

☎ (01287) 280799

Camerons Strongarm; guest beers Ⓗ

Old-fashioned community local, originally the first hotel in Guisborough, with railway connections. The bar features brasses and red leather upholstered furniture. A lounge/function room hosts entertainment throughout the week: bankhouse country & western (Mon), jazz night (Wed) and folk club (Fri). The large, rear yard doubles as a car park or garden. It supports local darts and dominoes teams; games played include shove-ha'penny, bar skittles and bagatelle. Snacks, tea and coffee are available all day. Q❀⊟♿♣P

Hampsthwaite

Joiners Arms

High Street, HG3 2EU (off A59)

⏲ 11.30-2.30, 5.30-11; 12-10.30 Sun

☎ (01423) 771673

Rudgate Viking; Tetley Bitter Ⓗ

Close to the A59 and Nidderdale Way, the lounge and tap room of this 200-year-old pub are connected by an unusual snug that was once the cellar and retains its original stone floor and vaulted ceiling. The no-smoking dining room displays a rare collection of gravy boats. Evening meals are served Wednesday-Saturday. Q◐◑⊟⊞P

Harrogate

Coach & Horses

16 West Park, HG1 1BJ (opp. The Stray)

⏲ 11-11; 12-10.30 Sun

Daleside Bitter, Blonde; Taylor Landlord; Tetley Bitter; guest beers Ⓗ

A central bar serves two guest beers from Yorkshire breweries. The pub is popular and maintains a friendly atmosphere with seating arranged into snugs and alcoves. The food is good: a curry night is held every Wednesday, while Tuesday is 'championship pie and peas' night, with the profits going to local charities. A well-attended quiz is held on Sunday evening. ◐⇌⊞⚟

Old Bell Tavern

6 Royal Parade, HG1 2SZ

⏲ 12-11; 12-10.30 Sun

☎ (01423) 507930

Black Sheep Best Bitter; Caledonian Deuchars IPA; Taylor Landlord; guest beers Ⓗ

Four changing guest beers, four regulars, including a Rooster's brew, and three continental draught beers are supplemented by an extensive range of foreign bottled beers. Dating back to 1846, the inn was expanded by extending into an old Farrah's toffee shop – see the memorabilia. Top quality food is available daily in the bar area, and a restaurant upstairs opens evenings (ring for times). The pub is no-smoking throughout. Q◐◑⇌⊞⚟

Tap & Spile

Tower Street , HG1 1HS (off West Park, opp. multi-storey car park)

⏲ 11.30-11 (flexible); 12-10.30 Sun

☎ (01423) 526785

Fuller's London Pride; Rooster's Yankee; Theakston Old Peculier Ⓗ

Well-established, quality ale house. A central bar links the three drinking areas, one of which is no-smoking. A mix of wood panelling and bare brick walls is used to display many old photographs of Harrogate. Popular with all ages, the pub stages folk sessions on Tuesday and rock on Thursday. A quiz is held on Monday evening and darts played alternate Tuesdays. Basic lunches are served Monday-Saturday. The cider is Westons Old Rosie. Some outdoor seating is provided. ❀◐⇌⊞♣●⚟

Winter Gardens

4 Royal Baths, HG1 2WH

⏲ 9am-midnight (1am Fri & Sat); 9am-midnight Sun

☎ (01423) 887010

Courage Directors; Greene King Abbot; Marston's Bitter, Pedigree; Theakston Best Bitter; guest beers Ⓗ

Magnificent Victorian building, impressively converted while retaining all its original grandeur, with modern additions that compliment the style. Five guest beers change often to provide excellent choice at reasonable prices. Food and beer are served from opening. Family friendly, the pub has an outdoor drinking area and baby changing facilities; children are welcome until 9pm. Q☋❀◐◑♿⇌⊞⚟

Woodlands

110 Wetherby Road, HG2 7AB (on A661, near Harrogate Town FC)

⏲ 11-11 (midnight Tue, Fri & Sat); 12-10.30 Sun

☎ (01423) 883396

John Smith's Bitter; Webster's Green Label; guest beer Ⓗ

Although first established in 1823 as a coaching inn, this pub has a modern feel. The layout is spacious: open plan with a bar down one side. The main entrance, which has wheelchair access, leads into a comfortable lounge area that doubles as a restaurant on Sunday lunchtime until 4pm. At the opposite end is a pool table and Sky TV. ❀◐♿♣P

Helwith Bridge

Helwith Bridge

BD24 0EH (off B6479, across the river)
⏲ 11-midnight; 12-midnight Sun
☎ (01729) 860220 🌐 helwithbridge.com
Greene King Old Speckled Hen; McEwan's 80/-; Webster's Bitter; Wells Bombardier; guest beers Ⓗ
Friendly, characterful, stone-flagged community pub. Backing onto the River Ribble and overlooking the Settle-Carlisle railway line, it affords good views of Pen-y-Ghent (one of the Three Peaks). The landlord's interests are reflected in the numerous paintings, photographs and railway memorabilia. A roaring fire in the main bar is guaranteed in winter. Guest beers are mainly from the Scottish Courage list. The pub is popular with members of a local caving club who meet regularly at their hostel nearby. ⛰Q❀◐◑▲🚌♣🍎P

Hemingbrough

Crown

Main Street, YO8 6QE (off A63, E of Selby)
⏲ 3 (12 Fri & Sat)-11; 12-10.30 Sun
☎ (01757) 638434 🌐 thecrowninn.net
Caledonian Deuchars IPA; John Smith's Bitter; guest beer Ⓗ
At the heart of the village, under the shadow of the elegant church spire, this is an unpretentious community pub that caters for local people. A central bar serves two rooms – the front room plays host to many sports teams, especially active darts enthusiasts. The rear room is used by families at the weekend and diners in the evenings (not Mon) when fresh local ingredients are prominent. Lunches are also served in summer. On Thursday evening the quiz draws a crowd. ❀◐◑🚌♣P

High Leven

Fox Covert

TS15 9JW
⏲ 12-11.30 (midnight Sat); 12-11 Sun
☎ (01642) 760033
Caledonian Deuchars IPA; Theakston Old Peculier Ⓗ
Long established as an inn, this old building of traditional longhouse style is easily recognisable as the farmhouse it once was. Whitewashed and nestling under a pantiled roof, it could be a pub in any village, but nearby Ingleby Barwick, which sounds like a village name, is in fact the largest housing estate in Europe. Run by the same family for many years, the pub has a strong food emphasis, with meals served all day, but the ales are also superbly kept. ⛰◐◑P⚡

Hubberholme

George Inn

Kirk Gill, BD23 5JE (1 mile NW of Buckden, off B6160) OS926782
⏲ 12-3, 6-11; closed Mon; 12-3, 6-11 Sun
☎ (01756) 760223 🌐 thegeorge-inn.co.uk
Black Sheep Special; Copper Dragon Scotts 1816; guest beer (occasional) Ⓗ
Sitting snugly alongside a river, this hamlet was named after a Viking chieftain called Hubba. This remote and unspoilt 18th-century inn was reputedly the author JB Priestley's favourite watering-hole. It boasts two rooms of genuine character with heavy oak beams and walls stripped back to the bare stone and hung with antique plates and photos. An open stove in a big fireplace welcomes visitors to the stone-flagged bar. Wholesome bar food is available at reasonable prices.
⛰Q❀🛏◐◑P

Hutton Rudby

King's Head

36 North Side, TS15 0DA
⏲ 12-11 (midnight Fri & Sat); 12-11 Sun
☎ (01642) 700342
Camerons Strongarm; Mansfield Cask; guest beer Ⓗ
Old-fashioned pub set in a pretty, historic village beside the River Leven. On the left is a U-shaped bar replete with a beamed ceiling and brasses. Across the corridor is a snug-cum-restaurant where children are welcome and meals are served every day except Monday. A quiz is staged on Tuesday.
⛰Q❀🛏◐◑♣⚡☐

Ingleton

Wheatsheaf

22 High Street, LA6 3AD
⏲ 12-11 daily
☎ (01524) 241275 🌐 wheatsheaf-ingleton.co.uk
Black Sheep Best Bitter, Special; Taylor Golden Best; Tetley Bitter Ⓗ
One long, narrow bar is divided into different areas: one end is used for games, the other leads into the restaurant, which is as large as the bar. The attractive garden is home to birds of prey. The pub is popular with tourists, who come especially for the accommodation and food. It is handy for the Waterfalls Walk. Ingleton is served by bus Nos. 80 and 80A from Lancaster and the 581 from Settle. ⛰❀🛏◐◑▲🚌♣P

Kettlesing

Queen's Head

HG3 2LB (off A59 W of Harrogate)
⏲ 11-3, 6.30-11; 11-3, 6.30-10.30 Sun
☎ (01423) 770263
Black Sheep Best Bitter; Theakston Old Peculier; guest beer Ⓗ
Located in a quiet village, the Queen's Head is noted for its good food. An entrance lobby, dominated by images of Queen Elizabeth I, leads to two bars, one decorated with cricketing memorabilia, presumably to baffle the regulars from the nearby American base. Benches are put out in front of the pub in summer and there is a large patio at the rear. ⛰Q❀🛏◐◑🚌P

Killinghall

Travellers Rest

Otley Road, HG3 2AP (at A59/B6161 jct)
⌚ 11-11 (1am Fri & Sat); 12-11 Sun
☎ (01423) 503518
Tetley Bitter; guest beer [H]
The current licensees reopened this pub in 2005 as their first venture into inn keeping and have developed a welcoming atmosphere, catering largely for local customers. The main entrance to the stone building gives access to a small public bar and an equally small lounge, both warmed by real fires. The guest ale is usually chosen after consultation with the regulars and is often an unusual beer from a distant part of the country. No evening meals are served Sunday. ⌂❀◑⊟⛺P

Kirby Hill

Shoulder of Mutton

DL11 7JH (2½ miles from A66, 4 miles NW of Richmond) OS140067
⌚ 12-3 (not Mon-Fri), 6-11.30; 12-3, 6-11 Sun
☎ (01748) 822772 ⊕ shoulderofmutton.net
Black Sheep Best Bitter; Daleside Bitter; Jennings Cumberland Ale; guest beer [H]
Ivy-fronted country inn in a beautiful hillside setting, overlooking Lower Teesdale and the ruins of Ravensworth Castle. Situated opposite the church, the pub consists of an opened-out front bar linking through to the lounge and no-smoking restaurant to the rear. The guest beer is chosen by the regulars. It hosts live music every Monday. Popular with walkers, there are also five en-suite guest bedrooms. Evening meals are served Wednesday-Sunday. ⌂Q❀⛟◑♿♣P⊬⊓

Kirklevington

Crown

Thirsk Road, TS15 9LT (on A67, near Crathorne A19 interchange)
⌚ 5 (12 Sat)-11; 12-10.30 Sun
☎ (01642) 780044
Draught Bass; John Smith's Magnet [H]
Transformed from a rundown Whitbread house by the present licensee into a highly regarded village pub where real ales feature prominently. The two bar areas have blazing log fires; the environmental health officer cited health and safety regulations when he failed to find the gas tap for the one in the lounge. Only the best fresh ingredients are used in the small but impressive menu served in the lounge where smoking is not permitted during mealtimes. Lunch is served on Sunday (booking essential). ⌂❀◑⊟♿♣P

Kirk Smeaton

Shoulder of Mutton

Main Street, WF8 3JY
⌚ 12-2, 6-midnight (phone for winter hours); 12-1am Fri & Sat; 12-midnight Sun
☎ (01977) 620348
Black Sheep Best Bitter; guest beer [H]
Traditional village pub, comprising a large lounge with two open fires and a cosy, dark-panelled snug. Popular with the local community and walkers from the nearby Went Valley and Brockadale Nature Reserve, it has good outdoor facilities for summer drinking. The beer is obtained direct from mainly local independent breweries and you will be able to appreciate the difference. A quiz is held on Tuesday evening. ⌂❀P

Knaresborough

Blind Jack's

18A Market Place, HG5 8AL
⌚ 4 (5.30 Mon; 3 Fri)-11; 12-11 Sat; 12-10.30 Sun
☎ (01423) 869148 ⊕ blindjacks.villagebrewer.co.uk
Black Sheep Best Bitter; Taylor Landlord; Village White Boar; guest beers [H]
When you enter, it is difficult to appreciate that this pub has only existed since the 1990s. The award-winning ale house is based around an existing Georgian building with dark wood panelling and bare floorboards. The small bar serves two downstairs rooms and two smaller rooms upstairs, one of which is no-smoking. A changing beer from Rooster's is always available. Q⇶⊬⊓

George & Dragon

9 Briggate, HG5 8BQ
⌚ 5-11 (midnight Fri); 12-midnight Sat & Sun
☎ (01423) 862792
John Smith's Bitter; guest beers [H]
Bright and comfortable town pub, popular with all ages. Its open-plan interior is effectively split by a large central bar. Four guest beers are offered, including one each from local brewers Daleside and Rooster's and two more from Yorkshire micros. The outside drinking area/car park to the rear is near Holy Trinity Church whose tall spire can be seen from miles around. Dominoes, darts and pool are played. Wheelchair access is via the back door. Well-behaved dogs are welcome. ❀⛟♿⇶♣P

Langdale End

Moorcock Inn

YO13 0BN (4 miles from Scarborough) OS938913
⌚ 11-2, 6.30-11 (phone for winter hours); 12-3, 6.30-10.30 Sun
☎ (01723) 882268
Beer range varies [H]/[G]
Sympathetically restored a few years ago, the pub is in an isolated, picturesque hamlet near the end of the Dalby Forest Drive. The beer, usually from Daleside and Wold Top, is served through a hatch to both bars. It can be busy in summer, especially when the village cricket team is playing. No-smoking throughout, it is well worth the effort to find this pub, but note that in winter it is usually closed early in the week and Sunday evening. ⌂Q◑⛺♣P⊬

Lastingham

Blacksmith's Arms

Front Street, YO62 6TL (4 miles N of A170 between Helmsley and Pickering)
⌚ 12-2.30 (not Tue), 6-midnight; 12-midnight Fri-Sun & summer

☎ (01751) 417247
Theakston Best Bitter; guest beers Ⓗ
Pretty pub in a conservation village opposite St Mary's Church, famous for its 11th-century Saxon crypt. It was once run by the vicar's wife, who had 13 children; they are gone, but you may encounter the ghost called Ella. The single bar has an old range, lit in winter; the adjoining room is served by a hatch. A snug and two dining rooms complete the interior but do not miss the secluded rear garden. Food is of the highest quality. ♨Q❀⇌◑◗

Lazenby

Half Moon
High Street, TS6 8DX (off A174 by Wilton works)
⏲ 11-11; 12-10.30 Sun
☎ (01642) 452752
Black Sheep Best Bitter; Greene King Old Speckled Hen; Taylor Landlord; guest beer Ⓗ
The pub is located beneath the Eston Hills and the view from the rear patio is spectacular. An Enterprise Inns house, this is a traditional village inn, with an excellent reputation for home-cooked food, which is served daily from 12 noon until 9pm. Visit the Half Moon to enjoy a meal or drink in a completely smoke-free environment; it offers four cask ales, one of which is a guest that varies regularly. Children are welcome in the restaurant. ♘❀◑◗♿P⚡

Leavening

Jolly Farmers
Main Street, YO17 9SA
⏲ 7 (6 Fri; 12 Sat)-11; 12-10.30 Sun
☎ (01653) 658276
John Smith's Bitter; Taylor Landlord; Tetley Bitter; guest beers Ⓗ
Former York CAMRA Pub of the Year, dating from the 17th century, lying between York and Malton on the edge of the Yorkshire Wolds. Despite extensions, the cosiness of its original multi-room layout has been retained, with two small bars, plus family and dining rooms. Guest ales often include stronger beers from independent breweries, while the restaurant offers a wide range of dishes and specialises in locally-caught game. It is well worth a visit for the beer and food. ♨♘❀◑◗🚌♣P🍷

Leyburn

Black Swan Hotel
Market Place, DL8 4AS
⏲ 11.30-11; 12-10.30 Sun
☎ (01969) 623131
Black Sheep Best Bitter; John Smith's Bitter; Taylor Landlord; guest beer Ⓗ
Centrally situated in the market place, the ivy-clad exterior opens into a neatly divided bar/dining area with a busy atmosphere. Dating back to 1713 and formerly known as the Corn Market, it retains many features and artefacts of local interest. A wide range of home-cooked food includes a Sunday carvery and steak night specials. The pub stages regular music nights.
♘❀⇌◑◗♿⇌(Wensleydale Rlwy)

Long Preston

Maypole Inn
Main Street, BD23 4PH
⏲ 11-3, 6-11; 11-11 Sat; 12-10.30 Sun
☎ (01729) 840219 🌐 maypole.co.uk
Jennings Cumberland Ale; Moorhouses Premier; Taylor Landlord; Wells Bombardier; guest beer (occasional) Ⓗ
Standing by the village green, where maypole dancing is still celebrated, this welcoming local has been in the same capable hands for 23 years. The cosy lounge displays old photos of the village and surrounding area and a list of all the licensees since 1695. Dogs are permitted in the tap room which has Victorian bench seating. The cider is Saxon Ruby Tuesday. ♨Q❀⇌◑◗⊟⇌🚌♣●P

Low Worsall

Ship
TS15 9PH
⏲ 11-11 (midnight Thu-Sat); 11-11 Sun
☎ (01642) 780314
Taylor Landlord; guest beer Ⓗ
This busy roadside inn is a welcome port of call for travellers on the road but is not accessible by public transport. Once a Nimmo's house, it serves food all day from 12 until 9pm (8pm Sun). The garden is home to rabbits and guinea pigs. Many years ago Low Worsall was the limit of navigation for commercial boats on the River Tees – hence a pub called the Ship so many miles inland. There is easy wheelchair access and a disabled WC. ❀◑◗♿♣P

Malham

Lister Arms
Gordale Scar Road, BD23 4DB
⏲ 12-3, 7-11; 12-11 Fri & Sat; 12-10.30 Sun
☎ (01729) 830330 🌐 listerarms.co.uk
Boddingtons Bitter; Caledonian Deuchars IPA; Taylor Landlord; guest beers Ⓗ
Built in the 17th century, this coaching inn takes its name from Thomas Lister, the first Lord of Ribblesdale. The tiled entrance opens to a main bar with a large inglenook and many other original features. Up to four guest ales are supplemented by a real cider or perry and a wide choice of British and foreign bottled beers, usually served in the correct glass. Internet access is available in the bar. Look out for the magnificent resident tabby cats. ♨❀⇌◑◗⛺🚌♣●P

Malton

Crown Hotel (Suddaby's)
12 Wheelgate, YO17 7HP
⏲ 11-11; 12-10.30 Sun
☎ (01653) 692038 🌐 suddabys.co.uk
Malton Double Chance, Golden Chance, Auld Bob, seasonal beers; John Smith's Bitter; guest beers Ⓗ
This Grade II listed market town-centre pub, in the Suddaby family for five generations, is celebrating 21 consecutive years in this Guide. At present no brewing takes place on the premises – beers are contract brewed at Hambleton and Brown Cow. It stages beer

festivals in July and September, plus a mini-fest at Easter. Malt'on Hops off-licence on the premises stocks over 350 bottled beers from around the world, plus wines. Accommodation includes two en-suite family rooms. Sandwiches are always available. ⛫Q❀⇌P

Manfield

Crown Inn

Vicars Lane, DL2 2RF (500 yds from B6275)
6 (12 Sat)-11.30; 12-11 Sun
☎ (01325) 374243
Village White Boar, Bull; guest beers Ⓗ
Yorkshire CAMRA Pub of the year 2005, this attractive, 18th-century pub in a quiet village consists of two bars, a games room and a no-smoking lounge. The mix of locals and visitors gives the pub a friendly atmosphere. Up to six guest beers come from micro-breweries countrywide; a rotating guest wheat beer on draft and one or two ciders or perries are also stocked. A regular local CAMRA Country Pub of the Year, it hosts two annual beer festivals. Dogs are welcome in this rural gem. ⛫Q❀◐♣●P⅟

Masham

Black Sheep Brewery Visitors Centre

Wellgarth, HG4 4EN (follow brown tourist signs on A6108)
10.30-3.30 (11 Thu-Sat); 10.30-4.30 Sun
☎ (01765) 680100 blacksheep.co.uk
Black Sheep Best Bitter, Special, Emmerdale, Riggwelter Ⓗ
This popular tourist attraction is housed in the spacious former maltings. As well as offering the opportunity to sample the brewery's products, there is a high quality cafe/bistro, serving snacks and full meals with an emphasis on local ingredients. A 'sheepy' shop stocks the bottled product and Black Sheep souvenirs and visitors can book for a 'shepherded' tour of the brewery. A small garden overlooks scenic Lower Wensleydale. ❀◐♿P⅟

White Bear

12 Crosshills, HG4 4EN (follow brown tourist signs on A6108)
12-11; 12-10.30 Sun
☎ (01765) 689319
Caledonian Deuchars IPA; Theakston Best Bitter, Black Bull Bitter, XB, Old Peculier; guest beer Ⓗ
The original White Bear, situated some 100 yards away, was bombed in 1941 and the current pub was converted from brewery cottages belonging to the former Lightfoot Brewery. The impressive stone building houses two bars: a spacious lounge offering meals (not Sun eve) and occasional live music, and a more traditional public bar. Both benefit from roaring fires in winter. Note the stained glass panels behind the bar depicting a cooper's shop. ⛫Q❀◐♣P

Maunby

Buck Inn

YO7 4HD (signed from A167 at South Otterington and Kirby Wiske)
12-2, 5-11; 12-11 Fri & Sat; 12-10.30 Sun
☎ (01845) 587777 buckinnmaunby.co.uk
John Smith's Bitter; guest beers Ⓗ
Slightly off the beaten track, it is well worth making the effort to find this thriving village local, with its warm, friendly atmosphere, oak beams and open fires. This former 18th-century dower house has two bars (one no-smoking) and an excellent restaurant (booking recommended). Quoits, darts and pool are played and children are welcome. If you like the pub you can even get married here. ⛫❀◐♣P⅟

Middlesbrough

Star & Garter

14 Southfield Road, TS1 3BZ
11-11 (1 am Fri & Sat); 12-10.30 Sun
☎ (01642) 245307
Beer range varies Ⓗ
Due to undergo refurbishment before this Guide is published, the plans involve creating a single room with soft furnishings, and an outside drinking area. While there will be a greater emphasis on food than at present, the four constantly-changing cask beers – often seasonal offerings and frequently from micro-breweries – will be retained, as will the cask cider. The pub can get busy at the weekend. ❀◐♿⇌●P

Muker

Farmers Arms

DL11 6QG
11.30-midnight (1am Fri & Sat); 11.30-midnight Sun
☎ (01748) 886297
Black Sheep Best Bitter; John Smith's Bitter; Theakston Best Bitter, Old Peculier; guest beer (summer) Ⓗ
Close to the head of Swaledale, this remote, former lead-mining village attracts ramblers on the Coast-to-Coast walk. The Dale's most westerly pub is a popular resting place, particularly the front patio in summer. Inside many old features remain, including the stone-flagged floor and the welcoming open fire. The pub may not take full advantage of its new licensing hours, particularly in winter. There is an infrequent bus service. ⛫Q❀◐▲♣P

Newall with Clifton

Spite

Roebuck Terrace, LS21 2EY (on B6451)
12-3, 6-11; 12-11 Thu-Sat; 12-10.30 Sun
☎ (01943) 463063
Copper Dragon Golden Pippin; Tetley Bitter Ⓗ
Good, honest country pub and restaurant where exposed beams enhance the friendly atmosphere. The tale goes that in days of yore, a second pub existed a few doors along. The clientele would never cross the threshold of the other and dastardly deeds were done to spite it. When the other pub was put up for sale it was bought and closed down out of spite and the name stuck. Meals are served in the restaurant area daily, except Monday. ⛫Q❀◐▲♣P

Northallerton

Tithe Bar & Brasserie

2 Friarage Street, DL6 1DP (off High St near hospital)
✪ 12-11 (midnight Fri & Sat); 12-11 Sun
☎ (01609) 778482
John Smith's Bitter; Taylor Landlord; guest beers Ⓗ
Lying between the High Street and the hospital, this bar offers the best choice of cask ales in town, with five constantly changing guest beers and an ambitious range of continental brews. Decorated in plain, but pleasant cafe-bar style, it has a brasserie upstairs. Ask at the bar for some of the unusual games to play. Owners Market Town Taverns became England's first entirely smoke-free pub group in 2006.
Q⊂◗♿⊟♣⚟

Norwood

Sun Inn

Brame Lane, Norwood, HG3 1SZ (on B6451 about ½ mile S of A59)
✪ 11-11; 12-10.30 Sun
☎ (01943) 880220 🌐 thesuninn.net
Greene King Old Speckled Hen; Theakston Best Bitter, Old Peculier; guest beer Ⓗ
Large, popular country inn. The original part of this stone building dates back to the 18th century. The extension, which includes the main dining area, blends in well, although it was added in the last century. The three regular real ales are supplemented by a changing guest beer. Two darts and two pool teams are based here. The garden provides an ideal opportunity to enjoy a beer in a truly rural setting. Meals are available all day Saturday, 12-5pm Sunday. ❀⊂◗♣P

Nun Monkton

Alice Hawthorn

The Green, YO26 8EW (off A59, York-Harrogate road)
✪ 12-2, 6-11; 12-10.30 Sun
☎ (01423) 330303 🌐 alicehawthorn.co.uk
Black Sheep Best Bitter; Caledonian Deuchars IPA; Taylor Landlord; guest beers Ⓗ
Isolated by the rivers Ouse and Nidd, the village is accessible only via a remote country lane. The cosy pub overlooks the village green, complete with a maypole and duckpond. Popular with the fishing and boating fraternity, walkers are also made welcome and details of local walks are available on request. A wide range of home-cooked food is served. The garden has patio furniture and a children's playground.
⛰Q❀⊂◗⊟⛺🚌♣P⚟

Old Malton

Wentworth Arms

Town Street, YO17 7HD
(200 yds off A64, Malton bypass)
✪ 11.30-2.30, 5-11; 11.30-11 Sat & summer; 12-10.30 Sun
☎ (01653) 692618
Black Sheep Best Bitter; Theakston Best Bitter; guest beers Ⓗ
Former coaching inn, situated just off the busy A64 halfway between York and Scarborough. The main bar area is a low, beamed, L-shaped room where food is served. A no-smoking restaurant has been converted from an adjoining barn, where good value, home-cooked meals are based on locally-sourced produce and feature daily specials. The Royal Oak just along the road is in the same ownership, but sells a different range of beers, so there is a choice of six between the two pubs. ⛰Q❀🛏⊂◗⛺♣P

Osmotherley

Golden Lion

6 West End, DL6 3AA (1 mile off A19, at A684 jct)
✪ 12-3.30, 6-11; 12-11 Sat & Sun
☎ (01609) 883526 🌐 goldenlionosmotherley.co.uk
John Smith's Bitter; Taylor Landlord; guest beer Ⓗ
On the edge of the moors, the pub overlooks the village cross. Splendid floral displays and tables out the front make it a winner with ramblers. The one-roomed bar with its whitewashed stone walls, mirrors and candlelight has atmosphere aplenty, and welcomes drinkers and diners alike. Produce for the meals is sourced locally. This CAMRA award-winner hosts an annual beer festival in November. Buses run in the daytime.
⛰❀🛏⊂◗⛺🚌

Patrick Brompton

Green Tree

DL8 1JW
✪ 12-3 (not winter Mon-Fri), 6.30 (7 Sat)-11; 7-10.30 Sun
☎ (01677) 450262
Black Sheep Best Bitter; Taylor Landlord; guest beer Ⓗ
Nestling next to the ancient village church at the foot of Wensleydale on the Bedale-Leyburn road, this simple, but welcoming, Grade II listed building comprises a small but pleasant public bar with an open fire and an adjoining dining room. Motorists entering the car park should beware the narrow entrance. ⛰Q❀⊂◗⊟🚌♣P

Pickering

Royal Oak

Eastgate, YO18 7DW
✪ 11-midnight; 12-midnight Sun
☎ (01751) 472718
John Smith's Bitter; guest beers Ⓗ
Friendly, popular pub situated next to a roundabout and bus stops, and five minutes' walk from the North York Moors steam railway station. Guest beers are sourced from the SIBA breweries initiative. An extensive car park and lawned garden lie to the rear, with a children's play area. Food is available 12-9pm daily. It hosts occasional live music and a beer festival over August bank holiday. Q❀⊂◗⛺≹(N York Moors Rlwy)♣P

Pickhill

Nag's Head

YO7 4JG (off A1, between Thirsk and Masham)
OS346835
✪ 11-11 daily
☎ (01845) 567391 🌐 nagsheadpickhill.co.uk

Black Sheep Best Bitter; Hambleton Bitter; Theakston Black Bull Bitter; guest beer H
This CAMRA award-winner has it all: a first-rate restaurant, bar meals in the cosy lounge and an atmospheric public bar frequented by locals; it succeeds in maintaining a perfect balance. Hambleton Ales' creator is a near neighbour and his company's beers are a regular feature on the bar. Games include quoits and even a putting green – but beware the bar draughts. The pub is handy for travellers on the A1.
♨Q❀⊭◐◑⊟♿⅄♣P⊬

Pool in Wharfedale

Hunter's Inn
Harrogate Road, LS21 2PS (on A658, Harrogate-Bradford road)
✪ 11-11; 12-10.30 Sun
☎ (0113) 284 1090
Fuller's London Pride; Tetley Bitter; Theakston Best Bitter; guest beers H
Roadside pub with the feel of a country lodge, enhanced by a balcony furnished with tables overlooking the surrounding fields of the lovely Wharfe Valley. Besides the three regular ales, the inn always has six guest beers from around the country that change often. Dogs are welcome, as are children until 9pm. The lunches are home cooked. Harrogate to Otley buses on route 653 and 904 stop outside. ♨❀◐⊟♣P⊬

Ribblehead

Station
LA6 3AS (on B6255)
✪ 11-11; 12-10.30 Sun
☎ (01524) 241274 🌐 thestationinn.net
Black Sheep Best Bitter; Copper Dragon IPA; guest beer H
Homely bar where you will find plenty of references to the Settle-Carlisle Railway, including a timetable for the nearby station. Lots of tourists and trippers visit of course, but at least a few regulars make it here most evenings, which is surprising, given the lack of houses around here. The path to Whernside from the pub passes close to the famous viaduct. The pub has a restaurant and bunkhouse accommodation is available. No buses serve this dog-friendly hostelry.
♨❀⊭◐◑⇌♣P

Richmond

Ship
93 Frenchgate, DL10 7AE
(near war memorial on A6108)
✪ 3 (12 Fri & Sat)-11; 12-11 Sun
☎ (01748) 823182
Black Sheep Best Bitter; Tetley Bitter; guest beer H
A warm welcome awaits at this much improved local, situated at the top of cobbled Frenchgate, just off the Scotch Corner road, in this fine Georgian market town. On two levels, the pub has recently been sympathetically refurbished but has retained its nautical theme featuring HMS Richmond, and its built-in fish tank. Two regular beers are supplemented by a guest that is often changed. Pool can be played here. ❀⊟♣

Ripon

One-Eyed Rat
51 Allhallowgate, HG4 1LQ (near bus station)
✪ 5 (12 Fri & Sat)-11; 12-10.30 Sun
☎ (01765) 607704 🌐 oneeyedrat.co.uk
Black Sheep Best Bitter; guest beers H
Five beers are always available in this cosy pub, situated in a row of terraced houses, dating back to the 17th century. Further up the street the workhouse, built in 1854, is now a museum. A true local, the pub is warmed by a roaring fire in winter and has a bar billiards table. A garden is hidden behind the pub for balmy summer days. ♨Q❀♣

Robin Hood's Bay

Dolphin
King Street, YO22 4SH
(foot of steep steps, just up from the sea)
✪ 11 (12 winter)-11; 12-10.30 Sun
☎ (01947) 880337
Caledonian Deuchars IPA; John Smith's Bitter; Theakston Old Peculier; guest beer H
Friendly, old-fashioned village pub boasting an open coal fire and beamed bar. The single, ground-floor room serves as a bar-cum-dining room, decorated with pump clips and old beer bottles – note the bottle from Roses of Malton. An upstairs room is used for families and further space for diners. Home-cooked food is available lunchtime and evening. Friday is folk night, while a quiz is staged on Sunday. Two benches at the front allow drinkers to sit and watch the world go by. ♨Q⛭❀◐◑⅄♣

Runswick Bay

Royal Hotel
TS13 5HT (off A174 at Hinderwell, down steep bank, then left)
✪ 11-3, 5.30-11; 11-11 Fri-Sun
☎ (01947) 840215 🌐 theroyal-runswickbay.co.uk
Black Sheep Best Bitter; Tetley Bitter; guest beer (summer) H
Old seaside hotel, snuggled against the cliffs and cottages, comprising a large front bar with an open fire, a quiet back bar, recently renovated in traditional Yorkshire style and an upstairs dining room, affording good views over the bay. You can enter via the patio where you can also enjoy fresh sea air (there is an outdoor heater for the British weather). Popular with walkers along the Cleveland Way; after a few drinks the walk up the bank appears less daunting.
♨Q⛭❀◐◑♣⊬

Ruswarp

Bridge Inn
High Street, YO21 1NJ (by bridge over River Esk)
✪ 12-3 (Sat); 7-midnight (1am Fri-Sat); 12-midnight Sun
☎ (01947) 602780
Caledonian Deuchars IPA; John Smith's Bitter H
Traditional village ale house of two bars,

with a pool room on the right. Step down from the pavement into the bar. The pub hosts occasional live music. In summer, take a trip on the Esk Valley Railway or the miniature steam trains, or row a boat to the Sleights. Alternatively, it is an easy walk across the fields to Whitby. Or you could simply relax in the garden and enjoy the views of the river.

Saltburn by the Sea

New Marine

Marine Parade, TS12 1DZ (on the top promenade)
12-11; 12-10.30 Sun
(01287) 622695
Hardys & Hansons Olde Trip; guest beer
Converted hotel with two bars, one has a juke box, TV and pool tables, the other is quiet; both are comfortably furnished and have a relaxed atmosphere. An upstairs restaurant doubles as a bar and function room. The patio overlooks the Durham coastline and the cliffs of North Yorkshire. Access to Saltburn's sandy beach is via steps or water-powered funicular railway, which also lead to England's most northerly pier. Parking is possible along the promenade. The grass area opposite is popular with paragliders. Q

Saltburn Cricket, Bowls & Tennis Club

Marske Mill Lane, TS12 1HJ (by leisure centre)
8 (2 summer Sat)-11; 12-3, 8-10.30 Sun
(01287) 622761
Beer range varies
Private sports club, fielding cricket, tennis and bowls teams; it is also used by divers for relaxation. Its spacious lounge overlooks the cricket field and Tees Bay, and can be divided for private functions. Casual visitors are welcome without joining, and may attend any of the many events. The club normally keeps a choice of two or three real ales. P

Saxton

Greyhound

Main Street, LS24 9PY
(W of A162, 5 miles S of Tadcaster)
11-3, 5.30-11; 11-11 Sat; 12-10.30 Sun
(01937) 557202
Samuel Smith OBB
Originally a teasel barn, nestling by the village church (it is said that some occupants of the graveyard still drop in for a quick one!), this picturesque, Grade II listed, 13th-century, whitwashed village inn, formerly listed in CAMRA's National Inventory for pubs with outstanding interiors, is favoured by locals and walkers. A low-ceilinged, stone-flagged corridor leads to a tiny bar. Real fires blaze in two of the three rooms in winter; admire the extensive collection of colourful wall plates in one bar. Q

Scaling Dam

Grapes

TS13 4TP (on A171, opp. reservoir)
11.30-3 (not winter Mon), 6.30-11; 12-3, 6-10.30 Sun
(01287) 640461
Black Sheep Special; guest beer (summer)
Old sandstone pub, comprising a small bar replete with exposed beams, brasses and collections of butterflies and old cameras, and a large restaurant. Situated at the heart of the moors Scaling is a popular venue for sailing and birdwatching, but it can be very quiet in the winter. The pub name has been reduced – it was formerly the Bunch of Grapes. P

Scarborough

Alma Inn

1 Alma Parade, YO11 1SJ
11.30-midnight; 12-11 Sun
(01723) 375587 almainn.co.uk
Malton Golden Chance; Tetley Bitter; Theakston XB; guest beers
Traditional, friendly local on a side street that runs parallel with Northway, the Alma is handy for the railway station and the main shopping centre. Antique bric-a-brac covers the walls and ceiling in all three serving areas. Good quality food is served at lunchtime, Monday-Saturday. Outside drinking is possible on the patio.

Cellars

35-37 Valley Road, YO11 2LX
12 (4 Mon)-11; 12-10.30 Sun
(01723) 367158 scarborough-brialene.co.uk
Beer range varies
Family-run pub, converted from the cellars of an elegant Victorian house. The busy bar area keeps four guest beers. It hosts live music Saturday evening and an 'open mike' night Wednesday, when the whole pub is no-smoking. Bar meals are available and there is a restaurant upstairs; all food is made on the premises from locally-sourced supplies. Beer festivals are staged in spring and autumn. The patio and gardens give a pleasant alfresco drinking experience. Guest accommodation is available.
P

Golden Ball

31 Sandside, YO11 1PG
11-11; 12-10.30 Sun
(01723) 353899
Samuel Smith OBB
Pub of striking mock Tudor appearance located on the seafront opposite the harbour, with fabulous sea views from the Harbour Bar. Multi-roomed, with a family room and garden, this is the only Samuel Smith's in the town. Popular in summer, it is a gem out of season, occasionally warmed by a real fire in winter and free of music. Lunches are served all year round, evening meals during the summer season.
Q

Indigo Alley

4 North Marine Road, YO12 7PD
4pm-2am daily
(01723) 381900
Beer range varies

Lively, popular, one-roomed pub, offering five constantly-changing real ales, including a regular Rooster's brew. Belgian Leffe blonde and brown beers as well as Hoegaarden are all sold on draught. Live music is performed several times a week. It was voted local CAMRA Pub of the Year for three consecutive years. An absolute cracker – not to be missed; note opening time, 4pm daily. ⇌

New Tavern

131 Falsgrave Road, YO12 5EY

12-3, 5.30-11.30; 12-midnight Fri & Sat; 12-11.30 Sun

☎ (01723) 366965

Camerons Bitter; guest beers [H]

Friendly, popular local with two rooms on the ground floor and a room and bar upstairs. Two big screens show all sporting occasions. A guest beer is always available, often from Marston's or Jennings, with a second on public holidays. There is live music on Wednesday evening, acoustic on Thursday, Irish on Friday and soul or covers bands on Saturday. ⊟♿⅄⇌♣P

North Riding Hotel

161-163 North Marine Road, YO12 7HY

12-midnight (1am Fri & Sat); 12-midnight Sun

☎ (01723) 370004

Caledonian Deuchars IPA; Taylor Landlord; Tetley Bitter; guest beers [H]

Not since the 1970s has this establishment (then a Camerons house) appeared in this Guide. Now a free house, new owners (CAMRA award winners) have given it a new lease of life. Located near the cricket ground on the north side, it consists of a public bar, lounge and upstairs dining room, serving home-cooked food. It stocks two (more in season) guest beers from micro-breweries and bottled Belgian beers. It hosts beer festivals and a weekly quiz (Thu). Q⇄◐◑⊟⅄♣

Old Scalby Mills

Scalby Mills Road, YO12 6RP

11 (12 winter)-11 daily

☎ (01723) 500449

Brains Rev James; Wychwood Hobgoblin; guest beers [H]

Favoured by walkers, tourists and locals, this seafront building was originally a watermill but has seen many uses over the years; old photographs and prints chart its history. Admire the superb views of the North Bay and castle from the sheltered patio or lounge. The Cleveland Way reaches the seafront here and there is a Sea Life Centre nearby. Children are welcome in the lounge until 11pm. It has a late licence but there is no admittance after 11pm. ♔Q♉❀◐◑⊟⅄♣⚟

Scholars

Somerset Terrace, YO11 2PW

12-3, 5.30-11; 12-11 Fri & Sat; 12-10.30 Sun

☎ (01723) 360084

Daleside Bitter; Durham White Amarillo; York Yorkshire Terrier; guest beers [H]

Situated in an elegant Regency crescent, and recently refurbished, Scholars has a warm, friendly atmosphere in its large front bar and games room to the rear. The three guest ales include regular offerings from Durham, York and Daleside breweries; Hoegaarden draught is also stocked. The Scarborough Jazz Club presents live performances on Tuesday evening and acoustic sets can be enjoyed on Wednesday. Home-cooked food is served. Q❀◐◑♿⇌♣

Valley

51 Valley Road, YO11 2LX

12-11; 12-10.30 Sun

☎ (01723) 372593 valleybar.co.uk

Theakston Best Bitter; Wold Top Mars Magic; guest beers [H]

Local CAMRA's Town Pub of the Year 2005, this family-run, multi-roomed pub has a popular cellar bar. Six handpumps feature beers from local micros as well as award-winners. The pub has a games room and a no-smoking dining room serving good quality meals all year at reasonable prices, including curry night on Friday (7-8.30pm) and a Sunday lunchtime carvery. The food is home-cooked from locally-sourced produce. A beer festival is staged every month from October to March. The Valley has 10 guest rooms. ❀⇄◐◑⅄⇌♣●⚟

Skipton

Cock & Bottle

30 Swadford Street, BD23 1RD

11.30 (11 Fri & Sat)-11 (midnight Fri; 12.30am Sat); 12-11 Sun

☎ (01756) 794734 cockandbottle.co.uk

Camerons Castle Eden Ale; Tetley Bitter; guest beers [H]

Former 18th-century coaching inn with a single, long, split-level bar, original exposed beams and fireplace. Note the unusual ground-floor beer 'cellar' visible through windows both from the bar and the street outside. Beware of the low beam above the step halfway along the bar. The three guest beers are from the Enterprise SIBA list, supplied by independent breweries in Lancashire and Yorkshire. Guide dogs are the only canines admitted. ♔❀◐⇌⊟

Narrow Boat

38 Victoria Street, BD23 1JE

(alley off Coach St near canal bridge)

12-11 daily

☎ (01756) 797922 markettowntaverns.co.uk

Black Sheep Best Bitter; Caledonian Deuchars IPA; guest beers [H]

Popular free house near the canal basin. The single no-smoking bar is furnished with old church pews and decorated with canal-themed murals, old brewery posters and mirrors; no piped music, juke box or gaming machines disturb the conversation. Six guest ales from northern independents usually include one from the local Copper Dragon Brewery; it stocks a selection of continental bottled beers. It hosts monthly jazz (first Tue) and folk (alternate Sun eves); Wednesday is quiz night. Children under 14 are admitted for meals. Q❀◐◑⇌⊟⚟

Snape

Castle Arms

DL8 2TB (off B6268, Bedale-Masham road)

⏲ 12-3, 6-midnight (2am Thu-Sat); 12-4, 6-midnight Sun

☎ (01677) 470270

Jennings Bitter, Cumberland Ale; Marston's Burton Bitter Ⓗ

Named after Snape Castle, once home of Catherine Parr, the Castle has an open, friendly bar with a stone-flagged floor and large fireplace. Known for its locally sourced food with a slight emphasis on fish, the restaurant is excellent. Accommodation is available in a converted barn to the rear that offers nine en-suite rooms. Quoits is played in summer. Camping and caravan facilities are available to CC members. ⩕Q❀⇌◐◗⅄♣P

Stainsacre

Windmill Inn

Mill Lane, YO22 4LT (off A171 from Whitby) OS912086

⏲ 12 (7 Tue)-11; 12-11 Sun

☎ (01947) 602671

Camerons Strongarm; Theakston Best Bitter (summer) Ⓗ

Traditional village local, with one large bar, a quiet, no-smoking dining room and a garden. It hosts bingo on Monday, pool is played on Tuesday, and Thursday is games night, with darts, pool and dominoes. It is popular with visitors to nearby Stainsacre Hall. Just off the old railway line, it is convenient for people walking and cycling from Whitby to Scarborough; cycles can be hired about three-quarters of a mile away. ⩕Q❀⇌◐◗♿⅄♣P⚟⊓

Staithes

Captain Cook Inn

60 Staithes Lane, TS13 5AD (off A174)

⏲ 11-midnight daily

☎ (01947) 840200 🌐 captaincookinn.co.uk

Rudgate Viking Bitter; guest beers Ⓗ

Built as the Station Hotel, renamed in the 1960s after the closure of the line, the pub affords views of England's highest cliffs, Boulby (660 feet). This lovely fishing village was the home of Captain Cook, commemorated by a museum. Meals are served Friday-Sunday evenings and Sunday lunchtime and the inn always offers at least two guest ales, often dark beers (mild, stout or porter). Children are welcome in the games room. It hosts a summer beer festival during Lifeboat Week.

⩕Q⚇❀⇌◐⊟⅄♣♣P

Staxton

Hare & Hounds

Main Street, YO12 4TA (on A64)

⏲ 12-11.30; 12-10.30 Sun

☎ (01944) 710243

Black Sheep Special; John Smith's Bitter; Wychwood Hobgoblin; guest beer Ⓗ

Busy roadside inn standing on the A64, seven miles from Scarborough, which served the coaching trade during the 19th century. The bar and lounge/dining area both feature low beams and open fires. Meals, served 12-8pm daily, are all cooked on the premises from fresh, locally-sourced produce. In summer drinkers can take advantage of tables at the front of the pub and a large grassed area to the rear. The extensive car park has easy access from the main road. ⩕Q❀◐◗⅄♣P

Stokesley

Spread Eagle

39 High Street, TS9 5AD (near town hall)

⏲ 11-11 (12.30am Fri &Sat); 12-11 Sun

☎ (01642) 710278 🌐 thespreadeagle.net

Camerons Strongarm; Marston's Pedigree; guest beers Ⓗ

Small, unspoilt, town-centre pub; this former coaching inn has friendly regulars and a relaxed atmosphere. Excellent, home-cooked food is available all day from an interesting menu with meat, game and poultry from the local butcher, real vegetables and imaginative salads (booking advisable). An enclosed rear garden leads down to the River Leven. In the front room, only the fire is permitted to smoke. Live music is performed Tuesday evening in this otherwise quiet pub – occasionally piped music is played at low volume. ⩕Q❀◐◗♿⚟

White Swan

1 West End, TS9 5BL (on road from centre towards Hutton Rudby)

⏲ 11.30-3 (not Tue), 5.30 (5 Fri)-11; 12-3, 7-10.30 Sun

☎ (01642) 710263

Camerons Castle Eden Ale; Captain Cook Sunset, Slipway, seasonal beers; guest beer Ⓗ

Old-fashioned town pub with a J-shaped bar, that is now mostly no-smoking. An outlet for the adjacent prize-winning Captain Cook's Brewery, no food is served here as it concentrates on brewing and selling quality craft ales. Just off West End, it stands in maybe the prettiest part of this fine little market town. No juke box or fruit machines disturb the peace. Served by buses from Hutton Rudby, Great Ayton, Redcar, Guisborough and Middlesbrough, it was local CAMRA's Pub of the Year 2003. ⩕Q⊟♣⚟

Tadcaster

Angel & White Horse

23 Bridge Street, LS24 9AW

⏲ 11-3, 5-11; 12-4, 7-11 Sat; 12-3, 7-10.30 Sun

☎ (01937) 835470

Samuel Smith OBB Ⓗ

Samuel Smith's brewery tap in the town centre is an old coaching inn with a late Georgian facade. At the front, large bay windows overlook the main street of this market town, while the side windows have views of the brewery yard and the stables famous for the grey dray shirehorses. Hot food is served at lunchtime in the large single bar that features fine wood panelling. The pub gets busy with drinkers enjoying the excellent, low-priced ale from their local independent brewery. ❀◐⊟

Thirsk

Golden Fleece Hotel

Market Place, YO7 1LL
✪ 11-3, 6-11; 12-3, 7-10.30 Sun
☎ (01845) 523108 🌐 goldenfleecehotel.com
Hambleton Bitter, Stud; Taylor Landlord ⊞
Hotel, overlooking the market place, a member of the Best Western group. The spacious Paddock Bar is on a split level and bears a strong horse racing theme. Thirsk is the real home of the literary vet, James Herriot. A musuem celebrating his work can be found a short distance from the hotel in the author's former surgery. ♛Q♨⇆◐◑P

Thixendale

Cross Keys

YO17 9TG OS842612
✪ 12-3, 6-11; 12-3, 7-10.30 Sun
☎ (01377) 288272
Jennings Bitter; Tetley Bitter; guest beers ⊞
Pub at the heart of Thixendale, a picturesque village in the Yorkshire Wolds at the junction of several typical dry glacial Wolds valleys. Inhabited since the Stone Age, many tracks established in Roman times are still used today by walkers in the dramatic surrounding countryside. The hostelry is an unspoilt, unpretentious village local with a single bar, serving guest beers from independent breweries and good value, home-cooked food. Children are welcome in the garden. ♛❀⇆◐◑♣

Thorganby

Ferryboat Inn

YO19 6DD (1 mile NE of village, SE of York) OS697426
✪ 7-11; closed Mon; 12-midnight Sat; 12-11 Sun
☎ (01904) 448224
Old Mill Bitter; guest beers ⊞
Set beside the River Derwent, this remote family-run inn is a haven of tranquillity, signposted from the main road down a narrow lane. It has only one small bar, but an excellent family room leads out to the large lawn that slopes down to the tree-lined river. Families, walkers, cyclists, boaters and anglers enjoy the varied guest beers from local breweries. Home to local dominoes and quiz teams, the inn hosts folk music nights. ♛Q♨❀♿▲⊟♣P⊡

Thruscross

Stone House Inn

Duck Street, HG3 4AH (2 miles N of A59 at Blubberhouses) OSSE1658
✪ 12-3, 6-11 (flexible); closed Mon; 12-5 Sun
☎ (01943) 880325 🌐 stonehouseinn.co.uk
Black Sheep Best Bitter; Taylor Landlord; guest beer ⊞
This rural pub, built 300 years ago, reopened in February 2005 after a period of closure. Family run and no-smoking throughout, it is characterised by exposed beams, a Yorkshire stone-flagged floor, settles and a stone-fronted bar. Two snug alcoves give a feeling of partial seclusion. The pub runs a darts team, with matches on alternate Tuesdays, and hosts a weekly open dominoes competition. The menu caters for vegetarians. Popular with locals and walkers, it is well worth a visit. ♛❀◐◑P⊬

Warthill

Agar Arms

YO19 5XW (off A166, 5 miles NE of York)
✪ 11.30-2.30, 6.30-11; 12-3, 7-10.30 Sun
☎ (01904) 488142
Samuel Smith OBB ⊞
On a bank overlooking the village pond, there is an air of indolence and tranquillity about this pub. In a traditional interior of low, timbered ceilings and panelled walls, a well in the floor is testament to the building's origins as a blacksmith's shop. A full range of the independent brewery's merchandise is available, but it keeps only one cask conditioned beer. Renowned for its generous helpings, food is served lunchtime and early evening. The pub is popular with locals and visitors alike. ♛Q♨❀◐◑♣P⊬

Wass

Wombwell Arms

YO61 4BE OS555794
✪ 12-2.30 (4 Sat), 6.15-11; closed winter Mon; 12-4, 6.15-10.30 (not winter eve) Sun
☎ (01347) 868280 🌐 thewombwellarms.co.uk
Black Sheep Best Bitter; Taylor Landlord; guest beers (summer) ⊞
Comfortable country inn built in the 18th century using stones from the ruined Byland Abbey nearby. The central bar serves a cosy area where diners meet and the newly restored Poacher's Bar where locals and visiting drinkers are made welcome. An ideal refreshment spot for visitors to the Hambleton Hills and Ampleforth School and Abbey, two dining rooms serve freshly cooked food that is based as far as possible on local produce. ♛Q❀⇆◐◑⊟♿▲♣P

Well

Milbank Arms

Church Street, DL8 2PX (dogleg S from B6268 Masham-Bedale road)
✪ 12-3, 6.30-11 (12.30am Fri & Sat); closed Mon; 12-3, 6.30-11 Sun
☎ (01677) 470411
Black Sheep Best Bitter; Rudgate Viking Bitter; guest beer ⊞
Traditional country inn, over 300 years old, the name derives from the original owners, the Milbank family. A recent major refurbishment has resulted in warm, comfortable surroundings and a relaxing atmosphere. A full menu is served daily except Monday when the pub is usually closed, although in summer the local quoits team plays its home games here on a Monday. Thorpe Perrow Arboretum is roughly a mile away; Bedale, Masham and Ripon are all a 15-minute drive. ♛Q❀◐◑♿♣P

West Witton

Fox & Hounds

Main Street, DL8 4LP (on A684)

⌚ 12-4, 6.30 (7 winter)-midnight daily (may open all day in summer)
☎ (01969) 623650 🌐 foxwitton.com
Black Sheep Best Bitter; John Smith's Bitter; guest beers Ⓗ
Genuine village free house, family run for 10 years. The welcoming bar is separated from the pool and darts area by the fireplace, while the dining room boasts an inglenook and other original features that are being restored. Good value meals are served all week, with a Sunday lunchtime roast. This CAMRA award-winning pub offers two guest beers, often from Yorkshire micro-breweries. It keeps an eclectic collection of games to choose from. 🏨❀◐▲♣P⊽

Whitby

Shambles

Shambles Market Place, YO22 4DD
⌚ 11-midnight; 12-midnight Sun
☎ (01947) 600306
Copper Dragon IPA; John Smith's Bitter; Theakston XB, Old Peculier; guest beers (summer) Ⓗ
Originally this building was a meat factory, hence the pub name, although it later became a Burberry factory outlet. Climb the steps from the market place into this relaxing pub: a central bar with a smoke-free family room and dining area. The main bar area retains the original 200-year-old beams and is furnished with large, comfortable chairs and sofas. Enjoy a beer on the balcony and admire the magnificent view of Whitby Harbour. The pub has a wheelchair lift. ❀◐♿⇌●⚡

York

Ackhorne

9 St Martins Lane, YO1 6LN (up cobbled lane by church at bottom of Micklegate)
⌚ 12-11 (midnight Thu-Sat); 12-11 Sun
☎ (01904) 671421 🌐 ackhorne.com
Caledonian Deuchars IPA; Rooster's Yankee; guest beers Ⓗ
Hidden up a cobbled lane is one of York's most popular inns – a former local CAMRA Pub of the Year. Converted to a pub from private dwellings in 1783, it reverted to its original name in 1993 after many years as the Acorn. At the same time, a major refurbishment resulted in the current layout of a bare boarded bar, with bench seating and a comfortable snug. Seek out the extended and refurnished suntrap garden. No meals are served Sunday. Q❀◐⇌🚌♣●

Blue Bell ☆

53 Fossgate, YO1 9TF
⌚ 11-11; 12-10.30 Sun
☎ (01904) 654904 🌐 bluebellyork.co.uk
Adnams Bitter; Caledonian Deuchars IPA; Greene King Abbot; Taylor Landlord; Tetley Mild; guest beers Ⓗ
Twice local CAMRA Pub of the Year, its generosity has made it Morning Advertiser fundraising Pub of the Year, too. There has been a pub on this site since 1798, with the entrance probably then at the rear. A 1903 refurbishment created the delightful hostelry it is now. Panelled throughout, the small front bar, lounge and drinking corridor have a relaxing timelessness. Sandwiches are sold until 5pm (not Sun) and tapas dishes daily until 8.30pm (5pm Wed and Sat) unless very busy. Q⊟🚌♣

Golden Ball ☆

2 Cromwell Road, YO1 6DU
⌚ 4 (12 Fri & Sat)-11 (11.30 Thu-Sat); 12-11 Sun
☎ (01904) 652211 🌐 goldenball-york.co.uk
Caledonian Deuchars IPA; Everards Tiger; Marston's Pedigree; John Smith's Bitter; Wells Bombardier; guest beers Ⓗ
A pub has existed on this corner site for more than 200 years but its current look and layout owes much to a 1929 refurbishment. This recent York CAMRA Pub of the Year is a fine community local, bearing an impressive glazed brick facade. The four public rooms include one converted recently from former living accommodation, and a tiny bar-side snug. The hidden, well-tended garden is delightful on sunny days. Q❀⊟▲⇌🚌♣

Golden Lion

9 Church Street, YO1 8BG
⌚ 11-midnight (1am Fri & Sat); 12-midnight Sun (may close earlier if quiet any eve)
☎ (01904) 620942
Greene King IPA; John Smith's Bitter; Taylor Landlord; Theakston Old Peculier; guest beers Ⓗ
The pub offers no fewer than five guest beers and often showcases the Wentworth Brewery – a rare occurrence in York. The pub's present layout resulted from the last major revamp, over 20 years ago. The striking exterior leads into a single, bare-boarded bar. On two levels, it is divided by pillars and screens into distinct areas; of particular note is the ornate wooden bar back that was salvaged from a pub in Stockton-on-Tees. Food is served all day until 9pm. ◐🚌⚡

Maltings

Tanners Moat, YO1 6HU (below Lendal Bridge)
⌚ 11-11; 12-10.30 Sun
☎ (01904) 655387 🌐 maltings.co.uk
Black Sheep Best Bitter; guest beers Ⓗ
Previously the Railway Tavern and Lendal Bridge, only since a revamp in 1992 has the pub achieved renown as the Maltings – it is now the first or last stop for many visitors to York. It continues to plough its own idiosyncratic furrow in the same capable hands. A fine selection of smaller breweries' beers is complemented by good value, wholesome food in generous portions (served until 2pm weekdays, 4pm weekends). The annual beer festival draws a cosmopolitan crowd. ◐⇌🚌●

Minster Inn

24 Marygate, YO30 7BH (off Bootham, A19, next to Museum Gardens)
⌚ 12 (11 Fri & Sat)-11; 12-11 Sun
☎ (01904) 624499 🌐 minsterinn.co.uk
Camerons Strongarm; Jennings Cumberland Ale; Marston's Burton Bitter; guest beers Ⓗ
This is a proper pub, not a bar, but a place to meet, to enjoy conversation and to relax. Locals converge here from all over for good

ale, bypassing pubs closer to home. Everyone receives a warm welcome. Little changed since it was built in 1903, it has three rooms (one no-smoking) off a central corridor, leading to an outside yard; dogs are welcome. Games include nine men's morris. ♨Q♉❀⊞⇌⊟♣⊬

Rook & Gaskill

12 Lawrence Street, YO10 3WP (near Walmgate Bar)
⌚ 12-11 (midnight Thu-Sat); 12-11 Sun
☎ (01904) 674067
Castle Rock Harvest Pale, Elsie Mo, seasonal beers; York Yorkshire Terrier; guest beers Ⓗ
Opened as a joint venture by York Brewery and Tynemill, York CAMRA's 2005 Pub of the Year is now wholly owned by the latter and is their most northerly outlet. Serving 12 beers, the regulars are augmented by an eclectic range of guests, providing a welcome outlet in the city for independent brewers, both local and from further afield. The single bar has terrazzo flooring, comfortable bench seating and sporting pictures, with a conservatory at the rear. No food is served Sunday. Q❀◐⊟♣

Saddle Inn

Main Street, Fulford, YO10 4PJ
(on A19, 2 miles S of York centre)
⌚ 11-midnight; 11-11 Sun
☎ (01904) 633317
Banks's Bitter; Camerons Bitter; guest beers Ⓗ
Although it has been on this site for more than 150 years, the original Saddle was across the street. A comfortable L-shaped lounge has an adjacent dining area, where children are welcome. Depending on demand meals are available at midday (not Mon) and in the evening. In the bar there are darts and pool; beyond the car park the attractive garden boasts a petanque terrain, to which the pub's enthusiastic team welcomes visitors at open sessions. ♨♉❀⊏◐⊟♣P

Sun Inn

The Green, Acomb, YO26 5LL (on B1224, York to Wetherby road)
⌚ 11.30-11; 12-10.30 Sun
☎ (01904) 798500
John Smith's Bitter; guest beers Ⓗ
In one of York's western suburbs, the Sun overlooks the village green and bears all the hallmarks of a real pub. Sensitively refurbished a few years ago, it has three drinking areas inside and patio tables outside to the front and rear. Displays of old local street scenes add interest. Quality home-made food, described as 'classic dishes with a modern twist' is served. The pub has good wheelchair access and WC. ❀◐⊞♿⊟♣P⊬

Swan Inn ☆

16 Bishopgate Street, YO23 1JH
⌚ 4 (12 Sat)-11 (midnight Fri & Sat); 12-10.30 Sun
☎ (01904) 634968
Caledonian Deuchars IPA; Taylor Landlord; Tetley Bitter; guest beers Ⓗ
One of three York pubs included in CAMRA's National Inventory as having outstanding historic interest, this Tetley Heritage Inn is a classic, street-corner local with a 'West Riding' layout, unusual for the city. The entrance leads to a drinking lobby with a servery, two other rooms with a hatch to the servery and a pretty, sunny, walled garden. Set just outside the city walls, it gets understandably busy at times; early evening and weekends are the quietest periods. ♨❀⊞⇌⊟♣

Tap & Spile

29 Monkgate, YO31 7PB
⌚ 12-11 (midnight Thu-Sat); 12-11 Sun
☎ (01904) 656158
Rooster's Yankee; guest beers Ⓗ
Imposing, Flemish-style house dating from 1897, built by then local brewers JJ Hunt of nearby Aldwark. Formerly the Black Horse, it was renamed in 1988 when it became one of the first Tap & Spiles of the chain. The spacious, split-level interior has a carpeted lounge area featuring bookshelves and an elegant fireplace. The four guest beers are mainly sourced from small, northern independents. The annual pork pie festival in September is popular. Lunch is served until 5pm Saturday and Sunday. ❀◐⊟♣●P

Three-Legged Mare

15a High Petergate, YO1 7EN
⌚ 11-11 (midnight Fri & Sat); 12-11 Sun
☎ (01904) 638246 🌐 thethreeleggedmare.co.uk
Castle Rock Harvest Pale; York Guzzler, Stonewall, Yorkshire Terrier, Centurion's Ghost Ale; guest beers Ⓗ
Known locally as the Wonkey Donkey, the pub is named after a wooden device that once stood on the York Knavesmire for the purpose of hanging three criminals simultaneously; take a look at the replica in the garden. Converted from a shop in 2001, this York Brewery pub, a stone's throw from the Minster, has the most modern appearance of its three tied houses. The single bar – free from electronic gimickry – leads to an airy conservatory. Toilets are down a spiral staircase. Q❀◐⇌⊟

Yorkshire Terrier

10 Stonegate, YO1 8AS
⌚ 11-11 (midnight Fri & Sat); 12-11.30 Sun
☎ (01904) 676722
York Guzzler, Stonewall, Yorkshire Terrier, Centurion's Ghost Ale; guest beers Ⓗ
York Brewery's latest pub in historic, touristy Stonegate won the 2005 CAMRA Pub Design award for best conversion to a pub. The frontage is the York Brewery shop; the pub entrance on the left leads to a single bar with two adjoining areas. A no-smoking room and disabled toilet are upstairs, accessed via a stairlift. Usually at least four York beers are supplemented by several local guests. Occasional live music is staged at this ale house hidden in the heart of the city. ◐♿⇌⊟⊬

YORKSHIRE (SOUTH)

Auckley

Eagle & Child

24 Main Street, DN9 3HS (on B1396)

⏲ 11.30-3, 5-11; 11.30-11 Sat; 12-4, 7-10.30 Sun
☎ (01302) 770406 🌐 Eagleauckley.co.uk
Black Sheep Best Bitter; John Smith's Bitter; Theakston Cool Cask; guest beers Ⓗ
The hub of the village, this inviting traditional inn was voted Doncaster CAMRA's Pub of the Year 2006. The present building dates back to 1820, although an inn is belived to have occupied the site for over 500 years. Handy for Doncaster's Robin Hood Airport, it is the perfect place to settle any butterflies prior to take off. Guest beers are usually from Yorkshire micro-breweries. Good quality food (which includes an excellent Sunday roast) is served daily.
Q❀◖◗⊟♣P⅟

Barnburgh

Coach & Horses ☆
High Street, DN5 7EP (follow signs from A635)
⏲ 1-5.30, 7.30-11.30; 12-1am Fri & Sat; 12-11.30 Sun
☎ (01709) 892306
John Smith's Bitter; guest beers Ⓗ
Imposing country inn at the centre of an old village. Its beautiful interior retains original features and it is a worthy entry in CAMRA's National Inventory. The main entrance leads to a lounge area on the right, with the left-hand room used for games. The side entrance opens onto the traditional unspoilt 'farmers' bar. The pub overlooks the Dearne Valley (but the best view is from nearby crags). The guest beers often come from Wentworth Brewery. Opening times may vary. ♨❀⊟♣P

Barnsley

Gatehouse
35 Eldon Street, S70 2JJ (by rail/bus interchange)
⏲ 11-11; closed Sun
☎ (01226) 282394
John Smith's Bitter; guest beers Ⓗ
New and very welcome addition (July 2005) to the town centre ale scene. A pub restored to life from various keg incarnations and too many name changes, its current title is due to the 'remaking Barnsley' project: the ale house stands prominently at a major entrance to the town centre. After an inaugural beer festival in February 2006, it now regularly features five real ales with at least two from small independent breweries, often local. It is handy for public transport.
◖◗⇌(Interchange)🚌⅟

George & Dragon
41-43 Summer Lane, S70 2NW
(follow signs from Town End to hospital)
⏲ 12-11 daily
☎ (01226) 205609
John Smith's Bitter; guest beers Ⓗ
Old, framed pictures of Barnsley are displayed in this busy, edge of town local. This brilliant white, roadside pub attracts a good mix of young and older drinkers. The open-plan area is well furnished with comfortable seating and stand around tables. Pool and darts are played in a smaller room up a few steps from the main area. The two changing guest beers are always popular and bank holiday barbecues on the patio are well attended. ❀⇌(Interchange)🚌(14, 44)♣P▯

Keel Inn
18 Canal Street, S71 1LJ
(next to Asda, 5 mins walk from centre)
⏲ 7-11; 12-4, 7-11 Sun
☎ (01226) 284512
Beer range varies Ⓗ
This true free house is well hidden off the busy Old Mill Lane, next to Asda. It stocks two changing guest beers from local micro-breweries. A nautical theme is a reminder of its location next to the now hidden remnants of the Aire and Calder Navigation Canal, which closed in the 1950s. The pub offers drinking areas of various size, from the lounge to the small conservatory/snug. The function room is used by local CAMRA for its beer festival here in October.
♨❀🛏⇌(Interchange)🚌(52, 59)♣P▯

Moulders Arms
49 Summer Street, S70 2NU
(off Summer Lane, heading to hospital)
⏲ 4.30 (2.30 Fri; 12 Sat)-11; 12-3.30, 7-11 (12-11 summer) Sun
☎ (01226) 215767
John Smith's Bitter; guest beer Ⓗ
This secluded little pub lies just off Summer Lane. Open-plan, three distinct areas are served by the small bar. A garden provides a secure drinking area for families. The name relates to the old foundry that once stood at this end of town. In a welcoming atmosphere locals play darts and exchange news. The small stage in the corner is where Friday night 'busking' takes place.
❀⇌(Interchange)🚌(14, 44)♣

Shaw Lane Sports Club (Barnsley RUFC)
Shaw Lane, S70 6HZ (next to Holgate School)
⏲ 5 (12 Sat)-11; 12-10.30 Sun
☎ (01226) 203509 🌐 barnsleyrufc.co.uk
Phoenix Wobbly Bob; guest beers Ⓗ
Just up the lane from a war memorial, this real ale haven is tucked away among the plethora of John Smith's outlets that exist in large parts of Barnsley. The plain exterior reveals a two-roomed clubhouse with a bar/lounge and function room. The larger second room houses the three handpulls serving a permanent strong ale and two rotating guests, all from micro-breweries. Deservedly a recent local CAMRA Club of the Year award winner, it welcomes sportsmen and women and spectators alike. ❀◖◗♿P

Bawtry

Turnpike
28-30 High Street, DN10 6JE (on A638)
⏲ 11-11; 12-10.30 Sun
☎ (01302) 711960
Caledonian Deuchars IPA; Greene King Ruddles Best Bitter; John Smith's Bitter; guest beers Ⓗ
Converted to a pub in 1986, the Turnpike, opposite the market place, celebrates 19 consecutive years in this Guide under the same landlord and has received five local CAMRA Pub of the Season awards.

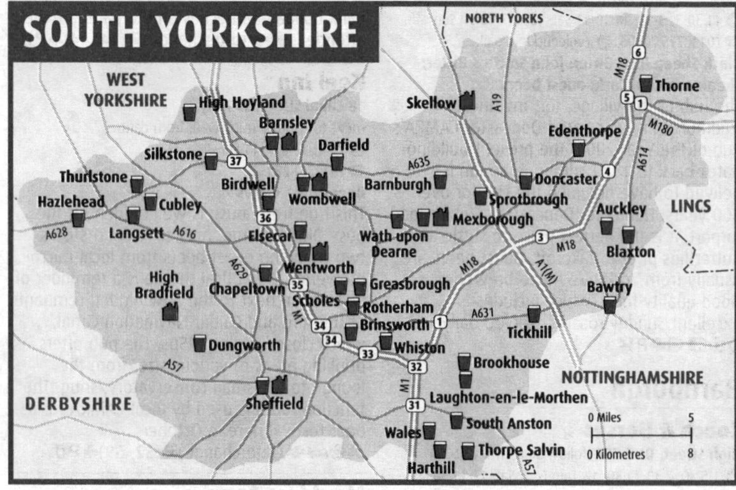

Arranged over three levels, it features glass and wood panelling, some flagstone floors, a cricket tie colllection and photos of the nearby RAF Finningley – now Robin Hood Airport. A good choice of food is served at lunchtime, plus Wednesday and Thursday evenings. Bus routes serve surrounding towns. ❀◑◗⊟

Birdwell

Cock Inn

Pilley Hill, S70 5UD (off A61 towards Pilley)
❂ 12-3, 5.30-11; 12-11 Sat; 12-10.30 Sun
☎ (01226) 742155
John Smith's Bitter; Stones Bitter; guest beers ⊞
This small, stone-built village pub, with its open coal fire, is very welcoming. The larger of the two rooms boasts a slate floor, exposed beams, much brassware and pictures of the old village. Home-cooked food, served daily, is popular and Sunday lunch must be booked (no meals Sun eve). The garden houses a children's play area and a summerhouse. A quiz is staged on Thursday and Sunday evenings at Barnsley CAMRA's Pub of the Season for autumn 2005. ⛫Q♉❀◑◗⊟(39)P

Blaxton

Blue Bell Inn

Old Thorne Road, DN9 3AL (at A614/B1396 jct)
❂ 12-11; 12-10.30 Sun
☎ (01302) 770424
John Smith's Bitter; Taylor Landlord; Theakston Old Peculier ⊞
This deceptively large, yet still cosy roadside inn offers a welcome to all: the local community, families and passing travellers, with a particular soft spot for dogs. The bar area, with an open fire and parquet floor, lies directly ahead on entering. The carpeted lounge to the left leads to the no-smoking restaurant (no food Mon). The pub is well decorated throughout, with prints of the village and nearby airfield on the walls. It is ideally situated for Robin Hood Airport. ⛫❀◑◗♿♣P

Brinsworth

Phoenix Sports & Social Club

Pavilion Lane, S60 5PA (off Bawtry Rd)
❂ 11-11; 12-10.30 Sun
☎ (01709) 363864
Wentworth Best Bitter; Worthington's Bitter; guest beers ⊞
Members of the public are welcome to be signed in at Rotherham's only club in this Guide. Set amid the club's 18-hole golf course, football and cricket pitches, the large, comfortable main bar features beers from Wentworth. A family room, TV room, snooker room with two full-sized tables and three function rooms complete the interior. The patio is especially popular in summer during the cricket season. No food is served on Monday. Q♉❀◑⊟(287)♣P⊬

Brookhouse

Travellers' Rest

Main Street, S25 1YA 1½ mile from Dinnington, near railway viaduct)
❂ 5-11; 12-11 Sat & Sun
☎ (01909) 562661
Hardys & Hansons Bitter, Olde Trip, seasonal beers ⊞
Bungalow-style pub in a picturesque farming village, originally built as a house, using stone from an old watermill that stood on the site until the 1960s. Handy for walks to Roche Abbey and Laughton, extensive gardens by the brook provide seats, an old boat, two bouncy castles and a children's ride. Duck races take place on bank holidays. Serving good value, home-cooked food, the pub is a rare outlet for Hardys' beers in the area and is popular with locals and walkers. ❀◑◗⊟♿♣P

Chapeltown

Commercial

107 Station Road, S35 2XF
❂ 12-3, 5.30-11; 12-11 Fri & Sat; 12-10.30 Sun
☎ (0114) 246 9066
Ward's Best Bitter; Wentworth Needles Eye,

WPA, Oatmeal Stout; guest beers Ⓗ
Former Stroutts Brewery pub, built in 1890, it now stocks regular Wentworth beers including specials, plus four changing guests and a rotating cider. An island bar seves the lounge, public/games bar and the refurbished no-smoking snug. Successful beer festivals are held in May and November. It has facilities for outdoor drinking to the side and rear of the pub. Children are welcome. No meals are served Sunday evening. Hot roast pork sandwiches are brought out at 10pm on Saturday. ⛰Q❀◑◗⊟♿⇌⊟♣●P⊬

Cubley

Cubley Hall Hotel

Mortimer Road, S36 9DF (2/3 of a mile S of Penistone)
⚙ 11-11; 12-10.30 Sun
☎ (01226) 766086
Tetley Bitter, Imperial, Burton Ale; guest beers Ⓗ
Spacious, multi-roomed former gentleman's residence. Much extended over the years, it has retained its elaborate ceiling cornices and mosaic tiled hallway. With a long, conservatory dining area it is as well known for its quality food as for its beers, and is frequently used for weddings and family functions. Usually one guest beer is on at a time. The surrounding area is crisscrossed by footpaths, and a 15-minute downhill walk takes you to Penistone. No. 22 bus runs Monday-Saturday, No. 20 on Sunday. ♉❀⊭◑◗♿⊟P⊬

Darfield

Darfield Cricket Club

School Street, S73 9EZ
⚙ 12-3 (not Mon-Fri), 7-11; (12-11 Sat in cricket season); 12-10.30 Sun
☎ (01226) 752194
Beer range varies Ⓗ
Staunchly Yorkshire cricket club that is determined to make the best of its resources – and what resources: a beautiful setting, fine food at the weekend and great beer. At least three changing guest beers, often from small local breweries, are augmented by mini beer festivals. Little wonder then that it was voted CAMRA Regional Club of the Year 2005. Card-carrying CAMRA members and visitors with this Guide are made most welcome. Q♉❀◑◗♿♣P⊟

Doncaster

Corner Pin

145 St Sepulchre Gate West, DN1 3AH (W of ring road)
⚙ 12-midnight daily
☎ (01302) 323159
John Smith's Bitter; guest beers Ⓗ
Traditional, street-corner pub, with a well-appointed lounge to the left and public bar area to the right. Of the four handpumps, three serve changing guest beers, mainly from small independent breweries via the SIBA scheme. At the rear an attractive decked area is ideal for alfresco drinking on a warm evening. The pub fields a football side and two darts teams. Oversized glasses are available on request. ❀⊟⇌♣⊟

Leopard

1 West Street, DN1 3AA (near station)
⚙ 11-midnight (1am Fri & Sat); 12-midnight Sun
☎ (01302) 363054 🌐 thegigguide.co.uk
Glentworth seasonal beers; John Smith's Bitter; guest beers Ⓗ
Recently refurbished, this classic, street-corner pub has adapted to modern times to appeal to all ages. Expect a comfortable lounge and a traditional bar, complete with pool, darts and sports TV, plus an upstairs concert room hosting a wide range of pop and rock music and occasional comedy nights. Real ale fans are treated to the town's only outlet for local Glentworth brewery and a choice of two guest ales that change frequently. The opening times may vary. Enjoy. ❀⊟⇌♣●P⊬

Masons' Arms

22 Market Place, DN1 1ND
⚙ 10.30-11 daily
☎ (01302) 364391
Taylor Landlord; Tetley Bitter; guest beer Ⓗ
Unpretentious, 200-year-old house next to the famous Doncaster market. The public bar at the front is frequented by the horse racing fraternity. For the moment the smoking room is appropriately named and very atmospheric. Children are admitted to the back room. Very friendly: call in for a quick pint and you may end up having five, chatting to people you have never met before. The lunchtime sandwiches are excellent value. ♉❀⊟♿⇌♣

Plough ☆

8 West Laith Gate, DN1 1SF (next to Frenchgate shopping centre)
⚙ 11-11 daily
☎ (01302) 738310
Acorn Barnsley Bitter; Draught Bass Ⓗ
One of the last truly traditional, multi-roomed pubs in the town centre, this popular drinkers' pub is handy for the Frenchgate centre. Long-standing hosts promote a comfortable, friendly atmosphere. Choose between the light, informal bar or the relaxing lounge. On warmer days, sit in the tiny, covered courtyard and admire the stained glass windows. Now in CAMRA's National Inventory for its well preserved interior, the Plough was last altered in 1934. ❀⊟⇌♣

Salutation Hotel

14 South Parade, DN1 2DR

INDEPENDENT BREWERIES

Abbeydale Sheffield
Acorn Wombwell
Bradfield High Bradfield
Concertina Mexborough
Crown & Wellington Sheffield
Glentworth Skellow
Kelham Island Sheffield
Oakwell Barnsley
Port Mahon Sheffield
Wentworth Wentworth

⏲ 12-11 (midnight Tue, Fri & Sat); 12-10.30 Sun
☎ (01302) 340705
Tetley Bitter; guest beers [H]
This 18th-century pub can be found just south of the town centre. It is divided into three interconnecting rooms where exposed beams contrast with two plasma screens. Upstairs is a function room. One of only two pubs in Doncaster to serve seven guest beers, generally from independent breweries, it also sells an ale brewed in aid of Doncaster Rovers FC. Food is available 12-9pm daily, the ever-popular quiz takes place Tuesday evening and folk music can be heard on Monday. ⛰❀◐◑♿♣P⊬▢

Tut 'n' Shive
6 West Laith Gate, DN1 1SF
(side of Frenchgate centre)
⏲ 11-midnight daily
☎ (01302) 360300
Black Sheep Best Bitter; Greene King IPA, Abbot; guest beers [H]
A Greene King house, this traditional pub features stone floors, boarded ceilings and walls decorated with hundreds of pump clips, all from beers that have been served here. It always stocks three guests that change frequently and has had Cask Marque accreditation for the last six years. It has one of the few remaining pub juke boxes in the area, with an emphasis on classic rock. ◐♿≹

Dungworth

Royal Hotel
Main Road, S6 6HF
⏲ 6 (12 Sat)-11; 12-4, 7-10.30 Sun
☎ (0114) 285 1213 🌐 royalhotel-dungworth.co.uk
Tetley Bitter; guest beer [H]
Dating back to the 19th century, this pub in a small rural village north of Sheffield benefits from panoramic views over the Loxley Valley and Vale of Bradfield. Comfortable lounge seating is arranged around a central bar with another room to the left. Children and walkers are welcome. Home-made pies are served evenings (not Sun) and weekend lunchtimes. Guest accommodation is in an adjoining lodge. Carol singing on Sunday lunchtime from mid-November until Christmas proves popular. Local buses run to Hillsborough Interchange. Q❀🛏◐◑🚌♣P⊬

Edenthorpe

Beverley Inn
Thorne Road, DN3 2JE (on A18)
⏲ 12-3, 5 (6 Sat)-11; 12-3, 7-10.30 Sun
☎ (01302) 882724 🌐 thebeverleyinn&hotel.co.uk
John Smith's Bitter; guest beers [H]
Welcoming, family pub with a no-smoking restaurant that serves mainly home-cooked food; the Sunday carvery is particularly popular. The owners put a great deal of effort into making your visit memorable. Sit in the lounge, sampling the guest ales – often from local breweries – and enjoy the Laurel and Hardy memorabilia, but do not get taken in by the backward clock. Accommodation is in 14 no-smoking rooms. ❀🛏◐◑P⊬

Eden Arms
Edenfield Road, DN3 2QR (off A18, next to Tesco)
⏲ 12-11 (midnight Fri & Sat); 12-11 Sun
☎ (01302) 888682
Taylor Landlord; guest beers [H]
Modern pub, where various seating areas include no-smoking sections, and a patio for fine weather. An extensive menu is served all day until 9pm by friendly staff. Three real ales are stocked – one guest is chosen by the licensee, the second by customers' votes. Two beer festivals are staged during the year, in May and October. A WC in the RADAR scheme is available. ⛰❀◐◑♿P⊬

Elsecar

Market Hotel
2-4 Wentworth Road, S74 8EP
(next to Heritage Centre)
⏲ 12 (11 Sat)-11; 12-11 Sun
☎ (01226) 742240
Beer range varies [H]
Unspoilt, multi-roomed pub: a wide corridor where drinkers can stand, a large games room and three more rooms give plenty of space to choose from. Many clubs and societies meet in the upstairs function room, while walkers, runners and cyclists use the pub as a start or finishing point. It takes just 10 minutes to walk to the Dearne and Dove Canal and the Trans-Pennine trail, and the pub is next to the Elsecar Heritage Centre. Q❀≹🚌(227, 325)♣

Greasbrough

Prince of Wales
9 Potter Hill, S61 4NU
⏲ 11-4, 7-11; 12-3, 7-10.30 Sun
☎ (01709) 551358
John Smith's Bitter; [P] **guest beers** [H]
Twelve consecutive years in the Guide, this popular street-corner pub has a spacious, well-decorated lounge and tap room. The friendly landlord is in his 27th year of tenancy and continues to provide cask beer from a wide range of breweries. The guest beer can change up to three times a day. Traditional pub games are available and in the summer tables and chairs allow customers to sit outside and watch the world go by. Q⊞🚌♣▢

Harthill

Beehive
16 Union Street, S26 7YH
(opp. church on road from Kiveton crossroads)
⏲ 12-3 (not Mon), 6 (6.30 Sat)-11; 12-3, 7-11 Sun
☎ (01909) 770205
Taylor Landlord; Tetley Bitter; guest beer [H]
Welcoming village pub with rooms for drinkers and diners (children welcome, if eating, until 9pm); last food orders are taken at 8.30pm. A full-sized snooker table is in the back room. Home to Harthill morris dancers and the local folk club, the function room upstairs can be reached by a chairlift. The pub is close to Rother Valley Country Park and is on the Five Churches and the Rotherham ring walks. Q◐◑♿♣P⊬

Hazlehead

Dog & Partridge

Bord Hill, Flouch, S36 4HH (2 miles from the Flouch roundabout, westbound A628)

🕘 12-3 (not Mon), 6-11; 12-11 Sat; 12-10.30 Sun

☎ (01226) 763173 🌐 dogandpartridgeinn.co.uk

Acorn Barnsley Bitter; guest beers 🄷

On the very edge of Barnsley's bit of the Peak District National Park, the bleak location belies the warm welcome to be found inside, abetted by quality food, open fires and, most importantly, cracking good ales. Four handpumps offer local micro-breweries' wares in regular rotation at Barnsley CAMRA's Pub of the Season winter 2006 winner. Moorland walks on the doorstep offer an opportunity to discover the raw wilderness of the area, but it is nearly two miles to the nearest bus stop. ♨Q☋❀🛏◑◗♿P⍁

High Hoyland

Cherry Tree

Bank End Lane, S75 4BB

🕘 12-3, 5.30-11; 12-11 Sat & Sun

☎ (01226) 382541

Black Sheep Best Bitter; E&S Elland Best Bitter, Beyond the Pale; John Smith's Bitter; Tetley Bitter 🄷

Fantastic views over Cawthorne and five real ales entice the visitor to this impressive rural pub. A long, beamed room with a central curved bar accommodates both drinkers and diners, to the left and right, in a cosy atmosphere. Regulars and visitors enjoy the sociable environment promoted by the attentive staff – every pub should be like this. Not to be missed, it is well worth the 25-minute ride on the No. 235 bus from Barnsley that drops you right outside. ❀◑◗♿🚌P⍁

Langsett

Waggon & Horses

Manchester Road, S36 4GY (on A616)

🕘 12-3, 6.30-11; closed Mon; 12-3 Sun

☎ (01226) 763147 🌐 langsettinn.com

Bradfield Farmers Bitter; Taylor Landlord 🄷

This family-run pub on the edge of the Peak District offers a wonderful welcome. In spring and summer you can enjoy fantastic views over the Langsett Reservoir from the garden, while in autumn and winter you can gaze into a roaring fire instead. With three individually-designed rooms, plus a 30-year reputation for its superb home-made meat and potato and bilberry pies, it is a perfect watering-hole for drinkers, walkers and holidaymakers. ♨Q❀🛏◑◗⇌(23, 24)P

Laughton-en-le-Morthen

St Leger Arms

4 High Street, S25 1YF (1 mile from B6463 at Dinnington)

🕘 10-2am daily

☎ (01909) 562940

Acorn Barnsley Bitter 🄷

Situated in a picturesque village near the magnificent parish church, this reputedly haunted pub was named after the famous Doncaster horse race, said to have been first run in the fields between Laughton and Firbeck as a wager between the Leger and Hatfield families. Popular with locals, tourists and ramblers, walks from the car park lead to Roche Abbey and Brookhouse. Children are welcome until 9pm in the restaurant where home-cooked food is served; the garden has a large play area. ❀◑◗♣P⍁

Mexborough

Concertina Band Club

9A Dolcliffe Road, S64 9AZ

🕘 12-4, 7.45 (7 Fri & Sat)-11; 7-10.30 Sun

☎ (01709) 580841

Concertina Club Bitter, Bengal Tiger; John Smith's Bitter; guest beer (occasional) 🄷

With the recent closure of the Federation Brewery, the Tina, as it is known, is the sole remaining club brewery. Photographs on the wall are a reminder of the days of the former band after which the club is named. Very much a traditional, old-fashioned place, it offers a warm, friendly welcome; show a CAMRA card or this Guide for entry. Occasional guest beers may be brewery specials or regular beers from independent brewers. ⇌♣⊔

Rotherham

Blue Coat

The Crofts, S60 2JD

🕘 9am-midnight (1am Fri & Sat); 9am-midnight Sun

☎ (01709) 539500

Greene King Abbot; guest beers 🄷

Situated behind the town hall, this Wetherspoon's house, formerly a school building, has gone from strength to strength. Under the direction of the now established manager, it offers nine beers and one cider on handpull. Rotherham's best pub by far, earning numerous CAMRA and in-house awards, it has now achieved the accolade of Rotherham CAMRA Pub of the Year 2006 and is well worth a visit. Children are welcome for meals. Q☋❀◑◗♿⇌🍎⍁

Scholes

Bay Horse

Scholes Lane, S61 2RQ (off A629, near M1 jct 35)
OS392954

🕘 5 (12 Sat & Sun)-11.30

☎ (0114) 246 8085

Kelham Island Pale Rider; Taylor Landlord; guest beer 🄷

Traditional village pub next to a cricket club. It serves good home-cooked food, including Dan's cow pie (earn a certificate if you eat everything on the plate) and popular curries. It hosts hog roasts four times a year. Other regular entertainment is provided by a pianist on Saturday, a choir on Thursday evening and two weekly quizzes. Local attractions include Scholes Coppice and Keppel's Column, Rotherham Roundwalk and a section of the Trans-Pennine Trail; Wentworth Woodhouse Hall is a pleasant if energetic walk. ♨Q❀◗♿P⍁

Sheffield: Central

Bath Hotel ☆

60 Victoria Street, S3 7QL

✪ 12-11; 7-10.30 Sun

☎ (0114) 249 5151

Abbeydale Moonshine; Acorn Barnsley Bitter; guest beers Ⓗ

Readers of the 2006 edition of this Guide will have seen on page 17 the adroit restoration this corner pub has received. Separate rooms provide the discerning drinker with a choice between the clear lines of the tiled lounge bar and the warmth of the well upholstered snug. After a sensible session supping fine cask beer, the drinker is faced with another choice – which of the single malt whiskies to round off the evening with.
◖⊖(University of Sheffield)🚌⚟

Devonshire Cat

49 Wellington Street, S1 4HG

✪ 11.30-11; 12-10.30 Sun

☎ (0114) 279 6700 🌐 devonshirecat.co.uk

Abbeydale Moonshine, Absolution; Caledonian Deuchars IPA; Theakston Old Peculier; guest beers Ⓗ

It would be hard to find a pub that caters for a more diverse clientele. A beacon for real ale, cider and continental products, it draws the after work, between lectures, pre-gig crowds and those simply wanting a drink. A near perfect compromise, no matter what qualities your friends seek in a pub (apart from 'unfrequented'). Good lighting and ventilation are real assets in such a busy establishment. Evening meals finish at 8pm. The house beer is brewed by Kelham Island.
◖◗♿⊖(West St)🚌●⚟

Fagans

69 Broad Lane, S1 4BS

✪ 12-11.30; 12-11 Sun

☎ (0114) 272 8430

Abbeydale Moonshine; Tetley Bitter Ⓗ

Away from the main drinking areas, this pub is hard to categorise and you feel it would be more at home down a side street than on one of the city's main arteries. Well dressed in green, red and dark wood panelling, the delightfully unspoilt, comfortable rooms have an intimacy that lends an air of gravitas to even the most workaday conversation. Rarely has 'snug' been a more descriptive term for part of a pub. ◖◗⊖(West St)🚌

Fat Cat

23 Alma Street, S3 8SA

✪ 12-3, 5.30-11; 12-11 Fri & Sat; 12-3, 7-10.30 Sun

☎ (0114) 249 4801 🌐 thefatcat.co.uk

Kelham Island Bitter, Gold, Pale Rider, seasonal beers; Taylor Landlord; guest beers Ⓗ

Possibly the most famous licensed establishment in Sheffield – certainly since Peter Stringfellow headed for the bright lights of London. Assuredly, nowhere else can boast as impressive a bar size:awards ratio. Even if you discount the plaques and certificates awarded to its neighbour and sister enterprise, the Kelham Island Brewery, the pub has received a breathtakingly broad range of recognition for its food, cellarmanship and hospitality. The home-cooked food is an ideal partner to a lunchtime pint. ♨Q⊃❀◖⊖(Shalesmoor)🚌●P⚟

Frog & Parrot

Division Street, S1 4GF

✪ 12-midnight (1am Fri & Sat); 12-11 Sun

☎ (0114) 272 1280

Boddingtons Bitter; Greene King Ruddles Best Bitter, County; Taylor Landlord; guest beers Ⓗ

Although at first glance this looks like any other generic city-centre pub, a closer investigation of the bar will reveal a commitment to excellent beer in all its forms. In contrast to the boutiques and trendy bars that surround it, the Frog is a welcome triumph of substance over style. Despite high ceilings, the multi-level interior and lighting give a surprisingly cosy feel. Substantial pub food is served all day. ◖◗♿⊖(West St)🚌

Kelham Island Tavern

62 Russell Street, S3 8RW

✪ 12-11; 12-3, 7-10.30 Sun

☎ (0114) 272 2482 🌐 kelhamislandtavern.co.uk

Acorn Barnsley Bitter; Pictish Brewers Gold; guest beers Ⓗ

Sheffield has a famous real ale trail, following the Upper Don Valley. The Kelham Island Tavern is one of the newer stops on the way. This oasis offers a warm welcome, diverse beer styles and evergreen foliage, tucked between the cutlers. After tackling the difficult job of choosing between the beers, you can relax and take in the decor, which runs the gamut from bonsai to baroque. Live music is performed on Sunday evening. Three times a winner of Sheffield CAMRA Pub of the Year.
Q◖♿⊖(Shalesmoor)🚌●⛉⚟

Museum

25 Orchard Street, S1 2GX

✪ 11-11.30; 12-10.30 Sun

☎ (0114) 275 5016

Beer range varies Ⓗ

While attempts to reform the British drinker in line with continental cafe culture may not have met with unqualified success, they have led to some places expanding their outdoor furniture collection. This gives the Museum a pleasant area for summer afternoon drinking. When you need to be indoors, several mezzanines provide contrasting areas to enjoy the edifying contents of the handpulls. Upstairs you get a fine view of Orchard Square's unusual ornamental clock.
◖◗♿≹(Midland)⊖(Cathedral)🚌⚟

Old Queen's Head

40 Pond Hill, S1 2BG

✪ 10-11.20; 11-10.30 Sun

☎ (0114) 279 8383

Thwaites Original, Lancaster Bomber, seasonal beers Ⓗ

At first sight, this appears to be a mocked up Tudor pub built into the side of an urban bus station. It is, in fact, a genuine Tudor hunting lodge that has had a bus station carelessly reversed into it. Its heritage is most evident in the timbered, no-smoking room, complete

with wall-mounted cuirasses. It is a convenient watering-hole, not just for the travel interchange, but also the international sports centre. Evening meals (not served Sun) finish at 6.50pm.
❀◐◑ ≹ (Midland) ⊖ (Ponds Forge) 🚌 ⚡

Red Deer

18 Pitt Street, S1 4DD
⏲ 11.30 (12 Sat)-11; 7.30-10.30 Sun
☎ (0114) 272 2890
Adnams Broadside; Black Sheep Best Bitter; Greene King Abbot; Taylor Landlord; Tetley Bitter; Wells Bombardier; guest beers Ⓗ
In a world where plastic 'traditional' pub decor can be purchased wholesale and fitted, this is the real thing – a hidden gem frequented by seekers of quality. Not for the flocks of lager sheep or alcopop goats who are happy with the local circuit, in this genuine article pub mirrors and a Guinness clock sit alongside prints and watercolours of local scenes, many of which are for sale. A terrace allows for outside drinking.
♣◐ ⊖ (West St) 🚌

Red Lion

109 Charles Street, S1 2ND
⏲ 11.30-11.30 (midnight Fri & Sat); 7-11 Sun
☎ (0114) 272 4997
Caledonian Deuchars IPA; Black Sheep Best Bitter; Taylor Landlord; Ward's Best Bitter Ⓗ
The Red Lion manages the feat of looking bright and cheerful while at the same time being full of interesting nooks and crannies, the main one being the intimate snug that has a bell to attract the attention of bar staff. Its situation in a side street of the Cultural Industries Quarter ensures a busy lunchtime crowd who often reappear to fill the pub in the evenings. The airy conservatory is popular all year, especially in summer.
❀◐ ≹ (Midland) ⊖ (Sheffield Station) 🚌

Riverside

1 Mowbray Street, S3 8EN
⏲ 12 (6 Sat)-11; 12-6 Sun & Mon
☎ (0114) 281 3621
Abbeydale Moonshine; Bradfield Farmers Bitter; Wentworth WPA; guest beers Ⓗ
This watering-hole, replete with stripped down wood and blackboards, boasts an impressive set of handpulls, despite calling itself a cafe-bar. It serves a range of ales with a distinctly local bias. Other highlights are the pleasant terrace overlooking the River Don, the Sunday carvery and the eclectic art on the walls. Live music is staged on Friday and Saturday evenings as well as other entertainment during the week. Evening meals are served on Thursday.
❀◐ ⊖ (Shalesmoor) 🚌

Rutland Arms

86 Brown Street, S1 2BS
⏲ 11.30 (12 Sat)-11; 12-3, 7-10.30 Sun
☎ (0114) 272 9003 🌐 rutlandarms-sheffield.co.uk
Adnams Bitter; Black Sheep Best Bitter; Cains Bitter; Caledonian Deuchars IPA; Greene King Abbot; guest beers Ⓗ
Many pubs display an abundance of ornaments, few however can match the Rutland's three feet tall golden cat staring at you from among the plethora of nick-nacks and ephemera gathered from the four corners of the world. But this is still not the most surprising aspect about this corner pub with its Gilmours' windows – that accolade goes to the award-winning back garden, a haven of colour, scent and shade, even in a city heatwave.
❀🛏◐◑ ≹ (Midland) ⊖ (Sheffield Station) 🚌 P

Sheffield: East

Carlton

563 Attercliffe Road, S9 3RA
⏲ 11-11; 7.30-10.30 Sun
☎ (0114) 244 3287
Marston's Pedigree; Wentworth WPA; guest beers Ⓗ
Built in 1862, this former Gilmours' house lies behind a deceptively small frontage. Carefully renovated over the last two years, it has been transformed from a typical east end workmen's pub to a thriving community local. The main room around the bar (salvaged from a recently closed country inn) is comfortably furnished in traditional style. To the rear is a newly extended games room and the garden. A strict no-swearing policy enhances the friendly atmosphere. Four guest beers are usually stocked.
❀◐◑ ⊖ (Attercliffe/Woodbourn Rd) 🚌 ♣ ⌂

Cocked Hat

75 Worksop Road, S9 3TG
⏲ 11-11; 11-3, 7-11 Sat; 12-2, 7-10.30 Sun
☎ (0114) 244 8332
Marston's Burton Bitter, Pedigree, seasonal beers; guest beer Ⓗ
Corner pub, dating from the 1840s, once at the heart of the steel industry, but now in the shadow of the Don Valley Stadium. One room set around a central bar has stalled seating at one end, reserved for diners for weekday lunches, and a raised area by the entrance occupied by the bar billiards table. This is a popular rendezvous for players and fans from the stadium and a refreshment stop on the Five Weirs walk. ⛰❀◐ ⊖ (Attercliffe) 🚌 ♣

Corner Pin

231-233 Carlisle Street, S4 7QN
⏲ 11-8 (11 Fri & Sat); closed Sun
☎ (0114) 275 2334
Abbeydale Moonshine; guest beers Ⓗ
This traditional, two-roomed local that once nestled among the steel works and the workers' houses, now stands isolated in an area of light industry. After careful restoration, it reopened as a free house in 2005 following a period of closure. The main bar is triangular in shape due to the angle of its street-corner site. On the left is the no-smoking lounge. Guest beers are mainly sourced fom Yorkshire micro-breweries.
❀◐ 🚌 ♣ ⚡

Sheffield: North

Cask & Cutler

1 Henry Street, Shalesmoor, S3 7EQ
⏲ 12-2 (not Mon), 5.30-11; 12-11 Fri & Sat; 12-3, 7-10.30 Sun

☎ (0114) 249 2295
Beer range varies Ⓗ
Multi-award winning, street-corner pub, fronting onto the supertram tracks. It serves an ever-changing range of nine excellent cask ales from micros and small independents (over 6,000 featured so far, and always including a mild and stout or porter), plus a range of continental bottled beers. House beers from the adjacent Port Mahon Brewery are sometimes available. This quiet pub retains many traditional features, including the original leaded windows; the no-smoking room has a real fire. A beer festival is staged in November.
⌂Q❀⊖(Shalesmoor)⊟●⅟⊡

Gardener's Rest

105 Neepsend Lane, S3 8AT
⊙ 3 (12 Fri & Sat)-11; 12-10.30 Sun
☎ (0114) 272 4978 ⊕ gardenersrest.co.uk
Bradfield seasonal beers; Wentworth Needles Eye, WPA; Ⓗ **guest beers** Ⓗ/Ⓖ
The tap for the Sheffield Brewery (due to open nearby in September 2006), the pub offers a range of 10 beers, including local brews and changing guests. The garden backs onto the River Don; trout are reared and released here. The main room, which hosts live music on Saturday and a quiz on Sunday, stages art and photographic exhibitions; a further small room displays brewery memorabilia. Popular with local groups, a chess club meets in the conservatory. A beer festival takes place in October. Q❀♿⊖(Infirmary Rd)⊟♣●⅟⊡

Hillsborough Hotel

54-58 Langsett Road, S6 2UB
⊙ 6 (4.30 Thu-Sat)-11; closed Mon; 6-10.30 Sun
☎ (0114) 232 2100 ⊕ edalebrewery.co.uk
Crown & Wellington HPA, Loxley Gold, Stannington Stout; Edale seasonal beers; guest beers Ⓗ
The hotel is home to the Crown & Wellington Brewery. Over 25 guest ales feature here each week. The conservatory and raised sun terrace overlook the Don Valley and the dry ski slopes beyond. On Tuesday quiz night participants are offered free roast potatoes. At other times, filled baguettes are available.
Q❀⊨⊖(Langsett/Primrose View)⊟♣P⅟

New Barrack Tavern

601 Penistone Road, Hillsborough, S6 2GA
⊙ 11-11 (midnight Fri & Sat); 12-11 Sun
☎ (0114) 234 9148
Abbeydale Moonshine; Acorn Barnsley Bitter; Castle Rock Harvest Pale, seasonal beers; guest beers Ⓗ
Imposing former Gilmours' house on Penistone Road, a short distance from Hillsborough, it is popular on match days with home and visiting fans, and offers pre-match meals. Food is a feature at other times, with late night takeaways available Friday and Saturday and parties catered for. Ten handpumps line the bar, while continental draught and bottled beers and a fine range of single malts add further choice. Live music at the weekend draws a crowd. The patio garden is a bonus.
⌂Q❀◐⊖(Bamforth St)⊟♣●⅟

Sheffield: South

Archer Road Beer Stop

57 Archer Road, S8 0JT
⊙ 11 (10.30 Sat)-10; 5-10 Sun
☎ (0114) 255 1356
Taylor Landlord; guest beers Ⓗ
Award-winning, small, but well stocked corner shop. A regular Guide entry, the shop is now approaching 25 years as a real ale off-licence. It stocks up to four draught beers mainly from local micro-breweries, such as Abbeydale, Bradfield and Kelham Island. On the shelves you will find as many as 200 bottled beers, including at least two dozen bottle-conditioned ales. Imported specialities include an extensive range of Belgian beers, German regional varieties and other world classics. ⊟

Sheaf View

25 Gleadless Road, Heeley, S2 3AA
⊙ 11-11; 12-11 Sun
☎ (0114) 249 6455
Highwood Shepherd's Delight; Kelham Island Easy Rider; Wentworth WPA; guest beers Ⓗ
This former John Smith's and Marston's house was rescued from dereliction and transformed into a genuine free house. A real ale oasis, it sells five rotating guests, selected by strength, with always a porter or stout available. It also stocks a large selection of continental bottled beers and over 50 malts. Pleasing features are a no-smoking conservatory and excellent disabled access. Backgammon and chess sets are available on request. Newcomers should ask for an introduction to the pub cat, Muggles.
Q❀♿⊟♣●P⅟

White Lion

615 London Road, Heeley, S2 4HT
⊙ 12-11 daily
☎ (0114) 255 1500
Marston's Pedigree; Taylor Landlord; Tetley Dark Mild, Bitter; guest beers Ⓗ
Former Tetley Heritage pub, retaining many original features. A tiled corridor leads to several small rooms, including a delightful snug. The concert room is the venue for live rock and blues on Thursday and monthly jazz (first Tue). A large-screen TV is available. Owned by Punch and leased to the Just Williams Group, it enjoys a good reputation for the consistency of its real ale, as reflected in the numerous local CAMRA Pub of the Month awards. Addlestones cider is sold. ❀⊟♣●⅟

Sheffield: West

Cobden View

40 Cobden View Road, Crookes, S10 1HQ
⊙ 4-midnight (1am Fri); 12-1am Sat; 12-midnight Sun
☎ (0114) 266 1273
Abbeydale Moonshine; Black Sheep Best Bitter; Caledonian Deuchars IPA, 80/-; guest beer Ⓗ
Named after Sir Richard Cobden, a 19th-century Sheffield industrialist, this busy community pub caters for a varied clientele, from students to retired folk. Although opened out, the original room layout is still apparent, with the bar serving a snug at the front, a

games area to the rear and a lounge to the right of the front entrance. It stages quizzes on Sunday and Tuesday, live music on Thursday and Saturday. Guest beers are usually from local micro-breweries. ❀♿⊟♣⁄

Fox & Duck
227 Fulwood Road, Broomhill, S10 3BA
⊙ 11-11.30 (midnight Fri & Sat); 12-11.30 Sun
☎ (0114) 263 1888
Abbeydale Moonshine; John Smith's Magnet; guest beers Ⓗ
Busy pub at the heart of the Broomhill shopping area. Although owned by the Students Union, it is popular with locals as well as students. Originally a two-roomed house, it was converted to its present open-plan format in the 1980s and more recently extended into an adjoining shop. No food is served, but drinkers may bring in their own from the many nearby takeaways. Beers, including four or five guests, come mainly from local brewers. The garden has a heated patio. ❀⊟⁄

Porter Brook
565 Ecclesall Road, S11 8PR
⊙ 11-midnight (1am Fri & Sat); 12-10.30 Sun
☎ (0114) 266 5765
Greene King IPA, Abbot, seasonal beers; guest beers Ⓗ
This 1990s conversion of a house on the bank of the River Porter originally opened as a Hogshead. Quickly established as the leading real ale outlet on the Ecclesall Road scene, it now usually has four or five beers from Greene King and three or four guests from regional brewers. Micro-breweries are sometimes featured, particularly at the periodic beer festivals. Furnished in typical ale house style, it attracts a broad clientele including students from the nearby campus. ◐◑♿⊟⁄

Ranmoor Inn
330 Fulwood Road, S10 3BG
⊙ 11.30-11; 12-10.30 Sun
☎ (0114) 230 1325
Abbeydale Moonshine; Black Sheep Best Bitter; Caledonian IPA; Taylor Landlord; guest beer Ⓗ
Renovated Victorian local, retaining its original etched windows, near Ranmoor Church in the leafy suburb of Fulwood. Now open-plan, seating areas reflect the old room layout. A friendly, old-fashioned pub, serving proper food Tuesday-Saturday, it attracts a diverse clientele, including choirs and football teams; the piano is often played by an enthusiastic regular. A small front garden is supplemented by the former stableyard that has been opened as a (largely) covered and heated outdoor drinking area. Q❀◐⊟♣⁄

Robin Hood
Greaves Lane, Stannington, S6 6BG
(off Myers Grove Lane)
⊙ 12 (5 Mon & Tue)-11; 12-10.30 Sun
☎ (0114) 234 4565
Bradfield Farmers Bitter, Blonde; guest beers Ⓗ
Large, secluded 200-year-old pub, retaining its original stone floor in the public bar. The split-level bar serves two rooms. Family-run, it is set in good walking country in the Loxley Valley, within easy reach of the Peak District National Park, and offers good food and accommodation. Booking is advised for the Sunday carvery. Muddy hiking boots and dogs (not necessarily muddy) are welcome. Q❀⊨◐◑⊟♣P⁄

Walkley Cottage
46 Bole Hill Road, S6 5DD
⊙ 11-11; 12-11 Sun
☎ (0114) 234 4968
Black Sheep Best Bitter; Greene King Abbot; Taylor Landlord; Tetley Bitter; guest beers Ⓗ
Spacious, roadhouse-style suburban local retaining two rooms. The good-sized tap room houses a snooker table and big-screen TV, while the comfortable lounge has a food servery and a no-smoking area for mealtimes. Built for Gilmours between the wars on a large site, the extensive garden affords panoramic views across the Rivelin Valley. A lively pub, with a quiz on Thursday evening, it offers at least two guest beers from regional and local brewers. ❀◐◑⊟⊟♣P

Silkstone

Ring O' Bells
High Street, S75 4LN (off A628)
⊙ 11-midnight daily
☎ (01226) 790298
Hardys & Hansons Bitter, Olde Trip, seasonal beers Ⓗ
Former cottages converted into an elongated pub in a picturesque village. The bar has a standing area, with a cosy tap room on the left and a large lounge leading to a pool table. An enclosed front drinking area is brightened by wonderful flower baskets and containers. A historic wagonway passes the back of the pub. Several clubs hold their meetings at local CAMRA's recent Pub of the Season winner. Bus Nos. 21 and 22 from Barnsley stop outside. ♨Q❀⛺⊟♣P

South Anston

Loyal Trooper
34 Sheffield Road, S25 5DT (off A57, 3 miles from M1 jct 31)
⊙ 12-3, 6-11; 12-11 Sat; 12-3, 7-10.30 Sun
☎ (01909) 562203
Adnams Bitter; Taylor Landlord; Tetley Bitter; guest beers Ⓗ
Friendly village local, twice local CAMRA Pub of the Year. Despite a recent change of landlord, the pub continues to sell a range of real ales and serves good, wholesome food (eve meals Mon-Thu). Parts of the pub date back to 1690 and it comprises a public bar, snug and lounge, with a function room upstairs used by many local groups, including yoga, folk music and birdwatchers. Children are welcome for meals until 8pm. The pub stands on the Five Churches walk. Q❀◐◑⊟P

Sprotbrough

Boat Inn
Nursery Road, Lower Sprotbrough, DN5 7NB
⊙ 11-11; 11-10.30 Sun
☎ (01302) 858500

Black Sheep Best Bitter; John Smith's Bitter; guest beers [H]
Deservedly popular pub owned by Vintage Inns. It has been modernised but retains an olde-worlde charm with exposed beams, farmhouse furniture and rustic decor. An extensive menu, served all day, attracts people from far and wide. Smoke-free areas are provided for drinkers and diners. Near Sprotborough Lock and the River Don, it is convenient for walkers on the Trans-Pennine Trail. The extensive courtyard drinking area is ideal for warm summer evenings. ♨❀◐◑⊟♿P⊬

Ivanhoe

Melton Road, DN5 7NS
⊙ 11-11; 12-10.30 Sun
☎ (01302) 853130
Samuel Smith OBB [H]
Imposing roadhouse, standing well back from Melton road, with a large front car park. It has a spacious lounge and public bar with pool and snooker tables, while the conservatory, partly no-smoking, is used by families. Convivial conversation can be enjoyed undisturbed by intrusive music. Good value meals (not served Sun eve) are a perfect accompaniment to the Sam Smith's bitter – possibly the cheapest in the country. The garden, with a safe play area, stands next to the cricket pitch. ♨Q☕❀◐◑⊟♿♣P⊬

Thorne

Punch Bowl Inn

Fieldside, DN8 4BE
(on A614, near Thorne North Station and M18)
⊙ 10.30-midnight; 12-11.30 Sun
☎ (01405) 813580
Old Mill Bitter, seasonal beers [H]
Refurbished to a high standard by Old Mill, the split-level layout offers a variety of pleasant drinking areas, including a smoke-free conservatory, a library room and a large function room. Children are welcome in some areas. Good quality, freshly cooked food is available all day. Bullion is often one of the three beers on sale. There are excellent facilities for the disabled at this popular hotel that specialises in good value accommodation. Boat moorings are available nearby. ❀⛟◐◑♿Ʌ⇌(Thorne North)♣P⊬

Victoria Inn

South End, DN8 5QN (next to Thorne South Station)
⊙ 1-11; 12-10.30 Sun
☎ (01405) 813163
Beer range varies [H]
Handy for Thorne South Station, this immaculate, multi-roomed pub offers two changing guest beers from mainly local independent breweries. Doncaster CAMRA Pub of the Season summer 2004, the Victoria boasts an unusually plush bar (apparently it was once the lounge). Open fires warm the cockles on a cold winter's night. Great value meals are served Thursday-Saturday evenings and Sunday lunchtime. Excellent outside drinking facilities and reasonably-priced accommodation are added attractions. ♨❀⛟◑⊟Ʌ⇌(Thorne South)♣⊬

Thorpe Salvin

Parish Oven

Worksop Road, S80 3JU
⊙ 12-2.30 (not Mon), 5.30-11; 12-11 Sat; 12-10.30 Sun
☎ (01909) 770685
Black Sheep Best Bitter; guest beers [H]
This award-winning pub is a popular venue for Sunday lunch (booking advisable) and evening meals, it offers a good choice of home-cooked food. The name is derived from the pub's location, on the site of a former communal bakery. There is a large outdoor play area for children, and well-behaved dogs are welcome in the bar – the pub stands on the Five Churches walk, close to Chesterfield Canal and Rotherham Ring walk. ❀◐◑♿♣P⊬

Thurlstone

Huntsman

136 Manchester Road, S36 9QW (on A628)
⊙ 6-11; 12-10.30 Sun
☎ (01226) 764892
Black Sheep Best Bitter; Clark's Classic Blonde; Taylor Landlord; Tetley Bitter; guest beers [H]
Multiple award-winning pub, at the side of the main Barnsley road (A628), it lies at the heart of its community. On quiz night or acoustic night – indeed on any night – it offers a warm welcome, with the added bonus of at least six real ales. Exposed beams and comfortable furnishings make it the ideal environment in which to enjoy a beer and conversation. ♨Q❀⊟(23, 24)⊬

Tickhill

Carpenter's Arms

Westgate, DN11 9NE
⊙ 12-11 (12.30am Sat); closed Mon;12-11 Sun
☎ (01302) 742839
Black Sheep Best Bitter; Jennings Cumberland Ale; John Smith's Bitter [H]
Appealing pub that has retained a cosy front room and adjoining bar despite the alterations that have taken place over the years. A large no-smoking conservatory doubles as a family room and leads to the garden. Traditional folk music sessions are held monthly (first Thu eve), while music quizzes and other live music are also staged regularly. The food is freshly cooked on the premises – weekend evening meals must be booked. ♨☕❀◐◑⊟♣P⊬

Scarbrough Arms

Sunderland Street, DN11 9QJ
(near Buttercross landmark)
⊙ 11 (12 Mon)-3, 6-11; 11-11 Sat; 12-10.30 Sun
☎ (01302) 742977
Courage Directors; Greene King Abbot; John Smith's Bitter; Wychwood Hobgoblin; guest beer [H]
A deserving Guide entry since 1990, this three-roomed stone pub has won several awards from CAMRA, including Doncaster Pub of the Year 1997 and 2003. Originally a farmhouse, the building dates back to the 16th century, although structural changes have inevitably taken place over the years. The pub's no-smoking snug is a delight, with

its barrel-shaped tables and real fire. This is one of the few pubs in the Doncaster district using oversized lined glasses. ⚚❀⊟♣P⊬▯

Wales

Duke of Leeds

16 Church Street, S26 5LQ (off A618 into School Rd)
✪ 12-3 (not Sat), 5-midnight; 12-midnight Sun
☎ (01909) 770301
John Smith's Bitter; Theakston Old Peculier; guest beer Ⓗ
Once the coaching inn of the Duke of Leeds, this old-fashioned country inn is more than 300 years old. It prides itself on its home-cooked food and welcoming atmosphere. On the Five Churches walk, ample parking space is provided behind the pub and the outdoor drinking areas afford views of the village. It is handy for the railway station.
Q❀◐♿⇌P⊬

Wath upon Dearne

Church House

Montgomery Square, S63 7RZ
✪ 9am-midnight (1am Fri & Sat); 9am-midnight Sun
☎ (01709) 879518
Marston's Pedigree, Old Empire; guest beers Ⓗ
This impressive Wetherspoon pub is set in a pedestrian square in the town centre. Serving a wide range of good value ales from around the country, with beers from Acorn and Wentworth making frequent appearances, the Church House is a quiet pub that is fully air conditioned over two floors. It is handy for the RSPB Wetlands Centre at Wombwell. Children are welcome for meals. ⚚Q❀◐♿⊟⊬

Wentworth

George & Dragon

85 Main Street, S62 7TN
✪ 10-11; 10-10.30 Sun
☎ (01226) 742440
Taylor Landlord; Wentworth WPA; guest beers Ⓗ
One of two pubs in the picturesque village of Wentworth, it is set back from the road to allow for generous gardens. This partly 16th-century house serves a range of ales from all over the country, featuring at least two beers from the nearby Wentworth Brewery, plus cask cider. Home-cooked food is an added attraction. ⚚Q❀◐⊟▲⊟(227)♣●P⊬

Rockingham Arms

8 Main Street, S62 7TL
✪ 11-11; 12-10.30 Sun
☎ (01226) 742075
Theakston Best Bitter, Old Peculier; Wentworth Needles Eye, WPA; guest beers Ⓗ
Country pub in the grounds of the Wentworth Estate, near Wentworth Brewery. Ideal for walkers, this pub offers accommodation, local entertainment, a range of home-cooked meals, and 'dogs' dinners' for canine companions at only £1. A crown green bowling green is attached. This pub is welcoming with real fires in winter and a patio and garden for the summer.
⚚Q❀◐⊟♿⊟(227)P⊬

Whiston

Chequers Inn

Pleasley Road, S60 4HB (on A618, 1½ miles from M1 jct 33)
✪ 12-11 (11.30 Fri & Sat); 12-11 Sun
☎ (01709) 829168
Taylor Landlord; Tetley Bitter; guest beers Ⓗ
Former coaching inn next to a 13th-century thatched barn, this friendly local has been transformed by the current tenant. One side has been turned into a tap room, while the large garden features a barbecue area and its own bar in summer. Quizzes are held three evenings a week and a jazz band plays on Wednesday evening. Children are welcome for meals until 7pm, except Sunday. In a picturesque village, this local CAMRA award winner is handy for Ulley Country Park. ❀◐♣P⊬

Golden Ball

7 Turner Lane, S60 4HY
(off A618, 1½ miles from M1 jct 33)
✪ 12-11 (midnight Thu-Sat); 12-11 Sun
☎ (01709) 726911
Caledonian Deuchars IPA; Taylor Landlord; Tetley Bitter; guest beers Ⓗ
Small cottage-style pub with a quiet snug at the back that was opened up during a recent refurbishment. Some parts of the building date back over 500 years. It boasts large gardens to the rear and sides and a big car park across the road. This Ember Inn offers an extensive menu, served until 9pm. Children are not admitted. Real fires create a warm atmosphere in winter. Whiston is a pretty, conservation village with a notable 13th-century manorial barn. ⚚❀◐♿P⊬

Sitwell Arms

Pleasley Road, S60 4HQ
(on A618, 1½ miles from M1 jct 33)
✪ 12-11 (midnight Thu-Sat); 12-11 Sun
☎ (01709) 377003
Acorn Barnsley Gold; Greene King Abbot; Tetley Bitter; guest beers Ⓗ
On the main road, this pub benefits from a large garden with a children's play area and a car park. Low ceilings and oak beams indicate the age of the building – parts are centuries old and it was a farm and ale house before becoming a coaching inn. Customers can enjoy the lively but friendly atmosphere that pertains in the restaurant and bar, and children are welcome. This local CAMRA Pub of the Season spring 2005 hosts a quiz three evenings a week. ❀◐♿♣P⊬

Wombwell

Horseshoe

30 High Street, S73 0AA (next to main post office)
✪ 9am-midnight (1am Fri & Sat); 9am-midnight Sun
☎ (01226) 273820
Acorn Old Moor Porter; Greene King Abbot; Marston's Burton Bitter, Pedigree; guest beers Ⓗ
Busy Wetherspoon outlet, selling keenly priced beer and equally good value food. The long bar has two banks of five handpulls offering an ever-changing choice of beers. Twice-yearly festivals provide a menu of ales from further

afield, while the local Acorn Brewery's beers are well represented at all times. The mostly open-plan layout includes a raised no-smoking area at the rear. The walled garden is a new feature. Q⚘◐◑♿🚌●⚡

YORKSHIRE (WEST)

Ackworth

Boot & Shoe

Wakefield Road, WF7 7DF
(on A638, ¼ mile N of A628 roundabout)
✪ 12-11 (midnight summer); 12-10.30 (11 summer) Sun
☎ (01977) 610218
Marston's Pedigree; John Smith's Bitter; Samuel Smith OBB; Taylor Landlord Ⓗ

Busy, non-food pub in the village of Ackworth, which supplied the grindstones for Sheffield's cutlery industry. The building dates back to the late 16th century, with some original features exposed. It offers a choice of cask ales and is a rare outlet for Samuel Smith in the free trade. It has a reputation for live music but no juke box. Behind the pub is the village cricket field. It makes a good start/finish for country walks. ♨⚘♿♣P

Baildon

Junction

1 Baildon Road, BD17 6AB (on Otley road, ½ mile from Shipley Station)
✪ 11.30 (10 Sat)-midnight (1am Fri & Sat); 12-midnight Sun
☎ (01274) 582009
Bob's White Lion; Fuller's ESB; Oakham JHB; Taylor Landlord; Tetley Bitter; guest beers Ⓗ

Traditional pub with a friendly atmosphere in its three rooms. Good quality ales are sold at low prices and change regularly as Bill and Chris listen to their customers' requests for different beers. Attractions here include a TV tuned to sport, a games room and a free juke box. Home-made pub food is served until 7pm every day; Tuesday is curry night. Jam sessions are staged most Sundays at Bradford CAMRA Pub of the Year 2006. The cider is from Saxon. ♉⚘◐◑♿⇌(Shipley) 🚌(653, 654, 658, 737)●P

Berry Brow

Berry Brow Liberal Club

6 Parkgate, HD4 7FN (on A616)
✪ 8 (12 Sat)-11; 12-10.30 Sun
☎ (01484) 662549
Jennings Cumberland Ale; guest beers Ⓗ

As CAMRA Yorkshire Regional Club of the Year 2004, this small, stone-built, CIU-affiliated club is no stranger to good beer. On entering, you will find the central bar that serves three open-plan areas. Hidden away upstairs is a snooker room and the club enjoys great views across the valley from the rear. Show your CAMRA membership card or this Guide to be signed in. Parking in surrounding streets is limited, but the club is on bus routes 310 and 313. ⇌🚌♣

Railway

2 School Lane, HD4 7LT (off A616)
✪ 3 (12 Sat)-11; 12-10.30 Sun
☎ (01484) 318052
Old Mill Bitter; guest beers Ⓗ

Three guest beers are normally available at this compact village free house, usually including a second beer from Old Mill and two more from micros such as Acorn, Cottage or Derwent. Games are popular here, with teams competing in local leagues for darts, dominoes and pool. Photos of bygone days in Berry Brow and commemorative plates adorn the walls. The pub operates a 'happy hour', Monday to Thursday 3-6pm. ♨⚘⇌🚌(306, 319)♣

Bingley

Brown Cow

Ireland Bridge, BD16 2QX (100 yds along B6429 from main street)
✪ 12-3, 5-11 (12-midnight Fri & Sat); 12-10.30 Sun
☎ (01274) 564345
Taylor Golden Best, Dark Mild, Best Bitter, Landlord, Ram Tam Ⓗ

This family-friendly, riverside pub provides the full range of real ales from local brewers, Timothy Taylor. Booking is advisable for meals, which can be served in a no-smoking area (where drinkers are also welcome). Food is available all day Friday-Sunday. Live music that appeals to a mature audience is staged on Saturday evening, with jam sessions on Wednesday, which is also curry night. Several bus routes pass the door. ♨⚘◐◑⇌🚌P⚡

Myrtle Grove

Main Street, BD16 1AJ
✪ 9am-midnight daily
☎ (01274) 568637
Greene King Abbot; Marston's Burton Bitter, Pedigree, Old Empire; Theakston Old Peculier; guest beers Ⓗ

Smaller than usual Wetherspoon outlet, this popular, one-roomed pub has built up a reputation for quality real ale, with five rotating guest beers often from West Yorkshire micro-breweries, including E&S Elland, Goose Eye and Old Bear. The large front windows are opened onto the street in warm weather. This Bradford CAMRA Pub of the Season 2005 winner is handy for public transport as well as town-centre car parks. Q◐◑♿⇌🚌(662, 760)⚡

Star Inn

York Street, BD16 2NL
(in a residential estate, E of station)
✪ 11-11; 11-10.30 Sun
☎ (01274) 568644
Black Sheep Best Bitter; Tetley Mild, Bitter; guest beer Ⓗ

Attractively decorated windows greet the visitor to this community local. The heavily ornamented lounge, games room and tap room (public bar) are all served by a central bar. While swearing is banned – as are dogs indoors – smoking is currently permitted throughout the premises, but conditions are ameliorated by four extractors. No food is

served on Tuesday. Bingley's 'hidden secret' rewards those who successfully seek it out. Buses from Bradford (662) and Leeds (760) to Keighley stop nearby. ❀◑⊟⇌⊟♣P

Birstall

Black Bull

5 Kirkgate, WF17 9PB (off A652, near A643)
⊙ 12-11 daily
☎ (01274) 873039
Boddingtons Bitter; Worthington's Bitter; guest beer Ⓗ
An important part of the local community since the 17th century, the pub boasts a well-preserved courtroom upstairs, which saw its last trial in 1839 and is now used for functions. This Grade II listed pub comprises several cosy areas, including a smoke-free snug that admits children. The guest beer changes daily, and may be any strength, mostly from well-known small breweries, although the regulars favour golden ales. Good value lunches are served daily, evening meals Tuesday-Saturday.
♨❀◑◐⊟♣P⚟

Bradford

Castle Hotel

20 Grattan Road, BD1 2LU (corner of Barry St)
⊙ 11-11; 12-10.30 Sun
☎ (01274) 393166
Mansfield Cask; Marston's Pedigree; guest beers Ⓗ
Imposing, castellated building, a former Webster's house that dates from 1898. It now sells a constantly-changing range of beers from an L-shaped bar in an open-plan single room. Among the breweries represented here you may find Cottage, Copper Dragon and Ossett as well as numerous others from around the country. A past local CAMRA Pub of the Year, it is close to the main shopping area and Bradford Colour Museum. Bus Nos. 617, 618 and 620 stop on Barry Street.
♿⇌(Interchange/Forster Sq)⊟

Cock & Bottle ☆

93 Barkerend Road, BD3 9AA (inner ring/Otley Rd jct)
⊙ 11-midnight daily
☎ (01274) 222305 🌐 williamgreenwood.com
Abbeydale Moonshine; Greenwood Fat Prop; Kelham Island Gold; Taylor Landlord; guest beers Ⓗ

INDEPENDENT BREWERIES

Anglo Dutch Dewsbury
Barearts Todmorden
Bob's Ossett
Briscoe's Otley
Clark's Wakefield
E&S Elland Elland
Empire Slaithwaite
Fernandes Wakefield
Fox & Newt Leeds
Golcar Golcar
Goose Eye Keighley
Greenwood Bradford
Halifax Hipperholme
Holme Valley Ales Honley
Linfit Linthwaite
Little Valley Hebden Bridge
Old Bear Keighley
Old Spot Cullingworth
Ossett Ossett
Riverhead Marsden
Ryburn Sowerby Bridge
Salamander Bradford
Saltaire Shipley
Sidecar Golcar
Taylor Keighley
Tigertops Wakefield
Turkey Goose Eye
WF6 Altofts

Restored to its former glory, this 19th-century Grade II listed pub is on CAMRA's National Inventory. The multi-roomed interior boasts its original Victorian mahogany bar back and counter as well as stained glass mirrors, etched windows, woodwork and fitted seating. William Greenwood's Brewery is attached to the pub, which plays host to the Topic Folk Club on Thursday. On the Bradford Heritage Trail, near the cathedral and Paper Hall, buses from Bradford Interchange (613, 614, 645 and 646) pass the door.
♨⊞⇌(Forster Sq)⊟P⊬

Corn Dolly
110 Bolton Road, BD1 4DE (near cathedral)
⏲ 11.30-11; 12-10.30 Sun
☎ (01274) 720219
Black Sheep Best Bitter; Everards Tiger; Taylor Landlord; guest beers Ⓗ
Popular, real ale oasis, a few minutes' walk from the city centre. Family run for many years, the four regular real ales are complemented by guests from the length and breadth of the country, and a house beer brewed by Moorhouses. The pub is split into two areas: a comfortable lounge one side, and a games area at the other. It is Bradford's most successful CAMRA award-winner – four times Pub of the Year to date. The food here is good value.
♨❀◐⇌(Interchange/Forster Sq)⊟(612, 641)♣P

Fighting Cock
21-23 Preston Street, BD7 1JE
(1 mile from city centre, off Thornton Rd)
⏲ 11.30-11; 12-10.30 Sun
☎ (01274) 726907
Copper Dragon Golden Pippin; Greene King Abbot; Old Mill Bitter; Phoenix White Monk; Taylor Golden Best, Landlord Ⓗ
Popular, unassuming pub, just a short walk or bus ride (615/6 or 636/7) from the city centre. Alongside 12 real ales, ciders, Belgian bottled beers and fruit wines are all served at this regular Bradford CAMRA award winner. It attracts a wide variety of customers, including loyal locals and well travelled real ale enthusiasts. Lunches are served Monday-Saturday. ♨◐⊟♣●

Haigy's
31 Lumb Lane, Manningham, BD8 7QU
⏲ 5-2 am; 12-4am Fri & Sat; 12-11 Sun
☎ (01274) 731644
Phoenix Arizona; Tetley Bitter; guest beers Ⓗ
Friendly local offering regular guest beers from Oakham, Ossett and Newby Wyke breweries. A cosy lounge, pool and music areas offer customers a choice. Try the unusual hexagonal revolving pool table. A Bradford CAMRA Pub of the Season on more than one occasion, it was Pub of the Year for 2005. Catch the No. 620 bus from Bradford Interchange.
❀⇌(Forster Sq/Interchange)⊟♣P

New Beehive Inn ☆
171 Westgate, BD1 3AA
⏲ 12-11 (2am Fri & Sat); 6-midnight Sun
☎ (01274) 721784
Archers Special IPA; Kelham Island Best Bitter; Taylor Landlord; guest beers Ⓗ
Gaslit pub on the edge of the city centre that fully merits its CAMRA National Inventory listing for its historic interior. The accommodation includes two main bars, a drinking area in the entrance hall, a games room and a no-smoking room. The cellar bar opens at weekends for live music. The range of guest beers often includes one from local brewer, Salamander. Buses run here from Bradford Interchange.
♨Q❀⇄⇌(Forster Sq)⊟(617, 618, 619)♣●P⊬

Prospect of Bradford
527 Bolton Road, BD3 0NW (opp. Wapping Rd jct)
⏲ 2.30-5.30 (11 Fri & Sat); 12-10.30 Sun
☎ (01274) 727018
Taylor Golden Best; Tetley Bitter Ⓗ
This Victorian pub has been run by Richard and Albina for almost 20 years. All customers, both regulars and visitors, are assured of the warmest of welcomes. There is a games room on the ground floor and a spacious bar area, where live music is a weekend speciality. The first-floor function room has its own real ale bar and catering can be provided for private parties. Take bus No. 612, 640 or 641 from Bradford Interchange.
♨⇌(Forster Sq)⊟♣P

Sir Titus Salt
Unit B, Windsor Baths, Morley Street, BD7 1AQ
(behind Alhambra Theatre)
⏲ 9am-midnight (1 am Fri & Sat); 9am-midnight Sun
☎ (01274) 732853
Greene King Abbot; Marston's Burton Bitter, Pedigree; guest beers Ⓗ
Splendid Wetherspoon's conversion of the original Windsor swimming baths, now named after the local industrialist and philanthropist. An upstairs seating area overlooks the main pub. Framed pictures feature the educational heritage, literature and art of the city. It draws a cosmopolitan clientele, including students from the university and college as well as theatregoers, clubbers and diners at nearby Indian restaurants. Handy for the National Museum of Photography, Film and Television, several buses serve the pub.
Q⇄◐◑♿⇌(Interchange/Forster Sq)⊟(610, 611, 612, 576)⊬

Bramhope

Fox & Hounds
The Cross, LS16 9AX
⏲ 11-11; 12-10.30 Sun
☎ (0113) 284 2448
Caledonian Deuchars IPA; Tetley Mild, Bitter; guest beers Ⓗ
Traditional stone village pub in a building dating from 1728, with typical low ceilings and exposed beams. The main room is decorated with a variety of pictures and boasts a grandfather clock in one corner. Evidence of the pub's sporting connections is clearly seen in the photos of various teams along the walls of the corridor that leads to the small tap room at the rear of the building. ❀◐◑⊞⊟♣P⊬

Brighouse

Red Rooster

123 Elland Road, Brookfoot, HD6 2QR (on A6025)
❂ 3 (12 Fri & Sat)-11; 12-10.30 Sun
☎ (01484) 713737
Caledonian Deuchars IPA; Rooster's Yankee; Taylor Landlord; guest beers Ⓗ
Small, stone pub on the inside of a sharp bend. Stone-flagged throughout, the former four-roomed layout is still apparent. The six guest beers always include one each from Ossett and Moorhouses, plus at least one dark beer. There is a small patio garden. Live blues is performed monthly (last Sun afternoon) and live music is a feature of charity week in mid-August. A beer festival is held in September at local CAMRA's Pub of the Year in 2005. Parking is limited. ❀♣P

Calverley

Thornhill Arms

18 Towngate, LS28 5NF (on A657, near parish church)
❂ 11.30-11; 12-11 Sun
☎ (0113) 256 5492
John Smith's Bitter; Taylor Landlord; Theakston Best Bitter; guest beers Ⓗ
Family-run village local where the stained glass on the windows and above the bar is thought to depict the crest of the Thornhill family. An active social programme includes two quiz nights (Tue and Thu), while the darts and dominoes teams play on Monday evening. Good, hearty meals are available at lunchtime (not Sun) – the mixed grill is not for the faint-hearted, but a vegetarian option is always available and there is a children's menu. The bistro opens 5-8pm. ❀◐◑♿🚌♣P

Castleford

Griffin

Lock Lane, WF10 2LB
❂ 2 (12 Fri & Sat)-midnight; 12-11.30 Sun
☎ (01977) 557551
John Smith's Bitter; guest beer Ⓗ
Small, two-roomed, traditional local on the northern outskirts of the town, 100 yards from the renowned Lock Lane ARLFC and new sports centre. The landlord regularly rotates a guest beer from the Enterprise list. The pub hosts quiz nights (Wed and Sun) and bingo on Wednesday. A friendly greeting is provided by the pub dog. Q❀◐⊟♣P

Shoulder of Mutton

18 Methley Road, WF10 1LX (off A6032)
❂ 11-4, 7-11; 12-4, 7-10.30 Sun
☎ (01977) 736039
Old Mill Old Curiosity; Tetley Dark Mild, Bitter; guest beer Ⓗ
A free house that started life as a farmhouse back in 1632. No juke box or pool table is to be found in this no-nonsense pub, just lively conversation and a landlord committed to real ale. The pub is the meeting place of the George Formby Society and also hosts frequent acoustic music sessions on a Sunday, when it stays open all day. Old-fashioned games played here include ring the bull and nine men's morris. ♨Q❀⊟♿⇌♣P

Chapel Allerton

Three Hulats

Harrogate Road, LS7 3NB
❂ 9am-midnight (1am Fri & Sat); 9am-midnight Sun
☎ (0113) 262 0524
Greene King Abbot; Marston's Pedigree; Theakston Old Peculier; guest beers Ⓗ
Formerly the Mexbrough and Foxy's night club, this is now a rare Wetherspoon's establishment away from the city centre. The pub name is connected to the Savile family, earls of Mexbrough – their coat of arms includes three owls or 'hulats'. The site of the present building was known as the Bowling Green. Demolished in the early 20th century it was renamed the Three Hulats and subsequently the Mexbrough Arms, perpetuating the family's association with Chapel Allerton. ❀◐◑🚌P⚟

Clayton Heights

Old Dolphin Inn

192 Highgate Road, BD13 1DR (on A647, Bradford side of Queensbury)
❂ 12-2.30 (not Mon), 5-11; 11-11 Sat; 12-10.30 Sun
☎ (01274) 882202
Beer range varies Ⓗ
This ancient coaching inn was built as a hospital during the War of the Roses and housed Cromwell's men in 1650. Note the Black Dyke Mills Band memorabilia. Mill owner, John Foster, performed here and cats eye inventor, Percy Shaw, was a regular visitor. The pub offers two guest beers, notably from Durham and the outstanding local micro-brewery, Halifax Steam. Good home-cooked food includes vegetarian options, large grills and steaks (no food Mon); the garden has a barbecue and play area.
♨Q❀◐◑🚌(576, 612)P

Cleckheaton

Marsh

28 Bradford Road, BD19 5BJ (200 yds S of bus station on A638)
❂ 12-11 (midnight Fri & Sat); 12-11 Sun
☎ (01274) 872104
Old Mill Mild, Bitter, Bullion, seasonal beers Ⓗ
Drinkers of all ages are drawn to this friendly, wedge-shaped pub, refurbished in Old Mill's house style. The popular games room features exposed brickwork with embedded bottles. The lounge has a dais and some attractive glass and woodwork. Darts, dominoes, pool and the Wednesday quiz are well supported. Old Mill's tasty dark mild has gained popularity and the seasonal beers change monthly. Located away from the bustle of the town centre, the pub is handy for the bus station. ❀🚌♣P

Dewsbury

Cedric Tapps

2 Bradford Road, WF13 1EL (between ring road and market)
❂ 12-midnight (1am Fri & Sat); 12-10.30 Sun
☎ (01924) 456284 🌐 cedrictapps.co.uk

Black Sheep Best Bitter; Boddingtons Bitter; Tetley Mild Ⓗ
This 19th-century pub, originally called the Railway Tavern, was renamed by new owners in 1997. A large, town-centre pub with a lively, friendly atmosphere, it attracts a mixed clientele and a good juke box caters for everyone's musical taste. The walls are littered with prints of old Dewsbury and other memorabilia. Darts and dominoes are played on Monday and pool leagues compete on Tuesday and Wednesday. No food is served Monday. ◑⇌🚌♣

Huntsman

Chidswell Lane, Shaw Cross, WF12 7SW (400 yds from A653/B6128 jct)
✪ 12-3 (not Mon), 7 (5 Thu & Fri)-11; 12-3, 7-11 Sun
☎ (01924) 275700
Taylor Landlord; guest beers Ⓗ
Overlooking open countryside on the edge of the village, the pub is frequented by walkers and cyclists as well as the friendly locals. The homely atmosphere is enhanced by exposed beams and horse brasses. The house beer is brewed by Highwood and guest ales are often from local breweries. Lunches are served Tuesday-Saturday. The village is on the route of the 202, 203 and 205 buses.
⛰❀◑🚌P

Leggers Inn

Robinsons Boatyard, Mill Street East, Saviletown, WF12 9BD (off B649, S of town centre)
✪ 12-11; 12-10.30 Sun
☎ (01924) 502846
Everards Tiger; guest beers Ⓗ
Converted from a hayloft, this bar overlooks a busy canal basin (follow the brown tourist signs). An ideal refreshment stop for walkers along the towpath, it stocks a rotating cider and many bottled beers. The handpumps always offer a good variety of beer styles from well-known brewers. Low, exposed beams are marked by dangling corks, strange nick-nacks and pub memorabilia. Pie and peas and sandwiches are served all day. The large canalside patio is perfect for relaxing in good weather. ⛰❀♣●P

Shepherd's Boy

157 Huddersfield Road, WF13 2RP
✪ 12-midnight (1am Sat); 12-midnight Sun
☎ (01924) 454116
Ossett Pale Gold, Excelsior; Taylor Landlord Ⓗ
Recent refurbishment by the new owners has emphasised the pub's best features, with some walls replaced to create further drinking areas. The original Webster's door leads to a snug on the right and the room to the left features comfortable long saddle seating fitted around the bay window. A brick arch accesses the stone-flagged no-smoking room. Eight handpulls serve a rotating mild, four Ossett beers and guests. Quality draught and bottled continental beers and good wines are also available. ❀♿⇌🚌P⅄

West Riding Licensed Refreshment Rooms

Railway Station, Wellington Road, WF13 1HF
(on platform 2 of Dewsbury Station)
✪ 11 (12 Mon)-11 (11.30 Fri & Sat); 12-11 Sun
☎ (01924) 459193 🌐 wrlrr.co.uk
Black Sheep Best Bitter; Taylor Landlord; guest beers Ⓗ
On platform two of Dewsbury Station, this Grade II listed pub is equally accessible by bus or car. Regular beers are supplemented by a rotating selection of guests to satisfy all tastes. One pump is dedicated to a rotating Anglo-Dutch brew and 'Yorkshire Wit' (Belgian style wheat beer) is always available. Excellent, home-cooked lunches are served Monday-Friday, pie night is Tuesday and curry night Wednesday, 6-9pm. It hosts occasional live music and an annual summer beer festival. ⛰❀◑♿⇌🚌P

Eccleshill

Royal Oak

39 Stony Lane, BD2 2HN
✪ 11-11; 11-10.30 Sun
☎ (01274) 639182
John Smith's Bitter; Taylor Landlord; Tetley Mild, Bitter Ⓗ
Comfortable, old urban village pub that attracts a loyal clientele. Although altered, it retains distinct drinking areas and a busy tap room that lends a traditional feel. Photos of old Bradford adorn the walls, alongside the landlord's many cellarmanship awards. Popular quizzes take place on Monday and Friday teatime and Tuesday evening. The covered patio to the rear is heated to extend the outdoor drinking season. Opening hours are likely to be extended in summer.
❀◐🚌♣P

Elland

Barge & Barrel

10-20 Park Road, HX5 9HP (on A6025)
✪ 12-11.30 daily
☎ (01422) 373623
Black Sheep Best Bitter; E&S Elland Bargee; Eastwood Best Bitter, Gold Award; Phoenix Wobbly Bob; guest beers Ⓗ
Large canal/roadside pub with a central horseshoe-shaped bar. Many interior walls have been removed, and some replaced by glazed screens. The decor features Victoriana and breweriana. The four guest ales come from micro-breweries and always include a dark beer. Beer festivals are held over the spring bank holiday and a weekend in late autumn. No food is served Monday. The pub is on the 537/8 bus route between Halifax and Huddersfield. ⛰❀◑🚌♣●P

Golcar

Rose & Crown

132 Knowle Road, HD7 4AN (off A62, into Milnsbridge, up Scar Lane)
✪ 11.30-2.30, 5-midnight; 11.30-midnight Fri & Sat; 12-10.30 Sun
☎ (01484) 460160
Golcar Mild, Bitter, Weavers Delight, seasonal beers Ⓗ
As the Golcar Brewery tap this picture postcard pub was voted local CAMRA 2003 winter Pub of the Season and is very much a

meeting place for the community. The lounge is warmed by a real fire in winter and houses a working model of a steam engine. The tap room has a pool table and Sky Sports TV; the pub fields its own football team. A play area for children is provided in the garden. Buses 301, 302 and 303 stop nearby. ⌂❀▭♣P

Greengates

Albion Inn

25 New Line, BD10 9AS

⊙ 12-midnight (11 Mon & Tue); 12-11.30 Sun

☎ (01274) 613211

Acorn Barnsley Bitter; John Smith's Bitter; Tetley Bitter Ⓗ

Busy roadside local near the Greengates crossroads and the stop for the Leeds-Keighley bus No. 760. It comprises an L-shaped lounge and a rare, traditional tap room where pub games are keenly contested. It gets packed on Sunday when it plays host to both men's and women's football teams. It holds popular quizzes on Thursday and Sunday evenings. The Albion is a rare outlet in this area for Barnsley Bitter. ❀▭▭♣P

Greetland

Greetland Community & Sporting Association

Rochdale Road, HX4 8JG (on B6113)

⊙ 5 (4 Fri; 12 Wed & Sat)-11 (midnight Fri & Sat); 12-11 Sun

☎ (01422) 370140

Beer range varies Ⓗ

Award-winning sports and social club, set back from the road at the top of Greetland village. A new wooden decked outside drinking area affords great views over Halifax. A growing display of pump clips adorns the lounge bar of CAMRA's national runner-up Club of the Year 2004. Five changing guest beers are stocked and you can sample the house beer – Coach House's, Duckworth's Delight (4.3% ABV). ❀▭P

Guiseley

Cooper's

4-6 Otley Road, LS20 8AH (opp. Morrisons on A65)

⊙ 12-11 daily

☎ (01943) 878835

Black Sheep Best Bitter; Caledonian Deuchars IPA; Taylor Landlord; guest beers Ⓗ

Modern café-bar bedecked with pre-war European posters. As one of the Market Town Tavern chain, it is no-smoking throughout. The large upstairs function room hosts regular music and comedy events. Meals are served until 9pm. All five guest beers are sourced from independent and micro-breweries, supplemented by a range of continental beers. ❀◐♿⇌⊬

Guiseley Factory Workers Club

6 Town Street, LS20 9DT (10 min walk from station)

⊙ 1-4 (5 Mon), 7-11; 1-11 Fri; 12-11 Sat & Sun

☎ (01943) 874793

Tetley Bitter; guest beers Ⓗ

CAMRA members gain entry on production of their card or this Guide to this small, friendly WMC in the Towngate area. The beers are a mix of local micro-brewers' and small regionals' products. A traditional three-room club, it has a snooker room with two tables. This community venue is home to a number of societies and Guiseley Ranger RLC. It hosts Saturday night concerts and big-screen sports on Friday and Saturday. The large walled garden is an added attraction. ❀♿⇌♣P

Ings

45A Ings Lane, LS20 9HR (off A65 near Guiseley Town FC)

⊙ 11-11; 12-10.30 Sun

☎ (01943) 873315

Taylor Landlord; Tetley Bitter Ⓗ

The pub affords scenic views from its rear window of the wet marshland area from which it derives its name. The three tiled fireplaces and suspended tabletop canopy lighting highlight a memorable collection of artefacts and pictures. Bus No. 97A drops passengers right outside the door. A music quiz (Tue) and general knowledge quiz (Thu) provide entertainment. ⌂❀⇌▭P

Halifax

Big Six

10 Horsfall Street, Savile Park, HX1 3HG (off A646, Skircoat Moor Lane at King Cross)

⊙ 5 (3.30 Fri; 12 Sat)-11; 12-10.30 Sun

☎ (01422) 350169

Greene King IPA; guest beers Ⓗ

Busy, friendly pub in a row of terraced houses, near the Free School Lane recreation ground. A through corridor divides two lounges from the bar, which has standing room and a cosy seating area. The decor features displays of beer related items on high shelves, including beer bottles from the Big Six Mineral Company that owned the premises a century ago. Now free of tie, the pub offers four interesting guest beers. ⌂Q❀♣⊬

George

66 Rochdale Road, HX2 7HA

⊙ 3.30 (2 Fri; 12 Sat)-11; 12-10.30 Sun

☎ (01422) 360500

Taylor Golden Best; guest beers Ⓗ

Free house, just five minutes' walk from King Cross shopping street, with a lounge area either side of the entrance – one with an ornate fire surround – and a bar with a standing area to the back. This local CAMRA award winner offers a house beer from Eastwood, a second ale from Taylor and three guests. Discreet lighting shows off the mirrored bar back, crowned with pump clips, while a high shelf encircling the pub displays bric-a-brac; pictures of old Halifax add interest. ▭♣P

Pump Room

35 New Road, HX1 2LH (250 yds from station)

⊙ 12-midnight (11 Mon-Wed); 12-11 Sun

☎ (01422) 381465

Caledonian Deuchars IPA; Taylor Golden Best, Landlord, Ram Tam; guest beers Ⓗ

Traditional, stone-built, two-bar ale house, between the station and the Shay, decorated with a collection of taps and other breweriana. A favourite with football and rugby league fans on match days, the wide range of real ales is supplemented with regular beer festivals and a guest cider. It hosts occasional live music and a quiz on Thursday evening. The car park is tiny. ❀⇌🚌●P

Three Pigeons ☆

1 Sun Fold, South Parade, HX1 2LX

⏲ 12 (3 Mon & Tue)-11; 12-10.30 Sun

☎ (01422) 347001

Ossett Pale Gold, Excelsior; Taylor Landlord; guest beers Ⓗ

This National Inventory listed pub was acquired in 2006 by the Ossett Brewery after many years as a free house. Three rooms radiate off a central octagonal drinking area/lobby, which boasts a ceiling painting depicting the birds that give the pub its name. The guest beers include an additional Ossett brew and a dark beer. The pub is served by the No. 530 bus. ⩕❀⇌🚌♣⅋

William IV

247 King Cross Road, HX1 3JL

⏲ 11-11; 12-10.30 Sun

☎ (01422) 354889

Tetley Bitter Ⓗ

Busy pub in the King Cross shopping street that draws a wide variety of customers – not just shoppers but sports fans too as there are TVs in most areas of the pub. The bar back has a hatch for service to the public bar. There is seating facing the bar with a standing area to one side and a lounge up a few steps on the other side. Picnic benches behind the pub allow for outdoor drinking. Lunches are served Monday-Saturday. ❀◗⊡🚌♣

Harecroft

Station Hotel

BD15 0BP (on B6144, opp. station)

⏲ 4-midnight; 12-midnight Sun

☎ (01535) 272430

Black Sheep Best Bitter; Greene King Old Speckled Hen; Taylor Landlord Ⓗ

The station at Harecroft was axed long ago, but other forms of transport will take you to this genuine local. The Great Northern Trail runs along the old railway line for cyclists and walkers, and bus Nos. 727 and 729 from Bingley or Cullingworth stop outside (not Sun). The pub has two good-sized rooms with open fires in winter, set around a central bar. The pool room to the rear overlooks an outside seating area. It is well worth a visit. ⩕❀🚌♣P

Haworth

Fleece Inn

67 Main Street, BD22 8DA

⏲ 11 (12 winter)-11; 12-10.30 Sun

☎ (01535) 642172 🌐 timothy-taylor.co.uk/fleeceinn

Taylor Golden Best, Best Bitter, Landlord, Ram Tam; guest beer Ⓗ

Former coaching inn, situated halfway down the cobbled main street. The large main room has a stone-flagged bar area, a section for drinkers and a spacious dining area, with comfortable furnishings throughout. This Taylor's tied house offers an extensive selection of its beers and good home-cooked food. It is convenient for many local tourist attractions, including the Keighley and Worth Valley steam railway. ⩕🛏◖◗♿⛺⇌🚌⅋

Haworth Old Hall Inn

8 Sun Street, BD22 8BP

⏲ 11-11 (11.30 Thu; midnight Fri & Sat); 12-11 Sun

☎ (01535) 642709 🌐 hawortholdhall.co.uk

Jennings Bitter, Cumberland Ale, Cocker Hoop, Sneck Lifter, seasonal beers; Tetley Bitter Ⓗ

Lovely Tudor manor house, full of charm and character, located close to the famous main street. On entering through the substantial, studded oak main door you will find stone floors, arches, mullioned windows, two huge fireplaces and a splendid wood-panelled bar. The pub is a Jennings tied house and a good showcase for its beers. Good quality home-cooked food is available. It can get very busy at weekends. ⩕Q🚸❀🛏◖◗⛺⇌🚌P⅋

Keighley & Worth Valley Railway Buffet Car

Haworth Station, BD22 8NJ

(join at any station on Worth Valley line)

⏲ 11.15-5.15 Sat & Sun Mar-Oct; Mon-Fri July, Aug & school hols; other dates as advertised (check timetable)

☎ (01535) 645214 🌐 kwvr.co.uk

Beer range varies Ⓗ

Volunteer-run railway whose bars on the trains serve draught beers decanted into tea urn-style containers. Normally one bar is in use, but up to three are pressed into service during busy periods and for special events, subject to staff availability. Views change from industrial to rural as the train progresses between stations – see how many film and TV locations you can recognise. Please note that a ticket to travel must be purchased. Q⛺⇌🚌P⅋

Heath

King's Arms ☆

Heath Common, WF1 5SL (off A655, Wakefield-Normanton road)

⏲ 11.30-3, 5.30-11; 11.30-11 Sat; 12-10.30 Sun

☎ (01924) 377527

Clark's Classic Blonde; Taylor Landlord; Tetley Bitter; guest beers Ⓗ

Built in the early 1700s and converted into a pub in 1841, the King's Arms is one of the small number of pubs owned by Clark's Brewery. The pub consists of three oak-panelled rooms lit by gas lighting. It enjoys a good reputation for food, which is served all day Sunday. Children are welcome in the conservatory. There is a wheelchair WC. A quiz is staged on Tuesday. ⩕Q🚸❀◖◗♿♣P

Hebden Bridge

Fox & Goose

9 Heptonstall Road, HX7 6AZ (on A646)

ENGLAND

11.30-3 (not Mon), 7-midnight; 11.30-midnight Fri & Sat; 12-11.30 Sun
(01422) 842649
Beer range varies H
A regular local CAMRA Pub of the Year winner, this family-owned, genuine free house has chalked up 16 consecutive years in this Guide. In three years the regulars have enjoyed over 1,200 different beers from 330 breweries and plans are in hand to extend the range to ensure a diversity of beer styles. The house beer, Slightly Foxed, is brewed by E&S Elland. The pub hosts two beer festivals a year and it can, and does, organise festivals elsewhere, too.
Q

Moyles Bar
6-10 New Road, HX7 8AD
11-11; 12-10.30 Sun
(01422) 845272 moyles.uk.com
Pictish Brewer's Gold; Purity Pure Gold; Taylor Landlord; guest beers H
Recently refurbished bar and restaurant in the vibrant mill town of Hebden Bridge. It has built up quite a reputation for its unusual range of European and American beers as well as its good food – a state of the art kitchen produces dishes from locally-sourced organic ingredients. The award-winning interior blends contemporary style with traditional comforts and a notable ceiling-high brass bar. Tables and chairs are put outside in summer. The accommodation (11 rooms) is recommended.

Holmfirth

Hervey's Bar
Norridge Bottom, HD9 7BB
4 (2 Sat)-12.30am; closed Mon; 2-11.30 Sun
(01484) 686925
Copper Dragon Black Gold, Golden Pippin; Scotts 1816; guest beer H
Hervey's is one of Holmfirth's hidden treasures. The licensees have gained Cask Marque accreditation and a reputation for good food that includes tapas. They offer a wide selection of bottled continental beers. The split-level floor has bare floorboards and the homely feel is enhanced in the back bar by a large white Aga range and kitchen furniture. The main bar opens out onto a paved area with tables and parasols for summer. Buses 310, 311, 312 and 313 all stop nearby.

Sycamore Inn
15 New Mill Road, HD9 7SH
(On A635, 1 mile from Holmfirth)
11.30-2.30 (not Mon), 4.30-11; 11.30-11 Sat; 12-10.30 Sun
(01484) 683458
Banks's Bitter; Black Sheep Best Bitter; Tetley Bitter; guest beers H
On the site of a 17th-century coaching inn, the present pub was built in 1880 and redeveloped seven years ago. This characterful hostelry imparts a convivial atmosphere throughout its three rooms (one no-smoking) and bar area. Two of the rooms are cosy and you can escape the sport on the large TV if you wish. Two excellent guest beers are sourced from various local micro-breweries. Buses (314/316) run hourly.
P

Horbury

Boon's
6 Queen Street, WF4 6LP (off High St)
11-3, 5-11; 11-11 Fri & Sat; 12-10.30 Sun
(01924) 280442
John Smith's Bitter; Taylor Landlord; Tetley Bitter; guest beers H
Centrally located, just off the High Street, this Clark's Brewery house caters for all age groups and is a real community pub. Needless to say, there is always one beer from the Clark's range among the guest beers. The pub has a sizeable outdoor drinking area where a beer festival is staged in summer.

Horbury Bridge

Bingley Arms
221 Bridge Road, WF4 5NL
12-midnight; 12-10.30 Sun
(01924) 281331
Black Sheep Best Bitter; Caledonian Deuchars IPA; Tetley Bitter; guest beers H
This two-roomed pub is bordered by the River Calder on one side and the Aire and Calder Navigation Canal on the other. It has its own moorings, so it is popular with boaters, particularly in the summer, when the large garden to the rear of the pub comes into its own. In winter, a fire is lit in both of the rooms. Meals are served 12-6pm (12-4pm Sat and Sun).
P

Horsforth

Town Street Tavern
16-18 Town Street, LS18 4RJ
12-11; 12-10.30 Sun
(0113) 281 9996
Black Sheep Best Bitter; Caledonian Deuchars IPA; Taylor Landlord; guest beers H
Once a shop on Horsforth's main street, this no-smoking pub offers a great range of British ales and bottled beers from around the world. An interesting menu is served in the upstairs brasserie from 6pm, while less upmarket, but just as good food is served daily in the bar. The cream and green walls are adorned with classy breweriana and an alcove displays Belgian beer glasses. The small bar is lined with handpumps, offering five guests that usually come from local micros. Q P

Huddersfield

Cowcliffe & Netheroyd Hill Liberal Club
181 Netheroyd Hill Road, Cowcliffe, HD2 2LZ
(Halifax Old Rd off A641, then Grimescar Ave)
7.30-11; 8-midnight Sat; 12-11 Sun
(01484) 514706
Taylor Golden Best, Dark Mild, Best Bitter; guest beer H
Voted by Huddersfield CAMRA as their Club

of the Year 2005, this popular little club is friendly and welcoming. The extensive bar area serves both the lounge and tap rooms. Home to bowling, snooker and pool teams, members also play dominoes and darts here. Live entertainment is sometimes staged in the lounge, which has Sky TV. Upstairs the snooker room opens out onto the bowling green that affords fantastic views across the valley. Show this Guide or CAMRA membership card for entry. 🚌(380, 381)♣P

Flyboat

6 Colne Street, Aspley, HD1 3BS (100 yds from A629, opp. marina)

🕘 5 (12 Fri & Sat)-11; 12-10.30 Sun

☎ (01484) 353494

Tetley Mild, Bitter 🄷

This quiet, back-street pub can be found just minutes from the town centre, not far from Aspley Marina. The lounge area, adorned with pictures of old Huddersfield, is served from a central bar. The large games room houses a pool table, TV and dartboard. Home to a pool team and the sub-aqua club, this former bargee's watering-hole is also a favourite for football and rugby fans. It hosts a well-attended quiz on Thursday. Local buses are 370, 371 and 372. ❀🚌♣

Rat & Ratchet

40 Chapel Hill, HD1 3EB (on A616, below ring road)

🕘 12 (1 Mon & Tue)-midnight (12.30am Fri & Sat); 12-11 Sun

☎ (01484) 516734

Ossett Pale Gold, Silver King, Excelsior; Taylor Best Bitter, Landlord; guest beers 🄷

Traditional, multi-roomed, former brew-pub, Ossett Brewery's second acquisition. The decor is enhanced by brewery adverts and music posters. The no-smoking back room is heated by a stove in winter. Usually 12 beers include four permanent and one rotated Ossett beer. Lunches are served Wednesday-Saturday. Several buses serve the pub: 306, 310, 313, 321 and 311. ❀◐≠🚌♣●P⚟

Slubber's Arms

1 Halifax Old Road, Hillhouse, HD1 6HW (off A641)

🕘 12-2.30 (3 Sat), 5.30-11.30; 12-3, 7-11.30 Sun

☎ (01484) 429032

Taylor Golden Best, Best Bitter, Landlord; guest beer 🄷

As the only Timothy Taylor tied house in Huddersfield, this wedge-shaped corner terrace pub dates back 150 years to the town's vibrant textile industry. Situated on the edge of the town centre, it offers a warm, friendly environment. Wherever you sit in this characterful pub you are invited to admire the relics of Huddersfield's past that adorn the walls. ⩩Q❀◐≠🚌(363, 328)♣⚟

Star Inn

7 Albert Street, Lockwood, HD1 3PJ (off A616)

🕘 5 (12 Sat)-11; closed Mon; 12-10.30 Sun

☎ (01484) 545443 🌐 thestarinn.info

Pictish Brewer's Gold; Taylor Best Bitter, Landlord; guest beers 🄷

Classic, back-street local enjoying deserved success since opening a few years ago. The emphasis is on quality ale, conversation and a friendly atmosphere, without juke boxes or games machines. A large, welcoming open fire warms this cosy pub during the winter months. A wide range of beers has been served here, through seven constantly-changing handpumps, one of which is dedicated to mild, stout or porter. Regular beer festivals (two or more yearly) are staged in the garden marquee.

⩩Q❀♿≠(Lockwood)🚌

Train Station Tavern

St George's Square, HD1 1JB (in station buildings)

🕘 11.30-11; 12-10.30 Sun

☎ (01484) 511058

Beer range varies 🄷

Situated in the Grade I listed railway station building, the Tavern is an established free house that supports the local and regional breweries by selling eight beers that are changed frequently. This open-plan, notoriously friendly pub features a mosaic tiled floor, a snug and a side room, housing a TV, piano and a large stage where live music is performed every Sunday. ◐≠

White Cross Inn

2 Bradley Road, Bradley, HD2 1XD (on A62)

🕘 11.45-11; 12-10.30 Sun

☎ (01484) 425728

Tetley Bitter; guest beers 🄷

Standing at the busy crossroads of the Leeds and Bradley roads, this popular local is a draw to both locals and passersby, many from the Huddersfield Narrow Canal and the Calder and Hebble Navigation. The large lounge extends on either side of a bare-boarded bar area that normally stocks five guest ales. Huddersfield CAMRA's Pub of the Year 2005 fields a pool team and hosts an annual beer festival in February. It is served by the 202 and 203 bus routes. ❀◐♿🚌♣P

Idle

Idle Working Men's Club

23 High Street, BD10 8NB

🕘 12-3 (not Tue-Thu), 7-11; 12-4, 7-10.30 Sun

☎ (01274) 613602 🌐 idleworkingmensclub.com

Tetley Bitter; guest beers 🄷

Club that attracts members because of its name – souvenir merchandise is sold. The concert room hosts live entertainment weekend evenings, while the lounge offers a quieter alternative. The downstairs games room houses two full-sized snooker tables, plus a large-screen TV for sports events. Show this Guide or CAMRA membership to be signed in. Parking is difficult. Bus Nos. 610, 611 and 612 pass close by. 🚌♣

Symposium Ale & Wine Bar

7 Albion Road, BD10 9PY

🕘 5.30 (12 Fri & Sat)-11; 12-2.30, 5.30-11 Wed & Thu; 12-10.30 Sun

☎ (01274) 616587

Taylor Landlord; guest beers 🄷

At the heart of Idle village, this popular bar is part of the no-smoking Market Town Taverns chain. A former restaurant, the food is of high quality and regular special food evenings are a feature. The Landlord is supported by five rotating guest beers often from northern England, but sometimes further afield, with one or two breweries represented at a time. It also stocks a wide range of foreign beers in bottles and on draught. The rear snug leads to a verandah. Q❀◐◗🚌⚟

Ilkley

Bar T'at

7 Cunliffe Road, LS29 9DZ

🕐 12-11 (11.30 Fri & Sat); 12-10.30 Sun

☎ (01943) 608888

Black Sheep Best Bitter; Caledonian Deuchars IPA; Taylor Landlord; guest beers Ⓗ

Popular, side-street pub renowned for its beer and food quality. Guest ales always include a Rooster's product and ales from Yorkshire micro-breweries. A good choice of proper foreign beers is available in bottles and on draught. Home-cooked food is on the menu every day. This three-storey building has a music-free bar area and is entirely no-smoking in line with Market Town Taverns' policy. It stands next to the main town-centre car park near the 963 bus stop. Q❀◐◗≠🚌⚟

Riverside Hotel

Riverside Gardens, Bridge Lane, LS29 9EU

🕐 11-11; 10-midnight Fri & Sat; 12-11.30 Sun

☎ (01943) 607338

Copper Dragon Best Bitter; Samuel Smith OBB; Tetley Bitter Ⓗ

Family-run hotel, with 10 bedrooms, set by the River Wharfe in a popular park; drink real ale while feeding the ducks. The adjacent fish and chip shop and ice cream servery also run by the hotel are popular in summer. Meals are served until early evening, and the bar has a 'happy hour' on weekdays, 4-8pm. The open fire is a welcome sight in cold weather. It is just 10 minutes' walk to the bus and train termini. ♨❀⇄◐◗≠(963)P

Keighley

Boltmakers Arms

117 East Parade, BD21 5HX (200 yds from station)

🕐 11-11 (midnight Fri & Sat); 12-11 Sun

☎ (01535) 661936

🌐 timothy-taylor.co.uk/boltmakers/

Taylor Golden Best, Best Bitter, Landlord; guest beer Ⓗ

Always a mecca for Taylor fans, this family-run pub lives up to its reputation under new licensees. Small, but warmly welcoming, the split-level pub is decorated with music memorabilia and whisky artefacts. Enjoy the quiz on Tuesday, live music on alternative Wednesdays and a smile and friendly banter at all times. The back yard serves as a tiny garden in summer. The guest beer and handpulled cider are from various sources, according to the licensee's whim. ♨❀≠🚌♣●

Brown Cow

5 Cross Leeds Street, BD21 2LQ

🕐 4 (12 Sat)-11; 12-10.30 Sun

☎ (01535) 602577 🌐 browncowkeighley.co.uk

Taylor Golden Best, Best Bitter, Landlord, Ram Tam; guest beers Ⓗ

At the opposite end of town from the other entries, this popular, friendly local is comfortably furnished and has a pool room. Among the local breweriana you will find the original sign from Bradford's Trough Brewery. The landlord is the town's official mace-bearer and steward. Guest beers are sourced mainly from local micros, often Brown Cow. Bad language and smoking are not tolerated at CAMRA's winter Pub of the Season 2005/06. ♨❀🚌♣●P⚟

Cricketers Arms

Coney Lane, BD21 5JE

🕐 11.30-midnight; 12-10.30 Sun

☎ (01535) 669912

Moorhouses Premier; guest beers Ⓗ

Welcoming, one-room pub on the quieter side of town, but still just 10 minutes' walk from the railway station and closer to the bus station. Serving five guest beers, real cider and a range of bottled beers, the guests showcase regional and micro-breweries rarely seen in the area. It hosts occasional beer festivals. ❀♿≠🚌●

Livery Rooms

89-97 North Street, BD21 3AA (nr Cavendish St jct)

🕐 9am-midnight (1am Fri & Sat); 9am-midnight Sun

☎ (01535) 682950

Greene King Abbot; Marston's Burton Bitter, Pedigree; guest beers Ⓗ

The pub has previously been used as stables, a Temperance hall, shop and bingo hall. Its history is displayed in various media, throughout the pub. A Moorhouses beer is always stocked and the guest ale policy offers strong support for local micros. Partly no-smoking, this rule is due to extend to the whole pub during 2006. Food is served all day until 11pm. ♨Q♉◐◗♿≠🚌●⚟

Leeds: City

Baroque

159 Headrow, LS1 5RG

🕐 11-11.30 (12.30am Sat); closed Sun

☎ (0113) 242 9674

Okells Bitter; guest beers Ⓗ

In addition to the Okells beer (of which more than one may be on offer), the pub usually stocks an ale from Copper Dragon and up to four guests that are pleasingly varied in their choice. It also hosts two or three beer festivals over the year. It comprises a large no-smoking room at the back, plus two seating areas and a stand-and-sup counter near the bar. It has won local CAMRA's Pub of the Season award. ◐≠🚌⚟

Duck & Drake

43 Kirkgate, LS2 7DR

🕐 11-11 (midnight Thu); 10-1am Fri & Sat; 11-11 Sun

☎ (0113) 245 9728

Taylor Landlord; Theakston Best Bitter, Old Peculier; guest beers Ⓗ

Basic, two roomed ale house with bare floorboards, serving the biggest range of real ale in Leeds. Regular live music is staged in the larger front room, while the back room houses the dartboard and no fewer than three TVs. A small outdoor drinking area is enlivened by murals drawn and painted by locals. It held its first beer festival in September 2005. ⋔❀⇌▭♣●

North Bar

24 New Briggate, LS1 6NU

12-1am (2am Wed-Sat); 12-10.30 Sun

☎ (0113) 242 4540 🌐 northbar.com

Beer range varies Ⓗ

A narrow frontage opens into a long building with the bar situated halfway down. The decor has a modern minimalist slant and the art for sale has been replaced by floor-to-ceiling panelling by the bar, displaying the beer menu. It keeps just one draught British ale, but it stocks an impressive range of foreign draught and bottled beers. Guest DJs perform on Friday and Saturday evenings. ⇌▭

Palace

Kirkgate, LS2 7DJ

11-11.30 (12.30am Fri & Sat); 12-11 Sun

☎ (0113) 244 5882

Draught Bass; Tetley Bitter; guest beers Ⓗ

Up to nine changing guest beers are sold here, always including a mild, plus a beer from the Rooster's/Outlaw stable. Set into the churchyard wall nearby you will find the East Bar Stone that marked the medieval city boundary. First recorded as an inn in 1841, it was once owned by the Melbourne Brewery. Food is served 12-7pm. ❀◐◑♿♣●⚟

Scarbrough Hotel

Bishopgate Street, LS1 5DY

11-midnight; 12-10 Sun

☎ (0113) 243 4590

Tetley Bitter; guest beers Ⓗ

Normally five guest beers are available, but sometimes seven in the joint Leeds CAMRA Pub of the Year 2004/5. The highlights of the year are the beer festival, held jointly with the Grove over the last week of January and the Yorkshire ale and produce festival (first week of Aug) to celebrate Yorkshire Day. This is the only pub in central Leeds to sell perry. ❀◐◑♿⇌●

Town Hall Tavern

17 Westgate, LS1 2RA

11.30-11; closed Sun

☎ (0113) 245 3966

Taylor Golden Best, Landlord; Tetley Bitter; guest beer Ⓗ

This is the third consecutive Guide entry for this Leeds CAMRA seasonal award-winner. The Tavern caters for the busy financial and legal sector of the city. A pleasant, open-plan venue, it is comfortably furnished and decorated with a changing display of memorabilia, photos, legal cartoons and other interesting collectables. It is probably the only permanent outlet for Golden Best in the city centre. Weekday lunches are served. ◐♿⇌▭

Victoria Family & Commercial

28 Great George Street, LS1 3DL

11-11 (midnight Thu-Sat); 12-6 Sun

☎ (0113) 245 1386

Black Sheep Best Bitter; Taylor Landlord; Tetley Mild, Bitter; guest beers Ⓗ

Fine example of a Victorian pub, the sign has lasted since the 1890s. Up to four guest beers are usually sold. The main bar is opulent, full of brass and glass, complete with snob screens. There is a comfortable, no-smoking room to the left of the entrance, and another room at the back of the main bar. Live jazz (Thu). ◐⇌▭⚟

Whitelock's First City Luncheon Bar ☆

Turks Head Yard, LS1 6HB (off Briggate)

11-11; 12-10.30 Sun

☎ (0113) 245 3950

Caledonian Deuchars IPA; John Smith's Bitter; Theakston Best Bitter, Old Peculier; guest beers Ⓗ

A hidden gem, boasting one of the largest pub gardens in the city centre. A frequent local CAMRA Pub of the Season winner, it serves ale from local breweries, such as York, Daleside and Wentworth and further afield. As one of the oldest pubs in Leeds, it has retained its traditional atmosphere and decor. The busy restaurant is warmed by a real fire. ⋔Q❀◐◑⇌▭

Leeds: North

Arcadia Ale & Wine Bar

Arndale Centre, Otley Road, Headingley, LS6 2UE

11-11; 12-10.30 Sun

☎ (0113) 274 5599

Black Sheep Best Bitter; Caledonian Deuchars IPA; Taylor Landlord; guest beers Ⓗ

Hidden away in a row of shops, Arcadia is an excellent conversion from a bank and has won a highly commended citation in CAMRA's Pub Design awards. It supplements the varied range of real ales with an interesting variety of bottled beers and draught fruit beer. The Arcadia eschews music and games machines and is no-smoking throughout. Q◐◑▭⚟

Bricklayers Arms

8 Low Close Street, Woodhouse, LS2 9EG

11-midnight (1am Fri & Sat); 11-11.30 Sun

☎ (0113) 245 8277

Caledonian Deuchars IPA; John Smith's Bitter; guest beers Ⓗ

Close to Leeds University and known locally as the Brickies, the management has created a true community pub by attracting a mix of locals and students. It sponsors student archery and hockey, and fields football, darts and dominoes teams. Guest beers are from local breweries via the SIBA scheme. ❀◐◑♣P

Eldon

190 Woodhouse Lane, LS2 9DX

11.30-11 (midnight Thu-Sat); 12-10.30 Sun

☎ (0113) 245 3591

Adnams Broadside; Greene King IPA, Abbot; Tetley Bitter; Wells Bombardier; guest beers Ⓗ

Sports-oriented, multi-level pub boasting no less than three big screens, ensuring you miss no sporting action. Located opposite Leeds University, the Eldon is at the forefront of promoting real ale to the student population. A wide range of guest beers is available, but there is less choice during student holidays. Meals are served until 7pm (5pm weekends).

Lord d'Arcy

618 Harrogate Road, LS17 8EH (on A61)

11.30-11; 12-10.30 Sun

☎ (0113) 237 0100

Hardys & Hansons Bitter, Olde Trip, seasonal beers Ⓗ

Large roadside pub on the busy A61. Although open plan, the interior is broken up by wood and glass panels. The decor, with a variety of artefacts including oil paintings and small statues, has the feel of a country house. A function room downstairs is available for hire. The extensive outdoor drinking area has patio heaters.

Leeds: South

Cross Keys

107 Water Lane, The Round Foundry, LS11 5WD

12-11; 12-10.30 Sun

☎ (0113) 243 3711 the-crosskeys.com

Beer range varies Ⓗ

Under the same ownership as the city centre North Bar, the pub offers a wider range of British ale, including a beer from Rooster's, a stout or porter and one or two guests, and places a greater emphasis on food (although remaining drinker-friendly). Two rooms (one no-smoking), both warmed by wood-burning stoves, are wrapped around a central bar. Exposed beams, stone flags, tiles and bare brickwork are much in evidence. Sunday meals are served 12-6pm.

Garden Gate ☆

Whitfield Place, Hunslet, LS10 2QB

11.30-11; 12-10.30 Sun

☎ (0113) 270 0379

Tetley Bitter Ⓗ

Victorian gem, hidden away in a modern housing estate. The pub has retained intact its multi-roomed layout, with a tiled drinking corridor, off which comes the tap room and two further rooms. Features include a mosaic in the entranceway, fine mirrors and stained glass panels. It also boasts a splendid tiled exterior.

Grove Inn

Back Row, Holbeck, LS11 5PL

12-11 (midnight Fri & Sat); 12-10.30 Sun

☎ (0113) 243 9254

Adnams Broadside; Caledonian Deuchars IPA, 80/-; Moorhouses Black Cat; Wells Bombardier; guest beers Ⓗ

Rare example of a West Riding corridor pub, now swamped by high rise buildings. This oasis of real ale stands minutes from Leeds train station. The changing guest beers are now selected from the Enterprise Inns SIBA list. Joint winner of the local Pub of the Year 2004/5 award, no food is served on Saturday. The car park is small.

Leeds: West

Jug & Barrel

56-58 Town Street, Stanningley, LS28 6EZ

12-midnight; 12-10.30 Sun

☎ (0113) 257 6877 jugandbarrel.com

John Smith's Bitter; Taylor Landlord; Theakston Old Peculier; guest beer Ⓗ

Once the Huddersfield Arms, a Strettons of Derby house, this pub lives up to its name with jugs, mugs, steins and even handpumps dangling from the ceiling, and a fine selection of cask ales on the bar. Decorated in traditional style, the single room encompasses several areas, including a darts alcove, a flag-floored 'conservatory' and a music room. The guest beer is usually Shepherd Neame Spitfire or Wells Bombardier.

Linthwaite

Sair

139 Lane Top, HD7 5SG (top of Hoyle Ing, off A62)
OS100143

5 (12 Fri & Sat)-11; 12-10.30 Sun

☎ (01484) 842370

Linfit Dark Mild, Bitter, Autumn Gold, English Guineas Stout, seasonal beers Ⓗ

Set on a hillside overlooking the Colne Valley, this brew-pub is a popular meeting place for locals and visitors alike. A central bar serves four rooms, including one for non-smokers. The real fires are a welcome sight in winter. Over the years the pub has won numerous awards, including CAMRA's national Pub of the Year in 1997. Up to 10 beers are normally available.

Liversedge

Black Bull

37 Halifax Road, WF15 6JR (on A649)

12-11.30 (12.30am Fri & Sat); 12-11.30 Sun

☎ (01924) 403779

Ossett Pale Gold, Excelsior; Taylor Landlord; guest beers Ⓗ

Dating back in part to the 18th century, Ossett's first pub is a no-nonsense delight for drinkers of all ages. It offers five drinking areas (two no-smoking), including the new room dubbed 'the chapel' by regulars, due to its handsome woodwork and stained glass. Four Ossett beers – one a house ale – and four others are stocked, always offering a variety of beer styles, including a mild. Classic German pils and weissbier are also available on draught.

Marsden

Tunnel End Inn

Waters Road, HD7 6NF (near Standedge Visitor Centre)

12-3 (not Mon-Wed), 5 (8 Mon)-11; 12-11 Sat; 12-10.30 Sun

☎ (01484) 844636

Black Sheep Best Bitter; Taylor Landlord; guest beers Ⓗ

Homely Pennine pub, near the Standedge tunnel – the longest, highest and deepest tunnel in this country. Surrounded by fine scenery, with several walking, cycling and canalside routes, the pub bears a country feel and attracts outdoor enthusiasts, while being within easy reach of the village. Patrons are assured of relaxing surroundings, good home-cooked food and the proprietors' 'personal touch'.

Marsh

Marsh Liberal Club

31 New Hey Road, HD3 4AL (on A640)
⏲ 12-2, 7-11; 12-11 Sat; 12-10.30 Sun
☎ (01484) 420152 🌐 marshlib.co.uk
Taylor Golden Best, Best Bitter; Theakston Best Bitter; guest beers 🄷
Popular, well-run club in a Grade II listed building west of the town centre. Facilities include snooker rooms, crown green bowling, a wheelchair ramp and disabled WC. Some rooms are no-smoking. Show this Guide or CAMRA membership card for entry. 🐴❀♿🚌♣P⊬

Mirfield

Navigation Tavern

6 Station Road, WF14 8NL
⏲ 11-11; 11-10.30 Sun
☎ (01924) 492476
John Smith's Bitter; Theakston Mild, Best Bitter, XB, Old Peculier; guest beer (occasional) 🄷
Congenial canalside pub, next to a boatyard on the Calder and Hebble Navigation near the centre of Mirfield and a stone's throw from the station. Comprising two open-plan rooms, a games room and the excellent New Lock restaurant, it is a haven for canal users and towpath walkers. Good quality meals are served in the restaurant (not Mon; 12-4 Sun). ❀🛏♿◗⇌🚌♣P

Old Colonial Club

Dunbottle Lane, WF14 9JJ (on A644, opp. fire station)
⏲ 4-midnight; 11.30-12.30am Sat; 11.30-midnight Sun
☎ (01924) 496920
Copper Dragon Best Bitter; guest beers 🄷
A club that welcomes all visitors (CAMRA members should show their cards). It has a large, but cosy room with a central bar and pleasing decor. The spacious, no-smoking conservatory-style annexe is used by families and hosts mid-week quizzes, games evenings and occasional live acts. The large garden houses an unusual living war memorial. Other attractions are the rare guest beers and great value Sunday lunch (eve meals served Thu-Sat). 🐴❀◗♿🚌P⊬

Mytholmroyd

Shoulder of Mutton

36 New Road, HX7 5DZ (on B6138 near station)
⏲ 11.30-3, 7-11; 11.30-11 Sat; 12-11 Sun
☎ (01422) 883165
Black Sheep Best Bitter; Camerons Castle Eden Ale; Greene King IPA; Taylor Landlord 🄷
Roadside village inn at the lower end of the attractively wooded Cragg Vale, tucked away between the stream and the railway line. It enjoys a strong local following from both drinkers and community sports teams, but it is more widely known for its excellent value food (not served Tue). The roomy main bar displays memorabilia relating to the Cragg Vale coiners, a group of 18th-century forgers. 🐴❀◖◗⇌♣P⊬

North Featherstone

Bradley Arms

98 Willow Lane, WF7 6BJ (on B6128)
⏲ 3-11; 12-midnight Fri & Sat; 12-10.30 Sun
☎ (01977) 792284
Black Sheep Best Bitter; John Smith's Bitter; Taylor Landlord; guest beer 🄷
Lovely old, ex-farm building with several rooms, including a candlelit lounge, this inn has a rich history. It was a key location in the infamous Featherstone massacre of 1893, the last occasion on which British troops shot and killed British citizens on English soil. Daleside, or another independent, supplies the guest beer. ♔Q🐴❀◘♣P

Ossett

Brewer's Pride

Low Mill Road, WF5 8ND
⏲ 12-3, 5.30-11; 12-11 Fri & Sat; 12-10.30 Sun
☎ (01924) 273865 🌐 brewers-pride.co.uk
Ossett Pale Gold, Excelsior; Taylor Landlord; guest beers 🄷
Genuine free house, on the outskirts of Ossett, five minutes' walk from the Calder and Hebble Canal. Good value lunches are served and on Wednesday evening, curry, pies and steak feature on subsequent weeks. The local folk club meets on Thursday evening and monthly live music is performed (first Sun). A summer beer festival is held annually. ♔Q❀◖🚌(121)♠

Otley

Bowling Green

18 Bondgate, LS21 3AB (near bus station)
⏲ 12-4 (not Mon & Tue), 7-11; 6-10.30 Sun
☎ (01943) 461494
Beer range varies 🄷
A Guide entry for many years, this solid-looking building dates from 1757. Set back from the road, it has an outdoor drinking area in front. Inside, there is an L-shaped drinking area with a pool table at one end. The walls are decorated with a bizarre array of artefacts. ♔❀♣

Junction

44 Bondgate, LS21 1AD (100 yds from bus station)
⏲ 11-11 (midnight Fri & Sat); 11-11 Sun
☎ (01943) 463233
Caledonian Deuchars IPA; Taylor Landlord; guest beers 🄷
Friendly, vibrant pub occupying a prominent corner site on the approach from Leeds. The single room features a central fireplace and pictures of bygone Otley alongside beer and brewery posters. The odd stuffed animal, antlers and a high shelf of beer bottles complete the decoration. It hosts live music on Tuesday. A former local CAMRA Pub of the Year. ♔❀

Oxenhope

Waggon & Horses Inn

Dyke Nook, Hebden Bridge Road, BD22 9QE
(on A6033, 1 mile from village)

12-2 (not Mon & Tue), 6-midnight; 12-11 Sun
(01535) 643302
Beer range varies H
Possibly the highest pub in West Yorkshire, it benefits from impressive views across Bronte country. Free of any tie, the beer range often includes a golden ale, sourced from northern micros. Oxenhope station on the Keighley Valley and Worth Valley line is just over a mile away. Fresh, home-cooked food is served. (500)P

Pontefract

Robin Hood

4 Wakefield Road, WF8 4HN
11.30-3.30 (4.30 Fri & Sat), 7-11; 12.30-3.30, 7-10.30 Sun
(01977) 702231
John Smith's Bitter; Tetley Bitter; guest beers H
Busy local near the notorious town end traffic lights, known locally as Jenkin's Folly. It has a public bar and three other drinking areas. It hosts quizzes twice weekly and fields darts and dominoes teams in the local charities league. Winner of several local CAMRA awards, including Pub of the Year, the Robin Hood stages a beer festival over August bank holiday weekend.
(Tanshelf/Baghill)

Pudsey

Fleece

100 Fartown, LS28 8LU
12-11; 12-10.30 Sun
(0113) 236 2748
Taylor Landlord; Tetley Bitter; guest beer H
Originally called the Smith's Arms, it has been known as the Fleece since the 1840s. To the left is the small tap room, rarely quiet and usually showing sport on TV. The more sedate lounge has plenty of comfortable seating. The guest beer is usually from Brown Cow, but may be from Timothy Taylor and is often a strong or dark beer. P

Rastrick

Roundhill Inn

75 Clough Lane, HD6 3QL (on A6107 400 yds from A643 jct, near M62)
5 (7 Sat)-11; 12-3, 7-10.30 Sun
(01484) 713418
Black Sheep Best Bitter; Taylor Golden Best, Landlord; guest beer H
This free house overlooks the unusual hill that gives the pub its name and it benefits from spectacular views of Rastrick cricket ground to Brighouse over a mile away, and beyond. A collection of racecourse tags hangs above the bar, alongside the pump clips from independent guest beers that have featured here. The small, quiet lounge is no-smoking. Parking can be difficult. Q(380/1)P

Ripponden

Beehive Inn

Hob Lane, Soyland, HX6 4NX (steep ½ mile walk up Royd Lane from A58) OS033199
4.30-2am; 12-2am Sun
(01422) 824670
Taylor Golden Best, Landlord; guest beers H
Rural pub, only half a mile from the centre of Ripponden; you can avoid the steep climb by taking the A532/3 bus. Formerly a small ale house, it has been opened out and extended over the years, but some flagstoned floors remain. The rear of the pub appears to be divided into dining alcoves, but in fact there are no strict divisions between drinking and dining areas. Sunday meals are served 12-8pm, other days 4.30-9.30pm. P

Butcher's Arms

143 Rochdale Road, HX6 4JU (on A58)
12-3 (not Mon), 5-midnight (12.30am Fri); 12-12.30am Sat; 12-10.30 Sun
(01422) 823100
Greene King Old Speckled Hen; Marston's Pedigree; Taylor Landlord; Tetley Bitter H
On the main road, just west of the village centre, overlooking the Ryburn Valley, this pub is set over three levels. The upper level is reserved for dining and pool is played on the lowest level. Extensive sports TV coverage is shown in the bar. Note the collections of old cigarette cards on display. P

Old Bridge Inn

Priest Lane, HX6 4DF (between A58 and B6113)
12-3, 5.30 (5 Fri)-11; 12-11 Sat; 12-10.30 Sun
(01422) 822595 porkpieclub.com
Taylor Golden Best, Best Bitter, Landlord; guest beers H
Whitewashed building on the opposite bank of the River Ryburn to the parish church, accessible via a 16th-century stone humpback bridge. One of the oldest pubs in Yorkshire, partly dating back to the 14th century, three rooms are spread over two levels, with the bar extending into all the rooms. The no-smoking room boasts an exposed cruck beam. On the route of the 50-mile Calderdale Way, lunchtime buffet and evening meals are served weekdays. A Black Sheep beer is always available. QP

Shipley

Fanny's Ale & Cider House

63 Saltaire Road, BD18 3JN (on A657, opp. fire station)
12 (5 Mon)-11; 12-midnight Fri & Sat; 12-10.30 Sun
(01274) 591419
Taylor Golden Best, Landlord; Theakston Old Peculier; guest beers H
Former shop, it was opened by the present owner firstly as a beer shop, then as a fully licensed free house, and has been a regular Guide entry since. The back room has a real fire and gas lighting, while the upstairs room provides more seating. Up to nine real ales include products from local breweries, such as Salamander. A selection of foreign beers is kept, both on draught and bottled.
Q(662, 760)

Shipley Club

162 Bradford Road, BD18 3PD (on A650 opp. Branch pub)
12-2 (not Mon, Tue or Thu), 6.30 (7.30 Fri)-11; 12-11 Sat; 12-2.30 Sun; hours may vary
(01274) 201842

Beer range varies ⊞
Formed in 1900 as Shipley Bowling Green Club; this thriving sports and social club has a steward devoted to real ale. The three ales often come from Yorkshire micros such as Litton and Salamander. Pub games and bowling are available, subject to club commitments. Children are welcome until 9.30pm. The outdoor drinking area is beside the bowling green. Show this Guide or CAMRA membership card to be signed in. ❀♿⊟♣P

Shipley Pride

1 Saltaire Road, BD18 3HH (on A657)
✪ 11.30 (11 Sat)-11; 12-10.30 Sun
☎ (01274) 585341
Taylor Landlord; Tetley Bitter; guest beers ⊞
This former free house, now owned by Punch, has recently extended its beer range from three to five ales. One guest beer is from the standard Punch list with two more from its 'finest ales' selection. This friendly, Victorian local has two rooms around the central bar, both boasting stained glass windows. The lounge is comfortably appointed, while the games room offers pool, darts and TV sport. Home-made food is served weekdays. ❀◑⇌(Shipley/Saltaire) ♣P

Sowerby Bridge

Alma Inn

Cottonstones, Mill Bank, HX6 4NS OS028215
✪ 12-11 daily
☎ (01422) 823334 🌐 almainn.com
Taylor Golden Best, Landlord; Tetley Bitter; guest beer (winter) ⊞
Rural pub, benefiting from splendid views from the patio, in excellent walking country, near the 50-mile Calderdale Way footpath. Exposed stone walls, flagstone floors, much wood and open fires characterise the pub that also has a 50-seat restaurant with authentic pizza oven. Meals are served all day and can be washed down with one of the 100 continental (mainly Belgian) bottled beers that are listed on a speciality menu, with tasting notes.
⛰❀⇆◑◐♿⛺⊟(532/3, 566/7)♣P⚟

Puzzle Hall Inn

21 Hollins Mill Lane, HX6 2RF (400 yds from A58)
✪ 12 (4 Mon & Tue)-11; 1-11 Sun
☎ (01422) 835547 🌐 puzzlehall.info
Greene King IPA; Taylor Landlord; guest beers ⊞
Lively, friendly pub nestling between the canal and the river. Opened in the 1700s, this former brew-pub is dominated by the tower of the old brewery. Although the pub is tiny, with just two rooms, it is a regular live music venue. Music festivals take place in May and August and beer festivals in March and September. Wednesday is curry and quiz night. ⛰❀◑◐⇌⊟♣P

Turk's Head

20 Back Wharf Street, HX6 2AD (off A58)
✪ 11-11 (11.30 Sat & Sun)
☎ (01422) 834216
Black Sheep Best Bitter; Taylor Landlord; Tetley Mild ⊞
This small, cosy, friendly pub is located just off the town centre, between the main shopping street and the River Calder. Its three small drinking areas, with flagged or timber floors, are traditionally furnished. Very much a pub for the local community, it can get busy on evenings when a big match is shown on TV. ⛰❀⇌

White Horse

Burnley Road, Friendly, HX6 2UG
(on A646, 3/4 mile NW of centre)
✪ 12-11; 12-10.30 Sun
☎ (01422) 831173
E&S Elland Beyond the Pale; Tetley Mild, Bitter ⊞
This white-painted pub stands just back from the busy A646 on the Halifax-Todmorden bus route. In summer the prize-winning window boxes can be stunning. This welcoming local has a tap room and a larger lounge bar – once two rooms and still partially divided. A strong local following includes members of Friendly football club, Friendly brass band, and a dominoes club. ❀⊟♣P

Works (in Progress)

12 Hollins Mill Lane, HX6 2QG (opp. swimming pool)
✪ 12-11; 12-10.30 Sun
☎ (01422) 834821
Taylor Golden Best, Best Bitter, Landlord; guest beers ⊞
The pub opened in August 2005 in a former joinery workshop that was only partly finished at the time – hence the name. Standing beside the Rochdale Canal on the western side of the town centre, this large, open-plan pub features exposed beams and floorboards. It has quickly established a reputation for the quality of its ale, with up to eight guests coming from the likes of Phoenix, Moorhouses, Newby Wyke, Copper Dragon and the local brewery, Little Valley.
⛰Q◑◐♿⇌⊟P⚟

Sowood

Dog & Partridge

Forest Hill Road, HX4 9LB (¼ mile W of B6112)
✪ 7-11; 12-4.30, 7-10.30 Sun
☎ (01422) 374249
Black Sheep Best Bitter; Taylor Landlord; guest beer ⊞
Once known locally as Mabel's after its long-standing landlady, this rare, rural gem is still run by her son. A simple, two-room local, it is totally lacking in frills; the peace is only disturbed by the conversation of the locals. A step ahead of the Government, the landlord imposed a smoking ban in 2005. You might be lucky enough to hear him play the piano.
Q❀♣P⚟

Stanbury

Friendly

54 Main Street, BD22 0HB (on Colne road)
✪ 12-11; 12-10.30 Sun
☎ (01535) 645528
Goose Eye Bronte Bitter; Tetley Bitter; guest beer ⊞
Pleasant village inn in scenic Bronte country that is easily accessible by car, bus or

footpath. Stanbury is just two miles from Haworth, but a million miles from its tourist hustle and bustle. Quite small, its main drinking area is split in two by a central bar, and there is a separate area for games, pool and TV. ❀◐♿⛺🚌♣P

Todmorden

Top Brink Inn

Brink Top, Lumbutts, OL14 6JB (near Lumbutts Mill activity centre) OS956236

⏲ 12-3 (not Mon-Fri), 6-11; 12-10.30 Sun

☎ (01706) 812696

Boddingtons Bitter; Camerons Castle Eden Ale; Flowers Original; Taylor Landlord; guest beer ⊞

Large rural inn, popular with family diners, it gets busy at the weekend. Set in spectacularly scenic countryside, it is handy for the Pennine Way and Stoodley Pike, and attracts outdoor enthusiasts, walkers, cyclists and riders. The guest beer changes on a regular basis and the food is recommended. Children are welcome. ❀◐◑⛺🚌P⚟

Wainstalls

Cat i' th' Well Inn

Wainstalls Lane, HX2 7TR OS041284

⏲ 12-3, 5.30-11; 12-11 Sat; 12-10.30 Sun

☎ (01422) 244841

Taylor Golden Best, Best Bitter, Landlord; guest beer ⊞

The 'Caty' lies in the attractive Luddenden Valley near Jerusalem Farm nature reserve and campsite (tel 883246) in superb walking country. Its garden affords delightful views. The cosy main bar and adjacent no-smoking/dining room feature wood panelling installed in 1964 from the former Castle Carr hunting lodge. You will often find a guest beer here from Old Mill, Copper Dragon, Phoenix, Black Sheep or Halifax Steam. ♨Q❀🛏◐◑⛺P⚟

Wakefield

Alverthorpe WMC

111 Flanshaw Lane, WF2 9JG (2 miles from city)

⏲ 11.30-4, 6.30-11; 11.30-11 Fri & Sat; 12-3.30, 6.30-11 Sun

☎ (01924) 374179

Tetley Mild, Bitter; guest beers ⊞

Multi-roomed, CIU-affiliated club, its cosy, arched interior features unusual glass. It stocks a wide selection of guest beers, mostly from local micros, and hosts a beer festival in October. This regular local CAMRA award-winner hosts live entertainment at the weekend, while weekday amusements include snooker, darts and a wide-screen TV for sports. It fields sports teams and boasts a floodlit bowling green. ❀♿♣P

Black Rock

3 Cross Square, WF1 1PQ (at top of Westgate)

⏲ 11-11 (midnight Sat); 12-10.30 Sun

☎ (01924) 375550

Tetley Bitter; guest beer ⊞

Compact, old-style, city-centre pub. Already enjoying a long-standing reputation for the quality of its Tetley's, it recently instigated a guest ale policy to offer greater customer choice, with the occasional appearance of Tetley's light and dark milds. Recently refurbished to a high standard, it is a pleasing alternative to the surrounding café-bars of Westgate. Old prints of Wakefield help create a relaxing ambience.

⇌(Westgate/Kirkgate)

Fernandes Brewery Tap

5 Avison Yard, Kirkgate, WF1 1UA

⏲ 5-11; 11-1am Fri & Sat; 12-midnight Sun

☎ (01924) 369547 🌐 fernandes-brewery.gowyld.com

Beer range varies ⊞

This pub is a regular local CAMRA award-winner. A friendly, one room bar, it offers a constantly changing range of excellent beers, with always two Fernandes brews and four guests. It also sells a good selection of Belgian beers. More unusual is the Genever gin bar. Q⇌(Kirkgate/Westgate)●

Flanshaw Hotel

Flanshaw Lane, WF2 9JD (400 yds from Dewsbury Rd)

⏲ 12-11; 12-10.30 Sun

☎ (01924) 290830

Acorn Barnsley Bitter; John Smith's Bitter; guest beers ⊞

Spacious 1930s community pub that enjoys a strong local following. The guest beers come from local micro-breweries. Heavily involved with local sports teams, the pub cellars are used as changing rooms. It hosts an auction on Monday. Unusual stained glass windows and a goldfish tank add a touch of individuality. ♨🏠❀⊟♿🚌(114)♣P⊓

Harry's Bar

107B Westgate, WF1 1EL (near Westgate Station)

⏲ 5-11 (midnight Fri & Sat); 12-11 Sun

☎ (01924) 373773

Ossett Silver King, Excelsior; Taylor Landlord; guest beers ⊞

Small, cosy, one-roomed pub that has a strong regular customer base of all ages. The blazing fire in winter is a much-appreciated rarity. The bare brick and wood interior shows what a modern conversion to a pub can achieve. Guest beers showcase newly-opened micro-breweries. The shady courtyard and south-facing terrace are popular for the views of the famous 99-arch viaduct. Live music is performed on Wednesday.

♨❀♿⇌(Westgate)

Henry Boon's

130 Westgate, WF2 9SR

⏲ 11-11 (1am Fri & Sat); 12-10.30 Sun

☎ (01924) 378126

Clark's Classic Blonde; Taylor Landlord; guest beers ⊞

The tap for Clark's Brewery, just behind the pub, it gets busy on weekend evenings as it is on the 'Westgate run'. Hogsheads are used for tables here and the thatched bar is a talking point, as are the many items of breweriana. Catering for drinkers of all ages, it stages regular live music.

⇌(Westgate/Kirkgate)♣

Labour Club (Red Shed)

18 Vicarage Street, WF1 1QX

12-5 (not Mon-Thu; 11-4 Sat), 7-11; 12-5 Sun
(01924) 215626 theredshed.org.uk
Acorn Barnsley Bitter; Ossett Pale Gold; guest beers H
One of a kind, the Red Shed is a former army hut that is still going strong, despite being threatened by city centre development. Four rotating ales, mostly from micros, are supplemented by bottled Belgian beers and the occasional Belgian draught. A winner of many local and national awards, the Shed plays host to trade union, Labour Party and many other local organisations' meetings. Staffed by volunteers, it stages two annual beer festivals, live music and barbecues. (Westgate/Kirkgate)P

Redoubt
28 Horbury Road, WF2 8TS
12 (11 Sat)-11.30; 11-11 Sun
(01924) 377085 theredoubt.co.uk
Taylor Landlord; Tetley Mild, Bitter H
One of the oldest pubs in Wakefield, this Tetley Heritage house has four small but cosy rooms and a drinking lobby. The Redoubt fields its own cricket and football teams and pictures of Wakefield's sporting history are displayed around the pub.
Q(Westgate)P

Six Chimneys
41-49 Kirkgate, WF1 1HY
11-midnight (1am Fri & Sat)
(01924) 239449
Greene King Abbot; guest beers H
Pleasant city centre Wetherspoon's catering for a wide clientele, with two family areas, one no-smoking. This large, open-plan pub was formerly a shop. Many different cask ales are offered including those from Yorkshire micros.
Q(Kirkgate/Westgate)

Talbot & Falcon
Northgate, WF1 3AP (just off Bull Ring)
11-11; 12-10.30 Sun
(01924) 201693
Greene King Old Speckled Hen; Taylor Landlord; Tetley Bitter; guest beers H
Convenient for the bus station and the Bull Ring, the pub is a listed building where workers and shoppers can enjoy a good value lunch and a chat over their beer. The cosy interior is a great place for taking refuge from the busy city centre.
(Kirkgate/Westgate)

Walton

New Inn
144 Shay Lane, WF2 6LA
12 (11 Sat)-11; 12-10.30 Sun
(01924) 255447
Caledonian Deuchars IPA; Jennings Cumberland Ale; John Smith's Bitter; Taylor Landlord; guest beer H
Traditional, 18th-century vernacular stone building under a flagstone roof, comprising several areas, including a restaurant that offers exceptionally good food (not served Mon) and a coffee shop that opens at 10am. This community-focused pub is in an ideal position for starting or finishing a walk along the route of the former Barnsley Canal. One of the five handpumps is dedicated to beers from local independent breweries. P

Wetherby

Muse Ale & Wine Bar
16 Bank Street, LS22 6NQ
12 (11 Sat)-11; 12-10.30 Sun
(01937) 580201
Beer range varies H
Part of the excellent Market Town Taverns chain, Muse has a small bar where four handpumps mainly serve beers brewed in Yorkshire. It also stocks an extensive range of foreign bottled beers. There is a small drinking area next to a large fireplace filled with plants and a larger section mainly used by diners. No-smoking is allowed anywhere on the premises which are also free of music and games machines. QP

Royal Oak
60 North Street, LS22 6NR
12 (4 Mon)-11; 12-3, 7-10.30 Sun
(01937) 580508
John Smith's Bitter; Tetley Bitter; guest beers H
Friendly local with a cosy atmosphere that draws a varied clientele. There is an L-shaped bar with two drinking areas, warmed by an open fire. The traditional feel is further enhanced by wooden panelling and internal stained glass. One of the guest ales usually comes from E&S Elland's extensive range.

Wintersett

Angler's Retreat
Ferry Top Lane, WF4 2EB OS382157
12-3, 7-11; 12-11 Sat; 12-3.30, 7-10.30 Sun
(01924) 862370
Acorn Barnsley Bitter; John Smith's Bitter; Samuel Smith OBB; Theakston XB; guest beer H
Locally known as the Sett, this is a superb example of a two-roomed rural beer house. Enjoying a strong local trade, it also offers a warm welcome to visitors. Close to the Anglers Country Park, it has a large garden. A regular CAMRA award-winner, where ale is dispensed through autovacs giving a tight, creamy head, the Sett is run by one of the longest-serving landlords in the area.
Q(195/6/7)P

Woodlesford

Two Pointers
69 Church Street, LS26 8RE (400 yds from A642)
3 (12 Fri & Sat)-midnight; 12-11.30 Sun
(0113) 282 3124
Black Sheep Best Bitter; John Smith's Bitter; guest beers H
Much improved, former coaching inn, it is comprised of a large, split-level lounge bar/function room and a panelled tap room with a pool table and dartboard. Table service is offered on Saturday evening and Sunday is quiz night. The pub has a spacious patio and hosts beer festivals in spring and autumn. P

Wales

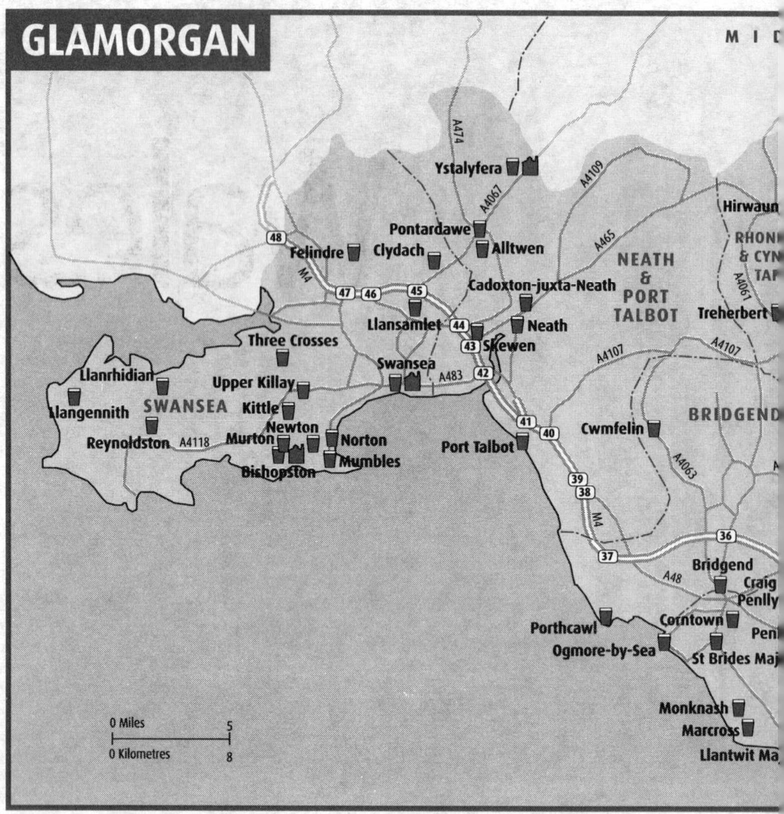

Authority areas covered: Bridgend UA, Caerphilly UA, Cardiff UA, Merthyr Tydfil UA, Neath & Port Talbot UA, Rhondda, Cynon, Taff UA, Swansea UA, Vale of Glamorgan UA

Aberdare

Cambrian Inn

60 Seymour Street, CF44 7DL

11-5, 7-11; 11-11 Fri & Sat; 12-10.30 Sun

(01685) 879120

Beer range varies H

Pleasant town pub just a short walk from the main shopping area. The comfy interior draws a mixed clientele. Only one ale is served, but this is invariably well sourced and changes frequently. The pub sign portrays a famous conductor from Aberdare, 'Caradog' or Griffith Rhys-Jones.

Whitcombe Inn

Whitcombe Street, CF44 7DA

2 (12 Fri & Sat)-11

(01685) 875106

Brains SA, Rev James; guest beer H

Making a welcome return to the Guide, this pub is situated just outside the town centre. Recently refurbished, its character still shows through in the pleasant, comfortable bar. Photographs of old Aberdare decorate the walls.

Aberthin

Farmers Arms

Cowbridge Road, CF71 7HB (on A4222)

12-3, 6-11; 12-2, 7-10.30 Sun

(01446) 773429

Wadworth 6X; guest beer H

Popular pub one mile north of Cowbridge on the main road towards Ystradowen. A changing guest keeps the 6X company on the bar, while the high quality food represents good value and brings many visitors from near and far. There is ample parking and extensive outdoor facilities in the pleasant grounds with a river running through. The current licensee was a local CAMRA Pub of the Year winner in his previous pub.

P

Hare & Hounds

Cowbridge Road, CF71 7HB (on A4222)

11.30 (3.30 Wed)-midnight; 12-midnight Sun

(01446) 774892

Hancock's HB; H **guest beers** H/G

Small, friendly, two-roomed village local: a traditional bar boasting wooden settles and a collection of photos of historic interest, and a larger lounge where children are welcome until 9pm. Two of the three guest ales are on gravity, lending an old-fashioned feel to the fine, comfortable pub. Cyril's bus (E1), between Cowbridge and Talbot Green, runs past the door. The hosts ran the Barn at Mwyndy for many years. They stage an annual beer festival here. Parking is limited.

Q P

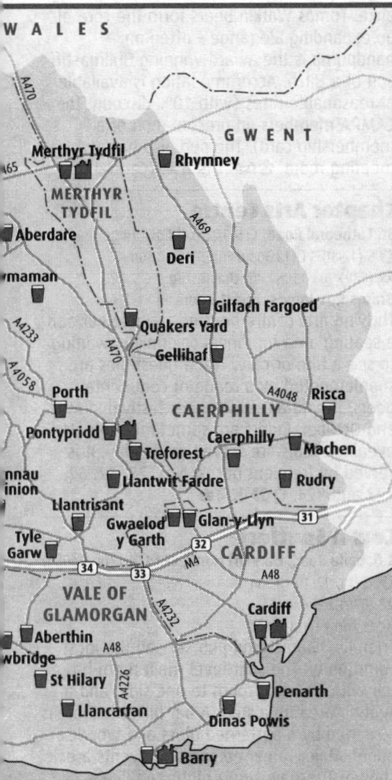

Alltwen

Butchers Arms

Alltwen Hill, SA8 3BP

✪ 12-midnight (12.30am Fri & Sat); 12-midnight Sun

☎ (01792) 863100

Beer range varies Ⓗ

Traditional village pub, set off the A474, between the Neath and Swansea valleys. A beautiful open hearth, wooden floors and furniture impart a truly homely character to the pub, while artefacts around the bar add interest. The pub's restaurant enjoys a good reputation locally and the food complements the excellent range of up to five guest beers served in the bar. Live music is performed here. ♨❀◑♿P

Barry

Castle Hotel

44 Jewel Street, CF63 3NQ

✪ 12-11.30 (midnight Fri & Sat); 12-11 Sun

☎ (01446) 408916

Brains Bitter, SA; guest beer Ⓗ

Welcoming, late Victorian pub, comprising a lounge, basic bar, 'cavern room', snooker room, skittle alley and a spacious function room. The etched windows of this former hotel advertise its original tea and coffee lounges. It once had strong links to the merchant navy and photographs of old Barry adorn the walls. The new landlord has a genuine enthusiasm for real ale and lovingly maintains this imposing building. Live music is staged Tuesday and Friday, and a quiz on Saturday. ❀⊟⇌(Dock)♣

Bishopston

Joiner's Arms

50 Bishopston Road, SA3 3EJ

✪ 11.30-11; 12-10.30 Sun

☎ (01792) 232658

Courage Best Bitter; Marston's Pedigree; Swansea Bishopswood, Three Cliffs Gold, Original Wood; guest beers Ⓗ

Attractive, stone village pub, dating from the 1860s; the Swansea Brewing Company is based here. Popular with locals and always busy, the food enjoys a good reputation. Beer festivals are held occasionally, further extending the range at local CAMRA's Pub of the Year 2002 and 2003, and regional winner in 1999. The bus from Swansea to Bishopston stops outside; the car park is small – if full try 100 yards down the hill. ♨Q❀◑⊟⊟♣P

Bridgend

Railway

Derwen Road, CF31 1LH

✪ 11-1am (2am Fri & Sat); 12-1am Sun

☎ (01656) 652266

Brains SA; Greene King Old Speckled Hen; guest beer Ⓗ

Previously known as the famous Pen-y-Bont Inn, this roomy free house has reverted to its original name. Much wood panelling is in evidence in this town-centre pub, which provides an extensive choice of lunchtime food (not Sun), including special offers for older people and a good children's selection. The open-plan layout features distinct drinking areas with low, beamed ceilings. Sports oriented, the TV relays events from opening through until the end of the evening. ◑⇌♣

Brynnau Gwynion

Mountain Hare

Brynna Road, CF35 6PG (between Pencoed and Llanharan turn off A473)

✪ 12-midnight; 12-11 Sun

☎ (01656) 860458 🌐 mountainhare.co.uk

Bullmastiff Welsh Gold; Evan Evans BB; guest beers Ⓗ

This family-owned village local is well worth a visit. It has a large, comfortable lounge and characterful bar. The two regular and two varying guest beers are always first class. There is ample parking space and the extensive lawned areas make it a popular

INDEPENDENT BREWERIES

Brains Cardiff
Bryncelyn Ystalyfera
Bullmastiff Cardiff
Otley Pontypridd
Rhymney Merthyr Tydfil
Swansea Bishopston
Vale of Glamorgan Barry
Tomos Watkin Swansea

choice in summer. In spring the pub hosts an Ales of Wales festival, which relies on a highly original system for cooling the casks invented by the locals. ❀⊟♿♣P

Cadoxton-juxta-Neath

Crown & Sceptre Inn

Main Road, SA10 8AP

⌚ 12-3 (not Mon), 5-11; 11-11 Fri & Sat; 12-10.30 Sun

☎ (01639) 642145 🌐 crownandsceptreinn.co.uk

Tomos Watkin OSB; guest beer Ⓗ

Built in 1835 as a tap for the nearby Vale of Neath Brewery, this former coaching inn has become very food oriented. The bar still serves two front rooms, but the old stables now house a fine restaurant that enjoys an excellent reputation for freshly-cooked food, such as its fillet steak and mushroom pie (no food Sun eve or Mon). A good refreshment stop for visitors to the Aberdulais Falls, there is ample space in the car park opposite. ❀◐⊟♿🚌P⚟

Caerphilly

Masons Arms

Mill Road, CF83 3FE

⌚ 12-11.30 (midnight Fri & Sat); 12-11.30 Sun

☎ (029) 208 83353

Adnams Bitter; Brains Bitter; guest beer Ⓗ

Traditional, friendly local, a short walk from the town centre. The bar houses a juke box and pub games in contrast to the large, comfortable lounge at the rear where food is food is served, and is partly no-smoking. The Masons offers a wider beer range than the town-centre pubs, as well as a welcome sanctuary from their weekend excesses. No-one is admitted here after 11pm. Q❀◐⊟♣P

Cardiff

Albany

105 Donald Street, Roath, CF24 4TL (off Albany Rd at post office)

⌚ 12-11; 11-11.30 Fri & Sat; 12-10.30 Sun

☎ (029) 203 11075

Brains Dark, Bitter, SA, seasonal beers; guest beers Ⓗ

This street-corner local goes from strength to strength. It was voted local CAMRA Pub of the Year in 2006 for the second year running, and has now introduced a regular guest beer. The public bar has a lively atmosphere, with a large-screen TV for sports events. The lounge is quieter and smoke-free during food service (no meals Sun). Added attractions are the skittle alley and large, pleasant garden where barbecues are held in summer. Q❀◐⊟🚌(57, 58)♣

Cayo Arms

36 Cathedral Road, CF11 9LL

⌚ 12-11; 12-10.30 Sun

☎ (029) 203 91910

Brains Rev James; Tomos Watkin Brewery Bitter, OSB, seasonal beers; guest beers Ⓗ

The single bar has a homely feel that appeals to locals, visitors and ale enthusiasts alike. Tomos Watkin beers form the core of an expanding ale range – often on handpump is the award-winning Bullmastiff Son of a Bitch. Accommodation is available at reasonable rates (with 10% discount for CAMRA members on presentation of a membership card). The pub also has a meeting room. ❀🛏◐♿▲≋(Central)P⚟

Chapter Arts Centre

36 Cathedral Road, CF5 1QE (off Cowbridge road)

⌚ 5 (1 Sat)-11 (12.30am Fri); 5-10.30 Sun

☎ (029) 203 11050 🌐 chapter.org

Brains Rev James; guest beers Ⓗ

Thriving arts centre housing a single bar and a seating area for diners or drinkers waiting to see a film or play. Three guest ales are supplemented by a range of continental beers; it hold a German beer festival in May and October. Ciders are sometimes sold. No evening meals are served on Sunday. It is served by frequent buses: Nos. 25, 32, 62, 122 and 124. Q◐♿🚌●

Cow n Snuffers

1 Gabalfa Road, Llandaff North, CF14 2JH (on A4054)

⌚ 12-11; 12-10.30 Sun

☎ (029) 205 64049

Beer range varies Ⓗ

Friendly, characterful pub serving the local community. The split-level main room has a bar with standing room to one side, and a seating area up a step. A bar billiards table is screened by a patterned glass and wood panel. Major televised sporting events are shown, Tuesday is quiz night and live entertainment is sometimes staged at the weekend. The beer changes frequently. Meals are available all day until 9pm. Buses Nos. 14, 25, 101 and 102 serve the pub. ❀◐≋(Llandaff)🚌

Deri Inn

Heol y Deri, Rhiwbina, CF14 6UH

⌚ 11-midnight; 12-11 Sun

☎ (029) 206 95050

Hancock's HB; Young's Bitter; guest beer Ⓗ

The bright modern decor incorporates displays of contemporary glassware and art works. A number of comfortable public areas surround a central bar. Beers are usually from large, established brewers. Take bus Nos. 21, 23, 18 or 22 to the pub, but if driving beware of the speed ramp at the car park entrance. 🔥❀◐♿🚌P⚟

Fox & Hounds

Old Church Road, Whitchurch, CF14 1AD

⌚ 12-11; 12-10.30 Sun

☎ (029) 206 93377

Brains Dark, Bitter, SA, Rev James; guest beers Ⓗ

Friendly, community pub. A wood-panelled interior houses one long bar, a large screen for sporting events and a quiet area for dining and drinking. Meals are served all day until 9pm (9.30pm Fri and Sat; 8.30pm Sun). The pleasant garden is a venue for outdoor events, while an extension around the corner is used for beer festivals. It offers two guest beers, with one pump giving priority to Brains special brews or seasonal ales. ◐♿≋(Whitchurch/Coryton)P

Glamorgan Council's Staff Club

17 Westgate Street, CF10 1DD (opp. entrance to Millennium Stadium)
9am-11 (11.30 Fri & Sat); 9am-11 Sun
☎ (029) 202 33216
Brains Bitter; guest beers Ⓗ
This city-centre members' club is noted for its varied choice of at least three guest beers at any time, from both local Welsh micro-breweries and further afield. There are bars on the ground and first floors of these premises that once accommodated the sheriff's offices, and are currently undergoing a programme of refurbishment. Production of this Guide or a CAMRA membership card will allow admission as a guest.
Q ⇌(Central)

Goat Major

33 High Street, CF10 1PU (opp. castle)
11-midnight; 12-11 Sun
☎ (029) 203 37161
Brains Dark, Bitter, SA; guest beer Ⓗ
This traditional local stands in stark contrast to many in the city centre. Its single bar has retained its Victorian character despite refurbishment. The beer is of a consistently high quality, and a guest or seasonal brew is regularly available. The menu majors on Welsh dishes and meals are served 12-8pm (5pm Sun). The pub still maintains strong links with the Royal Regiment of Wales – although sadly the goat no longer visits.
⇌(Central)

Heathcock Hotel

Bridge Street, Llandaff, CF5 2EN (at Cardiff Road jct)
12-11 (11.30 Fri & Sat); 12-10.30 Sun
☎ (029) 205 75005
Adnams Bitter, Broadside; guest beer Ⓗ
Friendly, popular local with distinct lounge and public bar areas. The pub has a pool table and skittle alley and there is a TV in the lounge. Entertainment is usually staged on Friday and Saturday, which may mean opening times vary, and evening meals finish early on these days (5.30-7pm). Several buses, including Nos. 24, 60 and 101, serve the pub. ⇌(Danescourt/Fairwater/Llandaff N)♣

Mochyn Du

Sophia Close, CF11 9HW
(near Welsh Institute of Sport)
12-11 (midnight Fri & Sat); 12-10.30 Sun
☎ (029) 203 71599
Brains Bitter, Rev James, seasonal beers; guest beers Ⓗ
This free house has gone from strength to strength since leaving the Wolverhampton & Dudley fold. Close to Glamorgan county cricket ground, and a leisurely 10-minute riverside amble from the city centre, this 'tafarn' is a firm favourite with local residents, city workers and students. Translated from the Welsh, its name is Black Pig and bi-lingual signage throughout encourages Welsh learners and interested foreign visitors to enjoy the 'hwyl' of a Welsh pub. The garden is well used.
⇌(Central)P

Old Cottage

Cherry Orchard Road, Lisvane, CF14 0UE
(100 yds W of Lisvane & Thornhill station)
12-11 (midnight Fri & Sat); 12-11 Sun
☎ (029) 207 64875
Wells Bombardier; Young's Bitter; guest beer Ⓗ
On the northern outskirts of the city, where the suburbs of Lisvane and Thornhill give way to the Caerphilly Mountain green belt, the pub stands near Parc Cefn Onn. The smart, comfortable lounge is partly split-level; behind it a designated dining section ensures that, while food forms a major part of the pub's business, it does not impinge on its traditional atmosphere.
Q ♿⇌(Lisvane & Thornhill)P⅄

Pendragon

Excalibur Drive, Thornhill, CF14 9BB (off A469)
11-11 (midnight Fri & Sat); 11.30-11 Sun
☎ (029) 206 10550
Brains Dark, Bitter, SA Ⓗ
Modern estate pub reached by a long driveway, with a garden and children's play area. It comprises three drinking areas: a lounge, pool room and a function room. Its elevated position provides fine views over Cardiff. The licensee continues to display a commitment to quality cask ale, while his wife shows a similar dedication to the provision of good food at reasonable prices. Keen supporters of local charities, customers and staff have raised thousands of pounds for worthwhile causes. Q ♿⇌ (Lisvane & Thornhill)(27, 28)♣P

Vulcan

10 Adam Street, CF24 2FH (opp. prison)
11.30-11; 12-4 Sun
☎ (029) 204 61580
Brains Bitter, SA Ⓗ
The last surviving example of a traditional, multi-bar local near the city centre, this pub, which opened in the 1850s, is the only Cardiff pub to have kept its original name throughout its existence. Sadly, however, it is now threatened with demolition and this may be its last appearance in this Guide. At the front is a public bar with a maritime theme and sawdust on the floor; a small lounge is accessed via a side passage. Good food is served at lunchtime. ⇌(Central)

Yard

42-43 St Mary's Street, CF10 1AD
10-1am; 11-12.30am Sun
☎ (029) 202 27517
Brains Dark, Bitter, SA, seasonal beers Ⓗ
Situated in the old brewery yard, the pub now forms part of a complex of restaurants and bars called the Old Brewery Quarter. A lively two-storey establishment, its somewhat unusual decor includes considerable use of steel for the staircase and other fittings. Outside drinking and dining are possible in a covered walkway. Convenient for the central rail and bus stations and the Millennium Stadium, it can be crowded, especially on Friday and Saturday evenings. ♿⇌(Central)

WALES

Clydach (Swansea)

Carpenters Arms

High Street, SA6 5LN (on B4603 through Clydach)
⏲ 11-midnight (1am Fri & Sat); 11-midnight Sun
☎ (01792) 843333 🌐 carpentersarmsclydach.co.uk
Adnams Broadside; Young's Bitter; guest beers Ⓗ
Popular, stone-fronted pub with a busy public bar and a split-level lounge/restaurant, serving a wide range of good quality meals. It has a patio garden and ample parking. Live music is played most Saturdays, and real ale festivals are held on bank holidays. It often stocks seasonal beers from Wye Valley. The pub is used by the local cycle group for meetings and events and it won a community pub award in 2004 from the trade paper, Morning Advertiser.
❀◑◐⊟♣P

Corntown

Golden Mile

Corntown Road, CF35 5BA (off A48, between Cowbridge and Bridgend) OS928774
⏲ 11.30-3, 5.30-11; 12-4, 7-10.30 Sun
☎ (01656) 654884
Evan Evans BB; guest beer Ⓗ
Set down below road level, this easily missed pub is well worth finding. The cosy lounge is warmed by a log fire, while in the bar you will receive a friendly welcome from Dave the dog. The dining room serves first class food at reasonable prices prepared by an award-winning chef; in summer meals can be taken on the patio, where you can enjoy fine rural views. The pub has ample parking. 🔥Q❀◑◐⊟P

Cowbridge

Vale of Glamorgan

53 High Street, CF71 7AE
⏲ 11.30-11; 12-10.30 Sun
☎ (01446) 772252
Draught Bass; Greene King Old Speckled Hen; Hancock's HB; Wye Valley Hereford Pale Ale; guest beers Ⓗ
Small, friendly, High Street pub in a busy, historic market town. The range and quality of its real ales are matched by the excellent food, comfortable surroundings and welcoming atmosphere. The pub's annual beer festival, held as part of the Cowbridge food and drink festival, is a particular highlight. Ales from the Vale of Glamorgan Brewery in Barry feature regularly as guests at local CAMRA's Pub of the Year 2006.
Q🚼❀🛏◑◐♣P

Craig Penllyn

Barley Mow

CF71 7RT
⏲ 12-11; 12-10.30 Sun
☎ (01446) 772555
Hancock's HB; guest beers Ⓗ
This cosy, atmospheric village pub enjoys a strong local following, but also extends a welcome to visitors, including families with children. The changing beer range often offers ales not usually found in this part of the country. The excellent food represents good value. There is a small garden behind the pub, but the car park is across the road. This is a marvellous pub for a cold winter's evening, but note that ringing mobile phones are not appreciated.
🚼❀◑◐⊟♣P

Cwmaman

Falcon Inn

1 Incline Row, CF44 6LU OS008998
⏲ 11-11; 12-11 Sun
☎ (01685) 873758 🌐 thefalcon.co.uk
Beer range varies Ⓗ
Although close to the village, this rural pub feels quite isolated at the end of a lane. It is popular in summer due to its riverside setting. Three beers are usually on offer. Well-appointed accommodation is available and touring caravans are welcome. A pub to visit and remember; note its large bar, built with wood from a local chapel.
❀🛏♿P

Cwmfelin

Cross Inn

Maesteg Road, CF34 9LB (on A4063)
⏲ 11.45-midnight (1am Fri & Sat); 11.45-midnight Sun
☎ (01656) 732476
Brains Bitter, seasonal beers; Wye Valley Butty Bach; guest beer (occasional) Ⓗ
Pleasant, comfortable and friendly local in a valley that is otherwise something of a real ale desert. It stands on a main road that is also a bus route, and it is a five-minute walk from Garth Station. Both the traditional bar and smart lounge have recently been refurbished. Children are welcome until 7pm and well-behaved dogs are permitted in the bar, but please ask first. The photographs in the little back room are worth a look.
❀⊟⇌(Garth)🚌

Deri

Old Club

93 Bailey Street, CF81 9HX
⏲ 4 (12 Sat)-midnight (2am Fri & Sat); 12-midnight Sun
☎ (01443) 830278
Beer range varies Ⓗ
A warm welcome awaits visitors to this independent social club. The beer range concentrates on tasty brews from small breweries, on three handpumps. It stocks a range of bottled continental beers and local cider is usually on offer. The upstairs function room has been refurbished and brought back into use. Bus No. 1 from Bargoed stops close by and also serves the nearby Cwm Darran Country Park. Last admission to the club is 11pm. ⛺🚌♣

Dinas Powis

Star Inn

8 Station Road, CF64 4DE
⏲ 11.30-11; 12-10.30 Sun
☎ (029) 205 14245
Brains Bitter, SA, Rev James Ⓗ

Following a recent refurbishment, this inn has become deservedly popular. The open-plan design provides cosy seating and dining areas. The ale is of excellent quality, while first class, reasonably-priced meals are served all day (12-4pm Sun) by friendly staff. There is a large car park and patio to the rear, from which disabled access to the pub is by wheelchair lift.
⅏Q❀◑◗♿⇌P

Felindre (Swansea)

Shepherds Country Inn

18 Heol-myddfai, SA5 7ND (2½ miles N of M4 jct 46)
✪ 12-3 (not winter Mon or Tue), 6-midnight; 12-midnight Fri-Sun
☎ (01792) 794715
Beer range varies Ⓗ
Pleasant, well-kept village pub: a single bar and a restaurant. This free house, usually offering two guest beers, also serves good quality meals at reasonable prices (eve meals Tue-Sat). It hosts a weekly curry evening and occasional live music. A large, decked patio overlooks a children's play area and benefits from country views. En-suite accommodation is ideal for visitors to the Lliw Reservoir Country Park nearby. There is a limited daytime bus service.
❀⇔◑◗🚌(142)P

Gellihaf

Coal Hole

Bryn Road, NP12 2QE (on A4049, S of Fleur de Lys)
✪ 12-3, 6.30-11; 11-11 Fri & Sat; 12-10.30 Sun
☎ (01443) 830280
Greene King Old Speckled Hen; Hancock's HB; guest beer Ⓗ
Set back from the road, this friendly, comfortable one-bar pub was converted from a farm during the 19th century. The bar, which occupies the former stables, offers a regularly-changing guest ale. Great food is served in the bar or no-smoking restaurant; on Sunday a three course roast lunch is served (no meals Sun eve or Mon). The Coal Hole is worth visiting for the extensive views over the Rhymney Valley, the warm welcome and good ale.
◑◗P

Gilfach Fargoed

Capel Hotel

Park Place, CF81 8LW
✪ 12-4, 7-11; 12-11.30 Fri & Sat; 12-12.30 Sun
☎ (01443) 830272
Brains SA; John Smith's Bitter; guest beers Ⓗ
This award-winning pub is among the finest for miles around. Many original features give a homely touch, and it would be easy to imagine the bar full of tired colliers as it once was. Today's customers enjoy up to three guest beers, plus a guest cider. Mid-Glamorgan CAMRA's Pub of the Year 2004 and 2005 displays an enthusiastic approach to real ale, with an annual beer festival held in early May. Note: the local station is a request stop.
Q⇔⇌♣●⅟

Glan-y-Llyn

Fagin's Ale & Chop House

8 Cardiff Road, CF15 7QD
(on A4054, 1 mile N of M4 jct 32)
✪ 11-midnight (1am Fri & Sat); 11-11 Sun
☎ (029) 208 11800
Brains Bitter; Felinfoel Double Dragon; Ⓗ **guest beers** Ⓖ/Ⓗ
A new licensee has brought the sparkle back to this roadside ale house. The welcome in the spacious, flagstoned bar is genuinely friendly and the ambience enhanced by fresh cut flowers on the tables and 'Wenglish' on the rafters. With five handpumps and room for eight casks in cooled stillage behind the bar, there is something to suit most palates (including local Gwynt y Ddraig Haymaker cider). Diners are well caterd for in the bar or restaurant (no meals Sun eve). ⅏❀◑◗⇌(Taffs Well)●

Gwaelod y Garth

Gwaelod y Garth Inn

Main Road, CF14 4HH (off A470 through Taffs Well)
✪ 11-11; 12-10.30 Sun
☎ (029) 208 10408
Felinfoel Dragon's Heart; Hancock's HB; guest beers Ⓗ
Pub in traditional style, with subdued lighting and open fires enhancing the friendly atmosphere. There is a dining area, plus a no-smoking restaurant upstairs, offering good food based on local produce. This welcoming local on the outskirts of Cardiff is worth a visit. A quiet, family-friendly pub, it stocks two guest ales that change regularly and bottled Gwynt y Ddraig cider. ⅏Q❀◑◗⇌(Taffs Well)🚌

Hirwaun

Glancynon Inn

Swansea Road, CF44 9PH
✪ 11-11; 12-10.30 Sun
☎ (01685) 811043
Greene King Abbot; guest beers Ⓗ
Large country pub with oak beams and a congenial atmosphere. Popular with drinkers and diners, it is the main real ale pub for a sizeable neighbourhood. Bookings are essential for Sunday lunch (no meals Sun eve). The pub offers a well-appointed and pleasantly decorated lounge and a split-level bar. A little way off the main roads, it is nonetheless easy to find. ❀◑◗⊟♣P

Kittle

Beaufort Arms

18 Pennard Road, SA3 3JS
✪ 11.30-11.30 (11 Tue-Thu); 12-11 Sun
☎ (01792) 234521
Brains Buckley's Best Bitter, Rev James, seasonal beers Ⓗ
Reputedly the oldest pub in Gower, the original part of the building, now the lounge, boasts a beamed ceiling and some early stonework. A Brains' tenanted house with three bars and a function room, it also offers outdoor seating, a covered decked area and

a children's playground. The pub has won various community and Gower in Bloom awards. A quiz is held on Monday and the pub hosts the local ladies' darts team. An extensive, home-cooked menu is served; meals are available all day Saturday and Sunday. ❀◑◗ ♣P

Llancarfan

Fox & Hounds
CF62 3AD
12-2.30, 6.30-11; 12-3, 7-10.30 Sun
☎ (01446) 781287
Brains Bitter, Rev James; guest beer H
Set deep in a rural vale, this is a traditional village local that, along with the nearby church, forms the heart of a close-knit community. Saved from closure some years ago when it was purchased by a consortium of locals, you can be sure of good hospitality whether visiting for a drink, a meal or B&B. The pub is cosy in winter, while in summer the riverside garden is lovely. No food is served Monday evening. Q❀◑◗ P

Llangennith

King's Head
SA3 1HX
11-11; 12-10.30 Sun
☎ (01792) 386212
Flowers IPA, Original; guest beers H
Historic pub on the village green, extended over the centuries as adjoining farm buildings have been incorporated. There are splendid views of nearby beaches that are within walking distance for the energetic. The pub is popular with visitors to nearby caravan and camping sites, especially in the holiday periods, and a games room is available. Good food is served all day. Note the old pictures in the bar, including those of Phil Tanner, the legendary Gower folk singer. Q❀◑◗ ♣P

Llanrhidian

Greyhound Inn
Oldwalls, SA3 1HA
11-11; 12-10.30 Sun
☎ (01792) 391027
Draught Bass; Flowers IPA; Wadworth 6X; guest beer (occasional) H
Free house with an excellent atmosphere situated on the main north Gower road. The food is popular – especially local fish and the Sunday carvery. Families are welcome in the games room and food is served all day in the bars and the restaurant. There is a function room, a garden and a welcoming fire in winter. Sometimes a guest beer replaces one of the regulars. Q❀◑◗ ♣P

Llansamlet (Swansea)

Plough & Harrow
57 Church Road, SA7 9RL (off A48, 200 yds N of traffic lights)
12-midnight (11.30 Mon & Tue; 1am Fri); 12-11.30 Sun
☎ (01792) 772263
Tomos Watkin OSB, seasonal beers; guest beers H
Semi-rural, Celtic Inns pub where the large bar has seating arranged in comfortable groups. It serves reasonably-priced bar meals and has a no-smoking dining/function room upstairs (eve meals Tue-Sat). Bench seating is provided in front of the pub for fine weather drinkers. Good disabled access and facilities are provided; family groups are welcome until 9pm. Local photos vie for wall space with breweriana. A charity quiz is run by the vicar from the church next door on Wednesday evening.
❀◑◗ (33)P

Llantrisant

Bear Inn
Heol-y-Sarn, CF72 8DA
11-11; 12-10.30 Sun
☎ (01443) 222271
Hancock's HB; guest beer H
Standing opposite the statue of Dr Price (who introduced cremation to Britain in the 19th century), the Bear offers a warm welcome to all. With two bars, a dining room and a partly walled garden, you will find a place to suit you. A guest beer may be kept on for a while, particularly if it proves popular. The food is of a good standard and includes the usual pub favourites.
Q❀◑◗

Llantwit Fardre

Bush Inn
Main Road, CF38 2EP
11-11; 12-10.30 Sun
☎ (01443) 203958
Hancock's HB; guest beers H
Busy village local that hosts regular quiz and darts evenings and occasional live music. The guest beers are often unusual for the area; the Hancock's may change but will always be replaced by something from a local brewer. ❀♣P

Llantwit Major

King's Head
East Street, CF61 1XY
11.30-11; 12-10.30 Sun
☎ (01446) 792697
Brains Dark, Bitter, SA; guest beer (occasional) H
Friendly, welcoming, two-bar local in the town centre, with a large public bar where various pub games are much in evidence. The smaller, comfortable lounge bar is normally quieter, but both bars are popular for televised sport. Good value meals can be enjoyed in the dining area. Families with children are welcome. Q❀◑ ♣P

Old Swan Inn
Church Street, CF61 1SB
12-11; 12-10.30 Sun
☎ (01446) 792230 oldswaninn.com
Beer range varies H
A changing range of local and national independent ales is sold at this fine pub (two on weekdays, four at weekends). In the old part of town, the large front bar is

popular with drinkers and those sampling the varied menu, while the smaller back bar attracts younger customers. It has an extensive outdoor drinking area. Various ciders are sold in summer and a beer festival is held late in the season at local CAMRA's Pub of the Year 2005. ⛰❀◐◑⊟⛺≉♣●

Machen

White Hart

Nant-y-Ceisiad, CF83 8QQ

(100 yds N of A468 at W end of village) OS203892

⏲ 11.30-2.30 (not winter Mon), 6-11.30; 12-10.30 Sun

☎ (01633) 441005

Beer range varies Ⓗ

Independent free house offering well-sourced guest beers. This rambling old pub has been much extended over the years, incorporating panels and fittings from the ocean liner Empress of France. A good range of food is served, but Sunday lunches are especially popular so booking is advisable. Occasional beer festivals are held. ❀⛟◐◑♣P

Marcross

Horseshoe Inn

CF61 1ZG

⏲ 12-11; 12-10.30 Sun

☎ (01656) 890568

Wye Valley Hereford Pale Ale; guest beers Ⓗ

Cosy, traditional, country pub, close to the beach and lighthouse at Nash Point. Previously known as the Lighthouse, it has reverted to its original name under new ownership. The two connecting bars both have comfortable seating and plenty of tables for dining or drinking with friends. The bar boasts six handpumps, with at least three in use at any time, more as throughput demands. ⛰Q❀◐♣P

Merthyr Tydfil

Rose & Crown

Morgan Street, CF47 8TP

(off Brecon Rd, follow signs to St Tydfils Well Church)

⏲ 12-midnight daily

☎ (01685) 723743

Brains Bitter; guest beers Ⓗ

Busy local, that also attracts many visitors – check for famous names in the visitors' book. Originally cottages, this many-roomed pub hosted prayer meetings in the 19th century. These days the locals have a strong interest in the modern religion of sport and the pub obliges with several TVs tuned to Sky. The former Giles & Harrap Brewery buildings are still standing nearby on Brecon Road. ❀◐♿≉♣

Monknash

Plough & Harrow

CF71 7QQ (off B4265, between Wick and Marcross)

⏲ 12-11; 12-10.30 Sun

☎ (01656) 890209

Archers Golden; Draught Bass; Worthington's Bitter; Wye Valley Hereford Pale Ale; guest beers Ⓗ

With the new licensee now fully established, this famous old pub has once again become a destination for drinkers from near and far. Set in a medieval grange, the building has seen many uses over the centuries, including a stint as a mortuary. Lounge customers are advised that the real ale is in the public bar. With between five and seven guest beers, Westons Old Rosie cider and tasty food, this is a must when in the area. ⛰❀◐◑⊟⛺♣●P

Mumbles (Swansea)

Mumbles Rugby Club

588 Mumbles Road, SA3 4DL

⏲ 6.30 (4 Sat)-11; closed Wed; 12-5 Sun

☎ (01792) 368989

Tomos Watkin OSB, seasonal beers; Worthington's Bitter Ⓗ

This popular club, established in 1887, welcomes non-members. Tomos Watkin's beers and seasonal ales are available at all times. The large function room upstairs gets lively on international match days. The club's 'cracker sevens' rugby tournament, held every year on August bank holiday weekend at nearby Underhill Park, coincides with the Mumbles beer festival. ⊟♣

Park Inn

23 Park Street, SA3 4DA

⏲ 4-11; 12-midnight Fri & Sat; 12-11 Sun

☎ (01792) 366738

Beer range varies Ⓗ

All ages of customers enjoy the convivial atmosphere at this perennially popular back-street local where five handpumps dispense a changing range of beers. Welsh and West Country independent breweries are highlighted and cider is sold in summer. There is a room for darts and a quiz is held on Thursday. Note the fine display of pump clips. Twice winner of Swansea CAMRA Pub of the Year. Q♣●

Murton

Plough & Harrow

88 Oldway, SA3 3DJ

⏲ 11.30-11; 12-10.30 Sun

☎ (01792) 234459

Courage Best Bitter, Directors; Greene King Abbot; guest beer Ⓗ

One of the oldest pubs in Gower, it has been enlarged and renovated in recent times but has retained its character. The pub combines a busy food trade with its tradition as a village local. The bar houses a TV and a pool table, which attract younger customers, while the lounge is a comfortable place to enjoy a quiet chat or a bar meal. Quiz night is Tuesday. Heaters in the garden are useful on chillier evenings. Q❀◐◑♣P

Neath

Borough Arms

New Henry Street, SA11 1PH

(side street in Melyn Cryddan)

⏲ 4 (12 Sat)-11; 12-3, 6.30-10.30 Sun

☎ (01639) 644902

Brains Dark; guest beers Ⓗ

Back-street ale house with a traditional feel.

The L-shaped bar offers a choice of up to four real ales, mainly from micro-breweries. The pub has a comfortable seating area in front of the bar and a corner games section for darts and nine-pin skittles. The TV is generally tuned to sport. A walk to this pub is a must when in Neath. Q🍀❀⇌🚌♣

David Protheroe
7 Windsor Road, SA11 1LS (opp. station)
⏲ 9am-midnight (1am Fri & Sat); 9am-midnight Sun
☎ (01639) 622138
Brains SA, Rev James; Greene King Abbot; Marston's Pedigree; guest beers 🄷
This spacious, busy Wetherspoon's was once a police station. Easily accessible from the train and bus stations and taxi rank, it comprises an open-plan bar with a family area at the back. A wide range of food is served; curry evening is Thursday and steak night is Tuesday. Drinks are sold at reduced prices on Monday and beer festivals are staged. The volume is turned off on the TV. Disabled provision is adequate.
Q🍀❀◐◑♿⇌🚌🗑

Oasis Bar
Neath Sports Centre, Cwrt Herbert, Neath Abbey Road, SA10 7BR
⏲ 5 (4.30 Thu & Fri; 11 Sat)-11; 11-11 Sun
☎ (01639) 635013
Beer range varies 🄷
Recently refurbished sports centre bar where the large open area is popular with local residents as well as those using the centre's facilities. A number of teams use it as a clubhouse. A large screen shows major sporting events. It keeps a single real ale, but it is well worth trying. Children are welcome until 8pm and it can get busy on match days. ❀♿🚌P

Star Inn
83 Pen-y-Dre, SA11 3HF
(near Fosters Gnoll rugby ground)
⏲ 12-midnight; 12-11 Sun
☎ (01639) 637745
Draught Bass; Brains SA; Rhymney Bitter; guest beers 🄷
Comfortable and traditional single-bar local divided into two distinct sections, one of which is no-smoking. Standing near the Gnoll, home of Neath RFC, it maintains strong rugby connections and can get crowded on match days. It is much quieter during the week and is a haven from the bustle of the town centre. The large enclosed garden has a children's play area and two boules courts and is the setting for summer barbecues. Q❀⇌🚌♣P⚟

Newton (Swansea)

Newton Inn
New Well Lane, SA3 4SR
⏲ 10-midnight; 12-midnight Sun
☎ (01792) 363226
Draught Bass; 🄷/🄶 **Fuller's London Pride; Greene King Abbot; Sharp's Doom Bar; Worthington's Bitter; guest beers** 🄷
Refurbished village local retaining the bar and lounge areas in a semi open-plan layout. The pub offers competitively-priced meals and is popular with diners at lunchtime and early evening. The bar has a big-screen TV, which is used for sporting events. The draught beers, particularly the Bass, can be drawn straight from the cask on request; the landlord regularly changes the guests. Quizzes are held on Monday and Wednesday. Roadside tables are placed outside for alfresco drinking.
❀◐◑🄿

Norton (Swansea)

Beaufort Arms
1 Castle Road, SA3 5TF
(turn by Norton House Hotel, off Mumbles Rd)
⏲ 11-11 (midnight Fri & Sat); 11-midnight Sun
☎ (01792) 401319
Draught Bass; Greene King Old Speckled Hen; Sharp's Doom Bar; Worthington's Bitter 🄷
This 18th-century village local comprises a public bar, housing a dartboard and TV, and a quiet, comfortable lounge; both rooms have real fires. A quiz is held every Tuesday, and many photographs show the pub's long-standing commitment to the annual Mumbles Raft Race, held in August. Good quality meals at reasonable prices are served at lunchtime, Monday-Saturday.
🔥Q❀◐🄿♣

Ogmore-by-Sea

Pelican in her Piety
Ewenny Road, CF32 0QP
⏲ 12-11; 12-10.30 Sun
☎ (01656) 880049
Draught Bass; Fuller's London Pride; Greene King Old Speckled Hen; Worthington's Bitter; guest beer 🄷
Although lying some way out of the relaxing seaside resort of Ogmore-by-Sea, this excellent roadside inn can now be considered as the local pub since the closure of the last licensed hotel in 2006. From the front of the pub, the view over the ruined castle and the estuary of the River Ogwr is quite stunning, especially on a warm summer's evening. A strong, welcoming, community feel is exemplified by the support given by the pub to local charities.
🔥Q❀◐◑⛺P⚟

Penarth

Bear's Head
37-39 Windsor Road, CF64 1JD
⏲ 10-11; 12-10.30 Sun
☎ (029) 207 06424
Brains SA; Bullmastiff Welsh Gold, Son of a Bitch; Marston's Burton Bitter; guest beers 🄷
This typical Wetherspoon's pub is popular and busy, attracting a wide cross-section of people, including brewers from the two nearest breweries. Upstairs is the family area, adorned with modern art. Downstairs offers a no-smoking section and a large selection of bottled beers from around the world. Westons cider is sold. Bear's Head is the English translation of Penarth.
Q🍀◐◑♿⇌(Dingle Rd/Penarth)●⚟

Windsor

93 Windsor Road, CF64 1JF
✪ 12-11.30 (midnight Wed & Sat); 12-11 Sun
☎ (029) 207 02821
Brains SA; Greene King Abbot; Hancock's HB; guest beers Ⓗ
A welcome return to this Guide for the pub that stocks the widest range of ales in town. Since Brains acquired the Windsor, there were concerns about a possible reduction in choice, but these proved to be unfounded due to the licensee's dedication. Fortunately, the new owners recognised a winning formula and did not change it. Framed pump clips of previous guest beers have a wall to themselves. Live music and morris dancers provide regular entertainment.
Q❀◑⊟≹(Dingle Rd)♣

Penllyn

Red Fox

CF71 7RQ
✪ 12-3 (not Mon), 6-11; 12-10.30 Sun
☎ (01446) 772352
Hancock's HB; Tomos Watkin OSB; guest beer Ⓗ
Seven years ago this fantastic rural pub faced imminent closure, but was saved by a vociferous campaign by Penllyn's residents, supported by CAMRA among others. It has since regained the reputation it enjoyed for many years, for its excellent food, beer and company. Popular with locals and visitors from further afield, it also attracts groups relaxing after a hard day at the nearby paintball facility. ♨Q❀◑♿♣P

Pontardawe

Pontardawe Inn

123 Herbert Street, SA8 4ED (near A4067 jct)
✪ 12-midnight (1am Fri & Sat); 12-midnight Sun
☎ (01792) 830791
Brains Buckley's Best Bitter, Rev James, seasonal beers; guest beers Ⓗ
Also known as the Gwachel, this typical village inn stands alongside the River Tawe and a cycle track. Catering for all ages, one bar displays notes and artefacts relating to local history, while the other has a TV for rugby and stages live entertainment on Friday and Saturday. Outside is a boules piste and children's play area. It also has a restaurant, open Monday-Saturday.
❀◑♿🚌♣P

Pontypridd

Bunch of Grapes

Ynysangharad Road, CF37 4DA
(off A4054, N of A470 jct)
✪ 11-midnight; 12-10.30 Sun
☎ (01443) 402934 🌐 bunchofgrapes.org.uk
Wye Valley Hereford Pale Ale; guest beers Ⓗ
A short walk from the town centre, this award-winning free house warmly welcomes both drinkers and diners. The former will find a comfortable bar, pool room and decked suntrap and a range of up to five ales, with usually two from the local Otley Brewery. Diners, whether they opt for the bar or the no-smoking restaurant, have a choice of home-produced fare from a seasonal menu or the specials board, whose standard justifies its 'gastropub' status (no meals Sun eve). ♨❀◑≹♣P⚟

Llanover Arms

Bridge Street, CF37 4PE
(opp. entrance to Ynysyngharad Park)
✪ 12-11 (midnight Fri & Sat); 12-11 Sun
☎ (01443) 402934
Brains Dark, Bitter; Felinfoel Double Dragon; guest beer Ⓗ
This free house is well sited for visitors to the town's historic centre and the renowned Ynysyngharad Park. The three rooms are festooned with a miscellany of bric-a-brac, including equine paintings, old mirrors, maps and (non-working) clocks. However, probably the most popular feature is the constantly-changing guest ale, which attracts a loyal following. Note: if using the car park obtain a ticket from the bar or risk clamping.
Q❀⊟≹♣P

Porth

Rheola

Rheola Road, CF39 0LF
(on A4058, 200 yds S of bus depot)
✪ 2 (1 Fri; 12 Sat)-11; 12-10.30 Sun
☎ (01443) 682633
Draught Bass; Butcombe Gold; guest beer Ⓗ
Comfortable, friendly pub with a lively bar and a smart lounge. Standing at the 'Gateway to the Rhondda' and only a short distance north of the Rhondda Heritage Park, this is a pub not to be missed. Both rail and bus stations are a short walk away.
❀⊟≹♣P

Porthcawl

Lorelei Hotel

36-38 Esplanade Avenue, CF36 3YU
(off the seafront)
✪ 12-2, 5-11; 11-11 Fri; 12-10.30 Sun
☎ (01656) 788342
Draught Bass; Ⓖ **Tomos Watkin OSB; guest beers** Ⓗ
Well hidden in a town not particularly well endowed with real ale outlets, this comfortable, friendly hotel comprises two bars and a dining room. It usually stocks two guest ales, supplemented by a range of foreign beers, plus a varying cider in summer. Two beer festivals a year help make this by far the best real ale pub in town. Children are welcome in the dining room. ♉❀⇔◑⛺●

Port Talbot

Lord Caradoc

69-73 Station Road, SA13 1NW
✪ 9am-midnight (1am Fri & Sat); 9am-midnight Sun
☎ (01639) 896007
Brains SA, Rev James; Greene King Abbot; Marston's Burton Bitter, Pedigree; guest beers Ⓗ
Typical Wetherspoon's situated in the town centre and easily accessible from the bus and train stations. The large, L-shaped, open-plan bar has an elevated drinking area, and

WALES

a patio allows for outdoor drinking; children are welcome throughout. Food is served all day, with steak night Tuesday, China Club Wednesday and curry night on Friday. It also stages beer festivals.
Q❀◑♿≠(Parkway)🚌⚡

Quaker's Yard

Glantaff Inn

Cardiff Road, CF46 5AH (off A4054)
⏲ 12-4, 7-11; 12-4, 7-10.30 Sun
☎ (01443) 410822
Courage Best Bitter; guest beers Ⓗ
Comfortable inn, where you can peruse a large collection of water jugs, boxing memorabilia, old photographs and other items of interest. The guest ales are popular with the locals, as well as walkers and cyclists travelling along the Taff Trail which runs from Cardiff to Brecon. No evening meals are served Sunday.
❀◑

Reynoldston

King Arthur Hotel

Higher Green, SA3 1AD
⏲ 11-11; 12-10.30 Sun
☎ (01792) 390775 🌐 kingarthurhotel.co.uk
Draught Bass; Felinfoel Double Dragon; guest beer Ⓗ
Imposing pub and hotel/restaurant, frequented by locals and tourists. The King Arthur is named after 'Arthur's Stone', a prehistoric monument situated on the nearby Cefn Bryn Hill. The hotel is in a most pleasant spot in the middle of the Gower Peninsula and benefits from a large outdoor area. It is reputedly haunted by two ghosts. Meals are served in the bar as well as the restaurant, the family room and outside. The hotel has recently been extended.
♨❀◑♿♣P

Rhymney

Farmers Arms

Brewery Row, NP22 5EZ
(off A465 at Rhymney jct then A469 for 1 mile)
⏲ 12-11; 12-3, 7-11 Sun
☎ (01685) 840257
Brains Bitter; Fuller's London Pride; guest beers Ⓗ
Local community pub furnished in traditional style to reflect the pub's history. It boasts a fine display of photographs and memorabilia of the former Rhymney Brewery and many ex-employees of the brewery drink here. A quiz night is held on Thursday and the function room can cater for up to 40 people. The lounge and dining area offer affordable food (eve meals served Tue-Sat).
❀◑≠♣P

Risca

Commercial

Commercial Street, Pontymister, NP11 6BA
(on B4591 at Brookland Rd jct)
⏲ 11-11.30 (midnight Fri & Sat); 12-11 Sun
☎ (01633) 612608
Beer range varies Ⓗ
Large, roadside pub in the Pontymister district of Risca, which is well served by buses from Newport, Blackwood and Brynmawr. Open plan, with pool and darts to the right and a lounge to the left, an extension is planned. The two ales on offer change often, which is much appreciated by the clientele, many of whom travel from Newport and the Valleys to sample them.
❀🚌♣

Fox & Hounds

Park Road, NP11 6PW (next to park)
⏲ 12-midnight; 12-10.30 Sun
☎ (01633) 612937
Beer range varies Ⓗ
Popular, open-plan pub at the southern end of Risca, by the park and shopping area and handy for buses. The pub has a large-screen TV, pool table, darts and a juke box. The ale on offer changes quickly, and is usually supplied by local micros or a regional brewery. It has a good-sized garden and in warmer months seating is provided at the front, overlooking the park.
♨❀🚌♣P

Rudry

Maenllwyd Inn

CF83 3EB (500 yds SW of village) OS201867
⏲ 12-11; 12-10.30 Sun
☎ (029) 208 82372
Courage Best Bitter; guest beers Ⓗ
Bustling Chef & Brewer restaurant, based around a former farmhouse and later, a Victorian inn. A pleasant rural retreat close to Rudry common, it is within easy reach of Cardiff and Caerphilly. Two guest beers are usually sourced from regional and family brewers. The menu is extensive; the restaurant serves meals all day and is supplemented by a bar menu at lunchtime.
♨Q❀◐P⚡

St Brides Major

Farmers Arms

Wick Road, Pitcot, CF32 0SE
⏲ 12-3, 6-11; 12-10.30 Sun
☎ (01656) 880224
Courage Best Bitter; Greene King Old Speckled Hen; Hancock's HB; Marston's Pedigree; Ushers Best Bitter Ⓗ
Extremely popular pub and restaurant situated directly across the road from the village pond, which is inhabited by a family of swans. The pub enjoys a reputation for the quality and value of its food, served in the restaurant and bar, and the beer is always superb. A collection of china jugs hangs from the beams and windows in the bar, which is always busy, but cosy.
♨Q❀◑♣P

St Hilary

Bush

CP71 7DP (off A48, E of Cowbridge)
⏲ 11.30-11; 12-10.30 Sun
☎ (01446) 772745
Draught Bass; Greene King IPA, Old Speckled

Hen; Hancock's HB; guest beer [H]
Beautiful thatched pub, dating back over 400 years, set opposite the church in a picturesque village in the Vale countryside. This stone-floored inn comprises three bars and a restaurant. Meals are served in one of the bars, and the pub enjoys a fine reputation for its cuisine (no meals Sun eve). The outdoor drinking area is well used in summer. Westons Old Rosie cider is stocked all year round.
⛫Q❀◐♣P

Skewen

Crown
216 New Road, SA10 6EW
12-midnight daily
☎ (01792) 411270
Brains Dark, Bitter, SA; guest beers [H]
Pleasant, centrally-located community pub consisting of a public bar, a lounge and an upstairs room for snooker and pool with full-sized tables. Televised horse racing in the bar is popular with the regulars. Live music is staged on Friday evening, karaoke on Saturday and a quiz on Thursday; the lounge displays some interesting music memorabilia. The pub is a regular meeting place for the local cricket and football clubs. An enclosed outside drinking area is a bonus.
❀♣

Swansea

Brunswick
3 Duke Street, SA1 4HS
(between St Helens Rd and Walter Rd)
11-11; 12-10.30 Sun
☎ (01792) 465676
Courage Best Bitter; [H] **guest beers** [H] /[G]
Good, well-maintained, side-street pub, resembling a country inn in an urban setting. Exposed beams and a comfortable seating arrangement provide a relaxing atmosphere. A recent innovation is the artwork on display that is for sale. A quiz is held on Monday and live acoustic music is staged three times a week. A frequently changed, seasonal guest beer, dispensed directly from the barrel adds variety. Evening meals are served Monday-Friday. ◐♿

Eli Jenkins Ale House
24 Oxford Street, SA1 4HS
10.30-11.30 (midnight Fri); 11-11 Sun
☎ (01792) 630961
Badger Tanglefoot; Brains Bitter; guest beers [H]
City-centre pub, 100 yards from the bus station, named after a character in Under Milk Wood by Dylan Thomas. Wooden alcoves with varied seating include a no-smoking area; prints of local views adorn the walls. Busy during the day, it is quieter in the evening. Two guest beers of consistently good quality, such as Fuller's ESB or Orkney Dark Island, supplement the two regulars. Meals are served 10.30am-8pm (11am-5pm Sun).
◐♿

Queen's Hotel
Gloucester Place, SA1 1TY (near museum)
11-11; 12-10.30 Sun
☎ (01792) 521531
Brains Buckley's Best Bitter; Theakston Best Bitter, Old Peculier; Tomos Watkin Cwrw Haf or Merlin Stout [H]
Vibrant free house, located between the city's main nightlife zone and the marina, handy for the newly opened Maritime Museum. Appropriately, the pub displays photographs depicting Swansea's maritime history. Queen's enjoys strong local support and home-cooked lunches are an added attraction. Entertainment includes a Sunday quiz and occasional live music. It offers a good range of ales and is a rare local outlet for Old Peculier. ◐♿

Rhyddings Hotel
Brynmill Avenue, SA2 0BT
(400 yds up hill from rugby and cricket ground)
11-11; 12-10.30 Sun
☎ (01792) 648885
Greene King Abbot; Webster's Yorkshire Bitter; guest beers [H]
Unusual red-brick and stone, two-roomed pub that draws a mix of students and locals, within five minutes' walk of the university and rugby and cricket ground. A room is set aside for the chess team and role-playing society based here. Darts and pool are popular. It hosts a quiz twice a week (Mon and Thu), while rugby and football matches are usually shown in the bar. Meals are served all day until 8pm (4pm Sun) and children are welcome until 8.30pm.
❀◐♿♣

Woodman Inn
120 Mumbles Road, Blackpill, SA3 5AS
12-11; 12-10.30 Sun
☎ (01792) 402700
Courage Best Bitter, Directors; Greene King Old Speckled Hen; guest beer [H]
Prominently situated on the main Mumbles road, the inn offers views over Swansea Bay. It has been extended over the years and the well-appointed restaurant now incorporates a conservatory, serving good food at reasonable prices. Beer festivals are sometimes held over bank holiday weekends. The nearby Clyne Gardens are worth visiting and the old LMS railway line is now a cycle path, providing links to Killay and Gowerton. Frequent buses (Nos. 2, 2A and 3A) run until late evening. ⛫❀◐♿P

Three Crosses

Poundffald Inn
Tirmynydd Road, SA4 3PB
12-11.30; 11-midnight Fri & Sat; 12-11.30 Sun
☎ (01792) 873428
Greene King Abbot, Old Speckled Hen; Worthington's Bitter [H]
This welcoming, two-roomed pub is an excellent example of a thriving village local. The comfortable lounge is a popular destination for diners who are attracted by good value meals based on local produce. The bar is favoured by drinkers who enjoy its

WALES

convivial atmosphere. A large garden at the front hosts well-attended barbecues in summer. The pub boasts an interesting collection of horse bits, and other rural implements. This is an ideal stop for visitors to the Gower. ⛰❀◐◑P

Treforest

Otley Arms

Forest Road, CF37 1SY (100 yds from station)
⏲ 11-midnight (1am Fri & Sat); 12-midnight Sun
☎ (01443) 402033
Bullmastiff Welsh Gold; Otley 01; guest beers [H]
Tardis-like, end-of-terrace pub where you will find locals rubbing shoulders with students from the nearby university. All enjoy the ambience, the range of guest ales, which may include other Otley beers, and the multiple TV screens that provide a wide choice for sports fans. Observant drinkers may spot the Terence Cuneo prints and other railway memorabilia. There are disabled toilet facilities, but at present access to the pub is difficult for an unaccompanied wheelchair user. Lunches are served 11-4pm, evening meals 6.30-9.30pm. ◐◑⇌♣

Treherbert

Baglan Hotel

30 Baglan Street, CF42 5AW
⏲ 11-11 (1am Sat); 11-11 Sun
☎ (01443) 776111
Brains Rev James, seasonal beer; guest beer [H]
Pleasant, single-bar Valley local at the top end of the Rhondda. In the same family since 1947, it has established itself as the real ale oasis in a veritable desert. Photographs of well-known visitors adorn the walls, while the bar is frequented by locals and travellers from afar. ❀🛏♣

Tyle Garw

Boar's Head

Coedcae Lane, Talbot Green, CF72 9EZ OS029891
⏲ 11-11; 12-4, 7-10.30 Sun
☎ (01443) 225400
Brains Rev James; RCH Pitchfork; guest beers [H]
This pub was built in 1845 to serve the local heavy industries, but now sits among modern light industry and housing. Regional CAMRA Pub of the Year 2003, it retains a country pub feel after extensive refurbishment. It stocks up to seven ales, while a good value, no-smoking restaurant serves fine fare (book for Sun lunch). Special deals are available on Tuesday (steak) and Wednesday (curry) evenings, but no meals are served Sunday or Monday evenings.
❀◐◑⊟P

Upper Killay (Swansea)

Railway Inn

553 Gower Road, SA2 7DS
⏲ 12-2, 4-11; 12-11 Sat; 12-10.30 Sun
☎ (01792) 203946
Swansea Deep Slade Dark, Bishopswood, Original Wood; guest beers [H]
This former CAMRA regional Pub of the Year dates back to 1864. It attracts all ages from students up, creating a good-humoured atmosphere that appeals to visitors. The former railway track is now part of the well-publicised network of cycleways, giving access to Swansea Bay seafront by bike (10 minutes) or foot (30 minutes). It normally offers three guest beers – some are rare for the area – but no food is served. Buses run to Killay Square, a five-minute walk away.
⛰❀⊟♣P

Ystalyfera

Wern Fawr Inn

47 Wern Road, SA9 2LY
⏲ 7 (6.30 Sat)-11; 12-3.30, 7-10.30 Sun
☎ (01639) 843625 🌐 bryncelynbrewery.co.uk
Bryncelyn Buddy Marvellous, Oh Boy, seasonal beers [H]
This fascinating pub is home to the Bryncelyn Brewery. The bar contains numerous old artefacts and needs to be seen to be believed. There is also a comfortable lounge. The beers, all named after Buddy Holly songs, are multiple CAMRA award winners. Polypins can be ordered at CAMRA's regional Pub of the Year 2005. This pub comes on beer buffs' 'must do before I die' lists.
⛰Q❀⊟🚌♣

New pub opening hours

The Licensing Act of November 2005 for England and Wales gave pub owners the ability to apply for more flexible and extended opening hours from the licensing authorities. The most obvious change has been that many pubs now stay open until midnight or later at weekends. The experience of the first 10 months of the new law has been that some pubs have scaled down their opening hours where they have found there is insufficient demand to remain open until midnight or later. The opening hours for pubs listed in the guide have been treble checked before going to press, but readers planning to make journeys to pubs are advised to phone and check current hours.

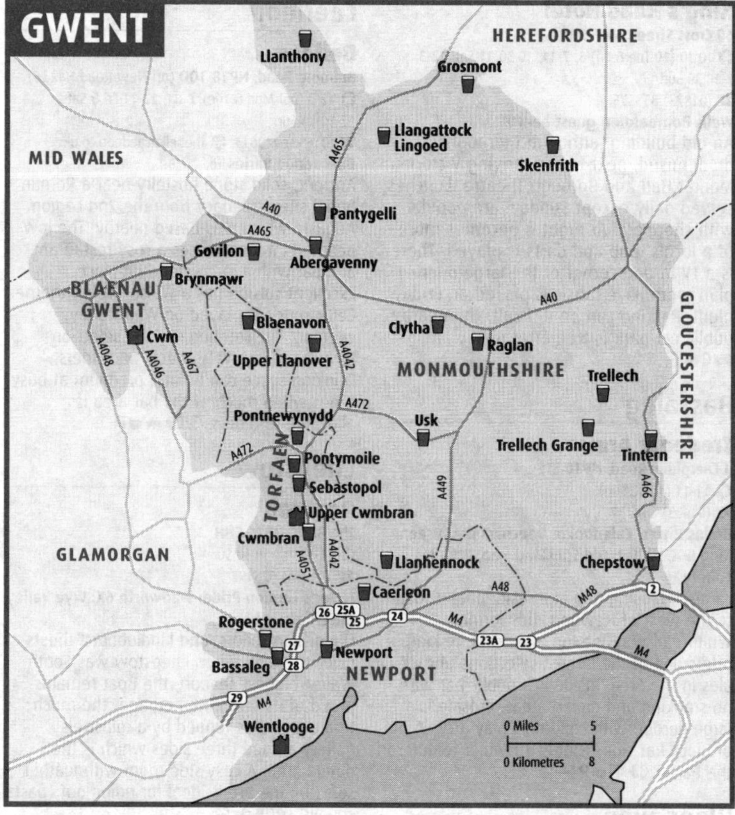

Authority areas covered Blaenau Gwent UA, Monmouthshire UA, Newport UA, Torfaen UA

Abergavenny

Angel Hotel

15 Cross Street, NP7 5EN

10-3, 6-11 (11.30 Fri & Sat); 12-3, 7-10.30 Sun

(01873) 857121 angelhotelabergavenny.com

Brains Rev James; Fuller's London Pride; guest beer Ⓗ

Independent town centre hotel providing good beer and food in a relaxed atmosphere. There are three drinking areas and a quality restaurant. The main bar has large tables and leather sofas, a quiet lounge off the lobby features interesting artwork. The sheltered patio area with large tables and umbrellas is delightful for alfresco dining and drinking.

Q❀P

Cantreff Inn

61 Brecon Road, NP7 7RA

12-2.30, 6-11; 12-3, 7-10.30 Sun

(01873) 855827

Beer range varies Ⓗ

Situated a short distance from the town centre on the road to Brecon and the hospital. Inside are two rooms, one for drinking, one for dining, either side of a central bar. Good value food is served in the dining room. The pub has grown in popularity since the current licensees introduced a rotating guest beer policy, sometimes including beers unusual for the area. A sheltered rear garden is busy in summer. Children under seven are not permitted.

❀P

Coliseum

Lion Street, NP7 5DR

9am-midnight (1am Fri & Sat); 9am-midnight Sun

(01873) 736960

Brains SA; Greene King Abbot; Marston's Pedigree; guest beers Ⓗ

Formerly the town's last surviving cinema, now part of the Wetherspoon chain, the pub offers the largest choice of beers in the area including ales from independent brewers. During the weekend evenings it is often very crowded as predominantly younger drinkers let their hair down, although at other times the clientele is more mixed. Standard Wetherspoon's food is served. Flexible licensing hours mean you can come for breakfast or supper.

INDEPENDENT BREWERIES

Cwmbran Upper Cwmbran
Kingstone Whitebrook
Warcop Wentlooge
Webbs Cwm

King's Head Hotel

60 Cross Street, NP7 5EU

10.30 (10 Tue & Fri)-3, 7-11; 10.30-11 Sat; 12-3, 7-10.30 Sun

(01873) 853575

Wells Bombardier; guest beer H

An old building, although thoroughly modernised, next to the thriving Victorian Market Hall and Borough Theatre. Lunches, served daily except Sunday, are popular with shoppers. At night it becomes more of a locals' pub and darts is played. There is a TV in one corner of the large open-plan room. Live music is played on Friday night. Parking can be difficult; the nearby public car park is free after 6pm.

Bassaleg

Tredegar Arms

4 Caerphilly Road, NP10 8LE

11-11 (10.30 Sun)

(01633) 894237

Brains Bitter; Caledonian Deuchars IPA; Greene King IPA, Abbot, Old Speckled Hen, Ruddles County H

Large, imposing pub in a residential district to the west of Newport, this former Whitbread Wayside Inn, now Greene King, offers one of the largest selections of cask ales in the area. Inside is a public bar with no-smoking and dining areas, outside is a large garden with children's play area. A pin of Black Rat cider is now a regular feature on the bar. P

Blaenavon

Queen Victoria Inn

Prince Street, NP4 9BD

11-11; 12-10,30 Sun

(01495) 791652

Brains Rev James; Rhymney Bitter; guest beer H

Part of Blaenavon's Book Town circuit, the pub's lounge is not only a family room but a dining room and book shop combined, with a wide range of titles for sale. A hatch separates the lounge from the small public bar. Guest accommodation and a reputation for tasty food make this homely inn an ideal base from which to explore local heritage sites.

P

Brynmawr

Hobby Horse Inn

30 Greenland Road, NP23 4DT (off Alma St)

12-2.30, 7-11; 12-11 Sat; 12-10.30 Sun

(01495) 310996

Beer range varies H

A distinctive hobby horse sign – logo of the old Rhymney Brewery – hangs outside this friendly back-street pub. The inn has a genuine community feel, with locals enjoying the cosy, low-beamed bar and dining area displaying models of sailing ships. With a restaurant and B&B accommodation this is also a comfortable base for visitors exploring the area.

P

Caerleon

Bell Inn

Bulmore Road, NP18 1QQ (off New Road B4236)

12-3 (not Mon & Tue), 6-11; 12-11 Fri & Sat; 12-10.30 Sun

(01633) 420613 thebellatcaerleon.co.uk

Beer range varies H

Ancient, solid stone hostelry near a Roman burial site – a legacy from the 2nd Legion Augusta which was based nearby. The low-beamed interior houses a cosy restaurant and bar with a large stone fireplace. Excellent cuisine has a Welsh-Breton theme. Celtic music is played on Wednesday evening. The rotating real ale selection includes many Welsh beers and ciders. Drinking space can be at a premium at busy times when much of the bar area is allocated to diners. P

Chepstow

Boat Inn

The Back, NP16 5HH

11-11; 12-10.30 Sun

(01291) 628192

Fuller's London Pride; Wadworth 6X; Wye Valley Bitter; guest beer H

Quenching sailors' and landlubbers' thirsts since the days when Chepstow was South Wales' biggest seaport, the Boat remains proud of its seafaring heritage. The much timbered bar is topped by a minstrels' gallery around three sides which is the dining area. A cosy side room with leather sofas by the fire is ideal for riding out coastal squalls.

Chepstow Athletic Club

Mathern Road, NP16 5JJ (off Bulwark Rd)

7-11; 12-midnight Sat; 12-2.30, 7-10.30 Sun

(01291) 622126

Brains SA; Flowers IPA; Rhymney Bitter; guest beers H

A beacon for real ale quality, this thriving club offers consistency, choice and value. Three regular cask ales are complemented by three guest beers, usually from smaller independents, typically changing twice a week, all at lower than average pub prices. The large, cheery lounge is home from home for sports players, fans, social members and local clubs and societies including Chepstow Male Voice Choir. CAMRA members are always welcome – show your card for free entry. The function room upstairs also serves real ale. P

Clytha

Clytha Arms

Old Raglan Road, NP7 8BW (on B4598 Abergavenny-Raglan road) OS368089

12-3 (not Mon), 6-11; 12-11 Sat; 12-4, 7-10.30 Sun

(01873) 840206 clytha-arms.com

Beer range varies H

Winner of Gwent local CAMRA Pub of the Year more times than any other pub, together with numerous other awards, this is an outstanding country pub. Formerly the Clytha estate's dower house, it is set in extensive, attractive grounds. Inside are two rooms and a high-quality restaurant. Six real ales, cider and perry are on offer, selected from far and wide. The accommodation here is recommended. ⌂Q❀⇌◑⊟♣●P

Cwmbran

Bush Inn

Graig Road, NP44 5AN
(off top of Upper Cwmbran Rd)
✪ 12-4, 7-11.30; 12-11.30 Sun (hours vary in winter)
☎ (01633) 483764
Cwmbran Crow Valley Bitter Ⓗ
An ideal hostelry to slake your thirst after some mountain walking, this popular pub in the shadow of Mynedd Maen lies close to Cwmbran Brewery. Situated in a pleasant residential area, formerly a mining community, it commands views of the Severn estuary from the front. The interior is divided between a bar and games area and a cosy parlour with dressers and a comfy sofa. Other Cwmbran beers may put in an occasional appearance. ⌂❀⊟♣P

Commodore Hotel

Mill Lane, Llanyravon, NP44 8SH (off Llanfrechfa Way behind Crow's Nest pub)
✪ 11-11; 12-10.30 Sun
☎ (01633) 484091 ⊕ commodorehotel.uk.com
Cwmbran Crow Valley Bitter; guest beer Ⓗ
Residential hotel now run by the third generation of the same family which has built up an excellent reputation over the last 30 years. High quality food prepared with seasonal ingredients can be enjoyed in the fine restaurant. Meals are also served in the lounge along with a choice of real ales. Outside is a decked patio for drinking and dining in fine weather. A function room is available. ❀⇌◑P

Govilon

Bridgend Inn

Church Lane, NP7 9RP
✪ 12-3, 7-12.30am (1am Fri & Sat); 12-3, 7-10.30 Sun
☎ (01873) 830177
Beer range varies Ⓗ
In the centre of the village just off the main road and handy for the Monmouthshire & Brecon Canal, popular with walkers, cyclists and boaters. The bar has a pool table and the lounge is no-smoking – the venue for live music on Friday evening. A range of beers, mainly from independent brewers, is on offer along with good value meals. ◑⊟♣P⊬

Grosmont

Angel Inn

NP7 8EP (off the A465 at Llangua)
✪ 12-2.30, 6-1am (2am Fri); 12-2am Sat; 12-11 (12-2.30, 7-11 winter) Sun
☎ (01981) 240646
Tomos Watkin seasonal beers; Wye Valley Hereford Pale Ale Ⓗ
A real success story – once CAMRA Gwent Pub of the Year, this pub went into a sad decline, eventually closing until a group of determined villagers bought the place and reopened it to much local rejoicing and positive publicity. Now back at the heart of community life, serving good food and drink, it is a welcome meeting place not just for villagers but for visitors to the Norman castle and medieval church. Lunches are served daily except Monday and evening meals Wednesday to Saturday evening. ⌂❀◑

Llangattock Lingoed

Hunter's Moon Inn

NP7 8RR (2 miles off B4521 at Llanvetherine)
✪ 12-3 (not Mon-Fri, Jan-Feb), 6.30-11; 12-3, 6.30-10.30 Sun
☎ (01873) 821499 ⊕ hunters-moon-inn.co.uk
Wye Valley Butty Bach; Ⓗ **guest beers** Ⓖ
Ancient pub in a tiny hamlet next to the renovated medieval church. Popular with walkers on the long-distance Offa's Dyke path which goes through the churchyard, it provides good quality food and accommodation. There are two outside spaces – raised decking overlooking the church and a grassy area around a natural pool with ducks. Inside, the small bar has handpumps for regular beer and draught cider; guests are on a stillage for gravity dispense. ⌂❀⇌◑●P

Llanhennock

Wheatsheaf Inn

NP18 1LT (turn right 1 mile along Caerleon-Usk road) OS353927
✪ 11-11 (closed 3-5.30 Wed winter); 12-3, 7-10.30 Sun
☎ (01633) 420468 ⊕ thewheatsheafllanhennock.co.uk
Draught Bass; M&B Brew XI; guest beer Ⓗ
Situated in a hamlet two miles outside the ancient Roman town of Caerleon (Isca Silurium), this is an excellent example of an unspoilt traditional country pub, with fine views to the north and south. Inside is a cosy lounge and a bar crammed with unusual memorabilia and old photographs. With its cosy log fire and enclosed garden, it is well worth a visit, whatever the season. ⌂❀◑⊟♣P

Llanthony

Half Moon

NP7 7NN (6 miles off A465 at Llanfihangel Crucorney) OS286279
✪ 12-3 (not Tue), 7 (6 Sat)-11; 12-3, 7-10.30 Sun (winter open Fri & Sat eves and Sun only)
☎ (01873) 890611
Bullmastiff Welsh Gold, Welsh Red, Son of a Bitch Ⓗ
A long way from the main road, situated in a small hamlet in idyllic countryside a few yards from the majestic abbey ruins. A rare outlet for Bullmastiff beers in this part of the country, the pub serves an isolated and remote community as well as providing a mecca for the many walkers and trekkers attracted by the wild beauty of the area. Note the framed CAMRA awards to Bullmastiff displayed by the brewery. ⌂Q⊃❀⇌◑⊟●P

Newport

Gladiator

Pillmawr Road, NP18 3QZ (off A4051) OS312907
☉ 11.30-11; 12-10.30 Sun
☎ (01633) 821353
Banks's Bitter; guest beers Ⓗ
Originally a small cottage but converted to a pub around 25 years ago. Situated on the outskirts of Newport just off the Ponthir road from Malpas, it has fine views of the countryside. Inside is a smart lounge and a large public bar, with an even larger function room hosting occasional live music. Meals are served Wednesday to Saturday and Sunday lunchtime. ❀◑◗⊟♿♣P⊬

Godfrey Morgan

158 Chepstow Road, Maindee, NP19 8EG
☉ 9am-11 daily
☎ (01633) 221928
Brains SA; Greene King Abbot, Old Speckled Hen; Marston's Burton Bitter, Pedigree; guest beers Ⓗ
Situated in a popular, bustling area about a mile from the city centre, this Wetherspoon pub is an attractive and welcoming conversion of a former cinema. The pub is named after Captain Godfrey Morgan who rode in the Charge of the Light Brigade. Furnished in Art Deco style, it is adorned with photographs of erstwhile stars of stage and screen with local connections. Both spacious bars have no-smoking areas.
Q☕◑◗♿P⊬

Old Murenger House

53 High Street, NP20 1GA
☉ 11-11; 7-10.30 Sun
☎ (01633) 263977 🌐 murenger.com
Samuel Smith OBB Ⓗ
Historic pub dating from Tudor times. Thanks to Sam Smith's respect for old premises, behind the impressive façade and old leaded window frame the interior is in keeping with the longevity of the building. High back settles and dark wood dominate the tasteful decor within several linked areas. Popular with all ages, it brings a comforting feel of tradition to an area dominated by 'superpubs'. Q◑⇌

Red Lion

47 Stow Hill, NP20 1JH
☉ 11-midnight (1am Fri & Sat); 12-11.30 Sun
☎ (01633) 264398
Beer range varies Ⓗ
A traditional ale house, this colourful pub draws a loyal clientele from various parts of the city and further afield. Popular with sports fans, rugby union memorabilia is on display and big matches are screened, especially international rugby, when the place is packed. Shove ha'penny is still played here. The founding place of Gwent CAMRA in 1974, it retains strong links as a meeting place and social venue. 🜂❀⇌♣

St Julian Inn

Caerleon Road, NP18 1QA
☉ 11.30-11; 12-10.30 Sun
☎ (01633) 243548
Banks's Bitter; John Smith's Bitter; Wells Bombardier; guest beers Ⓗ
Popular pub in a splendid location on the banks of the River Usk. The large balcony provides pleasant riverside views of rural tranquillity with historic Caerleon in the distance. The interior was opened out years ago but separate areas remain, some with a relaxing, cosy atmosphere, others livelier in feel, giving the pub wide appeal. A skittles alley and function room is available.
❀◑◗⊟♣P⊬

Pantygelli

Crown Inn

Old Hereford Road, NP7 7HR (off A465, 4 miles N of Abergavenny)
☉ 12-3 (not Mon), 6-11; 12-3, 6-10.30 Sun
☎ (01873) 853314
Draught Bass; Rhymney Bitter; Wye Valley Hereford Pale Ale; guest beer Ⓗ
Expanding facilities including disabled access are a sign of the increasing popularity of this pub, situated in a small hamlet but close enough to Abergavenny to attract a large number of regulars. The well-kept patio in front of the pub has fine views over the Skirrid Mountain and on warm days is a delightful place to enjoy a pint. The basic open-plan interior is divided into areas including a popular restaurant (booking recommended).
🜂❀◑◗♿♣P⊬

Pontnewynydd

Bridgend Inn

23 Hanbury Road, NP4 6QN (off Osborne Rd)
☉ 12-11; 12-10.30 Sun
☎ (01495) 757435
Beer range varies Ⓗ
The merger of two 17th-century cottages (with resident ghosts) created a pub to serve thirsty workers from local heavy industries. Today it is a pleasant community local also popular with walkers exploring the nearby disused railway track and surrounding countryside. Entry is below road level via a patio. The cosy interior has a bar and games area with a small lounge. Local micro-breweries are supported. Food is by prior arrangement only. 🜂❀♣

Pontymoile

Horse & Jockey

Old Usk Road, NP4 0JB (off A4042(T))
☉ 12-11; 12-10.30 Sun
☎ (01495) 762721
Adnams Broadside; guest beers Ⓗ
Pretty, 15th-century former coaching inn next to the ancient church and a short stroll from the Mon & Brec Canal (bridge 55). The single room interior is multi level and popular with diners. A varied range of good quality food includes vegetarian options (booking advisable). There is outside seating at the front and the rear garden provides views of the surrounding countryside. The guest beer is often from Archers. Q❀◑◗P

Raglan

Ship Inn
High Street, NP15 2DY
🕒 11.30-11; 12-10.30 Sun
☎ (01291) 690635
Beer range varies Ⓗ
Inside this former coach house are two bar areas and a dining room. The small cobbled courtyard at the front which is used by drinkers in summer has a disused water pump. Up to three constantly changing ales are dispensed, mostly from small breweries. Good food is freshly prepared and home cooked. ⛺Q🍃❀◑◗♣

Rogerstone

Tredegar Arms
57 Cefn Road, NP10 9AS
🕒 12-3, 5.30-11; 12-11 Thu-Sat; 12-4, 7-10.30 Sun
☎ (01633) 664999
Draught Bass; Courage Best Bitter; guest beer Ⓗ
Traditional pub popular with locals and visitors. Inside there is a public bar and a cosy flagstone-floored bar with dining area and family room. The pub has a good reputation for food, particularly Sunday lunch (booking advisable). As well as the two regular ales on handpull there is an ever-changing guest beer, often from a micro-brewery. Q🍃❀◑◗⊟P

Sebastopol

Open Hearth
Wern Road, NP4 5DR (off Austin Rd)
🕒 11.30-11; 12-10.30 Sun
☎ (01495) 763752
Caledonian Deuchars IPA; Greene King Abbot; guest beers Ⓗ
Standing alongside the Monmouthshire & Brecon Canal, this perennial favourite has an extensive garden and a towpath deck patio that are always busy in fine weather, particularly during canalside events and beer festivals. There are handpumps dotted throughout the three bars – check the blackboard for a choice of up to nine ales from regional and micro-breweries. A tempting menu offers a wide range of dishes which can be enjoyed in the bar or downstairs restaurant. ❀◑◗⊟♣P

Sebastopol Social Club
Wern Road, NP4 5DU (on jct with Austin Rd)
🕒 12-11; 12-10.30 Sun
☎ (01495) 763808
Hancock's HB; guest beers Ⓗ
Former UK CAMRA club champion with a clutch of regional awards too. The beer range usually includes ales from local brewers as well as guests from further afield. Note the colourful array of pump clip stickers decorating the servery. The main bar hosts bingo and live entertainment while the comfortable lounge is quieter with an unobtrusive TV for sporting events. Downstairs is a games room with skittle alley. Show your CAMRA membership card or a copy of this Guide to gain entry. ❀⊟♣P

Skenfrith

Bell
NP7 8UH (off B4521, midway between Abergavenny and Ross-on-Wye)
🕒 11-11 (not Mon Nov-Mar); 12-10.30 Sun
☎ (01600) 730235 🌐 skenfrith.co.uk
Breconshire Golden Valley; Freeminer Bitter; Taylor Landlord Ⓗ
Originally a coaching inn, the Bell was transformed into a high-quality independent hotel and restaurant a few years ago. To their credit the owners retained a separate bar serving beers from independent breweries for locals and visitors to enjoy. The pub is situated next to a low bridge over the river Monnow and under the walls of a Norman castle which was built as one of a chain intended to keep the Welsh at bay. Draught cider comes from a farm just over the border in Herefordshire.
⛺Q❀🛏◑◗⊟●P⚡

Tintern

Cherry Tree Inn
Forge Road, NP16 5TH (lane off A466 at Royal George Hotel)
🕒 12-11 (winter hours vary); 12-10.30 Sun
☎ (01291) 689292 🌐 thecherry.co.uk
Hancock's HB; guest beers Ⓖ
Enduring haven in an idyllic steep-sided valley just west of the village. A large patio with shelter for damp days is perfect for fine-weather drinking and dining. Part of the pub is the village shop and post office. Wales' only ever-present entry in the Guide, it offers a range of ales from smaller independents, numbering six or more in summer. Excellent home-cooked meals include tasty curries. Cask (Bulmers Traditional) and bottled ciders are always available. ⛺Q❀🛏◑◗●P⚡

Moon & Sixpence
Monmouth Road, NP16 5SG
🕒 11-11 (12-11 Oct-Easter); 12-10.30 Sun
☎ (01291) 689284 🌐 themoonandsixpence.co.uk
Beer range varies Ⓗ
Renowned throughout the area for his commitment to real ale, the landlord offers a range of brews from independents as well as good real food with influences from his native Hungary. Inside the pub are four charming interlinking rooms, one with an indoor spring fed by flow from the steep slopes above. Outside a terrace gives fine views across the beautiful Wye Valley. The annual beer festival has become a popular event and locally-made home-fermented cider makes an occasional appearance. ❀◑◗P⚡

Wye Valley Hotel
NP16 6SQ (on A466)
🕒 11-3, 6-11; 12-3, 7-10.30 Sun
☎ (01291) 689441 🌐 wyevalleyhotel.co.uk
Wye Valley Bitter, Butty Bach; guest beer Ⓗ
Tourists and locals alike are warmly welcomed to this distinctive multi-angled pub at the north end of the village. In recent years it has become a constant source of Wye Valley ales. A wondrous row of

commemorative beer bottles surrounds the two-part bar, with good food and conversation always on the menu. Tintern's Cistercian Abbey is a 15-minute stroll away while the hills above the pub hold a treasure-trove of waymarked paths for exploring many of the valley's scenic splendours.
❀⇌⊂▶P

Trellech

Lion Inn

NP25 4PA (on B4293, Chepstow-Monmouth Road)
12-3 (3.30 Sat), 6 (7 Mon; 6.30 Sat)-11 (midnight Thu-Sat); (12-midnight summer Sat); 12-4.30 Sun
☎ (01600) 860322 lioninn.co.uk
Beer range varies H
Open plan building with a bar area with a proper pub feel and a raised dining area offering an extensive menu. Up to four constantly changing ales are dispensed, usually from small breweries and micros. A beer festival is held in June and a bottled beer festival featuring many unusual foreign beers in November.
⩩❀⇌⊂▶⊟Å♣●P

Trellech Grange

Fountain Inn

NP16 6QW OS503011
12-3, 6.30-11; 12-11 Sat & Sun
☎ (01291) 689303 fountaininn-tintern.com
Beer range varies H
This 17th-century inn close to Tintern Abbey has gone from strength to strength since it was taken over by the new owner in August 2004. Inside is a small flagstone bar with dining areas leading off. Up to three ales are served with the emphasis on local breweries. The menu is extensive and food is popular but you are welcome to pop in for a pint and a game of darts, or maybe a tinkle on the tuned piano. ⩩❀⇌⊂▶Å♣P

Upper Llanover

Goose & Cuckoo

NP7 9ER (at end of narrow lane off A4042 at Llanover) OS292073
11.30-3, 7-11 (closed Mon); 11.30-11 Fri & Sat; 12-10.30 Sun
☎ (01873) 880277
Beer range varies H
Virtually unchanged for many years, this venerable pub is situated in a remote location within the Brecon Beacons National Park. It is advisable to take an Ordnance Survey map the first time you visit but the views when you get there are worth it. The landlord keeps binoculars behind the bar for bird-watching. The large garden is shared with the pub's ducks and goats. Hosting beer festivals a couple of times a year, it was Gwent CAMRA Pub of the Year in 2005.
⩩Q❀⇌⊂▶♣P⊬G☋

Usk

Usk Conservative Club

The Grange, 16 Maryport Street, NP15 1AB
12-3, 7-11; 12-3, 7-10.30 Sun
☎ (01291) 672634
Fuller's Discovery; Greene King IPA; guest beer H
Private members club in deceptively large premises. The old town house has a smart, comfortable lounge with a dining room on one side and games area on the other. At the rear is a function room large enough for dances. Decorated in shades of blue, photographs of Tory party notables hang on the walls including the real ale appreciating local MP. The guest ale changes every few weeks. Standard club entry restrictions apply.
❀⊂▶♣P

King's Head Hotel

18 Old Market Street, NP15 1AL
11-11; 12-10.30 Sun
☎ (01291) 672963
Fuller's London Pride; Taylor Landlord H
This 15th-century inn is a regular in the Guide. The bar has a pleasantly cluttered feel with subdued decor and a collection of books and interesting artefacts accumulated by the owner over the years. The great fireplace is a prominent feature of this cosy room with a dining room attached. A popular hostelry serving good, tasty food, there is also a restaurant and function room.
⩩⇌⊂▶P

Nag's Head Inn

Twyn Square, NP15 1BH
11-3, 5.30-11; 12-3, 6.30-10.30 Sun
☎ (01291) 672820
Brains Buckley's Best Bitter, SA, Rev James H
Old coaching inn that prides itself on the high quality of its locally-sourced cuisine. The menu is mouth-wateringly tempting with dishes that can be enjoyed with a glass of real ale. The charming front room with its intimate snug and etched glass windows is popular with diners. Note the fascinating collection of old cigarette cards, agricultural implements and local business memorabilia. The outside area is a blaze of floral colour in summer. Q☋❀⊂▶⊬

The Genuine Stunning

'What is your best – your very best – ale a glass?' 'Twopence-halfpenny,' says the landlord, 'is the price of the genuine Stunning Ale.'
'Then,' says I, producing the money, 'Just draw me a glass of the Genuine Stunning, if you please, with a good head to it.'

Charles Dickens, David Copperfield

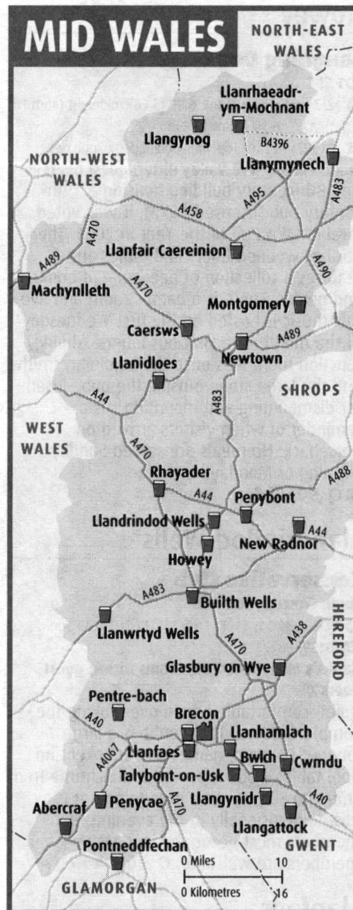

Abercraf

Copper Beech Inn

133 Heol Tawe, SA9 1XS (off A4067 Swansea-Brecon road)

11-11 daily

☎ (01639) 730269

Beer range varies Ⓗ

Large, friendly village pub near the Brecon Beacons National Park and the new Geopark. The meeting place for the local caving club, it is also frequented by cyclists and hikers. Cave Rescue is the main charity supported by the pub. It has a large bar, games room and upstairs function room. A wide selection of bar meals includes 10 curries of varying strengths. ⌂Q❀⇌◐♿⊟♣P

Brecon

Boar's Head

Ship Street, LD3 9AL

12 (11 Tue)-1am; 12-2am Thu-Sat; 12-1am Sun

☎ (01874) 622856

Breconshire County Ale, Golden Valley, Ramblers Ruin, seasonal beers; Fuller's London Pride; Greene King Abbot Ⓗ

The Breconshire Brewery tap is a lively and popular town centre pub. The wood-panelled front bar tends to be a little quieter than the larger back bar which houses the pool table and a large screen for showing major sporting events. Live music is hosted regularly and special events are held throughout the summer, particularly during the Brecon jazz festival. The patio garden gives fine views of the River Usk and over to the Beacons. ⌂❀◐⊟♣P

Black Bull

86 The Street, LD3 7LS

12-midnight daily

☎ (01874) 623900

Evan Evans BB, Cwrw, Warrior, seasonal beers Ⓗ

Popular pub now with a new name, layout and landlord dedicated to real ale (no smoothflow here!). The interior has been opened out and given a comfortable, contemporary feel. The central bar and pillars create separate areas for drinking and dining, while retaining a spacious, airy feel. Food is served until 8pm (6pm Sun). This pub has all the makings of a good, friendly, community ale house. ⌂Q◐

Clarence

25 The Watton, LD3 7ED

12-midnight (2am Fri & Sat); 12-midnight Sun

☎ (01874) 622810

Beer range varies Ⓗ

Recently refurbished by new owners, this town centre pub has two rooms separated by the central bar. Locals tend to frequent the front public bar while the back room, opened out and now with a contemporary feel, has tables and chairs for dining. A large screen shows major sporting events. Regular quiz nights are popular. Beers tend to be sourced from local breweries; cider is sold in summer. ❀◐⊟♣

Builth Wells

Greyhound Hotel

3 Garth Road, LD2 3AR

12-midnight (1am Fri & Sat); 12-11 Sun

☎ (01982) 553255 thegreyhoundhotel.co.uk

Fuller's London Pride; Greene King Abbot; guest beers Ⓗ

Early 20th-century hotel with open-plan bars, a restaurant and a large conference room. With ever-improving facilities, the hotel has a reputation for the high quality of its food – the Sunday lunchtime carvery is highly recommended. An engraved glass panel above the front door shows that a previous owner had a licence to brew. Guest beers are sourced mainly from smaller breweries including Cottage, RCH, Titanic and Orkney. A beer festival is held in the week before the Royal Welsh. ❀⇌◐♣P⚟

Bwlch

New Inn

LD3 7LQ (on A40 between Brecon and Crickhowell)

11-3, 6-11; 11-11 Sat & Sun

INDEPENDENT BREWERIES

Breconshire Brecon

WALES

☎ (01874) 730215
Brains Rev James; guest beers Ⓗ
Vibrant village-centre pub with a lively atmosphere. A large display of pump clips shows the landlord's commitment to real ales, along with a large selection of malt whiskies. Guest beers are usually sourced from local breweries. Note the panel on the bar relating the story of the landlord's dog, the paint pot and the spirits in the cellar, which explains the pub's sign. Good food, fine ales and accommodation make this an ideal base for exploring the surrounding area. ⌂Q❀⇌◐◑▲P

Caersws

Red Lion
Main Street, SY17 5EL (off A470)
⏲ 3 (12 summer)-11; 12-11 Fri-Sun
☎ (01686) 688023
Beer range varies Ⓗ
Friendly village local with a small, cosy bar and a lounge/restaurant area. The wood-beamed pub has a comfortable, relaxed feel and attracts a varied clientele of all ages. A good range of guest beers comes from independent breweries. Excellent home-cooked food is served and there is an attractive outdoor area for summer drinking. ⌂❀◐◑⊟⇌♣P

Cwmdu

Farmers Arms
NP8 1RU (on A470 between Crickhowell and Builth Wells)
⏲ 12-3, 6-11; closed Mon; 12-3, 6-11 Sun
☎ (01874) 730464
Shepherd Neame Spitfire; guest beers Ⓗ
Exposed beams and an impressive fireplace containing an iron wood-burning stove dominate the bar area of this village centre community pub. The hop-bedecked bar separates the bar room from the dining area at the front of the pub, where superb food is served. The menu ranges from locally-sourced black beef to regional specialities and old favourites. Guest beers are usually sourced from local breweries.
⌂Q❀⇌◐◑P

Glasbury on Wye

Hollybush Inn
HR3 5PS (on B4350 between Glasbury and Hay)
OS198403
⏲ 8am-midnight (closing time varies) daily
☎ (01497) 847371 🌐 hollybushcamping.co.uk
Breconshire Golden Valley; Greene King Abbot Ⓗ
Warm and friendly pub which has recently undergone renovation and refurbishment. The main bar has an annexe at one end and an additional dining area. Superb home-cooked food is served all day including dishes for vegans and vegetarians. The land between the pub's large garden and the River Wye has a spacious camping site, as well as woodland walks and an adventure area. Views of the Black Mountains and the Begwyn Hills mark the horizon. Weekend events are hosted regularly. ⌂Q❀◐◑▲●P⊬

Howey

Laughing Dog
LD1 5PT
⏲ 12-3 (not winter Mon), 6.30 (5 Fri)-midnight (1am Fri & Sat); 12-3, 6.30-midnight Sun
☎ (01597) 822406 🌐 thelaughingdog.ukpub.net
Wood Parish; Wye Valley Bitter; guest beers Ⓗ
An 18th-century building housing a 19th-century pub (licensed 1872), it was voted local CAMRA Pub of the Year in 2006. The bar has wooden floors and tables and features a collection of beer-related books and guides. There is a games room and live folk music is hosted on the first Wednesday of the month. The spacious lounge/dining/function room was once the adjoining smithy and the large stone outside the pub – used for dismounting and mounting – is a reminder of when visitors arrived on horseback. No meals are served Sunday evening or Monday lunchtime.
⌂Q❀◐◑⊟♣

Llandrindod Wells

Conservative Club
South Crescent, LD1 5DH
⏲ 11-2, 5.30-11; 11-11 Fri & Sat; 11.30-10.30 Sun
☎ (01597) 822126
Banks's Mansfield Cask; Brains Bitter; guest beers Ⓗ
Quiet, comfortable haven overlooking the Temple Gardens. The 'Con' has a large lounge, TV room, games bar, snooker and pool tables. Food is served at lunchtime from Friday to Sunday. Live entertainment is hosted occasionally in the evening. Non-members must be signed in; CAMRA members are welcome. Q❀◐♿⇌♣

Llanfaes

Drovers Arms
Newgate Street, LD3 8SN
⏲ 2-1am (2.30am Fri & Sat); 2-1.30am Sun
☎ (01874) 623377
Tetley Bitter; Wadworth IPA; guest beers Ⓗ
Lively community local. The main bar is L-shaped with a room to one side with its own servery. A big screen is available for viewing major sporting events. There is a secluded patio area at the rear for alfresco drinking. Guest beers are sourced from the nearby Breconshire Brewery and real cider is usually available in the summer. ❀◐◑♣●

Llanfair Caereinion

Black Lion
Parsons Bank, SY21 0RR
⏲ 8-midnight (2am Fri & Sat); 8-midnight Sun
☎ (01938) 810758
Brains Rev James; Worthington's Bitter; guest beer Ⓗ
Popular two-roomed town pub. The small, comfortable lounge is often crowded. The larger wood-beamed public bar has a big open fireplace, pool table, games machines and a darts area. Pictures of the local rugby team adorn the walls. Regular live music is staged. ⌂❀♣P

Goat Hotel
High Street, SY21 0QS (on A458)
11-11 (midnight Fri & Sat); 11-11 Sun
(01938) 810428
Beer range varies H
Excellent, beamed inn with a welcoming atmosphere. Popular with locals and tourists, the pub has a plush lounge with comfortable leather armchairs and sofas. Three real ales are available including one from the Wood Brewery. The lounge is dominated by a large inglenook with an open fire. There is a restaurant serving home-cooked food and a games room at the rear. P

Llangattock

Vine Tree
NP8 1HG OS215180
12-3, 6-11 daily
(01873) 810514
Breconshire Golden Valley; Fuller's London Pride H
Riverside pub where the emphasis is on excellent food. Drinkers are welcome in the cosy, copper-covered bar area, with its large fireplace, stone walls and flagged floors. Cider is produced locally, exclusively for the pub. The impressive food menu boasts locally sourced meat and vegetables, and ever-changing specials including fish, venison and game. Booking is advisable as the pub is often busy. The riverside garden is an added attraction. Q P

Llangynidr

Red Lion
NP8 1NT (just off B4558)
11.30-3 (not Mon), 6.30 (7.30 Mon)-midnight; 11.30-midnight Fri-Sun
(01874) 730223
Beer range varies H
Lively inn on the edge of the village – a real focus for the community with meetings and educational courses hosted regularly. The multi-roomed interior includes a cosy main bar with a games room and a dining room. Food is home cooked using local produce where possible, and the beers come from the nearby Breconshire Brewery. The pub, with a patio and garden, can be busy, particularly in summer. Q P

Llangynog

Tanat Valley Hotel
SY10 0BX (on B4391)
6-midnight; 12-11 Fri-Sun
(01691) 780210
Caledonian Deuchars IPA; St Austell Tribute H
Pleasant wooden-beamed hostelry with a stone fireplace, tiled floor and beamed bar adorned with hops. The lounge has a lower level providing a further drinking area and a pool table. Popular with locals, the pub has a friendly, relaxed feel. P

Llanhamlach

Old Ford
LD3 7YB (on A40 E of Brecon)
12-11 daily
(01874) 665220
Beer range varies H
Originally a coaching inn dating from the 12th century, the building has been much extended but retains its original character and charm. The central public bar has some unusual copper-work features and a collection of old half pint bottles from a number of British breweries. A larger room, used mainly for dining, affords superb panoramic views of the Brecon Beacons. Beers usually come from local breweries. Accommodation is available.
Q P

Llanidloes

Crown & Anchor Inn ☆
41 Long Bridge Street, SY18 6EF (on A470)
11-11; 12-10.30 Sun
(01686) 412398
Brains Rev James; Worthington's Bitter H
Traditional unspoilt town centre gem with a relaxed and friendly atmosphere. The pub appears in CAMRA's National Inventory of pubs with interiors of historic interest. It has been run by the same landlady, Ruby, for more than 40 years. Throughout that time it has remained unchanged, retaining its public bar, lounge, snug and two further rooms, one with a pool table and games machine. A central hallway separates the rooms.

Red Lion Hotel
Long Bridge Street, SY18 6EE (on A470)
11-midnight (1am Fri & Sat); 11-midnight Sun
(01686) 412270
Beer range varies H
Wood-beamed town centre hotel with a plush lounge featuring red leather sofas. The public bar is divided into two areas – the front with an interesting wood-panelled fireplace, the rear with a pool table and games machines. No food is served on Sunday. Three real ales are usually available.

Llanrhaeadr-ym-Mochnant

Plough Inn
SY10 0JR (on B4580)
3-midnight; 12-midnight Sat & Sun
(01691) 780654
Brains Rev James; guest beer H
Village local converted from a house. The many-roomed interior is wood beamed and tile-floored, with a stone-walled public bar boasting a large open fireplace and a back bar. Two real beers are stocked. Games areas to the rear of the pub offer pool, table football and darts.

Tafarn Llaw
SY10 0JJ (off B4580)
3 (12 Fri & Sat)-11; 12-10.30 Sun
(01691) 780413
Beer range varies H
Multi-roomed village pub with exposed beams and a tiled floor, frequented by friendly locals. The bar has a large inglenook with a real fire. The smaller,

cosy lounge has a second inglenook. There is an additional plush drinking area as well as a large function room along a corridor from the main bar.
⌂❀⇌◑◗⊟⛺♣P

Llanwrtyd Wells

Stonecroft Inn

Dolecoed Road, LD5 4RA
⏲ 5-midnight; 12-1am Fri-Sun
☎ (01591) 610332 🌐 stonecroft.co.uk
Brains Rev James; guest beers Ⓗ
Warm and friendly community pub with three areas for dining, drinking and games. A large riverside garden with aviaries is popular in good weather. Visitors in summer include walkers and mountain bikers – lodge accommodation is available. The pub hosts a major beer festival in November and is actively involved in the town's many and varied events: real ale walks, food festivals and the annual bog snorkelling world championships. Addlestones cider and a range of local ales are usually available.
⌂❀⇌◑◗⛺⇄♣●P

Llanymynech

Cross Keys

North Road, SY22 6EA (on A483)
⏲ 12-3 (not winter Mon & Tue), 4-midnight; 12-midnight Fri & Sat; 12-11 Sun
☎ (01691) 831585 🌐 crosskeyshotel.info
Greene King Abbot; guest beers Ⓗ
Roadside hotel now with a thriving trade in real ale. Full of character with real fires, the bar has a friendly atmosphere and a wide and varied clientele. Two changing guest beers are always available. There is a games room through an archway with a pool table and darts area. The restaurant offers good, reasonably priced food. The function room upstairs also serves real ale. ⌂⇌◑◗♣P

Machynlleth

Skinners Arms

Main Street, SY20 8EB (on A487)
⏲ 12 (11.30 Thu-Sat)-11; 12-11 Sun
☎ (01654) 702354
Burtonwood Bitter; guest beer Ⓗ
Town-centre pub where the plush lounge bar has exposed stone walls and a no-smoking dining area. The lounge is set around an impressive stone inglenook. The public bar is more basic and has a friendly, cosy feel with bare floorboards, subdued lighting and a pool table. A good selection of food is served in the lounge (not Sun eve) and snacks are available in the bar. There is a patio for summer drinking. ❀◑◗⇄♣🍺

Montgomery

Dragon Hotel

Market Square, SY15 6PA
⏲ 11-3, 6-11; 12-3, 7-10.30 Sun
☎ (01686) 668359 🌐 dragonhotel.com
Beer range varies Ⓗ
Small, cosy bar in a 17th-century coaching inn, situated in the centre of town. The beams and masonry are reputedly from the local castle which was destroyed by Cromwell. The bar walls are covered with bric-a-brac. The beer range usually includes an ale from the Wood Brewery. The hotel itself has good facilities with an indoor heated pool and a function room available to hire. Q❀⇌◑◗♣P

New Radnor

Radnor Arms

LD8 2SP
⏲ 12-3, 7 (5 Fri)-11 (midnight Fri); 11-midnight Sat; 12-10.30 Sun
☎ (01544) 350232
Beer range varies Ⓗ
Set in the Welsh Marches and close to the English border, this cosy pub offers accommodation, making it an ideal base for anyone looking for an outdoor activity break. Offa's Dyke is nearby, as are the border towns of Presteigne, Knighton and Kington. Food is served every day, with a popular Sunday carvery (booking advisable) and a takeaway service. The cask-conditioned beers are provided by Wood, Mayfields, Taylor, Six Bells, Wye Valley, Cottage and other small breweries. ⌂Q♨❀⇌◑◗⊟●P

Newtown

Buck Inn

High Street, SY16 2NP (off A483)
⏲ 11-11 (midnight Thu; 1am Fri & Sat); 11-midnight Sun
☎ (01686) 622699
Banks's Bitter; guest beer Ⓗ
Reputedly the oldest inn in Newtown, this town centre local often hosts live music at weekends and can be crowded and noisy. The comfortable beamed pub has a large stone inglenook and is divided into separate drinking areas, attracting a varied clientele. Patios at the front and back are available for outside drinking. ❀◑◗⇄♣

Railway Tavern

Old Kerry Road, SY16 1BH (off A483)
⏲ 12-2.30, 6-midnight; 11-1am Tue, Fri & Sat; 12-10.30 Sun
☎ (01686) 626156
Draught Bass; Worthington's Bitter; guest beer Ⓗ
Locals' bar with exposed beams and a rear stone wall, handy for the station. This unspoilt, compact one-bar hostelry has a good following due to its friendly atmosphere and welcoming landlord and landlady, who have been at the Railway for over 20 years. The pub has a successful darts team and match nights can be crowded. Guest beers come from a wide range of independent breweries. ❀⇄♣

Pentre-bach

Tafarn y Crydd (Shoemakers Arms)

LD3 8UB (follow signs to 'country pub' from Sennybridge) OS908328
⏲ 11.30-3 (not Tue), 5.30-11; 12-3, 6-11 Sun
☎ (01874) 636508
Brains Rev James; guest beers Ⓗ

Former CAMRA Powys Pub of the Year, this community-owned country pub lies close to the Eppynt firing ranges. However, as the signs on the approach road state, 'the road to Pentre-bach is always open'. A warm welcome, good food and fine ales make the journey here well worth the effort. Beers are sourced from local micros and regional brewers. The large garden with superb views and plentiful wildlife is a pleasant place to enjoy a pint in fine weather. Opening hours may vary depending on the time of year (it is often closed winter lunchtimes), so phone ahead to confirm.
⛰Q❀◐◑♿P

Penybont

Severn Arms

LD1 5UA

12-3, 6-11 (midnight Thu-Sat); 12-3, 7-10.30 Sun

☎ (01597) 851224

Brains Rev James; Courage Directors Bitter; Theakston Best Bitter; guest beers H

This 18th-century former coaching inn used to be a stop-off point on the route between Hereford and Aberystwyth. Although the journey is easier now, modern-day travellers will be just as pleased with the hospitality here. The public bar leads to spacious gardens overlooking the River Ithon – residents can fish for free on six miles of the river. Guest beers are sourced from a range of smaller breweries. A good selection of malt whiskies is an added attraction.
⛰Q❀🛏◐◑ 🎯 ▲♣P

Penycae

Ancient Briton

Brecon Road, SA9 1YY

10-1am (2am Fri & Sat)

☎ (01639) 730273

Beer range varies H

Swansea CAMRA Pub of the Year 2006 offers a kaleidoscope of up to six beers from far and wide plus a cider and a lager. The open plan pub is divided by screens into a games area, lounge and restaurant. Quality, home-made food is served including a choice of curries. There is a play area for children and camping facilities – all situated in the stunning Brecon Beacons National Park and world heritage status Fforest Fawr Geopark. The Dan-Yr-Ogof caves are nearby.
⛰❀🛏◐◑♿▲🚌♣🍎P

Pontneddfechan

Old White Horse Inn

12 High Street, SA11 5NP (off A465)

12-3, 6-11 (closed winter Mon); 12-11 Sat; 12-10.30 Sun

☎ (01639) 721219

Brains SA; guest beers H

Situated in waterfall country in Brecon Beacons National Park, with a tourist information centre nearby, this inn, built around 1600, has served as a coaching house, shop and B&B, before reverting to a pub in the early 1960s. It has a cosy public bar, lounge/restaurant and pool room. Good value food is served lunchtimes and evenings, except Sunday evening in winter. Three real ales are stocked in winter and five plus a cider in summer, when the pub holds its annual beer festival. Budget hostel accommodation is available. ⛰🐎❀🛏◐◑ 🎯♿🚌♣🍎P

Rhayader

Crown Inn

North Street, LD6 5BT

11-11 (midnight Fri & Sat); 12-10.30 Sun

☎ (01597) 811099

Brains Dark, Bitter, Rev James, seasonal beers; guest beers H

Interesting 16th-century pub that retains much charm despite major changes made to the interior in the 1970s. The walls of the bar and adjoining lounge are adorned with many photographs of local scenes and inhabitants. Look out for the interesting item referring to Major Stanscombe, a former owner. The Crown is a rare outlet for cask-conditioned mild. Most guest beers are seasonal and commemorative brews from Brains. Q❀🛏◐◑ 🎯⚡

Talybont on Usk

Star Inn

LD3 7YX (on B4558) OS114226

11-3, 6.30-11; 12-3, 7-10.30 Sun

☎ (01874) 676635

Beer range varies H

Large and lively pub beside the Brecon and Monmouth Canal. A vast display of pump clips reflects the enormous number of ales served by this CAMRA award-winning pub over the years. Beers are usually sourced from local breweries and real cider is available. The food here is recommended. Quiz nights and live music evenings are popular. The large garden overlooking the canal is very busy in summer.
⛰❀🛏◐◑ 🎯▲♣🍎

Your shout

We would like to hear from you. If you think a pub not listed in the guide is worthy of consideration, please let us know. Send us the name, full address and phone number (if known). If a pub in the guide has given poor service, we would also like to know. Write to Good Beer Guide, CAMRA, 230 Hatfield Road, St Albans, Herts, AL1 4LW or email **camra@camra.org.uk**

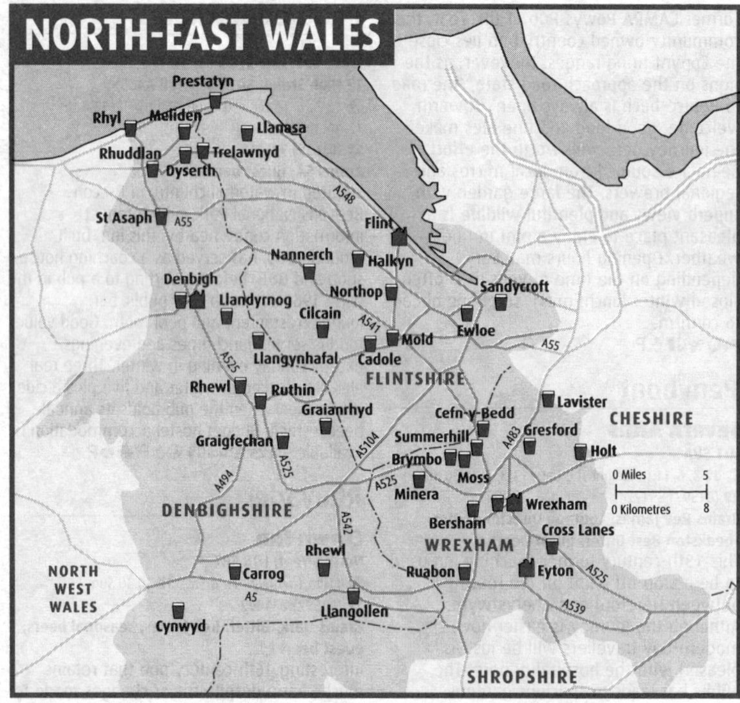

Authority areas covered Denbighshire UA, Flintshire UA, Wrexham UA

DENBIGHSHIRE

Carrog

Grouse Inn

LL21 9AT (jct of B5436/B5437) OS112436

⌚ 12-midnight daily

☎ (01490) 430272 🌐 thegrouseinn.webeden.co.uk

Lees Bitter, seasonal beers Ⓗ

Situated in a riverside location with spectacular views over the River Dee and the Berwyn mountain range. Close by is Carrog station, currently the western terminus of the Llangollen Railway. There is a campsite by the station (phone the pub for details). The single bar serves an open drinking area, leading to a dining room and games room. Meals are available throughout the day. ❀◐◑ ⇌(Llangollen Railway)♣P

Cynwyd

Blue Lion Hotel

Main Street, LL21 0LD (on B4401) OS057411

⌚ 12-3, 6-midnight; 12-midnight Fri-Sun

☎ (01490) 412106 🌐 bluelionhotel.co.uk

Marston's Burton Bitter; Plassey Bitter Ⓗ

Grade II listed building with three drinking areas. The bar serves two of the rooms directly and there is a cosy lounge and dining area. A third room is often used for meetings. The pub is an active centre for those fond of outdoor pursuits. Food is served between noon and 2.30pm and 7pm to 8.30pm but it is worth enquiring even outside these times. Last entry is 11.30pm. ⩩❀◐◑⛺♣

Denbigh

Railway

Ruthin Road, LL16 3EL (At A525/B4501 intersection and close to Denbigh Infirmary)

⌚ 12-11 (midnight Fri, 1am Sat); 12-11 Sun

☎ (01745) 812376

Bryn Bitter; guest beer Ⓗ

The Rhyl to Corwen railway once ran on an embankment – now a car park – behind this multi-roomed 19th-century establishment. Inside is a public bar, games room and two small lounges. Historic pictures, some railway-related, adorn the walls. Recently, the pub has concentrated on selling beers from the local Bryn Brewery. The pub gets busy when sport is shown on TV. Most bus routes serving Denbigh pass nearby, including a service to and from Rhyl station. ⊟⛺⊟♣

Dyserth

New Inn

Waterfall Road, LL18 6ET (On B5119 ¼ mile from A5151) OS055795

⌚ 12-11 daily

☎ (01745) 570482

Banks's Original, Bitter; Marston's Burton Bitter, Pedigree Ⓗ

This popular local has benefited from a large bar and dining extension along with facilities for the disabled. Real fires burn in two areas and old beams give a cosy feel. Behind the pub is a secluded beer garden. The old church and Dyserth waterfall are across the road. From the waterfall, a stream runs under the road and along the side of the inn. ⛰Q🍴❀◐◑♿⛺🚌(35, 36)♣P⅟

Graigfechan

Three Pigeons Inn

LL15 2EH (on B5429 3 miles S OF Ruthin) OS147545
5.30-11; 12-11 Sun
☎ (01824) 703178 threepigeonsruthin.co.uk
Draught Bass; Hancock's HB; guest beer 🄷
Situated on an old drovers' trail, this rural inn with outstanding views of the Clwydian range was rebuilt in 1777. Excellent meals are served in several areas including the no-smoking dining room. There are two beer terraces, both with far-reaching views of the countryside. As well as the regular beers, there are usually two guests in summer.
⛰Q🍴❀◐◑⛺🚌(76)♣P⅟

Graianrhyd

Rose & Crown

Llanarmon Road CH7 4QW (on B5430, off A5104)
4-11; 12-11 Fri & Sat 12-10.30 Sun
☎ (01824) 780727 theroseandcrownpub.co.uk
Flowers IPA; guest beers 🄷
Welcoming 200-year-old traditional pub with a friendly local feel. Popular with walkers as well as locals, the pub is split into two rooms both served from one compact bar – choose between a real fire and a wood burning stove in winter. Two ever-changing guest beers are mainly sourced from local breweries. The cheery landlord takes as much pride in his excellent pub food as he does with his ales. ⛰❀◐◑⊞⛺♣P

Llandyrnog

White Horse (Ceffyl Gwyn)

LL16 4HG (on B5429) OS108652
12-3, 6-11 daily
☎ (01824) 790582
Beer range varies 🄷
Before entering, visitors are recommended to glance up and read about a past licensee. The current hosts run a comfortable establishment offering a warm welcome with good quality food and drink. They have connections with Llandyrnog's nearby Golden Lion Inn, offering two further real ales. The bar has a real fire and its walls display pictures and news cuttings for those with an interest in local history. Lunches are not served on Monday. ⛰❀◐◑🚌(76)P

Llangollen

Corn Mill

Dee Lane, LL20 8PN
12-11, 12-10.30 Sun
☎ (01978) 869555 cornmill-llangollen.co.uk
Flowers Original; guest beers 🄷
Striking conversion of a former mill adjacent to the River Dee. A functioning water wheel is incorporated into the building and the interior comprises a number of distinct areas on several levels featuring heavy beams and pine flooring. In warmer weather you can relax on the extensive outdoor terrace and enjoy the views across the mill race and rapids to the restored railway station opposite. The four guest beers are predominantly from micros and imaginative well-prepared food is available all day.
Q❀◐◑♿⇌(Llangollen Rlwy)●⅟

Sun Inn

49 Regent Street
LL20 8HN (on A5 half mile E of town centre)
12-1am (2am Fri & Sat); 12-1am Sun
☎ (01978) 861043
Salopian Shropshire Gold; Thwaites Original; guest beers 🄷
Grade II listed corner house with six real ales and a selection of continental beers. Coloured glass doors open into a large green-walled room with a Welsh slate floor, three real fireplaces and school bench seating. A stage area hosts live music: folk, jazz and rock. Behind the small wood bar a small snug with large plasma screen leads to a covered courtyard for outdoor drinking. Wednesday to Saturday evenings may be busy when bands are playing. ⛰❀◐◑⊞♿♣

Wynnstay Arms

20 Bridge Street, LL20 8PF
12-11.30 daily
☎ (01978) 860710 wynnstay-arms.co.uk
Greene King IPA, Abbot; Tetley Burton Ale 🄷
Historic, popular, town centre pub and former coaching inn which remains largely unaltered. Opposite the main bar is a games room, served through a hatch. The rear rooms are for quiet drinking, dining and families. Accommodation ranges from en-suite rooms to bunkhouses for up to six people sharing. The steps at the front door originally provided a platform from which to mount a horse or carriage. Step-free access to the pub is available through the courtyard and rear door. ⛰Q🍴❀🛏◐◑♿

Llangynhafal

Golden Lion

LL16 4LN OS130635
6 (4 Thu)-12.30 (closed Mon); 4-2am Fri; 12-2am Sat; 12-11.30 Sun
☎ (01824) 790451 thegoldenlioninn.com
Holt Bitter; guest beer 🄷
At the foot of the Clwydian hills, close to Offa's Dyke path, Llangynhafal is one of the smallest and most peaceful hamlets in this part of north Wales. Popular with walkers, parts of the pub date back to the 18th century. A distinctive clock keeps time behind the brick and tiled bar counter and the restaurant features a timber fireplace. The licensee collects the Joseph Holt beers, served with pride, from the brewery.
⛰Q❀🛏◑⊞⛺🚌(76)♣●P⅟🗑

INDEPENDENT BREWERIES

Bryn Denbigh
Facer's Flint
Jolly Brewer Wrexham
Plassey Eyton

WALES

Meliden

Miners Arms

23 Ffordd Talaragoch, LL19 7TH (on A547 Prestatyn to Rhuddlan road) OS063810

✪ 11-11.30; 12-11 Sun

☎ (01745) 852005

Marston's Burton Bitter, Pedigree, Old Empire; guest beer ⊞

Village pub on the road between Prestatyn and Rhuddlan with a wood burning stove in the public bar and a snug to the right. The popular dining area has been extended and booking is advisable for meals at weekends. There are three beers from the Marston's range on offer as well as up to two guests. By the front door remains what was once the pay office for one of the last working lead mines in the area. ♨Q❀◑ ⊟P⊬

Prestatyn

Royal Victoria

Sandy Lane, LL19 7SG (at A548 Coast Rd traffic lights)

✪ 11.30-11 (11.30 Thu; midnight Fri & Sat); 12-11 Sun

☎ (01745) 854670

Marston's Burton Bitter; Tetley Bitter; guest beer ⊞

Originally part of a hotel and located close to the town centre opposite the railway station, this popular local has a raised seating area in the bar and a rear function room. The guest beer (usually two in summer) changes every few days. A beer festival is held as part of the local Jazz Festival each autumn. For walkers, this is the first or last pub on the Offa's Dyke path. ☋▲⇶♣

Rhewl (near Ruthin)

Drovers Arms

LL15 2HD (on A525 2 miles N of Ruthin) OS109604

✪ 11-midnight (1am Fri & Sat); 11-midnight Sun

☎ (01824) 703163 ⊕ thedroversarmsrhewl.co.uk

Fuller's London Pride; Young's Bitter ⊞

Roadside inn on a drovers' trail just north of Ruthin. Quality meals are served daily and booking is advisable at weekends. A large dining room and conservatory overlook the garden. Adjacent to the bar is a lounge area and a snug with sofas and there is a games area. From the outside are views of surrounding countryside. The Clwydian Way passes the front door. ☋❀◑▲⊟♣P⊬

Rhewl (near Llangollen)

Sun Inn

LL20 7YT (on B5103, follow signs from A542) OS178449

✪ 12-2.30, 6-10 (closed winter Mon); 12-10 Sun

☎ (01978) 861043

Beer range varies ⊞

This 14th-century former drover's cottage is a rural gem in delightful countryside overlooking the Dee Valley. As well as the splendid walking options in the immediate vicinity, the Horseshoe Falls and the attractions of Llangollen are nearby. The central bar serves three separate rooms each with its own character and charm. Children are allowed in two of the rooms and dogs are also welcome. The guest beer changes regularly; home-cooked meals are highly recommended. ♨Q☋❀◑ ⊟▲♣P⊡

Rhuddlan

King's Head

High Street, LL18 2TH

✪ 9.30am-11 (1am Fri & Sat); 9.30am-11 Sun

☎ (01745) 590345

Jennings Dark Mild; Marston's Burton Bitter; guest beer (summer) ⊞

Large corner pub in the centre of the village. The dining area is spacious and comfortable and can also be used as a function room. The walls of the cosy lounge bar are adorned with photos depicting local history and social events. The pub is within easy reach of the castle and ancient parliament building. Rhuddlan is well served by public transport with regular buses linking it to Rhyl, Denbigh and Prestatyn. Q❀◑ ⊟♿▲⊟♣P

Rhyl

Crown Bard

Rhuddlan Road, LL18 2RL (on A525 by retail park)

✪ 11-11 (11-3, 5-11 winter Mon-Fri); 12-11 Sun

☎ (01745) 338465

Greene King IPA; guest beer ⊞

Popular pub on the outskirts of town. The large, comfortable lounge doubles as a dining area; the cosy snug features a real coal fire. A smaller public bar has a pool table and dartboard. The landlord is keen to support local breweries from north Wales and north-west England. During the summer months a cask mild is available. A quiz is held every Sunday evening. ♨❀◐⊟P⊬

Swan

13 Russell Road, LL18 3BS

✪ 11-11 (11.30 Fri & Sat); 11-11 Sun

☎ (01745) 336694

Thwaites Dark Mild, Original, Lancaster Bomber ⊞

Popular town centre pub split into two distinct areas – a lively bar containing a pool table and numerous televisions, and a quieter lounge where meals are served. The lounge is attractively decorated with many interesting and historic photos. The Swan was the first pub to hold a public TV licence in 1951. The exterior of the pub still displays the name of a long defunct brewery, Wilderspool. ◐⊟⇶♣

Ruthin

Castle Hotel

St Peters Square, LL15 1AA

✪ 12-11 daily

☎ (01824) 702479 ⊕ castle-hotel-ruthin.co.uk

Greene King IPA, Old Speckled Hen; guest beer ⊞

Large hotel in the town square with a comfortable public bar at the rear. Ruthin is an historic town in the Vale of Clwyd with many attractions such as the Victorian gaol and medieval castle. The hotel has two restaurants, the Castle Grill serving Welsh meats and Globetrotters with dishes from around the world, plus Georgian tea rooms. Three beers are always available and food is served all day. ⇄◑P

St Asaph

Plough

The Roe, LL17 0LU (on A525 off jct 27 A55) OS033745
12-11 (1am Fri & Sat); 12-10.30 Sun
(01745) 585080
Plassey Bitter; guest beers H
A central bar serves several drinking areas. The ground floor has a horseracing theme, with tables named after racehorses. Plassey Bitter is available regularly and complemented by guests, including beers from other Welsh breweries. The first floor houses the Plough restaurant and, adjacent, a wine bar. Diners can choose from the bar menu or full restaurant fare. There is a no-smoking area and the back bar is no-smoking Monday to Friday.

Trelawnyd

Crown

London Road, LL18 6DN OS093797
12 (4 Mon)-11 (11.30 Thu-Sat); 12-11 Sun
(01745) 571580
John Smith's Bitter; Tetley Dark Mild; Young's Bitter; guest beer H
Following a change of ownership the Crown has been recently refurbished to a high standard. Fortunately it has retained much of its traditional village inn character, making it popular with locals and visitors alike. A centrally-situated bar serves a main drinking area supported by several alcove-like seating areas; dining is in an attractively furnished restaurant at the back.

FLINTSHIRE

Cadole

Colomendy Arms

Village Road, CH7 5LL (off A494, Mold-Ruthin road)
7 (6 Thu; 4 Fri; 12 Sat)-11; 12-10.30 Sun
(01352) 810217
Beer range varies H
Splendid red-brick local, convenient for the nearby Loggerheads Country Park. A regular local CAMRA Pub Of The Year, it has an ever-changing range of guest beers to satisfy the most ardent 'ticker'. The quarry-tiled floor in the thriving public bar is worn by the boots of cavers, walkers and runners who frequent this friendly community pub. You can also bring your dog along to enjoy the convivial atmosphere and the roaring real fire.

Cefn-y-Bedd

Ffrwd

Ffrwd Road, LL12 9TS (1 mile along B5102 from A541)
6.30 (12.30 Sat)-12.30am; 12.30-11 Sun
(01978) 757951
Beer range varies H
With its distinctive blue exterior, the Ffrwd is easily spotted nestling in the wooded valley of the River Cegidog. Built on top of a former pub which was buried when the ford across the river was replaced with a bridge, the Ffrwd has open-plan dining and bar areas served from a central, wood-panelled bar. The landlord-cum-chef, who can be seen busily preparing the excellent home-cooked food, constantly strives to provide something out of the ordinary among the three guest beers. Lunches are available at the weekend.

Cilcain

White Horse

The Square, CH7 5NN OS177652
12-11 daily
(01352) 740142
Banks's Bitter; guest beers H
Situated in the foothills of Moel Famau in the centre of a picturesque village, this inn welcomes walkers and cyclists in the flagstone bar. Note the old bank of three engines which have not been used for serving beer since 1977 and still show the original prices. The lounge has four areas displaying pictures of old Cilcain and houses a grandfather clock. Children over 14 are allowed in the pub. Four log fires in the winter provide a cosy welcome.

Ewloe

Boar's Head

Holywell Road, CH5 3BS
12-3, 5.30-11 (midnight Fri); 12-midnight Sat & Sun
(01244) 531065
Draught Bass; Tetley Mild, Bitter; guest beers H
Built in 1704, this traditional pub has copper-topped tables, black beams and a wealth of brassware and bric-a-brac. A splendid inglenook with a real log fire is the centrepiece of the cosy main bar. Unusually, the no-smoking side room is on a different level from the bar and is reached from the staircase that leads to the upstairs living quarters. A dining area is at the rear of the pub.

Halkyn

Blue Bell Inn

Rhosesmor Road, CH8 8DH (on B5123) OS209123
5-11 (midnight Fri); 12-11 Sat & Sun
(01352) 780309 bluebell.uk.eu.org
Beer range varies H
Situated on Halkyn Mountain, the Blue Bell offers a warm welcome to visitors and locals alike in a simple, relaxed environment. It is the focal point for organised walks around the surrounding countryside (see website for details) and dogs are welcome. The food is home made using local produce and the beer range usually features ales from local micro-breweries to complement the house beer brewed by Facer's. Unusually for the area, real cider and often a perry are also available.

Llanasa

Red Lion

Llanasa Road, CH8 9NE (signposted from A5151 at Trelawnyd) OS105815

WALES

12-11 (midnight Sat); 12-11 Sun
(01745) 854291
Webster's Yorkshire Bitter; guest beer Ⓗ
Traditional inn in a designated conservation area at the centre of this well cared for village. Popular with locals but offering an equally warm welcome to visitors and walkers, an unusual open fire divides the games room from the panelled and flag-stoned public bar. The restaurant becomes busy at weekends and booking is normally necessary.

Mold

Glasfryn

Raikes Lane, CH7 6LR (off A5119, signed to Theatr Clwyd)
11.30-11; 12-10:30 Sun
(01352) 750500 glasfryn-mold.co.uk
Bryn Bitter; Flowers Original; Taylor Landlord; Thwaites Bitter; guest beer Ⓗ
Originally built as a residence for circuit judges attending the courts opposite, the Glasfryn is situated in its own grounds near Theatr Clwyd. It was converted to its present use in 1999, following the successful Brunning and Price business model. The interior is spacious with separate areas and decorated with old books, prints, posters and other memorabilia. Food is served daily. Three guest beers from independent breweries supplement the regular range.
P

Gold Cape

8 Wrexham Road, CH7 1ES (30 yds S of Market Square)
9am-midnight (1am Fri & Sat); 9am-midnight Sun
(01352) 705920
Bryn Bitter; Marston's Burton Bitter; guest beers Ⓗ
Typical Wetherspoon conversion offering the best choice of cask beer in Mold town centre and named after a bronze age ancient find unearthed by local workmen in 1831. An impression of the gold cape stands in the foyer and a replica is on show in Mold Heritage Centre and Museum. The standard Wetherspoon interior has wall plaques telling stories of local interest to help confirm its local identity.

Nannerch

Cross Foxes

Village Road, CH7 5RD OS167695
6-11 (midnight Fri & Sat); 12-10.30 Sun
(01352) 741293
Beer range varies Ⓗ
Traditional local situated in a pretty village with a lounge and restaurant. On display are a 1920s wall-mounted telephone and a Liverpool tram bell in working order. Various copper and brass jugs hang from the ceiling. The bar itself features an old optic dispense and hops strung above. A free house, it offers two ever-changing beers. Curry and pint night is popular on Tuesday. The restaurant opens Friday and Saturday evening and Sunday lunchtime.
P

Northop

Boot Inn

High Street, CH7 6BQ OS243682
11.30-midnight; 12-11.30 Sun
(01352) 840247
John Smith's Bitter; guest beer Ⓗ
In the historic village of Northop, just off the A55, this is a quiet, traditional two-roomed pub with a no-smoking restaurant, a comfortable lounge with plush settees and lots of brasses on the walls. The smaller bar is busy with sports fans playing darts, dominoes or watching matches on television. Lancaster Brewery often supplies the guest beer. The village has a thriving cricket team.
Q P

Sandycroft

Bridge Inn

Chester Road, CH5 2QN (on B5129)
12-11 (11.30 Wed-Sat); 12-11 Sun
(01244) 538806
Caledonian Deuchars IPA; Jennings Cumberland Ale; Shepherd Neame Spitfire Ⓗ
Bright and airy real-ale oasis on the edge of the Deeside beer desert. Good-value home-cooked food is available and children are allowed in the family dining area. The pub is reached by a wooden footbridge from the car park and boasts a large garden. The open-plan lounge is adorned with photographs of old Chester. P

WREXHAM

Bersham

Black Lion

Y Ddol, LL14 4HN (off B5099 near Bersham Heritage Centre)
12-1am (1.30am Fri & Sat); 12-1am Sun
(01978) 365588 blacklionpub.co.uk
Hydes Mild, Bitter, Jekyll's Gold, seasonal beers Ⓗ
This friendly pub is set on a wooded hillside above the picturesque River Clywedog on the eight-mile Clywedog Industrial Trail. It is known by locals as the Hole in the Wall. A wood-panelled bar serves the front room and side lounge and there is also a games room. All rooms now have TV. A children's play area has been set up in the garden. Basic bar snacks are available all day.
P

Brymbo

George & Dragon

Ael-Y-Bryn, LL11 5BA (off High St, off B5101)
12-midnight (1am Fri & Sat); 12-10.30 Sun
(01978) 758515
Lees Bitter Ⓗ
Bright, basic no-frills pub situated up a side road in a dormitory town for Wrexham. Televised sport dominates the cosy bar although lovers of mainstream TV are catered for in the brightly lit lounge where there is also a juke box. Locals in the bar are kept entertained by the resident parrot. Live music is often played at weekends. A rare

local outlet for John Willie's Bitter.
♨❀⊟♣P

Cross Lanes

Kagan's Brasserie

Bangor Road, Marchwiel, LL11 0TF (on A525 1 mile from Marchwiel)
✪ 8am-2am; 11-midnight Sun
☎ (01978) 780555 ⊕ crosslanes.co.uk
Plassey Bitter; guest beer Ⓗ
This upmarket hotel lounge bar in a pleasant rural setting is a rare local outlet for Plassey. Served by a central bar, the drinking area comprises an airy, well lit and comfortably furnished front room along with a more rustic back room featuring slate floors, solid oak tables and a superb log fire. Next to this is a dining area decorated with old prints and photographs. Visitors should note the magnificent 17th-century oak panelling in the front hall.
♨Q⇌◐P

Gresford

Griffin Inn

Church Green, LL12 8RG (on B5373)
✪ 4 (7 Tue)-11 (11.30 Fri); 3-11.30 Sat; 3-11 Sun
☎ (01978) 582231
Beer range varies Ⓗ
A step back 30 years, this is the kind of local pub that is all too rare these days. Three irregular rooms run from the three-sided bar. Up to four real ales, normally from regional or small breweries, have been served by the friendly landlady for over 32 years. Polished brass figurines, a South African tortoise shell and domino clock account for some of the pub's character. Across the road is All Saints' Church whose bells are one of the seven wonders of Wales.
Q❀⊞(1)♣P

Pant-yr-Ochain

Old Wrexham Road, LL12 8TY (off A5156 follow sign to 'The Flash')
✪ 12-11 (10.30 Sun)
☎ (01978) 853525 ⊕ pantyrochain-gresford.co.uk
Caledonian Deuchars IPA; Flowers Original; Plassey Bitter; Taylor Landlord; guest beers Ⓗ
This splendid 16th-century manor house, overlooking a small lake, has been attractively refurbished and is now an elegant establishment offering cask ale and good food. The large open-plan eating area has groups of tables with wooden floors and a wealth of fittings and fixtures. The garden room has been newly rebuilt. The policy of supporting local suppliers is reflected in the quality of food and the presence of Plassey beer. The pub is completely no-smoking. Managed by the independent Brunning & Price group.
♨Q❀◐♿P⊁

Holt

Peal of Bells

12 Church Street, LL13 9JP (next to church)
✪ 12-11 daily
☎ (01829) 270411
Adnams Bitter; Banks's Bitter; Marston's Pedigree; guest beer Ⓗ
Popular, family friendly pub located next to St Chads Church on the English border. The open-plan layout, with three distinct areas, is served from a central bar. Look out for the original Wurlitzer organ, occasionally used for evening entertainment. At the rear of the pub is a no-smoking restaurant area overlooking the sizeable, fully enclosed garden with a good view of the River Dee.
❀◐⊞●P

Lavister

Nag's Head

Old Chester Road, LL12 8SN (on B5445, old Chester-Wrexham road)
✪ 12-3 (not Mon & Tue), 5.30-11.30; 12-1.30am Fri & Sat; 12-12.30am Sun
☎ (01244) 570486
Flowers IPA; guest beers Ⓗ
Large, extended inn with a small, welcoming lounge area and an open fire. A central bar serves the public bar, with pool table, darts and Sky TV. A plaque on the wall proclaims that the first CAMRA members were signed up here although locals from this pub actually conceived the idea in a pub in Ireland. One of the guest beers is often from a local micro such as Weetwood or Spitting Feathers. There is a large playground area at the rear of the pub.
♨❀◐⊟♿♣P⊁

Ruabon

Wynnstay Arms

High Street, LL14 6BL
✪ 12-1am daily
☎ (01978) 822187
Beer range varies Ⓗ
Late 18th-century coaching inn, enlarged and remodelled in 1841 into the grand public house and hotel that still exists to this day. The interior is split into many distinct rooms, each with its own character. The impressive library room is mainly for diners; drinkers can choose between the comfortable front lounge and the back bar with its dartboard and TV. A function room is available to hire for special occasions.
Q❀⇌◐⊟♿⇌♣P⊁

Minera

Tyn-y-Capel

Church Road, LL11 3DA (off B5426)
✪ 12-3, 5-11; 12-11 Sat & Sun
☎ (01978) 757502
Greene King Old Speckled Hen; guest beers Ⓗ
On an historic route once used by drovers and monks, the Tyn-y-Capel dates back over 400 years. The countryside below, part of the Eclusham Mountain, still bears traces of the lead mines that once supported the local community. A place to seek out for its cuisine along with its well-kept ales, the large spaces, high ceilings, dramatic plate glass windows, stripped floors and large open plan dining area all add to the appeal.
Q❀◐⊟♿⊞♣P⊁

Moss

Clayton Arms

Moss Hill, LL11 6ES
✪ 7-11 (not Tue & Wed); 3-11 Sat; 12-10.30 Sun
☎ (01978) 756444
Beer range varies Ⓗ
This newly refurbished pub is situated in Moss Valley, a local beauty spot and part of the Clwyedog Industrial Trail. The front part of the pub is furnished with cosy armchairs and settees, a lovely place to relax and enjoy delicious beer after a walk in Moss Valley. The single guest beer is usually an interesting choice from an independent brewery. ♔Q♉❀◑⊟♿♣P⅟⊓

Summerhill

Crown Inn

Top Road, LL11 45R (off Summerhill Rd, 1 mile from A483/A541 jct)
✪ 12-midnight daily
☎ (01978) 755788
Hydes Mild, Bitter, seasonal beers Ⓗ
Real ale drinkers receive a hearty welcome from the cheery landlord. The pub has a central bar with a lounge to one side, and a public bar with a pool table on the other. A Hyde's metal anvil can be seen in the lounge, and a collection of pump clips behind the bar shows the range of seasonal beers you have missed by not calling before. With stunning views of Alyn and Deeside, treat yourself – just ring the serving bell. Children are welcome until 7 pm. ♔Q♉◑⊟≠(Gwersyllt)♣P

Wrexham

Albion Hotel

1 Pen-y-Bryn, LL13 7HU
✪ 12-4, 7-11; 12-11 Thu-Sun
☎ (01978) 364969
Lees Bitter Ⓗ
Imposing corner Edwardian pub just out of the town centre heading south down Town Hill. A central bar serves the large, comfortable lounge and the basic public bar where pub games are played. Very much at the heart of the community, it has a strong local following and features live music at weekends. The accommodation here is good value. ⇌⊟≠(Central)♣

Horse & Jockey

Hope Street, LL11 1BD
✪ 10-midnight; 12-11 Sun
☎ (01978) 351081
Tetley Bitter; guest beers Ⓗ
Splendid old thatched pub in the heart of the town centre pedestrianised area. A central bar serves the main public bar to the front and lounge, dining and TV areas to the rear. Two guest beers are available, one usually from local brewer Plassey. The pub is always busy due to its central location near the shops during the day and its popularity as one of the few traditional town centre pubs in the evening. ◑⊟≠(Central/General)

Cask Marque

Cask Marque, whose symbol appears alongside many pubs in the Good Beer Guide, is an organisation financed by the brewing industry to improve the quality of cask beer in pubs. When a pub displays a Cask Marque plaque it means inspectors have been satisfied by the cleanliness and temperature of pub cellars and the quality of the beer at the bar. The plaque is removed if quality falls. The plaque is given to licensees and accreditation lapses when a publican leaves a pub.

The licensee of the Cherry Tree in Oxfordshire receives his plaque

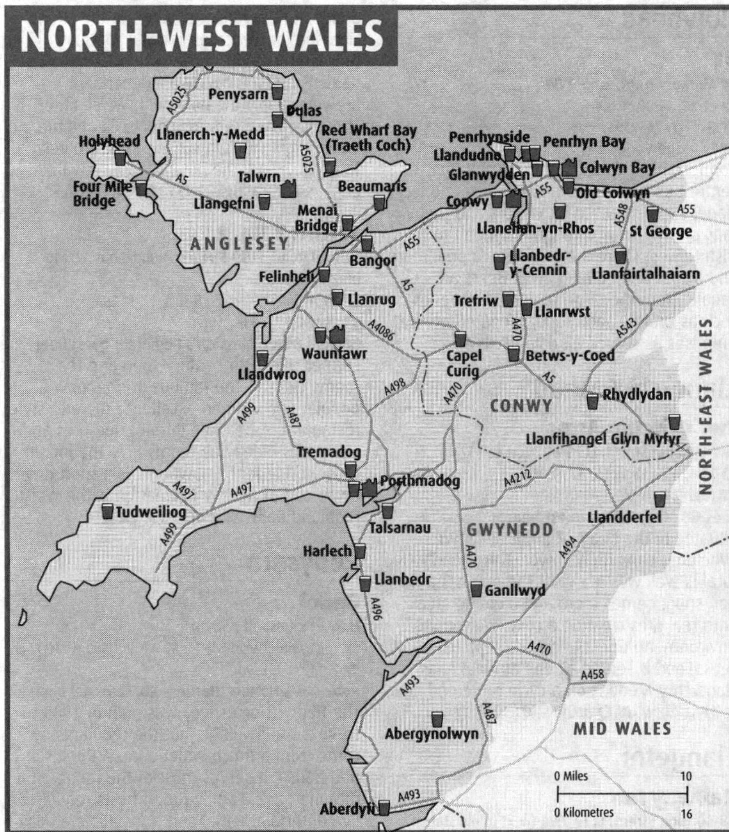

Authority areas covered: Anglesey UA, Conwy UA, Gwynedd UA

ANGLESEY/YNYS MÔN

Beaumaris

Olde Bull's Head Inn
Castle Street, LL58 8AA
11-11; 12-10.30 Sun
☎ (01248) 810329 bullsheadinn.co.uk
Draught Bass; Hancock's HB; guest beers Ⓗ
Grade II listed building that was the original posting house of the borough. In 1645 General Mytton, a parliamentarian, commandeered the inn while his forces lay siege to the castle, which is a mere stone's throw away. The Royalists surrendered on 25th June 1646. Dr Samuel Johnson and Charles Dickens were famous guests. The beamed bar has a large open fire and many antiques. Q P

Dulas

Pilot Boat Inn
LL70 9EX (on A5025)
11.30-11 daily
☎ (01248) 410205
Robinson's Unicorn Ⓗ
Friendly, rural, family pub with a play area and converted double decker bus to keep children amused. Originally a cottage-type building, now much extended, the lounge features an unusual bar created from half a boat. The pub is much used by walkers; the coastal path passes through the car park. It is worth visiting Mynydd Bodafon for its spectacular views and Traeth Lligwy for the sands. Meals are served all day.
Q P

Four Mile Bridge

Anchorage Hotel
LL65 3EZ (on B4545, just past bridge to Holy Island)
11-11 (midnight Thu-Sat); 12-11 Sun
☎ (01407) 740168
Taylor Landlord; Theakston Cool Cask; guest beer Ⓗ
This family-run hotel is situated on Holy Island close to Trearddur Bay. There is a large, comfortable lounge bar and a dining area serving a wide selection of meals all day. The hotel is close to some fine, sandy beaches and coastal walks. Its proximity to the A55 makes it a useful stopping off point for Holyhead Port. Q (4) P

INDEPENDENT BREWERIES

Conwy Conwy
Great Orme Colwyn Bay
Purple Moose Porthmadog
Snowdonia Waunfawr

Holyhead

79

79 Market Street, LL65 1VW
⏲ 11-11; 12-10.30 Sun
☎ (01407) 763939
Beer range varies [H]
Comfortable, attractively-furnished town-centre pub enjoying a good year-round local trade, supplemented by visitors and rugby fans on their way through Holyhead to the Irish ferries. There are two bars, a pool room and a split-level dining area. Beers are usually from the large regional breweries such as Brains. Good food, prepared on the premises, is served all day. ◑⇌♣

Llanerch-Y-Medd

Twr Cyhelun Arms

Twr Cyhelun Street, LL71 8DB (on B5112)
⏲ 7-11; 4-midnight Fri; 12-12.30am Sat; 12-11.30 Sun
☎ (01248) 470340
Lees GB Mild, Bitter; guest beer [H]
Situated in the heart of the island, Twr Cyhelun means Holly Tower. This friendly local is well worth a visit. The pub has a main bar, snug, games room and a dining area with real fires creating a cosy, welcoming environment. Guest beers are supplied by JW Lees. Food is served all day at weekends. Llanerch-y-Medd is on a cycle route and near to Llyn Alaw. ♨Q❀◑⊟⊞(32)P

Llangefni

Railway Inn

48-50 High Street, LL77 7NA (next to old station)
⏲ 7 (12 Sat)-11; 12-10.30 Sun
☎ (01248) 722166
Lees Bitter [H]
Classic, small-town pub next to the old railway station displaying plenty of railway memorabilia and old photographs of Llangefni. It is not far from the town centre and Oriel Môn (museum) where you can find out about the history of Anglesey and see Tunnicliffe's bird books and pictures. The main bar is hewn out of stone wall. The pub can get smoky. ♣

Menai Bridge

Auckland Arms

Water Street, LL59 5DD (50 yds from main square)
⏲ 3 (5 winter)-midnight; 3-2am Fri & Sat; 3-midnight Sun
☎ (01248) 712545 🌐 aucklandarms.co.uk
Greene King IPA; guest beers [H]
Around 120 years old, the hotel is in a superb location close to the pier and the Strait. The busy bar, popular with students, has two pool tables and a range of pub games. The conversion to cask bitters is quite recent. Check opening hours out of term time. ❀⛟◑▲♣P

Victoria Hotel

Telford Road, LL59 5DR
⏲ 11-11; 12-10.30 Sun
☎ (01248) 712309
Draught Bass; guest beers [H]
Situated 300 yards from the Menai suspension bridge, it has wonderful views of the Strait. Licensed for weddings, it has a spacious function room with wide-screen TV, extensive gardens and a patio. Two independent brewers supply the hotel with Welsh bitter. There is easy access to Snowdonia and the Welsh Highland Railway and ferries to Ireland from Holyhead. The hotel is popular with anglers and sailors. ♨Q❀⛟◑⊟♿▲P

Tafarn Y Bont

Telford Road, LL59 5DT (on roundabout next to bridge)
⏲ 11-midnight (1am Fri & Sat); 11-11 Sun
☎ (01248) 716888
Banks's Bitter; Marston's Pedigree; guest beers [H]
Former mid 19th-century shop and tea rooms close to the famous bridge, now a popular pub with an excellent brasserie-style restaurant. A beamed interior, log fires and numerous hideaway rooms give the inn an olde-worlde feel. Snowdonia is a short drive away and at nearby Caernarfon is the Welsh Highland Railway. ♨Q♉❀◑▲⚟

Penysarn

Bedol

LL69 9YR (just off A5025)
⏲ 12 (2 winter Mon-Fri)-11; 12-11 (2-10.30 winter) Sun
☎ (01407) 832590
Robinson's Hatters, Hartleys XB, seasonal beers [H]
The Bedol (Horseshoe) was built in 1985 to serve a small village, but the regulars now come from a much wider area. A Robinson's tied house, it serves most of the range on a rotating basis. Family run, it hosts regular live entertainment. Food is available all day except lunchtime in winter. Some of Anglesey's beautiful beaches are nearby. Q❀◑⊟▲⊞(62)♣P

Red Wharf Bay (Traeth Coch)

Ship Inn

LL75 8RJ (1½ miles off A5025 near Benllech)
⏲ 11-11 (later summer); 11-midnight (10.30 winter) Sun
☎ (01248) 852568 🌐 shipinnredwharfbay.co.uk
Adnams Bitter; Brains SA; guest beers [H]
Previously known as the Quay, this mid 17th-century pub has superb views over the bay. In the 18th century Red Wharf Bay was a busy port specialising in coal and fertiliser. Renowned for its excellent food including Sunday lunches, the upstairs restaurant has been revamped. Very busy in summer, it is popular with holidaymakers and the sailing fraternity. The garden has panoramic views. ♨Q♉❀◑⊟♿▲P⚟

CONWY

Betws-y-Coed

Pont-y-Pair

Holyhead Road, LL24 0BN (opp. Pont-y-Pair bridge over River Llugwy) OS791567
⏲ 11-11 (1am Thu-Sat); 12-midnight Sun
☎ (01690) 710407
Black Sheep Best Bitter; Greene King Abbot; Tetley Bitter; guest beer [H]
Traditional 10-roomed family-run hotel

situated near the centre of Betws-y-Coed opposite the famous Ponty-y-Pair bridge. A warm welcome is offered to locals, visitors and guests alike. Freshly-cooked meals are served in the bar and lounge area or the no-smoking dining room. The games room with pool table looks out onto the patio. Tiny car park. ❀⇌◑▲≠♣P

Capel Curig

Cobden's Hotel

Holyhead Road, LL24 0EE OS731576

☼ 11-11; 12-10.30 Sun

☎ (01690) 720243 ⊕ cobdens.co.uk

Conwy Castle Bitter, seasonal beers Ⓗ

Popular with walkers and climbers, this 200-year-old hotel has a large lounge and comfortable restaurant serving excellent meals made with local produce. The 16-bedroom hotel has built up a good reputation for its warm hospitality and relaxed informality. At the rear is a fascinating bar area built into the side of the mountain. The house beer, Cobden's Ale, is brewed especially for the pub by Conwy Brewery. ᗑQ❀⇌◑⊟▲≠♣P

Colwyn Bay

Pen-y-Bryn

Pen-y-Bryn Road, Upper Colwyn Bay, LL29 6DD (top of King's Rd) OS842783

☼ 11.30-11; 12-10.30 Sun

☎ (01492) 533360 ⊕ penybryn-colwynbay.co.uk

Thwaites Original; guest beers Ⓗ

Spacious, modern, open plan pub popular with all ages. Attractively furnished, it has oak floors and open fires in winter. Imaginative bar food changes daily; check the menu on the website. Six handpumps include five guest beers, mainly from independent breweries. Jazz is played on some Sunday evenings. The stunning garden and terrace provide panoramic views over the bay and Great Orme. Local CAMRA Pub of the Year 2006. ᗑQ❀◑♿⊟♣P⊁▯

Wings Social Club

Station Square, LL29 8LF OS850791

☼ 12-3 (11-4 Fri), 7-11; 11-11 Sat; 12-4, 7-10.30 Sun

☎ (01492) 530682

Lees GB Mild, Bitter Ⓗ

Popular social club across the road from the railway station and two minutes' walk from the main coast road bus services. Visitors and their families are welcome, particularly CAMRA members. Inside is a bar area and large L-shaped lounge with a small dance floor. Billiards, pool, snooker and darts are all played and there is a TV room. To be signed in as a guest take your CAMRA membership card or a copy of this Guide. ≠⊟♣

Conwy

Royal British Legion

Church Street, CC32 8AF (opp. Visitors Centre)

☼ 11-3.30, 7-11; 12-3, 7-11 Sun

☎ (01492) 593335

Tetley Dark Mild, Bitter; guest beer Ⓗ

Former CAMRA Abercolwyn branch Club of the Year situated within the medieval walls of the town close to the railway station. The central bar has a large concert room to the right and a function room upstairs. To the left is a lounge and games area with a TV room. Visitors are welcome, particularly CAMRA members. ≠⊟♣P

Glanwydden

Queen's Head

LL31 9JP (follow Penrhyn Bay sign from A470 1 mile, second right) OS817804

☼ 11-3, 6-11 (10.30 Mon); 12-10.30 Sun

☎ (01492) 546570 ⊕ queensheadglanwydden.co.uk

Adnams Bitter; guest beers Ⓗ

Formerly a wheelwright's cottage, in the centre of a quiet village on the outskirts of Llandudno, the pub is popular with locals and holidaymakers. A central bar serves a comfortable lounge which doubles as a dining area on one side and welcoming locals' bar on the other. The same chef and landlord have been here for over 20 years. The restaurant serves quality food using local Welsh produce in an olde-worlde pub atmosphere. ᗑQ❀⇌◑⊟▲⊟P

Llanbedr-y-Cennin

Olde Bull Inn

LL32 8JB (¾ mile from B5106 above Tal-y-Bont) OS761695

☼ 12-2.30 (not Mon), 6-11; 12-midnight Fri & Sat; 12-11 Sun

☎ (01492) 660508

Lees Bitter, seasonal beers Ⓗ

Small, 500-year-old drovers' inn on a steep incline above Tal-y-Bont (take lane off B5106 by side of Y Bedol) affording splendid views over the Conwy Valley. Push hard on the original entrance door to reveal an interior with a low-beamed ceiling and small copper-topped bar, where locals, walkers and birdwatchers gather. There is a no-smoking dining room at the rear. No food is served on Monday. ᗑ❀◑▲⊟♣P

Llandudno

King's Head

Old Road, LL30 2NB (next to Great Orme tramway) OS778827

☼ 12-midnight (11 Sun)

☎ (01492) 877993

Felinfoel Best Bitter; Greene King Abbot; guest beer Ⓗ

Over 300 years old, the King's Head is the oldest pub in Llandudno. It makes an ideal stop after walking the Great Orme or riding on Britain's only cable-hauled tramway. The traditional split level bar is dominated by a large open hearth. The suntrap patio with its award-winning flower display is a delightful place to watch the trams pass by. A popular quiz night is held on Wednesday evening. ᗑ❀◑▲⊖(Gt Orme Tramway)⊟P

Queen Victoria

4 Church Walks, LL30 2HD

☼ 11-11; 12-10.30 Sun

☎ (01492) 860952

Banks's Bitter; Marston's Pedigree, Old Empire; guest beers Ⓗ
Refurbished pub on the lower slopes of the Great Orme close to the pier. An attractive green-tiled bay frontage, with patio seating, leads to a large central bar with open-plan seating and dining areas. Many portraits of Queen Victoria decorate the walls. The pub attracts mostly a mature clientele. Upstairs is a no-smoking restaurant called Alberts.
❀◐♿⊖(Gt Orme Tramway)▣♣

Llanelian-yn-Rhos

White Lion Inn

LL29 8YA (off B583) OS863764
✪ 11.30-3, 6-11; 12-11 Sat; 11-midnight Sun
☎ (01492) 515807 ⊕ whitelioninn.co.uk
Marston's Burton Bitter, Pedigree; guest beer Ⓗ
Traditional 16th-century inn next to St Elian's Church in the hills above Old Colwyn. This attractive, family-run pub has a slate-floored bar area with antique settles and large, comfortable chairs by the real log fire. White lion pottery lamps feature in the windows. The spacious, no-smoking restaurant area has a collection of jugs hanging from the ceiling beams. ⌂Q♉❀◐⊟▲♣P

Llanfairtalhaiarn

Swan Inn

Swan Square, LL22 8RY
✪ 12-3 (not Wed), 6-11; 12-11 Sat; 12-10.30 Sun
☎ (01745) 720233
Banks's Original; Marston's Burton Bitter Ⓗ
In a peaceful village, this is an outstanding example of an unspoilt, welcoming, traditional inn that is said to date from the 16th century. At the front is a no-smoking dining room/bar, while the lounge bar has an open fire. The family room has a pool table, dartboard and juke box in the conservatory area and children are welcome. Watercolour paintings of village scenes adorn the dining room walls and are for sale.
⌂♉❀◐▣(48)♣⚡

Llanfihangel Glyn Myfyr

Crown Inn

LL21 9UL (on B5105 road, 3 miles from Cerrig-y-Drudion) OS992493
✪ 7-11 (closed Mon); 12 (4 winter)-11 Sat & Sun
☎ (01490) 420209
Beer range varies Ⓗ
Delightful old inn, a rural gem beside the Afon Alwen. The unspoilt interior of the front bar with its slate floor area and open fire is warm and welcoming. Across the corridor is the pool room with darts and TV. Monthly folk evenings are staged. Children are welcome in the pub and terraced gardens beside the river. Beers come from small independent breweries at this regular CAMRA award winner. ⌂Q❀▲♣P

Llanrwst

New Inn

Denbigh Street, LL26 0LL
✪ 11-1am (2am Fri & Sat); 12-2am Sun
☎ 01492 640467
Banks's Original; Marston's Burton Bitter; guest beers Ⓗ
Popular, traditional terraced town pub. One bar serves a comfortably furnished narrow lounge and corner snug with an open fire and TV. The rear games area has a pool table and juke box; in the evenings the volume can be unbelievably loud. Outside is a small partly-covered courtyard with a few picnic tables. Last entry is at 11.30pm.
⌂❀▲⇌▣♣

Pen-y-Bont

Bridge Street, LL26 0ET
✪ 11-11; 12-10.30 Sun
☎ (01492) 640202
Beer range varies Ⓗ
Genuine 14th-century family run free house overlooking the 17th-century stone bridge that crosses the River Conwy. Full of character, it has low beams and stone floors. A central bar between the congenial public bar and cosy lounge serves two frequently changing real ales from independent breweries. Rooms at the rear include a dining and family area as well a traditional pub games room. ⌂Q♉◐⊟▲⇌▣♣P

Old Colwyn

Plough

282 Abergele Road, LL29 9LN
✪ 12-11 (midnight Thu-Sat); 12-10.30 Sun
☎ (01492) 515387 ⊕ theplough.info
Courage Directors; guest beers Ⓗ/Ⓖ
Traditional town pub with a central bar in the comfortable lounge, a dining area and games and TV rooms. Up to six guest ales are offered including a mild and a cider. Two annual beer festivals are held over late May and August bank holidays featuring Welsh and Celtic ales respectively. The Colwyn Male Choir quenches its thirst here and the walls display a pictorial account of the choir's history. Sunday lunch is a speciality. Q❀◐⊟♿▣♣●

Red Lion

385 Abergele Road, LL29 9PL
✪ 5-11; 4-midnight Fri; 12-midnight Sat; 12-11 Sun
☎ (01492) 515042
Marston's Burton Bitter; guest beers Ⓗ
Ever-popular local serving up to seven beers from independent and local brewers including a regular guest mild. A genuine free house, it boasts many CAMRA awards for its real ale. The cosy L-shaped room is warmed by a real coal fire and features antique brewery mirrors and more breweriana. The traditional public bar has a pool table, darts and TV.
⌂Q❀⊟▣(12)♣

Sun Inn

383 Abergele Road, LL29 9PL
✪ 12-11 (midnight Fri & Sat); 12-11.30 Sun
☎ (01492) 517007
Jennings Dark Mild; Marston's Burton Bitter, Pedigree; guest beer Ⓗ
Dating from 1844, this is a typical beer drinker's local. The central bar serves a cosy lounge area with a welcoming real coal fire and paintings by a local artist on the walls.

CAMRA literature is displayed prominently on top of the piano. There is also a side bar with TV and juke box as well as a large games/meeting room with a dartboard and pool table. 🔥Q❀⊟🚌(12)♣

Penrhyn Bay

Penrhyn Old Hall

LL30 3EE OS816815
⏲ 12-3, 6-11; 12-3, 7-10.30 Sun
☎ (01492) 549888
Draught Bass; guest beer Ⓗ
The Hall is a 16th-century building with a wood-panelled Tudor bar serving a lounge area and restaurant at the rear. It has been owned by the same family since 1963. Note the stone dated 1590 above the large fireplace which conceals a priest hole. Good value meals are served daily in the restaurant including a traditional three-course Sunday lunch. The Hall has a baronial hall with a full-size skittle alley.
❀◐◑⛺🚌(12, 15)♣P

Penrhynside

Penrhyn Arms

Pendre Road, LL30 3BY (off B5115) OS814816
⏲ 5.30 (5 Thu)-midnight; 12-1am Fri & Sat; 12-11 Sun
☎ (01492) 541569 🌐 penrhynarms.com
Banks's Bitter; Marston's Pedigree; guest beers Ⓗ
Local CAMRA Pub of the Year 2005. The spacious L-shaped bar has a pool table, dartboard and wide-screen TV. The excellent website is updated regularly with a current list of beers and tasting notes. Framed pictures of notable drinkers such as George Best adorn the walls and an old Marston's mirror is above the fireplace. Real Welsh cider is served as well as up to three guest beers, including a mild and a winter ale on gravity at Christmas. 🔥❀⛺🚌♣🍎▯

Rhydlydan

Y Giler Arms Hotel

LL24 0LL OS892508
⏲ 11-2.30, 6-11 (12-2.30, 6.30-11 winter); 12-11 Sat; 12-10.30 (12-2.30, 6.30-10.30 winter) Sun
☎ (01690) 770612
Batham Mild, Best Bitter Ⓗ
Friendly country hotel just off the A5 in the Hiraethog – the hidden heart of north Wales. Set in six acres of grounds including a coarse fishing lake, small campsite and pleasant gardens beside the River Merddwr, it has a comfortable lounge with a large open stove and public bar with fireplace. There is a small pool room and a restaurant overlooking the lake. Popular with locals as well as visitors, children are welcome.
🔥Q❀🛏◐◑⊟⛺🚌(19)♣P

St George

Kinmel Arms

LL22 9BP (exit after Bodelwyddan, travelling W on A55) OS974758
⏲ 12-3, 6.30-11; closed Mon; 12-5 Sun
☎ (01745) 832207 🌐 thekinmelarms.co.uk
Tetley Bitter; guest beers Ⓗ
Former coaching inn dating from the 17th century set on the hillside overlooking the sea. An L-shaped bar serves a large dining and drinking area with a real log fire in the corner. The spacious conservatory at the rear is mainly for diners. Art by the owner Tim Watson adorns the walls. Two guest ales are from independent breweries and there is a selection of Belgian beers, bottled and draught. The pub has a reputation for good food. 🔥Q❀🛏◐◑♿P⊬

Trefriw

Old Ship/Yr Hen Llong

LL27 0JH (on B5106) OS781632
⏲ 12-3, 6-11; 12-11 Sat; 12-10.30 Sun
☎ (01492) 640013 🌐 the-old-ship.co.uk
Banks's Bitter; Marston's Pedigree; guest beers Ⓗ
Formerly a 16th-century customs house, now a busy village local. The small bar serves a cosy L-shaped lounge with an open fire and pictures of historical and nautical interest. The no-smoking dining room has an inglenook. This genuine free house serves a good range of guest beers and tasty home-cooked food.
🔥❀🛏◐◑🚌(19)P

GWYNEDD

Aberdyfi

Penhelig Arms Hotel

Terrace Road, LL35 0LT (on A493)
⏲ 11-11; 12-11 Sun
☎ (01654) 767215 🌐 penheligarms.com
Hancock's HB; guest beers Ⓗ
Small, friendly, seaside town hotel beside Penhelig harbour, affording superb views across the Dyfi estuary. The Fisherman's bar is located in a self-contained part of the building with a designated no-smoking area. Good food, including fish dishes and local meat, is served in the bar and restaurant.
🔥Q❀🛏◐◑♿⇌P⊬

Abergynolwyn

Railway Inn

LL36 9YN (on B4405)
⏲ 12-midnight (11 Sun)
☎ (01654) 782279
Tetley Bitter; guest beers Ⓗ
Friendly local in the centre of the village not far from Talyllyn Railway. There was once a connection for goods traffic from outside the door – you can still see the remains of the railway incline up the hillside opposite. An excellent range of food is served daily and there is a no-smoking dining area.
🔥Q❀◐◑⊟♿⇌(Talyllyn Railway)

Bangor

Belle Vue

Holyhead Road, LL57 2EU (in Upper Bangor Square)
⏲ 11-midnight (1am Fri & Sat); 12.30-11.30 Sun
☎ (01248) 364439
Flowers IPA; Marston's Pedigree; guest beer Ⓗ
Traditional town pub situated near the

university in upper Bangor. The bar boasts an old Welsh range and there is a wood-panelled lounge and piano. Regular quiz nights and outdoor summer music events are held. Generous helpings of home-made food are served at lunchtime when a no-smoking area is available. Check on pub opening hours outside term time.
❀◑⊟≹♣

Black Bull/Tarw Du

107 High Street, LL57 1NS
9am-midnight (1am Fri & Sat); 10am-midnight Sun
☎ (01248) 387900
Greene King Abbot; Marston's Burton Bitter, Pedigree; guest beers Ⓗ
Wetherspoon's pub in a converted church and presbytery at the top of the High Street. It offers spacious drinking areas including a large no-smoking section and a patio overlooking upper Bangor and the university. It is busy during term time. A lift is available for disabled access.
❀◑◗♿≹●⊬

Harp

80-82 High Street, LL57 1NS
11-1am; 11-11 Sun
☎ (01248) 361817
Brains Rev James; Greene King Abbot; Taylor Golden Best; Tetley Bitter Ⓗ
Recently refurbished, the Harp is one of the oldest pubs in Bangor. It has a large open-plan bar area with steps leading to a games room and a small snug to the side of the bar. Busy during term time and popular with students, there tends to be loud music playing in the evening. A pub quiz and live bands are hosted during the week.
♨♉❀◑◗≹♣⊬

Tap & Spile

Garth Road, LL57 2SW (off old A5, follow pier signs)
12-11.30 (midnight Tue, Fri & Sat); 12-11.30 Sun
☎ (01248) 370835
Draught Bass; guest beers Ⓗ
Popular split-level pub overlooking the renovated Victorian pier, offering superb views of the Menai Straits. The pub has a back-to-basics feel with old wooden tables and chairs and several church pews, but be prepared for the large-screen TV and fruit machines. The clientele is a mix of locals and university students. It was voted local CAMRA Pub of the Year 2004.
◑◗♣●

Union Tavern

Garth Road, LL57 2SF
11-11; 12-11 Sun
☎ (01248) 362462
Burtonwood Bitter; Marston's Burton Bitter; guest beer Ⓗ
Large multi-roomed pub in lower Bangor near Dickie's Boatyard. Each room is packed with local historic and racehorse pictures, brasses, wall plates and more. Part of the pub is now a well-appointed restaurant. The garden overlooks sailing boats and the sea. Bangor Pier is five minutes' walk away. A rare outlet for Burtonwood Bitter.
♨Q❀⛟◑◗⊟⊡(5, 5X, 9)P⊬

Felinheli

Gardd Fôn

Beach Road, LL56 4RQ (off main road by Menai Straits)
11-midnight daily
☎ (01248) 670359
Banks's Riding Bitter; guest beer Ⓗ
Nautically-themed, 18th-century, friendly pub that gets busy in summer and at weekends when locals are joined by numerous visitors. The bistro offers tasty food (booking is advisable at weekends). Splendid views of Anglesey and the Menai Straits can be enjoyed from the drinking area opposite the pub. The nearby marina is well worth a visit.
Q❀◑◗⊟♣

Ganllwyd

Tyn-Y-Groes Hotel

LL40 2HN (on A470 S of village)
11-11 (10.30 Sun)
☎ (01341) 440275 🌐 tynygroes.com
Flowers IPA; Purple Moose Madog's Ale; guest beers Ⓗ
Beautifully situated in the vale of Ganllwyd, this 16th-century coaching inn overlooks the Mawddach river. The building retains many original features and it is reputed that Gladstone stayed here. Mountain biking, fishing and hill walking are all popular in this unspoiled region. The beer range is limited in winter.
♨❀⛟◑◗⊟⊡P

Harlech

Lion Hotel

LL46 2SG
12 (11 Sat)-11; 12-10.30 Sun
☎ (01766) 780731
Boddingtons Bitter; Flowers Original; Taylor Landlord Ⓗ
Traditional small hotel and pub in the centre of the village just two minutes' walk from the legendary castle with its outstanding views. The lounge bar has an open fire with comfortable bench seating. A rear room has an electric stove in a large stone fireplace and the dartboard. The pub offers a warm and friendly welcome, serving good value food in the cosy bars.
♨Q❀⛟◑◗⊟♿≹⊡♣

Llanbedr

Ty Mawr Hotel

LL45 2NH (take Cwm Bychan turn in village centre)
11-11 daily
☎ (01341) 241440 🌐 tymawrhotel.org.uk
Worthington's Bitter; guest beers Ⓗ
Small country hotel set in its own grounds. The modern lounge bar has a slate flagged floor and cosy wood-burning stove. Unusual flying memorabilia reflect connections with the local airfield. French windows lead on to a verandah and landscaped terrace with outdoor seating. The pub is popular with locals, walkers and real ale enthusiasts. Dogs and children are welcome. Meals are served all day.
♨❀⛟◑◗♿⛺≹P

Llandderfel

Bryntirion Inn
LL23 7RA (on B4401 4 miles E of Bala)
☉ 11-11; 12-10.30 Sun
☎ (01678) 530205
Jennings Cumberland Ale; guest beer Ⓗ
Old coaching inn in a rural setting with views to the River Dee. Off the pleasant public bar is a family room and there is a no-smoking lounge where meals are served in a quiet environment. Bar snacks are also available. There is outdoor seating in the front car park; at the rear is a courtyard and a larger car park. Three bedrooms offer good value accommodation.
♨Q♉❀⛟◖◗⊟♣P⚟

Llandwrog

Harp Inn/Ty'n Llan
LL54 5SY
☉ 12-11 (12-2, 6-11 closed Mon winter); 12-10.30 (12-3 winter) Sun
☎ (01286) 831071 🌐 welcome.to/theharp
Beer range varies Ⓗ
Hidden on a back road to Dinas Dinlle and Caernarfon Airport, this beautiful old stone inn boasts many cosy rooms and a resident parrot called Dylan. The ever-changing beers come from small breweries, with one pump in use in winter and two in summer. Legend says that there was a tunnel from the cellar to the church, and in the churchyard look out for the pirate's grave.
♨♉❀⛟◖◗♿🚌(91)♣P⚟

Llanrug

Glyntwrog Inn
Caernarfon Road, LL55 4AN (on A4086)
☉ 11 (12 Sun)-midnight
☎ (01286) 671191
Greene King IPA; Young's Special Ⓗ
This spacious local is situated just outside the village. It offers a games room, comfortable no-smoking area and a children's playground. Open all year round, it is handy for Llanberis, Padarn Lake and Snowdonia National Park.
❀◖◗⛺🚌♣P⚟

Porthmadog

Spooner's Bar
Harbour Station, LL49 9NF
☉ 11-11; 11-10.30 Sun
☎ (01766) 516032 🌐 festrail.co.uk
Beer range varies Ⓗ
Local CAMRA Pub of the Year 2006, Spooner's offers an ever-changing range of ales from small independent breweries, including the new local brewery Purple Moose. Situated in the terminus of the world famous Ffestiniog Railway, steam trains are outside the door for most of the year. Food is served at lunchtime daily and most evenings – phone to check first in winter. Beer festivals are held at bank holidays and to coincide with special events on the railway.
Q♉❀◖◗♿⇌P⚟

Talsarnau

Ship Aground
LL47 6UB (on A496)
☉ 6-11; 12-midnight Sat; 12-11 Sun
☎ (01766) 770777
Purple Moose Glaslyn Ale; guest beer Ⓗ
Roadside pub in the centre of the village at the heart of the community. One central bar serves several drinking areas. The refurbished and extended restaurant serves excellent, good value food. With a pool table and large-screen TV the pub can become quite noisy. ♨❀◖◗⛺⇌♣P

Tremadog

Golden Fleece
Market Square, LL49 9RB (on A487)
☉ 11.30-3, 6-11; 12.30-3, 6-10.30 Sun
☎ (01766) 512421
Draught Bass; Purple Moose Glaslyn Ale; guest beer Ⓗ
Situated in the old market square, this former coaching inn is now a friendly local. Rock climbing and narrow gauge railways are nearby. The lounge bar has a no-smoking area at the rear and there is a snug which may occasionally be reserved for regulars. Outside, a covered area has decking and bench seats. Bar meals are good value and there is a bistro upstairs (booking advised). Guest beers come from small breweries. ♨Q♉❀⛟◖◗♿⛺🚌⚟

Tudweiliog

Lion Hotel
LL53 8ND (on B4417)
☉ 11-11 (12-2, 6-11 winter); 11.30-11 Sat; 11-10.30 (12-3 winter) Sun
☎ (01758) 770244
Beer range varies Ⓗ
Village pub on the glorious north coast of the Llyn Peninsula. The cliffs and beaches are a mile away over the fields, a little further by road. The origins of this free house go back over 300 years. Up to four beers are available including ales from Wye Valley and Purple Moose. Q♉❀⛟◖◗⊟♿🚌P

Waunfawr

Snowdonia Park
Beddgelert Road, L55 4AQ (on A4085 Caernarfon-Beddgelert road S of village) OS527588
☉ 11-11; 11-10.30 Sun
☎ (01286) 650409 🌐 Snowdonia-park.co.uk
Banks's Mansfield Dark Mild; Marston's Burton Bitter, Pedigree; Snowdonia Welsh Highland Bitter; guest beer Ⓗ
Home of the Snowdonia Brewery, you will usually find one of its brews here. Meals are served all day. There are children's play areas inside (separate from the bars) and outside. The large campsite gives a discount to CAMRA members. The pub adjoins the station on the Welsh Highland Railway; stop off here before going on to Rhyd Ddu on one of the most scenic sections of narrow gauge railway in Britain. Q♉❀◖◗⊟♿⛺⇌(Welsh Highland Railway)♣P⚟

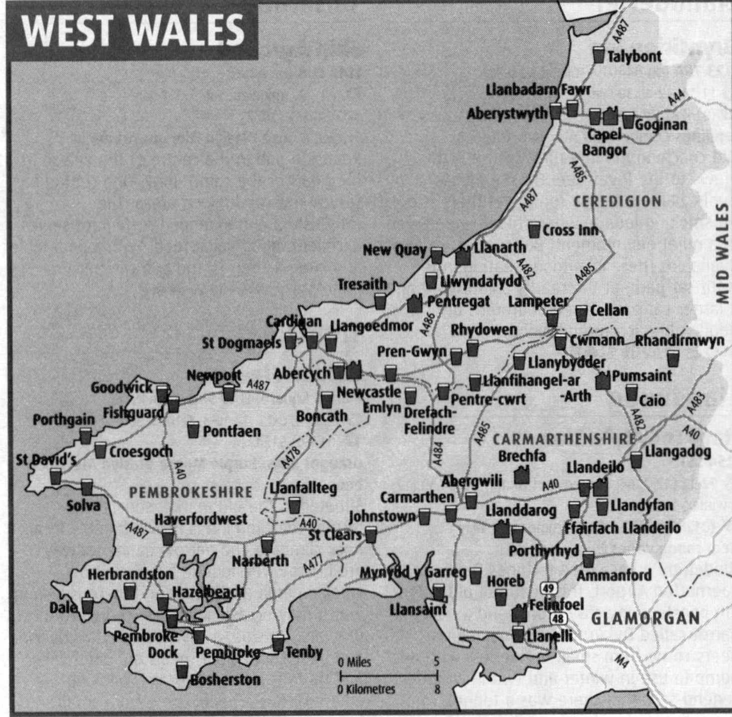

Authority areas covered: Carmarthenshire UA, Ceredigion UA, Pembrokeshire UA

CARMARTHENSHIRE

Abergwili

Black Ox

High Street, SA31 2JB

✪ 12 (5 Mon)-midnight (1am Sat); 12-11 Sun

☎ (01267) 222458

Beer range varies Ⓗ

Welcoming village local that has gained a reputation for its excellent home-cooked food. The bar is open plan but has three small, distinct drinking areas. The beer is often provided by a Welsh brewer. There is a dining room where children are welcome, but meals are also served in the bar (eve meals Tue-Sat). The former palace of the Bishop of St Davids – now a museum – is nearby.

❀◐◑♣P

Ammanford

Ammanford Hotel

Wernoleu House, 31 Pontamman Road, SA18 2HX

✪ 5.30-11; 1-midnight Sat; 12-10.30 Sun

☎ (01269) 592598

Brains Buckley's Best Bitter; guest beers Ⓗ

This hotel on the outskirts of Ammanford was originally a colliery manager's house. It is set in five acres of landscaped grounds and woodlands. The hotel bar is open to non-residents. A varied guest list of up to five beers is often chosen by regulars. The Victorian-style interior is enhanced by open log fires in winter. Families are welcome.

♨Q❀⇔◐◑⅄P

Caio

Brunant Arms

SA19 8RD (approx 2 miles off A482)

✪ 12-3, 6-midnight; 12-1am Fri-Sun

☎ (01558) 650483

Beer range varies Ⓗ

Traditional beamed pub dating from the 16th century not far from the Dolau Cothi gold mines. It is situated in the centre of the village near the church where a legendary Welsh wizard is buried. Hikers and pony-trekkers often find their way here. Pub games are popular here and quiz nights too. During the summer good food is served, from basic pub grub to exotic dishes (no food Mon). ♨❀◐◑⅄P

Carmarthen

Queen's Hotel

Queen Street SA31 1JR

✪ 11-11 daily

☎ (01267) 231800

Draught Bass; guest beers Ⓗ

Town-centre pub noted for the quality of the Bass. There are discounted meal offers in the late afternoon. The public bar has a large screen for viewing sporting events. An upstairs meeting room is available for small groups. A patio area at the back of the pub beneath the remnants of the old castle wall allows for alfresco drinking. ❀◐⇌♣

Stag & Pheasant

34 Spilman Street, SA31 1LQ

✪ 11-11; 12-10.30 Sun

☎ (01267) 236278
Worthington's Bitter; guest beers Ⓗ
Busy town pub, popular with locals and office workers. The pub was once part of a stable block belonging to a nearby hotel. The bar is a single, open-plan room where the welcome is warm and fine beer is served. There is no juke box or games machines and the TV in the corner is only used for sporting events. ⇌♣

Cwmann

Cwmanne Tavern
SA48 8DR (at A482/A485 jct near Lampeter)
⌚ 5 (12 Sat)-11; 12-10.30 Sun
☎ (01570) 423861 🌐 cwmanntavern.co.uk
Beer range varies Ⓗ
Built in 1720 on a drovers' route, a quarter mile from Lampeter. All age groups are welcome here. Three drinking areas around the bar feature wooden beams, posts and floors. The Dutch landlord has an impressive selection of bottled British and European beers (most bottle-conditioned). Live music, often blues, on Saturday evening draws a crowd. Quiz night is Tuesday. No food is served Monday. Q❀⇄◐♣●P

Drefach-Felindre

John y Gwâs
SA44 5XG (near St. Barnabus Church)
⌚ 2 (5 Mon; 12 Sat; 3 Sun)-12.30am
☎ (01559) 370469 🌐 johnygwas.co.uk
Beer range varies Ⓗ
John y Gwâs translates as John the Servant. Newly refurbished, it is a welcoming and friendly family pub. Three ales are always available. Local farm implements are on display in the main bar as well as historical photographs of the village – note the black and white photo of John the Servant. Play pool and you will notice the unusual green baize motif of the Welsh dragon. The no-smoking restaurant serves good home-cooked food made with mostly locally-sourced ingredients (Wed-Sat). ♔❀◐♣P⚟

Ffairfach Llandeilo

Torbay Inn
Heol Cennen, SA19 6UL
⌚ 6 (11 Sat)-11; 12-10.30 Sun
☎ (01558) 823140
Beer range varies Ⓗ
Friendly pub and restaurant situated by a railway crossing on the Heart of Wales line. The National Botanical Gardens and other attractions are nearby. The landlord is justly proud of the quality beer he serves. ❀⇌P

Horeb

Waunwyllt
Horeb Road, SA15 5AQ (off B4309 at Five Roads)
⌚ 11-11 daily
☎ (01269) 860209
Beer range varies Ⓗ
Excellent country pub and a previous local CAMRA Pub of the Year. The pub is close to the cycle path that runs to Llanelli, and is popular with passing cyclists. There are seats outside at the front and a garden to the rear. Live music is played occasionally. A genuine free house, four beers are usually available. Q❀⇄◐⛺P

Johnstown

Friends Arms
Old St Clears Road, SA31 3HH
⌚ 11-11; 12-10.30 Sun
☎ (01267) 234073
Tetley Burton Ale; guest beers Ⓗ
Lively and welcoming community local with a cosy, low-beamed bar. Adjoining a well-preserved toll house at the former western entry to Carmarthen, there has been a pub on this site for over 400 years. Regular quiz nights provide entertainment. An interesting selection of bottled beers is stocked. ♔❀♣⚟

Llandeilo

Salutation Inn
New Road, SA19 6DF
⌚ 12-midnight; 12-11 Sun
☎ (01558) 823325
Beer range varies Ⓗ
Vibrant pub just away from the centre of town. The central bar serves both the lounge and public bar. A large open fireplace is the focal point of the lounge area. Regular live music is staged – ring ahead for details. Large screens show major sporting events. ♔❀⊟♿⇌♣⚟

White Horse
Rhosmaen Street, SA19 6EN
⌚ 11-11; 12-10.30 Sun
☎ (01558) 822424
Evan Evans BB, Cwrw; guest beers Ⓗ
Grade II listed coaching inn dating from the 16th century. This multi-roomed pub is popular with all ages. There is a small outdoor drinking area to the front and a car park to the rear with access to the pub down a short flight of steps. ❀⇌🚌♣

Llandyfan

Square & Compass
SA18 2UD (midway between Ammanford and Trap)
⌚ 5 (1 Sat)-11; closed Mon; 12-6 Sun
☎ (01269) 850402
Beer range varies Ⓗ
This 18th-century building was originally the village blacksmith's, converted into a pub during the 1960s. Nestling on the western edge of the Brecon Beacons National Park, it

INDEPENDENT BREWERIES
Ceredigion Pentregat
Coles Llanddarog
Evan Evans Llandeilo
Felinfoel Felinfoel
Flock Brechfa
Gwynant Capel Bangor
Jacobi Pumsaint
Nags Head Abercych
Penlon Cottage Llanarth

offers magnificent panoramic views and plentiful walking opportunities. A traditional, family-oriented country pub, it also extends a warm welcome to visiting discerning drinkers. The pub has a wonderful rustic charm. Three guest beers, one from a local brewery, are usually available.
Q⚲◗♿⅄P⚟

Llanelli

Halfway House

Glyncoed Terrace, Halfway, SA15 1EZ (1 mile from town centre)
⏲ 11 (5.30 Mon)-11.30 daily
☎ (01554) 773571
Greene King Old Speckled Hen; guest beers Ⓗ
Roomy former coaching house with a splendid and spacious public bar. There has been a pub on this site from the 1840s or earlier and the landlord is a keen historian of his establishment. Two guest beers are usually dispensed. Children are welcome in the conservatory; afternoon teas are served.
♨⚲❀◐◗♣P⚟

Lemon Tree

2 Prospect Place, SA15 3PT
⏲ 12-11; 12-10.30 Sun
☎ (01554) 775121
Brains Buckley's Best Bitter; guest beer Ⓗ
End-of-terrace establishment near the site of the former Buckley's Brewery. Popular with locals, it has a strong sports following. The interior, although open plan, is split level, creating different drinking areas. What used to be a bowling green is now a partly covered outdoor drinking area. ❀♣

Llanfallteg

Plash Inn

SA34 0HN (off A40)
⏲ 12-10.30 (6-11 winter); 12-10.30 Sun
☎ (01437) 563472
Beer range varies Ⓗ
Terrace-style cottage pub with a large garden overlooking green fields and the River Taf. The regulars call it a 'talking pub'. The attractive bar was rescued from a local outfitter's shop. The landlord is keen to promote beers from smaller independent breweries. A small restaurant serves traditional home-made dishes. ♨Q❀◐◗♣P

Llanfihangel-ar-Arth

Cross Inn

Crossroads, SA39 9HX (on jct of B4459 and B4336)
⏲ 5-11; closed Tue; 12-10.30 Sun
☎ (01559) 384838 ⊕ crossinnwales.co.uk
Beer range varies Ⓗ
This popular local watering hole, known locally as pwll dwr (water place), was originally a 16th-century drovers' inn. It comprises a single main bar with open fire, a pool room and a restaurant serving wholesome good quality food. The specials menu and the themed evenings deliver a mouth-watering variety of dishes – the puddings are a delight. The annual Easter beer fest, now in its fifth year, offers over 14 beers sourced from micros near and far. The licensees organise regular events.
♨Q❀◐◗⊟⅄♣●P

Llangadog

Telegraph Inn

Station Road, SA19 9LS (off A40 by level crossing)
⏲ 4.30-11; 12-midnight Sat; 12-10.30 Sun
☎ (01550) 777727
Beer range varies Ⓗ
On the edge of the village, the inn is next to the railway station on the spectacular Heart of Wales line. Self-catering accommodation sleeps five. Built around 1830, the welcoming pub has a basic bar area and comfortable lounge. Food is served Wednesday to Saturday including takeaways. Curry night is Wednesday. ♨❀◗⅄⇌P

Llansaint

King's Arms

13 Maes yr Eglwys, SA17 5JE (behind church)
⏲ 12-2.30, 6.30-11 (closed winter Tue); 12-2.30, 6.30-10.30 Sun
☎ (01267) 267487
Brains Buckley's Best Bitter; guest beers Ⓗ
This friendly village local has been a pub for over 200 years. Situated near an 11th-century church, it is reputedly built from stone recovered from the lost village of St Ishmaels. Music and poetry nights are held every third Friday of the month. Children are welcome and good quality food is served. Carmarthen Bay holiday park is just a few miles away. Local CAMRA Pub of the Year in 2005. ♨Q❀⇔◐◗⅄♣P

Llanybydder

Albion Arms

Llansawel Road, SA40 9RN (off A485)
⏲ 5 (12 Sat)-11; 12-11 Sun
☎ (01570) 480781
Boddingtons Bitter; guest beers Ⓗ
Unpretentious and cheerful traditional Welsh market town pub. The restaurant is in the process of being restored. There has been a pub on this site for more than 200 years serving the village of Glanduar, now encompassed by the town of Llanybydder. The name Albion possibly comes from a ship-building connection. The spacious bar has a large-screen TV (no Sky) for sporting events and there is a pool room. Children and well-behaved dogs are welcome. ♨⊟⅄♣

Mynydd y Garreg

Prince of Wales

SA17 4RP (1½ miles from Kidwelly bypass)
⏲ 7 (5 Sat)-11; 12-3 Sun
☎ (01554) 890522
Bullmastiff Brindle, Son of a Bitch; guest beers Ⓗ
This little gem of a pub is well worth seeking out, both for its beer range and its ambience. As well as the two regular Bullmastiff beers there are at least four guests from a variety of small breweries. The cosy single-room bar is packed with movie memorabilia and the small no-smoking

restaurant offers good, reasonably priced food. Children under 14 are not admitted. Voted Pub of the Year by the local CAMRA branch in 2003. ⌂Q✿◐◑P

Newcastle Emlyn

Bunch of Grapes

Bridge Street, SA38 9DU (opp. clock tower)
⏲ 12 (5 winter Mon)-11; 12-3 Sun
☎ (01239) 711185
Courage Directors; guest beers Ⓗ
Well-kept pub in the town centre with original exposed beams and flooring. This 17th-century pub was voted Pub of the Year by local CAMRA members in 2004. An unusual small indoor garden features a grapevine and advertising memorabilia. The restaurant is just off the bar area. Pavement seating at the front gives a continental feel in summer. Three handpumps offer a range of real ales. ⌂✿◐◑

Ivy Bush

Emlyn Square, SA38 9BG
⏲ 11-11 (midnight Thu-Sat); 12-10.30 Sun
☎ (01239) 710542
Draught Bass; guest beer Ⓗ
Friendly village pub popular with locals. The snug has an open fire and there is a pool room and TV room with a large screen showing Sky Sports. Breakfast is served most mornings with bar snacks at lunchtime (not Sun). A delightful local with well-kept Bass and good old-fashioned pub grub. ⌂✿◐♣

Pentre-Cwrt

Plas Parke

Plas Parke, SA44 5AX (on B4335)
⏲ 4-11; 3-midnight Sat; 3-11 Sun
☎ (01559) 362684
Draught Bass; guest beer Ⓗ
Welcoming, friendly local with two cosy bars and another area for a quiet drink. In summer sheltered seating is provided in the garden under gazebos. It is popular for evening meals (not Tue). Close by is Altcafan Bridge, which spans the 'Queen of Welsh rivers', the Teifi, where fisherman catch salmon and sewin (sea trout). It is also handy for Llandysul Paddlers at the canoeing centre and the Teifi Valley narrow gauge railway two miles away at Henllan. The Welsh National Woollen Mill is within easy driving distance. ⌂✿◑Ⅹ♣P

Porthyrhyd

Mansel Arms

Banc y Mansel, SA32 8BS (off A48)
⏲ 6 (4 Sat)-11; 12-4 Sun
☎ (01267) 275305
Beer range varies Ⓗ
Dating from the 18th century, this former roadside coaching inn has wood fires burning in every room. The games room to the rear where pool and darts are played was originally used for killing pigs. The limestone slabs have been broken up and used in the fireplace. Low beams have been put in to enhance the traditional pub atmosphere, with a collection of jugs hanging from them. A welcoming and friendly pub well worth a visit. ⌂Q◑⊟Ⅹ⊞(129)♣P

Rhandirmwyn

Royal Oak

SA20 0NY
⏲ 12-3 (2 winter), 6-11; 12-2, 7-10.30 Sun
☎ (01550) 760201
Beer range varies Ⓗ
Remote, stone-flagged pub with excellent views of the Towy Valley. Originally built as a hunting lodge for the local landowner, it is now a focal point for community activities. Close to the RSPB bird sanctuary, it is popular with fans of outdoor pursuits. A good range of bottled beers and whiskies is stocked, and the good, wholesome food is recommended. ⌂Q✿⇌◐◑Ⅹ⊞♣P

St Clears

Corvus

Station Road, SA33 4BF
⏲ 11-midnight; 12-11 Sun
☎ (01994) 230965
Greene King IPA; guest beer Ⓗ
The bar area has recently been refurbished in this busy, two-bar local at the end of the village. The pub supports many of the local sports teams, particularly the village football squad. Caricatures of the pub's regulars adorn the walls of the bar. Lots of brass and beer jugs decorate the lounge. Friendly staff and locals welcome visitors to this inn which is reputed to have its own ghost. Q⊟

CEREDIGION

Aberystwyth

Downies Vaults

33 Eastgate, SY23 2AR
⏲ 11-11 (7-1am winter); 11-2, 7-11 Sat; 12-11 Sun
☎ (01970) 625446
Banks's Original, Bitter; Ⓟ **Mansfield Cask** Ⓗ
Livley town centre pub near the main shopping streets and seafront, decorated in Victorian style with old-fashioned mirrors and tiling. The Banks's beers are served by metered electric pumps – a small 'cask conditioned' inscription on the pumps distinguishing them from the keg fonts. TV screens show regular sport at the weekend. Popular with a young clientele, opening times in the afternoon and late evening may vary depending on university term times; no entry after midnight. Ⅹ⇌⊞♁

Fountain Inn

Trefechan, SY23 1BE (S end of Trefechan Bridge)
⏲ 12-midnight (11 Sun)
☎ (01970) 612430
Boddingtons Bitter; Brains Dark, SA Ⓗ
A warm, friendly atmosphere awaits visitors to this pub just outside the town centre. Divided into two, it has a lively public bar where conversation dominates and a comfortable lounge decorated with old photographs of the area. The lounge is also the place for excellent food. Located close to

the harbour and marina, it is also near the iron age hill fort at Pen Dinas, worth the climb for the fine views all over town.

Mill Inn

Mill Street, SY23 1HZ

3-midnight; 12-1am Sat; 2-midnight Sun

(01970) 612306

Beer range varies

Small, friendly pub on the edge of the town centre near the bus and railway station. A genuine free house, it serves one constantly changing beer chosen from micro and regional breweries across Britain. Popular with students and sports fans, Sky Sports is usually on TV and there is a pool table and juke box. Under the same management as the Ship & Castle, this is less of a specialist beer pub than its stablemate, although the quality of the ale is always superb.

Ship & Castle

1 High Street, SY23 1JG

2 (12 Sat)-midnight daily

Beer range varies

Set in the old part of town, this frequently bustling street corner ale house offers the widest range of quality draught beers in the area. A true free house, the four handpumps serve a constantly changing range that focuses, but not exclusively, on micro-breweries from Wales and the borders. Spring and autumn beer festivals extend the choice further. A dedicated handpump serves real cider. If you only have time to visit one pub in the town, this is the one to choose.

Capel Bangor

Tynllidiart Arms

SY23 3LR (on A44, 5 miles E of Aberystwyth)

11-3, 5-11; 12-11 Sun

(01970) 880248

Gwynant Cwrw Gwynant; Hancock's HB; guest beers

Dating from 1688, local CAMRA's Pub of the Year 2006 is unashamedly food-led – it is one the best places to eat in the area – but continues to offer its customers an enthusiastically received range of top quality draught beers. At the front stands the world's smallest commercial brew house, supplying necessarily restricted quantities of Cwrw Gwynant (usually weekends only). Two or three guest beers are sourced from a wide range of regional and micro-breweries. The decked garden overlooks the Rheidol Valley.

Cardigan

Black Lion/Llew Du

High Street, SA43 1JW

11-11; 12-10.30 Sun

(01239) 612532

Tomos Watkin Cwrw Braf, OSB; Worthington's Bitter

Historic coaching inn in a busy, characterful town. It dates back to the 12th century, but the present building is 18th century. There is a main drinking area, a small panelled snug and a rear dining section. It is a welcome outpost for Tomos Watkin beers. Good value food is available at this friendly meeting place.

Red Lion/Llew Coch

Pwllhai, SA43 1DB (behind bus station)

11-11; 12-10.30 Sun

(01239) 612482

Brains Buckley's Best Bitter; guest beer

Homely local where Welsh is the first language. Visitors are made to feel most welcome. The main bar area is complemented by a smaller private lounge and a restaurant area. Live music is a regular feature here. Snacks are available at most times. Tucked away behind the bus station, this pub is worth seeking out.

Cellan

Fishers Arms

SA48 8HU (on B4343)

4.30 (midnight Sat)-2am; 12-2am Sun

(01570) 422895

Tetley Mild; guest beer

Situated alongside the River Teifi, one of Wales' premier trout and salmon rivers, the Fishers dates from 1580 and was first granted a licence in 1891. The main bar has an open fire and flagstone floor, fly rods and antique guns hang from the beamed ceiling. The Tetley Mild is offered as a house beer and the guest usually comes from a Welsh brewery. Occasional buses from Lampeter and Tregaron stop nearby.

Cross Inn

Rhos-yr-Hafod

SY23 5NB (at B4337/B4577 crossroads)

12-2 (not winter), 6-midnight; closed Mon Jan & Feb; 12-3, 7-11 Sun

(01974) 272644

Boddingtons Bitter; guest beers

This sociable pub stands at a crossroads in the Ceredigion uplands. Small drinking areas cluster round the central bar. The back room, decorated with bird paintings and local photos, functions as a no-smoking family room; it also lacks loudspeakers, while the rest of the pub has quiet background music to set off the animated, bilingual conversation. There is a no-smoking restaurant (no eve meals Sun). Guest beers (usually two, one at quiet times) are from regional and micro-brewers. Beer festivals are regular events.

Goginan

Druid

High Street, SY23 3NT (on A44)

12-midnight (1am Fri & Sat) 12-midnight Sun

(01970) 880650

Banks's Bitter, Brains SA; guest beer

Commanding glorious views over the Melindwr Valley, this friendly family-run free house is the focus for village life and a handy stop-off for travellers. A guest beer is added in summer and other busy times, often from a micro-brewery in Wales and the borders. When quiet, ask to see the rock-hewn cellar. Local attractions include Llywernog Mining Museum, celebrating the area's industrial past, and Nant-yr-Arian Forest centre, famous for its red kites. ♨♘❀⇄◑⅄⊟♣P⁄

Lampeter

Black Lion Royal Hotel

High Street, SA48 7BG

⊙ 11-11.30; 12-11 Sun

☎ (01570) 422172

Draught Bass; Brains SA, Rev James Ⓗ

A much-needed outlet for real ale in Lampeter, this listed hotel has been recently purchased by Brains Brewery and completely refurbished in traditional style. A central bar serves the lounge and restaurant. Three real ales are offered – the Rev James alternates with a guest or seasonal beer. Sparklers can be removed on request. ♘❀⇄◑⅄P⁄

Llanbadarn Fawr

Black Lion

SY23 3RA

⊙ 12-midnight (11.30 Sun)

☎ (01970) 623448 ⊕ blacklion.info

Banks's Original, Bitter; Marston's Pedigree; guest beer Ⓗ

By the medieval church, the Black Lion attracts a wide range of customers including locals and students from the nearby university campus. The pub has one large main bar and a back bar where events including live music and the popular Friday quiz are hosted. Food is served at Sunday lunchtime and some other times during the summer. Guests and seasonal beers come from the Banks's list. ❀◑⊟♣P

Llangoedmor

Penllwyndu

SA43 2LY (on B4570, 4 miles E of Cardigan) OS241458

⊙ 3.30 (12 Sat)-11; 12-10.30 Sun

☎ (01239) 682533

Brains Buckley's Best Bitter; guest beers Ⓗ

Old-fashioned ale house standing on the crossroads where Cardigan's wrong-doers were hanged. The pub sign is worthy of close inspection. Cheerful and welcoming, the public bar has a slate floor and inglenook with wood-burning stove. Bar snacks are usually available and there is a restaurant area for more formal dining. In summer it is a treat to sit out in the garden and enjoy superb views of the Preseli Mountains. Two guest beers usually feature, one from the Cottage Brewery. ♨❀◑♣P

Llwyndafydd

Crown Inn & Restaurant

SA44 6BU (off A487, 1 mile S of A486 jct) OS371554

⊙ 12-3, 6-11; 12-3, 6-10.30 (not winter eve) Sun

☎ (01545) 560396 ⊕ thecrowninnandrestaurant.co.uk

Enville Ale; Flowers IPA, Original; guest beers (summer) Ⓗ

Among the loveliest pubs in Wales, it offers good food, fine ales and a garden/play area in an idyllic village setting. Exposed beams and low ceilings make this Dylan Thomas Trail pub an intimate, friendly place in which to savour expertly prepared local produce. Other Enville beers sometimes replace the Ale; summer guests come from a wide range of micros. See the landlord's photographic gallery of mainly local scenes. Q♘❀◑⅄♣P⁄

New Quay

Cambrian Hotel

New Road, SA45 9SE (on B4342)

⊙ 11 (12 Sun)-11

☎ (01545) 560295

Brains Buckley's Best Bitter; Felinfoel Double Dragon; guest beers Ⓗ

Cosy bar at the rear of the hotel, approached either through the dining room or an entrance up the lane. A guest beer, often from a micro-brewery or small family brewery, is available from Easter to late October and at other busy times. The TV lounge is now no-smoking. The pub's annual beer festival, usually in July, grows in popularity each year. Opening hours may vary at weekends when there is often live music. Q❀⇄◑⅄⊟♣P⁄

Pren-gwyn

Gwarcefel Arms

SA44 4LU (at A475/B4476 crossroads)

⊙ 12-midnight (1am Fri & Sat); 12-11 Sun

☎ (01559) 362720

Breconshire Brecon County; guest beers Ⓗ

Small country pub situated at the junction of five roads. The main bar has an open fire with cosy seating and a games area for pool and darts. A separate bar serves the restaurant which caters for functions and parties as well as lunchtime and evening meals. The recommended specials menu changes frequently. Guest beers include ales from Brains, Tomos Watkin, Brecon and Cottage. ♨❀⇄◑⅄♣P

Rhydowen

Alltyrodyn Arms

SA44 4QB (at B4459/A475 crossroads)

⊙ 3 (12 Sat)-11; closed Mon; 12-4 Sun

☎ (01545) 590319

Fuller's London Pride; guest beers Ⓗ

This family-run pub thrives in the small community of Rhydowen. With a warm welcome for all, it attracts locals and visitors alike. There are five handpumps although usually only three ales are dispensed – London Pride is a regular with a variety of guest ales from local breweries big and small. Food is served at Sunday lunchtime as well as occasional themed food evenings such as Chinese or Indian. Live music is a regular feature. ♨Q❀⊡⅄♣P

Talybont

White Lion/Llew Gwyn

SY24 5ER (7 miles N of Aberystwyth on A487)
☉ 11-1am; 12-midnight Sun
☎ (01970) 832245
Banks's Original, Bitter [H]
One of two pubs facing the village green, this refurbished local continues to delight. The flagstoned main public bar is the heart of the pub – note the local history display with fascinating photos. Across the corridor, the large family/games room has two dartboards; a no-smoking dining room is at the rear. The garden adjoins the Afon Ceulan stream. Fishing permits are sold over the bar. The menu features locally caught trout, crab and lobster. Live music is staged monthly. ♨Q❀◑♿▲♣⚡

Tresaith

Ship

SA43 2JL (lane leading to beach) OS279516
☉ 11-11 (11-3, 5-11 Jan-Feb if quiet); 12-10.30 Sun
☎ (01239) 810380
Hancock's HB; guest beers [H]
With a sea view to rival any in the country, this spacious pub comprises interlinked drinking and dining areas around a large central bar and servery. The conservatory overlooking the bay is a delightful place to enjoy the local seafood specialities. More than just a food pub, drinkers are very welcome and the bar is busy at weekends and early evening. Guest beers (usually two in summer) may include one from the Ceredigion Brewery. ♨❀◑♿▲♣P⚡

PEMBROKESHIRE

Abercych

Nags Head

SA37 0HJ (on B4332, between Cenarth and Boncath)
☉ 11-3, 6-11.30; closed Mon; 12-10.30 Sun
☎ (01239) 841200
Nags Head Old Emrys; guest beers [H]
Well restored old smithy with a beamed bar, riverside garden and children's play area. The bar area is furnished with collections of old medical instruments, railway memorabilia and clocks showing the time in various parts of the world. Space is also found for an extensive display of beer bottles. ♨Q❀◑P

Boncath

Boncath Inn

SA37 0JN (on B4332)
☉ 11-11; 12-10.30 Sun
☎ (01239) 841241
Salopian Shropshire Gold; Worthington's Bitter; guest beers [H]
Attractive pub at the centre of village life, dating back to the 18th century. Several distinct seating areas provide an intimate atmosphere. There is also a pleasant no-smoking restaurant serving home-cooked bar meals – try the steak and kidney pie. A wealth of local history is displayed in old pictures and photographs. Up to three guest ales are served. A beer festival is held on the August bank holiday. ♨❀◑♿▲♣P

Bosherston

St Govan's Country Inn

SA71 5DN (5 miles S of Pembroke on B4319)
☉ 11-3.30, 6-11.30; 12-11.15 Sun
☎ (01646) 661311
Fuller's London Pride; guest beers [H]
Modern single-roomed pub that takes its name from the saint who built a chapel on the cliffs nearby. It is close to the Pembrokeshire coast path, lily ponds and Broadhaven's sandy beach. The inn is popular with walkers and climbers, who find the local cliffs irresistible. ♨◑▲♣

Croesgoch

Artramont Arms

SA62 5JP (on A487)
☉ 6-11 (11-11 summer); 12-10.30 Sun
☎ (01348) 831309
Brains SA; Felinfoel Double Dragon; guest beer [H]
Appealing village local with a large public bar, lounge and conservatory dining area. There is a no-smoking area for drinkers and a pleasant garden. Good meals are offered lunchtime and evening from an imaginative menu. This community pub acts as a focus for village activities. ♨Q❀◑♿P⚡

Dale

Griffin Inn

SA62 3RB
☉ 12-2.30, 5-11 (12-11 summer); 12-11 Sat & Sun
☎ (01646) 636227
Tomos Watkins OSB; Worthington's Bitter; guest beers [H]
At the water's edge, close to the slipway, the Griffin is popular with visitors and locals alike. Some of the outside seats are right by the water. Inside have some fun with the table skittles. The pub is ideally located for walkers on the Pembrokeshire coastal path. ♨❀◑♣

Fishguard

Fishguard Arms

SA65 9HJ (on A487)
☉ 11-3, 6-midnight (12.30am Wed & Fri); 11-12.30am Sat; 12-11 Sun
☎ (01348) 872763
Beer range varies [G]
Small local behind a distinctive green painted exterior. There is no keg beer here, just a splendid rotation of guest ales. The main entertainment is conversation. A selection of speciality cheeses is offered on a Wednesday night to coincide with the darts match. The railway station for Fishguard is actually in nearby Goodwick. ♨Q▲

Royal Oak

Market Square, SA65 9HA (on A487)
☉ 10-2am; 12-10.30 Sun
☎ (01348) 872514
Brains Dark, Bitter, SA, Rev James; guest beer [H]

Charming, friendly pub with historic connections – the French forces landed here following the last invasion of mainland Britain in 1797. Note the fascinating memorabilia from this period on display. The pub is full of character with a public bar, dining area and garden. Home-cooked meals are served at affordable prices from a varied menu. Local folk singers meet here on Monday evenings. Q❀◐◑⅄⇌♣P

Goodwick

Rose & Crown

SA64 0BP

⊙ 11-midnight (1am Fri & Sat); 12-10.30 Sun

☎ (01348) 874449

Brains Bitter; Worthington's Bitter; guest beer Ⓗ

Picturesque pub, close to the ferry port and enjoying views of Goodwick harbour and the beach. It has a no-smoking dining area and offers meals at each session. The landlord is an active member of the Royal British Legion. The local lifeboat volunteers use the pub as a meeting place.

Q❀◐◑⅄⇌♣P

Haverfordwest

Hotel Mariners

Mariners Square, SA61 2DU

⊙ 12-11; 12-10.30 Sun

☎ (01437) 763353

Worthington's Bitter; guest beer Ⓗ

Established in 1625, this was formerly a grand coaching inn. It has a relaxed, informal atmosphere with quiet piped music. Modernisation has not detracted from its charm and character; large exposed beams and stone walls hint at its former glory. The food is high quality and imaginative.

⛫❀⇄◐◑⇌P

Pembroke Yeoman

Hill Street, St Thomas's Green, SA61 1QF

⊙ 11-11; 12-3, 7-10.30 Sun

☎ (01437) 762500

Draught Bass; Flowers IPA; guest beers Ⓗ

Popular and comfortable town local that attracts a wide range of customers. Conversation is the main entertainment here. A meeting place for many local organisations, it hosts a quiz night on Wednesday. Guest beers change regularly and are sourced from some unusual breweries. Food is excellent with generous portions. ⛫◐◑♣

Hazelbeach

Ferry House Inn

SA73 1EG (follow signs to Llanstadwell)

⊙ 12-3, 6-11; 12-3, 8-11 Sun

☎ (01646) 600270

Brains Bitter; Felinfoel Double Dragon; guest beer Ⓗ

Situated on the Milford Haven Waterway, on the famous coastal path, the pub is convenient for Neyland Marina. The conservatory restaurant overlooks the river, and the menu features local fresh fish. Good accommodation makes this an ideal base for exploring the area. The pub lies across the river from the town of Pembroke Dock.

Q⇄◐◑⊞P

Herbrandston

Taberna Inn

SA73 3TD

⊙ 12-midnight (1.30am Thu; 12.30am Fri-Sun)

☎ (01646) 693498

Beer range varies Ⓗ

Situated just off the Dale road three miles from Milford Haven. The pub publishes its own Good Beer Guide for all the guest ales it serves throughout the year. The atmosphere is pleasant and the locals are welcoming.

❀◐◑⊞♿P

Narberth

Angel Inn

High Street, SA67 7AS

⊙ 11-3, 5-11 (midnight Thu-Sat); 12-2, 7-10.30 Sun

☎ (01834) 860215

Brains Buckley's Best Bitter, Rev James; guest beer Ⓗ

Cosy, modernised, town-centre pub popular for its food. The lounge bar opens on to the split-level dining area. There is a public bar for customers who just want to drink. Narberth Station is 20 minutes' walk from the town and is on the Carmarthen-Pembroke Dock line. Q◐◑⊞⅄

Newport

Castle Hotel

Bridge Street, SA42 0TB (on A487 through road)

⊙ 11-11; 12-10.30 Sun

☎ (01239) 820742

Wadworth 6X; Worthington's Bitter; guest beer Ⓗ

This friendly, popular local has an attractive bar with a real fire and a wealth of wood panelling. Food is served at all sessions in the extensive dining area. A large off-street car park is situated to the side and rear of the hotel. ⛫♨❀⇄◐◑⊞P

Llwyngwair Arms

East Street, SA42 0SY (on A487)

⊙ 5 (11 summer)-11 (closed winter Mon); 12-10.30 Sun

☎ (01239) 820267

Draught Bass; guest beer Ⓗ

This popular local has not been altered for some considerable time. It has a dining area serving inexpensive food, with a focus on bar meals. Both food and ales have a distinctly Welsh emphasis. Parking is available through an archway on the opposite side of the road. ⛫Q◐◑⅄P

Pembroke

Royal George Hotel

9 Northgate, SA71 4NR (on bridge over millpond)

⊙ 11-midnight (1am Sat); 11-midnight Sun

☎ (01646) 682751

Worthington's Bitter; guest beers Ⓗ

Pleasant, cheery local situated on the old south quay, just on the edge of the town centre. The building, located directly below Pembroke Castle at what used to be the town's north gate, is part of the old town wall. The interior consists of one large, split-level, L-shaped room with a single bar. Current and future guest ales are listed on a blackboard by the bar. ⇆≹♣P

Pembroke Dock

Flying Boat Inn

6 Queen Street, SA72 6JL (off route 9 to dock)

⏲ 7am-12.30am; 12-10.30 Sun

☎ (01646) 682810

Beer range varies Ⓗ

This pub retains the same relaxed and friendly atmosphere that it had 50 years ago. The bar, with exposed stone and black beams, displays memorabilia from the heyday of the flying boats stationed at Pembroke Dock. Traditional pub games are played here including shove ha'penny. There is a TV for viewing Sky Sports. A summer beer festival is held in August. ♨Q⇆⊟♿≹♣●⚟

Station Inn

Hawkestone Road, SA72 6DN

⏲ 7-11 Mon; 11-3, 6-midnight (12.30am Fri & Sat); 12-3, 7-10.30 Sun

☎ (01646) 621255 ⊕ station-inn.com

Beer range varies Ⓗ

Housed in a Victorian railway station with the trains still running on the adjoining tracks, this town-centre pub is close to both the Irish ferry terminal and the coast path. It serves excellent value lunches and evening meals. Every Tuesday a new beer is sold. It holds a beer festival in June offering around 20 beers. Live music is performed on Saturday evening. Q◐◑♿≹P

Pontfaen

Dyffryn Arms ☆

SA65 9SG (off B4313 between Fishguard and Narbeth)

⏲ 11-midnight; 12-11.30 Sun

☎ (01348) 881305

Draught Bass; guest beer (occasional) Ⓖ

Fascinating bar that resembles a 1920s front room where time has stood still. The beer is served by jug through a sliding hatch. A relaxed atmosphere prevails and conversation is the main form of entertainment. The landlady is in her eighties. The pub lies at the heart of the scenic Gwaun Valley. It has featured in every issue of the Guide except the first one. ♨Q▲♣

Porthgain

Sloop Inn

SA62 5BN

⏲ 11.30-3, 6-11 (11-11 summer); 6-10.30 Sun

☎ (01348) 831449

Brains SA; Felinfoel Double Dragon; Worthington's Bitter Ⓗ

Sympathetically modernised old inn that has served both the locally-based fishing industry and the now-defunct quarrying and stone exporting industries. The pub displays quarrying and shipping artefacts as part of the decor. Holding hoppers for the stone can be seen on the opposite side of the harbour. Popular with both locals and visitors, it offers a good choice of beers and reasonably-priced food using local produce where possible. ♨Q❀◐◑♣P

St David's

Farmers Arms

Goas Street, SA62 6RF

⏲ 11-11; 12-10.30 Sun

☎ (01437) 720328

Brains Rev James; Worthington's Bitter; guest beer Ⓗ

Inviting, 19th-century stone hostelry that retains many original features. It is popular with local farmers, fishermen and young people, with many tourists calling in during the summer season. The pub serves an interesting range of good, wholesome, home-cooked food. Definitely worth a visit, there is often a singalong or folk sessions on a Sunday evening. ♨Q❀◐◑⊟▲

St Dogmaels

Ferry Inn

Poppit Road, SA43 3LF

⏲ 12-3, 7-11; 12-3, 7-10.30 Sun

☎ (01239) 615172

Brains Rev James; Greene King Old Speckled Hen; guest beer Ⓗ

An inn that sits on the very edge of the Teifi estuary. Boat trips are run from a nearby quay in summer. It has been sympathetically developed so that both the open deck and the enclosed dining area enjoy panoramic views over the estuary. As the name implies, the inn has always been closely associated with the river, and boating ephemera features in the decor. Q❀◐◑⊟▲

Solva

Harbour Inn

SA62 6RF (on A487, adjoining harbour car park)

⏲ 11-11; 12-10.30 Sun

☎ (01437) 720013

Brains Buckley's Best Bitter, Bread of Heaven; guest beer Ⓗ

This delightful harbourside hostelry retains a traditional atmosphere, having remained unaltered for a considerable time. It is used as a base for many community activities and is popular with the locals. Camping facilities close by cater for tents and caravans. Enjoy a quiet pint in this welcoming local. Entertainment is organised on an ad hoc basis. ♨Q❀⇆◐◑▲

Tenby

Hope & Anchor

St Julian Street, SA70 7AS

⏲ 11-11; 12-10.30 Sun

☎ (01834) 842131

Brains Rev James; guest beers Ⓗ

Near the harbour and close to the north beach, this friendly local caters for locals and tourists alike. An outside drinking and dining area is provided in summer. A range of bar snacks makes it an ideal place to take a break when walking to or from the harbour. The medieval town walls can be seen nearby. ♨❀◐◑▲≹♣

Scotland

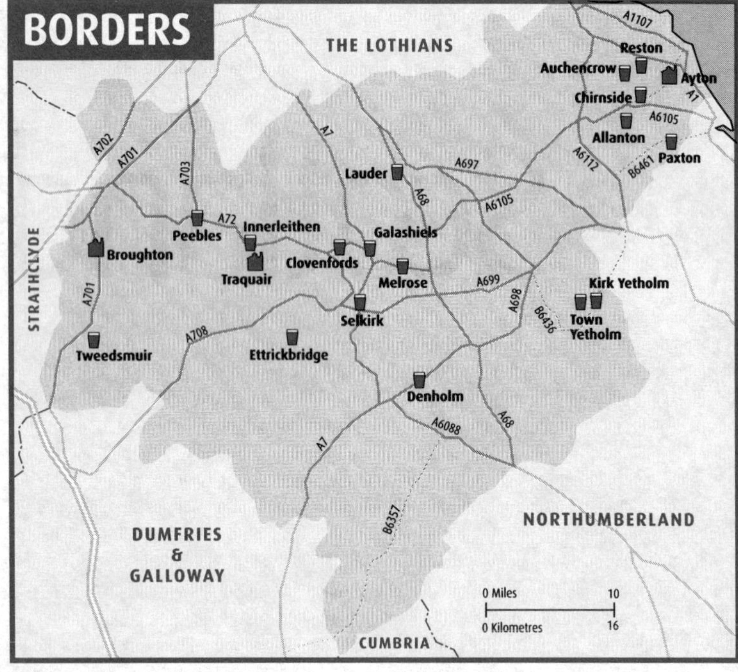

Authority area covered: The Borders UA

Allanton

Allanton Inn

TD11 3JZ (on B6437)
⏲ 12-2 (not Mon &Tue), 6-11 (10.30 Wed; 11.30 Fri & Sat): 12-2, 6-11 Sun
☎ (01890) 818260 🌐 allantoninn.co.uk
Beer range varies Ⓗ
Welcoming Borders coaching inn in a small village surrounded by rolling farmland. Hitching rings by the door are handy if you arrive by horse. The front rooms are a restaurant serving a good, varied menu, while the back bar offers an interesting selection of up to three real ales. There are plans for an extension which will open out onto the lovely rear garden, plus a shelter for smokers. ⛰Q❀🛏◐▶🚌♣P

Auchencrow

Craw Inn

TD14 5LS (signed from A1)
⏲ 12-2.30, 6-11 (midnight Fri); 12-midnight Sat; 12.30-11 Sun
☎ (01890) 761253 🌐 thecrawinn.co.uk
Beer range varies Ⓗ
Friendly village inn, circa 1680. The beamed bar has bench seating at one end and wooden tables, chairs and a church pew by the log-burning stove at the other. The two beers are usually from smaller breweries and change regularly. The rear of the inn is traditionally furnished, divided into a lounge/dining area and restaurant. Local produce features in many dishes on the wide ranging menu. Children are welcome. ⛰Q❀🛏◐▶♿🚌♣P

Chirnside

Waterloo Arms Hotel

Allanton Road, TD11 3XH (on A6105)
⏲ 12-midnight (1am Fri & Sat); 12.30-midnight Sun
☎ (01890) 818034 🌐 waterlooarms.com
Caledonian Deuchars IPA; Hadrian & Border Farne Island Pale Ale; guest beer (summer) Ⓗ
Comfortable village local, with bar and dining room, built circa 1820. The ceiling beams reflect its age, but the wooden panelling dates from the 1930s. The pub is reputed to be haunted by a farmer who was shot after a feud with his brother, who also died later from a fall. The real fire in the bar burns like a furnace on chilly winter days. Meals are served all day at weekends. Children are permitted until 9pm. ⛰❀🛏◐▶🚌(60, 260)♣P

Clovenfords

Clovenfords Hotel

1 Vine Street, TD1 3LU
⏲ 11-midnight; 12-11 Sun
☎ (01896) 850203
Beer range varies Ⓗ
A papier mâché statue of Sir Walter Scott outside this family-run hotel makes it easy to spot. The bar is uncluttered and has pictures of fish found in the Tweed and rugby memorabilia. It can be lively and

INDEPENDENT BREWERIES

Broughton Broughton
Peelwalls Ayton
Traquair Traquair

spontaneous music sessions occur. There is a comfortable lounge and conservatory restaurant. Children are welcome.
♨❀⇄◐◑⊟⛺🚌♣P

Denholm

Fox & Hounds Inn

Main Street, TD9 8NU (on A698)
⏲ 11-3, 5-midnight (1am Fri); 11-1am Sat; 12.30-midnight Sun
☎ (01450) 870247
🌐 foxandhoundsinndenholm.co.uk
Wylam Gold Tankard; guest beer 🄷
Village local, circa 1750, overlooking the green. The main bar is light and retains the original beams; a real fire gives it a cosy feel in winter. The rear lounge has a coffee house feel. The dining room is upstairs. In summer the courtyard is used for sheltered outdoor drinking, and is likely to become the all year smoking area. Children are welcome until 8pm and dogs are permitted. ♨❀⇄◐◑⊟🚌♣

Ettrickbridge

Cross Keys Inn

TD7 5JN
⏲ 12-2.30, 6.30-10.30 (11 Thu-Sat); closed Mon & Tue winter; 12.30-2.30, 6.30-10.30 Sun
☎ (01750) 52224 🌐 crosskeys-ettrickbridge.co.uk
Beer range varies 🄷
Dating from the 17th-century, the inn is located in the historic Ettrick valley. Stepping into the bar is like entering a time warp. It is crammed with all sorts of memorabilia, from water jugs and model trains to pipes and stuffed animals. Old photographs adorn the walls. The one real ale is ever changing and normally from a Scottish brewery. Quality food is served, with lunch and evening menus. There are outdoor benches for summer drinking. Children are welcome.
♨❀⇄◐◑♿♣P

Galashiels

Ladhope Inn

33 High Buckholmside, TD1 2HR (on A7, N of centre)
⏲ 11-3, 5-11; 11-11 Wed; 11-midnight Thu-Sat; 12.30-midnight Sun
☎ (01896) 752446
Caledonian Deuchars IPA; guest beer 🄷
Comfortable, friendly local with a vibrant Borders atmosphere. Originating circa 1792, the single room has been altered considerably inside and is decorated with whisky jugs. An alcove with a historical theme displays old photographs and a large inked map of the Galashiels area. The guest beer is often from Hadrian & Border but changes regularly. Toasties are available. Children and dogs are welcome. ❀⛺🚌♣

Salmon Inn

54 Bank Street, TD1 1EP (opp. the gardens)
⏲ 11-11 (midnight Thu, 1am Fri & Sat); 12.30-11 Sun
☎ (01896) 752577
Caledonian Deuchars IPA; guest beers 🄷
Comfortable, friendly pub with a mixture of old and modern decoration including historic photographs of the Galashiels area. The single room is split into two areas, with more seating and a games machine to the back of the bar. The guest beer, often from a smaller brewery, changes regularly. Good home-cooked meals are popular, but no food is served on Sundays. Children are welcome at lunchtime. ❀◐◑⛺🚌♣

Innerleithen

St Ronan's Hotel

High Street, EH44 6HF
⏲ 11-midnight (12.45am Fri & Sat); 12-midnight Sun
☎ (01896) 831487
Beer range varies 🄷
This village hotel takes its name from the local Saint who is also associated with a well. The functional public bar is long and thin and has a brick and wooden fireplace. There are two alcoves, one with seating, the other with a dartboard and a wide angled photograph of the village. A further room has a pool table. Food is only served in the summer. A pick up service is available for Southern Upland Way walkers. Children and dogs are welcome. ♨❀⇄◐◑⛺🚌♣P

Kirk Yetholm

Border Hotel

The Green, TD5 8PQ
⏲ 11-midnight (1am Fri & Sat); 12-midnight Sun (closes 1 hour earlier in winter)
☎ (01573) 420237 🌐 theborderhotel.com
Beer range varies 🄷
Built in 1750 as a coaching inn, situated at the end of the Pennine Way and on the St Cuthbert's Way, it is now popular with walkers. The wood beamed bar has a practical feel, with stone-flagged floor and red vinyl banquette seating. A warren of small rooms leads off, with two snugs, a pool room and a conservatory dining area. Dogs and children are welcome; the garden has a play area. ♨❀⇄◐◑⊟⛺🚌♣P

Lauder

Black Bull Hotel

Market Place, TD2 6SR
⏲ 12-11 (midnight Sat); winter 12-2.30, 5-11; 12-11 Sun
☎ (01578) 722208 🌐 blackbull-lauder.com
Beer range varies 🄷
An old coaching inn, now a smart country hotel, close to the Southern Upland Way. The interior includes a wood-panelled bar with an area for table seating, a half wood panelled lounge painted in neutral colours and a richly-decorated dining room. The walls throughout are festooned with sporting and historical prints. There are no electronic distractions. Children and dogs are welcome.
Q❀⇄◐◑♿⛺🚌(29)♣P

Melrose

Burt's Hotel

Market Square, TD6 9PL
⏲ 11-2, 5-11; 12-2, 6-11 Sun
☎ (01896) 822285

SCOTLAND

Caledonian Deuchars IPA, 80/-; guest beer Ⓗ
Elegant, family run hotel in the main square. The decor of this plush lounge bar reflects the country sporting interests of many of the clientele. The restaurant serves excellent food but is expensive. The bar menu offers cheaper options. Children are welcome. Melrose Abbey and the rugby ground are close by and National Cycle Route 1 passes the door. Real ale may not be available, and reservations are essential, during the Melrose 7's rugby week. ♨Q🛏◖◗▲🚌P

King's Arms Hotel
High Street, TD6 9PB
⏲ 11-midnight; 12-11 Sun
☎ (01896) 822143
Caledonian Deuchars IPA; Tetley Bitter; guest beer Ⓗ
Old coaching inn dating from 1793. The bar has a wooden floor and church pew seating, and is decorated with rugby memorabilia and old local photographs. There is a large-screen TV for sports events. The quieter lounge is comfortably furnished and has a lovely old carved door set into the ceiling. There are also dining rooms upstairs. National Cycle Route 1 passes the door. Children are welcome in the lounge until 8pm. ♨Q🛏◖◗⊟▲🚌♣P

Paxton

Cross Inn
TD15 1TE (off B6460)
⏲ 11-2.30, 6.30-midnight (closed Mon); 12.30-2.30, 6.30-midnight Sun
☎ (01289) 386267
Beer range varies Ⓗ
Pleasant, friendly village pub, circa 1870s, named after the recently restored old cross outside. The real ale is usually from Wylam, Mordue or Atlas. Planned changes in 2006 will link the bar and dining room by a shared bar; meals are served and children welcome in both areas. A covered, outdoor space provides refuge for smokers. ♨✿◖◗⊟♿🚌♣P

Peebles

Bridge Inn
Portbrae, EH45 8AW
⏲ 11-midnight; 12.30-midnight Sun
☎ (01721) 720589
Caledonian Deuchars IPA; guest beers Ⓗ
Cheerful, welcoming single-room town centre local, also known as the Trust. The mosaic entrance floor shows it was once the Tweedside Inn. The bright, comfortable bar is decorated with jugs, bottles, memorabilia of outdoor pursuits and photos of old Peebles. The Gents is superb, with well-maintained original Twyford Adamant urinals. The house beer is Atlas Three Sisters rebadged as Tweedside Ale. Awarded CAMRA Borders Pub of the Year 2004/05/06. ▲🚌(62)♣

Reston

Red Lion
Main Street, TD14 5JP
⏲ 12-2.30 (not Mon), 5.30-11; 12-1am Sat (summer); 12.30-11 (12.30-2.30, 5.30-11 winter) Sun
☎ (01890) 761266 🌐 a1redlionreston.co.uk
Beer range varies Ⓗ
Comfortable pub well signposted from the A1. An area is set aside for dining and the menu is good and varied. The lounge bar features wooden bench seating, a real fire and an intriguing collection of vintage cameras. The beer is usually from a Scottish brewery and is sometimes 1714, an exclusive ale from nearby Peelwalls. Wheat beers are also available. Children are welcome. Food availability in January is limited to Saturday and Sunday lunch. ♨Q✿🛏◖◗♿🚌(253)♣P

Selkirk

Heatherlie House Hotel
Heatherlie Park, TD7 5AL (½ mile W of centre)
⏲ 12-11 (midnight Fri & Sat); 12.30-midnight Sun
☎ (01750) 721200 🌐 heatherlie.freeserve.co.uk
Beer range varies Ⓗ
A family-run hotel in tranquil surroundings. Once a Victorian villa, it retains a stately air of grandeur with a magnificent hand-carved fireplace depicting barn owls in the entrance and beautiful cornices. The bar, which is also a dining area, is comfortable and airy, with views through the large bay windows to the gardens. In winter the single real ale is often from Broughton or Caledonian. In summer a choice is available. Children are welcome until 8pm. ♨✿🛏◖◗▲🚌♣P

Town Yetholm

Plough Hotel
High Street, TD5 8RF
⏲ 11-midnight (1am Fri & Sat); 11-midnight Sun
☎ (01573) 420215
Beer range varies Ⓗ
Friendly village local dating from 1710 set in idyllic surrounds near the end of the Pennine Way. The pleasant public bar has modern Tudor-style decor and a real fire. A functional games room has a pool table and video machine. There is also a small, pleasantly decorated dining room. Horse brasses and memorabilia of the gypsy king and queen adorn the walls. Children are welcome until 8.30pm. ♨✿🛏◖◗⊟♿▲🚌♣P

Tweedsmuir

Crook Inn ☆
ML12 6QN (on A701)
⏲ 11-11 (closed last 2 weeks Jan); 12-11 Sun
☎ (01899) 880272 🌐 crookinn.co.uk
Beer range varies Ⓗ
Originally dating back to 1604 and undergoing much change, the current building is a fine example of 1930s Art Deco, and listed in CAMRA's National Inventory. The bar, in the older part of the building at the back, retains its splendid fireplace, although the fire is now gas powered. Large, well appointed lounge areas are at the front. The beer is usually from Broughton Brewery. Children and dogs are welcome. ♨Q✿🛏◖◗⊟♣P

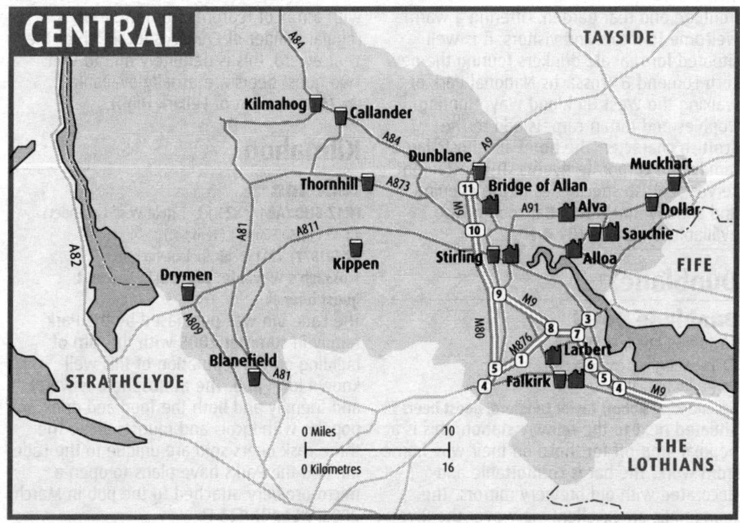

Authority areas covered Clackmannan UA, Falkirk UA, Stirling UA

Blanefield

Carbeth Inn

Stockiemuir Road, G63 9AY (on A809 N of Milngavie, near B821 jct) OSNS524791

11 (12.30 Sun)-11 (midnight Fri & Sat)

(01360) 770002

Beer range varies H

A busy pub with a sunny outside patio, popular with locals including fishermen and farm workers. The main bar has an unobtrusive TV screen, two wood-burning stoves and hosts regular live music and a Sunday quiz. There is a spacious restaurant which features occasional gastronomic events. The proximity to Glasgow makes it a convenient stop for bikers and those walking in nearby Mugdock Country Park or over the Whangie – a hill with impressive Loch Lomondside views. P

Callander

Waverley Hotel

88-92 Main Street, FK17 8BD

11-midnight (1am Fri & Sat)

(01877) 330245 thewaverleycallander.com

Beer range varies H

Renowned for its quality and range of good ales, the Waverley also hosts two beer festivals each year in September and December. There are usually four ales available, increasing to around eight, including some from mainland Europe, at the height of the season. Ideally sited for tourists, on the whisky trail in beautiful Perthshire, the pub is also well known for its good food using mainly local ingredients. Q

Dollar

Castle Campbell Hotel

11 Bridge Street, FK14 7DE

11-11.30 (1am Fri, midnight Sat); 12.30-11 Sun

(01259) 742519 castle-campbell.co.uk

Caledonian Deuchars IPA; Harviestoun Bitter & Twisted H

Pleasant hotel with a refurbished lounge bar and two further lounges, situated in the village of Dollar at the foot of the Ochil Hills. The historic Castle Campbell overlooks the village at the top of Dollar Glen and can be reached either by an excellent walk up the glen or via a steep road. The hotel is well presented with interesting wall decorations. A large range of whiskies is on offer in the lounge bar. Q P

Strathallan Hotel

6 Chapel Place, FK14 7DW (between Main Street and Dollar Academy)

12-2.30 (not Mon & Tue), 5-11.30; 12-midnight Sat & Sun

(01259) 742205

Harviestoun Bitter & Twisted; guest beer H

Small, country hotel situated in the lovely village of Dollar, close to the glen. The new owner has renovated the bar/restaurant and the patio garden to create a smoking area outside. The function room is suitable for up to 100 guests. National Trust Castle Campbell is a short walk away – dating back to the 15th century, it was burned by Cromwell's troops in mid 17th century and is still worth a visit. P

Drymen

Winnock Hotel

The Square, G63 0BL

11 (midnight Sun)-midnight (1am Fri & Sat)

(01360) 660245 winnockhotel.com

Caledonian Deuchars IPA, 80/-; guest beers H

An 18th-century coaching inn with a large

INDEPENDENT BREWERIES

Bridge of Allan Bridge of Allan
Devon Sauchie
Eglesbrech Falkirk
Harviestoun Alva
Stirling Stirling
Tryst Larbert
Williams Alloa

SCOTLAND

frontage and rear garden. Offering a warm welcome to locals and visitors, it is well situated for real ale drinkers touring the new Loch Lomond & Trossachs National Park or walking the West Highland Way. Hunting trophies and tartan carpets add to the Scottish character. The hotel also hosts large family and corporate events. The restaurant serves Scottish specialities in the evening and Sunday lunchtime. Bar food is also available. ⛰♉❀⇔◑♣P

Dunblane

Dunblane Hotel

10 Stirling Road, FK15 9EP
⏲ 11-midnight (1am Fri & Sat)
☎ (01786) 822178
Greene King Abbot; Taylor Landlord; guest beers Ⓗ
Situated next to the railway station, this is a popular stop-off for those on their way home from work. The bar is comfortable and decorated with old brewery mirrors. The lounge has an excellent view over the River Allan. A good range of national and micro beers are on offer. There are usually three frequently changing guest ales on tap, so it is always worth a visit just to try out what is on offer. Dunblane is well known for golfing and this is a relaxing place to stay if you like cosy surroundings. ❀⇔◑⊟♿⇌♣P

Tappit Hen

Kirk Lane, FK15 0AL (opp. cathedral)
⏲ 11 (12.30 Sun)-midnight (1am Fri & Sat)
☎ (01786) 825226
Caledonian Deuchars IPA; guest beers Ⓗ
Real old-fashioned pub, popular with locals and discerning drinkers, with eight ales on handpump during summer months. A single bar room, it is partitioned into smaller areas by the use of screens. The town, with an imposing cathedral, is in an ideal position to visit Gleneagles and the Highlands. A five-minute walk from Dunblane station. ◑♿⇌♣

Falkirk

Union Inn

Lock 16, Portdownie Road, Camelon, FK1 4QZ (next to lock 16 on the Forth-Clyde Canal)
⏲ 11-11.20 (12.30am Fri & Sat); 11-11.20 Sun
☎ (01324) 613839
Harviestoun Bitter & Twisted; guest beer Ⓗ
The Union Inn, situated on the Forth & Clyde Canal, lies just a mile from the Falkirk Wheel – the world's first and only rotating boat lift. This fine Georgian building stands on the point where the Union Canal used to join the Forth & Clyde canal. The Inn offers a good selection of meals and real ales.
❀⇔◑♿

Wheatsheaf Inn

16 Baxters Wynd, FK1 1PF
⏲ 11 (12.30 Sun)-11 (12.30am Sat)
☎ (01324) 623716
Caledonian Deuchars IPA; guest beers Ⓗ
A firm favourite with locals and real ale enthusiasts alike, this public house dates from the late 18th century and retains much of its character. The bar is wood panelled with a mix of features from the past. A regular winner of CAMRA's local Pub of the Year award, this is definitely one to visit. Two guest beers are usually available.
⇌ (Grahamston or Falkirk High)

Kilmahog

Lade Inn

FK17 8HD (A84/A821 jct, 1 mile W of Callander)
⏲ 12 (12.30 Sun)-11 (1am Sat)
☎ (01877) 330152 🌐 theladeinn.com
Trossach's Waylade, Ladeback, Ladeout; guest beer Ⓗ
The Lade Inn was purchased by the Park family in summer 2005 with the aim of building on the reputation of this well known local pub. The atmosphere is warm and friendly and both the food and drink are popular with locals and tourists alike. The three cask beers sold are unique to the Lade Inn and the Parks have plans to open a micro-brewery attached to the pub in March 2006. ⛰♉◑⊟♿P

Kippen

Cross Keys Hotel

Main Street, FK8 3DN (on B822)
⏲ 12 (12.30 Sun)-11
☎ (01786) 870293
Harviestoun Bitter & Twisted Ⓗ
A comfortable olde-worlde pub with a proper old-fashioned feel. The interior consists of a number of small rooms used mainly for dining, a small bar and a larger lounge/restaurant. Situated in an area surrounded by lovely countryside, it is ideally placed for tourists visiting Stirling.
⛰Q♉❀⇔◑⊟♿⛺♣P

Muckhart

Inn at Muckhart

Main Street, FK14 7JN
⏲ 11 (12.30 Sun)-11 (midnight Fri & Sat)
☎ (01259) 781324
Devon Original, Thick Black, Pride Ⓗ
Fine example of an old coaching inn operating as a pub and restaurant. The pub sells Devon Ales, brewed at its sister pub, the Mansfield in Sauchie, and has a reputation for good pub food. Located in a small country village at the edge of the Ochil Hills, this olde-worlde pub is ideal for hill walkers and tourists alike.
⛰Q❀◑♿⛺P⊡

Sauchie

Mansfield Arms

7 Main Street, FK10 3JR (25 yds off the main road through Sauchie)
⏲ 11 (12.30 Sun)-11.30 (12.30am Fri & Sat)
☎ (01259) 722020
Devon Original, Thick Black, Pride Ⓗ
The Mansfield Arms is located in the centre of Sauchie, a one-time mining town. Home of Devon Ales, the brewery stands behind the pub and tours can be arranged. The lounge/restaurant is frequented mainly by families and those looking for good value,

quality meals. The pub is located in a convenient part of the country for touring and golf. ◑⊟♿⛺P🍺

Stirling

Portcullis Hotel

Castle Wynd, FK8 1EG (next to Stirling Castle esplanade)
⏲ 11.30 (12.30 Sun)-midnight
☎ (01786) 472290
Orkney Dark Island; guest beer Ⓗ
Built in 1787 as a grammar school, the Portcullis is a quiet but popular bar, situated next to Stirling Castle. Reasonably priced food is served; booking is recommended for the evenings and weekends during the tourist season as it becomes very busy. A sheltered walled garden is available for dining and drinking alfresco. A peaceful pub that is popular with locals and tourists, the relaxed atmosphere is enhanced in the evening with candle-lit tables.
⚑❀⛟◑⇌P

Settle Inn

91 St Mary's Wynd, FK8 1BU
⏲ 3 (12 Sat & Sun)-midnight (1am Fri & Sat)
☎ (01768) 474609
Beer range varies Ⓗ
Dating from 1733, the Settle Inn lives up to its name – settle down with a pint next to the cosy fire and you may not want to leave, despite the ghosts that are rumoured to have made the pub their home! Situated on a route descending from the castle, this pub provides a friendly welcome to locals and visitors alike. Excellent community links, a Sunday night quiz and a Thursday night open mike session all contribute to a lively atmosphere. ⚑⇌

Thornhill

Lion & Unicorn Hotel

Main Street, FK8 3PJ
⏲ 12 (12.30 Sun)-midnight
☎ (01786) 850204
Beer range varies Ⓗ
A lovely old pub situated on the main street in the village. The interior is divided into a number of atmospheric lounges each with huge open fires, wood panelled walls and old furniture. The ale changes regularly, particularly in summer. Situated in a tourist area, it is close to Stirling and the Trossachs.
⚑Q⛟◑⊟⛺♣P

SCOTLAND

DUMFRIES & GALLOWAY

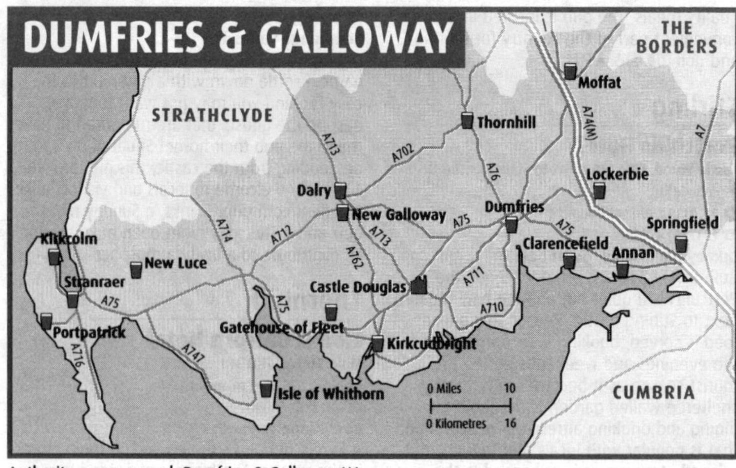

Authority area covered: Dumfries & Galloway UA

Annan

Bluebell Inn

10 High Street, DG12 6AG

11-11 (midnight Thu-Sat); 12.30-11 Sun

(01461) 202385

Caledonian Deuchars IPA; guest beer H

Fine old coaching inn retaining original panelling and features from its time as a Gretna & District State Management Scheme house. This friendly pub offers the best selection of beers between England and Dumfries, with three guest ales from both sides of the border. It also has pool, darts and a large-screen television. During the summer you can drink outside in the rear courtyard.

Clarencefield

Farmers Inn

Main Street, DG1 4NF (on B724)

11-2.30, 6-11.30 (12.30am Fri); 12-12.30am Sat; 12.30-11.30 Sun

(01387) 870675 farmersinn.co.uk

Beer range varies H

Late 16th-century coaching inn with a varied history. The current building opened in 1983 with the original bar area still in use. It was the post office and also housed the village's first telephone exchange. Robert Burns was a customer when he came on a visit to the Brow Well for health reasons. Nearby tourist attractions include the world's first savings bank at Ruthwell and the 8th-century Ruthwell Cross.

Dalry

Clachan Inn

8-10 Main Street, DG7 3UW (on A713)

11 (12 Sun)-midnight

(01644) 430241 clachaninn.com

Greene King Abbot; guest beer H

The Clachan Inn is set in the picturesque village of St. John's Town of Dalry, which straddles the A713. The area has a growing reputation for country pursuits and walkers are particularly welcome at this stopping off point along the Southern Upland Way. A year round special walkers' rate is available for accommodation. The pub has a varied menu and prides itself on using local produce as much as possible. There are usually two real ales on handpump. The bus service from Castle Douglas is limited.

Dumfries

Cavens Arms

20 Buccleuch Street, DG1 2AH

11-11 (12.30am Fri & Sat); 12.30-12.30am Sun

(01387) 252896

Caledonian Deuchars IPA; Greene King Abbot; guest beer H

The Cavens Arms is a welcome addition to the real ale scene in Dumfries. Four or more guests from all parts of the country supplement two regular ales. Beer festivals, held several times a year, are well publicised in the local area. Good value meals are available all day on Saturday, but not served on Monday. The pub hosts regular quiz nights and if you are lucky you may chance upon one of the occasional live traditional music sessions.

New Bazaar

39 Whitesands, DG1 2RS

11-11 (midnight Thu-Sat); 11-11 Sun

(01387) 268776

newbazaardumfries.co.uk

McEwan's 80/-; Sulwath Knockendoch; guest beer H

Traditional pub boasting a superb Victorian bar. The lounge is warmed by a welcoming fire during the winter months and benefits from great views across the River Nith. A back room is available for meetings. There is plentiful free parking in the nearby public car parks. It is conveniently located for a number of tourist attractions including the Camera Obscura and the Burns Centre.

INDEPENDENT BREWERIES

Sulwath Castle Douglas

Robert the Bruce

81-83 Buccleuch Street, DG1 IDJ

11 (12.30 Sun)-midnight

(01387) 270320

Caledonian Deuchars IPA; guest beer

Former Episcopalian church originally consecrated in 1817 and sold 50 years later to local Methodists. It remained empty and roofless for many years before a sympathetic conversion by Wetherspoon. With its relaxed atmosphere the Bruce has quickly established itself as a favourite meeting place, handy for the town centre. Beers from independent Scottish brewers can be found among the guests.

Gatehouse of Fleet

Masonic Arms

Ann Street, DG7 2HU

11.30-2.30, 5.30-11.30 daily

(01557) 814335 themasonic-arms.co.uk

Beer range varies

The Masonic Arms bar, brasserie and restaurant is in the picturesque town of Gatehouse. The coast is nearby with cliffs and sandy beaches to explore. Exposed beams are a feature in the comfortable bar area. Sulwath brews the house beer, Masonic Boom. Renowned for its food, meals are served in the bar as well as the conservatory and restaurant. Local CAMRA Pub of the Year in 2005.

Isle of Whithorn

Steampacket Inn

Harbour Row, DG8 8LL (on A750)

11(6 winter Mon-Thu)-11 (1am Fri; midnight Sat); 12-11 Sun

(01988) 500334

Courage Best Bitter; guest beer

This attractive harbourside inn caters for locals and tourists alike. There is a small public bar with stone-clad walls, a large fireplace and flagstone floor. The larger lounge has a tree trunk pillar. Picture windows give good views of the harbour which is popular with touring sailing craft. Both the Isle of Man and the Lake District can be seen from this attractive and historic village. There is a varied menu which features mainly local produce. Local Pub of the Year 2004.

Kirkcolm

Blue Peter Hotel

23 Main Street, DG9 0NL (on A718, 5 miles N of Stranraer)

6-11.30 (closed Wed in winter); 12-midnight Sat; 12.30-11.30 Sun

(01776) 853221 thebluepeterhotel.co.uk

Beer range varies

Since coming under new ownership this hotel has undergone major refurbishment of a high standard. Both lounge and public bars display beer memorabilia – look out for the model beer trucks and tankers. With rotating guest ales and a selection of over 70 malt whiskies, this is a real oasis in an ale desert. Kirkcolm is ideally situated for golfers, fishermen and bird watchers. It is served by NO. 408 bus from Stranraer.

Kirkcudbright

Masonic Arms

19 Castle Street, DG6 4JA

11 (12.30 Sun)-midnight

(01557) 330517

Beer range varies

This small, sociable bar is welcoming to both locals and visitors. The tables and bar fronts are made from old malt whisky casks from Islay's Bowmore Distillery. One real ale is available throughout the year with up to two more during the summer months. The Masonic also offers draught Budvar, a selection of 30 bottled beers from all over the world, and 100 malt whiskies. The town is picturesque with a variety of tourist attractions.

Lockerbie

Somerton House Hotel

35 Carlisle Road, DG11 2DR

11-11 daily

(01576) 202583 somertonhotel.co.uk

Caledonian Deuchars IPA

Situated on the B723 on the southern outskirts of this ancient royal burgh, the hotel is about a mile from the A74(M) northbound junction 18. The real ale can be found in the comfortable lounge bar and is available all year round. The atmosphere is quiet and relaxed. Meals are served in the restaurant.

Moffat

Balmoral Hotel

High Street, DG10 9DL

11 (12.30 Sun)-11

(01683) 220288 thebalmoralhotel-moffat.co.uk

Beer range varies

Traditional hotel with a long lounge bar serving a choice of ales, usually including one from the Broughton Brewery. Good value meals, served from noon until 9pm, include vegetarian options. Moffat is a good starting point for the scenic route to Edinburgh via the famous Devil's Beef Tub. There are good walking routes in the area and the Southern Upland Way passes nearby.

Black Bull Hotel

Church Gate, DG10 9EG

11-midnight (11 Sun)

(01683) 220206 blackbullmoffat.co.uk

McEwan's 80/-; Theakston Best Bitter; guest beer

Historic inn dating from the 16th century, with two bars both serving two regular ales plus up to two guests. The lounge bar with adjoining Burns Room is in the main building. Across the courtyard is the public bar, known as the Railway Bar, which is furnished with railway memorabilia. The hotel has 12 modern en-suite guest rooms. Ample parking is provided by nearby public car parks.

New Galloway

Cross Keys Hotel

High Street, DG7 3RN

12-2, 6-11; 12-10.30 Sun

☎ (01644) 420494 crosskeys-newgalloway.co.uk

Beer range varies Ⓗ

The Cross Keys has a warm, friendly and welcoming atmosphere. Situated close to the north end of Loch Ken and on the edge of the Galloway Forest Park, the secluded village and surrounding area offer many attractions including fishing, sailing and walking. Usually two real ales are stocked in winter and three in summer. Houston Brewery beers are regular guests.

⚠Q❀⇌◑▲P

New Luce

Kenmuir Arms Hotel

31 Main Street, DG8 0AJ (8 miles N of Glenluce along old military road)

5 (12 Wed & Thu)-11; 12-midnight Fri & Sat; 12.30-11.30 Sun (hours may vary in winter)

☎ (01581 600218) kenmuir-arms-hotel.com

Beer range varies Ⓗ

Small family-run hotel in a remote village on the River Luce. It is a popular stop for walkers on the nearby Southern Upland Way. Accommodation is available in the hotel or static caravans and there are camping facilities in the grounds. The bar serves up to two guest ales, one normally from the Houston Brewery range. An autumn beer festival is held every year. Q❀⇌◑▲♣

Portpatrick

Harbour House Hotel

53 Main Street, DJ9 8JW

11-11 (midnight Thu-Sat);12-10.30 Sun

☎ (01776) 810456 thedownshirearms.co.uk

Caledonian Deuchars IPA; guest beers Ⓗ

Classy lounge bar with a nautical theme overlooking the harbour. It has a fine selection of malt whiskies, a real fire, banquettes and fine large tables. Above the bar there is illuminated glass depicting local scenes. Seating outside in summer makes the most of the fantastic views.

⚠Q❀⇌◑▲P

Springfield

Queen's Head

Main Street, DG16 5EH

5 (12 Sat)-11 (midnight Thu & Fri); 12.30-11 Sun

☎ (01461) 337173

Caledonian Deuchars IPA Ⓗ

This single-room village pub, although slightly off the beaten track, is actually little more than a stone's throw from Gretna, wedding capital of the country. It is close to the A74(M) and about a mile from Gretna Green railway station. There is one real ale served in this friendly, unpretentious local. Note that there is no lunchtime opening on weekdays.

❀♣P

Stranraer

Ruddicot Hotel

London Road, DG9 8AJ (on A75, 400 yds E of centre)

12-2.30, 5-11 (midnight Thu-Sat); 12.30-2.30, 6.30-11 Sun

☎ (01776) 702684

Beer range varies Ⓗ

A former girls' school close to the Irish ferry terminal and Stranraer FC's football ground, this is now a small, friendly, family hotel. The bar retains traditional wooden screens that divide it into what were originally the eating and drinking areas. Popular with locals, it serves good value pub snacks and meals (lunches only).

Q❀⇌◐⇌(Harbour)P

Thornhill

Buccleuch & Queensberry Hotel

112 Drumlanrig Street, DG3 5LU

11 (12.30 Sun)-midnight (1am Thu-Sat)

☎ (01848) 330215 buccleuchhotel.co.uk

Caledonian 80/-; guest beer Ⓗ

You may well find yourself swapping stories with friendly locals or visitors from all over Europe and beyond in this cheery hotel. The food is always hearty – see the blackboard for special dishes. The nearby Drumlanrig Castle is worth a visit and regularly hosts special events. The area is an ideal location for country pursuits.

⚠Q⇌◑♿P

New pub opening hours

The Licensing Act of November 2005 for England and Wales gave pub owners the ability to apply for more flexible and extended opening hours from the licensing authorities. The most obvious change has been that many pubs now stay open until midnight or later at weekends. The experience of the first 10 months of the new law has been that some pubs have scaled down their opening hours where they have found there is insufficient demand to remain open until midnight or later. The opening hours for pubs listed in the guide have been treble checked before going to press, but readers planning to make journeys to pubs are advised to phone and check current hours.

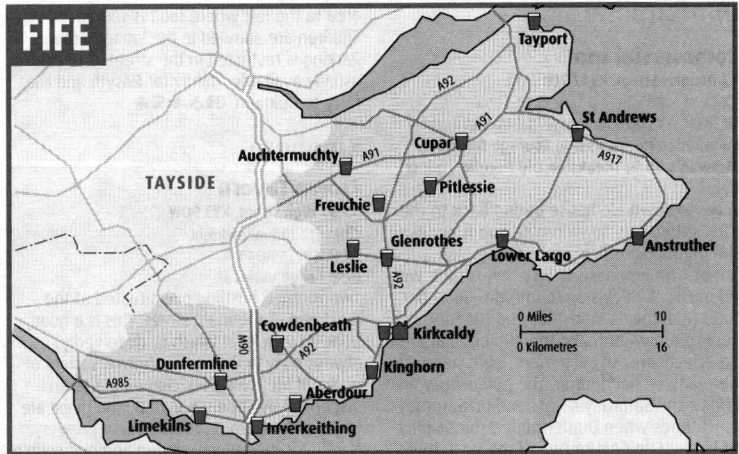

Authority area covered: Fife UA

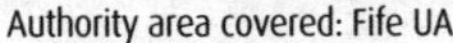

Aberdour

Aberdour Hotel

38 High Street, KY3 0SW
4-11; 3-11.45 Fri; 11-11.45 Sat; 12-11 Sun
☎ (01383) 860325 aberdourhotel.com
Caledonian Deuchars IPA; guest beer H
Small family-run hotel in a popular tourist town on the River Forth with separate public and lounge bars, the latter used mainly as a dining room. Originally a coaching inn, the old stables in the courtyard have been converted into bedrooms. One handpump is in constant use with a second serving occasional guest ales. Wheelchair access is from the courtyard.

Anstruther

Dreel Tavern

16 High Street, KY10 3DL
11 (12.30 Sun)-midnight
☎ (01333) 310727
Caledonian Deuchars IPA; Greene King Old Speckled Hen; guest beers H
Old stone building in the East Neuk of Fife with beamed ceilings, crow step gables and a pan tile roof. It started life as a coaching inn in the 16th century and was reputedly visited by James V. The public and lounge bars are separated by an open fire; the conservatory provides a pleasant dining and family area. The pub can be very busy at lunchtimes and early evenings when good quality meals, including locally caught fresh seafood, are served. One regular and two guest beers are dispensed from three handpumps at this previous CAMRA Fife Pub of the Year.
Q

Auchtermuchty

Cycle Tavern

75 Burnside, KY14 7AJ
11-11; 12.30-midnight Sun
☎ (01337) 828326
Caledonian Deuchars IPA; guest beer H
Friendly two-room pub in the town probably best known as the birthplace of Jimmy Shand and The Proclaimers. The bar has a pool table and a screen for sport. The sporting nature of the pub community is evident from the cabinets of trophies on show. The more comfortable lounge is busy at meal times, serving a good selection of keenly-priced home-made food.
P

Cowdenbeath

Crown Hotel

6 High Street, KY5 9NA
11 (12.30 Sun)-midnight
☎ (01383) 610540
Beer range varies H
Spacious single-roomed pub recently refurbished by new owners. It is situated at the west end of the High Street in this ex-mining town famous for being the home of the 'Blue Brazil' (the local football team so named, sarcastically, for its ineptitude). The bar has a raised, railed off area for a pool table. One beer, generally from Inveralmond Brewery, is usually available with a second handpump in use at busy times.
P

Cupar

Golf Tavern

11 South Road, KY15 5JF
11-midnight (1am Fri & Sat); 12.20-11 Sun
☎ (01334) 654233
Caledonian Deuchars IPA; guest beer H
Small traditional bar with a modern interior, part of a terrace on the main road south out of Cupar. The main room has a seating area to the right of the main entrance, with bar counter to the left. This friendly local usually offers one beer during the week, two at the weekend, with good quality home-cooked bar meals available at lunchtime. Q

INDEPENDENT BREWERIES

Fyfe Kirkaldy

SCOTLAND

Dunfermline

Commercial Inn

13 Douglas Street, KY12 7EB
11-11 (midnight Fri & Sat); 12.30-11 Sun
(01383) 733876 commercialinn.co.uk
Caledonian Deuchars IPA; Courage Directors; McEwan's 80/-; Theakston Old Peculier; guest beers H
A well-known ale house dating back to the 1820s, this cosy town centre pub is opposite the main post office, north of the high street. The emphasis is on conversation with no music or television to intrude. Good bar food (eve meals Mon-Thu) and friendly service are what make the pub popular with an eclectic mix of customers. Eight beers are normally on handpump. The pub is busy on Friday and Saturday nights and on Saturday lunchtimes when Dunfermline Athletic play at home. Fife CAMRA pub of the year 2005.

Freuchie

Albert Tavern

2 High Street, KY15 7EX
11-2, 5-11; 12-1am Fri & Sat; 12.30-11 Sun
(01337) 857192
Beer range varies H
Family friendly village local now under new management. The pub was reputedly a coaching inn when nearby Falkland Palace was a royal residence; an old photograph shows the property as a tavern in the 19th century. Both bar and lounge have beamed ceilings and the bar has wainscot panelling. A small restaurant upstairs seats 20. Three handpumps offer guest beers from around the UK. Winner of CAMRA Scottish Pub of the Year and national Pub of the Year runner up in 2002. Q

Glenrothes

Golden Acorn

1 North Street, KY7 5NA (next to bus station)
11 (12.30 Sun)-midnight
(01592) 751175
Caledonian Deuchars IPA; guest beers H
Recently refurbished, this JD Wetherspoon pub is situated next to the main shopping centre of the new town. The main bar area is split level with patio windows along one side, which are opened up during the summer. There is a smaller room and dining area to the left of the bar. A selection of five ales and one real cider are served from the six handpumps. Children are welcome for meals until 6pm.
P

Inverkeithing

Burgh Arms

16-22 High Street, KY11 1NN
11-11 (midnight Fri; 11.45 Sat); 12.30-11 Sun
(01383) 410384
Beer range varies H
Busy town centre bar with a friendly atmosphere. The bar is situated centrally with a pool area to the right and a lounge area to the left where food is served. Children are allowed in the lounge area. Parking is restricted in the street. One beer is usually available. Handy for Rosyth and the ferry to Belgium.

Kinghorn

Crown Tavern

55-57 High Street, KY3 9UW
11 (12.30 Sun)-midnight
(01592) 890340
Beer range varies H
Two-roomed bustling pub situated at the west end of the main street. This is a good, honest town local which is, deservedly, always busy with regulars from a variety of walks of life. Two ever-changing ales are dispensed by cheery bar staff. The guest ale is generally from a Scottish micro-brewery. Handy for the railway station and golf course.

Ship Tavern

2 Bruce Street, KY3 9JT
12 (12.30 Sun)-midnight
(01592) 890655 shiptavern.com
Caledonian Deuchars IPA; guest beer H
Now under new management, this is one of the older buildings in Kinghorn, originally built as a house for Bible John who printed the first bibles in Scotland. The unremarkable entrance door, facing the main road, opens into a fine timber-panelled interior with a long bar counter and ornate gantry. The small jug bar has probably one of the finest surviving traditional interiors in Fife. A brass pressure gauge at one end of the gantry is evidence of an old water engine for dispensing the beer. Meals are not served during the winter.

Kirkcaldy

Harbour Bar

471-475 High Street, KY1 1JL
11-3, 5-midnight; 11-midnight Thu-Sat; 12.30-midnight Sun
(01592) 264270 e-fife.com/harbourbar
Beer range varies H
Situated on the ground floor of a tenement building, the bar is described by regulars as a 'village local in the middle of town'. The public bar is decorated with murals depicting the town's whaling past and the comfortable lounge features model sailing ships in glass cases. Six handpumps sell up to 20 beers each week from micros all over Britain including those from the Fyfe Brewery which is situated to the rear of the pub. A fine selection of malt whiskies is also available. CAMRA Scottish Pub of the Year in 2000 when it was also a national runner up.

Leslie

Burns Tavern

184 High Street, KY6 7DD
12 (11 Fri & Sat)-midnight; 12.30-midnight Sun
(01592) 741345

Taylor Landlord; guest beers H
Typical Scottish two-room main-street local. The public bar is on two levels: the lower lively and friendly, the upper with a large-screen TV and pool table with football memorabilia on the walls. The lounge bar is quieter and more spacious. Pub quizzes are held on Wednesday and Thursday evenings and dominoes/darts/pool competitions on Sunday afternoon. One guest, sometimes two, generally from a small independent brewery, is available alongside Taylor's Landlord. A regular folk and blues music festival is held during the autumn.

Limekilns

Ship Inn

Halketts Hall, KY11 3HJ (on promenade)
11-11 (midnight Fri & Sat); 12.30-11 Sun
(01383) 872247
Beer range varies H
Excellent single-roomed pub in a historic village on the Forth. This ever-improving outlet offers an extensive and varied lunch menu as well as a good selection of beer mainly from Scottish micro-breweries and occasional real cider. The outdoor seating area provides wonderful views across the Forth.

Lower Largo

Railway Tavern

1 Station Wynd, KY8 6BU
11 (12.30 Sun)-midnight
(01333) 320239
Beer range varies H
Small two-room pub, close to the harbour, with a nautical theme. The beers usually rotate and include Caledonian Deuchars, Fuller's London Pride, Orkney Dark Island and Taylor Landlord. A focal point for this attractive coastal hamlet, the pub has a quiet room at the rear of the building, away from the main bar, suitable for meetings. Snacks are available lunchtimes and evenings. There is no longer a railway nearby – Dr Beeching saw to that in the 1960s. Q

Pitlessie

Village Inn

Cupar Road, KY15 7SU
11-2, 5-midnight; 11-midnight Fri & Sat; 12.30-midnight Sun
(01337) 830595
Caledonian Deuchars IPA; guest beer H
From the outside this is a typical Scottish village pub; inside the basic interior has the feel of a bothy with bare stonework, an open fire, candles on the tables and bare wooden tables for dining. Good restaurant-standard food is available at all times. Several rooms, one with an old Raeburn cooker, provide space for families and pub games; there is a large function room at the rear. Three handpumps offer an ever change range of beers.
Q P

St Andrews

Aikmans Cellar Bar

32 Bell Street, KY16 9UK
6-midnight; 1-1am Thu-Sat; 6-midnight Sun
(01334) 477425 cellarbar.co.uk
Beer range varies H
Basement lounge bar, a regular in the Guide since 1987, selling a good selection of real ales from all over the UK together with a variety of continental bottled beers. The rolled copper bar top was salvaged from the White Star liner Oceanic (the same shipping line as the Titanic). Opening hours outside term time can vary: the bar is closed most lunchtimes but cask ales are available on request in the bistro upstairs. Regular music and occasional beer festivals are held (see website for details). The pub can get very busy with students during term time.

Central Bar

77-79 Market Street, KY16 9NU
11-11.45 (11-1am Fri & Sat); 12.30-11.45 Sun
(01334) 478296
Caledonian Deuchars IPA; Greene King Old Speckled Hen; McEwan's 80/-; Theakston Best Bitter, Old Peculier; guest beers H
Student-oriented town-centre pub that is also popular with locals. It has a Victorian-style island bar, large windows and ornate mirrors creating a late 19th-century feel. This is the only pub in town that serves food after 9pm. Pavement tables are available, weather permitting.

Whey Pat Tavern

2 Argyle Street, KY16 9EX
11-11.30 (11.45 Fri & Sat); 12.30-11.30 Sun
(01334) 477740
Beer range varies H
Town centre pub on a busy road junction just outside the old town walls. There has been a hostelry on this site for several centuries, it was taken over by Belhaven in 2002 but minimal changes have been made. Unusually for St Andrews, this friendly, welcoming pub is popular with a mix of students, academics and townspeople. Superb sandwiches are freshly made to order at lunchtimes. Three handpumps offer an ever-changing range of beer from a wide variety of breweries.

Tayport

Bell Rock Tavern

4-6 Dalgleish Street, DD6 9BB
11-midnight (1am Thu-Sat); 12.30 to midnight Sun
(01382) 552388
Caledonian Deuchars IPA; guest beers H
Friendly, small town local opposite the picturesque harbour. This welcoming hostelry dispenses good cheer, fine ales and excellent value home-cooked meals such as mince and tatties at lunchtime. The bar is on three levels, each with a mainly nautical theme including old charts, photographs of ships and aircraft, old Dundee and the Tay ferries. One real ale served throughout the year increases to two in the summer and at busy times. An ideal stop-off for people on the Fife coastal path. Q

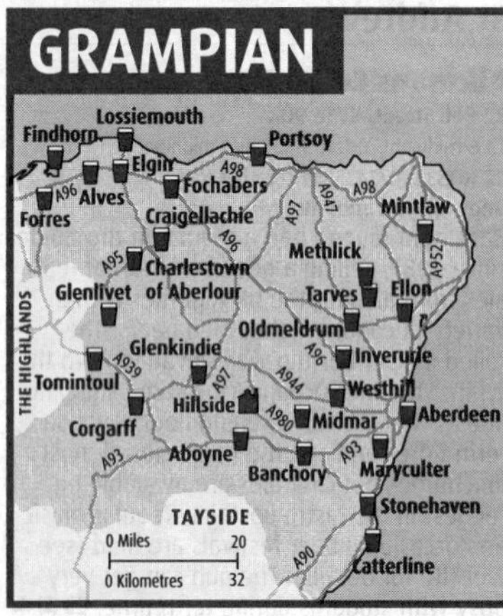

Authority areas covered: Aberdeenshire UA, City of Aberdeen UA, Moray UA

Aberdeen

Aitchies Ale House
11 Trinity Street, AB11 5LY
9am-10; 10-11 Fri & Sat; closed Sun
(01224) 575972
Orkney Dark Island H
Small street corner bar, renovated in 1994; the closest source of real ale you will find to the rail and bus stations in Aberdeen with hours to suit the early traveller. The service in here is of the old fashioned school and second to none, a reminder of how pubs used to be in the past. Food is of the snack variety but includes the recommended roast beef stovies. The top shelf holds a collection of whiskies including a variety of Bells special edition decanters. Wheelchair access to the toilets is by a slightly ramped incline within the small seated area.

Camerons Inn (Mas)
6-8 Little Belmont Street, AB10 9JG
11-midnight (1am Fri & Sat); 12.30-11 Sun
(01224) 644487
Caledonian Deuchars IPA; Greene King Abbot; Inveralmond Lia Fail; Orkney Dark Island H
Now part of Greene King's (formerly Belhaven's) Aberdeen empire and refurbished in 2002, this ancient inn boasts the most character-filled snug bar in the city, and is the longest serving outlet for real ale in Aberdeen since it returned to the area in 1976. The open plan rear lounge bar offers a contrast to the superb, tiny, listed public bar. There is now a small roof garden for smokers.

Carriages
101 Crown Street, AB11 6HH
11-2.30 (not Sat), 4.30-midnight; 6-11 Sun
(01224) 595440 brentwood-hotel.co.uk
Draught Bass; Boddingtons Bitter; Fuller's London Pride; guest beers H
One of Aberdeen's premier real ale outlets and multiple winner of the local CAMRA City Pub award. Part of the Brentwood Hotel, it has comfortable surroundings while avoiding the usual soulless nature of a hotel bar. The adjoining restaurant offers good food and lunches are also available in the bar. With 10 handpumps it offers an ever-changing selection of real ales. It can be busy midweek with business guests from the hotel, but weekends offers a more relaxed opportunity to enjoy the range of ales.

P

Grill ☆
213 Union Street, AB11 6BA
10-midnight (1am Fri & Sat); 12.30- midnight Sun
thegrillaberdeen.co.uk
Caledonian 80/-; guest beers H
A rare find in northern Scotland, this superbly preserved wood-panelled bar (the only CAMRA National Inventory pub north of Dundee) has slowly embraced the 20th century – it even has a ladies' toilet now! The largest local selection of malts can often be seen being sampled by touring musicians from the Music Hall across the road, popping in at half time from classical, rock or jazz gigs. A variety of snacks including stovies and pies is also available.

Old Blackfriars
52 Castle Street, AB11 5BB
10-midnight (1am Fri & Sat); 12.30-11 Sun
(01224) 581922
Belhaven Sandy Hunter's Ale; Caledonian Deuchars IPA, 80/-; Greene King Abbot; Inveralmond Ossian's Ale; guest beer H
Located on the Castlegate in the historic centre of the city, the pub has two levels, each with a bar, and plays unobtrusive background music, but there are no TV screens or sports coverage. Part of the Greene King chain (formerly Belhaven), it maintains a relatively independent choice of regular beers and normally serves one or two guest beers. The pub has a reputation for good food. Quiz night is the first Tuesday of the month. Themed beer festivals are held around four times a year.

Prince of Wales
7 St Nicholas Lane, AB10 1HF
10 (12 Sun)-midnight
(01224) 640597
Caledonian 80/-; Theakston Old Peculier; guest beers H
One of the oldest pubs in Aberdeen, the Prince maintains a friendly atmosphere with bare boards and flagstone floor in the bar, carpeted lounge and possibly the longest bar in Aberdeen. Eight handpumps serve a selection of ales with most Scottish micros and many English represented; the house beer is brewed by Inveralmond. Good value pub grub is available; folk music is played on Sunday evening. Despite a recent change of ownership this premier real ale pub maintains the high standards that have won it CAMRA City Pub award on several occasions. Q

INDEPENDENT BREWERIES
Hillside Hillside

Tilted Wig

55-56 Castle Street, AB11 5BA (opp. court house)
⏲ 12-midnight (1am Fri & Sat); 12.30-11 Sun
☎ (01224) 583248
Caledonian Deuchars IPA; Courage Directors; Marston's Pedigree; guest beer Ⓗ
Small city centre pub on the historic Castlegate, once called the Lang or Saloon Bar and, in the 1970s, the Welly Boot. The name comes from the proximity to the local Sheriff court, and the walls are adorned with pictures of wigged gentlemen with varying degrees of tilt. With a newly extended menu, food is now served until 10pm every day of the week. A large-screen television shows sporting events, with an alternative screen in an area to the front. The pub quiz is the first Tuesday of the month. Occasional live music is played.
◑◗ ⇌

Under The Hammer

11 North Silver Street, AB10 1RJ (off Golden Sq)
⏲ 5 (4 Fri; 2 Sat)-midnight (1am Thu-Sat); 6.30-11 Sun
☎ (01224) 640253
Caledonian Deuchars IPA; Inveralmond Ossian's Ale; guest beer Ⓗ
Atmospheric, comfortable and inviting subterranean wine bar situated next door to Auction House, hence the pub's name. Local artists' wares displayed on the walls are for sale if they take your fancy and the large noticeboard has posters advertising forthcoming events in town. Convenient for the Music Hall and His Majesty's Theatre, it may only open on Sunday if an event is on at either of these venues. An acoustic open mike session is held every second Monday. ⇌

Aboyne

Boat Inn

Charleston Road, AB34 5EL
(N bank of River Dee next to Aboyne Bridge)
⏲ 11-2.30, 5-11 (midnight Fri); 11-midnight Sat; 11-11 Sun
☎ (013398) 86137
Draught Bass; guest beers Ⓗ
Popular, riverside inn with a food-oriented lounge featuring a log-burning stove and spiral staircase leading to the upper dining area. Junior diners (and adults!) may request to see the model train, complete with sound effects, traverse the entire pub at picture-rail height upon completion of their meal. The local Rotary Club regularly meets here. Accommodation is provided in a self-catering flat. ♨Q⇆◑◗⊟♿⛺♣P

Alves

Crooked Inn

Burghead Road, IV30 8UU
⏲ 12-2, 5.30-11 (11.30 Fri; midnight Sat); 12.30-10.30 Sun
☎ (01343) 850646
Beer range varies Ⓗ
Food-led establishment, offering an extensive menu in the bar and restaurant. The bar is low-roofed and provides an ambience of cosy clutter. Popular with families from two nearby RAF bases, it can often feel busy. Beers tend to come from Scottish micros, especially Cairngorm.
♨◑◗🚌(10, 315)P

Banchory

Douglas Arms Hotel

22 High Street, AB31 5SR
⏲ 11-midnight (1am Fri & Sat) daily
☎ (01330) 822547 🌐 douglasarms.co.uk
Beer range varies Ⓗ
Small hotel with budget price accommodation. The public bar is a classic Scottish long bar with etched windows on to the High Street and vintage mirrors at either end. The lounge contains a large fireplace and a Chesterfield suite. It is in the east part of the hotel along with a function room and restaurant. Of the three ales, one is usually from a Scottish micro. There are benches outside overlooking the street for summer drinking. Pool is played here.
♨Q♉❀⇆◑◗⊟⛺🚌(201)♣P

Catterline

Creel Inn

AB39 2UL
(on coast off A92, 5 miles S of Stonehaven) OS868781
⏲ 12-3, 6-11 (midnight Fri & Sat); 12-11 Sun
☎ (01569) 750254 🌐 thecreelinn.co.uk
Beer range varies Ⓗ
Compact village inn in a stunning cliff-top position, built in 1838. It now incorporates adjacent cottages converted to enlarge the restaurant – an excellent menu is available with reservations recommended. Seafood is, naturally, a speciality and the same dishes are also served in the lounge. Up to three beers are available, mainly from a variety of Scottish micros, and a selection of more than 30 specialist bottled beers, mainly Belgian, is stocked. Crawton Bird Sanctuary lies two miles to the north. Best to phone in winter to check opening times before travelling.
♨Q❀◑◗P

Charleston of Aberlour

Mash Tun

8 Broomfield Square, AB38 9QP
⏲ 11-11 (11.45 Thu; 12.30am Fri & Sat); 11-11.45 Sun
☎ (01340) 881771
🌐 speyside.moray.org/Aberlour/mashtun.htm
Beer range varies Ⓗ
Built in 1896 as the Station Bar, this unusual, round ended building has a light interior with extensive use of timber. The Speyside Way runs past the door and patrons may drink their ales enjoying the view from the former station platform in summer (weather permitting!). A wide variety of bottled beers is available. Former local CAMRA Country Pub of the Year, it serves two beers during the tourist season and one in winter, mainly from local micros. ❀⇆◑◗⛺🚌(336)

Corgarff

Allargue Arms Hotel

AB36 8YP
⏲ 11 (12.30 Sun)-11

SCOTLAND

☎ (019756) 51410 🌐 allarguearmshotel.co.uk
Beer range varies Ⓗ
Overlooking historic Corgarff Castle, this pub is situated at the beginning of the ascent to the Lecht ski centre on the A939 at Cockbridge, a road infamous as the first to be closed every winter when the snow comes. However, it should still be accessible from the Strathdon side. It sells one ale, normally only from Easter to October, but a supply of varied Cairngorm bottles is also stocked. It makes an ideal base for hill walking, golf, pony trekking, clay pigeon, game shooting and mountain biking. As well as seven letting rooms, there is a bothy with six bunks and you may pitch your tent nearby.
ÄP

Craigellachie

Highlander Inn

10 Victoria Street, AB38 9SR
12-11 (12.30am Fri & Sat); 12-11 Sun
☎ (01340) 881446
Beer range varies Ⓗ
In the middle of Speyside's Whisky Trail, this cosy cellar bar boasts a good selection of malts and offers good value tasting sessions. An extensive food menu is offered, heavily featuring local produce. One beer, usually from Cairngorm, is available and supplemented by a second in the tourist season.
(336)♣P

Elgin

Muckle Cross

34 High Street, IV30 1BU
11-12.30am (midnight Wed & Thu; 1am Fri & Sat); 12.30-11.45 Sun
☎ (01343) 559030
Caledonian 80/-; Courage Directors; Theakston Best Bitter; guest beer Ⓗ
Typical small branch of Wetherspoon's converted from what used to be a bicycle repair shop and latterly a branch of Halfords. The long, wide bar offers a choice of up to five ales and can get very busy, especially at weekends. Opens at 10am for coffee.
(10, 305, 315)

Ellon

Tolbooth

21-23 Station Road, AB41 9AE
11-2.30, 5-11 (midnight Thu & Fri); 11-midnight Sat; 6.30-11 Sun
☎ (01358) 721308
Beer range varies Ⓗ
Comfortable and spacious lounge bar, on two levels, recently refurbished and extended, with a large conservatory on the lower level leading to an enclosed patio. An older customer base and lack of background music create a relaxing environment. The upstairs function room is much used by local organisations. The beers are mainly from the larger English regionals with the occasional Scottish micro brew.
(X50, 260)♣

Findhorn

Crown & Anchor Inn

44 Findhorn, IV36 3YF
12-11 (midnight Wed & Thu; 1am Fri & Sat); 12-11.30 Sun
☎ (01309) 690243 🌐 crownandanchorinn.co.uk
Cairngorm Trade Winds, Black Gold; Taylor Landlord; guest beer Ⓗ
Situated in the heart of a historic village, ideally positioned overlooking the bay, this is a fine base for visiting ornithologists or thirsty mariners from the Royal Findhorn Sailing Club. Just down the road is the internationally famous Findhorn Foundation community – its shop is worth a visit for the interesting selection of organic bottled beers from near and far.
Ä(336)♣P

Fochabers

Gordon Arms Hotel

80 High Street, IV32 7DH (A96 W end of village)
11 (12 Sun)-11
☎ (01343) 820508
Caledonian Deuchars IPA; Marston's Pedigree; guest beer Ⓗ
A rambling coaching inn with low ceilings on the main street of the village offering an upmarket restaurant and accommodation. It is home to many local societies. The real ale pumps are in the public bar but beer may be served in the lounge bar. The hotel is adjacent to Baxter's factory village and handy for the Speyside Way.
(10, 305, 315)P

Forres

Red Lion

2-6 Tollbooth Street, IV36 1PH
11-12.30am (1.30am Fri & Sat); 12-12.30am Sun
☎ (01309) 672716
Beer range varies Ⓗ
Dating from 1838 and known locally as the 'Beastie', this is one of the longest established real ale outlets in the north of Scotland going back to the 1970s and the long defunct Younger's XXPS. The modern lounge bar offers a solitary beer, generally from the Scottish & Newcastle portfolio. The public bar no longer sells ale but is worth a look as it is architecturally interesting.
(10, 336)

Glenkindie

Glenkindie Arms Hotel

AB33 8SX (on A97 at E edge of village)
12 (5 winter Mon-Fri)-11 (1am Fri; 11.45 Sat); 12-11 Sun
☎ (019756) 41288 🌐 theglenkindiearmshotel.com
Beer range varies Ⓗ
Tiny 400-year-old former drovers' inn in a listed building known as 'The Lodge' due to its former Masonic use, evidence of which is still visible on the outer walls. The hotel stands on the Castle Trail between Kildrummy and Corgarff Castles and is close to the Lecht ski centre. An extensive menu of local produce is offered plus a spicier

selection. One beer is served in winter, two in summer, usually from Scottish micros, as well as a changing range of malt whiskies and Belgian beers. It is best to check winter opening hours before travelling. ♨✿🛏◖◗P

Glenlivet

Croft Inn

AB37 9DP (on B9009 Dufftown-Glenlivet road)
⏲ 12 (5 winter)-11 (midnight Sat); 12.30-11 Sun
☎ (01807) 590361 🌐 croft-inn.co.uk
Beer range varies Ⓗ

Small, single-room bar with a conservatory restaurant. Originally an alms house, the building dates from 1770, and was used for crofting until 1973. It stands on the 'Whisky Trail', with more than 50 distilleries within a 15-mile radius, and stocks an extensive range of malts. Skiing and mountain biking trails are close by. Usually a light and a dark beer from either Cairngorm or Isle of Skye breweries are available. It is best to check hours in winter before travelling.
♨🛏◖◗♿♣P

Inverurie

Edwards

2 West High Street, AB51 3SA
⏲ 10-1am; 12.30-midnight Sun
☎ (01467) 629788
Beer range varies Ⓗ

This modern cafe bar has quickly become part of the town circuit since conversion from an old hotel several years ago. The upstairs function room doubles as a disco at weekends. Although light and modern, the decor has a hint of Art Deco about it and there is a series of comfortable snugs to relax in while having a snack and browsing the newspapers.
◖♿⇌🚌(10, 307, 737)

Lossiemouth

Skerry Brae Hotel

Stotfield Road, IV31 6QS
⏲ 11-11 (12.30am Fri & Sat); 11-11 Sun
☎ (01343) 812040 🌐 skerrybrae.co.uk
Beer range varies Ⓗ

Frequented by many RAF personnel (see the squadron stickers in the bar), this old granite hotel has views over the local golf club and the Moray Firth, which can be enjoyed from the patio. The three ales on offer, sourced from far and wide, are available in the spacious lounge bar with its modern dining area. Children are allowed in the conservatory, dining room and terrace until 9pm. ✿🛏◖◗🚌(329 from Elgin)P

Maryculter

Old Mill Inn

South Deeside Road, AB12 5FX (B979/B9077 jct)
⏲ 11-11 (midnight Fri & Sat); 12-11 Sun
☎ (01224) 733212 🌐 oldmillinn.co.uk
Draught Bass; Caledonian Deuchars IPA; Taylor Landlord Ⓗ

Family-run inn dating from 1797 situated on the banks of the River Dee, five miles west of Aberdeen and lying at the start of Royal Deeside. Close to Drum and Crathes Castle, numerous golf courses and, for the children, Storybook Glen is less than half a mile. Salmon fishing takes place within sight of the hotel. The large outside drinking area has an adjacent antique shop housed in the original mill building. The ales are served in the lounge and dining room.
✿🛏◖◗⛺P

Methlick

Kingscliff Sporting Lodge

AB41 7HQ (signed 1 mile W of village on B9005 Methlick-Fyvie road)
⏲ 12-11 (midnight Fri & Sat); closed Mon & Tue; 12-11 Sun
☎ (01651) 806375 🌐 kingscliff.co.uk
Orkney Dark Island; guest beer Ⓗ

Popular activities centre with an unexpected commitment to real ale. Why not arrange to have a day clay pigeon shooting or quad biking then retreat to the bar to unwind or enjoy a meal in the recently extended restaurant? The guest ale tends to come from the Atlas/Orkney ranges. Transport may be arranged by the centre's own mini-bus. ◖◗P

Ythanview Hotel

Main Street, AB41 7DT
⏲ 11-2.30, 5-11 (1am Fri); 11-12.30am Sat; 11-11 Sun
☎ (01651) 806235 🌐 ythanview.com
Beer range varies Ⓗ

Comfortable village local and relaxed restaurant with a welcoming fire. Fundraising events are held for various community teams including the village cricket side, the famous MCC (Methlick Cricket Club). Good quality local ingredients are used in the competitively priced food. Why not try Jay's special curry with whole chillies, if you dare!
♨Q🛏◖◗🍽🚌(290, 291, 294)♣P

Midmar

Midmar Inn

AB51 7LX (on B9119, 2 miles W of Echt)
⏲ 5-11; 11-midnight Thu-Sat; 12.30-midnight Sun
☎ (01330) 860515
Beer range varies Ⓗ

Small, welcoming locals' bar which, despite its lack of surrounding housing, can be especially busy at weekends and on Thursday's ceilidh night. The reasonably-priced meals are popular and booking, especially at weekends, is advisable. There is a games room at the back overlooking the grassy outside area.
Q✿◖◗🍽🚌(210)P

Mintlaw

Country Park Inn

Station Road, AB42 5EB
⏲ 11-11.30 (12.30am Fri-Sun)
☎ (01771) 622622
Beer range varies Ⓗ

Recently acquired by the Swallow Group, this was once the station hotel for the long gone

railway from Aberdeen to Peterhead which has been converted to a long distance walkway. A real ale oasis in the area, the inn is also sought out for its food, attracting families, especially at weekends. Convenient for Aden Country Park.
Q (267, 268)P

Oldmeldrum

Redgarth Hotel

Kirk Brae, AB51 0DJ (off A947 towards golf course)
11-2.30, 5-midnight; 12-2.30, 5-11 Sun
(01651) 872353 redgarth.com
Beer range varies H/G
Multiple local CAMRA award-winning pub with imposing views over the eastern Grampian mountains. At times, especially weekends, it is more like a restaurant but becomes more pub-like out of food hours. A dedicated core of regulars comes from miles around to sample the fare on offer, occasionally enticed by 'Brewers in Residence' evenings when the three hand-pumped ales are supplemented by many more on gravity.
Q (305)P

Portsoy

Shore Inn

Church Street, AB45 2QR (overlooking harbour)
10-11 (midnight Thu; 12.30am Fri & Sat); 10-11 Sun
(01261) 842831
Beer range varies H
This ancient, 18th-century coastal inn situated at the oldest harbour on the Moray coast exudes an old time atmosphere with its low ceilings and dark wooden bar fittings. The village hosts an annual boat festival for which the pub runs an outdoor bar – the Shore Out! Up to three ales are stocked (only one in winter) and the selection is unpredictable. (305)♣

Stonehaven

Marine Hotel

9-10 Shorehead, AB39 2JY (on harbour front)
11-11 (midnight Thu; 1am Fri & Sat); 11-midnight (11pm winter) Sun
(01569) 762155
Taylor Landlord; guest beer H
Former Scottish CAMRA Pub of the Year in a picturesque harbour-front location. Downstairs is a simple wood-panelled bar with five ever-changing ales selected from micro-breweries and the more enterprising regionals. The adjacent lounge is furnished with armchairs and settees and has a huge fire in winter – a comfortable contrast to the bustle of the small bar. Upstairs the main dining area specialises in fresh local produce, particularly seafood. Children are allowed upstairs only. The regular ale may be Taylor Landlord or house beer Inveralmond Dunottar Ale.

Ship Inn

5 Shorehead, AB39 2JY
11-midnight (1am Fri & Sat); 11-midnight Sun
(01569) 762617 shipinnstonehaven.com
Beer range varies H
Harbourside pub with a walled outside drinking area, which means you do not need to use dreadful plastic glasses (but you do if you wish to sit on the harbour wall). Note the original Devanha East India Pale Ale mirror on the wall in the long, three-sectioned pub, with great views of the harbour.
♣

Tarves

Aberdeen Arms Hotel

The Square, AB41 7GX
12-2.30 (not Mon), 5-11 (1am Fri); 12-11.45 Sat; 12.30-11 Sun
(01651) 851214
geocities.com/aberdeenarmshotel
Beer range varies H
Small, family-run community local in the middle of a conservation area. Very much a cheery regulars' establishment, it is also welcoming to visitors. It offers a wide choice of good value, inspired food, ranging from local specialities to far eastern cuisine. Convenient for visiting both Tolquhon Castle and Pitmedden Gardens which was laid out in the 17th century by Sir Alexander Seddon with elaborate flower beds, fountains and pavilions.
Q ♣

Tomintoul

Glen Avon Hotel

The Square, AB37 9ET
12-midnight daily
(01807) 580218 glenavon-hotel.co.uk
Cairngorm Trade Winds H
This wood-lined, rustic bar is part of a small family-run hotel in the highest village in the Highlands. Sit by the bar and exchange stories with the locals, or enjoy a game of pool. A wide range of home-cooked food features local produce, with vegetarian choices available. Nordic and downhill skiing are close by, as is an extensive range of mountain bike trails plus, of course, the distilleries of Speyside. The route over the A939 from Cockbridge is usually one of the first to be blocked during winter snow but alternate access via Dufftown is usually possible. ♣

Westhill

Shepherds Rest

10 Straik Road, Arnhall Business Park, AB32 6HF
11 (12.30 Sun)-11
(01224) 740208
Courage Directors; guest beer H
A typical example of one of Scottish and Newcastle's chain of custom built kit pubs, but with a manager who has a commitment to an interesting range of cask ale. More like a licensed restaurant than a pub, food is served all day; it is popular with families at weekends. Accommodation is provided in the adjacent Premier Travel Inn.
(215, 216, 217)P

Authority areas covered: Highland UA, Orkney Islands UA, Shetland Islands UA, Western Islands UA

Applecross

Applecross Inn

Shore Street, IV54 8LR (on unclassified road off A896) OS711445
✪ 11-11.30 (midnight Fri); 12.30-11.30 Sun
☎ (01520) 744262 ⊕ applecross.uk.com
Beer range varies Ⓗ

Owned by the same family since 1989, the pub is spectacularly situated on the shore of the Applecross Peninsula, enjoying views of the Isles of Skye and Raasay. It is reached by a single track road over the highest vehicular ascent in Britain, or by a longer scenic route. Two handpumps dispense beer from the Isle of Skye brewery and the food speciality is shellfish. It features regular ceilidhs and the area is ideal for climbing, walking and wildlife watching.
⛰❀⇌◑♿⛺P

Aviemore

Cairngorm Hotel

Grampian Road, PH22 1PE (opp. station)
✪ 11-midnight (1am Fri-Sat); 11.30-midnight Sun
☎ (01479) 810233 ⊕ cairngorm.com
Cairngorm Stag Ⓗ

The lounge bar of this 31-room privately owned hotel, though large, has a cosy feel, enhanced by two bay windows, distressed wooden furniture and a large coal effect fire. Though the trade is mainly holidaymakers, it is very popular with locals, with a large-screen TV showing only sport. There is a Scottish theme throughout the hotel with tartan wall coverings and Scottish entertainment on many afternoons and evenings.
❀⇌◑♿⛺⇄⊟♣P

Old Bridge Inn

Dalfaber Road, PH22 1PU
✪ 11-midnight (1am Fri); 12.30-midnight Sun
☎ (01479) 811137 ⊕ oldbridgeinn.co.uk
Beer range varies Ⓗ

Busy pub, popular with outdoor enthusiasts, serving good quality food. Originally a cottage and now greatly enlarged it lies on the road to the Strathspey Steam Railway. The three handpumps predominantly serve a range of Scottish beers. Children are welcome and there is a modern bunkhouse attached accommodating 40.
⛰Q❀⇌◑♿⛺⇄P

INDEPENDENT BREWERIES

An Teallach Dundonell
Atlas Kinlochleven
Black Isle Munlochy
Cairngorm Aviemore
Cuillin Sligachan
Far North Melvich
Hebridean Stornoway
Highland Birsay
Isle of Skye Uig
Orkney Quoyloo
Valhalla Baltasound

Badachro

Badachro Inn

IV21 2AA (S of Gairloch on B8056, 3 miles from A832)

12-midnight (4.30-11 Jan-mid March); 12-11 (12.30-6 Jan-mid March) Sun

(01445) 741255 badachroinn.com

Beer range varies H

Spectacularly situated on the shores of Loch Gairloch, this popular inn was converted from an old fishing station 120 years ago. With the adjacent jetty still in use, it provides a haven for the yachting fraternity as well as hill walkers. There is a thriving local trade and the two handpumps usually serve beers from An Teallach or Skye breweries. The menu includes fresh seafood with shellfish a speciality. Q P

Boat Of Garten

Boat Hotel

PH24 3BH

12-11; 12.30-11 Sun

(01479) 831258 boathotel.co.uk

Beer range varies H

This privately owned hotel is a haven for outdoor enthusiasts, situated close to the River Spey in the Cairngorm National Park near the Strathspey Steam Railway, Boat of Garten golf course and the famous RSPB Osprey centre at Loch Garten. Two handpumps in the Osprey Bar serve beers from the local Cairngorm Brewery. Bistro-style food is available and there is also a fine dining restaurant, The Capercaillie, accredited by EatScotland. Popular with locals, the small public bar has TV and a pool table. Q P

Cawdor

Cawdor Tavern

The Lane, IV12 5XP

11-11 (midnight Fri) (11-3, 5-11 Oct-April); 11-midnight Sat; 12.30-11 Sun

(01667) 404777 cawdortavern.com

Beer range varies H

Next door to a children's play park and a public bowling green at the heart of this conservation village, the pub is a short walk from the famous castle and within easy reach of historic Fort George and Culloden battlefield. Family owned, it is full of character, with a large lounge bar, cosy public bar and a 70-cover restaurant, Both bars are wood panelled with log fires. The public bar also features a splendid antique mahogany bar and a ceiling covered in old maps. The two handpumps serve beer from the Cairngorm Brewery. P

Drumnadrochit

Benleva Hotel

IV63 6UH

12-midnight (1am Fri; 11.45 Sat); 12.30-11 Sun

(01456) 450080 benleva.co.uk

Beer range varies H / G

Popular, friendly village hotel catering for locals and visitors. A 400-year-old former manse, it is convenient for Loch Ness monster hunting. The sweet chestnut was a former hanging tree. Four handpumps sell mainly Highland beers with one from the Isle of Skye and occasional beer from the wood. Good evening meals and lunches are available (limited in winter). It hosts the Loch Ness Beer Festival in September, occasional quiz nights and traditional music. Local CAMRA Pub Of The Year in 2003 and 2005. Q P

Fort Augustus

Bothy

Canalside, PH32 4AU

11-1am (12.30am Sat); 12.30-midnight Sun (hours vary in winter)

(01329) 366710 lochnessrestaurant.co.uk

Beer range varies H

In an ideal location in the centre of a tourist village beside the Caledonian Canal, Loch Ness and the Great Glen Way, this thick-stoned bothy has been put to many different uses, including a canal pay office, waiting room and exhibition centre. Two handpumps serve beer from the Isle of Skye and Cairngorm breweries with other guest ales appearing regularly. A cosy, friendly bar area with open fire leads to the conservatory where good food is served. P

Fort William

Grog & Gruel

66 High Street, PH33 6AE

11 (12 winter)-midnight (1am Thu-Sat); 5-midnight Sun

(01397) 705078 grogandgruel.co.uk

Beer range varies H

In the shadow of Britain's highest mountain, this bare-floored ale house with church pew seating keeps up to six beers in summer, with fewer in winter. Owned by the same family as the Clachaig Inn in Glencoe, it holds regular beer festivals. Busy with tourists in summer, it is also popular with locals. Home-cooked food is available in the upstairs dining room or from the more limited bar menu.

Nevisport Bar

Tweedale, PH33 6EJ

11.30-11.30 (1am Fri & Sat); 11.30-11.30 Sun

(01397) 704921 nevisport.com

Beer range varies H

The atmosphere is always very lively in this informal lounge-style bar, situated close to Ben Nevis, the Nevis Range ski resort and the end of the West Highland Way. It is a favourite meeting place for walkers, climbers and skiers. A collection of classic mountaineering photographs and gear adorns the walls to give an interesting insight into times gone by, and a warming log fire welcomes winter visitors. Mainly Scottish beers are served, often from the Isle of Skye brewery.

Fortrose

Anderson

Union Street, IV10 8TD

4 (11.30 Sat; 12.30 Sun)-11.30

(01381) 620236 theanderson.co.uk

Beer range varies 🄷
This cosy, homely bar, with a bare stone wall and two settees in front of an open fire, is part of a nine-bedroom hotel. The owner is an international beer writer and self-confessed 'beer geek'. Serving only independent brewery beers, this beer drinkers' mecca also offers 80 or more Belgian bottled beers, backed by over 200 malts. The food is reasonably priced and high quality, with international cuisine available in the lounge bar and restaurant. ♛♨❀⇌◑◗⊟⩓♣P

Gairloch

Old Inn

Flowerdale, IV21 2BD (opp. harbour) OSNG811751
✪ 11-1am (11.30 Sat); 12.30-11 Sun
☎ (01445) 712006 🌐 theoldinn.net
Beer range varies 🄷
This traditional family-run Highland coaching inn at the foot of the picturesque and historic Flowerdale Glen enjoys spectacular views across Gairloch harbour to Skye and the Western Isles. Up to eight mainly Scottish real ales are served to accompany the enticing menu of home-cooked game and locally caught seafood. Convenient for Loch Maree, the Beinn Eighe Nature Reserve, Inverewe Gardens, and Torridon, this is an ideal base for outdoor activities. Wester Ross CAMRA Pub-of-the-Year 2005. ♛♨❀⇌◑◗⊟⩓♣P🗍

Glencoe

Clachaig Inn

PH49 4HX (½ mile off A82 on old road to Glencoe going W) OSNN128567
✪ 11-11 (midnight Fri; 11.30 Sat); 12.30-11 Sun
☎ (01855) 811252 🌐 clachaig.com
Beer range varies 🄷
Set amid the rugged mountain beauty of Glencoe, the Clachaig attracts climbers, walkers and more adventurous tourists. The large, stone-floored public bar has spartan seating and is heated by iron stoves. There are more comfortable sitting rooms off it and a lounge. Beers are from Scottish micros and range from four to around 15 during beer festivals in February, June and October. The hearty bar meals are especially welcome after a hill walk. Live music is played most weekends. ♛♨❀⇌◑◗⊟♿⩓P

Inverie

Old Forge

PH41 4PL (100yds from ferry terminal)
✪ 11-midnight (1am Fri-Sat); 11-midnight Sun
☎ (01678) 462267 🌐 theoldforge.co.uk
Beer range varies 🄷
The most remote pub in mainland Britain can be reached only by ferry from Mallaig or a 15-mile hilly walk. In a spectacular setting on the shore of Loch Nevis, it provides an ideal location for hill walking the 'rough bounds' of Knoydart. Moorings welcome waterborne visitors. The two handpumps serve mainly Isle of Skye beers and food is served all day with specialities including locally caught seafood. The pub has an informal atmosphere, dress code being wellies, waterproofs and midge cream. The landlord can arrange local accommodation. ♛Q❀◑◗⩓

Inverness

Blackfriars

93-95 Academy Street, IV1 1LU
✪ 11-midnight (12.30am Fri; 11.45 Sat); 12.30-11 Sun
☎ (01463) 233881 🌐 blackfriars.50megs.com
Beer range varies 🄷
Traditional, town centre pub comprising one spacious room with a large standing area by the bar and ample seating in comfortable alcoves. Guest ales are usually from local Scottish breweries, often Isle of Skye and Cairngorm. Good-value meals are home cooked using local produce. A music-oriented pub, it features evenings of Scottish music and dancing with local bands often performing at weekends. Now back to its best under new owners. ◑◗≢

Clachnaharry Inn

17-19 High Street, Clachnaharry, IV3 6RB (A862 Beauly Road on outskirts of town) OSNH648466
✪ 11-11 (midnight Thu-Sat); 12.30-11.45 Sun
☎ (01463) 239806 🌐 clachnaharryinn.co.uk
Adnams Broadside; Caledonian Deuchars IPA; Isle of Skye Red Cuillin 🄷**; Blaven** 🄷/🄶**; McEwan's 80/-; guest beers** 🄷
Popular with locals and visitors alike, this lively 17th-century coaching inn is a regular local CAMRA Pub of the Year. An ever-changing selection of up to 10 real ales is served, including Isle of Skye Brewery ales by gravity from wooden casks. Bar meals to suit all tastes are served throughout the day and families are made welcome. Real log fires warm the cosy bars in winter. The lounge and garden afford fine views over the Caledonian Canal sea lock and Beauly Firth. ♛Q❀◑◗⊟⩓♣P

Snowgoose

Stoneyfield, IV2 7PA
(on A96, 1½ miles from city centre)
✪ 11-11; 12.30-10.30 Sun
☎ (01463) 701921
Draught Bass; Caledonian Deuchars IPA 🄷
One of Mitchell and Butler's Vintage Inns, this traditional dining house supports a popular bar trade. Though set next door to a Holiday Inn and a Travelodge, most of the customers are from the local area. The interior is one large L-shaped room, but alcoves and three log fires give it a more cosy and select feel. The building is a converted 1788 coach house and has part carpeted and part flagged flooring. A wide variety of food is offered all day at reasonable prices. ♛Q❀◑◗♿P

Kincraig

Suie Hotel

PH21 1NA
✪ 5-11 (1am Fri); 12-2.30, 5-1am Sat; 5-11 Sun
☎ (01540) 651344 🌐 suiehotel.com
Cairngorm Trade Winds; Isle of Skye Red Cuillin; guest beer 🄷
This cosy, wooden, self-contained extension to a seven-bedroom Victorian character hotel

is run by only the second owner in 103 years. Popular with locals as well as hill walkers and skiers, it is situated 200 yards or so from the River Spey and Loch Insh. The wooden floored bar features a large stove/open fire and has an alcove with a pool table and juke box. Traditional Scottish music is featured occasionally. A third handpump usually serves beer from the Cairngorm or Skye Breweries. ⌂❀⇄◑♣P

Kinlochleven

Tailrace Inn

Riverside Road, PA40 4QH (on B863)
⊙ 11-11.30 (12.30am Thu-Sat); 12-11.30 Sun
☎ (01855) 831777 ⊕ tailraceinn.co.uk
Beer range varies Ⓗ
Surrounded by the Mamore mountains, it lies midway between Ben Nevis and Glencoe, on the West Highland Way. Two handpumps sell beer from the Atlas brewery, just a short walk away. This modern inn serves food daily until 8pm in winter and 9pm in summer and features live music on Thursday and Friday. A bunkhouse is just up the road – an ideal base for outdoor enthusiasts with the new Ice Factor indoor climbing centre across the road. ❀⇄◐◑♿⊟P

Kirkwall

West End Hotel

14 Main Street, KW15 1BU
⊙ 11-11 (midnight Sat); 12.30-midnight Sun
☎ (01856) 872368 ⊕ orkneyisles.co.uk/westendhotel
Orkney Red MacGregor Ⓗ
The small, cosy bar on the first floor of what was originally a hospital from 1845 until 1927 is still a good place to recuperate. During the winter the open fire creates a cosy atmosphere while the garden, on the same level, is the place to be in summer. There is an adjoining restaurant. All the amenities of Kirkwall are within easy reach, including St Magnus Cathedral, and there is a busy shopping street, not dominated by national chains. ⌂Q❀⇄◐◑▲

Lochcarron

Rockvilla Hotel

IV54 8YB
⊙ 11.30-2.30 (not winter Wed), 5.30-11; closed winter Mon & Tue; 11.30-12.30am Fri; 11.30-midnight Sat; 12.30-3, 5.30-11 Sun
☎ (01520) 722379 ⊕ rockvilla-hotel.co.uk
Beer range varies Ⓗ
Situated on the shore of beautiful Lochcarron in the centre of the village, this hotel offers spectacular views of the loch and nearby mountains. It is an excellent base for exploring the Western Highlands. The lounge bar offers a range of ales, mainly from local breweries. Bar meals are available at all times. ⇄◐◑P

Newtonmore

Glen Hotel

Main Street, PH20 1DD (S end of village)
⊙ 11 (12.30 Sun)-midnight
☎ (01540) 673203 ⊕ theglenhotel.co.uk
Beer range varies Ⓗ
Set in 'Monarch of the Glen' country, the main bar of this small 10-room hotel has been fully refurbished and features a games room alcove. The bar has a good local trade and hill walkers and other visitors are well catered for. Two handpumps serve Glenbogle, a house ale from Isle of Skye, while the other two serve a variety of Scottish, usually Highland, guest ales. The extensive bar menu includes a good selection of vegetarian dishes. Phone to check opening times in winter.
⌂❀⇄◐◑♿▲≠⊟♣P

Onich

Corran Inn

Nether Lochaber, PH33 6SE (by east terminal of Corran ferry, 200 yds from A82)
⊙ 11-11 (midnight Fri & Sat); 12-11 Sun
☎ (01855) 821235
Beer range varies Ⓗ
Just a few yards from the busy A82, this cosy and welcoming little bar beside the slipway for the Corran Ferry is an ideal base for exploring the Ardnamurchan Peninsula. Once a temperance hotel and not allowed to serve alcohol on the premises, the bar was built at the rear of the building, only accessible from an outside door. Atlas and Isle of Skye beers are regularly served.
Q❀⇄◐◑▲♣P

Plockton

Plockton Hotel

Harbour Street, IV52 8TN
⊙ 11-midnight; 12.30-11 Sun
☎ (01599) 544274 ⊕ plocktonhotel.co.uk
Caledonian Deuchars IPA Ⓗ
This popular hotel is set in a row of whitewashed Highland cottages on the picturesque Plockton waterfront, and boasts spectacular views across Loch Carron. The award-winning menu includes the freshest seafood and locally reared beef. With a station on the Inverness to Kyle Railway, and close to Eilean Donan Castle and the Isle of Skye, the village has much to offer and is a regular haunt for outdoor enthusiasts. Palm trees take advantage of the Gulf Stream warmed coastline. Q☺❀⇄◐◑⊞♿≠♣P

Plockton Inn

Innes Street, IV52 8TW (50 yds from seafront)
⊙ 11-midnight (11 Sun)
☎ (01599) 544222 ⊕ plocktoninn.co.uk
Beer range varies Ⓗ
A friendly welcome is guaranteed at this busy family-run inn, set in the heart of the beautiful West Highland village of Plockton. Meals are served all day in the lounge bar and award-winning seafood restaurant, where locally caught shellfish and home-smoked fish take pride of place on the menu. There are regular, live traditional music sessions in the public bar and all are welcome to join in. Enjoy real log fires in winter or the outside seating in summer.
⌂Q☺❀⇄◐◑⊞♿≠♣P

Portree

Bosville Hotel

9-11 Bosville Terrace, IV51 9DG
⏲ 11 (12.30 Sun)-11
☎ (01478) 612846 🌐 bosvillehotel.co.uk
Isle of Skye Red Cuillin 🄷
Town centre hotel and bar, close to the bus station and picturesque harbour. The tastefully decorated bar with open fire has one handpump. Relax and unwind in the friendly atmosphere after your day's sightseeing, climbing or walking on the island. Enjoy the excellent bar food or try the delicious fresh food served in the award-winning restaurant. ♨🛏◑◗♿🚌P

Rosemarkie

Plough Inn

48 High Street, IV10 8UF
⏲ 11-midnight (1am Fri; 11.45 Sat); 12.30-11 Sun
☎ (01381) 620164
Beer range varies 🄷
Beautiful old country pub in a pretty seaside village just 100 yards from the beach. It has a cosy, wood-lined bar with an ancient marriage stone lintel (dated 1691) over the fireplace. A wide choice of beers is served from northern breweries including Orkney, Cairngorm, An Teallach and Hebridean. Food ranges from lunchtime bites to an a la carte menu featuring Black Isle produce such as lamb, beef and game. Booking is recommended especially in summer and weekends. ♨✿◑◗🂠⛺♣P

Roy Bridge

Stronlossit Hotel

PH31 4AG
⏲ 11-11.45 (1am Thu-Sat); 12.30-11.45 Sun
☎ (01397) 712253 🌐 stronlossit.co.uk
Cairngorm Trade Winds; Caledonian Deuchars IPA; Isle of Skye Red Cuillin; guest beer 🄷
This traditional Scottish inn is situated at the foot of the Nevis mountain range and makes an ideal base for outdoor activities or touring in the Highlands. In addition to a varied selection of Scottish and English ales and real cider, bar meals using local produce are available all day. ♨✿🛏◑◗⛺⇌●

Scourie

Scourie Hotel

IV27 4SX
(on A894 between Laxford Bridge and Kylesku)
⏲ 11-2.30, 5-11; 12-2.30, 6.30-10.30 Sun
☎ (01971) 502396 🌐 scourie-hotel.co.uk
Beer range varies 🄷
Popular with fishermen, this converted 1640 coaching inn overlooks Scourie Bay. It lies close to the bird reserve of Handa Island and the peaks of Arkle and Foinavon. The bar has a fishing theme with 1940s fishing nets as decoration. In addition to a fixed bar menu, the hotel dining room serves high quality four-course meals featuring seafood with the menu changing daily. The three handpumps serve a variety of beers from England and Scotland. Q✿🛏◑◗🂠⛺♣P

Scousburgh

Spiggie Hotel

ZE2 9JE (signed off A970)
⏲ 12-2, 5-11; 12-midnight Fri & Sat; 12-2, 5-11 Sun
☎ (01950) 460409 🌐 thespiggiehotel.co.uk
Beer range varies 🄷
The original terminus of the Northern Isles Ferries, this small, family run hotel situated above the Spiggie Trout Loch is convenient for exploring the archaeological sites of Scatness and Jarlshof as well as bird and whale watching from Sumburgh Head. The single bar is stone floored. There are usually four new beers each week – requests may be catered for if enough notice is given. Summer beers usually include at least one from the local Valhalla Brewery. Q✿🛏◑◗♿♣P

Shiel Bridge

Kintail Lodge Hotel

IV40 8HL
⏲ 12-11 (midnight Fri & Sat); 12.30-11 Sun; hours vary in winter
☎ (01599) 511275 🌐 kintaillodgehotel.co.uk
Beer range varies 🄷
Converted from a former shooting lodge, the hotel is situated on the A87 road to Skye at the foot of the Five Sisters of Kintail on the shores of Loch Duich and close to Eilean Donan Castle. Accommodation is available in the hotel or the adjacent bunkhouses. Excellent food is accompanied by one handpump serving Isle of Skye beers and a wide range of malt whiskies. Guided walks can be arranged from the hotel. ♨✿🛏◑◗P

Stornoway

Whaler's Rest

19 Francis Street, HS1 2ND
⏲ 11-1am (11 Sun & Mon)
☎ (01851) 701265
Hebridean Clansman Ale, Islander Strong Premium Ale; guest beer 🄷
Traditional local pub situated one minute from the centre of the largest town in the Outer Hebrides, providing an excellent base for touring Lewis and Harris. Thanks to popular demand from the locals the public bar has been left unchanged, though the lounge bar has been modernised and offers a raised seating area for diners. In addition to the regular beers, occasional guest beers are available. ✿🛏◑◗🂠⛺P

Stromness

Ferry Inn

John Street, KW16 3AA (100 yds from ferry terminal)
⏲ 9am-midnight (1am Thu-Sat); 9.30am-midnight Sun
☎ (01856) 850280 🌐 ferryinn.com
Highland Scapa Special; Orkney Red MacGregor, seasonal beers 🄷
Once a temperance hotel, the inn is easily spotted when arriving on the ferry from Scrabster; a welcoming sight especially after a rough crossing. It is popular all year round with locals and the clientele becomes more cosmopolitan during the season when the harbour is busy with dive boats which come to

SCOTLAND

the wrecks at Scapa Flow. It is also endorsed by the Cyclists Touring Club. It is particularly busy during the Folk Festival in May and Stromness Shopping Week in July.

Stromness Hotel

15 Victoria Street, KW16 3AA (opp. pier head; take Church St and Franklin Rd for car park)
11-11 (1am Fri & Sat); 12-11 Sun
(01856) 850298 stromnesshotel.com
Highland Scapa Special; Orkney Red MacGregor, Dark Island, seasonal beers H
The Hamnavoe Lounge, with a small balcony overlooking the harbour, is on the first floor of this hotel, which dominates the pier head. Sit in front of a roaring fire in the winter or, in fair weather, stand on the balcony watching the activities on the street and harbour below. Popular historic sites including Scara Brae, Ring of Brodger, and Maise Howe, are within easy reach. Annual events include jazz, folk and beer festivals plus the famous Stromness Shopping Week.

Uig

Uig Hotel

IV51 9YE (halfway down hill on approach to village)
OS397634
11 (12.30 Sun)-11; winter hours vary
(01470) 542205 uighotel.com
Beer range varies H
This attractive and imposing old coaching inn has spectacular views across Uig Bay to the ferry terminal for the Western Isles. The cosy lounge bar dispenses Isle of Skye beers from two handpulls in summer and one in winter. The friendly staff provide excellent service and meals are available in both the bar and adjoining restaurant. The hotel keeps its own highland cattle and is handy for a visit to the Isle of Skye Brewery. QP

Ullapool

Ferry Boat Inn

Shore Street, IV26 2UJ (on the waterfront)
11.30 (12.30 Sun)-11
(01854) 612366 ferryboat-inn.com
Beer range varies H
Small, comfortable 18th century inn, on the shore of Loch Broom just a short stroll from the Western Isles ferry terminal. A mix of locals and regularly returning visitors enjoy the friendly atmosphere in this busy old-fashioned bar, warmed by an open fire in winter. Local fresh produce is served in the bar (all year) and restaurant (open spring-late autumn) which afford glorious views across the sea loch to the mountains of Wester Ross. Q

Waternish

Stein Inn

Stein, IV55 8GA (N of Dunvegan on B886, 4½ miles from Fairy Bridge)
4-11; 11-midnight (1am summer) Fri; 12 (11 summer)-12.30am Sat; 12.30 (11.30 summer)-11 Sun
(01470) 592362 steininn.co.uk
Beer range varies H
This family-run hostelry, the oldest inn on the Isle of Skye, is located in a stunning setting on the shores of Loch Bay. Enjoy the warm fireside of the cosy bar in winter or the shore-side garden in summer. Locally caught seafood is served (Easter-October) in the bar and restaurant, which both have fine views over the sea loch to Rubha Maol. Facilities for seafarers include council moorings, showers, food supplies (by arrangement) and message relay services. QP

Wick

Alexander Bain

Market Place, KW1 4BS
10-midnight (1am Fri & Sat); 10-11.30 Sun
(01955) 609920
Greene King Abbot; guest beers H
This former telephone exchange is now a popular town centre Wetherspoon's pub with one large bar in the centre and several alcoves providing quieter areas. The large-screen TV is popular with sports fans. One regular ale is supplemented by two frequently-changing guests. Good value food is served and the Thursday evening curry club is a main attraction.

Wormadale

Westings Inn

ZE2 9LJ (on A971, 2 miles past Tingwall airstrip)
OS402464
12-3, 5-11; 12-midnight Fri & Sat; 12-3, 5-11 Sun
(01595) 840242 originart.com/westings
Beer range varies H
Friendly local pub, located centrally in the main island with stunning views over the islands to the west of Shetland. It is a convenient spot for visitors to stay and is close to Tingwall airstrip for those who wish to visit the outer isles. The local brewery's beers are also available in bottles and Shetland gin and vodka are stocked.
QP

Avoid lager

There is not a brewer who doesn't doctor his beer with something or other. Really something is in it. Four glasses made a Brooklyn man shoot down Dr Duggan in cold blood. Beer made a New York husband put a hole through his wife with a 22-calibre defender. Murder is in it. Who drinks lager beer is too apt to swallow the murder with it.

Elisha Chenery MD, 1889

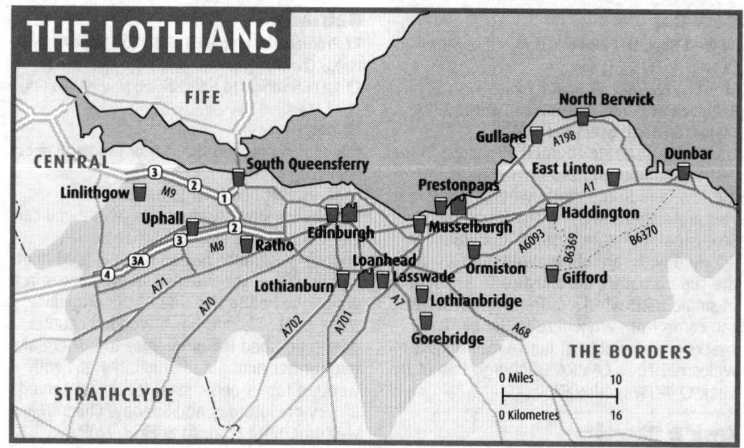

Authority areas covered: City of Edinburgh UA, East Lothian UA, Midlothian UA, West Lothian UA

Dunbar

Volunteer Arms

17 Victoria Street, EH42 1HP

12-11 (midnight Thu; 1am Fri & Sat); 12.30-midnight Sun

(01368) 862278

Beer range varies H

Overlooking Dunbar harbour, this is a friendly, traditional locals' pub. The cosy panelled bar is decorated with fishing and lifeboat memorabilia. Upstairs is a restaurant serving an excellent menu with the emphasis on seafood. Food is available all day until 9.30pm. Live folk music is played every fortnight. Children are welcome until 8pm and dogs after 9pm.

East Linton

Drovers Inn

5 Bridge Street, EH40 3AG

11-11 (1am Thu-Sat); 12.30-midnight Sun

(01620) 860298

Caledonian Deuchars IPA; guest beers H

Village pub full of character and rustic charm where food is the main priority. The cosy bar boasts a wooden floor, marble-topped counter and wood-burning stove. The wood-panelled and claret painted walls are adorned with memorabilia, with a stuffed goat's head taking pride of place. There is a restaurant upstairs and a bistro leading off the bar. The thirsty can find up to four serious ales. At weekends meals are served all day. Children and dogs are welcome.

Edinburgh

Barony Bar

81-85 Broughton Street, EH1 3RJ (E of new town)

11-midnight (1am Fri & Sat); 12.30-11 Sun

(0131) 558 2874

Caledonian Deuchars IPA, 80/-; Courage Directors; McEwan's 80/-; guest beers H

Full of character, this suburban pub has a number of fine internal features. Splendid tile work and stained wood are much in evidence while the bar and gantry are also noteworthy. Detailed cornices and a wooden floor add to the atmosphere in the L-shaped bar. Magnificent whisky mirrors adorn the walls. Food is served all day until 10pm (7pm Sun).

Bennets Bar ☆

8 Leven Street, EH3 9LG (SW of centre)

11-12.30am (1am Thu-Sat); 12-11.30 Sun

(0131) 229 5143 bennets.com

Caledonian Deuchars IPA; McEwan's 80/- H

Quite simply the zenith of late Victorian Edinburgh pub architecture, from the Jeffrey's Brewery etched door panels and window screens to the magnificent gantry. While the Bernard's Brewery mirror at the end of the bar is the most spectacular, the Taylor McLeod mirrors are the most significant – the last trace of the brewery that once stood on the site of the adjacent Kings Theatre. Children are welcome in the green room for meals until 9pm. No food is served on Sunday.

Blue Blazer

2 Spittal Street, EH3 9DX (SW of centre)

11 (12.30 Sun)-1am

(0131) 229 5030

Caledonian Deuchars IPA A**; guest beers** A/H

Two-roomed ale house nestling in the shadow of Edinburgh Castle. The interior window opposite the bar reflects the pub's previous life as a Bernard's Brewery house. Attracting a wide clientele, the atmosphere is cosmopolitan, and this is enhanced by the six guest beers that are often sourced from Scottish micros. A range of exotic rums is available. Dogs with well behaved owners are welcome.

INDEPENDENT BREWERIES

Caledonian Edinburgh
Fowler's Prestonpans
Innis & Gunn Edinburgh
McCowans Edinburgh
Stewart Loanhead

Bow Bar

80 West Bow, EH1 2HH (old town, off Grassmarket)
12-11.30; 12.30-11 Sun
(0131) 226 7667 bowbar.com
Belhaven 80/- Ale; Caledonian Deuchars IPA; Taylor Landlord; guest beers Ⓐ
Classic Scottish one-roomed ale house in the heart of Edinburgh's old town. This is one of the few bars in the world where all the real ales are dispensed using the traditional Scottish air pressure system. The walls are adorned with rare old brewery mirrors and the superb gantry does justice to a vast array of single malt whiskies. The five guest beers can come from anywhere in the UK. Bar snacks are available at lunchtime. Dogs are welcome. 2006 CAMRA Edinburgh Pub of the Year. Q ≠(Waverley)

Cask & Barrel

115 Broughton Street, EH1 3RZ (E edge of new town)
11-12.30am (1am Thu-Sat); 12.30-12.30am Sun
(0131) 556 3132
Draught Bass; Caledonian Deuchars IPA, 80/-; Hadrian & Border Cowie; guest beers Ⓗ
Spacious and extremely busy ale house drawing a mainly local clientele of all ages, ranging from business people to football fans. The interior features an imposing horseshoe bar, bare floorboards, a splendid cornice and a collection of brewery mirrors. Old barrels act as tables for those who wish to stand up or cannot find a seat. The guest beers, often from smaller Scottish breweries, come in a range of strengths. Sparklers can be removed on request. ≠(Waverley)

Clarks Bar

142 Dundas Street, EH3 5DQ (N edge of new town)
11-11 (11.30 Thu-Sat); 12.30-11 Sun
(0131) 556 1067
Caledonian Deuchars IPA, 80/-; McEwan's 80/-; guest beers Ⓗ
Basic tenement bar popular with locals and workers from the many offices nearby. The internal layout is interesting with two private rooms off the bar. Several brewery mirrors and some photographs from the days when trams ran outside adorn the main room. A trip to the toilets is a good test of sobriety as the stairs must be some of the steepest in the UK. Don't miss the interesting mural on the way. Dogs are welcome.

Cloisters Bar

26 Brougham Street, EH3 9JH (SW edge of centre)
12-midnight (12.30am Fri-Sat); 12.30-midnight Sun
(0131) 221 9997
Caledonian Deuchars IPA; Greene King IPA; Taylor Landlord; guest beers Ⓗ
A former parsonage, this bare-boarded ale house is popular with a broad cross section of drinkers. Large bench seats give the pub a friendly feel. A fine selection of brewery mirrors adorns the walls and the wide range of single malt whiskies does justice to the outstanding gantry, built using wood from a redundant church. A spiral staircase makes paying a visit an adventure. Food is served from midday until 8pm (4pm Fri & Sat, 6pm Sun). Dogs are welcome. Q

Dalriada

77 Promenade, Joppa, EH15 2EL (off Joppa Rd by St Philips Church)
11-11 (midnight Fri & Sat); closed Mon in Jan & Feb; 12-11 (7 winter) Sun
(0131) 454 4500
Caledonian Deuchars IPA; Taylor Landlord; guest beer Ⓗ
Long-established lounge bar on the Portobello/Joppa promenade where you can enjoy a pint and look out for seals. The imposing entrance has an original tiled floor and fireplace. The wooden-floored bar is in a wing attached to the side of the original stone built villa and has a wooden counter with a polished Italian granite top. There are two further dining and drinking areas with wooden tables and chairs. Meals are served all day on Saturday and Sunday. Children are welcome until 8pm. (26)P

Halfway House

24 Fleshmarket Close, EH1 1BX (up steps opp. station's Market St. entrance)
11-11.30 (1am Fri & Sat); 12.30-11.30 Sun
(0131) 225 7101
Beer range varies Ⓗ
Cosy little bar full of character hidden away halfway down an old town close. Old railway memorabilia and current timetables adorn the interior of this fairly small bar, which can get crowded. Usually there are three interesting guest beers from smaller Scottish breweries. Card-carrying CAMRA members get a discount on their first pint. Opening hours may extend to 1am at busy times. Dogs and children are welcome. Voted 2005 Scottish Pub of the Year. ≠(Waverley)

Leslies Bar ☆

45 Ratcliffe Terrace, EH9 1SU (Newington, 1½ miles S of centre)
11-11 (11.30 Thu; 12.30am Fri & Sat); 12.30-11.30 Sun
(0131) 667 7205
Caledonian Deuchars IPA, 80/-; Taylor Landlord; guest beers Ⓗ
Outstanding Victorian pub, listed in CAMRA's National Inventory of interiors of historic interest. It retains its fine ceiling, cornice, leaded glasswork and half-wood panelling. The island bar has a spectacular snob screen dividing the pub. Small ticket window hatches allow customers to order drinks. A plaque near the fire gives further details of this busy, vibrant but orderly pub. The three guest beers are usually from smaller breweries. Trad jazz is regularly played on Mon evenings. Q

Malt & Hops

45 The Shore, Leith, EH6 6QU
12-11 (midnight Wed & Thu; 1am Fri & Sat); 12.30-11 Sun
(0131) 555 0083
Caledonian Deuchars IPA; Marston's Pedigree; Tetley Burton Ale; guest beers Ⓗ
One-roomed public bar dating from 1749 in the heart of Leith's riverside restaurant district. Wood panelling gives an intimate feel with numerous mirrors, artefacts and a large oil painting adding interest. The superb collection of pump clips, many from now

defunct breweries, indicates the ever-changing interesting range of guest beers served. No meals are served on Saturday or Sunday. Children are welcome until 6pm. Dogs are welcome at any time. ⌂❀◑⊟♣

McCowans Brewhouse

Fountain Park Complex, Dundee Street, EH11 1AF (1 mile SW of centre)

⏲ 12-1am (midnight Mon); 12.30-midnight Sun

☎ (0131) 228 8198

Caledonian Deuchars IPA, 80/-; guest beers Ⓗ

American-style brew pub with working on-site brewery, providing a house beer, in a modern entertainment complex. Exposed metal roof beams and ventilation ducts give an industrial feel. On two levels, it has a glass front giving a light and airy interior, furnished with a mixture of tables and chairs and comfy armchairs. Regular entertainment is provided on Friday evening. Wireless internet access is available at £4.50 an hour. Food is served all day until 10pm. Children are welcome until 6pm. ❀◑◗♿≹(Haymarket)⊟P

Old Dock Bar

3-5 Dock Place, Leith, EH6 6LV

⏲ 12-11 (1am Fri-Sat); 12.30-11 Sun

☎ (0131) 555 4474 🌐 spidacom.co.uk/olddockbar/

Atlas Latitude; Caledonian 80/-; Taylor Landlord; guest beers Ⓗ

A true free house offering a mix of the old and the new. The traditional bar has an excellent selection of ales and the comfy bistro area offers food and fine wines. The walls are decorated with maritime prints and photographs of old Leith. The building has been a bar since 1813, and claims to be Leith's oldest. It is convenient for visitors to the Scottish Executive building and Ocean Terminal shopping centre, meals are served all day. ❀◑◗♿⊟♣

Oxford Bar ☆

8 Young Street, EH2 4JB (new town, off Charlotte Sq)

⏲ 11-1am; 12.30-midnight Sun

☎ (0131) 539 7119 🌐 oxfordbar.com

Belhaven 80/-; Caledonian Deuchars IPA; Edinburgh Brewing EPA; guest beers (summer) Ⓗ

Small, basic, vibrant New Town drinking shop decorated with Burns memorabilia. It is where the Professor holds court in Ian Rankin novels. The haunt of many famous and infamous characters over the years, you never know who you might bump into. Why not visit the website and contribute a story? A real taste of New Town past. Simple bar snacks are available. Dogs are welcome. ⊟♣

Railway Inn

542 Lanark Road, Juniper Green, EH14 5EL (on A70)

⏲ 11-11 (midnight Thu-Sat); 12.30-11 Sun

☎ (0131) 458 5395

Caledonian Deuchars IPA; Taylor Landlord; guest beer Ⓗ

Well-appointed, single-roomed lounge bar in a late 1800s building. The decor is attractive throughout, and a strong community spirit exists within the pub. The bar counter is mahogany and a more modern gantry is designed to match. Pictures of the old Balerno branch line provide interest. The food is freshly cooked to a high standard every day. A secluded patio and garden to the rear are popular in summer. ❀◑⊟

Regent

2 Montrose Terrace, EH7 5OL (¾ mile E of centre)

⏲ 11 (12.30 Sun)-1am

☎ (0131) 661 8198

Caledonian Deuchars IPA; guest beers Ⓗ

Large, comfortable tenement bar with two rooms (one music free), all on one level. Comfortable seating includes banquettes, leather sofas and armchairs. A new slant on pub games is a gymnastic pommel horse between the ladies' and gents' toilets. CAMRA LGBT group meets here on the first Monday of each month. Bar snacks are available and dogs are welcome. Orkney Dark Island is often a guest beer. ⊟

Scott's Bar

202 Rose Street, EH2 4AZ (off Charlotte Sq)

⏲ 11 (12.30 Sun)-1am

☎ (0131) 225 7401

Caledonian Deuchars IPA, 80/-; guest beers Ⓗ

Wooden floored ale house, a popular starting or finishing point on the Rose Street crawl. The single L-shaped room is dominated by a circular bar counter. Wooden tables and chairs predominate, giving a functional feel. Guest beers are usually from smaller breweries across the UK – the range may be reduced during weekdays. Meals are available all day. ❀◑◗≹(Waverley)⊟

Starbank Inn

64 Laverockbank Road, EH5 3BZ (foreshore near Newhaven)

⏲ 11-11 (midnight Thu-Sat); 12.30-11 Sun

☎ (0131) 552 4141 🌐 starbankinn.co.uk

Belhaven Sandy Hunter's Traditional Ale, 80/-; Caledonian Deuchars IPA; Taylor Landlord; guest beers Ⓗ

Bright, airy, bare-boarded ale house with a U-shaped layout extending into the conservatory dining area. Enjoy the superb views across the Firth of Forth to Fife. The pub is proud that it does not sell any keg ales but you can try a pint of prawns with your beer. Four interesting guest ales are usually available and the walls sport several rare brewery mirrors. Children are welcome until 8.30pm. Dogs are also welcome if on a leash. Occasional jazz is played on Sundays. Q◑◗♿⊟♣

Thomson's

182-184 Morrison Street, EH3 8EB (W edge of centre)

⏲ 12-11.30 (midnight Thu-Sat); 4-11 Sun

☎ (0131) 228 5700 🌐 thomsonsbar.co.uk

Caledonian Deuchars IPA, 80/-; Taylor Landlord; guest beers Ⓐ

An award-winning refurbishment of a pub modelled in the style of Glasgow's forgotten architect, Alexander 'Greek' Thomson, and dedicated to traditional Scottish air pressure dispense. The walls are liberally decorated with old adverts and rare mirrors from long defunct Scottish breweries. Up to five guest beers are available. Food is limited to pies on Saturday and is not served on Sunday. Dogs are welcome. Q❀◑≹(Haymarket)⊟

Winston's
20 Kirk Loan, Corstorphine, EH12 7HD (3 miles W of centre, off St Johns Rd)
✪ 11-11.30 (midnight Thu-Sat); 12.30-11 Sun
☎ (0131) 539 7077
Caledonian Deuchars IPA; guest beers [H]
Situated in Corstorphine in a small, modern building, this comfortable lounge bar is just over a mile from Murrayfield Stadium and close to the zoo. A warm and welcoming active community pub, it is popular with old and young alike and children are welcome until 3pm. The decor has golfing and rugby themes. Lunchtime meals include wonderful home-made pies. Simple bar snacks are served all day. Children and dogs are welcome. ◐♿🚌

Gifford

Goblin Ha' Hotel
Main Street, EH41 4QH
✪ 11-2.30, 4.30-11; 11-midnight Fri & Sat; 11-11 Sun
☎ (01620) 810244 🌐 goblinha.com
Caledonian Deuchars IPA; Hop Back Summer Lightning; guest beers [H]
Long-established inn near the village green with a colourful decor and light stained wood. The smart, contemporary lounge bar and conservatories focus on food, though an area is available for drinking. Drinkers may prefer the smaller and more rustic public bar with its half-wood, half-stone walls. A games room leads off the bar. The garden is a favourite in summer. Children are welcome in the lounge until 8pm or conservatory all day. Dogs are welcome in the bar. ♨Q✿⇄◐◑♿▲🚌♣

Gorebridge

Stobbs Mill Inn
25 Powdermill Brae, EH23 4HX (S edge of town)
✪ 11-3, 6-11 (11.30 Thu); 11-midnight Fri & Sat; 12.30-11.30 Sun
☎ (01875) 820202
Beer range varies [H]
Built in 1866 as a public house, this two-storey detached building resembles a private dwelling. The friendly locals' bar has three engraved wooden panels with sporting scenes separating it from an intriguingly tiny snug. Old photos of the town adorn the walls along with a selection of water jugs and bottles. The lounge is only open when food is served on Friday and Saturday evenings and Sunday lunchtime. Simple bar snacks are available at all times. Dogs are welcome. ◐◑🚌(3A, 29)♣P

Gullane

Old Clubhouse
East Links Road, EH31 2AF (W end of village, off A198)
✪ 11-11 (midnight Thu-Sat); 12.30-11 Sun
☎ (01620) 842008 🌐 oldclubhouse.com
Caledonian Deuchars IPA; Taylor Landlord; [P] **guest beers** [H]
Spacious, well appointed pub looking out over the golf links to the Lammermuir Hills. Decorated in natural woods, golfing memorabilia, stuffed birds and animals adorn the walls. Caricature-style statuettes, including the Marx Brothers and Laurel and Hardy, are among the many nick-nacks to be found. Food features highly and is served all day. An extensive menu and wine list is offered in both the bar and restaurant. Children are welcome until 8pm. Dogs are also welcome. ♨✿◐♿🚌

Haddington

Tyneside Tavern
10 Poldrate, EH41 4DA (A6137, ½ mile S of centre)
✪ 11-11 (midnight Thu; 12:45am Fri & Sat); 12.30-midnight Sun
☎ (01620) 822221 🌐 tynesidetavern.co.uk
Caledonian Deuchars IPA; Courage Directors; guest beer [H]
Cosy, convivial and popular community pub close to the River Tyne, attracting a mixed local clientele. The bar is long and narrow with a log fire in a fine stone fireplace beside the door. Rustic style woodwork fronts the bar counter, which boasts a mahogany top and gantry behind. The quieter lounge bar is being extended and will become a restaurant. Children are welcome until 8pm and dogs are also welcome in the bar. ♨✿◐◑♿🚌♣

Lasswade

Laird & Dog Hotel
5 High Street, EH18 1NA (on A768 near river)
✪ 11-11.30 (11.45 Thu; 12.30am Fri & Sat); 12.30-11.30 Sun
☎ (0131) 663 9219 🌐 lairdanddog.btinternet.co.uk
Beer range varies [H]
Comfortable village local catering for all tastes, from those who enjoy a quiet drink or meal to music loving pool players. The two real ales are usually from smaller breweries. Food is available all day with a good menu, daily specials and cheaper bar snacks. Pictures and horse brasses decorate the bar; there is an unusual bottle shaped well and a real fire surrounded by armchairs. Dogs are welcome. Children are also welcome until 8pm. ♨✿⇄◐♿🚌(31, 141, 77)♣P

Linlithgow

Four Marys
65-67 High Street, EH49 7ED
✪ 12-11 (11.45 Thu-Sat); 12.30-11 Sun
☎ (01506) 842171
Belhaven 80/-, St Andrew's Ale; Caledonian Deuchars IPA; guest beers [H]
Built around 1500 as a dwelling house, the pub was named after the four ladies-in-waiting of Mary, Queen of Scots, who was born in nearby Linlithgow Palace. The pub has seen several uses through the years; it was once a chemist's shop run by the Waldie family whose most famous member, David, established the anaesthetic properties of chloroform in 1847. Beer festivals are hosted in May and October when the handpumps are increased from eight to 18. ◐≹🚌

Platform 3
1a High Street, EH49 7AB
✪ 11-midnight (1am Fri & Sat); 12.30-midnight Sun
☎ (01506) 847405

Caledonian Deuchars IPA; guest beers [H]
Small, friendly pub on the railway station approach, originally the public bar of the hotel next door. It was purchased and renovated in 1998 as a pub in its own right and stages occasional live music. Note the interesting memorabilia displayed around the walls and look out for the train running above the bar. The guest ale rotates on one pump. ⇌🚌♣

Lothianbridge

Sun Inn

EH22 4TR (on A7, near Newtongrange)
⊙ 11 (12 Sun)-midnight
☎ (0131) 663 2456 🌐 thesuninndalkeith.com
Caledonian Deuchars IPA; guest beer [H]
Originally built around 1870, situated in the shadow of the impressive, currently disused, 23-span Waverley line viaduct. A friendly welcome is offered to both locals and travellers alike. The bar caters for drinkers and diners and is tastefully decorated throughout with a prominence of local art. Note the suspended model railway system. An additional dining area overlooks the garden. Food is served all day Friday-Sunday. Children and dogs are welcome.
🏨❀🛏◐◑♿⛺🚌(29)P

Lothianburn

Steading

118-120 Biggar Road, EH10 7DU (on A702, just S of bypass)
⊙ 11-midnight; 12.30-11 Sun
☎ (0131) 445 1128
Caledonian Deuchars IPA; Orkney Dark Island; Taylor Landlord; guest beer [H]
The pub was converted from farm cottages and has distinct areas for drinkers and diners. The popular restaurant now extends into a large conservatory and food is served all day. A simple menu is available in the bar area. The outside drinking area has excellent views of the Pentland Hills and the pub is ideally placed for a relaxing pint after walking in the hills or visiting the nearby dry ski-slope. Children and dogs are welcome.
🏨❀◐◑🚌(4)P

Musselburgh

Levenhall Arms

10 Ravensheugh Road, EH21 7PP (on B1348, 1 mile E of centre)
⊙ 12-11 (midnight Thu; 1am Fri & Sat); 12.30-midnight Sun
☎ (0131) 665 3220
Atlas Latitude; Caledonian Deuchars IPA [P]
This three-roomed hostelry dates from 1830 and is popular with locals and racegoers. The lively, cheerfully decorated public bar is half timber panelled and carpeted. A smaller area leads off with a dartboard and pictures of old local industries. The quieter lounge area has vinyl banquettes and tables for dining. Food is served all day until 8pm. Dogs are welcome. Children are also welcome until 8.30pm in the lounge.
Q◐◑🀫⛺⇌(Wallyford)🚌♣P

Volunteer Arms (Staggs)

81 North High Street, EH21 6JE (behind Brunton Hall)
⊙ 12-11 (11.30 Thu; midnight Fri); 12-midnight Sat; 12.30-11 Sun
☎ (0131) 665 9654
Caledonian Deuchars IPA [H]**, 80/-** [P]**; guest beers** [H]
Three-roomed pub run by the same family since 1858. The main bar is traditional with a lino-tiled floor, dark wood panelling, wood and glass screens and mirrors from defunct local breweries. A superb gantry is topped with old casks. The snug has a nascent history collection featuring local breweries. A more modern rear lounge opens at the weekend. The three guest beers, often pale and hoppy, change regularly. Dogs are welcome, but no children.
❀🀫🚌♣

North Berwick

Nether Abbey Hotel

20 Dirleton Avenue, EH39 4BQ (on A198, ½ mile W of town centre)
⊙ 11-11 (midnight Thu; 1am Fri & Sat); 12.30-11 Sun
☎ (01620) 892802 🌐 netherabbey.co.uk
Caledonian Deuchars IPA; guest beers [P]
Comfortable family-run hotel in a stone built villa. The ground floor is an open plan, split level room comprising a bar and dining area. It has a light and modern feel with pine and steel decor. The marble-topped bar counter has a row of modern chrome founts. The middle ones, with horizontally moving levers, dispense the real ales. The bar area can expand outside under a retractable canvas roof. Food is served all day in summer and at the weekend. Children are welcome until 9pm. Dogs are also permitted.
❀🛏◐◑♿⛺⇌🚌P

Ship

7-9 Quality Street, EH39 4HJ
⊙ 11-11 (midnight Thu-Sat); 12.30-11 Sun
☎ (01620) 890676
Caledonian Deuchars IPA; guest beers [P]
Open plan bar split into three areas by a glass partition and a twice pierced wall. It has pine floorboards, a mahogany counter and a dark wooden gantry. Real ale is dispensed from founts, which look similar to those dispensing the keg beers. Nautically themed throughout; note the dado tile work and maritime tableaux dotted on shelves around the bar. Popular for food, which is served until 3pm (4pm at weekends). Children are welcome until 8pm and dogs are also permitted.
❀◐⛺⇌🚌♣

Ormiston

Hopetoun Arms Hotel

Main Street, EH35 5HX
⊙ 11-11 (1am Fri & Sat); 12.30-11 Sun
☎ (01875) 610298
Caledonian Deuchars IPA; Taylor Landlord; guest beer [H]
Interesting village local where Hamish the west highland terrier holds court. Hops decorate the ceiling of the cosy public bar and on the walls are pictures of the village

SCOTLAND

and local sports teams, along with their trophies. Darts is played in a raised area at the end of the bar. The small lounge is mainly used for dining at weekends - evening meals are served Friday and Saturday. Children are admitted until 8pm and Hamish usually welcomes other dogs. ❀☾◗⊟♿⊟♣

Prestonpans

Prestoungrange Gothenburg ☆

227 High Street, EH32 9BE

⏲ 11-11 (midnight Fri & Sat); 12.30-11 Sun

☎ (01875) 819922 🌐 prestoungrange.org

Caledonian Deuchars IPA; Fowler's Prestonpans 80/-, Gothenburg Porter, guest beers Ⓐ

Superbly refurbished Gothenburg pub which was the winner of English Heritage's pub refurbishment award in 2005 and is CAMRA Lothian 2006 Pub of the Year. The ground floor comprises a micro-brewery, a restaurant and a public bar, which has to be seen to be appreciated. Upstairs is a lounge/function room and meeting room with superb views over the Forth. The walls throughout are covered in murals, paintings and prints depicting past local life. Meals are served all day until 8pm. Children are welcome but not in bar. ⛺☾◗⊟♿⊟P

Ratho

Bridge Inn

27 Baird Road, EH28 8RA (by canal)

⏲ 11.30-11 (midnight Fri & Sat); 12.30-11 Sun

☎ (0131) 333 1320 🌐 bridgeinn.com

Caledonian Deuchars IPA; guest beer Ⓗ

Old canalside inn, now with a modern extension. The older part, originally a farmhouse dating from around 1750, is used as a restaurant. The extension, called the Pop Inn, is a comfortable lounge bar with views over the canal where families are welcome. The original owner campaigned tirelessly for the restoration of the canal, part of the millennium link project. Regular cruises depart from the pub during the summer. Food is served all day until 8pm. ❀☾◗♿⊟♣P

South Queensferry

Ferry Tap

36 High Street, EH30 9HN

⏲ 11.30-11.30 (midnight Thu; 12.30am Fri & Sat); 12.30-11.30 Sun

☎ (0131) 331 2000

Caledonian Deuchars IPA, 80/-; Orkney Dark Island; guest beer Ⓗ

Ground floor bar in a 330-year-old building in the historic centre of a town overshadowed by mighty bridges. The one-room, L-shaped bar boasts an unusual barrel-vaulted ceiling. Dark wood gives an intimate feel and numerous artefacts, many from bygone breweries, add interest. A good selection of meals is served at lunchtime. Dogs are welcome but not children. Thursday is quiz night. ☾⇌(Dalmeny)⊟(43)

Uphall

Oatridge Hotel

2-4 East Main Street, EH52 5DA (jct of A899/B8046)

⏲ 11 (12.30 Sun)-midnight

☎ (01506) 856465

Beer range varies Ⓗ

Originally a 19th-century coaching inn, the hotel now serves the modern day traveller as well as thirsty locals. Real ale is dispensed in the public bar where up to three ales, mainly from Scottish micros, are available. The bar is stylish with an Art Deco feel and features a large mirror etched with a scene depicting life of yesteryear. TV sports are popular at the weekend and pool is also played. ❀⛺☾◗⊟⊟P

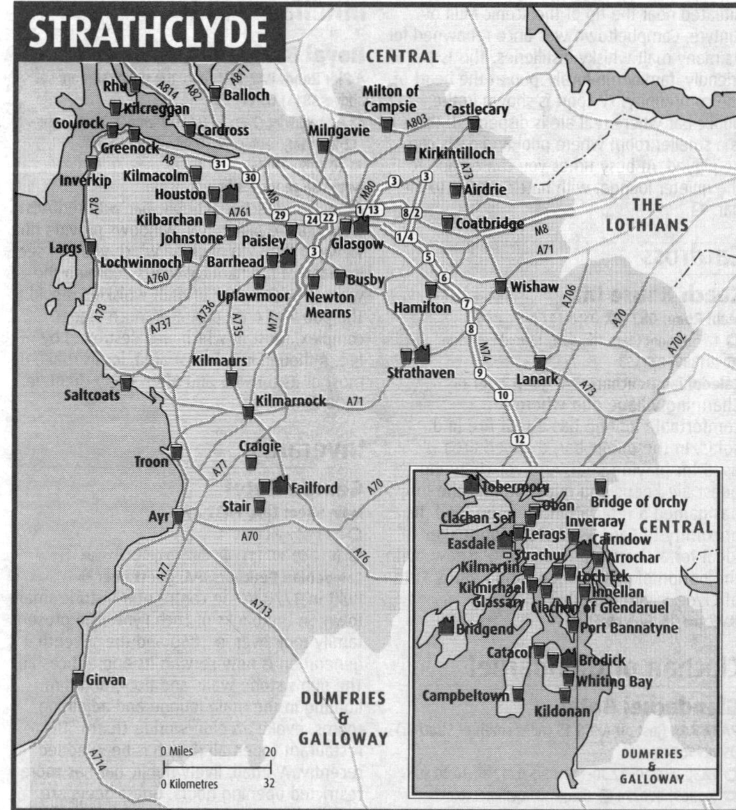

Strathclyde comprises Argyll and Bute, Ayrshire and Arran, Dunbartonshire, Glasgow, Lanarkshire and Renfrewshire

ARGYLL AND BUTE

Arrochar

Village Inn

Shore Road, G83 7AX (on A814, 3/4 mile S of A83 jct)
11-midnight (1am Fri & Sat); 12-midnight Sun
(01301) 702279 maclay.com/VillageInn.html
Beer range varies H

Set back from the main road, with a patio and garden amid mature trees, this idyllic inn offers impressive views over Loch Long, the Cobbler and Arrochar Alps. The bar and restaurant have solid wooden furniture and traditional Scottish country-style decoration. The friendly locals are joined by day trippers, hill walkers and tourists, some staying in the inn's well-appointed bedrooms. Food is served at lunchtime in the bar and garden and in the evening in the restaurant. ⌂Q❀⇌◐▮⊟&P

Bridge of Orchy

Bridge of Orchy Hotel

PA36 4AD (on A82, N end of Glen Orchy) OSNN298396
11 (12 Sun)-11 (midnight Fri & Sat)
(01838) 400208 bridgeoforchy.co.uk
Caledonian Deuchars IPA, 80/-; guest beers H

Located on the West Highland Way and route to Glencoe and Fort William, with a nearby rail station, this large, whitewashed hotel is easily accessible. There are impressive views of the glen and surrounding mountains from the comfortable bar and large restaurant to the rear. Popular with outdoor types who come for climbing, fishing, canoeing, rafting and kayaking; many stay in the bunkhouse. The interesting menu includes local Scottish produce. May close for three weeks in mid-winter. ⌂❀⇌◐▮≹P

Campbeltown

Commercial Inn

Cross Street, PA28 6HU (by town hall)
11-1am (2am Fri & Sat; 12.30am Sun)
(01586) 553703
Caledonian Deuchars IPA; guest beers H

INDEPENDENT BREWERIES

Arran Brodick
Clockwork Glasgow
Fyne Cairndow
Houston Houston
Islay Bridgend
Isle of Mull Tobermory
Kelburn Barrhead
Oyster Easdale
Strathaven Strathaven
West Glasgow
Windie Goat Failford

Situated near the tip of the scenic Mull of Kintyre, Campbeltown was once renowned for its many malt whisky distilleries. This is a friendly, family-run locals' pub at the heart of the community. TV sport is shown in the public bar where real ale is dispensed. There is a smaller room where pool and darts can be played. At busy times you can escape to the quieter lounge, with hatch service to the bar. 🀫

Cardross

Coach House Inn

Main Road, G82 5JX OSNS347775

✪ 12-midnight (1am Thu-Sat); 12-midnight Sun

☎ (01389) 841358

Caledonian Deuchars IPA; guest beer Ⓗ

Charming village pub where the comfortable lounge has a real fire and sofas. In the public bar, a raised area is used for playing pool. An ever-changing guest ale keeps you guessing and the inn has gained a reputation for good food. Its proximity to Cardross rail station makes it ideal for a short trip out from Glasgow, with the option of a walk along the nearby Firth of Clyde in fine weather.

⌂❀⇆◐◑⊟♿⇌P

Clachan of Glendaruel

Glendaruel Hotel

PA22 3AA (just off A886 15 miles south of Strachur) OSNR996842

✪ 12.30-2, 6-10; 12.30-11 Fri & Sat; 12.30-10.30 Sun

☎ (01369) 820274 🌐 theglendaruelhotel.co.uk

Beer range varies Ⓗ

The building has been a hotel since the 18th century, when the glen was the main route between Glasgow and the West Highlands. It lies on the Cowal Way with historic standing stones nearby. There is a small public bar with a bare wood floor and pool table, overlooked by a mounted stag's head, and a larger lounge/dining area. The hotel supplies shooting and fishing permits. The bar serves mainly locals, plus visitors, with beers often from Fyne Ales.

⌂Q❀⇆◐◑⊟♿⛺●P

Clachan Seil

Tigh-an-Truish

Isle of Seil by Oban, PA34 4QZ (on B844 just across the Atlantic via Clachan Bridge) OSNM785197

✪ 11 (12 Sun)-11 summer; 11-2.30, 5-11 winter daily

☎ (01852) 300242

Beer range varies Ⓗ

Tigh-an-Truish means 'House of the Trousers'. After Culloden, islanders changed from their forbidden kilts here, before crossing to the mainland. A pleasant adjacent beer garden and front patio seating afford views of the world famous 'Bridge over the Atlantic' (Clachan Sound). The pub has an unusual counter and possibly the world's only modern George Younger sign. Fyne and Atlas beers are usually available on rotation in the summer when food is available all day (no eve meals winter).

⌂Q♉❀⇆◐◑♣P

Innellan

Royal Bar

4 Pier Road, PA2 7TH (opp. the police station, set above A815) OSNS1470

✪ 12-midnight (2am Fri & Sat) summer; 2-midnight (12-2am Sat) winter; 12.30-midnight Sun

☎ (01369) 830742

Beer range varies Ⓗ

Attractive, functional public bar with red Ailsa Craig granite pillars. The windows provide fine views of the Firth of Clyde which you can see in many of the nautical charts adorning the walls. A wide range of malt whiskies is sold. The pub was once part of a much bigger complex, most of which was destroyed by fire. Although in a tourist area, locals make up most of its thriving and often lively clientele.

⌂◐◑⊟

Inveraray

George Hotel

Main Street East, PA32 8TT

✪ 11-midnight daily

☎ (01499) 302111 🌐 thegeorgehotel.co.uk

Caledonian Deuchars IPA; guest beer Ⓗ

Built in 1770 in the centre of a historic small town on the banks of Loch Fyne. The present family took over in 1860 and the seventh generation is now serving its apprenticeship. The pub's stone walls and floor, and dim lighting in the main lounge and adjoining rooms, evoke an olde worlde charm. The restaurant (open all day) has been added recently. A small, lively public bar has more restricted opening hours. Guest beers are usually from Fyne Ales at the head of the Loch. ⌂❀⇆◐◑⊟♿P

Kilcreggan

Kilcreggan Hotel

Argyll Road, G84 0JP (E of Kilcreggan near the pier) OSNS239805

✪ 12-midnight (1am Fri & Sat); 12.30-midnight Sun

☎ (01436) 842243

Beer range varies Ⓗ

Located at the southern tip of the Rosneath Peninsula, this stone Victorian mansion is accessible by bus from Helensburgh, passenger-only ferries from Gourock and the paddle steamer Waverley from Glasgow (Fridays in summer). A Daytripper ticket allows transport enthusiasts a circuit around the Firth of Clyde via trains, bus and ferry. The Hotel offers fine wood panelling, stained glass windows, ornate bargeboards and balconies, a curious gabled and battlemented tower and stunning views over the Clyde. ⌂❀⇆◐◑⊟🚌♣P

Kilmartin

Kilmartin Hotel

PA31 8RQ (on A816 10 miles N of Lochgilphead) OSNR835989

✪ 12-1am summer; 5-midnight (12-1am Fri & Sat) winter; 12-midnight Sun

☎ (01546) 510250 🌐 kilmartin-hotel.com

Atlas Three Sisters; Caledonian 80/-; guest beers (Summer) Ⓗ

A friendly, family-run hotel set in impressive

scenery, overlooking a glen with more than 5,000 years of history. Worth visiting are the churchyard, standing stones, stone circles, burial cairns, cup rings, an iron age fort and the museum that records the glen's history. Locals in the cosy, narrow bar room offer a warm welcome to visitors. There is a larger games room to the rear. The dining rooms serve good home cooking. Shinty is occasionally played on a nearby field. Q❀⇄◑ ΔP

Kilmichael Glassary

Horseshoe Inn

Bridgend, PA31 8QA OSNR852928
12 (6 Winter)-11 daily
☎ (01546) 606369
Caledonian Deuchars IPA; guest beers H

Large, pleasant inn, situated in a small village in the atmospheric Kilmartin Glen, three miles north of Lochgilphead. It offers a warm welcome to locals and tourists. The interior includes a variety of rooms and good value, fine food is available. Note the Art Deco coloured glass in a door panel. Pool and darts are played here. Nearby, stone circles, a fort and other archaeological artefacts can be seen, dating from 5,000 years ago. Q❀⇄◑ ♣P

Lerags

Barn

Cologin, PA34 4SE (at end of minor road off A816, three miles S of Oban) OSNM838245
11-midnight summer; phone to check in winter; 12-midnight Sun
☎ (01631) 564618 cologin.co.uk
Fyne Highlander; guest beers (summer) H

This converted barn poured its first pint in June 1978 and caters mainly for holidaymakers, staying in self-catering chalets. The family-friendly bar serves good food and can be very busy in summer. Located at the end of a three mile minor road, amid picturesque West Highland scenery, the Barn is worth making a detour for. Near the rugged Kilbride coast, it is an ideal starting point for walks to Loch Feochan or Minard Point. ❀⇄◑P

Loch Eck

Coylet Inn

PA23 8SG (on A815 at S end of Loch Eck) OSNS143885
11-11 (midnight Fri & Sat); 12.30-11 Sun
☎ (01369) 840426 coylet-locheck.co.uk
Caledonian Deuchars IPA; Fyne Highlander; guest beers H

Originally a coaching inn dating from 1650, this popular pub and restaurant attracts visitors from afar, with fine views of Loch Eck and yonder mountains. It claims a ghost, the unfortunate Blue Boy who drowned in the loch in the 1920s. Enjoy your ale in the cosy bar with a stone fireplace or in the restaurant before a meal. Close to Benmore Botanic Gardens and en-route to the Dunoon ferry. ❀⇄◑P

Oban

Oban Inn

1 Stafford Street, PA34 5NJ (near pier)
11 (12.30 Sun)-12.45am
☎ (01631) 562 484
Beer range varies H

Located near the harbour pier, which serves ferries to many islands, this is a traditional corner local, formerly a late 18th-century coaching inn. The public bar remains unspoilt and retains its dark wood panelling and old stone floors of Easdale slate. Maritime artefacts are displayed on the walls and currency notes from many nations cover the wooden beams. The upstairs lounge has a collection of stained glass panels, reputedly from an Irish monastery. ◑⇌

Port Bannatyne

Port Royal Hotel

37 Marine Road, PA20 0LW (2 miles N of Rothesay & ferry terminal) OSNS072672
12-1am (2am Sat); 12.30-1am Sun
☎ (01700) 505073 russiantavern.co.uk
Beer range varies G

Dag & Olga own this 'Russian tavern', the only Strathclyde pub serving ales on gravity, all from local micros. Real cider or perry, a range of foreign beers, Russian vodkas and real fruit drinks are also available. Distinctive dishes, prepared from local ingredients, are served all day. With fine views of the harbour, bay and mountains, the pub is popular with yachtsmen and recommended for visitors. It is sometimes closed for functions, so phone before you buy your train/ferry ticket.
⇄◑

Rhu

Ardencaple Hotel

Shore Road, G84 8LA (on A814)
11-11 (midnight Fri & Sat); 11-11 Sun
☎ (01436) 820200
Caledonian Deuchars IPA, 80/- H

This attractive white-painted, 250-year-old former coaching inn offers fine views over the Gareloch and Firth of Clyde. The Caple Bar caters for traditional pub games and has a large TV screen, regularly used for sporting events. This is the only bar with handpumps but real ale will also be supplied in the comfortable lounge bar.
❀⇄◑ ♣P

Rhu Inn

49 Gareloch Road, G84 8LA (near village church)
11-midnight (1am Fri & Sat); 12.30-11 Sun
☎ (01436) 821048 therhuinn.co.uk
Caledonian Deuchars IPA; guest beers H

Originally a coaching inn dating from 1648 and previously called the Colquhoun Arms, this gem of a pub has arguably the smallest public bar in Strathclyde. A popular community local, it has a wonderful mahogany gantry, Tiffany style windows and flagstone floor, plus an adjacent snug. Pictures of old village life and the football team adorn the walls. Refurbishment in 1998 added a modern lounge bar with Fyne Ales handpump. Live music is played at the weekend – guitars available.
⇄ ♣P

SCOTLAND

Strachur

Creggans Inn

PA27 8BX (on A815 Cairndow to Dunoon road)
OSNN087024
⌚ 11-11; 12.30-11 Sun
☎ (01369) 860279 🌐 creggans-inn.co.uk
Beer range varies Ⓗ
This whitewashed 18th-century coaching inn lies on a historic site with connections to Mary Queen of Scots. The old public bar has a modern extension and is home to the local shinty team. The dining room opens in the evening. There are warming real fires throughout. A single winter beer increases to two in summer, with Coniston beers often featured.
⛰Q❀⇌◑◐⊞P

AYRSHIRE AND ARRAN

Ayr

Balgarth

9 Dunure Road, Doonfoot, KA7 4HR (on A719, 2 miles S of town centre)
⌚ 11-11; 12.30-11 Sun
☎ (01292) 442441
Beer range varies Ⓗ
Imposing red sandstone building, set in its own grounds in a southern suburb of the town. Refurbishment of this former Brewers Fayre has resulted in a multi-roomed pub. Some areas are more akin to an upmarket restaurant, while others cater for drinkers. The garden features an excellent children's play area. The two beers on offer may be from regional or local micro-breweries.
❀◑◐♿🚌(A9)P

Chestnuts Hotel

52 Racecourse Road, KA7 2UZ
(on A719, 1 mile S of centre)
⌚ 11 (12 Sun)-midnight
☎ (01292) 264393 🌐 chestnutshotel.com
Beer range varies Ⓗ
The wood-panelled lounge of this family-run hotel features a large collection of water jugs and golfing memorabilia, reflecting its proximity to local courses. Three changing guest ales are offered with at least one from a local micro. High quality meals are available in the bar or adjoining restaurant. The garden has a children's play area.
⛰❀⇌◑◐🚌(A9)P

Geordie's Byre

103 Main Street, KA8 8BU
⌚ 11-11 (midnight Thu-Sat); 12.30-11 Sun
☎ (01292) 264925
Caledonian Deuchars IPA; guest beers Ⓐ
The landlord and landlady of this CAMRA award-winning pub have been in situ for over 25 years and nothing much has changed here during that time. Both the bar and lounge (open Thu-Sat evenings) feature a wealth of memorabilia. The three (sometimes four) guest ales come from a wide range of breweries, with both regionals and micros well represented. Over 100 malt whiskies and around 30 rums are also offered – ask for the menu. Q⊞⇌(Newton-on-Ayr)🚌

Old Racecourse Hotel

2 Victoria Park, KA7 2TR (on A719 1 mile S of centre)
⌚ 11 (12.30 Sun)-11
☎ (01292) 262873 🌐 oldracecoursehotel.co.uk
Beer range varies Ⓗ
The comfortable lounge bar of this small hotel features an unusual pot still-shaped fire as a centrepiece. Up to four ales from a wide range of breweries are offered. Good quality meals and snacks are available, either in the bar or the adjoining restaurant area. Golfing breaks can be arranged – the hotel is an ideal base for this pursuit. The Burns Heritage Park is nearby.
⛰❀⇌◑◐🚌(A9)P

Wellington's Bar

17 Wellington Square, KA7 1EZ
⌚ 11 (12.30 Sun)-11
☎ (01292) 269321
Beer range varies Ⓗ
Basement bar (look for the large Wellington boot advertisement outside) close to the seafront and local government offices. It caters mainly for office workers at lunchtime and features regular live music in the evening. One real ale is available, usually from a larger regional brewery. ◑◐⇌🚌

West Kirk

58a Sandgate, KA7 1BX
⌚ 11 (12.30 Sun)-midnight
☎ (01292) 880416
Beer range varies Ⓗ
Opposite the town's main post office, this Wetherspoon's conversion of a former church retains many original features, including the pulpit. The ales offered are this chain's usual mix of regionals and micros. It opens at 10am for breakfast and meals are available all day; children are welcome until 6pm. It gets crowded on Friday and Saturday evenings. ❀◑◐♿⇌🚌

Brodick

Brodick Bar

Alma Road, KA27 8BU
⌚ 11-11 (midnight Fri & Sat); 3-11 winter; 5.30-11 (summer only) Sun
☎ (01770) 302169
Caledonian Deuchars IPA; guest beers (summer) Ⓟ
This long white building next to the post office has two bars, one the main drinking bar and the other acts mainly a restaurant. Both have a light, airy and contemporary ambience. There is an extensive menu of freshly cooked, mainly local produce. The real ale founts are in the main bar and are unmarked, with the beer names written on a blackboard above them. Q❀◑◐⊞

Ormidale Hotel

Knowe Road, KA27 8BY (off A841 at W end of village)
⌚ 12-2.30 (not winter), 4.30-midnight; 12-midnight Sat & Sun
☎ (01770) 302293 🌐 ormidale-hotel.co.uk
Arran Ale, Blonde; guest beers Ⓐ
This fine sandstone building overlooking the sports field has a small, friendly bar plus a large greenhouse/conservatory, which is a

real suntrap. The original tall founts on the boat-shaped bar serve beers, including guests, from the nearby Arran Brewery, although the prices do not reflect the proximity. There are discos and folk music in the conservatory at weekends, and quizzes on Tuesday and Thursday evenings. Highly recommended home-cooked bar meals are served daily. Accommodation is available in summer. ⛫❀⊨◑⊟⊞♣P

Catacol

Catacol Bay Hotel

KA27 8HN

⚙ 11-midnight (1am Thu-Sat); 11-midnight Sun

☎ (01770) 830231 🌐 catacol.co.uk

Beer range varies Ⓗ

This free-standing white building nestles among the hills opposite the shore, with grand views across the Kilbrannan Sound towards Kintyre. It is adjacent to the Twelve Apostles, a listed terrace of former estate houses. Originally a manse, it has been run by the present owner for 27 years. Ideally situated for walking and climbing, there is a richness of wildlife: glimpses of red deer and golden eagles are not unusual. An Arran Brewery beer is often available.
⛫♨❀⊨◑⊟⊞(324)♣P

Craigie

Craigie Inn

KA1 5LY (signposted off B730)

⚙ 12-2, 5-midnight; 11-midnight Sat & Sun

☎ (01563) 860286 🌐 craigieinn.com

Caledonian Deuchars IPA; guest beers Ⓗ

Pretty village inn two and a half miles south of Kilmarnock where a well-appointed bar has dining and drinking areas and an open fire. Meals featuring local fish and game are served in the bar and restaurant. The outside seating area is extremely popular in summer. Live music is played on the last Friday of the month. A function room is available. ⛫Q❀◑♿⛺P

Failford

Failford Inn

KA5 5TF (on B743 Mauchline-Ayr road)

⚙ 12-midnight (12.30am Fri & Sat); 12.30-midnight Sun

☎ (01292) 540117 🌐 failfordinn.co.uk

Beer range varies Ⓗ

Country inn set on the banks of the River Ayr, with low ceilings and an old tiled range. Both restaurant and garden overlook the river. Meals are prepared by the chef/owner with an emphasis on freshly-cooked food. The inn is a good starting point for River Ayr gorge walks in a nearby nature reserve and the Source to Sea Footpath. There is very limited parking across the road. CAMRA local Pub of the Year 2005. ⛫Q❀◑⊟⛺⊞(43)

Girvan

Royal Hotel

36 Montgomery Street, KA26 9HE

⚙ 11-12.30am; 12.30-midnight Sun

☎ (01465) 714203 🌐 royalhotelgirvan.com

Beer range varies Ⓗ

Small hotel in a Clyde coast town still clinging to its fishing and tourist trades. The traditional public bar attracts locals as well as fishing, cycling and walking groups. The world-renowned Turnberry golf course is five miles away and the hotel is a good stopping off point for travellers to and from Irish ferries. The regular beer is from Houston Brewery, with a summer-only guest from another Scottish micro. A small but interesting range of bottled beers is also stocked. ❀⊨◑⊟♿⛺⇌⊞♣P

Kildonan

Breadalbane Hotel

KA27 8SE (on loop road through Kildonan)

⚙ 11-midnight (1am Thu-Sat); 11-midnight Sun

☎ (01770) 820284 🌐 breadalbanehotel.co.uk

Caledonian Deuchars IPA; guest beers Ⓗ

This white-painted hotel sits just behind the shore in a scattered village at the south end of the island. It enjoys extensive views, especially from the front sun lounge and new outside terrace, to Pladda and its lighthouse, Ailsa Craig, South Ayrshire and Loch Ryan. The main bar has a large stone fireplace, corner bar and pool table. The guest ale is often from a Scottish brewery and food is served all day. En-suite rooms and self-catering flats are available. The hotel is close to beaches renowned for seal spotting. Children are permitted up to 8pm. Closed second and third weeks in January.
Q❀⊨◑⛺⊞(323)♣P

Kilmarnock

Brass & Granite

53 Grange Street, KA1 2DD

⚙ 11.30-midnight (1am Thu-Sat); 12.30-midnight Sun

☎ (01563) 523431

Beer range varies Ⓗ

Modern, open-plan, town-centre pub situated in a quiet street behind the post office and popular with a varied mix of customers. Belgian fruit beers are available on draught and a variety of bottled beers are featured. There are several large-screen TVs, mostly used for sporting events. The pub also has a good food selection, with some speciality evenings including pasta on Wednesday and steak on Thursday. Quiz nights are Sunday and Monday. ◑⇌⊞♣

Wheatsheaf

Unit 5, Portland Gate, KA1 1JG

⚙ 10-11 (midnight Thu; 1am Fri & Sat); 10-11 Sun

☎ (01563) 572483

Caledonian Deuchars IPA; guest beers Ⓗ

Spacious, modern, Lloyds No.1, open-plan pub with a large, covered patio to the front affording views of the impressive railway viaduct. Food is available all day, from breakfast onwards. At the rear of the pub is the door to the original Wheatsheaf, which proclaims it to be the only licensed premises 'in the toun' to be visited by Rabbie Burns. Monday is quiz night and occasional food themed nights are held. The pub tends to be

SCOTLAND

busy Thursday to Saturday due to cut-price drinks and proximity to nightclubs. ❀◑♿⇌🚌

Kilmaurs

Weston Tavern

27 Main Street, KA3 2RQ
11 (12.30 Sun)-midnight
☎ (01563) 538805
Beer range varies Ⓗ
Built in 1740, this traditional pub in the centre of a village conservation area was originally a manse; the building has also served as a school and a smithy. The pub has been fully renovated over the last year with the previously unused rear lounge now a popular restaurant. The public bar has been altered to provide better seating while retaining the tiled floor and making a feature of the original stone walls. Real ale is from the Kelburn Brewery and a small range of Belgian bottled beers is available. In front of the pub is the historic 'Jougs' where criminals used to be shackled. ◑⇌🚌

Largs

Clachan

14 Bath Street, KA30 8BL
11-midnight (1am Thu-Sat); 12.30-midnight Sun
☎ (01475) 672224
Beer range varies Ⓗ
Single bar, town-centre pub with a good selection of whiskies. Refurbished two years ago, it hosts live music on Friday evening and a quiz on Monday evening. The back door leads to the seafront opposite the pier, from where the Cumbrae ferry leaves and the paddle steamer Waverley calls in summer. Largs is one of the main Costa Clyde resorts and boasts two good golf courses and the Vikingar Centre. ⇌🚌♣

Saltcoats

Salt Cot

7 Hamilton Street, KA21 5DS
10-11 (1am Thu-Sun)
☎ (01294) 465924
Beer range varies Ⓗ
A good conversion of a former cinema by Wetherspoon's, decorated with photos of the cinema in its heyday and of old Saltcoats. Children are allowed in one area and there is a family menu. Unusually for Wetherspoon's there are no regular beers but Theakston Old Peculier and Greene King Old Speckled Hen are frequently on handpump. The pub's name comes from the original cottages at the salt pans. Q◑♿⇌

Stair

Stair Inn

KA5 5HW
(on B730, 7 miles E of Ayr, 4 miles W of Mauchline)
12-11 (1am Fri & Sat); 12.30-11 Sun
☎ (01292) 591650 🌐 stairinn.co.uk
Beer range varies Ⓗ
Family-run inn nestling at the foot of a glen on the banks of the River Ayr. The bar, with an open log fire, has recently been refurbished with bespoke handmade furniture. The bedrooms are furnished in similar style. Built around 1700, it serves a widespread area and is close to the historic Stair Bridge. Houston beers are regulars and the food is recommended. The River Ayr Source to Sea footpath passes, but there is no public transport nearby. ⅏Q❀🛏◑♿⛺P

Troon

Ardneil Hotel

51 St Meddans Street, KA10 6NU
11-midnight; 12-midnight (11 winter) Sun
☎ (01292) 311611
Beer range varies Ⓗ
Situated next to Troon Station and close to the local municipal golf courses, this hotel's bar has recently been refurbished to a high standard. There are up to three changing ales with local breweries usually well-represented. The bar has a pool table and dartboard situated in a lowered seating area. There is a weekly quiz on Wednesday night. This hotel attracts golfers from Europe due to the proximity of Prestwick Airport. ❀🛏◑⇌🚌♣P

Lonsdale Bar

15 Portland Street, KA10 6AA
11-midnight (12.30am Thu-Sat); 12.30-midnight Sun
☎ (01292) 311355
Beer range varies Ⓗ
Popular bar in the centre of town with a carved gantry and flagstone floors in both bars. There are two handpumps in the public bar, but real ale is also available in the lounge. The ales are usually from Scottish breweries. There is a fine selection of malt whiskies. The public bar, dominated by two large TVs, regularly shows sport events and the lounge hosts regular karaoke nights. ◑⇌🚌♣

Whiting Bay

Eden Lodge Hotel

KA27 8QH
12.30-midnight (1am Thu-Sat); 12.30-midnight Sun
☎ (01770) 700357 🌐 edenlodgehotel.co.uk
Caledonian Deuchars IPA; guest beers Ⓗ
The Bar Eden is large, bright and airy with clear views across to Holy Island. The hotel is open all year round and its rooms have been refurbished to a high standard. Two rotating guest ales are served, although this can drop to one in the winter. There is a pool table in the bar. The hotel is handy for the 18-hole Whiting Bay Golf Club and for local walks, including the spectacular Glenashdale Falls. The village is eight miles south of Brodick ferry terminal. Q❀🛏◑🚌♣P

DUNBARTONSHIRE

Balloch

Balloch House Hotel

Balloch Road, G83 8LQ
11-11; 12.30-10.30 Sun
☎ (01389) 752 579

Caledonian Deuchars IPA; guest beer Ⓗ
Recently renovated hotel with a pleasing interior and a variety of areas to relax in. Popular with locals and tourists, good food is always available. In summer you can sit outside watching the wildlife on the banks of the River Leven flowing from Loch Lomond. Other diversions include the adjacent Balloch Country Park and the minor road north with impressive Lomond views, or the hills to the west. Near Balloch rail station, it is easy to reach from Glasgow.
♛❀⇌◐◑♿≠P

Kirkintilloch

Kirky Puffer

1-11 Townhead, G66 1NG (next to canal on main road through town)
⊙ 11 (12.30 Sun)-midnight
☎ (0141) 775 4140
Caledonian Deuchars IPA; Greene King Abbot; guest beers Ⓗ
This large Wetherspoon's lies next to the Forth & Clyde Canal and pictures of canal boats of old adorn the walls. The building was once a prison and there are several rooms, some possibly former cells. The main room is sub-divided with two rooms looking onto the canal. A cosy alcove has settees and coal-effect fire. Popular with locals, it is also handy for canal travellers and walkers on the nearby Roman Antonine Way. Breakfast is available from 10am.
Q☕◐◑♿🚌P

Milngavie

Talbot Arms

30 Main Street, G62 6BU
⊙ 11-11 (midnight Wed & Thu; 1am Fri; 11.45 Sat); 12.30-11 Sun
☎ (0141) 955 0981
Caledonian Deuchars IPA, 80/-; guest beer Ⓗ
Small corner locals' bar at the edge of Milngavie's pedestrianised shopping precinct and near the start of the West Highland Way. The single room is L-shaped and further divided by wooden panels including a cosy area with armchairs. The pub offers a good selection of beers and a wide choice of lunches and snacks. Entertainment includes pool and traditional pub games. Televised football is shown, quiz night is Wednesday and there is live music on Friday. ◐♿≠♣

Milton of Campsie

Kincaid House Hotel

Birdston Road, G66 8BZ (signed on B757, S of village at end of long, wooded drive) OSNS650759
⊙ 11-11.30 (1am Fri & Sat); 12.30-midnight Sun
☎ (0141) 776 2226 🌐 kincaidhouse.com
Caledonian Deuchars IPA; guest beers Ⓗ
Impressive Scottish country house at the end of a long driveway. Real ale is served in the public bar. The interior is decorated with numerous horse brasses and a fine Alloa Brewery mirror; it has a pool table and a dining area with open fire. Good for families, the safe, hedge-enclosed garden is busy in summer. Food is served all day. Popular with locals, tourists and walkers on the nearby Campsie or Kilsyth Hills.
♛❀⇌◐◑♿♣P

GLASGOW

Glasgow

1901 Bar & Bistro

1534 Pollokshaws Road, G43 1RF (Haggs Road jct)
⊙ 11.45-11 (midnight Fri & Sat); 12.30-11 Sun
☎ (0141) 632 0161
Caledonian Deuchars IPA; guest beer Ⓗ
Part of one of the first red sandstone tenements in Glasgow and originally opened in 1901 as The Old Swan Inn. The spacious, L-shaped room has a public bar area which leads via screened seating to the dining area. Popular with locals and regulars, food from the bistro is served in the bar. Beers are often from Scottish micros. Pollok Country Park and the world famous Burrell Collection are nearby. Live music is played at weekends.
◐◑♿≠(Pollokshaws West/Shawlands)

Babbity Bowster

16-18 Blackfriars Street, Merchant City, G1 1PE (in paved section between High St and Walls St)
⊙ 11 (12.30 Sun)-midnight
☎ (0141) 552 5055 🌐 babbity.com
Caledonian Deuchars IPA; Houston Peter's Well; Ⓟ **guest beer** Ⓗ
French meets Scottish in this distinctive hotel and pub. Watercolours and photographs decorate the walls of the bar serving mainly Scottish beers. The menu in both bar and upstairs restaurant uses local ingredients (oysters, mussels, venison). In summer, the garden (a Glasgow rarity) offers barbecues and boules. Located in a quiet side street, it is popular with local residents, business types and academics.
♛Q❀⇌◐◑≠(High St/Argyle St/Queen St) ⊖(Buchanan St)♣P

Blackfriars

36 Bell Street, Merchant City, G1 1LG
⊙ 12 (12.30 Sun)-midnight
☎ (0141) 552 5924 🌐 blackfriarsonline.co.uk
Courage Directors; Ⓗ **guest beers** Ⓗ/Ⓟ
Popular, lively pub in the heart of the Merchant City with an intimate atmosphere provided by low lighting and candles on the tables. The walls and pillars display posters advertising events in the local area. The bar downstairs is the venue for a comedy club at weekends, while upstairs hosts bands on Saturday and Sunday and a quiz on Monday. The bar offers four guest beers and a range of world beers from Peru to Estonia. ◐◑≠(High St/Argyll St/Queen St)⊖(Buchanan St)

Bon Accord

153 North Street, G3 7DA
⊙ 11-midnight; 12.30-11 Sun
☎ (0141) 248 4427 🌐 thebonaccord.freeserve.co.uk
Caledonian Deuchars IPA; Marston's Pedigree; guest beers Ⓗ
Famous Glasgow pub attracting real ale drinkers from the local area and beyond. Eight ever-changing guest ales are served from ten handpumps on the long counter, as

SCOTLAND

well as a good range of malt whiskies and foreign beers. Meals are served 12-7pm. The pub is close to the Mitchell Library and not far from the King's Theatre. Live bands play on Saturday night with an open stage on Tuesday and a quiz on Wednesday.
◐ ⇌ (Charing Cross/Anderston)

Clockwork Beer Co.

1153-1155 Cathcart Road, Mount Florida, G42 9BH
(Kings Park Rd jct, by rail bridge)
11-11 (midnight Thu-Sat); 12.30-11 Sun
☎ (0141) 649 0184
Caledonian Deuchars IPA, 80/-; guest beers Ⓟ
A distinctive pub near Scotland's national football stadium. The large bar room is separated by split levels and geometry. Upstairs, via a spiral staircase, there is regular live music. The five-barrel brewery is visible from the counter and supplies specialities such as ginger and lemon, plus conventional beers. Guest ales and Westons cider are supplemented by a wide range of bottled and draught foreign beers. The varied bar menu is popular with regulars and visitors.
◐ ♿ ⇌ (Mount Florida) P

Crystal Palace

36 Jamaica Street, G1 4QD
11 (12.30 Sun)-midnight
☎ (0141) 221 2624
Caledonian Deuchars IPA; Courage Directors; guest beers Ⓗ
Spacious Wetherspoon's pub with huge windows. The ground floor room has two raised areas and a quieter space behind the lift. A room upstairs with a novel patio style floor provides an escape from occasional big screen football; different beers are sometimes available here. Close to Central station and popular with travellers, city workers, and clubbers, it can be quiet after 10.30pm.
Q ◐ ♿ ⇌ (Central) ⊖ (St Enoch)

Doublet Bar

74 Park Road, G4 9JF (jct with Woodlands Rd, behind Kelvinbridge subway station)
11-midnight; 12.30-11 Sun
☎ (0141) 334 1982
Belhaven St Andrew's Ale; guest beer Ⓗ
Traditional corner pub with two small rooms. The bar is on the ground floor of an old tenement and cask ale is only available here. However, you can carry beer upstairs to the lounge, housed in an attached building to the rear. The bar is a 'quiet' room used mainly by locals; the lounge is popular with the young, including students, and has piped music. Foreign beers include Dark Budvar (rare in Glasgow).
Q ◐ ⊖ (Kelvinbridge)

Horseshoe Bar ☆

17-21 Drury Street, G2 5AE
11 (12.30 Sun)-midnight
☎ (0141) 229 5711
Caledonian Deuchars IPA, 80/-; Ⓗ **guest beers** Ⓗ/Ⓟ
Worth seeking out, the pub is in an obscure side street near Central station. The horseshoe-shaped island bar with tall gantry is reputedly Britain's longest. There are many decorative features of historical interest such as clocks and mirrors, plus more recent additions including photographs and gold discs of famous customers. A varying beer range is served to city workers and travellers. Several screens show football on weekday evenings. The food in the upstairs restaurant represents good value and is very popular.
◐ ⇌ (Central) ⊖ (St Enoch/Buchanan St)

Lismore

206 Dumbarton Road, G11 6AU
11 (12.30 Sun)-midnight
☎ (0141) 576 0103
Caledonian Deuchars IPA; Kelburn Red Smiddy; guest beer Ⓗ
Thanks to sensitive renovation this pub retains its distinctive character. In the public bar stone walls are combined with a dark wood gantry and fittings. Local artists were commissioned to create the stained glass windows depicting scenes from the Highland clearances – the urinals are dedicated to the villains responsible. The comfortable lounge features interesting modern art pieces. There are informal folk sessions most evenings. Over 100 malt whiskies are offered.
⇌ (Partick) ⊖ (Kelvin Hall)

Pot Still

154 Hope Street, G2 2TH
11 (6pm Sun)-midnight
☎ (0141) 333 0980 thepotstill.co.uk
Caledonian Deuchars IPA, 80/-; guest beers Ⓗ
Renovated several years ago, this small, cosy pub retains interesting original features. Stairs lead to a corner mezzanine area, an escape from the busy main room. The pub is renowned for its selection of around 540 malt whiskies, including many valuable rarities that attract devotees from afar. Popular at lunchtimes and early evening, particularly with city workers, it is recommended for visitors seeking a traditional Scottish pub. The kilted bar staff add to the effect.
⇌ (Central/Queen St) ⊖ (Buchanan St)

Samuel Dows

69-71 Nithsdale Road, G41 2PZ
11-11 (midnight Fri & Sat); 12.30-11 Sun
☎ (0141) 423 0107
Caledonian Deuchars IPA; guest beer Ⓗ
A busy locals' pub with a welcoming atmosphere. The bar has a dark wood finish with brewery mirrors behind the gantry, scenes from old Glasgow on the walls and big screen TVs showing football matches. The lounge upstairs hosts a varied social scene, from live bands on weekend evenings and sponsored jam sessions on Thursday to acoustic music on the first Sunday of the month and a folk club on the last, plus monthly writers' club meetings. ◐

State Bar

148 Holland Street, G2 4NG
11 (12.30 Sun)-midnight
☎ (0141) 332 2159

Caledonian Deuchars IPA, 80/-; Houston Killellan; Marston's Pedigree; guest beers Ⓗ
Little of the original decor of this 1902 pub remains, but a recent renovation retains its original style. Few would guess that the imposing island bar with brass fittings dates from the 1990s. Theatrical memorabilia and old photographs cover the panelled walls; note the wood-carved Glasgow coat of arms. Situated near the Kings Theatre and Centre for Contemporary Arts, this welcoming pub is used by theatregoers and is popular with office workers and students for its reasonably priced lunches.
(Charing Cross) (Cowcaddens)

Station Bar
55 Port Dundas Road, G4 0HF
11-midnight; 12.30-11.45 Sun
(0141) 332 3117
Caledonian Deuchars IPA; guest beer Ⓗ
The railways are long-gone but they are remembered in the pub name, pictures on the walls and glass panels behind the bar. Present day trades are depicted in adjacent panels. The pub is still very much a local, even though it is close to the hustle of the city centre and Concert Hall, and customers range from thirsty shoppers to concert-goers. Real ale fans can choose between two guest beers, often supplied by small local breweries.
(Queen St) (Cowcaddens/ Buchanan St)

Tennents
191 Byres Road, G12 8TN
11-11 (midnight Thu-Sat); 12.30-11 Sun
(0141) 341 1024
Broughton Old Jock; Cairngorm Wildcat; Caledonian Deuchars IPA; Harviestoun Bitter & Twisted; Taylor Landlord; guest beers Ⓗ
Large West End tenement corner pub with a long U-shaped counter lined with 12 handpumps, four with ever-changing guest beers. Admire the tall gantry and high ceiling, with original cornice work around the beams and pillars. Seating is arranged mainly along one wall, adorned with old paintings. Good value meals are served until 9pm. Popular with locals, city workers and staff and students from nearby Glasgow University, eight TV screens may show two top sports events simultaneously.
(Hillhead)

Three Judges
141 Dumbarton Road, G11 6PR
11-11 (midnight Fri & Sat); 12.30-11 Sun
(0141) 337 3055
Beer range varies Ⓗ
Friendly, traditional corner pub with a varied clientele from locals to commuters – visitors are made welcome. The counter in the sensitively refurbished bar room sports nine handpumps dispensing eight ever-changing micro-brewery beers and a farmhouse cider, attracting real ale devotees from afar. The only food is pork pies, but customers can bring in takeaways. A traditional jazz band plays on Sunday afternoon.
(Partick) (Kelvinhall)

LANARKSHIRE

Airdrie

Cellar Bar
79 Stirling Street, ML6 0AS
11-midnight (1am Fri & Sat); 12.30-midnight Sun
(01236) 764495 airdriecellarbar.co.uk
Beer range varies Ⓗ
A locals' bar with a traditional feel despite having formerly been a shoe shop. The bar area is small and intimate, with a flight of steps at the back leading down to a larger lounge area housing a pool table. Decorated with distillery scenes, this is a whisky pub – the quality of the range of 300 malts has earned the pub several awards. There is usually one Scottish brewery guest beer.

Castlecary

Castlecary House Hotel
Castlecary Road, G68 0HD
11-11 (midnight Thu-Sat); 12.30-midnight Sun
(01324) 840233 castlecaryhotel.com
Beer range varies Ⓗ
Private hotel in a village close to the restored Forth and Clyde Canal and Castlecary Viaduct. The main building houses three bars, one with a cosy fire. Up to three real ales can be found in any of the bars including the cocktail bar in the modern extension. The hotel has a reputation for quality bar and restaurant meals and holds a beer festival twice a year in April and October. P

Coatbridge

St Andrews Bar
37 Sunnyside Road, ML5 3DG
11-midnight (1am Fri & Sat); 12.30-midnight Sun
(01365) 423 773 standrewsbar.com
Beer range varies Ⓗ
The introduction of high quality real ale, plus sensitive renovation reversing some uninspired 20th century changes, has transformed a once run down bar into a popular corner pub. Visitors are assured of a warm welcome from both staff and locals in the small, lively, public bar where low-level music is drowned by conversation. There is a tiny, quieter lounge. A wide range of malt whiskies is sold. Handy for the renowned Summerlee Industrial Museum.
Q (Coatbridge Sunnyside)

Hamilton

George
18 Campbell Street, ML3 6AS
12 (11 Sat)-11.45 (1am Fri); 12.30-11.45 Sun
(01698) 424 225 thegeorgebar.com
Beer range varies Ⓗ
Welcoming, traditional corner pub. Owners Lynn and Colin are staunch supporters of cask ale, reflected by the numerous CAMRA awards on display. The ever-changing range of guest beers is appreciated by locals as well as drinkers from other parts of Lanarkshire. The main bar has an interesting central dark wood glasses stand, an alternative to the

SCOTLAND

seating around the walls. There is a small quieter room to the rear, a retreat on busy Friday nights. ❀◐♿⇌(Central)P

Lanark

Horse & Jockey

56 High Street, ML11 7ES

11-11 (1am Fri; 11.45 Sat); 12.30-midnight Sun

☎ (01555) 664 825

Beer range varies H

Welcoming bar in the centre of the oldest part of a historic town, popular with locals and visitors. The pub gets its name from the racecourse which used to be on the edge of town. The bar area is not large, but there is a restaurant upstairs. Typically for a building of its age, passageways and stairs are low and narrow, so take care. Beers, usually supplied by micro-breweries, change frequently. Lunches are served Monday to Saturday, evening meals Saturday only. ◐◗Ⲁ

Strathaven

Waterside Bar & Restaurant

31 Waterside Street, ML10 6AE

11-midnight (1.30am Thu-Sat); 11-midnight Sun

☎ (01357) 522 588

Beer range varies H

Family-run enterprise comprising a comfortable lounge bar with an adjoining restaurant. The building dates from the 19th century, although the interior has been thoroughly modernised and there are more recent extensions. As its name suggests, it is located by the burn running through the centre of town. A wide menu is available, from snacks and bar meals to three course dinners. Nevertheless, those 'only here for the beer' are equally welcome. ❀◐◗

Weavers

1-3 Green Street, ML10 6LT

4 (11 Mon)-midnight; 11-1am Fri & Sat; 7-1am Sun

Beer range varies H

This family-run pub is all that remains of the former Crown Hotel and takes its name from the traditional trade of the town. The old exterior now houses a modernised single room bar decorated with pictures of Hollywood film stars. A quiet pub by day, there is music at night, loud at weekends. Two beers are on offer, usually one from nearby Craigmill Brewery.

Wishaw

Wishaw Malt

62-66 Kirk Road, ML2 7BL

11-11 (1am Fri & Sat); 12.30-midnight Sun

☎ (01698) 358806

Beer range varies H

Modern Wetherspoon's pub with a large single room divided into many areas and levels. It is named after the local 19th-century distillery which made the critically acclaimed, but financially disastrous (due to the temperance movement) Clydesdale Single Malt. As well as its immediate local trade, it attracts drinkers from all over the real ale starved county of Lanarkshire. ⛾❀◐◗♿⇌●

RENFREWSHIRE

Barrhead

Cross Stobs Inn

4 Grahamston Road, G78 1NS (on B7712)

11-11 (midnight Thu; 1am Fri; 11.45 Sat); 12.30-11 Sun

☎ (0141) 881 1581

Kelburn Misty Law H

Inviting 18th-century coaching inn on the edge of town on the road to Paisley. The public bar has a real coal fire and retains much of its original charm with antique furniture and service bells, while the lounge has been recently refurbished. There is an outside drinking area at the front of the pub and an enclosed garden with a table tennis table at the rear. A self-contained pool room and function suite are also available. Children are allowed at lunchtime. A second beer from Kelburn is occasionally available. ⛫❀◐⊟⇌

Waterside Inn

Glasgow Road, The Hurlet, G53 7TH (on A736 near Hurlet)

11-11 (midnight Fri & Sat); 12.30-11 Sun

☎ (0141) 881 2822

Beer range varies H

Comfortable bar and lounge attached to a restaurant near the Levern Water, still famously known as Jeanie Gebbie's although the interior has been knocked through long since then. Cosy chairs round the real fire help to create a relaxed atmosphere. The friendly, efficient staff can sometimes be overwhelmed by diners over-spilling from the restaurant, which holds theme nights with musical accompaniment. A stained glass gantry and local pictures add to the ambience. ❀◐◗⊟♿P

Busby

White Cart

61 East Kilbride Road, G76 8HX (on A726, 100yds SE of station)

11 (12.30 Sun)-11

☎ (0141) 644 2711

Beer range varies H

A Chef and Brewer pub, the spacious interior is divided by large oak beams into several cosy nooks. The decor is from an earlier period incorporating a grandfather clock, dressing tables and a wealth of bric-a-brac. Part of the stone walls to the rear of the pub are thought to be from the stables that formerly stood on the site. Of the two beers, one is from the local Kelburn Brewery and the other from the Scottish Courage range. ⛫Q❀◐◗♿⇌P

Gourock

Spinnaker Hotel

121 Albert Road, PA19 1BU

11-11.30 (midnight Thu; 1am Fri & Sat); 12.30-midnight Sun

☎ (01475) 633107 spinnakerhotel.co.uk

Beer range varies H

Warm and friendly hotel popular with both locals and day trippers. Situated on the sea front, it offers great views across the Firth of Clyde from its bay windows and patio tables.

The food menu includes vegetarian and children's choices. It is handy for Gourock to Dunoon ferries and an ideal spot to watch the submarines heading up and down the Clyde. There are usually two real ales available, served from the cosy bar. Q❀⇄◖◗

Greenock

James Watt

80-92 Cathcart Road, PA15 1DD

⊙ 11-11 (midnight Thu; 1am Fri & Sat); 12.30-12.30am Sun

☎ (01475) 722640

Courage Directors; guest beer Ⓗ

Easy to find, town centre Wetherspoon's near the railway station, providing a much needed real ale outlet. It is named after the town's famous inventor and offers the usual JDW trimmings. There is good access for wheelchair users and a small garden and heated patio area for outside drinking. Guest ales from local breweries and regular English beers are served by the attentive, friendly staff. Families are welcome in a partitioned area of the bar and the all day food is popular with locals. Q❀◖◗♿⇌(Central)P

Houston

Fox & Hounds

South Street, PA6 7EN

⊙ 11-midnight (12.30am Fri & Sat); 12.30-midnight Sun

☎ (01505) 612448 🌐 houston-brewing.co.uk

Houston Killellan, Barochan, Peter's Well, Warlock Stout, seasonal beers; guest beer Ⓗ

This 17th-century coaching inn is also the home of the Houston Brewing Co, which can be viewed from a window in the recently decorated lounge. The spacious and comfortable lounge and public bars are decorated with hunting memorabilia. The Huntsman bar and restaurant upstairs has full a la carte and bar menus, served all day at weekends with Sunday traditional roast. The toilet is wheelchair accessible.

♨Q⚇◖◗⊟♿P

Inverkip

Inverkip Hotel

Main Street, PA16 0AS (off A78 Greenock-Largs road)

⊙ 11 (12.30 Sun)-11.30

☎ (01475) 521478 🌐 inverkip.co.uk

Caledonian Deuchars IPA; guest beers (summer) Ⓗ

Originally an old coaching inn, this two bar hotel sits by a marina in a small conservation village on the Clyde coast. It is warm and welcoming, offering diners locally sourced food in both the restaurant and lounge (booking recommended). Some guest ales arrive by boat and are served during the summer months to meet seasonal demand, in addition to the regular ale. Q⇄◖◗⊟⇌P

Johnstone

Coanes

26-28 High Street, PA5 8AH

⊙ 11-11.30 (1am Fri; midnight Sat); 12.30-11.30 Sun

☎ (01505) 322925

Boddingtons Bitter; Caledonian Deuchars IPA; guest beers Ⓗ

Friendly town centre pub with a welcoming atmosphere. The cosy bar has fake beams and bric-a-brac; part of the lounge doubles as a restaurant (Wed-Sat eve). No food is served on Sunday. Seven ales are normally on handpump including one from the local Kelburn Brewery. Q◖◗♿⇌

Kilbarchan

Glen Leven Inn

25 New Street, PA10 2LN (on A737 slip road)

⊙ 11-11 (midnight Wed & Thu; 1am Fri & Sat); 12.30-11 Sun

☎ (01505) 702481

Beer range varies Ⓗ

Traditional village pub with a warm and friendly atmosphere. The well stocked bar is run by helpful staff. The pub features original dark beams and plaster with nick-nacks and local pictures on display. A wide range of bar snacks is available. Entertainment is provided by local bands at the weekends plus quiz nights and a range of traditional pub games. Children are welcome during the daytime and for meals. ♨❀◖◗♿⊟(35)♣P

Trust Inn

8 Low Barholm, PA10 2ET (on A737)

⊙ 11.45 (11 Fri & Sat)-11.30 (1am Fri & Sat); 11.45-11.30 Sun

☎ (01505) 702401

Caledonian Deuchars IPA; guest beers Ⓗ

Pleasant and lively single-room, beamed village pub decorated in traditional style. It caters for a wide range of people and has friendly staff willing to accommodate particular needs. Two TVs, one widescreen which is folded away when not in use, provide entertainment along with local folk bands and quiz nights. Children are welcome. ◖◗♿⇌(Milliken Park)⊟(35)

Kilmacolm

Pullman Tavern

Eithinstone Court, Lochwinnoch Road, PA13 4LG

⊙ 11-11 (midnight Wed & Thu; 1am Fri & Sat); 12.30-11 Sun

☎ (01505) 874501

Beer range varies Ⓗ

Converted railway station on the Sustrans cycle path from Paisley to Gourock; the only pub in this conservation village. An outside seating area is a favourite spot for families, walkers and cyclists in summer. There are no handpumps in the public bar but staff will bring through your order from the pumps in the lounge bar. The beer range varies in this Mitchell & Butler pub, but Taylor Landlord appears regularly. ❀◖◗⊟P

Lochwinnoch

Brown Bull

33 Main Street, PA12 4AH

⊙ 12-11 (midnight Fri; 11.45 Sat); 12.30-11 Sun

☎ (01505) 843250

🌐 lochwinnoch.info/Business/brownbull/

Beer range varies Ⓗ

SCOTLAND

Friendly village pub with stone walls and oak beams situated in an old coach house, retaining all of its original charm. The old stone cellar is still in use. Popular with both visitors and locals due to its welcoming staff and warm atmosphere, this is a good place to seek out local information.

Newton Mearns

Osprey

Stewarton Road, G77 6NP (near M77 jct)

11 (12.30 Sun)-11

(0141) 616 5071

Boddingtons Bitter; Caledonian Deuchars IPA; guest beer H

Mitchell & Butler Vintage Inn with an olde worlde feel due to the judicious use of wood, brick and stone. The oak bar strewn with hops adds to the effect, along with the oak-beamed ceiling and stone-flagged floor. Quiet areas within the bar allow privacy while the main pub is oriented to family dining. Three handpumps serve two regular and one guest beer. Good food is popular here. Q

Paisley

Bull Inn ☆

7 New Street, PA1 1XU

11-midnight (1am Fri & Sat); 12.30-midnight Sun

(0141) 849 0472 maclay.com/MaclayInns.html

Caledonian Deuchars IPA; Kelburn Red Smiddy; guest beer H

Dating back to 1901, this pub, designed by local architect WD McLennan, is rich in art detail. The pillared back fitment acts as a support for elongated whisky barrels, now disused. There are three sitting rooms at the rear and a fourth is now the ladies toilet. The bar room would possibly benefit from less old curiosity shop clutter added under a previous owner, but don't let that put you off. (Gilmour St)♣

Gabriels

33-35 Gauze Street, PA1 1EX

11-midnight (1am Fri & Sat); 12.30-midnight Sun

(0141) 887 8204

Beer range varies H

A variety of real ales from local micro-breweries Kelburn and Houston is regularly available in this pub now owned by Greene King. It has an oval bar with two handpumps at the far side nearest the cellar. TV and music are kept at a reasonable volume and quiz nights are held on Tuesday evening. It is situated near Paisley Abbey. (Gilmour St)

Harvies Bar

83 Glasgow Road, PA1 3NU

11 (12.30 Sun)-midnight

(0141) 889 0911

Caledonian Deuchars IPA H

Large pub in a tenement building near the Barshaw Park. Friendly staff provide the mature and less mature with gentle 'banter' while plasma screens showing football keep eager punters from the bookies. This is the last pub in town before the Glasgow boundary. (Hawkhead)♣

Hogshead

45 High Street, PA1 2AH

11-midnight (1am Fri & Sat); 12.30-midnight Sun

(0141) 840 4150

Caledonian Deuchars IPA, 80/-; guest beer H

Open-plan, city-centre pub with a raised area for pool and private functions. Meals are served all day until 8pm and the efficient bar staff provide table service when quiet. Customers range from ale drinkers to students; four TVs provide football coverage and music videos so the pub can often be loud at weekends. (Gilmour St)

Wee Howff

53 High Street, PA1 2AN

11-11 (midnight Fri & Sat); closed Sun

(0141) 889 2095

Caledonian Deuchars IPA; guest beer H

Small town pub near the university frequented by students and other discerning cask ale drinkers, showcasing guest beers from Houston and Kelburn breweries. The present publican has been in the last 18 editions of this Guide and was the first Burton Master Cellarman in Scotland. (Gilmour St)

Uplawmoor

Uplawmoor Hotel

66 Neilston Road, G78 4AF (off A736)

12-2.30, 5-11; 12-midnight Sun

(01505) 850565 uplawmoor.co.uk

Beer range varies H

This hotel bar and restaurant, situated in the highest village in Renfrewshire, was originally opened in 1750 to serve travellers between Glasgow and the Clyde coast. It still performs that function admirably but also serves as a meeting place for locals – a true village pub. Try the public bar for homely atmosphere, the cocktail bar for something more upmarket and the restaurant for its excellent menu. Frequent diners can join the 'Smugglers Club' for a range of discounts. Beer choice is usually provided by local breweries. P

Your shout

We would like to hear from you. If you think a pub not listed in the guide is worthy of consideration, please let us know. Send us the name, full address and phone number (if known). If a pub in the guide has given poor service, we would also like to know. Write to Good Beer Guide, CAMRA, 230 Hatfield Road, St Albans, Herts, AL1 4LW or email **camra@camra.org.uk**

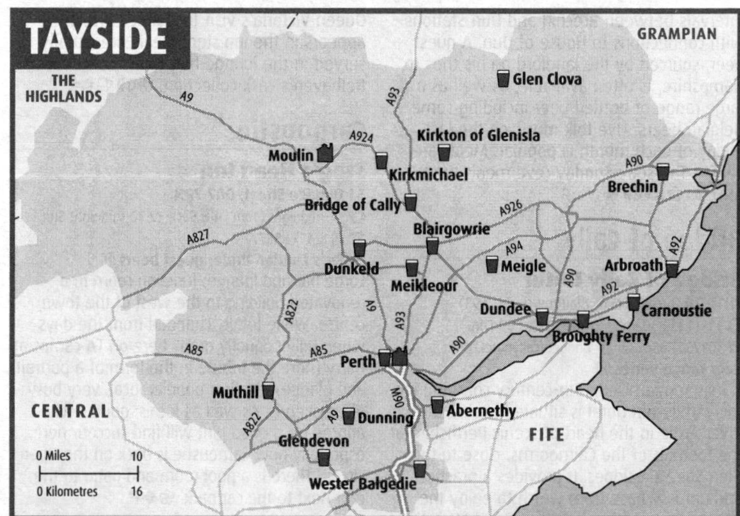

Authority areas covered: Angus UA, City of Dundee UA, Perth & Kinross UA

Abernethy

Crees Inn

Main Street, PH2 9LA

11-2.30, 5-11; 11-11 Sat; 12.30-11 Sun

☎ (01738) 850714 creesinn.co.uk

Beer range varies H

Warm, welcoming village local within the shadow of a Pictish watch tower (one of only two in Scotland) in the quiet village of Abernethy which was once the Pictish capital of Scotland. A former farmhouse, this listed building has been sympathetically renovated to provide a homely pub with a long L-shaped lounge and small restaurant area. Up to five ales are available with a good mix of regularly changing Scottish and English beers. A varied menu is provided at lunchtime and evening in the busy restaurant using fresh local produce. Q❀⇌◑&P

Arbroath

Corn Exchange

Market Place, DD11 1HR

11-midnight daily

☎ (01241) 432430

Greene King Abbot, Old Speckled Hen; Courage Directors; guest beer H

A typical Wetherspoon's conversion of a former corn exchange in the centre of the town. Arbroath is famous for the signing of the Declaration of Independence in 1320. The pub's interior is one large open plan room although there are a few quiet areas. It can get very busy during weekend evenings. Coffee is served from 10am. ◑&≠

Lochlands Bar

14 Lochlands Street, DD11 3AB

11-midnight (1am Fri & Sat); 12.30-midnight Sun

☎ (01241) 873286

Beer range varies H

Classic and busy street corner pub with strong sporting associations. The large public bar has a selection of sporting memorabilia adorning the walls plus two large TVs which dominate when football matches (and some rugby games) are shown. For those customers not interested in sport there is a smaller, quieter lounge area. Two ales are always on handpump. ⊟≠♣

Blairgowrie

Ericht Alehouse

13 Wellmeadow, PH10 6ND

11-11 (11.45 Fri & Sat); 12.30-11 Sun; times may vary

☎ (01250) 872469

Beer range varies H

Friendly, traditional town centre pub established in 1802. It has two seating areas split by a well stocked bar and the lounge area boasts a log-burning open fire. The range of up to six beers changes all the time, coming from Scottish and English breweries with Inveralmond a local favourite. Liefmans Frambozen is available on handpump and there is a good selection of bottled beers. Although no food is available customers are welcome to take in their own. Weekends can be busy with occasional live music. ♨Q&⊡

Brechin

Caledonian Hotel

43-47 South Esk Street, DD9 6DZ

(opp. Caledonian Station)

11.30-2 (not Mon), 5-11.30; 11.30-1am Fri & Sat; 12.30-11 Sun

☎ (01356) 624345

Inveralmond Thrappledouser; guest beer H

This hotel with a large bar and a function room/restaurant has been extensively refurbished. It takes its name from the privately run railway whose terminus is opposite. The Caledonian Railway closed in 1981 but now runs steam trains at regular

INDEPENDENT BREWERIES

Inveralmond Perth

Moulin Moulin

SCOTLAND

intervals between Brechin and Dun Stations with connections to House of Dun. A guest beer, sourced by the landlord on his trips to Hampshire, is often available, as well as a large range of bottled beer including some Belgian beers. Live folk music on the last Friday of each month is popular. Meals are served Thursday-Sunday (eve meals Wed, too). ♨❀⇌◐◑♣

Bridge of Cally

Bridge of Cally Hotel

PH10 7JJ (6 miles N of Blairgowrie on A93)
✪ 11-11 (12.30am Fri & Sat); 12-11.30 Sun
☎ (01250) 886232 ⊕ bridgeofcallyhotel.com
Beer range varies Ⓗ
A fully modernised 18th-century coaching inn, this family-run hotel is situated beside the River Ardle in the heart of scenic Perthshire at the foothills of the Cairngorms, close to the Glen Shee ski slopes. It provides a practical and unfussy base from which to enjoy the widest range of local pastimes and attractions including the 63-mile Cateran Trail, Scotland's newest long distance walk, which starts and finishes near Blairgowrie. Bar food is available for most of the day and evening, while the hotel restaurant offers home-grown vegetables for guests who prefer to dine in more formal surroundings. Two ales are available with Houston beers regularly on handpump. ♨Q☋❀⇌◐◑⊟♿♣P

Broughty Ferry

Fisherman's Tavern Hotel

10-12 Fort Street, DD5 2AD (by lifeboat station)
✪ 11-midnight (1am Fri & Sat); 12.30-midnight Sun
☎ (01382) 775941 ⊕ fishermans-tavern-hotel.co.uk
Beer range varies Ⓗ
First opened in the early 19th century as the Buckie Tavern by a fisherman who harvested buckies (whelks), the pub has expanded to a small hotel. The original atmosphere is largely maintained in the public bar, though the clientele is more upmarket, and there are three further rooms for drinking and dining. A long-standing Guide entrant, the 'Fish' continues to stock the biggest range of ales in Dundee. Local micros Inveralmond and Moulin appear regularly, also Caledonian and Harviestoun. Traditional music is played every Thursday evening, the pub quiz is the first Monday of the month. An annual beer festival is held. ♨Q☋❀⇌◐◑⊟♿⇌♣

Royal Arch

258 Brook Street, DD5 2DS (jct of Brook St/Gray St near station)
✪ 11-midnight; 12.30-11 Sun
☎ (01382) 779741
Caledonian Deuchars IPA; guest beer Ⓗ
Busy street-corner local with an impressive old gantry from the defunct Craigour Bar, Dens Road. Elaborately decorated, the walls feature a collection of sporting photographs and framed caricatures of worthies past and present. The name has almost certainly a Masonic association (linked to former premises over the road) despite the depiction of the former arch commemorating Queen Victoria's visit to Dundee which appears in the inn sign. Meals are usually served in the lounge bar. Beers come from Belhaven's cask collection. ❀◐◑⊟⇌

Carnoustie

Stag's Head Inn

61 Dundee Street, DD7 7PN
✪ 11-midnight (1am Fri & Sat); 12.30-midnight Sun
☎ (01241) 858777
Fuller's London Pride; guest beers Ⓗ
Large bar and lounge/function room in a renovated building to the west of the town centre. While totally changed from the days when Billy Connolly drank here on TA camps at Barry (note the tribute in the form of a portrait and plaque), this is a popular local, very busy at weekends. As well as locals, golfers who appreciate a good pint will find succour here, especially now Carnoustie is back on the Open circuit. There is a pool room and patio to the rear next to the car park. ❀♣P

Dundee

Counting House

67-71 Reform Street, DD1 1SP
✪ 11-midnight; 12.30-11 Sun
☎ (01382) 225251
Greene King Abbot; guest beers Ⓗ
This Wetherspoon's house is a large former bank with high ceilings opposite the McManus Galleries, decorated with Dundee memorabilia. The varying beer range includes Cairngorm, Caledonian and Stewart's. Quality cask ales at cheap prices ensure a busy atmosphere, with between three and six beers on handpump. ◐◑♿⇌

Drouthy Neebors

142 Perth Road, DD1 4JW (opp. art college)
✪ 11 (12.30 Sun)-midnight
☎ (01382) 633149
Caledonian Deuchars IPA; guest beers Ⓗ
'When.....drouthy neebors, neebors meet.' This quote from Tam o' Shanter by Scotland's favourite poet, Robert Burns, gives the pub its name. And it is an appropriate one, since the tongue in cheek warning against over-indulgence in fact celebrates the inn, good ale and good company. The bar is split level with a spiral stair leading to the toilets and function room; this gives a rambling effect, creating some cosy niches to 'sit bousing at the nappy' (strong ale). Beers include Belhaven and Cairngorm. ◐◑

Mickey Coyles

21-23 Old Hawkhill, DD1 5EU (by Hawkhill/West Port)
✪ 11-3, 5-midnight; 11-midnight Fri & Sat; 7-11 Sun
☎ (01382) 225871
Caledonian Deuchars IPA, 80/-; guest beers Ⓗ
A building that stood empty for many years after its eponymous owner died, this is now a busy, friendly town and gown establishment, offering good pub grub. Serving as a meeting place for several university clubs, it is also a trysting place for discerning Dundee drinkers – hence its Tayside CAMRA local Pub of the Year 2005 award. Traditional music is played on Monday, after 9.15pm. ◐◑⇌

Dunkeld

Taybank

Tay Terrace, PH8 0HY

✪ 11-11 (midnight Fri & Sat); 12-11 Sun

☎ (01350) 727340 ⊕ thetaybank.com

Inveralmond Ossian's Ale 🄷

Known as 'Scotland's Musical Meeting Place', the Taybank is a haven for lovers of traditional Scottish and Irish music often of a spontaneous nature. The small public bar is comfortable and full of character with an open fire; it is equipped with a large range of musical instruments including a piano for musicians who do not have their own. As well as the regular beer there is a small selection of bottled beer. The garden is located on the banks of the River Tay looking across toward Birnam Hill. A good base for a variety of outdoor pursuits, the pub is popular with locals, musicians and visitors from all over the world. There is a small music room where live events are regularly held.

⛫Q⚭❀⇄◐◑ ≉♣

Dunning

Kirkstyle Inn

Kirkstyle Square, PH2 0RR

✪ 11-2.30, 5-11 (midnight Fri); 11-midnight Sat; 12.30-11 Sun

☎ (01764) 684248

Caledonian Deuchars IPA; Greene King IPA; Harviestoun Bitter & Twisted; guest beer 🄷

Traditional village inn circa 1760 located in the centre of Dunning at the foothills of the Ochill range, dominated by the Norman steeple of St Serfs Church. It has a small public bar with a wooden floor and wood-burning stove where up to three ales are served (two in winter). Adjacent to the bar is a small snug area. There is a restaurant area serving excellent food, plus a downstairs room with pool table.

⛫Q❀◐◑⊟

Glen Clova

Clova Hotel

DD8 4QS (15 miles N of Kirriemuir)

✪ 11-11 (1am Fri & Sat); 12.30-11 Sun

☎ (01575) 550350 ⊕ clova.com

Caledonian Deuchars IPA, 80/-; guest beers 🄷

Comfortable country hotel offering its own fishing, hawking and shooting facilities. Once a drovers' inn, it has been upgraded and provides accommodation from bunkhouse to luxury four-poster bedrooms. Ales including Houston and Caledonian are served in the Climbers Bar. Beer festivals are held in spring and summer. ⛫Q❀⇄◐◑⊟▲P

Glendevon

Tormaukin Hotel

FK14 7JY

✪ 11 (12 Sun)-11

☎ (01259) 781252 ⊕ tormaukin.co.uk

Beer range varies 🄷

In a peaceful and rural setting surrounded by the Ochill Hills, this was originally an 18th-century drovers' inn (Tormaukin meaning 'hill of the mountain hare' in old Scots). It is an ideal base for a variety of outdoor activities such as walking, fishing and golf. It has two comfortable lounge bars in natural timber and stone, with log fires. An extensive menu offers traditional Scottish fare and international dishes. There is a separate restaurant with an a la carte menu. Up to three ales are available in the rear lounge, usually two from Harviestoun.

⛫Q⚭❀⇄◐◑P

Kirkmichael

Strathardle Inn

PH10 7NS (On A924 Bridge of Cally to Pitlochry road at E end of village)

✪ 12-2, 6-11 (11.30 Fri & Sat); times may vary

☎ (01250) 881224 ⊕ strathardleinn.co.uk

Beer range varies 🄷

Previously home to Aldchlappie, the smallest commercial brewery in Britain, the Strathardle is an old coaching inn on the route from Balmoral to Pitlochry dating back to the late 1700s. The inn retains the original barn and stables. It is an excellent base from which to explore central Scotland and the southern Highlands. The inn has a 700 yard beat of the River Ardle, offering salmon and trout fishing. The Cateran Trail passes nearby and the new Cairngorms National Park is a few miles north. Up to three ales are available, depending on season, with a strong commitment to Scottish micros.

⛫Q⚭❀⇄◐◑♿P

Kirkton of Glenisla

Glenisla Hotel

PH11 8PH (on B591 10 miles N of Alyth)

✪ 11 (12.30 Sun)-11 summer; winter hours vary, phone to check

☎ (01575) 582223 ⊕ glenisla-hotel.co.uk

Beer range varies 🄷

Former coaching inn, now an oasis for walkers and a centre for a variety of outdoor pursuits. Beers (one to three, depending on season) usually include Fyne Ales and Inveralmond brews. Home-cooked food is served in the oak and pine furnished rear bar and dining room. Traditional live music sessions are held. The pub is closed on Monday and Tuesday from October to March. Occasional beer festivals are held.

⛫Q❀⇄◐◑▲♣P

Meigle

Belmont Arms Hotel

PH12 8TJ (on A927 1½ miles S of Meigle)

✪ 12-11.30 (midnight Sat & Sun)

☎ (01828) 640232 ⊕ belmont-hotel.com

Caledonian Deuchars IPA; Inveralmond Ossian's Ale; guest beers 🄷

Welcoming small hotel standing on a bend on the Dundee-Alyth road, south of Meigle, with its famous Pictish Stone Museum. It was granted its first licence in 1831 to accommodate guests from nearby Belmont Castle and later served as a railway hotel for Alyth Junction station. Home cooking with fresh local produce has made the pub a popular dining place. ⛫❀⇄◐◑⊟♿🚌(57)P

SCOTLAND

Meikleour

Meikleour Hotel

PH2 6EB

11-3, 6-11 (midnight Fri); 11-midnight Sat; 12-11 Sun

(01250) 883206 meikleour-inn.co.uk

Beer range varies H

Warm, welcoming and pleasantly refurbished country village inn. There is a stone-flagged bar and comfortable lounge with two cask ales each. It is a popular venue for walkers and fisherman as well as those wanting a good meal or drink in a relaxing environment. The house beer, Lure, is brewed by Inveralmond. Nearby is the Meikleour Beech Hedge (100ft high and a third of a mile long) which was planted in 1745 and is recognised in the Guinness Book of Records as the tallest hedge in the world. Q P

Muthill

Muthill Village Hotel

6 Willoughby Street, PH5 2AB

12-2.30, 5.30-11 (11.45 Fri & Sat); 12.30-2.30, 5.30-11 Sun; summer open all day, hours vary

(01764) 681451 muthillvillagehotel.com

Beer range varies H

Located in the centre of the conservation village of Muthill, which has over 90 listed buildings, this 18th-century coaching inn is on the old drovers' road from the Highlands. The Bothy Bar is full of character with a large open fire and walls adorned with farming implements. The restaurant area has a hunting theme. Up to four ales are available depending on season with Scottish micros prominent. The house beer Tapsman's Yil (Drover's Ale) from Inveralmond reflects the hotel's historic links with cattle drovers (a tapsman is the head drover). Do not miss nearby Drummond Gardens – one of the finest formal gardens in Europe. Q P

Perth

Capital Asset

26 Tay Street, PH1 5TS

11-11 (11.45 Fri & Sat); 12.30-11 Sun

(01738) 580457

Caledonian Deuchars IPA; guest beer H

Large, open plan, modern but comfortable pub overlooking the River Tay. Perth was the ancient capital of Scotland and this building was originally a bank, hence the name. The ceilings are high and much of the original cornicing has been retained. A number of photographs of old Perth adorn the walls. Meals are served all day, and coffee from 10am. Up to five ales are available on handpump. Renowned for providing good value food and ale, this pub can be especially busy in the late evenings at weekends. It is handy for pre-theatre and concert meals. Q

Cherrybank Inn

210 Glasgow Road, PH2 0NA

11-11 (11.45 Fri & Sat); 12.30-11 Sun

(01738) 624349 cherrybankinn.co.uk

Inveralmond Independence, Ossian's Ale; guest beer H

Thought to be one of the oldest public houses in Perth, this former drovers' inn is located on the western outskirts of Perth. A popular local, it is also ideal for travellers, with accommodation in seven en-suite bedrooms. It has a small public bar with two adjacent rooms; lunches and evening meals are served in the well-appointed lounge. Up to four real ales are dispensed from Inveralmond and other Scottish micros. Q P

Greyfriars

15 South Street, PH2 8PG

11-11 (11.45pm Fri & Sat); 12-11 Sun

(01738) 633036 greyfriarsbar.com

Beer range varies H

This is one of the smallest lounge bars within the city centre. Popular with businessmen and office workers, it has a vibrant and friendly atmosphere. Good value lunches are served in the bar and a small upstairs seated area. Up to four ales are available including the house beer Friars Tipple brewed by local brewery Inveralmond. As a plaque above the bar says, this is 'More of a club without membership'. Various attractions nearby include the Victorian Theatre, Concert Hall, Art Gallery and Museum and walks along the banks of the 'silvery' Tay. Evening meals are served on Friday and Saturday, phone to check first.

Wester Balgedie

Balgedie Toll Tavern

KY13 9HE

11-11 (11.30 Thu; 12.30 Fri & Sat); 12.30-11.30 Sun

(01592) 840212

Harviestoun Bitter & Twisted; guest beers H

Welcoming and comfortable country tavern which, like many others built around the same time in Scotland, was situated at a road toll where travellers had to break their journey to make a payment before travelling on. The oldest part of the building is the original toll house at the southern end dating circa 1534. It has three seating areas plus a small bar with low ceilings, oak beams, horse brasses, wooden settles and works of art by a local painter. A good selection of meals and bar snacks is available. Q P

Timely advice

'I think now would be a good time for a beer' – **Franklin Delano Roosevelt**, 15 December 1933, on the day Prohibition ended.

Northern Ireland
Channel Islands
Isle of Man

NORTHERN IRELAND

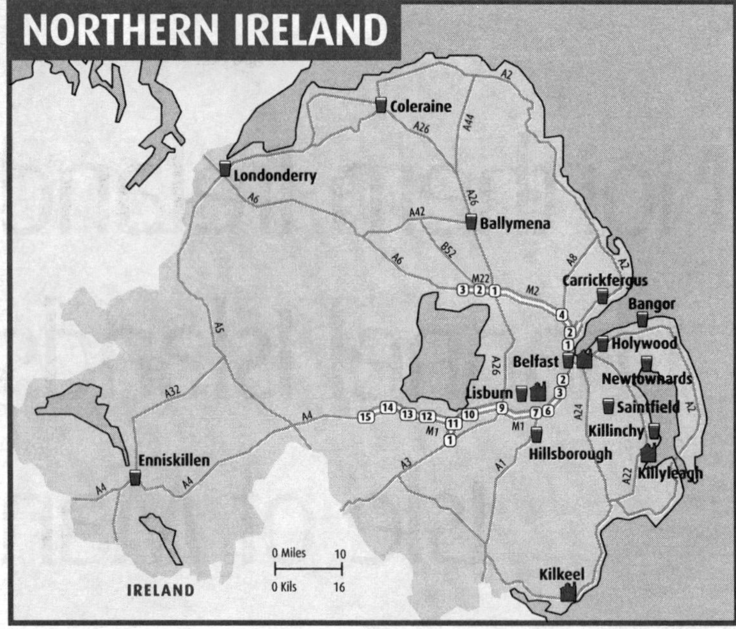

Ballymena

Spinning Mill

17-21 Broughshane Street, BT43 6EB

11.30-11 (midnight Thu; 1am Fri & Sat); 11.30-11 Sun

(028) 2563 8985

Beer range varies H

This building was a pub for over 100 years before it became Wetherspoon's first outlet in the province. Although extensively renovated, it retains a cosy, friendly atmosphere. Look out for all the fixtures and fittings from old churches. Mostly open plan, but with plenty of nooks and crannies, there is a pleasant family area upstairs.

Bangor

Gillespie's Place

12 Ballyhome Esplanade, BT20 5LZ

11.30-11; 12.30-10 Sun

(028) 9147 9584 gillespie-esplanade.com

Whitewater Glen Ale; guest beer H

Large seaside local a mile from the town centre. Inside is a bar, lounge, off-licence and restaurant. Recently refurbished, it now has an air exchange system in the bar and three TVs for sporting events. There are three handpumps in the bar and staff are willing to serve in the lounge and garden. One Whitewater and two UK guest beers are available. Excellent bar food is served. The garden affords beautiful views of Belfast Lough and Scotland. Q (B10)

Belfast

Botanic Inn

23-27 Malone Road, BT9 6RU

11.30-1am daily

(028) 9050 9740 thebotanicinn.com

Whitewater Belfast Ale H

The 'Bot' is near Queen's University and the Ulster Museum and is popular with sports fans and students. Sporting memorabilia bedeck the walls, especially in the more traditional front bar. A solitary handpump is located in the larger back bar. Tuesday is quiz night, with traditional music on Wednesday, live bands on Thursday and a DJ Friday to Sunday. The upstairs disco is nightly from Wednesday to Saturday. This is not a quiet bar.

Bridge House

37-43 Bedford Street, BT2 4HF

(opp. BBC, Ormeau Avenue)

10 (12 Sun)-midnight (1am Thu-Sat)

(028) 9072 7890

Greene King Abbot; guest beer H

Recently converted from a quiet Wetherspoon's into a far noisier Lloyds No 1, the Bridge House is a popular bar and can be busy at weekends. The TV screens are downstairs but the music is loud enough to be heard upstairs. The main attraction is the ale, usually from Scottish breweries, with occasional interesting guests. Food is served daily. (Gt Victoria St)

Crown Liquor Saloon ☆

46 Great Victoria Street, BT2 7BA (opp. Europa Hotel)

11.30-12.30am; 12.30-11.30 Sun

(028) 9027 9902

Whitewater Belfast Ale H

Dating from 1826 and owned by the

INDEPENDENT BREWERIES

College Green Belfast
Hilden Lisburn
Strangford Lough Killyleagh
Whitewater Kilkeel

National Trust, this is possibly the UK's most ornate pub. For some time the Crown has been due to undergo a sympathetic restoration to return it to its original glory, though this has not happened yet. The house beer, Whitewater Crown Glory, is usually accompanied by a second local brew. Good pub food is available and there is a restaurant upstairs. ◐◑ ⇌(Gt Victoria St)

John Hewitt

51 Donegal Street, BT1 2FH
(100 yds from St. Anne's Cathedral)
✪ 11.30 (12 Sat)-1am; Sun hours vary
☎ (028) 9023 3768 🌐 thejohnhewitt.com
Hilden Ale; guest beer ⊞
Named after a famous Belfast poet, the John Hewitt is a pub with a strong ethos, owned and run by the Belfast Unemployed Resource Centre. At the heart of local arts, literary and music festivals, it acts as an ever-changing gallery. Excellent food is served at lunchtimes. Layout is open plan with a snug, and there are plans for expansion. The single handpump serves mainly Hilden ales. ◐♿⚟

King's Head

829 Lisburn Road, BT9 7GY (opposite Kings Hall)
✪ 12-1am (midnight Sun & Mon)
☎ (028) 9050 9950 🌐 kingsheadbelfast.com
Whitewater Belfast Ale; guest beer ⊞
Large establishment extended and refurbished in 2004. On entering, there is a welcoming area with two handpumps (invariably dispensing Whitewater) and a cosy recess, behind this is a spacious, more modern area. A double fireplace splits the public bar. Stairs and a lift lead to an elegant restaurant. The comfortable L-shaped lounge is roomy and relaxed. A separate Live Lounge hosts entertainment, including bands, quizzes and salsa. In the summer, an outdoor patio area is popular. ❀◐◑ ⊟♿⇌(Balmoral)P

Kitchen Bar

36-40 Victoria Square, BT1 4DY (access off Ann St via Upper Church St)
✪ 11.30-11.30 (midnight Mon; 1am Fri & Sat); 12-6 Sun
☎ (028) 9032 4901
Whitewater Belfast Ale; guest beer ⊞
The new Kitchen is a single room bar with a more modern feel than the much-loved original. Situated in a converted shipping office, it features riveted steel columns and a double brick archway. Currently surrounded by a major building site, access is limited, so follow the directions above. Jazz music is played on Monday nights with a traditional set on Fridays. Paddy Pizzas are still available. Evening meals are served Wednesday to Friday. ◐◑⇌(Central)

McHugh's

29-31 Queens Square, BT1 3FG (near Albert Clock)
✪ 11.30-1am (midnight Mon); 12-midnight Sun
☎ (028) 9050 9999 🌐 mchughsbar.com
Whitewater Belfast Ale; guest beer ⊞
Busy city centre pub originally dating from 1711 which has recently been restored and extended. Families are welcome and excellent food is available. Two ales from Whitewater Brewery are usually served. The basement bar hosts live music. McHugh's is a good spot to take in the events held in the new Custom's House Square.
♨◐◑♿⇌(Central)🚌

Carrickfergus

Central Bar

13-15 High Street, BT38 7AN (opp. the castle)
✪ 10-11 (1am Thu-Sat); 12-midnight Sun
☎ (028) 9335 7840
Beer range varies ⊞
Basic, unpretentious pub overlooking the Norman castle, conveniently situated near the town centre and marina. The good-value food is typical Wetherspoon's fare, served all day. There is a family area upstairs. Like all Wetherspoon's pubs in the province, it has recently introduced television screens and music. Q♉◐◑⚟

Coleraine

Old Courthouse

Castlerock Road, BT51 3HP
✪ 11-11 (1am Thu-Sat); 12.30-midnight Sun
☎ (028) 7032 5820
Beer range varies ⊞
Converted, listed, former county courthouse dating from 1852. A wide mix of clientele mingles in the single bar. It serves an ever-changing range of beer, and Westons cider on gravity. An impressive staircase leads to the upstairs area. Monday is quiz night, occasional themed evenings are held at weekends. Unusual for a town pub in this area, there is a patio area outside. Good value food is served – try the Ulster fry.
♨♉❀◐◑🍎

Enniskillen

Linen Hall

11-13 Townhall Street, BT74 7BD
✪ 10-11 (1am Fri & Sat); 12.30-midnight Sun
☎ (028) 6634 0910
Beer range varies ⊞
Remote Wetherspoon's outlet in the far west of the province. Popular with locals and the large number of visitors drawn to this beautiful part of Northern Ireland, it makes a good base for the superb fishing that is available. Television screens and music have been introduced. ♨♉❀◐◑♿⚟

Hillsborough

Hillside

21 Main Street, BT26 6AE
✪ 12-11.30 (1am Fri & Sat); 12-11 Sun
☎ (028) 9268 2765
Whitewater Belfast Ale; guest beer ⊞
Two-roomed pub with two restaurants. Usually four ales are available in the main bar, two from Whitewater and two English guests. Meals are served in the bar and the refectory. The a la carte restaurant upstairs is open at the weekend. A major attraction is the annual beer festival, held in mid June. This is a popular pub with a varied clientele – CAMRA members, locals, bell-ringers and tourists. ♨Q❀◐◑⊟♿⛺⚟

Holywood

Dirty Duck Ale House

2-4 Kinnegar Road, BT18 9JW

⊛ 11.30-midnight (1am Fri & Sat); 12.30-midnight Sun

☎ (028) 9059 6666

Beer range varies ⊞

Cheery pub on the County Down side of Belfast Lough – a previous local CAMRA Pub of the Year. From the picture windows in the bar and recently-refurbished upstairs restaurant you can enjoy superb views across the Lough, taking in shipping and the County Antrim coast. Four handpumps dispense ales often from Inveralmond and Highwood breweries. The pub hosts live music from Thursday to Sunday and holds a late-August beer festival. ✿◐◑≢

Killinchy

Daft Eddie's

Sketrick Island, BT23 6QH (Whiterock Road, 2 miles N of Killinchy)

⊛ 11.30-11.30 (1am Fri); 12-10.30 Sun

☎ (028) 9754 1615

Whitewater Belfast Ale ⊞

An outstanding pub and restaurant situated at Whiterock Bay on the shores of Strangford Lough. The area is picturesque with a marina and the ruins of Skettrick Castle nearby. Despite being a little difficult to find it is very popular and it may be necessary to book the restaurant. Fresh local oysters are sold at the bar, and a piano player entertains on Saturday night. Q✿◐◑⊟♿P

Lisburn

Tap Room

Hilden Brewery, Hilden, BT27 4TY (5 minute walk from Hilden railway halt)

⊛ 12-2.30, 6-9 (not Mon-Thu eves); 12.30-3 Sun

☎ (028) 9266 3863

Hilden Molly Malone ⊞

This is the bar and restaurant belonging to Hilden Brewery and is an impressive place to visit. Good food and good beer is the approach – meals can be accompanied by ale from the adjoining brew house. The Tap Room often hosts events such as the increasingly popular annual beer festival held in August. Recently Hilden opened the new brewery/restaurant Molly's Yard in Belfast. ♨Q✿◐◑♿≢(Hilden)P

Tuesday Bell

Units 1 & 2 Lisburn Square, BT28 2TU (in shopping centre)

⊛ 11.30-11 (1am Fri & Sat); 12.30-11 Sun

☎ (028) 9262 7390

Courage Directors; guest beer ⊞

Large Wetherspoon pub spread over two floors in the centre of Lisburn. It can be very busy, particularly at weekends. Recently screens and music have been introduced in line with the chain's other pubs. There are usually two or more mainly Scottish ales available. The pub opens at 10am on Tuesday and Saturday to cater for the local markets, but alcohol is not served before 11.30am. ◐◑♿≢(Lisburn)⊬

Londonderry

Diamond

23-24 The Diamond, BT48 6HP

⊛ 11-11 (1am Thu-Sat); 12-midnight Sun

☎ (028) 7127 2880

Beer range varies ⊞

Large two-storey Wetherspoon pub in the centre of Northern Ireland's historic walled city. A converted department store, the pub is split level and there is a children's room upstairs with no smoking areas on both floors. It overlooks the city centre war memorial and has views towards the River Foyle. The food is typical Wetherpoon's good-value fare. Westons cider is available on handpump.

♘◐◑♿≢(Waterside)●⊬

Ice Wharf

Strand Road, BT48 7AB

⊛ 11-11 (1am Thu-Sat); 12-midnight Sun

☎ (028) 7127 6610

Beer range varies ⊞

Spacious, open-plan, glass fronted Lloyd's No.1 bar, the first one in Northern Ireland. This is a sizeable pub with a split-level main bar and a separate room for families. It caters for a wide mix of clientele. Westons cider is available on gravity. Standard Lloyd's food is served.

♘◐◑♿●⊬

Newtownards

Spirit Merchant

54-56 Regent Street, BT23 4LP

⊛ 10-11 (1 am Fri & Sat); 10-midnight Sun

☎ (028) 9182 4270

Beer range varies ⊞

Wetherspoon pub, quiet in daytime, featuring plasma TV screens at night. These play restrained soul music mid-week but at weekends can be noisy and attract a young crowd. The current manager is Scottish and offers a choice of ales from Scottish breweries. Recently, real cider has occasionally been available on handpump. Meals are served from breakfast onwards.

◐◑●

Saintfield

White Horse

49 Main Street, BT24 7AB

⊛ 11.30-11.30; 12-10 Sun

☎ (028) 9751 1143

Whitewater Mill Ale, Glen Ale, Belfast Ale; guest beer ⊞

The Horse, as it is known locally, is CAMRA's NI Pub Of The Year for 2006. Although it has been completely renovated, the pub is still a cosy, friendly place but is now more spacious, with a wood-burning fire. There is more seating and a carvery as well as the Oast House restaurant downstairs. Owned by Whitewater Brewery it dispenses various beers, as well as its own, from five pumps. There is an annual beer festival showcasing 15-20 beers usually held in March.

♨✿◐◑♿⊬

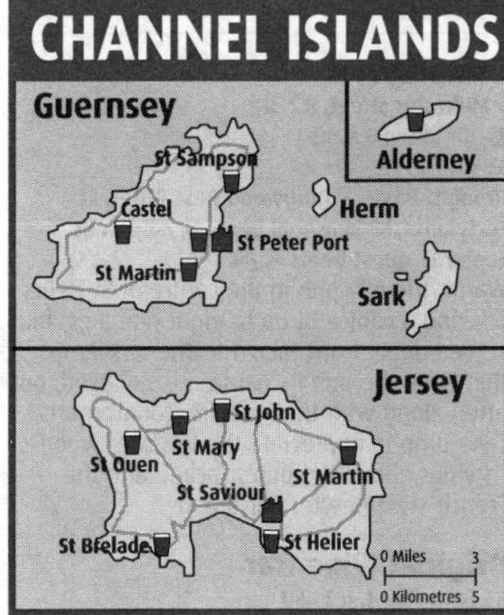

ALDERNEY

Alderney

Georgian House Hotel

Victoria Street, GY9 3UF

10-12.30am (winter 10-3, 6.30-midnight); 10-4 Sun

☎ (01481) 822471 georgianhousealderney.com

Randalls beer (varies) H

Situated on the main street, this imposing building extends a warm welcome to locals and visitors alike. It is a convenient location for enjoying a good pint or fine food from the extensive menu – from bar snacks to an a la carte meal. There is a good choice of seating in the bar area, the orangery or the gardens – the perfect place to while away a warm summer's afternoon.

❀⇄◑

GUERNSEY

Castel

Fleur du Jardin

Kings Mills, GY5 7JT

11.30-11.45 daily

☎ (01481) 257996 fleurdujardin.guernsey.net

Fuller's London Pride; Jersey Guernsey Sunbeam H

Country pub with a good-sized, sheltered garden in an attractive rural setting. There are two bars: one small and cosy, next to the restaurant, the other a larger room at the rear of the hotel. The menus in both the bar and restaurant feature fresh local produce. This popular pub can be busy at the weekend and throughout the summer.

♨Q❀⇄◑P

Rockmount Hotel

Cobo, GY5 7HB

10-11.45 (12.45am Fri & Sat); 12-10.30 Sun

☎ (01481) 256757

Randalls Envy H

This pub has two bars: a public to the rear of the building by the large car park and a lounge at the front by the road; with a warming fire in winter it is the perfect place to retreat from the gales. A good range of food is served in the lounge. The pub is just across the road from a beautiful sandy beach. At the end of the day why not relax with a good pint and enjoy one of the island's best views of Guernsey's legendary sunsets.

♨◑⊟P

St Martin

Ambassador Hotel

Route de Sausmarez, GY4 6SO

12-3, 6-11.45; 12-3.30 Sun

☎ (01481) 238356 ambassador.guernsey.net

Randalls beer (varies) H

The hotel is situated just down from Sausmarez Manor. A delicious range of meals is available, either in the bar, the restaurant or the Old Guernsey Conservatory. There is also a patio area to the rear of the bar for when the weather is fine. The bar is open only to hotel guests on Sunday; the accommodation is good value.

⇄◑P

Captain's Hotel

La Fosse, GY4 6EF

10-11.45; 10-4 Sun

☎ (01481) 238990

Fuller's London Pride H

In a secluded location down a country lane, this is a popular locals' pub with a lively, friendly atmosphere. There is a small outdoor area to enjoy in the summer. Meals can be eaten in the bar or bistro. A meat raffle is held on Friday. There is a car park but it fills up quickly. ❀⇄◑P

St Peter Port

Cock & Bull

Lower Hauteville, GY1 1LL

11.30-2.30, 4-12.45am; 11.30-12.45am Fri & Sat; occasional Sun

☎ (01481) 722660

Beer range varies H

Popular pub, just up the hill from the church. Five handpumps provide a choice of beers, including a brew created for the pub by Randalls called Sipping Bull. Beer festivals are hosted from time to time. Live music is performed, which on Monday may be baroque, salsa or jazz, and Tuesday night is live microphone. Seating is on three levels and a large-screen TV shows sporting events.

Cornerstone Café

2 La Tour Beauregard, GY1 1LQ

10 (8am Thu & Fri)-12.45am; occasional Sun

☎ (01481) 713832

Fuller's London Pride; Greene King Old Speckled Hen; Thwaites Lancaster Bomber H

Situated across the road from the States Archives, the café has a small bar area to the front with bar stools, and further seating to the rear. A Randalls beer is usually available. The menu offers a wide range of hot and cold meals, served all day. ◑

INDEPENDENT BREWERIES

Jersey St Saviour Jersey
Randalls St Peter Port Guernsey

ISLANDS

Randy Paddle

North Esplanade, GY1 2LQ
✪ 10-11.45 (12.45am Fri & Sat); closed Sun
☎ (01481) 725610
Fuller's London Pride; Wadworth 6X [H]
Across the road from the harbour and next door to the tourist board, the pub is in an ideal location for a drink before a meal at one of the varied restaurants surrounding it. The bar has a nautical theme and, although small, makes good use of the space, attracting a mixed crowd of regulars and visitors to the island.

Ship & Crown

North Esplanade, GY1 2NB (opp. Crown Pier car park)
✪ 10-12.45am; 12-10 Sun
☎ (01481) 721368
Fuller's London Pride; Greene King IPA; Shepherd Neame Spitfire; Wadworth 6X [H]
Newly refurbished, the pub has retained its nautical theme, with pictures of ships and a model of the 'Seven Seas', complete with tiny cannon balls, in a glass case. Situated across the road from the Victoria Pier (known locally as the Crown Pier), this busy pub attracts a varied clientele of all ages, including locals and tourists. Good quality bar meals are served in generous portions.
◐◗

St Sampson

La Fontaine Inn

Vale Road, GY2 4DS
✪ 10-11.45; 12-3.30 (6 summer) Sun
☎ (01481) 247644
Randalls Cynful, Envy [H]
Popular with the local community, the handpumps are located in the small public bar. Next to the bar is an L-shaped lounge and along one wall is a serving hatch, so you can obtain a drink wherever you are. Shove-ha-penny is played in the public bar and darts at the back of the lounge. A popular meat raffle is held on Friday. Cynful ale is named after Cindy, the landlady.
❀♣P

JERSEY

St Brelade

Smugglers Inn

La Mont du Ouaisne, JE3 8AW
✪ 11-11 daily (winter Mon-Fri 11-2.30, 5-11)
☎ (01534) 741510
Draught Bass; Greene King Abbot; [H] **guest beers** [G]
Set within a row of granite fishermen's cottages dating back to the 16th century, this is a fascinating pub set on many levels. Renowned for its excellent food, it can be busy despite its remote location. As one of the island's few free houses, it offers an ever-changing range of real ales and holds frequent mini beer festivals. It has been CAMRA's Jersey Pub of the Year every year since 2002.
♛Q◗

St Helier

Lamplighter

9 Mulcaster Street, JE2 3NJ
✪ 10 (11 Sun & Mon)-11
☎ (01534) 723119
Draught Bass; [G] **Ringwood Best Bitter,** [H] **Fortyniner,** [G] **seasonal beers** [H]/[G]**; Wells Eagle;** [H] **guest beers** [H]/[G]
Warm, friendly pub in the centre of St Helier offering a choice of up to eight real ales, four served direct from the cask. The gas lamps that gave the pub its name are still used, but often along with their electric counterparts. Take time to appreciate the intricate wood carvings above the pub's façade and the French-style pewter bar top. ◐

Original Wine Bar

86 Bath Street, JE2 4SU
✪ 11-11; 3-11 Sun
☎ (01534) 871119
Draught Bass; Ringwood Best Bitter; Jersey Jimmy's Bitter; guest beers [H]
The Original is renowned for its beer as well as its wine. The bar has five handpumps though often only three or four are in use. The interior has been sympathetically refurbished in recent years. Lunches are available every day except Sunday and there is a tapas bar if you fancy an evening snack. ◐

Prince of Wales Tavern

Hilgrove Lane, JE2 4SL
✪ 10.30-11; 12-2 (closed eve) Sun
☎ (01534) 737378
Draught Bass; Ringwood Best Bitter; Wells Bombardier; guest beers [H]
Situated close to the central market in a delightful cobbled street known locally as French Lane, this pub is popular with refugees from nearby offices. It offers five real ales served from a period six-pump beer engine (although only three of them work). Lunches are available in the summer and are served either in the bar or the secluded yard behind. Children are not allowed in the yard. ❀◐

St John

Les Fontaines Tavern

La Route de Nord, JE3 4AJ
✪ 11-11 daily
☎ (01534) 862707
Draught Bass; Wells Bombardier [H]
Converted Jersey farmhouse perched on the north coast. The Fontaine has a large oak-beamed bar (mind your head!) and plenty of charm. A family-friendly pub, outside there is a patio and children's play area. The food is popular here and the dining area is set on many levels. If the car park is full there is a large public car park nearby. Q❀◐◗P

St Martin

Royal

La Grande Route de Faldouet, JE3 6UG
✪ 11-11 daily
☎ (01534) 856289
Draught Bass; Ringwood Best Bitter [H]

A large village pub, the Royal is popular with locals and families, benefitting from a patio and children's play area. Good food is popular here and the large dining area is often full (no food summer Sun). There is a separate public bar, the Granite Bar, but real ale is not served here.
⚘Q❀◐◑⊟⅄P

Rozel Bay Hotel

La Vallee de Rozel, JE3 6AJ
✪ 11-11 daily
☎ (01534) 869801
Draught Bass; Courage Directors; Wells Bombardier Ⓗ
The hotel is tucked away in a picturesque valley on the north east corner of the island. It has two bars – cask ales are served in the smaller snug. Meals are served in the bar and in the excellent upstairs restaurant (no food Mon). Outside is a covered verandah and attractive garden. Parking is at a premium but there is a regular bus service from town. ⚘Q❀◐◑⊟⅄⊟P

St Mary

St Mary's Country Inn

La Rue des Buttes, JE3 3DS
✪ 12-11 daily
☎ (01534) 482897
Draught Bass; Jersey Jimmy's Bitter Ⓗ
At the heart of St Mary's village life, the inn has a spacious open-plan interior and welcomes all the family. The bar has a large open fire perfect for winter months. The pub has a good reputation for its food and the quality of its ale. It hosts live music, usually at the weekend. There is plenty of alfresco drinking and dining space.
⚘Q❀◐◑⊟P

St Ouen

Moulin de Lecq

La Mont de la Greve de Lecq, JE3 2DT
✪ 11-11 daily
☎ (01534) 482818
Greene King IPA, Abbot; Ringwood Best Bitter; Wells Bombardier; guest beers Ⓗ
Originally a 12th-century watermill, the Moulin de Lecq is a charming little pub tucked away in a picturesque valley. One of the few free houses on the island, it offers a range of ales and often Westons Old Rosie cider. The new oak-panelled restaurant serves excellent food. There is plenty of outdoor seating, a children's play area and free parking.
⚘Q❀◑●P

ISLANDS

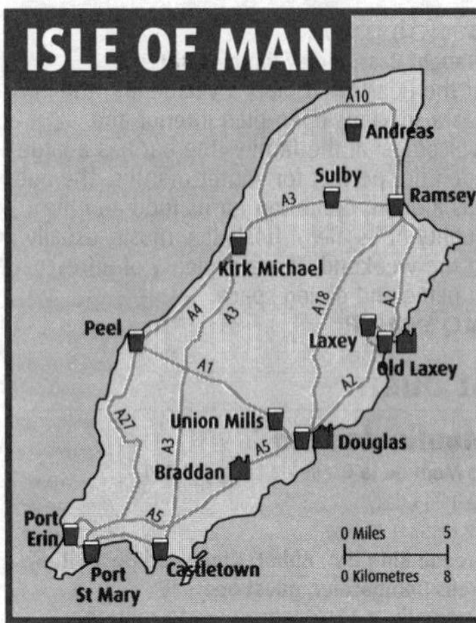

Andreas

Grosvenor Hotel

Kirk Andreas, IM7 4HE

✪ 12-3, 5-11 (midnight Fri & Sat); 12-4, 7.45-11 Sun

☎ (01624) 880576

Okells Bitter; guest beers Ⓗ

The most northerly pub on the island, it has a central bar serving two rooms and a dining area. The warm, friendly feel of this welcoming village pub makes the Grosvenor popular with real ale drinkers and diners alike. Reasonably-priced bar snacks are available all year round. Unusual for the Isle of Man, disabled access is good. Public transport to this part of the island is limited to daytime. Q❀◖◗⊟♿⊟♣P

Castletown

Castle Arms (Gluepot)

The Quay, IM9 1LP (between Castle Rushen and harbour)

✪ 12-11 (midnight Fri & Sat); 12-11 Sun

☎ (01624) 824673

Okells Bitter Ⓗ

For directions to the Gluepot, just look on the back of a £5 note – it is the gable-ended building in the bottom left-hand corner. Much effort and an extension of its public areas have restored the popularity of this historic building. The small patio outside allows you to sit overlooking the harbour and enjoy the maritime activities. A sea-going theme inside includes old photographs and models. No food is served Sunday.
❀◖≹(IMR)⊟

Sidings

Victoria Road, IM9 1EF (by station)

✪ 11.30-11 (midnight Fri & Sat); 11.30-11 Sun

☎ (01624) 823282

Bushy's Ruby Mild, Castletown Bitter; guest beers Ⓗ

The Sidings is a welcome sight when you arrive at the island's ancient capital by train. Still known to many as the Duck's Nest, its impressive and ornate wooden counter dispenses the regular ales at reasonable prices plus an ever changing variety of around 10 cask ales from Manx and British breweries. No food is served Sunday. A well-deserved CAMRA Pub of the Year in 2003 and 2005.
⛫❀◖≹(IMR)⊟♣

Douglas

Albert Hotel

3 Chapel Row, IM1 2BJ (near indoor market)

✪ 10-11 (midnight Fri & Sat); 12-10.30 Sun

☎ (01624) 673632

Okells Mild, Bitter Ⓗ

Close to the bus station and quayside, this busy local has a thriving social club. A central bar serves the spacious, wood-panelled lounge and smaller public bar. The colourful, lively atmosphere attracts locals and bikers. The house brew Jough (Manx Gaelic for beer) is supplied by Okells. Q⊟≹(IMR)⊟♣

Old Market Tavern

2 Chapel Row, IM1 2BJ

✪ 10-11; 12-4, 7-11 Sun

☎ (01624) 675202

Okells Bitter Ⓗ

Back-street local between the bus station and market hall with two small wood-panelled rooms served by a central bar. One of the few exterior-tiled pubs on the island, this is also one of the friendliest. Visitors are always made to feel welcome – it is more than likely that you will be quickly involved in the cheery banter.
⛫Q⊟≹(IMR)⊟♣

Prospect

Prospect Hill, IM1 1ES

✪ 12 (6 Sat)-11 (midnight Fri & Sat); closed Sun

☎ (01624) 616773

Okells Bitter; guest beers Ⓗ

Busy pub located within the business area of Douglas and popular with office workers. A large, single room with plenty of seating; one area is no-smoking. A wide range of beers is available from both on and off the island – guest beers change weekly. Food is served at lunchtime during the week and Thursday and Friday evening. Quiz night is Thursday. Be warned: after 5pm on Friday the pub becomes very crowded as the offices empty out. ◖◗≹(IMR)⊟⚟

Queens Hotel

Queens Promenade, IM2 4NL (on seafront)

✪ 12-11 (midnight Fri & Sat); 12-11 Sun

☎ (01624) 674438

Okells Bitter; guest beers Ⓗ

Established in 1853, this seafront pub has a pleasant façade and outdoor seating area. Recently refurbished, with a bar and games area and quieter wood-panelled lounge, the interior blends traditional and modern decor and furnishings. Popular all year round, if you want to enjoy the good, reasonably-priced menu it is advisable to get there early to find a table. A lively pub, particularly at weekends when there is live music.
❀◖◗⊟♿⊟♣

INDEPENDENT BREWERIES

Bushy's Braddan
Okells Douglas
Old Laxey Old Laxey

Rovers Return

11 Church Street, IM1 2AG (behind town hall)
⌚ 12-11 (midnight Fri & Sat); 12-11 Sun
☎ (01624) 676459
Bushy's Ruby Mild, Bitter, seasonal beers; guest beers Ⓗ
The Rovers has nine public rooms, two with real fires. There is now a downstairs bar stocking Bushy's, Archers and other real ales, and an area for bands with a video link to the bar. The Blackburn Rovers 'shrine' and snug have become no-smoking rooms. Note the unusual handpumps, fashioned from fire brigade brass branch pipes. Live music staged most weekends draws the crowds in the evenings and substantial portions of food make the pub a popular lunchtime venue. ♨❀☾⇶(IMR)⊟●⚡

Terminus Tavern

Strathallan Crescent, IM2 4NR
⌚ 12-11(midnight Fri & Sat); 12-11 Sun
Okells Bitter; guest beers Ⓗ
At the terminus for the electric and horse-drawn trams at the end of the promenade, this friendly pub is popular with drinkers and diners. The varied food menu is often themed. A large lounge and games room feature old photographs of the area in busier times. Enjoy the view through the bay windows as you relax with a pint and watch the trams pass by. ♨☎❀☾☽⊞♿⊟♣P

Woodbourne

Alexander Drive, IM2 3QF
⌚ 12 (2 Mon-Thu)-midnight daily
☎ (01624) 676754
Okells Mild, Bitter, seasonal beers Ⓗ
A little daunting from the outside, but inside is a cheerful but plainly furnished lounge and public bar. Unusually, there is also a gentleman's bar – although apparently this is no longer strictly enforced. Note that the pub is closed at lunchtime Monday to Thursday and no food is served at all. Q⊞⊟

Kirk Michael

Mitre

IM6 1AJ
⌚ 12-2.30 (not Mon), 5-11 (midnight Fri); 12-midnight Sat; 12-11 Sun
☎ (01624) 878244
Okells Bitter; guest beer Ⓗ
Recently reopened following extensive refurbishment, this cosy and welcoming pub has lost none of its original charm. One of the oldest pubs on the island, photographs of the TT and local area from years gone by decorate the walls. A wide selection of good-value home-cooked traditional pub food including Sunday lunches is available. Barbecue weekends are a speciality in summer. ♨❀☾☽⊞♿⊟♣P

Laxey

Bridge Inn

6 New Road, IM4 7BE
⌚ 11.30-11 (midnight Fri & Sat); 11.30-11 Sun
☎ (01624) 862414
Bushy's Mild, Bitter Ⓗ
Community pub in the centre of the village near Laxey Glen gardens, home to the Poetry and Pints society. The cellar was used as a morgue after the Snaefell mining disaster in 1897 in which 20 men perished. The inn is reputed to be haunted, with ghostly figures seen in the lounge. A wide-screen TV shows football. B&B and a function room are available. ♨☎⇌⊞⊖(MER)⊟(3)♣P

Queen's Hotel

New Road, IM4 7BP
⌚ 12-11 (midnight Fri & Sat); 12-11 Sun
Bushy's Ruby Mild, Castletown Bitter, Bitter; guest beers Ⓗ
Busy local sited on the edge of Laxey, popular with locals and bikers all year round. The interest in bikes is reflected in the numerous photos and pictures adorning the walls, including several of the late Joey Dunlop, famous TT rider. Live music is hosted every Saturday and barbecues are held on summer weekends on the patio. The large porch with seating and additional benches outside are perfect for watching the world go by, or even waiting for the bus to Douglas which stops outside. ❀⇌⊖(MER)⊟♣P

Old Laxey

Shore Hotel

IM4 7DA
⌚ 11-11 daily
☎ (01624) 861509
Old Laxey Bosun Bitter Ⓗ
Delightful village brew-pub near the harbour with outdoor seating along the riverside. The large single room has a nautical theme, with faded fishing boat pictures and fishing equipment. There is a real fire in winter and comfortable seating adds to the cosy atmosphere. Bosun Bitter from the adjacent micro-brewery is always available, supplemented by an occasional guest. ♨❀☾☽⊟P

Peel

Whitehouse Hotel

2 Tynwald Road, IM5 1LA (near bus station)
⌚ 11-midnight daily
☎ (01624) 842252
Bushy's Bitter, seasonal beers; Flowers Original; Okells Mild, Bitter; Taylor Landlord; guest beers Ⓗ
Multi-roomed, family-run town pub unaltered since the 1930s, with historic pictures of the local area on the walls. Three rooms including a snug are served by a central bar. Musicians meet most Saturday evenings to play Gaelic music. A delightful hostelry for real ales fans, it also stocks over 120 malt whiskies. ♨⊞⛺⊟♣P

Port Erin

Bay Hotel

Shore Road, IM9 6HC (on road to lifeboat house)
⌚ 12-11 daily
☎ (01624) 832084
Bushy's Ruby Mild, Bitter, Old Bushy Tail; guest beers Ⓗ
After many years of closure the Bay has been restored and the ground-floor bars are well worth a visit. Use of old and original materials gives the feel of a pub that has been around for

years. Frequent live music and gigs are hosted at the weekend. Excellent food is served by friendly, efficient staff. ♨♘◑◐⊟≑(IMR)♣●

Falcon's Nest Hotel

Station Road, IM9 6AF

⏲ 11-midnight daily

☎ (01624) 834077 ⊕ falconsnesthotel.co.uk

Bushy's Bitter; Okells Bitter; guest beers 🄷

Family-run, seafront hotel overlooking Port Erin bay and harbour with two bars, a function room and a large restaurant. The attractive lounge, with polished wood and stained glass, has recently been extended with a conservatory where you can enjoy panoramic views of the bay. Real ale is served in the lounge, not the bar. A wide range of meals is available including the popular Sunday carvery.
♨🛏◑◐⊟≑🚌P

Port St Mary

Albert Hotel

Athol Street, IM9 5DS (alongside bus terminal)

⏲ 11.30-midnight (1am Fri & Sat); 12-midnight Sun

☎ (01624) 832118

Bushy's Ruby Mild, Old Bushy Tail; Okells Bitter; guest beers 🄷

Traditional free house with a fine view over the inner harbour and bay. The busy public bar has pool, darts and a juke box. The cosy lounge has a nautical theme; both bars have real fires. There is a small restaurant across the hallway and bar meals are available. Food and accommodation are highly recommended.
♨❀🛏◑⊟🚌P

Shore Hotel

Shore Road, Gansey, IM9 5LZ (on main Castletown-Port St Mary road) OS220689

⏲ 12-11 (midnight Fri & Sat); 12-11 Sun

☎ (01624) 832269

Bushy's Bushy Tail; Okells Bitter; guest beer 🄷

Friendly free house with delightful views over Gansey bay. Traditional Manx ales along with a weekly guest beer are on dispense in the cosy bar. Bar snacks are available daily and good quality food is served in the restaurant. Themed Indian and Thai nights are popular, as well as Sunday lunches. Quiz night is Tuesday. Four bed and breakfast rooms are available. ❀🛏◑◐🚌(2)♣P

Ramsey

Ellan Vannin

West Quay, IM8 1JU (200 yds E of harbour swing bridge)

⏲ 12-11 (midnight Fri & Sat); 12-11 Sun

☎ (01624) 812131

Bushy's Castletown Bitter, Bitter, seasonal beers; guest beer 🄷

Small, cosy Bushy's pub on the corner of the bustling quay and market place. Ellan Vannin is the Manx name for the island. It offers a warm and friendly welcome to an eclectic mix of customers. Some foreign bottled beers are stocked, as well as Weston's traditional scrumpy on handpull. Occasional live music is performed at the weekend. It gets busy during the TT and Manx Grand Prix weeks.
♨♿⊖(MER)🚌♣●

Trafalgar Hotel

West Quay, IM8 1DW (E of harbour swing bridge)

⏲ 11-11 (midnight Fri & Sat); 12-3, 8-11 Sun

☎ (01624) 814601

Cains Mild, Bitter; Okells Bitter; guest beers 🄷

Friendly, freehold harbourside pub offering quayside drinking during warmer weather. Guest ales are sourced from throughout the UK. A regular finalist in the island's CAMRA Pub of the Year award, the Trafalgar is a well-established pub and can be very busy, particularly at the weekend. Popular during TT and Manx Grand Prix weeks due to its proximity to Parliament Square for an unrivalled view of these famous races.
⊖(MER)🚌♣

Sulby

Sulby Glen Hotel

Main Road, IM7 2HR (Sulby crossroads, A3)

⏲ 12-midnight (1am Fri & Sat); 12-11 Sun

☎ (01624) 897240

Bushy's Bitter; Okells Bitter; guest beers 🄷

Community pub and hotel on the famous Sulby Straight section of the TT course. A varied food menu and a good choice of ales are on offer at this large, multi-roomed pub. The bars display many photographs of riders through the ages. Look for the leaflets detailing forthcoming events including live bands, themed food nights and pub outings.
♨♘❀🛏◑◐⊟♿⛺🚌♣●P

Union Mills

Railway Inn

Main Road, IM4 4NE

⏲ 12-11 daily

☎ (01624) 853006 ⊕ iomrailwayinn.com

Okells Mild, Bitter; guest beers 🄷

Independent, historic pub dating back to 1841 with a welcoming, relaxed atmosphere. It is now in the fifth generation of ownership by the same family, all of them women. Frequented by a friendly crowd, this community pub at the centre of village life runs darts teams and a golfing society. Located on the TT circuit, it is a spectacular place to watch the racing. ❀🚌P🚭

Farmers' markets

Many small brewers cannot get their beers into pubs owned by large pub companies as a result of the deep discounts demanded. The same problem exists with supermarkets. The brewers have responded by looking for new outlets and have found them at farmers' market. For details of farmers' markets see www.farmersmarkets.net

The Breweries

How beer is brewed

Real ale is made by taking raw ingredients from the fields, the finest malting barley and hops, along with pure water from natural springs or the public supply, and carefully cultivated strains of brewers' yeast; in this exploded drawing by Trevor Hatchett of a classic British ale brewery, it is possible to follow the process that begins with raw grain and finishes with natural, living cask beer.

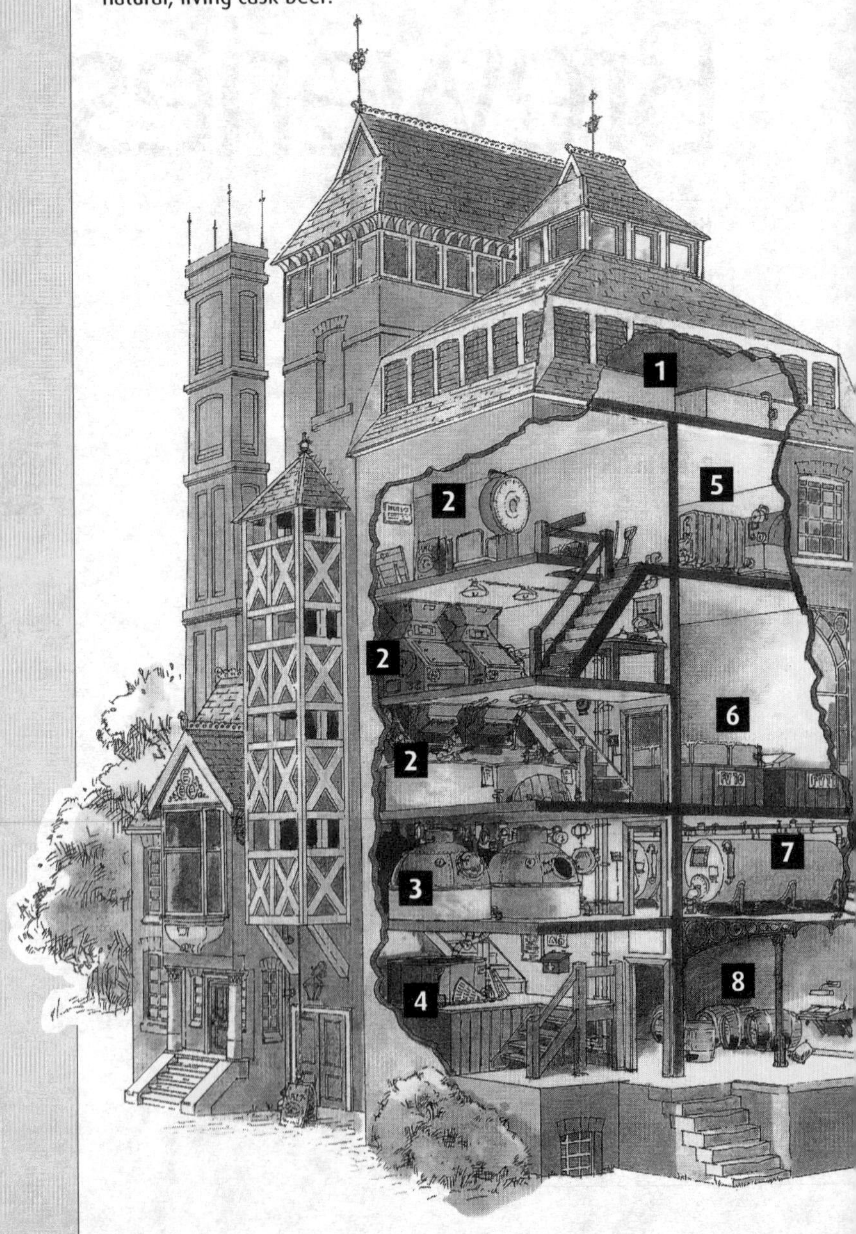

1 On the top floor, in the roof, are the tanks where pure water – called liquor by brewers – is stored. Soft water is not suited to ale brewing, and brewers will add such salts as gypsum and magnesium to replicate the hard, flinty waters of Burton-on-Trent, home of pale ale.

2 In the malt store, grain is weighed and kept until needed.The malt drops down a floor to the mills, which grind it into a coarse powder suitable for brewing. From the mills, the ground malt or grist is poured into the mash tuns along with heated liquor. During the mashing period, natural enzymes in the malt convert starches into fermentable malt sugars.

3 On the same floor as the conditioning tanks are the coppers, where after mashing, the wort is boiled with hops, which add aroma, flavour and bitterness.

4 At the end of the boil, the hopped wort is clarified in a vessel called the hop back on the ground floor. The clarified wort is pumped back to the malt store level where it is passed through a heat exchange unit. See 5.

5 The heat exchange unit cools the hopped wort prior to fermentation.

6 The fermenters are on the same floor as the mash tuns.The house yeast is blended or pitched with the wort.Yeast converts the malt sugars in the wort into alcohol and carbon dioxide. Excess yeast is skimmed off by funnels called parachutes.

7 Fermentation lasts for a week and the 'green' beer is then stored for a few days in conditioning tanks.

8 Finally, the fresh beer is run into casks on the ground floor, where additional hops for aroma and sugar to encourage a secondary fermentation may be added.The casks then leave for pubs, where the beer reaches maturity in the cellars.

How to use The Breweries section

Breweries are listed in alphabetical order. The Independents (regional, smaller craft brewers and brew-pubs) are listed first, followed by the Nationals, the Globals and finally the major non-brewing Pub Groups. Within each brewery entry, beers are listed in increasing order of strength. Beers that are available for less than three months of the year are described as 'occasional' or 'seasonal' brews. Bottle-conditioned beers are also listed: these are beers that have not been pasteurised and contain live yeast, allowing them to continue to ferment and mature in the bottle as a draught real ale does in its cask.

Symbols

A brew-pub: a pub that brews beer on the premises.

CAMRA tasting notes, supplied by a trained CAMRA tasting panel. Beer descriptions that do not carry this symbol are based on more limited tastings or have been obtained from other sources.
Tasting notes are not provided for brew-pub beers that are available in fewer than five outlets, nor for other breweries' beers that are available for less than three months of the year.

A CAMRA Beer of the Year in the past three years.

One of the 2006 CAMRA Beers of the Year, a finalist in the Champion Beer of Britain competition held during the Great British Beer Festival in London in August 2006, or the Champion Winter Beer of Britain competition held earlier in the year.

The brewery's beers can be acceptably served through a 'tight sparkler' attached to the nozzle of the beer pump, designed to give a thick collar of foam on the beer.

The brewery's beer should NOT be served through a tight sparkler. CAMRA is opposed to the growing tendency to serve southern-brewed beers with the aid of sparklers, which aerate the beer and tend to drive hop aroma and flavour into the head, altering the balance of the beer achieved in the brewery.

Abbreviations

OG stands for original gravity, the measure taken before fermentation of the level of 'fermentable material' (malt sugars and added sugars) in the brew. It is a rough indication of strength and is no longer used for duty purposes.

ABV stands for Alcohol by Volume, which is a more reliable measure of the percentage of alcohol in the finished beer. Many breweries now only disclose ABVs but the Guide lists OGs where available. Often the OG and the ABV of a beer are identical, ie 1035 and 3.5 per cent. If the ABV is higher than the OG, ie OG 1035, ABV 3.8, this indicates that the beer has been 'well attenuated' with most of the malt sugars turned into alcohol. If the ABV is lower than the OG, this means residual sugars have been left in the beer for fullness of body and flavour: this is rare but can apply to some milds or strong old ales, barley wines, and winter beers.

*The Breweries Section was correct at the time of going to press and every effort has been made to ensure that all cask-conditioned and bottle-conditioned beers are included.

The Independents

✲Indicates new entry since the last edition; SIBA indicates member of the Society of Independent Brewers; IFBB indicates member of the Independent Family Brewers of Britain; EAB indicates member of the East Anglian Brewers Co-operative

1648 SIBA

1648 Brewing Co Ltd, Mill Lane, East Hoathly, near Lewes, East Sussex, BN8 6QB
Tel (01825) 840830
Email brewmaster@1648brewing.co.uk
Website www.1648brewing.co.uk
Tours by arrangement

⊗ The 1648 brewery, set up in the old stable block of the King's Head pub in 2003, derives its name and some of the beer names from the time of the deposition of King Charles I. One pub is owned and more than 30 outlets are supplied. Seasonal beers: Three Threads (ABV 4.3%, April-July), Bee-Head (ABV 4.6%, May-Sept), Lammas Ale (ABV 4.2%, July-Oct), Armistice Ale (ABV 4.2%, Oct-Nov), Ginger Nol (ABV 4.7%, Oct-March), Winter Warrant (ABV 4.8%, Dec-March).

Original (OG 1040, ABV 3.9%)
Light, quaffable and easy drinking.

Signature (OG 1044, ABV 4.4%)
Light, crisp, medium hoppy clean beer with a bitter finish.

3 Rivers SIBA ✲

3 Rivers Brewing Ltd, Delta House, Greg Street, Reddish, Stockport, Cheshire, SK5 7BS
Tel (0161) 477 3333
Fax (0870) 285 1493
Website www.3riversbrewery.co.uk
Tours by arrangement

Mike Hitchen, previously at Beechams Bar in St Helens, launched 3 Rivers in 2004. There is a members' club on site and a purpose-built tasting area for brewery tours. Seasonal beers: Black Moon Stout (ABV 4.8%, Oct-Feb), Yummy Figgy Pudding (ABV 7.5%, December), Aquarian Ale (ABV 4%, Jan-Feb), Murphy's Law (ABV 4.5%, Wetherspoons festivals only).

GMT (ABV 3.8%)
Golden session bitter with an underlying malt character supported by moderate hop bitterness and a light floral finish.

Harry Jacks (ABV 4.1%)
A tawny-coloured ale with a fruity character supplemented by hints of roast malt in the finish.

Manchester IPA (ABV 4.2%)
A light russet/amber colour with a refreshing biscuit like flavour, supplemented by a complex citrus finish.

Pilgrims Progress (ABV 4.2%)
Light amber-coloured ale producing hints of coffee and caramel in the taste, complemented by a spicy hop character and a complex aroma.

Oxbow (ABV 4.5%)
Powerfully hoppy bitter; the initial dryness leads to a spicy character with a prominent aroma and notable citrus aftertaste.

Julie's Pride (ABV 5%)

Old Disreputable (ABV 5.2%)
A dark, malty brew with distinctive coffee and chocolate hints and a lasting bitter finish.

Suitably Irish (ABV 5.6%)
Full-bodied black stout.

For Beechams Bar, St Helens

Crystal Wheat (ABV 5%)
A spicy character with a floral aroma.

Abbey Ales SIBA

Abbey Ales Ltd, Abbey Brewery, Camden Row, Bath, Somerset, BA1 5LB
Tel (01225) 444437
Fax (01225) 443569
Email enquiries@abbeyales.co.uk
Website www.abbeyales.co.uk
Tours by arrangement

⊗ Abbey Ales is the first and only brewery in Bath for nearly 50 years. It supplies more than 80 regular accounts within a 20-mile radius of Bath Abbey while selected wholesalers deliver beer nationally. One tied house, the Star Inn, Bath, is listed on CAMRA's National Inventory of heritage pubs. The one regular cask beer, Bellringer, has won several CAMRA Beer of Festival awards and was a finalist in the 2001 Champion Beer of Britain competition. Seasonal beers: Bath Star (ABV 4.5%, spring), Chorister (ABV 4.5%, autumn), White Friar (ABV 5%), Black Friar (ABV 5.3%, winter), Twelfth Night (ABV 5%, Christmas).

Bellringer (OG 1042, ABV 4.2%) ◻ ◆
A notably hoppy ale, light to medium-bodied, clean-tasting, refreshingly dry, with a balancing sweetness. Citrus, pale malt aroma and dry, bitter finish.

Abbey Bells

Abbey Bells Brewery, 5 Main Road, Hirst Courtney, Selby, North Yorkshire, YO8 8QP
Tel (07940) 726658
Email enquiries@abbeybells.co.uk
Website www.abbeybells.co.uk
Tours by arrangement (for up to 12 persons only)

⊗ The brewery was launched by Jules Dolan in

2002 and was financed by the sale of his motorbike. The 2.5-barrel plant has cellar tanks from the defunct Brigg Brewery and other parts from a dairy maker in Congleton. Some 30 outlets are supplied. Seasonal beers: Santa's Stocking Filler (ABV 4.5%), Black Satin (ABV 6.2%, winter).

Monday's Child **(OG 1035, ABV 3.7%)**
An easy-drinking session beer, made with Maris Otter malt and Goldings hops. Pale and refreshing.

Amber Neck Tie **(OG 1040, ABV 4%)**

Hoppy Daze **(OG 1041, ABV 4.1%)**
Similar in colour to Monday's Child, the beer is hopped with Target, giving a hoppy tang.

Cordelia's Gift **(OG 1042, ABV 4.3%)**
The combination of Pearl and chocolate malts and Fuggles hops imparts a flavour reminiscent of dandelion and burdock.

Leper Squint **(OG 1045, ABV 4.5%)**

Grease **(OG 1045, ABV 4.6%)**

1911 Celebration Ale **(OG 1048, ABV 4.8%)**

Original Bitter **(OG 1050, ABV 5.1%)**
Made from Pearl malt with a dash of crystal and flavoured with Goldings hops.

Abbeydale SIBA

Abbeydale Brewery Ltd, Unit 8, Aizlewood Road, Sheffield, South Yorkshire, S8 0YX
Tel (0114) 281 2712
Fax (0114) 281 2713
Email abbeydale@mac.com
Website www.abbeydalebrewery.co.uk

⊗ A gradual yet sustained expansion programme has seen Abbeydale grow in its first decade to a point where it now supplies more than 250 outlets across the north and midlands. Late in 2005 the brewery acquired its first pub, the Rising Sun at Nether Green in Sheffield. Seasonal beers: Assumption (ABV 4.1%, August), Alchemy (ABV 4.2%), Black Bishop (ABV 4.2%), Devotion (ABV 4.4%), Wheat Beer (ABV 5.5%, summer), Belfry (ABV 4.5%), White Knight (ABV 4.5%), Stormbringer (ABV 4.7%), Reformation (ABV 4.8%), Epiphany (ABV 5.2%), Hells Bells (ABV 5.8%), Holy Water (ABV 6%, December).

Matins **(OG 1034.9, ABV 3.6%)**
Extremely pale and full flavoured, but light in alcohol; an excellent, hoppy session beer.

Brimstone **(OG 1039, ABV 3.9%)**

Moonshine **(OG 1041.2, ABV 4.3%)**
Pale premium beer balancing hints of sweetness and bitterness with full hop aroma. Pleasant grapefruit traces may be detected.

Absolution **(OG 1050, ABV 5.3%)**
Strong, pale, sweetish beer.

Black Mass **(OG 1065, ABV 6.6%)**
Strong black stout, quite bitter and dry but full flavoured with a characteristic hop aroma.

Last Rites **(OG 1097, ABV 11%)**
A pale, strong barley wine bursting with flavour.

Acorn SIBA

Acorn Brewery of Barnsley Ltd, Unit 11 Mitchells Enterprise Centre, Bradberry Balk Lane, Wombwell, Barnsley, South Yorkshire, S73 8HR
Tel (01226) 270734 Fax (01226) 270759
Email acornbrewery@tiscali.co.uk
Website www.acornbrewery.net
Shop Mon-Fri 9am-5pm
Tours by arrangement

Acorn Brewery started production in 2003 using a 10-barrel former Firkin plant. All beers are produced using the original Barnsley Bitter yeast strains. The brewery has 50 barrels a week capacity with current expansion taking this to 100 barrels. 400 outlets are supplied. Seasonal beers: Summer Pale (ABV 4.1%, March-Sept), Darkness (ABV 4.2%, spring/autumn), Winter Ale (ABV 4.5%, winter), 4th Noel (ABV 5.1%, Christmas).

Barnsley Bitter **(OG 1038, ABV 3.8%)**
A well-balanced, excellent session bitter. Fine, rewarding taste with hints of chocolate throughout.

Barnsley Gold **(OG 1041.5, ABV 4.3%)**
Fruit and hops carry throughout the whole drink. Crisp, dry and well-hopped.

Sovereign **(OG 1044, ABV 4.4%)**
Well-balanced bitter with plenty of fruit and malt. Excellent mouthfeel. A proper pint.

Old Moor Porter **(OG 1045, ABV 4.4%)**
Coffee notes on the aroma with hints of chocolate. Easy-drinking, creamy but dry with a balanced liquorice flavour.

IPA **(OG 1047, ABV 5%)**
A fruity and dry excellent IPA. Pleasant hoppy aroma with a zingy citrus flavour leading to a lingering crisp, dry finish.

Adnams IFBB

Adnams plc, Sole Bay Brewery, East Green, Southwold, Suffolk, IP18 6JW
Tel (01502) 727200
Fax (01502) 727201
Email info@adnams.co.uk
Website www.adnams.co.uk
Shop 10am-6pm daily

⊗ The earliest recorded brewing on the site of Adnams was in 1345. The present brewery was taken over by George and Ernest Adnams in 1872. The Adnams family was joined by the Loftus family in 1902, and a member of each family is still an active director of the company. New fermenting vessels were installed in 2001, 2003 and 2005 to cope with demand. Real ale is available in all 82 of its pubs. Seasonal beers: Regatta (ABV 4.3%, summer), Fisherman (ABV 4.3%, winter), Old (ABV 4.1%, winter), Oyster Stout (ABV 4.3%, winter), Tally Ho (ABV 7%, Christmas).

Bitter **(OG 1037, ABV 3.7%)**
Hops dominate the big nose of this tawny-coloured bitter. Citrus hop flavours give way to a long, lingering aftertaste.

Explorer **(OG 1042, ABV 4.3%)**
Brewed with American hops, hence the name. Citrus fruit in the mouth, with a long, sweet aftertaste.

Broadside (OG 1049, ABV 4.7%)
Grainy and dark brown; a complex, fruity beer. Rich fruity hop flavours and a long, fruity aftertaste.

Alcazar SIBA

Sherwood Forest Brewing Company Ltd, Alcazar Brewery, 33 Church Street, Old Basford, Nottingham, NG6 0GA
Tel (0115) 978 2282
Fax (0115) 978 9666
Email alcazarbrewery@tiscali.co.uk
Website www.alcazarbrewery.co.uk
Shop Tue-Wed 12-5pm; Thu-Sat 12-6pm
Tours by arrangement

Alcazar was established in 1999 and is located behind its brewery tap, the Fox & Crown. Alcazar means palace in Spanish, which relates to the crown in the pub name. The brewery is full mash with a 10-barrel brew length. Production is mainly for the Fox & Crown, with smaller quantities sold on demand to local free houses and beer festivals. The brewery shop opened in October 2005, selling a large range of bottle-conditioned beers, continental ales and other bottled English ales. Seasonal beers: Maple Magic (ABV 5.5%, winter), Mocha Stout (ABV 5%, winter), Black Fox (ABV 3.9%, spring), Desert Fox (ABV 4.3%, summer). Bottle-conditioned beer: Bombay Castle IPA (ABV 6.5%).

Alcazar Ale (OG 1040, ABV 4%)
A session ale made with a blend of English and North American hops; pale, full-flavoured with a fruity aroma and finish.

Nottingham Nog (OG 1042, ABV 4.2%)
An amber session ale.

New Dawn (OG 1045, ABV 4.5%)
Golden ale made with North American hops that give a unique fruity aroma and crisp, malty taste.

Foxtail Ale (OG 1050, ABV 4.9%)

Vixen's Vice (OG 1052, ABV 5.2%)
A pale, strong ale with a malt flavour balanced by a clean, crisp, hop taste.

Windjammer IPA (OG 1060, ABV 6%)
Traditional IPA brewed with five varieties of North American hops. Strong and hoppy.

Alehouse

(formerly Verulam)

Alehouse Pub & Brewing Company Ltd, Verulam Brewery, Farmers Boy, 134 London Road, St Albans, Hertfordshire, AL1 1PQ
Tel 07725 138243
Email contact@alehousebrewery.co.uk
Website www.alehousebrewery.co.uk
Tours by arrangement

Alehouse is owned by Kevin Yelland, co-licensee of the Lower Red Lion in St Albans. Alehouse took over the Verulam Brewery in February 2006. It continues to brew house beers for the Farmers Boy next door, to the original Verulam recipes, while producing beers under the Alehouse banner for the Lower Red Lion and other select local free houses. In total nine outlets are supplied.

Technician's Pale (OG 1040, ABV 4%)

Another Day, Another Dollar (OG 1042, ABV 4.3%)

Robust Porter (OG 1044, ABV 4.3%)

For Farmers Boy, St Albans

Best (OG 1037, ABV 3.8%)

Farmers Joy (OG 1043, ABV 4.5%)

Ales of Scilly SIBA

Ales of Scilly Brewery, Higher Trenoweth, St Mary's, Isles of Scilly, TR21 0NS
Tel/Fax (01720) 422419
Email mark@alesofscilly.co.uk
Tours by arrangement

Opened in 2001 as a two-barrel plant and expanded in 2004 to five barrels, Ales of Scilly is the most south-westerly brewery in Britain. Nine local pubs are supplied, with regular exports to mainland pubs and beer festivals. Seasonal ale: Old Bustard (ABV 4.2%). Bottle-conditioned beer: Scuppered (ABV 4.6%).

Natural Beauty (ABV 4.2%)

Scuppered (ABV 4.6%)

Allendale*

Allendale Brew Co Ltd, Allen Mill, Allendale, Hexham, Northumberland, NE47 9EQ
Tel/Fax (01434) 618686
Email info@allendalebrewco.co.uk
Website www.allendalebrewco.co.uk
Shop Mon-Sat 9am-5pm
Tours by arrangement

Allendale completed its first brew of Curlew's Return on Valentine's Day 2006. It is run by father and son team of Jim and Tom Hick. Their locally themed ales are on sale in nearby free houses and also in Newcastle and Carlisle. Seasonal beers: Black Grouse Bitter (ABV 4%, Aug-Jan), Curlew's Return (ABV 4.2%, Feb-July).

Best Bitter (OG 1037, ABV 3.8%)

Wolf (OG 1060, ABV 5.5%)

All Gates*

All Gates Brewery Limited, The Old Brewery, Brewery Yard, off Wallgate, Wigan, WN1 1JU
Tel (01942) 239444
Fax (01942) 824583
Email information@allgatesbrewery.com
Website www.allgatesbrewery.com
Tours by arrangement

All Gates was due to start brewing in summer 2006 in a Grade II listed building to the rear of the Last Orders pub in Wigan. It is the first town-centre brewery in Wigan since Moorfields closed in 1971. The building is an old tower brewery that has been lovingly restored but with a new five-barrel plant commissioned from Johnson Brewing & Engineering.

All Nations

See Worfield

Anglo Dutch SIBA

Anglo Dutch Brewery, Unit 12 Savile Bridge Mill, Savile Road, Dewsbury, West Yorkshire, WF12 9AF
Tel (01924) 457772
Fax (01924) 507444
Email mike@angdutchbrew.co.uk
Website www.anglo-dutch-brewery.co.uk
Tours by arrangement

Paul Klos (Dutch) set up the brewery with Mike Field (Anglo), who also runs the Refreshment Rooms at Dewsbury Station. The equipment came from the Rat & Ratchet in Huddersfield. Most beers contain wheat except for Spike and Tabatha, which contain lager malt. Seasonal beers: Devil's Knell (ABV 4.8%, January), Wild Flower (ABV 4.2%, September).

Best Bitter **(ABV 3.8%)**

Kletswater **(OG 1039, ABV 4%)**
Pale-coloured beer with a hoppy nose and a good hop and citrus fruit flavour.

Mild Rabarber **(ABV 4%)** ◆
Light-coloured brown mild with a malty, fruity flavour and moderate hop character. Refreshing and light bodied.

Spike's on 't' Way **(OG 1040.5, ABV 4.2%)** ◆
Pale bitter with citrus/orange flavour and dry, fruity finish.

Spikus **(OG 1040.5, ABV 4.2%)**
Made with organic lager malt and New Zealand hops.

Ghost on the Rim **(OG 1043, ABV 4.5%)** ◆
Pale, dry and fruity.

At 't' Ghoul and Ghost **(OG 1048, ABV 5.2%)** ◆
Pale golden bitter with a strong citrus and hoppy aroma and flavour. The finish is long, dry, bitter and citrus.

Tabatha the Knackered **(OG 1054, ABV 6%)** ◆
Golden Belgian-style Tripel with a strong fruity, hoppy and bitter character. Powerful and warming, slightly thinnish, with a bitter, dry finish.

Anker

See page 837

An Teallach

An Teallach Ale Co, Camusnagaul, Dundonnell, Garve, Ross-shire, IV23 2QT
Tel/Fax (01854) 633306
Email ataleco1@yahoo.co.uk
Tours by arrangement

An Teallach was formed in 2001 by husband and wife team, David and Wilma Orr, on Wilma's family croft on the shores of Little Loch Broom, Wester Ross. The business has grown steadily each year. Sixty pubs are supplied.

Beinn Dearg Ale **(OG 1038, ABV 3.8%)** ◆
Sweetish, fruity beer but can vary while the brewery is still experimenting. Some malt and hop character.

Ale **(OG 1042, ABV 4.2%)** ◆
Somewhat variable as the brewery is still in the experimental stage. Generally a sweetish pint in the Scottish 80/- tradition.

Crofters Pale Ale **(OG 1042, ABV 4.2%)**

Brew House Special **(OG 1044, ABV 4.4%)**

Kildonnon **(OG 1044, ABV 4.4%)**

Appleford *

Office: Appleford Brewery Company Ltd, Ironbridge House, St Peter's Court, Appleford-on-Thames, Oxfordshire, OX14 4YA
Brewery: Unit 14, Highlands Farm, High Road, Brightwell-cum-Sotwell, Wallingford, Oxfordshire, OX10 0QX
Tel/Fax (01235) 848055
Email sales@applefordbrewery.co.uk
Website www.applefordbrewery.co.uk

Appleford opened in June 2006 in converted farm units at Brightwell-cum-Sotwell on an eight-barrel plant.

River Crossing **(ABV 3.8%)**

Power Station **(ABV 4.2%)**

Archers

Archers Brewery, Penzance Drive, Swindon, Wiltshire, SN5 7JL
Tel (01793) 879929
Fax (01793) 879489
Email sales@archersbrewery.co.uk
Website www.archersbrewery.co.uk

⊗ Archers reached its 26th anniversary in 2005 and has continued to consolidate its position as one of the leading regional breweries in the south, with good growth through the free trade from its sales and distribution depots at Swindon, Warrington and Cambridge; regional brewers, micros and pub companies are also supplied. More than 2,000 free trade outlets are supplied direct; no wholesalers are used. Archers won two bronze medals in the 2005 International Brewing Awards.

Dark Mild **(OG 1036, ABV 3.4%)**
A dark beer with a well-balanced hop character, malty roast flavour and rich aftertaste.

Village **(OG 1036, ABV 3.6%)** ☐ ◆
A dry, well-balanced beer with a full body for its gravity. Malty and fruity in the nose, then a fresh, hoppy flavour with balancing malt and a hoppy, fruity finish.

Best Bitter **(OG 1040, ABV 4%)** ◆
Slightly sweeter and rounder than Village Bitter, with a malty, fruity aroma and pronounced bitter finish.

IPA **(OG 1042, ABV 4.2%)**
Pale golden, rich in citrus and grapefruit aroma and flavour with a crisp, bitter finish.

Special Bitter **(OG 1044, ABV 4.3%)**
Tawny in colour, full-flavoured and well-balanced.

Golden (OG 1046, ABV 4.7%) ◆
A full-bodied, hoppy, straw-coloured brew with an underlying fruity sweetness. A gentle aroma, but a strong, distinctive bitter finish.

Crystal Clear (OG 1050, ABV 5%)
Blonde in colour and packed with hop aroma and a subtle balanced finish. Originally introduced as a seasonal ale, it is now brewed permanently.

Swindon Strong Bitter/SSB (OG 1052, ABV 5%)
A copper-coloured ale, rich and full-flavoured. Brewed with Fuggles and East Kent Goldings hops.

Arkell's IFBB SIBA

Arkell's Brewery Ltd, Kingsdown Brewery, Upper Stratton, Swindon, Wiltshire, SN2 7RU
Tel (01793) 823026
Fax (01793) 828864
Email arkells@arkells.com
Website www.arkells.co.uk
Tours by arrangement

⊗ Arkells Brewery was established in 1863 and is still run by the family. The brewery continues to expand its estate and now owns 103 pubs in Berkshire, Gloucestershire, Oxfordshire and Wiltshire. Seasonal beers: Summer Ale (ABV 4.2%), JRA (ABV 3.6%), Noel Ale (ABV 5.5%). Bees Organic Beer (ABV 4.5%) is suitable for vegetarians and vegans.

2B (OG 1032, ABV 3.2%) ◆
Light brown in colour, malty but with a smack of hops and an astringent aftertaste. It has good body for its strength.

3B (OG 1040, ABV 4%) ◆
A medium brown beer with a strong, sweetish malt/caramel flavour. The hops come through strongly in the aftertaste, which is lingering and dry.

Moonlight (ABV 4.5%)

Kingsdown Ale (OG 1051, ABV 5%) ◆
A rich, deep russet-coloured beer, a stronger version of 3B. The malty/fruity aroma continues in the taste, which has a hint of pears. The hops come through in the aftertaste where they are complemented by caramel tones.

Arran SIBA

Arran Brewery Co Ltd, Cladach, Brodick, Isle of Arran, Strathclyde, KA27 8DE
Tel (01770) 302353
Fax (01770) 302653
Email info@arranbrewery.com
Website www.arranbrewery.com
Shop Mon-Sat 10am-5pm; Sun 12.30-5pm in summer, reduced hours in winter
Tours by arrangement

◎ The brewery opened in 2000 with a 20-barrel plant. Production has increased to 200 barrels a week with additional bottling capability. 50 outlets are supplied. Seasonal beers: Sunset (ABV 4.4%, Feb/March), Fireside (ABV 4.7%, Oct/Nov-Feb/Mar).

Ale (OG 1038, ABV 3.8%) ◆
An amber ale where the predominance of the hop produces a bitter beer with a subtle balancing sweetness of malt and an occasional hint of roast.

Dark (OG 1042, ABV 4.3%) ◆
A well-balanced malty beer with plenty of roast and hop in the taste and a dry, bitter finish.

Blonde (OG 1048, ABV 5%) ◫ ◆
A hoppy beer with substantial fruit balance. The taste is balanced and the finish increasingly bitter. An aromatic strong bitter that drinks below its weight.

Arrow*

♁ Arrow Brewery, c/o Wine Vaults, 37 High Street, Kington, Herefordshire, HR5 3BJ
Tel (01544) 230685
Email deanewright@yahoo.co.uk

Former Bridge Street brewer Deane Wright has built his five-barrel brewery at the rear of the Wine Vaults and re-started brewing for Christmas 2005. Occasional beer: Quiver (ABV 5%).

Arrow Bitter (OG 1042, ABV 4%)

Arundel SIBA

Arundel Brewery Ltd, Unit C7 Ford Airfield Industrial Estate, Ford, Arundel, West Sussex, BN18 0HY
Tel (01903) 733111
Fax (01903) 733381
Email arundelbrewery@dsl.pipex.com
Off-sales available Mon-Fri 9am-5pm at brewery
Tours by arrangement

⊗ Founded in 1992, Arundel Brewery is the historic town's first brewery in more than 60 years, marking the rebirth of a tradition dating back more than 200 years. Under new ownership since 2004, the brewery continues to improve its range of core brands and seasonal beers. In addition, Arundel also brew a range of occasional brands that are available in selected months; the first of a range of bottled beers was introduced in 2005. Seasonal beers: Footslogger (ABV 4.4%, spring), Summer Daze (ABV 4.7%, summer), Black Beastie (ABV 4.9%, autumn).

Gauntlet (OG 1035, ABV 3.5%) ◆
A copper-coloured Sussex bitter. Hops and fruit dominate the aroma. A sweet, tangy fruit-gum taste fades to leave clean, dry bitterness in the mouth, hops coming to the fore and ending with lemon notes.

Sussex Mild (OG 1037, ABV 3.7%) ◆
A dark mild. Strong chocolate and roast aromas, which lead to a bitter taste. The aftertaste is not powerful but the initial flavours remain in the dry and clean finish.

Castle (OG 1038, ABV 3.8%) ◆
A pale tawny beer with fruit and malt noticeable in the aroma. The flavour has a good balance of malt, fruit and hops, with a dry, hoppy finish.

Sussex Gold (OG 1042, ABV 4.2%) ◆
A golden-coloured best bitter with a strong floral hop aroma. The ale is clean-tasting and surprisingly bitter for its strength, with a tangy citrus flavour. The initial hop and fruitiness die quickly to a long, dry, bitter finish.

ASB (OG 1045, ABV 4.5%)
A special bitter with a complex roast malt flavour leading to a fruity, hoppy, bitter-sweet finish.

Stronghold (OG 1047, ABV 4.7%)
A smooth, full-flavoured premium bitter. A good balance of malt, fruit and hops comes through in this rich, chestnut-coloured beer.

Old Knucker (OG 1055, ABV 5.5%) ◆
A black coloured ale with a powerful bitter-sweet taste and a roasted burnt flavour coming at the end. Surprisingly clean aftertaste for a beer that has an oily mouthfeel. Long, tangy, sweet aftertaste.

Aston Manor

Aston Manor Brewery Co Ltd, 173 Thimble Mill Lane, Aston, Birmingham, West Midlands, B7 5HS
Tel (0121) 328 4336
Fax (0121) 328 0139
Email sales@astonmanor.co.uk
Website www.astonmanor.co.uk

Aston Manor owns the Highgate Brewery in Walsall (qv). Its own plant concentrates on cider. Beer is bottled at Highgate but is not bottle conditioned.

Atlantic

Atlantic Brewery, Treisaac Farm, Treisaac, Newquay, Cornwall, TR8 4DX
Tel (01637) 880657 / 880326
Email stuart@atlanticbrewery.com
Website www.atlanticbrewery.com

Atlantic started brewing in 2005. All beers are organic, Soil Association certified and suitable for vegetarians and vegans. They are now growing their own organic First Gold and Fuggles hops. Only bottle-conditioned beers are produced: Gold (ABV 4.6%, summer), Blue Dark Ale (ABV 4.8%), Red Celtic Ale (ABV 5%).

Atlas SIBA

Highlands and Islands Breweries Limited, Lab Road, Kinlochleven, Argyll, PH50 4SG
Tel (01855) 831111
Fax (01855) 831122
Email info@atlasbrewery.com
Website www.atlasbrewery.com/www.hibreweries.com
Shop open office hours
Tours by arrangement

⊗ Founded in 2002, Atlas is a 20-barrel brewery in a 100 year-old listed Victorian industrial building on the banks of the River Leven. It merged in 2004 with Orkney (qv) to form Highlands and Islands Breweries purely to improve distribution. Production will remain on both sites in order to preserve the beers' distinct and unique identities. Atlas uses Scottish malts and local Highland water with whole hops from five different countries. Around 150 outlets in Scotland are supplied direct and via wholesalers to the rest of Britain. Additional fermentation vessels were added in 2006 to increase weekly production capacity. Seasonal beers: Equinox (ABV 4.5%, spring), Wayfarer (ABV 4.4%, summer), Tempest (ABV 4.9%, autumn), Blizzard (ABV 4.7%, winter).

Latitude (OG 1036, ABV 3.6%) ◆
This golden ale has a light citrus taste with a hint of hops in the light, bitter finish.

Three Sisters (OG 1043, ABV 4.2%) ◆
A lightly malted beer with a short, hoppy, bitter finish.

Nimbus (OG 1050, ABV 5%) ◆
A well-balanced yellow/golden beer. Dry and fruity at the front, becoming slightly astringent with lasting fruit and a pleasant dry finish.

Atomic Brewery/ Alexandra Arms*

Atomic Brewery, c/o Alexandra Arms, 72-73 James Street, Rugby, Warwickshire, CV21 2SL
Tel Brewery: (01788) 542170; pub: (01788) 578660
Email sale@atomicbrewery.com
Websites www.atomicbrewery.com; www.alexandraarms.co.uk

CAMRA member Nick Pugh and his friend Keith Abbis planned their brewery for a year before launching their first beers in 2006. Atomic is housed in one of the outbuildings of the pub and supplies it with its ale. The landlord of the pub, Julian Hardy, uses the same kit to brew his own beers under the Alexandra Arms name.

Fusion (OG 1041, ABV 3.9%)

Reactor (OG 1047, ABV 4.5%)

Bomb (OG 1052, ABV 5%)

AVS

See Daleside

B&T SIBA EAB

B&T Brewery Ltd, The Brewery, Shefford, Bedfordshire, SG17 5DZ
Tel (01462) 815080
Fax (01462) 850841
Email brewery@banksandtaylor.com
Website www.banksandtaylor.com
Tours by arrangement

⊗ Banks & Taylor, founded in 1981, was restructured in 1994 under the name B&T Brewery. It produces an extensive range of beers, including monthly special brews together with occasional beers: see website for details. Three pubs are owned. Bottle-conditioned beers: Shefford Bitter, Goalden Hatter, Black Dragon Mild, Edwin Taylor's Extra Stout, Dragonslayer, SOS, SOD, Autumn Porter, Fruit Bat, Hoppy Turkey.

Two Brewers (OG 1036, ABV 3.6%)
Hoppy, amber-brown session beer.

Shefford Bitter (OG 1038, ABV 3.8%)
A pleasant, predominantly hoppy session beer with a bitter finish.

Shefford Dark Mild (OG 1038, ABV 3.8%) ◆
A dark beer with a well-balanced taste. Sweetish, roast malt aftertaste.

Goalden Hatter (OG 1040, ABV 4%)

Black Dragon Mild (OG 1043, ABV 4.3%)
Dark, rich in flavour, with a strong roast barley finish.

Dragonslayer (OG 1045, ABV 4.5%) ◆
A straw-coloured beer, dry, malty and lightly hopped.

Edwin Taylor's Extra Stout (OG 1045, ABV 4.5%) ◆
A pleasant, bitter beer with a strong roast malt flavour.

Fruit Bat (OG 1045, ABV 4.5%)
Raspberry flavoured, hoppy fruit beer.

Shefford Pale Ale/SPA (OG 1045, ABV 4.5%) ◆
A well-balanced beer with hop, fruit and malt flavours. Dry, bitter aftertaste.

SOS (OG 1050, ABV 5%) ◆
A rich mixture of fruit, hops and malt is present in the taste and aftertaste of this beer. Predominantly hoppy aroma.

SOD (OG 1050, ABV 5%)
SOS with caramel added for colour, often sold under house names.

Badger IFBB

Hall & Woodhouse Ltd, Blandford St Mary, Blandford Forum, Dorset, DT11 9LS
Tel (01258) 452141
Fax (01258) 452122
Email info@hall-woodhouse.co.uk
Website www.hall-woodhouse.co.uk
Shop Mon-Sat 9am-6pm; Sun 11am-3pm
Tours by arrangement (Call 01258 452141 to book)

⊗ Founded in 1777 as the Ansty Brewery by Charles Hall. Charles's son took George Woodhouse into partnership and formed Hall & Woodhouse in 1847. They moved from Ansty to their present site at Blandford St Mary in 1899. A new modern brewery is intended to replace the current brewery on part of the same site in late 2007 or early 2008. Trading under the Badger name, it owns 260 pubs in the south of England and supplies 700 free trade outlets. Hall & Woodhouse launched a visitor centre in 2002 and it is now a major attraction in Dorset. In 2000 Hall & Woodhouse bought King & Barnes of Horsham. The former K&B's 57 pubs now sell Badger beers, including Sussex Bitter, matching the K&B recipe. Seasonal beers: Festive Feasant (ABV 4.5%, Nov-Feb), Fursty Ferret (ABV 4.4%, March-Oct).

K&B Sussex Bitter (OG 1033, ABV 3.5%) ◆
A thin, malty session beer, with little of its traditional hop bitterness. Mid-brown in colour with a moderate bitterness that lasts into a bitter, somewhat sharp finish. A beer that bears little resemblance to that brewed by the former King & Barnes Brewery.

First Gold (OG 1039, ABV 4%)
A new beer that replaced Best Bitter in 2005. Well-balanced bitterness plus hints of orange and spice.

Tanglefoot (OG 1047, ABV 4.9%)
The beer was reformulated in 2004. The ABV has been dropped from 5.1% to 4.9%, crystal malt is now used and the beer is dry hopped in cask with Goldings hops.

For InBev

Flowers IPA (OG 1035, ABV 3.6%)

Flowers Original Bitter (OG 1043, ABV 4.3%)

Ballard's SIBA

Ballard's Brewery Ltd, The Old Sawmill, Nyewood, Petersfield, Hants, GU31 5HA
Tel (01730) 821301/821362
Fax (01730) 821742
Email info@ballardsbrewery.org.uk
Website www.ballardsbrewery.org.uk
Shop Mon-Fri 8am-4pm
Tours by arrangement

⊗ Launched in 1980 by Carola Brown, one of the founders of SIBA, at Cumbers Farm, Trotton, Ballard's has been trading at Nyewood (in West Sussex, despite the postal address) since 1988 and now supplies around 60 free trade outlets. Seasonal beers: Trotton Bitter (ABV 3.6%, spring), Wheatsheaf (ABV 5%, summer), On the Hop (ABV 4.5%, autumn), Old Bounder Series (ABV over 9%, winter). Bottle-conditioned beers: Old Bounder series, Best Bitter, Nyewood Gold, Wassail and Kings Table (ABV 4.2%).

Midhurst Mild (OG 1034, ABV 3.5%)
Traditional dark mild, well-balanced, refreshing, with a biscuity flavour.

Golden Bine (OG 1038, ABV 3.8%) ◆
Amber, clean-tasting bitter. A roast malt aroma leads to a fruity, slightly sweet taste and a dry finish.

Best Bitter (OG 1042, ABV 4.2%) ◆
A copper-coloured beer with a malty aroma. A good balance of fruit and malt in the flavour gives way to a dry, hoppy aftertaste.

Wild (ABV 4.7%)
A blend of Mild and Wassail.

Nyewood Gold (OG 1050, ABV 5%) ◆
Robust golden brown strong bitter, very hoppy and fruity throughout, with a tasty balanced finish.

Wassail (OG 1060, ABV 6%) ◆
A strong, full-bodied, fruity beer with a predominance of malt throughout, but also an underlying hoppiness. Tawny/red in colour.

Bank Top SIBA

Bank Top Brewery Ltd, The Pavilion, Ashworth Lane, Bolton, Lancashire, BL1 8RA
Tel/Fax (01204) 595800
Email john@banktopbrewery.com
Website www.banktopbrewery.com
Tours by arrangement

◎ Bank Top was established in 1995 by John Feeney and has enjoyed gradual expansion. It relocated in 2002 and in 2004 John formed a partnership with David Sweeney. The beers are supplied to around 100 outlets locally and throughout the north-west and Yorkshire. Seasonal beer: Santa's Claws (ABV 5%, Christmas).

Bikes, Trikes and Beer (OG 1036, ABV 3.6%)

Brydge Bitter (OG 1038, ABV 3.8%)

Game, Set and Match (OG 1038, ABV 3.8%)

Bad to the Bone (OG 1040, ABV 4%)

Dark Mild (OG 1040, ABV 4%) ◆
Dark brown beer with a malt and roast

aroma, rich mouthfeel and a complex taste, including roast malt and toffee. Roast, hops and bitterness in the finish.

Flat Cap (OG 1040, ABV 4%) ◆
Amber ale with a modest fruit aroma leading to a beer with citrus fruit, malt and hops. Good finish of fruit, malt and bitterness.

Gold Digger (OG 1040, ABV 4%) ◆
Golden coloured, with a citrus aroma, grapefruit and a touch of spiciness on the palate and a fresh, hoppy citrus finish.

Old Slapper (OG 1042, ABV 4.2%)

Samuel Crompton's Ale (OG 1042, ABV 4.2%) ◆
Amber beer with a fresh citrus-peel aroma. Well-balanced with hops and a zesty grapefruit flavour, and a hoppy, citrus finish.

Volunteer Bitter (OG 1042, ABV 4.2%)
Brewed with American hops.

Pavilion Pale Ale (OG 1045, ABV 4.5%)

Port O Call (OG 1050, ABV 5%)

Smokestack Lightnin' (OG 1050, ABV 5%)

For Barristers Bar, Bolton

Judges Chambers (OG 1043, ABV 4.3%)

For Strawbury Duck, Entwistle

Strawberry Duck (OG 1042, ABV 4.2%)

Banks's

See Wolverhampton & Dudley Breweries in New Nationals section

Barearts*

Barearts Brewery, c/o 110 Rochdale Road, Todmorden, West Yorkshire, OL14 7LP (gallery); brewery at 290-292 Rochdale Road, Todmorden, OL14 7PD
Tel (01706) 839305
Email trev@barearts.com
Website www.barearts.com
Shop Fri 3-7pm; Sat-Sun 2-5pm
Tours by arrangement

This four-barrel craft brewery is owned by Kathy and Trevor Cook and is named after their gallery, which is dedicated to nude art work. Its first brew was in November 2005. The gallery has an off-licence, which sells Barearts beers as well as those of other small, local breweries. The Cooks hope to expand into mail order and sales via their website.

Light Blonde (ABV 3.6%)

Cascade (ABV 4.8%)

Strong Bitter (ABV 5.9%)

First Brew (ABV 6%)

Old English Pale Ale (ABV 6.7%)

Keep your Good Beer Guide up to date by visiting www.camra.org.uk, click on *Good Beer Guide* then *Updates to the GBG 2007* where you will find information about changes to breweries.

Barefoot*

Barefoot Brewery, Unit 7, Whitehouse Farm Centre, Stannington, Morpeth, Northumberland, NE61 6AW
Tel (01670) 789988
Email barefootbeer@onetel.com

Formerly a partner in the now discontinued Font Valley Brewery, Michael Hegarty has used this experience as a platform to re-establish at the Whitehouse Farm Centre, which is near the thriving market town of Morpeth. Michael, with a background in biochemistry specialising in fermentation, has taken on David Wilson, a former business bank manager, as his new business partner. The 10-barrel brewery was set up in December 2005, with the first beers appearing January 2006.

First Foot (OG 1042, ABV 4.2%)
Fragrant citrus notes.

Milk of Amnesia (OG 1044, ABV 4.5%)
Ruby-red robust ale with a strong roasted toffee edge and pronounced hoppy finish.

Sole Beer (OG 1044, ABV 4.5%)
Equilibrium between Maris Otter malt and Syrian Goldings hops with a crisp wheat finish.

SB (OG 1048, ABV 5%)
Heady strong pale ale, with juicy malt and copious amounts of coriander; late hopped with Cascade. Bronze award winner at Newcastle Beer Festival 2005.

Barge & Barrel

See Eastwood

Barngates SIBA

Barngates Brewery Ltd, Barngates, Ambleside, Cumbria, LA22 0NG
Tel/Fax (015394) 36575
Email info@barngatesbrewery.co.uk
Website www.barngatesbrewery.co.uk
Tours by arrangement

⊛ Barngates Brewery started brewing in 1997 and initially provided only the Drunken Duck Inn with its own beers. It now supplies more than 200 outlets throughout Cumbria, Lancashire, Northumberland and Yorkshire. Seasonal beer: Chester's Strong & Ugly (ABV 5.2%)

Cat Nap (OG 1037, ABV 3.6%)
Pale, straw-coloured beer with a strong citrus hop aroma. Well-balanced bitterness leads to a long, dry finish. A fruity, zesty character throughout.

Cracker Ale (OG 1038, ABV 3.9%)
Copper-coloured with a subtle hoppy aroma, clean, smooth and refreshing, developing into a long bitter finish. A well-rounded ale.

Pride of Westmorland (OG 1042, ABV 4.1%)
Ruby red with a berry fruit aroma and

delicious malt and hop flavours. A polished, soft, bitter finish.

Westmorland Gold (OG 1043, ABV 4.2%)
Golden ale with a distinct fruity and hoppy nose. Crisp with a lingering, bitter-sweet palate.

Tag Lag (OG 1044, ABV 4.4%) ♦
Light, golden bitter, citrus hints in the flavour with a slight dry finish.

Red Bull Terrier (OG 1048, ABV 4.8%)

Barrowden SIBA

(formerly Blencowe)

Barrowden Brewing Company, c/o Exeter Arms, Barrowden, Rutland, LE15 8EQ
Tel (01572) 747247
Email info@exeterarms.com
Website www.exeterarms.com
Tours by arrangement

⊗ Set up in a barn behind the pub in 1998 by Peter Blencowe, the two-barrel plant was extended in 2001 with the addition of another fermenting vessel. The brewery and pub were sold in 2005 along with the beer recipes to the new owners who are committed to maintaining beer supply for the pub.

Beach Boys (OG 1040, ABV 3.8%)

Fun Boy Four (OG 1044, ABV 4.4%)

Bevin Boys (OG 1045, ABV 4.5%)

Danny Boys (OG 1046, ABV 4.5%)

Bartrams SIBA EAB

Postal Address: 23 Meadow Close, Felsham, Bury St Edmunds, Suffolk, IP30 9LZ
Brewery: Bartrams Brewery, Rougham Estate, Ipswich Road (A14), Rougham, Bury St Edmunds, Suffolk
Tel (01449) 737655 / 07790 596539
Email marc@captainbill007.plus.com
Website www.bartramsbrewery.co.uk
Shop Tue/Sat 12-6pm
Tours by arrangement

⊗ Marc Bartram moved his brewery to a new location on the same estate in 2004. It is signposted from the A14. There is a brewery shop stocking beers from EAB and brewers who trade with Bartrams, as well as a range of international specialist beers. Marc is seeking Soil Association accreditation for his organic beers. There was a Bartram's Brewery between 1894 and 1902 run by Captain Bill Bartram and a recreation of his image graces the pump clips. Beers are available in a selection of local pubs and there is a large amount of trade through local farmers' markets. Marld, Beltane Braces and all porters and stouts are suitable for vegetarians and vegans. Seasonal beers: September Ale (ABV 7%), Xmas Holly Daze (ABV 5%, Christmas), New Years Daze (ABV 5.2%), The Venerable Reed (ABV 5.6% – brewed for an annual medieval re-enactment on Rougham Airfield), Mother in Laws Tongue Tied (ABV 9%), Zodiac Beers range (ABV 4.2%).

Marld (ABV 3.4%)
A traditional mild. Spicy hops and malt with a hint of chocolate, slightly smoky with a light, roasted finish.

Rougham Ready (ABV 3.6%)
A light, crisp bitter, surprisingly full bodied for its strength.

Trial and Error (ABV 3.6%)
A full malty bitter, fruity with a lot of character.

Premier (ABV 3.7%)
A traditional quaffing ale, full-flavoured but light, dry and hoppy.

Little Green Man (ABV 3.8%)
A golden bitter with the peppery and delicate citrus tones of subtle coriander. Dry and bitter.

Red Queen (ABV 3.9%)
Typical IPA style, chocolate malt in the foreground while the resiny hop flavour lingers.

Grozet (ABV 4%)
Using Little Green Man as the base beer, gooseberries are added to give an appealing extra dimension.

The Cats Whiskers (ABV 4%)
A straw-coloured beer with ginger and lemons added; a unique flavour experience.

The Bees Knees (ABV 4.2%)
An amber beer with a floral aroma; honey softness on the palate leads to a crisp, bitter finish.

Catherine Bartram's IPA (ABV 4.3%)
A full-bodied malty IPA style; tangy hops lead the malt throughout and dominate the dry, hoppy aftertaste.

Jester Quick One (ABV 4.4%)
A sweet reddish bitter using the fruity American Ahtanum hops.

Beltane Braces (ABV 4.5%)
Smooth and dark.

Coal Porter (ABV 4.5%)
Plenty of body in this ruby beer, supported by ample hops.

Stingo (ABV 4.5%)
A sweetish, fruity bitter with a hoppy nose. Light honey softens the bitter finish.

Beer Elsie Bub (ABV 4.8%)
Originally brewed for a Pagan wedding, this strong honey ale is now brewed all year round.

Captain Bill Bartram's Best Bitter (ABV 4.8%)
Modified from a 100-year old recipe, using full malt and traditional Kentish hops.

Captain's Stout (ABV 4.8%)
Biscuity dark malt leads to a lightly smoked aroma, plenty of roasted malt character, coffee notes and a whiff of smoke.

Cherry Stout (ABV 4.8%)
Sensuous hints of chocolate leads to a subtle suggestion of cherries.

Damson Stout (ABV 4.8%)
A robust, full-bodied stout with the chocolate and smoky aroma giving way to a lingering finish.

Trafalgar Squared (ABV 4.8%)
Brewed using malt grown a few miles from Nelson's birthplace and Goldings hops.

Suffolk 'n' Strong (ABV 5%)
A light, smooth and dangerously potable

strong bitter, well-balanced malt and hops with an easy finish.

Comrade Bill Bartram's Egalitarian Anti-Imperialist Soviet Stout (ABV 6.9%)
A Russian stout by any other name, a luscious easy-drinking example of the style.

Barum SIBA

Barum Brewery Ltd, c/o Reform Inn, Pilton, Barnstaple, Devon, EX31 1PD
Tel (01271) 329994
Fax (01271) 378338
Email info@barumbrewery.co.uk
Website www.barumbrewery.co.uk
Tours by arrangement

⊗ Barum started brewing in 1996 at the Reform Inn. Distribution is primarily within Devon. Seasonal beers: Gold (ABV 4%, summer), Barnstablaster (ABV 6.6%, winter).

Basil's Best (OG 1040, ABV 4%)

Original (OG 1044, ABV 4.4%)

Breakfast (OG 1050, ABV 5%)

Firing Squad (ABV 5.3%)

Bateman IFBB SIBA

George Bateman & Son Ltd, Salem Bridge Brewery, Wainfleet, Lincolnshire, PE24 4JE
Tel (01754) 880317
Fax (01754) 880939
Email enquiries@bateman.co.uk
Website www.bateman.co.uk
Shop 11.30am-3.30pm daily
Tours by arrangement

⊗ Bateman's Brewery is an independent family-owned brewery, established in 1874 by the present chairman's grandfather. Bateman's is committed to brewing cask beer and a new brewhouse was opened in 2002. The beers were first brewed for the local farmers but they can now be found in pubs throughout Britain. Seasonal beers: Hop Bine Bitter (ABV 3.6%, January), Hooker (ABV 4.5%, February), Spring Goddess (ABV 4.2%, March-April), Miss Whiplash (ABV 4.2%, May), Summer Swallow (ABV 3.9%, July-Aug), Combined Harvest (ABV 4.4%, September), Victory Ale (ABV 5.9%, October), Miss Voluptuous (ABV 4.2%, November), Rosey Nosey (ABV 4.9%, December). Contract brews: Jesters IPA (ABV 3.5%), Bill Sutton's Bitter (ABV 3.7%).

Dark Mild (OG 1030, ABV 3%) ◘ ◆
Characteristic orchard fruit and roasted nut nose with hops evident. One of the classic mild ales, although the lasting bitter finish may not be entirely true to type; nevertheless, a ruby-black gem.

XB Bitter (OG 1037, ABV 3.7%) ◆
A mid-brown balanced session bitter with malt most obvious in the finish. The taste is dominated by the house style apple hop, which also leads the aroma.

Valiant (OG 1042, ABV 4.2%)
A delicious golden beer, clean, crisp and zesty.

Salem Porter (OG 1048, ABV 4.7%) ◘ ◆
Ruby black with a brown tint to the head. The aroma is liquorice with a subtle hint of dandelion and burdock; the initial taste is hoppy and bitter, with a mellowing of all the elements in the finish.

XXXB (OG 1048, ABV 4.8%) ◆
A brilliant blend of malt, hops and fruit on the nose with a bitter bite over the top of a faintly banana maltiness that stays the course. A russet-tan brown classic.

Bath Ales SIBA

Bath Ales Ltd, Units 3-7 Caxton Business Park, Tower Road North, Warmley, Bristol, BS30 8XN
Tel (0117) 947 4797
Fax (0117) 947 4790
Email hare@bathales.co.uk
Website www.bathales.com
Shop Mon-Fri 9am-5pm; Sat 9am-12pm
Tours by arrangement

⊗ Bath Ales started brewing in 1995, formed by two former Smiles brewers and a Hardington brewer. They began with rented equipment at the Henstridge Brewery near Wincanton, moved premises and upgraded to a full steam, 15-barrel plant in 1999. It now has a new, purpose-built site on the edge of east Bristol, with increased capacity of 50 barrels. Deliveries are direct to 260 outlets. Wholesalers are used in a limited way. Seven pubs are owned, all serving cask ale. Seasonal beers: Festivity (ABV 5%), Rare Hare (ABV 5.2%). Bottled beers: Gem Bitter (ABV 4.8%), Festivity (ABV 5%), Wild Hare (ABV 5%). Most beers are available for purchase from the website.

SPA (OG 1037, ABV 3.7%)
Gold/yellow in colour, this is a light-bodied, dry, bitter beer with a citrus hop aroma. Long, pale, malty, bitter finish with some fruit and a slight sweetness.

Gem Bitter (OG 1041, ABV 4.1%) ◆
Well-balanced and complex, this medium-bodied bitter is malty (pale and crystal with a tiny hint of chocolate), fruity and hoppy throughout. Amber-coloured, it is drier and more bitter at the end.

Barnstormer (OG 1047, ABV 4.5%) ◘ ◆
Malt (roast and chocolate), hop and fruit aroma, with a similar taste. Mid-brown, well-balanced and smooth, with a complex malty and bitter, dry finish.

Wild Hare (OG 1047, ABV 5%) ◆
Pale organic strong bitter. Toasted grapefruit aroma, hoppy/fruity taste developing into a long-lasting dry, fruity finish. Refreshing and clean on the palate.

Batham IFBB

Daniel Batham & Son Ltd, Delph Brewery, Delph Road, Brierley Hill, West Midlands, DY5 2TN
Tel (01384) 77229
Fax (01384) 482292
Email info@bathams.com
Website www.bathams.com

☺ A classic Black Country small brewery established in 1877. Tim and Matthew Batham represent the fifth generation to run the company. The Vine, one of the Black Country's most famous pubs, is also the site of the brewery. The company has 10 tied houses and supplies around 30 other outlets. Such is the demand for Batham's Bitter that the beer is delivered in 54-gallon hogsheads. Seasonal beer: XXX (ABV 6.3%, December).

Mild Ale (OG 1036.5, ABV 3.5%)
A fruity, dark brown mild with malty sweetness and a roast malt finish.

Best Bitter (OG 1043.5, ABV 4.3%)
A pale yellow, fruity, sweetish bitter, with a dry, hoppy finish. A good, light, refreshing beer.

Bathtub

Bathtub Brewery Co, Seven Stars Inn, Church Road, Stithians, Truro, Cornwall, TR3 7DH
Tel (01209) 860003

Bathtub is based in the back yard of the Seven Stars and started brewing in 2004. It produces only one cask per brew for the main bar on an intermittent basis from one of the two beers listed below; there is also a dark ale called Pete's Porter (ABV 5.2%), brewed for beer festivals only. The full range is supplied for the pub's two annual beer festivals in June and December. Longer term plans include upgrading the plant to two-barrel capacity.

Stithians Gold (OG 1040, ABV 3.8%)

Stithians Special (OG 1048, ABV 4.8%)

Battersea SIBA

Battersea Brewery Co Ltd, 43 Glycena Road, Battersea, London, SW11 5TP
Tel/Fax (020) 7978 7978
Email enquiries@batterseabrewery.com
Website www.batterseabrewery.com
Tours by arrangement

Battersea has been brewing close to the Thames by Battersea Power Station since 2001. The beers are all sold locally and in south-east England to the free trade and pub chains. The beers are made from hops and malt sourced as close as possible to the brewery and no additives are used. Bottle-conditioned beer: Power Station Porter.

Pagoda (OG 1038, ABV 3.7%)
Pale amber ale with a citrus fruit and sweet malt character.

Bitter (OG 1040, ABV 4%)
A refreshing, well-balanced, amber-coloured bitter with fruit throughout. The short, dryish finish has a trace of chocolate malt.

Power Station Porter (OG 1049, ABV 4.9%)
With caramelised fruit on the nose, this sweetish dark beer is surprisingly quaffable. Raisins, malt and a little roast are present on the palate and aftertaste.

Battledown *

Battledown Brewery, The Keynsham Works, Keynsham Street, Cheltenham, Gloucestershire, GL52 6EJ
Tel (07734) 834104
Email roland@battledownbrewery.com
Website www.battledownbrewery.com
Shop on site (please phone first)
Tours by arrangement

Established in 2005 by Roland and Stephanie Elliott-Beery, Battledown operates from an old engineering works and, following total renovation of the building, started production with an eight-barrel plant in September of that year, bringing brewing back to Cheltenham after an eight year gap caused by the closure of the Whitbread Flowers brewery. Battledown produces three beers and supplies 70 outlets.

Saxon (OG 1038, ABV 3.8%)
Fresh and crisp with a hoppy finish.

Turncoat (OG 1046, ABV 4.5%)
A deep red and smooth porter with a hint of bitterness.

Brigand (OG 1048, ABV 4.7%)
Rich in malt with a hint of spice from Challenger hops.

Bazens' SIBA

Bazens' Brewery, The Rees Bazen Brewing Co Ltd, Unit 6 Knoll Street Industrial Park, Knoll Street, Salford, Greater Manchester, M7 2BL
Tel (0161) 708 0247
Fax (0161) 708 0248
Email bazensbrewery@mac.com
Website www.bazensbrewery.co.uk
Tours by arrangement for CAMRA groups

Established in 2002, Bazens' moved to its present site in 2003, sharing plant and premises with Facer's Brewery (qv). Facer's has now relocated to Flintshire, North Wales. Output is expected to increase by 50% during 2006, with considerable investment in plant and casks.

Black Pig Mild (OG 1037, ABV 3.6%)
A dark brown beer with malt and fruit aromas. Roast, chocolate and fruit flavours, with an underlying bitterness, lead to a dry, malty aftertaste.

Pacific Bitter (OG 1039, ABV 3.8%)
Gold-coloured bitter with a fruity nose. Hops and citrus fruit dominate the taste and there is a bitter, hoppy finish.

Flatbac (OG 1042, ABV 4.2%)
Well-balanced, distinctive and refreshing blonde beer. A full hop character has pronounced citrus/floral notes.

Zebra Best Bitter (OG 1043, ABV 4.3%)
A complex premium bitter, loaded with full malt flavour and crisp fruity hop character.

Blue Bullet (OG 1045, ABV 4.5%)
Yellow in colour, this golden ale has a fruity

aroma. Hops, fruit and bitterness are found in the taste and linger in the finish.

Knoll Street Porter (OG 1055, ABV 5.2%)

eXSB (OG 1055, ABV 5.5%)
Full-bodied traditional strong bitter. Hints of orange peel and fruit overlie complex malt flavours.

Beartown SIBA

Beartown Brewery Ltd, Bromley House, Spindle Street, Congleton, Cheshire, CW12 1QN
Tel (01260) 299964
Fax (01260) 278895
Email headbrewer@beartownbrewery.co.uk
Website www.beartownbrewery.co.uk
Shop opening late 2006
Tours by arrangement (from late 2006)

Congleton's links with brewing can be traced back to 1272, when the town received charter status. Two of its most senior officers at the time were Ale Taster and Bear Warden, hence the name of the brewery. Both the brewery's Navigation in Stockport and the Beartown Tap have been named CAMRA regional pubs of the year. There are plans are to extend the tied estate to 15 outlets over the next two years. Beartown supplies 250 outlets and owns five pubs. A new 30-barrel plant is currently being installed. Seasonal beers: Santa's Claws (ABV 4.5%, December), Blarney Bear (ABV 4.8%, March), St Georges Bear (ABV 4.2%, April). Most of the beer range is now available in bottle-conditioned form.

Ambeardextrous (OG 1038, ABV 3.8%)
Dark mild.

Bear Ass (OG 1040, ABV 4%)
Dark ruby-red, malty bitter with good hop nose and fruity flavour with dry, bitter, astringent aftertaste.

Ginger Bear (ABV 4%)
The flavours from the malt and hops blend with the added bite from the root ginger to produce a quenching finish.

Kodiak Gold (OG 1040, ABV 4%)
Hops and fruit dominate the taste of this crisp yellow bitter and these follow through to the dryish aftertaste. Biscuity malt also comes through on the aroma and taste.

Bearskinful (OG 1043, ABV 4.2%)
Biscuity malt dominates the flavour of this amber best bitter. There are hops and a hint of sulphur on the aroma. A balance of malt and bitterness follow through to the aftertaste.

Bearly Literate (OG 1045, ABV 4.5%)

Pandamonium (OG 1048, ABV 4.8%)

Polar Eclipse (OG 1048, ABV 4.8%)
Almost black, thinnish stout with roast and coffee flavours to the fore. Lacks body for style and strength. Short fruity aftertaste.

Black Bear (OG 1050, ABV 5%)
Advertised as a strong mild, this beer is rather bitter for the style. Bitter and malt flavours are balanced and there is also a good roast character along with a hint of liquorice. Aftertaste is short and reasonably dry.

Bruins Ruin (OG 1050, ABV 5%)

Wheat Beer (OG 1050, ABV 5%)
A dry and bitter wheat beer. There is an initial fruitiness in aroma and taste with good wheat malt flavours. Long-lasting dry aftertaste.

Beckstones SIBA

Beckstones Brewery, Upper Beckstones Mill, The Green, Millom, Cumbria, LA18 5HL
Tel (01229) 775294
Email david@beckstonesbrewery.com

Beckstones started brewing in 2003 on the site of an 18th-century mill with its own water supply.

Leat (OG 1038, ABV 3.6%)
A floral, fruity, thirst quencher.

Black Dog Freddy (OG 1038, ABV 3.8%)

Iron Town (OG 1040, ABV 3.8%)
A well-balanced, malt and hops session ale.

Beer O'Clock (OG 1040, ABV 3.9%)
A golden, hoppy beer.

Border Steeans (OG 1042, ABV 4.1%)
Scottish Borders style, bitter-sweet with berry fruit undertones.

Hematite (OG 1058, ABV 5.5%)
Smooth with full malt throughout.

Beer Engine SIBA

The Beer Engine Ltd, Newton St Cyres, Exeter, Devon, EX5 5AX
Tel (01392) 851282
Fax (01392) 851876
Email peterbrew@aol.com
Website www.thebeerengine.co.uk
Tours by arrangement

The pub (of the same name) has been under new management since 2005, with Mike and Jan Tutty, but the brewery remains under the control of Peter Hawksley. He started brewing in 1983 next to the Barnstaple branch railway line. The brewery is visible behind glass downstairs in the pub. It uses malts from Tuckers of Newton Abbot and English hops from Charles Faram of Newland. Eight outlets are supplied regularly. Seasonal beer: Whistlemas (ABV varies, winter).

Rail Ale (OG 1037, ABV 3.8%)
A straw-coloured beer with a fruity aroma and a sweet, fruity finish.

Piston Bitter (OG 1043, ABV 4.3%)
A mid-brown, sweet-tasting beer with a pleasant, bitter-sweet aftertaste.

Sleeper Heavy (OG 1052, ABV 5.4%)
A red-coloured beer with a fruity, sweet taste and a bitter finish.

Belhaven

See Greene King in the New Nationals section

Bells

Bells Brewery & Merchants Ltd, The Workshop, Lutterworth Road, Ullesthorpe, Leicestershire, LE17 5DR
Tel (01455) 209940
Email jon@bellsbrewery.co.uk

Website www.bellsbrewery.co.uk
Shop Mon-Sat 9.30am-5pm; Sun 10am-4pm
Tours by arrangement (Wed/Thu daytime only)

Bells opened in 2004 and relocated from Bitteswell to Ullesthorpe in 2005 to premises within the Ullesthorpe Garden Centre complex. A brewery shop and farm deli opened in 2005, selling all Bells' beers along with a selection of other British micros products. 20 outlets are supplied. All the main beers are also available in bottle-conditioned form. Seasonal beer: Yule Fuel (ABV 4.8%, Christmas).

Cosbys (OG 1037, ABV 3.7%)

Rainmaker (OG 1041, ABV 4.1%)

Victor (OG 1041, ABV 4.1%)

Dreamcatcher (OG 1046, ABV 4.6%)

Vulcan XH558 (OG 1050, ABV 5%)

Belvoir SIBA

Belvoir Brewery Ltd, 6B Woodhill Industries, Nottingham Lane, Old Dalby, Leicestershire, LE14 3LX
Tel/Fax (01664) 823455
Email colin@belvoirbrewery.co.uk
Website www.belvoirbrewery.co.uk
Tours occasionally by arrangement

⊗ Belvoir (pronounced 'beaver') Brewery was set up in 1995 by Colin Brown, who previously brewed with Shipstone and Theakston. Long-term expansion has seen the introduction of a 20-barrel plant that can produce 50 barrels a week. Bottle-conditioned beers are now being produced using in-house bottling equipment. Up to 150 outlets are supplied. Seasonal beers: Whippling Golden Bitter (ABV 3.6%, spring/summer), Peacock's Glory (ABV 4.7%, spring/summer), Old Dalby (ABV 5.1%, winter). Bottle-conditioned beers: Star, Beaver Bitter, Peacock's Glory, Old Dalby.

Star Mild (OG 1034, ABV 3.4%) ◻ ◆
Reddish/black in colour, this full-bodied and well-balanced mild is at the same time both malty and hoppy with hints of fruitiness leading to a long, bitter-sweet finish.

Star Bitter (OG 1039, ABV 3.9%) ◆
Reminiscent of the long-extinct Shipstone's Bitter, this mid-brown bitter lives up to its name as it is indeed bitter in taste but not unpleasantly so.

Beaver Bitter (OG 1043, ABV 4.3%) ◆
A light brown bitter that starts malty in both aroma and taste, but soon develops a hoppy bitterness. Appreciably fruity.

Beowulf SIBA

Beowulf Brewing Co, Chasewater Country Park, Pool Road, Brownhills, Staffordshire, WS8 7NL
Tel/Fax (01543) 454067
Email beowulfbrewing@yahoo.co.uk
Tours by arrangement

Beowulf Brewing Company beers appear as guest ales predominantly in the central region but also across the country. The brewery's dark beers have a particular reputation for excellence and are now brewed throughout the year. Seasonal beers: Hurricane (ABV 4%, autumn), Glutlusty (ABV 4.5%, autumn), Blizzard (ABV 5%, winter), Grendel's Winter Ale (ABV 5.8%, winter), Wergild (ABV 4.3%, spring/summer), Wuffa (ABV 4.4%, spring/summer), Gold Work (ABV 5.1%, spring/summer). Bottle-conditioned beer: Dragon Smoke Stout (ABV 5.3%).

Beorma (OG 1038, ABV 3.9%) ◆
A pale session ale with a malty hint of fruit giving way to a lingering bitterness.

Noble Bitter (OG 1039, ABV 4%) ◆
Golden with a sweet malty aroma. Malty start becoming very hoppy then bitter, but not an over-long finish.

Wiglaf (OG 1043, ABV 4.3%) ◆
A golden bitter, with a malty flavour married to a pleasing bitterness, with three hop varieties used.

Chasewater Bitter (OG 1043, ABV 4.4%) ◆
Golden colour. Good hoppy aroma, even hoppier taste and hoppier aftertaste with a little malt and hints of citrus. Dry finish but not astringent.

Swordsman (OG 1045, ABV 4.5%) ◆
Pale gold, light fruity aroma, tangy hoppy flavour. Faintly hoppy finish.

Dark Raven (OG 1048, ABV 4.5%)

Dragon Smoke Stout (OG 1048, ABV 4.7%) ◼ ◆
Black and smoky as the name suggests. Full of roast flavours with a touch of fruit and hop. Bitterness develops supported by the full roast bitterness.

Finn's Hall Porter (OG 1049, ABV 4.7%)

Heroes Bitter (OG 1046, ABV 4.7%) ◆
Gold colour, malt aroma, hoppy taste but sweetish finish.

Mercian Shine (OG 1048, ABV 5%) ◆
Amber to pale gold with a good bitter and hoppy start. Plenty of caramel and hops with background malt leading to a great bitter finish with the caramel and hops lingering in the aftertaste.

Berrow SIBA

Berrow Brewery, Coast Road, Berrow, Burnham-on-Sea, Somerset, TA8 2QU
Tel (01278) 751345
Tours by arrangement

⊗ The brewery opened in 1982 and production is now around five barrels a week. Over the years, all the beers have won prizes at beer festivals. 15-20 outlets are supplied. Seasonal beers: Carnivale (ABV 4.7%, Oct-Nov), Christmas Ale (ABV 4.7%, Nov-Dec).

Best Bitter/4Bs (OG 1038, ABV 3.9%) ◆
A pleasant, pale brown session beer, with a fruity aroma, a malty, fruity flavour and bitterness in the palate and finish.

Porter (OG 1046, ABV 4.6%)

Sport (OG 1047, ABV 4.7%)

Topsy Turvy (OG 1055, ABV 5.9%) ◆
A gold-coloured beer with an aroma of malt and hops. Well-balanced malt and hops taste is followed by a hoppy, bitter finish with some fruit notes.

Betwixt*

Betwixt Beer Company, c/o Northern Brewing, Sandiway, Cheshire, WA7 4NQ
Tel (07792) 967414
Email brewer@betwixtbeer.co.uk
Website www.betwixtbeer.co.uk

The company was created in 2005 by brewer Mike McGuigan (ex-Brakspear and several micros and brew-pubs). He brews using spare capacity at Northern Brewing (qv) but plans to open a small brewery on the Wirral peninsula 'betwixt the Mersey and the Dee'. The beers are sold through farmers markets, festivals and in local pubs. Bottle-conditioned beer: Sunlight.

Sunlight (OG 1043, ABV 4.3%)

Big Lamp

Big Lamp Brewers, Grange Road, Newburn, Newcastle upon Tyne, NE15 8NL
Tel (0191) 267 1689
Fax (0191) 267 7387
Email admin@biglampbrewers.co.uk
Website www.keelmanslodge.co.uk
Tours by arrangement

Big Lamp started in 1982 and relocated in 1997 to a 55-barrel plant in a former water pumping station. It is the oldest micro-brewery in the north east of England. 30 outlets are supplied and two pubs are owned. Seasonal/occasional beers: Keelman Brown (ABV 5.7%), Old Genie (ABV 7.4%), Blackout.

Bitter (OG 1039, ABV 3.9%) ◆
A clean-tasting tawny bitter, full of hops and malt. A hint of fruit, with a good hoppy finish.

Double M (OG 1043, ABV 4.3%)

Summerhill Stout (OG 1044, ABV 4.4%) ◆
A rich, tasty stout, dark in colour with a lasting rich roast character. Malty mouthfeel with a lingering finish.

Prince Bishop Ale (OG 1048, ABV 4.8%) ◆
A refreshing, easy-drinking bitter, golden in colour, full of fruit and hops. Strong bitterness with a spicy, dry finish.

Premium (OG 1052, ABV 5.2%) ◆
A well-balanced, flavoursome bitter with a big nose full of hops. The sweetness lasts into a mellow, dry finish.

Embers (OG 1055, ABV 5.5%)

Blackout (OG 1100, ABV 11%) ◆
A strong bitter, fortified with roast malt character and rich maltiness. Try it for its mouthfeel and lasting bitterness.

Bitter End

Bitter End Pub & Brewery, 15 Kirkgate, Cockermouth, Cumbria, CA13 9PJ
Tel/Fax (01900) 828993
Email info@bitterend.co.uk
Website www.bitterend.co.uk
Tours by arrangement

The brewery opened in the back room of the Bitter End pub in 1995, using a one-barrel plant with former whisky casks as fermenters. The equipment was replaced in 2004 with a copper-clad system imported from the US. Beer is available only at the pub.

Cockermouth Pride (OG 1038, ABV 3.8%)
A pale brown, malty bitter, fruity and sweet beer with a slight astringency in the finish.

Wheat Beer (ABV 4.1%)

Call Out (ABV 4.2%)
Brewed to raise funds for Cockermouth Rescue Team.

Czechumberland (ABV 4.5%)

Cuddy Lugs (ABV 4.7%) ◆
A malty aroma and sweet start quickly lead to lingering bitter flavours.

Skinner's Old Strong (ABV 5.5%)

Blackawton SIBA

Blackawton Brewery, Unit 7 Peninsula Park, Moorlands Trading Estate, Saltash, Cornwall, PL12 6LX
Tel (01752) 848777 Fax (01752) 848999
Email info@blackawtonbrewery.com
Website www.blackawtonbrewery.com

Once Devon's oldest operating brewery, Blackawton relocated to Cornwall in 2000 and ownership changed in 2004. Some 50 outlets are supplied. Seasonal beer: Winter Fuel (ABV 5%, winter). Bottle-conditioned beers: Headstrong, Winter Fuel.

Original Bitter (OG 1036, ABV 3.8%)
A copper-coloured bitter brewed in the traditional English style. An ideal session beer with a fresh floral hop aroma.

Westcountry Gold (OG 1038, ABV 4.1%)
A light, golden, fresh-tasting summer beer with sweet malt flavours and delicate vanilla and fruit hints from Styrian Goldings hops.

44 Special (OG 1044, ABV 4.5%)
A premium full strength bitter that is rich and sweet with the aroma of ripe hops and fruit.

Peninsula Ale (OG 1046, ABV 4.6%)

Exhibition Ale (OG 1046, ABV 4.7%)
Pale in colour.

Headstrong (OG 1048, ABV 5.2%)
A deceptively smooth beer with a sweet malt taste.

Black Bull

See Redburn

Black Country

Black Country Ales, Old Bulls Head, 2 Redhall Road, Lower Gornal, Dudley, West Midlands, DY3 2NU
Tel (01384) 231516 / 07946 454150
Email info@blackcountryales.co.uk
Tours by arrangement (except Sundays)

The brewery was set up in 2004 by director Angus McMeeking and brewer Guy Perry. Guy was formally the brewer at nearby Sarah Hughes (qv). The brewery uses a new plant situated in part of the pub's original tower brewery, dating from 1834, which had last brewed in 1934. The already existing oak vessels that were installed in 1900 have been refurbished and brought into production. One-off beers are produced for distributors. Seasonal beer: English Winter (ABV 5.5%, winter).

Bradley's Finest Golden (OG 1040, ABV 4.2%)

Pig on the Wall (OG 1040, ABV 4.3%)

Fireside (OG 1047, ABV 5%)

Black Dog*

Black Dog Brewery, Foulsyke Farm, Fylingdales, Whitby, North Yorkshire, YO22 4QL
Tel (0845) 301 2337
Email info@blackdogbrewery.co.uk
Website www.blackdogbrewery.co.uk

☺ Black Dog Brewery started brewing in 1997 in the centre of Whitby, but closed in 2000. Since then beers under the Black Dog name had been contract brewed by Hambleton. However, Tony Bryars purchased the original Black Dog five-barrel plant, together with recipes, and re-established the brewery on his farm in April 2006 using local spring water. Three regular beers are brewed plus other occasional beers from the original Black Dog portfolio.

Whitby Abbey Ale (ABV 3.8%)

Schooner (ABV 4.2%)

Rhatas (ABV 4.6%)

Blackdown

Blackdown Brewery Ltd, Unit C6 Dunkeswell Business Park, Dunkeswell Airfield, Honiton, Devon, EX14 4LE
Tel (01404) 890096
Email info@blackdownbrewery.co.uk
Website www.blackdownbrewery.co.uk
Tours by arrangement (maximum of 20 people)

⊗ The brewery, established in 2002, is family-run and covers Devon, Dorset and Somerset. Some 160 outlets are supplied and two regular beers are produced.

Devon's Pride (OG 1038, ABV 3.8%)

Gold (OG 1043, ABV 4.3%)

Blackfriars*

Blackfriars Brewery Limited, Unit 4 Queens Road Business Centre, Great Yarmouth, Norfolk, NR30 3HT
Tel 07786 311301
Email w.russell@ntlworld.com

Established in 2004, the five-barrel plant began brewing in 2005. It is currently the only brewery in Great Yarmouth and plans to bottle its beers.

Yarmouth Bitter (OG 1036, ABV 3.8%)

Sygnus Bittergold (OG 1044, ABV 4%)

Old Habit (OG 1052, ABV 5.6%)

Black Hole*

Black Hole Brewery Ltd, Unit 63, Imex Business Park, Shobnall Road, Burton upon Trent, Staffs, DE14 2AU
Tel 0793 1823132
Email beer@blackholebrewery.co.uk
Wesbite www.blackholebrewery.co.uk

A new brewery in the capital of English brewing. It started operations in May 2006. The three beers listed below where in the planning stage as the guide went to press and the range is liable to change.

Bitter (ABV 3.8%)

Red Dwarf (ABV 4.4%)

No Escape (ABV 5.2%)

Black Isle SIBA

Black Isle Brewing Ltd, Old Allangrange, Munlochy, Ross-shire, IV8 8NZ
Tel (01463) 811871
Fax (01463) 811875

> Hardys & Hansons of Nottingham was bought in June 2006 by Greene King. The entry for the brewery now appears in the 'New Nationals' section. Gale's of Horndean was bought by Fuller's at the end of 2005. Gale's beers are now brewed at Fuller's brewery in London: see entry for Fuller's.

Email greatbeers@blackislebrewery.com
Website www.blackislebrewery.com
Shop 10am-6pm daily (closed Sundays in winter)
Tours by arrangement

⊗ Black Isle Brewery was set up in 1998 in the heart of the Scottish Highlands. The five-barrel plant is based in converted farm buildings on the Black Isle. The company concentrates on organic production: the beers have Soil Association certification, while the bottle-conditioned beers are certified by both the SA and the Vegetarian Society. Bottled beers are available by mail order to anywhere in mainland Britain. 20 outlets are supplied. Bottle-conditioned beers (all suitable for vegetarians and vegans): Wheat Beer (ABV 4.5%), Scotch Ale (ABV 4.5%), Porter (ABV 4.5%) ◻, Blonde (ABV 4.5%).

Yellowhammer (OG 1042, ABV 4%) ◆
A delicious, fruity, hoppy summer ale bursting with citrus fruit and hops, and with caramel on the nose. A hoppy taste with some bitterness but sweetness predominates.

Red Kite (OG 1041, ABV 4.2%) ◆
Light malt and some hop on the nose and with summer fruits on the palate. Not as sweet as it once was, with a more lasting bitterness.

Hibernator (ABV 4.5%)

Wagtail Porter (ABV 4.5%)

Black Sheep SIBA

Black Sheep Brewery plc, Wellgarth, Masham, Ripon, North Yorkshire, HG4 4EN
Tel (01765) 689227
Fax (01765) 689746
Website www.blacksheepbrewery.com
Shop 10am-5pm daily
Tours by arrangement

◎ Black Sheep was set up in 1992 by Paul Theakston, a member of Masham's famous brewing family, in the former Wellgarth Maltings. The company has enjoyed continued growth and now supplies a free trade of around 700 outlets, but owns no pubs. The brewery specialises in cask ale (70% of production). Over the past two years, £5 million has been spent on effectively doubling the capacity of the brewery and installing state of the art cask racking.

Best Bitter (OG 1038, ABV 3.8%) ◻ ◆
A hoppy and fruity beer with strong bitter overtones, leading to a long, dry, bitter finish.

Emmerdale (OG 1042, ABV 4.2%)

Black Sheep Ale (OG 1044, ABV 4.4%)

Riggwelter (OG 1059, ABV 5.9%) ◆
A fruity bitter, with complex underlying tastes and hints of liquorice and pear drops leading to a long, dry, bitter finish.

Blackwater

Blackwater Brewery, The Brewers Wholesale, Unit 18 Gainsborough Trading Estate, Rufford Road, Stourbridge, West Midlands, DY9 7ND
Tel (01384) 374050

Beers contract brewed by Salopian Brewery (qv).

Blanchfields SIBA

Blanchfields Brewing Co, 1 Southend Road, Rochford, Essex SS4 1HA
Tel (01702) 530053
Fax (01702) 543999
Email richlunn@btinternet.com
Website www.blanchfields-brewery.com
Tours by arrangement

⊗ The 2.5-barrel brewery was established in 1997 at the Bull in Fakenham, Norfolk – hence most of their beers have 'Bull' in their name. The brewery moved in 2003 to Rochford. The current brewery is in a unit on an industrial estate. The brewery has recently acquired its first brewery tap, Blanchfields Bar, in Rochford. Around 30 outlets are supplied.

IPA Twist (OG 1036, ABV 3.6%)

Black Bull Mild (OG 1040, ABV 3.6%) ◆
Light malty airs introduce this red-coloured, traditional mild. A dry fruity maltiness gives a hint of cocoa. The finish fades quickly although roasted malt remains.

Golden Bull (OG 1045, ABV 4.2%)

Porter Bull (OG 1042, ABV 4.2%)

White Bull (OG 1044, ABV 4.4%)

Raging Bull Bitter (OG 1048, ABV 4.9%) ◆
Fruity strong ale with a perfumed aroma and a reasonably bitter finish.

Blencowe

See Barrowden

Blindmans SIBA

Blindmans Brewery Ltd, Talbot Farm, Leighton, Somerset, BA11 4PN
Tel (01749) 880038
Fax (01749) 880379
Email info@blindmansbrewery.co.uk
Website www.blindmansbrewery.co.uk
Tours by arrangement

Blindmans brewery was established in 2002 with a five-barrel plant based between Frome and Shepton Mallet in a converted milking parlour. The brewery has its own exclusive water spring, giving the beer a clean, crisp natural taste. In early 2004 the brewery was purchased by owners Paul Edney (formerly head brewer of Ashvine) and Lloyd Chamberlain (chairman of the Rode Brewing Federation). A programme of investment and expansion has followed with several new ales introduced to complement the Blindmans range. Bottled beers were also introduced in 2006. Approximately 50 outlets are supplied. Seasonal beers: Eclipse (ABV 4.2%), Siberia (ABV 4.7%), Bah Humbug! (ABV 4.5%).

Buff (ABV 3.6%)
Amber-coloured, smooth session beer.

Golden Spring (ABV 4%)
Fresh and aromatic straw-coloured beer, brewed using selected lager malt.

Mine Beer (ABV 4.2%)
Full-bodied, copper-coloured, blended malt ale.

Icarus (ABV 4.5%)
Fruity, rich, mid-dark ruby ale.

Blue Anchor SIBA

Blue Anchor Inn, 50 Coinagehall Street, Helston, Cornwall, TR13 8EL
Tel (01326) 562821
Fax (01326) 565765
Email theblueanchor@btconnect.com
Website www.spingoales.com
Tours by arrangement

Dating back to the 15th century, this is the oldest brewery in Cornwall and was originally a monks' hospice. After the dissolution of the monasteries it became a tavern brewing its own uniquely flavoured beer called Spingo at the rear of the premises. Brewing has continued to this day and people travel from all over the world to sample the delights of this wonderful inn untouched by time. The brewery has undergone complete refurbishment and the pub is also due for improvement, with careful attention to preserving its special character. Five outlets are supplied. Seasonal beers: Spingo Bragget (ABV 6.1%, April-Oct), Spingo Easter Special (ABV 7.6%), Spingo Christmas Special (ABV 7.6%). All draught beers are available in bottle-conditioned form. Bragget is a recreation of a medieval beer style.

Spingo Jubilee (IPA) (OG 1045, ABV 4.6%)

Spingo Middle (OG 1050, ABV 5.1%)
A deep copper-red beer with a big fruity aroma of raisins and sultanas, a hint of vanilla and an earthy, peppery note from the hops. The palate is nutty, with a fruit cake note. The long bitter-sweet finish has a raspberry-like fruitiness balanced by the dryness of the hops.

Spingo Special (OG 1066, ABV 6.7%)
Darker than Middle with a pronounced earthy character on the nose balanced by rich fruit. Fruit and peppery hops dominate the mouth, followed by a big finish in which malt, fruit and hops vie for attention.

Blue Bell

Blue Bell Brewery, Cranesgate South, Whaplode St Catherine, Lincolnshire, PE12 6SN

Office: Blue Bell Brewery, Sycamore House, Lapwater Lane, Holbeach St Marks, Lincolnshire, PE12 8EX (all correspondence to this address)
Tel/Fax (01406) 701000
Email enquiries@bluebellbrewery.co.uk
Website www.bluebellbrewery.co.uk
Tours by arrangement

Alan and Emma Bell took over the Blue Bell Brewery in 2004 from original founder Mick Pilkington. The brewery operates as a separate business from the adjacent Blue Bell pub but the pub does act as the brewery tap. The brewery supplies some 40 outlets. The production of bottle-conditioned beer was planned for 2006. Seasonal beer: Mild (ABV 3.6%).

Old Honesty (OG 1040, ABV 4.1%)

Old Gold (OG 1045, ABV 4.5%)

Old Fashioned (OG 1045, ABV 4.8%)

Old Comfort (OG 1050, ABV 5%)

For Ivy Wall (Wetherspoons), Spalding:

Pain in the Glass (OG 1040, ABV 4.1%)

Blue Cow

Blue Cow Inn and Brewery, 29 High Street, South Witham, Lincolnshire, NG33 5QB
Tel/Fax (01572) 768432
Website www.thebluecowinn.co.uk
Tours by arrangement

Taken over in 2005, the brewery owners plan to develop the range of beers.

Best Bitter (OG 1039, ABV 3.8%)

Witham Wobbler (OG 1045, ABV 4.5%)

Blue Moon

Blue Moon Brewery, Cock Inn, Watton Road, Barford, Norfolk, NR9 4AS
Tel (01603) 757646

Pete Turner supplies the Cock and some 60 free trade outlets. A separate brewing company, Spectrum (qv), run by Andy Mitchell, usies the original Blue Moon kit.

Easy Life (OG 1040, ABV 3.8%)
A golden-hued brew with a complex character. A booming hop nose continues through to a hoppy, slightly astringent finish. Malt and caramel swirl in the background as lemon notes grow.

Sea of Tranquillity (OG 1042, ABV 4.2%)
A dry, malty character gives depth to this copper-coloured best bitter. A blackcurrant start fades as a long, ever-sweetening finish develops.

Moon Dance (ABV 4.7%)
A rich elderberry aroma is matched by a solid fruity taste in which the nutty malt flavours are slightly topped by well-defined hoppy overtones.

Dark Side (OG 1048, ABV 4.8%)
Slightly scented, with fruit, hops and malt, this dark brown strong mild has plenty of body. A caramel sweetness gives balance to the dominant malty foundation. A long finish maintains the rich blend of flavours.

Hingham High (OG 1050, ABV 5.2%)
This beautifully-balanced strong malty ale has something for everyone. Mellow fruitiness jostles for attention with chocolate, hops and toffee. The long, strong finish of a good vintage port.

Milk of Amnesia (OG 1055, ABV 5.2%)
A complex beer, mid-brown in colour but the light malty nose gives little away. The taste has a port-like note; cinnamon and ginger jostle with pepper and citrus as the flavours continue to hold up well.

Liquor Mortis (OG 1075, ABV 7.5%)
A heavy blackcurrant signature introduces this dark brown barley wine. A mature roast beginning counter-balances the fruity sweetness that carries through to a long, filling finish with more than a hint of hops.

Total Eclipse (ABV 9%)

Blythe SIBA

Blythe Brewery, Blythe House Farm, Lichfield Road, Hamstall Ridware, Rugeley, Staffordshire, WS15 3QQ
Tel 07773 747724
Email info@blythebrewery.plus.com
Website www.blythebrewery.co.uk
Tours by arrangement

Robert Greenway started brewing in 2003 using a 2.5-barrel plant in a converted barn on a farm. As well as specials, seasonal beers are produced on a quarterly basis. Fifteen outlets are supplied. Seasonal beers: Old Horny (ABV 4.6%, Sept-Nov), Johnson's Ale (ABV 4.4%, June-Aug). Bottle-conditioned beers: as for cask beers listed below.

Bitter (OG 1040, ABV 4%) ◆
Amber with a full hoppy aroma and fruity background. Immediate full hoppy taste that develops into an intense hoppy, lingering finish.

Chase Bitter (OG 1044, ABV 4.4%) ◆
Copper to tawny coloured, with a fruit and hop start with caramel sweetness developing; lingering bitterness with a sweet edge.

Staffie (OG 1044, ABV 4.4%) ◆
Sweet hoppy and citrus flower aroma from this amber beer. Gentle bitter start expands to a fresh fruity tang before the hops demand attention to the long bitter finish.

Palmer's Poison (OG 1045, ABV 4.5%) ◆
Malt and caramel are the first characteristics of this mid-brown beer. Liquorice roast develops; hoppy throughout with a long, bitter finish.

BMG Brewing

BMG Brewing Limited, c/o Tower Brewery, The Old Water Tower, Walsitch Maltings, Glensyl Way, Burton upon Trent, Staffordshire, DE14 1LX
Tel (01283) 561330

Beers are contract brews by Tower Brewery for Beer My Guest distributors.

Bob's

Bob's Brewing Company, c/o Red Lion, 73 Dewsbury Road, Ossett, West Yorkshire, WF5 9NQ
Tel (07789) 693597
Email bobwhitelion@yahoo.co.uk

The brewery was founded by Bob Hunter, formerly one of the partners in Ossett Brewery, in a tiny outbuilding behind the Red Lion pub on the outskirts of Ossett. Approximately 10 outlets are supplied.

White Lion (OG 1043, ABV 4.3%)
Pale, flowery, lager-style beer using American Cascade hops.

Yakima Pale Ale (OG 1045.5, ABV 4.5%)
A hoppy and bitter yellow beer that uses hops from the Yakima Valley in Washington State, US.

Chardonnayle (OG 1051.5, ABV 5.1%)
Complex, stylish strong pale ale with hints of lemongrass and fruits, with Willamette hops for aroma.

Boggart Hole Clough

Boggart Hole Clough Brewing Co, Unit 13 Brookside Works, Clough Road, Moston, Manchester, M9 4FP
Tel/Fax (0161) 277 9666
Email boggart@btconnect.com
Website www.boggart-brewery.co.uk
Tours by arrangement

⊛ The brewery was set up in 2001 by Mark Dade, former brewer at Marble (qv), next to Boggart Hole Clough Park in north Manchester. The park supplies timber from which the brewery's distinctive wooden pump clips are fashioned. Mark has increased the brew length to eight barrels. He has also set up the Workshop Brewery that enables visitors to design and produce beers to their own specifications on a dedicated 2.5-barrel plant. Boggart Distribution was launched in 2003 and this allows the beers to be sold to more than 250 free houses throughout the country. Monthly specials are produced. Bottle-conditioned beer: Steaming Boggart.

Best Bitter (ABV 3.9%)
An easy-drinking, light-coloured session beer with a hoppy, bitter aftertaste.

Dark Mild (ABV 4%)
A classic dark mild.

Standard Pioneer (ABV 4%)
A light-coloured session ale with lemon citrus taste and aroma.

Angel Hill (OG 1042, ABV 4.2%)
A premium, golden pale ale with an aromatic explosion of flavour.

Boggart Brew (OG 1043, ABV 4.3%)
A quaffable ruby-red beer.

Dark Side (OG 1044, ABV 4.4%)
A classic porter with a smooth roast finish and subtle hop aftertaste.

Sun Dial (OG 1047, ABV 4.7%)
A pale beer with a refreshing, fruity hop taste and aroma.

Borough Arms

Borough Arms, 33 Earle Street, Crewe, Cheshire, CW1 2BG
Tel (01270) 254999

A two-barrel brewery opened in 2005 at the Borough Arms pub. Up to six real ales were available until brewing ceased temporarily in December 2005. The licensee, John Webster, assisted by Martin Bond, owner of Barleycorns, a craft beer shop in Nantwich, restarted brewing in February 2006. They plan to offer two beers at the pubs; details were not available when the guide went to press.

Bottle Brook*

Bottle Brook Brewery, 10 Church Street, Kilburn, Belper, Derbyshire, DE56 0LU
Tel 07971 189915
Email tlc@leadmill.fsnet.co.uk

Work started on a 2.5-barrel plant in mid-2005 and brewing on a tower brewery system began in 2006 using only rare and limited hop varieties. Speciality beers will include a large number of milds. The plant is ex-Leadmill and the brewery is owned and operated by Richard Creighton, who is also the owner and brewer at Leadmill (qv). Two outlets are supplied.

Meandering Mild (OG 1044, ABV 4.3%)

Full Moon (OG 1044, ABV 4.6%)

Midnight Mash (OG 1050, ABV 5.1%)

Deep Well Bitter (OG 1051, ABV 5.2%)

Bowland SIBA

The Bowland Brewery, Bashall Town, Clitheroe, Lancashire, BB7 3LQ
Tel 07952 639465
Fax (01200) 428825
Email richardbakerbb@aol.com
Website www.bowlandbrewery.com
Tours by arrangement

Bowland originally started brewing in 2003 using a five-barrel plant that came from the Fuzz and Firkin in Southsea. Richard Baker now brews his award-winning cask ales in what was an old milking parlour close to the official geographical centre of the United Kingdom. 100 outlets are supplied throughout the north west. Small scale bottling started in 2005 with three of the regular beers and an ever-changing single cask variety being sold at the next door farm shop (please ring to check availability). At least one new beer is brewed each month and seasonal beers vary but include: Golden Trough, Sorceress, Headless Peg, Reviver, RLB, Sleigh Belle.

Sawley Tempted (OG 1038, ABV 3.7%)
A copper-coloured fruity session bitter with toffee in the mouth and a spicy finish.

Hunters Moon (OG 1039, ABV 3.7%)
A dark mild with chocolate, coffee and biscuit flavours.

Bowland Gold (OG 1039, ABV 3.8%)
A hoppy golden bitter with intense grapefruit flavours.

Chipping Steamer (OG 1040, ABV 3.9%)
A mid-gold bitter with hints of orange and a slightly floral finish.

Hen Harrier (OG 1040, ABV 4%)
A pale gold bitter with soft citrus, peach and apricot flavours throughout.

Bowland Dragon (OG 1043, ABV 4.2%)
A golden premium bitter with rounded fruit in the mouth and a refreshing finish.

Box Steam

Box Steam Brewery, Unit 2, Oaks Farm, Rode Hill, Colerne, Chippenham, Wiltshire, SN14 8AR
Tel (01225) 743622
Email marshallewart@ukonline.co.uk
Website www.boxsteambrewery.com
Tours by arrangement

The brewery was launched in 2004 on a farm between Bath and Box. The copper is fired by a steam boiler. One pub is owned and 15 outlets are supplied. Seasonal beers: Rev Awdry (ABV 3.8%, spring/summer), Figgy Pudding (ABV 5%, winter).

Tunnel Vision (OG 1041, ABV 4.2%)

Blind House (OG 1048, ABV 4.6%)

Bradfield

Bradfield Brewery, Watt House Farm, High Bradfield, Sheffield, South Yorkshire, S6 6LG
Tel/Fax (0114) 285 1118
Email info@bradfieldbrewery.com
Website www.bradfieldbrewery.co.uk
Shop Mon-Sat 12-4pm

◎ Bradfield Brewery is a family-run business, based on a dairy farm in the Peak District. Only the finest ingredients are used, along with clean, clear Peak District water from its own borehole at Millstone Grit. More than 200 outlets are supplied. Bottle-conditioned beers: Farmers 'Milk' Stout, Farmers Pale Ale.

Farmers Bitter (OG 1039, ABV 3.9%)

Farmers Blonde (OG 1041, ABV 4%)

Farmers Brown Cow (OG 1042.5, ABV 4.2%)

Farmers Milk Stout (OG 1045, ABV 4.5%)

Farmers Belgium Blue (OG 1048, ABV 4.9%)

Farmers Pale Ale (OG 1049, ABV 5%)

Brains IFBB

S A Brain & Co Ltd, The Cardiff Brewery, PO Box 53, Crawshay Street, Cardiff, CF10 1SP
Tel (029) 2040 2060
Fax (029) 2040 3324
Email brains@sabrain.com
Website www.sabrain.com

◎ S A Brain began trading at the Old Brewery in Cardiff in 1882 when Samuel Arthur Brain and his uncle Joseph Benjamin Brain purchased a site founded in 1713. The company has remained in family ownership ever since and in 1997 bought South Wales' other leading independent, Crown Buckley, formed from the merger of the Crown Brewery of Pontyclun with Buckleys of Llanelli. The full range of Brains Ales is now produced at the company's Cardiff Brewery (formerly Hancock's), bought from Bass in 1999. The company owns 230 pubs, has a sizeable free trade and a wholesale estate of more than 3,000 accounts since acquisitions of wholesalers James Williams of Narberth and Stedman's of Caerleon. Brains is the official sponsor of the Wales Rugby Union team. Bottle-conditioned beer: Brains Dark (ABV 3.9%).

Dark (OG 1035.5, ABV 3.5%)
A tasty dark brown mild, a mix of malt, roast, caramel with a background of hops. Bitter-sweet, mellow and with a lasting finish of malt and roast. An accomplished, classic mild.

Bitter (OG 1036, ABV 3.7%)
Amber coloured with a gentle aroma of malt and hops. Malt, hops and bitterness combine in an easy-drinking beer with a bitter finish.

Buckley's Best Bitter (OG 1036.5, ABV 3.7%)
Brewed with a combination of Challenger, Fuggles and Goldings hops. It has a light, fragrant nose with a hoppy character.

Bread of Heaven (OG 1040, ABV 4%)
Traditional cask ale with a distinctive reddish hue and rich hop aroma, finely balanced by a fruity finish.

SA (OG 1042, ABV 4.2%)
A mellow, full-bodied beer. Gentle malt and hop aroma leads to a malty, hop and fruit mix with a balancing bitterness.

Rev James (OG 1045.5, ABV 4.5%)
A faint malt and fruit aroma with malt and fruit flavours in the taste, initially bitter-sweet. Bitterness balances the flavour and makes this an easy-drinking beer.

Brakspear

Brakspear Brewing Co, Eagle Maltings, The Crofts, Witney, Oxon, OX28 4DP
Tel (01993) 890800
Fax (01993) 772553
Email info@brakspear-beers.co.uk
Website www.brakspear-beers.co.uk
Shop merchandise available on-line
Tours by arrangement

Brakspear brewing came back to Oxfordshire in 2004 and has its own fermenting room within Wychwood Brewery (qv). The major development of the Wychwood site in 2004 saw the installation of the original Brakspear copper and fermenting vessels, including the famous 'double drop' fermenters. All the regular and seasonal beers are now brewed at Witney. Bottle-conditioned beers: Live Organic (ABV 4.5%), Triple (ABV 7.2%).

Bitter (OG 1035, ABV 3.4%)
A classic copper-coloured pale ale with a big hop resins, juicy malt and orange fruit aroma, intense hop bitterness in the mouth and finish, and a firm maltiness and tangy fruitiness throughout.

Special (OG 1045, ABV 4.3%)
Rich malt, hops and fruit aroma; biscuity malt and hop resins in the mouth; long bitter-sweet finish with orange fruit notes.

Brancaster EAB

Brancaster Brewery, Jolly Sailors, Main Road, Brancaster Staithe, Norfolk, PE31 8BJ
Tel (01485) 210314
Fax (01485) 210414
Email jayatjolly@aol.com
Website www.jollysailors.co.uk

Brancaster opened in 2003 with a five-barrel plant squeezed into a converted ocean-going steel container adjacent to its own pub/restaurant. Occasional specials are produced. Bottle-conditioned beers: IPA, Old Les.

IPA (ABV 3.7%)

Old Les (ABV 5%)

Brandon*

Brandon Brewery, 76 High Street, Brandon, Suffolk, IP27 0AU
Tel (01842) 878496 / 07876 234689
Shop Mon-Sat 9am-1pm
Tours by arrangement

Brandon Brewery started brewing in 2005 in the old dairy of a 15th-century cottage. Visitors are welcome and encouraged to sample from the beer shop. 20 outlets are supplied. The entire range of beers is also available bottle conditioned.

Breckland Gold (OG 1037, ABV 3.8%)

Bitter (OG 1040, ABV 4%)

Moonshine (OG 1038, ABV 4%)

Gun Flint (OG 1041, ABV 4.2%)

Rusty Bucket (OG 1043, ABV 4.4%)

Slippery Jack (OG 1044, ABV 4.5%)

Nappertandy (OG 1047, ABV 4.8%)

Brandy Cask SIBA

Brandy Cask Pub & Brewery, 25 Bridge Street, Pershore, Worcestershire, WR10 1AJ
Tel/Fax (01386) 552602
Tours by arrangement

Brewing started in 1995 in a refurbished bottle store in the garden of the pub. It was run as a separate business until the retirement of the brewer in 1998. Brewery and pub now operate under one umbrella, with brewing carried out by the owner/landlord.

Whistling Joe (ABV 3.6%)
A sweet, fruity, copper-coloured beer that has plenty of contrast in the aroma. A malty balance lingers but the aftertaste is not dry.

Brandy Snapper (ABV 4%)
Golden brew with low alpha hops. Plenty of fruit and hop aroma leads to a rich taste in the mouth and a lingering aftertaste.

John Baker's Original (ABV 4.8%)
A superb blend of flavours with roasted malt to the fore. The rich hoppy aroma is complemented by a complex aftertaste.

Ale Mary (ABV 4.8%)
A rich malt and fruit aroma leads on to an equally complex taste with no one flavour dominating. A dry finish.

Branscombe Vale SIBA

Branscombe Vale Brewery Ltd, Great Seaside Farm, Branscombe, Devon, EX12 3DP
Tel/Fax (01297) 680511
Email branscombebrewery@yahoo.co.uk
Tours by arrangement

The brewery was set up in 1992 by former dairy workers Paul Dimond and Graham Luxton in cowsheds owned by the National Trust. Paul and Graham converted the sheds and dug their own well. The NT built an extension for the brewery to ensure future growth. Branscombe Vale currently supplies 60 regular outlets. Seasonal beers: Anniversary Ale (ABV 4.6%, Feb-March), Hells Belles (ABV 4.8%, regular occasional) Yo Ho Ho (ABV 6%, Christmas). Bottle-conditioned beer: Draymans.

Branoc (OG 1035, ABV 3.8%) ◆
A good session bitter. Pale brown in colour with a malt and fruit aroma and taste. A hoppy beer with a bitter finish.

Draymans (OG 1040, ABV 4.2%)
A mid-brown beer with hop and caramel notes and a lingering finish.

BVB Own Label (OG 1046, ABV 4.6%) ◆
Reddy/brown-coloured beer with a fruity aroma and taste, and bitter/astringent finish.

Summa That (OG 1050, ABV 5%)
Light golden beer with a clean and refreshing taste and a long hoppy finish.

Breconshire SIBA

Breconshire Brewery Ltd, Ffrwdgrech Industrial Estate, Brecon, Powys, LD3 8LA
Tel (01874) 623731
Fax (01874) 611434
Email sales@breconshirebrewery.com
Website www.breconshirebrewery.com
Shop Mon-Fri 8.30am-4.30pm
Tours by arrangement

⊗ The Breconshire Brewery was founded by Howard Marlow in 2002 as part of C H Marlow, a wholesaler and distributor of ales, beers, wines and spirits in the south Wales area for more than 30 years. The 10-barrel plant uses British Optic malts blended with a range of English whole hops. The beers are distributed throughout mid, south and west Wales and the west of England. Seasonal beers include: Winter Beacon (ABV 5.3%, Nov-Feb). Bottle-conditioned beers: Golden Valley, Brecknock Best, Red Dragon, Ramblers Ruin, Winter Beacon.

Brecon County Ale (OG 1037, ABV 3.7%) ◆
A traditional amber-coloured bitter. A clean hoppy flavour, background malt and fruit, with a good thirst-quenching bitterness.

Golden Valley (OG 1042, ABV 4.2%) 🏆 ◆
Golden in colour with a welcoming aroma of hops, malt and fruit. A balanced mix of these flavours and moderate, building bitterness lead to a satisfying, rounded finish. CAMRA Champion Beer of Wales 2004/05.

Brecknock Best (OG 1045, ABV 4.5%)
A tawny-coloured traditional best bitter, brewed with Bramling Cross and Pilot hops. First brewed to honour the Brecknockshire Agricultural Society's 250th Anniversary.

Red Dragon (OG 1047, ABV 4.7%)
A red-hued premium ale brewed with a complex grist of Optic and wheat malts and a blend of hedgerow hops for extra bite.

Ramblers Ruin (OG 1050, ABV 5%) ◆
Pale brown, full-bodied with rich biscuity malt and fruit flavours; background hops and bitterness round off the beer.

Brentwood*

Brentwood Brewing Co, c/o 372 Ongar Road, Brentwood, Essex, CM15 9JH
Tel/fax (01277) 375760
Email BrentwoodBrewing@aol.com
Website BrentwoodBrewing.co.uk

The 2.5-barrel plant was set up with the support of Felstar and Iceni breweries (qv). The address above is the office: the brewery address and beer portfolio were not available when the guide went to press.

Brewster's SIBA

Brewster's Brewing Co Ltd, Harby Lane, Stathern, near Melton Mowbray, Leicestershire, LE14 4HR
Tel (01949) 861868
Fax (01949) 861901
Email sara@brewsters.co.uk
Website www.brewsters.co.uk
Tours by arrangement

⊗ Brewster is the old English term for a female brewer and Sara Barton is a modern example. A Master of Brewing trained at Heriot Watt Brewing School in Edinburgh, she worked with Courage before striking out alone. Brewster's Brewery was set up in the heart of the Vale of Belvoir in 1998. Beer is supplied to some 250 outlets throughout central England and further afield via wholesalers. Seasonal beers: see website. Bottle-conditioned beer: Vale Pale Ale (ABV 4.5%).

Hophead (OG 1036, ABV 3.6%) ◆
As its name suggests, this amber beer caters for you if you delight in floral/hoppy brews; hops predominate throughout before finally yielding to grapefruit in a slightly astringent finish.

Marquis (OG 1038, ABV 3.8%) ◆
A well-balanced and refreshing session bitter with maltiness and a dry, hoppy finish. A SIBA award winner.

Daffys Elixir (OG 1042, ABV 4.2%)

Hop A Doodle Doo (OG 1043, ABV 4.3%)

Rutterkin (OG 1046, ABV 4.6%) ◆
A premium bitter with a golden appearance. A zesty hop flavour from American Mount Hood hops combines with a touch of malt sweetness to give a rich, full-bodied beer.

Wicked Woman Range (OG 1048, ABV 4.8%)
(Varies seasonally)

Belly Dancer (OG 1050, ABV 5.2%) ◆
Well-balanced, ruby-red ale having a full-bodied taste from crystal and roast malts, with a subtle hop finish from Bramling Cross and Fuggles. A beautifully smooth, warming beer.

Brew Wharf*

🍺 Brew Wharf Co Ltd, Brew Wharf Yard, Stoney Street, London, SE1 9AD
Tel (020) 7940 8333 Fax (020) 7940 8334
Website www.brewwharf.com

Brew Wharf opened in autumn 2005. It is adjacent to Borough Market in the arches behind Vinopolis, the wine exhibition and visitor centre, and has a bar plus a restaurant where dishes are matched with beer. The owners plan to produce seasonal ales.

Wharf Bitter (OG 1036.6, ABV 3.6%)

Wharf Best (OG 1041, ABV 4.2%)

Bridge of Allan SIBA

Bridge of Allan Brewery, The Brewhouse, Queens Lane, Bridge of Allan, Stirlingshire, FK9 4NY
Tel (01786) 834555
Fax (01786) 833426
Email brewery@bridgeofallan.co.uk
Website www.bridgeofallan.co.uk
Shop 12-5pm daily
Tours by arrangement

⊛ Bridge of Allan Brewery was founded in 1997 and is located in the Victorian spa town in the Forth Valley. In May 2006 the company became part of Traditional Scottish Ales Ltd with Stirling and Trossachs breweries (qv). Beer may be brewed at either Bridge of Allan or Stirling. The five-barrel plant was moved to Stirling Brewery (qv) in 2006 while the visitor centre is refurbished, with plans to acquire a public house licence. The brewery sells to pubs in Scotland and also distributes to England and abroad via wholesalers. There is a large number of seasonal beers: see website. Bottle-conditioned beers: Brig O'Allan, Dear Green Place, Porridge Oats, Organic Blonde, Ginger Organic, Wallace 700. Lomond Gold, Glencoe Wild Oat Stout and Ben Nevis are suitable for vegetarians and vegans.

Stirling Bitter (OG 1039, ABV 3.7%)
A full-flavoured beer with a nutty and fruity taste and a dry aftertaste.

Ben Nevis Organic (OG 1042, ABV 4%) ◆
A traditional Scottish 80 Shilling, with a distinctive roast and caramel character. Bitter-sweet fruit throughout provides the sweetness typical of a Scottish Heavy.

Stirling Brig (OG 1042, ABV 4.1%)
Brewed to commemorate the 700th anniversary of the Battle of Stirling Bridge in 1297. Classic rich, dark, ruby red ale; a typical Scottish 80 Shilling.

Bannockburn Ale (OG 1044, ABV 4.2%)
Pale golden coloured beer with a complex hoppy and fruity aroma.

Glencoe Wild Oat Stout Organic (OG 1048, ABV 4.5%) ◆
A sweetish stout, surprisingly not dark in colour. Plenty of malt and roast balanced by fruit and finished with a hint of hop.

Wallace Monument (ABV 4.8%)

Lomond Gold Organic (OG 1054, ABV 5%) ◆
A malty, bitter-sweet golden ale with plenty of fruity hop character.

Bridgnorth*

Bridgnorth Brewing Co Ltd, The Old Brewhouse, Kings Head Courtyard, Whitburn Street, Bridgnorth, Shropshire, WV16 4QN
Tel (01746) 762889
Email info@bridgnorthbrewing.com
Website www.bridgnorthbrewing.com

Brewing started in mid-2006 on two five-barrel brew plants from the Rising Sun in Audley. There are plans to add a further five-barrel plant to bring capacity up to 15 barrels. The brewery is on the site of an earlier brewery, which closed some 60 years ago. Some of the old equipment is still in place but not usable. The directors, Richard Beaman, Simon Lucas and Stephen Harris, are planning to open a real ale and wine bar called the Kings Head Stable Bar, which will act as the brewery tap.

Best Bitter (ABV 4%)

Brimstage*

Brimstage Brewing Company, Home Farm, Brimstage, Wirral, CH63 6LY
Tel (0151) 3421181 / (07870) 968323

Brewing started in June 2006 in a 10-barrel plant located in a redundant farm dairy in the heart of the Wirral countryside. This is Wirral's first brewery since the closure of the Birkenhead Brewery in the late 1960s.

Trappers Hat (ABV 3.8%)

Rhode Island Red (ABV 4%)

Scarecrow (ABV 4.2%)

Oystercatcher (ABV 4.6%)

Briscoe's

Briscoe's Brewery, 16 Ash Grove, Otley, West Yorkshire, LS21 3EL
Tel/Fax (01943) 466515
Email briscoe.brewery@virgin.net

The brewery was launched in 1998 by microbiologist/chemist Dr Paul Briscoe in the cellar of his house with a one-barrel brew length. Following a spell brewing on a larger scale at the back of a local pub, Dr Briscoe is currently doing just occasional brews on his original plant. Seasonal beers: Rombalds Reviver (ABV 3.8%), Runner's Ruin (ABV 4.3%), Shane's Shamrock Stout (ABV 4.6%), Chevinbrau Pilsner-style lager (ABV 5.2%), Puddled and Barmy Ale (ABV 5.8%).

Burnsall Classic Bitter (OG 1040, ABV 4%)
A full-flavoured, reddish-coloured bitter with a good hop flavour.

Chevin Chaser (OG 1043, ABV 4.3%)
A refreshing, pale-coloured, all-malt bitter with a distinct hop finish.

Dalebottom Dark (OG 1043, ABV 4.3%)
A smooth and malty strong dark mild with a good hop character.

Badger Stone Bitter (OG 1044, ABV 4.4%)
A classic English bitter, packed with the flavour of malt and hops.

Three Peaks Ale (OG 1045, ABV 4.5%)
A strong, pale premium bitter brewed with only pale malt and traditional hops.

Otley Gold (OG 1043, ABV 4.6%)
A pale, fairly full-flavoured but soft beer brewed in the style of a lager.

Victorian Velvet (OG 1049, ABV 4.9%)
A malty, fruity and smooth copper-coloured special bitter. Small amounts are available bottle-conditioned from the brewery at Christmas.

Bristol Beer Factory

Bristol Brewing Co Ltd, t/a Bristol Beer Factory, Unit A The Old Brewery, Durnford Street, Ashton, Bristol, BS3 2AW
Tel (0117) 902 6317
Fax (0117) 902 6316
Email enquiries@bristolbeerfactory.co.uk
Website www.bristolbeerfactory.co.uk
Tours by arrangement

The brewery was opened in the early 1800s by Thomas Baynton and was taken over in 1865 and registered as the Ashton Gate Brewing Co. There were a couple of name changes in the mid-to-late 1800s and in 1931 it was taken over by Georges & Co and was wound up in 1933. Bristol Brewing Co moved in and began brewing in 2004. The Beer Factory is a 10-barrel micro-brewery. The equipment has undergone major improvements. 25 outlets are supplied.

Red (OG 1038, ABV 3.8%)
Dark ale with slight roast barley taste, fruity aroma and ruby red tint.

No. 7 (OG 1042, ABV 4.2%) ◆
Mid brown, old-fashioned style, malty best bitter. Good body and mouthfeel, some apple-type fruit flavours, with a drying bitter and astringent finish.

Sunrise (OG 1044.5, ABV 4.4%) ◆
Pale, malty, traditional best bitter.

Gold (OG 1048.5, ABV 5%) ◆
Full-bodied and strong-flavoured golden ale. Complex aroma of pineapple and unripe pale fruits with hints of butterscotch and pear drops. A dry and bitter beer with a long, astringent finish and little sweetness.

Broadstone SIBA

Broadstone Brewing Co Ltd, Waterside Brewery, Rum Runner, Wharf Road, Retford, Nottinghamshire, DN22 6EN
Tel (01777) 719797
Fax (01777) 719898
Email broadstone@btconnect.com
Website www.broadstonebrewery.com
Tours by arrangement

Brewing suspended. Owner Alan Gill is looking for new premises.

Brothers*

Brothers Brewing Company Ltd, No. 1 Park Lodge House, Bagots Park Estate, Abbots Bromley, Staffordshire, WS15 3ES
Tel/Fax (01283) 840417
Email pam@brothersbrewing.co.uk
Website www.freedombeer.com
Tours by arrangement

No real ale. Established in 2005 by acquiring Freedom Brewery, Brothers Brewery specialises in lagers produced to the German Reinheitsgebot purity law. It currently produce three lagers. Freedom Organic is suitable for vegetarians and vegans. There are plans to produces cask beer in the future. (See also Bünker). Beers: Freedom Organic Lager (ABV 4.8%), Freedom Pilsener (ABV 5%), Freedom Soho Red (ABV 5%).

Broughton SIBA

Broughton Ales Ltd, Broughton, Biggar, Peebles-shire, ML12 6HQ
Tel (01899) 830345
Fax (01899) 830474
Email beer@broughtonales.co.uk
Website www.broughtonales.co.uk
Shop Mon-Fri 8am-5pm
Tours by arrangement only

⊛ Founded in 1979 in the Scottish Border country, Broughton Ales has been brewing cask beers for more than 25 years but more than 60% of production goes into bottle for sale in Britain and export markets. Seasonal beers: Summer Ale (ABV 3.6%, summer), Winter Fire (ABV 4.2%, winter), Scottish Oatmeal Stout (ABV 4.2%), The Ghillie (ABV 4.5%), Dr Johnson's Definitive (ABV 5%). All bottled beers are suitable for vegetarians and vegans.

The Reiver (OG 1038, ABV 3.8%)
A light-coloured session ale with a predominantly hoppy flavour and aroma on a background of fruity malt. The aftertaste is crisp and clean.

Clipper IPA (OG 1042, ABV 4.2%)
A light-coloured, crisp, hoppy beer with a clean aftertaste.

Bramling Cross (OG 1041, ABV 4.2)
A golden ale with a blend of malt and hop flavours followed by a hoppy aftertaste.

Merlin's Ale (OG 1041, ABV 4.2%) ◆
A well-hopped, fruity flavour is balanced by malt in the taste. The finish is bitter-sweet, light but dry.

Exciseman's 80/- (OG 1045, ABV 4.6%)
A traditional 80/- cask ale. A dark, malty brew. Full drinking with a good hop aftertaste.

Old Jock (OG 1070, ABV 6.7%)
Strong, sweetish and fruity in the finish.

Brown Cow

Brown Cow Brewery, Brown Cow Road, Barlow, Selby, North Yorkshire, YO8 8EH
Tel (01757) 618947
Email susansimpson@browncowbrewery.co.uk

Website www.browncowbrewery.co.uk

Set up by Susan Simpson in 1997, the original 2.5-barrel plant was replaced by a five-barrel unit in 2002. Joined by husband Keith in 2004, they installed additional fermenting vessels in 2006 and currently brew 15 barrels a week. In addition to the three well-established core beers, new one-off recipes are brewed regularly, selecting from the brewery hop stock of at least 20 varieties, especially the more unusual types. The beers are delivered throughout Yorkshire from the brewery and to a small number of outlets in the southern counties. Small-run specialist recipes, such as After Dark Coffee Porter, are also brewed for Suddaby's of Malton with other specialist brews planned. Seasonal beers: Nimbus Wheat Beer (suitable for vegans, ABV 4.8%, spring/summer), 1052 Celebration Ale (ABV 5%, winter). Various bottle-conditioned beers from both the Brown Cow and Suddaby's range are available. All bottle-conditioned beers are suitable for vegetarians.

Bitter (OG 1038, ABV 3.8%) ◆
A well-hopped traditional session bitter.

Old E'fer (OG 1042, ABV 4.4%)
Pale, refreshing bitter brewed with zesty American hops with a clean finish.

Simpsons No. 4 (OG 1043, ABV 4.4%) ◆
Dark and bitter-sweet, full of roast barley character.

For Malton Brewery

After Dark Coffee Porter (OG 1052, ABV 5%)
Full-flavoured porter with complex mix of malts and subtle hint of coffee.

Auld Bob (OG 1062, ABV 6%)
Deep ruby strong ale with rich velvet finish.

Brunswick SIBA

Brunswick Brewery Ltd, 1 Railway Terrace, Derby, DE1 2RU
Tel (01332) 290677
Fax (01332) 370226
Email grahamyates@work.gb.com
Tours by arrangement

⊗ The Brunswick is a purpose-built tower brewery that started brewing in 1991 and is now the city's oldest brewery. A viewing area allows pub users to watch production. Bought by Everards in 2002, it is now a tenancy supplying beers to local outlets and the Everards' estate. Seasonal beer: Rambo (ABV 7.3%, winter).

Mild (OG 1036, ABV 3.6%) ◆
A light-bodied, well-balanced Midlands dark mild with liquorice and hints of coffee on the nose and balanced fruit, caramel and roast in the taste.

Bitter (OG 1036, ABV 3.7%)
Brewed with a little crystal rye malt and flavoured with Styrian hops; a full bodied session bitter, malty with bitter undertones.

Triple Hop (OG 1038, ABV 4%) ◆
A pale gold colour and citrus hop bouquet promise sweetness but the hops deliver a firm, dry, lasting bitterness.

Second Brew (OG 1040, ABV 4%) ◆
This tawny best bitter, also known as The Usual, presents an aroma of sulphur and hops that continue throughout, accompanied by a striking bitterness and astringency.

Railway Porter (OG 1045, ABV 4.3%) ◆
A complex roast aroma can hint at coffee and vanilla, while roast malt dominates the taste, subsiding to a bitter aftertaste.

Triple Gold (OG 1045, ABV 4.5%) ◆
A smooth golden, full-bodied bitter with a pronounced hoppy aroma that develops into a complex fruity and hoppy taste with some sulphur. Long, astringent finish.

Pilsner (ABV 5%)

Old Accidental (OG 1050, ABV 5%)
A well-balanced, malty beer leading to a bitter finish with warming aftertaste. A light, vinous floral hop has underlying malt notes.

Father Mike's Dark Rich Ruby (OG 1055, ABV 5.8%) ◆
A smooth, near black mild with a hint of red. Well-balanced and filled with sweet roast flavours that conceal its strength.

Black Sabbath (OG 1058, ABV 6%)

Bryn

Bragdy'r Bryn Cyfyngedig, Unit 2, Vale Park, Colomendy Industrial Estate, Denbigh, Denbighshire, LL16 5TA
Tel /Fax (01745) 812266
Email info@bragdyrbryn.co.uk
Website www.bragdyrbryn.co.uk

Bryn was launched in 2005 with financial assistance from the Welsh Assembly. Geraint Roberts was a home brewer who then worked for Sharp's in Cornwall (qv) before setting up his own business. He has a five-barrel plant and will add to the beer range. Bottle-conditioned beers are planned for the near future. Some 40 outlets are supplied.

Bitter (OG 1039, ABV 4%) ◆
Full-flavoured bitter with a hoppy aroma leading to a refreshing hop flavour throughout. Good mouthfeel and satisfying finish. Sharp, clean-tasting and drinkable.

Special (OG 1044, ABV 4.5%) ◆
Fruity – blackcurrant – bitter premium beer with a hoppy aroma and a long, dry aftertaste.

Herald (OG 1060, ABV 6.2%) ◆
Classic IPA with citrus hop, bitterness and fruit coming through strongly in the flavour, leading to a long, dry, bitter aftertaste.

Bryncelyn

Bryncelyn Brewery, Wern Fawr Inn, 47 Wern Road, Ystalyfera, Swansea, SA9 2LX
Tel (01639) 843625
Email bryncelynbrewery@aol.com
Website www.bryncelynbrewery.co.uk
Tours by arrangement

⊛ A one-quarter barrel brewery was opened in 1999 by William Hopton (owner) and Robert Scott (brewer). Capacity was increased to its present three-quarter barrel capacity in the same year. As the beer names imply, the owner is fond of Buddy Holly: February 1959 commemorates the singer's death. One pub is owned; beer festivals and take away boxes are supplied. Seasonal beers: Feb 59 (ABV 3.7%), Peggy's Brew (ABV 4.2%, March), May B Baby (ABV 4.5%, May), That Will Be the Sleigh (ABV 6.6%, Dec-Jan).

Holly Hop **(ABV 3.9%)** ◆
Pale amber with a hoppy aroma. A refreshing hoppy, fruity flavour with balancing bitterness; a similar lasting finish. A beer full of flavour for its gravity.

Buddy Marvellous **(OG 1040, ABV 4%)** ◆
Dark brown with an inviting aroma of malt, roast and fruit. A gentle bitterness mixes roast with malt, hops and fruit, giving a complex, satisfying and lasting finish.

Buddy's Delight **(OG 1042, ABV 4.2%)**

Cwrw Celyn **(OG 1044, ABV 4.4%)**

CHH **(OG 1045, ABV 4.5%)** ◆
A pale brown beer with hints of red malt and an inviting hop aroma, with fruit and bitterness adding to the flavour. The finish is clean and hoppy-bitter.

Oh Boy **(OG 1045, ABV 4.5%)** ◆
An inviting aroma of hops, fruit and malt, and a golden colour. The tasty mix of hops, fruit, bitterness and background malt ends with a long, hoppy, bitter aftertaste. Full-bodied and drinkable.

Rave On **(OG 1050, ABV 5%)**

Buddy Confusing **(OG 1050, ABV 5%)**

Bryson's

Bryson's of Lancaster (Brewers) Ltd, Newgate Brewery, White Lund Industrial Estate, Morecambe, Lancashire, LA3 3PT
Tel (01524) 39481
Fax (01524) 382215
Email brysonbrews@supanet.com
Website www.brysonsbrews.co.uk

Bryson's closed in Heysham in 2004. The brewery moved to Morecambe and is now in partnership with Morecambe Bay Wines. The former brewer at Heysham, George Palmer, remains in charge of production. The brewery is planning to expand in 2006/07 to a 20-barrel plant.

Westmorland Bitter **(ABV 3.6%)**

Bryson's Bitter **(ABV 3.8%)** ◆
Light-bodied, easy-drinking session ale.

Shifting Sands **(ABV 3.8%)** ◆
Well-balanced, gold-coloured bitter with firm malt notes and a hoppy aroma.

Hurricane **(ABV 4.1%)**

Barrows Bitter **(ABV 4.2%)** ◆
Full-flavoured, well-balanced golden bitter.

Buffy's SIBA EAB

Buffy's Brewery Ltd, Rectory Road, Tivetshall St Mary, Norwich, Norfolk, NR15 2DD
Tel/Fax (01379) 676523
Email buffysbrewery@gmail.com
Website www.buffys.co.uk

⊠ Buffy's was established in 1993. The brewing capacity is 45 barrels, but a move to bigger premises is in hand. The brewery has one pub, the Cherry Tree at Wicklewood, and there are plans to buy a second pub: the brewery will eventually move to these premises. Some 150 outlets are supplied. Beers are now available in five litre mini kegs. Seasonal beers: Sleigher (ABV 4.1%, Nov-Dec), Hollybeery (ABV 6% December), Festival 9X (ABV 9%, winter), Birthstone Bitters (ABV 4.2%, changes every month).

Norwich Terrier **(OG 1036, ABV 3.6%)** ◆
A fragrant peachy aroma introduces this refreshing, gold-coloured bitter. Strong bitter notes dominate throughout as hops mingle with grapefruit to produce a long, increasingly dry finish.

Bitter **(OG 1039, ABV 3.9%)** ◆
A pale brown beer with a distinctly hoppy nose and grainy feel. A heady combination of bitterness and hops gives a dry astringent feel to the beer. A long, vinous finish.

Lite Relief **(OG 1041.5, ABV 4.1%)** ◆
Hop notes introduce a beer with a definitive dry, hoppy character. Malt fades quickly as the overall dryness develops to a lingering tartness. Pale brown with a chewy mouthfeel.

Mild **(OG 1042, ABV 4.2%)** ◆
A complex brew, deep red with a smooth but grainy feel. Caramel and blackcurrant bolster the heavy malt influence that is the main characteristic of this understated, deceptively strong mild.

Polly's Folly **(OG 1043, ABV 4.3%)** ◆
A jolly mixture of hoppiness, citrus fruit and malt gives this well-balanced offering a lively, satisfying feel. Grapefruit creeps into the flavour mix towards the end as the overall character becomes biscuity dry.

Mucky Duck **(OG 1044, ABV 4.5%)**
Porter style beer. Slightly sweet but with a good bitter edge.

Hopleaf **(OG 1044.5, ABV 4.5%)** ◆
Clean tasting with a pronounced hoppy signature. The singular hop bouquet wanes slightly in the initial taste as malt combines with a sweet fruitiness to give greater depth. Consistent dry finish.

India Ale **(OG 1046, ABV 4.6%)** ◆
Amber coloured with the distinctive hoppy nose of a classic IPA. A subdued malt background does little to diminish the raw hoppiness. An increasingly bitter finale accentuates a grainy mouthfeel.

Norwegian Blue **(OG 1049, ABV 4.9%)** ◆
A gentle hoppy nose belies the rich warming character of the pale brown taste explosion. A complex, ever-changing mix of malt, hops, bitterness and fruit. A long, lingering, bitter-sweet ending.

Festival 9X **(OG 1090, ABV 9.0%)**
A fine, old-fashioned ale, dark amber in colour.

Bull Box*

Bull Box Brewery, Oak Farm, Stradsett, Kings Lynn, Norfolk, PE33 9HH

Tel (01366) 385349/07920 163116
Email bullboxinfo@msn.com

Bull Box Brewery was launched early in 2006 and operates on a two-barrel plant based in Stradsett. They are plans for bottle-conditioned ales.

Bull Box Bitter (ABV 4%)

Mid Life Crisis (ABV 4.5%)

Kerb Crawler (ABV 5.2%)

Bull Lane

Bull Lane Brewing Company, The Clarendon, 143 High Street East, Sunderland, Tyne & Wear, SR1 2BL
Tel (0191) 510 3200

The brewery opened in 2005 in the cellar of the oldest pub in Sunderland, the Clarendon, on a 2.5-barrel plant. In addition to the Clarendon, beers are also supplied to the Beamish Mary and the Sun Inn at Beamish Museum in Co Durham. The beer names all have a strong Sunderland connection. There are plans to increase brewing capacity to meet the demand for the beers.

Nowtsa Matter (OG 1037, ABV 3.7%)

Black Barrel (OG 1038, ABV 3.8%)

Ryhope Tug (OG 1039, ABV 3.9%)

Jack's Flag (OG 1047, ABV 4.7%)

Bullmastiff SIBA

Bullmastiff Brewery, 14 Bessemer Close, Leckwith, Cardiff, CF11 8DL
Tel/Fax (029) 2066 5292

⊗ An award-winning small craft brewery run by brothers Bob and Paul Jenkins since 1987. The name stems from their love of the bullmastiff breed. They have no ambitions for expansion or owning any pubs, preferring to concentrate on quality control. 30 outlets are supplied. Seasonal beers: Summer Moult (ABV 4.3%), Mogadog (ABV 10%, winter).

Welsh Gold (OG 1039, ABV 3.8%) ◘ ◆
A hoppy and fruity aroma leads into the same strong juicy blend of flavours. Bitter-sweet initially, an easy-drinking and refreshing beer.

Jack the Lad (OG 1041, ABV 4.1%)

Thoroughbred (OG 1046, ABV 4.5%) ◆
A good hop aroma leads to a hoppy flavour with accompanying fruit, malt and balancing bitterness. There is a quenching hoppy bitterness in the finish of this amber brew.

Welsh Red (OG 1048, ABV 4.8%)

Welsh Black (OG 1050, ABV 4.8%)

Brindle (OG 1050, ABV 5.1%) ◆
A full-bodied, flavoursome pale beer. Good hop aroma with a mix of malt, hops, fruit and bitterness in the taste. A lasting and satisfying finish.

Son of a Bitch (OG 1062, ABV 6%) ◙ ◘ ◆
A complex, warming amber ale with a tasty blend of hops, malt and fruit flavours, with increasing bitterness. Champion Beer of Wales 2005/2006.

Bünker

Bünker Bar, 41 Earlham Street, Covent Garden, London, WC2H 9LD
Tel (020) 7240 0606
Fax (020) 7240 4422
Email info@bunkerbar.com
Website www.bunkerbar.com

A fully working micro-brewery brewing Freedom lager – see entry for Brothers Brewing Co.

Buntingford SIBA

Buntingford Brewery Co Ltd, Greys Brewhouse, Therfield Road, Royston, Hertfordshire, SG8 9NW
Tel (01763) 250749 / 07947 214058
Email catherine@buntingford-brewery.co.uk
Website www.buntingford-brewery.co.uk
Tours by arrangement

Buntingford Brewery started in 2001 and got going commercially in 2003 when production was temporarily transferred to Leicestershire. In autumn 2005 production started in its own custom-designed premises at the edge of Therfield Heath near Royston. A 15-barrel plant is in use, which is capable of producing up to 45 barrels a week. Locally grown barley is used whenever possible, including from the surrounding fields, all floor malted by Warminster Maltings. The brewery is located on a conservation farm: all brewery waste liquids are treated in a reedbed and plans are in hand to make full use of green energy sources. Beers are delivered over a wide area. Occasional and seasonal beers: Royston Red (ABV 4.8%), Grey Partridge (ABV 4%, autumn/winter), Night Owl Porter (ABV 4.2%).

Pargetters (ABV 3.7%)
A traditional style dark mild.

Challenger (ABV 3.8%)
Pale session beer with citrus hop flavours.

Royston Pale Ale (ABV 4.3%)
Golden best bitter.

Oatmeal Stout (ABV 4.4%)
A quaffing stout with oats and plenty of hop flavour.

Britannia (ABV 4.4%)
Light brown best bitter.

Silence (ABV 5.2%)
Lager malt and American hops combine with a strong citrus character.

Burrington SIBA

Burrington Brewery, Homelands Business Centre, Burrington, Devon, EX37 9JJ
Tel (01805) 622813 / 07986 009295
Email info@burringtonbrewery.co.uk

Website www.burringtonbrewery.co.uk
Tours by arrangement

Burrington is a traditional brewery in north Devon. It was established in a custom made building in 2003 by Craig Carter, proprietor and brewer. The five-barrel brewery supplies many outlets in north Devon and north east Cornwall and pubs further afield through wholesalers. Seasonal Beer: Barley Mow (ABV 3.8%, summer). Bottle-conditioned beers: Tippled Newt, Azza Newt, Newt 'n' Wriggly.

Ruby Newt Mild (ABV 3.6%)

Tippled Newt (ABV 3.8%)

Azza Newt (ABV 4%)

Alchemy (ABV 4.2%)

DNA (Dark Newt Ale) (ABV 4.4%)

Newt 'n' Wriggly (ABV 4.6%)

Newt-rition (ABV 5.2%)

Burton Bridge SIBA

Burton Bridge Brewery Ltd, 24 Bridge Street, Burton upon Trent, Staffordshire, DE14 1SY
Tel (01283) 510573
Fax (01283) 515594
Email bbb@burtonbridgebrewery.fsnet.co.uk
Website www.burtonbridgebrewery.co.uk
Shop Bridge Inn 11.30am-2pm, 5-11pm
Tours by arrangement

☺ A brewery established in 1982 by Bruce Wilkinson and Geoff Mumford, two refugees from Allied Breweries who finished up at Ind Coope of Romford. Burton Bridge now has four tenanted pubs in the town, including an enlarged, CAMRA award-winning brewery tap. It also supplies 300 outlets. There are many seasonal beers. Bottle-conditioned beers: Burton Porter (ABV 4.5%), Empire Pale Ale (ABV 7.5%), Bramble Stout (ABV 5%), Tickle Brain (ABV 8%).

Golden Delicious (OG 1037, ABV 3.8%) ◆
Golden as named, fruity as intended and tasty as anticipated. This beer is a Burton classic, with sulphurous aroma, well-balanced hops and fruit, and a mouth-watering bitter finish.

XL Bitter (OG 1039, ABV 4%) ◆
A golden, malty bitter, with fruity and hoppy aromas. Hoppy and bitter finish with a characteristic astringent aftertaste.

Bridge Bitter (OG 1041, ABV 4.2%) ◆
Pale brown and hoppy with a hint of roast and caramel. Complex taste with hops just dominating to provide a lingering hoppy finish.

Burton Porter (OG 1044, ABV 4.5%) ◆
Amazingly red with a pure white head. Sweet caramel aroma with some hops. Fruity taste combining with liquorice and hops develop an astringent bitterness but with lots of supporting flavours.

Stairway to Heaven (OG 1049, ABV 5%) ◆
Golden bitter. A perfectly balanced beer. The malty and hoppy start leads to a hoppy body with some astringency.

Top Dog Stout (OG 1049, ABV 5%) ◆
Black and rich with a roast and malty start. Very fruity and abundant hops give a fruity, bitter finish with a mouth-watering edge.

Festival Ale (OG 1054, ABV 5.5%) ◆
Pale brown with a fruity aroma. Fruity start reminiscent of Christmas pudding ingredients; sweet fruity finish that develops to bitterness.

Thomas Sykes (OG 1095, ABV 10%) ◆
Very rich and warming, fruity, heady and hoppy. A true barley wine to be handled with caution.

Burtonwood

Thomas Hardy Burtonwood Ltd, Bold Lane, Burtonwood, Warrington, Cheshire, WA5 4PJ
Tel (01925) 220022
Fax (01925) 224562
Website www.thomashardybrewery.co.uk
Tours by arrangement for a charge

Following the sale of 60% of its brewing operation to Thomas Hardy in 1998, Burtonwood sold the remaining 40% in 2004 to become solely a pub-owning group that was bought by Wolverhampton & Dudley (qv) in 2005. Burtonwood is now Thomas Hardy's only brewery, run by Peter Ward as a contract operation, principally for Scottish Courage.

For Scottish Courage:

Webster's Green Label (OG 1032, ABV 3.2%)

Webster's Yorkshire Bitter (OG 1035, ABV 3.5%)

Bushy's SIBA

Mount Murray Brewing Co Ltd, Mount Murray, Braddan, Isle of Man, IM4 1JE
Tel/Fax (01624) 661244
Email bushys@manx.net
Website www.bushys.com
Tours by arrangement

☺ Set up in 1986 as a brew-pub, Bushy's moved to its present site in 1990 when demand outgrew capacity. It owns four tied houses and the beers are also supplied to 25 other outlets. Bushy's goes one step further than the Manx Pure Beer Law, which permits only malt, hops, sugar and yeast, preferring the German Reinheitsgebot (Pure Beer Law) that excludes sugar. Seasonal beers are numerous – see website.

Castletown Bitter (OG 1035, ABV 3.5%)

Ruby (1874) Mild (OG 1035, ABV 3.5%)

Bitter (OG 1038, ABV 3.8%) ◆
An aroma full of pale malt and hops introduces you to a beautifully hoppy, bitter beer. Despite the predominant hop character, malt is also evident. Fresh and clean-tasting.

Old Bushy Tail (OG 1045, ABV 4.5%)

Piston Brew (OG 1045, ABV 4.5%)

Weiss Beer (OG 1040, ABV 4.5%)
Naturally cloudy.

Butcombe SIBA

Butcombe Brewery Ltd, Cox's Green, Wrington, Bristol, BS40 5PA

Tel (01934) 863963
Fax (01934) 863903
Email info@butcombe.com
Website www.butcombe.com
Shop Mon-Fri 9am-5pm; Sat 9am-12pm
Tours by arrangement

⊗ One of the most successful of the newer breweries, set up in 1978 by a former Courage Western director, Simon Whitmore, this West Country independent gained a considerable reputation for its quality beers. The brewery has doubled in size three times. Simon Whitmore sold the brewery to Guy Newell (the founder of the Beer Seller and now Butcombe's managing director) and friends in 2003. A new 14,000 sq ft brewery was built in 2004 on a new site. Butcombe has an estate of nine houses (although none are tied) and it also supplies 350 other outlets direct from the brewery, and a similar number via wholesalers and pub companies. Butcombe's beers contain no added sugars, colourings or preservatives, and are available from the brewery to outlets within a 50-mile radius and nationally via selected wholesalers and pub companies. Seasonal beer: Brunel (ABV 5%, Nov-March).

Bitter (OG 1039, ABV 4%) ◆
Amber-coloured, malty and notably bitter beer, with subtle citrus fruit qualities. Hoppy, malty, citrus and a very slightly sulphur aroma, and a long, dry, bitter finish with light fruit notes.

Blond (ABV 4.3%) ◆
Crisp and refreshing pale, hoppy best bitter. Floral and fruity hops predominate, balanced by a slight sweetness, followed by a clean and quenching finish.

Gold (OG 1047, ABV 4.7%) ◻ ◆
Aroma of pale malt, citrus hops and fruit. Medium bodied, well-balanced, with good pale malt, hops and bitterness. Yellow-gold in colour, it is quite fruity, slightly sweet, with an abiding dryness.

Butler's SIBA

Butler's Brewery Co Ltd, Whittles Farm, Mapledurham, Oxfordshire, RG4 7UP
Tel/Fax (0118) 972 3201
Email butlerbrew@aol.com
Website www.butlersbrewery.co.uk

The brewery was started by Mark and Sarah Butler in 2003. An old cart shed was converted into a brewery and a six-barrel plant was installed. Expansion plans are underway, including a new purpose-built building for a bottling plant. All hops are sourced from a local producer. 30-40 outlets are supplied. Bottle-conditioned beers: Whittles (ABV 5%), Old Specific (ABV 5.9%).

Oxfordshire Bitter (OG 1036.6, ABV 3.6%)

Butts SIBA

Butts Brewery Ltd, Northfield Farm, Wantage Road, Great Shefford, Hungerford, Berkshire, RG17 7BY
Tel (01488) 648133
Fax (01488) 648134
Email enquiries@buttsbrewery.com
Website www.buttsbrewery.com
Tours by arrangement

⊗ The brewery was set up in a converted Dutch barn in 1994. Apart from pubs, Butts also supplies a handful of local supermarkets with bottle-conditioned beers. In 2002, the brewery took the decision to become dedicated to organic production: all the beers brewed use organic malted barley and organic hops when suitable varieties are available. All beers are certified by the Soil Association. Some 60 outlets are supplied. Bottle-conditioned beers: Blackguard, Barbus Barbus, Golden Brown, Le Butts.

Jester Organic (OG 1035, ABV 3.5%) ◻ ◆
A pale brown session bitter with a hoppy aroma and a hint of fruit. The taste balances malt, hops, fruit and bitterness with a hoppy aftertaste.

Traditional (OG 1040, ABV 4%) ◆
A pale brown bitter that is quite soft on the tongue, with hoppy citrus flavours accompanying a gentle, bitter-sweetness. A long, dry aftertaste is dominated by fruity hops.

Blackguard (OG 1045, ABV 4.5%) ◆
A porter with caramel, malt, roast and fruit dominating the aroma. The taste is a combination of sweet, malt and roast undertones and a hoppy finish.

Barbus Barbus (OG 1046, ABV 4.6%) ◻ ◆
Golden ale with a hoppy aroma and a hint of malt. Hops dominate taste and aftertaste, accompanied by fruitiness and bitterness, with a hint of balancing sweetness

Golden Brown (OG 1050, ABV 5%)

Le Butts (OG 1050, ABV 5%)
Brewed with lager yeast and hops resulting in a crisp and refreshing European style beer.

Cains SIBA

Robert Cain & Co Ltd, Stanhope Street, Liverpool, Merseyside, L8 5XJ
Tel (0151) 709 8734
Fax (0151) 708 8395
Email info@cains.co.uk
Website www.cains.co.uk
Shop – Brewery Tap open during pub hours
Tours by arrangement

◎ The Dusanj brothers, Ajmail and Sudarghara, bought the brewery in 2002 and have invested heavily in the red brick Victorian plant. They have won many awards for their beers. Cains launched 2008 Ale in support of Liverpool's successful bid for European Capital of Culture, while Fine Raisin Beer won the 2003 Tesco Beer Challenge. In 2004 the brothers launched Cains Lager, which is lagered (cold conditioned) for 90 days. A cask version was launched in 2005. Twelve pubs are owned, more are planned, and around 400 outlets are supplied by the brewery. Seasonal beers: Raisin Beer (ABV 5%, Nov-Dec), Victorian Ale (ABV 6%, Jan-Feb), Triple Hop (ABV 4.5%, March-April), Sundowner (ABV 4.5%, July-Aug), Dragonheart (ABV 5%, Sept-Oct), Creamy Stout (ABV 4.1%).

Dark Mild **(OG 1034.5, ABV 3.2%)** ◆
A smooth, dry and roasty dark mild, with some chocolate and coffee notes.

IPA **(OG 1036, ABV 3.5%)**

Traditional Bitter **(OG 1041, ABV 4%)** ◆
A darkish, full-bodied and fruity bitter, with a good hoppy nose and a dry aftertaste.

Formidable Ale **(OG 1049, ABV 5%)** ◆
A bitter and hoppy beer with a good dry aftertaste. Sharp, clean and dry.

2008 **(OG 1049, ABV 5%)**

Cask Lager **(OG 1048, ABV 5%)**

Cairngorm SIBA

Cairngorm Brewery Co Ltd, Unit 12 Dalfaber Industrial Estate, Aviemore, Highlands, PH22 1ST
Tel (01479) 812222
Fax (01479) 811465
Email info@cairngormbrewery.com
Website www.cairngormbrewery.com
Shop Mon-Fri 9am-4.30pm (Online shop also available)
Tours by arrangement

Based in Aviemore in the shadow of the Cairngorms, the brewery has enjoyed much success since winning Champion Beer of Scotland in 2004 and 2005, and gold medals at GBBF in 2004 and 2005. Seven regular cask beers are produced along with a rolling programme of seasonal ales throughout the year. Expansion was completed in spring 2005 taking fermentation capacity to 90 barrels. The free trade is supplied as far as the central belt with national delivery via wholesalers. Seasonal beers (available for more than one month): White Lady (ABV 4.7%, spring), Blessed Thistle (ABV 4.5%, summer).

Stag **(OG 1040, ABV 4.1%)** ◆
A drinkable best bitter with plenty of hop bitterness throughout. This tawny brew has some malt in the lingering bitter aftertaste.

Trade Winds **(OG 1043, ABV 4.3%)** ◆
A truly intense, fruity, speciality beer with a strong hop character and grapefruit notes throughout. Bitter-sweetness does not come more intense than this Champion Beer of Scotland and winner of the Speciality class at GBBF 2004.

Black Gold **(OG 1044, ABV 4.4%)**

Nessies Monster Mash **(OG 1044, ABV 4.4%)** ◆
A good, traditional, English-type bitter with plenty of bitterness and with light malt to balance. The sweetness diminishes in the aftertaste but the bitterness lingers.

Cairngorm Gold **(OG 1044, ABV 4.5%)**

Sheepshaggers Gold **(OG 1044, ABV 4.5%)** ◆
A golden amber brew with some malt and hop character but balanced on the sweetish side.

Wildcat **(OG 1049.5, ABV 5.1%)** ◆
This brew has varied but it is now generally strong on bitterness and at its best is a fine strong bitter. Some malt and fruit but with an accent on hops and bitterness throughout.

Caledonian

Caledonian Brewing Company Ltd, 42 Slateford Road, Edinburgh, EH11 1PH
Tel (0131) 337 1286
Fax (0131) 313 2370
Email info@caledonian-brewery.co.uk
Website www.caledonian-brewery.co.uk
Tours by arrangement

The brewery was founded by Lorimer and Clark in 1869 and was run by them until being sold to Vaux of Sunderland in 1919. In 1987 the brewery was saved from closure by a management buy-out and the Caledonian Brewing Company was established. The brewery site was purchased by Scottish Courage in 2004 but is operated on their behalf by the Caledonian Brewing Company. The Caledonian Brewing Company Ltd is still an independently owned company, and owns and brews Deuchars IPA, Caledonian 80/- and a rolling programme of seasonal ales. CBC also brews the McEwans range of ales on behalf of Scottish & Newcastle. Early in 2006, CBC bought the Harviestoun Brewery (qv).

Deuchars IPA **(OG 1039, ABV 3.8%)** ◆
At its best, an extremely tasty and refreshing, amber-coloured session beer. Hops and fruit are evident and are balanced by malt throughout. The lingering aftertaste is delightfully bitter and hoppy.

Caledonian 80/- **(OG 1042, ABV 4.1%)** ◆
A predominantly malty, copper-coloured beer with underlying fruit. A Scottish heavy that now lacks the complex taste and hoppiness of old.

For Scottish & Newcastle

McEwan's 80/- **(OG 1042, ABV 4.2%)** ◆
This sweet, fruity beer has improved since its move from S&N's Fountainbridge site, but still lacks the body and complexity of a true 'heavy'.

Callow Top

See Haywood Bad Ram

Cambridge Moonshine

Cambridge Moonshine Brewery, 28 Radegund Road, Cambridge, Cambridgeshire, CB1 3RS
Tel (07906) 066794
Email mark.watch@ntlworld.com

A micro-brewery established in 2004. The first beers were launched at the 31st Cambridge Beer Festival where Mulberry Bitter was voted champion beer of the festival. A new self-built 2.5-barrel brewplant was installed in 2006. Plans for the future are to move to larger premises. The brewery concentrates on supplying CAMRA beer festivals, with two outlets supplied direct. Bottle-conditioned beers: Porter (ABV 5.8%), Red Watch, Mulberry Whale.

Harvest Moon Mild **(OG 1040, ABV 3.8%)**

Mulberry Whale Bitter **(OG 1040, ABV 4%)**

Red Watch Blueberry Ale (OG 1042, ABV 4.4%)

Black Hole Stout (OG 1044, ABV 4.5%)

Pigs Ear Porter (OG 1048, ABV 4.7%)

Cambrinus SIBA

Cambrinus Craft Brewery, Home Farm, Knowsley Park, Knowsley, Merseyside, L34 4AQ
Tel (0151) 546 2226
Email cambrinus@ukonline.co.uk

⊗ Established and run by John Aspinall since 1997, Cambrinus is housed in part of a former farm building on a private estate. It produces around 250 hectolitres a year on a five-barrel plant. Some 45 outlets are supplied on a regular basis in and around Lancashire, Cheshire and Cumbria. There were plans to supply own label beer to Knowsley Safari Park in filtered bottle form in 2006. Seasonal beers: Bootstrap (ABV 4.5%, spring), Fruit Wheat Beer (summer), St Georges Ale (ABV 4.5%, April), Clogdance (ABV 3.6%, May), Solstice (ABV 3.8%, June), Honeywheat (ABV 3.7%, July), Dark Harvest (ABV 4%, autumn), Hearts of Oak (ABV 5%, October), Parkin (ABV 3.8%, November), Lamp Oil (ABV 4.5%, winter), Celebrance (ABV 5.5%, Christmas).

Herald (OG 1036, ABV 3.7%)
Light summer drinking bitter, pale and refreshing.

Yardstick (OG 1040, ABV 4%)
Mild, malty and lightly hopped.

Deliverance (OG 1040, ABV 4.2%)
Pale premium bitter.

Endurance (OG 1045, ABV 4.3%)
IPA-style, smooth and hoppy, fermented with oak.

Camerons

Camerons Brewery Ltd, Lion Brewery, Hartlepool, Co Durham, TS24 7QS
Tel (01429) 266666
Fax (01429) 868195
Email martindutoy@cameronsbrewery.com
Website www.cameronsbrewery.com
Shop Tue-Sun 10am-4pm
Tours by arrangement

⊕ Founded in 1865, Camerons has had a topsy-turvy existence from the 1970s, owned in turn by Ellerman Shipping Lines, the Barclay Brothers, Brent Walker and Wolverhampton & Dudley. In 2002 the Castle Eden brewery bought Camerons and moved all production to Hartlepool. In 2003 a 12-barrel micro-brewery, known as the Lion's Den, was commissioned in a separate building. This gives the company the capability of brewing small batches of guest beers and includes a bottling line, recently upgraded. Nine pubs are owned, with four selling cask beer. Some 36 pubs are supplied. Seasonal beers: Spring Knights (ABV 4%), Summer Knights (ABV 4.2%), Autumn Knights (ABV 4.2%), Winter Royal Knights (ABV 5%).

Bitter (OG 1036, ABV 3.6%) ◆
A light bitter, but well-balanced, with hops and malt.

Strongarm (OG 1041, ABV 4%) ◆
A well-rounded, ruby-red ale with a distinctive, tight creamy head; initially fruity, but with a good balance of malt, hops and moderate bitterness.

Castle Eden Ale (OG 1043, ABV 4.2%) ◆
A light, creamy, malty sweet ale with fruit notes and a mellow dry bitterness in the finish.

Nimmos XXXX (OG 1045, ABV 4.4%) ◆
Light golden beer with a well-balanced character derived from English malt and Goldings hops.

Canavans*

Canavans Liverpool Brewery, Unit 29 Barclays Business Park, Wareing Road, Aintree, Liverpool, L9 7AU
Tel (07951) 210972
Tours by arrangement

Anthony Canavan has been brewing since October 2005. His five-barrel plant was purchased in 2004. 10 outlets are supplied direct. There were plans to expand the current range in 2006.

Two Churches Bitter (OG 1040, ABV 4.5%) ◆
Fairly bitter brown beer with malt and hop flavours balanced.

Dublin to Liverpool Stout (OG 1040, ABV 4.5%) ◆
Dry stout with a long, dry aftertaste. Sharp acidic bite leads to an intense roast flavour that follows through to the aftertaste.

Milligans Lager (OG 1042, ABV 4.7%)

Cannon Royall SIBA

⊄ Cannon Royall Brewery Ltd, Fruiterer's Arms, Uphampton, Ombersley, Worcestershire, WR9 0JW
Tel (01905) 621161
Fax (01562) 743262
Email info@cannonroyall.co.uk
Website www.cannonroyall.co.uk
Tours by arrangement (CAMRA only)

Cannon Royall's first brew was in 1993, in a converted cider house behind the Fruiterer's Arms. It has increased capacity from five barrels to more than 16 a week. The brewery supplies a number of outlets throughout the Midlands. Seasonal beers are regularly produced. Bottle-conditioned beers: Fruiterers Mild, King's Shilling, Arrowhead Bitter and Muzzle Loader.

Fruiterer's Mild (OG 1037, ABV 3.7%) ◆
This black-hued brew has rich malty aromas that lead to a fruity mix of bitter hops and sweetness, and a short balanced aftertaste.

King's Shilling (OG 1038, ABV 3.8%) ◆
A golden bitter that packs a citrus hoppy punch throughout.

Arrowhead Bitter (OG 1039, ABV 3.9%) ◆
A powerful punch of hops attack the nose before the feast of bitterness. The memory of this golden brew fades too soon.

Muzzle Loader (OG 1042, ABV 4.2%) ◆
The lingering aftertaste bears witness to this amber liquid's agreeable balance of malt and hoppy flavours that is evident in the aroma and palate.

Captain Cook SIBA

Captain Cook Brewery Ltd, White Swan, 1 West End, Stokesley, North Yorkshire, TS9 5BL
Tel (01642) 710263
Fax (01642) 714245
Email joonanbri@aol.com
Website www.thecaptaincookbrewery.co.uk
Tours by arrangement

The 18th-century White Swan concentrated on promoting real ale for 10 years before taking on the challenge of becoming a brew-pub. The brewery, with a four-barrel plant, started operations in 1999 and was opened by White Swan regular James Cook on his 79th birthday. Seasonal beer: Black Porter (ABV 4.4%, autumn/winter).

Sunset (OG 1040, ABV 4%)
An extremely smooth light ale with a good balance of malt and hops.

Slipway (OG 1042, ABV 4%)
A light-coloured hoppy ale with bitterness coming through from Challenger hops. A full-flavoured ale with a smooth malt aftertaste.

Castle Rock SIBA

Castle Rock Brewery, Queens Bridge Road, Nottingham, NG2 1NB
Tel (0115) 985 1615
Fax (0115) 985 1611
Email castle.rock@btconnect.com
Website www.castlerockbrewery.co.uk
Tours by arrangement

Castle Rock has been brewing next door to the Vat & Fiddle pub since 1998; the brewery is a trading division of the Tynemill pub group. Production now runs at around 80 barrels a week and is distributed on a local and nationwide basis through inter-brewery swaps and a network of wholesalers. It also supplies the Tynemill estate with its own and reciprocated beers. Work to complete a brewery visitor centre, which will provide a viewing area to allow Vat & Fiddle customers to watch the brewery at work, should be completed shortly. See website for full and up to date details. Seasonal beers: Nottingham Dark Stout (ABV 4.5%, winter), Snowhite (ABV 4.2%). Bottle-conditioned beer: Elsie Mo.

Black Gold (OG 1035, ABV 3.5%)
Hints of caramel and fruit balanced by bitterness in this dark mild.

Nottingham Gold (OG 1035, ABV 3.5%)
Full flavoured for its strength. A subtle toffee sweetness quickly gives way to a crisp dryness. Used as the house beer in many Tynemill pubs.

Harvest Pale (OG 1037, ABV 3.8%)
Assertive citrus hop bitterness with some underlying sweetness leading to a refreshing zesty finish that lingers.

Hemlock (OG 1040, ABV 4%)
Aromas of dried fruit enhance this well-rounded, bitter-sweet session beer.

Elsie Mo (OG 1045, ABV 4.7%)
Blond beer with a subtle floral nose and lemongrass freshness delivering a clean finish.

Caythorpe SIBA

Brewery: Caythorpe Brewery Ltd, c/o Black Horse, 29 Main Street, Caythorpe, Nottinghamshire, NG14 7ED
Office: Caythorpe Brewery Ltd, Trentham Cottage, Boat Lane, Hoveringham, Nottingham, Nottinghamshire, NG14 7JP
Tel (0115) 966 4933 / 07913 434922
Email johnsandrastachura@btinternet.com

Caythorpe was set up in 1997. Although there is a new owner who is being taught the brewing skills, founder Geoff Slack continues to head the brewing team. The beers are supplied to local outlets.

Cocker Beck (OG 1034.7, ABV 3.7%)

Dover Beck (OG 1037, ABV 4%)

Old Nottingham Extra Pale Ale (OG 1038.6, ABV 4.2%)

Stout Fellow (OG 1038.6, ABV 4.2%)

Ceredigion

Office: Bragdy Ceredigion Brewery, Bryn Hawk, New Quay, Ceredigion, SA45 9SB
Brewery: Bragdy Ceredigion Brewery, Unit 2 Wervil Grange Farm, Pentregat, Ceredigion, SA44 6HW
Tel (01239) 654888
Tours by arrangement

Bragdy Ceredigion (Cardigan Brewery) is situated on the coastal belt of West Wales and housed in a converted barn on Wervil Grange Farm. A family-run craft brewery established in 1997 by Brian and Julia Tilby, it produces bottle-conditioned and cask-conditioned ales. No chemical additives are used and the bottle-conditioned beers are suitable for vegans. A range of fruit beers is planned. Seasonal beer: Nadolig (ABV 6.2%, Christmas). Bottle-conditioned beers: as for cask beers, save for the Spirit of the Forest.

Ysbryd O'r Goeden/Spirit of the Forest (OG 1036, ABV 3.8%)

Gwrach Ddu/Black Witch (OG 1038, ABV 4%)

Draig Aur/Gold Dragon (OG 1039, ABV 4.2%)

Barcud Coch/Red Kite (OG 1040, ABV 4.3%)

Merlin (ABV 4.5%)
A dark premium bitter.

Morwen (ABV 5%)

Yr Hen Darw Du/Old Black Bull (OG 1058, ABV 6.2%)
A rich, dark stout.

Chalk Hill

Chalk Hill Brewery, Rosary Road, Norwich, Norfolk, NR1 4DA
Tel/Fax (01603) 477078

Run by former Reindeer brew-pub owner Bill Thomas and his partners Tiny Little and Dave Blake, Chalk Hill began production with a 15-barrel plant in 1993. It is developing plans for expansion and new brews, and supplies its own pub. The beers are also available nationwide via beer agencies. Occasional beer: IPA (ABV 5.3%).

Tap Bitter (OG 1036, ABV 3.6%) ◆
A pale brown brew with a gentle fruity nose. Lightly flavoured with swirling apple notes among a malty support. Steeply fading finish with a hint of bitterness.

CHB (OG 1042, ABV 4.2%) ◆
A copper-coloured brew with a dominant bitter flavour. Hops in the bouquet continue through to add to the prevailing bitterness and give a dry, lingering aftertaste. Background maltiness give balance.

Dreadnought (OG 1049, ABV 4.9%) ◆
A heavy malt-based, mid-brown beer with a slight hoppiness providing balance to the roast and caramel undertones. A subtle change in the ending creates a deeper roast finish.

Flintknapper's Mild (OG 1052, ABV 5%) ◆
Chocolate, stewed fruits, liquorice, hops and malt can all be found in this rich, red-coloured brew. The light malt nose belies the variety of flavours. Rich and sticky.

Old Tackle (OG 1056, ABV 5.6%) ◆
Red hued with a matching blackcurrant bouquet, this rich malty brew slowly subsides to a long dryish end. Roast notes remain consistent as initial caramel declines to an echo.

Cheriton SIBA

Cheriton Brewhouse, Cheriton, Alresford, Hampshire, SO24 0QQ
Tel (01962) 771166
Fax (01962) 771595
Email bestbeer1@aol.com
Tours by arrangement

⊗ The brewery closed at the end of April 2006 as a result of a legal dispute with the owner of the Flower Pots pub, for which it mainly brewed. The two working partners in the brewery, Ray Page and Martin Roberts, hope to start brewing again but under a different name.

Chiltern SIBA

Chiltern Brewery, Nash Lee Road, Terrick, Aylesbury, Buckinghamshire, HP17 0TQ
Tel (01296) 613647
Fax (01296) 612419
Email info@chilternbrewery.co.uk
Website www.chilternbrewery.co.uk
Shop Mon-Sat 9am-5pm
Tours by arrangement every Saturday at noon and weekdays for groups

⊗ The Chiltern Brewery is a second generation independent family brewery run by the Jenkinsons. Founded in 1980, the brewery produces a broad range of beers, both draught and bottled, using traditional methods with English ingredients. The spring of 2004 saw the culmination of 18 months of investment in the brewery, with a new brewhouse and brew-plant, a temperature-controlled cool room for conditioning and storing the beer, and improvements to the fermenting room. In 2005, the 25th anniversary year, they took over the running of the bar in the National Trust owned Kings Head in Aylesbury, while founders Richard and Lesley Jenkinson have handed over the day-to-day running of the business to their sons, George and Tom. George runs the Kings Head and organises sales of the beers at farmers' markets, while Tom is head brewer. Seasonal beers: Cobblestones (ABV 3.5%, summer), Glad Tidings (ABV 4.6%, winter). Bottle-conditioned beers: Glad Tidings, Bodgers Barley Wine (ABV 8.5%).

Chiltern Ale (OG 1037, ABV 3.7%) ◆
An amber, refreshing beer with a slight fruit aroma, leading to a good malt/bitter balance in the mouth. The aftertaste is bitter and dry but not overpowering.

Beechwood Bitter (OG 1043, ABV 4.3%) ◆
This pale brown beer has a balanced butterscotch/toffee aroma, with a slight hop note. The taste balances bitterness and sweetness, leading to a long bitter finish, but with slight initial sweetness.

Three Hundreds Old Ale (OG 1049, ABV 4.9%) ◆
A complex, copper-coloured, strong old ale. The mixed fruit/caramel aroma leads to a balanced taste, with sweetness slightly dominating. The finish starts sweet and leads to a long-lasting bitterness.

Church End SIBA

Church End Brewery Ltd, Ridge Lane, Nuneaton, Warwickshire, CV10 0RD
Tel (01827) 713080
Fax (01827) 717328
Shop during tap opening hours
Tours by arrangement
⊗ Stewart Elliot started brewing in 1994 in an old coffin shop next to the Griffin, Shustoke. He moved to the present site and upgraded to a 10-barrel plant in 2001. The

brewery tap was opened on the same site a year later. He has a sideline producing beers using fruit, herbs and spices. Future plans include building a small tied pub estate. Some 500 outlets are supplied. Seasonal beers: Without-a-Bix (ABV 4.2%), Pooh Bear (ABV 4.3%).

Poachers Pocket (ABV 3.5%)

Cuthberts (ABV 3.8%) ◈
A refreshing, hoppy beer, with hints of malt, fruit and caramel taste. Lingering bitter aftertaste.

Goat's Milk (ABV 3.8%)

Gravediggers Ale (ABV 3.8%) ◈
A premium mild. Black and red in colour, with a complex mix of chocolate and roast flavours, it is almost a light porter.

Hop Gun (ABV 4.1%)

What the Fox's Hat (ABV 4.2%) ◈
A beer with a malty aroma, and a hoppy and malty taste with some caramel flavour.

Vicar's Ruin (ABV 4.4%) ◈
A straw-coloured best bitter with an initially hoppy, bitter flavour, softening to a delicate malt finish.

Stout Coffin (ABV 4.6%)

Fallen Angel (ABV 5%)

City of Cambridge EAB

City of Cambridge Brewery Co Ltd, Ely Road, Chittering, Cambridge, CB5 9PH
Tel (01223) 864864
Email sales@cambridge-brewery.co.uk
Website www.cambridge-brewery.co.uk

⊗ City of Cambridge opened in 1997 and moved to its present site in 2002. In addition to prizes for its cask beers, the brewery holds a conservation award for the introduction of native reed beds at its site to naturally treat its brewery water. Seasonal ales (subject to availability): Jet Black (ABV 3.7%), Bramling Traditional (ABV 5.5%), Drummer St Stout (ABV 4.5%), Mich'aelmas (ABV 4.6%), Holly Heaven (ABV 5.2%). All beers are available in bottle-conditioned form.

Boathouse Bitter (ABV 3.8%) ◈
Copper-brown and full-bodied session bitter, starting with impressive citrus and floral hop; grassy fruit notes are present with finally a fading, gentle bitterness.

Rutherford IPA (ABV 3.8%) ◈
Satisfying session bitter with a soft hoppy, bitter-sweet balance and a light sulphury character after a fruity, malty start. This amber brew ends dry and bitter with a light balance of malt and hops.

Hobson's Choice (ABV 4.1%) ◻ ◈
A highly drinkable, golden brew with a pronounced hop aroma and taste, and a fruity, bitter balance in the mouth, finishing gently dry.

Sunset Square (ABV 4.4%)
A blend of two best-selling beers to create a unique smooth flavour. A pleasing, golden colour, with a refreshing aftertaste.

Atom Splitter (ABV 4.7%) ◈
Robust copper-coloured strong bitter with a hop aroma and taste, and a distinct sulphury edge.

Darwin's Downfall (ABV 5%)
A blended, ruby-golden coloured beer. Hoppy with a fruity character and a refreshing citrus aftertaste.

Parkers Porter (ABV 5.3%) ◈
Impressive reddish brew with a defined roast character throughout, and a short, fruity, bitter-sweet palate.

Bramling Traditional (ABV 5.5%)
Made with Bramling Cross hops, fruity and delicious.

City of Stirling

See Stirling

Clark's SIBA

HB Clark & Co (Successors) Ltd, Westgate Brewery, Wakefield, West Yorkshire, WF2 9SW
Tel (01924) 373328
Fax (01924) 372306
Email phillip.owen@hbclark.co.uk
Website www.hbclark.co.uk
Tours by arrangement

☺ Founded in 1905, Clark's ceased brewing during the 1960s and 1970s. It resumed cask ale production in 1982 and now delivers to more than 100 outlets. Clark's owns four pubs, all serving cask ale and are Cask Marque approved. Clark's is a micro-brewery but is often thought of as a regional due to its substantial wholesale business. Seasonal beers can be found on the website.

Classic Blonde (OG 1039, ABV 3.9%)
A light-coloured ale with a citrus and hoppy flavour, a distinctive grapefruit aroma and a dry finish.

No Angel (OG 1040, ABV 4%)
A bitter with a dry hop finish, well-balanced and full of flavour. Pale brown in colour with hints of fruit and hops from its aroma.

Classic Brunette (OG 1042, ABV 4.2%)
A hoppy, rich, deep coloured brew that is fruity and well-balanced in aroma with overtones of biscuit on the palate.

Rams Revenge (OG 1046, ABV 4.6%) ◈
A rich, ruby-coloured premium ale, well-balanced with malt and hops, with a deep fruity taste and a dry hoppy aftertaste, with a pleasant hoppy aroma.

Golden Hornet (OG 1050, ABV 5%) ◈
A crisp golden premium beer with a full fruity taste, with full hop aroma and dry hop aftertaste.

Mulberry Tree (OG 1050, ABV 5%)
A strong, distinctive and well-balanced brew, leading to a clean, fresh, fruity taste. Golden in colour with a hoppy aftertaste.

Clearwater SIBA

Clearwater Brewery, 2 Devon Units, Hatchmoor Industrial Estate, Torrington, Devon, EX38 7HP
Tel (01805) 625242
Tours by arrangement

⊗ Clearwater took on the closed St Giles in the

Wood brewery in 1999 and has steadily grown since. The brewery has a 10-12 barrel capacity and the owners plan to bottle their beers. Around 80 outlets are supplied.
Seasonal/occasional beers: Ebony & Ivory (ABV 4.2%, winter), 1646 (ABV 4.8%). Bottle-conditioned beers: Cavalier Ale, Oliver's Nectar.

Village Pride **(ABV 3.7%)**

Cavalier **(OG 1041, ABV 4%)** ♦
Mid-brown, full-bodied best bitter with a burnt, rich malt aroma and taste, leading to a bitter, well-rounded finish.

Torridge Best **(OG 1044, ABV 4.4%)**

Oliver's Nectar **(OG 1051, ABV 5.2%)**

Clockwork

◊ Clockwork Beer Co, 1153 Cathcart Road, Glasgow, G42 9HB
Tel (0141) 649 0184
Tours by arrangement

Clockwork is a micro-brewery in the middle of a bar. A wide range of beers, including fruit beers, wheat beers and lagers, are produced. Most beers are pressurised but there are two cask ales.

Amber IPA **(ABV 3.8%)**

Golden Ale **(ABV 4.1%)**

Coach House SIBA

Coach House Brewing Company Ltd, Wharf Street, Warrington, Cheshire, WA1 2DQ
Tel (01925) 232800
Fax (01925) 232700
Email info@coach-house-brewing.co.uk
Website www.coach-house-brewing.co.uk
Tours by arrangement for CAMRA groups

⊛ The brewery was founded in 1991 by four ex-Greenall Whitley employees. In 1995 Coach House increased its brewing capacity to cope with growing demand and it now delivers to some 250 outlets throughout England, Wales and Scotland, either from the brewery or via wholesalers. The brewery also brews a large number of one-off and special beers. Seasonal beers: Ostlers Summer Pale Ale (ABV 4%, summer), Squires Gold (ABV 4.2%, spring), Summer Sizzler (ABV 4.2%, summer), Countdown (ABV 4.7%, 6 December onwards), Taverners Autumn Ale (ABV 5%, autumn), Blunderbus Old Porter (ABV 5.5%, winter)

Coachman's Best Bitter **(OG 1037, ABV 3.7%)** ♦
A well-hopped, malty bitter, moderately fruity with a hint of sweetness and a peppery nose.

Gunpowder Mild **(OG 1037, ABV 3.8%)** ♦
Biscuity dark mild with a blackcurrant sweetness. Bitterness and fruit dominate with some hints of caramel and a slightly stronger roast flavour. Not as full-bodied as it used to be.

Honeypot Bitter **(OG 1037, ABV 3.8%)**

Farrier's Best Bitter **(OG 1038, ABV 3.9%)**

Dick Turpin **(OG 1042, ABV 4.2%)** ♦
Malty, hoppy pale brown beer with some initial sweetish flavours leading to a short, bitter aftertaste. Also sold under other names as a pub house beer.

Flintlock Pale Ale **(OG 1044, ABV 4.4%)**

Innkeeper's Special Reserve (OG 1044, ABV 4.5%) ♦
A darkish, full-flavoured bitter. Quite fruity, with a strong, bitter aftertaste.

Postlethwaite **(OG 1045, ABV 4.6%)** ♦
Thin bitter with a short, dry aftertaste. Biscuity malt dominates.

Gingernut Premium **(OG 1049, ABV 5%)**

Posthorn Premium **(OG 1049, ABV 5%)** ♦
Dry golden bitter with a blackcurrant fruitiness and good hop flavours leading to a strong, dry finish. Well-balanced but slightly thin for its gravity.

For John Joule of Stone

Old Knotty **(ABV 3.6%)**

Old Priory **(ABV 4.4%)**

Victory **(ABV 5.2%)**

Coles

◊ Coles Family Brewery, White Hart Thatched Inn & Brewery, Llanddarog, Carmarthen, SA32 8NT
Tel (01267) 275395
Tours by arrangement

⊗ Coles is based in an ancient inn built in 1371. Centuries ago beer was brewed on site, but brewing only started again in 1999. The brewery has its own water supply 320 feet below ground, free from pollution. Coles makes a large selection of cask ales due to a system that allows small-batch production. Two pubs are owned. Seasonal beers: Cwrw Nadolig (ABV 3%, Christmas), Summer Harvest (ABV 3.8%).

Nettle Ale **(OG 1039, ABV 3.8%)**

Amber Ale **(OG 1042, ABV 4%)**

Black Stag **(OG 1042, ABV 4%)**

Cwrw Betys Beetroot Ale **(OG 1042, ABV 4%)**

Liquorice Stout **(OG 1042, ABV 4%)**

Oaten Barley Stout **(OG 1042, ABV 4%)**

Roasted Barley Stout **(OG 1042, ABV 4%)**

Cwrw Llanddarog **(OG 1043, ABV 4.1%)**

Cwrw Blasus **(OG 1044, ABV 4.3%)**

Dewi Sant **(OG 1045, ABV 4.4%)**

College Green*

College Green Brewery, 1 College Green Mews, Belfast, BT7 1LW
Tel/Fax (028) 9032 2600
Tours by arrangement

College Green was set up in 2005 by Owen Scullion of Hilden Brewery, in Belfast's Botanic area, in conjunction with Molly's Yard Restaurant. Northern Ireland's newest, and now Belfast's only brewery, College Green hopes to chip away at the brewing monopoly that exists in Northern Ireland. The brewery was due to come on stream in the summer of 2006; until then, production was at Hilden (qv).

Molly's Chocolate Stout **(OG 1042, ABV 4.2%)**
A dark chocolate-coloured beer with a full-

bodied character due to the use of whole malted oats. A small amount of pure cocoa is added to give added credence to the name.

Headless Dog (OG 1042, ABV 4.3%)
A bright amber ale, using Munich malt. The well-hopped beer is named after the mural of a headless dog at the front door to the brewery.

Belfast Blonde (OG 1047, ABV 4.7%)
A natural blonde beer with a clean and refreshing character, derived from the use of lager malt along with a small proportion of maize.

Combe Martin*

Combe Martin Brewery, 4 Springfield Terrace, High Street, Combe Martin, Devon, EX34 0EE
Tel (01271) 883507

Combe Martin started by making country wine, then moved on to beer and cider. It operates from the kitchen and backyard of the owner's house on a one-barrel plant. Five outlets are supplied direct.

Past Times (OG 1036, ABV 3.9%)

Hangman's Bitter (OG 1044, ABV 4.5%)

Shammick Ale (OG 1062, ABV 6.2%)

Concertina SIBA

Concertina Brewery, 9a Dolcliffe Road, Mexborough, South Yorkshire, S64 9AZ
Tel (01709) 580841
Tours by arrangement

◎ The brewery started in 1992 in the cellar of a club once famous as the home of a long-gone concertina band. The plant produces up to eight barrels a week for the club and other occasional outlets. Other beers are brewed on a seasonal basis, including Room at the Inn at Christmas. 25 outlets are supplied.

Club Bitter (ABV 3.9%) ◆
A fruity session bitter with a good bitter flavour.

Old Dark Attic (OG 1038, ABV 3.9%)
A dark brown beer with a fairly sweet, fruity taste.

One Eyed Jack (OG 1039, ABV 4%)
Fairly pale in colour with plenty of hop bitterness. Brewed with the same malt and hop combination as Bengal Tiger, but more of a session beer. Also badged as Mexborough Bitter.

Bengal Tiger (OG 1043, ABV 4.6%) ◆
Light amber ale with an aromatic hoppy nose followed by a wonderful combination of fruit and bitterness. A very smooth finish.

Dictators (OG 1044, ABV 4.7%)

Ariel Square Four (OG 1046, ABV 5.2%)

Coniston SIBA

Coniston Brewing Co Ltd, Coppermines Road, Coniston, Cumbria, LA21 8HL
Tel (01539) 441133 Fax (01539) 441177
Email info@conistonbrewery.com
Website www.conistonbrewery.com
Shop 10am-11pm
Tours by arrangement.

◎ A 10-barrel brewery set up in 1995 behind the Black Bull inn, Coniston, it achieved national fame when it won the Champion Beer of Britain competition in 1998 for Bluebird Bitter. This was followed by SIBA North first prize in 2003. It is now brewing 30 barrels a week and supplies 30 local outlets while the beers are distributed nationally by wholesalers. One pub is owned. Bottle-conditioned Coniston beers are brewed by Ridgeway (qv) using Hepworth's Horsham plant: Bluebird in bottle is ABV 4.2%, Old Man Ale ABV 4.8%. Seasonal beer: Blacksmith's Ale (ABV 5%, Dec-March).

Bluebird Bitter (OG 1036, ABV 3.6%) ◆
A yellow-gold, predominantly hoppy and fruity beer, well-balanced with some sweetness and a rising bitter finish.

Opium (OG 1039, ABV 4%) ◆
Copper-coloured with distinctly fruity, hoppy aromas; a well-balanced flavour with malt, hops and fruit, and more bitter and astringent in the aftertaste.

Bluebird XB (OG 1042, ABV 4.2%) ◆
Well-balanced, hoppy and fruity golden bitter. Bitter-sweet in the mouth with dryness building.

Old Man Ale (OG 1042, ABV 4.2%) ◆
Delicious fruity, winey beer with a complex, well-balanced richness.

Consett Ale Works*

Consett Ale Works Ltd, Grey Horse, 115 Sherburn Terrace, Consett, Co Durham, DH8 6NE
Tel (01207) 502585
Email Kath@thegreyhorse.co.uk
Website www.thegreyhorse.co.uk
Tours by arrangement

A micro-brewery based in Consett's oldest surviving pub, 158 years old. The brewery opened in April 2006 and replaced the former Grey Horse brewery.

Steel Town Bitter (ABV 3.8%)

Red Dust (ABV 4%)

White Hot (ABV 4%)

Conwy

Conwy Brewery Ltd, Unit 17 Ffordd Sam Pari, Conwy Morfa Business Park, Conwy, LL32 8HB
Tel (01492) 585287
Email enquiries@conwybrewery.co.uk
Website www.conwybrewery.co.uk
Tours by arrangement

Conwy started brewing in 2003 and was the first brewery in Conwy for at least 100 years. The brewery has launched a home delivery service for its beers in 10-litre draught packs. Historic ale styles are planned as a regular feature; the first was Telford Porter. 40 outlets are supplied. Seasonal beers: Welsh Pride/Balchder Cymru (ABV 4.4%, spring), Sun

Dance/Dawns Haul (ABV 4%, summer), Telford Porter (ABV 5.6%, autumn/winter). All cask beers are available bottle-conditioned. Celebration Ale/Cwrw Gwledd (ABV 4.2%) is only available bottle-conditioned.

Castle Bitter/Cwrw Castell (OG 1037, ABV 3.8%)

Honey Fayre/Cwrw Mêl (OG 1044, ABV 4.5%)

Special/Arbennig (OG 1043, ABV 4.5%) ◆
Rich, fruity and smooth dark bitter. Fruit dominates the aroma leading into the flavour where malt is also prominent, as are some nuttiness and roasty hints. Dry aftertaste.

For Cobdens Hotel, Capel Curig

Cobdens Hotel Bitter/Cwrw Gwesty Cobdens (OG 1040, ABV 4.1%)

Copper Dragon SIBA

Copper Dragon Brewery Ltd, Snaygill Industrial Estate, Keighley Road, Skipton, North Yorkshire, BD23 2QR
Tel (01756) 702130
Fax (01756) 702136
Email post@copperdragon.uk.com
Website www.copperdragon.uk.com
Shop Mon-Fri 9am-5pm
Tours by arrangement

Copper Dragon began brewing in 2003 and now brews up to 250 barrels a week. There are 20 brewery employees and beer is produced on a German plant. The company supplies the free trade within a 100-mile radius of Skipton. The brewery is acquiring its own outlets in Lancashire and Yorkshire with plans to expand production. More than 1,200 outlets are supplied, with half as permanent stockists.

Black Gold (OG 1036, ABV 3.7%) ◆
A dark ale with subtle fruit and dark malts on the nose. Quite bitter with roast coffee flavours throughout and a long burnt and bitter finish.

Best Bitter (OG 1036, ABV 3.8%) ◆
A subtle hoppy/fruity aroma leads to an aggressively bitter and hoppy taste, with a bitter finish.

Golden Pippin (OG 1037, ABV 3.9%) ▣ ◆
This straw-coloured beer has an intense citrus aroma and flavour, characteristic of American Cascade hops. The dry, bitter astringency increases in the aftertaste.

Scotts 1816 (OG 1041, ABV 4.1%) ▣ ◆
A well-balanced, full-bodied, copper-coloured premium bitter with a fruity, hoppy and slightly nutty character. Bitterness increases in the finish to leave a dry, hoppy fruitiness.

Challenger IPA (OG 1042, ABV 4.4%) ◆
Amber coloured, this is a best bitter in the traditional style. Initial maltiness gives way to fruit, hops and a growing bitter, dry finish.

Corvedale SIBA

Corvedale Brewery, Sun Inn, Corfton, Craven Arms, Shropshire, SY7 9DF
Tel (01584) 861239
Email norman@suninncorfton.co.uk
Website www.suninncorfton.co.uk
Tours by arrangement

Brewing started in 1999 in a building behind the pub. Landlord Norman Pearce is also the brewer and he uses only British malt and hops, with water from a local borehole. Corvedale swaps its beer with those of other small craft breweries, making them available in many parts of the country. One pub is owned and 10 outlets are supplied. Seasonal beer: Teresa's Pride (ABV 4.5%, January). All beers are on sale in the pub in bottle-conditioned form and not fined, making them suitable for vegetarians and vegans. Beers have been in SIBA national finals for the past four years.

Katie's Pride (OG 1040, ABV 4.3%)

Norman's Pride (OG 1043, ABV 4.3%)
A golden amber beer with a refreshing, slightly hoppy taste and a bitter finish.

Secret Hop (OG 1045, ABV 4.5%)
A clear, ruby bitter with a smooth malty taste. Customers are invited to guess the hop!

Dark and Delicious (OG 1045, ABV 4.6%)
A dark ruby beer with hops on the aroma and palate, and a sweet aftertaste.

Cotleigh SIBA

Cotleigh Brewery Ltd, Ford Road, Wiveliscombe, Somerset, TA4 2RE
Tel (01984) 624086
Fax (01984) 624365
Email sales@cotleighbrewery.com
Website www.cotleighbrewery.co.uk
Shop 9am-4pm
Tours by arrangement for select CAMRA groups

Situated in the historic brewing town of Wiveliscombe, Cotleigh Brewery has become one of the most successful award-winning independent breweries in the West Country. The brewery, which started trading in 1979, is housed in specially converted premises with a modern plant capable of producing 165 barrels a week. 300 pubs and 100 retail outlets are supplied directly from the brewery; the beers are also widely available across the country through selected wholesalers. The business was sold in 2003 to Stephen Heptinstall and Fred Domellof. In 2005 a portfolio of six bottled beers was launched. Seasonal beers: Buzzard (ABV 4.8%, Oct-March), Buzzard Dark Ale (ABV 4.8%), Peregrine Porter (ABV 5%), Red Nose Reinbeer (ABV 5%, Sept-Dec).

Harrier Lite (OG 1035, ABV 3.5%)
A delicate floral and fruity aroma for a refreshing, sweet and slightly hopped finish.

Tawny Bitter (OG 1038, ABV 3.8%) ◆
Well-balanced, tawny-coloured bitter with plenty of malt and fruitiness on the nose, and malt to the fore in the taste, followed by hop fruit, developing to a satisfying bitter finish.

Cotleigh (OG 1040, ABV 4%)
Bright and golden-coloured. An explosion of flavours originating from American Cascade hops.

Golden Eagle (OG 1042, ABV 4.2%) ◆
A gold, well-hopped premium bitter with a flowery hop aroma and fruity hop flavour, clean mouthfeel, leading to a dry, hoppy finish.

Barn Owl (OG 1045, ABV 4.5%) ▣ ◆
A pale to mid-brown beer with a good

balance of malt and hops on the nose; a smooth, full-bodied taste where hops dominate, but balanced by malt, following through to the finish.

The Cotswold Brewing Co.
Premium Lager from the Heart of the Cotswolds

Cotswold*

Cotswold Brewing Company Ltd, Foxholes Lane, Foscot, Oxfordshire, OX7 6RL
Tel/Fax (01608) 659631
Email lager@cotswoldbrewingcompany.com
Website www.cotswoldbrewingcompany.com
Tours by arrangement

Cotswold Brewing Company is an independent producer of lager and speciality beers. The brewery was established in 2005 by Richard and Emma Keene with the intention of supplying quality lagers to the local Cotswold market. Inspiration is drawn from continental Europe. Richard studied brewing, distilling and microbiology at Heriot-Watt University and has worked as a brewer for a range of companies including Courage, Freedom and Archers. The brewery is housed in an old Cotswold stone barn, part of a working farm estate. The brewing equipment was sourced from a micro-brewery pub in Albany, USA. Plans for seasonal speciality beers are currently in the pipeline.

Premium Cotswold Lager **(OG 1044, ABV 5%)**

Cotswold Spring

Cotswold Spring Brewery Ltd, Dodington Ash, Chipping Sodbury, Gloucestershire, BS37 6RX
Tel (01454) 323088
Fax (08700) 527635
Email info@cotswoldbrewery.com
Website www.cotswoldbrewery.com
Shop Mon-Fri 9am-6pm; Sat 10am-1pm
Tours by arrangement

Cotswold Spring Brewery opened in 2005 with a 10-barrel refurbished plant that produces beers brewed using only the finest malted barley, subtle blends of hops and natural Cotswold spring water. All the beers are fermented in traditional vessels using specialist strains of yeast. They contain no artificial preservatives, flavourings or colourings. Seasonal beers: Christmas Old Ale (ABV 5%), Codrington Old Ale (ABV 4.8%), Codrington Winter Royal (ABV 5%).

Olde English Rose **(OG 1040, ABV 4%)**

Codrington Codger **(OG 1041, ABV 4.2%)** ◆
Mid-brown best bitter with the emphasis on malt. Nutty character.

Codrington Royal **(OG 1044, ABV 4.5%)** ◆
Ruby in colour with dark, sweet malt. Fruity with a hint of spices.

Cottage SIBA

Cottage Brewing Co Ltd, The Old Cheese Dairy, Hornblotton Road, Lovington, Somerset, BA7 7PP
Tel (01963) 240551
Fax (01963) 240383
Tours by arrangement

⊗ The brewery, which celebrated its 10th anniversary in 2003, was founded in West Lydford in 1993 and upgraded to a 10-barrel plant in 1994. Owned by former airline pilot Chris Norman and his wife Helen, the company got off to a flying start when Norman's Conquest won the Champion Beer of Britain title at the 1995 Great British Beer Festival. The brewery moved to larger premises in 1996, doubling the brewing capacity at the same time. In 2001, Cottage installed a 30-barrel plant. 1,500 outlets are supplied. The malt used is Maris Otter and hops come mainly from Kent. No pubs are owned but the beers are supplied as far away as Liverpool and Yorkshire. The names of beers mostly follow a railway theme. Seasonal beers: Goldrush (ABV 5%), Santa's Steaming Ale (ABV 5.5%, Christmas). Norman's Conquest is also available in bottle-conditioned form.

Southern Bitter **(OG 1039, ABV 3.7%)** ◆
Gold-coloured beer with malt and fruity hops on the nose. Malt and hops in the mouth with a long fruity, bitter finish.

Champflower Ale **(OG 1041, ABV 4.2%)** ◆
Amber beer with a fruity hop aroma, full hop taste and powerful bitter finish.

Somerset & Dorset Ale **(OG 1044, ABV 4.4%)**
A well-hopped, malty brew, with a deep red colour.

Golden Arrow **(OG 1043, ABV 4.5%)** ◆
A hoppy golden bitter with a powerful floral bouquet, a fruity, full-bodied taste and a lingering dry, bitter finish.

Norman's Conquest **(OG 1066, ABV 7%)** ◆
A dark strong ale, with plenty of fruit in the aroma and taste; rounded vinous, hoppy finish.

Country Life SIBA

Country Life Brewery, The Big Sheep, Abbotsham, Bideford, Devon, EX39 5AP
Tel (01237) 420808 / 07971 267790
Email countrylifebrewery1@tiscali.co.uk
Website www.countrylifebrewery.co.uk
Shop open 7 days a week
Tours by arrangement

⊗ Since moving to the Big Sheep tourist attraction, the brewery welcomes some 1,000 visitors in the summer. It offers a beer show and free samples in the shop during the peak season (April-Oct). A 14-barrel plant was installed in 2005, making Country Life the biggest brewery in north Devon. All bottling is now carried out on site. 30-50 outlets are supplied. All cask ales are also available in bottle-conditioned form. Bottle-conditioned only beers: The 8%-er (ABV 8%), The 10%-er (ABV 10%).

Old Appledore **(OG 1037, ABV 3.7%)**

Lacey's Ale **(OG 1042, ABV 4.2%)**

Pot Wallop **(OG 1044, ABV 4.4%)**

Golden Pig **(OG 1046, ABV 4.7%)**

Country Bum **(OG 1058, ABV 6%)**

Cox & Holbrook EAB

Cox & Holbrook, Manor Farm, Brettenham Road, Buxhall, Suffolk, IP14 3DY
Tel/Fax (01449) 736323
Tours by arrangement

First opened in 1997, the brewery concentrates on producing a range of bitters, four of which are available at any one time, along with more specialised medium strength beers and milds. There is also a strong emphasis on the preservation and resurrection of rare and traditional styles.

Crown Dark Mild (OG 1036-38, ABV 3.6%) ◈
Thin tasting at first but bags of malt, caramel and roast flavours burst through to give a thoroughly satisfying beer.

Shelley Dark (OG 1035-37, ABV 3.6%)
Full-flavoured and satisfying.

Beyton Bitter (OG 1037-40, ABV 3.8%)
A traditional bitter, pale tawny in colour, malty with classic Fuggles and Goldings hops.

Old Mill Bitter (OG 1037-39, ABV 3.8%)
Pale, hoppy and thirst quenching.

Bridge Road Bitter (OG 1042-44, ABV 4%)
Brewed exclusively for Grays Athletic FC. A robust malty bitter with a full hop flavour.

Rattlesden Best Bitter (OG 1042-44, ABV 4%)
A slightly darker than average, full-bodied and malty best.

JT's Superlative (OG 1042-44, ABV 4.2%)
Full-flavoured, mid-range ale bordering on amber in colour.

Goodcock's Winner (OG 1048-52, ABV 5%)
An amber ale, rather malty yet not too heavy, with a sharp hop finish.

Ironoak Single Stout (OG 1050-52, ABV 5%)
Full-bodied with strong roast grain flavours and plenty of hop bitterness plus a distinct hint of oak.

Remus (OG 1050-52, ABV 5%)
An amber ale, soft on the palate with full hop flavours but subdued bitterness.

Stormwatch (OG 1050-54, ABV 5%)
An unusual premium pale ale with a full, slightly fruity flavour.

Stowmarket Porter (OG 1055-58, ABV 5%)
Full-bodied with a soft rounded palate. Champion Beer at Ipswich Beer Festival 2005.

Uncle Stan Single Brown Stout (OG 1052-54, ABV 5%)
Unusual soft malt and fruit flavours in a full and satisfying bit of history.

East Anglian Pale Ale (OG 1058-60, ABV 6%)
Well matured, pale, well attenuated beer with a strong Goldings hops character.

Prentice Strong Dark Ale (OG 1082-84, ABV 8%)
A strong porter.

Crondall

Crondall Brewing Co Ltd, Lower Old Park Farm, Dora's Green Lane, Crondall, Surrey, GU10 5DX
Tel (01252) 319000
Email david@tarazsek.freeserve.co.uk
Shop Sat 10am-1pm
Tours by arrangement

David and Chrissy Taraszek converted an old granary barn into a 10-barrel micro-brewery and started brewing in 2005. The company sells directly to the general public in containers and to local free houses in the area. The brewery supplies around 50 outlets. Seasonal beer: Ghoulies (ABV 4.3%, Halloween).

Mr T's Anniversary Ale (ABV 3.8%) ◈
A malty nose that continues into an increasingly bitter flavour. A short, sharp and dry finish.

Sober as a Judge (ABV 4%) ◈
A best bitter but with many of the characteristics of a mild; dark brown, almost red in colour with a noticeably malty aroma. Roast and sharp, with some liquorice in the taste, but remaining predominantly malty throughout. Slightly spicy.

Rocket Fuel (ABV 4.5%)
Dark copper colour, rich malty flavour with plenty of hop aroma.

Cropton SIBA

Cropton Brewery, Woolcroft, Cropton, Pickering, North Yorkshire, YO18 8HH
Tel (01751) 417330
Fax (01751) 417582
Email info@croptonbrewery.co.uk
Website www.croptonbrewery.com
Tours by arrangement

Brewing returned to Cropton in 1984 when the cellars of the New Inn were converted to accommodate a five-barrel plant. The plant was extended in 1988, but by 1994 it had outgrown the cellar and a purpose-built brewery was installed in the grounds of Woolcroft Farm behind the pub. Production fluctuates between 35 and 50 barrels a week according to season. Cropton's additive-free beers are supplied to more than 100 independent outlets from the brewery and nationwide through wholesalers. One pub, the New Inn, is owned. All the beers, with the exception of Balmy Mild and Haunting Hanks, are available bottle conditioned and can be purchased from the visitor centre attached to the pub. All bottled beers are available all year round, regardless of the cask-conditioned version being permanent or seasonal, and are suitable for vegetarians and vegans (King Billy, Endeavour Ale, Two Pints, Yorkshire Moors Bitter and Monkmans Slaughter are all approved by the Vegetarian Society). Seasonal beers: Haunting Hanks (ABV 4.9%), Rudolph's Revenge (ABV 4.6%), Balmy Mild (ABV 4.4%), Uncle Sam's (ABV 4.4%), Scoresby Stout (ABV 4.2%).

King Billy (OG 1036, ABV 3.6%) ◈
A refreshing, straw-coloured bitter, quite hoppy, with a strong but pleasant bitter finish that leaves a clean, dry taste on the palate.

Endeavour Ale (OG 1038, ABV 3.6%)
A light session ale, made with the best

quality hops, providing a refreshing drink with a delicate fruity aftertaste.

Two Pints (OG 1040, ABV 4%) ◆
A good, full-bodied bitter. Malt flavours initially dominate, with a touch of caramel, but the balancing hoppiness and residual sweetness come through.

Honey Gold (OG 1042, ABV 4.2%) ◆
A medium-bodied beer, ideal for summer drinking. Honey is apparent in both aroma and taste but does not overwhelm. Clean finish with a hint of hops.

Yorkshire Moors Bitter (OG 1046, ABV 4.6%)
A fine ruby beer brewed with Fuggles and Progress hops. A unique hoppy beer with a fruity aftertaste.

Monkmans Slaughter (OG 1060, ABV 6%) ◆
Rich tasting and warming; fruit and malt in the aroma and taste, with dark chocolate, caramel and autumn fruit notes. Subtle bitterness continues into the aftertaste.

Crouch Vale SIBA

Crouch Vale Brewery Ltd, 23 Haltwhistle Road, South Woodham Ferrers, Essex, CM3 5ZA
Tel (01245) 322744
Fax (01245) 329082
Email info@crouch-vale.co.uk
Website www.crouch-vale.co.uk
Shop Mon-Fri 8am-5pm
Tours by arrangement

⊗ Founded in 1981 by two CAMRA enthusiasts, Crouch Vale is now well established as a major craft brewer in Essex, having moved to larger premises in 2006 to accommodate the needs of the business. The company is also a major wholesaler of cask ale from other independent breweries, which they supply to more than 100 outlets as well as beer festivals throughout the region. One tied (managed) house, the Queen's Head in Chelmsford, is owned, serving a range of Crouch Vale beers with additional guest ales. Seasonal beers: two beers are available each month, details on website.

Essex Boys Bitter (OG 1035, ABV 3.5%) ◆
Light-bodied pale bitter with a hoppy citrus aroma and a dry finish.

Blackwater Mild (OG 1037, ABV 3.7%) ◆
Dark, roasty and bitter with a dry finish.

Brewers Gold (OG 1040, ABV 4%) ◆
Golden ale with citrus hop aroma and a sweet, soft, fruity emphasis in the initial taste. The drying aftertaste sees a return of the lemon and orange noted on the aroma. Champion Beer of Britain 2005.

Crouch Best (OG 1040, ABV 4%) ◆
Dry, fruity bitter, with malt and hops. Well-balanced throughout.

Anchor Street Porter (OG 1049, ABV 4.9%) ◆
Roasty dark ale with a pleasing fresh hoppy character to the aroma. Coffee in the taste is balanced by dark fruits and a delicate sweetness.

Amarillo (OG 1050, ABV 5%)

Brewers Gold Extra (OG 1052, ABV 5.2%)

Crown & Wellington

Crown & Wellington Brewery, Hillsborough Hotel, 54-58 Langsett Road, Sheffield, South Yorkshire, S6 2UB
Tel (0114) 232 2100
Fax (0114) 250 0200
Tours by arrangement

The Hillsborough Hotel, where the Crown and Wellington beers are brewed, was bought by new owners in May 2006. The former owner, Richard Grimes, now runs the Edale Brewery (qv) as a separate business. The beer range at the hotel is liable to change.

Conviction (OG 1038, ABV 3.8%)

HPA (OG 1039, ABV 3.9%)

Mitigation (OG 1043, ABV 4.3%)

Loxley Gold (OG 1045, ABV 4.5%)

Sam Berry's IPA (OG 1050, ABV 5%)

Stannington Stout (OG 1050, ABV 5%)

Volenti (OG 1052, ABV 5.2%)

Beyond the Call (OG 1060, ABV 6%)

Copenhagen (OG 1080, ABV 8.2%)

Cuillin

Cuillin Brewery Ltd, Sligachan Hotel, Sligachan, Carbost, Isle of Skye, IV47 8SW
Tel (07478) 650204 / 07795 250808
Fax (01478) 650207
Email steve@cuillinbrewery.co.uk
Website www.cuillinbrewery.co.uk
Tours by arrangement

The brewery opened in 2004 and consists of a five-barrel plant originally from a Firkin pub. Four beers are produced and are available on the island and occasionally on the mainland. All beers are suitable for vegetarians and vegans. Seasonal beers: Black Face (Easter-Aug), Eagle Ale (Easter-Aug).

Skye Ale (ABV 4.1%)

Pinnacle (OG 1047, ABV 4.7%)

Cumbrian*

Cumbrian Legendary Ales Ltd, Old Hall Brewery, Hawkshead, Cumbria, LA22 0QF
Tel (015394) 36436
Website www.cumbrianlegendaryales.com

Partners David and Liz Newham and David and Gill Frost installed a 10-barrel plant in renovated farm buildings that date back to Tudor times and which are based in the Cumbria National Park. Brewing started in April 2006.

Wicked Jimmy (ABV 3.6%)

King Dunmail (ABV 4.2%)

Buttermere Beauty (ABV 4.8%)

Claife Crier (ABV 5%)

Custom

Custom Beers Ltd, Little Burchetts Farm, Isaacs Lane, Haywards Heath, West Sussex, RH16 4RZ
Tel (07799) 134188

Launched in 2005, Custom produces beers on

request from its customers. Head brewer Peter Skinner encourages customers to suggest new options for flavour, names and design. The custom service is complemented by a regular premium range.

Goldings Pale Ale (ABV 3.7%)

Smooth Mild (ABV 3.8%)

Chinook Best Bitter (ABV 4.2%)

Cascade Special Bitter (ABV 4.8%)

Dark Roast Porter (ABV 5.5%)

Cwmbran SIBA

Cwmbran Brewery, Gorse Cottage, Graig Road, Upper Cwmbran, Torfaen, NP44 5AS
Tel/Fax (01633) 485233
Email cwmbran.brewery@btopenworld.com
Website www.cwmbranbrewery.co.uk

◎ Cwmbran is a craft brewery on the slopes of Mynydd Maen in Upper Cwmbran in Gwent's eastern valley. Founded in 1994, it is sited alongside the brewer's cottage home. A mountain spring supplies the water used for brewing liquor. The brewery produces a range of cask beers, some with fruit flavours, using traditional methods and ingredients. An extension to the brewery has increased both capacity and flexibility. Seasonal beers: Easter Bunny (ABV 4.5%), Drayman's Gold (ABV 4.2%), Golden Wheat (ABV 4.5%), Four Seasons (ABV 4.8%), Pink Panther (ABV 4.8%), Plum Porter (ABV 4.8%, autumn/winter), Santa's Tipple (ABV 5.2%, Christmas). Bottle-conditioned beer: Crow Valley Bitter.

Drayman's Choice (OG 1041, ABV 3.8%)

Double Hop (OG 1039, ABV 4%)

Pure Welsh (OG 1045, ABV 4.5%)

Blackcurrant Stout (OG 1050, ABV 4%)

Crow Valley Bitter (OG 1042, ABV 4.2%) ◆
Faint malt and hops aroma. Amber coloured with a clean taste of malt, hops and fruit flavours. Bitterness builds with a lasting bitter finish.

Crow Valley Stout/Deryn Du (OG 1048, ABV 4.2%)

Nut Brown Premium Ale (OG 1044, ABV 4.5%)

Full Malty (OG 1047-49, ABV 4.8%)

Gorse Porter (OG 1048, ABV 4.8%)

Daleside

Daleside Brewery Ltd, Camwal Road, Harrogate, North Yorkshire, HG1 4PT
Tel/Fax (01423) 880022
Email enquiries@dalesidebrewery.plus.com
Website www.dalesidebrewery.com
Shop Mon-Fri 9am-4pm

◎ Founder Bill Witty opened the brewery in 1991 in Harrogate with a 20-barrel plant. The company is now owned by Eric Lucas and Alan Barker with Craig Witty as head brewer. Beer is supplied direct to some 200 outlets locally, via wholesalers nationally and to the London area through SIBA's direct delivery scheme. Seasonal beers: Pride of England (ABV 4%, spring/summer), St Georges Ale (ABV 4.1%, spring), Old Lubrication (ABV 4.1%, winter), Old Legover (ABV 4.1%), Starbeck Stout (ABV 4.2%, spring), Santa's Progress (ABV 4.2%, winter), Greengrass Old Rogue Ale (ABV 4.5%, summer), Monkey Wrench (ABV 5.3%, winter), Morocco Ale (ABV 5.5%, winter).

Bitter (OG 1039, ABV 3.7%) ◆
Pale brown in colour, this well-balanced, hoppy beer is pleasantly complemented by fruity bitterness and a hint of sweetness, leading to a moderately long, bitter finish.

Blonde (OG 1040, ABV 3.9%) ◆
A pale golden beer with a predominantly hoppy aroma and taste, leading to a refreshing hoppy, bitter but short finish.

Special Bitter/Shrimper (OG 1043, ABV 4.1%)

Danelaw

Danelaw Brewery Ltd, 9 St Peter's Road, Chellaston, Derby, DE73 6UU
Tel (07799) 607253
Email paul@danelawbrewery.co.uk
Website www.danelawbrewery.co.uk

The owners and equal partners of Danelaw are Paul Martin and Steve Twells. Both are full-time professional engineers and long-term CAMRA members who run the brewery as a part-time venture. Brewing started in 2005 on a former Leadmill 2.5-barrel plant to serve local free trade outlets and beer festivals. The brewery is named after the Viking occupation of the region, and the beer names continue this theme.

Danegeld (OG 1040, ABV 3.8%)

Golden Tears (OG 1042, ABV 4.3%)

Cnut (OG 1045, ABV 4.5%)

Valhalla (OG 1050, ABV 5%)

Rape & Pillage (OG 1057, ABV 5.7%)

Dark Star SIBA

Dark Star Brewing Company Ltd, Moonhill Farm, Burgess Hill Road, Ansty, West Sussex, RH17 5AH
Tel/Fax (01444) 412311
Email info@darkstarbrewing.co.uk
Website www.darkstarbrewing.co.uk
Tours by arrangement

⊗ Dark Star started brewing in 2001, since when growth has been steady. Three pubs are now owned, all of which serve a range of Dark Star and other micro-brewed beers. The brewery's range of beers is divided between permanent brews, seasonals and monthly specials. Some 70 outlets are supplied. Seasonal beers: English Pale Ale (ABV 4.5%), Golden Gate (ABV 4.5%), Sunburst (ABV 4.8%), Critical Mass (ABV 7.8%).

Hophead (OG 1039-41, ABV 3.8%) ◆
A golden-coloured bitter with a fruity/hoppy aroma and a citrus/bitter taste and aftertaste. Wonderfully hoppy and clean tasting with a refreshing mouthfeel. Flavours remain strong to the end.

Best (OG 1042, ABV 4%)

Espresso (OG 1040-42, ABV 4.2%)

Original (OG 1050-54, ABV 5%) ◆
Dark, full-bodied ale with a roast malt aroma and a dry, bitter stout-like finish.

Festival (OG 1050-52, ABV 5%)

DarkTribe

DarkTribe Brewery, Dog & Gun, High Street, East Butterwick, Lincolnshire, DN17 3AJ
Tel (01724) 782324
Fax (01724) 782324
Email dixie@darktribe.co.uk
Website www.darktribe.co.uk

⊗ The small brewery was built during the summer of 1996 in a workshop at the bottom of the garden by Dave 'Dixie' Dean. In 2005 Dixie bought the Dog & Gun pub and moved the 2.5-barrel brewing equipment there. The beers generally follow a marine theme, recalling Dixie's days as an engineer in the Merchant Navy and his enthusiasm for sailing. Local outlets are supplied. Seasonal beers: Dixie's Midnight Runner (ABV 6.5%, Dec-Jan), Dark Destroyer (ABV 9.7%, August onwards).

Dixie's Mild (ABV 3.6%)

Honey Mild (ABV 3.6%)

Full Ahead (ABV 3.8%) ◆
A malty smoothness is backed by a slightly fruity hop that gives a good bitterness to this amber-brown bitter.

Albacore (ABV 4%)

Red Duster (ABV 4%)

Red Rock (ABV 4.2%)

Sternwheeler (ABV 4.2%)

Bucket Hitch (ABV 4.4%)

Dixie's Bollards (ABV 4.5%)

Dr Griffin's Mermaid (ABV 4.5%)

Old Gaffer (ABV 4.5%)

Galleon (ABV 4.7%) 🗍 ◆
A tasty, golden, smooth, full-bodied ale with fruity hops and consistent malt. The thirst-quenching bitterness lingers into a well-balanced finish.

Twin Screw (ABV 5.1%) ◆
A fruity, rose-hip tasting beer, red in colour. Good malt presence with a dry, hoppy bitterness coming through in the finish.

Darwin SIBA

Darwin Brewery Ltd, 63 Back Tatham Street, Sunderland, Tyne & Wear, SR1 2QE
Tel (0191) 514 4746
Fax (0191) 515 2531
Email info@darwinbrewery.com
Website www.darwinbrewery.com
Tours by arrangement (including tasting at local venue)

⊜ The Darwin Brewery first brewed in 1994 and expanded with the construction of its Wearside brewery in central Sunderland in 2002 after a move from the Hodges brewhouse in Crook, Co Durham. The current brewery uses the plant from the former Butterknowle Brewery and produces a range of beers with the strong individual character of the North-east region. Darwin specialises in recreations of past beers such as Flag Porter, a beer produced with yeast rescued from a shipwreck in the English Channel. The brewery also produces trial beers from the Brewlab training and research unit at the University of Sunderland, and experiments in the production of novel and overseas styles for occasional production. Output from the brewery grew significantly in 2005. The brewery also produces the beers of the closed High Force Brewery in Teesdale. Seasonal beers: Richmond Ale (ABV 4.5%, summer/autumn), Saints Sinner (ABV 5%, autumn/winter). Bottle-conditioned beers: Richmond Ale (ABV 4.5%), Hammond's Porter (ABV 4.7%), Extinction Ale (ABV 8.2%), Hammond's Stingo (ABV 10%), Cauldron Snout, Forest XB.

Sunderland Best (OG 1041, ABV 3.9%)
A light and smooth-tasting session bitter, full of hop character and moderate bitterness. Amber malt provides a smooth body and creamy character typical of North-east beers.

Evolution Ale (OG 1041, ABV 4%)
A dark amber, full-bodied bitter with a malty flavour and a clean, bitter aftertaste.

Ghost Ale (OG 1041, ABV 4.1%)

Hop Drop (OG 1054, ABV 5.3%)

Killer Bee (OG 1054, ABV 6%)
A strong but light ale matured with pure, organic honey produced from Darwin's own hives.

Extinction Ale (OG 1084, ABV 8.3%)

For High Force Hotel

Forest XB (OG 1044, ABV 4.2%)

Cauldron Snout (OG 1056, ABV 5.6%)

De Koninck

See final entry in Independents section

Dent SIBA

Dent Brewery Ltd, Hollins, Cowgill, Sedbergh, Cumbria, LA10 5TQ
Tel (015396) 25326
Email paul@dentbrewery.co.uk
Website www.dentbrewery.co.uk

⊜ A brewery set up in a converted barn in the picturesque Yorkshire dales. Originally it brewed to supply the Sun Inn in Dent but, by popular demand, expansion has allowed the beer to be supplied throughout the country to some 50 free trade outlets. Monthly specials are produced, all at ABV 4.5%.

Bitter (OG 1035, ABV 3.7%) ◆
Fruity throughout and lightly hopped. This beer has a pervading earthiness that is evident to a lesser extent in other Dent beers. A short, bitter finish.

Aviator (OG 1039, ABV 4%) 🗍 ◆
This medium-bodied amber ale is characterised by strong citrus and hoppy flavours that develop into a long bitter finish.

Rambrau (OG 1042, ABV 4.5%)
A cask-conditioned lager.

Ramsbottom Strong Ale (OG 1042, ABV 4.5%) ◆

This complex, mid-brown beer has a warming, dry, bitter finish to follow its unusual combination of roast, bitter, fruity and sweet flavours.

Kamikaze (OG 1047, ABV 5%)
Hops and fruit dominate this full-bodied, golden, strong bitter, with a dry bitterness growing in the aftertaste.

T'Owd Tup (OG 1056, ABV 6%)
A rich, fully-flavoured, strong stout with a coffee aroma. The dominant roast character is balanced by a warming sweetness and a raisiny, fruitcake taste that linger on into the finish.

Derby

Derby Brewing Company Limited, Masons Place Business Park, Nottingham Road, Derby, DE21 6AQ
Tel (07887) 556788
Fax (01332) 242888
Email sales@derbybrewing.co.uk
Website www.derbybrewing.co.uk
Tours by arrangement

A purpose built brewery, established 2004, in the varnish workshop of the old Masons Paintworks by owner/brewer Trevor Harris, former brewer at the Brunswick Inn, Derby. Only the finest English whole hops with Maris Otter malted barleys from Warminster Maltings are used. Seasonal beer: White Christmas (ABV 5.5%, Dec & June).

Triple Hop (OG 1041, ABV 4.1%)

Business As Usual (OG 1044, ABV 4.4%)

Devilishly Dark (OG 1045, ABV 4.5%)

Old Intentional (OG 1050, ABV 5%)

For the Babington Arms, Derby

Penny's Porter (OG 1046, ABV 4.6%)

Taylor's Tipple (OG 1046, ABV 4.6%)

Derventio*

Derventio Brewery Limited, Trusley Brook Farm, Trusley, Derbyshire, DE6 5JP
Tel (07816) 878129
Email enquiries@derventiobrewery.co.uk
Website www.derventiobrewery.co.uk

Derventio Brewery was formed in 2005 by three railway engineers, all CAMRA members. The original site of the brewery fell through due to problems with utilities and the brewery is now located to the west of Derby city centre (approximately 10 miles) at Trusley. Their 5.5-barrel brewery plant was installed in March 2006 by Porter Brewing Company.

RPA (ABV 3.8%)

Centurion (ABV 4.7%)

Venus (ABV 5%)

Derwent

Derwent Brewery Co, Units 2A/2B Station Road Industrial Estate, Silloth, Cumbria CA7 4AG
Tel (016973) 31522
Fax (016973) 31523
Tours by arrangement

Derwent was set up in 1996 in Cockermouth by Hans Kruger and Frank Smith, both former Jenning's employees, and they moved to Silloth in 1998. Derwent supplies beers throughout the north of England, with outlets in Cheshire, Cumbria, Lancashire, Yorkshire and the north east. It organises the Silloth Beer Festival every September. It has supplied Carlisle State Bitter to the House of Commons, a beer that recreates one produced by the former state-owned Carlisle Brewery. Seasonal beers: Derwent Summer Rose (ABV 4.2%), Derwent Spring Time (ABV 4.3%), Harvesters Ale (ABV 4.3%), Bill Monk (ABV 4.5%), Auld Kendal (ABV 5.7%, winter).

Carlisle State Bitter (OG 1037, ABV 3.7%)
A light hoppy beer with underlying malt and fruit, and a dry, yeasty finish.

Parsons Pledge (OG 1040, ABV 4%)

Winters Gold (ABV 4.1%)

Hofbrau (ABV 4.2%)

W&M Kendal Pale Ale (OG 1044, ABV 4.4%)
A sweet, fruity, hoppy beer with a bitter finish.

Derwent Rose

See Consett Ale Works

Devon

Devon Ales Ltd, Mansfield Arms, 7 Main Street, Sauchie, Clackmannanshire, FK10 3JR
Tel (01259) 722020
Email john.gibson@btinternet.com
Tours by arrangement

Devon opened in 1992 and is still producing hand-crafted beer. Two pubs are owned and two outlets are supplied direct.

Original (OG 1038, ABV 3.8%)

Thick Black (OG 1042, ABV 4.2%)

Pride (OG 1046, ABV 4.8%)

Digfield*

Digfield Ales, North Lodge Farm, Barnwell, Peterborough, Cambridgeshire, PE8 5RJ
Tel (01832) 293295

With equipment from the Cannon Brewery, Digfield Ales started brewing in December 2005 as part of a farm diversification scheme. Digfield operates on a 10-barrel plant run by three partners. It supplies the local Barnwell pub, the Montagu Arms, as well as 10 other outlets. A bottling plant is planned.

Barnwell Bitter & Twisted (OG 1038, ABV 3.9%)
A light, refreshing beer, hoppy with an enjoyable bitter finish.

Barnwell Bitter (OG 1039, ABV 4%)
An easy to drink, traditional beer with a malty finish.

March Hare (OG 1046, ABV 4.7%)
A light, well-balanced strong ale.

Doghouse SIBA

Doghouse Brewery, Scorrier, Redruth, Cornwall, TR16 5BN
Tel (01209) 822022
Email stevewillmott@btinternet.com
Tours by arrangement

⊗ Established in 2001, this five-barrel brewery continues to brew in a former dog rescue kennel at Startrax Pets Hotel. The second-hand equipment was originally from the Fly and Firkin in Middlesbrough. Some 60 outlets are supplied. Seasonal beers: Staffi Stout (ABV 4.7%, Feb-March), Dingo Lager (ABV 5%, May-Oct), Christmas Tail/Winter's Tail (ABV 5.8%, Dec-Jan). Bottle-conditioned beers: all seasonal ales plus Biter, Dozey Dawg, Cornish Corgi, Bow Wow and Hot Dog Chilli Beer.

Wet Nose (OG 1038, ABV 3.8%)
A gold-coloured, quaffing bitter with plenty of hoppy bite in the aftertaste.

Retriever (OG 1039, ABV 3.9%)
A golden-coloured, easy-drinking beer.

Biter (OG 1040, ABV 4%)
A standard mid-brown bitter.

Snoozy Suzy (OG 1043, ABV 4.3%)
Copper-coloured, well hopped bitter.

Dozey Dawg (OG 1044, ABV 4.4%)
A light golden, refreshing beer.

Cornish Corgi (OG 1045, ABV 4.5%)
A golden premium ale brewed with Pilot hedgerow hops.

Seadog (OG 1046, ABV 4.6%)
Originally brewed to celebrate the 200th Anniversary of Nelson's victory and death at the Battle of Trafalgar.

Bow Wow (OG 1050, ABV 5%)
Dark ruby-coloured premium ale; well rounded maltiness gives way to a more bitter aftertaste.

Dolphin

Dolphin Bar & Brewery, 48 St Michael's Street, Shrewsbury, Shropshire, SY1 2EZ
Tel (01743) 350419

⊗ Dolphin was launched in 2000 and both bar and brewery changed hands in early 2006. Porter is suitable for vegetarians and vegans.

Best Bitter (OG 1043, ABV 4.2%)

Gold (OG 1044, ABV 4.5%)

Porter (OG 1045, ABV 4.6%)

Brew (OG 1046, ABV 4.8%)

Donnington IFBB

Donnington Brewery, Stow-on-the-Wold, Cheltenham, Gloucestershire, GL54 1EP
Tel (01451) 830603

⊗ Thomas Arkell bought a 13th-century watermill in idyllic countryside in 1827 and began brewing on the site in 1865. Today, it is owned and run by a direct family descendant, Claude Arkell, and the millwheel is still used to drive small pumps and machinery. Donnington supplies its own 15 tied houses and a number of free trade outlets.

BB (OG 1035, ABV 3.6%) ◆
A pleasant amber bitter with a slight hop aroma, a good balance of malt and hops in the mouth and a bitter aftertaste.

SBA (OG 1045, ABV 4.4%) ◆
Malt dominates over bitterness in the subtle flavour of this premium bitter, which has a hint of fruit and a dry malty finish.

Dorset SIBA

Dorset Brewing Co, Hope Square, Weymouth, Dorset, DT4 8TR
Tel/Fax (01305) 777515
Email dbcs@fineale.com
Website www.fineale.com
Shop at Brewers Quay 10am-5.30pm daily
Tours by arrangement via Timewalk at Brewers Quay

⊗ The Dorset Brewing Company, formerly the Quay Brewery, is the most recent in a long succession of breweries in one of the oldest sites in England, Hope Square, Weymouth. Brewing first started there in 1256 but in more recent times it was famous for being the home of the Devenish and Groves breweries. Brewing stopped in 1986 but restarted in 1996, when Giles Smeath set up Quay in part of the old brewery buildings. All the award-winning beers are brewed in the traditional manner with no artificial additives. They are available in local Weymouth pubs and selected outlets throughout the south west. Giles hopes to move to a new site as Hope Square is cramped and there is no room for expansion. Seasonal beers: Summer Knight (ABV 3.8%), Silent Knight (ABV 5.9%).

Weymouth Harbour Master (OG 1036, ABV 3.6%) ◆
Light, easy-drinking session beer. Well-balanced, with a long, bitter-sweet, citrus finish.

Weymouth Best Bitter (OG 1038, ABV 3.9%) ◆
Complex bitter ale with strong malt and fruit flavours despite its light gravity.

Weymouth JD 1742 (OG 1040, ABV 4.2%) ◆
Clean-tasting, easy-drinking bitter. Well balanced with lingering bitterness after moderate sweetness.

Steam Beer (OG 1043, ABV 4.5%) ◆
Citrus fruit and roasted malt dominate this complex best bitter, from the first aroma through to the long, lingering finish.

Jurassic (OG 1045, ABV 4.7%)
An organic premium bitter, pale golden colour; smooth with suggestions of honey underlying a complex hop palate.

Durdle Door (ABV 5%)
A full-bodied, clean-tasting, strong ale. Vanilla/citrus aroma; hints of marmalade on the palate.

Dow Bridge

Dow Bridge Brewery, 2-3 Rugby Road, Catthorpe, Leicestershire, LE17 6DA.
Tel/Fax (01788) 869121
Email dowbridge.brewery@virgin.net
Tours by arrangement

Established in 2002, increased demand has necessitated further building expansion. Traditional brewing methods, without the use of added sugars, adjuncts or additives, are adhered to. Beers are supplied to 117 outlets via the brewery's own distributor. Bottle-conditioned beers: Ratae'd Fosse, Porter. Beers are also contract brewed for Morgan Ales. Seasonal beers: Summer Light (ABV 3.6%), Porter (ABV 4.9%). Seasonal beers for Morgan Ales: Cuckoo Spit (ABV 4%), Beez Kneez (ABV 4.2%), Xmas Cracker (ABV 4.5%).

Bonum Mild (OG 1035, ABV 3.5%) ◆
Complex dark brown, full-flavoured mild, with strong malt and roast flavours to the fore and continuing into the aftertaste, leading to a long, satisfying finish.

Acris (OG 1037, ABV 3.8%)

Ratae'd (OG 1042, ABV 4.3%) ◆
Tawny-coloured, very bitter beer in which bitter and hop flavours dominate, to the detriment of balance, leading to a long, bitter and astringent aftertaste.

Fosse Ale (OG 1046, ABV 4.8%)

For Morgan Ales

Churchills Best (OG 1041, ABV 4.2%)

Olde Codger (OG 1042, ABV 4.4%)

Bishops Revenge (OG 1047, ABV 5%)

Downton

Downton Brewery Co Ltd, Unit 11 Downton Business Centre, Batten Road, Downton, Salisbury, Wiltshire, SP5 3HU
Tel (01722) 322890
Fax (01725) 513513
Website www.downtonbrewery.com
Tours by arrangement

The brewery was set up in 2003 with equipment leased from Hop Back (qv). The brewery has a 20-barrel copper and two 20-barrel fermenters. Seasonal beers: Maroonmaker Mild (ABV 3.3%, May), German Pale Ale (ABV 4.2%, October), All Rounder (ABV 4.4%, summer), Firedraught (ABV 4.5%, winter), Chimera Red (ABV 4.6%, autumn), Equinox (ABV 5%, spring/autumn), Dark Delight (ABV 5.5%, winter). Bottle-conditioned beer: Chimera IPA.

Chimera Quadhop (OG 1038, ABV 3.9%)

Chimera IPA (OG 1063, ABV 6.8%)

Driftwood

⌂ Driftwood Brewery, Driftwood Spars Hotel, Trevaunance Cove, St Agnes, Cornwall, TR5 0RT
Tel (01872) 552428 / 553323
Fax (01872) 553701
Email driftwoodspars@hotmail.com
Website www.driftwoodspars.com
Tours by arrangement

Gordon Treleaven started brewing in 2000 in this famous Cornish pub and hotel that dates back to 1660. The brewery is based in the former Flying Dutchman café across the road. The Old Horsebridge one-barrel plant has been replaced by a customised, five-barrel kit. Pale malt comes from Tuckers of Newton Abbot and the hops are Fuggles.

Cuckoo Ale (OG 1045, ABV 4.5%)

Dunkery*

Dunkery Ales Ltd, Edgcott Farm, Exford, Somerset, TA24 7QG
Tel 07769 676262
Email enquiries@dunkeryales.co.uk
Website www.dunkeryales.co.uk

After two years of planning, struggling with various authorities and applying for grants, Dunkery Ales opened in May 2006 in a converted cattle shed. The beers are available in local pubs as well as by mail order over the internet. The beer range was not available when the guide went to press.

Dunn Plowman SIBA

Dunn Plowman Brewery, Unit 1A Arrow Court Industrial Estate, Hergest Road, Kington, Herefordshire, HR5 3ER
Tel (01544) 231993
Fax (01544) 231985
Email dunnplowman.brewery@talk21.com
Tours by arrangement

⌂ The brewery was established in 1987 as a brew-pub, moved to Leominster in 1992, to Kington in 1993 and to its present site in 2002. It is run by husband and wife team Steve and Gaye Dunn, who also run the Olde Tavern in Kington. The brewery also supplies several freehouses within a 50-mile radius. Bottle-conditioned beers: Old Jake Stout, Kyneton Ale (ABV 5%), Golden Haze Wheat Beer (ABV 5%), Crooked Furrow.

Brewhouse Bitter (OG 1037, ABV 3.8%)

Early Riser (OG 1039, ABV 4%)

Sting (OG 1040, ABV 4.2%)

Kingdom Bitter (OG 1043, ABV 4.5%)

Old Jake Stout (OG 1046, ABV 4.8%)

Shirehorse Ale (OG 1053, ABV 5.5%)

Railway Porter (OG 1056, ABV 5.7%)

Crooked Furrow (OG 1063, ABV 6.5%)

Durham SIBA

Durham Brewery Ltd, Unit 5a Bowburn North Industrial Estate, Bowburn, Co Durham, DH6 5PF
Tel (0191) 377 1991
Fax (0191) 377 0768
Email gibbs@durham-brewery.co.uk
Website www.durham-brewery.co.uk
Shop open during business hours
Tours by arrangement

Established in 1994, Durham now has a portfolio of around 20 beers plus a bottle-conditioned range. Bottles can be purchased via the online shop and an own label/special message service is available. News from the brewery is delivered by email newsletter via free subscription on the website. Seasonal beers: Sunstroke (ABV 3.6%, summer), Frostbite (ABV 3.6%, winter). Bottle-conditioned beers: Cloister (ABV 4.5%), Evensong, Black Abbot, Saint Cuthbert (ABV 6.5%), Silver Chalice (ABV 7.2%), Benedictus (ABV 8.4%), Temptation (ABV 10%). All bottle-conditioned beers are suitable for vegans.

Gold (ABV 3.7%)

Green Goddess (ABV 3.8%)
English Goldings hops give a spicy, bitter flavour.

Magus (ABV 3.8%)
Golden, refreshing dry bitter. An excellent session and summer ale, with a medium fruity/dry aftertaste.

Bonny Lass (ABV 3.9%)
Ruby coloured but with the flavour of a white beer.

White Gem (ABV 3.9%)

White Herald (ABV 3.9%)

Black Velvet (ABV 4%)
Black like a stout but with the strength of a porter. Traditional English hops balance rich liquorice and roast flavours.

White Gold (ABV 4%)
Pale and aromatic, mouth-filling and thirst-quenching with citrus aromas and flavours.

White Amarillo (ABV 4.1%)
Named after the predominant hop (Amarillo is a light and floral American variety). The addition of Goldings hops add a little more spice. The result is a deliciously fragrant, light session beer.

Bede's Gold (ABV 4.2%)

Keltic (ABV 4.2%)

White Velvet (ABV 4.2%)
Smooth, golden bitter with a tangy hop and fruit taste. The aftertaste lingers with a pleasant fruitiness

Canny Lad (ABV 4.3%)
Rich, malty Scotch-type beer. Six malts make a complex body and ruby colour.

Dark Secret (ABV 4.3%)

White Crystal (ABV 4.3%)
Crystal is an aromatic American hop. The flavour is clean, spicy and refreshing.

Durham County (ABV 4.4%)

White Bullet (ABV 4.4%)

Prior's Gold (ABV 4.5%)

White Friar (ABV 4.5%)
A strong version of White Gold. All the aroma and rich grapefruit bitterness with a fuller body.

White Sapphire (ABV 4.5%)
Light and easy, aromatic and refreshing.

Bishop's Gold (ABV 4.6%)

Cuthberts Cross (ABV 4.7%)
Pale gold in colour but rich with grapefruit notes. This bitter is strong in alcohol and flavour, yet is thirst quenching. Named after St Cuthbert's Cross in Durham Cathedral.

White Bishop (ABV 4.8%)
A premium ale using lager malt. American fruity hops make this strong beer easy going and satisfying.

Evensong (ABV 5%)

Black Abbot (ABV 5.3%)

Magnificat (ABV 6.5%)

E&S Elland SIBA

E&S Elland, Eastwood & Sanders (Fine Ales) Limited, Units 3-5 Heathfield Industrial Estate, Heathfield Street, Elland, West Yorkshire, HX5 9AE
Tel (01422) 377677
Fax (01422) 370922
Email brewery@eandsbrewery.co.uk
Website www.eandsbrewery.co.uk
Shop in brewery office (normal office hours)
Tours by arrangement

Eastwood & Sanders was formed in 2002 as a result of the amalgamation of the Barge & Barrel Brewery and West Yorkshire Brewery. While the official company name remains Eastwood & Sanders, it now trades as E&S Elland. E&S has invested in additional vessels and equipment to meet increased demand with more than 100 outlets regularly supplied. As well as the core brands, there is a rolling programme of seasonal beers. Seasonal beers: Living in the Cask (ABV 3.6%), Born to be Mild (ABV 3.7%), Yorkshireman (ABV 4.1%), Maximum Darkness (ABV 4.3%), Night Porter (ABV 4.3%), Stocking Top (ABV 4.4%), Halifax Bomber (ABV 4.8%), Sam's Revenge (ABV 5%), Bark at the Moon (ABV 5.6%), True Leveller (ABV 5.7%). Bottle-conditioned beers: Beyond the Pale, 1872 Porter.

First Light (OG 1037, ABV 3.5%)
Refreshing, light golden-coloured beer with a fruity/honey flavour. Clean bitter aftertaste.

Bargee (OG 1038, ABV 3.8%)
Pale brown, grainy session bitter. Fruity

aroma and taste complemented by a bitter edge in the aftertaste.

Best Bitter (OG 1041, ABV 4%)
Made with a single malt and English and American hops, this is a straw-coloured bitter with a strong hoppy aroma and taste. Fruity and malty in character, the dry citrus, bitter flavour lingers to the end.

Beyond the Pale (OG 1042, ABV 4.2%) ◆
Gold-coloured, robust, creamy beer with ripe aromas of hops and fruit. Bitterness predominates in the mouth and leads to a dry, fruity and hoppy aftertaste.

Fireball (OG 1042, ABV 4.2%)
A copper-coloured bitter with crystal malt flavours and a long, hoppy finish.

Nettlethrasher (OG 1044, ABV 4.4%) ◆
A pale brown premium bitter brewed with three different malts and English and American hops. Fruity in nose and taste; dry, bitter aftertaste.

Elland Back (OG 1047, ABV 4.6%)
A pale premium bitter with grapefruit and citrus top notes in the nose, and a bitter yet fruity palate from the use of all American hops.

1872 Porter (OG 1065, ABV 6.5%) ◆
Prime, full-flavoured porter. Rich liquorice flavours with a hint of chocolate from the roast malt. Slightly sweet with surprisingly bitter aftertaste.

IPA (OG 1065, ABV 6.5%)

Eagles Bush

Eagles Bush Brewery, Salutation Inn, Ham, Berkeley, Gloucestershire, GL13 9QH
Tel (01453) 810284

The brewery moved to the Salutation in 2005 and brewing re-commenced in September that year. It was originally located at the Borough Arms, New Henry Street, Neath where it was first installed in 2004. The equipment used is a 3/4-barrel full mash with two fermenters, all self-made. Beers are only available from the Salutation.

Merlin (ABV 3.6%)

Kestrel Bitter (ABV 3.7%)

Osprey Dark (ABV 4%)

Golden Eagle IPA (ABV 4.2%)

Earl Soham SIBA

Earl Soham Brewery, The Street, Earl Soham, Woodbridge, Suffolk, IP13 7RT
Tel/Fax (01728) 684097
Email thebrewer@bjornson.fsnet.co.uk
Website www.earlsohambrewery.co.uk
Shop Village store Tastebuds next to brewery
Tours by arrangement

⊗ Earl Soham was set up behind the Victoria pub in 1984 and continued there until 2001 when the brewery moved 200 metres down the road. The Victoria and the Station in Framlingham both sell the beers on a regular basis and, when there is spare stock, it is supplied to local free houses and as many beer festivals as possible. Ten outlets are supplied and two pubs are owned. Seasonal beer: Jolabrugg (ABV 5%, December until finished). Most of the beers are bottle-conditioned for Tastebuds next door and are only available there.

Gannet Mild (OG 1034, ABV 3.3%)
An unusual, full-tasting mild with a bitter finish and roast flavours that compete with underlying maltiness.

Victoria Bitter (OG 1037, ABV 3.6%) ◆
A light, fruity, amber session beer with a clean taste and a long, lingering hoppy aftertaste.

Pale Ale (OG 1040, ABV 4%)

Sir Roger's Porter (OG 1040, ABV 4%)
Full-flavoured dark brown malty beer with bitter overtones and a fruity aftertaste.

Albert Ale (OG 1045, ABV 4.4%)
Hops dominate every aspect of this beer, but especially the finish. A fruity, astringent beer.

Empress of India Pale Ale (OG 1048, ABV 4.7%)

Eastwood

Eastwood the Brewer, Barge & Barrel, 10-20 Park Road, Elland, West Yorkshire, HX5 9HP
Tel 07949 148476
Fax (01422) 823909
Email eastwoodthebrewer@tiscali.co.uk
Tours by arrangement

The brewery, founded by John Eastwood at the Barge & Barrel pub, has a new brewer, Gary Mitchell. Some 35-50 outlets are supplied. Gary hopes to add bottled beers to the portfolio.

Best Bitter (ABV 4%) ◆
Creamy, yellow, hoppy bitter with hints of citrus fruits. Pleasantly strong bitter aftertaste.

England's Glory (ABV 4%)

Jollification (ABV 4%)

Gold Award (ABV 4.4%) ◆
Complex copper-coloured beer with malt, roast and caramel flavours. It has a hoppy and bitter aftertaste.

Mosquito (ABV 4.7%)
A strong tasting bitter with four types of malt and three hops.

Black Prince (ABV 5%)
Distinctive strong black porter, with a blend of pale and chocolate malts and roasted barley.

EPA (ABV 5%)
The big brother to Best Bitter.

Old Skool (ABV 5%)

Lilburne (ABV 5.7%)
Copper-coloured beer bursting with malt and hops.

Myrtle's Temper (ABV 7%)

Eccleshall

See Slater's

Edale

Edale Brewery Co, rear of Ruskin Villa, Hope Road, Edale, Derbyshire, S33 7ZE

Tel (01433) 670289
Fax (01433) 670134
Email info@edalebrewery.co.uk
Website www.edalebrewery.co.uk
Tours by arrangement

Edale started brewing in 2001 on a 2.5-barrel plant. It expanded by buying the Hillsborough Hotel in Sheffield, including the Crown Brewery in 2004, but that association ended in May 2006 when the Hillsborough brewery changed hands (see Crown & Wellington). Richard Grimes, ex-Hillsborough, now brews on a part-time basis at Edale. Seasonal beer: Kinder Wasaile (ABV 7%, Christmas). Bottle-conditioned beers: Downfall, Ringing Roger.

Kinder Right to Roam (OG 1039, ABV 3.9%)

Kinder Trespass (OG 1040, ABV 4%)

Backtor Bitter (OG 1042, ABV 4.2%)

Kinder Downfall (OG 1050, ABV 5%)

Kinder Stouter (OG 1050, ABV 5%)

Ringing Roger (OG 1060, ABV 6%)

Edinburgh

Edinburgh Brewing Co Ltd, Edinburgh. See Belhaven.

Eglesbrech

Eglesbrech Brewing Co, Behind the Wall, 14 Melville Street, Falkirk, FK1 1HZ
Tel (01324) 633338
Email info@behindthewall.co.uk
Website www.behindthewall.co.uk
Tours by arrangement

The brewery is part of an extension to the Ale House in Falkirk. Occasional special beers are made and a Falkirk Wheel Ale is planned to tie in with the area's newest tourist attraction, the Canal Boat Lift. Three pubs are owned, one of which serves cask beer although using gas pressure.

Falkirk 400 (ABV 3.8%)

Golden Nectar (ABV 3.8%)

Antonine Ale (ABV 3.9%)

Cascade (ABV 4.1%)

Stones Ginger Beer (ABV 4.2%)

Alt Bier (ABV 4.4%)

Elgood's IFBB SIBA

Elgood & Sons Ltd, North Brink Brewery, Wisbech, Cambridgeshire, PE13 1LN
Tel (01945) 583160
Fax (01945) 587711
Email info@elgoods-brewery.co.uk
Website www.elgoods-brewery.co.uk
Shop May-Sept 11.30am-4.30pm
Tours by arrangement

The North Brink Brewery was established in 1795 and was one of the first classic Georgian breweries to be built outside London. In 1878 it came under the control of the Elgood family and is still run today as one of the few remaining independent family breweries, with the fifth generation of the family now helping to run the company. The beers go to 42 Elgood's public houses within a 50-mile radius of Wisbech and free-trade outlets throughout East Anglia, while wholesalers distribute nationally. Elgood's has a visitor centre, offering the opportunity to combine a tour of the brewery and the magnificent gardens. Seasonal beers: Thin Ice (ABV 4.7%, Jan-Feb), Old Wagg (ABV 4%, March-April), Double Swan (ABV 4.5%, May-June), Mad Dog (ABV 4.4%, July-Aug), Barleymead (ABV 4.8%, Sept-Oct), Snickalmas (ABV 5%, December), Wenceslas Winter Warmer (ABV 7.5%, December).

Black Dog (OG 1036.8, ABV 3.6%)
Reddish black with liquorice rounded by hints of roast malt and a growing dry bitterness.

Cambridge Bitter (OG 1037.8, ABV 3.8%)
Thirst-quenching, copper-coloured bitter with a distinct biscuity malt presence throughout and a drying, bitter finish.

Golden Newt (OG 1041.5, ABV 4.1%)
Golden ale with floral citrus hop aroma and a satisfying soft hoppy palate ending with a spritzy bitterness.

Pageant Ale (OG 1043.8, ABV 4.3%)
A premium beer, with a good aroma of hops and malt, giving a well-balanced bitter-sweet flavour and a satisfying finish.

Greyhound Strong Bitter (OG 1052.8, ABV 5.2%)
Satisfying strong bitter with copper-red looks and a distinct malty aroma and palate. The malt is joined by soft berry fruits in the mouth and they are eventually subsumed by a powerful dry bitterness.

Elveden EAB

Elveden Ales, The Courtyard, Elveden Estate, Elveden, Thetford, Norfolk, IP24 3TA
Tel (01842) 878922

Elveden is a five-barrel brewery based on the estate of Lord Iveagh, a member of the ennobled branch of the Guinness family. The brewery is run by Frances Moore, daughter of Brendan Moore at Iceni Brewery (qv). Frances is a student and brews during holiday periods. The brewery produces three ales: Elveden Stout (ABV 5%) and Elveden Ale (ABV 5.2%), which are mainly bottled in stoneware bottles. The third ale is Charter Ale (ABV 10%) to mark the celebrations for the award of a Royal Charter for Harwich in 1604. The beer is based on a 19th-century style known as Arctic Ale, first brewed by Allsopps of Burton-on-Trent for Arctic explorers. The beer is available in cask and bottle-conditioned versions. The phone number listed above is shared with Iceni Brewery. Three more beers are planned and will be sold in pint size bottles and branded as Suffolk Pints.

Empire

Empire Brewing, The Old Boiler House, Upper Mills, Slaithwaite, Huddersfield, West Yorkshire, HD7 7HA
Tel (01484) 847343/07966 592276
Tours by arrangement

Empire Brewing was set up in a garage in 2004 by Russell Beverley with a five-barrel plant and relocated in 2006. All the beers are predominantly pale and hoppy. His first beer, Strikes Back, won Beer of the Festival at Huddersfield Festival. Beers are supplied to local free houses, CAMRA beer festivals and through specialist agencies.

Golden Warrior (ABV 3.8%)

Ensign (ABV 3.9%)

Strikes Back (ABV 4%)

Privateer (ABV 4.1%)

Longbow (ABV 4.3%)

Crusader (ABV 5%)

Enville SIBA

Enville Ales Ltd, Enville Brewery, Coxgreen, Enville, Stourbridge, West Midlands, DY7 5LG
Tel (01384) 873728
Fax (01384) 873770
Email info@envilleales.com
Website www.envilleales.com
Tours by arrangement for small groups only

☺ Enville is based on a picturesque Victorian farm complex. Using the same water source as the original Village Brewery (closed in 1919), the beers also incorporate more than three tons of honey annually, and recipes passed down from the proprietor's great-great aunt. Seasonal beers: Gothic (ABV 5.2%, Oct-March), Phoenix IPA (ABV 4.8%, April-Sept).

Chainmaker Mild (OG 1037, ABV 3.6%)

Nailmaker Mild (OG 1041, ABV 4%)

White (OG 1041, ABV 4.2%) ◆
Yellow with a malt, hops and fruit aroma. Hoppy but sweet finish.

Saaz (OG 1042, ABV 4.2%) ◆
Golden lager-style beer. Lager bite but with more taste and lasting bitterness. The malty aroma is late arriving but the bitter finish, balanced by fruit and hops, compensates.

Ale (OG 1044, ABV 4.5%) ◆
Golden ale with a sweet, hoppy aroma. Sweet start when the honey kicks in, but a hoppy ending with a whisky and heather blend; thirst-quenching.

Porter (OG 1044, ABV 4.5%) ◆
Properly black with a thick, creamy head and a sulphurous aroma. Sweet and fruity start with touches of spice in the taste. Incredible balance between sweet and bitter, but finally hops dominate the finish.

Ginger (OG 1045, ABV 4.6%) ◼ ◆
Golden bright with gently gingered tangs. Pleasing taste from the ginger. A drinkable beer with no acute flavours but a satisfying aftertaste of sweet hoppiness.

Evan Evans

Wm Evan Evans, The New Brewery, 1 Rhosmaen Street, Llandeilo, Carmarthenshire, SA14 6LU
Tel (01558) 824455
Fax (01558) 824400
Email info@evan-evans.com
Website www.evan-evans.com
Shop opens autumn 2006
Tours by arrangement

The brewery opened in 2004, owned by Simon Buckley, a member of the Welsh brewing family. The company has built a modern, purpose-built brewery, with a 20-barrel brew length and integrated fermenting room. Fifteen pubs are owned and 60 outlets are supplied. Seasonal beers: Sais Slayer (ABV 4%, January), Allez Rouge (ABV 4%, Feb-March), Easter Ale (ABV 4%, April), Cwrw Hâf (ABV 4.3%, May-July), Harvest Home (ABV 4.3%, August), Glyndwe (ABV 4.2%, September), Full Cry (ABV 4.3%, October), Bishops Revenge (ABV 4.2%, November), Cwrw Santa (ABV 4.4%, December).

BB (OG 1038, ABV 3.8%)

Cwrw (OG 1043, ABV 4.2%)

Warrior (ABV 4.5%)

Everards IFBB

Everards Brewery Ltd, Castle Acres, Enderby, near Narborough, Leicestershire, LE19 1BY
Tel (0116) 201 4100
Fax (0116) 281 4199
Email mail@everards.co.uk
Website www.everards.co.uk
Shop may be added to the Cash & Carry soon
Tours by arrangement

⊗ An independent, family-owned brewery run by the great-great grandson of the founder. The regular beers were re-branded with new pump clips in 2004 to underscore the company's commitment to cask. Based at Narborough on the outskirts of Leicester, Everards celebrated its 150th anniversary in 1999. A tenanted estate of approximately 160 pubs is based largely in Leicestershire and surrounding counties. Nearly all the pubs serve a full range of cask-conditioned beers and many serve guest ales. The principal beers are all dry-hopped and conditioned for a week prior to dispatch from the brewery. Daytime weekday tours can be arranged for CAMRA branches. Some 500 outlets are supplied. Seasonal/event beers are produced during the course of the year.

Beacon Bitter (OG 1036, ABV 3.8%) ◆
Light, refreshing, well-balanced pale amber bitter in the Burton style.

Sunchaser (ABV 4%) ◼ ◆
Brewed with ingredients usually used to produce lager, this golden ale has soft and subtle malt and hop flavours throughout, with hints of lemon in a pleasing, long, sweet finish.

Tiger Best Bitter (OG 1041, ABV 4.2%) ◻ ◆
A mid-brown, well-balanced best bitter crafted for broad appeal, benefiting from a long, bitter-sweet finish.

Original (OG 1050, ABV 5.2%) ◆
Full-bodied, mid-brown strong bitter with a pleasant rich, grainy mouthfeel. Well-balanced flavours, with malt slightly to the fore, merging into a long, satisfying finish.

Evesham

◊ S M Murphy Associates Ltd, t/a Evesham Brewery, rear of Blue Maze, Oat Street, Evesham, Worcestershire, WR11 4PJ
Tel (01386) 443462
Fax (01386) 443628
Email asumgold@aol.com

◎ The brewery opened in 1993 in the old bottle store at the Green Dragon pub (now the Blue Maze). The adjacent Gordon Hart pub was purchased in 2003 and incorporated with the Green Dragon to form the Blue Maze nightclub (Thursday-Sunday), pub, beer garden and function venue. The brewery supplies four other outlets locally and the Fish & Anchor, Offenham. Asum in the beer names is the local pronunciation of Evesham. Seasonal beer: Santa's Nightmare (ABV 5%, Christmas).

Asum (OG 1038, ABV 3.8%)

Asum Gold (OG 1052, ABV 5.2%) ◆
A well-balanced premium ale that has all the range of tastes from malt to a fruity hoppiness that make it a very satisfying drink.

For Fish & Anchor

Britain's Best (OG 1038, ABV 3.8%)

Exe Valley SIBA

Exe Valley Brewery, Silverton, Exeter, Devon, EX5 4HF
Tel (01392) 860406
Fax (01392) 861001
Email exevalley@supanet.com
Website www.siba-southwest.co.uk/breweries/exevalley
Tours by arrangement (charge made)

⊗ Exe Valley was established as Barron's Brewery in 1984. Guy Sheppard, who joined the business in 1991, continues to run the company. The beers are all brewed traditionally, using spring water, Devon malt and English hops. Direct deliveries are made to some 60 pubs within a 40-mile radius of the brewery; the beers are also available nationally via wholesalers. Seasonal beers: Devon Summer (ABV 3.9%, June-Aug), Spring Beer (ABV 4.3%, March-May), Autumn Glory (ABV 4.5%, Sept-Nov), Devon Dawn (ABV 4.5%, December), Winter Glow (ABV 6%, Dec-Feb). Bottle-conditioned beer: Devon Glory.

Bitter (OG 1036, ABV 3.7%) ◆
Mid-brown bitter, pleasantly fruity with underlying malt through the aroma, taste and finish.

Barron's Hopsit (OG 1040, ABV 4.1%) ◆
Straw-coloured beer with strong hop aroma, hop and fruit flavour and a bitter hop finish.

Dob's Best Bitter (OG 1040, ABV 4.1%) ◆
Light brown bitter. Malt and fruit predominate in the aroma and taste with a dry, bitter, fruity finish.

Devon Glory (OG 1046, ABV 4.7%)
Mid-brown, fruity-tasting pint with a sweet, fruity finish.

Mr Sheppard's Crook (OG 1046, ABV 4.7%) ◆
Smooth, full-bodied, mid-brown beer with a malty-fruit nose and a sweetish palate leading to a bitter, dry finish.

Exeter Old Bitter (OG 1046, ABV 4.8%) ◆
Mid-brown old ale with a rich fruity taste and slightly earthy aroma and bitter finish.

Exmoor SIBA

Exmoor Ales Ltd, Golden Hill Brewery, Wiveliscombe, Somerset, TA4 2NY
Tel (01984) 623798
Fax (01984) 624572
Email info@exmoorales.co.uk
Website www.exmoorales.co.uk
Tours by arrangement

⊗ Somerset's largest brewery was founded in 1980 in the old Hancock's brewery, which had been closed since 1959. It quickly won national acclaim, as its Exmoor Ale took the Best Bitter award at CAMRA's Great British Beer Festival that year, the first of many prizes. The brewery has enjoyed many years of continuous expansion and steadily increasing demand. Around 250 pubs in the south west are supplied and others nationwide via wholesalers and pub chains. Seasonal beers: Hound Dog (ABV 4%, March-May), Wild Cat (ABV 4.4%, Sept-Nov), Beast (ABV 6.6%, Oct-April ▪), Exmas (ABV 5%, Nov-Dec).

Ale (OG 1039, ABV 3.8%) ◆
A pale to mid-brown, medium-bodied session bitter. A mixture of malt and hops in the aroma and taste lead to a hoppy, bitter aftertaste.

Fox (OG 1043, ABV 4.2%)
Crafted from a blend of several malts and hops to produce a mid-brown beer of unusual subtlety and taste. The slight maltiness on the tongue is followed by a burst of hops with a lingering bitter-sweet aftertaste.

Silver Stallion (ABV 4.3%)
Chestnut-coloured best bitter with a full-bodied palate boasting a hint of blackcurrant; the initial grainy, malty finish is followed by a growing bitter finish.

Gold (OG 1045, ABV 4.5%) ◆
A yellow/golden best bitter with a good balance of malt and fruity hop on the nose and the palate. The sweetness follows through an ultimately more bitter finish.

Hart (OG 1049, ABV 4.8%) ◆
A mid-to-dark brown beer with a mixture of malt and hops in the aroma. A rich, full-bodied malt and fruit flavour follows through to a clean, hoppy aftertaste.

Stag (OG 1050, ABV 5.2%) ◆
A pale brown beer, with a malty taste and aroma, and a bitter finish.

Facer's SIBA

Facer's Flintshire Brewery, A8 Ashmount Enterprise Park, Aber Road, Flint, North Wales, CH6 5YL
Office: Tan-y-Coed, Bryn-y-Garreg, Flint

Mountain, North Wales, CH6 5QT
Tel (07713) 566370
Email dave@facers.co.uk
Tours by arrangement for CAMRA groups only

Facer's moved to its present location in January 2006 from Salford, where the equipment was shared with Bazens (qv). Future plans include expansion of production and the introduction of a new brew, Golden Ale. The plant is an eight-barrel brew length with total production of 250 barrels a year.

Twin City (OG 1035, ABV 3.3%) ◆
Red/brown in colour with a fruity nose. Quite complex with a warm spiciness adding to the roast, caramel and fruit flavours. Fairly short malty aftertaste.

Northern County (OG 1037, ABV 3.8%)

Jackdaw (OG 1041, ABV 4.3%)

This Splendid Ale (OG 1041, ABV 4.3%)

Dave's Hoppy Beer/DHB (OG 1041, ABV 4.3%)

Landslide 1927 (OG 1047, ABV 4.9%)

Fallen Angel*

Fallen Angel Micro-brewery, PO Box 95, Battle, East Sussex, TN33 0XF
Tel (01424) 777996
Fax (01424) 777976
Email custservice@fallenangelbrewery.com
Website www.fallenangelbrewery.com

The brewery was launched in 2004 by Tony Betts and his wife, who are first-time brewers. This is a one-barrel brewery making bottle-conditioned beers supplied to farmers' markets and pubs. Cask ales are planned for festivals. Seasonal beers are produced. Bottle-conditioned beers: St Patricks Irish Stout (ABV 3.1%), Englishmans Nut Brown Ale (ABV 3.2%), Cowgirl Lite (ABV 3.6%), Lemon Weissbier (ABV 3.7%), Fire in the Hole Chilli Beer (ABV 3.9%), Hickory Switch Porter (ABV 4.3%), Caribbean Lime (ABV 5.3%), Angry Ox Bitter (ABV 5.3%)

Falstaff

Falstaff Brewery, 24 Society Place, Normanton, Derby, DE23 6UH
Tel (01332) 342902
Email info@thefalstaffbrewery.co.uk
Website www.falstaffbrewery.co.uk
Tours by arrangement

⊠ The brewery dates from 1999 but was refurbished and re-opened in 2003 under new owners. Falstaff produces a range of themed Western and Shakespeare beers as well as a standard range for its own pub, the Babington Arms, Derby. Some 20 outlets are supplied.

Fist Full of Hops (OG 1044-45, ABV 4.5%)

Phoenix (OG 1045, ABV 4.7%) ◆
A smooth, tawny ale with fruit and hop, joined by plenty of malt in the mouth. A subtle sweetness produces a drinkable ale.

Smiling Assassin (OG 1050, ABV 5.2%)
A warm copper-coloured beer.

The Good, the Bad and the Drunk (OG 1058, ABV 6.2%)

Famous Railway Tavern

⌂ Famous Railway Tavern Brewing Co, 58 Station Road, Brightlingsea, Colchester, Essex, CO7 0DT
Tel (01206) 302581
Email famousrailway@yahoo.co.uk
Website www.geocities.com/famousrailway
Tours by arrangement

The brewery started life as a kitchen-sink affair. Crouch Vale Brewery assisted the development at Brightlingsea by obtaining two fermenters that gave the brewery a more professional appearance and increased production. A new hot liquor tank was added in 2005. The brewery only supplies the pub and beer festivals. Seasonal beers: Frog Ale (ABV 3.7%), Bladderwrack Stout (ABV 4.3%), Fireside Porter (ABV 4.4%), Nettle Ale (ABV 4.4%). Crab & Winkle Mild, Bladderwrack Stout and Fireside Porter are suitable for vegetarians.

Crab & Winkle Mild (ABV 3.7%)

Farmer's Ales EAB

(formerly Maldon Brewing Co)
Farmer's Ales, The Stable Brewery, Silver Street, Maldon, Essex, CM9 4QE
Tel (01621) 840925
Email info@maldonbrewing.co.uk
Website www.maldonbrewing.co.uk
Shop open for beer sales at the brewery
Tours by arrangement for small parties only

Situated in a restored stable block behind the ancient Blue Boar Hotel, the brewery started in 2002 and has enjoyed considerable success, including awards at the Maldon Beer Festival. The five-barrel plant has been recently extended with a new fermenter to allow for additional seasonal beers. Cask ale is always available at the Blue Boar Hotel and as a guest in an increasing number of local pubs. Bottled beers are now available in a number of local outlets as well as direct from the brewer. All cask beers are available in bottle-conditioned form.

A Drop of Nelson's Blood (OG 1038, ABV 3.8%) ◼ ◆
Brown, bitter session ale dominated by citrus hops.

Hotel Porter (OG 1041, ABV 4.1%) ◆
Powerful roasty bitterness is balanced by sweet fruit in this oatmeal stout.

Pucks Folly (OG 1042, ABV 4.2%) ◆
Pale golden ale with pineapple on the aroma and taste. The use of Goldings hops gives the beer a more spicy character than other golden ales.

Far North SIBA

⌂ Far North Brewery, Melvich Hotel, Melvich, Thurso, Caithness, KW14 7YJ
Tel (01641) 531206
Fax (01641) 531347
Email farnorthbrewery@aol.com
Website www.smoothhound.co.uk/hotels/melvich
Tours for hotel residents

⊠ The most northerly brew-pub in Britain. It originally brewed just one cask a week for hotel guests working at Dounreay power station. Far North now has a two-barrel plant from Dark Star's original brewery in Brighton. Owner Peter Martin plans to add a bottle-conditioned John O'Groats Ale for summer tourist outlets. One pub is owned and one outlet is supplied direct.

Real Mackay (OG 1038, ABV 3.8%)

Split Stone Pale Ale (OG 1042, ABV 4.2%)

Fast Reactor (OG 1048, ABV 4.8%)

John O'Groats Dark Ale (OG 1048, ABV 4.8%)

John O'Groats Porter (OG 1048, ABV 4.8%)

John O'Groats Wheat (OG 1050, ABV 5%)

Edge of Darkness (OG 1065, ABV 7%)

Fat Cat SIBA

Fat Cat Brewing Company, The Shed, 98-100 Lawson Road, Norwich, Norfolk, NR3 4LF
Tel (01603) 788508/624364/07816 672397
Email fatcol@hotmail.co.uk
Website www.fatcatpub.co.uk
Tours by arrangement

Fat Cat Brewery was founded by Colin Keatley, owner of the Fat Cat free house in Norwich, CAMRA National Pub of the Year 1999 and 2004. Brewing started in 2005 at the Fat Cat's sister pub, the Shed, under the supervision and management of former Woodforde's owner Ray Ashworth and head brewer David Winter. Four stock beers are brewed regularly, together with a range of seasonal and speciality beers.

Fat Cat Bitter (OG 1038, ABV 3.8%)

Alley Cat (OG 1042, ABV 4.2%)

Black Cat Stout (OG 1047, ABV 4.6%)

Top Cat (OG 1048, ABV 4.8%)

Felinfoel IFBB

Felinfoel Brewery Co Ltd, Farmers Row, Felinfoel, Llanelli, Carmarthenshire, SA14 8LB
Tel (01554) 773357
Fax (01554) 752452
Email info@felinfoel-brewery.com
Website www.felinfoel-brewery.com
Shop 9am-4pm
Tours by arrangement

Founded in 1830 by David John, the company is still family-owned and is now the oldest brewery in Wales. The present buildings are Grade II* listed and were built in the 1870s. Felinfoel was the first brewery in Europe to can beer in the 1930s. It supplies cask ale to half its 84 houses, though some use top pressure dispense, and to approximately 350 free trade outlets.

Felinfoel Best Bitter (OG 1038, ABV 3.8%)
A balanced beer, with a low aroma. Bitter-sweet initially with an increasing moderate bitterness.

Cambrian Best Bitter (OG 1039, ABV 3.9%)

Felinfoel Stout (OG 1041, ABV 4.1%)

Double Dragon Ale (OG 1042, ABV 4.2%)
This pale brown beer has a malty, fruity aroma. The taste is also malt and fruit with a background hop presence throughout. A malty and fruity finish.

Celtic Pride (OG 1043, ABV 4.3%)

Dragon's Heart (OG 1043, ABV 4.3%)

Fellows, Morton & Clayton

Fellows, Morton & Clayton Brewhouse Co Ltd, 54 Canal Street, Nottingham, NG1 7EH
Tel (0115) 950 6795
Fax (0115) 953 9838
Email sales@fellowsmortonandclayton.co.uk
Website www.fellowsmortonandclayton.co.uk

Nottingham's first brew pub since the 1940s, it was founded in 1980 as a Whitbread home-brew house but is now operated under a tenancy from Enterprise Inns (qv). The beers are brewed using malt extract with the exception of Original Strong Brew, which is full mash.

Fellows Bitter (OG 1039, ABV 3.8%)

Matthew Clayton's Original Strong Brew (ABV 4.4%)

Post Haste (OG 1048, ABV 4.5%)

Felstar EAB

Felstar Brewery, Felsted Vineyards, Crix Green, Felsted, Essex, CM6 3JT
Tel (01245) 361504 / 07973 315503
Fax (01245) 361504
Email felstarbrewery@supanet.com
Shop 10am-dusk daily
Tours by arrangement

The Felstar Brewery opened in 2001 with a five-barrel plant based in the old bonded warehouse of the Felsted Vineyard. A small number of outlets are supplied. Seasonal beer: Howlin' Hen (ABV 6.5%). Bottle-conditioned beers: all the cask beers plus Pecking Order (ABV 5%), Lord Kulmbach (ABV 4.4%), Dark Wheat (ABV 5.4%).

Essex Knight (OG 1039, ABV 3.8%)

Crix Gold (OG 1041, ABV 4%)

Hop-Hop-Hurray (OG 1042, ABV 4%)

Chick-Chat (OG 1043, ABV 4.1%)

Hopsin (OG 1048, ABV 4.6%)

Wheat (OG 1048, ABV 4.8%)

Good Knight (OG 1050, ABV 5%)

Lord Essex (OG 1056, ABV 5.4%)

Haunted Hen (OG 1062, ABV 6%)

Fenland SIBA

Fenland Brewery Ltd, Unit 2 Fieldview, Cowbridge Hall Road, Ely, Cambridgeshire, CB6 2UQ
Tel (01353) 699966

Fax (01353) 699967
Email enquiries@elybeer.co.uk
Website www.elybeer.co.uk
Tours by arrangement

⊗ The brewery opened in 1997 in Chatteris, but moved to new premises on the Isle of Ely. In 2003 the company was bought by David and Maria Griffiths. Beers are supplied to more than 100 outlets throughout Bedfordshire, Cambridgeshire, Lincolnshire, Norfolk, and Northamptonshire. Seasonal beers: Amber Solstice (ABV 4.1%), Winter Warmer (ABV 5.5%). Bottle-conditioned beers: Doctors Orders, Sparkling Wit, Smokestack Lightning, Babylon Banks.

Rabbit Poacher (ABV 3.8%)

St Audrey's Ale (ABV 3.9%)

Babylon Banks (ABV 4.1%)

Smokestack Lightning (ABV 4.1%)

Osier Cutter (ABV 4.2%)

Sparkling Wit (ABV 4.5%)

Doctors Orders (ABV 5%)

Fernandes SIBA

Fernandes Brewery, 5 Avison Yard, Kirkgate, Wakefield, West Yorkshire, WF1 1UA
Tel (01924) 291709/369547
Website www.fernandes-brewery.gowyld.com
Tours by arrangement

◎ The brewery opened in 1997 and is housed in a 19th-century malthouse. It incorporates a home-brew shop and a brewery tap. It has won Wakefield CAMRA's Pub of the Year every year since 1999 and has been awarded Yorkshire Regional Pub of the Year 2001 and 2002. One pub is owned and 10-15 outlets are supplied.

Malt Shovel Mild (OG 1038, ABV 3.8%)
A dark, full-bodied, malty mild with an abundance of roast malt and chocolate flavours, leading to a lingering, dry, malty finish.

Triple O (OG 1041, ABV 3.9%)
A light, refreshing, hoppy session beer with a lingering fruity finish.

Ale to the Tsar (OG 1042, ABV 4.1%)
A pale, smooth, well-balanced beer with some sweetness leading to a nutty, malty and satisfying aftertaste.

Wakefield Pride (OG 1045, ABV 4.5%)
A light-coloured and full-bodied, clean-tasting malty beer with a good hop character leading to a dry, bitter finish.

Empress of India (OG 1058, ABV 6%)
A strong, light-coloured, malty beer with a complex bitter palate. Fruit and malt dominate the aftertaste.

Double Six (OG 1062, ABV 6%)
A powerful, dark and rich strong beer with an array of malt, roast malt and chocolate flavours and a strong, lasting malty finish, with some hoppiness.

FILO SIBA

♁ FILO Brewing Co Ltd, First In Last Out, 14-15 High Street, Hastings, East Sussex, TN34 3EY
Tel (01424) 425079
Fax (01424) 420802
Email mike@thefilo.co.uk
Website www.thefilo.co.uk
Tours by arrangement

⊗ FILO Brewery was first installed in 1985, using old milk tanks. The current owner, Mike Bigg, took over in 1988 and remains in control of the pub and brewery business. In 2000, the brewery went through a complete overhaul, although it remains a small, five-barrel craft brewery with the First In Last Out pub as the only outlet apart from beer festivals.

Crofters (ABV 4%)

Ginger Tom (ABV 4.4%)

Cardinal (ABV 4.4%)

Gold (ABV 4.8%)

Flock Inn*

♁ Flock Inn Brewery, Ty Mawr Country Hotel, Brechfa, Carmarthen, SA32 7RA
Tel (01267) 202332
Email info@flockinnbrewery.co.uk
Website www.flockinnbrewery.co.uk
Tours by arrangement

Flock Inn Brewery was opened at Ty Mawr Country Hotel in South-west Wales in March 2006. As well as a 2.5-barrel plant, the site also has a tap room and bar that are open Friday to Monday (please ring for times). Full details of the beer range were not available but plans are for a session bitter, a stout/porter and a light summer beer.

Font Valley

See Barefoot

Four Alls

♁ Four Alls Brewery, Ovington, Richmond, Co Durham, DL11 7BP
Tel (01833) 627302
Tours by arrangement

The one-barrel brewery was launched in 2003 by John Stroud, one of the founders of Ales of Kent, using that name. In 2004 it became Four Alls, named after the pub where it is based, the only outlet except for two beers supplied twice yearly to Darlington beer festivals. Phone first to check if beer is available.

Bitter (OG 1035, ABV 3.6%)
A light-coloured beer from pale and crystal malts and hopped with Fuggles, Goldings and Styrian Goldings to give a lingering citrus bitterness.

Iggy Pop (OG 1036, ABV 3.6%)
A honey-coloured beer made from pale, crystal and wheat malts and hopped with First Gold and Goldings.

30 Shillings (OG 1039, ABV 3.8%)
A dark session ale made from pale, crystal and chocolate malts with First Gold and Fuggles hops.

Swift (OG 1038, ABV 3.8%)
A dark mild made with pale, crystal and chocolate malts. Hopped with Fuggles and

Goldings to give a smooth, pleasant character.

Red Admiral (OG 1041, ABV 3.9%)
A deep red beer that uses pale and crystal malts and is hopped with Fuggles. A malty beer with flowery notes.

Smugglers Glory (OG 1048, ABV 4.8%)
A black beer made with pale, crystal and chocolate malts and roast barley. Hopped with Fuggles and Goldings, it is a stronger and more bitter version of Swift.

Fowler's

Fowler's Ales (Prestoungrange) Ltd, 227-229 High Street, Prestonpans, East Lothian, EH32 9BE
Tel (01875) 819922s
Fax (01875) 819911
Email craigallan@prestoungrange.org
Website www.prestoungrange.org
Tours by arrangement

Fowler's opened in 2004. A new brewer, Craig Allan, joined in 2005 and introduced a new range of beers. The adjacent pub, the Gothenburg, offers all the beers and a few other outlets in the surrounding area also take them. There are plans to increase fermentation capacity and build a bigger brewery. Fowler's also offers brewsets (brewing courses). Seasonal beer: Winter Warmer (ABV 4.8%). Bottle-conditioned versions are available of all the beers (including Winter Warmer, Nov-Feb) except Prestonpans Pryde.

Prestonpans 80/- (OG 1041, ABV 4.2%)

Gothenburg Porter (OG 1042, ABV 4.4%)

Prestonpans Pryde (OG 1043, ABV 4.5%)

Fox EAB

Fox Brewery, 22 Station Road, Heacham, Kings Lynn, Norfolk, PE31 7EX
Tel (01485) 570345
Fax (01485) 579492
Email info@foxbrewery.co.uk
Website www.foxbrewery.co.uk
Tours by arrangement

Based in a successful free house, the 2002 conversion of an outbuilding into a brewery now supplies cask beer for the Fox & Hounds and a sizeable free trade. The brewery is keen on traceability and quality local ingredients. For example, all the Branthill beers are brewed from barley grown on Branthill Farm near Wells-next-the-Sea, home to the Real Ale Shop, and malted at Crisp's of Great Ryburgh. A major expansion was planned for 2006/07. Bottle-conditioned beers: all cask ales listed below. England Expects (ABV 3.8%) is a bottle-conditioned beer brewed for the Lord Nelson in Burham Thorpe, Nelson's home village. Seasonal beers: Nina's Mild (ABV 3.9%, spring/summer), Perfick (ABV 3.7%, summer), Wootton Wild (ABV 4.9%, autumn/winter).

Branthill Best (OG 1037, ABV 3.8%)
Old-fashioned best bitter.

Heacham Gold (OG 1037, ABV 3.9%) ◆
Straw-coloured, refreshingly hoppy bitter. Some caramel in the nose disappears under the dominance of the hops. A gentle, understated fruitiness gives some depth.

LJB (OG 1040, ABV 4%) ◆
A well-balanced malty brew with a hoppy, bitter background. Long finish holds up well, as a sultana-like fruitiness develops. Mid-brown with a slightly thin mouthfeel.

Red Knocker (OG 1043, ABV 4.2%)
Copper coloured and malty.

Branthill Norfolk Nectar (OG 1043, ABV 4.3%)
Slightly sweet. Brewed only with Maris Otter pale malt.

Cerberus Norfolk Stout (OG 1046, ABV 4.5%)
Dark, fruity and easy drinking.

Branthill Pioneer (OG 1050, ABV 5%)
Malty, fresh aroma. Hops are present in the background.

Nelsons Blood (ABV 5.1%)
A liquor of beers. Red, full-bodied; made with Nelsons Blood Rum.

IPA (OG 1051, ABV 5.2%)
Based on a 19th-century recipe. Easy drinking for its strength.

Punt Gun (OG 1056, ABV 5.9%) ◆
A dark brown, malt-based brew with solid fruity overtones. A distinctly roast aroma subsides in the flavour as a sweet prune character competes with the maltiness in the long ending.

Foxfield

Foxfield Brewery, Prince of Wales, Foxfield, Broughton in Furness, Cumbria, LA20 6BX
Tel (01229) 716238
Email drink@princeofwalesfoxfield.co.uk
Website www.princeofwalesfoxfield.co.uk
Tours by arrangement

Foxfield is a three-barrel plant run by Stuart and Lynda Johnson in old stables attached to the Prince of Wales Inn, across the road from the railway station. A few other outlets are supplied. The Johnsons also own Tigertops in Wakefield (qv). The beer range constantly changes, as Stuart tends to brew as the fancy takes him. The beers listed here may not necessarily be available. There are many occasional and seasonal beers. Dark Mild is suitable for vegetarians and vegans.

Sands (OG 1038, ABV 3.4%)
A pale, light, aromatic quaffing ale.

Fleur-de-Lys (OG 1038, ABV 3.6%)

Dark Mild (OG 1040, ABV 3.7%)

Brief Encounter (OG 1040, ABV 3.8%)
A fruity beer with a long, bitter finish.

Frankton Bagby

Frankton Bagby Brewery, The Old Stables, Green Lane, Church Lawford, Rugby, Warwickshire, CV23 9EF
Tel (02476) 540770 / (07977) 570779
Tours by arrangement

Frankton Bagby is a small independent brewery established in 1999 by three local families. The five-barrel plant is housed in an

18th-century stable block that has been carefully renovated by local craftsmen to preserve its original features. More than 150 outlets are supplied and the brewery has also built up a steady trade supplying private parties, beer festivals and special events with casks and polypins. Frankton Bagby is always pleased to welcome visitors to the brewery. Seasonal beers: XXXMAS (ABV 5%, Christmas), Spring Chicken (ABV 3.8%, spring), Dizzy Blonde (ABV 4%, summer), Fat Bob (ABV 4.8%, autumn).

Barnstormer (OG 1038, ABV 3.8%)
This light golden bitter has a clean, refreshing and delicate taste with a subtle floral aroma; brewed with Maris Otter malt and American Liberty hops.

Old Chestnut (OG 1040, ABV 4%)
A chestnut-coloured bitter with a distinctive nutty taste. The combination of Green Bullet and Fuggles hops gives the beer a mellow flavour while late hopping with Styrian Goldings imparts a fruity nose.

Squires Brew (OG 1042, ABV 4.2%)
A light-coloured beer, smooth on the palate and with a good hoppy aftertaste. A mix of Challenger and Fuggles hops is used for the main brew and Styrian Goldings for late hopping.

Rugby Special (OG 1045, ABV 4.5%)
A reddish-brown, full-bodied, well-balanced and pleasantly hoppy best bitter. First brewed in the borough of Rugby to celebrate Rugby Union's World Cup, the beer proved so popular it became a regular brew.

Freedom

See Brothers

Freeminer SIBA

Freeminer Brewery Ltd, Whimsey Road, Steam Mills, Cinderford, Gloucestershire, GL14 3JA
Tel (01594) 827989
Fax (01594) 829464
Email gbg@freeminer.com
Website www.freeminer.com

⊗ Founded in 1992, Freeminer has themed its cask ales on the local historic mining industry. It has won a number of awards including Champion Beer of Britain competition, Beauty of Hops, Gloucester Beer of the Year, Drinks Producer of the Year (Gloucs) and several retail awards for its packaging. Freeminer continues to develop bottle-conditioned beers, fair trade beers and intends to bring new concepts in bottle to the shelf. Seasonal beer: Strip And At It (ABV 4%, summer). Bottle-conditioned beers: Gold Miner (ABV 5%, for the Co-op), The Best (ABV 6%, for Morrisons).

Freeminer Bitter (OG 1038, ABV 4%) ◆
A light, hoppy session bitter with an intense hop aroma and a dry, hoppy finish.

Speculation Ale (OG 1046, ABV 4.8%) ◆
An aromatic, chestnut-brown, full-bodied beer with a smooth, well-balanced mix of malt and hops, and a predominately hoppy aftertaste.

Slaughter Porter (OG 1047, ABV 5%)

Frog Island SIBA

Frog Island Brewery, The Maltings, Westbridge, St James Road, Northampton, NN5 5HS
Tel (01604) 587772
Fax (01604) 750754
Email beer@frogislandbrewery.co.uk
Website www.frogislandbrewery.co.uk
Tours by arrangement to licensed trade only

⊗ Started in 1994 by home-brewer Bruce Littler and business partner Graham Cherry in a malt house built by the long-defunct brewery Thomas Manning & Co, Frog Island expanded by doubling its brew length to 10 barrels in 1998. It specialises in beers with personalised bottle labels, available by mail order. Some 40 free trade outlets are supplied, with the beer occasionally available through other micro-brewers. Seasonal beers: Fuggled Frog (ABV 3.5%, May), Head in the Clouds (ABV 4.5%, August). Bottle-conditioned beers: Natterjack, Fire Bellied Toad, Croak & Stagger. Bottled beers are available for sale in a shop on the brewery forecourt.

Best Bitter (OG 1040, ABV 3.8%) ◆
Blackcurrant and gooseberry enhance the full malty aroma with pineapple and papaya joining on the tongue. Bitterness develops in the fairly long Target/Fuggles finish.

Shoemaker (OG 1043, ABV 4.2%) ◻ ◆
An orangey aroma of fruity Cascade hops is balanced by malt. Citrus and hoppy bitterness lasts into a long, dry finish. Amber colour

That Old Chestnut (OG 1044, ABV 4.4%)
A malty, chestnut-brown ale brewed with Maris Otter pale malt, with a hint of crystal and malted wheat, and coloured with roast barley. Target is the bittering hop with Cascade as a late addition for aroma.

Natterjack (OG 1048, ABV 4.8%) ◆
Deceptively robust, golden and smooth. Fruit and hop aromas fight for dominance before the grainy astringency and floral palate give way to a long, dry aftertaste with a hint of lingering malt.

Fire Bellied Toad (OG 1050, ABV 5%) ◻ ◆
Amber-gold brew with an extraordinary long bitter/fruity finish. Huge malt and Phoenix hop flavours have a hint of apples. The pink grapefruit nose belies its punchy overall hit.

Croak & Stagger (OG 1056, ABV 5.8%) ◆
The initial honey/fruit aroma is quickly overpowered by roast malt then bitter chocolate and pale malt sweetness on the tongue. Gentle, bitter-sweet finish. A dark winter brew.

Frog & Parrot

Frog & Parrot Brewhouse, 94 Division Street, Sheffield, South Yorkshire, S1 4GF
Tel (0114) 272 1280
Email 7776@greeneking.co.uk
Tours by arrangement

Opened in 1982 by the brewers of Gold Label barley wine to regain the title of World's Strongest Beer, Roger and Out weighed in at 16.9%. The strength has since been reduced to 12.5%, though the recipe, handed down by word of mouth, remains the same. The brewery underneath the pub is now Sheffield's oldest surviving brewery since the demise of Wards.

Roger & Out (OG 1125, ABV 12.5%)

Front Street*

Front Street Brewery, 45 Front Street, Binham, Fakenham, Norfolk, NR21 0AL
Tel (01328) 830297
Email steve@frontstreetbrewery.co.uk
Website www.frontstreetbrewery.co.uk
Tours by arrangement

The brewery is based at the Chequers Inn and is probably Britain's smallest five-barrel plant. Brewing started in 2005 and three regular beers are produced as well as seasonal and occasional brews. Both cask and bottled beers are delivered to the free trade and retail outlets throughout East Anglia. Seasonal beers: China Gold (ABV 5%, winter), The Tsar (ABV 8.5%, winter). Bottle-conditioned beers: Callums Ale, Unity Strong, China Gold, The Tsar.

Binham Cheer (OG 1039, ABV 3.9%)

Callums Ale (OG 1043, ABV 4.3%)

Unity Strong (OG 1051, ABV 5%)

Fugelestou

Fugelestou Ales, Fulstow Brewery, 6 Northway, Fulstow, Lincolnshire, LN11 0XH
Tel (01507) 363642
Email fulstow.brewery@virgin.net
Website www.fulstowbrewery.co.uk
Tours by arrangement

Fugelestou operates on a 2.5-barrel plant. Some 30 outlets are supplied. One-off brews are produced regularly. Seasonal ales: Sumerheade (ABV 4.7%), Autumn Village (ABV 4%), Xmas Spirit (ABV 5%), White Xmas (ABV 4.6%). Bottle-conditioned beers: Fulstow Common, Northway IPA, Sledge Hammer Stout.

Fulstow Common (OG 1038, ABV 3.8%)

Marsh Mild (OG 1039, ABV 3.8%)

Northway IPA (OG 1042, ABV 4.2%)

Pride of Fulstow (ABV 4.5%)

Sledge Hammer Stout (OG 1077, ABV 8%)

Fuller's IFBB

Fuller, Smith and Turner plc, Griffin Brewery, Chiswick Lane South, London, W4 2QB
Tel (020) 8996 2000
Fax (020) 8995 0230
Email fullers@fullers.co.uk
Website www.fullers.co.uk
Shop Mon-Fri 10am-6pm; Sat 10am-5pm
Tours by arrangement

⊗ Fuller, Smith & Turner's Griffin Brewery in Chiswick has stood on the same site for more than 350 years and direct descendants of the founding families are still involved in running the company. Fuller's has won the Champion Beer of Britain award five times in the 25 years the competition has been staged. In 2005 beer production was around 200,000 barrels of which London Pride took up a significant proportion. Both Chiswick Bitter and ESB have undergone a change to their dry hopping regime to improve consistency. As a result of this and an overall general re-launch of ESB, cask sales of ESB have shown good growth and the new pale beer, Discovery, is succeeding in tempting drinkers away from lager. At the end of 2005 Fuller's announced an agreed acquisition of Hampshire brewer George Gale. This added 111 tied outlets to produce a combined estate of 361. Fuller's stopped all brewing at the Gales' Horndean site at the end of March 2006. The main Gales brands are now brewed at Chiswick. The company will continue to operate a full distribution and warehousing operation in Horndean. Some of Gales' seasonal beers are still brewed. Seasonal beers: London Porter (5.4% ■), India Pale Ale (ABV 4.8%), Organic Honey Dew (ABV 4.3%,), Jack Frost (ABV 4.5%). Bottle-conditioned beers: 1845 (ABV 6.3% ■ ▢), Vintage Ale (ABV 8.5% ▢), Prize Old Ale (ABV 9%, under the Gale's brand name).

Chiswick Bitter (OG 1034.5, ABV 3.5%) ▢ ◆
A pale brown bitter beer balanced by malt, citrus hops and a little sweetness. The finish is short and clean with a pleasant dry bitterness.

Discovery (ABV 3.9%) ◆
This dark gold beer has an aroma of citrus with slight perfume notes. The palate has the same fruit, complemented by malt and a dry bitterness.

London Pride (OG 1040.5, ABV 4.1%) ■ ▢ ◆
A fruity sweet malt nose with a hoppy edge that is also present on the palate and aftertaste; mellow peachy/orange notes give way to a lingering dry, bitter aftertaste.

ESB (OG 1054, ABV 5.5%) ■ ▢ ◆
The inviting complex aroma of this golden brown beer prologues flavours of fruity marmalade mixed with malt and hops, which remain in the dry finish with a hint of roast.

Under the Gale's brand name

Butser Bitter (OG 1034, ABV 3.4%)

HSB (OG 1050, ABV 4.8%)

Festival Mild (OG 1052, ABV 4.8%) ■

Full Mash

Full Mash Brewery, 17 Lower Park Street, Stapleford, Nottinghamshire, NG9 8EW
Tel (0115) 949 9262
Email karlwaring@yahoo.com

Full Mash started brewing in 2003 after Karl Waring had spent some years as an enthusiastic home brewer and thought he could make a commercial success if he went full time. The brewery has now expanded to a two-barrel plant and, with the addition of extra fermenters, six barrels a week are now produced. Plans are in hand to acquire premises to accommodate a five-barrel plant and a brewery tap. Trade is buoyant with two regular beers, a number of seasonal ales plus special one-off brews.

Séance (OG 1039, ABV 4%)

Apparition (OG 1044, ABV 4.5%)

Funfair

Funfair Brewing Co, 34 Spinney Road, Ilkeston, Derbyshire, DE7 4LH
Tel (07971) 540186
Email sales@funfairbrewingcompany.com
Website www.funfairbrewingcompany.com
Tours by arrangement

Funfair Brewing Company was launched in 2004 at the Wheel Inn in Holbrook, Derbyshire. The Wheel Inn was sold and the brewing equipment was relocated to its present site in Ilkeston. Plans include opening a bottling plant and increasing the size of the brewing plant to 10 barrels, which will mean relocating again. In the mean time, Dave Tizard and Gemma Simms continue to produce an ever-growing range of handcrafted ales. Seasonal beer: Christmas Cake Walk (ABV 6.5%).

Gallopers (OG 1038, ABV 3.8%)

Showman's Gold (OG 1044, ABV 4.4%)

Showman's Bitter (OG 1046, ABV 4.6%)

Dodgem (OG 1047, ABV 4.7%)

Brandy Snap (OG 1047, ABV 4.7%)

Showman's IPA (OG 1053, ABV 5.3%)

Cakewalk (OG 1060, ABV 6%)

Fuzzy Duck*

Fuzzy Duck Brewery, 11 Hillside Avenue, Preesall, Poulton-le-Fylde, Lancashire, FY6 0ES
Tel (01253) 811107 / 07904 343729
Email ben@fuzzyduckbrewery.co.uk
Website www.fuzzyduckbrewery.co.uk

The brewery has a half-barrel capacity and is run on a part-time basis. It began selling beers to local beer festivals in January 2006. Demand soon outstripped supply and there are plans to relocate and increase capacity to eight barrels.

Feathers (OG 1040, ABV 4%)

Stout (OG 1042, ABV 4%)

Fyfe SIBA

Fyfe Brewing Co, 469 High Street, Kirkcaldy, Fife, KY1 2SN
Tel (01592) 646211/264270
Fax (01592) 646211
Email fyfebrew@blueyonder.co.uk
Website www.fyfebrewery.co.uk
Tours by arrangement

Established in 1995 behind the Harbour Bar, Fyfe was the town's first brew-pub in the 20th-century. Most of the output is taken by the pub, the remainder being sold direct to 10 local outlets and to the free trade via wholesalers. One pub is owned and over 50 outlets are supplied. Seasonal beer: Cauld Turkey (ABV 6%, winter).

Rope of Sand (OG 1037, ABV 3.7%) ◆
A quenching bitter. Malt and fruit throughout, with a hoppy, bitter aftertaste.

Greengo (OG 1038, ABV 3.8%)

Torque Ale (OG 1039, ABV 3.9%)

Fidra (OG 1039, ABV 3.9%)

Auld Alliance (OG 1040, ABV 4%) ◆
A very bitter beer with a lingering, dry, hoppy finish. Malt and hop, with fruit, are present throughout, fading in the finish.

Lion Slayer (OG 1042, ABV 4.2%)

First Lyte (OG 1043, ABV 4.3%)

Lino Richie (OG 1045, ABV 4.5%)

Weiss Squad (OG 1045, ABV 4.5%)
Wheat beer

Fyre (OG 1048, ABV 4.8%)

J.P.S. Pilsner (OG 1050, ABV 5%)

Fyne SIBA

Fyne Ales, Achadunan, Cairndow, Argyll, PA26 8BJ
Tel/Fax (01499) 600238
Email jonny@fyneales.com
Website www.fyneales.com
Shop 10am-4pm daily
Tours by arrangement

Fyne Ales brewed for the first time on St Andrew's Day 2001. The 10-barrel plant was installed in a redundant milking parlour on a farm in Argyll. The brewery has an enthusiastic following in the central belt and the Highlands. A number of regular wholesalers also helped to build trade south of the border. Seasonal beers: Summerled (ABV 4%), Holly Daze (ABV 5%).

Piper's Gold (OG 1037.5, ABV 3.8%) ◆
An easy-drinking, golden session ale. Bitter-sweet taste with a hoppy finish.

Maverick (OG 1040.5, ABV 4.2%) ◆
Smooth, nutty session beer with a sweet, fruity finish.

Vital Spark (OG 1042.5, ABV 4.4%)
A rich, dark beer that shows glints of red. The taste is clean and slightly sharp with a hint of blackcurrant.

Highlander (OG 1045.5, ABV 4.8%)
A strong traditional ale with intense malt flavours and a citrus hop aroma.

Gale's

Closed March 2006. See Fuller's

Gargoyles*

Gargoyles Brewery, Court Farm, Holcombe Village, Dawlish, Devon, EX7 0JT
Tel (07773) 444501

Gargoyles Brewery was established in 2005. Seasonal and special brews are planned.

Best Bitter (ABV 4.2%)

Garton SIBA

Garton Brewery, Station House, Station Road, Garton on the Wolds, Driffield, East Yorkshire, YO25 3EX
Tel (01377) 252340
Email gartonbrewery@aol.com
Tours by arrangement

Garton was launched in 2001 by Richard Heptinstall with the aim of resurrecting some of the powerful beers of Dickensian times. Beers of a lesser magnitude are also brewed, but the big beers are the driving force of the brewery. Seasonal beers: Goodnight Vienna (ABV 8%), Stunned Mullet (5%).

Woldsman Bitter (OG 1048, ABV 4.5%) ◆
This refreshing bitter is gold in colour. The full-bodied beer has a mix of hops and fruit balancing the sweetness. A dry, crisp finish.

Old Buffer (OG 1050, ABV 4.5%)
A dark mild of a type brewed around the time of the First World War.

Chocolate Frog (ABV 8%)

Liquid Lobotomy Stout (OG 1080, ABV 8%)
Garston's flagship beer, its strength derived from grain without the aid of extracts and sugars.

George & Dragon

George & Dragon, Churchend, Foulness Island, Southend-on-Sea, Essex, SS3 9XQ
Tel (01702) 219460
Email fred.fara@gandpub.fsnet.co.uk
Website www.georgeanddragonpub.co.uk

A pub-brewery that came on stream in 2004 in the cellar of the pub. Nine gallons can be produced at a time. An occasional mild is brewed. Limited brewing.

Beaters Best Bitter (ABV 5%)

George Wright

See under Wright

Glastonbury SIBA

Glastonbury Ales, Unit 10 Wessex Park, Somerton Business Park, Somerton, Somerset, TA11 6SB
Tel (01458) 272244
Email glastonburyales@ukonline.co.uk
Tours by arrangement

⊗ Glastonbury Ales was established in 2002 by Greig Nicholls who had been a home brewer for many years. Production has increased to 15 barrels a week and is still rising. The five-barrel plant uses malt from Tuckers of Newton Abbot and hops from Charles Faram in Worcestershire. 60 outlets are supplied. Seasonal beers: Ley Line (ABV 4.2%, Jan-March), Pomparles Porter (ABV 4.5%, Feb-March), Spring Loaded (ABV 4.4%, Feb-June), Pilton Pop (ABV 4.2%, May-June), Brue (ABV 4%, May-Nov), Black As Yer 'At (ABV 4.3%, Sept-Nov), FMB (ABV 5%, Sept-Dec), Holy Thorn (ABV 4.2%, Oct-Dec), Excalibur (ABV 4%, Nov-May).

Mystery Tor (OG 1040, ABV 3.8%) ◆
A golden bitter with plenty of floral hop and fruit on the nose and palate, the sweetness giving way to a bitter hop finish. Full-bodied for a session bitter.

Lady of the Lake (OG 1042, ABV 4.2%) ◆
A full-bodied amber best bitter with plenty of hops to the forefront balanced by a fruity malt flavour and a subtle hint of vanilla, leading to a clean, bitter hop aftertaste.

Hedgemonkey (OG 1048, ABV 4.6%)
A ruby bitter with toffee/coffee undertones that give way to a medium hopped, spicy finish.

Golden Chalice (OG 1048, ABV 4.8%)
Light and golden best bitter with a robust malt character. Strong bitterness provided by Challenger hops gives way to a light floral aftertaste, due to the late addition of American Mount Hood.

Glentworth SIBA

Glentworth Brewery, Glentworth House, Crossfield Lane, Skellow, Doncaster, South Yorkshire, DN6 8PL
Tel (01302) 725555
Fax (01302) 724133

The brewery was formed in 1996 and is housed in dairy buildings. The five-barrel plant supplies more than 80 pubs. Production is concentrated on mainly light-coloured, hoppy ales. Due to demand, a second cold room has been added, doubling storage capacity. Seasonal beers (brewed to order): Oasis (ABV 4.1%), Happy Hooker (ABV 4.3%), North Star (ABV 4.3%), Perle (ABV 4.4%), Dizzy Blonde (ABV 4.5%), Whispers (ABV 4.5%).

Lightyear (OG 1037, ABV 3.9%)

Goacher's

P&DJ Goacher, Unit 8, Tovil Green Business Park, Burial Ground Lane, Tovil, Maidstone, Kent, ME15 6TA
Tel (01622) 682112
Tours by arrangement

⊗ A traditional brewery that uses only malt and Kentish hops for all its beers. Goacher's celebrated 21 years in the business in 2004. Phil and Debbie Goacher have concentrated on brewing good wholesome beers without gimmicks. Two tied houses and around 30 free trade outlets in the mid-Kent area are supplied. Special, originally a mix of Light and Dark ales, is brewed for sale under house names. Seasonal beer: Old 1066 (ABV 6.7%).

Real Mild Ale (OG 1033, ABV 3.4%)
A full-flavoured malty ale with background bitterness.

Fine Light Ale (OG 1036, ABV 3.7%) ◆
A pale, golden brown bitter with a strong, floral, hoppy aroma and aftertaste. A hoppy and moderately malty session beer.

Special/House Beer (OG 1037, ABV 3.8%)

Best Dark Ale (OG 1040, ABV 4.1%) ◆
A bitter beer, balanced by a moderate maltiness, with a complex aftertaste.

Crown Imperial Stout (OG 1044, ABV 4.5%)
A classic Irish-style stout with a clean palate

and satisfying aftertaste from Kent Fuggles hops.

Gold Star Strong Ale (OG 1050, ABV 5.1%) ♦
A strong pale ale brewed from 100% Maris Otter malt and East Kent Goldings hops.

Old/Maidstone Old Ale (OG 1066, ABV 6.7%)

Goddards SIBA

Goddards Brewery Ltd, Barnsley Farm, Bullen Road, Ryde, Isle of Wight, PO33 1QF
Tel (01983) 611011
Fax (01983) 611012
Email office@goddards-brewery.co.uk
Website www.goddards-brewery.co.uk

⊗ Housed in a converted 18th-century barn on a farm near Ryde, the brewery went into production in 1993. Sales of its award-winning beers have been rising steadily. Around 40 outlets are supplied. Seasonal beers: Ale of Wight (ABV 4%, spring), Duck's Folly (ABV 5%, early autumn), Iron Horse (ABV 4.8%, late autumn), Inspiration (ABV 5.2%), Winter Warmer (ABV 5.2%).

Special Bitter (OG 1038.5, ABV 4%) ▯ ♦
Well-balanced session beer that maintains its flavour and bite with compelling drinkability.

Fuggle-Dee-Dum (OG 1048.5, ABV 4.8%) ♦
Brown-coloured strong ale with bags of malt and hops.

Goff's SIBA

Goff's Brewery Ltd, 9 Isbourne Way, Winchcombe, Cheltenham, Gloucestershire, GL54 5NS
Tel (01242) 603383
Fax (01242) 603959
Email brewery@goffs.biz
Website www.goffs.biz

⊗ Goff's is a family concern that celebrated its 10th anniversary in 2004. Its ales are available regionally in more than 200 outlets and nationally through wholesalers. The addition of the seasonal Ales of the Round Table provides a range of 12 beers of which four or five are always available. Seasonal beers: Mordred (ABV 4.2%, Jan-Feb), Launcelot (ABV 4.5%, March-April), Guinevere (ABV 4.1%, May), Galahad (ABV 4.3%, June), Excalibur (ABV 3.8%, July), Lamorak (ABV 5%, August), Merlin (ABV 4.3%, Sept-Oct), Camelot (ABV 4.4%, Nov-Dec).

Tournament (OG 1038, ABV 4%) ♦
Dark golden in colour, with a pleasant hop aroma. A clean, light and refreshing session bitter with a pleasant hop aftertaste.

Jouster (OG 1040, ABV 4%) ♦
A drinkable, tawny-coloured ale, with a light hoppiness in the aroma. It has a good balance of malt and bitterness in the mouth, underscored by fruitiness, with a clean, hoppy aftertaste.

White Knight (OG 1046, ABV 4.7%) ♦
A well-hopped bitter with a light colour and full-bodied taste. Bitterness predominates in the mouth and leads to a dry, hoppy aftertaste.

Black Knight (OG 1053, ABV 5.3%) ▮ ♦
A dark, ruby-red tinted beer with a strong chocolate malt aroma. It has a smooth, dry, malty taste, with a subtle hoppiness, leading to a dry finish.

Golcar SIBA

Golcar Brewery, Swallow Lane, Golcar, Huddersfield, West Yorkshire, HD7 4HT
Tel (01484) 644241 / 07970 267555
Email golcarbrewery@btconnect.com
Tours by arrangement

⊛ Golcar started brewing in 2001 and production has increased from 2.4 barrels to five barrels a week. The brewery owns one pub, the Rose and Crown at Golcar, and supplies four other outlets in the local area.

Dark Mild (OG 1034, ABV 3.4%) ♦
Dark mild with a light roasted malt and liquorice taste. Smooth and satisfying.

Pennine Gold (OG 1038, ABV 3.8%)
A hoppy and fruity session beer.

Bitter (OG 1039, ABV 3.9%) ♦
Amber bitter with a hoppy, citrus taste, with fruity overtones and a bitter finish.

Weavers Delight (OG 1045, ABV 4.8%)
Malty best bitter with fruity overtones.

Winkle Warmer Porter (OG 1047, ABV 5%)
A robust all grain and malty working man's porter.

Goldfinch

⌂ Goldfinch Brewery, 47 High East Street, Dorchester, Dorset, DT1 1HU
Tel (01305) 264020

Goldfinch has been brewing since 1987 and is situated behind the Tom Brown public house.

Tom Browns (ABV 4%)

Flashman's Clout (ABV 4.5%)

Midnight Blinder (ABV 5%)

Goodmanham

⌂ Goodmanham Brewery, Goodmanham Arms, Main Street, Goodmanham, East Yorkshire, YO43 3JA
Tel (01430) 873849
Email info@goodmanhamarms.co.uk
Website goodmanhamarms.co.uk

Brewing stopped in October 2005 but there are plans to re-start.

Goose Eye SIBA

Goose Eye Brewery Ltd, Ingrow Bridge, South Street, Keighley, West Yorkshire, BD21 5AX
Tel/Fax (01535) 605807
Email goose-eye@totalise.co.uk
Website www.goose-eye.co.uk

⊛ Goose Eye has been run by Jack and David Atkinson for the past 13 years at Ingrow Bridge. They are brewing to capacity and are looking for bigger premises. The brewery supplies 60-70 regular outlets, mainly in West and North Yorkshire, and Lancashire. The beers are also available through national wholesalers and pub chains. It produces an ever-expanding range of occasional beers, sometimes brewed to order, and is diversifying into wholesaling and bottled beers (filtered but not pasteurised). No-Eye Deer is often re-badged under house names.

Barm Pot Bitter **(OG 1038, ABV 3.8%)**
The bitter hop and citrus flavours that dominate this amber session bitter are balanced by a malty base. The finish is increasingly dry and bitter.

Bronte Bitter **(OG 1040, ABV 4%)**
A malty amber best bitter with bitterness increasing to give a lingering dry finish.

No-Eye Deer **(OG 1040, ABV 4%)**
A faint fruity and malty aroma. Strong hoppy flavours and a long, bitter finish characterise this refreshing, copper-coloured bitter.

Golden Goose **(OG 1045, ABV 4.5%)**
A straw-coloured beer light on the palate with a smooth and refreshing hoppy finish.

Wharfedale **(OG 1045, ABV 4.5%)**
Malt and hops dominate the taste of this copper-coloured premium bitter. Bitterness comes through into the finish.

Over and Stout **(OG 1052, ABV 5.2%)**
A very dark palatable old ale.

Pommies Revenge **(OG 1052, ABV 5.2%)**
An extra strong, single malt bitter.

Grainstore SIBA

Davis'es Brewing Co Ltd (Grainstore), Grainstore Brewery, Station Approach, Oakham, Rutland, LE15 6RE
Tel (01572) 770065
Fax (01572) 770068
Email grainstorebry@aol.com
Website www.rutnet.co.uk/customers/grainstore
Tours by arrangement

⊗ Grainstore, the smallest county's largest brewery, has been in production since 1995. The brewery's curious name comes from the fact that it was founded by Tony Davis and Mike Davies. After 30 years in the industry, latterly with Ruddles, Tony decided to set up his own business after finding a derelict Victorian railway grainstore building. The brewery is designed traditionally, relying on whole hops and Maris Otter barley malt. 60 outlets are supplied. In 2005 they won awards for Rutland Panther and Springtime at Leicester Beer Festival, then Rutland Panther went on to win the Mild category in the Champion Beer of Britain competition and came second in the overall championship. Seasonal beers: Springtime (ABV 4.5%, March-May), Tupping Ale (ABV 4.5%, Sept-Oct), Three Kings (ABV 4.5%, Nov-Dec). Bottle-conditioned beer: Ten Fifty.

Rutland Panther **(OG 1034, ABV 3.4%)**
This superb reddish-black mild certainly punches above its weight with malt and roast flavours combining to deliver a brew that can match the average stout for intensity of flavour.

Cooking Bitter **(OG 1036, ABV 3.6%)**
Tawny-coloured beer with malt and hops on the nose and a pleasant grainy mouthfeel. Hops and fruit flavours combine to give a bitterness that continues into a long finish.

Triple B **(OG 1042, ABV 4.2%)**
Initially hops dominate over malt in both the aroma and taste, but fruit is there, too. All three linger in varying degrees in the sweetish aftertaste of this brown brew.

Gold **(OG 1045, ABV 4.5%)**
A refreshing, light beer with a complex blend of mellow malt and sweetness, balanced against a subtle floral aroma and smooth bitterness.

Ten Fifty **(OG 1050, ABV 5%)**
Full-bodied, mid-brown strong bitter with a hint of malt on the nose. Malt, hops and fruitiness coalesce in a well-balanced taste leading to a satisfying bitter-sweet finish.

Rutland Beast **(OG 1053, ABV 5.3%)**
A strong beer, dark brown in colour. Well-balanced flavours blend together to produce a full-bodied drink

Winter Nip **(OG 1073, ABV 7.7%)**
A true barley wine. A good balance of sweetness and bitterness melding together so that neither predominates over the other. Smooth and warming.

For Steamin' Billy Brewing Co (qv)

Country Bitter **(OG 1036, ABV 3.6%)**

Grand Prix Mild **(OG 1036, ABV 3.6%)**

Robert Catesby **(OG 1042, ABV 4.2%)**

Bitter **(OG 1043, ABV 4.3%)**
Brown-coloured best bitter. Initial malt and hops aromas are superseded by fruit and hop taste and aftertaste, accompanied by a refreshing bitterness.

Skydiver **(OG 1050, ABV 5%)**
Full-bodied, strong, mahogany-coloured beer in which an initial malty aroma is followed by a characteristic malty sweetness that is well balanced by a pronounced hoppy bitterness.

Grand Union SIBA

Grand Union Brewery Co, 10 Abenglen Industrial Estate, Betam Road, Hayes, Middlesex, UB3 1SS
Tel (020) 8573 9888
Fax (020) 8573 8885
Email info@gubrewery.co.uk
Website www.gubrewery.co.uk
Tours groups by arrangement

⊗ Grand Union Brewery started brewing in 2002 with a 10-barrel plant that came from Mash and Air in Manchester. Direct deliveries are made to Greater London and surrounding counties and the beers are available through selected wholesalers. The single varietal One Hop series of beers uses hop varieties from around the world. Some 200 outlets are supplied. Seasonal beers: Mild (ABV 3.6%, April-May), English Wheat Beer (ABV 4.4%, June-Sept), Autumn Ale (ABV 4.4%, Oct-Nov), Old Ale (ABV 6-8.5%, winter), Brass Monkeys (ABV 4.1%, Nov-Jan), WMD (ABV 5.2%, Feb-March), Heart of Gold (ABV 4.3%, Jan-Feb).

Bitter **(OG 1036, ABV 3.7%)**
Amber-coloured, easy-drinking beer with

hoppy citrus notes throughout and an increasing bitter dryness.

Gold (OG 1040, ABV 4.2%) ◆
Perfumed hops, present throughout, are complemented by a slight sweet maltiness and a bitterness that lingers in the aftertaste.

Liberty Blonde (OG 1041, ABV 4.2%)

One Hop (OG 1043, ABV 4.5%) ◆
This yellow-coloured beer has hops and fruit on the nose and palate, giving way to a dominating bitterness in the finish.

Special (OG 1044, ABV 4.5%) ◆
A copper-coloured beer with a sweet fruit aroma and a drinkable hoppy bitterness.

Stout (OG 1050, ABV 4.8%) ◆
A dark, roasty stout with kiwi fruit notes and a short, bitter, roast aftertaste.

Honey Porter (OG 1050, ABV 4.9%) ◆
Honey sweetness, fruit and roast notes dominate this smooth-tasting black beer. An undertone of caramel is also present.

Great Gable

Great Gable Brewing Co Ltd, Wasdale Head Inn, Gosforth, Cumbria, CA20 1EX
Tel (019467) 26229 Inn 26333
Fax (019467) 26334
Email info@greatgablebrewing.com
Website www.greatgablebrewing.com
Tours by arrangement

Great Gable brewery is situated at the famous Wasdale Head Inn, birthplace of British climbing. The inn is at the head of remote and unspoiled Wasdale, at the foot of Great Gable, one of England's highest mountains and near its deepest lake. The brewery was the brain child of Giles Holiday and Howard Christie, co-workers at the Wasdale Head Inn for many years and now brewmaster and director respectively. The Wasdale Head is the main outlet for the beers. Bottle-conditioned beer: Yewbarrow. All the beers are fined with isinglass; in addition, Yewbarrow contains a little honey.

Liar (OG 1037, ABV 3.4%)

Great Gable (OG 1035, ABV 3.7%)
Made from Thomas Fawcett's pale malt with a little dark crystal malt. High alpha Challenger hops for bittering and another hop for aroma.

Prickly Bee (OG 1037, ABV 3.9%)
Variant of Liar with addition of honey and gorse.

Wry 'Nose (OG 1039, ABV 4%)

Burnmoor Pale (OG 1040, ABV 4.2%)

Wasd'ale (OG 1042, ABV 4.4%)
Ruby in colour with a fine aftertaste.

Scawfell (OG 1046, ABV 4.8%)
Reminiscent of an old-fashioned ale, brewed with pale malt and a small amount of pale crystal. The hops are Bramling Cross.

Illgill IPA (OG 1048, ABV 5%)
A blend of pale malts, highly hopped with only aroma varieties.

Yewbarrow (OG 1054, ABV 5.5%)
A rich, dark, mellow, strong dark mild (some say stout) with an unusual fruit flavour.

Great Oakley

Great Oakley Brewery, Bridge Farm, 11 Brooke Road, Great Oakley, Northamptonshire, NN18 8HG
Tel (01536) 744888
Fax (01536) 742460
Email sales@greatoakleybrewery.co.uk
Website www.greatoakleybrewery.co.uk
Tours by arrangement

The brewery is situated in the village of Great Oakley and is housed in converted stables on a former working farm. Partners Mike Evans and Phil Greenway started production in 2005 and supply more than 50 outlets including the Malt Shovel Tavern, Northampton, which is the brewery tap.

Wot's Occurring (OG 1040, ABV 3.9%)

Harpers (OG 1045, ABV 4.3%)

Gobble (OG 1047, ABV 4.5%)

Tailshaker (OG 1052, ABV 5%)

Great Orme

Great Orme Brewery/Bragdy y Gogarth, Nant y Cywarch Farm, Glan Conwy, Colwyn Bay, Conwy, LL28 5PP
Tel (01492) 580548
Email info@greatormebrewery.co.uk
Website www.greatormebrewery.co.uk

Great Orme started brewing in 2005 on a hillside halfway up the Conwy Valley between Deganwy and Betws-y-Coed, with views of Liverpool Bay and Great Orme. Jonathan Hughes has based his brewery in a former cow shed on the family farm. A spring in the grounds provides pure Welsh water from the hills.

Best (ABV 3.8%)

Extravaganza Ale (ABV 4.4%)

Green Dragon

Green Dragon Brewery, Green Dragon, 29 Broad Street, Bungay, Suffolk, NR35 1EE
Tel/Fax (01986) 892681
Tours by arrangement

The Green Dragon pub was purchased from Brent Walker in 1991 and the buildings at the rear converted to a brewery. In 1994 the plant was expanded and moved into a converted barn across the car park. The doubling of capacity allowed the production of a larger range of ales, including seasonal and occasional brews. The beers are available at the pub and beer festivals. Seasonal beers: Mild (ABV 5%, autumn/winter), Wynnter Warmer (ABV 6.5%).

Chaucer Ale (OG 1037, ABV 3.7%)

Gold (OG 1045, ABV 4.4%)

Bridge Street Bitter (OG 1046, ABV 4.5%)

Strong Mild (ABV 5.4%)

Greene King

See New Nationals section

Greenfield

Greenfield Real Ale Brewery Ltd, Unit 8 Tanners Business Centre, Waterside Mill, Chew Valley Road, Greenfield, Saddleworth, Greater Manchester, OL3 7PF
Tel (01457) 879789
Email office@greenfieldrealale.co.uk
Website www.greenfieldrealale.co.uk
Tours by arrangement (call 07813 176121)

☺ Greenfield was launched in 2002 by Peter Percival, former brewer at Saddleworth. Tony Harratt joined Peter in 2005 as a partner. They plan to expand the delivery area and look into the possibility of producing bottled beer. Some 40-50 outlets are supplied.

Black Five (OG 1040, ABV 4%)

Celebration (OG 1040, ABV 4%)

Dovestones Bitter (OG 1040, ABV 4%)

Bill O' Jacks (OG 1041, ABV 4.1%)

Delph Donkey (OG 1041, ABV 4.1%)

Castleshaw (OG 1041, ABV 4.2%)

Evening Glory (OG 1041, ABV 4.2%)

Ice Breaker (OG 1041, ABV 4.2%)

Pride of England (OG 1041, ABV 4.2%)

Uppermill Ale (OG 1041, ABV 4.2%)

Brassed Off (OG 1044, ABV 4.4%)

Friezeland Ale (OG 1044, ABV 4.4%)

Icicle (OG 1044, ABV 4.4%)

Indians Head (OG 1044, ABV 4.4%)

Longwood Thump (OG 1050, ABV 4.5%)

Rudolph's Tipple (OG 1050, ABV 5%)

Green Jack

T Dunford t/a Green Jack Brewery, Triangle Tavern, 29 St Peters Street, Lowestoft, Suffolk, NR32 1QA
Tel (01502) 582711
www.bikeways.freeserve.co.uk/greenjack.htm
Tours by arrangement

Green Jack started brewing again in 2003. In 2005 awards were won at Leicester, Peterborough, Ipswich and Norwich CAMRA beer festivals. 20 outlets are supplied and two pubs are owned. Seasonal ales: Honey Bunny (ABV 4%, spring), Summer Dream (ABV 4%), Lurcher (ABV 5.9%, winter).

Canary (OG 1038, ABV 3.8%)

Orange Wheat (OG 1042, ABV 4.2%) ■ ◆
Citrus notes dominate the introduction to this deceptively interesting beer. Gold coloured with equal hints of hop and mandarin in the first impression. A dry bitterness develops as the fruit slowly melts away.

Grasshopper (OG 1045, ABV 4.6%)

Golden Sickle (OG 1047, ABV 4.8%)

Gone Fishing (OG 1052, ABV 5.5%)

Ripper (OG 1074, ABV 8.5%)

Raspberry Blower (OG 1074, ABV 8.5%)
Ripper with added raspberries, which impart a reddish colour and a strong, sweet flavour. Well balanced and not at all sugary.

Green Tye EAB

Green Tye Brewery Ltd, Green Tye, Much Hadham, Hertfordshire, SG10 6JP
Tel (01279) 841041
Fax (01279) 842956
Email info@gtbrewery.co.uk
Website www.gtbrewery.co.uk
Tours by arrangement

⊗ Established by brewer William Compton in 1999, in a village on the edge of the Ash Valley, it uses traditional Hertfordshire grown Maris Otter barley. It supplies the village pub and local free trade, as well as the south west, north west and East Anglia direct and/or by reciprocal arrangement with other micro-brewers. All cask ales are also available in bottle-conditioned form. Occasional speciality beers are also brewed. Seasonal beers: Snowdrop (ABV 3.9%, spring), Mad Morris (ABV 4.2%, summer), Autumn Rose (ABV 4.2%, late autumn), Conkerer (ABV 4.7%, early autumn), Coal Porter (ABV 4.5%, winter).

Union Jack (OG 1036, ABV 3.6%)
A copper-coloured bitter, fruity with a citrus taste and a hoppy, citrus aroma, with a balanced, bitter finish.

Mustang Mild (OG 1037, ABV 3.7%)

Green Tiger (OG 1042, ABV 4.2%)

XBF (OG 1042, ABV 4.2%)

Wheel Barrow (OG 1044, ABV 4.3%)
Amber-coloured beer with a soft, fruity nose and taste. Gentle malt, with underlying hop bitterness, with a fruity and slightly dry finish.

Greenwood

William Greenwood Brewing Co Ltd, Cock & Bottle, 93 Barkerend Road, Little Germany, Bradford, West Yorkshire, BD3 9AA
Tel (01274) 222305
Tours by arrangement

Greenwood started its days in an industrial estate in Thorton in 2004 and moved to the Cock & Bottle pub. Three Rugby League fans from the Keighley area – John Williams, Peter Fell and Rick Greenwood – produce beers with names based on the game. A range of Cock & Bottle themed beers is planned.

Flying Winger (ABV 3.6%)

Merlins Magic Touch (ABV 3.6%)

One Hop Drop (ABV 4.1%)

Drop Kick (ABV 4.4%)

Inn Touch (ABV 4.5%)

Fat Prop (ABV 5%)

New Jock Strap IPA (ABV 6.5%)

Old Jock Strap Stout (ABV 6.5%)

Gribble

🍺 **Gribble Brewery Ltd, Gribble Inn, Oving, West Sussex, PO20 6BP**

Tel 07813 321795
Email gribblebeers@hotmail.co.uk
Website www.gribblebrewery.co.uk

⊗ The Gribble Brewery is 25 years old. Until February 2005 it was run as a managed house operation by Badger (qv) but it is now an independent micro-brewery owned by Brian Olderfield, the previous manager. Brian and brewer Rob Cooper still brew K&B Mild for Badger and will continue to brew and sell the full range of Gribble beers for the free trade. Eight outlets are supplied and more are in the offing. Seasonal beer: Wobbler (ABV 7.2%).

Slurping Stoat (ABV 3.8%)

Toff's Ale (ABV 4%)

Ale (ABV 4.1%)

Reg's Tipple (ABV 5%)
Reg's Tipple was named after a customer from the early days of the brewery. It has a smooth nutty flavour with a pleasant afterbite.

Plucking Pheasant (ABV 5.2%)

Pig's Ear (ABV 5.8%)
A full-bodied old ale with a rich ruby-brown colour.

For Badger

K&B Mild Ale (ABV 3.5%) ◆
A truly dark mild with a toffee, roast malt character that is present throughout. Short aftertaste. Nothing like the old K&B Mild, but pleasant nonetheless.

Gwynant

◊ Bragdy Gwynant, Tynllidiart Arms, Capel Bangor, Aberystwyth, Ceredigion, SY23 3LR
Tel (01970) 880248
Fax (01970) 880929
Tours by arrangement

Brewing started in 2004 in a building at the front of the pub, measuring just 4ft 6ins by 4ft, with a brew length of nine gallons. Beer is only sold in the pub and there are no plans for expansion. The brewery has now been recognised as the smallest commercial brewery by the Guinness Book of Records (certificate on display in the Tynllidiart Arms). The small scale of the plant means that beer may not always be available; however, additional beers may be brewed occasionally.

Cwrw Gwynant (OG 1044, ABV 4.2%)

Hadrian & Border SIBA

Alnwick Ales Ltd t/a Hadrian & Border Brewery, Unit 11 Hawick Crescent Industrial Estate, Newcastle upon Tyne, Tyne & Wear, NE6 1AS
Tel (0191) 276 5302
Fax (0191) 265 5312
Email border@rampart.freeserve.co.uk
Tours by arrangement

⊛ Hadrian & Border is the result of a merger between Border Brewery of Berwick-on-Tweed and Four Rivers of Newcastle. The company is based at the ex-Four Rivers 20-barrel site in Newcastle. There are plans to move to a new site. The company's brands are available from Glasgow to Yorkshire, and nationally through wholesalers. They are hard to find on Tyneside, though the Sir John Fitzgerald group (qv) stocks them from time to time. Approximately 100 outlets are supplied.

Vallum Bitter (OG 1034, ABV 3.6%)
A well-hopped, amber-coloured bitter with a distinctive dry, refreshing taste.

Gladiator (OG 1036, ABV 3.8%) ◆
Tawny-coloured bitter with plenty of malt in the aroma and palate, leading to a strong bitter finish.

Farne Island Pale Ale (OG 1038, ABV 4%) ◆
A copper-coloured bitter with a refreshing malt/hop balance.

Flotsam (OG 1038, ABV 4%)
Bronze coloured with a citrus bitterness and a distinctive floral aroma.

Legion Ale (OG 1040, ABV 4.2%) ◆
Well-balanced, amber-coloured beer, full bodied with good malt flavours. Well hopped with a long bitter finish.

Secret Kingdom (OG 1042, ABV 4.3%)
Dark, rich and full-bodied, slightly roasted with a malty palate ending with a pleasant bitterness.

Reiver's IPA (OG 1042, ABV 4.4%)
Dark golden bitter with a clean citrus palate and aroma with subtle malt flavours breaking through at the end.

Centurion Best Bitter (OG 1043, ABV 4.5%) ◆
Smooth, clean-tasting bitter with a distinct hop palate leading to a good bitter finish.

Halifax Steam

Halifax Steam Brewing Co Ltd, Southedge Works, Brighouse Road, Hipperholme, Halifax, West Yorkshire, HX3 8EF
Tel (07974) 544980
Email davidearnshaw@blueyonder.co.uk
Website www.halifaxsteam.co.uk

⊛ David Earnshaw started brewing in 2001 in a converted garage, inspired by CAMRA's series of home-brewing books. He bought his five-barrel plant from the Fox & Firkin in Lewisham, south London, which he collected and installed himself in new premises. In addition to brewing, David supplies temporary bars for events and beer festivals. His beers are supplied to approximately 50 pubs locally and further afield via brewery swaps. A brewery tap was due to open in summer 2006.

Morning Glory (ABV 3.8%)

Jamaican Ginger (ABV 4%)

Lilly Fogg (ABV 4%) ◆
Yellow, creamy, full-flavoured beer, hoppy and fruity, very drinkable bitter. Clean and fresh bitter finish.

Pickel Hut Imposter (ABV 4%)
Cask lager.

Probably Organic (ABV 4%) ◆
Creamy golden ale. Easy-drinking and fruity with a grapefruit zest nose.

Bantam (OG 1043, ABV 4.1%)

Joker (ABV 4.1%)

Rio (ABV 4.3%)

Uncle John (ABV 4.3%)
A dark beer. Smooth and moody with a fruity finish.

Rhode Island Red (ABV 4.5%)
Ruby red in colour, lots of body.

Tokyo Joe (ABV 4.5%) ◆
Lighty-flavoured, lager-style beer. Rice is used, which means the beer has an unusual nose and taste.

Golden Rain (ABV 4.6%) ◆
Distinctive best bitter at a different end of the taste spectrum to other steam beers. Predominant exotic fruit flavour.

Luftkissenfahrzeug (ABV 4.6) ◆
Pale beer brewed with a lager recipe, with a good balance of flavours and slight bitter aftertaste.

Cock of the North (OG 1048, ABV 4.9%)

Rio Grande (ABV 4.9%)
Coffee porter.

Shirley Crabtree (ABV 4.9%)

Hambleton SIBA

Nick Stafford Hambleton Ales, Melmerby Green Road, Melmerby, North Yorkshire, HG4 5NB
Tel (01765) 640108
Email sales@hambletonales.co.uk
Website www.hambletonales.co.uk
Shop Mon-Fri 9am-4pm
Tours by arrangement

⊛ Hambleton Ales was established in 1991 by Nick Stafford on the banks of the River Swale in the heart of the Vale of York. Expansion of the brewery in 2005 resulted in the relocation to larger premises in view of the famous White Horse on the Hambleton Hills. Brewing capacity has increased to 100 barrels a week and a bottling line caters for micros and larger brewers, handling more than 20 brands. More than 100 outlets are supplied throughout Yorkshire and the North-east. The brewery has won a number of awards for its beers. Five core brands are produced along with an additional special brew each month. Hambleton is the only British producer of a gluten and wheat free bottled ale – GFA (ABV 4.2%). The company also brew beers under contract for the Village Brewer and Malton Brewery.

Bitter (OG 1037.5, ABV 3.6%) ◆
Rich, hoppy flavour rides through this light and drinkable beer. Taste is bitter with citrus and marmalade character and a solid body. Ends dry with a spicy mouthfeel.

Goldfield (OG 1041, ABV 4.2%) ◆
A light amber bitter with good hop character and increasing dryness. A fine blend of malts gives a smooth overall impression.

Stallion (OG 1041, ABV 4.2%) ◆
A premium bitter, moderately hoppy throughout and richly balanced in malt and fruit, developing a sound and robust bitterness, with earthy hops drying the aftertaste.

Stud (OG 1042.5, ABV 4.2%) ◆
A strongly bitter beer, with rich hop and fruit. It ends dry and spicy.

Nightmare (OG 1050, ABV 5%) ◆
Fully deserving its acclaim, this impressively flavoured beer satisfies all parts of the palate. Strong roast malts dominate, but hoppiness rears out of this complex blend.

For Village Brewer

White Boar (OG 1037.5, ABV 3.8%) ◆
A light, flowery and fruity ale; crisp, clean and refreshing, with a dry-hopped, powerful but not aggressive, bitter finish.

Bull (OG 1039, ABV 4%) ◆
A pale, full, fruity bitter, well hopped to give a lingering bitterness.

Old Raby (OG 1045, ABV 4.6%) ◆
A full-bodied, smooth, rich-tasting dark ale. A complex balance of malt, fruit character and creamy caramel sweetness offsets the bitterness. A classic old ale.

For Malton Brewery

Double Chance (ABV 3.8%)

Golden Chance (ABV 4.2%)

Auld Bob (ABV 4.5%)

Hammerpot*

Hammerpot Brewery Ltd, Unit 30 The Vinery, Arundel Road, Poling, West Sussex, BN18 9PY
Tel/Fax (01903) 883338
Email info@hammerpot-brewery.co.uk
Website www.hammerpot-brewery.co.uk

Brewing began in 2005. The brewery supplies beer to local pubs in Arundel, Littlehampton, Worthing, Shoreham-on-Sea and Brighton.

Vinery Mild (ABV 3.2%)

Meteor (OG 1038, ABV 3.8%)

Red Hunter (OG 1042, ABV 4.3%)

Hampshire SIBA

Hampshire Brewery Ltd, 6 Romsey Industrial Estate, Greatbridge Road, Romsey, Hampshire, SO51 0HR
Tel (01794) 830529
Fax (01794) 830528
Email online@hampshirebrewery.com
Website www.hampshirebrewery.com
Shop Mon-Fri 9am-4pm; Sat 10am-3pm
Tours by arrangement (for parties of 12-18)

⊗ Hampshire was founded in 1992 and merged with the Millennium Bottling Company in 2002. All the beers are also available in bottle-conditioned form. The brewery produces four core beers, 24 monthly specials at two per month, and three other seasonal beers over longer three to four month periods: see website for full details. Some 300 outlets are supplied. Seasonal beers: Lionheart (ABV 4.5%), Pendragon (ABV 4.8%), King's Ransom (ABV 4.8%, June-Aug), 1066 (ABV 6%).

King Alfred's (OG 1037, ABV 3.8%) ◆
A pale brown session beer featuring a malty aroma with some hops and fruit. Rather thin but well-balanced citrus taste with plenty of malt and a dry, bitter finish.

Strong's Best Bitter (OG 1037, ABV 3.8%) ◆
Named after the original Romsey Brewery,

this tawny-coloured bitter is predominantly malty. An initially hoppy aroma gives way to an increasingly bitter finish.

Ironside (OG 1041, ABV 4.2%)

A clean-tasting, flavoursome best bitter with a gorgeous fruit and hops aroma. Hops are predominant throughout but balanced by malt and fruit and some sweetness. The finish is long and dry.

Pride of Romsey (OG 1050, ABV 5%)

A strong citrus aroma leads to a beautifully-balanced mix of fruit and hops that continues to build in the aftertaste.

Hanby SIBA

Hanby Ales Ltd, Aston Park, Soulton Road, Wem, Shropshire, SY4 5SD
Tel/Fax (01939) 232432
Email info@hanbyales.co.uk
Website www.hanbyales.co.uk
Tours by arrangement

Hanby was set up in 1988 by Jack Hanby following the closure of the Shrewsbury & Wem Brewery. The aim was to continue the 200 year-old tradition of brewing in the area. In 1990 the brewery moved to its present home and has recently upgraded to 30-barrel production runs. Hanby supplies 300 outlets. Seasonal beer: Green Admiral (ABV 4.5%, Sept-Oct). Bottled beers: Rainbow Chaser, Golden Honey, Nut Cracker, Cherry Bomb.

Drawwell Bitter (OG 1039, ABV 3.9%)

A hoppy beer with excellent bitterness, both in taste and aftertaste. Beautiful amber colour.

Black Magic Mild (OG 1040, ABV 4%)

A dark, reddish-brown mild, which is dry and bitter with a roast malt taste.

All Seasons (OG 1042, ABV 4.2%)

A light, hoppy bitter, well balanced and thirst quenching, brewed with a fine blend of Cascade and Fuggles hops.

Rainbow Chaser (OG 1043, ABV 4.3%)

A pale beer brewed with Styrian Goldings hops.

Cascade (OG 1045, ABV 4.4%)

A very pale beer, brewed with Cascade hops, producing a clean crisp flavour and a hoppy finish.

Wem Special (OG 1044, ABV 4.4%)

A pale, straw-coloured, smooth, hoppy bitter.

Golden Honey (OG 1045, ABV 4.5%)

A beer made with the addition of Australian honey. Not over sweet.

Scorpio Porter (OG 1045, ABV 4.5%)

A dark porter with a complex palate introducing hints of coffee and chocolate, contrasting and complementing the background hoppiness.

Shropshire Stout (OG 1044, ABV 4.5%)

A full-bodied, rich ruby/black coloured stout. A blend of four malts produces a distinct chocolate malt dry flavour, with a mushroom-coloured head.

Premium (OG 1046, ABV 4.6%)

An amber-coloured beer that is sweeter and fruitier than most of the beers above. Slight malt and hop taste.

Old Wemian (OG 1049, ABV 4.9%)

Golden-brown colour with an aroma of malt and hops and a soft, malty palate.

Taverners (OG 1053, ABV 5.3%)

A smooth and fruity old ale, full of body.

Cherry Bomb (OG 1060, ABV 6%)

A splendid rich and fruity beer with maraschino cherry flavour.

Joy Bringer (OG 1060, ABV 6%)

Deceptively strong beer with a distinct ginger flavour.

Nutcracker (OG 1060, ABV 6%)

Tawny beer with a fine blend of malt and hops.

Hardknott*

Hardknott Brewery, Woolpack Inn, Boot, Holmrook, Cumbria, CA19 1TH
Tel (019467) 23230
Email brewery@woolpack.co.uk
Website www.woolpack.co.uk
Tours by arrangement

The Woolpack Inn, an ancient ale house, used to brew its own beer in the 18th and 19th century. The Hardknott Brewery opened in 2005 using a second-hand, two-barrel plant believed to have come from the Brigg Brewery. Local outlets and beer festivals are supplied as well as the Woolpack itself.

Black Sail (OG 1030, ABV 3.4%)

Hardknott Bitter (OG 1033, ABV 3.6%)

Woolpacker Ale (OG 1040, ABV 4.3%)

Tenacity (OG 1044, ABV 5%)

Hardys & Hansons IFBB

See Greene King in New Independents

Hart

Hart Brewery Ltd, Cartford Hotel, Cartford Lane, Little Eccleston, Preston, Lancashire, PR3 0YP
Tel (01995) 671686
Fax (01772) 797069
Tours by arrangement Tue-Thu evenings

The brewery was founded in 1994 in a small private garage in Preston. It moved to its present site at the rear of the Cartford Hotel in 1995. With a 10-barrel plant, Hart now supplies around 150 outlets nationwide and does swaps with other breweries. Seasonal beers: Gold Beach (ABV 3.8%, summer), Lord of the Glen (ABV 4%, summer), Snowella (ABV 4.3%, winter), Bat Out of Hell (ABV 4.5%, Halloween), Val Addiction (ABV 4.8%, winter).

Dishie Debbie (OG 1040, ABV 4%)

Ice Maiden (OG 1040, ABV 4%)

Hoppy, crisp, straw-coloured bitter with floral notes and a dry finish.

Squirrels Hoard (OG 1040, ABV 4%)

Nemesis (OG 1045, ABV 4.5%)

Harveys IFBB

Harvey & Son (Lewes) Ltd, The Bridge Wharf

Brewery, 6 Cliffe High Street, Lewes, East Sussex, BN7 2AH
Tel (01273) 480209
Fax (01273) 486074
Email maj@harveys.org.uk
Website www.harveys.org.uk
Shop Mon-Sat 9.30am-4.45pm
Tours by arrangement (currently two year waiting list)

⊗ Established in 1790, this independent family brewery operates from the banks of the River Ouse in Lewes. A major development in 1985 doubled the brewhouse capacity and subsequent additional fermenting capacity has seen production rise to in excess of 38,000 barrels a year. Harveys supplies real ale to all its 48 pubs and 450 free trade outlets in Sussex and Kent. Seasonal beers: Kiss (ABV 4.8%, February), 1859 Porter (ABV 4.8%, March), Knots of May Light Mild (ABV 3%, May), Copperwheat Beer (ABV 4.8%, June), Tom Paine (ABV 5.5%, July), Southdown Harvest Ale (ABV 5%, September), Star of Eastbourne (ABV 5.5%, October), Sussex XXXX Old Ale (ABV 4.3%, Oct-May), Bonfire Boy (ABV 5.8%, November), Christmas Ale (ABV 8.1%, December). Bottle-conditioned beer: Le Coq's Imperial Extra Double Stout (ABV 9% ■).

Sussex XX Mild Ale **(OG 1030, ABV 3%)**
A dark copper-brown colour. Roast malt dominates the aroma and palate leading to a sweet, caramel finish.

Hadlow Bitter **(OG 1033, ABV 3.5%)**
Formerly Sussex Pale Ale

Sussex Best Bitter **(OG 1040, ABV 4%)**
Full-bodied brown bitter. A hoppy aroma leads to a good malt and hop balance, and a dry aftertaste.

Armada Ale **(OG 1045, ABV 4.5%)**
Hoppy amber best bitter. Well-balanced fruit and hops dominate throughout with a fruity palate.

Harviestoun SIBA

Harviestoun Brewery Ltd, Alva Industrial Estate, Alva, Clackmannanshire, FK12 5DQ. A susbidiary of Caledonian Brewing Company
Tel (01259) 769100
Fax (01259) 763003
Email harviestoun@talk21.com
Shop Mon-Fri 9am-4.30pm

Harviestoun, winner of Champion Beer of Britain 2003, started in a barn in the village of Dollar in 1985 with a five-barrel brew plant. Winning awards has helped the company achieve great success: Champion Beer of Scotland twice; Tesco Beer Challenge Winner three times; Schiehallion three Golds and four Silver awards in CBoB since its launch nine years ago. Harviestoun has built a state-of-the-art 50-barrel brewery seven miles from the original site and has nationwide supermarket sales of bottled Bitter & Twisted, which won Supreme Champion Bottled Beer 2004 at the Brewing Industry International awards. The brewery supplies local outlets itself and nationwide through wholesalers. It was bought by Caledonian early in 2006 and the founders, Ken and Ingrid Brooker, have retired. Seasonal beers: Jack the Lad (ABV 4.1%, January), Ice Maiden (ABV 4.2%, February), Belgian White (ABV 4.3%, March), Spring Fever (ABV 3.8%, April), Navigator (ABV 4.3%, May), Dragonfly (ABV 3.6%, June), Natural Blonde (ABV 4%, July), Gold Rush (ABV 3.9%, August), Late Harvest (ABV 3.8%, September), Gremlin (ABV 4.3%, October), Old Manor (ABV 4.6%, November), Good King Legless (ABV 4.5%, December).

Bitter & Twisted **(OG 1036, ABV 3.8%)**
Refreshingly hoppy beer with fruit throughout. A bitter-sweet taste with a long bitter finish. A golden session beer.

Celebration Ale **(OG 1042, ABV 4.1%)**
A new beer brewed to celebrate 20 years brewing. 50/50 pale and wheat malts with Amarillo, Brewers Gold and Fuggles hops.

Ptarmigan **(OG 1047, ABV 4.5%)**
A well-balanced, bitter-sweet beer in which hops and malt dominate. The blend of malt, hops and fruit produces a clean, hoppy aftertaste.

Schiehallion **(OG 1048, ABV 4.8%)**
A Scottish cask lager, brewed using a lager yeast and Hersbrucker hops. A hoppy aroma, with fruit and malt, leads to a malty, bitter taste with floral hoppiness and a bitter finish.

Hawkshead SIBA

Hawkshead Brewery Ltd, Town End, Colthouse, Hawkshead, Cumbria, LA22 0JU
Tel (015394) 36111
Email info@hawksheadbrewery.co.uk
Website www.hawksheadbrewery.co.uk
Brewery and Visitors Centre at Staveley
Tours by arrangement

Hawkshead Brewery now has two working breweries in the heart of the Lake District. In early 2006 the brewery expanded on to a second site at Staveley Mill, beside the River Kent, near Windermere. It has a 20-barrel purpose built plant, sampling room and visitor centre. The original brewery, in a listed barn at the head of Esthwaite Water, just outside the village of Hawkshead, continues to brew on the seven-barrel plant it began with in 2002. Hawkshead Brewery was founded by former BBC journalist Alex Brodie, who remains head brewer of both operations. Five beers are regularly available. There are plans to add Damson Stout, an organic beer, and bottle-conditioned beers.

Hawkshead Bitter **(OG 1037, ABV 3.7%)**
A pale, hoppy and bitter session ale, with the distinctive aroma of Slovenian Styrian Golding hops.

UPA/Ulverston Pale Ale **(OG 1041, ABV 4.1%)**
A very pale ale, using three English hops.

Red (Best Bitter) **(OG 1042, ABV 4.2%)**
A red ale; malty and spicy, with a long dry finish.

Lakeland Gold **(OG 1043, ABV 4.4%)**
A hoppy, bitter, golden ale with complex fruit flavours. Champion Best Bitter, SIBA National awards 2005.

Brodie's Prime **(OG 1048, ABV 5%)**
A dark beer with an unusual medley of flavours, rich and malty, with a roasted stout-

like edge, yet also light and dry with spiciness and fruit.

Haywood Bad Ram

Haywood Bad Ram Brewery, Callow Top Holiday Park, Sandybrook, Ashbourne, Derbyshire, DE6 2AQ
Tel (01335) 344884 / 07974 948427
Fax (01335) 343726/344884
Email acphaywood@aol.com
Website www.callowtop.co.uk
Shop 9am-5pm (seasonal)
Tours by arrangement

The brewery is situated in a converted barn at Callow Top Holiday Park, adjacent to Haywood Farm. Dr Samuel Johnson Ale won a Gold award at the 2003 Peterborough beer festival. A bottling plant has been built next to the brewery to supply own label beers. One pub is owned (on site) and several other outlets are supplied. The brewery is not operational during the winter.

Dr Samuel Johnson (ABV 4.5%)

Bad Ram (ABV 5%)

Woggle Dance (ABV 5%)

Callow Top IPA (ABV 5.2%)

Hebridean SIBA

Hebridean Brewing Co, 18A Bells Road, Stornoway, Isle of Lewis, HS1 2RA
Tel (01851) 700123
Fax (01851) 700234
Email info@hebridean-brewery.co.uk
Website www.hebridean-brewery.co.uk
Shop open in summer months only
Tours by arrangement

⊜ The company was set up in 2001 by Andy Ribbens, whose family came from Lewis. The plant is steam powered with a 14-barrel brew length. A shop is attached to the brewery and the beers are also bottled (not bottle conditioned). The company owns one pub in Uig, Skye, beside the ferry terminal. Seasonal beers are produced for Mods, Gaelic festivals that are the Scottish equivalent of the Welsh Eisteddfod.

Celtic Black Ale (OG 1036, ABV 3.9%)
A dark ale full of flavour, balancing an aromatic hop combined with a subtle bite and a pleasantly smooth caramel aftertaste.

Clansman Ale (OG 1036, ABV 3.9%)
A light Hebridean beer, brewed with Scottish malts and lightly hopped to give a subtle bittering.

Seaforth Ale (ABV 4.2%)
A golden beer in the continental style.

Islander Strong Premium Ale (OG 1044, ABV 4.8%)
A deep ruby in colour, the beer is predominantly malty with a robust hopping to match. SIBA Bronze Medal and Beer of Scotland 2003, Premium Cask Ale category.

Berserker Export Pale Ale (OG 1068, ABV 7.5%)
Brewed using traditional methods and based on 19th-century recipes. Matured to develop a smooth, intricate flavour.

Hepworth SIBA

Hepworth & Co Brewers Ltd, The Beer Station, The Railway Yard, Horsham, West Sussex, RH12 2NW
Tel (01403) 269696
Fax (01403) 269690
Email mail@hepworthbrewery.co.uk
Website www.hepworthbrewery.co.uk
Shop 9am-6pm
Tours by arrangement

⊗ Four workers from King & Barnes started the brewery in 2001, bottling beer only. In 2003 draught beer brewing was started with Sussex malt and hops. In 2004 an organic lager was introduced in bottle and on draught. 20 outlets are supplied. Seasonal beer: Old Ale (ABV 4.8%, Nov-Jan), Super Horse (ABV 6.1%), Summer Ale (ABV 3.4%), Harvest Ale (ABV 4.5%). Bottle-conditioned beer: Christmas Ale (ABV 7.5%).

Traditional Sussex Bitter (OG 1035, ABV 3.6%) ◆
A fine, clean-tasting amber session beer. A bitter beer with a pleasant fruity and hoppy aroma that leads to a crisp, tangy taste that belies the beer's strength. A long, dry finish.

Pullman First Class Ale (OG 1041, ABV 4.2%) ◆
A sweet, nutty maltiness and fruitiness are balanced by hops and bitterness in this easy-drinking, pale brown best bitter. There is little aroma but a subtle bitter aftertaste.

Iron Horse (OG 1048, ABV 4.8%) ◆
There's a fruity, toffee aroma to this light brown, full-bodied bitter. A citrus flavour balanced by caramel and malt leads to a clean, dry finish.

Hereward

Hereward Brewery, 50 Fleetwood, Ely, Cambridgeshire, CB6 1BH
Tel (01353) 666441
Email michael.czarnobaj@ntlworld.com

A small home-based brewery launched in 2003 by Michael Czarnobaj who had brewed for several years before going on a Brewlab course in Sunderland. He has 10-gallon kit and brews two or three times a month in his garage. He mainly supplies beer festivals and also now brews festival specials (brewed to order). Seasonal beer: Uncle Joe's Winter Ale (ABV 5%). The entire range of beers is now also available in bottle-conditioned form.

Bitter (ABV 3.8%)

St Ethelreda's Golden Bitter (ABV 4%)

Porta Porter (ABV 4.2%)

Oatmeal Stout (ABV 4.5%)

Hesket Newmarket SIBA

Hesket Newmarket Brewery Ltd, Old Crown Barn, Back Green, Hesket Newmarket, Cumbria, CA7 8JG
Tel/Fax (016974) 78066
Email brewer@hesketbrewery.co.uk
Website www.hesketbrewery.co.uk
Tours via the Old Crown Inn (016974) 78288

⊛ The brewery was established in 1988 by Jim Fearnley. In 1999 it was bought by a co-operative of villagers, anxious to preserve a community resource when Jim retired. It is now managed on their behalf by Mike Parker, ex-Stones head brewer. Most of Jim's recipes have been retained, all named after local fells except for Doris's 90th Birthday Ale. A 10-barrel plant was installed in 2004 followed by bottling on a small scale in late 2005. Some 30 regular outlets are supplied. Seasonal beer: Autumn Chestnut (ABV 4.7%).

Great Cockup Porter **(OG 1035, ABV 3%)**
A refreshing, dark and chocolaty porter with a dry finish.

Blencathra Bitter **(OG 1035, ABV 3.2%)** ◆
A malty, tawny ale, mild and mellow for a bitter, with a dominant caramel flavour.

Skiddaw Special Bitter **(OG 1035, ABV 3.6%)**
An amber session beer, malty throughout, thin with a dryish finish.

Haystacks Refreshing Ale **(OG 1037, ABV 3.7%)**
A light, pale, refreshing beer with a zesty hop. Hint of grapefruit on the finish.

Doris's 90th Birthday Ale **(OG 1045, ABV 4.3%)** ◆
A full-bodied, nicely balanced malty beer with an increasing hop finish and butterscotch in the mouth.

Sca Fell Blonde **(OG 1047, ABV 4.5%)**
Pale with fruity hop notes. A good introduction to real ale for lager drinkers.

Catbells Pale Ale **(OG 1050, ABV 5%)** ◆
A powerful golden ale with a well-balanced malty bitterness, ending with a bitter and decidedly dry aftertaste.

Old Carrock Strong Ale **(OG 1060, ABV 6%)**
A dark red, powerful ale.

Hexhamshire SIBA

Hexhamshire Brewery, Leafields, Ordley, Hexham, Northumberland, NE46 1SX
Tel (01434) 606577
Fax (01434) 600973
Email ghb@hexhamshire.co.uk

⊛ Hexhamshire was founded in 1992 in a converted cattle shed. The brewery has been operated by one of the founding partners and his family since 1997. Five beers are brewed regularly for the Dipton Mill pub and 40 other outlets are supplied.

Devil's Elbow **(OG 1036, ABV 3.6%)** ◆
Amber brew full of hops and fruit, leading to a bitter finish.

Shire Bitter **(OG 1037, ABV 3.8%)** ◆
A good balance of hops with fruity overtones, this amber beer makes an easy-drinking session bitter.

Devil's Water **(OG 1041, ABV 4.1%)** ◆
Copper-coloured best bitter, well-balanced with a slightly fruity, hoppy finish.

Whapweasel **(OG 1048, ABV 4.8%)** 🗋 ◆
An interesting smooth, hoppy beer with a fruity flavour. Amber in colour, the bitter finish brings out the fruit and hops.

Old Humbug **(OG 1055, ABV 5.5%)**

Hidden SIBA

Hidden Brewery Ltd, Unit 1 Oakley Industrial Estate, Wylye Road, Dinton, Salisbury, Wiltshire, SP3 5EU
Tel (01722) 716440
Email sales@thehiddenbrewery.com
Website www.thehiddenbrewery.com
Shop/Off Licence Mon-Sat 10am-4pm
Tours by arrangement

Hidden Brewery was founded in 2003 and managed by head brewer Gary Lumber, previously at Oakhill. The brewery is named after its location, hidden away in the Wiltshire countryside. It currently supplies between 400-500 outlets. The brewery acquired the Bell at Wylye in 2005 as its first tied pub. Seasonal beers: Spring (ABV 4.5%), Fantasy (ABV 4.6%), Depths (ABV 4.6%), Treasure (ABV 4.8%).

Pint **(OG 1039, ABV 3.8%)**
A clean-tasting, tangy bitter with good hop content, and a citrus fruit and malt balance. Dry finish, mid-brown in colour; light hop aroma.

Old Sarum **(OG 1042, ABV 4.1%)**
A well-balanced bitter with a complex combination of malts and hops. The aroma is floral and spicy, full-flavoured with a dry bitterness. The colour is dark ruby-brown.

Quest **(OG 1042, ABV 4.2%)**
An amber-coloured bitter with a malt background, fruity aroma and a dry finish.

Pleasure **(OG 1049, ABV 4.9%)**
Traditional India Pale Ale, mid-brown in colour with a strong presence of Bramling Cross, Challenger and Progress hops.

Highgate SIBA

Highgate Brewery Ltd, Sandymount Road, Walsall, West Midlands, WS1 3AP
Tel (01922) 644453
Fax (01922) 644471
Email info@highgatebrewery.com
Website www.highgatebrewery.com
Tours by arrangement

⊛ Built in 1898, Highgate was an independent brewery until 1938 when it was taken over by Mitchells & Butlers and subsequently became the smallest brewery in the Bass group. It was brought back into the independent sector in 1995 as the result of a management buy-out and was subsequently acquired by Aston Manor (qv) in 2000. Some of the original equipment in the traditional Victorian brewery is still in use, but a new racking line and laboratory have been added along with a visitor facility. Highgate has now acquired 10 tied houses towards a target of 50, including the City Tavern, a restored Victorian ale house off Broad Street in Birmingham. Five of the tied houses serve cask-conditioned beer. Around 200 outlets are supplied. The company also has a major contract to supply Mitchells & Butlers pubs as well as contract brewing for Smiles Brewery. Seasonal beer: Old Ale (ABV 5.3%, winter).

Dark Mild **(OG 1036.8, ABV 3.6%)**
A dark brown Black Country mild with a good balance of malt and hops, and traces of roast flavour following a malty aroma.

Special Bitter **(OG 1037.8, ABV 3.8%)**

Davenports Bitter **(OG 1040.8, ABV 4%)**

Saddlers Best Bitter **(OG 1043.8, ABV 4.3%)**
A fruity, pale yellow bitter with a strong hop flavour and a light, refreshing bitter aftertaste.

Davenports Premium **(OG 1046.8, ABV 4.6%)**

For Coors

M&B Mild **(OG 1034.8, ABV 3.2%)**

For Smiles

Blonde **(ABV 3.8%)**

Best **(ABV 4.1%)**

Bristol IPA **(ABV 4.4%)**

Heritage **(ABV 5.2%)**

High House SIBA

High House Farm Brewery, Matfen, Newcastle upon Tyne, Tyne & Wear, NE20 0RG
Tel/Fax (01661) 886192
Email info@highhousefarmbrewery.co.uk
Website www.highhousefarmbrewery.co.uk
Tours by arrangement

The brewery was founded in 2002 by fourth generation farmer Steven Urwin on his 200-acre family farm. Steven set up the brewery and offices in his own Grade II listed converted farm buildings. High House Farm is unique in its area in using the farm to provide ingredients and helps the environment by returning all brewery waste products and water to the land. Two of the beers are named after the farm's collie dogs. The beers are distributed throughout Northumberland, Cumbria, Tyne & Wear and the Scottish border. A visitor centre, including shop, bar and café with function room, opened in May 2006.

Auld Hemp **(OG 1038, ABV 3.8%)**
Tawny-coloured ale with malt and fruit flavours and a good bitter finish.

Nel's Best **(OG 1041, ABV 4.2%)**
Golden hoppy ale full of flavour with a clean bitter finish.

Matfen Magic **(OG 1046.5, ABV 4.8%)**
Well-hopped brown ale with a fruity aroma, malt and chocolate overtones with a rich, bitter finish.

Highland

Highland Brewing Co Ltd, Swannay Brewery, Swannay by Evie, Birsay, Orkney, KW17 2NP
Tel (01856) 721700
Fax (01856) 721711
Email sales@highlandbrewingcompany.co.uk
Website www.highlandbrewingcompany.co.uk
Tours by arrangement

Highland Brewing was founded by Rob Hill, a brewer with 25 years' experience in the craft brewing sector. Brewing began in January 2006, breathing life back to an ancient farm steading. Further beers will be developed. 30 outlets are supplied direct. Seasonal beer: Orkney Blast (ABV 6.2%, winter).

Highland Best/Orkney Best **(OG 1038, ABV 3.8%)**

Scapa Special **(OG 1042, ABV 4.2%)**

St Magnus Ale **(OG 1045, ABV 4.5%)**

Strong Northerley **(OG 1055, ABV 5.5%)**

Highlands & Islands

See Atlas and Orkney

Highwood SIBA

Highwood Brewery Ltd, Grimsby West, Birchin Way, Grimsby, Lincolnshire, DN31 2SG
Tel (01472) 255500
Fax (01472) 255501
Email tomwood@tom-wood.com
Website www.tom-wood.com

Highwood, best known under the Tom Wood brand name, started brewing in a converted Victorian granary on the family farm in 1995. The brew-length was increased from 10 barrels to 30 in 2001, using plant from Ash Vine brewery. In 2002, Highwood bought Conway's Licensed Trade Wholesalers. It now distributes most regional and national cask ales throughout Lincolnshire and Nottinghamshire. More than 300 outlets are supplied. Seasonal beers: see website.

Dark Mild **(OG 1034, ABV 3.5%)**

Best Bitter **(OG 1034, ABV 3.5%)**
A good citrus, passion fruit hop dominates the nose and taste, with background malt. A lingering hoppy and bitter finish makes this amber bitter very drinkable.

Shepherd's Delight **(OG 1040, ABV 4%)**
Malt is the dominant taste in this amber brew, although the fruity hop bitterness complements it all the way.

Harvest Bitter **(OG 1042, ABV 4.3%)**
A well-balanced amber beer where the hops and bitterness just about outdo the malt.

Old Timber **(OG 1043, ABV 4.5%)**
Hoppy on the nose, but featuring well-balanced malt and hops otherwise. A slight, lingering roast/coffee flavour develops, but this is generally a bitter, darkish brown beer.

Bomber County **(OG 1046, ABV 4.8%)**
An earthy malt aroma but with a complex underlying mix of coffee, hops, caramel and apple fruit. The beer starts bitter and intensifies to the end.

Higson's*

Higson's Brewery, Unit 21, Brunswick Business Park, Liverpool, L3 4BD
Tel (0151) 228 2309. Fax (0151) 709 2684
Website www.higsonsbrewery.co.uk

The proud name of Higson's has been restored to Liverpool. The brewery was founded in 1780 and was taken over by Boddingtons in 1985. When Whitbread bought Boddingtons it closed Higson's. The new company currently has its beers brewed by Mayflower (qv) but will transfer to its own site once brewing equipment has been installed.

Bitter (ABV 4.1%)

Hilden

Hilden Brewing Co, Hilden House, Hilden, Lisburn, Co Antrim, BT27 4TY
Tel/Fax (02892) 660800
Email irishbeers@hildenbrewery.co.uk
Website www.hildenbrewery.co.uk
Tours by arrangement

☺ Hilden was established by Ann and Seamus Scullion in 1981 and is Ireland's oldest independent brewery. The brewing tradition remains in their family with their son Owen now taking over the reins. Hilden's exposure has been increased over the past two years and has become a regular fixture at CAMRA festivals. Hilden supplies beer to a large number of pubs throughout the UK and now has a range of bottled beers available through its own bottling plant.

Ale (OG 1038, ABV 4%) ◆
An amber-coloured beer with an aroma of malt, hops and fruit. The balanced taste is slightly slanted towards hops, and hops are also prominent in the full, malty finish. Bitter and refreshing.

Silver (OG 1042, ABV 4.2%)
A pale ale, light and refreshing on the palate but with a satisfying mellow hop character derived from a judicious blend of aromatic Saaz hops.

Molly Malone (OG 1045, ABV 4.6%)
Dark ruby-red porter with complex flavours of hop bitterness and chocolate malt.

Scullion's Irish (OG 1045, ABV 4.6%)
A bright amber ale, smooth initially with a slight taste of honey that is balanced by a long, dry aftertaste which lingers on the palate.

Halt (OG 1058, ABV 6.1%)
A premium traditional Irish red ale with a malty, mild hop flavour. This special reserve derives its name from the local train stop, which was used to service the local linen mill.

Hill Island

Michael Griffin t/a Hill Island Brewery, Unit 7 Fowlers Yard, Back Silver Street, Durham, County Durham, DH1 3RA
Tel 07740 932584
Email mike@hillisland.freeserve.co.uk
Shop most weekdays 10am-2pm (bulk purchasing only – phone before visit)
Tours by arrangement for groups of 10 or more

☺ Hill Island is a literal translation of Dunholme from which Durham is derived. The brewery began trading in 2002 and stands by the banks of the Wear in the heart of Durham City. Many of the beers produced have names reflecting local history and heritage. The brewer, Michael Griffin, produces a core range of six beers along with seasonal and occasional beers. Brews are also made exclusively for individual outlets, such as Silly Steps for the New Board Inn in Esh, near Durham. Some 40 outlets are supplied. Seasonal beers: Priory Summer Ale (ABV 3.5%), Festive Ale (ABV 4%), St Oswald's Xmas Ale (ABV 4.5%).

Peninsula Pint (OG 1036.5, ABV 3.7%)

Bitter (OG 1038, ABV 3.9%)

Dun Cow Bitter (OG 1039, ABV 4.2%)

Cathedral Ale (OG 1042, ABV 4.3%)

Griffin's Irish Stout (OG 1045, ABV 4.5%)

Hillside*

Hillside Brewery Limited, Hillside, Corse, Lumphanan, Aberdeenshire, AB31 4RY
Tel (01339) 883506
Email brewery@hillsidecroft.eclipse.co.uk
Website www.hillsidecroft.eclipse.co.uk

Business consultant and home brewer Rob James aims to turn his hobby into his full-time job. The first batch of the brewery's signature beer, Macbeth, went into local shops in January 2006. Rob aims to install a fully-functioning micro-brewery within the next year. Currently he is limited to around 100 litres a week, which is all bottle-conditioned and distributed to local quality food outlets. Bottle-conditioned beers: Brude (ABV 3.8%), Macbeth (ABV 4.1%), Broichan (ABV 4.5%).

Hobden's

See Wessex

Hobsons SIBA

Hobsons Brewery & Co Ltd, Newhouse Farm, Tenbury Road, Cleobury Mortimer, Worcestershire, DY14 8RD
Tel (01299) 270837
Fax (01299) 270260
Email beer@hobsons-brewery.co.uk
Website www.hobsons-brewery.co.uk

⊗ Established in 1993, Hobsons Brewery was conceived by the Davis family. Located in the village of Cleobury Mortimer, the premises originally used a former sawmill but relocated up the road to a farm site with more space, allowing more production capacity and greater storage. Beers are supplied within a radius of 50 miles. The most recent addition is a new brewery adjoining the existing one, including a bottling plant. Hobsons also brews and bottles for the local tourist attraction, the Severn Valley Railway (Manor Ale, ABV 4.2%). Seasonal beers: Old Henry (ABV 5.2%, Sept-April), Steam

No 9 (ABV 4.2%, September).

Mild (OG 1034, ABV 3.2%) ♦
A classic mild. Complex layers of taste come from roasted malts that predominate and give lots of flavour.

Best Bitter (OG 1038.5, ABV 3.8%) ♦
A pale brown to amber, medium-bodied beer with strong hop character throughout. It is consequently bitter, but with malt discernible in the taste.

Town Crier (OG 1044, ABV 4.5%) ▯
An elegant straw-coloured bitter. The hint of sweetness is complemented by subtle hop flavours, leading to a dry finish.

Hoggleys SIBA

Hoggleys Brewery, 30 Mill Lane, Kislingbury, Northampton, NN7 4BD
Tel (01604) 831762
Email hoggleys@hotmail.com
Website www.hoggleys.co.uk
Tours by arrangement (occasionally)

Hoggleys was established in 2003 as a part-time brewery. There were plans in 2006 to buy a new plant and relocate to larger premises. All four main brews are available bottle-conditioned. Approximately 20 outlets are supplied. Solstice Stout and Mill Lane Mild are suitable for vegetarians.

Mill Lane Mild (OG 1040, ABV 4%)
Brewed from mild, black and crystal malts and hopped with Challenger and Fuggles.

Northamptonshire Bitter (OG 1040, ABV 4%)
A straw-coloured bitter brewed with pale malt only. The hops are Fuggles and Northdown and the beer is late hopped with Fuggles for aroma.

Kislingbury Bitter (OG 1041, ABV 4%)

Solstice Stout (OG 1044, ABV 5%)

Hogs Back SIBA

Hogs Back Brewery Ltd, Manor Farm, The Street, Tongham, Surrey, GU10 1DE
Tel (01252) 783000
Fax (01252) 782328
Email info@hogsback.co.uk
Website www.hogsback.co.uk
Shop – see website
Tours by arrangement

⊠ The traditional-style, purpose-built brewery has occupied a range of 18th-century farm buildings since 1992. The popularity of its ales, the award-winning TEA in particular, has necessitated an expansion over the years. The strong A over T won the Champion Winter Beer of Britain award in 2006. Seasonal and commemorative ales are brewed throughout the year, from milds and porters to strong winter ales and barley wines. The brewery shop and visitor centre now sell more than 400 different bottled beers from around the world plus Hogs Back draught and bottled beers, along with brewery merchandise, either direct from the brewery or via mail order and e-commerce. There are regular guided tours and tastings by arrangement; please consult the website. Seasonal beers: Dark Mild (ABV 3.4%), Spring Call (ABV 4%), Summer This (ABV 4.2%), Easter Teaser (ABV 4.2%), Blackwater Porter (ABV 4.4%), Advent Ale (ABV 4.4%), X-hibition Stout (ABV 4.5%), Autumn Seer (ABV 4.8%), Rip Snorter (ABV 5%). Bottle-conditioned beers: TEA (ABV 4.2%), BSA (ABV 4.5% ◼), OTT (ABV 6%), Brewster's Bundle (ABV 7.4%), Wobble in a Bottle (ABV 7.5%), A over T (ABV 9% ◼).

Legend (OG 1040, ABV 4%) ♦
Complex and drinkable, this golden-coloured beer contains both wheat and lager malts, and has a dry, malty and bitter taste that lingers.

TEA or Traditional English Ale (OG 1044, ABV 4.2%) ▯ ♦
A pale brown best bitter with both malt and hops prominent in the nose. These carry through into a well-rounded bitter flavour, balanced by fruit and some sweetness. Hoppy bitterness grows in the aftertaste.

Hop Garden Gold (OG 1048, ABV 4.6%) ▯ ♦
Pale golden best bitter, full bodied and well balanced with an aroma of malt, hops and fruit. Delicate flowery-citrus hop flavours are balanced by malt and fruit. Hoppy bitterness grows in an increasingly dry aftertaste with a hint of sweetness. Dangerously drinkable.

Holden's IFBB

Holden's Brewery Ltd, George Street, Woodsetton, Dudley, West Midlands, DY1 4LW
Tel (01902) 880051
Fax (01902) 665473
Email holdens.brewery@virgin.net
Website www.holdensbrewery.co.uk
Shop Mon-Fri 9am-5pm
Tours by arrangement

⊛ A family brewery going back four generations, Holden's began life as a brew-pub when Edwin and Lucy took over the Park Inn (the brewery tap) in the 1920s; the inn has now been restored to its former Victorian heritage. Holden's also renovated a Grade II listed railway building in Codsall. The latest addition to the Holden's estate is the Waterfall in Blackheath. Holden's continues to grow with 21 tied pubs. It supplies some 60 other outlets.

Black Country Mild (OG 1037, ABV 3.7%) ♦
A good, red/brown mild; a refreshing, light blend of roast malt, hops and fruit, dominated by malt throughout.

Black Country Bitter (OG 1039, ABV 3.9%) ◼ ▯ ♦
A medium-bodied, golden ale; a light, well-balanced bitter with a subtle, dry, hoppy finish.

XB (OG 1042, ABV 4.1%) ♦
A sweeter, slightly fuller version of the Bitter. Sold in a number of outlets under different names.

Golden Glow (OG 1045, ABV 4.4%) ◼
A pale golden beer with a subtle hop aroma plus gentle sweetness and a light hoppiness.

Special (OG 1052, ABV 5.1%) ♦
A sweet, malty, full-bodied amber ale with hops to balance in the taste and in the good, bitter-sweet finish.

Holland

Holland Brewery, 5 Brown's Flats, Brewery Street, Kimberley, Nottinghamshire, NG16 2JU

Tel (0115) 938 2685
Email hollandbrew@btopenworld.com

Len Holland, a keen home-brewer for 30 years, went commercial in 2000, in the shadow of Hardys & Hansons. Seasonal beers: Holly Hop Gold (ABV 4.7%, Christmas), Dutch Courage (ABV 5%, winter), Glamour Puss (ABV 4.2%, spring), Blonde Belter (ABV 4.5%, summer).

Chocolate Clog **(OG 1038, ABV 3.8%)**

Golden Blond **(OG 1040, ABV 4%)**

Lipsmacker **(OG 1040, ABV 4%)**

Cloghopper **(OG 1042, ABV 4.2%)**

Double Dutch **(OG 1045, ABV 4.5%)**

Mad Jack Stout **(OG 1045, ABV 4.5%)**

Holme Valley

Holme Valley Ales, Upper Agbrigg Brewery, Unit 12 Honley Business Centre, New Mill Road, Honley, Holmfirth, West Yorkshire, HD9 6QB
Tel (01484) 660008
Fax (01484) 663359
Email info@homevalleyales.co.uk

⊛ Upper Agbrigg Brewery was founded in 2001 by Andrew Balmforth in the cellar of his house with a three-barrel brew length. The popularity of his beer was such that Andrew has now teamed up with Clive Donald of Brupaks, a leading supplier of brewing equipment and ingredients, and installed a brand new brewery in Brupaks' warehouse in Honley. The beers are sold under the Holme Valley Ales label. Monthy specials are available. Fifteen outlets are supplied. Seasonal beers: Kellerbier (ABV 4.8%), Oatmeal Stout (ABV 4.8%), Rauchbier (ABV 4.8%), Winterfest (ABV 5%).

Uncle Orinoco's Mild **(ABV 3.8%)**
A refreshing dark mild with a delicate hop flavour from Fuggles.

Graham's Gold **(ABV 3.8%)**
A golden bitter hopped with First Gold.

India Pale Ale **(ABV 4.5%)**
Deep copper in colour with a full malt flavour balanced by a massive Cascade hop character.

Premium Gold **(ABV 4.6%)**
A golden bitter ale with a malty profile and a long, dry finish from American Cascade hops.

Holt IFBB

Joseph Holt Ltd, The Brewery, Empire Street, Cheetham, Manchester, M3 1JD
Tel (0161) 834 3285
Fax (0161) 834 6458
Website www.joseph-holt.com
Tours Saturday mornings only for 10-15 visitors, £10 donation to Christie Hospital

⊛ The brewing company was established in 1849 by Joseph Holt and his wife Catherine. It is still a family-run business in the hands of the great, great-grandson of the founder. Holt's supplies approximately 80 outlets as well as its own estate of 128 tied pubs. It still delivers beer to many of its tied houses in large 54-gallon hogsheads. A recently established 30-barrel brew plant is ideal for seasonal beers: see website.

Mild **(OG 1033, ABV 3.2%)**
A dark brown beer with a fruity, malty nose. Roast, malt and some fruit in the taste, with strong bitterness for a mild, and a dry malt and hops finish.

Bitter **(OG 1040, ABV 4%)**
Copper-coloured beer with malt and hops in the aroma and taste. Uncompromisingly bitter.

Hook Norton IFBB

Hook Norton Brewery Co Ltd, The Brewery, Hook Norton, Banbury, Oxfordshire, OX15 5NY
Tel (01608) 737210
Fax (01608) 730294
Email info@hook-norton-brewery.co.uk
Website www.hooky.co.uk
Shop Mon-Fri 9am-5pm
Tours by arrangement

⊗ Hook Norton was founded in 1849 by John Harris, a farmer and maltster. The current premises were built in 1900 and Hook Norton is one of the finest examples of a Victorian tower brewery, with a 25hp steam engine for most of its motive power. The brewhouse is currently expanding, with new fermenters, copper, mash tun and racking plant. Hook Norton owns 45 pubs and supplies approximately 400 free trade accounts. All Hook Norton draught beers are cask conditioned and dry hopped. All the beers use water drawn from wells beneath the brewery, Maris Otter malt and English Challenger, Fuggles and Goldings hops. The visitor centre is open Monday-Friday 9am-5pm (01608 730384). Seasonal beers: First Light (ABV 4.3%, March-April), Copper Ale (ABV 4.8%, Sept-Oct), Double Stout (ABV 4.8%, Jan-Feb), Haymaker (ABV 5%, July-Aug), Twelve Days (ABV 5.5%, Nov-Dec).

Hooky Dark **(OG 1033, ABV 3.2%)**
A chestnut brown, easy-drinking mild. A complex malt and hop aroma give way to a well-balanced taste, leading to a long, hoppy finish that is unusual for a mild.

Hooky Bitter **(OG 1035, ABV 3.4%)**
A classic golden session bitter. Hoppy and fruity aroma followed by a malt and hops taste and a continuing hoppy finish.

303AD **(OG 1041, ABV 4%)**
A pale brown best bitter, predominantly hoppy but balanced with moderate malt and banana fruit. The fruit and malt decline to a relatively short, hoppy finish.

Old Hooky **(OG 1048, ABV 4.6%)**
A strong bitter, tawny in colour. A well-rounded fruity taste with a balanced bitter finish.

Hop Back SIBA

Hop Back Brewery plc, Unit 22 Downton Business Centre, Downton, Salisbury, Wiltshire,

SP5 3HU
Tel (01725) 510986
Fax (01725) 513116
Email info@hopback.co.uk
Website www.hopback.co.uk
Tours by arrangement

⊗ Started by John Gilbert in 1987 at the Wyndham Arms in Salisbury, the new 20-barrel brewery has expanded steadily ever since. It went public via a Business Expansion Scheme in 1993 and has enjoyed rapid continued growth. Summer Lightning has won many awards. The brewery has 11 tied houses and also sells to more than 200 other outlets. Seasonal beers are produced on a monthly basis. Bottle-conditioned beers: Summer Lightning, Taiphoon (ABV 4.2%), Crop Circle, Entire Stout.

GFB/Gilbert's First Brew (OG 1035, ABV 3.5%)
A golden beer, with the sort of light, clean quality that makes it an ideal session ale. A hoppy aroma and taste lead to a good, dry finish. Refreshing.

Odyssey (OG 1040, ABV 4%)
A new, darker beer with a blend of four malts.

Crop Circle (OG 1041, ABV 4.2%)
A refreshingly sharp and hoppy summer beer. Gold coloured with a slight citrus taste. The crisp, dry aftertaste lingers.

Entire Stout (OG 1043, ABV 4.5%)
A rich, dark stout with a strong roasted malt flavour and a long, sweet and malty aftertaste. A beer suitable for vegans. Also produced with ginger.

Summer Lightning (OG 1049, ABV 5%)
A pleasurable pale bitter with a good, fresh, hoppy aroma and a malty, hoppy flavour. Finely balanced, it has an intense bitterness leading to a long, dry finish. Though strong, it tastes like a session ale.

Hopdaemon

Hopdaemon Brewery Co Ltd, Unit 1 Parsonage Farm, Seed Road, Newnham, Kent, ME9 0NA
Tel (01795) 892078
Email hopdaemon@supanet.com
Website www.hopdaemon.com

Tonie Prins opened a 12-barrel plant in 2001 in Canterbury and within six months was supplying more than 30 pubs in the area, as well as exclusive bottle-conditioned, own-label beers for London's British Museum, Southwark Cathedral and Science Museum, and more recently for the Barbican and National Gallery. In 2005 the brewery moved to bigger premises in Newnham and some 100 outlets are now supplied. Bottle-conditioned beers: Skrimshander IPA, Green Daemon (ABV 5%), Leviathan, Barbican Beer (ABV 5%), British Museum Beer (ABV 5%), National Gallery Beer (ABV 4.5%). Green Daemon is brewed with organic ingredients and no finings and is suitable for vegetarians and vegans.

Golden Braid (OG 1039, ABV 3.7%)

Incubus (OG 1041, ABV 4%)

Skrimshander IPA (OG 1045, ABV 4.5%)

Leviathan (OG 1057, ABV 6%)

Hopstar

Hopstar Brewery, c/o Black Horse, 72 Redearth Road, Darwen, Lancashire, BB3 2AF
Email hopstar@theblackun.co.uk

Hopstar first brewed in 2005 on a half-barrel plant from Red Rose. A 2.5-barrel plant was then commissioned from Porter Brewing. Two new fermenters were added in 2006 to double capacity due to demand.

Dizzy Danny Ale (ABV 3.8%)

Spinning Jenny (ABV 4%)

Smokey Joe's Black Beer (ABV 4%)

Hoskins Brothers

Hoskins Brothers Ales, The Ale Wagon, 27 Rutland Street, Leicester, LE1 1RE
Tel (0116) 262 3330
Email mail@alewagon.com
Website www.alewagon.co.uk

Stephen and Philip Hoskins founded Hoskins and Oldfield in Leicester in 1984. This ceased operation in 2001 and the beers were contract brewed, most recently by Tower, and the name was changed to Hoskins Brothers. A seven-barrel plant is currently in the process of being installed at their pub, the Ale Wagon in Leicester. It is intended to use this to brew the full range of the former Hoskins and Oldfield beers. Two outlets are supplied direct.

Hob Best Mild (ABV 3.5%)

Brigadier Bitter (ABV 3.6%)

Hob Bitter (ABV 4%)

White Dolphin (ABV 4%)
Wheat beer.

Tom Kelly's Stout (ABV 4.2%)

EXS (ABV 5%)

Ginger Tom (ABV 5.2%)
Ginger Ale.

Old Navigation Ale (ABV 7%)

Houston SIBA

Houston Brewing Co, South Street, Houston, Renfrewshire, PA6 7EN
Tel (01505) 614528
Fax (01505) 614133
Email ale@houston-brewing.co.uk
Website www.houston-brewing.co.uk
Shop open pub hours, every day
Tours by arrangement

⊗ A well-established brewery attached to the Fox and Hounds pub and restaurant. Brewery tours include dinner and tastings. Gift packs and bottles are also available. 200 outlets are supplied. There is a rolling programme of seasonal beers: see website.

Killellan (OG 1037, ABV 3.7%) ◆
A light session ale, with a floral hop and fruity taste. The finish of this amber beer is dry and quenching.

Blonde Bombshell (OG 1040, ABV 4%)
A gold-coloured ale with a fresh hop aroma and rounded maltiness.

Barochan (OG 1041, ABV 4.1%) ◆
A red, malty beer, in which fruit is balanced by roast and hop overtones; dry, bitter-sweet finish.

Peter's Well (OG 1042, ABV 4.2%) ◆
Well-balanced fruity taste with sweet hop, leading to an increasingly bitter-sweet finish.

Warlock Stout (ABV 4.7%)

Howard Town

Howard Town Brewery Ltd, Unit 10 Howard Town Mill, Mill Street, Glossop, Derbyshire, SK13 8PT
Tel (01457) 869800
Email beer@howardtownbrewery.co.uk
Website www.howardtownbrewery.co.uk
Tours by arrangement

A serious fire in Howard Town Mill in March 2006 destroyed the entire building, forcing the brewery to move into temporary premises. Other local brewers produced the beers on a temporary basis. The phone number will stay the same. Howard Town was established in 2005 by partners Tony Hulme and Les Dove, with their wives. Four regular beers are brewed, interspersed with occasional seasonal beers. Approximately 30-40 outlets are supplied direct. Seasonal beer: Robins Nest (ABV 5.2%, Christmas).

Bleaklow (OG 1040, ABV 3.8%)

Wrens Nest (OG 1043, ABV 4.2%)

Dinting Arches (OG 1045, ABV 4.5%)

H.T.B. (OG 1044, ABV 4.7%)

Glott's Hop (OG 1048, ABV 5%)

Sarah Hughes

Sarah Hughes Brewery, Beacon Hotel, 129 Bilston Street, Sedgley, Dudley, West Midlands, DY3 1JE
Tel (01902) 883381
Fax (01902) 884020
Email andrew.brough@tiscali.co.uk
Tours by arrangement

⊛ A traditional Black Country tower brewery, established in 1921. The original grist case and rare open-topped copper add to the ambience of the Victorian brewhouse and give a unique character to the brews. New head brewer Andrew Brough has plans for monthly specials and to expand the fermenting space for the addition of bottling Dark Ruby Mild. One pub, the Beacon Hotel, is owned. Seasonal beers: Raucous (ABV 4.8%, summer), Scrupulous (ABV 4.6%, autumn), Snowflake (ABV 8%, winter).

Pale Amber (OG 1038, ABV 4%)
A well-balanced beer, initially slightly sweet but with hops close behind.

Surprise Bitter (OG 1048, ABV 5%) ◆
A bitter-sweet, medium-bodied, hoppy ale with some malt.

Dark Ruby (OG 1058, ABV 6%) ◆
A dark ruby strong ale with a good balance of fruit and hops, leading to a pleasant, lingering hops and malt finish.

Humpty Dumpty

Humpty Dumpty Brewery, Church Road, Reedham, Norfolk, NR13 3TX
Tel (01493) 701818
Fax (01493) 700727
Website www.norfolkbroadsbrewing.co.uk
Shop 9am-6pm daily
Tours by arrangement

⊗ Established in 1998 by Mick Cottrell, this 11-barrel brewery changed hands in 2006 and continues to operate in its Norfolk Broads location. The new owners, the Fermoys and Georges, plan to continue producing the Humpty Dumpty range as well as introducing new styles. The brewery shop sells a wide range of its own and other regional brewers' bottle-conditioned beers. All Humpty Dumpty beers are also available in bottle-conditioned form. Seasonal beer: Christmas Crack (ABV 4.4%).

Little Sharpie (OG 1040, ABV 3.8%) ◆
A delicate hoppy aroma is a forerunner to a sweet hoppy, lagerish flavour. A clean golden yellow bitter with a finish in which bitterness grows.

Lemon and Ginger Ale (OG 1041, ABV 4%)

Swallow Tail (OG 1041, ABV 4%)

Humpty Dumpty (OG 1043, ABV 4.1%) ◆
Amber coloured with an overtly hoppy nose and grainy feel. The balance of this brew is definitely on the bitter side. Underlying sweetness fades to leave a long, dry finish.

Claud Hamilton (OG 1043, ABV 4.1%) ◆
A well-rounded, red-brown beer with a distinct hickory stick aroma. The solid roast malt base lingers as the bitter-sweet beginning fades into a light hoppy dryness.

Reed Cutter (OG 1046, ABV 4.4%) ◆
A light, soft-flavoured beer with banana and toffee notes. A distinctly malted milk flavour in the first taste, and a shallow, sweetish, fruity follow through.

Cheltenham Flyer (OG 1048, ABV 4.6%)

Norfolk Nectar (OG 1048, ABV 4.6%)

Norfolk Punch (OG 1048, ABV 4.6%) ◆
A soft citrus aroma begets a sweet, smoky brew that is gentle on the palate. The deep red colour is at odds with the lightness of flavour that quickly disappears. Some liquorice may be detected.

Reedham Gold (OG 1048, ABV 4.6%)

Butt Jumper (OG 1049, ABV 4.8%) ◆
Toffee and malt dominate the aroma of

this tawny-hued ale. Full-flavoured, with malt vying with a fruity bitterness for dominance. The long, lingering finish does not fade as a nutty bitterness becomes prevalent.

Spark Arrester (OG 1049, ABV 4.8%)

Peto's Porter (OG 1051, ABV 5%)

Railway Sleeper (OG 1051, ABV 5%) ♦
Full-bodied tawny brew with a rich, fruity nature. Slight malt bouquet belies the strong plummy character where sweetness and malt counterbalance the background bitterness. A quick, spicy, bitter finish.

Hydes IFBB

Hydes Brewery Ltd, 46 Moss Lane West, Manchester, M15 5PH
Tel (0161) 226 1317
Fax (0161) 227 9593
Email mail@hydesbrewery.com
Website www.hydesbrewery.com
Tours by arrangement

In the past 12 months Hydes has consolidated its recent dramatic expansion. Eleven cask ales are now regularly brewed including contract brewing for Diageo and InBev UK. In 2005 Hydes expanded on to the site adjoining the brewery for its warehousing and packaging operations. Now with more than 200 trade accounts and 80 tied pubs, the brewery operates 24 hours a day to keep up with demand. Hydes is also diversifying and has a growing number of pub restaurants and café bars. The company is now the biggest volume producer of cask ales in the North-west, with further expansion planned. Seasonal beers: Free Spirit (ABV 4.8%, Jan-Feb), Heavenly Draft (ABV 4.2%, March-April), Dr's Orders (ABV 4.4%, May-June), Cutty Shark (ABV 4.1%, July-Aug), Hidden Treasure (ABV 4.5%, Sept-Oct), Stormtrooper (ABV 5%, Nov-Dec).

Light Mild (OG 1033.5, ABV 3.5%) ♦
A lightly-hopped, amber-coloured session beer with a fresh lemon fruit taste and a short, dry finish. Sold as 1863 Bitter is some outlets.

Traditional Mild (OG 1033.5, ABV 3.5%) ♦
A mid-brown beer with malt and citrus fruits in the aroma and taste. Dry, malty aftertaste.

Dark Mild (OG 1033.5, ABV 3.5%) ♦
Dark brown/red in colour with a fruit and malt nose. Complex taste, including berry fruits, malt and a hint of chocolate. Satisfying aftertaste.

Original Bitter (OG 1036.5, ABV 3.8%) ♦
Pale brown beer with a malty nose, malt and an earthy hoppiness in the taste, and a good bitterness through to the finish.

Jekyll's Gold (OG 1043, ABV 4.3%) ♦
Pale gold in colour, with a fruity nose. A well-balanced beer with hops, fruit and malt in the taste and the bitter finish.

XXXX (OG 1070, ABV 6.8%)

For InBev UK

Boddingtons Bitter (OG 1038, ABV 4.1%)

Iceni SIBA EAB

Iceni Brewery, 3 Foulden Road, Ickburgh, near Mundford, Norfolk, IP26 5BJ
Tel (01842) 878922
Fax (01842) 879626
Email icenibrewe@aol.com
Website www.icenibrewery.co.uk
Shop Mon-Fri 8.30am-5pm; Sat 9am-3pm
Tours by arrangement

Brendan Moore launched Iceni in 1995 and is now at the forefront of local brewing as a member of SIBA and a founder member of the East Anglian Brewers' Co-operative. Iceni was launched following Redundancy Plus help from a Rural Enterprise Grant. Equipment is ex-dairy and milk farm stock. The brewery has its own hop garden and barley plot aimed at amusing the many visitors that flock to the shop to buy the 28 different ales, stouts and lagers bottled on-site. Beer as a gift is an increasingly important trend at Iceni. 40 outlets are supplied and Brendan also targets local farmers' markets and the tourist shop in nearby Thetford Forest. Special beers are brewed for festivals. Seasonal beer: Winter Lightning (ABV 5%). All cask ales are also bottle conditioned; there are many additional bottle-conditioned beers: see website.

Elveden Forest Gold (OG 1040, ABV 3.9%) ♦
Forest fruits on the nose give way to strong hop bitterness in the initial taste. Residual maltiness provides balance at first but is swamped by a long, dry, bitter finish.

Fine Soft Day (OG 1038, ABV 4%) ♦
A swirling mix of understated malt, hop and bitter flavours. Amber-hued with a grainy feel, this essentially bitter ale has a hint of cranberry toward the end but little complexity.

Celtic Queen (OG 1038, ABV 4%) ♦
A golden brew with a light hoppy nose giving way to distinctly bitter characteristics throughout. A shallow mix of malt and hops adds some depth. A long, lingering finish.

Fen Tiger (OG 1040, ABV 4.2%)

It's A Grand Day (OG 1044, ABV 4.5%)

Raspberry Wheat (OG 1048, ABV 5%)

Men of Norfolk (OG 1060, ABV 6.2%) ♦
A superb chocolaty stout with heavy roast overtones from initial aroma to strong, solid finish. Malt and vine fruits counterbalance the initial roast character while a caramel undertone remains to the end.

Innis & Gunn

Innis & Gunn Brewing Co Ltd, PO Box 17246, Edinburgh, EH11 1YR
Tel (0131) 337 4420
Email dougal.sharp@innisandgunn.com
Website www.innisandgunn.com

Innis & Gunn produces one regular bottled (not bottle conditioned) product, Oak Aged Beer (ABV 6.6%).

Inveralmond SIBA

Inveralmond Brewery Ltd, 1 Inveralmond Way, Inveralmond, Perth, PH1 3UQ
Tel/Fax (01738) 449448
Email info@inveralmond-brewery.co.uk
Website www.inveralmond-brewery.co.uk

◎ Established in 1997, Inveralmond was the first brewery in Perth for more than 30 years. The brewery has gone from strength to strength, with some 150 outlets supplied and wholesalers taking beers nationwide. In 2005 the brewery expanded ino the next door premises, more than doubling floor space and output. Seasonal ales: Inkie Pinkie (ABV 3.7%), Special (ABV 3.7%, May-June), IPA (ABV 3.8%, Sept-Oct), XXX (ABV 4.4%, July-Aug), Brown Ale (ABV 4.6%, Nov-Dec), Sunburst Pilsner (ABV 4.8%, Jan-Feb), Export Pale Ale (ABV 5.6%, March-April).

Independence (OG 1040, ABV 3.8%) ◆
A well-balanced Scottish ale with fruit and malt tones. Hop provides an increasing bitterness in the finish.

Ossian's Ale (OG 1042, ABV 4.1%) ▯ ◆
Well-balanced best bitter with a dry finish. This full-bodied amber ale is dominated by fruit and hop with a bitter-sweet character.

Thrappledouser (OG 1043, ABV 4.3%) ◆
A refreshing amber beer with reddish hues. The crisp, hoppy aroma is finely balanced with a tangy but quenching taste.

Lia Fail (OG 1048, ABV 4.7%) ◆
The name is the Gaelic title for the Stone of Destiny. A dark, robust, full-bodied beer with a deep malty taste. Smooth texture and balanced finish.

Islay

Islay Ales Co Ltd, The Brewery, Islay House Square, Bridgend, Isle of Islay, PA44 7NZ
Tel/Fax (01496) 810014
Email info@islayales.com
Website www.islayales.com
Shop Mon-Sat 10.30am-5pm
Tours by arrangement

Brewing started on a four-barrel plant located in a converted tractor shed within Islay House Square in 2004. The brewery shop is next door. Paul Hathaway, Paul Capper and Walter Schobert set up the brewery on an island more famous for its whisky, but it has quickly established itself as a must-see place for those visiting the eight working distilleries on the island. Four outlets are supplied. All the beers are available in bottle-conditioned form.

Finlaggan Ale (OG 1039, ABV 3.7%)

Black Rock Ale (OG 1040, ABV 4.2%)

Saligo Ale (OG 1044, ABV 4.4%)

Dun Hogs Head Ale (OG 1044, ABV 4.4%)

Ardnave Ale (OG 1048, ABV 4.6%)

Nerabus Ale (OG 1048, ABV 4.8%)

Isle of Arran

See Arran

Isle of Mull

Isle of Mull Brewing Co Ltd, Ledaig, Tobermory, Isle of Mull, Argyll, PA75 6NR
Tel (01688) 302830
Fax (01688) 302046
Email isleofmullbrewing@btinternet.com

Brewing started in 2005 using a five-barrel plant supplied by Brewing Solutions. There are plans to relocate to a larger, custom-built brewery in Tobermory. The brewery currently supplies Macgochans Bar and a number of local outlets on Mull, Oban and surrounding areas and a variety of pubs in Edinburgh and Glasgow. Seasonal and bottled beers are planned.

Island Pale Ale (OG 1038, ABV 3.9%)

McCaig's Folly (OG 1042, ABV 4.2%)

Terror of Tobermory (OG 1045, ABV 4.6%)

Galleon Gold (OG 1048, ABV 5%)

Isle of Purbeck

☼ Isle of Purbeck Brewery, Manor Road, Studland, Dorset, BH19 3AU
Tel (01929) 450225
Fax (01929) 450307
Tours by arrangement

The 10-barrel brewing equipment from the former Poole Brewery has been installed in the grounds of the Bankes Arms Hotel that overlooks the sweep of Studland Bay. There are plans to add new brews and the size of the plant will enable the brands to be sold to other pubs. 50 outlets are supplied. Seasonal beer: Thermal Cheer (ABV 4.8%, winter).

Fossil Fuel (OG 1040, ABV 4.1%)

Solar Power (OG 1043, ABV 4.3%)

Studland Bay Wrecked (OG 1044, ABV 4.5%)

IPA (OG 1047, ABV 4.8%)

Isle of Skye

Isle of Skye Brewing Co (Leann an Eilein) Ltd, The Pier, Uig, Isle of Skye, IV51 9XP
Tel (01470) 542477
Fax (01470) 542488
Email info@skyebrewery.co.uk
Website www.skyebrewery.co.uk

Shop Mon-Sat 10am-6pm; Sun 12.30-4.30pm (Apr-Oct)
Tours by arrangement

◎ The Isle of Skye Brewery was established in 1995, the first commercial brewery in the Hebrides. Originally a 10-barrel plant, it was upgraded to 20-barrels in 2004, including a 22-barrel copper by Macmillans of Prestonpans, who supply many of the whisky stills in Scotland. Fermenting capacity now stands at 80 barrels, with plans to further increase this and upgrade bottling facilities. The brewery is owned by former Business Studies teacher Angus MacRuary while Pam Jones, a former chef, is head brewer. Seasonal beers: Skye Light (ABV 3.8%), X (ABV 4.3%), Oyster Stout (ABV 4.6%), Skye's Grand (ABV 5.5%). Bottle-conditioned beers: Misty Isle (ABV 4.3%), Am Basteir (ABV 7%).

Young Pretender (OG 1039, ABV 4%) ◆
Predominantly hoppy and fruity, this golden amber ale has hops and fruit on the nose. The bitter taste is also dominated by fruit and hop, with the hops lingering in to the long, bitter finish.

Red Cuillin (OG 1041, ABV 4.2%) ◆
This tawny-reddish beer has a light fruity, malty nose that leads to a deliciously bitter-sweet palate and a long, dry aftertaste.

Hebridean Gold (OG 1041.5, ABV 4.3%) t
Oats are used to produce this golden beer. Nicely balanced, it has a refreshing, bitter, fruity flavour. Thirst-quenching and drinkable.

Black Cuillin (OG 1044, ABV 4.5%) ◆
A complex, tasty brew worthy of its many awards. Full-bodied malts hold sway but there are plenty of hops and fruit to be discovered in its varied character. A truly delicious Scottish old ale.

Blaven (OG 1047, ABV 5%) ◆
Sweetish amber ale with orange fruit notes. There is plenty of hop bitterness to balance the fruitiness. The malty aroma gives way to a bitter-sweet finish.

Cuillin Beast (OG 1061.5, ABV 7%) ◆
Sweet and fruity, and much more drinkable than the strength would suggest. Plenty of caramel throughout with a creamy, dry mouthfeel.

For Devanha Brewery

XXX (OG 1043, ABV 4.4%)

Itchen Valley SIBA

Itchen Valley Brewery, Unit B, Prospect Commercial Park, 4 Prospect Road, New Alresford, Hampshire, SO24 9QF
Tel (01962) 735111
Fax (01962) 735678
Email info@itchenvalley.com
Website www.itchenvalley.com
Shop Mon-Fri 8am-4pm; Sat 9am-1pm
Tours by arrangement

⊗ Itchen Valley Brewery, under the successful management of Matthew Nye and head brewer Rob Dupre has moved to new premises and now produces six award-winning core beers and up to 30 seasonal ales to more than 250 pubs in Berkshire,Hampshire, London, Surrey and Sussex. Local and national wholesalers are used for further distribution. Seasonal beers: Green Jackets (ABV 4.5%), Watercress Line (ABV 4.2%), Father Christmas (ABV 5%), Rudolph (ABV 3.8%). Bottle-conditioned beers: Pure Gold, Wat Tyler, Wykehams Glory (ABV 4.3%), Hampshire Rose, Father Christmas.

Godfathers (OG 1038, ABV 3.8%) ◆
A citrus hop character with a malty taste and a light body, leading to an increasingly dry, bitter finish. Pale brown in colour.

Fagin's (OG 1041, ABV 4.1%) ◆
Enjoyable copper-coloured best bitter with a hint of crystal malt and a pleasant bitter aftertaste.

Hampshire Rose (OG 1042, ABV 4.2%)
A golden amber ale. Fruit and hops dominate the taste throughout, with a good mouth feel.

Winchester Ale (OG 1042, ABV 4.2%)

Pure Gold (OG 1046, ABV 4.6%) ◆
An aromatic, hoppy, golden bitter. Initial grapefruit flavours lead to a dry, bitter finish that leaves you wanting more.

Wat Tyler (OG 1048, ABV 4.8%)

Jacobi*

Jacobi Brewery of Caio, Penlanwen Farm, Pumsaint, Carmarthenshire
Tel (01558) 650605
Email justin@jacobibrewery.co.uk

Brewing started in May 2006 on an eight-barrel plant in a converted barn. Brewer Justin Jacobi is also the owner of the Brunant Arms in Caio, which will be a regular outlet for the beers. The brewery is located 50 yards from the Dolaucothi mines where the Romans dug for gold and which is now a major visitor attraction. Justin plans at first to sell to pubs within a 20-mile radius before expanding.

Light Ale (ABV 3.8%)

Original Bitter (ABV 4.4%)

Jarrow SIBA

Jarrow Brewery, The Robin Hood, Primrose Hill, Jarrow, Tyne & Wear, NE32 5UB
Tel/Fax (0191) 483 6792
Email jarrowbrewery@btconnect.com
Website www.jarrowbrewing.co.uk
Tours by arrangement

◎ Brewing started in 2002 and during the first year the brewery won five CAMRA awards. Owners and brewers Jess and Alison McConnell own three pubs on South Tyneside: the Albion Inn, Bill Quay; the Robin Hood, Jarrow; and the recently acquired Maltings, South Shields. Some

125 outlets are supplied. 2005 was a good year for the brewery with the flagship beer Rivet Catcher winning Champion Beer of the North East and a silver award in the Champion Beer of Britain competition. Brewing was set to start at the Maltings during 2006. Seasonal beers: Red Ellen (ABV 4.4%, Feb-Oct), Venerable Bede (ABV 4.5%, April-Sept), McConnells Irish Stout (ABV 4.6%, March-Nov), Old Cornelius (ABV 4.8%, Jan-Dec).

Jarrow Bitter (OG 1037.5, ABV 3.8%)
A light golden session bitter with a delicate hop aroma and a lingering fruity finish.

Palmers Resolution (OG 1037.5, ABV 3.8%)

Rivet Catcher (OG 1039, ABV 4%) 🗍
A light, smooth, satisfying gold bitter with fruity hops on the tongue and nose.

Joblings Swinging Gibbet (OG 1041, ABV 4.1%)
A copper-coloured, evenly balanced beer with a good hop aroma and a fruity finish.

Westoe IPA (OG 1044.5, ABV 4.6%)

Jennings

See Wolverhampton & Dudley in New Nationals

Jersey SIBA

Jersey Brewery, Tregear House, Longueville Road, St Saviour, Jersey, JE2 7WF
Email paulhurley@victor-hugo-ltd.com
Tours by arrangement

Following the closure of the original brewery in Ann Street during 2004, the Jersey Brewery is now located within an old soft drinks factory using a Canadian-built 40-barrel plant and the eight-barrel plant from the former Tipsy Toad brewery at the Star in St Peter. Most cask beers are produced on the smaller plant, though the bigger, which usually produces keg beer, can also be used for cask production. Cask Special was originally produced as a one-off for the 2005 Jersey beer festival but, after receiving the Beer of the Festival award, the brewery has continued to produce it. The other cask ale, Sunbeam, is produced for the Guernsey market following the closure of the Guernsey Brewery in 2002.

Guernsey Sunbeam (OG 1042, ABV 4.2%)

Jimmy's Bitter (OG 1042, ABV 4.2%)

Special (OG 1045, ABV 4.5%)

Horny Toad (OG 1050, ABV 5%)

Jolly Brewer

Jolly Brewer, 1 College Street, Wrexham, LL13 8LU
Tel (01978) 263338
Email pene@jollybrewer.co.uk
Website www.jollybrewer.co.uk
Shop Mon-Sat 9.30am-6.30pm

Penelope Coles has been brewing for the past 25 years. Some 10 years ago she decided to open a craft brewing shop and five years later added a real ale off-licence, the Jolly Brewer. She then decided to become a registered brewer in order to sell her beer in the shop. The brewing plant is based in Penelope's home and produces 10 gallons a day with the help of her assistant, Matthew McGivern. A full range of bottle-conditioned beers are made and cask beers are supplied to order. All beers are suitable for vegetarians and vegans.

Taid's Garden (OG 1040, ABV 4%)

Cascade Ale (OG 1045, ABV 4.6%)

Jolly Brewer Bitter (OG 1045, ABV 4.6%) ◆
Fruit and bitterness dominate the flavour of this gold-coloured beer. Hops are also proment. Dry aftertaste.

Lucinda's Lager (OG 1045, ABV 4.6%)

Diod y Gymraef (OG 1048, ABV 5%)

Taffy's Tipple (OG 1050, ABV 5%)

Y Ddraig Goch (OG 1050, ABV 5%)

Dark Lager/Strange Brew (OG 1060, ABV 6%) ◆
Powerful, fruity, black lager-style beer. Dry, crisp, vinous and sharp with a sweetish aftertaste.

Jollyboat

Jollyboat Brewery (Bideford) Ltd, The Coach House, Buttgarden Street, Bideford, Devon, EX39 2AU
Tel (01237) 424343

⊗ The brewery was established in 1995 by Hugh Parry and his son, Simon. In 2004, Contraband became Reserve Champion Beer at the SIBA South-west Festival at Tucker's Maltings, Newton Abbot. Jollyboat currently supplies some 16 outlets. A Jollyboat is a sailors' leave boat that brings them ashore. All the beer names have nautical connections.

Grenville's Renown (ABV 3.8%)

Freebooter (OG 1040, ABV 4%)

Mainbrace (OG 1041, ABV 4.2%) ◆
Pale brown brew with a rich fruity aroma and a bitter taste and aftertaste.

Plunder (ABV 4.8%)

Contraband (ABV 5.8%)
An award-winning ale based on a Victorian porter recipe.

Juwards

Juwards Brewery, Unit 14 Tonedale Business Park, Wellington, Somerset, TA21 0AW

Ted Bishop started brewing in 1994 in a former woollen mill at Tonedale Business Park in Wellington on a six-barrel brewplant. In 1999 a 10-barrel plant was purchased to allow further expansion. Brewing ceased in 2001 as Ted had a serious accident and the brew plant was sold to Moor Brewery. But during 2005 Ted decided to restart brewing on a part-time basis and a small plant was put together. Four firkins are brewed at a time, once or twice a week, and all beer is sold through the Moor Beer Company to whom all enquiries should be directed (qv Moor). Seasonal beer: Juwards Winter Brew (ABV 4.3%), Juwards Stout (ABV 4.6%).

Bishops Special Mild (ABV 3.8%)

Bitter (ABV 3.8%)

Bishops Somerset Ale (ABV 4%)

Juwards (ABV 4%)

Amber (ABV 4.1%)

Premium (ABV 4.3%)

Kelburn SIBA

Kelburn Brewing Co Ltd, 10 Muriel Lane, Barrhead, East Renfrewshire, G78 1QB
Tel (0141) 881 2138
Fax (0141) 881 2145
Email info@kelburnbrewery.com
Website www.kelburnbrewery.com
Tours by arrangement

⊗ A family business run by Derek Moore, who started brewing in 2002. In the first four years of business, Kelburn beers have won 19 awards. Goldihops was voted Best Beer of Glasgow 2002 and Cart Blanche SIBA Best Strong Beer of Scotland 2004 and 2005. Beers are available in bottle and take-away polypins. Five brews are available throughout the year and there is currently one seasonal ale, Ca'Canny (ABV 5.2%, winter ■).

Goldihops (OG 1038, ABV 3.8%) ◻
Well-hopped session ale with a fruity taste and a bitter-sweet finish.

Misty Law (ABV 4%)
A dry, hoppy amber ale with a long-lasting bitter finish.

Red Smiddy (OG 1040, ABV 4.1%) ■
A smooth ale with a reddish hue and a citrus, fruity aftertaste.

Dark Moor (OG 1044, ABV 4.5%)
A dark, fruity ale with undertones of liquorice and blackcurrant.

Cart Blanche (OG 1048, ABV 5%)
A golden, full-bodied ale with a dry aftertaste.

Kelham Island SIBA

Kelham Island Brewery Ltd, Alma Street, Sheffield, South Yorkshire, S3 8SA
Tel (0114) 249 4804
Fax (0114) 249 4803
Email sales@kelhambrewery.co.uk
Website www.kelhambrewery.co.uk
Tours by arrangement

⊛ The brewery opened in 1990 on land adjoining the Fat Cat public house. Due to its success in its early years, the brewery moved to new purpose-built premises at Kelham Island in 1999, with five times the capacity of the original brewery. Kelham Island has won awards at beer festivals nationwide and Pale Rider became Supreme Champion Beer of Britain in 2004 at the Great British Beer Festival. Seasonal beers: Golden Eagle (ABV 4.2%, July-Aug), Harvest Gold (ABV 3.8%, September), Grande Pale (ABV 6.6%, November), Red Rudolph (ABV 5%, December), Fat Cat Bitter (ABV 4.4%).

Bitter (OG 1038, ABV 3.8%) ◻ ◆
A clean, characterful, crisp, pale brown beer. The nose and palate are dominated by refreshing hoppiness and fruitiness, which, with a good bitter dryness, lasts in the aftertaste.

Gold (OG 1038, ABV 3.8%)
A light golden ale, a hoppy nose and finish, a smooth drinking bitter.

Easy Rider (OG 1041.8, ABV 4.3%) ◆
A pale, straw-coloured beer with a sweetish flavour and delicate hints of citrus fruits. A beer with hints of flavour rather than full-bodied.

Pale Rider (OG 1050, ABV 5.2%) ◻ ◆
A full-bodied, straw pale ale, with a good fruity aroma and a strong fruit and hop taste. Its well-balanced sweetness and bitterness continue in the finish.

Fat Cat IPA (OG 1050, ABV 5.5%)

Keltek SIBA

Keltek Brewery, Candela House, Cardrew Industrial Estate, Redruth, Cornwall, TR15 1SS
Tel (01209) 313620
Fax (01209) 215197
Email sales@keltekbrewery.co.uk
Website www.keltekbrewery.co.uk
Shop Mon-Fri 9am-6pm

⊗ Keltek Brewery moved to Lostwithiel in 1999 and in 2006 moved again to purpose-built premises in Redruth. Keltek won its first gold medal in 1998 and many awards have followed. Five outlets are currently supplied. Seasonal ales and custom beers are available. Bottle-conditioned beers: as for cask beers listed below.

4K Mild (OG 1038, ABV 3.8%)

Golden Lance (OG 1038, ABV 3.8%)

Special IPA (OG 1040, ABV 4%)

Kornish Nektar (OG 1042, ABV 4.2%)

Magik (OG 1042, ABV 4.2%) ◆
A rounded, well-balanced and complex beer.

Mr Harvey's Golden Sunshine Ale (OG 1050, ABV 5%)

King (OG 1051, ABV 5.1%)

Uncle Stu's Famous Steak Pie Stout (ABV 6.5%)

Kripple Dick (ABV 7%)

Beheaded '76 (ABV 7.6%)

Kemptown SIBA

⌂ Kemptown Brewery Co Ltd, 33 Upper St James's Street, Brighton, East Sussex, BN2 1JN
Tel (01273) 699595
Fax (01932) 344413
Email bev@kemptownbrewery.co.uk
Website www.kemptownbrewery.co.uk
Tours by arrangement

⊗ A brewery established in 1989 and built in

the tower tradition behind the Hand in Hand, which is possibly the smallest pub in England with its own brewery. It takes its name and logo from the former Charrington's Kemptown Brewery 500 yards away, which closed in 1964. Three free trade outlets are supplied. Seasonal beer: Old Grumpy (ABV 6.5%, winter). Occasional brews include Tippers Tipple, Trailblazer and Crewsaver.

Black Moggy Mild (OG 1038, ABV 3.8%)

Kemptown Bitter (OG 1040, ABV 4%)

Ye Olde Trout (OG 1045, ABV 4.5%)

S.I.D./Staggering in the Dark (OG 1050, ABV 5%)

Keswick*

Keswick Brewing Co, The Old Brewery, Brewery Lane, Keswick, Cumbria, CA12 1JN
Tel (07792) 156489
Fax (0870) 1202948
Email enquiries@keswickbrewery.co.uk
Website www.keswickbrewery.co.uk
Shop – call for details
Tours by arrangement

Phil and Sue Harrison set up their 10-barrel brewery in April 2006. Local sheep wool is used for insulation and the copper heater can run on reclaimed vegetable oil. They intend to extend their range of beers using high-quality organic materials and trying to provide vegetarian products where possible. The brewing plant has been designed and manufactured by George Thompson of Brewing Solutions. Both beers are available in bottle-conditioned form.

Best Bitter (ABV 3.8%)

Organic Best Bitter (ABV 3.8%)

Keynsham*

Keynsham Brewing Co Ltd, Brookleaze, Stockwood Vale, Keynsham, Bristol, BS31 2AL
Tel (0117) 986 7889
Email jonfirth@blueyonder.co.uk
Website www.keynshambrewery.co.uk
Tours by arrangement

Keynsham opened in 2005 using the equipment of the former Nursery Brewery. The brewer is John Firth, a long-term CAMRA member and a craft brewer for many years. A wide variety of hops and grains is used. Some 30 outlets are supplied. Seasonal beers are available quarterly.

Pixash (OG 1042, ABV 4.1%)
A mid-brown beer using Goldings hops, with a distinct roast malt accent.

Somerdale Golden (OG 1046, ABV 4.5%) ◆
Interesting floral bitter, with fresh minty aroma. Hoppy, full-bodied and bitter-sweet.

Keystone*

Keystone Brewery, Old Carpenters Shop, Berwick St Leonard, Salisbury, Wiltshire, SP3 5SN
Tel (01747) 870307/07920 004145
Email info@keystonebrewery.co.uk
Website www.keystonebrewery.co.uk

Keystone Brewery opened in early summer 2006, using a 10-barrel plant from La Brasserie de Soif in Brittany and fermenters from Wickwar Brewery (qv). Water is used from a borehole in the chalk beneath Fonthill Bishop.

Large One (OG 1042, ABV 4.2%)

Khean

See Woodlands

King SIBA

W J King & Co (Brewers), 3-5 Jubilee Estate, Foundry Lane, Horsham, West Sussex, RH13 5UE
Tel (01403) 272102
Fax (01403) 754455
Email office@kingfamilybrewers.co.uk
Website www.kingfamilybrewers.co.uk
Shop Sat 10am-2pm
Tours by arrangement (limited to 15)

⊗ Launched in 2001 by former King & Barnes managing director Bill King, with a 20-barrels a week ex-Firkin plant, the brewery had expanded to a capacity of 50 barrels a week by mid-2004. In 2004 the lease of premises next door was taken over to give more cellar space and to enable room to stock more bottle-conditioned beers. One pub is owned and approximately 200 regular and occasional outlets are supplied. Seasonal beers: Kings Old Ale ◘, (ABV 4.5%, winter), Summer Ale (ABV 4%, summer), Merry Ale (ABV 6.5%, Christmas). Bottle-conditioned beers: Red River (ABV 5%), Kings Old Ale (ABV 4.5%) ◘, Cereal Thriller (ABV 6.3%), Five Generation (ABV 4.4%), Merry Ale (ABV 6.5%), Mallard Ale (ABV 5%), Winter's Tale (ABV 4.2%). All the bottled beers are suitable for vegetarians as no isinglass finings are used.

Horsham Best Bitter (OG 1038, ABV 3.8%) ◆
A predominantly malty best bitter, brown in colour. The nutty flavours have some sweetness with a little bitterness that grows in the aftertaste. Crystal malt and three different hops are used.

Red River (OG 1048, ABV 4.8%) ◆
A full-flavoured, mid-brown beer with a red tinge. Using the same ingredients as Horsham Best Bitter, this is very malty with some berry fruitiness in the aroma and taste. The finish is reasonably balanced with a sharp bitterness increasingly coming through.

Kings Head

⚲ Kings Head Brewery, Kings Head, 132 High Street, Bildeston, Ipswich, Suffolk, IP7 7ED
Tel (01449) 741434
Email enquiries@bildestonkingshead.co.uk
Website www.bildestonkingshead.co.uk
Tours by arrangement

⊗ Kings Head has been brewing since 1996 in the old stables at the back of the pub. The plant has approximately five barrels' capacity and brewing takes place twice a week. The brewery stages a beer festival in May (Late Spring Bank Holiday) every year where most of the 40 beers on offer are from other micros around the country. Six other pubs and many beer festivals are supplied. Seasonal beer: Dark Vader (ABV

5.4%, winter). Bottle-conditioned beers: Blondie, Apache, Crowdie and Dark Vader.

Not Strong Beer/NSB (OG 1030, ABV 2.8%)

Best Bitter (OG 1040, ABV 3.8%)

Blondie (OG 1041, ABV 4%)

First Gold (OG 1044, ABV 4.3%)

Apache (OG 1046, ABV 4.5%)

Crowdie (OG 1050, ABV 5%)

Kingstone*

Kingstone Brewery, Kinsons Farm, Whitebrook, Monmouth, NP25 4TX
Tel/Fax (01600) 860778

Kingstone Brewery is located in the Wye Valley, an area of outstanding national beauty. Brian and Jilly Austwick were growing raspberries and rhubarb on their small farm, with most of the production going for winemaking. They then decided to utilise surplus farm buildings to make some of the wine themselves, but the lead times were such that they decided brewing was a better prospect. They ordered a four-barrel plant from Dave Porter and their first brew was produced in December 2005. Three beers are produced and are available in both cask and bottle-conditioned forms.

Three Castles (ABV 3.8%)

Classic (ABV 4.5%)

Gatehouse (ABV 5.1%)

Kinver

Kinver Brewery, Unit 2 Fairfield Drive, Kinver, Staffordshire, DY7 6EW
Tel (07715) 842679 / 07906 146777
Email kinvercave@aol.com
Website www.kinverbrewery.co.uk
Tours by arrangement

Established in 2004 by two CAMRA members, Kinver Brewery consists of a five-barrel plant bought from Brewsters, producing three regular beers, seasonals and one-off brews. Brewing once a month initially, they are now up to twice a week, supplying over 30 pubs and clubs throughout the Midlands including two locally in Kinver. Seasonal beers: Maybug (ABV 4.8%), Over the Edge (ABV 7.6%, Nov-March).

Edge (OG 1041, ABV 4.2%) ◆
Hoppy aroma from this copper-coloured ale, which has a full hop taste with fruity and flowery asides. Bitterness develops with a great hoppy, lingering mouthfeel.

Pail Ale (OG 1044, ABV 4.4%)
Very pale bitter ale with a citrus, hoppy flavour.

Caveman (OG 1050, ABV 5%) ◆
Pale brown with a caramel start, sweet and fruity middle, fruity finish going bitter with satisfying astringency.

Lancaster

Lancaster Brewery Ltd, Unit 19 Lansil Industrial Estate, Caton Road, Lancaster, LA1 3PQ
Tel (01524) 844610
Fax (01524) 844621
Email sales@lancasterbrewery.co.uk
Website www.lancasterbrewery.co.uk
Tours by arrangement

Lancaster Brewery opened in 2005 and brews three main beers with monthly seasonals. There are plans to relocate in 2007 to larger premises with room for a brewery tap and visitor centre.

Duchy (OG 1040, ABV 3.9%) ◆
Smooth-tasting bitter with a delicate sweetness balanced by firm hop notes. A sweet, hoppy finish.

Blonde (OG 1042, ABV 4.1%)

JSB (OG 1044, ABV 4.3%) ◆
Dry yet mellow-tasting bitter with a good balance of malt and hops.

Langham*

Langham Brewery, The Old Granary, Langham Lane, Lodsworth, Petsworth, West Sussex, GU28 9BU
Tel (01798) 860861

Langham Brewery opened in May 2006 using a 10-barrel ex-Wickwar Brewery plant. It is owned by Steve Mansley and James Berrow. The portfolio was not available when the guide went to press.

Langton

♀ Langton Brewery, Grange Farm, Welham Road, Thorpe Langton, Market Harborough, Leicestershire, LE16 7TU
Tel (07840) 532826
Website www.thelangtonbrewery.co.uk
Tours by arrangement

⊛ Langton Brewery is run by three partners, Alistair Chapman, Dave Dyson and Derek Hewitt. Using a four-barrel plant in a barn that has been converted to industrial use, they brew Caudle Bitter (named after the range of local hills) and Bowler, which marks the nearby Bell Inn's long association with Langton Cricket Club. The Bell was the brewery's first home. Boxer Heavyweight is named after Jack Gardner, British Heavyweight champion, who was resident in the Langtons. The beers are available for take-away. Seasonal beers: Buzz Light Beer (ABV 4.2%), Bankers Draught (ABV 4.2%), Langton Belle (ABV 4.5%), Boxer Heavyweight Porter (ABV 5.2%).

Caudle Bitter (OG 1039, ABV 3.9%) ◆
Copper-coloured session bitter that is close to pale ale in style. Flavours are relatively well-balanced throughout with hops slightly to the fore.

Plane Bitter (OG 1042, ABV 4.2%)

Bowler Strong Ale (ABV 4.8%)
A strong traditional ale with a deep red colour and a hoppy nose.

Larkins SIBA

Larkins Brewery Ltd, Chiddingstone, Edenbridge, Kent, TN8 7BB
Tel (01892) 870328
Fax (01892) 871141

Tours by arrangement Nov-Feb

⊗ Larkins Brewery was founded in 1986 by the Dockerty family, farmers and hop growers, who bought the Royal Tunbridge Wells Brewery. The company moved to Larkins Farm in 1987. Since then the production of three regular brews and Porter in the winter months has steadily increased. Brews are made using only Kentish hops, yeast and malt; no sugars or brewing adjuncts are added to the beers. Larkins owns one pub, the Rock at Chiddingstone Hoath, and supplies around 70 free houses within a radius of 20 miles.

Traditional Ale (OG 1035, ABV 3.4%)
Tawny in colour, a full-tasting hoppy ale with plenty of character for its strength.

Chiddingstone (OG 1040, ABV 4%)
Named after the village where the brewery is based, Chiddingstone is a mid-strength, hoppy, fruity ale with a long, bitter-sweet aftertaste.

Best (OG 1045, ABV 4.4%) ◆
Full-bodied, slightly fruity and unusually bitter for its gravity.

Porter (OG 1052, ABV 5.2%) ◆
Each taste and smell of this potent black winter beer (Nov-April) reveals another facet of its character. An explosion of roasted malt, bitter and fruity flavours leaves a bitter-sweet aftertaste.

Leadmill

Leadmill Brewery Ltd, Unit 1 Park Hall, Park Hall Road, Denby, Derbyshire, DE5 8PX
Tel/Fax (01332) 883577
Email tlc@leadmill.fsnet.co.uk
Website www.leadmillbrewery.co.uk

⊗ Originally set up in a pig sty in Selston, the brewery moved to Denby in 2001/02 and now has a four-barrel plant. The company has bought the Old Oak pub in Horsley Woodhouse. The Old Stables Bar at the brewery functions as a visitor centre and offers up to 12 Leadmill beers and guest ales. Leadmill is in the process of finalising the purchase of its latest pub, the William IV at Milford. Three pubs are owned and some 20 outlets are supplied. Owner Richard Creighton has set up a second brewery (see Bottle Brook) that will specialise in using hop varieties from rare sources. Stronger Leadmill beers and porters will soon be available in bottles and presentation packs. Seasonal beers: Jersey City (ABV 5%, autumn), Ginger Spice (ABV 5%, summer), Autumn Goddess (ABV 4.2%), Get Stuffed (ABV 6.7%%, Christmas)

Mash Tun Bitter (OG 1036, ABV 3.6%)

Old Oak Bitter (OG 1037, ABV 3.8%)

Duchess (OG 1041, ABV 4.2%)

Strawberry Blonde (OG 1042, ABV 4.4%)

Rolling Thunder (OG 1043, ABV 4.5%)

Curly Blonde (OG 1044, ABV 4.6%)

Maple Porter (OG 1045, ABV 4.7%)

Snakeyes (OG 1045, ABV 4.8%)

Agent Orange (OG 1047, ABV 4.9%)

Born in the USA (OG 1048, ABV 5%)

Rampage (OG 1050, ABV 5.1%)

B52 (OG 1050, ABV 5.2%)

Destitution (OG 1051, ABV 5.3%)

Ghostrider (OG 1052, ABV 5.4%)

The Beast (OG 1053, ABV 5.7%)

Nemesis (OG 1062, ABV 6.4%)

Old Mottled Cock (OG 1041, ABV 4.2%)

Dream Weaver (OG 1042, ABV 4.3%)

WMD (OG 1065, ABV 6.7%)

Leatherbritches SIBA

Leatherbritches Brewery, Bentley Brook Inn, Fenny Bentley, Ashbourne, Derbyshire, DE6 1LF
Tel (01335) 350278
Fax (01335) 350422
Email all@bentleybrookinn.co.uk
Website www.bentleybrookinn.co.uk
Tours by arrangement

◎ The brewery was started by 'Steamin' Billy Allingham in the 1990s and is now owned and run by his brother Edward, who is expanding the site from two-barrel capacity to 14 barrels. The brewery is on the site of the family-owned Bentley Brook Inn and will stay there even though the pub has been sold. Some 100 outlets are supplied. Bottle-conditioned beers: Hairy Helmet, Bespoke, Porter (ABV 5.5%), Blue (ABV 9%).

Goldings (OG 1036, ABV 3.6%)
A light golden beer with a flowery hoppy aroma and a bitter finish.

Ginger Spice (OG 1036, ABV 3.8%)
A light, highly-hopped bitter.

Ashbourne Ale (OG 1040, ABV 4%)
A pale bitter brewed with Goldings hops for a crisp lasting taste.

Belter (OG 1040, ABV 4.4%)
Maris Otter malt produces a pale but interesting beer.

Belt-n-Braces (OG 1040, ABV 4.4%)
Mid-brown, full-flavoured, dry-hopped bitter.

Dovedale (OG 1044, ABV 4.4%)
Copper-coloured.

Hairy Helmet (OG 1047, ABV 4.7%)
Pale bitter, well hopped but with a sweet finish.

Ginger Helmet (OG 1047, ABV 4.7%)
As above but with a hint of China's most astringent herb.

Bespoke (OG 1050, ABV 5%)
Full-bodied, well-rounded premium bitter.

Bentley Brook Bitter (OG 1050, ABV 5.2%)
Pale, dry and crisp.

Leek

Leek Brewing Co Ltd t/a Leek Brewers Co, Units 11 & 12 Churnet Court, Churnetside Business Park, Cheddleton, Leek, Staffordshire, ST13 7EF
Tel (01538) 361919
Email leekbrewery@hotmail.com

Tours by arrangement

Brewing started in 2002 in a 4.5-barrel plant located in outbuildings behind the owner's house, before moving to the current site in an industrial unit in 2004. All the beers are available in bottle-conditioned form and are suitable for vegetarians. The brewery also produces special one-off beers during the year, occasionally using speciality ingredients such as pumpkin.

Staffordshire Gold (ABV 3.8%) ◆
Light, straw-coloured with a pleasing hoppy aroma and a hint of malt. Bitter finish from the hops, making it easily drunk and thirst-quenching.

Danebridge IPA (ABV 4.1%)

Staffordshire Bitter (ABV 4.2%) ◆
Amber with a fruity aroma. Malty and hoppy start with the hoppy finish diminishing quickly.

Black Grouse (ABV 4.5%)

Hen Cloud (ABV 4.5%)

St Edwards (ABV 4.7%)

Rudyard Ruby (ABV 4.8%)

Double Sunset (ABV 5.2%)

Danebridge XXX (ABV 5.5%)

Cheddleton Steamer (ABV 6%)

Tittesworth Tipple (ABV 6.5%)

Lees IFBB

J W Lees & Co (Brewers) Ltd, Greengate Brewery, Middleton Junction, Manchester, M24 2AX
Tel (0161) 643 2487
Fax (0161) 655 3731
Email mail@jwlees.co.uk
Website www.jwlees.co.uk
Tours by arrangement

Lees is a family-owned brewery founded in 1828 by John Lees and run by the sixth generation of the family. Brewing takes place in the 1876 brewhouse designed and built by John Willie Lees, the grandson of the founder. All 170 pubs (most in north Manchester) serve cask beer. Seasonal beers: Greengate (ABV 3.4%, March-May), Scorcher (ABV 4.2%, June-Aug), Ruddy Glow (ABV 4.5%, Sept-Nov), Plum Pudding (ABV 4.8%, Dec-Feb).

GB Mild (OG 1032, ABV 3.5%) ◆
Red-brown beer with malt and fruit aroma. Creamy mouthfeel with chocolate malt and fruit flavours and a malty finish.

Bitter (OG 1037, ABV 4%) ◆
Pale brown beer with a malty, hoppy aroma. Distinctive malty, dry flavour and aftertaste.

Moonraker (OG 1073, ABV 7.5%) ◆
A reddish-brown beer with a strong, malty, fruity aroma. The flavour is rich and sweet, with roast malt, and the finish is fruity yet dry. Available only in a handful of outlets.

Leith Hill

Leith Hill Brewery, c/o Plough Inn, Coldharbour, nr Dorking, Surrey, RH5 6HD
Tel (01306) 711793
Fax (01306) 710055
Email theploughinn@btinternet.com
Website www.ploughinn.com
Tours by arrangement

Leith Hill was formed in 1996 using home-made equipment to produce nine-gallon brews in a room at the front of the pub. The brewery moved to a purpose-built storeroom at the rear of the pub in 2001 and increased capacity to 2.5-barrels in 2005. All beers brewed are only sold on the premises.

Hoppily Ever After (OG 1036, ABV 3.6%) ◆
Initially hoppy and citrussy with a sharp, hoppy/malty taste, slightly lacking in body. A hoppy, dry finish.

Crooked Furrow (OG 1040, ABV 4%) ◆
A tangy, bitter beer, with strong malt and some balancing hop flavours. Pale brown in colour with an earthy, malty aroma and a long, dry and bitter-sweet aftertaste.

Tallywhacker (OG 1048, ABV 4.8%) ◆
A dark, full-bodied old ale with an aroma of malt and toffee. An initial burst of blackcurrant fades into a vinous flavour with malt and caramel and an underlying sweetness. A sweet, fruity finish but a noticeable lack of bitterness throughout.

Leyden SIBA

Leyden Brewing Ltd, Lord Raglan, Nangreaves, Bury, Greater Manchester, BL9 6SP
Tel/Fax (0161) 764 6680
Tours by arrangement

The brewery was built by Brian Farnworth and started production in 1999. Additional fermenting vessels have been installed, allowing a maximum production of 12 barrels a week. One pub is owned and 30 outlets are supplied. Raglan Sleeve and Forever Bury are available in filtered bottled form.

Balaclava (ABV 3.8%)

Black Pudding (ABV 3.8%)
A dark brown, creamy mild with a malty flavour, followed by a balanced finish.

Nanny Flyer (OG 1040, ABV 3.8%)
A drinkable session bitter with an initial dryness, and a hint of citrus, followed by a strong, malty finish.

Light Brigade (OG 1043, ABV 4.2%) ◆
Copper in colour with a citrus aroma. The flavour is a balance of malt, hops and fruit, with a bitter finish.

Forever Bury (ABV 4.5%)

Raglan Sleeve (OG 1047, ABV 4.6%) ◆
Dark red/brown beer with a hoppy aroma and a dry, roasty, hoppy taste and finish.

Crowning Glory (OG 1069, ABV 6.8%)
A surprisingly smooth-tasting beer for its strength, ideal for cold winter nights.

Lichfield

Lichfield Brewery Co Ltd, Upper St John Street, Lichfield, Staffordshire
Email robsondavidb@hotmail.com
Website www.lichfieldbrewery.co.uk

Does not brew; beers mainly contracted by Blythe, Tower and Highgate breweries (qv).

Lidstones

See Wensleydale

Linfit

Linfit Brewery, Sair Inn, 139 Lane Top, Linthwaite, Huddersfield, West Yorkshire, HD7 5SG
Tel (01484) 842370

A 19th-century brew-pub that started brewing again in 1982, producing an impressive range of ales for sale at the pub. The beer is only available at the Sair Inn. Seasonal beer: Xmas Ale (ABV 8%). Dark Mild and English Guineas Stout are suitable for vegetarians and vegans as isinglass finings are not used.

Dark Mild (OG 1032, ABV 3%)
Roast grain dominates this straightforward dark mild, which has some hops in the aroma and a slightly dry flavour. Malty finish.

Bitter (OG 1035, ABV 3.7%)
A refreshing session beer. A dry-hopped aroma leads to a clean-tasting, hoppy bitterness, then a long, bitter finish with a hint of malt.

Gold Medal (OG 1040, ABV 4.2%)
Very pale and hoppy. Use of the new dwarf variety of English hops, First Gold, gives an aromatic and fruity character.

Swift (OG 1040, ABV 4.2%)
Pale and hoppy with a smooth mouthfeel and a slightly malty finish.

Special (OG 1041, ABV 4.3%)
Dry-hopping provides the aroma for this rich and mellow bitter, which has a very soft profile and character: it fills the mouth with texture rather than taste. Clean, rounded finish.

Autumn Gold (OG 1045, ABV 4.7%)
Straw-coloured best bitter with hop and fruit aromas, then the bitter-sweetness of autumn fruit in the taste and the finish.

English Guineas Stout (OG 1050, ABV 5.3%)
A fruity, roast aroma preludes a smooth, roasted barley, chocolaty flavour that is bitter but not too dry. Excellent appearance; good, bitter finish.

Old Eli (OG 1050, ABV 5.3%)
A well-balanced premium bitter with a dry-hopped aroma and a fruity, bitter finish.

Leadboiler (OG 1060, ABV 6.6%)
Powerful malt, hop and fruit in good balance on the tongue, with a well-rounded bitter sweet finish.

Enoch's Hammer (OG 1075, ABV 8%)
A straw-coloured beer with malt, hop and fruit aromas. Mouth-filling, smooth malt, hop and fruit flavours with a long, hoppy bitter finish. Dangerously drinkable.

Lion's Tail*

Lion's Tail Brewery, Red Lion, High Street, Cheswardine, Market Drayton, Shropshire, TF9 2RS
Tel (01630) 661234
Email cheslion@btinternet.com

The building that houses the brewery was purpose-built in 2005 and houses a 2.5-barrel plant. Jon Morris and his wife have owned the Red Lion pub since 1996.

Lion Bru (ABV 4%)

Little Valley

Little Valley Brewery Ltd, Turkey Lodge Farm, New Road, Cragg Vale, Hebden Bridge, West Yorkshire, HX7 5TT
Tel (01422) 883888
Fax (01422) 883222
Email info@littlevalleybrewery.co.uk
Website www.littlevalleybrewery.co.uk
Tours by arrangement for CAMRA branches only

The brewery opened in 2005 and is based in the Upper Calder Valley high above Cragg Vale. The 10-barrel plant was installed by Porter Brewing in a converted pig shed. All beers are organic and approved by the Soil Association. Seasonal beer: Moor Ale (ABV 5.5%, autumn/winter). All the cask beers are also available in bottle-conditioned form.

Withens IPA (OG 1039, ABV 3.9%)
Creamy, gold-coloured, light IPA. Floral hops, spice and citrus aroma. Clean, bitter aftertaste.

Cragg Vale Bitter (OG 1041, ABV 4.2%)
Rich red-brown colour with a full rounded body and a crisp and fruity character with spices and lemon.

Hebden's Wheat (OG 1043, ABV 4.5%)
Yellow coloured, hazy, fruity beer. Aromas of coriander and lemon.

Stoodley Stout (OG 1046, ABV 4.8%)
A rich, black stout with a creamy roasted flavour.

Tod's Blonde (OG 1047, ABV 5%)
Gold coloured with a citrus hoppy start and a dry finish. Very fruity with a hint of spice. Similar in style to a Belgian blonde beer.

Moor Ale (OG 1051, ABV 5.5%)
Copper in colour with a full-bodied taste. Strong malty nose and taste with hints of heather and smoked peat malt. Well balanced with a bitter finish.

Litton

Litton Ale Brewery, Queens Arms, Litton, Skipton, North Yorkshire, BD23 5QJ
Tel (07834) 622632
Email queensarmslitton@amserve.net
Website www.yorkshirenet.co.uk/stayat/queensarms
Tours by arrangement

Brewing started in 2003 in a purpose-built stone extension at the rear of the pub. Brewing liquor is sourced from a spring that provides the pub with its own water supply. The brew length is three barrels and all production is in cask form. Some 90 outlets are supplied, mainly in Yorkshire, but now moving further afield. Seasonal beer: Dark Star (ABV 4%). There are plans to produce beer in bottle-conditioned form.

Litton (OG 1038, ABV 3.8%)

Leading Light (OG 1038, ABV 3.8%)

Dark Star (OG 1040, ABV 4%)

Potts Beck (OG 1043, ABV 4.2%)

Lizard

Lizard Ales Ltd, Unit 2a St Keverne Rural Workshops, St Keverne, Helston, Cornwall, TR12 6PE
Tel/Fax (01326) 281135
Email lizardales@msn.com

Launched in autumn 2004 by partners Richard Martin and Mark and Leonora Nattrass, Lizard Ales has some 12 regular outlets in the local area plus others on a guest basis. Bottle-conditioned beers are an important part of the business and are available at approximately 50 outlets between Land's End and Truro.

Helford River Bitter (1035, ABV 3.6%)

Kernow Gold (OG 1036, ABV 3.7%)

Lizard Bitter (OG 1041, ABV 4.2%)

An Gof Strong Cornish Ale (OG 1049.5, ABV 5.2%)

Loddon SIBA

Loddon Brewery Ltd, Dunsden Green Farm, Church Lane, Dunsden, Oxfordshire, RG4 9QD
Tel (01189) 481111
Fax (01189) 481010
Email loddonbrewery@aol.com
Website www.loddonbrewery.co.uk
Shop Mon-Fri 8am-5pm; Sat 9am-2pm
Tours by arrangement

Loddon was established in 2003 by Chris and Vanessa Hearn between Reading and Henley-on-Thames. Extensive rebuilding work on a 240-year-old brick and flint barn was required in order to house the 17-barrel showpiece brewery that produces distinctive beers made from Maris Otter barley and whole hops. Chris has been in the brewing industry since 1976 and head brewer Steve Brown has 25 years' experience, most recently at Brakspear. Some 190 accounts are supplied. There are plans to improve the brewery site to allow for additional storage and a possible new fermenting room. In addition to the regular range, four seasonal beers are produced together with a monthly special in a range of styles: see website. Seasonal beers: Bloomin' Eck (ABV 4%, Feb-March), Flight of Fancy (ABV 4.2%, April-Aug), Russet (ABV 4.5%, Sept-Nov), Hocus Pocus (ABV 4.6%, Dec-Jan). Bottle-conditioned beer: Ferryman's Gold (ABV 4.8%).

Hoppit (OG 1035.5, ABV 3.5%) ◆
Hops dominate the aroma and taste of this drinkable, light-coloured session beer. A hint of malt and fruit accompanies and a pleasant bitterness carries through to the aftertaste.

Dragonfly (OG 1040, ABV 4%)

Hullabaloo (OG 1043.8, ABV 4.2%) ◆
A hint of banana in the initial taste develops into a balance of hops and malt in this well-rounded, medium-bodied tawny bitter with a bitter aftertaste.

Ferryman's Gold (OG 1044.8, ABV 4.4%) ◆
Golden coloured with a strong hoppy character throughout, accompanied by malt in the aftertaste.

Bamboozle (OG 1048.8, ABV 4.8%) ◆
Full-bodied and well-balanced amber ale. Distinctive bitter-sweet flavour with hop character to accompany. Very drinkable.

Lovibonds*

Office: Lovibonds Brewery Ltd, Greys Green Farm, Henley-on-Thames, Oxon, RG9 4QG
Tel (07761) 543987
Email henleybeer@lovibonds.com
Website www.lovibonds.com
Tours by invitation

Lovibonds Brewery was founded in 2005 by Jeff Rosenmeier, a long-time home brewer, graduate of the School of Brewing in the United States and an active member of CAMRA. He was keen to maintain Henley's brewing traditions following the closure of Brakspear. Lovibond's beers are hand-crafted in small batches and distributed to the local free trade and festivals.

OHB/Ordinary Henley Bitter (OG 1035, ABV 3.4%)
An amber session bitter using Maris Otter malt and three British hop varieties. A blend of roasted malts gives a complex profile that battles the hop flavour and bitterness.

Henley Gold (OG 1042, ABV 4.2%)
A golden ale with Maris Otter malt balanced with a blend of English and Continental hops, giving it a citrus hop aroma and a long, clean bitterness.

Lovibonds Lager (OG 1049, ABV 5%)
Crafted from Continental malt and Saaz hops.

Lowes Arms

🍺 Lowes Arms Brewery, Lowes Arms, 301 Hyde Road, Denton, Manchester, M34 3FF
Tel (0161) 336 3064
Fax (0161) 285 9015
Email info@lowesarms.co.uk
Website www.lowesarms.co.uk
Tours by arrangement

⊛ The brewery, known as The Lab, was set up by Peter Wood, landlord of the Lowes, who had brewed as a student, and Anthony Firmin, a keen home-brewer. The brewery is located in the cellars of the pub. It produces a range of five beers named after local landmarks and sites of interest. The brewery is a 2.5-barrel system, but two new fermenting vessels have been added to enable The Lab to brew four times a week. There are plans to wholesale the beer.

Jet Amber (OG 1040, ABV 3.5%)
Brewed for the Stockport and Manchester Mild Challenge.

IPA (ABV 3.8%)

Frog Bog (OG 1040, ABV 3.9%)
A light, easy-drinking bitter with an orange aroma and a light hoppy taste.

Sweaty Clog (ABV 4%)

Wild Wood (OG 1043, ABV 4.1%)

A spicy session bitter with a malty and fruity aroma, and spicy hop taste.

Broomstairs (OG 1043, ABV 4.3%)
A dark best bitter with distinct roast flavours and a hoppy aftertaste.

Haughton Weave (OG 1043, ABV 4.5%)
Distinct tangerine aromas in this light-coloured beer are followed by lots of bitterness and hoppy tastes in the mouth.

Loweswater

Loweswater Brewery, Kirkstile Inn, Loweswater, Cumbria, CA13 0RU
Tel (01900) 85219
Fax (01900) 85239
Email info@kirkstile.com
Website www.kirkstile.com
Tours by arrangement

Loweswater Brewery was re-established at the Kirkstile Inn in 2003 by head brewer Matt Webster. Brewing took place in the inn 180 years ago. Brewing now takes place twice a week to keep up with demand. The plant can produce six barrels a week. The beers are available at the inn and at local festivals.

Melbreak Bitter (OG 1038, ABV 3.7%)
Pale bronze with a tangy fruit and hop resins aroma, and a long, bitter finish.

Rannerdale (OG 1042, ABV 4%)
A fruity beer made with Styrian Goldings hops.

Kirkstile Gold (OG 1042, ABV 4.3%)
Pale lager-style beer with masses of tropical fruit flavour. Brewed with German hops.

Grasmoor Dark Ale (OG 1043, ABV 4.3%)
Deep ruby red beer with pronounced chocolate malt on the aroma, and hop resins, roast malt and raisin fruit on the palate.

Ludlow*

Ludlow Brewing Co Ltd, Kingsley Garage, 105 Corve Street, Ludlow, Shropshire, SY8 1DJ
Tel (01584) 873291
Website www.theludlowbrewery.co.uk
Tours by arrangement

Ludlow Brewing opened in June 2006 and has a six-barrel plant. It is housed in a converted old malthouse. At least three beers will be available.

Maclay

See Belhaven in New Nationals section

McCowans

McCowans Brewhouse, 134 Dundee Street, Edinburgh, EH11 1AF
Tel (0131) 228 8198
Fax (0131) 228 8201
Email mikelangan@hotmail.com

Opened in 1998 by Scottish & Newcastle, McCowans brewed until 2003 and was then sold to the Spirit Group. After a long fight, the pub management convinced Spirit that brewing should start again and it recommenced in 2004 with a range of Domnhul – pronounced Donnel – ales.

Domnhul Ban (ABV 3.8%)

Domnhul (ABV 4.5%)

Domnhul Dubh (ABV 4.5%)

McGuinness SIBA

Thomas McGuinness Brewing Co, Cask & Feather, 1 Oldham Road, Rochdale, Greater Manchester, OL16 1UA
Tel (01706) 711476
Fax (01706) 669654
Email tonycask@hotmail.com
Website www.mcguinnessbrewery.com
Tours by arrangement

McGuinness opened in 1991 and now averages 15-20 barrels a week. It supplies beer to its own pub and several other outlets. There are seasonal beers at ABV 3.8-4.2% plus Tommy Todd's Porter (ABV 5%, winter).

Feather Pluckers Mild (ABV 3.4%)
A dark brown beer, with roast malt dominant in the aroma and taste, with hints of chocolate. Satisfying bitter and roast finish.

Best Bitter (ABV 3.8%)
Gold in colour with a hoppy aroma: a clean, refreshing beer with hop and fruit tastes and a hint of sweetness. Bitter aftertaste.

Utter Nutter (ABV 3.8%)

Special Reserve Bitter/SRB (ABV 4%)
A tawny beer, sweet and malty, with underlying fruit and bitterness, and a bitter-sweet aftertaste.

Junction Bitter (ABV 4.2%)
Mid-brown in colour, with a malty aroma. Maltiness is predominant throughout, with some hops and fruit in the taste and bitterness coming through in the finish.

McMullen IFBB

McMullen & Sons Ltd, 26 Old Cross, Hertford, SG14 1RD
Tel (01992) 584911
Fax (01992) 500729
Email fjmcmullen@aol.com
Website www.mcmullens.co.uk

McMullen, Hertfordshire's oldest independent brewer, founded in 1827, has recovered well from the dispute that threatened the future of the company in 2003. It remains controlled by a series of trusts and its future, as an integrated brewery and pub business, is assured. The company benefits from reductions in duty under the government's Progressive Beer Duty. A new brewhouse opened in 2006 giving McMullen greater flexibility to produce its regular cask beers and small volume special brews. Cask ale is served in all but one of its 135 pubs in Hertfordshire, Essex and London, although many managed houses use cask breathers on all their cask beers, as do some of the tenanted pubs. McMullen also delivers to more than 50 free houses. The company's chain of Baroosh bars is expanding into town centres outside of the traditional McMullen trading area. Seven or eight seasonal beers are produced each year, though these are not always available in all pubs.

AK (OG 1036, ABV 3.7%) ♦
A pleasant mix of malt and hops leads to a distinctive, dry aftertaste that isn't always as pronounced as it used to be.

Country Best Bitter (OG 1042, ABV 4.3%) ♦
A full-bodied beer with a well-balanced mix of malt, hops and fruit throughout.

Magpie*

Magpie Brewery, Unit 4 Ashling Court, Ashling Street, Nottingham, NG2 3JA
Tel (0115) 9611556
Email info@magpiebrewery.com
Website www.magpiebrewery.com

A six-barrel brewery was launched in June 2006 some six metres from the perimeter of the Meadow Lane Stadium, home of Notts County FC (the Magpies).

Fledgling (ABV 3.8%)

Two4Joy (ABV 4.2%)

Thieving Rogue (ABV 4.5%)

Maldon

See Farmers Ales

Mallard SIBA

Mallard Brewery, 15 Hartington Avenue, Carlton, Nottingham, NG4 3NR
Tel/Fax (0115) 952 1289
Email phil@mallard-brewery.co.uk
Website www.mallard-brewery.co.uk
Tours by arrangement

⊗ Phil Mallard built and installed a two-barrel plant in a shed at his home and started brewing in 1995. The brewery is a mere nine square metres and contains a hot liquor tank, mash tun, copper, and three fermenters. Since 1995 production has risen from one barrel a week to between six or eight barrels, which is the plant's maximum. Phil has no plans at present to expand and now supplies around 12 outlets, of which seven are on a regular weekly basis. Seasonal beer: Waddlers Mild (ABV 3.7%, spring), DA (ABV 5.8%, Jan-March), Quismas Quacker (ABV 6%, December).

Duck 'n' Dive (OG 1039, ABV 3.7%)
A light, single-hopped beer made from the hedgerow hop, First Gold. A bitter beer with a hoppy nose, good bitterness on the palate and a dry finish.

Quacker Jack (OG 1040, ABV 4%)

Feather Light (OG 1040, ABV 4.1%)
A very pale lager-style bitter with a floral bouquet and sweetness on the palate. A light, hoppy session beer.

Duckling (OG 1041, ABV 4.2%) ◼
A crisp refreshing bitter with a hint of honey and citrus flavour.

Spittin' Feathers (OG 1044, ABV 4.4%)
A mellow, ruby bitter with a complex malt flavour of chocolate, toffee and coffee, complemented with a full and fruity/hoppy aftertaste.

Drake (OG 1045, ABV 4.5%)
A full-bodied premium bitter, with malt and hops on the palate, and a fruity finish.

Owd Duck (OG 1048, ABV 4.8%)
A dark ruby bitter with a smooth mellow smoky flavour and fruity finish.

Friar Duck (OG 1050, ABV 5%)
A pale, full malt beer, hoppy with a hint of blackcurrant flavour.

Duck 'n' Disorderly (OG 1050, ABV 5%)

Malton SIBA

Malton Brewery t/a Suddabys (Malton) Ltd, Crown Hotel, 12 Wheelgate, Malton, North Yorkshire, YO17 7HP
Tel (01653) 697580
Fax (01653) 691812
Email enquiries@suddabys.co.uk
Website www.suddabys.com

Malton is not currently brewing while a bigger site is sought. The main beers are brewed at Hambleton (qv) while Brown Cow (qv) brews short run and speciality beers.

Malvern Hills SIBA

Malvern Hills Brewery Ltd, 15 West Malvern Road, Malvern, Worcestershire, WR14 4ND
Tel (01684) 560165
Fax (01684) 577336
Email mhb.ales@tiscali.co.uk
Website www.malvernhillsbrewery.co.uk
Tours by arrangement

⊗ Founded in 1997 in an old quarrying dynamite store on the northern slopes of the Malvern Hills, the business had gained about 40 regular outlets by the start of 2006, mostly as direct sales with little use made of wholesalers. But a new era began as owner and head brewer Julian Hawthornthwaite gave up his other employment to run the brewery full time. Considerable expansion is expected in terms of both output and outlets. Seasonal beer: Dr Gully's Winter Ale (ABV 5.2%).

Red Earl (OG 1037, ABV 3.7%) ♦
A very light beer that does not overpower the senses. With a hint of apple fruit, it is ideal for slaking the thirst.

Moel Bryn (OG 1039, ABV 3.9%)

Swedish Nightingale (OG 1040, ABV 4%)

Worcestershire Whym (OG 1042, ABV 4.2%)

Priessnitz Plsen (OG 1043, ABV 4.3%) ♦
A mix of soft fruit and citrus give this straw-coloured brew its quaffability, making it ideal for quenching summer thirsts.

Black Pear (OG 1044, ABV 4.4%) ◆
A sharp citrus hoppiness is the main constituent of this golden brew that has a long, dry aftertaste.

Black Country Wobble (OG 1045, ABV 4.5%) ◆
A sharp, clean-tasting golden beer with an aroma of hops challenged by fruit and malt, which hold up well in the mouth. A bitter dryness grows as the contrasting sweetness subsides.

Mr Phoebus (OG 1047, ABV 4.7%)

Mansfield

See Wolverhampton & Dudley in New Nationals section

Marble SIBA

Marble Beers Ltd, 73 Rochdale Road, Manchester, M4 4HY
Tel/Fax (0161) 819 2694
Email enquiries@marblebeers.co.uk
Website www.marblebeers.co.uk
Tours by arrangement

Designed by legendary brewmaster Brendan Dobbin, the Marble Brewery was opened at the Marble Arch Inn in 1997. Its success prompted a request from the Manchester Food Festival to brew an organic beer. This resulted in the brewery going totally organic and vegan, registered with the Soil Association and the Vegetarian Society. It has a five-barrel plant that operates at full capacity, producing four regular beers and a number of seasonal ales. Marble currently own two pubs and supplies four outlets with its brews. Seasonal beers: Marble Bitter (ABV 3.9%), Roadrider (ABV 4.3%), Festival (ABV 4.4%), Summer Marble (ABV 4.5%), Port Stout (ABV 4.7%), Uncut Amber (ABV 4.7%), Chocolate (ABV 5.5%).

GSB/Gould Street Bitter (OG 1037.5, ABV 3.8%)
A pale, hoppy brew dominated by the flavour of Goldings hops and a slight fruitiness.

Manchester Bitter (OG 1042, ABV 4.2%) ◆
Yellow beer with a hoppy aroma. A balance of malt, hops and fruit on the palate, with a hoppy and bitter aftertaste.

Ginger Marble (OG 1045, ABV 4.5%)
Intense and complex. Full-bodied and fiery with a sharp, snappy bite.

Lagonda IPA (OG 1048, ABV 5%)
A golden, dry bitter. A quadruple addition of hops gives it depth and complexity.

Marches

Marches Brewing Co, The Old Hop Kiln, Claston, Dormington, Hereford, Herefordshire, HR1 4EA
Tel (01584) 878999
Email littlebeer@totalise.co.uk
Tours by arrangement

⊗ Brewing restarted at Marches in 2004. The brewery is now housed in two converted hop kilns. Beer is mostly brewed for owner Paul Harris's shop in Ludlow although he does supply some 20 local outlets. Paul works closely with hop growers to develop traditional beer styles and produces single-varietal beers using new varieties of hops. A new bottling line is now operational. Bottle conditioned beers: Ludlow Gold, St Lawrence Ale.

Forever Autumn (ABV 4.2%)

Ludlow Gold (ABV 4.3%)

Dormington Gold (OG 1044, ABV 4.5%)
A light golden bitter brewed using First Gold hedgerow hops. It has an intense bitterness with a citrus zest.

St Lawrence Ale (ABV 4.5%)
A ruby premium bitter brewed with Boadicea hops.

Marston Moor

Marston Moor Brewery Ltd, PO Box 9, York, North Yorkshire, YO26 7XW
Tel (01423) 359641
email info@marstonmoorbrewery.co.uk

⊛ Established in 1983 in Kirk Hammerton, the brewery had a re-investment programme in 2005, moving brewing operations to nearby Tockwith, where it shares the site with Rudgate Brewery (qv). Based upon the original recipes, the brewery offers five original beers along with a mild. Two special beers are also available each month, based either on the English Civil War theme or on rural England. Some 150 outlets are supplied.

Cromwell Bitter (OG 1036, ABV 3.8%) ◆
A golden beer with hops and fruit in strong evidence on the nose. Bitterness as well as fruit and hops dominate the taste and long aftertaste.

Matchstick Mild (OG 1038, ABV 4%)

Mongrel (OG 1038, ABV 4%)

Brewers Pride (OG 1039, ABV 4.2%) ◆
A light but somewhat thin, fruity beer, with a hoppy, bitter aftertaste.

Merriemaker (OG 1042, ABV 4.5%)

Brewers Droop (OG 1045.5, ABV 5%)
A pale, robust ale with hops and fruit notes in prominence. A long, bitter aftertaste.

Marston's

See Wolverhampton & Dudley in New Nationals section

Mash SIBA

Mash Ltd, 19-21 Great Portland Street, London, W1W 8QB
Tel (020) 7637 5555
Fax (020) 7637 8446
Website www.mashrestaurantandbar.co.uk
Tours by arrangement

The micro-brewery is the centrepiece of the Mash bar and restaurant. The American-style brewery can be toured to inspect the process at close hand and the restaurant provides a tutored lunch or dinner where the beers are matched to food. The beers are not cask conditioned but are stored in cellar tanks using a CO2 system. Regular beer: Mash Wheat (ABV 5.2%). Other beers include a Blackcurrant Porter, Scotch, IPA, Peach, Extra Stout and Pils.

Matthews*

Matthews Brewing Company Ltd, Unit 7 Timsbury Workshop Estate, Hayeswood Road, Timsbury, Bath, BA2 0HQ
Tel (01761) 472242
Email info@matthewsbrewing.co.uk
Website www.matthewsbrewing.co.uk
Tours by arrangement

Matthews Brewing was established in 2005 by Stuart Matthews and Sue Appleby, with the aim of brewing high-quality cask-conditioned ales on a five-barrel plant. The emphasis is on the use of traditional techniques and quality ingredients, such as floor-malted barley from the nearby Warminster Maltings. Around 25 outlets are supplied and the ales are distributed more widely by wholesalers. Seasonal beers: Pit Pony (ABV 5.5%, autumn), Davey Lamp (ABV 5%, winter).

Brassknocker (OG 1037, ABV 3.8%) ◆
Pale session bitter with light malt and citrus flavours. Thirst-quenching with a dry, astringent finish.

Bob Wall (OG 1041, ABV 4.2%) ◆
Fruity best bitter; roasty hint with intense forest fruit and rich malt flavour continuing to a good balanced finish.

Mauldons SIBA EAB

Mauldons Ltd, The Black Adder Brewery, 13 Churchfield Road, Sudbury, Suffolk, CO10 2YA
Tel (01787) 311055
Fax (01787) 379538
Email sims@mauldons.co.uk
Website www.mauldons.co.uk
Shop Mon-Fri 9.30am-4pm
Tours by arrangement

⊗ The Mauldon family started brewing in Sudbury in 1795. The brewery with 26 pubs was bought by Greene King in the 1960s. The current business, established in 1982, was bought by Steve and Alison Sims – both former employees of Adnams – in 2000. They relocated to a new brewery in 2005, with a 30-barrel plant that has doubled production. There is also a brewery shop. Some 200 outlets are supplied. There is a rolling programme of seasonal beers: see website. Bottle-conditioned beers: Suffolk Pride, Bah Humbug (ABV 4.9%), Black Adder.

Micawber's Mild (OG 1035, ABV 3.5%) ◆
A smooth, dark, East Anglian mild, easy drinking despite its body.

Bitter (OG 1036, ABV 3.6%)
A traditional session bitter with a strong floral nose and lingering, bitter finish.

Moletrap Bitter (OG 1038, ABV 3.8%) ◆
A well-balanced session beer with a crisp, hoppy bitterness balancing sweet malt.

Pickwick (OG 1042, ABV 4.2%)
A best bitter with a rich, rounded malt flavour and ripe aromas of hops and fruit. A bitter-sweet finish.

Suffolk Pride (OG 1048, ABV 4.8%) ◆
A full-bodied, copper-coloured beer with a good balance of malt, hops and fruit in the taste.

Black Adder (OG 1053, ABV 5.3%) ◆
A grainy, roast mouthfeel. The tastebuds are almost overwhelmed by caramel, malt and vine fruit.

White Adder (OG 1053, ABV 5.3%) ◆
A pale brown, almost golden, strong ale. A warming, fruity flavour dominates and lingers into a dry, hoppy finish.

Suffolk Comfort (OG 1066, ABV 6.6%)
A powerful peppery Goldings aroma with malt notes. There is a rich balance of crystal malt and hops in the mouth with a long, malty finish.

Mayfields

Mayfields Brewery, Bishop Frome, Herefordshire, WR6 5AS
Tel (01531) 640015
Fax (01885) 490428
Email themayfieldsbrewery@yahoo.co.uk
Tours by arrangement

Established in 2005, the Mayfields Brewery resides in an 18th-century hop kiln, located in the heart of one of England's major hop growing regions, the Frome Valley. The head brewer insists on using only Herefordshire hops, many of which are grown on the brewery farm. The brewery also produces real cider and perry to complement its beer range. Around 25 outlets are supplied. Seasonal beer: Crusader (ABV 4.3%, St George's Day/Trafalgar Day).

Pioneer (ABV 3.9%)
Straw-coloured ale with a fruity finish.

Naughty Nell's (ABV 4.2%)
Smooth, copper-coloured ale with a malty body and citrussy hop finish.

Conqueror (ABV 4.3%)
Amber, full-bodied ale with a strong, hoppy zing.

Mayflower

Mayflower Brewery, Mayflower House, 15 Longendale Road, Standish, Wigan, Greater Manchester, WN6 0UE
Tel (01257) 400605
Email info@mayflowerbrewery.co.uk
Website www.mayflowerbrewery.co.uk

Mayflower was established in 2000 at the Worthington Lake industrial estate in Standish. Due to the demolition of the original site, the brewery has been relocated to the Royal Oak in Wigan. The premises are much smaller but the original vessels and casks are still used. The Royal Oak is supplied as well as a number of other outlets in and around Wigan. Seasonal beers: Oakey Cokey (ABV 8%, winter), Cuckoo Spit (ABV 4.4%, spring).

Black Diamond (OG 1033.5, ABV 3.4%)

Dark Oak (OG 1034, ABV 3.5%)

Myles Best Bitter (OG 1036, ABV 3.7%)

Light Oak (OG 1038, ABV 4%)

Special Branch (OG 1038, ABV 4%)

Premiership (ABV 4.1%)

Wigan Bier (OG 1039.5, ABV 4.2%)

Black Oak (ABV 5%)

Maypole SIBA

Maypole Brewery Ltd, North Laithes Farm, Wellow Road, Eakring, Newark, Nottinghamshire, NG22 0AN
Tel (07971) 277598/07947 242683
Email maypolebrewery@aol.com
Website www.maypolebrewery.co.uk
Tours by arrangement

⊗ The brewery opened in 1995 in a converted 18th-century farm building. After changing hands in 2001 it was bought by the former head brewer in 2005. Increased demand has seen the installation of a fourth fermenting vessel with a fifth vessel planned for 2006/2007. Maypole beers are always available at the Eight Jolly Brewers, Gainsborough, and at the Beehive Inn, Maplebeck. Several new beers have been introduced over the past year to complement the existing Maypole range. Seasonal beers can be pre-ordered at any time for beer festivals. Seasonal beers: Mayday Mild (ABV 3.5%, April-May), Cockchafer (ABV 4.1%, May-June), Flanagans Extra Stout (ABV 4.5%, Feb-March), Ghost Train (ABV 4.7%, Sept-Oct), Wonky Donkey (ABV 5.2%, Nov-Dec).

Mayfly Bitter (OG 1038, ABV 3.8%)

BXA (OG 1039, ABV 4%)

Mayfair (OG 1039, ABV 4.1%)

Maybee (OG 1040, ABV 4.3%)

Major Oak (OG 1042, ABV 4.4%)

Mae West/Wellow Gold (OG 1044, ABV 4.6%)

Mayhem (OG 1048, ABV 5%)

Meantime SIBA

Meantime Brewing Co Ltd, 2 Penhall Road, Greenwich, London, SE7 8RX
Tel (020) 8293 1111
Fax (020) 8293 4004
Email info@meantimebrewing.com
Website www.meantimebrewing.com
Tours by arrangement

⊗ Meantime Brewing celebrated its fifth birthday in 2005 and was the only British brewery to win medals at the World Beer Cup in 2004. Meantime specialises in properly matured beers and brews traditional, unpasteurised Continental styles as well as innovative new flavours. One pub is owned in Greenwich and three outlets are supplied. Meantime launched its first cask ale in 2003. Bottle-conditioned beers: Porter, IPA, Chocolate, Coffee (ABV 6%). Meantime Organic Pilsner is suitable for vegetarians and vegans.

Late Hopped Blonde Ale (OG 1050, ABV 5%)

Meesons

See Old Bog

Melbourn

Melbourn Bros Brewery, 22 All Saints Street, Stamford, Lincolnshire, PE9 2PA
Tel (01780) 752186
Email info@melbournbrothers.co.uk
Website www.melbournbrothers.co.uk

A famous Stamford brewery that opened in 1825 and closed in 1974, it re-opened in 1994 and is owned by Samuel Smith of Tadcaster (qv). Melbourn brews spontaneously fermented fruit beers primarily for the American market but which can be ordered by the case in Britain by mail order. The beers are Apricot, Cherry and Strawberry (all ABV 3.4%). The brewery is open for tours Wednesday to Sunday 10am-4pm and there are open evenings for brewery tours, and beer and food tastings: prior booking essential.

Mersea Island

Mersea Island Brewery, Rewsalls Lane, East Mersea, Colchester, Essex, CO5 8SX
Tel (01206) 385900
Fax (01206) 383600
Email beer@merseawine.com
Website www.merseawine.com
Shop/café 11am-4pm daily, closed Tuesday
Tours by arrangement

The brewery started production at Mersea Island Vineyard in 2005, producing cask and bottle-conditioned beers. The beers are available from an on-site shop and also served in a café. Take-home sales in beer-in-a-box format is available. The brewery supplies a growing number of pubs and clubs on a guest beer basis as well as most local beer festivals.

Mud Mild (OG 1035, ABV 3.6%)
Dark from the use of black and chocolate malts. Fuggles hops add a distinctive flavour.

Yo Boy Bitter (OG 1038, ABV 3.8%) ◆
Pale beer with a juicy malt character and a fierce bitterness in the finish.

Skippers Bitter (OG 1047, ABV 4.8%) ◆
Fruity, malty beer with a moderate hop character. Bitterness is more dominant in the aftertaste.

Monkeys (OG 1049, ABV 5.1%)
A porter first brewed by a group of Colchester CAMRA members, known as the Monkeys, for local beer festivals. The beer has proved popular and is now more widely available. It has deep and lasting malt and hop flavours.

Mighty Oak SIBA

Mighty Oak Brewing Co Ltd, 14b West Station Yard, Spital Road, Maldon, Essex, CM9 6TW
Tel (01621) 843713 Fax (01621) 840914
Email moakbrew@aol.com
Tours by arrangement

⊗ Mighty Oak Brewing Co was formed in 1996 by John Boyce and Ruth O'Neill and was originally based in Hutton, near Brentwood, Essex. In January 2001 the brewery moved to Maldon, Essex and at the same time its capacity was increased to 67.5 barrels a week from 37.5 barrels. Another increase in capacity is planned for late 2006 to 85.2 barrels a week. Mighty Oak supplies around 200 outlets plus a small number of wholesalers each year. Twelve monthly ales are brewed based on a theme; for 2006 there was a maritime theme including Lost at Sea, Tiller Girl and Jolly Grog.

IPA (OG 1035.1, ABV 3.5%)
Light-bodied session ale with a light malty taste and a dry, bitter finish.

Oscar Wilde (OG 1039.5, ABV 3.7%)
Dry, roasty mild with a dark red hue. The taste is dominated by coffee and chocolate, with a pleasant suggestion of blackberry.

Maldon Gold (OG 1039.5, ABV 3.8%)
Rather bitter golden ale with a floral aroma and hints of lemon peel. Earthier hop tones are off-set by sweet vanilla in the taste.

Burntwood Bitter (OG 1041, ABV 4%)
Tawny bitter with a roast grain character. Sharp citrus hops are balanced by sweet vanilla and a lasting maltiness.

Simply The Best (OG 1044.1, ABV 4.4%)
Complex and fruity best bitter with a solid, meaty taste.

English Oak (OG 1047.9, ABV 4.8%)
Fruit, hops and malt are well-balanced throughout this copper-coloured bitter, with bitterness increasing in the finish.

Saxon Strong (OG 1063.6, ABV 6.5%)

Milestone

Milestone Brewing Co, Great North Road, Cromwell, Newark, Nottinghamshire, NG23 6JE
Tel (01636) 822255
Fax (01636) 822200
Email info@milestonebrewery.co.uk
Website www.milestonebrewery.co.uk
Tours by arrangement

The brewery has been in production since 2005 on a 12-barrel plant purchased from the Dwan Brewery in Tipperary, Ireland. It was founded by Kenneth and Frances Munro with head brewer Dean Penney. Around 150 outlets are supplied. Seasonal beers: Cool Amber (ABV 6%, May-Aug), Donner & Blitzed/Christmas Cracker (ABV 5.4%, Nov-Dec).

Lions Pride (ABV 3.8%)
Full-bodied session ale.

Classic Dark Mild (ABV 4%)
A rich, creamy mild.

Normanton IPA (ABV 4.1%)
A crisp, refreshing dry ale.

Loxley Ale (ABV 4.2%)
Rich golden ale with a subtle hint of honey.

Black Pearl (ABV 4.3%)
Irish stout with a full flavour.

Crusader (ABV 4.4%)
Blonde ale with citrus overtones.

Rich Ruby (ABV 4.5%)
Celtic ale, smooth, rich and creamy.

Olde Home Wrecker (ABV 4.9%)

Harry Porter (ABV 5.2%)
Rich, peat-smoked dark porter

Milk Street SIBA

Milk Street Brewery, The Griffin, 25 Milk Street, Frome, Somerset, BA11 3DB
Tel (01373) 467766
Email rjlyall@hotmail.com
Website www.milkstreet.5u.com
Tours by arrangement

The brewery was commissioned in 1999 and has a capacity of 20 barrels a week. Four beers are brewed, with seasonal brands every two months. Milk Street owns three pubs and plans to expand. 50 other outlets are supplied. (NB The Griffin, home to the brewery, is not open until 5pm.) Beer and Funky Monkey won awards at CAMRA beer festivals in 2005. Seasonal beer: Zig-Zag Stout (ABV 4.5%, Oct-Feb).

Gulp (OG 1036, ABV 3.5%)
An amber beer that is fresh and lively on the palate. The aroma is reminiscent of grapefruit peel and freshly-picked hawthorn leaves.

Funky Monkey (OG 1040, ABV 4%)
Copper-coloured summer ale boasting fruity flavours and aromas. A dry finish with developing bitterness and an undertone of citrus fruit.

Mermaid (OG 1041, ABV 4.1%)
Amber-coloured ale with a rich hop character on the nose, plenty of citrus fruit on the palate and a lasting bitter and hoppy finish.

Amarillo (OG 1043, ABV 4.3%)
Brewed with American hops to give the beer floral and spicy notes. Initially soft on the palate, the flavour develops to that of burnt oranges and a pleasant herbal taste.

Nick's (OG 1045, ABV 4.4%)
A malty best bitter with a rich nose of toffee and nuts, while the palate delivers plenty of rich chocolaty flavours. A dry finish with a slight sweetness.

Beer (OG 1049, ABV 5%)
A blonde beer with musky hoppiness and citrus fruit on the nose, while more fruit surges through on the palate before the bitter-sweet finish.

Elderfizz (OG 1051, ABV 5%)

Millis

Millis Brewing Co Ltd, St Margaret's Farm, St Margaret's Road, South Darenth, Dartford, Kent, DA4 9LB
Tel (01322) 866233
Email john@millis-brewing.com
Website www.millis-brewing.co.uk

⊗ John Millis started with a half-barrel plant at his home in Gravesend. Demand outstripped the facility and Millis moved in 2003 to a new site – a former farm cold store – with a 10-barrel plant. John now supplies some 40 pubs and clubs within a 50-mile radius. Seasonal beers: Gravesend Guzzler (ABV 3.7%, April-Sept), Winter Witch (ABV 4.8%, Oct-March).

Tuggies Dark Mild (ABV 3.5%)
A traditional dark mild with chocolate and roasted notes.

Oast Shovellers Bitter (ABV 3.9%)
A copper-coloured ale with a pale and crystal malt base, ending with a distinctive, clean finish.

Dartford Wobbler (ABV 4.3%)
A tawny-coloured, full-bodied best bitter with complex malt and hop flavours and a long, clean, slightly roasted finish.

Kentish Red Ale (ABV 4.3%)
A traditional red ale with complex malt, hops and fruit notes.

Thieves and Fakirs (ABV 4.3%)
A full-bodied beer with fruit, hops and malt notes, with a long, clean finish.

Millstone SIBA

Millstone Brewery Ltd, Unit 4 Vale Mill, Micklehurst Road, Mossley, Greater Manchester, OL5 9JL
Tel/Fax (01457) 835835
Email info@millstonebrewery.co.uk
Website www.millstonebrewery.co.uk
Tours by arrangement

Established in 2003 by Nick Boughton and Jon Hunt, the brewery is located in an 18th-century textile mill. The range now includes four regular and five seasonal/occasional beers; most are available in bottles. More than 70 outlets are supplied. Seasonal beers: A Miller's Ale (ABV 3.8%), Summer Daze (ABV 4.1%), Autumn Leaves (ABV 4.3%), Millstone Edge (ABV 4.4%), Christmas Ruby (ABV 4.7%).

Three Shires Bitter (OG 1040, ABV 4%)
A very pale, hoppy bitter with a full hop aroma and crispy fruit taste followed by a smooth, bitter finish.

Windy Miller (OG 1041, ABV 4.1%)
Pale in colour with crisp, hoppy aromas and a bitter taste.

Grain Storm (OG 1042, ABV 4.2%)
A golden bitter with a full hop aroma and crisp pine and citrus notes followed by a balanced dry, bitter finish.

True Grit (OG 1050, ABV 5%)
A well-hopped strong ale using only the Chinook hop; the mellow bitterness makes way for a distinctive citrus/grapefruit aroma.

Milton SIBA EAB

Milton Brewery Cambridge Ltd, 111 Norman Industrial Estate, Cambridge Road, Milton, Cambridgeshire, CB4 6AT
Tel (01223) 226198
Fax (01223) 226199
Email enquiries@miltonbrewery.co.uk
Website www.miltonbrewery.co.uk
Tours by arrangement

⊗ The brewery has grown steadily since it was founded in 1999. More than 100 outlets are supplied. The flagship beer, Pegasus, was a CAMRA Beer of the Year for 2003. Now with three tied houses (Peterborough and London), further expansion is being carried out to cope with demand. Seasonal beer: Mammon (ABV 7%, from Dec)

Minotaur (OG 1035, ABV 3.3%)
Impressive full-flavoured, reddish-brown mild ale. Distinctly malty with a smoky roast layer and touches of liquorice. A delicate bitter-sweet balance becomes dry and bitter.

Jupiter (OG 1037, ABV 3.5%)
A light malty aroma and a delicate hoppy palate lead to a bitter finish. A light barley sugar aroma and taste underpin this amber session bitter.

Neptune (OG 1039, ABV 3.8%)
Delicious hop aromas introduce this well-balanced, nutty and refreshing copper-coloured ale. Good hoppy finish.

Pegasus (OG 1043, ABV 4.1%)
Malty dark brown best bitter with a butterscotch aroma and taste. Hints of hops and fruit appear in the mouth and the malt/hop balance remains in the bitter ending.

Electra (OG 1046, ABV 4.5%)
A restrained bitter and hoppy backbone with short, sweet, fruity undertones and a light malt flavour after a gentle, fruity aroma. This full-bodied amber premium bitter ends with a persistent hop bitterness.

Cyclops (OG 1055, ABV 5.3%)
Deep copper-coloured ale, with a rich hoppy aroma and full body; fruit and malt notes develop in the finish.

Moles SIBA

Moles Brewery, Merlin Way, Bowerhill Trading Estate, Melksham, Wiltshire, SN12 6TJ
Tel (01225) 704734/708842
Fax (01225) 790770
Email sales@moles-cascade.co.uk
Website www.molesbrewery.com
Shop Mon-Fri 9am-5pm
Tours by arrangement

⊗ Moles has been brewing at Bowerhill since 1982 and has bought two pubs in its home town of Melksham. The traditionally brewed, all-Wiltshire malt beers, balanced with bitterness from Kent hops, can now be drunk within shouting distance of the brewery, as well as nationwide. 13 pubs are owned, all serving cask beer. 150 outlets are supplied. Seasonal beers: Barleymole (ABV 4.2%, summer), Molegrip (ABV 4.3%, autumn), Holy Moley (ABV 4.7%, spring), Moel Moel (ABV 6%, winter), Mole Slayer (ABV 4.4%, St Georges Day).

Tap Bitter (OG 1035, ABV 3.5%)
A session bitter with a smooth, malty flavour and clean bitter finish.

Best Bitter (OG 1040, ABV 4%)
A well-balanced, amber-coloured bitter, clean, dry and malty with some bitterness, and delicate floral hop flavour.

Landlords Choice (OG 1045, ABV 4.5%)
A dark, strong, smooth porter beer, with a rich fruity palate and malty finish.

Molennium (OG 1045, ABV 4.5%)
There are fruit, caramel and malty overtones in the aroma of this deep amber-coloured ale, balanced by a pleasant bitterness in the taste.

Rucking Mole (OG 1045, ABV 4.5%)
A chestnut-coloured premium ale, fruity and malty with a smooth bitter finish.

Molecatcher (OG 1050, ABV 5%)
A copper-coloured ale with a delightfully spicy hop aroma and taste, and a long bitter finish.

Moonstone

☼ Moonstone Brewery (Gem Taverns Ltd), The Ministry of Ale, 9 Trafalgar Street, Burnley, Lancashire, BB11 1TQ
Tel (01282) 830909
Email meet@ministryofale.co.uk
Website www.moonstonebrewery.co.uk
Tours by arrangement

☺ A small, 2.5-barrel brewery, based in the Ministry of Ale pub. Brewing started in 2001 and beer is only generally available in the pub. Owner Mick Jaques occasionally brews other beers. Seasonal beer: Red Jasper (ABV 6%, winter).

Black Star (OG 1037, ABV 3.4%)

Blue John (ABV 3.6%)

Tigers Eye (OG 1037, ABV 3.8%)

MPA (ABV 4%)

Moonstone Darkish (OG 1042, ABV 4.2%)

Moor SIBA

Moor Beer Co, Whitley Farm, Ashcott, Bridgwater, Somerset, TA7 9QW
Tel/Fax (01458) 210050
Email arthur@moorbeer.co.uk
Website www.moorbeer.co.uk
Tours by arrangement

⊠ Moor has been brewing since 1996 when farmer Arthur Frampton and his wife Annette swapped beef for beer and set up a brewery on their former dairy farm. It is now a 10-barrel operation with Arthur's daughter Holly doing the brewing. The brewery also runs a successful beer wholesaling business. They upgraded their brew plant in 2006. Seasonal beers: Santa Moors (ABV 4%). There are many monthly specials with a rail theme. Bottle-conditioned beers: Old Freddy Walker, Peat Porter, Merlin's Magic.

Withy Cutter (OG 1040, ABV 3.8%) ◆
A lightly malty, pale brown beer with a moderately bitter finish.

Avalon (OG 1041, ABV 4%)

Merlin's Magic (OG 1044, ABV 4.3%) ◆
Dark amber-coloured, complex, full-bodied beer, with fruity notes.

Peat Porter (OG 1045, ABV 4.5%) ◆
Dark brown/black beer with an initially fruity taste leading to roast malt with a little bitterness. A slightly sweet malty finish.

Somerland Gold (OG 1052, ABV 5%)

Old Freddy Walker (OG 1074, ABV 7.3%) ☐ ◆
Rich, dark, strong ale with a fruity complex taste, leaving a fruitcake finish.

Moorcock

Moorcock Brewing Co, Hawes Rural Workshop Estate, Brunt Acres Road, Hawes, Cumbria, DL8 3UZ
Tel (01969) 666188
Email info@moorcockbrewing.co.uk
Website www.moorcockbrewing.co.uk

The brewery was launched in 2005. The plant was originally located at the Moorcock inn in Garsdale, but has been moved five miles away to an industrial unit in Hawes. Mark Owens was the landlord of the Moorcock for three years and was always keen to brew. He opened with a 2.5-barrel kit from Moss Brew but within five months had to upgrade to five barrels. He currently supplies only the Moorcock.

Garsdale (ABV 3.2%)

OPA (ABV 3.8%)

Mescan's Porter (ABV 4.3%)

Hail Ale (ABV 4.8%)

1888 (ABV 5%)

Moorhouses SIBA

Moorhouses Brewery (Burnley) Ltd, The Brewery, Moorhouse Street, Burnley, Lancashire, BB11 5EN
Tel (01282) 422864/416004
Fax (01282) 838493
Email info@moorhouses.co.uk
Website www.moorhouses.co.uk
Tours by arrangement

☺ Established in 1865 as a drinks manufacturer, the brewery started brewing cask-conditioned ale in 1978 and has achieved recognition by winning more international and CAMRA awards than any other brewery of its size. Two new additional 30-barrel fermenters were installed in 2004, taking production to 320 barrels a week maximum. The company owns six pubs, all serving cask-conditioned beer, and supplies some 250 free trade outlets. There is a selection of seasonal ales throughout the year: see website. The brewery celebrated 140 years of brewing in June 2005 with a steam train extravaganza.

Black Cat (OG 1036, ABV 3.4%) ☐ ◆
A dark mild-style beer with delicate chocolate and coffee roast flavours and a crisp, bitter finish.

Premier Bitter (OG 1036, ABV 3.7%) ◆
A clean and satisfying bitter aftertaste rounds off this well-balanced hoppy, amber session bitter.

Pride of Pendle (OG 1040, ABV 4.1%) ◆
Well-balanced amber best bitter with a fresh initial hoppiness and a mellow, malt-driven body.

Blond Witch (OG 1045, ABV 4.5%)
A pale coloured ale with a crisp, delicate fruit flavour. Dry and refreshing with a smooth hop finish.

Pendle Witches Brew (OG 1050, ABV 5.1%) ◆
Well-balanced, full-bodied, malty beer with a long, complex finish.

Mordue SIBA

Mordue Brewery, Units D1 and D2, Narvic Way, Tyne Tunnel Estate, North Shields, Tyne & Wear, NE29 7XJ
Tel (0191) 296 1879
Fax (0191) 270 8426
Email enquiries@morduebrewery.com
Website www.morduebrewery.com
Tours by arrangement

The original Mordue Brewery closed in 1879 and the name was revived in 1995 by two brothers, Garry and Matthew Fawson. Workie Ticket won the Champion Beer of Britain competition in 1997. In 1998, a 20-barrel plant and a move to bigger premises allowed production to keep pace with demand. By 2005 the business had expanded to the point where another move became necessary. Mordue is now located on a large estate that will enable the brewery to realise its potential. The full range of Mordue beers is distributed nationally and 200 outlets are supplied by the brewery. An export market in Denmark is opening up. Seasonal beers: Summer Tyne (ABV 3.6%), Millennium Bridge Ale (ABV 3.8%), Spring Tyne (ABV 4%), Autumn Tyne (ABV 4%), A'l Wheat Pet (ABV 4.1%), Headmasters Xmas Sermon (ABV 5.2%), Zehn Dunkel (ABV 5.8%).

Five Bridge Bitter (OG 1038, ABV 3.8%) ◆
Crisp, golden beer with a good hint of hops. The bitterness carries on in the finish. A good session bitter.

Geordie Pride (OG 1042, ABV 4.2%) ◆
Well-balanced and hoppy copper-coloured ale with a long, bitter finish.

Workie Ticket (OG 1045, ABV 4.5%) 🏆 ◆
Complex, tasty bitter with plenty of malt and hops and a long, satisfying, bitter finish.

Radgie Gadgie (OG 1048, ABV 4.8%) 🏆 ◆
Strong, easy-drinking bitter with plenty of fruit and hops.

IPA (OG 1051, ABV 5.1%) 🏆 ◆
Easy-drinking, golden ale with plenty of hops. The bitterness carries on into the finish.

Moulin

🍺 Moulin Brewery, 2 Baledmund Road, Pitlochry, Perthshire, PH16 5EL
Tel (01796) 472196
Fax (01796) 474098
Email enquiries@moulinhotel.co.uk
Website www.moulinhotel.co.uk
Shop 12-3pm daily
Tours by arrangement

☺ The brewery opened in 1995 to celebrate the Moulin Hotel's 300th anniversary. Two pubs are owned and four outlets are supplied. Bottle-conditioned beer: Ale of Atholl.

Light (OG 1036, ABV 3.7%) ◆
Thirst-quenching, straw-coloured session beer, with a light, hoppy, fruity balance, ending with a gentle, hoppy sweetness.

Braveheart (OG 1039, ABV 4%) ◆
An amber bitter, with a delicate balance of malt and fruit and a Scottish-style sweetness.

Ale of Atholl (OG 1043.5, ABV 4.5%) ◆
A reddish, quaffable, malty ale, with a solid body and a mellow finish.

Old Remedial (OG 1050.5, ABV 5.2%) ◆
A distinctive and satisfying dark brown old ale, with roast malt to the fore and tannin in a robust taste.

Nags Head

🍺 Nags Head Inn & Brewery, Abercych, Boncath, Pembrokeshire, SA37 0HJ
Tel (01239) 841200

Pub-brewery producing just one beer for its own customers and two other outlets.

Old Emrys (OG 1038-40, ABV 3.8-4%)

Nailsworth*

Nailsworth Brewery Ltd, The Cross, Bath Road, Nailsworth, Gloucestershire, GL6 0HH
Tel (01453) 839343 / 07738 178452
Email jonk@nailsworth-brewery.co.uk
Website www.nailsworth-brewery.co.uk
Shop Mon-Sat 12-2pm
Tours by arrangement

The original Nailsworth Brewery closed in 1908. After a gap of 98 years, commercial brewing has returned to Nailsworth in the form of a six-barrel micro-brewery. This is the brainchild of Messrs Hawes and Kemp, whose aim it is to make the town of Nailsworth once again synonymous with quality beer. They intend to supply the whole range of beers in bottle in the near future.

The Artist's Ale (ABV 3.9%)

The Mayor's Bitter (ABV 4.2%)

The Dudbridge Donkey (ABV 4.5%)

The Town Crier (ABV 4.5%)

Naylors

Naylor's Brewery, c/o Old White Bear, 6 Keighley Road, Crosshills, Keighley, West Yorkshire, BD20 7RN
Tel (01535) 637451/632115
Fax (01535) 634875
Email info@naylorsbrewery.co.uk
Website www.naylorsbrewery.co.uk
Tours by arrangement

Naylors started brewing early in 2005, based at the Old White Bear pub and is in North Yorkshire despite the postal address. The range has increased to seven regular beers and occasional seasonals. Expansion was planned for 2006/7 with relocation likely. Around 40 outlets are supplied.

Sparkey's Mild (OG 1035, ABV 3.4%)
This delicious, full-flavoured, dark brown, malty mild has rich roast flavours with chocolate and fruity undertones, and a dryish, bitter finish.

Eric's Well Read (OG 1038, ABV 3.7%)

Mother's Best (OG 1039, ABV 3.9%)
Well-balanced with plenty of malt and hop character, this mid-brown bitter has a pleasantly fruity aroma and bitter aftertaste.

Dave's Waterloo Sunset (OG 1044, ABV 4.2%)

Stoney's Trippel S (OG 1046, ABV 4.5%)
An amber beer with a hoppy aroma, a bitter-sweet palate and a lingering hoppy, bitter finish.

Roger's Challenger (OG 1049, ABV 4.8%)
Easy-quaffing for its strength, this gold-coloured strong bitter is rich and hoppy with a fruity nose and dry, bitter aftertaste.

Gonzo's Black Porter (OG 1058, ABV 5.5%)
Jet black with a rich roast character throughout, a sweetish palate with raisin and liquorice flavours, and a roast bitter finish.

Nelson

Nelson Brewing Co Ltd, Unit 2, Building 64, Historic Dockyard, Chatham, Kent, ME4 4TE
Tel (01634) 832828
Fax (01634) 832278
Email sales@nelsonbrewingcompany.co.uk
Website www.nelsonbrewingcompany.com.uk
Shop Mon-Fri 10am-5.30pm
Tours by arrangement

⊗ Nelson Brewing is located in Chatham's preserved Georgian dockyard and distributes to 150 regular outlets with further supplies available via wholesalers and other breweries. Seasonal beers: Spring Pride (ABV 4%), Powder Monkey (ABV 4.4%), Frigging Yuletide (ABV 5.5%).

Victory Mild (OG 1036, ABV 3.5%)
A dark mild with smooth malt and hop flavour and roast aftertaste.

Rochester Bitter (OG 1038, ABV 3.7%)
A refreshing pale and hoppy bitter.

Admiral's Bitter (OG 1037, ABV 3.8%)
A flavoursome session ale with added chocolate malt and well-rounded with hops to give a mellow bitterness and good hop aroma.

Trafalgar Bitter (OG 1039, ABV 4.1%)
A light, easy drinking ale with balanced malt and hop flavour and hints of honey and nuts to finish.

Hardy's Kiss (OG 1038, ABV 4.2%)
A fruity ale with a good balance of malt and hops.

Spanker (OG 1039, ABV 4.2%)
Fruity ale with smooth predominance of hops giving a refreshing feel in the palate.

Friggin in the Riggin (OG 1048, ABV 4.7%)
Drinkable premium bitter with smooth malt flavour and bitter-sweet aftertaste.

Dover Patrol (OG 1055, ABV 5.5%)
Golden brown beer with a sweet, hoppy yet bitter aftertaste.

Nelson's Blood (OG 1062, ABV 6%)
Malty with mellow roast tones, slightly nutty and fruity.

Nethergate SIBA EAB

Nethergate Holdings Ltd t/a Nethergate Brewery, The Street Brewery & Wine Cellars, Pentlow, Sudbury, Suffolk, CO10 7JJ
Tel (01787) 283220
Fax (01787) 283221
Email orders@nethergate.co.uk
Website www.nethergatebrewery.co.uk

⊗ Nethergate Brewery was established at Clare, Suffolk, in 1986. Production tripled in the 1990s, but the brewery was unable to meet demand and in 2005 moved four miles away to a new site to enable production to double. Some 400 outlets are supplied. Seasonal beers are brewed monthly.

IPA (OG 1036, ABV 3.5%)
This amber-coloured session bitter is clean, crisp and very drinkable. Plenty of malt and hoppy bitterness together with some fruit are pleasing to the palate. Bitterness lingers in a long dry aftertaste.

Priory Mild (OG 1036, ABV 3.5%)
Distinctive, full-flavoured, very dark mild. Pronounced lingering roast and dry hop aftertaste.

Umbel Ale (OG 1039, ABV 3.8%)
Pale bitter infused with coriander. Hops and malt are evident in the taste, which is followed by a powerfully bitter finish.

Three Point Nine (OG 1040, ABV 3.9%)
A delicate session beer, well-hopped with a floral finish.

Suffolk County Best Bitter (OG 1041, ABV 4%)
A pleasant brown bitter in which fruity and malty tones dominate over hop character.

Augustinian Ale (OG 1046, ABV 4.5%)
A pale, refreshing, complex best bitter. A fruity aroma leads to a bitter-sweet flavour and aftertaste with a predominance of citrus tones.

Old Growler (OG 1052, ABV 5%)
A complex and satisfying porter, smooth and distinctive. Sweetness, roast malt and fruit feature in the palate, with bitter chocolate lingering. The finish is powerfully hoppy.

Umbel Magna (OG 1052, ABV 5%)
The addition of coriander to the Old Growler wort completes the original 1750s recipe for this distinctive dark beer. The powerful spiciness only adds to this porter's appeal.

Stour Valley Strong/SVS (OG 1063, ABV 6.2%)
A dark ruby red porter, brewed using a blend of amber, black and chocolate malts.

Newby Wyke SIBA

Newby Wyke Brewery, Willoughby Arms Cottages, Station Road, Little Bytham, Lincolnshire, NG33 4RA

Tel (01780) 411119
Fax (01780) 411240
Email newbywyke.brewery@btopenworld.com
Website www.newbywyke.co.uk
Tours by arrangement

⊗ The brewery is named after a Hull trawler skippered by brewer Rob March's grandfather. After starting life in 1998 as a 2.5-barrel plant in Robert's converted garage, growth has been steady and the brewery moved to premises behind the Willoughby Arms in Little Bytham. Current brewing capacity is 50 barrels a week. Some 180 outlets are supplied. Seasonal beers: Sidewinder (ABV 3.8%, April-Oct), Summer Session Bitter (ABV 3.8%, April-Sept), Festive Ale (ABV 3.9%, December), Kingston Topaz (ABV 4.2%, Oct-March), England Expects (ABV 4.6%, brewed for national sporting events such Six Nations, Ashes and World Cup), Black Funnel Mild (ABV 5%, May), White Sea (ABV 5.2%, Oct-March).

HMS Revenge (OG 1039, ABV 4.2%)
A single-hopped ale with floral undertones.

Red Squall (OG 1042, ABV 4.4%)
A full, rich red ale, full of fruit with a hoppy finish.

Bear Island (OG 1044, ABV 4.6%)
A blonde beer with a hoppy aroma and a crisp, dry citrus finish.

Black Squall Porter (OG 1044, ABV 4.6%)
A subtle taste of coffee and chocolate with a hoppy finish.

White Squall (OG 1045, ABV 4.8%)
A pale blonde ale with a full hop taste and a citrus finish.

Chesapeake (OG 1050, ABV 5.5%)
Strong, pale, complex hoppy ale.

For Nobody Inn, Grantham

Grantham Gold (OG 1039, ABV 4.2%)

Newmans SIBA

Newmans Brewery, 107 Wemberham Lane, Yatton, Somerset, BS49 4BP
Tel/Fax (01934) 830638
Email sales@newmansbrewery.com
Website www.newmansbrewery.com

Newman's Brewery has developed new branding for all of its beers as part of a drive to spread sales further afield. Tom Newman has also started to buy nearby freehold property to convert into new brewing premises. The company also owns a bar/bistro, the Castle Tavern, at Kewstoke, Weston-Super-Mare. 100 outlets are supplied. Seasonal beer: Hoppy Gristmas (ABV 5%, Christmas).

Red Stag Bitter (ABV 3.6%)

Cave Bear Stout (ABV 4%)

Wolvers Ale (ABV 4.1%) ◈
Well-rounded best bitter with good body for its strength. Initial sweetness with a fine malt flavour is balanced by a slightly astringent, hoppy finish.

Woolly Mammoth Weis (ABV 4.5%)

Bite IPA (ABV 4.6%)

Nobby's

Nobby's Brewery, 3 Pageant Court, Kettering, Northants, NN15 6GR
Tel (01536) 521868
Email info@nobbysbrewery.co.uk
Website www.nobbysbrewery.co.uk
Tours by arrangment

Paul Mulliner (Nobby) commenced commercial brewing in 2004 with a 2.5-barrel plant brewing three times at week. It is installed at the rear of the Alexandra Arms in Kettering, which also serves as the brewery tap. He supplies more than 20 outlets and planned to expand to a five-barrel plant in 2006 with bottle-conditioned ales being added to the portfolio of 14 cask ales already brewed throughout the year. Seasonal beers: T'owd Navigation (ABV 6.1%, winter), Wet Spell (ABV 4.2%, summer), Dark Spell (ABV 4%, autumn), Santa's Secret (ABV 4.7%, Christmas), Merlin's Magic (ABV 3.4%, spring).

Best (OG 1039, ABV 3.8%)

Tressler XXX Mild (OG 1039, ABV 3.8%)

Monster Mash (OG 1045, ABV 4.3%)

Wild West Ale (OG 1046, ABV 4.6%)

Landlords Own (OG 1050, ABV 5%)

Norfolk Cottage SIBA

Norfolk Cottage Brewing, The Shed, 98-100 Lawson Road, Norwich, Norfolk, NR3 4LF
Tel (01603) 788508/270520
Fax (01603) 270349
Email norfolkcottagebrewing@ntlworld.com

Launched in 2004 by Ray Ashworth, founder of Woodforde's, Norfolk Cottage undertakes consultancy brewing and pilot brews for the Fat Cat Brewing Co at the same address. One best bitter is available to the trade plus bespoke ales in small quantities to order. Three outlets are supplied direct.

Norfolk Cottage Best (OG 1042, ABV 4.1%)

North Cotswold

North Cotswold Brewery/Pilling Brewing Company, Unit 3 Ditchford Farm, Stretton-on-Fosse, Warwickshire, GL56 9RD
Tel/Fax (01608) 663947
Email jon@pillingweb.co.uk
Website www.northcotswoldbrewery.co.uk
Shop – please ring first
Tours by arrangement for a charge

⊛ North Cotswold Brewery started in 1999 as a 2.5-barrel plant, which was upgraded in 2000 to 10 barrels. In 2005 the brewery was purchased by Jon Pilling. The plant is on the estate of Lord Willoughby de Broke and has a visitor centre and shop. The brewery specialises in bottle-conditioned beers and also distributes real cider and perry under the Happy Apple Cider Company. Around 50 outlets are supplied. Seasonal beers: Hung Drawn n Portered (ABV 5%, Jan-Feb), Stour Stout (ABV 5%, March), Mayfair (ABV 4.1%, May), Summer Solstice (ABV 4.5%, July-Sept), Winter Solstice (ABV 4.5%, Oct-Dec), Blitzen (ABV 6%, December). There are other specials available for one month only in different styles and strengths.

Bottle-conditioned beers: Stour Stout, Summer Solstice, Blitzen.

Pig Brook (OG 1038, ABV 3.8%)

North Yorkshire

North Yorkshire Brewing Co, Pinchinthorpe Hall, Guisborough, North Yorkshire, TS14 8HG
Tel/Fax (01287) 630200
Email sales@nybrewery.com
Website www.nybrewery.co.uk
Shop 10am-5pm
Tours by arrangement

◎ The brewery was founded in Middlesbrough in 1989 and moved in 1998 to Pinchinthorpe Hall, a moated and listed medieval estate near Guisborough that has its own spring water. The site also includes a hotel, restaurant and bistro. More than 100 free trade outlets are currently supplied. A special monthly beer is produced together with three beers in the Cosmic range. All beers are organic and most of the range is bottled.

Best Bitter (OG 1036, ABV 3.6%)
Clean tasting, well hopped, pale-coloured traditional bitter.

Prior's Ale (OG 1036, ABV 3.6%) ◆
Light, refreshing and surprisingly full-flavoured for a pale, low gravity beer, with a complex, bitter-sweet mixture of malt, hops and fruit carrying through into the aftertaste.

Boro Best (OG 1040, ABV 4%)
Northern-style, full-bodied beer.

Ruby Ale (OG 1040, ABV 4%)
A full-bodied beer with a malty aroma and a balanced malt and hops taste, with vanilla notes.

Crystal Tips (OG 1040, ABV 4%)

Love Muscle (OG 1040, ABV 4%)

Honey Bunny (OG 1042, ABV 4.2%)

Cereal Killer (OG 1045, ABV 4.5%)

Fools Gold (OG 1046, ABV 4.6%)
Hoppy, pale-coloured premium beer.

Golden Ale (OG 1046, ABV 4.6%) ◆
A well-hopped, lightly-malted, golden premium bitter, using Styrian Goldings and Goldings hops.

Flying Herbert (OG 1047, ABV 4.7%)
Full-flavoured premium bitter, smooth and well balanced.

Lord Lee (OG 1047, ABV 4.7%) ◆
A refreshing, red/brown beer with a hoppy aroma. The flavour is a pleasant balance of roast malt and sweetness that predominates over hops. The malty, bitter finish develops slowly.

White Lady (OG 1047, ABV 4.7%)

Dizzy Dick (OG 1048, ABV 4.8%)

Rocket Fuel (OG 1050, ABV 5%)

Northern SIBA

Northern Brewing Ltd, Blakemere Brewery, Blakemere Craft Centre, Chester Road, Sandiway, Northwich, Cheshire, CW8 2EB
Tel/Fax (01606) 301000
Email sales@norbrew.co.uk
Website www.norbrew.co.uk
Tours by arrangement

Northern first brewed in 2003. The five-barrel plant was formerly located at Orchard Brewery Bar, Barnsley, then in Runcorn. It relocated to a larger unit at Blakemere Craft Centre near Northwich in 2005. The original plant has been augmented by the addition of a third fermenter and six conditioning tanks. An adjacent cold store houses the conditioning tanks and hop storage area. A hospitality/bar area is being fitted out for use during brewery tours. Brewery and beer names are mainly based on the Northern Soul theme. Monthly specials appear under both Northern Brewing and Blakemere Brewery names.

All-Niter (ABV 3.8%) ◆
Full-bodied, pale bitter beer with caramel overtones. Good hoppy nose and aftertaste.

All-Dayer (ABV 3.9%)

Soul Rider (ABV 4%)

Spellbinder (ABV 4.1%)

Dancer (ABV 4.2%)

Star (ABV 4.3%) ◆
Well-hopped clean and bitter straw-coloured beer. Crisp and fruity hop flavours.

Soul Master (ABV 4.4%)

'45 (ABV 4.5%) ◆
Soft, light and malty pale brown beer. Fairly sweet with fruit to the fore on the nose and in the flavour. Soapy hop flavour leads into the aftertaste.

Northumberland

Northumberland Brewery Ltd, Earth Balance, Bomarsund, Bedlington, Northumberland, NE22 7AD
Tel/Fax (01670) 822112
Email dave@northumberlandbrewery.co.uk
Website www.northumberlandbrewery.co.uk
Tours by arrangement

◎ The brewery has been in operation for 10 years using a six-barrel brew plant on the Earth Balance organic farm and visitor centre. Some 200 outlets are supplied. The brewery tap, the Lakeshore, is an integral part of the Earth Balance project . Seasonal beers: Summer Gold (ABV 3.7%), Spring Gold (ABV 4%), Autumn Gold (ABV 4.1%), Winter Gold (ABV 4.5%), Blaydon Races (ABV 4%, June), Dracula's Soup (ABV 4.5%, October), Rudolph's Balls (ABV 4.5%, December). Bottle-conditioned beers: Gateshead Gold, Fog on the Tyne, Sheepdog.

Castles Bitter (ABV 3.8%)
A golden, full-flavoured beer with a hoppy aftertaste.

Holy Island (ABV 3.8%)

Byker Bitter (ABV 4%)

Highway Robbery (ABV 4%)

Fog on the Tyne (ABV 4.1%)

Ashington (ABV 4.2%)

Newcastle Pride (ABV 4.3%)

Sheepdog (ABV 4.7%)
An old-fashioned tawny beer, with fruit and malt throughout and a hoppy finish.

McCrory's Irish Stout (ABV 4.8%)

Gateshead Gold (ABV 5%)

Whitley Wobbler (ABV 5%)

Nottingham SIBA

Nottingham Brewing Co Ltd, The Plough Inn, 17 St Peter's Street, Radford, Nottingham, NG7 3EN
Tel (0115) 9422649 / 07815 073447
Fax (0115) 9422649
Email philip.darby@nottinghambrewery.com
Website www.nottinghambrewery.com
Tours by arrangement

Founded in 2001, the brewery produces classic beers in the style of the original historic Nottingham Brewery that closed in 1960. Successful awards have included gold, silver and bronze in the SIBA East Midlands Championship and a bronze medal in the 2004 Champion Beer of Britain competition for Extra Pale Ale. Owners Niven Balfour and Philip and Peter Darby have expanded the brewing plant and have entered into a bottling enterprise. There are also plans to widen the customer base in the Midlands. 60 outlets are supplied and one pub is owned. Occasional beers: Cock & Hoop (ABV 4.3%, for Pub People Co), Olympic Flame (ABV 4.3%).

Rock Ale Bitter Beer (OG 1038, ABV 3.8%)

Rock Ale Mild Beer (OG 1038, ABV 3.8%)

Legend (OG 1040, ABV 4%)

Extra Pale Ale (OG 1042, ABV 4.2%)

Dreadnought (OG 1046, ABV 4.5%)

Bullion (OG 1048, ABV 4.7%)

Sooty Stout (OG 1050, ABV 4.8%)

Supreme Bitter (OG 1055, ABV 5.2%)

For Wetherspoons

Spoon & Arrow (OG 1047, ABV 4.7%)

O'Hanlon's SIBA

O'Hanlon's Brewing Co Ltd, Great Barton Farm, Whimple, Devon, EX5 2NY
Tel (01404) 822412
Fax (01404) 823700
Email info@ohanlons.co.uk
Website www.ohanlons.co.uk

Since moving to Whimple in 2000, O'Hanlon's has continued to expand to cope with ever increasing demand for its prize-winning beers. More than 100 outlets are regularly supplied, with wholesalers providing publicans nationwide with access to the cask products. A new bottling plant has increased production and enabled O'Hanlon's to contract bottle for several other breweries. Export sales also continue to grow with Thomas Hardy's Ale now being available in Japan, Canada, Denmark and Chile. Bottle-conditioned beers: Port Stout, Double Champion Wheat Beer, Royal Oak, Thomas Hardy's Ale (ABV 11.7%).

Firefly (OG 1035, ABV 3.7%)
Malty and fruity light bitter. Hints of orange in the taste.

Double Champion Wheat (OG 1037, ABV 4%)
1999 and 2002 SIBA Champion Wheat Beer of Britain has a fine citrus taste.

Dry Stout (OG 1041, ABV 4.2%)
A dark malty, well-balanced stout with a dry, bitter finish and plenty of roast and fruit flavours up front.

Yellowhammer (OG 1041, ABV 4%)
A well-balanced, smooth pale yellow beer with a predominant hop and fruit nose and taste, leading to a dry, bitter finish.

Original Port Stout (OG 1041, ABV 4.8%)
A black beer with roast malt in the aroma that remains in the taste but gives way to hoppy bitterness in the aftertaste.

Royal Oak (OG 1048, ABV 5%)
Well-balanced copper-coloured beer with a strong fruit and malt aroma; a malty, fruity and sweet taste; and bitter aftertaste.

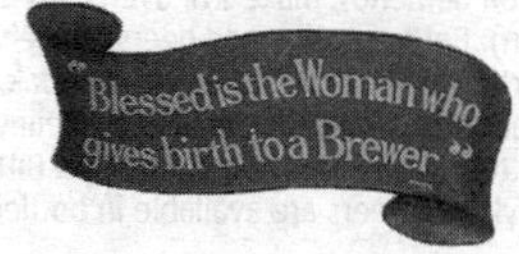

Oakham SIBA EAB

Oakham Ales, Unit 2 Maxwell Road, Woodston Industrial Estate, Peterborough, Cambridgeshire, PE2 7JB
Tel (01733) 358300
Fax (01733) 394300
Email oakhamales@aol.com
Website www.oakhamales.com
Tours by arrangement

The brewery started in 1993 in Oakham, Rutland and expanded to a 35-barrel plant from the original 10-barrel in 1998 after moving to Peterborough. This was the brewery's main brewhouse until 2006 when a new 70-barrel brewery was completed at Maxwell Road, designed to brew more than 700 barrels a week. Some 80 outlets are supplied direct and three pubs are owned. Seasonal beers: Black Hole Porter (ABV 5.5%), Kaleidoscope (ABV 4.7%), Inferno (ABV 4%), Harlequin (ABV 4.9%), Mompessons Gold (ABV 5%), Helter Skelter (ABV 5%), JHB Extra (ABV 4.2%), Five Leaves Left (ABV 4.5%), Gravity (ABV 5.1%), Oblivion (ABV 5.7%).

Jeffrey Hudson Bitter or JHB (OG 1038, ABV 3.8%)
An assault of aromatic citrus hop, a hoppy, fruity and grassy bitter-sweet palate and an uncompromising dry, bitter aftertaste characterise this impressive straw-coloured ale.

White Dwarf Wheat Beer (OG 1042, ABV 4.3%)
Straw-coloured hoppy brew with a powerful citrus hop aroma and a zesty hop bitterness, ending with a powerful dry bite.

Bishops Farewell (OG 1046, ABV 4.6%)
Intensely hoppy and full-bodied golden best bitter. Tropical fruit flavours provide a counterpoint to the grapefruit hoppy character. An abiding dryness develops.

Oakleaf SIBA

Oakleaf Brewing Co Ltd, Unit 7, Clarence Wharf Industrial Estate, Mumby Road, Gosport, Hampshire, PO12 1AJ
Tel (023) 9251 3222
Fax (023) 9251 0148
Email info@oakleafbrewing.co.uk
Website www.oakleafbrewing.co.uk
Tours by arrangement

Ed Anderson, a former Firkin brewer, set up Oakleaf with his father-in-law, Dave Pickersgill, in 2000. The brewery stands on the side of Portsmouth Harbour. Bottled beers are sold in the Victory Shop at the historic dockyard in Portsmouth. Some 150 outlets are supplied. Seasonal beers: Green Gold (ABV 4.3%, September), Reindeer's Delight (ABV 4.5%, Christmas), Piston Porter (ABV 4.6%, Oct-Nov), I Can't Believe It's Not Bitter (ABV 4.9%, May-Sept), Stoker's Stout (ABV 5%, Jan-Feb), IPA (ABV 5.5%, on demand), Blake's Heaven (ABV 7%, Dec-Jan). Bottle-conditioned beers: Blake's Gosport Bitter, Hole Hearted, Heart of Oak, Oakleaf Bitter, Maypole Mild, I Can't Believe It's Not Bitter, Blake's Heaven, Eichenblatt Bitte. All Suthwyk Ales beers are available in bottled form.

Oakleaf Bitter (OG 1038, ABV 3.8%)
A pale brown beer with a hoppy and malty aroma that leads to an intensely hoppy and bitter flavour, with some balancing lemon and grapefruit and a long, dry finish. Full-tasting for its strength.

Maypole Mild (OG 1040, ABV 3.8%)
This dark mild has a gorgeous full biscuity aroma. A lasting mix of flavours, roast and toffee lead to a slightly unexpected hoppiness. A roast, bitter finish.

Nuptu'ale (OG 1042, ABV 4.2%)
A full-bodied pale ale, strongly hopped with an uncompromising bitterness. An intense hoppy, spicy, floral aroma leads to a complex hoppy taste. Well balanced with malt and citrus flavours making for a very refreshing bitter.

Heart of Oak (OG 1044, ABV 4.5%)

Hole Hearted (OG 1048, ABV 4.7%)
An amber-coloured strong bitter with strong floral hop and citrus notes in the aroma. These continue to dominate the flavour and lead to a long, bitter-sweet finish.

Blake's Gosport Bitter (OG 1053, ABV 5.2%)
Packed with berry fruits and roastiness, this is a complex strong bitter, almost Belgian in style, with a superb hoppy bitterness. Malt, roast and caramel are prevalent as sweetness builds to an uncompromising, vinous finish. Warming, spicy, well balanced and delicious.

Eichenblatte Bitte (OG 1052, ABV 5.4%)
Smoked wheat beer.

For Suthwyk Ales:

Bloomfields Bitter (ABV 3.8%)

Skew Sunshine Ale (ABV 4.6%)
An amber-coloured beer. Initial hoppiness leads to a fruity taste and finish. A slightly cloying mouthfeel.

Liberation (ABV 4.2%)

Oakwell

Oakwell Brewery, PO Box 87, Pontefract Road, Barnsley, South Yorkshire, S71 1EZ
Tel (01226) 296161
Fax (01226) 771457

Brewing started in 1997 and there are plans for expansion. Oakwell supplies some 30 outlets.

Old Tom Mild (ABV 3.4%)

Barnsley Bitter (OG 1036, ABV 3.8%)

Odcombe*

Odcombe Ales, Masons Arms, 41 Lower Odcombe, Odcombe, Yeovil, Somerset, BA22 8TX
Tel (01935) 862591
Email paula-drew@masonsarmsodcombe.wanadoo.co.uk
Website www.the-masons-arms.co.uk
Brewery tours by prior arrangement

Odcombe opened in 2000 and closed a few years later. It re-opened in 2005 with assistance from Shepherd Neame. Brewing takes place every week and more beers and seasonal brews are planned.

No 1 (OG 1040, ABV 4%)

Spring (OG 1042, ABV 4.1%)

Offa's Dyke*

Offa's Dyke Brewery Ltd, Chapel Lane, Trefonen, Oswestry, Shropshire, SY10 9DX
Tel (01691) 831680
Fax (01691) 656889
Tours by arrangement

Offa's Dyke started in 2006 with brewing plant from Fisherrow. Trial brews began in early 2006 and the company has taken on the management of the pub next door to the brewery, which will act as the brewery tap. Three permanent beers will be on offer as well as seasonals and the brewers are experimenting with a relatively new hop from New Zealand.

ODB (OG 1046, ABV 4.6%)

Okells SIBA

Okell & Son Ltd, Kewaigue, Douglas, Isle of Man, IM2 1QG
Tel (01624) 699400
Fax (01624) 699476
Email mac@okells.co.uk
Website www.okells.co.uk
Tours by arrangement

Founded in 1874 by Dr Okell and formerly

trading as Isle of Man Breweries, this is the main brewery on the island, having taken over and closed the rival Castletown Brewery in 1986. The brewery moved in 1994 to a new, purpose-built plant at Kewaigue to replace the Falcon Brewery in Douglas. All the beers are produced under the Manx Brewers' Act 1874 (permitted ingredients: water, malt, sugar and hops only). 36 of the company's 48 IoM pubs and four on the mainland sell cask beer and some 70 free trade outlets are also supplied. Seasonal beers: Spring Ram (ABV 4.2%), Autumn Dawn (ABV 4.2%), Summer Storm (ABV 4.2%), St Nick (ABV 4.5%), Aile (ABV 4.8%, winter).

Mild (OG 1034, ABV 3.4%) ◆
A genuine, well-brewed mild ale, with a fine aroma of hops and crystal malt. Reddish-brown in colour, this beer has a full malt flavour with surprising bitter hop notes and a hint of blackcurrants and oranges. Full, malty finish.

Bitter (OG 1035, ABV 3.7%) ◆
A golden beer, malty and superbly hoppy in aroma, with a hint of honey. Rich and malty on the tongue, it has a wonderful, dry, malt and hop finish. A complex but rewarding beer.

Maclir (OG 1042, ABV 4.4%)
Beer with resiny hops and lemon fruit on the aroma, banana and lemon in the mouth and a big, bitter finish, dominated by hops, juicy malt and citrus fruit.

Dr Okells IPA (OG 1044, ABV 4.5%)
An extremely light-coloured beer with a surprising full-bodied taste. The sweetness is offset by a strong hopping rate that gives the beer an overall roundness with spicy lemony notes and a fine dry finish to counteract the initial sweetness.

Old Bear

Old Bear Brewery, Unit 4b Atlas Works, Pitt Street, Keighley, West Yorkshire, BD21 4YL
Tel/Fax (01535) 601222
Email sales@oldbearbrewery.com
Website www.oldbearbrewery.com
Tours by arrangement

◎ The brewery was founded in 1993 by Bryan Eastell as a brew-pub at the Old White Bear and is now in the hands of Ian Cowling. The brewery moved to Keighley in 2005 to a purpose-designed unit to cater for increased production. The original 10-barrel plant was kept and there is now a one-barrel plant for specials. 60 outlets are supplied.

Bruin (OG 1035, ABV 3.5%)
A mix of three malts, one being dark chocolate, giving a soft bronze colour. The combination of English Fuggles and Goldings hops give a sharp blackcurrant aftertaste.

Original (OG 1039, ABV 3.9%) ◆
A refreshing and easy-to-drink bitter. The balance of malt and hops gives way to a short, dry, bitter aftertaste.

Black Mari'a (OG 1043, ABV 4.2%)
A jet black stout, smooth on the palate. Brewed with Maris Otter malt and roasted barley and a blend of two English hops producing a strong roast malt flavour with a fruity finish.

Honeypot (OG 1046, ABV 4.4%)
Straw-coloured beer enhanced with golden honey from Denholme Gate.

Goldilocks (OG 1047, ABV 4.5%)
A light, golden ale with a pungent, hoppy taste and a lemon tangy fruit aroma, which comes from the blend of four hops, leaving a clean, wheaty, citrus flavour on the palate.

Hibernator (OG 1055, ABV 5%)
A strong, dark ale, ruby red in colour with a powerful malt and light liquorice aroma.

Old Bog*

Old Bog Brewery, Masons Arms, 2 Quarry School Place, Oxford, Oxfordshire, OX3 8LH
Tel (01865) 764579
Email theoldbog@hotmail.co.uk
Website www.masonsquarry.co.uk

Brewing started in 2005 on a one-barrel plant from Bitter End Brewery in Cockermouth. At present Old Bog brews once a week. The beers, when available, are sold at the Masons Arms and occasionally at beer festivals.

Quarry Gold (ABV 4%)

Quarry Morris (ABV 4%)

Munt's Pit (ABV 4.6%)

Quarry Wrecked (ABV 5.5%)

Old Cannon

Old Cannon Brewery Ltd, 86 Cannon Street, Bury St Edmunds, Suffolk, IP33 1JR
Tel (01284) 768769
Fax (01284) 701137
Website www.oldcannon.co.uk
Tours by arrangement

⊗ St Edmunds Head pub opened in 1845 with its own brewery. Brewing ceased in 1917, and Greene King closed the pub in 1995. It re-opened in 1999 complete with a unique state-of-the-art brewery housed in the bar area. There are plans for bottling, further off-sales, more seasonal beers and the acquisition of a further pub. Ten outlets are supplied. Seasonal beers: Blonde Bombshell (ABV 4.2%), Old Chestnut (ABV 4.2%), Grapeshot (ABV 4.4%), Black Pig (ABV 4.8%).

Best Bitter (OG 1037, ABV 3.8%) ◆
An excellent session bitter brewed using Styrian Goldings, giving a crisp grapefruit aroma and taste. Very refreshing and full of flavour.

Gunner's Daughter (OG 1052, ABV 5.5%) ◆
A well-balanced strong ale with a complexity of hop, fruit, sweetness and bitterness in the flavour, and a lingering, pleasant, hoppy, bitter aftertaste.

Old Chimneys

Office: Old Chimneys Brewery, The Street, Market Weston, Diss, Norfolk, IP22 2NZ
Brewery: Hopton End Farm, Market Weston, Diss, Norfolk, IP22 2NX

Tel Office (01359) 221411/Brewery (01359) 221013
Fax (01359) 221843
Shop Fri 2-7pm, Sat 11am-2pm
Tours by arrangement

⊗ A craft brewery opened in 1995 by former Vaux/Greene King/Broughton brewer Alan Thomson. In 2001 the brewery moved to larger premises in a converted farm building in the same village. Despite the postal address, the brewery is in Suffolk. The beers produced are mostly named after endangered local species. Old Chimneys currently supplies 30 outlets. Seasonal beers: Corncleavers Ale (ABV 4.3%, summer), Golden Pheasant (ABV 4.5%, summer), Natterjack (ABV 5%, winter), Winter Cloving (ABV 6%, winter). Bottle-conditioned beers: all cask ales listed below plus Hairy Canary (ABV 4.2%), IPA (ABV 5.6%), Brimstone Lager (ABV 6.5%), Redshank (ABV 8.7%). In bottled form, Military Mild is known as Meadow Brown and bottled Good King Henry is marketed as Special Reserve and is stronger than its draught version at ABV 11%; it is also bottle-conditioned for two years before going on sale. All bottle-conditioned beers are suitable for vegetarians and all except Black Rat and Hairy Canary are suitable for vegans.

Military Mild (OG 1035, ABV 3.3%) ◆
A rich, dark mild with good body for its gravity. Sweetish toffee and light roast bitterness dominate, leading to a dry aftertaste.

Great Raft Bitter (OG 1040, ABV 4%)
Pale copper bitter bursting with fruit. Malt and hops add to the sweetish fruity flavour, which is nicely rounded off with hoppy bitterness in the aftertaste.

Polecat Porter (OG 1043, ABV 4.2%)

Black Rat Stout (OG 1046, ABV 4.4%)

Good King Henry (OG 1107, ABV 9%)

Old Cottage

Burton Old Cottage Beer Co, Unit 10 Eccleshall Business Park, Hawkins Lane, Burton upon Trent, Staffordshire, DE14 1PT
Tours by arrangement

⊗ Old Cottage was installed in the old Heritage Brewery, once Everard's production plant in Burton. When the site was taken over, Kevin Slater was evicted and set up in a modern industrial unit. Kevin sold the brewery in 2005 to three friends, Mick and Dave Machin and Paul Makelin. Mick and Paul previously worked at the nearby Coors Brewery, both with more than 30 years' experience, Mick in process and Paul as an engineer. All the old beers will remain and they hope to introduce a summer seasonal called Pale.

Oak Ale (OG 1044, ABV 4%) ◆
Tawny, full-bodied bitter. A sweet start gives way to a slight roast taste with some caramel. A dry, hoppy finish.

Chariot Ale (OG 1045, ABV 4.5%)

Stout (OG 1047, ABV 4.7%) ◆
Dense black but not heavy. Sweet with lots of caramel, hints of liquorice and a roast and bitter finish.

Pastiche (OG 1050, ABV 5.2%)

Halcyon Daze (OG 1050, ABV 5.3%) ◆
Tawny and creamy with touches of hop, fruit and malt aroma. Fruity taste and finish.

Oldershaw SIBA

Oldershaw Brewery, 12 Harrowby Hall Estate, Grantham, Lincolnshire, NG31 9HB
Tel (01476) 572135
Fax (01476) 572193
Email oldershawbrewery@btconnect.com
Website www.oldershawbrewery.com
Tours by arrangement

⊗ Experienced home-brewer Gary Oldershaw and his wife Diane set up the brewery at their home in 1997. Grantham's first brewery for 30 years, Oldershaw now supplies 60 local free houses. It concentrates on delivering direct to outlets and is enjoying steady growth. The Oldershaws have introduced small-scale bottling and have an application with the council to sell bottled beer direct from the brewery. They are members of the CAMRA Real Ale in a Bottle scheme. Seasonal beers: Sunnydaze (ABV 4%, May-Aug), Topers Tipple (ABV 4.5%, Nov-Feb), Yuletide (ABV 5.2%, Nov-Dec).

Mowbrays Mash (OG 1037, ABV 3.7%)

High Dyke (OG 1039, ABV 3.9%)
Golden and moderately bitter. A predominantly hoppy session beer.

Newton's Drop (OG 1041, ABV 4.1%) ◆
Balanced malt and hops but with a strong bitter, lingering taste in this mid-brown beer.

Caskade (OG 1042, ABV 4.2%)
Pale, golden beer brewed with American Cascade hops to give a distinctive floral, hoppy flavour and aroma, and a clean lasting finish.

Ermine Ale (OG 1042, ABV 4.2%)
Golden brown with a fruity hop the dominant feature on nose and taste giving bitterness that lasts; malt plays a supporting role.

Ahtanum Gold (OG 1043, ABV 4.3%)
A gold-coloured, fruity, hoppy beer balanced with some maltiness. Moderately bitter.

Grantham Stout (OG 1043, ABV 4.3%) ⌂
Dark brown and smooth with rich roast malt flavour, supported by some fruit and bitterness. A long, moderately dry finish.

Regal Blonde (OG 1043, ABV 4.4%) ◆
Straw-coloured, lager-style beer with a good malt/hop balance throughout; strong bitterness on the taste lingers.

Isaac's Gold (OG 1044, ABV 4.5%)

Old Boy (OG 1047, ABV 4.8%) ◆
A full-bodied amber ale, fruity and bitter with a hop/fruit aroma. The malt that backs the taste dies in the long finish.

Alchemy (OG 1052, ABV 5.3%)
A golden, premium hoppy beer brewed with First Gold hops.

Olde Swan

Olde Swan Brewery, 87-89 Halesowen Road, Netherton, Dudley, West Midlands, DY2 9PY
Tel (01384) 253075
Tours by arrangement

A famous and much-loved brew-pub, best known as 'Ma Pardoe's', after the matriarch who ruled it for years. The pub has been licensed since 1835 and the present brewery and pub were built in 1863. Brewing continued until 1988 and restarted in 2001. The plant brews primarily for the on-site pub with some beer available to the trade. Some 20 outlets are supplied. Seasonal beer: Black Widow (ABV 6.7%, winter). In addition, monthly specials are available together with various commemorative beers for sporting events.

Original **(OG 1034, ABV 3.5%)**
Straw-coloured light mild, smooth but tangy, and sweetly refreshing with a faint hoppiness.

Dark Swan **(OG 1041, ABV 4.2%)**
Smooth, sweet dark mild with very late roast malt in the finish.

Entire **(OG 1043, ABV 4.4%)**
Faintly hoppy, amber premium bitter with sweetness persistent throughout.

Bumble Hole Bitter **(OG 1052, ABV 5.2%)**
Sweet, smooth amber ale with hints of astringency in the finish.

Old Laxey

Old Laxey Brewing Co Ltd, Shore Hotel Brew Pub, Old Laxey, Isle of Man, IM4 7DA
Tel (01624) 863214
Email shore@mcb.net
Tours by arrangement

Beer brewed in the Isle of Man is brewed to a strict Beer Purity Act. Additives are not permitted to extend its shelf life, nor are chemicals allowed to assist with head retention. Most of Old Laxey's beer is sold through the Shore Hotel alongside the brewery.

Bosun Bitter **(OG 1038, ABV 3.8%)**
Crisp and fresh with a hoppy aftertaste.

Old Luxters SIBA

Old Luxters Brewery, Hambleden, Henley-on-Thames, Oxfordshire, RG9 6JW
Tel (01491) 638330
Fax (01491) 638645
Email david@oldluxters.co.uk
Website www.oldluxters.co.uk
Shop Mon-Fri 9am-6pm (5pm winter), Sat-Sun 11am-6pm (5pm winter)
Tours by arrangement

A traditional, full-mash, independent farm brewery established in 1990 and situated in a 17th-century barn alongside the Chiltern Valley vineyard. The craft brewery retails three cask ales through the brewery shop. The brewery is in Buckinghamshire despite the postal address. Old Windsor Gold (ABV 5%) and Old Windsor Dark Ale (ABV 5%) are brewed for the Royal Household farm shops (Balmoral, Sandringham, Windsor etc). Fortnum & Mason Ale (ABV 5%) and several others are brewed under contract. Bottle-conditioned beers: Barn Ale (ABV 5.4%), Damson Ale (ABV 7%), Dark Roast Ale, Luxters Gold (ABV 5%), Winter Warmer (ABV 4.5%).

Barn Ale Bitter **(OG 1038, ABV 4%)**
A fruity, aromatic, fairly hoppy, bitter beer.

Barn Ale Special **(OG 1042.5, ABV 4.5%)**
Predominantly malty, fruity and hoppy in taste and nose, and tawny/amber in colour. Fairly strong in flavour: the initial, sharp, malty and fruity taste leaves a dry, bitter-sweet, fruity aftertaste. It can be slightly sulphurous.

Dark Roast Ale **(OG 1048, ABV 5%)**
The use of chocolate and crystal malts give this ale a nutty, roasty bitter flavour.

Old Mill

Old Mill Brewery Ltd, Mill Street, Snaith, East Yorkshire, DN14 9HU
Tel (01405) 861813
Fax (01405) 862789
Email mail@oldmillbrewery.co.uk
Website www.oldmillbrewery.co.uk
Tours by arrangement to organisations and customers only

Old Mill is a craft brewery opened in 1983 in a 200-year-old former malt kiln and corn mill. The brew-length is 60 barrels. The brewery is building a tied estate, now standing at 17 houses. Beers can be found nationwide through wholesalers and around 80 free trade outlets are supplied by the brewery. There is a rolling programme of seasonal beers (see website) and monthly specials.

Mild **(OG 1034, ABV 3.4%)**
A satisfying roast malt flavour dominates this easy-drinking, quality dark mild.

Bitter **(OG 1038.5, ABV 3.9%)**
A malty nose is carried through to the initial flavour. Bitterness runs throughout.

Old Curiosity **(OG 1044.5, ABV 4.5%)**
Slightly sweet amber brew, malty to start with. Malt flavours all the way through.

Bullion **(OG 1047.5, ABV 4.7%)**
The malty and hoppy aroma is followed by a neat mix of hop and fruit tastes within an enveloping maltiness. Dark brown/amber in colour.

Old Poets'*

Old Poets' Corner Brewery, Butts Road, Ashover, Chesterfield, Derbyshire, S45 0EW
Tel (01246) 590888
Email enquiries@oldpoets.co.uk
Website www.oldpoets.co.uk

Husband and wife team Kim and Jackie Beresford took a private lease on the Old Poets' Corner pub in 2004, with an option to buy. The plan was to set up a brewery in the spacious cellars once they had acquired the freehold. This was achieved in 2005 and the brewery was due to be installed during 2006. The brew length will be five barrels and beers will only be available from the Old Poets' Corner and local beer festivals. The beer range will be initially limited to four regulars and four seasonals.

Old Spot*

Old Spot Brewery Ltd, Manor Farm, Station Road, Cullingworth, Bradford, West Yorkshire, BD13 5HN
Tel (01525) 691144
Fax (01535) 609677
Email jp.hargreaves@lineone.net
Tours by arrangement

Old Spot started brewing in 2005 and is named after a retired sheepdog on Manor Farm. Ten outlets are supplied direct.

Ruby Lu (ABV 3.8%)

Dog's in't Barrel (ABV 4.5%)

Hunter Hill (ABV 5%)

Organic SIBA

Organic Brewhouse, Unit 1 Higher Bochym Workshops, Cury Cross Lanes, Helston, Cornwall, TR12 7AZ
Tel (01326) 241555
Fax (01326) 241188
Email orgbrewandy@tiscali.co.uk
Tours by arrangement

⊗ Laid out as a mini 'tower' system, Organic's production has increased to six regular beers. It was established by Andy Hamer in 2000 and is dedicated to supplying exclusively organic beer, using its own source of natural mineral water. Some 20 local outlets are supplied regularly and the beers occasionally head north with wholesalers. Bottle-conditioned beers: Lizard Point, Serpentine, Black Rock, Wolf Rock. All beers are Soil Association certified and bottled beers are suitable for vegetarians.

Halzephron Gold (OG 1033, ABV 3.6%)

Lizard Point (OG 1038, ABV 4%)

Serpentine (OG 1042, ABV 4.5%)
A big malty nose, a bitter-sweet palate and a finish balanced by rich malt and tangy hops.

Black Rock (OG 1044, ABV 4.7%)
Hop and apple aroma masked by complex roast overtones.

Wolf Rock (OG 1047, ABV 5%)

Charlie's Pride Lager (OG 1048, ABV 5.3%)

Orkney SIBA

Orkney Brewery, Highlands & Islands Breweries Ltd, Quoyloo, Stromness, Orkney, KW16 3LT
Tel (01856) 841802
Fax (01856) 841754
Email info@orkneybrewery.com
Website www.orkneybrewery.com

◎ Set up in 1988 in an old school building in the remote Orkney hamlet of Quayloo, the brewery was modernised in 1995 with new buildings and brewing equipment. Capacity is now 120 barrels a week, all brewed along strict ecological lines from its own water supply. All waste water is treated through two lakes on the brewery's land, which in turn support fish and several dozen mallard ducks. There are plans for additional fermenting capacity and a visitor centre by the end of 2006. Along with Atlas (qv), Orkney is part of Highlands & Islands Breweries; the combined business distributes to some 350 outlets across Scotland and via wholesalers to the rest of Britain. The extra distribution has improved chances of finding Orkney's more specialist beers such as Dragonhead and Skullsplitter. Seasonal beer: White Christmas (ABV 5%, December).

Raven Ale (OG 1038, ABV 3.8%)
A well-balanced, quaffable bitter. Malty fruitiness and bitter hoppiness last through to the long, dry aftertaste.

Dragonhead Stout (OG 1040, ABV 4%)
A strong, dark malt aroma flows into the taste in this superb Scottish stout. The roast malt continues to dominate the aftertaste, and blends with chocolate to develop a strong, dry finish. Hard to find.

Northern Light (OG 1040, ABV 4%)
A straw-coloured beer, hoppy and refreshing. Fruity hop notes can develop a true lager nose. A late copper hop is intense without being cloying.

Red MacGregor (OG 1040, ABV 4%)
Generally a well-balanced bitter, this tawny red ale has a powerful smack of fruit and a clean, fresh mouthfeel. A thoroughbred from a successful stable.

Dark Island (OG 1045, ABV 4.6%)
An excellent brew with many accolades and awards. The amount of roast and chocolate malt character varies, making it hard to categorise this beer as stout or old ale. Generally a sweetish roast malt taste leads to a long-lasting roasted, slightly bitter finish.

Skullsplitter (OG 1080, ABV 8.5%)
An intense velvet malt nose with hints of apple, nutmeg and spice. Hops to the fore are balanced by satiny smooth malt with fruity, spicy edges leading to a long dry finish with a hint of nut.

Ossett SIBA

Ossett Brewing Co Ltd, Kings Yard, Low Mill Road, Ossett, West Yorkshire, WF5 8ND
Tel (01924) 261333
Fax (01924) 261356
Email brewery@ossett-brewery.co.uk
Website www.ossett-brewery.co.uk
Tours by arrangement

◎ Brewing began at Ossett in 1998 and the company has gone from strength to strength since then. The brewery moved premises in 2005 — less than 50 metres — and now has a capacity of approximately 100 barrels a week. Ossett delivers to all points between Newcastle and Peterborough and the beers are also available through most wholesalers. The tied pub estate now numbers six outlets. For a full listing of seasonal and special beers, see the website.

Pale Gold (OG 1038, ABV 3.8%)
A light, refreshing pale ale with a light, hoppy aroma.

Black Bull Bitter (OG 1039, ABV 3.9%)
A dark, dry bitter.

Silver King **(OG 1041, ABV 4.3%)**
A lager-style beer with a crisp, dry flavour and citrus fruity aroma.

Fine Fettle **(OG 1048, ABV 4.8%)**
A strong yet refreshing pale ale with a crisp, clean flavour and citrus aroma.

Excelsior **(OG 1051, ABV 5.2%)**
A strong pale ale with a full, mellow flavour and a fresh, hoppy aroma with citrus/floral characteristics.

Otley*

Otley Brewing Co Ltd, Unit 42 Albion Industrial Estate, Cilfynydd Road, Pontypridd, Mid Glamorgan, CF37 4NX
Tel/Fax (01443) 480555
Email info@otleybrewing.co.uk
Website www.otleybrewing.co.uk
Tours by arrangement

Otley Brewing was set up during the summer of 2005. The brew plant was originally from Moor Beer Co in Somerset. Six regular beers are brewed and there are plans to introduce bottling.

Dark O **(OG 1036.8, ABV 3.8%)**
A light, easy-drinking mild stout with chocolate malt flavours and Fuggles hops.

01 **(OG 1038.8, ABV 4%)** ◆
A pale golden beer with a hoppy aroma. The taste has hops, malt, fruit and a thirst-quenching bitterness. A satisfying finish completes this beer.

CO2 **(OG 1040.7, ABV 4.2%)**
Golden-brown in colour, fruity with heavy floral aromas from Cascade and Centennial hops.

OBB **(OG 1043.6, ABV 4.5%)**
A tawny-red coloured ale that is a gentle blend of pale, wheat and crystal malts bittered with Centennial hops and aromas from Mount Hood.

OG **(OG 1052.3, ABV 5.4%)**
A golden, honey-coloured ale, extremely smooth; steeped in Progress and Bramling Cross hops.

08 **(OG 1077.5, ABV 8%)**
A pale and strong ale, deceptively smooth and friendly.

Otter SIBA

Otter Brewery Ltd, Mathayes, Luppitt, Honiton, Devon, EX14 4SA
Tel (01404) 891285
Fax (01404) 891124
Email info@otterbrewery.com
Website www.otterbrewery.com
Tours by arrangement

⊗ David and Mary Ann McCaig (both with Whitbread connections) set up Otter Brewery in 1990 and it has grown into one of the West Country's major producers of beers. The brewery is located in the Blackdown Hills, between Taunton and Honiton. An 80-barrel plant, built in exactly the same style as the old brewery, was commissioned in 2004 and has proved invaluable in supplying demand. The beers are made with local spring water. Otter Beers are delivered to more than 500 pubs across the South-west including the brewery's first pub, the Holt, in Honiton.

Bitter **(OG 1036, ABV 3.6%)** ◻ ◆
Well-balanced amber session bitter with a fruity nose and bitter taste and aftertaste.

Bright **(OG 1039, ABV 4.3%)** ◆
Fruit and hop aroma in a straw-coloured bitter with a strong bitter finish.

Ale **(OG 1043, ABV 4.5%)** ◻ ◆
A full-bodied best bitter. A malty aroma predominates with a fruity taste and finish.

Head **(OG 1054, ABV 5.8%)**
Fruity aroma and taste with a pleasant bitter finish. Dark brown and full-bodied.

Oulton

Oulton Ales Ltd, Lake Lothing Brewery, Harbour Road, Oulton Broad, Lowestoft, Suffolk, NR32 3LZ
Tel (01502) 587905
Fax (01502) 583387
Email wayne@oultonales.co.uk
Website www.oultonales.co.uk
Tours by arrangement

⊗ Several new names have been added to the range to reflect the nautical history of Oulton Broad and Lowestoft. The capacity of the brewery is now 30 barrels a week due to expansion in 2005. 20 outlets are supplied as well as its own three pubs. Five of the brands are brewed throughout the year. Bottle-conditioned beers: Nautilus, Gone Fishing, Roaring Boy, Sunrise, Cormorant Porter.

Bitter **(OG 1037, ABV 3.5%)**

Mutford Mild **(OG 1038, ABV 3.7%)**

Beedazzled **(OG 1040, ABV 4%)**

Sunrise **(OG 1040, ABV 4%)**

Nautilus **(OG 1042, ABV 4.2%)**

Sunset **(OG 1041, ABV 4.2%)**

Wet and Windy **(OG 1044, ABV 4.3%)**

Windswept **(OG 1044, ABV 4.5%)** ◆
Fairly full-bodied with an intense elderflower aroma and flavour. Quite sweet but with a hint of bitterness, particularly in the finish.

Excelsior **(OG 1045, ABV 4.6%)**

Gone Fishing **(OG 1049, ABV 5%)**

Cormorant Porter **(OG 1050, ABV 5.2%)** ◆
An initial rich, plummy fruitiness gives way to bitter-sweetness and a long, sweet aftertaste.

Keelhaul **(OG 1060, ABV 6.5%)**

Roaring Boy **(OG 1075, ABV 8.5%)**

Outlaw

See Roosters

Owl

Owl Brewing Co Ltd, Unit 41 The Acorn Centre, Barry Street, Oldham, Lancashire, OL1 3NE

Tel 07889 631366
Fax (01706) 840356
Email gordon@owlbrew.co.uk
Website www.owlbrew.co.uk
Shop Thu-Fri 2-5pm
Tours by arrangement

Brewing started at the Hope Inn, Oldham, in 2004. The brewery relocated to the Acorn Centre in 2006 and the Hope Inn was sold. After 20 years designing bar and cellar equipment for the brewing industry, Gordon Potts is happily settled as a micro-brewer. In its new location, the brewery can concentrate on free trade supplies with room for expansion. It also specialises in Party Pig carry-out packs and nine-gallon firkins. Seventeen outlets are supplied. Seasonal and special event ales are brewed occasionally.

Russett Owl **(OG 1038, ABV 3.8%)**

Owl OB Bitter **(OG 1041, ABV 4%)**

YPA **(OG 1041, ABV 4%)**

OPA **(OG 1042, ABV 4.2%)**

Night Owl **(OG 1044, ABV 4.2%)**

Lancashire Hop Pot **(OG 1048, ABV 5.4%)**

Oxfordshire Ales

Bicester Beers & Minerals Ltd, 12 Pear Tree Farm Industrial Units, Bicester Road, Marsh Gibbon, Bicester, Buckinghamshire, OX27 0GB
Tel (01869) 278765
Fax (01869) 278768
Email bicesterbeers@tiscali.co.uk
Tours by arrangement

The company first brewed in 2005. The five-barrel plant was previously at Picks Brewery but has now been upgraded to a 10-barrel plant with the purchase of a larger copper. It supplies 30-40 outlets as well as several wholesalers. Triple B and Marshmellow are also available in bottles but not in bottle-conditioned form. Future plans are to produce seasonal beers and an organic beer.

Triple B **(ABV 3.7%)** ◆
This pale amber beer has a huge caramel aroma. The caramel diminishes in the initial taste, which changes to a fruit/bitter balance. This in turn leads to a long, refreshing, bitter aftertaste.

IPA **(ABV 4.1%)** ◆
An amber beer, the aroma is butterscotch/caramel, which carries on into the initial taste. The taste then becomes bitter with sweetish/malty overtones. There is a long, dry, bitter finish.

Marshmellow **(ABV 4.7%)** ◆
The slightly fruity aroma in this golden-amber beer leads to a hoppy but thin taste, with slight caramel notes. The aftertaste is short and bitter.

Oyster

Oyster Bar & Brewery, Ellenabeich, Easdale, Oban, Argyll & Bute, PA34 4RQ
Tel (01852) 300121
Email gascoignea@tiscali.co.uk
Website www.oysterbrewery.com

The brewery was built in 2004 and came on stream in the spring of 2005. Head brewer Andy Gascoigne brought the state-of-the-art brewery north after first installing it in his pub in West Yorkshire.

Easd'ale **(ABV 3.8%)**
Golden smooth bitter with a dry aftertaste.

Thistle Tickler **(ABV 4%)**
Amber, fruity session bitter using Fuggles hops and Vienna malt.

Red Pearl **(ABV 4.5%)**
Traditional red-hued Scottish ale brewed with a blend of malts and roasted barley with First Gold hops. Toffeeish aftertaste.

Old Tosser **(ABV 5%)**
Strong dark ale brewed with roasted barley and American Cascade hops to give a rich, full-bodied character.

Palmer IFBB SIBA

JC & RH Palmer Ltd, The Old Brewery, West Bay Road, Bridport, Dorset, DT6 4JA
Tel (01308) 422396
Fax (01308) 421149
Email enquiries@palmersbrewery.com
Website www.palmersbrewery.com
Shop Mon-Sat 9am-6pm
Tours by arrangement (Please ring 01308 427500)

⊠ Palmers is Britain's only thatched brewery and dates from 1794. It is based in an idyllic location by the sea in west Dorset. The company is run by John and Cleeves Palmer, great-grandsons of Robert Henry and John Cleeves Palmer, who bought the brewery in 1896. Palmers enjoys sustained growth in real ale sales. Heavy investment is made in free trade ale dispense. 56 pubs are owned and a further 240 outlets are supplied.

Copper Ale **(OG 1036, ABV 3.7%)** ◆
Well-balanced session ale. Gentle fruit and caramel on the nose lead through a sweetish taste with hop bitterness developing.

Traditional Best Bitter IPA **(OG 1040, ABV 4.2%)** ◆
A deep copper beer that is hoppy and bitter throughout. Fruit and malt undertones give some balance in the aroma and taste, and there is a lingering bitter aftertaste.

Dorset Gold **(OG 1046, ABV 4.5%)**
A golden premium ale, refreshing and thirst-quenching, full and fruity.

200 **(OG 1052, ABV 5%)** ◆
Full-bodied: caramel sweetness and fruity aroma are balanced with a dry finish; not excessively bitter; a deep-copper ale. First brewed to mark the brewery's 200th anniversary.

Tally Ho! **(OG 1057, ABV 5.5%)**
A strong, nutty, full-strength dark beer with a distinctive and long-lasting taste.

Paradise SIBA

Paradise Brewing Co, Unit 2 The Old Creamery, Station Road, Wrenbury, Nantwich, Cheshire, CW5 8EX
Tel/Fax (01270) 780916

Email paradisebrewery@uwclub.net
Tours by arrangement

In 2003 the brewery came under the sole ownership of John Wood, one of its founders. An annual beer festival is held, featuring local micro-breweries. The brewery is located at the side of Wrenbury Railway Station. Ten outlets are supplied, varying with the season. 70% of beer is now in bottle-conditioned form, sold at local farmers' markets. John Wood is now looking for new premises, possibly in a different area.

Mild (OG 1036, ABV 3.6%)

Farmers Favourite (ABV 4%)

Dabbers (OG 1048, ABV 5%)

Nantwich Ale (ABV 5.6%)

Parish

Parish Brewery Ltd, 6 Main Street, Burrough on the Hill, Leicestershire, LE14 2JQ
Tel/Fax (01664) 454801
Tours by arrangement

Parish began in 1983 in a 400-year-old building next to the Stag & Hounds pub. It moved to Somerby in 1990 before returning home four years ago. The 20-barrel brewery supplies local outlets, notably with bottle-conditioned Baz's Bonce Blower.

Mild (OG 1038, ABV 3.8%)

Special Bitter/PSB (OG 1040, ABV 4%)

Somerby Premium (OG 1041, ABV 4.2%)

Farm Gold (OG 1042, ABV 4.2%)

Burrough Bitter (OG 1048, ABV 4.8%)

Poachers Ale (OG 1060, ABV 6%)

Baz's Bonce Blower (OG 1120, ABV 12%)

Peak Ales SIBA

Peak Ales, Barn Brewery, Chatsworth, Bakewell, Derbyshire, DE45 1EX
Tel (01246) 583737
Email info@peakales.co.uk
Website www.peakales.co.uk

Peak Ales opened in 2005 in converted former derelict farm buildings on the Chatsworth estate, with the aid of a DEFRA Rural Enterprise Scheme grant with support from trustees of Chatsworth Settlement. The brewery supplies local outlets and wholesalers for national distribution. Seasonal beer: Noggin Filler (ABV 5%, winter). Bottled beer: Gardner's Tap (ABV 5%, for Chatsworth Estate).

Swift Nick (OG 1037.5, ABV 3.8%) ◆
Traditional English session bitter with a slight fruit and hop aroma. Balanced flavours of malt and hops lead to a dry, bitter finish.

Dalesman (OG 1039, ABV 4%)

Bakewell Best Bitter (OG 1040.5, ABV 4.2%) ◆
Refreshing, copper-coloured bitter beer with little aroma. Initial sweetness leads to a complex but balanced hop and malt flavour. Bitterness is present throughout, ending in a dry, fruity finish and aftertaste.

Peakstones Rock

Peakstones Rock Brewery, Peakstones Farm, Cheadle Road, Alton, Stoke-on-Trent, Staffordshire, ST10 4DH
Tel 07891 350908
Email dfedwards@fwi.co.uk

David Edwards, a keen CAMRA member, started brewing in 2005 on a purpose-built, five-barrel plant on a dairy farm. Around 20-30 outlets are supplied. Seasonal beer: Black Hole (ABV 4.8%, winter).

Nemesis (ABV 3.8%) ◆
Pale brown with a liquorice aroma; roast but not burnt. Pleasing lingering bitter finish.

Oblivion (ABV 5.5%)

Peelwalls

Peelwalls Brewery, Peelwalls Farmhouse, Ayton, Eyemouth, Berwickshire, TD15 5RL
Tel (01890) 761357/781885
Email peelwallsbrewery@aol.com

The enterprise started as a winery in 2004 with beer production a year later. 2005 saw the move to newly renovated buildings on the same site, purpose-built for wine, cider and beer production. It has its own heating and water treatment plant to make full use of the water drawn from an underground spring. An on-site shop was due to open in late 2006. The cask beer range is available in bottle-conditioned form.

Golden Harvest (ABV 3.8%)

The Good Swallow (ABV 3.8%)

Eight Minute Link (ABV 4.2%)

Emperor (ABV 4.8%)

Pipe Major Stout (ABV 5%)

Old Aitoun IPA (ABV 5.2%)

Penlon Cottage

Penlon Cottage Brewery, Pencae, Llanarth, Ceredigion, SA47 0QN
Tel (01545) 580022

Email beer@penlon.biz
Website www.penlon.biz

Penlon Cottage Brewery started in 2004 and is located on a working smallholding in the Ceredigion coastal region of West Wales. Hops and malting barley are part of a programme of self-sufficiency, with grain, yeast and beer fed to pigs, sheep and chickens on the holding. Only bottle-conditioned beers were brewed at first but cask beers to local pubs were due to come on stream in summer 2006. Brewing is traditional and simple, using only malt and barley grains, whole hops, yeast and water, making all beers suitable for vegans. Seasonal beers: Autumn Harvest (ABV 3.2%, Sept-Nov), Shepherds Delight Christmas Ale (ABV 5.6%, Christmas). Bottle-conditioned beers: Lambs Gold Light Ale (ABV 3.2%), Tipsy Tup Pale Ale (ABV 3.8%), Stock Ram Stout (ABV 4.6%), Twin Ram IPA (ABV 4.8%), Ewes Frolic Lager (ABV 5.2%), Ramnesia Strong Ale (ABV 5.6%).

Phoenix

Phoenix Brewery, Green Lane, Heywood, Greater Manchester, OL10 2EP
Tel (01706) 627009
Fax (01706) 623235
Email tony@phoenixbrewery.fsnet.co.uk

⊜ A company established as Oak Brewery in 1982 at Ellesmere Port, it moved in 1991 to Heywood and changed its name in 1992 to Phoenix (after the original name of the brewery it occupies). It now supplies 400 to 500 free trade outlets mostly in North-west England as well as several national pubcos and suppliers. A vast range of seasonal beers is brewed; for details, contact the brewery via email.

Bantam (OG 1035, ABV 3.5%) ◆
Light brown beer with a fruity aroma. Balance of malt, citrus fruit and hop in taste. Hoppy, bitter finish.

Navvy (OG 1039, ABV 3.8%) ◻ ◆
Amber beer with a citrus fruit and malt nose. Good balance of citrus fruit, malt and hops with bitterness coming through in the aftertaste.

Best Bitter (OG 1039, ABV 3.9%)

Monkeytown Mild (OG 1039, ABV 3.9%)

Arizona (OG 1040, ABV 4.1%) ◻ ◆
Yellow in colour with a fruity and hoppy aroma. A refreshing beer with citrus, hop and good bitterness, and a shortish dry aftertaste.

Pale Moonlight (OG 1042, ABV 4.2%)

Black Bee (OG 1045, ABV 4.5%)

Old Oak Ale (OG 1045, ABV 4.5%) ◆
A well-balanced brown beer with a multitude of mellow fruit flavours. Malt and hops balance the strong fruitiness in the aroma and taste, and the finish is malty, fruity and dry.

White Monk (OG 1045, ABV 4.5%) ◻ ◆
Yellow beer with a citrus fruit aroma, plenty of fruit, hop and bitterness in the taste, and a hoppy bitter finish.

Thirsty Moon (OG 1046, ABV 4.6%) ◆
Tawny beer with a fresh citrus aroma. Hoppy, fruity and malty with a dry, hoppy finish.

West Coast IPA (OG 1046, ABV 4.6%)

Double Dagger (OG 1050, ABV 5%) ◆
A pale brown, malty brew, more pleasantly dry and light than its gravity would suggest. Moderately fruity throughout; a hoppy bitterness in the mouth balances the strong graininess.

Double Gold (OG 1050, ABV 5%)

Wobbly Bob (OG 1060, ABV 6%) ◆
A red/brown beer with a malty, fruity aroma. Strongly malty and fruity in flavour and quite hoppy, with the sweetness yielding to a dryness in the aftertaste.

Pictish

Pictish Brewing Co Ltd, Unit 9 Canalside Industrial Estate, Rochdale, Greater Manchester, OL16 5LB
Tel/fax (01706) 522227
Email mail@pictish-brewing.co.uk
Website www.pictish-brewing.co.uk

⊜ The brewery was established in 2000 by Richard Sutton, formerly senior brewer for the north with the Firkin Brewery group. The brewery supplies 60 free trade outlets in the North-west and West Yorkshire. Seasonal beers: Northern Dawn (ABV 4.3%, Jan-Feb), Claymore (ABV 4.5%, Feb-March), Dolmen (ABV 4%, March-April), Maelstrom (ABV 5%, April-May), Black Diamond (ABV 3.5%, May-June), Summer Solstice (ABV 4.7%, May-Aug), Ginger Ale (ABV 3.9%, June-July), Siren (ABV 4.1%, July-Aug), Corn Dolly (ABV 5%, Aug-Sept), Staddle Stone (ABV 4.5%, Sept-Oct), Aztec Gold (ABV 4.8%, November), Z-Rod (ABV 4.8%, Nov-Dec), Porter (ABV 4.4%, Nov-March), Winter Solstice (ABV 4.7%, Dec-Jan).

Brewers Gold (OG 1038, ABV 3.8%) ◆
Yellow in colour, with a hoppy, fruity nose. Soft maltiness and a strong hop/citrus flavour lead to a dry, bitter finish.

Celtic Warrior (OG 1042, ABV 4.2%) ◆
Tawny beer with malt and hops dominant in aroma and taste. Good bitter finish.

Alchemists Ale (OG 1043, ABV 4.3%)

For Crown Inn, Bacup

Crown IPA (OG 1050, ABV 5%)

Pilgrim SIBA

Pilgrim Ales, The Old Brewery, West Street, Reigate, Surrey, RH2 9BL
Tel (01737) 222651
Fax (01737) 225785
Email david@pilgrim.co.uk
Website www.pilgrim.co.uk

⊗ Set up by David Roberts in 1982 and based in Reigate since 1985, Pilgrim has gradually increased its capacity and its beers have won both local and national awards, although sales are mostly concentrated in the Surrey area (around 60 outlets). Seasonal beers: Autumnal (ABV 4.5%, Sept-Oct), Excalibur (ABV

4.5%, March-May).

Surrey Bitter (OG 1037, ABV 3.7%) ◆
Pineapple, grapefruit and spicy aromas in this well-balanced, quaffing beer. Initial biscuity maltiness with a hint of vanilla give way to a hoppy bitterness that becomes more pronounced in a refreshing, bitter-sweet finish.

Porter (OG 1040, ABV 4%) ◆
Black beer with a good balance of dark malts with hints of berry fruit. Roast character is present throughout to give a bitter-sweet finish.

Progress (OG 1040, ABV 4%) ◆
A well-rounded, tawny-coloured bitter. Predominantly sweet and malty, with an underlying fruitiness and a hint of toffee. The flavour is well balanced overall with a subdued bitterness. Little aroma and the aftertaste dissipates quickly.

Crusader (OG 1049, ABV 4.9%)

Talisman (OG 1049, ABV 5%) ◆
A strong ale with a tawny red colour. Little aroma but a sweet malty flavour, with a noticeable bitterness but no discernible hoppiness and somewhat lacking in aftertaste.

Pitfield

Pitfield Brewery, The Nurseries, London Road, Great Horkesley, Colchester, Essex, CO6 4AJ
Tel (0845) 833 1492
Email sales@pitfieldbeershop.co.uk
Website www.pitfieldbeershop.co.uk

⊗ After 24 years in Hoxton, London, both Pitfield Brewery and its sister business, the Beer Shop, left the capital in January 2006 on the expiry of their lease. Pitfield found a temporary home with Custom Beers in West Sussex where Andy Shore, Pitfield's brewer, continued to produce their ales while a new permanent home was found. In summer 2006, Pitfield moved to new premises in Essex with its own vineyard. The Beer Shop has now become a virtual retailer with a new delivery service. Bottle-conditioned beers: see website.

Original (ABV 3.7%)

Singhboulton/Pitfield Special (ABV 3.7%)
Brewed for the Singboulton organic pub in London.

Shoreditch Stout (OG 1040, ABV 4%) ◆
Chocolate and a raisin fruitiness on the nose lead to a fruity roast flavour and a sweetish finish with a little bitterness.

East Kent Goldings (ABV 4.2%) ◆
A dry, yellow beer with bitter notes throughout and a faint hint of honey on the palate.

Eco Warrior (ABV 4.5%) ◆
This pale golden beer has a hoppy citrus aroma and flavour that is balanced by some sweetness and a bitterness that builds on drinking.

Hoxton Best Bitter (ABV 4.8%) ◆
A well-balanced beer with a malty sweetness that lingers in the bitter, dry aftertaste.

Black Eagle (ABV 5%) ◆
A light-drinking strong old ale, black with red hues, with a lasting roast malt flavour and a malty, dryish aftertaste.

Plassey SIBA

Plassey Brewery, Eyton, Wrexham, LL13 0SP
Tel (01978) 781111 / (07050) 327127
Fax (01978) 781219
Email plassey@globalnet.co.uk
Website www.plasseybrewery.co.uk
Shop open office hours
Tours by arrangement

The brewery was founded in 1985 on the 250-acre Plassey Estate, which also incorporates a touring caravan park, craft centres, a golf course, three licensed outlets for Plassey's ales, and a brewery shop. Some 30 free trade outlets also take the beer. Seasonal beers: Ruddy Rudolph (ABV 4.5%, Christmas), Lager (ABV 4%). Bottle-conditioned beer: Fusilier.

Welsh Border Exhibition Ale
(OG 1036, ABV 3.5%)

Bitter (OG 1041, ABV 4%) ◆
Full-bodied and distinctive best bitter. Good balance of hops and fruit flavours with a lasting dry bitter aftertaste.

Offa's Dyke Ale (OG 1043, ABV 4.3%) ◆
Sweetish and fruity refreshing best bitter with caramel undertones. Some bitterness in the finish.

Owain Glyndwrs Ale (OG 1043, ABV 4.3%)

Fusilier (OG 1046, ABV 4.5%) ▯

Cwrw Tudno (OG 1048, ABV 5%) ▯ ◆
A mellow, sweetish premium beer with classic Plassey flavours of fruit and hops.

Dragon's Breath (OG 1060, ABV 6%)
A fruity, strong bitter, smooth and quite sweet, though not cloying, with an intense, fruity aroma. A dangerously drinkable winter warmer.

Poachers

Poachers Brewery, 439 Newark Road, North Hykeham, Lincolnshire, LN6 9SP
Tel (01522) 807404 / 07956 229638
Email george@poachersbrewery.co.uk
Website www.poachersbrewery.co.uk
Tours by arrangement

Poachers Brewery opened in 2001 as a five-barrel plant in an industrial unit and has moved to a converted barn at the rear of brewer George Batterbee's house, using a 2.5-barrel kit. All the beers brewed are also available in bottle-conditioned form.

Trembling Rabbit (OG 1034, ABV 3.4%)
Rich, dark mild with a smooth malty flavour and a slightly bitter finish.

Shy Talk (OG 1037, ABV 3.7%)
Clean-tasting session beer, pale gold in colour; slightly bitter finish, dry hopped.

Poachers Pride (OG 1040, ABV 4%)
Amber bitter brewed using Cascade hops that produce a fine flavour and aroma that lingers.

Poachers Trail (OG 1042, ABV 4.2%) ♦
A flowery hop-nosed, mid-brown beer with a well-balanced but bitter taste that stays with the malt, becoming more apparent in the drying finish.

Billy Boy (OG 1044, ABV 4.4%)
A mid-brown beer hopped with Fuggles and Mount Hood.

Poachers Dick (OG 1045, ABV 4.5%)
Ruby-red bitter, smooth fruity flavour balanced by the bitterness of Goldings hops.

Black Crow Stout (OG 1045, ABV 4.5%)
Dry stout with burnt toffee and caramel flavour.

Jock's Trap (OG 1050, ABV 5%)
A strong, pale brown bitter; hoppy and well-balanced with a slightly dry fruit finish.

Trout Tickler (OG 1055, ABV 5.5%)
Ruby bitter with intense flavour and character, sweet undertones with a hint of chocolate.

Porter

Porter Brewing Co Ltd, Rossendale Brewery, Griffin Inn, 84 Hud Rake, Haslingden, Lancashire, BB4 5AF
Tel/Fax (01706) 214021
Email dporter@porterbrewing.fsnet.co.uk
Website www.pbcbreweryinstallations.com
Tours by arrangement

⊗ The company has two tied pubs and all sell a minimum of five cask beers. The beers are suitable for vegans. Seasonal beers: Timmy's Ginger Beer (ABV 4.2%, March/Aug), Stout (ABV 5.5%, Sept-Oct), Sleighed (ABV 6.5%, Dec-Jan), Celebration Ale (ABV 7.1%, July-Aug).

Dark Mild (OG 1033, ABV 3.3%) ♦
A plain, well-made dark mild with a faint fruity aroma and a hint of roast in the finish.

Floral Dance (OG 1035, ABV 3.6%)
Pale and fruity.

Bitter (OG 1037, ABV 3.8%) ♦
Unusually dark for a standard bitter, this beer has a dry and assertively bitter character that develops in the finish.

Railway Sleeper (OG 1040, ABV 4.2%)
Intensely bitter and hoppy.

Rossendale Ale (OG 1041, ABV 4.2%) ♦
A malty aroma leads to a complex, malt-dominated flavour supported by a dry, increasingly bitter finish.

Porter (OG 1050, ABV 5%)
A rich beer with a slightly sweet, malty start, counter-balanced with sharp bitterness and a noticeable roast barley dominance.

Sunshine (OG 1050, ABV 5.3%) 🏆 ♦
A hoppy and bitter golden beer with a citrus character. The lingering finish is dry and spicy.

Port Mahon SIBA

🍺 Port Mahon Brewery, c/o Cask and Cutler, 1 Henry Street, Sheffield, South Yorkshire, S3 7EQ
Tel (0114) 2492295

⊗ Brewing started in 2001 in a purpose-built brewery behind the Cask and Cutler, using a one-barrel plant. There are plans to install a four-barrel kit. The brewery produces one-off beers mainly for festivals and special occasions. It is planned to brew a permanent house bitter and a range of beer styles that will alternate with the other guest ales in the pub. The beer range is yet to be established.

Potbelly

Potbelly Brewery Ltd, 25-31 Durban Road, Kettering, Northamptonshire, NN16 0JA
Tel (01536) 410818 / 07834 867825
Email toni@potbelly-brewery.co.uk
Website www.potbelly-brewery.co.uk
Tours by arrangement

Potbelly started brewing in 2005 on a 10-barrel purpose-built plant behind a leather fashion accessories factory. It has won a Gold award at Peterborough beer festival with Inner Daze and Gold at Nottingham beer festival with Beijing Black. Sawyers in Kettering acts as a brewery tap and some 100 other outlets in the area are supplied.

Aisling (ABV 4%)

Beijing Black (ABV 4.4%)

Inner Daze (ABV 4.6%)

Redwing (ABV 4.8%)

Sunny Daze (ABV 5.5%)

Potton SIBA

Potton Brewery Co Ltd, 10 Shannon Place, Potton, Sandy, Bedfordshire, SG19 2SP
Tel (01767) 261042
Fax (01767) 631693
Email info@potton-brewery.co.uk
Website www.potton-brewery.co.uk
Shop 8.30am-5pm
Tours by arrangement

⊗ Set up by Clive Towner and Bob Hearson in 1998, both former managers at Greene King's now closed Biggleswade Brewery, they resumed brewing in Potton for the first time since 1922. They expanded from 20 barrels a week to 50 in 2004. Some 150 outlets are supplied. Seasonal beers: Bunny Hops (ABV 4.1%, March-April), No-Ale (ABV 4.8%, Nov-Dec). Bottle-conditioned beers: Butlers Ale (ABV 4.3%); for the National Trust, Wimpole Hall, Shambles Bitter.

Shannon IPA (OG 1035, ABV 3.6%)
A well-balanced session bitter with good bitterness and fruity late-hop character. SIBA Eastern Region class winner 2003.

Gold (OG 1040, ABV 4.1%)
Golden-coloured, refreshing beer with a spicy/citrus late-hop character.

Village Bike (OG 1042, ABV 4.3%) 🍺
Classic English premium bitter, amber in colour, heavily late-hopped. CAMRA Bedfordshire champion beer 2003.

Shambles Bitter (OG 1043, ABV 4.3%)
A robust pale and heavily hopped beer with a subtle dry hop character imparted by Styrian Goldings.

Pride of Potton (OG 1057, ABV 6%) ♦

Impressive, robust amber ale with a malty aroma, malt and ripe fruit in the mouth, and a fading sweetness.

Princetown SIBA

Princetown Breweries Ltd, The Brewery, Station Road, Princetown, Dartmoor, Devon, PL20 6QX
Tel (01822) 890789
Fax (01822) 890798
Email info@jailale.com
Website www.jailale.com
Tours by arrangement

⊗ The highest brewery in England at 1,400 feet above sea level moved into a new purpose-built building in 2005 with equipment manufactured in Germany. The capacity is now 150 barrels a week with scope for further expansion. Established in 1994 by a former Gibbs Mew and Hop Back brewer, local demand has allowed the brewery to expand production of its cask beers. Bottle-conditioned beer: Jail Ale.

Dartmoor IPA (OG 1039, ABV 4%) ◆
There is a flowery hop aroma and taste with a bitter aftertaste to this full-bodied, amber-coloured beer.

Jail Ale (OG 1047, ABV 4.8%) ◆
Hops and fruit predominate in the flavour of this mid-brown beer, which has a slightly sweet aftertaste.

Purity*

Purity Brewing Co Ltd, The Brewery, Upper Spernall Farm, Spernal Lane, Great Alne, Warwickshire, B49 6JF
Tel (01789) 488007
Fax (01789) 488666
Email sales@puritybrewing.com
Website www.puritybrewing.com
Shop Mon-Fri 9am-5pm; Sat 10am-1pm
Tours by arrangement

The brewery is based in converted farm buildings in countryside in the heart of Warwickshire. The plant was installed in 2005 and the beers were officially launched in January 2006.

Pure Gold (OG 1039.5, ABV 3.8%)

Pure UBU (OG 1044.8, ABV 4.5%)

Purple Moose SIBA

Bragdy Mws Piws Cyf/Purple Moose Brewery Ltd, Madoc Street, Porthmadog, Gwynedd, LL49 9DB
Tel/Fax (01766) 515571
Email beer@purplemoose.co.uk
Website www.purplemoose.co.uk
Shop Mon-Fri 9am-5pm
Tours by arrangement

A 10-barrel plant opened in 2005 by Lawrence Washington in a former saw mill and farmers' warehouse in the coastal town of Porthmadog, famous for the Ffestiniog Railway and the adjoining harbour. The names of the beers reflect local history and geography. The brewery now supplies around 70 outlets. Seasonal beers: X-Mws Llawen/Merry X-Moose (ABV 5%). All beers are also available in bottle-conditioned form.

Cwrw Madog/Madog's Ale (OG 1037, ABV 3.7%) ◆
Full-bodied session bitter. Malty nose and an initial nutty flavour but bitterness dominates. Well balanced and refreshing with a dry roastiness on the taste and a good dry finish.

Cwrw Glaslyn/Glaslyn Ale (OG 1041, ABV 4.2%) ◆
Refreshing light and malty amber-coloured ale. Plenty of hop in the aroma and taste. Good smooth mouthfeel leading to a slightly chewy finish.

Ochr Tywyll y Mws/Dark Side of the Moose (OG 1045, ABV 4.6%) ◆
Dark, mellow strong mild with good roast and Bramling Cross hop flavours.

Quartz

Quartz Brewing Ltd, Archers, Alrewas Road, Kings Bromley, Staffordshire, DE13 7HW
Tel (01543) 473965
Email info@quartzbrewing.co.uk
Website www.quartzbrewing.co.uk
Tours by arrangement

The five-barrel brewery was set up in 2005 by Scott Barnett, a brewing engineer previously with Bass, and his wife Julia, a master brewer from Carsberg-Tetley. Brewing started in the second half of the year. Around 20 outlets are supplied.

Blonde (ABV 3.8%) ◆
Light amber bitter. Slightly sweet and fruity with a pleasant bitter finish.

Crystal (ABV 4.2%) ◆
Copper with a caramel aroma with a touch of hops. Fruity tasting with a hedgerow bitterness and short hoppy finish.

Quay

See Dorset

Rainbow

⌂ Rainbow Inn & Brewery, 73 Birmingham Road, Allesley Village, Coventry, West Midlands, CV5 9GT
Tel (02476) 402888
Tours by arrangement

⊛ Rainbow was launched in 1994 by the then landlord, Terry Rotherham. The current landlord, Jon Grote, took over the pub in 2001. Output is through the pub although firkins and polypins can be ordered for home use or beer festivals.

Piddlebrook (OG 1038, ABV 3.8%)

Ramsbury

Ramsbury Estates Ltd, Priory Farm, Axford, Marlborough, Wiltshire, SN8 2HA
Tel (01672) 520647/541407
Fax (01672) 520753
Email dgolding@ramsburyestates.com
Tours by arrangement

Ramsbury started brewing in 2004. Ramsbury Estates is a farming company covering approximately 5,500 acres of the Marlborough Downs in Wiltshire. It grows malting barley for the brewing industry including Optic, which the brewery also uses. Additional fermenters have been purchased and contract bottling taken on. Some 90 outlets are supplied.

Bitter (OG 1036, ABV 3.6%)
Amber-coloured beer using traditional malted Optic spring barley from the farm. Goldings hops are used to give a smooth, delicate aroma and flavour.

Kennet Valley (OG 1040, ABV 4.1%)
A light amber, hoppy bitter with a distinctive Goldings aroma, using a blend of malted spring barley and a small amount of crystal malt. A complex beer with a long, dry finish.

Flintknapper (OG 1041, ABV 4.2%)
A blend of Optic and chocolate malts give a rich amber colour and malty taste. Goldings hops produce a smooth hoppy character.

Gold (OG 1043, ABV 4.5%)
A rich golden-coloured beer produced by blending Optic malt, crystal malt and a small amount of torrefied wheat. Goldings and Styrian Goldings hops give a light hoppy aroma and taste.

Ramsgate SIBA

Ramsgate Brewery Ltd, 1 Hornets Close, Pyson's Road Industrial Estate, Broadstairs, Kent, CT10 2YD
Tel/Fax (01843) 580037
Email info@ramsgatebrewery.co.uk
Website ramsgatebrewery.co.uk
Tours by arrangement

⊗ Ramsgate was established in 2002 by Lois and Eddie Gadd in a derelict restaurant on the sea front. The beers are brewed with Kentish hops and English malts only. In 2006 the brewery moved to its current location, allowing for increased capacity and bottling. Seasonal beers: Doctor Sunshine's Special Friendly English Wheat Ale (ABV 4.2% summer), Gadds Dogbolter Winter Porter (ABV 5.6%, winter), Gadds Old Pig Ramsgate Brown Ale (ABV 4.8%, autumn).

Gadds No. 7 Ramsgate Bitter (OG 1037, ABV 3.8%)
Satisfying session bitter using local Fuggles hops.

Gadds Dark Mild (OG 1041, ABV 4%)
Traditional easy-drinking mild, packed with roast and chocolate flavours.

Gadds No. 5 Ramsgate Best (OG 1043, ABV 4.4%)
Complex, easy-drinking best bitter using East Kent Goldings and Fuggles hops.

Gadds No. 3 Ramsgate Pale Ale (OG 1048, ABV 5%)
A light and refreshing, full-strength pale ale, brewed with locally-grown East Kent Goldings hops.

Randalls SIBA

RW Randall Ltd, Vauxlaurens Brewery, St Julian's Avenue, St Peter Port, Guernsey, GY1 3JG
Tel (01481) 720134
Fax (01481) 713233
Shop Mon-Fri 9.30am-5pm; Sat 9.30am-1pm
Tours by arrangement

⊗ Randalls was in danger of closing early in 2006 when members of the family wanted to sell up. But in March the company was bought by a consortium, the Guernsey Pub Company, that includes local publicans and Ian Rogers, former managing director of Wycwhood Brewery in Oxfordshire. Ben Randall of the Randall family will remain with the company. Seventeen pubs are owned, 10 serving cask-conditioned beer, and 18 further outlets are supplied. A new site is being sought.

Cynful (OG 1035, ABV 3.5%)

Island Gold (ABV 4.2%)

Wycked (OG 1038, ABV 4.2%)

Envy (OG 1048, ABV 4.8%)

Guilty (OG 1034, ABV 5.2%)

For the Cock & Bull, Guernsey

Sipping Bull (OG 1042, ABV 4.2%)

RCH SIBA

RCH Brewery, West Hewish, Weston-Super-Mare, Somerset, BS24 6RR
Tel (01934) 834447
Fax (01934) 834167
Email rchbrew@aol.com
Website www.rchbrewery.com
Shop Mon-Fri 8.30am-4pm

⊗ The brewery was originally installed in the early 1980s behind the Royal Clarence Hotel at Burnham-on-Sea. Since 1993 brewing takes place on a commercial basis in a former cider mill at West Hewish. A new 30-barrel plant was installed in 2000. RCH supplies 75 outlets and the award-winning beers are available nationwide through its own wholesaling company, which also distributes beers from other small independent breweries. Seasonal beers: see website. Bottle-conditioned beers: Pitchfork ⊡, Old Slug Porter, Double Header, Firebox, Ale Mary (ABV 6%).

Hewish IPA (OG 1036, ABV 3.6%) ⊡ ◆
Light, hoppy bitter with some malt and fruit, though slightly less fruit in the finish. Floral citrus hop aroma; pale/brown amber colour.

PG Steam (OG 1039, ABV 3.9%) ⊡ ◆
Amber-coloured, medium-bodied with a floral hop aroma with some fruit. Hoppy and bitter to taste, with some malt, fruit and subtle sweetness. The finish is similar.

Pitchfork (OG 1043, ABV 4.3%) ⊡ ◆

Floral citrus hop aroma with pale malt. Yellow/gold in colour, hops predominate in a full-bodied taste, which is slightly sweet. Long finish – a class act.

Old Slug Porter (OG 1046, ABV 4.5%)
Chocolate, coffee, roast malt and hops with lots of body and dark fruits. A complex, rich beer, dark brown in colour.

East Street Cream (OG 1050, ABV 5%)
A superb premium ale, pale brown in colour, it tastes malty with chocolate hints, hoppy, fruity and bitter-sweet. All flavours vie for dominance in what is a notable and well-crafted ale.

Double Header (OG 1053, ABV 5.3%)
Light brown, full-bodied strong bitter. Beautifully balanced flavours of malt, hops and tropical fruits are followed by a long, bitter-sweet finish. Very refreshing and easy drinking for its strength.

Firebox (OG 1060, ABV 6%)
An aroma and taste of citrus hops and pale crystal malt are followed by a strong, complex, full-bodied, mid-brown beer with a well-balanced flavour of malt and hops.

Rebellion SIBA

Rebellion Beer Co, Marlow Brewery, Bencombe Farm, Marlow Bottom, Buckinghamshire, SL7 3LT
Tel (01628) 476594
Fax (01628) 476617
Email info@rebellionbeer.co.uk
Website www.rebellionbeer.co.uk
Shop Mon-Fri 8am-5.30pm; Sat 9am-5pm
Tours by arrangement (1st Tuesday of the month – £8)

⊗ Established in 1993, Rebellion has bridged the void left when Wethereds ceased brewing in 1998 at Marlow. A steady growth in fortunes led to larger premises being sought and, following relocation in 1999, the brewery has gone from strength to strength and maximised output. Rebellion's nearby Three Horseshoes pub is the brewery tap. Rebellion Mild is exclusive to this pub. Around 200 other outlets are supplied. Seasonal beers: Overdraft (ABV 4.3%, Jan-Feb), Blonde (ABV 4.3%, summer), Roasted Nuts (ABV 4.6%, winter), Zebedee (ABV 4.7%, spring), Red (ABV 4.7%, autumn). Bottle-conditioned beer: White (ABV 4.5%).

Mild (OG 1035, ABV 3.5%)

IPA (OG 1039, ABV 3.7%)
Copper-coloured bitter, sweet and malty, with resinous and red apple flavours. Caramel and fruit decline to leave a dry, bitter and malty finish.

Smuggler (OG 1042, ABV 4.1%)
A red-brown beer, well-bodied and bitter with an uncompromisingly dry, bitter finish.

Mutiny (OG 1046, ABV 4.5%)
Tawny in colour, this full-bodied best bitter is predominantly fruity and moderately bitter with crystal malt continuing to a dry finish.

Rectory SIBA

Rectory Ales Ltd, Streat Hill Farm, Streat Hill, Streat, Hassocks, East Sussex, BN6 8RP
Tel (01273) 890570
Email rectoryales@hotmail.com
Tours by arrangement (Easter to Sept)

⊗ Rectory was founded in 1995 by the Rector of Plumpton, the Rev Godfrey Broster, to generate funds for the maintenance of his three parish churches. 107 parishioners are shareholders. The brewing capacity is now 20 barrels a week. All outlets are supplied from the brewery. Seasonal beer: Christmas Cheer (ABV 3.8%, December).

Rector's Bitter (OG 1040, ABV 4%)

Rector's Best Bitter (OG 1043, ABV 4.3%)

Rector's Strong Ale (OG 1050, ABV 5%)

Redburn

Redburn Brewery, Redburn, Bardon Mill, Northumberland, NE47 7EA
Tel/Fax (01434) 344656
Email redburnbrewery@btinternet.com

Redburn Brewery in the heart of Hadrian's wall country supplies beer to a number of local free houses. The brewery, set up in 2003, brews regular ales as well as four seasonal beers. There are usually five or six bottle-conditioned beers at any one time available locally.

Ebrius Bitter (ABV 3.7%)

1555 (ABV 4.1%)

Haltwhistle Pride (ABV 4.2%)

Fortis Stout (ABV 4.3%)

Summus Best Bitter (ABV 4.4%)

Bishop Ridley Ale (ABV 4.8%)

Optimus (ABV 5%)

Red Rock*

Red Rock Brewery Ltd, Higher Humber Farm, Bishopsteignton, Devon, TQ14 9TD
Tel (01626) 778535
Email john@redrockbrewery.co.uk
Website www.redrockbrewery.co.uk

Red Rock was set up by two teachers, one of whom was a keen home-brewer. The four-barrel plant, which went into production in the summer of 2006, has a maximum output of 12 barrels a week. The brewery is housed in a renovated barn on a working farm. The water for brewing comes from a spring on the site while some of the barley the farmer grows is malted at Tucker's in Newton Abbot. All the beers are named after local landmarks and planned bottled beers will be bottle conditioned.

Back Beach (ABV 3.8%)

Red Rock (ABV 4.2%)

Red Rose SIBA

Red Rose Brewery, Unit 4 Stanley Court, Heys Lane Industrial Estate, Great Harwood, Lancashire, BB6 7UR
Tel (01254) 877373/883541
Fax (01254) 877375
Email beer@redrosebrewery.co.uk
Website www.redrosebrewery.co.uk
Tours by arrangement

⊛ Red Rose Brewery was launched in 2002 by microelectronic design engineer Peter Booth to supply the Royal Hotel, Great Harwood. A 2.5-barrel capacity plant was installed to replace the pilot 0.75 kit and to allow for sales to other pubs. Demand for the ales outstripped capacity and the brewery expanded to four fermenting vessels, bringing production up to more than 10 barrels a week. Further expansion in to a new unit in 2005 has allowed production to grow further and as a result the beers are now available nationwide. Red Rose uses English malted barley and English hops. No extracts or adjuncts are used. Seasonal beers: Blackpool Belle Golden Age Ale (ABV 4%), Pissed Over Pendle Halloween Ale (ABV 4.4%), 34th Street Miracle Beer (ABV 4.9%), 65 Special Celebration Ale (ABV 3.9%). Special beers are available throughout the year.

Bowley Best (ABV 3.7%)
Darkish northern bitter. Malty, yet sharp with hoppy citrus finish.

Quaffing Ale (ABV 3.8%)

Treacle Miners Tipple (ABV 3.9%)

Felix (ABV 4.2%)
Dry, pale and remarkably hoppy with a keen nose, yet rounded and smooth with a lingering finish.

Old Ben (ABV 4.3%)
Pale, clean-tasting, crisp beer with a strong hop presence and no sweetness.

Lancashire & Yorkshire Aleway/Steaming (ABV 4.5%)
Copper-coloured, strong beer. Initially sweet and malty, though with a good hop aroma. Full and fruity.

Older Empire (ABV 5.5%)

Care Taker of History (ABV 6%) ◆
A dark, strong ale with a roast malt aroma. The taste is complex, rich and warming. Well-balanced and drinkable.

Red Shoot

Red Shoot Inn Brewery, Toms Lane, Linwood, Ringwood, Hampshire, BH24 3QT
Tel (01425) 475792

The brewery, owned by Wadworth, was commissioned in 1998 with Forest Gold as the first brew. Tom's Tipple was introduced in 1998 as a winter brew and is now a permanent brand. Red Shoot would like to expand but the size of plant (2.5 barrels) makes this difficult, though some occasional beers are produced. The pub was refurbished in 2006.

Forest Gold (ABV 3.8%)

Tom's Tipple (ABV 4.8%)

Red Squirrel

Red Squirrel Brewery, 14b Mimram Road, Hertford, Hertfordshire, SG14 1NN
Tel (01992) 501100
Fax (01992) 500660
Email gary@redsquirrelbrewery.co.uk
Website www.redsquirrelbrewery.co.uk
Tours by arrangement

⊛ Red Squirrel started brewing in 2004 with a 10-barrel plant. There are plans to expand the brewery and product range, including adding bottled beers and speciality American-style beers. More than 70 outlets are supplied. Seasonal beer: Old Age (ABV 5%).

Dark Ruby Mild (OG 1036, ABV 3.7%)

Conservation Bitter (OG 1040, ABV 4.1%)

Gold (OG 1041, ABV 4.2%)

Irish Stout (OG 1044, ABV 4.5%)

Pilzen Bier (OG 1044, ABV 4.5%)
Lager.

Liquorice Stout (OG 1047, ABV 4.9%)

Michigan Ale (OG 1048, ABV 5%)

Reepham

Reepham Brewery, Unit 1 Collers Way, Reepham, Norwich, Norfolk, NR10 4SW
Tel (01603) 871091
Tours by arrangement

⊗ Reepham has completed 22 years of continuous brewing on the same premises. A beer in the style of Newcastle Brown Ale was introduced (Tyne Brown), to show support for the Tynesiders' brewery. S&P Best Bitter was launched in 2005 to celebrate Norwich's brewing heritage: the beer is named after Steward & Patteson, bought and closed by Watneys. Some 20 outlets are supplied. Bottle-conditioned beer: Rapier Pale Ale.

Granary Bitter (OG 1038, ABV 3.5%) ◆
A gold-coloured beer with a light hoppy aroma followed by a malty sweetish flavour with some smoke notes. A well-balanced beer with a long, moderately hoppy aftertaste.

S&P Best Bitter (OG 1038, ABV 3.7%)

Rapier Pale Ale (OG 1043, ABV 4.2%) ◆
Pale brown beer with a swirling citrus and malt nose. A complex mix of bitter hoppiness and lemon is bolstered by a smoky malt background. The long-lasting finish becomes refreshingly dry.

Velvet Sweet Stout (OG 1044, ABV 4.5%) ◆
There is a heavy roast influence in aroma and taste. A smoky malt feel to the taste produces an interesting combination that is both creamy and well-defined. Initial fruit and hop contributions indicate a subtle sweetness that soon fades to leave a growing dry bitterness.

Tyne Brown (OG 1046, ABV 4.6%)

St Agnes (OG 1047, ABV 4.8%) ◆
Fund-raising brew for a local church. Smooth and creamy with bananas to the fore in aroma and taste. Smoky malt overtones

subside as increasing bitterness dominates a gently receding finish.

Rhymney

Rhymney Brewery Ltd, Unit A2 Valleys Enterprise Centre, Pant Industrial Estate, Dowlais, Merthyr Tydfil, CF48 2SR
Tel (01685) 722253
Fax (01685) 723323
Email marc@rhymneybreweryltd.com
Website www.rhymneybreweryltd.com
Shop Sat 10am-2pm
Tours by arrangement

Rhymney first brewed in 2005. The 75-hl plant, sourced from Canada, is capable of producing both cask and keg beers. Around 220 outlets are supplied. Seasonal beer: Rhymney Christmas Special (ABV 4.1%).

1905 Centenary Ale (OG 1040, ABV 3.9%)

Bevans Bitter (OG 1043, ABV 4.2%)

Premier Lager (OG 1046, ABV 4.5%)

Bitter (OG 1044, ABV 4.5%)

Ridgeway SIBA

Ridgeway Brewing, Beer Counter Ltd, South Stoke, Oxfordshire, RG8 0JW
Tel (01491) 873474
Email peter.scholey@beercounter.co.uk

Ridgeway was set up by ex-Brakspear head brewer Peter Scholey. It specialises in bottle-conditioned beers but equivalent cask beers are also available. At present Ridgeway beers are brewed by Peter using his own ingredients on a plant at Hepworth's of Horsham (qv) and occasionally elsewhere. All beers listed are available cask and bottle-conditioned. Six strong (ABV 6-9%) bottle-conditioned Christmas beers are produced annually, principally for export to the US and available in Britain from September onwards.

Ridgeway Bitter (OG 1040, ABV 4%)
Uses Challenger and the new Boadicea hop.

Ridgeway Organic Beer/ROB (OG 1043, ABV 4.3%)

Ridgeway Blue (OG 1049, ABV 5%)
Tesco Challenge winner 2006, exclusive to Tesco for 2006.

Ivanhoe (OG 1050, ABV 5.2%)
Scandinavian designed red ale.

Ridgeway IPA (OG 1055, ABV 5.5%)

For Coniston Brewing

Coniston Bluebird (ABV 4.2%)

Coniston Old Man (ABV 4.8%)

Coniston XB (ABV 4.4%)

Ridleys

See Wolverhampton & Dudley in New Nationals section

Ring O' Bells SIBA

Ring O' Bells Brewery Ltd, Pennygillam Way, Pennygillam Industrial Estate, Launceston, Cornwall, PL15 7ED
Tel/Fax (01566) 777787
Email enquiries@ringobellsbrewery.co.uk
Website www.ringobellsbrewery.co.uk

⊗ Ring O'Bells started trading in the 13th century as a cider farm-cum-alehouse for the stonemasons of St Torney Church, North Hill. It closed in 1918 and after 79 years of neglect new owners set about restoring the old ale house and rebuilding the cider press and vat. Intensive research with the help of micro-biologists re-cultured the original yeast strain that was trapped within the walls of the old vat. The culture is now used to ferment today's ales, some 600 years later. The success of the beers when launched in 1999 led to the brewery moving to new premises in Launceston in 2001. Some 300 outlets are supplied. Monthly seasonal ales are also available. Bottle-conditioned beer: Scuttled.

Porkers Pride (OG 1036, ABV 3.8%)
A light, refreshing ale that is well-balanced with a hoppy, malty, clean, finish.

Celtic Blonde (OG 1038, ABV 4%)
A golden ale with hints of citrus and pine fortified with Cornish heather and gorse.

Grays Best Bitter (ABV 4%)

Grays Honey Pot (ABV 4%)

Wipeout (ABV 4%)
A golden-coloured wheat beer with a pronounced hoppy aroma and a clean, bitter finish.

Bodmin Boar (OG 1041.5, ABV 4.3%) ◆
Apple and aromatic nose, heavy and fruity in the mouth with a long bitter finish.

One & All (OG 1042, ABV 4.4%)
A light, clean ale with a good hoppy aroma and dry finish. Proceeds go to the Pirate Trust.

Grays Premium Ale (ABV 4.5%)

Dreckly (OG 1046, ABV 4.8%)
A warm, ruby-coloured, strong ale fortified with gorse and heather. Rich in malt with a spicy aroma and good malty aftertaste.

England's Glory (ABV 4.8%)

Grays Champion Ale (ABV 5.1%)

Tipsy Trotter (OG 1048.3, ABV 5.1%)
A strong, dark ale with a good malty taste, a wheaty aroma, clean finish and a pleasant bite.

Scuttled (ABV 5.5%)

Sozzled Swine (OG 1051.8, ABV 5.5%)
A rich, ruby-coloured strong ale with a good flowery aroma, well balanced with a malty aftertaste.

Ringwood IFBB SIBA

Ringwood Brewery Ltd, Christchurch Road, Ringwood, Hampshire, BH24 3AP
Tel (01425) 471177
Fax (01425) 480273
Email enq@ringwoodbrewery.co.uk
Website www.ringwoodbrewery.co.uk
Shop Mon-Fri 9.30am-5pm; Sat 9.30am-12pm

Tours by arrangement

⊗ Ringwood opened in 1978 as a tiny micro and moved in 1986 to the former Tunks Brewery site in the town. Some 650 outlets are supplied from the brewery and seven pubs are owned. A major new development in 2005/06 saw the addition of seven new conditioning tanks. The brewery also plans to instal a new 120-barrel fermenting vessel to allow for the increase in growth. Seasonal beers: Boondoggle (ABV 4%, summer), Bold Forester (ABV 4.2%, spring), Huffkin (ABV 4.4%, autumn), XXXX Porter (ABV 4.7%, winter). Bottle-conditioned beers: Bold Forester, Huffkin, Fortyniner, XXX Porter.

Best Bitter (OG 1038, ABV 3.8%) ◆
Easy-drinking, predominantly malty session beer. A malty aroma leads to a malty taste with some toffee and hops to balance an underlying sweetness. A short malty and bitter finish.

Fortyniner (OG 1049, ABV 4.9%) ◆
A mid-brown beer. A fruity aroma with some malt leads to a sweet but well-balanced taste with malt, fruit and citrus hop flavours all present. The finish is bitter-sweet with some fruit.

Old Thumper (OG 1055, ABV 5.6%) ◆
A powerful mid-brown beer. A fruity aroma preludes a sweet, malty taste with soft fruit and caramel, which is not cloying and leads to a surprisingly bitter bitter-sweet aftertaste, with malt and hops.

Riverhead

◊ Riverhead Brewery Ltd, 2 Peel Street, Marsden, Huddersfield, West Yorkshire, HD7 6BR
Tel (01484) 841270
Email info@riverheadbrewery.co.uk
Website www.riverheadbrewery.co.uk
Tours by arrangement

Riverhead is a brew-pub that opened in 1995 after conversion from an old grocery store. The seven beers are named after local reservoirs, with the height of the reservoir relating to the strength of the beer. Occasional specials such as Jazz Bitter (ABV 4%, for Marsden Jazz Festival), and Ruffled Feathers Bitter (ABV 4.2%, for Marsden Cuckoo Day) are brewed. The brewery also supplies three local outlets on an occasional basis. Black Moss Stout is suitable for vegans and vegetarians.

Sparth Mild (OG 1038, ABV 3.6%) ☐ ◆
A light-bodied, dry mild, with a dark ruby colour. Fruity aroma with roasted flavour and a dry finish.

Butterley Bitter (OG 1038, ABV 3.8%) ◆
A dry, amber-coloured, hoppy session beer.

Deer Hill Porter (OG 1040, ABV 4%)
A dark brown bitter with the characteristics of stout, but not as strong.

Cupwith Light Bitter (OG 1042, ABV 4.2%)
A very pale bitter with a distinctive bitter aftertaste.

Black Moss Stout (OG 1043, ABV 4.3%) ◆
Roast malt and fruit aromas arise from a lightly hopped dry stout with a chocolaty finish.

March Haigh (OG 1046, ABV 4.6%)
A smooth, rounded flavour is created by the complex selection of hops.

Redbrook Premium (OG 1055, ABV 5.5%) ◆
A rich and malty strong beer, with malt and fruit in the taste, and a sweet, fruity finish.

Riverside

Riverside Brewery, Unit 1 Church Lane, Wainfleet All Saints, Lincolnshire, PE24 4BY
Tel (01754) 881288
Website www.wainfleet.info/shops/brewery-riverside.htm

Riverside started brewing in 2003, almost across the road from Bateman's, using a five-barrel plant supplied by Rob Jones of Dark Star. Owner John Dixon had not previously brewed but he was assisted by his father Ken, who had been head brewer at several breweries, including Bateman's. Eight barrels a week are produced for local trade, with some 15-20 outlets supplied. Seasonal beer: Dixon's Good Swill (ABV 5.8%, Nov-Dec).

Dixon's Major Bitter (OG 1038, ABV 3.9%)

Dixon's Light Brigade (OG 1038, ABV 3.9%)

Dixon's Desert Rat (OG 1048, ABV 4.8%)

John Roberts

See Three Tuns

Robinson's IFBB

Frederic Robinson Ltd, Unicorn Brewery, Stockport, Cheshire, SK1 1JJ
Tel (0161) 480 6571
Fax (0161) 476 6011
Email brewery@frederic-robinson.co.uk
Website www.frederic-robinson.com
Tours by arrangement

⊗ Robinson's has been brewing since 1838 and the business is still owned and run by the family. Recent investment at the packaging centre and a greater demand for contract brewing means Robinson's look set for a busy future. It has an estate of more than 400 pubs. Wards Bitter (ABV 4%) is brewed under contract.

Hatters (OG 1032, ABV 3.3%) ◆
A light mild with a fruity aroma, and biscuity malt and a fresh fruitiness in the taste and finish. A darkened version is available in a handful of outlets and badged Dark Mild.

Old Stockport (OG 1034, ABV 3.5%) ◆
A beer with a refreshing taste of malt, hops and citrus fruit, a fruity aroma, and a short, dry finish.

Hartleys XB (OG 1040, ABV 4%) ◆
An overly sweet and malty bitter with a bitter citrus peel fruitiness and a hint of liquorice in the finish.

Cumbria Way (OG 1040, ABV 4.1%)
A pronounced malt aroma with rich fruit notes. Rounded malt and hops in the mouth, long dry finish with citrus fruit notes. Brewed for the Hartley's estate in Cumbria.

Unicorn (OG 1041, ABV 4.2%) ☐ ◆
Amber beer with a fruity aroma. Hoppy,

bitter and quite fruity to taste, with a bitter finish.

Double Hop (OG 1050, ABV 5%) ◆
Pale brown beer with malt and fruit on the nose. Full hoppy taste with malt and fruit, leading to a hoppy, bitter finish.

Old Tom (OG 1079, ABV 8.5%) ▣ ▢ ◆
A full-bodied, dark beer with malt, fruit and chocolate in the aroma. A delightfully complex range of flavours includes dark chocolate; full maltiness, port and fruits lead to a long, bitter-sweet aftertaste.

Rockingham SIBA

Rockingham Ales, c/o 25 Wansford Road, Elton, Cambridgeshire, PE8 6RZ
Tel (01832) 280722
Email brian@rockinghamales.co.uk
Website www.rockinghamales.co.uk

⊗ A part-time brewery established in 1997 that operates from a converted farm building near Blatherwycke, Northamptonshire (business address as above). The two-barrel plant produces a prolific range of beers and supplies half a dozen local outlets. The regular beers are brewed on a rota basis, with special beers brewed to order. Seasonal beers: Fineshade (ABV 3.8%, autumn), Sanity Clause (ABV 4.3%, December), Old Herbaceous (ABV 4.5%, winter).

Forest Gold (OG 1040, ABV 3.9%)
A hoppy blonde ale with citrus flavours. Well-balanced and clean finishing.

Hop Devil (OG 1040, ABV 3.9%)
Six hop varieties give this light amber ale a bitter start and spicy finish.

A1 Amber Ale (OG 1041, ABV 4%)
A hoppy session beer with fruit and blackcurrant undertones.

Saxon Cross (OG 1041, ABV 4.1%)
A golden-red ale with nut and coffee aromas. Citrus hop flavours predominate.

Fruits of the Forest (OG 1043, ABV 4.2%)
A multi-layered beer in which summer fruits and several spices compete with a big hop presence.

Dark Forest (OG 1050, ABV 5%)
A dark and complex beer, similar to a Belgian dubbel, with numerous malty/smoky flavours that give way to a fruity bitter finish.

Rodham's

Rodham's Brewery, 74 Albion Street, Otley, West Yorkshire, LS21 1BZ
Tel (01943) 464530

In 2005 Michael Rodham put 25 years of home-brewing to use by going commercial with a one-barrel plant in the cellar of his house. Plans are underway to increase capacity. All beers produced are malt-only, without sugars or cheaper cereals. Six outlets are supplied.

Bitter (OG 1033, ABV 3.5%)
Straw-coloured session beer with a sharp, citrus, hoppy taste, underlying malt and a dry, bitter finish.

Rubicon (OG 1039, ABV 4.1%)
Amber-coloured with a nutty, malt and light fruit taste. A dry, peppery and bitter aftertaste.

Old Albion (OG 1048, ABV 5%)
Ruby black premium beer with a complex mix of roasted malt, liquorice and tart fruit with a balancing bitterness.

Rooster's SIBA

Rooster's Brewing Co Ltd, Unit 3 Grimbald Park, Wetherby Road, Knaresborough, North Yorkshire, HG5 8LJ
Tel/Fax (01423) 865959
Email sean@roosters.co.uk
Website www.roosters.co.uk

⊜ Rooster's Brewery was opened in 1993 by Sean and Alison Franklin. Its sister company, Outlaw Brewery Co, started in 1996. In 2001 the brewery relocated to larger premises at Knaresborough. Production is close to 80 barrels a week. Under the Rooster's label, Sean and Alison make six regular beers while Outlaw produces experimental beers. They change materials or process or both to make a new beer every two months. Sean Franklin is a devotee of hops and uses many varieties, including North American, in his brews. 500 outlets are supplied. Occasional beers: Oyster Stout (ABV 4.7%, winter), Nector (ABV 5.2%, winter).

Special (OG 1038, ABV 3.9%) ▢ ◆
Yellow in colour, a full-bodied, floral bitter with fruit and hop notes being carried over in to the long aftertaste. Hops and bitterness tend to increase in the finish.

Leghorn (OG 1042, ABV 4.3%)
A pale-coloured bitter with fruity aromas and a long finish.

YPA (OG 1042, ABV 4.3%)
A pale-coloured beer with pronounced raspberry and flower aromas.

Yankee (OG 1042, ABV 4.3%) ◆
A straw-coloured beer with a delicate, fruity aroma leading to a well-balanced taste of malt and hops with a slight evidence of sweetness, followed by a refreshing, fruity/bitter finish.

Hooligan (OG 1042, ABV 4.3%) ◆
Pale and aromatic bitter, with a citrus fruit aroma with hints of tangerine. The palate has pronounced fruit and hops with a hint of sweetness. Bitterness and hops linger in the aftertaste, accompanied by a background of fruit flavours.

Cream (OG 1045, ABV 4.7%) ◆
A pale-coloured beer with a complex, floral bouquet leading to a well-balanced, refreshing taste. Fruit lasts throughout and into the aftertaste.

Rother Valley SIBA

Rother Valley Brewing Co, Gate Court Farm, Station Road, Northiam, East Sussex, TN31 6QT
Tel (01797) 253535
Fax (01797) 253550
Tours by arrangement

⊗ Rother Valley was established in Northiam

in 1993 with the brewhouse situated between hop fields and the oast house. Hops grown on the farm and from Sandhurst Hop Farm are used. Brewing is split between cask and an ever-increasing range of filtered bottled beers. Around 50 outlets are supplied. Seasonal beers: Summertime Blues (ABV 3.7%, summer), Copper Ale (ABV 4.1%), Holly Daze (ABV 4.2%, Christmas), Blues (ABV 5%, winter).

Smild (OG 1038, ABV 3.8%)

Level Best (OG 1040, ABV 4%)
Full-bodied tawny session bitter with a malt and fruit aroma, malty taste and a dry, hoppy finish.

Hoppers Ale (OG 1044, ABV 4.4%)

Boadicea (OG 1046, ABV 4.6%)

Rudgate SIBA

Rudgate Brewery Ltd, 2 Centre Park, Marston Moor Business Park, Tockwith, York, North Yorkshire, YO26 7QF
Tel/Fax (01423) 358382
Email sales@rudgate-beers.co.uk
Website www.rudgate-beers.co.uk

Rudgate Brewery was founded in 1992 and is located in an old armoury building on a disused World War II airfield. It has a 15-barrel plant and four open fermenting vessels, producing more than 40 barrels a week. Rudgate uses local maltsters and English hops. Around 300 outlets are supplied. Seasonal beers: Rudolphs Ruin (ABV 4.6%, Xmas), Crimble Ale (ABV 4.2%, Xmas). Other seasonal beers are produced on a monthly basis.

Viking (OG 1036, ABV 3.8%)
An initially warming and malty, full-bodied beer, with hops and fruit lingering into the aftertaste.

Battleaxe (OG 1040, ABV 4.2%)
A well-hopped bitter with slightly sweet initial taste and light bitterness. Complex fruit character gives a memorable aftertaste.

Ruby Mild (OG 1041, ABV 4.4%)
Nutty, rich ruby ale, stronger than usual for a mild.

Special (OG 1042, ABV 4.5%)

Well Blathered (OG 1046, ABV 5%)

Rugby

Rugby Brewing Co Ltd, Units 2-6 Upton Road, Rugby, Warwickshire, CV22 7DL
Tel (0845) 0091626
Website www.rugbybrewingco.co.uk

Rugby started brewing in 2005 and is owned by the Pig Pub Company. All the beer names are connected to the town or Rugby Union football. The brewery supplies beer to a number of local outlets in Warwickshire and Leicestershire and is a permanent fixture in the Pig Pub estate. Seasonal beer: Cement (ABV 6.8%, winter).

1823 (ABV 3.5%)
A chocolate mild.

Twickers (ABV 3.7%)
A traditional Yorkshire bitter.

Webb Ellis (ABV 3.8%)
A straw-coloured, hoppy beer.

Victorious (ABV 4.2%)
A reddish-coloured bitter.

No 8 (ABV 5%)
A strong ale.

Ryburn SIBA

Ryburn Brewery, 26 Wakefield Road, Sowerby Bridge, Halifax, West Yorkshire, HX6 2AZ
Tel (01422) 835413
Fax (01422) 836488
Email ryburnbrewery@talk21.com
Tours by arrangement

The brewery was established in 1989 at Mill House, Sowerby Bridge, but has since been relocated to the company's sole tied house, the Rams Head. Some business is done with the local free trade but the chief market for the brewery's products is via wholesalers, chiefly JD Wetherspoon.

Best Mild (OG 1033, ABV 3.3%)
A traditional northern-style mild with chocolate in evidence. Smooth, bitter aftertaste.

Best Bitter (OG 1038, ABV 3.8%)
Amber-coloured, fresh, fruity session bitter. Lightly flavoured with a bitter aftertaste.

Numpty Bitter (OG 1044, ABV 4.2%)
Pale brown beer with a sweeter, vinous flavour than Best Bitter.

Luddite (OG 1048, ABV 5%)
Intensely flavoured black, creamy stout. Well balanced with strong chocolate, caramel and liquorice flavours tempered by sweetness.

Stabbers (OG 1052, ABV 5.2%)
Pale brown, creamy, fruity, sweet and vinous bitter. Its drinkability belies its strength.

Saddleworth

Church Inn & Saddleworth Brewery, Church Lane, Uppermill, Oldham, Greater Manchester, OL3 6LW
Tel (01457) 820902/872415
Tours by arrangement

Saddleworth started brewing in 1997 in a brewhouse that had been closed for around 120 years. The first brew, Saddleworth More, sold for £1 per pint; it now sells at £1.20. Brewery and inn are set in a historic location at the top of a valley overlooking Saddleworth and next to St Chads Church, which dates from 1215. Seasonal beers: Ayrton's Ale (ABV 4.1%, April-May), Robyn's Bitter (ABV 4.6%, Nov-Dec), Christmas Carol (ABV 5%, Dec-Jan), Harvest Moon (ABV 4.1%, Aug-Sept), Bert Corner (ABV 4%, summer), Indian Z Pale Ale (ABV 4.1%, summer).

Clog Dancer (ABV 3.6%)

More (ABV 3.8%)

St George's Bitter (ABV 4%)

Honey Smacker (ABV 4.1%)

Hop Smacker (ABV 4.1%)
A golden, refreshing bitter, brewed with five different varieties of hops.

Shaftbender (ABV 5.4%)
A black porter/stout bitter.

Saffron*

Saffron Brewery, Unit 2 Pledgdon Hall Farm, Henham, Bishops Stortford, Hertfordshire, CM22 6BJ
Tel (01279) 850923
Fax (01279) 851922
Email tonyb@datatrustee.com
Website www.saffronbrewery.com
Tours by arrangement

Founded in 2005, Saffron is a traditional, independent full-mash brewery situated on Pledgdon Hall Farm near to the historic East Anglian town of Saffron Walden, famous for its malting industry in the 18th century. The five-barrel plant, designed and built on split-levels, started commercial production in spring 2006. A full range of cask, bottle-conditioned and bespoke beers will be available through local outlets and an online store. The range had not been finalised when the guide went to press.

St Austell IFBB SIBA

St Austell Brewery Co Ltd, 63 Trevarthian Road, St Austell, Cornwall, PL25 4BY
Tel (01726) 74444
Fax (01726) 68965
Email info@staustellbrewery.co.uk
Website www.staustellbrewery.co.uk
Shop Mon-Fri 9am-5pm
Tours by arrangement

St Austell Brewery celebrated 150 years of brewing in 2001. Founded by Walter Hicks in 1851, the company is still family owned and run, with Walter Hicks's great-great-grandson, James Staughton, at the helm as managing director since 2000. He leads a young team, with head brewer Roger Ryman, and there is a powerful commitment to cask beer. The beer range has been overhauled, with new branding and pump clips in pubs. Cask beer is available in all 160 licensed houses, as well as in the free trade throughout Cornwall, Devon and Somerset. An attractive visitor centre offers guided tours and souvenirs from the brewery. The brewery hosts its own Celtic Beer Festival late in the year (see website). Bottle-conditioned beers: Admiral's Ale (ABV 5%), Clouded Yellow (ABV 5%), Proper Job IPA (ABV 5.5%).

St Austell IPA (OG 1035, ABV 3.4%)
Copper/bronze in colour, the nose blossoms with fresh hops. The palate is clean and full bodied with a hint of toffee caramel. The finish is short and crisp.

Tinners Ale (OG 1038, ABV 3.7%) ◆
A deservedly popular, golden beer with an appetising malt aroma and a good balance of malt and hops in the flavour. Lasting finish.

Dartmoor Best (OG 1039, ABV 3.9%)
A delicately hopped, golden bitter. Originally brewed at the now-closed Ferguson Brewery in Plymouth, DBB was brewed by St Austell for Carlsberg, but is now owned by the brewery and is spearheading the company's increased presence in Devon.

Black Prince (OG 1041, ABV 4%) ◆
Little aroma, but a strong, malty character. A caramel-sweetish flavour is followed by a good, lingering aftertaste that is sweet but with a fruity dryness.

Tribute (OG 1043, ABV 4.2%) ◆
A pale brown best bitter. The aroma is of fruity Oregon hops and malt with a trace of tangy ester. Refreshing and crisp taste with a balance of malt and fruity hops. The finish is malty and moderately dry with a hint of sweetness towards the end.

Hicks Special Draught/HSD (OG 1052, ABV 5%) ◆
An aromatic, fruity, hoppy bitter that is initially sweet and has an aftertaste of pronounced bitterness, but whose flavour is fully rounded. A good premium beer.

St George's

St George's Brewing Co Ltd, Bush Lane, Callow End, Worcester, WR2 4TF
Tel/Fax (01905) 831316
Email andrewsankey@tiscali.co.uk
Tours by arrangement

⊗ The brewery was established in 1998 and is now owned by Brian McCluskie and managed by Andrew Sankey. They have a strong commitment to traditional brewing. The five-barrel plant produces a range of monthly specials, as well as bespoke beers on request. St George's supplies some 100 outlets and uses wholesalers for wider distribution.

Maiden's Saviour (ABV 3.9%)
Light and refreshing, brewed using traditional English barley and hops.

Paragon Steam (ABV 4%)
Styled on California steam beer, this amber thirst-quencher features a marked maize and hop character.

War Drum (ABV 4.1%) ◆
A sharp, bitter taste with a hint of sweetness. Afterwards the memory is of bitter hops.

WPA/Worcerstershire Premium Ale (ABV 4.3%) ◆
Straw-coloured and medium-bodied with a gentle fruity nose and a combination of bitterness with malt on the palate and finish.

St Peter's SIBA EAB

St Peter's Brewery Co. Ltd, St Peter's Hall, St Peter South Elmham, Bungay, Suffolk, NR35 1NQ
Tel (01986) 782322
Fax (01986) 782505
Email beers@stpetersbrewery.co.uk
Website www.stpetersbrewery.co.uk
Shop Mon-Fri 9am-5pm; Sat-Sun 11am-5pm
Tours by arrangement

⊗ St Peter's was launched in 1996 by marketing expert John Murphy. The brewery concentrates in the main on bottled beer (80% of capacity) but has a rapidly increasing cask market. Brewery developments include an in-house rotary bottling line and an increase in brewing capacity from 100 barrels a week to 175 barrels. Two pubs are owned and 75 outlets are supplied. Seasonal beers: Ruby Red (ABV 4.3%), Wheat Beer (ABV 4.7%), Summer Ale (ABV 6.5%), Winter Ale (ABV 6.5%), Spiced Ale (ABV 6.5%), Cream Stout (ABV 6.5%).

Mild (OG 1037, ABV 3.7%)
Sweetness balanced by bitter chocolate malt

to produce a rare but much sought after traditional mild.

Best Bitter (OG 1038, ABV 3.7%) ◈
A complex but well-balanced hoppy brew. A gentle hop nose introduces a singular hoppiness with supporting malt notes and underlying bitterness. Other flavours fade to leave a long, dry, hoppy finish.

Organic Best (OG 1041, ABV 4.1%)
Hop and vanilla aroma. Hoppy and astringent first taste remains constant. Initial fruit and malt notes soon fade to leave a persistent dry astringency.

Organic Ale (OG 1045, ABV 4.5%)
Soil Association standard, light malted barley from Scotland, with organic Target hops create a refreshing ale with a delicate character.

Golden Ale (OG 1047, ABV 4.7%) ◈
Amber-coloured, full-bodied, robust ale. A strong hop bouquet leads to a mix of malt and hops combined with a dry, fruity hoppiness. The malt quickly subsides, leaving creamy bitterness.

Grapefruit Beer (OG 1047, ABV 4.7%)
Wheat Beer is the base for this refreshing, zesty/pithy beer.

Lemon and Ginger Spiced Ale (OG 1047, ABV 4.7%)
A traditional English ale with a light citrus aroma and a delicate ginger aftertaste.

Salamander

Salamander Brewing Co Ltd, 22 Harry Street, Bradford, West Yorkshire, BD4 9PH
Tel (01274) 652323
Fax (01274) 680101
Email salamanderbrewing@fsmail.net
Website www.salamanderbrewing.com
Tours by arrangement

⊗ Salamander first brewed in 2000 in a former pork pie factory. It is mainly composed of ex-dairy plant with some equipment from Mitchells of Lancaster. Further expansion during 2004 took the brewery to 40-barrel capacity. There are direct deliveries to more widespread areas such as Cumbria, East Yorkshire and Lancashire in addition to the established trade of about 100 outlets throughout Lancashire, Manchester, North Yorkshire and Derbyshire.

Mudpuppy (OG 1042, ABV 4.2%) ◈
A well-balanced, copper-coloured best bitter with a fruity, hoppy nose and a bitter finish.

Golden Salamander (OG 1045, ABV 4.5%) ◈
Citrus hops characterise the aroma and taste of this golden premium bitter, which has malt undertones throughout. The aftertaste is dry, hoppy and bitter.

Stout (OG 1045, ABV 4.5%) ◻ ◈
Rich roast malts dominate the smooth coffee and chocolate flavour. Nicely balanced. A dry, roast, bitter finish develops over time.

Salopian SIBA

Salopian Brewing Co Ltd, 67 Mytton Oak Road, Shrewsbury, Shropshire, SY3 8UQ
Tel (01743) 248414
Tours by arrangement

⊛ The brewery was opened in 1995 in an old dairy on the outskirts of Shrewsbury. Owner Wilf Nelson has developed cask sales locally and nationally through wholesalers. Capacity has increased to 72 barrels. The brewery has acquired a brewery tap, the Star at Market Drayton. More than 100 outlets are supplied.

Shropshire Gold (OG 1037, ABV 3.8%)

Icon (OG 1041, ABV 4.2%)

Heaven Sent (OG 1044, ABV 4.5%)

Lemon Dream (OG 1043.5, ABV 4.5%)

Golden Thread (OG 1048, ABV 5%)

Saltaire*

Saltaire Brewery Limited, Dockfield Road, Shipley, West Yorkshire, BD17 7AR
Tel (01274) 594959
Fax (01274) 595010
Email info@saltairebrewery.co.uk
Website www.saltairebrewery.co.uk
Tours by arrangement

Launched in February 2006, Saltaire Brewery is a 20-barrel brewery situated in an impressive Victorian industrial building that formerly generated electricity to the local tram system. A mezzanine bar within the brewery provides visitors with views of the whole brewhouse equipped with specially-commissioned vessels, built by Moeschle, a leading German manufacturer. Saltaire plans a range of bottled beers and the full range will be available through direct deliveries and wholesalers.

Bitter (OG 1036, ABV 3.8%)

Golden Ale (OG 1040.7, ABV 4.2%)

Special Bitter (OG 1050, ABV 5.2%)

Sawbridgeworth

Sawbridgeworth Brewery, 81 London Road, Sawbridgeworth, Hertfordshire, CM21 9JJ
Tel (01279) 722313
Email the.gate.pub@dial.pipex.com
Website www.the-gate-pub.co.uk
Tours by arrangement

⊗ The brewery was set up in 2000 by Tom and Gary Barnett with equipment from the Alford Arms, Frithsden, at the back of the Gate pub. One pub is owned. Tom is a former professional footballer whose clubs included Crystal Palace. Special or one-off brews are occasionally brewed.

Selhurst Park Flyer (ABV 3.7%)

Is It Yourself (ABV 4.2%)

Stout (ABV 4.3%)

Brooklands Express (ABV 4.6%)

Piledriver (ABV 5.3%)

Scattor Rock

Scattor Rock Brewery Ltd, Unit 5 Gidley's Meadow, Christow, Exeter, Devon, EX6 7QB
Tel (01647) 252120
Email inquiries@scattorrockbrewery.com
Website www.scattorrockbrewery.com
Tours by arrangement

⊗ The brewery was set up in 1998 on the edge of Dartmoor National Park and is named after a local landmark. The brewery has expanded its business and now supplies some 300 outlets on a regular basis. There is a monthly rotation of seasonal brews, with two or three available in addition to the regular beers at any one time. Point of sale from the brewery is planned, with polypins for home delivery.

Scatty Bitter (OG 1040, ABV 3.8%)

Teign Valley Tipple (OG 1042, ABV 4%)
A well-balanced, tawny-coloured beer with a hoppy aroma.

Skylark (OG 1043, ABV 4.2%)
A refreshing, light brown session ale.

Devonian (OG 1045, ABV 4.5%)
A strong, fruity, light-coloured ale.

Golden Valley (OG 1046, ABV 4.6%)
A golden refreshing ale.

Valley Stomper (OG 1051, ABV 5%)
Light brown and deceptively drinkable.

Selby

Selby (Middlebrough) Brewery Ltd, 131 Millgate, Selby, North Yorkshire, YO8 3LL
Tel (01757) 702826

Not currently brewing but there are plans to restart.

Severn Vale*

Severn Vale Brewing Co, Woodend Lane, Cam, Dursley, Gloucestershire, GL11 5HS
Tel (01453) 547550
Email severnbrew@gmail.com
Website www.severnvalebrewing.co.uk
Shop Mon-Fri 10am-4pm; Sat 10am-12pm
Tours by arrangement

Severn Vale started brewing in 2005 in a redundant milking parlour using a new five-barrel plant designed and installed by Dave Porter from Lancashire. The brewer, Steve McDonald, had previous brewing experience at Wickwar Brewing Co. Some 50 outlets are supplied direct.

Vale Ale (OG 1041, ABV 4%)
Traditional bitter using four different hop varieties to flavour a quaffable session ale.

Dance (OG 1046, ABV 4.5%)
Light and refreshing, straw-coloured best bitter.

Monumentale (OG 1047, ABV 4.6%)
Designed as a porter but not dissimilar to a strong mild. Dark and warming with plenty of hop aroma and flavourf.

Shakespeares

Shakespeares Brewery Ltd, 9 Smallbrook Business Centre, Bidford-on-Avon, Warwickshire, B50 4JE
Tel (0845) 838 1564
Email info@shakesbrew.co.uk
Website www.shakesbrew.co.uk

Shakespeares started brewing on a 2.5-barrel plant in 2005 and almost immediately won a gold medal for Tempest at the SIBA Nottingham beer festival. The beers are currently sold in local free houses and at local farmers' markets. There were plans to start bottling the beers in late 2006 and the company hopes to achieve organic certification in the near future. Seasonal beers: You're Bard (ABV 4.2%, March-May), Twelfth Night (ABV 5%, Nov-Jan).

Noble Fool (OG 1040, ABV 3.9%)
Light, fruity and aromatic.

Taming of the Brew (OG 1043, ABV 4.3%)

The Scottish Ale (OG 1046, ABV 4.6%)
Malty, bold, traditional Scottish beer.

The Tempest (OG 1055, ABV 5.5%)
Dark, hoppy, robust porter.

Shardlow

Shardlow Brewing Co Ltd, The Old Brewery Stables, British Waterways Yard, Cavendish Bridge, Shardlow, Leicestershire, DE72 2HL
Tel (01332) 799188
Tours by arrangement

⊗ On a site associated with brewing since 1819, Shardlow delivers to outlets throughout the East Midlands. It deals with other craft brewers and as a result its beers are sold in East Anglia, the West Midlands, Yorkshire, Cumbria and Wales. Reverend Eaton's Ale is named after a scion of the Eaton brewing family, Rector of Shardlow for 40 years. The brewery tap is the Blue Bell Inn at Melbourne, Derbyshire, where four cask ales including a mild are regularly available, together with other guests. Seasonal beers are produced, including strong winter beers up to ABV 7%. Bottle-conditioned beers: Special Bitter, Golden Hop, Narrow Boat, Reverend Eaton's Ale, Five Bells, Whistle Stop.

Chancellors Revenge (OG 1036, ABV 3.6%)
A light-coloured, refreshing, full-flavoured and well-hopped session bitter.

Cavendish Dark (OG 1037, ABV 3.7%)

Special Bitter (OG 1039, ABV 3.9%)
A well-balanced, amber-coloured, quaffable bitter.

Golden Hop (OG 1041, ABV 4.1%)

Narrowboat (OG 1043, ABV 4.3%)

A pale amber bitter, with a short, crisp hoppy aftertaste.

Reverend Eaton's Ale (OG 1045, ABV 4.5%)
A smooth, medium-strong bitter, full of malt and hop flavours with a sweet aftertaste.

Five Bells (OG 1050, ABV 5.2%)

Whistle Stop (OG 1050, ABV 5.2%)
Maris Otter pale malt and two hops produce this smooth and surprisingly strong pale beer.

Sharp's SIBA

Sharp's Brewery Ltd, Pityme Business Centre, Rock, Wadebridge, Cornwall, PL27 6NU
Tel (01208) 862121
Fax (01208) 863727
Email enquiries@sharpsbrewery.co.uk
Website www.sharpsbrewery.co.uk
Shop 9am-5pm weekdays
Tours by arrangement for groups of 5-30

⊗ Sharp's Brewery was founded in 1994 by Bill Sharp. Within 10 years the brewery had grown from producing 1,500 barrels annually to selling 25,000. Sharp's has no pubs and delivers beer to more than 1,000 outlets across the south of England. All beer is produced at the brewery in Rock and is delivered via temperature controlled depots in Cornwall, Bristol and Reading. 2007 will see more expansion of the Rock brewery to facilitate a 25% increase in fermentation and conditioning capacity.

Cornish Coaster (OG 1035.2, ABV 3.6%) ◆
A smooth, easy-drinking beer, golden in colour, with a fresh hop aroma and dry malt and hops in the mouth. The finish starts malty but becomes dry and hoppy.

Cornish Jack (OG 1037, ABV 3.8%)
Light candied fruit dominates the aroma, underpinned with fresh hop notes. The flavour is a delicate balance of light sweetness, fruity notes and fresh spicy hops. Subtle bitterness and dry fruit notes linger in the finish.

Doom Bar Bitter (OG 1038.5, ABV 4%) ◆
A tawny beer with little aroma but a smooth and moderately fruity and malty taste, it can be quite bitter, masking other flavours. The finish is long but pleasantly bitter.

Eden Pure Ale (OG 1042, ABV 4.4%)
Hops dominate the aroma complemented by light fruit esters. In the mouth hops are again the centrepiece with a dry bitterness and a hint of malty sweetness. The finish is dry and hoppy.

Own (OG 1042.5, ABV 4.4%) ◆
A deep golden brown beer with a delicate hops and malt aroma, and dry malt and hops in the mouth. Like the other beers, its finish starts malty but turns dry and hoppy.

Atlantic IPA (OG 1045, ABV 4.8%)
Lightly sweet and fruity. The finish is sweet at first then becomes dry and lingering.

Nadelik Lowen (OG 1046, ABV 4.8%)
An aroma of spicy, almost piny hops and candy floss with toffee notes.

Special (OG 1048.5, ABV 5.2%) ◆
Deep golden brown with a fresh hop aroma. Dry malt and hops in the mouth; the finish is malty but becomes dry and hoppy.

Shaws

Shaws Brewery, The Old Stables, Park Road, Dukinfield, Greater Manchester, SK16 5LX
Tel (0161) 330 5471
Fax (0161) 343 1879
Email windfab@aol.com

The brewery is housed in the stables of William Shaws Brewery, established in 1856 and closed by John Smiths in 1941. Brewing restarted in 2002 with a five-barrel plant, designed and commissioned by brewers Neil Hay and Phillip Windsor. Beer is supplied to more than 30 local free trade outlets and beer festivals. Monthly guest beers are produced.

Best Bitter (OG 1038, ABV 4%)

Golden Globe (OG 1040, ABV 4.3%)

IPA (OG 1044, ABV 4.8%)

Shepherd Neame IFBB

Shepherd Neame Ltd, 17 Court Street, Faversham, Kent, ME13 7AX
Tel (01795) 532206
Fax (01795) 538907
Email company@shepherdneame.co.uk
Website www.shepherdneame.co.uk
Shop Mon-Fri 11am-3pm
Tours by arrangement

⊗ Kent's major independent brewery is believed to be the oldest continuous brewer in the country (since 1698), but records show brewing began on the site as far back as the 12th century. The same water source is still used today and 1914 teak Russian mash tuns are still operational. A visitor centre, which is being refurbished in 2006, is housed in a restored medieval hall. In 2004/5 Shepherd Neame invested £3.1 million in the brewery, boosting production to more than 200,000 barrels a year. The company has 370 tied houses in the South-east, nearly all selling cask ale. More than 2,000 other outlets are also supplied. All Shepherd Neame ales use locally sourced ingredients. The cask beers are made with Kentish hops, local malted barley and water from the brewery's own artesian well. Seasonal beers: Early Bird (ABV 4.3-4.5%, spring), Goldings (ABV 4.3-4.7%, summer), Whitstable Bay (ABV 4.1%, summer), Late Red (ABV 4.5%, autumn), Original Porter (ABV 4.8%, winter). Bottle-conditioned beer: 1698 (ABV 6.5%).

Master Brew Bitter (OG 1032, ABV 3.7%) ◆
A distinctive bitter, mid-brown in colour, with a hoppy aroma. Well-balanced, with a nicely aggressive bitter taste from its hops, it leaves a hoppy/bitter finish, tinged with sweetness.

Kent's Best Invicta Ale (OG 1036, ABV 4.1%)

Spitfire Premium Ale (OG 1039, ABV 4.5%)
A commemorative Battle of Britain brew for the RAF Benevolent Fund's appeal, now the brewery's flagship ale.

Bishops Finger (OG 1046, ABV 5%)
A cask-conditioned version of a famous bottled beer.

Sherborne*

⚲ Sherborne Brewery Ltd, 16 Old Yarn Mills, Westbury, Sherborne, Dorset, DT9 3RQ
Tel (01935) 815444
Email stephen@walshg82.freeserve.co.uk
Website www.sherbornebrewery.co.uk

Sherborne Brewery started in late 2005. At present only one beer is brewed for its own pub. The brewery plans to upgrade from the current 2.5-barrel plant to a five-barrels one when it supplies other outlets.

257 (OG 1039, ABV 3.9%)

Sherwood Forest

See Alcazar

Shoes SIBA

⚲ Shoes Brewery, Three Horseshoes Inn, Norton Canon, Hereford, HR4 7BH
Tel/Fax (01544) 318375
Tours by arrangement

Landlord Frank Goodwin was a keen home brewer who decided in 1994 to brew on a commercial basis for his pub. The beers are brewed from malt extract, stored in casks and dispensed under a blanket of mixed gas. Each September Canon Bitter and Norton Ale are brewed with green hops. Bottle-conditioned beer: Canon Bitter, Norton Ale, Farriers Ale.

Norton Ale (OG 1038, ABV 3.6%)

Canon Bitter (OG 1040, ABV 4.1%)

Peploe's Tipple (OG 1060, ABV 6%)

Farriers Ale (OG 1114, ABV 15%)

Shugborough

Shugborough Brewery, Shugborough Estate, Milford, Stafford, ST17 0XB
Tel (01782) 823447
Fax (01782) 812349
Tours by arrangement

Brewing in the original brewhouse at Shugborough, former home of the Earls of Lichfield, recommenced in 1990 but a lack of expertise led to the brewery being a static museum piece until Titanic Brewery of Stoke-on-Trent (qv) began helping in 1996. Since then, the brewery has produced many one-off brews under Titanic's guidance. Plans are now being prepared to brew more regularly with Keith Bott of Titanic as head brewer. Ten outlets are supplied.

Miladys Fancy (OG 1048, ABV 4.6%)

Coachmans Tipple (OG 1049, ABV 4.7%)

Gardeners Retreat (OG 1049, ABV 4.7%)

Farmers Half (OG 1049, ABV 4.8%)

Butlers Revenge (OG 1053, ABV 4.9%)

Lordships Own (OG 1054, ABV 5%)

Sidecar*

Sidecar Brewery, c/o The Golcar Brewery, Swallow Lane, Golcar, Huddersfield, West Yorkshire, HD7 4HT
Tel 07814 568473

The brewery was launched in 2005 by Andrew Moorhouse, former brewer at the Rat & Ratchet brew-pub. The Sidecar Brewery shares the plant at the Golcar Brewery when not in use. The beers are named after types of motorcyle sidecars. Beers are supplied to local free houses and CAMRA beer festivals. Recipes are different to Golcar beers and are pale golden bitters.

Formula II (ABV 3.8%)

Spyder (ABV 4%)

Golden Spyder (ABV 4.4%)

Busmar (ABV 4.8%)

Six Bells SIBA

⚲ Six Bells Brewery, Church Street, Bishop's Castle, Shropshire, SY9 5AA
Tel (01588) 638930
Fax (01588) 630132
Website www.bishops-castle.co.uk/SixBells/brewery.htm
Tours by arrangement

⊗ Neville Richards – 'Big Nev' – started brewing in 1997 with a five-barrel plant and two fermenters. Alterations in 1999 included two more fermenters, a new grain store and mashing equipment. He supplies a number of customers both within the county and over the border in Wales. Seasonal beers: Old Recumbent (ABV 5.2%, Oct-spring), Spring Forward (ABV 4.6%, March-May), Seven Bells (ABV 5.5%, Christmas), Festival Pale (ABV 5.2%, June-July — for town's annual beer festival).

Big Nev's (OG 1037, ABV 3.8%)
A pale, fairly hoppy bitter.

Roo Brew (OG 1038, ABV 3.8%)
Brewed exclusively for the Kangaroo Inn, Aston on Clun, to the publican's recipe. Copper-coloured, hoppy and heavily late hopped with Goldings.

Goldings (OG 1040, ABV 4.2%)
Made entirely with Goldings hops; moderately hoppy with a distinctive aroma.

Cloud Nine (OG 1042, ABV 4.2%)
Pale amber-colour with a slight citrus finish.

Duck & Dive (OG 1044, ABV 4.6%)
Pale and hoppy.

Brew 101 (OG 1048, ABV 4.8%)
A dark, fruity beer.

Skinner's SIBA

Skinner's Brewing Co Ltd, Riverside, Newham Road, Truro, Cornwall, TR1 2DP
Tel (01872) 271885
Fax (01872) 271886
Email info@skinnersbrewery.com
Website www.skinnersbrewery.com
Shop Mon-Sat 10am-5pm
Tours by arrangement

⊗ Skinner's brewery was founded in by Steve and Sarah Skinner in 1997.The brewery moved to bigger premises in 2003 and now employs 25 people. A brewery shop opened in 2003 and a visitor centre and brewery tours were added in 2005. The brewery has enjoyed success, winning numerous awards at both CAMRA and SIBA festivals with different beers. Seasonal beers: Christmas Fairy (ABV 3.9%), Pennycomequick (ABV 4.5%), Davey Jones Knocker (ABV 5%), Skilliwidden (ABV 5.1%), Jingle Knocker (ABV 5.5%), Green Hop (ABV 4.2%), Hunny Bunny (ABV 4.5%).

Spriggan Ale (OG 1038, ABV 3.8%) ◆
A light golden, hoppy bitter. Well-balanced with a smooth bitter finish.

Betty Stogs (OG 1040, ABV 4%) ▢ ◆
Pleasant session beer with well-balanced hop and fruit in the taste, and a lasting, bitter finish.

Heligan Honey (OG 1040, ABV 4%)
A slightly sweet amber bitter, brewed with West Country malt and Heligan Garden honey.

Keel Over (OG 1041, ABV 4.2%)
A classic Cornish bitter, amber in colour, beautifully balanced with a smooth finish.

Cornish Knocker Ale (OG 1044, ABV 4.5%) ◆
Refreshing, golden beer full of life with hops all the way through. Flowery and fruity hops in the mouth and malt undertones, with a clean and lasting malty, bitter-sweet finish.

Figgy's Brew (OG 1044, ABV 4.5%) ◆
A classic, dark, premium-strength bitter. Full-flavoured with a smooth finish.

Cornish Blonde (OG 1048, ABV 5%)
A combination of wheat malt and English and American hops makes this light-coloured wheat beer deceptively easy to drink.

Slater's SIBA

Slater's Brewery, St Albans Road, Stafford, Staffordshire, ST16 3DR
Tel (01785) 850300
Fax (01785) 851452
Email information@thegeorgeinn.freeserve.co.uk
Website www.thegeorgeinn.freeserve.co.uk
Tours by arrangement

The brewery was opened in 1995 and in 2006 moved to new, larger premises. It has won numerous awards from CAMRA and currently supplies 600 outlets direct throughout the country. One pub is owned, the George at Eccleshall, which is also the brewery tap. Occasional beer: Slater's Monkey Magic Mild (ABV 3.4%). Seasonal beers are available.

Bitter (OG 1036, ABV 3.6%) ◆
Golden bitter with a hop and malt aroma. Bitterness develops to a long, pleasant astringency.

Original (OG 1040, ABV 4%) ▢ ◆
Amber looks with a creamy head; great caramel aroma, hops and fruit tastes, and a long, bitter finish.

Top Totty (OG 1040, ABV 4%) ▢ ◆
Hoppy aroma with tangerine notes. Marmalade fruits and generous hops provide a strong, bitter finish.

Premium (OG 1044, ABV 4.4%) ▢ ◆
Pale brown with a caramel, malt and hop aroma. Complex hop and fruit with hints of roast develop into a bitter finish with a malty background.

Shining Knight (OG 1045, ABV 4.5%) ◆
No dominant flavours but hops and fruit combine in the bitter finish. A good session beer for its strength.

Supreme (OG 1047, ABV 4.7%) ▢ ◆
Copper-coloured bitter with a fresh fruity and hoppy aroma; sweet start and a dry, bitter finish.

Slaughterhouse SIBA

Slaughterhouse Brewery Ltd, Bridge Street, Warwick, Warwickshire, CV34 5PD
Tel/Fax (01926) 490986
Email enquiries@slaughterhousebrewery.com
Website www.slaughterhousebrewery.com
Tours by arrangement

Production began in 2003 in an old slaughterhouse. The four-barrel plant is the original Church End equipment. Some 30 outlets are supplied direct. Seasonal beers: Summer Daze (AVB 3.9%), Hogwort Special (ABV 4.2%), Stout Snout (ABV 4.4%), Black & Tan (ABV 4.5%), Wild Boar (ABV 5.2%), Anniversary Ale (ABV 5%).

Saddleback Best Bitter (OG 1038, ABV 3.8%)
Amber-coloured session bitter with a distinctive Challenger hop flavour.

Hog Rider (OG 1039, ABV 4%)
A pale, refreshing bitter, brewed using Maris Otter malt, Goldings and Progress hops.

Hog Mix Special (OG 1043, ABV 4.3%)
A light brown bitter, created by blending Hog Rider and Hog Goblin.

Hog Goblin (OG 1045, ABV 4.6%)
A well-balanced, mid-brown premium bitter.

For the Waterman, Hatton

Arkwright's Special Bitter (ABV 3.8%)

Smiles

See Highgate

Samuel Smith

Samuel Smith Old Brewery (Tadcaster), High Street, Tadcaster, North Yorkshire, LS24 9SB

Tel (01937) 832225
Fax (01937) 834673
Tours by arrangement

⊜ Although related to the nearby John Smith's, this fiercely independent, family-owned company is radically different. Tradition, quality and value are important, resulting in traditional brewing without adjuncts, with real ale supplied in wooden casks. Sadly, nitro-keg beer has crept in, especially in London. A fine range of bottled beers is produced, though they are not bottle conditioned. A filtered draught wheat beer is a recent addition. Some 200 pubs are owned.

Old Brewery Bitter/OBB (OG 1040, ABV 4%) ◆
Malt dominates the aroma, with an initial burst of malt, hops and fruit in the taste, which is sustained in the aftertaste.

Snowdonia SIBA

Snowdonia Brewery, Snowdonia Parc Brewpub & Campsite, Waunfawr, Caernarfon, Gwynedd, LL55 4AQ
Tel (01286) 650409
Email info@snowdonia-park.co.uk
Website www.snowdonia-park.co.uk

Snowdonia started brewing in 1998 in a two-barrel brewhouse. The brewing is now carried out by the new co-owner, Carmen Pierce. The beer is brewed solely for the Snowdonia Park pub and campsite.

Station Bitter (OG 1040, ABV 4%)

Snowdonia Gold (OG 1050, ABV 5%)

Welsh Highland Bitter (OG 1048, ABV 5%)

Somerset (Electric)

See Taunton Vale

South Hams SIBA

South Hams Brewery Ltd, Stokeley Barton, Stokenham, Kingsbridge, Devon, TQ7 2SE
Tel (01548) 581151
Fax (01548) 581010
Email info@southhamsbrewery.co.uk
Website www.southhamsbrewery.co.uk
Tours by arrangement

⊗ The brewery, formerly Sutton Brewing Co, moved to its present site in 2003, with a 10-barrel plant and plenty of room to expand. It supplies more than 60 outlets in Plymouth and south Devon. Wholesalers are used to distribute to other areas. Two pubs are owned. Seasonal beers: Wild Blonde (ABV 4.4%), Hopnosis (ABV 4.5%), Porter (ABV 5%), Knickadroppa Glory (ABV 5%). Bottle-conditioned beer: Porter.

Devon Pride (OG 1039, ABV 3.8%)

XSB (OG 1043, ABV 4.2%) ◆
Amber nectar with a fruity nose and a bitter finish.

Sutton Comfort (OG 1045, ABV 4.5%) ◆
Hoppy-tasting, mid-brown beer with a bitter hop finish underscored by malt and fruit.

Eddystone (OG 1050, ABV 4.8%)

Pandamonium (OG 1050, ABV 4.8%)

Southport

Southport Brewery, Unit 3 Enterprise Business Park, Russell Road, Southport, Merseyside, PR9 7RF
Tel 07748 387652
Email southportbrewery@fsmail.net

The Southport brewery opened in 2004 as a 2.5-barrel plant and supplies around 30 pubs in the North-west. It also supplies the free trade via Boggart Brewery. The owner, Paul Bardsley, is working flat out and intends to install a five-barrel plant to cope with demand. Seasonal beers: Old Shrimper (ABV 5.5%, Nov-Feb), Tower Mild (ABV 3.7%, May-Sept).

Sandgrounder Bitter (OG 1039.5, ABV 3.8%)
Pale, hoppy session bitter.

Bothy Beer (ABV 3.9%) ◆
Creamy, gold-coloured bitter. Well balanced, malty and refreshing with a hint of sweetness and moderate hop coming through on the flavour and aftertaste.

Carousel (OG 1041.5, ABV 4%)
A refreshing, floral, hoppy best bitter.

Natterjack (OG 1043.5, ABV 4.3%)
A premium bitter with fruit notes and a hint of coffee.

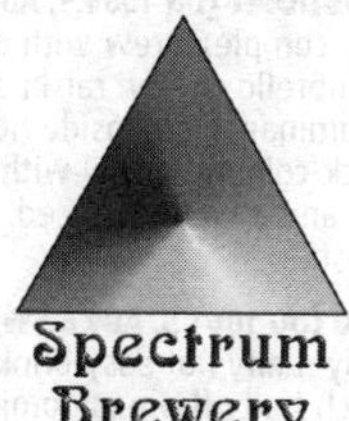

Spectrum SIBA EAB

Spectrum Brewery, c/o 23 Briton Way, Wymondham, Norfolk, NR18 0TT
Tel 07949 254383
Email info@spectrumbrewery.co.uk
Website www.spectrumbrewery.co.uk

⊗ After escaping from the IT industry, proprietor and founder Andy Mitchell gained experience working for a number of East Anglian brewers, as well as gaining an MSc in brewing and distilling, before establishing Spectrum Brewery in 2002. It's the only East Anglian brewery to brew exclusively from organic malt and hops. The brewery shares plant and premises with Blue Moon Brewery. Seasonal beers: Spring Promise (ABV 4.5%, Jan-Feb), Autumn Beer (ABV 4.5%, Sept-Oct – names and formulations vary). All dark beers produced (Dark Fantastic, Black Buffle, Old Stoatwobbler) are suitable for vegans.

Light Fantastic (OG 1035.5, ABV 3.7%) ◆
A sulphurous nose introduces this jaunty, refreshing bitter. The initial hoppy bitterness continues to a dry grapefruit finish that slowly becomes more astringent. Yellow hued with a coarse grainy feel.

Dark Fantastic (OG 1041, ABV 3.8%)
A very dark red, malty mild.

Bezants (OG 1038, ABV 4%)
A well-hopped, clean-tasting bitter. Although some maltiness can be detected in both the aroma and taste, it is hops that dominate. A residual bitterness adds to a long aftertaste that ends in a lingering dryness.

42 (OG 1039.5, ABV 4.2%)
An interesting mix of flavours. Blackcurrant fruitiness vies for dominance with a strong malty base. Undercurrents of hops, caramel and bitterness give a woody feel to this pale brown brew.

Black Buffle (OG 1047, ABV 4.5%)
A dark brown brooding stout. Roast and malt are the dominant characteristics, which, allied to a rich chocolate background, produce a dry traditional beer. Sustained ending with liquorice hints.

XXXX (OG 1045, ABV 4.6%)
A deep copper strong bitter, first brewed for the proprietor's 40th birthday.

Wizzard (OG 1047.5, ABV 4.9%)
Malt combines with a sultana fruitiness to produce a warming, full-flavoured ale. Copper coloured with a fruity aroma, the richness of flavour continues to a sustained, uplifting finish.

Old Stoatwobbler (OG 1064.5, ABV 6%)
Wonderfully complex brew with dark chocolate, morello cherry, raisin and banana vying for dominance alongside hops and malt. A black-coloured brew with a solid fruity nose, and a well-balanced, smooth but soft finish.

Trip Hazard (OG 1061.5, ABV 6.5%)
Exceptionally malty but easy-drinking for its strength. Rich fruity flavours dominate throughout, date and sultana to the fore. A growing bitterness in the finish.

Solstice Blinder (OG 1079, ABV 8.5%)
Strong IPA. Brewed twice a year, dry-hopped and left to mature (unfined) for at least three months before release in time for the solstices.

Spinning Dog SIBA

Spinning Dog Brewery, 88 St Owen Street, Hereford, Herefordshire, HR1 2QD
Tel (01432) 274998
Tel/Fax (01432) 342125
Email jfkenyon@aol.com
Website www.spinningdogbrewery.co.uk
Tours by arrangement

The brewery was built in a room of the Victory in 2000 by Jim Kenyon, following the purchase of the pub. Initially only serving the pub, it has steadily grown from a four-barrel to a 10-barrel plant. In 2005 the brewery commissioned its own bottling plant, capable of producing 80 cases a day. It now supplies some 300 other outlets as well as selling bottle-conditioned beer via the internet. Seasonal beers: Mutleys Mongrel (ABV 3.9%), Harvest Moon (ABV 4.5%), Santa Paws (ABV 5.2%). Bottle-conditioned beers: Hereford Organic Bitter, Organic Oatmeal Stout.

Chase Your Tail (OG 1036, ABV 3.6%)
A good session beer with an abundance of hops and bitterness. Dry, with citrus aftertaste.

Hereford Organic Bitter (ABV 3.9%)
Light in colour with a distinctive fruitiness from start to finish.

Herefordshire Owd Bull (ABV 3.9%)

Hereford Cathedral Bitter (OG 1040, ABV 4%)
A crisp amber beer made with local hops, producing a well-rounded malt/hop bitterness throughout and a pleasing, lingering aftertaste.

Mutleys Dark (OG 1040, ABV 4%)
A dark, malty mild with a hint of bitterness and a touch of roast caramel. A smooth drinkable ale.

Herefordshire Light Ale (ABV 4%)
Brewed along the lines of the award-winning Mutleys Pitstop. Light and refreshing.

Top Dog (OG 1042, ABV 4.2%)
A hoppy beer with both malt and fruit flavours.

Organic Oatmeal Stout (OG 1044, ABV 4.4%)
The subtle blend of organic oats and barley along with New Zealand hops produce a complex mixture of flavours.

Celtic Gold (OG 1045, ABV 4.5%)

Mutleys Revenge (OG 1048, ABV 4.8%)
A strong, smooth, hoppy beer, amber in colour. Full-bodied with a dry, citrus aftertaste.

Mutts Nuts (OG 1050, ABV 5%)
A dark, strong ale, full bodied with a hint of a chocolate aftertaste.

Spire*

Spire Brewery, Unit 3 Gisbourn Close, Ireland Business Park, Staveley, Chesterfield, Derbyshire, S43 3JT
Tel (01246) 410005 / 07904 638550
Email enquiries@spirebrewery.co.uk
Tours by arrangement

The brewery opened in spring 2006 with a 10-barrel plant offering a range of three permanent beers. It is run by an ex-Scots Guards musician, David, and his brewing partner, Andy Bolton. They plan to offer a musically themed range of seasonal beers in the near future.

Encore Session Bitter (OG 1040, ABV 4%)

Land of Hop and Glory (OG 1045, ABV 4.5%)

Chesterfield Best Bitter (OG 1048, ABV 4.8%)

Spitting Feathers*

Spitting Feathers Brewery, Common Farm, Waverton, Chester, Cheshire, CH3 7QT

Tel/Fax (01244) 332052
Email info@spittingfeathers.org
Website www.spittingfeathers.org
Tours by arrangement

Spitting Feathers was established in 2005. Two new beers were due to be added to the range during 2006. Around 50 outlets are supplied.

Thirstquencher (OG 1038, ABV 3.9%) ◆
Powerful hop aroma leads into the taste. Bitterness and a fruity citrus hop flavour fight for attention. A sharp, clean golden beer with a long, dry, bitter aftertaste.

Special Ale (OG 1041, ABV 4.2%) ◆
Complex tawny-coloured beer with a sharp, grainy mouthfeel. Malty with good hop coming through in the aroma and taste. Hints of nuttiness and a touch of acidity. Dry, astringent finish.

Old Wavertonian (OG 1043, ABV 4.4%) ◆
Creamy and smooth stout. Full-flavoured with coffee notes in aroma and taste. Roast and nut flavours throughout, leading to a hoppy, bitter finish.

Basket Case (OG 1046, ABV 4.8%) ◆
Smooth, refreshing tawny beer with good citrus hop notes throughout and a lasting dry finish.

Springhead SIBA

Springhead Fine Ales Ltd, Old Great North Road, Sutton-on-Trent, Newark, Nottinghamshire, NG23 6QS
Tel (01636) 821000
Fax (01636) 821150
Email steve@springhead.co.uk
Website www.springhead.co.uk
Tours by arrangement

⊛ Springhead Brewery opened in 1990 and was at the time the smallest micro in England (2.5 barrels). In 1993 the brewery moved to bigger premises and, to meet increased demand, expanded to a 50-barrel plant in 2004. Some 500 outlets are supplied. Many of the beer names have a Civil War theme.

Surrender 1646 (OG 1038, ABV 3.6%)
A burnished, copper-coloured bitter with a good combination of malt and hops. Long dry finish.

Springhead Bitter (OG 1041, ABV 4%)
A clean-tasting, easy-drinking, hoppy beer.

Puritans Porter (OG 1041, ABV 4%)
A porter, dark but not heavy. Smooth with a lingering finish of roasted barley.

Roundhead's Gold (OG 1042, ABV 4.2%)
Golden beer made with wild flower honey. Refreshing but not too sweet with the glorious aroma of Saaz hops.

Rupert's Ruin (OG 1042, ABV 4.2%)
A coppery, complex beer with a fruity aroma and a long, malty aftertaste.

Goodrich Castle (OG 1044, ABV 4.4%)
Brewed following a 17th-century recipe using rosemary: a pale ale, light on the palate with a bitter finish and a delicate flavour.

Oliver's Army (OG 1044, ABV 4.4%)

Charlie's Angel (OG 1045, ABV 4.5%)

Sweet Lips (OG 1046, ABV 4.6%)
A light, smooth and refreshing beer with some grapefruit notes from American Cascade hops.

The Leveller (OG 1047, ABV 4.8%)

Newark Castle Brown (OG 1049, ABV 5%)

Willy's Wheatbeer (OG 1051, ABV 5.3%)

Roaring Meg (OG 1052, ABV 5.5%)
Smooth and sweet with a dry finish and citrus honey aroma.

Cromwell's Hat (OG 1056, ABV 6%)

Stanway

Stanway Brewery, Stanway, Cheltenham, Gloucestershire, GL54 5PQ
Tel (01386) 584320
Website www.stanwaybrewery.co.uk

⊗ Stanway is a small brewery founded in 1993 with a five-barrel plant that confines its sales to the Cotswolds area (15 to 20 outlets). The brewery is the only known plant in the country to use wood-fired coppers for all its production. Seasonal beers: Morris-a-Leaping (ABV 3.9%, spring), Cotteswold Gold (ABV 3.9%, summer), Wizard (ABV 4%, autumn), Lords-a-Leaping (ABV 4.5%, Christmas).

Stanney Bitter (OG 1042, ABV 4.5%) ◆
A light, refreshing, amber-coloured beer, dominated by hops in the aroma, with a bitter taste and a hoppy, bitter finish.

Star*

Star Beermaking Co, Mystique Too, Steeple, Essex, CM0 7RT
Tel 07980 530707

James Adams launched Star in 2006 after working in the print and mail industries. He started home-brewing in 2004 and moved to advanced brewing. He gained experience at Blanchfields and Mighty Oak breweries before setting up his own one-barrel plant at his home. James plans to add to his beer range and hopes to move to new premises that he will share with Blanchfields, though both will remain independent concerns.

Gold Star (ABV 3.6%)

IPA (ABV 4.5%)

Station House

Station House Brewery, Unit 1 Meadow Lane Industrial Estate, Meadow Lane, Ellesmere Port, Cheshire, CH65 4TY
Tel/Fax (0151) 356 3000
Email enquire@stationhousebrewery.co.uk
Website www.stationhousebrewery.co.uk
Tours by arrangement

Station House opened in 2005. Barry Davidson was a keen home brewer who worked for a local authority and went on a Brewlab course in

Sunderland to perfect his brewing skills. His site is close to Ellesmere Port station. The plant has a 5-7 barrel brew length and is powered by electricity and propane gas. Approximately 60 outlets are supplied.

Less is More (ABV 3.5%)

1st Lite (ABV 3.8%) ◆
Light, hoppy bitter with clean lemon/grapefruit hop flavours and the trademark Station House bitterness and dry aftertaste. Clean and refreshing.

Lady of the Stream (ABV 3.9%) ◆
Fruit dominates the aroma, leading into the characteristic brewery strong bitterness and lip-puckering aftertaste. Good hops throughout in this gold-coloured bitter.

4 All That (ABV 4%)

Ode 2 Joy (ABV 4.1%) ◆
Clean, bitter beer in which citrus fruit dominates. Strong bitterness in flavour and an astringent, dry finish.

Buzzin' (ABV 4.3%) ◆
Golden beer dominated by a honey sweetness; other flavours are rather low-key. Has a tendency to be rather thin.

3 Score (ABV 4.5%)

Steamin' Billy

Registered Office: Steamin' Billy Brewing Co Ltd, 5 The Oval, Oadby, Leicestershire, LE2 5JB
Tel (0116) 271 2616
Email enquiries@steaminbilly.co.uk
Website www.steaminbilly.co.uk

In spite of the name, Steamin' Billy doesn't brew and its beers are contracted to Grainstore (qv) in Oakham. Six outlets are supplied and two pubs are owned. Seasonal beers: Lazy Summer (ABV 4.5%), Spring Goldings (ABV 4.5%), Knock Out (ABV 7.1%). Bottle-conditioned beer: Skydiver.

Stewart

Brewery: Stewart Brewing Ltd, 42 Dryden Road, Bilston Glen Industrial Estate, Loanhead, Midlothian, EH20 9LZ
Mail Address: Stewart Brewing Ltd, 33 Montague Street, Newington, Edinburgh, EH8 9QS
Tel (0131) 440 2442
Fax (0131) 667 0242
Email steve.stewart@stewartbrewing.co.uk
Website www.stewartbrewing.co.uk

Steve Stewart is a qualified master brewer with the Institute of Brewing who, after 10 years in the brewing industry worldwide, returned to Edinburgh to launch Stewart Brewing. The company specialises in the production of premium cask ales in a variety of styles, all made from natural ingredients. Beer for home can be purchased in a variety of packages direct from the brewery for collection or delivery in the Edinburgh area.

Pentland IPA (OG 1041, ABV 4.1%) ◆
Delightfully refreshing hoppy IPA. Hops and fruit announce their presence on the nose and continue through the taste and lingering bitter aftertaste of this full-flavoured beer.

Copper Cascade (OG 1042, ABV 4.2%)
Deep red colour, full bodied and rounded with a generous addition of American Cascade hops.

Edinburgh No.3 Premium Scotch Ale (OG 1043, ABV 4.3%) ◆
Traditional dark Scottish heavy. The pronounced malt character is part of a complex flavour profile, starting sweet yet with a bitter, dry, creamy finish.

Edinburgh Gold (OG 1048, ABV 4.8%) ◆
Full flavoured and full-bodied golden ale in the continental style. Plenty of hops are enjoyed throughout the drinking experience and give the beer a bitter profile.

Stirling

(Formerly City of Stirling)
Stirling Brewery, Unit 7c Bandeath Industrial Estate, Stirling, FK7 7NP
Tel (01786) 817000
Fax (01786) 833426
Tours by arrangement

A custom-built, 20-barrel brewery based in a former torpedo factory. It started brewing in 2004 in the historic Royal Burgh of Stirling, Scotland's newest city. It is now part of Traditional Scottish Ales along with Bridge of Allan (qv) and Trossachs. A range of traditional ales is available, including regular seasonals. A bottling line was due to be installed during 2006. All beers are available in bottle-conditioned form. Stirling's beers are made with organic ingredients and pure Scottish mountain water.

Copper (ABV 4%)

Silver (ABV 4.5%)

Gold (ABV 5%)

Jugs (ABV 7%)

For Trossachs Craft Brewery

Waylade (OG 1040, ABV 3.9%)
A good-flavoured blonde bitter with a malty, fruity nose and lightly-hopped aftertaste.

LadeBack (OG 1048, ABV 4.5%)
A sweet, refreshing amber ale that is well balanced with a hop-dominated dry finish.

LadeOut (OG 1055, ABV 5.1%)
A robust, satisfying ale with a complex flavour of dark chocolate and liquorice.

Stonehenge SIBA

Stonehenge Ales Ltd, The Old Mill, Mill Road, Netheravon, Salisbury, Wiltshire, SP4 9QB
Tel (01980) 670631
Fax (01980) 671187
Email stonehengeales@onetel.com
Website www.stonehengeales.co.uk
Tours by arrangement

⊗ The beers are brewed in a mill built in 1914 to generate electricity for the new military airfield nearby, using the water power of the River Avon. The building was put to a variety of uses after power generation stopped and was sold by the Ministry of Defence in 1983. The site was converted for brewing in 1984 (then

Bunce's Brewery), and in 1994 the company was bought by the Danish master brewer Stig Anker Anderson, who took up the challenge of making English beer. Cask-conditioned beers are delivered to more than 300 free trade outlets in the south of England and several wholesalers are also supplied. Seasonal beers: Sign of Spring (ABV 4.6%, March-May), Second-to-None (ABV 4.6%, summer), Old Smokey (ABV 5%, autumn), Rudolph (Christmas, ABV 5%)

Spire Ale (OG 1037, ABV 3.8%)
A light, golden, hoppy bitter.

Pigswill (OG 1040, ABV 4%)
A full-bodied beer, rich in hop aroma, with a warm amber colour.

Heel Stone (OG 1042, ABV 4.3%)
A crisp, clean, refreshing bitter, deep amber in colour, well balanced with a fruity blackcurrant nose.

Great Bustard (OG 1046, ABV 4.8%)
A strong, fruity, malty bitter.

Danish Dynamite (OG 1050, ABV 5%)
A strong, dry ale, slightly fruity with a well-balanced, bitter hop flavour.

Storm

Storm Brewing Co, 2 Waterside, Macclesfield, Cheshire, SK11 7HJ
Tel/Fax (01625) 431234
Email thompsonhugh@talk21.com

Storm Brewing Co was founded in 1998 by Hugh Thompson and David Stebbings. They operated from an old ICI boiler room until 2001 when the brewing operation moved to the current location, which until 1937 was a public house known as the Mechanics Arms. Storm supplies more than 60 outlets in Cheshire, Manchester and the Peak District. Seasonal beers: Summer Breeze (ABV 3.8%), Looks Like Rain Dear (ABV 4.8%, Christmas). All cask beers are also available in bottle-conditioned form.

Beauforts Ale (OG 1038, ABV 3.8%)
Golden brown, full-flavoured session bitter with a lingering hoppy taste.

Bitter Experience (OG 1040, ABV 4%)
A distinctive hop aroma draws you into this amber-coloured bitter. The palate has a mineral dryness that accentuates the crisp hop flavour and clean bitter finish.

Desert Storm (OG 1040, ABV 4%)
Amber-coloured beer with a smoky flavour of fruit and malt.

Twister (OG 1041, ABV 4%)
A light golden bitter with a smooth fruity hop aroma complemented by a subtle bitter aftertaste.

Bosley Cloud (OG 1041, ABV 4.1%) ◻ ◆
Dry, golden bitter with peppery hop notes throughout. Some initial sweetness and a mainly bitter aftertaste. Soft, well-balanced and quaffable.

Brainstorm (OG 1041, ABV 4.1%)
Light gold in colour and strong in citrus fruit flavours.

Ale Force (OG 1042, ABV 4.2%) ◆
Amber, smooth-tasting, complex beer that balances malt, hop and fruit on the taste, leading to a roasty, slightly sweet aftertaste.

Downpour (OG 1043, ABV 4.3%)
A combination of Pearl and Lacier malts produces this pale ale with a full, fruity flavour with a hint of apple and sightly hoppy aftertaste.

Tornado (OG 1044, ABV 4.4%) ◆
Fruity premium bitter with some graininess. Dry, satisfying finish.

Hurricane Hubert (OG 1045, ABV 4.5%)
A dark beer with a refreshing full, fruity hop aroma and a subtle bitter aftertaste.

Windgather (OG 1045, ABV 4.5%)
A gold-coloured beer with a distinctive crisp, fruity flavour right through to the aftertaste.

Storm Damage (OG 1047, ABV 4.7%)
A light-coloured, well-hopped and fruity beer balanced by a clean bitterness and smooth full palate.

Silk of Amnesia (OG 1047, ABV 4.7%) ◆
Smooth premium, easy-drinking bitter. Fruit and hops dominate throughout. Not too sweet, with a good lasting finish.

Typhoon (OG 1050, ABV 5%) ◆
Copper-coloured, smooth strong bitter. Roasty overtones and a hint of caramel and marzipan. Drinkable despite the gravity.

Stowey*

Stowey Brewery, The Old Cider House, 25 Castle Street, Nether Stowey, Somerset,TA5 1LN
Tel (01278) 732228
Website www.stoweybrewery.co.uk

Stowey was due to come on stream in spring 2006. The beer range had not been finalised when the guide went to press.

Strangford Lough

Strangford Lough Brewing Co, 22 Shore Road, Killyleagh, Downpatrick, Northern Ireland, BT30 9UE
Tel (028) 4482 1461
Fax (028) 4482 1273
Email contact@slbc.ie
Website www.slbc.ie

Beers for this company are contract-brewed by a number of breweries in Northern Ireland and Britain, though there are plans to build a plant in Northern Ireland. Bottle-conditioned beers: St Patrick's Best (ABV 3.8%), St Patrick's Gold (ABV 4.5%), St Patrick's Ale (ABV 6%), Barelegs Brew (ABV 4.5%), Legbiter (ABV 4.8%).

Strathaven*

Strathaven Ales, Craigmill Brewery, Strathaven, ML10 6PB
Tel (01357) 520419
Fax (01357) 528695
Email info@strathavenales.co.uk
Website www.strathavenales.co.uk
Shop Mon-Sat 2-4pm
Tours by arrangement

Strathaven Ales is a 10-barrel brewery on the River Avon close to Strathaven. The town has a long history of brewing but the last brewery closed around 1848 after a serious fire, which also wiped out a large part of the town. Craigmill was established as a brewery about 10 years ago by renovating and converting a 16th-century mill and was then successfully operated for about eight years until the facility was outgrown. The building lay empty for almost two years until three local businessmen decided to resurrect the brewery and upgrade the plant. It is hoped to add a visitor centre. Fifty outlets are supplied. Seasonal beers: Duchess Anne (ABV 3.9%, spring/summer), Trumpeter (ABV 4.2%, autumn/winter).

Clydesdale IPA (ABV 3.8%)

Old Mortality (ABV 4.2%)

Claverhouse (ABV 4.5%)

Stroud* SIBA

Stroud Brewery Ltd, 141 Thrupp Lane, Thrupp, Stroud, Gloucestershire, GL5 2DQ
Tel 07891 995878
Email greg@stroudbrewery.co.uk
Website www.stroudbrewery.co.uk

Brewer Greg Pilley spent four years in the late 1990s researching a book on traditional alcoholic drinks of Africa. He was a keen home-brewer since his university days and on his return to Britain he started to plan a brewery. He went on a Brewlab course and then assembled a five-barrel plant that came on stream in spring 2006.

Redcoat (ABV 3.9%)

Budding (ABV 4.5%)

Five Valleys (ABV 5%)

Stumpy's

Stumpy's Brewery, Unit 5 Lycroft Farm, Park Lane, Upper Swanmore, Hampshire, SO32 2QQ
Tel (01329) 664902 / 07771 557378
Fax (01329) 664902
Email info@stumpysbrewery.com
Website www.stumpysbrewery.com
Tours by arrangement

⊗ A five-barrel brewery opened in 2004 in a converted hen house on a farm so remote than an Ordnance Survey map and reference (SU 588185) are essential to find it. The owner and brewer is CAMRA member Brian 'Stumpy' Lewis. Brian brewed for several months at Yates' on the Isle of Wight and the acclaim for his brews there encouraged him to set up on his own. Some 20 outlets are supplied. All cask ales are available bottled. Seasonal beer: Silent Night (ABV 5%, autumn/winter).

Dog Daze (OG 1040, ABV 3.8%) ◆
A light-tasting golden beer with a strong malty aroma. The taste is predominantly sweet rather than bitter; tastes rather thin and sweet and lacking in bitterness. A sweet malty finish.

Hop a Doodle Doo (OG 1040, ABV 4%)

Hot Dog (ABV 4.5%)

Old Ginger (ABV 4.5%)

Old Stumpy (OG 1045, ABV 4.5%) ◆
Grassy best bitter with a strong hoppy and fruity aroma. Some malt and bitterness in the flavour lead to a harsh finish.

Bo'sun's Call (ABV 5%)

Haven (OG 1050, ABV 5%)
Creamy and deceptively strong.

Sulwath SIBA

Sulwath Brewers Ltd, The Brewery, 209 King Street, Castle Douglas, Dumfries & Galloway, DG7 1DT
Tel/Fax (01556) 504525
Email allen@scottdavid98.freeserve.co.uk
Website www.sulwathbrewers.co.uk
Shop Mon-Sat 10am-4pm
Tours by arrangment

☺ Sulwath is a small, privately-owned company that started brewing in 1995. Maris Otter malts are used in each full mash brew, with the addition of whole hop flowers from the Hereford area. The beers are now supplied to markets as far away as Devon in the south and Aberdeen in the north. The brewery has a fully licensed brewery tap open 10am-4pm Monday-Saturday. Cask ales are sold to some 100 outlets and three wholesalers. Seasonal beer: Solway Mist (ABV 5.5%, May-Oct).

Cuil Hill (OG 1039, ABV 3.6%) ◆
Distinctively fruity session ale with malt and hop undertones. The taste is bitter-sweet with a long-lasting dry finish.

Black Galloway (OG 1046, ABV 4.4%)
A robust porter/stout that derives its colour from the abundance of Maris Otter barley and chocolate malts used in the brewing process.

Criffel (OG 1044, ABV 4.6%) ◆
Full-bodied beer with a distinctive bitterness. Fruit is to the fore of the taste with hop becoming increasingly dominant in the taste and finish.

Galloway Gold (OG 1049, ABV 5%) ◆
A cask-conditioned lager that will be too sweet for many despite being heavily hopped.

Knockendoch (OG 1047, ABV 5%) ◆
Dark, copper-coloured, reflecting a roast malt content, with bitterness from Challenger hops.

Summerskills SIBA

Summerskills Brewery, 15 Pomphlett Farm Industrial Estate, Broxton Drive, Billacombe, Plymouth, Devon, PL4 7BG
Tel (01752) 481283
Email info@summerskills.co.uk

Website www.summerskills.co.uk

⊗ Originally established in a vineyard in 1983 at Bigbury-on-Sea, Summerskills moved to its present site in 1985 and has expanded since then. National distribution is carried out by experienced wholesalers. Twenty outlets are supplied by the brewery.

Cellar Vee (OG 1037, ABV 3.7%)

Hopscotch (OG 1042, ABV 4.1%)

Best Bitter (OG 1043, ABV 4.3%) ◆
A mid-brown beer, with plenty of malt and hops through the aroma, taste and finish. A good session beer.

Tamar (OG 1043, ABV 4.3%)
A tawny-coloured bitter with a fruity aroma and a hop taste and finish.

Menacing Dennis (OG 1045, ABV 4.5%)

Whistle Belly Vengeance (OG 1046, ABV 4.7%) ◆
A red/brown beer with a beautiful malt and fruit taste and a pleasant, malty aftertaste.

Indiana's Bones (OG 1056, ABV 5.6%)
A mid brown beer with a good balance of fruit and malt in the aroma and taste and a sweet, malty finish.

Surrey Hills SIBA

Surrey Hills Brewery Ltd, Old Scotland Farm, Staple Lane, Shere, Guildford, Surrey, GU5 9TE
Tel (01483) 212812
Email info@surreyhills.co.uk
Website www.surreyhills.co.uk

Surrey Hills is based in an old milking parlour and produced its first commercial beers in 2005. The beers are sold in a number of local outlets – check the website for current stockists. The beers have already won a number of awards. Seasonal beers: Albury Ruby (ABV 4.6%, winter), Gilt Complex (ABV 4.6%, summer).

Ranmore Ale (ABV 3.8%) ◆
A light session beer with bags of flavour. An earthy hoppy nose leads into citrus grapefruit and a hoppy taste, and a clean, bitter finish.

Shere Drop (ABV 4.2%) ◆
Well-balanced and hoppy, with a pleasant citrus aroma and a noticeable fruitiness in the taste. The finish is dry, hoppy and bitter.

Suthwyk

Suthwyk Ales, Offwell Farm, Southwick, Fareham, Hampshire, PO17 6DX
Tel (02392) 325252
Email mjbazeley@suthwykales.com
Website www.suthwykales.com / www.southwickbrewhouse.co.uk

Barley farmer Martin Bazeley does not brew himself. The beers are produced by Oakleaf Brewing (qv) in Gosport, using Martin's Optic malt. The beers listed are also available in bottle-conditioned form and can be bought by mail order or from a shop and steam brewery museum.

Bloomfields (ABV 3.8%)

Liberation (ABV 4.2%)

Skew Sunshine Ale (ABV 4.6%)

Sutton

See South Hams

Swan on the Green

Swan on the Green Brewery, West Peckham, Maidstone, Kent, ME18 5JW
Tel (01622) 812271
Fax (01622) 814977 / 0870 0560556
Email info@swan-on-the-green.co.uk
Website www.swan-on-the-green.co.uk
Tours by arrangement

⊗ The brewery was established in 2000 to produce handcrafted beers. Major developments have taken place to include lager production and standard British bitters. The beers are not filtered and no artificial ingredients are used. There are plans to expand the plant. One pub is owned and other outlets and beer festivals are occasionally supplied.

Fuggles Pale (OG 1037, ABV 3.6%)
A session bitter, traditionally hoppy, using local Fuggles hops.

Whooper (OG 1037, ABV 3.6%)
Straw coloured and lightly hopped with American Cascade for a subtle fruity aroma.

Trumpeter Best (OG 1041, ABV 4%)
A copper-coloured ale hopped with First Gold and Target.

Porter (OG 1045, ABV 4.5%)

Bewick (OG 1051-1054, ABV 5.3%)
A heavyweight premium bitter hopped with Target for bite and softened with Kentish Goldings for aroma.

Swansea SIBA

Swansea Brewing Co, Joiners Arms, 50 Bishopston Road, Bishopston, Swansea, SA3 3EJ
Office: 74 Hawthorne Avenue, Uplands, Swansea, SA2 0LY
Tel (01792) 232658 brewery / (01792) 290197 office
Email rorygowland@fsbdial.co.uk
Tours by arrangement

⊗ Opened in 1996, Swansea was the first commercial brewery in the area for almost 30 years and is the city's only brew-pub. It doubled its capacity within the first year and now produces four regular beers and occasional experimental ones. The founder, Rory Gowland, learnt his trade working in the Chemistry Department of Swansea University. Four regular outlets are supplied along with other pubs in the South Wales area. Seasonal beers: St Teilo's Tipple (ABV 5.5%), Barland Strong (ABV 6%), Pwll Du XXXX (ABV 4.9%).

Deep Slade Dark (OG 1034, ABV 4%)

Bishopswood Bitter (OG 1038, ABV 4.3%) ◆
A delicate aroma of hops and malt in this pale brown colour. The taste is a balanced mix of hops and malt with a growing hoppy bitterness ending in a lasting bitter finish.

Three Cliffs Gold (OG 1042, ABV 4.7%) ◆

A golden beer with a hoppy and fruity aroma, a hoppy taste with fruit and malt, and a quenching bitterness. The pleasant finish has a good hop flavour and bitterness.

Original Wood (OG 1046, ABV 5.2%)
A full-bodied, pale brown beer with an aroma of hops, fruit and malt. A complex blend of these flavours with a firm bitterness ends with increasing bitterness.

Tarka

Tarka Ales, Yelland Manor Farm, Yelland, Barnstaple, Devon, EX19 8SN
Tel (01837) 811030

A five-barrel plant was recommissioned after being mothballed in 2004. It is under new management with new beer recipes. Two pubs are supplied on a regular basis. Seasonal beer: Cockle Warmer (ABV 5.7%, Dec-Feb). Bottle-conditioned beers: Tom Noddy, Golden Pool, Black Hen (ABV 5.7%), Stock Ale (ABV 8%), Barley Wine (ABV 8.7%).

Tom Noddy (OG 1041, ABV 4.2%)
A dark ruby-coloured beer with a rich malt taste; dry in the mouth.

Golden Pool (OG 1042, ABV 4.3%)
A light, aromatic beer with strong hop character.

H.W. (OG 1048, ABV 4.9%)
A dark copper-coloured beer with a hint of roast barley.

Taunton Vale

Taunton Vale Brewery, New Inn, Halse, Taunton, Somerset, TA4 3AF
Tel (01823) 432352
Website www.newinnhalse.com

The brewery was established in 2003 in the cellar of the New Inn, Halse by former landlord Mark Leadeham. The pub and brewery are now under new management and were completely renovated in 2006. The beer range had not been finalised when the guide went to press.

Timothy Taylor IFBB

Timothy Taylor & Co Ltd, Knowle Spring Brewery, Keighley, West Yorkshire, BD21 1AW
Tel (01535) 603139
Fax (01535) 691167
Website www.timothy-taylor.co.uk

One of the classic brewers of pale ale, Timothy Taylor is an independent family-owned company established in 1858. It moved to the site of the Knowle Spring in 1863. Its prize-winning ales, which use Pennine spring water, are served in all 24 of the brewery's pubs as well as 300-plus other outlets. In 2003 the brewery was given planning permission for a £1 million expansion programme that included a new brewhouse. Draught beer uses isinglass finings but bottled beers are suitable for vegans and vegetarians. Seasonal beer: Ram Tam (ABV 4.3%, winter).

Golden Best (OG 1033, ABV 3.5%)
A clean-tasting and refreshing traditional Pennine light mild. A little fruit in the nose increases to complement the delicate hoppy taste. Background malt throughout. A good session beer.

Dark Mild (OG 1034, ABV 3.5%)
Malt and caramel dominate the aroma with hops and hints of fruit leading to a dry finish.

Best Bitter (OG 1038, ABV 4%)
Hops and citrus fruit combine well with a nutty malt character in this drinkable bitter. Bitterness increases down the glass and lingers in the aftertaste.

Landlord (OG 1042, ABV 4.3%)
An increasingly dry, hoppy, bitter finish complements the spicy, citrus character of this full-flavoured and well-balanced amber beer.

Teignworthy SIBA

Teignworthy Brewery, The Maltings, Teign Road, Newton Abbot, Devon, TQ12 4AA
Tel/Fax (01626) 332066
Email john@teignworthy.freeserve.co.uk
Website www.siba-southwest.co.uk/breweries/teignworthy/
Shop 10am-5pm weekdays at Tuckers Maltings
Tours available for trade customers only

Teignworthy Brewery was established in 1994 by John and Rachel Lawton and is located in part of the historic Tuckers Maltings. The brewery is a 15-barrel plant and production is now up to 50 barrels a week, using malt from Tuckers. It supplies around 120 outlets in Devon and Somerset. Some of the beers are bottled on site and are available from the Tuckers Maltings shop and mail order. A large range of seasonal ales is available: see website. Bottle-conditioned beers: Reel Ale, Springtide, Old Moggie, Beachcomber, Martha's Mild (ABV 5.3%).

Reel Ale (OG 1039.5, ABV 4%)
Clean, sharp-tasting bitter with lasting hoppiness; predominantly malty aroma.

Springtide (OG 1043.5, ABV 4.3%)
An excellent, full and well-rounded, mid-brown beer with a dry, bitter taste and aftertaste.

Old Moggie (OG 1044.5, ABV 4.4%)
A golden, hoppy and fruity ale.

Beachcomber (OG 1045.5, ABV 4.5%)
A pale brown beer with a light, refreshing fruit and hop nose, grapefruit taste and a dry, hoppy finish.

Teme Valley SIBA

Teme Valley Brewery, The Talbot, Bromyard Road, Knightwick, Worcester, WR6 5PH
Tel (01886) 821235
Fax (01886) 821060
Email enquiries@temevalleybrewery.co.uk
Website www.temevalleybrewery.co.uk
Tours by arrangement

Teme Valley Brewery opened in 1997. In 2005, new investment enabled the brewery to expand to a 10-barrel brew-length. It maintains strong ties with local hop farming, using only Worcestershire-grown hops. Some 30 outlets are supplied. Seasonal beers: Talbot Porter (ABV 4.4%, Nov-Jan), Heartwarmer (ABV 6%,

December), The Hops Nouvelle (ABV 4.1%, Sept-Oct), Spring's First (ABV 4.7%, Feb-March), Dark Stranger (ABV 4.4%, June-July), 3 Pears (ABV 3.9%, July-Aug). Bottle-conditioned beers: This, That, The Hop Nouvelle, Wotever Next? (ABV 5%), Heartwarmer (ABV 6%).

T'Other (OG 1035, ABV 3.5%) ◈
Refreshing amber offering with an abundance of flavour in the fruity aroma, followed by a short, dry bitterness.

This (OG 1037, ABV 3.7%) ◈
Dark gold brew with a mellow array of flavours in a malty balance.

That (OG 1041, ABV 4.1%) ◈
A rich fruity nose and a wide range of hoppy and malty flavours in this copper-coloured best bitter.

Theakston

T&R Theakston Ltd, The Brewery, Masham, Ripon, North Yorkshire, HG4 4YD
Tel (01765) 680000
Fax (01765) 689921
Email info@theakstons.co.uk
Website www.theakstons.co.uk
Tours by arrangement

⊛ After 20 years under the control of first Matthew Brown and then Scottish & Newcastle, Theakstons returned to the independent sector in 2003 when S&N sold the company back to the family. It is run by four Theakston brothers. The brewery is one of the oldest in Yorkshire, built in 1875 by the brothers' great-grandfather, Thomas Theakston, the son of the company's founder. The Theakston's range, with the exception of Best Bitter, is brewed at Masham but as a result of restraints on capacity the company has contracted Scottish Courage to brew Best Bitter at John Smith's in Tadcaster. In 2004 a new fermentation room was added to provide additional flexibility and capacity.

Mild Ale (OG 1035, ABV 3.5%) ◈
A rich and smooth mild ale with a creamy body and a rounded liquorice taste. Dark ruby/amber in colour, with a mix of malt and fruit on the nose, and a dry, hoppy aftertaste.

Black Bull Bitter (OG 1037, ABV 3.9%) ◈
A distinctively hoppy aroma leads to a bitter, hoppy taste with some fruitiness and a short bitter finish. Rather thin.

Hogshead Bitter (ABV 4.1%)
A robust ale with striking aroma and palate.

Lightfoot Bitter (ABV 4.1%)
Special malt produces a pronounced peach-like note to the aroma and palate, complemented by a floral hop character.

Cool Cask (OG 1042, ABV 4.2%)
A beer served through special cooling equipment at 10°C.

Grouse Beater (ABV 4.2%)
A golden bitter with moderate hop bitterness.

Paradise Ale (ABV 4.2%)
A light, fruity flavoured ale.

Cooper's Butt (ABV 4.3%)
Full-bodied, amber-red classic IPA.

XB (OG 1044, ABV 4.5%)
A sweet-tasting bitter with background fruit and spicy hop. Some caramel character gives this ale a malty dominance.

Old Peculier (OG 1057, ABV 5.6%) ◫ ◈
A full-bodied, dark brown, strong ale. Slightly malty but with hints of roast coffee and liquorice. A smooth caramel overlay and a complex fruitiness leads to a bitter chocolate finish.

Masham Ale (OG 1065, ABV 6.5%)
Deceptively smooth, full-bodied strong ale. Beautifully rich and balanced.

Abraham Thompson

Abraham Thompson's Brewing Co, Flass Lane, Barrow-in-Furness, Cumbria, LA13 0AD
Tel 07708 191437
Email abraham.thompson@btinternet.com

Abraham Thompson was set up in 2004 by John Mulholland, a long-standing CAMRA member, with a mission to return Barrow-brewed beers to local pubs. This was achieved in 2005 after an absence of more than 30 years following the demise of Case's Brewery in 1972. With a half-barrel plant, Abe's nano-brewery has concentrated almost exclusively on dark beers, reflecting the tastes of the brewer. As a result of the small output, finding the beers outside the Low Furness area is difficult. The only frequent stockist is the Black Dog Inn between Dalton and Ireleth.

Dark Mild (ABV 3.5%)

Lickerish Stout (ABV 4%)
A black, full-bodied stout with heavy roast flavours and good bitterness.

Porter (ABV 4.1%)
A deep, dark porter with good body and a smooth chocolate finish.

Extra Stout (ABV 5.8%)

Letargion (ABV 9%)
Black, bitter and heavily roast but still very drinkable. A meal in a glass.

John Thompson

⚲ John Thompson Inn & Brewery, Ingleby, Melbourne, Derbyshire, DE73 7HW
Tel (01332) 852469
Fax (01332) 865647
Email nick_w_thompson@yahoo.co.uk
Tours by arrangement

John Thompson set up the brewery in the 1970s. The pub and brewery are now run by his son, Nick. Seasonal beers: Gold (ABV 4.5%, summer), Rich Porter (ABV 4.5%, winter), St Nicks (ABV 5%, Xmas).

JTS XXX (OG 1041, ABV 4.1%)
Porter (OG 1045, ABV 4.5%)

Thornbridge SIBA

Thornbridge Hall Country House Brewery, Thornbridge Hall, Ashford in the Water, Bakewell, Derbyshire, DE45 1NZ
Tel (01629) 640617

Fax (01629) 640039
Email info@thornbridgehallbrewery.co.uk
Website www.thornbridgebrewery.co.uk
Tours by arrangement

Operations began at the 10-barrel brewery, housed in a converted joiners' and stonemasons' workshop in the grounds of Thornbridge Hall, in 2004. The first year of brewing saw considerable success with Jaipur IPA winning several awards, including Sheffield CAMRA's champion beer award, Leeds CAMRA Beer of the Festival, and a gold medal in the strong ale section of the SIBA Midlands Beer Competition. Jaipur is one of five regular beers produced, which are available in 60 local outlets. The plan is to continue to brew a small number of regular beers while developing new brews through innovation in approach and use of ingredients. The two young brewers are from Scotland – Martin Dickie – and Italy – Stefano Cossi. Seasonal beers: Treason (ABV 4.6%), Saint Petersburg Imperial Russian Stout (ABV 7.7%), Bohemia Cask Lager (ABV 5.6%), De Longsdon (ABV 4.8%). Bottle-conditioned beers: Jaipur IPA, Saint Petersburg Imperial Russian Stout.

Foxwood (OG 1035, ABV 3.5%) ◆
A pleasant low-gravity session beer, brewed with a blend of five different malts. Well-balanced mix of malt and hops, becoming increasingly dry, leading to a bitter aftertaste.

Lord Marples (OG 1041, ABV 4%)
An easy-drinking, copper-coloured, fruity session beer. Malty, with a citrus finish and long bitter aftertaste.

Brock (OG 1040, ABV 4.1%) ◆
A velvety dark, exceptionally smooth and creamy stout. With soft treacle and smoky flavours and a full body.

Blackthorn Ale (OG 1044, ABV 4.4%)
Clear golden ale with a slight aroma of floral hops. Nicely balanced flavours of hops, citrus and sweetness lead to a lingering fruit and hops aftertaste.

Jaipur IPA (OG 1055, ABV 5.9%) ◆
Complex, well-balanced IPA with a fine blend of citrus and other fruit flavours, mixed with a slight sweetness and ending with a lingering bitter finish. Hoppy and dangerously drinkable.

Three B's

Three B's Brewery, Unit 5, Laneside Works, Stockclough Lane, Feniscowles, Blackburn, Lancashire, BB2 5JR
Tel/Fax (01254) 207686
Email info@threebsbrewery.co.uk
Website www.threebsbrewery.co.uk
Tours by arrangement

Robert Bell designed and began building his two-barrel brewery in 1997 and in 1998 he obtained premises in Blackburn to set up the equipment and complete the project. It is now a 10-barrel brewery. 20 outlets are supplied. Bottle-conditioned beers: Shuffle Ale, Doff Cocker, Knocker Up, Tackler's Tipple.

Stoker's Slake (ABV 3.6%) ◆
Lightly roasted coffee flavours are in the aroma and the initial taste. A well-rounded, dark brown mild with dried fruit flavours in the long finish.

Bobbin's Bitter (ABV 3.8%)
Warm aromas of malt, Goldings hops and nuts; a full, fruity flavour with a light dry finish.

Tackler's Tipple (ABV 4.3%)
A best bitter with full hop flavour, biscuit tones on the tongue and a deep, dry finish. A darker coloured ale with a fascinating blend of hops and dark malt.

Doff Cocker (ABV 4.5%) ◆
Yellow with a hoppy aroma and initial taste giving way to subtle malt notes and orchard fruit flavours. Crisp, dry finish.

Pinch Noggin' (ABV 4.6%)
A luscious balance of malt, hops and fruit, with a lively, colourful spicy aroma of citrus fruit. A quenching golden beer.

Knocker Up (ABV 4.8%) ◆
A smooth, rich, creamy porter. The roast flavour is foremost without dominating and is balanced by fruit and hop notes.

Shuttle Ale (ABV 5.2%)
A strong pale ale, light in colour with a balanced malt and hop flavour, a Goldings hops aroma, a long dry finish and delicate fruit notes.

Three Rivers

See 3 Rivers

Three Tuns SIBA

John Roberts Brewing Co Ltd, Three Tuns Brewery, 16 Market Square, Bishops Castle, Shropshire, SY9 5BN
Tel/Fax (01588) 638392
Email tunsbrewery@aol.co.uk
Tours by arrangement

Brewing started on the site more than 300 years ago. In the 1970s, the Three Tuns was one of only four brew-pubs left in the country. Nowadays the brewery and Three Tuns pub are separate businesses. Plans to increase the brew length are in progress. More than 100 outlets in the Shropshire area plus one in Croydon (Beer Circus) are supplied direct. Seasonal beers: Solstice (ABV 4.7%, summer), Old Scrooge (ABV 6.5%, Christmas).

Golden Nut (OG 1036, ABV 3.4%)

Three 8 (OG 1042, ABV 3.8%)

XXX (OG 1046, ABV 4.3%) ◆
A pale, sweetish bitter with a light hop aftertaste that has a honey finish. Very drinkable.

Castle Steamer (ABV 4.4%) ◆
A very dark and well-roasted porter/stout with coffee tastes and a hop finish.

Cleric's Cure (ABV 5%)
A pale beer with strong hopping to resemble old IPAs.

Thwaites IFBB

Daniel Thwaites plc, Star Brewery, PO Box 50, Blackburn, Lancashire, BB1 5BU
Tel (01254) 686868
Fax (01254) 681439
Email marketing@thwaites.co.uk
Website
www.thwaites.co.uk/www.thwaitesbeers.co.uk
Tours by arrangement

⊕ Thwaites will celebrate its 200th anniversary in 2007 and is still controlled by the Yerburgh family, descendants of founder Daniel Thwaites. The company has refocused on cask beer mainly by promoting Lancaster Bomber with a campaign featuring England and Lancashire cricketer Andrew Flintoff. Cask beer is available in around two-thirds of the company's 430 pubs but Dark Mild is hard to find. Seasonal beers: Bloomin' Ale (ABV 3.9%, spring), Craftsman (ABV 4.2%, Aug-Sept), Liberation (ABV 4.5%, Oct-Nov), Good Elf (ABV 4.9%, Christmas). Daniel's Hammer (ABV 5%) is an occasional brew.

Dark Mild (OG 1036, ABV 3.3%) ◆
A tasty traditional dark mild presenting a malty flavour with caramel notes and a slightly bitter finish.

Original (OG 1036, ABV 3.6%) ◻ ◆
Hop driven, yet well-balanced bitter with subtle apple flavours and a long crisp finish.

Thoroughbred (OG 1040, ABV 4%) ◆
A copper-coloured best bitter with a dry hop aroma. It has a balanced taste with is a rather thin finish.

Lancaster Bomber (OG 1044, ABV 4.4%) ◆
Hop driven yet well-balanced copper-coloured best bitter with firm malt flavours and autumn fruit notes and a long, dry finish.

For Carlsberg

Ansells Mild (ABV 3.4%)

Tigertops SIBA

Tigertops Brewery, 22 Oaks Street, Flanshaw, Wakefield, West Yorkshire, WF2 9LN
Tel (01229) 716238 / (01924) 897728
Email tigertopsbrewery@hotmail.com

⊕ Tigertops was established in 1995 by Stuart Johnson, a former chairman of the Wakefield branch of CAMRA, and his wife Lynda and they still own the brewery as well as running the Foxfield brew-pub in Cumbria (qv). Tigertops is run on their behalf by Barry Smith. Five outlets are supplied. Seasonal beers: Billy Bock (ABV 7.9%, Nov-Feb), May Bock (ABV 6.2%, May-June).

Axeman's Block (OG 1036, ABV 3.6%)
A malty beer with a good hop finish.

Dark Wheat Mild (OG 1036, ABV 3.6%)
An unusual mild made primarily with wheat malt.

Thor Bitter (OG 1038, ABV 3.8%)
A light, hoppy bitter.

Charles Town Best Bitter (ABV 4%)

Blanche de Newland (OG 1044, ABV 4.5%)
A cloudy Belgian-style wheat beer.

Ginger Fix (OG 1044, ABV 4.6%)
A mid-amber ginger beer.

White Max (OG 1044, ABV 4.6%)
A light, German-style wheat beer.

Uber Weiss (OG 1046, ABV 4.8%)
A dark, German-style wheat beer.

Big Ginger (OG 1058, ABV 6%)
A strong, amber ginger beer.

Tindall EAB

Tindall Ales Brewery, Toad Lane, Seething, Norwich, Norfolk, NR35 2EQ
Tel (01508) 483844/07795 113163
Fax (01508) 483844
Email greenangela5@aol.com
Tours by arrangement

⊗ Tindall Ales opened in 1998 and is a family-run business with the main objective of producing good quality ale made from local malt and Kentish hops. Various outlets are supplied. Seasonal beers: Summer Loving (ABV 3.6%), Autumn Brew (ABV 4%), Lovers Ale (ABV 4%, Valentine's), Christmas Cheers (ABV 4%). All the beers listed below, except IPA, are available in bottle-conditioned form.

IPA (OG 1036, ABV 3.6%)
A smooth-tasting pale ale. The Goldings hops lead to a delicate, refreshing finish, without lacking in flavour.

Best Bitter (OG 1037, ABV 3.7%) ◆
A distinctly sulphurous aroma introduces this copper-coloured bitter. A gentle blend of malt and bitterness makes for a good session beer. Bitterness lingers well into the long, slowly-drying finish.

Fuggled Up! (ABV 3.7%)

Mild (OG 1037, ABV 3.7%)
A good dark mild.

Liberator (OG 1038, ABV 3.8%) ◆
Named after the warplanes that flew from the former airfield that now houses the brewery. A jaunty, undemanding bitter with a hoppy citrus nose and tumbling mix of hop, citrus, malt and sweetness.

Alltime (OG 1040, ABV 4%) ◆
A well-balanced, traditional English bitter. The blend of hop and malt is reflected in both the bouquet and taste. The residual bitterness increases towards the end of a long, sustained finish.

Mundham Mild (ABV 4%)

Ditchingham Dam (OG 1042, ABV 4.2%) ◻ ◆
Strong ginger and malt notes fight for supremacy in the swirling bouquet of this

mid-brown brew. The flavours linger on the tongue to produce a refreshingly clean finish. As the malt slowly wanes, the ginger notes continue in full flow.

Seething Pint (ABV 4.3%)

Norfolk 'n' Good (OG 1046, ABV 4.6%) ◆
Amber coloured with a strawberry nose and creamy mouthfeel, this beer has a well-balanced gentle mix of flavours. Fruitiness eventually takes precedence over hops, malt and bitterness. Short, sharp ending.

Norwich Dragon (ABV 4.6%)

Honeydo (OG 1050, ABV 5%) ◆
Honey dominates the taste and aroma. Some bitterness takes the edge off the inherent sweet fruitiness but quickly subsides, taking the faint hop and malt background with it.

Tipples EAB

Tipples Brewery, Unit 6 Damgate Lane Industrial Estate, Acle, Norwich, Norfolk, NR13 3DJ
Tel/Fax (01493) 741007
Email brewery@tipplesbrewery.com
Website www.tipplesbrewery.com

The owner's name really is Tipple, Jason Tipple in full. He worked in the financial services and the food industry but was clearly destined to get involved in brewing. Jason has a six-barrel plant built by Porter Brewing Co and his first beer came on stream in autumn 2004. There are nine regular beers as well as seasonal brews, details of which can be found on the brewery website, along with an online shop.

Longshore (ABV 3.6%)

Ginger (ABV 3.8%)

The Hanged Monk (ABV 3.8%)

Lady Evelyn (ABV 4.1%)

Redhead (ABV 4.2%)

Battle (ABV 4.3%)

Topper (ABV 4.5%)

Moon Rocket (ABV 5%)

Jacks' Revenge (ABV 5.8%)

Tipsy Toad

See Jersey

Tirril SIBA

Tirril Brewery Ltd, Red House, Long Marton, Appleby-in-Westmorland, Cumbria, CA16 6BN
Tel (017683) 61846
Fax (017683) 61841
Email chris@tirrilbrewery.co.uk
Website www.tirrilbrewery.co.uk
Tours by arrangement

⊛ Tirril started brewing for the award-winning Queen's Head at Tirril in 1999, 100 years after Siddle's Brewery had been bought and closed in 1899. The brewery moved after the 2001 foot-and-mouth epidemic to Brougham Hall, to the original 1823 brewing rooms. A 20-barrel plant at Long Marton will be functional by summer 2006. Two pubs are owned and 50-plus outlets are supplied. Special ales are also produced for the Fox Inn at Ousby and the Shepherds Inn at Langwathby.

Bewsher's Best Bitter (OG 1038.5, ABV 3.8%)
A lightly-hopped, golden brown session beer, named after the landlord and brewer at the Queen's Head in the 1830s.

Brougham Ale (OG 1039, ABV 3.9%)
A gently hopped, amber bitter.

Old Faithful (OG 1040, ABV 4%)
Pale gold, aromatic and well-hopped.

1823 (OG 1041, ABV 4.1%)

Academy Ale (OG 1041.5, ABV 4.2%)
A dark, full-bodied, traditional rich and malty ale.

Titanic SIBA

Titanic Brewery Co Ltd, Unit 5 Callender Place, Burslem, Stoke-on-Trent, Staffordshire, ST6 1JL
Tel (01782) 823447
Fax (01782) 812349
Email titanic@titanicbrewery.co.uk
Website www.titanicbrewery.co.uk
Tours by arrangement

⊛ Founded in 1985, the brewery is named in honour of Captain Smith who hailed from the Potteries and had the misfortune to captain the Titanic. A monthly seasonal beer provides the opportunity to offer distinctive beers of many styles, each with a link to the liner. Titanic supplies 300 free trade outlets throughout the country. One pub is owned. A new 50-barrel brew plant was installed in 2005. Bottle-conditioned beer: Titanic Stout (ABV 4.5% ■) ▢.

Best Bitter (OG 1036, ABV 3.5%) ◆
Straw-coloured bitter with a sulphurous nose, a fruity start, a well-hopped middle and a dry finish.

Mild (OG 1036, ABV 3.5%) ◆
Roast and malt aroma in this red-brown ale. Hops give a dry finish after a smooth, sweet body.

Fullkiln Ale (OG 1040, ABV 4%)

Lifeboat (OG 1040, ABV 4%) ◆
A fruity and malty beer, dark red with a fruity finish.

Iceberg (OG 1042, ABV 4.1%) ▢ ◆
Gold coloured, with a hoppy and fruity aroma leading to a fruity and hoppy taste with tones of honey and grass. Bitterness develops in the long finish.

Anchor Bitter (OG 1042, ABV 4.1%) ◆
Copper-coloured with a sulphurous aroma parting to reveal fruit and hops. A robust bitterness relaxes in to a long, dry, hoppy finish.

Stout (OG 1046, ABV 4.5%) ◆
Good and black! Full roast aroma with fruit and malt tones. Roast dominates with a bitter, fruity finish and mouth-watering liquorice flavours.

White Star (OG 1050, ABV 4.8%) ◆
Golden bitter with some hop and fruit aromas. Touches of honey and citrus begin

the taste. Malty sweetness arrives but quickly gives way to a bitterness that lingers to perfection.

Captain Smith's Strong Ale (OG 1054, ABV 5.2%) ◆
Red with a hoppy aroma plus malt and a touch of sulphur. Fine balance of hop and caramel with roast and hints of malt and fruit. Sweet to start then a hoppy, bitter finish with a fruity layer.

Toll End

◘ Toll End Brewery, 131 Toll End Road, Tipton, West Midlands, DY4 0ET
Tel 07843 717933
Tours by arrangement

A four-barrel brewery that opened in 2004. With the exception of Phoebe's Ale, named after the brewer's daughter, all brews commemorate local events, landmarks and people. Toll End is brewing to full capacity and produces around 300 gallons a week. Four outlets are supplied.

Horace Bitter (ABV 3.8%)

Lost City Mild (ABV 4%)

Darby Ginger (ABV 4.2%)

William Perry (ABV 4.3%)

Great Escape (ABV 4.4%)

Upper Cut (ABV 4.5%)

PA/Phoebe's Ale (ABV 4.7%)

Power Station (ABV 4.9%)
Cask-conditioned lager.

Coal Ole (ABV 5.1%)

Tollgate*

Tollgate Brewery, Unit 8 Viking Business Centre, High Street, Woodville, Derbyshire, DE11 7EH
Tel/Fax (01283) 229194
Email tollgatebrewery@tiscali.co.uk

Tollgate is a six-barrel brewery in one of the 12 units on the site of the old Brunt & Bucknall Brewery, which was bought out and closed by Bass in 1927. Seasonal beer: Woodville Winter Warmer (ABV 5.4%, Nov-Feb).

Special/TGS (OG 1043, ABV 4.3%)

Light/TGL (OG 1045, ABV 4.5%)

Red Star IPA (OG 1045, ABV 4.5%)

Topsham & Exminster

Topsham & Exminster Brewery, Lions Rest Industrial Estate, Exminster, Exeter, Devon, EX6 8DZ
Tel (01392) 823013
Website www.topexe.co.uk
Tours by arrangement

The brewery was established in 2003 and is located in the Exminster Marshes, a popular bird sanctuary on the River Exe. The brew run is now 10 barrels and while Ferryman is the regular brew others occasionally appear in a few selected local pubs and clubs.

Ferryman (OG 1041, ABV 4.4%)

Tower SIBA

Tower Brewery, The Old Water Tower, Walsitch Maltings, Glensyl Way, Burton upon Trent, Staffordshire, DE14 1LX
Tel/Fax (01283) 530695
Email towerbrewery@aol.com
Tours by arrangement

Tower was established in 2001 by John Mills, previously the brewer at Burton Bridge, in a converted derelict water tower of Thomas Salt's maltings. The conversion was given a Civic Society award for the restoration of a Historic Industrial Building in 2001. Tower has 20 regular outlets. Seasonal beers: Sundowner (ABV 4%, May-Aug), Spring Equinox (ABV 4.6%, March-May), Autumn Equinox (ABV 4.6%, Sept-Nov), Winter Spirit (ABV 5%).

Thomas Salt's Bitter (OG 1038, ABV 3.8%)

Bitter (OG 1042, ABV 4.2%) ◆
Gold coloured with a malty, caramel and hoppy aroma. A full hop and fruit taste with the fruit lingering. A bitter and astringent finish.

Malty Towers (OG 1044, ABV 4.4%) ◆
Yellow with a malty aroma and a hint of tobacco. Strong hops give a long, dry, bitter finish with pleasant astringency.

Pale Ale (OG 1048, ABV 4.8%)

Tower of Strength (OG 1076, ABV 7.6%)

Townes SIBA

◘ Townes Brewery, Speedwell Inn, Lowgates, Staveley, Chesterfield, Derbyshire, S43 3TT
Tel (01246) 472252
Email curly@townes48.wanadoo.co.uk
Tours by arrangement

⊗ Townes Brewery started in 1994 in an old bakery on the outskirts of Chesterfield using a five-barrel plant. It was the first brewery in the town for more than 40 years. After a period of steady progress, the Speedwell Inn at Staveley was bought and the plant was moved to the rear of the pub. Brewing at Staveley started in 1997 and, after a period of renovation, the pub opened a year later. It was the first brew-pub in north Derbyshire in the 20th century. Bottling is now established and there are plans to extend this part of the operation. More than 40 outlets are supplied on an occasional basis. Seasonal beers: Stargazer (ABV 5.5%, winter), Sunshine (ABV 3.7%, summer). A monthly special is available under the Real Gone motif. Two seasonal milds are produced to increase interest in the style: Golden Bud (ABV 3.8%, summer) and Muffin Man (ABV 4.6%, winter). Staveley Cross, IPA, Oatmeal Stout and Staveleyan are also available in bottle-conditioned form and are suitable for vegetarians and vegans.

Speedwell Bitter (OG 1039, ABV 3.9%)

Lockoford Best Bitter (ABV 4%)

Lowgate Light (OG 1041, ABV 4.1%)

Staveley Cross (OG 1043, ABV 4.3%)

IPA (OG 1045, ABV 4.5%) ◘

Oatmeal Stout (OG 1047, ABV 4.7%)

Staveleyan (OG 1049, ABV 4.9%)

Town House

Town House Brewery Ltd, Units 1-4 Townhouse Studios, Townhouse Farm, Alsager Road, Audley, Staffordshire, ST7 8JQ
Tel 07976 209437 / 07812 035143
Email j.nixon2@btinternet.com
Tours by arrangement

⊛ Town House was set up by Tony Nixon in 2002 with a 2.5-barrel plant. It mainly supplied the Plough at Bignall End and a few other local outlets. In 2004 the brewery scaled up to a five-barrel plant. Demand is growing rapidly and in early 2006 two additional fermenting vessels were added. Bottling is planned for the future. Some 30 outlets are supplied.

Audley Bitter (OG 1038, ABV 3.8%)
A pale, well-balanced session bitter with a citrus hop character.

Flowerdew (OG 1039, ABV 4%) ◆
Golden with a wonderful floral aroma. Fabulous flavour of flowery hops delivering a hoppy bite and presenting a lingering taste of flowery citrus waves.

Dark Horse (OG 1042, ABV 4.3%)
A dark ruby ale with malt character and late hoppy finish.

Audley Gold (OG 1043, ABV 4.5%) ◆
Golden premium bitter with a spicy, fruity hop character.

Armstrong Ale (OG 1045, ABV 4.8%)
A rich, fruity ruby red beer with a hoppy, dry finish.

Monument Ale (OG 1048, ABV 5%)
A copper-coloured, well-balanced strong ale with a pronounced malt character.

Traquair SIBA

Traquair House Brewery, Traquair House, Innerleithen, Peeblesshire, EH44 6PW
Tel (01896) 830323
Fax (01896) 830639
Email enquiries@traquair.co.uk
Website www.traquair.co.uk
Shop Easter-Aug 12-5pm daily (June-Aug 10.30am-5pm)
Tours by arrangement

⊛ The 18th-century brewhouse is based in one of the wings of the 1,000-year-old Traquair House, Scotland's oldest inhabited house, visited by Mary Queen of Scots and Prince Charles Edward Stuart. The brewhouse was rediscovered by the 20th Laird, the late Peter Maxwell Stuart, in 1965. He began brewing again using all the original equipment, which remained intact, despite having lain idle for more than 100 years. The brewery has been run by Peter's daughter, Catherine Maxwell Stuart, since his death in 1990. The Maxwell Stuarts are members of the Stuart clan, and the main Bear Gates will remain shut until a Stuart returns to the throne. All the beers are oak-fermented and 60 per cent of production is exported, mostly bottled Traquair House Ale and Jacobite Ale. Some five outlets take the cask beer. Seasonal beers: Stuart Ale (ABV 4.5%, summer), Bear Ale (ABV 5%, winter).

House Ale (ABV 7%)

Tring SIBA

Tring Brewery Co Ltd, 81-82 Akeman Street, Tring, Hertfordshire, HP23 6AF
Tel (01442) 890721
Fax (01442) 890740
Email info@tringbrewery.com
Website www.tringbrewery.com
Shop Mon-Fri 9am-6pm; Sat 9am-12pm
Tours by arrangement (evenings only)

⊗ Founded in 1992 by Richard Shardlow, Tring Brewery is based on a small industrial estate and brews 35 barrels a week. In 2000 Andrew Jackson joined the company and took over the running of the brewery, enabling Richard to concentrate on his other business of building new breweries: he built the new Butcombe (qv) plant for example. Most of the beers take their names from local myths and legends. In addition to the regular, traditional and seasonal ales, Tring brews a selection of specials. Polypins and nine-pint mini-casks are available for collection from the small brewery shop by prior arrangement. There are plans to move the brewery to larger premises in the near future. Seasonal beers: Walter's Winter Ale (ABV 4%), Tapsters (ABV 4%), Fanny Ebbs Summer Ale (ABV 3.9%), Huck-Me-Buck (ABV 4.4%), Santa's Little Helper (ABV 4.8%).

Side Pocket for a Toad (OG 1035, ABV 3.6%)
Citrus notes from American Cascade hops balanced with a floral aroma and a crisp, dry finish in a straw-coloured ale.

Brock Bitter (ABV 3.7%)
A light brown session ale with hints of sweetness and caramel, gentle bitterness and a hop aroma from Styrian hops.

Mansion Mild (ABV 3.7%)
Smooth and creamy dark ruby mild with a fruity palate and gentle late hop.

Ridgeway (OG 1039, ABV 4%)
Balanced malt and hop flavours with a dry, flowery hop aftertaste.

Jack O'Legs (OG 1041, ABV 4.2%)
A combination of four types of malt and two types of aroma hops provide a copper-coloured premium ale with full fruit and a distinctive hoppy bitterness.

Tea Kettle Stout (ABV 5%)
Rich and complex traditional stout with a hint of liquorish and moderate bitterness.

Colley's Dog (OG 1051, ABV 5.2%)
Dark but not over-rich, strong yet drinkable, this premium ale has a long dry finish with overtones of malt and walnuts.

Triple fff SIBA

Triple fff Brewing Co Ltd, Magpie Works, Station Approach, Four Marks, Alton, Hampshire, GU34 5HN
Tel (01420) 561422
Email sales-triplefbrewery@tiscali.co.uk
Website www.triplefff.com
Shop Mon-Fri 9am-5pm; weekends to be confirmed
Tours by arrangement

⊗ The brewery was founded in 1997 with a five-barrel plant. It is now under the sole ownership of Graham Trott, who also owns the Railway Arms and Leathern Bottle in Alton. Triple fff has enjoyed increasing national success over the years, winning more than 50 awards including Champion Best Bitter and Champion Mild at the Great British Beer Festival. In 2006 the brewery moved to the historic village of Selborne, increasing the plant from 18 barrels to 50 barrels. More than 200 outlets are supplied. Seasonal beers: Apache Rose Peacock (ABV 4.2%, April-May), Snowblind (ABV 4.2%, Dec-Jan), Little Red Rooster (ABV 5%, March-May), Comfortably Numb (ABV 5%, Nov-Feb), Sumer is Icumin (ABV 6%, May-Sept), Witches Promise (ABV 6%, December), I Can't Remember (ABV 6.8%).

Alton's Pride (ABV 3.8%)
Excellent, clean-tasting, golden brown session bitter, full-bodied for its strength. A glorious aroma of floral hops. An initial malty flavour fades as citrus notes and hoppiness take over, leading to a lasting hoppy, bitter finish.

Pressed Rat & Warthog (ABV 3.8%)
Complex hoppy and bitter mild; not in the classic style but nevertheless delicious. Ruby in colour, a roast malt aroma with hints of blackcurrant and chocolate lead to a well-balanced flavour with roast, fruit and malt vying with the hoppy bitterness and a dry bitter finish.

Moondance (ABV 4.2%)
A pale brown-coloured best bitter; less intense than in the past, but still wonderfully hopped, with an aromatic, citrus hop nose balanced by bitterness and a hint of sweetness in the mouth. Bitterness increases in the finish as the fruit declines.

Stairway (ABV 4.6%)
An aroma of pale and crystal malts introduces this pale brown beer with a flavour of summer fruits. Well-balanced, with a dry, strong, hoppy finish. Predominantly bitter with some sweetness and malt.

I Can't Remember (ABV 6.8%)

Trossach's Craft

Trossach's Craft Brewery, Lade Inn, Kilmahog, Callender, FK17 8HD

Not currently brewing. The kit has been removed and the beers listed are being produced by Stirling Brewery (qv).

Tryst

Tryst Brewery, Lorne Road, Larbert, Stirling, FK5 4AT
Tel (01324) 554000
Email johnmcgarva@tinyworld.co.uk
Tours by arrangement

John McGarva, a member of Scottish Craft Brewers, started brewing in 2003 in an industrial unit near Larbert station. Some 35 outlets are supplied. All beers are now also available bottle-conditioned since Carronade IPA won Champion Bottle-conditioned Beer of Scotland in 2005.

Brockville Dark (OG 1039, ABV 3.8%)

Brockville Pale (OG 1039, ABV 3.8%)

Festival Red (OG 1041, ABV 4%)

Buckled Wheel (OG 1043, ABV 4.2%)

Carronade IPA (OG 1043, ABV 4.2%)

Tunnel SIBA

Tunnel Brewery Limited, Lord Nelson Inn, Birmingham Road, Ansley, Nuneaton, Warwickshire, CV10 9PQ
Tel (02476) 394888
Email info@tunnelbrewery.co.uk
Website www.tunnelbrewery.co.uk
Shop open Sat & Sun mornings
Tours by arrangement

Bob Yates and Mike Walsh started brewing in 2005, taking the name from a rail tunnel that passes under the village. Maris Otter malts and local and international hops are used. Pub and brewery are independent of one another but the beers are available in the pub as well as being supplied to more than 40 outlets. A shop at the brewery is planned. Seasonal beers: Meadowland (ABV 3.8%, spring), Fields of Gold (ABV 5%, summer), Boston Beer Party (ABV 5.6%, autumn), Winter Storm (ABV 6%, winter). Bottle-conditioned beers: Late Ott, Sweet Parish Ale, Trade Winds, Nelsons Column, Boston Beer Party.

Late Ott (OG 1040, ABV 4%)
Dark golden session bitter with a fruity nose and perfumed hop edge. The finish is dry and bitter.

Trade Winds (OG 1045, ABV 4.6%)
An aromatic, copper-coloured beer with an aroma of Cascade hops and a clean, crisp hint of citrus, followed by fruity malts and a dry finish full of scented hops.

Sweet Parish Ale (OG 1047, ABV 4.7%)
A reddish-amber, malty ale with a slight chocolate aroma enhanced by citrus notes on the nose. It becomes increasingly fruity as the English hops kick in. Smooth, gentle hop bitterness in the finish.

Nelsons Column (OG 1051, ABV 5.2%)
A ruby red, strong old English ale.

Turkey

Turkey Brewery, Turkey Inn, Goose Eye, Oakworth, Keighley, West Yorkshire, BD22 0PD
Tel (01535) 681339
Tours by arrangement

Turkey is a purpose-built brewery with walls four feet thick, built into the hillside at the back of the pub. Some of the beers are named after local caves. Brewery trips are free, with a small donation to Upper Wharfdale Fell Rescue. Beer festivals are staged every May Bank Holiday.

Bitter (ABV 3.9%)

Black Shiver (ABV 4.3%)

Twickenham

Twickenham Fine Ales Ltd, The Crane Brewery, Ryecroft Works, Edwin Road, Twickenham, Middlesex, TW2 6SP
Tel (020) 8241 1825
Fax (020) 8241 2815
Email info@twickenham-fine-ales.co.uk
Website www.twickenham-fine-ales.co.uk
Tours by arrangement

The brewery was set up in the autumn of 2004 by Steve Brown, with many small investors. It was the first brewery in Twickenham since the 1920s. The 10-barrel plant was purchased from Springhead Brewery. In the summer of 2005 former Grand Union brewer Tom Madeiros joined the company. The brewery supplies some 100 pubs and clubs in west London. Bottling was due to start during 2006. Seasonal beers: Spring Ale (ABV 4.3%), Strong & Dark (ABV 5.2%, Oct-March).

Crane Sundancer (OG 1037, ABV 3.7%)
Amber bitter with a citrus fruity hop nose that flows through to the taste, leaving a short, sharp, bitter finish.

Advantage Ale (OG 1040, ABV 4%)
A copper-coloured beer with citrus notes throughout. Malt notes are slightly caramelised and a hoppy bitterness is present in both taste and aftertaste.

Original (OG 1042, ABV 4.2%)
Malt is prevalent with an overlaying bitterness producing a smooth, easy-drinking pale brown beer.

IPA (OG 1045, ABV 4.5%)
An amber beer that has a spicy hop aroma giving way to citrus hops on the palate and faintly in the short, bitter finish.

Ufford

Ufford Ales Ltd, White Hart, Main Street, Ufford, Cambridgeshire, PE9 3BH
Tel (01780) 740250
Tours by arrangement

Ufford Ales opened in 2005 and in 2006 additional fermenting vessels gave the brewery four times its original capacity. Beers are currently available at the Periwig and the Crown Hotel in Stamford as well as Smith's of Bourne and the White Hart, Ufford. Seasonal ales are also produced.

Idle Hour (OG 1040, ABV 3.9%)
Amber-gold bitter with a light malty aroma. The malt is supported in the mouth by a gentle hoppy bite as the bitterness grows.

Setting Sun (OG 1050, ABV 5.2%)

Snow Storm (OG 1053, ABV 5.6%)

Uley

Uley Brewery Ltd, The Old Brewery, 31 The Street, Uley, Gloucestershire, GL11 5TB
Tel/Fax (01453) 860120
Email chas@uleybrewery.com
Website www.uleybrewery.com
Shop open Sat morning
Tours by arrangement

Brewing at Uley began in 1833 at Price's Brewery. After a long gap, the premises were restored and Uley Brewery opened in 1985. It has its own spring water, which is used to mash with Tucker's Maris Otter malt and boiled with Herefordshire hops. No sugar or additives are used. Uley serves 40-50 free trade outlets in the Cotswold area and is brewing to capacity. Expansion is not an option as the brewery is a listed building. Seasonal ales: Harping Hog (ABV 5%).

Hogshead PA (OG 1038, ABV 3.8%)
A pale-coloured, hoppy session bitter with a good hop aroma and a full flavour for its strength, ending in a bitter-sweet aftertaste.

Bitter (OG 1040, ABV 4%)
A copper-coloured beer with hops and fruit in the aroma and a malty, fruity taste, underscored by a hoppy bitterness. The finish is dry, with a balance of hops and malt.

Laurie Lee's Bitter (OG 1045, ABV 4.5%)

Old Ric (OG 1045, ABV 4.5%)
A full-flavoured, hoppy bitter with some fruitiness and a smooth, balanced finish. Distinctively copper-coloured, this is the house beer for the Old Spot Inn, Dursley.

Old Spot Prize Ale (OG 1050, ABV 5%)
A distinctive full-bodied, red/brown ale with a fruity aroma, a malty, fruity taste, with a hoppy bitterness, and a strong, balanced aftertaste.

Pig's Ear Strong Beer (OG 1050, ABV 5%)
A pale-coloured beer, deceptively strong. Notably bitter in flavour, with a hoppy, fruity aroma and a bitter finish.

Ulverston*

Office: Ulverston Brewery, 59 Urswick Road, Ulverston, Cumbria, LA12 9LJ
Brewery: Diamond Buildings, Pennington Lane, Lindal in Furness, Cumbria, LA12 0LE
Tel (01229) 584280 / 07840 192022
Email paulandanita@brewery.e7even.com

Anita Garnett and Paul Swann purchased the ex-Whitley Bridge four-barrel plant in 2005 and, following test brews, went into full production in March 2006.

Harvest Moon (ABV 3.9%)

Laughing Gravy (ABV 4.1%)

Lonesome Pine (ABV 4.3%)

Bad Medicine (ABV 6%)

Uncle Stuarts EAB

Uncle Stuarts Brewery, Antoma, Pack Lane, Lingwood, Norwich, Norfolk, NR13 4PD
Tel (01603) 211833/07732 012112
Email stuartsbrewery@aol.com
Website www.unclestuartsbrewery.com
Tours by arrangement

The brewery started in 2002, selling bottle-conditioned beers and polypins direct to customers and by mail order. Since 2003, all the beers have also been available in nine-gallon casks. Seasonal beer: Xmas (ABV 7%).

Pack Lane **(OG 1038, ABV 4%)**

Excelsior **(OG 1042, ABV 4.5%)**

Church View **(OG 1050, ABV 4.7%)**

Buckenham Woods **(OG 1051, ABV 5.6%)**

Upper Agbrigg

See Holme Valley Ales

Ushers

See Wadworth and Wychwood

Vale SIBA

Vale Brewery Co, Thame Road, Haddenham, Buckinghamshire, HP17 8BY
Tel (01844) 290008
Fax (01844) 292505
Email valebrewery@yahoo.co.uk
Website www.valebrewery.co.uk
Tours by arrangement

⊗ After many years working for large regional breweries and allied industries, brothers Mark and Phil Stevens opened a small, purpose-built brewery in Haddenham. This revived brewing in a village where the last brewery closed at the end of World War II. The plant was expanded in 1996, 1999 and 2005 and now has a capacity of 60 barrels. All the beer is traditionally brewed without adjuncts, chemicals, or preservatives. A bottling line was added in 1997, which produces a range of 10 different ales plus own label beers in short runs. In 2003 the brewery took over an additional unit on the estate to give it larger storage for conditioning beer, a reception area and a brewery shop. Vale now runs five pubs and around 250 local outlets take the beers. Seasonal beers: Hadda's Spring Gold (ABV 4.6%), Hadda's Summer Glory (ABV 4%), Hadda's Autumn Ale (ABV 4.5%), Hadda's Winter Solstice (ABV 4.1%), Good King Senseless (ABV 5.2%). Bottle-conditioned beers: all regular cask beers except Notley Ale. All are suitable for vegetarians and vegans.

Black Swan Dark Mild **(OG 1033, ABV 3.3%)**

Notley Ale **(OG 1033, ABV 3.3%)** ◆
A refreshing, copper-coloured session bitter with some malt in the aroma and taste, and an uncompromisingly dry finish.

Best Bitter **(OG 1036, ABV 3.7%)** ◆
This pale amber beer starts with a slight fruit aroma. This leads to a clean, bitter taste where hops and fruit dominate. The finish is long and bitter with a slight hop note.

Wychert Ale **(OG 1038, ABV 3.9%)**
A full-flavoured beer with nutty overtones.

Black Beauty Porter **(OG 1043, ABV 4.3%)** ◆
A complex, black-coloured porter with little aroma and a thin, balanced bitter-sweet taste with roast flavours dominating. The finish is dry and bitter.

Edgar's Golden Ale **(OG 1043, ABV 4.3%)** ◆
A golden, hoppy best bitter with some sweetness and a dry, bitter-sweet finish. An unpretentious and well-crafted beer.

Special **(OG 1046, ABV 4.5%)**
Deep brown-coloured premium ale brewed with Maris Otter, crystal and chocolate malts blended with choicest hops.

Grumpling Premium Ale **(OG 1046, ABV 4.6%)**

Hadda's Headbanger **(OG 1050, ABV 5%)**

Vale of Glamorgan*

Vale of Glamorgan Brewery Ltd, Unit 8a Atlantic Trading Estate, Barry, Vale of Glamorgan, CF63 3RF
Tel/Fax (01446) 730757
Email info@vogbrewery.co.uk
Website www.vogbrewery.co.uk
Tours by arrangement

Vale of Glamorgan Brewery started brewing in 2005 on a 10-barrel plant. Future plans are to bottle some beers and produce seasonal brews. More than 30 outlets are supplied direct.

The Session VoG **(OG 1034, ABV 3.7%)**

The Original No.1 VoG **(OG 1039, ABV 4.2%)**

The Special VoG **(OG 1047, ABV 4.8%)**

Valhalla

Valhalla Brewery, Shetland Refreshments Ltd, Baltasound, Unst, Shetland, ZE2 9DX
Tel/Fax (01957) 711658
Email mail@valhallabrewery.co.uk
Website www.valhallabrewery.co.uk
Tours by arrangement

The brewery started production in 1997, set up by husband and wife team Sonny and Sylvia Priest. A bottling plant was installed in 1999. The Priests plan a new brewery/visitor centre within the next two years. One outlet is supplied direct.

White Wife **(OG 1038, ABV 3.8%)** ◆
Predominantly malty aroma with hop and fruit, which remain on the palate. The aftertaste is increasingly bitter.

Old Scatness **(OG 1038, ABV 4%)**
A light bitter, named after a famous archaeological dig at the south end of Shetland where early evidence of malting and brewing was found. One of the ingredients is an ancient strain of barley called Bere which used to be common in Shetland until the middle of the last century.

Simmer Dim **(OG 1039, ABV 4%)** ◆
A light golden bitter, named after the long Shetland twilight. The sulphur features do not mask the fruits and hops of this well-balanced beer.

Auld Rock (OG 1043, ABV 4.5%) ◆
A full-bodied, dark Scottish-style best bitter, it has a rich malty nose but does not lack bitterness in the long dry finish.

Sjolmet Stout (OG 1048, ABV 5%) ◆
Full of malt and roast barley, especially in the taste. Smooth, creamy, fruity finish, not as dry as some stouts.

Ventnor SIBA

Ventnor Brewery Ltd, 119 High Street, Ventnor, Isle of Wight, PO38 1LY
Tel (01983) 856161
Fax (01983) 530960
Email sales@ventnorbrewery.co.uk
Website www.ventnorbrewery.co.uk
Shop Mon-Fri 9am-5pm; Sat 10.30am-1pm (Online shop also available)

⊛ Beer has been brewed on the site since 1840. The beers today are still made with St Boniface natural spring water that flows through the brewery. Ventnor has a 10-barrel plant and supplies pub chains, wholesalers and supermarkets nationwide. Some 90 outlets are supplied. Seasonal beers: Antifreeze (ABV 5.2%), De-Icer (ABV 4.5%, Nov-Jan), Old Ruby (ABV 4.7%, February), Molly Downer (ABV 4.2%, March), Druid Fluid (ABV 4.5%, May), Samphire, Hooray Henry, BestivAle (ABV 4%, September). Bottle-conditioned beer: Old Ruby Ale (ABV 4.7%). Hygeia Organic Ale is suitable for vegetarians and vegans.

Ventnor Golden Bitter (OG 1040, ABV 4%) ◆
Creamy, light bitter with hints of honey and gorse persisting through to the aftertaste.

Sunfire (OG 1043, ABV 4.3%) ◆
A generously and distinctively bittered amber beer that could be toned down if pulled through a sparkler.

Hippy High Ale (ABV 4.4%)
A light, hoppy beer brewed especially for Radio 1 DJ Rob Da Bank's first Bestival 2004 on the Isle of Wight.

Pistol Night (OG 1043, ABV 4.4%) ◆
Deceptive light, flowery, professionally-crafted hoppy bitter with scents and flavours of early spring that continue through to a pleasant and satisfying finish.

Oyster Stout (OG 1045, ABV 4.5%) ◆
Rich, sugary, malty but watery dark brown beer.

Hygeia Organic Ale (OG 1046, ABV 4.6%) ◆
A malty but refreshing beer.

Wight Spirit (OG 1050, ABV 5%) ◆
Predominantly bitter, hoppy and fruity strong and very pale ale.

Sandrock Smoked Ale (OG 1056, ABV 5.6%)
A smoked beer created to commemorate the famous Sandrock Inn in Niton, tragically destroyed by fire in 1985. Brewed using peated malt and a combination of hops.

Verulam

See Alehouse

Village Brewer

See Hambleton

Wadworth IFBB

Wadworth & Co Ltd, Northgate Brewery, Devizes, Wiltshire, SN10 1JW
Tel (01380) 723361
Fax (01380) 724342
Email sales@wadworth.co.uk
Website www.wadworth.co.uk
Shop (reception) Mon-Fri 9am-5pm
Tours: Trade April-Oct; Public September (by prior arrangement)

⊗ A market town brewery set up in 1885 by Henry Wadworth, it is one of few remaining producers to sell beer locally in oak casks; the brewery still employs a cooper. Though solidly traditional, with its own dray horses, it continues to invest in the future and to expand, producing up to 2,000 barrels a week to supply a wide-ranging free trade, around 300 outlets in the south of England, as well as its own 256 pubs. All tied houses serve cask beer. Wadworth 6X is still handmade in Devizes and sold nationally through wholesalers, pubcos and regional brewers. Wadworth also has a 2.5-barrel micro-brewery used for brewing trials, speciality brews and the production of cask mild. Seasonal beers: Old Father Timer (ABV 5.8%, Nov-Dec), Malt n' Hops (ABV 4.5%, Oct-Nov), Summersault (ABV 4%, May-Sept), Bishops Tipple (ABV 5.5%, winter).

Henry's IPA (OG 1035, ABV 3.6%)

6X (OG 1041, ABV 4.3%) ◆
Copper-coloured ale with a malty and fruity nose, and some balancing hop character. The flavour is similar, with some bitterness and a lingering malty, but bitter finish. Full-bodied and distinctive.

JCB (OG 1046 ABV 4.7%)
A deep amber, robust but perfectly balanced, traditional English ale with a rich, malty body, complex hop character and a hint of tropical fruit in the aroma and taste. A gentle barley sugar sweetness blends wonderfully with smooth nutty malt and rounded hop bitterness before a dry, biscuity, bitter finish.

Wagtail*

Wagtail Brewery, New Barn Farm, Old Buckenham, Attleborough, Norfolk, NR17 1PF
Tel (01953) 887133
Email markandjo2@tesco.net
Shop open Sun (ring for times)

Wagtail brewery opened in March 2006, producing only bottle-conditioned beers at present. There are plans to make it the first brewery to be turbine powered and to brew using rainwater. Bottle-conditioned beers: Coopers Best (ABV 4.2%), April Fool (ABV 4.7%).

Wapping

◊ Wapping Beers Ltd, Baltic Fleet, 33A Wapping, Liverpool, Merseyside, L1 8DQ
Tel/Fax (0151) 707 2242

⊛ Established in 2002 using the former

Passageway plant, Wapping has expanded by installing another two fermenting vessels, increasing capacity by half. The brewery delivers to trade in the local area. Seasonal beers: Winter Ale (ABV 6.5%, Nov-Feb).

Bitter (OG 1036, ABV 3.6%)
Light, easy-drinking session beer with a good, bitter finish.

Bow Sprit (OG 1036, ABV 3.6%)

Baltic Gold (OG 1039, ABV 3.9%) ◈
Hoppy golden ale with plenty of citrus hop flavour. Refreshing with good body and mouthfeel.

Summer Ale (OG 1042, ABV 4.2%)
Golden/straw coloured, thirst-quenching with a bite in the finish.

Stout (OG 1050, ABV 5%) ◈
Classic dry roasty stout with strong bitterness balanced by fruit and hop flavours. The flavours follow through to a pleasantly dry finish.

Warcop

Warcop Country Ales, 9 Nellive Park, St Brides Wentlooge, Gwent, NP10 8SE
Tel/Fax (01633) 680058
Email william.picton@tesco.net
Website www.warcopales.com

A small brewery based in a converted milking parlour, serving 30 outlets and others supplied by two wholesalers. Cask ales are also available bottle conditioned. The beers below are made on a cyclical basis, the full repertoire normally being made twice a year. Five to six beers are normally in stock at any one time. There is also a stock of four to eight bottled beers. Seasonal beers (normally brewed for Christmas or beer festivals): Red Hot Furnace (ABV 9%), Dark Furnace (ABV 7.5%), Furnace Fire (ABV 7.2%), Spinners (ABV 6.4%), Oil Fire (ABV 6-6.7%), Crushers (ABV 6.7%), War Paint (ABV 8%).

Pit Shaft (ABV 3.4%)
Dark mild.

Pitside (ABV 3.7%)
A malty beer with a delicate taste.

Arc (ABV 3.8%)
Light session beer with a dry, hoppy taste.

Pit Prop (ABV 3.8%) ◈
Fruit and roast aroma, dark brown in colour. A mixture of roast, malt, caramel and fruit in taste and aftertaste. The bitterness builds, adding to the character.

Black and Amber (ABV 4%)
A traditional pale ruby bitter, lightly hopped and full of flavour.

Casnewydd (ABV 4%)
Light, easy-drinking beer.

Drillers (ABV 4%)
A lightly hopped, golden-yellow ale.

Hackers (ABV 4%)
Pale yellow, lightly-hopped bitter.

Hilston Premier (ABV 4%)
Rustic coloured, medium dry, autumnal beer.

Steeler's (ABV 4.2%)
Light red, malty-tasting brew.

Brokers (ABV 4.3%)
A lightly-hopped golden bitter.

Raiders (ABV 4.3%)
A lightly hopped, strong yellow ale.

Rollers (ABV 4.3%)
A light ruby-coloured, well hopped bitter.

Cutters (ABV 4.4%)
A pale yellow, hoppy ale.

Zen (ABV 4.4%)
A light yellow ale with a dry finish.

Furnace (ABV 4.5%)
A ruby-coloured malty beer with a dry finish.

Honeyed Stout (ABV 4.5%)
Stout with honey provided by local bees.

Refuge (ABV 4.5%)
A well hopped, golden-yellow strong ale using Fuggles hops.

Riggers (ABV 4.5%)
A strongly hopped golden beer with body.

Printers (ABV 4.6%)
Pale yellow strong ale.

Forgers (ABV 4.8%)
A strong, golden ale.

Rockers (ABV 4.8%)
A pale yellow, refreshing strong ale.

Tanners (ABV 4.8%)
A strong ale.

Deep Pit (ABV 5%)
Ruby, full-bodied beer with distinctive taste.

Dockers (ABV 5%)
Golden, fruity, full-bodied beer with real taste.

Painters (ABV 5%)
Pale yellow, full-bodied strong ale.

Blasters (ABV 5.4%)
A yellow strong ale.

Caspa (ABV 5.4%)
A strong lager with an aftertaste of citrus/grapefruit.

Shunters (ABV 5.4%)
A strong, golden ale.

Fulcrum (ABV 5.6%)
A stronger version of Deep Pit.

QE2 (ABV 6%)
A pale yellow, full-bodied, strong ale.

Warrior

Warrior Brewing Co, 4 Old Matford House, Old Matford Lane, Alphington, Exeter, Devon, EX2 8XS
Tel (01392) 221451
Email warrior@warrior.go-plus.net

James and Jude Warrior started brewing in 2004. James has been a professional actor for more than 30 years and has to suspend brewing from time to time when he is called away to work in the theatre or appear before the cameras. The brewery has a five-barrel plant and supplies around 12 outlets, three of which are on a regular weekly basis. James plans a small-scale bottling enterprise within the next year. Seasonal beer: Custer's Last Stand (ABV 6.8%, Dec-Feb).

Tomahawk (OG 1042, ABV 4%)
A full-bodied bitter with lots of hops.

Geronimo (OG 1049, ABV 4.9%)
A hoppy, refreshing amber bitter.

Warwickshire

Warwickshire Beer Co Ltd, The Brewery, Queen Street, Cubbington, Leamington Spa, Warwickshire, CV32 7NA
Tel (01926) 450747
Fax (01926) 450763
Email info@warwickshirebeer.co.uk
Shop Sat 8am-12pm (ring first)
Tours by arrangement

Warwickshire is a six-barrel brewery operating in a former village bakery since 1998. Brewing takes place four times a week and, in addition, some beer is produced under licence by Highgate Brewery. The cask beers are available in approximately 80 outlets as well as the brewery's two pubs, the Market Tavern in Atherstone and the Market Tavern in Southam. Polypins and bottles are available from the brewery shop. Seasonal beers: Xmas Bare (ABV 4.9%), Thunderbolt (ABV 8.5%). Bottle-conditioned beers: Best Bitter, Lady Godiva, Churchyard Bob, King Maker.

Shakespeare's County (OG 1034, ABV 3.4%)
A very light session ale.

Best Bitter (OG 1039, ABV 3.9%)
A golden brown session bitter flavoured with First Gold hops.

Lady Godiva (OG 1042, ABV 4.2%)
Blond, gentle, and full-bodied.

Falstaff (OG 1044, ABV 4.4%)
A mahogany-coloured bitter flavoured with Cascade and First Gold hops.

Golden Bear (OG 1049, ABV 4.9%)
Golden in colour with well-balanced bitterness and spicy/fruity notes.

Churchyard Bob (OG 1049, ABV 4.9%)

King Maker (OG 1055, ABV 5.5%)

Watermill*

Watermill Brewing Company, Watermill Inn, Ings, nr Staveley, Kendal, Cumbria, LA8 9PY
Tel (01539) 821309
Fax (01539) 822309
Email doggiebeer@tiscali.co.uk
Website www.watermillinn.co.uk
Tours by arrangement

Watermill was established in 2006. The five-barrel plant and equipment were originally at the Hops Bar & Grill opposite Daytona International Speedway, USA. The beers are named with a 'play on words' to do with dogs, which are allowed in the main bar of the pub.

Collie Wobbles (ABV 3.9%)

A Bit'a Ruff (ABV 4.4%)

W'Ruff Night (ABV 5%)

Tomos Watkin SIBA

Hurns Brewing Company Ltd t/a Tomos Watkin, Unit 3 Century Park, Valley Way, Swansea Enterprise Park, Swansea, SA6 8RP
Tel (01792) 797300/797264
Fax (01792) 797281
Email beer@hurns.co.uk
Website www.hurnsbeer.co.uk
Shop Mon-Fri 9am-5pm
Tours by arrangement

Brewing started in 1995 in Llandeilo using a 10-barrel plant in converted garages. Tomos Watkin moved to larger premises in Swansea in 2000 and the plant increased to a 50-barrel capacity. HBC Ltd was formed in 2002 when the Swansea Brewery was purchased from Tomos Watkin. The addition of bottled beers has allowed successful entry into several major national supermarket chains. Plans are under way to build a state-of-the-art, interactive visitor centre with shop and brewery tap. Some 100 outlets are supplied. Seasonal beers: Cwrw Ceridwen (ABV 4.2%, spring), Cwrw Haf (ABV 4.2%, summer), Owain Glyndwr (ABV 4.2%, autumn), Cwrw Santa (ABV 4.6%, winter).

Cwrw Braf (OG 1037, ABV 3.7%)

Brewery Bitter (OG 1041, ABV 4%)
Dark amber with a malt and hop aroma. A rounded blend of malt, hops and fruit with a building bitterness.

Merlin Stout (OG 1043, ABV 4.2%)
Dark brown with a malty and roast aroma. Pleasing blend of malt, roast, caramel and background hop flavour with a balancing bitterness and a similar lasting finish. A rounded and satisfying beer.

Old Style Bitter/OSB (OG 1046, ABV 4.5%)
Amber with an inviting aroma of hops and malt. Full bodied, a mix of hops, fruit, malt and bitterness with a balanced bitter finish.

Waveney

Waveney Brewing Co, Queen's Head, Station Road, Earsham, Norfolk, NR35 2TS
Tel (01986) 892623
Email lyndahamps@aol.com

Established at the Queens Head in 2004 by landlord and landlady John and Lynda Hamps with the aid of Tom Knox, head brewer at Nethergate (qv), the five-barrel brewery produces three beers, regularly available at the pub along with free trade outlets. Occasional beers are brewed and there are plans to bottle beers in the near future. Seasonal beer: Raging Bullace (ABV 5.1%, Dec-Jan).

East Coast Mild (OG 1037, ABV 3.8%)
A traditional East Anglian mild with distinctive roast malt aroma and red-brown colouring. A sweet, plummy malt beginning quickly fades as a dry roasted bitterness

begins to make its presence felt.

Lightweight (OG 1039, ABV 3.9%) ◆
A gentle concoction with a light but well-balanced hop and malt character. A light body is reflected in the quick, bitter finish. Golden hued with a distinctive strawberry and cream nose.

Great White Hope (OG 1047, ABV 4.8%) ◆
A well-balanced golden brew with a dry, bitter character. Grapefruit in both aroma and taste gives depth and contrast. A long, slightly hoppy ending lingers on.

WC BREWERY
CHESTER

WC*

WC Brewery, 3 Micklegate, Mickle Trafford, Chester, Cheshire, CH2 4TF
Email thegents@wcbrewery.com
Website www.wcbrewery.com

Ian Williams and Steve Carr founded the brewery in 2003, initially to produce beers for friends and family. The local CAMRA branch got wind of the strong SBD though and the first public brew was donated to the Chester Charity beer festival in 2005. The 10-gallon plant is operated part time and is one of the smallest commercial breweries in the country. The best place to seek out one of the exclusive ales is either at the Bunbury Arms in Stoak or the Mill Hotel in Chester. Seasonal beers: B'Day (ABV 3.8%, June), Yellow Snow (ABV 5.5%, January).

IPA Ale (ABV 3.8%)
A pale beer, heavily hopped for extra bitternesss and a lingering citrus finish.

Gypsy's Kiss (ABV 4.1%)
A copper-coloured ale brewed to produce a well-balanced session bitter.

SBD (ABV 5%)
A premium ale; rich, fruity and deceptively strong.

Wear Valley*

Wear Valley Brewery, The Grand Hotel, South Church Road, Bishop Auckland, County Durham, DL14 6DU
Tel 07810 751425
Email mail@the-grand-hotel.co.uk
Website www.the-grand-hotel.co.uk
Tours by arrangement

The brewery was established in 2005 by partners Simon Gillespie and Ian Boyd. It is a four-barrel plant situated at the rear of the Grand Hotel. It was opened by the Bishop of Durham and the first brew was named Bishop's Blessing in his honour. Fifteen outlets are supplied. All beers are suitable for vegetarians and vegans.

Grand Canny'Un (ABV 3.8%)

Excalibur (ABV 3.9%)

Amos Ale (ABV 4.1%)

Auckland Ale (ABV 4.3%)

Morning After Stout (ABV 4.8%)

Weatheroak

Weatheroak Brewery Ltd, Coach & Horses Inn, Weatheroak Hill, Alvechurch, Birmingham, B48 7EA
Tel 07798 773894 (day) / (0121) 445 4411 (eve)
Email dave@weatheroakales.co.uk
Website www.weatheroakales.co.uk

⊠ The brewery was set up in 1997 in an outhouse at the Coach & Horses by Dave and Pat Smith by arrangement with pub owners Phil and Sheila Meads. The first brew was produced in 1998. A real ale off-licence has been opened in nearby Alvechurch. Weatheroak supplies 40 outlets. Seasonal beer: Miss Stout (ABV 4.7%, winter).

Light Oak (ABV 3.6%) ◆
This straw-coloured quaffing ale has lots of hoppy notes on the tongue and nose, and a fleetingly sweet aftertaste.

Ale (ABV 4.1%) ◆
The aroma is dominated by hops in this golden-coloured brew. Hops also feature in the mouth and there is a rapidly fading dry aftertaste.

Redwood (ABV 4.7%) ◆
A rich tawny strong bitter with a short-lived sweet fruit and malt balance.

Keystone Hops (ABV 5%) ◆
A golden yellow beer that is surprisingly easy to quaff given the strength. Fruity hops are the dominant flavour without the commonly associated astringency.

Webbs*

Webbs Brewery Ltd, Unit 12 Cwm Small Business Centre, Cwm, Ebbw Vale, NP23 7ST
Tel (01495) 370026
Email info@webbsbrewery.co.uk
Website www.webbsbrewery.co.uk
Tours by arrangement

The brewery was set up in 2006 with an 18-

Keep your Good Beer Guide up to date by visiting www.camra.org.uk, click on *Good Beer Guide* then *Updates to the GBG 2007* where you will find information about changes to breweries.

barrel plant. There are plans to bottle the beers in the near future. Around 35 outlets are supplied.

Huntsman (ABV 3.6%)

Black Widow (ABV 4.5%)

Tarantula (ABV 4.8%)

Arachnaphobia (ABV 5.1%)

Weetwood

Weetwood Ales Ltd, Weetwood Grange, Weetwood, Tarporley, Cheshire, CW6 0NQ
Tel (01829) 752377
Email sales@weetwoodales.co.uk
Website www.weetwoodales.co.uk

The brewery was set up at an equestrian centre in 1993. In 1998, the five-barrel plant was replaced by a 10-barrel kit. Around 200 regular customers are now supplied.

Best Bitter (OG 1038.5, ABV 3.8%)
Pale brown beer with an assertive bitterness and a lingering dry finish. Despite initial sweetness, peppery hops dominate throughout. A clean quaffing bitter that is well-balanced and robust.

Cheshire Cat (ABV 4%)
Pale, dry bitter with a spritzy lemon zest and a grapey aroma. Hoppy aroma leads through to the initial taste before fruitiness takes over. Smooth creamy mouthfeel and a short, dry finish.

Eastgate Ale (OG 1043.5, ABV 4.2%)
Well-balanced and refreshing clean amber beer. Citrus fruit flavours predominate in the taste and there is a short, dry aftertaste.

Old Dog Bitter (OG 1045, ABV 4.5%)
Robust, well-balanced amber beer with a slightly fruity aroma. Rich malt and fruit flavours are balanced by bitterness – the latter dominating the aftertaste. Some sweetness and a hint of sulphur on nose and taste.

Ambush Ale (OG 1047.5, ABV 4.8%)
Full-bodied malty, premium bitter with initial sweetness balanced by bitterness and leading to a long-lasting dry finish. Blackberries and bitterness predominate alongside the hops. Marzipan hints also present.

Oasthouse Gold (OG 1050, ABV 5%)
Straw-coloured, crisp, full-bodied and fruity golden ale with a good dry finish.

Wellington

See Crown & Wellington

Wells & Young's IFBB

Wells & Young's Brewing Co, Eagle Brewery, Havelock Street, Bedford, MK40 4LU
Tel (01234) 272766
Fax (01234) 279000
Email postmaster@charleswells.co.uk/sales@youngs.co.uk
Websites www.charleswells.co.uk/www.youngs.co.uk
Shop Mon-Thu 7.30am-10pm
Tours by arrangement

In May 2006, Charles Wells and Young & Co of Wandsworth, London, announced the creation of a new company, Wells & Young's Brewing. In October 2006 Young's planned to close its brewery and move production to Bedford. Young's had to find a new site as Wandsworth Council wants to redevelop the area, which has become too cramped for the brewery. Young's also needed additional capacity for its successful cask and bottled beers, and the brewery had been unable to find a suitable alternative site in London. Wells & Young's Brewing will jointly own the Eagle Brewery and will have a combined sales team to expand such key brands as Bombardier, the fastest-growing premium cask beer in Britain, and Young's Bitter, the fastest-growing standard cask bitter. Charles Wells and Young's will continue as separate companies and will operate their own pub estates. The brewing company will become the third in size to Greene King and Wolverhampton & Dudley.

Wells

Charles Wells was established in 1876 and is still run by descendants of the founder. The brewery has been on the current site since 1976 and owns 255 pubs, of which 230 serve cask beer. Wells also supplies a large number of other outlets, while wholesalers distribute the beers nationally. Seasonal beers: Summer Solstice (ABV 4.1%, June), Lock, Stock and Barrel (ABV 4.3%, September), Banana Bread Beer (ABV 4.5%, Jan/June), Winter Cheer (ABV 5.5%, Nov-Dec).

Eagle IPA (OG 1035, ABV 3.6%)
A refreshing, amber session bitter with pronounced citrus hop aroma and palate, faint malt in the mouth, and a lasting dry, bitter finish.

Bombardier (OG 1042, ABV 4.3%)
Gentle citrus hop is balanced by traces of malt in the mouth, and this pale brown best bitter ends with a lasting dryness. Sulphur often dominates the aroma, particularly with younger casks.

Young's

Charles Young and Anthony Bainbridge bought the Wandsworth brewery in 1831 where brewing had taken place continuously since 1581. The business was continued by the Young family and remains very much a family affair even though it is now a public company. Young's tied estate numbers 206 pubs and the company supplies 500-600 free trade accounts. Bottle-conditioned beers: Special London Ale (ABV 6.4%), Champion Live Ale (ABV 5%).

Bitter (OG 1036, ABV 3.7%)
A light brown bitter beer that is well balanced by fruity citrus hop notes and some malt, finishing with a refreshing dryness.

Special (OG 1044, ABV 4.5%)
Sweet citrus on the nose follows through into a malty, hoppy flavour with a dry bitter aftertaste and a touch of toffee.

Waggledance (OG 1052, ABV 5%)
An amber beer with some honey on the nose

and palate, but the sweetness is well balanced by hops, leaving a rich, fruity finish.

Winter Warmer (OG 1055, ABV 5%)
A full-flavoured, ruby-black-brown beer with raisins, caramel and dark roast notes throughout, giving way to a typical Young's pleasant dry finish.

*These notes refer to beers brewed at Wandsworth and may change.

Welton's SIBA

Welton's Brewery Ltd, 1 Mulberry Trading Estate, Foundry Lane, Horsham, West Sussex, RH13 5PX
Tel (01403) 242901/251873
Email sales@weltons.co.uk
Website www.weltons.co.uk
Tours by arrangement

Ray Welton moved his brewery to a factory unit in Horsham in 2003, which has given him space to expand. Bottled beers were due to come on stream in 2006. The beers are available through some 400 outlets in the South-east.

Pride 'n' Joy (ABV 2.8%)
A light brown bitter with a slight malty and hoppy aroma. Fruity with a pleasant hoppiness and some sweetness in the flavour, leading to a short malty finish. Well balanced and drinks well for its strength.

Kid & Bard (OG 1036, ABV 3.5%)
Mid-brown session beer. Some fruit and hops in the aroma lead to a well-balanced beer with hops dominating, but malt and fruit prevalent. Bitterness grows in to a pleasant hoppy, bitter finish.

Horsham Bitter (ABV 3.8%)

Sussex Pride (ABV 4%)

Old Cocky (OG 1043, ABV 4.3%)

Horsham Old (OG 1046, ABV 4.5%)
Roast and toffee flavours predominate with some bitterness in this traditional old ale. Bitter-sweet with plenty of caramel and roast in a rather short finish.

Old Harry (OG 1051, ABV 5.2%)

Wensleydale

Wensleydale Brewery Ltd, Manor Farm, Bellerby, Leyburn, North Yorkshire, DL8 5QH
Tel (01969) 625250
Fax (01969) 825251
Email info@wensleydalebrewery.com
Website www.wensleydalebrewery.com
Tours by arrangement

Set up in 2003, Wensleydale Brewery (formerly Lidstone's Brewery) bought its first pub, the Forester's Arms, in Yorkshire Dales National Park, with in-house ales being produced on a two-barrel plant. A year later the pub was leased with a beer tie and the brewery relocated to larger premises six miles away. Most beers are available as bottle-conditioned ales. About 30 outlets are supplied.

Lidstone's Rowley Mild (OG 1037, ABV 3.2%)
Chocolate and toffee aromas lead into what, for its strength, is an impressively rich and flavoursome taste. The finish is pleasantly bitter-sweet.

Forester's Session Bitter (OG 1038, ABV 3.7%)
Intensely aromatic, straw-coloured ale offering a superb balance of malt and hops on the tongue; an ideal session beer by any standards.

Semer Water (OG 1041, ABV 4.1%)
Golden ale with a hint of banana on the nose. The taste is clean, crisp and hoppy, with grapefruit flavours also present.

Coverdale Gamekeeper (OG 1042, ABV 4.3%)
A light copper best bitter with a lingering aftertaste.

Aysgarth Falls (ABV 4.4%)
A thirst-quenching cloudy wheat beer with tart apple and banana fruit.

Black Dub Oat Stout (OG 1044, ABV 4.4%)
Black beer brimming with roasted chocolate taste and aroma.

Coverdale Poacher IPA (OG 1049, ABV 5%)
Citrus flavours dominate both aroma and taste in this pale, smooth, refreshing beer; the aftertaste is quite dry.

Hardraw Force Strong Ale (ABV 5.6%)
A well-balanced premium ale with a fine malty, hoppy character.

Barley Wine (ABV 8.5%)
A rich, complex, strong ale with a lingering bitter-sweet aftertaste.

Wentworth SIBA

Wentworth Brewery Ltd, The Power House, Gun Park, Wentworth, Rotherham, South Yorkshire, S62 7TF
Tel (01226) 747070
Fax (01226) 747050
Email info@wentworth-brewery.co.uk
Website www.wentworth-brewery.co.uk
Tours by arrangement

Wentworth was built during the summer of 1999, using equipment from two defunct Sheffield breweries, Stones and Wards. Brewing started in 1999 and the first brew, WPA, won Best Beer of the Festival at CAMRA's Sheffield festival. Wentworth has installed three 15-barrel fermenters, boosting production to 70 barrels. One pub is owned and the owners plan to create a small tied estate. Approximately 300 outlets are supplied.

Needles Eye (OG 1035, ABV 3.5%)
A session bitter with a rather bitter taste that dominates the aftertaste.

WPA (OG 1039.5, ABV 4%)
An extremely well hopped IPA-style beer that leads to some astringency. A very bitter beer.

Best Bitter (OG 1040, ABV 4.1%)
A hoppy, bitter beer with hints of citrus fruits. A bitter taste dominates the aftertaste.

Early Fruits (ABV 4.1%)

A fruity, dark red beer; bitter with a sweet aftertaste.

Bumble Beer (ABV 4.3%)
A pale golden beer, made using local honey.

Rock Spalt (OG 1045, ABV 4.5%)
Straw-coloured, aromatic, dry and drinkable. Spalt is the German variety of hop used.

Black Zac (OG 1046, ABV 4.6%)
A mellow, dark ruby-red ale with chocolate and pale malts leading to a bitter taste, with a coffee finish.

Oatmeal Stout (OG 1050, ABV 4.8%) ◻ ◆
Black, smooth, with roast and chocolate malt and coffee overtones.

Rampant Gryphon (OG 1062, ABV 6.2%) ◆
A strong, well-balanced golden ale with hints of fruit and sweetness but which retains a hoppy character.

Whistle Jacket (ABV 8.4%)
A dark, extremely strong ale with sweet overtones.

Wessex SIBA

Wessex Brewery, Rye Hill Farm, Longbridge Deverill, Warminster, Wiltshire, BA12 7DE
Tel (01985) 844532
Email wessexbrewery@tinyworld.co.uk
Tours by arrangement

⊗ The brewery went into production in 2001 as Hobden's Wessex Brewery and moved to a more easily maintained building in 2004, at which time the name Wessex Brewery was adopted. Seven outlets are supplied by the brewery with most distribution via wholesalers. Around two occasional beers a month are also brewed.

Naughty Ferret (OG 1035, ABV 3.5%)
A session bitter with full flavour. Tawny colour, spicy bitterness and citrus hop aroma.

Truth Decay (OG 1038, ABV 3.9%)

Crockerton Classic (OG 1041, ABV 4.1%)
Full bodied, tawny, full flavoured; bitter, fruity and malty.

Kilmington Best (OG 1041, ABV 4.2%)
Sweet, hoppy bitter.

Old Deverill Valley Pale (OG 1042, ABV 4.2%)

Deverill's Advocate (OG 1045, ABV 4.5%)

Warminster Warrior (OG 1045, ABV 4.5%)
Premium bitter.

Wylye Warmer (OG 1058, ABV 6%)

Russian Stoat (OG 1080, ABV 9%)

West Berkshire SIBA

West Berkshire Brewery Co Ltd, The Old Bakery, Yattendon, Thatcham, Berkshire, RG18 0UE
Tel/Fax (01635) 202968
Email info@wbbrew.co.uk
Website www.wbbrew.co.uk
Shop Mon-Fri 10am-4pm; Sat 10am-1pm
Tours by arrangement

⊗ The brewery quickly outgrew its five-gallon plant when it started business in 1995 in out-buildings attached to the Pot Kiln pub, Frilsham, and the owners converted an old bakery into an additional 25-barrel brewery in nearby Yattendon. With a staff of six, weekly production in both sites now regularly exceeds 50 barrels, supplying the free trade throughout Berkshire and Oxfordshire. At least one different additional beer is brewed every month, usually in the range of 4.2 to 4.8% ABV, and including stouts and porters as well as bitters. Beers are brewed as one-off commissions for festivals and other special events. Full Circle gained a silver award for Best Bitter at GBBF 2003. Brick Kiln Bitter (ABV 4%) is brewed solely for the Pot Kiln pub. Bottled beer: Decadence (ABV 4.5%), to celebrate the 10th brewing anniversary.

Old Father Thames (OG 1038, ABV 3.4%)
A traditional pale ale with a full flavour despite its lower strength.

Mr Chubb's Lunchtime Bitter (OG 1040, ABV 3.7%) ◆
A drinkable malty session bitter. A malty caramel note dominates aroma and taste and is accompanied by a nutty bitter-sweetness and a hoppy aroma.

Maggs' Magnificent Mild (OG 1041, ABV 3.8%) ◆
Silky, full-bodied dark mild with a creamy head. Roast malt aroma is joined in the taste by caramel, sweetness and mild, fruity hoppiness. Aftertaste of roast malt with balancing bitterness.

Good Old Boy (OG 1043, ABV 4%) ◆
Well-rounded, tawny bitter with malt and hops dominating throughout and a balancing bitterness in the taste and aftertaste.

Dr Hexter's Wedding Ale (OG 1044, ABV 4.1%) ◆
Fruit and hops dominate the aroma and are joined in the bitter-sweet taste by a hint of malt. The aftertaste has a pleasant bitter hoppiness.

Full Circle (OG 1047, ABV 4.5%) ◆
A golden ale with a pleasing aroma and taste of bitter hops with a hint of malt. The aftertaste is hoppy and bitter with a rounding note of malt.

Dr Hexter's Healer (OG 1052, ABV 5%) ◆
Amber strong bitter with malt, caramel and hops in the aroma. The taste is a balance of malt, caramel, fruit, hops and bitter-sweetness. Caramel, fruit and bitter-sweetness dominate the aftertaste.

West Brewing*

West Brewing Co Ltd, Binnie Place, Glasgow Green, Glasgow, G40 1AW
Tel/Fax (0141) 550 0135
Email gordon@westbeer.com
Website www.westbeer.com
Tours by arrangement

West Brewing opened in March 2006 and produces a full range of European-style beers. The two brewers are both German-trained in Munich and their copper-clad system, visible from the 300-seat bar and restaurant, is a fully-automated German one with an annual capacity of 1.5 million litres. Brewing is in strict accordance with the Reinheitsgebot, the German purity law, importing all malt, hops and yeast from Germany. Beers: Hefeweizen (ABV 4.9%); Munich-Style Helles (ABV 5%); Dunilles (ABV 5.1%); U-Bier (ABV 5.2%); Dunkel Hefeweizen (ABV 5.3%)

Westbury

Westbury Ales, Horse & Groom, Alfred Street, Westbury, Wiltshire, BA13 3DY
Tel 07771 976865
Email brewing@westburyales.com
Website www.westburyales.com
Tours by arrangement

Brewing started in 2004, using a 2.5-barrel plant and expanded a few months later to 10-barrel production. The brewery supplies some 40 outlets, including its own pub, the Horse & Groom. Seasonal beers: Faith, Hop & Charity (ABV 3.7%), Holly Daze (ABV 4.2%), Pale Storm (ABV 4.3%), Dark Horse (ABV 3.7%), PSZ (ABV 4%).

Amber Daze **(OG 1038, ABV 3.8%)**

Early Daze **(OG 1040, ABV 4.1%)**

Bitham Blonde **(OG 1044, ABV 4.5%)**

Midnight Mash **(OG 1048, ABV 5%)**

Westerham SIBA

Westerham Brewery Co Ltd, Grange Farm, Pootings Road, Crockham Hill, Edenbridge, Kent, TN8 6SA
Tel/Fax (01732) 864427
Email sales@westerhambrewery.co.uk
Website www.westerhambrewery.co.uk
Shop Mon-Fri 9am-5pm
Tours by arrangement

Robert Wicks set up the brewery in 2004, trading in a top job in the City of London to brew on modern copper and stainless steel equipment imported from Canada and the US. He has restored brewing in Westerham that was lost when the Black Eagle Brewery was taken over by Ind Coope of Burton and Romford in 1959 and closed in 1965. Black Eagle's beers were enjoyed by Sir Winston Churchill, who lived close by at Chartwell, and by airmen at RAF Biggin Hill during World War II. Two of Black Eagle's yeast strains were deposited at the National Collection of Yeast Cultures and are being used to recreate the true flavour of Westerham beers. The new brewery is based at the National Trust's Grange Farm in a former dairy and uses the same water supply as Black Eagle. Around 100 free trade outlets are supplied in Kent, Surrey and Sussex. Seasonal beers: General Wolfe Maple Ale (ABV 4.3%, autumn), God's Wallop Christmas Ale (ABV 4.3%), Puddledock Porter (ABV 4.3%, winter), Summer Perle (ABV 3.8%), Little Scotney Bitter (ABV 4.3%, summer). Bottle-conditioned beer: British Bulldog.

Grasshopper Kentish Bitter **(OG 1039, ABV 3.8%)**

Black Eagle Special Pale Ale **(OG 1039, ABV 3.8%)**

British Bulldog **(OG 1042, ABV 4.3%)**

India Pale Ale **(OG 1047, ABV 4.8%)**

Sevenoaks Bitter 7X **(OG 1046, ABV 4.8%)**

Special Bitter Ale 1965 **(OG 1048, ABV 5%)**

WF6

WF6 Brewing Co, c/o 21 Rose Farm Approach, Altofts, West Yorkshire, WF6 2RZ
Tel 07876 141336
Email info@wf6brewingcompany.co.uk
Website www.wf6brewingcompany.co.uk

Rob Turton and Bryan Guy founded WF6 Brewing Company in 2004 with the brand name Birkwoods. The brewery is in a converted milking parlour on the outskirts of Altofts village. A custom-made five-barrel plant allows them to produce a varying portfolio of seasonal beers, which are supplied to distributors, pubs and festivals. In 2006 the beers were due to include: Birkwoods Mad March (ABV 4.2%), Birkwoods Headache (ABV 4.2%), Birkwoods Legless (ABV 4.2%), Birkwoods Hammered (ABV 4.2%), Birkwoods April Showers (ABV 4.2%).

Whalebone

Whalebone Brewery, 163 Wincolmlee, Hull, East Yorkshire, HU2 0PA
Tel (01482) 226648
Tours by arrangement

The Whalebone pub, which dates from 1796, was bought by Hull CAMRA founding member Alex Craig in 2002. He opened the brewery the following year and his beers have names connected with the former whaling industry on the adjoining River Hull. Two or three outlets are supplied as well as the pub. Seasonal beers: Truelove Porter (ABV 4.7%), Joseph Allen (ABV 5%), Moby Dick (ABV 8%), Full Ship (ABV 8.4%).

Diana Mild **(OG 1037, ABV 3.6%)**

Neckoil Bitter **(OG 1037, ABV 3.9%)**

Wharfedale SIBA

Wharfedale Brewery Ltd, Coonlands Laithe, Hetton, Skipton, North Yorkshire, BD23 6LY
Tel/Fax (01756) 730555
Email nigel@follyale.com
Website www.follyale.com
Tours by arrangement

Opened in 2003 by the Duke of Kent, the brewery is based in an old hay barn within the Yorkshire Dales National Park. Water comes from its own 56 metres-deep borehole. Three beers are permanently available, plus one special each month and are supplied to free houses and distributors throughout Yorkshire, Lancashire and the West Midlands. All permanent beers are also available in bottle. A range of monthly seasonals is also available throughout the year.

Folly Ale **(OG 1038, ABV 3.8%)** ◆
A pale brown beer with crystal malt character throughout. Bitterness dominates the taste while hops increase in the bitter finish.

Executioner (OG 1046, ABV 4.5%) ◆
A complex reddish brown ale, more akin to a strong mild than a best bitter. Malt and roast flavours predominate with background fruit, leading to a bitter finish.

Folly Gold (OG 1051, ABV 5%) ◆
A full-bodied pale golden premium strong bitter with a bitter, hoppy and malty palate. The dry character extends into the finish.

Whim SIBA

Whim Ales Ltd, Whim Farm, Hartington, near Buxton, Derbyshire, SK17 0AX
Tel/Fax (01298) 84991

⊗ A brewery opened in 1993 in outbuildings at Whim Farm by Giles Litchfield who bought Broughton Brewery (qv) in 1995. Whim's beers are available in 50-70 outlets and the brewery's tied house, the Wilkes Head in Leek, Staffs. Some one-off brews are produced. Occasional/seasonal beers: Kaskade (ABV 4.3%, a lager), Snow White (ABV 4.5%, a wheat beer), Easter Special (ABV 4.8%), Stout Jenny (ABV 4.7%), Black Christmas (ABV 6.5%).

Arbor Light (OG 1035, ABV 3.6%)
Light-coloured bitter, sharp and clean with lots of hop character and a delicate light aroma.

Hartington Bitter (OG 1039, ABV 4%) ◻
A light, golden-coloured, well-hopped session beer. A dry finish with a spicy, floral aroma.

Hartington IPA (OG 1045, ABV 4.5%)
Pale and light-coloured, smooth on the palate allowing malt to predominate. Slightly sweet finish combined with distinctive light hop bitterness. Well rounded.

White SIBA

White Brewing Co, 1066 Country Brewery, Pebsham Farm Industrial Estate, Pebsham Lane, Bexhill-on-Sea, East Sussex, TN40 2RZ
Tel (01424) 731066
Fax (01424) 732995
Email whitebrewing@fsbdial.co.uk
Tours by arrangement

The brewery was founded in 1995 by husband and-wife team David and Lesley White to serve local free trade outlets and some wholesalers. White has expanded production threefold with the addition of seasonal and occasional ales. Some 25 to 30 outlets are supplied. Seasonal beers: White Gold (ABV 4.9%, summer), Chilly Willy (ABV 5.1%, winter), Old White Christmas (ABV 4%), Heart of Rother (spring).

1066 Country Bitter (OG 1040, ABV 4%)
Amber-gold in colour, a light, sweetish beer with good malt and hop balance, and a bitter, refreshing finish.

Dark (OG 1040, ABV 4%)

White Horse

White Horse Brewery Company Ltd, 3 White Horse Business Park, Ware Road, Stanford in the Vale, Oxfordshire, SN7 8NY
Tel/Fax (01367) 718700
Website www.whitehorsebrewery.com
Tours by arrangement

White Horse Brewery was founded on a modern industrial estate in 2004 by Andy Wilson and Stuart Wastie, both previously employed by Wychwood Brewery (qv). The second-hand brewing plant was manufactured in Belgium and has a brew-length of 7.5 barrels. The beers are mainly available in plastic nine-gallon firkins, but some 18-gallon kilderkins are also used. Some 80 outlets are supplied. Seasonal beers: Dragon Hill (ABV 4.2%), Flibbertigibbet (ABV 4.3%), Village Idiot (ABV 4.1%), Christmas Ale (ABV 4.8%).

White Horse Bitter (OG 1040, ABV 3.7%)

Wayland Smithy (OG 1049, ABV 4.4%)

For Turf Tavern, Oxford

Turf Tavern Summer Ale (OG 1044, ABV 4.1%)

Guv'nor (OG 1066, ABV 6.5%)

White Star SIBA

White Star Brewery Ltd, 5 Radcliffe Court, Radcliffe Road, Northam, Southampton, Hampshire, SO14 0PH
Tel (02380) 232480
Fax (02380) 232580
Email info@whitestarbrewery.com
Website www.whitestarbrewery.com
Tours by arrangement

⊗ The 10-barrel plant was set up in 2003 by brothers Andy and Chris Ingram on a small industrial estate next to the main railway line and close to Southampton FC's St Mary's Stadium. The name comes from the White Star Shipping Line of Southampton, whose most famous liner was the Titanic. It is the first brewery in Southampton for 53 years. The brewing equipment came from the closed Woodhampton Brewery. Bottling started in 2004. There are seven regular brews with distribution throughout the country. Seasonal beers: Black Panther Stout (ABV 4.4%), Royal Standard (ABV 4.3%), Battleaxe (ABV 4.6%), Steamer (ABV 5%), Frostbite (ABV 4.5%), Afrodizzysack (ABV 7.2%). The full range of beer is also available in bottle-conditioned form.

Best Bitter (ABV 3.5%)
Copper-coloured session bitter, thirst-quenching and well hopped with a malty finish.

U-X-B (ABV 3.8%) ◆
Session bitter with little aroma and some hops and malt in the flavour and finish. Rather sulphurous throughout.

Crafty Shag (ABV 4.1%)
A Pilsner-style beer, brewed using German hops.

Majestic (ABV 4.2%) ◆
A Burton-style best bitter, sulphurous and sharp but with some malt and biscuit character. Quite bitter, becoming hoppy and increasingly astringent in the finish.

Dark Destroyer (ABV 4.7%)
Roasted malts produce a rich, dark ale blended with English hops. A good thirst quencher.

Starlight (ABV 5%) ◆
Gentle aroma in this hoppy strong bitter, with hints of toffee and fruit. A light body and a sharp finish.

Capstan Full Strength (ABV 6%) ◆
A smooth, dark ale, with a spicy aroma of blackberries and blackcurrants. Strong fruit flavours dominate but with hops and malt providing some balance. The finish is bitter-sweet and vinous.

Whitewater

Whitewater Brewing Co, 40 Tullyframe Road, Kilkeel, Co Down, Northern Ireland, BT34 4RZ
Tel/Fax (028) 4176 9449
Email bernard@whitewaterbrewing.co.uk
Tours by arrangement

⊛ Set up in 1996 and nestling in the heart of the Mourne Mountains, Whitewater is now the largest brewery in Northern Ireland. The brewery has a 15-barrel brew length and produces 14 different ales and a real lager. Currently, Whitewater supplies 14 outlets and owns one pub, the White Horse, Saintfield, Co. Down. Future plans include producing bottle-conditioned beers. Seasonal beers: Solstice Pale (ABV 4%, summe), Nut Brown Ale (ABV 4%, winter), Snake Drive (ABV 4.3%, spring), Sanity Claus (ABV 4.5%, Christmas), Bee's Endeavour (ABV 4.8%, autumn).

Mill Ale (OG 1038, ABV 3.7%)

Blonde Lager (OG 1040, ABV 4%)

Glen Ale (OG 1043, ABV 4.2%)

Belfast Ale (OG 1046, ABV 4.5%)

For Strangford Lough Brewing Co (qv)

Barelegs Brew (ABV 4.5%)

Whitstable

Whitstable Brewery, The Brewery, Little Telpits Farm, Woodcock Lane, Grafty Green, Kent, ME17 2AY
Tel (01622) 851007
Fax (01622) 859993
Email whitstablebrewer@btconnect.com
Tours by arrangement

⊗ Whitstable Brewery was created when the Swale and North Weald Brewery was sold in 2003 to the Green family who initially produced beer for their own outlets in Whitstable (a hotel and two restaurants) and beer festivals. The company has now decided to supply beer further afield and is looking for potential outlets. There are plans to open a new bar next to the East Quay Restaurant in the summer of 2006. Twelve regular outlets across Kent are supplied direct. Seasonal beer: Smack Ale (ABV 5.5%, winter).

Native Bitter (OG 1037, ABV 3.7%)

East India Pale Ale (OG 1040, ABV 4.1%)
A light, refreshing pale ale with floral hop aroma and bitterness that give a well-balanced flavour.

Bohemian (OG 1044, ABV 5.2%)
Dry-hopped, cask-conditioned lager.

Oyster Stout (OG 1047, ABV 4.5%)
Rich and dry with deep chocolate and mocha flavours.

Raspberry Wheat (OG 1049, ABV 5.2%)

Wheat Beer (OG 1049, ABV 5.2%)

Whittington's SIBA

Whittington's Brewery, Three Choirs Vineyard Ltd, Newent, Gloucestershire, GL18 1LS
Tel (01531) 890555
Fax (01531) 890877
Email info@whittingtonbrewery.co.uk
Website www.whittingtonbrewery.co.uk
Shop 10am-5pm daily
Tours by arrangement

Whittington's Brewery started in 2003 using a purpose-built five-barrel plant producing 20 barrels a week. Dick Whittington came from nearby Gloucester, hence the name and feline theme. All beers are bottled and available from the onsite shop, online and from local outlets. There are plans to introduce a winter beer. Seasonal beer: Summer Pale Ale (ABV 4%, May-Aug). Bottle-conditioned beer: Cats Whiskers.

Nine Lives (OG 1035, ABV 3.6%)

Cats Whiskers (OG 1041, ABV 4.2%)

Why Not*

The Why Not Brewery, 17 Cavalier Close, Thorpe St Andrew, Norwich, NR7 0TE
Tel (01603) 300786
Email colin@thewhynotbrewery.co.uk
Website www.thewhynotbrewery.co.uk

The Why Not Brewery opened in January 2006 with equipment located in a shed and custom-made by Brendan Moore of Iceni Brewery. The brewery can produce up to 200 litres per brew. All cask ales are also available in bottle-conditioned form.

Wally's Revenge (OG 1040, ABV 4%)

Cavalier Red (OG 1047, ABV 4.7%)

Chocolate Nutter (OG 1056, ABV 5.5%)

Wicked Hathern

Wicked Hathern Brewery Ltd, The Willows, 46 Derby Road, Hathern, Loughborough, Leicestershire, LE12 5LD
Tel (01509) 842585
Email beer@hathern.com
Website www.wicked-hathern.co.uk/brewery
Tours by arrangement (£3 charge – includes beer tasting)

⊛ Opened in the first month of the new millennium, the 2.5-barrel brewery is owned and operated by John and Marc Bagley, John Worsfold and Sean O'Neill, in their spare time. They generally supply beer on a guest basis to many local pubs and beer festivals, and brew commissioned beers for special occasions, such as beer festivals. Since 2002 they have bottled their beers to supply mainly their local shop, as the policies of owners of the pubs in Hathern preclude the brewery having a regular village outlet. Seasonal beers: Gladstone Tidings (ABV 5.1%, Christmas). All beers are available in bottles from selected off-licences (see website) and from Hathern Village shop. Bottled beers are brewed exclusively for Alexander Wines off-licence in Earlsdon, Coventry, namely Restoration Ale, Lazy Bones and Barking Mad.

WHB/Wicked Hathern Bitter (OG 1038, ABV 3.8%)
A light-tasting session bitter with a dry palate and good hop aroma.

Cockfighter (OG 1043, ABV 4.2%)
A pale bitter with a pronounced maltiness offset by a delicate hop flavour.

Hawthorn Gold (OG 1045, ABV 4.5%)

Derby Porter (OG 1048, ABV 4.8%)

Soar Head (OG 1048, ABV 4.8%) ◆
A dark ruby-coloured strong bitter with a cocktail of distinctive flavours.

For the Albion, Loughborough:

Albion Special (OG 1041, ABV 4%)
A light, copper-coloured bitter with a nutty aroma and smoky malt taste, hops leading through.

Wickwar SIBA

Wickwar Brewing Co Ltd, The Old Brewery, Station Road, Wickwar, Gloucestershire, GL12 8NB
Tel (0870) 777 5671
Fax (0870) 777 5672
Email bob@wickwarbrewing.co.uk
Website www.wickwarbrewing.co.uk
Shop Mon-Fri 9.30am-4.30pm; Sat 10am-12pm
Tours by arrangement

⊗ Since setting up Wickwar in 1990 in the cooper's shed of the old Arnold, Perrett & Co Brewery, Ray Penny's ambition had been to move into the main brewery building across the road. This was achieved in 2004 with the installation of a 50-barrel plant. A new beer was introduced, IKB (Isambard Kingdom Brunel), to mark the fact that Brunel built the railway tunnel that runs at the rear of the old brewery. The original brewery was built around 1840 but spent most of the 20th century as a cider factory and latterly as a bonded warehouse. Wickwar Brewery supplies some 350 outlets and is considering further expansion of its pub estate. Seasonal beers: Premium Spring Ale (ABV 3.8%, April-May), Sunny Daze (ABV 4.2%, June-Aug), Christmas Cracker (ABV 4.3%, December), Autumnale (ABV 4.5%, Sept-Nov). Rite Flanker (ABV 4.4%) is brewed during all major rugby competitions. Bottle-conditioned beer: Brand Oak Bitter.

Coopers WPA (OG 1036.5, ABV 3.5%) ◆
Golden-coloured, this well-balanced beer is light and refreshing, with hops, citrus fruit, apple/pear flavour and notable pale malt character. Bitter, dry finish. A crisp and quenching ale.

Brand Oak Bitter (BOB) (OG 1039, ABV 4%) ◆
Amber-coloured, this has a distinctive blend of hop, malt and apple/pear citrus fruits. The slightly sweet taste turns into a fine, dry bitterness, with a similar malty-lasting finish.

Cotswold Way (OG 1043, ABV 4.2%) ◆
Amber-coloured, it has a pleasant aroma of pale malt, hop and fruit. Good dry bitterness in the taste with some sweetness. Similar though less sweet in the finish, with good hop content.

Rite Flanker (ABV 4.3%)
Amber in colour with a big malt taste and fruit notes and a hoppy finish. Brewed originally for major Rugby Union games, it is now available throughout the year.

IKB (OG 1045, ABV 4.5%)
A ruby-red ale with a complex hop aroma and flavour derived from the use of three hop varieties. Flowery but well balanced.

Mr Perretts Traditional Stout (OG 1059, ABV 5.9%) ◆
Aroma and taste of smoky chocolate malts and peppery hops. Dark fruits of black cherry and blackcurrant give hints of sweetness to the dry, quite bitter, slightly spicy, well-balanced taste.

Station Porter (OG 1062, ABV 6.1%) ◆
This is a rich, smooth, dark ruby-brown ale. Starts with roast malt; coffee, chocolate and dark fruit then develops a complex, spicy, bitter-sweet taste and a long roast finish.

Wild's

Wild's Brewery Ltd, Unit 6 Whitehill Park, Weobley, Herefordshire, HR4 8QE
Tel (01544) 319333
Website www.wildsbrewery.com
Tours by arrangement

After an eight-year break, Pete and Wendy Wild returned to brewing in 2005 after many months of taste-testing. Seasonal beer: Wild Summer (ABV 4.2%).

One (OG 1041, ABV 4.1%)

SX (OG 1042, ABV 4.2%)

Blonde (OG 1045, ABV 4.5%)

Night (OG 1045, ABV 4.5%)

Williams SIBA

Williams Brothers Brewing Co/Heather Ale Ltd, New Alloa Brewery, Kelliebank, Alloa, FK10 1NT
Tel (01259) 725511
Fax (01259) 725522
Email fraoch@heatherale.co.uk
Website www.heatherale.co.uk
Tours by arrangement

Bruce and Scott Williams started brewing Heather Ale in the West Highlands in 1993. A range of indigenous, historical ales were added over the following 10 years. The Williams Bros now have their own 40-barrel brewery and bottling line and produce a range of hoppy beers under the Williams Bros banner as well as continuing with the range of historical ales. Around 30 outlets are supplied. Seasonal beers: Ebulum (ABV 6.5%, winter), Alba (ABV 7.5%, winter).

Williams Gold (OG 1040, ABV 3.9%)

Fraoch Heather Ale (OG 1041, ABV 4.1%) ◆

The unique taste of heather flowers is very noticeable in this beer. A fine floral aroma and spicy taste give character to this drinkable speciality beer.

Black (OG 1042, ABV 4.2%)

Roisin-Tayberry (OG 1042, ABV 4.2%)

Red (OG 1045, ABV 4.5%)

Grozet (OG 1047, ABV 5%)

Joker (OG 1047, ABV 5%)

Willy's SIBA

Willy's Wine Bar Ltd, 17 High Cliff Road, Cleethorpes, Lincolnshire, DN35 8RQ
Tel (01472) 602145
Tours by arrangement

The brewery opened in 1989 to provide beer for its two pubs in Grimsby and Cleethorpes. It has a five-barrel plant with maximum capacity of 15 barrels a week. The brewery can be viewed at any time from pub or street.

Original Bitter (OG 1038, ABV 3.8%)
A light brown 'sea air' beer with a fruity, tangy hop on the nose and taste, giving a strong bitterness tempered by the underlying malt.

Burcom Bitter (OG 1044, ABV 4.2%)
Sometimes known as Mariner's Gold, although the beer is dark ruby in colour. It is a smooth and creamy brew with a sweet chocolate-bar maltiness, giving way to an increasingly bitter finish.

Last Resort (OG 1044, ABV 4.3%)

Weiss Buoy (OG 1045, ABV 4.5%)
A cloudy wheat beer.

Coxswains Special (OG 1050, ABV 4.9%)

Old Groyne (OG 1060, ABV 6.2%)
An initial sweet banana fruitiness blends with malt to give a vanilla quality to the taste and slightly bitter aftertaste. A copper-coloured beer reminiscent of a Belgian ale.

Winchester

Winchester Brewery Ltd, Unit 19 Longbridge Industrial Park, Floating Bridge Road, Southampton, Hampshire, SO14 3FL
Tel/Fax (02380) 710131
Email info@winchesterbrewery.com
Website www.winchesterbrewery.com

The brewery was launched in 2004 by David Wealleans and brewing started a year later. The brewery was intended to be located in Winchester but problems with premises at the last minute meant it is located in the heart of Southampton. The plant was built from scratch by David to enable him to be in direct control. In 2006 he took on Nick Harper as a partner in the business. Four regular beers are produced alongside a small but growing range of seasonals. Trusty Servant has won two awards, including overall winner at the Southampton Beer Festival 2005. Around 30 outlets are supplied. All cask ales are also available in bottle-conditioned form.

Best Bitter (OG 1038, ABV 3.7%)
An amber beer with strong hop flavours.

Summer '76 (OG 1045, ABV 3.7%)
A golden ale, more delicately hopped than many of the genre.

West Window (OG 1048, ABV 4.5%)

Trusty Servant (OG 1052, ABV 4.7%)

Windie Goat*

Windie Goat Brewery, Failford Inn, Failford, South Ayrshire, KA5 5TF
Tel (01292) 240117
Fax (01292) 540331
Email enquiries@windiegoatbrewery.co.uk
Website www.windiegoatbrewery.co.uk
Tours by arrangement

The brewery was due to come on stream during 2006, located in the old cellar of the Failford Inn, supplying the pub and local beer festivals. The name comes from an area of woodland down river from the brewery and pub. Three beers are planned.

Windrush*

Windrush Brewery Ltd, Downs Road, Witney, Oxfordshire, OX28 0SY
Tel (01993) 703333
Fax (01993) 703319
Email windrushbrewery@yahoo.co.uk

Husband and wife team Nigel and Susan Harrison started brewing in late 2005 in a purpose-built unit hidden away on a small industrial park on the outskirts of Witney in the Windrush Valley. A five-barrel plant is used. Local free houses and beer festivals are supplied. One regular beer is produced with plans to brew a summer ale.

Windrush Ale (ABV 4.3%)

Keep your Good Beer Guide up to date by visiting www.camra.org.uk, click on *Good Beer Guide* then *Updates to the GBG 2007* where you will find information about changes to breweries.

Windsor Castle

Windsor Castle Brewery Ltd t/a Sadler's Ales, 7 Stourbridge Road, Lye, Stourbridge, West Midlands, DY9 7DG
Tel (01384) 897809
Fax (01384) 893666
Email johnsadler@windsorcastlebrewery.com
Website www.windsorcastlebrewery.com
Shop 11am-11pm daily
Tours by arrangement

Nathaniel Sadler opened the original brewery in 1900 adjacent to the Windsor Castle Inn, Oldbury. Although brewing ceased in 1927, his son passed on all he knew. John Sadler and his son Chris have reopened the brewery in its new location, continuing the brewing tradition of the Sadler family. The tap house, the Windsor Castle, opened early in 2006, offering six beers plus two or three from other local breweries. Some 120 outlets are supplied. Bottle-conditioned beer: Sadler's IPA.

Jack's Ale (OG 1037, ABV 3.8%)
Light, hoppy beer with a crisp and zesty lemon undertone.

Best Bitter (OG 1040, ABV 4.1%)

Worcester Sorcerer (OG 1042, ABV 4.3%)
Pale beer, light and refreshing yet smooth and fruity with hints of mint and lemon. Floral aroma and crisp bitterness combine to make a balanced and clean-tasting beer.

1900 Original (OG 1043, ABV 4.5%)
Dark malty bitter with a light hoppy aroma and a dry, lingering finish.

Thin Ice (OG 1043, ABV 4.5%)

IPA (OG 1046, ABV 4.8%)
Classic India Pale Ale, light, tangy and bitter with a distinctive refreshing aftertaste.

Winter's SIBA

Winter's Brewery, 8 Keelan Close, Norwich, Norfolk, NR6 6QZ
Tel/Fax (01603) 787820
Email sales@wintersbrewery.com
Website www.wintersbrewery.com

⊗ David Winter, who had previous award-winning success as brewer for both Woodforde's and Chalk Hill breweries, decided to set up on his own in 2001. He purchased the brewing plant from the now defunct Scott's Brewery in Lowestoft. The local free trade is supplied.

Mild (OG 1036.5, ABV 3.6%) ◆
A gentle roast aroma introduces this dark brown, softly-flavoured mild. The gentle blend of hops and roast lingers to a long finish and a dry, fruity background.

Bitter (OG 1039.5, ABV 3.8%) ◆
A gentle hop aroma greets the drinker and leads to a gentle bitter introduction. Malt and hops mingle with the basic bitterness in a well-balanced but muted blend of flavours.

Golden (ABV 4.1%) ◆
Amber hued with a strong bitter backbone dominating the initial flavour and the lingering finish. Background malt notes soften the grapefruit dryness that develops as the beer progresses.

Revenge (OG 1047, ABV 4.7%) ◆
Blackcurrant notes give depth to the inherent maltiness of this pale brown beer. A bitter-sweet background becomes more pronounced as the fruitiness gently wanes.

Storm Force (OG 1053, ABV 5.3%) ◆
Booming malt notes in both aroma and flavour. Pale brown with a blackcurrant fruitiness that adds to the richness that is both sustained and filling. Gentle bitterness lightens the load.

Tempest (OG 1062, ABV 6.2%) ◆
A deep sultana fruitiness holds this copper-coloured old ale together. Maltiness can be detected over the hoppy bitterness of background flavours. A solid fruity finish dwells on the tongue.

Wissey Valley

Wissey Valley Brewery, Grey House, Lynn Road, Stoke Ferry, Norfolk, PE33 9SW
Tel (01366) 500767

The brewery was launched in 2002 as Captain Grumpy and in 2003 moved to Stoke Ferry and was re-established as Wissey Valley. Around 15 outlets are supplied direct as well as wholesalers and beer festivals. Captain Grumpy's Best Bitter and Khaki Sergeant Strong Stout have both recently won awards. Fruit and vegetable beers are also produced as well as custom beers made to order. Only bottle-conditioned beers are produced.

Wild Widow Mild (ABV 3.5%)

Captain Grumpy's Best Bitter (ABV 3.9%)

Old Grumpy's Porter (ABV 4.1%)

Busted Flush (ABV 4.5%)

Golden Rivet (ABV 5.1%)

Khaki Sergeant Strong Stout (ABV 6.7%)

Wizard SIBA

Wizard Ales, The Hops, Whichford, Shipston on Stour, Warwickshire, CV36 5PE
Tel (01608) 684355/684621
Email brewery@thenormanknight.co.uk
Website www.thenormanknight.co.uk/wizard_brewery
Tours by arrangement

⊗ Brewing started in 2003 on a 1.25-barrel plant, previously used by Swaled Ale Brewery in Gunnerside. A new five-barrel plant is now fully operational. One pub is owned and more than 20 local outlets are regularly supplied. Seasonal beer: Bah Humbug (ABV 5.8%, Christmas).

Apprentice (OG 1038, ABV 3.6%)

One For The Toad (OG 1041, ABV 4%)

Black Magic (OG 1040, ABV 4%)

Mother in Law (OG 1043, ABV 4.2%)

Sorcerer (OG 1044, ABV 4.3%)

White Witch (OG 1045, ABV 4.5%)

Bullfrog (OG 1047, ABV 4.8%)

Druid's Fluid (OG 1048, ABV 5%)

Wold Top SIBA

Wold Top Brewery, Hunmanby Grange, Wold Newton, Driffield, East Yorkshire,YO25 3HS
Tel (01723) 892222
Fax (01723) 892229
Email enquiries@woldtopbrewery.co.uk
Website www.woldtopbrewery.co.uk
Tours by arrangement (summer only)

Wold Top started brewing in 2002 in a converted granary on a farm. The brewery grows its own barley, uses its own water and would like to grow its own hops. A 10-barrel plant is used. One pub, the Falling Stone in Thwing, is owned. 300 outlets are served. A bottling plant was installed in 2003 and all beers are now available in bottled form from off-licences and via mail order.

Bitter (OG 1037, ABV 3.7%)
Maris Otter pale malt and a small amount of crystal malt form the basis of the beer, with Northdown hops for aroma and bitterness.

Falling Stone (OG 1042, ABV 4.2%)
A full-bodied and well-rounded beer. The rich colour is produced by adding a small amount of chocolate malt to the mash, which is based on Maris Otter pale malt. Progress hops are used for aroma.

Mars Magic (OG 1044, ABV 4.6%)
Dark beer with red hue from the roast barley used. Progress hops are used for both bittering and aroma and give a well-balanced flavour with a hint of caramel.

Wold Gold (OG 1046, ABV 4.8%)
Light-coloured summer beer. Maris Otter, wheat and cara malts, along with Goldings and Styrian hops, make this very drinkable with a hint of spice.

Wolf

WBC (Norfolk) Ltd, t/a Wolf Brewery, Rookery Farm, Silver Street, Besthorpe, Attleborough, Norfolk, NR17 2LD
Tel (01953) 457775
Fax (01953) 457776
Email info@wolfbrewery.com
Website www.wolfbrewery.com
Tours by arrangement

The brewery was founded by Wolfe Witham, the former owner of the Reindeer Brewery, in 1996, using a 20-barrel plant housed on the site of the old Gaymer's cider orchard. 200 outlets are supplied. All the beers are also sold in bottle-conditioned form. In the 2005 SIBA national cask beer championships Wolf won the supreme championship with Granny Wouldn't Like It, a silver for Golden Jackal and a bronze for Woild Moild. Seasonal beer: Timber Wolf (ABV 5.8%, winter).

Golden Jackal (OG 1039, ABV 3.7%) ◆
Flavoursome golden ale with a hoppy, citrus nose. Lemon notes enhance the dominant hop flavour that soars above a sweet malty background. Long-lasting with hops to the end.

Wolf In Sheep's Clothing (OG 1039, ABV 3.7%) ◆
A malty aroma with fruity undertones introduces this reddish-hued mild. Malt, with a bitter background that remains throughout, is the dominant flavour of this clean-tasting beer.

Bitter (OG 1041, ABV 3.9%) ◆
Well-balanced mix of flavours. Hops blend with malt and bitterness in a grainy first impression. Some citrus notes in the background fade quickly.

Coyote Bitter (OG 1044, ABV 4.3%) ◆
Citrus notes introduce this amber-coloured bitter. The first impression is of a distinctive mix of malt and bitterness side by side with a dry hoppiness. The flavours are distinctive but none is initially dominant.

Newshound 2001 (ABV 4.5%) ◆
Copper coloured with a light hop and malt nose. Malt takes the edge off the bitter backbone of this solid tasting beer. Vanilla and citrus hints can be detected as the long finish grows into a dry hoppiness.

Straw Dog (ABV 4.5%)

Woild Moild (OG 1048, ABV 4.8%) ◆
Dark brown and creamy with overall roast-dominated flavour. Molasses and caramel add to the depth with more than a hint of sweetness also present. Finish somewhat more bitter and drier.

Granny Wouldn't Like It (OG 1049, ABV 4.8%) ◆
Well-rounded strong ale with a robust mix of malt and cherry fruitiness. The aroma matches the taste with the fruity malt character looming large throughout. A hoppy biterness gives an understated contrast.

Lupus Lupus (ABV 5%) ◆
A soft blackcurrant nose introduces this red-coloured brew. Hops vie with bitterness in the initial taste. Fruity malt notes soon fade to leave a long bitter finish with just a hint of blackcurrant fruitiness.

Wolverhampton & Dudley

See Banks's, Jennings and Marston's in the New Nationals section

Wood SIBA

Wood Brewery Ltd, Wistanstow, Craven Arms, Shropshire, SY7 8DG
Tel (01588) 672523
Fax (01588) 673939
Email mail@woodbrewery.co.uk
Website www.woodbrewery.co.uk
Tours by arrangement

The brewery opened in 1980 in buildings next to the Plough Inn, still the brewery's only tied house. Steady growth over the years included the acquisition of the Sam Powell Brewery and its beers in 1991. Building extension was completed in 2003 to enlarge fermentation, storage and office space. 2005 marked the brewery's silver anniversary. Production averages 70 barrels a week. 200 outlets are supplied. Seasonal beers: Summerthat (ABV 3.9%, June-Aug), Woodcutter (ABV 4.2%, Sept-Nov), Hopping Mad (ABV 4.7%, March-May), Christmas Cracker (ABV 6%, Nov-Dec). A monthly beer is also brewed.

Quaff (ABV 3.7%)
A pale and refreshing light bitter with a clean, hoppy finish.

Craven Ale (ABV 3.8%)
An attractively coloured beer with a pleasant hop aroma and a refreshing taste.

Parish Bitter (OG 1040, ABV 4%) ◆
A blend of malt and hops with a bitter aftertaste. Pale brown in colour.

Special Bitter (OG 1042, ABV 4.2%) ◆
A tawny brown bitter with malt, hops and some fruitiness.

Pot O' Gold (OG 1044, ABV 4.4%)

Shropshire Lad (OG 1045, ABV 4.5%)
A strong, well-rounded bitter, drawing flavour from a fine blend of selected English malted barley and traditional English Fuggles and Golding hops.

Old Sam (OG 1047, ABV 4.6%)
A dark copper ale with a ripe, rounded flavour and hop bitterness.

Wonderful (OG 1048, ABV 4.8%) ◆
A mid-brown, fruity beer, with a roast and malt taste.

Tom Wood

See Highwood

Wooden Hand

Wooden Hand Brewery, Unit 3 Grampound Road Industrial Estate, Grampound Road, Truro, Cornwall, TR2 4TB
Tel (01726) 884596
Fax (01726) 884579
Email mel@woodenhand.co.uk
Website www.woodenhand.co.uk

Wooden Hand took over the plant from the former Ventonwyn Brewery. The company is run by Anglo-Swedish businessman Rolf Munding, who also owns the Zatec Brewery in the Czech Republic. The brewery moved to Unit 3 in 2005. That year also saw a major expansion into bottling. Some 20 outlets are supplied.

Smugglers Gold (OG 1036, ABV 3.6%)

Black Pearl (OG 1039, ABV 4%)

Cornish Buccaneer (OG 1039, ABV 4.3%)

Cornish Mutiny (OG 1048, ABV 4.8%)

Woodforde's SIBA

Woodforde's Norfolk Ales, Broadland Brewery, Woodbastwick, Norwich, Norfolk, NR13 6SW
Tel (01603) 720353
Fax (01603) 721806
Email info@woodfordes.co.uk
Website www.woodfordes.co.uk
Shop Mon-Fri 10.30am-4.30pm; Sat-Sun 11.30am-4.30pm
Tours by arrangement (Tue & Thu evenings)

⊠ Founded in 1981 in Drayton near Norwich, Woodforde's moved to Erpingham near Aylsham in 1982, and then moved again to a converted farm complex, with greatly increased production capacity, in the picturesque Broadland village of Woodbastwick in 1989. A major expansion of Broadland Brewery took place in 2001-2002 to more than double production capacity and included a new brewery shop and visitor centre. Woodforde's brews an extensive range of beers and runs two tied houses with some 600 other outlets supplied on a regular basis. Bottle-conditioned beers: Wherry Bitter, Great Eastern, Nelson's Revenge ■, Admiral's Reserve, Norfolk Nog, Headcracker, Norfolk Nip. Admiral's Reserve was added to the range in 2002 to celebrate Woodforde's 21st anniversary.

Mardler's (OG 1035, ABV 3.5%) ◆
A traditional Norfolk dark mild. A somewhat light blend of roast malt and chocolate sweetness with little body. Roast notes heighten as other flavours fade.

Wherry Best Bitter (OG 1037.4, ABV 3.8%) ■ □ ◆
A well-balanced bitter with floral citrus notes in aroma and taste. A good blend of malt and hops engender a light but flavoursome feel. Amber coloured with a sustained finish.

Great Eastern (OG 1039.8, ABV 4.3%) ◆
A light citrus bouquet introduces this gentle blend of toffee sweetness and dry hoppiness. Hop flavours fade quickly to leave a heavy, sweet fruitiness.

Nelson's Revenge (OG 1042.7, ABV 4.5%) ■ □ ◆
A glorious mix of vine fruit, malt and hops give a rich Christmas pudding feel. Malt begins in the nose and remains to the end. Sultana-like fruitiness blunts the hop background throughout.

Norfolk Nog (OG 1046.8, ABV 4.6%) □ ◆
Dark red, with a deep roast character. Little bitterness in the dominant roast body. Liquorice appears in both flavour and nose. Lingering finish dominated by dried fruit.

Admiral's Reserve (OG 1050, ABV 5%) ◆
Light tasting for its strength but well balanced throughout. Malt and caramel on the nose and initial flavour with a growing hop influence. Quick finish with a gentle bitterness.

Headcracker (OG 1065.7, ABV 7%) □ ◆
Surprisingly clean-tasting for a barley wine. A booming, plummy aroma buttressed with malt continues to become the dominant taste throughout. A pleasant winey bitterness provides a counterpoint. A dry sultana plumminess provides a fitting finale.

Norfolk Nip (OG 1076, ABV 8.5%) ■ □
Dark mahogany in colour, this intensely flavoured beer has a stunning range of malts and hops enveloped by a warming balanced bitterness. This traditional dark barley wine is matured in the cask to develop the rich and robust flavours that give it a personality of its own. This beer benefits from long storage.

Woodlands

Woodlands Brewing Co, Unit 5 Creamery Industrial Estate, Station Road, Wrenbury, Nantwich, Cheshire, CW5 8EX
Tel (01270) 620101

Email woodlandsbrewery@aol.com
Shop 8am-5pm daily
Tours by arrangement

The brewery opened in 2004 with a five-barrel plant from the former Khean Brewery. The beers are brewed using water from a spring that comes to the surface of a peat field on nearby Woodlands Farm. Consideration is being given to adding a still to enable the production of spirits. Some 100 outlets are supplied. Bottle-conditioned beers: Woodlands Bitter, Oak Beauty, Midnight Stout, Woodlands IPA, Old Willow, Lager-Beer, Gold Brew.

Drummer Bitter (OG 1039, ABV 3.9%) ◆
Clean, malty session bitter with lasting dry finish and increasing bitterness in the aftertaste.

Lager-Beer (OG 1041, ABV 4.1%)

Old Willow (OG 1041, ABV 4.1%)

Oak Beauty (OG 1042, ABV 4.2%) ◆
Malty, sweetish copper-coloured bitter with toffee and caramel flavours. Long-lasting and satisfying bitter finish.

IPA (OG 1043, ABV 4.3%) ◆
Pale, dry and very bitter beer with sharp initial tartness leading to a moderate fruitiness. Good citrus hop throughout but not strong enough for an IPA. Good dry aftertaste.

Midnight Stout (OG 1044, ABV 4.4%) ◆
Classic soft, creamy stout with caramel and roast flavours to the fore. Well-balanced with bitterness and some hops on the taste and a good dry, roasty aftertaste. Some sweetness. Very drinkable.

Bitter (OG 1044, ABV 4.4%)

Gold Brew (OG 1050, ABV 5%) ◆
Strong malty nose with fruit and sweetness balanced in the flavour. Hint of caramel and a dry finish.

Worfield

Worfield Brewing Co, All Nations Brewhouse, Coalport Road, Madeley, Shropshire, TF7 6DP
Tel (01746) 769606
Email mike@worfieldbrew.fsbusiness.co.uk

Worfield began brewing in 1993 at the Davenport Arms and moved to Bridgnorth in 1998. Following the reopening of the All Nations in Madeley, the brewery produced Dabley Ale for the pub and in 2004 relocated to the All Nations from Bridgnorth. Around 200 outlets are supplied. Seasonal beers: Winter Classic (ABV 4.5%, January), Spring Classic (ABV 4.5%, March), Summer Classic (ABV 4.5%, June), Autumn Classic (ABV 4.5%), Ironfounders (ABV 4.6%), Bedlam Strong Bitter (ABV 5.2%), Redneck (ABV 5.5%, Christmas).

Coalport Dodger Mild (OG 1034, ABV 3.5%)

Dabley Ale (OG 1039, ABV 3.8%)

OBJ (OG 1043, ABV 4.2%) ◆
A light and sweet bitter; delicate flavour belies the strength.

Shropshire Pride (OG 1045, ABV 4.5%)

Dabley Gold (OG 1050, ABV 5%)

George Wright

George Wright Brewing Co, Unit 11 Diamond Business Park, Sandwash Close, Rainford, Merseyside, WA11 8LU
Tel (01744) 886686
Fax (01744) 886694
Email sales@georgewrightbrewing.co.uk
Website www.georgewrightbrewing.co.uk
Tours by arrangement

George Wright Brewery started production in 2003. The original plant consisted of a 2.5-barrel system, but this proved to be too small and a five-barrel plant was installed. This has now been upgraded to 25 barrels with production of 200 casks a week and is fully computer controlled.

Drunken Duck (ABV 3.9%) ◆
Fruity gold-coloured bitter beer with good hop and a dry aftertaste. Some acidity.

Longboat (ABV 3.9%) ◆
Good hoppy bitter with grapefruit and an almost tart bitterness throughout. Some astringency in the aftertaste. Well-balanced, light and refreshing with a good mouthfeel and long, dry finish.

Midday Sun (ABV 4.2%)

Winter Sun (ABV 4.2%) ◆
Thinnish bitter with strong fruit aroma. Hops and bitterness dominate the flavour along with caramel. Flavours follow through to a sharp finish.

Pipe Dream (ABV 4.3%)

Kings Shillin' (ABV 4.5%) ◆
Amber bitter with a hoppy aroma leading to a sharp, almost tart initial taste with citrus fruit notes. This full-flavoured malty beer has a good dry finish.

Cheeky Pheasant (ABV 4.7%)

Roman Black (ABV 4.8%)

Black Swan (ABV 3.8%)

Blue Moon (ABV 4.9%) ◆
Easy-drinking strong, gold-coloured beer. Good malt/bitter balance and well hopped.

Icebreaker (ABV 5.5%)
A regular beer brewed at eight-weekly intervals

Wychwood SIBA

Wychwood Brewery Ltd, Eagle Maltings, The Crofts, Witney, Oxfordshire, OX28 4DP
Tel (01993) 890800
Fax (01993) 772553
Email info@wychwood.co.uk
Website www.wychwood.co.uk
Shop Sat 2-6pm
Tours by arrangement

Wychwood Brewery is located in the Oxford Cotswolds on the fringes of the ancient medieval forest, The Wychwood. The brewery was founded in 1983 by two local characters, Paddy Glenny and Chris Moss, on a site dating back to the 1800s, which was once the original maltings for the town's brewery. The brewery, now owned by Refresh UK, has recently been renovated and expanded, and the site also includes the Brakspear Brewery (qv). The beers contain local water from the river Windrush and no additives are used. A range of seasonal beers is also produced, including the infamous Dog's Bollocks.

Shires Bitter (OG 1035, ABV 3.7%) ◆
A copper-coloured session beer with a fruity and malty aroma and admirable hop character. Good body for its strength. Fruit declines to a dry finish.

Fiddler's Elbow Bitter (OG 1042, ABV 4.5%) ◆
A spicy amber beer, complex, with a spicy hop aroma and a suggestion of cinnamon. Easy to drink, with a crisp and refreshing finish.

Hobgoblin (OG 1050, ABV 5%) ◆
Powerful, full-bodied, copper-red, well-balanced brew. Strong in roasted malt, with a moderate bitterness and a slight fruity character.

Wye Valley SIBA

Wye Valley Brewery, Stoke Lacy, Herefordshire, HR7 4HG
Tel (01885) 490505
Fax (01885) 490595
Email enquiries@wyevalleybrewery.co.uk
Website www.wyevalleybrewery.co.uk
Shop Mon-Fri 10am-4pm
Tours by arrangement

⊗ Wye Valley was founded in 1985 in Canon Pyon, Herefordshire. The following year it moved to the old stable block of the Barrels pub in Hereford and 2002 saw another move to Stoke Lacy in the north of the county. During this move the plant was expanded and upgraded and has a capacity to brew 80 barrels a day. Two pubs are owned, with plans for more over the next few years. Some 400 outlets are supplied. Seasonal beers: DG Springtime Ale (ABV 4%, Feb-April), DG Summertime Ale (ABV 4.2%, May-July), DG Autumn Ale (ABV 4.4%, Aug-Oct), DG Winter Tipple (ABV 4.7%, Nov-Jan). Twelve monthly guest beers and occasional specials are also available. Bottle-conditioned beers: DG Golden Ale, Butty Bach, DG Wholesome Stout ■ ⊡, Country Ale (ABV 6%).

Bitter (OG 1037, ABV 3.7%) ◆
A beer whose aroma gives little hint of the bitter hoppiness that follows right through to the aftertaste.

Hereford Pale Ale (OG 1040, ABV 4%) ◆
A pale, hoppy, malty brew with a hint of sweetness before a dry finish.

Dorothy Goodbody's Golden Ale (OG 1042, ABV 4.2%)
A light, gold-coloured, refreshing ale with a hint of malty sweetness from the pale crystal malt, balancing well with the aroma and flavour of the classic English hop varieties used.

Butty Bach (OG 1046, ABV 4.5%) ■
A burnished gold, full-bodied premium ale.

Dorothy Goodbody's Wholesome Stout (OG 1046, ABV 4.6%) ⊡ ◆
A smooth and satisfying stout with a bitter edge to its roast flavours. The finish combines roast grain and malt.

Wylam SIBA

Wylam Brewery Ltd, South Houghton Farm, Heddon on the Wall, Northumberland, NE15 0EZ
Tel/Fax (01661) 853377
Email admin@wylambrew.co.uk
Website www.wylambrew.co.uk
Tours by arrangement

⊗ Built by John Boyle and Robin Leighton in 2000, Wylam started with a 4.5-barrel plant, which increased to nine barrels in 2002. New premises and brew plant (20 barrels) are being installed on the same site during 2006. The brewery delivers to more than 200 local outlets and beers are available through wholesalers around the country. Seasonal beers: Spring Thing (ABV 3.4%), Hopping Mad (ABV 4.2%, autumn).

Hedonist (OG 1038, ABV 3.8%)

Bitter (OG 1039, ABV 3.8%) ◆
A refreshing, copper-coloured, hoppy bitter with a clean, bitter finish.

Gold Tankard (OG 1040, ABV 4%) ◆
Fresh, clean flavour, full of hops. This golden ale has a hint of citrus in the finish.

Magic (OG 1042, ABV 4.2%) ◆
Light, crisp and refreshing. Floral and spicy with a good bitter finish.

Whistle Stop (OG 1046, ABV 4.4%)

Bohemia (OG 1046, ABV 4.6%) ■ ⊡ ◆
Tawny in colour with a heady bouquet of malt and hops, and a deep finish of fruit.

Haugh (OG 1046, ABV 4.6%) ◆
A smooth velvet porter packed with flavour. Roast malt and a slight fruitiness provide a satisfying pint with a smooth finish.

Landlords Choice (OG 1046, ABV 4.6%)

Silver Ghost (OG 1050, ABV 5%)

Wyre Piddle

Wyre Piddle Brewery, Highgrove Farm, Peopleton, near Pershore, Worcestershire, WR10 2LF
Tel/Fax (01905) 841853

⊗ A brewery established in a converted stable by a former publican and master builder in 1992. Some 200 pubs in the Midlands take the beer. The brewery relocated and upgraded its equipment in 1997 and has now moved again to Highgrove Farm. It also brews for Green Dragon, Malvern: Dragon's Downfall (ABV

3.9%), Dragon's Revenge (ABV 4%). For Severn Valley Railway: Royal Piddle (ABV 4.2%). Seasonal beers: Piddle in the Sun (ABV 5.2%, summer), Yule Piddle (ABV 4.5%, Christmas).

Piddle in the Hole (OG 1039, ABV 3.9%) ♦
Copper-coloured and quite dry, with lots of hops and fruitiness throughout.

Piddle in the Dark (ABV 4.5%)
A rich ruby-red bitter with a smooth flavour.

Piddle in the Wind (ABV 4.5%) ♦
This drink has a superb mix of flavours. A hoppy nose continues through to a lasting aftertaste, making it a good, all-round beer.

Piddle in the Snow (ABV 5.2%) ♦
A dry, strong taste all the way through draws your attention to the balance between malt and hops in the brew. A glorious way to end an evening's drinking.

Yates

Yates Brewery Ltd, Ghyll Farm, Westnewton, Wigton, Cumbria, CA7 3NX
Tel (016973) 21081
Email enquiry@yatesbrewery.co.uk
Website www.yatesbrewery.co.uk
Tours by arrangement

◎ Cumbria's oldest micro-brewery, established in 1986. The brewery was bought in 1998 by Graeme and Caroline Baxter, who had previously owned High Force Brewery in Teesdale. Deliveries are mainly to its Cumbrian stronghold and the A69 corridor as far as Hexham. A new brewhouse and reed bed effluent system have been completed on the same site. Around 40 outlets are supplied. Seasonal beers: Spring Fever (ABV 4.7%), Best Cellar (ABV 5.8%, Christmas), IPA (ABV 4.9%), Genius (ABV 4.1%)

Bitter (OG 1035, ABV 3.7%) ♦
A well-balanced, full-bodied bitter, golden in colour with complex hop bitterness. Good aroma and distinctive flavour.

Fever Pitch (OG 1039, ABV 3.9%)
An extremely pale-coloured beer. Fully rounded, smooth, hoppy flavour, using lager malt and hops.

Sun Goddess (OG 1042, ABV 4.2%)
A lager-style cask beer, light and fruity with agreeable bitterness.

Solway Sunset (OG 1042, ABV 4.3%)

Yates' SIBA

Yates' Brewery, The Inn at St Lawrence, Undercliff Drive, St Lawrence, Ventnor, Isle of Wight, PO38 1XG
Head Office: Unit 6 Dean Farm, Whitwell Road, Whitwell, Isle of Wight, PO38 2AB
Tel/Fax (01983) 731731
Email info@yates-brewery.fsnet.co.uk
Website www.yates-brewery.co.uk
Tours by arrangement

David Yates previously worked for the original Burts Brewery in Ventnor, which went into receivership in 1992. He then moved to the Island Brewery in Newport, working for Hartridges. When Hartridges sold out to Ushers, David was made redundant. He then decided to start up on his own, installing a five-barrel plant at the Inn at St Lawrence. Brewing started in 2000. Yates' now has 40 regular outlets. Bottling started in 2003 and in 2004 the brewery won Bronze in the Champion Beer of Britain competition with Yates' Special Draught. All the draught beers are also available in bottle-conditioned form. Seasonal beer: Yule B Sorry (ABV 5.5%, Christmas).

Bugle Best (OG 1039, ABV 3.8%)
A light, refreshing session bitter.

Undercliff Experience (OG 1040, ABV 4.1%)
An amber-copper ale with a bitter-sweet malt and hop taste with a dry lemon edge that dominates the bitter finish.

Blonde (OG 1045, ABV 4.5%)
A light beer with a fruity, citrus nose and a dry, hoppy finish.

Holy Joe (OG 1050, ABV 4.9%) ♦
Strongly bittered golden ale with pronounced spice and citrus character, and underlying light hint of malt.

Wight Winter (OG 1050, ABV 5%)
A ruby ale with malty milk chocolate at first in the nose, then plenty of orange fruit. It has a smooth roasted taste.

Special Bitter (YSD) (OG 1056, ABV 5.5%) ◫ ♦
Easy-drinking strong, amber ale with pronounced tart bitterness and a refreshing bite in the aftertaste.

Yeovil*

Yeovil Ales, Unit 5 Bofors Park, Artillery Road, Lufton Trading Estate, Yeovil, Somerset, BA22 8YH
Tel (01935) 414888 Fax (01935) 355439
Email rob@yeovilales.co.uk.
Website www.yeovilales.co.uk

Rob Sherwood, a civil engineer and keen home-brewer, turned his hobby into a business in May 2006. He bought an 18-barrel plant from Triple fff (qv) when that brewery upgraded to a larger plant.

Yeovil Pride (ABV 3.8%)

Summerset (ABV 4.1%)

Glovers Gold (ABV 4.6%)

IPA (ABV 5.4%)

Yetman's

Yetman's Brewery, c/o 37 Norwich Road, Holt, Norfolk, NR25 6SA
Tel (01263) 713320
Email peter@yetmans.net
Website www.yetmans.net

A 2.5-barrel plant built by Moss Brew was installed in restored medieval barns in 2005. The brewery supplies local free trade outlets. Bottle-conditioned beer: Orange.

Yellow (OG 1036, ABV 3.6%)

Red (OG 1038, ABV 3.8%)

Orange (OG 1042, ABV 4.2%)

Green (OG 1048, ABV 4.8%)

York SIBA

York Brewery Co Ltd, 12 Toft Green, York, North Yorkshire, YO1 6JT
Tel (01904) 621162
Fax (01904) 621216
Email info@yorkbrew.co.uk
Website www.yorkbrew.co.uk
Shop Mon-Sat 12-6pm
Tours by arrangement (please ring for times)

⊛ York started production in 1996, the first brewery in the city for 40 years. It has a visitor centre with bar and gift shop. It is designed as a show brewery, with a gallery above the 20-barrel plant and viewing panels to fermentation and conditioning rooms. The brewery opened the Yorkshire Terrier Inn on Stonegate in 2004, fronted by its own gift shop. In 2005, York and Tynemill amicably dissolved their pub partnership and the Rook & Gaskill became a Tynemill pub. The Three-Legged Mare in High Petergate and the Last Drop Inn on Colliergate are now York Brewery pubs. Work is in hand to increase capacity by 20-barrels a week. More than 400 pubs take the beers. Seasonal beers: see website.

Guzzler (OG 1036, ABV 3.6%) ◆
Refreshing golden ale with dominant hop and fruit flavours developing throughout.

Stonewall (OG 1038, ABV 3.8%) ◻ ◆
Balanced amber bitter where maltiness underlines strong hop and fruit aromas and flavours.

Wild Wheat (OG 1040, ABV 4.1%)

Yorkshire Terrier (OG 1041, ABV 4.2%) ◻ ◆
Refreshing and distinctive amber/gold brew where fruit and hops dominate the aroma and taste. Hoppy bitterness remains assertive in the aftertaste.

IPA (OG 1049, ABV 5%)

Centurion's Ghost Ale (OG 1051, ABV 5.4%) ◼ ◆
Dark ruby in colour, full-tasting with mellow roast malt character balanced by light bitterness and autumn fruit flavours that linger into the aftertaste.

Yorkshire Dales*

Yorkshire Dales Brewing Co Ltd, Seata Barn, Elm Hill, Askrigg, North Yorkshire, DL8 3HG
Tel/Fax (01969) 622027
Email info@yorkshiredalesbrewery.com
Website www.yorkshiredalesbrewery.com

Situated in Askrigg in the heart of the Yorkshire Dales, brewing started in 2005 on a 1.25-barrel brew plant previously used by Wizard Ales and prior to that by Swaled Ale. Expansion plans for 2006 included the installation of new plant in a converted milking parlour. Four beers are regularly produced with seasonal ones also available. Around 20 outlets are supplied.

Herriot Country Ale (OG 1041, ABV 4%)

Gunnerside Gold (OG 1043, ABV 4.4%)

Nappa Scar (OG 1045, ABV 4.8%)

Whernside ESB (OG 1056, ABV 5.8%)

Young's

See Wells & Young's

Zerodegrees SIBA

London: Zerodegrees Microbrewery, 29-31 Montpelier Vale, Blackheath, London, SE3 0TJ
Tel (020) 8852 5619/Fax (020) 8852 4463
Bristol: Zerodegrees Microbrewery, 53 Colston Street, Bristol, BS1 5BA
Tel (0117) 925 2706/Fax (0117) 934 9420
Reading: 2-4 Gun Street, Reading, Berkshire, RG1 2JR
Email info@zerodegrees.co.uk
Website www.zerodegrees.co.uk
Tours by arrangement

Brewing started in 2000 in London and incorporates a state-of-the-art, computer-controlled German plant, producing unfiltered and unfined ales and lagers, served from tanks using air pressure (not CO2). Four pubs are owned. All beers are suitable for vegetarians and vegans. All branches of Zerodegrees follow the same concept of beers with nothing added and nothing taken away. There are regular seasonal specials including fruit beers.

Fruit Beer (OG 1040, ABV 3.8%)
The type of fruit used varies during the year.

NEW BREWERIES

The following new breweries have been notified to the Guide and should come on stream during 2006/2007:

Amber Valley, Hammersmith, Derbyshire
Beeston Brewery, Beeston, Norfolk: www.beestonbrewery.co.uk
Blackbeck, Blackbeck, Cumbria
Blue Bear, Kempsey, Worcs: www.bluebearbrewery.co.uk
Clarion, Derbyshire
Crown Inn, Little Staughton, Beds
Dobbins & Jackson Newport Brewing Co, Shaftesbury, Newport
Enfield Brewery, Enfield, Mddx
Fifield Farm, Oxon
Fox & Newt, Leeds
Geltsdale, Brampton, Cumbria
Glenfinnan, Inverness
McLaughlin, London
Plockton, Ross & Cromarty: www.theplocktonbrewery.com
Rosebridge, Wigan
St Jude's, Ipswich
Sheffield Brewery, Sheffield
Teesdale Brewing Co Ltd, Barnard Castle. Co Durham

Wheat Beer (OG 1045, ABV 4.2%) ◆
Refreshing wheat ale with spicy aroma; banana, vanilla and sweet flavours; dry, lasting finish.

Pale Ale (OG 1046, ABV 4.6%) ◆
American-style IPA with complex fruit aroma and peach flavours. Clean bitter finish with long aftertaste.

Black Lager (OG 1048, ABV 4.8%) ◆
Light, Eastern European-style black lager brewed with roasted malt. Refreshing coffee finish. An interesting variation on a stout theme.

Pilsner (OG 1048, ABV 4.8%) ◆
Clean-tasting refreshing Pilsner with a malty aroma and taste, accompanied by delicate bitterness and citrus fruits.

FROM OVERSEAS

Anker

Brouwerij Het Anker, 49 Guido Gezellelaan, 2800 Mechelen, Belgium
Tel (0032) 15 28 71 47 Fax (0032) 15 28 71 48
Email het.anker@pandora.be
Website www.hetanker.be

The Anchor Brewery has been in production since the 14th century. It was seriously damaged during the two world wars of the 20th century. It achieved fame from the 1960s when it introduced Gouden Carolus, a strong dark ale named after a coin from the reign of Emperor Charles V. The brewery was updated in the 1990s and the beer range extended. As with De Koninck below, the beer is served under pressure in Belgium but a cask version is on sale in selected outlets of the Wetherspoons chain of pubs.

Gouden Carolus Ambrio (ABV 8%)

De Koninck

Brouwerij De Koninck NV, 291 Mechelsesteenweg, 2018 Antwerp, Belgium
Tel (0032) 3 218 4048
Email info@dekoninck.com
Website: www.dekoninck.be

Legendary Belgian brewer of a classic pale ale, founded in 1833. In its home territory the beer is served under pressure but a cask-conditioned version is now available in Wetherspoon's pubs in Britain. The beer is sent in tankers to Shepherd Neame in Faversham (qv) where it is fined and racked into casks. It is called Ambrée in Britain but is known simply as De Koninck in Belgium.

Ambrée (ABV 5%)

R.I.P.

The following breweries have closed, gone out of business, suspended operations or merged with another company since the 2005 Guide was published:

Blackpool
Bridge Street
Cheriton
Clark's Organic
Egyptian Sand & Gravel
Fantasy
Font Valley
Gale's
Lass O'Gowrie
Merlin
Old Stables
Ramsbottom
Ridley's
Scarecrow
Trossachs Craft
Walsh's Bakehouse
Wheal Ale
Whitley Bridge
Yns Mon

The soul of beer

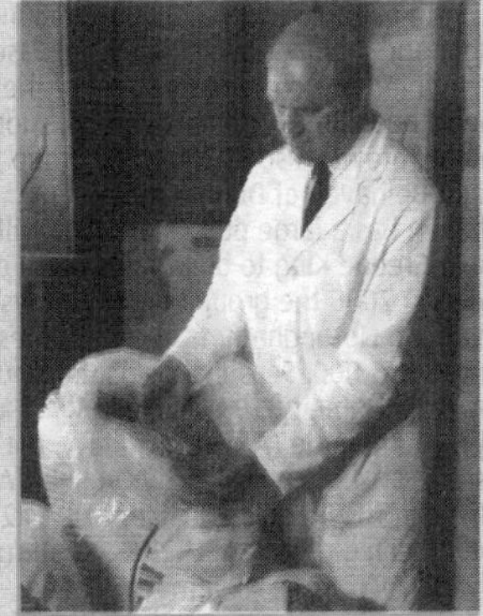

Brewers call barley malt the 'soul of beer'. While a great deal of attention has been rightly paid to hops in recent years, the role of malt in brewing must not be ignored. Malt contains starch that is converted to a special form of sugar known as maltose during the brewing process. It is maltose that is attacked by yeast during fermentation and turned into alcohol and carbon dioxide. Other grains can be used in brewing, notably wheat. But barley malt is the preferred grain as it gives a delightful biscuity/cracker/Ovaltine note to beer. Unlike wheat, barley has a husk that works as a natural filter during the first stage of brewing, known as the mash. Cereals such as rice and corn/maize are widely used by global producers of mass-market lagers, but craft brewers avoid them.

New nationals

The rapid growth of Greene King and Wolverhampton & Dudley Breweries since 2000 has given them the status of national breweries. They do not match the size of the global brewers but they do reach most areas of Britain as a result of both their tied and free trade activities. Unlike the global producers or the old national brewers who disappeared in the 1990s, Greene King and W&D are committed to cask beer production. Greene King IPA is the biggest-selling standard cask beer in the country while Marston's Pedigree now outsells Draught Bass in the premium sector. There is a down-side to this progress: in some parts of the country, the choice of real ale is often confined to the products of the two groups, and their continued expansion, seen in the takeovers of Belhaven, Hardys & Hansons, Jennings and Ridley's, is cause for concern for drinkers who cherish choice and diversity.

Greene King

Greene King plc, Westgate Brewery, Bury St Edmunds, Suffolk, IP33 1QT
Tel (01284) 763222 Fax (01284) 706502
Email solutions@greeneking.co.uk
Website www.greeneking.co.uk
Shop Mon-Sat 10-5, Sun 12-4
Tours 11am, 2pm and evening by arrangements

⊗ Greene King has been brewing in the market town of Bury St Edmunds in the heart of rural Suffolk since 1799. It closed its Biggleswade brewery in Cambridgeshire in the late 1990s, where it brewed only lager, in order to concentrate on cask beer production. In the 1990s it bought the brands of the former Morland and Ruddles breweries and promotes them with some fervour, Old Speckled Hen in particular; the Ruddles beers bear little relationship to the former brews, either in taste or strength. As a result of buying the former Morland pub estate, the company acquired a major presence in the Thames Valley region. But it has not confined itself to East Anglia or the Home Counties. Its tenanted and managed pubs, which include Old English Inns and Hungry Horse, total more than 2,100 while the assiduous development of its free trade sales, totalling more than 3,000 outlets, means its beers can be found as far away from its home base as Wales and the north of England. In 2005 Greene King bought and rapidly closed Ridley's of Essex. In spite of pledges to maintain some of the Ridley's beers, they are now just occasional or seasonal brews. Also in 2005, the group bought Belhaven of Dunbar in Scotland. Belhaven has a large pub estate that will enable Greene King to build sales north of border. In 2006 the group bought Hardys & Hansons in Nottingham, taking its pub estate to close to 3,000. Seasonal beers: Rumpus (ABV 4.5%, January), Prospect (ABV 4.1%, May), Triumph Ale (ABV 4.3%, May), Ale Fresco (ABV 4.3%, June), Tolly Original (ABV 3.8%, August), Ruddles Orchard (ABV 4.2%, September), Old Bob (ABV 5.1%, September), Firewall (ABV 4.5%, November). Bottle-conditioned beer: Hen's Tooth (ABV 6.5%).

XX Mild (OG 1035, ABV 3%)
Brewed under licence at Ridley's until 2005; now back at Bury St Edmunds.

IPA (OG 1036, ABV 3.6%)
A light, uncomplicated session bitter. Copper coloured with a subtle malty nose and just as hint of hops. A light bitter introduction with a sweetish, malty undertone give a refreshing, lemonade-type feel. A long, tapering finish turns drier and increases bitterness.

Ruddles Best Bitter (OG 1037, ABV 3.7%)
An amber/brown beer, strong on bitterness but with some initial sweetness, fruit and subtle, distinctive Bramling Cross hop. Dryness lingers in the aftertaste.

Morland Original Bitter (OG 1039, ABV 4%)

Ruddles County (OG 1048, ABV 4.3%)
Richer and slightly darker than Ruddles Best, this premium ale shares similar characteristics. Sweetness and fruit on the palate give way to bitterness and a distinctly hoppy, dry finish. Good body for its strength.

Abbot Ale (OG 1049, ABV 5%)
A full-bodied, distinctive beer with a bitter-sweet aftertaste.

Old Speckled Hen (OG 1050, ABV 5.2%)
Rich and cloying in both nose and taste, with an intense malty nose and plummy overtones. The flavour spectrum matches this with rich spicy maltiness overwhelming the latent bitterness. A solid mouthfeel helps retain the fruity sweetness as the heavy malt framework slowly turns to a light dryness.

Belhaven

Belhaven Brewing Co Ltd, Spott Road, Dunbar, East Lothian, EH42 1RS
Tel (01368) 862734 Fax (01368) 869500
Email info@belhaven.co.uk
Website www.belhaven.co.uk
Shop open during tours
Tours by arrangement

Belhaven is located in Dunbar, some 30 miles east of Edinburgh on the East Lothian coast. The company claimed to be the oldest independent brewery in Scotland but it lost that independence when Greene King bought it. Belhaven owns 275 tied pubs and has around 2,500 direct free trade accounts. Seasonal beers: Fruit Beer (ABV 4.6%, July), Fruity Partridge (ABV 5.2%, December).

60/- Ale (OG 1030, ABV 2.9%)
A fine but virtually unavailable example of a Scottish light. This bitter-sweet, reddish-brown beer is dominated by fruit and malt with a hint of roast and caramel, and increasing bitterness in the aftertaste.

70/- Ale (OG 1038, ABV 3.5%)
This pale brown beer has malt and fruit and some hop throughout, and is increasingly bitter-sweet in the aftertaste.

Sandy Hunter's Traditional Ale (OG 1038, ABV 3.6%) ◆
A distinctive, medium-bodied beer named after a past chairman and head brewer. An aroma of malt and hops greets the nose. A hint of roast combines with the malt and hops to give a bitter-sweet taste and finish.

80/- Ale (OG 1040, ABV 4.2%) ◆
One of the few remaining Scottish 80 Shillings, with malt the predominant flavour characteristic, though it is balanced by hop and fruit. Roast and caramel play a part in this complex beer. The soubriquet 'the claret of Scotland' hints at the depth and complexity of the flavours.

St Andrew's Ale (OG 1046, ABV 4.9%)
A bitter-sweet beer with lots of body. The malt, fruit and roast mingle throughout with hints of hop and caramel.

For Maclay pub group (qv)

Signature (OG 1038, ABV 3.8%)
A pronounced malty note is followed by a digestive biscuit flavour. The beer has a late addition of Goldings and Styrian hops.

Kane's Amber Ale (AV 4%)
A hoppy aroma gives way to a malty yet slightly bitter flavour.

Wallace IPA (ABV 4.5%)
A classic IPA in both colour and style, with a long, dry finish.

Golden Scotch Ale (ABV 5%)
Brewed to an original Maclay's recipe, the emphasis is firmly on malt.

For Edinburgh Brewing Co (qv)

Edinburgh Pale Ale (ABV 3.4%)

Hardys & Hansons

Hardys & Hansons plc, The Brewery, Kimberley, Nottingham, NG16 2NS
Tel (0115) 938 3611
Fax (0115) 945 9055
Email info@hardysandhansons.plc.uk
Website www.hardys-hansons.co.uk
Tours by arrangement

⊛ The company and its 262 tied pubs were bought by Greene King in June 2006. Greene King has refused to say whether or not it will close the Kimberley brewery, which is brewing at well below capacity as a result of stopping the production of beers produced under contract. It is not known if Greene King has sufficient capacity at Bury St Edmunds to add the H&H brands to the Greene King, Morland, Ridley's and Ruddles beers produced there. Hardys and Hansons were established respectively in 1832 and 1847 and competed vigorously until merging in 1930. The combined company continued to be run by members of both families until they were made an offer of £271 million by Greene King. The offer was considered within the brewing industry to be generous but it gives Greene King a foothold in the Midlands where its arch-rival Wolverhampton & Dudley is a major force. The tragedy of the loss of H&H is that the company had survived the collapse of the local mining industry in the 1980s – the brewery supplied beer to many miners' clubs – and had rebranded its cask beers and added the premium Olde Trip to mark its acquisition of the historic Olde Trip to Jerusalem pub in Nottingham. In addition to its tied trade, H&H supplies some 300 free trade accounts. Seasonal beers are produced (see website) with a rotation of new beers every month. However, the entire range of beers could change and it is likely that East Midlands drinkers may soon be introduced to Greene King IPA and other Bury-brewed beers.

H&H Mild (OG 1035, ABV 3.1%) ◆
Traditional rich ruby mild with roasted malt to the fore. The fruitiness and caramel provide the sweetness, which is balanced in the faint hoppy finish.

H&H Bitter (OG 1038, ABV 3.9%) ◆
Well-balanced bitter with good bitterness, although the malt is never far away. A pleasant and satisfying finish.

Olde Trip (OG 1043, ABV 4.3%) ◆
Premium ale with hops to be found in the aroma and taste although balanced with maltiness and fruitiness to give a full flavour.

Wolverhampton & Dudley

Wolverhampton & Dudley Breweries plc, PO Box 26, Park Brewery, Wolverhampton, West Midlands, WV1 4NY
Tel (01902) 711811 Fax (01902) 429136
Website www.wdb.co.uk

Wolverhampton & Dudley has grown with spectacular speed in recent years. It became a 'super regional' in 1999 when it bought both Mansfield and Marston's breweries, though it quickly closed Mansfield. In May 2005 it bought Jennings of Cockermouth. In June 2005 the group announced it would invest £250,000 at Cockermouth to expand fermenting and cask racking capacity. In total, W&D owns some 2,200 pubs and supplies some 3,000 free trade pubs and clubs throughout the country. It no longer has a stake in Burtonwood Brewery (qv) but brews Burtonwood Bitter for the pub estate, which is owned by W&D (see Pub Groups). It added a further 70 pubs in March 2006 when it bought Celtic Inns for £43.6 million.

Banks's and Hanson's

Banks's Brewery, Park Brewery, Wolverhampton, West Midlands, WV1 4NY
Contact details as above.

Banks's was formed in 1890 by the amalgamation of three local companies. Hanson's was acquired in 1943 but its Dudley brewery was closed in 1991. Hanson's beers are now brewed in Wolverhampton, though its pubs retain the Hanson's livery. Banks's Original, the biggest-selling brand, is a fine example of West Midlands mild ale but the name was changed to give it a more 'modern' image. Beers from the closed Mansfield Brewery are now brewed at Wolverhampton.

Hanson's Mild Ale (OG 1035, ABV 3.3%) ◆
A mid-to-dark brown mild with a malty roast flavour and aftertaste.

Mansfield Dark Mild (OG 1035, ABV 3.5%)

Riding Bitter (OG 1035, ABV 3.6%)

Original (OG 1036, ABV 3.5%) ◆
An amber-coloured, well-balanced, refreshing session beer.

Bitter (OG 1038, ABV 3.8%) ◆
A pale brown bitter with a pleasant balance of hops and malt. Hops continue from the taste through to a bitter-sweet aftertaste.

Mansfield Cask Ale (OG 1038, ABV 3.9%)

For Burtonwood pub group

Bitter (OG 1036.8, ABV 3.7%) ◆
A well-balanced, refreshing, malty bitter, with a good hoppiness. Fairly dry aftertaste.

Jennings IFBB

Jennings Bros plc, Castle Brewery, Cockermouth, Cumbria, CA13 9NE
Tel 0845 1297185 Fax 0845 1297186
Website www.jenningsbrewery.co.uk
Shop 9-5 Mon-Fri, 10-4 Sat, 10-4 Sun (July & aug)
Tours by arrangement

⊛ Jennings Brewery was established as a family concern in 1828 in the village of Lorton. The company moved to its present location in 1874, in the historic market town of Cockermouth, in the shadow of Cockermouth Castle, at the point where the rivers Cocker and Derwent meet. Pure Lakeland water is still used for brewing, drawn from the brewery's own well, along with Maris Otter barley malt and Fuggles and Goldings hops. A distribution centre in Workington services the brewery's estate of 127 pubs and 350 free trade houses. Seasonal beers: Wards (ABV 4%, Jan-Feb), Crag Rat (ABV 4.3%, March-April), Golden Host (ABV 4.3%, March-April), Redbreast (ABV 4.5%, Oct-Jan).

Dark Mild (OG 1031, ABV 3.1%) ◆
A well-balanced, dark brown mild with a malty aroma, strong roast taste, not over-sweet, with some hops and a slightly bitter finish.

Bitter (OG 1035, ABV 3.5%) ◆
A malty beer with a good mouthfeel that combines with roast flavour and a hoppy finish.

Cumberland Ale (OG 1039, ABV 4%) ◆
A light, creamy, hoppy beer with a dry aftertaste.

Cocker Hoop (OG 1044, ABV 4.6%) ◆
A rich, creamy, copper-coloured beer with raisiny maltiness balanced with a resiny hoppiness, with a developing bitterness towards the end.

Sneck Lifter (OG 1051, ABV 5.1%) ◆
A strong, dark brown ale with a complex balance of fruit, malt and roast flavours through to the finish.

Marstons

Marston, Thompson & Evershed, Marston's Brewery, Shobnall Road, Burton upon Trent, Staffordshire, DE14 2BW
Tel (01283) 531131 Fax (01283) 510378
Website www.wdb.co.uk

⊛ Marston's has been brewing cask beer in Burton since 1834 and the current site is the home of the only working 'Burton Union' fermenters, housed in rooms known collectively as the 'Cathedral of Brewing'. Burton Unions were developed in the 19th century to cleanse the new pale ales of yeast. Only Pedigree is fermented in the unions but yeast from the system is used to ferment the other beers.

Burton Bitter (OG 1037, ABV 3.8%) ◆
Overwhelming sulphurous aroma supports a scattering of hops and fruit with an easy-drinking sweetness. Suddenly the taste develops from the sweet middle to a satisfyingly hoppy finish.

Pedigree (OG 1043, ABV 4.5%) ◆
Sweet beer with a slight sulphur aroma. Has the hoppy but sweet finish of a short session beer.

Old Empire (OG 1057, ABV 5.7%) ◆
Sulphur dominates the aroma over malt. Stylish, copper-coloured beer, malty and sweet to start but developing bitterness with fruit and a touch of sweetness. A balanced aftertaste of hops and fruit leads to a lingering bitterness.

For InBev UK

Draught Bass (OG 1043, ABV 4.4%) ◆
Pale brown with a fruity aroma and a hint of hops. Hoppy but sweet taste with malt, then a lingering hoppy bitterness.

Over the bridge

The Sunday morning convention of going to see the trout jumping was well known in the village. In Wales, on Sundays, none of the pubs were open, but only three miles away, where the border river curved in towards the village, lay England, and just across the bridge was the Silver Fox. To go to see the trout jump under the bridge had become something of a habit.

Raymond Williams, Border Country. 1960

Global giants

Eight out of ten pints of beer brewed in Britain come from the international groups listed below. Most of these huge companies have little or no interest in cask beer. Increasingly, their real ale brands are produced for them by smaller regional brewers

Anheuser-Busch UK

Anheuser-Busch UK, Thames Link House, 1 Church Road, Richmond, Surrey, TW9 2QW. Tel (020) 8332 2302

The company brews 'American' Budweiser at the Stag Brewery, Lower Richmond Road, Mortlake, London SW14 7ET, the former Watneys plant, which is now run as a joint operation with Scottish & Newcastle (qv). Budweiser in bottle, can and keg is brewed from rice (listed first on the label), malt and hops, with planks of wood – the famous beechwood chips – used to clarify the beer. Not to be confused with the classic Czech lager, Budweiser Budvar.

Carlsberg UK

Carlsberg Brewing Ltd, PO Box 142, The Brewery, Leeds, West Yorkshire, LS1 1QG
Tel (0113) 259 4594 Fax (0113) 259 4000
E-mail via website
Website www.carlsberg.co.uk/carlsberg.com

Tetley, the historic Leeds brewery with its open Yorkshire Square fermenters, now answers to the name of Carlsberg UK: Carlsberg-Tetley was unceremoniously dumped in 2004. A wholly-owned subsidiary of Carlsberg Breweries of Copenhagen, Denmark, Carlsberg is an international lager giant. In Britain its lagers are brewed at a dedicated plant in Northampton, while Tetley in Leeds produces ales and some Carlsberg products. Some 140,000 barrels are produced annually. Tetley's cask brands receive little or no promotional support outside Yorkshire, most advertising being reserved for the nitro-keg version of Tetley's Bitter.

Tetley's Dark Mild **(OG 1031, ABV 3.2%)**
A reddish, mid-brown beer with a light malt and caramel aroma. A well-balanced taste of malt and caramel follows, with good bitterness and a satisfying finish.

Tetley's Mild **(OG 1034, ABV 3.3%)**
A mid-brown beer with a light malt and caramel aroma. A well-balanced taste of malt and caramel follows, with good bitterness and a satisfying finish.

Ansells Best Bitter **(OG 1035, ABV 3.7%)**

Tetley's Cask Bitter **(OG 1035, ABV 3.7%)**
A variable, amber-coloured light, dry bitter with a slight malt and hop aroma, leading to a moderate bitterness with a hint of fruit, ending with a dry and bitter finish.

Tetley's Imperial **(ABV 4.3%)**

Draught Burton Ale **(OG 1047, ABV 4.8%)**
A beer with hops, fruit and malt present throughout, and a lingering complex aftertaste, but lacking some hoppiness compared to its Burton original. Carlsberg-Tetley also brews Greenalls Bitter (ABV 3.8%) for former Greenalls pubs supplied by wholesalers. Greenalls Mild has been discontinued.

Coors

Coors Brewers Ltd, 137 High Street, Burton upon Trent, Staffs, DE14 1JZ.
Tel (01283) 511000
Fax (01283) 513873
Website www.coorsbrewers.com

Coors of Colorado established itself in Europe in 2002 by buying part of the former Bass brewing empire, when Interbrew (now InBev) was instructed by the British government to divest itself of some of its interests in Bass. Coors owns several cask ale brands. It brews 110,000 barrels of cask beer a year (mainly under licensing arrangements with other brewers) and also provides a further 50,000 barrels of cask beer from other breweries. Coors closed the Mitchells & Butlers brewery in Birmingham in 2002.

M&B Mild **(OG 1034, ABV 3.2%)**
Brewed under licence by Highgate Brewery, Walsall

Stones Bitter **(OG 1037, ABV 3.7%)**
Brewed for Coors by Everards

Hancock's HB **(OG 1038, ABV 3.6%)**
A pale brown, slightly malty beer whose initial sweetness is balanced by bitterness but lacks a noticeable finish. A consistent if inoffensive Welsh beer brewed for Coors by Brains.

Worthington's Bitter **(OG 1038, ABV 3.6%)**
A pale brown bitter of thin and unremarkable character.

M&B Brew XI **(OG 1039.5, ABV 3.8%)**
A sweet, malty beer with a hoppy, bitter aftertaste, brewed under licence by Brains of Cardiff.

Worthington's White Shield
(ABV 5.6%)

Brewed virtually unchanged since 1829. A bottle-conditioned IPA with a clean fruit aroma and a fruity/nutty taste.

White Shield Brewery

Horninglow Street, Burton upon Trent, Staffs, DE14 1YQ
Tel (0845) 6000598 Fax (01283) 513509
E-mail via website
Website www.coorsvisitorcentre.com
Shop (in Museum of Brewing) 9.30-4.30
Tours by arrangement

The White Shield Brewery – formerly the Museum Brewing Co – based in the Museum of Brewing, is part of Coors. Confusingly, while it brews White Shield, the beer is now a Coors brand (see above). The brewery opened in 1994 and recreates some of the older Bass beers that had been discontinued. The brewery dates from 1920 with some equipment going back to 1840. It has a maximum capacity of 60 barrels a week. Production is divided 50:50 between cask and bottled beers. P2 Imperial Stout and No 1 Barley Wine are now brewed on an occasional basis and in bottle only, though draught versions are supplied to CAMRA festivals when supplies are available.

St Modwen (OG 1037.5, ABV 4.2%)

Worthington E (OG 1043, ABV 4.8%)
Cask version of Bass's 1970s keg beer.

P2 Imperial Stout (ABV 8%) ◆
Christmas pudding aroma, sweet and full bodied, with a dry liquorice finish that is dry, hoppy, mouth-watering and astringent.

No 1 Barley Wine (ABV 10.5%) ◆
Unbelievably fruity! Thick and chewy, with fruit and sugar going in to an amazing complex of bitter, fruity tastes. Brewed in summer and fermented in casks for 12 months.

Guinness

Guinness Brewing GB, Park Royal Brewery, London, NWl0 7RR

An Anglo-Irish giant, part of the Diageo drinks group, with worldwide brewing operations and distribution. It closed its London brewery in 2005. All Guinness keg and bottled products on sale in Britain are now brewed in Dublin.

InBev UK

InBev UK Ltd, Porter Tun House, 500 Capability Green, Luton, Beds, LU1 3LS
Tel (01582) 391166
Fax (01582) 397397
E-mail name.surname@interbrew.co.uk
Website www.inbev.com

A wholly-owned subsidiary of InBev of Belgium and Brazil. Interbrew of Belgium became the world's biggest brewer in 2004 when it bought Brazil's leading producer, Ambev, leapfrogging Anheuser-Busch in the production stakes. Its international name is now InBev and it is a major player in the European market with such lager brands as Stella Artois and Jupiler, and internationally with Labatt and Molson of Canada. It has some interest in ale brewing with the cask- and bottle-conditioned wheat beer, Hoegaarden, and the Abbey beer Leffe. It has a ruthless track record of closing plants and disposing of brands. In the summer of 2000 it bought both Bass's and Whitbread's brewing operations, giving it a 32 per cent market share. The British government told Interbrew to dispose of parts of the Bass brewing group, which were bought by Coors (qv). Draught Bass has declined to around 100,000 barrels a year: it once sold more than two million barrels a year, but was sidelined by the Bass empire. It is now brewed under licence by Marston's (see W&DB in New Nationals section). Only 30 per cent of draught Boddingtons is now in cask form and this is brewed under licence by Hydes of Manchester (qv Independents section). InBev closed the Boddingtons plant despite stiff resistance from the trade unions and CAMRA.

Scottish & Newcastle

Scottish & Newcastle UK, 2-4 Broadway Park, South Gyle Broadway, Edinburgh, EH12 9JZ
Tel (0131) 528 1000
Website www.scottish-newcastle.com

Scottish & Newcastle UK is the new name for Scottish Courage and is Britain's biggest brewing group with close to 30 per cent of the market. S&N joined the ranks of the global brewers in 2000 when it bought Brasseries Kronenbourg and Alken Maes from the French group Danone; Kronenbourg is the biggest French beer brand and is exported internationally. Alken Maes is a major Belgian group that produces lagers and the Grimbergen abbey beer range. The group also has extensive brewing interests in Russia and the Baltic States through a consortium, BBH, formed with Carlsberg. BBH owns the biggest brewery in Russia, Baltika. S&N also has brewing interests in China, India and Portugal. The group has focused on Kronenbourg and its Baltic operations to such an extent that a major rationalisation of its brewing operations in Britain was announced in 2004, with the closure of both the Fountain and Tyne breweries in Edinburgh and Tyneside respectively. Scottish & Newcastle was formed in 1960, a merger between Scottish Brewers (Younger and McEwan) and Newcastle Breweries. In 1995 it bought Courage from its Australian owners, Foster's. Since the merger that formed Scottish Courage, the group has rationalised by closing its breweries in Nottingham, Halifax and the historic Courage [George's] Brewery in Bristol. The remaining beers were transferred to John Smith's in Tadcaster. It bought the financially stricken Bulmer's Cider group, which included the Beer Seller wholesalers, now part of WaverleyTBS. In 2003, S&N sold the Theakston's Brewery in Yorkshire back to the original family (see Theakston's entry in Independents section) but still brews some of the beers at John Smith's. In February 2004, S&N entered into an arrangement with the Caledonian brewery in Edinburgh that gave S&N a 30% stake in Caledonian and 100% control of the brewery's assets (see Caledonian in the Independents). S&N's sole Scottish cask beer, McEwan's 80/-, is now brewed at Caledonian. S&N also owns a leased pub estate: see Pub Groups.

Berkshire

Berkshire Brewery, Imperial Way, Reading, Berkshire, RG2 0PN
Tel (0118) 922 2988

No cask beer

Federation

Federation Brewery, Lancaster Road, Dunston, Gateshead, Tyne & Wear, NE11 9JR

The former co-operative brewery run by workingmen's clubs. S&N transferred production to Dunston when it closed its Tyneside plant in 2004 and bought Federation. 'Newcastle' Brown Ale is now brewed in Gateshead. No cask beer.

Royal

Royal Brewery, 201 Denmark Road, Manchester, M15 6LD
Tel (0161) 220 4371

Massive brewery in Manchester capable of producing 1.3 million barrels of beer a year. No cask beer.

John Smith'S

John Smith's Brewery, Tadcaster, North Yorkshire, LS24 9SA
Tel (01937) 832091
Fax (01937) 833766
Website: as for S&N above
Tours by arrangement.

The brewery was built in 1879 by a relative of Samuel Smith (qv). John Smith's became part of the Courage group in 1970. Major expansion has taken place since the formation of Scottish Courage, with 11 new fermenting vessels installed. Traditional Yorkshire Square fermenters have been replaced by conical vessels.

John Smith's Bitter (OG 1035.8, ABV 3.8%) ◆
A copper-coloured beer, well-balanced but with no dominating features. It has a short hoppy finish.

Courage Best Bitter (OG 1038.3, ABV 4%) ◆
Pale brown beer with hops throughout and a bitter aftertaste.

Courage Directors Bitter (OG 1045.5, ABV 4.8%) ◆
Fruity, medium-bodied, pale brown beer with hoppy and yeasty notes throughout.

For Theakston's of Masham (qv)

Theakston Best Bitter **(OG 1038, ABV 3.8%)**

S&N also runs the Stag Brewery in Mortlake, London, as a joint venture with Anheuser-Busch (qv).

Brewery organisations

There are three organisations mentioned in the Breweries section to which breweries can belong.

The Independent Family Brewers of Britain (IFBB) represents around 35 regional companies still owned by families. As many regional breweries closed in the 1990s, the IFBB represents the interests of the survivors, staging events such as the annual Cask Beer Week to emphasise the important role played by the independent sector.

The Society of Independent Brewers (SIBA) represents the growing number of small craft or micro brewers: some smaller regionals are also members. SIBA is an effective lobbying organisation and played a leading role in persuading the government to introduce Progressive Beer Duty. It has also campaigned to get large pub companies to take beers from small breweries and has had considerable success with Enterprise Inns, the biggest pubco.

The East Anglian Brewers' Co-operative (EAB) was the brainchild of Brendan Moore at Iceni Brewery. Finding it impossible to get their beers into pub companies and faced by the giant power of Greene King in the region, the co-op makes bulk deliveries to the genuine free trade and also sells beer at farmers' markets and specialist beer shops.

Pub Groups

Pubs groups or 'pubcos' [pub companies] dominate beer retailing in Britain but, with the exception of Wetherspoon, tend not to brand their outlets. If you can break the code of Mitchells & Butlers' various brand names, you may be able to spot one of that group's pubs. The global brewers – with the exception of S&N – have disengaged from running pubs, preferring to sell beer to the pub groups. As a result of the deep discounts demanded by the pubcos, most sell beers mainly from the globals, thus restricting drinkers' choice, and forming a barrier to regional and micro-breweries. The market is dominated by three giant pub companies: Enterprise, which acquired the Unique chain, Mitchells & Butlers (the former Bass managed pubs), and Punch, which merged with Pubmaster and in 2005 bought Avebury Taverns and the Spirit Group, a managed pub estate. This made Punch, with more than 10,000 pubs, the biggest in the country. The national pub groups act like supermarkets: buying heavily-discounted national brands in large volumes and selling them at inflated prices. However, as a result of a Direct Delivery Scheme developed by the Society of Independent Brewers (SIBA), a number of pubcos, including Admiral Taverns, Enterprise, New Century and Punch, now stock beers from micro-breweries in selected outlets. Nevertheless, as this section shows, there is a depressing tendency for many pubcos to take their beers mainly or exclusively from the global brewers, with a devastating impact on drinkers' choice. There are some independent companies that are committed to cask beer: *after a company's name indicates it's an independent pub group that focuses on cask.

Admiral

Admiral Taverns, Penn House, 30 High Street, Rickmansworth, Herts, WD3 1EP
Tel (01923) 726300 Fax (01923) 726301
Email info@admiraltaverns.co.uk
Website www.admiraltaverns.com

Admiral was formed in 2004 and has rapidly become a major player in the pubco market, with 801 pubs, some bought from Enterprise, Punch and Globe. Its main beer suppliers are Carlsberg, Coors, InBev and S&N.

Avebury Taverns.

Bought by Punch (qv) in 2005.

Barracuda

Barracuda Group Ltd, Lunar House, Globe Park, Fieldhouse Lane, Marlow, Bucks, SL7 1LW
Tel (0845) 345 2528 Fax (0845) 345 2527
Email info@barracudagroup.co.uk
Website www.barracudagroup.co.uk

Barracuda was formed in 2000. It runs 181 managed outlets. The main pub brands in Barracuda are the 20-strong Smith & Jones chain,Varsity student bars and 44 Juniper Inns. It takes its main cask beers from Adnams, Coors, Interbrew, Greene King, and S&N.

Barter

Barter Inns, 132 Gypsy Hill, London, SE19 1PW
Tel/fax (020) 8670 7001.
Email barterinns@aol.com

Barter was formed in 1993 and operates in South-east England with 25 managed pubs. It takes beer from InBev and S&N, but its best-selling beer is Fuller's London Pride.

Bold

Bold Pub Company, Unit 13, Bold Business Centre, Sutton, St Helens, Merseyside, WA9 4TX
Tel (01925) 228999 Fax (01925) 295999

Bold was set up in 2003 and operates in the North-west and Wales. It has 30 managed pubs and runs 16 of them as community locals under the Value Inns name. It takes its beers mainly from Coors and Carlsberg.

Botanic Inns

Botanic Inns Ltd, 261-263 Ormeau Road, Belfast, North Ireland, BT7 3GG
Tel (0289) 0509 700

Botanic runs nine bars, two hotels and two off-licences. It takes extremely limited amounts of cask beer from unspecified suppliers.

Brakspear

W H Brakspear & Sons plc, The Bull Courtyard, Bell Street, Henley-on-Thames, Oxon, RG9 2BA.
Tel (01491) 570200 Fax (01491) 570201
E-mail information@brakspear.co.uk
Website www.brakspear.co.uk

Brakspear is the pub company that emerged from the ashes of a much-loved Henley brewery. The directors quit brewing in 2002, selling the prime site in Henley for £10 million to make way for luxury apartments overlooking the Thames. It sold the brands to Refresh UK: see Brakspear in Independent Breweries section. The company runs 102 pubs. The only cask beers sold are the Brakspear brands now brewed at Witney.

Brunning & Price*

Brunning & Price, Yew Tree Farm Buildings, Saighton, Chester, CH3 6EG.
Tel (01244) 333100 Fax (01244) 333110
Website www.brunningandprice.co.uk

Brunning & Price runs 12 managed pubs in the North-west. The company is committed to cask beer; its managers and tenants are free to choose their beers but are encouraged to support independents and micros. Customers may find Hydes, Ossett, Robinsons, Rooster and Phoenix and the company says 'You won't find keg or smoothflow bitters in any of our pubs'. See website for the company's beer page.

Bulldog

Bulldog Pubs Co, 6 Bridge Street, Boston,

Lincolnshire, PE21 8QF
Tel (01205) 355522 Fax (01205) 355534
Email kevin.charity@bpcgroup.co.uk
Website www.bpcgroup.com

Formed in 1996, Bulldog runs 16 pubs in the Midlands and East Anglia.

Burtonwood

Burtonwood plc, Bold Lane, Burtonwood, Warrington, WA5 4PJ
Tel (01925) 225131 Fax (01925) 229033
Email seyles@burtonwood.co.uk
Website www.burtonwood.co.uk

Burtonwood's 480 pubs, the majority of which are traditional tenancies, were sold to Wolverhampton & Dudley Breweries in 2005. The brewery is owned by Thomas Hardy Burtonwood but Burtonwood Bitter is now brewed by W&D. Fewer than half the Burtonwood pubs stock cask beer but the number is expected to increase under the new owner.

Caledonian Heritable

Caledonian Heritable, 4 Hope Street, Edinburgh, EH2 4DB.
Tel (0131) 220 5511 Fax (0131) 225 6546
Email ga@caleyheritable.co.uk
Website www.caley-heritable.co.uk

A group with 292 pubs, all in Scotland. Beers come mainly from S&N, but the best-selling ale is Caledonian Deuchars IPA.

Camelot

Camelot Inns & Taverns, 22 Bancroft, Hitchin, Hertfordshire, SG5 1JS
Tel (01462) 455188 Fax (01462) 455099
Email mikek@camelotinns.fsnet.co.uk

Formed in 1993, Camelot runs 12 managed pubs in Hertfordshire and North-east London.

Capital*

Capital Pub Co, 1 Relton Mews, London SW7 1ET
Tel (020) 7589 4888 Fax (020) 77581 9854
Email enquiries@capitalpubcompany.com
Website www.capitalpubcompany.com

Formed in 2000 by veteran pub owner David Bruce of Firkin brew-pub fame, Capital runs 26 managed pubs in London. In 2005 it bought 10 pubs from Spirit just before the group was sold to Punch. The company is funded through the Enterprise Investment programme, which allows small investors to back companies. Most of the pubs in the estate, which includes the famous Anglesea Arms in SW7, serve cask beer from independent brewers.

Cascade

Cascade Public House Management, 5 Merlin Way, Bowerhill, Melksham, Wiltshire, SN12 6TJ
Tel (01225) 704734) Fax (01255) 790770
Email cascade@blueyonder.co.uk

Formed in 1993, it runs 14 managed pubs in South-west England.

Catmere

Catmere Group, Bridge House, Station Road, Scunthorpe, Lincolnshire, DN15 6PY
Tel (01724) 861703 Fax (01724) 861708

Catmere owns 10 pubs in Leicestershire and Lincolnshire. Five serve cask beer from both national and regional brewers.

CCT Group

CCT Group/Jack Beard, 76 Mitcham Road, Tooting, London, SW17 9NG.
Tel (020) 8767 8967 Fax (020) 8767 3675
Email admin@jackbeards.co.uk

A South-east based company with 40 managed pubs operating under the Jack Beards name. Beer is supplied by S&N and Greene King.

Celtic Inns

Bought by Wolverhampton & Dudley Breweries (qv) in March 2006.

Chapman

Chapman Group, Syon House, High Street, Angmering, West Sussex, BN16 4AG.
Tel (01903) 856744 Fax (01903) 856816)
Email vicki@thechapmansgroup.co.uk
Website www.thechapmansgroup.co.uk

Formed in 1978, Chapman runs 44 pubs in southern England and Gloucestershire. Its main beer supplies come from S&N but it also sells cask beers from Harvey's of Lewes.

Churchill

Churchill Taverns Group, Avon House, Tithe Barn Road, Wellingborough, Northamptonshire, NN8 1DH
Tel (01933) 222110 Fax (01933) 277006
Email frwpjm@churchilltaverns.freeserve.co.uk

Formed in 1997, Churchill runs 17 managed pubs in Northamptonshire.

CI Hospitality

CI Hospitality, 19 Royal Square, St Helier, Jersey, JE2 4WA
Tel (01534) 764000 Fax (01534) 618282
Website www.indulgence.co.uk

CI Hospitality is the trading name of Citann, part of CI Traders, which bought the Ann Street Brewery in 2002, now known as Jersey Brewery (qv). The group runs 81 pubs in the Channel Islands, which sell beer from its own brewery and Coors.

Clark

Clark Pub Co, 6a Western Corner, Edinburgh, EH12 5PY
Tel (0131) 466 7190 Fax (0131) 466 7074
Email info@clarkpubco.co.uk
Website www.clarkpubs.com

Formed in 1997, Clark runs four pubs in Scotland. It sold eight outlets to London & Edinburgh in 2003.

Conquest Inns

14 Theobald Steet, Borehamwood, Hertfordshire, WD6 4SE

A company owned by CI Traders (qv) with 66 pubs in London, the South-east and East Anglia, it was bought by Punch for £261 million.

County Estate

County Estate Management, 79 New Cavendish Street, London W1G 6XB
Tel (020) 7436 2080 Fax (020) 7436 1040
Email mail@countyestate.co.uk
Website www.countyestate.co.uk

County Estate runs 640 pubs nationwide. It works hand-in-glove with Pubfolio (qv) on pub acquisitions. It takes beers from Carlsberg, Coors, InBev, S&N and W&D, and has its own supply company. Many houses serve cask beer.

Daisychain

Daisychain Inns, Chesterton Way, Eastwood Trading Estate, Rotherham, South Yorkshire, S65 1ST
Tel (01709) 820073 Fax (01709) 820112

Daisychain operates 90 pubs across the Midlands, north of England, Wales and Scotland and also acts as a holding company for other pub operators. It takes beers from Coors, InBev and S&N.

JT Davies

JT Davies & Sons Ltd, 7 Aberdeen Road, Croydon, Surrey, CR0 1EQ
Tel (020) 8681 3222 Fax (020) 8760 0390
Email postbox@jtdavies.co.uk
Website www.jtdavies.co.uk

Wine merchants now controlling 46 tenancies and leased houses in the South-east. Its main suppliers are InBev and S&N, with some beers from Fuller's and Harveys. In June 2002, the company bought a 28% share in Henley pub company W H Brakspear.

Davy's Wine Bars

Davy & Co, 59-63 Bermondsey Street, London, SE1 3XF
Tel (020) 7407 9670 Fax (020) 7407 5844
Email info@davy.co.uk
Website www.davy.co.uk

Wine merchants and shippers since 1870, Davy has been opening wine bars and restaurants in the London area since 1965, taking previously unlicensed properties and creating a Dickensian, sawdust, nooks-and-crannies type of establishment. Its Davy's Old Wallop (ABV 4.8%) is a re-badged brew of undeclared origin (though Courage Directors fits the bill). This is usually served in pewter tankards or copper jugs. The company currently runs around 45 outlets, including a few pubs.

Dorbiere

Dorbiere Public Houses, Green Lane, Patricroft, Eccles, Manchester, M30 0RJ
Tel (0161) 707 7787 Fax (0161) 789 6713
Email robin.gray@LWC-drinks.co.uk

Dorbiere is part of LWC – Licensed Wholesale Company – a major drinks wholesaling group. It runs 40 managed pubs in the North of England. It takes beers form InBev and S&N and has only a marginal interest in cask beer.

Dukedom

Dukedom Leisure, Blenheim House, Falcon Court, Preston Farm Industrial Estate, Stockton-on-Tees, TS18 3TD.
Tel (01642) 704930
Email enquiries@dukedom.co.uk

Dukedom runs 32 managed pubs and nightclubs in North-east England.

Eldridge Pope

Eldridge Pope & Co plc, Weymouth Avenue, Dorchester, ST1 1QT
Tel (01305) 251251 Fax (01305) 258300
Email enquiries@eldridge-pope.co.uk
Website www.eldridge-pope.co.uk

Founded as the Green Dragon Brewery in 1837, Eldridge Pope divorced itself from brewing in 1996 when it split into two wings, the brewing side becoming known as Thomas Hardy Burtonwood, with breweries in Burtonwood and Dorchester; Dorchester closed in 2003. The pub company, with 158 outlets, was bought in 2004 by Michael Cannon, who valued the business at £42.3 million. Cannon has a long track record in the industry of buying groups of pubs and eventually selling them on. EP has supply agreements with Coors, Interbrew and S&N.

Elizabeth Inns

Elizabeth Inns, Merchant House, 33 Fore Street, Ipswich, Suffolk, IP4 1JL
Tel (01473) 217458 Fax (01473) 258237
Email info@elizabethholdings.co.uk
Website www.elizabethhotels.co.uk

Formerly Ryan Elizabeth Holdings, the company runs 45 pubs in East Anglia, many bought from national brewers. Some pubs are tied to InBev. Other suppliers are Adnams, Greene King and Nethergate.

English Inns*

English Inns, 5 Mill Meadow, Langford, Bedfordshire, SG18 9UR
Tel (01462) 701750
Email burlisoninns@aol.com

Formely Burlison Inns, English owns seven pubs in Bedfordshire, Cambridgeshire, Hertfordshire and Warwickshire. Its main cask beer supplier is Everards and it also takes beers from B&T, City of Cambridge, Nethergate, and Tring.

Enterprise Inns

Enterprise Inns plc, 3 Monkspath Hall Road, Solihull, West Midlands, B90 4SJ
Tel (0121) 733 7700 Fax (0121) 733 6447
Email enquiries@enterpriseinns.plc.uk
Website www.enterpriseinns.com

Formed in 1991 with an initial acquisition of 372 pubs from Bass, the company has grown rapidly and is now Britain's second biggest pub group. In 2002 it bought the former Whitbread tenanted pub estate known as Laurel Inns, and it has consolidated its position by adding the Unique pub estate from Nomura. Enterprise previously purchased pubs from John Labatt Retail, Discovery Inns, Gibbs Mew, Mayfair Taverns, Century Inns (Tap & Spile), and Swallow Inns.

Enterprise added to this number by buying 439 former Whitbread pubs, and then in 2001 bought 432 managed houses from Scottish & Newcastle. Its current estate numbers 8,637 and it has a war chest of £100 million for further acquisitions. A range of cask beers from all the major brewers, as well as many of the regionals and some micros through the SIBA Direct Delivery Scheme, is available.

Festival Inns

Festival Inns, PO Box 12288, Loanhead, Midlothian, EH20 9YF
Tel (0131) 440 3290 Fax (0131) 440 3231
Email headoffice@festival-inns.co.uk
Website: www.festival-inns.co.uk

Festival Inns was founded in 1997 and now has 26 pubs in Scotland, with plans to buy three more in Edinburgh during 2006. The main beer suppliers are Carlsberg, InBev and Greene King.

Fitzgerald*

Sir John Fitzgerald Ltd, Cafe Royal Buildings, 8 Nelson Street, Newcastle upon Tyne, NE1 5AW
Tel (0191) 232 0664 Fax (0194) 261 4509
Website www.sjf.co.uk

Long-established, family-owned property and pubs company. Its pubs convey a free house image, most offering a good choice of cask beers, including guest ales from smaller craft breweries. The 28 pubs are mainly in the North-east but there are also outlets in Edinburgh, Harrogate and London.

G1

G1 Group, 62 Virginia Street, Glasgow, G1 1DA.
Tel (0141) 552 4494. Fax (0141) 552 3730.
Email info@1group.co.uk
Website www.g1group.co.uk

G1 owns 37 managed pubs in Scotland in Aberdeen, Dundee, Edinburgh, Glasgow and Perth. The main beer supplier is S&N.

Globe

Globe Pub Company, c/o Scottish & Newcastle Pub Enterprises, 2-4 Broadway Park, South Gyle Broadway, Edinburgh, EH12 9JZ.
Tel (0131) 528 2700 Fax (0131) 528 2890
Website www.pub-enterprises.co.uk

Globe owns leasehold pubs bought by Robert Tchenguiz, owner of Laurel (qv), through his R20 investment company. Ten pubs are leased through S&N Pub Enterprises (qv). Not surprisingly the beer is supplied by S&N.

Gray*

Gray & Sons (Chelmsford) Ltd, Rignals Lane, Galleywood, Chelmsford, Essex, CM2 8RE
Tel (01245) 475181 Fax (01245) 475182
Email enquiries@grayandsons.co.uk
Website www.grayandsons.co.uk

Former Chelmsford brewery that ceased production in 1974 and which now supplies its 49 tied and tenanted houses in Essex with a choice of cask beers from Adnams, Greene King and Mighty Oak. The tenants are also free to choose from a monthly guest list that features at least 10 different ales.

Great British Pub Co

Great British Pub Company, Redhill House, Hope Street, Salthey, Cheshire, CH4 8BU
Tel (01244) 678780 Fax (01244) 682667
Email info@gbpubco.co.uk

Formed in 1998, the company runs an estate of 35 managed pubs in Yorkshire. It sold 25 pubs in 2003.

Head of Steam*

Head of Steam Ltd, Manesty, Leazes Lane, Hexham, Northumberland, NE46 3AE.
Tel/Fax (01434) 607393
Email tony@theheadofsteam.co.uk
Website www.theheadofsteam.com

Founded by CAMRA activist Tony Brookes, Head of Steam has pubs based on railway station concourses at Huddersfield, Newcastle-on-Tyne and Liverpool. All the outlets serve a wide range of cask beers and they stage regular beer festivals. The Euston Head of Steam has been sold to Fuller's but serves beers from other breweries as well.

Heavitree

Heavitree Brewing, Trood Lane, Matford, Exeter, EX2 8YP
Tel (01392) 217733 Fax (01392) 229939

A West Country brewery, established in 1790, which gave up production in 1970 to concentrate on running pubs. The current estate, which is mainly confined to Devon, stands at 102. The pubs are tied to beers from Coors and InBev.

Herald Inns

Herald Inns and Bars, Sagar House, Eccleston, Chorley, Lancashire, PR7 5SH
Tel (01257) 452452 Fax (01257) 454274
Website www.brannigansbars.com

Herald runs 41 managed pubs and bars nationwide, including the Brannigans bar chain. The group is owned by leisure tycoon Trevor Hemmings, whose interests include Blackpool Tower and Pleasure Beach. The range of suppliers is wide and includes Arkells and Charles Wells as well as Anheuser-Busch, InBev and S&N.

Heritage

Heritage Pub Co, Donnington House, Riverside Road, Pride Park, Derby, DE24 8HY
Tel (01332) 384808 Fax (01332) 384818
Email firstname@heritagepubs.com

Heritage runs 65 tenanted pubs in the East Midlands. Its main suppliers are Hardys & Hansons and InBev. Its best-selling cask beer is Marston's Pedigree.

Honeycombe*

Honeycombe Leisure, Marian House, Beech Grove, Preston, Lancashire, PR2 1DU
Tel (01772) 723764 Fax (01772) 722470
Email firstname.surname@honeycombe.co.uk
Website www.honeycombe.co.uk

Formed in 1976, Honeycombe bought the Devonshire Pub Co in 2000 and now has

95 houses. Beers are supplied by the nationals plus Burton Bridge, Eccleshall, Moorhouses, Phoenix and Timothy Taylor, and most micro-brewers in the North-west. It is one of the biggest sellers of Black Sheep.

Inns & Leisure

Inns & Leisure, 20-24 Leicester Road, Preston, Lancashire, PR1 1PP.
Tel (01772) 252917 Fax (01772) 204543
Email innsleisure@btconnect.com
Website www.innsandleisure.co.uk

Inns & Leisure, formed in 1970, runs 28 pubs in Cumbria, Lancashire and Yorkshire. Beer is supplied by S&N.

InnSpired

See Pubfolio

Interpub

Interpub, c/o the Stag, Hawthorn Lane, Burnham Beeches, Buckinghamshire, SL2 3TA.
Tel (01753) 647603 Fax (01753) 647604
Email office@interpub.co.uk
Website www.interpub.co.uk

Formed in 1996, Interpub runs 14 pubs in London, Cornwall and Scotland.

Inventive

Inventive Leisure, 21 Old Street, Ashton-under-Lyne, Tameside, Lancashire, OL6 6LA
Tel (1061) 330 3876
Email enquiries@revolution-bars.co.uk
Website www.revolution-bars.co.uk

Runs 'vodka bars' aimed at young people.

Kingdom

Kingdom Taverns, Dean House, 191 Nicol Street, Kirkcaldy, Fife, KY1 1PF
Tel (01592) 200033 Fax (01592) 200044

Formed in 1972, Kingdom has a pub estate of 38 in Scotland. Major beer suppliers are InBev and S&N.

Laurel

Laurel Pub Co, Porter Tun House, 500 Capability Green, Luton, Bedfordshire, LU1 3LS
Tel 07002 528735 Fax (01582) 540698
Website www.laurelpubco.com

Laurel was created in 2001 by Morgan Grenfell/Deutsche Bank, who bought the Whitbread pub estate. Laurel sold the tenanted pubs to Enterprise Inns (qv) a year later, but kept the managed houses, including the Hogshead chain. They have been re-branded as Hogs Head and no longer specialise in cask beer. Other brand names include Litten Tree and Slug & Lettuce. The company was bought in 2005 by Robert Tchenguiz who then added the Yates's estate of 149 pubs for £202 million. See also Globe. Main suppliers are Coors, Diageo, InBev and S&N. Mr Tchenguiz is not cask beer-friendly; fortunately his bid for Mitchells & Butlers in spring 2006 failed.

Lionheart

Lionheart Inns, Porter Black Holdings, 7 Market Street, Newton Abbot, Devon, TQ12 2RJ
Tel (01626) 882000 Fax (01626) 882001
Email admin@lionheartinns.co.uk
Website www.lionheartinns.co.uk

Lionheart runs 33 managed pubs throughout the country.

London & Edinburgh

London & Edinburgh Swallow Group, 5th Floor, Meadow House, Medway Street, Maidstone, Kent, ME14 1HL
Tel 0870 770 0777 Fax 0870 950 1716
Website www.londonandedinburghinns.com

Formed in 1996, London & Edinburgh has an estate of 890 pubs nationwide. It bought Swallow Hotels from Whitbread in 2003 and plans to expand its estate. Some of the smaller Swallow Hotels trade as Swallow Inns. Its main beer supplier is S&N but some outlets sell Greene King IPA in cask form.

Luminar

Luminar, Luminar House, Deltic Avenue, Rooksley, Milton Keynes, Bucks, MK13 8LL
Tel (01908) 544 100 Fax (01908) 394 721
Email mailbox@luminar.co.u
Website www.luminar.co.uk

Formed in 1987, Luminar runs 245 bars and nightclubs and has no interest in cask beer.

Maclay*

Maclay Group plc, The e-Centre, Cooperage Way Business Village, Alloa, FK10 3LP
Tel (01259) 272 087 Fax (01259) 272 088
Website www.maclay.com

Maclay, founded in 1830, stopped brewing in 1999. It owns 23 managed pubs and supplies them with cask ales under the Maclay name brewed by Belhaven (qv).
It also serves Caledonian Deuchars IPA.

McManus

McManus Taverns, Kingsthorpe Road, Northampton, NN2 6HT
Tel (01604) 713601 Fax (01604) 7902209
Email enquiry@mcmanuspub.co.uk
Website www.mcmanuspub.co.uk

Company formed in 1970 with 22 pubs in the East Midlands. Half serve cask beer mainly from S&N and Wadworth.

Market Town Taverns*

Market Town Taverns, 6 Green Dragon Yard, Knaresborough, North Yorkshire, HG5 8AU.
Tel (01423) 866100
Email office@markettaverns.co.uk
Website www.markettowntaverns.co.uk

Run by CAMRA member Ian Fozard, the group owns eight pubs in North and West Yorkshire. It concentrates on beers from independent and micro-breweries, including Black Sheep and Timothy Taylor.

Massive

Massive Pub Co, Central House, 124 High Street, Hampton Hill, Middlesex, TW12 1NS
Tel (020) 8977 0633 Fax (020) 8288 1502
Website www.massivepub.com

Formed in 1993, Massive owns 68 bars in London, Surrey and Hampshire.

Mercury

Mercury Management (UK) Ltd, Mercury House, 19-20 Amber Business Village, Amington, Tamworth, Staffordshire, B77 4RP
Tel (01827) 62345 Fax (01827) 64166
E-mail headoffice@mercurymanagement.co.uk
Website www.mercurymanagement.co.uk

Mercury Management is the result of a 1999 buy-out of Mercury Taverns. It has slimmed down its estate from 45 pubs to 16.

Mill House

Mill House Inns, Berkeley House, Falcon Close, Quedgeley, Gloucestershire, GL2 4LY
Tel (01452) 887200 Fax (01452) 887333
Website www.millhouseinns.co.uk

Mill House has 84 managed pubs nationwide, ranging from town bars to country pubs and family pub-diners. It bought 50 Pioneer pubs in 2005. Its main suppliers are Coors, InBev and S&N.

Mitchells & Butlers

Mitchells & Butlers plc, 27 Fleet Street, Birmingham, B3 1JP
Tel 0870 609 3000 fax (0121) 233 2246
Email communications@mbplc.com
Website www.mbplc.com

When the Bass brewing and pub empire was sold off in 2000, Coors closed the giant M&B Brewery in Birmingham but a year later the name resurfaced as a pub company. M&B owns some 1,800 pubs, bars and restaurants. Its brands include Ember Inns, Goose, Harvester, Nicholson's, O'Neill's, Toby Carvery and Vintage Inns. Some of the pubs serve cask beer and Ember also holds mini-beer festivals. Most pubs stock Draught Bass and also offer a choice of cask beers from Coors and some regional breweries. Ember specialises in regional brewers' beers.

Mitchells*

Mitchells of Lancaster, 11 Moor Lane, Lancaster, LA2 6AZ
Tel (01524) 596000 Fax (01524) 596036
Email sales@mitchellspubs.co.uk
Website www.mitchellsoflancaster.co.uk

Mitchells stopped brewing in 1999 and now runs 60 pubs in North-west England. Its leading cask beer brand, Lancaster Bomber, is leased to Thwaites of Blackburn (qv). The pubs take cask beers from Everards, Moorhouses and Thwaites.

Morrells

Morrells of Oxford Ltd, Ferry Hinskey Road, Osney Mead Industrial Estate, Oxford, OX2 0ES
Tel (01865) 263000 Fax (01865) 791868

Morrells of Oxford was bought by Greene King in June 2002 for £60 million. The 132 pubs are all that remain of the once much-loved Oxford brewery that closed in 1998 following a boardroom split and the eviction of two members of the Morrell family.

New Century

New Century Inns, Belasis Business Centre, Coxwold Way, Billingham, TS23 4EA
Tel (01642) 343415 Fax (01642) 345729
Email NCI@newcenturyinns.co.uk
Website www.newcentury inns.co.uk

Formed in 1999, New Century owns 48 pubs in Yorkshire and the North-east. Its main beer suppliers are Coors, InBev and S&N.

Noble House

Noble House, 580 Ipswich Road, Slough, Berks, SL1 4EQ.
Tel (01753) 515250 Fax (01753) 537225
Email mail@noblehouseleisure.com
Website www.noblehouseonline.net

Noble House has retreated from owning pubs to concentrate on oriental-style bars and restaurants plus the Arbuckles American diner chain.

Old English

Old English Inns was bought by Greene King in 2001.

Passionate

Passionate Pub Company, Belasis Business Centre, Billingham, Stockton-on-Tees, TS23 4EA
Tel (01642) 345639 Fax (01642) 345659
Email postmaster@passionatepub.co.uk
Website www.passionatepub.co.uk

In spite of sharing the same address, Passionate and New Century (qv) are separate companies that 'work alongside' one another. Passionate was founded in 1999 and runs 30 pubs in the North-west, East Midlands and East Anglia. Beers are sourced via Enterprise Inns and include Caledonian Deuchars IPA.

Pathfinder

Pathfinder Pubs is the managed pubs division of Wolverhampton & Dudley Breweries (qv in New Nationals section). See also Union.

Peninsula

Peninsula Inns, Peninsula House, Castle Circus, Torquay, Devon, TQ2 5QQ
Tel (01803) 200960 Fax (01803) 200990
Email office@peninsula.co.uk
Website www.peninsulainns.co.uk

Peninsula has 28 managed pubs in the South-west. It takes its beer supplies from Coors and S&N but some pubs offer Sharp's Doom Bar.

Pub Estate

Pub Estate Co Ltd, Blenheim House, Foxhole Road, Ackhurst Park, Chorley, Lancashire, PR7 1NY
Tel (01257) 238800 Fax (01257) 238801
Email info@pub-estate.co.uk
Website www.pub-estate.co.uk

A company established with the purchase of 230 pubs from Scottish & Newcastle, it currently has 510 pubs nationwide. The pubs offer beers from Carlsberg, Coors, InBev, Carlsberg and S&N.

Pubs 'n'Bars

Pubs 'n' Bars, Sandwood House, 10-12 Weir Road, London, SW12 0NA
Tel (020) 8228 4800 Fax (020) 8675 1950

Formed in 1990, the group owns 66 pubs within the M25, Wales and the West Country.

Pub People*

Pub People Company, Morewood House, Broadmeadows Business Park, South Normanton, Alfreton, Derbyshire, DE55 3NA
Tel (01773) 510863 Fax (01773) 819299
Website www.pubpeople.com

The company has 72 managed pubs based in the Midlands and the North-east. Its main suppliers are Carlsberg, Coors, InBev and S&N but some pubs offer ales from Castle Rock, Greene King and Hardys & Hansons with regular micro-brewed beers from the likes of Acorn and Milestone.

Pub Support

Pub Support Company, Unit 13, Bold Business Centre, Sutton, St Helens, Merseyside, WA9 4TX
Tel (01925) 228999 Fax (01925) 295999

Pub Support has the same management as Bold (qv) but operates its own outlets. It has 40 managed pubs and they are supplied by S&N.

Pubfolio

Pubfolio, Wiltshire Drive, Trowbridge, Wilts, BN4 0TT
Tel (01225) 763171
Website www.pubfolio.co.uk

Pubfolio grew out of the Innspired pub company, the former tied estate of Ushers of Trowbridge. The pubs were taken over by Punch and then sold to Pubfolio, which works closely with County Estate (qv) on tenant recruitment. Pubfolio has 540 tenanted pubs and takes its supplies from Carlsberg, Coors, InBev and Wolverhampton & Dudley.

Punch Group

Punch Taverns, Jubilee House, Second Avenue, Burton upon Trent, Staffordshire, DE14 2WF
Tel (01283) 501600 Fax (01283) 501601
Email firstname.lastname@punchpubs.co.uk
Website www.punchtaverns.com

Punch was formed in 1998 by a team led by Hugh Osmond, founder of Pizza Express, with the purchase of the Bass leased pub estate. In 1999, Punch, with the backing of Bass, bought Allied Domecq's pub estate. It sold 550 former managed houses to Bass, now Mitchells & Butlers (qv). In 2004, Punch merged with Pubmaster, creating an estate of more than 8,000 pubs. In December it leapfrogged Enterprise (qv) and became Britain's biggest pubco when it bought the Spirit Group of managed outlets for £2.7 billion. It also acquired Avebury Taverns. The group now owns around 10,000 pubs though some of the recent acquisitions that are not suitable for conversion to tenancy or lease will be disposed of. It trades under such brand names as Chef & Brewer, John Barras and Qs. Punch claims its lessees are free to take guest beers, but brewers who supply the group are closely monitored and have to offer substantial discounts to be accepted. The main suppliers of beer are Carlsberg, Coors, Greene King, InBev and S&N with guest ales from a number of regionals, including Adnams. It takes some micro-brewed beers via the SIBA Direct Delivery Scheme.

Pyramid

Pyramid Pub Co Ltd, Suite H3, Steam Mill Business Centre, Steam Mill Street, Chester, CH3 5AN
Tel (01244) 321171 Fax (01244) 317665
Email admin@pyramidpub.co.uk
Website www.pyramidpub.co.uk

Pyramid manages 410 tenanted pubs. It was formerly known as Paramount and bought its estate from Royal Bank of Scotland. The pub estate is widely spread, mainly in towns and cities in the North-west, North-east, Midlands and Wales. Beers are supplied by InBev, S&N and Wolverhampton & Dudley. Banks's is the leading cask ale.

Randalls Vautier

Randalls Vautier Ltd, PO Box 43, Clare Street, St Helier, Jersey, JE4 8NZ
Tel (01534) 836700 Fax (01534) 836703
Email lequesne@randalls.je
Website www.randallsjersey.com

A brewery that ceased production in 1992. It now runs 58 pubs on Jersey selling beers from InBev and S&N as well as the Jersey Brewery. Not to be confused with Randalls of Guernsey (see Independents).

Regent Inns

Regent Inns plc, 77 Muswell Hill, London, N10 3PJ
Tel (020) 8375 3000 Fax (020) 8375 3001
Email info@regent-inns.plc.uk
Website www.regentinns.co.uk

Founded in 1980, Regent owns 71 managed bars in London and the Home Counties under such names as Bar Risa, Jongleurs and Walkabout. The company has contracts with Coors, InBev and S&N.

S&N Pub Enterprises

Scottish & Newcastle Pub Enterprises, 2-4 Broadway Park, South Gyle Broadway, Edinburgh, EH12 9JZ
Tel (0131) 528 2700 Fax (0131) 528 2890
Website www.pub-enterprises.co.uk

The pub-owning arm of global brewer S&N, it has 1,170 leased pubs throughout Britain and also operates a further 470 pubs on behalf of Globe (qv). It is developing river and canalside pubs through the Waterside Pub Company, a joint venture with British Waterways. Unsurprisingly, S&NPE takes its beer supplies from the parent company and its other subsidiary, WaverleyTBS. A regular cask beer is Theakston Best Bitter.

SFI

Now part of Laurel (qv).

Spirit

See Punch.

Tadcaster Pub Company

Tadcaster Pub Co, Commer Group Ltd, Commer House, Station Road, Tadcaster, North Yorkshire, LS24 9JF
Tel (01937) 835020 Fax (01937) 834236
E-mail info@tadpubco.uk
Website www.tadpubco.co.uk

The company has 57 pubs in the North-east. Beers are supplied by Carlsberg, Coors, InBev and S&N.

Tattershall

Tattershall Castle Group, Regus House, Windmill Hill Business Park, Whitehill Way, Swindon, Wilts, SN5 6QR
Tel (01793) 441429
Website www.tattershallcastlegroup.com

Tattershall was created when the Spirit Group, now part of Punch (qv), sold 178 managed city-centre pubs for £177 million in 2005. Tattershall is backed by the private equity group Alchemy Partners, headed by the former boss of Innspired, Peter Brook. It plans to spend £40 million on the estate and has such powerful brands as Rat & Parrot, Bar 38 and Henry's in the group. Pubs and bars are owned throughout Britain but the main concentration is in London and the South-east. The main beer supplier is S&N.

Taverna Inns

Taverna Inns, Marquis of Granby, Main Street, Hoveringham, Nottinghamshire, NG14 7JR
Tel (0115) 966 5566
Email tavernainns@freuk.com

Formed in 1990, Taverna owns 30 pubs in the Midlands, Lincolnshire and NE England.

Thorley Taverns

Thorley Taverns, The Old Police Station, 60 Gladstone Road, Broadstairs, Kent, CT10 2HZ
Tel (01843) 602010 Fax (01843) 866333
Email ho@thorleytaverns.com
Website www.thorleytaverns.com

Founded in 1971, Thorley operates 36 managed pubs in Kent and London. Beers are supplied by S&N.

Trust Inns

Trust Inns, Blenheim House, Ackhurst Park, Foxhole Road, Chorley, Lancs, PR7 1NY
Tel (01257) 238800 Fax (01257) 238801
Email info@trustinns.co.uk
Website www.trustinns.co.uk

Trust Inns runs 510 pubs throughout Britain and has a war chest of £5 million to improve the estate. The main beer suppliers are Carlsberg and S&N.

Tynemill*

Tynemill Ltd, 2nd Floor, Victoria Hotel, Dovecote Lane, Beeston, Nottingham, NG9 1JG
Tel (0115) 925 3333 Fax (0115) 922 6741

Founded by former CAMRA chairman Chris Holmes, Tynemill has been established in the East Midlands for more than 20 years, and now owns 17 pubs. It has a 'pubs for everyone' philosophy, avoiding trends and gimmicks, and concentrating on quality cask ales and food in good surroundings, including public bars where space permits. It sold more than 1,500 different cask ales during 2000, thought to be more than anyone else in the industry. Managers have complete autonomy on guest beers they sell. Tynemill is now the sole owner of the Castle Rock Brewery in Nottingham (qv). Regional and micro-brewers make up the bulk of Tynemill's products.

Ultimate Leisure

Ultimate Leisure, 26 Mosley Street, Newcastle upon Tyne, NE1 1DF
Tel (0191) 261 8800 Fax (0191) 221 2282
Email enquiries@ultimateleisure
Website www.ultimateleisure.com

Ultimate, a North-east based bar operator, expanded into Northern England and Northern Ireland in 2005. Its venues are branded Coyote Wild, Blue Bambu and Chase and, not surprisingly, have little or no interest in cask.

Union

Union Pub Company, The Brewery, Shobnall Road, Burton upon Trent, Staffs, DE14 2BW
Tel (01902) 711811 Fax (01283) 507857
Email info@theunionpubcompany.co.uk
Website www.tupuc.co.uk

Union is the tenanted and leased division of Wolverhampton & Dudley Breweries (qv). It operates 1,750 nationwide and added to its number with the acquisition of the pub estates of Burtonwood and Jennings. Cask beers come from the W&D portfolio, with lagers from Carlsberg, InBev and S&N.

Wellington

Wellington Pub Co, c/o Criterion Asset Management Ltd, Beechwood Place, Thames Business Park, Wenman Road, Thame, Oxfordshire, OX9 3XA
Tel (01844) 262200 Fax (01844) 262237
Website www.criterionasset.co.uk

A private company running 840 leased pubs nationwide. It is chaired by Hugh Osmond, founder of Pizza Express, who also formed the Punch Group.

Wetherspoon*

JD Wetherspoon plc, Wetherspoon House, Reeds Crescent, Central Park, Watford, Hertfordshire, WD11 1QH
Tel (01923) 477777 Fax (01923) 219810
Email customersservices@jdwetherspoon.co.uk
Website www.jdwetherspoon.co.uk

Wetherspoon is a vigorous and independent pub retailer that currently owns 670 managed pubs. No music is played in any of the pubs, all offer no-smoking areas – some are completely non-smoking – and food is served all day. Each pub stocks regional ales from the likes of Cains, Fuller's, Greene King and Wolverhampton & Dudley, plus at least two guest beers. There are usually two beer festivals a year, one in the spring, the other in the autumn, at which up to 30 micro-brewery beers are stocked over a four-day period. Wetherspoon joined the Cask Marque scheme in 2000 and now enjoys CM accreditation in more than 435 pubs. The group also owns the Lloyds No 1 chain.

Wharfedale

Wharfedale Taverns Ltd, Highcliffe Court, Greenfold Lane, Wetherby, West Yorkshire, LS22 6RG
Tel (01937) 580805 Fax (01937) 580806
E-mail post@wharfedaletaverns.co.uk
Website www.wharfdaletaverns.co.uk

A company set up in 1993 by former Tetley employees to lease 90 pubs from that company, it currently owns 30 pubs, mainly in the north. The main beers come from Carlsberg; guest beers are from the Tapster's Choice range.

Whitbread

Whitbread Court, PO Box 77, Dunstable, Bedforshire, LU5 5XG
Tel (01582) 424200
Website www.whitbread.com

Once a mighty power in the world of brewing and pub retailing, 670 managed pubs are all that are left of the empire. They operate under such banners as Beefeater, Brewers Fayre, Out & Out and TGI Friday's. There was repeated speculation in 2006 that the estate might be sold, with Greene King and Mitchells & Butlers thought to be interested. Beers are supplied by InBev.

Yesteryear

Yesteryear Pub Company, Grimes Arcade, 22-24 King Street, Wigan, WN1 1BS
Tel (01942) 823980
Email enquiries@yesteryearpubco.co.uk
Website www.yesterydearpubco.co.uk

Yesteryear operates 31 managed pubs in North-west England and is busily expanding its estate. The main beer supplier is S&N.

Zelgrain

Zelgrain, PO Box 85, Brighton, East Sussex, BN1 6YT
Tel (01273) 550000 Fax (01273) 550123
Email info@zelnet.com
Website www.zelnet.com

Zelgrain was formed in 1995 and operates 31 managed pubs in South-east England. Beers are supplied by S&N and WaverleyTBS.

*This list does not include regional brewers with tied estates. See the Independents section.

Watch out, there are pub vandals about

The manner in which Britain's pub heritage is under attack can be seen in St Albans in Hertfordshire, where CAMRA's head office is based. St Albans has both Roman remains – Verulamium – as well as the great Abbey Cathedral around which many pubs are sited as they were originally built to provide food, drink and accommodation for workers constructing the church.

In recent years, St Albans has lost the Mile House on London Road and the Ancient Briton on the Harpenden Road. The Mile House stood on the site of an ale house where pilgrims paused for refreshment before walking the last mile to the abbey. The modern Mile House, sold by Whitbread to developers, served a large housing community that no longer has a pub in the vicinity. The Ancient Briton stood opposite Beech Bottom Dyke, a pre-Roman settlement of enormous historic importance: when Verulamium was built, Boudicca's Iceni joined the Celtic tribe based at the dyke to sack the Roman city. The Ancient Briton has been turned by Mitchells & Butlers into a Harvester eaterie: all that remains of the pub is a polystyrene 'stone' announcing the Ancient Briton road junction.

In the summer of 2006, the owners of the Fleur-de-Lys in French Row, within the shadow of the abbey and the medieval Clock Tower, announced they planned to rename the 15th-century tavern the Snug Bar. As a result of local protests, the plan has been dropped and, as the guide went to press, an apologetic sign in the pub window says, 'We have no plans to change the name of the pub'. The 19th-century Harrow in Verulam Road has not been so lucky. It is now a bar called Mokoko, which is believed to be Japanese for 'vandal'.

The beers index

More than 2,800 beers are listed in this index. They refer to the beers in bold type in The Breweries section (beers in regular production) and so therefore do not include seasonal, special or occasional beers that may be mentioned in the text. Also omitted are beers that are easy to identify, because they share the same name as the brewery (e.g. Humpty Dumpty), or because they are just simply named after beer styles (e.g. Bitter, Stout, Wheat Beer, etc.).

D

E

F

H

N

O

P

Q

R

T

X

Y

Z

Global brewers' beer dumping hits pubs

The activities of the global brewers in the supermarket trade is hitting pubs hard. Consider the following offers from Budgens in the summer of 2006: 10 x 250ml bottles of Stella Artois for £5.99; 20 x 300ml bottles of Kronenbourg for £10.99; and 12 x 440ml cans of Foster's for £7.49. The supermarket helpfully explains that these prices are the equivalent of £2.40 a litre for Stella, £1.83 a litre for Kronenbourg and £1.42 a litre for Foster's. A litre is the equivalent of 1¾ pints. There isn't a pub in the land where you could buy almost two pints of premium lager for £1.42.

The annual prices survey produced by CAMRA shows that the average price of a pint of lager is now £2.45. In London and the South-east the average price is £2.61. The figures are stark: a pint of lager in a South-east pub will cost only 20 pence less than a litre – almost twice as much – bought from a supermarket. How can beer be sold so cheaply? A former chief beer buyer for a major supermarket chain told the guide that the global brewers make zillions of pounds from supermarket sales. The profit per bottle or can may be marginal but the pennies add up when so much beer is being shifted.

The problem can only be tackled if pubcos pass on the benefits of the discounts they get from brewers to their tenants – which would enable tenants to reduce the price of their pints – and by the government taking seriously the call from SIBA, the small brewers' association, to reduce the duty on beer sold in community and rural pubs. Unless these demands are taken up, more pubs will close and the future will be Foster's.

Readers' recommendations

Suggestions for pubs to be included or excluded

All pubs are surveyed by local branches of the Campaign for Real Ale. If you would like to comment on a pub already featured, or any you think should be featured, please fill in the form below (or copy it), and send it to the address indicated. Your views will be passed on to the branch concerned. Please mark your envelope with the county where the pub is, which will help us to sort the suggestion efficiently.

Pub name:

Address:

Reason for recommendation/criticism:

Pub name:

Address:

Reason for recommendation/criticism:

Pub name:

Address:

Reason for recommendation/criticism:

Your name and address:

Pub name:

Address:

Reason for recommendation/criticism:

Pub name:

Address:

Reason for recommendation/criticism:

Pub name:

Address:

Reason for recommendation/criticism:

Pub name:

Address:

Reason for recommendation/criticism:

Your name and address:

Please send to: [Name of county] Section, Good Beer Guide,
230 Hatfield Road, St Albans, Hertfordshire AL1 4LW

Books for Beer Lovers

CAMRA Books, the publishing arm of the Campaign for Real Ale, is the leading publisher of books on beer and pubs. Key titles include:

Good Beer Guide Belgium

EDITOR: TIM WEBB

Now in its 5th edition and in full colour, this book has developed a cult following among committed beer lovers and beer tourists. It is the definitive, totally independent guide to understanding and finding the best Belgian beer and an essential companion for any beer drinker visiting Belgium or seeking out Belgian beer in Britain. Includes details of the 120 breweries and over 800 beers in regular production, as well as 500 of the best hand-picked cafés in Belgium.

£12.99 ISBN 1 85249 210 4 / 978 1 85249 210 6

300 Beers To Try Before You Die!

ROGER PROTZ

300 beers from around the world, handpicked by award-winning journalist, author and broadcaster Roger Protz to try before you die! A comprehensive portfolio of top beers from the smallest microbreweries in the United States to family-run British breweries and the world's largest brands. This book is indispensable for both beer novices and aficionados.

£14.99 ISBN 1 85249 213 9 / 978 1 85249 213 7

The Big Book of Beer

ADRIAN TIERNEY-JONES

Everything you could ever want to know about the world's favourite drink; this beautifully illustrated book is an eye-opener to the world of beer articulated by well-known beer experts and those who brew it. A perfect gift for the 'real beer' connoisseur.

£14.99 ISBN 1 85249 212 0 / 978 1 85249 212 0

Good Beer Guide Germany

STEVE THOMAS

The first ever comprehensive region-by-region guide to Germany's brewers, beer and outlets. Includes more than 1,200 breweries, 1,000 brewery taps and 7,200 beers. Complete with useful travel information on how to get there, informative essays on German beer and brewing plus beer festival listings.

£16.99 ISBN 1 85249 219 8 / 978 1 85249 219 9

Good Pub Food

SUSAN NOWAK & JILL ADAM

This fully revised sixth edition of Good Pub Food singles out over 600 real ale pubs in England, Wales, Scotland and Northern Ireland, which also specialise in fine cuisine. All are highlighted on easy-to-use maps and have a full description of their location, ales, menus, prices, vegetarian selections and facilities. Both Susan Nowak and Jill Adam have been involved in editing and compiling CAMRA guides for over 20 years.

£14.99 ISBN 1 85249 214 7 / 978 1 85249 214 4

Good Beard Guide

GREG GRAHAM

This light-hearted but informative pack provides all you need to know to keep your beard growing, groomed and gorgeous. It includes a fake beard for beginners, together with an 80-page full-colour book to guide you through the history, myth and magic of facial hair, from a Garibaldi to a goatee and a Van Dyke to a Soul Patch. Weird beards, famous beards and recommendations for beers to suit your beard colour are combined with invaluable tips on grooming and upkeep and a useful glossary, making this the only book of beards you will ever need.

£5.95 ISBN 1 85249 228 7 / 978 1 85249 228 1

Good Bottled Beer Guide

JEFF EVANS

This award-winning book is the bible for all aficionados of real ale in a bottle. It is a comprehensive guide to the huge number of beers now available in supermarkets, off-licences and via the internet in the UK, from bitters and milds to wheat beers, stouts, porters, fruit beers and barley wines. This fully updated and expanded sixth edition profiles nearly 800 bottle-conditioned beers with tasting notes, ingredients and brewery details.

£10.99 ISBN 1 85249 226 0 / 978 1 85249 226 7

Beer, Bed & Breakfast

JILL ADAM & SUSAN NOWAK

Beer, Bed & Breakfast singles out over 500 real ale pubs in England, Wales and Scotland, which also offer quality overnight accommodation and tasty breakfasts. Each entry gives all contact details, type and extent of accommodation, a list of beers, meal types, and an easy to understand price guide so you can plan your budget. Published April 2007.

£14.99 ISBN 1 85249 230 9 / 978 1 85249 230 4

Order these and other CAMRA books online at **www.camra.org.uk/books**, ask at your local bookstore, or contact:
CAMRA, 230 Hatfield Road, St Albans, AL1 4LW. Telephone **01727 867201**

An offer for CAMRA members

GOOD BEER GUIDE Annual Subscription

Being a CAMRA member brings many benefits, not least the big discount on the Good Beer Guide. Now you can take advantage of an even bigger discount on the Guide by taking out an annual subscription.

Simply fill in the form below and the Direct Debit form opposite (photocopies will do if you don't want to spoil your book), and send them to CAMRA at the usual St Albans address.

You will then receive the *Good Beer Guide* automatically every year. It will be posted to you before the official publication date and before any other postal sales are processed.

You won't have to bother with filling in cheques every year and you will receive the book at a lower price than other CAMRA members (for instance, the 2006 Guide was sold to annual subscribers at only £8.50).

So sign up now and be sure of receiving your copy early every year.

Note: This offer is open only to CAMRA members and is only available through using a Direct Debit instruction to a UK bank (use the form opposite, or copy it if you do not want to spoil your book). This offer applies to the 2007 *Guide* onwards.

Name

CAMRA Membership No.

Address and Post code

I wish to purchase the *Good Beer Guide* annually by Direct Debit and I have completed the Direct Debit instructions to my bank which are enclosed.

Signature

Date

Instruction to your Bank or Building Society to pay by Direct Debit

Please fill in the form and send to: Campaign for Real Ale Ltd. 230 Hatfield Road, St. Albans, Herts. AL1 4LW

Name and full postal address of your Bank or Building Society

To The Manager — Bank or Building Society

Address

Postcode

Name (s) of Account Holder (s)

Bank or Building Society account number

Branch Sort Code

Reference Number

Originator's Identification Number

9	2	6	1	2	9

FOR CAMRA OFFICIAL USE ONLY
This is not part of the instruction to your Bank or Building Society

Membership Number

Name

Postcode

Instruction to your Bank or Building Society
Please pay CAMRA Direct Debits from the account detailed on this Instruction subject to the safeguards assured by the Direct Debit Guarantee. I understand that this instruction may remain with CAMRA and, if so, will be passed electronically to my Bank/Building Society

Signature(s)

Date

Banks and Building Societies may not accept Direct Debit Instructions for some types of account

detached and retained this section

This Guarantee should be detached and retained by the payer.

The Direct Debit Guarantee

- This Guarantee is offered by all Banks and Building Societies that take part in the Direct Debit Scheme. The efficiency and security of the Scheme is monitored and protected by your own Bank or Building Society.
- If the amounts to be paid or the payment dates change CAMRA will notify you 7 working days in advance of your account being debited or as otherwise agreed.
- If an error is made by CAMRA or your Bank or Building Society, you are guaranteed a full and immediate refund from your branch of the amount paid.
- You can cancel a Direct Debit at any time by writing to your Bank or Building Society. Please also send a copy of your letter to us.

CAMRA, the Campaign for Real Ale, is an independent, not-for-profit, volunteer-led consumer organisation. We actively campaign for full pints and longer licensing hours as well as protecting the local pub and lobbying government to champion pub-goers' rights.

CAMRA has 85,000 members from all ages and backgrounds, brought together by a common belief in the issues that CAMRA deals with and their love of good quality British beer. For just £18 a year, that's less than a pint a month, you can join CAMRA and enjoy the following benefits:

- A monthly newspaper informing you about beer and pub news and detailing events and beer festivals around the country.
- Free or reduced entry to over 140 national, regional and local beer festivals.
- Money off many of our publications including the Good Beer Guide.
- Access to a members' only section of our national website, www.camra.org.uk, which gives up-to-the-minute news stories and includes a special offer section with regular features saving money on beer and trips away.
- The opportunity to campaign to save pubs under threat of closure, for pubs to be open when people want to drink and a reduction in beer duty that will help Britain's brewing industry survive.

Do you feel passionately about your pint? Then why not join CAMRA?

Just fill in the application form (or a photocopy of it) and the Direct Debit form on the previous page to receive three months' membership FREE! If you wish to join but do not want to pay by Direct Debit, please fill in the application form below and send a cheque, payable to CAMRA, to: CAMRA, 230 Hatfield Road, St Albans, Hertfordshire AL1 4LW.

Please tick appropriate box   Direct Debit rates below. Visit www.camra.org.uk/joinus for non-Direct Debit payers rates.

Single Membership (UK &EU)	**£18** ☐	**From 1st Jan 2007 £20** ☐
Under 26 membership	**£10** ☐	**From 1st Jan 2007 £11** ☐
Over 60 membership	**£10** ☐	**From 1st Jan 2007 £11** ☐

■ For joint membership add £3 (or £5 after 1st January 2007) – For concessionary rates both members must be eligible for the membership rate. ■ Life membership information is available on request.

If you join by Direct Debit you will receive three months' membership extra free!

Title ______ Surname ______

Forename (s) ______

Address ______

______ Post Code ______

Date of Birth ______ E-mail address ______

Signature ______

Partners details if required

Title ______ Surname ______

Date of Birth ______ E-mail address ______

☐ Please tick here if you would like to receive occasional e-mails from CAMRA, (at no point will your details be released to a third party).

Find out more about CAMRA at www.camra.org.uk